D1733128

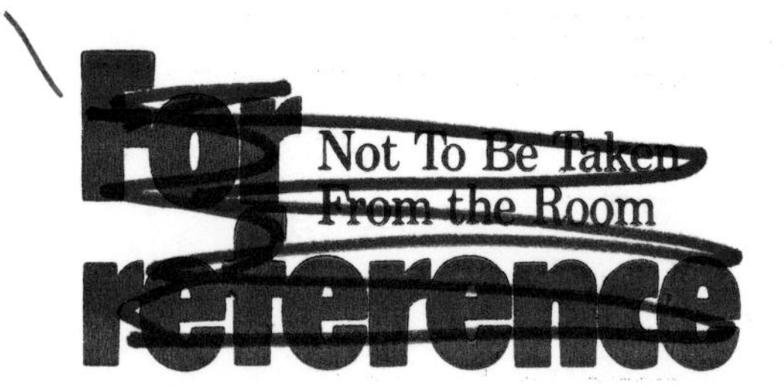
For
Not To Be Taken
From the Room
reference

WORLD ENCYCLOPEDIA
of Library and Information Services

WORLD ENCYCLOPEDIA *of Library and Information Services*

Third Edition

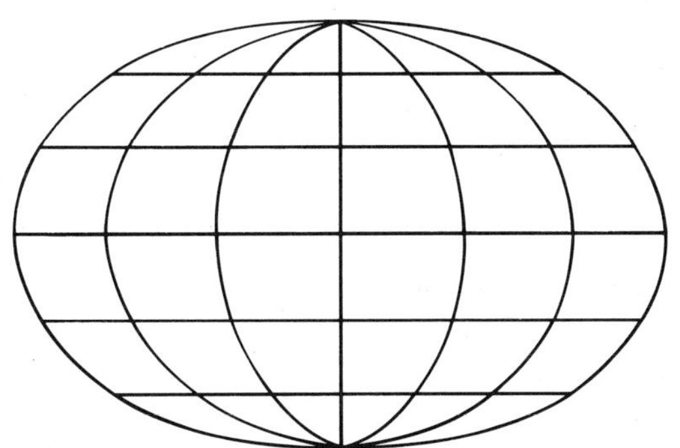

1993 AMERICAN LIBRARY ASSOCIATION *Chicago*

The paper used in this publication meets the minimum requirements of American National Standard for Information Sciences—Permanence of Paper for Printed Library Materials, ANSI Z39.48-1984. ∞

Cover designed by Gordon Stromberg

Composed by Clarinda Company

Printed on 50-pound Phoenix Opaque, 16-page insert 80-pound Sterling Litho Gloss paper, a pH-neutral stock, and bound in Roxite B-grade cloth by Edwards Brothers

Library of Congress Cataloging-in-Publication Data

World Encyclopedia of library and information services / [Robert Wedgeworth, editor]. 3rd ed.
p. cm.
Includes index.
ISBN 0-8389-0609-5 (alk. paper)
1. Library science—Encyclopedias. 2. Information science—Encyclopedias. I. Wedgeworth, Robert.
Z1006.W67 1993
020′.3—dc20 93-25159

Printed in the United States of America.

97 96 95 94 93 5 4 3 2 1

Contents

Editor's Preface

The First Edition of this work in 1980 brought to fulfillment the long-term objective of the Editor to establish a firm basis for the comparative study of librarianship internationally. Previous efforts to understand and analyze the respective circumstances of librarianship in many countries of the world have been limited by the lack of descriptive and statistical information as a starting point for more in-depth study. For many countries current information on the status and condition of libraries and librarianship is not readily accessible or does not exist.

The *World Encyclopedia* attempts to fill this fundamental gap in the literature of library and information services through a one-volume overview of the history, the major institutions and the distinguished personalities that have shaped the field as we know it. Its historical articles trace the development of the field, an overview enriched by current descriptions of library and information services in countries around the world. Professional concepts and principles are explained and analyzed in articles ranging from Abstracting and Indexing to Young Adult Services. Biographies emphasize major achievements in the lives of distinguished persons who have led the field.

Plans for the Third Edition developed by the editors called for a 70 percent revision of the work including both new and revised contributions. Of the 437 contributors many are new. A number of articles have been updated by contributors to previous editions or the editors, and a few have been reprinted from the Second Edition. The illustrations give a fresh look to the work with a new sixteen-page color section, "A Portfolio of Great Libraries." Many new photos and charts accompany the text. An entirely new and more comprehensive index gives greater access to the content of the work.

The Third Edition of the *World Encyclopedia* follows the editorial plan of the previous editions. Its categories of articles are organized under five principal divisions. The Library and Society covers the history and role of libraries from ancient times to the present. In addition to nine major articles on historical periods, 160 articles cover libraries and librarianship in separate articles on countries of the world. Appearing in alphabetical order in the text, they are usually accompanied by comprehensive statistical information and tables. Two hundred and sixteen biographies complete this division.

The Library as an Institution comprises thirteen major articles on the principal types of libraries and archives. Articles emphasize North America, but examples are drawn from other parts of the world as well. Five entirely new articles focus on institutions that, because of their size and scope, have been selected for special treatment including the special color photo section: Bibliothèque Nationale, Paris; British Library, London; Harvard University Libraries, Cambridge, Massachusetts; Library of Congress, Washington, D.C.; and New York Public Library, New York.

Theory and Practice of Librarianship covers the heart of the field. Fifty-five articles explain and analyze the principles and practices that define library and information services.

Education and Research, eight major articles, covers the history, practices and issues surrounding education and research for librarianship, information science and archival administration.

International Library, Information, and Bibliographical Organizations comprises thirty-one articles that describe the growth and development of key institutions and international organizations that have a sustaining influence on the field.

The articles, which range in length from one thousand words to over 30,000 (Medical Libraries, for example), were designed to provide enough space to treat significant aspects of each topic, including the hundreds of tables and illustrations that enrich and enliven the text.

Not enough can be said about the 437 contributors who gave their experience, knowledge and extraordinary cooperation in the production of this work. Given the many changes that occurred in the world during the production of this work, many had to submit substantial revisions of their texts to reflect new conditions. Nevertheless, in some instances it was not possible to provide completely updated information on countries where internal strife and rapidly changing conditions made it difficult to determine what could be reported.

The period since the Second Edition has been marked by worldwide recession plus revolutionary technological and political change. These pages reflect the achievements of individuals, institutions and the field as a whole under trying circumstances as best we could determine it. The editors acknowledge the contributions of the authors with sincere gratitude.

Grateful acknowledgments also go to the editorial and production team for this Third Edition. Mary Ellen Chijioke and Olha Della Cava shared the major editorial responsibilities, while Diana Zimmerman updated the illustrations, Chung-Kyun Wedgeworth maintained the contributor files and Bettie Jane Third created the index. Don Ludgin, whose experience as copy editor with the Second Edition guided us through the production phase, also deserves special mention. To the translators and editorial writers, production specialists and especially to David Epstein, Dianne Rooney and Mary Huchting we are also very grateful for assistance and support.

The experiences, achievements, failures, hopes, aspirations, strengths and weaknesses of the library and information services world reflected in the pages of this Third Edition of the *World Encyclopedia of Library and Information Services* continue to build upon the conception and execution of the previous editions of this work. The editors were encouraged by the response to previous editions and hope our efforts to improve the work will be received similarly.

ROBERT WEDGEWORTH
Editor

June 14, 1993
University Library
University of Illinois
at Urbana-Champaign

Contributors

Constantin Ivanovich Abramov (retired)
Moscow State Institute for Culture. *Lev Tropovsky*

Thomas R. Adams (deceased)
Brown University Library, Providence, R.I. *Benjamin Franklin*

N.M. Adhikari
National Library of Bhutan. *Bhutan*

Simeon B. Aje (retired)
National Library of Nigeria. *Felice Adetowun Ogunsheye*

M. Shaheed Akhand
Bangladesh Central Library. *Bangladesh*

Mohammed Hamar Al Nassr
Qatar National Library. *Qatar*

Krissiamba Larba Ali
Documentation Center, Ougadougou. *Burkina Faso*

S. Nazim Ali
University of Bahrain Library. *Bahrain*

Laura Alpern
Association of International Libraries, Geneva. *Association of International Libraries*

R.C. Alston
University College, London, School of Library, Archive and Information Studies. *British Library*

Mohammed M. Aman
University of Wisconsin-Milwaukee, School of Library and Information Sciences. *Bibliotheca Alexandrina (Modern), Egypt, Sha'ban Khalifa, Sudan*

Norma Y. Amenu-Kpodo
Commonwealth Library Association, Jamaica, W.I. *Commonwealth Library Association*

Ogo N. Amucheazi
University of Nigeria Library, Nsukka. *Beatrice O. Aboyade*

Beryl Anderson (retired)
National Library of Canada. *Canada*

Margaret Anderson
University of Toronto, Canada, Faculty of Library and Information Science. *George Locke*

Hedwig Anuar (retired)
National Library of Singapore. *Singapore*

Alan Asaf (deceased)
Grolier Club of New York. *Joseph Sabin*

Tetiana Arseenko
Vernadsky Central Research Library, Kiev. *Ukraine*

C. Wesley Armstrong
University of Liberia. *Liberia*

Diana Astle
Clemson University Library, Clemson, S.C. *Serials*

Kwami E. Avafia
University of Namibia Library. *Namibia*

Henriette D. Avram (retired)
Library of Congress, Washington. *MARC*

Augusta Baker (retired)
University of South Carolina, Columbia, S.C., College of Library and Information Science. *Anne Carroll Moore*

John P. Baker
New York Public Library. *Conservation and Preservation of Library Materials*

K.G.B. Bakewell
Liverpool Polytechnic, School of Librarianship and Information Studies. *S.C. Bradford, S.R. Ranganathan*

E. Bejide Bankole
Lagos, Nigeria. *Standing Conference of African University Libraries*

Peggy Barber
American Library Association, Chicago. *Public Relations*

Maria Alice Barroso
Formerly, National Library of Brazil, Rio de Janeiro. *Brazil*

Anabela Barroso
Historical Archives of Sao Tome and Principe. *Sao Tome and Principe*

Daniel W. Barthell
Northwestern University Library. *Honduras*

Susan Shattuck Benson
Organization of American States, Washington. *Organization of American States*

Emilia Bernal-Rosa (retired)
University of Puerto Rico, Rio Piedras. *Puerto Rico*

Jean Wilfred Bertrand
National Archives of Haiti. *Haiti*

Russell L. Bidlack (retired)
University of Michigan. *Rudolph Gjelsness*

Mary Biggs
Trenton State College Library, New Jersey. *Bibliographic Instruction*

Judy Blackman
National Library Service, Barbados. *Barbados*

Bruno Blasselle
Bibliotheque Nationale, Paris. *Bibliotheque Nationale*

George S. Bobinski
State University of New York, Buffalo, School of Information and Library Studies. *Andrew Carnegie, Edward G. Holley*

David W. Boilard
Medical College of Ohio Library, Toledo. *Medical Libraries: Library Cooperation*

Mary Elizabeth Bouscarle
International Center for Medical Research, Gabon. *Gabon*

T.H. Bowyer
Formerly, University of London, Queen Mary College Library. *K.W. Humphreys*

Alex Boyd
Newark Public Library, New Jersey. *Public Libraries*

Patrick W. Brennen
Medical College of Wisconsin Library, Milwaukee. *Medical Libraries: Governance, Finance and Management*

Estelle Brodman (retired)
Washington University Medical Library, St. Louis. *Frank Bradway Rogers*

Barry S. Brook
International Association of Music Libraries. *Archives and Documentation Centers*

Gloria Primm Brown
Carnegie Corporation of New York. *Frederick Paul Keppel*

Robert E. Brundin
University of Alberta, Edmonton, Faculty of Library Science. *Justin Winsor*

Mary Lynn McCree Bryan
Duke University, Durham. *Ernst Posner*

Frank G. Burke
University of Maryland, College Park, College of Library and Information Services. *Archives: Nature, Goals and Principles, Archives: Organization and Description, Archives: Electronic Records*

Redmond A. Burke
University of Wisconsin Library, Oshkosh. *Saint Benedict, Cassiodorus, Bartolomeo Platina*

C.A. Burmester (retired)
National Library of Australia. *Sir John Alexander Ferguson, Edward Augustus Petherick*

Charles H. Busha
Censorship and Intellectual Freedom

Ana Maria Magaloni de Bustamente
National Council for Culture and the

Arts, Public Libraries of Mexico. *Mexico*

Gary Byrd
Health Sciences Library, University of North Carolina, Chapel Hill. *Medical Libraries: Purpose and Objectives*

Maria Luisa Cabral
Formerly, National Library of Portugal. *Portugal*

Kenneth E. Carpenter
Harvard University, Widener Library. *Harvard University Libraries*

Michael Carpenter
Louisiana State University, Baton Rouge, School of Library and Information Science. *Seymour Lubetzky*

Elizabeth Carvalho
Rio de Janeiro, Brazil. *Brazil*

Edwin Castagna (deceased)
Joseph L. Wheeler

Octavio Castillo
University of Panama, School of Librarianship. *Panama*

Cordelia R. Cavalcanti
University of Brasilia, Brazil. *Maria Luisa Monteiro de Cunha*

Roderick Cave
University of Wellington, New Zealand. *Arundell Esdaile, Andrew Maunsell*

Sten Cedergren
Gothenburg Public Library. *International Association of Metropolitan City Libraries (INTAMEL)*

Rosemarie Chait
National Library of Algeria. *Algeria*

Peter Nkangafack Chateh
University of Yaounde, Cameroon. *Cameroon*

Marc Chauveinc
Ministry of Education, Libraries. *France*

Mary K. Chelton
Milltown, NJ. *Margaret C. Scroggin*

Elin B. Christianson
Library Consultant, Hobart, Indiana. *Special Libraries*

Jul Christophory
National Library of Luxembourg. *Luxembourg*

Charles D. Churchwell
Clark Atlanta University. *Charles C. Williamson*

Jean-Pierre Clavel (deceased)
Switzerland

Paul Cohen
New York Historical Society. *Isadore Gilbert Mudge*

Lois Ann Colaianni
National Library of Medicine, Bethesda. *Martin M. Cummings*

John Y. Cole
Center for the Book, Library of Congress, Washington. *Archibald MacLeish, Herbert Putnam, Ainsworth Rand Spofford*

John P. Comaroni
Library of Congress, Washington. *Melvil Dewey*

Barbara Commissiong
University of the West Indies. *Trinidad and Tobago*

Michael G. Cook
University of Liverpool. *Archives: Professional Training*

Ishvari Corea
Sri Lanka National Library Services Board. *Sri Lanka*

David Cornelius
Ghana Library Board. *Ghana*

Antonio M.B. Costa e Silva
National Library of Mozambique. *Mozambique*

Caroline Coughlin
Drew University Library, Madison, N.J. *Academic Libraries: Purposes, Goals and Objectives, Academic Libraries: Laws and Regulations*

Timothy J. Crist
Donald Goddard Wing

Prudenciana C. Cruz
National Library of the Philippines. *Congress of Southeast Asian Librarians (CONSAL)*

Maria Manuela Cruzeiro
New University of Lisbon, Portugal. *Cape Verde*

Clifford Currie (retired)
Robert Shackleton

Frank Kurt Cylke
National Library Service to the Blind and Physically Handicapped, Washington. *Services to Users with Disabilities*

Doris Cruger Dale
Southern Illinois University, Carbondale. *Sarah Bogle*

Phyllis Dain
Columbia University, New York. *Scholarly and Research Services*

Helen Dalrymple
Library of Congress, Washington. *Library of Congress*

Charles H. Davis
Indiana University, Bloomington, IN, Graduate School of Library and Information Science. *Library and Information Science Research*

Donald G. Davis, Jr.
University of Texas, Austin, School of Library and Information Science. *Mary Wright Plummer*

Anthony Debons (retired)
University of Pittsburgh, School of Library and Information Science. *Information Science*

Andrew N. DeHeer
Ghana Library Board. *Ghana*

Virginia W. Dike
University of Nigeria, Nsukka, Department of Library Service. *Simeon B. Aje, School Libraries and Media Centers, Standing Conference of African University Libraries (SCAUL)*

Zhi-Gang Ding
China Society of Library Science. *China, Peoples Republic of*

Dang Ngoc Dinh
Central Institute for Scientific and Technical Information, Hanoi. *Vietnam*

Oumar Diowara
National Library, Nouakchott. *Mauritania*

Julien C. Djosse
National Library of Benin. *Benin*

Mahir Domi
Council of Libraries, Tirana. *Albania*

Keith Doms (retired)
Free Library of Philadelphia. *Ralph Munn*

Michel Duchein
National Archives, Paris. *Archives: Legislative Foundations*

Frederick Duda (retired)
Warren J. Haas

Domingos van Dunem
National Library. *Angola*

Truong Thai Dung
Vietnam

Nguyen Van Dung
Vietnam

Mary Dykstra
Dalhousie University, School of Library and Information Studies. *PRECIS*

Harry East
City University, London, Department of Information Science. *Brian Vickery*

Ivi Eenma
National Library of Estonia. *Estonia.*

Lawrence D. Eicher
International Standards Organization, Geneva. *International Organization for Standardization (ISO)*

Mohammed M. El Hadi
Computer Consultants (CCH), Saudia Arabia. *Kuwait, Saudi Arabia, Yemen*

Roger Ellis (retired)
Public Records Office, London. *Sir Hilary Jenkinson*

Deidre Ellis-King
Dublin City County Public Libraies. *Ireland*

Lina Ernesta
National Library of Seychelles. *Seychelles*

Hipolita-Escolar-Sobrino
National Library of Spain. *Spain*

William R. Eshelman
The Press at Camperdown Elm, Wooster, OH. *Lawrence Clark Powell*

John R.T. Ettlinger (retired)
Dalhousie University, Halifax, N.S., School of Library and Information Studies. *Middle Ages, Libraries in the*

Charles W. Evans
University of Mississippi. *Library Education: Education and Training of Library Employees*

Frank B. Evans (deceased)
Theodore R. Schellenberg

John A. Evans
University of Papua New Guinea, Department of Library and Information Studies. *Kiribati, Papua New Guinea, Solomon Islands*

Elaine Fain (deceased)
Mary Eileen Ahern

Emily Gallup Fayen
University of Pennsylvania Libraries, Philadelphia. *Circulation Services*

E.A. Fenelonov (retired)
Russian State Library, Moscow. *O.S. Chubarian*

Stephney Ferguson
University of the West Indies, Department of Library Studies. *Joyce Robinson*

Meyer Fishbein
National Archives and Records Service. *Archives: Records Management and Appraisal*

Richard Fitzsimmons
Pennsylvania State University Library, Scranton. *J.B. Lippincott*

Nancy Fjallbrant
Chalmers University of Technology Library, Gothenburg, Sweden. *International Association of Technological University Libraries (IATUL)*

Marisol Floren
Central University of the East Library, San Pedro de Macoris. *Dominican Republic*

Georgij Fonotov (retired)
Russian State Library. *Nadezhda Krupskaya*

Edson Nery da Fonseca
University of Brasilia, Brazil. *Rubens Moraes*

Jody Bales Foote
Cornell University Library, Ithaca, NY. *Bangladesh*

John B. Forbes
National Agricultural Library. *Food and Agricultural Organization*

Vincent Forshaw
Lesotho National Library Service, Maseru. *Lesotho*

Barbara Foster
Hunter College Library, New York. *Netherlands Antilles*

D.J. Foskett
University of London Library. *Sir Frank Francis*

Sir Frank Francis (deceased)
Donald John Urquhart

Yoshiko Moriya de Freundorfer
National University of Asuncion, Paraguay. *Paraguay*

Stephen E. Furth (deceased)
Hans Peter Luhn

Ervin J. Gaines (deceased)
William Howard Brett

Richard K. Gardner
University of Montreal. *Association Internationale des Ecoles des Sciences de l'Information*

Gloria Gasperini
University Library School, Montevideo. *Uruguay*

Barbara Gates
Brown University Library, Providence, R.I. *Minnie Earl Sears*

Mary V. Gaver (deceased)
Ralph Shaw

Stanley Gillam (retired)
Thomas Carlyle

Marion Gilroy
University of British Columbia, School of Library, Archival and Information Studies. *Elizabeth Homer Morton*

Margaret Knox Goggin (retired)
Certification of Librarians

B.R. Goordyal
University of Mauritius Library. *Mauritius*

Martha Gorman
Boulder, CO. *Ecuador, Peru*

Else Granheim (retired)
National Library Service of Norway. *Margreet Wijnstroom*

Chandler B. Grannis (deceased)
Daniel Melcher

Belver Griffith
Drexel University, Philadelphia, School of Library and Information Science. *Eugene Garfield*

Laurel A. Grotzinger
Western Michigan University. *Adelaide Hasse, Katharine L. Sharp*

Seydou Gueye
National Library of Ivory Coast. *Ivory Coast*

Hussein Habaili
Faculty of Medicine of Tunis. *Tunisia*

Alfred D. Hagle
National Library Service to the Blind and Physically Handicapped, Washington. *Services to Users with Disabilities*

Charles A. Hamaker
Louisiana State University Library, Baton Rouge. *Serials*

Robert E. Handloff
Ivory Coast

Jane Anne Hannigan (retired)
Columbia University, New York. *Frances E. Henne*

Kenneth C. Harrison (retired)
Librarian of Westminster, London. *Frank Gardner, Sir Harry Hookway, Library Association, Lionel R. McColvin, W.A. Munford, W.C. Berwick Sayers*

Dan C. Hazen
Harvard College Library, Cambridge, MA. *Seminar on the Acquisition of Latin American Library Materials (SALALM)*

Timothy S. Healey (deceased)
New York Public Library. *New York Public Library*

Fred Heath
Academic Libraries: Administration

Veslemoy Heintz
International Association of Music Libraries, Archives and Documentation Centers

John B. Hench
American Antiquarian Society, Worcester, MA. *J. Frank Jameson, Waldo Gifford Leland*

Donald D. Hendricks
University of New Orleans Library, Louisiana. *J. Pierpont Morgan, Eugene Morel*

Dan Henke
University of California, San Francisco, Hastings College of Law. *Law Libraries: Services to Users*

Carol Henry
International Federation of Library Association and Institutions, The Hague. *International Federation of Library Associations and Institutions (IFLA)*

Hernandono
Indonesian National Scientific Documentation Center. *Winarti Partaningrat*

Peter Hernon
Simmons College, Graduate School of Library and Information Science. *Measurement and Evaluation of Libraries*

Jose Tamayo Herrera
University of Lima, Peru. *Peru*

M. Teresa Herrero de Alvarez
Chilean-North American Institute of Culture, Santiago. *Chile*

Joe A. Hewitt
University of North Carolina Library, Chapel Hill. *F. Wilfred Lancaster*

Doralyn J. Hickey (deceased)
Paul S. Dunkin

Blanca Hodge
Philipsburg Jubilee Library, St. Maarten. *Netherlands Antilles*

Bernardine E. A. Hoduski
U.S. Congress, Joint Committee on Printing. *Official Publications*

Edward G. Holley
University of North Carolina, Chapel Hill, School of Information and Library Science. *American Library Association, Lester E. Asheim, Charles Evans*

Oliver W. Holmes (deceased)
Philip M. Hamer

Virginia H. Holtz
University of Wisconsin, Madison, Center for Health Science Library. *Medical Libraries: Measurement and Evaluation*

Norman Horrocks
Scarecorw Press, Metuchen, N.J. *Library Education: History*

Warren Horton
National Library of Australia. *Australia*

P. Lim Pui Huen
Institute for Southeast Asian Studies, Singapore. *Hedwig Anuar*

Gregory S. Hunter
Long Island University, Palmer School of Library and Information Science. *Reprography*

Toshio Iwasura (retired)
Kansei University. *Keitaro Amano, Fujio Mamiya*

Sara Jean Jackson
University of Texas, Houston, M.D. Anderson Cancer Center Library. *Medical Libraries: Laws and Regulations*

Sidney L. Jackson (deceased)
Alexandrian Library, Byzantine Libraries, Egypt (Ancient), Greece (Ancient), Near East (Ancient), Rome

William Vernon Jackson
Rosary College, Illinois. *Louise-Noelle Malcles*

Roger E. Jacobs
Notre Dame University, Law School. *Law Libraries: Laws and Legislation*

Jean-Frederic Jauslin
National Library of Switzerland, Bern. *Switerzerland*

Duane F. Johnson
Kansas State Library, Topeka. *Extension Services*

Stephen C. Johnson
Behavioral Images Inc. *Audiovisual Materials*

H.G. Jones
University of North Carolina, Chapel Hill. *Robert D.W. Connor*

William Goodrich Jones
University of Illinois Library, Chicago. *Academic Libraries: Collections*

Milbrey L. Jones (deceased)
Formerly, U.S. Department of

Education Library. *Mary V. Gaver*

Alma Jordan (retired)
University of the West Indies Library. *Trinidad and Tobago*

E.J. Josey
University of Pittsburgh, School of Library and Information Science. *Eliza Atkins Gleason*

Gladys M. Jusu-Sheriff
University of Sierra Leone, Freetown, Institute of Library Studies. *Sierra Leone*

Paul Kaegbein (retired)
University of Cologne, Germany. *Germany, Horst Kunze, Fritz Milkau*

Leif Kajberg
Royal School of Librarianship, Copenhagen. *Preben Kirkegaard*

Margaret Kaltenbach (retired)
Case Western Reserve University. *Jesse H. Shera*

Lai-Bing Kan
University of Hong Kong Libraries. *Hong Kong*

David Kaser
Indiana University, Graduate School of Library and Information Science. *Frederick G. Kilgour, Library Buildings, Keyes D. Metcalfe*

U. Thaw Kaung
Universities Central Library, Rangoon. *Myannar*

E.E. Kaungamno
Tanzania National Library Service. *Tanzania*

Boniface M. Kawesa
Makere University Library, Kampala. *Uganda*

Charles Keclemeti
International Council on Archives, Paris. *International Council on Archives (ICA)*

Charles Kecskemeti
International Council on Archives, Paris. *International Council on Archives*

Stella Keenan
Formerly, International Federation for Documentation, The Hague. *International Federation for Documentation*

D.G. Keswani
University of Ghana, Accra. *J.M. Akita*

M.T. Khafagi
Arab League Department of Documentation and Information. *Arab League Educational, Cultural and Scientific Organization*

Sha'ban Khalifa
Cairo University. *Sudan*

Anis Khurshid (retired)
University of Karachi. *Pakistan*

Amer Ibrahim Kindilichie
Al-Mustansiriya University, Baghdad, Department of Library and Information Science. *Iraq*

Mary E. Kingsbury
University of North Carolina, Chapel Hill, School of Information and Library Science. *Effie Louise Power*

Jeno Kiss
Metropolitan Ervin Szabo Library, Budapest. *Hungary*

Therese Kleindienst
Bibliotheque Nationale, Paris. *Julien Cain*

Asgerdur Kjartansdottir
University of Iceland, Reykjavik. *Iceland*

Philip A. Knachel
Folger Shakespeare Library, Washington. *Henry Clay Folger*

Hans-Albrecht Koch
State and University Library, Bremen. *LIBER*

Al Hady Koita
Ministry of Communication and Culture, Bamako. *Mali*

Helena Kolarova-Palkova
Ministry of Culture, Libraries, Bratislava. *Czechoslovakia*

Madoko Kon
Chuo University, Faculty of Literature. *Japan*

Elena Kosinskiene
National Library of Lithuania. *Lithuania*

Jean Thibodeaux Kraemer
University of Western Louisiana, Media Center. *Audiovisual Materials*

Richard L. Kort
Boston Public Library. *Yugoslavia*

Miroslav Krek
Brandeis University, Waltham, MA. *Islamic Libraries*

Joe W. Kraus (retired)
Illinois State University, Bloomington, IL. *Robert B. Downs*

D.W. Krummel
University of Illinois, Urbana-Champaign, Graduate School of Library and Information Science. *Conrad Gessner*

Patricia Kuhr
H.W. Wilson Co., New York. *Abstracting and Indexing*

N.H. Kulkarnee
National Archives of India, New Delhi. *S.N. Prasad*

A.R. Kulkarni
University of Poona, India. *Vishwanath Kashinath Rajwade*

Alex Ladenson (deceased)
William Frederick Poole

Ghassan Lahham
Assad National Library, Damascus. *Syria*

F. Lalande-Isnard (retired)
Amadou A. Bousso. *Guinea*

F. Wilfred Lancaster (retired)
University of Illinois, Urbana-Champaign, Graduate School of Library and Information Science. *Cyril Cleverdon*

Charles T. Laugher
Dalhousie University, Halifax, N.S. *Thomas Bray*

Giovanni Lazzari
Chamber of Deputies Library, Rome. *Italy*

Renee Lemaitre (retired)
United States Information Service, Paris. *Henri Lemaitre*

Tomas Lidman
Stockholm University Library, Sweden. *Sweden*

Herman Liebaers (retired)
National Library of Belgium. *Margarita Ivanova Rudomino*

Emma Linares
Formerly, Center for the Study of Publications Library, Buenos Aires. *Carlos Victor Penna, Josefa Sabor*

Maurice B. Line (retired)
Information and Library Consultant, U.K., Formerly, British Lending Library, Boston Spa. *National Libraries*

Max Liniger-Goumaz
School of Economics and Business Administration, Lausanne. *Equatorial Guinea*

Jill L. Locke
University of North Carolina, Greensboro, Department of Library and Information Science. *Children's Services*

Wolfgang Loehner
UNESCO, General Information Program, Paris. *UNESCO*

Carla M. Lont
Ministry of Education, Documentation Center. *Suriname*

Guadelupe Lopez
National Library of Venezuela, Caracas. *Venezuela*

John G. Lorenz (retired)
Library of Congress, Washington. *L. Quincy Mumford*

Jean E. Lowrie (retired)
International Association of School Librarianship, Kalamazoo, MI. *International Association of School Librarianship (IASL)*

Mary Jo Lynch
American Library Association, Chicago. *Academic Libraries: Measurement and Evaluation, Margaret Hutchins, Constance M. Winchell*

Beverly P. Lynch
University of California, Los Angeles, Graduate School of Library and Information Science. *Academic Libraries: Purposes, Goals and Objectives*

Mary Niles Maack
University of California, Los Angeles, Graduate School of Library and Information Science. *Suzanne Honore, Eugene Morel*

Stan M. Made
University of Zimbabwe Library, Harare. *Zimbabwe*

Leena Maissen
International Board on Books for Young People, Basel. *International Board on Books for Young People*

S.G. Malshe
A.K. Priolkar

Seth Manaka
University of the North, Sovenga, Department of Library and Information Science. *South Africa*

Salifa Mane
Cheikh Anta Diop University of Dakar, School of Librarians, Archivists and Documentalists. *Senegal*

Pramad B. Mangla
University of Delhi, New Delhi,

Department of Library and Information Science. *India*
K.A. Manley
University of London. *E.W.B. Nicholson*
Farouq Mansour
University of Jordan Library. *Jordan*
Julius J. Marke
St. John's University Law Library. *Law Libraries: Purposes and Objectives*
Albert P. Marshall (retired)
Virginia Lacy Jones
J. Marton-Lefevre
International Council of Scientific Unions, Paris. *International Council of Scientific Unions*
David J. Martz, Jr.
Bowling Green State University Library. *Peter Force*
Thomas G. Mathews
Association of Caribbean University, Research and Institutional Libraries, San Juan, Puerto Rico. *Association of Caribbean University, Research and Institutional Libraries (ACURIL)*
A.H.H.M. Mathijsen
University of Utrecht, Faculty of Veterinary Medicine. *Netherlands*
Charles R. McClure
Syracuse University, School of Information Studies. *Measurement and Evaluation of Libraries*
Lucretia W. McClure
University of Rochester Medical Library, Rochester, NY. *Medical Libraries: Services to Users*
Donald R. McCoy
University of Kansas, Lawrence. *Wayne C. Grover, Solon Justus Buck*
Stanley McElderry (deceased)
Herman Howe Fussler
Neil McHugh
Northwestern University, Evanston, IL. *Chad*
Brian McKeon
Wellington Public Library, New Zealand. *New Zealand*
Haynes McMullen (retired)
University of North Carolina, Chapel Hill, School of Information and Library Science. *R.R. Bowker*
Marilyn G. McSweeney
Massachusetts Institute of Technology Library. *Acquisitions*
Jean Medioni
Cantonal and University Library of Lausanne. *Switzerland*
Victor Ubalde Mendieta Ortiz
University of Panama, El Dorado. *Panama*
Roy M. Mersky
University of Texas, Austin, School of Law. *Law Libraries: Administration*
Colette Meuvret
Gabriel Henriot
Marion A. Milczewski (deceased)
Carl H. Milam
Marilyn L. Miller
Department of Library and Information Science, University of North Carolina, Greensboro. *May Hill Arbuthnot*
Francis L. Miksa
University of Texas, Austin, School of Library and Information Science. *Charles Ammi Cutter, John Eaton*
Betty L. Milum
Ohio State University Library. *Luther Evans*
Shanti Mishri
Tribhuven University Library, Kathmandu. *Nepal*
Thornton W. Mitchell (retired)
North Carolina State Archives, Raleigh. *Margaret Norton*
O.N. Mohamedali
University of Zambia, Department of Library Studies. *Zambia*
Foster E. Mohrhardt (deceased)
Fred C. Cole
R. Kathleen Molz
Columbia University, School of International and Public Affairs. *Library Management and Administration*
Margaret E. Monroe (retired)
University of Wisconsin, Madison, School of Library and Information Studies. *Douglas Waples*
Paul M. Mosher
University of Pennsylvania Libraries. *Academic Libraries: Collections*
Julie Glienna Mueller
University of Chicago, Illinois. *Henry Bliss*
W.A. Munford (retired)
Formerly, National Library for the Blind, U.K. *Theodore Besterman, George Birkbeck, James Duff Brown, Edward Edwards, John Passmore Edwards, Richard Garnett, Kenneth C. Harrison, Sir John Young Walker MacAlister, United Kingdom*
Jafred S. Musisi
Moi University Library. *Kenya*
Steve S. Mwiyeriwa
University of Malawi Libraries. *Malawi*
S.P.C. N'jie
Central Bank of Gambia Library. *Gambia*
Aida Naaman
Beirut University College Library. *Lebanon*
William Z. Nasri
University of Pittsburgh, Graduate School of Library and Information Science. *Copyright*
Ildar K. Nazmutdinov
Union of Soviet Socialist Republics
Waly Ndiaye
National Archives of Senegal. *Senegal*
May Brookings Negrao
Rio de Janeiro. *Brazil*
Diane M. Nelson and Robert B. Nelson
Boston, MA. *Li Ta-chao*
Polycarpe Ninteretse
University of Burundi Library. *Burundi*
Danuta Nitecki
University of Maryland Libraries, College Park. *Academic Libraries: Services to Users*
Ock-Soon Noh
Ewha Womans University Library, Seoul. *Korea*
Bart U. Nwafor
University of Jos Library, Jos. *Nigeria*
Donald E. Oehlerts
Clark Atlanta University Library. *Stephen McCarthy*
F.A. Ogunsheye (retired)
University of Ibadan. *Simeon B. Aje*
James G. Olle (retired)
University of Technology, Loughborough, U.K. *Louis Stanley Jast, Gabriel Naude, Sir Anthony Panizzi, Ernest A. Savage, A.J. Walford*
Larry R. Orberg
Academic Libraries: Library Cooperation
Robin Osborne
Columbia University Libraries, New York. *Henry Lewis Bullen*
Alois Ospelt
Liechtenstein National Library. *Liechtenstein*
Cyril O. Packwood
Bermuda Library. *Bermuda*
Guillermo Palma R.
Institute of Nutrition of Central America and Panama. *Guatemala*
Anne Pellowski
New York, NY. *UNICEF*
Gunther Pflug (retired)
German National Library. *Germany*
Harold Pinkett
National Archives and Records Service. *Archives: Services to Users*
Peter A. Poole
Old Dominion University, Norfolk, VA. *Laos*
Vladimir Popov
Cyril and Methodius National Library, Sofia. *Bulgaria*
Alain-Michel Poutou
Champs sur Marne, France. *Central African Republic*
Mary Luella Powers (deceased)
Carleton B. Joeckel
Luwarsih Pringgodisurjo (retired)
National Scientific Documentation Center, Jakarta. *Indonesia*
Serafin Quiason (retired)
National Library of Philippines. *Philippines*
Naimuddin Qureshi
Fullerton, CA. *Anis Khurshid*
Winifred Ragsdale (retired)
Claremont College Graduate School, Altadena, CA, George C. Stone Center for Children's Books. *Frances Clarke Sayers*
Ruth R. Rains
University of Illinois, Urbana-Champaign, University Film Center. *Audiovisual Materials*
T.N. Rajan
Indian National Scientific Documentation Center, New Delhi. *B.S. Kesavan*
H.Kay Raseroka
University College of Botswana, Gaborone. *Botswana*
Neil Ratliff
International Association of Music Libraries, Archives and Documentation Centers
Pongpan Rattanabusit
IFLA Regional Office, Bangkok. *Thailand*
W. Boyd Rayward
University of New South Wales,

Sydney, School of Information, Library and Archive Studies. *International Library and Bibliographical Organizations, John Wallace Metcalfe, Andrew D. Osborn, Paul-Marie-Ghislain Otlet*

Cornelius Reedijk (retired)
Royal Library of the Netherlands. *Leendert Brummel*

Christian Relly
Pestalozzi Library, Zurich. *International Association of Metropolitan City Libraries (INTAMEL)*

Paulina Retana
Technical Institute of Costa Rica, Cartago. *Costa Rica*

James R. Rettig
College of William and Mary Library. *Reference and Information Services*

Dennis Reynolds
CAPCON Library Network, Washington. *Library Automation*

James B. Rhodes (retired)
International Council of Archives

Daniel T. Richards
Dartmouth College, Dana Medical Library. *Medical Libraries: Collections*

Phyllis A. Richmond (deceased)
Eva Verona

Constance Rinchart
University of Michigan, School of Library and Information Studies. *Margaret Mann*

Alma Beatriz Rivera-Aguilera
Centroamerican University, San Salvador. *El Salvador*

Jane Robbins-Carter
University of Wisconsin, Madison, School of Library and Information Studies. *Library Education*

David D. Roberson
James River Paper Company, Richmond, VA. *William J. Barrow*

Frank Bradway Rogers (deceased)
John Shaw Billings

Gary O. Rolstad
State Library of Louisiana, Baton Rouge. *Adult Services*

Samuel Rothstein (retired)
University of British Columbia. *Elizabeth Homer Morton*

Gotthard Rueckl (retired)
Central Institute for Librarianship, Berlin. *Germany.*

Steffen Rueckl (retired)
Humboldt University, Berlin, Institute for Librarianship and Scientific Information. *Germany*

Bendik Rugaas
Royal Library of Norway. *William Munthe, Norway*

James E. Rush
Powell, OH. *Library and Information Science Research*

Ibrahim Sabir
Islamic Center Library, Maldives. *Maldives*

Paul Saenger
Newberry Library, Chicago. *Renaissance Libraries*

Armando Samper
Sugar Cane Research Center of Colombia. *Daniel Samper Ortega*

Lars Erik Sanner (retired)
Stockholm University Library. *Scandinavian Federation of Research Libraries*

D. Gail Saunders
Ministry of Education, Nassau. *Bahamas*

Edith Scott
Library of Congress, Washington. *J.C.M. Hanson, Charles Martel*

Hans Georg Schulte-Albert
University of Western Ontario, London. *Gottfried Wilhelm Leibniz*

Eileen Searls
St. Louis University Law Library. *Law Libraries: Library Cooperation*

JoAn S. Segal (retired)
American Library Association, Chicago. *Bibliographic Networks and Utilities*

Emmanuel Serugendo
National University of Rwanda Library. *Rwanda*

Shmuel Sever
University of Haifa. *Israel*

Russell Shank (retired)
University of California, Los Angeles. *Charles Coffin Jewett, Robert G. Vosper*

Spencer G. Shaw (retired)
University of Washington, Seattle, Graduate School of Library and Information Science. *Augusta Baker*

Gerald R. Shields (deceased)
David H. Clift

Jesse H. Shera (deceased)
Pierce Butler, Philosophy of Librarianship

Ritva Sievanen-Allen
Central Medical Library, Helsinki. *Finland*

Ian Simons
Sultan Qaboos University Library, Muscat. *Oman*

Ivan Sipkov
International Journal of Legal Information, Washington. *International Association of Law Libraries (IALL)*

A.E. Skinner (deceased)
H.W. Wilson

Richard P. Smiraglia
Long Island University, Palmer School of Library and Information Science. *Classification*

Geoffrey Smith
T.C. Farries and Company, Ltd. *Frederick A. Thorpe*

Malcolm Smith
British Library Document Supply Centre, Boston Spa. *Resource Sharing*

Wilfred Irvin Smith
Public Archives of Canada. *Archives: Technical Aspects*

Soemartini
National Archives of Indonesia. *Harsya W. Bachtiar*

Poori Soltani
National Library of Iran, Teheran. *Iran*

Joseph S. Soosai (retired)
Rubber Research Institute of Malaysia Library, Kuala-Lumpur. *Malaysia*

Jutta Sorenson
Royal School of Librarianship, Denmark. *Derek Austin*

Lola Souad
School of Information Science, Rabat. *Morocco*

Claud Glenn Sparks
University of Texas, Austin, School of Library and Information Science. *William Warner Bishop*

Costas D. Stephanou
Ministry of Education, Nicosia. *Cyprus*

Yvonne V. Stephenson
University of the West Indies Library, St. Augustine. *Guyana*

Gordon Stevenson (deceased)
Karl Dziatzko

Ian Stoica
Central University Library, Bucharest. *Romania*

Elizabeth W. Stone (retired)
Catholic University of America, School of Library and Information Science. *Library Education: Continuing Professional Education*

Margaret R. Strassnig-Bachner
Austrian National Library. *Austria*

Basil Stuart-Stubbs
University of British Columbia, Vancouver School of Library, Archival and Information Studies. *W. Kaye Lamb, Guy Sylvestre*

Reinaldo Jose Suarez
Buenos Aires, Argentina. *Argentina, Domingo Faustine Sarmiento, Aurelia Zlatko Tanodi*

F. William Summers
Florida State University, Tallahassee, School of Library and Information Studies. *Accreditation, Francis R. St. John*

Ray R. Suput
Ball State University, Muncie, IN. *E.I. Shamurin*

Ron G. Surridge (retired)
Formerly, Borough of Islington Library, U.K. *Lorna Paulin*

Thein Swe
Louisiana State University Library. *Myannmar*

Nasser M. Swaydan
Iman Muhammed Ibn Saud Islamic University, Riyadh. *Saudi Arabia*

Richard J. Talbot
University of Massachusetts Library. *Academic Libraries: Measurement and Evaluation*

G. Thomas Tanselle
John Simon Guggenheim Memorial Foundation. *Frederick G. Melcher*

Ruth Tarbox (retired)
American Library Association, Chicago. *Mildred Batchelder*

Arlene G. Taylor
University of Pittsburgh, School of Library and Information Science. *Cataloguing*

Betty W. Taylor
University of Florida, Gainesville, College of Law. *Law Libraries: Collections*

Marta Terry
Jose Marti National Library of Cuba. *Cuba*

Dennis Thomison
Theresa Wright Elmendorf

Marta V. Tome
Organization of American States, Washington. *Jorge Aguayo, Organization of American States, Carmen Rovira*

Anabel Torres
National Library, Bogota. *Colombia*

Helen Welch Tuttle (retired)
Princeton University Library, NJ. *William S. Dix*

John de Belfort Urquidi
Afghanistan

Ernesto de la Torre Villar
National University of Mexico. *Maria Teresa Chavez Campomanes*

Daniel Traister
University of Pennsylvania, Philadelphia. *Rare Books and Special Collections*

Alphonse Trezza (retired)
Florida State University, Tallahassee, School of Library and Information Studies. *Library Cooperative Systems*

Nilifer Tuncer
Hacetteppe University, Ankara, Department of Library Science. *Turkey*

Rosa M. Vallejo
University of the Philippines, Quezon City, Institute of Library Science. *Gabriel A. Bernardo*

D.J. Van Der Berg
International Association of Agricultural Librarians and Documentalists

Willy Vanderpijpen
Royal Library, Brussels. *Belgium*

Carlos Vernimb
Commission of the European Communities, Luxembourg. *Euronet*

L.G. Vernon
National Library Service, Belize City. *Belize*

Jacqueline Viaux
Gabriel Henriot

Morton Laursen Vig
National Library Authority, Copenhagen. *Denmark*

Andris Vilks
National Library of Latvia, Riga. *Latvia*

Rose L. Vormelker (retired)
Kent State University. *John Cotton Dana*

Robert G. Vosper (retired)
University of California, Los Angeles, Graduate School of Library and Information Science. *Herman Liebaers, Foster E. Mohrhardt*

Linda Waddle
American Library Association, Chicago. *Young Adult Services*

Bruno Wambi
Darien Ngouabi University Library, Brazzaville. *Congo*

Chen-Ku Wang
National Taiwan Normal University, Taipei. *Taiwan (Republic of China)*

Chi Wang
Library of Congress, Washington. *Yuan T'ung-li*

Frances A. Weaver
University of North Carolina Archives, Chapel Hill. *Louis Round Wilson*

Robert Wedgeworth
University of Illinois Library, Urbana-Champaign. *Censorship and Intellectual Freedom, Germany, T.P. Sevensma*

Hans H. Wellisch
University of Maryland, College of Library and Information Services. *Classification*

Leonard Wertheimer (retired)
Toronto Public Library. *Multicultural Populations, Services to*

Paul Gabrielle Weston
Vatican Library, Rome. *Vatican Library*

Herbert S. White
Indiana University, Bloomington, IN, Graduate School of Library and Information Science. *Mortimer Taube*

Yoke-Lam Wicks
National Library of Singapore. *Singapore*

Wayne A. Wiegand
University of Wisconsin, Madison, School of Library and Information Studies. *United States*

D.E.K. Wijasuriya (retired)
National Library of Malaysia, Selangor. *Malaysia*

Billy R. Wilkinson (deceased)
Baltimore, MD. *Academic Libraries: Services to Users*

Howard W. Winger (retired)
University of Chicago, Illinois. *Leon Carnovsky*

Francis J. Witty
Catholic University of America, School of Library and Information Science. *Jean-Paul Bignon*

Jan Wolosz
Poland

Pat Woodrum
Tulsa City-County Library. *Allie Beth Martin*

William A. Wortman
Miami University Library, Oxford, OH. *Collection Management*

Margaret Wright
John Rylands University Library, Manchester, U.K. *A.W. Pollard*

H. Curtis Wright (retired)
Brigham Young University. *Assurbanipal, Callimachus*

Paul Xuereb
Malta

Abby Yochelson
Library of Congress, Washington. *National Bibliographies*

Arthur P. Young (retired)
University of Rhode Island Libraries, Kingston. *Ernest C. Richardson, Arthur Fremont Rider*

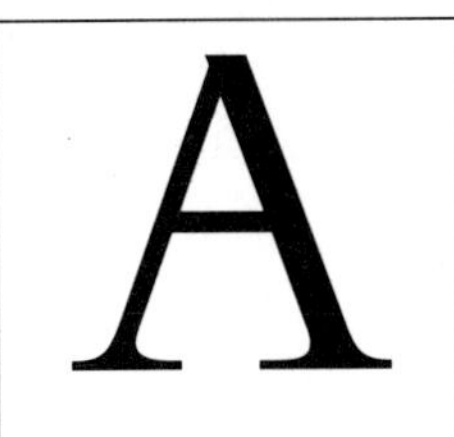

Aboyade, Beatrice O.

(1935–)

Beatrice Olabimpe Aboyade, Nigerian library pioneer, worked as a university librarian, taught Library Science at the University of Ibadan, and directed RUDIS, the Rural Development Information System, which focused the efforts of a major African library school on the information needs of rural people.

She was born August 24, 1935, in Ogun State, Nigeria, and attended a primary school in her home town, Porogun, Ijebu-Ode. She received her high school education at Queen's College, Lagos (1948–51), and Queen's School, Ede (1952–53). She went on to University College, Ibadan (1955–60), for a B.A. Honours degree in English, then earned the M.L.S. degree from the University of Michigan (1963–64), and finally returned to Ibadan, where the University College was now the University of Ibadan, for her Ph.D. in English (1967–70). She married Ojetunji Aboyade, a Professor of Economics, and they have four children.

Aboyade worked briefly at the Nigerian Broadcasting Corporation (now the Federal Radio Corporation of Nigeria) before she started her career as a librarian as an Assistant Librarian at the University of Ibadan Library (1962–63). Next she became the Chief Cataloguer at the University of Ife (now Obafemi Awolowo University) Library at Ibadan (1965–68). She moved back to the University of Ibadan Library as Head of Readers' Services (1968–72). In 1972 she joined the Department of Library Science as Lecturer, rose to the rank of Senior Lecturer, and in 1978 became Professor. She served as head of the Department of Library, Archival, and Information Studies.

In that post, Aboyade developed RUDIS, a pilot rural library service project, at Badeku, a predominantly Moslem agricultural village near Ibadan in Oyo State. Experience with the RUDIS project revealed that villagers could become quite interested in information on issues that affect their daily lives: where to obtain fertilizers, loans, and credit facilities for their farms or trading activities; health; ways of improving the quality of life in their village through such social amenities as electricity, pipe-borne water, and good access roads; how to find employment outside the village; where to get information on governmental activities; and how to become literate through adult education classes. The project revealed that the villagers needed mainly functional information.

The RUDIS project provided information to the nonliterate and semiliterate villagers using a wide variety of communications media: print media such as posters, books, newspapers, and pamphlets; audiovisual media such as filmstrips, slides, and audio and video cassettes; and live activities such as drama, oral narratives, songs, folktales, and group discussions. The project also revealed gaps and deficiencies in rural information transfer that can be improved through a rural library service by such means as reinforcing specific messages, repackaging information, acquiring and organizing specialized materials, filling an identified information vacuum, and coordinating all information transfer activities in rural areas.

Aboyade served in various other capacities, as a member of the Federal Government Commonwealth Scholarship Board (1968–71), and as a consultant to a variety of organizations associated with information work. She was a member of the Nigerian Association of University Women and a member of the Nigerian English Studies Association.

Her publications include *Nigerian Contribution to Humanistic Studies, 1948–1975,* a bibliographical survey (1978); *A Student Companion to the Library* (1979); *The Provision of Information for Rural Development* (1987); *Can the Humanities Survive?* (1988); and articles in local and international library journals.

OGO NANCY AMUCHEAZI

Abstracting and Indexing

INDEXING

The volume of mankind's intellectual output and the limitations of human memory have long necessitated a guidance system to the body of current and historic information that exists worldwide. Two sciences have evolved to provide access to this vast amount of data: *classification,* a hierarchical, often numerical system that groups items into broad disciplines and then into subdivisions of those disciplines, and *indexing,* a language-based system that describes the contents of a work, resulting in a list of subjects or topics referred to as an *index.* (Indexing can also mean the process of assigning a smaller number of topical headings to an entire item, which is more commonly referred to as subject cataloguing.)

Hans Wellisch gives a fine etymology of the word *index.* Basically, the term comes from the Latin verb *dicare,* meaning *to show,* and, when used with the prefix *in,* means a pointer from outside. In its broadest sense, an index can be a pointer to other than published material. Street signs and directories can be considered indexing systems as well. Dictionaries generally define indexes in the more specific sense, an alphabetic list of names, places, or subjects derived from a text with references to their location in it. The American National Standards Institute (ANSI) in the 1984 standard *Basic Criteria for Indexes* (under revision in the early 1990s) defines an index as

> a systematic guide to items contained in or concepts derived from a collection. These items or concepts are represented by entries arranged in a searchable order, such as alphabetical, chronological, or numerical. This order is normally different from that of the items or concepts within the collection itself.

History. Perhaps the earliest known systematized access to document collections was developed by the scholars of the Alexandrian Library, about 300 B.C., who customarily listed titles and occasionally wrote abstracts for the manuscripts in the collection. These were noted on "tags" that hung from the scrolls, so one could ascertain the contents without having to unroll the parchment.

The next major advance in the history of indexing was the concordance. Probably the most common concordances were those to various translations of the Bible that were reported to exist in the 7th and 8th centuries. Harold Borko and Charles L. Bernier note one prepared by a Cardinal, Hugo de Saint Caro, sometime before the year 1300. Concordances, however, merely indicate the use of words in a text (much like the "indexes" emanating from modern word-

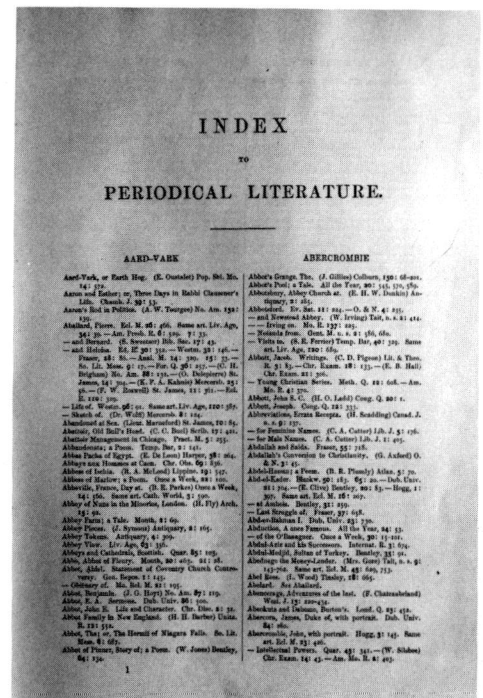
INDEX
TO
PERIODICAL LITERATURE.

AARD-VARK | ABERCROMBIE

1

The Boston Athenaeum

Poole's Index to Periodical Literature, *1882. Subject entries were created from keywords in titles of journal articles indexed.*

processing programs) rather than synthesizing the ideas or concepts in a text and grouping them together under a specific topic or term.

The development of printing from movable type in the mid-1400s made possible identical copies of books in large numbers, rather than unique handwritten copies, and therefore identical copies of indexes to those books as well. The first index that approaches the form and concept of an index as we know it today, as noted by Borko and Bernier, was an "Index of Alphabetical Table containing the principal matters in this history" in Speed's *History of Great Britaine* published in 1611. Speed's concept of alphabetizing brought indexes to the next stage of their development. Early Latin indexes had been arranged by grouping entries under a letter of the alphabet, but with no particular order within the letters.

The rise of universities in the 13th and 14th centuries fostered the need to locate and refer to written authorities, but such reference was basically to books or manuscripts. The 17th century saw the growth of journal literature, used to disseminate current information about the great strides being made in the sciences during this period. Scholars who desired to keep abreast of these advances needed a guide to this documentation, a need that continues to drive the current "Information Age."

Developments in information science during the 19th century, such as the codified subject cataloguing principles of Charles Ammi Cutter, and the classification system of Melvil Dewey, had an impact on the development of systematic subject indexing of documents. This century gave rise to truly professional indexing that spanned entire fields of knowledge and included the periodical literature as well as books.

During the 1800s, the growing need to locate journal literature reporting on legal precedence contributed to the development of a variant form of index known as the *citation index*. Such indexes are not subject oriented, although they may contain a non-bibliographic subject listing. They are, instead, lists of bibliographic items, usually arranged alphabetically by author, and followed by entries for later articles or documents that have cited the lead item. In this way research can be traced forward from first reporting to the most recent scholarship. *Shepard's Citations,* which began publication in 1873, was the first example. These indexes stand apart from the subject-oriented indexes covered here.

In 1876 the newly founded American Library Association at its first meeting took up a discussion of the need for periodical indexing. In 1882 *Poole's Index* appeared with subject entries created from keywords in the titles of the journal articles indexed. In 1896 the Cleveland Public Library began the *Cumulative Index to a Selected List of Periodicals* (later merged with *Readers' Guide*). In 1901 the H. W. Wilson Company began *Readers' Guide to Periodical Literature,* still in existence today. Indexing for periodical literature expanded in the 20th century as journal titles proliferated, while indexing for books, long the predominant format for published information, lagged.

As noted by Robert L. Collison, Lord Campbell "considered an index to be essential to every book, and proposed to bring a Bill into Parliament to 'deprive an author who published a book without an index of the privilege of copyright, and, moreover, to subject him for his offences to a pecuniary penalty'." This effort failed to materialize, and, as Cleveland has written, "until the 20th century . . . the presence of an index in a book was generally taken for granted, its absence generally ignored, its quality rarely the subject of comment by publishers or users."

Automation. The introduction of computers in the 1950s challenged the traditional methods of subject development and retrieval (covered below) and eventually gave rise to the addition of electronic formats for many heretofore printed indexes. *Readers' Guide,* still printed, can also be accessed by computer. Often referred to as *online databases* rather than electronic indexes, many exist only in the newer format.

Indexing reached a new plateau in the 1980s. Advances in computer technology enabled large indexing firms to develop proprietary database programs for use in indexing periodicals. At the same time, commercially available computer software became available designed to aid in indexing books.

H.W. Wilson Company

Indexer for Readers' Guide to Periodical Literature, *first published in 1901.*

These programs, which are regularly reviewed in the *ASI Newsletter,* differ dramatically from the "automatic indexing" touted by publishers of word-processing software. They alleviate the clerical aspects involved in book indexing, such as alphabetization, indentation, and other layout chores. Some specialists have experimented with natural language processing and true automatic indexing, but research in artificial intelligence has not yet progressed to the point where computers can supplant the intellectual process of indexing.

This intellectual process has been recognized in another way since the mid-1980s. Based on the Supreme Court case *Feist v. Rural* (1989), which, Mulvaney writes, "clearly discusses the importance of selection, arrangement, originality, creativity, and authorship in regard to copyright . . . it is my opinion that authored subject indexes satisfy the requirements . . . regarding copyright." In fact, book indexes have been submitted to, and awarded copyright by, the U.S. Copyright Office. The creative process of indexing thus recognized adds considerable weight to the long-standing argument for indexing as an art rather than a science.

The future holds continued challenges for book publishers and indexers. They will have to cope with designing indexes for electronically published "books on demand," most frequently textbooks, that will vary from copy to copy depending on the chapters included or excluded for a particular purchaser—a process somewhat akin to creating an index for a unique handwritten manuscript of the Middle Ages.

Process. The process of indexing involves just two basic actions: analyzing the material for its conceptual contents and translating those concepts into a particular set of index terms. This process of analysis and translation has also been referred to as understanding and expression, as selection and representation, and as almost any combination of these terms. The terminology developed during the translation process includes the terms used as headings and those used as cross references: *see* references that lead the user from the non-preferred entry term to the preferred term; and *see also* references that indicate additional terms related in meaning or narrower in scope that might be of interest to the user.

The development of this vocabulary is dependent on a number of factors, including the physical form of the document, the audience for whom it was written, the scope of the material, and, where appropriate, the method of storage and retrieval.

The physical form of the document—book or serial—has been demonstrated to be the most significant factor in the approach to indexing. A book is a self-contained volume of information, usually limited to a specific subject and written with a particular audience in mind. The index similarly will be self-contained, never changing once printed, will use the vocabulary of the author for subject terms (called *derivative indexing*), will be as specific as needed by the scope of the book, and generally will be created by one person.

Serial, or periodical, indexing, however, is an open-ended process and may involve either one journal over a period of years, a number of journal titles with similar subject content over a period of time, or a number of journal titles with a wide range of subject material. Each variable in this list requires a different approach to indexing. In addition, the ongoing nature of periodical indexing and the employment of more than one indexer, simultaneously or successively, requires the use of a controlled vocabulary to ensure consistency in subject terms. This use of a subject heading list or a thesaurus is called *indexing by assignment*. Exhaustivity of indexing—how many terms will be assigned to a specific article—is a further issue in periodical indexing.

Natural Language Systems. The two-step process of indexing has remained constant over the last century, but the need to improve the translation of concept into retrievable terminology, particularly in periodical indexing, has spawned a variety of types of index, many employing "natural language"—that is, the language contained in the document itself. In the 1950s Mortimer Taube devised the *Uniterm* system, in which a card is created for each term and each card contains a notation for every document employing this term. Taube believed that the user's selection and combination of terms, which he called "post-coordination," would yield the desired documents. Hans Peter Luhn of IBM created the *Keyword-in-Context* or KWIC system, in which a computer rotates the words of a title so each significant word appears in the alphabetic list generated. This system is similar to concordances, in that it uses adjacent words to convey meaning from text. The *Keyword Out-of-Context* or KWOC system is a variation in which the significant words in the title are displayed in an alphabetic column to the left of the remainder of the title. Other derivative indexing systems include *faceted* indexes, such as the bibliography published by the Modern Language Association, derived from the faceted classification system of S. R. Ranganathan of India, and the *Preserved Context Index System* (PRECIS) developed in England. Most have not gained wide acceptance. Periodical indexing today continues to rely on controlled, pre-coordinated terms contained in lists of subject headings such as *Library of Congress Subject Headings* (LCSH), *Medical Subject Headings* (MeSH), and *Sears List of Subject Headings,* or on controlled, post-coordinated terms contained in thesauri such as *The Art and Architecture Thesaurus* and the *CAB Thesaurus* of the Commonwealth Agriculture Bureaux.

Controlled Vocabulary. The benefit of a controlled vocabulary, whether pre- or post-coordinated, has been proven time and again, even with the development of computer technology. Research in the late 1980s and early 1990s points out that attempts to rely on keywords and Boolean searching is inefficient and frustrating. Boolean logic, like Taube's uniterms, combines words found in the title or text of a document. But this search strategy produces an unacceptable number of "false drops"—documents containing the right terms but not having the desired meaning—and fails to retrieve relevant documents that contain variant terms.

The growth of electronic technology and its use by bibliographic services has brought these controlled vocabularies into question, however. Because they deal with a more heterogeneous audience with computer access to multiple indexing systems, database searchers have begun demanding a more unified, if not uniform, terminology. Traditionally, the quality of periodical indexes and indexing systems has been measured by how well the subjects match the scope of the literature indexed and the audience for whom the index is provided. Over the course of time, the effort to design such terminology has resulted in a plethora of specialized and unique vocabularies. This proliferation is now considered a hindrance to searching and has become a challenge to subject development in periodical indexing, one that will not easily be resolved.

Controlled vocabularies exist in basically two forms: the subject heading list and the thesaurus. The National Information Standards Organization (NISO) *Standard for the Construction, Format, and Management of Monolingual Thesauri* (under revision in the early 1990s) defines a thesaurus as "the controlled vocabulary of an indexing language designed for postcoordination." It further states that the standard "is particularly concerned with means for establishing and displaying certain kinds of relationships between terms." These relationships—hierarchical (broader or narrower), associative (related), or equivalence (synonymous)—distinguish a thesaurus from a subject heading list. Subject lists, while they may use such designations as BT and NT, rather than the more traditional see and see also, are not necessarily constructed with scrupulous attention to semantic accuracy, but may include references to terms deemed useful to the searcher. A subject list, in other words, may contain a see also to terms that are not hierarchically or associatively related. A second difference between a subject heading list and a thesaurus is the construction of the terms or descriptors. A subject list used as a controlled vocabulary is usually a precoordinated list—that is, concepts can be joined together as a main heading and subheadings and displayed as a whole. A thesaurus is usually a postcoordinated vocabulary—that is, single concepts (though they may be expressed as phrases, such as nervous system) are linked together either at the indexing stage, by the indexer, or at the retrieval stage, by the user.

ABSTRACTING

In the decades since Soviet scientists launched Sputnik in 1957, the world has been faced with what has generally been known as the information explosion—vast amounts of scientific research and writing about that research. Borko and Bernier (1975) refer to a 1964 report that states that the biomedical press alone has been estimated to publish two million papers each year. Read at the rate of two per day, one reader would need 27.4 centuries to read the output of one year's research. Since the 1960s this annual output has grown exponentially, exacerbating the problem of keeping abreast. The availability of abstracts, while not solving the problem of volume, at least helps to reduce the amount of reading necessary to keep informed.

ANSI/NISO in its *Standard for Writing Abstracts* defines an abstract as "an abbreviated, accurate representation of the contents of a document, preferably prepared by its author(s) for publication with it." An abstract should state the "purpose, methodology, results, and conclusions presented in the original document" and additionally should note any specialized contents such as tables or charts. Although NISO recommends author-written abstracts, many abstracts have been written by experts in the discipline covered or by professional abstractors. Abstractors should be widely read and should have considerable thinking, writing, and editing skills.

Perhaps the two most important qualities of an abstract are clarity and brevity. Ashworth defines clarity as the ability of an abstract "to stand as a readable and complete item in its own right. . . ." Brevity, of course, is dependent on the length of the original document and is usually described as a percentage of the original rather than as so many sentences. Another factor governing the length of the abstract is the complexity of the information conveyed in the article. Complex ideas cannot always be distilled briefly and remain coherent. An abstractor should also consider physical accessibility in determining the length of an abstract. A foreign-language publication or material that would be difficult to obtain in full text might require a more expansive abstract, in order to make retrieval less necessary.

Abstracting, like indexing, dates back several thousand years. In early times often abstracts were oral, rather than written. In Greek plays of the 500s B.C. a Chorus recited brief summaries, often in verse, before the action began. Scribes in the Middle Ages gave oral abstracts of long ambassadorial missives to sometimes illiterate kings. The 17th century, which gave rise to scientific scholarship, also saw the beginnings of abstract journals such as *Le Journal des Scavans*. These journals were the beginnings of periodical literature as we know it today.

The intent of these abstract journals was, of course, to disseminate information about scientific research. This need for "current awareness" continues to be the leading purpose of abstracts. In addition, abstracts facilitate selection. Based on the information in the abstract, the user can choose which materials to read in full text form. This pre-selection function has become even more important in this computerized era, when abstract retrieval precedes full-text retrieval, saving computer usage costs. Abstracts written in the language of the retriever allow access to foreign-language materials, overcoming language barriers. Lastly, an accurate abstract, written prior to indexing, facilitates that process, cutting time needed for reading and concept selection and thereby cutting indexing costs.

The two-step indexing process of analysis and translation also applies to abstracting. Although conceptual analysis—skimming the text for concepts—remains the same, the concepts are translated into accurate and readable text rather than indexing terminology. This translation, while using the vocabulary contained in the text, is not merely an extraction of sentences but, in fact, a synthesis of information.

F. W. Lancaster describes three types of abstracts. The first and most prevalent is the *indicative* abstract, one that simply describes what is contained in the original. Next is the *informative* abstract, "which attempts to summarize the substance of the document, including the results." The third type, the *critical* abstract, adds an evaluation of "the quality of the work of the author and perhaps contrasts it with the work of others."

An abstract's quality can be judged on whether it notes major points of the document and whether it conveys these points accurately. Lancaster notes that "the ultimate test of a good abstract is simply 'does it allow a reader to predict accurately whether the item abstracted is relevant to his present interests or not?' "

ORGANIZATIONS
Several organizations are involved in the fields of indexing and abstracting. Two major library groups, the American Library Association and the Special Libraries Association, have general interest in the field. Other groups are more specifically involved. Foremost of these is the American Society of Indexers (ASI), which includes among its objectives improving the quality of indexing, acting as an advisory body on the qualifications and remuneration of indexers, and sponsoring seminars and workshops. The ASI publishes a *Register of Indexers,* listing freelance indexers and their subject specialties; a bimonthly newsletter; and occasional monographs on topics related to the field. It presents an award funded by the H. W. Wilson Company for the best index produced in the United States each year. It keeps its members informed on issues of copyright, contracts, and technological developments. The ASI is affiliated with the Society of Indexers in the United Kingdom, the Australian Society of Indexers, and the Indexing and Abstracting Society of Canada. Jointly they sponsor publication of *The Indexer.*

The National Federation of Abstracting and Information Services (NFAIS) and the American Society for Information Science (ASIS) also have interests in indexing. Members of NFAIS, an umbrella group, include major commercial indexing and abstracting services, online vendors, and related organizations. Its goals include facilitating communication among members, conducting research related to abstracting and indexing, and providing educational programs. ASIS seeks to improve the information transfer process through research, development, application, and education. Both organizations publish regularly and include directories and conference proceedings among their publications.

All five organizations mentioned are voting members of NISO, entrusted with setting standards for the information industry in the U.S. NISO is affiliated with the American National Standards Institute (ANSI) and formerly its Z39 committee, and through them with the International Standards Organization (ISO).

REFERENCES

W. Ashworth, "Abstracting as a Fine Art," *The Information Scientists* (1973). Harold Borko and Charles L. Bernier, *Abstracting Concepts and Methods* (1975).

Borko and Bernier, *Indexing Concepts and Methods* (1978).

Donald Cleveland and Ana D. Cleveland, *Introduction to Indexing and Abstracting,* 2nd edition (1990).

Robert L. Collison, *Indexes and Indexing* (1959).

F. W. Lancaster, *Indexing and Abstracting in Theory and Practice* (1991).

Nancy C. Mulvany, "Copyright for Indexes, Revisited," *ASI Newsletter* (1991).

Hans Wellisch, *Indexing from A to Z* (1991).

PATRICIA S. KUHR

Academic Libraries

PURPOSES, GOALS, AND OBJECTIVES
Academic libraries support the development of the colleges and universities of which they are a part. These libraries, integral parts of the institutions they serve, design their collections and services to meet the instructional and research programs of their parent institutions. The program of the academic library varies by type of institution; the library services offered in a doctoral-granting university will differ from the services developed to support the offerings of a two-year college. Other differences may evolve as a result of the distinctive research practices, pedagogy, and information needs of the disciplines and professions taught at the university. In some countries, particularly countries in Africa and Latin America, university libraries have a responsibility to serve as national libraries in addition to the role of service to the faculty and students of the institutions. Other academic libraries play a role in national scholarly developments when they acquire and organize world-class collections in particular subjects.

In the United States and Canada, libraries with more than a million volumes in institutions with a research orientation may choose to join the Association of Research Libraries (ARL), an organization established in 1932 to help these libraries develop in a sound fashion, supported by one another and by the availability of grants when possible. Other libraries and most academic librarians join the Association of College and Research Libraries (ACRL), a division of the American Library Association, for many of the same reasons—academic librarians find that belonging to professional organizations helps them strengthen the libraries for which they are responsible.

The basic assumption governing the growth and development of all academic libraries is that the library plays a significant role in the instructional and scholarly life of the college or university. This assumption is one that some seek to validate by demonstrating the value of the collections to the researchers on campus, while others focus on the benefits derived from the delivery of reference service to the campus community by liberally educated librarians who are involved in educational matters. In his 1966 report to the American Council on Education, Allan M. Carter wrote,

> The library is the heart of the university; no other single non-human factor is as closely related to the quality of graduate education. . . . But institutions strong in all areas invariably have major national research libraries.

Ernest Boyer, a leader in higher education in the U.S., made similar observations about the importance of quality collections in college libraries in his well-received report on undergraduate education in the country. He also recognized the value of a welcoming library with a staff that encouraged students to pursue independent reading.

The U.S. has about 2,800 institutions of higher education; about 200 are research universities granting doctoral degrees, about 800 are comprehensive universities offering some doctoral and master's degrees, 700 or so are four-year colleges offering bachelor's degrees, and the remaining 1,100 are two-year colleges, many called community or junior colleges, offering

University Library, Graz

Main reading room of the University Library, Graz, Austria, the second largest library in the country.

associate's degrees, often in technical subjects. There is great variety in the mix of institutions: a research university also offers undergraduate instruction and many colleges offer programs through the master's degree level. Two-thirds of all students are enrolled in publicly supported institutions, but more than half the colleges and universities in the U.S. are privately supported. In other countries the pattern of support for higher education is more centralized, and both access to higher education and the definitions of types of institutions and the degrees an institution can offer are tightly regulated by national agencies in charge of higher education.

Theodore F. Welch

Decorated with mosaics by Diego Rivera, the Universidad Nacional Autónoma de México, is one of the world's most striking library buildings.

Many universities began as colleges to train ministers or as professional schools of law, theology, or medicine, law being more often true in the U.S. and theology or medicine the genesis of some of the great universities of Europe. In Europe each faculty gathered its books to itself, and the pattern of many departmental libraries was established, with a university library emerging as the locus for collections and services of general interest. In the U.S. concerted efforts have been made to centralize collections and services with the argument that centralized services give the greatest access to the greatest number in the most cost-effective and efficient manner. Central libraries are supplemented by departmental libraries, and all libraries work to offer services that facilitate the use of recorded information in all formats. The records that permit access to the collections are designed to be complete, consistent, and in conformity with national bibliographic standards. The collections in academic libraries are designed to support the instructional and research needs of the students and faculty, with the level of support for research varying greatly, both as a goal and as an actuality, in various types of libraries. With the continued growth of knowledge and the rapid increase in the scholarly literature that results from such growth, no university library is now able to possess in its collections all of the recorded information that faculty members and students may need as they pursue their research; therefore, academic libraries have developed formal and informal arrangements for sharing resources.

The central goal of every academic library remains, however, to offer to the students and faculty of the institution collections of broad scope and depth and specialized assistance in the use of library resources. Any academic library must seek to attain the level of self-sufficiency that is essential to the health and vigor of the parent institution and its academic programs. The library will supplement this service by making available to its clientele the resources and collections of other libraries through various cooperative programs.

There are differences among types of academic libraries in terms of collections. Libraries in research universities build comprehensive and retrospective collections, while college libraries make available standard works representing the heritage of civilization and works that keep the faculty apprised of the latest advances in their fields, while seeking to discard out-of-date material on a regular basis. Two-year colleges may place greater emphasis on including nonprint resources such as film, filmstrips, and audio and video recordings, perhaps because the curriculum may feature training for work as technicians and require demonstrations of various techniques. When the two-year college offers the basic courses of a liberal arts curriculum, its library collection will be similar to that of a four-year college in this area. Libraries in two-year schools are often called learning resource centers, a name that both honors their use of a variety of media and recognizes the close ties between these institutions and the local school system. In many countries the system of higher education includes a group of two-year institutions, and often they are responsible for training teachers for the primary levels. Some offer terminal degrees; others develop curricula that permit students to transfer to the university level on satisfactory completion of a degree, especially if the degree program includes basic liberal arts courses.

Historical Background. Before 1900 American colleges resembled the secondary schools of Europe more than European universities; generally, the libraries in the colleges reflected the same—an uneven growth in collections and a limited service pattern, with collection growth dominated by a reliance on gifts and services contributed by a faculty member assigned to maintain the library as part of his full complement of duties. Many new colleges survived for only a few decades, but others, including the state-based land-grant colleges established with federal funds under the Morrill Acts, developed rapidly in the late 19th century. Specializations emerged, with land-grant colleges and universities concentrating on applied sciences, including engineering and agriculture, and state and private universities developing programs in the traditional academic disciplines. Colleges sought to educate future leaders of the society. At first, this focus meant an emphasis on the classics and theology; later it evolved into a curriculum that stressed appreciation for the best in both classic and modern scholarship and included some elective courses and the development of a major.

Library growth paralleled the growth of the parent institutions. Harvard College, which developed into one of the finest universities in the world, started its library with a collection of books variously estimated at from 260 to 370 volumes bequeathed to the college by John Harvard. It grew to 226,650 volumes in 1876, 901,000 in 1900, and many millions now. The collections of Harvard, like those of other major university and independent research libraries, are so rich that the purpose of the library includes extending the use of its collections to the broad community of scholars outside the institution.

The collections of the great American university libraries such as Harvard, Yale, and the universities of Illinois, Michigan, and California are prominent and impressive. In some cases, such as the Africana collection at Northwestern University, the collection may rival the collections of one or more national libraries. Also strong are the special collections of rare books and manuscript materials at some of the leading liberal arts colleges: Oberlin College is known for its anti-slavery collection; Amherst College has Robert Frost and Emily Dickinson collections; and Bowdoin College has Nathaniel Hawthorne and Henry Wadsworth Longfellow collections. Some of the collections relate to the original mission of the college, notably the Women's Studies collections at Smith and Wellesley colleges, the collections of Quaker materials at Haverford and Swarthmore colleges, and the Methodistica collection at Drew University.

In the late 19th century desires for improvements in academic librarianship came from several directions, and the leaders of the various reform movements often worked in concert. The emergence of library science as a discipline led to the establishment of goals relating to systematic collection development programs, organization of materials, and provision of reference service. The emergence of other disciplines with research agendas determined the collection development goals of university libraries and led to the rapid building of important collections in the new U.S. universities. The aspirations of students who wanted free access to the library's collections supported the development of service goals, and the needs of both faculty and students for materials to support their research helped integrate the library into the intellectual life of the institution.

Much of this impetus for improvement in U.S. librarianship was supported by private foundations, especially the Carnegie Corporation of New York. In 1928 it developed a program to encourage the integration of the library into the educational program of the liberal arts college, sponsored several studies of college libraries, and funded other studies to encourage improvement in library education. Among these studies was a survey of the American college library by William Randall, which described major inadequacies in the book collections of college libraries, as well as in their funding, staffing, and physical facilities. His study prompted the Carnegie Corporation to award 83 grants, for a total of $1,011,000, to college libraries for the improvement of their book collections. Most university libraries had stronger support from their university administration and faculty, and many university libraries experienced tremendous growth between 1890 and 1980, even allowing for declines during the Great Depression and the two World Wars. Collaboration between representatives of the leading libraries and the key foundations was then and is now a preferred method for developing and testing agendas for improvements in service. If the demonstrations are successful, the leaders in the field, those who ran the demonstration sites, promote the new concepts to the

Central Library, Chulalongkorn University

Central Library of Chulalongkorn University, Thailand.

profession, the concepts become accepted practice in many libraries, and they are incorporated into basic documents. Standards are a case in point.

Standards. Randall and the librarians advising the Carnegie Corporation sought but did not find either reliable standards for college libraries or definite and comprehensive statistics, so they prepared their own sets of standards. These efforts led to further work on library standards. The *Standards for College Libraries* were first published by the American Library Association (ALA) in 1959 and were reviewed and revised in 1975 and 1986. *Standards for Junior College Libraries* were published by ALA in 1960; they were reviewed, revised, and published as *Guidelines for Two-Year College Learning Resources Programs* in 1972 and as *Standards for Community, Junior, and Technical Colleges Learning Resources Programs* in 1990. *Standards for University Libraries*, prepared jointly by the Association of College and Research Libraries (ACRL, a division of ALA) and the Association of Research Libraries (ARL), were published in 1978; a revised document, *Standards for University Libraries: Evaluation of Performance,* was approved by ACRL in 1989. Each of these standards addresses the essential questions of the adequacy of library collections, services, staff, physical facilities, finance, and governance, placed in the context of the educational program and objectives of the individual institution the library serves. Each also addresses the question of evaluation, although the approaches differ, as will be seen in a later section of this article.

The development and application of standards for academic libraries in the U.S. has become a major activity of the ALA and other organizations. Adoption of the standards and voluntary use of them in evaluating American academic libraries have led to significant improvement in the quality of collections and services in many academic libraries. Colleges measure themselves against the standards, set goals for improvement, and then seek funds to accomplish the goal. Other standards, also voluntary, are the standards of accreditation for the parent institution developed and promulgated by regional accrediting agencies. Adherence to these standards and acceptance of a college as an accredited institution brings status to the college. Accreditation standards tend to be widely accepted and serve as a carrot-and-stick method of making improvements in institutions with limited resources.

Standards developed for the U.S. have influenced the library standards developed internationally by Unesco. The International Federation of Library Associations and Institutions (IFLA) Section for University Libraries and other General Research Libraries issued *Standards for University Libraries* in 1985. In Japan and some countries of Europe, standards have been developed and adopted by ministries of education; application of the standards may be a requirement for academic institutions, not voluntary, as in the U.S., and may be included in national legislation concerning academic institutions.

Academic librarians have sought even better and more objective methods of measurement and evaluation of library services than the expert opinion reflected in the standards. Much of the early work emphasized size of collections, staff, and budget as indicators of quality. More recently, sophisticated techniques have been applied to academic libraries to assist librarians and others in the assessment of the quality of library programs.

Support and Governance. Institutions of higher education in the U.S. are usually grouped according to whether they are funded by private or public monies; about half the colleges are funded privately, many with the original source of funding a particular religious group. Many continue as denominational colleges; others are now secular but still private, receiving funds from tuition and endowment earnings. In the U.S. the constitutional requirement for the separation of church and state has prohibited the use of public funds for direct support of private colleges and universities. Indirect support is available through federal and, sometimes, state programs supporting faculty research, student financial aid and scholarships, and low-cost loans for the construction of facilities. Most funding for public institutions comes from the states, not the federal government, and some states place more emphasis on the need for strong systems of higher education than others. There is a high degree of autonomy at the local level in U.S. higher education, and federal and state agencies for higher education have the greatest influence on the issues of program definition and articulation prior to the establishment of a new degree program, definitions of appropriate staffing levels, and formulas for funding.

The structure and governance of the library is based on the legal status and governance pattern of the parent institution. Colleges and universities have charters and bylaws that define the rights and responsibilities of the trustees, officers, faculty, and staff in a manner deemed acceptable and legally binding by both the institution and the state or nation. Governance flows both from the organization's structure and its history; written documents state the general practices with regard to decision making. National control of an institution may bring with it a formalized and hierarchical system of decision making, as may state control of publicly funded universities. Size, local custom, the preferences of leading administrators, and the issue of the moment itself may all influence the pattern of decision making with respect to a given topic. In any case there are established channels for authorizing programs, disbursing funds, and, perhaps, offering faculty and staff advice on academic policy issues, particularly the curriculum and, usually, the design of library service. For example, most academic libraries have faculty library committees designed to advise the director of libraries on matters pertaining to the budget and the collection.

In the U.S. librarians at all levels of responsibility in the organization have sought greater participation in the library's internal decision-making process, and organizational structures have modified accordingly. In the aftermath of the velvet revolution in the countries of eastern Europe and the former Soviet Union, many libraries, like other agencies in those societies, are experiencing a transition from leadership authority based on political realities to leadership centered in professional competence and management ability. Some libraries include representation from the library staff in the regular administrative staff meetings. Others have tried to eliminate administrative staff meetings and replace them with collegially based groups. Variations in these governance arrangements result as much from personalities and individual styles as from campus tradition. Librarians on a given campus may study several models before adopting one for their use and then, over time, modify the model selected. The literature of academic librarianship reflects this diversity in the debate over whether academic librarians are or should be considered faculty—a debate that continues despite the existence of an official ACRL policy favoring full faculty status.

A fundamental issue in the internal governance of academic libraries is the need to establish consensus about which issues are appropriately decided by the administration, which are decided in the forum of the whole (that is, the entire staff of librarians), and which are appropriately resolved in organizational units, such as reference, collection development, public services, or technical services.

Facilities and Growth. Nancy McAdams reported that 445 academic library buildings were constructed in the U.S. in the years 1967–71, another 202 in 1972–76, 143 in 1977–81, and 133 in 1982–86. Funds authorized under the federal Higher Education Facilities Act went into some of the early building projects, but the bulk of funding came from state appropriations and private sources, especially foundations and donors willing to support a particular institution.

The academic library buildings constructed in North America after World War II show a marked change in architectural style from earlier buildings. Modular planning was accepted, and a shift occurred from fixed-function buildings to buildings with functional flexibility—that is, without load-bearing interior walls, with open-stack shelving, and with comfortable furniture near the collection itself.

Growth in size of collection, staff, and budget require new and additional library space. The predictions of Fremont Rider and others that an academic library's collection would double every 15 years have

University of Washington Libraries, Seattle

Library of the University of Washington, Seattle, in 1896—6,780 titles in the attic of the school's only building.

been fairly accurate for North American libraries, and many now seek to build new libraries with enough space for a 20-year growth in collections. Realistically, most libraries will face several years of severe overcrowding before a new facility is funded. Given the ever-present need for judicious use of scarce financial resources and the need not to be overtaken by the dynamics of the world's publishing explosion, academic librarians are seeking reliable electronic storage options for materials and cooperative programs for collection development. These approaches will reduce but not eliminate the need for new buildings; academic library buildings put up in the coming decades may have different configurations and emphasize only selected functions. Harvard and the University of California system have built library storage facilities to house little-used materials; these facilities are designed for minimal access, maximum use of compact shelving, and predictable patterns of non-use. Other facilities are being built to house rare materials with special security and temperature controls. Some libraries, built to serve branch campuses with a majority of undergraduates, are designed to support extensive use of electronic access devices and a collection of printed materials that is of a fixed and limited size.

The economic recession of the late 1980s forced many U.S. librarians to reduce staffing levels and the rate of current acquisitions; other economic and political realities caused declines in the purchasing abilities of academic libraries in Africa, eastern Europe, and the former Soviet Union. Many see the reductions not as temporary downturns but as permanent changes that will alter expectations about future growth rates of collections and increase demand for electronic access mechanisms and cooperation among libraries.

Library cooperation takes several forms. One major program emphasizes bibliographic access, the development of standards of bibliographic control, and the automation of bibliographic records. Efforts in these areas have resulted in the creation of a bibliographic network with more than 20 million records and options for electronic transmission of interlibrary loan requests. Another method of cooperation features establishing shared responsibility for collection development in one or more subject areas among a few universities, either complete with budgets and governance protocols or less formally managed. A third approach is represented by the program of the Center for Research Libraries, a research library of little-used material in selected subject areas, supported by the membership fees of other research libraries. When library cooperation includes provision for equitable sharing of burdens and provides patrons with the materials they need in a timely fashion, access as a goal is accepted by both libraries and patrons and becomes, for some libraries, an important component in designing future patterns of service. Private foundations have been instrumental in helping libraries develop these access mechanisms, notably the Council on Library Resources, the W. K. Kellogg Foundation, and the Andrew W. Mellon Foundation.

Specific services and aspects of collection development are described in sections that follow. Also included are detailed descriptions of the administration and financing of academic libraries, the measurement and evaluation of these libraries, cooperation among academic and research libraries, and the laws and regulations pertaining to academic libraries in the U.S.

REFERENCES

Ernest Boyer, *College, the Undergraduate Experience in America* (1987).

Caroline M. Coughlin and Alice Gertzog, *Lyle's Administration of the College Library* (1992).

Beverly Lynch, editor, *Academic Library in Transition: Planning for the 1990s* (1989).

Louis Shores, *Origins of the American College Library, 1638–1800* (1935).

Allen B. Veanor, *1985–1995: The Next Decade in Academic Librarianship* (1985).

CAROLINE M. COUGHLIN;
BEVERLY P. LYNCH

SERVICES FOR USERS

The primary functions of academic libraries are to fulfill both the needs of the instructional programs of their parent institutions and the research needs of students, faculty, other staff members, and people outside the academic community. The public services designed by academic librarians to serve their clienteles have developed over many years, based on technical services that provide for an organized collection. After first gathering a reference collection exclusively for the on-site use of officers and faculty of the academic institution, the library next allowed use by undergraduate students.

Services have continued to develop into the myriad of activities now found in most academic libraries. In addition to the original sole service—circulation of materials, including interlibrary loan—the other major services are reference/information services, including general and specialized user assistance; bibliographic instruction; and provision of space and facilities. Delivery of services to users has developed to include not only those services provided in the library building, but also those available to remote users accessing information sources through automated network channels and document delivery options.

Circulation Services. The decision to lend books to undergraduates was really a major philosophical shift from conservator to purveyor; American academic librarians have loaned countless volumes to users and have devised record systems to control the daily flow. Manual systems of ledgers and card files formed the first circulation records. By the mid-1970s automated systems were in use in various types and sizes of libraries. Larger, integrated computer systems (with circulation as one module) were installed in the 1980s academic libraries, predominantly in large and medium-sized ones. These systems facilitate the labor-intensive record-keeping required to keep track of the whereabouts of borrowed materials, as well as the production of associated notices to users to recall items requested by others, to remind borrowers of overdue loans, and to alert people to the availability of specific titles requested that were previously on loan or being acquired for the collection. Dependency on the efficiencies of automated record-keeping and user notification has raised expectations for speed and accuracy in making library materials available when and where needed, while also creating impatience and disappointment at the service desk when the occasional malfunction occurs. Many libraries still rely on manual systems and, depending on the rate of circulation or the availability of workers, find the system cost-effective or at least satisfactory, given the large initial investment needed for automated library systems.

Academic libraries have also extended borrowing privileges to unaffiliated persons. The most formal, if not the earliest, method of serving the unaffiliated is through interlibrary loan, as guided by the American Library Association's *National Interlibrary Loan Code*. Building on the medieval European idea of the community of scholars in which each member felt the responsibility to make his own or others' works available to a serious fellow scholar, American librarians in 1917 first formally codified the process of lending unusual volumes not available in the requesting library. This interlibrary loan system, as it was designed and has developed, did place restrictions on the kinds of materials lent to other libraries; for example, manuscripts, rare books, current issues of magazines and newspapers, and low-cost in-print volumes were excluded. The system once excluded interlibrary lending to undergraduate students, reserving this particular service for faculty members and graduate students.

Perhaps learning from their users, who have developed their own informal means of access to the holdings of libraries with which they are not affiliated, contemporary academic libraries have designed simple but effective reciprocal borrowing plans. These plans include a range of examples such as parochial agreements among a small number of nearby libraries to lend directly to students and faculty from their institutions on presentation of proper identification; state and regional consortium commitments of similar direct borrowing privileges; free photocopy services or otherwise expedited document delivery services among the group's participants; and the nationwide reciprocal library borrowing agreement for faculty members from universities participating in programs sponsored by OCLC and the Association of Research

Libraries (ARL). The development of automated online bibliographic systems, begun by OCLC in the 1970s, led to an even greater and more extensive direct sharing of resources, no longer limited by geographic proximity to the user's home library. While these forms of reciprocal borrowing are increasing at a rapid rate in most North American academic libraries, the programs still account for a small percentage of each library's total circulation.

No matter how rapid, sophisticated, and universal circulation services in academic libraries become in the future, these services rest on a manual system—the exact shelving of thousands or millions of individual books and other library materials. The training and supervision of shelving staff and the maintenance of an accurate and continuous shelf-reading program will always play a large and essential part in this most basic service. Collection maintenance responsibilities may expand as libraries increasingly use compact shelving and remote storage facilities; users' retrieval patterns will need articulation. A new form of stack maintenance will emerge as more materials appear in electronic formats that require periodic tape restoration and screening for possible user-introduced computer viruses or erasures. Information packages that come in multiple formats, such as a CD-ROM with both disc and printed guide, will require multiple storage formats and locations for the various components.

Reference/Information Services. A public librarian, Samuel Green of the Worcester Free Library, made the first formal proposal in the U.S. for a program of assistance to readers, but Melvil Dewey, then the Librarian at Columbia University, actually appointed the first full-time reference librarians, George Baker and William G. Baker, in 1884, as members of the reference department. It is clear that the "reference department" meant organized personal assistance—in answer to a questionnaire in 1885, Columbia responded that two reference librarians were on the staff specially to aid inquirers.

Louis Kaplan for the period 1876–93 and Samuel Rothstein for 1850–1950 recorded the growth and development of reference services in academic libraries. Rothstein is particularly thorough, describing the practices as well as the policies and theories of service. After presenting the conservative (minimal assistance or guidance only), the moderate, and the liberal (full information service) theories of reference service and the continuing professional debate over them, Rothstein concludes that assistance on the scale of the librarian as a collaborator in the research process was not common through 1940. The chief problem was the heterogeneous nature of the demands placed on the library, making it hard to differentiate between services for scholars and services for the more numerous general users. In larger libraries, with thousands of general readers, the great service load often resulted in limited capacity for offering more than minimal aid.

Three trends dominate the development of reference service in North American academic libraries after about 1970. These are the expansion of automation, the development of library and bibliographic instruction, and the extension of service to diverse users.

Automation. Since the early 1970s reference service has been altered most drastically by the introduction of automated resources. The first wave of change

T. Charles Erickson, Yale University, Office of Public Information

Circulation desk at Sterling Memorial Library, Yale University.

came with online databases, typically offered to users through fee-based bibliographic search services, with the searches mediated by librarians. Commercial vendors of online services introduced billing systems dependent on the amount of online use and the number of records retrieved or printed, making library costs for online services impossible to predict and library budgets almost impossible to manage. Some librarians wanted to offer the service, but could not see their way clear to funding it. Discussions on the topic, known as the "fee or free" controversy, included much debate about the philosophical and economic issues of charging users for services offering access to information. The controversy subsided in the late 1980s, in part because the economically depressed campus climate made recovery of cost from departmental users difficult, in part because the increasing costs of publications in print format made electronic access more cost-effective, and in part because the technology changed, offering more options, some for every library budget. In the mid-1980s reference tools in optical disk formats, such as CD-ROM and laser discs, were typically offered to users at no cost and with the expectation that users would perform the searches themselves. Fixed costs, without variable rates for telecommunications connections, database access time, or royalties for retrieved records, presented these new reference tools as resources within

Reference stacks, Main Library of Sultan Qaboos University, Oman's largest library.

the budget and planning parameters of many academic libraries.

New resources led to new demands for service, including higher demands for reference assistance (estimated to be at least a 35 percent increase in some libraries), more requests for library instruction, and requests for adaptations of space and equipment to accommodate the new technology. The next stage of development is occurring in those libraries able to provide users with bibliographical data, and occasionally full-text documents, through online catalogue terminals and personal computers, sometimes called scholars' workstations, linked to both campus and worldwide electronic networks. The amount of information available on these networks is increasing rapidly, presenting new challenges to reference librarians in academic libraries, who will need to design new approaches for local library service and remote access.

Instruction. Academic library service has for many years included instructional support of the curriculum. At present there is heightened interest in training users to search electronic databases effectively and to develop ways to address future information retrieval needs. On some U.S. campuses courses on library use or information literacy are offered for college credit, but most academic librarians teach skills during guest appearances in courses, through library guides and publications, or occasionally through developed video, slide, or online tutorials. Library instruction has shifted from being an introduction to the library and its facilities to emphasizing the development of competencies needed to function successfully in an information-rich society. The importance of such knowledge as part of a university education is coming to be recognized by accrediting agencies as they promulgate criteria for colleges to consider when developing institutional goals and programs.

Extension. Library reference services are tailored to diverse users at many academic libraries, though the practice is not always explicitly stated. Most academic reference staff give more attention to administrators and faculty researchers on their campuses, often providing in-depth information delivery service. Graduate students and faculty typically receive consultation on strategies to search for relevant information in their areas of research. Undergraduate students are encouraged to learn research strategies for retrieving information in the future, but some liberal arts college libraries encourage research strategy consultations as a matter of course to support curricula that stress independent research at the undergraduate level. Reference librarians in larger academic libraries may manage specialized information services beyond their primary clientele—business people, workers in government agencies, or high-school students. Given demographic projections, academic reference librarians in the U.S. expect to serve more older students, a more culturally diverse student body, students with physical challenges, and students for whom English is a second language.

One-on-one, in-person reference assistance; compilation of bibliographies; supervision of professional and nonprofessional staff members; telephone information services; care of periodicals, government publications, or curriculum materials; interlibrary borrowing or lending; and design of help screens for a new integrated library system are among the responsibilities of the reference staff.

The profession has strongly believed it was wrong to define reference work as only what goes on in a reference room. Although questions of specialization versus nonspecialization of staff and of centralization or decentralization have concerned academic librarianship, and there have been some descriptions of library service that provide reference/information services to supplement those offered in the local unit, the profession still lacks a strong knowledge base about the various kinds of library users, their information needs, and the uses to which information is put. Often the study of these questions is linked to the analysis of the research or publications practices of the members of one discipline, and the study results inform collection development practices and reference service, but do not transform them.

Space and Facilities for Users. The provision of an environment in which the use of library materials for instruction and research can flourish has traditionally been a major goal for academic librarians. In the 1960s and 1970s successfully designed academic library buildings could be found on each continent, and many major academic libraries moved to new quarters. Some institutions provided separate buildings to house undergraduate library collections, following the lead of Harvard, which opened its Lamont Library for undergraduates in 1947. Other campuses focused on the needs of their particular clientele and developed branch libraries for the sciences or the arts, or to house rare books or special collections. Since the founding of Johns Hopkins University in the 1870s, American universities have always looked to the German model of scholarship with respect to graduate study, and the German model of seminar (or discipline-specific) libraries is no exception. This model is less successful when the area of study is interdisciplinary or when budget realities intrude on the desire to have items important in more than one discipline duplicated in several seminar libraries. Progress in the electronic transmission of text and bibliographic information may cause this perennial issue to be less evident, or even to become less important. As with many issues, local conditions, as well as local politics, provide the appropriate answers.

The worth of an academic library in support of higher education has been measured since at least the 1960s in terms of the size of its collection. This emphasis on possession of physical items has resulted in the creation of some of the world's greatest collections of knowledge, housed in close proximity to scholars and students of one institution. However, problems of lack of space to house these growing collections have also emerged. Many librarians struggle with the dilemma of whether they can best serve their academic communities by maintaining collections in overcrowded stack areas at the price of reduced seating, but with relative convenience for browsing, or by preserving research seating and storing collections at remote sites. Some academic libraries have rented or cooperatively established storage facilities that require timely retrieval and delivery services to accommodate user needs; some operate them with provision for selected readers to browse in these facilities. Several have introduced compact shelving to house both less frequently used materials and the general circulating collections; these movable shelving ranges eliminate aisles, reducing the number of simultaneous browsers, a situation which at some libraries has resulted in new restrictions on patron use patterns.

Other alternatives to acquiring information in print format have been utilized both to preserve materials and to save space. Technologies such as microformats, optical storage disks, and electronic tapes may address some of these goals, but present other challenges, including adequate facilities to access their content. Microfilm and microfiche readers and printers are standard equipment in most academic libraries; librarians are familiar with the service issues of machine maintenance, user education, and special space allocation, as well as the benefits of having materials available in these formats at reasonable costs. Each new technology brings similar issues to the fore. The number of computer workstations with modems for access to remote files or with compact disc readers for using CD-ROMs has increased rapidly since the mid-1980s. Many academic libraries have extended their study and research facilities by adding personal computer work stations, many linked to networks for far-reaching communications, and at times offering files of licensed software packages for individual use, especially software useful to students writing papers. From such workstations, as well as similar ones located in homes, campus offices, and dormitories, library users are able to discover library holdings, learn whether desired items are available, request that the items be held for them, request purchases or interlibrary loans for items not held, and search the catalogues of other libraries and various electronic databases in nearly all fields of knowledge.

The Future. Academic library service will continue the traditions of assisting users to identify and locate needed information, of instructing them in how to retrieve and evaluate information, and of ensuring the availability of materials from both local and remote sources. The growth of electronic sources of information will probably continue to have the greatest impact on expanding the variety of services within these basic traditions. Automation has proven to be evolutionary—improving some library services and creating some previously unimagined ones, but seldom completely replacing established ones.

By the year 2000 the multiplicity of sources of information and of various techniques to use them are likely to be even greater than they were in 1990. Perhaps progress will be made in the area of standard-

George Don

Public Terminal Room, part of the student computer facilities in the Margaret Clapp Library at Wellesley College, Massachusetts.

ization of retrieval languages, a constant concern of librarians and other users of these systems; more likely many competitive and creative producers will bring a variety of new and unique products to market, paying limited attention to the issue of compatibility with existing systems. The result will be a vast array of resources in a variety of print and electronic formats, requiring different equipment and, often, different software protocols for use. Recognition of the problem is emerging and attention is being paid to identifying, organizing, and distributing these resources. Library online catalogues and new menus on electronic networks are slowly expanding to organize paths for interested users to locate resources in various formats, but agreements and standards are lacking in many key areas.

Library staff will be challenged to motivate users to consider the array of information resources in terms of their needs, to help them navigate through appropriate directories and indexes to locate those of potential interest, to show them how to use unfamiliar resources, and finally to assist them to assimilate their findings into their own personal information systems. The future service librarian will need skills to search electronic and print information sources effectively, understanding of the organization of knowledge in general and of specific subject resources, and the ability to interview and interact with users in person and through remote channels.

Assistance to users in academic libraries may more clearly differentiate among levels of reference services than is typically seen today. Services will need to be personalized while working with sources that may seem more impersonal. Some libraries already offer several service sites from which users can seek various kinds of help. For example, some assistance desks, many staffed by student employees or support staff, offer quick ready reference help with simple problems, such as finding directory information or locating resources in the library. Others may provide more in-depth consultation in a given subject area, such as humanities, social sciences, or sciences; in using particular formats, such as automated reference tools, microforms, or nonprint materials; or in discov-

Foto Estudio Callado

Reading room in the library of the Universidad Católica Madre y Maestra in Santiago, Dominican Republic.

ering unique collections, such as government documents or manuscripts. New services are emerging to meet the needs of users overwhelmed by the explosion of information and of the variety of sources in which it can be obtained. Some librarians have experimented with a partnership model to deliver information to researchers; others have developed programs to merge retrieved information into specially constructed files and then tailored their programs to the needs of individual researchers. Even the approaches to library staff are changing: users now seek assistance not only in person, by phone, and by mail, but also through electronic mail, telefacsimile (fax) requests, televised conferences, and prearranged appointments.

The emphasis in library instruction is shifting from orientation to a particular library to developing information-seeking strategies for lifelong learning. The challenges are twofold at least. Graduates of such programs should not only have a reasonable expectation of what libraries offer and how to use their materials and services, but also be competent in understanding how knowledge is organized, how to seek it, how to evaluate it, and how to use it. In the coming years there will be greater interaction among academic librarians, teaching faculty, and students as new information literacy curricula are designed and as all three groups seek to take full advantage of the emerging technologies and the research about them to understand, evaluate, and improve the information-seeking process. In countries where independent inquiry has not been the common practice, there will be greater interest in such an approach as it supports the goals of technological advancement and democracy. The common goals will be the creation of a literate adult population equipped to utilize information throughout their lifetimes.

Before the age of microcomputers, document delivery services consisted of maintenance and service support of circulation and browsing of collections in a library; interlibrary loan borrowing (and lending) for items not locally owned; and, on occasion, purchase of tailor-made bibliographies (the product of online searches) or photocopies of specific articles from other libraries or commercial sources. The future will witness a dramatic increase in the delivery of textual information by microcomputers. For example, fax transmissions, either from other libraries as interlibrary loans or from local collections, can be sent to remote locations. Reference questions and responses to them can be transmitted through electronic mail systems. Data from machine-readable databases, not just bibliographic ones, can be downloaded. There will be a dramatic increase in provision of specific information as opposed to provision of sources in which that information can be found. This development will be facilitated by improved digital data storage. It will be more cost-effective for libraries to purchase large databases in digital formats for local use than to have access to information on remote computer systems. Library budgets will need to accommodate the increasing crossover between what are traditionally called *materials* and *services*. Information needs that were once satisfied by buying a book may be better satisfied by providing a terminal with access to a database. Already, online versions of major periodical indexes are competing successfully with their printed counterparts. Both the criteria by which a library is judged to be excellent and the budget categories used in the library must be flexible enough to accommodate alternative systems for information access and retrieval. Budgets for major capital expenditures (such as the significant costs of wiring a campus so all its microcomputers can be networked together) will be required; finding these large sums is a challenge that libraries will need to meet in concert with, not in competition with, academic computer centers and networks as they share in the technological revolution.

These changes in service are being accompanied by shifts in management attitudes among service staff in academic libraries. A nonprofit entrepreneurial attitude to managing academic library services is emerging, whereby the library user is seen as a central client of a marketed service; the impressions and satisfactions of users are among measures of success; and the effectiveness of an operation is viewed in terms of cost-efficiencies of personnel and resources used to run it. At the Library of the Technological University of Budapest this shift has led to mounting mini-trade shows of the output of U.S. publishers specializing in management; at several large state universities in the U.S., it has meant the development of fee-based specialized services to local industries. Customer-centered goal-setting augments traditional emphases on collection growth and preservation. Advisory groups composed of various stakeholders in the library's future, such as students and special interest groups, as well as faculty, are being formed on campuses to advise library and university administrations, as well as to play an advocacy role in campus political arenas. Feedback from users, both informally and systematically obtained, is valued and incorporated in service evaluations and development. Notwithstanding the philosophical implications of the decision for the concept for the free delivery of information, limited financial resources at a time of increased opportunities for providing specialized information services have led some academic libraries to charge for some services as an alternative to denying users any chance of having them. These decisions are made reluctantly, and after examination of the relationship of the fee to the value of the additional information being made available through repackaging or the addition of supplemental material. The managerial skills required to be an effective nonprofit entrepreneur are creating new specializations in the service segment of the academic library, placing greater reliance on cost recovery, accountability, quality control, and meeting customer expectations.

Because of these changes, and the changes made possible with the increased availability of microcomputers to process and deliver information, it may be possible in the 21st century to move beyond traditional definitions of reference work to a new configuration of service. The early writers always discussed services *to* patrons or *to* faculty and students. *Reference work* became *reference service* and then *reference/information service*. Later, the literature shows concern about services *for* readers or *for* users. It is not too much to read into this language a change in attitude from paternalism to service. We may hope that library services will be characterized by one preposition as we reach the 21st century. It should be librarians *with* students and faculty—librarians really in touch and truly working *with* users.

REFERENCES

Patricia Senn Breivik and E. Gordon Gee, *Information Literacy: Revolution in the Library* (1989).

Mary W. George, "Instructional Services," in *Academic Libraries: Research Perspectives*, edited by Mary Jo Lynch and Arthur P. Young (1990).

Louis Kaplan, *The Growth of Reference Service in the United States from 1876 to 1893* (1952).

Samuel Rothstein, *The Development of Reference Services* (1955).

DANUTA NITECKI;
BILLY R. WILKINSON

COLLECTIONS

"The powerful and steady growth of book collections in individual American university libraries, particularly during the mid-twentieth century, has been a major achievement in American cultural and educational history, it has both matched and fostered the ebullient and questing intellectual life of the universities themselves, and it has been a marvel to many foreign observers."

These words of Robert Vosper are no less valid today than when they were written in 1971, even if some of the ebullience has been tempered by changes in the U.S. economy that led to reduced budgets for many academic institutions in the 1990s. After a spectacular spurt in the number of new colleges in the U.S. between the end of World War II and the mid-1960s, that growth came to an end, and developments in the 1990s dealt more with retrenchment than growth. Greater attention is being paid to linkages between and among institutions, including international exchanges for faculty, students, and curriculum development. The basic infrastructure of higher education in North America includes steady support for libraries; the steadiness of this support over time has permitted the establishment of some great collections, as well as many good collections. These collections will not disappear in difficult times, but the growth rate will not pertain. The average two-year national increase in state funding in 1991 was only 3 percent,

University Library of Uppsala

First reading room, University Library of Uppsala, Sweden.

the lowest in the 33 years that data has been collected and down from the highs of the mid-1980s, when two-year increases ranged between 13 and 19 percent. Various studies of quality in higher education have been made over the years, and they have all shown a high correlation between the highest ranking for graduate programs in the humanities and the presence of a large library collection on the campus. Scholars need good libraries, and good libraries attract, and help to retain, good scholars.

Collection Growth. The academic library collections of North America are the largest and richest the world has ever known. U.S. academic libraries spent more than $890 million on library materials in 1987–88 and their total operating expenditures in that year were more than $2.7 billion. Some other statistics are also revealing: the total holdings in U.S. academic libraries at the end of 1987–88 were 365,452,000 books and bound serial volumes and more than 6.4 million periodical subscriptions; at the end of the academic year 1989–90 the 107 U.S. and Canadian academic members of the ARL possessed 355,700,000 volumes. When this number is compared to estimates of total world book production by the same date (70 to 80 million volumes—no accurate figures exist), the unparalleled strength and scale of North American academic library research resources becomes evident. Similar collections exist in the great universities of Europe, although amassed over several centuries, and not as the result of the rapid building of institutions and collections, as has been the pattern in North America. Until recently U.S. libraries were known for building collections by mass purchases, while European methods stressed selection of individual items.

The growth of academic library collections has paralleled the development of graduate programs and professionalism as major developments in American universities. These two trends have had an enormous impact on higher education, scholarship, and the evolution of knowledge as an industry in the U.S. In 1876—one hundred years after the nation's founding—collections were still very small. Yale, which now has more than 8 million volumes, then had 114,000; the University of Illinois at Urbana-Champaign and the University of California at Berkeley, each now possessing more than 6.5 million volumes, then held 10,600 and 12,000 respectively, while the University of Michigan, now holding more than 5.5 million, possessed 27,500.

By the third decade of the 20th century, graduate programs had begun to transform higher education, many colleges were becoming universities, new universities—such as Chicago, Stanford, Duke, and Texas—had been founded, and pressures to expand inadequate academic library collections began in earnest. By the beginning of World War II, academic library holdings, especially in universities, had increased manyfold; after the war universities resumed and indeed accelerated the growth of their collections and colleges found the resources to strengthen their holdings. For research universities the goal became to acquire as substantial a part of the world's new publications as possible; for colleges the goal was to develop a collection that supported the curriculum and the independent work of the faculty and students.

Local budget restrictions and a decline in the strength of the dollar overseas have reduced the ability of U.S. academic libraries to purchase books and journals. Factors that contributed to this decline include reductions in federal funding for higher education, declining income from endowments and tax revenues, pricing policies of some publishers who may charge libraries more than individual subscribers or raise prices precipitously, and the increasing need to share acquisitions budgets with electronic technologies. As a result, research libraries estimate that they collectively purchased 450,000 fewer titles a year in the early 1990s than they had in the mid-1980s.

In the late 1980s and early 1990s in the U.S. institutions of higher learning suffered from some redirection of both state and private funding to primary and secondary education, from scandals connected with overcharges to the federal government for research, and from controversies over whether the standard curriculum contains enough or too much material about the works of dead white males. Each of these debates influences the development of many college and university library collections in macro and micro detail. In Africa academic library collection development is influenced by the high cost of importing materials, the limited amount of local publishing, and the decision in many countries to stress funding for primary and secondary education. In China, eastern Europe, and the former Soviet Union, political change and uncertainty about the government as a source of support have brought with them an increased desire to effect exchange programs with libraries in countries previously considered unacceptable trading partners. Faculty members engaged in top-level research experience the true globalization of our society, including access to rapid communication of research results and acceptance of one or more languages as the media of communication for findings in a particular discipline; they also expect to find in their local collections the publications that report their research, regardless of cost. However, if funding for research is reduced, expectations for collection development will probably need to be adjusted as well.

Evolution of Academic Library Collections. Library collections acquire their characteristics over time as the result of many thousands of decisions, some categorical and others individual. The history and nature of collections is largely the result of the cumulation of methods by which the collections have been developed. These methods have varied depending on the public or private nature of the institution, the differing character of academic programs, the degree of local support and funding for library collection development, and the pattern and level of staff support for collection development programs.

Most academic libraries were characterized by the accretion of gifts, both great and small, and the active guidance and contributions of faculty members. Before the 1930s most major collections were shaped by gifts and by emphasis on European techniques of collecting, which reflected curricular need and a focus on "serious scholarly material," mostly monographic and serial in nature and quite rigidly defined. The library in this scheme was usually the passive repository of materials thus selected, though university librarians were often active participants in identifying and soliciting major gifts or purchases of materials en bloc. In addition, many academic departments developed their own library collections over the years, under more-or-less direct faculty control. These collections, since the 1950s, have increasingly devolved to the central library system.

From the 1930s on, the nature of collecting and collections in universities changed, largely in response to the new needs of graduate and research programs in the humanities and social sciences. There was increasing emphasis on primary and original source materials, and after World War II on information that could be accumulated, abstracted, quantified, manipulated, and analyzed. Older materials were often as valuable as current materials, increased emphasis on area studies created new need for foreign titles from nontraditional sources, and the increased study of popular and traditional cultures called for collecting more ephemeral, popular, "gray," or other elusive materials previously excluded from the serious academic library's collecting purview. As the 1960 annual report of one major academic library put it, "Selection of books for a library like this calls for an attempt to foresee the future course of research and to obtain publications that, though they may seem insignificant today, will be wanted by scholars tomorrow." New methods were developed to assist in this effort, notably approval plans. Working with the library staff and, perhaps, university faculty, representatives of book jobber firms would profile the collecting interests of a given library and then supply copies of relevant materials to the library without order requests for individual items. Libraries would review the materials and return the items that did not meet their needs.

College libraries focused their collections on the curriculum, and the collections expanded along with course offerings in the areas of African and African-American studies, women's studies, Asian studies, Hispanic studies, and interdisciplinary studies. As majors in business and computer science enjoyed a high degree of popularity, collections in these areas increased in size. The goal was not to develop research collections, but to offer students timely and, to some extent, timeless collections of the scholarly materials of greatest usefulness to undergraduates. Both faculty and librarians select the materials, supported by the joint efforts of faculty and librarian reviewers who critique current scholarship in the pages of *Choice,* the reviewing journal published by the Association of College and Research Libraries (ACRL).

Since the 1960s librarians in academic libraries have gradually assumed primary responsibility for library selection and collection management, most often with the advice and counsel of interested faculty. This assumption of the selection function by library subject specialists was a significant development in the postwar years; it has had an enormous impact on the nature and quality of research library collections in the U.S. and has helped academic librarians in their quest for professional recognition. It has also helped academic librarians create closer and more reciprocal relationships with the faculties of their institutions. These bibliographers have combined American and European theories of collection development, formed collection development policies to guide their work systematically over time, and codified the links between library collecting and academic program needs. Bibliographers have made collection development in American libraries more conscious, selective, and consistent; they have studied, systematized, and regularized other collection management functions, such as weeding, analyzing, or evaluating the utility of collections, the systematic study of collection use and users, and the allocation of acquisition funds.

Collection Management. Over the years there has been a growth of the concept of librarians as stewards of the collections housed in their libraries. Where once librarians were regarded as the keepers of the books in their possession, they have now become managers of their collections of library materials in a wide variety of formats. Collection development librarians have come to apply a number of the tools of the social and behavioral sciences to the study of library collections and their users, in order to manage more effectively not only the development of library collections, but also the collections themselves.

The literature of library science now contains a substantial bibliography of studies on the functions of collection development and management, including (1) collection analysis or evaluation, (2) the preparation and use of collection development policy statements, (3) the study of library use and library users, (4) pruning collections and identifying and moving materials to auxiliary storage, (5) library materials budgeting and budget allocation, and (6) selection of materials for preservation and conservation treatment. While it is generally recognized that the most effective pruning, storage, or preservation decision is made at the time of purchase, the often unsystematic early growth of library collections and the high cost of maintaining titles in active collection space have made review of existing collections an important part of the collection manager's job.

Leaders in research librarianship have recognized the importance of such work: they have encouraged the development of the Research Libraries Group (RLG) conspectus program as a tool for developing collection profiles and using them in cooperative collection development or preservation management programs. RLG's collection development officers devised the conspectus methodology in the late 1970s. The conspectus itself is a detailed overview or summary in Library of Congress (LC) classification of a library's existing collection strengths and future collecting intensities. The North American Collections Inventory Project (NCIP) expanded the use of the conspectus in an attempt to create an online inventory of collection strengths and weaknesses in North American research libraries.

Other collection management initiatives of the 1980s and 1990s have centered on preserving existing collections. In the mid-1980s the Council on Library Resources (CLR) established the Commission on Preservation and Access to help the libraries of the U.S. and the world deal with the crisis of brittle books, books that were deteriorating because they had been printed on paper with high acidity and stored in conditions not conducive to long life. The issue gained worldwide attention: in the U.S. Congress provided funds for preservation microfilming of as many as two million titles in a 20-year period. Many academic libraries implemented preservation programs designed to protect the deteriorating segment of their collections, a segment estimated to be as much as 35 percent of the collections developed prior to 1950. Statistics on preservation activities at member libraries of ARL show considerable growth. Other indicators include the Brittle Books program of the National Endowment for the Humanities (NEH), increased NEH funding for microfilming, federal legislation in 1990 requiring use of alkaline paper in government publications, and an increase in research and publication on preservation problems. Deciding to preserve an individual title is not an individual act; it is a rich example of the complex nature of collection management as it is practiced in academic libraries. The librarian concerned with an individual brittle book consults members of the faculty to ascertain the worth of the scholarship of the title in question, or to gather candidates for preservation, and then works with other libraries in all parts of the world to coordinate preservation filming and to determine the best of the current preservation technologies.

Another issue for collection specialists is the burgeoning of electronic sources, both bibliographic and full-text, and their availability in several formats. Popular with users, but not necessarily equally available to all users, these expensive sources strain budgets already hard pressed and raise issues of access and appropriateness of format for various contents. A number of electronic journals have been created, some for purchase, some distributed without charge, and they raise difficult questions about access, ownership, and archiving. Several professional organizations, including ALA and ARL, joined together in 1990 to form a new organization, the Coalition for Networked Information, to seek answers to these questions. While awaiting advice from the Coalition, individual libraries continued to utilize electronic sources within their funding and policy limitations and sought ways to enhance access. Such access becomes a form of temporary collection ownership, different from the permanent ownership options of the past.

Collection development reflects the academic programs of the institutions served. Among the probable consequences are that collections will become less topically diverse as smaller, less profitable departments and programs are eliminated or absorbed. The increasing diversity of undergraduate populations will require more introductory-level materials, possibly at the expense of materials supporting more advanced scholarship. Disagreements about what constitutes the canon may contribute to the dissolution of traditional collection strengths, and diminished levels of staffing will require greater reliance on approval programs.

The economic environment will lead to closer scrutiny of the maintenance of branch collections and specialized research collections, and libraries will have no choice but to give greater consideration to offsite storage of lesser-used resources. Campus planners and faculty visionaries are inclined to believe that reliance on electronic information will reduce the demand for storage for book collections, but the staggering investment required to make even a modest portion of texts electronically accessible make this an unrealistic expectation in most situations at this time. Additionally, individuals tend to want multiple options, including access to both the electronic and print versions of a document, and even the pure electronic environment brings its own needs for terminals, other equipment, and space for users.

Cooperative Acquisition Plans. American academic librarians have long recognized that the concept of the entirely self-sufficient library is a myth and that the resources of any single research library, much less the resources of a typical academic library, cannot satisfy the entire need of that institution's researchers and students, now or in the future. The evolution of the *National Union Catalog* and the bibliographic utilities of OCLC and RLG are testimony to this fact, and also evidence that cooperation has often focused on acquiring and cataloguing materials from other countries, especially materials in languages other than English.

The Interdepartmental Committee for the Acquisition of Foreign Publications, established during World War II to provide important library materials to war agencies, was followed by the Cooperative Acquisitions Project (CAP) for Wartime Publications which sought, during the immediate postwar years, to provide materials published during the war years to U.S. academic and research libraries. The project distributed nearly 820,000 book and periodical volumes to participating research libraries. It not only demonstrated the capacity of major U.S. libraries to collaborate in acquiring elusive foreign publications, but also demonstrated LC's capacity to lead such cooperative national efforts.

The ARL, which had promoted CAP, also helped form and support its successor, the Farmington Plan. Stemming from a meeting of LC's Librarian's Council in Farmington, Connecticut, in 1942, the Farmington Plan divided foreign collecting among American libraries. Adopted by ARL in 1947, the program continued until 1972 and strengthened foreign collections in ARL libraries. It ended only when weakened budgets and an inability to accommodate academic program changes on individual campuses limited its collective focus.

The Farmington Plan was replaced in the U.S. by a program in which Congress allowed the use of foreign surplus funds to acquire library materials from foreign countries for selected U.S. research libraries. The emphasis of the program was on non-Western countries, and the program sought to acquire nontrade or ephemeral items as well as trade monographs. The program provided much material, as well as its own set of challenges, notably the problem of processing the collections. Further cooperation led to the establishment of the National Program of Acquisitions and Cataloging (NPAC), authorizing LC to acquire and catalogue such materials on behalf of the research library community. Funding for this program ran until the mid-1980s; since then the work of building strong and useful cooperative acquisitions and cataloguing programs for foreign-language material has clustered around the bibliographic utilities, OCLC and RLG's RLIN, and relied on the contributions of some key research libraries as well as LC. In addition, the Center for Research Libraries has served as a source for collecting other foreign materials, including newspapers, international documents, and dissertations.

The RLG Conspectus has been influential in these endeavors. It allows improved local and cooperative collection planning and management options through clearer understanding of the collections, collecting efforts, and commitments of other research libraries for more than 5,000 subjects and fields. The presence of Conspectus typologies, undergirded by the availability of the bibliographic utilities for rapid and shared communication and access to fax equipment, has provided a basis for a variety of cooperative efforts in distributed cataloguing of less common foreign publications and in distributing preservation and acquisitions activities among major academic and research libraries.

Cooperation among academic libraries often centers on nearby institutions. Many long-standing cooperative collection development programs exist throughout the U.S. For example, Duke University and the University of North Carolina began cooperating in collection development as early as 1933. North Carolina State University at Raleigh joined this effort in 1978. Today, the libraries assign subject responsibility at the research level and work to avoid duplication in their collections.

In 1976 Stanford University and the University of California at Berkeley began a broad program of cooperation sponsored initially by the Sloan and Mellon foundations. By 1992 the program included formal cooperative collection development arrangements in both East Asian and Latin American studies. Informal arrangements exist in many other subject areas and between individual selectors. Because of the vagaries of the materials budgets over the years, these arrangements have proven difficult to formalize. During the period of extreme fiscal stringency in the early 1990s, emphasis was placed on coordinating serials cancellations.

The University of California Shared Collections Acquisitions Program (SCAP) was formed in 1976 to allow statewide purchase and sharing of low-use research materials. All nine campus libraries pool 3 percent of their materials budgets for these purchases. Stanford University joined as a full participant in 1979.

Since the late 1980s SCAP has funded the cost of mounting periodicals index tapes on MELVYL, the shared statewide online catalogue. As a result, a high percentage of these shared funds has been spent for high-use, rather than low-use, purchases. Local union lists of periodicals have been a popular cooperative effort, and these efforts are enhanced by the availability of local networks supporting rapid transmission and delivery of interlibrary loan requests. The system is supported by the state library, which funds the main academic library in the state as a backup for the others.

Other forms of formal cooperation, such as shared purchases of expensive items, are less common. What is typical is to rely informally on the collection strengths of the colleges in an area and to avoid building duplicate collections in specialized subjects. In these libraries the use of OCLC for cataloguing has expanded options for sharing considerably; for example, it is estimated that 90 percent or more of the cataloguing done in college libraries is not original, but copied or "borrowed" from another library, such as LC. The presence of holdings records from academic libraries other than the major research libraries in the OCLC database has meant that the burden of interlibrary loan work need not fall exclusively on the larger libraries, and smaller academic libraries can offer much to the ongoing process of the timely distribution of scholarly materials to the users who seek them.

Future efforts at collaboration in collection development and management can be expected to heed the problems of local funding and to be clear about local commitments, to rely on the infrastructure of the bibliographic utilities in designing cooperative programs, and to seek cost recovery for services rendered (even if the cost recovery is simply a mutual agreement not to charge one another for services). Scholars will continue to lead in defining emerging subject areas for collecting efforts, and librarians will demonstrate ever-increasing proficiency with and reliance on computerized systems for delivering information. What Hendrik Edelman and Marvin Tatum wrote about university libraries in 1976 is also true for college libraries today:

> The collections of American university libraries have been built with vision, ambition, knowledge, dedication, and large amounts of money. The influence of pace-setters has been great, yet each university library reflects very much the particular academic history of its institution and especially the influence of a relatively small number of scholars and librarians. On balance, it has always been the scholar who has provided the impetus. The librarian has made it possible.

REFERENCES

J. Periam Danton, *Book Selection and Collections: A Comparison of German and American University Libraries* (1963).

Hendrik Edelman and G. Marvin Tatum, Jr., "The Development of Collections in American University Libraries," *College and Research Libraries* (1976).

Charles B. Osburn and Ross Atkinson, editors, *Collection Management: A New Treatise* (1991).

WILLIAM GOODRICH JONES;
PAUL H. MOSHER

ADMINISTRATION

Patterns of organization and finance for academic libraries in the U.S. tend to be more diverse and less uniform than was the case prior to 1970. A dual pattern common since World War II still predominates—all library activities are described as either reader services or technical services, and each service has in it function- or format-based departments. However, many variations can be found in the design of libraries. Columbia University Libraries underwent a widely publicized major change in 1973, its activities organized into a resources group, a services group, and a technical support group, and still another well-publicized change when it modified its structure to have libraries and information systems report to one vice president in the mid-1980s.

Other patterns, such as a subject division plan initiated at the University of Colorado, although not new, continue to be effective. Some of the new patterns of organization are similar in that reader services are no longer grouped under a single manager. The major departure from the dual organizational pattern is based on the reality in many academic libraries that the responsibilities of the public services director have become too extensive. The effect of automation on library activities has also influenced administrative structure in the library and on the campus. Another characteristic of new patterns of organization is that libraries have relatively flatter structures, with fewer levels in the administrative hierarchy. Academic library managers share many of the concerns confronting other administrators in higher education and the public sector generally. Accordingly, they are affected by the same broad forces that shape public policy formulation and the allocation of resources. The years since 1980 have witnessed the convergence of several factors that have affected universities and their libraries, placing a premium on management skills.

Key Issues. Changes in demographics and the size of the traditional college-age pool in the U.S. have slowed the growth of the college population. Limited growth, in turn, has reduced the increments to institutional budgets, in both public and private institutions, that are associated with a steady increase in credit-hour production. With an upturn in the numbers of 18-year-olds not expected until the year 2000, administrators must seek to fill classes from sources other than the traditional ones or anticipate meeting costs from revenue sources other than credit-hour production.

At the same time colleges and universities have been assailed with huge increases in the costs of maintaining their human resources. Many have had to extend pension benefits and other perquisites once reserved for faculty and certain other classes to all categories of university employees. Even more significant have been the escalating costs of health maintenance and health insurance.

In addition, most state governments in the U.S. have been affected by severe revenue problems of their own since the late 1980s. They have had to find new funds to address a wide range of pressing social problems with roots in demographic fundamentals, including crime, drugs, and health. Even states where education has remained a priority have concentrated on primary and secondary schools. There is little broad-based support for enhanced funding of higher education in general or of libraries specifically.

To these general forces that have affected higher

education, American library managers have had to add a specific problem of their own: responding to the pressures of runaway prices for serial subscriptions. Occasioned in large measure by the devaluation of the dollar against world currencies between 1987 and 1991, the sharp increase in journal costs hit research libraries especially hard, but no library was immune to its sting.

To maintain the quality of their programs and to advance the mission of the library within the university, academic library managers have reviewed a wide array of solutions to their problems. They have considered experimenting with formal organizational structures, applying information technologies, and networking as ways to deal with the challenges confronting them.

The Role of the Library Manager. In the organizational structure that characterizes higher education in the U.S. in the 1990s, most library managers report to the central academic officer and need to influence that individual and other key academic administrators. At some distance from the epicenter of academic decision making, they may face difficulties in communicating the needs of libraries to those making decisions on resource allocations. To make those needs known, library managers must be effective and knowledgeable spokespersons.

In order to be a contributing member of the university administrative team, the library manager must understand issues affecting higher education and know the place of the library in the university. For the chief administrative officer of one of the largest and most costly units in the institution, the ability to describe clearly and compellingly the requirements of the library is an obvious prerequisite. Equally important is an ability to communicate clearly with the library staff. Here the administrator serves as the connecting link between the external decision-making structure and the library organization.

Maintenance of academic excellence in times of scarce resources and competing demands requires careful planning. To be successful, library planning should be strategic in outlook and must incorporate comprehensive involvement of staff. Budgeting is one aspect of planning where library managers must excel. As fixed costs rise and programs proliferate, resource-allocation decisions on all campuses become more complex. In the midst of the fiscal problems afflicting higher education in the U.S., libraries are in the first decades of the full bloom of information technology. Participating in that revolution and harnessing technology to the service mission of the library, while maintaining the performance indexes of other measures of library quality, requires considerable skills. The circumstances require that the library administrator enjoy the confidence of campus planners who must make tough budgetary decisions. At the same time, they require that the library administrator have an understanding of alternative funding sources and a willingness to work hard to secure external funds to support the development of library programs.

Productivity and efficiency are important considerations in the public sector today. Higher education and libraries are no exception. In that context, libraries and universities that place staff development and staff welfare as priorities are more likely to be successful in the pursuit of their missions than those that do not. A major goal of the modern chief administrator must be to create the kind of open environment in which work can take place and to establish the high standards that connote the professional nature of the undertaking.

The effective library manager must also be an agent of change, able to create a library that is responsive to the many disparate demands made upon it. Further, the manager must be willing to use the central place of the library in the intellectual life of the community to advance the concerns and needs of the constituency it serves. Currently, significant strides are being made in many academic libraries to address the concerns of increasingly ethnically diverse student bodies and expanding curricula. Similarly, exemplary programs are in place to identify managerial skills in the library workforce generally, without regard to gender or ethnicity. Thanks to the efforts of advocates in a number of universities, the field of library management is certainly more open today than it was in the 1970s.

REFERENCES

Fred Heath, "Administrative Styles," *The Smaller Academic Library: A Management Handbook,* edited by Gerard B. McCabe (1988).

David W. Lewis, "Organizational Paradigm for Effective Academic Libraries," *College and Research Libraries* (1986).

Rutherford D. Rogers and David C. Weber, *University Library Administration* (1971).

FRED HEATH

MEASUREMENT AND EVALUATION

Traditionally, library administrators have relied on library surveys, crude rules of thumb, and internal audits vis-a-vis standards to measure and evaluate academic libraries. Library surveys were for much of the 19th century and half of the 20th century the most popular form of library evaluation, and indeed still are, when reports from accreditation visits are included in this category. In 1939 Louis Round Wilson formalized the survey when he designed an instrument to be used by an outside team. The questions he included are still common today. They are:

1. Are the library's collections adequate to support the objectives of the university?
2. Is the staff sufficient and does it have the appropriate training to carry out the library's programs?
3. Are the library's materials organized effectively?
4. How adequate are the physical equipment and plant?
5. What kinds of administrative relationships exist among the library, the faculty, and the administration?
6. Is the library adequately financed?
7. Does the library engage in cooperative ventures with other libraries in the state and region?

A library survey is intended to provide an authoritative assessment of a library. It is based on easily gathered countable data, on which the judgment of the surveyors is to be based. Such techniques are common in academe and elsewhere, but they are inevitably Delphic or prescriptive. They have little empirical foundation, and their credibility depends largely on the prestige of the surveyors. However, such assessments are often just what academic or government officials want, even though, with their weak empirical base, they provide a very uncertain guide for library management.

Rule of thumb measures are another approach. Examples include: (1) the library should receive 6 percent of the institution's educational and general expenditures (E & G) budget—less if established, more if new; and (2) its own budget should be divided into 30 percent for acquisitions, 60 percent for personnel, and 10 percent for everything else—give or take as much as 10 percent in any category, so long as the total remains 100 percent. Such measures really beg the question of measurement because they fail to justify why these rules are valid in the first place. The rules of thumb do influence library administrators as they allocate funds in their control, and are used to argue for further funding, but the rationale is not rigorous, even if cloaked by the use of comparisons with other institutions. At times the comparisons are further institutionalized and presented in the form of standards—preferably quantitative standards.

Quantitative Standards. The history of the effort to develop quantitative standards for libraries is long and complex, but the most obvious reason for developing them was best stated by Verner W. Clapp and Robert T. Jordan. "When . . . standardizing authorities omit or refuse to set standards in quantitative terms, the budgeting and appropriating authorities, who cannot avoid quantitative bases for their decisions, are compelled to adopt measures which, though perhaps having the virtue of simplicity, may be essentially irrelevant." This statement was written in 1965; it is still germane, even with the work done in the Association of College and Research Libraries (ACRL) in the 1980s to revise standards and develop performance measures.

The problem is multifaceted, but it tends to resolve itself into three issues: (1) the question of whether quantitative standards for libraries can be created at all; (2) the difficulty of obtaining adequate data; and (3) the necessity to reconceptualize the meaning of library measures to change their focus from a consideration of inputs to a consideration of outputs—that is, from additions to services and collection to measures of performance.

ACRL has addressed these issues in different ways in each of the three sets of standards developed since 1986, and the very differences among the approaches reveal that the problem has not yet been solved in a definitive fashion. First in point of time is *Standards for College Libraries, 1986.* These standards are addressed to "institutions defined by the Carnegie Commission on Higher Education as Liberal Arts Colleges I and II and Comprehensive Universities and Colleges I and II." Three evaluation formulas are included: formula A for collection size, formula B for size of staff, and formula C for space. For the second and third formulas the standard specifies a grading scheme from A through D, depending on the percentage of the formula requirement the library meets.

The 1990 *Standards for Community, Junior and Technical College Learning Resources Programs,* developed in cooperation with the Association for Educational Communications and Technology, takes a different approach to evaluation. Instead of formulas and grading levels, this document offers several tables that specify quantities needed for either "minimum" or "excellent" programs, depending on full-time equivalent (FTE) student enrollment. The tables cover staffing, dollar expenditures, services, collections, and space.

A good number of academic librarians reject the formula approach to evaluation embodied in these standards documents. Instead, they prefer to compare their libraries to libraries in groups of peer institutions. Several statistical reporting systems have been developed to facilitate such comparisons.

The annual Association of Research Libraries (ARL) and the biennial ACRL "University Library Statistics" are the best-known reports of such data collection efforts. Both are available, currently and retrospectively, in machine-readable form. Others, such as the Tufts University data set for private colleges and universities, are circulated only to member institutions that have supplied the data. John Minter Associates of Boulder, Colorado, has used data from the biennial surveys of academic libraries conducted by the National Center for Educational Statistics (NCES) to display ranges of management statistics and ratios in *Statistical Norms for College and University Libraries.* The 1990 edition of this work, based on NCES data collected in the autumn of 1988, provided these data by Carnegie Classification category in hard copy and on disk.

The third ACRL standards document, *Standards for University Libraries: Evaluation of Performance,* approved in 1989, eschews such formulas, tables, and comparisons to others. Instead it specifies that "each university library system is unique and therefore should determine its own criteria for performance and evaluation." After recommending how university libraries should go about "setting goals and objectives" (Section A), the document suggests "factors to be considered in developing goals" (Section B) and ends with a description of "measuring achievements and forming a statement of expectations" (Section C). The final section, under the heading Evaluation Criteria, is really a list of 62 questions "suggested as a means of reaching a proper assessment of the library." The differences between this list and the questions used in Wilson's first survey indicate the increasing complexity of academic library service in the years from 1939 to 1989.

In the light of this complexity, the 1986 *Standards for College Libraries* may seem somewhat simplistic. But these standards also pointed the way toward a very different method of evaluation. The Foreword mentions that "the committee discussed extensively the topic of performance measures," but decided it could not provide them. Instead, it urged the profession to monitor and support ACRL's Ad Hoc Committee on Performance Measures. The work of that committee came to fruition in 1990 with the publication of *Measuring Academic Library Performance,* developed under contract to ACRL by a team headed by Nancy Van House, who was also senior editor of *Output Measures for Public Libraries,* 2nd edition. Though quite different in detail, the academic library volume is like the public library volumes in its focus on clear directions for realistic measures developed by researchers and practitioners working together and based on trials in the field.

It is too early to tell whether the performance measure approach will avoid the problems associated with other measures. For example, what would be

Central Library, State University of Campinas, São Paulo, Brazil.

regarded only as a minimal standard for librarians and scholars is a sufficient standard for budget officers, particularly in less well-supported institutions. Wealthy institutions find that standards couched in minimal terms weaken their search for excellence in collections and services. The adequacy of the data used in describing library operations is another persistent problem, whether the data be used to detail input or output operations. There have been improvements in the definitions used in many Higher Education General Information Survey (HEGIS) data elements, but there are still unresolved issues relating to definitions and measures of access (as opposed to ownership). The Committee on ARL Statistics, the NCES, and the Advisory Committee of the American Library Association's Office for Research and Statistics are all working together to make improvements in this area, but the literature had not reflected the results of this work by 1992.

Comparative and Internal Measures. Ultimately, whether the issue is input or output measures, two kinds of measures are necessary: a comparison between similar institutions and a yardstick or set of yardsticks for internal measures. The first is necessary to orient the evaluation within the universe of academic libraries. It is a common habit in higher education to compare one institution with another, and libraries are usually one of the features of comparison. At times the inadequacy of comparative data is troublesome, and the counting methods used by most libraries might better be replaced by standardized sampling methods that would be both easier and cheaper to apply. But aggregations of volumes, and so on, do have a raw power, and tabulations by groups such as ARL and ACRL will provide base data to use in comparisons, especially if the comparisons are selected carefully and like institutions are matched.

Once a comparison is made, simple inspection of the data thus isolated, aided by ranking, ranges, averages, and medians, can provide useful insights for both library managers and senior administrators seeking evidence of the worth of their investment in libraries. If desired, a further reduction of data into ratios can occur. Some of those that provide useful insights into library operations are the ratio of professional to nonprofessional staff, expenditure for library materials as a percent of total library operating expenditures, and the ratio of salary expenditures to library material expenditures.

Most academic libraries appear to have a ratio of one professional to between two and three nonprofessional staff members. They expend 30 percent of their total budget on library materials, with perhaps 15 percent on operational expenditures and the remainder on staffing in a library with an integrated library system. But these figures are not static; they have meaning only in relation to a comparison group and as part of an institution's history. They are not benchmarks at which every institution should aim, but they do provide a relative standard, a framework for comparisons with like institutions.

A more extended form of ratio analysis is Allan M. Carter's Library Resources Index, which is an average of three indexes: total volumes held, volumes added, and periodicals received. Carter used this measure and found a high correlation between excellence of graduate schools and a high position of the parent institution's library on the index. Similar correlations exist in ranking and perception studies of quality institutions at both undergraduate and graduate levels.

Baumol and Marcus extended the comparative analysis of libraries by the use of regression techniques; Kendon Stubbs, by applying factor analysis to ARL library data, discovered a library factor that underlies most library input variables. Both regression and factor analysis provide more synthetic forms of data reduction and enable the analyst to inspect the interaction of a number of variables. Given the easy availability of computer programs to perform these statistical techniques, they should become more widely used. They remain dependent, however, on the collection of suitable and accurate data by individuals who care to ask important questions. Most studies rely on some variation of the basic input figures, such as total number of volumes held, or expenditures, and there are other library variables that may be more explanatory, or at least measure other activities. Performance measures can help to address these issues, as can detailed studies of one or more areas of performance, such as book availability.

In many instances, library staff only dimly understand what they are trying to measure, and continuing education of staff becomes a part of the research program. As the name implies, performance measures attempt to determine how well a library (and its staff) performs: Can it deliver a particular item when needed? How fast can it do so? and so forth. Performance measures provide librarians with a completely new kind of measure—a feedback response mechanism that permits a standard of performance to be set, a means of comparison to determine adherence to the standard, and a method for correcting performance if it fails to meet the standard.

In an ideal world every well-meaning public-service organization would welcome such measures, especially if they are cost-beneficial to apply. As of 1990 college libraries had such an option, and it will be instructive to see which of the eligible libraries seek out this approach as a management strategy. Certainly the rapid changes in the information delivery environment should encourage fresh thinking in the design, delivery, and evaluation of library services.

Future Trends and Goals. Changes in social objectives and economic conditions have produced a decline in the financial resources available to the parent institutions of academic libraries. At the same time governmental concerns about the quality of the performance of typical graduates of each level of schooling have led to calls for greater accountability in educational institutions. As higher education proves its worth and examines each facet of its operations to justify its existence and demonstrate its cost-effectiveness, library programs will face increasingly rigorous evaluations. The number of accredited library schools declined in the 1980s; some of them closed after university-wide internal evaluation committees raised questions of all academic programs about their relative quality and cost and determined that library schools on particular campuses were no longer feasible. While some fear the merger of academic computing centers and libraries, with a corresponding diminution of the programs of the libraries, no one seriously suggests eliminating libraries. They will not be phased out, the way a library science department can be, but they should expect to face unrelenting difficulty in maintaining their traditional share of the institution's E & G budget. At the same time, libraries are being driven to ask for more funds to cover the persistent pressures of inflation, new scholarship, and new media for information.

Typically an institution has a self-imposed limit on the fraction of its total budget that it devotes to the library. When the parent institution is unable to raise its total budget, two trends collide: the inflationary costs of library materials and the lack of movement to address the problem in the parent institution's budget. All this is familiar, but what seems to be misunderstood is that these trends, together with the proliferation of other means of information delivery, will provoke a fundamental change in what libraries can be. Basically, libraries can continue to reduce their collections gradually, satisfying fewer and fewer of the demands made upon them, or they can attempt to redefine their roles, to shift their emphasis from collecting materials to providing information. And they need to validate this shift with adequate measures of performance that will attest to the fact that libraries both deliver necessary information and teach students how to become information literate. The goals will differ from the goals of the present, and so will the objectives. Uniform standards will not exist, because there is no generally accepted set of empirical standards by which libraries can be judged; institutions develop along different paths, based on the great variety of needs to which they respond.

Academic libraries are going to be redefined by the pressures on institutions to cope with the information revolution. If they are to survive as more than repositories for books seldom used, they must be effectively managed. Effective management of complex library processes depends on measurement; library managers of the future should expect their performance to be evaluated in part on how they facilitate the work of measuring the ongoing performance of the library.

REFERENCES

William J. Baumol and Matityahu Marcus, *Economics of Academic Libraries* (1973).

F. W. Lancaster, *The Measurement and Evaluation of Library Services* (1977).

Mary Jo Lynch and Arthur P. Young, editors, *Academic Libraries: Research Perspectives* (1990).

New Social Science Library, Tel-Aviv University, Tel-Aviv, Israel.

K. Stubbs, "University Libraries: Standards and Statistics," *College and Research Libraries* (1981).

Nancy A. Van House, Beth Weil, and Charles R. McClure, *Measuring Academic Library Performance* (1990).

MARY JO LYNCH;
RICHARD J. TALBOT

LIBRARY COOPERATION

Cooperation between libraries has occurred throughout much of recorded history. Joseph J. Branin notes that as far back as 200 B.C. there are references to the great library at Alexandria lending material to Pergamum. David C. Weber reminds us that by 1876 library cooperation was a primary concern of the newly formed American Library Association (ALA). The second half of the 20th century has witnessed a considerable increase in the variety and scale of cooperative library ventures. Today, new technological means of storing and disseminating information are creating rising expectations, heightened demand, and new possibilities for interlibrary cooperation and even collection coordination.

Library cooperation may be defined as the banding together of individual libraries into mutually beneficial arrangements, particularly those that facilitate sharing resources. Today academic, public, and special libraries are forming a wide range of cooperative ventures at a quickening pace. Branin points out that most networks and library consortia have grown up since the 1960s, "with over 90 percent having been established since 1960 and 75 percent since 1975."

Several forces account for this move toward cooperation, including the publication explosion, the prolonged economic slowdown of the late 1980s and early 1990s, the general contraction of higher education in the U.S., and the increased application of technology to library processes. Static or declining materials budgets have become routine, and individual libraries are hard pressed to build or maintain local collections that satisfy the needs of their clientele.

Cooperative library programs range from informal local agreements to formal state, regional, national, and even international protocols. Since the 1970s, libraries that chose to cooperate, particularly those that joined in multitype library ventures, benefitted from the financial and technical support of private foundations and various state and federal agencies. Cooperative academic library ventures include reciprocal borrowing privileges, standardized loan periods and borrowing rules, centralized technical processing, cooperative storage and preservation of materials, joint purchases, cooperative staff training, shared technology, and coordinated cooperative collection development.

Nonetheless, Branin notes that tension often exists between local autonomy and shared network and consortial responsibilities. Although it is unlikely that fully self-contained library collections ever existed, the traditional desire of many librarians for self-sufficiency and decentralized library governance, he suggests, may be in conflict with the goals of many cooperative library efforts. But, in the changing information environment at the end of the 20th century, libraries and cooperation are difficult to separate, and Michael Gorman suggests that "the ongoing technological revolution will support and encourage desirable changes in attitudes toward cooperation."

At the same time, innovations in communications and computing technology and evaluation methodology provide librarians with the means they require to accomplish the three primary goals that most cooperative programs aim to achieve: (1) expanded bibliographic access to collections and other information resources, (2) improved physical access to library and information resources, and (3) coordinated cooperative collection development.

Bibliographic Access. Without comprehensive bibliographic data or other measures of local, regional, and national collection strengths and weaknesses, most cooperative library activities are doomed to remain abstractions. Many of the most successful cooperative efforts, both past and present, involve sharing bibliographic data to improve physical access. The importance of shared bibliographic data was recognized early on, certainly by the early decades of the 20th century, when the first union catalogues were established. Today, vast regional, national, and international bibliographic utilities form the electronic backbone of most cooperative cataloguing, resource-sharing, collection development, and preservation efforts.

The National Union Catalog was established in 1901, the year the Library of Congress began selling galley proofs and copies of its printed catalogue cards. Many librarians filed these cards directly into their catalogues, creating early rudimentary union lists. The availability of printed LC catalogue cards, however, encouraged not only the development of union catalogues, but also the standardization of bibliographic description and data. These early efforts were precursors of the now nearly universal MARC format and a growing number of internationally shared bibliographic protocols. Although the U.S. has no official national library, the LC has assumed a leadership role in providing bibliographic services.

One of the largest and most successful cooperative projects to benefit from LC's involvement is CONSER (Cooperative Online Serials Program). It is designed to provide a reliable and authoritative online serials database of North American serials and supports many union-listing and serials cataloguing programs. It will certainly function as an indispensable element of any emerging national or international database. CONSER has about two dozen members and is managed by an Executive Committee composed of representatives of the LC, the Online Computer Library Center (OCLC), the National Library of Medicine, the National Agricultural Library, the National Library of Canada, and one full-level CONSER organization. The CONSER database is resident on OCLC. Started in 1973 with funding from the Council on Library Resources (CLR), it was originally called the conversion of serials project, with the same acronym.

Two related projects, the CONSER Abstracting and Indexing (A&I) Coverage Project and the U.S. Newspaper Program (USNP), are designed to expand and complement the CONSER database. The A&I project, begun in 1983, involves participants from outside the library community by establishing direct links between serials entries in catalogues and individual articles from commercial abstracting and indexing services. USNP contributes bibliographic and holdings records for newspapers to the CONSER database. As specialized members of the program, the U.S. and Canadian national centers for the International Serials Data System (the National Serials Data Program and ISDS/Canada) add International Standard Serial Numbers (ISSN) and maintain their accuracy in the database.

By the mid-1960s the information explosion, the application of computer technology to library processes, and the availability of high-speed telecommunications systems had created the conditions that gave rise to the bibliographic utilities that now serve most North American libraries and many others throughout the world. These utilities foster cooperative cataloguing, interlibrary loan, and exchange of bibliographic and holdings information. The major utilities serving North America are OCLC; the Research Libraries Information Network (RLIN), developed by the Research Libraries Group; the Washington Library Network (WLN); and the University of Toronto Library Automation Systems (UTLAS). Libraries in the European Community developed DIANE (Direct Information Access Network for Europe) as part of Euronet. OCLC provides service in Japan and other countries, especially in Asia. Australia and other countries have licensed WLN software to support their national systems. For further information, *see* Bibliographic Networks and Utilities.

The bibliographic utilities have profoundly affected the ways libraries conduct their operations. The rapid provision of cataloguing copy and the standardization of bibliographic records that the utilities made possible have allowed, for example, many once innovative but now routine cataloguing and acquisitions tasks to migrate from professional to support staff.

Bibliographic utilities support the retrospective conversion of a library's records from manual to machine-readable MARC format and enable librarians to build databases of their holdings for later retrieval in magnetic tape format. These tapes are then used as the foundation of local online catalogues and circulation and serials control systems.

Three major players—LC, WLN, and RLG—began the Linked Systems Project (LSP) in 1980 as a cooperative venture. OCLC joined the project in

1984. The LSP aims to provide computer-to-computer connections to support resource-sharing activities. The initial application is for maintaining the National Authority File, an integrated, consistent file built jointly by LC and other libraries under the aegis of the National Coordinated Cataloging Operations (NACO) and partially funded by CLR. The LSP was expected to grow beyond this initial phase to encompass links between bibliographic records and additional systems.

The developing network of bibliographic utilities made possible by the LSP is intended to support many new cooperative sharing, collection development, and preservation projects. Nonetheless, the records these databases contain remain surrogates for the documents themselves. The challenge facing the information community in the 1990s is to move beyond bibliographic citation and begin providing access to primary research data, research findings, commentaries on findings, and the texts of the derivative secondary instructional sources.

Physical Access. Traditionally, academic librarians have sought to provide physical access to research materials by building comprehensive collections and supplementing them with marginal and judicious use of interlibrary loans. But, by the 1990s, most academic librarians recognized that an individual academic library can no longer acquire and store resources that anticipate and satisfy all client demands. Academic librarians place increasing emphasis on access rather than ownership and speak of obtaining materials "just in time," rather than purchasing them "just in case." Under these circumstances, physical access assumes increased importance.

One of the oldest established forms of library cooperation is interlibrary lending, often abbreviated to ILL. In 1907, Weber notes, LC issued an interlibrary lending policy "and lent to such an extent that by 1909 it loaned 1,023 volumes to 119 libraries." The first ALA interlibrary lending code was published in 1916. By the 1990s interlibrary lending had become the primary mode of resource sharing between individual libraries in a system. Estimates of ILL activity in the U.S. vary—some range as high as 25 million per year—but most observers agree that it is increasing. Between 1982 and 1991 the number of transactions on the ILL subsystem of OCLC grew from more than one million to more than five million.

Several factors account for this rise in ILL, including static or declining materials budgets, the availability and popularity of the electronic ILL subsystems available on most bibliographic utilities, the increasing number of library holdings records that became available as libraries completed the retrospective conversion of their catalogues, and the increasingly routine use of fax transmission to deliver some types of materials, particularly journal articles. Most observers expect ILL to grow as document delivery mechanisms improve.

In the past, most librarians relied on the postal service or proprietary delivery services when exchanging documents, but fax transmission began playing an increasingly important role in the late 1980s. In a typical ILL transaction, a librarian at a borrowing institution requests a journal article through the ILL module of a bibliographic utility; a librarian at the lending library faxes a copy of the article to the borrower without charge, rather than shipping it. Fax has rapidly become a standard method of document transmission, as well as a means of communication.

Facsimile itself may be supplanted by another technological innovation. In 1991 the RLG began marketing Ariel, a software package for microcomputers that is faster, more reliable, and less expensive than fax. At the lending library a staff member scans documents and images electronically, including photographs, charts, formulas, and tables, stores them on disk, and transmits them rapidly over the Internet network as highly compressed files. At the receiving library, staff members produce high-resolution copies on laser printers. Unlike fax, Ariel uses nondedicated equipment, corrects for transmission error, scans the original source, sends and receives simultaneously, and, because data transmission over the Internet is free to nonprofit research institutions, promises significant cost savings.

Bibliographic utilities, union lists, and improved document delivery systems have increased awareness of information sources and reduced turnaround time. The result has been increasing demand for interlibrary loan services. Many librarians have difficulty coping with the number of requests they receive and have erected institutional barriers to borrowing in the form of fees or restricted participation. Others have entered into exclusive expedited cooperative arrangements with one or more peer institutions. Opportunities and problems abound.

As book and serials budgets decline and access to certain materials becomes difficult and time-consuming, for-fee document delivery systems have begun to proliferate. In 1991, for example, UnCover2 became available. UnCover is the journal index of the CARL (Colorado Alliance for Research Libraries) system and contains citations from more than 10,500 journals. UnCover2 is an add-on service that allows individuals or libraries both online ordering for journal articles and online credit-card payment. The service promises either one-hour or 24-hour turnaround by fax. UnCover2 and other for-fee document delivery systems enable library patrons to order locally unavailable journal articles and other materials themselves and bypass entirely the library's ILL service.

The most far-reaching cooperative development to affect academic libraries in the U.S., however, is NREN, the National Research and Education Network. As it was being planned in the early 1990s, NREN promised to move us beyond even the most advanced document-based delivery systems toward more broadly defined information services. It promised innovation in information access techniques and even the transformation of knowledge management. It offered to move us further toward the virtual library or toward what Eldred Smith described as a "single, complete archive of scholarship, controlled by a comprehensive, consistent index, and available [from] office, laboratory, or home."

Cooperative Collection Development. Coordination of resources between groups of libraries promises benefits to users, reduced costs to participants, and a level of information sufficiency that a single library cannot achieve. Collection coordination also forces librarians to focus on client need, not on their traditional preoccupation with collection building. It is likely that only a coordinated national effort will ensure the adequacy of the resources required to support the basic and applied research that is essential to continued social and economic development.

After the 1980s several factors contributed to the feasibility of coordinating local, state, regional, and national collection development. The increasing use of the conspectus method of evaluating collections by large and even small libraries, for example, contributes to the elaboration of a comprehensive national portrait of subject strengths and weaknesses. And the participation of most libraries in the growing databases created by the bibliographic utilities promises an exhaustive title-by-title census of the national bibliographic patrimony of the U.S.

Yet coordinated cooperative collection development is a concept that has proven difficult to implement, as described above. Perhaps the most important past national cooperative collection development effort was the Farmington Plan. Most libraries today are members of several associations and consortia at the local, state, regional, and national levels. The cooperative resource sharing and collection development activities of these groups are wide-ranging. An excellent example at the local level is the VALNet project in the Lewiston-Clarkston valley of northern Idaho and eastern Washington. VALNet links small high school, college, public, and county libraries in a common effort to ensure information adequacy for regional development. Formed in 1983, during an economic downturn, VALNet was successful in meeting many of its original goals.

In 1992 VALNet consisted of eight agencies and 28 library locations. Members shared a common online catalogue, extended reciprocal borrowing privileges to all patrons, and established a jitney service. Participating libraries shared more than 100,000 volumes between 1986 and 1992. During the same period, VALNet received more than $1 million in grants for collection building in the health sciences, business, and education. The traditional model of cooperative collection development—a single library assuming primary responsibility in a particular subject area—was not feasible, but strong collections were developed, distributed throughout the member libraries.

The impetus for VALNet grew out of individual member library participation in the Library and Information Resources for the Pacific Northwest (LIRN). LIRN was an ambitious regional program in the early 1980s to assess, coordinate, and deliver information resources in Alaska, Washington, Oregon, Idaho, and Montana. LIRN participants developed the Pacific Northwest Conspectus, a version of the RLG conspectus worksheets designed to accommodate the region's smaller libraries. Many of these libraries assessed hundreds or even thousands of Dewey or LC subject subdivisions in their collections. In addition to providing small libraries with an assessment instrument suited to their needs, LIRN encouraged multitype library cooperation by sponsoring training workshops, offering small grants, and reviewing the document delivery capability of the region.

Both the VALNet and LIRN projects are examples of the kinds of local and regional cooperative programs that have long existed in the U.S. Many other cooperative collection development efforts have been successful. Alaska, with underdeveloped library resources to serve more than 400,000 people scattered over a land area a fifth the size of the 48 contiguous states, needs multitype library cooperative efforts to assure service. Other states with strong statewide cooperative programs include Colorado, Illinois, Minnesota, and New York. At the national level the RLG/NCIP collection evaluation programs have profoundly influenced cooperative collection development in large research libraries.

By the early 1990s the conspectus methodology was used by public and academic libraries of all sizes in all parts of the U.S. and in many other countries as well. Many regional networks (perhaps misnamed because few operate their own computer networks) exist in the U.S. and facilitate cooperation and even coordinated collection development among libraries. Most, but not all, were formed to broker OCLC in their regions. Their primary focus has been OCLC access, training, and support services, contract work on LC record preparation, online reference searching services, retrospective record conversion, group purchase plans, reclassification, and a variety of other library automation products and services that vary from network to network.

A not-for-profit organization, AMIGOS, is one of the largest regional networks, serving more than 340 members, primarily in the southwestern states. In addition to the standard network services, AMIGOS offers a collection analysis service that enables a single library or group of libraries to compare holdings with the holdings of other peer groups and produces quantitative data in the form of basic record counts, proportional counts, overlap percentages, gap measures, and uniqueness measures. Other regional networks affiliated with OCLC include BCR, ILLINET, INCOLSA, MINITEX, NELINET, OHIONET, PALINET, and SOLINET.

The decade of the 1980s was marked by compelling progress in preservation. Cooperation in preservation is important because of the magnitude of the problem and the need to assure the continued existence of our common cultural heritage. The Commission on Preservation and Access, founded in 1986, played a key role in coordinating and promoting national and international preservation programs. Public awareness of the preservation problem was enhanced by the widespread dissemination of such films as *Slow Fires* and *Turning to Dust*.

Technology and dwindling resources mandate change. The impact of automation and the trend toward providing information in electronic, as well as print, format will drive academic library cooperation in the 21st century in directions that are, as yet, difficult to predict. Although these changes do not guarantee the free sharing of resources, they do promise to alter dramatically the ways in which libraries cooperate. Librarians have done well in developing collaborative programs for describing and preserving resources, but have not yet developed models for changing the ways academic institutions develop collections or share resources. The process of assuring equality of access to our combined information resources promises to remain an intensely political, yet essential, process.

REFERENCES

Joseph J. Branin, "Cooperative Collection Development," in *Collection Management: A New Treatise,* edited by Charles B. Osburn and Ross Atkinson (1991).

Jasper G. Schad, "The Future of Collection Development in an Era of Fiscal Stringency: A Symposium," *Journal of Academic Librarianship* (1992).

David C. Weber, "A Century of Cooperative Programs among Academic Libraries," *College and Research Libraries* (1976),

LARRY R. OBERG

LAWS AND REGULATION

Librarians need to understand the kinds of legislative issues they may have to respond to. In order to do so, they need to understand the nature of the legislative context in which academic libraries operate.

Academic libraries are bound by the general legislative context of the country in which they exist; not all academic libraries are free to collect aggressively the publications of other countries, able to negotiate their own purchasing arrangements with vendors, or bound by international copyright conventions. The national government articulates a framework for access to information and ownership of intellectual property and establishes systems for exchanging mail, including library materials, and collecting national revenues, including, perhaps, some revenues generated by taxes on imported items such as books. The national government also establishes a rationale for distributing the revenues raised through taxation, and this rationale guides the administration of any governmental programs that provide funding for academic libraries. In some countries, the majority of the control and funding emanates from the national sector; in other countries, the central government delegates control to a state or local government or to the institution itself, retaining some powers at the national level.

Legislation for academic libraries is both broad and narrow; it is as broad as a policy of censorship can be in its rejection of materials in many disciplines, and it is as narrow as a ruling by the courts in the state of Pennsylvania that academic libraries in that state are exempt from a newly levied tax on journal subscriptions. The range of concerns includes funding for a stable and economical postal system to foster delivering materials to and among libraries, establishing national collections, supporting a national system for cataloguing materials, providing for education for professionals to serve as librarians in the country, and funding for buildings, collections, and technology.

In democratic societies, academic librarians often use the power of their professional associations to garner support for desired legislation. Librarians attempt to demonstrate to legislators both the benefit of the existing legislation and the necessity of any additional legislation by reference to the good the legislation offers to library users in a variety of arenas. Other groups may have opposing opinions, and the legislation, when finally enacted, reflects the compromises made during the process. The doctrine of *fair use,* the part of U.S. copyright law that permits librarians and scholars to make some use of materials under copyright, is a case in point. Librarians maintain systems to ensure that they do not violate the law in the course of providing library service; they also inform users about the requirements of the law.

Online public access catalog and CD-ROM area, located in the new wing of the Main Library, University of Hong Kong, completed in 1991.

During the years that the legislation was being drafted, librarians were forceful in defending the needs of scholars to have a system of fair use, and they were often in the position of opposing publishers, many of whom wished to eliminate or severely limit the custom.

One type of material, U.S. federal government publications, offers many examples of the impact of legislation on the availability of information and library materials. When the framers of the U.S. government decided that the best government was a government of the people and that, therefore, the people needed both to be educated and to have access to information about their government, they established or affirmed several important institutions. One was the system of public education, a responsibility of local governments in the U.S.; another was the system of publishing the work of the federal government and making the publications available to the citizens. This process is now part of the Federal Depository Library System. Many academic libraries are accorded the status of depository library and accept the obligation to house documents from a number of federal agencies and make them available to citizens, in return for receiving the materials at no cost. During the administrations of Ronald Reagan and George Bush, the government reduced the scope of the federal publications program, with corresponding gaps in the information available to citizens. In 1992 the Office of Management and Budget issued a proposed policy guideline stating the belief that government functions do not normally include gathering information and that libraries and cafeterias are examples of functions not inherently governmental. The ALA and other professional associations opposed this view and sought the support of legislators and citizens interested in the free flow of government information. Such policy differences are usually resolved after negotiations between the political parties, and clarifying legislation is enacted.

Several pieces of federal legislation affect most

Rear view of the Walter Royal Davis Library, the University of North Carolina at Chapel Hill. Since 1931 the University of North Carolina and Duke University have had a cooperative agreement for collection development, reciprocal borrowing and delivery of materials.

L. C. Scarborough

academic libraries in the U.S.; one of the most important is the legislation that maintains the programs of the Library of Congress and the other national libraries. The collection development and collection organization work of these national institutions undergird the work of all academic libraries, especially the LC programs for cataloguing materials in a machine-readable format (MARC). Other legislation, notably the Higher Education Act, provided funds for research libraries seeking to acquire and catalogue specialized collections, as well as funds for institutions that are less affluent and funds dedicated to certain goals. The grant programs are competitive, and public and private academic libraries in all 50 states seek these scarce funds as a way to introduce innovative ideas on their campuses, to fund the purchase of newer technologies, or to catalogue important older collections. Other funds for academic libraries are available through the legislation supporting the National Endowment for the Humanities; these funds provided the bulk of the support for efforts to microfilm master and service copies of significant copies of endangered brittle books. Some dollars are made available for research activities, others for fellowships for educating future librarians. In many cases the legislation needs renewal after a set term, and hearings on reauthorization provide an opportunity to testify on the good impact of the legislation and to suggest modification of priorities. With the growth of the federal deficit has come concern for the proliferation of federal programs, and each library program faces scrutiny as to its worth. In many cases a program is authorized, but not funded at a level that would allow it to reach its goals with ease or in a short time. New legislation is a result of agreement that the legislation will help meet a national priority.

One federal law that illustrates this focus on funding important priorities and also demonstrates the expectation of linkages between the federal and state governments is the High Performance Computing Act. Passed in 1991, this act authorized $2.9 billion over five years for two interrelated technological efforts of importance to all academic libraries, not just those in the U.S. The first part, the National High-Performance Computing Program, established goals and priorities for federal high-performance computing research, development, networking, and related activities.

The second part is the National Research and Education Network (NREN), designed to link research and educational institutions, government, and industry in every state. The act directed federal agencies to work with private network service providers, state and local agencies, libraries, educational institutions, and other organizations to ensure that researchers, educators, and students have appropriate access to the high-performance computing systems, electronic information resources, and other research facilities through the network. Building on such existing computer networks as Merit, NSFNET, and the global Internet, the multigigabit NREN was designed to link researchers in government, industry, and higher education to a formidable international array of databases, supercomputers, and research services through a high-capacity, high-speed electronic superhighway.

NREN marked a clear progression from such earlier research networks as the Department of the Army's ARPANET, the NSFNET, and even the global Internet. NREN culminated a move from closed to open user groups, from serving basic science to serving applied science, and from proprietary to generic software platforms. It was designed to serve a broader base of users because the underlying assumption of the builders of the original networks, that they would serve mainly computational, not communications, traffic, proved not to be accurate. Quite the opposite proved to be the case: on Internet, for example, electronic mail and packet routing account for more than half the traffic.

The many individuals who have already experienced some of the power of electronic networking, through the use of OCLC or Bitnet, are the primary customers for these new services—services that rely to some extent on the astute leadership of the present generation of academic librarians and the illustrious history of cooperation and technological innovation in the field of academic librarianship. Closely linked to NREN is the Coalition for Networked Information. A joint project of ARL, CAUSE, and EDUCOM, the Coalition was formed to promote the creation of and access to information resources in networked environments.

In many cases librarians have sought legislation for a public good and thereby facilitated the preservation of a nation's heritage, the education of its citizens, and the growth of scientific knowledge on a worldwide basis. Most academic librarians in the U.S., except those in some denominationally supported colleges, maintain a policy of neutrality for their libraries and expect all points of view to be available in the collection or to be expressed in the library's public meeting rooms. Librarians in the U.S. also demonstrate an eagerness to make all libraries useful to all citizens and often seek the support of legislators to that end. While public libraries are by definition the best example of this tradition, academic libraries share in it. The NREN legislation is an example of this ideology in action; it is predated by other examples, many of them still in effect.

State and local governments are the primary sources of funding for academic libraries, providing more than 90 percent of all funds to all but a few academic libraries. As state funding declined, academic institutions, including their libraries, redefined their programs. Reductions were a part of most redefinitions, and library collections and services grew at a slower rate than previously. Where growth occurred, it was usually in concert with legislative support for a newer priority, such as internationalizing the curriculum or increasing the enrollment of disadvantaged students.

State funding supports the work of the state library, an important node in the network delivering information to the citizens; state funding is also often a source of support for cooperative ventures among academic libraries. Other state regulations establish personnel classification systems in state colleges, regulate union organizing activity, establish penalties for theft or mutilation of library materials, protect the privacy of library users, develop systems for distributing state documents, and authorize new colleges or new programs at existing colleges. Not the least of these activities are the regular appropriations bills that fund state-supported academic libraries and provide some financial support for private colleges.

Future Trends. Legislation is no longer only a local, state, or national issue; it is often an international issue. With the growth of the European Community, many activities in the countries of Europe were coordinated on a regional level. Unesco now talks of Education sans Frontiers; voluntary collaboration, long a hallmark of librarianship, is enhanced by bilateral and multinational educational exchange agreements and by the power of satellite transmission and computer networks. Legislation to fund such exchanges has been available for decades—what is new is that more than a token number of institutions pay attention to it. Some programs at some academic libraries will need partial redirection as a result. Efforts toward regional cooperation are taking place at the same time that nationalism is gaining importance in many countries previously under the domination of the former Soviet Union. The two trends are not necessarily in collision; rather, new regional groupings based on language, not politics, may develop, as in the Baltic states. In each of these political decisions there is usually an educational exchange agreement of interest to academic libraries. While the legislation is vague and the funding may be temporary and insufficient, the goals are germane to the goals of academic librarianship, long a profession with a desire for universal bibliography and a worldwide network for scholars.

There is a reality and urgency to information that transcends the barriers of countries, even countries at war or countries in the midst of natural disasters. Language and legislation are temporary obstacles, overcome if the need for the information is great. Academic librarians concerned about eliminating barriers to information around the globe may choose to support the International Federation of Library Associations and Institutions and the work of its committees. Or they may choose to make their contributions in the area of collection development; through staff exchanges and/or participation in the work of Unesco, the Fulbright Program, or the ALA/Book Fellows program; or through supporting technological advances that further the availability of electronic networks to all academic institutions or permit distance learning by satellite. But, lest academic librarians think that they have solved the problems of international, national, and regional access by virtue of their good will to their neighbors, they should remember that in 1992 it was still easier to cross the border from one country to another than to check out a book at an academic library other than their own.

CAROLINE M. COUGHLIN

Accreditation

Accreditation of educational institutions and programs, based on peer evaluation and judgment, developed as a North American alternative to the European pattern of control of education by a government agency or the church. No provision was made in the U.S. Constitution for national involvement in education, and only in New York was there a State Board of Regents that was required to report annually to the Legislature on every college in the state.

Introduced late in the 19th century with the creation of the New England Association of Colleges and Secondary Schools, the concept of accreditation spread first to other regions of the United States and then to subject disciplines as professional associations assumed responsibility for monitoring educational programs in their respective fields. Initially, the purpose of accreditation was to improve communication between postsecondary educational institutions and secondary schools in order that students entering college might arrive with more nearly equal academic preparation. Closely allied with this purpose was the goal of standardizing the quality and measurement of learning experiences so that credits earned in one institution could be transferred to another with the assurance that the student's prior education would meet the expectations of the new school.

Another factor in the accrediting movement has been of such increasing importance that it sometimes overshadows the initial primary purposes. This is the social demand that accreditation should protect the public against incompetent and/or poorly educated graduates of educational institutions. While the health professions come most immediately to mind, the same principle applies to all professionals, including librarians. Professional self-regulation in North America begins with the accreditation of professional schools and educational programs. In no sense, however, may an association use accreditation as a device to limit access to the profession in order to reduce competition for jobs. A common misconception is that accreditation should constitute a device to control the number and the geographical distribution of educational programs within a profession. The granting of accreditation to a program signifies that that program meets or exceeds the quality expressed in the written standards for that area of study and thus meets its responsibilities to its constituency.

Accreditation falls into two categories: "general or institutional" and "specialized or programmatic." There is much overlapping, of course, as illustrated by the fact that every library education program currently accredited in the U.S. exists in an institution that is recognized by one of the six regional accrediting associations. In fact, regional accreditation of the institution is a prerequisite for even the consideration of a program in library education in the U.S. However, because the Canadian Library Association (CLA) many years ago arranged with the American Library Association (ALA) to accredit programs in Canadian library schools, this requirement does not apply in Canada, where regional accreditation does not exist.

During the early decades of the 20th century, as more and more professional associations assumed responsibility for monitoring educational programs in their fields, it was inevitable that this power to accredit would become a matter of dispute among associations. Furthermore, because much of the cost of accreditation must be borne by the institution or program seeking accreditation, university and college administrators became increasingly concerned with the number of professional associations demanding the right to accredit. In 1949 the National Commission on Accrediting (NCA), supported by some 640 U.S. institutions of higher education, was created not only to determine which professional associations would have the power to accredit educational programs but also to monitor the procedures and standards used by these associations.

In 1964, in response to a growing concern for "regionalism" in the accrediting process, the accrediting commissions of the six regional associations in the U.S. were brought together under the Federation of Regional Accrediting Commissions of Higher Education (FRACHE). The goal of FRACHE was to assure "quality education" on a nationwide basis.

In 1975 the National Commission on Accrediting merged with the Federation of Regional Accrediting Commissions of Higher Education to form the Council on Postsecondary Accreditation (COPA). A nongovernmental and nonprofit body, COPA fosters and facilitates the roles of both institutional and specialized accrediting agencies in promoting and ensuring the quality and diversity of American postsecondary education. COPA recognizes agencies that accredit educational programs in various fields and reviews those agencies periodically. COPA receives a portion of its financial support from the accrediting bodies it recognizes.

The concept of accreditation developed in the United States because the founders had deliberately avoided the imposition of government control of education. In the 1950s the provision of federal aid to higher education introduced the question of institutional eligibility for aid. The U.S. Commissioner of Education turned to the accrediting bodies to help determine that eligibility. The Department of Education now makes this determination by periodically reviewing the standards and processes used by accrediting agencies and publishing a list of approved accrediting bodies. It deems acceptable any institution or program accredited by an approved accrediting agency. The federal government's involvement in accreditation has not been without controversy. In the 1970s critics charged that the government was using its review mechanism to encourage social policies of which it approved; in 1991–92 critics charged that it was using its review mechanism to discourage policies on multiculturalism with which the administration did not agree. In a different sphere, critics charge that the government is using accreditation review to encourage institutions to be more rigorous in their pursuit of student loan defaulters.

Today, like other accrediting agencies, the ALA Committee on Accreditation (COA) must undergo periodic review of its procedures and practices by both COPA and the Department of Education in order to retain its authority as a recognized accrediting body. There will probably be constant tension over the federal government's use of accreditation as a criterion for various kinds of aid programs in higher education among those who believe that these decisions should be based solely on academic standards rather than social or administrative policy.

Accreditation in library education had its beginning in 1924 when the ALA created a Board of Education for Librarianship (BEL). This action was prompted by the publication one year earlier of the famous "Williamson Report," which painted a distressingly bleak picture of the 15 library schools then in existence. In 1956, with a general reorganization of the ALA, the COA was created to replace the Board of Education for Librarianship.

As a standing committee of ALA, the COA consists of 12 members appointed by the Executive Board, with one designated to chair. Appointments are for two years; the Association's President-elect nominates individuals to fill approaching vacancies. Broad representation on the Committee is sought among practicing librarians and educators, along with two lay members to represent the public interest. The Committee's formal charge is "to be responsible for the execution of the accreditation program of the American Library Association, and to develop and formulate standards of education for librarianship for the approval of the Council."

In 1969, supported by a substantial grant from the H. W. Wilson Foundation, COA appointed a ten-member subcommittee to draft new standards to replace those adopted in 1951. Those standards were developed after a period of open discussion, and after early drafts had been published for comments from the library community.

The six standards in the 1972 documents differ from earlier requirements in that the first and overriding standard requires that a school establish clearly defined goals and specific objectives for the program for which accreditation is sought. The interpretation of the five remaining standards depends on what the school determines to be its goals and program objectives. The latter five standards treat curriculum; faculty; students; governance, administration, and finance; and physical resources and facilities.

For many years, concerns had been expressed that the field was increasingly specialized, yet interdisciplinary responsibility continued to remain solely the responsibility of the COA. In 1984 the Association for Library and Information Science Education (ALISE), with the support of the H. W. Wilson Foundation, sponsored a conference on accreditation that brought together representatives of 17 organizations to discuss the topic of accreditation in the field and whether the accreditation program could be broadened to provide for specific participation and governance by organizations acting in concert. The conference concluded that such an effort was both desirable and feasible.

At the close of the ALISE/H. W. Wilson conference, Robert M. Hayes, then Chair of COA, announced that ALA had received a grant from the Department of Education to "explore procedures and guidelines for participation of a variety of associations in the accreditation of programs of library and information science education." The final report of this project, issued in 1986, endorsed the idea of cooperative accreditation and recommended that ALA fund an Inter-Association Advisory Committee on Accreditation. As the report was discussed, it became clear that many associations were interested in participating in the governance and operation of accreditation, but few, if any, were willing to assume a share of the costs. The idea of cooperative accreditation did not progress beyond this point.

Despite ongoing concerns in Canada over the appropriateness of accrediting Canadian library education programs through the ALA, the arrangement has continued. A Canadian always sits on the COA, and when a Canadian program is visited, at least one member of the visiting team is a Canadian; the CLA is invited to send an observer on the site visit. Many Canadians expected a more direct benefit from ALA accreditation in the late 1980s and early 1990s as new treaties facilitating the immigration of Canadians to the U.S. took effect.

In 1988 the COA created a subcommittee to advise it on whether the 1972 Standards needed revision. The subcommittee recommended a revision in 1989 and COA adopted it, along with a work plan for carrying it out. In creating a subcommittee to work on the revisions, chaired by Jane Robbins, the COA sought nominations from many organizations. The subcommittee produced successive drafts of the Standards and forwarded them to all interested groups for comment; it also held public hearings on the drafts. The COA anticipated presenting the Standards to the ALA Council at the Annual Conference in June 1992. However, when Charles Bunge, Chair of COA, presented the proposed Standards to the Council at the 1992 Midwinter Conference for information, there was such agreement that the Council adopted them at that time.

During the work on revising the Standards it became clear that there was general dissatisfaction, especially among the schools, with the processes the COA used to consider schools for accreditation. These processes involve creation of a detailed and lengthy Self-Study, an on-site visit by a team of at least four persons, and subsequent consideration of the site visit report by the COA. The schools indicated that the process had become too intrusive, focused on matters of detail rather than significance, and was far too costly. As part of the process of implementing the 1992 Standards, COA committed itself to a substantial revision of this process and created an Ad Hoc Advisory Panel on the Revision of the Accrediting Process.

In 1992 there were 59 schools accredited by the ALA, including 7 in Canada. However, two U.S. schools, at Brigham Young and Columbia universities, were identified as admitting no new students and were in the process of closing.

REFERENCES

Accreditation: A Way Ahead: Executive Summary (1986).

Edward G. Holley and Muriel Howick, "The Accreditation Process: What the Task Force Learned," *Journal of Education for Librarianship* (1977).

Patricia O. Rice, *The Accreditation of Library and Information Science Education: A Content Analysis of COA Recommendations, 1973–1985* (doctoral dissertation, State University of New York at Buffalo).

F. WILLIAM SUMMERS

Acquisitions

The term acquisitions refers to the function of obtaining all materials to be added to a library's collection. This definition is limited primarily to the processes that occur after the decision on which materials are to be ordered has been made. (For the selection process itself, *see* Collection Development.)

In a small library one individual may handle all phases of the acquisitions process and other functions as well, while in larger libraries one person may work only on acquisitions; in the largest libraries many may be assigned acquisitions duties. Staff devoted to acquisitions are usually placed organizationally with those who handle the other technical operations required to prepare library materials for the shelf (such as cataloguing, serials check-in, and binding). They work closely with those who select the library materials, those who handle the accounting of the library materials budget, and those who catalogue and classify the material received.

Acquisitions Procedures. The acquisitions process may be divided into six major steps:

Bibliographic Verification. Before ordering, acquisitions staff (or collections staff) determine whether the item to be ordered is available. Such verification helps ensure accuracy in budget encumbrances and speeds receipt of materials by providing the bookdealer with accurate information. The existence of a title may be verified by finding its bibliographic description in national or trade bibliographies, locating a complete record in a bibliographic utility, or contacting the ordering source.

Pre-order Searching. Acquisitions staff must search library files to make sure that the item to be ordered is not already in the collection. Searching includes checking the catalogue, all on-order and in-process files, and serials records. Acquisitions staff are often required to record information discovered during the searching process (such as call numbers, related editions, or series information) for later use in cataloguing.

Placing the Order. The acquisitions librarian must select the bookdealer (middleman, vendor, or publisher) to receive the purchase order. The order is transmitted to the dealer as a brief bibliographic description (author, title, place, publisher, date, series) in paper or electronic format. The acquisitions librarian strives for an economy of effort, going into only as much detail as is required for the type of library and level of specificity demanded.

Receiving the Item. When the item arrives, all elements of its bibliographic description must be carefully checked against the order. Acquisitions staff must investigate any inconsistency to be sure that the item received is indeed the item wanted. The invoice must be reviewed to make sure that the charges are correct. If the order, item received, and invoice are correct, the invoice is approved for payment and the piece is forwarded for cataloguing.

Resolving Problems. Acquisitions staff must solve the problems that arise during the ordering process. They may seem to be as varied as their number, but generally can be categorized as: incorrect items received, items received damaged or incomplete, and billing inaccuracies.

Related Processes. Acquisitions staff record the bookdealers' reports on why an item may be delayed or unavailable, send claims to dealers for those items not received in a specified time and for which no reports have been received, and cancel acquisitions records for items that cannot be supplied.

Types of Acquisitions. Most libraries obtain materials in two ways, by purchase or as gifts. In addition, some libraries obtain materials through exchange.

Purchases. Many bookdealers populate the international marketplace of bookselling. These bookdealers act as middlemen in providing not only books and periodicals, but also various special services tailored to library needs. Libraries find it efficient to use these bookdealers, because they can obtain through one source materials that they would otherwise have to order from many sources. Thus they can send orders to one place instead of many, process one invoice instead of many and resolve problems with one firm instead of many. A bookdealer purchases far more titles from a publisher than most individual libraries would and, as a result of such a large volume, may receive and pass along a greater discount than the library would realize by ordering the title directly from the publisher.

Librarians can identify bookdealers through advertisements in library literature; through direct mailings sent to libraries; through exhibits during state, regional, national, and international meetings; through dealer sales representatives who visit libraries; through communication with colleagues responsible for acquisitions in other libraries; and through publications such as *International Subscription Agents* (American Library Association, 5th edition, 1986; 6th edition scheduled for 1993) or *Buy Books Where—Sell Books Where: A Directory of Out-of-Print Booksellers and Their Author-Subject Specialties, 1990–91* (Morgantown, West Virginia, Ruth E. Robinson Books, 7th edition, 1990).

It is important for an acquisitions librarian to do business with bookdealers who offer services that match the library's needs. The spectrum of services is wide. Some dealers specialize in a particular subject matter (such as scientific and technical) or cater to a specific type of library (such as academic or special). Some maintain large warehouses so they are able to supply many titles immediately. A dealer may concentrate on certain types of materials: monographs, serials, government documents, maps, out-of-print items, rare materials, or such nonbook formats as microforms, sound recordings, slides, films, music scores, CD-ROM products, or video tapes or discs. Services may include providing customized invoices and management reports in paper or electronic format, paying shipping costs, allowing automatic returns for unmarked items, supplying processing forms, and making immediate communication possible with toll-free telephone lines, fax transmission, or electronic mail addresses.

A library may place many kinds of orders with a bookdealer. The most common are:

a *firm order*— for a single monographic title; may be for multiple copies.

a *subscription or continuation*—an order for a title that appears over a long period of time; includes titles with a specified number of volumes, not all published simultaneously, as well as serials titles, which theoretically have no end in sight.

a *blanket order*—an order for all titles produced by a specific publisher.

an *approval plan*—an order for current titles answering a library's customized specifications (often called a profile) based on all or a combination of the following: subject, level of complexity, publisher, country of imprint, format, edition types, and language. Approval plan shipments may come as frequently as once a week. Only those that meet the "approval" of designated library staff are purchased. Items not accepted are returned to the bookdealer.

Ordering directly from the publisher may be preferred under certain circumstances, such as a special price discount offer, the need to fulfill a user's request quickly, or a publisher's policy of not selling through bookdealers. A first step in acquiring out-of-print material is to query the publisher before sending an order to a specialized dealer or trying the secondhand market. If no copy is available in out-of-print sources, the acquisitions staff must obtain the publisher's permission before making any interlibrary loan request for a photocopy. Some publishers of CD-ROMs or electronic publications require signed lease agreements before they supply materials. Even though many products can be ordered through vendors who pass along the lease forms, the acquisitions staff will deal directly with the publisher over questions or negotiations.

The Publications Committee of the Acquisitions of Library Materials Section of the ALA's Association for Library Collections and Technical Services (ALCTS) produced guidelines to assist acquisitions librarians in purchasing library materials and in running their acquisitions operation. The Acquisitions Committee of the ALCTS Serials Section drafted guidelines for evaluating the performance of serials vendors (scheduled for publication in 1993).

The Bookdealer Library Relations Committee, a committee of American Library Association's Resources and Technical Services Division, Resources Section, produced guidelines to assist acquisitions librarians in purchasing library materials. (For published Guidelines, see References.) A guideline to aid librarians in evaluating the performance of bookdealers, *Guide to Performance Evaluation of Library Materials Vendors,* was published by ALA in 1989.

Gifts. A second source of library materials is the individual donor or group that wishes to give books to the library. It is important for library staff to apply their standard selection guidelines to gift materials, because the administrative cost of adding a gift title to the collection is comparable to the cost for adding a purchased title. Because many gifts are older materials, it is imperative to consider their condition as well as their subject matter. It is usually not worthwhile to go to the expense of adding a brittle book unless it is a rare or antiquarian item.

Many donors ask library staff to evaluate the worth of a gift. As the recipient, the library should have a policy against providing such appraisals, because appraisal for the donor would usually be regarded as a conflict of interest. The donor may engage a specialist consultant or bookseller to appraise donated collections. A library's written acknowledgment of the gift is not only a courtesy, but also a record of the donation for the donor.

Some donors ask the library to agree to certain stipulations placed on the gift (such as housing all the items in a gift together or creating a special room named for the donor). Such restrictions must be carefully weighed against the real value of having the gift as a part of the library collection. It is considered good policy to accept gifts with no strings attached.

Exchanges. Some larger or specialized libraries use exchanges as a method of acquisition. An exchange arrangement is a partnership between libraries, a two-way relationship based on an expectation of sending and receiving future publications. Each library must have publications to offer, either published by its parent institution or purchased to send to its partner library. Some titles are available only on exchange because of the economic or political situations of the countries in which the exchange partners reside. Titles received on exchange should be selected with the same criteria used for purchased items, because processing and storage costs are identical for both.

Although it is more economical to exchange serials than it is to barter monographs, there are many costs associated with maintaining an exchange program beyond the usual purchase procedures—labor-intensive activities such as maintaining partner records and corresponding with or on behalf of partners. Care should be taken to ensure that exchanges are balanced in the sense that each half of the exchange partnership is receiving equal benefit from the arrangement. Exchanges should be reviewed periodically to assure that they are still providing valid additions to both library collections involved.

Automation. For many years, libraries maintained their acquisitions files on paper, and the organization and procedures of most acquisitions operations centered on paper files. Many libraries now rely on computers to provide files in automated form. As their files evolve from paper to electronic format, acquisitions librarians should rethink their organizational design and procedural workflows and, in some cases, redefine appropriate functions for acquisitions. Tasks traditionally associated with cataloguing, such as record selection, copy cataloguing, and authority work, are now sometimes incorporated into the acquisitions workflow.

In the 1960s libraries began using computers to assist with their acquisitions processes. These acquisitions programs were costly, cumbersome batch operations run on mainframe computers and relying on punched cards for input. In the 1970s acquisitions librarians in the U.S. first had the opportunity to simplify their verification procedures by using bibliographic databases such as OCLC and RLIN. Some libraries elected to use the automated acquisitions subsystems offered by the bibliographic utilities, thus relying on a large bibliographic network for computer support. In the 1980s, as microcomputers became more common in libraries, acquisitions librarians were able to utilize automation to maintain files and produce reports. In addition, library system vendors developed modules that not only generated paper orders, but also integrated acquisitions operations and records into online catalogues and circulation systems.

Some acquisitions procedures have been difficult to fit into standard automated systems, leading many libraries to create local microcomputer files and databases to automate specialized files, forms, exchange and gift donor lists, out-of-print files, form letters, and mailing labels, for example. As data storage and transmission technologies improve, there is growing potential for linking local databases and larger automated systems.

By the 1990s, electronic ordering became a reality for many libraries. Some libraries send their orders to vendors by electronic mail, tape transfer, or direct transmission. Some vendors in turn use similar methods of automated communication with their regional or branch offices and with publishers. As more libraries have automated their acquisitions processes, they have demanded more collaboration between materials vendors and systems vendors to enable them to make the most effective combination of the increasingly sophisticated components available in the marketplace.

Proliferation of software and hardware for transmission of acquisitions data has led to recognition of the need for standards to support electronic transmission of bibliographic information among publishers, vendors, and libraries. Several organizations in the U.S. have worked on these standards, most notably the Book Industry Systems Advisory Committee (BISAC) and the Serials Industry Systems Advisory Committee (SISAC). For example, SISAC published a draft standard X12 for electronic data interchange (EDI) of invoices. The National Information Standards Organization/American National Standards Institute's work on standards for computerized book ordering, serials ordering, claiming, cancellations, and acknowledgments are codified in ANSI standards Z39.49 and Z39.45.

As more libraries, vendors, and publishers increase their automation activities, and as interfaces among systems improve, the speed and accuracy of acquisition of library materials will increase in direct proportion to the increased ease of communication.

REFERENCES

Richard W. Boss, Hal Espo, and Susan Harrison, "Automating Acquisitions," *Library Technology Reports* (1986).

Alfred H. Lane, *Gifts and Exchange Manual* (1980).

Rose Mary Magrill and John Corbin, *Acquisitions Management and Collection Development in Libraries,* 2nd edition (1989).

MARILYN G. McSWEENEY

Adult Services

Adult services is the programmatic and organizational expression of the public library's role as an educational institution in its community. Although closely related to reference services, it emphasizes an active stance through such services as adult education programs, including literacy training; readers' advisory services; and a variety of community and cultural programs. Adult services is the modern expression of the 19th-century vision of the public library as "the people's university."

Adult services benefits from all the functional activities of libraries—selection of materials, cataloguing and classification, direct assistance to library users, encouragement of library use through targeting individuals or organized groups, even administrative and technical work. The great diversity in the public library's clientele produced another type of specialization, however, by type of user: children, adults, young adults, handicapped, business people, and so on. Adult services has always considered the individual as a member of a larger public. As one study stated, "The enduring focus of a generic adult user . . . has been the active transformation of collections, resources, and staff into programmatic responses relevant to the community served." (Heim and Wallace, 1990.)

Institutional Development. The library, once the exclusive receptacle of the official documents of governments, the religious and philosophical manuscripts of the church, or military and commercial records, developed dramatically in the 19th century with the onset of literacy resulting from mass public education. The printing and publishing industries responded to this growth in readership and hunger for learning by creating materials of the widest possible variety.

The Argentinian politician and educator Domingo Faustino Sarmiento wrote in the mid-19th century of the "potential of the public library as an instrument for the continuing education and self-development of the people." (Krzys, 1983.) But perhaps the most identifiable developments in adult services have been centered in the United States, thanks to the establishment and progress of public education and public libraries there. Robert Ellis Lee's *Continuing Education for Adults through the American Public Library, 1833–1964* describes stages in the evolution of library services with relation to adult education. The background on public library growth is significant. Institutional goals in American libraries from 1833 to 1875 were focused on collecting and preserving materials. The next 20 years were typified by the organization of these resources for wider use. Early in the 20th century collections were activated by extending services to special groups, by intentional information services, and by establishing an educational role for the public library.

The educational objective of public libraries was articulated as early as 1876, when Samuel Swett Green wrote a report for the U.S. Office of Education covering personal assistance to users and indicating direct promotion of library collections. In 1877 Charles Frances Adams declared the basic purpose of the library to be a means of continuing self-education. Henry Munson Utley, Librarian at the Detroit Public Library, declared the public library to be purely and wholly educational—"truly the people's university."

In the United Kingdom the Mechanics' Institutes, founded in the early 19th century to spread education among members of the working classes, were provided with libraries that catered to the needs of institute students and served as precursors of public libraries.

The migration of peoples from all continents into the U.S. in the late 19th and early 20th centuries placed great demands on libraries. Adults were hungry for a new language and a new life. The reading rooms of urban public libraries were popular places of adult education, meetings, and respite. This is a major

Carnegie Library of Pittsburgh Photo by Ray Fleming

Job and Career Education Center, Carnegie Library of Pittsburgh.

reason why Lee describes the period up to 1920 as one "associated with a theory of democratic library service which emphasized the indeterminate idea of the observance of the rights of the library user." Also, "informational reference service, increasing in scope and importance, became a highly specialized service representing a substantial claim on the librarian's time and on the library budget."

During these years, current fiction, formerly a low-priority portion of public library collections, was supplied and circulated systematically and in quantity. In other words, more diversity and specialization was offered in services to adults. Both of these areas of interest—reference and current fiction—represented early phases of actual book promotion, or active support of parts of the collection. Library manuals, such as Jennie Flexner's *Circulation Work in Public Libraries* (1927), describe a broad range of educational, recreational, and cultural services for adults.

Adult Education. An important factor in the development of adult services is the link to the adult education movement. Malcolm S. Knowles contends that the American Library Association's Commission on Library and Adult Education in its 1926 report, *Libraries and Adult Education,* "enunciated a philosophy and set forth directional guidelines which exerted a powerful influence on the development of the library as an educational institution."

Another similar and important declaration of the 1920s was William S. Learned's *American Public Library and the Diffusion of Knowledge* (1924). A new dimension of adult services was being explored, he suggested, where "knowledge and understanding [may be] derived from sources other than print," including lectures, museum services, motion pictures and radio, and the fine arts. Programs in the form of lectures, discussions, displays, exhibits, and demonstrations took hold among library adult services. Audiovisual collections and concomitant programming were established, growing to widespread adult programming in the ensuing decades.

A classic work by Margaret E. Monroe, *Library Adult Education: The Biography of an Idea,* describes the extraordinary elements of a growing service in public libraries tied to adult education. Through case studies of several libraries and accounts of the organizational maneuvering of the ALA, Monroe tells how adult education became firmly grounded among adult services and how it was also embodied in a particular service: readers' advisory.

Readers' Advisory. Librarians created models of certain adult services, described them for their colleagues, and promoted them as a core to serving adults. Foremost among them was a system to guide readers through great literature or areas of knowledge. Some libraries, especially large urban institutions, even maintained readers' advisory "offices."

Lynn Birge says "readers' advisory service gradually faded from the forefront of the library's adult education program" after World War II. The courses and alcoves that had appeared in libraries disappeared. However, readers' advisory made a comeback in the 1980s, and the professional literature and studies of an earlier generation are enjoying a new life. ALA published *Readers' Advisory Service in the Public Library* by Joyce Saricks and Nancy Brown in 1989.

The importance of this movement was and is that it shows a new, specific, individualized turn toward a user population. The "offices" provided organizational structure, and librarians were designated on its behalf.

Lincoln City Library, Oregon

Senior citizens at a community center in Lincoln, Oregon, are reached through Lincoln City Library's extension services.

ALA Involvement. The ALA nurtured adult services under the concept of "library adult education" continuously from the Enlarged Program at the end of World War I through the lectures and discussion groups of the People's Institute collaboratively developed in the New York Public Library in the 1920s. The Carnegie Corporation supported an ALA project called "Reading with a Purpose." A subcommittee on Readable Books initiated new forms in published books for the layman in the 1930s. The Ford Foundation's Fund for Adult Education in the 1950s stressed discussion of public issues, political philosophy, and classics in the humanities.

For a generation, ALA, in cyclical ups and downs, provided the status, the funds, the consulting expertise, and the training in workshops and conference programs that brought adult services to maturity on a national scale. John Chancellor, Grace T. Stevenson, Helen Lyman, Eleanor Phinney, Margaret E. Monroe, and Ruth Warncke were among a number of ALA leaders whose work in the field of adult services gave it the professional status it needed.

ALA sponsored research and development in adult services performance and analysis, as in two major studies, one by Helen Lyman Smith, *Adult Education Activities in Public Libraries* (1954), and a general work, *Studying the Community: A Basis for Planning Adult Education Services* (1960). The earlier study identified 37 variables, or possibilities, among adult services. It asked how programs were committed, how groups were served, how reading was promoted, and even how reading was taught. The underlying philosophy of adult services was no longer subsumed in mere extension or outreach attempts.

Instead, adult services had a dominant definition among all library services.

The ALA committees and boards supervising adult service projects were complemented by a growing membership structure for adult services. The Adult Education Section of the Public Library Association in the early 1950s was transformed in 1957 into the Adult Services Division, reflecting a vigorous leadership in the field. But the dominance of the information function over the educational, cultural, and recreational functions was reasserted in 1972, with the merger of the Reference Services Division with the Adult Services Division.

Library Education. Few library schools have classes in adult services. However, workshops, training institutes, and manuals have been created. The Allerton Park Conference in 1950 was devoted to "Training Needs of Librarians Doing Adult Education Work." The teaching of Miriam Tompkins for 30 years, at Emory University and then at Columbia University, was probably a greater influence during the 1930s and 1940s than any other single educational factor in building the cadre of adult services specialists who gave leadership to the field.

On the other hand, staff training in major public library systems provided significant dissemination of adult services skills and understanding throughout the U.S. as staff who benefitted from training in major libraries were dispersed to other public library positions. Often staff training was built around the learning needed to carry out staff projects in adult services. The Columbus-Franklin County library system in Ohio provides an intensive training program in which adult services librarians work in many sections of the main library and in branch libraries as well before they are permanently assigned to the day-to-day challenge of adult services.

Literacy. Literacy education in libraries has been the cause of considerable debate among librarians. Resistance has most often been generated by the feeling that librarians cannot take on a direct educational role. However, most agree that the strategy of involvement is one of support, not teaching. Furthermore, the great interest in making active readers of the general population is reason enough to provide space, purchase appropriate materials, and facilitate programs for illiterates and adult new readers. The pervasiveness of the problem of illiteracy has generated response from thousands of librarians throughout the world.

Among the many works on this service, several stand out. Bernice MacDonald of the New York Public Library wrote *Literacy Activities in Public Libraries* in 1966. Helen Lyman Smith wrote *Library Materials in Service to the Adult New Reader* (1973), *Reading and the Adult New Reader* (1976), and *Literacy and the Nation's Libraries* (1977).

Although the federal government created programs in the 1970s and 1980s, no significant official program has survived. Title VI of the Library Services and Construction Act provided funding for programs beginning in the 1980s, notably the California Literacy Campaign in 1984, a $2 million start-up that became an important part of the effort of the State Library of California.

ALA spearheaded the Coalition for Literacy in 1981. Eleven national agencies and volunteer organizations helped to promote the establishment of programs and to create a national referral center for literacy education. Literacy persists as a central adult service, fundamental to all others.

Recent Trends. The Adult Education Act of 1966 began the organization of potential library users into special classes and groups so that libraries could turn their attention to targets in the community. In the 1980s the National Endowment for the Humanities (NEH) and the ALA jointly sponsored many reading and discussion programs. One notable collaboration was the "Let's Talk About It" series that drew 30,000 adults into 300 libraries in all parts of the country for scholar-led book discussion groups. A similar effort, the "Voices and Visions" series, focused on poetry. These programs provide examples of the need for informal but structured settings for adults to discuss what they read outside the normal educational milieu. NEH and ALA published a guide, *Planning Library Programs,* to facilitate the concept of programming that grew out of adult services and book promotion.

Librarians in Denmark promoted Danish culture with activities, meetings, adult education programs, and exhibitions in libraries. In Papua New Guinea a librarian likens the library to a "traditional *kobo* (men's house) where knowledge is being passed on to others." Libraries in many countries face the challenge of multilingual and multiethnic adult users, with the added complication of providing materials for these diverse communities when funds are limited.

Helen Lyman Smith's study was repeated and updated in the 1980s. The "Adult Services in the Eighties" project received funding from the Bailey K. Howard/World Book Encyclopedia Award. The questionnaire covered 64 programmatic efforts in public libraries, allowing for variations in each to be reported upon. The diversity and creativity of the findings documented in this huge study provide a convenient summary of the status of resources and programming for adults in libraries throughout the U.S. and augur well for the indispensability of adult services in libraries in years to come.

GARY O. ROLSTAD

Afghanistan

Afghanistan, a republic in south-central Asia, is bordered by Turkmenistan and the Uzbek and Tadzhik republics on the north, Pakistan on the east and south, and Iran on the west. Population (1989 est.) 18,136,000; area 652,090 sq.km. The official languages are Dari (Afghan Persian) and Pashto. The peasant-tribal society is composed of various ethnic groups (Pashtuns, Tadjiks, Hazaras, Uzbeks, Baluchs, Turkoman, and Kirghiz, among others), with a 90 to 95 percent nonliterate population.

History. In Afghanistan, as in many Asian countries, what libraries there were in the past were created, organized, and supported by an elite group of rulers and religious leaders for their own use. Only comparatively recently did the concept of libraries as institutions of preservation give way to a more modern concept of libraries as sources of knowledge and information service. However, the progress made in the late 1960s and early 1970s was stalled by the coup d'état of 1978, the Soviet occupation of the country, and years of warfare. Following a UNmediated Soviet withdrawal in 1988, rebels overthrew the government in 1992. Reliable information about libraries was scarce after 1978.

National Library. There is no national library in Afghanistan, but some functions of one are performed by certain institutions, such as the Kabul University Library, the Ministry of Education Reference Library, and the Public Library of the Ministry of Information and Culture. A national bibliography is issued irregularly by the Kabul University Library.

Academic Libraries. The most important and largest library in Afghanistan is the Kabul University Library. Kabul University (Kabul Pohantun) was founded in 1932. Small faculty libraries came into existence but were accessible only to faculty members. In 1967 an Indiana University team reorganized the structure of the university system, and the present library was organized at that time. (Betty White, an American librarian, is remembered for organizing the present University Library.) Its collection totals about 130,000 volumes, arranged by the Library of Congress Classification. It holds special collections dealing with material on Afghanistan and Islamic civilization.

At 13 teacher training institutions, high school graduates are given one to two years of training and then sent to the provinces in a program to eradicate illiteracy. The provincial teacher training institutions have small libraries numbering at the most 500 books. These small collections were augmented regularly by small gifts of books from foreign philanthropic and cultural organizations.

Most of these collections, largely in English, were entrusted to teachers untrained in librarianship. The three teacher training institutions in Kabul fare much better. The Higher Teacher's College, a two-year institution for training college-level teachers, has a library of approximately 10,000 volumes with a professionally trained librarian. The Academy for Teacher Education and the Dar'ul Mo'alamein training schools have libraries of approximately 1,000 volumes. The greater portion of the collections is in English, a language not usually known by the students.

Public Libraries. The Public Library of the Ministry of Information and Culture, usually referred to as the Kabul Public Library, is in the central part of the city facing Zarnegar Park. The Library has its own Reading Garden, a pleasant plane tree grove with reading benches along the public paths, and popular with Kabul students who use the area as an outdoor reading-study room. Its collection numbers 120,000 volumes; a large portion is in English. Efforts were made to increase the books in the two national tongues, Pashto and Dari. There is a Children's Section, an Afghan room housing material pertaining to Afghanistan, and a periodical room containing a complete collection of Afghan periodical publications. The Library is under the direct jurisdiction of the Ministry of Information and Culture. Not all books circulate, but all may be used on the premises. The Library is housed in a two-story building that was once a private mansion, and has five branches. There are 36 other public libraries in the country, but all have far smaller collections.

School Libraries. In Kabul, Habiba High School, subsidized at one time by the United States, has a library with a collection of 5,000 books, supervised by a teacher. The Isteqlal Lycée, subsidized by the French government, has a library of approximately 10,000 volumes in French. The "Russian" Polytechnic Institute has a library, but it is not open to the public. It has approximately 10,000 volumes on science and technology. The "German" High School, subsidized to some extent by the German government, also has a library, primarily in German. In elementary schools libraries are practically nonexistent, though a few have small collections of 50 to 100 books, usually administered by a *tawildar* (keeper), who discourages lending because he or she is held financially responsible for all books lost. There was no government assistance to libraries at the elementary school level.

Special Libraries. The Historical Society of Afghanistan Library, in the Shar-e-Nau section of Kabul, has a collection of approximately 40,000 volumes. This specialized collection deals exclusively with anthropology, ethnology, prehistory, archaeology, genealogy, history, and folklore of Afghanistan. It contains all publications of the Délégation Archeologique Française en Afghanistan (DAFA), which excavated sites at Ai Khanoum and Hadda. Other special libraries include the Afghan Institute of Technology, the Anjumane Tareekh, and the Goethe Institute. All are in Kabul, and all have small collections.

Other Libraries. The Ministry of Education Reference Library and Book Distribution Center in Kabul holds about 28,000 books on education, open to teachers and employees of the Ministry. It acts as a central cataloguing agency for books distributed to schools, providing some 40,000 books to teacher training institutions and some high schools. The open-shelf libraries of the British Council, American Center, and French Cultural Center were used by students needing materials and study centers.

Libraries in Afghanistan (1990)

Type of library	Number of administrative units (main libraries)	Number of service points (branches, mobile stops, etc.)	Volumes in collections	Population served
Academic* Higher Education	18	18	191,000	11,331
Public*	55	55	350,000	30,802

*1984 data

Source: Unesco, *Statistical Yearbook,* 1991.

The Profession. The Anjuman Ketab-khana-e-Afghanistan (Afghanistan Library Association) was organized in 1971 by a former Kabul University Librarian, Abdul Rasul Rahim, to promote literacy and libraries in Afghanistan as its basic objective; it works to improve the status of librarians and to lobby for a national library system and for a School of Library Science in Kabul University. It sponsored training workshops and seminars for teacher-librarians in the teacher training schools and irregularly published the *Afghan National Bibliography*.

JOHN DE BELFORT URGUIDI

ALA

Jorge Aguayo

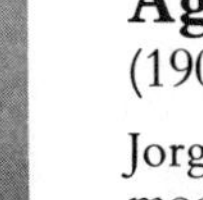

Aguayo, Jorge
(1903–)

Jorge Aguayo is considered the founding father of modern library procedure and library education in Cuba. He also contributed to the library development in other parts of Latin America, to furthering library cooperation through the Pan American Union and the American Library Association, and to scholarship in Spanish-language classification.

Born in Havana, Cuba, December 4, 1903, Aguayo received his early schooling in the capital. At the University of Havana he received degrees in Civil Law in 1925 and in Diplomatic and Consular Law in 1927. Aguayo entered the library field, following a strong interest in books and learning.

In 1937 he began a long and fruitful association with the General Library of the University of Havana, serving as Assistant Director until 1959, when he assumed the post of Director. The Rockefeller Foundation awarded him a one-year fellowship to study at Columbia University's Library School in 1941, and Aguayo took a concentrated curriculum with emphasis on cataloguing problems and university administration. In the years following his return to the University of Havana, the General Library pioneered in the use of fundamental tools such as the dictionary catalogue with subject headings translated and adapted from the Sears and Library of Congress lists, the Dewey Decimal System, the ALA cataloguing rules, the use of Library of Congress printed cards, the establishment of a separate reference collection, and many other services previously unknown to Cuban library users. The results of Aguayo's work are summarized in three manuals written in the 1940s: *Reglas para la Ordenación del Catálogo Diccionario de la Biblioteca General de la Universidad* ("Rules governing the dictionary catalogue of the General Library of the University," Havana, 1940); *Manual Prático de Clasificación y Catalogación de Bibliotecas* ("Practical manual of classification and cataloguing for libraries," Havana, 1943; 2nd ed., 1951); and *Modelos de Fichas* ("Model cards," Havana, 1942; 2nd ed., 1949). The latter two have been used as textbooks by a number of Latin American library schools.

In 1940 Aguayo and three associates initiated the teaching of library science at the Havana Lyceum. All four served as Cuba's first professional faculty of library science, offering a variety of courses lasting three and six months. In 1946 the formal teaching of library science began with the establishment of Cursos de Técnica Bibliotecaria at the Summer School of the University of Havana under Aguayo's direction. He served as Director of the summer courses until 1952 and assumed the professorship of cataloguing and classification in the University's School of Librarianship from its founding in 1950 until his departure from Cuba in 1960.

Aguayo's involvement in library development in individual Latin American countries and the region as a whole went hand in hand with his ambitious program in Cuba. In 1944 the U.S. State Department, the ALA, and the Rockefeller Foundation invited him to teach the first library science course in Peru after a fire destroyed the National Library in Lima. In 1947 he attended the First Assembly of Librarians of the Americas. He served as a consultant to the Regional Conference of National Commissions of the Western World, held in Havana in 1950, and to the Conference on Development of Public Library Services in São Paulo in 1951. He was President of the first Cuban Library Workshop in 1953.

Aguayo served as a prominent spokesman for Latin American librarians on cataloguing matters in the ALA. He was a member of the Canadian and Latin American Subcommittee of the ALA's Special Committee on Dewey Classification from 1944 to 1947. He then served on the ALA's Standing Committee on Cooperation with Latin American Catalogers and Classifiers from 1953 to 1958.

After the Castro revolution in 1960, Aguayo went to the United States and worked for two years at Syracuse University as bibliographer in charge of the Farmington Plan for Uruguay, Paraguay, and Argentina. In 1962 he became the Branch Librarian of the Pan American Union (PAU) and served as the Head Librarian of the PAU's central Columbus Library from 1968 until 1973. During that time he was also consultant to the Spanish translation of the Anglo-American Cataloging Rules (1970) and together with Carmen Rovira compiled the PAU-sponsored *Lista de Encabezamientos de Materia para Bibliotecas* ("Subject heading list for libraries," 1967), a milestone work that served libraries throughout the Spanish-speaking world as the basic subject heading list. Aguayo was named Editor and Director of the translation into Spanish of the 18th edition of the Dewey Decimal Classification System, which appeared in 1980.

Aguayo wrote more than 50 articles on a variety of library subjects, published in journals in the United States, Peru, Cuba, Bolivia, and Argentina. In addition, he served as Contributing Editor to *Libri,* 1949–50. Aguayo also translated into Spanish *The University Library, Its Organization, Administration and Function,* by Louis R. Wilson and Maurice F. Tauber.

MARTHA TOMÉ

Ahern, Mary Eileen
(1860–1938)

Mary Eileen Ahern was the Editor of the U.S. journal *Public Libraries* (later just *Libraries*) from its beginning in 1896 to its demise in 1931. In its editorial pages, readers can find Ahern's ideas about the public library movement, ideas that she believed in and fought for throughout her career. "There is only one solution of all social problems," she proclaimed in the opening issue, "—an increase in intelligence, a gradual education of the people." "The public library," Ahern went on to say in the same editorial, "is the broadest of teachers, one may almost say the only free teacher. It is the most liberal of schools, it is the only real people's college." She saw a librarian "as a teacher on all proper occasions."

Born in Indiana on October 1, 1860, Ahern was the daughter of Irish immigrants, William and Mary O'Neil Ahern. She attended high school and normal college in Indiana, taught in public schools in various small Indiana towns, and became Assistant State Librarian of Indiana in 1889. While in that office, she helped organize the Indiana Library Association, served as its first Secretary, and was later President. She was elected State Librarian by the Indiana Legislature in 1893, but the job ended in 1895 after the Democrats, who had supported her, lost the elections of 1894.

Aware that the State Librarian's job was a political football, Ahern mounted a campaign to take the State Library away from the Legislature and assign it to an independent Library Board. From the election until her position ended, she made special efforts to provide library materials and services to all the newly elected legislators. Each time she delivered materials and was told, "It's too bad that you cannot stay on here," she brought up her proposal for an independent library board and an independent state librarian. As it turned out, an independent library board was out of the question politically. Ahern did manage to promote a compromise in which the State Library was transferred from the Legislature to the State Board of Education. Part of that compromise was that Ahern would not seek reappointment as State Librarian, but she had already decided in any case to enroll in library school.

Ahern attended the library school at the Armour Institute of Technology in Chicago, 1895–96. During her time there, she was offered the editorship of *Public Libraries,* a new journal sponsored by the Library Bureau. The journal was subsequently taken over by the Illinois Library Association, an organization in which Ahern took an active part. A missionary for state and local library association organization and activity, she constantly urged her readers to get involved in the library movement. She was three times elected President of the Illinois Library Association (1908, 1909, and 1915), served on the ALA Council for many years, attended every ALA conference from 1893 to 1931, and was named a Charter Member of the American Library Institute. She was also Secretary for many years of the Library Department of the National Education Association, an organization whose formation she had heralded in the pages of *Public Libraries.*

The relationship between the schools and the public libraries, library training in the normal schools, the role of the school library, and the teaching function of the public librarian were topics with which Ahern was constantly concerned. She wrote on these subjects in *Public Libraries,* gave talks before library associations and civic groups, and contributed articles and reports to other publications. The school, the church, and the library were—in Ahern's view—linked together in a great mission: the education of the American people. She was an enthusiastic supporter of Andrew Carnegie's public library philanthropy. In the high-minded manner so characteristic of public librarians of her period, Ahern emphasized educational work, deplored the vulgarity of the popular newspaper press, and worried about the problems American public libraries experienced because of the publication of so many indelicate French novels.

Ahern gave up the editorship of *Libraries* in 1931; she was more than 70 years of age, and her eyesight had become so poor that she could not continue in editorial work. The Illinois Library Association decided to end the journal, rather than continue it without her. In the last issue, many colleagues paid tribute to Ahern and the journal. All agreed that *Libraries* had been a voice for small public libraries and had provided an important forum for the more practical aspects of library work. "The loan desk and the field trip," commented Frank K. Walter, Librarian of the University of Minnesota, "have been nearer her heart than the private study or the complicated problem of bibliographic research."

Even after retirement, Ahern continued to travel and to take a keen interest in library affairs. She died on a train near Atlanta, Georgia, on May 22, 1938.

ALA

Mary Eileen Ahern

REFERENCE

Doris Cruger Dale, "Ahern, Mary Eileen," *Dictionary of American Library Biography* (1978).

ELAINE FAIN (d. 1980)

Aje, Simeon Babasanya
(1927–)

National Library Association

Simeon Babasanya Aje

Simeon Babasanya Aje, Director of the National Library of Nigeria from 1971 to 1985, contributed in no small measure to the national public image of the librarian and put Nigeria on the international librarianship map. He worked for professional development through IFLA and Unesco activities.

Aje was born June 11, 1927, in Ondo State, Nigeria. He attended primary schools in his hometown, Ijurun, and Ijero in Ekiti from 1935 to 1941 and attended Christ's School, Ado-Ekiti, from 1942 to 1945, after which he took the Cambridge School Certificate and a Nigerian teachers' examination in 1948. From 1946 to 1954 Aje was a teacher in primary and secondary schools in what was then the Western Region.

He was a teacher/librarian in the Iwo District Council in 1955 and 1956. In 1957 he moved to the Western Regional Library and obtained leave and a scholarship to study at Loughborough College in England. At Loughborough Aje successfully completed the Great Britain Associateship of the Library Association Examination and obtained the Fellowship of the Library Association in 1959. Before returning to Nigeria, Aje was an Assistant Librarian at the National Central Library London (January–April 1960) and a cataloguer at the British National Bibliography later in the year. He then returned to the Western Regional Library.

Aje went to the United States for postgraduate professional education in 1962 at the University of Chicago Graduate School of Library Science, where he obtained an M.A. in 1963. During his stay in Chicago, Aje was also Social Science and Documents Librarian and Head of the Modern Languages Library at the University of Chicago Libraries. He returned as a Librarian in Western Regional Library services in 1964 and became Senior Librarian in 1967. In his post as Regional School Librarian, he was instrumental in promoting school library service and ran training programs for library assistants in primary and secondary schools. In the same year Aje was appointed Principal Librarian in the National Library of Nigeria, in Lagos. He was Acting Deputy Director from May 1967 to November 1969 and was then appointed Deputy Director. He became Director of the National Library in September 1971 and held the post until he retired in 1985.

As Director of the Library, Aje contributed significantly to the development of librarianship at the national level. He initiated considerable expansion of the National Library services with the establishment of branches located in the states. He also initiated the process for recognition of the profession of librarianship and the publication of a decree establishing a register of librarians. Aje also introduced the application of national standards in bibliographical description and the use of standard book numbers and standard serial numbers. He continued the publication of the *National Bibliography of Nigeria,* which was taken over in 1970 from the University of Ibadan Library.

Aje made available his wealth of professional experience in library education and training in Nigeria. He was a Visiting Lecturer at the University of Ibadan from 1960 to 1976 and Associate Lecturer from 1977. He helped to develop programs and courses on the National Library and on national bibliographic control.

Aje became well known in professional library circles in Europe and the U.S. He served as a regular member of IFLA and attended Council meetings from 1971. He served as a member of various IFLA-connected committees. Aje also contributed to the work of Unesco through membership in various conferences and councils.

As Director and President of the Nigerian Library Association, Aje influenced the acceptance of library boards and the establishment of state libraries as an essential service to the Nigerian public. He was appointed Chairman of the Ondo State Library Board after his retirement from the National Library.

Aje wrote *A Biography of Dr. Albert Schweitzer* in Yoruba and prepared a Yoruba translation of Chinua Achebe's *Things Fall Apart.* He also contributed to the library professional literature.

F. A. OGUNSHEYE;
VIRGINIA W. DIKE

Akita, J. M.

(1921–)

During the three decades of his stewardship of the National Archives of Ghana (1949–76), Jeremias Mama Akita, more than any other individual, shaped the development of the archival profession in his country in particular and Africa in general. He attacked almost all the problems that confront the modern archivist and invariably found happy and logical solutions.

Born May 11, 1921, in Teshi, Accra, Akita had his initial schooling in Ghana. He then proceeded to Queen's College, Cambridge, in 1945 and graduated in 1948. He did a year's training in Archives Administration at the School of Librarianship and Archives, University of London. Back in Ghana in 1949, he became Chief Archivist of Ghana, a post he held until his retirement in 1976.

His most signal service to Ghana was the founding of the National Archives. He started concentrating the records that were lying about, scattered in the government offices, corridors, and attics. At the same time he drew up plans for a new archival building. The construction work, which started in 1959, was completed by 1962. Akita went on to establish regional archival offices in Kumasi (1959) and in Cape Coast (1964), for which permanent buildings were constructed later. He also made building plans for other regional archives offices at various administrative capitals of Ghana.

To give his archival establishments legitimacy and security, he was instrumental in piloting an archival law through the then colonial legislature in 1955. The law envisages taking over all record groups and documents, both historical and administrative, and also those of the future. The procedures of evaluation and appraisal of records before their transfer to the National Archives have also been clearly enunciated.

Akita was a member of the Executive Committee of the International Council on Archives from 1968 to 1976. In recognition of his contributions to the International Council on Archives, he was made an honorary member of the Council for life.

When the question of establishment of a Unesco-sponsored training center for archivists for anglophone countries of Africa was raised in 1967, Akita was naturally closely associated with the project. He was in no small measure responsible for the location of the center at the Department of Library and Archival Studies of the University of Ghana in 1975. On retirement from the National Archives in 1976, he was invited to head the center. He thereafter worked as Senior Lecturer and Acting Director of the training center.

Akita's professional knowledge and extensive travels made him uniquely qualified to write on archival and ancillary problems, and he wrote numerous articles in professional journals.

Akita shared his specialized skills generously with the neighboring countries. He was appointed Archival Adviser by the Commonwealth Secretariat to the UN Institute for Namibia in Lusaka, Zambia, in 1977 and drew up a report on the establishment of an archival service for Namibia. In 1978 Unesco sent him on a consultancy mission to Uganda to prepare short- and long-term plans for the development of archival services there.

D. G. KESWANI

Albania

Albania, a republic, lies on the Balkan Peninsula in southeastern Europe. It is bounded by Montenegro on the north, Serbia on the east, Greece on the south, and the Adriatic and Ionian seas on the west. Population (1990 est.) 3,250,000; area 28,748 sq.km. The official language is Albanian.

National Library. The National Library was founded in Tirana in 1922 with a stock of 6,000 volumes. The liberation of the country in 1944 found it with a stock of 15,000 volumes. In 1986 it had 883,000 volumes.

Under law the National Library receives free of charge 15 copies of all publications produced in the country. Its stock is also enriched with purchases, exchanges, and loans of books and periodicals from other countries.

Library service is free. The National Library keeps readers informed about its stock through a wide information network including reference files, catalogues, bibliographies, and bulletins. The annual circulation of books among readers is about 250,000 copies. The National Library is also the archive for Albanian books, preserving one copy of each publication. It is also the center for study of practice and methods of library science and bibliography.

As the bibliographical center of the country, the National Library publishes the national bibliography on Albanian books (quarterly; first published in 1959) and the national bibliography of articles in Albanian periodicals (monthly; it appeared as a quarterly from 1961 to 1964 and as a bimonthly in 1965). The Library also publishes an annual catalogue of the foreign periodicals entering the country.

The National Library has a stock of about 30,100 publications on the history, linguistics, ethnography, and folklore of Albania. Its collections of books and manuscripts on Albanology are considered the richest and most important in the world. It also has a rich stock of books on the history and culture of the other countries of the Balkans.

The National Library has an exchange system with the other libraries of the country and with many libraries abroad. In 1982 it had such relations with 480 foreign libraries, institutions, and international organizations and with scholars in the sciences from some 70 countries.

Academic Libraries. The Library of the Academy of Sciences of Albania is the country's largest academic library. It was founded in 1975 with a stock of about 10,000 volumes. It annexed the stock of the Albanological branch of the University of Tirana in 1976, increasing the number of volumes to about 117,000; by 1986 the stock of that library numbered 812,000 volumes. It covers all branches of science and has incunabula on history and linguistics. The Library increases by about 4,000 books a year through purchases, exchanges, or borrowings. The Library receives three copies of each publication of the Academy free of charge.

The Library of the Academy provides free service for students and scholars in all fields of science; it also maintains relations with and serves district libraries. The circulation of books among readers is more than 50,000 volumes a year. It publishes informative bulletins on the foreign literature entering the country, covering history, geography, and economics. It also publishes the catalogue of foreign scientific magazines received by the Library as well as a number of other informative lists.

The Library of the Academy of Sciences maintains relations with 820 foreign academies, universities, scientific institutions, and libraries, and persons in the sciences and friends of Albania.

Other important academic libraries are those of the University of Tirana and of the Higher Agricultural Institute of Tirana.

The Scientific Library of the University of Tirana was founded in 1957 with an initial stock of about 40,000 volumes. In 1982 its stock numbered 500,000 volumes, 80 percent of which are technical and scientific books in foreign languages. The library receives three copies of all scientific, teachers', and periodical publications of the University free of charge. Its stock is enriched with Albanian and foreign books purchased, exchanged, or borrowed at a rate of 10,000 a year. It maintains relations with 422 foreign university libraries and scientific institutions and with individuals in 90 countries.

The Library of the University provides free service for the teachers, scientific workers, and students of the University as well as for all the specialists and workers of the country, maintaining regular contact with the libraries of the districts, scientific institutions, and production centers.

The Library of the University keeps readers informed about its stock through reference files, informative bulletins, reference bulletins, catalogues, bibliographies, lists of new books, and other ways. It publishes periodical informative bulletins on the entire technical-scientific literature entering the country for 12 fields of science and reference bulletins on foreign literature for eight main fields of science and production.

The Library of the Higher Agricultural Institute is the main library specializing in agriculture. It was founded in 1951 with a limited bookstock. By 1955 its stock had grown to 27,898 volumes, in 1959 to 41,260, and in 1976 to 88,000. In 1982 the library stock numbered 105,200 volumes. The library receives three

Libraries in Albania (1990)

Type of library	Number of administrative units (main libraries)	Number of service points (branches, mobile stops, etc.)	Volumes in collections	Annual expenditures (lek)	Population served	Professional staff (with certificate, diploma, etc.)	Total staff
National[a]	1	--	883,000	--	8,710	--	--
Academic[b]	2	15	812,000	--	--	--	--
Public[c]	45	3,633	4,072,000	--	228,786	--	--
School[b]	1,847	--	4,268,000	--	391,696	--	--
Other[a] (non-specialized)	40	--	2,344,000	--	116,755	--	--

[a]1986 data.
[b]1984 data.
[c]1988 data.

Source: Unesco, *Statistical Yearbook,* 1991

copies of each publication of the Higher Agricultural Institute free of charge and enriches it stock with about 3,000 Albanian and foreign books and periodicals a year through purchases, exchanges, or borrowings. It provides free service for teachers, scientific workers, and students of the University as well as for all specialists and working people of the agricultural institutions of the country. It maintains regular contact with district libraries, scientific agricultural institutions, and centers of production. In 1982 the Scientific Library of the Higher Agricultural Institute had regular relations with 111 foreign agricultural libraries and institutions in 29 countries. The Library keeps readers informed about its stock through bulletins, bibliographies, catalogues, and other methods comparable to those of the other major libraries. Each year it publishes the bibliographical bulletin "Agricultural Science and the Advanced Experience in Our Country"; a bulletin on new foreign agricultural literature entering the country; reference bulletins on foreign agricultural literature for branches of agriculture; a catalogue on the foreign agricultural periodicals entering the country; and a series of subject bibliographies on the various branches of agriculture.

Public Libraries. Public libraries function in all the districts of the country. The first public library was opened in Elbasan in 1934. In 1935 another was opened in the city of Shkodra, and in 1938 a similar one was opened in Korça. After the liberation of the country in 1944, three public libraries were opened in 1945 in the cities of Durrës, Vlora, and Berat. Four public libraries were opened in 1950, in Gjirokastra, Peshkopia, Fier, and Pogradec. Another five were set up in 1958 in Lushnja, Kukës, Erseka, Saranda, and Tepelena. In 1966 the number of public libraries reached 25 (new ones were opened in Kruja, Lezha, Puka, Tropoja, Përmet, Gramsh, Burrel, Rëshen, Skrapar, and Librazhd). In 1980 there were 45 public libraries altogether, with a stock of 2,175,248 volumes as against 202,000 volumes in 1950. The biggest public libraries by the early 1990s were in the cities of Shkodra (more than 250,000 volumes), Korça (139,000 volumes), Elbasan (288,000 volumes), Berat (107,000 volumes), and Durrës, including Shijak and Kavaja (234,000 volumes). The increase of the public library stocks is subsidized by the state. Service in these libraries, as well as the postal service for remote zones, is free.

Excluding the National Library and the Library of the Academy of Sciences, the library of the city of Shkodra is the richest in works on Albania and the Balkans and collections of manuscripts for the study of the development of Albanian national history.

School Libraries. In 1984 there were 1,847 school libraries with 4,268,000 volumes in Albania (both in city and countryside). They provide free service for the teachers and students and lend both Albanian and foreign books. The stocks are subsidized by the state.

Special Libraries. A network of specialized libraries has been set up for each institution and work center. In 1982 there were 519 such libraries with 1,107,736 volumes. They provide free service for the specialists and employees of the institution or enterprise and offer publications in Albanian and foreign languages. Subsidized by the state, these libraries regularly increase their stock with the specialized literature they need.

Other Libraries. Each House and Hearth of Culture in the city and the countryside has its own library rich in all kinds of literature. In 1982 there were 1,803 such libraries with 2,674,651 volumes. Subsidized by the state, these libraries increase their stocks mainly with Albanian books of all kinds. The libraries of the Houses and Hearths of Culture provide free service for all the residents of towns and villages. They have the right to exchange books with all the libraries of the country free of charge in order to serve their readers.

MAHIR DOMI

Alexandrian Library (Ancient)

The Eastern Mediterranean coast and the Near East generally were divided after the death of Alexander the Great (323 B.C.) among his generals, who, along with many of their associates and successors, were educated individuals. Committed to maintaining Greek culture, which they regarded as justification for their rule over other peoples, they stressed a well-rounded education called *paideia*; by 323 B.C. the written word was vital to it. When faced with a foreign cultural tradition, despite whatever merits it had, the occupying Greek community felt obliged to demonstrate the superiority of its own. Such was the purpose of the Museum and the libraries in Alexandria, Egypt, initiated by Ptolemy I Soter with the help of the Athenian scholar Demetrius of Phaleron.

The collections seem to have been developed on the principle that the library should have a proper copy of every title in Greek; before long that objective was expanded with efforts to acquire translations of significant works in other languages, such as the Hebrew Torah. The procurement process embraced not only the standard dealings with book collectors and book dealers but also the practice notorious in the days of Ptolemy III Euergetes (as related by Galen) of obliging ships dropping anchor in the harbor to yield their books so that copies could be made for the library. There is some evidence of the existence of a rapid-copying shop to do the royal bidding, and Galen also notes that the books copied were identified as being "from the ships." Assembled were not only classic and other literary materials but also cookbooks, magic books, and oddities. A case can certainly be made for regarding the Alexandrian Library as the national library of Greek Egypt, not dominated by the publications or commitments of any one school of philosophy as had been common in the scholarly collections in Greece.

According to the most informative witness—the 12th-century Byzantine savant John Tzetzes, whose reports were critically reviewed by modern authority Rudolf Blum—the library in the Brucheion founded by Ptolemy I Soter was enlarged most significantly by his son, Ptolemy II Philadelphus. Demetrius of Phaleron was brought from Athens in the early 3rd century B.C. to develop the collection in Greek tragic and comic poetry, a responsibility that also included preparation of scholarly correct editions. Maintenance of the collections and supervision of library service soon became tasks of equal importance and were placed in the hands of Zenodotus of Ephesus, a Homer scholar and initially junior to Demetrius. Zenodotus seems to have been the first, around 291 B.C. to have been designated Director (*bibliophylax*), at a time when cataloguing and translation were recognized as part of the library routine under the beneficent eye of Ptolemy II Philadelphus.

Just as Zenodotus apparently made his mark first as a textual critic and then as an administrator, the cataloguing achievements of Callimachus, 25 years his junior, evidently enhanced the luster of his literary skills in about 250 B.C. His high repute may have facilitated the appointment of his fellow-Cyrenian, Eratosthenes, scholar in several fields and celebrated by posterity as a geographer, as the next Director. During the ensuing century the library continued to be managed by a succession of persons distinguished in science, Fellows of the Museum as it were. After 145 B.C. the record is silent.

When the first of several catastrophes struck, the fire at the Alexandria docks in 47 B.C. during Caesar's invasion, the Brucheion and its "daughter" library (possibly built for overflow), the Serapeum, held jointly some 532,800 rolls. The normal papyrus roll constituting a book was about 20 feet long unrolled and 10 to 12 inches high. Such a roll would contain, for instance, Plato's *Symposium* inscribed on 56 "pages" of 36 lines apiece, each line being 3.4 inches long. Quite a few papyrus rolls had writing on both sides. They were probably arranged in subject groups and utilized only on the premises. There is no proof of that arrangement or of how anything was located; available data are scattered and frequently incomplete. From the *Pinakes* of Callimachus it is known that subject, descriptive, and even evaluative features had been developed rather elaborately. Other surviving testimony is much more limited; notable is the inscribed catalogue found on Rhodes, taken to be the library of a gymnasium of the 2nd century B.C. In this catalogue the writers' names are in alphabetical order, but what order (if any) prescribes the listing of individual titles is not clear.

Information on architecture or furnishings does not exist beyond what archaeologists and chroniclers estimate on the basis of reputations and remnants of other Hellenistic library sites. Strabo the geographer visited Egypt about 24 years after the Brucheion fire and later mentioned the Museum's area with seats for discussion and mess hall for the scholarly staff, but he said nothing of books or library activities. From other sources, such as archaeological studies at Pergamum, it can be deduced that the large central area originally provided for sacred or prestige purposes gradually disappeared from libraries; by the time of the Romans all was practical, and libraries comprised a group of rooms of moderate size.

Alexandrian scientists flourished during the Roman Empire and perhaps utilized the library as before. Not very clear is the possible relationship between the library and the university developed in Alexandria by the Neo-platonists. Only too obvious, unfortunately, is the record of damage in the later 4th century, a by-product of religious conflict that went as far as street riots. By the time the Christians were finished fighting the pagans and each other, there was not a great deal left for the Islamic conquerors of the mid-7th century to maltreat.

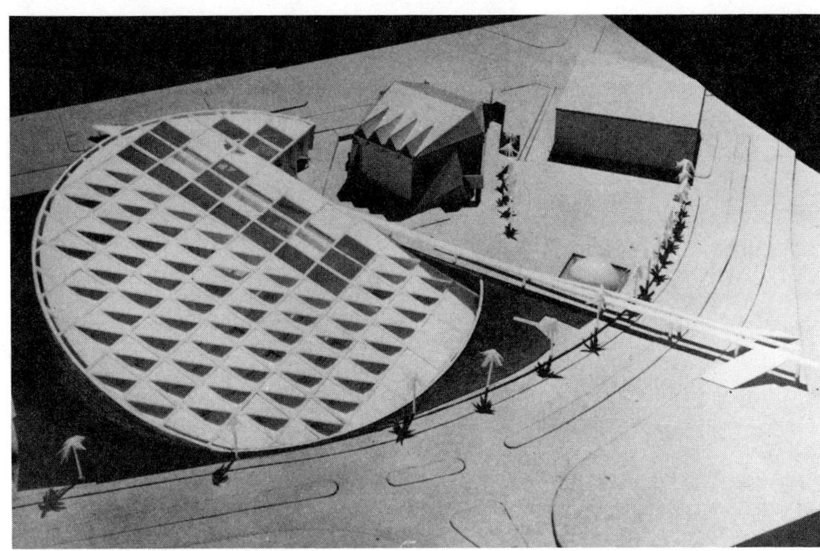

Snohetta Landskap Arkitektur, Oslo, Norway

Architectural model of Bibliotheca Alexandrina, scheduled to open in 1995, will be located near the site of the ancient Alexandrian Library.

Legacy. Yet the legacy of the Alexandrian Library was very substantial. For lack of surviving records one cannot produce details, but doubtless many writings of classical Greece and some other cultures were initially preserved for posterity by finding a home in that great repository. Indeed, the scholar hammering out the practices of textual criticism had to be working with numerous copies of many a work. And it is reasonable to assume that, with so much activity for unknown legions of scribes, there must have been considerable standardization of copying and manuscript handling, produced by supervision if not by formal instruction. We have very few precise comments by visitors and no official reports, but there are enough allusions in ancient and early medieval writings to indicate that word about many features, from architecture to the cataloguing implied by Callimachus' *Pinakes,* circulated rather widely. Moreover, for many who had no tangible data there was inspiration in the idea of the physically imposing, comprehensive scholar-library, an inspiration still voiced in Renaissance writings.

To a limited degree, the development of these traditions owed something identifiable to other libraries of the Hellenistic Age. The Attalids began in the latter half of the 3rd century B.C. to enhance their capital of Pergamum (now in northwestern Turkey, a few miles inland from Lesbos) with attractive installations, including a library. The archaeological testimony is scanty, but the literary traditions do touch on the fate of Aristotle's books on the one hand and the misadventures of the Alexandrian Library on the other. Perhaps the clearest record is the statement by late 1st century B.C. scholar Dionysius of Halicarnassus, working in Rome, that in preparing a biography he had used the *pinakes* of both Callimachus and Pergamum.

Other scholarly collections may have been established in the last two centuries of the Roman Republic in the Hellenistic East, because at least three turn up regularly in the histories of Roman conquest as war booty: at Pella, Macedonia, taken by Aemilius Paulus after the battle of Pydna in 168 B.C.; at Athens, whence about 86 B.C. Sulla carried off "Aristotle's Library"; and at Sinope, on the Black Sea, after Lucullus defeated Mithridates in 70 B.C. Scraps of archaeological and literary evidence indicate that there were founded also during that epoch, if not earlier, numerous secondary schools, *gymnasia,* teaching the seven liberal arts, and a few medical schools and law schools; all have been thought likely to have had book collections, but proof is rare.

The institutions built during the Roman Empire have understandably left more traces, and certain features, such as housing in a temple, can be attributed at least partly to the influence of Egypt and the ancient East. One cannot assume, however, that the numerous libraries established in all parts of the Empire were shaped decisively, let alone exclusively, by Hellenistic models; Roman and local influences were present as well.

For information on the modern library at Alexandria, *see* Bibliotheca Alexandrina.

SIDNEY L. JACKSON (d. 1979)

Algeria

Algeria, a republic in northern Africa, is bordered by the Mediterranean Sea on the north, Tunisia and Libya on the east, Niger, Mali, and Mauritania on the south, and the Spanish Sahara and Morocco on the west. Population (1990 est.) 24,961,000; area 2,381,741 sq.km. The official languages are Arabic and French.

History. Algeria possesses a variety of written documents for each epoch of its history from the most distant past to the present. On the rocks in the Tassili Mountains and in the Saharan Atlas Mountains there are paintings and stone engravings that bear witness to the life and culture of the first inhabitants of the country. Later the Carthaginians and Numidians left written messages on stone throughout the regions where they lived. These epigraphs in the Lybico-Berber alphabet are valuable resources for scholars.

Façade of the National Library of Algeria, constructed in 1958. Established in 1835, the Library is Algeria's oldest cultural institution.

B. Ben

Even the Romans who colonized Algeria from the 2nd century B.C. to the 5th century used stone for writing. The ruins of Roman cities such as Djamila, Timgad, and Tipaza still contain many inscriptions.

The rarest documents are perhaps the Tablettes Albertini, private transactions from the period of Vandal rule in Algeria (429-533). These tablets of cedar wood are covered with a cursive Latin script written with a sharpened reed dipped in ink made from a base of dried carob. In 1928 these 45 tablets, which make up 34 documents, were discovered in a sealed terra-cotta jar buried in the Tebessa region.

Following the Arab conquest of Algeria in 682, paper was incontestably the most used writing material, although vellum and parchment were also used in rare instances. The arts and sciences flourished by the 11th century, when two Berber dynasties, the Almoravides and later the Almohades, ruled in North Africa. Great kings such as Ibn Tumart and Abd al Mumin owned important private libraries. Much later, Ibn Khaldoun (1332-1406), an Arab historian famous for his *Mugaddima* (Prolegomena), maintained a large library during the many years he lived in Algeria. The Emir Abdelkader (1808-1883), an Algerian statesman who fought against France for 17 years, also possessed a remarkable personal library.

From their earliest existence in Algeria, the mosques and *medersas* (schools) played the role of libraries. Mosques and schools thus became the veritable guardians of manuscripts throughout many centuries, until France colonized Algeria and created libraries in the modern sense.

National Library. The National Library of Algeria, a public institution under the Ministry of Culture from 1982, was established in 1835 on the initiative of the civil administrator of the Regency of Algiers, Genty de Bussy. The National Library is the country's oldest cultural institution. Its first home was a state-owned building; it was moved into the Janissaries' barracks in 1838. After other moves, it settled in 1863 in the palace of the Dey (Janissarry commander) of Algiers, Mustafa Pasha. The National Library moved into the building it now occupies, a building constructed for it, in 1958.

The first four directors of the National Library were remarkable individuals. Adrien Berbrugger, who served from 1835 to 1869, was the author of several works including *L'Algérie Historique, Pittoresque et Monumentale.* He was also in charge of the *Revue Africaine* and the Algerian Historical Society. Oscar MacCarthy (served 1869–1890) was a geographer and an explorer. Thanks to him, the explorer and missionary Father Charles de Foucauld (1858–1916) was able to launch his Moroccan expedition. Émile Maupas (served 1890–1916), a biologist, was known in Europe for his work on the sexuality of the Rotifera, a class of microscopic animals with moving cilia, and the reproduction of Infusoria. Gabriel Esquer (served 1916–1948) was known for his works on Algerian history.

Although the Library collects in all fields, its humanities holdings are the strongest. Two notable private donations were the personal libraries of archaeologist Stéphane Gsell (1864–1932) and African explorer Pierre Sovorgnan de Brazza (1852–1905).

The National Library has a special collection of approximately 70,000 volumes on Algeria, Morocco, and Tunisia called the Maghreb Collection. In the 1950s, manuscripts concerning the history of Algiers in the 17th and 18th centuries (such as Pétis de la Croix's 1695 work "Description Abrégée de la Ville et Estat d'Alger" and General O'Reilly y las Casas's 1709 work "Nuevo Topographía de Argel") were acquired at sales of private libraries. The printed works in the Maghreb Collection include works of the 17th, 18th, and 19th centuries on the history of Algeria before 1830, when it became a French colony. Post-1830 materials are gathered together and include rarities such as the "Tableau de la Situations des Établissements Français dans l'Algérie, 1838–1868" and "L'Exploration Scientifique de l'Algérie," a 32-volume work (1844–54). Also included are certain old periodicals such as the *Moniteur Algérien* and *El-Akbar.* Since the independence of Algeria in 1962, the National Library has brought together in this collection extensive documentation on the War of National Liberation (1954–62).

The Library also has a loan collection of approximately 25,000 books and a large reading room seating 450.

The Library's 3,500 manuscripts, mostly in Arabic, cover various disciplines such as theology, legislation, Arabic grammar and language, poetry, history and geography, medicine, philosophy, and astronomy. These manuscripts are valuable because of their age (11th–13th centuries), their rarity, or their illustrations. Examples are "Al-Muwatta," a collection of moral precepts in a magnificent copy executed in 1194 by the Almohad Abu Yusuf Yakub; and the Quràn (Koran) in minuscule octagonal script, gilt-edged with blue and gold border, written in 1607 by the Persian Imad ben Ibrahim.

In 1958 the National Library owned a collection of 400,000 volumes and 1,200 current periodicals. By 1966 the collection had grown to 600,000 and by 1976 to 700,000 volumes, most in French, plus 150,000 Arabic-language works as well as 1,504 current periodicals in all languages. In 1981 the collections of the National Library numbered 765,850 volumes in foreign languages, 181,739 volumes in Arabic, 2,000 reels of microfilm, 4,250 phonodiscs, 360 maps, and 2,000 periodicals, of which 980 were current. The Library served 5,868 readers. By 1986, total holdings had reached 1,040,000 (38,180,000 meters) with 13,970 registered users.

The National Library, as the beneficiary of legal deposit, publishes the *Bibliographie de l'Algérie,* a twice-yearly publication that registers publications received by the Office of Legal Deposit. The Library also publishes certain specialized bibliographies. The Library runs a large exchange service and participates in interlibrary loan.

Academic Libraries. The law pertaining to higher education in Algeria (December 20, 1879) led to the creation of the Library of the University of Algiers. It is the major academic library in Algeria of the 75 academic libraries surveyed in 1982.

After occupying several buildings, the University Library found a permanent home in 1888 in the main part of the building of the University of Algiers. At that time the library owned 15,000 volumes. At the end of the Algerian War, in June 1962, the University Library burned down, destroying 112,510 volumes. The Library was rebuilt and reopened in 1968. The Library of the University of Algiers is foremost among the various departmental and institute libraries. It is rich in foreign dissertations and has major humanities, legal, scientific, medical, and pharmacy collections. By 1976 its collections comprised 600,000 works and 1,550 periodical titles, as well as 12,326 Arabic-language works on microfilm or fiche. By the end of 1982, the library contained 641,800 volumes.

Special Libraries. Almost every ministry, firm, bank, and institution has its own library or documentation center for its own specific purposes. A national survey (1975–76) showed 300 in the country.

School Libraries. More and more primary and secondary schools are equipped with libraries serving students and teachers. The National Library assists by sending them gifts of books (500 volumes on the average). No statistics were published on the number or size of such libraries in the mid-1980s.

Public Libraries. Since independence, Algeria has built city libraries in all the *wilayate* (*départements,* or "counties"). These libraries, like the cultural center libraries, report to the Ministry of the Interior through the *wali* (prefects). In Algiers there are at present 12 city libraries, the oldest and biggest of which was opened in 1951. In 1976 it had 68,182 works and 30 current periodicals; by 1982 the collection had increased to 80,100 volumes.

The Profession. The training of research assistants and documentalists and the granting of a technical diploma in libraries and archives are regulated by decree 64-135 (April 24, 1964). Each candidate must have a high school diploma and take a 12-month program of theory and practice. The directorate of

Libraries in Algeria (1990)

Type of library	Number of administrative units (main libraries)	Number of service points (branches, mobile stops, etc.)	Volumes in collections	Annual expenditures (dinar)	Population served	Professional staff (with certificate, diploma, etc.)	Total staff
National[a]	1	1	998,459	10,736,000	DA 15,000,000	26	116 + 17 vacataires
Academic[b]	127	--	--	--	--	--	--
Public[b]	47	--	--	--	--	--	--
School[b]	ca 100	--	--	--	--	--	--
Special[b]	159	--	--	--	--	--	--

[a]1990 data
[b]1989 data

books, libraries, and public reading is in charge of this program.

The training of librarians occurs at two levels. Persons with a high school diploma take a four-year program at the University's Library Science School and receive a library science degree (decree 75-90, July 24, 1975). Research assistants may take a professional examination after five years of experience and receive the title of Librarian.

The same procedures are used for *conservateurs* (curators). After five years of experience, a librarian may take a professional examination in order to become a curator. If not successful, the librarian must study for two more years before obtaining an advanced library degree.

Algeria did not have a library association in the mid-1980s.

R. CHAIT;
translated by CHARLES S. FINEMAN
and MARY NILES MAACK

Amano, Keitaro
(1901–)

Keitaro Amano

Keitaro Amano is recognized by many as the creator of modern bibliography in Japan. Born in November 1901 in Kyoto, Amano took a position in the Law Library of Kyoto University in 1922. In 1927 he published *Hosei, Keizai, Shakai Ronbun Soran* ("Index of Articles on Law, Politics, Economics, and Sociology"), which showed at once his brilliant ability as a bibliographer. It was followed by *Honpo Shoshi no Shoshi* ("A Bibliography of Japanese Bibliographies"; 1933), which won him a leading position in the Japanese bibliographical world.

In 1948 Amano moved to the Kansai University Library, where he took an active part in processing work as head of the Technical Service Division. He also compiled a great variety of bibliographies; among them were "A Bibliography of Dr. Hajime Kawakami" (1956), "Bibliography of the Classical Economics" (1961–64), "Index of All Contents of Journals" (1966), and "A Bibliography of Max Weber in Japan" (1969). Articles collected in his *Shoshi Sakuin Ronko* ("A Study on Bibliography and Index"; 1979) represent his deep knowledge of the subjects.

Also an excellent cataloguing theorist, Amano wrote many books and articles on cataloguing, including *Yosho-Mokuroku no Tsukurikata* ("Guide to Cataloguing Books in European Languages"; 1949) and *Yosho-Mokurokuho Nyumon* ("Introduction to Cataloguing Books in European Languages"; 1951). In 1959 he represented Japan at the Preliminary Meeting of the International Cataloguing Conference held in London under the auspices of IFLA.

He retired from the Kansai University Library in 1967 and served as a professor in the Social Science Department of Tokyo University until 1971. After returning to his hometown, Kyoto, he continued his life work, *Nihon Shoshi no Shoshi* ("A Japan Bibliography of Bibliographies"), the completely revised and augmented edition of *Honpo Shoshi no Shoshi,* published in 1933. The first volume covers *Generalia,* the second and third contain subject entries, and the fourth, compiled in 1991, is the index.

A detailed chronology and comprehensive list of his works appear in a book issued in honor of his 70th birthday, *Toshokan- gaku to sono Shuhen* ("On and around Library Science"; 1971).

TOSHIO IWASARU

American Library Association

The American Library Association (ALA) was founded in Philadelphia, Pennsylvania, in 1876, the centennial year of the United States. Among its founders were three major figures in American librarianship: Justin Winsor, William Frederick Poole, and Melvil Dewey, the latter relatively young and unknown at the time. The first Conference numbered 103 persons, 90 men and 13 women. From these small beginnings the Association had grown to a membership of over 54,000 by 1992. The ALA annual summer conferences have also attracted an average of more than 12,000 persons; the largest number, 14,566, attended the New York City Conference in 1980. Summer Conferences are primarily devoted to educational and professional programs. The business of the Association has become a responsibility of the Midwinter Meetings, usually held in January.

The ALA has had its headquarters in Chicago, Illinois, since 1909. In 1946 ALA occupied its own building at 50 East Huron Street. A new building was constructed on that site in 1963. Further expansion occurred in 1981 when the Association occupied additional space in a newly built adjoining building, Huron Plaza, in which it owns an interest.

In addition to the Chicago headquarters, the Association has a Washington Office, which provides legislative liaison with the Congress and departments in the executive branch of government, and editorial offices in Middletown, Connecticut, for *Choice,* the book selection guide for academic libraries.

Total staff in the three locations numbered more than 230 in 1992. The chief operational officer of the Association is the Executive Director. In 1992 the Association had total revenues of more than $26 million.

Purposes. According to the 1879 Charter, the ALA was founded for "the purpose of promoting the library interests of the country by exchanging views, reaching conclusions, and inducing cooperation in all departments of bibliothecal science and economy; by disposing the public mind to the founding and improving libraries; and by cultivating good will among its own members . . . ." This charter has been amended only once, in 1942, when (1) "promoting library interests of the country" was changed to read "promoting library interests throughout the world," thus giving a broader dimension to the Association's work, and (2) the phrase "and such other means as may be authorized from time to time by the Executive Board and Council of the American Library Association" was added.

The ALA Constitution states that the "object of the American Library Association shall be to promote library service and librarianship." This objective is further elaborated in a series of "Goals and Priorities" in the ALA Policy Manual; priorities are listed as (1) Access to Information, (2) Legislation/Funding, (3) Intellectual Freedom, and (4) Public Awareness.

History. Since its founding ALA has promoted libraries and librarianship in various ways. During its first quarter-century the Association grew slowly.

Often its major problem was staying alive. Justin Winsor served as President for the first nine years, followed by William Frederick Poole and Charles A. Cutter for two years each. Only two subsequent Presidents served more than one term: Melvil Dewey and Herbert Putnam, both for a year and a half-year on separate occasions. Dewey was also Secretary of the Association from 1879 to 1890 and in 1897 and 1898. He was, and is, the best known librarian among the American public generally.

Much was accomplished in the first 25 years despite the small membership. The Association launched a publications program; encouraged the cooperative development and publication of catalogues, indexes, and book selection guides; and promoted libraries at the World's Columbian Exposition in Chicago in 1893. Perhaps its greatest political accomplishment was the appointment of Herbert Putnam as Librarian of Congress in 1899, a position he would hold for the next 40 years and from which he would develop the Library of Congress into a truly national library.

As academic, public, and school libraries expanded, the need for trained librarians became more pressing. Dewey opened the first library school at Columbia University in January 1887. While not an ALA project, the school under Dewey's leadership was tied closely to the Association and its graduates had a far-reaching influence on the profession.

The second quarter-century was marked by Association growth and consolidation. The 1904 conference in St. Louis reflected dynamism, missionary zeal, and scholarship that, together, would continue throughout the next 75 years. This period also saw the rapid expansion of Carnegie libraries and the emergence of women as a major factor in American librarianship. ALA elected its first woman President, Theresa West Elmendorf, in 1911–12. World War I saw the ALA involved in an effort to provide books and library services to the U.S. armed forces, a highly successful effort that resulted in the permanent establishment of military libraries. Publishing was expanded with the establishment of the *ALA Bulletin* as the Association's official publication in 1907 and the *ALA Booklist,* with Carnegie help, in 1905.

Other library professional associations also began to emerge. A few state library associations had developed in the late 19th century. Some groups that began meeting informally at ALA conferences became independent: the Bibliographical Society of America (1904), the American Association of Law Libraries (1906), and the Special Libraries Association (1909). Subunits of ALA had earlier come into existence, including state librarians and college and reference librarians (1889), trustees (1890), and children's librarians and catalogue librarians (1900).

At the celebration of ALA's 50th anniversary in 1926, the Carnegie Corporation announced a $4 million program in grants to improve library education and to place ALA on a sound financial footing. Major topics for ALA in the next two decades would be adult education, library education, further development of library and professional standards, library legislation, and intellectual freedom.

In the years that followed, Carl H. Milam, who served as Executive Secretary from 1920 to 1948, dominated the Association as no one had since Melvil

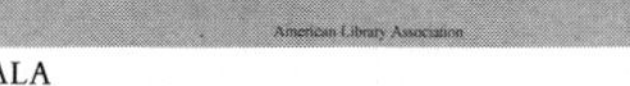

ALA

ALA

ALA posters promote libraries and reading, a principal objective of the Association since its inception.

Dewey's time. His biographer, Peggy Sullivan, notes that Milam became ALA Secretary in a time of controversy and postwar unrest and left the position in a similar climate. Like his successors, he was a strong leader and an articulate spokesperson for library development and the library profession.

The Great Depression saw not only decreased revenues for libraries and for the Association, but also internal dissension. A Junior Members Round Table was formed in 1931, the Association of Research Libraries was established as a separate organization in 1932, and a far-reaching Third Activities Committee report set the Association on a path to providing more autonomy for its various units, especially the academic librarians, whose Association of College and Research Libraries (1938) was to become the largest of all ALA Divisions (9,158 members in 1985).

Three activities of the 30s became major foci for ALA during the rest of the century: a push for federal aid for libraries, support of intellectual freedom, and movement toward racial equality.

Many academic and public libraries benefited from federal funding through various relief agencies of the Roosevelt administration. ALA became heavily involved in national planning, but the only result of a permanent nature was a library position in the U.S. Office of Education. Public library funding had to await passage of the Library Services Act (1956) under the Eisenhower administration. Other federal legislation for libraries was the product of the Johnson administration's Great Society programs (1963–68).

The coming of World War II, especially events in Europe, brought the issues of censorship and propaganda to the fore. ALA adopted its first Library Bill of Rights in 1939. Concern for free access was to become a major topic for the Association in the postwar years during attacks upon library materials by Senator Joseph McCarthy. In 1953 ALA and other organizations issued a "Freedom to Read Statement" which had a significant impact on the defense of intellectual freedom. The Association fought further battles for freedom of the mind in the 60s and 70s.

Racial issues in the Association became a concern at the Richmond, Virginia, conference in 1936, as a result of hotel discrimination against ALA's black members. Afterward ALA adopted a policy that it would not again meet in cities where Conference accommodations could not be provided equally for all its members. For another 20 years ALA did not meet in the U.S. South. Progress was painfully slow. Even by the late 60s few blacks had achieved prominence in ALA positions. In the 1970s Robert Wedgeworth became the first black chosen as Executive Director (1972) and Clara S. Jones became the first black to be elected President (1976–77).

At the end of the 1960s the Association went through another period of turmoil and reorganization. Members were unhappy that the Association had not addressed the issues of a changing society. There was also a concern that the large organization was remote and impersonal. Divisions—membership units of the Association that serve special professional interests—were restive and wanted more autonomy. The new Executive Director and the Executive Board addressed such issues, along with problems posed by declining fiscal resources and an inflation rate that threatened all voluntary organizations. In 1974 the membership approved a change in the personal dues structure that gave Divisions more control over their own programs. Publishing was revitalized. New space was acquired. And the Association celebrated its centennial in 1976 with a mixture of cultural events, intellectual substance, nostalgia, and more unity than it had enjoyed for a number of years.

The years after 1976 saw all parts of the Association grow and develop. Its membership passed 50,000 and its revenues doubled, to more than $24 million. It appointed its first female Executive Director, Linda Crismond, in 1987 and expanded its publishing activities to included electronic information sources. Crucial issues remain: the professionalism of librarianship in the face of attacks on credentials; the right of every citizen to have maximum access to information in a democratic society; the improvement of opportunities for women and minorities; the continued attacks on intellectual freedom; the change in sources of financial support for libraries; the emergence of information science as a discipline; and the need for revitalization of professional education to meet needs posed by the new technology. These challenges continue as ALA promotes the cause of librarians and librarianship "throughout the world."

Organization and Structure. The ALA has been described as a "collaborative organization" or "an association of associations."

The policy-making or legislative body of the Association is the Council, presided over by a President elected for a one-year term. The Council in 1992 consisted of 100 members elected at large by a mail ballot of personal members for four-year terms; one member elected by each of the 11 ALA Divisions; a chapter representative elected by each of the 51 state and regional associations; eight members of the Executive Board elected by the Council; the Association's elected officers (President, Vice-President and President-Elect, Past President, and Treasurer); and the Executive Director, a nonvoting member.

The Executive Board acts for the Council in the administration of policies and programs, serves as the ALA management board, and oversees headquarters operations.

Eleven divisions exercise responsibility in their own designated areas. Each of these Associations or Divisions has its own officers, plans its own programs, manages its own budget, and has its own Executive Director. They all publish newsletters or journals. Much of the work of these units, as of ALA, is accomplished through a committee structure of volunteers who are rarely reimbursed by the Association for their expenses.

In addition to the Divisions, there are 16 Round Tables, "established to promote a field of librarianship not within the scope of any single division." Round Tables have no formal authority to act for the Association, but they exercise considerable unofficial power. Each has a staff liaison person, officers, and committees. Many issue newsletters, reports, and other publications.

There are also other small groups, such as Membership Initiative Groups and ALA Student Chapters (at library schools). Formal ALA Chapters are state and regional library associations, which are independent organizations. There are also 21 affiliated organizations, among them the American Association of Law Libraries, Association of Research Libraries, and Medical Library Association.

Carrying out general ALA programs that cut across divisional lines is the responsibility of major Offices at ALA headquarters. These offices, which have membership advisory committees to assist them, are the Office for Intellectual Freedom, Office for Outreach Services, Office for Library Personnel Resources, Office for Research, and the Washington Office. Other major units at headquarters include Administrative Services, Communication Services, Fiscal Services, and Publishing Services. ALA also has a Headquarters Library and an Accreditation Officer who administers the process for accreditation of library education programs.

Critics have often charged that ALA's structure is too complex. As an umbrella organization, the ALA has had difficulty creating structures that can accommodate both general programs of benefit to all librarians and specialized programs of benefit to particular groups of librarians. Charts 1 and 2 show the organizational structure for governance and the organizational structure for the ALA staff.

Programs. The wide range of programs carried out by the ALA has been suggested in the review of its history and structure. Throughout its history the Association has promoted an awareness of libraries through its standards, publications program, legislative activities, defense of intellectual freedom, and preparation of library personnel. Priorities of the 1990s reflect that historic tradition: access to information, legislation and funding, intellectual freedom, and public awareness. Cooperative enterprises in cataloguing and classification, bibliographic control, indexing, bibliographic tools, automation, and networking have been encouraged and promoted by various units of the Association. Divisions and Round Tables address the

Membership, Organization, Mission

Membership

The American Library Association, founded in 1876, is the oldest and largest national library association in the world. Its concern spans all types of libraries: state, public, school and academic libraries; special libraries serving persons in government, commerce and industry, the arts, the armed services, hospitals, prisons, and other institutions. With a membership of libraries, librarians, library trustees, and other interested persons from every state and many countries of the world, the Association is the chief advocate for the people of the United States in their search for the highest quality of library and information services. The Association maintains a close working relationship with more than 70 other library associations in the United States, Canada, and other countries, and it works closely with many other organizations concerned with education, research, cultural development, recreation, and public service.

On August 31, 1991, the Association had 3,141 organization members and 49,752 personal members—a total of 52,893.

Organization

Council, the governing body of ALA comprised of 100 members elected at large, 52 by chapters, 11 by divisions, and the 12 members of the Executive Board.

Executive Board, central management board of ALA comprised of the elected officers, the immediate past president, and 8 members elected by Council from among the members of that body.

ALA *committees,* appointed by the president, responsible for areas affecting all library and Association concerns. Number varies from year to year.

11 *divisions,* each responsible for a specified area of concern; each with an elected board of directors, and such committees and sections as are required to accomplish the division's goals.

17 *round tables,* each with an elected governing body, composed of members of the Association interested in the same field of librarianship not within the scope of any division.

57 *chapters,* autonomous units, each with its own elective structure, responsible for the promotion of library service and librarianship within its geographic area.

22 *affiliated organizations,* autonomous national or international organizations having purposes similar to ALA's and requesting affiliation.

Headquarters staff of approximately 260 employees, under the direction of an Executive Director who serves at the pleasure of the Executive Board.

Mission

The mission of the American Library Association is to provide leadership for the development, promotion, and improvement of library and information services and the profession of librarianship in order to enhance learning and ensure access to information for all.

(See ALA Policy Manual, Section One for Priority Areas and Goals.)

Source: *ALA Handbook of Organization and Membership Directory, 1992/1993.*

specific concerns indicated by their titles. Most libraries in the U.S., and many libraries in other countries, have been affected by the activities of ALA.

The larger world of libraries outside the U.S. has actually involved relatively few members of the Association (except the Canadians, a large number of whom have long been ALA members). Nonetheless, international librarianship has been a concern of the ALA leadership since the beginning. The 1877 London International Conference, from which the Library Association of the United Kingdom (LA) emerged, had a large representation of librarians from America. Still, what had begun auspiciously did not take hold until the St. Louis Conference in 1904, which attracted large numbers of foreign visitors. World War I stimulated American interest in other countries and the 50th anniversary Conference of ALA in 1926 marked the first steps toward an international library organization. The following year the International Federation of Library Associations (IFLA) came into being at the 50th anniversary Conference of the LA, with ALA as one of the founding members.

Dennis Thomison, in his history (1978), describes ALA's international role as "strong and significant . . . with an almost missionary spirit in carrying the American methods of librarianship to other nations . . . ." Much of this ALA activity has been funded by American foundations or the U.S. government. An office devoted to international relations existed for quite a long time—1943–49 and 1956–72— but it was financed in large part by outside grants and was closed because of ALA's fiscal problems in the early 1970s. Since 1986 ALA has administered the Library Book Fellows program, funded by the U.S. Information Agency, which provides opportunities for U.S. librarians to work in other countries. ALA committees and boards on international relations have been and continue to be important avenues for the promotion of library interests in the areas of bibliographic control, library education, librarian exchanges, and sharing of ideas about professional development. These activities are coordinated through the Committee on International Relations and promoted by the International Relations Round Table.

The IFLA Conference in Chicago in 1985 was a cooperative enterprise of the six IFLA member associations (American Association of Law Libraries, ALA, Art Libraries Society/North America, Association of Research Libraries, Medical Library Association, and Special Libraries Association), the U.S. IFLA member libraries, and the National Commission on Libraries and Information Science. Delegates from

American Library Association

ALA Membership Organization

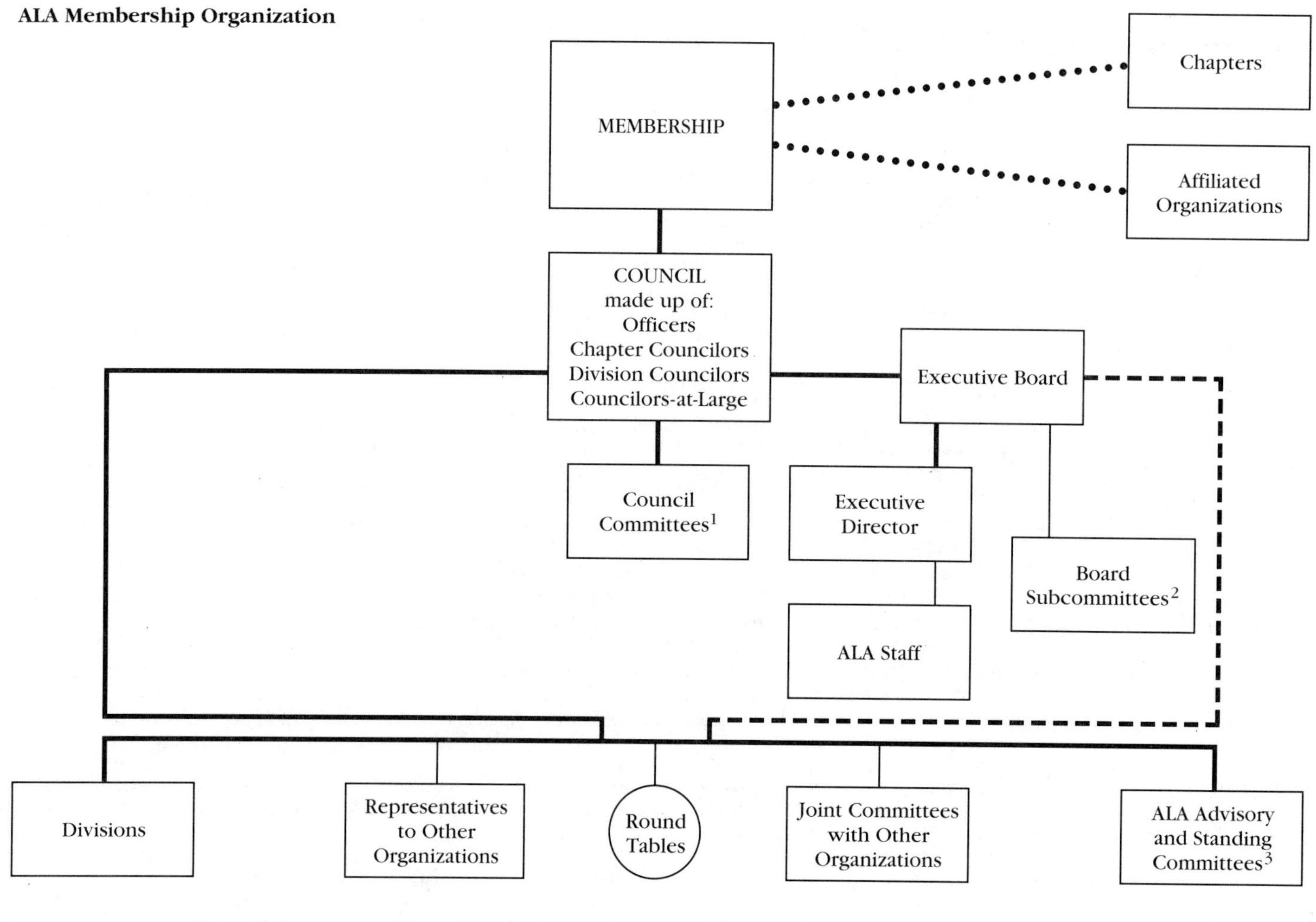

- - - Central Management. For explanation, see Constitution, Article VII, Sec. 3.
• • • • • Special relations. For explanation, see Constitution, Article X.
——— Reporting Relationship

1. Committee on Committees; Council Orientation; Intellectual Freedom; International Relations; Legislation; Library Education; Minority Concerns; Organization; Pay Equity; Planning; Policy Monitoring; Professional Ethics; Program Evaluation and Support; Publishing; Resolutions; Women in Librarianship, Status of.

2. Administrative; Directions and Program Review; Finance and Audit; Office Program Reviews; Personnel.

3. Accreditation; "American Libraries"; Appointments; Awards; Chapter Relations; Conference Program; Constitution and Bylaws; Endowment Campaign, to Develop; Library Outreach Services, Office for; Library Personnel Resources, Office for, Membership; Nominating; Public Information; Research and Statistics; Review, Inquiry, and Mediation; Standards; User Instruction for Information Literacy.

Source: *ALA Handbook of Organization and Membership Directory, 1992/1993.*

more than 86 countries attended programs of intellectual substance and practical significance. They toured special exhibits of products and services available to libraries primarily in North America.

Publications. One of ALA's significant contributions to the profession is its publishing program. At first ALA publications were printed and distributed by other organizations, including Dewey's Library Bureau, Houghton Mifflin, and the U.S. Government Printing Office. Early in the 20th century the Association began developing its own publishing services and now has one of the strongest publications programs of any library association. The first edition of *Guide to Reference Books* appeared in 1902. Under the editorships of Alice B. Kroeger, Isadore G. Mudge, Constance Winchell, and Eugene Sheehy, the *Guide* became known by the names of its editors ("Check its listing in Sheehy"), and over the years has been the best selling and most profitable of ALA publications. *American Libraries,* successor to the *ALA Bulletin,* with a circulation of more than 50,000, is one of the most widely read general library periodicals. The Divisional journals are major contributors to the research literature in their fields. Through *The ALA Yearbook* (first edition, 1976; later retitled *The ALA Yearbook of Library and Information Services,* the last edition was published in 1990) the Association provides "an annual review of information about library events, activities,

ALA REVENUE MIX 1992
$25,331,000

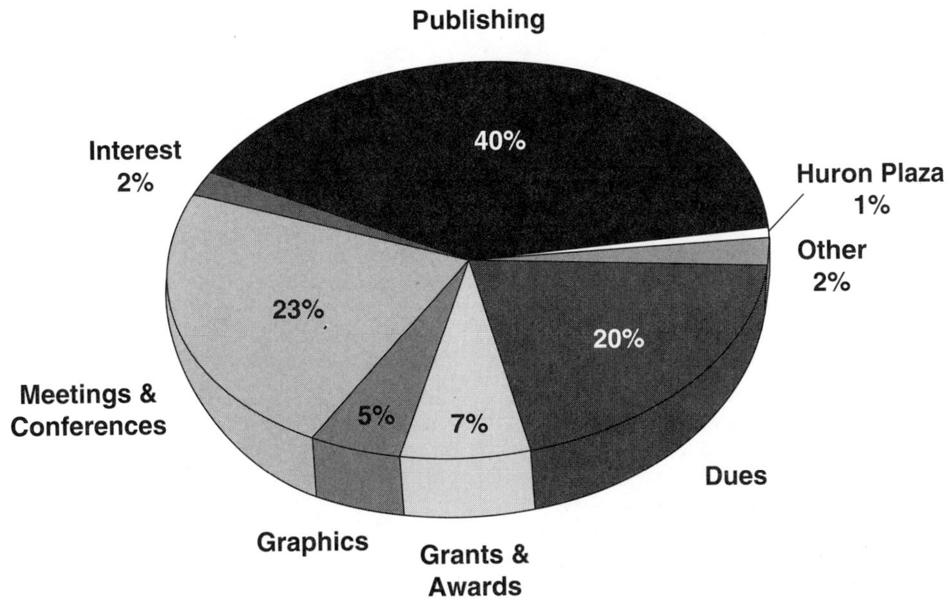

Source: ALA Treasurer, Carla J. Stoffle, Report to Council, January 27, 1992

ALA EXPENSE MIX 1992
$25,033,000

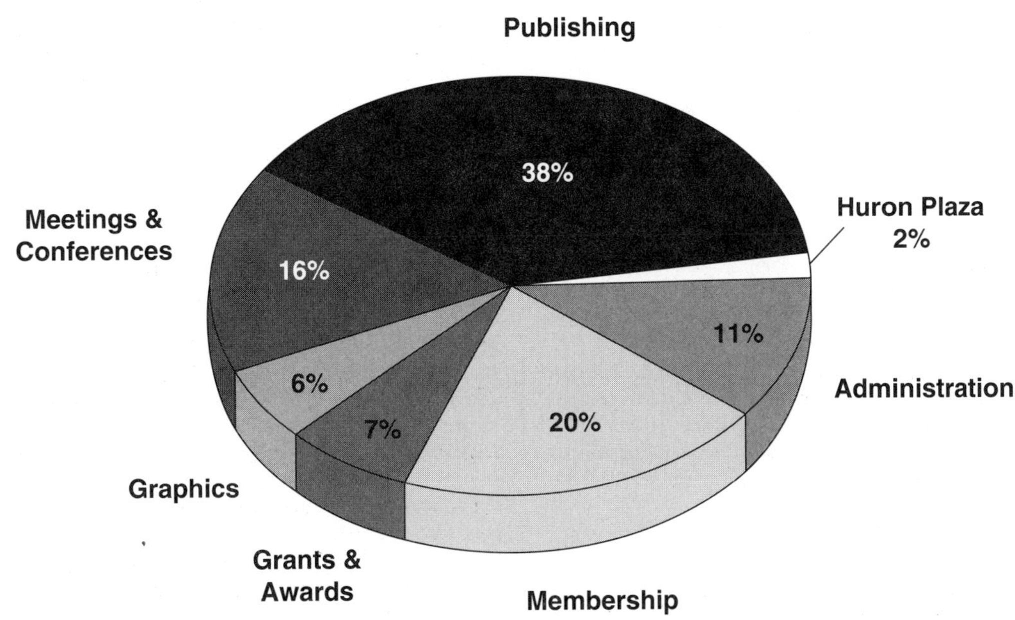

Source: ALA Treasurer, Carla J. Stoffle, Report to Council, January 27, 1992

ALA Books Financial Results 1986–1990

	1986	1987	1988	1989	1990	Growth	5-Year Avg.
Revenues	$1,772,448	$1,895,557	$2,644,112	$2,617,775	$2,195,466	24%	$2,225,076
Expenses	1,765,325	1,875,129	2,178,492	2,029,659	1,939,302	10%	1,975,581
Contribution Margin	7,123	20,328	465,620	588,116	256,164		267,495
% to Revenue	.4%	1.0%	17.6%	22.5%	11.7%		12.0%
Overhead	159,034	163,597	203,202	385,620	367,392	131%	255,769
% to Revenue	8.9%	8.6%	7.7%	14.7%	16.7%		11.5%
Net Revenue	$(151,911)	$(143,169)	$262,418	$202,496	$(111,228)		$11,726

NOTE: Because the method for calculating overhead has been changed several times in the last five years, comparing the net revenue from one year to the next is not a meaningful indication of financial return to the Association. The Contribution Margin is a better indicator. The overhead itself is composed not only of indirect costs incurred by the Books operation, but also covers some of the indirect costs of non-revenue generating units or components of ALA such as Council, Executive Board, Executive Office, etc.

Source: ALA Publishing Services Evaluation: Books ALA Publishing Committee, 1991

and personalities." *The ALA World Encyclopedia* (first edition, 1980), now in its third edition, provides "background information essential for comprehension of current issues and problems." *Booklist* is an important selection journal for thousands of libraries. The Association and its units also publish a variety of books, pamphlets, bibliographic tools, standards, and reading and audiovisual lists.

In the early 1990s ALA Publishing Services was responsible for producing more than 300,000 copies of books and pamphlets. The Association also produced 47 periodicals with a combined circulation of more than 360,000. Publishing revenue, including that of Divisional publications, was more than $11 million.

Relations with Other Organizations. Chapters have a special relationship to the Association because they elect voting members of the ALA Council. Yet they are independent organizations and some—California, New York, and Texas—have memberships larger than some ALA Divisions.

Affiliates, including library associations in information science, library education, law, medicine, music, and theater, may share a kindred purpose with ALA, but their participation in ALA is less direct than that of the chapters.

The Association has for many years sent representatives to organizations outside the library and information science field, such as the American Council on Education, the National Council of Teachers of English, and the U.S. National Commission for Unesco.

Relations with other major national library associations can best be described as "cooperative." ALA worked closely with the Association of Research Libraries, the American Association of Law Libraries, the Medical Library Association, the Music Library Association, and the Special Libraries Association on copyright legislation in the 1970s. Through the ALA Washington Office the Association maintains liaison with many organizations that have common interests in federal legislation.

REFERENCES

Edward G. Holley, *Raking the Historic Coals: The ALA Scrapbook of 1876* (Beta Phi Mu, 1967).

Holley, "ALA at 100," *The ALA Yearbook,* Centennial Edition (1976).

Kathleen Molz, *National Planning for Library Service, 1935–1975* (1984).

Peggy Sullivan, *Carl H. Milam and the American Library Association* (1976).

Dennis Thomison, *The American Library Association, 1876–1972* (1978).

ALA Handbook of Organization (issued annually).

"ALA Report," *The ALA Yearbook of Library and Information Services* (1984–90).

EDWARD G. HOLLEY

Angola

Angola, a republic in southwestern Africa, is bordered by Zaire on the north, Zambia on the east, Namibia on the south, and the Atlantic Ocean on the west. Population (1990 est.) 10,015,000; area 1,246,700 sq.km. The official languages are Portuguese and various Bantu languages.

History. Colonized by the Portuguese in the late 16th century, Angola did not receive significant numbers of Portuguese settlers until the 20th century. Guerrilla war against the Europeans broke out in 1961 and ended when the country gained its independence in 1975. Civil war followed, with forces from other countries supporting the Marxist government and its opponents. The war ended in 1991 and foreign troops withdrew. Reliable information about libraries after the early 1980s is scarce.

National Library. The National Department of Libraries was created in 1977 with the task of forming a national network of libraries, archives, and documentation centers. (Academic and school libraries, of the Ministry of Education, were excluded.) In that reorganization of the information community, the National Central Library in Luanda was founded, taking advantage of the collection and facilities of the former National Library (1968), a part of the National Library of Lisbon, Portugal. Its collection was formed in part from materials outside the areas of specialties of the Library of the National Museum of Angola and the Institute for Scientific Investigation of Angola, and also included the Library of Education of the Provincial Secretariat of Education. Legal deposit functioned from Lisbon, which distributed materials through the national libraries of its provinces. The National Central Library was enriched by the recovery of various private and official libraries that had been abandoned. In 1978 a statute was approved to organize and regulate the National Department of Libraries and to establish the National Central Library, and in 1979 a legal deposit law was passed.

The national network also covers archives and documentation centers, with the exception of those in history, which are the charges of the National Department of Museums and Monuments. The most important center for archives is in the Museu de Angola, in Luanda.

Academic Libraries. The University of Angola maintains a General Library, which also serves as a center for documentation and as the National Center for Scientific Investigation. The Library's holdings are divided into special collections and are distributed in the cities of Luanda, Lubango, and Huambo. Individual departments maintain their own specialized collections. Taken together, the several university libraries contain several thousand volumes. At Luanda, the Library holds about 75,000 volumes.

Public Libraries. The largest public library is the Municipal Library in Luanda. After independence the National Department of Libraries moved, in keeping with a national literacy campaign, to extend the network of libraries to the rural areas, further expanded by the creation of committees of party militants functioning in such production units as farms and factories. Through these efforts people's libraries had been established in more than 50 locations by the late 1970s, serving a literate population of more than 2,500,000 (plus a student population of 2,000,000). Whether this progress continued during the country's political problems is not known.

School Libraries. School libraries are under the direction of the Ministry of Education.

Special Libraries. Under the direction of the National Department of Libraries, Angola's special libraries are administratively linked to the ministries they serve, such as Agriculture, Industry and Energy, Justice, and Petroleum. The largest, in Huambo, Luanda, and Lubango, specialize in agriculture and animal husbandry. Others are in localities throughout the country.

DOMINGOS VAN-DUŃEM

Anuar, Hedwig
(1928–)

Hedwig Aroozoo Anuar, Singapore librarian and administrator, did much to promote and shape the development of Singapore libraries. Her career and interests involved her in many aspects of library development as well as library-related fields. She brought an intellectual quality and sense of vision to her work as head of the National Library and to other interests that proved unique.

She was born in the Malaysian town of Johor Bahru on November 19, 1928, and was graduated from the University of Malaya, Singapore, in 1951 with first class honors. She joined the University of Malaya Library in 1952 and was awarded an Inter-University Council Fellowship to study at the Northwestern Polytechnic in London. She obtained the Associateship of the Library Association in 1956 and the Fellowship two years later. She returned to the University of Malaya Library at its new campus in Kuala Lumpur, was assigned to the National Library of Singapore, and eventually became its Director in 1965, a position she held thereafter.

Hedwig Anuar

The Library had its beginnings in colonial Singapore as the Raffles Library, a subscription library serving a largely expatriate and English-reading public. It became the Raffles National Library in 1957 but was unable to break into a new pattern of service until 1962, when the New Zealand government sent A. Priscilla Taylor and J. R. Cole to Singapore as library consultants under the Colombo Plan. Taylor subsequently stayed on as Director until 1964 to do the initial planning and lay the groundwork for the development of the National Library. Under Anuar's directorship, these plans were realized and further extended.

Book collections amount to more than 2,000,000 volumes and include material in all four official languages—English, Chinese, Malay, and Tamil. Extension services were first provided through mobile libraries but later through branch libraries housed in attractive new buildings, as in Queenstown (1970), Toa Payoh (1974), Marine Parade (1978), and Bukit Merah (1982). Two more branch libraries opened in 1985 and two more in 1988.

National bibliographical activities include the publication of the *Singapore National Bibliography* (1967–), the *Singapore Periodicals Index* (1969/70–), and *Books about Singapore* (1962–). The National Library acts as the Singapore center for regional projects such as the International Serials Data System (ISDS) and the National Libraries and Documentation Center, Southeast Asia Consortium (NLDC-SEA).

Anuar's report *Blueprint for Public Library Development in Malaysia* (1968) was accepted as the basis for the development of public library services there. She served the Library Association of Singapore in many capacities, including the office of President. She chaired the LAS Joint Standing Committee on Library Cooperation and Bibliographical Service, 1965–75, and continued as the Vice-Chairman of its successor, the Committee on Bibliographical and Library Cooperation.

Other positions include Director (concurrent), National Archives and Records Center, 1969–78; Honorary Secretary, National Book Development Council of Singapore, 1965–80; and Chairman of the Council, 1980– . She was awarded the Public Administration Gold Medal in the National Day Honours in 1969 for her work in developing the National Library. She retired in 1988 but remained active in the National Book Development Council, consultancies, and other professional matters. She was granted Honorary Fellowship of the Library Association (London) in 1985.

LIM PUI HUEN

Arab League Educational, Cultural and Scientific Organization

The Arab League Educational, Cultural and Scientific Organization (ALECSO) was established on July 25, 1970, after the first meeting of the Organization's General Conference in Cairo. Its Information Department plays an active role in the development and promotion of information services in the Arab region. At the beginning the work was planned to include collecting selected documents; facilitating the exchange of information; supporting the research work of other departments of ALECSO; publishing journals, newsletters, guides, bulletins, and bibliographies; holding meetings, seminars, and conferences; and preparing statistics related to the fields served by ALECSO.

Four main activities took place in 1971 that paved the way for the Information Department of ALECSO to fulfill its goals. The first was a Seminar on Promoting Library Services in the Arab World, held in Damascus in October 1971. The second was the Seminar on Cultural Statistics held in Khartoum in December 1971. The third was the formulation of several questionnaires covering the fields of education, culture, and science to collect data related to those fields in the Arab world. The fourth was the effort to encourage the Arab states to apply legal deposit laws to their national libraries or other institutions with similar functions and roles.

As a result of those efforts, the Information Department carried out several projects in 1972–73, including (1) preparing guides and directories containing available data on information institutions, publishing houses, and periodicals in the Arab region; (2) issuing annual bulletins on Arab publications and educational statistics, a periodical entitled *The Arab Culture Magazine,* and a newsletter in Arabic and English; (3) holding a conference on the development of information services in the Arab region, the First Arab Bibliographical Conference (Riyadh, 1973), and a seminar on the Circulation of the Arabic Book (Doha, Qatar, 1972); and (4) organizing three-month training courses for librarians and documentation officers in the Arab world.

In 1974 ALECSO moved to a further stage. Programs and projects were planned to cover four major areas of activities: (1) developing technical, traditional, and mechanized tools used in information; (2) providing advanced bibliographical services in the fields covered by ALECSO; (3) raising the standards of personnel through training courses; and (4) collecting and publishing basic information on the Arab states in the fields of interest to ALECSO.

Several projects were initiated, including the *Bibliographical Guide to Reference Books in the Arab World;* a subject bibliography; new issues of the bulletins of statistics, Arab publications, *Arab Culture,* and the *ALECSO Newsletter;* organizing training courses; and holding a seminar on the use of computers in bibliographical works. The recommendations of the Riyadh Conference were carried out through a manual of Arab cataloguers, including Arabization of ISBD; a list of unified entries of Arab authors; studies on Arabic amendments to the Dewey Decimal Classification system; and experiments with an Arab classification system for Islamic disciplines. An experimental study was conducted on the rules to be adopted in preparing and using an Arab subject heading list. A model part of this list related to Islamic disciplines was produced and tried in some specialized libraries in the Arab states.

According to the results of these programs and the evaluation of the work achieved through them, ALECSO planned further projects that included a meeting on mechanical techniques in the field of information, held in Cairo in 1976, and the Second Arab Bibliographical Conference, in Baghdad in 1977. Several studies on information sciences and the application of modern techniques were published in Arabic. A subject bibliography in education was prepared, covering Arab specialized periodicals, and a bibliographical guide to Arab works in library science and documentation was also compiled. Training courses were continued, and a meeting of Arab experts in educational statistics was held in Baghdad in 1977. This meeting played an important role in developing the annual bulletin of educational statistics.

In 1978 the new information program included preparing the draft Arabic subject heading list, the Arabization of the modified edition of ISBD, and a manual containing models for the application of the Arabized rules. A guide to Arab works in social sciences and anthropology and a guide to documentation centers were also prepared, along with a new bulletin, the *Arab Journal of Information Sciences.*

The project FRARABI (First Arab Bank of Information) was completed by mid-1985. Three databases serve the objectives of the Organization: (1) the SAIB database deals with statistical information and research studies relating to education, culture, and science; (2) the SADOC database serves library and documentation functions; and (3) the SAFA database covers financial and administrative matters.

All three databases were to be connected with relevant databases of organizations and bodies related to the Arab League or ALECSO offices present in most Arab countries. Interconnections with international as well as inter-Arab national commissions affiliated to ALECSO, which operate in all the Arab countries, were to follow.

M. T. KHAFAGI

Arbuthnot, May Hill
(1884–1969)

May Hill Arbuthnot

May Hill Arbuthnot was not a librarian but, because of her contributions to education, as teacher, lecturer, children's literature specialist, reading consultant, and writer, children's librarianship in the United States is richer. In recognition of her efforts on behalf of literature and libraries for children, the Children's Services Division (now Association for Library Service to Children) of the American Library Association established in 1969 the May Hill Arbuthnot Honor Lectureship, sponsored by Scott, Foresman and Company.

Born in Mason City, Iowa, August 27, 1884, May Hill Arbuthnot received a baccalaureate degree from the University of Chicago in 1922 and her Master's degree from Columbia University in 1924. In 1927 she joined the faculty at Western Reserve University, Cleveland, Ohio (now Case Western Reserve University), from which she retired in 1949 as Associate Professor. Her teaching interests were in the general fields of nursery school and elementary education and the special field of children's literature. Her contributions in these areas were substantial. During her early years at Western Reserve, she was a pioneer in the nursery school movement. In 1929 she opened the University Nursery School, which became a successful model of a laboratory for teachers, doctors, nurses, parents, and other adults concerned with child development. Thousands of American children learned to read from the "Basic Curriculum Readers," which she wrote with William Scott Gray in 1951. Many of these children undoubtedly remember those readers as the "Dick and Jane" books.

Arbuthnot was a popular teacher on children's literature. A sought-after speaker throughout the country on children's books and reading, she spoke out firmly on topics related to the evaluation and selection of good books to meet children's developmental needs and reading tastes. In acknowledging the creation of the Honor Lectureship in 1969, she remembered "that long stretch of years when I was dashing from one end of the country to the other, bringing children and books together by way of the spoken word." She also offered her opinion that "a forthright, vigorous lecture can set fire to a piece of literature that had failed to come to life from the printed page."

She wrote extensively about children's books. For ten years she was Review Editor of children's books for *Childhood Education* and later for *Elementary English* (now *Language Arts*). In 1947 the first edition of her exhaustive textbook for children's literature courses, *Children and Books,* was published by Scott, Foresman; she provided historical background on the development of children's literature, giving many examples of the best books of each genre and type, selections from illustrators, and advice on developing a child's reading tastes. While her textbook emphasized excellence in its approach to selecting and using books with children, she also stated as a cautionary, "Two facts we need to keep constantly before us: a book is a good book for children only when they enjoy it; a book is a poor book for children, when adults rate it a classic, if children are unable to read it or are bored by its content." This text, which reached its sixth edition in 1981, was rewritten and reorganized by Zena Sutherland and other contributors.

Her other books include many anthologies in which she brought together, by genre, excellent examples of fine children's literature and provided advice on its selection and use with children. Those anthologies, all published by Scott, Foresman, include *Time for Poetry* (with Shelton L. Root, Jr; 3d ed., 1968), *Time for Stories of the Past and Present* (with Dorothy M. Broderick, 1968), *Time for Biography* (with Dorothy M. Broderick, 1969), *Time for Old Magic* (1970), *Time for New Magic* (with Mark Taylor, 1971), and *Time for Discovery* (with Evelyn Wenzel, 1971). Three of her other books—*The Anthology of Children's Literature* (4th ed. rev., 1976, by Zena Sutherland); a bibliography, *Children's Books Too Good to Miss* (7th ed., 1979); and *Children's Reading in the Home* (1969)—are still used in college courses and by others concerned with children's reading.

Arbuthnot's honors included the Constance Lindsay Skinner Award (1959) and the Catholic Library Association's Regina Medal (1964).

Arbuthnot died October 2, 1969, in Cleveland. Three months before her death, the May Hill Arbuthnot Honor Lectureship was announced. It provides for the annual selection of an outstanding author, critic, librarian, historian, or teacher of children's literature to prepare and give a lecture in the United States "which shall be a significant contribution to the field of children's literature." The lecture is presented annually, usually in April, and is subsequently published in an issue of *Top of the News.* (For lecturers, see *The ALA Yearbook,* 1976– , "Awards" and "Biographies.")

REFERENCE

Marilyn Miller, "Arbuthnot, May Hill," *Dictionary of American Library Biography* (1978).

MARILYN L. MILLER

Archives

NATURE, GOALS, PRINCIPLES

Nature of Archives. Archives constitute one of the world's primary information sources. They arise and grow uniquely out of the activities of any organization or institution, a family or even an individual. *Records* are the sum total of all documentary materials—regardless of their physical form or characteristics—created or received, and maintained, by an organization or other entity in connection with the transaction of its business and its other activities. An entity's records are the whole, the universe, from which its archives are selected. *Archives,* then, are those records of an organization, institution, or other entity that have been selected for preservation because they possess enduring value. The comparable records of an individual or family are often called *papers* or *manuscripts,* but there is no essential difference in the nature or handling of these materials.

Physically, a wide variety of media have been used for record keeping during the course of human history. Included are clay tablets, papyrus, palm leaves, and parchment; in modern times paper documentation of various kinds has evolved from the medieval parchments—the so-called "textual" records. In addition, many nontextual documentary forms have been brought into being by the new technologies of the 19th and particularly the 20th centuries: still photographs, motion picture films, videotapes, sound recordings, magnetic tapes, and related machine-readable forms. All of these, regardless of their special physical characteristics, are considered to be records, and therefore are potentially archives, if used by an organization or other entity for record keeping.

Types of Archival Agencies. The term *archives* is used to refer not only to records of archival value but also to the agencies—generally public or private institutions or organizational units—responsible for selecting, preserving, and making these records available. These agencies, as a rule, correspond to and serve the various types of record-creating and record-keeping organizations. Chief among the latter are public bodies, governmental agencies at every level (national or federal, regional, state or provincial, and local), attached to which, in a pattern that varies according to the structure of government in various countries, are the public archival agencies. The National Archives and Records Administration and the 50 independent state archives in the United States, and the Archives de France, a centralized system encompassing both the Archives Nationales and the archives

Hugh Talman/National Archives and Records Administration (NARA)

The National Archives in Washington, D.C., the National Archives and Records Administration Service (NARA) became an independent agency in 1985.

services of all the départements, are examples. The term *archives* also has a third meaning; it is used to refer to a building, or part of a building, where archives are housed.

Nonpublic archival agencies consist mainly of "institutional archives" attached to and providing archival services for business firms, trade unions, universities, scientific, social, and philanthropic organizations, religious bodies, and other institutions, both profit and nonprofit. Related to these are archival agencies, not associated with particular creating institutions, that serve as custodians of the archives of classes of such institutions, such as businesses, unions, and churches. Archives of institutions are also to be found among the manuscript holdings of public or private libraries and historical societies. Family and personal archives are usually maintained informally by the families concerned but, when prominent people are involved, are often deposited in and administered by libraries and historical societies as "papers" or manuscript collections. Similarly, such papers may find their way to public or private archival agencies attached to organizations with which the families or individuals have been connected.

Purposes and Functions. Among archival agencies, those serving public organizations were the first to emerge and still make up the predominant category. Today, as in the past, the overriding purpose of these public archival agencies is to identify the relatively small proportion of government records having archival value and to effect their regular transfer to archival custody, so they may be preserved for future use.

Such preservation is justified by the information contained in the archival sources, which are valuable alike (1) to the government entities that initially produced them as evidence of their origin, organization, policies, programs, and principal operations over time and for long-term legal, financial, and other administrative purposes; (2) to private individuals and unofficial bodies in order to safeguard rights of various kinds and to assist in meeting their obligations; and (3) to scholars working in the fields of history, the other humanities, and the social sciences primarily, but also in the natural sciences, in pursuing their research.

Having developed programs for the systematic acquisition of records of archival value, based upon the application of professionally determined evaluation or appraisal standards, the archival agency provides for their physical preservation under the best possible conditions; perfects their organization and arrangement; describes them in guides, inventories, lists, and other finding aids designed to open them to potential users; and, finally, makes them available for consultation—either directly, or through the medium of publication, originally by letterpress exclusively but later in microform and electronic formats as well—by the government itself and by the scholarly and general public.

Since World War II public archival agencies, led by those in the U.S., have increasingly expanded their function to the closely interconnected field of records management. Here the archival agency establishes standards of good practice with respect to the creation, organization, maintenance, and retrieval of the current records of government, as well as to their eventual disposition when they cease to be current by transfer to archival custody or by destruction; and seeks to promote the adoption of these standards by government bodies. Following the lead of government at the national level, state and local governments, as well as major businesses, have embraced the concept of records management as a tool for efficiency and economy. Art museums, banks, communications companies, fraternal organizations, labor unions, religious bodies, and many other entities have adopted records management for their internally created records. Although the involvement of archival agencies in records management was initially motivated by the need to facilitate the transfer to them of the archival core of government records, there has been the concomitant result of more efficient and effective administration of agencies and the entities just mentioned that is also vitally important.

Institutional archives of all kinds have the same basic purposes and functions as public archival agencies, although they generally operate on a smaller scale, and are becoming more and more involved in the records management practices of the organizations they serve. Similarly, archival agencies, including archives, libraries, and historical societies, that are not associated with the organizations, families, and individuals that created the archives they hold, play no records management role. Otherwise, however, they share the essential purposes and functions associated with other archival agencies.

Basic Principles and Terminology. A key characteristic of archives, as of the records from which they have been selected, is their organic character. This refers to the fact that they are not collected, in the usual sense of the term, by the originating organization or other entity but rather grow naturally—are created or received—out of its own activities and operations. Thus the individual documents that make up an organization's archives do not exist independently but instead are integrated in an overall structure of documentation that is essential to their significance.

The organic character common to all archival documentation leads logically to the fundamental principle of *provenance,* in its original French formulation. This concept, which implies "belonging," holds that since the archives of a given organization belong to and constitute an organic whole, they must not be intermingled with those of any other organization. For the same reason, the corollary principle of *respect des fonds,* which derives essentially from archaeology and has the sense of "not disturbing the ground," requires that the archives of an organization should be maintained in their original internal structural pattern, and in their original filing arrangement, in order to preserve intact the close interrelationships between the individual component units. Otherwise, the meaning of the substantive informational content that they share as an organic whole would be seriously impaired or even destroyed. The implications of these principles for archival arrangement and classification on the one hand, and for archival description (that is, the preparation of finding aids) on the other, are most important: they have resulted in practices in these areas that are fundamentally different from analogous library practices, which are typically concerned with discrete items.

For purposes of control in the archival agency, all the records of an organization, and the archives subsequently selected from them, compose its *fonds* (a classic French term used widely in Europe) or, in Anglo-Saxon parlance, its *record group* or *archives group.* (There are certain technical differences between the fonds and the record group concepts, but they are essentially comparable.) The contents of a record group normally subdivide into *subgroups,* corresponding to the primary subordinate administrative branches of the organizations concerned. Where an organization has inherited records of a predecessor organization, these would also form a subgroup. There may be other special situations in a given record group that call for the recognition of subgroups.

The primary physical unit in the record group and its subgroups is the *document,* a single item on which information is recorded that may take one of many varied forms, such as a letter or memorandum, a report, the minutes of a meeting, a map or chart, a photograph, a sound recording, or a reel of microfilm or magnetic tape. Documents rarely exist alone; they tend to be associated with other related documents in *file units* (for example, the folder, the dossier or case file, the bound volume in earlier centuries), which themselves are grouped in series.

As the basic archival grouping for all purposes, particularly for arrangement and description as well as reference control, the *series* is of paramount importance. It consists of a body of file units, multi-document and/or single document in nature, that are interdependently linked together (1) in accordance with some filing system, or (2) because they concern a particular physical character, or share a mutual relationship arising out of their creation, accumulation, or use. In the record group and its subgroups, the pattern of association of the constituent series reflects the hierarchical structure of the originating organization.

Against this background, the following sections deal with the principal functional aspects of archives administration, preceded by a description of their legislative foundations. The functional aspects covered are: records management and records appraisal; organization and description; services to users; archives management; technical aspects (building, custodial services, and technical services); electronic records; and professional training for archivists.

National Archives of Brazil

Aerial view of the National Archives of Brazil in Rio de Janeiro, established by imperial decree in 1838.

REFERENCES

Sir Hilary Jenkinson, *A Manual of Archive Administration,* 2nd edition (1965).

James M. O'Toole, *Understanding Archives and Manuscripts* (1990).

T. R. Schellenberg, *Modern Archives: Principles and Techniques* (1956).

Frank B. Evans, François-J. Himly, and Peter Walne, compilers, *Dictionary of Archival Terminology,* ed. by Peter Walne (1984).

FRANK G. BURKE

LEGISLATIVE FOUNDATIONS

What Is Archival Legislation? Archival legislation is probably as old and universal as archives themselves. Since archives are, according to a Unesco definition, "all noncurrent records of an institution or organization (those no longer needed in the conduct of current business) that are or should be preserved because of their permanent value," their preservation and use have long been regulated by the public powers. We know of the existence of laws on the subject as early as ancient Greece and the Roman Empire. In medieval Europe even the Popes and their Councils issued regulations on church archives, with threats of excommunication for offenders.

But the idea of comprehensive, systematic legislation on the whole matter of the conservation and use of archives is comparatively recent. The first country to conceive of it was France, in 1789–96, as a consequence of the French Revolution. Even now several countries throughout the world (especially developing countries) have no general archival legislation but only partial regulations of limited scope.

National Archives of Zimbabwe

Librarians in the map room of the National Archives of Zimbabwe.

Such differences from country to country can be explained by the fact that archives are closely linked with the entire legal, administrative, and socioeconomic system of each country. For example, in the United Kingdom and other countries with Anglo-Saxon legal traditions, documents derive legal value from the fact that they are kept in a public archival repository, whereas this is not the case in countries of Latin culture; legislation thus varies on this point. Another difference in the scope of archival laws is whether they are concerned with archives only after they have been transferred from the agency where they originated or also deal with the management of current records; the American and Canadian records management legislation has no equivalent in many countries. For all these reasons, it would be unrealistic to propose an "ideal" model for archival legislation. Many parts of a Russian or Chinese archival law would be meaningless in the U.S. or Japan, while many requirements useful in industrialized countries would be useless in developing ones.

Public and Private Archives. In the eyes of the legislator, the distinction between public and private (that is, "nonpublic") archives is fundamental. Unfortunately, there is no consensus of definition in this matter. Definitions vary widely from one country to another, according to differences in socioeconomic and political systems. In some countries private ownership of archives is strictly limited to personal and family papers, whereas in other countries most business, society, trade union, university and school, hospital, church, and other institutional archives are largely considered private archives, with many variations from one country to another.

In many countries one of the main points of uncertainty is the legal status of papers of heads of state, ministers, and senior public servants. A certain amount of confusion is inevitable between the private, personal correspondence and official papers of these individuals. In some countries the government may be able to seize the papers of deceased or dismissed ministers and senior public servants, but this is seldom fully implemented, except for top-ranking army officers and diplomats.

The designation "public" applies to the legal status of these archives and not necessarily to their accessibility. Some public archives may not be accessible to the public (for example, "security-classified" diplomatic or military records), while some private archives may be freely open to inspection. Nor do "private" archives always become public when they are given, bequeathed, or sold to the state or to public institutions. In many countries they retain their private status even when they are public property, the distinction between private and public archives being more in their origin than in their actual ownership.

Public archives are universally declared to be imprescriptible (that is, not subject to claims or the assertion of customary rights by private parties) and inalienable. They can never cease to be public property, and they can be destroyed only according to official regulations. In some countries, such as the U.S., the legal designation of "archives" is even limited to documents that have a permanent value, while in some others, such as France, it applies to all documents, whether of permanent or temporary value. (There the distinction made between "records" and "archives," in the section *Archives: Nature, Goals, Principles,* does not exist.)

As to private archives (which in the U.S. are frequently referred to as manuscript collections or papers), the law really began to be interested in them, with a few exceptions, only at the end of the 19th century and the beginning of the 20th. Even now there is no legal protection for them in some countries, but generally there are at least laws prohibiting the exportation of private archives of historical interest and giving to the government a right of preemption should they be sold.

Administrative Organization of Public Archives. Always a matter of legislative concern, the organization of public archives is closely related to the administrative system of each country. In countries with a centralized system, such as France, Italy, Spain, or the Scandinavian counties, archives are also generally centralized under one supreme authority (or a limited number of authorities). In such cases there is an integrated hierarchy of national (central), regional (provincial, departmental, or district), and local archives, as well as of specialized archives such as audiovisual, scientific, literary, diplomatic, military, and educational archives, all subordinate to a central governmental office.

On the other hand, in noncentralized countries, especially in countries with a federal structure such as the U.S., Brazil, Germany, and Switzerland, each level of archival responsibility is independent of every other level (for example, the federal and state levels in the U.S.). For this reason it is difficult to compare archival organization, for example, in France and the U.S., because in one case laws and regulations apply to the whole of archives in the country, while in the other case separate federal and state laws and regulations exist.

In the past, archives and libraries were often confused with each other and placed under one single authority. In the 20th century advanced countries became aware of the basic differences between archives and libraries and created separate organizations for each of them. This was not the case everywhere, however, and in a number of countries there still remains a confusion that is highly prejudicial both to archives and to libraries, since the nature and use of the holdings of each, and the requirements for their administration, are significantly different.

The governmental authority under which archives are placed also varies from one country to another. In Russia the General Directorate of State Archives depends directly on the Council of Ministers; in the U.K. the Public Record Office is under the Lord Chancellor; in France, Italy, and some other countries, archives are a responsibility of the Minister of Culture; elsewhere they belong to other ministries, such as Education, Interior, or Justice, or they come directly under the authority of the President or the Prime Minister.

No system can be said to be ideal, but it seems that, at least in developing countries, only placement at the highest level of authority can give to the archival administration a sufficient degree of legal and administrative effectiveness.

Accessibility of Public Archives. Public access to archives is a relatively modern concern; it is linked with the progress of both democracy and objective historical research. The French law of 1794, which opened all public archives to public investigation, was, for a long time, nothing more than window dressing. The duration of the period during which access is restricted has been steadily diminishing. The term has come to be, in most countries, from 30 to 50 years, with special provisions to ensure the protection of individual privacy and state security. In several countries there are no time restrictions at all on access to public archives, except for certain categories and bodies of archives for which limited access is deemed a public necessity. However, despite an evident (but not universal) trend toward liberalization, access to public archives is still restricted in many countries, either by specific laws and regulations (especially when the searcher is a foreigner) or by sheer inertia and bureaucratic red tape. Of course, the "freedom of information" laws enacted in a number of countries since the 1960s have resulted in opening many recent records to public inspection. But these laws sometimes conflict with "right of privacy" legislation, and the matter of accessibility has become one of the most controversial and complex issues in the archival field.

Basic Elements of Archival Legislation. This broad survey of archival legislation and its background throughout the world enables us now to define what basic elements should figure in any archival legislation, regardless of the national political, administrative, and/or socioeconomic systems involved:

(a) Definitions of archives (and of records where the distinction is relevant), both public and private, and of the nation's responsibility concerning their preservation for legal, administrative, evidential, and research needs. Special emphasis, where necessary, should be put on the distinction between archives, libraries, and documentation centers.

(b) Definitions of the organization and functions of public archival agencies, whether centralized or not, including their right to inspect public archives and records wherever they are located, to establish standards (preferably mandatory) of good current records management practice, and to operate intermediate records centers for the storage and maintenance of noncurrent records.

(c) Provisions granting to the archival agency the sole power and responsibility to appraise the value of public records for purposes of disposition (either destruction or preservation).

(d) Provisions governing the controlled destruction of noncurrent public records that have been appraised as lacking further value.

(e) Provisions governing (i) the transfer of noncurrent public records, selected as permanently valuable in the appraisal process, to the custody of archival repositories, and (ii) their subsequent arrangement and description.

(f) Standards for access to public records.

National Archives of Zimbabwe

The reading room of the National Archives of Zimbabwe in Salisbury provides workspace for researchers.

(g) Definitions of the duties and responsibilities of record managers and archivists and the requirements for their professional training.

(h) Provisions for the protection of private archives having historical interest.

REFERENCES

The archival legislation of more than 90 countries throughout the world has been published in vols. 17, 19–21, and 28 of *Archivum*.

MICHEL DUCHEIN

RECORDS MANAGEMENT AND RECORDS APPRAISAL

Before the Great Depression of the 1930s, records management was limited, with rare exceptions, to systems for controlling correspondence and devising methods of classifying centralized files. Chief clerks, then the administrative officers of most governmental agencies, and corporate secretaries or comptrollers in business and other private organizations, rarely concerned themselves with the disposition of noncurrent records. Though World War I had generated large volumes of records in most national governments, the problems of disposition were barely perceived. Filing operations were delegated to poorly paid clerks, and the cost of space for files was not deemed sufficiently high to justify managerial attention.

The public officials and archivists who were influential in establishing modern archives in France, Germany, the Netherlands, the United Kingdom, and several other European countries had scant conceptions of records retirement and neglected any systematic approach to the appraisal of records values. Disposition was limited to the transfer of very old records to the archives. As these records had been produced when documentation was relatively scarce, archivists were inclined to accept all that were offered by the departments. Even records relating to housekeeping activities (personnel management, supplies, and minor fiscal operations) were accepted for preservation. By the latter half of the 19th century, however, small quantities of routine records were being culled from accessions. This weeding operation was not given much professional attention until World War I. During the war, waste paper was used in making bullets, and occasionally important records were reduced to pulp without any opportunity for archival intervention. This loss alerted European archivists to the problem of preserving recent records; nonetheless, they failed to develop an appropriate methodology.

One exception to this neglect of systematic records disposition appeared in Poland in the early 1930s. As a result of the country's partition in the late 18th century, old and valuable Polish records were in the custody of Austria, Germany, and the U.S.S.R. Archivists, in order to establish a prestigious national archives, were compelled to concentrate on preserving valuable recent records. As a result, Poland pioneered in developing a theoretical approach by scheduling records disposition, that is, the itemization of discrete bodies of records, each accompanied by specific retention or disposal recommendations. The other European nations did not adopt similar programs until the end of World War II.

In the United States, railroads, banks, and insurance companies were among the first to try to rationalize records programs. They produced relatively large accumulations of records, many required for a number of years for administrative needs and regulatory compliance. Railroads led the reforms at the turn of the 20th century because of the need to manage information about real estate, rights of way, rolling stock, train movements, and the administration of extensive networks. Furthermore, the Interstate Commerce Commission issued regulations concerning the maintenance of their varied records. Thus by World War I railroads had adopted prescribed filing systems and designated records for permanent or long-term retention. Banks and insurance companies instituted similar procedures and practices in the years immediately after the war. With the exception of a few railroads, these firms did not, however, establish institutional archival units like those emerging in Europe between 1901 and 1930.

The U.S. National Archives. When the U.S. National Archives began operations in 1935, the Archivist of the United States recruited, in addition to a managerial and an advisory staff, persons deemed qualified to appraise records for permanent preservation. These appraisers were selected on the basis of some experience with manuscript materials but, more important, because of their subject matter expertise; for example, scholars who specialized in military and diplomatic history and in the westward movement were delegated responsibility for appraising noncurrent records of the defense agencies, the Department of State, and the Department of the Interior, respectively. These archivists (Deputy Examiners) found that the records were in a chaotic state. Trivial materials were intermixed with records required to conduct essential public business, to protect the rights of individuals, and to serve scholarly research needs. Storage areas were inadequate for efficient access to records; some lacked even elemental fire protection.

To avoid uneconomical large-scale weeding operations, the appraisers had to accept or reject massive files of both temporary and permanent records. The National Archives Building was empty, so they could, in good conscience, lean heavily in the direction of conservation. They nevertheless deplored the state of records management and provided some counsel for reforms.

Enabling legislation authorized the Archivist of the United States to submit to Congress proposals by agencies for the destruction of specific bodies of noncurrent records that he deemed unworthy of permanent preservation by the federal government. The task of reviewing the proposals was delegated to the Special Examiners. The Deputy and Special Examiners thus gained considerable experience in past and current records management methods. While most agencies lacked any systematic control over their documentation, the departments of State, War, Navy, and the Treasury had developed classification schemes for some logical arrangement of their records. They had not yet devised rational systems for retiring or destroying records, though units with certain archival functions had been established.

With the start of World War II in Europe in 1939, the national archivists took an increasingly active role

National Archives and Records Administration (NARA)

An architectural rendering of the new National Archives Building at College Park, Maryland. The 1.7 million-square-foot structure is scheduled for completion in 1993.

in advising agencies about reforms. They were especially effective, first, in the War and Navy departments and, later, in the war regulatory agencies. Some of the leading archivists actually transferred to records management positions in these agencies after they demonstrated how to organize files for more efficient access and how to rid files of records that were no longer needed for administrative purposes. They formed the nucleus of the records management profession that was to develop during and after the war.

These professional records managers worked in close association with their colleagues in the National Archives in developing efficient methods of providing for the orderly retirement of records. Together they successfully petitioned Congress in 1943 to authorize the National Archives to process agency recommendations for scheduling disposal of records after specific periods of time or after the occurrence of specific events. Two years later Congress authorized the National Archives itself to propose to Congress the disposal of records common to all or several agencies (General Records Schedules). The 1950s saw the emergence of the comprehensive records control schedule by means of which agencies or major subdivision of agencies proposed the retirement of all of their records, either by disposal or by transfer to archives custody.

Growth of the Profession. During this period, about 1943 to 1970, the records management profession expanded greatly its responsibility for generally controlling records and communication channels. The Hoover Commission of 1948 gave considerable attention to efficient means for reducing the costs of managing records. It proposed centralizing responsibility for developing records management standards. Agencies would be required to appoint records management staffs to implement the standards. The recommendations led in 1950 to the incorporation of the National Archives into the National Archives and Records Service (NARS) in the newly established General Services Administration. NARS was delegated the centralized responsibility for records management recommended by the Commission.

This broad mandate led to the expansion of records management from simply developing filing techniques and retiring records to the management of mail, reports, directives, forms, reprography, and correspondence. To facilitate records retirement, NARS organized Regional Records Centers based on agency-controlled centers established during World War II for the temporary storage of noncurrent records. While the records in the centers remained under the legal custody of the creating agencies, reference service and the destruction of disposable records were carried out by center personnel. The centers also facilitated transferring to the National Archives the records designated for preservation.

As records managers and archivists became familiar with the rapidly changing technology for processing information, they promoted the use of various microfilm techniques and the use of electronic devices. They were thus in the forefront of the emerging information revolution. Some, in fact, are now designated information managers rather than paperwork or records managers.

Most of the information-oriented efforts of these managers concerned miniaturization of records. Roll microfilm had been the leading form of miniaturization for storage of records, but in the 1970s they experimented with and increasingly used microfiche and computer output microfilm (COM). Though there was an initial separation between managers of records and of automated equipment, some cooperated to deal with the massive quantities of information in machine-readable form and in the resultant increases in hard-copy documentation and printouts. Like other types of records, machine-readable records and their

Maryland State Archives

Research Room, Maryland State Archives, Annapolis

by-products are scheduled for preservation or disposal. In 1984 NARS was separated from the General Services Administration and became an independent agency, the National Archives and Records Administration (NARA); it now shares with the General Services Administration responsibility for government-wide records management.

These innovations had significant domestic and foreign spinoffs. The states developed similar programs, and many foreign governments sent archivists and records managers to the U.S. to study techniques for managing current and noncurrent records. Most states and many foreign governments organized records centers adapted to their special needs. The practice of scheduling the disposal of valueless records, as well as the transfer of permanent records to the archives, became common first in the industrialized nations and more recently in developing nations. Many private organizations, such as businesses, labor unions, universities, and churches, have to a greater or lesser extent developed similar records management and archival programs.

For the most part, public archives in other countries and private institutions generally do not differentiate between records managers and archivists; records management is still limited largely to advising on file management and retirement methods. In most private institutions, on the one hand, the records managers serve as archivists to the degree that they store records deemed of sufficient value for preservation as long as the organization exists. In some foreign countries, on the other hand, archivists have become directly involved in making decisions about the disposition of public records. The activity common to all these organizations, now recognized as essential to efficient operations of agencies and to preserve resources of research, is the disposition process whereby a valuable core of records is selected for permanent retention and the remainder is eventually destroyed.

Appraisal. In their initial experience in appraising records, the founders of the National Archives benefited to some extent from the theories and practices of senior archivists elsewhere. The Polish archivist who recommended scheduling as a retirement technique, Gustaw Kalenski, also wrote of a selection process based on the values of records for continuity in government and for scholarly and other research. German archivists emphasized records that are required as evidence of the origin and administration of major governmental activities (evidential values). Other records deserve preservation for secondary purposes, that is, for the information of substantial value they contain for studies about people, places, events, and things (informational values).

The Archivist of the state of Illinois in the 1930s, Margaret Cross Norton, stressed the legal value of certain records as an essential element in selecting records for permanent preservation. Her emphasis on legal values was a direct extension of Germanic concerns about evidential values of basic records. About the same time Sir Hilary Jenkinson, Keeper of the Public Record Office in London, stated that records must have remained in unbroken official custody to assure their legal and evidential values. He also asserted that archivists should not intervene in records management and that archives should simply accept or reject the noncurrent records offered by administrative agencies.

While these views were helpful in developing their appraisal policies, the archivists in the National Archives decided that new concepts were desirable or necessary. The long neglect of records had left them in a poor state, and the frequent alienation of important documentation led these archivists to the conclusion that unbroken custody was secondary to the need to bring valuable records under archival control. While they agreed that archivists are obligated to preserve records that document important governmental policies and decisions, they became more concerned about the value of records for research in history and the other humanities, the social sciences, and, to a lesser extent, the physical sciences. While the identification of records having evidential value for the history of governmental or private organizations is based on specific or concrete criteria, the appraisal of records for their informational values depends on subjective judgments about the likelihood of important research use of them in the future.

Records having evidential value may be classified, in the main, as follows: (1) those that show the origin and organization of agencies and their programs; (2) delegations of authority; (3) regulatory materials; (4) minutes of meetings and other records that document policy determinations; (5) documentation on the allocation of resources; and (6) selected records that deal with the procedures and the general administration of basic functions. It should be noted that these kinds of records can also be used for research on topics other than the history of the agency; for example, regulatory materials may provide valuable information about business operations, and policy records of the Department of State may be sources for research on foreign countries, as well as on U.S. relations with them.

Few concrete criteria for selecting records of informational value have evolved. Basically, archivists seek records containing unique data for research on important topics. Within reason, they should be convinced that researchers will eventually avail themselves of the records. Generally speaking, to judge informational values appraisal archivists must, by extensive study, master broad subject fields and familiarize themselves with related research needs and trends. In many countries they must have the concurrence of leading academicians before approving disposal.

While all records by their nature contain information of some evidential and informational value, more often than not it may be of such marginal interest that the costly preservation of the records involved is unwarranted. Furthermore, the preservation of records relating to minor subjects would so burden researchers as to impede research on significant ones. American and, increasingly, other archivists use aggregate techniques to deal with massive accumulations of records. They judge the values of each series or file on the basis of the total content. Among voluminous records on minor topics there may be some documents of interest. Seeking them would normally not be cost-effective, but records of certain agencies are so significant that an effort to find key documents is justified. In the case of large subject-classified central files, it is often possible to eliminate by class most housekeeping records and other papers that concern minor transactions.

A leading problem in appraisal involves decisions regarding voluminous case and survey files, also known as dossiers in France and as single-instance files in the U.K. Many such files contain unique information for demographic, social, economic, and genealogical research. For research other than that which requires data about all individuals, institutions, or places documented in the series, archivists have used sampling techniques. This methodology assumes that the preservation of significant, typical, or random case files will provide sufficient information on the most important research topics to which the series relates. For functionally significant programs that generate quite routine documentation in the form of case files, appraisers have authorized the retention of another type of sample—a procedural one consisting of only a few cases to illustrate program operations.

Most sampling criteria for the disposal of case and survey files involve subjective judgments about the number of files to be retained and about their contents. To achieve objectivity, archivists and records managers have increasingly used statistical sampling based on a random selection of cases to reflect the contents of the aggregate files. This solution also has its limitations, since certain files with significant research value may not be part of the sample selected for preservation. One method used to overcome this deficiency is to create a stratified sample that includes all files at the high level of a scale and reduced percentages at lower levels of the scale. Sampling has also been used as the appraisal technique itself for case files of a governmental investigative body. Concerned researchers have challenged the proposed disposition in a judicial proceeding, and the rulings to 1992—the case had not yet been decided—constitute one of the most copiously documented explanations of the selection process.

The information and computer revolution has greatly increased pressures on archivists for the preservation of source documents for social, economic, and political research. Before the widespread use of electronic media, detailed research about individuals, institutions, and phenomena generally in large numbers was impeded by the slowness and tedium of manual tabulations. But with computers, researchers can easily undertake the kind of research involving voluminous data that had not been envisioned during the early years of the 20th century.

Social and economic data of great variety are now being recorded in machine-readable form. The electronic media used for the purpose have the advantage of miniaturizing the information and of providing it to researchers in a mode susceptible of rapid, efficient manipulation. Evaluation of these media for permanent preservation, or disposal by erasure of the media, is conducted in Canada, Sweden, the U.K., and the U.S. according to the same standards as for conventional records—that is, that records should have sufficient evidential or informational value to justify permanent retention. As a consequence, librarians, archivists, and records managers are increasingly including substantial training in electronic data processing as part of their professional education and training.

REFERENCES

M. H. Fishbein, "Appraisal of Twentieth Century Records," *Illinois Libraries* (February 1970).

Gustaw Kalenski, "Record Selection," *American Archivist* (January 1976), edited by M. H. Fishbein, from *Archivwum Dawynch* (1934).

P. Lewinson, "Archival Sampling," *American Archivist* (October 1957).

Theodore R. Schellenberg, "The Appraisal of Modern Records," *National Archives Bulletin* (1956).

National Archives and Records Service, *Appraisal of the Records of the Federal Bureau of Investigation,* 2 vols. (1981).

C. P. Waegemann, *Handbook of Records Storage and Space Management* (1983).

MEYER H. FISHBEIN

ORGANIZATION AND DESCRIPTION

The theory and practice of archival arrangement and description are of relatively recent origin. Historically, neither the volume, complexity, nor use of archives posed particular problems for either their custodians or their users. When no longer needed for the conduct of current business, most older documents, such as charters or treaties, were maintained in a basic chronological arrangement, while other noncurrent records, such as accounts and correspondence, tended to be maintained in the order in which they were transferred to the treasuries and strong rooms that served as archival repositories. Archives were conceived of primarily as "arsenals of law" for their parent institutions, and no general principles were needed to govern their arrangement.

At least from the days of Callimachus at the Alexandrian Library, custodians of book and document collections have been searching for the perfect organization of increasingly complex holdings. During the 18th century, the holdings of archival repositories were subjected to a variety of reorganizations. In accordance with the predominant ideas of the Age of Reason, the merits of chronological, subject-matter, and geographical arrangement of all documents were vigorously debated, and many archives were rearranged with no regard for their organic structure or

National Photography Collection, Public Archives of Canada

The enormous volume of governmental records creates special challenges in housing, processing, and using public archives.

functional relationships. With the development of the historical sciences, archives had come to be regarded primarily as "arsenals of history," and their custodians, intending to facilitate their use for historical research, adopted various schemes derived chiefly from library experience. Individual dossiers and documents were removed from the series in which they had originally been filed as part of administrative transactions (and for which they furnished the evidence) and were artificially rearranged, usually under specific subject headings.

For many archives, the results of this policy were disastrous. The removal of documents and files from the organizational and functional context in which they were created or received, and from the administrative context in which they had been maintained and used, not only obscured or compromised the official and legal character of the records but also destroyed the context necessary for their evaluation and effective use as historical sources. In addition, such rearrangement rendered useless or seriously impaired the value of existing finding aids, such as indexes and lists, and required that the archival repository undertake the expensive and time-consuming preparation of new and detailed classification schemes and indexes in order to locate and retrieve the incidental subject content that was the focus of many of the new systems. During the last half of the 19th century, however, the unfortunate consequences of artificial subject arrangement, as well as the development of a fuller understanding of the nature and character of archives, led to the formulation of the two basic principles that today are universally recognized as the sole appropriate basis for the arrangement of archives: the principle of provenance and the principle of respect for original order, defined above. (*See* Archives: Nature, Goals, Principles.)

Organization. Because the arrangement and description of archives are so closely related to the administrative structures and procedures and the record-keeping systems of the institutions in which they originated, and because these vary so greatly from country to country and historically within the same country, even a brief account for each country would require a treatise far beyond the scope of this article. The following summary is limited to current practice in the United States and, to a lesser extent, in Canada.

The Record Group. In modern archival practice the function of arrangement refers to the process and the results of organizing archives in accordance with the principle of provenance and the principle of respect for original order at as many as necessary of the following levels: repository, record group (or comparable control unit), subgroup(s), series, file unit, and document. The process is intended to achieve physical (or administrative) control and basic identification of the total holdings of a repository, and usually also includes packing arranged archives into containers and labeling and shelving the containers. This summary of the function assumes a general archival repository that receives the permanently valuable noncurrent records of many administrative units or offices of a parent institution, such as a government. Although hierarchically the repository level precedes the record group level, in practice the record group level must be given priority in arrangement. The process then proceeds from the repository level down to the individual item or document level.

Arrangement at the record group level consists of allocating new accessions of records on the basis of provenance to existing record groups or, if necessary, to newly established record groups. However, in establishing a record group, the concept of provenance, though fundamental, may be modified by other pragmatic considerations, particularly the administrative history, the complexity, and the volume of the records involved. In the U.S. National Archives, for example, all archives of the Department of State, on the grounds of common provenance, could theoretically be established as a single record group, but their considerable volume and complexity would serve to impede effective arrangement, description, and reference service. Thus these records have been divided into a number of record groups generally corresponding to the former bureaus of the Department, which exercised considerable autonomy in their operations. The records of the office of the head of the Department, the records of other units concerned with matters such as finance and personnel that affected the Department as a whole, and, in some cases, the records of predecessor agencies that had been incorporated into central files are then usually allocated to a separate "general" record group for the entire Department.

A further modification of the record group concept is the "collective" record group. To avoid creating an unmanageable number of record groups, the records of a number of small or short-lived, though separate, agencies that have an administrative or functional relationship (such as records of district courts or claims commissions) are assigned to a single record group. In such a record group the records of each constituent agency form a separate and distinct subgroup. Under the record group concept, any particular body of records can belong to only one record group, and, except for subgroups or series consisting predominantly of cartographic, audiovisual, machine-readable, or other special physical types, an effort is made to keep together in the stack areas all records belonging to the same record group.

The value and flexibility of the record group concept have been demonstrated by its adaptation not only to the complex archives of governments at every level and for every period, but also to the archives of a wide range of private organizations. Although broadly defined, the concept, when consistently applied, enables a repository to establish effective control over documentary materials of every type received from many sources.

The unit in personal papers comparable to the archival record group is the collection. A collection can be formed around a person, a subject, a geographical area, a format, or other identifying characteristics. Collections of literary manuscripts, correspondence, diaries, photographs, or other assembled materials do not have the organic nature of a record group and may or may not be capable of division into a hierarchical structure. In large collections of the papers of individuals or families, however, it is possible to identify, organize, and describe series based on archival principles.

The Repository. Once a decision has been made at the record group level, the records constituting that group are then allocated to an appropriate custodial unit for placement in the stacks of the repository. This is arrangement at the repository level, which necessarily will vary with the type of repository and, in the same repository, with the growth in the volume and character of its holdings. Allocation of record groups to custodial units may be made initially on the basis of a distinction between public records and nonpublic manuscripts (including personal papers), or it may be based, in a public repository, on broad functional or hierarchical divisions. Many legislative and judicial archives are maintained separately from those of executive agencies; many diplomatic and military archives are maintained as separate units; and county and municipal record groups are generally separate from the records of state agencies in a state archival repository. Another basic division may be made between "open" and "closed" record groups, the latter consisting of the records of discontinued agencies to which no further accessions are expected. As indicated above, separate custodial units are generally established for significant holdings of cartographic, audiovisual, and machine-readable records. Other basic considerations that play a part in arrangement at the repository level include the size and physical layout of the stack areas, the number and type of personnel needed to work with certain bodies of records, the degree of security required for particular holdings, and the character and frequency of reference and research use of certain record groups.

Subgroups. The third level of arrangement is that of subgroups within record groups. The subgroup concept is intended to distinguish between and to control the records of all primary subordinate offices or other administrative units that together constitute the record group, including any records of predecessor agencies. Each subgroup, in turn, is divided into as many levels as are necessary to accommodate the successive subordinate organizational units that make up the administrative hierarchy of the subgroup. For example, a bureau may be divided into divisions, each of which has several branches, each of which has several sections, and so on. The typical arrangement of subgroups is thus by administrative structure—the hierarchy of the offices of origin of the records—but where successive reorganizations or the consolidation of records series between offices obscures hierarchical origins, subgroups and subordinate levels therein may be established in terms of functional, geographical, or chronological relationships, or, if necessary, on the basis of the physical forms of the records.

The Series. Arrangement at the series level then takes place in the framework of subgroups in each record group. A series in the archival sense consists of documents in file units that are normally already structured or arranged, by the office that originated, maintained, and used them, in accordance with a filing system, or that were otherwise maintained as a collective unit by that office because they relate to a particular function or subject, result from the same activity, have a particular form, or have some other unifying relationship arising out of their creation, receipt, or use. Their hierarchical provenance ordinarily determines the specific subgroups in which series are included, but in cases where subgroups have been formed on nonhierarchical bases, the subgroup position of affected series varies accordingly. Since modern decentralized record-keeping systems do not establish a set order of series within agencies or their individual offices, the archivist, on the basis of study of the administrative history, structure, and functions of the institution concerned, and also on the basis of study of the records themselves, must give to the series a meaningful physical order in the subgroup structure. Because research access to archival stack areas is almost universally prohibited, the physical order of record groups, collections, subgroups, series, and subseries is not relevant to access, so long as the custodial unit maintains accurate location registers.

There is thus no one perfect or correct arrangement sequence for all series, but generally, in each subgroup level, series relating to policy formulation and program direction are placed before series documenting program execution, and series of program or substantive records are placed before series of housekeeping or facilitative records. Particular attention is given to the functions of the organization corresponding to the subgroup: as far as possible the series are grouped according to the logical order of those functions and, with respect to each function, according to the logical sequence of actions taken to carry it out. However, regarding older records, which tend to provide more centralized and general coverage of the organization's functions and actions, it may be necessary to group and arrange series according to major breaks in the filing system or according to chronological periods. In each case agency-created indexes or other finding aids are placed close to and usually precede the series to which they apply. Arrangement at the series level is thus intended to facilitate the use of archives while at the same time preserving their integrity in the organizational and functional context from which they emerged.

File Units. Once the series have been arranged in the subgroup structure of a particular record group, arrangement then proceeds to the file unit level. Since most series are already arranged in accordance with filing systems used by the originating agencies, arrangement at this level usually consists of simply verifying the correct placement of each file unit in that system and of correcting obvious misfiles. Only where there is no original arrangement, or where it has been irretrievably lost, or where it cannot be reconstructed without an excessive expenditure of time, is the archivist justified in imposing a new internal arrangement on the series, and in such cases a full explanation of what has been done and the reasons for it should be included in the appropriate finding aid to inform and assist the users of the records.

Documents. The final level of arrangement is the document level. This involves checking the individual documents, enclosures, and annexes, and the individual pieces of paper making up multipage documents, that collectively constitute the file unit, and correcting their placement when necessary. Because of the volume of modern archives, arrangement at this level remains an ideal rather than actual practice in most major repositories. It is a necessary preliminary, however, for series involved in microfilming or other photoduplication.

This summary of the sequence of actions involved in arrangement eventually culminates in the transfer of the records from temporary to permanent containers, which are then labeled with the designations of the appropriate record group, subgroups, series, and contents, and finally shelved. Control down to at least the series level must first be achieved before descriptive work is possible, since finding aids must refer to specific units in an established arrangement and the series is the basic unit of description.

Personal Papers. Conditions under which most personal papers collections are created or grow require handling different from that demanded by large, organic corporate record groups. Such collections are traditionally smaller, because the productive literary life of an individual is much shorter than the lives of most government or corporate entities. Personal papers collections also tend to be ad hoc, because an individual must decide to save them, rather than follow the procedures established in an office. These collections do not usually have files organized according to some structured filing scheme, nor separation of material by function, because the collector may simply accumulate materials in some arrangement that seems logical at the time. The idiosyncratic nature of such collections requires, in most cases, that the archivist impose order on it. Thus, while the archivist dealing with corporate records may attempt to verify and reflect the original organization and structure of a record group, the manuscript curator is often attempting to create a system that reflects the multiple activities and interests of the person or persons represented in the collection. Such an effort may result in a collection with identifiable series, subseries, and files, but the archivist will have established them, not merely accepted them.

Description. The theory and practice of archival description—the process of establishing intellectual control over holdings through the preparation of what are collectively called finding aids—are less developed than that of arrangement. In addition to the finding aids prepared for their own use by the offices of origin—which are properly part of the records and are accessioned and maintained with them—archival repositories produce a wide variety of published and unpublished finding aids that exhibit a lack of general agreement on either terminology or descriptive methodology. Published finding aids generally include guides and catalogues, inventories and registers, special lists, calendars, and indexes. In addition to such published finding aids, most archival repositories also prepare unpublished checklists, accession and location registers, and box and shelf lists. Finally, there are appraisal reports, record and manuscript group registration statements, and, for machine-readable records, software documentation, which serve incidentally as finding aids. Entries that can best be described as "catalogue entries" are also produced in the major bibliographic utilities, such as the Research Library Information Network (RLIN) and the Online Computer Library Center (OCLC). In recent years, however, there has been a trend toward the development of three basic types of published finding aids in which an increasing uniformity of descriptive practice may be discerned. The three types are inventories (registers for manuscript groups and collections), guides, and what may be called detailed lists.

Inventories. Just as the record group level provides the critical key to the collective arrangement of archives, the inventory is the basic finding aid in their collective description. An inventory is prepared for each record group or major subgroup, in which the unit of entry is the series. An introduction defines the limits of the record group and provides a general description of the structure and functions of the agencies and offices whose records are involved and of the characteristics and general contents of the records themselves. The body of the inventory or register consists of individual series entries organized in the framework of the subgroups in the record group. Since the terms used by the people in an office of origin to identify their "files" are usually meaningless to anyone outside that office, archivists must devise series titles that are unique and that convey the maximum information to the user about the types of records that constitute the series, the functions and activities they reflect or to which they relate, the inclusive dates within which the series was created, and its quantity. Under each series title there is usually a brief descriptive paragraph that indicates the arrangement of the constituent file units, any gaps in the series, further details of importance on the functions and activities that produced or are documented by the series, an indication of the major subject content of the records, and an indication of any restrictions on access and use. Series created by archivists for personal papers collections are traditionally quite simple and generally relate to the form of the material in the series, rather than the function. "Correspondence," "diaries," "lecture notes," "speeches and writings," and similar identifiers tend to make up the bulk of series titles in such collections. Whether the archivist subdivides "correspondence" into "family," "business," "professional," or other subgroups or considers each of these as a series in and of itself is a personal or institutional option. Many inventories and registers include in appendixes indexes, lists, or file titles or headings relating to particular series that would facilitate their use. Manuscript registers also include a descriptive level below the series, where box lists, consisting of the titles of all folders in each box of the collection, are provided. In small or extremely significant collections, archivists may list each document in each folder, but item lists are extraordinarily labor-intensive products, even when created with computer assistance, and the practice has generally fallen into disuse.

Guides. When holdings have been placed under basic intellectual control through a series of inventories or registers, the repository is then in a position to prepare and publish a general guide to its holdings. In such a guide the basic unit of entry is the record group or manuscript collection. The guide summarizes the administrative history, structure, and functions of the particular agency that corresponds to each record group, or biographical information about the persons represented in personal papers collections, and collectively characterizes the records that constitute the record group in terms of physical types and forms, inclusive dates, quantity, and general subject content. The guide also emphasizes organizational and functional relationships between record groups, or personal and professional relationships between individuals, in order to provide a general orientation to the scope and character of the total holdings of the repository. For the same reason, the guide directs attention to any restrictions on access or use of the records, and the entries also contain bibliographical data on published finding aids and relevant documentary or other publications.

In addition to repository guides, the term *guide* is also used to refer to finding aids that describe the holdings of one or more repositories relating to a particular geographical region, chronological period, or historical event, or to holdings of a particular physical type, such as cartographic or audiovisual. Although they are also sometimes called guides, finding aids that briefly describe the holdings of all repositories on the national, regional, or state level might more appropriately be termed *directories*.

Detailed Lists. The third type of finding aid, detailed lists of various kinds such as catalogues, calendars, and indexes, is usually prepared for records whose historical significance or research value and use justify the time and expense involved in their preparation. They may describe individual file units or documents from more than one record group, subgroup, or series that relate to particular subjects, but they are usually confined to the contents of single series or subseries. Such detailed lists are of particular value in assisting users of series whose original arrangement is unknown or that lacked any original arrangement. It should be noted, however, that microfilm publication has largely superseded the calendaring of archives.

As in the arrangement of archives, the principle of provenance remains the basis for all archival descriptive work. Faced with the wealth of major and peripheral subject content in modern public and institutional archives, obviously unable to foresee all future research trends and interests, and lacking the staff and budget necessary to create special subject-oriented finding aids to serve even the present range of research interests, archivists place primary reliance and emphasis on the structure and functions of the creating agencies in the closely related tasks of collectively arranging and describing archival holdings. In so doing they preserve the integrity of archives and protect their official and legal character. They also enable any present or future researcher on any subject to use archives effectively, because the experience of both archival repositories and users attests that knowledge of the organization and functions of their originating agencies serves as the best guide to the widely varied subject content of archives. As archivists experiment with automated techniques to establish better administrative and intellectual control over their holdings, it has become increasingly clear that the techniques developed by related disciplines must be adapted and modified to accommodate the unique and organic character of archives if automation is to improve or replace existing controls.

Automation and Archives. Archival automation began in the late 1950s with two major indexing projects: the Presidential Papers Project at the Manuscript Division of the Library of Congress and a project to index the papers of the prime ministers of Canada at the Public (now National) Archives of Canada. The two projects were institution- and collection-specific and had little impact on archival automation activities elsewhere. But the use of computers by archivists had a progressive effect, as those engaged in the two projects applied their knowledge of techniques to other tasks in the broad field of archival description.

Out of the Presidential Papers Project developed a parallel project in the Manuscript Division, to capture information about the holdings at the collection level, known as the Master Record of Manuscript Collections, and some experimentation with computerizing the Division's registers or finding aids. The Master Record has developed to the point where all accessions are now entered into the computer software ProCite, and all collections in the Division have been entered retrospectively, enabling users to search on a variety of fields and to print out collection catalogues.

In 1985 the archival community, through a National Information Systems Task Force (NISTF) of the Society of American Archivists, in cooperation with the LC, completed work on a format for archives and manuscripts within the USMARC family of formats. MARC (MAchine-Readable Cataloguing) had been developed starting in 1968 for use in processing information about books; modifications were made to produce formats suitable for maps, serials, music, video, and other materials. The format for archives and manuscripts control (AMC) was initially adopted by RLIN and later by OCLC. The Master Record in the Manuscript Division of LC is now in the USMARC/AMC format.

Network automation, especially in the large bibliographic utilities, requires strict adherence to standard formats and usage within those formats, and archivists were for the first time faced with the requirement to develop such standards to describe their holdings. The process was assisted when LC published Stephen L. Hensen's *Archives, Personal Papers, and Manuscripts* (APPM), a cataloguing manual that brought archival descriptive practice into line with acceptable library practices, at least in certain descriptive fields, such as headings and uniform titles. Both LC and the Society of American Archivists adopted the second edition of APPM as an official standard. Archivists also began to pay attention to recognized authority lists for names, geographical locations, and subjects. Initially, they applied standards for automated description at the collection level only, and manuscript collection descriptive formats were more compatible with library practices than were record group formats, but the permissive nature of the RLIN database led them to experiment with the formats, entering record groups and manuscript collection descriptions at all levels, including subgroups, series, subseries, folders, and even items. Similar work on standards occurred in Canada and the U.K.

Expansion of the USMARC format through the AMC application has in many ways revolutionized the original concept of MARC and has opened up the format to permit expanded access to materials. Whereas the book format for USMARC may display two or three name and/or subject entries per record, a USMARC/AMC record may have 10 or 20 names and/or subjects. Additionally, the summary, abstract, annotation, scope, and so on note field of the format (tag 520) and the biographical or historical note field (tag 545) can run to lengthy narratives of 10 or more lines each. The USMARC/AMC format also permits the entry of a wide variety of nontextual materials, because most archives and many manuscript collections include photographs, audiovisual materials, maps, and documents in electronic formats. The fact that archivists became engaged in the MARC process so late in its development enabled them to take immediate advantage of the progress in computer technology from the time when the original format was being developed for books. A side effect of the development of MARC formats and the APPM manual, relating in part to the Anglo-American Cataloguing Rules, as well as the use of standard authority lists for entering archival information, has been an increased need for library science training for staff members at major archives. Archival training has traditionally been thought of in terms of an education in history or one of the related humanities. While such a basis remains important, especially in appraisal and reference functions, library training in the organization of knowledge, description, and the application of computerization of these processes is now almost imperative for archivists. Applicants for archival positions who have cross-disciplinary education and training are those most sought after in today's employment market.

REFERENCES

Frank B. Evans, "Modern Methods of Arrangement of Archives in the United States," *American Archivist* (1966).

David B. Gracy II, *Archives and Manuscripts: Arrangement and Description* (1977).

T. R. Schellenberg, *The Management of Archives* (1965).

Richard C. Berner, *Archival Theory and Practice in the United States: A Historical Analysis* (1983).

FRANK G. BURKE

SERVICES TO USERS

Types of Service. The fundamental purpose of archival work is to preserve valuable records permanently and make them available for use. Together, the activities involved in providing access to records constitute the archival institution's reference service, which consists of furnishing records for use in search rooms, providing information from or concernin records, making copies of records, lending records to certain users, and exhibiting records. Complementing these direct reference services is the provision of indirect access by means of documentary publication.

Search Rooms. In the search rooms of archival repositories, which are analogous to library reading rooms, inquirers are able to examine records under the supervision of repository staff members. The inquirers are usually asked to complete an identification form giving their names and addresses and the purposes of their examination of the records. If necessary, repository personnel can advise inquirers about records that seem pertinent to their research and explain to them how the records are arranged and what guides, inventories, lists, or other finding aids are available. They can also make recommendations concerning information that should be included in footnotes or other references to records being examined and indicate what facilities exist for reproduction of records. Search room regulations governing the use of records typically require that their arrangement be left undisturbed; that they not be mutilated or destroyed by improper handling; that users avoid any actions likely to damage them, such as smoking, eating, or drinking; and that they be returned to search room attendants after their use. There are also regulations to prevent theft of records by requiring examination of objects carried out of the search room. These security measures, however, are often accompanied by increasingly liberal arrangements for the use of search room facilities during hours when repository stack areas are closed.

Information Services. On a limited basis, archivists provide information from the records in response to written and oral inquiries. They often furnish specific facts, such as the date or place of an event and the names of principal participants. They may furnish more extensive information for administrative and legal purposes to the agencies that created the records and as a courtesy to high-ranking public officials. They try to keep written replies reasonably concise and responsive to the inquiries and may use form letters or standard wording to reply to recurrent types of inquiries.

Information about records may also be provided orally or in writing, and inquirers are encouraged to seek such information before visiting archival search rooms. If their requests involve consulting large bodies of records, they are informed of the titles of the pertinent record groups or other subdivisions of the records and of the inclusive dates and quantities thereof. Often such information can be furnished by supplying copies of published finding aids or reproductions of pertinent pages of finding aids. Archivists may feel obliged to furnish more information to inquirers engaged in major research that will be useful to the general public. In supplying any information from or concerning records, they strive to make factual statements and to avoid interpretation.

Copying. Photoreproduction has increasingly expanded the availability of records for research and other uses. With reproduction services, archivists need not cull information from records and inquirers need not transcribe or take detailed notes on them. These services generally provide electrostatic, photostatic, or microphotographic copies of records at nominal cost. Electrostatic and photostatic methods are especially useful for furnishing full-size paper copies and reproducing selected records from scattered file locations. Such copies offer advantages in that they can be easily read; arranged, like research notes, in various ways; and examined together with related sources of information. Photographic and diazo prints of nontextual (that is, other than conventional paper documents) records are also furnished by an increasing number of archival repositories. Microphotography is generally preferred and used for reproducing a great quantity of records arranged in sequence. This process produces copies that are less expensive per item than full-size paper copies and have the great advantage of compactness. Such copies, however, require the use of reading devices. Copies of sound recordings and machine-readable records are increasingly being made, in keeping with the growth of these forms among archival holdings.

In the United States the copyright status of records, as defined under the Copyright Law of 1976, determines whether or how copies of them can be made in reference service. Records of the U.S. government, with some exceptions, have no copyright protection and can be freely reproduced by archival repositories. Such reproductions can also be certified if required. Copyrighted materials that have found their way into the custody of public repositories can be reproduced in limited quantities for research, provided there is no contrary agreement with the copyright holders. Such copies must carry a notice of the copyright status of the originals. This arrangement is supported by the accepted legal rule of *fair use,* whereby certain uses are not considered an infringement of copyright.

Lending. The lending of records by archival repositories takes place only under special circumstances. Normally it occurs when organizations that created the records, or their successors, need them for administrative or legal purposes or exceptionally when such organizations give related organizations official permission to use them. Regulations usually provide that requests for loans be made only by specific officials of the creating organization, and for relatively short periods. Archivists oppose lending records in fragile condition and normally, in such cases, will provide photocopies instead. Records in public archival repositories may be lent to nongovernment organizations for exhibition only under what are considered to be fully protective conditions. Loans are not made to individuals outside of repositories. Some American state archival agencies have established a network of regional archival repositories, usually at state universities, where state records may be sent on loan to be used for research. Archival loans are also made in response to subpoenas but, as far as possible, certified photocopies are furnished instead.

Exhibits. Exhibiting records is still another way of making them available to users. Archival repositories plan both long-term and short-term exhibits as an important part of their public outreach programs. The National Archives Building in Washington, for example, has on permanent display the three fundamental charters of the United States: the Declaration of Independence, the Constitution, and its first ten amendments (the Bill of Rights). This repository also mounts temporary exhibits celebrating the anniversary of historical events in American history or documenting unusual national or international developments. In general, exhibits enable archival institutions to publicize their holdings and develop popular appreciation of historical records as cultural resources.

Documentary Publication. Documentary publication is an extension of reference service because it disseminates in published form a part of the holdings of archival institutions. Originally, publication was by printing exclusively, the contents consisting of documents of importance selected from larger bodies of archives or manuscripts. Since World War II the concept of complete publication of these larger bodies has developed, in order to preclude the danger of subjectivity in selection. A concomitant development has been the adoption of microfilming as an alternative, and far less costly, means of publication by the national archives of such countries as the U.S., Canada, Spain, and the U.K. Microfilm publication involves preparing a master negative microcopy of the concerned body of records, usually a series, and incorporating in it an extensive editorial apparatus analogous to that to be found in the conventional printed publication. Upon receipt of orders, positive prints are run off. In recent decades it has been U.S. National Archives policy to publish by microfilm all of the principal series in its custody for worldwide sale through a periodically updated catalogue.

Policies Governing Service. The use of records in the several types of archival reference service described above is controlled by access policies that vary nationally and, to some extent, within nations. As indicated in *Archives: Legislative Foundations,* the basic closed period has been considerably reduced over the years to the current level of 30 to 50 years. For this development much credit must go to the International Council on Archives (ICA), whose 1966 and 1968 Congresses in particular made strong recommendations for such liberalization of access. Also under the stimulus of ICA, archivists in many countries are working to ensure access for foreigners on equal terms with nationals.

In making records available to a growing variety of users, archivists must consider two competing rights: the right to know and the right to privacy. In the United States the first right is protected by a national Freedom of Information Act (first passed in 1966), which provides free public access to information in the records of federal executive agencies except for specified categories exempted from disclosure, primarily relating to national defense and foreign policy secrets, confidential commercial and financial data, investigations, personal affairs, and other matters specifically restricted by law.

Similarly, Canadian national government records more than 30 years old are open to the public unless they fall into specifically exempted areas, such as records whose release would constitute a breach of faith with a foreign government, be contrary to law, violate individual privacy, or be harmful to national security. The 30-year rule for access to public records has also been adopted in the U.K., with exempted records similar to these in Canada. Many U.S. states have enacted "sunshine" or open record laws, which make information in state records more liberally available to the public.

The Federal Privacy Act of 1974 limits access to records relating to individuals in federal agencies

American Folklife Center, Library of Congress

Archivist and staff at the American Folklife Center, Library of Congress, organize an unprocessed collection. Ethnographic collections frequently include a wide variety of non-textual materials including still photographs, sound recordings, video tapes and film negatives.

generally but does not apply to the holdings of the National Archives. However, with respect to the latter, the right of privacy is upheld by certain of the exempted categories in the Freedom of Information Act, as well as restrictions imposed by the Archivist of the United States. These restrictions deny general access to records less than 75 years old containing information concerning the physical or mental health or medical or psychiatric treatment of individuals, and records concerning investigations of persons or groups of persons by investigative authorities of the federal executive branch. Efforts to protect privacy are also being made by archivists in administering nonfederal records containing personal data on such matters as medical treatment, legal representation, labor-management relations, and welfare benefits. Similar concern for protection of privacy is evident in regulations of the Public Record Office of the U.K., which restrict access to certain records less than 75 years old, such as land revenue records concerning confidential transactions with private individuals and certain classes of police records. Also exemplifying this concern is the regulation of the Public Archives of Canada providing that personnel records may be used for research only 90 years after the birth of the individual involved.

Trends in Service. Archival reference service makes records available for several principal purposes. For the creators of the records, or their successors, it furnishes information needed to show administrative or legal precedents and fiscal accountability. For citizens it provides documentary evidence often essential for the protection of various rights. For the researcher, official and academic alike, it supplies data extensively used in all branches of learning—traditionally history and the other humanities; increasingly the social sciences; and, to a more limited extent, the physical sciences as well. Reference for these purposes constitutes by far the greatest part of all reference service, and the records involved are preponderantly in the custody of public archival institutions.

These government sources have long been used in writing political, diplomatic, and military history, since they were early recognized as basic for the purpose. As government functions and activities have expanded, especially in the 20th century, in various ways that touch closely the day-to-day life of the people and the operations of the national economy, government records have become more highly valued and more greatly used for research not only in social and economic history but also in political science, economics, sociology, anthropology, geography, and other social sciences. These studies have in recent decades been facilitated by the development of automation and automated records processes, symbolized by the computer and the machine-readable record. Increased use of public records has also been stimulated in recent years by mass media presentations of genealogical subjects, such as Alex Haley's *Roots* (1976), emphasizing the value of these records as sources for personal and family history.

Reference service in nongovernment archival repositories also supports important research. In such repositories records of educational, religious, business, labor, professional, civic, and other organizations are being relied upon increasingly for studies (of, for example, intellectual trends, population characteristics, urban and industrial life, and humanitarian causes) in a way similar to the expanded and unconventional use of public records today.

Archival repositories customarily maintain certain statistics on the quantity and performance of reference service. In providing records to the search room, on loan, for reproduction, or for exhibit, the unit employed for reporting is an item such as a single document, folder, bound volume, roll of microfilm, or archival container. In furnishing written information from or concerning records, the unit is the transmitting letter or report. In supplying oral information, the unit is the telephone call or personal conference. In most archival repositories statistics of reference service tend to show increases year after year. At the U.S. National Archives, for example, since about 1940 total units of reference service have increased annually from a few thousand to some three million. The increases result largely from expanded and diversified holdings of repositories, liberalization of access to them, and publicity given to their subject matter and value by publications, archives-sponsored scholarly conferences, and other informational methods. This trend seems likely to continue, since there is a growing appreciation of archives not only as cultural resources but also as major components of national and international information systems.

REFERENCES

Robert L. Clark, Jr., editor, *Archive-Library Relations* (1976).

Sue E. Holbert, *Archives and Manuscripts: Reference and Access* (1977).

William L. Joyce, "Archivists and Research Use," *American Archivist* (1984).

Ernst Posner, *American State Archives* (1964).

Mary Jo Pugh, "The Illusion of Omniscience: Subject Access and the Reference Archivist," *American Archivist* (1982).

Alfred Wagner, "The Policy of Access to Archives: From Restriction to Liberalization," *Unesco Bulletin for Libraries* (1970).

HAROLD PINKETT

TECHNICAL ASPECTS

The technical aspects of archives administration help to fulfill the main obligation of the archivist: to preserve archival material for posterity and to make it available for use by the administration, by the scholarly community, and by the public. These aspects are necessarily based on the nature of archival materials and on the functions served by archives. Archival materials—stores of information now predominantly recorded on paper—accumulate, organically, in an administration or other organization as a by-product of its activities. Consequently documents are physically heterogeneous and exist either uniquely or in only a few copies each. Unlike modern books issued in planned editions and prepared by professionals, documents accumulate over time with little control over their physically diverse properties. Moreover, the modern media increasingly introduced by administrations, such as various audiovisual forms and the digital records associated with data processing, bring about even greater diversity.

Archives must serve their parent administrations as well as the scholarly and general publics, and thus have to absorb materials for both their administrative and legal values on the one hand and their informational values on the other. Since materials possessing such values are created constantly and must be preserved permanently, the potential for archival institutions' physical expansion is unlimited. The uniqueness of records, the diversity of forms, the duties to the administration and the public, and the unlimited growth—all leave their mark on archival buildings and facilities, conservation of materials, microphotography, and automation.

Archival Buildings and Equipment. The need to provide suitable housing for archives has played an important role in the establishment and design of archival buildings. This need is evident in the report of the parliamentary committee of 1836 in the U.K. as well as in the discussions leading to the establishment of the U.S. National Archives in 1934. The main purposes of an archival building are: to provide safe storage for an ever-increasing amount of valuable material, to keep the material indefinitely, and to make it available for use.

Safety and security considerations, as well as the prospect of unlimited growth, have in the 20th century led to a clear-cut separation between storage space and public reading rooms. Modern archives should be planned with an eye to expansion or decentralization. The need for expansion as well as the high cost of urban properties tends to drive archives to the urban periphery (as in the case of the new Public Record Office in the U.K.). The developed countries may have to choose between separating the urban service areas from the extraurban storage areas and decentralizing the archives themselves. In both cases, transportation and communication problems will have to be solved.

Storage specifications are dictated by the need to store vast amounts of material and to protect it from damage, natural or man-caused. In some countries the tendency is to build underground storage facilities, probably as a result of World War II experience (for example, the Riksarkivet in Oslo and the National Archives in Tokyo). Underground storage requires artificial lighting and air conditioning and thus larger expenditure. It also makes construction dependent on soil conditions. In other countries construction is both above and below ground. Some of the underground specifications are also applicable to above-ground construction, including artificial lighting and climate control.

New York State Archives and Records Administration (SARA)

Electronic back-up tapes for State offices, New York State Records Center. Archivists are developing a new sub-profession geared to the special requirements of machine-readable records.

It is now widely recognized that control of temperature, humidity, and radiation is most important for inhibiting deterioration caused by factors inherent in the documents, while filtering of the air is necessary to protect against pollution. Temperatures of 10°–14° C and 40 percent relative humidity are believed to be optimal conditions for most kinds of archival material. These conditions are, however, unsuitable for humans, and material kept under these conditions has to be preconditioned before it is transferred to reading-room environments. The accepted compromise is, therefore, 18°–20° C and about 50 percent relative humidity. Dust, aerosol, and hydrosol filtering should be introduced in most regions. In some countries, mostly tropical, the air-conditioning systems are used for fumigation. Light should be free from ultraviolet rays, since they are harmful to paper (and to other polymers). The issue of incandescent versus fluorescent lighting is still undecided; the safety and economy of both are still under discussion.

Fire protection is a cardinal problem of planning. To facilitate isolation of fires, storage areas are divided into compartments no larger than 200 square meters (about 2,000 square feet) and no higher than 2.4 meters (about 8 feet). Electrical wiring, switches, and outlets should be reinforced (the European term is "Panzer"); metal fuse boards with automatic fuses are preferable. Fire detection and alarm systems are considered essential, and a direct alarm connection to a fire station is desirable. Water-sprinkler extinguishing systems are not universally recommended since water may cause considerable damage to archival material. Automatic extinguishing systems employing nontoxic gases,

Riksarkivet/Solly Sannerud

Strongroom in the solid rock, four-story underground National Archives of Norway. The stacks on either side of the passageway are mobile.

aerosols, and hydrosols are gradually being introduced.

Efficient use of storage space leads to rectangular compartments with shelves usually running parallel to the long side of the rectangle. Internal planning depends on shelf size and aisle size. Though bodies of archives are heterogeneous, and many still consist of large series of bound volumes in various sizes, most modern archival material is loose and boxed in containers, usually of standard cardboard, corrugated cardboard, and lately of plastics. The size of such containers varies, ranging from about 30 by 40 by 28 centimeters (about 12 by 16 by 10 inches, or a volume of about 1 cubic foot) to one-third that amount. This requires a shelf size of around 80 centimeters (32 inches) deep and a length of some multiple of 35 centimeters (13 inches). Aisle width runs from 80 centimeters for side aisles to 100 centimeters (3 feet) for main aisles. Mobile stacks or compact stacks (known as "compactus") are becoming widely used, and although they are considerably more expensive than stationary shelves, they save space up to almost 50 percent. Floor load is around 700 kilograms per square meter (145 pounds per square foot) for stationary stacks and as high as 1,000 kilograms per square meter (about 200 pounds per square foot) for mobile or compact stacks. All shelving nowadays is metal and is rustfree or properly protected.

Since archival materials sometimes include extremely valuable documents and classified records, most institutions therefore have vaults for protection against fire and theft. The large amounts of nonpaper documentation, such as tapes, films, microforms, and sound recordings, call for metal cans, small boxes, racks, air conditioning, and other special facilities.

Many archival institutions place documents on exhibition, posing the specially complex problem of preserving documents while making them accessible to the public. One of the most elaborately protected exhibits, at the National Archives Building in Washington, houses the Declaration of Independence, the Constitution, and the Bill of Rights; it is displayed in a case that is simultaneously a vault and an elevator.

While search rooms in archives are not essentially different from reading rooms in libraries, they have certain requirements of their own: readers' desks should be large enough to accommodate archives and records; special research rooms for researchers working on long-term projects are needed; more room for micro-readers is required; and space and equipment for playing sound recordings, viewing films and video recordings, and working with machine-readable records should be provided.

Records centers are, in their essence, physically similar to archives buildings. However, they are generally smaller, because they do not require as much reading room space and, given their function of accepting materials for limited periods only, are not meant to expand indefinitely. A typical feature of records centers is the loading platform needed for receiving (and sending out) large consignments of records. Adjacent to the loading platforms are usually rooms for the cleaning and fumigation, the primary arrangement, and, in some centers, the boxing and labeling of records. These features have all been inherited from the modern archives building.

Conservation of Archival Material. Conservation comprises *preservation,* preventative measures, and *restoration,* remedial measures. Preservation starts with the arrival of records at the archives. Unlike books, usually bought in new condition, records are deposited in the archives after years of frequent handling. Preliminary treatment (dry cleaning and fumigation) is necessary before they can be transferred to the stacks. Other preventative measures have been described above.

Document conservation presents some problems not encountered in book conservation. For instance, black printing ink, used in books, has remained virtually unchanged since the invention of printing. Documents, on the other hand, were first written with india ink (similar in stability to printing ink), then with ferrous ink—a stable material whose acidity, however, weakened the paper and even corroded it. The 20th century brought unstable and washable fountain-pen inks and ball-point pens. The typewriter (patented in 1714 and put on the market in 1874) and carbon paper produced additional forms of unstable writing found in documents. Other features contributing to the problems of documentary conservation are paper clips, seals, and rubber bands and the most recent nuisance, adhesive tapes used for repairs.

In the 1930s the process of silking (to prevent documentary damage or to stabilize it once it has occurred) gave way to lamination with cellulose acetate, first practiced on a large scale by the U.S. National Archives. Yellowing and brittleness of the first laminates led to William J. Barrow's work, which resulted in the recognition of the importance of paper acidity and the necessity of deacidification. In the 1950s polyethylene was introduced for lamination in Eastern Europe, and in the 1960s Kathpalia initiated "cold lamination" (by cellulose acetate and acetone) in India. Lamination raised the problem of the reversibility of restoration where required. It is still a controversial issue, as are some new techniques that have been developed, such as encapsulation, introduced in the 1970s.

The vulnerability of modern inks encouraged research into nonaqueous deacidification, such as Bains-Cope's barium hydroxide in methanol. Gaseous deacidification by ammonia has been practiced in

Germany since the 1950s but is not widely accepted since it is considered unstable. Various vapor-phase-deacidification methods have been rejected, either because of unsatisfactory results or because of toxicity (for example, cyclohexilamine-carbonate). While experimentation goes on, the important problem of nonliquid deacidification has not yet been solved satisfactorily.

Paper casting, introduced in the 1960s, is not suitable for documents with unstable inks. The only way to reduce damage to ink is to fix it, the most popular fixer being soluble nylon sprayed on the document. The results of such fixing, however, are not altogether satisfactory.

The International Council on Archives, through its Conservation Committee, is trying to set standards for archival conservation and to help train archival conservators.

Microphotography. Microphotography may be applied in archives for a number of purposes: (1) Security copies: copying the most valuable documents to ensure against loss or destruction. These copies are usually deposited in vaults, preferably separate from the main storage area. (2) Supplementary material: copying records in other custody, mainly in foreign countries, of interest to the copying institution; this is especially important for countries formerly under colonial rule. (3) Publication: microphotography is considered, nowadays, the cheapest way to publish documents, especially in limited editions (see *Archives: Reference Services*). (4) Preservation: microcopies of documents in bad physical condition are substituted in reference service for the originals, thus protecting the originals from further damage.

Microforms present special preservation problems. The silver halide films, although the most durable of photographic materials (if properly processed), are not durable enough on the archival time-scale; periodic film-to-film copying is considered essential for long-term preservation until more lasting materials are introduced. Past problems concerning the admissibility of microcopies as legal evidence of the existence of the originals have been solved in most countries.

The earlier notion that microphotography automatically solves archival space problems, once widely believed, is now regarded more skeptically since the cost of filming is often greater than that of storing the originals, even for a long period.

The International Council on Archives' Microfilm Committee is concerned with the archival aspects of microfilming and publishes a bulletin on the subject.

Computers and Archives. Archives are affected by the electronic revolution in two ways. Being themselves information systems, archives first used the new tools for more efficient information retrieval. Many archives employ automated techniques for registering and indexing archival material, though online systems are still rare in search rooms.

Second, since automation has penetrated into administration, records are increasingly kept on magnetic media, and archives have to preserve the valuable part of such records. Machine-readable tapes are extremely unstable, and even when kept under optimal conditions (that is, complete environmental control, dust control, and protection from magnetic

Northeast Document Conservation Center (NEDCC), Andover, Massachusetts

Preservation of a rare wall map at Northeast Document Conservation Center, Andover, Massachusetts.

fields), they do not last more than about 15 years. Regular recopying procedures are therefore essential. It is hoped that Computer Output Microfilm (COM) and Computer Input Microfilm (CIM) may ease the problem to some extent. Other magnetic media, such as microcomputer disks, are more stable than magnetic tapes, and optical formats, such as CD-ROMs, appear to be more stable still.

In order to make effective use of the magnetic media, it is necessary to preserve, together with them, the complete documentation associated with their creation. The International Council on Archives' Automation Committee is guiding archivists in these subjects by conducting seminars, publishing manuals, and issuing a bulletin.

REFERENCES

Yash Pal Kathpalia, *Conservation and Restoration of Archives: A Survey of Facilities* (1978).

Louis A. Simon, "Some Observations on Planning Archives Buildings," in *Building and Equipment for Archives,* Bulletin of the National Archives no. 6 (1944).

A. ARAD

ARCHIVES MANAGEMENT

Archives management is a subject that has been virtually ignored in archival literature, but there is some evidence that its importance is beginning to be recognized. Management is the utilization of human, financial, and material resources to perform the functions for which an organization exists. Indeed, good management is particularly important for archives. Because of the traditionally low priority given to archives in the allocation of public funds, it is necessary to make the most effective use of the resources available, and, if additional resources are

National Archives and Records Administration (NARA)

Assistant Archivist, Office of the National Archives, explains archival policy to government agency administrators as part of a program to involve Federal officials in records management issues.

required, the justification should be documented and presented in a manner that will convince legislators, budget officials, and the general public that such expenditures will produce measurable benefits to the community that is served.

While archives are universal in the sense that all human activity produces them, there exist a wide variety of archival institutions concerned with various types of archives: government archives (national, state, and municipal); the archives of businesses, universities, and other corporate bodies; and specialized archives for particular subject-matter areas (labor, immigration, or science) or particular physical types of archival material (films or sound recordings). The place of archives in an administrative structure varies even for similar types of archives. For example, some state archives are a part of a government department, while others are a part of state libraries or historical societies. Whatever the place of an archives in an administrative structure, it is desirable that it have a distinct identity, with a separate budget, staff, accommodation, and direct relationships with creators of records; and that the director have authority to control the complete operations of the archives and its available resources.

The main functions of management are planning, evaluation, organization, staffing, and external relations.

Planning. While the general objectives of archives are formulated in legislation, they are not precise enough to meet planning needs. Long-term plans should include objectives and goals to be achieved in, for example, a period of five years. For each year operational plans should have precise targets and the allocation of precise resources that can be translated into an operating budget. While managers are subject to constraints such as regulations and management systems that apply to an entire government jurisdiction or other organization of which the archival institution is a part, they have the primary responsibility for the definition of objectives for the archives and the development of plans to meet them. The approval of long-term plans implies a commitment of the resources that are necessary to attain them, and annual budgets as stages in the implementation of an approved plan are more likely to be adopted than if they were based on ad hoc increments to programs antedating the plan. Planning is a cooperative exercise in which all concerned managers should participate, but the particular objectives and plans of subunits should be in the context of a comprehensive plan for the institution as a whole. Factors that are important in archival planning are the requirements for services to users; necessary accommodation, including space for expansion; the emphasis on conservation; the adaptation of technology to archival operations; and the commitment of a rational allocation of resources that will ensure the execution of all archival operations.

Evaluation. Plans are based on priorities at a point in time and on the information that is available at that time. Even if the elements in the plan are valid and conditions that affect its implementation do not change, it is essential to be able to assess and measure the progress in achieving the objectives for which the plan was developed. This requires performance measurement, based on quantifiable indicators that will indicate production or work accomplished. On the basis of information obtained by monitoring implementation, of changing priorities, and of other modifications arising from the allocation of resources, plans must be evaluated periodically and appropriate changes made in objectives and programs. To use the example of conservation, if all the resources called for in a particular year are not provided, if production is more or less than was projected, or if technological innovations affect the original program, these factors, considered in the evaluation of the program, will result in the revision of the original plans. Management control, then, requires a plan, the measurement of activity, the comparison of actual to planned activity, analysis of results, and corrective action. Important elements in evaluation are the promotion of economy, efficiency (the ratio of input to output), effectiveness (the extent to which the objectives are achieved), and the quality and level of service (which user surveys should test).

It is recognized that statistics are essential for planning, organizing, directing, and controlling. Most archives compile statistics for their own purposes on holdings, accessions, arrangement and description, reproduction, and reference services. But they tend to lag behind libraries in the standardization of statistics (which is necessary for comparison with similar activities in other institutions) and in using statistical data for planning. For example, a plan for protective microfilming should take into consideration all the elements in the program and their costs. Although the quantity of material and salaries of the various types of staff involved are known, it is difficult to project the cost of such a program without information concerning time norms for prefilming preparation of material and microfilming rates. The use of statistical information is necessary not only in the costing of programs and decisions on various options but also in planning every aspect of an archival service from accommodation to reference services, establishing priorities, ensuring the most effective utilization of available resources, and justifying additional resources.

Organization. While libraries and archives have, in the words of Robert L. Clark, Jr., a common purpose, "to collect, maintain and make available the written and graphic record of man's intellect and experience," differences in the origin and nature of the sources with which they are concerned impose differences in organization and methodology. Since archives are the official records of a corporate body, the relationship between the originating body and the archival institution is an essential concern of archives management. Indeed, archives are not collected but are accumulated, as records, through a process of creation or reception by the originating body. The doctrine of continuous custody (between the originating body and the archival institution that serves it), which has been put forward by Sir Hilary Jenkinson, a former Director of the Public Record Office in the United Kingdom, has been extended, particularly in North America, to the concept of the integrated records/archives life cycle that encompasses the entire existence of records from the creation to permanent preservation of their valuable nucleus as archives and destruction of the valueless remainder.

Under the general direction of the chief archivist, there are two distinct major operational units in the archival institution, one for current records management and retirement, and the other for archival operations, each with appropriate subdivisions. Separate units also exist for conservation, reprography, and general administration. There are two basic elements in records management operations: advisory services to originating departments, and services for records centers, intermediate repositories housing noncurrent records prior to their destruction upon expiration of residual values, or to transfer of their valuable segments to the archival institution.

Several factors, including the unique nature of archival materials, the principle of *respect des fonds,* and the need for knowledge of the content of records, affect the organization of internal archival operations. While libraries are usually organized on functional lines with divisions and separate staff for accessioning, cataloguing, and reference, it is not unusual for individual archivists to be involved in all functions with respect to particular bodies of archives: appraisal, acquisition, arrangement, description, reference, and even the preparation of publications and exhibitions. Subdivisions are usually established on the basis of broad subject-matter areas—for example, foreign or military affairs—deriving from the functions of the originating bodies, or of significant chronological periods, or a combination of both. When an archival institution, in addition to receiving the official records of its parent body, accepts related corporate or personal records from external sources, these records should be maintained in a separate section or division. Other special units are required for nontextual types of archival materials—machine-readable archives, maps, photographs, films, and sound and video recordings. Special units are required for conservation and reprography. The institution should also have its own archival reference library.

No special organization is required for basic administrative functions such as personnel, financial, and materials management. Arrangements depend to some extent on the degree of autonomy of individual institutions, which ranges from separate archives departments, with all the staff required for administration, to archives divisions within a government department or library that provides administrative services for the archives as well as its other components. These services, however, must be responsive to the special requirements of archives with regard to specialized staff and training, special accommodation and equipment, and the essential purposes of the archival institution.

National Archives of Zambia

National Archives Building in Lusaka, Zambia.

Staffing. The most important resources in archival operations are human. Since these operations are labor-intensive in nature, a major proportion of a budget (perhaps 75 percent) is for salaries. One could gain the impression from publications relating to archival functions that most of these functions are carried out uniformly by professional archivists. On the contrary, in any archival organization that has a staff of more than one there is a degree of specialization that increases with its size and scope. Indeed, the operations of an archival institution require a variety of specialized skills, and an important task of its management is recruiting and allocating personnel possessing these skills—at the appropriate levels and in the appropriate numbers—in order to ensure the collective achievement of the objectives of the institution.

For statistical as well as functional purposes the archival staff usually comprises professional, professional support, clerical, technical, and administrative categories. While in North America the qualifications of a professional archivist are not as precise as in European countries, which typically have uniform preappointment training, a minimum educational qualification is a university degree, usually in history or a related field. Professional functions require a combination of academic knowledge, professional skills, and the exercise of judgment. To make the most effective use of staff, a "professional support" category (the archives assistant), between the professional and clerical categories, is most important. A proportion of two professional, one professional support, and three clerical positions has been suggested as most suitable for archival operations. As mentioned earlier, specialists are required to deal with such record media as maps, photographs, film, and machine-readable materials. It is advisable, however, to train professional archivists to work in the first and last of these media areas rather than to recruit the corresponding media specialists, that is, cartographers and computer specialists. The reason is that substantive archival considerations are more important in these areas than are technical ones. On the other hand, conservation and reprography are entirely technical support areas for which trained technical specialists are essential. Similarly technical specialists are needed in such areas of administration as financial and personnel management. But in all of these areas it is indispensable that senior management direct all operations, approve policies, set priorities, and ensure the maintenance of acceptable standards. Staff requirements should be identified in the context of the budgetary cycle.

External Relations. A former Archivist of the United States, Robert H. Bahmer, insisted that one of the most important functions of archival management is interpreting the archives to "a variety of publics." This is more than public relations in the conventional sense. An archives does not operate in isolation, and the effectiveness of its operations depends to a considerable extent on the quality of its relationships with many elements in society. The archival manager should miss no opportunity to interpret "archival work to the public as a necessary factor in an enlightened society" through speeches, interviews, conferences, publications, and so on.

A number of specific "publics" require special attention. One is the authority from which the financial resources supporting the archives are obtained, usually a legislature, and particularly the responsible cabinet officer. Another is the officialdom throughout the records-creating departments responsible for managing records there; still another, in the case of archival institutions that accession materials from the private sector, is the body of donors, potential donors, or friends of potential donors. The users of archives and their professional associations make up another important public with which close relationships must be maintained. Among them are the historians, about whom a great deal has been said and written, but the support and approval of many other bodies of users, in academic and nonacademic fields alike, is also vital. Close connections must be cultivated as well with related institutions such as libraries and historical societies, and with national and international professional archives associations.

REFERENCES

Robert E. Bahmer, "The Management of Archival Institutions," *The American Archivist* (1963).

B. Delmas and J. A. d'Olier, *Planning National Infrastructures for Documentation, Libraries and Archives* (1975).

Frank B. Evans and Eric Ketelaar, *A Guide for Surveying Archival and Records Management Systems and Services: A RAMP Study* (1983).

James B. Rhoads, *The Role of Archives and Records Management in National Information Systems* (1983).

Michael Swift, "Management and Technical Resources," Paper, 10th International Council on Archives, Bonn (1984).

W. I. SMITH

ELECTRONIC RECORDS

Government, corporate, and academic records managers and archivists now confront the problems associated with a newly emerging form of record material: electronically created documents, sometimes referred to as machine-readable records. The age of some of the earlier forms of electronic records now dictates an archival decision on their disposal, and archivists are developing a new subprofession geared to the special requirements of the new record forms. For electronic records archivists, many traditional processes and terms are proving inadequate.

The organization and description of nontextual records, and those dependent on a machine for interpretation, are not totally new experiences for archivists. Audiovisual records, including video, require special understanding and special equipment, much of which is nonstandard. Various forms of recordings—wax and vinyl cylinders and discs, open reel and cassette tapes, audio compact discs, strands of recording wire, video tapes and discs, and motion-picture film—all demand specialized equipment and handling because of nonstandardized recording and playback techniques and environmental storage requirements. Just as archives have employed or trained specialists in these media, so they are entering the field of electronic records.

Archival practices in handling such records have not yet settled down to accepted universal procedures, but some generalities can be applied to them.

Organization of Computerized Records. Although there may be a computerized records structure that relates to the traditional archival hierarchy of record group, subgroup, series, file, and document, the concept and terminology of automated records structure differ from those used in textual records. To differentiate these terms from those associated with traditional records, the electronic record in databases is sometimes referred to as the *logical record* and the file is referred to as the *data file* or even the *machine-readable data file* (MRDF). These structures exist in various electronic media, including magnetic tape, magnetic floppy disks, hard or fixed disks, optical digital disks, and others.

The life-cycle concept, wherein records are monitored and controlled from their initial creation until their final retirement from use, is especially important in administering electronic records. During the early stages of the life-cycle, electronic records are updated frequently to include changes in an account, a student's courses and grades, and similar transactions. However, at the end of the student's schooling, the master file is, for all practical purposes, frozen; it forms the permanent record, which can be archived and used for reference, but cannot be changed. Records that are continually updated, without an anticipated terminal point—such as sales reports, demographic data, or meteorological observation—must be "broken" at some point if they are to be retained for archival purposes. The archival record thus becomes a "snapshot" in time, which is not uncommon in paper records that document similar activities.

From time to time there have been movements to abandon the idea of retaining records in their electronic form and for converting them to paper formats, which can then be kept according to traditional archival principles. Although such a process would be acceptable for some records (the student's final academic record, for example), the advantage of automation would be lost if other types of records were frozen in paper. Demographic or meteorological records, for instance, probably consist of micro-data that is aggregated, sorted, and printed in various reports during the output process. The ability to manipulate the micro-data for other reports, perhaps even combining databases (to determine whether weather conditions in an area relate to population, for example), is lost if the micro-data electronic records are not maintained. Some early archival databases, such as the indexes to the papers of individual presidents at the Library of Congress, were destroyed after a printed product was published, limiting any further analysis of the data assembled. A school might even decide to keep the data files of closed student records so they could be processed for comparison, analysis, and statistical compilations.

The archivist must confront the medium on which archival information is captured and stored in order to facilitate information retrieval; thus the archival equipment must be able to operate with the storage medium. But the archivist is concerned with access to the data, which implies having access to software that will process the data stored in the medium. Therefore, equipment or software obsolescence is a special concern for archivists, as opposed to operating units that create and maintain current machine-readable records. Archival retention implies long-term storage and accessibility of recorded information, and therefore some way must be found to maintain thousands, and perhaps hundreds of thousands, of data files created on equipment that has become obsolete in software that has been continually modified or whose use has been abandoned.

The concepts of maintenance of original physical order or respect for a physical representation of organizational hierarchy that archives apply to textual and other traditional records have little meaning in electronic files. Although it is important to know the structure of the institution that produced computer records, and how those records relate to the organization and function of the agency or institution, the maintenance of the logical record in its original form becomes less important than changing the nature of the record so that it is hardware independent and software neutral. Since such changes will require reference to the documentation for the program in which the record was created, as well as auxiliary files, such as input documents and products from the electronic file, the archivist may determine that such peripheral materials, even though on paper, are pertinent to an understanding of the records and should be kept. Record layouts, codebooks, source documents, flowcharts, narrative data descriptions, and a list of reports produced from the data are but a few examples of paper records accompanying a data file.

When evaluating or appraising old, inactive electronic records or data systems, the archivist may find that the records have become essentially unusable (inaccessible) and decide not to keep them if these peripheral materials are not available. The archivist must therefore work closely with the government or corporate records manager to assure the preservation of all documentation associated with files identified for retention. Maintaining an electronic archive does not mean that paper records are no longer kept.

Appraisal of electronic records is in part based on the traditional archival values of content information and secondary research use. In computerized files, however, content information may depend on the file's relationship to other record files, and perhaps even on the interaction among them. Anticipating or forecasting secondary research use is as subjective a decision in machine-readable records as in traditional forms, but is more affected by the form and structure of the machine files related to future accessibility. There are also parallels in the appraisal of machine-readable and paper records in the area of levels of data aggregation. Just as the traditional record archivist must determine how much preliminary and related documentation must be kept with records—rough notes, drafts, preliminary data analyses, and so on—so must the archivist of machine-readable records make such determinations. However, whereas the archivist in paper may discount micro-level data in favor of summaries and aggregates, the machine-readable archivist may determine that the micro-level data are more important to preserve because they are manipulable in machine-readable form, and can therefore provide summaries, analyses, and aggregations not provided in the initial reports from the databases. Such micro-data become "virtual records," assembled from the database for whatever "report" the researcher wants.

From this brief overview, it should be clear that today's archivist faces problems that did not confront those of yesteryear. Considerations of records linkage, auxiliary applications, accompanying documentation, data readability, software and hardware dependence, standards for information technology, and data security and preservation over time are moving some professional archivists out of the stacks and search rooms, and away from the disciplines of history and librarianship, and closer to combining these fields with computer studies. By the year 2000 we should know whether the profession will delegate many of these activities to professional specialists who will be chosen based on a different educational and training background than archivists dealing with traditional research materials.

REFERENCES

Margaret L. Hedstrom, *Archives and Manuscripts: Machine-Readable Records* (1984).

Steven L. Hensen, *Archives, Personal Papers, and Manuscripts: A Cataloging Manual for Archival Repositories, Historical Societies, and Manuscript Libraries*, 2nd edition (1989).

Frederic M. Miller, *Arranging and Describing Archives and Manuscripts* (1990).

Nancy Sahli, *MARC for Archives and Manuscripts: The AMC Format* (1989).

Frank G. Burke

PROFESSIONAL TRAINING

Professional training for archivists in the strict and formal sense began in Western Europe in the first half of the 19th century. Five types or traditions have developed.

The European Tradition. Here the training offered was originally based mainly on the historical auxiliary sciences, in particular paleography and diplomatics (generally relating to studying, deciphering, and authenticating historical documents and manuscripts), which during the 19th century and after were among the central disciplines of "scientific" history. The first formal training schools for archivists were the École Nationale des Chartes in Paris and the Bayerische Archivschule München (Munich), both founded in 1821. These were followed during the next half-century by eminent schools in many European

Theodore F. Welch

Entrance to the Yomei Bunko, Kyoto, containing historical records of the Fujiwara-Konoye families.

countries, such as the Institut für Österreichische Geschichtsforschung, Vienna, founded in 1854. Some of the leading institutes of this period no longer exist, but all those remaining were radically reorganized in the period immediately after World War II, at which time a number of new schools were set up. Today virtually all European countries have centers of some type in which the archivists for their national archives services at least (if not for other institutions) are trained. The older traditions are still carried on to a certain extent by most of the countries of Central and Eastern Europe, for example by the State Institute of History and Archives at Moscow.

The training schools of the European tradition are usually either autonomous institutes, financed by government (like the French École des Chartes), or are attached to principal archives services (like the Archivschule Marburg, Germany), or are associated with the historical faculty of a university (like the Institute of History and Archivistics, Nicholas Copernicus University, Torun, Poland). Among these training schools a distinction is possible between those in which students are already staff members of the national archives services, or in which successful graduates are guaranteed appointments in those services on completion of the course, and those in which the students compete in an open job market. A distinction is also possible between those schools that take students at about the age of 18 years, on completion of their secondary school education, and those that take students on completion of their university education. The former courses are naturally longer than the latter, usually three or four years as opposed to one or two years, but there are great variations from country to country both in the length and the weight of courses, practical requirements, and so on. The most extreme case of prolonged training is found in Germany, where students are recruited at the postdoctoral stage and then given another two years of training. Such students will be at least 27 years old before starting employment. The average starting age in most European countries, however, would be 22 or 23.

Relatively little attention was given until recent years to professional subjects, as distinct from the historical sciences, so much so that in France the National Archives has had to institute a second training course, known as the Stage Technique International des Archives. All its new staff members must attend this course, which may be attended by external and foreign students also. It has had a potent influence in disseminating professional standards and knowledge in many countries.

The Italo-Hispanic Tradition. The second of the main traditions in archival training may be termed the Italo-Hispanic. In Italy there are no fewer than 17 government-financed schools of archivistics, paleography, and diplomatics, one in each province. Together, these schools turn out more than 3,000 students a year, only a tiny proportion of whom actually become archivists. In Spain, and even more in Latin America, there is a similar phenomenon. In Latin America there are at least 18 archival schools or courses in 12 countries, most of them attached to universities. Particularly notable is the Interamerican Center for Archival Development at the Escuela Nacional de Archiveros in Córdoba, Argentina, which acts as a regional training school. Most courses in this tradition offer first degrees in archival science or in librarianship and archival science. In the Spanish and Portuguese traditions, a close link is maintained between archival and library training; indeed it is difficult to differentiate them in such schools as that of the Faculty of Letters, University of Coimbra (Portugal), or the School of Documentalists, National Library of Spain, Madrid. In these first-degree courses, a large number of the students do not intend to follow archival careers.

The British Tradition. A third model is provided by the British tradition. Here there is no specialization until students have taken their first degree, usually at the age of 21, by which time they have completed their general education. They may then be recruited into an established archive service and trained by apprenticeship in-house, or, more usually, will follow a one-year postgraduate course leading to a Diploma (in some cases a Master's degree) in Archives Administration. These courses are offered by four universities (Dublin, Liverpool, London, and Wales). They concentrate on technical and professional subjects, give practical instruction, and can be closely associated with historical researchers and research methodology. Small numbers of students (between six and twenty per course) are normal. A similar pattern of training may be seen elsewhere in the world where the British tradition in education is important, particularly in the Commonwealth countries, in Africa, Asia, and Australasia, and, most recently, in Canada. For Britain itself, the Society of Archivists has a system of distance education for unqualified archivists who are in post.

North America. In the U.S. and Canada there is no universally established method of initial training. The Society of American Archivists issues an *Education Directory*, periodically updated, which lists courses and institutes in archival subjects. The 1983 issue lists 43 multi-course offerings, 19 single-course offerings, and 6 institutes and workshops at universities, archival institutions, or historical societies. None of these courses constitutes a full-time specialized training program, and many of them are not accredited academically. Normally, local archivists provide the teaching staff. Professionals in North America complain about the inability of the region to establish either a professional training institute on the European model, or a regular full-time course on the British model, but despite this the U.S. has achieved a flexible and economic system, which makes maximum use of the teaching potential of practicing archivists and local archives services and which can respond quickly to local demand. In many cases the academic and professional standing of these courses is high, and they have made substantial contributions to the theory and practice of archives administration. The development of short, comprehensive summer institutes—often held in library schools, open to all comers, and a characteristic feature of North American training methods—is associated initially with Ernst Posner (who taught 1939–61) and later with T. R. Schellenberg (who taught 1963–70). In recent years the Society of American Archivists has promoted studies of training requirements and is seeking to develop systems of accreditation of training programs and of certification of qualified archivists.

The Third World. In the Third World there has been a natural tendency to continue the traditions of the former imperial countries. This is particularly true in Latin America. The 1970s saw the emergence of a movement towards regional training, sponsored in large part by Unesco and the International Council on Archives. In Senegal (University of Dakar), the regional school for French-speaking African countries runs a two-year course to train archives assistants; students at a higher level must seek training overseas, mainly in Europe. A one-year postgraduate program has been set up at the University of Ghana, but has not succeeded in giving a training provision for English-speaking countries.

Proposed regional schools for Southeast Asia, first mooted in 1968, and for the Caribbean, were planned to start in 1983, but as of the mid-1980s they had failed to take shape. In South Asia, by contrast, the Indian national training school at New Delhi caters to students from the region as a whole and from other regions. Despite the initiative of Iraq's training school in Baghdad, which operated for some years in the late 1970s, there is no regional facility for the Arab world. The tendency now is for the more advanced countries to propose new training courses to cover their own needs; such proposals exist for Nigeria, Kenya, Zambia, the Philippines, Indonesia, and no doubt others. Although the Indian training school is associated with the National Archives, the tendency today is for new schools to be projected as components of established university schools of librarianship.

Unesco has directed much effort to promoting the harmonization of curricula between the archives courses and those provided for students of library or information studies.

World Problems. The variety of these traditions notwithstanding, no country or region has as yet achieved a system of archival training that meets with general approval. There is a widespread feeling that existing facilities are inadequate and, at least in part, inappropriate. In particular, even when established training schools produce a sufficient number of trained archivists to staff the public, government-supported archives services, many do not attempt to serve the archives services in the private sector. In many cases the curriculum is directed toward old-fashioned and inappropriate goals, that is, biased toward teaching historical sciences at the expense of professional subjects, modern methodology, and practical training. Where courses are attached to library schools, there are complaints that library subjects predominate unduly.

A new directory of archival training courses published by the ICA in 1985 lists 80 such courses, but there is as yet no satisfactory list. An informed guess might be that there are some 150 worldwide. The number of student places they provide is certainly in excess of 3,000 (excluding the Italians mentioned previously). An attempt made in 1979 to calculate the numbers of archivists at work produced an estimate, certainly much too low, of some 7,000; a guess here might be that there are perhaps twice that number. The same survey suggested that there was an immediate training need of 6,000 places worldwide. The evident immediate shortage does not necessarily mean that the long-term requirement is anything like so great. Calculations of the provision of student places is made more difficult by the numbers of general students who do not intend to enter the profession. There is a serious imbalance from region to region. Latin America is relatively well supplied with schools of indifferent reputation, while the remaining regions of the Third World are seriously undersupplied. For them, the places available in the training schools of the Third World itself, plus those of the developed countries of Europe, North America, and Australia, amount only to about 25 professional and 40 subprofessional trainees a year—about enough to supply the archival needs of one large country.

An important characteristic of archival training schools is the wide variety of subjects that must be taught. There are three main subject areas: professional studies (archives administration, records management, managerial and administrative studies, research methodology); auxiliary historical or interpretative sciences; and administrative or institutional history. It is probable that a complete course of training that limits itself strictly to these subjects and does not include any element of general education or languages would require about eight professors. To render a teaching body of this size possible, there would have to be a student enrollment of 80 to 100, but so large a training school would exceed the requirements of most countries and would demand a considerable investment. Hence there exists the problem of providing professional training to a student body of beginning archivists that typically numbers only between 10 and 30.

Consequently, most specialized archival training schools are associated with larger institutions. These are usually (1) a large archives service, such as that to which the German Archivschule Marburg is attached; (2) a school of historical studies at a university; or (3) a library school. There is much debate within the profession as to the relative merits of association with each of these. Schools dependent on archival services are probably the most effective in terms of teaching practical skills, and they can provide, better than others, for periods of supervised practical laboratory work. But few national or other archives services have the standing or the resources to undertake this work (although many larger archives systems do in fact offer training programs, and these are not usually strictly limited to their own novice staff members). Archives schools associated with historical studies have the advantage that archivists trained there may easily become, in their professional practice, members of the research communities of their countries. In the exercise of their professional skills archivists should represent research interests in the world of administration and should apply their knowledge of research methodology and of research findings to the basic archival function of appraisal. The main drawback of associating archival training with historical studies, however, is the tendency of the archivists so trained to withdraw from active administration and from involvement in the fundamental day-to-day professional, as opposed to scholarly, functions of the archival institution.

The tendency today, and one that was given powerful backing by the leading theorist of archival science, T. R. Schellenberg, is to associate archival with library training. This has been done in the most recently established archival schools, in Senegal, Ghana, and Australia (University of New South Wales, Sydney). The benefits to be obtained from this association are considerable, and particularly so since the likely future development of technology in both archives and libraries is likely to increase the area of common skills. Conservation, reprography, computer technology, and documentation services are important fields in which both professions are operating increasingly. However, there are and will remain considerable differences in methodology inherent in the different media with which archivists and librarians work, and so far no attempt to devise common curricula for training has been practicable. Apart from technical areas shared with librarians, such as conservation, reprography, and automation, archival training courses that are situated in library schools will still have to maintain a distinct syllabus and teaching staff and inculcate a distinct professional ethos.

Technical Training. So far only peripheral mention has been made of the technical fields of conservation, reprography, and automation with the fundamentals of which professional archivists must be familiar if they are to plan and administer the technical aspects of archival programs and operations. The degree of attention professional training schools give these subjects varies considerably, but generally speaking it can be described as inadequate. Similarly, facilities for training the actual practitioners—the technicians themselves—are inadequate as well; most technicians either learn on the job or receive prior training in a nonarchival setting. In recognition of this deficiency initiatives are being taken, both in the archivally advanced countries and in the developing world, to provide improved technical training. In particular, concrete efforts are being made to organize technical training centers on the Third World regional level.

REFERENCES

Statistical data are from a report by Michael Cook, *The Education and Training of Archivists,* made to the Unesco meeting of experts on archival training programs, November 1979.

Frank B. Evans, "Post-Appointment Archival Training: A Proposed Solution for a Basic Problem," *American Archivist* (1977).

"La Formation des Archivistes en Europe," *Archives et Bibliothèques de Belgique* (1975).

Morris Rieger, "The Regional Training Center Movement," *American Archivist* (1972).

MICHAEL COOK

Argentina

A federal republic and the second largest country of South America, Argentina is bounded by Bolivia and Paraguay on the north, Brazil, Uruguay, and the Atlantic Ocean on the east, and Chile on the west. Population (1990 est.) 32,322,000; area 2,766,889 sq.km. on the continent; Argentina also claims 969,464 sq.km. in Antarctica and the islands of the southern Atlantic. The official language is Spanish.

History. Most of the national libraries in Latin America had their origins in collections of the Jesuits, the order expelled from the Spanish colonies in 1767. These collections later became the bases for the first public libraries of the region. By decree of September 7, 1810, the First Junta, which had arisen from the Revolution of May 25, founded the Biblioteca Pública, later known as the Biblioteca Nacional. The decree was published in the *Gazeta de Buenos Ayres* on September 13, which has been observed in Argentina as "Librarians' Day" since 1942. The library was inaugurated on March 16, 1812; its first librarians were Fray Cayetano Rodríguez and Saturnino Segurola. Its first director, the priest Luis José Chorroarín, served as director until 1821.

National Library. On August 29, 1884, the library was nationalized, and from September 9 it was called the National Library. Its first collections consisted of works from the libraries of the Colegio San Carlos, the Jesuit library of Córdoba, the library of Bishop Manuel de Azamor y Ramírez of Buenos Aires, and donations from General Manuel Belgrano and others. The public also provided assistance in the form of books and financial contributions.

Materials are acquired through purchase, donations, exchange, and legal deposit. Its holdings consist of books, pamphlets, newspapers, manuscripts, maps, illustrations, musical compositions, photographs, and reproductions from the Archivo de Indias. Among its special collections are the library of Mariano Balcarce, son-in-law of José de San Martín, and the libraries and archives of Ezequiel Leguina, Pedro Denegri, Félix Frias, and Pastor Obligado, as well as manuscripts of Rubén Darío and other well-known writers. Paul Groussac served as director from 1885 to 1929. José

Libraries in Argentina (1990)

Type of library	Number of administrative units (main libraries)	Number of service points (branches, mobile stops, etc.)	Volumes in collections	Population served	Professional staff (with certificate, diploma, etc.)	Total staff
National (1986)	1[a]	1[a]	1,800,000[a]	67,250	16	90
Special (1984)	63[a]	64[a]	1,645,000[a]	645,288[a]	--	--

[a]1991 data

Source: Unesco, *Statistical Yearbook,* 1991

Maria Castineira de Dios was appointed director in 1989.

The National Library operated from 1901 to 1992 from a building constructed for the National Lottery. A new building was dedicated in 1992 as a place to store Argentina's bibliographic patrimony and as a center for information networks throughout the country.

The National Library has been the site of the Escuela Nacional de Bibliotecarios and the Comisión Nacional Protectora de Bibliotecas Populares (National Commission on Popular Libraries) since 1958. The Library published the national bibliography until 1956, when that role was assumed by the Camara Argentina del Libro (Argentine Book Council). The Council also serves as the official agency for registering International Standard Book Numbers (ISBN) and publishes *Argentine Books: ISBN.*

Academic Libraries. Argentina has 28 national universities, 2 provincial ones, and 23 private ones. The national university libraries are coordinated in a network, the Red Nacional de Bibliotecas Universitarias (RENBU). RENBU is coordinated by the Junta de Biblioteas Universidades Nacionales (JUBIUNA; the Council of National University Libraries). Its headquarters, the Sistema de Bibliotecas y de Información (SISBI), serves specific programs and projects such as library holdings, user training, library student internships, the Catálogo Colectivo Nacional Universitario de Libros (CCNUL), and Catálogo Colectivo National de Revistas (CCNR). It coordinates the purchase of library materials nationwide, the automation of catalogues, and professional training.

SISBI, together with the Consejo Nacional de Investigaciones Científicas y Técnicas and the UN Program for the Development of Libraries, published a "Guía de las Bibliotecas de la Universidad de Buenos Aires" (preliminary edition), which lists 116 libraries serving university faculties, laboratories, institutes, and departments, with approximately 1,600,000 volumes. Their total staff of more than 400 includes 150 technicians and 265 administrative employees.

Public Libraries. Public libraries are known in Argentina as popular libraries. These libraries began in 1870, during the term of President Domingo F. Sarmiento, and the law which brought them into being is known as the Sarmiento Law for the Development of Popular Libraries. Sarmiento believed strongly in a close relationship between public and school libraries and saw the two as complementary.

The coordinating organization for public libraries is the National Commission on Popular Libraries, established in Buenos Aires in coordination with the National Library. Public libraries are found throughout the country and, for the sake of classification, are divided into categories according to the numbers of volumes they possess. Though most of the approximately 1,500 public libraries are supported by private institutions, official support for operating expenses is provided through the provision of books, salaries for librarians, and purchase of equipment and furniture. The provincial and municipal governments also contribute to the development of these libraries, which are grouped into five geographic regions.

In the province of Buenos Aires, provincial laws and decrees determine the organization of the Sistema Provincial de Bibliotecas (provincial library system), which includes 190 institutions. The Dirección de Bibliotecas controls the system and plans, organizes, and implements effective library and cultural services. Popular libraries work in cooperation and cultural exchange with one another, comprising a regional network. Among the benefits member libraries receive are salaries for librarians, funds for new services

Photo Archive of *La Nación*

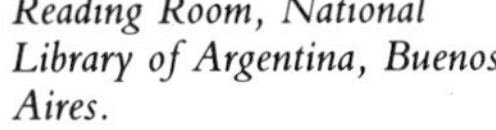

Reading Room, National Library of Argentina, Buenos Aires.

Photo Archive of *La Nación*

New National Library building in Buenos Aires.

for mobile libraries in rural areas, and funds for buying library materials. The Dirección also develops courses and meetings designed to upgrade the education of library employees and works to promote reading in every way.

Some popular libraries in the province of Buenos Aires are more than a hundred years old; the Popular Library of Baradero was founded in 1872 and the Museum and Popular Library of San Fernando in 1873. The popular library Bernardino Rivadavia, in Bahía Blanca, was established in 1882.

The Biblioteca Pública José de San Martín was founded in the city of La Plata (province of Buenos Aires) in 1950 as a lending library in which readers have full access to all available materials. Its new building was inaugurated in 1973. It has a department for the blind, a lending service, and audiovisual materials and interlibrary loans, with priority for the province of Buenos Aires. It has a children's library and provides for handicraft activities and story hours. It also provides photocopy service, telephone directory service, bibliographic and reference information, and bibliographic orientation for students. It houses the Archivo Sonoro de la Palabra (an archive of the spoken word), the Colección de Autores Bonaerenses, and the unpublished papers of Platense writers. Its holdings include local newspapers and journals, including about 500 titles. Altogether, its holdings number about 70,000 volumes. and its staff includes ten professionals.

The Dirección General de Bibliotecas, with jurisdiction over 25 libraries, a periodical and newspaper library, and three mobile units, operates throughout the city of Buenos Aires. Its collections number about 500,000 volumes and its staff includes four professionals and more than 200 other employees.

School Libraries. In spite of Sarmiento's ideas for cooperation, public and school libraries tend to go their own ways. No one agency coordinates school libraries, and action is not coordinated between school and public libraries. However, in Buenos Aires and several other parts of the country, there are teachers' libraries and centers for documentation and research.

The city of Buenos Aires is divided into 20 school districts, in which there are more than 600 schools with a total attendance of more than 140,000 students. In order to provide for the needs of the students, 61 bibliotecas populares have a total of more than 900,000 volumes.

There is no professional librarian in charge of every school library. In most cases teachers take library training as well as their teaching degrees. Provincial rules regulate the position of teacher-librarian, requiring the degree of school librarian granted by the Institutos Superiores or the elementary teaching degree and the librarian's degree granted by the Universidades or Institutos Terciarios Officiales y Privados. The Instituto Superior de Formación Docente in La Plata trains personnel for the position of teacher-librarian.

Special Libraries. Included among these libraries are government and private agencies, such as the libraries of ministries, institutes, national planning offices, museums, banks, businesses, medical laboratories, and other organizations. These libraries serve as information centers in such specialized areas as municipal affairs, biomedicine, biochemistry, science and technology, agriculture, nuclear technology, and law. Most of them belong to the Asociación Argentina de Bibliotecas y Centros de Información Científicos y Tecnológicos (Argentine Association of Scientific and Technical Libraries and Information Centers), with headquarters in Buenos Aires. The Asociación de Bibliotecas Bio-Médicas (Association of Argentine Biomedical Libraries) includes more than a hundred member institutions.

The Centro Argentino de Información Científica y Tecnológica (CAICYT), a member of the Consejo Nacional de Investigaciones Científicas y Técnicas (CONICET), works jointly with SISBI on services, programs, and projects related to specialized libraries, such as catalogue automation, International Standard Serials Numbers (ISSN), and bibliographic record holdings. The Sistema Nacional de Información y Documentación Científica y Tecnológica (SIDCYT) prepared and published the *Formato Comun para el Ingreso de Información en Bases de Datos Bibliográficos* ("Common Format for the Input of Information in Bibliographic Databases") in 1988. Subsequently the system was renamed the Programa Nacional de Información y Comunicación Científica y Tecnológica (PNICCYT).

The 22 libraries of the Comision Nacional de Energía Atómica (CNEA) provide access throughout the country to the International Nuclear Information System (INIS). To facilitate catalogue automation, CNEA in 1988 published *PERSIS: Manual de Referencias,* dealing with periodicals, and *DOCSIS: Manual de Referencias,* dealing with bibliographic documents.

The Profession. The Asociación de Bibliotecarios Graduados de la República Argentina (ABGRA; Association of Graduate Librarians of the Argentine Republic) was founded in 1953, first calling itself the Association of Librarians of the Federal Capital. It succeeded the Center for Library Studies of the Argentine Social Museum (1943–53). ABGRA is a member of the International Federation of Library

Associations (IFLA). To become a member of ABGRA—which had about 1,000 members in 1991—one must be officially recognized as a professional librarian.

ABGRA's primary activities concentrate on its national meetings, the first of which took place in 1962; the 25th took place in 1990. It publishes a *Boletín Informativo* (first series, 1968–75; second series, 1984–), as well as occasional documents and proceedings of meetings. In 1979 it began publishing the *Revista de Bibliotecología y Documentatión* ("Review of Library Science and Documentation"). At the international level, it sponsored the Eleventh National and First Ibero-American Meeting of Librarians in Buenos Aires in 1974 and the Regional Meeting of the Professional Library and Information Science Associations of Latin America and the Caribbean in 1983. ABGRA offers postgraduate courses in library training. It also gives grants to students selected from places without library schools.

Other library associations dedicated to professional concerns can be found in Córdoba, La Plata, Rosario, and other localities throughout Argentina.

To be admitted to a library school, a student must have graduated from secondary school. Programs do not vary much among the schools. Programs take from three to five years to complete, depending on the degree sought. There are 24 library schools in Argentina, 9 connected with the faculties of humanities and social sciences of the universities and the other 15 subordinated to the directorate of higher education and the provincial directorates for secondary education. The Instituto Superior de Formación Docente at La Plata, in Buenos Aires province, specializes in library science and archival and museum work. It trains teaching personnel to be appointed teacher-librarians at school libraries in the province and trains librarian assistants and professional librarians at provincial public libraries, depending on whether they take one-, two-, or three-year courses.

REINALDO JOSÉ SUAREZ; translated by JOSEFINA TRELLES-SOLOMON and GLADYS MARKOFF-SOTOMAYOR

Asheim, Lester E.

(1914–)

Lester Eugene Asheim contributed to North American librarianship in many ways, through writing, teaching, and work with the American Library Association. He helped to define the principles of book selection, to establish criteria for library education and personnel, and to foster communication among librarians in all parts of the world.

Asheim was born in Spokane, Washington, January 22, 1914. Except for a short period in Idaho, he grew up in Seattle, where he received from the University of Washington an A.B. in English in 1936, along with a Phi Beta Kappa key; a B.A. in Librarianship in 1937; and an M.A. in American Literature in 1941. Asheim began library work as a page in the Seattle Public Library, and from 1937 to 1941 he served as Junior Reference Assistant at the University of Washington while he continued his work on his Master's degree.

For the year 1941–42, Asheim served as Librarian of the Prison Library at McNeill Island, Washington. During World War II he served for three years in the U.S. Army Signal Intelligence Corps, chiefly in Alaska.

Upon his return to civilian life in 1945, Asheim organized a library for the Federal Public Housing Authority in Seattle. Taking advantage of a fellowship and the G.I. Bill, he enrolled at the Graduate Library School (GLS) of the University of Chicago, from which he received a Ph.D. in 1949. His doctoral dissertation, *From Book to Film: A Comparative Analysis of the Content of Novels and the Films Based on Them,* demonstrated his interest in both literature and non-print media, an interest that he maintained throughout his career. His dissertation was published in an edited version in four installments of *Hollywood Quarterly* (1951) and *The Quarterly of Film, Radio and Television* (1951–52).

At the GLS Asheim's talents were early recognized. He assisted Bernard Berelson in writing *The Library's Public: A Report of the Public Library Inquiry* (1949) and then edited the papers of the GLS conference on the Inquiry, *A Forum on the Public Library Inquiry* (1949). This was only the first of a number of GLS conference volumes for which he was to serve as Editor, including *The Core of Education for Librarianship* (1954), *The Future of the Book* (1955), *New Directions in Public Library Development* (1957), *Persistent Issues in American Librarianship* (1961), and *Differentiating the Media* (1975).

Asheim was appointed Assistant Professor at the GLS, 1948–52; Dean of Students, 1951–52; and Dean and Associate Professor, 1952–61. During the decade of his deanship he continued to study library education, but his most important work was probably his now classic article "Not Censorship but Selection" (1953), which has been widely reprinted. *Wilson Library Bulletin* published his reappraisal of this landmark article in 1983. In 1957 he published *The Humanities and the Public Library,* which has been widely used in library schools as a guide to selection and use of humanities materials.

In 1961 Asheim became Director of the International Relations Office (IRO) of the ALA. In his five years in that post he visited 44 countries and shared his experience in American librarianship with students and practicing librarians throughout the world. One result of his IRO activities was an invitation to deliver the Phineas Lawrence Windsor Lectures at the University of Illinois. These lectures, subsequently published as *Librarianship in the Developing Countries* (1966), were a major contribution to the study of comparative librarianship and brought him the Scarecrow Press Award for "an outstanding contribution to library literature" in 1968.

In 1966 Asheim resigned his IRO post to accept the directorship of ALA's new Office for Library Education. The rapid expansion of libraries during the period of Great Society programs placed serious strains on library education, which was urged to produce not only more librarians but also better-trained librarians. Much of Asheim's work was concentrated on the development of a statement defining the titles, basic requirements, and responsibilities of library personnel—both professional and support. His

University of North Carolina

Lester E. Asheim

statement on "Library Education and Manpower" (often known as the Asheim Paper or Statement) was adopted as the official policy of the ALA on June 30, 1970. In the spring of 1976 that document, without substantive change, was renamed "Library Education and Personnel Utilization." It remains the major position on personnel development of the American library community.

While Director of the ALA Office of Library Education, Asheim continued to write and speak on library education and other topics. He had earlier chaired ALA's Committee on Accreditation and over the years frequently served as a consultant for library education programs. He was President of the Library Education Division of ALA, 1976–77.

In 1971 Asheim returned to the University of Chicago as Professor in the Graduate Library School and in 1972 became the Editor of *Library Quarterly,* the major scholarly journal in American librarianship, a post he held for the next three years. He was William Rand Kenan, Jr., Professor of Library Science at the University of North Carolina at Chapel Hill from 1975 until he retired in 1984.

In honor of Asheim's 65th birthday, colleagues presented him with a Festschrift, *As Much to Learn as to Teach* (1979). As is apparent from the topics treated in this series of essays—such as intellectual freedom, library service to the public, library education, professional associations, international and comparative librarianship, and mass communications—Asheim showed interest in many areas of librarianship, and to most he has made significant contributions. Many testify that this diligent researcher and writer is an excellent teacher and a delightful colleague.

Asheim was selected as the 1973 recipient of the Beta Phi Mu Award for Distinguished Service to Education for Librarianship. At the ALA Centennial Conference he was given the Joseph W. Lippincott Award for distinguished service to the profession of librarianship. The University of Washington School of Librarianship gave him its Distinguished Alumnus Award in 1966 and the Illinois Library Association its Intellectual Freedom Award the same year. He was named a member of the Advisory Committee to the Center for the Book at the Library of Congress in 1978. At the time of his retirement, ALA conferred on him its highest award, Honorary Membership.

REFERENCE

Joel M. Lee and Beth A. Hamilton, editors, *As Much to Learn as to Teach: Essays in Honor of Lester Asheim* (1979), includes biographical information and a bibliography of Asheim's writings.

EDWARD G. HOLLEY

Asociación Latinoamericana de Escuelas de Bibliotecología y Ciencias de la Información

The Asociación Latinoamericana de Escuelas de Bibliotecología y Ciencias de la Información (ALEBCI; the Latin-American Association of Schools of Library and Information Science) was founded in September 1970 during the International Congress of Documentation in Buenos Aires, Argentina, to promote library education in Latin America. The Association was temporarily housed at the Colegio de Bibliotecología, Universidad Nacional Autónoma de México.

Membership is open to individuals and institutions interested in sharing information and exchanging publications related to library education in Latin American countries. The entire membership meets every two years.

The official journal is *ALEBCI: Boletín Informativo,* published four times a year. The Association is affiliated with IFLA and FID.

Association Internationale des Écoles des Sciences de l'Information

The Association Internationale des Écoles des Sciences de l'Information (AIESI; International Association of Schools of Information Science) was founded in 1977 in Geneva, Switzerland. Representatives from library and information science schools in eight countries were present at the founding meeting: Algeria, Belgium, France, Morocco, Senegal, Switzerland, Tunisia, and French Canada (Quebec). The original impetus for the creation of this organization came from the Université de Montréal's École de Bibliothéconomie, the only French-language library school that was accredited by the American Library Association and that had experienced the benefits of participating in the work of the English-speaking Association for Library and Information Science Education (ALISE). Membership in AIESI is limited to those schools, university departments, and other organizations engaged in educating librarians, documentalists, and information scientists at the university level (or its equivalent) that use French, entirely or in part, as their language of instruction. Schools or organizations that do not meet all of these requirements may be admitted as associate members. Most of the associate members do not offer university-level instruction. A change in the bylaws in 1984 created the category of individual member. French-speaking professors at non-French-language schools may join their colleagues from AIESI-member schools as individuals. The Association attempted through this change to broaden participation in its activities without losing its French-language character.

AIESI is formally attachted to the Association des Universités Partiellemen ou Entièrement de Langue Française (Association of French-language Universities), which provides it with secretarial help and financial aid, largely from funds obtained from FICU, the International Fund for Inter-University Cooperation. The Association's administrative structure consists of a General Assembly in which each institutional member has one vote. The Assembly meets every two years. An Executive Board, consisting of five elected members, who in turn choose their own President, Vice-President, Secretary, and Treasurer, runs the affairs of the Association between Assembly meetings.

The Association has the following objectives: to encourage the development of library and information science education and to assist in raising the quality of persons engaged in such activities; to establish and maintain continuing liaison among the various institutions offering French-language instruction in library and information science; to encourage cooperative programs among these institutions; to plan and organize periodic international meetings (colloquia, seminars, and workshops); to stimulate original French-language research in the area; to encourage by all possible means, financial and otherwise, the publication in French of needed textbooks, journals, and the results of research undertaken; to speak on topics of mutual interest; and to issue opinions and recommendations on questions having to do with the education of librarians and information scientists.

In conjunction with the meetings of its General Assembly every two years, the Association sponsors three- or four-day workshops. They covered the teaching of management (Lyons, France, 1978); the teaching of information science (Montréal, 1980); nonbook materials and documentation (Liège, Belgium, 1982); teaching methods and the information sciences (Rabat, Morocco, 1984); continuing education (Bordeaux, France, 1986); and relating theory and practice (Montreal, Canada, 1988). AIESI publishes the proceedings of these workshops. It published a directory of French-language library and information science programs throughout the world in 1979 and again in 1985. The 1985 edition included all known programs, whether their host institutions were members of AIESI or not. The directory also gave detailed information about the content of the individual programs, much more than is to be found in the average directory, so that each member might better understand the elements to be found in the programs of schools in other countries where the educational system might be different.

Creation of the Association has greatly stimulated the exchange of information and expertise throughout the French-speaking world. No longer do individual schools exist in a vacuum. Increasing amounts of funds have been obtained from various governmental agencies (international and national) to facilitate such exchanges. An expansion in the French-language research and publications program was seen as much needed in a discipline in which 80 percent of the publications used in French-language schools are printed in English.

RICHARD K. GARDNER

Association of Caribbean University, Research and Institutional Libraries

The Association of Caribbean University, Research and Institutional Libraries (ACURIL) originated as part of a movement for Caribbean cooperation at the university level that was initiated during the 1960s by Sir Philip Sherlock, the Vice-Chancellor of the University of the West Indies.

In 1967, when the Association of Caribbean Universities (UNICA) was formed, the need for close cooperation among university and research libraries in the region was also recognized. The Association therefore sponsored the first Caribbean Conference of Librarians in University and Research Libraries in Puerto Rico in 1969. At that conference, an independent Association of Caribbean University and Research Institute Libraries (ACURIL) was voted into existence. Delegates elected Alma Jordan, then Deputy Librarian of the University of the West Indies Library at the St. Augustine Campus, Trinidad, as the first president of the Association and Albertina Perez de Rosa, then Chief of the Department of Latin American Studies and Exchange at the José M. Lazaro Library of the University of Puerto Rico, San Juan, as the first Vice-President.

Later, in 1976, the Association changed its name slightly, but kept the acronym. "Institutional" was substituted for "Institute," to reflect accurately the Association's membership, which from the beginning included public and special libraries in the region.

There are three categories of membership: (1) institutional: open to libraries, archives, and schools conducting programs of library or archival education in the Caribbean archipelago and those mainland countries (including the United States) that border on the Caribbean Sea or Gulf of Mexico; (2) organizational: open to national library associations and regional or other special organizations or associations; and (3) personal: open to librarians, archivists, and other employees interested in archival and library services. An associate membership is available in each category for organizations or persons living outside the geographic area. All categories of membership are represented on the Executive Council. In 1991 the membership stood at 112 institutional members, 14 organizational members, and 70 personal members.

ACURIL's constitution outlines its aims: to facilitate the development and use of libraries and archives and the identification of library collections in support of the whole range of intellectual and educational endeavors throughout the Caribbean area; to strengthen the profession of librarianship in the region; and to promote cooperative library activities in pursuit of these objectives.

The Constitution provides for a 15-member Executive Council, with four members elected each year to three-year terms. The Treasurer and the Executive Secretary are permanent members. The Council endeavors to meet at least twice a year, once at the annual meeting and again six months later.

The Standing Committees are Acquisitions, Bibliography, Indexing, Constitution and Bylaws, Education, Microforms, Planning and Research, and Publications. The first three Committees operate in language groups: English-, Spanish-, and French-speaking. Committee activities are reviewed during the annual conference.

The program of the annual conference is developed around a theme of interest to library and information services in the Caribbean. The papers presented for discussion and the proceedings are published. A newsletter in Spanish and English, *ACURIL: Carta Informativa/Newsletter,* is also published. ACURIL has maintained its affiliation with UNICA and is a member of the International Federation of Library Associations (IFLA).

The ACURIL Secretariat, headed by an executive secretary, is located in San Juan at the Caribbean Regional Library in the José M. Lázaro Library of the University of Puerto Rico.

THOMAS MATHEWS

Association of International Libraries

The Association of International Libraries (AIL) was created in Sofia, Bulgaria, in 1963 by a group of librarians from international organizations and curators of international documents collections, during the annual meeting of the International Federation of Library Associations (IFLA). Its aim is to promote cooperation among international libraries. For many years the AIL was active in representing the interests of these libraries in a wider framework, particularly in IFLA. It organized international symposia on the subject of documentation of the United Nations and other international organizations (Geneva, 1972, and Brussels, 1980); these and other activities attracted participants from major libraries around the world. During that period, the AIL held annual general assembly meetings around the annual IFLA meetings, which further facilitated contacts. In those years of activity at the international level, the AIL made many recommendations to improve coordination of processing of the mass of documentation produced by international organizations.

In the mid-1980s, however, because of limited resources, the AIL has limited its activities to the Geneva area. The high concentration of international or internationally oriented libraries in the Geneva area (more than 70 members representing 35 libraries) has made it possible for the association to have an active program at the local level. Members maintain contacts between libraries through study visits, lectures, presentations, and round table discussions on subjects of common interest. An informal network enables members to share helpful information among libraries.

During the 1990s, the AIL hopes to expand its role. One project will produce a directory of libraries of the main international organizations, including internationally oriented research and special libraries in the Geneva area. Other activities will aim to produce an inventory of training needs, a local electronic mail network, and a union list of information management periodicals. Joint activities with the Swiss professional associations will be undertaken. Training activities will be expanded and participation in training events will be open to libraries outside the Geneva area. Eventually, it is hoped, contact will be renewed with other international libraries and the scope of AIL will become, once again, truly international.

REFERENCE

Laura Alpern, "L'Association de Bibliothèques Internationales," in *La Documentation Internationale* (Paris, La Documentation française, forthcoming).

LAURA ALPERN

British Museum

Assurbanipal

Assurbanipal
(fl. 7th century B.C.)

Assurbanipal (Ashurbanipal), the last important king of Assyria (7th century B.C.), helped create both its Golden Age of literature and its sudden destruction. He organized coteries of scribes, sending them to all parts of the empire to find and copy Sumero-Babylonian documents, and even learned the scribal art himself, in order to assemble the Assyrian "Library of Congress" at Nineveh. The resulting library operation represents the basic content, and possibly the complete corpus, of the Mesopotamian scribal tradition. But it does not represent the realities of librarianship for several reasons.

Assurbanipal was first of all a warrior, then an administrator, and finally a librarian. Like most imperialists, he was overly pragmatic, preferring to manage things and people rather than ideas. Accordingly, he reduced librarianship to housekeeping routines for creating and maintaining the order arrangements of clay tablets in the only library of Mesopotamia. The literatures of Sumer and Old Babylon were thus preserved by "the Assyrian gift for arranging and systematizing," not by any "marked advance in thought." There was no contemporary literature or science because the Assyrians were better consumers than producers of information. Their only original contributions were archival grist for the future historians of Assyria, but the Assyrians themselves were not concerned with "scholarly accuracy" or with "the truth."

Assurbanipal was the first ultrapragmatic librarian to exhibit "a complete absence of any speculative or reasoning effort." Not ability, mind you, but *effort.* When his bibliographical methods arrived in Alexandria, the Greeks simply accepted them as folksy procedures for running a library and turned to substantive issues—like inventing the higher and lower criticisms for managing the literary tradition itself. Thus, they avoided the unresolved problems of bibliographic organization and control, which passed through the Romans to Western Europe. The resultant utter lack of Greek influence in bibliographical matters is essentially what is wrong with librarianship today: it has never been able to get Assurbanipal off its back.

H. CURTIS WRIGHT

Audiovisual Materials

Audiovisual materials are defined by the media of their expression. The classic library drew its name and character from the medium that formed the basis of its collections—the printed book and its cousin, the serial. Archives also concentrated their collecting efforts on the written word, though frequently in manuscript form.

Taken literally, the term *audiovisual materials* encompasses all those information media that convey their messages without the mediation of the written word. In practice, the boundaries of the term are elastic, and the designation of specific materials as audiovisual in any particular institution may depend more on administrative convenience than abstract definition.

Nontextual materials share certain characteristics that, while not defining, cause them to be treated as a special, generally troublesome category by most libraries and archives. Virtually all audiovisual materials come in forms, shapes, and sizes quite different from the codex book, requiring special storage facilities and other terms of description than those developed for cataloguing printed material. Many cannot be used without separate, specialized hardware. Many are created by processes quite different from traditional notions of authorship; they are distributed in manners only roughly analogous to publishing. All these traits have forced librarians striving to integrate the full range of information media into their collections to revise their book-oriented methods of organization, access, and service.

Types of Materials. Historically, the visual materials were the first nontextual materials frequently collected in libraries; prints, graphics, photographs, charts, flash cards, even maps can be included in this category. These materials are all exceptions to the generalization about dependency on separate hardware for their use—all can be consulted with the naked eye. Visual materials were, however, strongly affected by changing technology. Even before the invention of photography, experimenters were developing techniques for simulating movement, beginning in 1832 with Plateau's Phenakistiscope. By 1839 Louis Daguerre had achieved formal recognition for his photographic process. In a now familiar pattern, successive advances in image-timing, projection, and photography led to Étienne Marey's invention of the first practical cinema camera in 1887. Silent pictures ruled Hollywood until 1927, and a simpler form of silent projection, the filmstrip, continued as a mainstay of school libraries into at least the 1960s.

Thomas Edison patented the phonograph in 1877. By 1904 Eugène-Augustin Lauste had succeeded in recording both sound and picture on the same film, ushering in the audiovisual age. Since then, sound and vision technologies have interacted closely.

The phonograph, from Edison's wax cylinder to the stereophonic vinyl disk, records sound by the mechanical impression derived from sound waves on a smooth surface. A Danish engineer, Valdemar Poulson, demonstrated an alternative approach, using an electromagnet to create a magnetized "map" of sound waves on a wire. A sensitized film quickly replaced the wire, and tape recordings existed side-by-side with phonograph disks. Until the 1960s, tapes were generally restricted to direct recording of sounds, with phonograph records dominating the mass-distribution market. The Philips Corporation introduced the tape cassette, with the tape permanently fixed to its reels in a package that could be simply dropped into a player, providing an alternative to the vinyl disk that was inexpensive, less subject to damage through use, and easily portable.

Elmer Holmes Bobst Library, New York University

The Avery Fisher Center for Music and Media, Elmer Holmes Bobst Library, New York University. The Center houses 43 video carrels and over 1,000 videotapes.

The motion picture long remained the standard medium for recording both visual images and sound, in three sizes: 35mm film for commercial theater projection, 16mm for institutional use, as in schools, and 8mm (and super-8) for home movies. Broadcast television, which had been introduced in the United Kingdom and the United States in the late 1930s, continued to depend on photographic film for recording its programs until the 1960s, when magnetic video tape, first demonstrated by the Ampex Corporation in 1956, entered full-scale commercial use. Philips introduced a home video recorder in 1972 and, by the 1980s, a videocassette recorder (VCR) was a standard companion to the home television set in many countries. Even the simplest VCR could both record from broadcasts and play back those broadcast tapes, amateur efforts recorded on portable video cameras, and "published" cassettes of everything from feature films to documentaries.

All the media described above record an analog—a proportional "map" of the original visual or sound energy captured by the equipment. The revolution of the 1980s was the application of digital technology, already in use for computers and telecommunications, to video and aural recordings. Digitization has been applied to phonograph disks, audio tapes, and video tapes. Optical technology, in which lasers (super-focused light beams) are used both to etch a master and to read the resulting coded pattern, has been married to digitization in the compact disc

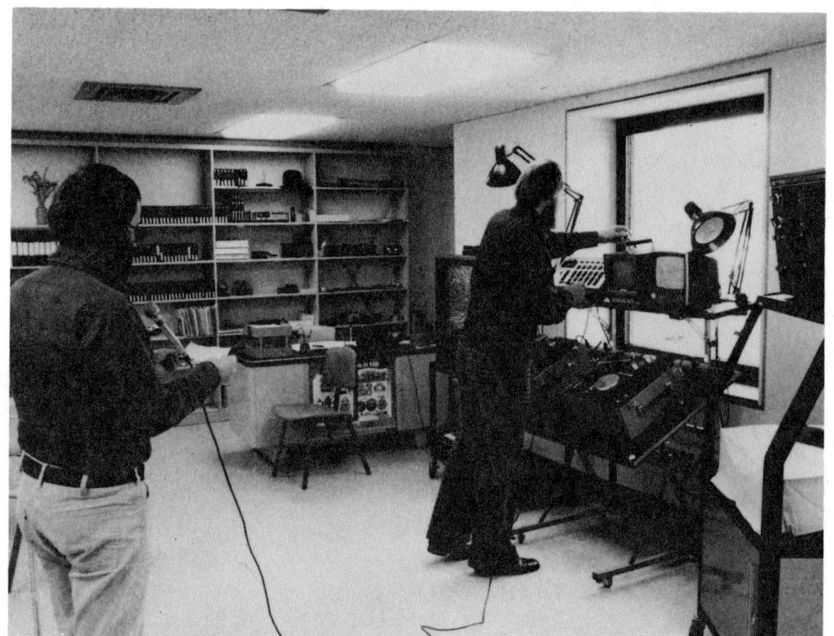

St. Paul Public Library

Editing room at the St. Paul Public Library's Video Communications Center. The Center lends equipment and offers training in production.

(CD), introduced jointly by Philips and the Sony Corporation in 1980. By 1990, the CD had largely displaced the vinyl phonograph record in the home market. Videodiscs were still largely confined to institutional use. In 1992, Kodak introduced a photo-CD for displaying photographs on television monitors.

Personal computers and computer software occupy one of the ill-defined boundary zones of library materials, in part because of their multiple uses. Originally developed as business machines, computers now serve as platforms for business applications, interactive learning programs, arcade-style games, and multimedia displays of information. Whether computer programs are considered just another variety of audiovisual material (even when they actually display text) and computers a new companion to the slide projector depends largely on how expertise in dealing with the hardware is divided among an institution's staff. Many libraries with specialized staff in charge of automated systems for library operations will leave to the same specialists control and maintenance of all computer-based library materials. Without such staff, the audiovisual librarian is generally assumed to have the greatest aptitude for dealing with the technical problems of computers.

In the 1970s and 1980s libraries, especially school media learning centers, began collecting another form of library material little connected with technological advance but long considered the preserve of museums—realia. Libraries collected both classes of objects, such as shells or cultural artifacts, and educational toys and games. Public libraries included recreational toys and even stuffed animals in their lending collections.

The Impact of Technology. The impact of technology on printed materials has largely been on the side of production. The codex book of 1992 looks remarkably like that of 1492. The same could be said, to some degree, of flat graphic materials, including prints and maps. While some advances in audiovisual technology only improve a known product or economize on production, many introduce new products based on new hardware for their use.

The first problem facing libraries aspiring to significant collections of audiovisual materials is simply to keep up with the introduction of media, formats, and equipment. Collections of historical materials have the reciprocal problem of retaining and maintaining the hardware necessary to make use of the wide variety of obsolete formats represented in their collections.

Standardization is always a problem with new types of material. In the 1970s, Panasonic and Sony introduced competing formats for videocassettes; libraries that invested heavily in Sony's Betamax system looked like poor gamblers when the 8mm VHS format emerged as the de facto standard for home VCRs by the late 1980s. Variation in television broadcast standards also restricts the international exchange of video recordings. One reason for the rapid success of the audio CD was prior agreement on standards by the major producers.

Personal computers have also been plagued by problems of standardization and compatibility. The first home computers used a wide variety of operating systems, and most programs were specifically written for specific brands of machines. The importance of the IBM personal computer meant that its Microsoft Disk Operating System (MS-DOS) became another de facto standard; competing manufacturers began advertising their equipment or programs as "IBM-compatible," actually meaning "MS-DOS-compatible." The Apple Corporation, an important exception, used its own operating system for its Macintosh personal computers. In 1991 IBM and Apple announced joint ventures to develop compatible operating systems. Major shifts in operating systems render obsolete the programs designed to run on them. Applications software is a quagmire of shifting standards—there is little compatibility between brands of the same type of program, and each producer constantly revises its products.

Collection Development. Librarians responsible for choosing audiovisual resources for libraries are confronted with a bewildering array of selection tools, specialized by medium, subject, and audience. Traditional book selection tools such as *Booklist* and *Library Journal* include reviews of audiovisual materials, especially videos. Media organizations and vendors publish directories and review journals. Because commercial publishers were slow to develop selection tools for nonprint media, many educational and library organizations took up the slack.

Audiovisual materials also present special preservation problems. Most arise from the rigors of use, but audiovisual media can deteriorate simply while sitting on the shelf. Many, including films and photographs, are especially liable to damage from high heat and humidity. Analog magnetic media are subject to "print through" and loss of information content over time, especially if not rewound on a regular basis. No one knows the life expectancy of a compact disc. Digitized information has an advantage over analog in that any information coding greater than 0 is taken as 1, both eliminating the creeping deterioration of analog coding and allowing re-recording through successive generations without significant loss of content.

Organization and Access. Physical organization of audiovisual materials in libraries is a product of their varying shape and size, their unsuitability for browsing, and/or their intolerance of frequent handling.

The videocassette is one audiovisual item that lines up quite nicely on standard library shelving; in this it is a rarity. Graphic prints, 35mm slides, and audio cassettes all require their own special storage facilities. There is no regularity to the physical characteristics of realia. If media are to be used in the library, the library must have the equipment necessary for their use, either as individual user stations (such as audio listening stations) or for staff operation (the 16mm projector). Libraries in larger institutions may also stock equipment for loan to other departments, with or without the technicians to operate it.

Whether or not the library allows free patron access to materials in any given medium will depend largely on the balance between browsability and fragility. Most libraries allow free browsing of cased phonograph records, because the object itself is fairly tough and its jacket probably includes extensive descriptive information. Videocassettes are likewise tolerant of handling, although the labels seldom include more information than is contained in the catalogue. Prints and graphics are usually kept under closer control, not because bibliographic control systems provide adequate access, because they seldom do, but because of the need to limit casual handling. Motion picture films are both fragile and unsuitable for browsing and are seldom left in open stacks.

These factors, together with the constraints of staffing, all influence the design of space and storage facilities for audiovisual materials and the institution's policies regarding open or closed access.

Bibliographic Control. Cataloguers of audiovisual materials frequently point out that the standards for description and subject access to library materials were developed for books, with a nod to serials. Microforms, when added, were treated simply as variant forms of the print publication.

Until the 1980s, most general libraries holding audiovisual materials relied on separate card files, with one sequence for each format, minimal description, and often no subject access. The increase in importance of audiovisual materials in all kinds of libraries and the effort to establish the online catalogue as the single focus of bibliographic control for all library materials led to a reevaluation of cataloguing standards as they apply to nonbook materials. Jean Withs and the Canadian Library Association broke new ground in 1973 with her book *Nonbook Materials,* the first real manual for integrating bibliographic control of textual and audiovisual materials. The second edition of the *Anglo-American Cataloguing Rules* (AACR2; 1978), which specified general rules of description, then applied them to each medium in turn, was the first set of rules to accord audiovisual materials theoretical parity with books. AACR2 failed to satisfy audiovisual librarians because most of the general rules were still derived from the model developed for books. There were many problems with physical description. More important, intellectual responsibility for the creation of a motion picture film, for example, is usually much more diffuse than the traditional notion of authorship; many cataloguers object to main entry under the producer, whose chief responsibility is organizing the resources for the other participants. The traditional functions of publisher are thus split between producer and distributor. The chapter relating to computer files was so unsatisfactory that it required complete replacement. Many of the changes consolidated in the 1988 revision of AACR2 dealt with audiovisual materials.

Automated library systems have also demonstrated anew the importance of subject access to library collections. Audiovisual materials pose special problems in this regard. Some educational materials clearly have an "aboutness" analogous to that of monographs, but subject access is an even more complicated concept for materials such as historical photographs: Is the picture "about" the place where an event happened, the people shown, the building behind them, the clothes they wore, the social problems in which they were involved, or the history of photography? A single picture could easily be consulted for all these reasons. To try to provide for the widest range of possibilities, cataloguers have developed a number of specialized indexes with their own controlled vocabularies, such as the *Art & Architecture Thesaurus*.

The mechanism for providing an integrated online catalogue is the MARC format, developed initially for books. The need to deal with other media led the Library of Congress to develop a series of US-MARC formats: books, serials, maps, music (including scores and sound recordings), visual materials, computer files, and the archives and manuscript control format. Because the same field, subfield, or tag could be defined differently in each format, full integration of the catalogue has been limited. The LC and the American Library Association's Committee on Representation in Machine-Readable Form of Bibliographic Information (MARBI) worked through the late 1980s to approve an integrated US-MARC format, scheduled for implementation in 1994.

The multiplication of information media has also presented a new problem for bibliographic control: linking records representing multiple manifestations of the same work. An example might be a motion picture film issued simultaneously or sequentially in 35mm and 16mm film, videocassette, book transcription, and soundtrack recording on audio cassette and CD. In one sense, these items all represent the same "edition" of the work, but the user clearly needs to be able to distinguish among the various media.

Services to Users. The range of audiovisual media, services, and facilities provided by a given library may depend on a number of factors. The predominant criterion *should* be the library's statement of its goals and the needs of its clientele. Many school and junior college libraries articulate the importance of audiovisual media in the educational programs of their parent institutions through their names—school media center or learning resources center. But many desired services may be lacking because of shortages of space, facilities, or staff.

The simplest service a library or media center can provide is simply to lend materials for patrons to use in their own homes or offices. Audiovisual media present special problems for lending. Vinyl records

Fernandez C. Rodrigo/Biblioteca Central Pontificia. Universidad Catolica de Chile

Music room of the Audiovisual Center at the Pontificia Universidad Católica de Chile.

were easily scratched, but at least they could be checked for damage before charging out and at return. Damage to magnetic media is likely to go undetected until the next person tries to use them. Games with many pieces require strict control if they are to remain useful. Fragile or unique materials, such as photographs or posters, may be limited to consultation in the library.

Most audiovisual media require specialized facilities for in-library use by individual patrons. Full access implies sufficient individual viewing/listening stations for each medium to satisfy expected concurrent demand. The library may also provide group facilities, especially if it collects media that cannot easily be used in an individualized setting, such as motion picture films. All such facilities imply that the library can afford not only the space, specialized furniture, and equipment, but also the staff to maintain the equipment and to instruct patrons in its use.

Many libraries in larger institutions, especially educational institutions, bear responsibility for maintaining the establishment's entire stock of audiovisual equipment, lending it to departments as needed. Teaching staff cannot all be expected to be competent in the use and care of all types of equipment, and this loan often implies provision of technicians to run the equipment at specified times and places. Some integrated library automation systems now include capabilities for managing such a booking service.

Many library outreach programs make use of audiovisual materials. Always popular with audiences, they can be included in educational, cultural, and recreational programs of all sorts.

Continuing discussions about the range of audiovisual materials suitable for public libraries reflect the long-standing argument over whether the library is primarily an educational or recreational facility. Especially in times of scarce resources, most librarians would agree that the library should not compete with the local video store, but should concentrate on supplying those cultural works that the commercial sector may not provide. Others point out that media such as videos attract whole new categories of users, including those previously unable to use the library because they cannot read. Certainly, public demand for video recordings has been unmistakable.

Professional Organizations. The earliest American organization formed to support the interest of libraries in nonprint media is the Educational Film Library Association (EFLA), sponsor of the annual American Film Festival in New York City. The relationships EFLA developed for librarians with both the commercial film production-distribution community and the government-art-foundation community are significant.

Indicative of the close relationship between audiovisual materials and education is the importance of the Association for Educational Communications and Technology (AECT), which began as the Department of Audio-Visual Instruction of the National Education Association. AECT works closely with NAVA, the International Communications Industries Association (formerly the National Audio-Visual Association), holding joint exhibits. Its Division of Technology (DOT), Division of Instructional Development (DID), Division of Educational Media Management (DEMM), and Association for Special Education Technology (ASET) all run programs related to audiovisual media.

Several ALA Divisions have ongoing committees focusing on audiovisual materials. The Editorial Board of *School Library Media Quarterly* is a committee of the American Association of School Librarians (AASL). The Audiovisual Committee of the Association for Library Collections & Technical Services (ALCTS) has subcommittees on AV Producer/Distributor-Library Relations and on AV Standards. The Association for Library Service to Children (ALSC) has committees to evaluate computer software, films and videos, filmstrips, and audio recordings. A number of interest groups of the Library and Information Technology Association (LITA) concern themselves with the problems of digital and optical media and telecommunications issues affecting library services. The Young Adult Library Services Association (YALSA) has committees on Computer Applications to Young Adult Service, Media Selection and Usage, and Selected Films and Videos for Young Adults.

There is no reason to believe that the role of audiovisual materials in library collections will do anything but grow. In a visual age, librarians will have to provide the same level of care in selecting, organizing, maintaining bibliographic control, preserving, and providing user services for audiovisual media as they do for their traditional mainstay, printed books. Providing this welcome to new media will be a major challenge to librarians in an age combining technological change with budgetary constraint.

REFERENCES

John W. Ellison and Patricia Ann Coty, editors, *Nonbook Media: Collection Management and User Services* (1987).

Sheila Intner and Richard Smiraglia, editors, *Policy and Practice in Bibliographic Control of Nonbook Media* (1987).

Jean Withs, with Shirley Lewis, *Nonbook Materials: The Organization of Integrated Collections,* 3rd edition (1989).
American Association of School Librarians and Association for Educational Communications and Technology, *Information Power: Guidelines for School Media Programs* (1988).

JEAN T. KREAMER
RUTH R. RAINS
STEPHEN C. JOHNSON

Austin, Derek

(1921–)

Derek William Austin made significant contributions to the field of indexing through his work with the Classification Research Group and the development of the PRECIS (PREserved Context Index System).

Austin was born in London, August 11, 1921. He started his library career in 1938, joining the staff of his local public library directly from grammar school. He spent most of the period 1941–46 on army service in India, Burma, China (with a commando unit), and Germany. After being demobilized he applied for an ex-serviceman's grant to study at Loughborough Library School and achieved the Associateship of the Library Association in 1948, passed the LA final examination (with honors) in 1949, and was elected a Fellow of the Library Association in 1950.

Most of his early career was spent in public libraries (Enfield, Hertfordshire, and Tottenham), usually in the capacity of reference librarian, readers' adviser, or subject specialist. Service of this kind, requiring a constant use of indexes as tools for relating queries to answers, is a necessary background, Austin became convinced, for anyone who intends to produce an index or attempts to design an indexing system.

He became involved in index production when he joined the staff of the *British National Bibliography* as a Subject Editor in 1963. He was seconded from *BNB* in 1967 to work on the NATO-supported research, directed by the Classification Research Group (London), into a new library classification based on faceted principles. Although the CRG classification had not materialized when the NATO funds ran out, Austin came to consider that such an innovation was no longer necessary. The general principles of subject analysis formulated during that research were the critical starting point for his later research into subject indexing.

The need for a fresh approach to indexing arose when the editors of *BNB* decided that all its issues from the start of 1971 should be produced by computer from MARC records. With just over a year to go, Austin was appointed to lead a team with the task of designing a new subject index. The goal was a controlled-language, precoordinated indexing system conceived from the outset with the computer in mind. The system had to satisfy the following main criteria: (1) all index entries, and their supporting cross-references, should be generated, filed, and printed entirely by the computer; (2) the indexer would prepare only an input string of terms and coded instructions, which would then be manipulated by standard algorithms into index entries under any selected term; and (3) all entries should be meaningful and equally coextensive, and the mechanical generation of entries should not entail any loss of information, nor any distortion of the subject. All these goals were achieved by PRECIS—a name that has become almost a synonym for Derek Austin.

Although Austin's work on classificatory theory formed a necessary basis for his later ideas on indexing, PRECIS has taken the concept of subject analysis and concept organization in a new direction: away from relative significance as the organizing principle and toward general linguistic principles and an order of terms in index entries which is directly concerned with the clear expression of meaning. Thus, an explanation of PRECIS mainly calls for reference to grammatical categories and general logical relations.

Although PRECIS is still a relatively young system (what might be called the definitive version for the English language was adopted by *BNB* in 1974), it is now employed by a number of indexing agencies in Britain, Australia, and Canada, and experimental indexes were produced in several other countries. The logic on which the system is based, and on which the production of meaningful entries depends, appears to be language-independent, and the system has been applied successfully in a range of European languages.

In the course of his researches, Austin necessarily had to reexamine many facets of the total indexing operation. Several of the techniques developed originally for PRECIS are capable of standing in isolation, and many indexers who have no intention of adopting PRECIS have nevertheless benefited from a study of its approach to concept analysis, the treatment of compound terms, and the construction of a machine-held thesaurus. The general applicability of these techniques is mentioned only occasionally in Austin's own writing on PRECIS, but they appear, nevertheless, in two documents that would otherwise, by their very nature, remain anonymous; Austin was the principal author of a Draft International Standard on techniques for document analysis and of the current British Standard on the construction of a monolingual thesaurus.

In 1976 Austin received the first Ranganathan Award presented by the FID for original contributions to classification (defined in its widest sense). This was followed by the Margaret Mann Citation for 1978.

REFERENCES

Hans Wellisch, editor, *The PRECIS Index System: Principles, Applications, and Prospects* (1977).
Derek Austin, PRECIS: A Manual . . . (1974).

JUTTA SØRENSON

Australia

Australia is an independent nation formed in 1901 from the federation of six states: New South Wales, Queensland, South Australia, Tasmania, Victoria, and Western Australia. Two later creations, the Northern Territory and the Australian Capital Territory, are to all intents and purposes states as well. Australia is both the world's largest island and its smallest continent. It lies in the Southern Hemisphere, between the Pacific and Indian oceans. Population (1991 est.) 17,300,000; area 7,713,364 sq.km. The official language is English.

European settlement dates from 1788, but Australia now has a strongly multicultural population because of a major immigration program since World

Melbourne Public Library in Victoria, opened to the public in 1856.

La Trobe Collection/State

War II. Almost 42 percent of the people living in Australia were born overseas or of at least one parent born overseas. The Aborigine peoples, who are thought to have been in Australia for at least 40,000 years, have been in a troubled political and social relationship with the European settlers since 1788. The question of reconciliation between the two peoples is seen as of major importance in the events leading to the centennial of federation in 2001.

History. Library development in Australia has been strongly influenced by the small population compared to the size of the country, the concentration of that population in cities and overwhelmingly on the southeast coast (known to many as the "Koala Triangle"), and the harsh climatic conditions pervading much of the continent. The provision of library services has been strongly influenced by the state governments; responsibility for providing library services to the public is shared by the Commonwealth (federal), state, and local governments. The Commonwealth government has taken strong financial initiatives in supporting higher education and some other library services since the late 1960s.

General reference library reading room of the State Library of New South Wales, one of Australia's largest libraries.

State Library of New South Wales

National Library. The National Library of Australia was established in 1902 as the Library of the first Commonwealth Parliament and in 1960 as an autonomous institution governed by its own Council. The archives function was subsequently separated into what is now the Australian Archives.

From the beginning the Parliament had grand aspirations for the National Library, stating that it should be developed on the lines of the Library of Congress in the United States. The Library's main tasks are to be a major provider of information services, the central agency for collecting and disseminating bibliographic data and other library services; the hub of the Australian library network, providing and supporting a wide range of resource-sharing and other cooperative services; and a national heritage institution, acquiring and preserving a comprehensive collection of Australian library material. Its holdings in 1991 included more than 2,700,000 monographs, about 2,000,000 microform equivalents, 105,000 current serials, and extensive collections of manuscripts, oral history, and pictorial and other heritage materials. It published a new collection development policy in 1990.

A major achievement of the Library was the establishment of the Australian Bibliographic Network (ABN) in 1981. ABN is a national resource-sharing network, providing cataloguing data to Australian libraries and enabling them to share their cataloguing effort to achieve significant cost savings. It also provides online access to nationwide information about the location of library materials and supports interlibrary loans. By 1991 more than 1,100 libraries used ABN, which had almost eight million bibliographic records in its database and thirteen million locations for items in Australian libraries.

The National Library has played a strong leadership role since the early 1980s. It convened an Australian Libraries Summit meeting in 1988 to reach agreement on the most effective structures and processes for delivering library and information services throughout the nation to the year 2000. Its "Towards Federation 2001" conference of 1992, based on a similar planning process, was expected to formulate a similar agenda for improving control and access to

Libraries in Australia (1990)

Type of library	Number of administrative units (main libraries)	Number of service points (branches, mobile stops, etc.)	Volumes in collections	Annual expenditures (Australian dollar)	Population served	Professional staff (with certificate, diploma, etc.)	Total staff
National	1	1	4,850,000	38,000,000	17,300,000	224	589
Academic	67	209	30,000,000	200,000,000	420,000	n.a.	4,250
Public	n.a.	1,400	27,600,000	212,000,000	17,300,000 (6.3 mill. registered)	n.a.	5,160
School	10,000	10,000	65,000,000	233,000,000	3,200,000	2,745	6,100
Special	1,100	1,100	n.a.	n.a.	n.a.	n.a.	n.a.
Other							
State/ Territory	8	8	6,772,000	72,000	17,300,000	705	1,500

Australia's heritage collections. Aboriginal access will be a key element of that agenda.

State Libraries. State governments founded their own libraries before federation, and the state libraries were the most important libraries in the country until the mid-20th century. The rapid growth of the National Library and of academic libraries reduced the relative importance of the state libraries in terms of the bibliographic resources of the nation, but all are the prime repositories for state heritage materials. The Australian collections of the State Library of New South Wales are of particular national importance. There has been a major resurgence of the state libraries since 1980, partly because of new buildings for them in Western Australia, New South Wales, and Queensland. Technological developments have enabled them to play a much stronger role in coordinating the public library systems in their states.

Academic Libraries. As a result of a report of a government inquiry in 1957, the Commonwealth government committed itself to a massive funding program for universities, colleges of advanced education, and institutes of technical and further education which led to a great expansion of academic libraries in Australia. At that time there were nine universities whose libraries had a total stock of 1,500,000 volumes. By 1982 there were 19 universities with 15,400,000 volumes. Dramatic changes in higher education in the late 1980s replaced the previous system of universities and colleges of advanced education with a unified national system of universities. By 1990 there were 35 university libraries with an estimated total bookstock of 30,000,000 and about 300,000 serials subscriptions.

The two oldest university libraries, those of the University of Sydney (founded 1851) and the University of Melbourne (1853) remain the largest, with collections (including microform equivalents) totalling approximately 4,200,000 and 2,500,000 volumes. Several other university libraries have considerable strength, but many are comparatively new. An inquiry into library services in higher education in 1990 made major recommendations for further development.

The 300 Technical and Further Education (TAFE) colleges were estimated in 1990 to hold about 2,500,000 items; these colleges serve about a million users. The Commonwealth government proposed taking over funding for the TAFE colleges from the states in 1991.

Resource-sharing has traditionally been a subject of great interest to academic libraries, and the Committee of Australian University Librarians (CAUL) is responsible for promoting cooperation and the exchange of statistical and policy information. CAVAL (Cooperative Action by Victorian Academic Libraries) in Victoria was established in 1976 as a consortium of the academic libraries and the State Library of Victoria to encourage resource sharing. UNISON is the latest in a series of such consortia among academic libraries in New South Wales. The development of regional databases, and their relationship to the ABN, is a subject of keen interest.

Public Libraries. The provision of public library service is largely the responsibility of local government authorities and the state governments. Administrative patterns and service arrangements vary widely from one state to another. In the common pattern in the mainland eastern states, local governments own and provide public library services, with the states providing some coordination and financial support. By contrast, the Library and Information Service of Western Australia (LISWA) provides the bookstock for all public libraries, with local governments providing the buildings. In Tasmania the state government operates an integrated public library service with strong local government involvement.

Two key issues in the development of public library services in Australia are the question of possible federal support and a continuing debate over whether all services should be free. A public inquiry of 1975–76 recommended significant Commonwealth funding for public library services, a proposal repeated by a Parliamentary inquiry in 1991. The Commonwealth government held fast to its belief that the other two levels of government should support funding for public library services.

The Australian Libraries Summit of 1988 recommended a distinction between the concept of free core services and value-added services that could be charged for; this idea has been the subject of bitter debate in the professional community. Several state governments accepted the idea, but others strongly supported the principle of totally free public library services.

School Libraries. Commonwealth funding assistance starting in the 1960s led to sustained improvement in school libraries, in both state and private school systems. But federal funding came to an end in

1986. School libraries have been hit by the economic recession. One remaining federal/state funding project is the curriculum corporation (formerly ASCIS) database that is the basis for the nationwide shared cataloguing program for school libraries.

There were at least fifty million volumes in the more than 10,000 school libraries in 1990. The country has about 80 *joint-use* libraries, most of them school-housed public libraries in South Australia. The success of this program, which began in 1977, has attracted international attention. Since the mid-1980s there has been an increased emphasis on the need for students to become information literate if they are to function effectively in the information society of our times. This shift has led to a redefinition of the role of the teacher-librarian from a resource manager to a partner with classroom teachers in helping students to acquire the information skills they will need in order to become lifelong learners.

Special Libraries. Australia's special libraries are not well documented, but there are more than 1,500 of them serving the needs of government departments, commercial, professional, and religious organizations, and other bodies. The importance of their resources has become clear since the 1980s as they have become better known through inclusion in the Australian Bibliographic database operated through ABN. The Commonwealth and state Parliaments all have strong Parliamentary libraries with a wide range of functions. The Commonwealth Parliamentary Library, with a continuous history since 1902, has developed a strong legislative research service since the 1970s. The information and library services of the Commonwealth Scientific and Industrial Research Organization (CSIRO), based not only on central services but also on a strong network of branch libraries throughout Australia, is particularly important in providing scientific and technical information. It is not a de facto national scientific and technological library, because its primary purpose is to meet CSIRO's needs, but its holdings, along with those of the university libraries and the National Library, are central to meeting Australia's research needs in science and technology.

The libraries of government departments and agencies at both the federal and the state level are an important part of the nation's library resources. Organizational details vary from one unit to another, but the usual pattern is for these libraries to be administratively the responsibility of the department or agency concerned. Up to about 1970, some state libraries provided coordinating mechanisms and provided staffs for these libraries.

Librarians working in special libraries have traditionally played a strong role in professional activities in Australia, in part because geographic and employment isolation encourages such activities. Australian special libraries, especially those in the business, health, and law sectors, have actively incorporated advanced computing and telecommunications technologies into their services.

The Profession. The Australian Library and Information Association (ALIA) is the major professional body in Australia, with membership open not only to professional librarians but also to others working in libraries or interested in the development of librarianship in the country. It was founded as the Australian Institute of Librarians (AIL) in 1937, succeeded by the Library Association of Australia in 1949, and changed its name to ALIA in 1990 after a review of its structure and policies in the mid-1980s. The change of name signals the Association's interest in broadening its membership to include other interested information professionals. Its membership in 1992 stood at 8,000, including about 4,500 professional members. After considerable debate, the Association moved in 1990 from its traditional location in Sydney to a prestigious new purpose-built headquarters in Canberra.

ALIA has always had a strong interest in education for librarianship in Australia, which was developed originally on the British pattern of an examination system conducted by the professional association. This system was finally phased out in 1981, with professional education now embedded in university schools of librarianship and education for library technicians in the TAFE system. In 1992 there were 15 institutions offering professional education and 19 providing library technical education.

There are a wide range of other professional associations and special interest groupings in Australia. The Australian School Libraries Association (ASLA), a federation of state associations of school librarians, works closely with ALIA. The Australian Council of Libraries and Information Services (ACLIS) is a voluntary cooperative association representing the interests of Australian libraries. It has more than 600 members, including almost all the major research libraries and a significant number of special and public libraries. Its main responsibilities are representing the interests of Australian libraries to governments and encouraging national cooperation among libraries.

ACLIS was established in 1988 by the amalgamation of the Australian Libraries and Information Council (ALIC), formed by all governments in 1981 to provide advice on library development, and the Australian Advisory Council on Bibliographical Services (AACOBS), funded by the National Library since 1956 to promote cooperation among libraries.

REFERENCES

ALIAS: Australia's Library, Information and Archives Services: An Encyclopedia of Practice and Practitioners, 3 volumes (1988–91).

Australia, Parliament, House of Representatives, Standing Committee for Long-term Strategies, *Australia as an Information Society: Grasping New Paradigms* (1991).

Australia, Parliament, House of Representatives, Standing Committee for Long-term Strategies, *Australia as an Information Society: The Role of Libraries/Information Networks* (1991).

WARREN C. HORTON

Austria

A federal republic in central Europe, Austria is bounded by Germany and Czechoslovakia on the north, Hungary on the east, Yugoslavia and Italy on the south, and Switzerland and Liechtenstein on the west. Population (1990 est.) 7,712,000; area 83,853 sq.km. The official language is German.

History. The Austrian library scene, like that of other old European nations, originates in a few monastic centers. Salzburg, the oldest library on Austrian territory, was founded about 700 and Mondsee in 748. More than 100 others followed. The most famous still are Kremsmünster (777), St. Florian (1071), Admont (1074), Göttweig (1083), Melk (1089), St. Paul (1091), Klosterneuburg (1108), Heiligenkreuz (1136), Zwettl (1138), and Altenburg (1144). They house an abundant and precious stock of manuscripts (up to 1,300) and incunabula (up to 2,000) in libraries with wonderful baroque halls.

The early Hapsburgs laid the basis for the great Imperial Court Library in the 14th century. In 1365 the University Library of Vienna was founded; Graz, Innsbruck, and Salzburg followed.

In the 18th century, Empress Maria Theresa (ruled 1740–80) effected a series of library reforms. Following the dissolution of the Jesuit Order in 1773 and of many monasteries by Joseph II, a number of rare book collections were transferred to Studienbibliotheken (university libraries). Other collections went to newly established research libraries. Library affairs were centralized and a nationwide library network was created. The Ministry of Education took responsibility for research libraries, including the Austrian National Library, in 1918.

In the 19th and 20th centuries a great variety of new ministries, governmental bodies, universities, unions, chambers, institutes, and associations developed and with them new libraries with rapidly growing book collections. Old buildings have been remodeled and new ones constructed. Present emphasis is given to the preservation and conservation of the old stock, introduction of microforms, and especially the implementation of an integrated, computerized library system. The first result was the Austrian Periodical Data Base. Two further online networks followed, linking the pedagogical academies with the libraries of the working chambers and the federal research libraries.

The legal basis for research libraries is defined under two laws. The Universitäts-Organisationsgesetz (UOG) of 1975 altered the structure of university libraries, centralizing library operations in each main institution. The Forschungsorganisationsgesetz (FOG) of 1981 defines the main objectives of the Austrian National Library: the collection of "Austriaca," central planning of library concerns for the country, and training of research librarians.

National Library. The Österreichische Nationalbibliothek (Austrian National Library) began as the Kaiserliche Hofbibliothek (Imperial Court Library) of the Hapsburgs. Its earliest manuscript was acquired by Duke Albrecht III in 1368. Emperor Frederick III (reigned 1440–93) and his son Maximilian I (reigned 1493–1519) were devotees of the arts and sciences and avid book collectors. In 1575 Hugo Blotius became the collection's first full-time librarian. By 1590 the collection held 9,000 volumes. It grew to be the largest library of the German-speaking world, a position it held until the 19th century.

Austrian National Library

Prunksaal (State Hall) in the Austrian National Library, built by Johann Bernard Fischer von Erlach and his son Emmanuel in the early 1700s.

After the dissolution of the Austro-Hungarian Empire in 1918, the Library became the property of the Republic, gradually being transformed into a modern research library. It now has more than 2,500,000 printed books and periodicals, but it is most famous for its special collections, including manuscripts (about 100,000, more than 16,000 of which are dated before 1600), incunabula (about 8,000), autographs (305,454), maps (234,850), globes (145), printed music (106,036), papyrus (194,038, of which more than 100,000 were catalogued in the 1980s), portraits (721,129), photographs (722,376), and theatrical items (figures included in other counts). An Austrian Theatre Museum was founded in 1991.

Libraries in Austria (1990)

Type of library	Number of administrative units (main libraries)	Number of service points (branches, mobile stops, etc.)	Volumes in collections	Annual expenditures (schilling)	Population served	Professional staff (with certificate, diploma, etc.)	Total staff
National	1	--	2,737,433	10,733,340	438,539	139.4	270.9
Academic	21	--	15,591,448	214,558,973	3,185,535	1,938.5	8,370
Public	1,216	2,374	8,195,315	n.a.	869,292	683	4,665
School	9	--	574,832	3,904,860	25,861	21	37
Special	32	--	6,248,157	42,217,119	191,246	166.3	353.6

Austrian National Library

Main Reading Room, Austrian National Library.

As the central library of the nation, it houses the Planning Center for Research Libraries; the Österreichische Zeitschriftendatenbank (ÖZDB; Austrian Periodicals Database); a Union Catalogue for all new foreign monographs acquired by research libraries since 1930 (Büchernachweisstelle); the fortnightly Austrian National Bibliography (since 1946), which listed for 1987 a total of 9,642 titles; the final stage of professional training for research librarians; the Institute for Restoration; the Vereinigung Österreichischer Bibliothekare (VÖB; Association of Austrian Librarians); and the Austrian Literature Archive (founded 1990). It is a depository library for all Austrian publications.

The library building was erected on the premises of the court in Vienna in 1723 and is still expanding. The most recent important expansion is a four-floor underground library designed to hold about four million books. The library's showcase is the magnificent baroque Prunksaal (State Hall).

Academic Libraries. Under the UOG of 1975, Austrian university libraries have taken a prominent role. There are four full universities, at Vienna, Graz, Innsbruck, and Salzburg; two general technical universities, at Graz and Vienna; and 14 schools and academies for the study of special fields such as theology, educational sciences, social sciences, design, music, art, commerce, mining, agriculture, and veterinary medicine. The oldest academic library is the University Library of Vienna (founded 1365). Under the terms of the UOG, it is the largest library of Austria, with combined holdings of 4,753,014 volumes, including those of more than 100 faculties and institutes; next is Graz (1573), with a total of 2,098,773 volumes. Almost all the universities have had to expand their library buildings or build new ones. Prominent are the University Library of Salzburg and the Technical University Library in Vienna.

Public Libraries. Public library services are about 100 years old in Austria. Initiated by religious and political bodies in Vienna, they developed particularly after World War II. There are more than 2,000 such libraries. The main groups are: municipal libraries (672 branches with 3,550,666 volumes); religious libraries (Österreichisches Borromäuswerk, 443 branches with 1,018,409 volumes); trade unions (442 branches with 1,355,135 volumes); and smaller groups such as reading societies, provincial libraries, infirmaries, and prisons. Most are run by volunteers, a few by professional librarians.

Special Libraries. Austria has a great variety of special libraries. Each of the nine provinces has a main library (Landesbibliothek) with the legal right of deposit; they range in size from 75,000 to 570,000 volumes. A number of libraries serve government bodies, ministries, chambers, museums, and scientific agencies, the most comprehensive collections of which are those of the Ministry of Defense (570,000 volumes), the Federal Chancellery (460,000), the Ministry of Education and the Ministry of Science and Research (354,000), the Patent Office (308,700), and the Museum of Natural History (389,400). Nongovernmental agencies and industrial and commercial enterprises also have significant collections. A modern special library is that of the International Atomic Energy Agency (80,000 books, 551,000 technical reports, and 1,024,000 documents).

School Libraries. Each province has a pedagogical academy, others are under the aegis of the church, and there are a few specialized schools (graphic arts and music, for example). Their libraries range in size from about 20,000 to 70,000 volumes. School libraries for elementary and higher education (about 6,000) are maintained by teachers. Some of them are used by teachers and pupils alike; some function as public libraries.

The Profession. Austria has no library school, nor any library science program at the university level. Regulations issued in 1979 provide for training at the professional (academic) and paraprofessional (secondary) levels, and a new *Fachdienst* (clerical) level has been added. Practical experience at one of six training libraries is followed by theoretical lectures at the Austrian National Library, with examinations at each stage.

Public librarians receive one year of practical training at training libraries, also with examinations. Continuing education is offered in the form of seminars, symposia, and various programs at professional meetings.

The Association of Austrian Librarians dates back to 1896. It had 901 certified members in 1987. Its official journals are *Mitteilungen der Vereinigung Österreichischer Bibliothekare* and *Biblos*. The proceedings of the biennial meetings are published in *Biblos-Schriften*.

The Verband der Österreichischen Volksbüchereien und Volksbibliothekare (Association of Austrian Public Libraries and Public Librarians) has more than 1,000 members. It issues *Erwachsenenbildung*. Other important associations are: Verein Österreichischer Archivare (Austrian Association of Archivists), with 333 members; Österreichische Gesellschaft für Dokumentation und Information (Austrian Society for Documentation and Information); and Österreichische Gesellschaft für Öffentlichkeitsarbeit des Informationswesens (Austrian Society for Publicity of the Information Sciences).

MARGARET R. STRASSNIG-BACHNER

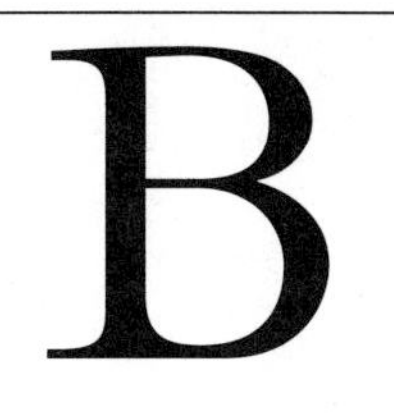

Bachtiar, Harsya W.
(1934–)

Harsya Wardhana Bachtiar, Indonesian educator, sociologist, anthropologist, and historian, was Dean of the Faculty of Letters, University of Indonesia, 1969–75. Concerned about the acquisition, storage, and accessibility of information, he actively involved himself in programs to increase the capacity of library, documentation, and archival centers in Indonesia to provide improved services.

Born in Bandung, Indonesia, May 3, 1934, he studied at the Faculty of Social and Political Science, University of Amsterdam, 1953–55; at the College of Arts and Sciences and then Graduate School of Arts and Sciences, Cornell University, 1955–59; and later at the Graduate School of Arts and Sciences, Harvard University, 1963–67. Bachtiar earned a Ph.D. in sociology from Harvard with a dissertation on "The Formation of the Indonesian Nation." He lectured at the Faculty of Letters, University of Indonesia, from 1959, becoming a full Professor of Sociology and Social History in 1976.

He served as Acting Director of the National Institute of Economic and Social Research (LEKNAS), Indonesian Institute of Science (LIPI), 1969–75. On the national level, he took an active part in the development of higher education and research in the social sciences as Coordinator of the Consortium of Social Sciences and Humanities, an advisory body to the Minister of Education and Culture, 1971–75, and then, among other work, as Executive Secretary of the Interdisciplinary Consortium, one of 11 consortia maintained to assist the Director General of Higher Education. Bachtiar served as a member of various official Indonesian delegations, such as the delegation to the annual conferences of the Southeast Asian Ministers of Education Organization (SEAMEO) at Kuala Lumpur, 1971, Saigon, 1972, and Vientiane, 1973; the delegation to the Unesco General Conference in Paris, 1974, when he was elected Vice-Chairman of Commission V (Social Science, Humanities, and Culture); in Nairobi, 1976, in Paris, 1983, and in Sofia, 1985. From 1975 he also served as Chairman of the Indonesian Steering Committee, Dutch-Indonesian Cooperation for the Promotion of Indonesia Studies.

He participated in many conferences on archives and worked closely with the Director of the National Archives of the Republic of Indonesia, particularly in matters of archival professional training, archival cooperation among Southeast Asian countries, archival cooperation between Indonesia and the Netherlands, and oral history.

In 1983 he became Head of the Office of Educational and Cultural Research and Development, Ministry of Education and Culture, Republic of Indonesia.

Among his many publications is a *Directory of Social Scientists in Indonesia* (Jakarta, 1976).

SOEMARTINI

Bahamas

An independent state off the southeast coast of the United States in the Atlantic Ocean, the Bahamas comprises 700 islands, of which only about 30 are inhabited. Population (1990 est.) 253,000; area 13,878 sq.km. The official language is English.

National Library Plan. Plans called for a library that would maintain a national union catalogue, national bibliography, national and international loan service, and strong local history collection. In the 1980s arrangements were envisaged for the library to become the official depository for all government and other publications of the Bahamas, as well as for copyrighted works. It would also possess audiovisual material and equipment, periodicals, and microforms and would include a high percentage of children's materials. The national library, it was hoped, would open with a minimum of 440,000 volumes (or 2 volumes per capita), with an increase of 100,000 over a 20-year period. The National Archives in the mid-1980s had holdings totaling about 2,300 linear feet and a staff of 21, including seven professionals.

Academic Libraries. The College of the Bahamas Library is the principal academic library in the Bahamas. It was established in 1975 and incorporated the Bahamas Teachers' College Library (now defunct), the Technical College Library, and the San Salvador Teachers' College Library. Its general collection numbers about 30,000 volumes and three special collections and includes Bahamian, African, and West Indian works; materials on teaching practice; and theses by students.

Public Libraries. There are five public libraries in Nassau and some 32 in the Family Islands (those outside Nassau). Public libraries, which operate as independent units under their respective boards of trustees, were established under the Nassau Public Library Act (1847) and the Out Island Public Library Act (1909). The public libraries were included in the portfolio of the Minister of Education from 1964. In 1972 the Government appointed a committee to raise funds to establish a Public Library Service.

School Libraries. The majority of the schools in the Bahamas (both government and private) possess libraries; comparative information and statistics on their collections were not available in the late 1980s.

Special Libraries. The Ranfurly Out Island Library, founded in Nassau in 1954, is a branch of an international charitable and voluntary organization with headquarters in London and branches in 63 countries. It is a nonsectarian and nonracial organization, primarily interested in building up school libraries. It sends free boxes of both adults' and children's books to Family Island head teachers, who make them available to the community. Approximately 200,000 volumes were donated in some 25 years. Some government departments have libraries in their agencies that serve the department and the Public Service (such as the Department of Statistics and the Public Service Training Centre).

REFERENCES

Enid Baa and Mary Heneghan, "Report to the National Library Committee on the Proposal for Establishing a Public Library Service in the Bahama Islands" (1973).

D. G. Reid, *Bahamas—Public Library Service* (1973).

D. GAIL SAUNDERS

Bahrain

Bahrain, an independent country in the Middle East, lies between Saudi Arabia and the Qatar Peninsula. It occupies 36 islands; Manama, the capital, is on the largest, Bahrain Island. Population (1990 est.) 503,000, including 325,000 Bahrainis and 164,000 expatriates; area 678 sq.km. The official language is Arabic, though English is widely used.

Bahrain does not have national library. There were almost 250 libraries in 1990, of which 14 were public, 4 academic, 170 school, and 60 special libraries. A total of 421 personnel were employed in the libraries, of whom only 76 held diplomas or degrees in library science. Almost all libraries are working to increase their professional staffing and to improve their collections. As in western countries, the use of microcomputers and information technologies is high on the agenda for most libraries.

Academic Libraries. There are four academic libraries: the University of Bahrain (UB), Arabian Gulf University (AGU), College of Medicine and Medical Sciences (CMMS) of AGU, and College of Health Sciences (CHS).

The University of Bahrain library, the largest academic library, was established in 1987 when the two largest academic institutions were merged. They were the University College of Arts, Science, and Education (formerly the Teachers Training College, founded in 1962) and the Gulf Polytechnic (formerly the Gulf Technical College, founded in 1968). UB has more than 5,000 students, with 1,000 faculty and staff. It offers undergraduate and postgraduate programs in five colleges: arts, business, education, engineering, and science. The UB library has more than 110,000 volumes of Arabic and non-Arabic material. It has about 18,000 periodical titles, both Arabic and non-Arabic. It is a depository library for United Nations and World Bank publications. The UB library makes extensive use of CD-ROM technology, subscribing to more than 50 frequently used bibliographic databases in CD format.

The Arabian Gulf University is sponsored by the Arab Bureau of Education in Riyadh, a regional body representing Bahrain, Iraq, Kuwait, Oman, Qatar, Saudi Arabia, and the United Arab Emirates. AGU's main campus, in newly constructed buildings in Saquer, has faculties in special education and applied technology, offering postgraduate degree and diploma programs. Its library has 10,000 volumes in Arabic and non-Arabic languages.

The College of Medicine and Medical Sciences is AGU's oldest college, founded in 1983 and situated at the Salmanya Medical Center in Manama. Its library has a total of 15,000 volumes and its periodical holdings include more than 700 titles. It offers online database searching services through DIALOG.

The College of Health Sciences was founded in 1976 as the School of Nursing. It trains students to work in hospitals and health centers as paramedical professionals, primarily nurses and lab technicians. Its library is a depository for World Health Organization publications. It has 20,000 catalogued volumes and 535 periodical subscriptions. Two main CD-ROM database systems have been installed: BiblioFile for cataloguing and MEDLINE for reference.

Although cooperation among academic libraries exists, insufficient backruns of periodicals require most libraries to rely on the British Library Document Supply Centre for interlibrary loan. Librarians at UB began work in the early 1990s on a new edition of the *Bahrain Union List of Serials and Standing Orders.* Prepared by UB staff, it includes academic, special, and school libraries. Academic libraries also handle and distribute textbook orders.

Public Libraries. The first public library was established in 1946. Today Bahrain has a Manama Public Library with 11 branch libraries. It is a depository for Unesco and government publications. Public libraries are part of the Ministry of Education, which has a Directorate of Libraries for overall public library operations. The system has almost 125,000 volumes, more than 600 periodical subscriptions, and almost 2,000 audiovisual items. In the early 1990s, the library circulated more than 330,000 volumes annually to about the same number of patrons.

The Manama Public Library (MPL) has assumed responsibility for acquiring five deposit copies of each book published in Bahrain. The MPL is the headquarters for the public library system, providing centralized purchasing, cataloguing, and processing for all public libraries. MPL has a music library and a mobile library. MPL and other branch libraries have children's sections equipped with AV equipment and materials.

The director is the chief executive officer of the

Libraries in Bahrain (1990)

Type of library	Number of administrative units (main libraries)	Number of service points (branches, mobile stops, etc.)	Volumes in collections	Annual expenditures (dinar)	Population served	Professional staff (with certificate, diploma, etc.)	Total staff
National	0	--	--	--	--	--	--
Academic	3	5	190,000	--	8,500	7	75
Public	1	11[a]	199,000[a]	--	700,000	1	50
School	170	170	186,000[b]	--	92,862[b]	3	--
Special	65	70	14,000[c]	--	11,800[c]	5	--

[a]1986 data
[b]1987 data
[c]1983 data

Source: Unesco, *Statistical Yearbook,* 1991, and author.

public library system, with two key assistants, the Chief of the Central Library (MPL) and Chief of Branch Libraries. A total of 90 staff work in the system, of whom 21 have the title of librarian. Of these, 10 hold Bachelor's degrees in library science and 11 hold Bachelor's degrees in other disciplines.

School Libraries. The Ministry of Education operates 147 elementary, intermediate, and secondary schools, 69 for females and 78 for males. By the end of the 1980s, total student enrollment was almost 91,000. Bahrain also has nearly 30 private schools supported by various organizations and embassies. Each school must have a library in order to be accredited. Among government schools, the best libraries are found in secondary schools.

Of the 100 persons staffing the government school libraries, 40 have Bachelor's degrees, some in library science. A few elementary school libraries are staffed with voluntary part-time staff; all secondary school libraries have qualified librarians. The Ministry of Education has a centralized acquisition and processing department that distributes books to schools. Individual schools can also purchase materials through their own administration using private funds.

Among the 30 private schools, the largest is the Indian School, with an enrollment of more than 5,000 students. It has two qualified librarians and a collection of 12,000 volumes and 120 periodical titles. Bahrain School, an American school, received the U.S. Presidential award in 1985 as one of the outstanding overseas American educational institutions. Its library contains 27,000 volumes and 160 periodicals and has a fully equipped media center. The Saint Christopher's School, a British school, has a library of 11,000 volumes. Ibn Khuldun School and Al-Bayan School have good library facilities with qualified librarians. Other private schools with libraries include the Sacred Heart School, Pakistani School, Urdu School, Asian School, and Habara School.

The Educational Technology Center (formerly Audiovisual Aid Center) was established in 1984 under the Ministry of Education to provide AV equipment for government school libraries. It has nearly 1,000 films. With its help, the role of school libraries has expanded, and they are now being called Learning Resource Centers or School Media Centers.

Special Libraries. Bahrain has some new special libraries, but government libraries represent the largest category. The 16 government ministries and several government organizations have their own libraries. Bahrain Center for Studies and Research (BCSR), a government institute, supports research in social and applied sciences; it is the equivalent of the U.S. National Science Foundation. The BCSR library has 4,000 volumes and subscribes to 200 journals. It offers online search facilities through DIALOG and has direct links with the Kuwait Institute of Scientific Research (KISR) through DIAL-IN. This link provides direct access to the KISR database, which consists of KISR Library holdings.

Bahrain Document Center was established under the Crown Prince's Office. It has a collection of 5,000 volumes and a large collection of manuscripts and documents related to Bahrain and other Gulf countries. It issues *Al-Watheeqa,* a scholarly journal of Bahrain.

The newly constructed University of Bahrain Library is the country's largest academic library.

Bahrain Defence Forces (BDF) has a Central Library and three branch libraries, one of them a medical library attached to BDF hospital. Other medical libraries include those attached to the American Mission Hospital and the International Hospital.

The British Council Library (BCL) has more than 12,000 volumes and several journals of wide interest. The U.S. Embassy has a commercial library and a student advisory service. Dawa and Irshad library, sponsored by the Saudi Arabian Educational Mission in Bahrain, has a good collection of books on Islam, Hadith, and related topics. In 1977 a regional United Nations Information Center (UNIC) was established in Bahrain. Its aim is to provide information on the UN and its agencies to Bahrain, Qatar, and United Arab Emirates, which all gained UN membership in 1971. UNIC is open to the general public as well. It has 10,000 items, including periodicals from all UN agencies and a large section of documentary films.

Bahrain is a center for off-shore banking and has libraries and information centers attached to many banks. The Bahrain Monetary Agency (BMA) library has a collection of 5,000 volumes and subscribes to 50 periodicals. The Arab Banking Corporation, Gulf International Bank, National Bank of Bahrain, Bank of Bahrain and Kuwait, and Arab Insurance Group have libraries or information centers.

Bahrain Petroleum Company (BAPCO) has two libraries: technical and recreational. The recreational library has 13,000 volumes and 75 periodical subscriptions. Bahrain Aluminium, Gulf Petrochemical Industries Corporation, Bahrain National Gas Company, and others also have technical libraries. A number of training centers, such as the Bahrain Bankers Training Center, Management Consulting Group, BATELCO Training Center, and Bahrain Institute of Finance, have their own libraries.

Such groups as the Bahrain Historical and Archaeological Society, Bahrain Medical Association, Bahrain Arts Society, and Bahrain Society for Engineers have libraries for their members. Beit Al-Qur'an (Koran) (Qur'an House) Library, housed in an attractive building in downtown Manama, has a collection on Holy Qur'an and its associated literature. Its materials include translations of the Qur'an from all parts of the world. The newly constructed headquarters of Bahrain National Museum has a library containing 8,000 volumes and a special collection related to Bahrain.

The Profession. The University of Bahrain has a postgraduate diploma program in Learning and Information Resources, the first library professional program in the country. It is jointly sponsored by the Department of Education and the University Library. The Ministry of Education sponsored 33 working librarians under this program in its first years of operation. Students must complete 30 credit hours. By the late 1980s, six Bahrainis had completed their studies abroad and returned with MLS degrees and postgraduate diplomas in library and information science from Canada, the United Kingdom, and the United States. They have assumed a leadership role in the profession. Most local library staff received their library qualifications in Saudi Arabia, Egypt, Qatar, or the United Arab Emirates.

There is still no professional body or association of librarians or information specialists. Discussion on forming a Bahrain Library Association led to an outline of bylaws and activities in 1985, but little progress has been made since.

REFERENCES

Central Statistical Organization, *Statistical Abstract 1988.*

Directorate of Public Libraries, *Facts and Figures about Public Libraries, 1989.*

S. NAZIM ALI

Baker, Augusta

(1911–)

Ronald Bright

Augusta Baker

Augusta Baker, distinguished American librarian, administrator, educator, author, raconteur, and folklorist, won a preeminent place in library service to children. She was born April 1, 1911, in Baltimore, Maryland, and received a Bachelor of Arts in Education from the State University of New York in 1933 and a Bachelor of Science in Library Science from the same institution in 1935. From 1937 to 1974 Baker was a staff member of the New York Public Library, where her career was marked by notable contributions in service to children in the areas of administration, collection development, programs, and services.

As a children's librarian in the Countee Cullen Regional Branch from 1937 to 1953, she pioneered in the momentous task of bringing to the children of Harlem a knowledge of and appreciation for their cultural heritage and background. Working closely with Arthur Schomburg, whose unique collections of materials relating to the black experience were housed in the Branch Library, and with certain Harlem women interested in black culture, she established the James Weldon Johnson Memorial Collection for children because of Johnson's interest in the children and the Library. Enriching experiences for children and adults were made possible and augmented through her programs of storytelling, concerts, reading clubs, visits of school classes, and guest appearances of eminent black artists, writers, dramatists, and other specialists from various professions.

Entering into the administration of library service to children in the New York Public Library, Baker served as Assistant Coordinator and Storytelling Specialist from 1953 to 1961. Her established reputation as a storyteller and folklorist enabled her to continue the great tradition of the Library in utilizing the art form of storytelling in bringing together children and books. Creative and gifted, she shared her talents with others in and outside the Library through inspired instruction and guidance.

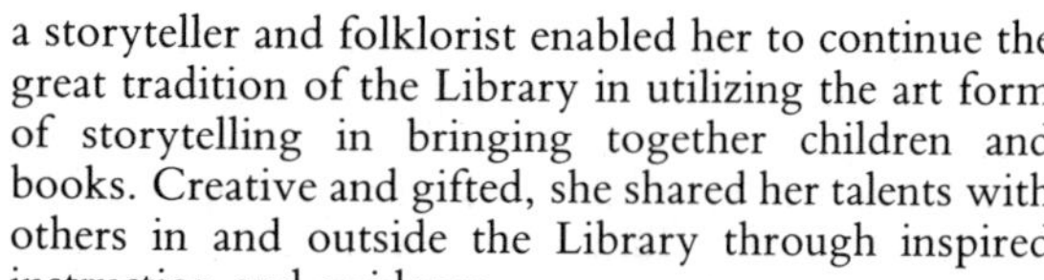

Administratively, she furthered the work of library service to children with the renowned Coordinator of the Children's Department, Frances Lander Spain. Recognized as an authority in the field of black literature for children, Baker continued her research in the area with a Dutton-Macrae Award, given to her in 1953 by the American Library Association. Her subsequent publication, *Books about Negro Life for Children* (1963), was a landmark and became a prototype for several revised editions under the new title *The Black Experience in Children's Books.* During this same year she accepted an invitation to organize children's library service for the Trinidad Public Library, Port of Spain, Trinidad. She began a teaching career in 1955 as a Visiting Lecturer in the Columbia University School of Library Service.

The year 1961 was significant for the New York Public Library when Baker was appointed Coordinator of Children's Services. The Library's administrators established a precedent for large urban library systems by elevating a member of an ethnic minority group to a high-level policy-making position. Extending the traditional boundaries of service in the Library's 82 branches and six bookmobiles in Manhattan, the Bronx, and Staten Island, Baker expanded the children's collections to include recordings; she enlarged the annual bibliography of children's books to include special juvenile materials. Utilizing the media of television and radio, she initiated the series of weekly broadcasts "The World of Children's Literature" on WNYC in 1971 and moderated the television program "It's Fun to Read." She also served as a consultant and bibliographer of materials for the television program "Sesame Street" and later produced programs for South Carolina instructional and educational television.

A member of the adjunct faculty in the College of Library and Information Science, the University of South Carolina, she was appointed Storyteller-in-Residence in 1980. Her activities include giving statewide lectures and workshops related to the art of storytelling, the preservation of the oral tradition, and the study of folklore for all age and interest groups.

Baker's influence as a librarian, storyteller, and authority on materials for children is national and international in scope. She lectured or taught at many universities, including Rutgers (1965–67), Syracuse (1955–60), and Texas Woman's University (1975–), and the universities of Nevada at Las Vegas, Southern Florida, and Washington. She lectured before the Australian Library Association in 1973 and participated in conferences of the International Board on Books for Young People (IBBY). Active in the ALA from 1953, she served as Councillor (1965–72), member of the ALA Executive Board (1968–72), chair of the ALA Advisory Committee to the Westinghouse Broadcasting Company, and member of various committees in the Public Library Association. In ALA's Association for Library Service to Children (formerly the Children's Services Division or CSD), she was a member of the Board of Directors (1958–61 and 1966–69), Vice President and chair of the Newbery/Caldecott Awards Committee (1966), President (1967), member of the Notable Books Committee, and member of the CSD Advisory Committee for Library U.S.A. at the New York World's Fair (1964–65); member of the ALA/Children's Book Council Joint Committee; member of the Hans Christian Andersen Award Committee (1974–78); and representative to UNICEF for the ALA/International Board on Books for Young Children. Recognizing her many years of service, ALA extended to her its highest award, Honorary Life Membership, in 1975.

Other professional activities included co-founder and co-chair of the Friends of (New York Public Library) Children's Services (1975) and delegate to the 1950 and 1970 White House Conferences on Children. She also served as a consultant to the Council on Library Resources, the Teen Age Book Club of Scholastic Books, and *Children's Digest* magazine.

Baker received many awards and honors, including the *Parent's Magazine* Medal (1966); ALA Grolier Foundation Award (1968); Constance Lindsay Skinner Award of the Women's National Book Association (1971); Clarence Day Award (1974); Distinguished Alumna Award of the State University of New York at Albany (1974); and Regina Medal of the Catholic Library Association (1981). In 1989 she received the first Zora Neal Hurston Award from the Association of Black Storytellers. She received honorary degrees from Saint John's University, Queens, New York (1978) and the College of Library and Information Science, University of South Carolina (1986), where she is honored annually by the presentation "A Baker's Dozen."

Among the publications she authored are *Talking Tree* (1955), *Golden Lynx* (1960), *Young Years* (1960), and *Readings for Children* (1964). She compiled *The Black Experience in Children's Books* (1971) and co-authored, with Ellin Green, *Storytelling: Art and Technique* (1977; 2nd edition, 1987). She wrote chapters in six monographs and introductions or forewords in seven publications. Her journal articles appeared in the *Horn Book, Junior Libraries, Modern Maturity, Top of the News,* and *Wilson Library Bulletin*. Her reviews of materials for children were published in many professional periodicals. Her preeminence in the field of public library service to children was recognized nationally and internationally.

SPENCER G. SHAW

Bangladesh

Bangladesh, a people's republic and member of the Commonwealth in the northeastern Indian subcontinent on the Bay of Bengal, is one of the most densely populated countries in the world. Population (1990 est.) 115,594,000; area 143,998 sq.km. The official language is Bangla (Bengali).

History. Prior to 1972, the area was East Pakistan; before the partition of India in 1947, it was the province of East Bengal and the Sylhet district of Assam. Libraries suffered great losses during the Bangladesh War in 1971, and the young country, hindered by lack of financial resources, is still struggling to rebuild its collections.

Only 5 percent of the people in Bangladesh live in Dhaka, the capital, yet more than 75 percent of the library resources are there. Dhaka houses the premier academic library, the National Library, and nearly all of the special libraries. Most of the libraries in Bangladesh have noncirculating collections, limiting their use to nearby residents.

A key factor in the development of libraries in Bangladesh is the infusion of support from donors in the developed countries. Most Western nations have active aid programs operating in Bangladesh and a few of those resources are directed to libraries. The most sophisticated libraries in the country are those specialized collections financed partly from external sources. While modern technology was available to only a few libraries in Bangladesh in the 1980s, professional librarians, especially those with training from abroad, were eager to automate and computerize their operations.

National Library. In 1972 the Directorate of Archives and Libraries established the Bangladesh National Library and the Bangladesh National Archives. Both were still small and developing in the 1980s, but the Bangladeshi government targeted the National Library as one of its core projects.

The Copyright Ordinance of 1974 mandated that the National Library receive copies of all books published in Bangladesh. (Only 616 books were published in Bangladesh in 1983.) The 75,000-volume collection consists of Bengali, Urdu, and English-language materials. The Library also collects journals and newspapers published in Bangladesh. No circulation of materials is permitted. From 1973 the Library published the annual *Bangladesh National Bibliography* in both English and Bangla.

The Archives of East Pakistan were housed in Lahore, in West Pakistan. Therefore, after independence the new country was left with virtually no official records. In the years after 1971 the National Archives surveyed materials from the divisional government offices around the country and trained archivists to prepare the materials. In November 1985 the National Library and the National Archives moved to a seven-story air-conditioned permanent building that provides 60,000 square feet of working space.

Academic Libraries. Six academic libraries serve Bangladesh's 42,800 university students: Dhaka University (established 1921), 500,000 volumes; Rajshahi University (1953), 230,000 volumes; Bangladesh University of Engineering and Technology (1962), 87,800 volumes; Chittagong University (1966), 117,000 volumes; Mymensingh Agricultural University (1966), 123,700 volumes; and Jahangirnagar University (1970), 50,000 volumes. All six libraries are staffed with professional librarians, have varied collections of foreign and domestic journals and newspapers, and offer reference services and bibliographic instruction to their patrons. There is no formal interlibrary loan arrangement among the university libraries, but materials are made available to students and faculty through informal contacts. Most of the academic libraries have established interlibrary loan arrangements with the British Library Lending Division.

Because textbooks are expensive for individuals to buy and not readily available in Bangladesh, most of the university libraries have large textbook collections. At Bangladesh University of Engineering and Technology, students borrow textbooks from a lending library. Circulation of nontextbooks is limited in most libraries to faculty and graduate students. The majority of materials are in English, with Bangla, Urdu, Arabic, and Persian comprising the remainder of the collections.

The Dhaka University Library is the premier library in the country. Its collection of 500,000 volumes is the largest in Bangladesh and covers all academic disciplines except engineering, technology, and medicine. The Library has a professional staff of 57 librarians. In addition to its direct role in serving Dhaka University faculty and students, the library has assumed a significant role in collecting and preserving the archives of Bangladesh. It houses 25,000 handwritten manuscripts, many from the 14th and 15th centuries, reflecting the literature and culture of Bengal. Among its rare book collection is the periodical *Dhaka Prakash,* a major periodical of local news from 1890 to 1914. The Library also microfilms local journals and newspapers.

Public Libraries. The Bangladesh Central Public Library (BCPL), Dhaka, is the headquarters of the Public Library Department and administers the government-sponsored divisional and district public libraries. Part of the Dhaka University Library before 1963, BCPL has a collection of 100,00 volumes and is the focal point of all public libraries in Bangladesh. It also sponsors cultural exhibits and has a children's library.

In addition to the Central Public Library in Dhaka, divisional public libraries of approximately 30,000 volumes each are located in Chittagong, Khulna, and Rajshahi. There are 65 district level public libraries around the country, each with approximately 4,000 volumes. Thirty-six professional librarians staffed the 69 public libraries in the country in the mid-1980s.

The focus of the public libraries in Bangladesh is on textbooks, because the majority of patrons are students. Public libraries do not allow books to circulate, nor did they offer bookmobile or audiovisual services in the mid-1980s.

School Libraries. Library services to the 8,900,000 pupils attending 44,000 primary schools and 2,600,000 students attending the 9,000 secondary schools are limited. Most primary schools have no libraries; some secondary schools have library facilities, with teachers serving as librarians. The government made a strong effort to train school librarians in the 1980s. The school library collections range in size from 500 to 5,000 books, but most libraries are at the lower end of the scale. English, Bangla, and Urdu materials can be found in the libraries. Because audiovisual materials are not available and because media centers do not exist in school libraries, the Dhaka Teacher Training College Audio-Visual Education Center provides a mobile unit of audiovisual services to visit schools around the country.

Special Libraries. Special Libraries, both government and privately funded, play an important role in Bangladesh and are an integral part of the library system of the country. Most are associated with scientific organizations, research institutes, and government departments, and are staffed by professional librarians. The libraries of the Bangladesh Agricultural Research Council (BARC) and the International Center for Diarrhoeal Disease Research (ICDDR) are two examples of well-staffed special libraries receiving resources from Western countries. They offer reference services, literature searching, compilation of bibliographies, current awareness service, indexing and abstracting, and selective dissemination of information to their patrons.

BARC had eight professional librarians (1985), five of whom had training abroad. The Library uses a microcomputer database management system to publish subject bibliographies. BARC created the National Agricultural Library and Documentation Centre (NALDOC), which serves as the national center for AGRIS (Agricultural Research Information Service) and CARIS (Current Agricultural Research Information Service).

The ICDDR Library, part of a well-financed internationally acclaimed medical institute, has an 18,000-volume collection, collects 525 medical journal titles, and has a reprint collection of more than 12,000 articles, reports, and documents. The BARC and ICDDR libraries represent the most sophisticated operations in the country and show how external support can substantially upgrade collections and services in a developing country. Other special libraries of interest are the Bangladesh National Scientific and Technical Documentation Center (BANSDOC) and the National Health Library and Documentation Center and libraries of the Bangladesh Institute of

Libraries in Bangladesh (1990)

Type of library	Number of administrative units (main libraries)	Number of service points (branches, mobile stops, etc.)	Volumes in collections	Annual expenditures (taka)	Population served	Professional staff (with certificate, diploma, etc.)	Total staff
National[a]	1	1	75,000	800,000	--	25	73
Academic[a]	6	14	1,108,492	--	42,800	--	--
Public[b]	1	63	384,000	7,000,000	--	36	346
Special[a]	125	--	--	--	--	--	--

[a]1984 figures
[b]1986 figures

Source: Unesco, *Statistical Yearbook,* 1991 and *ALA World Encyclopedia,* 2nd ed. (1985)

Development Studies, Bangladesh Atomic Energy Commission, and Bangladesh Bank.

Some foreign governments also provide library services in Bangladesh. Most are in Dhaka and are heavily used by college and university students. The British Council Library has a collection of 50,000 volumes and more than 100 subscriptions to British journals and newspapers. More than a third of its books are textbooks for the use of college and university students. In addition, the Council offers English-language classes, cultural programs, and scholarships for study abroad. The American Cultural Center Library's 6,300-volume collection and 150 journals and 4 newspapers are used by about 175 students daily. Like the British Council, the American Cultural Center sponsors films, speakers, and cultural presentations, and promotes the idea of free public library services in Bangladesh.

The Profession. The Department of Library Sciences at Dhaka University, founded in 1959 with the introduction of a Diploma in Library Science, offered the only academic program for professional librarians in Bangladesh. In 1962 the Master of Arts degree program began. The Department offers the following degrees: Post-graduate Diploma in Librarianship, Master of Arts in Library Science, and Master of Philosophy in Library Science.

Nearly all librarians in Bangladesh are graduates of the Dhaka University program. The curriculum is traditional, but efforts are being made to expand it into several new areas of information science.

The Library Association of Bangladesh, founded in 1956, is the professional organization of librarians in the country. Total membership was 560 in 1985, with approximately 500 holding professional degrees. Meetings are held monthly. The association's journal, *The Eastern Librarian,* discontinued publication in 1978. While continuing education opportunities are limited for librarians in Bangladesh, several librarians have been awarded grants and fellowships from private sources for advanced training and education in other countries.

REFERENCES

East Pakistan Library Association and the British Council, *The Need for Public Library Development* (Dacca, 1966).

M. A. Syed, *Public Libraries in East Pakistan: Yesterday and Today* (1967).

JODY BALES FOOTE

Barbados

Barbados, an independent parliamentary state and member of the Commonwealth in the southern Caribbean Sea, is the easternmost island of the West Indies. Population (1990 est.) 255,000; area 430 sq.km. The language spoken is English.

History. Barbadian librarianship began in the 18th century with subscription libraries. An Act of 1847 established a Public Library and the Barbados Museum, but the system only took root in the 1920s. The entire library service has undergone changes since the mid-1980s, particularly libraries that were government-funded.

In 1980 the Minister of Information created a National Council on Libraries, Archives, and Documentation Centers (NACOLAD) to develop plans and make recommendations for a National Library Service. Two reports were eventually submitted to the Government—*A National Library and Information Service System in Barbados* (1981), by a consultant, Carl Keren, and the NACOLAD *Final Report.* As a result, the Barbados Library, Archives, and Information Center Network (BLAIN) was established in 1982, then replaced in 1985 by the National Library Service.

Barbados Government Information Service

The headquarters of the Public Library in Bridgetown, Barbados.

The National Library Service has direct responsibility for planning, developing, and administering public library services and for coordinating and supervising government department libraries. It is engaged in computerizing certain of its public library operations. It publishes the semi-annual *National Bibliography of Barbados,* which is compiled largely from receipts of legal deposit materials.

The National Library Service is associated with the Caribbean Network of Regional Information Systems and with local nongovernmental libraries for the purpose of sharing resources.

Academic Libraries. The University of the West Indies (U.W.I.) group of libraries comprise the major academic libraries. They are the Main Library (established 1963), the Library of the Faculty of Law (1971), the Library of the Institute of Social and Economic Research (Eastern Caribbean) (1962), and the Library of the Faculty of Education (1973). Other academic libraries are the Barbados Community College Library; the Medical Library of Queen Elizabeth Hospital, a teaching hospital for medical students of the University of the West Indies; Erdiston Teachers' Training College Library; and the Library of the Samuel Jackman Prescod Polytechnic.

Public Libraries. By the late 1980s public libraries included a main library, seven branches, and two mobile libraries. Services are free to all residents over five years of age. Its focus of activity is on lending and reference services. It publishes the popular quarterly *West Indian Collection: Additions.*

School Libraries. School libraries continue to be neglected. There were 21 secondary schools in the late 1980s serving approximately 50,000 pupils. Since 1985, many small primary schools have been amal-

Libraries in Barbados (1990)

Type of library	Number of administrative units (main libraries)	Number of service points (branches, mobile stops, etc.)	Volumes in collections	Annual expenditures (Barbados dollar)	Population served	Professional staff (with certificate, diploma, etc.)	Total staff
National*	1	10	159,000	--	--	--	--
Academic	7	8	215,990[a]	2,381,166[b]	5,500[a]	17[c]	65[d]
Public	2	76	131,135	3,360,160	257,000	15	73
School	23	89	--	--	48,940	1 Known	34
Special	13	13	145,919[e]	255,000[e]	1,216[e]	12[f]	21[e]

[a]Figures for 3 libraries
[b]Figures for 2 libraries
[c]Figures for 5 libraries
[d]Figures for 4 libraries
[e]Figures for 7 libraries
[f]Figures for 9 libraries
*1989 data

Source: Unesco, *Statistical Yearbook,* 1991, and author.

gamated and replaced by larger units. In theory each secondary school has a library; in reality, pupils rely on the public and university libraries. In the primary schools, there are "library corners" supplemented since 1968 by a basic service provided by the Public Library. Fortnightly visits by two mobile units to 70 primary schools fall short of remedying the deficiencies of the service. NACOLAD and the Ministry of Education began to address the problem in the late 1980s.

Special Libraries. Most of the special libraries are well run. They include the libraries of the Caribbean Development Bank (1970) and the Central Bank of Barbados (1974). Others of note are Christian Action for Development in the Caribbean (1971); Caribbean Meteorological Institute (1967); Barbados Development Bank (1980); and the Barbados Museum (1933). Some government departments have strong special collections. Since 1984 a number of new special libraries have sprung up in large corporations and regional and international agencies. These will be the future growth area in Barbadian librarianship.

The Profession. Librarianship is a growing profession in Barbados, continuing to gain in numbers and strength. In the past, training was sponsored by the National Library Service, but recently there have been private initiatives. The Humphrey Fellowship, established in 1987, and occasional Organization of American States grants assist students to obtain the master's degree.

Education is provided principally by the University of the West Indies (U.W.I.) in Jamaica, which offers two programs: a three-year course for nongraduates and a post-graduate fifteen-month course.

The Library Association of Barbados (1968) is the sole organization for the profession. It includes librarians, archivists, documentalists, and other interested persons. It publishes *Update,* an occasional newsletter.

REFERENCE

Carl Keren, *A National Library and Information Service System . . .: Report of a Consultancy Mission (September 1981)* (1981).

JUDY BLACKMAN

William J. Barrow Restoration Shop
William J. Barrow

Barrow, William J.
(1904–1967)

William James Barrow's research into the factors that cause paper to deteriorate resulted in the development of processes to restore and preserve precious library and archival materials. His work forms the basis for the increasing attention to the conservation and preservation of library resources in the United States and elsewhere.

Barrow was born December 11, 1904, in Brunswick County, Virginia, the son of a rural physician. After graduation from Randolph-Macon Academy in 1923, he attended Randolph-Macon College. For a time he was employed by a relative's company that manufactured overalls, but when the business faltered he turned his attention elsewhere.

In 1932 he became interested in document preservation and began to study bookbinding and the preservation techniques then in use at the Library of Congress. The Virginia State Library (VSL) gave him workshop space and document restoration assignments.

During the late 1930s Barrow operated a shop at the Mariners Museum in Newport News, Virginia, where he developed the first practical roller-type laminator for the lamination of weakened and disintegrating documents, using the cellulose acetate film that had been approved for the purpose by the National Bureau of Standards. In this laminator the document and the acetate film were preheated together and fed through the nip of two synchronously driven steel rolls. Not long after, Barrow began to add strong long-fibered tissue to his laminates, which made them stronger without sacrificing legibility. The acetate filled the interstices of the tissue in such a way that there was little light scattering, and the added layers were quite transparent.

In 1940 Barrow was back at the Virginia State Library operating a restoration shop and speculating on the causes of deterioration. It seemed likely that degradation of the paper would continue even after lamination if it were not stopped. Concluding that the major cause was acidity in the paper itself, he completed by the end of 1945 the development of a deacidification process in which solutions of calcium hydroxide and calcium and/or magnesium bicarbonate are used to neutralize acidity. Subsequent events have substantiated his judgment that paper acidity is the most important single cause of paper deterioration. Barrow now had the means of greatly reducing paper's rate of deterioration and restoring integrity and strength to paper already damaged. His laminators and techniques have since been obtained by more than 30 institutions throughout the world.

Barrow recognized early that much of his restoration work was on papers manufactured after 1875 and that many papers, much older, had no need of it. This was often ascribed to the use in modern papers of wood pulp, which came into fairly common use about that time, while some blamed it on an increasingly polluted industrial atmosphere. In 1957, with the sponsorship of the VSL and the support of the Council on Library Resources (CLR), he undertook a testing program involving papers from 500 books published between 1900 and 1949. Although it is true that the early wood pulps were not as good as they could have been and that atmospheric pollution is a deteriorative factor, this study showed that the poor condition of most of the papers examined was caused by acidity resulting from the use of alum-rosin sizing in their manufacture.

With the continued involvement of CLR and VSL and the advice of A. L. Rothschild and other paper industry people, Barrow planned a series of experiments, begun in the laboratories of the Herty Foundation in Savannah, Georgia, to determine whether modern methods and materials could be used to make an affordable long-lasting paper. This work culminated in December 1959 in the production of such a paper at Standard Paper Manufacturing Company in Richmond. Only chemical wood pulps were used; Aquapel sizing, which is compatible with mild alkalinity, replaced alum and rosin, and calcium carbonate was added to ensure that the paper would remain alkaline for many years.

Barrow then published tentative specifications for long-life paper, setting minimum performance at high but demonstrably attainable levels. At that time only his paper met those criteria, but in 1972 eight commercially available papers were identified that could meet similar requirements. Such papers have the physical strength to withstand handling and use (durability) and the chemical stability that makes their deterioration very slow (permanence).

In 1961 the CLR under the leadership of Verner W. Clapp, who was always interested and involved in Barrow's research, provided a grant that made possible the establishment of the W. J. Barrow Research Laboratory in the Virginia Historical Society Building. There Barrow studied polyvinyl acetate binding adhesives and defined the properties required for long useful life. Testing equipment was designed, and experimental work for the development of library binding performance standards was performed for the American Library Association. One study resulted in better catalogue card stock. Archival materials are protected from the migration of impurities by the acid-free file folders developed there. Barrow's test facilities and experience were brought to bear in the selection of paper for the ALA National Union Catalogue.

Barrow believed the two physical tests most relevant to printing and records paper durability were folding endurance and tear resistance. Extensive testing of a variety of papers at many temperatures showed that these two properties usually decline according to a predictable pattern and that the rate of decline is related to temperature in a specific and consistent way. This work gives credibility to predictions of paper's useful life at natural temperatures, which are based on test results from oven-aged samples. The research was also the basis of his suggestion that materials of great lasting value should be stored at low temperature.

The results of Barrow's research and the techniques he developed were reported in a number of publications. The restoration process is described in *The Barrow Method of Restoring Deteriorated Documents* (1965), and the research into the structure and materials of books was published in the five-part *Permanence/Durability of the Book* (1963–65). These and other publications form the basis for contemporary practice in restoration of deteriorating print materials.

Barrow died in Richmond, Virginia, August 25, 1967. The Laboratory continued its research until 1977. The Restoration Shop in the Virginia State Library continued in operation until the mid-1980s under Barrow's son, James A. Barrow, President.

DAVID D. ROBERSON

Batchelder, Mildred Leona
(1901–)

Mildred Batchelder

In July 1966 the Grolier Award was presented to Mildred Leona Batchelder, American children's librarian and library association executive, the citation praising her years of "devoted attention to children's reading and books for younger readers. Throughout her career she has emphasized the values of selectivity in books. . . . Her influence has been an international one, reaching children's and school librarians, and through them the children from coast to coast in America and also in foreign lands where she has lectured and traveled. Her judgment, her knowledge, her wit, her persuasive leadership have made her a national figure in the world of books."

Batchelder was born September 7, 1901, in Lynn, Massachusetts. She received a B.A. degree from Mt. Holyoke College in 1922 and a B.L.S. from New York State Library School, Albany, in 1924. She began her professional career as Head of the Children's Department, Omaha Public Library, Nebraska (1924–27), and served as Children's Librarian, State Teachers College, Saint Cloud, Minnesota (1927–28). She was Elementary and Intermediate School Librarian at the Haven School in Evanston, Illinois (1928–36).

In 1936 she joined the headquarters staff of the American Library Association as School Library Specialist, becoming Chief of the School and Children's Library Division in 1938. In 1946 she was named Acting Chief, Department of Information and Advisory Service, and a year later Chief of that department, a position she held until 1949, when a headquarters reorganization took place. Batchelder then became Executive Secretary of the Division of Libraries for

Children and Young People (DLCYP), which included the School Librarians Section. When the School Libraries Section achieved division status in 1951, Batchelder became half-time Executive Secretary for the DLCYP and half-time Special Assistant to the ALA Executive Secretary on Special Membership Promotion. She held those positions until 1954, when the DLCYP executive secretaryship was made a full-time position. With reorganization in 1957, she became the Executive Secretary of the Children's Services Division (CSD) and the Young Adult Services Division (YASD); she retired from that position in 1966.

During 30 years of service on the ALA staff, Batchelder made many significant contributions to the profession. The development, growth, and accomplishments of the units she worked with are evidence of her skill as a leader. A division president described her as "a catalyst of magical proportions." Many programs and projects begun under her direction were continued, including the Frederic G. Melcher Scholarship and the divisional journal, *Top of the News.*

Batchelder initiated working relationships with many people and organizations outside the library profession in the U.S. and abroad that continue to benefit libraries and librarians today. In 1960 the first edition of *Let's Read Together,* a family reading list, was published by ALA, the work of a Special Committee of the National Congress of Parents and Teachers and the Children's Services Division.

She represented ALA at the White House Conference on Children and Youth in 1950 and 1960 and participated in the planning. An active member of the Council of National Organizations for Children and Youth (CNOCY), she served as its Secretary and was a member of the National Committee on Children and Youth (NCOCY).

At a ceremony in 1966 held during the annual National 4-H Club Conference in Washington, D.C., Batchelder was one of seven leaders in business, education, and industry commended for outstanding contributions to 4-H Club work.

Batchelder held that children's books can be an aid to international understanding and worked toward that end in many ways. In 1949 the International Youth Library was established in Munich by Jella Lepman. The U.S. portion of the funds given during the launching of that unique project was a Rockefeller Foundation grant, administered by the CSD Office (1949–57) under Batchelder's direction.

She recognized the need for thoughtful selection of books to be translated, and a list of 100 children's books published from 1930 to 1954 "recommended for translation" was prepared by CSD in 1955 and distributed to Unesco, the U.S. Information Agency, library contacts in other countries, publishers, and others. Annual lists were prepared from 1955.

During a five-month sabbatical in 1964, Batchelder visited 11 European countries and studied the translation of children's books. She wrote later, "To know the classic stories of a country creates a climate, an attitude for understanding the people for whom that literature is a heritage. . . . Interchange of children's books between countries, through translation, influences communication between the people of those countries, and if the books chosen are worthy books, the resulting communication may be deeper, richer, more sympathetic, more enduring. I accept and believe these assumptions."

CSD established the Mildred L. Batchelder Award in 1966; the first award was given in 1968. A citation to an American publisher, the award is intended to encourage international exchange of quality children's books by recognizing publishers of such books in translation.

The Constance Lindsay Skinner Award of the Women's National Book Association was given to Batchelder in 1967.

RUTH TARBOX

Belgium

Belgium, a constitutional monarchy of Europe, is bounded by the North Sea on the northwest, the Netherlands on the north, the Federal Republic of Germany and Luxembourg on the east, and France on the south and southwest. Population (1990 est.) 9,845,000; area 30,519 sq.km. Languages are Dutch, French, and German. The Flemings of the northern provinces speak Dutch, the Walloons of the southern provinces speak French, and a small group in the southeast speak German. The capital, Brussels, is officially bilingual (Dutch and French).

History. The earliest library collection in what is now Belgium is probably the collection of illuminated manuscripts known as the *librarie de Bourgogne,* which became part of the holdings of the royal library, established in 1559. But there were probably significant collections in Antwerp around 1480, when printing was established in the city. In 1772 the Royal Library was made accessible to the public. Three popular libraries were established in the 1840s (at Furnes, Antwerp, and Ardenne), precipitating a sudden desire for this sort of collection; by 1884 there were 571 in the country. University libraries were also well established by this time, having taken over the collections of the city libraries in the cities of Ghent and Liège at the beginning of the 19th century.

National Library. The National Library in Brussels (Koninklijke Bibliotheek Albert I; Bibliothèque Royale Albert Ier) originated from the 15th-century library of the Dukes of Burgundy and was established as the Royal Library of Belgium in 1837. It performs the twofold function of a national library and a central research library. The act of Parliament instituting the Copyright Deposit (April 8, 1965), obligating each Belgian publisher to deposit one copy of each work, enables it to operate as a national library. The monthly issues of the Belgian Bibliography *(Belgische Bibliografie; Bibliographie de Belgique)* are published on the basis of the deposit copies. As a central research library, the Royal Library in Brussels has a number of specialized divisions and documentation centers. The divisions cover prints, manuscripts, precious works, music, the numismatic collection, and the collection of maps. The documentation centers are the National Center for Scientific and Technical Documentation, the Center for American Studies, the Center for African Documentation, and the Documentation Center for Tropical Agriculture and Rural Developmental Works. The Royal Library holds about 3,362,000 volumes, 26,000 current periodicals,

43,000 precious works, 305,000 government documents, 37,000 manuscripts, 180,000 coins and medals, 700,000 prints, 35,000 rare books, and 4,000 records. Although the Royal Library is a reference collection—all documents can be used on the premises only—it participates in interlibrary loans with Belgian and foreign research libraries.

Academic Libraries. The six great universities in Belgium all have general academic libraries, each of them possessing a fairly extensive collection. The universities of Ghent and Liège are state universities founded in 1816. The central library of the University of Liège contains 1,700,000 volumes, nearly 4,700 current periodicals, and more than 4,000 manuscripts, that in Ghent 2,000,000 volumes, 5,900 current periodicals, and 5,000 manuscripts. The Catholic University of Louvain, founded in 1425, the oldest university in Belgium, was split into two separate, autonomous universities in 1968: the Katholieke Universiteit Leuven (KUL) and the Université Catholique de Louvain. Since 1970 the original library has also been split. The Dutch section possesses 1,000,000 volumes, the French section 1,300,000. The Faculteit der Godgeleerdheid library at the KUL also has an important collection of archives from Vatican II in its library of 500,000 volumes.

The Free University of Brussels was established in 1834. Since 1970 this institution has been split into two autonomous universities. The library of the Dutch section, the Vrije Universiteit Brussel, contains 160,000 volumes; the French section, the Université Libre de Bruxelles, 1,414,000.

Apart from the six complete universities in Belgium, there exist also a number of college institutions with one or more integral or partial faculties. Antwerp has three such centers. The Universitaire Faculteiten Sint-Ignatius (the University Faculties Saint Ignatius) were founded in 1852. The disciplines taught are philosophy and arts, social and political sciences, law, and economics. The Rijksuniversitair Centrum Antwerpen (Antwerp State University) was established in 1965 and specializes in applied economics and exact sciences. In these institutions, only the first study-cycle is taught (two years of "candidatures"). In the Universitaire Instelling Antwerpen (Antwerp University Institution), founded in 1971, the second study-cycle (two years of "licentiate" studies) and the third study-cycle (doctoral studies) are taught in the sciences, medicine, philosophy and arts, law, and social and political sciences. The number of volumes in the specialized libraries of the three institutions amounts to 700,000.

A department of the faculties of medicine, exact sciences, law, and philosophy and arts of the KUL was founded in 1965 in Courtray (first cycle). Its library possesses 56,000 volumes. From 1968–69 economics was taught in the Limburgs Universitair Centrum (Limburg University Center) in Diepenbeek near Hasselt (three cycles). From 1971–72 the first study-cycle of sciences and medicine could also be followed there. The library of that university possesses 50,000 volumes. The Facultés Universitaires Saint Louis (the University Faculties Saint Louis), founded in 1858, specializes in philosophy and arts, law and economics, and social and political sciences (first study-cycle). The library contains 120,000 volumes.

The library of the Universitaire Faculteiten Sint Aloysius (University Faculties Saint Aloysius), where from 1968 the first study-cycles in law, philosophy and arts, and economics were taught, has 69,000 volumes. Mons has three university institutions: the Université de l'Etat à Mons (the State University at Mons), founded in 1965, offering lectures in sciences, applied economics, psychology, and pedagogy; the Faculté Polytechnique de Mons (the Mons Polytechnic Faculty), founded in 1837 and specializing in applied sciences; and the Faculté Universitaire Catholique de Mons (the Mons Catholic University Faculty), founded in 1965 and specializing in economics. Volumes in the libraries of the three colleges in Mons total 540,000. The Facultés Universitaires Notre Dame de la Paix in Namur, founded in 1831, teaches philosophy and arts, law, economics, exact sciences, and medicine. The library holds a collection of 720,000 volumes.

The Faculté des Sciences Agronomiques de Gembloux (Faculty of Agronomic Sciences at Gembloux), established in 1947, has 32,000 volumes. The Faculté de Théologie Protestante de Bruxelles (the Faculty of Protestant Theology of Brussels), founded in 1942, possesses about the same number.

Many university colleges are institutions of a comparatively recent date, and their libraries, more than others, employ modern and economical library techniques. In applications of modern automation they are unrivaled. Online services such as DIALOG, ESA, QUESTEL, INKA, SDC, LIBIS, and EURONET are all used.

Public Libraries. As is the case with Belgian librarianship viewed as a whole, Belgian public librar-

Libraries in Belgium (1990)

Type of library	Number of administrative units (main libraries)	Number of service points (branches, mobile stops, etc.)	Volumes in collections	Annual expenditures (franc)	Population served	Total staff
National[a]	1	1	3,366,000	345,952	8,099	265
Public[a]	2,351	--	24,140,000	1,731,256	--	--
Special[b]	717	717	21,780	--	--	--

[a]1980
[b]1985

Source: Unesco, *Statistical Yearbook,* 1991 and *ALA World Encyclopedia,* 2nd ed. (1985)

ianship is not well organized. Considerable improvement was anticipated, however, under two decrees that passed both the Dutch and French Councils of Culture in 1978. Up to that time all public libraries in Belgium came under the "Law Destrée" (1921), which did not effectively deal with the obligation to establish public libraries, the definition of such institutions, their financial support, and their general organization. The two decrees of 1978, however, defined a logical structure that meets contemporary demands for local public libraries. Their activities and operations are coordinated by central public libraries. A national center of public libraries (in both Flanders and Wallonia) studies problems concerning the public library and provides for some special (noncommercial) central services. The decree promulgated by the Dutch Council of Culture requires the municipalities to establish public libraries. This obligation is less rigidly formulated in the decree of the French Council of Culture (the king *can* put the municipalities under an obligation to establish public libraries). Subsidization is satisfactory.

The method used for shelving books in public libraries is nearly always open-access. Works are arranged in classified order: usually UDC in French libraries; in Dutch libraries a system called SISO (system for the arrangement of the classified catalogue in public libraries). The important public libraries have special departments: sound library, media center, a center for pictures, and even a department of toys.

There was a 50 percent increase in the number of readers at public libraries over a single decade (1965–1975) while the population grew at only 3 percent during that time. This trend was more marked among Dutch-speaking Belgians than among French-speaking Belgians.

School Libraries. School librarianship in Belgium remains underdeveloped. On the level of secondary education, few schools have librarians. At best there were a few class libraries set up by teachers of subject specialties. On the level of higher, nonuniversity education are some important libraries, many of them administered by librarians. Most of them are inadequately catalogued, however. The Royal Conservatory in Brussels, for example, possesses a significant library containing 700,000 volumes, but it was not adequately staffed for cataloguing.

Special Libraries. The government departments have libraries containing documents related to their specific subjects. The Ministry of Economic Affairs, for instance, possesses an important collection of 630,000 volumes (Fonds Quetelet). This library takes a leading position in Belgium in automation. The parliamentary library, containing 1,500,000 volumes on law and social and political sciences, possesses a significant collection of documents of several European parliaments.

Various research institutions have well-organized libraries. The Royal Institute of Natural Sciences of Belgium, for example, possesses about 800,000 volumes.

Many libraries of business companies are well-structured centers of documentation. The best example can be found in the library and documentation service of Agfa-Geevaert in Mortsel, where books and articles in the field of photography and related sciences are abstracted.

Some cities also have "city-libraries" operating independently of the public libraries. Usually they are very old, humanistic, books-preserving libraries that perform some of the functions of "national libraries" in their own regions. The city-library of Antwerp, for example, which was founded in 1607, possesses 650,000 volumes.

The Profession. Belgium has a great number of associations of librarians and libraries. The Vereniging van Archivarissen en Bibliothecarissen van België—Association des archivistes et bibliothécaires de Belgique (Belgian Association of Archivists and Librarians), founded in 1907, serves all persons who perform scientific functions in a record office or library. The Association publishes *Archief- en Bibliotheekwezen in België—Archives et Bibliothèques en Belgique*.

The Vlaamse Vereniging van Bibliotheek-, Archief-, en Documentatiepersoneel (Flemish Society of Archive, Library, and Documentation Staff) was founded in 1921 and assembles the staff of libraries and archives in Flanders. Its organ is *Bibliotheekgids*. The monthly publication *Bibinfo* contains up-to-date information on the society and on activities outside it.

The Katholiek Centrum voor Lektuurinformatie en Bibliotheekvoorziening (Catholic Center for Reading-Information and Library-Supplies) publishes criticism in its monthly annotated bibliographical review *Boekengids en Jeugdboekengids*. Its monthly publication *Openbaar* includes general information.

The Nationaal Bibliotheekfonds (National Funds of Libraries) groups Flemish socialist libraries and librarians and publishes criticism in *Lektuurgids*.

Librarians in the French-speaking part of the country are chiefly grouped in three associations: the Association Nationale des Bibliothécaires de'Expression Française (National Association of French-speaking Librarians), the Association des Bibliothécaires-Documentalistes de l'Institute Supérieur d'Etudes Sociales de l'Etat (Association of Librarian-Documentalists of the Higher State Institution for Social Studies), and the Association Professionelle des Bibliothécaires et Documentalistes (Professional Association of Librarians and Documentalists). The Belgische Vereniging voor Documentatie (Belgian Society for Documentation) serves Dutch-speaking documentalists.

The Vlaamse Bibliotheek Centrale (Flemish Library Center) is a central service that provides a large assortment of library-technical and bibliographical material.

WILLY VANDERPIJPEN

Belize

Belize, long known as British Honduras but an independent nation since September 1981, lies on the east coast of Central America, bounded by Mexico on the north and by Guatemala on the west and south. Its coastline is fringed by the second largest coral reef in the world. Population (1990 est.) 188,000; area 22,965 sq.km. The official language is English.

History. As early as 1825 a library service existed, and between that time and 1902 there were seven libraries and reading rooms. The Jubilee Library, from which the idea of public library service spread in Belize, opened in 1935 with assistance from the Carnegie Corporation of New York. The central government undertook to provide funds for the library service.

National Library Service. The National Library Service came under the direction of the Minister of Education in 1960. A statutory library board administers the service. It has its headquarters in the Bliss Institute in Belize City. The service's bookstock totalled 125,000 in the late 1980s. The National Library Service extends full library services to all government departments and other institutions. It also acts as the national library.

The main lending library, also in the Bliss Institute in Belize City, offers some 15,000 volumes in English. A National Collection comprises about 2,000 volumes and includes books primarily on Belize or by Belizeans, a West Indian collection, and a Central American collection, including works on Maya civilization. Apart from the Bliss Institute, which was only partly designed for library use, there are three other library buildings in the country designed for that purpose. These are in three main towns: Punta Gorda, Orange Walk, and Corozal. All other library services are housed in rented or borrowed accommodations.

There are 58 service points or sub-libraries throughout the country, administered by a staff of 2 professional librarians, 14 paraprofessionals, 15 clerical workers, a bookbinder, and a host of part-time volunteers in the villages (1987). A bookmobile service has been in operation since 1979. Other sections of the service include a children's library and a reference library.

Membership at any service point of the National Library Service is free. Any child who is able to read may join a library and on reaching age 16 may register as a member of the adult library. Members total 18,200, the majority of them children; books issued average 75,000 annually.

Academic Library. The University of the West Indies maintains a university center in Belize. Its library consists of some 3,000 volumes and other printed material. The University College of Belize opened in 1989 and has a collection of 8,000 volumes.

Special Libraries. All departments and ministries of government have collections of printed materials, and many private industrial firms also have libraries.

L. G. VERNON

National Library Service of Belize

Belize's main lending library and the headquarters of the National Library Service are located in The Bliss Institute, Belize City.

Benedict, Saint

(*c.* 480–*c.* 546)

Saint Benedict, Abbot of the monastery at Monte Cassino, who is considered the father of Western monasticism, made his main contribution through the constitution of monasticism, the Benedictine Rule, written at Monte Cassino (*c.* 530–540). It became the most influential factor in the spread of Western monasticism. He also made provision for the care of books, and it is difficult to overestimate his contributions to reading.

In the 6th century all was in a state of civil war, confusion, and looting, on the decline of the Roman Empire. Benedict provided the will, the means, and the men to bring some degree of cultural order out of chaos. After spending 35 years at Subiaco, he founded a monastery at Monte Cassino, about 70 miles southeast of Rome. The Rule of Benedict rapidly circulated among European monasteries with far-reaching cultural influence and has been practiced ever since.

In the tradition of Eastern monasticism, the individual monk's career was largely of a solitary kind, whereas under the Benedictine Rule the labors of the

Libraries in Belize (1990)

Type of library	Number of administrative units (main libraries)	Number of service points (branches, mobile stops, etc.)	Volumes in collections	Annual expenditures (Belize dollar)	Population served	Professional staff (with certificate, diploma, etc.)	Total staff
National	1	35	130,000	442,000	175,000	2	34
Academic	2	--	6,000	70,000	--	1	5
Public[a]	1	34	125,000	--	--	22,000	--
School	200	--	35,000	--	39,000	--	--
Special	17	--	14,000	--	6,000	--	20

[a]1989 data

Source: Unesco, *Statistical Yearbook,* 1991, and author.

community were determined not only for its collective good but likewise for service to the world at large. Monasticism was no longer regarded so much as a life of austerity but as one of service, philanthropy, and Christian charity. The main occupations of the monks were the work of God, devotion, and physical labor. Benedict made special provision in his Rule for the illiterate but imposed the obligation of devotional reading upon the literate monks.

Reading was not so much an intellectual activity as a means to the contemplation of God and self-improvement in the life of grace. As a remedy for idleness, the life of the monk was to be devoted to physical labor and the study of sacred subjects. The Rule added:

> From Easter to the Calends of October, . . . From the fourth hour until close upon the sixth let them apply themselves to reading.

The Rule mentioned the siesta following the sixth hour, important to Italians during the hot season of the year. Those who preferred to read were encouraged to do so, but in a low voice. After the seasonal labors in the fields were concluded in October, work was concentrated inside the monastery. The Rule canceled siestas and set out changes in the manual labor and in the time for reading. From morning until the close of the second hour, the monks were to devote their time to reading.

During the third and final period of the year, the Lenten season, the Rule made some changes in the daily schedule and paid special attention to a systematic program of additional reading. Benedict reflected a certain severity when communal ownership did not permit personal property ("neither a book, nor tablets, nor a pen . . ."), but in no way did he intend privation for any monk. Provisions were to be made for an adequate collection of manuscript codices so that each monk could have one for his personal reading. Though Benedict was silent on intellectual study or scribal work, the reading requirements of his Rule necessitated a monastic book collection that was essentially spiritual. The monastic library was to have sufficient books for the ceremonial distribution of books at the beginning of Lent.

The reading program discouraged skipping through pages or reading at random in a perfunctory manner. The Rule did not prescribe a definite time for loans, nor did it seem to imply that the book must be completely read by the close of Lent. But certain disciplinary measures were established to encourage individuals who felt little attraction for deciphering or other distractions. Surely some preferred working in the field to reading sermons or biblical commentators. These points are carefully detailed in the following passage:

> Let one or two seniors be deputed to go round the monastery at the hours when the brethren are engaged in reading, and see that there be no slothful brother . . . not applying himself to his reading.

On Sundays the monks did only essential work such as kitchen duty. The most desirable use of time was to read books of devotion, but monks who found the task too difficult were to be assigned other duties so they would not be idle. Bible reading was mentioned several times in the Rule. Benedict also recommended biblical commentaries of the Church Fathers to help the monks devotionally. This was an impressive list for monks of the 6th century, and latitude on the selection of other books was also expressed in the Rule: "or something else that may edify the hearers," for those public readings were to be held every evening.

The monks assembled in the oratory at stated hours of the day and night for choral recitation of the Divine Office. The service was fixed in its general outlines, and the recitation of the psalms was its main substance.

The Rule set forth Benedict's program for beginners in the monastic life. Only its final chapter opens up horizons beyond the elementary reading program for monks aspiring to the advanced stages of perfect life. For such members of the monastic community he intended that his Rule would be complemented by a range of books that were the special heritage of monastic ideals and that would bring his followers to the summit of Christian perfection. Among prescribed books were the *Rule* of Saint Basil; the *Conferences* and *Institutes* of John Cassian, an author from Gaul who wrote around 435; and the "Lives of the Fathers," that is to say, the biographies of Anthony of Egypt, Pachomius, and Macarius of Alexandria.

The Rule of Silence. It was the monastic idea that silence was golden. Benedict laid down rules on the subject and, for the most part, only three hours of speaking time was allowed in each day. This severe rule was mitigated by the provision that a brother could read aloud from a "common book." Singing was differentiated from speaking and thus allowed, provided the singer not sit too near a silent reader. Such restraints were, in practice, softened somewhat. An elaborate code of signs to allow silent communication was developed, for example; it was essentially the same for all monasteries and indispensable to the monk who used the library in a silent hour. For example:

> If one wants a book, he shall make the general sign, *i.e.,* extend his hand in a movement of turning the leaves of a book. For the sign of a missal, make the same movement adding the sign of the fingers as though flying. For the sign of a tract, lay one hand on the abdomen and the other across the mouth. For the sign of a sequence or hymn, raise the hand bent and, moving it away from the breast, invest it so that what was before up shall be under. For a book containing a lesson for Sundays and feast days make the sign of a book, add the sign of reading, and, clenching the fist, place the arm over the shoulder, imitating the action of him that carries a burden, on account of the size of the book.

The books called for above are strictly liturgical. For a secular author such as Ovid, the sign was different. For such pagan authors, after making the general sign, "Scratch your ear with your finger, even as a dog when itching does with his foot, for pagans may be compared with such an animal." It is not necessary to read library catalogues to infer that monkish ears itched often.

REFERENCES

The Rule of Saint Benedict, translated by Dom Justin McCann (1961), best English translation.

E. C. Butler, *Benedictine Monachism,* 2nd edition (1961).
L. J. Daly, *Benedictine Monasticism* (1961).
Jean Decarreaux, *Monks and Civilization,* translated by Charlotte Haldane (1964).

REDMOND A. BURKE

Bénin

Bénin, a republic in West Africa, is bordered by Togo on the west, Burkina Faso and Niger on the north, Nigeria on the east, and the Gulf of Guinea on the south. It gained independence from France as Dahomey in 1960 and was the People's Republic of Bénin from 1975 to 1990. Population (1990 est.) 4,041,000; area 112,622 sq.km. The people use about 60 national languages; the official language is French.

National Library. The National Library was established in the capital, Porto Novo, in 1975. It is responsible for collecting all national oral and printed matter (acquired by copyright registration or by gift or bequest) and all foreign publications about Bénin; stimulating reading through the use of mobile libraries; and coordinating activities at public reading libraries throughout the country. Under the jurisdiction of the Ministry of Popular Culture, Youth, and Sports, it is part of the Department of National Culture.

The National Library has three major technical divisions. That of public reading has a staff of about 40, of whom 10 are professionals. Its collection is estimated at about 8,500 volumes. It does not have its own budget, so its new acquisitions come from gifts and copyright registrations.

The National Library produces the National Bibliography. The first three issues covered the period from 1976 through 1988. The National Library has good relations with other libraries throughout the country and with foreign cultural institutions.

The Department of National Archives was established in 1976. It is responsible for collecting and safeguarding all written works and documents from all social strata; handling requests for documents; and planning the official journal. Access to the archives is public and free. At first dependent on the Ministry of Culture, the Department is now under the direct administration of the President of the Republic. Its four collections cover the four periods of Bénin's history: the colonial period (1860–1958), independent Dahomey (1960–72), the revolutionary period (1972–90), and the democratic revival (since March 1990).

The National Library of Bénin, Porto Novo.

Academic Libraries. The Central University Library was founded in 1962, when the Institute of Higher Learning began a literary foundation course for first-year students. The Institute became the University of Dahomey in 1970 and the National University of Bénin in the mid-1970s. The Central University Library moved to new buildings on the Abomey-Calavi campus in 1975. The Library coordinates all collections of the seven university entities that have their own libraries. It is subject to the Chief Education Officer in the Ministry of National Education, whereas the faculty libraries are under the authority of the Deans of the faculties or Directors of the institutes or schools. The academic libraries together have a collection of more than 91,000 volumes, more than half of them in the Central University Library. They have their own budgets, but cannot meet the needs of the 8,000 students

Public Libraries. The National Library coordinates the work of a network of public reading libraries in the six departments and most of the 80 subprefectures of the country. There are six departmental libraries, four municipal libraries, and four reading centers. Four other municipal libraries are in the planning stage. In addition to this network, subsidized by France, the Agency of Cultural and Technical Cooperation subsidizes a network of centers for reading and cultural activities in 20 subprefectures. The two networks have altogether about 60,000

Libraries in Bénin (1990)

Type of library	Number of administrative units (main libraries)	Number of service points (branches, mobile stops, etc.)	Volumes in collections	Annual expenditures (C.F.A. franc)	Population served	Professional staff (with certificate, diploma, etc.)	Total staff
National	1	1	11,000	--	60,000	12	35
Academic	1	8	100,000	--	8,000	15	--
Public	16	39	99,000	--	100,000	5	30
School	--	3	12,000	--	10,000	--	--
Special	10	19	95,500	--	--	12	--
Non-specialized[a]	4	4	40,000	--	--	--	--

[a]1989 data

Source: Unesco, *Statistical Yearbook,* 1991, and author.

volumes. Both networks suffer from critical financial, material, and staffing problems.

Four additional public reading centers are provided by the French, United States, Russian, and Chinese embassies in Cotonou, Bénin's commercial capital. They have contributed greatly to the efficient development of reading in Bénin.

School Libraries. Only two high schools and one junior high school have libraries of more than 1,500 volumes each. School libraries in the country have a combined collection of more than 12,000 volumes.

Special Libraries. There are only 19 special libraries whose collections exceed 1,000 items, 14 of them government-sponsored. They cover agriculture, the arts, culture, economics, education, health, and law. Few of them are computerized. Their joint holdings are about 95,500 volumes.

The Profession. A university-based training program for managing scientific and technical information was created in 1980. This program, originally connected with the National School of Administration, was designated the Center for Training for Information Careers in 1989. Another training program was planned for non-professional library staff seeking professional status.

Library professionals established the Association for the Development of Documentation Activities in Bénin. The association, managed by a general assembly and a permanent secretariat, is funded by the Conference of Officials of Documentation Services and Units (CRID). CRID also organizes meetings where professionals can discuss how to handle the varying tasks at their documentation sites.

JULIEN C. DJOSSE
translated by MIRKA DETTA CAVA

Bermuda

Bermuda is a self-governing dependent territory of the United Kingdom and comprises a group of islands in the western part of the North Atlantic Ocean. Population (1990) 61,000; land area 53 sq.km. The official language is English.

History. Library service in Bermuda is provided by the Bermuda Library, a department of the Bermuda Government, and by a number of smaller, specialized libraries. The Bermuda Library was officially established in 1839 as a subscription library, but there were at least two "public" libraries in existence before that. In 1765 the families living around Somerset Bridge got together a collection of useful books and formed a society that circulated reading materials; it was known as the Somerset Bridge Club. Some of its books can still be found on the shelves of the Bermuda Library, as can books from the Hamilton Club, another "public" library.

The act establishing a public library (1839) provided for a Board of Trustees, which was presided over by the Governor until passage of the Library Act in 1921. Under that act, the President of the Legislative Council became Chairman of a Board made up of colonial and city legislators. The Head Librarian acted as Secretary to the Board. With little change, this system remained in operation until the implementation of the new Bermuda Constitution in June 1968. Today the Head Librarian serves under the policy direction of the Minister for Community and Cultural Affairs. The Board of Trustees, renamed the Library Committee, acts in an advisory capacity only.

National and Public Libraries. The Bermuda Library provides both national and public library services, including legal deposit. Headquarters are at 13 Queen Street, Par-la-Ville, in Hamilton, the capital city, with the Youth Library a few blocks away and branches at St. George's and Somerset. The service is free to all residents of Bermuda. A free mailing service has operated since 1855. In 1990 total bookstock stood at 150,700 and the annual circulation was more than 110,800. While circulation figures declined compared with previous years, visitors to all libraries increased to 162,000.

Videocassettes, compact discs, cassettes, long-playing records, talking books, and slides are provided. The Main Library presents slide/lecture travelogues, "Meet Bermudian Authors" evenings, and Bermudian crafts demonstrations. The Youth Library holds regular story hours and film shows, presents seasonal and special programs, and provides a Dial-a-Story service.

The Reference Department maintains a Bermuda collection of books and articles on and about Bermuda. A Rare Book Room was established in 1982. There is a nearly complete file of the *Royal Gazette* newspaper. Microform and photocopy services are offered, as well as a Dialog database search service.

The Bermuda National Bibliography, published quarterly with annual cumulations and available on a subscription basis, was launched in 1984.

Archives. The Bermuda Archives collects and preserves Bermuda's historical records and makes them available for research. It provides records management services to all government departments, advising them on the care and retention of records and providing storage and retrieval facilities for semi-current records. The Archives' holdings are listed in the *Guide to the Records of Bermuda*.

Libraries in Bermuda (1990)

Type of library	Number of administrative units (main libraries)	Volumes in collections	Annual expenditures (Bda dollar)	Population served	Professional staff (with certificate, diploma, etc.)
National & Public	1	150,701	1,003,000	58,616	8
Archives	1	--	302,600	58,616	1
Academic	1	26,063	100,000	--	1
School	23	--	--	7,605	2
Special	--	--	--	--	5

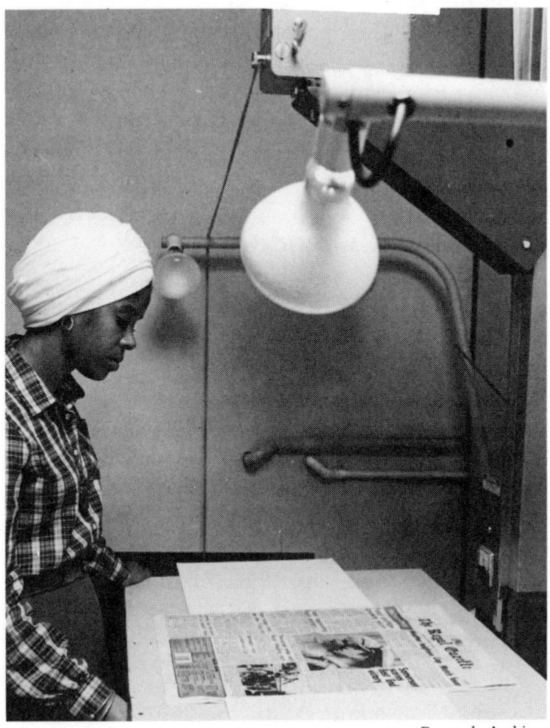

Bermuda Archives

At the Bermuda Archives in Hamilton, microfilm operator photographing the Royal Gazette.

Academic Libraries. Bermuda College is a two-year junior college geared to the courses offered by the departments of Academic Studies, Commerce and Technology, and Hotel Technology. Its library contains 26,000 volumes and 150 periodicals. Bermuda does not have a university. Undergraduate extension students are served by the Bermuda Library and the libraries of the Bermuda College and the U.S. Naval Air Station.

School Libraries. There are libraries in all government secondary schools and most primary schools, although a few of the latter are still only classroom collections. Standards of the Library Association (U.K.) in facilities and bookstock are attempted, but there is a need for more professionally qualified staff. Library service in private schools is comparable.

Special Libraries. Among the larger and more formally organized government libraries are those of the Supreme Court, the departments of Education, Agriculture and Fisheries, and Health and Social Services, and the two hospitals. The E. L. Mark Memorial Library at the Bermuda Biological Station provides research facilities in marine and environmental sciences; it has a stock of 20,000 volumes and 150 current periodicals acquired by subscription, gift, and exchange. Large professional and business office libraries specialize in such areas as accounting, banking, insurance, and oil and gas.

Bermuda boasts a number of significant private libraries and some rare book collectors. Community organizations such as churches and youth centers also maintain small collections.

The Profession. The first Bermudian known to have taken library science courses was Katherine G. S. Seon, who studied at the school started by Andrew Carnegie in Atlanta, Georgia. She served as Librarian-Secretary of the Bermuda Library from 1912 to 1940. By the mid-1960s the Bermuda Library had a professional staff of four librarians. By 1990 there were 17 professionally trained librarians serving in public, college, school, archival, hospital, law, and other special libraries on the island. Bermudians wishing to enter the profession study abroad, usually in the United States, the United Kingdom, or Canada.

The Library Association of Bermuda was established in 1983 and Bermuda maintains ties with such international and national professional bodies as the International Federation of Library Associations and Institutions, the Commonwealth Library Association, the International Council on Archives, and the national associations of Great Britain, Canada, the United States, and the Caribbean. Two major surveys were completed in the 1980s. In 1983 K. C. Harrison was commissioned to survey the country's resources with a view to establishing a national library and information systems network. Aaron Cohen Associates did an information center/library needs assessment for the Bermuda Library in 1988, analyzing and justifying short- and long-range plans.

CYRIL O. PACKWOOD

Bernardo, Gabriel A.

(1891–1962)

Gabriel Adriano Bernardo, father of Philippine librarianship, was a bibliographer, scholar, librarian, writer, folklorist, and teacher and mentor of Filipino librarians for half a century. Bernardo was interested in everything Philippine: the country's language and literature, paleography, Tagalog literature, music and fine arts, numismatics, archives, and history. His works, both published and unpublished, show the breadth of his interest.

Bernardo was born in Barasoain, Malolos, March 14, 1891, during the last decade of the Spanish rule in the Philippines. The second of six children of Mauricio Bernardo, a carriage-maker and painter, and Engracia Adriano, a meat dealer in the Malolos market, he spent his elementary schooling at the Malolos Elementary School and his secondary education at the Bulacan High School. He studied at the University of the Philippines and, working his way through college, earned the Bachelor of Arts degree in 1916. He attended the University of Wisconsin from 1918 to 1920 as a government scholar in library science and bibliography and was awarded the Certificate in General Library Services. When he returned to the Philippines, he resumed his studies while working at the Philippine Library and Museum as Assistant Librarian and Researcher. In 1923 he earned the Master of Arts in English and Bibliography. At the same time, he was a lecturer in library science and bibliography at the University of the Philippines, where he taught various courses. Later he became a full-time member of the University library staff as a cataloguer, and successively became Assistant Librarian and Instructor of Library Science. When Mary Polk, then university librarian, died in 1924, Bernardo became the Librarian of the University of the Philippines Library and head of the Department of Library

Science, which was then under the College of Liberal Arts.

In 1929, as a University of the Philippines Fellow, he went to Germany and took advanced courses in library science at the University of Berlin. He also worked in various library departments at the University of Leipzig and the Prussian State Library in Berlin. While he was in Germany his initiative led to the Philippine Library Association's joining the International Federation of Library Associations in 1930.

Bernardo's career as a librarian was almost totally spent in the service of the University of the Philippines Library, where he served as University Librarian from 1924 until he retired in 1957. He was responsible for the construction of the library building in Manila, the first building planned and equipped solely for library purposes there. When it was destroyed in the battle of Manila in 1945, he immediately went to work on the construction of another library building, a bigger one on a new site in Diliman, Quezon City.

In 1945 he made a survey of the destruction of libraries in the Philippines wrought by World War II. His report became the basis for the creation of a special committee to draw up plans for the rehabilitation of war-devastated libraries and other cultural agencies in the Philippines. In 1946 Bernardo went to the United States as technical adviser to the Philippine Foundation of America to campaign for overseas aid for the rehabilitation of libraries and cultural agencies. As a result of that campaign, book donations from America poured in.

Bernardo's far-reaching influence was expressed not only through the classroom, where he trained hundreds of librarians, but also in his leadership of the Philippine Library Association. He was cofounder and charter member and served as Vice-President and Acting President (1927–31), then as President (1933–34, 1949–53, and 1957–62). He was responsible for abolishing voting by proxy and helped raise the association's professional standards.

Bibliographical Works. Bernardo pursued bibliography vigorously up to his death. He believed that bibliographies are important to research and deplored the absence of an up-to-date national bibliography for the Philippines. He engaged himself in producing exhaustive studies of individual titles and subject bibliographies representing his main interests—folklore, history, anthropology, language and literature, and librarianship. He always insisted on accuracy in entries and annotations. Of the many bibliographical works he produced, noteworthy are *Bibliography of Philippine Bibliographies, 1593–1961* (1968) and *Philippine Retrospective National Bibliography, 1523–1699* (1974). Both works were published after his death in Quezon City on December 5, 1962. He produced some 88 works and, at the time of his death, left 13 bibliographical works unfinished. Tributes from public figures, scholars, and librarians recognized his special contributions as "doyen of Filipino librarians" (*Manila Times*) and "pioneer, a devoted professor" (Carlos P. Romulo).

REFERENCES

Mauro Garcia, editor, *Gabriel A. Bernardo: Librarian, Bibliographer and Scholar* (Bibliographical Society of the Philippines, 1974).

Carlos P. Romulo, "In Memoriam: Gabriel A. Bernardo; March 14, 1891–December 5, 1962," *University of the Philippines Library Bulletin* (April 15, 1963).

Natividad P. Verzosa, "Gabriel A. Bernardo: A Memoir," *Philippine Studies* (October 1963).

ROSA MENGUITO VALLEJO

Besterman, Theodore

(1904–1976)

Theodore Deodatus Nathaniel Besterman was an eminent bibliographer, Voltaire scholar, and good friend to libraries and librarians. Polish-born and brought up in Britain, he was a true European.

He was born in Poland November 18, 1904, and, after his family moved to London, was educated mostly at home, receiving little formal education at school and none at college or university. A teenage flirtation with youth movements coincided with interest in and membership of the theosophical movement and, initially, with admiration for its leader at the time, Annie Besant (1847–1933). Besterman's first book, published at the age of 20, was *A Bibliography of Annie Besant*. She had been prominent in and had published widely on a succession of interests prior to theosophy, including secularism, birth control, the status of women, and trade unionism, all, including theosophy, leading to her later concern for Indian nationalism; Besterman's bibliography included more than 400 items. His *Mind of Annie Besant,* an appreciation by a devoted admirer in honor of her 80th birthday, came in 1927. But his *Mrs. Annie Besant: A Modern Prophet* (1934) was the work of a disillusioned and lapsed theosophist who condemned her "monstrous authoritarianism."

Besterman's involvement with theosophy had encouraged a near-parallel interest in the paranormal, and from 1927 to 1935 he was one of the investigating officers of the Society for Psychical Research; he became editor of its journal and its librarian, publishing a catalogue and four supplements. Further consequences were his *Some Modern Mediums* (1930), his editorship of and contribution to BBC talks, "Inquiry into the Unknown" in 1934, and his *Bibliography of Sir Oliver Lodge* in 1935. Prior to these, however, had come more specialized books introduced by *Crystal Gazing: A Study in the History, Distribution, Theory and Practice of Scrying* in 1924, which suggested "a latent and unknown faculty of perception." *The Divining Rod: An Experimental and Psychological Investigation,* prepared when Besterman was assistant to Sir William Barrett but published in 1926, after Barrett's death, was partly supplemented by *Water-Divining: New Facts and Theories* (1938), the books together claiming, rather more plausibly, "the impossibility of finding any normal explanation of the phenomena of dowsing."

Another interest, this time in anthropology, manifested itself in Besterman's revised 1927 edition of Ernest Crawley's *The Mystic Rose: A Study of Primitive Marriage,* first published in 1902 but now provided with a much more comprehensive index and a new bibliography of some 800 references. The revision was dedicated to Sir J. G. Frazer, of *Golden Bough* fame; Besterman's *Bibliography of Sir James George Frazer* followed in 1934. The success of the revision encouraged him to bring together a number of Crawley's essays, previously unpublished in book form, as *Studies of Savages and Sex* (1929) and *Dress, Drinks and Drums* (1931). He then attempted to bridge the gap between primitive and modern with *Men against Women: A Study of Sexual Relations* (1934), a brief historical survey.

Besterman displayed a more explicit interest in bibiliography by becoming a lecturer in the School of Librarianship at University College, London, in 1931, and by publishing, four years later, *The Beginnings of Systematic Bibliography* (second edition 1936, third edition; in French, *Les Débuts de la Bibliographie Méthodique,* 1950). This book, which examines bibliographies published up to and during the 17th century, may be regarded as one introduction to his *World Bibliography of Bibliographies,* but there were others. Prominent among them was his paper "A New Bibliography of Bibliographies," read at the (British) Library Association's conference in 1936. A slightly revised version was published separately later that year and a further revision prefaces the first volume of the *World Bibliography*. Meantime, however, there were other publications of bibliographic interest. *The Publishing Firm of Cadell and Davies: Select Correspondence and Accounts 1793–1836, Edited with an Introduction and Notes,* is a revealing presentation of the company that published Robert Burns and rejected Jane Austen's *Pride and Prejudice*. Also in 1938 came *The Travellings and Sufferings of Father Jean de Brébeuf among the Hurons of Canada as Described by Himself, Edited and Translated from the French and Latin,* an account of the checkered life and martyrdom by the Iroquois in 1649 of the French Jesuit missionary. A year later came *The Pilgrim Fathers: A Journal of Their Coming in the Mayflower to New England and Their Life and Adventures There, Edited with Preface and Notes,* and reprinted from the rare 1622 edition, which "remains the only detailed source of information for the first settlement of New England." A further Anglo-American link was provided by Besterman's own Guyon House Press—named after his London house in Hampstead, set up in 1937 but destroyed by a bomb in 1940—which published a translation of *Magna Carta and other Charters of English Liberty:* a copy was exhibited at the Library of Congress during World War II, together with the original Charter sent to the United States for safety.

Besterman's World Bibliography of Bibliographies and of Bibliographical Catalogues, Calendars, Abstracts, Digests, Indexes and the Like was first published in 1939–40, the second edition in 1947–49 (reprinted 1950), the third in 1955–56 (reprinted in reduced facsimile 1960), and the fourth in four volumes with a separate index volume in 1965–66. It is arranged alphabetically by subjects and, in the fourth edition, is brought down to 1963. It is limited to separately published bibliographies and aims to be international and comprehensive in scope. It excludes only lists in, but not on, oriental languages, and contains more than 117,000 entries. Compilation of the immense work involved the personal handling of more than 80,000 volumes in the Library of Congress and the Library of the British Museum (now the British Library); the work is dedicated to the staff of the latter. Entries for African and Oriental subjects, published separately from 1939 onward, were updated to 1973 by J. D. Pearson and published in 1975; the main arrangement here is by geographical division. A decennial supplement to the *World Bibliography* is planned: the first, covering the years 1964–74 and published in two volumes in New Jersey in 1977, was compiled by Alice F. Toomey.

The time gap between the first and second editions of the *World Bibliography* was explained by Besterman's British war service and, until 1949, by a period at Unesco, where he became head of a department for the international exchange of information. He had prepared the way for this activity by his work for Aslib during the 1930s, by his general editorship of its publications from 1944 to 1946, by the establishment and temporary editorship in 1945 of its *Journal of Documentation,* and by the planning of the *British Union Catalogue of Periodicals* (BUCOP).

Besterman expressed his feeling for Voltaire, the great French philosopher and man of letters, at the end of the preface to his own ambitious biography published in 1960 (third revised edition 1976): "I have been his lifelong admirer this side idolatry. I have spent many years in close and critical study of his life and works, for over a decade I lived in his house, worked in his library, slept in his bedroom. It would be absurd for me to pretend to cold impartiality." He had been collecting Voltaire material for many years and, after an abortive attempt to establish a Voltaire center in France, turned alternatively—and so appropriately in view of Voltaire's own experience—to Switzerland. Following prolonged negotiations the Institut et Musée Voltaire was created in Voltaire's own house, Les Délices, in Geneva, and officially opened in 1954. From it, under Besterman's personal direction, poured an amazing output of impeccably produced books, including in particular 107 volumes of the correspondence, edited for the first time mostly from manuscript sources. Other notable publications included the first "Studies on Voltaire and the 18th century," which total nearly 200 volumes.

Besterman eventually moved his Voltaire publishing activities to England and established the Voltaire Foundation in Oxford. He bequeathed the Foundation to the Taylor Institution of the University with the residue of his estate. The primary aims of the Foundation are to continue his work and notably to complete the definitive edition of the collected works, including the correspondence, in approximately 150 volumes, and to undertake other publications and related research on 18th-century studies and the Enlightenment. There is an attractive Voltaire Room in the Taylorian building; publishing is directed and controlled from offices nearby.

In his Arundell Esdaile lecture, "Fifty Years a Bookman," read to a joint meeting of the Library Association and the English Association in 1973, Besterman referred to himself as "a man who has conducted a life-long and passionate affair with books," an appropriate epitaph for one whose bibliographical and literary activities verge on the unbelievable. He died at Banbury, near Oxford, November 10, 1976.

Honorary degrees had been conferred on him by Oxford and other universities. The Library Association, which had made him an Honorary Fellow in 1969, remembers him through its Besterman Medal, awarded annually for an outstanding bibliography or guide to the literature first published in the United Kingdom during the preceding year.

REFERENCES

Theodore Besterman, *Fifty Years a Bookman* (1974).

Edward J. Carter, "Theodore Besterman: A Personal Memoir," *Journal of Documentation* (1977).

W. A. MUNFORD

Bhutan

In the Great Himalayan Range, Bhutan is bounded by the Tibetan Autonomous Region of China on the north and by India on the south. Its area is approximately 47,000 sq.km. Its population, chiefly of Tibetan and Nepalese origin, was estimated at about 1,517,000 in 1990; of these, 95 percent depend on agriculture for their livelihood. The national language is Dzongkha, but English is used for instruction and much official correspondence.

History. The country has been independent since time immemorial but was considerably influenced by the British during their rule in India. The country became known to the outside world as a sovereign kingdom only after the ascent to the throne of the Wangchuk dynasty in 1907, when Ugyen Wangchuk was crowned as the first hereditary king of Bhutan by civil and monastic representatives. Since then, Bhutan has made great efforts to modernize and to improve the living conditions of its people.

The development of a comprehensive education system was initiated in 1961. Prior to that, there were virtually no modern educational facilities in the country, apart from the traditional monasteries. Today an extensive network of schools and other educational institutions spreads throughout the country. The literacy rate had risen to 22 percent by 1989.

National Library Service. The National Library of Bhutan was established in 1967 with the objective of collecting and preserving ancient Bhutanese and Tibetan literary and scriptural documents dealing with the religion, culture, traditions, and history of the country. It has a Branch Library at Kungarabten Dzong, Tongsa district, and a Public Library in the capital, Thimpu. The National Library acquires material in three ways: purchase, exchange, and gift. Purchase remains the most important method, but the others contribute significantly to the collection. For example, in 1978 the National Library acquired the Tibetan Buddhist Canon (Kanjur and Menjur) from the Beijing edition of the complete works of the Sakyapa Masters by exchange with the Reiyukai Library in Tokyo. Also, E. G. Smith, Field Director of the Library of Congress in New Delhi, over the years donated more than 800 volumes of current Tibetan publications.

The government is making efforts to develop the National Museum at Paro, one of the prominent cities of the country, where a large collection of national archival materials is being organized.

School Libraries. Almost all schools and educational institutions in the country have their own libraries, which collect materials depicting the history, culture, and religion of Bhutan and neighboring countries.

N. M. ADHIKARI

Bibliographic Instruction

Whenever and wherever information seeker comes together with information keeper, something resembling instruction tends to occur. For this reason, it is often difficult to isolate "bibliographic instruction" as an activity separate from more traditional public services, which themselves overlap: bibliography, research assistance, reference, or readers' advisory. As currently used, however, the term usually denotes formal, group instruction in library use. More ambitiously, it may seek to acquaint users with the world of recorded knowledge, not limited by the walls that contain it: its nature, organization, economics, and politics. But ultimately the goal of all bibliographic instruction is to bring information seekers together with the information they need. Differences in instructional programs, and controversies among those who run them, center on which skills and understandings will foster attainment of that goal and how best to impart them.

Bibliographic instruction, like reference, has developed most fully and self-consciously in the United States, though librarians in all parts of the world have written about it.

Libraries in Bhutan (1987)

Type of library	Number of administrative units (main libraries)	Number of service points (branches, mobile stops, etc.)	Volumes in collections	Annual expenditures (lakhs)	Population served	Professional staff (with certificate, diploma, etc.)	Total staff
National	1	3	12,000	20	5,000	24	35
Public	1	1	6,000	8	5,000	2	3
School							
Each	--	1	ca 500 to 1,200	--	above 500	--	--
All	--	--	ca 10,000	--	--	1–3	3
Special[a]	1	2	10,000	--	150	--	--

[a]1983 data

Source: Unesco, *Statistical Yearbook,* 1991, and author.

Philosophically, librarians' professional turf was tilled for teaching in 1876, near the very beginning of the modern librarianship movement, when Melvil Dewey wrote in the first issue of the first professional library journal, "The time *is* when a library is a school, and the librarian is in the highest sense a teacher."

Formal reference service developed in the late 1800s and early 1900s as standardized cataloguing and classification systems spread, relatively sophisticated reference works were published, and the public library movement found much of its justification in democratic principles: patrons were to be spoken to, advised, and assimilated into American life through books. No longer passive "keepers," librarians were to be active guides.

Not surprisingly, however, formal education in library use was advocated principally by academicians—a trend that continues to this day. Articles began to appear, written by authors as diverse as the philosopher Ralph Waldo Emerson, federal higher education official Kendric C. Babcock, and academic librarians Azariah Smith Root and Raymond C. Davis, promoting credit-bearing courses in library use or "bibliography."

However, the most striking intellectual forebear of the contemporary bibliographic instruction movement was probably Louis Shores, who indefatigably wrote articles over four decades explicating his notion of the "library-college." Central to it were independent study as the primary learning mode and librarians as equal partners with classroom faculty.

In the late 1950s, Patricia B. Knapp conceptualized a progressive program of bibliographic instruction that apparently owed much to Shores's ideas. Piloted at Wayne State University's experimental Monteith College in the early 1960s, the program was not an unqualified success. However, Knapp's report on it and her proposed model program, which emphasized "unity and coherence," teaching the research process, and thorough integration of bibliographic instruction with the broader curriculum, were extremely influential.

No one was more influenced, or more influential in his turn, than Evan Ira Farber, chief librarian at Earlham College in Indiana, a small, selective, conspicuously informal school affiliated with the Society of Friends. Blessed with particularly fertile soil for the development of an effective program, Farber and his colleagues Thomas Kirk and James R. Kennedy, Jr., (all of whom later spoke and wrote about their experiences) instituted "library instruction throughout the curriculum." Its linchpin was "course-related" or "course-integrated" instruction, which began in the required freshman Humanities course and continued in subsequent more specialized courses.

Fostered by the Earlham group's almost messianic fervor and, in several cases, by funding from the U.S. National Endowment for the Humanities and the Council on Library Resources, somewhat similar programs sprang up at many other undergraduate colleges throughout the 1970s. Prominent among them were initiatives at the University of Wisconsin-Parkside (Carla J. Stoffle), Wabash College (John Mark Tucker), Sangamon State University (Patricia Senn Breivik), and the University of Evansville. Miriam Dudley, College Librarian at the University of California-Los Angeles, moved in another direction with a "self-paced, self-directed" library skills program that depended on a standardized workbook. Less labor-intensive than course-related instruction, it was more feasible for large institutions and was widely copied.

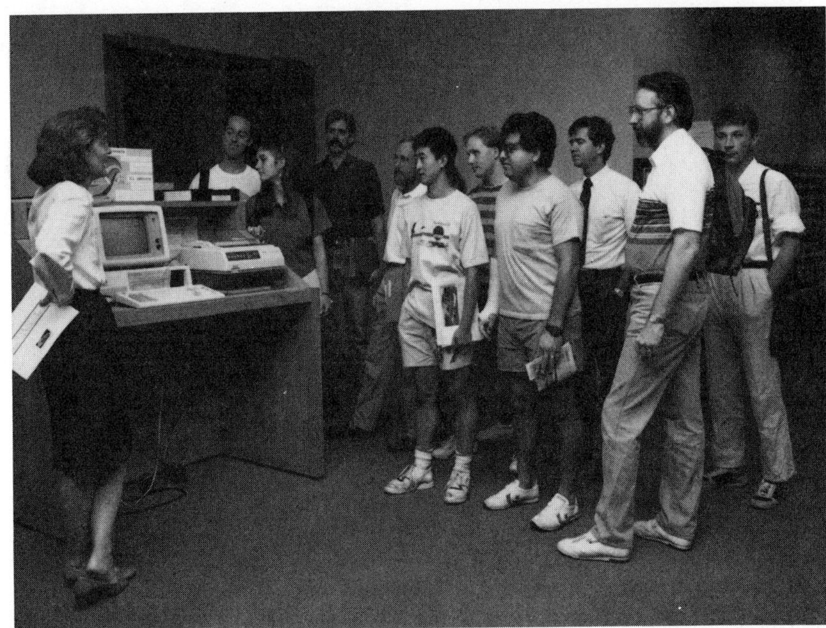

University of Tennessee, Knoxville

University of Tennessee librarian explains INTERNET access to university catalogs nationwide to a group of new graduate students.

Bibliographic instruction as a formal service concept, though variously manifested, won remarkably rapid and wide acceptance—at least in academe. Probable contributing factors included: its congruence with public service traditions of librarianship and with professional self-definitions of librarians; the support it seemed to lend librarians' concurrent drive for enhanced prestige, as evidenced in the faculty status movement; the relatively high availability of necessary resources in the 1960s and early 1970s, which were financially favorable years for colleges and universities; and the era's general dissatisfaction with the status quo, which generated broad educational experimentation.

But for whatever combination of reasons, bibliographic instruction advanced rather quickly from innovation to established practice. Evidence of its institutionalization included the decision by librarians at Eastern Michigan University to found LOEX at the start of the 1970s. An invaluable clearinghouse for information about instructional programs, LOEX manifested in its very name the quick development of the service. First called the Library Orientation EXchange, it soon became Library Orientation/Instruction Exchange in an attempt to transcend the limited scope implied by the word "orientation" without changing its acronym. Pierian Press published the proceedings of the resulting LOEX conferences. The 70s also saw the Association of College and Research Libraries creating formal "Guidelines for Bibliographic Instruction in Academic Libraries"; the ALA Council adopting a "Policy Statement: Instruction in the Use of Libraries"; *The Journal of Academic Librarianship* including a regular column on bibliographic instruction edited by LOEX director Carolyn A.

Librarian conducts a class in bibliographic instruction at Fiorello G. La Guardia Community College, City University of New York.

Kirkendall; many professional associations founding bibliographic instruction "round tables" or subdivisions; and schools of library and information science establishing formal "methods" courses. In 1983 a journal devoted to bibliographic instruction commenced: the enigmatically titled *Research Strategies*.

Meanwhile, the terminology used to denote bibliographic instruction stirred controversy and kept changing. Just as "library orientation" quickly seemed too limited to describe the ambitious aims of the programs, so "library instruction" seemed too restrictive in its emphasis on the contents of a building. "Bibliographic instruction" came into vogue, was routinely shortened to "b.i.," and approached the status of a standard term, which is why it is used here. But "instruction" often sounded limiting, and "bibliographic" referred, literally, only to books and writing, an anachronism in the computer age. Both "bibliographic education" and "user education" are used today as well.

But to what exactly do they refer? In the 1990s as in the 1960s, most writing on the subject emanates from academic institutions in the United States and assumes instruction that is, directly or indirectly, course- or assignment-related.

However, as the service has become taken for granted as a routine part of librarianship, increasing numbers of articles have appeared that focus on educating users of special and public libraries. School librarians have written less about bibliographic instruction than might have been expected, perhaps because it seems less a novelty, a special service, to them than to librarians in other environments. That is, school librarians tend to hold qualifications comparable with those of their classroom-teaching colleagues and to be in close contact with them as library-use assignments are developed and administered. It seems likely that wherever school libraries or media centers exist, the professionals in them tend to undertake relatively vigorous endeavors that can roughly be described as bibliographic instruction. Still, the documentation is relatively slim. Of course, it may be that the coincidence of the academic-library faculty status movement with the proliferation of writing about bibliographic instruction is not accidental: that the pressure to publish bearing on academic librarians since the 1960s has spawned more articles on all subjects than would otherwise have appeared. School, public, and special librarians are not similarly pressed, and their silence may reflect this fact more than the absence of instructional efforts.

Internationally, especially among British librarians, there has been increasing interest in bibliographic instruction, though it seems much less widespread than in the United States. This fact may result from differential degrees of professional pressure to publish, as well as the comparatively large number of American journals and publishing houses available to present librarians' writings.

There have, however, been notable shifts in the instructional services offered and concerns expressed by bibliographic instruction professionals, mirroring their growing sophistication as educators, as well as obvious changes in the larger worlds of librarianship and information distribution.

First of all, the array of instructional techniques available to librarians has broadened. One of the oldest, the library tour, remains nearly ubiquitous, even though it is much maligned for its physical awkwardness and the facts that students are bored by it and retain little information from it. Then, too, it is usually detached from any immediate need to use the library (such as a looming term paper). One variation is the tape- or handout-assisted self-guided tour.

The separate course in library skills, long ago assumed to be the only logical format, has been and continues to be used in colleges and universities. However, its labor intensiveness and relative inefficiency (educating few students in depth rather than many superficially), combined with its usual divorce from a broader, obviously meaningful context, limit its popularity.

Course-related or -integrated instruction, regarded as the almost self-evidently superior format by Knapp, Farber, and those they influenced, was thought to overcome all the separate-course problems except, perhaps, labor intensiveness, and to be unassailably sound from a pedagogical standpoint. It remains widely used by academic and school librarians. But, since the 1970s, critics have questioned its effectiveness, noting that it tends to be an insubstantial add-on geared to a single assignment, is often repetitive for some students while over-sophisticated for others, and resists valid evaluation.

Less complex and highly pragmatic formats abound, such as videotapes, audiotapes, and slide shows; term-paper clinics; workshops or seminars geared to specific reference tools or subject areas; and handbooks, handouts, and point-of-use guides. With all their limitations, they are more readily adapted to special and public libraries than are course-based efforts.

Starting in the 1980s, concerns raised by information technology have dominated much of the literature about bibliographic instruction. The question of how best to prepare users for searching online public-access catalogues and other online sources, as well as sources in CD-ROM, has forced reconsideration of what a reference source is; what the real challenges of seeking information are; whether there are qualitative differences between seeking information on paper and on a computer and, if so, what they are; and how best to develop students' information technology skills. Increasingly, stand-up lectures are de-emphasized and hands-on sessions favored. While slides and other old audiovisual formats may seem static and outdated, terminal screen projection and other computer-related technologies seem increasingly essential.

As librarians have become skeptical of the effectiveness of both traditional and new teaching methods, they have written extensively about evaluation, though it can usually yield only "soft" (or meretriciously "hard") information. Techniques have included reviewing completed student library assignments, distributing attitudinal surveys to students or classroom faculty, peer observation, and, perhaps most prominently, testing. The tests are usually in simple "objective" format, but are administered in various ways and may include comparison of various teaching methods, use of control groups, pre- and post-testing, freshman entry testing, college exit competency testing, and so forth. Finally, there seems to be agreement that evaluation of bibliographic instruction, like that of all other teaching endeavors, should be aggressive and continuous but may never be definitive.

In summary, bibliographic instruction, by whatever name, is a well-established service in most college and university libraries, though it is not without critics. School librarians also seem to provide much instruction, though their efforts are probably not as fully documented in the professional literature. Public and special libraries pose greater challenges and, arguably, lesser need by their very nature. Even in those environments, however, librarians and information specialists are increasingly aware of the desirability of educating users and are devising a variety of procedures for doing so.

REFERENCES

Melvil Dewey, "The Profession," *American Library Journal* (1876).

Patricia B. Knapp, *The Monteith College Library Experiment* (1966).

John Lubans, Jr., editor, *Educating the Library User* (1974); *Educating the Public Library User* (1983).

Constance A. Mellon, editor, *Bibliographic Instruction: The Second Generation* (1987).

Louis Shores, "Library-College: Prototype for a Universal Higher Education," *Encyclopedia of Library and Information Science,* volume 14 (1975).

Arthur P. Young, "And Gladly Teach: Bibliographic Instruction and the Library," *Advances in Librarianship* (1980).

MARY BIGGS

Bibliographic Networks and Utilities

In the library context, *network* may have several meanings: (1) The informal links that help people make contacts, transact business, and find out what they need to know. It may be used as a verb, "to network," and is most frequently seen in its gerund form, "networking." (2) *Bibliographic "utilities,"* probably most accurately called networks, since they are the most complete networking systems, including database, hardware, and telecommunications systems.

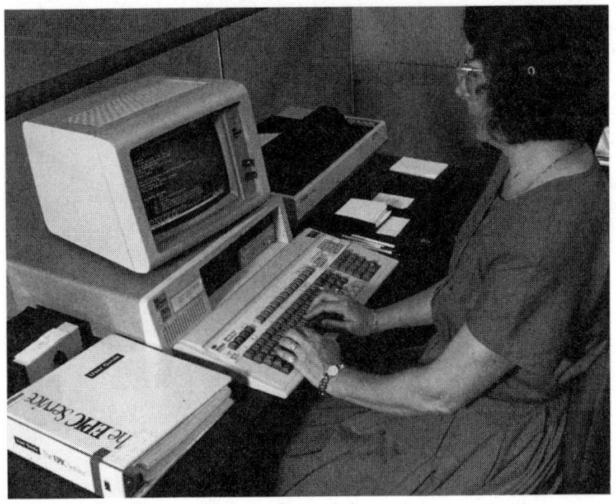

OCLC (Online Computer Library Company)

OCLC has grown from a cooperative of Ohio academic libraries into a bibliographic "utility" providing a giant national network of libraries with a variety of products and services. In 1990 OCLC introduced EPIC service, a new online reference system.

(Perhaps the term ought to be reserved for them alone.) (3) *Systems for online bibliographic searching,* including such database vendor systems as DIALOG, BRS, or SDC. (4) *Telecommunications systems* used to link libraries with utilities and database vendor systems. (5) *Organizations of libraries for assistance in the use of computerized library services,* such as utilities and database vendor systems. These usually involve several types of libraries and may be organized on a single- or multi-state basis. (6) *Organizations of libraries in a single area of specialization,* such as law or medicine, similarly linked to each other and to one or more national databases for the retrieval of technical and reference information. (7) *Library cooperatives of any kind.* This increasingly common usage for years seemed to be inaccurate, but more and more cooperatives, systems, and consortia are adding telecommunications links to improve their service to members, making the synonymous use more appropriate.

In the 1970s, a reference to library networks usually involved definition 5 above; specifically, the affiliates of OCLC, the Online Computer Library Center; AMIGOS, BCR, CAPCON, FEDLINK, ILLINET, INCOLSA, MINITEX, MLC, MLNC, NEBASE, NELINET, OHIONET, PALINET, PRLC, SOLINET, SUNY, and WILS; plus the OCLC service center, PACNET; and CLASS. Norman D. Stevens's definition of networks is limited to those meeting the following criteria: *geographical level:* state, multi-state, or national; *(financial) support:* primarily from payments for services from participating libraries; *direction:* having a full-time, specialized staff; *governance:* by an independent body including a high level of involvement by members, usually through a board of directors or trustees; and *services:* use of a large-scale cooperative database in machine-readable form, available through a telecommunications network.

The use of the term "bibliographic utility," disliked as it has been by those to whom it has been applied, has become increasingly standardized in the library community. A *bibliographic utility* is a nonprofit organization serving as a source of bibliographic data stored in machine-readable form, which data are available to those affiliated with the utility (usually library members) for such purposes as online cataloguing and interlibrary loan through a telecommunications network. Commercial vendors have been "designated" as utilities by at least one state government for contractual purposes, but, by the late 1980s, the generally accepted list of utilities included only four organizations in North America: OCLC, Dublin, Ohio; the Research Libraries Information Network (RLIN), Stanford, California; UTLAS (formerly the University of Toronto Library Automation System) Toronto, Ontario; and the Western Library Network (WLN), Olympia, Washington. UTLAS, which started as a nonprofit operation, later moved into the private sector, indicating that flexibility in the definition may be necessary.

This article covers the utilities and networks cited in definitions 2 and 5. See further articles on Electronic Data Sources, Library Cooperative Systems, and Resource Sharing.

FUNCTIONS

The differentiation between "utilities" and "networks" is historically defined at a functional level.

Utilities. The organizations that would be called utilities came into being in various ways: OCLC as a cooperative endeavor among academic libraries in Ohio; WLN as a state-library-sponsored automation system in Washington and later as an independent not-for-profit corporation; and RLIN and UTLAS as single library systems that grew and expanded in California and Ontario respectively. The historical development of these organizations altered their original functions and led to the use of the term "utility" to define them.

OCLC's origin as a cooperative of Ohio academic libraries is legendary. Its development through the affiliation of networks representing libraries in other regions of the country, and its subsequent addition of its own service centers in the United States and abroad, led to a demand for a governance structure representative of all users. By the time that had been accomplished, the organization's functions had been transformed from providing cataloguing information, cards, and interlibrary loan locations for a homogeneous group of libraries in a small geographical region, to that of providing a giant national, multitype library network with an increasing variety of products and services.

The Western Library Network's state library origins defined its functions: to serve libraries in the state of Washington with high-quality cataloguing information and related products for resource sharing. The function has not altered significantly, although the region served has been enlarged to include the Pacific Northwest, and the sale of WLN software has carried the system to the Southeastern U.S. through SOLINET; to Missouri, Arizona, and other regions of the United States; and to Australia as well. The form of the organization became that of an independent not-for-profit corporation in 1990.

RLIN is based on BALLOTS, the automated system of the Stanford University Libraries. Acquired by the Research Libraries Group (RLG) in 1978, BALLOTS sharply changed in function from a single library's automation system with a few regional users into a vehicle to support the sharing of cataloguing, acquisitions, interlibrary loans, preservation, and other activities among a selected group of research libraries throughout the United States.

Similarly, the University of Toronto Library Automation System was later called UTLAS and began to make its services available throughout Canada and internationally, providing a gigantic database supporting cataloguing and acquisitions. Purchased by the International Thompson Organization (ITO) in November 1984, UTLAS was the first utility to surrender its nonprofit status.

Networks. The function networks have commonly shared has been brokering automated services to libraries, usually in a geographically defined area. Each of the networks has had unique functions, however, depending on its origins. These functions generally fall into five categories:

1. Older cooperatives linked with a utility to replace an inefficient manual union catalogue; for example, BCR and PALINET

2. Organizations formed to automate their library members, then joined with a successful utility; for example, NELINET and SOLINET

3. Organizations formed with another purpose, for whom brokerage was a means to reach that end; for example, MINITEX and WILS

4. Organizations formed explicitly for automation brokerage; for example, AMIGOS and MLC

5. Independent organizations affiliating only loosely with a utility, such as CLASS.

Despite the historical differences among the OCLC-affiliating networks, they developed similarly in relation to OCLC. At first (PRLC was the trailblazer) they entered into innovative joint ventures; but before long they took on responsibility for serving as the link between their members and OCLC. Because individual libraries outside Ohio had no rights of membership in OCLC before 1978, the networks and their directors had a primary role in representing the user-members' interests. After the 1978 change in governance, when all user libraries were designated OCLC members, the liaison function altered perceptibly. Furthermore, shifts in management at OCLC and technological developments made it increasingly difficult for OCLC and networks to agree on network functions and roles, leaving the networks in a state of transition.

At the same time, the networks had been developing their range of products and services, occasionally offering competition to OCLC. Several networks also entered into brokerage relationships with other vendors, sometimes competing with OCLC (such as REMARC). In a few cases, OCLC entered into competition with networks in markets they first entered (as in the case of database brokerage, which OCLC later abandoned). Agreements about levels of service to be provided by OCLC networks reduced the conflicts between OCLC and the networks.

Finally, increasing attention to member needs has become the driving motivation of most networks. Indeed, for almost all of them, the primary goal is the satisfaction of member needs.

TYPES AND STRUCTURES

Governance. The governance of library networks has been defined by Huntington Carlile as "the structure and administration of the power relationships among the various organizational stakeholders (members or constituents) within the shared activity or network."

Types. Three major network types are: (1) governmentally affiliated agencies, including state-government-related agencies such as INCOLSA and NEBASE; the federal agency FEDLINK; and organizations that are part of a state's higher education structure, such as MINITEX and SUNY; (2) quasi-governmental agencies, such as CLASS; and (3) not-for-profit corporations, including small regional networks, covering parts of several states but relatively small geographical areas (such as CAPCON and PRLC); single-state networks (MLNC and OHIONET); and multi-state regional networks (such as AMIGOS and BCR).

Carlile extolled the benefits of the nonprofit corporate form, citing advantages (among others) such as relative ease of creation, existence of a separate legal entity, availability of central management, continuity of life or existence, limited liability, a favorable tax structure, and flexibility.

Boards. A significant role in the governance of a network is played by its board. Stevens cites the importance of the board as a member-representative body with close control over the network's operations. Boards have responsibility for identifying network mission, goals, and objectives, approving long- and short-range plans, and setting and monitoring network budgets. The board also hires—and fires—management.

Members who serve on network boards have fiduciary responsibility and most are covered by liability insurance. Although they do have responsibility to their immediate constituents, most serve at-large, rather than as representatives of narrow constituencies. They may face serious conflict-of-interest problems, in that they are both governors of the network and users of its service. Their sizable time commitment and their loyalty represent major assets of library networks.

Levels of Networking. Because of technological, economic, and political developments, networking activity has become increasingly common, and libraries have tended to group together at various geographical levels:

Institution. A number of decentralized libraries at one institution may be linked for various purposes, including catalogue searching and resource sharing; multi-campus institutions are particularly appropriate examples.

Consortium. A group of institutions, usually geographically close, may link databases for shared acquisitions, circulation, or interlibrary loan, and for broadened bibliographic access.

Sub-state. Libraries in one region within a state may join a library system for shared cataloguing, interlibrary loan, sharing of special collections (such as film, materials for the blind and physically handicapped, and audiovisual materials and equipment.)

State. Government-related or independent systems may be created to broker database searching, to use a bibliographic utility, or to perform any of the functions cited above, or to create and maintain a statewide database in microform or CD-ROM format.

Multi-state. Government-related, quasi-governmental, or private not-for-profit networks may exist

UTLAS, Inc.

Computer room at UTLAS, Inc., Toronto. UTLAS provides a database supporting cataloguing and acquisitions.

for contracting with a bibliographic utility, brokering online searching, and providing technical assistance and training.

National. These may consist of single types of libraries, such as the Regional Medical Library Network, or may include many types of libraries with some common feature (for example, the FEDLINK network, comprised of federal libraries of all types and sizes throughout the United States). These networks may similarly offer a broad range of services.

Relationships among networks at different levels pose an interesting problem in library cooperation. Deciding what services are appropriately provided at each level is exceedingly important, because trends toward decentralization lead to proliferation of networks and to potentially counterproductive duplication of services. It is reasonable for a library to expect to receive certain services at the institution level, others from a local cooperative, still others from a sub-state system, further ones at the state level, and still more from a regional network. Identifying the services that should be provided at each level is an important task.

Financing. One of the principles of networking is that the affiliation should work to the financial benefit of the library members. This means that—at least for the nonprofit networks—the libraries should pay less than if they operated independently, and the vendor should find it advantageous to use the network to market and distribute its services and products, but the network should also receive sufficient revenue to operate successfully.

The financial savings obtained by government-subsidized networks mean that they can offer their members a great bargain. They represent a sizable investment on the part of the agencies that underwrite them. Where they operate in direct competition with nonprofits, they have the advantage (much as the nonprofits have an advantage over tax-paying businesses), because networks must first justify their prices to their members; indeed, many require member approval of prices on a regular basis.

In its financial aspects, a nonprofit network is more like a small business than like a library. It is a revenue-driven operation, dependent on market forces, with little leeway in which to operate. With neither allocations nor free overhead from a parent institution, the network must pay rent, salaries, and other operating costs from its revenues, a hard reality not always understood by members. Libraries must fare better within the network than outside it, or they will withdraw their membership; unless vendors continue to see an advantage in using networks to distribute their products and services, they will cease to do so. Thus, networks must try to persuade their members of the value of the entire package represented by their membership, rather than offer only products on which they can make enough revenue to support themselves. And, increasingly, they must convince vendors that networks are successful marketing and promotional agents for their products and services.

SERVICES AND BENEFITS

Program Development. Networks must constantly plan for services they will offer and both the governing body—the board—and management—the staff—must be involved in this process. Selection of a package of products and services suited to the particular network will be based on a knowledge of the field and of products and services available and on a familiarity with the market of present and future network members.

Financial considerations also rank high in decisions about service offerings. Start-up costs of new services may include staff (regular, part-time, and consultants); capitalization; market surveys; promotion; space; and support services and equipment. Therefore, new products and services often require several years to break even. Some valuable network services may be offered as part of the service package even if they never contribute to equity. Decisions about discontinuing unsuccessful services may be based on financial considerations alone, but may also take other factors into account.

Networks, however, must be able to move quickly to fill perceived gaps, to provide needed services on relatively short demand, and to gear up (or down) with flexibility; flexibility in comparison with its member institutions is one of the network's major strengths.

Services. Specific services provided by the networks considered in this article—and not all networks provide all these services—include: shared cataloguing, acquisitions, serials control, union listing, and interlibrary loan, via brokerage of a major bibliographic utility's services and products; database access, via brokerage of major database vendors; technical assistance and service in the use of the various brokered services; training and continuing education activities directly and indirectly related to brokered services; consulting services in library automation and related fields; direct provision of certain computerized services (such as AMIGOS' SHARES program); document delivery, either from a central collection at a parent institution or among member institutions; hardware and software sales, service, and training for microcomputer and CD-ROM applications; advocacy in the library networking and government environment for all types and sizes of member libraries; and provision of information about library cooperation and technology, through a newsletter or program of publications for members.

Benefits of Network Membership. Libraries that belong to networks receive certain benefits in addition to the specific products they purchase. They share the costs of developing products and services, can save money through group contracts, and have a forum in which to interact with other libraries. They enjoy the advantage of network flexibility, especially in financing. The network can order items quickly and submit to the library a single bill for a variety of services. Finally, having the network handle all contractual arrangements with all vendors, while the library has one contract with the network, is a great advantage, especially in view of the increasingly complex contracts for computerized services.

TECHNOLOGY

Library networking is based on three major areas of technology: encoding bibliographic information in machine-readable format for storage and retrieval (database building and management); machines (hardware) and instructions (software) to manipulate the information; and telecommunications mechanisms to transmit the information.

Database Building and Management. Although there were successful computerized library projects earlier, the development of networking really began when Henriette Avram and others at the Library of Congress created the MARC communication format in 1966. This format instructs the computer on how to read and handle bibliographic information.

The MARC record identifies the elements that librarians and others may use, to the level of detail desired, to perform such library operations as cataloguing, acquisitions, and interlibrary loan, without any need for operators to be highly sophisticated about computers. Users must follow a set of rules supplied by the utility (and often learned in training sessions offered by networks) for entering and modifying data.

One of the problems of networks and utilities is to control the quality of the records input: to see that they adhere to cataloguing standards, such as the *Anglo-American Cataloguing Rules,* Second Edition, and that exact duplicates and errors are eliminated. Efforts at quality control range from RLIN's dependence on institutional prestige to WLN's daily revision of member input. OCLC's Bibliographic Maintenance Section revises records upon notice from members, who are enjoined to report errors. Networks use peer councils, advanced training sessions, and even rewards for low error rates to encourage quality database building.

Hardware and Software. The MARC record for a typical monograph is some 550 characters in length—rather long. Libraries also usually want a great number of access points to each record, and database indexes also tend to be very large. Library systems, therefore, tend to require very large amounts of computer storage. For years, this meant that even a moderate-sized library needed a mainframe computer. By 1990, however, most network nodes used minicomputers, CD-ROM technology was widely used in storing large bibliographic databases for microcomputer use, and library workstations consisted of PCs with CD-ROM drives and communications software.

The trend in computers in and out of libraries in the mid-1980s seemed to be toward a mix of centralized databases of up-to-the-minute currency, many on CD-ROM discs, used at microcomputer workstations. OCLC and UTLAS offer CD-ROM products to help reduce telecommunications costs.

Telecommunications. Telecommunications technology allows the movement of voice and data from one point to another by means of electrical and optical transmission systems. The most common systems move data from remote terminals to a central point, where it can be operated upon by a computer, stored, and later retrieved. For libraries, this technology has primarily allowed the sharing of bibliographic information and the speedy transmission of interlibrary loans.

Several network configurations have been used by libraries. The *star* is the most common form for a centralized network; a *tree,* or hierarchical, network has been common among noncomputerized library networks. With trends toward decentralization, mixed networks and configurations such as the *ring* are becoming more common.

Whatever the configuration, data transmitted over the network must be transformed from ordinary language into a machine-readable form, so that the computer at the other end of the transmission channel can read it. It must then be put into a form the transmission channel can handle. In the case of bibliographic data, first the MARC communications format translates the data into machine-readable format; then the machine-readable (digital) data are changed into analog (wave) form for transmission over communication lines (using a modem); finally, the signal is demodulated so that it can be read in its digital form by the computer at the other end of the line.

Earlier in the development of library networking, telecommunication was relatively inexpensive. More recently, however, and especially since the breakup of AT&T, increasing telecommunications costs have pushed toward decentralization. New techniques in telecommunications, such as more sophisticated multiplexing, satellite refinements, and increased use of fibre optics, may have a strong influence on the library networks of the future. Each major bibliographic utility upgraded its telecommunications network in the late 1980s to improve response time and reduce cost.

While these three technologies formed the basis of library networking in the 1970s and 1980s, others will have an impact on its future. Remote laser printing may allow printing at remote sites of accession lists, orders, shelf lists, or other centrally produced products. Telefacsimile blossomed in the late 1980s and is now a major factor in transmitting interlibrary loans.

Specific library applications facilitated by networks include online catalogues, interlibrary loan bulletin board and message systems, and shared processing. Future possibilities include library management systems based on shared statistical information, cooperative consortium development, and availability to home computers of library databases such as the Wilson indexes and catalogues of neighboring libraries.

ISSUES

Some issues of importance in library networking include identifying levels appropriate for certain kinds of activity; home delivery of services and the need for library networks to satisfy the needs of the computer-sophisticated user; and decentralization in political and economic life and its implications for library resource sharing and cooperation.

Several other key issues can also be identified. Networks and their constituents are concerned about the respective roles of the private and public sectors and about the provision of information to those who cannot afford to pay for it. They wish to overcome the delays in actually delivering information to users, since one can now immediately identify and locate materials online and transmit interlibrary loan requests electronically. Networks want to make their services available to all types and sizes of libraries. New barriers to cooperation can also be observed, including an individualistic attitude fostered by the availability of microcomputers, which relieve the economic pressure to share computer resources. Such attitudes could lead to short-sighted isolationism on the part of libraries. Another issue concerns competencies needed for library networking, not only to develop a cadre of professionals to work in networks, but also to educate librarians so that they can provide informed leadership in the use and governance of networks.

Networks will survive and prosper to the extent that they provide needed services to their members at an affordable price. Technological developments, broad swings in the library automation marketplace, inter-vendor competition and conflict, and rapid changes in the information profession characterize their highly volatile environment. To survive, networks must be soundly based upon the needs of their members, but their responses to member needs must reflect judgments about the future that, in turn, grow out of a well-founded understanding of library technology, economics, and politics. The most significant trend facing the networks in the 1990s will be the centrifugal pull toward decentralization. To the extent that they can create reasonable service configurations, combining both political and technological separateness and the strong library tradition of cooperation, then the networks and their constituent libraries will move successfully into the next phase of library networking.

REFERENCES

Norman D. Stevens, "Network Organization: Current Status and Concerns," *Resource Sharing and Library Networks* (1981).

Huntington Carlile, "The Diversity Among Legal Structures of Library Networks," *Networks for Networks: Critical Issues in Cooperative Library Development* (1980).

JO AN S. SEGAL

Bibliotheca Alexandrina (Modern)

Momentum toward building a new library to revive the spirit and function of the ancient Library of Alexandria was boosted at a meeting in Aswan,

Egypt, in February 1990, convened by the Director General of Unesco, Federico Mayor, and the President of Egypt, Hosni Mubarak. They met to launch an international fund-raising campaign for the Bibliotheca Alexandrina, scheduled to open in 1995. Contributions of $65 million, primarily from oil-producing Arab countries such as Saudi Arabia and the United Arab Emirates, provided funds to begin construction in the early 1990s.

The Bibliotheca Alexandrina will be a public research library, located in the vicinity of the ancient library (*see* Alexandrian Library). Its sponsors intend to have it become a seat of learning with a reputation like that of its predecessor as a center for scholarship and knowledge, used by scholars and researchers from Alexandria, from Egypt, from the Mediterranean region, and from the rest of the world.

The new Library will initially emphasize the social sciences, arts, and humanities, for which no adequate library exists in the region. It will concentrate on branches of learning that relate directly to the historical heritage of the region. Its preservation and conservation laboratory will facilitate restoration of old and rare books and manuscripts scattered throughout Egypt. The faculty of the International School of Information Studies (ISIS), housed in the Library complex, will also use the laboratory for teaching and research.

The Site. On June 26, 1988, President Mubarak laid the cornerstone for the new Library on a 35,000 sq.m. site in the center of modern Alexandria, on the waterfront of the eastern port, north and west of the university. It lies between Port Said Street, main access to the Library, and El-Gaish Avenue, called the Corniche, the main traffic artery of the city. Plans call for expanding the site onto a peninsula that stretches out to the sea beyond the Corniche, facing the old Mameluke fortress of Qait Bey, built in 1480 on the site of the lighthouse that was one of the seven wonders of the world. A Conference Center has been completed on the site, with a seating capacity of 2,500.

The Architecture. Snohetta Arkitektur Landskap of Oslo, Norway, won an international competition to design the complex. The competition attracted more than 500 designs from architects in 58 countries. A key consideration was the environment of Alexandria's beautiful circular harbor. Snohetta's design features a circular shape, partly submerged in the ground, encircled by the water of a reflecting pool. The roof, inclined toward the sea, will let in natural light and offer views of the sea. Staff areas will have balconies overlooking the bay. Enclosing the building on the west is a stone wall decorated with carvings of the world's scriptures. The site will also house a planetarium, a calligraphy exhibit, and permanent and changing exhibits.

Holdings. The Bibliotheca Alexandrina was planned with collections that would enrich the heritage and encourage the cultural development of Egypt, the Mediterranean region, Africa, and the Arab world. It was designed to provide a link with the major research libraries of the world. Planners hoped for a collection of nearly 200,000 books and 1,500 periodical titles when the library opens, but allowed space for four to five million volumes. The Library is designed to include printed materials, microforms, archives, manuscripts, maps, and other forms of information sources. Its first subject areas include: Egyptian art history from the Ptolemaic era to the present; Greco-Roman archeology and history, epigraphy and papyrology, and languages and literature; oriental monachism; Hellenistic antiquity and oriental patrology; the marriage of Egyptian and Greek civilizations; transmission of the classical heritage; the history of science and medicine in the ancient world; the birth of Coptic Christianity; the influence of Islam; Arabic and Islamic literature; the culture and civilization of the Mediterranean region; Middle Eastern geography; and modern and contemporary history of the region.

Organization. The Library will be an autonomous public organization with a director general and an administrative council. A chief librarian will be responsible for internal functioning. The University of Alexandria, which donated the site, will provide technical and academic support.

Computerization. Planners intend that the Library should use the most advanced tools of information technology, able to handle Arabic, Greek, Hebrew, and Roman characters and conform to internationally acceptable standards. The system is designed to create a computerized union catalogue of the holdings of all faculty libraries in the University of Alexandria as well as the Municipal Library of Alexandria. The integrated system will combine cataloguing, acquisitions, circulation, serials, OPAC, reference and information, and administration.

ISIS. As part of the process of reviving the tradition of librarianship, the Library will contain an autonomous graduate school of information studies, which will confer degrees up to the doctorate in various aspects of information and communication sciences. The dean of this school will come directly under the authority of the rector of the University of Alexandria.

Support. The project was endorsed by Unesco, the UN Development Program, and the American Library Association. An international network of Friends of the Bibliotheca Alexandrina is linked to the ALA International Relations Committee.

REFERENCES

Mohammed M. Aman, *The New Bibliotheca Alexandrina: A Link in the Historical Chain of Cultural Continuity* (1991).

David Raitt, "The Electronic Library Manager's Guide to the New Library of Alexandria," *The Electronic Library* (1990).

Jacques Tocatlian, "Bibliotheca Alexandrina—Reviving a Legacy of the Past for a Brighter Common Future," *International Library Review* (1991).

MOHAMMED M. AMAN

Bibliothèque Nationale

Situated in the center of Paris, along the right bank of the River Seine, the Bibliothèque Nationale (BN) occupies a prime location at the center of a triangle whose points are the Bourse, the gardens of the Tuileries, and the Opera. Heir to a long history, the library is one of the oldest cultural institutions in France. The variety and quality of its collection place it among the most important libraries in the world.

History. The Bibliothèque Nationale began as the personal collection of the kings of France. Charles V (who reigned from 1364 to 1380), a great bibliophile and scholar, gathered an important collection of nearly a thousand manuscripts at his palace, the site of the modern Louvre. His Librarian, Gilles Malet, set up a cataloguing system that is still in use today. This library did not survive the Hundred Years War intact. Louis XI (reigned 1461–83) passed on to his successors a collection that has grown ever since. Military expeditions in Italy under Charles VIII and Louis XII led to confiscations of important foreign collections.

François I (reigned 1515–47) made two significant contributions to the development of the Library. He gave it Greek manuscripts he had gathered at his palace at Fontainebleau. More important, in the Edict of Montpellier (1537), he established the principle of *dépôt légal* (copyright deposit), requiring publishers and printers to provide copies of every book printed in France for the royal library, then housed at the château of Blois in the Loire valley. This requirement, so closely linked to the idea of a national library, took time to become effective—by 1645, the royal library held only 1,324 printed books.

The royal library was formally installed in Paris, initially in the Latin Quarter, in the late 1500s. Colbert, Louis XIV's chief minister, moved it across the Seine to the Rue Vivienne, near its current site, in 1666. He expanded it considerably (the bequest of Marolles in 1667 added 123,000 prints alone) and improved its organization (Nicolas Clément provided a new classification of printed books).

The 18th century was one of the great periods in the history of the Bibliothèque Nationale. It has been open to the public since 1720. It moved to its current site, the palace of Cardinal Mazarin (chief minister during Louis XIV's childhood) in the Rue Richelieu, in 1743. There it was divided into five departments: manuscripts; printed books; medals, coins, and cameos; prints; and genealogy and titles. Under the direction of the Abbé Bignon, the library became a center of intellectual life, frequented by the great philosophers and writers of the time, including Diderot, Rousseau, and Voltaire. Acquisitions made abroad enriched the collection. The first printed catalogue appeared in 1739.

During the French Revolution, the National Assembly abolished the office of Bibliothèquaire du Roi, modified the law of copyright deposit, renamed the Library the Bibliothèque Nationale, and entrusted it to a conservator. The Library itself was not vandalized; indeed, its collection experienced tremendous growth. More than 300,000 books and manuscripts, confiscated from the private libraries of the clergy and from those who fled the Revolution, were added to the Bibliothèque Nationale. During the wars of the Revolution and of Napoleon, the Library gained important foreign acquisitions.

The premises became overcrowded during the early 1800s and the staff moved collections around to try to gain space. Some parts of the building were rebuilt. The staff also tried to catalogue the huge number of acquisitions. But significant reforms did not occur until the 1850s, when a Director General was appointed to run the Library. Partial reconstruction took place under the supervision of the architect Henri Labrouste, who built the bookshops and reading room (1861) still in use today. Publication of the catalogue of printed books began with books on the history of France. At the end of the century, Leopold Delisle initiated publication of the author catalogues—the 231st volume appeared in 1981.

Bibliothèque Nationale

Inauguration of the Bibliothèque Nationale's Main Reading Room, designed by Henri Labrouste, 1868.

In the 20th century, the growth of the collections and the addition of new types of acquisitions brought about the need for new departments: music (1942) and theater arts, sound archives, and audiovisual materials (1976). Expansion in Paris included the Oval Periodical Room (opened in 1936), the Vivienne Annex (1985), and renovation of the departments for maps, prints, and coins. The BN also expanded services to the environs of Paris (at Versailles) and to the provinces (Sablé and Provins).

Organization. The Bibliothèque Nationale is a national public body with financial autonomy and a civil service staff. Since 1981 it has been under the supervision of the Ministry of Culture. Its mission, organization, and financial system were established by a decree issued on March 22, 1983.

Mission. The BN is to collect, preserve, and impart the national information heritage through legal deposit and to publish the French National Bibliography. The national information heritage consists of books, periodicals, prints, photographs, maps and charts, coins and medals, musical scores, sound recordings, video recordings, and multimedia entries. By purchase, gift, bequest, or exchange, the heritage is enriched by other works that traditionally include the following categories: manuscripts, coins and antiques, and works pertaining to the lyric and theater arts, such as costumes and designs for stage sets. It also holds foreign reference collections on literature and the social sciences, as well as documents of interest to specialized departments. The BN also conducts research in these areas.

Administration. A Director General appointed by the President of the Republic heads the Bibliothèque Nationale. It is administered by a Council of 15 members representing the government and cultural, economic, and scientific communities. The Council confers on matters of the Library's direction and votes on its budget. A Scientific Council of 23 members consults on all the Library's research plans.

Under the Director General, a Managing Director is assisted by the heads of the administrative and financial services departments and by three Directors who serve not only as heads of departments, but also as advisors to the departments of preservation and information. The Director of Research supervises the departments of bibliographic entry and processing and all international lending and exchange services. The Technical Director oversees reproduction, preservation, and restoration. The Director of Development and Information handles commercial circulation, exhibitions, internal communication, public relations, and publications, including the *Bibliothèque Nationale Review*. The Library has ten departments of preservation and information, each headed by a director.

Facilities. Holder of some of the world's richest artistic and documentary treasures, the Bibliothèque Nationale is privileged to manage this trove at its many prestigious sites and buildings. Including its facilities in Paris and the provinces, its physical domain extends over 125,000 sq.m., 77,000 of them in the heart of Paris.

Budget. About 80 percent of the Library's funds come from the Ministry of Culture to cover operations, acquisitions, specific research, and equipment and supplies. The remaining 20 percent comes from the Library's own operations, such as fees, sales of publications and reproductions, and sales of tickets to exhibitions. The Library's budget includes neither the payroll for its permanent staff nor funds provided for specific major projects, both of which come from the national budget and are managed by the government. In the early 1990s the BN's budget neared 160 million French francs a year, of which about 20 million was allocated to acquisitions, 20 million to preservation, and 20 million to data processing. The payroll is estimated at about 150 million French francs a year.

Personnel. The BN has a permanent staff of 1,250 employees. Those performing library duties come under the Ministry of National Education; those in administration, restoration, and support functions come under the Ministry of Culture. The library staff is responsible for gathering, cataloguing, and preserving the collection and making it available for use. It is divided into research personnel (230 employees), technical personnel (230), and warehouse staff (360).

Collections. The collections of the Bibliothèque Nationale are divided into ten departments of information and preservation:

Printed Books. This department includes 110 km. of shelving and nearly 10 million volumes of books, official publications, and periodicals prior to 1959. The classification system is an adaptation of a system instituted by Nicolas Clément at the end of the 18th century. At the heart of this department is the Rare Books Collection, which houses about 150,000 works, of which nearly 12,000 are incunabula.

Periodicals. Created in 1945, this department holds daily newspapers and all periodicals published after 1959 on 53 km. of shelving. It receives about 40,500 titles a year, including 32,000 edited in France and covered by legal deposit. The other 8,500 serial titles come from more than 125 other nations and appear in more than 100 languages.

Manuscripts. This department has two divisions, Western and Eastern; works are arranged according to language. In the Western Division (51,000 French, 21,800 Latin, and 5,000 Greek manuscripts), Carolingian and medieval illuminated manuscripts are grouped with an exceptional collection of literary manuscripts of classical and contemporary French writers. The Eastern Division houses 30,000 manuscripts (7,200 in Arabic, 4,300 in Chinese, and 3,100 in Tibetan) and 160,000 wood engravings.

Prints and Photographs. This department has received copyright deposit engravings since the 18th century and photographs since the 19th century. It has also acquired large specific collections, which explains the variety of its 15-million-piece stock (including drawings, postcards, and posters) and the presence of a significant number of engravings.

Maps and Charts. Created in 1828 by the geographer Jomard, this department houses more than 600,000 maps and 10,000 atlases. Its collection of globes of the earth and heavens dates back to the 16th century.

Coins, Medals, and Antiques. This department has amassed more than 350,000 coins, classified by geographic area and chronological period. Its museum displays a spectacular series of archaeological finds dating back to ancient times, most notably Greek vases. Its library has 35,000 numismatic pieces.

Music. This department brings together books, periodicals, scores, inconographic documents, and some composers' manuscript scores, such as Mozart's *Don Giovanni*. The Library/Opera Museum has been affiliated with the BN since 1935.

Sound Archives and Audiovisual Materials. Part of the BN since 1976, this department gained much of its collection since 1938 from copyright deposit of sound recordings. Legal deposit was extended to video recordings in 1975. The department has more than a million sound recordings, 20,000 videotapes, and 10,000 multimedia works.

Theater Arts. Since 1920, when the collector Auguste Rondel bequeathed his collection to this department, it has continued to grow. Located in the Bibliothèque de l'Arsenal, its wide assortment of works (more than three million, including books, periodicals, photographs, costumes, and models for stage sets) represents mostly contemporary theater and set design. The department has a branch, the Jean Vilar house, in Avignon, where it sponsors an annual theater festival.

The Bibliothèque de l'Arsenal. Near the Place de la Bastille, the Bibliothèque de l'Arsenal has been part of the Bibliothèque Nationale since 1935. Its collections on literary history are both old and wide, including 15,000 manuscripts, 100,000 prints, and a million printed books.

Collection Development. Departments of French and foreign acquisitions are responsible for the collection and bibliographic treatment of printed works acquired by legal deposit or by purchase, gift, or exchange, even though this function is integrated into all other departments. By law, publishers must register printed matter of all types (books, engravings, maps, pamphlets, periodicals, posters, and prints), musical works, photographs and films, and sound recordings. For every book and periodical, the publisher must deposit four copies and the printer must deposit two copies.

In 1990, legal deposit added to the Bibliothèque Nationale's collections almost 42,000 books and pamphlets, more than 1,570,000 issues of periodicals, more than 2,100 maps, almost 17,250 photographs, 273 medals, and more than 1,500 scores. Items purchased for the BN amounted to almost 30,000 books, more than 45,000 microfiches, and more than 12,000 official documents. Most came from Europe and North America and were concentrated in the humanities and social sciences. The BN also acquired nearly 6,800 items through exchange.

Legal deposit items are listed in the French National Bibliography. A cumulative edition on CD-ROM includes all items entered since 1970. Books and periodicals acquired by purchase or exchange are listed in the database BN-OPALE, which by 1991 had more than 1,300,000 bibliographical citations. Continued progress in computerizing the card and printed catalogues is expected to raise this figure to 7,000,000. Specialized departments contribute to the BN-OPALE database.

Conservation. In 1980 the Bibliothèque Nationale began work on a plan to safeguard and preserve its collection. According to the plan, the Library had as many as a million threatened documents. Two conservation centers, one at Sablé for books and one at Provins for periodicals, handle such tasks as deacidifying paper, repairing and reinforcing bindings, and making photographic reproductions. More than 15,000 books are available on microfiche and 1,600 newspapers on microfilm. This plan has been extended to all departments. Some of the preservation projects are handled at the central conservation laboratory or at laboratories set up in various departments. Other projects are assigned to independent conservation specialists.

Information. The diversity of the BN's missions and the range of its collections assure a diverse public. Access to the Reading Room (more than 42,400 passes were issued in 1990) is subject to qualifications. Applicants must prove that they are conducting professional research or postgraduate studies that require access to collections not available at other libraries in Paris. Access for readers depends less on their professional status than on the nature of their study needs and on the Library's ability to provide them with appropriate materials. The public is largely drawn from the Université de Paris (70 percent), with a substantial number of foreigners (26 percent). On-site information service is characterized by at least one reference office per department. With 945 seats, the Bibliothèque Nationale each year welcomes about 400,000 patrons; they access nearly 1,300,000 documents. More than half of them use the Department of Printed Books.

The BN's loan services department responded to nearly 48,000 requests in 1990, a third of them from overseas. Photocopying is growing: nearly 2,000,000 photocopies were made each year in the early 1990s. The photography service department handled more than 1,200,000 new images a year.

Research and Development. The depth and breadth of the collection justify the importance the Bibliothèque Nationale has always given to research. Its established programs lead to thematic research, inventories of specialized collections, and technical and professional studies. It conducts most research programs in collaboration with other agencies, such as the Centre Nationale de Récherche Scientifique. The BN uses exhibitions to introduce the diversity of its collections to a vast public. The 22 exhibitions organized in 1990 drew 170,000 visitors to the Rue Richelieu. The BN publishes exhibition catalogues aimed at a wide audience, as well as specialized works for scholarly use.

The Future. With storage space reaching its limit, most departments faced major decisions on how they could continue to grow and to serve the public. In 1987 the Director General, Emmanuel Le Roy Ladurie, proposed creating a second Bibliothèque Nationale, a Bibliothèque "Bis" (encore). In his Bastille Day address to the nation on July 14, 1988, the President of the Republic, François Mitterand, announced plans for a new national library, the Bibliothèque de France. The government produced a report defining the project's major objectives and proposing a new site along the Seine in the 13th arrondisement in southeastern Paris. The architect Dominique Perrault was appointed to design the new structure.

Plans called for a group of collections currently held in the departments of printed books, periodicals, and sound archives to be moved to the new facility. The move was scheduled to begin in 1994. Printed matter at the Bibliothèque de France was to be organized into four departments: philosophy, history, humanities, and social sciences; political science, law, and economics; science and technology; and literature and the arts. The new site was planned to include a rare and precious works department holding about 400,000 items and a bibliographic research room.

Starting in 1990, the BN began a number of activities in preparation for the move, including conversion of its catalogues into machine-readable form. This four-year project, the first since 1947 to cover the total collection, was designed to make a computerized inventory of all items scheduled to move and to allow patrons to access bibliographic citations for the full collection either on-site or from a distance. In addition, the BN undertook measures to improve the protection of fragile works and to ensure the reproduction of tens of thousands of them on microfiche and microfilm. Finally, a portion of the acquisitions budget for the Bibliothèque de France was transferred to the BN so it could immediately begin building foreign and open-shelf collections for the new institution.

When the printed materials and audiovisual collections were moved, the Bibliothèque Nationale, renamed the Bibliothèque Nationale des Arts, was to be reorganized at the Rue Richelieu to house collections with history and art in common, such as those of the Art Library and of the archaeologist Jacques-Doucet.

BRUNO BLASSELLE;
translated by MIRKA DELLA CAVA

Bignon, Jean-Paul
(1662–1743)

Jean-Paul Bignon oversaw the French Royal Library during the reign of Louis XV, and, as *Bibliothècaire du Roi* (King's librarian), introduced a new golden age into the history of the collection.

He was born at Paris, September 19, 1662, to a family prominent in public affairs and closely associated with the management of the Bibliothèque du Roi. He received his early formal education at the College of Harcourt, where Bossuet directed his thesis in philosophy. Since his cultural tastes seemed to point toward the priesthood, he began his sacerdotal studies at the Séminaire de S. Magloire. In 1684 he was received as a priest into the Congregation of the Oratory, where, in the same year, he published his first work, a life of a Father Levêque of the same order. Seeking a retreat where he could pursue the primary sources for his literary and historical studies, the Abbé Bignon retired to a country manor, but because of its lack of resources he returned to Paris, where he found a suitable residence and library in the Maison de S. Honoré.

In 1691 he left the Oratory so that he could pursue his scholarly interests completely. In that year he was appointed to the Académie Royale des Inscriptions et Belles-Lettres. Ten years later he was named Conseiller d'État, although he continued both his scholarly and priestly activities, even acquiring a reputation for his occasional sermons.

His extensive studies, of course, led him to acquire a sizable library; thus it is not surprising that in 1718 he was appointed by Louis XV to oversee the Royal Library. Shortly after his appointment he saw to it—like Naudé with the Bibliothèque Mazarine—that the Library was opened to the public (1720). Thus, as Hessel observes, the leading scholars of the Enlightenment were able to utilize the collection for their studies.

Under the Abbé's direction the Library was divided into five sections: printed books, manuscripts, genealogical titles, engravings, and medals, and the holdings were significantly enlarged. During his administration the 6,645 manuscripts acquired by Colbert, along with the Louvre and Fontainebleau collections, were added. Following the precedent of Colbert, he acquired books and manuscripts through the diplomatic corps on an even larger scale than did his predecessors. In 1739 he supervised the initial publication of the printed catalogue, which was completed 10 years after his death, in six folio volumes. His four-volume catalogue of Oriental, Greek, and Latin manuscripts (1739–44) prefigured similar undertakings of the late 19th and early 20th centuries. During his term as *Bibliothècaire du Roi* he continued his wide-ranging studies, producing an extended commentary on the *Bibliotheca* of Apollodorus, a primary source for the study of Greek mythology.

His personal life seems to have been austere; rising at 4:00 A.M. to pursue his scholarly interests until 8:00 A.M., he then went to his regular duties as librarian and academician. In 1741, about to enter his 80th year, he began to suffer from a violent abdominal disorder and surmised that death was close at hand. Accordingly he had his Royal Library position transferred to his nephew, Jérôme Bignon. The Abbé's health steadily deteriorated and, on March 14, 1743, he died. To the day of his death, according to Fréret, he retained his "reason, not to mention the sweetness and equanimity that he had displayed" throughout his life.

REFERENCE

Jack A. Clarke, "Sir Hans Sloane and Abbé Jean-Paul Bignon: Notes on collection-building in the 18th century," *Library Quarterly* (1980).

FRANCIS J. WITTY

Billings, John Shaw
(1838–1913)

John Shaw Billings, North American physician and librarian, was active in many fields and played a leading role in most of them. He made significant contributions in hospital design and construction, in the public hygiene and sanitation movement, in the reform of medical education, and in the development of vital statistics. His most enduring accomplishments were in the field of librarianship and bibliography, as the creator of two great U.S. research libraries—what became the National Library of Medicine and the New York Public Library.

Billings was born in Switzerland County, Indiana, April 12, 1838. His family moved to Rhode Island in 1843 and returned in 1848 to Allensville, Indiana, where his father, James Billings, ran a country store and served as postmaster and shoemaker. The young Billings attended a country school for three months each winter and read everything he could lay his hands on; by the age of eight he had read the Bible through verse by verse and had finished *Pilgrim's Progress,* Plutarch's *Lives, Robinson Crusoe,* and *The Deerslayer.* With the help of a grammar, a dictionary, and the local clergyman, he taught himself Latin and a little Greek and managed to pass the entrance examination for the subfreshman class at Miami University, Oxford, Ohio, in the fall of 1852. Miami was a typical western college of the period, with a small faculty and student body, a fixed and limited curriculum, a religiously oriented administration, and a library of 8,000 volumes that was open on Sundays from 9 A.M. to 12 noon. Billings graduated in 1857, second in his class.

He then spent an interim year as a tutor and as a lecturer with a traveling lantern show, saving his earnings to enter the Medical College of Ohio at Cincinnati in 1858. "In those days," he said later, "they taught us medicine as you teach boys to swim, by throwing them in the water." He attended a course of lectures for five months and then attended the identical course of lectures for another five months in the following year, graduating with his M.D. degree in 1860. He said that he practically lived in the dissecting room and in the clinics; when he wrote his thesis on the *Surgical Treatment of Epilepsy,* he found that even after ransacking public and private libraries in Cincinnati and searching in the libraries of Philadelphia and New York, he was unable to make a complete survey of the pertinent literature. This experience formed the kernel of his resolve to try to establish a fairly complete medical library with catalogues and indexes to match, should the opportunity appear.

After graduation he stayed on at the school—one of a faculty of nine—as demonstrator of anatomy. On the April day in 1861 when the guns fired on Fort Sumter, Billings was celebrating his 23rd birthday. In September 1861 he went to Washington and took the three-day examination for admission to the Medical Corps of the Army; he passed first on the list and was immediately hired as a contract surgeon until his commissioning as First Lieutenant and Assistant Surgeon in April 1862. He was placed in charge of Cliffburne Hospital, which he set up in an old cavalry barracks on the hill above Georgetown. In August 1862 he was transferred to Philadelphia as Executive Officer of the West Philadelphia Hospital. On September 3, 1862, he married Katherine Mary Stevens of Washington.

In March 1863 he reported for duty with the Army of the Potomac; by May he was performing field surgery at Chancellorsville; in July he joined the 7th Regiment of the Second Division, V Corps, at Gettysburg; and in August he was in New York City in the aftermath of the Draft Riots.

He was eventually reassigned to hospital duty on Bedloe's Island, and in February 1864 he was given command of an extraordinary secret expedition to Haiti to rescue some 371 survivors of a group of freed slaves who had been resettled there and swindled in the process. The rescue was successful, and by the end of March Billings had been reassigned as Acting Medical Inspector of the Army of the Potomac. In August he was reassigned to duties in Washington, and in December he was transferred to the Surgeon General's Office.

The war over, Billings settled down to a routine of office duties involving "arid drudgery among invoices and receipts, requisitions and bills of lading, treasury drafts and auditors' decisions. His days were filled with routine office work, with questions of bookkeeping and pecuniary responsibility." He also began to study German and undertook to teach himself something about microscopy, eventually publishing four papers on fungi between 1869 and 1872. He was detailed to the Secretary of the Treasury to conduct a survey of the Marine Hospital Service, 1869–70, and he prepared a reorganization plan that set the Service, later renamed the Public Health Service, on a new course.

During the period 1870–75 he prepared long reports on army hospitals and army hygiene. Beginning in 1875 he became closely involved in the development of the new Johns Hopkins Hospital and Medical School. His plans were chosen for the new Hospital, which was begun in 1877 and opened in 1889. He arranged the curriculum of the school and was instrumental in bringing William H. Welch and William Osler to the faculty. Shuttling by train between Baltimore and Washington, he gave his advice and delivered his lectures in the history of medicine—which he repeated in Boston, New York, and abroad.

Billings served as Vice-President of the National Board of Health in 1879, and in that year surveyed and reported on the sanitary condition of Memphis following that summer's devastating yellow fever epidemic. In 1880 he served as President of the American Public Health Association and began his long consulting association with the U.S. Census Bureau, stressing the need for collecting statistics on disease, not just mortality, and striving for standardized reporting. In that capacity he suggested to Herman Hollerith the desirability of developing a mechanical tabulating machine. In the decade or so after 1880 Billings published dozens of papers on vital statistics, on sanitation and sewage disposal, and on heating and ventilation. He also found time to be President of the Philosophical Society of Washington in 1886; Treasurer of the National Academy of Sciences from 1887 to 1898; and Treasurer of the Cosmos Club, 1878–79, and its President, 1886–87.

The wonder is that in the midst of all these activities his major task for the 30 years from 1865 to 1895 was directing the Library of the Surgeon General's Office, which he organized and developed into the foremost medical library in the world. For a staff Billings had a dozen civilian employees, most of them former army hospital stewards; they were dependable and reliable, if not learned, and Billings trained them in the rudiments of bibliographic procedure. He instituted exchanges with medical societies and institutions; wrote begging letters to private individuals at home and abroad; and amassed duplicates for exchanging. Reference services were not neglected; Billings and his small staff answered in a typical year about 2,000 inquiries. He also instituted an interlibrary loan system; physicians were required to make a deposit before borrowing books. And the collections kept growing—1,800 volumes in 1865, 6,000 volumes in 1868, 50,000 titles in the three-volume catalogue of 1873–74.

In 1876 Billings published the renowned *Specimen Fasciculus of a Catalogue of the National Medical Library*. The title itself is noteworthy, with "National Medical Library" appearing in large, bold type. (The letterheads of the Library at this time bore the same legend, foreshadowing the transformation to the National Library of Medicine in 1956.) The *Specimen* set forth in dictionary order both books and periodical articles; the books were listed by author and by subject, the periodical articles by subject only, in a single alphabet. On this model the first volume of the great *Index-Catalogue of the Library of the Surgeon General's Office* appeared in 1880; the first series was completed in 16 volumes in 1895, listing 300,000 books and pamphlets and 500,000 periodical articles.

The bibliographic workflow was arranged so that library clerks copied out titles on cards, which then went to Billings and to Robert Fletcher, his assistant from 1876, who penciled a single appropriate subject rubric across the top of each card. Those cards dealing with current materials were utilized, beginning in 1879, as the substance of the *Index Medicus,* "A Monthly Classified Record of the Current Medical Literature of the World," published by Frederick Leypoldt. Thus Billings provided both a bibliographic service for current awareness, the *Index Medicus,* and a service designed primarily for retrospective search, the *Index-Catalogue,* from the same database.

From 1876 to 1896 Billings made eight European trips. In 1884 he received the degree of LL.D. from the University of Edinburgh, in 1889 the degree of Doctor of Civil Laws from Oxford, and in 1892 an honorary M.D. from Dublin. Especially noteworthy are the address he gave at the 7th International Medical Congress, London, 1881, on "Our Medical Literature," and his address before the British Medical Association in 1886, "Medicine in the United States, and Its Relations to Co-operative Investigation."

In 1895 Billings retired from the Army and went to Philadelphia to become Professor of Hygiene at the University of Pennsylvania and Director of its laboratory of hygiene, which he had opened in 1892. In November 1895 his English and American friends held a great banquet in his honor, at which they presented him with a check for $10,000 and the Surgeon General announced that Billings's portrait was to be painted and hung at the Library. Just at that time he was offered the directorship of the New York Public Library, which had been formed earlier that year through a merging of the Astor Library, the Lenox Library, and the Tilden Trust. Billings remained in Philadelphia through spring 1896, then went to London as a delegate to the Royal Society's International Conference on a Catalogue of Scientific Literature. When he returned at the end of summer, he settled in New York, where he was to remain for the last 17 years of his life as Director of the New York Public Library.

In its emergent and as yet indeterminate state, the New York Public Library presented some heavy challenges. Billings set to work. He drew up a classification scheme; he reorganized the chaotic cataloguing situation and brought in a system that was much like that of the *Index-Catalogue,* with periodical articles carded among the books. He set up two miles of temporary wooden shelving in the Astor building and installed artificial lighting in both buildings. He successfully bargained for a site for a new building on the land occupied by the old Croton Reservoir at Fifth Avenue and 42nd Street. The cornerstone of the new building was laid in 1902 and the building opened to the public in May 1911. The staff was augmented and reorganized; the collections grew from 500,000 volumes in 1901 to more than 1,000,000 in 1913; and the 40 branch libraries that Billings established held another million volumes.

In 1902 Billings was President of the American Library Association. From the founding of the Carnegie Institution of Washington in 1902 Billings served on its Executive Committee and from 1903 on as Chairman of its Board of Trustees. Between 1905 and 1908 Billings was engaged in drawing up plans for the Peter Bent Brigham Hospital in Boston.

On March 11, 1913, Billings died in New York City. He was buried at Arlington National Cemetery.

REFERENCES

Fielding H. Garrison, *John Shaw Billings, a Memoir* (1915).

Harry M. Lydenberg, *John Shaw Billings, Creator of the National Medical Library and Its Catalogue, First Director of the New York Public Library* (1924).

Dorothy Schullian and Frank B. Rogers, "The National Library of Medicine," *Library Quarterly* (1958).

Selected Papers of John Shaw Billings, compiled, with a life of Billings, by Frank Bradway Rogers (1965), contains a bibliography of Billings.

Phyllis Dain, "Billings, John Shaw," *Dictionary of American Library Biography* (1978).

FRANK BRADWAY ROGERS

Birkbeck, George

(1776–1841)

George Birkbeck was a "founding father" of the Mechanics' Institutes, which were the closest predecessors of public libraries in Britain.

Courtesy of the Newberry Library

George Birkbeck

He was born at Settle, North Yorkshire, January 10, 1776. He came of a Quaker banking family but, having decided on a scientific career, was trained in what was then the only satisfactory medium, medicine. By the time he received his degree at the University of Edinburgh in 1799, he had rubbed shoulders with Walter Scott, Francis Jeffrey, and many of the other great literary figures then associated with "the Athens of the North." At the age of 23 he was appointed Professor of Natural Philosophy at the Glasgow Institution and began to lecture there on physics and chemistry.

The Glasgow Institution, which had been founded as a rival to the University of Glasgow, functioned at the beginning of the 19th century as a kind of early technical college. Birkbeck was impressed by the keen interest in scientific and technical matters displayed by some of the *mechanics,* the skilled and semiskilled manual workers employed to make his medical apparatus, and he organized an evening class in elementary science for them. He moved to London, however, in 1804 and established himself there, not as a scientist, but as a medical man in general practice. That practice was soon fashionable and successful and included many of his distinguished neighbors, such as the Grotes, the Mills, and the Ricardos.

In the meantime, his class at the Glasgow Institution was kept going by his successor, Andrew Ure. It continued to flourish, and its members built up a small scientific library; in 1823 it was reestablished as a semiautonomous association, the Mechanics Class of the Glasgow Institution, which by head-and-tail abbreviation became known as the Mechanics' Institute. Birkbeck continued to be keenly interested and supported the movement to establish a similar institution in central London despite his earlier opinion that the lower standards of elementary education ill-prepared students for mechanics' classes. The London Mechanics' Institute, of which Birkbeck became and remained President until his death on December 1, 1841, started classes and began to accumulate a small scientific library in temporary premises. It then built its own new headquarters, but these proved much too ambitious for its finances, since its only income, apart from the gifts of a few wealthy benefactors, was from the small subscriptions of its members. Birkbeck himself lent nearly £54,000 toward the building fund. Thus, the library grew slowly and was heavily dependent on gifts.

The mechanics' institute movement spread rapidly; by the middle 1830s institutes had been established in such provincial towns as Birmingham, Dundee, Liverpool, Manchester, and Newcastle-upon-Tyne, and in other districts of London. The classes and library facilities, however limited, began to appeal more to middle-class than to working-class people. Subjects such as English grammar, elementary mathematics, and foreign languages were soon included in the London Institute's curriculum. Birkbeck continued his interest in the national expansion and visited many of the provincial institutes. By the time of his death there were institutes in many of the smallest towns and villages throughout the country. It was abundantly obvious, of course, that if those in the larger towns found financial viability difficult, the situation elsewhere was nearly hopeless. Dickens satirized small MI's in his *Uncommercial Traveller*.

Despite the continuing problems of the institutes, influential people in addition to Birkbeck continued to interest themselves in them, notably Lord Brougham and his Society for the Diffusion of Useful Knowledge. The Society was responsible for the publication of *A Manual for Mechanics' Institutes* in 1839, which was especially interesting and revealing because, following a careful survey of existing institutes, it included a model building plan with two rooms for a library. The library was to be systematically arranged and catalogued and satisfactorily administered with the aid of a model code of rules and regulations. Several paragraphs were devoted to the bookstock, and in these the risks of relying on gifts were suitably emphasized and the risks to readers relying on "miscellaneous perusal of books" suitably underlined. The fiction problem raised its ugly head as it has continued to do during the succeeding century and a half; the manual expressed the view that persistent novel reading was "an abuse of the library of a M.I." The select list of recommended subjects, authors, and titles appended nevertheless included some fiction, although no works by the questionable if standard 18th-century novelists such as Fielding, Richardson, Smollett, and Sterne. The nonfiction subjects and authors included were heavy, although a few lighter books on such perennially popular subjects as disasters at sea had managed to creep in. The MI's had always sought most assiduously to exclude any political or religious books that might be regarded as in any way controversial; most of their libraries must have been extremely dull places.

The available evidence suggests that by 1850, the beginning of the movement for public libraries supported by *rates* (local taxes) in Britain, only a small number of MI's had been able to build up bookstocks likely to attract many readers. There were happy exceptions; the Brontë sisters, for example, made good use of the library of nearly 2,000 volumes accumulated by the Keighley MI. Some of these MI's, with or without their bookstocks, were taken over by the early public libraries, and the debt of the latter to the former should not be underestimated.

Birkbeck's own pioneer institute in central London, popularly known as the Birkbeck Institute, grew finally, after a long period of stagnation, into Birkbeck College of the University of London. It has continued to provide evening classes and lectures, supported by a good library, for several generations of students employed during normal working time.

REFERENCES

T. Kelly, *George Birkbeck: Pioneer of Adult Education* (1957).

W. A. Munford, "George Birkbeck and Mechanics' Institutes" in C. B. Oldman and others, *English Libraries 1800–1850: Three Lectures Delivered at University College, London* (1958).

W. A. MUNFORD

ALA

William Warner Bishop

Bishop, William Warner
(1871–1955)

Through his writings and speeches, William Warner Bishop furthered the adoption of enlightened practices in North American libraries and promoted ideals of technical performance, new in the early part of the 20th century but now taken for granted. He promoted international intellectual cooperation and, as an articulate advocate of cooperative and specialized acquisitions, union catalogues, and other forms of cooperation, he led his contemporaries in thinking of library adequacy for research on a regional and national basis.

Bishop was born July 20, 1871, in Hannibal, Missouri. When his father, William Melancthon Bishop, died in 1878, his mother, Harriette Anna Warner Bishop, returned to her native Detroit with the boy and his two sisters. Bishop attended the University of Michigan, where he earned the A.B. degree in classics in 1892 and the Master's degree a year later. He taught one year at Missouri Wesleyan College and one year at the Academy of Northwestern University before spending three years as Instructor of Greek and Assistant Librarian at Garrett Biblical Institute in Chicago.

A year at the American School of Classical Studies in Rome (1898–99) was followed by service as Librarian and Latin teacher at the Polytechnic Preparatory School in Brooklyn (1899–1902) and five years at Princeton, first as Cataloguer (1902–05) and then as Reference Librarian (1905–07). At Princeton he began to mature professionally, laying foundations under the tutelage of Head Librarian Ernest Cushing Richardson for his later prominence in national and international library affairs. His professional growth continued (1907–15) during service as Superintendent of the Reading Room at the Library of Congress, then ably administered by Herbert Putnam.

From 1915 until he retired in 1941, Bishop was Director of Libraries at the University of Michigan. During his administration the library grew into one of the largest and best selected research collections in the country. His efforts in promoting library education culminated in 1926 in the formation of the Department of Library Science, which he administered as Chairman until 1941. A thorough scholar himself, Bishop insisted on a scholarly approach to education for librarianship at Michigan and elsewhere.

Bishop joined the American Library Association in 1896. He was Chairman of the Cataloging Section (1906–07) and of the College and Reference Section (1908–09; 1917–18); for five years beginning in 1912 he served on Council. These, along with some committee work, were his major ALA activities until he was elected President for 1918–19, the fifth academic librarian to serve in that capacity since formation of the organization in 1876. During his tenure the ALA War Service received much of his attention, but the end of World War I came during his year in office; the net effect of Bishop's presidency was a strong effort to set the stage for postwar organizational change and progress.

Having served as President comparatively early in his career, before the age of 50, Bishop had many years left to provide leadership in the ALA as a knowledgeable senior statesman. Chief among his assignments were those related to the international affairs of the organization, and for over two decades he played a multifaceted role in that realm. He was active in the 1920s on the Executive Board (as Chairman of the Subcommittee on Foreign Affairs), on the Committee on Library Cooperation with Other Countries, and in the planning groups concerned with the celebration in 1926 of ALA's 50th anniversary. He was Chairman of the Committee on International Relations (1926–34) and a committee member (1935–37), then consultant to the ALA Board on International Relations from 1942 to 1949. From 1928 to 1945 he was ALA's first representative in the International Federation of Library Associations, serving as President of IFLA (1931–36). He gave stimulating, responsive leadership to IFLA, both in the formation and conduct of the organization itself and in the action taken on matters that came before it for consideration.

Bishop saw in the entire area of international intellectual cooperation an opportunity and duty to influence library development worldwide, to diminish the influence of nationalism in the library field, to promote the pursuit of knowledge, and to advance research in the world at large. He did not, therefore, limit his efforts to ALA assignments with international import. At the request of League of Nations officials, he served on their Library Planning Committee (1928–37). As a frequent adviser to the Carnegie Endowment for International Peace, the Carnegie Corporation, and the Rockefeller Foundation, he took part in a number of the international projects sponsored by those organizations in the 1920s, 1930s, and early 1940s. One of the most significant and interesting of his foundation activities resulted in his being the principal adviser to the Vatican Library in its reorganization and modernization, financed by the Carnegie Endowment for International Peace. Under his general direction, from 1927 through 1934, bibliographic records for the Vatican Library were planned and initiated, opening its great manuscript and printed-book collections for modern scholarship.

Throughout the United States significant improvements resulted from his work as Chairman of several advisory groups formed by the Carnegie Corporation to help selected college libraries with gifts of suitable books and by endowment of several college librarianships. From 1928 through 1943, Bishop headed advisory groups concerned with four-year liberal arts colleges, junior colleges, teachers colleges, Negro colleges, state colleges, and technological colleges. In all, grants totaling more than $2,000,000 were made. Out of the project grew the first qualitative standards for libraries in four-year colleges and junior colleges, as well as lists to be used for selection of basic books for collections in them. The body of doctrine on college libraries, inadequate in the literature of librarianship, was substantially increased. The books distributed under Bishop's guidance no doubt helped to raise standards of teaching in many institutions, to promote the development of reading habits among college students, and to inform college administrators of the real significance of their institutional libraries.

Bishop died in Ann Arbor, Michigan, on February 19, 1955.

REFERENCES

Claud Glenn Sparks, "William Warner Bishop: A Biography," Ph.D. dissertation, University of Michigan, 1967. Includes complete bibliographies of sources of information about Bishop and of Bishop's writings.

Claud Glenn Sparks, "Bishop, William Warner," *Dictionary of American Library Biography* (1978).

Claud Glenn Sparks, *William Warner Bishop: A Tribute* (1941).

CLAUD GLENN SPARKS

Bliss, Henry
(1870–1955)

The American Henry Evelyn Bliss, a notable figure in library classification, was associated with the City College of New York (CCNY) for more than half a century. He devoted his life to the development, testing, and implementation of the Bibliographic Classification system (Bliss Classification). He wrote several significant works on library classification theory and practice and many journal articles. He was also Editor of the *Bliss Classification Bulletin*.

Bliss was born in New York City January 29, 1870, the son of Henry Hale and Evelina Matilda Davis Bliss. The family lived for several years in New York and later at the Davis's New Jersey estate. Bliss settled in New York, where in 1901 he married Ellen de Koster (d. 1943), a teacher at Hunter College.

Bliss received no formal education until he was 15. He was educated at home by his mother, who taught him to read and write, and by governesses who taught him French, Latin, arithmetic, and grammar. Bliss entered the classics department of CCNY in 1885 but was dissatisfied with the program. In 1889, at his father's suggestion, he left college without finishing to pursue a business career.

For the next three years, he embarked on a variety of clerical positions in merchandising houses in New York. Following that, he taught school in New York until he accepted a position as Assistant Librarian at CCNY in 1892. Bliss had found his true vocation and began his life's work. He devoted the remaining 63 years of his life to librarianship and to library classification.

His work culminated in the Bibliographic Classification system, popularly known as the Bliss Classification. Bliss was a thoughtful and conscientious librarian and his ideas were carefully developed and constantly tested against the College's collection. Bliss was a contemporary of John Dewey, Charles A. Cutter, and S. R. Ranganathan, and of the development of their classification systems, but his aspirations and goals for library classification were different. Bliss saw relationships between things—and saw that the key to these relationships was classification. His classification system reflects a profound study of knowledge and library theory.

Bliss began working on his classification scheme in early 1900. He found none of the currently available classification systems adequate for his library's needs, so he proceeded to develop his own system. In 1908, when the College moved to a new location, Bliss had an opportunity to reclassify the entire collection using his Bibliographic Classification. In 1910 he published an article entitled "A Modern Classification for Libraries with Simple Notation, Mnemonics, and Alternatives," the first public description of his scheme. Over the next few years Bliss contributed articles to library literature while on leave from his position at the College. He presented some of his views on classification. His criticism of the Dewey Decimal Classification system, the most widely used system at the time, was considered shocking by some of his more conservative colleagues.

In 1928 he returned to active duty and was appointed Associate Librarian. In 1929 he published his theoretical work, *The Organization of Knowledge and the System of the Sciences,** which John Dewey lauded as "monumental." This book laid the groundwork for his major publication, in 1935, *A System of Bibliographic Classification*. The two-volume work outlined the techniques for implementing the system, including instructions for using the main schedules and subdivisions. Bliss's work met with favorable response in the library community. Scholars called the classification system "truly impressive" and suggested that his work would help to establish librarianship as a true scholarly discipline. For the next 20 years, Bliss continued to develop, refine, and publish schedules to the classification scheme. He remained active at the College until he retired in 1940. His other activities at the College included the consolidation of several department libraries and work as coeditor of the *City College Quarterly*. He also published a small volume of his poems, *Better Late Than Never* (1937). His finished classification scheme was published in 1953.

In early 1954 the *Bliss Classification Bulletin* was established to improve cooperation among libraries using the system. The *Bulletin* provides librarians with updated schedules and corrects some of the minor defects of the system. Bliss served as the first editor of the *Bulletin,* and his estate ensured the future of the publication.

The Bliss Classification scheme emphasizes a subject approach to information. The main outline of the scheme clusters topics under broad headings, then subdivides those headings hierarchically. It makes use of facet analysis and was one of the first systems to have alternative placements of some subjects. For this reason, it is considered one of the most flexible classification systems ever developed. Bliss favored short notation. The notation was designed so that book numbers rarely exceed four digits. A comprehensive index with more than 20,000 entries provides access to the main classes as well as to the subdivisions. This classification system compares most closely with the Library of Congress system, but has greater flexibility.

The Bliss Classification system has been used successfully in school, government, and special libraries, primarily in Britain and the Commonwealth. More than 80 libraries in Australia, Nigeria, and New Zealand use this scheme. The editorship of the *Bulletin* was continued in Britain. Many of the schedules have been updated and republished. An abridged edition of the system was published in 1967 for British school libraries.

Although the system continues to be used and updated, it is not included on LC or British Library MARC records, which is unfortunate, because Bliss Classification may have interesting computer applications. In his later years Bliss was intensely interested in computer applications of his classification system. Facet indexing, a major feature of the Bliss Classification system, is implicit in most, if not all, machine systems. Schedule revisions are being developed around many of the principles underlying the automated PRECIS system, which emphasizes subject access and has been proven to be easily manipulated by computer.

Bliss died in Plainfield, New Jersey, on August 9, 1955.

His major publications include *The Organization of Knowledge and the System of the Sciences* (1929), *A System of Bibliographic Classification* (1936), *The Organization of Knowledge in Libraries and the Subject Approach to Books* (1939), and *A Bibliographic Classification,* Vols. 1–4 (1940, 1947, 1952, 1953).

REFERENCE

Eugene Garfield, "The 'Other' Immortal: A Memorable Day with Henry E. Bliss," *Wilson Library Bulletin* (1969).

JULIE GLIENNA MUELLER

Bodley, Sir Thomas
(1545–1613)

Thomas Bodley, English diplomat, was the founder of the Bodleian Library of Oxford University. He wrote in his autobiography of the elements that made the establishment of the Library possible: knowledge of literature, ability to finance the project, friends for assistance, and the leisure in which to work. He had all of those elements under his control and established the Library on a strong foundation that has allowed it to continue as a strong center of learning and research.

He was the son of John Bodley, a Protestant who fled to Germany and Switzerland during the reign of the Catholic Queen Mary I. The family lived among other Protestant refugees until 1558, when they returned to London. In 1559 Bodley entered Magdalen College, Oxford, where he was tutored by Lawrence Humphrey, another former Protestant refugee. Bodley earned his B.A. in 1563 and went on to Merton College, where he was elected Fellow and began lecturing in Greek and natural philosophy. In 1566 he received his M.A. and was elected a Proctor, a chief university administrative officer elected annually by colleges in rotation. He also acted as Deputy Public Orator.

Sir Thomas Bodley

Bodley's ambition was to be in state service, so he left Oxford in 1576 to become fluent in foreign languages. He traveled in Italy, France, and Germany for four years, then returned to England to accept an appointment at Court. Beginning in 1585 he was in the diplomatic service on missions to Denmark, Germany, and France, and in 1588 he became English Resident in the United Provinces. He retired in 1596 after gaining a high reputation for his service in Holland.

In 1598 Bodley wrote to the Vice-Chancellor of Oxford to explain his plan for restoring the former public library to use by the university. He rarely visited Oxford during his project but kept up a detailed correspondence with Librarian Thomas James, beginning in December 1599; they discussed, among other details, whether to chain books and how to combat woodworms, as well as more general topics such as classification and cataloguing. He also corresponded on questions of building and furnishing. Bodley acquired books through his public service contacts, including such men as the Earl of Dorset, Sir Walter Raleigh, Lord Hunsdon, and Lord Southampton, who contributed money for their purchase. The Earl of Essex contributed the Bishop of Faro's library, which he had seized in 1596 when he landed the English army in Portugal. Notable antiquarians and collectors, such as William Camden, Sir Robert Cotton, and Lord Lumley, gave gifts of manuscripts. Other manuscripts were received from ecclesiastical bodies, among them the Chapters of Exeter and Windsor.

The Library was also furnished with standing presses of a medieval pattern, similar to those in Merton College Library. (They are still in use.) By 1602 the original library room had been refurnished and housed books by major Protestant writers. On November 8, 1602, it opened to serve the University.

Bodley's great success in acquiring books for the Library led to a need for expansion. The year 1610 marked the opening of the Arts End extension, which Bodley supervised and financed. He also saw that there would be further need for book storage room, so he urged the University to restore the lecture rooms adjacent to the Library. On his death in 1613, Bodley left his fortune to the Library, in part to build the storage extensions he had proposed. The top floor of the Schools Quadrangle was the first to be completed, in 1620. It now contains the main series of reading rooms.

REFERENCE

Sir Thomas Bodley, *The Life of Sir Thomas Bodley: The honourable founder of the publique library in the University of Oxford: written by himselfe* (Folcroft Library Editions, 1972).

STAFF

Bogle, Sarah
(1870–1932)

Sarah Comly Norris Bogle, Assistant Secretary of the American Library Association from 1920 to 1931, was an influential figure in the activities of the ALA, in library development overseas, and in the growth of library education.

She was born in Milton, Pennsylvania, November 17, 1870, to John Armstrong Bogle, a chemical engineer, and Emma Ridgway Norris Bogle. In a tribute to her at the 1932 annual conference of the American Library Association in New Orleans, Harrison Craver described her education as "the typical training then in vogue for women of leisure." This consisted of attendance at Miss Stevens' School in Germantown, Pennsylvania, and extensive foreign travel. She attended Drexel Institute Library School in Philadelphia, receiving a certificate of proficiency in 1904; that year she joined the American Library Association.

She began her library career as Librarian at Juniata College in Huntingdon, Pennsylvania, where she remained for three years. After another year of study she became a branch librarian for the Queens Borough Public Library. In spring 1909 she was invited by Craver to join the staff of the Carnegie Library of Pittsburgh, where she spent the next 10 years, first in a branch library, then as the Principal of the library school and as the chief children's librarian.

In 1920 she joined the staff of the ALA in Chicago and soon became Assistant Secretary to Carl Hastings Milam. Her work at Headquarters reflected her previous interests in library education and library services for children. Her writings also reflected these interests; of the 16 articles written by her and indexed in the first two compilations of *Library Literature* (1921–32 and 1933–35), over half express her thoughts and experiences in library education and her work as Secretary to the Temporary Library Training Board and its succes-

ALA

Sarah Bogle

sor, the Board of Education for Librarianship. Sample titles are: "A Survey of the Library School Situation in the Southern States," "Training for Negro Librarians," "Trends and Tendencies in Education for Librarianship," and "Education of School Librarians in America." Two articles reflect her interest in children's library services: "The Child and the Book" and "A Conception of the Children's Librarian." Three relate her experiences as Director of the Paris Library School and her interest in the library movement in France: "The Fascination of the New Library Movement in France," "Library Development in France," and "The Future of the Paris Library School."

She traveled extensively, attending 18 ALA annual conferences and many state library association conferences, as well as library meetings abroad, such as those of the (British) Library Association and the British Institute of Adult Education. Besides her interest in library development in France, she conducted a survey of library needs for the Virgin Islands under a Carnegie Corporation grant in 1929 and represented ALA at the meetings of the International Library Committee in Stockholm in 1930.

At Headquarters Bogle was second in command to Milam and remained loyal to him and ALA. She had a special competence in supervising staff and dealing with people. Harold Brigham called her the "balance wheel" and the "power behind the throne." Milam called her his "tower of strength." Emily Danton said: "They were a great team during the twenties. Her vision and her personal connections, antedating her service at headquarters, must never be forgotten. She knew her way around in international relationships and she did much to help her younger chief gain background in these aspects of his work. They supplemented each other in many ways, and both were highly stimulating to their associates."

Her special interests at ALA included the selection of staff; work with foundations, especially the Carnegie Corporation; education for librarianship; and the direction of the Paris Library School. In addition there was the daily routine of work at Headquarters.

Everett Fontaine, ALA publishing officer, described her as a grande dame—erect, well-groomed, with perfectly set blond-gray hair, and with a velvet or beaded band high up on her throat.

She served on the ALA Council (1917–20) and was a member of many library and educational groups, including the Association of American Library Schools (she was President, 1917–18), the Keystone State Library Association, the Pennsylvania Library Association, the Illinois Library Association, the Illinois Chapter of the Special Libraries Association, the American Library Institute, the American Woman's Association, the American Association for Adult Education, the National Education Association, and the Chicago Library Club (President 1922–23).

Bogle died on January 11, 1932, in White Plains, New York, and was buried in Milton, Pennsylvania. In 1951 she was selected by *Library Journal* for a "Library Hall of Fame for the 75th Anniversary" of the American Library Association.

REFERENCES

Harrison Warwick Craver, "Sarah C. N. Bogle: An Appreciation," *ALA Bulletin* (1932).

Emily Miller Danton, "Mr. ALA: Carl Hastings Milam," *ALA Bulletin* (1959).

Peggy A. Sullivan, *Carl H. Milam and the American Library Association* (1976).

Peggy A. Sullivan, "Bogle, Sarah Comly Norris," *Dictionary of American Library Biography* (1978).

DORIS CRUGER DALE

Bolivia

Bolivia, a republic in central South America, is bounded by Brazil on the north and east, Paraguay and Argentina on the south, and Chile and Peru on the west. Population (1990 est.) 7,400,000; area 1,098,581 sq.km. The official language is Spanish.

National Library. The National Library—founded on June 23, 1821, by Mariscal Andrés de Santa Cruz and reorganized in 1938—is in Sucre, the official capital of the country (La Paz in the political capital). It houses about 150,000 volumes. The main part of the collection is made up of 19th-century publications. The National Archive, founded in 1883, is at the National Library. The National Depository Library is in La Paz and functions as the legal depository.

Academic Libraries. Libraries are located in all 10 Bolivian universities. During the colonial period the most important academic library was at the Universidad San Francisco Javier, founded in Sucre in 1624. It housed the Colonial Academy, founded in 1776, which provided much of the intellectual stimulus for the independence of Latin America.

The most important academic libraries are the Universidad Mayor de San Andrés, with 150,000 volumes, 1,300 current periodicals, 2,500 manuscripts, and a complete collection of the country's leading newspapers; and the Universidad Mayor de San Simón, with 45,000 volumes, 510 current periodicals, 800 dissertations, and 900 audiovisual materials. Collections in the other university libraries range from

Libraries in Bolivia (1990)

Type of library	Number of administrative units (main libraries)	Volumes in collections	Annual expenditures (peso)	Population served	Professional staff (with certificate, diploma, etc.)	Total staff
National[a]	1	150,000	61,000,000	60,000	1	10
Academic[b]	17	220,000	20,000[d]	750,000[a]	1[a]	70[a]
Public and School[c]	70	345,000	--	1,000,000	2	72
Special[c]	15	450,000	--	75,000	3	48
Non-specialized	13	220,000	--	--	--	--

[a]1983
[b]1982
[c]1976 data
[d]excludes salaries

Source: Unesco, *Statistical Yearbook,* 1991 and *ALA World Encyclopedia,* 2nd ed. (1985)

10,000 to 35,000 volumes, with strengths in the humanities and the social sciences. Cataloguing in all the academic libraries is insufficient because there are so few library school graduates in the country.

Public and School Libraries. In 1968 the Book Bank (Banco de Libro) was created to organize public and school libraries throughout the country. The Organization of American States began to provide technical assistance to the Book Bank in 1976 in its effort to establish a National Technical Processes Center in La Paz. In all, 55 branches of the Book Bank were founded throughout the country, with pilot centers in Sucre, Tarija, Cobija, and Trinidad. The branches serve both students and the general public. Book Bank branches are in each town's House of Culture, and cooperation between the local community and the Bolivian Institute of Culture is a necessary link in providing Book Bank services. Collections in the branches range from 800 to 1,500 volumes.

The largest public library in Bolivia is the Municipal Library in La Paz, founded in 1838 by Mariscal Andrés de Santa Cruz, with current holdings of 90,000 volumes. The Municipal Library set up 12 branches in various parts of the city. Another branch serves as a special library for students at the Medical School at the Universidad Mayor de San Andrés, and a book bus serves the schools in zones without libraries.

A unique aspect of Bolivia's municipal library system is a procedure whereby bookstores pay their municipal taxes with books selected by staff of the municipal library in amounts equal in value to what the stores would have otherwise paid in taxes.

Special Libraries. Most of Bolivia's special libraries are located in La Paz. The largest is the Biblioteca de la Dirección General de Cultura, with a collection of about 130,000 volumes. Libraries are also found in the Documentation Center, Ministry of Mines and Hydrocarbons; Documentation Center, National Office of Standards and Technology, Ministry of Industry and Tourism; Military School; and Central Bank.

The Profession. The Bolivian Association of Librarians is headquartered in La Paz. Its members include both practicing librarians and students enrolled in the country's only library school, at the Universidad Mayor de San Andrés.

JULIO AGUIRRE QUINTERO

Boorstin, Daniel J.
(1914–)

Daniel Joseph Boorstin, North American author and 12th Librarian of Congress, built a national and international reputation as a teacher, scholar, and historian with an attractive writing style and an army of fresh, provocative ideas.

Boorstin was born October 1, 1914, in Atlanta, Georgia. When Boorstin was two his parents moved to Tulsa, Oklahoma, where his father, Samuel A. Boorstin, practiced law and the family prospered in the midst of the local oil boom. The precocious younger Boorstin also did well, excelling in academic studies at Tulsa Central High School. Largely at the prompting of his mother, Dee Olson Boorstin, who "was extremely ambitious for me," he entered Harvard in 1930. There his mentor was F. O. Mathiessen, internationally known professor of history and English literature. Boorstin wrote editorials for the Harvard *Crimson,* was elected to Phi Beta Kappa, and wrote a senior honors thesis on Gibbon's *Decline and Fall of the Roman Empire* that won the Bowdoin Prize. He was graduated *summa cum laude* in 1934.

The next three years he spent studying law in England as a Rhodes Scholar at Balliol College, Oxford, where he earned first-class honors in two degrees, a B.A. in jurisprudence in 1936 and a Bachelor of Civil Laws in 1937. In 1937 he returned to America as a Sterling Fellow at Yale Law School. He received a Doctor of Juridical Science degree in 1940 and was admitted to the Massachusetts bar in 1942. In the interim he began teaching American history and literature at Harvard; he published his first book, *The Mysterious Science of the Law,* in 1941.

After a few months as senior attorney in the U.S. Lend-Lease Administration in 1942, Boorstin returned to academe as Assistant Professor of History at Swarthmore. Two years later he accepted an offer from the University of Chicago to join the faculty of an experimental interdisciplinary program in the social sciences. In the next 25 years his reputation as a scholar and writer grew, and he eventually became Preston and Sterling Morton Distinguished Professor of American History at Chicago.

Certain themes connect Boorstin's many publications. At the center is a conviction that the United

States is unique because the social and political institutions it built over the centuries were a practical response to its peculiar environment, not to a set of abstract ideas that European countries experienced. This belief surfaces in *The Lost World of Thomas Jefferson* (1948) and *The Genius of American Politics* (1953), but finds its fullest development in a trilogy entitled *The Americans*. The first volume, subtitled *The Colonial Experience* (1958), concentrates on scores of previously slighted subjects in everyday life, including the "Culture" and "Decline of the Book," the "Rise of the Newspaper," and "The Publick Printer." *The Colonial Experience* won the Bancroft Prize in 1959. A second volume, subtitled *The National Experience* (1965), extends coverage from the Revolutionary to the Civil War. It received the Parkman Medal in 1966. The third volume, *The Democratic Experience* (1973), won the Pulitzer Prize for History in 1974.

Boorstin's return to this theme frequently led him to laud the entrepreneurial spirit evident in American history and to admire "the unprecedented opportunities" presented by American democracy. Conservative thinkers applaud this spirit. J. W. Lukacs, for example, once called Boorstin one of a "small but honorable group of principled, liberty-loving American thinkers who aim to restore American conservative cornerstones." But liberal thinkers often question his interpretations and criticize him for glossing over some of the sinister episodes in American history and undervaluing the power of ideology.

In *The Image* (1962), Boorstin argues that the mass media invent events and create illusions that rob Americans of the reality of national experience. In an essay entitled "The New Barbarians" (1968), he draws a distinction between *disagreement,* which he believes is a constructive way to reform society from within, and *dissent,* which he thinks is destructive of the consensus necessary to strengthen the nation. He criticizes dissenters for retarding rather than accelerating social progress. He openly criticized student anti-war demonstrators at the University of Chicago in 1968.

These views and actions did little to endear Boorstin to liberal critics, who also recalled his 1953 testimony before the House Un-American Activities Committee. When the Committee questioned him about a membership he had held in the American Communist Party in 1938 and 1939, he blamed youthful exuberance and a misplaced hope that the Soviet Union could check Nazi anti-Semitism. But the German-Soviet Non-Aggression Pact of 1939 had permanently soured him on Communism, he said. He also identified other people who were party members at the time and agreed with several committee members that active party members should not be allowed to teach in American schools and colleges because membership militated against intellectual freedom. "The most effective way to fight communism [and] the one effective way in which I may have some competence," he told the Committee, "is by helping people to understand the virtues of our institutions and their special values as these emerged from our history, and that I have tried to do."

In 1969 Boorstin left Chicago to become Director of the National Museum of History and Technology of the Smithsonian Institution. There he reconfigured an entire floor to consolidate a group of exhibits on printing, photography, and postal history into a coordinated "communications" display, then added a "news reporting" exhibit at the center. He also rebuilt the Hall of Numismatics and Medallic Arts and renamed it the Hall of Money and Medals. He pressed the Smithsonian to concentrate a Bicentennial display called "A Nation of Nations" on American pluralism, improved the museum's collecting policy and procedures, and encouraged scholars to study museum objects. He expanded the museum's public services by reconstructing an old but still functional post office inside the Smithsonian and by negotiating an agreement with McGraw-Hill to fund and run the Smithsonian Bookstore. In 1973 he was appointed Senior Historian, which allowed him more time for research and writing.

Daniel J. Boorstin

In the spring of 1975 President Gerald R. Ford asked Boorstin if he would accept nomination as Librarian of Congress, a post recently vacated by the retiring L. Quincy Mumford. Boorstin asked for a month to think it over. While contemplating the offer, Boorstin visited the Library's Manuscript Reading Room, which coincidentally had an exhibit on the selection of previous Librarians of Congress. A letter from Felix Frankfurter to Franklin D. Roosevelt in 1939 caught Boorstin's eye. In response to FDR's question about whom he should pick to succeed Herbert Putnam, Frankfurter wrote, "What is wanted in the directing head of a great library [is] imaginative energy and vision. He should be a man who knows books, loves books, and makes books." Roosevelt picked poet Archibald MacLeish, who eventually became an excellent Librarian. The precedent was instructive. ". . . to be *the* Librarian, you don't have to be *a* librarian," Boorstin later concluded. On June 20, 1975, Ford nominated Boorstin to succeed Mumford.

The hearings on Boorstin's nomination were hardly routine. While many influential Congressmen supported Boorstin precisely because of his scholarly credentials and his desire to bring what he perceived as the best in American culture to a much wider audience, several important groups objected. The American Library Association argued that Boorstin did not have enough experience as an administrator and that the Library of Congress needed a professional librarian who understood the world of librarianship. Members of the Capital Area Council of Federal Employees, the American Federation of State, County, and Municipal Employees, and the Black Employees of the Library of Congress objected that Boorstin's past showed soft attitudes toward affirmative action. Since the Library had traditionally been slow to correct discriminatory hiring and promotion practices, they argued, Boorstin would not be an appropriate nominee. Others pointed to Boorstin's brief flirtation with Communism, his 1953 testimony before the House Un-American Activities Committee, and a Jack Anderson column accusing him of misusing $65,000 in taxpayers' money for manuscript preparation on the last volume of his *Americans* trilogy. Since Boorstin owned the copyright, he was also awarded royalties, and thus the government had not been reimbursed, Anderson had charged.

Undaunted, Boorstin directly addressed all objections, emphasized his intention to be a full-time Librarian, and noted that he would probably continue to research and write in his free time. That he was sufficiently convincing, on the one hand, and that his credentials were a match for Congress's perceptions of what its Librarian ought to be, on the other, was obvious from Congressional reaction. The Senate's Committee on Rules and Administration unanimously reported the nomination to the Senate floor, where Boorstin was promptly confirmed on September 26, 1975, as the nation's 12th Librarian of Congress.

Librarian of Congress. Within months of becoming Librarian, Boorstin appointed a staff Task Force on Goals, Organization, and Planning, and supplemented it with eight outside advisory groups to review Library activities and recommend improvements. The groups reported a year later. In the interim Boorstin took several steps that forecast the direction he wished to take and that capitalized on the strength of his convictions and the influence of his scholarly contacts. He quickly opened the front doors to the Library and provided the public with direct access to the impressive Great Hall (where he had been sworn in) and replaced a guard's office with an orientation room. He placed tables on the Neptune Plaza in front of the Library and scheduled lunchtime cultural events to entertain visitors and staff. He also made the reference staff more accessible to users of the Library's domed Main Reading Room. He invited prominent members of the scholarly, publishing, and cultural communities to a series of formal dinners in the Great Hall to enlist their support as LC "ambassadors." He created a Council of Scholars to advise him on improving links with the scholarly world. In 1977 he persuaded Congress to authorize the Library to establish a Center for the Book to help concentrate more attention on the book's role in the process of communication. Since its creation, the Center has arranged various programs and seminars, promoted a series of "Read More About It" television spots after CBS television specials, sponsored an ABC cartoon character named O. G. Readmore, conducted a survey entitled "Books Make a Difference," and helped persuade the U.S. Postal Service to issue a commemorative stamp in 1984 that celebrated "A Nation of Readers."

Boorstin also altered the way in which the Library approached its holdings by promoting them as a "multimedia encyclopedia" and structuring lines of Library services to introduce users to all information formats in the Library's collections. He moved a substantial performing arts collection to Washington's Kennedy Center, inaugurated a series of traveling exhibits based on Library holdings, and expanded the LC publications list. Several of his proposals failed. He was not allowed to turn the LC Law Library into a subject department, and his recommendation that the Library move its foreign language collections to ethnic population centers around the nation was rejected for fear of damaging the Library's value as a central source for all types of materials.

Boorstin retired from the Library of Congress in 1987. He accepted a position as editor-at-large at Doubleday and Company.

It is too early to measure Boorstin against his predecessors at the Library of Congress. Some perceive his administrative style as arrogant, but most objections raised at the hearings on his nomination have quieted, and he formed working relationships with all communities vitally interested in the LC. In addition, he raised the institution's profile and forged new ties with scholars, cultural leaders, and various sectors of the communications industry.

REFERENCE

Daniel J. Boorstin, *The Republic of Letters,* edited by John Y. Cole (1989).

WAYNE A. WIEGAND

Botswana

Botswana, a landlocked republic in southern Africa, is bounded by Zimbabwe on the northeast, South Africa on the east and south, and Namibia on the west and north. Population (1991 est.) 1,300,000; area 581,730 sq.km. The Kgalagadi (Kalahari) occupies about 80 percent of the country, making communication difficult. The official languages are English and Setswana.

History. The people of Botswana, then called Bechuanaland, were first introduced to reading through the translation of parts of the Bible by Robert Moffat in 1826. In 1841 David Livingstone took 500 copies of the New Testament in the Tswana language to the country. The written literature of the Tswana, however, was produced only in the middle of the 20th century.

The first known reading room was provided in Serowe by the London Missionary Society, probably for the use of students and converts. In 1938 the Carnegie Trust provided a grant of U.S. $1,000 to establish libraries for Africans in Bechuanaland, in keeping with its activities in neighboring South Africa. The Government used the money to finance the Travelling Library, consisting of book boxes distributed to seven centers around the country. Each book box contained 25 titles, of which a third were reference and the rest were for loan. The service was free and was administered by the Education Department. The book boxes were to move among the centers every fourth month, but the process stopped in 1941 and was formally ended in 1950.

From 1950 to 1963 there were many unsuccessful attempts to establish public library facilities. Libraries were available only in government departments or in schools and colleges. The Government of Bechuanaland in 1963 requested assistance from the British Council, which prepared a blueprint for library development in Botswana. The Government accepted that plan and made a financial commitment for capital, administration, and recurring book costs.

National and Public Library Services. The Botswana National Library Services (BNLS) is both the national library and the national public library service. Its headquarters are in the capital, Gaborone. It was established by the National Library Service Act in 1967 and officially opened on April 8, 1968. The BNLS, headed by a Director, is a department of the Ministry of Labor and Home Affairs, which also includes archives and museums. The BNLS has a Board that advises the Director and speaks for the BNLS management when required, particularly on matters related to finance. Members of the Board are drawn from significant sections of the community, including a member of Parliament, a top civil servant, an academic, and outstanding members of the public.

In the early 1990s the BNLS had five divisions, two for central support and three for major functions,

Libraries in Botswana (1990)

Type of library	Number of administrative units (main libraries)	Number of service points (branches, mobile stops, etc.)	Volumes in collections	Annual expenditures (rand)	Population served	Professional staff (with certificate, diploma, etc.)	Total staff
National*	1	1	21,640	286,360*	930,000*	94*	300*
Academic							
(University)	1	1	150,000	1,837,455	5,000	34	73
Colleges	10	13	75,000	205,700	3,000	8	38
Public*	1	54	18,500	--	--	--	--
School		147	328,692	547,600	57,795	8	25
Special	1	35	--	--	--	22	38
Other							
Archives	1	1	13,236 (books) 143,290 files	--	9,335	5	17

*National and Public Libraries are administered centrally by the Botswana National Library Service.

each headed by a senior professional librarian. The Administrative Support Services Division is responsible for planning, finance, training, personnel, and liaison with other ministries on library-related matters. The Bibliographic and Research Services Division controls the book budget, purchases library materials for all public and school libraries, and processes and distributes them. It also manages interlibrary loans. The National Reference and Special Libraries Division collects books submitted for legal deposit and publishes the Botswana National Bibliography. It also oversees the development of special libraries in Government ministries. The Public Library Services Division is responsible for 22 branch libraries, 14 mobile library service points, 20 village reading rooms, and the postal library service. Its total bookstock in 1987 was more than 168,000 volumes. The Educational Libraries Division is responsible for school libraries.

Academic Libraries. The University of Botswana in Gaborone was inaugurated in 1982, having been a college of the University of Botswana and Swaziland (1975–82) and of the University of Botswana, Lesotho, and Swaziland (1971–75). The Library supports undergraduate and graduate programs in education, the humanities, sciences, and social sciences. By 1990 the collection included more than 150,000 volumes and 1,100 periodical titles. The Library is adding back issues as well as current works and has invested in abstracting and indexing tools, both in print and on CD-ROM. The first phase of a new library building was completed in 1986, providing seating for 600 readers.

Within the University, but independent of the University Library, is the Documentation Unit and Library of the National Institute of Development and Cultural Research. It has a collection of 12,000 documents and 1,000 newspaper clippings (1990). It produces *Devindex-Botswana,* an index to literature on economic and social development in the country, which supplements the Botswana National Bibliography.

Botswana also has an agricultural college, a polytechnic, six teacher training colleges, and five health worker training institutes. All these post-secondary institutions have libraries, some with as few as a thousand books. The best has more than 20,000 volumes in its library.

School Libraries. The Ministry of Education has more than 150 secondary schools, almost all of them with libraries, and controls the book budgets for them. The Educational Libraries Division of BNLS cooperates with the Ministry in supervising these libraries. School librarians, in the few schools that have them, must persuade their principals to use the book budgets for the libraries, instead of just returning the money to the treasury. In a school without a trained librarian, or a school in which the principal does not want to spend the money, a specialist from the BNLS may try to improve the situation.

The Educational Libraries Division of the BNLS provides a book box service to more than 150 primary schools administered by local government authorities, seeking to show the local governments the advantages of libraries in schools. It also oversees newly established school libraries, providing centralized acquisition and cataloguing services. It assigns professionals to help train the staffs. After the libraries are properly staffed, the BNLS offers advice when necessary.

The Profession. The University of Botswana has a Department of Library and Information Studies, established in 1979. It was intended primarily to provide trained library personnel in Botswana, Lesotho, and Swaziland, but now attracts students from about a dozen countries. At first it offered only certificate and diploma courses, but now offers a postgraduate diploma in library studies, a step toward a more prestigious Master's degree from a library school in another country. In 1990 the Department began offering courses in a Bachelor's degree program to candidates holding nongraduate diplomas.

The Department offers regional vacation courses in information technology and in information studies as part of its program of continuing education. Cooperating with the Deutsche Stiftung für Internationale Entwicklung, it publishes *Information Trends,* covering developments in eastern and southern Africa.

The Botswana Library Association was inaugurated in 1978 and its headquarters are in Gaborone. Membership is open to practicing librarians, information specialists, students of librarianship, persons interested in libraries, and institutions. Its major aim is to develop libraries and protect the interests of librarianship. It had more than 35 individual members in the early 1990s. It publishes the *Botswana Library Association Journal* and a newsletter. The Association hosted a meeting of the Standing Conference of Eastern, Central, and Southern African Libraries in 1986 and published its proceedings, *Libraries and Literacy*.

H. KAY RASEROKA

Bousso, Amadou A.

(1933–)

Amadou Alassane Bousso initiated and organized formal library education in Senegal and worked for professional training and support in other African countries.

He was born in 1933 at Kenel in the Senegal Valley to a family with a tradition of Islamic learning. His postprimary education was at the Ponty school, the only full teacher-training school for the whole of French West Africa, from which he was graduated in 1956. He then taught in primary and secondary schools in the Dakar area and attended Dakar University, where he took a degree in literature.

Appointed counterpart to the Unesco expert in charge of setting up EBAD (Ecole de Bibliothécaires, Archivists et Documentalistes) in 1963, he undertook 18 months of specialized studies in library science in France, Switzerland, Denmark, and Britain and was appointed Director of the Centre Régional de Formation de Bibliothécaires (CRFB, 1963–1967) and then Director of EBAD, which replaced the Centre (1967–81). The school was intended to address the need for trained librarians in former French colonies of Africa; before independence, none had been trained locally or overseas. It first took as students existing library personnel, most of whom had certificates for four years of secondary school education, which was the level Africans were usually allowed to reach, and some younger trainees with full secondary schooling. The first program crammed training into one school year. Bousso participated in a number of international meetings and traveled extensively in other countries, persuading a number of governments to send students to the school and urging them to organize the profession of librarianship so that the graduates could find suitable posts on returning home. His work proved difficult because library support by various governments often lagged.

EBAD in 1979 offered a two-year course and annually enrolled 50 or more pupils with full secondary education. It became part of Dakar University, was housed in handsome new buildings, and, more important, established a full-time staff of teachers. A Master's degree course was offered starting in the mid-1980s.

Bousso chaired various national commissions on library science, archives, and documentation, and held many international positions before being appointed to Unesco, where he became Assistant to the Director of the General Information Programme. Chairman of the African branch and Chairman of the Division of Regional Activities of the International Federation of Library Associations and Institutions (IFLA), Chairman of the Committee on Professional Training and Education of the International Council on Archives (ICA), and a member of the Management Committee for the Prix Noma du Livre Africain, he often acted as adviser to African states in the development of their national information policy.

He wrote a sociological study on the Toucouleur family and various articles on library science and technical reports for Unesco, the Association of Partially or Wholly French-Language Universities (AUPELF), and IFLA.

F. LALANDE ISNARD

Bowker, R. R.

(1848–1933)

Richard Rogers Bowker, Publisher and Editor of the American periodicals *Library Journal* and *Publishers' Weekly,* was noted as a friend of libraries and as a political reformer.

He was born September 4, 1848, in Salem, Massachusetts, to proper and prosperous parents, Daniel and Theresa Maria Savory Bowker. The panic of 1857 brought business reverses to his father, who was never really successful afterward despite a move to New York City and several attempts to start again. Before Rogers was 20, he provided the main financial support for his mother, father, and younger sister, Carolyn.

Bowker enrolled as a student at the Free Academy in New York City in 1863; it became the City College of New York before he graduated in 1868. He had an excellent academic record and formed several lasting friendships. For a while he operated single-handedly one of the first student newspapers in the country and was influential in establishing one of the earliest student government organizations. Neither of these enterprises found favor with the college administration; when Bowker helped start a chapter of Phi Beta Kappa, the President of the College prevented the young activist's membership.

Bowker's experience in operating the student newspaper led directly into one of his several careers. While he was still in college, he reported some events for the New York *Evening Mail* and he began working full-time for that paper on the day after his commencement. He became Literary Editor of the *Mail* in 1870; as one of the many pieces he wrote for outside papers and periodicals, he contributed a series of articles reviewing American literature in 1871 that appeared early in 1872 in Frederick Leypoldt's *Publishers' and Stationers' Weekly Trade Circular* and in the third edition of Leypoldt's *Annual American Catalogue*. The *Weekly Trade Circular* became *Publishers' Weekly* in 1873 with Bowker as part-time Assistant; he began to work on *PW* full-time in 1875 and bought it from Leypoldt in 1878. He owned *PW* until his death, exercising varying degrees of editorial control through the years, and was listed as its Editor for most of his life.

In his early years Bowker was intensely interested in the contemporary literary scene. Since many authors and publishers were his friends, he was deemed the perfect choice when the Harper firm needed a representative in London to make contacts with British authors and to launch a transatlantic version of *Harper's Magazine*. He spent two happy and successful years in England, from 1880 to 1882, but wished to come home for many reasons; he missed his family, his friends, and the chance to take part in liberal political movements.

One of his favorite causes was closely related to his work in the book world: the movement for international copyright. Bowker's innate sense of fairness and his lifelong habit of expressing his convictions through actions made it natural for him to support this cause through the pages of *Publishers' Weekly,* through his position as Chairman of the Executive Committee of the American Copyright League, and through continual efforts at personal persuasion. He was perhaps as influential as any other individual in obtaining the copyright acts in 1891 and 1909.

It is difficult to determine when Bowker first became interested in libraries. Leypoldt's *Publishers' and Stationers' Weekly Trade Circular* had carried some news of libraries before Bowker's association with the firm, and *Publishers' Weekly* continued this practice after Bowker became a member of its staff. He joined Leypoldt and Melvil Dewey in 1876 in establishing the *Library Journal* and in the planning that preceded the meeting at which the American Library Association was formed.

The *Library Journal* lost money regularly in the early years, partly because Dewey, its Editor, had struck a hard financial bargain, demanding 20 percent of gross receipts from subscriptions and advertisements. Publishing the periodical was a great nuisance to Leypoldt and Bowker because Dewey was dilatory and careless. Bowker, however, continued to support the library movement, keeping the *Library Journal* alive after Dewey's departure in 1881 and Leypoldt's death in 1884. Bowker wrote editorials and articles for *LJ* throughout his life; they were always informative, positive in tone, and sometimes quite laudatory of good works. Typical of the articles are "The Work of the Nineteenth-Century Librarian for the Librarian of the Twentieth" (September-October 1883), in which he saw the librarian as a liberator rather than a keeper of books; "The Formation and Organization of Public Libraries" (March 1887), in which he demonstrated a good knowledge of library legislation and suggested some practical ways to start a public library; "Making the Most of the Small Library" (March 1915), practical advice on the operation of a public library too small to hire a professional librarian; and "Women in the Library Profession," a three-part article in 1920, in which he pointed out gains made by women in the profession and described the contributions of a number of leading women librarians.

Bowker's friendship for libraries was expressed in another way: he was an active member of the ALA, serving on the Council for more than 20 years and as Chairman of the Committee on Public Documents for some time. He refused the presidency of the Association three times, believing that a librarian should hold the post, but was made Honorary President when he was in his seventies.

He promoted the welfare of several individual libraries in a number of ways. He was one of the two people who were most influential in persuading President McKinley to appoint Herbert Putnam as Librarian of Congress and later gave several thousand dollars to the LC Trust Fund. In Brooklyn, where he lived for many years, he worked hard in the movement that culminated in the formation of the Brooklyn Public Library in 1902; he then served as one of its trustees until his death. He was also President of the Library Association in Stockbridge, Massachusetts, where he had a summer home, from 1904 until 1928. He wrote articles for the *Library Journal* about the work of public library trustees.

ALA

R. R. Bowker

Bowker's bibliographic work also helped libraries. He carried on Leypoldt's *Publishers' Weekly* and *American Catalogue* and inaugurated a few bibliographic enterprises of his own, most notably three features added to the *American Catalogue* that he felt were needed by librarians: a list of federal government publications (1885), a list of society publications (1885), and a list of state publications (1891). But Bowker was not the innovative bibliographer that Leypoldt had been, nor was he in his later years as inventive and as quick to sense the needs of librarians as was his younger rival, H. W. Wilson.

Perhaps Bowker did not change or develop his bibliographical work further because throughout his life his basic interest had been broadly humanitarian, not bookish and bibliographic, and he directed much of his tremendous energy into fighting bravely and intelligently for almost every liberal cause. He was a part of a small group of men who founded the "Mugwumps," a liberal group in the Republican Party, though he may not have been, as some have said, *the* founder of that movement. He fought against corrupt politicians and for civil service. A supporter of tariff reform, he felt that existing U.S. tariffs protected special interests at the expense of the public. His concern for the welfare of mankind in general led him to oppose imperialistic and militaristic tendencies in the government. He also worked for the benefit of minorities in the United States. He wrote articles strongly advocating the establishment of settlement houses, vigorously opposed tendencies toward anti-Semitism at City College, gave generously to colleges for blacks, and opposed the persecution of conscientious objectors in World War I.

Bowker held liberal, humanitarian views about the conduct of business and put them into practice. He believed that owners and managers should voluntarily hold down profits and should show concern for their employees and for consumers. He accepted the position as Executive Officer of the Edison Electric Illuminating Company in New York in 1890 partly in order to put his ideas about the proper conduct of a business into practice on a larger scale than he could at *Publishers' Weekly*. For a while he was successful, managing to reduce the cost of electricity to consumers while raising wages and paying a fair return to stockholders, but he resigned in 1899 when a group of stock manipulators, planning to establish a monopoly, managed to gain control of the company.

When Bowker left Edison, he was beginning to have serious eye trouble, and he became completely blind in a few years. His failing sight would have prevented him from giving close personal supervision to the development of new bibliographic or indexing services, a situation that may have prevented the diversification of the Bowker Company's services during his later life.

Around the time Bowker was adjusting to the loss of his eyesight, he surprised his friends by marrying Alice Mitchell on New Year's Day, 1902, when he was 53 and she was 38. The couple had known each other for several years.

Although Bowker had lost his sight, his general health was good, and his concern for other human beings was undiminished; for many years he wrote and spoke in favor of a variety of causes. He remained active until November 12, 1933, when he died, after a short illness, at the age of 85. At the time of his death, Herbert Putnam surely expressed the feeling of librarians when he wrote in the special December 1, 1933, issue of *Library Journal,* "Our profession has had no friend who, without the professional obligation, has aided so greatly to define its aims, maintain its dignity, and promote its fellowship."

REFERENCE

E. M. Fleming, *R. R. Bowker, Militant Liberal* (1952). The largest collection of Bowker's manuscripts is in the New York Public Library; others are listed in Fleming's bibliography.

HAYNES McMULLEN

Bradford, S. C.
(1878–1948)

Samuel Clement Bradford, British librarian and writer on the classification of scientific literature, was a supporter of moves to improve the control of scientific and technical information and contributed to the development of the field of documentation.

Bradford was born in London, January 10, 1878. He trained as a chemist, and a former colleague related that Bradford obtained his first degree by study at night school and his doctorate by research in his office in the Science Museum Library. He was fond of roses, and sandwiched between his many writings on chemistry and documentation was a book on the science of roses.

He joined the staff of the Science Museum in 1899 and worked in its library from 1901 until his retirement in 1938, becoming Assistant Keeper in 1922, Deputy Keeper in 1925, and Keeper in 1930. During his tenure he devoted his vision and energy to turning the Science Museum Library into the National Science Library. D. J. Urquhart observed that his great achievement was that he managed to change a small scientific library into the largest collection of scientific literature in Europe.

Bradford enthusiastically supported the adoption of the Universal Decimal Classification (UDC) throughout the world, with a view to the production of a world bibliography, and is well remembered for his advocacy of UDC as superior to any other system of classification and to alphabetical systems. He introduced UDC into the Science Library and was a keen supporter of the International Institute of Bibliography, later to become the International Federation for Documentation (FID). Largely to further the use of UDC, Bradford formed, in 1927, with A. F. C. Pollard, the British Society for International Bibliography (BSIB) as the British Committee of FID, and BSIB became one of the main channels of communication about UDC in Britain. He edited the *Proceedings of the British Society for International Bibliography* from its inception in 1939 until the amalgamation of BSIB with Aslib (then the Association of Special Libraries and Information Bureaux) in 1948. He followed Pollard as President of BSIB in 1945 and was elected a Vice-President of FID and Chairman of its International Committee on Classification in 1947.

One of the reasons for Bradford's strong support of UDC was his concern that scientific literature should be fully documented and well organized. In *Documentation* (1948), he refers to experiments conducted at the Science Library that showed that less than half the useful papers published were being covered by abstracting journals. He then investigated the manner in which articles on one subject would often appear in periodicals not primarily concerned with that subject. He deduced a common pattern in this "bibliographical scatter," which led him to formulate his "Law of scatter." "Bradford's Law" has received a great deal of attention from writers on scientific documentation—too much, according to Bradford's successor, Urquhart, who wrote, "Bradford's Law . . . was but a small element in his propaganda war," and suggested that "Bradford would be appalled by the academic discussion which has taken place about his law. He was interested in much more practical things."

Bradford published 35 contributions to documentation, but he also wrote many papers on chemistry and other scientific subjects. He will be best remembered by librarians as a writer for the collection of essays published as *Documentation,* which Margaret Egan, reviewing the book in *Library Quarterly* (1950), said "should be useful in directing the attention of American librarians to the importance of bibliographic control in some form and the need for further investigation of this neglected aspect of librarianship." The conclusion to her review showed that Bradford was human and that he did not always practice what he preached: "One cannot conclude, however, without expressing surprise that Mr. Bradford, who argues so convincingly for more adequate indexing services, should be so inconsiderate as to give us this book without an index, organized according to either the UDC or even the abhorred concealed classification of subject headings." It is interesting to note that an index *was* provided for the reprint, published five years after Bradford's death, to which Egan and Jesse Shera contributed a 35-page introductory essay calling for librarianship and documentation to be regarded as a unity.

Urquhart remarks that Bradford seemed to him at first "a very fussy man." The official support given to the National Lending Library for Science and Technology (now incorporated in the British Library Lending Division) owed a great deal to Bradford's pioneering propaganda efforts, and Urquhart observes, "That to me is how Bradford should be remembered—as one who sought to convince others of the importance of scientific information and who did a great deal despite the odds against him to make scientific information available. The fussy little man I once met was really a giant in disguise."

REFERENCES

E. M. R. Ditmas, "Dr. S. C. Bradford," *Journal of Documentation* (1948).

D. J. Urquhart, "S. C. Bradford," *Journal of Documentation* (1977). M. Gosset, "S. C. Bradford, Keeper of the Science Museum Library 1925–1937," *Journal of Documentation* (1977).

K. G. B. BAKEWELL

Bray, Thomas

(1658–1730)

Because of his own activities and those of the societies he founded, Thomas Bray was one of the greatest single cultural influences at work in the American colonies during the 18th century.

He was born in Marton, Shropshire, England, in 1658. Edward Lewis, Vicar of the nearby town of Chirbury, noticed Bray's aptitude for learning and made available his notable collection of chained books. Through Lewis's influence, Bray's parents sent him to Oswestry Grammar School. He matriculated at All Souls College, Oxford, in 1674 as a *puer pauper,* supporting himself through service to the fellows, and receiving his Bachelor of Arts degree in 1678. He later took Bachelor of Divinity and Doctor of Divinity degrees from Magdalen College.

Bray's first appointment was to a parish near Bridgnorth, Warwickshire, in 1681. A few months later he was asked to preach the annual assize sermon. One of the members of the congregation was Simon, Lord Digby. Impressed with the young priest's presentation, he persuaded his brother, William, to offer Bray the parish of Over Whitacre. In 1690 William presented Bray with the living at Sheldon, which he continued to hold until his death, although an appointed curate actually served the parish for over 25 years while Bray labored in London on his various schemes.

Through his friendship with the Digbys, Bray came to the notice of Bishop Compton of London, who had been concerned for some time with the lack of spiritual leadership in the colonies. He had appointed James Blair as Commissary of Virginia in 1689, and in 1696 he offered Bray a comparable position in Maryland.

Bray, who was concerned with the intellectual as well as the spiritual life of the colonists, developed a scheme to provide libraries for all the parishes of Maryland; he agreed to accept the position if Compton would support his plan. With Compton's approval, he began collecting books and interviewing missionaries for service in the colony. He was so successful that Governor Nicholson suggested Compton appoint Bray Commissary for New York, Pennsylvania, and New England as well.

At the start, Bray's primary concern was for Maryland, but as he began to hear from ministers in the New World about the lack of books in other colonies, he expanded his plan to provide libraries for each of the colonies. By 1697, 16 libraries had been established in Maryland and 7 in the other colonies, and plans were under way for 6 more.

In his *Bibliothecae Americanae Quatripartidiae,* Bray outlined his colonial library system. A large provincial library would be established in the major city of each colony. A parochial library would be established in each parish. And a layman's library would be comprised of certain religious books that would be loaned by the minister. A number of tracts would be given free to the people.

When he presented his final report on the libraries to the Society for the Propagation of the Gospel in Foreign Parts in 1704, Bray could claim the establishment of provincial libraries in Boston, New York, Philadelphia, Annapolis, Charleston, and Bath, North Carolina. He had provided 29 parochial libraries for Maryland and at least one such library in each of the other colonies, as well as providing more than 35,000 volumes for the layman's libraries in all the colonies.

Some of Bray's library ideas were surprisingly modern. In his *Memorial to the Clergy of Maryland,* published in 1700, he outlined two ideas for increasing and preserving the libraries. First, each library would provide a catalogue of its collection to the others so that they might exercise a primitive system of interlibrary loan. Second, a small annual subscription would be assessed on the borrowers to enlarge the collections.

Given his personal involvement in establishing libraries, it is certain that had Bray been able to return to America, he would have promoted their growth and development. Because he could not return, they were left to struggle on their own. Without support and encouragement from the colonists, they gradually diminished as an intellectual force in the life of the people.

In addition to providing libraries and missionaries for the colonies, Bray steered a bill through Parliament for the establishment of the Church of England in Maryland. At the same time, in order to further his library plans, he founded the Society for the Promotion of Christian Knowledge, the Society for the Propagation of the Gospel in Foreign Parts, and the Bray Associates. The Act of Establishment of the Church remained in force throughout the colonial period, and the societies still exist today, active in missionary enterprise, publishing, and education.

Bray died in London on February 15, 1730. Although Bray had the satisfaction of seeing legislative protection given to libraries in three colonies during his lifetime, he failed in his attempts to secure public support for their growth and continued development. Nearly a century and a half had to pass before the support necessary for the growth of the library as a public institution would develop. Had he lived in the 19th century, Bray would have been one of the driving forces in that development.

REFERENCES

Charles T. Laugher, *Thomas Bray's Grand Design* (1973).
Henry Thompson, *Thomas Bray* (1954).

CHARLES T. LAUGHER

Brazil

Brazil, a federal republic, is the largest country in South America. It is bordered on the north, west, and south by every South American country except Chile and Ecuador; the Atlantic Ocean lies to the east. Population (1990 est.) 150,368,000, area 8,511,965 sq.km. The official language is Portuguese.

History. The first libraries in Brazil were school libraries, maintained by the Jesuits in the

The National Library in Rio de Janeiro.

schools they founded in São Vicente (1550), Rio de Janeiro (1567), and Bahia (1568). The most important was that of Bahia, which had European librarians.

In 1808 the Portuguese royal family, fleeing Napoleon's troops, sailed to Brazil, carrying with them many of the precious books of Portugal. This Royal Library formed the basis for the collection in the National Library, which was founded in 1810. Many public libraries were founded, the first in Bahia, in 1811, modeled along the lines of the subscription public libraries that arose in the United States and in Britain in the 18th century. After Brazil became independent in 1822, other Brazilian states opened public libraries.

Government support for public libraries waned after the 1950s, when technological developments encouraged the creation of academic and special libraries. The Brazilian Institute for Information in Science and Technology (IBICT) was founded in 1954. It has contributed greatly to the development of academic and special libraries and to the implementation of information systems. The national and state governments took renewed interest in public libraries in the late 1970s and throughout the 1980s, while academic and special libraries benefited from wide use of new technologies.

National Libraries. The Biblioteca Nacional (National Library) began with the royal family's collection of books when the Court moved to Brazil in 1808–09. The royal family first housed the Library in the Hospital of the Third Order of Carmelites, moving it to a new building in 1859. The Library continued to grow and had outgrown that building by the early 1900s. It has added to its rich collections by means of Brazil's legal deposit system as well as by purchase, gift, and exchange. The Library's holdings include approximately 7,000,000 volumes, 650,000 manuscripts, and 60,000 volumes of rare books.

The National Library became a Foundation in 1990, incorporating the former National Book Institute as one of its four departments. The National Library Foundation is the repository of Brazilian bibliographic production, the center for international interlibrary exchanges, and the Brazilian agency for International Standard Book Numbers (ISBN).

National Archives. The basic functions of the National Archives were established by an imperial decree in 1838. The National Archives has collected the records of the executive, legislative, and judicial branches, as well as documents from individuals and businesses that are of historical interest. It houses more than 25 linear kilometers of manuscripts, printed materials, cartographic works, and audiovisual items, from the 16th century to the present. The National Archives has a 20,000-volume library specializing in the areas of history, law, and archival studies, including some rare books. It also has a laboratory for preservation and restoration.

Academic Libraries. The Programa Nacional de Bibliotecas Universitárias (PROBIB; National Program of University Libraries) of the Secretariat of Higher Education of the Ministry of Education was created in 1986 to support cooperative programs among academic libraries and to develop policies for both public (government-funded) and private university libraries.

Among state universities, the Library of the University of São Paulo has the largest collection in Brazil. Among private universities, the Library of the Pontifical Catholic University in Rio de Janeiro is noted for its excellent services and the currency of its holdings.

Most universities have decentralized library facilities. The Federal University of Rio de Janeiro estab-

Libraries in Brazil (1985)

Type of library	Number of administrative units (main libraries)	Number of service points (branches, mobile stops, etc.)	Volumes in collections *books only*	Annual expenditures (cruzeiro)	Population served *registered readers*	Professional staff (with certificate, diploma, etc.)	Total staff
National	1	1	1,057,024*	--	110,190	--	472
Academic	907	--	8,472,343	--	1,664,276	--	7,105
Public	4,174	--	11,517,031	--	3,696,977	--	12,766
School	12,914	14,334	19,072,191	--	15,085,314	--	21,280
Special	1,166	--	4,926,478	--	397,682	--	5,007
Children & adult libraries	154	--	--	--	185,266	--	635

*In 1990, of which 45,358 are rare books.

lished SIBI, a system of information for its libraries, in 1990. The Central Library coordinates the decentralized library system, which includes 7 university center libraries and 38 departmental libraries. Total holdings amount to almost 975,000 volumes and more than 37,000 periodical titles. The University publishes a *SIBI Library Guide*, a quarterly bulletin, and "Current Summaries in Information Science" (1990–). The staff includes 124 librarians and 165 clerical workers. The libraries of the federal universities of the states of Rio Grande do Sul, Paraná, Santa Catarina, Minas Gerais, Espírito Santo, Pernambuco, and Ceará have similar organizations.

Public Libraries. All public libraries in Brazil are state libraries except the Municipal Library of São Paulo, founded in 1925. This public library—today called the Mario de Andrade Library in honor of a great Brazilian author—opened a major new building in 1938 under the directorship of Rubens Borba de Moraes. Renewed emphasis on public libraries followed, and some state libraries were reorganized.

The Instituto Nacional do Livro (INL; National Book Institute), founded in 1937 to foster reading and library development, played an important part in public library renewal. But it did not try to implement a program for a national system of public libraries until 1977. INL helped publish professional handbooks and journals, sponsored congresses and meetings, and distributed books to municipalities willing to spend matching funds for book purchases. The INL program, focusing on a library in each municipality, planted the seeds of a public library system in the states. Some of these public libraries have been successful, but they continue to depend on politicians and on the leadership of their head librarians to obtain financial support from local governments. As a result of changes in federal law, many municipalities have been able to increase their budgets and have accepted the idea of building cultural centers with libraries at their core. INL was merged into the National Library Foundation in 1990.

School Libraries. In Brazil, education is a responsibility shared by federal, state, and local governments. Despite support from international organizations, the idea of a library in each school, or in the main school for a given area, is not as widely accepted as the idea of a library in each municipality. In fact, most students look for information and material for homework at their local public libraries. Fewer than 10 percent of public schools have libraries, but some states are working toward implementing public library systems. Most good private schools, by contrast, have libraries or multimedia centers. The federal government promotes reading rooms in public schools, a concept that has been accepted by some states and municipalities.

Special Libraries. Brazil has important special libraries in many fields. For example, the Ministry of Agriculture has an office called Coordenação e Documentação Agrícola (Coordination and Documentation on Agriculture) and the Empresa Brasileira de Perquisa Agropecuária (EMBRAPA; Brazilian Enterprise for Research in Farming and Cattle-Raising). Petróleo Brasileiro sponsors an information network, the Sistema de Informação e Documentação Técnica em Petróleo (SINPETRO; Petroleum Information and Technical Documentation System). The Sistema de

René Vergara

The modern State Library of Rio de Janeiro.

Informação em Geociências e Tecnologia Mineral (GEOCINF; Information System in Geosciences and Mining Technology) serves the mining industry. And the Centro de Informaçãoes Nucleares (CIN; Center for Nuclear Information) in the National Commission for Nuclear Energy supports Brazilian and other Latin-American scientists specializing in nuclear and alternative sources of energy. Government ministries also have special libraries. The Government created a Programa de Apoio ao Desenvolvimento Científico e Tecnológico (PADCT; Program of Support for Scientific and Technological Development) to help finance information and documentation systems.

IBICT, the Instituto Brasileiro de Informação em Ciência e Tecnologia, has been actively engaged in training personnel and in working with scientific and technological information systems. In association with the Federal University of Rio de Janeiro, IBICT offers specialization in library science and scientific documentation and a graduate program in information science leading to a Master's degree. It also offers access to international databases for small and medium-sized private enterprises.

The BIBLIODATA network, coordinated by the Getulio Vargas Foundation, is designed to establish a cooperative infrastructure for libraries and documentation centers that would speed up technical processing, avoid duplication in cataloguing and classifying, and foster standardization, reducing costs. It also conducts research on software for information science. By the early 1990s it dealt with 64 institutions with a total of 210 libraries and had a total of almost 400,000 records that can be examined through several telecommunications networks or on diskettes.

The Government sponsors the Programa de Comutação Bibliográfica (COMUT; Bibliographic

Exchange Program) to locate documents in the many Brazilian libraries and make them available to those who need them. In the early 1990s COMUT provided more than a million copies of articles from periodicals to users in some 900 libraries.

The Biblioteca Regional de Medicina (BIREME; Regional Library of Medicine), located in São Paulo, covers literature in the health sciences produced by Latin-American authors and published since 1980. It is linked to the Pan American Health Organization, which is affiliated with the World Health Organization. With subcenters in several Brazilian universities, it maintains an efficient biomedical information system.

The Profession. The National Library offered the first library science course in 1911, concentrating mainly on book preservation. The first library service program to reflect new developments in librarianship was inaugurated in 1936. It was sponsored by the City of São Paulo, which needed trained personnel to work in its Municipal Public Library. Among its teachers were Adelfa Figueiredo, who had been trained at the Columbia University School of Library Service, and Rubens Borba de Moraes. This program marked the beginning of North American influence on Brazilian librarianship, an influence that lasted until the 1970s.

In 1938 graduates of the São Paulo program founded the Paulista Association of Librarians, the oldest association of librarians in Latin America. In 1959 librarians meeting at the Second Brazilian Congress of Library Science and Documentation founded the Federação Brasileira de Asociaçãoes de Bibliotecários (FEBAB; Brazilian Federation of Library Associations). With headquarters in the city of São Paulo, FEBAB coordinates the professional work of the local library associations. It has permanent commissions on such topics as public and school libraries, technical processing, and university libraries. FEBAB publishes the *Revista Brasileira de Biblioteconomia e Documentação* and sponsors the Brazilian Congress of Library Science and Documentation. The congress, organized by one of the state associations, is held every two years.

The Federal Council of Librarianship was created in 1962, when the profession was legally recognized. The Asociação Brasileira de Ensino de Biblioteconomia e Documentação (Brazilian Association of Teachers of Librarianship and Documentation) was founded in 1967.

REFERENCE

Cavan M. McCarthy, "Achievements and Objectives in Brazilian Librarianship," *International Library Review* (1983).

MARY ALICE BARROSO;
ELISABETH CARVALHO;
MAY NEGRAÕ BROOKING

ALA

William Howard Brett

Brett, William Howard

(1846–1918)

William Howard Brett was librarian of the Cleveland Public Library and a library educator. Few American librarians, even among that remarkable group who were his contemporaries, displayed more virtuosity or made more contributions to disparate parts of the profession than Brett.

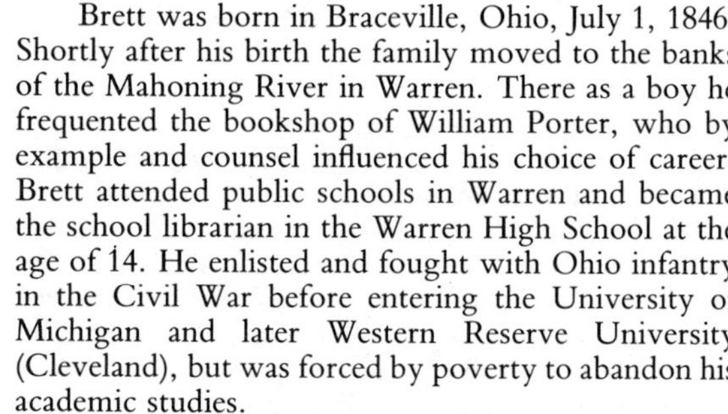

Brett was born in Braceville, Ohio, July 1, 1846. Shortly after his birth the family moved to the banks of the Mahoning River in Warren. There as a boy he frequented the bookshop of William Porter, who by example and counsel influenced his choice of career. Brett attended public schools in Warren and became the school librarian in the Warren High School at the age of 14. He enlisted and fought with Ohio infantry in the Civil War before entering the University of Michigan and later Western Reserve University (Cleveland), but was forced by poverty to abandon his academic studies.

Brett settled in Cleveland. He worked for a Cleveland bookdealer, Cobb and Andrews Company, and expanded his acquaintanceship among bibliophiles, including John Griswold White, who was instrumental in appointing him Librarian of the Cleveland Public Library in 1884.

Brett soon distinguished himself for his contributions to cataloguing in the traditions set by Cutter and Dewey. By 1890 he was developing the concept of the open-shelf library, which led among other things to his being invited to London to deliver a paper on his ideas of free access to library collections.

Brett continued to grow and expand in almost every aspect of librarianship. Andrew Carnegie depended much on Brett's advice during the most fruitful years of his philanthropy. Brett was expert in the design of buildings. He published the first issue of his *Cumulative Index to the Selected List of Periodicals* in 1896, a publication that after several metamorphoses became the familiar *Readers' Guide to Periodical Literature*. In the same year he was elected President of the American Library Association.

Brett campaigned vigorously for libraries for children and established an alcove for juvenile books in the Cleveland Public Library. Under his leadership the first branch libraries were opened in Cleveland.

Staff training came to occupy a large place in Brett's thinking, and he came to realize the importance of specialized education to the work of librarians. His interest in this idea developed eventually into a plan for a library school at Western Reserve University, where in 1904 he was present at the birth of that school. He was its first dean even as he remained head of the public library.

Brett died on August 24, 1918, in Cleveland. During his last years, he developed plans for the main library building on Superior Avenue in Cleveland, which, although not opened until 1925, bears the imprint of his thought.

REFERENCES

Linda A. Eastman, *Portrait of a Librarian: William Howard Brett* (1940).

C. H. Cramer, "Brett, William Howard," *Dictionary of American Library Biography* (1978).

ERVIN J. GAINES

British Library

If the sum of human knowledge can be said to be located anywhere, it would probably be the British Library. No other library can match the riches and variety of its resources for research into every aspect of human thought and achievement. Books and manuscripts contain the DNA of civilization. Those who

British Library

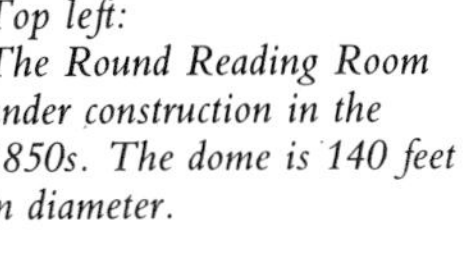

The British Library Board

Top left:
The Round Reading Room under construction in the 1850s. The dome is 140 feet in diameter.

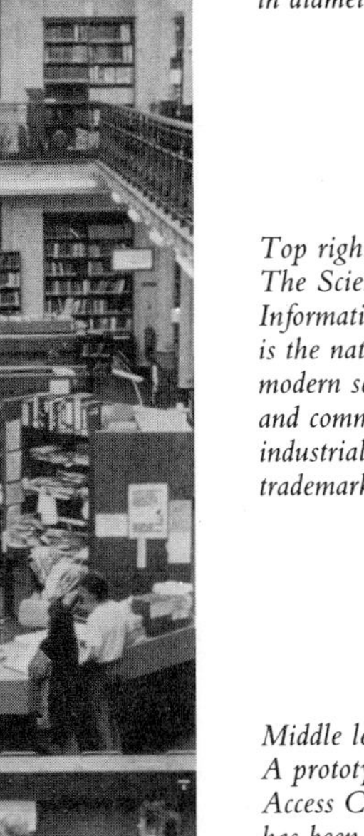

The British Library Board

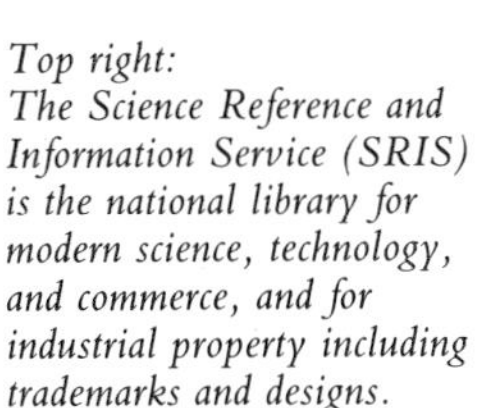

Top right:
The Science Reference and Information Service (SRIS) is the national library for modern science, technology, and commerce, and for industrial property including trademarks and designs.

The British Library Board

Middle left:
A prototype Online Public Access Catalogue (OPAC) has been available for trials by staff and users in the Round Reading Room since 1990. At the new British Library at St. Pancras now under construction, access to the collections will be primarily through a dedicated OPAC system.

The British Library Board

Bottom right:
The science, technology and business area of the new British Library at St. Pancras under construction.

The British Library Board

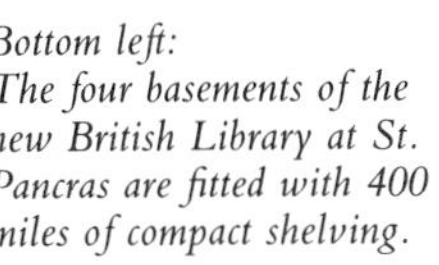

Bottom left:
The four basements of the new British Library at St. Pancras are fitted with 400 miles of compact shelving.

seek to understand the past and shape the future, from almost every country, employ the resources of the British Library every day by personal visit, by telephone, by post, and by internationally linked computer networks. It is one of the world's few general and universal libraries with sufficiently comprehensive collections to satisfy the specialist. Among the many communities of researchers the British Library serves are scientists, industrialists, and businessmen, writers, teachers, and historians, academics in British and overseas universities, and hosts of individual researchers applying their initiative and energy to new topics of research. Remote users in all parts of the world rely on the British Library for information unobtainable elsewhere and for services unavailable locally.

History. The British Library Act, passed by Parliament in 1972, was a public renewal of faith in the ideas that inspired the foundation and growth of its oldest component, the Library of the British Museum. The scientist Sir Hans Sloane left his books, manuscripts, and specimens of natural history and ethnography to the nation in 1753; they became the nucleus of the British Museum. Other collectors followed his example and within a century the munificence of monarchs and the support of public funding had expanded Sloane's remarkable working library and "cabinet of curiosities" into a great cultural and scientific institution. Within another century further private benefaction and enlightened legal deposit legislation had built up in this museum a library indispensable to the world of learning and to those for whom information is a precondition of successful enterprise.

An institution may be created by Act of Parliament, but its potential can be realized only by the vision, energy, and determination of individuals. The reasons for the British Library's greatness lie not only in the foresight of the intellectual architects who gave the Museum and Library form and direction, but also in the ceaseless growth of its collections, whether by purchase, legal deposit, or donation, and in the work of generations of skilled and highly motivated members of its staff who have believed passionately in the importance of knowledge.

Determination to provide ready access to information on every aspect of human thought and activity was the vision that led to the creation of the British Library in 1973 as a merger of the British Museum Library, the National Central Library, the National Lending Library for Science and Technology, the Patent Office Library, the Science Reference Library, and the staff of the *British National Bibliography*. It has become not only a storehouse of the written record but also a vital repository of information serving the current needs of scientists, engineers, inventors, industrialists, lawyers, and commercial companies, upon whose activities the economic strength of the nation depends. On a typical day the British Library supplies information to more than 30,000 users: in the various reading rooms, by post, by telephone, by telex, and by online computer access. Of these 30,000 users, a quarter are nationals of other countries or work in foreign institutions.

The library Sir Anthony Panizzi made famous in the mid-1800s (the great Reading Room was opened to the public in 1857) now has collections of more than 100 million items dispersed in 19 buildings in London and in Yorkshire. Faced with the enormous problems of continuing to satisfy the demands of its varied users with such dispersed collections, at the same time ensuring that they are preserved, senior members of the staff recognized that they needed a new building in London to hold them.

Within 20 years after creating the British Library, the Government recognized that the Library needed a new home. The significance of the building, scheduled to open in 1994, extends beyond the awesome statistics of its construction and the magnitude of the collections it was designed to house. By bringing together on one site all its incomparable resources, scattered when they could not all fit in the British Museum building, the British Library will be taking a leading role in making possible the kinds of research that future generations will require. The enabling power of the concept of the new building lies in bringing together resources for all disciplines. The doctor whose collection (on all subjects and in many languages) formed the nucleus of the British Museum Library established a tradition that the British Library still honors in providing access in one building to information on science, technology, and industry, as well as the humanities and social sciences. The new building was designed to allow for new services made possible by advances in technology, in addition to providing a physical environment constructed to ensure the preservation of the collections. These facilities, and the services they offer, are without parallel in any other national library.

Organization. The British Library is governed by a Board responsible to the Minister for the Arts and Libraries. The Board consists of four permanent members and ten part-time members who serve limited terms. The four permanent members are the Chairman, the Chief Executive, and two Directors General. They administer a staff that included in 1991 more than 2,250 members, a number they planned to cut by 1996. The total operating expenditure was more than £5100 million in the early 1990s, including £570 million in direct grants from the Government and revenue from some profit-making services.

Before completion of the new building in London, the Library was organized partly on a geographic basis and partly on a collection basis. Boston Spa, in Yorkshire, houses services associated with providing documents and bibliographic data to remote users (the *Document Supply Center* and the *National Bibliographic Service*), publishing, and administration. London also has some administrative offices, including the offices of the Chief Executive, the Board, and staff members who handle the press and public relations. London services are divided between those for science, technology, and industry (the *Science Reference and Information Services*) and those for the humanities, including *Humanities and Social Sciences*, the *Newspaper Library*, *Special Collections*, the *British Library Information Sciences Service*, and the *National Sound Archive*. Planners hoped to accommodate all London services and most London collections in the new building by 1997.

Humanities and social sciences comprise all the collections other than those specifically designated for science and technology and include all the traditional departments of the British Museum Library. They are administered by four directorates. *Humanities and*

Social Sciences includes the general collections (formerly the Department of Printed Books), the library and information science collections (formerly the Library Association Library), the Newspaper Library at Colindale, and the National Sound Archive. *Special Collections* includes four historically independent departments: maps, music, oriental, and philatelic. *Collection Management* includes such departments as storage and delivery, preservation, and photographic. *Public Services* includes exhibitions and education.

Collections. The Foundation Collections of the British Museum Library (1753) included the books and manuscripts of Sir Hans Sloane; what was left of the Old Royal Library, then housed at St. James's; the manuscripts owned by Robert Harley; and the historic collections of medieval and Renaissance manuscripts formed by Sir Robert Cotton. Other great collections were added: Clayton Cracherode (1800), Colin's French Revolution tracts (1817), Sir Joseph Banks (1820), George III (1823), and Thomas Grenville (1847). By the time Antonio Panizzi became Keeper of Printed Books in 1837, the Library was second in size only to the Bibliothèque Nationale in Paris. While Panizzi was Keeper and then Principal Librarian (1856–66), the collections expanded dramatically to cover all subjects in all languages, but with particular emphasis on various parts of the British Empire. When he retired, Panizzi left an institution without equal anywhere in the world for the scope of its collections. His philosophy has guided successive generations of librarians who have been responsible for the Library's collection development. This encyclopedic philosophy suffered from dwindling resources in the 1970s and 1980s, an affliction shared by other great libraries everywhere.

After 1973 the British Library added enormous collections, notably by absorbing the printed books, manuscripts, and archives of the India Office Library (now amalgamated with the Department of Oriental Manuscripts and Printed books, founded in 1892, and designated the *Oriental and India Office Collections*), the sound recordings of the British Institute of Recorded Sound (now designated the *National Sound Archive*), and the Library of the Library Association (now designated the *British Library Information Sciences Service*). The number of items contained in the various departments can only be guessed: they probably exceed 100,000,000. Merely to list the catalogues and finding aids, published and unpublished, would require a substantial volume, and the task has never been attempted. The collections have never been systematically re-catalogued to modern standards, and every year scholars report the discovery of items of extraordinary importance. Most discoveries made by members of the staff are reported in *The British Library Journal*.

Services. In addition to the normal services provided by all large research libraries, the British Library is unique in providing loan and photocopy services to remote customers in every country. Institutions subscribing to this service (more than 15,000 in the early 1990s) can request photocopies of any documents in the collections, including some materials held only in London. This service responded to more than three million requests a year in the early 1990s, of which 30 percent came from overseas. In London readers now have access to most of the major computer networks in Europe and the United States. The various departments of the former humanities and social sciences division deal with more than 500,000 inquiries every year by post, telephone, fax, and personal visit.

Users. The Library is used by researchers worldwide on almost every working day of the week, personally or from a distance. The reading rooms in London can accommodate 1,450 readers and are generally full, especially in the summer months. A survey in the early 1990s showed that on an average day between May and October, nationals of 20 countries were using the collections.

New Building. The new building at St. Pancras, scheduled to be completed in 1997, was designed to hold most of the collections now scattered across London. Plans called for the four basements, each the size of the football pitch at Wembley, to be fitted with more than 400 miles of compact shelving, with automated services controlling all operations involving requests for and retrieval of materials. The designers incorporated adequate space for exhibitions, lectures, and conferences and provided a controlled environment for the storage of printed and manuscript materials, thereby ensuring that, in the words of the Act of 1752, its prodigious collections could be preserved "for public use and posterity."

ROBIN ALSTON

Brown, James Duff
(1862–1914)

Library Association
James Duff Brown

From about 1890 until 1914 the best-known initials in British librarianship were those of J. D. B., James Duff Brown. Brown was a library pioneer of outstanding importance.

Brown was born November 6, 1862, in Edinburgh into a working-class family that was unusually musical and in which books counted for much. He was educated at an excellent normal school but only up to the age of 12, when he was apprenticed to a local bookselling firm. Moving with his family in 1876 to Glasgow, he found temporary employment there with another bookseller but began his real library career at the age of 16 when appointed to a junior post in the Mitchell Library. The library, named after its founder, Stephen Mitchell, a Glasgow tobacco magnate, had opened its doors for the first time only one year before Brown joined its staff. Its founder had endowed it with the then very large sum of £570,000 to enable it to function as a large public library. Its origins were therefore comparable with those of the New York Public Library and, like its American counterpart, it provided an outstanding reference service that did not originally form part of a normal municipal system.

J. D. B. spent 10 formative years at the Mitchell and saw its bookstock increase to 80,000—a period of growth that provided good bibliographical training for a young librarian. In 1888 he was appointed the first Librarian of Clerkenwell, one of the increasing number of London parishes that were adopting the Public Libraries Acts and initiating municipal libraries. Brown's early years at Clerkenwell established him as an apparently orthodox but unusually gifted librarian of the period, but in 1894 he became a pioneer by converting his library to "safe-guarded open access."

Prior to this date British public libraries, unlike

many American ones, had not admitted readers to the shelves; books were requested at counters and fetched for readers by members of the staff. Although J. D. B. manifested throughout his life a marked antipathy to American library methods and indeed to American librarianship generally, there can be little doubt that his attendance at the ALA Congress at Chicago (1893) and visits to many libraries in the eastern states prepared the way for "open access." It remained a highly controversial issue for many years following 1894, although after 1920 British public libraries remaining "closed" could be safely regarded as extremely old-fashioned.

In 1905 J. D. B. moved from Clerkenwell, or rather from the Metropolitan Borough of Finsbury, into which his London parish had been absorbed, and became Borough Librarian of next-door Islington. His years at Clerkenwell/Finsbury had been very happy—an exceptional librarian being supported and encouraged by an understanding, progressive, and forward-looking committee. Although by contrast his governing body at Islington proved obstructive, unsympathetic, and parsimonious, J. D. B., struggling with every conceivable discouragement, built up a public library service that was regarded at the time as a model.

Despite the excellence of the two municipal library systems for which J. D. B. was successively responsible and for which, to avoid using the much disliked Dewey Decimal, he created no fewer than three systems of "Brown" classification, much of his reputation was gained outside London, mostly as journalist and author. He was the main public library contributor to MacAlister's *The Library* from 1890, and when it became clear that the Library Association would be discontinuing its recognition as the "official organ" and instead establishing its own *Library Association Record,* he ensured his own continuing independence by founding another monthly magazine, *The Library World;* the first number appeared in 1898.

This new journal not only provided a useful medium in which many librarians began and continued their journalistic careers but also enabled J. D. B. himself to write and print his own material, which he could subsequently revise and use in one or another of his many books. The best known of these was his *Manual of Library Economy*. This should have provided British librarianship, and particularly British public librarianship, with its basic textbook. The second and substantially revised edition of 1907 assuredly did; the first edition of 1903 was excessively opinionated. The third (1920) and subsequent editions were edited and rewritten by W. C. Berwick Sayers and others.

Other notable books by J. D. B. were his *Subject Classification* (first edition, 1906; second edition, 1914; third edition [by J. D. Stewart], 1939); *Library Classification and Cataloguing* (1912), the successor to his *Manual of Library Classification and Shelf Arrangement* of 1898; *The Small Library: A Guide to the Collection and Care of Books* (1907); and *Manual of Practical Bibliography* (1906) based primarily on lectures delivered at the pioneer school of librarianship at the London School of Economics. J. D. B. was always a keen advocate of better education and better opportunities for young librarians and was also largely responsible for beginning the system of correspondence courses and classes upon which most British librarians depended for their professional studies until at least the later 1930s.

Brown's membership in a musical family had lifelong influence. He published *Biographical Dictionary of Musicians* (1886) and *British Musical Biography* (1897) and edited *Characteristic Songs and Dances of All Nations* (1910). This special musical interest also manifested itself in his keen desire to encourage and improve the provision of music and musical literature in public libraries, early symbolized by his *Guide to the Formation of a Music Library* (1893).

He exercised profound influence on British public library thinking during his lifetime and long after his death, in London, on February 26, 1914. That influence had at least two shortcomings; it stimulated irrational prejudice against the methods of American librarianship and against the methods of types of British librarianship other than the municipal. He was a keen admirer of the pioneer work of Edward Edwards (1812–86), the great British librarian of the mid-19th century, and ranks with him as one of the makers of modern British librarianship.

REFERENCES

W. A. Munford, *James Duff Brown 1862–1914: Portrait of a Library Pioneer* (1968).

V. Malhan, "James Duff Brown and his Contributions," *Herald of Library Science* (1978).

W. A. MUNFORD

Brummel, Leendert
(1897–1976)

Leendert Brummel was Chief Librarian of the Royal Library at The Hague, Netherlands, from 1937 to 1962.

Brummel was born August 10, 1897, at Arnhem. He received his grammar school education at The Hague and in 1916 enrolled as a student at Leiden University, where he read history and Dutch literature. Under the supervision of the famous historian Johan Huizinga, he wrote a thesis on the philosopher Franciscus Hemsterhuis, on the strength of which he received his doctorate *cum laude*. His book, *Frans Hemsterhuis: een filosofenleven* ("Frans Hemsterhuis: a Philosopher's Life," 1925), has proved to be a contribution of lasting value to the history of European thinking in the later decades of the 18th century.

In 1926 Brummel was appointed Librarian of the Royal Netherlands Academy of Sciences and Letters at Amsterdam. In 1927 he joined the staff of the Royal Library and on September 1, 1937, he succeeded P. C. Molhuysen as Chief Librarian.

When he took over, Brummel could in reason count on 25 years in which to strengthen the potential of the library and to enhance its usefulness to the community. In the event, he had considerably less time at his disposal. During the German occupation all he could do was to improvise measures for protecting the most valuable collections and to evade ideological interference on the part of the Germans and their Dutch henchmen. The war was followed by a period of great national poverty, in which libraries were decidedly not regarded as a priority.

Nevertheless, during his remaining, more prosperous years of office, Brummel succeeded in carrying

Koninklijke Bibliotheek

Leendert Brummel

out the major part of the improvements he had had in mind from the outset. He established a more efficient division of labor by freeing members of the academic staff from clerical duties. Thanks to this and to an increase of the number of subject specialists and of the budget, the quality and diversity of acquisitions were improved. The effectiveness of the union catalogue was raised. Many valuable items were added to the collections of manuscripts and early printed books. A severe lack of space was alleviated—for the time being—by the construction of an annex.

As Chairman of the State Advisory Committee on Library Affairs, of which both university librarians and the directors of some of the larger public libraries were members, Brummel did much to reconcile the sometimes conflicting views of his colleagues. His efforts to further a reasonable degree of harmony within the profession at large were sustained by the healthy mixture of idealism and pragmatism characteristic of his personality.

As Superintendent (*Hoofdbestuurder*) of the Rijksmuseum Meermanno-Westreenianum in The Hague, another ex-officio function of the Royal Librarian, Brummel brought about a symbiosis of that venerable institution and a new creation of his own: the Museum of the Book.

In 1953 the Museum and Documentation Center for Dutch Literature was founded. Brummel was its first Director and contributed much to its success.

Brummel felt very much at home on the international scene. His first contact with IFLA took place in July 1939, when the International Library Committee met in The Hague, just before the outbreak of the war. He was greatly impressed by Marcel Godet's courageous speech on the ideological rift that for years had been dividing German librarians from their colleagues. After the war he played an active role in IFLA. He was a Vice-President from 1961 to 1964 and in 1965 was made Honorary Vice-President. Together with E. Egger he published a *Guide to Union Catalogues and International Loan Centers* (1961), and he was the moving force of the team that prepared *Libraries in the World, A Long-term Programme for the International Federation of Library Associations* (1963).

Brummel was a prolific writer. His *Geschiedenis der Koninklijke Bibliotheek* ("History of the Royal Library," 1939) is still regarded as one of the best examples of library history ever produced in the Netherlands. He advocated the principle that library history should not limit itself to a mere recording of facts and events, but should include research into the political, social, and cultural forces that may have influenced the destiny of a library. Applying this principle to his own work, Brummel succeeded in producing a well-balanced and very readable work.

The dilemmatic role of the librarian as a scholar, the debate on the fundamentals of library science—those were theoretical problems which interested him to a certain extent without unduly disturbing him. In his paper *The Librarian as a Scholar,* read as a special University Lecture at the University of London in 1956 and published in *Miscellanea Libraria,* a selection from his studies presented to him on the occasion of his 60th birthday (1957), he wrestled manfully with these and related problems; yet one is left with the impression of having witnessed a mimic battle ending in a draw. When he gave his inaugural address after being appointed in 1960 to the chair of library science at the University of Amsterdam, he declared his preference for a pragmatic approach.

He retired as Royal Librarian in 1962, but continued to teach with great enthusiasm. After retiring from teaching, he kept on writing and publishing. Until a few months before his death in The Hague on February 1,1976, he was an assiduous visitor of the Royal Library.

REFERENCE

Frank C. Francis, "Leendert Brummel: 1897–1976," *IFLA Journal* (1976).

C. REEDIJK

Brunet, Jacques-Charles
(1780–1867)

Louisiana State University Library

Jacques-Charles Brunet

A bookseller and bibliographer, Jacques-Charles Brunet was born November 2, 1780, the son of Thomas Brunet, in Paris, where he would spend virtually his entire life. His formal education was scanty even by the standards of his day and was terminated by the revolutionary events of 1792; thereafter he was self-educated.

His private life and work in bibliography and classification are so entwined that to separate them is to falsify them. He never married, and his close friends were few; although created Chevalier of the Legion of Honor in 1845, he functioned largely outside the literary and political worlds. The sole biography devoted to Brunet was done for an antiquarian book exposition in 1960—a pastiche of obituaries and contemporary literary commentaries.

Brunet's current reputation is founded upon two complementary aspects of his bibliographical work: he was a pioneer in library classification from literary warrant and, more concretely, he compiled a massive, meticulously detailed, and often charming rare-book bibliography (each edition expanding its predecessor) that has become a mainstay of rare-book librarians and dealers.

To supplement this work and provide an ordering for lesser works, Brunet conceived a classification set forth most fully in the final volume of his *Manuel du libraire et de l'amateur de livres* ("Bookdealer's and Book Lover's Handbook"). This scheme, reportedly based upon the commerce-tested logic of the successful bookseller, was taken up and used with various modifications by many libraries. The entire scheme, along with Brunet's historical introduction (a somewhat biased history of cataloguing), was made available for the first time in English in 1976.

The most salient feature of Brunet's scheme is its a posteriori character; in contrast to most of his predecessors, he eschewed a priori theoretical structures and founded his arrangements on pragmatism. Although the weighting of the divisions (Theology: 7.3 percent; Jurisprudence: 3 percent; Arts and Sciences: 22.7 percent; Literature; 28.2 percent; History: 38.8 percent) is quite inappropriate today and reflects the tastes of his classically educated clientele, its principle that a library's content and purpose should govern its arrangement was a forerunner of modern library classification for use.

The first known direct use of the Brunet scheme in the United States was at Harvard College in 1830. At various times, it was also used by the Saint Louis Mercantile Library, the Philadelphia Library, and others.

Among Brunet's publications, his *Manuel* perpetuates his name (a reprint edition is currently available); his remaining production consisted chiefly of contemporary articles. He was perhaps the last of the individual polyhistors to work alone on such massive works of bibliography. The last expansion of his *Manuel* was completed after his death by his friends P. Deschamps and Gustave Brunet.

He passed away peacefully in his own armchair on November 17, 1867, in his 87th year, surrounded by the books that had been the friends of his life.

REFERENCE

D. B. McKeon, *The Classification System of Jacques-Charles Brunet* (Louisiana State University Graduate School of Library Science Occasional Papers no. 1, 1976).

DONALD BRUCE McKEON

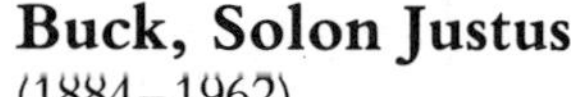

Buck, Solon Justus
(1884–1962)

Records of the National Archives
Solon Justus Buck

Solon Justus Buck, Archivist of the United States and writer, achieved outstanding success as a scholar, teacher, archivist, and historical administrator.

He was born in Berlin, Wisconsin, August 16, 1884. Buck received B.A. and M.A. degrees from the University of Wisconsin in 1904 and 1905 and took a Ph.D. at Harvard University in 1911.

A leading protégé of the eminent historian Frederick Jackson Turner, Buck early reached prominence as a publishing scholar. In quick succession he produced *The Granger Movement* (1913), *Illinois in 1818* (1917), and *Agrarian Crusade* (1920), all of which were widely and favorably noted. Buck taught at Indiana University, 1908–09, and indeed was an outstanding

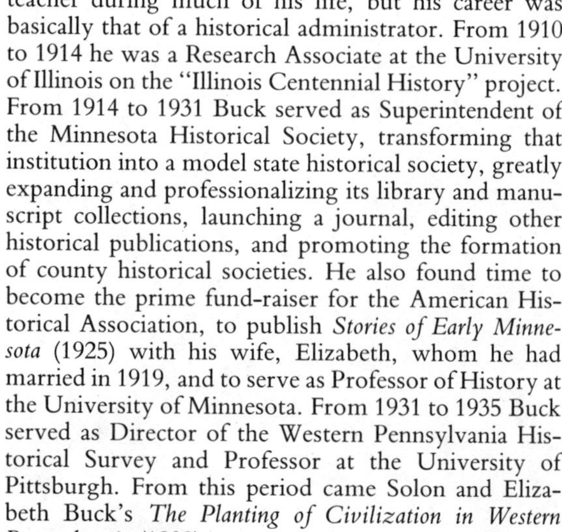

teacher during much of his life, but his career was basically that of a historical administrator. From 1910 to 1914 he was a Research Associate at the University of Illinois on the "Illinois Centennial History" project. From 1914 to 1931 Buck served as Superintendent of the Minnesota Historical Society, transforming that institution into a model state historical society, greatly expanding and professionalizing its library and manuscript collections, launching a journal, editing other historical publications, and promoting the formation of county historical societies. He also found time to become the prime fund-raiser for the American Historical Association, to publish *Stories of Early Minnesota* (1925) with his wife, Elizabeth, whom he had married in 1919, and to serve as Professor of History at the University of Minnesota. From 1931 to 1935 Buck served as Director of the Western Pennsylvania Historical Survey and Professor at the University of Pittsburgh. From this period came Solon and Elizabeth Buck's *The Planting of Civilization in Western Pennsylvania* (1939).

In 1935 Buck became one of the four chief assistant administrators of the new National Archives. His title was Director of Publications, but that belied the scope of his activities. He had found a new stage upon which to act out his career and took full advantage of it. He became the chief envoy of the National Archives to historical associations, especially as Treasurer of the American Historical Association (1936–57) and a representative in 1938 to the International Committee of Historical Sciences. He was one of the founders of the Society of American Archivists in 1936 and was active in the formation of the American Documentation Institute. At Columbia University in 1938 he inaugurated the first professional course in archival administration in the United States; he refined this instruction at the American University in 1939, so that it became the model for archival courses offered over the country during the following generation. Among the many other successful projects he initiated or headed at the National Archives was the Finding Mediums Committee of 1940–41, the report of which greatly changed archival administration with its recommendations for organizing archives on the basis of record groups and for providing a variety of guides to them, most notably the preliminary inventory. Ironically, Buck was unable to make any significant progress as Secretary of the National Historical Publications Commission (NHPC), his most visible job at the Archives.

As a result of Buck's imaginative and usually successful work at the National Archives, President Franklin D. Roosevelt appointed him to head the agency as Archivist of the United States in 1941. Buck's work during his almost seven years in that position was often brilliant, though mixed in results. Despite severe shortages of staff and equipment, he expanded the services of the National Archives. Buck plunged his agency into the work of records management, achieving more efficient and economical government control over its burgeoning records. One by-product of this work was the Archives' role in developing the new records management profession and in encouraging archivists to take a broader view of their work. Buck also played the leading role in founding the International Council on Archives (1948). In addition to his continuing interest in archival training and professional organization, he found a variety of war-related research, technical, and consulting tasks for archivists to perform. He forwarded the earlier programs of his agency, especially the accessioning of older federal archives, the microfilming program, the *Federal Register,* and the Franklin D. Roosevelt Library.

Buck's frequent experiments with reorganizing the National Archives made the agency more efficient, but at the cost of considerable staff unhappiness and congressional criticism. He made the Archives into a more nearly perfect servant of the state, but only at the price of the agency's becoming too acquiescent in restrictions on the private use of federal records. Buck's authoritarian leadership and his sometimes abrasive personality, moreover, contributed to problems among his staff and with Congress, in effect jeopardizing appropriations for the support of the National Archives. By 1948 it was clear that Buck—tired, aging, and having recently suffered serious illness—was unlikely to improve his staff's morale and to gain appropriations for new programs.

Later Career. Buck resigned that year as Archivist of the United States and accepted the position of Chief of the Manuscripts Division of the Library of Congress. Three years later he became Assistant Librarian, a job he held until his retirement in 1954. Although his vitality was gone, he functioned satisfactorily at the Library of Congress, performing a number of administrative and intellectual tasks as an elder statesman of research and information management, including membership on the reinvigorated NHPC. He served as Acting Director of the Minnesota Historical Society, 1954–55, and occasionally as a consultant to the Library of Congress.

The University of Minnesota conferred an honorary LL.D. degree upon him in 1954. Throughout his career he had been an officer in a variety of historical, archival, and research organizations, serving as President of the Mississippi Valley Historical Association, the Agricultural History Society, and the Society of American Archivists. In addition to his several books, he was the author of many historical and archival articles. His was a remarkably broad career. Buck died in Washington, D.C., May 25, 1962.

REFERENCES

Donald R.McCoy, *The National Archives: America's Ministry of Documents, 1934–1968* (1978).

Theodore C. Blegen, "Solon Justus Buck—Scholar–Administrator," *The American Archivist* (1960).

Ernst Posner, "Solon Justus Buck—Archivist," *The American Archivist* (1960).

DONALD R. McCOY

Bulgaria

Bulgaria, a republic in southeastern Europe, lies in the eastern Balkan Peninsula. Romania lies to the north, the Black Sea to the east, Turkey and Greece to the south, and Yugoslavia to the west. Population (1990 est.) 9,011,000; area 110,912 sq.km. The official language is Bulgarian.

History. The first Bulgarian state was created in A.D. 681, in the northeastern part of the Balkan Peninsula. By the second half of the 10th century it was one of the mightiest states in Europe. After the acceptance of Christianity as the official religion in 864 and the introduction of the Cyrillic alphabet, invented by the learned brothers Cyril and Methodius, in 893, Bulgaria experienced a period of astounding cultural growth known as the Golden Age of Bulgarian Literature. Two great cultural centers emerged: one in the capital, Preslav, the other in the region of Ochrid.

The National Library of Bulgaria in Sofia

These centers produced the first Bulgarian libraries of significance. King Simeon established one of them, perhaps the largest of all, in his palace under his direct supervision. It contained a large collection of old Greek and Byzantine manuscripts and all Bulgarian writings produced at the time. The literature created in the 10th century spread to other countries, especially to Kievan Rus, fostering its cultural development.

After the liberation of Bulgaria from Byzantine domination, which lasted for almost two centuries (1018–1186), Bulgaria experienced a new period of cultural revival and expansion, reaching a climax in the 14th century during the reign of King Ivan Alexander. A flourishing literary school emerged in the capital, Tărnovo, and several major libraries were established in the King's palace, at the Patriarchate of the Bulgarian Orthodox Church, at monasteries and churches, and in the palaces of feudal rulers.

During the five centuries of Ottoman domination (1393–1878), all Bulgarian libraries were destroyed, except those of some 300 monasteries. The monastic librarians preserved the literary heritage of Bulgaria, copied Bulgarian manuscript books, translated foreign books, and compiled historical chronicles. The most important were those of the Rila, the Bachkovo, and the Zograph monasteries.

The first Bulgarian public libraries in the Ottoman Empire began to appear after 1840 during the Bulgarian national and cultural revival. They were school libraries and libraries of the *chitalishta* ("reading clubs"), and they rapidly increased in number. Thanks to them, Bulgarian writings and cultural traditions have been preserved.

After liberation from Ottoman domination (1878), public libraries played an important role in assisting the nation's education and were the most important cultural centers in the country. Research libraries also began to appear, the first being the Library of the Bulgarian Literary Society (which developed into the Bulgarian Academy of Sciences) and the National Library. The revolutionary changes after World War II gave a strong impetus to the development of libraries.

National Management. In 1970 the Council of Ministers decreed a Unified Library System for Bulgaria governed by the Ministry of Culture and professionally guided by the National Library. The National Library, the Library of the Bulgarian Academy of Sciences, the Library of the University of Sofia (the country's largest university library), as well as the central research libraries of medicine, science and technology, and agriculture form a closely integrated group of libraries, managed by a Council of Directors of Central Research Libraries and aimed at providing an overall high-quality, comprehensive library and documentation service. Each of these central research libraries guides and coordinates the activities of the libraries in its network. Central regional libraries guide the public libraries and coordinate all library activities in the regions.

New library legislation sought to revise and improve the organization and functions of the library system, introducing measures such as regulations for funding libraries by parent bodies; stricter requirements for creating new libraries; compulsory centralization of public library services; and establishing a National Council on Librarianship at the Ministry of Culture, presided over by the first Deputy Minister of Culture and consisting of prominent public figures and library experts with advisory and guiding powers.

National Library. The Cyril and Methodius National Library (founded 1878) in Sofia possesses a complete collection of the national production of printed materials, an important selection of foreign publications in all fields, and the country's largest collection of foreign periodicals—about 9,500 current titles in the late 1980s. It has a full collection of UN publications and the basic publications of other international organizations. Its holdings total more than 6,000,000 accessioned items, including a significant collection of Bulgarian and foreign manuscripts and old and rare books. It also preserves over 3,500,000 national and oriental historical documents and serves as National Archives for documents pertaining to Bulgarian history to 1900. (The State Archives is responsible for the preservation of documents relating to the 20th century.)

Since 1897 the National Library has been the national center of legal deposit, and it publishes the national bibliography. The national bibliography consists of separate accessions lists for books, maps, sheet music, and other items (issued biweekly); official publications and dissertations (monthly); articles from journals and collective works (biweekly); articles from newspapers (monthly); Bulgarian periodicals (annually); Bulgarica (quarterly); and the "Bibliography of Bulgarian Bibliography" (annually). There are also four annual cumulations: books and other materials, dissertations, sound recordings, and Bulgarica.

The National Library is an active bibliographic information center with emphasis on the fields of culture, ecology, economy, and law. It functions as a research institute in the fields of library science, bibliography, and book science, employing in 1990 about 40 full-time research fellows and 15 research students.

As a national methodological center it provides help and guidance to regional and central research libraries and their networks. Since 1970 it has coordinated the basic library processes in the country's library system.

Academic Libraries. Twenty-eight academic libraries at universities and other institutions of higher education held more than 6,000,000 volumes in the late 1980s. The largest libraries are the Library of Sofia University and the Central Medical Library at the Higher Medical Institute in Sofia.

Public Libraries. Chitalishta libraries, those in village or town reading clubs or houses of culture, number about 3,800. Each town or village community has one or more of them serving the entire population free of charge. Next in importance are more than 1,800 libraries organized at industrial and trade enterprises and public agencies, which serve their staffs. They are sponsored by the trade unions and funded by their parent bodies. There are also several city libraries directly governed by the state. The most important

Libraries in Bulgaria (1989)

Type of library	Number of administrative units (main libraries)	Number of service points (branches, mobile stops, etc.)	Volumes in collections	Annual expenditures (lev)	Population served	Professional staff (with certificate, diploma, etc.)	Total staff
National	1	1	6,496,260	333,658	26,000	315	508
Academic	29	51	6,616,000	6,121,431	142,000	498	610
Public	3,820	4,521	48,319,000	20,775,505	1,551,000	2,673	3,007
School	3,268	3,268	17,399,000	5,986,867	815,000	902	902
Special	866	792	21,084,000	9,306,731	206,000	760	852
Other*	1,563	1,731	9,573,000	3,098,542	357,000	498	498

*Libraries at industrial and trade enterprises, rapidly diminishing in number, to be abolished.

Source: Central Statistical Agency, Sofia

trend in the development of public libraries in the 1980s has been their gradual centralization. In order to preserve the autonomy of the *chitalishta* organizations, the centralization follows the line of functional concentration of the basic library processes in the main chitalishta libraries of the towns. The second important trend has been the steady reduction of the number of public libraries, mainly affecting very small and unviable libraries.

Central Regional Libraries. The 27 central regional libraries are the most accessible libraries, but they should not be considered public libraries because they have assumed the status and functions of central research libraries for their regions. They have large holdings of indigenous and foreign publications and unique collections of publications and other documents pertaining to their regions.

Special Libraries. Special scientific libraries are organized in academies of sciences, other research institutes, learned societies, industrial enterprises, business firms, museums, and editorial boards, and have total holdings of about 21,000,000 items (including more than 18,000,000 patents, standards, and other special technical publications). The most important are the Library of the Bulgarian Academy of Sciences (with a central library and over 40 branch libraries), the Central Agricultural Library (heading a network of specialized agricultural libraries), and the Central Technical Library (coordinating the work of specialized technical libraries).

A notable trend is the constant reduction in the number of special libraries (704 in 1976, 677 in 1982, and 652 in 1988), which reflects a policy of centralization and abolition of unviable institutions.

School Libraries. Every school in Bulgaria has its own library. There are more than 3,500 school libraries with total holdings of 17,300,000 volumes (about 30 percent of which are children's books). About 80 percent of the country's enrolled students are registered readers of the school libraries.

The Profession. Four institutions provide courses of formal library education: the University of Sofia (which has chairs of library science and information science), the State Institute of Librarians in Sofia (two years after secondary education or three years extramural), and the National Library (six-month training courses on completion of university education). The University of Sofia and the National Library also provide postgraduate doctoral dissertation programs.

The National Library, the central research libraries, and the central regional libraries regularly organize short courses, seminars, and other undertakings to improve the professional qualification and skills of librarians.

A Union of Library and Information Workers was founded in 1990. It has individual, institutional, and associate memberships, as well as local associations in the regions. Its main tasks are to speak for the profession, to foster development of librarianship and information theory and practice, to arrange seminars, conferences, publications, and similar efforts, to promote professional qualification and education, and to study and publicize achievements of foreign library and information institutions that can benefit Bulgaria's librarians.

REFERENCES

Alexander Kazandzief, *Libraries in Bulgaria* (1987). Elena Savova et al., *Research Libraries: Theory and Practice* (1980), In Bulgarian.

VLADIMIR POPOV

Bullen, Henry Lewis
(1857–1938)

Henry Lewis Bullen

Henry Lewis Bullen was a printer by trade but, more important, a daring and determined archivist and librarian of that trade. His efforts to preserve historical specimens and literature of printing culminated in the creation of the American Type Founders' Company Library, one of the world's outstanding collections dealing with printing and graphic arts.

Bullen was born in 1857 in Australia, to which his father had emigrated from New England. When he was 14, he left school to become a printer's apprentice. During his four-year apprenticeship, he began writing articles for trade magazines. In 1875 Bullen set off to the United States, where he worked as a printer and studied new printing technologies. He lived for ten years in Boston, making frequent visits to libraries in New York City to study the history of typography and printing. Bullen became editor of *Printers' Review,* a trade paper, for which he wrote articles on printing history. He wrote for other trade journals as well, among them *Inland Printer,* where his most important articles appeared. In 1891 Bullen moved to New York City to work for a printing supplier that later became part of an amalgamation of type foundries called the American Type Founders' Company (ATF). He remained at ATF for most of the rest of his career as a printer.

Bullen had started collecting books about printing in his years in Boston. At ATF he began to assemble books and other items that had belonged to the small foundries that merged with the company. Indeed, he would later refer to this gathering as the beginning of the ATF Library, but the Library was not formally started until after Bullen wrote a series of articles in 1906 called "Discursions of a Retired Printer," using the pseudonym "Quadrat." In these articles Quadrat urged ATF to develop a collection of artifacts and documents of the printing trade, well aware that the company already had many such items in its possession. Quadrat then offered to donate his personal library to such a collection and suggested that ATF find someone to create and manage it (while hinting that he, Quadrat, had been unemployed for some time).

The general manager of ATF, Robert Wickham Nelson, received this series of articles with great interest. He had no idea that the writer was actually in his employ. Nelson lent his support, both philosophically and financially, to the creation of such a collection. Bullen began to amass materials in 1907 and the ATF Library and Museum was created at the company's New Jersey plant in 1908.

Bullen served as librarian without pay. In 1908 he issued a statement of the Library's purposes, one of which was "to perpetuate the memory and honor the achievements of all persons who in any period and in any country have advanced the printing arts." Given this statement, it is perhaps no surprise that the scope of the ATF Library is enormous. The Library contained at its peak more than 16,000 items, including books, periodicals, ephemera, and artifacts of the trade. They were catalogued under headings ranging from pre-typographic records to archives of famous printers to "liberty of printing, comprising an extensive collection of laws, edicts, and narratives of trials and oppression relating to attempts to regulate and repress the powers and efforts of printers." The Library's holdings include two early polyglot Bibles, a specimen book of the Vatican printing office issued in 1628, and an early (1511) edition of Albrecht Dürer's *Apocalypsis cum Figaris* with 16 full-page woodcuts.

Printers and librarians appreciated Bullen's creation and visited it, even though its New Jersey location was difficult to reach. Visitors included Pierce Butler, John Cotton Dana, and Alfred Knopf; Bullen took an exhibition from the ATF Library called "An Exhibition of the Evolution of the Art of the Book and in Praise of Printing" to display at Dana's Newark Free Public Library.

Bullen retired as a printer in 1923 and, with a fund of more than $40,000 provided by ATF, left for Europe for two years to acquire rare books. The trip was financed largely through the efforts of Nelson, Bullen's unflagging supporter throughout his tenure at ATF. Nelson's backing resulted in the construction of a new building for the Library in 1925.

Nelson's death in 1926, along with the declining economy, signaled the end of the golden age for the ATF Library. The company filed for bankruptcy in 1933 and Bullen was forced to sell duplicates from the Library to maintain its existence. When the company decided to relocate, it sought a new home for the collection. After a great deal of negotiation with various institutions, the ATF Library was deposited at Columbia University in 1936; Bullen was appointed honorary librarian and curator of the typographic collection. He died on April 27, 1938. The ATF Library at Columbia is now divided into two smaller collections, Graphic Arts and Book Arts. The catalogue of the holdings of the ATF Library is evidence of Bullen's devotion to the art of printing.

REFERENCES

The History of Printing from Its Beginnings to 1930: The Subject Catalogue of the American Type Founders' Company Library in the Columbia University Libraries (1980).

David Walker Mallison, "Henry Lewis Bullen and the Typographic Library and Museum of the American Type Founders' Company," thesis, Columbia University (1976).

ROBIN OSBORNE

Burkina Faso

Burkina Faso, a republic of West Africa, is bounded on the north by Mali and Niger and on the south by Benin, Togo, Ghana, and the Ivory Coast. Population (1990 est.) 9,001,000; area 274,200 sq.km. The official language is French; the dialect More is widely spoken. The country, called Upper Volta when it became independent in 1960, was renamed Burkina Faso in 1984.

Burkina Faso does not have a national library. A National Commission for Libraries, Archives and Documentation was established in 1969 but little was accomplished. The Centre National de la Recherche Scientifique et Technologique (CNRST), founded in 1950, receives copies of all publications on and about the country, including those published outside Burkina Faso. Its Library specializes in research in the humanities and natural sciences and holds more than 6,000 volumes. The Centre publishes a quarterly "Notes and Documents" and other publications on an irregular basis, and is responsible for the compilation of a current national bibliography. The first volume was issued in 1967, the *Bibliographie générale de la Haute-Volta,* covering the years 1956 through 1965.

A National Center for Archives was organized in 1973. It conducted a survey of the archives of all administrative districts of the country and drew plans for a central depository at Ouagadougou.

Burkina Faso has one university. The Université de Ouagadougou was founded in 1970 and was granted university status in 1974. The university's Library holds approximately 55,000 volumes, 100 periodicals, and 1,400 maps. There are many smaller libraries affiliated with colleges in Ouagadougou. The academic library of the Lycée Philippe Zinda Kabore de Ouagadougou has a small library primarily for the use of teachers and secondary students.

There is no public library system in Burkina Faso. Library facilities are available to the public primarily through the cultural centers in Ouagadougou, most notably those of Germany, the United States, France, Libya, and Russia.

The Documentation and Information Center of the Interafrican Committee for Hydraulic Studies (CIEH) in Ouagadougou houses 11,000 documents, including books, technical reports, proceedings of conferences, maps, aerial and satellite photographs, and periodical articles. The Center receives approximately 135 journals and compiles bibliographical bulletins, which are sent to more than a thousand recipients on five continents. The Center published two catalogues in 1977: *An Index of Authors* and a *Geographical Index* representing a total of 6,000 documents. Bulletins deal with documents selected and analyzed after the 1977 publication date.

Other documentation centers include one in Bobo-Dioulasso, which specializes in public health and tropical medicine; the Institut National de la Statistique et de la Démographie in Ouagadougou, with 2,200 volumes, primarily in the field of economics, 50 periodicals, and statistical bulletins from various countries; and the Institut National d'Education in Ouagadougou, with approximately 15,000 volumes and 237 periodicals on educational theory and psychology.

In 1972 the Association Voltaïque pour le Développement des Bibliothèques, des Archives et de la Documentation (AVDBAD) was founded at Ouagadougou. Its primary purpose is to aid in the development of libraries, archives, and documentation centers in the country. The Association is governed by an executive committee elected by its members and is affiliated with IFLA.

KRISSIAMBA LARBA ALI

Burundi

Burundi, a republic in central eastern Africa, is bordered by Rwanda on the north, Tanzania on the east and south, Lake Tanganyika on the southwest, and Zaire on the west. Population (1990) 5,356,000;

area 27,834 sq.km. The official languages are Kirundi and French; Swahili is also widely spoken.

History. A kingdom since the 16th century, Burundi was a Belgian colony called Urundi (often associated with Ruanda) until it gained its independence in 1962. A military coup overthrew the monarchy in 1966 and established a republic.

National Library. The national library and archives are combined and located in Bujumbura, the capital. They offer a wide range of services and facilities for research, but they are not professionally organized, nor are the collections properly housed, because the institutions lack professional staff and funds. They do have book and card catalogues of their holdings and a reading room.

Academic Libraries. Major academic libraries in Burundi are those of the University of Burundi (150,000 volumes and 600 current periodicals), the theological college of Bujumbura (15,000 volumes), and the higher military institute (4,600 volumes). The University of Burundi has a central library and several departmental and institute libraries on the main campus in Bujumbura and one library at the Institute of Agriculture in Gitega. The central library is housed in a two-story building with seats for about 1,500 readers. The university libraries are designed to help students and faculty conduct research on a wide range of subjects. They also offer their services to the general public for a small fee. The university libraries offer library tours and bibliographic instruction to new students at the beginning of each academic year.

Public Libraries. National cultural centers were created in the provinces starting in 1989; by the early 1990s, 10 of the 15 provinces had them. Their holdings average 15,000 volumes of general-interest books and small collections of audiovisual materials. There are three major libraries open to the public in Bujumbura: the American cultural center (4,000 volumes and 50 periodicals), the French cultural center (21,000 volumes and 50 periodicals), and the United Nations information center (almost 6,400 volumes and more than 200 periodicals). They are used mainly by high school students and civil servants.

School Libraries. Many secondary schools throughout the country have school libraries. However, these libraries are not supported by the government, but by the local schools themselves. The quality and the number of their collections vary according to the budgets provided by local school boards.

Special Libraries. Most government ministries maintain important technical and historical collections, including the National Center for Statistical Documentation in the Ministry of Planning, the Library of Agronomic Sciences in the Ministry of Agriculture, the library of the Department of Scientific Research in the Ministry of Education, and the library of the Continuing Education Center in the Ministry of Public Administration. In many cases the documents, though useful for research, are not well used, because most libraries are not well organized and few have professional staffs.

Universitè du Burundi, Bibliothèque

Library at the University of Burundi/in Bujumbura. It was built in 1981 and formally dedicated in 1985.

The Profession. Librarianship is a new profession in Burundi. For many years, library services were provided by non-professional staff. The first professional librarians, who had been trained in France and Sénégal, began working in the country in the 1980s. The country now has about 20 librarians with professional degrees in library science. The Department of Library Science at the University of Burundi offers a two-year program for assistant librarians, evidence of the government's commitment to develop and strengthen librarianship in the country.

POLYCARPE NINTERETSE

Butler, Pierce

(1886–1953)

Pierce Butler, American library educator and scholar, was not concerned with the technology of librarianship, which he left to others, but with its philosophy, the basic principles that give it unity and cohesiveness.

Libraries in Burundi (1990)

Type of library	Number of administrative units (main libraries)	Number of service points (branches, mobile stops, etc.)	Volumes in collections	Annual expenditures (franc)	Population served	Professional staff (with certificate, diploma, etc.)	Total staff
National	5	--	--	--	--	2	7
Academic	81	9	169,000	24 million[a]	5,500	16	106
Public	12	--	--	--	--	3	15[b]

[a]Acquisitions only, University of Bujumbura, 199 FBU = 1 US $
[b]Bujumbura only

He was a historian and humanist, though he did not discredit the contribution that science has made to our culture and could make to librarianship. This point of view was the central theme of Butler's major course on the history of scholarship and of his *Introduction to Library Science* (1933).

The work begins with an introductory essay on the nature of science followed by an analysis of three major problem areas in librarianship—the sociological, the psychological, and the historical. The book concludes with a summary chapter on "Practical Considerations." In the literature of librarianship, which is characterized mainly by its ephemera, Butler's little volume stands out as a true landmark in the development of library thought.

Pierce Butler was born December 19, 1886, at Clarendon Hills, Illinois. As a child he suffered a severe attack of scarlet fever that left him with seriously impaired hearing, and he relied on a hearing aid throughout his lifetime. He received a Ph.B. from Dickinson College, Carlisle, Pennsylvania, in 1906, taught for one year at the Virginia Military Academy, and from 1907 to 1909 studied at the Union Theological Seminary, New York. The following year he returned to Dickinson for an A.M., and he received the B.D. from the Hartford Theological Seminary, in Connecticut, that same year. He was also a Fellow in Medieval History at Hartford, and in 1912 he was awarded the Ph.D.

Butler joined the Newberry Library staff in 1916, after holding a clerical position in the offices of the Burlington Railroad. For the first year at Newberry he was a Reference Assistant. Within a year he was promoted to Head of the Order Department and Bibliographer and Custodian of the John Wing Foundation on the History of Typography and the Printed Book. He continued in those capacities until his resignation in 1931. While at the Newberry he published a checklist of its holdings of books printed in the 15th century, issued in revised form in 1924. In 1926 he married Ruth Lapham, who was the Newberry's Curator of the Ayer Collection on the American Indian and a productive scholar in her own right.

In 1928 Butler was appointed part-time lecturer on the history of books and printing at the University of Chicago's Graduate Library School (GLS). In 1931, at the insistence of Douglas Waples and William Randall, he joined the full-time faculty of the School. He spent the remainder of his professional life at the GLS, until his retirement in 1952.

Butler's books are relatively few in number, the *Check List,* the *Introduction,* and *The Origin of Printing in Europe* (1940). In his unorthodox study of printing, he espoused the belief that Gutenberg was not the inventor of printing from movable type but that the technology was the product of many men working in various cities beginning as early as the 1440s. Butler saw Gutenberg as a shadowy figure whose primacy in the printing craft was the result of myth and the tendency of earlier generations to attribute innovation to a single figure who had caught the popular imagination.

His little pamphlet *Scholarship and Civilization,* "published as proof" by the University of Chicago in 1944, is a synopsis of his course on the history of scholarship and a tantalizing essay—tantalizing because it shows what a major work on that subject the pamphlet could have been had he but persisted in carrying it to completion. It still remains valuable to all who would seek insight into the sociological and anthropological relationships to the development of the library. One gains from it a deepening understanding of the origins of the library and its intellectual roots.

At the time of his death he was preparing a work on the management and administration of rare book collections, a subject on which he was well qualified to speak. He wrote many articles on librarianship and its philosophy and was a popular speaker. He was an excellent raconteur and always enjoyed a good story.

During his Chicago years he made an impression on cultural thought and the philosophy of librarianship that, as he confessed, exceeded his expectations. He was convinced that it was his role to recognize and interpret the social history of the library in terms that would validate it for our own age. Thus he linked the philosophical approach to the intellectual and technical problems of librarianship. "I wrote my *Introduction,*" he said, "to persuade my professional colleagues to be more scientific. Now I have to struggle to keep them from being too damned scientific."

Butler's breadth of knowledge was little short of phenomenal—a true polyhistor of the 20th century. He was a superior teacher. The other teachers at Chicago's Graduate Library School taught students how to *be* librarians, and they taught well. However, Butler taught what librarianship *could be.* In his favorite course on the history of scholarship he gave students, almost without their knowing it, an intellectual heritage to which many have returned as experience has reinforced its significance.

In the library profession, Butler was as controversial a figure as was his intellectual antagonist, Douglas Waples. Despite the handicap of defective hearing, he enjoyed a fruitful social life. He reveled in an audience and was at his best on a public platform.

Jesse Shera, writing in the First Edition of this Encyclopedia, told the following story about his relation with Butler: "The writer's own association with him was marked by frequent arguments. These discussions were often heated but never acrimonious, and were always suffused with mutual respect and the warmth of friendship. At the end of the summer quarter of 1952, when Butler was retiring and the writer was leaving Chicago for another academic post, he finally burst out, 'Pierce, before we part company I do hope you will realize that I *am* on your side. I, too, am a humanist, despite my defense of science.'

"'Oh, I know that, Shera; I know that,' he replied, 'but I sometimes feel about you as I do about Bob Hutchins; your heart is in the right place, but you are forever saying things that give aid and comfort to the enemy.'"

Less than a year later, on March 28, 1953, Butler died in an automobile accident while returning from the dedication of a new library building in Winston-Salem, North Carolina.

REFERENCE

Lee Ash, "Butler, Pierce," *Dictionary of American Library Biography* (1978).

JESSE H. SHERA
(d. 1982)

Byzantine Libraries

Knowledge of Byzantine libraries is scattered and uncertain. Because of turbulent political change and major fires and even earthquakes, there is hardly any archaeological evidence pertaining to the major centers. The student is heavily dependent upon inferences from such literary testimony as the 5th-century writings of Stobaeus (John of Stobi, Macedonia), the 9th-century "Library" of Patriarch Photius, the 10th-century encyclopedic miscellany known to the admiring West as Suidas, and the massive collection of quotations presented in poetic form by John Tzetzes in the 12th century. Some direct documentation, mainly theological, is extant in either the original locations or Western research collections, in the form of Greek codices from the Byzantine era, presumably used for study and argumentation in the churches and monasteries of the Near East, Egypt, Greece, and the Aegean islands.

The outstanding library was reportedly the imperial collection in Constantinople (capital of the Eastern Empire, 395–1453); it was founded in 353 and favored administratively by such steps as were ordered in 372 by Emperor Valens, incorporated in the Theodosian Code. It may have held 100,000 "volumes," the largest assemblage at that time known to Western records; most, if not all, were apparently consumed in the fire of 475(?). There are references to higher studies in the 6th and 7th centuries with tantalizingly unclear hints of book collections. It is indeed known that in the years 607–10 the Patriarch of Constantinople built a library in his palace—burned in 870. Further, it is plausible that library support existed during the 8th century despite the discouragements of the Iconoclasts because a renaissance flowered in the 9th century. In any case, Benedictine-like copying began in 789 at the Constantinople abbey directed by the reformer Theodore of Studium.

The "Library" of Patriarch Photius helps to illuminate the question of what reading matter was apparently available to career men and able women of privilege in 9th-century Constantinople and the Eastern Empire, although not such particulars as where one obtained a desired book or whether it could be borrowed. Concerning Stobaeus, for example, Photius reports the author's stated purpose, the contents of the 208 chapters organized into four books, and the numerous philosophers, poets, orators, historians, kings, and generals from whom he has drawn his material. The list of "philosophers" includes Aristotle, Euclid, and Zoroaster; among the poets are Homer and Sappho. The last list, more varied, includes orator Demosthenes, physician Hippocrates, and historian Thucydides. Photius recommends Stobaeus's encyclopedia as "obviously" a great help for those who have read the writings referred to, as a painless way for others to get acquainted with their essential contributions, and as a bag from which a speaker or writer can pull an apt quotation. R. Henry, who edited Photius (Paris, 1960), can vouch for Photius's care with attributions and copying from some 300 texts but withholds any assurance as to what the Patriarch read in the original and what was picked up in anthologies. Nor is there a shred of evidence as to contacts between Photius and any library.

Hellenic culture continued to be promoted in both the new imperial schools at the capital and several established elsewhere. Considering the centralization that so sharply differentiated Byzantine civilization from Western conditions, benefit likely flowed from the advances at the imperial court. The 10th century was marked by the broad interests of Constantine Porphyrogenitus (i.e., "of the breed of Porphyry," influential promoter of Aristotle); the 11th by Constantine Monomachos, reorganizer of the university, and the philosopher Michael Psellos; and the 12th by several dictionary and encyclopedia compilers and by Princess Anna Comnena, who reputedly took good advantage of her opportunities in learning.

The Crusaders arrived in the early 13th century. Driving out the existing regime, they also wrecked its libraries on some infamous days in 1204. The defeated retired to Nicaea and assembled, among other things, a new library. By 1263 they were able to return to Constantinople, where they remained for two centuries. When the Turks ended Christian domination in 1453, the Greek manuscript treasures, with their remarkable illumination and bindings, had long since migrated westward. The copying still conducted in the East had settled in monasteries such as those at Patmos and Mount Athos; around 1200, at least, many libraries of the North Aegean borrowed liturgical items from Patmos. The city of Byzantium, renamed Istanbul, later regained fame for its wealth in book collections. Its Suleiman Library cherished thousands of Arabic, Persian, and Turkish codices.

REFERENCES

S. K. Padover, "Byzantine Libraries," in J. W. Thompson, *Medieval Libraries* (1939).

Handbuch der Bibliothekswesen III-1 (1955).

Daphne I. D. Kyriaki, *The Role of Libraries and Monastic Centres in the Development of Eleventh Century Byzantine Humanism* (1987). Microform.

SIDNEY L. JACKSON
(d. 1979)

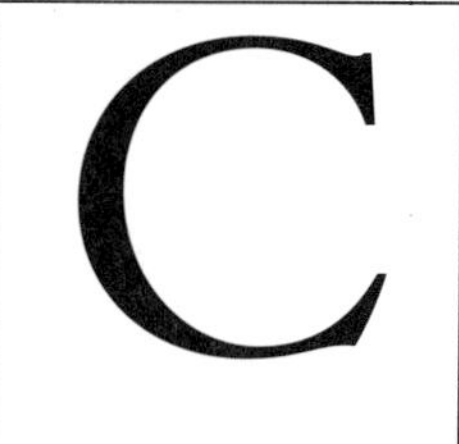

Cain, Julien
(1887–1974)

As director of the Bibliothèque Nationale for 34 years, Julien Cain exerted an enormous influence on the development of modern librarianship in France. His contributions touched virtually every aspect of the field, from modernizing library buildings and creating new services to increasing the public's appreciation for the rich artistic and literary heritage contained in French books. Cain's own deep knowledge of art also gained him the friendship of writers and artists and assured his reputation as a leading figure in the world of cultural affairs.

Cain was born in Montmorency (Val d'Oise), France, May 10, 1887. He was descended from printers through his maternal grandfather, Napoléon Alexandre, a Parisian, and through his father, Sylvain Cain (1865–1937), who had left Lorraine after the Franco-Prussian War in 1870. Julien Cain attended secondary school in Paris, first at the Collège Rollin, then at the Lycée Condorcet, where he studied under the philosopher Alain (Emile Chartier, 1868–1961). After completing his military service in Amiens in 1907, Cain had his interest in bibliography awakened at the Sorbonne by Charles-Victor Langlois, the author of a well-known textbook on historical bibliography (*Manuel de Bibliographie Historique,* 1896). In 1911, after qualifying as a teacher in history, Cain taught for a year at the Lycée de Toulon (Var). He then obtained a leave to study at the École du Louvre, where he undertook research on the painter Jean-François Millet (1814–75).

Bibliothèque Nationale, Paris

Julien Cain

During World War I, Cain was serving as a lieutenant when he was gravely wounded on February 12, 1916. Not able to return to military service, he was assigned to the Information Office (then attached to the Ministry of War but later made part of the Ministry of Foreign Affairs). There he was involved with editing daily and periodic bulletins of the foreign press as well as editing collections of foreign documents *(Recueils de Documents Étrangers)*. In 1918 he also published the second edition of the guide to periodicals used in compiling those bulletins.

From June 10, 1919, to September 30, 1920, Cain received another leave to complete his studies at the École du Louvre. He was then assigned to the Ministry of Foreign Affairs, where he worked for several years in the cultural relations division. Cain left his post in the ministry in 1927 to take over the direction of the Cabinet of the President of the Chamber of Deputies.

Appointed Administrator-General of the Bibliothèque Nationale on May 1, 1930, Cain undertook the physical renovation of the buildings—notably the construction of an annex in Versailles (1934) and the construction of two basement floors for stacks in the department of printed books in the central library (1936). He also began the interior renovation of the 17th-century Hôtel Tubeuf for the department of engravings (1937). Between 1930 and 1939 there was also an increased pace of production of the printed catalogue *(Catalogue Général des Livres Imprimés);* 61 volumes appeared (or one-quarter of the total set issued between 1897 and 1981). A microfilm department was also created (1937–39) and in 1938 a national record library, the Phonothèque Nationale, was established. The Bibliothèque Nationale also began to meet the needs of other French libraries through the creation of joint services to provide for information, purchase, and cataloguing of periodicals and through the establishment of the Catalogue Room (Salle des Catalogues), which was conceived in 1935 as a national center for documentation and bibliography. In addition, Cain served as President of Class II (Libraries and Literary Manifestations) of the 1937 International Exposition in Paris, where he set up a Museum of Literature. He also edited volume 8, "Written Civilization," of the topical *Encyclopédie Française.*

In November 1939, the writer Jean Giraudoux (1882–1944), then commissioner general of information, called upon Cain to become secretary general of the Ministry of Information on April 9, 1940; in June he had to leave Paris with the government. Dismissed from his duties at the Bibliothèque Nationale on July 23, 1940, he nonetheless returned to Paris. The following February he was arrested by the Germans and was deported to Buchenwald in 1944. Liberated by the American army, he returned to Paris on April 18, 1945.

By October 1945 he had effectively resumed his duties as Administrator-General of the Bibliothèque Nationale; on April 18, 1946, he was also placed in charge of the national directorate of libraries created at the time of the liberation. As head of the Direction des Bibliothèques, Cain carefully followed the elaboration of civil service statutes for library personnel, which served as a key element in standardizing appointment and advancement procedures in French libraries. Between 1948 and 1963 Cain also oversaw important construction projects that affected nearly 200 municipal libraries, including the war-damaged libraries in Douai (opened in 1956) and in Brest, Tours, Chartres, and Lorient (in progress in 1963). At the same time, construction work was undertaken for many academic libraries; in some instances departments *(sections)* of the university library were moved to the central campus (as in Bordeaux-Talence, Lyon-La Doua, Toulouse-Rangueil), while in other cases they were newly created, as in Nice and Reims.

Always in favor of coordination, Cain set up a union list of foreign works *(Catalogue Collectif des Ouvrages Étrangers)* in 1952 and created an ongoing inventory of current foreign periodicals *(l'Inventaire Permanent des Périodiques Étrangers en Cours)* in 1953. That same year he got the *Bibliographie Annuelle de l'Histoire de France* established under the auspices of the Centre National de la Recherche Scientifique (CNRS) and got the future center for research on the conservation of graphic records set up with the sponsorship of CNRS and the Muséum National d'Histoire Naturelle. Cain also had several directories of libraries and agencies for documentation published (1950–51, 1963) and in 1958 he served as the first President of the Association pour la Conservation et la Reproduction Photographique de la Presse (Association for the Conservation and Photographic Reproduction of the Press).

At the Bibliothèque Nationale, Cain carried out 15 construction projects between 1945 and 1964; among them were the installation of the map library division in the central portion of the Hôtel Tubeuf and the construction of a second building in Versailles in 1954. Other building projects undertaken during that period included the extension of the central stacks in the department of printed books (1958); the excavation of Sully hall at the Bibliothèque de l'Arsenal (1959); and the construction of quarters for the music department and the national record library at 2 rue Louvois.

Many private collections had been acquired by the national library, and in 1960 an exhibit presented the notable acquisitions of the Bibliothèque Nationale during the preceding 15 years. On display were items drawn from the legacy of Atherton Curtis (which contained 7,000 engravings); manuscripts, drawings, and valuable editions of French authors bequeathed by Henri de Rothschild (1872–1934); and items on the history of photography drawn from a collection assembled by Nadar (1820–1910).

Altogether Cain inaugurated more than a hundred exhibits, including the great retrospective exhibits on the history of the book, such as those on French manuscript painting (the 7th to the 12th century in 1954 and the 13th to the 16th century in 1955–56). Other exhibits commemorated specific artists from Pisanello, the engraver of medals (1932), to the painter Georges Braque (1960), or honored writers and composers, from François Rabelais (1932) to Maurice Maeterlinck and Claude Debussy (1962).

Cain's activities extended beyond libraries to participation in many societies concerned with the book arts (Amis de la Bibliothèque Nationale; Peintres-Graveurs Français; La Reliure Originale) and included service on national committees that dealt with illustrated French books and with engraving. As director of the Bibliothèque Nationale, Cain also served as ex officio member of national boards and commissions that dealt with archives and archival training; museums; belles-lettres; research; historical monuments; and radio and television broadcasting. In 1952 Cain was chosen a personal member of the Académie des Beaux-Arts (one of the five Académies of the Institut de France) and in 1961 he became a member of the advisory board of the Comédie Française.

Cain also served on the French National Commission to Unesco until 1972; he became President in 1967 and chaired the Committee on Libraries and Museums. In addition he served as a member (1958–64) and then as Vice-President (1960–62) of the Executive Council of Unesco; he presided over the Consultative Committee on Bibliography, which became the International Consultative Committee on Documentation, Libraries and Archives in 1967. He also served as Vice-President of both the International Federation of Library Associations (1949–51) and of the International Federation for Documentation (1954–56). The creation of the International Association of Bibliophily (1959–63) was one of Cain's last initiatives in his capacity as head of the Bibliothèque Nationale and of the Direction des Bibliothèques. He retired in 1964.

In 1963 Cain began serving as curator of the Musée Jacquemard-André, which was administered by the Institut de France. There he organized many important exhibits from 1964, when he presented the works of Millet, to 1974, when he opened an exhibit on the designer Paul Poiret. Beginning in 1964 Cain presided over the national commission charged with preparing a general inventory of the monuments and artistic treasures of France, and in 1971 he became President of the French national committee for International Book Year.

He died in Paris on October 9, 1974. His honors had included Knight of the Legion of Honor (World War I); the Grand-Croix of the Legion of Honor (1957); designation as Knight Commander of the Order of the British Empire; and honorary doctorates from the University of Glasgow (1950) and the University of Stockholm (1960). His guiding principle was "to maintain a well-considered balance between two equally necessary points of view—the respect for the values of the past and the willingness to respond to the exigencies of the present."

REFERENCES

"Hommage à Julien Cain," *Gazette des Beaux-Arts* (1966).

Bernard Gavoty, *Notice sur la Vie et les Travaux de Julien Cain* (1976).

"Hommage à Julien Cain," *Bulletin de la Bibliothèque Nationale* (1976).

THÉRÈSE KLEINDIENST;
translated by MARY NILES MAACK

Callimachus

(fl. 3rd century B.C.)

Callimachus, who rose from the obscurity of schoolteaching to become the lynchpin of Hellenistic poetry in its Golden Age (290–240 B.C.), worked as a bio-bibliographer at the Alexandrian Library, where he compiled the *Pinakes*, a *catalogue raisonné* of Greek literature in 120 volumes. Beyond that, we know only a few details of his life, mostly of his childhood; a critical biography cannot be written.

Homer and Callimachus represent the traditional and modern viewpoints of ancient Greece. The traditional culture, which prevailed from Homer through Aristotle, was born of the Greek oral past; it was created in the absence of writing and maintained against the encroachments of literacy as long as possible. But Callimachus, less than 20 years after Aristotle, stood on the threshold of a new age whose culture was created by the book. The oral and literary cultures of Greece thus found expression in the two differing poetries of Homer and Callimachus.

Homer produced poetry spontaneously in live performances before a native audience; his was an oral art addressed to the ear, a matter of arranging preestablished musical formulas without fishing for the right word or adjusting it to the meter. Callimachus, however, composed poetry in the study, carefully selecting his words and working them into a few impeccable lines each day. He strove for technical perfection, regarding the ideal poem as a tiny jewel to be cut, polished, and admired by experts, and addressed an esoteric audience of educated connoisseurs in the artificial climate of Alexandria. He always looked things up before rehashing them.

Callimachus, finally, should not be regarded as the patron saint of cataloguers, even though he completed the bibliographical projects initiated by Zenodotus, which culminated in the higher and lower criticisms and in exegesis. The result of his work was a massive catalogue, the *Pinakes,* based on the *pinax*, the annotated list underlying all antiquarian writing in the 5th century B.C. It contained much more information than a library catalogue, providing for each writer a brief biographical sketch and a list of his or her works, including lost ones; any doubts about the authenticity of the book were also noted. It was apparently arranged according to large categories such as epic, oratory, and history. Not merely a library catalogue, the *Pinakes* was actually a critical inventory of Greek literature, the first scientific literary history, attempting no less than a complete record of all Greek literature as it then existed.

Despite the availability of Oriental cataloguing techniques, Callimachus had no real model for his immense project because his bibliographical aims were typically Western: he wanted to make the *ideas* of Greek literature available for the use of scholars. The Orient, on the other hand, which regarded books as *things*, had invented a complicated system of cataloguing for keeping track of them, but it focused not on scholarship but on descriptive notes and parallel glossaries, which served only the practical needs of the archives, libraries, and schools of temples. These conflicting aims have created permanent bibliographical ambivalence. Do cataloguers deal primarily with the physical "body" of a book, or with its metaphysical "spirit" as a complex of meanings? Should they perpetuate the ancient cataloguing practices devised for managing things, or invent new procedures capable of managing ideas? The *Pinakes* of Callimachus constitutes an experiment that failed, for its influence on libraries is difficult to trace beyond the Byzantine period. But the work does raise for the Western cataloguer the bothersome question of bibliography as bookology—an issue that helps to explain, at least partially, why the problems of bibliographic organization and control continue unresolved.

REFERENCES

K. J. McKay, *The Poet at Play: Kallimachos, the Bath of Pallas* (1962).

H. Curtis Wright, *The Oral Antecedents of Greek Librarianship* (1978).

H. CURTIS WRIGHT

Cambodia

Cambodia (the Khmer Republic, formerly Kampuchea) is a republic of Southeast Asia in the southwest part of the Indochinese Peninsula. It is bounded on the northeast by Laos, on the east and southeast by Vietnam, on the southwest by the Gulf of Thailand, on the west and northwest by Thailand. Population (1990 est.) 8,246,000; area 181,035 sq.km. The official language is Khmer; French is widely spoken.

History. During the four-year period of Communist rule (1975-79) and after the Vietnamese conquest of Cambodia in 1979, library services were reported to be effectively eliminated. There was no evidence that any were functioning at the end of the 1970s, and little sign of recovery even by the 1990s. The University of Phnom Penh was reported totally inactive in April 1979 but had reopened by 1990. Several public and university libraries, as well as the collections in museums and temples, were destroyed. Except for academic libraries, the information below applies to libraries before 1975.

National Library. The Archives et Bibliothèque Nationales was founded in 1923 in Phnom Penh as a national deposit library that housed more than 31,000 volumes. An ordinance of 1956 required publishers to deposit five copies of all works published there. Printers were obliged to deposit three copies. No law required that every administrative document be forwarded to the National Archives, although a decree of 1918 required public departments to deposit such documents periodically. Some departments deposited no documents.

No national bibliography was established for Cambodia, although the National Archives and Library compiled catalogues of its holdings, including books, pamphlets, official publications, university dissertations and theses, maps, atlases, and standards.

A national exchange center, the Bibliothèque Centrale in Phnôm Penh, was created in 1972 to collect works in all fields of knowledge and to establish contacts with foreign libraries. An exchange system was developed among the university libraries, which included the Université des Beaux-Arts, the Université de Phnôm Penh, the Université Bouddhique, the Université des Sciences Agronomiques, and the Université Technique, all in Phnom Penh.

Academic Libraries. By 1990, the universities were all opened, though with limited facilities. The Université Phnôm Penh reported an academic staff of 350 serving a student body of 8,400. Total holdings of five faculty libraries (Letters and Human Sciences, Science, Law and Economics, Medicine, and Commerce) stood at 36,500. The Université Technique had no library for its 1,000 students. The other institutions fared slightly better: Université des Sciences Agronomique (100 students, 1,000 volumes); Université Buddhique (180 students, 10,000 volumes), and Université des Beaux Arts (9,420 volumes for 50 staff and an unknown number of students).

Other Libraries. The Bibliothèque de l'Institut Bouddhique, founded in 1923 in Phnom Penh, housed books and manuscripts in French, English, Thai, Burmese, Sinhalese, Chinese, Tibetan, and Mongolian, as well as documents in Khmer and Pali on Khmer folklore and Buddhism. The library built a collection of about 40,000 volumes and 16,200 manuscripts on palm leaves.

The Institut National de la Statistique et des Recherches Économiques, founded in 1963 in Phnom Penh under the Ministère du Plan, became a documentation center holding more than 300 volumes. The Institut compiled national and international statistical and economic data and published the *Bulletin Trimestriel de Statistique, Annuaire Statistique,* and *Comptes Economiques.*

The Library of the Association des Écrivains Khmers, founded in 1962 in Phnom Penh, housed 4,525 volumes. The association was created to aid writers and promote literature in the Khmer language; it published a monthly literary review. There was no official library association, although a governmental department, the Office National de Planification et de Développement des Bibliothèques, was established in 1975 to coordinate library and archival activity in Cambodia.

PETER A. POOLE

Cameroon

Cameroon, a republic in western Africa, is bounded on the north and east by Chad and the Central Africa

Republic, on the south by Congo, Gabon, and Equatorial Guinea, and on the west by the Gulf of Guinea and Nigeria. Lake Chad links it to Niger. Population (1990 est.) 11,834,000; area 475,442 sq.km. The official languages are English and French, but there are more than 200 Cameroonian languages.

History. Before the coming of the written word, people passed on stories, messages, and other information by word of mouth. The drum was also widely used. Oral tradition will play a key role for a long time to come. The Regional Centre for the Collection of Oral Traditions and Literatures collects and stores much "knowledge" from the "old wise people." It is said that "when an old man dies, it is a library burning."

After the partition of Africa in 1884, the Germans introduced their language as the lingua franca in Cameroon. There is now little German spoken except by the old men who still pride themselves in it. In 1971 Max Dippold published a bibliography of documents in the German language in Cameroon that lists 6,216 titles. Most of these are in the National Archives in Yaoundé. But a student using documents in the German language still has to go to Germany. The Germans left fortresses and archives in Cameroon, but no libraries. After World War I, the French and British ruled parts of Cameroon. The French colonial administrators established *bibliothèques de brousse* (rural libraries) but these libraries served only as reading centers for officers who had to work far from the urban centers. There is no evidence in the French-speaking part of Cameroon of any deliberate aim to open libraries for the people.

In the English-speaking part of the country, following the British tradition, all secondary schools had libraries. Some of these have grown but have not reached the dimensions of real school libraries. Many people still take pride in saying, "I was the school librarian." In fact, these people were students in charge of the libraries. Even though the libraries did not receive many books, and although the growth has been rather slow, all the secondary schools, especially those run by missionary bodies, have libraries. It would be an overstatement to say that all secondary schools had libraries in English-speaking Cameroon. Before independence (1961), only the government and missionary bodies ran secondary schools. Later many private secondary schools were opened, most of them with libraries.

Some public libraries existed in the larger towns, although most of them in the capital city were opened around 1960 by foreign bodies. Those opened by foreign embassies are called cultural centers. The few public libraries that existed in the 1960s were those of Garoua and Douala in French-speaking Cameroon and Bamenda and Limbe (formerly Victoria) in English-speaking Cameroon. None of these libraries had more than a few hundred volumes, in poor condition. Urban centers had a great influx of people after about 1968 because of the availability of schooling and greater opportunities for jobs. A major hurdle in the development of public libraries was the lack of trained librarians.

National Library Service. The Cameroon National Library was established in 1966. It is attached to the Ministry of Information and Culture. It has three sections: Acquisition and Legal Deposit, Classification and Cataloguing, and National Bibliography. By 1990 it had 20,000 books, 130 periodicals, and 150 reports. The book collection grew because of French government donations in the 1980s. The National Library is now called Service du Livre et des Bibliothèques (Book and Library Services). The National Library is supposed to produce the National Bibliography, but no volumes had been issued by 1990. The National Archives was also attached to the Ministry of Information and Culture.

Serials Department, University of Yaoundé Library.

Academic Libraries. The largest academic library is that of the University of Yaoundé. It was established in 1966 when the University (founded in 1962–63) moved to its present site. It brought together a number of small book collections scattered over the whole campus. It did not comprise a large collection; in 1973 it totaled 52,000 books, 620 serials, and small collections of slides, tapes, and microfilms. By 1990 the book collection had increased to 93,000 and the serials to about 900.

Efforts were made to increase reading facilities for the students at the University of Yaoundé. Planning for a new building started in 1975 and construction began in 1983. It was planned as a modern library, with space for at least 500,000 books, facilities for about 600 readers, and modern equipment, including an IBM 4331 computer acquired in 1985.

Other academic libraries include those of the School of Journalism, opened in 1971 to train journalists for work in central Africa. By 1990 it held almost 5,000 books, 130 journal titles, and 400 reports. The Polytechnic School, opened in 1971 to train engineers mainly in road construction, building construction, architecture, and electrical engineering, had about 90 sitting places, almost 6,000 books, and 70 current serials in 1990. The Advanced Teacher College, opened in 1961 and the oldest institute in the University of Yaoundé, held by 1990 nearly 30,000 books and 180 serial titles. The Medical School, opened in 1969, held more than 25,000 books, 250 journal titles, and 440 reports, representing the largest collection outside the main University Library. The School of International Relations, opened in 1972, has about 12,000 books, 200 serials, and 130 reports, including United Nations documents. There are libraries at the University Centers at Buea, Douala, Dschang, and Ngaoundéré.

Public Libraries. The few that exist are in Bamenda, Limbe, Douala, and Garoua. A public library existed in Bamenda long before 1960. Although most of the books are old, the seating space attracted some patrons to study and relax. It was transferred to what is called the Cultural Center attached to the Ministry of Information. The libraries in Douala and Garoua have trained staff. The Limbe Public Library is attached to the Youth Center. Built by the Presbyterian Mission in a busy part of the town, it is heavily used.

Libraries attached to foreign cultural centers function as public libraries, accessible to the general public. The Centre Culturel Français (French Cultural Center) in Yaoundé, created just after independence in 1960, was the largest public library in the country in the late 1980s, with 20,000 volumes, nearly 70 journal titles, and more than 90 reports. It was the first library in the country to have a children's section. Heavy users include students of all grades. The French Cultural Center in Douala, Cameroon's largest city, has a large library with a children's section.

In the late 1980s the French government began promoting "lecture publique" (public libraries) throughout the Francophone world, donating thousands of books to libraries in such countries as Cameroon. The Cameroon government made intense efforts to set up libraries, first at the provincial level and then at lower levels. It planned libraries in Yaoundé, Garoua, Bertoua, Douala, Bafoussam, and Bamenda. A second plan, for libraries built on a joint venture basis among the British, French, and Germans, with collections in the three languages, has not yet been realized. An American nonprofit organization, Books for the World, began donating books to Cameroon in the late 1980s. A local organization, Cameroon Educational Resource Committee (CEREC), was set up to distribute them. It identifies viable libraries and sends books to them on request. When the first 20,000 books arrived, most went to public libraries.

School Libraries. Libraries in secondary schools are more developed in the English-speaking than the French-speaking parts of Cameroon and vary greatly in holdings. Almost all secondary schools run by religious organizations have rooms set apart and called "libraries." The number of books range from a few hundred to a few thousand. Those with more than 5,000 books include St. Joseph's College, Sasse; Queen of the Holy Rosary College, Okoyong, Mamfe; Cameroon Protestant College, Bali; St. Augustine's College, Nso; and Sacred Heart College, Mankon Bamenda. Few have audiovisual equipment and facilities.

In French-speaking Cameroon, libraries are less developed. Few have more than 200 books. Among those with more than 3,000 books are the Lycée de Bagangte, Lycée de Foumban, and Lycée de Bafoussam.

St. Pius Teacher Training College, Tatum, has about 10,000 books. It built a new library and sought American books from Books for the World through CEREC.

Special Libraries. Research libraries, which fall under the Ministry of Higher Education and Scientific Research, are likely to develop rapidly in the 1990s. The oldest special library in the country, the Library of the Institute of Social and Human Sciences, was founded in 1935. By the 1990s it had about 25,000 books and 60 current journals. This library has some rare material on the social sciences in Cameroon. Other libraries that fall under the Ministry of Higher Education are the Library of the Institute of Man and Biosphere (MAB), founded in 1977 (about 1,100 books); the Library of the Institute of Zootechnical Research (IRZ), founded in 1979 (350 books and 98 journals); and the Library of the Institute of Medicinal Plants (IMPM), founded in 1981 (650 books and 89 serial titles).

The Library of the National Assembly was opened in 1960. It covers the human sciences, politics, economics, law, and literature. It moved to a new building built specifically for it. Although the Library had only about 4,000 books in the late 1980s, it was expected to grow. It is used not only by members of the legislature but also by university students. The library of the Ministry of Planning and Industry is mainly concerned with economics. Its 39,000 volumes are used by those who work on national economic plans and also by university students. It is the largest single library of any ministry in Cameroon.

The Profession. As of the end of the 1980s there was no library school in Cameroon. Librarians are trained in Britain, Canada, France, Nigeria, and the United States. Because of the increasing demand for trained librarians, many people recognized the need for a library school. Following a survey by the author of this article and a series of meetings with the

Libraries in Cameroon (1991)

Type of library	Number of administrative units (main libraries)	Number of service points (branches, mobile stops, etc.)	Volumes in collections	Annual expenditures (C.F.A. franc)	Population served	Professional staff (with certificate, diploma, etc.)	Total staff
National	1	1	21,000	300,000	560,000	6	20
Academic	9	11	171,000	181,750,000	40,000	19	103
Public	6	6	10,500	700,000	500,000	1	17
School	43	43	81,000	60,000,000	600,000	--	49
Special	5	5	n.a.	20,500,000	400	2	22

Ministry of Higher Education, plans were made in 1986 to establish a library school. An economic crisis in the late 1980s forced its abandonment.

By 1990 there were about 30 graduate librarians in Cameroon. There were about the same number of sublibrarians, practically all of them trained at the library school in Dakar.

On a limited basis, junior staff are trained in the University Library to work in various ministries in Yaoundé. The duration of the training has been generally three to six months, but a few have stayed on for a year.

The Cameroon Association of Librarians, Archivists, Documentalists, and Museum Curators (ABADCAM) was founded in 1975. Its main aims are to encourage the establishment of libraries at all levels and in all parts of the country and to promote the training of personnel for libraries, archives, museums, and documentation centers. Peter N. Chateh was its founder and first President. But, with more than 40 members and a roster of 120 potential candidates for membership, the Association lapsed.

PETER NKANGAFACK CHATEH

Canada

The largest country in area in the Western Hemisphere and the second largest in the world, Canada stretches from the Arctic Ocean on the north to the United States on the south and from the Atlantic Ocean on the east to the Pacific Ocean and Alaska on the west. It is a federation of ten provinces and two territories; its government follows the British parliamentary tradition, and Canada is a member of the Commonwealth of Nations. Population (1990 est.) 26,522,000; area 9,976,139 sq.km. Official languages are English and French, but the presence of aboriginal peoples and a large influx of immigrants means that many more languages are spoken.

HISTORY

In Canada, as elsewhere, geographic, demographic, economic, political, and historical factors have affected library development. Most of the people in this vast country live in a narrow, 300 km.-wide corridor stretching for more than 5,500 km. from coast to coast north of the U.S. border. Communications may still be difficult in spite of the advances in technology; provision of library service has been, and to some extent still is, a problem in sparsely populated areas.

Canada's population, like that of the U.S., is mixed, and has grown both through immigration and by natural increases in the birth rate. Large influxes of people in the aftermath of two world wars have enriched the Canadian mosaic, but have given public libraries the problem of providing materials for them in their own languages. The difficulties have been mitigated—for smaller libraries in particular—by the work of the National Library's Multilingual Biblioservice, which supplies shelf-ready foreign language books on long-term loan to provincial agencies for distribution in the provinces.

Natural resources are rarely distributed equally in any country; Canada is no exception. The economic development of the provinces has been uneven, and library development has also been uneven, because the British North America Act, under which Canada was formed, put education—and, tacitly, libraries—under provincial jurisdiction. The province of Ontario, with large resources and strong British traditions, had libraries supported by local communities from an early

Libraries in Canada (1990)

Type of library	Number of administrative units (main libraries)	Number of service points (branches, mobile stops, etc.)	Volumes in collections	Annual expenditures (Canadian dollar)	Population served	Professional staff (with certificate, diploma, etc.)	Total staff
National							
National Library of Canada	1	1	1,461,485	36,471,699	26,512,100	197[a]	500
CISTI	1	14	2,251,914	25,896,000	26,512,100	73[a]	213
Academic							
University[b]	68(est.)						
CARL members only	27	--	79,914,000	312,303,000	520,364[c]	1,424[a]	6,185
College	166 (est.)						
Public	847[d]	5,821	59,886,915	585,339,791	23,961,423 (est.)	2,548[e]	13,161
School	n.a.						
Special	2,600 (est.)						

[a]May include other professionals in addition to librarians
[b]Includes 12 degree-granting colleges federated or affiliated with another university
[c]FTE students
[d]Excludes 143 boards in Ontario which contract with other boards for services
[e]Includes 318 other professionals (FTE) in addition to librarians

Sources: National libraries: annual reports; ARL Statistics 1989–90. University libraries: *Corpus Almanac . . . 1991;* Canadian Association of Research Libraries, 1989/90 statistics. Public libraries: Statistics Canada, Education, Culture and Tourism Division, 1989/90 statistics.

The National Library of Canada in Ottawa. Established with the passage of the National Library Act of 1952, it did not occupy these permanent quarters until 1967.

The National Library of Canada

date. In 1884 it took the next step and passed the first law in Canada allowing tax support for public libraries. Quebec, on the other hand, with slower economic development and a religious rather than secular library tradition, relied mainly on libraries of religious educational institutions, some going back to the 17th century, and did not pass a comparable law until 1959. Thereafter development was rapid, spurred by provincial funding to aid municipalities willing to set up libraries. The Territories, in contrast, with less accessible resources and a sparse and scattered population, funded and administered their libraries centrally.

Jurisdictional differences have kept the federal government from trying to equalize public library service countrywide by direct funding, although its grants to the provinces for higher education have been of indirect benefit to university libraries. Jurisdictional differences have also prevented any federal measures for library improvement, and any advances in research, cooperation, and development of standards have had to depend on local and provincial government support. Canada has indeed been fortunate that usually such support has been forthcoming and that the high standard of living in the country has enabled libraries of all types to improve services by utilizing advanced technologies to automate procedures, facilitate communication, and make possible the interconnections and resource sharing that budgetary restrictions made imperative given the fiscal constraints of the 1980s.

One other factor in Canadian library development has been very important: the influence of U.S. models. American libraries and library associations have been generous in sharing knowledge with their Canadian counterparts. Canadians in turn have freely adapted American models to suit local situations. This pattern of joint Canadian-U.S. library development has mitigated local differences in Canada and has produced a North American library context in which librarians and users can move with familiarity.

Canada Institute for Scientific and Technical Information

Canada Institute for Scientific and Technical Information, which has developed a national automated information network.

NATIONAL LIBRARIES

Canada has two libraries that serve the nation: the National Library of Canada, founded in 1953, and CISTI, the Canada Institute for Scientific and Technical Information, founded in 1974 when the National Research Council amalgamated its technical information services with the National Science Library, founded in 1966 as a successor to library of the National Research Council (1924).

National Library of Canada. Until the end of World War II, libraries were too few and too weak to lobby for a national library. Postwar developments, among them the formation of the Canadian Library Association (1946) and the findings of the Royal Commission on National Development in the Arts, Letters, and Sciences (1949–51), led to increased pressure on the federal government to set up a national library. Kaye Lamb, the Dominion Archivist, was given responsibility for planning it. In 1953 the National Library came into being. Its chief responsibilities were to compile a national bibliography and a national union catalogue of holdings of major Canadian library collections. Lamb served as both Dominion Archivist and National Librarian. Under the National Library Act of 1952, the Library was given the status of a department reporting to Parliament through a minister (in the 1990s the Minister of Communications).

Until 1967 the National Library staff struggled along in temporary quarters. In that year the Library moved into its own building, shared with the Public (now National) Archives. Both institutions have long outgrown the space and have had to transfer holdings and operations to other buildings in the area of Ottawa, Ontario, and Hull, Quebec, but they still share the main building.

Lamb retired in 1968 and the posts of National Librarian and Dominion Archivist were separated. Guy Sylvestre succeeded Lamb as National Librarian. Under his leadership the National Library Act was revised in 1969 to include legal deposit. The revision spelled out more clearly the National Library's coordinating role among federal government libraries and its potential for coordinating bibliographic services for the country.

Sylvestre recognized, too, the importance of new computer and telecommunications technologies for libraries. DOBIS (the Dortmunder Bibliothekssystem), an integrated, automated system originally acquired in 1976, was adapted to meet the bilingual needs of Canada. *Canadiana* and the national union catalogue (covering monographs, serials, and special-format materials) were the first major automation projects. The resulting database is now used by more than 500 libraries across Canada as well as by the National Library's own staff and clientele. Today the National Library is recognized as a world leader in applying the open systems interconnection model to library functions, including interlibrary loan and file transfer. In the areas of automation and standards, the Library cooperates closely with other national libraries and international bodies.

Other national services maintained by the Library include a Canadian Book Exchange Center, the Multilingual Biblioservice, and manual and automated reference, information, and advisory services, with emphasis on the Canadiana collections, such as government documents, newspapers, theses, music (sheet music, sound recordings, manuscripts, and papers), children's literature, and literary manuscripts. A program of exhibitions, cultural events, and publications complements the core activities.

The Library also coordinates a Cataloguing-in-Publication program and provides secretariats for advisory groups on services to disabled persons and for federal libraries. The Library Development Center offers a unique information service on Canadian and foreign library developments.

In 1984 Marianne Scott, formerly director of libraries at McGill University, succeeded Sylvestre as National Librarian. She fostered close relations with the Canadian library community and continued the policy of holding the Library's Advisory Board meetings outside Ottawa.

Like other government departments, the National Library suffered serious staff cuts in the 1980s that may limit new as well as older programs. In *Orientations: A Planning Framework for the 1990s,* the Library reaffirmed its commitment to preserving Canada's printed

National Library of Quebec, established in 1968.

heritage, resource sharing, and library development. It pursued the first goal by establishing a preservation collection of Canadian materials at the Library itself, continuing a mass deacidification program that began in 1981, and coordinating a major preservation microfilming study undertaken with five university libraries. It worked toward the second goal by convening a series of meetings in each province to discuss strategies and models for resource sharing, coordinating a national inventory of Canadian newspapers, and applying systematic efforts to identify Canadian collection strengths. It pursued the third goal through its information service and its involvement in international activities important to Canadian libraries.

CISTI, the Canada Institute for Scientific and Technical Information. CISTI houses an outstanding collection of books, serials, and technical reports in science and technology and makes them available to users through interlibrary loan and photocopy. It provides reference and referral services using printed materials and access to hundreds of scientific and technical databases, among them its own CAN/OLE (Canadian Online Enquiry System, an online bibliographic reference database) and CAN/SND (Canadian Scientific Numeric Databases, an online source of scientific data). CISTI's *Union List of Scientific Serials in Canadian Libraries* has long been a standby for Canadian libraries in its print form and is now online, and CAN/SDI is a current selective dissemination of information service based on CAN/OLE. CISTI also operates a Health Sciences Resource Center; is the Canadian coordinator for MEDLARS, the U.S. National Library of Medicine database; and maintains the Canadian Index of Scientific Translations. Like other federal libraries, CISTI experienced a series of staff cuts in the 1980s, but it remains an unparalleled resource in its fields for all Canadian libraries.

ACADEMIC LIBRARIES

Canada has two groups of academic libraries: the libraries of some 60 universities and degree-granting colleges, many of the latter affiliated with universities, and about 170 post-secondary, non-degree-granting institutions variously named colleges or institutes,

Laurentian University/Université Laurentienne

The new J. N. Desmarais Library/Bibliothèque J. N. Desmarais.

which offer two- or three-year diploma courses. Both types of institutions derive most of their support from government; few are privately supported, although some universities have substantial endowments.

University Libraries. Before World War II the largest Canadian universities were in the Maritimes, Quebec, and Ontario. They had professional schools such as law, medicine, and theology, but did not in general offer graduate work at the doctoral level; for that most Canadians went to the U.S. or the United Kingdom. University libraries were correspondingly small and many were poorly staffed. As late as 1949 only McGill University Library in Montreal could claim more than 500,000 volumes in its collection. But Canada came out of World War II conscious of itself as a nation; this determination, combined with a postwar increase in population and an expanding economy, led to a determination to prepare at home the highly trained people the country needed. In the 1960s the provinces and indirectly the federal government began to pour money into the universities, enlarging older ones and starting many new ones. University libraries benefited: staffs, service outlets, and collections increased; new buildings were constructed; and the library proportion of total university budgets reached a median of 7.5 percent. Internal changes included conversion from outmoded classifications to the Library of Congress system and the use of automated systems to speed the process. The University of Toronto, Laval University in Quebec, and the University of British Columbia were leaders in this respect; the Toronto bibliographic system, UTLAS (the University of Toronto Library Automation System), developed into an independent organization serving users in Canada, Japan, and the U.S.

The 1970s saw the end of the period of rapid growth, but university libraries for the most part held their own; collections grew to a total of almost 50 million volumes by 1982. By 1987, for the 27 largest libraries alone, the total was more than 74 million volumes. But, by the mid-1980s, mounting economic difficulties in the country were reflected in the universities and in their libraries. Collections, particularly in the area of serials, were cut back and staffs decreased. Support staff tended to meet job uncertainty through unionization; librarians tended to join faculty associations and many fought for, and obtained, faculty status.

Directors of Canadian libraries sought to effect economies through cooperation in acquisitions and processing. They tried to achieve "rationalization of collections," notably in Ontario and British Columbia. These attempts failed with respect to collections, but left an important legacy of reciprocal borrowing rights (between universities and between provinces in some cases), interuniversity transit (still facilitating interlibrary lending), and shared cataloguing. UTLAS became the chief supplier of computer-based cataloguing products and services in Canada. It also became a major component in a developing decentralized Canadian bibliographic network of union files that technological advances made feasible.

Laurent Denis and Ethel Auster studied the effects of the retrenchment of the late 1970s and early 1980s in Canadian university libraries using 22 members of the Canadian Association of Research Libraries (CARL). They found that between 1972–73 and 1982–83 adjusted budget allocations per student dropped in all parts of the country; the proportion of budget spent on materials declined, although net volumes increased (except in Quebec, which did not report these figures); and total positions and the number of full-time equivalent professionals increased (except in Ontario), but staff per 100 FTE students declined in all regions. The picture would probably not be improved if figures for the smaller universities were available as well. CARL statistics for 1986–87 indicate that the median percentage of university budgets for its members dropped from 7.5 percent to 6.7 percent.

The 1980s brought three other major developments. One is the continuing and increasing use of automation to support library functions other than cataloguing. For example, some university libraries

Library of Parliament in Ottawa primarily, which serves as a legislative reference service, and also houses extensive scholarly collections.

The National Film Board of Canada

cooperated with the National Library in experiments on automated file transfer and machine-readable reporting to the National Library's union catalogue. Second, as their parent universities moved to support distance learning and to broaden their student base to include older members of the population, libraries began learning to apply new methods of training users unfamiliar with libraries in how to use library resources. They also designed new ways to deliver documents and information to such users. Finally, as a partial answer to financial stringency, some libraries began offering, for a fee, information search services to local businesses and industries that lacked their own special libraries. In short, Canadian university libraries began learning how to adapt to an environment characterized by fast-changing technology, rising service demands from within and outside the universities, and declining financial support.

College Libraries. In Canada the term "college" usually means a tertiary or post-secondary institution that does not confer degrees, but offers two- or three-year courses designed to provide technical and vocational education, to meet the needs of the local community for continuing education, and to allow later transfer to a university. Most of the colleges functioning in the 1990s were formed after 1965; their booming enrollments testified to the need for them, but meant that many of their libraries were hard put to keep up with student numbers and service to multiple campuses. In 1986–87 college libraries spent more than $100 million, roughly 3 percent of total college expenditure, with acquisitions taking about $10 million of the total.

The distinctive features of Canadian college libraries are their emphasis on audiovisual materials (including involvement in production in some cases); their close cooperation with faculty; and their support for services their institutions offer their local communities. Provincial variations remain. Ontario colleges function fairly independently but cooperate closely. For example, they sponsored a joint ordering and cataloguing service. Quebec colleges operate under somewhat more central control. Enrollment in the Anglophone colleges of Quebec declined markedly. In the Atlantic provinces the trend seems to be toward systems: Newfoundland established one college with eight campuses, and Nova Scotia revamped its vocational institutes into a provincial community college system. In British Columbia, three community colleges were upgraded to university college status in order to provide university education beyond the three existing universities.

Standards for college libraries were a major concern in the 1980s. Committees in Nova Scotia and New Brunswick proposed standards and guidelines for their provincial systems. At the national level, the Community and Technical College Libraries Section of the Canadian Association of College and University Libraries worked on draft Canadian standards modelled on work done in the U.S.

A national study of college libraries in 1989 found that librarians were most concerned about automation—ahead of budgets, staffing, and collections. Administrators gave equal priority to resource sharing, cooperation, and networking (also a concern of university libraries); changes in curriculum and program delivery; and clear articulation of the role and

North York Central Library, Canada

Interior of recently completed North York Central Library.

value of the library (a concern shared by special libraries). These issues seemed likely to continue to engage college librarians throughout the 1990s.

Research Libraries. Except for the specialized libraries of research institutes, many of them on university campuses and with access to university libraries as backup, Canada has no research libraries as such. But the collections of the Bibliothèque Nationale du Québec make it a valued source for researchers in addition to its wider responsibilities. Founded in 1968, it duplicates some of the National Library's functions for Quebec writing and publishing. Its collection is based on that of the old St. Sulpice Library, enriched by gift, purchase, and the legal deposit of books published in Quebec. It has an active bibliographic program covering materials published in or about Quebec or by Quebec writers, both retrospective and current. It also publishes an index to French-language materials and has produced a number of excellent retrospective bibliographies of Quebec materials.

PUBLIC LIBRARIES

The British North America Act (1867) assigned jurisdiction over education—and thereby libraries—to the provinces, with the result that public libraries operate under the legislation of nine provinces and two territories. (Prince Edward Island has no specific library act.) The first province to pass legislation establishing free, tax-supported libraries was Ontario, in 1884; the last, Quebec, in 1959. In the Territories, the Yukon act was passed in 1987. The provincial acts have been revised over the years, with major changes ensuing in Ontario (1984) and Newfoundland (1988), and movements for revisions in British Columbia, Saskatchewan, and Quebec. A strategic plan for public libraries was issued in Ontario in 1990.

One effect of the relatively small size and the scattering of Canadian communities has been to foster cooperation among groups of smaller units in order to improve service. In the larger metropolitan areas, such as Toronto and Vancouver, cooperation and coordination have been achieved through systems of various types; elsewhere, regional libraries have developed. Regional systems were first tried in British Columbia; they have long been established in Nova Scotia and Saskatchewan, and are found as well in Newfoundland, Alberta, and Manitoba. In these provinces the provincial library or some other government unit coordinates library service. In Prince Edward Island, the Provincial Library is responsible for both school and public library systems. In Ontario, by contrast, county library systems are the main library units, and two provincially funded services, one in the south and one in the north, facilitate cooperation and coordination. The northern unit also offers some direct services, such as interlibrary loan, to libraries in its area.

In most provinces library governance is by boards of interested citizens. But in Quebec, libraries have been made municipal departments in larger communities. Service in smaller communities is provided by 11 provincially funded Bibliothèques de Prêt (central lending libraries) that emphasize collections and "animation culturelle" (popular culture).

Local support is still of prime importance, but provincial government grants have become important for public libraries as well. An infusion of provincial funding enabled the percentage of the population served in Quebec to rise from some 20 percent in 1959 to 86 percent by 1987. In 1986–87, in the Territories, New Brunswick, Newfoundland, and Nova Scotia, government grants formed 58 to 100 percent of library budgets; in the other provinces, provincial grants formed from 12 to 16 percent of library revenue.

From the 1960s through the mid-1980s Canadian public libraries held their own: bookstocks increased, audiovisual materials were introduced, automation became more common, and new buildings were built. The Metropolitan Toronto Reference Library and the North York Public Library in particular gained wide attention for their innovative designs. Older services were maintained and new cultural initiatives, such as writers in residence and authors' reading tours, and strong support for literacy programs were added.

There were stresses as well: unionization, which in some cases led to strikes; and budgets that did not keep up with inflation or expand to meet new demands on the libraries, such as serving immigrants with materials in their own languages, providing materials and equipment to assist disabled readers, and offering video materials. Nevertheless, progress was made in these areas.

New pressures and problems faced libraries in the 1990s. They included the effects of revisions to the Copyright Act if they did not allow libraries a "fair dealing" exemption for copying; of the Goods and Services Tax; and of a groundswell of demand from some local governments that users be charged for services.

An interior view of the Faculty of Library and Information Science Library, University of Toronto.

Faculty of Library and Information Science, University of Toronto

SCHOOL LIBRARIES

Schools in Canada are a provincial matter, and whether or not they have centralized, well-equipped, and well-staffed libraries or merely collections of unorganized materials scattered around the classrooms and corridors largely depends on provincial regulations and the degree of compliance required by them.

Like other Canadian libraries, school libraries before World War II were few and marginal, sources of supplementary reading or study halls rather than active libraries. Postwar changes in educational theory that stressed individual learning meant that schools needed more and better libraries. As in the college libraries, there was considerable emphasis on audiovisual materials, and school libraries were variously renamed learning resource centers or materials resource centers. To advise and assist the school librarians, departments of education and sometimes district school boards hired library consultants. Some boards also set up local processing centers to enable staff in the individual schools to spend more time working with students. These staff unfortunately were not always either fully trained librarians or teachers with courses in librarianship. Data for 1978–79 indicated that (excluding Quebec and the Territories) less than nine percent of full-time school library staff were trained librarians.

The 1980s were a bad time for school libraries. Often regarded as one of the frills to be cut as budgets decreased, many libraries were closed or lost trained staff. Yet national and provincial studies all directly or indirectly made the case for the importance of school libraries in educating students for the world in which they will live and work.

Training of the staff for school libraries is a major concern. The Canadian School Library Association worked to have library courses included in teacher-training programs, whether in regular or summer sessions, and to develop a specialization in school librarianship in M.L.S. programs.

SPECIAL LIBRARIES

Although special libraries in Canada can be traced back as far as 1725, their chief development followed World War II. Beryl L. Anderson's definitive study, "Special Libraries in Canada," in *Canadian Libraries in Their Changing Environment* (1977), estimated that 75 percent of Canadian special libraries had been established after

1946. The development of this type of library can almost be considered a reflection of Canadian economic and social development: libraries before 1949 were concentrated in Montreal, Toronto, and Ottawa, respectively the national business, industrial, and government centers of the time. As Canadian branch plants became more important and as independent businesses developed, business and industrial libraries were set up in other centers. A prime example is the phenomenal growth of special libraries in Calgary during the oil boom in Alberta.

Montreal and Toronto still have the greatest concentrations of special libraries. Their directories for 1986 and 1988 show that growth continued among nongovernment libraries more actively in Toronto than in Montreal. Growth also continued elsewhere in the country; the *Canadian Library Yearbook* for 1990 lists 2,600 special libraries.

The federal government has always maintained a large number of departmental and agency libraries, with well over 200 in the early 1990s. The Library of Parliament, the largest federal library, is particularly rich in parliamentary and other government publications. Because it functioned for many years in place of a national library, it is also rich in early Canadiana. Its mandate to serve only Parliament restricts use by outsiders, but qualified researchers can sometimes be accommodated.

As other governments moved more vigorously into social and economic affairs, provincial government libraries increased in number. Alberta is one example, but growth in Quebec has been even more spectacular. As of 1987 fully 70 percent of the government libraries in Quebec had been established since 1970, 22 percent since 1980. Other provincial governments in both East and West have also seen increases. One result of this growth in almost all the provinces has been the formation of government library councils to share expertise and promote service. Two of these councils, in Manitoba and Alberta, arranged formal inter-provincial exchange of information.

Hospital libraries also increased to become another major group of special libraries. Many are organized into associations cooperating closely with local medical schools, but also cooperating nationally through the Canadian Health Libraries Association (founded 1976). A third group that has shown substantial growth in numbers since the 1970s is law firm libraries. They cooperate with government and university colleagues through the Canadian Association of Law Librarians (founded 1960).

Most special libraries are fairly small in terms of materials held, but they now average two staff members, although a number of one-person libraries remain. Trained staff are now also apparently the norm rather than the exception in any but the smallest libraries.

While many Canadian special librarians belong to American organizations and value highly the contacts so gained, they have had their own national association, with local chapters, since 1972: the Canadian Association of Special Libraries and Information Services (CASLIS), a division of the Canadian Library Association (CLA). Like health science and law librarians, map, parliamentary, and music librarians have national associations to address their specifically Canadian as well as subject concerns. The Special Libraries Association has three chapters in Canada, in Toronto, Montreal, and Calgary. Those in Toronto and Montreal were for years the major groups in Canada addressing special library concerns.

THE PROFESSION

As in the U.S., the Canadian library profession has no national legal mechanisms governing qualifications for entrance to the profession or for quality control in the practice of the profession. Generally speaking, however, a professional librarian must be a graduate of one of the seven Canadian programs accredited under American Library Association standards or their equivalent.

Education. The first library school course in Canada was given at McGill University in 1904, as was the first full-year postgraduate program, in 1931. The University of Toronto followed in 1937. But, with the expansion of libraries in the 1960s, these two schools could no longer meet the demand. Others were started at the University of British Columbia (1961), the University of Montreal (1961; French-language), the University of Western Ontario in London (1968), the University of Alberta in Edmonton (1968), and Dalhousie University in Halifax, Nova Scotia (1969). The schools initially offered the Bachelor of Library Science (B.L.S.) as the first professional degree (equivalent to the M.L.S. in the U.S.).

Because of the rapid increase in the amount of knowledge needed to equip librarians for their jobs, McGill in 1964 adopted a two-year (four-term) program with the M.L.S. as the first degree. By 1976 the other six schools had also changed to the two-year degree. It is one of the longest training periods for the first postgraduate degree now in effect, and several U.S. programs have adopted it.

Other developments in the 1970s were the establishment of doctoral programs at Toronto and the University of Western Ontario; the demise of the bilingual school at the University of Ottawa; the growth of the two Ontario schools; and the completion of a large and well-equipped building at Toronto designed specifically for the library school.

The seven graduate library schools awarded about 500 master's degrees in 1981–82, but by 1990–91 the figure had dropped to about 360. During this period most schools changed their names to reflect the growing importance of information science components in their courses, and the Toronto school instituted a Master of Information Science program.

Undergraduate courses in librarianship are offered at Concordia University (Montreal) and Lakehead University (Thunder Bay, Ontario). Library science courses for teacher-librarians are given by some university faculties of education. Library technician programs are offered at more than 20 community colleges and universities. Quebec CEGEPs *collèges d'enseignement général et professionel* prefer the term "techniques de la documentation" for their programs because their courses may cover automation and archives as well as strictly library topics. Programs outside Quebec tend to follow *Guidelines for the Training of Library Technicians* developed by the Canadian Library Association. In addition to these formal programs, various provinces have distance education programs to help library assistants and staff in charge of small rural collections function more knowledgeably. The Rural Library Training Project developed in Alberta has been particularly successful.

Library Associations. The 1990 *Canadian Library Yearbook* lists almost 200 library associations, exclusive of their divisions, chapters, and branches. The 1979 *Directory of Library Associations in Canada* indicated that 90 percent of the ones listed had been established since 1960, and the percentage is not likely to have fallen. Association growth reflects not only the greater number of libraries and librarians today but also the greater complexity of the library scene and the regionalism that has characterized Canadian library development. The earliest library associations were provincial: the Ontario Library Association (1900) and the British Columbia Library Association (1911). There were provincial or regional associations in all parts of the country by 1936, but the Canadian Library Association/Association Canadienne des Bibliothèques (CLA/ACB) was not formed until 1946. Until then the only opportunity for national meetings had been at ALA conferences in the U.S.

Canadian Library Association and ASTED. From its inception, CLA tried to meet the needs of both Francophone and Anglophone members. In 1968, however, CLA yielded representation of Francophone librarians to the national French-speaking library association, ACBLF (Association Canadienne des Bibliothécaires de Langue Française), which in turn was reorganized in 1973 as ASTED (Association pour l'Avancement des Sciences et des Techniques de la Documentation). CLA and ASTED maintain a liaison committee and cooperate closely in areas of mutual concern.

In the early 1990s CLA had about 4,200 personal members. It is governed by an elected Executive Council that includes the Executive Director and the Convenor of the CLA-ASTED Liaison Committee. Close liaison is maintained with provincial association presidents to ensure joint action when necessary. There are four major type-of-library divisions (public, school, university and college, and special) and a trustee division that has provision for committees and a number of small interest groups with less formal structures. The associations constitute an umbrella organization for the widely varying members of the Canadian library community—librarians and others—and enables them to speak with one voice when it is possible to present their case to government on such matters as copyright, taxes on books, and legislation on pornography.

Another type of association, the professional librarians' association, limiting membership to those holding stated professional qualifications, has existed in Canada, but attracted too few members to achieve licensing powers. Of these only the Corporation des Bibliothécaires Professionels de Québec/Corporation of Professional Librarians of Quebec and the Institute of Victoria Librarians (British Columbia) survive.

Considering their small numbers and generally limited resources, the associations in Canada may seem unwise in proliferating. But they are a channel for sharing expertise among the groups concerned and an essential means of communication among peers, especially in the absence of a strong commercial library press. They obviate some of the isolation in which many librarians must work and, if they forget parochial concerns and cooperate in a common cause, they can make their voices heard for the good of the profession as a whole.

REFERENCES

Canadian Library Handbook/Guide des Bibliothèques Canadiennes.

Laurent Denis, editor, "Libraries and Librarianship in Canada," *IFLA Journal* (1982).

Laurent Denis and Ethel Auster, *The Management of Retrenchment in Canadian Academic Libraries* (1988).

Elizabeth Frick, editor, *A Place to Stand: User Education in Canadian Libraries* (1988).

BERYL L. ANDERSON

Cape Verde

Cape Verde, an independent African republic, is an island archipelago in the Atlantic Ocean approximately 620 km. off Africa's west coast. Population (1990 est.) 370,000; area 4,033 sq.km. The official language is Portuguese.

National Library. Cape Verde gained its independence from Portugal in July 1975. A National Library, with headquarters in the capital of Praia, was established to play an important role in coordinating educational activities and directing new initiatives. Coordination is especially crucial because the nation is spread among a collection of small islands.

Public Libraries. Facilities for the general public center in the nation's two major cities; both the capital of Praia on the island of Santiago and Mindelo on the island of São Vicente operate relatively small libraries.

School Libraries. Libraries in the public schools provide the broadest coverage in library service to the islands. Fifteen school libraries are found in all the major islands of the archipelago.

Special Libraries. The Government Statistics Service maintains a technical library for the use of government administrators. The Service's library serves as a center for documentation, maintaining census and other statistical records.

MARIA MANUELA CRUZEIRO

Carlyle, Thomas
(1795–1881)

Thomas Carlyle, British essayist and historian, was responsible for founding the London Library.

Carlyle was born at Ecclefechan, Dumfriesshire, Scotland, December 4, 1795. He entered Edinburgh University in 1809 and studied mathematics, of which he became a teacher. Later on he also read law at Edinburgh, but he is best remembered today as a writer.

Carlyle moved to London in 1834, but two years earlier he had written in his journal: "What a sad want I am in of libraries, of books to gather facts from! Why is there not a Majesty's library in every county town? There is a Majesty's gaol and gallows in every one." This cry from the heart came almost 20 years before the Public Libraries Act of 1850 was passed. Carlyle's only source of books in London was the British Museum, but to one who was extremely sensitive to

Courtesy of The Newberry Library

Thomas Carlyle

physical discomforts, the Museum was an unfriendly place and its principal librarian, Sir Anthony Panizzi, totally unhelpful. Moreover, the journey from Chelsea to Bloomsbury was tedious, the Museum closed at five in the afternoon, and books could not be taken away.

Carlyle, therefore, decided to explore the possibility of forming a library containing the sorts of books that would be useful to him and that he could take home. He canvassed his many influential friends and acquaintances, called a public meeting, and formed a committee. The London Library opened its doors on May 3, 1841, with 500 subscribers and 3,000 books.

The Earl of Clarendon was elected President, and he persuaded the Prince Consort to become patron of the Library, which has enjoyed the privilege of royal patronage ever since. Once the Library was on its feet, Carlyle took little interest in its day-to-day affairs, although he was greatly concerned about finding the right librarian. Eventually he secured the election of John George Cochrane, already 60 years of age and with no library experience, although he had recently compiled the catalogue of the Scott library at Abbotsford. Cochrane died after 11 years in office and Carlyle, who in the intervening years had seldom attended Committee meetings, once more became active. There were more than 200 candidates for the vacant post. Gladstone, who was on the Library Committee, supported the application of Neapolitan émigré Giacomo Lacaita, but Carlyle was determined that he should not be appointed. In the end he had his way. The committee chose William Bodham Donne, who received 16 votes, while Lacaita received only 4.

Carlyle's final appearance in the Committee Room took place five years later, when Donne resigned and the question of a successor arose, but no record remains of the discussions that took place. Carlyle remained on the Committee until 1870, when he was invited to fill the vacancy on the death of the President, the Earl of Clarendon. He accepted on the strict understanding that he must never be asked to preside, and he remained in office until his death in London, February 5, 1881.

REFERENCES

Frederic Harrison, editor, *Carlyle and the London Library* (1907).

Simon Nowell-Smith, "Carlyle and the London Library," in *English Libraries 1800–1850* (1958).

STANLEY GILLAM

Carnegie, Andrew

(1835–1919)

Andrew Carnegie, often referred to as the "Patron Saint of Libraries," made new library buildings available to hundreds of communities in all parts of the world. He donated $56,162,622 for the construction of 2,509 library buildings throughout the English-speaking parts of the world. He gave more than $41,000,000 of this amount for the erection of 1,679 public library buildings in 1,412 communities in the United States. And he gave another $4,283,000 toward the construction of 108 academic library buildings in the U.S. After 1911 library grants were made by the Carnegie Corporation rather than by Andrew Carnegie personally, although he was president of the Corporation until his death.

This library philanthropy was actually only a small part of Carnegie's benefactions. The "Steel King" spent more than $333,000,000 (90 percent of his fortune) for what he termed "the improvement of mankind." The range of Carnegie's philanthropy was great and included the Simplified Spelling Board, more than 7,000 church organs, the Carnegie Hero Fund, the Carnegie Institute in Pittsburgh, the Carnegie Institution of Washington, the Foundation for the Advancement of Teaching, and the Carnegie Endowment for International Peace.

ALA

Andrew Carnegie

Andrew Carnegie was born November 25, 1835, in a weaver's cottage in Dunfermline, Scotland. Because of the rapid industrialization of the textile trade, his father was forced to sell out his business, the boy's formal education came to an end, and the family moved to the United States in 1846. They settled in Allegheny, Pennsylvania, a suburb of Pittsburgh.

Carnegie's first job, at the age of 13, was that of a bobbin boy for $1.20 per week. After a year he became a messenger boy for a local telegraph company, where he taught himself the art of telegraphy and met important people. Carnegie eventually worked his way up in the Pennsylvania Railroad, made many wise investments, and built up the Carnegie Steel Company until he sold it to J. P. Morgan in 1901 for nearly $500,000,000. Then at the age of 66—healthy, alert, and keenly interested in politics and literature—Carnegie retired to devote the rest of his life to philanthropy and to securing international peace. He had married Louise Whitfield in 1887 and their daughter, Margaret, was born in 1897. Carnegie died in New York City on August 11, 1919.

A memorandum found among Carnegie's papers after his death revealed that as early as 1868, at the age of 33, he made plans to use the surplus of his income for the benefit of others. But he did not formally declare his philosophy of the trusteeship of wealth or, as it came to be called, the Gospel of Wealth, until 1889.

In his first essay on the subject, "Wealth," Carnegie declared that wealthy men were to live without extravagance, provide moderately for the legitimate needs of their dependents, and then consider all the remainder as surplus funds that they as trustees should distribute in their lifetime for the best promotion of welfare and happiness of ordinary people. The main consideration was to help those who would help themselves—but only to assist and never or rarely to do all, because neither the individual nor the group was improved simply by almsgiving.

In his second essay, entitled "The Best Fields for Philanthropy," Carnegie lists seven fields to which the wealthy could devote their surplus in the following order: universities, libraries, medical centers, public parks, meeting and concert halls, public baths, and churches. The best gift that could be given to a community was a free library, "provided the community will accept and maintain it as a public institution, as much a part of the city property as its public schools, and, indeed, an adjunct to these."

Carnegie Public Library Philanthropy. Why did Carnegie select libraries to be among his first and foremost benefactions? One reason was given by a friend of the philanthropist who said that all of

Carnegie's gifts were dedicated to causes and movements with which he was personally concerned. Libraries and books seemed to be of special importance to him. His father had led his fellow weavers in Dunfermline to pool their contributions for the purchase of books and delegated one of their number to read aloud while the others worked. This collection became the first circulating library in town. And Carnegie gave his first library to Dunfermline in 1881.

In 1850, while Carnegie was still a working boy in Pittsburgh, a Colonel Anderson of Allegheny established the J. Anderson Library of Allegheny City to furnish reading matter for the mechanics and workingmen in the trades. Young Andrew wrote a letter to the newspaper requesting that the library be opened to all working boys, and he was invited to use it. In later years he recalled awaiting Saturday afternoons with intense longing, "and it was when reveling in the treasures which he opened to us that I resolved, if ever wealth came to me, that other poor boys might receive opportunities similar to those for which we were indebted to that noble man."

Carnegie's confidence in the value of free libraries as a wise object of philanthropy may also have been stimulated by earlier and contemporary library philanthropists. He praised Ezra Cornell for beginning the distribution of his wealth by establishing a public library in Ithaca, New York, in 1857. He also had a high regard for Enoch Pratt's gift to Baltimore of $1,000,000 with a requirement that the city pay 5 percent of this sum annually to the library trustees for the support of the main library and branches.

Perhaps Carnegie's library philanthropy was also influenced by his business background. He once told an audience that, far from being a philanthropist, he was making the best bargains of his life. For instance, when he gave money to a city for library buildings, he succeeded in obtaining a pledge that the city would furnish sites and maintain the libraries forever. The city's investment was greater than his. "This was not philanthropy but a clever stroke of business." To all of these motivations must be added one with which Carnegie was frequently charged. His accusers claimed that he built libraries as monuments to himself for posterity.

Evaluation. The procedure for obtaining a Carnegie public library building grant was fairly simple. A community in need of a library structure had to have its mayor and council promise to provide a site. The city had to pledge to support the new library through local taxation in an annual amount that would be at least 10 percent of the sum given for the library building. That sum was usually based on about $2 per capita of local population.

The importance of Carnegie public library philanthropy lies in its perfect timing, coming in the best possible period—during the height of library expansion in the U.S. Beginning in the 1890s, states began to play active roles in organizing public libraries in each community. The need for library buildings was desperate, and Carnegie's gifts helped to fill the void. The provision of new buildings created an avid interest in and enthusiasm for libraries in their early, crucial years of development. Carnegie dramatized the value of libraries and stimulated other philanthropists to provide library benefactions.

An even more important point is that Carnegie's philanthropy widened the acceptance of the principle of local government responsibility for the public library. The method of giving was not perfect; many poor sites were selected, and the 10 percent support pledge was sometimes broken or more often not surpassed. Nevertheless, it was a wise provision, placing indirect pressure on government and the public to accept the organization and maintenance of the public library as a governmental service.

Actually, about two-thirds of the communities receiving funds for one or more Carnegie library buildings already had free public libraries or were in the process of organizing them when the Carnegie gift was offered. To be sure, many had just been organized or were being organized as a result of the stimulation of Carnegie benefactions and with the hope of obtaining new buildings. The incentive of Carnegie's gifts was enough to accelerate the library movement to a stampede. Some 188 public libraries in 1876 grew to 3,873 by 1923.

Carnegie's philanthropy continued to benefit public libraries and librarianship long after the formal termination of building grants. This extended library philanthropy is still in evidence today; in many ways it is even more important than the original bequest of Carnegie buildings, which ended after World War I.

Carnegie Corporation and Libraries. In 1918 the Carnegie Corporation asked Charles C. Williamson to make a study of library training. His report recommended that librarians should receive their education in universities rather than in training schools sponsored by public libraries and other agencies. Williamson also recommended the establishment of a graduate library school for advanced study, a national accrediting and certification system for library schools, and numerous fellowships. His study was a monumental work that resulted in a complete revision of the curriculum in library schools.

A Carnegie Corporation-sponsored study in 1924 by William S. Learned centered on the role of the library as a medium for spreading information. It called for expanded services to be provided by the American Library Association and for local and regional experiments and demonstrations leading to better ways of getting books to the people.

In 1926 the Corporation embarked on a 10-year Library Service Program, for which the trustees approved $5,000,000 in financial support. The aim of this program was to strengthen the library profession by supporting the activities of the ALA, by improving training opportunities, and by supporting certain centralized library services and projects.

ALA. Carnegie provided $100,000 in endowment funds to the ALA in 1902, and the Corporation gave $549,500 for the general support of the Association from 1924 to 1926; in 1926 it added $2,000,000 in endowment funds. During this period the Corporation also provided financial assistance to the Library of Congress and to bibliographic centers and regional catalogues such as those at the Denver and Philadelphia public libraries.

Other Benefactions. Gifts for the endowment and support of library schools and the establishment of the first graduate library school at the University of Chicago totaled $3,359,550. Fellowships for library training and the sponsorship of conferences, studies, and publications were also provided.

The Corporation also provided funds for several demonstrations of methods and techniques for bringing books to people of all ages who were living in rural areas far from the major population centers.

Following World War II, the Corporation provided $212,170 to the Social Science Research Council for the Public Library Inquiry. The idea of a study of the library's actual and potential contribution to American society was suggested by the ALA. The appraisal was made in sociological, cultural, and human terms.

Again, financial assistance from the Carnegie Corporation helped the ALA in 1956 to formulate and publish what popularly became known as the Public Library Standards. The Public Library Inquiry discovered the failings of the public libraries, and the Standards presented what they should be doing by setting up minimum guidelines for good service. Public libraries were urged to cooperate, federate, or consolidate into library systems for better library service. The Corporation's financial support of demonstration centers for extension of library service in rural areas, of the Public Library Inquiry, and of the Standards was an important factor in bringing about federal aid for public libraries beginning in 1956.

Carnegie's benefactions have played a major role in American public library development and have had a significant impact in all areas of American librarianship as well as those throughout the English-speaking world.

REFERENCES

Andrew Carnegie, *Autobiography of Andrew Carnegie* (1920).

Burton Hendrick, *The Life of Andrew Carnegie* (1932).

George Bobinski, *Carnegie Libraries: Their History and Impact on American Public Library Development* (1969), contains extensive bibliography.

George Bobinski, "Carnegie, Andrew," *Dictionary of American Library Biography* (1978).

Carnegie Corporation of New York, *Carnegie Corporation Library Program, 1911–1961* (1963).

GEORGE S. BOBINSKI

Carnovsky, Leon
(1903–1975)

Leon Carnovsky, a member of the faculty of the Graduate Library School of the University of Chicago, excelled in teaching, writing, editing, and service to the profession of librarianship in the United States.

Carnovsky was born to Isaac and Jennie Stillman Carnovsky in St. Louis, Missouri, November 28, 1903. Appointed Instructor at Chicago in 1932, he advanced to the rank of Professor in 1944. He continued active service until 1971 when as Professor Emeritus he moved to his retirement home in Oakland, California. He died there on December 6, 1975.

His parents fostered his intellectual interests from early boyhood. His father had been a Talmudic scholar before emigrating from Lithuania, and his mother also came from a rabbinical family. In St. Louis they ran a small grocery store, which provided for them and their seven children, and they encouraged Leon to frequent the public library. After high school he worked for two years as a secretary, then entered the University of Missouri. Graduating with an A.B. in philosophy in 1927, he entered the training school of the St. Louis Public Library, going on in 1928 to become Assistant to the Librarian at Washington University. In 1929 he received a fellowship in the newly established Graduate Library School at the University of Chicago, where he earned his Ph.D. in 1932, the same year he joined the faculty.

ALA
Leon Carnovsky

As a teacher he conducted courses on the library and society, research methods, public libraries, comparative librarianship, and education for librarianship. His lectures, logical and coherent, were presented in a vibrant and resonant voice. He exerted a warm and dynamic presence within and without the classroom, and large numbers of his students regarded him as a confidant and friend. Foreign students were particularly drawn to him. He was both rigorous and skillful in directing theses and dissertations, and he was exceptionally adept at eliciting publishable papers from members of his classes.

His bibliography of published writings includes more than 160 items, all clearly and gracefully written. Their quality matches their quantity, and their range is far-reaching. Lester Asheim described the scope of this writing in a memorial tribute rendered Carnovsky in 1976:

> His doctoral dissertation was only one of his many contributions to the seminal studies of reading that marked the early years of GLS's innovative research program. His many library surveys, and studies of public libraries, became guides to action, as well as models for other professional appraisals. His writings on intellectual freedom, which anticipated by many years the themes which are now watchwords on this always contemporary issue, led to his chairmanship of ALA's Committee on Intellectual Freedom and subsequently built upon that experience. His long list of writings on library education cover developments from the early defensive days . . . through his chairmanship of the ALA's Committee on Accreditation, and after. His studies and reports on aspects of international librarianship reflect his foreign travels, as a Fulbright Fellow and on assignments for ALA, Unesco, and the American government.

Through 18 years, from 1943 to 1961, Carnovsky edited *The Library Quarterly*. In this work he maintained a standard of content and style that made the *Quarterly* the leading learned journal in its field, a model for both creative and careful editing. The work absorbed a huge amount of his energy and concentration. He devoted detailed attention to every phase of the publication process, from judging and editing manuscripts to proofreading and surveying the subscription list. Equally well edited were the many conference volumes he planned and prepared for the Graduate Library School.

His many library surveys and consultations throughout the world strongly represent his service to the profession. A notable example of their influence is his *Report of a Program for Library Education in Israel,* prepared for Unesco in 1957, which led to the founding of the library school at Hebrew University. Also active in library associations, he was President of the Association of American Library Schools (1942–43) and Chairman of the ALA Committee on Intellectual Freedom (1944) and of the Committee on Accreditation (1963–65). He received the Melvil Dewey Medal in 1962 "for creative professional achievement of a high order," the Beta Phi Mu Award in 1971 for "distinguished service to education for librarianship," and the Joseph W. Lippincott Award in 1975 for "distinguished service in the profession of librarianship."

Carnovsky was a connoisseur of music, the ballet, drama, literature, and fine food. He married Marian Satterthwaite, a librarian and author of a book on public libraries, in August 1939. She died in January 1965. In June 1967 he married Ruth French Strout, a colleague on the Graduate Library School faculty. His homes were distinguished by their genial hospitality.

REFERENCES

"The Brothers Carnovsky: A Profile, a Monologue," *University of Chicago Magazine* (1970); his brother, Morris, gained public notice as a distinguished actor.

William Converse Haygood, "Leon Carnovsky: A Sketch," *Library Quarterly* (1968).

Frederick A. Schlipf, "Leon Carnovsky: A Bibliography" *Library Quarterly* (1968).

Howard W. Winger, "Carnovsky, Leon," *Dictionary of American Library Biography* (1978).

HOWARD W. WINGER

Cassiodorus

(*c.* 485–after 580)

Flavius Cassiodorus Senator, writer and monk, was noted for his direction of his library at Vivarium. He was born in southern Italy around 485 and died after 580. Though his contemporaries called him Senator, later writers refer to him as Cassiodorus. From the scholarship displayed in his writings it can be inferred that he received the customary liberal arts training for public service. Besides giving orations, he found time while in public service at Ravenna to produce a number of writings: *A History of the Goths,* his *Chronicle,* and several other treatises.

The Gothic kingdom virtually came to a close in 540, when the royal city Ravenna fell before the onslaught of Belisarius. About the same time, and possibly as a result of it, Cassiodorus relinquished his position. He first proposed to Pope Agapetus the creation of a university at Rome on the pattern of the schools of Alexandria and of Nisibus in Syria, a plan that had to be abandoned because of unfavorable conditions. Evidently it caused the Pope to create a library in Rome.

Cassiodorus then returned to southern Italy, where he found time to establish and govern a monastery. The sacred retreat he established was by no means a cheerless prison. At his estate, Squillace, overlooking a beautiful bay, it included luxuries and various attractions, such as elaborate baths and fishponds. From the latter extravagance the monastery derived its name; it was called *Vivarium,* or the fish pond. Cassiodorus's ideal was complete literacy among the monks, because he believed reading was basic to education. The written word was an instrument to develop one's individual perfection and to lead to a deeper understanding of the Bible. His *Introduction to Divine and Secular Readings* outlined the general monastic educational program. Devotional reading naturally held the highest place and comprised the content of the first of two books. The goal was a thorough knowledge of the Bible, and because the Psalms were recited in common, the Psalter was to be memorized. The total number of 1,399 lines is divided as follows: logic (dialectics) 37 percent, rhetoric 17 percent, arithmetic 16 percent, music 14 percent, astronomy 7.5 percent, grammar 5 percent, and geometry 3.5 percent. The proportion of emphasis probably reflects the chiefly literary content that constituted the curriculum of schools of his day.

Special provisions were made for those not intellectually gifted to follow the regular liberal arts program of study. It would be sufficient for them to study the outlines and usefulness of the seven liberal arts. For them Cassiodorus recommended practical training on the material needs of the monastery, including a reading program of such selected writers as Gargilius Martial, Columella, and Emilianus on the cultivation of farms, gardens, bees, birds, and fish and the study of herbs.

These two books constituted training in the correct understanding of the Bible, an art in which the liberal arts led the way. Cassiodorus drew up his study program to develop methods in appreciation of the Bible: how to read it, how to understand it, how to interpret it in the light of recommended commentators, how to treat the manuscript text, and how to edit and transcribe it so that authentic writings could be preserved intact and passed on to coming generations. The last portion of the first book treated the techniques of literary transcriptions.

Cassiodorus saw the possibility of including intellectual labor within the sphere of monastic duties. Under his direction the multiplication, translation, and correction of manuscript texts was to become part of the daily routine of qualified monks. The Scriptorium was equipped with mechanical devices such as a sundial and a water clock to indicate the hours for the convenience of copyists, editors, and binders. It was lighted by self-filling lamps so that not even a cloudy day or nightfall should interrupt their tasks. Through his methodical directives, Cassiodorus made available for copyists a guidebook with rules for scribal work.

In addition to furnishing practical rules, he provided complete bibliographical references to allied fields in the reproduction of manuscripts. He recommended some knowledge of geography, abbreviations, and other secular studies as an aid to correct reading and understanding of handwritten texts. And because correctness of spelling was of high importance, he reminded them of the standard works and of his own book on the subject, *De Orthographia.* Some monks were trained for more advanced work in the Scriptorium. Since not all the monks could read Greek, some undertook Latin translations. Questions of textual criticism were reserved for emendators *(notarii),* who compared variant copies and added rubric notes and punctuation marks.

The craft of bookbinding was viewed as important to manuscript book production. Cassiodorus equipped a staff of binders to attire the books or, as he phrased it, provide "wedding garments for the heavenly feast," for the external decoration was intended to express the beauty of its content. Those assigned to the bindery were provided with a manual of sample bindings to assist them in selecting appropriate bindings.

Though our knowledge of the library collection at Vivarium is limited, a key to the reconstruction of its holdings is to be found in his Manual. Cassiodorus referred to 123 authors, including Greek and Roman classical writers such as Artistotle, Homer, Hippocrates, Dioscorides, Euclid, Archimedes, Galen, Plato, Ennius, Terence, Lucretius, Varro, Cicero, Virgil, Horace Columellam Fortunatius, Valerius Probus, Seneca, Pliny, Quintilian, and Macrobius. Some of the manuscript books that lined the shelves of the library at Vivarium are extant; these are listed by D. M. Cappuyns. The library was arranged in nine bookcases with all Greek books put together in the eighth case. The classification scheme was based on subject matter rather than authors. In some cases several works on the same subject were bound together in a single volume.

REFERENCES

D. M. Cappuyns, "Cassiodore," *Dictionaire d'Histoire et Geographie Ecclesiastiques* (1948), vol. 2, pp. 1349–1408, excellent for identification and location of books housed in the Library of Cassiodorus.

Cassiodorus, *Institutiones,* edited by R. A. B. Mynors (1937).

L. W. Jones, *Cassiodorus Senator: An Introduction to Divine and Human Readings* (1946), superb introduction to Cassiodorus in English and a translation of his *Institutes.*

REDMOND A. BURKE

Cataloguing

The users of libraries sometimes assume that the staff who serve them should be able to recall immediately whether any particular book, recording, or magazine is in the library's collection. Because librarians cannot in reality remember the authors, titles, and subjects of all the materials in their care, they create lists of the materials. The process of preparing such lists is called cataloguing.

Curators of ancient as well as modern repositories have regularly developed at least rudimentary lists of their holdings, if only to serve as an inventory device to determine whether all the materials that are supposed to be in the collection are actually present. Most early lists recorded the title or *incipit* (first words of the text) of a work, its author (if known), the extent of the work (such as the number of scrolls, tablets, or codices required to transcribe it), its location in the library, and perhaps its provenance (history of creation and ownership) and the name of the scribe who copied it. After the invention of printing from movable type and the subsequent growth of libraries, accompanied by an increase in the scholarly use of libraries, librarians began to find it useful to have fuller descriptions, predictable first words of catalogue entries—usually only one entry per item—and some references from alternative entry points. The resulting "finding lists" became known as catalogues.

During the last half of the 19th century new demands began to be made on catalogues. Users wanted not only to be able to locate a specific known item but also to be able to find all works by one author, all editions of a work, and all works on particular subjects. In order to provide such access, catalogues had to have multiple entries for each item the library owned, and those entries had to be given consistent headings. Catalogues thus became "collocating devices" as well as finding lists.

Modern catalogues are organized sets of bibliographic records that represent the holdings of a particular collection. The representation of holdings is one factor that distinguishes cataloguing from the more general discipline called *bibliography.* While bibliographers attempt to identify all items relevant to a particular subject field, produced in a given nation, or issued during a certain period of time, cataloguers normally direct their attention to the contents of a

Carnegie Library of Pittsburgh

Catalogue card production in 1907: a library assistant works the press.

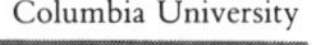

Catalogue Room in a public library, Louisville, Kentucky, ca. 1905.

Columbia University

single repository. The two disciplines were often almost indistinguishable during the Middle Ages, but the separation of cataloguing from bibliography became common with the development of printed books that could be duplicated in large numbers and become parts of many libraries. During the mid-20th century the two disciplines have moved closer together again. The impact of computer and photocopying technologies and the development of comprehensive library collections, particularly at the national level, have combined to cause some large library catalogues to function also as major bibliographies.

Cataloguing is usually also distinguished from the activity called *indexing*. Indexing is a term often applied to the provision of access to parts of larger bibliographic items (such as articles in serials, poetry in collections, or chapters in books), while cataloguing usually involves provision of access to larger entities (such as whole books or entire serials). Modern libraries typically engage in cataloguing and leave indexing to be done by other agencies, usually commercial ones. In the late 19th and early 20th centuries, indexing was often a library activity, but economic constraints eventually dictated that only whole items owned and housed in a particular location could be catalogued. This distinction is becoming invisible to users as libraries begin to provide access to commercial journal indexes through their online catalogs.

Forms of Catalogues. In one ancient library, workers are reported to have inscribed its catalogue on the walls of the building. More commonly, the catalogue was recorded in a form similar to that of the library materials themselves: on clay tablets, on scrolls, in a book (called a *codex*). After the invention of movable type, it became common to issue catalogues in printed form. During the latter part of the 19th century, however, many librarians abandoned these expensive printed book catalogues for a more easily updated loose-leaf format, including sheaf catalogues and guard books. During the first half of the 20th century, cards—eventually standardized to 7.5 × 12.5 centimeters (3 × 5 inches)—became the dominant medium for transmitting cataloguing information.

Although improvements in photographic and duplication techniques made the production of cards easier and faster, which in turn led to the development of centralized services that permitted many libraries to benefit from the cataloguing performed by a national library or a commercial organization, these same techniques also encouraged the reintroduction of the book catalogue, since photolithography provided a flexible and relatively inexpensive means of reproducing cataloguing data. By the 1960s, librarians began to take advantage of data processing techniques to produce catalogues. Machine-readable catalogue records were first used to produce book catalogues and then, increasingly, COM (computer-output microform) catalogues. In the 1980s the online computer catalog, often referred to as an online public access catalogue (or OPAC), rapidly increased in popularity. In an online catalogue, bibliographic records—stored in computer memory or on CD-ROM—are displayed on a video screen in response to a request from a user. CD-ROM technology makes online catalogues available in places that were not able to take advantage of earlier technological advances because of unreliable telephone connections, environmental factors such as heat and humidity, or unavailability of machine parts such as the light bulbs for microform readers.

OCLC Photo by Rick Skopin

Users consult the online catalogue at Texas Medical Center Library, Houston Academy of Medicine.

The variety of new catalogue formats has stimulated experimentation with new configurations of data. In online catalogues, displays of records may comprise whole records or only parts of them, as needed. Research in the 1990s focused on ways in which the online catalogue could be made more responsive than its earlier counterparts to the needs of users.

Arrangements of Catalogues. A printed catalogue, unlike an online one, must be arranged according to some plan. Over the centuries various arrangements of library catalogues have been devised, with formats and arrangements dictated mainly by the context that they were designed to serve. Broad groupings of materials by their forms (such as literature or music) or by their discipline (such as philosophy, religion, or science) were used to organize certain catalogues; others were designed to emphasize such characteristics as authorship and titles of the works and specific topics covered. The amount of detail shown in these catalogues and the order in which descriptive elements were presented, however, often varied, sometimes quite markedly, from library to library.

Even the cultural setting of the library influenced the arrangements of catalogues that appeared. In Europe, for example, they tended, especially after the Renaissance, to focus on personal authorship as the primary access to each item in the collection and to use the Roman alphabet as the principle of arrangement. In contrast, many of the catalogues in the Orient used the title of the work as the key element and arranged the records in a sequence according to the number of strokes in the initial character of the title.

Subject and Classified Arrangements. Library catalogues organized according to subject or topic proved to be popular, especially when only fragmentary or inconsistently developed subject bibliographies were available. Such catalogues have the distinct advantage of revealing materials immediately accessible to library users, whereas bibliographies identify but often do not specify a location for the items listed.

One form of subject arrangement catalogue, called *classified* or *classed,* gained popularity especially in Europe. Although subject catalogues can be sequenced alphabetically according to the words or phrases chosen to express the topics of the material, classed catalogues are arranged according to symbols representing a logical, hierarchical system that moves from general classes to specific subclasses in an orderly fashion. To make use of such a catalogue, a person must either recognize and be comfortable with the classification pattern or begin with the alphabetical index that will lead to the relevant sections of the classed catalogue. One strength of the classed catalogue is its "browsability," in that it can display a variety of materials either broadly or more specifically pertinent to a field of interest, without forcing its user to move back and forth among entries that are juxtaposed merely because they begin with the same letter of the alphabet. A weakness, however, is that many classification systems used to organize the catalogue are unfamiliar to the library's clientele and may be awkward to use.

In an effort to make the classified catalogue easier to consult, the *alphabetico-classed* list was invented. In it, materials are categorized first by the name of a general discipline, then further by the names of classes and subclasses. The general disciplines, classes, and subclasses, however, are not arranged according to a classification system. The subclasses are listed alphabetically within each class; the classes are arranged alphabetically within each discipline; and the disciplines themselves are sequenced alphabetically. This system requires some understanding of hierarchical relationships among subject fields but has the advantage of lessening the user's dependence upon knowledge of a particular classification scheme and to some degree reduces the need to consult a separate index to the catalogue.

A classified or an alphabetico-classed catalogue is actually only the subject part of a *divided* catalogue, as described in the next section. It must be accompanied by a name/title catalogue.

Alphabetical Arrangements. A popular catalogue during the first half of the 20th century was the *dictionary* list, in which all types of entries are arranged in a single alphabetical sequence. Such a catalogue is generally based on a unit of descriptive information about each item in the collection; the unit can then be reproduced as many times as required to provide access to various aspects of the material, with each reproduced unit headed by the name of an individual or a group associated with the work, its title, and each subject or form represented in it. Dictionary catalogues do not need separate indexes. Because the dictionary principle was used mainly to arrange card catalogues, its popularity began to wane toward the middle of the 20th century as the increasing complexity and size of the card files caused problems for the easy location of appropriate cataloguing information.

In an effort to overcome the filing problems of the large dictionary catalogue, a number of libraries constructed *divided* catalogues in which various types of entries were separated according to their function. Some combined author and title entries in one section, placing subject entries in another; others created a three-part file: author (or name), title, and subject. These same patterns of division have also been used for other types of catalogues, such as those issued as books, as microforms, or as computer printouts.

Online catalogues do not have to be arranged in a linear fashion, and the internal arrangements of machine-readable records make little difference to a user. What does matter is the way in which the catalogue can be searched and the manner in which the responses are displayed. Most online catalogues are, in effect, divided catalogues, because the user must choose to search through one of the indexes: author, title, subject, and sometimes classification or other numbers. The results may be displayed in alphabetical order by main entry or by title, or they may be displayed in chronological order or some other fashion that the user must decipher.

State Historical Society of Wisconsin Photo by Robert Granflaten

Film archivist at the State Historical Society of Wisconsin uses a Steenback flatbed film viewing machine to catalogue television newsfilm.

The Cataloguing Process. Modern cataloguing usually begins with descriptive cataloguing and continues with subject analysis; the process of authority control is intertwined throughout both phases. Descriptive cataloguing is concerned with the identification and description of an item and the selection and formation of access points (such as names of persons or groups associated with a work and names of titles). Subject analysis involves determining what subject concept is covered by the work, selecting subject headings to represent the concept, and choosing one or more classification notations. (*See also* Classification.) Authority control is the process of maintaining consistency in the verbal form used to represent an access point and the further process of showing the relationships among names, works, and subjects.

Arthur Plotnik

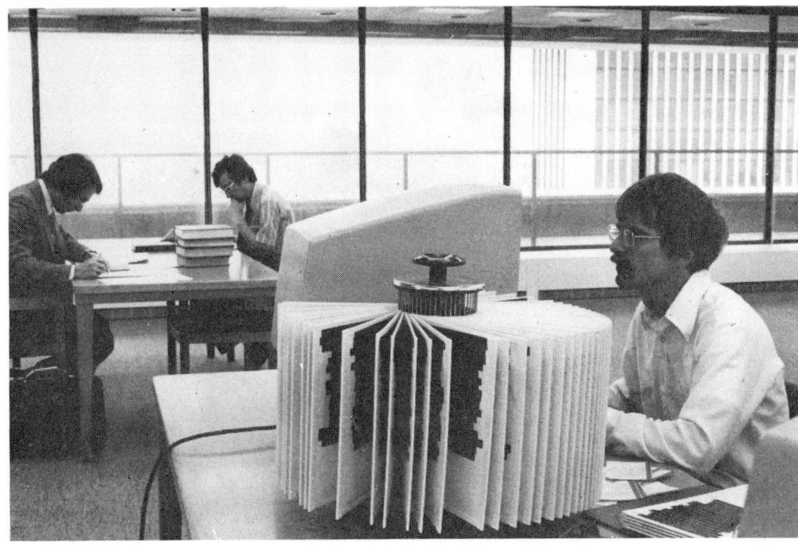

Microfiche catalogue at the State University of New York at Albany.

National Archives of Japan

Book catalogues in the National Archives of Japan.

Standardization. Increased emphasis on sharing cataloguing data has stimulated the development of systems that can result in greater uniformity in recording such data. Standardization of basic descriptive data elements—their order, content, and punctuation style—has been seen as a way to enable cataloguers in one library to construct records usable by a variety of others and permit a library user to obtain information from several facilities without having to learn the cataloguing peculiarities of each.

Cataloguing Codes. In order to bring about standardization of cataloguing practice, a number of individuals as well as groups of librarians developed manuals detailing their procedures. These manuals specified what data should be included in the cataloguing record (such as name of author, title, edition, place of publication, publisher, date, extent and characteristics of the physical item, and series relationship), how to select access points (such as names of persons or groups, titles of works, and series connections), and how to regularize the heading forms by which the access points are listed (authority work). Some guides also offered rules for determining subject access and for the physical construction of the cataloguing medium.

A few of these cataloguing manuals, though initially designed for limited purposes, became the basis of later cataloguing codes. Such noted works as the 1791 *Instruction pour proceder à la confection du catalogue* . . . issued from Paris for those libraries taken over during the French Revolution, the "91 Rules" of Antonio Panizzi designed in the 1830s for the printed book collection of the British Museum, and the "Prussian Instructions" of 1908 were crucial in establishing cataloguing standards.

The contributions in Britain of Panizzi and in the United States of such imaginative thinkers as Charles C. Jewett, Melvil Dewey, and Charles A. Cutter led the way to the cooperative development of the first Anglo-American rules, published as *Catalog Rules: Author and Title Entries* in 1908 under the auspices of the American Library Association and the Library Association of Britain. The effects of World War II prevented much meaningful cooperation in the production of the preliminary second edition in 1941 (issued as *A.L.A. Catalog Rules*) or the 1949 *A.L.A. Cataloging Rules for Author and Title Entries,* with its companion volume, *Rules for Descriptive Cataloging in the Library of Congress.* International efforts were again stimulated when the International Federation of Library Associations and Institutions (IFLA) sponsored a seminal conference in 1961 to try to achieve some compromise among rule differences, particularly between the Anglo-American and German traditions. The results of this International Conference on Cataloguing Principles, held in Paris, seemed to bode well for reducing the differences, but an American review of the expected consequences for the card files in large libraries caused dissension. Lack of agreement concerning especially the rules for the formation of corporate entry headings finally resulted in the publication of two versions of the *Anglo-American Cataloguing Rules* (AACR) of 1967: the North American text and the British text.

In the 1970s IFLA developed the International Standard Bibliographic Descriptions (ISBDs), designed to facilitate the international exchange of bibliographic information by standardizing the elements to be used in the bibliographic description, assigning an order to these elements in the entry, and specifying a system of symbols to be used in punctuating these elements.

The stimulation generated by the development of the ISBDs and the increased use of computer-based systems in many national libraries suggested that AACR might be revised to bring the two texts together, including the ISBD as a coordinating principle for the description of all types of library materials produced anywhere in the world. The introduction of the *Anglo-American Cataloguing Rules,* Second Edition (AACR2) in 1978 occasioned a break with some traditional entry patterns and heading forms and caused considerable agitation among librarians using the older cataloguing codes. AACR2 did, nonetheless, help to advance international cooperation by encouraging the extension of "shared cataloguing," whereby librarians in one country can use the cataloguing output of another without significant alteration. The publication of the *Anglo-American Cataloguing Rules,* Second Edition, 1988 Revision (AACR2R), represented a continuation of efforts on the part of the Joint Steering Committee for Revision of AACR (consisting of members from Australia, Canada, the United Kingdom, and the United States) to resolve differences of opinion and understanding and to refine the rules.

MARC. The Library of Congress developed its *MA*chine *R*eadable *C*ataloging (MARC) system in the late 1960s. Because of the increased use of computer-based systems in many national libraries, use of MARC expanded rapidly, with development of UK-MARC in the United Kingdom, CANMARC in Canada, and many others. The UNIMARC format, developed by IFLA and officially adopted by the International Organization for Standardization (ISO), is in use in many countries and is used for international exchange of machine-readable data.

The ability to store cataloguing data in a standardized format gave rise to regional and national bibliographic utilities. These organizations maintain and/or provide access to huge databases of bibliographic records that member libraries can use for cataloguing, interlibrary loan, and other activities. A cataloguer in a member library locates a record to match the item to be catalogued, edits to local standards, and then causes it to be printed on a set of cards, transmitted electronically to the local system, or otherwise produced for the local catalogue. The process causes the library's symbol to be attached to the record so that others will know that the item is held by that library. As cataloguing has become more standardized, less and less local editing is being done on these systems.

CIP. The development of Cataloguing-in-Publication programs by a number of national libraries throughout the world has also contributed to standardization. In these programs, a publisher sends information about a book to the national library just prior to its publication. The library returns cataloguing data to the publisher, who then publishes it in the book. The cataloguing data can be used by cataloguers as the basis for local catalogue records.

Authority Control. The adoption of AACR2 occasioned much discussion of dealing with heading changes resulting from rule changes. Many librarians saw for the first time the need to keep a separate record of all heading forms used in the catalogue, along with a record of references from unused forms and a record of conflict resolutions. The 1980s saw a rapid increase in the development of authority control, especially in machine-based systems. There has also been increased interest in design of an international authority system so that access points to library materials might be equated among the various languages and national practices.

With the proliferation of media has come a necessity for more authority control of works. For example, a work can now appear not only in more than one print edition, but also in more than one format, including optical disk, sound recording, and motion picture versions. There are also multiple ways in which works can be related to other works. Providing ways of dealing with such relationships in catalogues became a project of the 1990s.

Language Scripts. For many years works in languages not using the roman alphabet had to be "romanized" or transliterated before they could be entered into catalogues in Europe and America. In the 1980s systems were developed to enter non–roman-alphabet languages online in MARC-formatted records. Systems developed by the early 1990s include the means for entering Arabic, Chinese, Cyrillic, Greek, Hebrew, Japanese, Korean, and Persian, among others.

Subject Access. International agreement on standards for subject analysis (subject terminology and classification procedures) has been much more difficult to achieve. Even where there is supposedly no language barrier, as between the United States and the United Kingdom, or between one part of the United States and another, there are language usage differences. In addition, various types of libraries, such as a public library and a medical library, differ in their need for specialized language. There are many other examples of non-agreement. Nevertheless, work on achieving some control over the terms used in subject catalogues has proven to be useful. Without controlled vocabulary, materials covering the same concept are scattered among numerous synonyms and near synonyms. In addition, materials that are more general or more specific than the term at hand cannot be related to it.

The first lists of subject headings were drawn up in the late 19th century, soon after Charles Cutter set down rules for construction of such headings, and several of the lists intended for general use continue to be maintained and updated, such as Library of Congress Subject Headings (LCSH). In the mid-20th century, lists of terms for specialized use (each one called a *thesaurus*) began to proliferate. Most of these lists are especially intended for use with machine-readable databases of indexed articles in specialized subject areas, and many of these, too, continue to be maintained and updated. In the 1970s, Derek Austin developed PRECIS (Preserved Context Indexing System) at the British Library. Neither a subject heading list nor a thesaurus, PRECIS is a set of established procedures for creating pre-coordinated, context-dependent strings of terms in which each term is semantically defined and syntactically related to synonyms and other associated terms. (*See also* Abstracting and Indexing; PRECIS.)

None of these approaches has drawn even national agreement. But in the late 1980s there began to be calls for a "subject code." The desired content for such a code has not become clear. Should it be a set of rules for creating a consistent list of headings? Or a set of principles on which to base verbal subject analysis? These questions were debated in the 1990s, and research focused on improving subject access.

While the basic intent of cataloguing has not been essentially altered by advances in technology and standardization, the methods of constructing catalogues and presenting them to the public have been significantly transformed. Bibliographic utilities are connecting the libraries of the world so that users can now learn what is held not only in the local library but also in libraries at great distances. As interfaces become more transparent, the definition of a catalogue as representing the holdings of a particular collection will change. Soon users will expect immediate access to the works identified through these expanded catalogues. As more full texts of works are stored online, one of the next frontiers for cataloguing will be the provision of effective bibliographic control for online texts that are accessible from the same computer terminal as is the catalogue.

REFERENCES

A. C. Foskett, *The Subject Approach to Information,* 4th ed. (1982).

Ronald Hagler, *The Bibliographic Record and Information Technology,* 2nd ed. (1991).

Kathryn Luther Henderson, "'Treated with a Degree of Uniformity and Common Sense': Descriptive Cataloging in the United States, 1876–1975," *Library Trends* (1976).

Sally H. McCallum and Winston D. Roberts, editors, *UNIMARC in Theory and Practice: Papers from the UNIMARC Workshop, Sydney, Australia, August 1988* (1989).

Elaine Svenonius, editor, *The Conceptual Foundations of Descriptive Cataloging* (1989). Papers from a conference held at the University of California, Los Angeles, February 4–15, 1987.

ARLENE G. TAYLOR

Censorship and Intellectual Freedom

In a general sense censorship is placing restrictive controls on the dissemination of ideas, information, or images transmitted through any communication medium. More specifically, censorship is commonly a prohibitive act directed against the original forms of information or materials conveyed—or intended to be conveyed—on the printed page, on television, in motion pictures, on the radio, in works of art, in sound recordings, or in a variety of electronic data transfer or communication devices. Censorship may also be directed toward the contents of such live events as staged plays, musicals, dances, public speeches, or art exhibits. Some restraint is applied before the objectionable content is disseminated and is called *preventive* censorship or *prior restraint*. Restraint applied after publication is called *punitive* or *post-publication* censorship.

Throughout recorded history censorship has been used in many attempts to bolster existing institutions, political systems, religions, or social systems. It has often been practiced to restrain free discussion, criticism, or analysis of doctrines or systems that particular censors have attempted to sustain, protect, or preserve. Censorship played a major role in the conflict between scientific inquiry and religious doctrines. Scientific inquiry won, marking a significant turning point in intellectual history.

Censorship in all parts of the world tends to be based on matters of religion, race, sex, violence, politics, and combinations thereof. The most common bases for censorship are, perhaps, moral objections, when individuals or groups attempt to impose their moral values on others, or government restrictions for military or political reasons, to protect military secrets in war or to restrict access to sensitive policy documents in peacetime.

Censorship for political or state reasons is common in nondemocratic societies at both ends of the political spectrum: military dictatorships and "people's democracies." After the Nazis took control of Germany in 1933, they rigidly censored books by Jewish and communist authors. They also staged public book-burnings of works they objected to as another type of political censorship. Religious or church-sponsored censorship may be practiced when ecclesiastical bodies are allowed to control certain public communications. The Roman Catholic Church maintained the *Index Librorum Prohibitorum,* a list of publications Catholics were not supposed to read.

Historical Background. There is evidence that censorship in one form or another has been practiced in almost all civilizations. Assurbanipal (c. 668–627 B.C.), the Assyrian king who developed a collection of more than 30,000 clay tablets that formed one of the greatest libraries of the ancient world, practiced a simple form of censorship. His librarians removed from the library whatever the king found disagreeable.

Censorship also existed in Roman public libraries, where the works of Julius Caesar were removed on order of the Emperor Augustus (63 B.C.–14 A.D.). The Emperor Julian (361–363), founder of Roman libraries in Constantinople and Antioch, attempted to destroy Christian texts. As a result of censorship in the classical world, many works by some authors were lost forever.

The term *censor* is rooted in Roman antiquity. Various magistrates were selected to take censuses of the Roman population and to determine citizens' responsibilities. These officials, called censors, were also charged with protecting traditional values. Among the renowned censors of the Roman Empire was Cato the Elder, elected to his office in 198 B.C., who worked diligently to erase immorality and promote the prevailing understanding of what virtuous Roman character should be. His great-grandson, Marcus Porcius Cato, or Cato the Younger, also functioned as an effective Roman censor after 65 B.C.

The censors of antiquity were regarded by Roman officials as protectors of high moral principles, integrity, and acceptable lifestyles among the citizenry. Thus, the modern concept of censorship derived from an ancient office of responsibility. It is significant to note, however, that free speech in the Roman Empire was primarily a privilege of members of the Senate and that many ordinary citizens who spoke out too freely were prosecuted and punished by officials of the government. Some poets, notably Ovid (43 B.C.–17 A.D.) and Juvenal 65–128 A.D.), were banished from their homeland because of their unorthodox literary works. Ovid's *Ars Amatoria,* devoted to the art of making love, and Juvenal's remarkable satires, which dealt with the follies and vices of imperial Roman society, became objects of the censors' scorn.

Johann Gutenberg's introduction of a new technique of printing from movable type in the mid-15th century in Germany stimulated the censorship of books, when Roman Catholic authorities initiated prepublication censorship of printed books in an effort to control heretical ideas. In the 16th century the Reformation was a period of intense censorship, when Roman Catholic and Protestant church leaders alike sought to control the spread of religious ideas that were in conflict with their favored theological teachings. The punishment of heresies was quite common during the Reformation. In England the Act of Supremacy (1534) gave Henry VIII authority to punish heretics. Church authorities were required to submit their books to higher officials for prior approval before publication; John Milton's *Areopagitica* (1644) was a protest against such licensing of printed books. The dissolution of monasteries and religious orders in England during the Reformation resulted in the wanton destruction of many thousands of irreplaceable manuscripts and books.

Philosophies of Intellectual Freedom. Ironically, the philosophers who first formulated both a theory of censorship and a theory of intellectual freedom lived as contemporaries in ancient Greece, where democracy was first conceptualized and initially practiced in Athens. Socrates (c. 470–399 B.C.) promoted freedom of the mind and refused to allow his teaching to be censored. Although Socrates respected Athenian law, the philosopher was regarded with suspicion by some public officials because he attributed vice to ignorance and promoted the notion that virtue is knowledge. Falsely charged with neglecting traditional Greek gods and of corrupting the morals of the young by alienating them from their government, the philosopher was convicted and executed. By promoting his faith in the value and benefits of free discussion, Socrates became the first person to express a profound philosophy of intellectual freedom.

On the other hand, Plato (c. 428–347 B.C.), a disciple of Socrates, formulated a defense of censorship for the control of certain undesirable religious, artistic, and intellectual ideas. In the *Republic,* Plato discussed the nature of justice and the presumed benefits of certain kinds of censorship. He argued that artistic works believed to be capable of undermining morality should be banned, works supposedly promoting heresy should be censored, and objectionable folktales should not be told to young persons.

Although dictatorships have routinely practiced censorship, most nations with democratic forms of government have limited such repressions through laws and have established legal reviews and appeals for certain repressive censorship decisions handed down by courts. For example, the Constitution of the United States outlines citizens' free-speech guarantees. The Supreme Court has ruled on many cases where constitutional law has been violated by restraints on freedom of speech or freedom of the press.

When citizens are allowed to govern themselves, intellectual freedom—freedom of the mind—takes on the role of the major sustaining right for that self-government. In a democracy, freedom of speech and of the press are sustained by the belief that citizens desire the actual truth and that, once truth has been found, it will guide human action. Citizens have the legal right in a truly free society to write articles or books for publication without first having to obtain a censor's approval. Of course, freedom of speech and intellectual freedom are not without their risks; they can be used to convey and sustain both truth and distortions of truth. However, freedom of speech and intellectual freedom have been used many times to expose falsehoods and other distortions of truth.

In writing the U.S. Declaration of Independence, Thomas Jefferson expressed the notion that natural right takes precedence over prescriptive law. That idea was embedded in the French Declaration of the Rights of Man and the Citizen (1789) and it became the preamble of the French Constitution of 1791. The emphasis on natural right was also incorporated in the basic laws that govern the U.S. For example, it is implicit in the First Amendment to the Constitution:

> Congress shall make no law . . . abridging the freedom of speech, or of the press; or the right of the people peaceably to assemble, and to petition the government for a redress of grievances.

Freedom of expression internationally is embodied in Article 19 of the United Nations Universal Declaration of Human Rights:

> Everyone has the right to freedom of expression and opinion; this right includes freedom to hold opinions without interference and to seek, receive, and impart information and ideas through any media and regardless of frontiers.

Although history shows that nations founded on democratic principles tend to allow their citizens the right of access to all forms of human expression with few restrictions, all governments tend to censor.

Censorship Problems. In many countries censorship occurs with respect to restrictions on certain religious practices, the expression of beliefs, or the expression of objections to religious beliefs or practices. Some Islamic countries require that teaching materials be consistent with the religious dogma approved by the government. In several Latin American countries, difficulties between a government and members of a religious group have led to restrictions. Mexico, for example, prohibits members of religious orders from voting or from criticizing government actions. When the British author Salman Rushdie published *The Satanic Verses* in 1989, the government of Iran considered the book an insult to Islam and condemned the author to death. The book was subsequently banned in 25 countries. Rushdie went into hiding to avoid threats to himself and his family.

Legal limitations on the expression of racist views are enforced in many countries, consistent with Article 20 of the International Covenant on Civil and Political Rights. Although Article 18 of the Covenant guarantees freedom of conscience, religion, and belief, and Article 19 protects freedom of expression, Article 20 prohibits propaganda for war and incitement to national, racial, or religious hatred. The 1980s saw many governments in Europe and North America prosecute extremist groups for expressions of racial and religious hatred. An international boycott of South Africa was prompted by the government's systematic repression of its black majority population through a series of *apartheid* (racial separation) laws. These laws banned publications that were inconsistent with government policies and banned organizations and individuals who advocated political beliefs contrary to its racial policies. By the early 1990s the government had rescinded most of these laws, but it continued to censor publications.

The Obscenity Problem. For the purpose of controlling publications and other materials deemed to be obscene or pornographic, all state legislatures in the U.S. have enacted legislation restricting sexually oriented public expression. Furthermore, federal laws currently prohibit the importation of obscene materials, their shipment across state lines, and their transmission through the mails.

Some critics of laws designed to regulate so-called obscene, lascivious, or immoral materials in the U.S. feel that such controls are acts of censorship and, when enforced, violate First Amendment provisions for freedom of expression or freedom of the press. In the opinion of these critics, both the lack of a precise legal definition for obscenity and the vague and indefinite nature of many laws passed to control sexually oriented materials fail to ensure due process of law for persons accused of crimes relating to such materials. Moreover, critics of obscenity legislation claim that it is often difficult—if not impossible—to prove that alleged offensive materials of a sexual nature cause criminal behavior; thus, they claim that free-press guarantees can be violated in some cases that involve the censorship of so-called obscenity. Another objection is that obscenity laws violate freedom of speech; however, it should be noted that obscene expression is presently not protected by the First Amendment, according to interpretations of constitutional law handed down in recent decades by the Supreme Court.

Many incidents of censorship are currently based on the assumption that exposure to certain ideas, words, images, or sounds will produce undesirable or illegal behavior on the part of persons who have read, seen, felt, or heard them. But the results of many scientific studies have failed to provide definitive answers to this question. Responses and reactions to materials deemed to be objectionable or obscene have often been unique; they have varied from one group of research subjects to another. Moreover, many complex sociological and psychological variables have been shown to be associated with both the desirable and undesirable internal meanings that many research subjects have gleaned from exposure to various sexual materials. Furthermore, only inconclusive research data have been produced relating to the degree and permanence of deviant behavior attributed in a cause-and-effect relationship to exposure to highly questionable sexual materials.

In the U.S., many cases involving the censorship of books or other publications, films, videotapes, or other media presently focus on, or relate to, the alleged obscene nature of media content. Another characteristic of contemporary censorship is that printed materials are usually allowed greater latitude or freedom of content than some of the newer electronic media, particularly television. Some observers have explained this difference by noting that television is a popular vehicle of mass communication and entertainment—and that the more popular or pervasive a communication vehicle is, the more closely its contents are likely to be scrutinized by censors and would-be censors. The motion picture industry in the U.S. practices some degree of self-censorship, rating popular, mass-produced films according to their intended audience. As another popular entertainment and communication medium, films have long been subject to the watchful scrutiny of censors.

In 1970, the President's Commission on Obscenity and Pornography, responding to its charge to study the obscenity problem, and after examining results of many scientifically conducted research studies, concluded that no substantial evidence existed to link obscene materials to criminal behavior. But President Richard M. Nixon rejected the Commission's conclusions and recommendations for both legislative and nonlegislative action. In addition, the Senate rejected the Commission's report by a vote of 60 to 5. Almost three years after the commission's report was released, the Supreme Court issued a decision on obscenity that also reflected the Court's legal and philosophical disagreement with the Commission.

In its report, the Commission on Obscenity and Pornography observed that the inability or reluctance of people in the U.S. to deal with sexual matters in an open and direct manner was responsible for many contemporary problems relating to sexually explicit materials. As to its recommendations, the Commission also stated that "accurate, appropriate sex information provided openly and directly through legitimate channels and from reliable sources in healthy contexts can compete successfully with potentially distorted, warped, inaccurate and unreliable information from clandestine, illegitimate sources." But these conclusions and recommendations on sexual materials have remained quite controversial; they have also generated a long debate about the question of obscenity and its real or assumed effects on people. The Department of Justice authorized a new commission on obscenity in 1985 to conduct another investigation of how obscenity and pornography might be better controlled. The national debate about whether sexually explicit materials produce adverse social effects and whether obscenity laws should be strengthened is likely to continue for many years.

In 1973 and 1974, the Supreme Court strengthened the censorship powers of governments of the 50 states by allowing the states to tighten their controls on so-called obscene works. The Court's decision delegated to the local area, rather than to the national level, the responsibility for deciding what is or is not obscene—a question that eluded the nation's highest tribunal for many years. At the same time, the Court put the states on notice to rewrite their censorship laws concerning sexually oriented materials. For more than a decade after the Court's last major decision on obscenity laws, state legislatures tried to reform their obscenity and pornography laws to bring them into conformity with the Supreme Court's three-part test for obscenity: (1) whether the average person, applying contemporary community standards, would find the work, taken as a whole, as an appeal to prurient interests; (2) whether the work depicts or describes, in a patently offensive way, sexual conduct specifically defined by the applicable state law; and (3) whether the work, taken as a whole, lacks serious literary, political, or scientific value.

Censorship Trends. Since the 1980s a group in the United Kingdom called Article 19, the International Center on Censorship, documented increases in the number of incidents and types of censorship and restrictions on freedom of expression. Its studies were confirmed by reports from the Fund for Free Expression and its Watch Committees in the U.S. Most prevalent during this period were government efforts to restrict access to information, protests against government policies, and restrictions on the media.

Governments justified these restrictions by citing reasons of national security and the public interest. The Israeli government acted to repress Arab publications for printing articles on its activities and policies in the Occupied Territories that had already appeared in Hebrew publications. The U.K. government prohibited the publication in newspapers of extracts from *Spycatcher* by Peter Wright, a former British spy, for reasons of national security. It further banned all media reporting on allegations in the book based on injunctions originally obtained against *The Observer* and *The Guardian*. The Chinese government imposed severe restrictions on newspapers, journalists, and the media after the violent confrontations with students and workers advocating freedom of assembly in Tiananmen Square led to more than a thousand deaths and thousands of injuries. The government justified its actions as being in the public interest. Interestingly, demonstrators who were suppressed by the declaration of martial law had justified their actions as guaranteed by the 1982 Constitution, which sanctioned demonstrations, freedom of assembly, and freedom of expression.

Libraries and Censorship. Although the International Federation of Library Associations and Institutions (IFLA) adopted several measures, including Article 19 of the Universal Declaration of Human Rights, during its 1989 Council Meeting in Paris, the most comprehensive set of policies and procedures to guide librarians and libraries in resisting censorship evolved in the U.S. in the American Library Association. The Library Bill of Rights, adopted by the ALA in 1939 and systematically reviewed and revised since that time by the organization's Intellectual Freedom Committee, outlines philosophical guidelines for the protection of library users' freedom of access to uncensored library collections. It is ALA's official policy statement regarding the right of citizens to both current and historical information on all subjects and issues. The intellectual freedom statement serves as a guide to the desired professional behavior of librarians regarding freedom of speech; it also challenges librarians to resist "abridgments of free expression and free access to ideas." Although widely viewed in the profession as a standard by which practicing librarians can gauge their actions concerning the preservation of intellectual freedom and the resistance to censorship, the Library Bill of Rights is not a binding legal document, such as the Bill of Rights of the Constitution of the U.S. The complete text of ALA's fundamental statement on intellectual freedom is as follows:

Library Bill of Rights

The American Library Association affirms that all libraries are forums for information and ideas, and that the following basic policies should guide their services.

1. Books and other library resources should be provided for the interest, information, and enlightenment of all people of the community served. Materials should not be excluded because of the origin, background, or views of those contributing to their creation.

2. Libraries should provide materials and information presenting all points of view on current and historical issues. Materials should not be proscribed or removed because of partisan or doctrinal disapproval.

3. Libraries should challenge censorship in the fulfillment of their responsibility to provide information and enlightenment.

4. Libraries should cooperate with all persons and groups concerned with resisting abridgments of free expression and free access to ideas.

5. A person's right to use a library should not be denied because of origin, age, background, or views.

6. Libraries which make exhibit spaces and meeting rooms available to the public they serve should make such facilities available on an equitable basis, regardless of the beliefs or affiliations of individuals or groups requesting their use.

Various written interpretations of the Library Bill of Rights have been adopted by the ALA Council to bolster the maintenance of intellectual freedom in libraries. These carefully developed and widely publicized statements are as follows: How Libraries Can Resist Censorship; Free Access to Libraries for Minors; Sexism, Racism, and Other -isms in Library Materials; Exhibit Spaces and Meeting Rooms; Expurgation of Library Collections; Reevaluating Library Collections; Resolution on Challenged Materials; Intellectual Freedom Statement; The Freedom to Read; School Library Bill of Rights; and Resolution on Government Intimidation.

The ALA's Office for Intellectual Freedom works to implement ALA policies on intellectual freedom as embodied in the Library Bill of Rights. It publishes the *Newsletter on Intellectual Freedom* and the *Intellectual Freedom Manual*.

Many attempts to censor library collections have become public issues, and many librarians have struggled vigorously to maintain the rights of library users to intellectual freedom. On the other hand, there is evidence that some librarians tend to compromise and cooperate with censors. But the Library Bill of Rights and related interpretative statements are designed to help all librarians resist the forced curtailment of the purchase, use, or circulation of library materials, simply because someone finds them to be objectionable. Similarly, these principles are designed to prevent self-censorship by librarians, whereby negative selection policies are applied to screen purchases so carefully that anything likely to become the object of public controversy is not acquired or made available.

In the U.S. and elsewhere librarians are increasingly committed to resisting censorship and to promoting the maximum use of libraries as institutions of freedom where citizens can seek truth without restriction in an uncensored repository of information, knowledge, and entertainment.

REFERENCES

Charles H. Busha, editor, "Censorship in the Eighties" (1982).

Article 19, "Information, Freedom, and Censorship: World Report 1991" (1991).

American Library Association, *Intellectual Freedom Manual,* 4th edition (1992).

CHARLES H. BUSHA;
ROBERT WEDGEWORTH

Central African Republic

The Central African Republic, a former territory of French Equatorial Africa, is bounded by Chad on the north, the Sudan on the east, Zaire and Congo on the south, and Cameroon on the west. Population (1990 est.) 3,039,000; area 622,984 sq.km. The official language is French. The national language is Sango.

History. The location of Ubangi–Shari, the earlier name of the Central African Republic, in the heart of Africa was an obstacle for the first French explorers. As a result, modern institutions were established quite late in what had been an oral-tradition society. Libraries, archives, and documentation services are fairly recent in the Central African Republic.

The first libraries came into being with educational institutions at the beginning of the 20th century. They were not separate institutions, just collections of books that supported the curriculum. Several decades were to pass and independence achieved (1960) before small libraries were set up in high schools and professional schools.

Archives first appeared with the French colonists who kept daily records and logs, sent reports to France, and received directives back. Ubangi–Shari was one of the countries of French Equatorial Africa (FEA) that did not keep its historical archives. The capital of FEA was Brazzaville, and the government's records were held there. Before the countries achieved independence, the archives were in large part transferred to Aix-en-Provence. The aim of the Central

Libraries in Central African Republic (1990)

Type of library	Number of administrative units (main libraries)	Number of service points (branches, mobile stops, etc.)	Volumes in collections
Special*	2	2	21,000

*1985 data

Source: Unesco, *Statistical Yearbook,* 1991

African Republic was the repatriation of those parts of the archives that concern the country.

The establishment of colonial institutions in the French Overseas Territories was followed by various local studies aimed at resource development. The accumulation of such research led gradually to the creation of documentation services, first in Brazzaville, then in Ubangi–Shari. The setting up of an agricultural research center in Boukoko and of others in the early 1940s marks the beginning of documentation services.

National Library. A decree of 1981 created a National Library in the Central African Republic. The government department in charge of culture took steps to ensure that this institution would come into being and a legal deposit law was adopted in 1986.

Public and Private Archives. The National Archives, which reports to the office of the President of the Republic, was created by law in 1969. Legislation establishing an archives law in the Central African Republic was signed in 1983.

A large draft conservation plan exists for historical archives still dispersed throughout the country, but no real work had been started as of the early 1990s because of a lack of funds. In the meantime, the Director of the National Archives undertook a campaign of public talks, radio interviews, and other public activities, in order to increase public awareness of the problems of archives.

The most important private archives are those of members of the clergy, former political figures, and old business firms. These remain the exclusive property of their owners.

University Library. Since 1981 the University Library, founded in 1970, at the same time as the University of Bangui, has been in a building that houses its science, literature, and law collections; the medical school has its own library. The same is true for certain other segments of the University: the Institut Supérieur de Développement Rural at M'Bai'ki and the École Normale Supérieure, which became a university institute in 1982. There is seating for only 100 (out of a student body of 2,000) in the main building of the University Library.

Public Libraries. The public library system in the country is run by the government's Culture Department, assisted by the towns and cultural institutions such as the Protestant Youth Center and the cultural centers of certain embassies in Bangui. An objective of a new National Library is to play a major role in the promotion of reading throughout the country. In certain areas of Bangui and in the larger towns outside of Bangui, youth centers offer art programs and set space aside for reading. There was, in fact, no building housing a public library in the late 1980s. Users are for the most part elementary and secondary school students.

School Libraries. School libraries have not been developed for a good number of years. In the larger schools there are small libraries, but they do little more than distribute books to students at the beginning and the end of the school year. Nevertheless, small reading rooms were being created here and there in the 1980s.

Special Libraries. Special libraries are connected with international organizations whose main offices are in Bangui and with research institutes. Among these are the libraries of the Organisation Commune Africaine et Mauricienne (OCAM), the Central African Customs and Economic Union (UDEAC), and the Bureau Interafricain des Sols et de l'Économie Rurale.

The Profession. In 1990 the Central African Republic had no library, archives, or documentation school. Training in those fields was given by schools elsewhere in Africa and in Europe, notably the University of Dakar (Senegal), the École Nationale Supérieure de Bibliothécaires, the École des Chartes, and the Institut National des Techniques Documentaires in France, and the École des Sciences de l'Information in Morocco.

There was no librarians', archivists', or documentalists' association in the Central African Republic in the late 1980s.

ALAIN-MICHEL POUTOU;
translated by CHARLES S. FINEMAN

Certification of Librarians

A major characteristic of any profession is the concern its members exhibit for the quality of the services provided to its clientele. Every field sets standards of quality for those practicing in the profession and establishes some means by which those entering the profession can be qualified to practice. Several means for establishing credentials have been developed.

DEFINITIONS

Accreditation, licensure, and certification are three ways in which professions recognize the competency of those practicing in professional fields.

Accreditation is the process of examining the educational programs that prepare persons for entrance into the profession and attesting that the programs meet certain predetermined and prescribed standards. The professional association has the responsibility for setting standards and for designing the process whereby individual programs are examined and reviewed. By publicly acknowledging that the program is accredited, the profession, through its professional accrediting agency, states that the education is of sufficient quality to develop practitioners qualified to perform acceptably the functions of the profession. For the United States and Canada, the American Library Association (ALA) has chosen accreditation as the method to establish credentials for librarians, and through its Committee on Accreditation (COA) has set standards for the accreditation of graduate educational programs leading to the first professional degree. The COA regularly examines schools and accredits those programs which measure up to its standards.

Licensure is the legal requirement that each person wishing to practice in a profession must obtain a license. A license gives the person the right to perform the duties of that profession, and anyone who attempts to perform them without a license can be prosecuted. Issued by government agencies, licenses are most often required in fields in which the health and welfare of the public might be affected by unqualified practitioners; medical doctors and dentists, for example, are required to obtain licenses to practice in a given nation, state, or province.

Certification is the process by which a professional organization or an independent agency recognizes a person who has successfully completed certain prescribed requirements of education and experience and has demonstrated certain skills or competencies, and declares that person qualified to practice that profession. Certification is accorded to the individual, rather than to the program of study or the institution. More than 425 professional associations have established standards and certification processes for their members in the U.S.

Certification of librarians may be *mandated* by laws or regulations; it may be *permitted* by law, but not required; or it may be *voluntary* under a plan developed by a professional group on a nationwide basis or by professionals working at the state, regional, or local level. In general, school librarians/media specialists are certified under law or education department regulations; public librarians may have certification that is required, permitted, or voluntary; academic librarians may be certified under law applying to all librarians employed in a given jurisdiction or, more generally, are not certified but rather are employed as graduates of ALA-accredited library science programs; and librarians working in specific special library groups, such as law and medicine, are certified through voluntary certification programs developed by their professional associations.

SCHOOL LIBRARIANS/ MEDIA SPECIALISTS

The certification of those who provide library and audiovisual services in U.S. elementary and secondary schools has for many years been linked with the teaching profession and governed by state education departments in each state. Generally, the requirements for library certification are attached as endorsements to teaching certificates and in most states carry a certification to practice for kindergarten through 12th grade rather than one limited to practice in only elementary or secondary schools.

There is little consistency or uniformity in certification requirements for professionals in school libraries or learning resource centers. School librarians are certified under a wide variety of titles, from "school librarian" to "media generalist," "media professional," "learning resource specialist," and "school media specialist (library)." As varied as the nomenclature is, the same variety is evident in the number of hours of course work required and the subject content of the program. Requirements range from six semester hours of preparation in librarianship to be certified to work in a school with fewer than 75 pupils, to education at the master's degree level and beyond. A majority of states require 27 or more semester hours for regular certification, and many require the master's degree.

Most states do specify certain required courses, often stipulating that they be at the graduate level. While the subjects may vary, there is some consensus that the study should include courses in administration, cataloguing and classification, reference, selection of materials, and audiovisual/instructional media production or use. Twenty-two states require a practicum.

There has recently been increased activity in state library and media associations in reviewing and updating certification requirements. Results can be seen in the added requirement of computer study in some states and a course in public relations in another. Some states have introduced tests as a part of the certification process, such as the California Basic Education Test, the Criterion Referenced Test in Georgia, and the National Teacher Exam in Virginia and South Carolina. By the late 1980s, one state also recognized the movement toward competency-based programs for certification.

At the national level, the American Association for School Librarians, a Division of ALA, has for many years taken an active role in developing model certification programs for school/media specialists and in working with the Association for Educational Communications and Technology to raise the standards of school library/media services.

PUBLIC LIBRARIANS

Certification of public librarians in the U.S. can be traced back to a 1909 California law requiring certification of the head librarian of each county library, and to similar laws in Texas in 1919 and in Wisconsin in 1921. Some form of certification for librarians occupying certain positions in public library systems has since been adopted into law in about half of the states. Certification plans may be either mandatory or voluntary; in a few states, voluntary certification plans have been developed and implemented by state library associations.

Because there is no clear pattern, it is difficult to generalize on the qualifications required for certification of public librarians or on the positions that require certified librarians. Some states (such as Georgia, Virginia, and Washington) require certification of all librarians in public libraries serving populations of more than 5,000, and in every library operated by the state or its authority, including institutions of higher learning; county or city law libraries and public schools are specifically exempt. In states with this inclusive certification, the law generally provides for withholding state funds from libraries that do not comply.

A larger number of states exempt the libraries of educational institutions, applying certification to public libraries supported by public funds. Other states (Maryland, for example) require each appointee to a professional library staff of a county library to hold a certificate, while other states restrict the requirement to heads of county libraries or library systems. The law may briefly state that certification is required, or it may, as in New Mexico and Michigan, describe in detail the degrees and experience that earn the certificate. In states where the public librarians are part of the state civil service system, there is specific attention to grades or ranks and their appropriate requirements. In some states, certification is given automatically or by library school verification to those who possess a library degree from an ALA-accredited program. Other candidates for certification may offer equivalencies for consideration.

Whatever the certification requirements, most plans also provide for equivalencies to be presented for the educational requirements, often substituting experience for education, or a test over courses in specified subjects. In many states, persons with degrees from unaccredited programs may authenticate their studies with examinations, while those with foreign degrees or study in countries outside the U.S. may request an analysis of their credits for equivalency.

State library agencies, divisions of library service in state governments, and state professional library associations were in the 1980s reexamining certification rules and regulations. Wisconsin, for example, replaced the lifetime certificate with a five-year one, renewable upon evidence of suitable continuing education and professional development activity. Tests were added to the certification requirement in some states, while in others specific courses were identified.

ACADEMIC LIBRARIANS

A few states of the U.S. have general library certification plans for all librarians in libraries receiving state money; in those states, the basic requirement is the master's degree from an ALA-accredited program. The majority of states have no provision for certification of academic librarians, so requirements for employment are determined according to the needs of the library or the personnel regulations of the university or college system.

SPECIAL LIBRARIANS

Medical librarianship has led the way toward special certification in a library specialty in the U.S. As early as 1948 the Medical Library Association (MLA) adopted a Code of Training and Certification of Medical Librarians. This voluntary certification, developed and implemented by the professional association rather than by an outside authority, was directed toward improving medical librarianship through basic standards for education and training and by certifying qualified librarians. This Code, with revisions, remained in effect from 1949 to 1977, and 3,200 individuals were certified.

MLA adopted a new Code for the Certification of Health Sciences Librarians in 1978, with revisions in 1981. The librarian seeking MLA certification must not only have graduated from a ALA-accredited program, but also pass an examination administered by the Association to test the entry-level competencies required of health sciences librarians; two years' post-library-degree experience as a health sciences librarian in the past ten years is also required, but provisional certificates may be issued to candidates lacking only the two years' experience. Recertification by MLA is required every five years and is obtained through continuing education activities approved by the Association or by successful completion of the current certification examination.

Another example of a national voluntary certification plan for a special area in librarianship is that adopted in 1965 by the American Association of Law Libraries (AALL). The AALL preferred standard for all law librarians is Category I, which requires a library science degree from an ALA-accredited program, an accredited law degree or admission to the Bar, and two years of professional library experience, half of which must be in a law library. Category II substitutes four years of library experience for the library degree, and Category III substitutes six to ten years of library experience for the law degree.

The programs in both law and health sciences are examples of successful voluntary national certification that have raised the standards of library service in these fields.

NATIONAL CERTIFICATION

Certification and licensing have different meanings outside North America. In most European countries, for example, an agency such as the Ministry of Education grants licenses or certificates within the terms of the educational programs it authorizes.

One national plan for certification of librarians, in the United Kingdom, was extensively revised in the late 1970s. It offers at least a model for the planning process if not for a certification plan itself. The Library Association (LA) formed a Working Party on the Future of Professional Qualifications to "determine appropriate levels of registration and certification in relation to the present and future needs of the profession; to consider and define the nature of and to identify the principles underlying professional education and registration and how these should be attained and regulated, in the light of available evidence; and to assess the resources required from employers, training boards, educational institutions, and the Association, and to determine priorities." The document the Working Party produced, referred to as the Paulin Report, was the result of more than four years of study, work, and discussion. After its adoption in 1977 by the Library Association Council, an Implementation Board was formed to develop a plan of action and implement the program by the beginning of 1981.

The Paulin Report affirms the belief that the LA should "formulate a positive education policy aimed at producing the kinds of staff needed to operate the library and information services required by the community in the latter part of the twentieth century." While the plan as accepted retains two-year undergraduate courses, it recommends that "all those wishing to enter schools of librarianship should be clearly advised of the advantages of achieving graduate status." After completing the course of study, students must spend a year in a planned and supervised training program in a library agency. Candidates who complete this year with positive written assessments from their supervisors are admitted to the LA as Licentiates.

For the next step, the Licentiate must complete three additional years of appropriate service and professional development and submit a written report to the LA. If successful, the Licentiate becomes an Associate of the Library Association (A.L.A.) and a Chartered Librarian.

"Fellow" is the Library Association's highest classification. While retaining the requirement of a thesis and five years of library service as an Associate, the Paulin Report adds alternative routes to achieve this classification, such as submission of published work demonstrating original thought, or a carefully written account of professional achievement contributing to the field of librarianship.

With the implementation of the recommendations of the Paulin Report, the LA abolished external examinations, becoming more a validating agency than an examining one. In each classification the LA clearly affirms its belief in the importance of continuing education. The longer and more carefully prescribed period of training for chartered librarians strengthens library services, gives prestige to the profession, and may possibly bring the added benefit of improving salaries. The effects of the reforms stimulated by the Paulin Report have been obscured by financial pressures that led to a general restructuring of higher education in the U.K. and by an oversupply of library and information workers.

TRENDS

Certification of U.S. librarians has been discussed within the profession for many years. The Williamson Report of 1923, commissioned by the Carnegie Foundation to examine the preparation of librarians for professional practice, recommended the establishment of a national certification plan. After much discussion, ALA chose to accredit library education programs, leaving certification for the states to address.

Ambivalence toward certification in Canada was indicated in 1985, when one province, British Columbia, decided to discontinue certification of librarians, which had been the practice since 1944. In the profession, only the library educators raised any significant objections.

The library literature of the 1980s and early 1990s reveals a growing interest in reexamining the potential of national certification for the profession in the U.S. Proponents identify a number of advantages from a national certification plan. First, certification would guarantee to the public that practitioners have attained a certain accepted code of professional behavior and ethics, a recognizable level of knowledge and job responsibility, and standards of acceptable performance. By developing competency-based exams, the profession would clearly define the characteristics of the professional librarian and would provide a national uniform standard of competency. Such exams might be instrumental in validating the MLS degree.

Certification would further provide employers with objective criteria by which to measure those applying for beginning professional positions, thereby reducing biased and discriminatory hiring practices. Some assert that certification could improve the public image of librarians and, therefore, help to recruit a high level of intelligent, qualified persons into the profession. It could improve the quality of professional education and provide incentives for continuing education and professional advancement. It could also enhance job security for librarians by preventing the hiring of unqualified persons.

Those opposing national certification observe that there are many incompetents in fields that do have certification as an entry requirement. They point to the high cost of developing and implementing certification programs and to the belief that librarianship is too diverse a profession to be entered through one certification plan.

Whether national certification could or would become a reality for librarians in the U.S. was still unclear by the early 1990s. It was certain that discussions of certification would continue at state and national levels and within the entire profession.

REFERENCES

Barry Bratton and Myrene Hildebrand, "Plain Talk about Professional Certification," *Instructional Innovator* (1980).

Peter Havard-Williams, "Library and Information Education Today: From the British Point of View," *Library and Information Science Education* (1987).

Holly G. Willet, "Certification and Education for Library and Information Science," *Journal of Education for Library and Information Science* (1984).

Elizabeth H. Woellner, "Requirements for Certification, for Elementary Schools, Secondary Schools, Junior Colleges," 49th ed. (1984).

MARGARET KNOX GOGGIN

Chad

Chad, a republic in central western Africa, is bordered by Libya on the north, Sudan on the east, the Central African Republic on the south, and Cameroon, Nigeria, and Niger on the west. Population (1990 est.) 5,679,000; area 1,284,000 sq.km. The official language is French.

Academic Libraries. The library of the University of Chad, in N'Djaména, was founded with the university itself in 1971 and consists of three collections: the central University Library with just over 12,000 volumes and 41 current periodicals; the Library of the Institut Universitaire des Sciences, in Farcha, which offers some 1,500 volumes relating to the physical and biological sciences; and the collection of the Institut Universitaire des Techniques de l'Élevage with its 500 volumes and 20 periodicals.

Public Libraries. While there is no centralized and uniform system of public libraries, most of the major towns have at least one library, falling within one of several classifications. Cultural centers are in Abéché, Am Timan, Ati, Biltine, Doba, Fianga, and Oum Hadjer. Mission libraries with general collections number about 30 throughout the country. Five other larger libraries are particularly noteworthy: the Municipal Library of Sarh, the library established by the Alliance Française in Moundou, the American Cultural Center (a bilingual collection in English and French), the Libyan Cultural Center (Arabic), and the French Cultural Center (the largest collection in Chad—some 24,847 volumes with a lending rate of

Libraries in Chad (1990)

Type of library	Number of administrative units (main libraries)	Number of service points (branches, mobile stops, etc.)	Volumes in collections	Population served
Academic[a] (Higher Education)	1	1	10,000	350
Public[b]	1		4,000	250
Special[c]	1		4,000	
Non-specialized[c]	2		3,000	6,150

[a]1987 data
[b]1985 data
[c]1984 data

Source: Unesco, *Statistical Yearbook*, 1991

8,000 per month) in the capital. The French Cultural Center also offers a film collection.

Special Libraries. The Institut National pour les Sciences Humaines, primarily a research institution, was founded in 1961 and has a library of some 3,000 volumes and 3,000 documents relating to Chadian ethnology, archaeology, geography, history, and linguistics. A similar range of subject matter is covered in the collection of the Bibliothèque Afrique et Tchad of the Archdiocese of N'Djaména. The Office de la Recherche Scientifique et Technique Outre-Mer (ORSTROM), also in the capital, has a library of 3,100 volumes, with 100 current periodicals, 713 manuscripts, and 230 maps.

Materials on problems of development are housed in the library of the Centre d'Etude et de Formation pour le Développement (CEFOD). The Centre de Documentation Pédagogique (3,300 volumes), founded in 1962, offers materials on education in French and Arabic. The American Cultural Center keeps about 4,500 volumes, with some current periodicals, records, and tapes. Other small library collections are those of the Institut d'Élevage et de Médecine Vétérinaire du Pays Tropicaux (in Farcha), the Central Hospital, and the Laboratoire de Recherche Vétérinaires et Zootechniques.

NEIL McHUGH

Chavez Campomanes, Maria Teresa
(1890–)

Mexican Library Association
Maria Teresa Chavez Campomanes

Mexican library educator Maria Teresa Chavez Campomanes contributed significantly to the education of Mexican librarians, the improvement of teaching methods, and steps toward the goal of making libraries an extension of the classroom.

Born in Puebla de los Ángeles, Mexico, August 1, 1890, Maria Teresa Chavez studied at the School for Librarians in Mexico City under the direction of Emilio Baz. She traveled to the United States for further study, graduating from Pratt Institute, and did postgraduate work in library science in Detroit and at Columbia. Later she was employed in the New York Public Library and the Library of Congress in Washington.

After returning to Mexico, she continued to study Spanish literature in the Faculty of Philosophy and Letters of the National University. She received the degree of Doctor of Literature in 1953 with a thesis on books that became classics. She was director of the Franklin Library and Subdirector (later Director) of the Library of Mexico from its establishment under José Vasconcelos, a philosopher. The progress of that library was due in great measure to her perseverance, and she became one of the few to serve youth of the metropolis with vigor and efficiency.

Chavez Campomanes came to be regarded as the very foundation of teaching at the National School of Archivists and Librarians of the Secretariat of Education and a similar school of the Faculty of Philosophy and Letters of the National University. The great majority of Mexican librarians learned at her side, gaining as much from her teaching as from the effective manuals of classification and cataloguing that she wrote. As a teacher, she was a model of clarity and patience. She was named Teacher Emeritus of the Secretariat of Education and won wide respect as one of the most distinguished women of Mexico.

ERNESTO DE LA TORRE VILLAR

Children's Services

Children in many countries have access to two types of libraries: the school library and the public library. In general, the school library relates to the curriculum of the institution it serves and the public library meets the informational, educational, recreational, and cultural needs of the community it serves. The systems are at various stages of development in various countries and even in various communities in one country, but their common goal is to offer children access to materials that will help them become literate, lifelong learners, able to obtain access to information in a reasonable time in their local area. This article deals primarily with children's services in public libraries. *See also* School Libraries/Media Centers.

The development of children's services in different countries varies greatly, depending on political support, funding, legislation, educational priorities, language, book publishing, the availability of specially trained librarians, and the attitudes of families and children themselves. In the United States, for example, political pressure led to a National Library Card campaign in 1987 that sought to provide every child

Library Association

Mime time in the weekly story period, Shard End Library, Birmingham, England.

with a library card and to ensure that he or she used it. Hundreds of thousands of young people signed up in the first few years, and a National Library Card month now occurs each autumn.

Traditional library services to children have included providing circulating materials, reference services, and reader's advisory services; helping children and adults use the library; and promoting the enjoyment of reading. Children's librarians have always carried the extra responsibility of being advocates for children in such areas as access to information, intellectual freedom, and networking with other youth agencies.

A number of authors have studied the changes in society in the last decade of the 20th century—the centennial decade of library services for children in the U.S.—that public library services must adapt to. Some of these changes involve society as a whole: its racial composition, its age structure, its overall literacy, and its response to expanding technology. Some of these changes are specific to children: their need for childcare, their survival in families at risk, and their survival in increasingly violent times. And some of these changes are specific to libraries and other educational institutions: the need to provide more services during a time of shrinking financial resources and the need to attract more and better professionals.

In 1989, in an effort to define the role of the librarian serving children in the public library, the Association for Library Service to Children (ALSC) of the American Library Association (ALA) identified seven competency areas: knowledge of the client group; administrative and management skills; communication skills; materials and collection development skills; programming skills; advocacy, public relations, and networking skills; and professionalism and professional development.

COLLECTIONS

The book collection is a major part of library service to children throughout the world. In more affluent countries it includes books for infants, beautifully

Phil Moloitis

Children watching chicks hatch at Woodson Regional Library, Chicago, part of a farm study project planned with the assistance of Illinois 4-H Cooperative Extension Service.

Greensboro Public Library

Young people enjoying their favorite books at Greensboro Public Library, North Carolina.

illustrated picture books, easy readers, folk and fairy tales, fiction of all types, biographies, and other nonfiction titles. Some children's libraries provide textbooks, special collections for parents or caregivers, foreign language or bilingual collections, changing book displays, and racks or bins of paperback and other popular titles. Many developing countries, however, do not have such resources and are faced with large populations of children speaking numerous languages. Librarians in Thailand are coping with the problem of more children than books by using portable libraries, consisting of three or four compartments of books that travel the country. Ghana has nine regional libraries and nine mobile libraries serving an increasing number of children in a country in which 49 languages are spoken. Few children see books other than textbooks.

Photo by Hiroshi Urushibara, Tokyo

A young patron with his book bag provided by the library. (Japan)

Besides book collections, today's public librarians work to provide periodicals, computer hardware and software, sound recordings (phonograph records, cassettes, and compact discs), video recordings, realia, and other items that provide contemporary information. Films and disk recordings are being replaced by videotapes and compact discs. Advances in computer technology, electronic communications, new software, and CD-ROMs and databases all require con tinual updating and education on the part of youth librarians.

In the U.S., children's book publishing has seen a great increase in production as many members of the baby-boom generation begin raising families of their own. Many parents and grandparents are well educated and demand books and library services as they raise their children. They remember books they loved as children, some of them winners of the Newbery or Caldecott awards of the ALA, and want excellent materials for their own families. Publishers are responding, and bookstores are flourishing. Series books have proliferated, especially for the older and middle-school-age child. The demand for multicultural books and characters is increasing as the population shifts, with large increases in the numbers of Hispanic and Asian-American children. Publishers are increasing the numbers of translated books as access barriers fall and as such events as the Bologna Book Fair grow.

In Egypt, library service to children has been greatly strengthened because of support for children's libraries from the Integrated Care Society and from Suzanne Mubarak, who chairs the Egypt Section of the International Board on Books for Young People. The Society now sponsors about 20 children's libraries in various parts of the country. Public government schools have 45 more, including libraries for disabled children. A mobile library staffed by librarians and child counselors travels to the remote areas of Cairo.

PROGRAMS AND ACTIVITIES FOR CHILDREN

One of the most visible services of children's librarianship in public libraries is the activity planned and sponsored by the library relating to books, library materials, and reading. Since the beginning of children's services in the U.S. in the 1890s, such activities have included story hours and reading clubs, and later preschool programs. Today, programs range from computers to cooking, realia to read-to-me clubs.

In the Winter 1987 issue of *Library Trends,* Alice Naylor identified the five traditional services for children: story hour, preschool story hour, reference and reader's advisory service, summer reading club, and a quality book collection. She added that these services have not changed over the years except for the lowering of age level served.

The first national survey of U.S. public library services and resources for children, "Services and Resources for Children in Public Libraries, 1988–89," was issued in 1990 by the National Center for Educational Statistics. Some of the highlights of the report were that 37 percent of public library users in the autumn of 1988 were children 14 years old or younger; children of this age comprise only 22 percent of the total population; the mean circulation of children's materials in libraries was 43 percent; the book budget mean was 35 percent for children's materials. The services that most often reported moderate or heavy use by children in 1988–89 were summer reading programs (89 percent), story hours (78 percent), and reader's advisory service (72 percent). Public libraries in that year offered an average of 9 group programs for infants through two-year-olds, an average of 43 group programs for three- to five-year-olds, an average of 25 group programs for school-age children, and an average of 5 programs for children of unspecified ages. Group programs included such activities as story hours, puppet shows, and book talks. A full 83 percent of public libraries cooperated with schools enrolling children of 14 and under, as did 62 percent with preschools or daycare centers. Cooperation included such programs and services as book talks, class visits and tours, and meetings with staff. More than half the public libraries—58 percent—do not have children's librarians.

In the former Soviet Union, children's libraries served as cultural centers and resource centers for children from preschool to age 15, as well as parents, teachers, and other adults. Most children's libraries are in separate buildings, except in small communities. They were designed as total cultural experiences that encourage talking and thinking, by displaying works of art and sculpture and presenting music, dance, opera, puppet plays, films, and readings. They also sought to create warmth in reading rooms by using plants and soft music. Most library programs for Soviet children involved literary clubs that focused on such topics as cinema after school, drawing, fantasy, foreign languages (most children learn at least three), young diplomats, and nature. Specialists conducted the clubs; some were paid and others were volunteers. Much of this emphasis seems likely to continue in the Commonwealth of Independent States.

Library service to children in Australia depends on where the children are. Children in or near the urban centers have access to traditional library services, such as storytelling and film and video shows. Rural services provided for isolated children may be books that travel on the weekly mail plane, dial-ups on electronic mail services, or fax transmissions of questions and responses.

Many libraries have activities for toddlers and their parents, designed both to expose children to the library and to literature and to expose parents to the possible uses of library materials with their children. The San Francisco Public Library calls its parent-toddler story hours "Lapsits." Now that a majority of preschoolers have working parents, libraries have reached out to serve preschool and daycare centers. The library service in Prince George's County, Maryland, has identified home daycare programs as an area needing library materials in its outreach program, "Wee Care." In Denver, Colorado, a "Magic Bus" tours the city, providing library services.

Editions of books specifically for reading aloud have encouraged literacy efforts in family and classroom reading. In an effort to increase the availability of books, the library services in Port Chester, New York, and Greenwich, Connecticut, have established portable reading collections called "Books to Go." In Pittsburgh, Pennsylvania, Joan Friedberg and Elizabeth Segel started "Beginning with Books" as a pilot project funded with a grant to serve six well-baby clinics of the Allegheny Health Department. It has since grown and expanded and is now a service of the Carnegie Library of Pittsburgh.

Carnegie Library of Pittsburgh. Photo by Jane Freund

A family participates in the Beginning With Books program, Carnegie Library of Pittsburgh, Pennsylvania.

In Greensboro, North Carolina, "The Community of Readers" is a campaign to promote reading in Guilford County. Established by the Greensboro Public Library, the program was developed by a task force including representatives from schools, community agencies, government agencies, and the media. Each month an activity is featured to celebrate the joy of reading for everyone. The Community offers such services as "Welcome the New Baby" (a kit for all new babies born in the county), "Catch 'Em in the Cradle" (programs for parents and caregivers to encourage pre-reading activities with young children), a traveling "Literary Resources Fair" set up in local

National Library of India

Special children's section in India's National Library, Calcutta.

Amman Public Library

Children's reading hall in the Amman Public Library, Jordan.

factories and offices, Family Storytimes, and "Soar to the T.O.P." (Teenage Opportunity Programs), and more.

Librarians and educators in Kenya have approached the problem of literacy by developing ways to help illiterate mothers teach their babies the alphabet. An important part of women's clothing in Kenya is the cloth wrap called kanga cloths. The International Board on Books for Young People in Kenya is printing alphabet kanga cloths for mothers and babies to use together to promote the importance of reading—and future library use.

Library programs have been referred to in many ways, from a way to make learning fun, to the most effective way to introduce children to the library. Margaret M. Kimmel wrote, "If children's services goes beyond housing materials, if, indeed, it is to provide an opportunity for an individual child to go beyond what he thinks he wants to what he *might* want, stimulating, effective programming should be developed as a basic part of a library's service. And the program must be regularly evaluated and revised, because the program itself is a service, not an end."

Children's reading corner of the Kapsala Community Library, Viejas Indian Reservation, San Diego County, California.

Indian Library Services Project, San Diego County Library

PERSONNEL

The profession faces a shortage of children's librarians, school librarians, and youth library educators. The shortage is made critical by a number of trends that have come together: some library schools have closed; others do not teach courses in these competencies; still others do not have full-time faculty with the skills to do so. At the same time, library schools need to attract new students to the profession, which is "graying" noticeably.

Writing in 1987, Immroth and Somerville identified several factors as exacerbating this shortage. Although children's circulation represents 30 to 50 percent of the total library circulation, budgets for children's services materials show, as Somerville put it, "that Mother Goose can't compete with Shakespeare, or even Danielle Steel." Some youth librarians are more interested in literature, public relations, and children than in statistics, budgeting, and goal setting. They face low salaries, few opportunities for advancement, and better salaries and benefits in school libraries. Other demonstrated prejudices can be a lack of respect for the skills required to work with young people and the fact that many coordinator positions are not line positions in management and lack authority. Many library schools are apathetic to children's services, burnout is a serious problem, and the field needs more minority representation. Some of these prejudices are true not only in the field of youth librarianship, but in children's specialties in fields such as medicine and law.

Studies of recruitment in the 1980s suggest the increasing difficulty of recruiting bright young students into service occupations that pay little and are perceived as having low status because they involve working with children. Research also shows that the majority of students entering the field of librarianship are older and found out about the profession from working in libraries. The profession has promoted the "each one reach one" concept. Job satisfaction, however, is related to more than salary and status. Loriene Roy, in a study for the University of Illinois in 1986, found that 97 percent of the respondents to a survey of children's librarians in Illinois declared that if they were to start their careers over, they would choose the same jobs again.

CONTINUING ISSUES

Staffing. Among the many negative factors raised are reduced offering of youth service courses in some library school curricula, distances students must travel from states that do not have ALA-accredited library schools, the fact that 58 percent of public libraries did not have any librarian whose primary job is serving children, and the shortage of personnel. This situation is not unique to the U.S. Lack of easy access to training, the high cost of studying at some distance from home, and understaffing are concerns found in many parts of the world.

On the other hand, the field does have many interested, dedicated, and talented professionals, new and experienced, who are both aware of the problems and determined to serve children.

Access. Guaranteeing children access to information remains a challenge for librarians. Censorship is ever present and will always be an issue. Adoption of textbook series in the U.S. has become a constant and intensifying battle. Librarians *must* know their collections and their community, and they must have a well-developed and endorsed selection policy.

Another aspect of access is what is being termed "the haves and the have nots," the information rich and the information poor. Is new technology available to children on an equal basis in public libraries? Are microcomputers and online services available to children? Many children have access to computers at their schools and some have access to computers at home, but many public libraries lag in providing new technologies, especially to children. Are children allowed to check out videos? Do children understand how to use the technology? If not, are staff trained and available to assist them? Are children's special needs being considered? Are the children of working parents able to get to the public library? These are a few of the issues concerning access that the professionals who work with children must constantly assess.

Many speak of children and young adults as the future of the nation, but the actions and funding patterns of many library managements do not demonstrate that belief. New impetus is needed for examination and thought about the field of public librarianship for youth as we pass the centennial decade of these services in the U.S.

JILL L. LOCKE

Chile

Chile occupies the southern Pacific coast of South America. Comprising 756,945 sq.km. in its continental zone, and claiming 1,250,000 sq.km. in Antarctica, it is bounded by Peru, Bolivia, and Argentina. Pop. (1990 est.) 13,173,000. The inhabitants are distributed between the Andes Mountains and the Pacific Ocean. About one-third of the people live in the capital city, Santiago. The official language is Spanish.

History. The early inhabitants of Chile kept no written records. The Spaniards entered the area in 1535, but they were not interested in books or reading—they were constantly at war with the Araucanian Indians. Some few written works by Europeans living in Chile, mainly epic poems and chronicles, were published in Europe. During the 17th and 18th centuries, the influence of religious orders on the cultural life of the colony was evident and many private libraries were formed. Ecclesiastical collections were the largest. In 1767, when the Jesuits left Chile, they had 20,000 books in their schools throughout the country.

The book trade was started in 1807 by Manuel Riesco. The National Library was created in 1813; the government gave its first impulse to public libraries under President Manuel Montt (1851–61) by creating 43 public libraries annexed to schools. In 1863 an educational reform required the creation of school libraries.

Central children's library at the Public Library in Bridgetown, Barbados.

During the 1900s Chilean governments have shown a marked interest in the development of both school and public libraries. However, geographical configuration and economic conditions have hindered a steady progress. The introduction of new technologies has meant an accelerated development of academic and special libraries.

José Toribio Medina (1852–1930), distinguished bibliographer, was commissioned by the government to visit archives and libraries in South America and Europe in order to obtain historical documents related to Chile. His works and his own library are preserved in the National Library.

National Library. The National Library was founded on August 13, 1813, during the first years of Chile's independence. Its basic collection consisted of 8,000 volumes that belonged to the colonial library of the Jesuits and had been preserved in the University of San Felipe until they were transferred to the National Library. Ten years later, its holdings had increased to 12,000 volumes. By the late 1980s its collection totaled more than 4,000,000 volumes. One of the most important sources for the increase has been the legal deposit requirement established by decree in 1825. Publishers are required to deliver 15 copies of every book or pamphlet printed in Chile to the National Library.

The Library is distinguished for its collection of Chilean literature. It maintains a manuscript collection and is a depository library of United States government publications. Since 1877, it has published the important national bibliography, the *Anuario de la Prensa Chilena* (Yearbook of the Chilean Press), which changed its name to *Bibliografía Chilena* (Chilean Bibliography) in 1976.

The National Library began implementing NOTIS (Northwestern Total Integrated System) in the

La Biblioteca Central de la Universidad de Chile

Central Library of the University of Chile, Santiago.

1980s. Using MARC tapes, the project was designed to include the National Library's collection as well as the collections of Chilean universities.

Academic Libraries. A decree of 1981 introduced a profound reform in the higher educational system. This reform allows for the creation of autonomous and private universities, as well as professional and technical institutes of higher education. Careers considered not university professions were transferred to technical institutes.

Before 1981 there were 8 universities, some of them with branches in major cities. By 1983, there were 24 institutions of higher education in the country: 11 universities, 2 academies of pedagogical sciences, 5 professional institutes receiving government support, and 6 private establishments. These institutions have well-organized libraries that served more than 127,000 students in the late 1980s.

The University of Chile, created in 1738, has 64 autonomous libraries that serve the university community and the general public. The Pablo Neruda Library (donated by the poet), Andrés Bello manuscripts, and Chilean imprints to 1849 are among the special collections maintained at the main library. Libraries of the faculties of Agriculture, Medicine, and Sanitary Engineering and Environmental Sciences are active participants in national and international information programs. The Information Systems Service provides access to several national and international databases and compiled, in a joint venture with the School of Library Science, a "Union Catalog of Periodical Publications" at the University of Chile.

The Catholic University has a centralized library administration with 21 libraries. In a new building, the main library had modern audiovisual resources and excellent facilities in the 1980s. The central administration was engaged in creating a bibliographic database using the MARC format and automating circulation processes. The library also had access to the Dialog retrieval service.

Public Libraries. The public library system is administered by the Department of Libraries, Archives, and Museums in the Ministry of Education. In 1977 the government initiated a National Plan for Libraries to create more public libraries. A coordinating office establishes agreements with municipalities, rural community centers, and penitentiaries for the creation of new libraries. The Coordinating Office provides books and technical assistance and the institutions, their facilities and personnel. These libraries extend free borrowing privileges to patrons living in their areas. The increase of this type of library has been remarkable. Before 1976, there were 56 public libraries. By 1982 there were 188, with more than 3,344,000 registered borrowers.

School Libraries. A decree of 1813 stated that every school should have funds for books to serve students. In 1863 a decree ordered that a library be established in the main school of every major city. Although the legal evidence shows that since Chile's independence government authorities have understood the importance of school libraries, development has been poor and slow. In 1962 only 259 out of 5,831 schools had library facilities. In 1972 there were 7,845 schools, yet only 295 had some kind of library service. In 1982 there were 9,848 schools, with 2,819,000 enrolled students, but only 634 had library service.

School libraries in Chile can be classified as those

Libraries in Chile (1990)

Type of library	Number of administrative units (main libraries)	Number of service points (branches, mobile stops, etc.)	Volumes in collections	Population served
National[a]	1	2	3,514,000	--
Academic[b]	169	--	4,883,000	--
Public[a]	293	293	1,054,000	27,450
School[b]	820	--	3,586,000	--
Special[c]	4	6	86,000	--

[a]1989 data
[b]1987 data
[c]1985 data

Source: Unesco, *Statistical Yearbook,* 1991

in public schools that possess a small book collection and offer a few hours of library service and those that have a well-rounded book collection with at least one person—a teacher or a librarian—in charge of the library.

In 1976 the Ministry of Education designed and approved a national system of school libraries, which was being developed in the 1980s.

Special Libraries. Special libraries are well organized and equipped in Chile. They offer their services to patrons in the government, national and international organizations, professional and learned societies, industry, banks, and binational institutes. They showed a significant development in services. In 1976 there were 299 and in 1983, 272, excluding the special university libraries.

The use of computers in the libraries of the Institute of Natural Resources, National Development Corporation, Ministry of Housing, National Telecommunications Company, and others has allowed them to create databases and participate in a nationwide information and documentation network designed and coordinated by the National Commission for Science and Technology (CONICYT).

The National Commission of Nuclear Energy and international organizations such as the United Nations Economic Commission for Latin America (ECLA), the Center for Latin American Demographic Studies (CELADE), and the Institute of Latin American Iron and Steel (ILAFA) maintain databases providing information in their fields.

The Institute of Technology (INTEC), the Corporation of Computer and Information Technology (ECOM), and the Chilean North American Institute provide online information from international commercial databases.

The Profession. In 1946 the University of Chile retained Edward Martin Heiliger of the U.S. to help establish a school of library science. In 1947 the Central Library for the University of Chile inaugurated a Library School, which was officially sanctioned by a Ministry of Education decree in 1959. Approximately 940 students were graduated from 1947 to 1980.

Ten continuing education courses on automation, information systems, organization of archives, statistics, and *American Cataloguing Rules,* Second Edition, were offered to practicing librarians from 1977 to 1981. Similar courses are offered by the Colegio de Bibliotecarios and the National Center for Information and Documentation.

Library students developed various projects, among them a University Union Catalogue, a survey of national and international databases, and a national bibliography entitled *Bibliografía de Chile* (Chilean Bibliography), published in 1982.

The University of Chile also offered courses in some of its southern and northern headquarters during the period 1965–80. The University of Concepción offered a Library Science program from 1975 to 1979.

Chilean librarians are represented by the Colegio de Bibliotecarios, an organization that superseded the Asociación de Bibliotecarios, established in 1953. The Colegio de Bibliotecarios, created by a 1969 law, had more than 1,300 members in the 1980s and has prepared several publications, including a "Code of Professional Ethics," "Standards for Chilean Public and School Libraries," and "Chilean Standards for Documentation."

REFERENCES

Alejandro Burgos and Héctor Gómez, *Bases de Datos Bibliográficos en Chile* (1982).

Juan R. Freudenthal and Héctor Gómez, *Library Education in Chile* (Libri, 1983).

M. TERESA HERRERO DE ALVAREZ

China

The People's Republic of China covers a total area of about 9,596,961 square kilometers in eastern Asia on the western shores of the Pacific Ocean, with a continental land boundary of more than 20,000 kilometers. China adjoins Tadzhikistan, Kirgizia, Russia, and Mongolia on the north; Korea on the east; and Vietnam, Laos, Burma, India, Bhutan, Nepal, Pakistan, and Afghanistan on the south. The continental coastline is more than 18,000 kilometers long. More than 4,000 islands are scattered along China's coastline. China is divided into 31 provinces, 5 autonomous regions, and 3 municipalities. Population (1990 est.) 1,139,060,000. It is a unified multi-national country with 56 ethnic groups, among which the Han nationality is the largest. The official language is Chinese.

History. Ancient inscriptions, cast, engraved, or impressed on permanent materials, are hardly to be considered "books." But we may say Chinese books originated from ancient literal records and archives.

The oracle-bone inscriptions are the earliest known Chinese documents preserved in their original form today. They were inscribed on tortoise shell and ox bone about 3,500 years ago. Early inscriptions cast or engraved on bronze have also been found; some have been preserved for about 3,200 years. As for the inscriptions on stone, some ancient stone drums with inscriptions engraved on them were made about 2,200 years ago.

The direct ancestors of Chinese books are believed to have been the tablets made of bamboo or

A view of the new building of the National Library of China, opened in June 1990.

wood that were connected by strings and used like paper books. They appeared from the 14th century B.C. to the 3rd or 4th century A.D. and prospered from the 8th century B.C. to the 2nd century A.D. Another kind of book written on silk rolls appeared in the 5th or 4th century B.C. down to the middle of the 3rd century A.D. In A.D. 105 paper made from the bark of trees, old rags, and fishing nets was invented by T'sai Lun, a man of talent in charge of government manufacture of the East Han Dynasty. During the 2nd and 3rd centuries A.D., paper was more and more used as a writing material. During that period, bamboo, silk, and paper were simultaneously used as writing materials. Writing tools, such as various forms of Chinese brush-pens and black ink, had been used, of course, along with the various writing materials.

The technique for multiplication of written works before the invention of block printing involved taking inked impressions from stone or other inscriptions by pressing paper on their surfaces. Moreover, seals, cast from metal or cut in stone or jade, were impressed on soft and sticky clay— and later, on silk and paper—to make duplicate inscriptions. Such techniques have been considered forerunners of mass production of early writings and eventually led to the invention of block printing.

Printing from engraved wood block appeared in the first years of the T'ang Dynasty or even earlier (about the 8th century A.D.). At the beginning of the 9th century, calendars were printed in that way. And an extant book, the *Diamond Sutra,* which was printed in 868, with the printing date in it, shows very nice printing technique. It can be presumed that the invention of block printing must have been much earlier than the time the book was printed.

In the middle of the 11th century, during the Northern Sung Period, Bi Sheng invented movable type for printing. It was not necessary to print many copies of books at that time, so the former method of printing from engraved wood block was still often used. With the further development and application of movable-type printing, the number of books printed by the method grew in successive generations.

In 213 B.C. the first emperor of China of the Chin Dynasty ordered the burning of a great many books except those in certain categories and in the possession of learned officials. Large-scale recovery of ancient works was not begun until the reign of Emperor Wu (ruled 180–140 B.C.), during the Han Dynasty. And for the first time in Chinese history a centralized imperial library was established where a wide range of materials was systematically collected and well kept.

In 26 B.C., under the reign of Emperor Cheng of the Han Dynasty, a decree was issued to collect books again and designated Liu Hsiang (81–8 B.C.), a state counselor, to examine the collection with his assistants. Liu recorded the headings of the chapters and wrote a summary for each book to be presented to the emperor. The result of these summaries was a collection of critical bibliographies known as *Pieh-lu,* or "Separate Record." After he died with the task unfinished, his son, Liu Hsin (d. A.D. 23) succeeded him in the work. He arranged all the books then in the imperial library into seven categories and compiled a classification catalogue known as *Chi-lüeh,* or seven summaries. Liu Hsiang's work is the earliest known bibliography in China and Liu Hsin's scheme is the first system of subject classification and descriptive cataloguing of Chinese books.

A modified fourfold scheme made in the 3rd century A.D. and revised again and again afterward has been used by Chinese bibliographers for more than 1,500 years. Even now many libraries in China still use such a revised scheme to classify the ancient Chinese books in their collections.

In A.D. 1407, under the decree of the Emperor Cheng Zu of the Ming Dynasty, the compilation of the famous *Yong Le Encyclopedia* was finished and the imperial library called the Wen Yuan Pavilion was founded. *Yong Le Encyclopedia* was the largest encyclopedia in China, including a total of 11,919 volumes. They were arranged according to phonetic rhymes, reproduced from more than 7,000 extant books. At that time only one set of a handwritten master copy was prepared; afterward another set was copied. The original set was unfortunately destroyed and of the second set only a little more than 200 volumes were preserved, most of which are kept in the National Library of China.

Wen Yuan Pavilion was the imperial library of the Ming Dynasty (1369–1644). The remainders of the ancient books from the preceding Sung (960–1279) and Yuan Dynasties (1279–1368) provided its basic collection. There also were the books of the Ming Dynasty that were especially rich in local chronicles.

In the last years of the Emperor K'ang-hsi (ruled 1661–1722) in the Ch'ing (Qing) Dynasty, compila-

Libraries in China, People's Republic of (1990)

Type of library	Number of administrative units (main libraries)	Number of service points (branches, mobile stops, etc.)	Volumes in collections	Annual expenditures (Renminbi)	Population served	Professional staff (with certificate, diploma, etc.)	Total staff
National	1	1	15,980,000	35,500,000	1,692,347	1,159	1,689
Academic(1)	1,162	--	374,000,000	177,300,000	4,407,000	32,560	38,130
Public	2,527	--	290,640,000	302,710,000	6,030,000	26,900	40,247
Special(2)	4,500	--	225,000,000	--	--	--	--

Notes: (1) Including libraries of universities or colleges as well as military universities or military colleges in 1990
(2) Including libraries or Documentation and Information Centers of Chinese Academy of Sciences and its institutes, of Chinese Academy of Social Sciences and its institutes, of Chinese Academy of Agricultural Science, of Chinese Academy of Geological Science and of Chinese Academy of Medical Science, etc.

tion of another encyclopedia, "A Collection of Books of Ancient and Modern Times," was begun. It was completed in 1725 and was later printed with movable type. This giant work consisted of 10,000 volumes with about 100,000,000 words together with many fine pictures. At the end of Ch'ing Dynasty it was copied twice.

During the rule of the Emperor Tsien Long (1736–1795) in the Ch'ing Dynasty, "The Complete Library of the Four Treasures" had its beginning in 1772 and was completed a decade later. It consisted of 3,502 titles bound into 36,000 volumes. It was the largest collection of books in the history of China. It was copied by hand in four copies at first and three more copies afterward. Now there are only four copies left.

The collection of the Wen Yuan Pavilion of the Ming Dynasty was inherited by the Cabinet Library of the Ch'ing Dynasty, but a lot of the collection was lost. In 1910 the remaining part was transferred to the Metropolitan Library of Peking and thus it became the first collection of rare books for the National Library of China.

National Library. The National Library's predecessor was the Metropolitan Library of Peking, opened in 1912. Apart from inheriting the books from the imperial libraries, the National Library, when opened, got a number of important and famous publications collected and donated by the government. All these laid the foundation for the collection of books. Up to 1949, it had already had more than 1,400,000 volumes (items) and 120 staff members. After the establishment of the People's Republic of China in 1949, its collections were mainly augmented through channels such as sample copies from domestic publishers, selective purchase of both old and new domestic publications, donations and allocations from institutions and individuals, selection and ordering of foreign publications, international exchange of publications, and so on. By 1987 the National Library of China had 14,270,000 books, magazine issues, and other items, and more than 1,685 staff members. It is a comprehensive research library under the leadership of the Ministry of Culture of China. It seeks to perform the functions required of other national libraries throughout the world. A new building for the library covering a floor space of 140,000 square meters and capable of providing for modern equipment was completed in 1987. The computer had begun to be used in some professional work by the mid-1980s and further applications of computer technology to library service were adopted and developed.

Academic Libraries. Under the leadership of the National Commission of Education of the State Council and relevant administrative offices of the provincial governments or those of the same level, the Commissions of University and College Libraries lead the nationwide or regional university and college libraries respectively. There are more than 1,060 such libraries in all parts of the country. Some of them belong to the national key universities, such as the Library of Beijing (Peking) University and the Library of Qinghwa (Tsinghua) University. The former was established as early as 1902. In the early years of the 20th century, the Chinese revolutionary pioneers and Marxists Lee Da-zhao and Mao Tse-tung worked in it. In 1987 the Library had a total collection of more than 4,000,000 volumes (items). A new building was opened in 1975 with 24,500 sq.m. of floor space. In 1987 the Library of Qinghua University held more than 2,300,000 volumes (items) in its collection, concentrating on natural science and technology. These two libraries and some other university or college libraries used computers in their work.

A front view of the new building of the National Library of China, opened in June 1990.

Public Libraries. Under the leadership of the Ministry of Culture, the libraries of the cities, including those of their streets and lanes, and the libraries of counties or districts, including those of their inferior districts and villages, are all public libraries. They serve many readers, offering help in various subjects and striving to raise their working abilities in production and management. Although the libraries of provinces, autonomous regions, and municipalities and other large cities or some medium-sized cities with comparatively large populations also serve the public, their main service is seen as meeting the needs of economic construction and scientific research. They are research libraries or in some degree close to research libraries.

The Shanghai Library (about 7,370,000 items in 1987) is a notable city library; the largest public library in China, it is renowned for its collection of 1,500,000 classical Chinese books. Others include Nanking Library (about 6,410,000 items in 1987) for Jiangsu (Kiangsu) Province and Wuhan for Hubei (Hopei) Province.

School Libraries. Apart from the many libraries or reading rooms of primary and middle schools, separate children's libraries were established in some places. Under the leadership of the Ministry of Culture alone, there were 45 city or regional children's libraries in the late 1980s and most of the county, district, and city libraries have children's reading rooms, large or small. Children's Palaces or Children's Activities Centers in some cities also have their own libraries or reading rooms. All of the children's libraries or reading rooms outside the schools are used by students and their teachers and sometimes they are open for children before school age.

Special Libraries. Libraries in the system of the Chinese Academy of Sciences, including the

Academy Library, the regional libraries of the Academy, and the institutional libraries, total 142. The Library of the Chinese Academy of Sciences is a major comprehensive scientific and technological library. It collects books, periodicals, scientific reports, patents, proceedings, professional publications, and other materials. In 1987 it had a collection of 5,420,000 volumes (items) and a staff of more than 430. In that library the Scientific Information Office was established in order to combine library service with information service. This library and others in the system of the Chinese Academy of Sciences have used computer technology to process and retrieve data from foreign source documents in the sciences.

Other academic or special libraries are under the leadership of the Chinese Academy of Social Sciences and the ministries and commissions of the State Council, such as the Library of the Chinese Academy of Agricultural Sciences, the Library of Medical Sciences, the Library of Geology, and the Library of Nationalities.

The Profession. Some 50 universities or colleges have departments or specialities of library science. One of the two oldest departments of library science was established in Wuhan University (now merged into the College of Library and Information Science of that university). The other is in Beijing University. In some universities and a few research libraries, graduate students continue to study for the master's degree and some students are sent abroad to study as graduate or undergraduate students or visiting scholars. Many libraries established schools or classes for vocational training: for example, the Spare-time Professional College for Staff Members in the National Library of China has enrolled classes of students through entrance examination. The National Library, other libraries, and the Administrative Bureau of Library Affairs of the Ministry of Culture also run many short training classes for staff members on various subjects. In addition, there are some library vocational middle schools or library vocational classes in the middle schools.

The China Society of Library Science was established in July 1979. The members of its third council were elected for a term of four years by the representatives at the third plenary session in November 1987. Its journal is the *Bulletin of China Society of Library Science* (quarterly). The Society holds meetings for discussion on library science or exchange of experience and provides seminars or training classes on special topics. The Society had registered more than 8,000 members on the national level by the 1987. Under the Society, 30 more Societies of Library Science are scattered in provinces, autonomous regions, and municipalities. They are enthusiastic in pursuing professional activities and most of them publish society journals of their own. Sometimes the societies of several neighboring areas unite to carry on their professional activities.

Beijing has hosted a number of international meetings of librarians, including seminars of the International Federation of Library Associations and institutions and meetings of the directors of national libraries in Asia and Oceania.

DING ZHIGANG

Chubarian, O. S.
(1908–1976)

Ogan Stepanovich Chubarian was a specialist in library science who greatly stimulated the development of library science and practice in the former U.S.S.R. through his many-sided scientific, pedagogical, and administrative activities.

He was born in Rostov-on-Don on October 8, 1908, and received professional training at Advanced Bibliographic Courses, which functioned at the State Book Chamber of the R.S.F.S.R. Chubarian prepared a candidate dissertation on "The Technical Book in Russia during the Reign of Peter the Great." He was granted a Doctor's degree for his monograph "General Library Science."

Chubarian began his career as a rank-and-file librarian and in 1963 became one of the senior officers of the National Library of the Soviet Union. He published over a hundred works dealing with various problems of librarianship, bibliography, and bibliology. "General Library Science," one of his most important works, gave contemporary interpretations of the role of librarianship in Soviet society. This work formulated and revealed in detail the main principles of library development in the U.S.S.R.: the state character of librarianship, the availability of libraries for all, planned organization of the library network, centralization, and the drawing of representatives of the population into the work of libraries and their management. Chubarian was the first Soviet library specialist to cover the essence and place of library science in the general system of sciences from a Marxist standpoint.

Many works by Chubarian were devoted to the study of current problems of library development and the activities of libraries, such as problems of centralization of librarianship, cooperation of libraries and information centers, surveys of readership, development of national libraries of the Union republics, and acquisitions. Chubarian laid stress on the common goals and tasks of libraries that should not be ignored by any library institution, regardless of its specific character.

Chubarian gave much of his time and effort to bibliography; he advocated the recommendatory bibliography as an efficient instrument in the guidance of reading. His idea that library and bibliographic activities should be carried out in close cooperation represents one of the leading concepts in defining the role of Soviet libraries. In his studies theoretical propositions and pragmatic conclusions interlace, and the examination of problems is closely connected with the practice and tasks of libraries.

For many years he guided the activities of important Soviet library institutions such as the Moscow State Institute of Culture, the State Public Technical and Scientific Library, and the State Lenin Library. He was also Vice-Chairman of the Council for Coordination of Research in Library Science and Bibliography attached to the U.S.S.R. Ministry of Culture.

He was one of the founders of two periodicals—*Sovetskoye Bibliotekovedeniye* ("Soviet Library Science") and *Nauchniye i Tekhnicheskiye Biblioteki SSSR* ("Scientific and Technical Libraries of the U.S.S.R."), which greatly stimulated research in the field.

He had many students, whom he helped to write dissertations and become library specialists. He also directed many important surveys, and through his efforts the following studies were published: *The Soviet Reader* (1968), *The Book and Reading in the Life of Towns* (1973), and *The Book and Reading in the Life of the Soviet Village* (1978).

He edited many collections of articles such as *Lenin and Contemporary Problems of Library Science; History of Librarianship in the U.S.S.R.: Documents and Materials; Problems of Sociology and Psychology of Reading;* and a *Dictionary of Library Terms.*

Chubarian did much in the way of acquainting foreign librarians with the state of library science and practice in the Soviet Union. He worked persistently to exchange information on problems of library development; he took part in organizing many international conferences, discussions, and joint research projects and in developing international book exchange. He participated in many IFLA sessions and worked on a number of reports. In 1966 he was elected Chairman of the IFLA Bibliographic Committee, and later he headed the Committee on Library Science.

His works have been translated into many foreign languages. The U.S.S.R. Ministry of Culture and party and state authorities of the country frequently invited him to act as adviser when important documents concerning librarianship were drawn up.

Chubarian was granted the title of Professor and the honorary title "Merited Worker of Culture of the R.S.F.S.R." He was also granted state awards; a library in Artashat, in the Armenian S.S.R., was named after him. He died in Moscow on January 7, 1976.

E. A. FENELONOV

Circulation Services

Circulation services is the term used to describe many of the most important and visible activities of today's libraries. Circulation services, broadly defined, include all activities that are involved in making library books, journals, and other materials directly available to the people who need them. Thus, check-out and check-in (or charge-out and charge-in, as these activities are sometimes called) is the central function of these services.

Almost all libraries, except those whose collections comprise especially rare and valuable material, *circulate* (lend) library materials for use outside the library. Circulation is sometimes called "home use." Library policy varies widely from institution to institution with respect to the types of materials that are circulated, the length of time patrons may borrow an item, whether the loan period may be extended, and whether patrons may *reserve* (place a hold on) an item for future use.

History of Circulation Services. Circulation of library materials, a common practice throughout the world today, is a relatively recent development in the history of libraries. Building large collections of library materials has been a major focus for centuries, but the use of the collections was much more limited in the past than it is today. It must be remembered in this day of comparatively inexpensive, expendable paperbacks (at least in the Western world) that books were a nearly priceless possession, especially before Gutenberg.

The library of the past, much like rare books libraries and archives of today, was primarily regarded as a safe repository for books and the other priceless and nearly irreplaceable materials entrusted to its care, rather than as a facility designed to foster use of the materials. A common name for the library in an early monastery or cathedral was *armorium,* literally the book chest or press where the books were kept. A librarian of the day was known as the *bibliothecarius* or *custos librorum,* keeper of the books.

Books could be loaned for copying and also just for reading. Interlibrary loan was used to extend the range of materials available to the library's patrons. Although materials were usually exchanged between neighboring collections, loans were sometimes made between countries such as France and Greece or England and Austria.

The librarian's primary duties in caring for these collections of books were to protect the volumes, to increase the number of holdings, and to ensure that no volumes be lost or damaged. Volumes were loaned, of course, but the librarian was admonished to "Let not a book be given to anyone without a proper and sufficient voucher and let this be entered on the roll."

As the number of volumes making up a library's collection increased, the armoria gave way to shelves and later to reading rooms. In many cases the collection was separated into two parts, one for public use and another for private use. Books in the public collections were the first to be chained to the desks, rather than the more valuable reference volumes. By the 18th century, after printed books became more common, the manuscript volumes were usually chained solely for their protection.

Early Systems. Circulation rules varied widely from place to place but in general followed guidelines

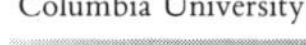
Columbia University

Circulation Desk, Brooklyn Public Library, Brownsville Branch, 1919. (Brooklyn, New York)

Guelph University

Circulation attendant at Guelph University Library, Ontario, Canada, scanning a patron's badge to charge out a book.

set by monastic libraries. In the Sorbonne Library in the 14th century, for example, books were to be used only in the building in which the library was housed and, if taken from the library, had to be returned the same day. If anyone other than a professor or student took a book from the library, a deposit of equal value was required. In some other libraries students could check out a book for a year; in others, the more valuable books were kept under triple lock and key, so that the presence of more than one keeper was required before a volume could even be seen.

The first public circulating libraries were the commercial circulating libraries and subscription libraries that began in England and on the Continent in the 18th century. The commercial circulating libraries were generally established by booksellers or groups of readers and would generally be called "rental collections" today. Most of these collections consisted of popular fiction and nonfiction. At about the same time, subscription libraries came into being. Readers in a community would form a society with a library for use by members only. In general, the quality of the materials available in these libraries was much better than in the commercial collections. As one example, the Library Company of Philadelphia, founded in 1731 by Benjamin Franklin and others, continues to operate as a research collection of early Americana.

The modern public library began about 1850 with the establishment of free public circulating libraries. By this time, collections were larger, the number of patrons had increased, and the need to manage borrowing records became more pronounced. (*See also* Public Libraries.)

Almost all early libraries used some sort of ledger system or daybook to keep track of borrowers and the materials they checked out. The daybook consisted of a set of line entries to record each day's transactions. Thus one entry would be made in the daybook for each item checked out to a patron. When a book was returned, either a new entry would be made for it or the old one crossed out. The ledger system usually involved creating a page for each patron on which loans and returns could be recorded. The borrower's identification number was attached to the book so that the proper ledger sheet could be located when the book was checked in.

The ledger system made it possible to monitor use of the collections, to know a patron's preferences, and to suggest other materials that might be of interest. In small school libraries, a ledger enabled teachers to monitor a child's reading progress. Today, at a time of concern about privacy, such detailed records of a patron's library use are seldom kept. Instead, patrons who wish to do so may have interest profiles created for them to guide the library staff both in acquiring new material and in recommending items from the collection.

The main problems with the ledger system were the difficulties encountered in searching for overdue materials or in placing holds on items checked out to other patrons. In spite of those drawbacks, however, the ledger system had some advantages and remained a popular way to handle circulation. Aside from its simplicity and ease of use, the ledger system provided quite a bit of additional information to the librarian. Although ledger systems and daybooks have largely been replaced by more modern methods, they are still occasionally used in small, specialized collections.

Another early method of keeping track of circulating materials was the "dummy," whereby a piece of paper, block of wood, or other placeholder was inserted on the shelf in place of the item on loan. The patron's name and the item borrowed were recorded in a diary. This method is still sometimes used, not for circulation, but to indicate large blocks of materials that are shelved elsewhere. It also survives in some vertical files, where a user records name, date, and materials borrowed on a loan form and puts that form in the file in place of the materials.

Modern Systems. As the size of the collection, number of patrons, and volume of transactions grew, ledger or daybook systems became unwieldy, and other, more flexible systems were developed. Temporary slips containing the borrower's name, address, and registered number were made for each item checked out. These slips could be filed by call number, due date, or borrower's name, and would be destroyed when the item was returned. In some libraries, multiple slips were made for each loan, each of which could be stored in a separate file. Obviously these systems required careful discharging to make sure that returned items were properly credited. While these systems made it somewhat easier for librarians to detect overdue materials and to place holds, they created additional paperwork and are seldom used today except in some non-automated libraries.

The permanent slip or card, prepared at the time the book is accessed, is an outgrowth of the temporary slip. Identifying information for the book is printed on the card, which is removed from the book and filed by due date when the book is borrowed. This approach is still often used in libraries, although some problems may result from illegible or forged patron information, but it is quick and efficient. It is particularly widely used at academic library reserve desks, where the transaction volume is high and the loan period short.

An extension of the basic idea was developed by the Newark Public Library in 1900 and is now marketed by several vendors. When a patron registers at a library, a metal plate is created showing the borrower's name, address, registration number, and any other information the librarian wants to have on file, such as borrower class (J for Juvenile, for example), expiration date, and so forth. This information is imprinted on the book card at the time the item is checked out. The process works exactly like the permanent card system, except that there is less chance for error in recording the borrower information, and the device can set due dates automatically for various classes of materials and borrowers. One drawback of this method is that the anonymity provided by recording only the patron's registration number is lost. The saving in library staff time resulting from not having to look up patron names and addresses is a bonus, however. There have been several variations on the permanent card system, primarily designed to provide additional access points and to save labor, but as computer-based systems became ever more affordable, card systems are less and less commonly used.

Automated Systems. With the advent of electronic data processing in the late 1940s, it was natural that librarians should investigate and apply this technology to circulation services. Most of the early efforts at automating circulation services were batch processing systems, in many cases using punched cards. These systems were fast and reliable, eliminated the need for filing, and could produce overdue notices on demand. But, helpful as they were, they did not meet all of the librarians' needs for circulation information. It was still not possible to tell patrons what titles were charged out to them without a special computer run and, because most early systems posted changes overnight, it was not possible to know the status of a given item between runs.

Further, many of the early automated circulation systems were based on exceptions—that is, records were kept in the circulation system only for those materials that were checked out. There was no information about other materials that were supposedly in the collection, and it was difficult to locate items in order to place holds on them.

Librarians are still concerned about issues of privacy, and today's systems are generally designed to preserve the item-patron links only while the material is actually checked out. Nevertheless, most automated circulation systems are able to provide much better management information than the earlier manual systems could deliver. Although no item-patron link is preserved, aggregate statistics on collection use can be generated according to a variety of criteria, such as patron types, call numbers, collections, locations, and so forth.

Great advances in computing power, rapid declines in the cost of data storage, and much better file-handling techniques gave rise to development of the first online circulation systems in the early 1970s. Some were developed by librarians themselves, while others were developed and marketed by vendors. These systems now range from simple microcomputer-based systems designed (and priced!) to meet the needs of even the smallest school or public libraries to very large networks of interconnected systems designed to support multiple institutions in a geographic area or sharing a particular focus.

Scanning technology has also revolutionized circulation services. Early systems depended on mechanical devices to identify library patrons. Today's systems depend on labels or codes that can be scanned electronically to identify both items and patrons. Optical character recognition (OCR) and bar code scanners have both been used, although bar code scanning is by far the most commonly used technique today.

Although many automated circulation systems were designed and developed as relatively straightforward single-function systems, today they are rarely used in isolation. Instead, automated circulation is generally viewed as one tool to support circulation services and is also usually viewed as just one component of an integrated library system. These integrated systems enable a librarian to keep track of an item from the time a decision is made to acquire it, during its entry into the collection, throughout many long years of its use, and, finally, to the time of its withdrawal or disappearance from the collection through loss, damage, or other mishap.

The characteristics of such systems change rapidly as new technology appears that makes better support possible at ever-decreasing costs, thus widening the range of institutions that may be considering automating their circulation services to include libraries of virtually every size and type. The newest systems provide many functions that library users can perform themselves, such as requesting an item for purchase, placing a hold on an item, and, in some cases, renewing circulating materials electronically. They also provide greatly expanded management information statistics and reporting features.

Circulation Functions. Circulation activities include one or more of the following:

Blocks. A block is used to prevent a patron from checking out any additional library materials for a variety of reasons, such as too many items checked out already, fines owed, lost books, or other problems. In a manual or an automated system, library staff members may override a block with the proper authorization.

Queens Borough Public Library

Laminated card with individual bar code, part of the computerized circulation system in the Queens Borough Public Library.

Calendar. Every circulation system—whether automated or manual—must have a calendar for calculating loan periods and for stipulating when materials are due. Library policies vary widely, and consequently flexibility in maintaining the calendar is very important. For example, the calendar needs to be able to allow for holidays, "snow days," and other anomalies.

Check-Out. Library materials are temporarily loaned to patrons for a predefined period of time, the "loan period." Whether the process is manual or automated, some identifying information about the patron is recorded and linked with information identifying the particular item being checked out, such as its call number and title, bar code number, or other unique identifier. Check-out is sometimes called *charging*.

Check-In. Library materials are returned to the collection and reshelved in the home library. In most systems, any link between the patron and the library materials is broken. That is, no record of a patron's circulation transactions is retained once the materials have been returned to the library. Check-in is sometimes called *discharging*.

Facilities Booking. Many libraries—especially public ones—have conference rooms and other facilities that patrons may use. The process is usually similar to circulation of library materials, except that patrons may reserve a facility for a specific date and time.

Fines. Most libraries levy fines or other penalties to encourage timely return of materials. In a manual system, circulation desk personnel will calculate any fines due, based on the type of material, the patron category, and the calendar. In automated systems, the computer uses the same information to calculate the amount due. In both manual and automated systems, members of the library staff can use their own discretion in reducing fines, waiving them, forgiving them altogether, or other methods of handling problems.

Interlibrary Loan. This activity is sometimes included as part of circulation services, but more often is treated as a separate function. The primary difference between interlibrary loan and other charge-out/charge-in activities is that the loan is made to another library or other institution, which assumes responsibility for the actions of its patron.

Materials Booking. In addition to circulating books and other conventional library materials, many libraries also loan items such as movie projectors, overhead projectors, computers, computer software, and videocassette recorders. Circulation of these materials is similar to circulation of other library materials, except that the loan period is usually shorter and the patron can reserve a particular item for a specific date and time, as in booking facilities.

Overdue Notification. Both manual and automated systems notify patrons when they have failed to return items borrowed by the date due. Automated systems generate the notices automatically, based on the library's loan policies and calendar information stored in the system. In a manual system, members of the circulation desk staff periodically check a file of materials in circulation to see whether any are overdue.

Patron File. Whether manual or automated, circulation services require an up-to-date list of library users. The information may be stored in a computer file or a card file, but it must be updated frequently to ensure that addresses, phone numbers, and patron category and status information are correct.

Renewal. Users may arrange to keep one or more items for a second loan period or an even longer period. Some libraries allow more or less unlimited renewals, but others control the process more closely.

Reserve. This term is used for two entirely separate circulation functions with different meanings.

In most libraries, users may "reserve" or "place a hold on" materials that they want to borrow but that are at present unavailable because they are in use by another patron, at the bindery, or not yet catalogued. Most automated circulation systems produce notices to send to patrons notifying them that the items they have placed on hold are now available. Items that have been placed on hold but are not claimed within a specified period of time are returned to the collection or given to the next person in the hold queue. In some systems, the list of users who have placed a hold on a particular item can be reordered or manipulated.

In academic libraries, faculty members may make specific materials available to members of a certain class by putting these materials "on reserve." The materials may come from the library's holdings or from their own collections. Students may borrow these items for limited amounts of time (perhaps two hours) and may not take them out of the library building. The penalties for not returning reserve materials when due are usually heavier than for regular materials.

Tracers. Circulation systems can place markers in the records for lost or missing items. In this way, if an item turns up, it can be returned to its proper shelving location. Tracers are useful in letting patrons know that an item the library owns is unavailable for loan because it is lost or missing.

As modern circulation systems evolve, new features and functions are added, including patron profiles, notification systems, and many other patron-initiated activities, such as requesting a purchase, checking on items borrowed, and various methods of overriding, forgiving, or waiving fines and fees. Because circulation systems are so visible, they are often given priority when new systems enhancements are made.

REFERENCES

Elmer D. Johnson, *A History of Libraries in the Western World* (1965).

Frank R. Bridge, "Automated System Marketplace 1991," *Library Journal*, April 1, 1991.

EMILY GALLUP FAYEN

Clapp, Verner W.
(1901–1972)

One of the most influential and productive American librarians of his generation, Verner Warren Clapp was a Library of Congress administrator, writer and consultant, leader in professional organizations, and foundation head.

Clapp was born on June 3, 1901, in Johannesburg, South Africa. His father, George Herbert Clapp, was a native of New Hampshire who had gone to Johannesburg on business. His mother, May Sybil

Helms, was of Danish descent. The Clapps met in Johannesburg and were married there in 1898 but left Johannesburg for Poughkeepsie, New York, in 1905, after the Boer War.

Clapp attended the public schools in Poughkeepsie and earned an A.B. at Trinity College in Hartford, Connecticut, where he captained the track team, joined Sigma Nu fraternity, and was elected to Phi Beta Kappa. Following his graduation in 1922, he joined his parents in Washington, D.C., where they then lived, and found temporary summer employment cataloguing manuscripts at the Library of Congress. In the fall he left the Library to study philosophy at Harvard, but at the close of the academic year he decided to return to the Library of Congress and was employed as a reference librarian in the main reading room. His great energy, intelligence, and wide-ranging interests impressed his superiors, and in 1928, when the Library's Congressional Unit was organized, he was placed in charge. At that time he also met Dorothy Devereux Ladd; they were married on August 24, 1929. She shared many of his diverse interests.

In 1931 Clapp was promoted to the post of Special Assistant to the Superintendent of the Reading Rooms. Six years later he became Assistant Superintendent of the Reading Rooms and was given additional responsibility for the Division for the Blind. Under his administration the production of braille and talking books was increased, and regional libraries were established to improve services to the blind.

In 1940, shortly after Archibald MacLeish's appointment as Librarian, the Library of Congress was reorganized and a Department of Administrative Services was established. Clapp became its first Director and undertook a reform of the Library's fiscal management. When the United States entered World War II, he was given responsibility for the evacuation to Fort Knox of the nation's cherished documents—the Declaration of Independence, the Constitution of the United States, and the Articles of Confederation—and, also, the copy of Magna Carta which the British Government had sent to Washington for safekeeping.

After helping plan the organization of an Acquisitions Department in 1943, Clapp was named its first Director. With his usual vigor and vision he revamped the Library's acquisitions program to make it more comprehensive and responsive to the new and increased informational needs of the government. His contributions during this period were not limited to development of the Library's collections, however. His ideas were influential in the organization of the Library's Reference Department, in the shaping of its personnel policies, in proposals for the revision of the Copyright Act, in efforts to develop interlibrary cooperation in microfilming, and in various other areas of library activity.

Immediately after World War II, Clapp entered into a new period of noteworthy and varied activity. During the war years the flow of publications to the U.S. from Germany and other countries of Europe had been cut off. With the cessation of hostilities, Clapp helped plan, and was made responsible for, a vast undertaking, the Cooperative Acquisitions Project, which involved the procurement of some 2,000,000 European publications for the Library of Congress and 112 other American research libraries

Arthur Plotnik

Verner W. Clapp

and the distribution of these publications on an equitable basis. Additionally, in 1946 his talent for diplomacy was tested in successful negotiations in Berlin with representatives of the U.S.S.R. to effect the release of books and journal issues that had been ordered before the war by U.S. libraries and were being held in storage in East Germany. In 1945 and 1946 he was given the assignment of collecting and making useful disposition of a vast quantity of books published in special wartime editions for the use of the military. Even finding temporary storage for these publications was a monumental task, but the project was carried out to the satisfaction of all concerned. The books were distributed to colleges and universities, whose rapidly increasing enrollments were creating a demand for scarce teaching materials.

Of quite a different order was his assignment in 1945 to organize a library and provide a reference service for the United Nations Conference at San Francisco; he did so with great skill, working under extreme pressure. The United Nations turned to him on many occasions thereafter for advice on UN library matters, and from 1959 to 1962 he served, with three other librarians, as a consultant to the Secretary General of the United Nations and the architects employed in planning the UN Library building.

In 1947 the Librarian of Congress decided to appoint a deputy, and it was no surprise to anyone in the profession when, on March 5 of that year, Clapp was named Chief Assistant Librarian of Congress. Before he had been in that position a year, he was asked to chair a U.S. Library Mission to Japan to assist in the establishment of a National Diet Library. In two months he and Charles Harvey Brown, Director of the library of Iowa State College, produced a plan for the organization and services of the proposed library as well as drafts of the legislation needed for its implementation. Their ideas were accepted, and the necessary legislation was enacted promptly by the Diet. At the celebration of the 20th anniversary of the National Diet Library in 1968, he was honored by Japan with the Order of the Sacred Treasure.

When Luther Evans resigned as Librarian of Congress to become Director General of Unesco, Clapp assumed the duties of Acting Librarian and served in that capacity from July 4, 1953, until September 1954.

Over the years of its existence the Ford Foundation had been the recipient of many grant requests from research libraries. In 1955 it asked Louis B. Wright (Director of the Folger Library), Leonard Carmichael (Secretary of the Smithsonian Institution), and L. Quincy Mumford (Librarian of Congress) to call a meeting of librarians and scholars to advise it on how it might assist in the solution of library problems. Two conferences were held at the Folger Library that year on the problems of research libraries and the possibility of using new scientific and technological developments in solving them. At the second meeting it was decided that a new and independent organization was needed. In September 1956 the Council on Library Resources, Inc., was established with a $5,000,000 grant from the Ford Foundation, and, on the advice of many librarians and others whose opinions had been solicited, Clapp was persuaded to serve as President. He threw himself into the work of the Council with all the energy and enthusiasm he had displayed throughout his career for every venture that engaged his interest.

Under his direction the Council sponsored a variety of highly productive projects. Among many other undertakings, it supported the study that stimulated the automation of the Library of Congress; the preliminary work that led to the mechanization of the production of the *Index Medicus;* the work of the Barrow Laboratory on the deterioration of book paper, the development of a formula for "permanent/durable" paper, an aerosol process for the deacidification of deteriorating books, and performance standards for library binding; development of the *National Union Catalog of Manuscript Collections;* the third edition of *The Union List of Serials;* production by the American Historical Association of a *Guide to Photocopied Historical Manuscripts;* the establishment of the *National Register of Microform Masters;* the production of the International Inventory of Musical Sources; a system for searching statute law by computer; the American Library Association's Library Technology Project; the book-selection journal *Choice; Books for College Libraries*; and Cataloging in Publication.

Clapp was quick to assist, through Council grants, various national and international library conferences, as well as cooperative library undertakings, surveys, studies, and extensions of worthwhile existing programs. Council support made possible the first publication of a scientific journal exclusively in microform and the production of such notable publications as Keyes Metcalf's *Planning Academic and Research Library Buildings* and Robert Hayes and Joseph Becker's *Handbook of Data Processing for Libraries.*

In 1967 Clapp retired from the Presidency of the Council on Library Resources but continued until 1972 to give the Council, as a full-time consultant, the benefit of his long experience and encyclopedic knowledge.

The range of Clapp's interests is exemplified by the many varied organizations in which he maintained membership: the American Antiquarian Society; the American Association for the Advancement of Science; the American and Canadian Bibliographic Societies; the American Institute of Graphic Arts; the American, Canadian, and District of Columbia Library Associations; the Abstracting Board of the International Council of Scientific Unions; the American Society for Information Science; the Columbia Historical Society (Washington, D.C.); the National Microfilm Association; and the Special Libraries Association.

He was also a member of the National Advisory Commission on Libraries and the Science Information Council. He served for 18 years as a Director of the Forest Press, Inc., and, for the last 12 years of his life, as its President. He was a Trustee of the Lake Placid Club Education Foundation from 1955 until his death. It is not entirely coincidental, perhaps, that one of the most important contributors to librarianship since Melvil Dewey should have had such close affiliation with projects that continued Dewey's work.

Clapp served during his career on many committees and published extensively. His writings, always lucid and lively, exhibit an astonishing range of knowledge. They number more than 200 but represent only a fraction of the subjects that engaged his interest.

Few librarians have been as honored as he in their lifetimes, nor have many been so nobly eulogized in death. The American Library Association awarded him the Lippincott Award and the Melvil Dewey Medal and made him an Honorary Life Member. The Special Libraries Association gave him a Special Citation, and the Association of Research Libraries, at the time of his retirement from the Council on Library Resources, honored him with a citation for his "selfless dedication to the cause of librarianship and the service of scholarship," his service "to the United Nations and to foreign governments, to library organizations" and "to scholarly associations." It called him "an honored spokesman for the library profession" who had exerted "a more beneficent influence on research librarianship" than any other man of our time, and it named him the "Librarian's Librarian."

When Clapp retired from the Library of Congress, Mumford said of him, "His contributions to the Library of Congress and to the library world are so varied and numerous that one is staggered at the knowledge that a single person in his lifetime could accomplish this and at the same time manage to be a loving husband, father, and friend." He died on June 15, 1972, in Virginia. At the memorial tribute to him held in the Coolidge Auditorium of the Library of Congress on June 20, David C. Mearns, the former Assistant Librarian of Congress and Honorary Consultant in the Humanities, said of him, "Verner was . . . indomitable, exuberant, prodigious, passionate, inexhaustible, a polymath, and a fellow of infinite zest. . . . He was generous with his patience, with his counsel, with his consideration. . . . his friends were legion; his admirers a mighty host."

REFERENCES
Verner W. Clapp, 1901–1972: A National Tribute (1977).
William J. Crowe, "Verner Clapp and Preservation of Library Materials: The Years at the Council on Library Resources," in *Academic Librarianship, Past, Present, and Future* (1989).
Foster E. Mohrhardt, "Clapp, Verner Warren," *Dictionary of American Library Biography* (1978).

FREDERICK H. WAGMAN

Classification

The book of Genesis tells us that the world was created out of chaos when "God divided the light from the darkness." Thus the idea of classification, literally "the making of classes," was thought, by Westerners at least, to be the origin and essence of the world since ancient times. The ability to classify is indeed a fundamental faculty without which no living organism can function. We must, for example, distinguish between edible and inedible things, or animals that are (or may be) dangerous to us and those that are not. Everyone goes through life constantly making distinctions between things that are like and those that are unlike while at the same time also grouping them into larger containing classes or into smaller subclasses and perceiving relationships between classes. The farmer keeps cattle, horses, and poultry apart, but together thinks of them as livestock, and each class of animals may at times have to be further subdivided into milch and beef cows, riding and draft horses, and chickens, turkeys, and geese. The mechanic sorts fasteners into nuts and bolts and puts each of these into separate bins according to shape, size, threading, and so on. All our physical sense impressions are transformed into concepts by a process of classification, and abstract ideas as well do not float haphazardly in our minds but are thought of as being related to each other in an orderly way.

The human race's greatest achievement was the discovery that concepts expressed by words could be transmitted to other people in distant places and preserved for those living in other times by means of writing. Ever since human knowledge was first recorded in more or less durable form, the resulting documents have been gathered to form collections, but such collections become libraries only when they are arranged in systematic patterns. In a larger sense, all arrangements of documents, whether by author, title, subject, or physical form, are based on some kind of classification, but in a more restricted sense only the systematic arrangement of documents by *subject* is commonly understood to be the purpose of library classification.

It is important to distinguish between three different but interrelated meanings of the term *classification* in library practice: in its most literal and basic sense it is the act of *classifying* or *making a classification scheme* (the resulting scheme often being called a classification for short); second, it is the act of *classing* or assigning class marks to documents that indicate subject content; third, it is the resulting *physical arrangement* of documents (books as well as other materials) on shelves or the related but not necessarily identical arrangement of document surrogates (catalogue entries) in a classified subject catalogue.

The first of these, making a classification scheme, is obviously the fundamental one, the others being dependent on it. It has been defined by the International Federation for Documentation (FID) as follows:

> By classification is meant any method creating relations, generic or other, between individual semantic units, regardless of the degree of hierarchy contained in the systems and of whether those systems will be applied in connection with traditional or more or less mechanized methods of document searching.

A classification scheme consists generally of three interrelated parts:

(1) A *schedule* or *table* listing the classes in a sequence perceived by the makers of the scheme as a logical or useful one, normally subdivided in hierarchical order from the most general to the most specific topics. The phrase "relations, generic or other" in the FID definition means that a classification scheme should be able to express not only hierarchic (genus-species) relations but also others, such as whole-part or agent-action. These are known as *paradigmatic* relations—that is, they follow a known pattern and are independent of the treatment of the subject in a document. For example, a book on cars deals implicitly also with motor vehicles and vehicles in general. There are also associative and correlative or *syntagmatic* relations, namely those dealt with in specific documents in a relationship determined by the author (such as a book on accidents caused by cars in the U.S. versus the U.K.), and classification schemes should allow for the clear and specific expression of such relations. Recurrent features, such as place-names, time periods, languages, personal characteristics, or forms of presentation (such as "bibliography" or "periodical"), which are applicable throughout all or most of a scheme, may be listed separately in *auxiliary schedules*.

(2) A *notation* that mechanizes the order of schedules by means of symbols that have a generally known order, namely either numerals or letters, or a combination of both; other marks, such as mathematical symbols or punctuation marks, may also be used, although those do not have a universally agreed-upon and known order.

(3) An *alphabetical index* that lists subjects by their names and synonyms and shows distributed aspects (their relationship to other subjects), in each case indicating through the notation their place in the schedules. Nineteenth-century classification schemes were arranged almost entirely on enumerative hierarchical principles, resulting in fixed "pigeonholes" for preconceived subjects. Modern classification schemes are both hierarchical and synthetic, providing for individual "facets" or aspects of subjects that can be combined at will to express the conceptual content of a document, thus avoiding the rigidity of older schemes and readily accommodating entirely new subjects and their various relationships.

Early Library Classifications. The clay tablets found in one of the world's oldest libraries, the large royal archives of Assurbanipal (7th century B.C.), contained a catalogue that divided the works into main classes (Grammar, History, Law, Natural History, Geography, Mathematics, Astronomy, Magic, Religion, and Legends), each being subdivided into several subclasses. No actual classification scheme from Greek and Roman libraries has survived, but the catalogue of the great Alexandrian library, the *Pinakes* ("tables") compiled by Callimachus (3rd century B.C.) was apparently classified into Poets, Lawmakers, Philosophers, Historians, Rhetoricians, and Miscellaneous writers; further subdivisions were by form, subject, and time. The libraries of China at the end of the Western Han period (1st century A.D.) were classified into seven large groups: Encyclopedias, the Six Arts, Philosophy, Poems and Songs, Military Art, Soothsaying, and Medicine. During the later Wei and Tsin dynasties (3rd to 5th centuries), a system was designed that survived practically unchanged until the 20th century. It consisted of four main classes, retaining several of the older classes as subdivisions: (1) Classics; (2) Philosophy, Military Art, Mathematics, and Theology; (3) History, Government, and Miscellanea; and (4) Literature.

Medieval Library Classification. Early monastic libraries were so small that they had no need for a classification, but later it became common practice to divide the holdings of such libraries into three large groups, Theological Works, Classical Authors of Antiquity, and Contemporary Authors on the Seven Arts. The latter were also the backbone of classification in the university libraries, where books were arranged according to the classical division of the curriculum into the Trivium (Grammar, Rhetoric, and Logic) and the Quadrivium (Arithmetic, Geometry, Music, and Astronomy).

Philosophical and Pragmatic Classifications. Since the Renaissance two main types of classifications can be distinguished: those that are based on a philosophical scheme or an ideal order of knowledge, and those that aim merely at a practical arrangement of books on shelves. Outstanding among the former is the Swiss polyhistor Conrad Gesner's *Pandectarum . . . libri xxi,* the classified part of his *Bibliotheca Universalis* that listed most learned books known at the time (1548). The system arranged books according to their subjects by 21 major classes, each with a number of subdivisions. Gesner's scheme marked the beginning of modern library classification and served as a model for the arrangement of many libraries until the end of the 18th century. Another philosophical scheme was contained in Francis Bacon's *Advancement of Learning* (1605); though it was not intended for library use, it influenced many later classifiers, among them Thomas Jefferson and Melvil Dewey. A practical scheme, first developed in the mid-17th century by Paris booksellers and ascribed to Ismael Bouilleau, was further elaborated by the French bibliographer Jacques-Charles Brunet in the early 19th century; the scheme was quite simple and had only five main classes—Theology, Jurisprudence, Sciences and Arts, Literature, and History—each with a moderate number of subdivisions. It is still used in part by the Bibliothèque Nationale and some other large French libraries, and an adaptation of the scheme is used in the British Library.

A classification scheme that combined philosophical principles of arrangement with practical applicability was designed in the 1840s by the German Orientalist and librarian A. A. E. Schleiermacher for the court library at Darmstadt. It comprised 25 main classes (A/Z) with some 13,000 subdivisions and was the most detailed scheme of the 19th century. It was remarkably modern in its use of auxiliary tables for recurrent geographical and other features, and it had a fully developed relative index. The scheme was used in some German national and university libraries well into the 20th century.

The Dewey Decimal Classification (DDC). Melvil Dewey designed his scheme for the small library at Amherst College (Massachusetts) in 1873 and first published it in 1876. It grew from a slim booklet containing less than 1,000 subdivisions on 12 pages (at the time criticized as excessively detailed!) and an alphabetical index of 18 pages to a four-volume work of more than 3,200 pages, comprising schedules for several thousands of classes and their subdivisions, supplemented by seven auxiliary tables, a comprehensive relative index, and a manual. It had gone through 20 full and 12 abridged editions by 1990. DDC has been translated into several dozen languages and is used in thousands of libraries throughout the world. It is also used for the arrangement of a number of national bibliographies, foremost among them the *British National Bibliography*.

The success of DDC results from several features. It has a simple notation that is independent of language or script and based on the principle of decimal fractions (incorrectly called "numbers") as class marks, which are infinitely expandable for further subdivision of any existing class "horizontally" (though "vertical" expansion, the intercalation of a new subject into a hierarchy, is not possible when all nine subdivisions at the same notational level are already utilized). The notation has excellent mnemonic features and has some flexibility through auxiliary tables for forms, areas, literatures, languages, racial, ethnic, and national groups, and persons, which are applicable throughout the schedules (though not for all class marks). The principle of "number building" allows subdivision of one basic class mark by all or part of another, thus indicating certain aspects of relationships between subjects, while at the same time not burdening the schedules with an excessive number of subdivisions. These last two features are Dewey's most important contribution, and they formed the nucleus for the later development of faceted classifications. Finally, and perhaps most important, the DDC is backed by its own organization, the Forest Press (a division of the Online Computer Library Center, Inc.), and is supported by the Library of Congress, thus assuring its continued existence and revision to keep the scheme up to date.

Among the shortcomings of the scheme are its sequence of main classes, reflecting the world outlook of the late 19th century; the allocation of only one main class each to science and technology, resulting in overcrowding and long notations and in separation of the basic sciences from their technological applications; the separation of history from social sciences; the separation of political geography from other geographical topics; and the strict adherence to the principle of "integrity of numbers," which often prevents the restructuring of old schedules to accommodate new topics and sometimes even the proper application of general facets. To a certain extent, the latter deficiency has been remedied by the successive introduction of so-called Phoenix schedules, which are completely redesigned sections of the schemes.

In the U.S. the DDC is used almost exclusively for shelf classification of books, mainly in school, public, and college libraries. Some subject bibliographies, notably the *American Book Publishing Record,* are also classified by DDC. The Library of Congress provides DDC class marks for some 70 percent of books catalogued in the MARC database. In the U.K. and several European countries, and also in many Asian and African libraries, the DDC is widely used not only for shelf classification but also for the construction of classified subject catalogues and bibliographies, in which the detailed (and sometimes long) notations made possible by number building can be used to much better advantage than as mere call numbers on the spines of books.

With the increasing use of online catalogues in the U.S. it has been recognized that searching a DDC classified sequence is an important complement to searching by keywords or subject headings, especially for generic searches ("up" or "down" a hierarchy). For this purpose, too, long notations, far from being a hindrance, become useful in pinpointing specific subjects.

The Universal Decimal Classification (UDC). In the 1890s two Belgian lawyers, Paul Otlet and Henri LaFontaine, conceived the idea of a worldwide bibliography on cards of all recorded knowledge, not only in book form but also in articles, reports, patents, and so on. To achieve this goal they needed a highly specific classification. The DDC had by then become known in Europe, and the two men considered it suitable for their project, although it was not sufficiently detailed. In 1895 they asked for and received Dewey's permission to adopt, translate, and further develop his scheme (then in its fifth edition). Otlet and LaFontaine proceeded to translate the schedules into French, made some changes in religion, the social sciences, and technology, and thus developed with the help of subject specialists the *Classification Décimale Universelle* (for some time known as the "Brussels Expansion").

Although the UDC was and still is based on the DDC, it differs from it in several respects. The basic structure of 10 main classes and most of the first 1,000 three-digit notations were retained (except for final 0's, which were dropped), but a much larger number of sometimes very minute subdivisions were introduced. Dewey's form and place auxiliaries were indicated by means of mathematical symbols or punctuation marks. Finally, the colon sign was introduced to link two or more UDC codes so as to indicate relationships, a device that makes the notation highly flexible: a document on "Use of computers in the management of hospital personnel" is classed as 362.1:658.3:519.68 (Hospitals: Personnel management: Computers); each of the three codes can be used as an access point.

The full UDC tables were first published in 1905 under the title *Manuel du Repertoire Bibliographique Universel,* followed later by full editions in German, English, Russian, Spanish, Japanese, and eight other languages. These full editions contain about 150,000 subdivisions. Medium editions (about 30 percent of the full tables) exist in English, German, French, Japanese, and 13 other languages. Abridged editions (about 10 to 15 percent of the full tables) exist in 17 languages and 5 alphabets. In addition there are special editions for certain subject fields in which the codes for the special subjects are given in full, while codes for fringe subjects are listed only in abbreviated form.

Although the idea of a worldwide bibliography had to be abandoned in the 1920s as impractical, the UDC was rapidly adopted throughout the world by many libraries, abstracting services, and journals, especially for scientific and technical subjects, and it is still a widely used general system of classification, with an estimated 100,000 institutional and individual users. In the U.S. the UDC is used by several specialist subject bibliographies, a large abstracting service, and several libraries. In the former Soviet Union, the UDC was made mandatory in 1963 for all scientific and technical libraries, as well as for abstracting services, foremost among them *Referativnyi Zhurnal;* all scientific and technical books also carry UDC numbers. Consequently, in eastern European countries the UDC is also widely used, and is employed on a large scale in Japan, in Brazil, and in other Latin American countries.

Although the basic structure of the UDC still follows DDC's 10 main classes (except for class 4, which is presently empty, Language having been amalgamated with Literature in class 8), it is no longer fully compatible with the DDC because many subjects are now classed by notations that are quite different. The responsibility for the revision and development of the UDC lies with the FID, working through committees of specialists or interested individuals. *Extensions and Corrections* is published semi-annually; each issue contains many hundreds of new, corrected, or deleted codes, thus keeping the scheme continuously up to date.

The Expansive Classification (EC). While Dewey conceived the DDC in the traditions of the pragmatic classifications, his older colleague Charles Ammi Cutter designed in the 1880s a scheme that was influenced by the then current philosophy of "evolutionary order in nature." The EC consisted of seven different but related schemes (the last of which remained unfinished). The first was rather broad, comprising only seven classes, each subsequent "expansion" being more finely subdivided and intended to be used by increasingly larger libraries. The notation for main classes consisted of letters, while auxiliary tables used digits; a period or full stop was also used as a notational device. Unfortunately, EC's notation had to be changed throughout the seven expansions, necessitating constant reclassification when a library grew and wished to move from one expansion to the next. Only a small number of American libraries ever used the scheme, and after its inventor's death in 1903 it was soon almost entirely abandoned. Both Cutter's notation and his ideas of an order of subjects suggested by a scientific consensus had a decisive influence on two other American schemes—the Library of Congress Classification and Bliss's Bibliographic Classification.

The Library of Congress Classification (LC). When the Library of Congress moved into a new main building in 1897, it needed a new classification scheme because the one originally devised by Thomas Jefferson (an adaptation of the Baconian scheme) had become inadequate. In 1899 the DDC was considered, but Dewey could not agree to some major changes the Library requested. The Library then decided to design its own scheme, taking many features from Cutter's EC but essentially producing a pragmatic system primarily based on its own holdings. The LC is in fact not one system but a loosely coordinated series of 21 special classifications, each with its own structure, notation, auxiliary tables, and index, occupying 34 volumes with a total of more than 10,600 pages. One class, P (Language and Literature), occupies more than 3,200 pages (30 percent of the whole scheme), whereas all of science and technology constitutes only 13 percent; Class K (Law) is still incomplete.

The notation is mixed, consisting of one or two letters for main classes followed by ordinal numbers up to a maximum of four digits for subdivisions. Gaps are left between numbers for future expansion, but where these have been filled, decimal subdivision, generally by one or two digits, is used. Beyond (or instead of) decimal subdivision, further subdivision of a subject is alphabetical, often by the English name of a subject expressed by "Cutter numbers" (a letter plus one or more digits); this feature results in dispersion of closely related subjects. No use is made of synthesis or mnemonics. Where geographical, historical, or form subdivisions are necessary, they are specially developed for each subject without regard to similar subdivisions in the same or in other classes.

Revision of the schedules is carried out individually for each class; whole blocks of numbers may be canceled, the subjects classed there moved to an entirely different schedule, and the former numbers used for different subjects. Sometimes added subjects are arbitrarily inserted just where a vacant number exists and without regard to collocation of related subjects.

Several hundred American libraries have switched from DDC to LC since the 1960s, primarily because of the administrative advantages of centralized classification and the universal availability of LC class marks on cards and in machine-readable (MARC) catalogue records. A few university libraries outside the U.S. also adopted LC for similar reasons, though they often make their own adaptations and expansions for topics not covered by the scheme at all or not in sufficient detail.

The Bibliographic Classification (BC). Henry Evelyn Bliss, the most eminent of American classification theorists, devoted a lifetime to the design of a scheme that would reflect the "scientific consensus" on the order of things and ideas. It was considered by many to be far superior to all other general schemes both in structure and notation, but by the time it was published by the H. W. Wilson Co. (1935–53), most American libraries had already been classified by either DDC or LC and could not or would not change to a new and unproved system. In the U.K., however, about a hundred libraries adopted the BC. The scheme consists of 26 main classes (A/Z) and an "anterior class" (1/9) for form subdivisions that are applicable throughout the schedules. A characteristic feature is the provision of alternative locations or treatments for many subjects, depending on the point of view of the book or the needs of a particular library. Thus a book on economic history may be classed under History at LGE or under Economics at T9. The notation uses all letters of the alphabet (as many as four capital letters), lowercase letters for geographical subdivisions, and digits for forms. For example, BOV3 is History of broadcasting; JCAe is Educational research in England.

After Bliss's death in 1955, upkeep and revision of the BC ceased for almost 15 years, and several libraries abandoned the scheme. In the 1970s it was revived in England under the editorship of Jack Mills; the first new BC2 schedules began to appear in 1976, but progress has been slow, and by 1990 less than one-half of the new BC2 schedules had been published. BC2 is in fact a new classification based on BC1 but with a faceted structure and a revised notation. Whether it will meet with more success than BC1 remains to be seen.

The Colon Classification (CC). This is the last universal scheme designed by one person and actually used in libraries. The Indian mathematician-turned-librarian S. R. Ranganathan published the first version of the CC in 1933. It constituted an almost complete break with traditional methods of classifying, relying on an analytico-synthetic approach. Instead of enumerating classes of things and ideas and their ever more minute subdivisions, the CC lists only relatively simple objects and ideas as well as general properties and characteristics, or "facets," whose class marks can be combined to express exactly the subject of a document. It thus abandoned the method of creating fixed pigeonholes for preconceived and precoordinated subjects that had bedeviled earlier classification schemes. The backbone of the scheme is formed by 43 main classes (denoted by one or two capital letters and two Greek letters), roughly corresponding to traditional disciplines but not extensively subdivided. All detail is provided by the facets, which are combined according to the formula PMEST, where P stands for Personality (generally the primary or central aspect of a subject), M for Material, E for Energy (any kind of action or process and its results), S for Space (place), and T for Time. Each facet is set off from others by punctuation marks (originally only the colon sign from which the scheme takes its name and which was itself adopted from the UDC). When constructing a class mark, not all facets may have to be used, whereas others may appear more than once. Thus a work on "Attempts to eradicate poverty in Scotland in the 1940s" would first of all be put into main class Y Sociology, because it deals with a social phenomenon. Analyzing the work, we find that it is concerned with Poverty, :434 in the E facet and its Eradication, :64, also in E; Scotland is .563 in S, and the 1940s are 'N4 in facet T, so that the complete class mark becomes

Y : 434 : 64 .563 'N4

P E 2E S T

(In this case, no Material facet is involved, but two Energy facets are used.)

The alphabetical index to the scheme is also constructed along new lines, the "chain indexing" principle invented by Ranganathan.

Though the seeds of generally applicable facets were sown by Dewey, and the idea was further developed in the UDC, it was fully applied and systematized only in the CC, which reached its seventh edition in 1987. Schedules for specific topics not dealt with in sufficient detail in the general scheme are also published from time to time. Although the

CC is used in relatively few libraries in its homeland, and almost nowhere else, its underlying theory has had a major impact on classification. Since the 1950s, the structure and revision policy of all existing or newly devised classification schemes (with the exception of the LC) have been more or less affected by Ranganathan's ideas.

The Bibliothecal-Bibliographic Classification (BBK). A classification system for the libraries of the U.S.S.R., the BBK was elaborated by the Lenin Library in Moscow and published in 30 volumes from 1960 to 1968. An abridged edition in six volumes was published in 1970–75; an abridgement for public libraries in four volumes was published in 1980–83; and a one-volume abridgment for very small libraries appeared in 1975, with updated editions in 1984 and 1986. The BBK consists of 21 main classes, each of which is indicated by one of the 28 letters of the Cyrillic alphabet. First is Marxism-Leninism, followed by the Sciences, Technology (eight classes), Agriculture, Medicine, Social Sciences (seven classes), Literature, Art, Religion, Philosophy, and Generalia. The 21 classes are further subdivided into a total of about 45,000 main headings. The notation is mixed, the letter of the main class being followed by digits expressed in decimal fractions, with points after every three digits. General auxiliary tables are provided for geographical areas and for other facets, most of which are modeled on those in the UDC (though the notation is different). Each class has its own index, and there is no general index. Most class marks are enumerative and they are often precoordinated (similar to LC), but some combinations are possible.

The BBK was mandatory in general and university libraries in the Soviet Union and in those dealing primarily with the social sciences. It was also introduced in eastern European countries, where it was used for classified catalogues but not for shelf arrangement; in the German Democratic Republic, it was used for the classified arrangement of the *Deutsche Nationalbibliographie*. Given the heavy Marxist-Leninist emphasis in the BBK and the general abandonment of such emphasis in eastern Europe after the collapse of the Soviet Union in 1991, the future of the BBK remains uncertain.

Modern Chinese Classification Schemes. In the early years of the 20th century the classification scheme used for almost 2,000 years proved to be unsuitable for modern Chinese literature. Some libraries began to use DDC in 1907, and during the 1920s LC was also tried. Neither scheme was adequate for Chinese topics, and local adaptations were made. After the establishment of the People's Republic of China, an entirely new general classification scheme was designed, the first version of which was published in 1953. It had 17 main classes with many subdivisions, the first of which in each class was always devoted to the Marxist-Leninist and Maoist view of a subject, and its notation used only Arabic digits. A revised version, *Zhongguo Tushu Ziliao Fenlei Fa* ("Classification System for Chinese Libraries"), appeared in 1975 and a second updated edition appeared in 1980. A third edition appeared in 1989. The scheme has more than 25,000 main headings in 22 main classes with a notation consisting of one or two Roman capital letters; subdivisions have a decimal numerical notation, general auxiliaries use lowercase Roman letters, and special auxiliaries are expressed by hyphens and digits (such as -0). Complex subjects can be expressed by coloning (as in UDC); for example, O29: TB11 is Mathematics for engineering (the first unit is the letter O, not the digit zero). The index follows traditional Chinese methods—the logograms expressing the names of the subjects are arranged by number of strokes.

The Broad System of Ordering (BSO). The most recent general classification scheme, commissioned by Unesco in 1971 and elaborated by FID as a "roof classification," was published in 1978. It was intended to be used as a "switching language" between existing classification systems, thesauri, and other information-retrieval systems, centers, or organizations, not in order to supplant any of these, but to make them mutually compatible on a general level. As its name implies, it provides only about 4,000 not very detailed subdivisions. BSO features an entirely new system of notation based on digits that are used in groups of millesimal and centesimal fractions, separated by commas, thus ensuring a maximum of hospitality and flexibility in a pattern of 3,2,2 digits. For example:

716	Building construction & services
.40	Parts of buildings
.45	Walls

Complex subjects can be expressed by combinations of class marks from different parts of the scheme, separated by a hyphen; under BSO, for example, "Environmental aspects of building construction" is 716-390, where 390 is Environment.

Although the BSO was not designed for classification of books in libraries, it could very well be employed for broad shelf classification, which is all that is needed in many open-shelf browsing collections. It has not yet achieved its stated goal as an international switching language.

Special Classification Schemes. The universal classifications described above are useful for general collections, but many specific subject collections or databases require special classifications that provide detailed subdivisions and other features not offered by any of the general schemes. Some examples are the W schedules for Medicine developed by the National Library of Medicine (employing a letter not used in LC), a scheme for physics designed by the American Institute of Physics, and one designed for the *British Catalogue of Music* by E. J. Coates.

Research on Classification. In 1952 a Classification Research Group (CRG) was founded in England to study the theoretical foundations of classification. Members of the CRG later constructed several special classification schemes, and some were also instrumental in the design of the BSO. Similar research groups were founded in other countries during the 1960s, and their work attracted much interest on the part of philosophers and linguists.

The FID has a standing Committee on Classification Research (FID/CR), concerned with maintaining a register of current research on classification, promoting the education and exchange of researchers, organizing meetings, and publishing research reports. The American Society for Information Science has a Special Interest Group on Classification Research

(SIG/CR) whose members are active in research on classification and indexing by human beings and machines. The journal *International Classification,* founded in 1974, carries articles and research reports on classification and indexing and contains a current awareness bibliography of books, reports, and papers on these subjects.

Efforts to employ classification for information retrieval have led to theoretical developments that would appear to indicate a potential symbiosis of classification and verbal subject analysis. It has become apparent that the hierarchical and enumerative qualities of the majority of the universal schemes described above, which are the very qualities that recommend them for shelf arrangement of documents, render them inflexible for sophisticated information retrieval, which is better served by synthetic approaches. It has been suggested that prevailing Western notions of order that have driven the development of classification must be broadened considerably.

Classification for Information Retrieval. During the 1980s many researchers undertook experiments utilizing classifications for subject retrieval in online catalogues. Because of its highly faceted structure and largely expressive notation, the UDC has been used successfully in computerized information retrieval and has been used as a switching language between subject heading lists and thesauri. Both DDC and LC have been tested as enhancements to subject searching in online catalogues. By and large the results of this experimentation have been somewhat indifferent, indicating potential for enhancement of subject searching using classification, but also indicating the many problems that face designers and users of classifications in online catalogues. Success has been sufficient, however, to fuel the development of a MARC format for classification, which can be used to store classification information in online systems.

Another major area of classification research has been the development of methods for classifying documents automatically. Early experiments tested machine algorithms that assigned each document to a predetermined class based on terms found in the abstract of the document. Later experiments were devoted to techniques for clustering documents based on similarities in their contents. Automatic classification methods have been found to be advantageous for information retrieval in part because the class description subsumes the individual document descriptions. Automatically generated clusters have been found to be more effective than library-assigned classes for the retrieval of books. Tentative experiments have suggested that classification clusters can be used to provide relevance information in the information retrieval process that can then be used to enhance precision by calculating the probability of relevance of any document to a particular query. These experiments into the potential uses of classification for information retrieval suggest that the long-neglected power of classification to organize knowledge rather than documents might be within our grasp after all.

REFERENCES

K. G. B. Bakewell, *Classification and Indexing Practice* (1978).

"Classification: Theory and Practice," *Drexel Library Quarterly* (1974).

Ingetraut Dahlberg, "Major Developments in Classification," *Advances in Librarianship* (1977).

Wolfgang Dahlberg, "Natural Law and Evolution: Toward a Natural Classification of Order," *International Classification* (1986).

International Classification and Indexing Bibliography (1982–85) 5 volumes. Volume 1 lists 2,250 general and special classification schemes.

Ray R. Larson, "Classification Clustering, Probabilistic Information Retrieval, and the Online Catalog," *Library Quarterly* (1991).

Leo La Montagne, *American Library Classification* (1961).

W. C. B. Sayers, *A Manual of Classification for Librarians,* 5th edition, revised by Arthur Maltby (1975).

E. I. Shamurin, "History of Library and Bibliographical Classification" (1955–59). In Russian. German translation: *Geschichte der Bibliothekarisch-Bibliographischen Klassifikation* (1967–68).

Dagobert Soergel, *Organizing Information: Principles of Data Base and Retrieval Systems* (1985).

HANS H. WELLISCH
RICHARD P. SMIRAGLIA

Cleverdon, Cyril
(1914–)

Cyril Cleverdon, British librarian and information scientist, is best known for his work in information retrieval.

Cleverdon was born in Bristol, England, September 9, 1914, and served on the staff of Bristol Public Libraries from 1932 to 1938. From 1938 to 1946 he was the Librarian of the Engine Division of the Bristol Aeroplane Co. Ltd. In 1946 he was appointed Librarian of the College of Aeronautics at Cranfield (later the Cranfield Institute of Technology), where he remained until his retirement in 1978. He also served there as Professor of Information Transfer Studies from 1976 to 1978. He served as Executive Secretary of the European Association of Information Services (EUSIDIC) from 1978 to 1983.

Cleverdon became a leader in the evaluation of information systems. In 1957 the National Science Foundation awarded a grant to Aslib for an evaluation of indexing systems, to be undertaken under Cleverdon's direction at the College of Aeronautics. Thus began the Aslib Cranfield Research Project. "Cranfield 1," 1957–62, compared the performance of four index languages: UDC, alphabetical subject catalogue, Uniterms, and a special faceted classification. The study was large, involving 18,000 documents and 1,200 search topics. The twin measures of recall ratio and precision ratio assumed major significance for the first time in the experiments. In comparing the systems, Cleverdon studied many performance variables, including type of document, indexing time, qualifications of the indexers, and number of index terms assigned. The results indicated surprisingly little difference in the performance of the systems. Human errors in indexing and searching were more serious than failures due to file organization. Cleverdon concluded that specificity of vocabulary and exhaustivity of indexing are much more important than file organization as factors affecting the performance of information systems.

Cranfield 1 was important because it revealed which factors significantly affect the performance of retrieval systems and which do not. It also developed methodologies that could be applied successfully to evaluation of experimental, prototype, and fully operating information systems. The Cranfield techniques were subsequently used in the evaluation of a number of operating systems, including the extensive evaluation of MEDLARS (1966–68).

The second stage of the studies ("Cranfield 2") began in 1963. The major objective was to investigate the components of index languages and their effects on the performance of retrieval systems. In Cranfield 2 the various index language devices were each evaluated according to their effect on the recall and precision of a retrieval system. Altogether 29 index languages, consisting of various combinations of the several devices, were evaluated, using a test collection of 1,400 documents and 221 test searches. The results again were rather unexpected because the index languages that performed best were natural-language systems based on words occurring in document texts.

Cleverdon wrote many reports and journal articles on information retrieval, the most important being the detailed reports on the two phases of the Cranfield studies: *Report on Testing and Analysis of an Investigation into the Comparative Efficiency of Indexing Systems* (College of Aeronautics, 1962) and *Factors Determining the Performance of Index Languages* (Aslib Cranfield Research Project, 1966), the latter written with Jack Mills and E. Michael Keen.

Cleverdon served on the Council of Aslib for most of the period from 1952 to 1977 and was its Chairman in 1958 and from 1975 to 1977. He became a Fellow of the Library Association, an Honorary Fellow of the Institute of Information Scientists, of which he was President in 1980, and an Honorary Member of Aslib.

Cleverdon's contributions were widely recognized in North America, Europe, and elsewhere. He received the Professional Award of the Special Libraries Association in 1962, the Award of Merit of the American Society for Information Science in 1971, and an award from the Special Interest Group on Information Retrieval of the Association for Computing Machinery in 1991.

F. W. LANCASTER

Clift, David H.

(1907–1973)

David Horace Clift, American librarian and association director, served as the chief executive of the American Library Association from 1951 to 1972. He led the association in expanding its membership and program and in organizing its headquarters.

Born on June 16, 1907, in the bluegrass hills of Washington, Kentucky, the eldest of six children, Clift was a reader all his life. He loved books and went out of his way to be involved with them. By the time he had finished high school in 1925, he had decided to attend the University of Kentucky in Lexington. He saved money by boarding with friends of the family while taking any part-time job he could find. By his junior year he had won a student assistant job in the university library. Using that experience as a springboard, he was able to obtain summer work in the Lexington Public Library.

He knew where he wanted to go by then. At that time the evolving library profession offered a fifth-year Bachelor's degree. Clift secured a loan from the Masonic Order of DeMolay and went to New York City in 1930 to attend the Columbia University School of Library Service. He found part-time work in the university library until he finished his degree in mid-1931.

Instead of returning to Kentucky during the Great Depression, he stayed in New York, working in the famous "reference" Room 315 of the New York Public Library. He was among many famous librarians to emerge from the same room; Keyes D. Metcalf, L. Quincy Mumford, Robert B. Downs, and Ed Freehafer are just a few of the people with whom he worked. He married Eleanore Flynn, a children's librarian for the Brooklyn Public Library. Their six years in the New York system were happy ones for both of them, but Clift could not resist the blandishments of Charles C. Williamson, Director of the Columbia University Library, and joined him as his assistant at Columbia in 1937. For the next five years Clift sharpened his personnel skills and managerial talent; Frederick G. Kilgour came to know Clift at Columbia and to appreciate his quiet and sure way with organization and personnel supervision.

In 1942 Clift was drafted into the Army and assigned as an orderly in a hospital. He was soon transferred into the Office of Strategic Services (OSS), where intelligence-gathering activity was growing under the Interdepartmental Committee for the Acquisition of Foreign Publications. Clift became the Deputy to the Executive Director—who happened to be Frederick G. Kilgour. Clift soon found himself supervising a staff of 140 people.

Following his honorable discharge in 1945, Clift became Associate Librarian at Yale. There he became a Fellow of Trumbull College and developed for the library a position classification and pay plan that was an admired model of academic librarians.

During this period he led a delegation of the Library of Congress Mission to Germany (1945–46) and served as President of the Connecticut Library Association (1950–51).

Clift became Executive Secretary of ALA in September 1951. He moved into the crowded old McCormick Mansion on Huron Street in Chicago, which had served as headquarters for the Association for far too long. The membership was 19,701 and the general funds budget was $191,129. The outlook was bleak, but Clift's strong points were administration, personnel work, and subtlety. When once asked what he felt was required of an association executive, he replied that it was to administer the policies decided by membership and leave the leadership to those elected by the membership. He went to work on reorganizing headquarters staff and creating an equitable pay plan that enabled ALA to recruit some of the most able and dedicated people in the field.

David H. Clift

Successful dealings with the professional leadership contributed to his long tenure as ALA chief. He was able to encourage consensus and compromise, thus avoiding some of the divisive in-fighting that had marked some previous headquarters administrations. When Clift retired in 1972 as Executive Director of ALA, the membership stood at 30,592 and the general funds budget was $2,262,971. During his 20 years of service some $15 million in grants came to ALA, making possible the establishment of national library standards and advances in professional library education. Among other achievements were advances in making a place for libraries in schools. *Choice* was founded as a review medium for undergraduate collection development, under the auspices of the Association for College and Research Colleges, an ALA division. The official *ALA Bulletin* changed from a journal primarily of record to a lively magazine called *American Libraries*. A series of nationwide adult education programs were conducted in libraries, and goals set for public library service. New emphasis was placed on the defense of intellectual freedom in library service. Further, the ALA Washington Office emerged as an important agency, resulting in the successful involvement of the federal government in support and assistance programs for libraries.

Clift was returning from a European trip collecting data for a study on comparative librarianship when he died on October 12, 1973. Grace Stevenson, his longtime associate at ALA, said of Clift, "He was never selling a bill of goods—or himself—just libraries."

REFERENCE

Gerald R. Shields, "Clift, David Horace," *Dictionary of American Library Biography* (1978).

GERALD R. SHIELDS

Council on Library Resources, Inc.

Fred C. Cole

Cole, Fred C.

(1912–1986)

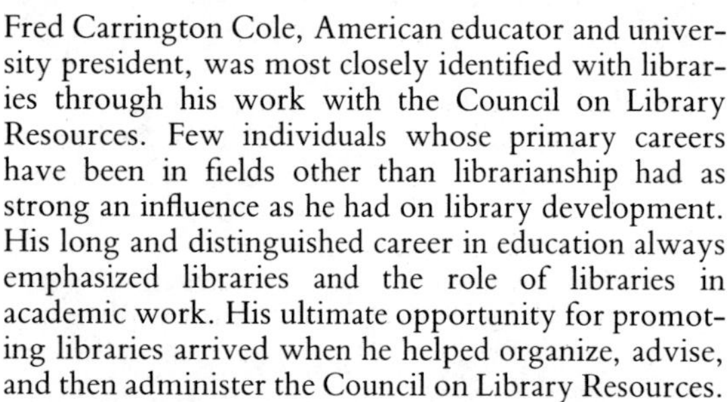

Fred Carrington Cole, American educator and university president, was most closely identified with libraries through his work with the Council on Library Resources. Few individuals whose primary careers have been in fields other than librarianship had as strong an influence as he had on library development. His long and distinguished career in education always emphasized libraries and the role of libraries in academic work. His ultimate opportunity for promoting libraries arrived when he helped organize, advise, and then administer the Council on Library Resources.

Cole was born in Franklin, Texas, April 12, 1912. His first close connection with libraries came when he occupied an office in the Louisiana State University Library while serving as an editor for activities connected with the university. L.S.U. awarded him an A.B. degree in 1934 and an A.M. in 1936. He so impressed the faculty with his scholarship and his writing ability that he was chosen to serve as Editorial Associate of the *Journal of Southern History*, 1936–41, and Managing Editor, 1941–42, and as Co-editor of the Southern Biography Series, 1938–45. He was History Editor for the Louisiana State University Press (1938–42). During those years he also worked on his Ph.D. in history, which he received in 1941. During World War II he saw extensive sea duty as a gunnery officer with the U.S. Navy. Later, at the Office of the Surgeon General of the Navy, he revised the Manual of the Medical Department. Before leaving the Navy in 1946, he was awarded a special commendation by the Surgeon General. A brief period as a civilian historian and editor for the Air Force followed.

He resumed his academic career in 1946 at Tulane University. He was associate professor, professor, dean, and vice-president there, and in 1959 he became President of Washington and Lee University, Lexington, Virginia. He received national recognition for his success in raising academic standards at both universities and in stimulating the integration of the libraries into the educational programs.

Within and without higher education, he won notice as a leader in academic administration, and he was called upon to serve as an adviser to many government and nongovernment organizations, including the College Entrance Examination Board, the American Council on Education, various foundations, and the National Science Foundation.

A strong proponent of international cooperation in education and in the broad field of information, he served as an official U.S. representative to international conferences in Europe and Asia and was a leader in international library activities. The American Library Association in 1976 presented him with a special Centennial Award for, in part, his "skill in making Ford Foundation dollars for libraries achieve maximum impact," and for "his support of the best in the past in librarianship as well as his interest in the world of the future." He was also honored with the medal of the International Federation of Library Associations and the medal of the International Council on Archives.

In 1954–55, on leave from his post as Vice-President of Tulane University, Cole served as a full-time consultant to the Ford Foundation. He joined with other scholars, educators, and librarians in developing plans for the Council on Library Resources, which was established in 1956 with Ford Foundation funding. Cole became a member of the CLR board in 1962. When Verner Clapp, the first President of the Council, retired in 1967, Cole succeeded him. In 1977, when Cole retired from CLR, Whitney North Seymour, for many years Chairman of the CLR Governing Board, said: "Dr. Cole has shown extraordinary imagination and skill in marshaling the Council's efforts to meet the problems of libraries head-on. Under his leadership, the Council has engaged in several long-range programs aimed at increasing the effectiveness of academic library management, enhancing library services to undergraduates, and improving the skills of librarians in their own and other scholarly fields. Such programs as the Academic Library Management Intern Program, the College Library Program, the Fellowship Program, and the Library Service Enhancement Program in large measure owe their existence and success to Fred Cole."

The ALA Citation of 1976 pointed out that Cole's contributions were accomplished by a gentleman of dignity and vision whose "quiet manner and self-effacing personality belie a progressive attitude and serious concern with the library's role in the future of American society."

Cole retired from the CLR in 1977 and moved to Chapel Hill, North Carolina, where he died in May 1986.

FOSTER MOHRHARDT

Collection Management

Library collections are our primary concern, and effective management of them is the heart of our profession. From the individual selector, preservation specialist, or student shelver to the administrator defining mission and winning budgets or to professional associations promulgating standards and sponsoring workshops, most of our professional knowledge and skill are directed toward selecting and providing the right books and information at the right time for our users. S. R. Ranganathan's Five Laws accurately describe the principles on which collection management is based (*see also* Shigali Ramamrita Ranganathan); this article describes the scope of issues and practices involving collections worldwide in the early 1990s.

Tradition and Change. The traditional collection consists of print and nonprint materials, developed and maintained for the benefit of users, whose information and reading needs and interests we have recorded and analyzed. This collection includes a broad range of materials and information services as well as the resources of other libraries beyond ours, and yet it is a coherent whole, its pieces collected and maintained according to plan. It is dynamic: users' needs change, materials wear out, contents of some materials grow obsolete, and new formats and services appear. Most of all, however, the traditional collection is a place—perhaps a small room with a few books and tattered magazines in a remote, dusty corner of the country, or perhaps the arena of a huge research library with floor upon floor of books and offices humming with computers—where students and scholars wrestle information into knowledge.

New technologies of digitization and telecommunications, however, challenge the continuing relevance of this traditional model as the metaphorical "library without walls" is transformed into an actual electronic library. Automated systems in libraries offer enhanced bibliographic control and access, linking acquisitions, cataloguing, indexing, circulation, and communication operations; they also link local libraries with other libraries in consortia and networks, nationally and internationally, and so create massive databases rich with accurate, detailed bibliographic data.

Further, the new technologies actually provide texts and information in new ways. Computerized databases accessible online, on CD-ROMs, and on optical disks seemingly transform collections as we have known them. They offer huge files of text and information that are the raw material of research or that contain a precise bit of crucial information or simply the latest news, and these files of scientific and social data, current political and financial news, and full texts of literary works, historical records, and legal documents can be accessed, manipulated, and selectively downloaded or printed. They can be accessed from virtually any place in the world (or beyond). They can be accessed in the library or at individual workstations independent of libraries, giving us the new ability to access the information without having to own the documents. In future editions of this *Encyclopedia,* this article may well be titled "Information and Text Management."

Problems and Opportunities. Libraries deal with abundance and austerity. They are flooded with printed materials as publication rates increase in all countries; new technologies offer new information in a bewildering number of forms; information itself has become the basis of modern society, and libraries the center at which it and people meet. Yet there are an increasing array of restrictions hampering us as we struggle to collect the information and materials. The costs of materials, of lease and fee-for-use rates, and of competition for highly educated and skilled librarians skyrocket, while public and institutional funds dwindle. In particular, scholarly and scientific serials, which have become the key medium in research and scholarly communication, are priced beyond the budgets of most libraries. The influx of new materials demands more space, while the materials already on hand must be preserved, repaired, and renewed. Information, once thought to be something we all have a right to, lies buried in government bureaucracies or is sold to the highest bidder in a market economy. Libraries fear being excluded from this market and fear that control over what is produced and sold has shifted from buyer to seller and that information has become a commodity produced and sold by for-profit concerns.

Fortunately, some opportunities are intertwined with these problems. Austerity forces us to focus our thinking and more clearly define our collecting efforts, while new technologies enable us to provide access without always owning materials. We can distinguish materials we need to own and keep on hand from information services we can lease or tap; with fax, wide-area networks, and electronic mail we can provide better collection services to patrons in distant libraries and can better coordinate our collection management efforts with other libraries; indeed a new era of cooperation and coordinated planning may be imminent. As for our patrons, increasing literacy and familiarity with new technologies make them more sophisticated and demanding users who are open to more innovative ways of accessing information and materials.

The Collection Management Program. To continue to provide for the traditional collection, to control changes already occurring, to deal with new problems, and to develop opportunities into realities, any library should establish an effective collection management program. The elements of the full program are the same in all types, sizes, and locations of libraries, and in the new electronic library no less than in the traditional library: they are actions (such as selecting new books), processes and systems (such as a weeding project and a system of storage facilities), knowledge and understanding (as of users' needs and circulation records), and the financial realities of budgets and allocations. Development and maintenance of the collection take place in a context of information, evaluation, and policy that requires careful management by both individual librarians and the administrators who coordinate their work, with support from professional associations.

Users' Needs. We build collections to meet our users' needs, but individual users are complex and user communities even more so. We must not simply recognize their interests but also understand their needs. In academic libraries, in addition to knowing the subjects taught and the degree programs offered, we must also understand the kind of teaching and learning engaged in and the nature of scholarly communication. In public libraries we must know the demographics of our communities, the local social and political issues, and the kinds of personal needs that we can provide information and reading for. In the area of popular reading we must be especially alert to users' demands and actual use, while in other areas users rely on our judgment of quality and expect us to anticipate their needs and acquire appropriate materials and information. Collections are built to meet demand and provide quality.

Collection Assessment. In most cases a library is already well established with an existing collection: does it satisfy users' expectations and is it of good quality? Users' interest and satisfaction are indicated by their use of the collection, revealed by circulation records, materials picked up and reshelved, reference questions asked, and requests for materials and information not held. We can judge the quality of the collection itself in part by measuring it against professional standards and authoritative bibliographies and judging its potential for meeting specified kinds of needs. Through user-based and collection-based assessment we can identify strengths to be built upon and weaknesses to be remedied and devise a collecting policy that will meet our users' interests and needs.

Mission and Collection Development Policy. A mission statement defines broadly the users we intend to serve and the range of needs we expect to meet. Knowing our users and our collections, we are able to direct our efforts explicitly. A collection development policy, whether a generalized statement of the library's collecting intentions or a specific, subject-by-subject and form-by-form statement of collecting priorities based on our understanding of how materials and information will meet users' needs, lets the public know what we propose to do and guides us as we do it. In North America, use of the *conspectus* developed by the Research Library Group, with its definition of collection levels, provides a common language in which libraries can communicate among themselves about the quality of their collections and about their collecting policies.

Alternatives to Purchase. Users identified, mission defined, and collecting policies set, we can consider alternatives to purchasing materials. Traditional alternatives—interlibrary loans, union catalogues, shared collections such as that of the Center for Research Libraries, local networks that serve all users from member libraries and provide delivery services—show that resource sharing and cooperation have an honored history. New technologies of the electronic library build on this thinking. Access without ownership is possible, but it requires cooperation among libraries, coordination of local, national, and international efforts, and the ability of individual librarians to recognize when and how these new technologies actually provide viable alternatives.

Budgets and Allocations. In the ideal world budgets will be based on needs we can identify and costs we can calculate; in our real world, however, budgets typically come first and limit our collection building. Budget requests by library administrations should be based on a reasonable projection of future costs derived from analysis of past costs and justified by known use in the past and an understanding of likely need. Whatever budget figure the library administration can achieve, the funds received are then allocated among several aspects of the collection program, including the various acquisitions activities (such as serials and direct orders), subject areas, and formats, and other library departments or operations. These allocations are a management decision that reflects the library's mission, its collecting policies, and its priorities.

Selection Process. Selection may be the quintessential professional act; it is neither an art nor a science, but a set of complex professional decisions performed in the context of a complex library situation. The actual process of selection involves an acquisitions system and an individual selector. The acquisitions system incorporates several ways of acquiring materials: subscriptions to periodicals and serials such as annuals and monographic series; leases on information services (looseleaf, CD-ROMs, or online); depository arrangements with governments and other organizations; gifts; endowed funds earmarked for specific subjects or types of materials; buying plans with book vendors; and of course direct orders for single items such as new books, audio cassettes, a single issue of a periodical, and so forth. The individual librarian makes specific selections in the framework of the total acquisitions system in that library, so that, for example, new books are selected with the knowledge of the library's standing order and periodical lists, its depository arrangements, and its established buying plans.

Selectors must identify the range of what is relevant, distill out those that are truly pertinent, and finally prioritize and make decisions according to a collecting plan (the practical application of a collection development policy) and within the confines of budget allocations. As selection tools, selectors use trade and national bibliographies, publishers' catalogues, wholesalers' and retailers' lists or book slips, agency and association lists of new or relevant publications, and the less current but more selective lists provided in the bibliographies of other publications. At the same time, selectors need some means of evaluating quality. While past experience tells us much about specific authors and publishers and about our users' interests, we do need reviews, and for these there exist a range of private, commercial, and professional or scholarly association publications, from newspapers and magazines to newsletters to specialized reviewing periodicals, indexes to reviews, and digests of reviews. Selectors' collecting plans provide short-term and long-term direction, enabling them to prioritize the materials they identify and to plan their selection activity throughout the fiscal year.

As selectors scan their lists, sort through notification slips, and read reviews, they simultaneously consider subject, treatment of the subject, audience level addressed, quality of contents, format and physical quality, ready availability, and, not least, cost related to potential use. Expensive materials that will be used may be selected while inexpensive materials that will not be used may not be selected. We look not only at what is coming in but also at what is here already and know that the dead weight of unused items on our shelves has its own cost. Increasingly, use has become the critical factor in the selector's decisions.

Access. Well-managed selection develops good collections, but our efforts will have been wasted unless we can maintain the accessibility and availability of the materials we collect. Our first responsibility is to provide bibliographic access at a level that is appropriate for our users, but, if bibliographic access is to be universal and consistent, we should also participate in national and international cooperation and standards for cataloguing and indexing. Physical access is a second responsibility. It is achieved through effective arrangement of materials in the library, diligent reshelving and shelf maintenance, and a storage system that puts little-used, obsolete materials in remote sites and keeps important, highly used materials closer to users. Architectural standards and building codes must be followed, of course; they are designed partly for user safety and comfort but also for adequate accessibility. Stack maintenance operations in libraries provide quick reshelving of materials brought back from circulation or picked up after in-house use, keeping materials straight on the shelves and in proper order.

Adequate physical space is a problem worldwide: collections have outgrown their buildings and construction costs have outrun libraries' ability to fund them. New technologies offer some hope for reducing the need for deep collections in most libraries by substituting fast interlibrary loans, faxed pages, and full-text online, but even so the existing materials must be dealt with. The most effective way to do so is to distribute them over a storage system that includes a central building, nearby branch libraries, close-in storage facilities, and remote warehouse-style facilities, perhaps shared among several libraries. Our core collection—identified by high use, need, or particular quality—should be in the central facility so as not to inconvenience users and not to run up costs delivering materials from distant or remote facilities to the central one.

Availability. Collections are dynamic, most so in their physical condition. Whether from the slow fires consuming acidic paper, the ravages of use, or sudden disasters, many materials are unavailable or unusable: conscientious selection and precise bibliographic access are useless if the materials cannot be found or used. To improve availability, we need effective shelving arrangements and storage systems, appropriate (and flexible) circulation policies, efficient binding, mending, and preservation operations, along with continuous updating and replacement of lost or obsolete materials. As in setting up storage systems, we must identify the core materials that most need attention and justify the expense entailed in assuring that they remain available.

Circulation policies allow users to take materials out of the library but also let them recall and put holds on materials they need, trying thus to reconcile competing needs. Length of loan period is the key factor in assuring availability, supported by means for recovering loaned items quickly. Various materials, various types of users, and various times of the year can all be considered in setting and revising loan periods. Circulation systems provide data on use that can be important in collection management: one apparent law in libraries is that those materials that have circulated are more likely to circulate again than those that have not. While acknowledging that circulation figures do not measure in-house use and so are indicative, not determinative, we can still use data about circulation by subject class and by individual items to gain information useful in setting budget allocations, defining the core of high-use materials, and identifying items needing additional copies and areas needing additional support.

Preservation, Repair, and Replacement. We manage an inherently fragile resource. Libraries bind periodicals and paperbacks to strengthen them; mend torn pages, headbands, and spines; and rebind broken books; some go farther and clean off marginalia, smudges, and debris. This is item-by-item work, but there are whole segments of the collection that require constant attention. Books by popular authors or on popular subjects need multiple copies, frequent repair, and replacement; popular periodicals and newspapers must be microfilmed (and even this must in many cases be replaced); and the whole collection of late 19th and early 20th century print materials, virtually 150 years of the world's print heritage, must be considered for conservation treatment. This last is a large-scale problem now receiving coordinated attention from libraries, scholarly societies, commercial firms, and governments, but whether we will be able to preserve more than a fraction of this material is still in doubt. We have at least learned the specifications of acid-free paper, binding standards, and controlled environment. Through our efforts production quality has improved, governments have set appropriate standards through regulations, users better understand the problem, and people are being trained. In individual libraries, budgets now include allocations for conservation costs and mending operations, additional training for librarians, and proper heating and ventilating equipment. Even if the past is lost, we may be able to preserve the future.

Renewal. As with physical, there is intellectual obsolescence. Factual information goes out of date, scholarly methods change, readers' interests shift, and once-useful materials languish unused, although users' interests can circle around and come back on subjects once abandoned. Collections must be renewed. Adding new items does not necessarily renew a collection, so in developing collections we want to find reprints, new editions, and back runs of periodicals to retain the intellectual coherency of the existing collection while infusing it with as much of the new as truly embodies new thinking and best quality.

Weeding and Deaccesssioning. Some of our materials, however, are simply no longer wanted or needed; they take precious space and their presence probably obscures the more useful materials. Out-of-date, incorrect information, worn-out and unusable items, and materials no longer of interest to users can probably be discarded. Weeding, however, can be controversial and must be conducted openly, according to clear policies and procedures, and limited to materials not needed (as opposed to materials that are simply little used). It must be combined with active willingness to replace, to borrow, and to refer, and librarians should cooperate with colleagues in other libraries to ensure that so-called last copies in a network or consortium are retained. Policies, plans, and procedures are as important in deaccessioning materials as in selecting them.

Collection Review and Analysis. The process of development and maintenance rounds off and comes full circle through regular collection review and analysis. Monitoring the physical condition of our materials and the physical conditions in which they are stored and carrying out weeding, inventory, and storage projects ensures that those materials needing attention get it and that availability levels are maintained. This review takes us into the stacks to look at the books on the shelves; it sends us to retrospective bibliographies and to vendor and acquisition reports to analyze our accessions and expenditures. We spend as much time with the existing collection as with new materials, as we should, and the insight and information we gain are crucial in our management. Collection management is not simply doing, it is also thinking. The information and data gathered in collection review and analysis, along with data about users and user communities, about production of materials and services, and about new developments in digitization and telecommunications, are crucial for effective management decisions. Library administrations have a responsibility to create databases of relevant information, and individual librarians to be sure that the information is used.

The Future. If our best collections have been built and maintained for the benefit of users, whose complex needs we have tried to interpret accurately, then certain management concerns have been fulfilled. We emphasize use, access, and availability, and we think in terms of the whole collection and the whole process of developing and maintaining it. The traditional collection will be altered as technological developments enable us to provide what is needed as faxed documents, computer printouts, and downloaded files. But this change is more one of form than one of substance: future collections will be technology-based, but they must continue to be user-centered.

REFERENCES

G. Edward Evans, *Developing Library and Information Center Collections,* 2nd edition (1987).

G. E. Gorman and B. R. Howes, *Collection Development for Libraries* (1989).

Rose Mary Magrill and John Corbin, *Acquisitions Management and Collection Development in Libraries,* 2nd edition (1989).

David Spiller, *Book Selection: Introduction to Principles and Practices,* 4th edition (1988).

William A. Wortman, *Collection Management: Background and Principles* (1989).

WILLIAM A. WORTMAN

Colombia

Located on South America's northwest tip, Colombia is a republic bordered on the north by the Caribbean Sea, on the east by Venezuela and Brazil, on the south by Peru and Ecuador, on the west by the Pacific Ocean, and on the northwest by Panama. Population (1990 est.) 32,987,000; area 1,138,914 sq.km. Spanish is the official language. About 50 indigenous tongues and dialects are still in use.

History. During the 18th century, under Spanish rule, the capital, then Santa Fé de Bogotá, was a thriving cultural center. It had universities, women's private schools, printing houses, the first newspaper worth mentioning (the *Papel Periódico Ilustrado,* 1791), and the Royal Library, now Biblioteca Nacional (BN; National Library). Leaders of the movement for independence, among them Simón Bolívar, Francisco Santander, Camilo Torres, and Antonio Nariño, all born in the Western Hemisphere, were without exception highly educated men, familiar with European enlightenment ideas, and booklovers.

Academic and private libraries developed first, and, except for the BN, were always open to the public. Public libraries historically sprang from scattered local efforts, generally on a small scale, and many with government support. Today there are few adequately serviced towns, and hardly any lending libraries. As a result, most books are acquired by a selected few. Sometimes private collections are donated to found public libraries, yet there is an almost total absence of reading materials in many homes.

Efforts made by the Instituto Colombiano de Cultura (COLCULTURA, 1969), the government office that runs the BN and coordinates public libraries, achieved unparalleled development of public libraries during the decade 1976–85. In 1976 Colombia had 200 public libraries in 174 towns (out of a total of 990 towns and cities). The number was increased to 436 in 341 towns in 1983. By 1985 there were 780 libraries, counting Casas de Cultura (Cultural Centers) that have book collections, in 537 towns.

Colombia was the first Latin-American country to create a Sistema Nacional de Información (SNI, 1973), coordinated by the Fondo Colombiano de Investigaciones Científicas y Proyectos Especiales "Francisco José de Caldas" (COLCIENCIAS). Even though it has not fulfilled its original expectations, the SNI has promoted the creation of several subsystems and networks, mainly scientific and technical, and contributed to the development and preservation of public libraries and archives.

The Asociación Nacional de Bibliotecas Públicas (National Public Library Association), created during the Seminario Nacional de Bibliotecas Públicas in Bogotá in 1985, announced that it would work to promote local and regional networks and eventually achieve national integration. COLCULTURA planned a national program for the use of 33 bookmo-

Libraries in Colombia (1990)

Type of library	Number of administrative units (main libraries)	Number of service points (branches, mobile stops, etc.)	Volumes in collections
Academic*	225		1,143,000
Public*	974	1,036	2,381,000

*1985 data

Source: Unesco, *Statistical Yearbook,* 1991

biles and 37 jeeps with lending libraries bought in Spain to cover areas, mainly rural, with few library services.

National Library. The BN was founded in 1777 with books confiscated from the Jesuits when they were ordered to leave by Charles III of Spain. Francisco Moreno y Escandón, Royal Auditor Fiscal, is considered its founder. The first Director of great merit was a Cuban, Manuel del Socorro Rodríguez, also the father of Colombian journalism. The BN has about 600,000 volumes, with 28,000 in the Rare Books Section, including 40 incunabula. Its Newspaper and Magazine Room receives around 1,000 titles and is the country's most complete collection, dating to Colonial times. In the early 1980s the budget was five million pesos, not counting regular staff and running costs.

The 1946 Book Law contributed to accumulation of a representative national bibliography, although not everyone complies with it. The one person who contributed the most to the BN's progress in the 20th century was Daniel Samper Ortega, BN Director from 1931 to 1938. Samper persuaded the national government to build the BN headquarters in Bogotá, the capital. During his administration the BN published a collection of books called *Biblioteca Aldeana* ("Village Library") and *Senderos,* ("Paths"), a magazine. Jorge Eliécer Ruiz was Director of the BN from 1979 to 1982, when Eddy Torres succeeded him. Torres put in motion a plan to reorganize the BN, involving its automation, microfilming, and space and service expansion. He managed to obtain from the town government land adjoining the present building that would allow the BN to grow substantially. Torres died in January 1983. Conrado Zuluaga, writer and professor, who succeeded him, took up the plans outlined in 1982 and advanced them with enthusiasm, in spite of great financial difficulties.

The Archivo Nacional de Colombia, directed by Pilar de Angel, is lodged temporarily in the BN. Its headquarters were under construction in the mid-1980s. It has a Colonial document collection. The Instituto Caro y Cuervo, another independent official institute, publishes the "Colombian Bibliographical Annual" and also edits works of historic, linguistic, or literary merit. COLCULTURA launched important publications from the time it was founded.

Academic Libraries. The Instituto Colombiano para el Fomento de la Educación Superior (ICFES; Colombian Institute for the Promotion of Higher Education) is the government office in charge of coordinating actions, services, and technical processes in academic libraries by means of the University Libraries Network. All higher education centers, whether universities, technological schools, or intermediate professional ones, private or public, must provide information services to their students. There are 300 information units, sponsored by some 225 schools. One-third of these services are run by professional librarians, especially in universities. There is uneven distribution and low mobility of professionals; about three-quarters work in Bogotá, Medellín, and Cali.

The national average per enrolled student is four books. A great number of these libraries have no separate budgets, and almost all the funds they receive are spent for managing and personnel. Very few have adequate buildings. The services offered vary, but the most common are reading rooms, book circulation, reservations, interlibrary loans, bibliographic guidance, instructions on how to use information, and selective dissemination of information. There are central libraries, specialized faculty libraries, and information centers. Most use manual means, but about a fourth of them, especially at universities, had undergone or were in the process of undergoing automation in the 1980s. The Library of the Universidad de Antioquia, for example, automated control of its 1,500,000 books.

The Sistema de Información y Documentación para la Educación Superior (SIDES; Higher Education Information and Documentation System) is the government's major effort toward the development of modern means of controlling and using scientific and technical information. One of its aims is to create a bibliographical database to register national production and all previous documents owned by the libraries making up the network. To implement the program, the Sistema Colombiano de Información Bibliográfica (SCIB; Colombian Bibliographic Information System) was developed.

Public Libraries. In May 1978 the Red Colombiana de Bibliotecas Públicas (Colombian Public Library Network) came into being as a component of SNI and coordinated, though not financed, by COLCULTURA and its Public Library Section. The starting point was a National Inventory of Information Resources and Services in Public Libraries. COLCULTURA began training, consultancy, library furnishing, and centralized technical processes in 1977. A development plan for 1979–82 was made to broaden the range of the network. Its aim was to have direct participation in structuring and running departmental networks. The most advanced are in Antioquia, Bogotá, Valle, and Tolima.

One of the three best public libraries is the Biblioteca Pública Piloto para Latinoamérica (Pilot Public Library for Latin America), founded in 1954 with Unesco support; it offers the greatest variety of services to readers and has branches in Medellín, where it is headquartered, and in some nearby towns in Antioquia. Another is the Biblioteca Luis Angel Arango (BLAA), founded and funded by the Banco de la República (the National Bank of Colombia), also with branches in several cities. The BLAA bought the NOTIS system from Venezuela and Northwestern University. The Biblioteca Gabriel Turbay, the most recent of the three leading libraries (1982), is in Bucaramanga, Department of Santander, where it has been crucial in the region's development. Its creation is almost entirely the work of its founder, Jorge Valderrama.

There are few children's library services in Colombia. The work carried out by the Cajas de Compensación Familiar (compulsory, privately run organizations that must be created for the social benefit of all kinds of workers) in library development is outstanding, and they often make up for government deficiencies.

School Libraries. The public school system is run by the Ministerio de Educación Nacional (MEN), which also coordinates and supervises private schools and regulates curriculum. Libraries are required by law in secondary and vocational schools, but many schools do not have them. MEN itself has insufficient funds to equip and run libraries in all its schools. Many of the reported libraries do not exist, and MEN did not establish the financial means to change conditions. Perhaps the plight of school libraries is the most dramatic in the country. There is no census to determine the number of public and private school libraries. The Programa de Bibliotecas Escolares (School Library Program) began as part of the broader Plan de Mejoramiento Cualitativo de la Educación (Plan for Qualitative Improvement of Education, 1976). It is geared to communities with less access to sources of information and attempts to cover the greatest possible number of underprivileged groups, rural zones, and sparsely populated areas.

Despite national efforts, most public libraries are still forced by the circumstances to double as school libraries, sometimes assigning to school users practically all resources. Even the BN has a 70 percent school reader frequency rate. This still leaves many students without library services at all, both in primary and secondary schools.

Special Libraries. There are about 300 special library and information centers, favored in funding and recognition. The network is run by COLCIENCIAS and has developed subsystems in the areas of agriculture, health, education, industry, marine studies, and environment. Its principal sites are in Bogotá, Medellín, and Cali. The Servicio Nacional de Aprendizaje (SENA; National Craftsman Service) created a technical information network in metalworking, welding, and small industries. The Departamento Administrativo Nacional de Estadísticas (DANE; National Statistics Department) has a database that supports the work of many government offices. Many of the existing organizations are recognized throughout Latin America and form part of international information programs such as AGRINTER or UNISIST.

The Profession. Three library science schools have contributed to the development of libraries. The Escuela Interamericana de Bibliotecología (Interamerican Library School), attached to the Universidad de Antioquia, was founded in Medellín (1956), the city with the highest development of library networks. The Facultad de Bibliotecología y Archivística of the Universidad de La Salle, Bogotá, was founded in 1971, and the Facultad de Ciencias de la Información, Universidad Javeriana, Bogotá, in 1972. The President of the Republic inaugurated in 1982 the Centro Latinoamericano de Informatica (Latin American Computerized Information Center), across the street from the Presidential Palace; grade and high school students may receive free training in computers there.

There are several associations, among them the Asociación Colombiana de Archivistas (ACAR), and the Asociación Colombiana de Bibliotecarios (ASCOLBI, 1958), which played a significant role in getting the profession approved and regulated by law. Perhaps the most interesting one to appear in the 1980s is the Asociación Colombiana del Libro Infantil y Juvenil (ACLIJ, 1982), which serves librarians, writers, teachers, editors, and bookdealers concerned with children and books. This Children's and Juveniles' Book Association is a national chapter of the International Board on Books for Young People (IBBY), and its most ambitious project, inaugurated in 1985, is the Centro Experimental del Libro Infantil y Juvenil, an experimental center that planned to sponsor workshops, a children's library, publications, and research.

ANABEL TORRES

Commonwealth Library Association

The Commonwealth Library Association (COMLA) was inaugurated in 1972 in Lagos, Nigeria, with 20 founder members—national library associations in the countries of what was formerly the British Commonwealth. Membership in 1991 comprised 52 national library organizations, of which 40 were library associations and 12 were library institutions in countries where a national association has not yet been formed. In addition, 140 library schools and libraries were affiliated organizations (Commonwealth) or newsletter subscribers (non-Commonwealth). Each member and affiliate is required to appoint a personal member of the organization to be its representative to COMLA and to exercise its vote.

The principal objects of COMLA are to improve libraries in the Commonwealth; to forge, maintain, and strengthen professional links between libraries of the Commonwealth; to support and encourage library associations; to promote the status and education of librarians and the reciprocal recognition of qualifications in librarianship; to initiate research projects designed to promote library provision; and to further technical developments in libraries in Commonwealth countries.

COMLA is one of 29 Commonwealth Professional Associations (CPOs) receiving ongoing financial support from the Commonwealth Foundation, an agency established in 1966 by the Commonwealth Heads of Government "to promote professional cooperation within the Commonwealth." The Foundation's mandate was extended in 1979 to voluntary nongovernmental organizations and its functions broadened to include culture, the role of women, rural and social development, the disabled, and the media and information. COMLA has benefitted from the Foundation's support of regional and pan-Commonwealth meetings on matters of common professional concern and from travel grants to professionals for participation in conferences, workshops, study visits, and training programs within the Commonwealth.

Organization. The Commonwealth Library Association is governed by a General Council representing the members proportionately (it meets every three or four years) and an Executive Committee that meets more frequently. After Nigeria (1972), the Council met in Jamaica (1975), Fiji (1979), Kenya (1983), Canada (1986), and Malta (1990). The Executive Committee met in Britain (1974, 1977, 1980, and 1987), in Jamaica (1976), in Singapore (1985), and in Australia (1988).

K. C. Harrison (UK) was the founding President of COMLA from 1972 to 1975. He was succeeded by J. C. Harrison (Canada) from 1975 to 1978, Paul Xuereb (Malta) from 1978 to 1983, John Stringleman (New Zealand) from 1983 to 1986, Stephaney Ferguson (Jamaica) from 1986 to 1990, and Michael Wooliscroft (New Zealand) from 1990. The first Executive Secretary, Mrs. C. P. Fray, served from 1973 to 1979.

She was succeeded by K. C. Harrison from 1980 to 1983, Joan E. Swaby (Jamaica) from 1983 to 1990, and Norma Amenu-Kpodo (Jamaica) from 1990.

The Executive Committee comprises the three officers elected by the General Council (President, Vice-President, and Honorary Treasurer); six Vice-Presidents elected regionally (representing East, Central, and Southern Africa; West Africa; the Americas and the Caribbean; Asia; Europe; and the South Pacific); and the immediate Past President. Members hold office for the period between meetings of the General Council. Under the chairmanship of its Vice-President, each region has a Council that arranges its program and submits it for approval to the Executive Committee.

Programs. COMLA's activities fall into four categories: conferences, including training seminars and workshops in various regions in turn; practical projects; occasional publications; and maintaining professional contacts throughout the Commonwealth, chiefly through its quarterly *COMLA Newsletter.* There is an annual subscription, kept low to encourage membership but thereby insufficient to cover costs of these activities. When members host conferences, COMLA relies on regional support funds and on grants from agencies such as the Commonwealth Fund for Technical Cooperation (CFTC). In Jamaica the government supports the COMLA Secretariat, which was located there from its inception, the first of the CPOs to be accommodated in a developing country.

COMLA conferences have included an Asia region workshop in Singapore on research methodology in librarianship (1977); a South Pacific region seminar in Brisbane on electronic systems for librarians (1984, in association with the Library Association of Australia); a Europe region workshop in Malta on bibliography (1984), and one in Malta on automation (1990); and a West Africa region workshop in Ghana on rural resource centers (1991).

Publications. Most COMLA publications have resulted from conferences and workshops. They include reports on *National Bibliographies for the English-speaking Caribbean* (1974); *Exchanges, Attachments, and Internships* (1975); *Reciprocity of Qualifications and Training for Librarianship* (1975); *Information for Development* (1984); *Government Libraries for the Nation: Services and Training* (1986); and *Rural Libraries and Community Resource Centres* (1990). In Fiji COMLA cooperated with CFTC in a workshop that resulted in publication by the Commonwealth Secretariat of *Training Modules for Non-Professional Library Staff* (1981). *COMLA Newsletter* was published continuously from 1973. The organization planned a *COMLA Manual* for 1991 and a *COMLA Directory of Training and Education Opportunities in Library and Information Studies in Commonwealth Countries.*

Ties with Other Associations. The Commonwealth Library Association is a member of the International Federation of Library Associations and Institutions (IFLA) and of the Association of Caribbean University, Research and Institutional Libraries (ACURIL). It has close relations with the Standing Conference of East, Central, and Southern African Librarians (SCECSAL), the Congress of Southeast Asian Librarians (CONSAL), the Standing Congress of Pacific Librarians (SCOPAL), the Cooperative Association of Librarians in the Mediterranean (CALM), and the Pacific Information Centre (PIC).

REFERENCES

Ken Williams, editor, *A Guide to Commonwealth Professional Associations* (1983).

The Commonwealth Foundation, *Aims and Achievements 1966–1984* (1984).

Directory of Commonwealth Organizations (1991).

NORMA AMENU-KPODO

Congo

The People's Republic of the Congo (République Populaire du Congo; not to be confused with Zaire, formerly Belgian Congo) was, up to 1960, a French colony as part of French Equatorial Africa. Located on the equator, the country is bounded by the Central African Republic on the north, Zaire on the east and south, Angola on the southwest, the Atlantic Ocean and Gabon on the west, and Cameroon on the northwest. Population (1990 est.) 2,271,000; area 342,000 sq.km. The official language is French; Bantu dialects are spoken. The national languages—Lingala and Kikongo—do not possess any real written literature.

History. Before independence, the library of the General Government of French Equatorial Africa (FEA) had a collection of some 2,500 volumes; the library of the Institute of Central African Studies, a collection of 8,000 volumes and approximately 250 periodical titles; and the library of the Institute of Congo Studies, about 3,040 volumes. All these libraries specialized in the ethnology, history, geography, and economy of FEA as well as in botany, entomology, soil science, and sociology.

The Board of Libraries, Archives, and Documentation (DSBAD) is the central management, coordination, and supervision organ for library, archive, and documentation services in the Congo. The DSBAD, which reports to the Ministry of Culture and Arts, was created by decree in 1971. It has the basic functions of planning and organizing the development of all documentary structures in the country and setting national standards suited to ensure the efficacy of those structures. However, contrary to the spirit of the decree, the DSBAD at present supervises only the People's National Library, the National Documentation Center, and the National Archives, which are the core of the Center. The DSBAD did not control other documentary units as of the mid-1980s, whether they be public libraries, the University Library, or other special libraries. Furthermore, its budget is woefully inadequate.

National Library Services. The People's National Library, established in 1971, is not a national library in the classical sense. It is a deposit and research library but at the same time serves as the main locus of public reading, whence its title as a people's library. The People's National Library benefits from a type of legal deposit obligation placed on bookstores that import books. (There are no publishing houses.) Its collections (some 5,500 volumes) comprise principally novels, paperback books, and some research and popular works. The library also has 53 periodical titles, plus some films and prints. The areas repre-

Libraries in Congo (1990)

Type of library	Number of administrative units (main libraries)	Number of service points (branches, mobile stops, etc.)	Volumes in collections	Population served
National[a]	1	1	8,000	995
Academic[b]	1	9	78,000	12,000
Public[a]	1	4	15,000	22,365
Special[c]	1	--	20,000	--

[a]1989 data
[b]1987 data
[c]1986 data

Source: Unesco, *Statistical Yearbook,* 1991

sented are literature, humanities, social sciences, and science.

The National Documentation Center was established in 1971 but began real operation only in 1978. It plans and carries out the national documentary policy. It is charged with research, collecting, processing, and use of all information relating to the Congo, with setting up and coordinating all documentary activity in the country, and with organizing documentation centers and furthering international cooperation through exchanges. It publishes an analytical guide to the articles it reviews.

The National Archives Service was established in 1971. It has as its task the preservation of files from all central services, territorial organizations, and state enterprises as well as the supervision of municipal archives and, according to appropriate rules, of notarial papers and certain other private archives. In 1974 the National Archives received on deposit a segment of the archives of the General Government of FEA, most of the colonial archives being housed in the French National Archives in Aix-en-Provence. The Archives also received on deposit the archives of retired civil service employees and contract workers.

Public Libraries. Generally speaking, the DSBAD, cultural centers of foreign countries, and certain private individuals look after public reading. However, national efforts still remain weak. There are public libraries in Makelekele (2,241 volumes), Moungale (2,234), and Ouénzé (3,557), and a pool regional library (1,500 volumes), all administered by the DSBAD.

Private Libraries. Private libraries include those of the Abraham de Bacongo Home (3,500 volumes), of the American Cultural Center (2,450 volumes, 28 periodical titles), of the Angolan Cultural Center (632 volumes), of the French Cultural Center in Brazzaville (25,000 volumes), of the French Cultural Center in Pointe-Noire (13,331 volumes), and of the Russian Cultural Center (18,500 volumes). All but two of these libraries are located in Brazzaville; there is free access.

University Library. Open to students, university teachers, and researchers, the University Library is the largest in the country. It receives most of its support from the state and employs the most professionals. After the breakup of FEA, the collection of the old library of the general government of FEA as well as the collection of the Alliance Française library (5,000 volumes) became the basis of the Library of the Center for Higher Education in Brazzaville (1959), which then became the Foundation for Higher Education in Central Africa (1961), the University of Brazzaville (1971), and Marien Ngouabi University (1977). Marien Ngouabi University does not have a single campus; parts of it are scattered throughout Brazzaville and indeed throughout the entire country. Each part of the university has its own library, resulting in ten libraries; the Library of the School of Letters and Humanities and of the Advanced Institute of Economic, Juridical, Administrative, and Management Sciences (which is still called the Central Library) is the most important. It arose from the ashes of the library of the general government of FEA and the Alliance Française. The law, economics, literature, humanities, and social science library houses an encyclopedia collection. The collections of the Central Library cover colonial literature and accounts of explorers and missionaries as well as various scientific studies on Central Africa (45,000 volumes and 252 current periodical titles). The Library of the School of Science has 11,200 volumes and 141 current periodical titles. There is a special science library. The Library of the Advanced Institute of Education contains 12,665 volumes and 41 current periodical titles. The Library of the Advanced Institute of Health Sciences has 3,890 volumes and 55 current periodical titles; it collects in the areas of medicine and pharmacy and receives grants from the World Health Organization. The Library of the Institute of Physical and Sports Education contains 400 volumes and 8 journal titles. The Library of the Institute of Rural Development has 3,750 volumes and 32 current periodicals; it collects predominantly in the fields of agronomy, education, and management. The Library is a depository for FAO publications. The Library of the Management Department has 2,500 volumes. The Library of the Advanced Normal School of Technical Education (400 volumes) covers mostly applied sciences. The 400 volumes of the Library of the National Administration and Magistrateship School cover political economy, public finance, and law. The Library of the Advanced Education Institute of Loubomo is a general education and polytechnic library. Many schools are quite new and their libraries are new.

Special Libraries. Most are organized and run by international groups. The Library of the National Institute of Research and Educational Action was established in July 1962 and has 8,500 volumes and 35 current periodical titles. The ORSTOM library in Brazzaville, established in 1947, in 1961 received as a gift the collection of the defunct library of the Office pour la Recherche Scientifique Outre-Mer (ORSTOM, Institute of Central African Studies, a French research organization). There are 17,000 volumes and 831 periodicals, 1,400 microfilms, and 2,000 topographic maps. Principal subjects covered include botany, entomology, ethnology, psychology, sociology, geography, soil science, and hydrology. The ORSTOM library at Pointe-Noire contains 6,000 volumes; its main subject is oceanography. The Library of the World Health Organization was established in 1963 and contains 45,000 volumes and 200 current periodicals; its main interest is medicine and pharmacy. The Library of the National Economic Documentation Center contains 1,100 volumes and 30 periodicals. The Library of the General Scientific and Technical Research Board has 2,600 volumes and 45 periodicals.

School Libraries. These are almost nonexistent. High schools are supposed to have libraries, but they are poor and out-of-date. School libraries contain mainly textbooks. The staffs of such libraries are generally not credentialed.

The Profession. The Congo has neither a library school nor a professional training center. Its professional workers receive their education at the library, archives, and documentalists school in Dakar, in Russia, and in France. The Congolese Association for the Development of Documentation, Libraries, and Archives (ACDBA) was established in 1984. The Congo in the late 1980s had about 70 trained professionals: 15 archivists, 15 documentalists, and 40 librarians, though all were not employed in libraries. Many change to other professions after earning their professional diplomas.

BRUNO WAMBI

Congress of Southeast Asian Librarians

The Congress of Southeast Asian Librarians (CONSAL) was founded at the First Conference of Southeast Asian Librarians, in Singapore, August 14–16, 1970, with a theme of regional cooperation. CONSAL is a nongovernmental organization with the following objectives, as specified in its constitution: to establish and strengthen relations among librarians, libraries, library schools, library associations, and related organizations in the region; to promote cooperation in the fields of librarianship, library education, documentation, and related activities in the region; and to cooperate with other regional and international organizations and institutions in the fields of librarianship, library education, documentation, and related activities.

Themes chosen for CONSAL conferences have revolved around issues and concerns of librarians, libraries, and information centers in the region, although matters of international professional concern have also been addressed. CONSAL II (Manila, December 10–14, 1973) discussed library education. CONSAL III (Djakarta, December 1–5, 1975) dealt with integrated library and documentation services. CONSAL IV (Bangkok, June 5–9, 1978), discussed the development of national information services. CONSAL V (Kuala Lumpur, May 25–29, 1981) covered access to information. CONSAL VI (Singapore, May 30–June 3, 1983) discussed the issue of the library in the information revolution. CONSAL VII (Manila, February 15–21, 1987) focused again on regional problems and the role of libraries in rural development. CONSAL VIII (Djakarta, June 11–14, 1990) discussed new challenges to library services in the developing world.

CONSAL is an independent regional body that functions according to the provisions of its original constitution, ratified by the delegates to the first conference, held in Singapore in 1970. The constitution was amended in Djakarta in 1975 to change the name from "Conference" to "Congress." It was amended again, in Bangkok in 1978, to provide for national membership comprising national library associations and national and other libraries and other related organizations, in both member countries and non-member countries, as well as individuals interested in the objectives of the organization. CONSAL conferences are hosted on a rotating basis among the member countries every three years. The Secretariat of CONSAL also rotates according to the country hosting the conference.

CONSAL publishes the proceedings of each conference. In some instances, the host country publishes a newsletter, primarily to inform members of the progress of plans and programs for the forthcoming conference. Bangkok was selected as the host for CONSAL IX in 1993.

The Association of Southeast Asian Nations (ASEAN) considers CONSAL an important regional organization that projects to the international library community the development of librarianship and information services in the region.

REFERENCE

D. E. K. Wijasuriya, "CONSAL: An Assessment," *Proceedings of the 7th Congress of Southeast Asian Librarians* (1987).

PRUDENCIANA C. CRUZ

Connor, Robert D. W.
(1878–1950)

North Carolina State Archives
Robert D. W. Connor

Robert Digges Wimberly Connor, historian and educator, was the first Archivist of the United States.

Connor was born in Wilson, North Carolina, September 26, 1878, one of 12 children of Henry Groves and Kate Whitfield Connor. He attended the local public schools and in 1899 received a Ph.B. from the University of North Carolina at Chapel Hill. For four years he was engaged in public school work; then from 1904 to 1907 he served as Secretary of the state educational campaign committee. In 1903 Connor was appointed by Governor Charles B. Aycock to membership on the newly created North Carolina Historical Commission; for four years he served as the Commission's unpaid Secretary.

In 1906 Connor published a booklet, *A State Library and Department of Archives and Records,* an ambitious plan for the revitalization of the State Library and the establishment of a state archival agency. In response to his prodding, the General

Assembly the following year broadened the authority of the Historical Commission and gave it an increased appropriation. Thereupon Connor accepted the salaried secretaryship and during the next 14 years developed one of the nation's outstanding state historical agencies. In addition, he was Secretary of the North Carolina Teachers Assembly for six years, President of the North Carolina Literary and Historical Association for a year and its Secretary for seven, member of the University of North Carolina's Board of Trustees for seven years and its Secretary for five, President of the General Alumni Association of the University from 1917 to 1921, and member of the National Board of Historical Service during World War I.

After a leave of absence to study at Columbia University, 1920–21, Connor resigned from the Historical Commission to accept the Kenan Professorship in History and Government at the University of North Carolina. His lectures, characterized by their clarity and wit, made him an unusually popular teacher.

In 1934, with the strong endorsement of the American Historical Association, Connor was appointed the first Archivist of the United States by President Franklin D. Roosevelt. His tasks were monumental: the National Archives building was unfinished; a 150-year backlog of public records crowded offices throughout the federal government; and there were only a few people in the entire country acquainted with European archival principles. For the next six years Connor presided over the completion and occupation of the new building, the organization and training of a large staff, and the establishment of policies and procedures for the transfer, repair, arrangement, description, and use of the nation's archives. He gathered around him other historians of high standing, encouraged the formation in 1936 of the Society of American Archivists (SAA), and insisted that the National Archives share its growing expertise with records custodians at the state level. He also worked closely with the President in establishing the Franklin D. Roosevelt Library, the first of a number of similar archival institutions administered by the National Archives.

Connor resigned as Archivist in 1941 and returned to Chapel Hill as Craige Professor of Jurisprudence and History. He maintained his interest in archival administration, however, serving as President of the SAA, 1941–43, and as Chairman of the North Carolina Historical Commission and its successor, the Executive Board of the State Department of Archives and History, from 1942 until his death.

Connor's most notable published work was his two-volume history, *North Carolina: Rebuilding an Ancient Commonwealth, 1584–1925* (1929). Among other books were *History of North Carolina: The Colonial and Revolutionary Periods, 1584–1783* (1919); *The Life and Speeches of Charles Brantley Aycock* (1912); *Race Elements in the White Population of North Carolina* (1920); and *The Story of the United States, for Young People* (1916). *The North Carolina Manual 1913,* which he compiled, was for 60 years a standard reference work.

He died February 25, 1950, in Durham and was buried in the Chapel Hill Cemetery. The Historical Society of North Carolina presents each year the Robert D. W. Connor Award for the best article published in the *North Carolina Historical Review*.

H. G. JONES

Conservation and Preservation of Library Materials

Preservation of library materials is part of a broader concern that is sometimes referred to as the preservation of cultural property. Some authorities trace the beginnings of preservation to the Age of Enlightenment and the discoveries of the ruins at Pompeii and Herculaneum. Others claim that preservation is as old as civilization itself, rooted in the idea that mankind learns from what has gone before, and that the evidence of earlier times is important and worth saving. Libraries and other institutions whose collections serve an archival function play a primary role in collecting and preserving the human record; not everything worth preserving is collected by libraries, nor is everything they collect necessarily worth preserving.

Preservation and *conservation* are often used interchangeably, and there seems to be no clearcut distinction between the two terms. Conservation seems more specific and object-oriented, whereas preservation is a broader concept that embraces conservation as well as protection, maintenance, and restoration in its meaning. It also carries a connotation of official policy and perhaps for that reason is the preferred term to describe the entire constellation of administrative and technical activities that bear on collection management in libraries and archives.

With the encouragement of several professional organizations, government agencies, and private foundations, the early 1980s witnessed a proliferation of preservation programs in the United States and abroad. In the U.S., important contributions are being made by the Society of American Archivists (SAA), the American Library Association (ALA), the Association of Research Libraries (ARL), the Council on Library Resources (CLR), and the National Preservation Program Office of the Library of Congress. Additional impetus is provided by direct grants to individual libraries in support of specific projects from such agencies as the National Endowment for the Humanities (NEH), the National Historic Publications and Records Commission (NHPRC), and the Department of Education (under Title II-C of the Higher Education Act). The Andrew W. Mellon Foundation has provided generous support to libraries in such areas as internships for conservators and preservation program administrators, establishment of treatment facilities, and support for cooperative microrecording programs.

In 1984 alone, a dozen major libraries and library consortia established administrative positions to guide expanding institutional programs; among them were Northwestern University, the University of Chicago, Cornell University, Ohio State University, the New York State Library, and the Southeastern Library Network (SOLINET). In 1983 the British Library consolidated its preservation activities under one administrative officer, and in 1984 created a National Preservation Office to promote the better conservation of library collections throughout the United

Kingdom. Landmark legislation in New York State in 1984 provided annual grants of $90,000 for five consecutive years to 11 comprehensive research libraries in the state.

Preservation of library and archival materials was not viewed by most research libraries as a matter of great urgency until the 1960s. Perhaps the greatest influence on the future development of the field in the U.S. was William J. Barrow's alarming assertion—based on his investigations reported in *Deterioration of Book Stock: Causes and Remedies: Two Studies on the Permanence of Book Paper* (1959)—that most library books printed in the first half of the 20th century will be in unusable condition by the next century. Further stimulus came from two disasters that occurred in 1966—a fire at the Jewish Theological Seminary in New York City that consumed 70,000 volumes and damaged an additional 150,000, and the flood of the Arno River in Florence, Italy, that inundated a million volumes stored in the cellar and ground floor of the Biblioteca Nazionale Centrale, including 150,000 volumes in the Magliabecchiana Collection, gathered during the 17th century by Florentine Humanists to create Italy's first public library. These events, vivid reminders of the vulnerability of books, particularly those that are also cultural artifacts, contributed to the development of emergency salvage techniques for water-damaged materials and jolted libraries into action in such areas as planning for disaster preparedness and formulating recovery procedures for water-damaged materials.

Characteristics of the Field. Library preservation may be characterized as follows. (1) It is highly technical and is concerned with such complicated topics as the chemistry of materials, the monitoring of environmental control systems, and the design of book structures. (2) The ethical and philosophical framework within which preservation decisions must be made is not well developed. (3) The problems of library preservation are highly diverse as a result of the wide range of physical formats found in library collections and the difficulty of distinguishing materials of an artifactual nature from those of value solely for their intellectual content. (4) The need for preservation of library materials is both massive and urgent. (5) Preservation is expensive—given the quantity of material that is deteriorating, microfilming and conservation treatment are frighteningly costly, as is the development, testing, and implementation of such alternate technologies as mass deacidification and optical disk storage. (6) Library preservation is a developing field—there are few comprehensive training programs; the literature of the field is growing rapidly, and some of it is redundant or of varying quality; there are few standards; and numerous technical questions still demand solution. (7) Preservation is an interdisciplinary enterprise and demands close cooperation of the library profession, the conservation profession, the suppliers of materials and services, and the scientific community, including chemists and computer specialists.

Nature and Extent of Deterioration. Present-day collections are composed largely of books printed on unstable paper, and libraries will continue to acquire significant works printed on poor paper.

Scientists have defined deterioration as a process of transition from a higher to a lower energy level.

Sequential steps in preserving the typescript of Richard Wright's Native Son:

(1) Examining and documenting the condition of the untreated leaves.

(2) Testing the stability of the inks in order to determine the most appropriate deacidification treatment.

Cellulose, the principal component of most library materials, is remarkably stable in its pure form, but under certain conditions it tends to break down into simpler molecules, returning eventually to carbon dioxide. Natural oxidation is accelerated by two chemical reactions—hydrolytic attack on cellulose fibers by acid in the paper itself, and photochemical degradation caused by light and other forms of radiant energy. Environmental factors (such as the polluted air present in most urban centers and widely fluctuating levels of temperature and relative humidity) and biological factors (mold, insects, and even human beings) also contribute to the process of deterioration.

In order to quantify the extent of deterioration in their collections, and to develop resources and strate-

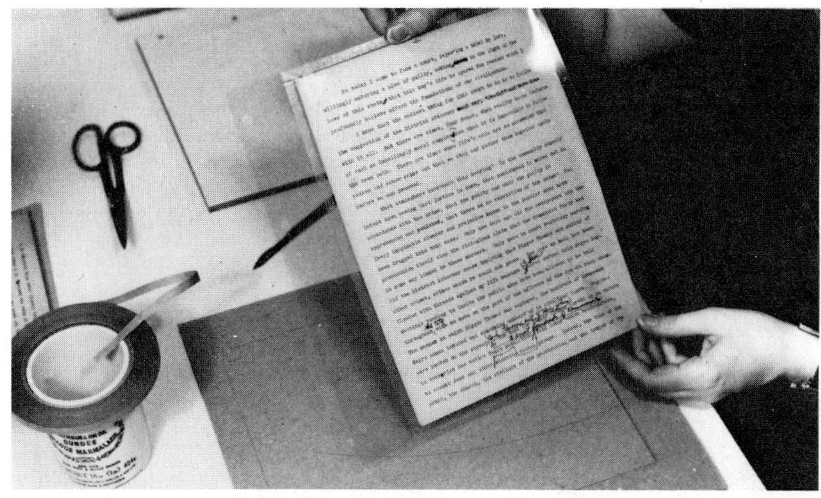

(3) *A single leaf, deacidified, mended, and encapsulated in stable polyester film (Mylar) preparatory to being placed in a post binding.*

(4) *The completed volume.*

(5) *The project completed: bound volumes of the encapsulated leaves preserved for scholarly research.*

Schomburg Center for Research in Black Culture, New York Public Library.

gies for addressing the problem, several research libraries in the U.S. completed surveys by the early 1980s, among them Yale University Libraries, the Library of Congress (LC), and the New York Public Library (NYPL). Results of these surveys corroborated Barrow's predictions; for example, Yale determined that 44.3 percent of the books sampled had brittle paper that broke after four folds or less, and 82.7 percent had highly acidic paper and would eventually require some form of treatment. The LC and NYPL surveys yielded similar findings.

Preventive Measures. Preventive preservation—that is, action taken *before* damage has occurred, that will retard further deterioration—has emerged as a basic concept in the field. The single most effective measure libraries can take to slow the deterioration process is to reduce the temperature in book storage areas. The higher the temperature, the faster chemical reactions accelerate; conversely, paper scientists generally agree that for every 10 degrees Celsius the storage temperature can be reduced, the life of paper can be approximately doubled.

There are several immediate steps libraries can take to prolong the useful life of their collections. Smaller libraries with limited funds and small staffs can identify brittle books that are too poor to rebind and insert them into acid-free paper wrappers until they can be repaired or replaced. Such flat paper objects as manuscripts and drawings can be interleaved with alkaline-buffered tissue available from conservation supply houses and stored in archival-quality folders and boxes. Extremely fragile paper objects in single-sheet format can be placed in envelopes of polyester film available in the U.S. under such trade names as Mylar, Scotchpar, and Melinex; it is essential that order specifications clearly indicate that film appropriate for preservation uses is required. Volumes can be cleaned and a program of minor repairs begun using procedures such as those described in Carolyn C. Morrow's *Conservation Treatment Procedures* (1982).

Spurred by a dialogue that began in the mid-1970s between preservation librarians, representatives of library binding firms, and members of the Library Binding Institute, a growing number of firms offer a wide variety of binding methods and other preservation treatment options. For example, several firms now supply custom-made preservation cases that may be used as an alternative to rebinding for volumes that have become brittle.

In large libraries faced with massive deterioration problems, a preservation program can be developed using a phased approach, doing the easier, less expensive things first and leaving costlier and more complex tasks until later. A key element is to undertake administrative planning *before* embarking on a course of action. Initial steps should include inspecting the physical storage facilities to identify particular problems, conducting a survey to determine the extent of deterioration among the various formats of material in the collection, framing a realistic plan of action tailored to the budgetary and staffing realities of the particular library, and planning a disaster preparedness and recovery program.

Early in 1980 the Association of Research Libraries embarked on an ambitious preservation project designed to encourage individual libraries to expand

and improve preservation efforts. A number of planning tools and procedural manuals were produced, and a planning procedure was developed that provides a structured approach to the numerous administrative and organizational decisions that must be made, consistent with the libraries' service goals and present and potential resources.

Training. In the library preservation field, development of educational programs is needed in four areas: programs for new and practicing librarians, archivists, and curators; programs for training professional conservators; programs for educating administrators of preservation programs; and programs for training conservation technicians who work under the supervision of professional conservators.

A growing number of library schools in North America and Europe offer courses on preservation of library materials. In North America the *Preservation Education Directory*, published by ALA, is an important source of information. Until 1981 there was no postgraduate degree program for the education and training of book conservators and preservation administrators. That year the School of Library Service at Columbia University began both programs, leading to M.S. degrees and postgraduate certificates in the specialization. By 1992, when the School was closed, the program had produced almost a hundred graduates who were actively working in the field. Paul N. Banks, founding Director of the programs, described them in *The History and Future Directions of Conservation Training in North America* (1984). The programs moved to the University of Texas, Austin, in 1992.

As a result of the Columbia programs, the number of apprenticeships and internships in library and archival facilities expanded significantly in the U.S. and elsewhere. Some, such as the Center for Book Arts in New York City and the Copernicus School of Bookbinding and Restoration in Berkeley, California, offer short courses on paper deacidification techniques, paper cleaning and repair, bookbinding, and box-making. The Deutsche Bucherei in Leipzig, as part of the new Deutsche Bibliothek, began adding to these programs in the early 1990s.

Research. Despite growing awareness of the magnitude of the preservation problem, expenditures for basic and applied research have been disturbingly small. The high cost of staffing and equipping research facilities has obliged most libraries to place their emphasis on microrecording and physical treatment programs rather than on analysis and research. Such laboratories as do exist are usually in a museum or other institution caring for a wide variety of cultural properties.

A worldwide directory of conservation research centers was still not available in 1990, although such facilities were known to exist in several countries. An indirect means of identifying such facilities, as well as individuals conducting research and the areas of their investigations, is available through journals serving the field. Among them are *The Abbey Newsletter: Bookbinding and Conservation; Conservation Administration News; Art and Archaeology Technical Abstracts; Conservation Studies;* and the *Journal of the American Institute for Conservation.*

Future Technologies and Trends. Significant strides are being made in the development of new technologies and in the adaptation of existing technologies to alleviate the preservation problems of libraries and archives. Typical of recent progress is the work of Todor Stambolov and others at the Central Research Laboratory for Objects of Art and Science, Amsterdam, The Netherlands, in the conservation of leather; the investigations of Bruce J. Humphrey of the Nova Tran Corporation, Clear Lake, Wisconsin, into the application of parylene conformal coating technology as a means of strengthening paper; the achievement of Richard D. Smith in developing the Wei T'o Nonaqueous Book Deacidification System in use in the Public Archives of Canada; and of Chicago book restorer William Minter, who, with Peter Malosh, pioneered in the development of an ultrasonic welder

Orszagos Széchényi Konyvtar

Library employee restoring maps at the National Széchényi Library, Budapest, Hungary.

National Library of Japan

Fumigation station used in the preservation of the National Library of Japan.

for polyester encapsulation that seals and protects fragile documents more efficiently than traditional techniques.

Sensing a potential market in preservation techniques, several commercial firms announced plans to offer deacidification services based on such technologies as treating book paper with diethyl zinc vapor (DEZ). However, by the early 1990s, only one firm, Akzo Chemicals, Inc., remained. It worked with the LC on offering services based on the DEZ process.

The British Library in cooperation with the Optronics Group of Cambridge, England, developed a book scanner and digitizer that allows the conversion of books and other library materials into digital electronic form for storage in computers and transmission to remote destinations. This conversion is quick and is accomplished without damage to the original material.

Through its Optical Disk Pilot Program, begun in 1982, the LC is evaluating the use of optical disk technology for preserving and managing its collections and is determining the cost and benefits of such technology when used in a production setting. The first of six analogue videodisks with its player and video monitor is now installed in the Prints and Photographs Reading Room; with it, a library patron can sort quickly through or study any one of almost 40,000 photographs, posters, and other high-use pictorial items.

In another phase of the program, a system is now being implemented on an experimental basis that uses digital optical disks for computerized mass storage, preservation, and retrieval of printed materials, including text and halftone illustrations.

An important landmark in the development of standards was set with publication of the American National Standard "Permanence of Paper for Printed Library Materials" (American National Standard Z39.48-1984). It grew out of the work of the Committee on Production Guidelines for Book Longevity, sponsored by the CLR (1979–82), with funding from the Mellon Foundation. Work on a second important standard, "Standard Practice for Storage of Paper-Based Library and Archival Documents," is in progress. It was sponsored by the National Institute for Conservation under a grant from the NHPRC.

Following the *Final Report on Preservation* of the Association of American Universities (AAU) and the CLR (1981), a new Commission on Preservation Access was established to organize and coordinate an international strategy for preservation activities. Patricia Battin was appointed its first President. The Commission sponsored studies, hosted conferences, and funded many preservation projects.

REFERENCES

Book Longevity: Reports of the Committee on Production Guidelines for Book Longevity (1982).

Carolyn Clark Morrow, *The Preservation Challenge: A Guide to Conserving Library Materials* (1983).

U.S. National Association of Government Archives and Records Administrators, *Guide and Resources for Archival Strategic Preservation* (1990).

JOHN P. BAKER

Copyright*

The term "copyright" has a double meaning stemming from its etymology. It denotes both the right "to own and control a work of authorship" and the right "to copy it." The English term does not, for historical reasons, identify the beneficiary in the rights; the beneficiary is clearly identified, however, in usage in other languages, such as the French *droit d'auteur,* the German *Urheberrecht,* and the Spanish *derecho de autor,* all of which mean "the right of the author."

LEGAL NATURE OF COPYRIGHT

Copyright is a property right that pertains to original works of authorship. It is one part of what is known as intellectual property, which also includes patents and trademarks. In general, copyright rewards authors for their contributions to society and entices them to contribute to the advancement of knowledge. Others who seek to use an author's copyrighted work have to ask permission and, in some cases, to pay a fee called a *royalty*. Copyright protects only the author's expressions and arrangements in relation to an idea. Copyright does not extend to the idea itself; thus, ideas are free and can be built upon and be expressed differently or more fully. Accordingly, the new explanation or the fuller treatment can also be protected without violating the copyright on the original expression of the same idea. Patents, by contrast, protect both the idea and its expression in any given invention, provided that the invention is novel, useful, and not obvious to an expert in the field. A patentee has a monopoly right (for 17 years in the U.S.) to prevent others from using the invention, in part or in entirety, even if others made the same discovery independently. Trademark protection, on the other hand, is based on the investment and skill in creating a symbol the public will readily identify with particular goods or services.

There are two major schools of thought concerning the legal nature of copyright. One considers copyright as a type of alienable property such as real estate and goods and advocates unlimited, perpetual rights to the owner of copyright. The second school believes that copyright is a monopoly and that the author should be given as limited protection as possible. Some Western European countries (such as France) recognize copyright as a unique form of property right with strong personal elements at its base. These countries recognize this personal right in their laws and grant the author an inalienable "moral right" that assures his or her identification with the work and protects against its distortion or any alteration that might be prejudicial to the author's reputation or honor. This approach underlies the Berne Convention.

HISTORY

The copyright concept began in England after William Caxton introduced the technique of printing from movable type in 1476. Before that historic event, ideas had to be recorded by hand on parchment or paper, and making a copy of a book involved copying each word, again by hand. Printing from movable type revolutionized the production of books, because any work could easily be produced in quantity. The printing press thus came to have well-documented religious, social, and economic impacts. The printing press also created a threat for the publisher of the works, whose original work could be reproduced easily by "pirates" who incurred none of the costs involved in producing the first copy.

To protect themselves, publishers, booksellers, and printers created a trade association, the Stationers' Company, chartered in 1557 by Queen Mary. In accordance with this Charter, the Stationers maintained a register in which the members recorded the title of each book they bought from an author or from another member. An entry in the register granted the registrant perpetual rights to the registered book and determined claims of piracy. A decade later, most regulations—including the Stationers' rules to control the press—had proven ineffective and unenforceable. By 1710 the Statute of Anne was enacted as the first English copyright law. This statute granted protection against unauthorized printing or copying of published works for a limited period of time. Unpublished works were covered by common law and not protected by the Statute of Anne.

U.S. Copyright Laws. One might consider the Statute of Anne the prototype of all subsequent copyright laws. For example, it was in concept the basis for Article I, Section 8, of the U.S. Constitution, which vested in the Congress the power to create a law to give authors and inventors exclusive rights to their writings and discoveries, for a limited time, for the purpose of the "advancement of science and useful arts." In 1790 the first U.S. copyright law was enacted; it applied only to books, maps, and charts. It granted protection only to U.S. citizens, and foreign authors—Charles Dickens is an example—were so fully pirated by U.S. publishers that more costly American authors were excluded. In 1891 Congress passed the Chase Act, granting protection to foreign authors under certain conditions, and thus protecting American authors from the unfair competition of royalty-free, pirated English works.

The 1790 law was amended several times, mainly to expand the subject matter protected by its provisions; for example, in 1802 Congress extended copyright protection to prints; in 1831 to public performances; and in 1870 to fine arts and to the rights to dramatization and translation. A major revision took place in 1909. It included still more categories of protected work, such as "plastic works of scientific or technical character," and gave the author the right to make derivations (such as abridgments) from an original work. The period of protection under the 1909 law was 28 years, renewable for a similar period. In 1947 the law was codified and enacted as Title 17 of the U.S. Code. In 1971 sound recordings were added as the seventh category of protected works of authorship.

Copyright Act of 1976. Dramatic changes in society and vast advances in technology after World War II dictated the necessity to review the 1909 law. Congress passed a general revision in 1976 that had a profound effect on the copyright system. This revision, which took effect in 1978, preempted common law copyright (that is, unpublished works are now protected for a period of 100 years from the date of creation and not in perpetuity). The period of protection for works created after 1978 was changed from the 28 years plus 28-year renewal to the life of the author and 50 years after the author's death. As to corporate ownership, copyright protection extends to 75 years from date of publication. The new law also created a Copyright Royalty Tribunal to deal with compulsory licensing for public broadcasting, cable television, and jukeboxes.

The 1976 act included two important changes: the concept of "fair use," a 19th-century court-created rule of reason, in Section 107; and specific provisions for library photocopying and use of copyrighted works, in Section 108. Section 108 applies only to libraries whose collections are accessible to the public or to researchers in their specialized fields, and when the reproduction of copyrighted material is made for no direct or indirect profit. The new law also liberalized the strict requirements and formalities of the copyright notice. As it stands now, the omission of the notice (© or the abbreviation "copr.") does not result in the forfeiture of statutory copyright protection, provided that the unintentional omission is corrected within five years.

From 1891, the copyright law included one provision, the Manufacturing Clause, designed to protect American printers against the competition of cheap printing abroad. The Clause deals with works in the English language produced abroad by U.S. citizens or residents. The 1976 revision included a provision that would have abolished the Manufacturing Clause in 1982. The ALA and publishers favored abolition, but American printers, who feared loss of U.S. jobs, lobbied strongly to have the Clause extended. They won an extension to 1986, but could not win a further one, and the Clause died.

Despite significant revisions in the copyright law in 1976, Congress fell short in dealing with issues relating to computers and technology in general. Section 117 of the new law in essence preserved the protection status quo of information systems and reflected a lack of sufficient knowledge at the time of passage to deal with technological issues. Therefore, a National Commission on New Technological Uses of Copyright Works (CONTU) was created to look into

Library of Congress

Seal of the United States Copyright Office is applied to new patent.

questions relating to interlibrary loans, computer software, and databases. CONTU was instrumental during its three-year existence in securing an agreement on guidelines between copyright owners (publishers and authors) and librarians on permissible amounts of copying for interlibrary loan and on what constitutes the aggregate number of copies obtained through interlibrary loans that is not permissible (that is, copying anything beyond five copies of one title in one year is generally not permissible without permission of the copyright owner). CONTU recommended that computer software programs should be accorded statutory copyright protection. As a result, Congress amended the copyright law in 1980 to include software under the category of "literary works" (Section 102). It also amended section 117 to include provisions to allow the purchaser of any software package to modify it to fit its intended use and to copy it for preservation.

Fair Use. Authors have exclusive rights to control how their work is produced; the development of any works derived from it; the right to the first sale of the work; and the right to control any public performance or display of it. It is easy to see that the author's right to control and benefit from a work might at some point collide with society's right to know. The question was raised in the case of Folson v. Marsh and the U.S. Supreme Court decided in 1891 that the defendant's use of the plaintiff's work without authorization was "fair use." The concept was invoked in many subsequent cases challenging various types of uses of copyright work and was eventually included as Section 107 of the 1976 copyright law. According to the law, if the use is "fair," then it is permissible without authorization or payment of royalties. Fairness is determined by meeting four criteria: the purpose of the use; the nature of the work used; the substantiality of the use; and the effect of the use on the actual and potential market for the work used.

In passing the revised law, Congress acknowledged in House Report No. 94–1476 that the concept of "fair use" is vague and that the parties involved should come to an agreement as to what constitutes fair use of copyrighted material. As a result, representatives of publishers, authors, and an Ad Hoc Committee of Educational Institutions and Organizations on Copyright Law Revisions met several times and reached agreement on guidelines for classroom copying of copyrighted works for nonprofit educational institutions. Under these guidelines, a teacher or teacher's agent (such as a librarian) may make one copy of a copyrighted work for research or teaching. Multiple copying for classroom use is allowable only if it meets tests of *brevity, spontaneity,* and *cumulative effect.* Similar guidelines were developed first with music educators and later with educators in general regarding taping copyrighted programs off the air for educational purposes. These various guidelines, however, are not a part of the copyright law and are technically not enforceable. Yet they would carry substantial weight in litigation, because Congress included them in the published House Report and considered them to be representative of the legislative intent regarding fair use. While the CONTU guidelines for interlibrary loans are applicable to all types of libraries, the guidelines for educational uses of copyrighted material are only applicable to libraries in nonprofit educational institutions.

The Guideline for Classroom Use includes a list of uses that are not permitted under any circumstances. One of these prohibitions is the creation of anthologies, such as collections of copies of articles and sections of books, bound together and sold as reading material for classroom use. Harper and Row and seven other publishers sued a photocopying service, Kinko's Graphics Corporation, in 1989, claiming that it was producing photocopied anthologies of copyrighted works without permission. A federal district court found that the photocopier had violated the copyright law, and it settled the suit out of court, at considerable cost.

A related question, involving quotation from unpublished material, had not been resolved in the early 1990s. Several decisions of a federal appeals court seemed to make quoting even a limited amount of unpublished material without permission extremely difficult, in effect limiting fair use to published material. The ALA strongly supported proposed legislation that would have clarified Section 107, but the bill was not passed.

INTERNATIONAL COPYRIGHT LAW

Before the 19th century, national copyright laws of countries throughout the world were concerned mainly with protecting the works of the country's own nationals and denied foreign authors any protection. Some exceptions did exist, based on bilateral treaties mandating reciprocal treatment. In 1852 France extended its copyright protection to all works regardless of nationality, a move that led to the establishment of the Association Littéraire et Artistique Internationale. In 1883 this group presented a treaty for a multilateral system of international copyright. The proposed treaty provided the basis for the Berne Convention of September 9, 1886.

The Berne Convention. The objective of the Berne Convention was to give foreign authors in any of the 14 countries that signed the Convention the same protection accorded to their native authors. The Convention was revised and amended more than seven times, most recently in 1971. The Berne Convention was broadened to include, among other items, motion pictures, architecture, choreography, pantomime, and photographs. In the 1948 revision, known as the Brussels Protocol, the author's "moral right" was introduced as a mandatory part of the author's right to be protected in signatory countries. Two additional major requirements were introduced: the establishment of a minimum term of copyright protection for the life of the author plus 50 years after the author's death (a "Unionist Treatment"); and the abolition of any registration formalities as prerequisites for copyright protection. Therefore, according to the Berne Convention, any published work, regardless of nationality or membership, receives copyright protection automatically without the need for registration or for a copyright notice—© or the word "copyright"—affixed to it, provided the work is first published in a "Berne Union" country or published in a nonmember country and simultaneously in a member country.

The U.S. did not sign the original Berne Convention because of conflicts with U.S. copyright law. However, U.S. works are protected under the Berne Convention if they are published simultaneously (within approximately 30 days) in Canada, the United Kingdom, or other member countries. This partially explains why many U.S. publishers maintain offices in Berne Union countries and affix their names on the title pages of their publications. Differences between U.S. and Berne provisions were greatly reduced in the copyright law of 1976, and the U.S. finally signed the Berne Convention in 1988. As a result, the copyright notice is no longer mandatory in U.S. publications, although the law provides incentives for voluntary notice. But an author could not protect copyright ownership in court in the U.S. unless the work had been registered.

Signing the Convention involved the U.S. in two other changes in law. Congress included architecture and constructed design of buildings as categories covered by copyright. It also passed the Visual Artists' Rights Act of 1990, giving visual artists the right to claim authorship of their works, to disclaim authorship of distorted or mutilated works, and to bring civil claims for destruction of such works. The law applies only to signed and numbered limited editions of 200 copies or fewer of paintings, drawings, prints, sculpture, and still photographs. One of the problems that still must be resolved is a retroactive effect that might require copyright protection under the Berne Convention for works that are already in the public domain in the U.S. since their term of protection (28 years plus one 28-year renewal) has already expired according to the 1909 U.S. Copyright law.

Moral Right. The Berne Convention requires signatories to recognize that authors have the moral right to authorize or prohibit any alterations to their works or to prohibit publishers from releasing works if they have experienced a change of conviction about ideas expressed in them. Some U.S. publishers feared that adherence to the Berne Convention might encourage intolerable interference by authors during the publishing process and that it might lead to more litigation. Most publishers felt that they could use the added advantage of adherence in their fight against growing international piracy of copyrighted materials.

Universal Copyright Convention. In the late 19th century, many attempts were made to secure copyright agreements in the Western Hemisphere. These attempts produced several "Pan-American" copyright conventions. The United States was a signatory only to the Buenos Aires Convention in 1910, which provides that the copyright in a work will be protected in a member country if it was copyrighted in another member country and bears a copyright notice to that effect. It soon became obvious that a middle ground had to be established between the Pan-American Convention and the Berne Convention, and the Universal Copyright Convention (UCC) was established in 1952. It was eventually signed by more than 70 countries, including the U.S.S.R. But, as U.S. law and the Berne Convention drew closer, the UCC seemed less and less necessary.

CURRENT ISSUES IN THE U.S.

Reproduction and Distribution. The copyright law states that the librarian's right to reproduce and distribute copies of copyrighted material extends only to the isolated and unrelated production or distribution of a single copy of the same material on separate occasions. The "one copy at a time rule" is extended only to libraries, and it seems that this rule exemplifies fair use as practiced by librarians. Consequently, substantial or multiple reproduction of a copyrighted work is not considered fair, and therefore is not permitted. The "one copy at a time rule" does not extend to the parent institution which the library serves, whose copying is governed by sections 106 and 107, not section 108, of the copyright law.

The first American lawsuit against a library for copyright infringement came in 1972, when Williams and Wilkins, a medical journal publisher, sought damages from the National Library of Medicine (NLM) and the National Institutes of Health (NIH) for excessive photocopying. An even split on the Supreme Court let stand the Court of Claims ruling that the NLM and NIH were providing services within the scope of fair use. The ruling was explicitly based on the particular mission of the libraries concerned and the legislative process then underway to revise the copyright law; it cannot be used as a precedent under the new law. Fair use cases since 1978 have been judged individually, each on its own merits.

Interlibrary Loans. The Library's right of copying and distribution as stated in Section 108d does not extend to cases in which the library "engages in systematic reproduction or distribution of single or multiple copies" of copyrighted material. Though "systematic reproduction" is not formally defined, the phrase does not seem to apply to a library's "system" for handling copying requests from its own patrons. Rather, the clause seems to be intended for interlibrary loan transactions that might substitute photocopies for subscriptions or purchases. A library is allowed to obtain copies through interlibrary loan if these copies are not in such aggregate quantities as to substitute for purchases.

At the request of Congress, CONTU developed guidelines for interlibrary loan photocopying that, in essence, allow a library to receive five photocopies per calendar year from copyrighted books and from periodicals published within the preceding five years. The library may disregard the "rule of five" if it has a subscription or purchase order in force for the work. Interlibrary loan records must be retained for three years. These guidelines are not part of the law itself, but they have been acknowledged by Congress as representing the legislative intent and would carry considerable weight in any litigation. They apply only to interlibrary loan photocopying for libraries covered by Section 108. The situation is still evolving, with publishers wanting further limitation and regulation.

Section 108. The law requires the Register of Copyright to report to Congress every five years about how Section 8 is working, including suggestions for changes in the law. For the first five-year review, the Register commissioned a survey of educators, library users, librarians, publishers, and authors to find out how they thought the law was working. In his report, submitted to Congress in January 1983, he included "non-statutory" and "statutory" recommendations. Non-statutory recommendations included sharing "new collective library agreements" between libraries and copyright owners and "new guidelines" in light of new technologies and present photocopying practice, as well as a number of specific steps to compensate copyright owners.

The statutory recommendations included incentives for both libraries and publishers to join a "qualified licensing system" and the requirement that libraries be compelled to reproduce the work's copyright notice on every photocopy they make. The Report made clear the Register's view that the balance between publishers' and libraries' rights had not been achieved and that library photocopying exceeded what the law allowed, a view that many in the library community felt was biased toward the publishers' interests. Congress felt little pressure to respond quickly.

The Register submitted his second report in January 1988, concluding that consensus had been reached among the parties involved and that "a reasonable balance" exists between the competing interests concerning library photocopying. He noted that suggestions made in the first report had been ignored and that "the general reaction to the 1983 report was far [less] than earthshattering." He asked Congress to allow the Copyright Office to study the effects of new technology on the intended statutory balance. Behind this concern is the expansion of document delivery services, use of optical disks, and further development of networks and consortia. He recommended that, if the scope of the third review in January 1993 were not expanded as suggested, Congress should increase the time between reviews to 10 years or more.

Technology. The 1976 copyright law passed with virtually no provisions concerning emerging technologies. CONTU was asked to look into such copyright issues as protecting computer software and databases. Following the recommendations of the 1979 CONTU final report, Congress in 1980 amended Sections 101, 102, and 117, giving computer software the same protection as "literary works." The change allows the user of a lawfully owned software package to adapt it for the purpose of its intended use and to duplicate it for safekeeping. Litigation and case law can be expected to refine this area of copyright throughout the 1990s.

Among such issues is the use of "shrink-wrap agreements," by which software producers print on packaging visible through clear plastic wrapping the conditions (such as use, copying, and transfer) under which the package is sold. Opponents have questioned the validity of such unilateral agreements. In 1992, only Louisiana had a law endorsing shrink-wrap agreements, but the Fifth Circuit Court of Appeals held that such agreements were unenforceable because the state law was preempted by the federal copyright law.

The Semiconductor Chip Protection Act (1984) created a new form of industrial intellectual property and explicitly protected the patterns on semiconductor chips against unauthorized reproduction. The act grants ten-year proprietary protection to "mask works" for semiconductor chip products and authorizes the use of an Ⓜ as a notice of copyright on such chips. Congress opted for a *sui generis* rather than a copyright approach for protecting computer chips. This law covers only the mask work itself, not the computer program on the chip, which is protected under the copyright law.

Nonprint Material. Under the 1976 law, librarians' right to reproduce copyrighted material does not apply to audiovisual works in general, only those dealing with news. The law is silent on the questions of classroom use of audiovisual works and about off-air taping by libraries, and Congress encouraged all parties to discuss the issues. Following a two-year series of meetings, representatives of audiovisual professionals, media producers, and teachers in 1981 issued "Guidelines for Off-Air Taping for Educational Use," which were officially recognized by insertion in the *Congressional Record* (October 14, 1981). The guidelines permit taping off the air for educational purposes at nonprofit educational institutions under conditions that represent an appropriate balance between the rights of the copyright owner and the instructional needs of educational institutions.

The Guidelines covered only educational off-the-air taping. In the Betamax case, brought by Universal City Studios against Sony Corporation of America, the Supreme Court held in 1984 that noncommercial home videotaping of television programs does not constitute copyright infringement because such home taping is generally done for the purpose of "time-shifting," that is, for later viewing, and thus is a legitimate fair use. The Court also held that manufacturing and selling videotape recorders does not constitute contributory infringement. Libraries are still permitted to copy programs off the air only if they are a part of a nonprofit educational institution and act within the 1981 Guidelines.

Software. The Computer Software Amendments Act of 1990 extended the limited exception of the "first sale doctrine," initially granted to sound recordings, to include computer programs. The first sale doctrine refers to the copyright owner's loss of control over the physical form of a work when it is sold to others, so that, for example, someone who has bought a copy of a book is free to use or dispose of it. Sound recordings and computer programs may not be rented, leased, or lent for the purpose of direct or indirect commercial advantage. Certain exceptions are made for nonprofit libraries and educational institutions. The Register of Copyright is required to record and publish information about computer "shareware" as a way to encourage individuals to permit unrestricted use of their software. They need only file documents to that effect with the Copyright Office.

Databases. Another issue referred to CONTU was that of "downloading," that is, an individual user's recording onto an in-house computer all or part of a commercial database that has been accessed through outside sources. In its final report CONTU recommended that a database is simply a compilation, to be protected in the same way as dictionaries and encyclopedias, in which the arrangement of information constitutes the original work. Copyright of the compilation is distinct from that of its components.

Users subscribing with a vendor or producer to use a numeric, textual, or bibliographic database may wish to download some or all of the data in a file, recording it on their own computer disks for further work offline. Most frequently, such downloading is used to produce edited and formatted search results, but it also permits preserving search results in personal databases, implying the loss of revenues the producer and supplier could expect from repetitive searches.

A database created by a private producer such as Chemical Abstracts Service is obviously the property of the producer, which can copyright it. A supplier who does not create the content can copyright only the format. The OCLC database is a complicated case, because it contains both Library of Congress MARC tapes, which are in the public domain because they are the work of the federal government (Section 105), and data created by libraries participating in the OCLC cooperative which own the data they produce. OCLC, however, claimed copyright on the entire file, creating a heated debate over its ownership. OCLC's copyright pertains only to the format of its data file, not to its content.

While some consider downloading in the absence of explicit permission a violation of copyright, many believe that it can be considered fair use in certain circumstances, evaluated on the standard criteria of purpose, nature of the original, substantiality of copying, and effect on the market. Downloading of a small segment of data from a large general database for noncommercial teaching and research might be permissible as fair use, provided the downloaded data are erased from the computer memory after the research project is over. However, there is no working definition of a permissible "fair" amount of downloaded data, and the hardest criterion to apply in fair-use judgments is the effect of downloading on the actual and potential market of the database.

Since downloading is hard to monitor or detect and fair use is an ambiguous concept, most database vendors negotiate contractual agreements, particularly collective ones, with users. Most contracts are based on either subscription arrangements for high-volume downloading or unrestricted downloading for other applications.

State Immunity. Legislation passed in 1990 holds states and state agencies liable for violation of the Copyright Act and of the Semiconductor Chip Protection Act. All remedies for copyright infringement apply to the states as they would to private citizens.

CURRENT ISSUES IN OTHER COUNTRIES

Many countries, particularly countries in eastern Europe, were working to establish their first copyright laws in the 1990s or to seek significant improvements through revised and strengthened copyright laws. China adopted its first national copyright law, which went into effect in 1991, but implementation will require a long period of adjustment and refinement before the country will be able to sign an international copyright convention. The government of the then Soviet Union negotiated an agreement with the Copyright Clearance Center in the U.S. in 1990, allowing it to photocopy all Russian published works. A reciprocal agreement for photocopying American works in Russia was under consideration in 1992.

Piracy in countries without copyright laws continued to be a major problem for authors and publishers in countries with strong copyright laws. For example, U.S. copyright industries (book publishers, chipmakers, film and recording producers, and software publishers) claimed that they lost more than four billion dollars in 1990 because of piracy, which continues in 22 identified countries in violation of international copyright agreements. Attempting to curb such illegal activities, the Association of American Publishers took legal action against copyright violators in such countries as Korea, Malaysia, Singapore, and Taiwan. In one action, for example, the Taiwanese Supreme Court in 1991 found a medical bookstore guilty of pirating American medical textbooks.

CONCLUSION

Dealing with copyright is like aiming at a moving target. Technology continues to introduce new ways to select, store, search, display, transfer, and disseminate information. Copyright is affected by such developments, which occur faster than we can keep up with them legislatively. The only practical and possible solution to this lasting controversy is in the hands of the many parties involved. Each special interest group, including librarians, should know its rights and obligations, but all should also be willing to agree on common grounds that will contribute to the advancement of knowledge for the benefit of the general public.

WILLIAM Z. NASRI

Costa Rica

Costa Rica, a Central American republic on the isthmus between North and South America, lies between the Pacific Ocean and the Caribbean Sea and is bounded by Nicaragua on the north and Panama on the southeast. Population (1990 est.) 2,994,000; area 51,100 sq.km. The official language is Spanish.

History. The indigenous Indians in the northwest, under Meso-American influence, wrote in hieroglyphs on deerskin parchment. They used vegetable inks in red and black. They also traced their inheritances. After conquest by the Spaniards (1563), the few

Libraries in Costa Rica (1990)

Type of library	Number of administrative units (main libraries)	Number of service points (branches, mobile stops, etc.)	Volumes in collections	Population served
National[a]	1	1	7,000	190,419
Academic[b]	1	3	227,000	17,000
Public[a]	81	87	321,000	293,615

[a]1986 data
[b]1983 data

Source: Unesco, *Statistical Yearbook,* 1991

Indian survivors came under strong European influences. Independent from 1821 and a republic from 1848, Costa Rica achieved recognition for its democratic tradition.

National Library. Created in 1887, the Library of the University of Saint Thomas, in the capital, San José, became the National Library when that university was closed. Under a law instituted in 1910, the National Library became the depository for the national bibliography, and publishers were required to deposit their publications with it. From 1980 the National Library became the center of a system of libraries forming part of a national plan designed to centralize cataloguing and classification. Access is provided in the Library, through loans between the various libraries of the system, and through loans for home use. The National Library maintains a National Register of authors' rights and associated matters as well as the National ISBN Agency. It publishes an "Index of Newspapers and Weeklies" and a "National Analytic Index of Periodicals."

Public Libraries. By the late 1980s there were more than 80 public libraries. Before 1980, there were only 18. The newer public libraries are canton and district libraries whose collection growth depends on community effort and the help of the national system. In 1983 a law providing financing for the libraries was approved and the construction of 15 buildings for public libraries was planned. Efforts were also made to provide adequate library staff.

Public materials are available for internal use in a library and are lent among libraries.

The system uses two mobile units that visit distant zones of the Central Valley.

School Libraries. Under the Development Plan for the School Library System of 1975, programs for these libraries were initiated and a department was established under the Ministry of Public Education. Initial actions emphasized technical services through organization of a center for processing materials. Attention was also given to improving qualifications of library personnel through courses offered by the Asesoría Nacional de Bibliotecas Escolares in coordination with the state universities.

In 1978 Costa Rica began a school library pilot study under auspices of the Multinational Project of School Libraries OEA–MEP (Organización de Estados Americanos–Ministerio de Educación Pública). Costa Rica's experience provided information for Latin American librarians on concerns about school libraries. The goal has been to transform the libraries into resource centers, so that the school library can be integrated totally in the curriculum.

Children's Libraries. In 1971 the Municipality of San José established the Carmen Lyra Library for Children. In 1978 and in 1983 two new libraries for children opened. Besides offering books for use in the library and lending books for home use, children's libraries have other activities, such as story hours, film programs, and puppet shows. Costa Rican librarians provided help to other Latin American librarians on the organization of libraries for children.

University Libraries. The country has four state universities. The Commission of Directors of University Libraries was founded in 1983 to coordinate contacts among them. The commission works to rationalize the use of resources, especially in the acquisition of bibliographic material. In these libraries, plans and projects of automation are developed.

Special Libraries. Hospital libraries, which numbered five in the 1970s, were combined into one, the Biblioteca Nacional en Ciencias de la Salud (the National Library of Health Sciences). Many specialized libraries had been consolidated by the late-1980s, offering their special services in many areas. Examples are the Library of the Legislative Assembly, the Documentation Center of the Latin American Institute of the United Nations for the Prevention of Crime, the Library of the Central Bank, and the Documentation Center of the National Council of Scientific and Technological Investigations. Some of these have developed automation in support of their work.

The Profession. The Colegio de Bibliotecarios de Costa Rica, established in 1971, is the professional umbrella association for all librarians. Its role is to improve professional qualifications of members through courses, seminars, and various programs, and to represent and protect professional interests of librarians.

PAULINA RETANA

Cuba

The Republic of Cuba occupies the largest island in the Greater Antilles. The Cuban archipelago consists of several thousand small islands, islets, and cays. Population (1990 est.) 10,609,000; area 110,861 sq.km., including the Cuban archipelago. The official language is Spanish.

History. The Biblioteca de la Sociedad Económica de Amigos del País (Library of the Economic Society of the Friends of the Country) was founded in 1793 to "contribute to the promotion of the moral and economic interests of Cuba and to stimulate culture and popular instruction in all their manifestations." The Library has the most important collection of

Libraries in Cuba (1990)

Type of library	Number of administrative units (main libraries)	Number of service points (branches, mobile stops, etc.)	Volumes in collections	Annual expenditures (U.S. dollar)	Population served	Professional staff (with certificate, diploma, etc.)	Total staff
National	1	--	2,173,943	1,200,000	500,000	207	359
Academic	82	46	2,353,000	4,500,000	213,269	289	657
Public	368	5,164	4,861,200	8,500,000	8,722,400	1,305	2,096
School	3,636	--	17,376,900	--	5,109,435	395	4,878

Cuban books and periodicals. The Real y Pontificia Universidad de San Jerónimo was created on January 5, 1728, by Pope Innocent XIII with provision for a Library, though it took many years for the Library to work as such.

The Constitution of the Republic issued in 1940 called for a public library in each municipality, but the law needed to enforce that obligation was never passed. A Decree of 1954 created the Organización Nacional de Bibliotecas Ambulantes (ONBAP) with the goal of founding 50 small public libraries; each library was to have a collection of approximately 1,000 volumes; by 1958, 21 of those libraries were created with modest monthly allocations. In 1958, out of a population of 6,700,000, a million were illiterate, 600,000 children had no opportunities to obtain any kind of education, and 10,000 teachers were jobless. In 1959 there were about 30 public libraries; by 1983 there were more than 300. But those libraries did not provide any of the features nor meet the standards of service that make an adequate modern public library. Only two of those libraries could be counted as such—the Lyceum Lawn Tennis Club Public Library and the Sociedad de Amigos del País Public Library.

The Lyceum Lawn Tennis Club was a women's liberal and cultural society whose public library made contributions toward shaping the literary taste of the generations of the 1930s through the 1950s. It also supported interest in librarianship.

During the 19th century and the first half of the 20th, some academic libraries were founded, such as those of the Academy of Sciences, Academy of Arts, and Academy of History. Some professional societies, such as the Engineers Society and the Architects Society, also founded important libraries. The sugar industry has been the main economic resource of Cuba, and one of the first research libraries of the country was that of the industry's Asociación de Técnicos Azucareros.

National Library. In 1901, by a military order during the United States occupation of Cuba, a director to the National Library was appointed. In 1936 a Cuban writer and historian, Emilio Roig de Leuchsenring, who was Historian of the City of Havana, denounced the poor condition of the National Library through his articles in the weekly magazine *Carteles* and called urgently for improvement. The Asociación de Amigos de la Biblioteca Nacional (Association of Friends of the National Library) was founded. Many distinguished writers and historians were members, with Emilio Roig de Leuchsenring as President.

In 1935 the Foreign National Association, based in New York, published a report entitled "Problems of the New Cuba," which cited the National Library's "shameful conditions. Its shelves were drawn off during the President Machado administration and the books were packed into boxes and stored in a facility belonging to a state prison, and even though they have already been returned to the library, the deplorable state of the building and the shelves made possible the unpacking [of only] a few volumes; in addition a fire took place in the building and a great deal of books were burned to ashes."

In 1938 the government decided to move the Library to the Castillo de la Fuerza and to tear down the building that housed it and build a police station

Biblioteca Nacional José Martí

Facade of Biblioteca Nacional José Martí, Havana.

instead. The books were packed again with haste and transferred to their new place.

The lack of resources and qualified personnel led to deteriorating conditions that became so obvious that the government appointed a Cuban writer and diplomat, José Antonio Ramos, as the library technical adviser, giving him power over cataloguing and classification. Ramos implemented a system of classification on his own, based on the Universal Decimal System and adapted to Cuban needs. His was undoubtedly the most significant attempt to organize the bibliographic resources of the institution up to that time. After struggling to improve the National Library, Ramos resigned in 1946, shortly before his death.

In 1941 the government imposed a one-half cent tax on each 325-pound sugar bag in order to raise funds to build a National Library. Construction of the National Library's new building began in 1952. It was named after José Martí (1853–95), the Cuban national hero who was a poet, a thinker, a warrior, and a "symbol of the National Liberation against colonialism and imperialism."

After the Cuban Revolution of 1959, sweeping changes took place in the Library as well as in the rest of the country. María Teresa Freyre de Andrade, Cuban librarian and long a fighter for the development of librarianship in Cuba, was appointed Director of the institution. She started intense efforts to move the National Library toward modern goals and to make libraries reach everyone. She also encouraged the reform of library science studies at both university and technical levels.

The government resolved that all books that belonged to dictator Fulgencio Batista (1901–73), to his associates, and to people leaving the country should be transferred to the National Library. These "rescued libraries" played an important role in filling out the collections of the National Library and in starting collections in the new libraries in various parts of the country.

Because of the shortage of libraries, the National Library has served as a public library. Its Department of Bibliographic Research created a Union Catalogue of Scientific and Technological Periodicals and a Union Catalogue of Social Sciences and Humanities. A special service of the National Library is the Children and Young Adult Department. Its activities,

ALA

Havana University Library, founded in 1728. This building was constructed in 1937.

including storytelling, painting, literature, philately, and others, have been the model for other children's and juvenile libraries in the country. At the international level, the National Library has an information exchange agreement with the Centro de Información Científica Técnica Humanística (CICH) of the Universidad Nacional Autónoma de México. It coordinates the cultural information exchange work of several cultural institutions in Cuba.

In 1989, as part of a restructuring of the Ministry of Culture, the Biblioteca Nacional José Martí became the National Methodological Center for the Public Library Network, head of a network for culture and arts information with as its main objective the present and prospective condition of public libraries in the country. It became responsible for promoting reading among adults and children through the Programa Nacional de la Lectura. It also assumed responsibility for collecting the official documents of the Ministry of Culture into the Archivo General de Cultura and for organizing the Biblioteca Memorial Juan Marinello, honoring a Cuban leader who bequeathed his library to the National Library.

National Bibliography. In the 19th century the Cuban scholar Antonio Bachiller y Montes published his *Apuntes para la Historia de las Letras y la Instrucción Pública en Cuba.* The second volume of that work includes the first account of periodicals edited in Cuba; the third makes the most important contribution to the field of bibliography of that time. It was titled *Catálogo de Libros y Folletos Publicados en Cuba desde la Introducción de la Imprenta hasta 1840.*

Some Cuban and foreign authors worked to compile the national bibliography during the first half of the 20th century. Carlos M. Trelles was the most important of the group, because of the completeness and accuracy of his *Bibliografía Cubana del Siglo XX,* published in 1917. From 1937 to 1958 the *Anuario Bibliográfico Cubano,* compiled and edited by Fermín Peraza, tried to continue the work of Trelles.

In 1959 the National Library was appointed to compile and publish the Cuban National Bibliography. It published the bibliographies for the following years: 1917 to 1920 (published 1960); 1921 to 1936 (1979); 1959 to 1962 (1968); 1963 and 1964 (1967); and yearly from 1965.

National Archives. The Archivo General de la Isla de Cuba was founded by an order of the Queen of Spain in 1840. In 1888 the Captain General of the Island, by order of the Madrid government, sent to Spain 2,300 documents of great historical value. An official decree of December 20, 1904, established the island institution as the National Archives.

From 1921 to 1956 an outstanding Cuban historian, Joaquín Llaverías y Martínez, was its Director. He had "a constant preoccupation [with] the search for and conservation of valuable documents that are in the collection of the institution." From 1945 to 1958 it published the periodical *Memorias.* In 1963 the National Archives was attached to the Academia de Ciencias de Cuba. It succeeded in forming a network of provincial and regional archives.

Academic Libraries. The history of the Library of the University of Havana reflects the history of the main institution, which had scant resources until the late 1930s, when a new building was constructed and a new organization was adopted as a result of the revolutionary movement of that time. After 1959, the University of Havana Library evolved toward the concept of a Biblioteca Central (Central Library), providing the conditions for better development of the particular libraries of the University faculties.

The Central Library of the University of Havana was named after Rubén Martínez Villena, a revolutionary leader of the 1930s. The complete holdings of the Central Library total 150,500 volumes with a reference collection of 10,200 volumes and a natural sciences periodical collection with 10,800 titles.

Higher education was expanded in order to reach more people and improve its overall quality. In 1976 a scientific and technical information network for higher education was organized to serve the universities and research centers attached to the Ministry of Higher Education. The system includes 19 scientific and technical information centers and 46 libraries. The network provides a system of storage and retrieval for unpublished documents such as theses and papers (*informe de investigación*), and a printed union catalogue of scientific and technical periodicals in the network.

Public Libraries. In 1961 the Dirección General de Bibliotecas (General Library Board) was created as part of the National Council for Culture with the task of establishing a national network of public libraries under the technical guidance of the National Library. In 1977 the Ministry of Culture was established, and within it was created the Dirección de Bibliotecas with the aim of continuing and broadening public libraries' work. There are almost 375 libraries of this kind in all parts of the country. The system is organized with the National Library at the head, main libraries in the provinces, and libraries and branch libraries in the municipalities.

By the early 1990s, there were 13 main libraries in the provinces, one for each province, except for the City of Havana province, which does not have its own provincial library; more than 200 municipal libraries in the main towns; and more than 150 municipal branch libraries, 65 of them in sugar mill areas and 12 in new rural communities. The system also has six bookmobiles that make almost 300 stops in rural communities without libraries and about 1,500 minilibraries in factories, mass organization offices, hospitals, and other institutions.

School Libraries. There are no available statistical data on school libraries prior to the Revolution in 1959. A statute issued on July 6, 1960, mandated that a school library service was to be organized. It was the first official step toward reaching the goal of having a library in every primary and secondary school. Unesco had helped in the late 1950s with technical assistance through a School Library Pilot Project. After that experience was adapted to the new and growing demands of Cuban society, the school library system started to work.

The main objectives of the school library are to contribute to the formation of "a scientific conception of the world and a communist morale" in the students through "systematic reading of socio-political as well as scientific and recreational literature linked to the curricula." The school libraries have circulation and reference services.

Special Libraries. Each of the central administrative bodies of the government, research institutes in the various branches of the economy, and the services has its own information center or special library. Among them are the ministries of the Sugar Industry, Foreign Commerce, Public Health, Agriculture, and Construction, the Central Planning Board, and many others.

The National Information Center for Medical Sciences, founded in 1965, is the main body for the scientific information system in the field of public health in Cuba. The system is structured into a network formed by the national center and other health centers. The National Center provides services for administrative and technical leaders and for scientists and research personnel in the medical disciplines. It also serves as the National Medical Library for physicians, students, and other users.

Personnel requirements for the various levels of medical libraries are as follows: for minilibraries at the "bookcase" level, nontechnically qualified employees with minimum training; at hospital library level, graduates of the Medium Technical Medical Librarianship School; and at the provincial centers, Medium Technical graduates and university graduates. At the National Center librarians must have university degrees not only in librarianship but also in medical specialty fields.

The José A. Echeverría Library is part of the Casa de las Américas, an institution set up "to put into practice measures and initiatives which would contribute to cultural unity among the Latin American and Caribbean countries, as well as situating these regional cultural expressions in the context of universal culture." This institution was guided and directed until her death in 1980 by Haydée Santamaría, one of the two women who participated in the attack on Moncada Barracks (July 26, 1953), later a member of the Central Committee of the Cuban Communist Party and the country's Council of State. The Library serves all those interested in Latin American culture, history, and sociology. It houses almost 100,000 volumes and more than 6,000 periodical titles.

The Pedagogic Documentation Centers form a network founded in 1960. It is composed of the Centro Nacional de Documentación e Información Pedagógicas, 162 centers, and 15 Provincial Departments of Research, Documentation, and Pedagogic Information.

The Junta Central de Planificación (Central Planning Board), the Cuban government institution that deals with the main economic affairs of the country, has a Scientific and Technical Information Center. At the first experts' meeting held at Havana in 1979 under the auspices of the Comité de Desarrollo y Cooperación del Caribe (CDCC; Caribbean Committee on Development and Cooperation), planners agreed to establish an information network whose coordinating center would be the Centro de Documentación del Caribe (CDC). The International Development Research Center (ICRD) of Canada granted financial aid for the project. The Scientific and Technical Information Center of the Junta Central de Planificación coordinates the work of the economic institutions of the country as participants. Among those institutions are the Banco Nacional de Cuba, Comité Estatal de Estadística, Comité Estatal de Finanzas, Instituto de Investigaciones Económicas, Ministeria de Comercio Exterior, and Oficina Nacional de Diseño Industrial. Among the main accomplishments were advances in bibliographic indexing and abstracting, the use of a thesaurus for economic information indexing, and the definition of the kinds of documents the system should process.

The Profession. Many attempts were made to establish the study of library science in Cuba prior to 1960. The most significant was the foundation in 1950 of the Escuela de Bibliotecarios (Library School) in the Faculty of Philosophy and Letters of the University of Havana. Many librarians holding leading positions in Cuba in the 1980s and 1990s were graduated from that center. From an enrollment of about 10 students with five professors in 1956, the school had grown to 700 students and more than 20 professors by the early 1990s.

The Department of Scientific and Technical Information at the University of Havana was created in 1970 by the Ministry of Higher Education as a part of new approaches to university studies. Subjects added to the curriculum include computing, bibliographic research, information storage retrieval systems, and

Biblioteca Nacional José Martí

Children's Room at the Biblioteca Nacional "José Martí" in Havana.

organizing and managing information institutions. This Department played an important role in fostering scientific research and in publishing textbooks written by Cuban authors.

After passing the five-year university course, a graduate receives the degree of Licenciado. A university graduate may obtain the Doctor in Library Science degree. For library technicians, undergraduate programs are conducted at the Escuela de Técnicos Medios under the Ministry of Culture. By examination, graduates may enroll as students in the evening courses offered by the University of Havana.

MARTA TERRY

National Library of Medicine
Martin M. Cummings

Cummings, Martin M.
(1920–)

As its 18th director, Martin Marc Cummings expanded the U.S. National Library of Medicine (NLM) from a conventional medical research library into an institution pioneering the most sophisticated technology in information exchange and established it as an international biomedical communications center. Under his leadership medical library resources throughout the United States were enhanced, specialized information and medical audiovisual services were developed, and an international online bibliographic retrieval network was created. Cummings's vision and direction created and expanded the information resources that provided the biomedical research community with the necessary tools to transfer the results of research effectively and efficiently to health care practitioners.

Cummings was born in Camden, New Jersey, September 7, 1920. After graduating with a B.S. degree from Bucknell University, Pennsylvania, in 1941, he received his M.D. degree in 1944 from Duke University, where he became interested in microbiology and infectious diseases, especially tuberculosis. He accepted a Public Health Service (PHS) internship followed by a residency at the Boston Marine Hospital, after which the PHS provided him with specialized training programs in pulmonary medicine at the Grasslands Hospital in Valhalla, New York; at the University of Minnesota; at the Michigan State Department of Health; and at the State Serum Institute of Denmark. On his return from Denmark he was given the responsibility of establishing the first tuberculosis laboratory in the Public Health Service at the Communicable Disease Center in Atlanta, where he pursued his research interests and held a faculty appointment in medicine at Emory University. Two years later the Veterans Administration (VA) invited him to head the Tuberculosis Service at Lawson VA Hospital in Atlanta, where he organized a control laboratory for tuberculosis studies. He also developed a systematic methodology for the analyses of large numbers of medical records of veterans with pulmonary diseases.

In 1953 the VA selected him to become Director of Research Services in Washington, D.C. He was responsible for administering the VA's extensive medical research program and coordinating it with research initiatives at the National Institutes of Health (NIH), the Department of Defense, and the National Science Foundation. In addition to his administrative duties, he continued his research, saw patients, lectured in microbiology at George Washington University School of Medicine, and continued a growing interest in medical history.

In 1959 he accepted the position of Professor and Chairman of the Department of Microbiology at the University of Oklahoma. He was persuaded by James Shannon, Director of NIH, to return to Washington in 1961 as Chief of the Office of International Research at NIH and Shannon's principal staff adviser. That position provided an important opportunity to examine medical problems internationally, as well as nationally, and to learn firsthand the powerful and positive impact that the political process can have on public health. During these years of rapid growth at NIH, he took on the additional duties of Associate Director for Research Grants, advising the Director on related policy and administrative matters.

In 1963, following the resignation of Frank Bradway Rogers as Director of NLM, Surgeon General Luther Terry selected Cummings for the directorship. Cummings brought to the position a background of diverse and relevant experiences as a user of medical information, an understanding and familiarity with how public policy is made, a respect for the contribution of individual researchers, and a vision for the age of new communication technologies and their potential application to libraries. In his remarks to the NLM Board of Regents following his introduction in December 1963, he noted that "The Library has an unmatched opportunity to serve national and international needs in the health communications areas. It will be my responsibility to maintain the very high standards of this Library. At the same time I recognize a need to broaden our interests to provide a creative, imaginative contribution to the increasing complexities of communications."

On January 1, 1964, when Cummings officially assumed the directorship, the Library was already engaged in the pioneering effort of implementing MEDLARS, the MEDical Literature Analysis and Retrieval System. The Library had been engaged in indexing the medical literature since 1897, but publication was a laborious process. MEDLARS was designed to store the indexed citations of the current literature in electronic format. The data on magnetic tape could then be manipulated by a computer, producing an output designed to be used by a high-speed photocomposition device for preparing copy for *Index Medicus,* recurring bibliographies, and special individual subject searches. The initial implementation of MEDLARS required many internal changes at NLM as computerized processing replaced some of the Library's well-established manual traditions with a state-of-the-art automated system.

In the Library's external relationships, extensive change also occurred under Cummings's leadership. John Shaw Billings, the Library's first director, had personally selected the journals to be included in *Index Medicus,* and journal selection had been continued through the years by a small number of library staff. Cummings sought advice from consultants, researchers, educators, administrators, and practitioners on many areas of the Library's operations, including the journals selected to be indexed in *Index Medicus* and the subject headings used in indexing. He was quick to seek the recommendations of his staff and outside experts as the Library continued to use the newest technology to upgrade its overall operation and MEDLARS specifically. Searches of the MEDLARS databases were originally run in batch mode at the Library. Advances in telecommunications technology enabled remote users with terminals and modems to access the databases online. Up-to-date medical bibliographical information became available throughout the entire United States and many other parts of the world through international MEDLARS centers in 14 countries.

In the 1960s most medical libraries had insufficient facilities, staff, or budgets to acquire, process, house, or provide access to the information needed by users. Rogers had made progress toward federal legislation authorizing grants to aid medical libraries, and Cummings gave the task his immediate attention. His articulate advocacy resulted in the introduction and passage of the Medical Library Assistance Act (MLAA) of 1965. MLAA was extended over the years and has been used to finance construction of medical libraries, training of librarians and other information specialists, expansion and improvement of medical library resources, stimulation of research and development in medical library sciences, biomedical publications, and the establishment of a resource-sharing network of more than 4,000 health science libraries through the regional medical library program.

Spurred on by the awareness of the unexpected adverse effects of drugs such as thalidomide and the harmful effects of chemical contaminants in the environment, the Library undertook programs for collecting, organizing, and disseminating information on drugs and the toxic effects of chemicals. Cummings established a major division at the Library, the Specialized Information Services, to take responsibility for such activities.

Through the National Medical Audiovisual Center, the Library cooperated with professional societies and medical schools to improve instruction. Audiovisuals were produced and a database listing peer-reviewed audiovisuals (AVLINE) was developed and added to the MEDLARS family of databases.

Cummings had a vision of the Library as an active information center that was part of a network for communicating biomedical information. In 1965 he proposed the establishment of a Center for Biomedical Communications at the Library, set up in 1968 as the Lister Hill National Center for Biomedical Communications. The Lister Hill Center building was dedicated in 1980 as the research and development division of NLM. Projects at the Lister Hill Center pioneered in such areas as Abridged Index Medicus-Teletypewriter Exchange System (AIM-TWX) and those involving computer-assisted instruction, educational television, satellite communications, medical informatics, and interactive videodisks.

Cummings listened carefully to teachers and colleagues over the years. He evidenced a deep appreciation of the people whose accomplishments resulted in medical progress. This philosophy is most evident in the History of Medicine Division of the Library, especially in the oral history program and modern manuscript collections.

Cummings encouraged cooperation among the U.S. national libraries, meeting often with the directors of the Library of Congress and the National Agricultural Library to discuss issues of mutual interest and ways to avoid redundancy. In 1965 the directors of the three national libraries established the Federal Library Committee, an ongoing mechanism through which to pursue their common goals. His interest in biomedical communication also extended beyond the U.S. He established the position of Special Assistant to the Director for International Programs, providing both a focus and an impetus for NLM to expand its international cooperation.

During his tenure at the Library, Cummings addressed many public policy issues, two of which consumed considerable time and energy: (1) copyright and (2) the role of a tax-supported institution in providing information services. In 1968 a publisher of medical journals filed suit against the government, alleging that the NLM and NIH infringed on its copyright by photocopying articles from its journals. The case was finally decided in the government's favor in 1975. (*See* Copyright.) In this long legal battle, Cummings championed the rights of scholars and libraries everywhere for the judicially created doctrine of "fair use."

The appropriate role of NLM in providing information to health professionals is an equally complex public issue. Cummings considered that biomedical information was a public resource and should not be treated solely as a market commodity. He argued forcefully that NLM was "fulfilling its Congressionally mandated function . . . when the fees the Library charged for its products and services recover only the costs of providing access to them."

Cummings complemented his administrative achievements with superb scholarship; he published more than a hundred scientific and historical publications. He gained a reputation as a forceful and articulate speaker and received seven honorary degrees and many special awards. He retired in January 1984 after 20 years as Director to pursue his interest in reviewing the papers of the first Director of the Library, John Shaw Billings. He also published a work on the economics of libraries and served as a consultant to the Council on Library Resources.

REFERENCES

Martin M. Cummings, *The Economics of Research Libraries* (1986).

N. E. Davies and E. J. Huth, "Martin M. Cummings and the National Library of Medicine," *Annals of Internal Medicine* (1983).

Wyndham D. Miles, *A History of the National Library of Medicine* (1982).

LOIS ANN COLAIANNI

Cunha, Maria Luisa Monteiro da

(1908–1980)

Maria Luisa Monteiro da Cunha, Brazilian librarian and cataloguing specialist, was active in national and international library affairs. Her country came to rely heavily on her expert advice.

She was born in Santos (São Paulo), September 14, 1908. She received a Bachelor's degree in dentistry (1928); later, she registered at the Library School of the Fundação Escola de Sociologia e Política (São Paulo) and received a Bachelor's degree in library science in 1940. She won a special scholarship granted by the American Library Association and, during the academic year 1946–47, studied at Columbia University School of Library Service. She prepared a term paper that, translated into Portuguese, contributed to the development of cataloguing practice in Brazil. She represented Columbia University at the First Conference of Librarians of the Americas (Washington, D.C., 1947).

From 1942 to 1949 she worked at the São Paulo Municipal Public Library. She was Director of the University of São Paulo Central Library from 1949 to 1970 and of the Documentation and Library Division from 1970 to 1978.

In 1965 she was appointed one of the members of a Special Committee nominated to study the creation and organization of an Institute devoted to the professional teaching of communication media, including journalism, theater, the movies, radio, television, librarianship, documentation, and public relations. The Committee activities resulted in the Communications and Arts School. A member of its faculty from 1967 to 1972, she gave courses on librarianship and cataloguing.

Cunha became an active member of specialized committees, mainly the Brazilian Committee on Library Technical Services. She was one of the members of the Working Group on Coordination of Cataloguing Principles (created in 1959 by IFLA under a grant from the Council on Library Resources) for the organization and follow-up of the International Conference on Cataloguing Principles (Paris, 1961). She participated in the first Seminar on University Libraries (Monticello, Illinois, 1961), the International Meeting of Cataloguing Experts (Copenhagen, 1969), and the Revision Meeting for International Standard Bibliographic Description-M (Grenoble, 1973).

From 1954 she was an invited participant at Brazilian library conferences. In 1973 she received a gold medal from the Seventh Brazilian Documentation and Librarianship Congress (Belém, Pará). Cunha died in São Paulo on July 28, 1980.

She wrote *Treatment of Brazilian and Portuguese Names* (Paris, IFLA, 1961), *Formación Profesional* ("Professional Training," 1965), *Controle Bibliográfico Universal* ("Universal Bibliographical Control," Brasíla, 1975), and *Bibliotecas Universitárias em Sistemas Nacionais de Informação* ("University Libraries in National Information Systems," Porto Alegre, 1977).

CORDELIA R. CAVALCANTI

Cutter, Charles Ammi
(1837–1903)

One of the most important of all contributors to U.S. librarianship, Charles Ammi Cutter was librarian of the Boston Athenaeum, 1869–93, a leader of the developing U.S. library profession in the second half of the 19th century, and the author of notable works on cataloguing and classification.

Cutter was born on March 14, 1837, in Boston. He lived with his grandfather and his three aunts in West Cambridge, Massachusetts, where he was raised in a strong Unitarian religious atmosphere. He was sent to the Hopkins Classical School, a school designed to prepare young men for Harvard College. By 10 he had also become acquainted with the West Cambridge town library as both a patron and occasional assistant to his aunt, Charlotte Cutter, who served as its Librarian from 1849 to 1851.

Cutter enrolled in the fall of 1851 at Harvard College, where he applied himself diligently to his studies, winning several prizes and graduating third in his class. He studied French literature, science, and mathematics with great interest and was thoroughly exposed to the philosophy of Scottish Common Sense Realism through the teaching of Francis Bowen. His interest in scientific studies was such that for a semester after he graduated in 1855 he attended the Lawrence Scientific School as a special student in mathematics.

Cutter was ambivalent about pursuing a scientific career, however, and in the fall of 1856 he enrolled in the Harvard Divinity School, again distinguishing himself in scholarship by winning the Bowdoin prize dissertation competition in 1857. His course of studies trained him for the Unitarian ministry, but the experience that had the most influence on him while in the Divinity School was his tenure as the School's student librarian for the period 1857–59. He not only discharged his regular duties but also directed the writing of a new catalogue and the complete rearrangement of the books on the shelves. His work as a librarian also brought him into contact with Ezra Abbot, the College Library's cataloguer. This relationship was significant, not only for the personal influence that Abbot had over Cutter, but also because several months after Cutter graduated from the School in 1859, Abbot successfully obtained Cutter's appointment as his assistant in the College Library. Thus, on May 11, 1860, Cutter formally entered the career that would occupy him throughout the remainder of his life.

Cutter's years at the Harvard College Library from 1860 to the end of 1868 were formative in several ways. He experienced first-hand the growth and administrative problems of a large academic library, then under the direction of John Langdon Sibley. He learned from Abbot a systematic approach to the organization of knowledge in catalogue form, the chief characteristic of which was its basis in the classificatory theory that was inherent in the Scottish realists' view of mental processes. He also learned the techniques of cataloguing, for he not only helped Abbot to plan the alphabetico-classed card catalogue that bears Abbot's name but also assumed supervisory control over the project.

In May 1863 Cutter married Sarah Fayerweather Appleton, and by the summer of 1868 three sons had been born to them. His growing family responsibilities made it necessary for him to supplement his regular wages through a variety of special projects. These included assisting Joseph Sabin as a bibliographer on the *Bibliotheca Americana;* working as a part-time cataloguer at the Boston Public Library (1866–68), where he came into personal contact with Charles Coffin Jewett; indexing scholarly books in preparation for their publication; and writing reviews and articles for the *North American Review* and for the *Nation.* He was able to dispense with much of that activity, however, when he accepted the position of Librarian of the prestigious Boston Athenaeum on January 1, 1869.

Years of Success, 1869–80. The years from 1869 to 1880 were for Cutter ones of great success and undoubted personal satisfaction. His work at the

Athenaeum consisted of a thoroughgoing and continuous systematization of the library's programs. His ideal, gained from his scientific and philosophical training, was that all elements and processes of the library should together form an integrated whole that efficiently reached stated goals at the most reasonable cost—much like a finely tuned machine. In carefully reaching toward that systematization, Cutter captured not only the confidence of his trustees but also the admiration of the new but advancing profession of librarianship.

The confidence and admiration that he gained was due in no small part to his special accomplishments; the most notable were in the realm of cataloguing. He planned and published between 1869 and 1882 a monumental five-volume dictionary catalogue of the Athenaeum's collections that was not only a testament to his ideals of systematization but also so artfully executed and convenient to use that it brought general esteem to both Cutter and the library. Moreover, Cutter presented to the wider library world both the theory and procedures he used in making the catalogue in the form of an essay, "Library Catalogues," and his *Rules for a Printed Dictionary Catalogue,* both important parts of the Bureau of Education's important special report of 1876, *Public Libraries in the United States of America, Their History, Conditions, and Management.* The *Rules* were afterward published in three more editions, the last and most notable issued posthumously in 1904. The second of his accomplishments consisted of his classification work; by the end of 1880 he had circulated the first copies of his author tables, later published in three separate formats (a two-figure author table, 1887; the *Cutter-Sanborn Three-Figure Author Table,* 1896; and Cutter's own three-figure expansion of his earlier two-figure table, 1901). By 1880 Cutter had also worked out the general plan and had circulated the first schedules of his "Boston Athenaeum Classification."

Concurrent with these activities and accomplishments, Cutter also took part directly in the formal rise of the library profession. He worked closely with Melvil Dewey and others in the establishment of the American Library Association in 1876. Preferring the shadows more than the limelight, he became one of ALA's most active committee workers, chairing the important Cooperation Committee from its inception in 1877.

His literary contributions also increased in number. Though he was shy and somewhat reticent in public, he was able in his writing to express with great logic and clarity, as well as with occasional sharpness, the forcefulness of his views. His writings included major articles and reviews on library matters in the *Library Journal;* many literary pieces in the *Nation,* notable for their pithiness and wit; and the bibliography columns that he compiled and edited for the *Library Journal.* Finally, Cutter also joined with Dewey and others in 1879 in the formation of the Readers' and Writers' Economy, a speculative business venture Dewey designed to profit from the new commercial market arising with the growing library field. But that venture proved to be short-lived and engendered a financial imbroglio that cast a pall over an otherwise bright and energetic period.

ALA Leadership from 1881. One important result of the financial imbroglio of 1880 was the realignment of some of the ALA leadership responsibilities. For example, Dewey—the forceful if unofficial leader of the ALA—relinquished his editorship of the *Library Journal,* which Cutter then assumed in January 1881 and eventually continued until late in 1893. Cutter also worked on most of the Association's important new committees during the following decade and, from 1887 to 1889, served as its President. But Cutter, along with others, represented an essentially conservative approach to professional library leadership. He was content to view the meetings of the ALA and the pages of the *Journal* as a forum in which librarians shared their insights, debated their differences, and gained general inspiration. Colleagues could then apply to their own situations whatever techniques seemed appropriate. Dewey, however, represented a rising bureaucratic spirit, seeing the future of the profession in the exercise of its organizational power: the formation of explicit standards; centralized control of library processes, methods, and leadership where possible; and simple, pragmatic solutions to library programs. From his vantage point in New York, Dewey offered an increasingly attractive alternative to the regular leadership of the profession. The force with which he presented his program not only brought him the presidency of the Association twice during the early 1890s but also changed the character of the Association and its general purposes.

ALA

Charles Ammi Cutter

Cutter's response to the changes taking place, especially after 1885, was ambivalent. On the one hand, he agreed with Dewey in many matters, particularly those related to classification and education. And because of his good-natured humor, his patience, and the esteem in which others held his judgment, he was able to play a mediating role, defending Dewey's work and standing between Dewey and others who opposed him. On the other hand, Cutter found himself increasingly uncomfortable with Dewey's tendency to oversimplify library problems and their solutions and with his emphasis on the exercise of organizational power to achieve what were clearly Dewey's own goals. By the early 1890s Cutter was taking decided stands against some of Dewey's measures and in the editorials of the *Journal* increasingly emphasized the more conservative interpretation of the role of the Association. But he recognized that the ALA was changing dramatically and, as bewildering as it may have appeared, accepted it as inevitable.

Changes in the Association during that period were paralleled by changes at the Athenaeum. Cutter finished the dictionary catalogue and began the arduous task of applying his classification scheme to the Athenaeum's collections. The latter dragged on for 10 years, however, and its cost and disruption brought criticism from Athenaeum members. Furthermore, the Board of Trustees of the Athenaeum underwent a significant turnover in membership during the mid-1890s. The new members, bringing with them a growing sense of protectiveness against outsiders, criticized Cutter's openness in administration and willingness to use the Athenaeum for what they considered expensive experiments on behalf of the wider library world. In 1892 the conflict over administration priorities broke into the open when the trustees unofficially censured him. Cutter began to search for another library position, but his search was unsuccessful. In April 1893 he resigned his Athenaeum post and traveled to Europe for a rest. He returned in the summer to attend the Columbian Exposition library meetings, but his subsequent search for a new position was likewise unsuccessful. In October 1893 he again returned to Europe, severing most of his ties with the American library scene until the following summer.

Forbes Library, 1894–1903. While in Europe, Cutter was asked by the trustees of the new Forbes Library in Northampton, Massachusetts, to purchase books for their library. After subsequent negotiations, he moved to the Forbes in August 1894 as its first Librarian. Cutter's accomplishments during the next 10 years were considerable; he increased the Forbes collections to nearly 90,000 carefully selected volumes, built large circulating collections of art reproductions and music, and began a medical collection for the area's physicians, a children's section in the Library, and a branch library system for the area surrounding Northampton. But the administration of the Forbes brought him grief as well, for while generous funds were available for purchases and building needs, severe limitations were constantly imposed on the funds necessary for the administration of the Library. As a result, Cutter was unable to hire highly trained assistants, and those he trained himself left the Forbes for better-paying positions elsewhere. This factor made it impossible, for example, to catalogue and classify the collection in any more than a rudimentary manner.

The application of the shelf classification was of great concern to Cutter. During the late 1890s, he had remodeled his Boston Athenaeum classification into his much better known *Expansive Classification*. By 1893 he had published the first six expansions of the scheme. Believing it to be the best arranged and most adaptable classification available, he hoped that it might overtake Dewey's Decimal Classification as the scheme most used by all libraries. To that end he promoted his classification scheme tirelessly, presenting its merits whenever he could. In 1897 this effort took him as far as the International Conference of Librarians in London and the Institut Internationale de Bibliographie in Brussels. But his inability to apply it fully to the Forbes and the enormous work of singlehandedly editing it, supervising its printing, promoting it, and distributing it slowed to a snail's pace his progress on the seventh and final expansion. At his death it remained unfinished, although its use as a fundamental pattern for the Library of Congress's classification extended its influence immeasurably.

Cutter's last years brought, as a result, a mixture of accomplishments and frustrations. Given to selfless labor on behalf of libraries, he constantly took on arduous projects. Between 1901 and early 1903, besides his Forbes work, he participated without reserve in the demanding work of the catalogue code revision committee of ALA, addressed local library groups, and lectured at library schools. He died in New Hampshire on September 6, 1903.

REFERENCES

W. P. Cutter, *Charles Ammi Cutter* (1931).
W. E. Foster, "Charles Ammi Cutter: A Memorial Sketch," *Library Journal* (1903).
Francis L. Miksa, editor, *Charles Ammi Cutter: Library Systematizer* (1977).
Francis L. Miksa, "Cutter, Charles Ammi," *Dictionary of American Library Biography* (1978).
Francis L. Miksa, *The Subject in the Dictionary Catalog from Cutter to the Present* (1983).

FRANCIS L. MIKSA

Cyprus

Cyprus, the third largest island of the Mediterranean Sea, lies in the eastern Mediterranean, south of Turkey and close to Syria and Israel. Population (1990 est.) 702,000; area 9,251 sq.km. The official languages are Greek and Turkish. English is the second language widely spoken. A republic, Cyprus is a member of the Commonwealth of Nations.

History. The island has been inhabited at least since the 6th millennium B.C., but Cypriot library history begins in the Classical Greek period. The earliest libraries and archives were attached to such temples as the sanctuary of Aphrodite at Paphos, the temple of Apollo at Curium, and the temple of Cybele at Soli. The earliest known public library (*bibliophylakion*, "place where books are kept") in Cyprus was in the city-state of Soli: a man called Apollonius was in charge. Nicocrates the Cypriot is also mentioned for his private library.

Cyprus was an early center of Christianity. Many early Christian codices and manuscripts from Cyprus can be found in major libraries abroad, including the Vatican Library, the Bibliothèque Nationale in Paris,

Libraries in Cyprus (1990)

Type of library	Number of administrative units (main libraries)	Number of service points (branches, mobile stops, etc.)	Volumes in collections	Annual expenditures (Cyprus pound)	Population served	Professional staff (with certificate, diploma, etc.)	Total staff
National	1	--	60,000[a]	--	--	3	5
Academic	16	--	300,000	n.a.	15,000	6	15
Public	160	50	500,000	n.a.	450,000	3	150[c]
School	149[b]	--	500,000	n.a.	65,000	--	149[c]
Special	15	--	200,000	n.a.	--	3	14

[a]1991 data
[b]Excludes elementary schools
[c]Most are part-time

and the British Library in London. These are the only surviving evidence of the libraries that must have been associated with churches and monasteries.

In the Frankish period (1191–1571), there were libraries in the court of Lusignan kings and in churches, monasteries, and abbeys. During the Turkish occupation (1571–1878), nearly all works of art were destroyed and the Catholic cathedrals of Saint Sophia (Holy Wisdom) in Nicosia and Saint Nicholas in Famagusta were converted to mosques. The books kept in churches and other places were destroyed. Only a few books were saved in isolated small churches and monasteries.

After 1821 a small library was formed by the Archbishopric in Nicosia, where most of the books saved from ancient collections in churches, monasteries, and bishoprics were collected. The library of the Archbishopric of Cyprus originates from those collections. In 1982 the library of the Makarios III Foundation was amalgamated with the library of the Archbishopric of Cyprus in Nicosia and the Phaneromeni Library.

At the beginning of the 19th century the Ottoman government in Cyprus set up a small library, the library of Sultan Mahmut II, with Turkish, Arabic, and Persian works. Originally housed in a medieval building behind Saint Sophia Cathedral in Nicosia, it is now in a building owned by Evkaf, a Turkish charitable trust.

After the cession of Cyprus to the British in 1878, there was an increase in book imports, mainly from Greece and the United Kingdom. New libraries were started, mainly in government offices. In July 1878 a Greek Cypriot began operating the first printing press, at Larnaca. The first newspaper in Cyprus, *Kypros,* was issued at that time in Greek and English.

In 1887 a legal deposit law was passed and a depository set up in the office of the Chief Secretary. Two copies of each book were also sent to the Keeper of the Department of Printed Books at the British Museum. After independence (1960), the law was amended to require deposit of three copies in the library of the Public Information Office at Nicosia. The State Library is now the depository library for Cyprus. Nearly all libraries in Cyprus, except those already mentioned, started functioning after 1927, most of them after independence in 1960.

In July 1974 Turkey invaded Cyprus and occupied 40 percent of the island. Many library collections were either damaged or destroyed. Two large private libraries with many codices and rare books about Cyprus were seized also, and no information is available about their fate. The library service thereafter faced many difficulties, including a reduction of stock and library facilities. The situation improved by the mid-1980s.

National and Public Libraries. The Public Library of Nicosia, established in 1927 and transferred to Nicosia Municipality in 1936, acted as a kind of National Library (with a gap in operations from 1953 to 1977) until 1985, when the State Library of Cyprus opened. The library of the Ministry of Education, established in 1960, is housed in the same building. These two libraries are run by the same library committee and administration. The library is open to every citizen of Cyprus. Patrons can borrow books in person or by mail. The library has two regional libraries in other parts of Nicosia—one an educational library and the other a children's library. The library has about 60,000 volumes of bound books and periodicals, not only in Greek and English but also in other languages.

Public Information Office, Nicosia, Cyprus

Paphos Municipal Library, Cyprus.

The main towns of Cyprus have public libraries run by the municipalities. There are also 120 communal libraries in large villages, run by the Cultural Service of the Ministry of Education. The Cultural Service also runs three mobile libraries serving the districts of Nicosia, Larnaca, Limassol, and Paphos and part of Famagusta.

There was no national bibliography before 1985. Since 1960 C. D. Stephanou has published the Cyprus Bibliographical Bulletin; it records the publications of Cyprus in the original language and is classified according to Dewey Decimal Classification. In 1985 the Bibliographical Society of Cyprus in Nicosia started publishing a bibliographical bulletin that records all published books of Cyprus of the previous year.

Press and Information Office, Nicosia

The library at the Nicosia Pedagogical Academy.

Academic Libraries. The University of Cyprus began accepting students in September 1992. Its Library opened two years earlier with a staff of two professionals and three assistants. The country's five other tertiary-level government-run institutions of higher education are the Pedagogical Academy (College of Education), the Higher Technical Institute, the Forestry College, the School of Nursing, and the Hotel and Catering Institute. Each of these institutions has its own library, with from 10,000 to 30,000 volumes. There are also eight private institutions of tertiary education that have their own well-organized libraries.

School Libraries. All 435 primary schools of Cyprus had their own lending libraries of varying size in the late 1980s. All secondary schools (high schools and technical schools) had libraries ranging from 3,000 to 45,000 volumes. Most of the high school libraries are run by assistant librarians or teachers who act as part-time librarians. School libraries are supported by the Ministry of Education, which contributes an allowance for the purchase of books based on the number of pupils.

Special Libraries. All ministries and departments of the government have special libraries. Among them are the library of the Archeological Museum, with an excellent collection of books on the archeology of Cyprus; the Cyprus Research Center, with a fine collection on Cyprus history and folklore; and the library of the Institute of Agriculture Research. The Public Record Office library, opened in 1972, houses all public records and archives.

The Profession. The Cyprus Library Association in Nicosia was founded in 1962. It is a member of IFLA and a founding member of the Commonwealth Library Association (COMLA), established in 1972.

COSTAS D. STEPHANOU

Czechoslovakia

The Czech and Slovak Federal Republic lies in central Europe, with Germany on the west and north, Poland on the northeast, Ukraine on the east, and Hungary and Austria on the south. Population (1990 est.) 15,662,000; area 127,876 sq.km. The official languages are Czech and Slovak.

History. The area now called Czechoslovakia was part of the Holy Roman Empire, then the Austrian Empire, and finally the Austro-Hungarian Empire until it achieved independence after World War I. It was occupied by German troops during World War II and became a people's republic in 1948. After the "Velvet Revolution" of 1989, the Czech and Slovak peoples began pulling away from one another. By 1993, they had established separate, independent republics. Information given in this article is based on the situation before the breakup.

Prague was a center of learning from the Middle Ages on. The Charles University, the first in central Europe, was founded in 1348. The University Library grew with it; it is now part of the National Library in Prague. The Academia Istropolitana in Bratislava was established in 1467. Its Library has grown to become part of the University Library in Bratislava. Universities and libraries were established in Olomouc (1568), Irnava (1635), and Košice (1657). In 1863 Matica Slovenská was established in Martin. There were libraries attached to churches and schools and, later, public libraries. Book clubs played a significant role in democratizing library services.

The first Czechoslovak Library Act (1919) called for public libraries throughout the country. The Second Library Act (1959) defined the mission, tasks, administrative structure, and mutual relations of libraries. After the federative state was set up in 1969, the libraries have worked in two independent national systems, Czech and Slovak.

National Libraries. There are two national libraries, the National Library in Prague for the Czech Republic and Matica Slovenská in Martin for the Slovak Republic.

National Library, Prague. The origins of the Library date back to 1348. As the oldest depository library, it has vast holdings (more than 5,750,000 volumes in 1987), including unique collections of manuscripts, incunabula, rare printed items, and printed music. The Library is the center of international exchange and of interlibrary lending and is a UN and Unesco depository library. The Library publishes the Czech National Bibliography in four series (books, periodicals, articles, and printed music). From 1989 it served as the seat of the ISBN Group Agency for the Czech and Slovak republics and the ISBN National Agency for the Czech Republic. It is both a center of book research and methodology and a public lending library.

Matica Slovenská, Martin. Founded in 1863, the Matica Slovenská is a depository library of Czech and Slovak literary production from 1945 on. The Library is the central Slovak archive of literature and music. Its holdings (more than 5,000,000 volumes in 1987) include manuscripts, incunabula, rare printed items, an archival collection of 1,800,000 items, and special

Libraries in Czechoslovakia (1990)

Type of library	Number of administrative units (main libraries)	Number of service points (branches, mobile stops, etc.)	Volumes in collections	Annual expenditures (Koruna)	Population served	Professional staff (with certificate, diploma, etc.)	Total staff
National	1	--	3,324,240	6,500,000	3,054	181	194
Research	10	--	12,828,218	70,161,076	114,948	637	932
Academic	1	--	484,266	5,990,000	11,066	52	54
Public	2,627	--	20,290,956	134,691,760	952,867	2,918	3,393
School	5,503	--	16,004,739	40,250,813	697,209	5,413	5,758
Special	687	--	5,303,880	28,913,286	111,153	913	975

collections (printed music, picture postcards, and posters). The Library has published the Slovak National Bibliography with computers since 1977. In 1989 it became the ISBN National Agency for the Slovak Republic. It is charged with caring for and protecting its collection, further education for experts, and the development of library theory and research. The Library provides lending and information services for the public.

Academic Libraries. In 1989 the two republics had 59 universities and colleges (technical, economic, agricultural, and artistic) with their own faculty or central libraries. In all they serve more than 180 faculties, 140,000 students, and 24,000 teachers. Academics also use the general and specialized independent research libraries in their regions. The most important academic libraries are the University Library in Bratislava (with more than two million volumes in 1987), the State Technical Library in Prague (1,764,000 volumes), the State Technical Library in Bratislava (specialized collections of more than 3,300,000 volumes), and the Basic Library–Science Information Center of the Czechoslovak Academy of Science (more than 900,000 volumes).

Public Libraries. Public libraries in the regional capitals are the centers of bibliography, information, research, and lending services. Their holdings are general in nature, and fiction represents the highest percentage of all loans. Public libraries have separate departments for children and youth. These libraries have a well-organized library network.

School Libraries. Almost all primary and secondary schools have libraries, but most lack professional staff and suitable space and equipment. They cannot serve the pupils' needs, and most students turn to their public libraries. Many public libraries cooperate with the schools through mutual agreements.

Special Libraries. Special libraries exist as dependent units in scientific institutions, medical facilities, industrial and agricultural plants, and museums and galleries. They provide bibliographic and information services for the staffs they serve.

The Profession. Education of specialists and information workers in the republics begins at the secondary level in library schools at Prague, Brno, and Bratislava. The course of study lasts four years after basic secondary education.

Education for specialists is provided at two universities: the Department of Information Science and Librarianship of the Faculty of Arts of Charles University in Prague and the Department of Librarianship and Information Science of the Faculty of Arts of Comenius University in Bratislava. Information science is also taught at the College of Economics in Prague. The course of study lasts eight terms after secondary school.

Continuing education of workers and specialists is offered at the Center for Further Education of Librarians attached to the Slovak National Library in Martin, at the Center attached to the Slovak Technical Library in Bratislava, and at the National Library in Prague. Continuing professional education is also provided at the Departments of Librarianship and Information Science in Prague and Bratislava.

In the Czech Republic, the Association of Librarians and Information Workers was revived in 1990. It acts as a trade union, with its main objective to increase the level and social prestige of library and information work. The Association has its headquarters in Prague.

Slovak National Library, Martin Photo by Philip Asut

Slovak National Library in Martin, opened in 1975.

In the Slovak Republic, the Society of Slovak Librarians was founded in 1968 as the Association of Slovak Librarians and Information Scientists; it changed its name in 1990. It is a voluntary professional organization of librarians, bibliographers, and information workers. It has its headquarters in Bratislava.

EDITOR'S NOTE: On January 1, 1993, Czechoslovakia separated into its constituent Czech and Slovak republics.

HELENA KOLAROVA-PALKOVA

State Library of the Czech Socialist Republic

Baroque Hall of the Czech National Library, Prague, formerly the State Library of the Czech Socialist Republic.

D

Dana, John Cotton
(1856–1929)

John Cotton Dana, public librarian for four decades, notable for his innovations in offering and promoting library services and public education, was a leader of the library profession who served as President, and sometimes critic, of the American Library Association and was an organizer and President of the Special Libraries Association.

Born on August 19, 1856, in Woodstock, Vermont, Dana spent his early life in Woodstock, where he was reared in a home in which education and reading were emphasized. He received an introduction to business there also, working in his father's general store "on the green," a store originally opened by his grandfather in 1802. He maintained strong ties with Woodstock throughout his life and spent many summer vacations there. In 1874 Dana entered Dartmouth College. There he had a good academic record and was elected to Phi Beta Kappa in 1878.

ALA

John Cotton Dana

In June 1878 he returned home and began the study of law in the firm of French and Southgate in Woodstock. In addition to his study of law, he found time to read widely from the classics, biography, travel, and metaphysics. Less than two years later, threatened with tuberculosis, he sought a higher and drier climate. One of his college friends, Frank Wadleigh Gove, had gone to Colorado in 1879 and had become a deputy United States land and mineral surveyor in the mining section of the state. Dana joined him at Rico, Colorado, in 1880 and continued his study of law there. He was admitted to the Colorado bar later that year. Mostly, however, he worked with Gove as a surveyor until 1882.

Dana returned to Woodstock for a brief time before moving to New York City. There he lived with his brother Charles, a doctor, while he continued his study of law and also did some tutoring. Dana passed the New York State Bar examinations in May 1883. About the same time health problems surfaced again, and in March 1884 he went to Fergus Falls, Minnesota, where another college friend, William D. Parkinson, lived. From there he moved to Ashby, Minnesota, where he practiced law and in July 1884 became Editor, for a short time, of the local newspaper, the *Avalanche.* After a few months he returned to Colorado and again engaged in work as a surveyor and later as construction superintendent for the Colorado Midland Railroad, living in construction camp tents a good deal of the time. He also began to make public appearances as a lecturer on religious and social questions. For one month he occupied the pulpit in a Unitarian church, and there he met Adine Rowena Waggener, a native of Russellville, Kentucky, whom he married in November 1888.

For a while after marriage the couple lived on a Colorado ranch, where Dana began to write articles for publication on a variety of subjects including travel and educational and sociological matters. He also wrote letters to the editors of newspapers. An article entitled "The Public School," critical of the public school system in the United States, was published in the *Denver Arbitrator* for February 16, 1889, and attracted wide attention. To a degree it may well have been this very article that was responsible for Dana's eventual entrance into the library profession. Other influences, however, may have played a part also. Aaron Gove, Superintendent of the Denver Public School system, was Frank Wadleigh Gove's brother. For some time he and his Board had hoped to establish a library for the high school that could be open to the public and function as a public library also. The tax levied for educational purposes in Colorado included a provision that made this plan legal. Dana's article in the *Denver Arbitrator* spurred Gove on toward accomplishment of that hope. Gove made the recommendation to his Board to vote for the establishment of the library to serve the school and the public and to appoint John Cotton Dana as the Librarian. It was so voted. Dana accepted and in 1889 began a career in librarianship that lasted four decades.

Denver. Dana began at once to organize the Denver Public Library, gather a staff, acquire materials in books, magazines, newspapers, and pamphlets, supplementing the 2,000 books in the school library, which he inherited upon his appointment, and to initiate service. Most significant of all, he began to advertise it. His idea about libraries was to get them used. He sent notices about the new library to the editors of every newspaper in Colorado and to national educational and religious journals, and he made personal visits to many of the editors. He sought their cooperation and help in making the services, planned for everyone, known and specifically indicated to them how he was sure the library could be of use to them too.

Advertising a library had not been the custom in the profession, and Dana's first moves in that direction were frowned upon by many in it. Other libraries were giving many of the services Dana inaugurated for Denver, but publicizing and advertising them was Dana's unique contribution. He also sought a sharing of experiences from fellow librarians.

He proceeded at once to issue a monthly library bulletin entitled *Books* (the first issue was dated October 1889); he invited educational and civic leaders to give lectures in the public library open to the public; and he gave many talks himself before business, educational, and other professional groups, many of which have been published. He followed William Howard Brett's innovative policy of open access to shelves. In 1894 Dana opened the very first children's room in a public library—a room with suitable furniture, decoration, and a supply of children's literature for their enjoyment, information, and personal development.

His library flourished. Its resources and use, as determined by circulation figures, grew significantly. Visitors numbered a thousand daily. He assembled a collection of business books and related materials and placed it in the Chamber of Commerce, thus becoming one of the entrepreneurs, among librarians, attempting to provide service in the field of business information. A special collection of medical books was developed in cooperation with the Colorado Medical Library Association that later formed the nucleus of the Denver Medical Library.

With all this he also started a library training class for his staff. As procedures and forms became established, he took great pains to put them in writing for frequent review. Some of these became part of a book, the *Public Library Handbook,* in 1893. He took an active part in professional associations as a member and also officer, being elected President of the Colorado Library Association in 1895 and Chairman of its Convention Committee for the forthcoming conference of the American Library Association to be held in Cleveland the next year.

Dana began to look elsewhere for an opportunity to pursue his vocation. A controversy had arisen concerning his policy of providing library materials on both sides of the free silver matter, a policy Dana defended earnestly; the School Board was criticized by Denver's Chamber of Commerce for using part of its tax appropriation to finance the business library there, even though the action was definitely within the law. Dana became the Librarian of the City Library of Springfield, Massachusetts, effective January 1, 1898.

Springfield. The City Library of Springfield, Massachusetts, was already established with a collection over four times larger than the one Dana left in Denver and a staff already organized and at work. Dana saw possibilities for making the library better known in the community and more usable and inviting physically. He put into effect policies found successful in Denver, such as providing easier access to the shelves and a special corner for children's books and removing all devices—bars, gates, or anything else—that deterred direct contact of the public with the library staff. Because the library building was on a hill, and access to the entrance necessitated climbing flights of stairs up that hill, he had an elevator installed. He also started library training classes to provide qualified assistants for the library. The interest shown in his classes prompted him to invite the librarians in the northwestern part of the state to a meeting to discuss mutual library problems. An outgrowth of these sessions was the organization of the Western Massachusetts Library Club.

Dana wrote a series of articles entitled "A Library Primer," which were published in the first six issues of *Public Libraries* in 1896. Later he revised, rewrote, and extended the original draft for publication in book form. He included additional material selected from many sources, written by other library pioneers, for *A Library Primer* (the same title as his 1893 book), published in 1899.

Dana resigned his post in Springfield on December 18, 1901, to become Librarian of the Free Public Library of Newark, New Jersey, succeeding his friend and fellow Dartmouth graduate, Frank P. Hill.

Newark. Dana joined the Free Public Library of Newark, New Jersey, as Librarian, on January 15, 1902, and remained there the rest of his life. The new building had been completed the year before. The resources for reference and lending were comprehensive. The staff was capable, qualified, and interested. Beatrice Winser, who had been Assistant Librarian under Hill, and who was appointed Acting Librarian when Hill left, had administered the Library capably for seven months. Dana with Winser as Assistant Librarian formed a dynamic team. He did much writing, planned policies, edited Newark library publications, e.g., *The Newarker, The Library,* prepared broadsides, gave numerous talks to alert the public on the contribution the Library could and did make to the social structure of the community, and directed preparation of various book lists. He provided new activities for the Library, such as the hospital library service, a special collection of foreign language books for the immigrants coming to the city, and branch libraries. All of these developments provided news items for the newspapers and business, professional, and other journals, and gave Dana opportunities to keep the library in the public eye. He was spectacularly successful in doing so.

Always searching for new ways to make the Library more meaningful, he became deeply involved in museums. His philosophy, expressed in one of the Library's booklists, was, "Libraries and museums exist to furnish the knowledge that leads to understanding." Though there were no museums in Newark, he saw possibilities in creating some museum activities within the Library, e.g., preparing exhibits that could be displayed there, and proceeded to borrow materials from citizens of Newark, from department stores, and from other museums for that purpose. He organized exhibits on American art and on science.

On April 29, 1909, the Newark Museum Association was formed with Dana as its Secretary. Almost four years later he was appointed the Association's first Director, holding that position as well as his Library post until his death. In this capacity he began to see his dream of a museum building and museum service for Newark come true. And so it did, but not without controversy over location and other delays. Finally, on March 17, 1926, the Newark Museum of Art, Science, and Industry was opened near the Library.

Perhaps Dana's most famous contribution to the library profession was establishment of what became the Business Library of the Newark Public Library. He had been aware of the possibilities of library service to the business community in Denver and in Springfield and initiated services there, working with business groups such as Chambers of Commerce and with community business leaders. But the information needs of business were not very clearly defined at that time, and very little printed documentation of what was defined was available to libraries. In Newark, he was fortunate in recognizing a member of his staff, Sarah B. Ball, who shared his enthusiasm for seeking ways to make the Library of genuine use to business. She was the Librarian of Branch 1, opened in October 1904 and located in Newark's business district. In reporting to him of the use being made of the branch by businessmen, she suggested a change of name to Business Men's Library and began collecting as much material as could be found on anything relating to business. No one could have been happier about this than Dana. The Business Men's Library flourished largely because of the tremendous dedication and enthusiasm of Ball, who had the wholehearted support of Dana and Richard C. Jenkinson, one of the Trustees, and also because the flood of business print had started from the presses.

At the Business Men's Library emphasis was put on providing exact information needed—specific facts and figures. Lists of book and periodical references for specific business subjects were issued frequently, and a regular bulletin entitled "Business Literature" had subscribers throughout the country. The Library became a model for other public libraries seeking to extend similar services for their communities.

Dana's work as Librarian of the Denver Public Library brought him to the attention of members of the American Library Association, some of whom stopped on the way to a San Francisco convention to meet Dana and see the Denver Public Library. The visit led to his first ALA Conference, and in 1895 he became its President-Elect.

Association Leadership. His concern with some of the country's and world's great problems made a number of the ALA's topics for discussion seem puerile to him, and he was soon in controversy with some of its members and officers. Dana, however, was willing and anxious to identify with library and education associations as a member even when he differed with them or was actively opposed to some of their activities. He was elected or appointed to many committees of national, state, and local organizations: President of the American Library Association, 1895–96; member of its Council, 1896–1902; and President of the New Jersey Library Association, 1904–05 and 1910–11. He also became President of the Special Libraries Association, which he helped organize, 1909–10.

The group whose efforts finally resulted in the formation of the Special Libraries Association had started really with Sarah B. Ball and Anna Sears, Librarian of the Merchant's Association of New York. They had invited librarians doing special library research work outside public libraries, as well as those specializing in business information and other specialties within public libraries, to meet together informally while they were in attendance at ALA meetings. When this fact was brought to Dana's attention, he started the action that brought together about 56 librarians working in such fields as law, insurance, chambers of commerce, engineering, public utilities, museums, and municipal research.

Largely through Dana's help, this group organized themselves into the Special Libraries Association (1909), a name suggested by Dana.

Dana hoped to get the new Association under the umbrella of the ALA, and his failure to accomplish this because of reluctance, or misunderstanding on both sides, increased his dissatisfaction with the ALA. He remained an active member of the Association, however, and continued vocal in his criticism when he disagreed in its decisions.

Shortly before his death on July 21, 1929, he wrote to Matthew S. Dudgeon of the Milwaukee Public Library:

> I have been for years, now and then, the down-right critic of the A.L.A. During these same years I hope I have been of assistance to A.L.A. in all its good work. My criticism is what I'm remembered for, I assume, and I cannot help feeling that I have been, not infrequently, unfairly judged concerning it (Chalmers Hadley, *John Cotton Dana—A Sketch,* ALA, 1943).

Dana had many interests in his life—politics, education, business, art, music, printing: in fact, anything that affected mankind concerned him.

Publications. Dana was a prolific writer and speaker. Many of his talks and addresses were printed in library, business, and other professional journals, often in more than one. A comprehensive list, chronologically arranged, compiled by Hazel Johnson and Beatrice Winser, was published with Hazel Johnson's article on Dana in *The Library Quarterly* (1937). *Literature of Libraries in the Seventeenth and Eighteenth Centuries* (1906–07), edited by J. C. Dana and Henry W. Kent, was reprinted in 1967 by Scarecrow.

His family's Elm Tree Press in his home in Woodstock, Vermont, operated mainly by two of his brothers, was used frequently to print works written or edited by him or in collaboration with others. Edmund Lester Pearson's *The Old Librarian's Almanack* (1909) was printed there for many years, as were Dana's translations of 17th- and 18th-century classics on librarianship.

Newark recognized him as "the First Citizen of Newark" and celebrated the 100th anniversary of his birth with a Centennial Convocation on October 17, 1956.

Dana's philosophical approach to librarianship is best revealed in his book *Suggestions,* published by F. W. Faxon in 1921. It consists of extracts from his papers and essays. They were selected by him to help the beginner in library work look at the profession with fresh interest and make it seem deserving of careful thought. They contain those nuggets of thought that, through the years, have been quoted over and over again on reading, books, and business.

ROSE L. VORMELKER

DeGennaro, Richard

(1926–)

A U.S. university librarian, Richard DeGennaro has been a thoughtful library director, a perceptive writer, and a pioneer in the application of computers to library operations.

Born March 2, 1926, in New Haven, Connecticut, he left high school to join the U.S. Navy at the age of 16, serving with distinction in the Pacific during World War II on the *USS Montpelier* and the *USS San Juan.* He achieved the rank of Radioman First Class and earned ten battle stars and a Navy commendation.

After completing high school, he enrolled in Wesleyan University in Middletown, Connecticut, where he earned a B.A. in Government in 1951 and an M.A. in Liberal Studies in 1960. In the time between the two degrees he spent four years traveling in Europe, studying at the Sorbonne and the universities of Madrid, Barcelona, Poitiers, and Perugia. He met his wife, Birgit, a native of Sweden, while studying at the Sorbonne.

After a brief period teaching French, DeGennaro sought the counsel of the librarian at Wesleyan and decided to enter the School of Library Service at Columbia University, where he received an M.S. in 1956. His first library position was as a Reference Librarian at the New York Public Library, where he worked from 1958 to 1961 in the Economics, Science, and Technology Division, at the Main Information Desk, and in the American History Division.

He moved to Harvard University Library in 1958 and in 12 years rose to the position of Senior Associate University Librarian (1969–70). During this period he gained national recognition as the Associate University Librarian for Systems Development for initiating efforts to create machine-readable records of the Harvard shelflist and introducing a computerized acquisitions system.

DeGennaro left Harvard in 1970 to become the

Director of Libraries and Adjunct Professor of English at the University of Pennsylvania in Philadelphia, where he remained until 1986. During this period he was elected President of the Association of Research Libraries (1975). He served on the Board of Governors of the Research Libraries Group from 1979 to 1990 and was its chairman in 1984–85. He returned to the New York Public Library as its Director in 1987, then returned to Harvard as the Roy E. Larsen Librarian of Harvard College in 1990.

In 1967, as a founding member of the Information Science and Automation Division of the American Library Association (which became the Library and Information Technology Association), he began to articulate in speeches and contributions to the professional literature the problems and opportunities presented by the application of computers and other new technologies to library management and operations. His perspective on the costs of library automation, the conflicts with publishers over intellectual property rights, and his understanding of the increased demands on library management as resources began to erode in the 1970s helped to educate a whole generation of academic librarians to the realities of the profession.

Honored for his leadership and his writings, he received the ALA's Melvil Dewey Award in 1986. He was named Academic Librarian of the Year by the Association of College and Research Libraries in 1991. He also received distinguished alumni awards from both Columbia and Wesleyan universities.

DeGennaro and his wife have two sons, Ralph and George, and a daughter, Christina. He lives in Cambridge, Massachusetts.

REFERENCE

Richard DeGennaro, *Libraries, Technology, and the Marketplace* (1987).

ROBERT WEDGEWORTH

Denmark

Denmark, a constitutional monarchy, lies between the North and the Baltic seas in north-central Europe. It consists of the greater part of the Jutland Penisula and a number of islands, the largest of which is Zealand. Copenhagen, the capital and largest city, is on Zealand. Population (1990 est.) 5,140,000; area 43,077 sq.km. The official language is Danish.

History. The earliest libraries in Denmark belonged to churches and monasteries, but they have all been lost. The oldest existing library is the University Library of Copenhagen, founded in 1482. After the Reformation, most libraries were private collections; a few have survived, mostly integrated into present-day collections such as the University Library and the Royal Library. The emergence of new academic institutions during the 19th and especially the 20th century has brought about a number of university and other academic libraries.

The public libraries in Denmark can be traced back to the late 18th century; during the 19th century, small parish libraries, funded through private donations, appeared throughout the country. In 1882 the state began to make grants to public libraries; local authorities increasingly contributed to their maintenance. Under the first public library law (1920), all libraries became entitled to state grants proportional to local funding. The law established the State Inspectorate of Public Libraries to ensure that quality, balance, and professional standards were maintained.

National Library. The Royal Library in Copenhagen (1665), originally the king's personal library, but open to the public since 1793, is the national library and the largest in Denmark. A legal deposit library since 1697, it has the most complete Danish collections in existence, including translations of Danish works into other languages and foreign books dealing with Denmark, as well as manuscripts, maps, photographs, and musical scores. It also serves as the national book museum.

The Royal Library is the main library of the University of Copenhagen for theology, the social sciences, and the humanities, where it holds the most extensive collections in Denmark. It also has several special collections, notably Judaica (one of the world's finest) and Oriental Books and Manuscripts.

The National Archives consist of the Central Record Office in Copenhagen and four provincial archives, with holdings that occupied 201,000 running meters in 1988. Total staff numbered 149 (about a third of them professionals), and annual expenditures totaled almost 45,720,000 Danish kroner. The Na-

Libraries in Denmark (1990)

Type of library	Administrative units	Service points	Volumes in collections	Annual expenditures (DKK)	Population served	Professional staff	Total staff
National	1	4	3,447,148	111,450,600	--	143	305
Academic	17	50	7,799,511	298,172,300	53,273**	375	830
Public	250	1,031	34,285,411	1,895,218,000	5,146,469	2,339	5,707
School	275	1,815	32,235,388	242,677,000	586,654*	n.a.	n.a.
Special	120	144	3,735,206	110,018,500	--	213	431

*1989
**Teachers and students; teachers = full-time equivalents; students = active (not registered)

Sources: *Biblioteksårbog* '90. Statistik for folke- og skolebibliotekerne. Statistik for forskningsbibliotekerne [*Library Yearbook* '90. Statistics for Public and School Libraries. Statistics for Research Libraries.] *Skolebiblioteksårbog* 1989–90 [*School Library Yearbook* 1989–90]. *Statistisk Årbog* 1991 [*Statistical Yearbook* 1991].

tional Danish Business History Archives in Aarhus had a staff of 12 and a budget of more than 4,200,000 Danish kroner.

Academic Libraries. Apart from the Royal Library, there are 18 libraries serving degree-granting institutions. In 1989 the University Library of Copenhagen became the Danish National Library of Science and Medicine and its humanities section was merged with the Royal Library. The State and University Library of Aarhus (founded 1902) also fulfills some national functions as a legal deposit library, as a national media archive holding the main national collection of newspapers, and as a central lending library for public libraries. Other important libraries are the National Technological Library of Denmark, the Danish Veterinary and Agricultural Library, the Library of the Copenhagen School of Economics and Business Administration, the National Library of Education, and the university libraries of Odense, Roskilde, and Aalborg.

All major academic libraries are open to the general public without any restrictions. During the 1930s a division of work among the research libraries developed, each library assuming the responsibility for maintaining adequate collections in its subject areas and making them universally available. Although this system was never formalized, it is still one of the basic elements of library cooperation in Denmark.

Public Libraries. According to an act of Parliament, each of the country's 275 municipalities is obliged to provide library services that meet certain minimum standards. But two or more local authorities can establish a joint library system, and one municipality may buy library service from a neighbor. Most of the public libraries circulate music records and tapes and provide facilities for other cultural activities. In each of the country's 14 counties, one library, in addition to serving its local community, also acts as a central library for the county (amtsbiblioteker), especially in interlibrary loan. County authorities fund this function.

Until 1983, a percentage of the expenses of public libraries was reimbursed by the state. In return, the Ministry of Cultural Affairs exercised fairly direct control over the libraries through the State Inspectorate of Public Libraries (Bibliotekstilsyn). This office was instrumental in bringing about the high professional level of Danish public libraries.

The Royal Library, which serves as Denmark's national library and traces its beginning to the 16th century. It also serves as the main library of the University of Copenhagen for the humanities, theology, and social sciences.

Royal Library of Denmark

In 1986 the Office of the National Librarian (originally established in 1943) was separated from the Royal Library. A number of functions as well as the title of National Librarian were transferred to the head of the new institution, which acts as a coordinating body and adviser to the government in matters concerning research libraries. It also maintains a central database, ALBA. In 1990 the State Inspectorate was abolished and its remaining functions were merged with those of the Office of the National Librarian, now renamed the National Library Authority.

School Libraries. The Library Act requires each primary school to have its own library. School libraries offer books and periodicals as well as non-book materials. They are also used for library instruction, with the aim of making the children familiar with the use of library facilities.

Special Libraries. In Denmark academic and special libraries are known collectively as research libraries, without any sharp distinctions. National library statistics register about 110 libraries, mainly small, serving non-academic professional or special institutions.

The Profession. The Royal School of Librarianship, located in Copenhagen and with a branch at Aalborg, provides four-year basic programs in librarianship. Since 1990 it has offered academic degrees in information science.

In the Danish Library Association, the oldest in the country, representatives of the local authorities concerned with libraries predominate, whereas institutional representatives and staff members make up the membership of the Danish Research Library Association. The Union of Danish Librarians is the trade union for non-academic professional librarians. Other associations serve school libraries, school librarians, and other specialized branches of the profession.

REFERENCES

State of the Art of the Application of New Information Technologies in Libraries and Their Impact on Library Functions: Denmark (1987).

Jens Thorhauge, *New Trends in Scandinavian Public Libraries* (1988).

The Royal Library Today and in the Future (1990).

MORTEN LAURSEN VIG

Dewey, Melvil
(1851–1931)

At an early age Melvil Dewey concluded that knowledge was better than ignorance, that education was the surest means to knowledge, and that, beyond schooling, reading was the surest means to an education—to reach understanding one needed only diligence and a book. The young American also concluded that he would have to see to it that the best means to bring person and book together be found and employed. Librarianship did not exist when Dewey set out on his self-assigned task. To be sure, there were libraries, and people worked in them, but no unified body of

ALA

Melvil Dewey

purpose and practice (which we call librarianship) existed to guide them.

From 1873 to 1906 he was to devise and construct almost singlehandedly the forms and substance of librarianship (Charles Ammi Cutter providing the other hand on occasion). To achieve what he did Dewey had to play many roles:

organizer: of the ALA and other professional associations; of a classification scheme (the Dewey Decimal Classification); and of a library school.

advocate: for professionalism in librarianship; for the education of its members; for an equal role for women.

standardizer: of supplies, equipment, tools, methods, education.

librarian: of one of the first modern university libraries (Columbia); of the foremost state library of its day (New York).

teacher: through editing and writing for *Library Journal* and *Library Notes;* through the establishment of apprentice programs and a library school; through promoting the role of the college library in academic pursuits; through pursuing always the role of the library as the "People's University"; and through inspiration and example.

Melvil Louis Kossuth Dewey was born on December 10, 1851, in Adams Center, New York, to Joel and Eliza Dewey. He gathered his early education in bits and pieces, entering Amherst College, Amherst, Massachusetts, in 1870. While there he launched his career in librarianship, the first step being to examine exemplary libraries of the Northeast in order to determine the methods libraries should use in carrying out their roles. This quest led him to his most lasting achievement in librarianship.

Libraries normally arranged their collections by the fixed location method—a book's physical location was fixed on a specific shelf in a specific range. Dewey pondered the inevitable costs of such a system: works on the same subject did not shelve near each other, and when a library grew beyond its four walls, its collection had to be renumbered on book and in catalogue—an expensive business. (Two cornerstones of Dewey's lifelong activities were his concerns for time and cost.) To prevent the unwanted effects of fixed location, Dewey conceived relative location, using decimal fractions to number the contents of books rather than the physical books themselves. That stroke of genius led to the Dewey Decimal Classification, published in 1876, in its 20th edition in the late 1980s and the most widely used library classification in the world. From it was to stem the Universal Decimal Classification, also widely used, and itself one of the bases of information science through S. C. Bradford's *Documentation* (1948).

The year 1876 saw Dewey lay other foundations for the profession. (1) He was the motive force in bringing together the Conference of Librarians in Philadelphia at which the American Library Association was born (and dominated by him for 30 years). (2) By approaching Frederick Leypoldt and R. R. Bowker on the need for a journal in librarianship, Dewey assured the future publication of the *Library Journal* and subsequently helped direct it for its first five years (1876–81). (3) He established the Library Bureau, a firm that took major steps toward standardizing supplies, equipment, and library methods.

Dewey moved to Boston in 1876 and for six years cultivated his slowly growing garden. During this time the DDC was being developed toward the epochal second edition; the Library Bureau was founded; and he contributed greatly to the modernization of the profession through the *Library Journal*. He also suggested, and with Cutter and Justin Winsor guided, the abortive but brilliant idea of cataloguing data accompanying a book—title-slip registry. We have the idea in practice today—the justly appreciated Cataloging-in-Publication. Dewey had taken that idea originally from one suggested by Natale Battezzati in 1871—colored catalogue cards would accompany a book to booksellers so that they could compile various catalogues of their inventory and better serve their patrons. Dewey's borrowing here is a good example of his capacity to recognize a useful idea when he saw one and to meld it with other ideas to produce a method or tool that, though not original in its parts, was new in its totality. Predictably, some resented this capability as much as Dewey's originality.

On October 26, 1878, Dewey married Annie Godfrey, his companion and adviser for the next half century and mother to his only child, Godfrey Dewey (1887–1977), himself important in librarianship (primarily in his association with the DDC). He also contributed to the success of the 1932 Winter Olympics in Lake Placid, New York.

In 1883 Columbia College offered Melvil Dewey the opportunity to develop its library. In doing so he epitomized the schism between scholar and librarian that lasts to this day in strongly centralized academic libraries. Dewey believed—and convinced Columbia's administration—that the library is the heart of the college. His belief led to the growth of the central library that gathers as many books (and therefore as much power) to itself as it can. Many scholars believe, on the other hand, that books in their specialty (preferably just down the hall) promote the scholarship of a faculty that in turn is the heart of a college.

The Columbia faculty waited as Dewey combined the diverse subject collections and integrated them through the DDC, created a classed catalogue, extended library service to other users, initiated instruction of users through the reference department, and formulated strict and often restrictive rules for the use of the library. When, in the establishment of a library school at Columbia, 17 of the 20 students to matriculate in the first class in 1887 were women, Dewey's critics saw the chance to rid themselves of the pest in the library. Late in 1888 the trustees voted to suspend him from his duties in the Library but not in the school.

His work done at Columbia, Dewey moved to the next opportunity awaiting him. After being impressed by Dewey's views on the educational role of the library delivered in a speech before them, and being in need of a state librarian, the Regents of the University of the State of New York offered him the post. They were so impressed by his vigor and accomplishments that they also offered him the responsibilities of another vacant post—thus he became both Secretary and Treasurer of the Board, as well as Director of the State Library.

If there was one aspect of life that Dewey loved more than work, it was power. His new positions gave him power and the means to gain more. He used power not primarily for personal gain (except to the extent that he equated himself with his projects) but to further the role of the library as the "People's University." Every action Dewey took furthered the library's role in the schools, colleges, cities, states, and nation (the Library of Congress).

One of Dewey's first acts at Albany was to obtain permission for the transfer of his library school from Columbia to the State Library. There instruction and supervision could be given the students for the work they did in the Library, thus maintaining the means to develop a unified profession through standard methods and a cadre of people to convey them, as well as facilitating the development of the collection and services of the State Library.

While at Albany, Dewey continued to develop the purposes and methods of the profession. (1) Just as he had founded the New York Library Club in 1885, he now was the prime mover in establishing the New York Library Association in 1890, the first of the state associations and the model for those to come. (2) The State Library became a reference center and "collection of last resort." (3) He instituted special collections and services for physicians, the blind, women, children, individuals with an interest in social matters and concerns, and even traveling libraries to provide support to libraries throughout the state and to carry libraries to people otherwise without access to books. He also proposed bookmobiles ("book-wagons") for the isolated, especially farmers. (4) He extended acquisitions to materials other than books; pictures, slides, and other media began to flow into the Library. (5) He advocated depository libraries for seldom-used books, centralized cataloguing by the Library of Congress, and national library status for the Library of Congress, to which the nation's libraries could turn for guidance. (6) He pioneered and advocated the use in libraries of such new equipment as the typewriter and the telephone. (7) He served in many professional offices, among them as President of the Association of State Librarians from 1889 to 1892 and as President of ALA in 1890 and 1892–93. For ALA he was instrumental in the success of an excellent library exhibit at the World's Columbian Exposition of 1893. (8) And with his able lieutenants—Walter Stanley Biscoe, Evelyn May Seymour, and Dorcas Fellows—he developed the DDC through its sixth edition. With them he was instrumental in producing the *A.L.A. Catalog: 8,000 Volumes for a Popular Library, with Notes* (1904), yet another standardized and standardizing tool for the profession.

Many of his dreams achieved and many dawning, the profession now well on its way to success in bringing education to the people who cherished and sought it, Dewey was forced to resign his positions as Director of the State Library, the Home Education Department, and the Library School. He had lost a power struggle with Andrew S. Draper, a man who admired neither Dewey nor his views and who had become his superior in 1904. The ostensible cause for his resignation on January 1, 1906, was the flap over the anti-Semitism of the Lake Placid Club, an organization that Dewey had been instrumental in founding and guiding. The actual cause, however, was that Draper sought to strengthen the position of schools at the expense of libraries regardless of the role Dewey wanted them to fulfill. Dewey had to leave or be discredited. Though he did not bring on the adverse criticism himself, Draper did let the criticism take its course, and Dewey was forced to leave.

Dewey was a visionary. Capable of perseverance and extreme dedication, he cared more for results than the particular means and not only was willing to adopt readily new materials and methods but also expected such things to change continually. (Note his attitude toward books and other media for communicating ideas to people and his adoption of the typewriter, the telephone, and other mechanical improvements. He would have equally easily adopted the computer if he were working now. It is important to note that he would have used mechanical means for his ends—he did not adapt his ends to suit the exigencies of the means, a response seen too often in today's library world.) In his writings and speeches he advocated virtually every process that librarianship has come to or is coming to: standardization and cooperation in cataloguing (he envisioned networking); standardization of cataloguing rules (the rules not to be changed unless overwhelming improvement results); the Library of Congress to be the national library; centralized storage; and "fee for service."

Dewey stood for the needs of the user above all; these included the need for information, education, and recreation. Libraries, though they change in nature, should tell the news, answer what and how and why, tell a story, and sing a song.

Scholars of library history have not truly grasped the nature of Melvil Dewey. They refer to him as being complex, charismatic, and any of a host of other terms that tell us little about anyone. The matter is not so complex: Dewey was simply a genius confident in his capacity, a demon for work, and one who took pleasure in acquiring and using power. Those who would be leaders resented or hated him; those who would follow admired or adored him. He was a master politician despite his abrasive nature; rarely did he not bring people to do what he wanted them to do—the battles he lost (Columbia, Albany) were to overwhelming odds. Nor did he accept defeat or frustration ungraciously. He did not like to lose, but he was too smart to let it show; there would always be another day. But after January 1, 1906, there was not another day. Dewey died in Lake Placid, New York, December 26, 1931.

Though Dewey never fully left his work in librarianship, his semiretirement to the Lake Placid Club removed from librarianship its strongest advocate, its most original designer, and its most effective organizer. Perhaps his leaving was not so great a loss as it was a shame; his work may have been done. One may believe, however, that had he continued, libraries would have become more central to education than they were to come to be. Dewey knew that knowing was better than not knowing, that any means to knowledge were good means if they produced enlightened leaders and citizens, and that the profession had to work hard and together to bring knowledge through books or other media. Where we work hard and together, Dewey lives.

REFERENCES

Sarah K. Vann, *Melvil Dewey, His Enduring Presence in Librarianship* (1978).

Gordon Stevenson and Judith Kramer-Greene, editors, *Melvil Dewey: The Man and the Classification* (1983).

Francis L. Miksa, "Melvil Dewey: The Professional Educator and His Heirs," *Library Trends* (1986).

Sarah K. Vann, "Dewey, Melvil," *Dictionary of American Library Biography* (1978).

JOHN P. COMAROMI

Dix, William S.

(1910–1978)

William Shepherd Dix, Librarian of Princeton University from 1953 until 1975, was honored widely for contributions to library and academic communities in the United States. He did not have a library science degree, but he *became* a librarian by *being* one. His character and scholarship fitted him peculiarly to bridge the gap between the user and the library. He matched the tradition of gentleman with a strong sensitiveness to each individual's needs.

Born on November 19, 1910, in Winchester, Virginia, Dix grew up in Berryville, Virginia, and Hagerstown, Maryland. In 1931 he graduated with honors from the University of Virginia and took his M.A. in English there the following year.

He began his career in the Darlington School for Boys in Rome, Georgia, as a teacher of English from 1932 to 1939 and went on to teach at Western Reserve University (now Case Western Reserve University), Cleveland, and Williams College, Williamstown, Massachusetts, before going to Harvard in 1944 on the staff of the wartime Radio Research Laboratory. When the Laboratory was disbanded in 1946, he taught for one year at Harvard and completed his Ph.D. in American Literature at the University of Chicago.

In 1947 Dix became an English instructor at Rice Institute (now Rice University) in Houston and the next year accepted the additional assignment of directing the school's library. He was an Associate Professor of English and Librarian when he left Rice in 1953 to head the Princeton University Library. He was Princeton's 22d Librarian and had served 22 years when he retired in 1975.

Princeton University Library

William S. Dix

Dix's considerable activities outside his daily obligations were apparent early. During his two years at Western Reserve he became Director of the Committee on Private Research. His book, *The Amateur Spirit in Scholarship* (Western Reserve University Press, 1942), describes the work of that body, whose purpose was to promote amateur activities in scholarly and creative research.

During the Princeton years, he served the campus, the Association of Research Libraries, the American Library Association, the New Jersey Library Association, library causes in Washington and in other countries, and other libraries in advisory capacities. In 1970 he was called on to preside over disciplinary hearings at Princeton following campus disruptions protesting U.S. involvement in the Vietnam War. He kept the hearings on course through angry turmoil with a clear sense of the fundamental purposes of a university.

He served the Association of Research Libraries in a variety of capacities, including a part-time appointment from 1957 to 1959 as its first Executive Secretary when it was moving toward permanent headquarters and a full-time Executive Director. In the 1960s, in a service of lasting importance to library users, he chaired the ARL Committee on Shared Cataloging, which influenced Congress to include Title II-C in the Higher Education Act of 1965. This provision enables the Library of Congress under the National Program for Acquisitions and Cataloging to assist libraries by acquiring and cataloguing promptly the world's scholarly publications. His skill in appearing as a witness before Congressional committees was useful on other occasions in fostering legislation of value to library service.

Dix carried out a wide range of assignments in ALA and its units. As Chair of the ALA Intellectual Freedom Committee during the divisive and fearful McCarthy period, he was the principal drafter of the Association's declaration on "The Freedom to Read," a statement adopted jointly by the American Book Publishers Council (now the Association of American Publishers) and subsequently endorsed by 21 other organizations. The importance he attached to a free society is stated there:

> Freedom has given the United States the elasticity to endure strain. Freedom keeps open the path of novel and creative solutions, and enables change to come by choice. Every silencing of a heresy, every enforcement of an orthodoxy, diminishes the toughness and resilience of our society and leaves it the less able to deal with stress.

His chairing of the ALA International Relations Board was the beginning of a number of international assignments: Consultant to the Ford Foundation, Baghdad, 1958; member of the U.S. Delegation to the Unesco General Conference, Paris, 1958 and 1960, serving as Vice-Chairman of the Delegation, 1960; U.S. Delegate to the Conference of Asian National Commissions for Unesco, Manila, 1961; Asian-American Assembly, Kuala Lumpur, 1963; and U.S. Department of State Government Advisory Committee on International Book and Library Programs, 1967–69.

Dix's longtime involvement in library matters reached a climax with his service as the ALA President, 1969–70, a crucial year. It was a time of national conflict between the complacency of the old ways and the new demands for meeting social obligations. To the task of preserving the Association while providing for change, he brought his propensity to see each side of a controversy, his firmly based belief in tolerance for differing viewpoints, his concern for the individual, and his evenhanded leadership.

He was a member of the American Council of Learned Societies committee to propose programs to meet the needs of American research libraries and of the Boards of Directors of the H. W. Wilson Company and of the Franklin Book Programs. He served on advisory bodies for the New Jersey State Library, Rutgers University Graduate School of Library and Information Studies, the libraries of Duke and Harvard Universities, and the Association of American University Presses. At the time of his death, he was a member of the Board of Directors of the Council on Library Resources and of the National Commission on New Technological Uses of Copyrighted Works, the latter body working for agreement among divergent interests relating to copyright.

Dix's deportment and his public addresses probably influenced his colleagues as much as his many published articles, convincing others through the force of his well-reasoned positions. Although ill with terminal cancer during the last ten months of his life (he died in Princeton on February 22, 1978), he worked diligently on his retirement project of writing the history of the Princeton University Library—work that he had often put aside to meet his commitment to public groups. He was able to complete "The Princeton University Library in the Eighteenth Century," which was published as volume 40, number 1 (Autumn 1978), of *The Princeton University Library Chronicle,* and as a separate monograph by the Library. It is a worthy legacy, embodying his scholarship and his felicitous way with words.

Many honors came to him: honorary doctorates from the University of Florida and Washington College; the New Jersey Library Association's Distinguished Service Award; ALA's Melvil Dewey and Lippincott Awards and its highest honor, an Honorary Membership.

HELEN WELCH TUTTLE

Djibouti

The Republic of Djibouti, formerly French Somaliland and then the French Territory of the Afars and the Issas, became independent in June 1977. It lies south of a narrow strait linking the Gulf of Aden to the Red Sea and is bordered on the southeast by Somalia and on the south, west, and northwest by Ethiopia. Population (1990 est.) 490,000; area 23,200 sq.km. The official language is Arabic; French is widely spoken.

The only significant libraries open to the public are one in the French Cultural Center and the Arab Maritime Academy library. The former opened in the capital of Djibouti in June 1978 with a collection of 8,000 books. The Arab Maritime Academy has about 8,500 volumes and 180 current periodicals. There is also a Documentation Center with a collection of materials relating to Djibouti; the collection consists primarily of periodical articles. There are small working library collections in some government ministries.

STAFF

Dominican Republic

The Dominican Republic occupies the eastern section of the island of Hispaniola in the Caribbean Sea. Haiti occupies the western section, with a chain of mountains in between. Population (1990 est.) 7,170,000; area, 48,734 sq.km. The official language is Spanish.

History. The Spaniards were the first Europeans to inhabit the Caribbean Islands, and many people assume that they first used the printing press there, but such was not the case. In all probability, they utilized the printing facilities on the mainland or in Spain itself. Nothing related to the colonies at that time could be printed without the permission of the Indies Council.

No one knows for sure the date of the introduction of the printing press on the island of Hispaniola. Some historians believe that a press was used in the 17th century, but no evidence exists to that effect. The first references come from Moreau de Saint-Mery, who, in 1783, mentioned the existence of a printing press, located in the Royal Court of Justice, "the place designated by law as the residence of the President of the Royal Court of Justice, depository of the royal seal, the archives of the Secretariat, and also the printing press and the prison." The first extant imprint dates from the year 1800 and was produced by a Frenchman, Andres Josef Blocquerst, who had come to the island around 1782: *Novena para implorar la protección de María Santísima por medio de su imagen de Altagracia*.

Little is known of libraries during the colonial era. The first reference to a public library appeared in 1860, slightly more than 15 years after the founding of the Republic (1844). The library in question was organized in the Government Palace through the donation of the private library of Rafael María Baralt, a Venezuelan jurist and writer who lived for a time in the city of Santo Domingo. But his bibliographical treasures were not destined for good fortune: in 1876 they were removed to the Saint Thomas Aquinas Seminary, under the protection of the "Friends of the Nation Society," and by 1904 they had been scattered. That public library was followed in the city of Santiago de los Caballeros by the libraries of the Amantes de la Luz Atheneum (1874) and the Alianza Cibaeña (1888), and by the library of the atheneum in San Pedro de Macoris (1890).

In June 1884 the National Congress created a depository for the conservation of editions produced by the state—the first known reference to a legal depository law. On September 26 of the same year, the National Congress created the position of Public Archivist based on the principle that "it was necessary to create a public office through which could be deposited all of the works, documents, and certificates that constitute the Archives of the Secretariats of State and of the other offices." The Archives were located in the main hall of the Municipal Council Building.

The founding of libraries throughout the country continued in the 20th century. The Gabriel A. Morillo Public Library was established in the town of Moca

(1904), followed in other cities by the Baní Public Library (1920), the Santo Domingo Municipal Library (1922), and the Restoration Society Public Library in Puerto Plata (1928). The year 1927 saw the founding of the National Museum and Library, considered as one unit.

The period from 1930 to 1960, encompassing the 30-year dictatorship of Rafael L. Trujillo, was an important one for library development in the country. The General Archives of the Nation appeared in 1935. In 1939 the first professional librarian arrived in the Dominican Republic: the Spaniard Luis Florén Lozano (1913–1973). Florén lived in Santo Domingo from 1939 until 1953, during which time he was Director of the Library of the University of Santo Domingo. He gave a technical stamp to library development in the Dominican Republic. With his arrival came a resurgence of public libraries, bibliographic activities that resulted in the first national bibliographies, the first training courses for archivists and librarians, and the first book fairs in the country.

By 1956 there were 110 public libraries in the country that served 425,874 users. The period of greatest growth, the late 1950s, saw a total of 136 libraries serving 569,903 users.

The 1960s were a period of political and economic instability in the Dominican Republic. After the death of Trujillo in 1960 and the civil war that followed in 1965, the country underwent a recession that was keenly felt in the nation's libraries. The number of libraries decreased and their collections deteriorated rapidly—heavy use and looting characterized the period. The lack of economic assistance made it difficult to keep book collections up to date.

The decade of the 1970s marked a new era for Dominican librarianship. Beginning in 1970, the first group of Dominican professional librarians, 10 in number, returned to the country. Florén, who had directed the Interamerican School of Librarianship in Medellín, Colombia, from 1959, was named as adviser to the recently created National Library. Courses for library assistants were begun and the Dominican Association of Librarians was created. The first special libraries began to emerge, but public and school libraries continued without support because of lack of interest on the part of the government. All in all, this was one of those crucial periods in library development when, little by little, the importance of library services in national development came to be appreciated.

The National Library and National Archives. The National Library was originally founded in 1927 as the National Museum and Library. From its beginning it maintained a precarious existence; it was the National Library in name only because its functions were actually carried out by the Library of the University of Santo Domingo for the period 1947–71. The Copyright Law of 1948 required the deposit of two copies of all printed materials in the Central Library of the University of Santo Domingo and two copies in the General Archives of the Nation.

In 1969 the National Library received authorization to construct its own building, which was inaugurated in 1971. A law on Legal Deposit was promulgated, overturning the law of 1948 and designating the National Library as the only depository for the national printed output. The law mandates the deposit of two copies of periodicals, monographs, and similar printed materials, and one copy of phonograph records, under penalty of fine. In 1982 the National Congress modified the legal deposit law to include the Libraries of the National Congress and the National Archives in addition to the National Library.

The National Library reports to the Presidency of the Republic. It is organized into five departments: Administrative Services, Technical Processes, Periodicals, National Bibliography, and Public Services. It maintains a collection of 345,424 volumes and publishes a current national bibliography entitled *Anuario Bibliográfico* (No. 1, 1978–).

Although the position of General Archivist dates from the year 1884, the modern organization of the General Archives of the Nation began with the promulgation in 1935 of a law designed to ensure the orderly conservation of all documents published by the state, which constitute an important source of historical data on the country.

The mission of the General Archives is the conservation, organization, and diffusion of all documents and certificates emanating from the various offices and branches of the state, as well as all the relevant historical documents that can be acquired. Its role is determined by decrees that establish the system of organization and conservation of its holdings and regulate the transfer of documents to it.

The Archives consists of seven departments: Administration, Research, Dissemination, Archives, Pre-Archives, Library and Periodicals, and Technical Services. The dates of its holdings range from 1600 to 1979. Colonial documents are represented by the valuable collections of the Royal Archives of Bayaguana and Higüey. The Periodicals Section contains a valuable collection of Dominican newspapers, including the first to be published in the country: *El Telégrafo Constitucional de Santo Domingo* (1821) and *El Duende* (1821). The Archives publishes the *Boletín del Archivo General de la Nación* (No. 1, March 1938–).

Two other important archives should be mentioned: the Historical Archives of Santiago, located in the city of Santiago de los Caballeros and containing documents pertaining to that city, and the National Archives of Music.

Academic Libraries. There are eight institutions of higher learning with libraries. The largest and oldest is the Universidad Autónoma de Santo Domingo (UASD), formerly the University of Santo Domingo, which was founded as far back as 1538, although its present library dates from 1927. As of 1983, the library contained 260,000 volumes of books and pamphlets and 5,000 periodical titles. Its period of greatest growth was from 1940 to 1960, due in part to the Copyright Law of 1948 that called for the deposit of two copies of all works published in the Dominican Republic. From 1948 to 1971 it functioned, for all practical purposes, as the National Library. During the period 1944–52 it averaged 40,000 titles in annual acquisitions. It maintains an exchange program with the Library of Congress of the United States and is the official depository for U.S. government publications.

Under the direction of Florén, the UASD library became the National Bibliographic Center, publishing a number of bibliographies, including the *Bibliografía dominicana, Bibliografía histórica dominicana,* and *Bibliografía de los profesores universitarios*. Its collection of journals, newspapers, books, theses, and pamphlets is one of the richest in the country, especially in materials relating to the Dominican Republic.

Of the 65 employees in the UASD library, 7 were professionals in 1985. In addition to the Central Library, the university has five other departmental libraries: Economics, Engineering and Architecture, Agronomy and Veterinary Science, Humanities, and Law and Political Science. The university also maintains libraries at the four regional campuses: the Northwest Regional University Center (CURNO), located in Mao, with an extension in the city of Santiago Rodríguez; Southwest Regional University Center (CURSO) in Barahona; Northeast Regional University Center (CURNE) in San Francisco de Macorís; and Eastern Regional University Center (CURE) in Higüey.

Some 60 percent of the nation's professional librarians work in university libraries, and this concentration is reflected in both the services offered by the university libraries and the importance assigned to them. A good sign is the increasing number of library buildings that have already been constructed or are under construction; these buildings represent large investments in furniture and equipment. The most notable of these is the modern building of the Central Library of the Eastern Central University (UCE) in San Pedro de Macorís. Inaugurated in 1981, this library had a collection of 45,000 volumes in 1985 as well as modern audiovisual equipment.

The library of the Pedro Henríquez Ureña University (UNPHU), founded in 1966, has 45,000 volumes and publishes an acquisitions bulletin entitled *Biblionotas*. The Santo Domingo Technical Institute (INTEC) maintains a collection of 35,000 volumes, and the quality of its materials and services is considered outstanding. Among those services is selective dissemination of information (SDI) in the areas of pure sciences, technology, humanities, social sciences, and biomedical sciences. Three other institutions—the Catholic University, Mother and Teacher (UCMM); the World University; and the Institute of Advanced Studies—maintain collections of 70,000, 5,300, and 12,000, respectively.

Public Libraries. The government of the Dominican Republic showed little interest in the creation and development of public libraries, with the exception of the city of Santo Domingo. The mayor in the early 1980s, José Francisco Peña Gómez, promised to build 50 public libraries for the *barrio*. After assuming office, Peña Gómez created an Office for Public Libraries in the municipal government to carry out his electoral promises. In 1982 and 1983, 15 such libraries were founded in various neighborhoods, with collections ranging from fewer than 400 to more than 1,000 volumes. The Office for Public Libraries is responsible for planning, organizing, and directing this system of libraries. All materials are centrally processed by a classification system developed by the Office. The collections consist of school textbooks ranging from the first grade through the first year of college, as well as small general collections made up of encyclopedias and dictionaries.

The private sector contributed to library development through the founding, in 1979, of the Children's Pilot Library, directed by a women's group called the Bibliophile Circle. It has a collection of 3,900 volumes and by 1983 had been visited by 27,600 children. It has a small permanent staff.

In the city of Puerto Plata the Restoration Society carries out a number of cultural activities involving the public library, including the preservation of the city's historical monuments.

School Libraries. The Dominican Republic is almost completely lacking in school libraries. The few there are tend to be small and dependent on the goodwill of donors, and therefore do not relate to the curricula or reflect principles of good selection. Those who tend these libraries rely, in large part, on their own experience; since they have had no training in library science, both technical processes and public services suffer accordingly. Of the 5,200 educational institutions in the country, only 115 (2.2 percent) had libraries in the mid-1980s.

In 1983 the State Secretary of Education, Fine Arts, and Culture carried out a study that provided the following results: (1) not a single collection can be considered up to date; (2) without specially constructed facilities of their own, the libraries have to operate out of classrooms or administrative offices; (3) the collections consist almost entirely of textbooks, most of them ranging between 125 and 5,000 volumes with only one at more than 7,000 volumes; (4) no library has adequate furniture or open stacks; and (5) the librarians have no professional preparation. As for technical processes, no collection is processed systematically; no library maintains a file of users; and no one maintains control over book acquisitions. As for services, the basic function of these libraries is to lend books only within the reading room.

A national system of school libraries was proposed as a project of international technical assistance. A beginning point has been that of providing school library training to 276 persons to assume responsibility for organizing and providing modern services in the proposed network. Also under way in 1985 was a system of mobile libraries designed to reach unserved populations and to support curriculum and teaching in the frontier areas of the country.

Special Libraries. This type of library began to appear in the Dominican Republic around 1975 and since then a number of important special libraries have emerged. One of them is the Scientific and Technical Information Center (CENICIT) of the Dominican Institute of Industrial Technology (INDOTEC), which is part of the Central Bank of the Dominican Republic, specializing in industrial technology with special emphasis on the technology of food production. CENICIT consists of two divisions: the Library, with 6,000 books and 600 periodical titles; and the Division of Technical Information, which contains documents, a database, reference services for technical questions, an area on standards and patents, an area on publications, and a section dealing with catalogues and directories of equipment and machinery. CENICIT is the Dominican representative of the National Technical Information Service (NTIS).

The Dominican Center for Export Promotion (CEDOPEX), which specializes in international commerce, maintains an information center with 8,104 books and 400 periodical titles and uses the commercial information system of the International Commerce Center of the United Nations.

The National Center for Agricultural Information (CENADOA) belongs to the Department of Information, Statistics, and Computation under the Secretary of Agriculture and was created in 1978. CENADOA is the national coordinator of the Interamerican System for Agricultural Information on Latin America and the Caribbean (AGRINTER/IICA) and the International Information System on Agricultural Science and Related Technologies (AGRIS/FAO). Its information center has a collection of 4,575 volumes and 712 journal titles. It offers a program of training and technical assistance to agricultural libraries belonging to the National Network of Agricultural Information.

The Enrique Apolinar Henríqez Library of the Dominican Society of Bibliophiles maintains a collection consisting of 3,279 volumes, specializing in Dominican history, literature, and related fields. The Society publishes a collection on Dominican culture, featuring previously unpublished works and first editions that have special significance for Dominican history and culture.

The Dominican Financial Company maintains a library that specializes in finance and agro-industry, with a collection of 2,463 books and 6,789 documents and journals.

Libraries also exist in the National Office of Statistics (ONE), the Advanced Institute of Agriculture (ISA) in Santiago, the Central Bank of the Dominican Republic, the Dominican Electric Corporation (CDE), and the Reserve Bank of the Dominican Republic.

The Profession. Library education in the Dominican Republic dates from the decade of the 1940s, when the Faculty of Philosophy of what is now the Autonomous University of Santo Domingo included librarianship as an area of study in the undergraduate and graduate studies in philosophy. A number of outstanding professionals set out on the long road of organizing the nation's libraries and compiling bibliographies. A large number of them were concentrated in the library of the Autonomous University of Santo Domingo.

A School of Librarians and Archivists was created as part of the Faculty of Philosophy and Education in 1960. It was abolished in 1966 as one of a number of changes in academic units. Although the School never actually functioned, its creation reflected an awareness of the need for such a program.

Beginning in 1967 the same university and the Catholic University sponsored the professional training of a group of young people to study at the Interamerican School of Librarianship in Medellín, Colombia, thus providing the first large group of professional librarians for the country.

In the 1970s formal courses were offered at the national level by the Catholic University, the Eastern Central University, the National Office of Personnel Administration, and the Dominican Association of Librarians. In addition, the School of Librarianship was created in the Dominican World University in 1979. It offers the Licenciate in Librarianship.

A total of 17 courses were offered for library paraprofessionals for no less than 450 persons by the mid-1980s. The General Archives of the Nation offered two courses for paraprofessionals in archives for some 40 persons. They attained the title of Technical Assistant in Archives.

The Dominican Association of Librarians, Inc. (ASODOBI), was founded on November 28, 1974. Its primary objective is to promote the extension of library services throughout the country. It consists of a General Assembly and an Executive Committee of five persons. As of 1978 it had 32 members. It publishes *El Papiro* (1976–) and has its headquarters in the National Library. Membership is open to both paraprofessionals and professional librarians.

The Association of University Libraries was formed upon a resolution of the National Council of Institutions of Higher Education (CONIES) on October 3, 1978. Its objective is the creation of a system to coordinate the development of university library collections by avoiding duplication of effort and resources and establishing channels of communications among the member libraries.

MARISOL FLORÉN;
translated by EDWIN S. GLEAVES

Downs, Robert B.
(1903–1991)

ALA

Robert B. Downs

Robert Bingham Downs combined the careers of American library administrator and library educator with outstanding leadership in professional library organizations and a remarkable publication record of books and articles.

Downs was born May 25, 1903, on a farm near Lenoir, North Carolina, where he attended a one-room country school for seven years. In 1917 his family moved to Asheville, North Carolina, where he discovered the Asheville public library and started a lifelong addiction to reading. But a career in librarianship had no place in his plans then, and formal education was abandoned after one year of high school. After a variety of jobs—including construction worker, fire ranger, telephone repairman, and ranch hand in Wyoming—he returned to graduate from Trinity High School in Durham.

He entered the University of North Carolina at Chapel Hill in 1922. As a student assistant in the University Library, he came under the influence of Louis Round Wilson. Receiving his A.B. in 1926, Downs enrolled in the School of Library Service at Columbia, where he received his B.S. in L.S. degree in 1927 and his M.S. in 1929. From 1927 to 1929 he was a reference assistant in the New York Public Library.

In 1929 he became Librarian of Colby College and two years later returned to the University of North Carolina to become Assistant Librarian under Louis R. Wilson. When Wilson became Dean of the Graduate Library School at the University of Chicago in 1932, Downs was made Acting Librarian and the following year was appointed University Librarian and Professor of Library Science. During the next five years he developed strong library collections, instituted a program of duplicate exchanges, and taught bibliography, history of books, and reference in the library school. He also began his studies in the cooperative development of library resources and, with Harvie Branscomb of Duke University, developed a plan for sharing responsibility for collecting research materials between the neighboring university libraries. His first major book, *The Resources of Southern Libraries,* was published in 1938.

The same year he was appointed Director of Libraries of New York University with the task of coordinating seven quasi-independent libraries of the University. There he centralized the technical services departments, developed a union catalogue, and reorganized the staff and services of the Washington Square Library. During this period he published his *Resources of New York City Libraries* (1942), a series of three annual surveys of "Notable Materials Added to American Libraries" in *Library Quarterly* (1940–42), and *Union Catalogs in the United States* (1942).

In 1943 he was appointed Director of Libraries and of the Library School at the University of Illinois, a dual appointment he held until his retirement 27 years later. He was designated Dean of Library Administration in 1958. At Illinois he reorganized the library staff and secured faculty rank and status for librarians, a task that earlier directors had attempted unsuccessfully. The book collection, already a notable one in many fields, grew to more than 4,000,000 volumes. Under his direction, the Library School introduced a doctoral program, a series of Windsor Lectures (honoring Director-Emeritus P. L. Windsor) to bring outstanding bookmen to the campus, the annual Allerton Park Institutes, and two serial publications, *Library Trends* (1952–) and *Occasional Papers* (1949–).

Downs served the University in many extralibrary activities: Chairman of the Land Grant Centennial Committee, Vice-Chairman of the University Centennial Committee, Chairman of the Senate Committee on Honorary Degrees, Chairman of the University Concert and Entertainment Board, and President of the University Chapters of Phi Beta Kappa and Phi Kappa Phi.

Downs's continuing interest in the definition and description of library resources led to the publication of his *American Library Resources: A Bibliographical Guide* in 1951, with supplementary volumes in 1962, 1972, and 1981. *Resources of Canadian Academic and Research Libraries* appeared in 1967, and after his retirement a Guggenheim Fellowship enabled him to spend a year in England to gather information for his *British Library Resources* (1973). A similar survey of Australian and New Zealand library resources was published in 1979.

Downs conducted more than 30 surveys of libraries and groups of libraries, beginning with the survey of Cornell University Libraries (with Louis R. Wilson and Maurice F. Tauber) in 1948. He was responsible for surveys of the libraries of the University of Utah (1965), the University of Georgia (1966), Purdue University (1967), and Brigham Young University (1969). He conducted state library surveys for North Carolina, Missouri, Arkansas, and Illinois and shorter reports on libraries ranging from the Library Company of Philadelphia (1940) to the libraries of the Kansas City Regional Council for Education (1964).

At the end of World War II Downs served as a consultant to libraries and library schools overseas. In 1948 he went to Japan as adviser to the U.S. Military Government on the establishment of the National Diet Library and two years later returned to help establish a library school at Keio University. In Mexico he was consultant to the National Library and the University of Mexico in 1952. He served in a similar capacity in Turkey in 1955, 1968, and 1971; in 1963 he was consultant for a new library at Kabul University, Afghanistan. He lectured at Brazilian libraries and library schools at São Paulo, Rio de Janeiro, and Belo Horizonte in 1961 and was adviser to the Interamerican Library School at Medellín, Colombia, in 1964. He was consultant to the Library of the University of Puerto Rico for the establishment of its library school, 1964–65, and in 1973 he was consultant for the University of Tunis.

Active in professional organizations throughout his career, Downs served as President of the Association of College and Research Libraries (1940–41) and as President of the American Library Association (1952–53). He was also President of the Illinois Library Association (1955–56).

In addition to his professional writings, which cover most areas of librarianship, Downs wrote eight popular books, all of which link books and reading with notable persons. His *Books That Changed the World* (ALA, 1956) was translated into a dozen languages. Later books include *Famous Books Ancient and Modern* (1964), *Books That Changed America* (1970), *Books That Changed the South* (1977), *In Search of New Horizons* (1978), *Landmarks in Science* (1982), and *Memorable Americans* (1983, with John T. Flanagan and Harold W. Scott).

His interest in American humor and folklore led to an early booklet on *American Humor* (1938), written with Elizabeth Downs; one on *American Humorous Folklore* (1950); one of the Windsor Lectures published in 1958 as *The Family Saga;* and a collection of stories, *The Bear Went Over the Mountain* (1964). Later he wrote *Horace Mann* (1974), *Heinrich Pestalozzi* (1975), *Henry Barnard* (1977), and *Friedrich Froebel* (1978). *The First Freedom Today,* a revision of his 1960 book, was published by ALA in 1984.

Honors came to him from many quarters. The Association of American Publishers gave him the Clarence Day Award in 1963. The ALA conferred its Joseph W. Lippincott Award in 1964 and its Melvil Dewey Award in 1974. He received the Illinois Library Association's Librarian of the Year Award in 1972 and the Syracuse University Centennial Medal. He was awarded honorary degrees by Colby College, the University of North Carolina, Ohio State University, Southern Illinois University, and the University of Illinois. In 1979 he shared the first ACRL Academic Research Librarian of the Year Award with Keyes D. Metcalf. Downs died on February 24, 1991.

REFERENCES

Jerrold Orne, editor, *Research Librarianship: Essays in Honor of Robert B. Downs (1971),* contains a biography by Robert F. Delzell and a bibliography of Downs's publications.

Arthur Young, "Bestriding the Profession: Robert Bingham Downs and Academic Librarianship," *Leaders in American Academic Librarianship* (1983).

Robert B. Downs, *Perspectives on the Past: An Autobiography* (1984).

JOE W. KRAUS

Dunkin, Paul S.

(1905–1975)

As a library practitioner of merit, a philosopher of cataloguing theory and practice, a writer of pithy commentary, and a stimulating teacher, Paul Shaner

Dunkin earned the recognition and respect of the American library profession. His ability to strip away pretense and lay bare a problem in simple, direct fashion served the profession well during the period of library growth after World War II.

Born on September 28, 1905, in Flora, Indiana, he eventually traveled throughout the United States and abroad, and lived much of his life on the Atlantic Coast. But Dunkin remained true to his midwestern heritage, returning finally to Indiana to live after retirement from his active career. Dunkin's undergraduate work at DePauw University in Indiana led to an A.B. degree in 1929. As a Phi Beta Kappa student, he found his greatest interests to lie in English literature and the classics. Dunkin pursued classical studies further in the completion of an M.A. in 1931 and a Ph.D. in 1937, both awarded by the University of Illinois. The relatively long interval between those two advanced degrees is explained by Dunkin's move in 1935 from Graduate Assistant in classics to Cataloger for the University of Illinois Library. He obtained the B.S. in Library Science from the University in that year.

Dunkin was able to combine his classical scholarship and love of English literature with his interest in librarianship through an appointment in 1937 as Senior Cataloger at the Folger Shakespeare Library in Washington, D.C., a position he held until 1950, when he was promoted to Chief of Technical Services. Those who recognized Dunkin's continued interest in academe were perhaps not so startled as some of his other colleagues when he decided to leave the Folger Library in 1959 to assume responsibilities as Professor in the Graduate School of Library Service at Rutgers. Although the move signaled a dramatic change in focus, Dunkin's scholarly bent continued to be served as he directed masters' studies and doctoral research at Rutgers. He taught during the deanship of Ralph R. Shaw, as well as during portions of the terms of Lowell Martin and Neal Harlow. Under Shaw's leadership, the Ph.D. program in library service was initiated at Rutgers, thus allowing the Dunkin imprint to be felt by a number of the subsequent administrators and teachers in librarianship and information services.

In addition to his teaching, Dunkin became increasingly active in the work of the library profession, especially through his responsibilities in the American Library Association. While still at the Folger Library, he had completed his first library monograph, *How to Catalog a Rare Book* (1951), and had begun his critique of the approach proposed by Seymour Lubetzky for the development of the *Anglo-American Cataloging Rules* while Lubetzky was serving as Editor of the code. Dunkin's 1956 paper, "Criticisms of Current Cataloging Practice," written for the 21st conference of the Graduate Library School of the University of Chicago, initiated a series of discussions and reflections that appeared under his name during the 1950s and 1960s.

Among the more significant of Dunkin's writings were his commentary on Lubetzky's *Code of Cataloging Rules* (1960), his "year's work" papers in *Library Resources & Technical Services* reviewing the developments in cataloguing and classification (1958–66), and his book *Cataloguing U.S.A.* (1969). Although his commentaries tended to focus on the American scene, he participated in the International Conference on Cataloguing Principles in Paris in 1961 and continued to reflect on the impact of the "Paris Principles" throughout his subsequent writings.

Carleton F. Smith

Paul S. Dunkin

Dunkin's style was filled with classical allusions as well as references to homely, everyday events. He was especially fond of making satirical comments about the pretensions of librarians and the preoccupations of cataloguers—a predilection that endeared him to some and caused others to react in annoyance and sometimes hostility. Despite the sharpness of his wit and the barbs ever present in his papers, Dunkin was a gentle companion and in later life gave the impression of being somewhat frail. The keen analytical mind was sometimes betrayed by the body; for example, a badly broken bone caused by a fall prevented him from serving an active term as President of the Resources and Technical Services Division of ALA.

As a result of his visibility in the field of cataloguing, Dunkin was elected and appointed to many posts in the ALA. When Esther Piercy, the founding editor of *Library Resources & Technical Services,* died in 1967, Dunkin was selected to assume her responsibilities. Meanwhile, he was also contributing the "Viewpoint" column for *Library Journal.* Not surprisingly, then, Dunkin became the recipient of the Margaret Mann Citation in 1968, awarded by the Cataloging and Classification Section of ALA. Noted as "elder statesman with a refreshingly young perspective," Dunkin was commended for his "modestly-worn erudition, grace and wit."

There is some difficulty in assessing the peculiar quality of Dunkin's contributions to library service and particularly to cataloguing. He was more of an interpreter than an innovator. He tried to codify, simplify, and encourage iconoclasm among his students and colleagues. By sometimes amusing and occasionally outraging his readers, he hoped to make them reflect upon their activities and avoid taking themselves too seriously. Dunkin also rejected the "cataloguing manual" mentality, preferring to recapture the philosophical approach that he so much appreciated in the works of Charles Ammi Cutter. Interestingly, in *Cataloguing U.S.A.* Dunkin quietly avoided mention of the plethora of cataloguing texts published in the 1940s and 1950s, perhaps in the hope that they might not even warrant a footnote in cataloguing history.

After retiring in 1971, Dunkin was designated Professor Emeritus at Rutgers. He told his friends, however, that he intended to take no further role in professional organizations and to make no postretirement speeches. His collected essays, *Tales of Melvil's Mouser; or Much Ado about Librarians,* had appeared in 1970 at the end of his teaching career. In 1973 the second edition of *How to Catalog a Rare Book* was published. Then, in 1975, his final work, *Bibliography: Tiger or Fat Cat?,* was released; Dunkin's death in Indianapolis, Indiana, on August 25, 1975, preceded the official publication of that last volume.

REFERENCES

Doralyn J. Hickey, "Paul Shaner Dunkin, 28 September 1905–25 August 1975: An Appreciation," *Library Resources & Technical Services* (1975).

Doralyn J. Hickey, "Dunkin, Paul Shaner," *Dictionary of American Library Biography* (1978).

Norman D. Stevens, "The Writings of Paul S. Dunkin: A

Review Article," *Library Resources & Technical Services* (1978).

DORALYN J. HICKEY

Dziatzko, Karl

(1842–1903)

Karl Franz Otto Dziatzko was a prominent figure in the reform of Prussian librarianship that took place under the aegis of Friedrich Althoff (1839–1908), the Prussian Minister of Culture. The centralized authority of the libraries of the 10 Prussian universities was such as to facilitate cooperative projects such as union catalogues, cataloguing standards, interlibrary loan networks, standard administrative procedures, and requirements for the education and certification of professional librarians. Besides doing extensive research in the history of the book, printing, and philology, Dziatzko was deeply involved in these library developments.

Dziatzko was born on January 27, 1842, in Neustadt, a small town in Upper Silesia, then part of Prussia. He was educated at the Catholic Grammar School (*Gymnasium*) in Oppeln (now Opole in Poland). An early enthusiasm for language and mathematics gave way to what was to become a lifelong devotion to classical philology. He entered the University of Breslau (now University of Wroclaw) in 1859. After three years he moved to the University of Bonn, where he was influenced by the philologist and librarian Friedrich Ritschl (1806–76). A student in Ritschl's seminar, Dziatzko also worked in the library under Ritschl's direction. Graduating in 1863, with a dissertation on Plautus and Terence, he began his professional career as a teacher.

His early academic career was a restless one that first took him back to Oppeln and then to Lucerne, Switzerland. For a very brief period he was Director of the University Library at Freiburg (Baden) and then Director of a grammar school in Karlsruhe. The decisive turning point in his career came in 1872 when he was appointed Director of the University Library in Breslau. In 1886 he was appointed Director of the Library and Professor of Library Science at the University of Göttingen.

His administrative reforms at Breslau were regarded as a model for other German universities. His rules for the revision of the catalogue at Breslau subsequently became the basis of the *Prussian Instructions (Preussische Instruktionen),* which was first published in 1899, revised in 1908, and reprinted by Harrossowitz in 1966. It was translated into English by Andrew D. Osborn (University of Michigan Press, 1938). He was a key figure in the founding of the German Library Association (Verein Deutscher Bibliothekare) in 1900. His lectures and seminars on librarianship at Göttingen were the beginning of library education in Germany. He founded and edited the series *Sammlung Bibliothekswissenschaftlicher Arbeiten,* which was remarkable for the broad scope of its definition of library sciences. When, in 1893, by Althoff's decree, professional certification became mandatory in Prussia, Dziatzko was appointed Chairman of the examining committee.

Dziatzko's interests and reputation were international. He visited London and toured Italy to study methods of library organization. In 1900 he became a contributing editor to *The Library,* an English periodical. He died on January 13, 1903. With a singular dedication to the intellectual and scholarly dimension of librarianship that, at the same time, took into account practical matters of administration, service, and bibliographic control, Dziatzko made contributions in his lifework—the perfection of librarianship and the advancement of learning—that are still a part of modern German librarianship.

REFERENCES

Alfred Schneider, bibliography in *Sammlung Bibliothekswissenschaftlicher Arbeiten,* (1904).

Robert Langker, "The Earliest Professor of Librarianship: Karl Dziatzko of Göttingen," *The Australian Library Journal* (1960).

Joseph Becker, "Karl Dziatzko," in *Der Schlesier des 17. bis 18. Jahrhunderts* (Breslau, 1928) (*Schlesische Lebensbilder,* vol. 3).

GORDON STEVENSON

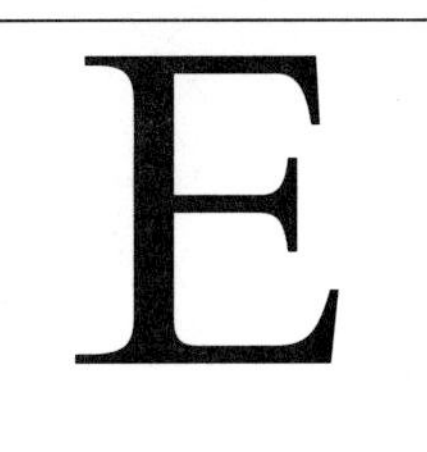

Eaton, John
(1829–1906)

John Eaton served as U.S. Commissioner of Education from 1870 to 1886. During his tenure he provided support for libraries through the compilation of statistics and the publication of reports and library aids, including the landmark 1876 *Public Libraries in the United States of America*.

Eaton was born December 5, 1829, near Sutton, New Hampshire, the oldest in a family of nine children. His early formal education was at first delayed and scanty, but he eventually earned his way through Dartmouth College, from which he received an A.B. in 1854. He worked as a public school administrator, first in Cleveland and then in Toledo, Ohio (1856–59), where he served as the Superintendent of public schools. In 1859 he enrolled at the Andover Seminary. When he graduated in 1861, he entered the Civil War as a chaplain with the 27th Ohio Volunteer Infantry. In 1862 U. S. Grant placed him in charge of the many ex-slaves who were coming to the Union Army for refuge. He continued that work until the end of the war, earning the rank of Brigadier General. While in that post Eaton developed educational and humanitarian ideals that coalesced into a strong overall view of the central importance of public education as the key agency of social renewal that would ensure an enlightened democracy. After five postwar years of newspaper and educational work in Tennessee, Eaton won another appointment from Grant, now President, as the U.S. Commissioner of Education, a position in which he was able to promote his educational goals.

Eaton viewed the proper work of the Bureau of Education to be the promotion of general education through gathering and publishing educational statistics, informative reports, and other writings; presenting educational programs at public expositions; and exchanging information with other countries on the establishment of educational systems. Eaton also considered libraries to be a component of the national educational program, as essential auxiliary aids to education and culture. He had first been involved in library work in Ohio. As Superintendent of Public Instruction in Tennessee (1867–69), he insisted that each school district have a library for the aid of teachers and campaigned for each county to have a library for the general citizenry.

As Commissioner of Education he began immediately to incorporate library statistics in the annual reports of the Bureau. His interest in compiling a library census (1874–76) led him to publish and distribute freely the special Bureau report, *Public Libraries in the United States of America: Their History, Condition and Management,* in which a variety of statistical tables were combined with a large number of general articles written by librarians to form what served for years as a fundamental handbook of library management. Eaton also correlated publication of the report in 1876 with the initial meeting of the American Library Association, which he helped to promote.

Between 1876 and 1885 he provided annual supplements to the 1876 library statistical data and in the Bureau's 1884–85 annual report issued a fully revised library census. During this period the Bureau also published and freely distributed special circulars of information on college libraries (1880), library buildings (1881), and general library aids (1882), each written by prominent librarians. In 1884 he committed the Bureau to issuing the *A.L.A. Catalog,* a promise that kept alive the Association's interest and work on the project.

By 1885 Eaton's work had set a pattern of cooperation between the library profession and the Bureau that would continue permanently. Eaton, however, found the greatly expanded work of the Bureau to be overtaxing, and in 1886 he resigned his post. He remained active in educational concerns until his death in Washington, D.C., on February 9, 1906.

REFERENCES

P. W. Alexander, *John Eaton, Jr.—Preacher, Soldier, and Educator,* Ph.D. dissertation, George Peabody College for Teachers (1939).

Francis L. Miksa, "The Making of the 1876 Special Report on Libraries," *Journal of Library History* (1973).

Francis L. Miksa, "Eaton, John," *Dictionary of American Library Biography* (1978).

G. Smith, "John Eaton, Educator, 1829—1906," *School and Society* (1969).

M. S. Williams, "The Library Work of the Bureau of Education," *Library Journal* (1887).

FRANCIS L. MIKSA

Ecuador

The Republic of Ecuador lies on the west coast of South America, with Colombia on the north and Peru on the east and south. Population (1990 est.) 10,782,000; area 283,561 sq.km. The official language is Spanish, but Indian languages are common.

History. The earliest libraries in Ecuador were the extensive collections of Jesuit and Franciscan clergy. When a royal ordinance from Spain resulted in the confiscation of Jesuit property in 1776, these libraries became the property of the state. The Jesuits had established universities and even a printing press, and these were taken over as well. But a demand for libraries did not spread until the middle of the 19th century. Between 1862 and 1925, 40 public libraries were established in cities around the country. In 1869 a decree for public support of the National Library was issued.

The year 1968 marked a renewed effort to upgrade libraries in general, much of the momentum having been derived from the Universidad Central, which hired its first professional librarian as Director of the General Library. Decisions were made to prepare a national union catalogue, to promote the Unesco UNISIST Project, to create a NATIS (National Technical Information System), and to update the professional statutes, revise the salaries of professionals, and prepare a Professional Defense Law.

National Library. The Biblioteca Nacional del Ecuador, in Quito, was founded in 1792. It contains about 60,000 volumes, many dating from the 16th and 17th centuries. A number of cooperative programs with the 97 municipal or public libraries have been instituted. The National Bibliography is published by the Biblioteca General of the Universidad Central on a bimonthly basis and cumulated annually. Support is given by the professional community and the Asociación Ecuatoriana de Bibliotecarios (AEB; Ecuadorian Library Association).

Libraries in Ecuador (1990)

Type of library	Number of administrative units (main libraries)	Number of service points (branches, mobile stops, etc.)	Volumes in collections	Population served
Academic[a]	128	128	531,000	224,517
Public[b]	210	210	142,000	--
Special[c]	1	1	2,000	230

[a]1987 data
[b]1988 data
[c]1983 data

Source: Unesco, *Statistical Yearbook,* 1991.

Academic Libraries. There are 51 academic libraries serving more than 200,000 students and faculty in Ecuadorian institutions of higher education. Perhaps the largest and most noteworthy of these is the Biblioteca General de la Universidad Central (General Library of the Central University), founded in 1826 and possessing a collection of more than 170,000 volumes. Almost all academic libraries have closed stacks; most give only registered students borrowing privileges.

Public Libraries. Public libraries in Ecuador are called bibliotecas municipales (municipal libraries), and many regions lack them, because of limited resources and lack of trained personnel. The Biblioteca Pública Municipal de Cuenca (Cuenca Public Library) has offered many short courses to train personnel for public and school libraries, as has the Ecuadorian Library Association, which has sponsored 42 multi-leveled training programs in the capital of each province. The Biblioteca Municipal de Quito was founded in 1886 and possesses more than 13,000 volumes; the Biblioteca Municipal de Guayaquil, founded in 1862, offers a collection of more than 120,000 volumes.

Other major libraries open to the public are the Biblioteca Ecuatoriana Aurelio Espinosa Pólit, in Quito, with about 120,000 volumes, 2,880 current periodicals, 14,000 manuscripts, 83 incunabula, 7,000 government documents, and 20,000 other materials; and the Biblioteca de Autores Nacionales Fray Vincente Solano in Cuenca, with about 40,000 volumes in its collection.

Of the 97 public libraries presently serving the Ecuadorian population, the majority struggle to survive and offer minimal services that generally do not include borrowing privileges. Most are closed collections that depend heavily on donations for growth. Many public libraries must double as school libraries in the absence or inadequacy of such institutions.

School Libraries. School libraries constitute more than 80 percent of all libraries in Ecuador, numbering almost 1,600. The majority are in private schools or offer rudimentary collections and services. Many double as public libraries, and most have irregular and insufficient hours. Generally speaking, one or several teachers with full-time class activities are assigned to library work. The government is actively promoting improvements in the public schools, but funding continues to be a problem. The Library Association has done much to promote the concept of school libraries, and training courses are directed toward the teachers in charge of these libraries.

Special Libraries. As in the majority of Latin American countries, special libraries and information centers are the most advanced in information management and enjoy the best funding and personnel. The largest are probably the Biblioteca Hispano-Americana in Cuenca (55,000 volumes) and the library of the Instituto Nacional Mejia in Quito (25,000). CIESPAL, the Centro Internacional de Estudios Superiores de Comunicación para América Latina (International Center of Higher Studies in Communications for Latin America) deserves special mention, having pioneered in modern information-handling techniques. CENDES, a technical information center specializing in food industry documentation, has also played a major role in the field. The Junta Nacional de Planificación (National Planning Department) has endeavored to set up a National Technical Information System. It organized the Seminario Nacional de Información Científica y Técnica (National Seminar on Scientific and Technical Information) in 1975.

The Profession. The Asociacíson Ecuatoriana de Bibliotecarios was founded in 1944 by Alfredo Chávez Granja, the first professional librarian in Ecuador. It has its headquarters at the Casa de Cultura Ecuatoriana (Ecuadorian Cultural Center) and has received a great deal of support from it. The Universidad Católica (Catholic University) has also been a staunch supporter of the AEB. After a number of periods of little activity after its inception, the AEB was revived in 1965 when four professional librarians returned from the Interamerican Library School in Colombia and initiated the publication of the *Boltín Bibliográfico Ecuatoriano*. Many courses and conferences have been offered, and the Association has been very active in promoting the development of the profession in Ecuador.

MARTHA GORMAN

Edwards, Edward
(1812–1886)

Edward Edwards, British librarian and author, held posts at the British Museum, 1839–50, in the Manchester municipal library system, 1851–58, and thereafter at Oxford. His permanent library reputation derives, however, not from work done in salaried posts held; Melvil Dewey put his finger on basic essentials when he referred to him as "foremost writer and thinker." During March 1877 Dewey wrote to Edwards— a lonely, unemployed, and impecunious librarian living in Oxford—inviting him to become the new *American Library Journal*'s Associate Editor for England:

> It seems eminently fitting that you to whom we have so long looked as the foremost writer and thinker in the library world should be associated with the leading librarians of the country in carrying forward this work. . . . I feel a strong personal interest in the matter because on several vital points I agree wholly with you and differ from most of our American librarians. . . . Your name on our list will vouch for your interest in our work. (Dewey's unpublished letter is now in the Edwards collection in Manchester Central Library.)

Edwards was born in Stepney, in the East End of London, December 14, 1812. His father, Anthony, was a bricklayer. Probably encouraged by his wife, Charlotte, a woman of some education, he unsuccessfully expanded his business activities to become "builder, chapman, and dealer" and was adjudged bankrupt in 1832. Mrs. Edwards's encouragement of her only son was more successful. She was very ambitious for him and probably taught him much herself; no record of his attendance at any school has been traced. Edwards also owed much to Thomas Binney, who became Minister of King's Weigh House Chapel in the City of London in 1829, and to Edwin Abbott, a teacher who was appointed Headmaster of Marylebone Grammar School in 1827. Edwards's education obviously continued steadily and successfully during his seven years' apprenticeship to his father, and by his early 20s he was easily able to hold his own with men of similar age who had been more formally educated.

In 1834 Edwards became a reader in the library of the British Museum, then the only large and freely available library open to the general public in London, and remained closely associated with it for the next 16 years. Following commissioned authorship on such varied subjects as coins, seals, and medals, and the state, constitution, and future of New South Wales, he joined the library staff in 1839 as one of the additional cataloguers temporarily employed to prepare a new catalogue.

Until 1850 his professional life was lived on three levels. He worked on the catalogue; became extremely active in the movement to establish free public libraries, publishing many pamphlets and articles in periodicals; and during at least the later years of the period did little or nothing to alleviate what would now be termed a serious personality clash with the head of his department in the British Museum, Antonio Panizzi. This clash was regrettable, not only because it led ultimately to Edwards's dismissal from his post but even more because both he and Panizzi were deeply concerned with making vast improvements in the Library's service to readers.

Although various proposals to establish freely available public libraries, supported wholly or in part from public funds, had been made in England earlier in the 19th century, the task of providing the authorizing legislation fell to a private Member of Parliament, William Ewart (1798–1869). Edwards acted as his information officer and was the chief witness to testify before a Select Committee of the House of Commons, chaired by Ewart, in 1849. The Committee's Reports prepared the way for the first Public Libraries Act in 1850. This Act, which, with numerous safeguards, empowered town councils to establish libraries and to finance them up to the limit of a local rate of one halfpenny in the pound (raised to one penny by the amending Act of 1855), was adopted most readily in large towns with substantial industrial populations.

The lead was taken by Manchester, which appointed Edwards as its first Principal Librarian in 1851. He did much during the next seven years to lay sound foundations for what has become one of the greatest of British municipal library systems but, once again, did little or nothing to alleviate serious personality clashes with the members of his own governing body; Manchester dismissed him in 1858. During the remaining 30 years of his life he found salaried occupation mostly in Oxford. He was employed, primarily as a cataloguer, in the library of Queen's College from 1870 to 1876 and in the Bodleian Library from 1877 to 1883.

While in Manchester Edwards had also been working assiduously on *Memoirs of Libraries, Including a Handbook of Library Economy,* which was published in London by Trübner three months after his dismissal. It provides a history of libraries from the earliest evidences in Egypt and Assyria up to 1857, the second volume including an account of American libraries from the beginnings at Harvard in 1632 to the New York Public Library and the Smithsonian of 1854. Edwards's approach may also be regarded as propagandist, the libraries of the past being viewed as the predecessors of what the author regarded as the highest and most socially significant form, the municipal free public library. The second half of the second volume, "Economy of Libraries," covers book acquisition, buildings, classification and cataloguing, and "internal administration and public service," and provided librarians of the second half of the 19th century with their most comprehensive treatise. *Memoirs* can also be regarded as visionary because Edwards not only pioneered scientific book classification in England, but also speculated on such possibilities as national bibliographies, library associations, and even staff pension schemes.

References and discussions at the ALA's inaugural conference at Philadelphia in 1876 and at the LA's in London in 1877 make clear the continuing high reputation of *Memoirs* 20 years after first publication. By 1876, however, Edwards had supplemented it with two later works, both also published by Trübner in London: *Free Town Libraries* (1869), a mostly historical treatment in 14 chapters of which 6 cover the libraries of North America; and *Lives of the Founders of the British Museum* (1870). These two works may be regarded as contributions toward the second and substantially revised edition of *Memoirs,* which the author earnestly desired but of which only a few other chapters ever found their way into print.

During the years between his dismissal from Manchester Public Library and his appointment to Queen's College, Oxford (from 1858 until 1870), Edwards had to earn his living mostly by authorship and journalism and to take advantage of whatever opportunities came his way. His publications were mostly on subjects other than librarianship. Outstanding among them was the two-volume life of *Sir Walter Raleigh* (1868), which still holds its place in the bibliography of the great Elizabethan because, as an eminent 20th-century Elizabethan scholar, A. L. Rowse, has explained: "It is admirable for its steady good judgment and is still indispensable for it contains the Letters" (*Raleigh and the Throckmortons,* [London, 1962]).

Edwards also edited a volume in the Rolls Series, *Liber Monsaterii de Hyda; Comprising a Chronicle of the Affairs of England from the Settlement of the Saxons to the Reign of King Cnut; and a Chartulary of the Abbey of Hyde in Hampshire, A.D. 455–1023,* which was welcomed on its publication as a scholar's book for scholars. He was responsible for a variety of articles in the later volumes of the Eighth Edition of the *Encyclopaedia Britannica* (1852–60) on subjects as diverse as Police, Post Office, Alexis de Tocqueville, and Wool. His *Britannica* article on Libraries had been written while he was still at Manchester.

Edwards was an outstanding example of Victorian "self-help." But he was always opinionated and frequently arrogant; he made enemies much too easily and often of people who, handled differently, might have befriended and helped him. He was a bad manager, of his own life, of his personal finances, and certainly of his own writing, since he was seldom able to conform to limits and patterns previously agreed with his publishers. He married Margaretta Hayward, who was nine years older than himself, in 1844. Their marriage was tolerably happy for the most part, granted that Margaretta was a much more gregarious person than her husband. They had no children. He died in poverty at Niton, on the Isle of Wight, on February 7, 1886, 10 years after his wife, and is buried in the parish churchyard at Niton. The Library Association maintains his grave.

REFERENCE

W. A. Munford, *Edward Edwards, 1812–1886: Portrait of a Librarian* (1963).

W. A. MUNFORD

Edwards, John Passmore

(1823–1911)

John Passmore Edwards, British businessman, philanthropist, and library benefactor, became a successful publisher of newspapers and periodicals, including a pioneer halfpenny daily, and *Mechanics Magazine,* which had itself helped to pioneer mechanics institutes, regarded in Britain as the most important and influential predecessors of public libraries.

He was born of poor parents in Blackwater, Cornwall, March 24, 1823. Edwards was much influenced by the Transcendentalism of Channing and Emerson, became a disciple of Cobden and Bright, and supported the full program of their Manchester School. He advocated moderate liberal reform throughout his life and by the age of 60 was a rich man with much money to spend on causes appealing to him. He decided to spend largely on the welfare of the working class.

During the 1890s he made generous gifts for hospitals, homes for the handicapped, museums and art galleries, a public park, schools of art and science (including a notable gift to the then-new London School of Economics), and even an Oxford scholarship. But he remains best known for his public library benefactions. His library gifts were given mostly to places in his native Cornwall, where, in the later 19th century, a substantial working class population was still dependent on the declining extractive industries of tin and copper mining, and to the working class areas of east and southeast London. Recipient towns in Cornwall included Camborne and Redruth, Falmouth, Truro, Bodmin, and Launceston; districts in London included Limehouse, Poplar, Whitechapel, Southwark, West Ham, Shoreditch, and Edmonton. Edwards presented approximately 30 library buildings and also gave public and other libraries nearly 100,000 books. His British library benefactions may be regarded as standing midway between those of local philanthropists such as Michael Bass at Derby, John Gulson at Coventry, Edmund Harris at Preston, and William Brown at Liverpool and the much greater nationwide contribution of Andrew Carnegie.

Edwards died in London on April 22, 1911.

REFERENCES

J. Passmore Edwards, *A Few Footprints* (1905).
T. Kelly, *A History of Public Libraries in Great Britain 1845–1975* (1977).
J. J. Macdonald, *Passmore Edwards Institutions* (1900).

W. A. MUNFORD

Egypt (Ancient)

The principal known, written records of ancient Egypt were fixed as inscriptions, paintings, or reliefs on the walls of tombs and columns of temples; those that were portable were first entered on rolls of papyrus (or leather) but were customarily restricted to tombs and temple archive rooms. The main practices were developed in the 3rd millennium B.C. under the Old Kingdom. They may account for such testimony as the sandstone stele declaration by Neferhotep (18th century B.C.) that before dispatching agents up the Nile to Thebes to begin building a temple, he consulted the ancient writings in the Atum Temple at Heliopolis (in the Delta).

The use of papyrus for writing also may have begun during the Old Kingdom, but because of its fragility nothing is extant older than the 3rd century B.C., and little has been determined beyond doubt. Ernest C. Richardson (1860–1939) thought he had identified 21 libraries in the texts of the Book of the Dead and other sources, but Karl von Vogelsang and others, after checking the originals, concluded that Richardson had misunderstood or mistranslated key terms. There were indeed archives but no known libraries before the Ptolemaic period. (As Mogens Weitmeyer put it in *Libri* (1955–56), archival materials were stored by their nature and date; library materials were gathered into subject-related series, bore colophons including regulations of a library character, and were listed in separate catalogues.)

The three "houses of writings" and the House of the Chief of Taxation in the care of a principal courtier in the 4th and 5th dynasties (c.2613–c.2345 B.C.) have not been shown to be other than archives. The same holds for the celebrated 370 cuneiform tablets found at El-Amarna, mainly international correspondence of the busy 14th century B.C., in Akkadian. Verification of a sort is provided by the wall painting in the late-13th-century grave of a Ramesside high official: scribes are depicted at work in the left panel, the chief checking and signing documents in the center, and the wooden storage chests of the "Records Depository" on the right—all under the supervising eye of Thoth, god of knowledge and patron of scribes, who is represented as a baboon.

Ramses himself (II, 1304–1237 B.C.) figures in the venerable tales of the "sacred library" of "King Osymandias," renowned for its entrance inscription, "Nourishment of the Soul." Portions of the story appear to go back to the historian Diodorus Siculus (1st century B.C.), as well as later authorities such as Galen, philosopher-physician of the 2nd century A.D.

Diodorus' recital was studied in the mid-19th century by Karl R. Lepsius, who found near the tomb of Ramses II the graves of two "librarians," father and son, which apparently encouraged him to identify the "sacred library" and "King Osymandias" with Ramses. No "sacred library" has been established beyond doubt, but the suppositions are considered reasonable because there were by that time numerous temple "libraries." The "Nourishment of the Soul" inscription, however, has never had archaeological support and is perhaps to be explained by Galen's remark that he found in the "sacred library" a medical recipe he described in terms of "nourishment."

The origins of the temple of Isis on the island of Philae, near the First Cataract, are not certain, but it is known that the building was further developed by the Ptolemies and Romans partly to attract pilgrims. A doorpost inscription referred to a bookroom designed to preserve the life-giving writings of Isis, and below the wall recesses for papyrus rolls—or for wooden jars containing them—was a life-size relief of Thoth-as-baboon with a papyrus roll.

Possibly owing something to the ideas of Imhotep, 27th-century B.C. architect-courtier, reputedly expressed in the original temple of Edfu, somewhat north of Philae, was the new Horus temple built there by the Romans as an instrument of reconciliation with the Egyptian priests. Its library is the only one in Egypt whose existence enjoys archaeological verification. The titles of 37 works were painted on a wall; their presence has been established. They are regarded as having been a sort of ready-reference collection for the staff.

SIDNEY L. JACKSON
(d. 1979)

Papyrus Collection, Special Collections Library, The University of Michigan

Dating from the 22nd Dynasty (940–717 B.C.), this papyrus fragment of the Book of the Dead contains the passwords or "passport" to the underworld. It was probably written in the city of Thebes for use in a burial in the Fayum, a fertile region in Northern Egypt where it was found.

Egypt

The Arab Republic of Egypt in northeast Africa is bounded on the north by the Mediterranean Sea, on the east by Israel, the Gulf of Aqaba, and the Red Sea, on the south by the Sudan, and on the west by Libya. Population (1990 est.) 53,153,000; area 1,001,449 sq.km. The official language is Arabic; French and English are widely spoken.

History. Libraries in Egypt can be traced back to the time of the Pharaohs, and are reported to have existed for 6,000 years. Small private collections were housed in schools, palaces, and temples. The library of King Ramses II (Ozymandyas), c. 1304–1237 B.C., may have been the largest in Egyptian antiquity, numbering as many as 20,000 papyrus rolls, including works on agriculture, astronomy, history, and irrigation, as well as poetry and fiction. *See also* Egypt (Ancient).

Libraries in Egypt (1990)

Type of library	Number of administrative units (main libraries)	Number of service points (branches, mobile stops, etc.)	Volumes in collections	Annual expenditures (pound)	Population served	Professional staff (with certificate, diploma, etc.)	Total staff
National[a]	1	11	1,343,000	83,000[b]	24,490[c]	160[c]	800[c]
Academic[d]	214	214	2,591,000[c]	--	879,000	432[c]	805[c]
Public[c]	836	--	1,329,000	--	--	--	--
School[c]	4,565	--	8,150,000	1,220,000	1,100,000	--	--
Special[a]	380	--	1,639,000	--	--	--	851[c]

[a]1983 data
[b]acquisition only, 1982
[c] 1982 data
[d]1987 data
[e]1988 data

Source: Unesco, *Statistical Yearbook,* 1991. *ALA World Encyclopedia,* 2nd ed., 1986.

During the Arab-Islamic Renaissance, mosque libraries were founded in Cairo, and supported by princes and private persons for the preservation of Islamic culture. In the 9th century, the mosques became inadequate to house the growing collections and to accommodate students. The *madrasah,* a school or college resembling medieval European colleges, came into existence. The first madrasah and its library were founded in Cairo by the Fatimid Caliph al-Hakim. The library collection included works on mathematics, astronomy, medicine, and grammar.

The Seljuk period (10th and 11th centuries) was one of great prosperity in Egypt, and important colleges and university libraries were founded. This tradition continued under the Ayyubid emirs and during the Mameluke period. In 1517 Egypt came under Ottoman rule and was isolated from the rest of the world until the late 18th century. This intellectual isolation ended with the introduction of French and English publications and particularly with the introduction of the printing press.

Modern librarianship in Egypt began with the establishment of the Khedieval Library (now the National Library) in 1870. Library activity expanded in Egypt between 1945 and 1965 when many libraries, as well as the first Arab library school, were established in Cairo. The era after the Six-Day War with Israel in 1967 witnessed a decline in the library movement in Egypt, but the government in the late 1980s began planning a magnificent modern edifice, the Biblioteca Alexandrina, near the site of the ancient Alexandrian Library.

National Library. The National Library of Egypt (Dar el-Kutub Al-Misriyyah) was established in 1870 through the endeavors of Ali Moubarak, the Minister of Education at that time. Moubarak collected the scattered manuscripts and printed books from mosques, schools, archives, ministries, and other governmental departments. The formation of this library helped preserve what was left of Arabic books, manuscripts, and rare books from being lost or sold to foreign collectors. The library was in the palace of Khedive Isma'il until transferred to a new building in 1904.

In 1971 the National Library was combined with the National Archives and the National Publishing House to form the General Egyptian Book Organization. In 1970 the National Library ceased to be a circulation library. It concentrates on scholarly collections, research, and preservation programs. The National Library is the legal deposit for every publication printed in Egypt. It is also responsible for compiling and publishing the *Egyptian Publications Bulletin,* which can be considered the official national bibliography of the country. Since 1955 the Library has served as the secretariat for the Egyptian National Committee for Bibliographic Services, which is responsible for developing plans for a national bibliographic organization.

There are about 1,000,000 volumes in the National Library. Only a small number of the Library's staff of approximately 800 have library science degrees.

Academic Libraries. Egypt has 9 national universities and about 100 technical colleges and teacher training institutes. Cairo University, which was established in 1908, is the oldest national university. It has an enrollment of 113,800 students. Ain Shams University, just east of the center of Cairo, has an enrollment of 122,000. In addition to national universities there are two institutions that are not part of the national system: al-Azhar University, the world's oldest university, established in A.D. 970; and the American University in Cairo, a private institution established in 1920.

There are more than 200 academic libraries in the country. Most of the universities have main libraries to house the large library collections in the humanities and social sciences and many faculty libraries, which contain the more specialized materials in science and technology. Cairo University has a building designed basically to be a library, and it is the sole exception of all university libraries.

All the university and college libraries in Egypt suffer from a shortage of qualified librarians. The country often loses its finest librarians to institutions in other Arab countries that offer better positions and salaries. A lack of cooperation is evident among university and college libraries. There is minimal interlibrary loan. Libraries at the same university do not share library resources, and no central processing exists. Students suffer from restrictive library regulations. Open access is limited, with libraries usually open only during the hours when students are attending classes.

Staffing patterns in most academic libraries depend on the size of the institution. The library can have from 25 to 200 workers, divided into professionals, staff, library assistants, and technicians. Most libraries are inadequate for the number of students and faculty they serve.

Public Libraries. Although there are 836 public libraries in Egypt, only one-third have holdings of 25,000 to 100,000 volumes and are supervised by qualified librarians. The rest are in cultural centers, which were set up to attract young men and women who may be interested in reading or in any other social or cultural activities. Most of these centers include theaters, film projection rooms, music rooms, and reading rooms with small collections of books, ranging from 500 to 3,000 volumes. At least one professional librarian is in charge of each cultural center.

Public library services have been extended to farmers and the rural population in an attempt to reduce illiteracy and to educate the villagers on the best ways of maintaining healthy communities. Other public library services do not go far beyond the traditional services, such as lending books outside the library and allowing readers to read in the building. Reader assistance is limited. The libraries come under several jurisdictions, so there is no general or systematic plan for developing public libraries in the country and no way to coordinate their services.

School Libraries. The systematic establishment of school libraries in Egypt began in 1955, when the Ministry of Education founded the Department of School Libraries to supervise and promote school libraries in all parts of the country. This department recommends to the Minister of Education new regulations to improve school library service; it inspects school libraries in all parts of the country and provides standards for furniture and equipment to be used in school libraries. Until 1970 the Department of School Libraries in the Ministry of Education also operated a centralized acquisition and book-processing center that selected, purchased, and distributed books for all the school libraries in the country. Each library thereafter purchased its own books, but most of these were chosen from the selection tools prepared by the Department. Therefore, there is a kind of similarity between collections in all school libraries of the same level not only in the quality of books but also in the quantity. In many instances the collections do not correspond with the needs of pupils or teachers. School library services are traditional: they are restricted to lending books. Collections comprise only books and a few local newspapers and magazines. In 1961 the concept of school-community libraries was introduced in Egypt, and they provide services to the general public as well as to the students.

There are more than 4,500 school libraries, with holdings of approximately 8,150,000 volumes. These estimates, provided by the government, include all schools that have even a handful of books. The actual number of school libraries is closer to 1,000, and they serve only about 14 percent of the population.

Special Libraries. Egypt entered the 1990s with 7 information centers and 380 special libraries, most of them in ministries and other governmental agencies and smaller numbers in learned societies and in institutions and corporations. The special library in Egypt corresponds in collections and size with the needs of the institution it serves. The size of the collections depends entirely upon the history of the institution and the available budget. Governmental libraries contain government documents, laws, archives, and foreign materials not easily available elsewhere. In many instances services are limited to lending materials only to those who work in the institution. Information centers were established to serve researchers and scientists in government and semigovernment organizations. They are considered special libraries, although they are superior to most special libraries in the country. They go beyond traditional services and provide new kinds of services that represent modern thinking in special librarianship and information services. Among the services these centers provide are indexing and abstracting, translation, bibliographic activities, and current awareness services; some provide computerized information storage and retrieval. Information centers are recognized at the Institute of Public Administration, Iron and Steel Company, Atomic Energy Establishment, National Information and Documentation Center (NIDOC), Education Documentation and Research Center of the Ministry of Education, National Planning Institute, and Ministry of National Planning. Each special library or information center varies. A library may have as few as four staff members, or it may have a staff of a hundred. Some libraries or centers concentrate their holdings on books, others on periodicals or documents. They may have from 3,000 to 180,000 volumes in their collections.

The Profession. The Egyptian Library and Archives Association (ELAA), established in 1946 as the Cairo Library Association, works toward improvement of professional standards of librarianship. Other activities include the development of library collections and increased publication of Arabic library literature. The Association is affiliated with IFLA.

MOHAMMED M. AMAN;
SHA'BĀN KHALIFA

Electronic Data Sources

Electronic data sources, like general reference sources, provide answers or references to answers, but with greater flexibility, precision, and speed than similar print resources can. They open comprehensive stores of information to anyone with a computer terminal. It is no coincidence that such sources were first used and nurtured by libraries and are still associated with the provision of reference services in libraries. By the late 1980s, the proliferation of electronic databases had created a new market for specialized directories. What follows is not a comprehensive listing but a review of historical highlights in the development of electronic information services.

HISTORY

Electronic data sources for libraries were developed as a means to facilitate the search of bibliographic citations. In "Online Systems: History, Technology, and Economics," in the *Journal of the American Society for Information Science* (May 1980), Charles Bourne observed that "an investigation of online bibliographic searching was first made by Bagley in 1951" with the development of a program for a computer at the Massachusetts Institute of Technology "to search encoded abstracts." Bourne noted that "application of the computer to bibliographic searching was first demonstrated in 1954 in the form of batch searching."

Over the next 10 years, many research and development efforts culminated in the development of "batch" searches of bibliographic databases offered by a limited number of special libraries. Search analysts coded requests sent to them for literature searches. Several searches were then batched, or run consecutively, to make the most efficient use of the computer's time. Several weeks generally passed before the requestor received any result. One batch retrospective search service, the Medical Literature Analysis and Retrieval System (MEDLARS) of the National Library of Medicine (NLM), was made available to the general public in 1964.

Several years and a complete generation of computing ability would pass before the powerful systems that people can immediately interact with were introduced. Subsequent developments enabled users to search databases on CD-ROM (compact disc read-only memory disks) at their own workstations or microcomputers. Through the use of CD-ROM "jukeboxes," libraries can provide remote access over a network to a large number of databases. Another alternative becoming more popular in the 1990s is to tape-load commercial bibliographic databases into the library's online catalog. With some products and systems, the user is able to switch directly between the citation of an article to information on the availability of the article in the user's library. By the early 1990s, libraries were experimenting with systems that further allow the user to order an electronic or paper copy of

Dialog Information Services, Inc.

Section of the Dialog computer room showing cassette tape drives used for database updates.

the full article. Librarians in developed countries are increasingly called upon to help users navigate through a confusing array of local databases, CD-ROMs, online services, and networked electronic bulletin boards and file servers.

SDC Information Services. Systems Development Corporation (SDC) demonstrated the first interactive online system, Protosynthex, developed by Robert Simons and John Olney, in 1960. Using a terminal wired directly to the computer, Protosynthex allowed access to the full text of the *Golden Book Encyclopedia* with the ability to search for the occurrence of terms in proximity with each other and to search for truncated forms of words, but not to combine terms with the use of Boolean logic.

Another online retrieval system was developed at SDC in late 1964 by Harold Borko, H. P. Burnaugh, and W. H. Moore. The system, Bibliographic Organization for Library Display (BOLD), was developed for browsing literature citations on magnetic tapes. It was first publicly demonstrated about a year later and was one of the first systems capable of displaying an online thesaurus. In November 1964 SDC first demonstrated an online system that nearly achieved the interactive capability today's users enjoy, Language Used to Communicate Information System Design (LUCID), developed for SDC by E. Franks and P. A. DeSimone.

"The first demonstration of an online retrieval network, on a national scale," according to Bourne, "was probably made in 1965 by SDC in an experiment . . . to provide 13 organizations with access to some 200,000 bibliographic records on foreign technology." This work was done by SDC-Dayton for the Foreign Technology Division of Wright-Patterson Air Force Base, Ohio.

SDC was instrumental in the development of NLM's online information service, MEDLINE (MEDLARS ON-LINE). In late 1967 NLM experimented with SDC's Online Retrieval of Bibliographic Information Timeshared (ORBIT) retrieval language to search NLM's database of 10,000 citations on neurology. In May 1970 SDC began operating the Abridged Index Medicus (AIM)/TWX online information system on behalf of NLM. In October 1970 NLM introduced MEDLINE as a free service on its own computer facilities with a database of more than 400,000 citations while allowing the AIM/TWX service to continue with SDC. In February 1972 NLM utilized TYMNET, the first public telecommunication network, for access to MEDLINE.

NLM introduced a modified version of ORBIT for the ELHILL retrieval language used in MEDLINE; the H. W. Wilson Company also adopted a version of ORBIT for the retrieval language used in its WILSONLINE service, inaugurated in 1984.

SDC Search Services was made commercially available in December 1972 as an online information service using the ORBIT retrieval language, Carlos A. Cuadra serving as its manager for several years. The service, later named SDC Information Services, offered more than 60 databases in the late 1980s with strengths in petroleum, energy, patents, chemistry, and science and technology.

DIALOG Information Services. Roger K. Summit of Lockheed Missiles and Space Corporation first demonstrated the ability to search an in-house database of the Lockheed library catalogue file in 1961. Summit designed the DIALOG language in 1962 at the Lockheed Information Sciences Laboratory in Palo Alto, California, while "working on only the third IBM 360 produced," according to Marjorie Hlava in an article "The NASA Information System":

> In 1964, after some discussion with Mel Day of NASA, Summit prepared a proposal to NASA to use DIALOG for the automation of the NASA information system. NASA responded by issuing a Request for Proposal to develop a NASA/RECON prototype. Lockheed and several other companies bid the proposal.

Although it lost the first bid, in July 1966, Lockheed won a contract to demonstrate an online system for searching and retrieving more than 300,000 bibliographic citations of NASA, an effort that utilized the DIALOG retrieval language. Lockheed began providing a regular online search service to the NASA Ames Laboratory in November 1966 and later to other NASA facilities. "By 1970," Bourne notes, "a version of the DIALOG system was being operated by NASA, the system serving 24 terminals in NASA facilities across the country from a file that had grown to 700,000 records." NASA's Remote Console Information Retrieval Service (RECON) was installed at its Scientific and Technical Information Facility in Maryland to serve all major NASA research centers through a telephone communication network.

Subsequent contracts resulted in application of the DIALOG language to bibliographic databases of the Atomic Energy Commission, the European Space and Research Organization, the U.S. Office of Education, and the National Technical Information Service. In March 1969, for example, the ERIC Clearinghouse at Stanford demonstrated the use of DIALOG with an ERIC database of 415,000 citations. In the same year, DIALOG was installed on the European Space Agency's online system.

Lockheed's information service became commercially available in 1972 under the name of its retrieval language, DIALOG Information Retrieval Service, with two bibliographic databases of scientific and technical information. By 1985 DIALOG had become the most comprehensive online information service in the world, with more than 200 separate databases in business and economics, chemical, patent and trademark information, science and technology, medicine and the biosciences, news and current events, education, directories, energy and the environment, law and government, computer science and microcomputers, books, the social sciences, and the humanities.

Mead Data Central (MDC). Mead is primarily associated with the full-text, online information services it created for primary sources in law and legal research. This service was introduced commercially in 1972 as LEXIS. Mead introduced NEXIS, a full-text information service for news and current events, in 1980, and MEDIS, for medicine, in 1985.

LEXIS was the product of an effort funded by the Ohio Bar Association between 1968 and 1970 to make Ohio case law searchable online. This effort of the Ohio Bar Automated Research (OBAR) group and the Data Corporation developed the first extensive full-text search capability. In 1968 Data Corporation was acquired by the Mead Corporation; in 1970 Mead Data Central, Inc. (MDC), was formed as a subsidiary of the Mead Corporation with Don Wilson and Gerry Rubin as its chief executive officers.

Mead initially fostered the use of its full text databases through dedicated, custom terminals. It later allowed them to be searched with such microcomputers as the IBM PC and the Apple Macintosh, using software it specifies.

Mead also offers full-text databases licensed from other producers such as the *Encyclopaedia Britannica,* the New York Times Online, and the National Automated Accounting Research System (NAARS). In 1985 Mead also introduced several bibliographic databases through its Reference Service.

Bibliographic Retrieval Services (BRS). BRS had its origins in the State University of New York (SUNY) Biomedical Communications Network (BCN). During a conference in Oxford, England, on the mechanization of library services in June 1966, Irwin Pizer described plans for the SUNY online information network. BCN began in October 1968, with online searches of the MEDLARS database for nine medical libraries, using a modified version of the IBM Document Processing System as the basis of its retrieval system. "In 1973," according to Bourne, "BCN adopted the IBM STAIRS system, added additional databases in subject areas other than medicine, and expanded to incorporate 32 member libraries." In May 1977 BRS became commercially available and BCN ceased.

BRS took a direct approach to soliciting suggestions from its user community through its User Advisory Board and its subcommittees on database selection and technical features. BRS grew by 1985 to include 73 separate databases in the life sciences, medicine and pharmacology; the physical and applied sciences; education; the social sciences and humanities; and business.

CAS ONLINE. This service is an outgrowth of the publishing efforts of one of the largest professional societies in the U.S. The American Chemical Society (ACS) began publishing its index to the chemical literature, *Chemical Abstracts,* in 1907. The Society founded the Chemical Abstracts Service

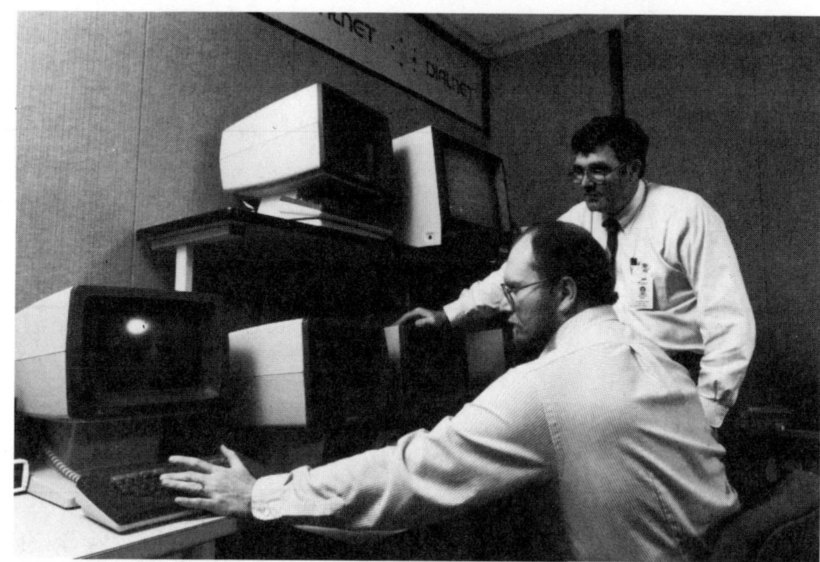

Dialog Information Services, Inc.

DIALNET Operations Center.

(CAS) division in 1956 to manage the publication. In the late 1960s CAS developed an automated processing system and began building a database to improve text editing and formatting. CAS introduced CAS ONLINE in November 1980 as an online dictionary of chemical substances; it expanded in late 1983 to include the database of *Chemical Abstracts* citations dating back to 1967. CAS made available several million unlicensed abstracts for citations in that database on CAS ONLINE only. In 1984 ACS and Germany's Fachinformaszentrum Energie, Physik, Mathematik (FIZ Karlsruhe) joined their online information services to form STN International (the Scientific and Technical Information Network).

Pergamon INFOLINE. In the late 1970s a consortium of British producers of scientific, technical, and patent databases created INFOLINE, unsuccessfully planning to develop it as an online information service. INFOLINE was purchased by Pergamon Press, a British publisher of scientific journals and catalogues. After its advent as Pergamon INFOLINE in 1981, the service grew to include 33 separate databases by 1985. INFOLINE's strength is patent, scientific and technical, and business information, especially for companies in the U.K. Its typesetting and index production capability have enabled it to undertake comprehensive database production, such as the conversion to a bibliographic database of the British Patent Office Archives dating back to 1910.

WilsonLine and WilsonDisc. The H. W. Wilson Company was a pioneer publisher of indexes and abstracts for libraries. (*See* Wilson, H. W.) In the late 1980s, Wilson began issuing its publications in electronic format. By the 1990s, the company provided online access not only to all its own publications but also served as a gateway to other bibliographic databases like the *MLA Bibliography, LC MARC,* and the *GPO Monthly Catalog.* H. W. Wilson publications illustrate the management choices thrust upon libraries by the multiplication of electronic media as the same indexes and abstracts became available simultaneously in paper, CD-ROM, and online format, and as tapes to be mounted on the local library system.

OCLC and RLIN. The Online Cooperative

Chemical Abstracts Service

STN Express software enables researchers to create structure diagrams on a personal computer for rapid uploading to the REGISTRY and BEILSTEIN databases on STN International and the DARC system on Questal.

Library Center, Inc. (OCLC), developed primarily as a bibliographic utility for library cataloging. Only in 1990 did it begin to provide general reference to its own union catalog through its Epic service. Thereafter, OCLC quickly moved to provide gateway services to other major bibliographic services like *ERIC* (the Educations Resources Information Center database). In 1991, OCLC field-tested its end-user search system. It has marketed its reference systems in a unique manner, allowing libraries to purchase search credits in passworded groups of as little as ten searches. Libraries can then distribute passwords to individual users either free or for a charge according to local policy. Much like photocopy cards, a fixed amount of service has been pre-paid, solving the problem of open-ended costs usually associated with online services.

From its inception, the Research Libraries Group (RLG) intended its RLIN online system to provide member access to more than an online union catalog. The specialized RLIN databases, such as the *RLG Conspectus Online* and the *Eighteenth-Century Short Title Catalogue,* have been a major component of the cooperative focus of RLG. In the late 1980s, RLIN began providing access to other bibliographic databases through its CitaDel service. Unlike the broad coverage of a service like DIALOG, RLIN's CitaDel includes a limited number of databases of special interest to academic researchers, such as ABI-INFORM, Dissertation Abstracts, and the History of Technology Index. Institutions that are not RLG members can open search-only accounts, connecting to RLIN by direct dial, public telecommunications network (SprintNet), or the Internet. (*See* Bibliographic Networks and Utilities.)

BIBLIOGRAPHIC AND FULL-TEXT DATABASES

The mechanics of online information services involve use of a computer terminal or microcomputer to interact with a remote database, or an organized collection of information in machine-readable form, through a telecommunications line or enhanced phone connection. The wider distribution in recent years of terminals and telecommunication services has channeled online information services into such nonlibrary environments as offices, hospital emergency rooms, and homes. High-density, low-cost data storage devices now also permit users to load large databases "online" in a local area network or even at a single work station. Librarians and information specialists, along with economists, financial analysts, business planners, engineers, chemists, researchers in the social sciences, educators, lawyers, physicians, and a host of other professional people, now rely on online information services.

Online information services may be defined simplistically as the use of computer technology to facilitate reference work. The service offered is unchanged from that of general reference services in libraries; expectations concerning a reference tool as set forth by William Katz in the first volume of his *Introduction to Reference Work* apply equally to online information services:

> When the layman thinks in terms of a reference work, it is in terms of questions and answers. He has a question. He expects the librarian to give him an answer or, at a minimum, show him where the answer may be found. Disengaged from the necessary variables, reference work may be defined simply as the process of answering questions.

Proponents of online information services such as Ron Dunn and Harry Boyle offer the same explanation in their article "On-Line Searching: Costly or Cost-Effective?" outside the context of reference services:

> Online services are not valuable in and of themselves. They merely add value to existing information through improved packaging and distribution. . . . online services are used because they provide access to information, and it is information that users want and need (*Journal of Chemical Information and Computer Sciences,* May 1984).

Databases available through online information services fall roughly into the two categories of *bibliographic* databases (which at a minimum show where the answer can be found) and databases in which the source document itself or even raw data files can be found.

Bibliographic Databases. Bibliographic databases individually offer hundreds of thousands of references to several years of published literature in a subject discipline. References cite the author, title, and source; many include indexing and an abstract that serve to identify an article, book, or paper. Many references also cite other forms of literature, such as patents, in which the inventor serves as the author and the primary claim serves as the abstract.

An information need can sometimes be satisfied by bibliographic databases alone if sufficient summary information has been extracted from the source document into the abstract; however, document ordering services have also emerged as a growing service industry, supplying copies of original source documents to users of bibliographic databases. Pre-search interviews continue to be held as a matter of policy between the librarian and the requestor to emphasize, among other things, that searches of bibliographic databases yield references to source documents rather than the source documents themselves.

The image of online information services has suffered to some extent from overidentification with bibliographic databases. For example, in his 1977 essay "Libraries in the Information Marketplace" in the book *Libraries in Post-Industrial Society,* Kas Kalba wrote:

> The online retrieval services that exist today are essentially in the accessing business rather than in the convenience business. What they offer is rapid access to citations and abstracts from a particular data base.

Kalba's remark reflects the popularity and availability of bibliographic databases among search service vendors at that time. Source databases, such as numeric databases, have been equally available, but their distribution has not been as wide as that of bibliographic databases. Ching-chih Chen observed in *Numeric Databases* (1984) that "at present, librarians have not demonstrated the same acceptance and enthusiasm for numeric databases as they have expressed for bibliographic ones." Susan Meschel observed in her paper "Numeric Databases in the Sciences" that "many of the services that make numeric databases available market 1 to 5 files on the average" (*National Online Meeting Proceedings,* 1984). Other types of source databases, such as those offering directory information for business and marketing research and those offering the complete text of source documents, were emerging at the time of that observation. Since then, data files have become a staple feature of both popular and academic networks, such as Prodigy, Compuserv, BITnet and Internet.

Full-Text Databases. Full-text databases provide the complete text of a source document in addition to the citation and indexing found in bibliographic databases. Full-text databases offer the obvious advantage of immediate availability of the complete text of a source document. However, the ability to search the complete text of documents online for names, terms, or concepts not identified in the citation or indexing is often the greatest asset of these databases as vehicles to locate information.

Mead Data Central first made the full text of cases and statutes related to state and federal law available in 1973 through its LEXIS service. LEXIS is one of several online services that offer the complete text of important source documents in law and legal research, along with the full text of Shepard's Citations and Matthew Bender's legal treatises. The West Publishing Company offers WESTLAW, with the full text of those sources and West's own indexing. The impetus for the development of such services did not arise out of a need for the ready availability of the source documents, but rather, as Allan Onove explained in "A Comparison of the LEXIS and WESTLAW Databases" (*Legal Economics,* April 1983), "from the legal profession's need for more effective, less time-consuming ways of locating relevant precedents."

The demand for the complete text of sources for news and current events was first addressed by the New York Times Company. The New York Times Information Service first offered the complete text of the newspaper online with the June 1, 1980, issue, as part of its INFORMATION BANK online service. In February 1983 MDC offered the complete text of the *Times* through its NEXIS service, modeled after its full-text LEXIS service. NEXIS had been offering the full text of other newspapers, as well as magazines, wire services, and newsletters, since 1980. By 1985 the complete text of newspaper and magazine articles and newswires was offered not only by NEXIS but also by Information Access Corporation through its MAGAZINE ASAP and TRADE AND INDUSTRY ASAP databases on DIALOG. The Associated Press (AP) made the complete text of its wire services available through vendors such as DIALOG and Dow Jones.

Three major news companies, Knight-Ridder, Times Mirror, and Gannett, were the first to have produced their own online information services. Knight-Ridder's VU/TEXT contains the full text of many major newspapers, stock quote services, and bibliographic databases in business. Gannett's USA TODAY UPDATE offers national and international news, business and financial information, and industry reports in technology, banking, law, energy, insurance, and travel. In April 1985 the British Broadcasting Corporation (BBC) introduced WORLD REPORTER, which features the full text of the BBC and AP news services.

NewsNet began its venture into electronic publishing in 1982 by offering 17 online newsletters; it would be a misnomer to refer to this as a full-text service insofar as the newsletters have no printed counterparts. Approximately 250 newsletters were available by May 1985; an *IDP Report* of 1984 listed telecommunications, investment, electronics and computers, and publishing and broadcasting as the subject headings that appear most often among these newsletters.

In business and financial information, DIALOG introduced the complete text of financial research reports from leading investment banking firms through the INVESTEXT database in 1984. In the same year MDC began offering the complete text of research reports written by security analysts and economists through its EXCHANGE service. The complete text of *Commerce Business Daily,* a major publication for any business or organization that does business with the U.S. government, is available on DIALOG. The complete text of the *Harvard Business Review* dating back to 1976, with citations as far back as 1971, is produced in machine-readable form by John Wiley and Sons, and is offered by DIALOG and BRS.

In the sciences and medicine, BRS announced in April 1980 that it was experimenting with a "private test database of the full text of approximately 1,000 articles from the *Journal of Medicinal Chemistry*" in cooperation with the American Chemical Society (ACS). In 1983 BRS offered the full text of 32 medical journals in its IRCS MEDICAL SCIENCE database and the full text of 18 chemistry journals in its ACS JOURNALS FULLTEXT database. In the same year, BRS introduced the full text of the 24-volume Kirk-Othmer *Encyclopedia of Chemical Technology*.

Early in 1984 BRS began offering the complete text of reference books and journals in internal medicine, pharmacology, and critical care and emergency medicine as part of its COLLEAGUE service, targeted toward physicians and other health care professionals. The Critical Care Medical Library of COLLEAGUE contains the full texts of 18 medical textbooks.

Many standard encyclopedias, including the *Academic American, Everyman's,* and *Encyclopaedia Britannica,* are also online or, increasingly, on CD-ROM.

OTHER DATABASES

Numeric Databases. Numeric databases, also variously known as *fact, source,* and *nonbibliographic databases, datafiles,* and *databanks,* provide organized numeric data such as statistics, time series, demographic reports, corporate financial records, stock market quotations, chemical and physical properties, and chemical nomenclature and graphic structures. Most of these databases are used to support business or financial research; the smaller percentage of numeric databases of physical and chemical properties are used in the physical and biological sciences.

Most numeric databases can be manipulated interactively by their users. In economic forecasting or market research, these data are *post-processed,* or manipulated after the information has been identified and captured from an online service, generally on a microcomputer. In the sciences, however, the key to retrieving the information is *pre-processing* the data, as in identifying three-dimensional structures and plotting physical data.

Business Numeric Databases. Numeric databases that support economic forecasting and market research are found on major online services and feature the ability to post-process this information. They include Dow Jones News/Retrieval, I. P. Sharp Associates Limited, Chase Econometrics/Interactive Data Corporation, Data Resources, Inc., and DIALOG.

Dow Jones News/Retrieval, which began in 1974 as a stock-quote service for brokers and professional investors, offers such information as current and historical stock quotes, current and historical Dow Jones averages, a weekly survey of U.S. money market and foreign exchange trends, and earnings forecasts for U.S. companies. Dow Jones has developed software packages to manipulate such data by collecting and storing it, performing any of 17 standard technical analyses on it, and transferring it into spreadsheet programs.

I. P. Sharp, a Canadian computer time-sharing company, began offering online databases in 1970. Sharp has more than 100 databases in aviation, economics, energy, finance, and actuarial information. The databases include text only where needed to clarify the numeric data. Sharp's software allows data to be manipulated and is also available for use on microcomputers.

Chase Econometrics/Interactive Data Corporation was established in 1971 to produce economic forecasts based on econometric models and has expanded its services to offer economic, financial, and demographic data from nearly every country in the world. Subscribers to Chase services can receive software developed by Chase for simulations, forecasting, and analysis of these data.

Data Resources, Inc. (DRI), offers national economic models of countries throughout the world and 17,000,000 time series covering U.S. national and regional, international, industrial, energy, and financial data. DRI offers its software for report writing, analytic data manipulation, and graphic display of these data. Portions of these data are sold separately on disk for manipulation with spreadsheet software.

Business numeric databases on DIALOG include time series, forecasts, and census-related data. Databases of time series or tables of historical data and projected forecasts of data for the economies of the U.S. and for other countries are produced by Predicasts. The Bureau of Labor Statistics offers three databases of time series for the U.S. (the producer price index, the consumer price index, and employment, hours of work, and earnings information) on DIALOG. Data from the 1990 census, current estimates, and five-year projections for demographic characteristics of geographic regions of the U.S. are offered through the Donnelley Demographics database on DIALOG.

Nonbibliographic Databases in Chemistry. Questions raised in chemical and patent information depend heavily on nonbibliographic data for utmost precision in searching bibliographic databases. The large number of numeric databases in the physical sciences identify chemical compounds by structure, mass spectra, and other properties. In "A Review of Online Physical Sciences and Mathematics Databases. Part 2: Chemistry," (*Database,* June 1985), Donald Hawkins explained that "chemical name dictionaries and substructure searching systems are important because of the wide variety of chemical substances that exist and because classes of substances with similar structures are often of interest to chemists." Keyword searches of bibliographic databases in chemistry are effective in locating citations where the search terms are found in the title or indexing. However, the location of citations dealing with specific chemical substances is best achieved through the use of databases that serve as dictionaries of unique chemical substances, identified in the chemical literature and indexed by the American Chemical Society (ACS).

DIALOG made a significant contribution to the effective use of chemical information online as the first service to create large-scale dictionary databases containing every class of chemical substances. The registry numbers uniquely identify a substance in these dictionary databases and can be transferred to the bibliographic databases to identify citations indexed with the registry number for the substance in question.

Graphics capabilities have been introduced for microcomputers and terminals, allowing for display of two- or three-dimensional chemical structure diagrams to identify chemical substances and the bibliographic citations that deal with those substances. In her previously cited paper, Susan Meschel explained the significance of graphic-display capability:

> One of the primary concerns in chemistry is identifying an active core of a compound regardless of additional groups connected to the molecules. This type of problem cannot usually be solved completely by word-segment searching. The best recent developments in this area are the QUESTEL system's DARC database and CAS ONLINE marketed by Chemical Abstracts. In these files one can graphically draw the desired active core as a fragment and probabilistically match it against the over 6,000,000 compounds in these databases.

CAS has addressed the problem of online identification of indeterminate chemical substances, or those that are incapable of exact definition, known as Markush structures, previously out of reach of both print and online services. In March 1985 CAS announced the ability to identify Markush structures; as many as 20 variable groups of atoms can be combined in a single search for a structure, and a variable number and type of attachments of atoms in a molecule may also be specified.

The utility of graphics-based retrieval in chemical information is a topic of some debate, focusing on issues of speed, cost of terminals, and technical problems. CAS ONLINE has made graphics searching possible with specific software on more common terminals and microcomputers.

The graphics-based search services permit constructing the active core fragment of the chemical compound and matching it against the substances indexed in the dictionary databases. DARC Questal employs graphic or alphanumeric input of structures to allow each molecule to be described by a graph, the nature of the atoms, and the types of bonds, eliminating the relative ambiguity that results from the use of chemical codes and nomenclature in the identification of substances.

The largest number of science-related numeric databases are offered by the NIH-EPA Chemical Information System (CIS), a cooperative project of the National Institutes of Health, the Environmental Protection Agency, and several other U.S. and European organizations. The Structure and Nomenclature Searching System of CIS allows chemical compounds to be identified by a two-dimensional structure in addition to identification by chemical or chemical fragment name, name fragment, molecular weight, or fragment codes. Meschel observed that "through CIS it is possible to build a compound practically bond by bond graphically and request the interactive system to retrieve the partial or full formula from their field."

Among the services offered by the Mass Spectral Search System are mass spectral data and a numerical evaluation score to assess the quality of the spectra. Several databases can perform calculations on mathematical models of organic and inorganic molecules. The Man Lab-NPL Materials Databank can retrieve thermodynamic data as well as perform calculations on the thermodynamic functions, useful for chemists and metallurgists; the database can also plot phase diagrams.

To assist in the design and identification of chemical substances among local in-house databases, software producers such as Molecular Design Ltd. have developed such programs as MACCS, which allows users to draw chemical structures with light pens, add their own data, and display the results on the screen. The displays can rotate or show stereo-pairs.

Directory Databases. Directory databases offer the information of published directories or serve a purpose similar to that of published directories without having published equivalents. These are not full-text databases, although they may represent the complete text of a publication in machine-readable form. Nor are they numeric databases, although they contain numeric information. And they are definitely not bibliographic databases, because they provide primary sources, or source documents, for the users.

The Electronic Yellow Pages (EYP), for example, are databases created from telephone books and specialized directories in the U.S. by Market Data Retrieval, Inc. The databases cannot be said to reflect the full text of their 4,800 published counterparts. Business activity is described for each listing in the database by Standard Industrial Classification (SIC) codes. Intra-corporate relationships are identified for each listing, along with codes that represent the number of employees and net worth of the company. Potential applications exist for these databases which could not be imagined with their published counterparts. In addition to being able to search the equivalent of 4,800 yellow page directories simultaneously by the business name, state, city, or county of location, users can restrict searches to businesses with specific zip codes, telephone exchanges, or ranges of SIC codes to reflect a certain type of business activity.

The TRINET databases offer more detailed information, including a listing of the headquarters for each business, sales figures, and percentage share of the market. In addition to many of these features for locating businesses, various Dun & Bradstreet databases provide number of employees, base sales figures, intra-corporate identification numbers, Standard Metropolitan Statistical Area (SMSA) information, and sales growth and trends. The most detailed and substantive directory of U.S. businesses, DISCLOSURE II, has much of the directory information mentioned for other databases as well as information extracted from reports filed with the U.S. Securities and Exchange Commission (SEC).

Reference Directories. Databases such as the Encyclopedia of Associations, produced by Gale Research Company, correspond to the published directories of the same names. The Books in Print database corresponds to the most current edition of several published directories of books published by R. R. Bowker Company. Directories of microcomputer software such as .MENU–The International Software Database, or Business Software Database publish no print counterparts. The number or existence of published counterparts to these online databases is not significant; the differences in published format cannot compare to the convenience and enhanced capabilities for locating desired information that is offered by online databases.

Dictionary Databases. Dictionary databases, such as the chemical substance dictionaries mentioned earlier, are similar to directory databases insofar as each record identifies something. The purpose of some dictionary databases, such as the online version of the *Oxford English Dictionary,* is apparent to the user. Other dictionary databases serve also to provide a measure of control in the use of bibliographic databases. For example, the chemical registry numbers contained in the chemical substance dictionary files can be mapped to identify bibliographic citations that have been indexed with these numbers. The H. W. Wilson Company developed three separate databases to provide control over the bibliographic databases in WILSONLINE, including a Publishers Directory, a Journal Directory, and a Name Authority File, used as a means for bibliographic control of names.

ADMINISTRATION OF ONLINE SERVICES IN LIBRARIES

Pricing Structures. Of all library services, the direct costs for online information services may be among the most elusive to budget for, because they do not represent fixed costs. There are basically three charges assessed for use of online information services:

connect-hour charges, print or display royalties, and telecommunication charges. The connect-hour cost for such services as DIALOG, SDC, and INFOLINE represents the combination of royalties paid to the database producer and those paid to the vendor on whose system the database is available. The full-text information services offered by MDC are priced in connect-hour units. An additional, separate cost for each search is added to the connect-hour price. Services such as WILSONLINE and CAS ONLINE have databases that are produced and made available through in-house online systems; prices for both are structured in connect-hour units. BRS presents the royalties paid to the database producer and those paid to itself as the vendor as separate connect-hour charges.

Lesser incremental royalty charges may also be assessed when the user displays or prints a portion or all of a record while still online or when the user requests the service to print it offline and mail it to the user.

Most vendors charge separately for telecommunication services. A majority of vendors contract with at least two and possibly three public vendors of telecommunication services, including GTE TELENET, Tymshare's TYMNET, or United Technology Corporation's UNINET. Three services—DIALOG, I.P. Sharp, and MDC—have their own dedicated networks. These services enable users to make the distant connection with a remote database more cheaply and reliably than would be possible over public telephone lines. The cost for telecommunications is usually expressed as a separate connect-hour charge paid to the database vendor.

The highest prices for online information services result from infrequent use. Discounts on connect-hour costs are available in exchange for annual subscription deposits or for commitments to a certain level of connect-hour usage throughout a year. DIALOG and SDC offer discounts through subscription or commitment agreements; SDC also offers automatic volume discounts for connect-hour usage at certain levels during a month. H. W. Wilson offers a discount for subscriptions to WILSONLINE alone, or for subscriptions to both WILSONLINE and the printed Wilson indexes. ACS, publisher of CAS ONLINE, also offers lower connect-hour costs in exchange for subscriptions to print indexes. Discounts given in exchange for subscriptions to the printed *Chemical Abstracts* also apply toward the royalty charges incurred for printing or displaying citations in CAS ONLINE and toward the file entry fee for the CA file on that service. Although BRS does not use commitment agreements, it offers discounts through subscription agreements or through small group subscriptions, in which several users can consolidate their usage to obtain a discount. MDC discounts search costs according to the volume of searches per month.

The time of day that one uses a service can affect the cost of a search session. The price for MDC and Dow Jones varies during prime and nonprime hours of service; charges for an MDC search conducted during off-peak hours are half the prime-time costs. Weeknight and weekend rates for Dow Jones are significantly less than those charged during the day. BRS reduced its connect-hour rate by half for its BRKTHRU service during off-peak hours. Dow Jones introduced DOWQUOT in mid-1984 as an off-peak service offering securities quotes and business news at a reduced flat-rate cost.

BRS and DIALOG introduced AFTER DARK and KNOWLEDGE INDEX, respectively, in late 1982 as flat-rate or lower-priced simplified versions of their more popular databases. Self-instructional manuals replaced the need for training in both cases; AFTER DARK is optionally menu-driven. Both were made available during off-peak hours, on weeknights and weekends, and with fewer system capabilities than their regular counterparts.

The unpredictability of cost for online searching makes CD-ROM especially attractive as the means of gaining access to electronic information. CD-ROM can be acquired by purchase or subscription, much as with print publications, and cost is unaffected by the degree of subsequent use. Library users can be allowed to search CD-ROM databases for themselves, without worries about the cost of errors and inefficient search strategies. Some services, like DIALOG and WILSONLINE are available both online and in CD-ROM. The library can then depend on the CD-ROM for most general searches, turning to the online version online for materials too recent to have been included in the last CD-ROM. Access to multiple databases through a network can usually be provided by mounting CD-ROMs in a "jukebox," but most vendors charge an additional licensing fee for network access.

Tapes mounted on local library systems share the same benefit of fixed cost, at least once mounted. (Like networked CD-ROMs, prices are a combination of a fixed charge for the database and a "licensing fee" determined by the number of users having access to the database.) Although more expensive than CD-ROMs tape-loaded databases have the benefit of being accessible through any terminal linked to the public catalog. They became increasingly popular in the early 1990s as library system vendors (1) developed "gateway" software allowing users to search the database using the same menus and commands as for the catalog; and (2) created links between the tape-mounted indexes and the library catalog, so that a user could not only identify a relevant article but determine whether the library held it. Some systems allow the library (or the user) the option of only displaying those items represented in the library's holdings. As can be expected, such features add to the cost of the system. Evaluating shifts in capabilities and pricing structures has become a major aspect of the library manager's art.

Contracts. Libraries most commonly contract with the vendors or producers of online services either directly or indirectly, through group contracts. Library networks make group contracts on behalf of member libraries, offering vendors substantial subscriptions in return for high rates of discount, a portion or all of which is passed on to participating libraries. These networks may be multi-type library networks on a regional, state, or local scale, such as BCR (the Bibliographical Center for Research), INCOLSA (Indiana Cooperative Library Services Authority), or MELSA (Metropolitan Library Service Agency). Such networks may also be organized by type of library, such as the School Practices Information Network (SPIN) or the renascent Biomedical Communications Network (BCN). Group contracts are also arranged by federal or state agencies responsible for library services, such as FEDLINK. Libraries that are either unable or unwilling to make an individual commitment can obtain some discount on their costs through a network's group contract for online services.

Commercial sources of access to multiple online information services are made possible through what are commonly referred to as "gateway" services. A gateway links an online information service to such products or services as communication software or electronic mail to online information services. ITT DIALCOM is an electronic mail service that also serves as a gateway to several online databases. DIALCOM conveniently allows for use of online information services without the need for the user to secure a separate account and password for each service. Other gateways exist between online information services, such as that from MDC to DIALOG or from DIALOG to the *Official Airline Guide* and the U.S. Department of Commerce database, CENDATA. Communication software packages that serve as gateways to online information services also feature menu-driven prompts to obviate the need for system training and documentation among end-users of these services.

Funding. The costs described previously are all direct costs, incurred as a result of an online search session. All other expenses involved in running an online search service are indirect. Nancy Grimes, in her article "Costs, Budgets, and Financial Management" in *Online Searching Technique and Management* (1983), divides these indirect costs into one-time expenditures and recurring costs. The purchase or lease of equipment and their maintenance contracts are only a few examples of one-time, indirect costs.

> Documentation and supplies must also be purchased. System manuals, database thesauri, and other user aids will compose the search service's own reference collection, together with system newsletters and subscriptions to relevant journals. If the equipment includes a printer, paper will be needed; if the printer is an impact type, new ribbons will be needed.

Personnel, training, promotion, and overhead account for a variety of recurring indirect costs for a search service. Grimes suggests that the cost for these expenses will vary according to the specific circumstances of a library.

> For example, searcher and coordinator may be one and the same person, or coordination may consume a quarter of a department head's time. Training sessions may take place onsite, or may require travel and overnight lodging. Promotion may include newsletters, brochures, or complementary searches; the facility may need modification, and so on.

Two budget options for starting an online search service, one representing a low-cost and another a more expensive approach, were developed by the Costs and Financing Committee of the Machine-Assisted Reference Section (MARS) of the Reference and Adult Services Division of ALA. The document entitled "Online Reference Services: Costs and Budgets" (1985) illustrates how the indirect costs of the service can vary according to circumstance.

Approaches to funding a search service also vary according to circumstance. The Committee observes in its "Online Reference Services: Funding Methods" (1984) that "Libraries often seek external sources of funding for start-up costs and internal sources for ongoing services." It found that the sources of funding most frequently referred to in the literature are "new money, a reallocation of existing funds, and charging end-users for searches."

New money is obtained through requests for new and ongoing funds from the budgeting agency or from outside sources such as library agencies, federal agencies, and private donors and foundations. According to the Committee, these are usually "one-time, fixed-fund sources."

Existing funds can be reallocated to support a search service in a number of ways. Funds can be transferred from other library service or material budgets to pay for the online service or can be reallocated from other units in the larger organization of which the library is a part, such as academic departments or laboratories. There is usually an implicit reallocation in the library budget for professional, clerical, and business office staff time allotted a search service and a reallocation of intangible library resources such as overhead, space, and utilities. CD-ROM and tape-loaded databases may not noticeably reduce indirect cost, merely shifting professional time from searching to user training.

Charges to users for their searches may fund the online service. The amount of the assessment in a cost-recovery scheme can range anywhere from partial recovery of direct costs to full recovery of those costs plus additional charges to account for overhead. OCLC's Epic service charge system is designed to provide maximum flexibility to libraries in allocating use and charges. The Committee cites case studies as helpful models in deciding on a combination of funding approaches best suited to matching service goals with funding realities.

Training. There are a number of options for training library staff in the use of online information services. Many vendors and database producers offer one-day or half-day training sessions to introduce their own services. Such courses may present instruction in the mechanics of online searching and some theory in formulating search strategies and using Boolean logic. Trainees should have opportunities for hands-on experience with the instructor present. In some cases, free connect time is provided through training passwords for the trainees' use after the course.

Some vendors and producers offer training databases to complement and enhance their courses. DIALOG, for example, offers several ONline Training and Practice (ONTAP) databases in a variety of subject areas at greatly reduced flat rates so users can practice economically. ONTAP databases contain small portions of regular DIALOG databases. CAS ONLINE offers a practice *Chemical Abstracts* database.

The introductory training offered by some vendors is also often complemented by one-day seminars that address more advanced search techniques and search strategy preparation. Such seminars ideally build upon prior training and search experience. Typical one-day introductory and advanced seminars may orient system instruction to the interests of people in business, the chemical industry, law, or medicine, for example.

There are various approaches to offering training. All database vendors and producers control the format and content of their training session and materials;

many vendors and producers are the exclusive sources of the training. In 1983 BRS adopted a cooperative approach to the distribution of its training through qualified library networks, permitting the Bibliographical Center for Research (BCR) and the Cooperative Library Agency for Systems and Services (CLASS) to represent it as agents. BRS controls the content, materials, and price of the course and monitors the effectiveness of the presentation. DIALOG's own customer services staff, field offices, and foreign representatives train the equivalent of the total enrollment of main campuses of some state universities each year, but DIALOG has also sanctioned qualified library networks to use its training materials in network-sponsored DIALOG training.

Training is also available through qualified programs of academic instruction. Database vendors such as BRS, CAS ONLINE, DIALOG, and MDC offer most or all of their services at reduced rates to allow faculty to expose their students to the service. Graduate schools of library and information science have offered this training for many years, and professional schools in law, business, education, and the sciences also offer it as part of their instruction in research methods.

Local and regional online user groups provide continuing education in the use of online information services by hosting training seminars by database producers. These groups also foster an awareness of applications of these services through presentations by members. National associations such as the American Library Association, the Special Libraries Association, and the American Chemical Society sponsor programs, publications, and committee activity that serve as additional sources of continuing education.

Self-instruction and in-house training by experienced staff members are alternative training methods. The quality of a searcher's negotiating skills with a patron and performance online can be developed through continuous peer evaluation of searches and through attendance at seminars or online user group meetings that highlight use of specific databases. As of the mid-1980s, WILSONLINE's Tutorial and the DIALOG Basics Manual provided opportunities for self-instruction. Computer-assisted instruction (CAI) in the use of these services, in a simulated environment, was realized by Elaine Caruso at the University of Pittsburgh through her TRAINER program, developed in the late 1970s. Observers anticipated that database vendors would develop many more CAI programs.

Enhanced communications software packages are offered by database vendors, producers, and software companies to enable online information services to be used in an environment as close to that of natural language as possible. These software packages also offer simplified ways to log on to the services, and, in many cases, the ability to build and edit personal files of information produced from online searches. SEARCH HELPER, produced by Information Access Corporation (IAC), allows for convenient log-on, search, sort, and downloading of the results of searches conducted on IAC's databases on DIALOG. Two software packages, SCI-MATE, produced by the Institute for Scientific Information (ISI), and SEARCH MASTER, produced by SDC, translate a searcher's responses to a series of questions and prompts into search statements that can be executed on any of the databases on DIALOG, BRS, SDC, or NLM. In addition to allowing a search strategy to be formulated in advance of the online connection, SCI-MATE enables search results to be downloaded and edited with additional information added by the searcher. Disclosure, Inc., offers a software package, MicroDISCLOSURE, to enable end-users to conduct a menu-driven search of the DISCLOSURE-II database on DIALOG. This package also allows financial and company information to be downloaded, to analyze that information and prepare reports, and to use the data with microcomputer spreadsheet programs.

In early 1984 the Menlo Corporation introduced a communication software package, In-Search, primarily to enable untrained end-users to search DIALOG. In 1985 Menlo introduced an enhanced version, Pro-Search, for experienced searchers, with the same capacity to download and edit search results, plus accounting report features, and the ability to search both DIALOG and BRS.

The Business Computer Network (BCN) sells communication software (Super-Scout) that offers electronic mail and single-keystroke access to many online services in business information. BCN offers a gateway to 14 online information services, but does not simplify search system protocols.

BRS created BRKTHRU to provide optional menu-driven prompts and instructions for searching many BRS databases during all hours of standard BRS service. BRS encouraged librarians to offer BRKTHRU to end-users "for those day-to-day searches that use your time but not your expertise."

EasyNet was introduced in 1984 as a menu-driven service offering simplified access to BRS, DIALOG, SDC, INFOLINE, Questel, VU/TEXT, and NewsNet. The service features options for those with no previous knowledge of online services, such as system selection of the databases to be searched.

End-user searching, whether by CD-ROM, library system, or online (such as OCLC's Epic), requires another level of training. Bibliographic instruction in academic libraries gained a whole new lease on life in the late 1980s and 1990s as reference librarians found themselves spending an increasing proportion of their time teaching search languages and strategies to students and faculty. School and academic libraries often try maximize efficiency by providing group instruction in basic searching techniques. Public libraries must rely more exclusively on individualized, on-demand training.

Service Location and Staffing. In his overview of "Library Organizational Patterns in Online Retrieval Services" in *Online Searching Technique and Management* (1983), Peter G. Watson addressed the problems and options in deciding upon centralized or dispersed authority over the online search service in a library, describing the advantages of integrating the service with the library's full reference services or separating it from them. Physical location of the service is often a secondary question, decided in the context of the library's service goals and objectives, the degree of centralized authority, and the funding options open to the library.

The centralized authority of metropolitan public library systems is often manifest in the decision to centralize the search service in one location for all its libraries. State libraries offer centralized search services to public libraries throughout the state but in many cases also encourage development of search services among these libraries. Main and departmental libraries among academic institutions and school district offices and learning centers all face the same question of search service location in this context. Some geographically dispersed corporations have autonomous libraries with their own search service contracts, policies, and procedures. Other dispersed corporations channel search requests through central search services for all the corporate libraries.

Visibility of the service is also dependent on the service goals and objectives of the library. The service is highly visible when all or part of it is available at the reference desk, either for ready-reference searches providing short, quick answers or for comprehensive searches. A more subtle but equally important consideration is promotion of the service. Traditionally, the service is made available in rooms closed to the public. Security considerations, the need to conduct interviews with patrons before and after the search, and the need to store documentation conveniently are strong arguments for maintaining that tradition.

Staffing is largely a matter of reallocating staff resources among those professional reference staff who are trained in the use of online services. Accommodating the service in a one-person special library involves the creative redesign of a schedule to eliminate less productive and time-consuming research activity in favor of the use of online services. Staffing for the service among libraries with reference staffs is often an extension of the subject specialization already in place. One staff person is generally appointed to coordinate the use, training, billing, and documentation activity associated with the service.

TRENDS

Growth of Online Information Services. The growth of online information services has been consistently strong each year since their introduction. The Cuadra Associates *Directory of Online Databases* (Fall 1984) listed 2,453 databases available from 1,189 producers through 362 online information services; the Fall 1979 issue had listed only 400 databases available from 221 producers on only 59 online services. According to the *Friday Memo* of June 14, 1985, a study concluded that "the online database industry could very well maintain a 23%/year average growth rate through the next decade."

Growth of Microcomputer Applications. The growth in the number and variety of online databases has been accompanied by an equally impressive growth in the distribution of microcomputers. In the February 1, 1985, *Library Journal,* John N. Berry concluded from the results of a research report released in late 1984 by the R. R. Bowker Company that "it is obviously safe to predict that microcomputers have found a home and utility throughout the nation's libraries. Not only are they in place, but many more will arrive in the next few months." The survey indicated that nearly 5,000 public libraries, 1,600 academic libraries, and more than 7,000 special libraries own and are using more than 45,000 microcomputers. More than 140,000 micros are in use among elementary and high school libraries in the U.S. The libraries sampled in this survey planned to purchase nearly 128,000 new micros by the end of 1986. An article in *Business Week* (August 27, 1981) had predicted a similar pattern of growth in the shipment of desktop computer systems for education. With a base rate of 70,000 units shipped in 1980, a 31 percent growth rate was predicted in shipments through 1985, when 270,000 were expected to have been shipped to educational institutions.

Microcomputers have added a significant dimension to the use of online information services by facilitating downloading, reformatting, and editing (or post-processing) of search results. Microcomputers have also introduced a new channel of distribution of online information to the library.

Distribution of Local Databases. Database producers have distributed the machine-readable versions of their products either directly to the consumer or indirectly through vendors or host services. Direct distribution has taken two forms: producers such as Chemical Abstracts Service, H. W. Wilson, and the Institute for Scientific Information (ISI) have developed their own online information services; a longstanding method is to distribute products on machine-readable tape, to be read on the user's mainframe computer.

Many in the information industry have expressed optimism about the potential of microcomputers as a distribution channel for online information services. John Blair, Jr., a columnist on microcomputer applications in *Database,* observed (December 1982) that "the microcomputer could serve as an important step toward making more of the information already stored in the large databanks or remote mainframes accessible to local centers of distribution." In his guest editorial in the September 1980 *Database,* ISI President Eugene Garfield predicted that "it is not unreasonable to expect by the end of the decade, central online databases may be replaced by local databases stored on and manipulated by microcomputers. By that time we may be sending out floppy disks or whatever, instead of printed volumes." BRS President William Marovitz voiced his optimism about the potential of videodisk and microcomputer technology to foster "a boom in local/regional database distribution" in a January 1983 column in *Online.*

CD-ROM and videodisks have amply borne out the accuracy of these predictions. A single CD-ROM disk can make large amounts of information equivalent to large portions or all of a database available for use on microcomputers. Applications of this technology include InfoTrac, introduced in January 1985 by IAC, a menu-driven system enabling as many as four people to search nearly half a million fully indexed citations to articles from business, technical, legal, and general-interest publications stored on a single 12-inch videodisk on a microcomputer. IAC keeps the service current with monthly updates.

The English-language portion of the complete Library of Congress MARC database is available on compact disk for use with a personal computer or an OCLC M300 Workstation. This product of the Library Corporation allows editing of catalogue records and ordering of catalogue card sets and labels.

International Thompson Information (which owns the University of Toronto Library Automation System, UTLAS), Carrollton Press (producer of the

REMARC database), and Cuadra Associates (producer of the microcomputer data entry and retrieval software STAR, System To Automate Records) developed a CD-ROM, microcomputer-based system that offers the 6,500,000 records in the MARC and REMARC databases with the capacity for Boolean searching and current and retrospective cataloguing.

The video and optical disk industry showed promise in the mid-1980s as a distribution channel for database producers and suppliers. In September 1984 Reference Technology announced Clasix, which offers replicable, prerecorded optical disks and a minicomputer-based premastering system to enable publishers to organize and prepare their data for the actual mastering by 3M and other companies. In January 1985 BRS announced its commitment to produce databases on videodisk as part of a laser-optic publishing project with Reference Technology. Clasix is distributed through BRS, and the BRS Search Software, which can be used to search databases stored on videodisk, is marketed by Reference Technology.

In February 1985 SDC and Sony announced discussion of a joint venture to develop videodisk applications for online information services. In March 1985 Reference Technology announced "a complete data delivery service to publishers and information providers," a more complete premastering service that includes videodisk equipment and software. In April 1985 a Japanese firm announced a programmable version of CD-ROM that allows for the production of videodisks without an outside mastering process. The trend in this technology is toward greater convenience for database producers to provide (and distribute) their products on video or optical disk. Robert November, a managing consultant at LINK Resources, a market research firm for the information industry, predicted greater storage capacity for data on compact optical disks for use with home computers. With this technology, "publishers have the option of circumventing the costs of printing and paper for multi-volume reference works" such as encyclopedias.

Standard microcomputer floppy disks store only a fraction of the information that can be stored on video or optical disks, but represent a less complicated channel for the direct distribution of information by the producer. For example, NTIS offers portions of its complete database on floppy disks for use on IBM PCs and compatible microcomputers. BIOSIS offers a similar service complete with periodic updates through its BIOSIS Information Transfer Service (BITS). Cuadra Associates made *The Directory of Online Databases* available on floppy disks. The December 1984 *Database* reported that NLM is making subsets of MEDLINE available on floppy disks defined by subject, time, language, journal title, and so on, and with optional monthly or quarterly updates to the database on disk. Companies such as Knowledge Access designed software that emulates the command logic of DIALOG's KNOWLEDGE INDEX to support the use of such databases as Microcomputer Index on floppy disk.

A rich potential for locally created databases exists among library vertical file collections. Microcomputer data entry and retrieval software such as STAR and the Micro/Mini Version of BRS/SEARCH allow for the creation and search of in-house databases on sophisticated microcomputers. The January 1981 issue of *Online* reported that STAR is also used "by publishers to support the production and management of small- to medium-sized databases that are distributed to one or more online services." A March 1981 issue of *Database* reported that firms such as Cuadra Associates and InfoMart optionally package their data-entry and retrieval software "with the small computer and all the necessary peripheral equipment" needed to enter data in-house or by data-conversion companies. On a smaller scale, software packages such as Newsdex and Bookdex are used to prepare databases of literature references that one accumulates as a result of conducting research.

The Internet/NREN. From its beginnings in the 1970s as a link among defense research establishments in the United States, the Internet has grown into a worldwide telecommunications web linking computers in academic, research, government, communications, commercial and private non-profit organizations. Its electronic mail system allows not only the rapid transfer of personal messages but also dissemination of electronic "bulletin board" messages to large numbers of individuals. Standard file transfer protocols allow subscribers to retrieve large information files, including full-text documents, from remote sources. The telecommunications network also allows individuals in one institution to search databases, including library catalogs, in any other institution's computer that has been made available for such use.

By the early 1990s, two factors became clearly apparent. First, the power of the Internet was clearly established, while access was also clearly uneven and often inefficient, especially in the United States, which lacked a national network development policy. Congress recognized this situation in 1992 by passing legislation to create a National Research and Educational Network (NREN). Librarians have been active in negotiating with other interests (information suppliers, computer specialists, private research organizations, etc.) to determine the direction of NREN development. The speed of development will depend primarily on the level of government funding.

With the explosion of information sources available through the Internet, "bibliographic control" was becoming a significant problem. Individuals faced "information overload" and had increasing difficulty identifying the resources they needed while screening out the vast amount that were of no interest. To librarians and information retrieval specialists, these problems were just another manifestation of the classic issues of recall and precision. The division of services and expertise between library and computing centers became increasingly unclear, forcing a not-always-comfortable collaboration between the professionals staffing the two units within an institution.

Non-print media. Data suppression techniques and high-density storage devices developed in the 1980s led in the 1990s to the increased use of electronic media for storing and transmitting digitized still images, moving pictures, and sound. By 1992, several libraries were conducting pilot projects for the use of digital scanning and photo-CDs for providing access to their collections of visual materials. Publishers were developing multi-media products in digital formats (CD, videodisk, and other). Librarians have been participating actively in the development of standards to ensure these technologies develop in a manner to maximize access.

The Role of Artificial Intelligence. Seminal developments in artificial intelligence (AI) will contribute to the use of online information services by end-users. Howard Weber defined AI during the 1984 Information Industry Association conference on that subject as "a machine process that manages information so as to replicate the function of elements of human cognition more efficiently than they may function naturally." Steven Sieck observed in his article "Artificial Intelligence: Its Promise for the Information Industry" that AI will contribute to the use of natural language in the use of online information services "to allow end-users to retrieve information from databases without needing to know the specific commands used by the underlying database management software." Brattle Research applied AI to enable natural language to be used in monitoring new information added to a database. Sieck explained that "These alert rules are stored in a knowledge base—a network of attributes and relationships through which the machine can recognize and relate important concepts when they appear in incoming documents, whether or not they are expressed in the same semantic terms." The system is capable of isolating key concepts embodied in the document and automatically adding an appropriate phrase to the alert rule, once the user has identified that document as highly relevant.

Another form of AI known as *expert systems* is in use by the British chemical company ICI to give its agrochemical dealers and distributors a more sophisticated means to help farmers decide which chemicals can be used to treat crops to give the best yields. The article "Expert Systems Meet the Mass Market?" in the February 1985 issue of *Information Today* reported that the system "gives the dealer online expert help when a farmer asks him what he recommends to treat his crops." The dialogue with the system is query-based, and the user can ask the system to explain why it has asked a question or made a recommendation.

In "Intelligence in the 1980s" in *The Information Society* (1981), former CIA director William Colby argued for the use of AI in the management of intelligence information "to relate not only relevant but even apparently unrelated facts." While these applications of AI are limited, they point to a trend to use computer resources to simplify the use of online information services for the end-user.

Evaluation. Electronic information sources have come of age as full reference tools in the library and have made significant strides toward becoming recognized as such in the home and the office. These services are increasingly relied on as an effective and, in some cases, the only, source to satisfy the need for information conveniently. There is evidence that growth in the use of these services both in and outside the library is redefining the library's view of itself as an information provider and of the users to whom its services are delivered. At a minimum, the view that "Books Are Us," displayed on the cover of, and editorialized in, a 1985 issue of *American Libraries,* is eroding in favor of a broader view of information and its delivery, regardless of whether the mechanism for its storage has a binding or is a silver platter.

REFERENCES

Charles P. Bourne, "On-Line Systems: History, Technology, and Economics," *Journal of the American Society for Information Science,* May 1980.

Greg Byerly, *Online Searching: A Dictionary and Bibliographic Guide* (1983).

Gale Directory of Databases (semi-annual).

Donald T. Hawkins, "A Review of Online Physical Sciences and Mathematics Databases," *Database,* 1985.

Brendan P. Kehoe, *Zen and the Art of the Internet: A Beginner's Guide.* 2nd ed. (1993).

John E. Kinsock, *Legal Databases Online: LEXIS and WESTLAW* (1985).

James J. Maloney, editor, *Online Searching Technique and Management,* (1983).

Elmendorf, Theresa West

(1855–1932)

In March 1951 the *Library Journal* selected Theresa West Elmendorf for its new Library Hall of Fame in recognition of her contribution to librarianship in America. In commenting on the choice, *LJ* took note of her exceptional knowledge of books and of her ability to interest others in reading literature. Her selection was a fitting reminder of an early library pioneer with rare ability, vision, and high ideals.

Theresa Hubbell West was born in Pardeeville, Wisconsin, on November 1, 1855; six years later her family moved to Milwaukee, primarily to ensure educational opportunities for the four children. She graduated from Milwaukee's public schools and then from a school for girls in 1874. In 1877 she began her long library career as an assistant at the Young Men's Association of Milwaukee, a library that was soon to form the basis for a new municipal library. While waiting for the state legislature to pass the enabling act effecting this transfer, she kept the library open as a reading room and found time to read the 1876 report of the U.S. Bureau of Education, *Public Libraries in the United States of America.* This milestone in library literature was to form the basis of her knowledge of library theory and practice, and perhaps even the inspiration for her ideas about library service. She was appointed to the staff of the new Milwaukee Public Library and in 1880 became Deputy Librarian. Following a scandal involving the embezzlement of city funds by the head Librarian, K. A. Linderfelt, West was appointed to the post in 1892. Her four years at the helm of Milwaukee's library were important, at a time when a new library-museum was planned and built. She also developed her executive abilities, and the library became known as a carefully administered, patron-oriented institution.

She resigned her position in 1896 upon her marriage to Henry L. Elmendorf, then Librarian of the public library at Saint Joseph, Missouri, and a Vice-President of the American Library Association. For about a year the couple lived in London, where he managed the branch of the Library Bureau. The library profession beckoned, however, and in mid-1897 Henry Elmendorf became the head of the newly established Buffalo Public Library, a position he held until his death nine years later. While having no official connection with the library during this time, Theresa Elmendorf acted as a silent partner and frequent adviser. She had had more experience as an administrator than he, and it seems likely she was instrumental in developing the library. At a time when public libraries traditionally closed their bookshelves to the public, Buffalo began what was called the Open Shelf Room. The Elmendorfs also started the "Buffalo Plan," a program that included public library service to the schools of the city. Evidence of her role in the plan is her address before the New York State Teachers Association, which was later expanded into a booklet called "Buffalo's System of Public School and Public Library Cooperation."

As an unpaid worker, she found time to do research, to write, and to serve in various organizations. She produced a *Descriptive Catalogue of the Gluck Collection of Manuscripts and Autographs in the Buffalo Public Library* in 1899 and in 1904 served as the Selection Editor of the ALA's *Catalogue of Books for Small Libraries.* Elmendorf as Editor was a logical choice since she was recognized as an authority on book selection. Her contributions appeared in *Library Journal* and *Public Libraries,* as well as magazines outside the profession. In 1903–04 she served as President of the New York Library Association, at which time she was also a member of the American Library Institute.

The death of her husband in 1906 forced Theresa Elmendorf to end her unpaid status, and for the next 20 years she held the position of Vice-Librarian at the Buffalo Public Library. Her new role also meant an increased participation in ALA; in 1911–12 she served as its President, the first woman to hold that position. She presided at the Ottawa conference, the second meeting held by the Association in Canada. Although she made the political mistake of suggesting a closer alliance between the two countries—at a time when Canadians were especially sensitive to such a suggestion—ruffled feelings were smoothed over, and the meetings resulted in increased cooperative library development.

She probably made her greatest contribution in the area of popular bibliography. Her exceptional knowledge of books, and her enthusiasm in encouraging appreciation of reading in others, led her to produce a variety of reading lists and bibliographies. In 1917 *Poetry: The Complementary Life,* a selection made for Buffalo's Open Shelf Room, was published, and in 1921 a short reading list of popular books entitled *The United States* was reprinted by ALA. Her *Classroom Libraries for Public Schools,* published by the Buffalo Library in 1923, was a valuable selection aid. Even mandatory retirement in September 1926 failed to bring a halt to her efforts. In 1928 she prepared the bibliography of poems and poets for Joseph Auslander and F. E. Hill's *Winged Horse,* published by Doubleday, Doran. This was enlarged three years later into the ALA publication *Poetry and Poets: A Readers List.* Appreciation of poetry was one of her strongest characteristics, and so it was especially appropriate that this would be her last contribution to the world of books. She died at her home in Buffalo on September 4, 1932.

Theresa Elmendorf was a woman of unusual ability who made a major contribution to the profession and to its Association. She had high ideals and a vision of expanding library service well before its time. After her death, Mary E. Hazeltine of the University of Wisconsin Library School wrote, "Many librarians in important positions today have carried on because she awakened their appreciation of books and opened up for them insight into new realms. She was a stimulating guide and a vitalizing teacher, as well as a great librarian."

DENNIS THOMISON

El Salvador

El Salvador, the smallest republic in Central America, is bordered by Honduras on the north and east, the Pacific Ocean on the south, and Guatemala on the west. It gained independence from Spain in 1821. Population (1990 est.) 5,252,000; area 21,041 sq.km. The official language is Spanish; the local Nahuat and Lenca languages have almost disappeared.

The country endured a 12-year civil war (1979–91) and libraries suffered along with most Salvadoran institutions. An overview of Salvadoran libraries in the early 1990s primarily comprises plans and projects for the new era of peace.

National Library. The National Library of El Salvador was created by presidential decree in 1870 with an initial collection of 6,000 works on theology, philosophy, law, and classical literature purchased from Rome by the family of the librarian of Pope Gregory XVI. It was administered by the National University (1871–87), when it was opened to the general public. In 1962 the National Library became the General Directorate of Libraries and Archives and together with the holdings of the National Archives moved to the first library building constructed in El Salvador.

The National Library is the depository library under Salvadoran copyright law; it also holds documents of international organizations. The majority of its holdings come from donations and exchanges with Latin American countries and with learned societies of the United States and Europe.

In the early 1990s, despite serious budget and operational problems, the National Library staff worked on a retrospective national bibliography, the current national bibliography, preservation, and replacement of lost periodicals. With support from the Organization of American States, it worked to open a National Documentation Center.

Academic Libraries. For more than a century the Central Library of the National University of El Salvador (UES) was the leading Salvadoran library in higher education. Established in 1854, it suffered three natural disasters: fires in 1865 and 1955 and an earthquake in 1986. It also suffered from military interventions in 1972 and 1980 and was abandoned for long periods. Almost two-thirds of the items were lost from a collection of about 200,000 volumes. In 1992 UES began working on a library system adequate to the university's needs, with new buildings, automation, and training.

The main academic library is that of the Central American University (UCA), established along with the first private university in the nation in 1965. In the early 1990s its holdings included about 100,000 monographs and 1,225 current periodicals. It serves UCA faculty and students and also serves students at some of the institutions of higher education established in the 1970s and 1980s that do not have adequate libraries.

Public Libraries. Since the 19th century the National Library and some municipal libraries in urban areas offered limited public library services. In 1973 Unesco supported the development of a national network of Casas de la Cultura (Houses of Culture) that offered library services to the communities. The service became politicized and funding declined. In 1991 the Ministry of Education began a Public Libraries Network supported by the Mexican government. The first library in this network opened in June 1992 in San Miguel. Planners hope to establish 14 libraries, one in each department of the country. At the same time, the Catholic Church worked to develop a network of Popular Libraries in areas affected by the civil war.

School Libraries. Except for some libraries in private schools and a few in public schools (mainly supported by parent organizations), there have not been effective efforts to support library service to primary and secondary schools. In 1992 the Ministry of Education sponsored an experimental project as a part of its Outreach Support for Basic Education (SABE), working with 18 school libraries in rural, urban, and mixed sites. Planners hoped to organize about 1,500 new libraries in the first years of the project. They consider that a national policy commitment and effective leadership will be more important for its success than material resources.

Special Libraries. These libraries have been the best developed and the best funded in the country. Along with the traditional special libraries in banks, government offices, private enterprises, and professional associations, documentation centers were organized, especially in the social sciences, in the 1980s as support centers for research and the media. With increased access to microcomputers, bibliographic descriptions of the holdings of some special collections are being stored in machine-readable form. The most accepted bibliographic format is CEPAL.

The Profession. Librarianship has not been an attractive career in El Salvador because of the low salaries and low social status of librarians. The only library school in the country was founded at UES in 1973 with a three-year program. Few librarians are trained overseas and the rest are self-educated on the job. Visitors from other countries (mostly from Spain, the United States, and Mexico), sponsored by foreign universities and international agencies, have developed seminars and training sessions. UES began considering a new curriculum for a five-year program at the bachelor's level. New professionals will be expected to have a solid cultural background, social commitment, and knowledge of new technology and information science trends.

The Salvadoran Association of Librarians, founded in 1947, is the large professional organization. The Association of Agricultural Librarians is also active. Members of both groups have been a constant stimulus to the library life of the country.

ALMA B. RIVERA-AGUILERA

El Sheniti, El Sayed Mahmoud
(1920–)

El Sayed Mahmoud El Sheniti, Egyptian library educator and administrator, participated in many important library projects and conferences around the world and contributed to significant library achievements in Egypt.

El Sheniti was born in Egypt on November 25, 1920. He earned a B.A. degree from Cairo University in 1940, a higher diploma in social sciences from Alexandria University in 1953, and a Ph.D. in Library Science from the University of Chicago in 1960.

El Sheniti served the Egyptian and international library profession in several capacities. He was Librarian of Alexandria University Library, 1949–51; Assistant Librarian of the Unesco Fundamental Education Center in Sirs El Layyan, Egypt, 1952–54; Director of the American University in Cairo Library, 1958–63; Unesco Documentation and Publications Expert Stationed at the Unesco Regional Center of Community Development for the Arab States in Sirs El Layyan, Egypt, 1963–68; Under Secretary of State for the Egyptian National Library and Archives, 1968–71; Senior Under Secretary of State for the Ministry of Culture and Chairman of the General Egyptian Book Organization, 1971–77; and Deputy Minister of Culture and Chairman of the General Egyptian Book Organization (GEBO), a post he held until his retirement in December 1978.

El Sheniti contributed largely to library education in Egypt as a visiting professor to the Department of Librarianship and Archives of the Faculty of Arts, Cairo University. He also worked as an expert and consultant to numerous organizations in Egypt and in other Arab countries. From 1964 to 1970 he presided over the Egyptian Library Association.

He contributed to several Unesco meetings. From 1966 to 1974 he served as a member and Chairman of the Unesco International Advisory Committee for Libraries, Documentation and Archives. He was elected President of the Unesco Intergovernmental Conference on National Planning of Documentation and Archives Infrastructure, Paris, 1974; Vice-President of the International Congress on National Bibliography, Paris, 1977; and member of the International Book Committee and the International Book Year Support Committee.

El Sheniti wrote or edited many articles and books dealing with various aspects of library science. Noteworthy are "Book Cataloging Rules for Arabic Materials" (Cairo, 1961), "Authority List of Arabic Names" (Cairo, 1962), and "Arabic Adaptation of Dewey Decimal Classification" (Cairo, 1961).

As an administrator, El Sheniti contributed to library achievements in Egypt. Among them are centralized library activities focused around the book, i.e., public library services, national library and archives, and the state publishing industry under the umbrella of the GEBO; a new modern building for the National Library and Archives; and the establishment of various centers within the framework of the GEBO, such as the Arabic Book Development Center, the Bibliographic Center, the Arab Heritage Center, and the Computer and Microfilming Center.

MOHAMED M. EL HADI

Equatorial Guinea

Equatorial Guinea is a republic in West Africa, comprising Rió Muni—between Cameroon on the north and Gabon on the south and bordered by the Atlantic Ocean on the west—and the islands of Fernando Po (Bioco) and Annobon. Population (1990 est.) 348,000; area 28,051 sq.km. The official language is Spanish.

History. Equatorial Guinea, former Spanish Guinea, became independent in October 1968. The few libraries left by Spain were closed or had been evacuated by 1979 when Macías Nguema's dictatorship was ended in a military coup d'état led by his nephew, Obiang Nguema. Few were reopened during the second dictatorship, 1981–91. Few official sources documenting library services in Equatorial Guinea after 1968 are available.

Oral tradition—arising out of legends—has not yet been documented in any detail. First accounts of the area go back to the 15th century. From 1827, with Protestant missions, and from 1856 with Catholic missionaries, some small libraries were started.

An American, Sanford Berman, published the first annotated bibliography of the country in 1961. Between 1974 and 1991, a Swiss Africanist, Max Liniger-Goumaz, published a seven-volume bibliography containing 13,120 entries.

National Library. The country had no National Library until 1982. In that year, the Biblioteca Pública of Santa Isabel (Malabo) was transformed into the National Library. It merged with the Library of the Hispano-Guinean Cultural Center. Books were again available for loan after 1990.

Most documents published on Spanish Guinea are available in Spanish libraries. In the early 1990s, the main Equatoguinean sources could be found in libraries in Madrid, among them the Biblioteca Nacional, Biblioteca del Instituto de Estudios Africanos, Hemeroteca Nacional, Centro de Documentación Africana, and Biblioteca de los Misioneros Claretianos; in Rome, at the Biblioteca del Vaticano; in Geneva, Switzerland, at the United Nations Library; and in the United States at Northwestern University (Evanston, Illinois), at its Melville J. Herskovits Library of African Studies, and at the Library of Congress.

Academic Libraries. In 1963 the Escuela de Magisterio (Teacher Training College) in Bata was created with a library for students' use only. In 1971 the library's collection numbered about 3,000 volumes, covering mostly Spanish literature, books on pedagogy, and almost all publications on Guinea of the Instituto de Estudios Africanos. In 1973 the library was absorbed by the Centro de Desarrollo de la Educación, a teacher-training center created with Unesco's assistance (after many books had been burned by the Youth Movement of Macías Nguema). In 1974 there were 2,400 volumes. The government closed the library; it was reopened partially in 1976, but after deportation or exile of most of the students and the departure of Unesco's experts, the library was not in use from 1978 to 1982.

In Santa Isabel the Library of the Escuela Superior Indígena (later called Escuela Superior Provincial) was established in 1946 for training auxiliary primary school teachers and auxiliary administrators. In 1946 its stock numbered 1,400 volumes, for students' use only.

Shortly before independence, the Dirección General de Enseñanza y Inspección began to organize a pedagogical library with the help of the Spanish Dirección General de Plazas y Provincias and the Instituto Pedagógico San José de Calasanz (Madrid). Its aim was to create circulation libraries for teachers and pupils in remote districts, but they did not work.

There were also some small libraries in the four Catholic seminaries, two seminarios mayores (clerical training colleges) in Banapa and Nkuefulan, and two seminarios menores (clerical-staffed secondary schools) in Concepción and Mikomeseng.

Public Libraries. The Biblioteca Pública of Santa Isabel, created in 1942 by the Ministry of Education, opened to the public in 1945. It counted 3,000 volumes at inception; the Library is in the building of the Instituto Cardenal Cisneros (presently Instituto Rey Malabo, the main secondary school of the country). Books were supplied by the Gobierno General de la Colonia, the Administración de Intercambios y Compras de Libros (Madrid), the Dirección General de Marruecos y Colonias (later de Plazas y Provincias), and the Ministry of Foreign Affairs, as well as by private sources. Under the supervision of the Governor General of the Colony (later Province), the Library was directed by the Archivist of the Gobierno General. The Library administered two

Libraries in Equatorial Guinea (1990)

Type of library	Number of administrative units (main libraries)	Volumes in collections	Population served	Professional staff (with certificate, diploma, etc.)	Total staff
National	1	7,000	400	10	10
Academic	7	5,000	1,000	--	--
Public[a]	10	3,000	10,000	23[c]	23[c]
Special	4	2,000	1,000	4	4
Parliament[b]	1	100	50	--	1

[a]The Public Library of Santa Isabel (Malabo) became the National Library in 1982.
[b]1984 data.
[c]Inlcudes state libraries—Spanish and French Cultural Centers—Libraries in rural areas.

small circulation libraries in San Carlos (Fernando Po) and Bata (Rió Muni). In 1967, for 11,600 volumes there were 25,750 loans. By 1990 there was still no air conditioning in the Library. The Director in 1991 was Silvestre García Sobé.

Under the authority of the Ministry of Information, Tourism, and Culture, the General Department of Archives, Libraries, and Museums planned the establishment of 13 libraries in rural areas. By 1990, the first 10 were functioning.

Other Libraries. In 1955 Father Jesus Morras founded a small private library in the Claretian Mission (Hijos del Inmaculado Corazón de Maria—missionaries established in Spanish Guinea from 1883). The Library collected rare documents on archaeology, history, ethnology, and natural sciences, and complete collections of various newspapers. The Library's African Museum preserved some 5,000 prehistoric stones. In response to opposition to Roman Catholicism under the Macías Nguema government, the whole Library was evacuated from Fernando Po in 1974, then out of the country.

The library of the Museo Etnográfico of Santa Isabel (about 500 volumes), managed by the Ministry of Education, was abandoned after the Ministry of Education was closed in 1977 and the Minister and other officials were assassinated. From 1981, an expert of the Baha'i faith worked toward restoring the Museum and the Library.

The French Cultural Center (Santa Isabel) offers a library for children and students of about 3,000 books. After donating 2,000 books to the Biblioteca Infantil in 1986–87, the Spanish government decided to open nine libraries for children with about 200 volumes each. It also provided a bus for film projections. Its cooperation program for 1988–90 donated 500 books to the Hispanic Cultural Center of the capital, as well as a thousand books to the cultural centers and teleclubs of Baney, Ebebiyin, Nkogo, Niefang, and Annobon.

The Dirección de Archivos, also in Santa Isabel and a very understaffed service since independence, was supported by the Ministry of Education. Most Equatoguinean archival materials have to be consulted in Spain and in other countries, principally the Archivo de las Cortés, Archivo del Consejo de Estado, Archivo de la Dirección General de Promoción del Sahara, Archivo del Ministerio de Asuntos exteriores, and Archivo Histórico Nacional, all in Madrid; Archivo General de Simancas, in Valladolid; and Archivo de Indias, in Sevilla. Besides Spanish archives are the colonial archives of Portugal, France, the United Kingdom, and Germany. The Berlin archives are famous for the study of the Fang, the indigenous people of the mainland of Equatorial Guinea. Finally, the Vatican archives are also a rich resource.

In the early 1990s there were no library associations.

REFERENCES

Max Liniger-Goumaz, *Guinea Ecuatorial, Bibliografía General,* 7 volumes (1974–91).
Max Liniger-Goumaz, *Historical Dictionary of Equatorial Guinea* (1988).
Max Liniger-Goumaz, *Small Is Not Always Beautiful: The Story of Equatorial Guinea* (1989).

MAX LINIGER-GOUMAZ

Esdaile, Arundell
(1880–1956)

Edmond Esdaile
Arundell Esdaile

An exemplar of the old style of scholar-librarian who spent his whole professional career in the service of the British Museum (BM), Arundell James Kennedy Esdaile made significant contributions to bibliography, library practice, and library education both in Britain and internationally.

Born in London April 25, 1880, and educated at Lancing and at Magdalene College, Cambridge, Esdaile joined the staff of the British Museum Department of Printed Books in 1903. Under the inspiration of Robert Proctor and the direction of Alfred Pollard, work on the BM *Catalogue of XVth Century Books* had recently begun, and for the next few years, in company with such scholars as Henry Thomas and Victor Scholderer, Esdaile was occupied with the cataloguing of incunabula. His own research interests were much more concerned with English literature, and with time his duties became concentrated on the purchase and particularly the cataloguing of early English books. Besides his Museum work, he was engaged in work for the Malone Society, the Bibliographical Society, and others, contributing the section on "The Age of Elizabeth" to *English History Source Books* (G. Bell & Sons Series, 1912) and assisting Caroline Spurgeon with her *Five Hundred Years of Chaucer Criticism and Allusion* (1914–25). His authority in this field was recognized in his invitation in 1926 to give the Sandars Lectures at Cambridge, published as *The Sources of English Literature* (Cambridge, 1928).

Relations between the British Museum and the Library Association, though at one time close, had become very weak by the time of World War I. Esdaile was one of the first Museum men to strive to bring the National Library and the profession closer together. He was closely associated with the first British School of Librarianship at University College London from its establishment in 1919, creating the course in Bibliography and Historical Bibliography, which he taught for the next 20 years. His *Students Manual of Bibliography,* first published in 1931 as the first volume in the "Library Association Series," was for many years an essential textbook. His work in library education did much to change the negative attitudes toward formal library education that had been prevalent in learned libraries in Britain.

From 1923 until an illness in 1935 compelled him to resign the editorship, he directed the *Library Association Record,* injecting a new, more professional, and more scholarly tone into the journal. He was responsible for the Library Association's starting publication of the *Year's Work in Librarianship,* himself editing the annual volumes from 1928 to 1938. His work in setting up the University and Research Section of the Association in 1927 helped ensure that the gap between learned libraries and other parts of the profession could not reopen.

In 1926 Esdaile moved out of the Department of Printed Books to the Director's office at the British Museum, to the post of Secretary, which had lain dormant for many years. In that position he was able to represent the Museum in many external activities, including the Library Committee of the League of Nations Institute of Intellectual Cooperation. He was closely involved in the formation of the International Library and Bibliographical Committee, later to become the International Federation of Library Associations and Institutions (IFLA), at the Library Association's 50th conference, Edinburgh 1927. He subsequently served as a Vice-President of IFLA from 1931, taking an active part in its deliberations until ill health caused him to resign in 1936.

Esdaile was elected President of the Library Association in 1939. His term in office was much longer than the normal one-year period. As a consequence of the outbreak of war that year, normal conduct of the Association's affairs was suspended, and he remained as President until 1945, working unobtrusively with the Emergency Committee to consolidate the Association's progress after the end of hostilities. An Honorary Fellowship of the Association was conferred on him in 1946, in recognition of this and his earlier services for the library world.

With "ambassadorial" visits to North American libraries in 1933 and again in 1941, his work with IFLA, and publication of his important *National Libraries of the World* (1934), Esdaile did much sound work to improve international links in the library world. A second volume, which he had planned as a sequel to his *National Libraries,* surveying some of the great non-national libraries (Bodleian, Boston Public Library, El Escorial, and others) was completed by Margaret Burton as *Famous Libraries of the World* (1937). His final substantial book was his excellent study *The British Museum Library,* written in retirement (1946). His interest in libraries and the health of the library profession continued right up to his death in London on June 22, 1956.

Esdaile's role in bringing together the British Museum and the library profession in Britain and in forging links with libraries abroad was of key importance in the interwar years. He may not have been a profound scholar, but his skills as a teacher, his friendliness, and his enthusiasm in building bridges were of real importance for facilitating the significant changes and major improvements in library service after World War II.

RODERICK CAVE

Estonia

Founded as an independent state in 1918, the Republic of Estonia was annexed by the U.S.S.R. in 1940 and called the Estonian Soviet Socialist Republic. It then regained its independence in 1991. The Baltic Sea lies to the west and north, Russia to the east, and Latvia to the south. Population (1991 est.) 1,576,000; area 45,215 sq.km. The official language is Estonian.

History. The first Estonian libraries were in the monasteries and churches of the 13th century. The Reformation produced the first public library in Tallinn, the library of the Olevist church, established in 1552. The first known book containing the Estonian language was published in 1525, but has not survived. The fragments of the Catechism by Wanradt and Koell, published in 1535, are considered parts of the oldest existing book in Estonian.

The first university, Academia Gustaviana, was founded in Tartu in 1632. Although the library had more than 3,300 volumes by the end of the 17th century, it was moved to Sweden during the Great Northern War (1700–21). Reopened as Tartu University Library in 1802, it is the oldest operating library in Estonia. Other early libraries include the library of Tallinn Gymnasium (1632), the General Public Library of Estonia, also in Tallinn (1825), and the library of the Estonian Learned Society (1839).

In the 19th century Lutheran ministers and schoolteachers founded public libraries containing Estonian literature. By the 1880s there were at least 125 public libraries in the country, but Russification and legal limits on public libraries cut the number to 79 by 1900. Further surges in public library development came in the early 1900s and after independence. After the Soviet occupation, libraries suffered both the ravages of war and the destruction of books considered ideologically unsound. Postwar development began in the 1950s on the Soviet library model, and centralization was complete by the mid-1970s. With national independence, libraries regained their autonomy.

National Library. The Estonian State Library, established in Tallinn in 1918 as a parliamentary library, gained depository right in 1919 to a copy of every item printed in Estonia. It was named the State Library of the Estonian S.S.R. (1940–53), the F. R. Kreutzwald Library (1953–88), and the National Library of Estonia (1988–). The National Library of Estonia Act of 1990 lists its tasks: to collect, preserve, and make accessible printed matter published in Estonia, in the Estonian language, or about Estonia; to introduce world culture; to compile and publish the national bibliography; to conduct research in library science, bibliography, and information science; and to receive and preserve literature that is valuable but not widely used. The Library also serves as a parliamentary library, providing reference service for deputies and government officials. Its holdings in 1990 included 2,100,000 books, 6,000 cartographic items, 99,400 musical manuscripts and printed works, 93,000 graphic items, and 1,600 musical recordings. The National Archival Collection was founded in 1935.

Academic Libraries. Each of Estonia's six universities has its own library. Tartu University Library, the oldest, has had deposit rights since 1919. Its holdings of 4,500,000 volumes are especially rich in literature about the Baltic states, including manuscripts and rare printed works from the 15th century. The collections are open to readers outside the university. The Tallinn Technical University Library (founded 1919) contains more than 1,200,000 volumes, chiefly in the natural sciences and technology. The collections reflect the development of the school's curriculum over time. The libraries of the other institutions—the Estonian Agricultural University, Estonian Art University, Tallinn Conservatory, and Tallinn Teacher Training Institute—are considerably smaller, and most are open only to their own faculty and students.

Public Libraries. Estonia has a network of more than 560 libraries, including 21 central libraries in towns and counties, 64 other town and county libraries, 464 village libraries, and 14 children's libraries. They have broad collections of fiction and nonfiction in Estonian and other languages, with a total of more than 11 million volumes in 1990. Libraries for

Libraries in Estonia (1990)

Type of library	Number of adminstrative units (main libraries)	Number of service points (branches, mobile stops, etc.)	Volumes in collections	Annual expenditures (kroon)	Population served	Professional staff (with certificate, diploma, etc.)	Total staff
	1990	1990	1990	1990	1990	1990	1990
National	1	1	4,284,808	2,965,900	--	174	563
Academic	16	18	4,844,260	--	21,054	70	167
Public	627	1,019	11,099,372	--	386,226	760	1,319
School	500	--	9,854,300	--	224,918	--	600
Special	155	--	2,934,516	--	91,496	38	118
Other	124	--	10,123,457	--	456,100	--	659

special audiences include 43 for trade unions, 3 for collective farms, and 17 for institutions for the aged and handicapped.

School Libraries. Each of Estonia's 80 vocational schools has a library emphasizing its specialty. The 600 comprehensive secondary schools have libraries. Most village primary schools depend on nearby public libraries for library services.

Special Libraries. The Archival Collection of the F. R. Kreutzwald Museum of Literature, established in Tartu in 1909 as the library of the Museum of the People of Estonia, has major holdings of literature in Estonian, by Estonians, and about Estonia and the other Baltic and Finno-Ugric peoples.

The library of the Estonian Academy of Sciences, established in Tallinn in 1947, has a large current collection of scientific literature in foreign languages and a collection on the Baltic states. It is the coordinating center for scientific libraries in Estonia, with collections totalling 3,400,000 items. Its historical holdings, built from the language holdings of the oldest libraries of Estonia, include the only remaining copies of the oldest books printed in Estonia.

The Estonian Medical Library, established in Tallinn in 1944, holds more than 400,000 items and serves specialists in the medical and allied sciences. The Estonian Pedagogical Library, established in 1892, has about 180,000 volumes and coordinates school libraries in the country. From 1968 to 1992, the Estonian Technical Library controlled more than 4,000 technical libraries, mostly in industrial enterprises. Parts of its collection were given to the Tallinn Technical University and the Department of Standards. The Library of Patents holds 10 million patents.

The Profession. Professional library training in Estonia began in 1927 when library science and bibliography were added to the curriculum of the Department of Philosophy at Tartu University. Bibliography was taught as an independent subject from 1944 to 1965, when professional training was transferred to the Tallinn Teachers Training Institute. A new curriculum was introduced, based on the compulsory programs of the U.S.S.R., offering specialization in public, scientific, or technical library work. Adaptation of the curriculum to Estonian conditions began in 1980. The program, which lasts five years and leads to a diploma, covers both general cultural subjects and technical courses in library and information science. It includes compulsory internship in libraries. Programs leading to the Master's and Doctor's degrees were introduced in 1991. Since 1952 the secondary school in Viljandi has offered a three-year program with a specialization in librarianship.

IVI EENMAA

Ethiopia

Ethiopia, in northeastern Africa, is bordered by the Red Sea on the north, Djibouti and Somalia on the east, Kenya on the south, and Sudan on the west. Population (1990 est.) 49,241,000; area 1,221,900 sq.km. The official language is Amharic.

History. Ethiopia's ancient civilization had a script of its own that goes back as far as the 5th century B.C. The Ethiopian civilization is a genuine African civilization born and developed on African soil, not transplanted from the other side of the Red Sea. The Hamitic peoples that have inhabited Ethiopia since ancient times lived on both sides of the Red Sea. Their settlements in the coastal lands of ancient southern Arabia were known and called by the Arabs of the time as Habashat, from the word *habash,* signifying individuals or tribes not organized in the usual Arab, Semitic tribal organization they were familiar with. There were constant and prolonged economic, social, cultural, and physical contacts between the peoples of the two continents. The resultant cultural and linguistic mix gives an Afro-Asian or Ethio-Semitic flavor to the present-day literary culture of Ethiopia. Added is the rich centuries-old heritage of the peoples of Ethiopia.

Ethiopia developed its own ancient alphabet, which manifested itself first in its Sabean form, followed in the Geez (liturgical language), Amharic, Tigrigna, Tigre, Oromo, and other languages and now in the various vernaculars. It was restricted to the temple and the court before Christianity and to church and court afterward up to the threshold of the 20th century.

The earliest literary records consist of inscriptions written on hard surfaces. Monumental writings on granite steles and walls of rock and religious votive writings on clay vessels, iron implements, gold, silver, bronze, and iron coins were the main media, during both the pre-Christian and Christian eras. When Christianity was introduced to the country in the 4th

Libraries in Ethiopia (1990)

Type of library	Number of administrative units (main libraries)	Number of service points (branches, mobile stops, etc.)	Volumes in collections	Population served
National[a]	1	10	100,000	--
Public[a]	4	17	124,000	11,680
Non-specialized	5	13	530,000	9,400

[a]1986 data

Source: Unesco, *Statistical Yearbook,* 1991.

century A.D., the Bible was translated into Geez from Greek. Gradually other religious texts were translated and adapted from Greek, Coptic, and Arabic. Parchment, imported by Christian missionaries from the Hellenized Middle East, was developed for writing as the only soft medium and spread at the end of the 5th century when a group of missionaries arrived in northern Ethiopia to found monasteries. Manuscript (known as *branna* from the Greek *membrana*) collections flourished with the growth and strength of Christian monasticism. There are tens of thousands of churches and monasteries throughout the country, mainly in the northern half plus southern Showa, holding all kinds of manuscript collections and manuscripts. The worth and full extent of these have not yet been established despite Unesco and other projects to begin to microfilm and catalogue collections in the second half of the 20th century. The manuscripts are scattered throughout some estimated 12,500 churches and 800 monasteries. The content is not exclusively religious, and the literary, linguistic, and historical importance, among other things, should not be underestimated. Royal collections were also important and a number of emperors were great manuscript collectors and patrons of religious and scholarly arts and centers.

Hundreds of Ethiopian manuscripts were expropriated by adventurers, diplomats, missionaries, and soldiers and taken to libraries in Europe. The tradition of gathering and maintaining collections was carried forward in modern times by the Emperor Yohannes IV (1871–89), Menelik (1889–1913), and Haile Selassie (1930–74). Menelik collected manuscripts in his palace by copying ancient manuscripts found in the Zway island monastery, by recovering some from Europe, and by other methods. There was a good scriptorium in his palace in Addis Ababa.

Before the printing press was introduced in the country in the 19th century, Geez and Amharic books were printed in Europe. A book of Psalms was printed in Geez in Rome (1513) by a German typographer from Cologne with the active help of Ethiopian monks. Learned religious men, such as Abba Tesfatsion of Malabso, an Ethiopian pilgrim monk who settled in a hospice provided to pilgrims by the Pope, were instrumental in making type fonts for small printing machines with Geez characters. They aroused European curiosity in Ethiopian studies and Ethiopia, and they made scholarly contributions on their own. Various linguistic and literary works were printed in Europe, chiefly in Rome. A missionary bishop, Lorenzo Biancheri, of the Lazarists, imported a small printing press to Massawa in October 1863. It became not only the first permanent printing press on Ethiopian soil (Massawa was then under Egyptian suzerainty) but the first in Eastern Africa (the press was introduced into Tanzania in 1875 and Kenya in 1877). Biancheri's press began operation on May 10, 1867. It was transferred to Keren in 1879 and on to Asmara in 1912. There were other famous missionary presses, such as the Swedish Evangelical Mission's at Emkullu and a Roman Catholic press at Harar. Menelik imported a government printing press from Europe in 1906, and the Ethiopian Printing Press started production in 1908. Private commercial presses came soon to the scene and began to produce much needed literature, newspapers, government ordinances, regulations, religious texts, textbooks, journals, and pamphlets. Gradually their impact was felt, printed books for libraries were produced, and public interest in literacy and knowledge was increased.

The first modern library was established under Haile Selassie and was inaugurated on the occasion of his coronation in 1930. Named the National Library of Ethiopia, it consisted of a sort of national and public library cum museum. The collections included selected Geez manuscripts and printed books in French, English, and Russian. The museum section included priceless ancient objects from various parts of the country. A prestige showpiece to impress European dignitaries during the coronation festivity, it was not much frequented by the public. The Library did not survive after Italian forces entered Addis Ababa on May 5, 1936. The Italians set up a public library for themselves in Massawa that later was transferred to Asmara. That Library grew to be comparatively large, its collection at one time reaching 10,000 volumes. During the Italian occupation there were several well-run school and special libraries for the colonial community, and in Addis Ababa an Italian East Africa Central Library was set up for Italians in 1936. It too reached 10,000 volumes. But the Italian occupation brought a halt to Ethiopian education and modern librarianship. Damage to cultural and intellectual property was considerable. Fires in Addis Ababa and expropriation of irreplaceable treasures to Italy proved a severe loss to the country.

National Library. Founded, together with a National Museum, by Haile Selassie in 1944, the National Library offers loan and reference facilities to the public, acting as a central public library and as the national repository of Ethiopiana. A proclamation conferring depository privileges was enacted in 1975, a year after the Revolution.

The Library's valuable collection of several hundred Ethiopian Christian Orthodox manuscripts, some finely illuminated and dating from as early as the 14th century, also includes Ethiopian "incunabula" from the period when local printing began in the 19th century. In the 1960s the Library opened branches in several provincial centers, notably Debre Zeit, Yrgalem, and Harar, stocking them with volumes from its own collection. Collections total more than 90,000 volumes. A national bibliography had not been issued by the early 1990s, though efforts toward its creation had been made, and plans were under way to house a national archives at the National Library.

Academic Libraries. The principal resource is the library system of the University of Addis Ababa. Founded in 1961 and building on the collections of the University College of Addis Ababa established 11 years earlier, the University Library has a number of branches, including law, medical, engineering, science, agriculture, and public health. The collections were developed extensively with Ford Foundation and U.S. AID assistance. Exceeding 500,000 volumes in the early 1990s, they include a unique library of Ethiopiana at the Institute of Ethiopian Studies, where the holdings of more than 25,000 volumes are made up of a comprehensive collection of books about Ethiopia and the Horn of Africa; some 10,000 books, mostly in Amharic, printed in the country; and a collection of about 1,000 manuscripts and scrolls. The Library, together with the Institute, publishes *Ethiopian Publications* (1965–), a classified list of books and periodical articles published in Ethiopia.

The University of Asmara Library was founded by Italian nuns and added collections in English after the institution gained university status in 1967.

Although events of the 1970s and early 1980s—including increasing enrollments not matched by sufficient growth of collections—led to a system weakened by pressures of demand and insufficient support, academic library service remained by far the best of the library sector in the early 1990s.

Public Libraries. Responsibility for public library service is carried by the National Library, with its inadequate funding. A number of municipal and community libraries have grown, in addition, mainly through local initiative. In 1973 a books-by-mail service was launched by the University Library, initially to provide recreational paperback reading to students on university service in the provinces, but it was later made available to the public. The service expanded after the 1974 Revolution, in cooperation with the Ethiopian Library Association, to serve students and teachers on the National Campaign for Development and Work 1974–1976, which included intensive literacy drives. Books were distributed through school or public libraries wherever these existed.

Generally speaking, the public library system is poor and the least developed service. There are only a small number of libraries but more than 6,000 reading rooms. Libraries range from one-room collections to reasonably well organized small ones. Detailed statistics are not available.

School Libraries. Modern secular education was advanced significantly in Ethiopia by Emperor Menelik, who opened the first modern government school in 1908. The Teferi Makonnen school, opened in 1925, was a landmark in educational history; it was the first school provided with a library in accord with a plan based on a European model.

National Library of Ethiopia

Main reading room of the National Library, Addis Ababa.

In the 1960s and 1970s the Ministry of Education attempted to improve library services in secondary schools. Courses were held to train school librarians and, with AID assistance, books were purchased and distributed. School libraries continued to lack adequate bookstocks and qualified staff in the 1990s.

Special Libraries. The most important special library in Ethiopia is that of the UN Economic Commission for Africa (1958). It has a strong collection of African government and agency documents, periodicals, and some 60,000 books on African development. Other libraries serve government agencies. The National and Commercial banks, the Institute of Public Administration, and the Police and Air Force colleges have libraries of long standing. Among libraries sponsored by other countries are the British Council Library and the libraries of the French, German, Italian, and Russian cultural centers.

After the Revolution of 1974, many new special libraries were created. Several organizations imported computers in the 1980s, but modern information systems had not been widely applied by the 1990s.

For centuries thousands of churches and monasteries in Ethiopia have served as repositories of religious manuscripts used in services, teaching, and scholarship. It is estimated that some 50,000 manuscripts are housed in these churches. A project for recording them on film, initiated in 1973 by the Ethiopian Orthodox Church and Saint John's University, Collegeville, with funding from the National Endowment for the Humanities, led to microfilming thousands of manuscripts. They are kept in the Ethiopian Manuscripts Microfilm Library, Addis Ababa, and the Hill Monastic Manuscripts Microfilm Library, Collegeville (1976–).

The Profession. The Ethiopian Library Association, founded in 1967, achieved official status as a registered society in 1969. It has been active in campaigning for better public library facilities and in training librarians. Training is provided by a small staff with limited resources at Addis Ababa University, which offers diplomas in library science.

ADHANA MENGSTE-AB

Euronet

The Euronet communications network, jointly set up by the European Commission and the Post, Telegraph, and Telephone departments of the member states of the European Community (EC), provides access to more than 500 databases. Thanks to work done on the Euronet system as a result of three triennial scientific and technical information and documentation action plans (1975–83), the Community developed the basis of an information industry. Euronet's functions have been assumed by interconnected national networks. The Community has largely reduced the disparity between the comparatively few EC databases and those available in the United States by encouraging the development of an access system, most of which is used by private industry.

The European Commission worked in the early 1990s to encourage further development of computer-based information services that could supplement Euronet in the EC. DIANE (network for direct access to information for Europe) is the acronym under which online information services in Europe are being promoted. Trends in the development of the Euronet DIANE network include: developing new aids to assist the large community of network users to make the greatest possible use of the system and to encourage new users; exploring prospects for export; and developing the infrastructure of an information industry concerned with document delivery, multilingual problems, and other matters.

A complete guide to databases is issued by Euronet DIANE, Luxembourg. A database containing information on all the databases is made available by ECHO, the organization of the European Community's host computer.

CARLO VERNIMB

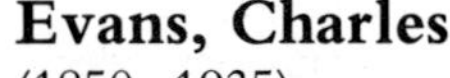

Evans, Charles
(1850–1935)

ALA

Charles Evans

Charles Evans, U.S. librarian and bibliographer, served a number of libraries from 1866 to 1901; from 1902 he devoted the rest of his life with single-minded dedication to his *American Bibliography*, the fundamental resource for early American imprints, which secures his place in library history.

Evans was born November 13, 1850, in Boston. After the deaths of both parents, he was placed in 1859 in the Boston Asylum and Farm School, where he received rigorous training in religion, manual labor, and academic studies. At the age of 16 Evans became an assistant at the Boston Athenaeum, the distinguished private library then under the direction of William Frederick Poole. The Athenaeum proved to be Evans's bibliographical "alma mater" and Poole his lifelong mentor.

Evans was an effective library organizer and internal administrator and a leader in developing library services. But he failed to work well with supervising boards and administrators. That failure led to an uneven career as a librarian despite his achievements. He was the first Librarian of the new Indianapolis Public Library from late in 1872 until disagreements led to the end of his employment in August 1878. (He was to serve in Indianapolis again, from 1889 to 1892, but he again failed to sustain his board's support.)

Evans worked outside the library profession from 1878 to 1884. The following year he went as Assistant Librarian to the Enoch Pratt Free Library in Baltimore, but he resigned in December 1886 after difficulties with the Head Librarian. At the Newberry Library in Chicago, he worked in classification and reference from July 1892 to January 1895 and in the next year began to organize the collections of the Chicago Historical Society on a part-time assignment. Evans was Secretary and Librarian of the Society from July 1896 until the trustees dismissed him in 1901. His career as a librarian ended, but a new one was to begin.

In January 1902 Evans announced to a skeptical library community an ambitious project—a chronological, annotated record of publications printed in the U.S. from the beginning of printing in 1639 through 1820. Thereafter Evans set about achieving his objective with total commitment. By that time he had married Lena Young (1884), and they had three children (one of whom, Chick, became a golfer). But family and all ordinary social obligations and pleasures were to be displaced by his relentless pursuit of his goal. He took on not only the editorial and scholarly roles that the work demanded but also all production and printing—selecting his own paper, looking for the most economical printer, and directly overseeing all the work, including his own order fulfillment from his home. His plan was to offer separate volumes at $15 each to an initial 300 subscribers.

He began his editorial work for each period in the Newberry and Chicago Public libraries, carefully preparing annotated slips from bibliographies and printed catalogues. Then he would visit the Library of Congress and many other libraries in the East, often discovering stacks of publications that had not been previously organized. He worked long hours to bring out his first volume (covering the years 1639–1729), published in November 1903, and did not let up in his prodigious efforts in subsequent years. With characteristic energy and devotion, he managed to issue at fairly regular intervals the next eight volumes, carrying the work through the period 1790–92 by 1915. He had about 375 subscribers at the beginning of World War I. Evans won a reputation for his bibliographical achievement and benefited from cooperation with other bibliographers and librarians who provided information. He saw his work recognized by professional peers when he was elected to membership in the American Antiquarian Society in 1910.

Increased costs and the loss of foreign subscribers during World War I interrupted his publishing program for the next decade. With the support of Theodore Wesley Koch, Northwestern University Librarian, and an ALA committee, enough sales were generated to permit continuation of the work—volume 9 (1793–94), priced now at $25, was published in 1926 and volume 10 (1795–96) in January 1929. During the Depression of the 1930s grants from the American Council of Learned Societies made possible publication of volume 11 and volume 12, covering the years 1796 and through the letter *M* of 1799. He had given up his original goal of 1820 to settle for 1800, but he did not live to complete the final volume in his revised plan. He died in Evanston, Illinois, on February 8, 1935.

Evans attended the first meeting of the American Library Association in October 1876. He served as ALA's first Treasurer until 1878, but he was not active in the Association thereafter. ALA named him an honorary member at its Conference in 1926, and in 1934 Brown University awarded him an honorary Doctor of Letters degree.

Evans's revised plan was eventually completed in 1955 when volume 13 (*N* 1799–1800) was published by the American Antiquarian Society under the editorship of Clifford K. Shipton. The American Antiquarian Society also issued volume 14, a cumulative Index, by Roger P. Bristol, in 1959. Bristol's index to printers, publishers, and booksellers in the series appeared in 1961. After another decade of work, Bristol issued his *Supplement to Charles Evans' American Bibliography* (1970), adding 11,000 titles to Evans's original 39,000. Thus Evans's original work continues to serve as the foundation stone of American bibliographic effort.

REFERENCES

Edward G. Holley, *Charles Evans, American Bibliographer* (1963), includes a complete list of Evans's works and other Evans materials.

Edward G. Holley, "Evans, Charles," *Dictionary of American Library Biography* (1978).

EDWARD G. HOLLEY

Evans, Eve
(1910–)

Evelyn Jane Alice Evans, British-born public librarian, developed the national library service of Ghana and contributed to library service in many other developing countries.

Born March 22, 1910, in Coventry, England, she served the Public Library there from 1927 to 1941. She became an Associate of the Library Association (LA) in 1931 and a Fellow in 1933. She worked in the University of Michigan Library in Ann Arbor in 1935 and 1936.

Evans was British Council Librarian in the then Gold Coast from 1945 until 1949, when she was transferred to the Gold Coast Library Board. The Board became a statutory body in 1950, and she became its first Chief Librarian and later its first Director of Library Services.

In 1945 there were no significant public library services in the Gold Coast. By 1965, when she left Ghana, there were 21 libraries and various services, including mobile units. Her philosophy was to use local resources when possible, and she early saw that she would one day have to make way for indigenous librarians. She also gave emphasis to the development of children's libraries.

In November 1961 Evans made a world tour to study library cooperation and national libraries. She traveled extensively in Africa and other developing areas, served as an expert on public libraries for Unesco, and advised Nigeria and Sierra Leone. In Ghana she was one of the pioneers who formed the West African Library Association in 1954, and she became its President in 1959.

In 1955 she was decorated as a member of the Order of the British Empire (M.B.E.) and in 1960 as a Commander of the Order (C.B.E.). She was made Honorary Fellow of the LA in 1965.

A Unesco consultant to Liberia in 1967, Evans was in Ceylon from 1967 to 1970, and she drew up legislation for the Ceylon National Library Services Board.

In 1975 she was invited by the Ghana Library Board to participate in the 25th anniversary celebration of the service that she had created from scratch and which she left intact, a monument to herself, to Ghana, and to African librarianship.

ANDREW N. DEHEER

Evans, Luther
(1902–1981)

Library of Congress

Luther Evans

Luther Evans, tenth U.S. Librarian of Congress and third Director-General of Unesco, is remembered especially for his wide participation in international activities.

He was born near Sayersville, Texas, October 13, 1902. After earning a B.A. in 1924 and an M.A. in 1925 at the University of Texas, he completed a Ph.D. at Stanford in Political Science in 1927 with a dissertation on the mandate system of the League of Nations. Short-term instructorships ensued, at New York University (1927) and Dartmouth (1928–30), followed in 1930 by an appointment as Assistant Professor of Politics at Princeton, where he remained until 1935.

In October 1935 Evans was appointed Director of the Historical Records Survey in the Washington office of the Works Progress Administration. The American Imprints Inventory was perhaps its most significant project, as later edited by the Library of Congress and incorporated into the *National Union Catalog*. Evans remained with that office until joining the staff of the Library of Congress (LC) in 1939 as Director of the Legislative Reference Service. He was soon promoted to Chief Assistant Librarian under Archibald MacLeish and served concurrently as Director of the Reference Department. He served as Acting Head (1940–45) during MacLeish's frequent wartime absences and after his resignation in 1944. Evans succeeded MacLeish in December 1945 as the tenth Librarian of Congress. His was one of the rare appointments to be made from within the ranks.

Most significant of Evans's many accomplishments at the LC include the program to publish the *Cumulative Catalog of Library of Congress Printed Cards* (1947), the issuance of *Rules for Descriptive Cataloging in the Library of Congress* (1949) and *New Serial Titles* (1953), a greatly expanded readership, a 28 percent collection increase despite mounting budgetary restraints, and a democratic philosophy of management that greatly expanded the involvement of library staff in advisory groups.

In November 1945 MacLeish, then Assistant Secretary of State, invited Evans to join the U.S. delegation to the London Conference, which was ultimately responsible for the establishment of Unesco, the United Nations Educational, Scientific and Cultural Organization. In July 1953 Evans was elected Director-General of Unesco and resigned from the LC. This move brought an end to mounting congressional criticism of Evans's continuing extension of services to noncongressional patrons and of his heavy participation in international affairs. He served Unesco until 1958 and was actively involved in such major issues as the 1956 agreement on the protection of cultural property in wartime, peaceful use of nuclear energy, and the establishment of the Universal Copyright Convention.

After leaving Unesco, Evans served as an international studies consultant at the University of Texas and directed studies for the Brookings Institution on federal department libraries and the National Education Association on educational implications of automation. He assumed directorship of the international and legal collections at Columbia University in 1962, retiring in 1971 to an ongoing professional involvement in the American Library Association, World Federalists U.S.A., the United States Committee for Refugees, U.S. People for the United Nations, and the United Nations Association of the United States of America.

Evans died in San Antonio, Texas, on December 23, 1981.

REFERENCES

William J. Sittig, "Luther Evans: Man for a New Age," *Librarians of Congress, 1802-1974* (1977).

Walter F. Bell, "Luther Evans: Librarian for the Nation," *Texas Library Journal* (1988).

BETTY L. MILUM

Extension Services

Extension service is the activity of lending or delivering books and other forms of information to users who are distant from a library or who may be relatively near it but unable to travel to it. Effective extension has been developed through the commitment and experimentation of librarians in a variety of types and sizes of libraries, but the larger units of service have been encouraged to implement the most ambitious programs. Urban and rural systems, state library agencies, and, in at least one notable example, a federal library agency have pioneered in extension service. The concept and practice of library extension in the United States received dramatic support in the federal Library Services Act of 1956, for the extension of service to rural areas. Extension support continued when LSA was renewed and expanded by Congress in 1964 as the Library Services and Construction Act.

In a well-developed urban, suburban, or rural library system, extension is provided as a convenience to user populations for whom travel to a central library is difficult or expensive. Extension service may be a necessity to significant numbers of users who find travel to the central library impossible because they have physical disabilities, are institutionalized or homebound, or lack transportation. Because of these human and economic considerations, extension is a necessary and important specialization in public library service. Extension may also be provided in special, academic, and school district libraries, but the service is most frequently associated with public library operations.

Extension service is a part of many library organizations, but it does have limitations. Because of logistical and financial considerations, it cannot normally provide complete information service. Compared to centralized service, on a per user basis extension is usually an expensive means of providing information delivery. In many cases funding required for branch operations will reduce the funding otherwise available for central library services. In spite of these limitations, extension is accepted as an essential component of effective library and information service.

Special considerations include the logistics and mechanical means for delivery, human and safety factors related to delivery systems, achieving balance between the expense of the information resources to be made available and their relative value to extension users, and the application of information and communications technology to assist extension.

Library extension began as a means of delivery of traditional lending service to users in growing cities and to dispersed populations in rural areas. Extension techniques were further developed to respond to the needs of special populations such as the visually handicapped, the homebound, and the economically disadvantaged. In the 1980s the concept of library extension took on additional new meaning as library uses of computers and improved telecommunications were employed to meet the demands of increasingly sophisticated information users.

Branch Libraries. Strategically located branch libraries form the network through which traditional library services have been most effectively extended in major city and suburban areas. The services of each branch library in the network are designed to meet the cultural and information needs of the people in the neighborhood. The cultural background of the branch's staff and other factors that affect the staff's ability to relate to users in the community should be strong considerations in the branch's design.

A branch network may be organized around a large central library, or the system may be composed entirely of relatively strong branches with central support functions performed in an administrative center or in one or more of the individual branches. There are advantages for users in having at least one library in a system where they can have access to a comprehensive materials collection and reference service; this encourages a system organization comprised of a central library with carefully planned branch locations. While such a system will have special adult collections and specialized reference services centralized, basic adult services will continue to be a feature in the branch program. Children's and young adult services are likely to be emphasized in the branch locations convenient to the younger users, who are less likely to be able to travel to the central library.

The ideal branch location would be a carefully designed, permanent library building with convenient patron access, ample parking, on a well-selected site. As this ideal is frequently not achievable, there have been relatively successful branch locations in storefront buildings originally designed for uses other than as libraries, in portable buildings designed for library service but movable as changing demographics require, and even in accessible, visible areas of operating businesses or in shopping malls where pedestrian traffic is high. A branch emphasizing reference information service as well as lending may be supported with terminals for computer communications with the central library and with other specialized information sources.

The service area of a branch is usually defined geographically, but it may also be identified as the center for a special subject or service emphasis. Each branch will rely upon the support services of a central library or administrative center, but there should also be the capability for communication and exchange of materials between branches. Thus effective communications and courier service are important to the successful operation of a branch system. These features must be added to the administrative, staff development, facility maintenance, technical service, public service, and public relations responsibilities that are basic components of any individual library's operation. The complete effectiveness of extension through a branch network will depend upon the integration of all branches with these basic support services.

Service extension through branch libraries is also characteristic of large colleges and universities and school districts. The outlying libraries may operate under a designation other than "branch," but the basic service objective and many of the support service relationships are the same as those that occur among the units of a city or suburban library system. The important differences are primarily in the background and training of staff and in the specialized nature of the information resources and services maintained for the special clientele.

Mobile Services. Librarians motivated by their concern to provide service to citizens without access to central or branch libraries have devised an interesting variety of delivery methods.

The bookmobile, with a one-person or several-person staff, carrying a few hundred volumes or several thousand, has proven to be an effective means of delivering materials for loans to areas where a complete branch library is not affordable. City and suburban library systems have used bookmobile service, with scheduled stops at specified locations, as service test sites, or as a permanent but flexible method of extension. Bookmobile stops can be changed as traffic patterns and demographics change, and in developing suburban areas a bookmobile can provide service until the installation of a branch can be justified. Bookmobile service has been used as a principal form of extension for large rural areas. In riverine areas, the bookmobile may be a boat, rather than a wheeled vehicle.

A bookmobile has the advantage of being driven to a shopping center, nursing home, community center, or other location convenient to groups of users. Over a period of time, its staff can learn and supply materials for the personal interests of those who consistently visit the bookmobile at its various stops. Books for study and popular reading are the materials most frequently supplied, but requests for special-interest materials such as recorded music, videocassettes, or talking books are not unusual. The staff may also provide limited reference services or convey patron requests back to central reference staff, who can then respond to the patron by telephone or mail, or through the bookmobile staff at the next scheduled visit.

The bookmobile can also be used for the delivery of special programs for neighborhood children. Librarians have shown much creativity in the development of bookmobile story hours, puppet plays, exhibits, and other interest-generating outreach programs. In some jurisdictions a bookmobile and its staff have served as a voter-registration site.

An effective bookmobile operation is complex because it requires all of the basic support services from the administrative center and, in addition, vehicle maintenance, facilities for the exchange and loading of materials, a specially trained staff, and a process of public relations and communications with the administrators of the sites visited. A special electrical supply may be required at each stop if the vehicle is not equipped with an onboard generator. The bookmobile staff must maintain intense awareness for the safety of all users around the vehicle.

Other less frequently used forms of mobile service include rotating book collections and deposit book collections. Rotating collections are a support for small community libraries provided by a library system or cooperative. A rotating service librarian using a truck or van moves collections of books from one community library to the next on a specified schedule and in a regular sequence until the individual collections have been held for the deposit period in all libraries of the cooperative. The rotating service van usually carries new materials for the librarian to add to the individual collections as they are left at each community library. Books still on loan to patrons at the collection change date are placed in the collection on hand as they are returned to the library.

In an alternative form of extension, a rural library cooperative may maintain a central collection from which deposit collections of a few dozen to several hundred titles may be selected by community librarians participating in the cooperative. The deposit collection is held at the borrowing library for a period of several months to supplement the small library, until the deposit collection is returned and exchanged for another deposit. The objective of rotating book service or deposit collections is to give a small community library a variety of library materials it otherwise could not afford to buy and that may not have lasting value to the small population of users. In extension to a community without a library, system staff may place a deposit collection in a store or other business where it will be visible and where a volunteer will be on hand at least part-time to process loans from the collection.

Librarians use whatever affordable systems are at hand for the delivery of service. An example of determination to provide service is shown by the airplane delivery used by the State Library of Alaska to reach outlying areas.

Books by Mail and Telephone. As extension service has been developed to reach widely dispersed populations in rural areas, it has become common practice to use the mail and the telephone to receive requests from users and to deliver books and other forms of information in response to those requests. It is not unusual for materials to be loaned through the mail with only minimal lending records and circulation control.

Books-by-Mail is a lending service to rural families, people in institutions, and the homebound based upon a "department store catalogue" approach to merchandising. A family or individual receives a catalogue of books with a brief description of each item available for loan. A request card in the catalogue is used to mail in the book request. The central library packages the book or books requested in a protective mailer, includes a return mailing label and perhaps promotional information about available library services, and then sends the package to the borrower; books are usually returned by mail in the same mailer. Attractive catalogues for this service and related book collections and mailing supplies are available from commercial library suppliers, or, with considerable effort, can be produced locally.

Dial-A-Book and Dial-A-Fact have also been formalized as extension services. Dial-A-Book is more likely to be used in rural service extension where a library or library system is willing to receive an information request by telephone and then respond to that request with a book or other material sent to the borrower by mail along with a return mailing label. Dial-A-Fact is an extension of reference information service by telephone; it allows a patron to call the library for needed statistics, bibliographic information, recipes, or other forms of factual information. Availability of call-in reference service of this kind has come to be a standard and well-used service in many types of libraries.

Special Populations. The extension service best known in the U.S. is the recorded book and braille book distribution program of the National Library Service for the Blind and Physically Handicapped, Library of Congress, popularly known as the Talking Book Service. The National Library Service, working with state and local libraries throughout the U.S., has operated an effective extension service to visually and physically handicapped users that has also served as a model for other forms of library service extension. The materials of this program are identified to users in large print and on recorded catalogues. Requests for materials are received from users by telephone and mail. Materials and the special equipment to use them are supplied to the user by mail or by personal delivery by a librarian or trained volunteer.

Extension service by personal delivery can also be effective in reaching homebound individuals who are elderly, temporarily ill, or physically handicapped or who for other reasons have limited mobility. It is not unusual for a public library to have a well-organized group of trained volunteers, or of assigned library staff, to give personalized extension service to the homebound or to individuals in institutions.

New Technology and Library Extension. As the uses of microcomputers and other computer systems in homes and libraries become commonplace, it is inevitable that these technologies, supported by improved telecommunications, will influence the traditional approaches to library service extension. Communication with online library catalogues is available for personal computer users at home and in offices over telephone lines. Full-text databases of reference and research information are available online to more and more home users and others away from the library, as well as to users at the library.

There has been experimentation in the provision of full-text video from the library to home users, in support of reference information service. Improvements in local mass data storage, such as databases on CD-ROM, will allow large files of bibliographic or textual information to be loaned by mail in disk or cassette units for use at home on personal computers.

All of these refinements in new information technology indicate that information users will see a growing capability to use library resources from remote locations. Librarians and the library's extension services will be important participants in these new, developing information systems.

REFERENCES

Eleanor F. Brown, *Modern Branch Libraries and Libraries in Systems* (1970).

Laura M. Janzow, editor, *The Library Without Walls, Reprints of Papers and Addresses* (1927). With its interesting and extensive collection of articles, this volume is possibly the earliest to gather together the varied concepts in library service extension.

Carleton B. Joeckel, editor, *Reaching Readers: Techniques of Extending Library Services* (1949).

Robert T. Jordan, *Tomorrow's Library: Direct Access and Delivery* (1970).

DUANE F. JOHNSON

Ferguson, Sir John Alexander
(1881–1969)

Sir John Alexander Ferguson, bibliographer and book collector, compiled the great *Bibliography of Australia 1784–1900.* The *Bibliography* is an important tool of the historian, the book collector, the librarian, and the dealer in rare and out-of-print books. Ferguson was by training a lawyer and industrial court judge.

Ferguson was born in Invercargill, New Zealand, December 15, 1881. His family went to Australia when his father was appointed as minister to Saint Stephen's Church in Sydney. Attending William Street Superior Public School and later studying with a private tutor, Ferguson matriculated to the University of Sydney and earned a B.A. with First Class Honours and the University Medal in Logic and Mental Philosophy. In his law school he earned the George Wigram Allen scholarship for most distinguished arts graduate entering the school and later was awarded the Pitt Cobbet Prize for international law.

Admitted to the Bar on May 27, 1905, he practiced first in equity and continued in that jurisdiction despite a developing and important practice in industrial law. By the early 1930s he was regarded as the leading barrister in the industrial jurisdiction in New South Wales and was appointed Lecturer in Industrial Law at the University of Sydney. In 1936 he was elevated to the bench of the Industrial Commission of New South Wales. During the 17 years before his retirement he made an important contribution to the industrial affairs of his state.

Early in life Ferguson began to collect and to describe materials relating to Australia, New Zealand, and the Pacific Islands, regarding collection and description as complementary activities. His personal and scholarly interests found emphasis in collections on bibliography, law, imaginative literature, social reform, military history, church affairs, the mission fields, and publishing. The influence of his father and his own lifelong association with the church led to a collecting interest in the church and missions in the Pacific areas and to the development of one of the most comprehensive collections of its vernacular publications. His *Bibliography of the New Hebrides* appeared in three parts between 1917 and 1945.

Ferguson set aside a number of other bibliographical compilations to devote himself to the *Bibliography of Australia 1784–1900,* the first volume of which appeared in 1941; his work on the seventh and final volume continued, despite frailty of health, into his 80th year, the checking of the proofs completed just a week or so before his death.

As a bibliographer and collector, Ferguson saw his primary purpose to be the service of scholarship and research. Neither vanity nor greed led him to depart from a rational attitude to collecting by purchasing unique items at outrageous prices; his object was not to ornament his collection with priceless gems but to gather a substantial body of material of value for research.

As early as 1909 Ferguson had begun a relationship with the National Library that continued throughout his life. In 1937 he made the first transfer to the Library of part of his collection: "newspapers and periodicals illustrating the growth of all forms of political, social, economic and industrial thought in the Commonwealth." Further transfers included a large group of pamphlets in the same subject area, his "sociological pamphlets," arranged in the chronological order that he regarded as being of great importance. The collection finally totaled some 34,000 items; even with continuing transfers of other subject groups, there was still a considerable amount in his home in Sydney at his death on May 7, 1969. The Library purchased it from the Ferguson Estate and some time later, in 1975, acquired the copyright of the *Bibliography of Australia,* of which it published a new edition between 1975 and 1977. The Ferguson Room in the National Library is named in his honor.

Ferguson served from 1935 to 1965 as a Trustee of the Public Library of New South Wales. His university honored him in 1955 with the degree of Doctor of Letters, and in 1961 he was knighted for services to Australian literature, bibliography, and history.

C. A. BURMESTER

National Library of Australia

Sir John Alexander Ferguson

Fiji

Fiji comprises more than 320 islands in the South Pacific Ocean. It lies approximately 3,200 km. east of Australia and 5,200 km. south of Hawaii. Population (1990 est.) 765,000; area 18,274 sq.km. Fiji gained its independence from Great Britain in 1970 and became a republic in 1987. The official language is English, but Fijian, Hindi, and Chinese are commonly spoken and are the primary languages at village level.

History. Missionaries established the first libraries as early as 1855. British sugar interests established Fiji's first lending libraries on a subscription basis. The Ramakrishna Library at Nadi, founded in 1928, and Suva's Carnegie Library provided the islands' major source of reading materials for many years. During the period 1944–65, reports, plans, and proposals for national library schemes were put forward, but little positive action resulted. After that, development was erratic and generally short-lived. Proposals for restructuring special libraries were left in abeyance; school libraries did not receive the attention they deserve; public libraries, the responsibility of the Library Service of Fiji (LSF), pushed on regardless, with the town councils assisting in limited ways; the academic and tertiary institution libraries, especially the University of the South Pacific Library, forged ahead; but still there is no national library plan.

National Library Service. The LSF was established in 1964 and is currently a department of the Ministry of Education, Youth, and Sport. It moved from one ministry to another four times in its first 25 years. The LSF operates public branches in all the major towns, two bookmobiles, postal loan services, and a book box service. A restructuring in 1987 made the LSF fully responsible for school libraries and departmental or special libraries.

Academic Libraries. The University of the South Pacific (USP), established in 1968, is the only university in Fiji. It is based in Suva, the capital, and has the largest library in Fiji. A new library of 6,500 square meters and seating capacity for 600 readers opened in May 1988. The library houses 320,000 volumes, 13,405 current periodicals, 5,000 maps, 6,000 microforms, a special Pacific collection with 40,000 volumes, and a Pacific music archive with 4,800 tapes. The Library is computerized and uses the

Libraries in Fiji (1989)

Type	Administrative units	Service points	Volumes in collections	Annual expenditures (Fiji dollar)	Population served	Professional staff	Total staff
Academic	8	5	443,000	400,000[a]	10,000[b]	19	70
Public	13	13	190,000	30,000[a]	40,000[b]	3	33
School	500	--	300,000	125,000[a]	--	2	50
Special	120	60[b]	100,000	--	1,200[b]	4	20
Media units	25	25	10,000	--	--	1	--

[a]Acquisitions only.

[b]Estimate.

Source: *Fiji Library Association Newsletter 1989–90;* Annual reports of libraries for 1989

URICA library automated system. The University Library cooperates with other tertiary institutions in Fiji which have smaller collections, including the Fiji School of Agriculture (25,000 volumes), Fiji Institute of Technology (20,000), Pacific Theological College (20,000), Pacific Regional Seminary (15,000), Fiji School of Medicine (12,000), Fiji School of Nursing (5,000), and Lautoka Teachers College (5,000).

Public Libraries. The main libraries are the Western Regional Library (150,000 volumes), Suva City Library (40,000), Labasa Town Council Library (8,000), Nadi Town Council Library (6,000), and Levuka Community Center (4,000). After 1980 small public library collections were established with the support of the LSF and the town councils and the assistance of trained paraprofessional librarians.

School Libraries. The Library Service of Fiji is responsible for developing school libraries. It provides an advisory service to schools for design and planning and conducts workshops for teacher-librarians with the aim of incorporating library and information services into the curriculum. In the late 1980s there were 681 primary schools and 141 secondary schools in Fiji, some with good libraries, others with classroom or cupboard libraries, and some with no libraries at all. LSF provides reading materials for these schools as best it can. Access to libraries is especially limited for rural students. LSF has established 25 media centers in the rural areas to alleviate this problem to some degree.

Special Libraries. The number of special libraries has increased since the mid-1980s as a direct result of a growing awareness of the importance of libraries and information to national development and good decision making. Fiji has about 120 special libraries in various stages of development. A few that have developed good collections and offer good services include the Ministry of Primary Industry Information Unit, Fiji Fisheries (6,000 volumes), Mineral Resources Library, Fiji National Training Council Library, Ministry of Energy Library, and Economic Planning Library. The Reserve Bank of Fiji, United Nations offices based in Suva, and various embassies also have libraries.

Main section of the sprawling University of the South Pacific Library, Fiji's largest library, opened in 1988.

Training. The USP Library offers a Certificate in Librarianship, a distance learning course, and, beginning in 1990, a Diploma in Library and Information Studies. In the 1980s, 91 students received the certificate and took jobs in libraries in Fiji and other countries in the South Pacific.

The Profession. The Fiji Library Association (FLA) was founded in 1972. Its membership stood at 155 in the late 1980s, including 35 school librarians. The FLA organizes workshops as well as its annual National Library Week and convention. It also has an active publishing program.

ESTHER BATIRI WILLIAMS

Finland

Finland, a republic in northern Europe, is bounded by Norway on the north, Russia on the east, and the Gulf of Bothnia and Sweden on the west. Population (1990 est.) 4,902,000; area 338,127 sq.km. The official languages are Finnish and Swedish.

History. Finland's geopolitical site between East and West, Russia and Sweden, has strongly influenced its culture. In the 12th century people were baptized into the Roman Catholic faith by the Swedes, and the country became a Swedish province. In 1810, as a result of the Russo-Swedish War, Finland was made into a Grand Duchy of the Russian Empire, and in 1917 it became independent: a Western-European democracy with a President and a Diet with 200 members.

Accordingly, the history of Finnish libraries and librarianship can be divided into three periods: from the Middle Ages to the 1820s, from the 1820s to 1917, and from 1917 onward.

The first library established in Finland was the library of Turku Academy, the first university in the

Libraries in Finland (1987)

Type of library	Number of administrative units (main libraries)	Number of service points (branches, mobile stops, etc.)	Volumes in collections	Annual expenditures (markka)	Population served	Professional staff (with certificate, diploma, etc.)	Total staff
National	1	--	1,996,000	19,896,000FIM	--	57	126
Academic	20	--	13,301,100	153,546,000	--	235	485
Public	1,265	824	31,579,846	799,340,000	4,902,125	3,622	5,104
School	--	--	--	--	--	--	--
Special	26	--	2,261,400	36,373,700	--	117	215

country, founded in 1640. There were book collections in the churches, schools, and monasteries before that time, but they were modest in size. The academy library grew slowly, but, thanks to donations and deposit copies, it had a collection of about 3,500 volumes by the middle of the 18th century. The most important librarian was Henrik Gabriel Porthan (1739–1804), a prominent scholar, who also introduced the idea of a national "Fennica" collection. The library grew to 40,000 volumes, and it was a great loss when the collections were almost totally destroyed in the Great Fire of Turku in 1827.

When Finland became a Grand Duchy, Helsinki was made the capital of the country and the university was moved there. It was given many more resources than before, such as new buildings in the heart of the city. Even the university library received a building of its own. Designed by Carl Ludwig Engel, it is considered one of the most representative neoclassical buildings in the country. The Chief Librarian, Fredrik Wilhelm Pipping (1783–1868), worked hard to reestablish and organize the collections, which grew quickly thanks to liberal gifts and allowances. In 1844, when the new building was ready, there were more than 50,000 volumes, and in 1857 about 100,000.

By the beginning of the 20th century the building was too crowded, and an annex was built. Other scientific libraries were formed in the 19th century, mainly to serve the publishing and exchange activities of the scientific societies, and new institutions of higher education, such as the Institute of Technology (Helsinki Technical School), founded in 1849.

The public library movement in Finland started in the middle of the 19th century on the initiatives of the clergy and the students and was linked with nationalistic ideas and achievements. The beginning of Finnish literature dates from the period of the Lutheran reformation, when the first books were printed in the vernacular. The educational system was part of the church, and the clergy played a central role in the spread of reading. During the Swedish regime, however, Finnish book production was small: only about 1,500 titles altogether. The main language was Swedish; Finnish gained its leading position toward the end of the 19th century. At that time almost the total population was literate: 97.9 percent in 1890, thanks to the public school system, which was established by the Public Education Decree in 1866.

When the country became independent, the educational level was significantly raised. New schools and universities were founded, statutes governing compulsory education were issued, and in 1921 public libraries began to receive regular government aid.

World War II interrupted the development, but in the later 1940s and the 1950s a new boom took place. More resources were given to the libraries and several new library buildings were designed and constructed. The most important example of Finnish library architecture, Viipuri Public Library, designed by Alvar Aalto and built in the late 1930s, was surrendered, however, to the Soviet Union.

A new Library Law was passed in 1962, supporting small libraries and libraries in institutions in particular, and one in 1986, dealing with new information and communications technology. These laws, however, cover only public libraries.

Most academic and special libraries are parts of other organizations. Their development is mainly the result of so many new universities being founded after World War II and of international information networks that have been established.

National Library. The National Library of Finland is the Helsinki University Library, established in 1640 in Turku as the Turku Academy Library and transferred to Helsinki in 1828 together with the Academy, which then became the Helsinki University. Its tasks include those of a national library and of a general research library. It collects all publications printed in Finland and publications written by Finns or dealing with Finland but published elsewhere, in addition to foreign literature for the study and research needs of Helsinki University. It also collects manu-

Töölö branch of the Helsinki City Library, designed by Aarne Ervi, opened in 1970.

Töölö Library

scripts dealing with Finnish cultural history and compiles the Finnish national bibliography and the union catalogue of Finnish research and university libraries. It receives publications on legal deposit and distributes them to other libraries. Among its resources is a special collection of Slavonic literature, started in 1820 when Finland became a grand duchy of Russia and the library received deposit copies of publications printed in that country. The library's holdings totaled 1,996,000 in 1987, making it not only the oldest but also the largest library in Finland.

The National Archives of Finland, with a total staff of 83, of whom 37 are professional, includes seven Provincial Archives. Holdings in 1987 occupied some 37,183 linear meters of shelving, and annual expenditures were about 1,296,500 Finnmarks.

Academic Libraries. There are 20 academic libraries in Finland, a great number for a small country. Helsinki University was the only university until 1919, when Åbo Akademi, a Swedish university, was founded in Turku. Two years later a Finnish university was also founded in Turku. From their beginnings they were both remarkable, with national as well as foreign collections. In 1987, there were 1,713,500 volumes in Turku University Library and 1,401,000 volumes in the Åbo Akademi Library.

The first technical library in Finland was founded in 1849 in the Helsinki Technical School; it later became the Helsinki Technical University, and its library had a collection of 912,700 volumes in 1987. The Helsinki School of Economics Library was founded in 1911; it had 237,200 volumes in 1987.

After World War II several institutions of higher education were founded, among them the universities of Jyväskylä, Oulu, and Tampere. Only the Oulu University was actually a new institution; in Jyväskylä the Teachers' College was made into a university, and Tampere got a university when the School of Social Sciences was transferred from Helsinki and later became a university. In 1987 the Jyväskylä University Library had a collection of 1,050,900 volumes, the Oulu University Library 1,189,900 volumes, and the Tampere University Library about 912,700. These universities and other academic institutions worked together with special libraries to provide new forms of information service, and some function as central libraries in their respective fields under a Cabinet Statute of 1972. In the early 1990s the academic and some special libraries will join an integrated automatic system (VTLS).

A special feature in the history of Finnish academic libraries was the student libraries. The student unions established libraries of their own; some of them, such as the Library of the Student Body of Helsinki University, were quite remarkable. Founded in 1858, it had its own building and a collection of 200,000 volumes when in 1974 it became a part of the Helsinki University Library. The student libraries have merged with university libraries.

Public Libraries. The oldest public library in Finland is the library of the Regina School in Anjala, established in 1804. Its collection is now in a museum at the Central Board of Schools, where the government office for public libraries is housed. Public libraries, in the true sense of the word, came into being in the middle of the 19th century through the initiative of students and clergy. From the beginning public libraries were local municipal institutions, and state aid was not given to them until 1921. The State Library Bureau was set up with Helle Kannila (1896–1972) as its energetic and effective Director, and a group of library inspectors was elected to direct library activities. The first Public Library Act was passed in 1928 and the second in 1962, giving strong support to rural municipalities and to libraries in hospitals and social institutions. The second act also made it possible to found central regional libraries, whose main task is to serve as interlibrary lending centers, borrowing material from research and university libraries for the public libraries. Many small public libraries have been replaced by bookmobiles; thus the number of public libraries was 4,007 in 1960 and 2,903 in 1970, while the number of home loans was 15,300,000 in 1960 and 32,400,000 in 1970. There were 1,265 public libraries in 1987. Public libraries in Finland have taken on the functions of cultural centers, arranging, for example, for concerts, exhibitions, and puppet theater performances.

School Libraries. There is no organized system of school libraries in Finland, although school libraries were included in plans for a comprehensive school system; these plans had not been totally carried out by the late 1980s.

Special Libraries. The oldest special libraries in Finland were the libraries of the scientific societies, founded in the early and middle 19th century. Most special libraries are now part of private firms and institutions. Typical of their activity are information service and documentation; documentation started in Finland in the 1940s in industrial libraries, where the first documentalists were engineers. Among Finland's special libraries are such large libraries as the Parliament Library, founded in 1872 and having a collection of 521,400 volumes, and the remarkable Central Medical Library, established in 1966 and holding some 300,000 volumes. Most of the special libraries are small, however, forming a part of bigger organizations. Several of these libraries belong to an international information network and compile special bibliographies in their fields.

The Profession. The Finnish Library Association dates back to 1910; it publishes a Finnish library journal, *Kirjastolehti*. The Finnish Research Library Association dates from 1929; it publishes the journal *Signum*. The Finnish Association for Documentation (1948) also has a journal, *Tietopalvelu*. All three associations arrange meetings, seminars, and courses; national meetings of librarians are held every second year. There are other associations in the field of librarianship and documentation, including professional unions.

Financed by funds from a private cultural foundation, the first professional course in librarianship was organized in 1920. When the State Library Bureau was founded, it took upon itself the responsibility for training librarians. In 1945 the professional education of librarians was started on a regular basis at the School of Social Sciences, later Tampere University, where a course leading to a librarian's certificate was included in the curriculum. It was valid for service in all public libraries and in most scientific libraries. At the Helsinki University Library an Amanuensis Examination was arranged as early as the beginning of the 20th century; later it was also offered at other academic libraries.

In 1971 a remarkable change took place: a professorship of library and information science was founded in the Faculty of Social Sciences at Tampere University, and thereafter it was possible to include library and information science in programs leading to Master's and Doctor's degrees. In 1982 another professorship, at the Swedish University of Turku, Åbo Akademi, was established; the training of librarians for the Swedish-speaking minority takes place there. A third professorship was established in 1988 at Oulu University.

Continuing education is partly organized by the Finnish Library Association, the Finnish Research Library Association, the Finnish Association for Documentation, and other library associations. Centers for continuing education at Tampere University and Helsinki Technical University also offer courses for librarians; the latter is responsible for the training of information scientists for libraries, information services, and various posts in industry, business, and administration. In spite of the many-sided supply of courses and degrees in librarianship, many libraries were without professional staff in the late 1980s, legislative support lagged, and libraries were still in many cases seen as little more than book depositories. Modern methods of information service have not been easily accepted.

RITVA SIEVÄNEN-ALLEN

Folger, Henry Clay
(1857–1930)

Henry Clay Folger, U.S. businessman who headed Standard Oil Company of New York, was one of the great book collectors of the late 19th and early 20th centuries. With invaluable assistance from his wife, he brought together a remarkable collection of books, manuscripts, art objects, and other materials relating to Shakespeare, his works, and his age. Folger and his wife founded the Folger Shakespeare Library in Washington, D.C., to house their collection and to make it accessible to an international community of researchers.

Folger belonged to a family with distinguished American antecedents. Peter Folger, the first of the name to settle in America, emigrated from England and settled on Nantucket Island in 1635; his daughter was the mother of Benjamin Franklin. Several generations later another descendant, Charles James Folger, served President Chester Arthur as Secretary of the Treasury. Henry Folger's father was a resident of New York City who built up a prosperous wholesale millinery business and sent his son to grammar and high school in the New York area.

Folger entered Amherst College in 1875. For a time his continuation at Amherst was threatened by his father's financial reverses, but timely loans from two classmates permitted him to complete his course of studies there, and he graduated in 1879. A career in business seemed tempting; with the help of his college roommate, Charles Pratt, whose father headed one of the affiliates of Standard Oil, Folger accepted a clerkship in the company. He also enrolled in the Columbia University Law School and two years later obtained an LL.B. degree. A steady climb up the corporate ladder rewarded Folger for his shrewd business sense and industrious dedication to the growth of the company. He became President of Standard Oil of New York and held that post until 1923, when he was made Chairman of the Board. He retired from active involvement in the company in 1928.

Despite his corporate responsibilities, Henry Folger retained a keen interest in the world of letters. The published address by Ralph Waldo Emerson on the "Tercentenary of Shakespeare's Birth," which Folger had read as an undergraduate, fired him with an enthusiastic appreciation for Shakespeare that never waned. Indeed, his marriage to Emily Clara Jordan intensified it. She was a Vassar graduate who went on to graduate school after her marriage and wrote a Master of Arts thesis on "The True Text of Shakespeare."

Their shared interest in Shakespeare led the Folgers quite early into book collecting. They started in 1885 with a relatively cheap facsimile of the 1623 First Folio edition of Shakespeare's works, and their pursuit of Shakespeareana accelerated as their financial means to satisfy their hobby increased. Soon they were combing bookshops on both sides of the Atlantic. Rare quarto editions of Shakespeare's plays and the first folio edition of his collected works were those most sought by the Folgers, but they also looked for later editions of the plays and materials reflecting Shakespeare production down to modern times, including printed texts, promptbooks, playbills, paintings and illustrations, costumes, and memorabilia of all sorts. They wisely realized that Shakespeare could best be understood in the context of the times in which he lived; they purchased books that reveal the sources for plots and ideas contained in his plays, the works of his contemporaries in the literary world, and a wide spectrum of rare books and manuscripts depicting the society of Elizabethan and Jacobean England and, more generally, Western Europe and America in the early modern period.

Folger Shakespeare Library
Henry Clay Folger

The Folgers amassed a collection of some 93,000 books, 50,000 prints and engravings, and thousands of manuscripts that, for lack of space, they carefully inventoried and then stored in bank vaults and warehouses. Shortly after World War I they determined to unite their collection in a library dedicated to Shakespeare. The site they selected in Washington, D.C., was directly across from the Library of Congress, whose resources they knew would enhance the value of their own Library. The cornerstone for their Library was laid May 28, 1930. Two weeks later, on June 11, Folger died in Brooklyn, New York.

Mrs. Folger was present for the opening of the Library on April 23, 1932, and she was involved closely with its operation until her death in 1936. Under the terms of Folger's will the administration of the Library was entrusted to the Trustees of Amherst College. Folger and his wife left the bulk of their estates to serve as endowment to defray the operating costs of their Library.

Following the lines laid out by its founders, the Folger Shakespeare Library has become an international center for the study of Shakespeare and of the Renaissance and early modern period. The Library's exhibition gallery attracts thousands of visitors each year to view items from the original Folger Collection as well as many later acquisitions. An Elizabethan theater, which is an integral part of the Library, provides thousands more with an opportunity to enjoy theatrical productions both Shakespearean and modern, concerts of Renaissance music, lectures, and conferences.

REFERENCE

Betty Ann Kane, *The Widening Circle— The Story of the Folger Shakespeare Library and Its Collections* (Folger Library, 1976).

PHILIP A. KNACHEL

Food and Agriculture Organization

The Food and Agriculture Organization of the United Nations is an autonomous agency of the UN. It is made up of member nations pledged to raising the levels of nutrition and standards of living of their peoples, to improving the production and distribution of all food and agricultural products, and to improving the condition of rural people. FAO functions simultaneously as a development agency, an information center, an adviser to governments, and a continuing forum for the discussion of food and agriculture issues.

Established in October 1945 at a conference in Quebec, Canada, FAO has headquarters in Rome. It established regional offices for Africa in Accra, Ghana; for Asia and the Pacific in Bangkok, Thailand; for Europe in Rome; for Latin America and the Caribbean in Santiago, Chile; and for the Near East in Rome. There is an FAO Liaison Office for North America in Washington, D.C., and a Liaison Office with the UN in New York.

The work of the organization is conducted by an international Secretariat under the leadership of a Director-General. The supreme governing body is the Conference, which meets every two years and elects as an interim governing body a Council of 49 member nations.

As a development agency, the FAO gives direct help in the developing world through technical assistance projects in all areas of food and agriculture. These projects strengthen local institutions, assist research and training, and develop and demonstrate new techniques. The technical assistance projects are financed chiefly by the UN Development Program and trust funds of national governments.

Investment in agriculture is covered by FAO's Investment Support Program, which helps developing countries find the external capital needed to build up their agriculture. The World Bank is the single most important financing institution for investment projects prepared by FAO.

As a focal point for world agriculture, FAO serves as a clearinghouse for information and makes it available in almost every medium: print, film, radio and TV, video, filmstrips, and computer tapes. It acts as the coordinating center for the Worldwide Network of Agricultural Libraries (AGLINET), an international cooperative that ensures the availability of global information not held by participating libraries.

Major periodical publications include yearbooks on world production, trade, fertilizers, forest products, and fishery statistics. Others include reports on world food supply, commodity reviews, and the *FAO Plant Protection Bulletin* and *FAO Monthly Bulletin of Statistics. Ideas and Action* is a publication of the Freedom from Hunger/Action for Development program.

Major databases and systems include AGRIS (International Information System for the Agricultural Sciences and Technology), a bibliographic database online in the U.S. since 1985 (also used to produce the monthly bibliography *AGRINDEX*); CARIS (Current Agricultural Research Information System), data on current research projects; ICS (Interlinked Computer Storage and Processing System of Food and Agricultural Commodity Data); ASFIS (Aquatic Sciences and Fisheries Information System); FISHDAB (Fisheries Database); and FORIS (Forest Resources Information System).

JOHN B. FORBES

Force, Peter

(1790–1868)

Courtesy of The Newberry Library

Peter Force

Peter Force compiled historical documents and was a bibliophile and collector, printer, editor, bibliographer, librarian, and archivist. An American, he created research tools that became models for subsequent generations.

Force was born near Little Falls, Essex County, New Jersey, November 26, 1790. His family moved several times before settling in New York City in 1794, where he received limited schooling. Early in his teens he became an apprentice in the printing business of William A. Davis and assumed the responsibilities of printshop foreman at about the age of 16. The New York Typographical Society elected him its President in 1812. He won a militia commission during the War of 1812 and served as marshal of printers.

Force moved to Washington, D.C., in 1815, when Davis secured a government printing contract, and they operated a lending library of more than 3,000 volumes out of their printery until debts compelled them to sell the books in 1825. From 1823 to 1831 Force published a newspaper, the *National Journal,* aligned with Adams's administration. A Whig, Force participated in District of Columbia politics, sitting on the city council and winning the mayorality for two terms (1836–40). He also edited directories of government personnel, commercial statistics, and historical data intermittently from 1820 to 1836. His industriousness notwithstanding, creditors in 1830 nearly seized his property, which already included another substantial library.

Financial motives, along with a genuine veneration of America's past, inspired Force to propose in 1831 publishing for the federal government a multivolume compilation of historical documents. The idea was not original, but Force and his partner, Clerk of the House Matthew St. Clair Clarke, promised unprecedented thoroughness. Congress authorized the project in 1833. Sadly, the lucrative contract left unclear the exact scope and cost of the work and the *American Archives,* as it became known, thus suffered repeated attacks by the frugal as well as by the politically antipathetic.

Force supervised researchers and dealers dispersed through the 13 original states and England in transcribing or purchasing pamphlets, books, newspapers, maps, government documents, and manuscripts. His preference for printed sources may reflect his lack of scholarly training. His eye for ephemeral pieces, however, preserved a number of texts from historical oblivion. Copyists received instructions on careful handling of archival materials that were exemplary for their time. Publication commenced in 1837; showing a canny sense of patriotic appeal, Force started with the fourth and fifth series (covering 1774–76) of the six (1492–1787) he scheduled to complete the work. In 1853 the Democrats deprived the Whigs of the presidency, and Secretary of State William L. Marcy refused to approve the contents of the next two volumes, and subsequent changes of administration failed to revive the *American Archives.* Truncation of the project left Force holding a huge collection of rare Americana, with obligations to match.

Even in its abbreviated form the *American Archives* was an impressive undertaking. Major bibliographies on colonial America still cite its more than 16,000 folio pages as a basic resource. Historians also continue to use Force's *Tract and Other Papers Relating . . . to . . . the Colonies of North America* (1836–46). This four-volume work reproduced 52 pamphlets, some of which Force had already reprinted separately. Most were 17th-century London imprints, scarce even by 1836, when the *Tracts* began to appear. The set reveals Force's personal bibliophilic leanings better than the *American Archives.* "Whenever I found a little more money in my purse than I absolutely needed," he later recalled, "I printed a volume of Tracts."

Loss of income from the *American Archives* transformed Force's matchless collection into a passion he could ill afford during the last 15 years of his life. Librarian of Congress Ainsworth R. Spofford for years visited the reclusive old man, surrounded in his Washington residence by crude tables and shelves bearing his treasures. Spofford and others yearned to relieve the owner of them; Force finally agreed for a price of $100,000. The New-York Historical Society could not raise the sum, but Spofford managed with difficulty to extract the money from a wartime Congress. So the "Force Library" in 1867 became a primary foundation for future development of Americana holdings at the Library of Congress. Force died less than a year after the collection left his home, on January 23, 1868, in Washington, D. C.

Force made several noteworthy contributions to library and archival science. He created research tools that remain useful almost a century and a half later. With Spofford's good offices, he furthered the growth of the Library of Congress. Most importantly, he communicated to a young nation the vitality of his concern about collecting and preserving records of its past. His *American Archives* mark a giant step toward federal recognition of a public responsibility to assist in the dissemination of historical information. Force's publications became models that local governments and historical organizations before long emulated with happy results.

REFERENCES

The main body of Force's personal papers now resides in the Manuscript Division of the Library of Congress.

Newman F. McGirr, compiler, *Bio-Bibliography of Peter Force 1790–1868* (1941).

Ainsworth R. Spofford, "The Life and Labors of Peter Force, Mayor of Washington," *Records of the Columbia Historical Society* (1899).

Richard W. Stephenson, "Maps from the Peter Force Collection," *Quarterly Journal of the Library of Congress* (1973).

DAVID J. MARTZ, JR.

Foskett, D. J.
(1918-)

D. J. Foskett

One of the most prominent figures in contemporary British library and information science, Douglas John Foskett made many, varied, and important contributions to library and information science. Classification was always one of Foskett's major interests, and in 1952 he was one of the founders of the Classification Research Group in Britain. But he proved equally influential in the fields of comparative librarianship and library education and in the development of the Library Association (LA).

Foskett was born in London on June 27, 1918. He had hardly begun his professional career in the Ilford (Essex) Public Libraries when World War II intervened; from 1940 to 1946 he served first in the Royal Army Medical Corps and later in the Intelligence Corps.

In 1948 Foskett left Ilford to become Librarian of the Metal Box Co. Ltd., a post he held until 1957. He served as Librarian of the University of London Institute of Education (1957–78), then was promoted to the position of Director of Central Library Services of the University of London (1978–83). He thus had wide experience in public, special, and academic libraries.

A member of the Council of the Library Association for many years, he was Chairman (1962–63), a Vice-President (1966–73), an Honorary Fellow (1975), and President (1976). A vigorous protagonist for the unity of the profession, he consistently supported the idea of a confederation among the LA, Aslib, the Institute of Information Scientists, and other related bodies. He was for some time Chairman of the LA Education Committee.

Foskett also became an internationalist, undertaking many missions for Unesco and the British Council and traveling on lecture and observation study tours in most parts of the world. From 1968 to 1973 he was a member and rapporteur of Unesco's International Advisory Committee on Libraries, Documentation, and Archives; he was also a consultant on documentation to the International Labour Organisation. In addition he worked on a classification scheme for the European Packaging Federation and was later a committee member of the UNISIST/Unesco and the EUDISED/Council of Europe projects.

An engaging speaker, Foskett served as Visiting Professor at the Universities of Michigan, Ghana, Ibadan, and Iceland and at the Brazilian Institute of Bibliography and Documentation. He made observation tours to Czechoslovakia and the People's Republic of China. Latterly he was courier and leader of many tours to China.

Foskett is a Freeman of the City of London. A prolific writer on library and information topics, he wrote, among other works, *Assistance to Readers in Lending Libraries* (1952), *Information Service in Libraries* (1958), *Classification and Indexing in the Social Sciences* (1963), *Science, Humanism, and Libraries* (1964), *Reader in Comparative Librarianship* (1976), and *Pathways to Communication* (1984). With B. I. Palmer he edited *The Sayers Memorial Volume* (1961).

K. C. HARRISON

France

see also Bibliothèque Nationale

France, a republic in northwestern Europe, is bounded by the English Channel, Belgium, and Luxembourg on the north, Germany, Switzerland, and Italy on the east, the Mediterranean Sea and Spain on the south, and the Bay of Biscay on the west. Population (1990 est.) 56,440,000; area 551,500 sq.km. The official language is French.

History. *Middle Ages.* In France as in other countries of Europe, the first libraries after the Dark Ages were parts of monasteries and reserved for the monks. They were linked to *scriptoria* (copyists' workshops) where manuscripts borrowed from other monasteries were transcribed by hand. Such manual reproduction was the only means by which Latin and Greek texts were brought from classical antiquity to modern times. A scriptorium can still be seen at the Abbey of Cîteaux (Bourgogne). Monastic libraries had very small collections—for example, 300 at Saint Riquier (Somme)—and were housed in single rooms or in wall niches near the *scriptorium*, such as those in Le Thoronet (Var), Silvanès (Aveyron), Luxeuil (Vosges), and Saint Martin de Tours.

From the 13th century, the development of universities led to the creation of university libraries. Each had its own scriptorium. In those libraries, books were kept on lecterns and chained to them. The Sorbonne was one of the largest, with 1,017 books in 1290. The library of the Chapter House in Le Puy (Massif Central) is the last remaining example of this type of library in France. At the same time, private libraries flourished, created by the king, princes, and other noblemen. The kings of France all had private libraries, going back to Charlemagne. Among the princes, the Comte d'Angoulème, for example, had a rich library that was later partly transferred to the king's library.

Naudé and the Bibliothèque Mazarine. When Cardinal Mazarin, Richelieu's successor as first minister of France, arrived in Paris in 1640, he brought with him a personal library of 5,000 volumes that he had collected in Rome. In 1642 he purchased the Hôtel Tubeuf on the corner of the Rue Neuve des Petits Champs and Rue de Richelieu and decided to establish a large library there. To carry out the project he chose Gabriel Naudé (1600–53), who had been Richelieu's Librarian. Naudé was a scholar and a book lover. Although his studies had been in medicine, his career was in books: he was, in turn, the Librarian of Cardinal Bagni, of Cardinal Barberini, and in 1642 of Cardinal Richelieu. After Richelieu's death that same year, Naudé became Mazarin's librarian, buying large collections of books (12,000 volumes and 400 manuscripts) and compiling a catalogue. In 1627 he published *Advis pour dresser une bibliothèque* (Advice on Establishing a Library), in which he put forward the first rules of modern librarianship (a library must be open to all who need it).

The library at the Hôtel Tubeuf (where the Bibliothèque Nationale is now) was opened to the public every Thursday beginning in 1643 and every day beginning in 1647, with 100 readers each open day. Naudé traveled throughout Europe buying for the collection, and Mazarin built several additions to house the 40,000 volumes handsomely bound and emblazoned with his arms.

During the Fronde (civil war, 1648–1653), the collection was dispersed in public sales. Naudé died in 1653. After Mazarin's return to France that year, he rebuilt his library with the help of François Lapoterie, his new Librarian. Mazarin's library was reconstituted and new collections, including Naudé's personal library, were bought. Mazarin, who died in 1661, left his library to the Collège des Quatre Nations, founded, according to his will, for students from four provinces conquered by France; thus began the Bibliothèque Mazarine.

Bibliothèques Communales and Impact of the French Revolution. Before 1789, most French libraries were private. Exceptions included the Bibliothèque Mazarine, the Royal Library, and a few collections of the 13th and 14th centuries, open only to scholars. The municipal library of Grenoble was opened in 1772 thanks to a public subscription, and some noblemen gave their private libraries to towns (including Aix-en-Provence and Carpentras) or academies (such as the one at Bordeaux).

The first network of public libraries was established by the Revolution. Property that had belonged to the aristocracy and to the Church, including numerous libraries, was confiscated; from dispersed private collections, the Revolution made a national patrimony; the libraries thus created became the

Libraries in France (1991)

Type	Administrative units	Service points	Volumes in collections	Annual expenditures (franc)	Population served	Professional staff	Total staff
National	1	15	10,000,000	334,000,000	42,500	467	1,245
Academic	67	195	21,000,000	922,000,000	1,300,000	1,526	3,583
Municipal	1,600	2,500	72,400,000	3,200,000,000	30,594,000	4,577	12,652
Central Lending	96	33,000	15,000,000	350,000,000	27,000,000	672	1,397
Paris	1	57	4,000,000	163,500,000	2,188,918	362	854
School	7,828	6,674	--	--	4,591,000	--	6,971
Special	10,000	10,000	--	--	--	--	25,000

Photopress

University of Grenoble Library.

nucleus of a widespread public library system. Clerical properties were put "at the Nation's disposal" on November 2, 1789, and some months later the property of émigrés and of persons condemned by the Terror was sequestered. In a report to the Convention dated April 11, 1794, the Abbé Grégoire estimated that the confiscations amounted to 10,000,000 books and 26,000 manuscripts. (By comparison, the Royal Library contained 300,000 volumes.)

In order to classify the mass of documents, an inventory had to be taken. Lefèvre d'Ormesson in 1790 put forward the idea of a national union catalogue, so each library would know what the others had. The catalogue was actually written on playing cards. Then a Conservation Committee picked out for sale some of the books on theology, religion, and asceticism. Books not put up for sale were stocked in "literary depots" in Paris and other cities, then divided among existing libraries (the Bibliothèque Nationale received 300,000 volumes). They also served to create new libraries (for example, that of the Assemblée Nationale). The rest was given to central schools newly formed in each département in 1795. When those schools became high schools in 1803, the books were given to the communes, provided that they pay for their maintenance, to create municipal libraries.

But there was a contradiction between the intentions of the authorities and their methods. The Revolutionary project was to set up libraries to serve as "schools for all citizens," but the collections confiscated from the nobility and the Church consisted mainly of works on theology, jurisprudence, and ancient literature—not what was required for popular education. Inertia prevailed, and the public library system that could have come into being did not. A hundred years after the Revolutionary period, many large libraries in France had not been inventoried, and their custodians were concerned more about ensuring the security of their collections than increasing them or opening them to the public. No acquisitions policy came to balance the enormous mass of ancient documents for which the public authorities became responsible. The dominating influence of the past was the most striking feature of French public libraries until the 20th century.

Some private initiatives, however, attempted to encourage reading among the masses. Booksellers organized *Cabinets de lectures* to lend books at nominal annual fees. The bourgeoisie opened *Bibliothèques populaires* to educate the workers and save them from "evil reading."

Bibliothèque Nationale. The Bibliothèque Nationale is an outgrowth of the Royal Library, which dates back to the reign of Charles V (1364–80). Appreciating the manuscript treasures he inherited from his royal ancestors, he put them in the Louvre and appointed a scholar, Gilles Malet, to catalogue them; the first catalogue of the Bibliothèque Nationale is a manuscript dated 1380. The library was dispersed, but was enthusiastically rebuilt by Francis I (reigned 1515–47), who, with the help of his ambassadors (notably in Germany, Venice, and the Middle East), bought numerous manuscripts. He housed them in Blois, then in Fontainebleau, and named Guillaume Budé *Maître de la Librarie du Roy* ("Master of the King's Library"). The King's Library comprised around 2,000 volumes; only 200 were printed books.

Budé's successors continued to buy collections, to receive gifts (for example, that of Gaston de France, duc d'Orléans [1608–1660]), and to seize private libraries, among them the libraries of Nicolas Fouquet (finance minister of Louis XIV, imprisoned for embezzlement), La Vallière (a mistress of Louis XIV who fell into disfavor), and of the Jesuits, who were the object of frequent attacks in France. Nicolas Clément drew up a classification scheme in 1684 that is still in use today. Jean-Paul Bignon separated the collection into five departments in 1720: Manuscripts, Printed Books, Titles and Genealogy, Prints, and Coins. He also opened the King's Library to the public. The library found a permanent home on the Rue de Richelieu in 1743. Bignon published its first catalogue in 1739.

The King's Library possessed 300,000 volumes in 1789. The revolutionary government renamed it the Bibliothèque Nationale. Major improvements in the

Bibliothèque Nationale

Municipal library at Pantin, France.

building and its reading room were made from 1856 to 1868 by the architect Henri Labrouste. A new building in the Rue Vivienne, almost 190,000 sq. ft. of office space, opened in 1985.

The Library is funded through the Ministry of Culture. It also relies on gifts, legacies, and the sale of documents. In 1991 the budget amounted to 334,000,000 French francs, of which 25,000,000 francs were for acquisitions. The staff comprised 1,245 persons, 235 of them professional librarians (*conservateurs*), 232 assistant librarians, and 394 stack attendants.

Legal Deposit. Legal deposit in France stems from Francis I, who in his Montpellier regulation of December 28, 1537, provided that one copy of every book published in France be deposited in the Royal Library to qualify for the King's authorization. A law of June 21, 1943, requires two deposits of printed books. Printers must send two copies to the municipal library in their region, one of which is passed on to the Bibliothèque Nationale; publishers must send four copies to the Bibliothèque Nationale and one to the Ministry of the Interior. Deposit rules for sound recordings were added in 1963, for audiovisual materials in 1975, and for films in 1977. The number of items deposited each year averages 40,000 books, 16,000 brochures, 17,000 official publications, 32,000 serial titles (with 1,700,000 issues), 2,000 maps, 10,000 engravings, 6,000 posters, 2,400 musical works, 1,500 films, 2,000 cassettes, and 15,000 records.

Services. In 1897 the Library began publishing its general catalogue of authors; the final volume was published in 1981. A new catalogue was issued covering the period 1960–1969; the period 1970–1980 was prepared on cards, then converted to machine-readable form for inclusion in the BN database, BN-OPALE. Other catalogues cover manuscripts, maps, engravings, and other materials. In 1921 the Bibliothèque Nationale took over the weekly publication of the *Bibliographie de la France* (1811). This national bibliography became automated in 1975.

Bibliothèque de France. A new era began for the BN in 1988 when François Mitterand, President of the Republic, announced plans to construct "one of the largest and most modern libraries in the world." The architect Dominique Perrault designed a huge structure for a site in Tolbiac, in the eastern part of Paris, providing space for 4,200 seats and stacks for 15 million books in 260,000 square meters. The four main departments of the BN were scheduled to move their collections to Tolbiac in 1995. An open-access public library with 400,000 documents, an audiovisual department, a rare book collection, and a reference department were to be added there.

To prepare for the move, the staff began a number of major projects, including a complete inventory of the BN's collections (the first since 1945), an automated circulation system, a national union catalogue, a program for preservation, a Technical Center for the Book, and a new integrated computer system. To prepare the union catalogue, the staff began a retroconversion program at the BN and in a few university and public libraries in France. Some of these libraries will be associated with the Bibliothèque de France in a national network for document delivery.

Central Administration in Paris. France has always been a centralized country, and the organization of the library system reflects this pattern. In 1945, a Direction des Bibliothèques was created in the Ministry of Education; it controlled the BN, university libraries, département lending libraries, and some important municipal libraries. The Directorate was divided in 1975, in 1981, and again in 1986. University libraries remained under the Ministry of Education and the Bibliothèque Nationale and public libraries came under the Ministry of Culture. Its Direction du Livre (the book) et de la Lecture (reading) (DLL) is responsible for the Bibliothèque Publique d'Information (BPI) at the Centre Georges Pompidou, for the Bibliothèque Nationale, and for national library policy. The départements took responsibility for provincial lending libraries and the communes took charge of municipal libraries. The DLL subsidizes some projects submitted by départements or cities, such as buildings, automation, and preservation; it supervises training; and it keeps statistics.

Decentralization is less visible for university libraries, although they have come increasingly under the jurisdiction of their own universities. For example, their budgets must be approved by the University Council. In the Ministry of Education, the Sous-Direction des Bibliothèques is responsible for university libraries, allocating 85 percent of their budgets, nominating staff, developing cooperative projects such as union catalogues, and defining policies. The Ministry also appoints and pays the professional librarians in some scientific institutions, such as the École Polytechnique, the Paris Observatory, the Institut de France, and the Museum d'Histoire Naturelle. The Sous-Direction des Bibliothèques publishes a monthly journal, the *Bulletin des Bibliothèques de France*.

Personnel in university libraries are nearly all civil servants. In public libraries, the central government provides about ten percent of the staff and local authorities recruit the rest. The Ministry of Education recruits conservateurs, assistant librarians, and stack attendants through competitive national examinations, evaluates them, promotes them, and arranges transfers. Civil service staff are able to move from one library to another (public, university, or national) without losing seniority.

Finally, the central administration has General Inspectors who visit libraries of all categories, university and public, to check the quality of their operation and the efficiency of their staff, to advise local governments on building projects, to assess requests for grants, and to provide other services.

The Conseil supérieur des Bibliothèques (National Council for Libraries), long awaited, was finally created in 1989. It advises the government on library matters with the aim of creating an efficient library network. For example, it provides guidance on the national union catalogue, a proposed law on public libraries, and education. André Miquel, former head of the Bibliothèque Nationale, was the first president of the Conseil.

Special Libraries (Documentation Centers). Besides scientific sections of university libraries, which are entirely state-supported, there are numerous scientific and technical libraries for which state participation varies from total to none. Some depend on government departments, such as the Army (École Polytechnique), the Ministry of Justice, the Ministry of Industry (Médiathèque de la Villette), and the Ministry of Research (INIST, the Institut Nationale de l'Information Scientifique et Technique). Others are entirely private, serving industrial companies such as Elf-Aquitaine and L'Oréal. A few receive subsidies from both the government and private industries (such as the libraries at the Institut Pasteur or Electricité de France). About 25,000 professionals work in these libraries, which number about 10,000. Most are called *documentation centers* and are supposed to have objectives slightly different from those of libraries. French libraries have traditionally concentrated on conservation; documentation centers are managed for efficient services to readers, primarily reference work. By the 1990s their objectives became more and more similar, but a distinction remained in staffing: conservateurs work in state libraries, while *documentalistes* work in private industry.

Parliamentary Libraries. The Library of the Assemblée Nationale, founded in 1789, received its first collection of books from the Revolutionary literary depots. It now holds about 670,000 books, 1,500 periodical titles, and 1,800 manuscripts. It is open to members of the Assemblée Nationale and to authorized readers. Bibliographies and reports are prepared on request. Use of the Senate Library is reserved for its members. Like the Library of the Assemblée Nationale, it contains mostly works on law, economics, and history, though it also has a number of special collections coming from donations. It, too, goes back to the Revolution, and it possesses 500,000 books and 600 periodicals.

University Libraries. Created by a decree of 1879 that merged the libraries of the faculties and institutes, university libraries had their structure and rules defined first in 1886 and then in 1962. Until 1970, universities comprised four or five faculties (law, humanities, science, pharmacy, and medicine) to which were attached specialized institutes (chemistry and mathematics among others). In 1970 the former large universities (30,000 students) were split into several smaller specialized ones and new universities were created in medium-sized towns. The old encyclopedic university libraries had already been split into "sections" during the period 1950–70 when numerous buildings were erected on new campuses. The main reason for all these changes is the steady increase in the number of students, which rose from 150,000 in 1950 to 1,300,000 in 1991.

For 73 universities there were 67 university libraries in the early 1990s, 16 of them serving two or more universities in one town. Taken as a whole, they were organized in 195 sections by subject and had 65,000 seats.

Organization. Starting in 1985, the Ministry of Education began transforming university libraries into one of two forms: *Services Commun de la Documentation* (SCD, Common Documentation Services) or *Services Interétablissements de Coopération Documentaire* (SICD, Interuniversity Library Cooperation Services). Former institute and laboratory libraries, some of which had means equal to the university libraries, may be associated with or merged with the SCD or SICD at their university. Each university is now responsible for the organization and budget allocation for all its libraries. A professional librarian, director of the SCD or SICD, answers to the university president and is aided by a Board including faculty members, students, and library staff. Since 1962, university libraries have been divided into (1) an open-access collection, classified according to UDC, for undergraduate students, and (2) a collection for graduate students and faculty using both open access and closed stacks.

Buildings. From 1950 to 1975 French university libraries expanded considerably. New campuses were created and 120 library buildings were constructed, totaling 4,500,000 sq.ft., but the vast growth in numbers of students meant that even the new libraries provided only a little more than seven square feet for each student. In 1988 the government asked André Miquel to report on the state of university libraries; he proposed that another 4,100,000 sq.ft. of library space be built. By 1992, nine universities had received money for new construction.

Staff. In 1991 the personnel in academic libraries totalled 3,583, 1,520 of them professionals. The ratio of staff to students, 2.75 per 1,000 in 1991, was down from the 4 per 1,000 of 1970, partly as the result of years of economic difficulties from 1973 through 1988. Recruitment began to rise again in 1990.

Budget. The total budget for French academic libraries followed the same pattern, down in the 1970s and 1980s and rising again in the 1990s. It was estimated at 922 million francs for 1991, including 786 million francs from government grants (467 million for personnel and 319 million for operations). Other sources of income include student fees, sales, gifts, and grants from local governments.

Collections. Varying in quantity and quality, some collections have several millions books plus incunabula and manuscripts (both the Sorbonne and the Bibliothèque Sainte Geneviève have three million), whereas the more recent ones, such as Le Havre, Mulhouse, and Toulon have fewer than 100,000 volumes. But none has the old, rich collections typical of the municipal libraries created by the Revolution. University libraries totaled 21,500,000 volumes in 1991, 350,000 periodical titles (110,000 current), and

1,000,000 microforms, plus the collections of faculty libraries, which may run as high as 10,000,000 volumes. Their annual intake of books runs to about 572,000 volumes. They record about 10 million loans to 730,000 readers on site and another million interlibrary loans.

Automation. The central administration has always favored cooperation and networking among libraries, but automation has had a number of failures. Four national projects from the late 1980s and early 1990s should eventually be merged: an interlibrary loan system, PEB, linking 200 institutions and handling about a million transactions a year; an online union catalogue of periodicals, CCN, which contains some 550,000 titles; an online catalogue of theses, *Téléthèses;* and an online union catalogue of books, PANCATALOGUE. Individual academic libraries use a wide variety of automated systems for circulation. For cataloguing, 25 libraries use OCLC, 17 use SIBIL, and 15 BN-OPALE. All cataloguing records from the three systems are integrated in PANCATALOGUE.

The Ministry of Education designated 23 libraries as *Centres d'sAcquisition et de Diffusion de l'Information Scientifique et Technique* (CADIST), giving them responsibility for collecting documents worldwide in a particular field and for making them available to others. The libraries receive separate grants for this work. Examples include the chemistry collection at the University of Lyons, physics at Grenoble, theology at Strasbourg, and history at the Sorbonne.

Municipal Libraries. Created and operated by the communes, more than 1,600 municipal libraries existed in France in 1991, almost twice as many as in 1980. Of the 834 towns with more than 10,000 inhabitants, all but 100 have their own libraries.

Many municipal libraries were created by a decree of January 28, 1803, that handed the central school collections over to the cities. Many of those libraries, however, were not well maintained by the communes, and some were completely abandoned. The central government instituted tighter control over them in 1839, and in 1897 issued a regulation proclaiming that pre-1789 books and manuscripts were state property that could not be sold or removed without government permission. A decree of 1931 introduced the concept of *bibliothèques municipales classés,* libraries containing important state collections that had come from the confiscations of the French Revolution. There are 54 libraries of this kind; the state appoints professional librarians to manage them and allocates grants to them. A National Committee on Patrimony authorizes interlibrary loan of rare books and gives advice on preservation. Other municipal libraries are staffed by personnel appointed by the municipalities. Library inspectors visit all municipal libraries and report to the Ministry of Culture.

After World War II, many municipal libraries began to shed their 19th-century style under the leadership of the Direction des Bibliothèques headed by Julien Caen. The change intensified after 1964 under Etienne Dennery. The new institutions are well-lighted, pleasant *médiathèques* (multimedia libraries) with open access, sections for adults and for children, and various media. Besides their main research collections housed downtown, the large, long-established libraries in major cities have set up networks of branches or have started bookmobiles in order to stimulate reading among the population in their areas. Bordeaux and Lyons have 14 branch libraries, Grenoble 17, Toulouse 21, and Paris 59.

Buildings. Municipal library floor surfaces doubled in a 10-year period from 1970 to 1980 and nearly doubled again from 1980 to 1990. Modern buildings now serve the people of such cities as Bordeaux, Aix-en-Province, and Nantes, as well as many smaller towns. Some towns preferred to renovate old buildings, such as churches, monasteries, or even palaces, in order to obtain working libraries. Avignon, Beauvais, Chaumont, and Colmar are examples.

The municipalities pay for their libraries, but they can receive grants from the Ministry of Culture for building (50 percent), for specific acquisitions, for automation (25 percent), or for current operations (provided they spend more than 40 francs per inhabitant). The staff serving these libraries numbers more than 12,600.

French municipal libraries have remarkable prerevolutionary collections, including 162,000 manuscripts and 10,000 incunabula, but they are now growing by 4 million books a year. The total collection of municipal libraries amounts to 72 million books. Collections of special significance are in Aix-en-Provence, Bordeaux, Carpentras, Dijon, Grenoble, Lyons, Rouen, Toulouse, and Troyes. Automation has been introduced in 400 municipal libraries. Municipal libraries provided almost 111 million loans in 1989, an average of almost 3.5 books per inhabitant.

Paris. Municipal libraries in Paris have a special status. Created in 1865, well after the Revolution, they have no state collections, and, despite their location at the center of a centralized state, they are not under state control. Their funds are allocated by the city of Paris, augmented by grants from the Ministry of Culture. They have 2,500,000 books in their loan collections, 1,500,000 volumes in their research collections, and 2,000,000 prints and posters. They have a staff of 854. They are administered by a Library Bureau and their professional staff is recruited through a special competitive examination.

Parisian libraries are of two kinds: research libraries, such as the Historical Library of the City of Paris, in the Hôtel Lamoignon, or the Forney Library, in the Hôtel de Sens, specializing in arts and crafts techniques; and standard public libraries. Since 1971, the 52 public libraries have been organized in a network consisting of one large district library (20,000 sq.ft.) in each of the Paris *arrondissements* and smaller libraries (5,000 sq.ft.) for every 35,000 inhabitants. In 1990 Parisian libraries lent out 8 million items to more than 270,000 users.

Of note is the Bibliothèque Publique d'Information (BPI) at the Pompidou Center in Paris. It is not a municipal library, but depends directly on the Direction du Livre et de la Lecture. Opened in 1977, it offers a new style of library service—anyone can enter without a card and can use freely its open-access non-circulating collection of 500,000 volumes and a large collection of audiovisual materials, including slides, films, and tapes. More than 13,000 visitors use it daily, mostly students who work there because they cannot find seats in their own university libraries. BPI studies its readers' habits and use of new media to weed its collection and serves as a laboratory to test new products, such as its catalogue on CD-ROM.

Another unique library is the *Médiathèque de la Cité des Sciences et de l'Industrie de la Villette* (Multimedia Library in the City for Science and Industry), part of a new science center housed in the former Paris slaughterhouse. Intended to popularize science and technology, it offers a multimedia science collection for children and adults. Its collection, unlike that of the BPI, circulates freely. It also has a major collection of scientific films and of educational computer programs.

Provincial Lending Libraries. Because smaller towns might not be able to support libraries, the government decided in 1945 to establish *Bibliothèques Centrales de Prêt* (BCP, Central Lending Libraries) in each of the 96 administrative *départements* (more or less the equivalent of counties). These libraries, usually set up in the département capital city, were intended to serve communes of fewer than 10,000 inhabitants with bookmobiles. Some now offer direct loans from their bookmobiles, some provide collections chosen by local librarians (often part-time volunteers) deposited at various points in the district, such as town halls, and some drop off book boxes at various deposit points. Schools served as deposit points for many years, but the DLL in 1985 ordered the BCPs to find places where all members of the community could find books easily. Each bookmobile takes a collection of 300 to 5,000 books to each deposit point and changes it three times a year. Book deposits are also made in factories, homes for the elderly, and cultural centers. Bookmobiles visit each town four times a year, with stocks of 3,000 books on their shelves. In 1987 there were 336 bookmobiles, with a staff of 1,397, giving access to 15 million books. Loans numbered 40 million in 1987.

School Libraries. Before 1958, primary and high-school libraries existed, but only for teachers or for classroom use. They were old and not kept up to date. From 1958, and mainly from 1968 on, teachers' and classroom libraries were progressively brought together to form larger units, one for each school, called, since 1974, Centres de Documentation et d'Information (CDI) in high schools and Bibliothèque Centre Documentaire (BCD) in primary schools. They are financed by the schools and staffed by teachers who may have received short introductory courses in library work at best, but who have the same status as other teachers. France's 7,828 high schools have 6,674 CDIs.

The Profession. The library profession in France is divided between civil servants and documentalists. Civil servants (*conservateurs, bibliothécaires,* and *bibliothécaires adjoints*) are recruited by national competitive examinations and work in libraries managed by the government. Documentalists are trained at the *Institut Nationale des Techniques de la Documentation* (INTD) or at one of a few private schools. The associations reflect this division, even though they cooperate on many joint projects.

Associations. There are seven library associations. The *Association des Bibliothécaires Français* (ABF; Association of French Librarians), founded in 1906, is the oldest and one of the largest library associations in France (2,700 individual members and 422 institutional members in 1991). Its funds come from membership fees and government grants. Its objectives are to defend the profession in a very broad sense; to further librarianship by promoting studies, conferences, and reports; and to bring together all those interested in librarianship. The association is open to professional librarians and to those professionally concerned with libraries, such as publishers, bookdealers, and software and equipment manufacturers.

The ABF is organized in four sections by type of library (national, university, general public, and special) and in 17 regional groups that meet between annual national conferences. The structure is the same at all levels: a Council elects a Board that elects the President, the Secretary-General, four Vice-Presidents, and a Treasurer.

The ABF played an important role in promoting libraries before the government began providing services in 1945. Its inadequate resources do not permit it to undertake extensive activities at the national level, but the regional groups are very active. They organize conferences, library visits, and training courses, and foster cooperation among members. Nationally, the Association organizes working groups on professional topics (such as training, automation, and conservation) and colloquia, but its main activity is the Annual Congress on a professional theme (such as the public image of libraries or decentralization). It has organized training courses for first-level librarians in small public libraries and grants diplomas. Its *Manuel du Bibliothécaire* (handbook on librarianship) first appeared in 1966 and is updated every four or five years. The Association publishes a quarterly *Bulletin d'Informations de l'ABF* and an informal *Note d'Information.*

The *Association des Documentalistes et Bibliothécaires Spécialisés* (ADBS; Association of Documentalists and Special Librarians) was founded in 1963 to bring together information and documentation specialists. It had about 4,600 members in 1990, mainly from private documentation centers. Funding comes from membership fees, grants, and fees for training courses. The Association is structured in sections by subject (such as electronics or transportation) and in seven regional groups. A council elects the Board, which is composed of the President, two Vice-Presidents, the Secretary General, and the Treasurer. Activities emphasize improving electronic information handling and transfer by means of visits, round tables, seminars, and a national congress every two years. One of its main activities is training: its members, isolated in private enterprises, need special courses to improve their skills and gain promotions. It is the only library association that offers one- or two-week courses. The ADBS publishes a quarterly bulletin, *Le Documentaliste,* a monthly information sheet, and a series of monographs.

The *Association de l'École Nationale Supérieure des Bibliothèques* (AENSB; Association of the National School for Libraries), founded in 1967, is composed, as its name indicates, of alumni of the national school for librarians in Lyons. It had about 500 members in 1990. Its funds come from membership fees and from grants. It is concerned with all library activities, especially library education. It seeks to improve the library school and the status of civil service librarians.

The Association publishes an internal *Note d'Information* and is a founding member of the Presses de l'ENSB, which publishes books on professional librarianship. The AENSB holds seminars and an annual meeting.

The *Association des Diplomés de l'École des Bibliothécaires et Documentalistes* (ADEBD; Association of Graduates of the School of Librarians and Documentalists), founded in 1936, is composed of alumni of the library school of the Catholic University in Paris. It had about 500 members in 1990; their fees constitute the main financial resources of the Association. It finds employment in the private sector for new graduates of the school. It publishes a semiannual bulletin.

The *Fédération des Associations de Documentalistes-Bibliothécaires de l'Éducation Nationale* (FADBEN; Federation of Associations of Documentalist-Librarians in public schools) was set up to bring together school librarians from CDI and BCD. By 1990 it had about 1,500 members.

The *Amicale des Directeurs de Bibliothèques Universitaires* (ADBU; Association of Directors of University Libraries) was founded in 1971 to address problems specific to the organization and management of academic libraries, to coordinate policies and technical procedures, and to deal with public authorities. It is a closed association of about 100 members; their dues are its only financial resources. The ADBU meets once a year; its board meets often with government representatives to discuss specific problems.

The *Association des Directeurs de Bibliothèques Centrales de Prêt* (ADBCP; Association of Directors of Central Lending Libraries) consists of about 60 members, all of them heads of provincial lending libraries. Because of decentralization, they are willing to share their experiences and develop standards for their work.

Library Education. The teaching of librarianship in France reflects the three categories of professional librarians: (1) civil servants in most of the state-supported libraries, (2) civil servants in local and regional institutions, and (3) documentalists working in private or semi-private documentation centers. All three have their own training, with, of course, some overlap among them.

The *École Nationale Supérieure des Sciences de l'Information et des Bibliothèques* (ENSSIB) in Lyons prepares civil servants for the position of conservateur. It was called École Nationale Supérieure des Bibliothèques (ENSB) until 1991. It is a public institution with university status supported by the Ministry of Education. At the Master's level, it can confer doctorates in conjunction with the University of Lyons. It has two kinds of students. Those who pass the competitive entrance examination are paid during their study and become civil servant conservateurs; the others, *élèves associés,* are French or foreign regular students who are not paid, do not become civil servants, and have no guaranteed posts after their diploma. Since 1991, the curriculum has lasted 18 months, including periods of work in libraries. Each candidate presents a paper to complete the course.

Some conservateurs may come from the École des Chartes, the school for historians and archivists. This school, located in the Sorbonne and entered through a competitive examination at the "baccalauréat" (end of secondary school) level, offers a three-year course in history, Latin, and paleography.

Library Association

Sir Frank Francis

Local authorities seek staff for town or département libraries who have earned the *Certificat d'aptitude aux fonctions de bibliothécaires* (CAFB). The ENSSIB organizes this program, but teaching for the diploma is given in 12 regional centers in universities (*Centre Régional de Formation aux Carrières des Bibliothèques, du Livre, et de la Documentation*). A two-year course prepares professionals for public libraries and for private documentation centers. The CAFB was due for revision in the early 1990s, following changes in the status of civil servants.

Several schools prepare documentalists for their work, the two main ones being the Institut National des Techniques de la Documentation (INTD), part of the Conservatoire National des Arts et Métiers, and the Catholic University in Paris. Opened in 1950, the INTD offers a two-year course in documentation and information retrieval oriented toward industrial documentation centers. The Catholic University also has a library school with several levels of training, including evening courses, which prepare candidates for work in private libraries and documentation centers. These schools graduate about 1,200 students each year.

Many universities began offering courses in documentation and in information sciences (but not in librarianship) beginning in the mid-1970s. At the lower level, the Instituts Universitaires de Technologie (IUT) offer a two-year course in documentation, usually linked to communication. At the upper level, some universities, such as Lyons, Paris, Grenoble, and Lille, offer graduate degrees in documentation and information sciences—Diplome d'études supérieures (DESS) and the doctorate. The Fondation Nationale des Sciences Politiques follows the same structure and offers a DESS in documentation.

REFERENCES

Association des Bibliothécaires Français, *Le Métier de Bibliothécaire* (1988).

Graham Keith Barnett, *Histoire des Bibliothèques Publiques* (1987).

André Masson and Denis Pallier, *Les Bibliothèques* (1982).

André Miquel, *Les Bibliothèques Universitaires: rapport au Ministre d'État, Ministre de l'Éducation Nationale* (1989).

André Vernet, Claude Jolly, Dominique Varry, et al., *Histoire des Bibliothèques Françaises,* three volumes published (1988).

MARC CHAUVEINC

Francis, Sir Frank

(1901–1988)

Sir Frank Francis, one of the outstanding figures on the British library scene for many years, contributed to the library profession and to scholarship over an unusual range as bibliographer and editor, teacher, administrator, and statesman.

Francis was born October 5, 1901, in Liverpool. After graduating from Liverpool and Cambridge, he became a schoolmaster in 1925. The following year he entered the service of the British Museum, where he spent the whole of his career. In 1946 he became Secretary in succession to Arundell Esdaile, whose contributions to bibliographical scholarship he had already followed with his own. Promoted to Keeper in the Department of Printed Books in 1948, he became in 1959 Director and Principal Librarian, holding that office until his retirement in 1968. He was created Companion of the Order of the Bath (C.B.) in 1958 and knighted (K.C.B.) in 1960.

Bibliographical and editorial work came early in his career with a regular flow of studies for the Library Association, the Bibliographical Society, and the British Museum; from 1936 to 1953 he edited *The Library,* and from 1947 to 1968 he jointly edited the *Journal of Documentation.* During those years he laid the foundations of his renowned course in bibliography at the School of Librarianship of University College, London (1945–59), and also for the numerous lectures he gave throughout the world. As Keeper and Director of the British Museum, he initiated and successfully carried out a number of projects for publications based on its unique collections, culminating in the third edition of the *General Catalogue of Printed Books,* which marked an epochal advance in printing technology. He was a leading figure in the discussions that led to the founding of the *British National Bibliography* in the British Museum and lent it the full weight of his support in its early years; his authority and influence were instrumental in ensuring its success.

As a statesman of the profession, Francis set a record that is unmatched. He was President of the major associations: the LA, the Museums Association, Aslib, the Bibliographical Society, and the International Federation of Library Associations. He helped to set up the advisory committee on bibliography and documentation in Unesco and, as Chairman of the Trustees of the National Central Library, guided its course until its merger with the British Museum and other libraries to form the British Library.

In addition he proved an enthusiastic and energetic member of many committees and working parties, and many leading British librarians have had cause to be grateful for his friendship and wise counsel. In long and controversial discussions about the nature and role of librarianship and information work, Francis constantly strove for unity among professional bodies and their members. His assertion of the value of professional qualifications was recognized by the award of the Honorary Fellowship by the LA, but he never neglected the value of high scholarship for all librarians. Thus, he was able in the early 1950s to give full recognition to the growing importance of information services in science and technology and played a significant role in the Committee of the Science Advisory Council.

His own interests demonstrated the same extraordinary range, testified by his membership and honorary rank in many scholarly bodies and his collection of honorary doctorates. Perhaps his major attention was given to the classics and especially to Scandinavian studies, in which he achieved international fame. Even in retirement his activity continued unabated. As Consultant to the Council on Library Resources, he became a familiar figure in the United States and, as Master of the Clockmakers' Company, he fulfilled a role in the functions of the City of London.

Sir Frank Francis died September 15, 1988.

D. J. FOSKETT

Benjamin Franklin plaster bust by Jean Jacques Caffiéri, ca. 1779–84.

The Library Company of Philadelphia

Franklin, Benjamin
(1706–1790)

Benjamin Franklin stands at the beginning of the history of America's public libraries. As founder of the Library Company of Philadelphia, he initiated the first subscription library in the United States, a precursor to the modern public library.

Franklin was born on January 17, 1706, in Boston, which had the largest concentration of bookshops in British America; over half of the booksellers active between 1700 and 1725 were within a quarter-mile of his birthplace. Ideally situated for one who was to be almost entirely self-educated, he received two years of formal schooling. At the age of 12 he was apprenticed to his brother James, a printer. Franklin, who said of himself, "I do not remember when I could not read," began with his father's "little library consisting chiefly of Books in polemic Divinity," which he found of little use. Lending libraries were unknown, but Matthew Adams, a merchant, gave him access to his "pretty Collection of Books." Franklin went one step further, persuading fellow apprentices to borrow books from their masters' book shops, which he read and returned. His reading was eclectic, ranging from classical authors in translation through philosophy, logic, grammar, navigation, and arithmetic. *The Spectator* especially pleased him, and he used it as a model for his own writing. Franklin was vigorous in mind and body and developed a high opinion of his own ability.

In 1722 a series of letters signed Silence Dogood

appeared in James Franklin's *The New England Courant.* Written by Benjamin, the letters were favorably received, much to James's annoyance. On two occasions when James was in trouble with the authorities, Benjamin had the full responsibility for the newspaper. The already existing strain between the two grew to the point where Benjamin was eager to break his apprenticeship, which still had three years to run. In the autumn of 1723 he secretly left Boston for New York.

Printer. Unable to find work with William Bradford in New York, Franklin continued on to Philadelphia. There he was employed by Samuel Keimer, who had opened a printing shop in competition with Bradford's son Andrew. Once settled, Franklin "began now to have some acquaintances among young people of the Town, that were Lovers of Reading with whom I spent my Evenings very pleasantly." His abilities attracted the attention of Governor William Keith, who promised him assistance and arranged for him to go to London to buy a press and type to open a shop of his own. Franklin arrived in England in 1724, only to find himself a victim of Keith's habit of making promises he did not keep. He found employment almost immediately with Samuel Palmer, a printer of some note, and later moved to John Watts's shop, where many successful printers had been trained. Franklin satisfied his need for books by making "an Acquaintance with one Wilcox a Bookseller. . . . Circulating Libraries were not then in Use; but we agreed that on certain reasonable Terms . . . I might take, and return any of his Books."

When he returned to Philadelphia in 1726 at the age of 20, Franklin had completed what amounted to his formal education, although he never stopped learning. He taught himself French, Italian, Spanish, and Latin. Opening his own printing shop in 1728, he embarked on one of the most successful business careers of any printer in pre-Revolutionary America. He started a stationer's store, made arrangements with binders, bought a lampblack house, set up as a wholesale paper merchant, and imported books. The business arrangements he entered into with printers in Newport, New Haven, New York, Charleston, and the West Indies provided a network for distributing his work. The largest part of his printing was for colonial governments; at various times he was printer to Pennsylvania, Philadelphia, Delaware, and New Jersey. Of almost equal importance were his publications on religious subjects, many of which were also subsidized. These two groups make up more than half of the output of his press between 1728 and 1748, when he went into partnership with David Hall and retired from active participation in the business.

His most successful publications were the Poor Richard's almanacs and the *Pennsylvania Gazette;* the distribution of the latter was greatly helped in 1737 when Franklin became Deputy Postmaster at Philadelphia. He scarcely ever undertook the publication of a book or pamphlet on his own. His most successful such venture was the 16 editions of George Whitefield's writing and other controversial tracts occasioned by his visit to America in 1740.

Franklin's best-known and handsomest piece of printing, James Logan's translation of *M. T. Cicero's Cato Major,* was a financial loss. Franklin could execute a piece of fine printing when he felt he could afford it, but in general he confined himself to sound workmanlike productions at reasonable prices. At one time he boasted of having the smallest typeface in America.

The Library Company. Parallel and frequently a part of his business career was Franklin's role in founding institutions and organizations for the public good. The first was the Library Company of Philadelphia. The Junto, which he had formed in 1727 for "mutual Improvement," failed in its attempt to form a small library. Soon afterward, in 1731, Franklin created the Library Company. The inspiration for it may have had its origins in Franklin's practice of borrowing books from booksellers in Boston and London, but the idea of a subscription library, owned by its members, for the purpose of circulating books of general interest to those who could not afford to build their own collections, seems to belong to Franklin. There was no counterpart in Great Britain during his stay there; the first British subscription library appeared in Scotland in 1741, the year in which Franklin printed the second *Catalogue* of the Library Company with 375 titles, and the London Library was not founded until 1785. Circulating books was not a new idea, but it had been narrowly oriented, usually around some religious interest.

The founders of the Library Company were almost all in trade, practical men who wanted useful information for self-improvement. Most of the original books were in English, and theology was held to a minimum. The Library's functions were soon expanded; it was given an air pump, followed by electrical instruments, a telescope, artifacts from the Arctic, a cabinet of fossils, and other objects appropriate to a museum. On a number of occasions its rooms were used for demonstrations and lectures. The directors saw their Library as taking an active part in making practical and scientific knowledge readily and cheaply available. Until he left for England in 1757, Franklin played an active role in the Library's affairs. He was briefly acting librarian when in 1734 the Library was opened to all who would pay a rental fee. From 1746 to 1757 he was the Secretary, the principal officer. By 1776 there were at least 18 subscription libraries in America, almost all of which bore some trace of influence from the Library Company.

Other Contributions. Although a number of other institutions with which Franklin's name is associated developed libraries, he was not closely involved. He was on the committee that selected the first books for the College of Philadelphia in 1750, but various factors, including the hostility between Provost William Smith and Franklin, meant that he had little to do with its small library. The American Philosophical Society, which he founded in 1743, did not take its present form until 1769, when Franklin was in England; until 1800 its books were all donated. After the appearance of the first volume of the Society's *Transactions* in 1771, Franklin used it to solicit gifts from the scientific writers of Europe and, even more important, to establish exchange arrangements with learned societies in Britain and on the Continent, to 20 of which he belonged. Likewise the Pennsylvania Hospital, founded in the early 1750s, did not decide to develop a medical library until 1762, and Franklin's only participation seems to have been an offer to seek gifts in England. His part in beginnings of the Pennsylvania State Library was more direct; in 1752 he was the member of the Assembly who was directed, along with the Speaker, to purchase books for the newly erected library room.

With the exception of two brief periods, Franklin spent the 28 years between 1757 and 1785 in England or France representing the interests of his country. His achievements, particularly his electrical experiments, made him a welcome addition to the literary and intellectual worlds of both countries. He continued to encourage the bookish interests of the organizations he left behind and acted as their agent in acquiring books. In London he became a close friend of England's leading printer, William Strahan, and in Paris picked up his old craft, establishing his own press in Passy. As always he bought and was given books.

On his return to Philadelphia in 1785, he set about putting his library in order and designed a ladder-chair and an arm to reach books on high shelves. At his death there on April 17, 1790, he left his library of 4,276 volumes to his family. They sold it at an 1803 auction that was the largest and most important to have taken place in America.

Appraisal. Franklin's position in the history of American public libraries is well known; that some of the ideas he brought to librarianship may have predated their appearance in the mother country is not as widely recognized. Certainly the Library Company's view of itself as an active force in the educational and intellectual life of Philadelphia would seem to be one of the earliest examples of what is now taken for granted—that libraries have a responsibility that goes beyond passively providing books.

REFERENCES

Quotes and other material are from Franklin's *Autobiography*, edited by Leonard W. Labaree et al. (1964).

Austin K. Gray, *Benjamin Franklin's Library: A Short Account of the Library Company of Philadelphia* (1937).

Margaret Barton Korty, "Benjamin Franklin and Eighteenth Century Libraries," *Transactions of the American Philosophical Society* (1965).

Carl Van Doren, *Benjamin Franklin* (1938).

Michael H. Harris, "Franklin, Benjamin," *Dictionary of American Library Biography* (1978).

THOMAS R. ADAMS

Fussler, Herman Howe

(1914-)

Herman Howe Fussler, North American university library administrator, scholar, and teacher, made major contributions to the improvement of library services to scholars and labored successfully to increase the general understanding of the tasks and problems of research libraries.

A practicing library administrator for 35 years (23 of them as Director of the University of Chicago Library), he pioneered in the development and application of new technologies and service concepts, beginning with his early contributions to library microphotography and culminating in the conception and design of the Joseph Regenstein Library of the University of Chicago, which opened in 1970. The Regenstein Library is widely recognized as an attractive and efficient environment remarkably well adapted to the activity of scholarship. Known as a stimulating and provocative teacher, Fussler gained a comprehensive familiarity with the literature of librarianship and with the library practitioners of his generation, and as a student and scholar distinguished himself for penetrating and balanced analyses of the major issues confronting the academic research library. He wrote or edited many significant books, articles, and reports on academic libraries, on the technologies applicable to libraries, on the ways in which the products of scholarship are disseminated, and on the management of scholarly resources. He was frequently consulted by librarians, scholars, academic administrators, and foundation officers because of his experience and perspective.

Fussler was born in Philadelphia on May 15, 1914, the son of a physics professor. His family, after living in various parts of the country, settled in Chapel Hill, where Fussler attended the University of North Carolina. He received an A.B. degree in mathematics in 1935 and, a year later, a bachelor's degree in library science. Shortly thereafter he began studies at the Graduate Library School (GLS) of the University of Chicago, where he earned the M.A. degree in 1941 and the Ph.D. in 1948.

He began his library career in 1936 at the New York Public Library as a library assistant in the Science and Technology Division. After a brief period of service there he was invited to the University of Chicago Library to establish and direct its pioneering Department of Photographic Reproduction, with the specific mission of developing operating and technical processes, particularly in microreproduction, that would be of utility to research libraries generally. He served in that capacity from 1936 to 1946, added concurrent responsibilities as Science Librarian in the University Library from 1943 to 1947, became Assistant Director and then Associate Director, 1947–48, and later in 1948 was appointed Director, serving in that position until 1971, when he resigned to devote full time to research and teaching in the GLS. Twice during his service in the University Library his abilities were made available to other important enterprises: during 1937 he served as Head of the Demonstration of Microphotography at the Paris International Exposition, under the auspices of the Rockefeller Foundation and the American Library Association; and from 1942 to 1945 he was detached from his primary responsibilities to serve the Manhattan Project as Assistant Director of the Information Division and Librarian of the Metallurgical Laboratory.

The University of Chicago
Herman Howe Fussler

His career in library research and in education for librarianship paralleled his career in the University Library. He became an Instructor in 1942, was promoted to Assistant Professor in 1944, and was made Professor in 1948, the year he became Director of the Library. For the period 1961–63 he served, in addition, as Acting Dean of the GLS. His contributions to library scholarship and to the scholarly work of the University were formally acknowledged in 1974 when he was named the Martin A. Ryerson Distinguished Service Professor of Library Science. In 1977 he was Visiting Professor at Monash University in Australia.

Fussler influenced thought and action in many areas through his diligent and effective service on the boards and committees of library associations and learned societies. He served on the ALA Council from 1956 to 1959 as well as on a number of committees. He was a member of the board of the Association of Research Libraries from 1961 to 1964 and in 1970 and 1971. He was one of the initial three-man team selected to study the feasibility of a Midwest storage facility for academic libraries and was active in the planning and establishment of the resulting Midwest Interlibrary Center (now the Center for Research Libraries), served on its board from 1950 to 1967, was Vice Chair of the board in 1954–55, and was Chair, 1959–60. He was a member of the Board of Regents of the National Library of Medicine (1963–67) and served on the visiting committees of various academic libraries. He was appointed by President Lyndon B. Johnson to the National Advisory Commission on Libraries in 1966.

Fussler received the Melvil Dewey Medal from ALA in 1954 and the Ralph R. Shaw Award for library literature in 1976.

Fussler served as Associate Editor for the *Journal of Documentary Reproduction* (1938 to 1942) and the *Library Quarterly* from 1949. His principal publications include *Photographic Reproduction for Libraries: A Study of Administrative Problems* (1942) and *Characteristics of the Research Literature Used by Chemists and Physicists in the United States* (1949); he edited *Library Buildings for Library Service* (1947), *The Function of the Library in the Modern College* (1954), and *The Research Library in Transition* (1957); he was co-author, with Julian L. Simon, of *Patterns in the Use of Books in Large Libraries* (revised edition 1969) and Editor of *Management Implications for Libraries and Library Schools* (1973) and *Research Libraries and Technology* (1973).

STANLEY McELDERRY

G

Gabon

On the west coast of Africa, Gabon is a republic bounded on the north by Equatorial Guinea and Cameroon, on the east and south by the Congo, and on the west by the Atlantic Ocean. Population (1990 est.) 1,172,000; area 267,667 sq.km. The official language is French.

History. Among the 40 ethnic groups of Gabon, oral traditions kept alive the social codes and taboos, the tales, proverbs, and riddles, and the family-by-family genealogies of the people. The Gabonese were once matrilineal in the south and patrilineal in the north, but they have become more and more patrilineal. Local language and traditions, including the oral transmission of cultural history, have receded in the face of the Westernized French model, with village life and older people dying out.

National Library. In 1969 the National Archives in Libreville was begun, including a library department that serves as the National Library. In 1972 it became the official depository for Gabonese documents; it also receives dissertations dealing with the country.

In 1978 Amoughe M'Ba Pierre returned from study overseas as the first highly trained Gabonese librarian. He developed and catalogued the National Library collections. While the population served increased, the shortage of space worsened.

In 1982 the government decided to establish CICIBA, a Bantu civilizations international institute. Amoughe was named a member of the advisory board. The ambitious scheme, some observers felt, could impede library development in Gabon.

Academic Libraries. The largest university library, the Bibliothèque Centrale of the Université Omar Bongo, was established in 1972. Special collections are located off campus at the Medicine Faculty, Law School, and Teachers' College, and at the Computer Sciences and Forest Studies Institutes.

Public Libraries. There were no public libraries in Gabon in the mid-1980s. Experiments in providing services in working-class districts of Libreville and Port Gentil were conducted between 1968 and 1975. The National Library and the Gabonese Librarians Association in the mid-1980s planned reading facilities for everyone by the year 2000.

School Libraries. Four schools in Libreville and two denominational schools in the country maintain small libraries.

Special Libraries. Among the 26 special libraries in 1984, the oldest one was established in 1938 at the Chamber of Commerce of Libreville. Ten are attached to research institutions and four to ministries. Both the French and the American Cultural Centers have special libraries, as does the United Nations office in Libreville. The most advanced library opened in 1979 at Franceville as part of the International Center for Medical Research (CIRMF), specializing in human reproduction.

The Profession. Trained archivists or librarians numbered 35 in 1984 and most of them belong to the Gabonese Librarians Association, initiated in 1981 by Amoughe M'Ba Pierre. Most of them went to a Unesco-sponsored school in Dakar, Senegal. But in 1981 Amoughe organized a three-year professional course with university teachers and librarians. In 1984 eight archivists and librarians were graduated in Libreville. In 1985 a master's degree in information sciences was offered on the opening of a fourth-year course.

REFERENCES

Hubert Deschamps, *Traditions orales et archives du Gabon* (Paris, 1962).

Danielle Haeringer, *Documentation et planification au Gabon* (Libreville, 1981).

Marie Elizabeth Bouscarle, *Les Bibliothèques au Gabon* (1982).

MARIE ELIZABETH BOUSCARLE

Gambia, The

The Republic of Gambia, on the Atlantic coast of West Africa, is the smallest country on the African continent. It lies on a strip of land on the banks of the Gambia River; Senegal surrounds The Gambia on the north, east, and south. Population (1990 est.) 861,000; area 11,295 sq.km. The official language is English.

National and Public Library Services. The Gambia government did not have a public or national library service of its own until April 1962, when the British Council closed its office and handed its library in the capital city of Banjul to the government. The British Council, which ran a subscription library service in The Gambia from 1946, had provided the only public library in the country apart from smaller

Libraries in The Gambia (1990)

Type of library	Number of administrative units (main libraries)	Number of service points (branches, mobile stops, etc.)	Volumes in collections	Annual expenditures (dalasi)	Population served	Professional staff (with certificate, diploma, etc.)	Total staff
National	1	4	2,500	D15,000	23,000	3	4[a]
Academic	3	3	33,000	D206,000	1,530	5	14[a]
Public	1	35	60,000	D100,000	100,000	3	16[a]
School	61	61	11,500	D25,000	30,100	2	62[b]
Special	3	3	14,000	D125,000	1,300	2	14[a]
Other describe	2	2	15,000	D45,000	700	--	6[a]

[a]ancillary included
[b]60 teacher/librarians

Extension services are provided by The Gambia National Library's Mobile Library.

libraries in schools, government departments, mission houses, and clubs, whose materials were loaned only to members or clients. When the book stock was transferred, it numbered 25,000 volumes and a total of 500 phonograph records, films, and filmstrips.

In 1971 the name was changed from the British Council Library to The Gambia National Library. Before the change, Roy Flood had been sent from the British Council in London to evaluate and recommend a library service suitable for The Gambia. His recommendations for a complete reorganization of The Gambia library service were accepted.

In 1974 the British government provided 300,000 dalasis (£575,000) for the building, books, furniture, and equipment. When the new library was opened in 1976, the collection totalled more than 54,600 volumes—it had doubled in the period 1962–76. Books, manuscripts, films, recordings, and other items added thereafter made the collection more extensive.

Under an act of Parliament, the National Library was made the legal depository library and the Bibliographic Center. More than 2,000 volumes of archival material are stored there. Its departments are the National Collection (mainly materials by and about The Gambia and the Gambians); Adult Lending; School Library Service (bulk loans to primary schools); Children's Lending; and Mobile and Bookbox services. The National Library, in summary, serves dual purposes—as a National Reference and Lending Library and also as the public library of the nation.

A branch of the National Library was opened at Brikama, Western Division, in 1990. By the early 1990s the National Library had a bookstock of 75,000 volumes and 3,000 archival items.

Academic Libraries. The three academic institutions in Gambia are the Gambia College, at Brikama, formerly the Teachers' Training College at Yundum; the Gambia Technical Training Institute; and the Management Development Institute. The Gambia College offers courses up to the Higher Teacher's Certificate. The institutes offer vocational and paraprofessional training. All planned to offer degree-level programs in the early 1990s. Each has a library, with total holdings of 33,000 volumes.

S. P. C. N'JIE

ALA

Frank Gardner

Gardner, Frank
(1908–1980)

Frank Matthias Gardner, British public librarian, editor, and writer, was a leader of the Library Association (LA) and was noted for his international library service.

Gardner was born in Sheffield, Yorkshire, January 13, 1908, and throughout his life he demonstrated the tough, hardy, blunt determination characteristic of Yorkshire folk of the North Country. But he gained his professional successes and reputation in London and the south of England.

Gardner was educated at Firth Park Grammar School in Sheffield. In 1927 he became an assistant in the Sheffield Public Libraries, staying there for three years before moving on to a more senior position in the Leeds Public Libraries, where he remained until 1933. Sheffield and Leeds were, and still are, rival Yorkshire cities, vying with each other in the fields of industrial, social, and municipal progress. During his formative years in librarianship, Gardner served under two dynamic city librarians, J. P. Lamb of Sheffield and Richard Gordon of Leeds, and these early professional experiences colored his whole future. He never forgot the library philosophies and techniques inculcated into him at Sheffield and Leeds between 1927 and 1933.

From the industrial north of England, where unemployment was rife in the 1930s, many young people were beckoned by the more affluent London and the south. Gardner was one of those who responded to the call, and in 1933 he became a branch librarian at Willesden, then a municipal borough in northwest London and now part of the London borough of Brent. He remained there from 1933 to 1938, a period that witnessed the flowering of his professional life. His new job not only widened his experience but brought him into contact with many other librarians in London and the south, librarians of his own and earlier generations. He became a member of the Council of the Association of Assistant Librarians and soon was editor of its official monthly journal, *The Library Assistant,* now *The Assistant Librarian*. Through it he became friendly with other contemporary library journalists, among them Stanley Snaith, F. Seymour Smith, T. E. Callander, W. B. Stevenson, and J. T. Gillett. Among them, and under Gardner's editorship, they gave *The Library Assistant* a reputation and a readability second to none in the 1930s.

By 1938 Gardner had carved for himself a considerable reputation and it came as no surprise when, in that year, he was appointed Borough Librarian of Luton, a town of more than 100,000 about 30 miles north of London. Two years earlier he had married a children's librarian, Lysobel Margaret Watt-Smith. The war came at just the wrong time for Gardner: it prevented him from carrying out many much-needed reforms in the Luton Public Libraries, and it also meant that by 1945 he had missed many opportunities for professional advancement. He stayed on at Luton until his retirement in 1972. By that time, however, he had provided Luton not only with new branch libraries, but also with a fine new central library, which Queen Elizabeth II opened in 1962.

During and after the war Gardner became a member of the Council of the LA. He was Chairman of the LA Publications Committee for a number of years, later becoming Chairman of the Association's Executive Committee and finally President in 1964.

Before that time, he had become interested in international library affairs. In 1950 Unesco asked him to direct the Delhi Public Library pilot project, which he did successfully, and his name will long be honored in India. In 1954 he revisited Delhi to direct a Unesco seminar on public libraries in Asia. Meanwhile, at home, he was one of the leaders of the LA's efforts to secure much-needed legislation for public libraries in England and Wales. It was fitting that his efforts were rewarded during his LA Presidential year with the passing of the Public Libraries and Museums Act, which came into force on April 1, 1965.

During his Presidential year Gardner inaugurated "The President's Page" in the *LA Record,* presided over a memorable LA Conference at Rothesay in Scotland, and visited Nigeria and other Commonwealth countries in Africa. From then on he attended IFLA General Council meetings on a regular basis, and from 1969 to 1973 was chairman of the Public Libraries Section Committee of IFLA. He pressed for the adoption and publication of international standards for public libraries during his term of office. This meant the formation of a special committee to study and prepare the standards, and involved additional meetings in London, Luton, Bremen, East Berlin, Lund, Liverpool, and elsewhere. As chairman, Gardner handled a difficult task with great finesse, with the result that the IFLA *Standards for Public Libraries* were published in time for the IFLA General Council meeting in Grenoble in 1973. Since then they have been widely adopted, and revisions have taken place.

At home Gardner was a member of the Libraries Advisory Council from 1965 to 1971 and chairman of the Books and Libraries Panel of the British Council from 1966 to 1972. He remained on the LA Council until his retirement in 1972. He was also prominent in the field of library cooperation, having served as honorary secretary of the South Eastern Regional Library System, and was also a member of the Executive Committee of the National Central Library until it was merged into the British Library in 1973. Gardner was also a great supporter of the idea of National Library Weeks and was a member of the Joint Organizing Committee for NLW in the 1960s.

Gardner contributed many articles to the British and overseas library press, though his books were relatively few. He compiled *Sequels* in 1947, which came out in revised editions periodically, and he followed it with *Junior Sequels,* produced in 1977 in collaboration with Lisa-Christina Persson. He also wrote *Letters to a Younger Librarian* (1948), *Public Library Legislation: A Comparative Study* (1971), for Unesco, and *Reading Round the World* (1969), in collaboration with M. Joy Lewis. He was made an Honorary Fellow of the LA in 1966 and was honored by the Queen with the award of the CBE (Companion of the Order of the British Empire) in the following year.

Gardner was in later life in demand as a lecturer at library schools and contributed to many conferences, national and international. He mingled freely and happily with librarians from other countries, but they sometimes found his low-pitched voice and his flat Northern accent difficult to understand. He remained a popular and certainly an influential figure in British and international library circles.

REFERENCE

K. C. Harrison. "Frank Gardner: Internationalist." *IFLA Journal* (1980).

K. C. HARRISON

Garfield, Eugene

(1925–)

Drexel University

Eugene Garfield

The library and information world has many entrepreneurs; American Eugene Garfield earned a special place in that his success was based upon early and deep insights regarding the structure of science literatures and the nature of scientific communication.

Eugene Garfield was born September 16, 1925, in New York City. He was raised in a Jewish-Italian family in which he, in retrospect, rejoiced, according to his warm memoir (1978) relating his experiences with his Italian stepfather to those with his intellectual mentor, Chauncey Leake. He was educated at Columbia University, earning a B.S. in Chemistry in 1949 and an M.S. in Library Service in 1954 while working at a variety of jobs to pay for his education. Self-employment began almost immediately after the last degree, first as a consultant to Smith, Kline and French, the pharmaceutical company, and then as the founder of a tiny company producing the predecessor to *Current Contents,* started first as a cottage industry in a converted chicken coop.

Critical years were 1960 and 1961; his small firm took on its current name, Institute for Scientific Information (ISI). He received a Ph.D. in Structural Linguistics from the University of Pennsylvania (1961). (His dissertation applied modern linguistics to the indexing of chemical information.) The most important event in 1961 was that he brought out the first citation index to a broad spectrum of science literature, genetics.

A variety of products, ideas, and special techniques and services can be identified with Garfield and his associates, but just two products, *Current Contents* and *Science Citation Index,* and their conceptualization and development, their implementation and successful management, would stand alone as major monuments to his skills, energy, and intellect. *Current Contents* capitalizes upon the researcher's urgent needs for current research information, particularly in the life sciences, and a person's enormous ability to scan text skillfully. *Science Citation Index* identified citation behavior, a means of acknowledging intellectual debt and assigning credit, as the key to a basic organizational feature of the scientific literatures, useful for retrieval, for research on the nature of science, and for science policy.

ISI marketed many products and employed hundreds of people in the 1990s; Garfield continued as President following the sale of the company.

REFERENCES

Eugene Garfield, *Essays of an Information Scientist* (1977).
Eugene Garfield, *Citation Indexing* (1979).

BELVER GRIFFITH

Garnett, Richard

(1835–1906)

Richard Garnett, English librarian and man of letters, was a major figure in British librarianship in the late

The British Library

Richard Garnett

19th century. Perhaps best known for his work in the British Museum, he was also a respected literary scholar, poet, and translator.

Garnett was born February 27, 1835, at Lichfield, near Birmingham. His father, Richard, a distinguished Celtic scholar, then Priest-Vicar of the Cathedral there, moved to London in 1838 to become Assistant Keeper of Printed Books in the British Museum. Following his death in 1850, and as a compliment to him, his son was appointed to an assistantship at an exceptionally early age.

The younger Garnett became an expert cataloguer and classifier and gained thereby, and by exceptionally wide personal reading, vast knowledge of his library's stock. This knowledge earned him unprecedented renown following his promotion to Assistant Keeper of Printed Books and Superintendent of the Reading Room in 1875. As one example, when the Library Association (LA) held its inaugural conference in 1877, he arranged to facilitate Charles Ammi Cutter's researches in connection with his bibliography of the devil.

Garnett became an outstanding, active, and highly valued member of the LA and served as President in 1893, after he succeeded George Bullen (1816–1894) as Keeper of Printed Books. His LA activities brought him into the controversies of the late 1870s and early 1880s on the various proposals for universal and specialist bibliographies, and he never overlooked the desirability of printing a catalogue of the Library of the British Museum—the manuscript version in more than 2,000 pasted-up volumes was becoming increasingly unmanageable. Once the decision had been taken to print the catalogue (subsequently famous as GK1) Garnett, if at first unofficially, became its editor and in 1884 was relieved of his Reading Room responsibilities to concentrate on the vast task. It was eventually completed nearly two years after his retirement in 1899.

David Garnett, in his *Golden Echo* (1953), described his grandfather as

> tall, round-shouldered, stooping . . . by no means a well-dressed man . . . with gentleness, perfect courtesy and slyly hidden humour.

He was also a great cat lover and something of an amateur astrologer. He built up a second reputation as a man of letters with his own poems and translations of poetry from several languages; with contributions to many periodicals and to the *Dictionary of National Biography* and the *Encyclopaedia Britannica*; with numerous short biographies—for example Milton (1887), Emerson (1888), William Blake (1895); with prefaces and introductory essays to many reprints of English classical works; with a history of Italian literature (1897); and mostly, and lastingly, with *The Twilight of the Gods,* first published in book form in 1888 with a new and enlarged edition in 1903. This is a beguiling collection of 28 satirical stories of East and West which originally appeared in a wide variety of periodicals and in *The Yellow Book.* The first story provides the book with its title. It concerns the release of Prometheus from his rock at a time when the old Gods were being dethroned by the early Christians and his subsequent adventures in the company of the maiden Elenko. Others of the stories have titles such as "The Demon Pope" and "Alexander the Ratcatcher." In his introduction to an illustrated reprint of 1924, T. E. Lawrence rightly insisted:

> It wants not learning to enjoy *The Twilight of the Gods* but the more learning you have the more odd corners and hidden delights you will find in it.

Garnett edited George Allen's "Library Series," which provided British librarianship at the turn of the century with some of its best working textbooks and other guides. Titles included were Henry Ogle's *The Free Library* (1897), F. J. Burgoyne's *Library Construction: Architecture, Fittings and Furniture* (1897), and his own *Essays in Librarianship and Bibliography* (1899)—he was also a member of the Bibliographical Society and served as its President from 1895 to 1897. His book contains 24 pieces, half of them reprinted papers read originally at LA meetings and conferences between 1877 and 1898. Those on the B.M.'s catalogues are specially revealing in that they trace, indirectly, the evolution of his own thought on the printed catalogue—initially cautious and critical, then assured, supportive, and determined. Others on such subjects as the future of municipal libraries, mobile shelving, the practical applications of photography, and even the possibilities of telex are exceptionally farsighted. The book ends with brief biographies and appreciations of the three Principal Librarians under whom Garnett had served—Sir Anthony Panizzi (1797–1879), the creator of the modern B.M., John Winter Jones (1805–1881), and Sir Edward Bond (1815–1898), under whose auspices GK1 was produced and financed. Also included is a biography of Henry Stevens (1819–1885), the "Green Mountain Boy," whose "happy union of bibliographical attainments and social qualities," as Garnett aptly put it, did much to link the librarians of America and Europe.

Garnett's *Essays of an Ex-Librarian* (1901) comprises 12 contributions to literary history and criticism on Emerson, Shelley, Coleridge, Thomas Love Peacock, and other writers. An occasional footnote reminds the reader of the author's broad literary insights:

> Though the scenic resources of Shakespeare's age were limited, they were sufficient to be troublesome on a private stage. Tombs, rocks, hell-mouths, beacons and trees are found in lists of properties.

Garnett died at his Hampstead home in London on April 13, 1906.

REFERENCES

Barbara McCrimmon, *Power, Politics and Print: The Publication of the British Museum Catalogue, 1881–1900* (1981).

Barbara McCrimmon, *Richard Garnett: The Scholar as Librarian (1989).*

W. A. MUNFORD

Gaver, Mary

(1906–)

Mary Virginia Gaver, American librarian, educator, researcher, editor, writer, and publisher, developed school library programs that were far in advance of her times, conducted major research on effectiveness of school libraries, assisted in developing standards for school libraries, and conceived and organized a brilliant effort to facilitate implementing those standards.

Gaver was born in Washington, D.C., December 10, 1906. She received an A.B. degree from Randolph-Macon Woman's College in 1927, where she earned a Phi Beta Kappa key, and the B.S. and M.S. at Columbia in 1932 and 1938. She was a Carnegie fellow in 1937 and continued graduate study at Teachers College, Columbia (1947–50). Her early professional experience included service as an English teacher and librarian, George Washington High School, Danville, Virginia (1927–37); Technical Director, State-Wide Library Project, W.P.A. of Virginia (1938–39); Librarian, Scarsdale (New York) High School (1939–42); Librarian and Associate Professor of Library Service, New Jersey State Teachers College, Trenton (1942–54); Visiting Professor, University of Teheran, and leader-specialist, International Information Administration in Iran (1952–53). Between 1934 and 1942, she was a Visiting Professor at the University of Virginia and Emory University.

Gaver made her most important contributions for the advancement of libraries during her years as Associate Professor (1954–60) and Professor (1960–71) at the newly established Graduate School of Library Service at Rutgers University. In 1959–60, under the sponsorship of the U.S. Office of Education, she directed a major research project, *Effectiveness of Centralized School Library Services (Phase I)*. She assisted Frances Henne in completing *Standards for School Library Programs* (published by the American Library Association in 1960). The 1960 standards were enormously influential in individual schools and school districts, primarily because of the extensive and highly successful national promotion campaign Gaver conceived. She chaired the advisory committee to the School Library Development Project of the American Association of School Librarians, which worked through state associations to improve professional leadership among school librarians.

In 1962 she was named chair of an ALA advisory committee to administer a $1,130,000 grant from the Knapp Foundation. The committee organized a five-year program, the Knapp School Libraries Project, to demonstrate good school library service throughout the United States.

Gaver's greatest impact during her Rutgers years was felt through the students who came from far and wide to attend her classes on school library administration, collection building for libraries, and children's literature. She taught and advised many doctoral students and directed a number of dissertations, and later maintained a wide correspondence with her former students.

Gaver worked productively for her objectives through professional organizations, including IFLA. She represented the New Jersey Library Association (NJLA) on the ALA Council (1956–60) and served as a member at large (1961–65). She served NJLA as Vice-President (1947–48) and President (1954–55). The New Jersey School Library Association honored her with a testimonial luncheon in March 1965 in appreciation of her 20 years of achievement in the development of the state's libraries. She served as President of ALA's Library Education Division (1949–50); President of the American Association of School Librarians (1959–60); and President of ALA (1966–67). In 1980 the American Association of School Librarians presented Gaver with the third annual President's Award, cosponsored by AASL and the Baker and Taylor Company, to honor an individual for "outstanding work in school librarianship and school library development."

Compson

Mary Virginia Gaver

Other recognitions include the Rutgers Research Council Award, conferred in 1962, which recognized her "outstanding contributions to the development of service to children and young people in school and public libraries"; the Randolph-Macon Woman's College Achievement Award; and the Beta Phi Mu Award of Good Teaching in 1964. One of the highest honors in librarianship, the Herbert Putnam Honor Award of the ALA, conferred only rarely since its inception in 1939, was presented to Gaver in 1963. The citation referred to her "significant contributions to the profession of librarianship in the areas of professional leadership in library development and organization, research, children's and school library work, library education, and her professional and educational writing."

Other awards include the Constance Lindsay Skinner Award of the Woman's National Book Association (1973) and research grants from the Rutgers University Research Council (1968–69 and 1969–70). C. W. Post College awarded her an honorary LL.D. in 1967; Mount Holyoke College gave her an LL.D. in 1968.

In addition to *Effectiveness of Centralized School Library Services (Phase I)* (2nd edition, 1963), Gaver published *Every Child Needs a School Library* (1957); *The Research Manual* (3rd edition, 1963) with Lucille Hook; *School Libraries of Puerto Rico, A Survey and Plan for Development* (privately published, 1963) with Gonzalo Velasquez; *Libraries for the People of New Jersey; or Knowledge for All* (1964) with Lowell A. Martin; *Patterns of Development of Elementary School Libraries Today* (3rd edition, 1969); *Services of Secondary School Media Centers* (1970); and *A Survey of the Educational Media Services of Calgary Public Schools* (with others) (1971).

She retired from the faculty of the Rutgers Graduate School of Library Science in 1971 and joined Bro-Dart, Inc., as Consultant for Library and Publisher Relations. She was named a Vice-President of the firm in 1973. She was General Editor of *The Elementary School Library Collection* (ESLC) (1st–8th editions, Bro-Dart Foundation, 1965–73), and continued to evaluate fiction for the ESLC until 1984.

In 1975 she moved back to Danville, Virginia. She organized a local arts association and Friends of the Public Library there, and also developed a book review series for the local Young Women's Christian Association.

In 1976, at the ALA Centennial Conference, Gaver received the highest award the Association can give, Honorary Membership.

MILBREY L. JONES

Germany

Germany is a federal republic in central Europe, bordered on the north by the North Sea, Denmark, and the Baltic Sea; on the east by Poland and the Czech Republic; on the south by Austria and Switzerland; and on the west by France, Luxembourg, Belgium, and the Netherlands. Population (1991 est.)

79,879,000; area 356,910 sq.km. The official language is German.

EDITOR'S NOTE: The German Democratic Republic (East Germany) merged with the Federal Republic of Germany (West Germany) on October 3, 1990, to form a unified state after more than 40 years of separate development following World War II. The two reports that follow outline how the two library communities developed from the 1940s to 1990. The final section highlights major changes made and anticipated as a result of the merger.

FEDERAL REPUBLIC OF GERMANY (1946–90)

History. The foundation of contemporary librarianship in Germany dates back to the Reformation, but the development of modern librarianship in Germany—as well as in other large European nations—began in the early 19th century, a result of attempts during the Romantic period to maintain ecclesiastical libraries that had been abandoned because of political events. Many rare book collections, particularly from monasteries, were transferred to libraries of ruling nobilities, and in turn became part of regional and state libraries—the central research libraries of the individual states of the German Empire—in the course of the 19th century. Meanwhile, university libraries gained greater prominence after the reform of German universities during the first decades of that century. The University of Göttingen—already in possession of an efficient library during the 18th century—was a model for new university libraries in already established and newly founded universities. Regional, state, and university libraries assumed guiding functions in library work in Germany.

During most of the 19th century a university library was run by a university professor, but later it was headed by a library professional, as library science came into being. However, the *professor-librarian,* as represented by Friedrich Ritschl (classical philology), Karl Richard Lepsius (Egyptology), and Adolf von Harnack (theology), still existed into the beginning of the 20th century.

In addition to academic and research libraries, public libraries, originally financed by private contributions, were established in the 19th century. Later the Anglo-American model influenced German public library development with the *Bücherhalle* (book hall). During the second decade of the 20th century, the Bücherhalle's emphasis on instruction was replaced by an emphasis on the education of its readers, as shown especially in the work of Walter Hofmann. After World War II German libraries again turned toward the Anglo-American public library tradition.

The Former German State Library (East Berlin), founded in 1661 as part of the court library of the Lector of Brandenberg, is now part of the new German National Library.

Tschuschke

World War II marked a significant turning point in the Germany library system. In the course of the ravages of war, many libraries were destroyed. The largest German library, the Preussische Staatsbibliothek (Prussian State Library) in Berlin, was divided among the German *länder* (states). The reconstruction of academic and research libraries after 1945 was based on the traditional patterns of library administration as described in the *Handbuch der Bibliothekswissenschaft* ("Handbook of Library Science," 2nd ed. 1952–65), edited by Fritz Milkau and Georg Leyh (1931–42). It guided academic and research libraries for almost 40 years.

German university libraries at the end of the 19th century felt restricted because of the better-financed libraries of the university institutes, which the directors of the university libraries could not influence. Also the number of personnel in academic libraries was generally insufficient up to the middle of the 1960s. Central services, such as cataloguing by a national library, did not exist in Germany, so that libraries with only a small number of employees had to handle a considerable amount of work.

The reestablishment of German sciences after the World Wars created a strong demand for foreign literature. In order to assure that the required literature for research would be available in the Federal Republic, the Deutsche Forschungsgemeinschaft (German Research Society) founded a system of special collections in the German academic and research libraries whereby approximately 40 libraries collect newly published foreign literature relevant for scientific research in their specific fields of science. Since 1949 this literature has been made available to all users through a more and more developed interlibrary loan system.

In the early 1960s a trend toward new universities brought about changes in academic libraries. These changes included open access, centralized library systems, professors working with specialists in book selection, and the introduction of electronic data processing. Data processing also led in the 1970s to the establishment of regional library centers, which provide data processing services for the libraries of individual regions.

After the war the public libraries became oriented to the Anglo-American library system. In a short period the public library replaced the German *Volksbücherei* (people's library) first in the large cities and somewhat later in smaller cities and towns. Closed stacks were opened and comprehensive information services were developed. Efficient library centers with large collections were founded, and the collections of the Volksbüchereien, which had been restricted mainly to belles lettres, were significantly enlarged with other types of informational materials.

National Libraries. A single comprehensive national library has never existed in Germany; however, beginning in 1912 the Deutsche Bücherei (German Library) in Leipzig collected all German publications and published a national bibliography. After the partition of Germany, a new library, the Deutsche Bibliothek, was founded for these tasks in the Federal Republic in 1946. It became a federal government institution in 1969. One of its tasks was the comprehensive collection and bibliographic registration of German literature—not only publications of the Federal Republic but also German-language publications of the German Democratic Republic, Austria, Switzerland, and Luxembourg, as well as of non-German-speaking countries in all parts of the world.

Besides collection and bibliographic registration, the Deutsche Bibliothek handled central services for all libraries. It maintained the German office of the International Serials Data System, a CIP-Service for central cataloguing of new German publications, and the online database Biblio-Data for bibliographic search, containing all German titles from 1972.

Central Special Libraries. There were four central special libraries—for medical sciences in Cologne, technology in Hannover (TIB), worldwide economics in Kiel, and agricultural sciences in Bonn. Organized step by step from 1959, they were modeled after similar national libraries in the United States, with foremost concentration on foreign literature.

State Libraries. Two large state libraries, the Bayerische Staatsbibliothek (Bavarian State Library) in Munich and the Staatsbibliothek Preussischer Kulturbesitz (State Library "Prussian Cultural Heritage") in Berlin, handled some central services for the Federal Republic. The Staatsbibliothek Preussischer Kulturbesitz was jointly financed by the federal and state governments; the Bayerische Staatsbibliothek was an agency of the state of Bavaria. These two libraries handled the collections of ancient and foreign literature and were the largest libraries in the Federal Republic. Along with the Deutsche Bibliothek, they carried out central functions for all German libraries. The ISBN agency was affiliated with the Staatsbibliothek Preussischer Kulturbesitz, which established the serials database for German libraries. The Bayerische Staatsbibliothek took care of the German communications format for electronically stored title entries and the cataloguing of 15th- and 16th-century publications.

Other State Libraries. There are state libraries in the individual German states (Staats- und Landesbibliotheken), which supply materials in a state or region. Some of these libraries additionally serve as university libraries, such as the Staats- und Universitätsbibliothek Hamburg (State and University Library of Hamburg). All these libraries have the right of legal deposit for their respective regions and in most cases publish regional bibliographies.

Regional Library Centers. In order to meet the data processing needs of libraries, specific regional library centers were established, such as those in North Rhine-Westphalia (University Library Center), in Lower Saxony (Göttingen), and in Berlin, where the Deutsches Bibliotheksinstitut (German Library Institute) also performed these tasks at the supra-regional level. These centers operate online databases for the libraries of their regions, make their services available to all libraries, and are responsible for centralized planning of data processing for the region's libraries.

City Libraries. The city research libraries have an old tradition, traceable to the late Middle Ages in many cases. But the largest and most important ones received new responsibilities in the 20th century because of their integration into universities, as in Cologne, Frankfurt, Hamburg, Bremen, and Düsseldorf. The trend toward public libraries after World War II also affected city research libraries, and in many cases they were consolidated with public libraries to create new and efficient library systems, as in Hannover, Essen, Munich, and Wuppertal.

Staatsbibliothek Preussischer Kulturbesitz

Staatsbibliothek Preussischer Kulturbesitz, Berlin, one of the nation's largest and most ambitious post-World War II library buildings, completed in 1978.

Academic Libraries. University libraries play a dominant role in German librarianship; next to the public libraries of the large cities, they have the greatest number of readers. The expansion of universities in the Federal Republic from 1960 had a considerable influence on the number and structure of university libraries. The number of universities and technical institutes in 1964 totaled 25. By 1984 the number had more than doubled. In addition, a completely new type of university, the *Fachhochschule* ("professional university"), specializing in more practical education, was created. There were about 60 of these institutions in the Federal Republic.

The structure of university libraries also changed. The library system of the old universities was characterized by a central university library and a number of independent institute libraries (often more than a hundred in one university). Most of the newer university libraries simultaneously manage a few departmental libraries; this type is referred to as a "single-line" university library.

Public Libraries. This type of library developed to quite an extent after World War II. By the 1990s all cities had big city-financed libraries with many branches that housed comprehensive literature selections for the public. Since the beginning of the 20th century, the library development in smaller towns and provinces had been supported by Staatliche Büchereistellen (advisory offices for public libraries); these institutions had advisory functions and kept bookstocks available for smaller libraries for completing their collections.

Special Libraries. The Federal Republic had a great number of special libraries, many with quite comprehensive holdings. About 1,500 important special libraries ranged in size from several thousand to several hundred thousand volumes. Parliamentary and administrative libraries existed at state as well as federal level, the largest being the Bibliothek des Deutschen Bundestages (Library of the House of Parliament).

Larger industrial firms and business associations also maintained significant libraries. Both established churches (Roman Catholic and Protestant) also maintained library systems that included public and research libraries.

Beginning in 1962 the Federal Republic developed a documentation and information system financed jointly by the federal and state governments. Under the Government Program for Advancement of Information and Documentation (I & D Program), a central institution for research and development was established, the Gesellschaft für Information und Dokumentation (Institute for Information and Documentation) in Frankfurt. In addition, some central documentation centers in specific fields worked jointly with their area libraries to supply needed materials.

The Profession. Most librarians were in the civil service and paid according to rank on three levels: as subject specialists, certified librarians, and library assistants. They prepared for service in public libraries and for service in academic and research libraries as well as in documentation centers. Passing a state examination was a prerequisite to entering the service. Certificates for state examinations were provided by library schools after a study of three or two years respectively. The library schools mostly belonged as so-called *Fachhochschulen* to the lower level of German universities, which award only the Diploma degree to their students. Library science could be studied at the University of Cologne leading to the master's degree (in a four-year course) and the doctorate (with at least two supplementary years).

Continuing education was offered by the library schools in close cooperation with library associations.

Associations. The six large library associations of the Federal Republic were united in the *Deutsche Bibliothekskonferenz* (German Library Conference), the official partner of the federal government and the states regarding all general library affairs. The President was the chairman of one of the member associations and served a one-year term.

The *Deutscher Bibliotheksverband* (German Library Association) comprised libraries and their financing institutions. Until the foundation of the German Library Institute in 1978 this association was responsible for all library development in the Federal Republic. The library foreign office (Bibliothekarische Auslandsstelle) was part of this association. This office was responsible for international contacts, particularly for inviting foreign librarians to visit German libraries and arranging trips by German librarians to foreign countries.

Librarians in academic and research libraries were members of the *Verein Deutscher Bibliothekare* (Association of German Librarians) and *Verein der Diplombibliothekare an Wissenschaftlichen Bibliotheken* (Association of Certified Librarians in Research Libraries). The Verein Deutscher Bibliothekare had been responsible for the official work of academic and research libraries for almost 75 years. The new German cataloguing rules (RAK) and new rules for interlibrary loan are examples of these initiatives. These associations also organized meetings of the Deutsche Bibliothekartag (German Librarian's Conference). After the founding of the Deutsches Bibliotheksinstitut, these associations concentrated on professional tasks. The official periodical of these associations is the *Zeitschrift für Bibliothekswesen und Bibliographie.*

The *Verein der Bibliothekare an Öffentlichen Bibliotheken* (Association of Librarians in Public Libraries) was a personnel-oriented organization for librarians of public libraries. It dealt mainly with professional matters and published the journal *Buch und Bibliothek* (Book and Library).

The *Arbeitsgemeinschaft der Spezialbibliotheken* (German Special Libraries Association) represented the special libraries in the Federal Republic. It held a congress every two years to deal with problems of special libraries.

Bayerische Staatsbibliothek

Bayerische Staatsbibliothek, Munich, constructed in 1840.

REFERENCES

Gisela von Busse, Horst Ernestus, and Engelbert Plassmann, *Libraries in the Federal Republic of Germany*, 2nd ed. (1983).

Studies on the Organizational Structure and Services in National and University Libraries in the Federal Republic of Germany and in the United Kingdom (1979).

GÜNTHER PFLUG;
PAUL KAEGBEIN

GERMAN DEMOCRATIC REPUBLIC (1949–90)

History. Before 1945 Germany had large and efficient academic libraries but few general public libraries, and there was only limited state planning or guidance in library work. As a result there were no libraries in a majority of towns, villages, and enterprises. Further, many libraries were destroyed or badly damaged during the war.

After the establishment of the GDR in 1949, development took place in several stages. From 1949 to 1957 a library network was created in the towns and rural communities, in the large enterprises, in all universities and colleges, and in the research institutes of the academies. The next stage involved attaining higher quality in all fields of librarianship and all phases of library work. An important step was the foundation in 1964 of the Library Association of the German Democratic Republic, open to libraries in all fields and of all types.

In 1968 Council of Ministers promulgated the *Bibliotheksverordnung der DDR* (Library Ordinance of the GDR). The first inclusive legal instrument for the whole library system of a German state, it laid down the basic tasks for all libraries in the GDR. It also summarized the principles and requirements necessary for the further development of the branches and types of libraries and for individual libraries.

Public discussion preceded publication of the 11 implementation regulations issued by the mid-1980s. The integrated library system, working in close connection with the information and documentation systems of the GDR, involved several types of libraries. They included libraries with state-wide functions; state public libraries and other public libraries; libraries of universities, colleges, and academies; libraries in enterprises (specialized and trade union libraries); and specialized libraries for research, administration, and other activities. Libraries in the GDR embraced a wide range of objectives, among them contributing to development of scientific-technical progress; greater efficiency in production; research work in all fields and the rapid implementation in practice of research findings; development of a rich intellectual-cultural life; and increase in the educational standard of citizens.

About 32,000 libraries of various types and sizes made some 110 million volumes available to readers in the mid-1980s. More than a third of the citizens of the GDR were regular library users. Every citizen was entitled to borrow books, to use library reading rooms, and to use the many library services. No fee was charged for borrowing books and other library stock, for using reading rooms, or for playing records or tapes. A small fee was charged for some services, such as photocopying and the provision of bibliographical information.

Library Policy and Administration. Central state bodies held final responsibility for library service. The Council of Ministers set basic policy; the Ministry of Culture coordinated the system. It had an Advisory Council on Librarianship, with representatives of various fields and library interests, including the Library Association. The Ministry implemented the Library Law and issued detailed regulations on use, interlibrary lending, and similar topics. The Ministry of Higher Education was responsible for academic libraries.

Central Institutions were set up for important areas of the library system. The central scientific-methodological institutions included the *Zentralinstitut für Bibliothekswesen* (ZIB; Central Institute for Librarianship), which dealt with basic issues; the *Methodisches Zentrum für Wissenschaftliche Bibliotheken und Informations-/Dokumentationseinrichtungen des Ministeriums für Hoch- und Fachschulwesen* (Methodological Center for Scientific Libraries and Information and Documentation Institutes of the Ministry of Higher and Technical Education), which coordinated the work of special libraries; and the *Zentralbibliothek der Gewerkschaften* (Central Library of the Trades Unions).

National Libraries. Two major libraries in the GDR shared the functions of a national library. They were the Deutsche Staatsbibliothek in Berlin and the Deutsche Bücherei in Leipzig.

German State Library. The Deutsche Staatsbibliothek dates back to 1661. It was the central academic library of the GDR and collected all German literature up to 1913. Its 6,550,000 titles in the late 1980s included many treasures of German-language literature from many centuries. It held the largest collection of foreign literature in the GDR. It also collected manuscripts and autographs, sheet music, maps, portraits, and other nonprint material. Stocks were enlarged through deposit copies and wide-ranging exchange agreements with libraries and institutes in some 85 countries; in addition, it was library of deposit for UN publications.

The Library included departments for music, Asia, Africa, maps, incunabula, and books for children and young people; the manuscript department/literature archive; the department for rare and precious prints; and, in addition, the Theodor Fontane Archive in Potsdam. It performed central functions in the fields of interlibrary loan, union catalogues, and manuscripts and incunabula. In addition, it worked closely with other libraries in various fields, particularly in the coordination of new acquisitions. It published the union catalogue of incunabula, a register of all known incunabula in the world.

German Library. The Deutsche Bücherei in Leipzig was established in 1912 by the Börsenverein der Deutschen Buchhändler (German Book Trade Association). From 1913 it collected all German publications and after 1945 continued to do so, covering the GDR, the Federal Republic, and West Berlin, as well as all varieties of German-language writing appearing in all parts of the world. In addition to books and periodicals, it collected university theses, music, art, prints, cards, patent specifications, and other classes of publications. From 1976 it collected musical records produced in the GDR. The Museum of Books and Writings was part of the German Library. The Library held about 7,500,000 titles. As the bibliographic information center for German-language literature, the Library published the *Deutsche Nationalbibliographie* ("German National Bibliography") and basic bibliographies on music and translations, among others.

Academic Libraries. The nine university libraries were among the oldest libraries in the GDR and held wide-ranging and valuable historic bookstocks in addition to modern scientific literature. They were the Library of Humboldt University, Berlin, founded 1831 (4,500,000 volumes); University and Sachsen-Anhalt Province Library of Martin Luther University, Halle-Wittenberg, founded 1696 (3,900,000); Library of Karl Marx University, Leipzig, founded 1543 (3,500,000); Library of Friedrich Schiller University, Jena, founded 1858 (2,800,000); Library of Ernst Moritz Arndt University, Greifswald, founded 1604 (2,400,000); Library of Wilhelm Pieck University, Rostock, founded 1569 (2,000,000); Library of the Technical University, Dresden, founded 1828 (1,600,000); Library of the Technical University, Chemnitz (formerly Karl-Marx-Stadt), founded 1836 (700,000); and Library of the Technical University, Magdeburg, founded 1953 (600,000).

Each university library was organized as a unitary system, integrating services for literature, information, and documentation. In structure the university libraries consisted of main libraries to which were attached the branch libraries in the departments and other academic sections of the university.

College and Technical College Libraries. Among the most important of the more than 60 college libraries were the libraries of the Technical College, Leuna-Merseburg (180,000 volumes); the Mining Academy, Freiberg (482,000); the College of Transport, Dresden (330,000); the College of Economics, Berlin (232,000); the College of Architecture and Civil Engineering, Weimar (204,000); and the College of Physical Training and Sport, Leipzig (100,000). These libraries functioned much like the university libraries. In addition, the approximately 240 technical and specialized colleges of the GDR maintained libraries for their special requirements.

Academy Libraries. The libraries of the six academies of the GDR—Academy of Pedagogic Science, Academy of Architecture, Academy of Agricultural Science, Academy of Arts, Academy for Advanced Medical Training, and Academy of Sciences—held important stocks of scientific literature. The library of the Academy of Sciences was the most important.

Sächsische Landesbibliothek, the Saxon Regional Library, in Dresden, operated directly under the Ministry for Higher and Technical Education as a scientific general library and a specialized central library for the arts. It maintained the regional central catalogue for Dresden, Chemnitz, and Cottbus. It was founded in 1556 as the Saxon Court Library, and had valuable historic bookstocks, including incunabula.

Special Libraries. All ministries, central state departments, and institutions maintained special libraries. The most important special libraries of state bodies were the Library of the People's Chamber (Parliament), the Central Library in the House of the Ministries, the Library of the Supreme Court of the GDR, the Library of the Office for Inventions and Patents, and the Central Library of the Ministry of Transport.

Social Organizations. The parties, mass organizations, and other associations maintained special libraries. In addition, the museums of the GDR, more than 600 in number, had special libraries, some of considerable importance, as did archives and many scientific societies.

Networks. Cooperative networks of technical libraries grew up in the 1980s, specialized both by theme and bookstocks, including heavy engineering, mining and metallurgy, the chemical industry, agriculture, education, and medicine. The more than 400 medical libraries in the state hospitals, medical research centers, and training centers worked together in one specialized network with the medical information centers. The network was directed by the Institute for Scientific Information in Medicine (IWIM). The network is organized on a geographic basis for medical care and on a subject basis for medical research.

Public Libraries. The *Staatliche Allgemeinbibliotheken* (StAB; state general libraries) were the basic libraries in the national library system of the GDR. Their functions and tasks extended to all sections of the population and to all parts of the country. The ruling principle was that they served the general and specific needs for literature and information services of all citizens. Their mission was to awaken, foster, and satisfy the needs of adults, young people, and children for educational, recreational, and vocational or professional information and library services. Their bookstocks were general in nature, and they were linked through interlibrary loans with other libraries. As a rule, in communities with more than 3,000 inhabitants, they were administered and directed by full-time staff; in smaller communities, staffing was on a part-time basis. They were organized in local networks on the pattern of main library, branch library, lending center.

Networks existed for each of the 190 rural districts. The urban and rural libraries in each district center functioned as advisory and bookstock centers for the library networks. Rural central libraries, with extensive collections and full-time staff, served as bookstock centers for a number of communities with part-time libraries. The library system in East Berlin maintained a main library in each of the nine city boroughs; the Berlin City Library acted as the bookstock center and scientific-methodical guidance center.

In the late 1980s the GDR had about 14,000 public libraries. Those staffed full-time consisted of about 1,000 main libraries, 700 branch libraries, and 5,000 lending stations. Those staffed part-time consisted of 6,000 community libraries and 1,000 lending stations.

Children's Services. Two-thirds of all children and young people up to the age of 18 used these libraries. For children between 6 and 14, special separate collections were made available, including both print and audiovisual materials. Available either in special branch libraries or in separate departments, they were sorted according to age groups and school grades. At branch libraries or children's departments, children could borrow books, read in the library, and play records and tapes. Guided tours of the library and instruction on library use were provided for the various ages and school grades.

A 1975 agreement between the Ministry of Culture and the Ministry of Education provided that library services for children in the GDR would be provided by the public libraries. As a result the ten-grade general polytechnic schools in the GDR did not maintain their own school libraries, but only grade selections with materials pertaining to the curriculum. But many children's branches of public libraries were established in schools.

Young Adults. For young people above the age of 14, selections particularly suited for that group were offered in the adult section of the library. Apart from that, young people were free to use the entire adult collection.

Trade Union Libraries existed in all sectors of the economy, and in state institutions, administrative offices, houses of culture, and holiday homes. They performed functions similar to those of the public libraries. Their main task was to provide access to information among those employed in an enterprise, in trade union groups, and in work teams. Their basic tasks and the general rules for their activities were determined by the central board of the Federation of Free German Trades Unions (FDGB). In enterprises with more than 1,000 employees, the libraries had full-time staff and in smaller enterprises, part-time staff. Of the nearly 4,000 trade union libraries in the late 1980s, almost 3,000 had full-time staff. The trade union libraries were not organized in a general library network, but they worked closely with the libraries in their regions.

The Profession. Trained library personnel in the GDR were classified in three groups: *Bibliotheksfacharbeiter* (trained library workers), *Bibliothekar* (graduate librarians), and *Diplombibliothekar* or *Wissenschaftlicher Bibliothekar* (academic librarians). Library workers received two years of theoretical and practical training in a library and vocational school. Graduate librarians took either three years of full-time study or four and a half years of part-time study at a training college. Academic librarians could study library and information science with another subject in five years, library science only in four years, or library or information science for two years after their first degrees in other subjects.

Institutions that provided library training were the Vocational School for Trained Library Workers in Sondershausen; the Training College for Librarians and Training College for Scientific Librarianship in Leipzig; and the Training College for Scientific Information and Scientific Librarianship and Institute for Library Science and Scientific Information of the Humboldt University in Berlin.

Association. The Bibliotheksverband (BV; Library Association) of the GDR, established in 1964, had about 2,000 institutional members. It was divided into 15 county groups on a geographic basis (the basic organizations of the association) and professionally into sections for libraries with the same specialization and working groups on such topics as education.

The Association held its General Assembly every five years to elect a President and a Präsidium (executive board) to direct its activities and decide on its professional program. The BV drafted proposals and recommendations for the development of the library system for state bodies and advised those directing these bodies. In addition it undertook wide-ranging educational publicity work. It had working relationships with the library associations of other countries and was a national member of IFLA.

Research. Various institutions participated in library research, primarily the scientific-methodical centers, central libraries, and training centers. The Institute for Library Science and Scientific Information of the Humboldt University in Berlin drew up plans for library research and coordinated research activities. The results of library research found their expression in dissertations, diploma theses, training college theses, research reports, and publications.

Publications. There were many library publications in the GDR, issued by publishing houses, library institutions, libraries, and the VB. The VEB Bibliographisches Institut in Leipzig specialized in monographs on library subjects and on information/documentation. Library monthlies were *Zentralblatt für Bibliothekswesen* and *Der Bibliothekar.* Both periodicals had a joint editorial staff in Berlin and both published supplements related to special themes. Specialized library information was provided by the annotated *Informationsdienst Bibliothekswesen,* published every two months by the Central Office for Information and Documentation in Librarianship and attached to the Central Institute for Librarianship.

REFERENCES

Das Bibliothekswesen in der Deutschen Demokratischen Republik: Jahresbericht 1988 (1989).

Wilfried Kern, *Librarianship in the German Democratic Republic* (1981).

GOTTHARD RÜCKL;
STEFFEN RÜCKL

REUNIFYING THE LIBRARY SYSTEMS

The separate development of libraries and librarianship in the Federal Republic and the German Democratic Republic presented great difficulties for the reunification of the two countries in 1990. Considerable discussion and consultation took place prior to reunification and a joint newsletter, *Bibliotheksinformationen: Ost-West,* was established in June 1990 to report current developments and to stimulate contacts between the two communities.

The national libraries in Frankfurt and Leipzig were merged into a new institution under the old title, Deutsche Nationalbibliothek. The Leipzig library planned to concentrate on bibliographic services to the German book trade, preservation and conservation processes, and a planned museum for books and writing. The Frankfurt library planned to compile and publish the national bibliography and sponsor other information and communication activities, including hosting the IFLA Universal Bibliographic Control–International MARC (UBC-IM) program.

The national bibliographies, *Deutsche Nationalbibliographie* (Leipzig, 1913–) and *Deutsche Bibliographie* (Frankfurt, 1947–), were combined under the management of the Frankfurt library, which had pioneered in the automation of its compilation, but retained the original title, *Deutsche Nationalbibliographie,* from January 1991.

The Berlin libraries, the Deutsche Staatsbibliothek (East) and Staatsbibliothek Preussicher Kulturbesitz (West), were merged under the name Deutsche Staatsbibliothek as one institution with two locations. The library in the eastern sector was designated to collect primarily pre-1945 materials; the library in the western sector concentrated on more modern materials. This division resolved the historic split between the old and rare materials that had been relocated to the west during World War II for security and their catalogue descriptions, which remained in the east.

The Zentralinstitut für Bibliothekswesen and the Methodisches Zentrum were merged with the Deutsches Bibliotheksinstitut in Berlin. The two major professional journals, the *Zentralblatt für Bibliothekswesen* and the *Zeitschrift für Bibliothekswesen,* merged under the latter name. The major book trade associations merged as the Borsenblatt für den Deutschen Buchhändel.

Initial assessment of libraries in the former GDR revealed significant deficiencies in the range and scope of their collections resulting from both ideological orientations and censorship, but there is some evidence that the public libraries contained a surprising amount of what might have been considered subversive or anti-government literature. Many library buildings were found to be in poor condition and in need of major renovation, and most institutions lacked such equipment as photocopy machines. The new German government promised funds to upgrade the libraries and sought book donations from institutions and individuals to help fill gaps in their collections.

Discussion in the professional literature suggested the need to standardize German library education in order to minimize or eliminate variances and also to prepare for the need to harmonize professional education in Germany with that of the European Community.

REFERENCES

Gert Kreusel, "Gleichgeschalet oder subversiv? Oeffentliche Bibliotheken am Beispiel DDR," *Buch und Bibliothek* (1991).

Diann Rusch-Feja, "Reciprocity of Qualifications in Practice: Equivalency Issues Affecting the Librarian and Documentation Professions in Germany after Reunification," *The International Information and Library Review* (1992).

Mathilde V. Rovelstad, "East German Libraries in a Reunified Germany: The Adaptation Process," *Journal of Academic Librarianship* (1992).

ROBERT WEDGEWORTH

Conrad Gesner

The Newberry Library

Gesner, Conrad
(1516–1565)

Conrad Gesner, Swiss Humanist scholar, discovered in bibliography an appropriate expression for his profound intellectual adventurousness. It is hardly correct to see Gesner as the "father of bibliography," since Tritheim, Erasmus, Nevizzano, Leland, and Champier all did important work before him, but the dimensions of Gesner's achievements are many times more vast. The logical planning that was called for, no doubt, was conspicuous in first inspiring the monumental efforts behind the *Bibliotheca Universalis,* his best-known work.

Born into a large Zurich family on March 16, 1516, he was assigned to live with two family friends, both of whom encouraged his studies. One was Johann Jacob Amman, a friend of Erasmus. Amman taught him Latin. The Battle of Kappel in 1531, which took the life of Zwingli, also claimed Gesner's father, and Conrad returned home to support his mother. In 1533 he traveled to Bourges on a fellowship but returned home the next year following the strong French reaction to Protestantism. He married in 1535, at the age of 19.

His first published book, a Greek-Latin dictionary (1537), coincided with his appointment as Professor of Greek at the newly founded university in Lausanne. Four years later he left for a chair in physics and natural history at the Collegium Carolinum in Zurich, where he lived until his death. Honors were bestowed on him by nearby royalty; scholars visited him and contributed to his vast correspondence. He died on December 13, 1565, during one of the frequent plagues of Zurich.

Gesner produced 72 "books" that were published in his lifetime and left 18 more unfinished. Alongside the *Bibliotheca Universalis* is the *Historia Animalium,* four volumes of which appeared 1551–58 and a fifth posthumously in 1587. His work in botany began with an edition of Valerius Cordus of 1561 and was not completed in print until the *Opera Botanica* of 1751–71. In both zoology and botany, his work was mostly that of a collector and organizer; he remains the leading modern scholar up to the time of Linnaeus. In philology, his several dictionaries take second place to the *Mithridates* of 1555, in which parallels in 130 languages are presented and the Romany language is discussed for the first time. His medical studies were collected in the *Epistolarum Medicinalium* of 1577, while his culinary insights are seen in his 1563 edition of Willich's cookbook, *Ars Magirica.* He also worked and published extensively in geology and mineralogy; his studies of fossils were probably the result of his love for mountain climbing, the reports that he did the latter for exercise and amusement notwithstanding.

Gesner's *Bibliotheca Universalis* was issued in four folio volumes by a friend, the Zurich publisher Christopher Froschauer. The first volume (1545) is the author catalogue. Next come the *pandects,* a classified subject-index to the first volume, with 21 subdivisions of the world of knowledge. The second volume (1548) contains 19 subjects; theology alone comprises the third volume (1549); while the material on medicine was never published. The fourth volume (1555) is an appendix with additional titles. Gesner's colleagues soon discovered the importance of this work. Two abridgments quickly appeared (1551, 1555); supplements were issued as early as 1555; and expanded new editions were assembled by his pupils Josias Simler (1574) and Johann Jacob Frisius (1583). Gesner's entries include not only author and title information but also in many cases imprints, chapter and section headings or other contents descriptions, and occasional critical observations. Gesner both cites the published editions he knew about and in many cases gives credit to authors for their unpublished or unfinished works, even for works that were known to have been projected.

REFERENCES

J. Christian Bay, "Conrad Gesner (1516–1565), the Father of Bibliography: An Appreciation," *Papers of the Bibliographical Society of America* (1916).

Hans Fischer, "Conrad Gessner [sic] (1516–1565) as Bibliographer and Encyclopedist," *The Library,* 5th series (1966).

D. W. KRUMMEL

Ghana

The Republic of Ghana, known before independence in 1957 as the Gold Coast, lies on the Gulf of Guinea.

It is bounded by Ivory Coast on the west, Burkina Faso on the north, and Togo on the east. Population (1990 est.) 15,028,000; area 238,533 sq.km. The official language is English, and the government sponsors 11 other languages, including Akan, Dagbani, Ewe, Ga, and Nzema.

History. All libraries in Ghana look back to two founding collections. One was that of John Onfeur Anglionby, the Anglican Bishop of Accra, established in 1928 with a collection of nearly 6,000 volumes. It was later taken over by the British Council and finally became part of the public library service of Ghana. The other was the collection held by the Achimota College Library. The college was at one time the center for training librarians in the country. The collections of the Bishop Boys School Library and the British Council Library became the core of the stock of the Ghana Library Board. Ghana was the first black African country to create a nationwide public library system.

National Library. The Research Library on African Affairs in Accra, the capital, functions as the National Library of Ghana. Kwame Nkrumah founded the Library in 1961 as the Padmore Research Library in memory of his friend and adviser George Padmore, a West Indian and Pan-Africanist, to support research on African affairs. Governed by the Ghana Library Board, it changed its name in 1966.

The Library acquires and conserves copies of all significant publications produced in the country and functions as a legal deposit library; produces a national bibliography; and keeps up to date a large representative collection of foreign literature, including books about Ghana. It has a good collection of newspapers and periodicals on microfilm and a collection of photographs of historical and political events. It serves as the bibliographic control center for publishers in the country.

The Research Library cooperates actively with other Africana libraries in Ghana in order to pool library resources. It has an active international lending and exchange program. It keeps union lists of certain types of library materials. The Library has an active program for collecting and preserving oral tradition. It covers not only oral literature but also history, music, and dance, on film, tapes, and records.

Academic Libraries. Achimota Training College, founded in the 1920s, became Achimota College in 1948. It had the first academic library in the country, and its collections seeded other libraries throughout the 1950s and 1960s.

Jean E. Lowrie

The Balme Library of the University of Ghana, Legon, Accra, is the largest academic library in Ghana.

The Balme Library, the main library of the University of Ghana in Legon, is the oldest and largest academic library in Ghana. It moved into its permanent buildings in 1959 and now has 336,000 volumes and more than 5,000 periodical subscriptions, including an Arabica collection. It has been a depository of documents for the UN Economic Commission for Africa since 1963; a World Bank Documents Library was in development in the early 1990s. A Braille Library was opened in 1989. The Africana Library was established to complement the efforts of the Institute of African Studies Library. The faculties of law and agriculture and other departments have smaller collections.

The University of Ghana Medical School Library was founded in 1967 and inherited the resources of the Ministry of Health Library, successor to the Medical

Libraries in Ghana (1989)

Type of library	Number of administrative units (main libraries)	Number of service points (branches, mobile stops, etc.)	Volumes in collections	Annual expenditures (cedi)	Population served	Professional staff (with certificate, diploma, etc.)	Total staff
National[a]	1	1	35,000	--	--	3 Prof. 2 Sub-Prof.	23
Academic*	9	9	180,000	56,000,000	2,953	10	50
Public	12	40	1,168,892	102,000,000	85,000	15	404[b]

*For University of Cape Coast only.
[a]Research library.
[b]including Research Library on African Affairs

Research Library (1909) and the erstwhile National Institute of Health and Medical Research. Its stock is about 27,000 volumes.

The University of Science and Technology Library at Kumasi, developed from the Achimota Training College, has a total stock of more than 145,000 volumes, 300 current periodicals, and more than 1,600 dissertations. Many departments of the University have libraries attached to them.

The Library of the University of Cape Coast started as a college library when the University College of Cape Coast was established in 1962 to train teachers. The library has about 180,000 volumes and more than 1,100 serials. It inherited about 650 volumes from the Kumasi College of Technology in the early 1960s.

Public Libraries. Public librarianship is the concern of the Ghana Library Board. Its function is to establish, equip, and maintain a network of public libraries and to promote and make available books, periodicals, and other reading materials. It set out to establish temporary libraries in the regional capitals and has established nine regional libraries and 40 branches. It provides children's library services in all its outlets except the Research Library on African Affairs. Some branch libraries emphasize children and youth more than adults.

The Board, established in 1950, adopted the pattern of countrywide service initiated by the British Council and inherited some 27,000 books from its Library. The Council made available to the Board the services of its Librarian, Evelyn J. A. Evans. The Board now has a bookstock of almost 1,170,000, including a fair number of books on the arts and sciences for general readers, and a number of periodical subscriptions. It offers consultancy services to public and private organizations, including training programs, assistance in organizing libraries, and professional advice.

School Libraries. In Ghana school libraries rank lowest in the hierarchy of libraries that serve the public, although there has been increased awareness of the importance of libraries in education since 1960.

In 1968–69 the Board, in association with the Ministry of Education and the British Council, appointed a committee to study school library service in the country. The committee reported in 1970 that it found unsuitable accommodations, poor furniture, and a dependence on the interest and enthusiasm of the headmaster or principal. The greatest defect was the lack of proper organization. Practices varied widely, and there was no consistency of library procedure. A total bookstock of 350,000 volumes was found in the 245 schools in the country.

Following these revelations, the committee recommended that the Ghana Library Board be asked to run the libraries in these schools with additional grants for books and services. The School and College Department of the Board, established in 1972, is responsible for ordering, cataloguing, and providing books for schools. It also arranges regular visits to offer professional guidance in using the library. It prepares booklists and conducts seminars for teacher/librarians and library clerks in the schools and colleges in the country.

Special Libraries. In Ghana special libraries support scientific and social research in various institutions or are built around special collections. The Central Reference and Research Library of the Council for Scientific and Industrial Research (CSIR), founded in 1964, has a collection numbering about 12,000 volumes It coordinates and supplements collections and services of the Council's institute libraries, including the Animal Research Library (founded 1951), the Cocoa Research Institute Library (1960), the Forest Products Research Institute Library (1960), the Institute of Aquatic Biology Library (1965), and the Soils Research Unit Library (1968). These libraries have collections ranging from 2,500 volumes to about 20,000 volumes each.

Among other special libraries are the Ministry of Agriculture Library and those in 18 other government ministries. Prominent among them are the Ministry of Lands and Mineral Resources, the Central Bureau of Statistics, and the Volta River Authority. The Ghana Institute of Management and Public Administration Library and Documentation Center (1961) acquired in 30 years some 30,500 monographs and 150 periodical titles. It has a strong collection of Gold Coast and Ghana official documents and documents from international organizations. It is a depository for World Bank and World Health Organization publications. Some banking and financial institutions and a few government boards, such as the Ghana Standards Board and the National Energy Board, have established libraries.

REFERENCES

Evelyn J. A. Evans, *A Tropical Library Service: The Story of Ghana's Libraries* (1964).

Ghana Library Board, "The Ghana Library Board Silver Jubilee Brochure 1950–1975" (1975).

John Harris, *Patterns of Library Growth in English-speaking West Africa* (1970).

DAVID CORNELIUS

Gjelsness, Rudolph H.
(1894–1968)

Rudolph H. Gjelsness, American library educator, consultant, and scholar, was the first recipient (1954) of the Beta Phi Mu Award for distinguished service to education for librarianship.

ALA

Rudolph H. Gjelsness

He was born in Reynolds, North Dakota, October 18, 1894. Following his graduation from the University of North Dakota in 1916, Gjelsness became a high school principal in Adams, North Dakota, but resigned a year later to join the American Expeditionary Force (AEF) in World War I. His interest in librarianship had its origin following the Armistice in 1918 when he was detached from the Army to serve as Reference Librarian with the AEF in Beaune, France.

Returning to the United States in 1919, Gjelsness enrolled in the University of Illinois's library school and received the B.L.S. degree in 1920. His first professional library position was as Order Librarian for the University of Oregon; in 1922 he became Senior Bibliographer at the University of California. A fellowship from the American Scandinavian Foundation in 1924 permitted him to spend a year in Norway, the home of his ancestors.

Gjelsness's first contribution to library literature appeared in the July 1925 issue of *Public Libraries* and was entitled "A Librarian's Year in Norway." Writing from Norway, he closed the article with, "When I return, I shall be interested in a position where I could develop or organize something." That opportunity came quickly with his appointment by William Warner Bishop as Assistant Librarian and Chief Classifier for the University of Michigan. In the summer of 1927 Gjelsness was given his first opportunity to contribute to library education, teaching a course in national and regional bibliography in Michigan's new library school.

From 1929 to 1932 Gjelsness was Chief of the Preparation Division of the New York Public Library and a Lecturer in library science at Columbia University. From 1932 to 1937 he was Head Librarian at the University of Arizona. In 1937 he consented to return to Michigan as Professor of Library Science with the tacit understanding that in due course he would succeed Bishop as head of the Library School, a position he held from 1940 until his retirement in 1964. During the 24 years that Gjelsness chaired the Department of Library Science, the University conferred 2,269 degrees in Library Science, including 47 doctorates.

Active in association work, Gjelsness chaired the ALA Committee on Cataloging and Classification from 1930 to 1933, and from 1935 to 1941 he headed the Catalog Code Revision Committee. He was Editor-in-Chief of the *A.L.A. Catalog Rules: Author and Title Entries* (1941). He was Treasurer of ALA from 1941 to 1947 and President of the Association of American Library Schools, 1948–49.

Strongly committed to international librarianship, Gjelsness co-directed a summer school at Bogotá, Colombia, in 1942 and spent a year away from Michigan (1943–44) as Director of the Benjamin Franklin Library in Mexico City. A sabbatical year (1962–63) was spent as Library Consultant to the President of the University of Baghdad in Iraq.

Following his retirement in 1964, Gjelsness returned to the University of Arizona Library to head its Special Collections Division. After a summer teaching assignment at Michigan in 1968, he went to the University of Puerto Rico to assist in founding the Graduate School of Librarianship. He was killed by an automobile in a hit-and-run accident on his second day in Rio Piedras, August 16, 1968.

Luther College and the University of North Dakota awarded him honorary degrees, and in 1966 a Festschrift was published in his honor by the University of Virginia, *Books in America's Past*. His articles and books, which number more than 80, pertain largely to issues in library education, international and comparative librarianship, cataloguing and classification, the history of books and printing, and Norwegian literature. He translated a number of Norwegian short stories and novels into English.

REFERENCE

Russell E. Bidlack, "Gjelsness, Rudolph H.," *Dictionary of American Library Biography* (1978).

RUSSELL E. BIDLACK

Gleason, Eliza Atkins
(1909–)

Atlanta University Center Library Archives Department, Atlanta University

Eliza Atkins Gleason

Eliza Atkins Gleason, American librarian and educator, was the first Dean of the School of Library Service, Atlanta University, and the architect of a library education program that trained more than 90 percent of all black librarians in the United States.

She was born in Winston-Salem, North Carolina, December 15, 1909, to Simon Green and Oleona Pegram Atkins. Her father was the founder and first President of Slater State College, now Winston-Salem State University, and her mother was a teacher.

After graduating from Fisk University in 1930 as a member of Phi Beta Kappa, Eliza Atkins received the Bachelor of Science degree from the Library School of the University of Illinois in 1931. In 1936 she received the Master of Arts in Library Science from the University of California at Berkeley. She studied at the University of Chicago Graduate Library School and in 1940 became the first black person to receive the Ph.D. in Library Science. She was married to Maurice F. Gleason, a physician, in 1937.

The Dean of the School of Library Service, Atlanta University (1940–46), which opened in 1941, Gleason was aware that the success of the program, even in a period of segregation and rampant discrimination against black persons, depended on a philosophy that was responsive to current human needs but at the same time capable of being remodeled and reshaped when necessary. She wrote, "these objectives are enunciated with the full recognition that no institution can long remain an active force unless it is sensitive to contemporary life, which implies a willingness to accept change. A program of this kind, therefore, predisposes that the objectives of the School of Library Service of Atlanta University are not static but that they may be altered according to the best judgment of the school in what seems to be the present and long-term needs of library service with special reference to the Negro" (*Library Quarterly*, July 1942).

Gleason's professional career was distinguished, wide, varied, and productive. In 1931 and 1932 she was Librarian of the Louisville Municipal College. In 1932 she accepted the position of Head of the Reference Department and Assistant Professor at Fisk and served there until 1936. In 1936–37 she was Director of Libraries at Talladega College, where she became aware of the lack of public library service to black people in the South and began to open the college library resources to black citizens in the surrounding communities. Her interest in access to public libraries for black Americans is reflected in her landmark dissertation, *The Southern Negro and the Public Library* (1941).

In 1953 Gleason became Head of the Reference Department of the Wilson Junior College Library in Chicago. In 1953–54 she was Associate Professor and Head of the Reference Department of the Chicago Teachers College Library. She was Associate Professor of Library Science, Illinois Teachers College, Chicago, from 1954 to 1963. From 1964 to 1967 she was Assistant Librarian at John Crerar Library in Chicago. She was Professor of Library Science, Illinois Institute of Technology, from 1967 to 1970. In 1970 she became Assistant Chief Librarian in charge of the regional centers, Chicago Public Library.

Writing in *Illinois Libraries* (April 1972) about the establishment of the Chicago Public Library's regional library centers, Gleason manifests her continuing interests in students and education:

> In planning for Regional Center service, what potential users did the Chicago Public Library have in mind? It had in mind "students"—students of all kinds. Can one imagine a greater boon for the high school teen-agers who are in honors or accelerated courses, or for junior college students whose programs are terminal, or for junior and senior college students whose own college libraries may be inadequate or on the wrong side of town when they have time to study? And finally, there is that vast hoard of "students" who are not enrolled in formal courses but who wish to pursue a subject in depth.

In the 1974–75 academic year she again returned to library education and served as Professor of Library Science at Northern Illinois University.

Active in professional associations, Gleason was the first Afro-American to serve on the ALA Council; she was a member from 1942 to 1946. In 1964 Fisk bestowed upon her its Alumni Award for outstanding accomplishments.

In addition to her book on *The Southern Negro and the Public Library: A Study of the Government and Administration of Public Library Service to Negroes in the South* (1941), she wrote *A History of the Fisk University Library* (1936) and a large number of journal articles.

A woman of great energy and resourcefulness, Gleason led an active community life. She was elected and appointed to many positions of leadership. In 1978, for example, she was appointed to the Chicago Public Library Board. While most people are in or considering retirement as they begin their 70th year, she demonstrated her vitality by beginning a new career for the benefit of humankind—in the fall of 1978 she was appointed Executive Director of the Chicago Black United Fund.

E. J. JOSEY

Greece (Ancient)

Libraries of public character are attributed by ancient writers to certain 6th-century tyrants of Greek cities, notably Polycrates of Samos and Peisistratus of Athens. Much more is known of the latter than of the former, but we lack the original documents that might have described Peisistratus' supposed library of papyrus rolls of contemporary poetry and drama. Leading scholars believe that any progress in library organization that may have been made under Peisistratus can be determined only by checking the practices of the later libraries of the Ionian cities, which were so important in Greek commerce and culture. Of note during the 5th century were such private libraries as those of the celebrated playwright Euripides, who collected works of poets, dramatists, and philosophers. His passion for books was ridiculed publicly by his rival, Aristophanes. Some writers argue that at least the theater public of that day was conscious of the book but nothing certain is known about these libraries.

By contrast, when one considers philosophical schools, some encouraging deductions become possible. Socrates is understood to have worked exclusively through oral discourse. His pupil Plato likewise believed that the written word was a burden on free discussion and creative thinking, although it seems probable from the testimony of his writings that much material referred to by him and his students was being checked in a book collection of some sort even though none is mentioned. Besides, Plato's own prose is indebted to some of the very poets he banned from his ideal society, and at least one of his (and Isocrates') students established a library.

Furthermore, if one relies on a modern translation (McKeon edition), Aristotle, speaking briefly of writers on husbandry and household economy in *The Politics,* explains that he did not go into detail because "any one who cares for such matters may refer to their writings." This seems to imply the presence of one or more libraries accessible to the student, or of stores selling such works at prices within student means, but this is not certain. The sole established fact is that Aristotle's personal library was not a part of his Lyceum in either a physical or legal sense.

In the later case of Zeno, the founder of Stoicism, the personal library may have been perceived as an integral part of teaching. In any case, Antogonos Gonatas, who seized power in Macedonia in 276 B.C., tried to attract the septuagenarian Zeno to court and offered him slaves to copy books; but, reportedly, Zeno felt physically unable to leave Athens.

The question of libraries arises also in connection with a number of other educational institutions of pre-Alexandrian Greece. Medical teaching was established by Hippocrates and his associates early in the 4th century, and the early 3rd century witnessed the intellectual enrichment of the gymnasium curriculum. Both enterprises may have had "book" collections among their resources, but there is no evidence as yet.

Most vexing are the uncertainties regarding the books owned by Aristotle, thanks to his prominence and the gaps and contradictions in the record. That he left them (d. 323 B.C.) to his disciple Theophrastus is accepted by scholars on the basis of ancient writers' testimony; it is also known that Theophrastus (d. 288 B.C.) bequeathed his collection (including the Aristotle legacy) to his pupil Neleus. Though these facts promote little argument, one must be cautious, since Aristotle's will says nothing of either his school or books, while his legal status as a "metic" (alien resident) prevented him from owning real property in Athens. Did Neleus take the books (which ones?) to his hometown, Skepsis, less than 50 miles north of Pergamum? Were they hidden in a cellar to conceal them from energetic agents seeking books for Pergamum? Did they deteriorate from neglect until found and bought by a rich young Athenian, Appelicon, or were they actually stolen by him right in Athens, or were they in the meantime purchased by representatives of Ptolemy II Philadelphus (reigned 285–247 B.C.) for the great library in Alexandria? It seems fairly clear that when Sulla conquered Athens in 86 B.C., he took to Rome what came to be labeled "Aristotle's library," which was confiscated from the late Appelicon's property; that some blundering efforts were made to restore the documents and the texts they contained; and that sometime in the middle of the 1st century B.C. they were properly edited by the scholarly Andronicus of Rhodes, usually referred to as the 11th Director of the Lyceum. Finally, it is clear—and distressingly important—that a danger of misinterpretation awaits every step, thanks to the dual meaning of *biblia:* when did the author refer to the writings of Aristotle or Theophrastus and when to their entire libraries?

SIDNEY JACKSON
(d. 1979)

Greece

Greece, a republic in the southern Balkan Peninsula, is bounded by Albania on the northwest, Yugoslavia and Bulgaria on the north, and Turkey on the northeast; it extends into the Mediterranean Sea, lying between the Ionian Sea on the west and the Aegean Sea on the east, and occupies most of the islands in the Aegean. Population (1990 est.) 10,048,000; area 131,990 sq.km. The official language is Greek.

History. From ancient times the Greeks were interested in the collection of manuscripts and papyri. In Athens Peisistratus (d. 527 B.C.) was the first to build a collection of Homeric epics and other works of literature to preserve for future generations. Aristotle followed in collecting manuscripts for his private use and systematically catalogued them for more efficient use. The Roman Emperor Hadrian later created a large and beautiful library in Athens in the old Agora. *See also* Greece (Ancient).

During the Middle Ages, a great number of libraries were established in Byzantium by individual and religious institutions. After the fall of Constantinople (A.D. 1453), many important manuscripts found their way to the West.

During the Turkish occupation of Greece (1453 to 1821), many libraries were founded to preserve the culture of the Greek nation. After the 16th century and the introduction of the printing press, many monastic libraries were enriched with rare editions of important works in theology and other disciplines that are preserved until the present day.

In modern Greece, since independence in 1821, the first public library created for research and public use was that of the National Library of Greece, which was donated by the wealthy Cephallonian brothers Vallianos in 1828–29 and was designed by the Danish architect Christian Hansen. The second library to be created in modern Greece was that of the Parliament in 1845.

In 1914 the General Archives of the Nation was established and is housed in the Academy of Athens. It has a rich collection of archives of eminent personalities of 1821 and the following period.

National Library. The inspiration to establish a national library in modern Greece was John Mager, the Swedish publisher of the Greek Chronicles of Messologhi. The first Prime Minister, John Kapodestrias, was instrumental in establishing what became the National Library. He was assisted by the educator and bibliophile George Gennadius. The first collection was housed in the National Museum and the Center for Educational Institutions of Greece in Aegina. In 1832 it moved to Naphlion and through legislation was named Public Library. It had a collection of 1,844

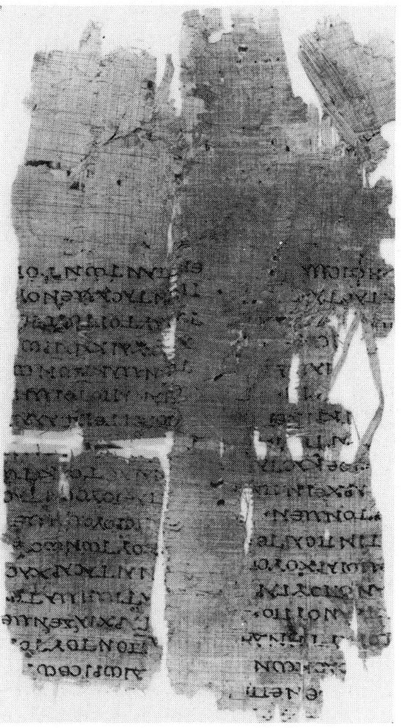

Papyrus Collection, Special Collections Library, The University of Michigan

Leaf of papyrus from ca. 100 A.D. containing text from The Politics *by Aristotle.*

volumes, and the first Librarian was George Gennadius. The National Library was moved to Athens in 1834. A law was passed that required one copy of all published books to be given to the National Library. In 1867 by law it was named "National Library."

In 1888 groundbreaking took place for the erection of a new library edifice. This magnificent, beautiful building was completed in 1903. The Library is open to the public on all working days. It contains books in Greek and several European languages, ancient and modern, and Asian languages. The strength of the library is in the area of papyri, Byzantine manuscripts, manuscripts in several European and Asian languages, Byzantine documents, Patriarchal sigillia, a great wealth of historical archives of the Turkish domination, the revolution for independence and modern Greece, first-edition printed books, including the famous Greek grammar by Laskaris printed in Milan in 1476, and many old and rare books from the 16th century. The Library collection was especially enriched by gifts from Greeks and philhellenes who endowed the National Library with their collections. It contains more than 2,000,000 volumes and 4,500 manuscripts.

Library of Parliament. The second library to be created in modern Greece is that of the Parliament (Vivliotheke tes Voules). It was established by law in 1845. In the beginning the collection was housed in the Old House of the Parliament. In 1935 the greater part of the collection was moved to the second floor of the Old Palace. The Library of the Parliament is open to the public on all working days and is partially a lending library. By special permission of the Director, students may borrow books. It sponsors lectures and book displays. The strongest collection is that of law. It has the most complete collection of periodicals and newspapers in Greece.

Arthur Plotnik

National Library of Greece, established in 1829 in Aegina and moved to Athens in 1834.

Academic Libraries. The University of Athens does not have a central library but each school or department has its specialized collection to support its curriculum.

The University of Thessaloniki, created in 1926, has an academic central library that has more than 1,000,000 volumes.

The University of Crete was created in 1977 and organized its library according to the Library of Congress cataloguing system, the only institution in Greece that is completely organized on the basis of the LC classification.

In addition, there are many special archaeological libraries of various archaeological institutions such as the American, Austrian, British, French, German, and Italian, among others. Also, many local libraries throughout Greece are of significant importance.

Public and School Libraries. In Greece the idea of school libraries and modern public libraries did not exist until after World War II. There were attempts to create media centers for the schools in Greece.

Special Libraries. The most important special library in Athens is the Gennadius Library. It was established by the generous gift of 24,000 volumes by John Gennadius to the American School of Classical Studies. The Greek government donated the land and the Carnegie Corporation provided the funds for the construction of the library building. The collection is specialized in Greek history and culture, mainly before 1900. It is a research library and well organized with more than 60,000 volumes. In 1985 it published a *Guide to the Gennadius Library*.

Religious Collections. The most significant collections in Greece are those of the religious institutions. Some of these libraries, especially in monasteries, were established during the Byzantine era. One of the oldest libraries in Greece was established in 1088 in the monastery of St. John the Evangelist on the island of Patmos. The monk Christodoulos willed his library to the monastery in 1093. Valuable collections of manuscripts are found in the monasteries of Mount Athos from the 10th century. Each of the 20 monasteries has a library of valuable manuscripts.

The libraries in Greece are making strenuous efforts toward cataloguing their rich collections. Most libraries in Greece use the Dewey Decimal System with some modification to accommodate the Greek language.

The Profession. Library personnel receive minimal training in Greece, and their preparation is not on a par with university-level education for other intellectual pursuits. Schools for technical training of librarians have been founded in several cities throughout Greece, and certification from those schools is required for employment in libraries in Greece. Many library personnel receive library science education in Europe or America, however.

In 1968 the Greek Library Association was organized in Athens to promote library science and librarianship in Greece. It also encourages bibliographic dissemination and information and keeps in close touch with international library associations. It is a member of IFLA.

Librarianship in Greece in the late 1980s was in a state of development. Newer methods and library procedures were only slowly implemented and refined. The library profession in Greece needed to be appropriately recognized. This can be accomplished by implementing a university-level degree for librarianship. Also, librarians needed to make greater use of contemporary techniques for manuscript preservation. And finally there was need for the computerization of information about library collections through a central database that would serve scholars in and outside Greece. In some academic libraries recognition of the importance of such changes for the future of libraries led to the application of computer technology.

GEORGE C. PAPADEMETRIOU

Grover, Wayne C.
(1906–1970)

Wayne Clayton Grover, Archivist of the United States from 1948 until 1965, was the architect of the many-faceted organization that was to become the National Archives and Records Service.

Grover was born in Garland, Utah, September 16, 1906. Graduated from the University of Utah in 1930, he received the M.A. (1937) and Ph.D. degrees (1946) from the American University, Washington, D.C. In 1935 he married Esther Thomas, the daughter of U.S. Senator Elbert Thomas (Democrat, Utah).

Grover worked as a journalist and as a congressional aide between 1930 and 1935. He joined the staff of the National Archives in 1935, during its first year. One of the first persons to receive training as an archivist, he was given a variety of assignments at the Archives. He served as a Records Consultant in 1941–42 with the Office of Strategic Services. In 1943 Grover was commissioned a Captain in the Army, and he became Chief of its records management branch in the Adjutant General's Office. As such he was the War Department's principal staff officer for its pioneering records management program, and he inaugurated the Army's system of records centers. Although he was discharged a Lieutenant Colonel in 1946, he remained in his job as a civilian. He was decorated with the Legion of Merit for his work.

In 1947 the National Archives was confronted with a reduction in staff, a great preservation backlog, and the need to bring the records glut of the federal government under control. The Archivist of the United States, Solon J. Buck, decided to make use of Grover's demonstrated ability by naming him his deputy as Assistant Archivist. Grover was responsible for mending his agency's relations with Congress and getting the Archives to work more efficiently within its slender resources. When Buck resigned as Archivist in 1948, he proposed Grover as his successor.

During his first year as Archivist, Grover managed to improve his agency's funding and to reduce the backlog of material needing preservation. Nevertheless, the long-range outlook for proper support of the National Archives's programs was poor. Grover was able to get the Hoover Commission on the Organization of the Executive Branch of the Government to champion the establishment of a comprehensive federal records management program. Only that, he believed, would lead to efficiency, economy, and effectiveness in the use of federal records and would assure a smooth flow of records of enduring value to the Archives. The Hoover Commission, however, recommended that the National Archives lose its status as an independent federal agency and that a new bureau deal with records management. In 1949 Congress did place Grover's agency, as the National Archives and Records Service (NARS), under the General Services Administration (GSA), but Congress also clearly intended that NARS become the government's records management service and provided increased funding for that purpose.

Previously, his agency had been chiefly concerned with archives, although it also operated the Franklin D. Roosevelt Library and the Federal Register Division and was involved in promoting records management. Grover's first important step was to gain enactment of the comprehensive Federal Records Act of 1950, which officially made NARS into the government's records management agency. This step enhanced the likelihood of preserving federal archives for research use, as well as the improved management of records by government agencies. It was most important for the information sciences and for research that Grover won his fight to have records dealt with during their life span on the basis of archival as well as managerial principles.

Grover was responsible for more than the enduring—though occasionally rocky—marriage of archivists and records managers. He upgraded NARS's display program, the centerpieces of which were the Declaration of Independence and the Constitution, which he procured from the Library of Congress in 1952. He inaugurated a facsimile program and expanded his agency's outstanding micropublications and film preservation operations. In 1950 he resuscitated the National Historical Publications Commission, the work of which has enriched the nation's documentary publications.

Under Grover's sponsorship the Federal Register Division in 1957 began a valuable new series, the *Public Papers of the Presidents of the United States*. Grover guided the systematization of the acquisition and administration of the papers of recent Presidents and their associates in the Presidential Libraries Act of 1955. Moreover, under his supervision NARS made considerable progress in solving its problems of preservation and description. His agency grew from 341 employees when he became Archivist to 1,716 by the time of his retirement in 1965.

Grover did not deal easily with the General Services Administration. Although it provided NARS with increased resources, GSA, with its management orientation, was increasingly criticized for posing a threat to archival professionalism. Grover used the occasion of his retirement to argue for his agency's return to independent status. Although his campaign was unsuccessful, it resulted in better funding for NARS and expansion of its programs. The issue continued to be raised by archivists and historians until 1985, when NARS became independent as the National Archives and Records Administration. Grover remained active in other ways after his retirement, including advising President Lyndon B. Johnson on the development of his Presidential Library.

In recognition of Grover's services, Brown (Providence, Rhode Island) and Bucknell (Lewisburg, Pennsylvania) universities and Belmont Abbey College (North Carolina) bestowed honorary degrees upon him. He received the GSA's Distinguished Service Award in 1959 and one of the National Civil Service League's Career Service Awards in 1961. Grover was President of the Society of American Archivists, Vice-President of the International Council on Archives, and a member of the United States Commission of Unesco. He was the author of articles in a wide array of professional publications. Yet the real monument to his vision was the remarkably broad-based institution that NARS became during his tenure as Archivist of the United States. Grover died in Silver Spring, Maryland, June 8, 1970.

Records of the National Archives
Wayne C. Grover

REFERENCE

Donald R. McCoy, *The National Archives: America's Ministry of Documents, 1934–1968* (1978).

DONALD R. McCOY

Guatemala

Guatemala, a republic in northern Central America, is bordered by Mexico on the west and north, Belize on the northeast, the Caribbean Sea on the east, Honduras and El Salvador on the southeast, and the Pacific Ocean on the south and southwest. Population (1990 est.) 9,197,000; area 108,889 sq.km. The official language is Spanish.

History. Although the Mayan civilization was a rich one, no evidence has been found of library collections in pre-Columbian times. The earliest collections, in fact, date from the colonial period, in convents and monasteries founded by the conquerors. The opening of the University of San Carlos in 1677 marked the first time since the arrival of printing presses (1659) that any institution cultivated special collections of books. Yet the idea of public libraries did not take root until the founding of the National Library in 1879, with its 15,000 volumes. The greatest expansion of libraries took place in the 1960s.

National Library and Archives. The National Library of Guatemala was founded in Guatemala City. A dependent of the Ministry of Public Education, it preserves the national bibliographic heritage and also functions as a public library, the

Central Library, University of San Carlos

Reading Room of the Central Library, University of San Carlos, Guatemala.

largest in the country. It occasionally produces and publishes works of national significance. Service is provided to more than 125,000 readers annually and includes a special service for children. The total collection of volumes in the National Library is 350,000, including that of the periodicals in the library, which operates independently in the same building. The national archives are held in the Archivo General de Centro América in Guatemala City. It holds almost 100,000 documents relating to Costa Rica, El Salvador, Guatemala, Honduras, Nicaragua, and Chiapa (a state of Mexico). There are also periodicals pertaining to the colonial period and independence, historical volumes, and microfilm.

Public Libraries. Ninety-three small public libraries exist throughout the republic. Of these libraries, 64 in various parts of the country fall under the direction of the National Library; the remaining 29 are under the direction of the Bank of Guatemala, which sponsors them. Their total collection is about 74,000 volumes. Service is provided to approximately 232,500 readers annually throughout the republic.

Academic Libraries. The Central Library of the Universidad de San Carlos, the autonomous state university, is the largest academic library in the country. It was established at the new university city in 1966; however, as the faculties that had continued to function in other areas of the capital moved to the new site, their libraries were also incorporated into the Central Library, beginning in 1974. The collection comprises 150,000 volumes.

The Library of the Universidad Rafael Llandivar (1963) has 20,000 volumes and 60 journals and serves 30,000 readers. The library of the Universidad Francisco Marroquín (1972) has almost 9,800 volumes, serving 37,500 readers. The library of the Universidad José Cecilio del Valle provides service to 37,500 readers. Founded in 1966, it holds more than 16,500 volumes and 373 journals. The library of the Universidad Mariano Gálvez (1966) contains 5,000 volumes, serving 5,000 readers. All five of these libraries are in Guatemala City.

School Libraries. In some educational institutions, especially at the secondary level and in state schools, there are small libraries. However, the largest collection does not exceed 3,000 volumes, and they lack professional personnel. The use of these libraries is restricted to faculty and students. These institutions are not required by law to have libraries.

Special Libraries. The most important special libraries are in the capital. The Library of the Bank of Guatemala, founded in 1946, serves interests in banking, currency, and economics. Its collection totals 31,000 volumes and 320 journals. It provides service to 60,000 readers, including the Bank's officials and the general public. The Library of the Instituto de Nutrición de Centroamérica y Panamá (INCAP), founded in 1949, specializes in nutrition and allied sciences. Its basic functions are research, teaching, and providing technical assistance to the area countries, and it also serves the general public. Its collection numbers 70,000 volumes. Almost half of its collection was destroyed by fire resulting from the earthquake of February 1976, but this material has since been replaced.

The Library and Documentation Center of the Instituto Centroaméricano de Investigación y Tecnología Industrial (ICAITI), founded in 1956, serves industry and business; it also functions as the regional coordinator of the OAS Program of Information and Technical Assistance for Business in Central America

Libraries in Guatemala (1990)

Type of library	Number of administrative units (main libraries)	Number of service points (branches, mobile stops, etc.)	Volumes in collections
National[a]	--	100	1,824,000
Academic[b]	1	1	133,000
Special[c]	16	16	500,000

[a]1983 data
[b]1987 data
[c]1986 data

Source: Unesco, *Statistical Yearbook,* 1991.

and the Caribbean. It conducts training in documentation services. Its collection totals 20,000 volumes and 300 journals. Service is provided to approximately 10,000 readers. Other institutions that contribute to the economic development of Guatemala, and whose holdings include important collections of journals and documents, are the Instituto Técnico de Capacitación y Productividad (INTECAP), the Centro Nacional de Promoción de las Exportaciones (GUATEXPRO), and the Secretaría Permanente del Tratado General de Integración Económica Centroaméricana (SIECA).

GUILLERMO PALMA R.

Guinea

Guinea, a republic of West Africa, on the Atlantic Ocean, is bounded by Guinea-Bissau on the northwest, Senegal and Mali on the north and northeast, Ivory Coast on the east, and Liberia and Sierra Leone on the south. Population (1990 est.) 5,756,000; area 245,857 sq.km. It was a French colony until it gained independence in September 1958, then a single-party state under Sekou Touré until his death in 1984. French is the official and teaching language, though it was superseded by African languages from 1967 to 1980.

The National Library was officially founded in 1958, but that was but renaming what had been the library of the local Institut Français d'Afrique Noire (IFAN) in the capital city, Conakry. An attempt was made to turn it into a public library, but it had neither trained personnel nor budget. By 1961 it had a trained librarian (the only one in the country), new and trainable personnel, and money appropriated by the government. It grew in size and effectiveness so that by the end of 1967 the stock had reached 11,000 books and 300 current periodicals, as well as exchanges, purchases, and gifts. It was moved to a more central but smaller and older building in 1968, about the time a French-trained Guinean librarian took over. But librarians trained in Dakar and Paris were promoted out of the Library into political appointments and the National Library ground to a standstill in its unsuitable premises. Political and financial difficulties led to an increase in untrained personnel and a decrease in the buying budget; by 1985 the National Library received nothing but gifts and exchanges.

The main academic library, at the Institut Polytechnique, appointed its first professional librarian in 1965, but never got a regular budget. Book-hungry students helped themselves whenever they could, and its stock decreased in number and usefulness.

The French and Guinean governments decided to set up a Centre d'Étude et de Documentation Universitaire, Scientifique et Technique (CEDUST) to lend books, documents, and films to academics and professionals. They also planned to create a French-Guinean library to fill the niche occupied in other francophone countries by the libraries of French Cultural Centers.

F. LALANDE ISNARD

Libraries in Guinea (1990)

Type of library	Number of administrative units (main libraries)	Number of service points (branches, mobile stops, etc.)	Volumes in collections	Population served
Academic[a]	6	7	1,235,000	10,957
School[b]	6	6	585,000	7,756

[a]1988 data
[b]1987 data

Source: Unesco, *Statistical Yearbook,* 1991

Guinea-Bissau

Guinea-Bissau, an independent republic of West Africa, is bounded by Senegal on the north, Guinea on the east and south, and the Atlantic Ocean on the west. Population (1990 est.) 965,000; area 36,125 sq.km. The official language is Portuguese.

Long governed as an overseas province of Portu-

Libraries in Guinea-Bissau (1990)

Type of library	Number of administrative units (main libraries)	Number of service points (branches, mobile stops, etc.)	Volumes in collections	Population served
Non-specialized[a]	1	1	60,000	200

[a]1986 figures

Source: Unesco, *Statistical Yearbook,* 1991.

gal (Portuguese Guinea), Guinea-Bissau gained its independence in 1975. At that time the Museum and Public Library of Bissau was the only significant library. Its restricted schedule of hours and out-of-date collections limited use. The Center of Scientific Investigation, under the Ministry of Culture, was founded after independence; it received the collections previously held by the Museum and Public Library. It then entered a period of reorganization. The Biblioteca National da Guiné-Bissau holds 25,000 volumes and 4,000 current periodicals.

Three secondary and eight primary schools operate libraries in the capital of Bissau.

Two special libraries are the Library of Legal Sciences, which planned to become part of a new university, and the library of the Statistics Service, under the Ministry of State for Planning. However, the only significant special libraries to date are the Centro de Estudos da Guiné-Bissau (14,000 volumes) and the library at the Museu da Guiné-Bissau (10,000 volumes). The most important library activities center in Bissau.

MARIA MANUELA CRUZEIRO

Guyana

Guyana, a republic on the Atlantic coast of South America, is bounded by Suriname on the east, Brazil on the south, and Venezuela on the west. Population (1990 est.) 796,000; area 214,969 sq.km. It was known as British Guiana until it gained independence in 1966. The official language is English.

History. The Amerindians, the earliest inhabitants of Guyana, are associated with centuries-old marks and figures found engraved on many huge rocks in the mountainous interior of the country and called Timehri writings. Guyana developed as a plantation society in the 17th century in which most of the people were slaves, working for Dutch and later British plantation owners.

Following emancipation in 1834, the introduction of popular education gradually led to the development of a literate society. A few private subscription libraries such as the Berbice Reading Society (1843) and the Royal Agricultural and Commercial Society (1864) were established, but they served only exclusive groups. A few church and Sunday school libraries offered limited service to selected groups of persons. The first public library service became available in 1909 with the opening of the Carnegie Free Library. Pioneered by the early librarians Emily Murray (served 1909–1940) and Ruby Franker (1942–1962) and later significantly expanded by Stella Merriman (1962–1972), this service laid the foundation for what has become a nationwide public library service.

General expansion of library services in the country has been blocked by a persistent lack of adequate financial resources, an inadequate supply of professional personnel, and foreign currency crises. Yet the University of Guyana Library can boast of having developed an extensive collection of research material on Guyana, unsurpassed by any other known collection of material on this subject.

National and Public Library Services. The National Library of Guyana in Georgetown had its origin in the Carnegie Free Library. In 1950 an act of the British Guiana Legislative Council empowered the Library Authority to extend its service beyond the city of Georgetown, giving impetus to the rapid development of a nationwide service. The Law Revision Act of 1972 created the National Library, assigning to it the responsibility for performing the functions of both a national and a public library. The Act also designated the National Library as a legal deposit library entitled to one copy of every local imprint. It has published the Guyanese National Bibliography since 1972.

The National Library provides nationwide service through the operation of several service units. The Adult Reference and Lending Departments, a phonograph records service, the Juvenile Department, a toy library service, and one Branch Library serve Georgetown. Two Branch Libraries outside Georgetown, the Rural Services Department comprising 17 Rural Library Centers, two bookmobiles, and deposit collections in three prisons jointly provide a service to the rest of the country. The resources of the National Library totaled an estimated 220,000 items in the late 1980s; they include rare historical documents, manuscripts, and a valuable special collection of research material on Guyana. It is also a depository of Unesco publications.

The John F. Kennedy Library provides additional public library services with collections devoted exclusively to works published in the United States, including videotape recordings. It provides CD-ROM searches, the first such service in Guyana. It also sponsors a number of public activities that include video shows, lectures, and professional and cultural discussion groups.

Libraries in Guyana (1990)

Type of library	Number of administrative units (main libraries)	Number of service points (branches, mobile stops, etc.)	Volumes in collections	Annual expenditures (Guyanese dollar)	Population served	Professional staff (with certificate, diploma, etc.)	Total staff
National	2	40	235,000	700,000	200,000	4	60
Academic	3	--	250,000	1,000,000	3,500	8	80
Public	1	--	30,000	--	380,000	1	8
School	18	--	--	--	--	--	--
Special	28	--	150,000	--	20,000	7	53

The National Archives of Guyana was in 1972 designated a legal depository for all local publications. It had a staff of four in the mid-1980s and its holdings totaled 510,000 linear feet. The economic decline has caused a decline in archival services.

Academic Libraries. The University of Guyana Library, established in 1963, is the only academic library in the country. A substantial extension to its original building was added in 1983. Organized on a subject divisional arrangement, it supports the teaching and research programs of seven faculties and one research institute with a total collection of some 200,000 items including manuscripts and nonprint materials. The Library is a partial depository for the publications of the United Nations and its agencies, and in 1972 it was designated a legal deposit library for Guyanese imprints.

Of special importance is the Library's Caribbean Research Collection. An extensive collection of material on Guyana and the Caribbean, it is considered, because of its many unique holdings, the world's largest collection of material on Guyana.

The University Library operates an international gifts and exchange program and is the local center for international interlibrary loan activities through the British Lending Library. It is also responsible for coordinating local input to CARISPLAN, a regional database for Caribbean economic and planning information. The University Library in the late 1980s began planning for automation and developing an audiovisual resource center.

Special Libraries. The libraries of the Bank of Guyana, Geology and Mines Commission, Guyana National Resource Agency, Medical Sciences Library, National Agricultural Research Institute, Public Service Ministry Library, and State Planning Secretariat are the largest and best organized special libraries in the country; although primarily committed to serving the organizations to which they are attached, these libraries also provide limited services to the wider community. Most other special libraries are small units of unorganized collections attached to government departments and to corporations. Efforts toward developing those libraries were under way in the late 1980s.

The Library of the Caribbean Community Secretariat (CARICOM) in Georgetown is a regional institution that supports the needs of an estimated 80 specialists and researchers concerned with the development of the English-speaking Caribbean. Limited service is given to researchers and students in the Guyanese community. Its stock comprises an estimated 25,000 monographs and pamphlets and a large collection of unpublished reports and conference documents. The library began a program of computerization in the late 1980s.

School Libraries. The organized libraries in 18 of the largest secondary schools in the country indicate a modest development of libraries at that level, but it could still be said that school libraries are underdeveloped, particularly at the primary level. There were six libraries in the post-secondary colleges such as colleges of education, most of which consist of relatively small collections of books, journals, and, in some cases, audiovisual materials.

The Profession. Professional librarians in Guyana were trained exclusively in the United Kingdom, the United States, or Canada, until the Department of Library Studies was established at the University of the West Indies, Jamaica, in 1972. Continuing education programs depend heavily on courses available in the U.K., U.S., and Canada, and at U.W.I. In addition, some short courses are also pursued in European countries, among them Denmark and Russia. Programs with a focus on regional activities are sometimes available under the sponsorship of organizations such as Unesco and the Organization of American States.

The Guyana Library Association (GLA), established in 1972 with a membership of 17 professionals and 42 non-professionals, promotes the professional interests of all personnel in libraries. It sponsors lectures, seminars, and workshops on a range of topics concerning the library and information field. Its principal publication is the *Guyana Library Association Bulletin,* published quarterly. The Association also publishes a *Directory of Library and Information Services.*

YVONNE V. STEPHENSON

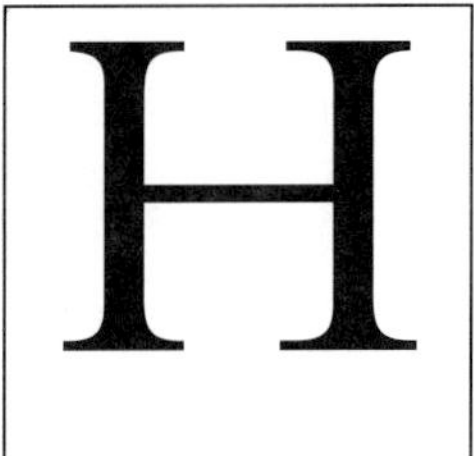

Haas, Warren J.
(1924-)

Warren James Haas, U.S. university library director and administrator and President of the Council on Library Resources (CLR) from January 1978 through January 1991, served at the center of some of the most innovative and successful efforts to reshape research libraries in an era marked by revolutionary technological change. At the CLR he gained increased support of private foundations in the research library enterprise, particularly in the areas of computer and communications technology; scholarly communications; library resources, preservation, and access; and library education, management, and cooperation.

Born on March 22, 1924, in Racine, Wisconsin, Haas received a B.A. degree from Wabash College, in Indiana, in 1948, after serving in the U.S. Air Force from 1943 to 1946. He received a B.L.S. degree from the University of Wisconsin in 1950. His first library position was as Head of Branch Libraries for the Racine Public Library. In 1952 he went to Johns Hopkins University, where he served first as Acquisitions Librarian and then as Assistant Librarian. In 1959 and 1960 he was Library Consultant for the Council of Higher Educational Institutions of New York. In 1961 he began his first association with Columbia University when he was appointed Associate Director of Libraries, a position he held until he was appointed Director of the University of Pennsylvania Libraries in 1966.

ALA

Warren J. Haas

Haas returned to Columbia as University Librarian in 1970. In 1972 he was made Vice-President for Information Services with responsibilities for both libraries and the university's computer center, the first such designation in a major university. The Columbia that Haas returned to in 1970 had been the scene of massive student demonstrations, the resignation under fire of senior university administrators, and the unionization of supporting staff in the Library. Haas faced serious fiscal constraints. He was among the first administrators of major research libraries to experience drastic budgetary cuts at a time when user demands were increasing and emerging technology was promising many advantages but at enormous costs.

Recognizing the need for a reorganization and redefinition of academic librarianship, he devised a two-track system of professional ranks and position categories that recognized both the management responsibilities of librarian positions and the professional achievements of the individuals who filled them. He subtly modified the structure introduced for the Columbia Libraries after a pilot management study by the Association for Research Libraries. The success of these organizational ventures was directly attributable to Haas's personal philosophy of upgrading the profession of research librarianship by raising the sights of individual members, encouraging higher standards of performance, and identifying ways for librarians to contribute effectively to the academic purposes of higher education.

With Douglas Bryant of Harvard, Richard Couper of the New York Public Library, and Rutherford Rogers of Yale, Haas was a major force in the establishment of the Research Libraries Group in 1974. RLG's transformation from a regional association of four major research libraries into a national partnership of some 30 owner-members and a number of associate and special members and associates owes much to Haas's vision and to his early recognition of the need to promote a comprehensive computerized bibliographic system for the U.S.

As President of the Council on Library Resources from 1978 to 1991, Haas introduced a number of new projects while continuing to support major programs in networking, preservation, and library management and education. His view of the role of the Council is that it is "one of a few library organizations focused on the future rather than the past." In carrying on the traditions of the Council, Haas attracted the interests of a growing number of private foundations.

Haas's memberships on the American Library Association's International Relations Advisory Committee on Liaison with Japanese Libraries and on the Library subcommittee of the Japan–U.S. Conference on Cultural and Educational Interchange indicate active involvement on the international library scene. The Council assisted the International Federation of Library Associations and Institutions for many years, an effort that Haas continued. In 1984 the CLR, along with the NATO Scientific Affairs Division, the Commission of the European Communities, the European Cultural Foundation, and the Council of Europe, sponsored an advanced research workshop in Luxembourg on the impact of new information technologies on library management, resources, and cooperation. The reports presented at that workshop cover cooperative efforts, education and training, and a European equivalent of the CLR. The Haas imprimatur is evident.

Haas was a workshop leader in Beijing and Shanghai in 1980, providing some 300 Chinese librarians with their first exposure to advances in librarianship after 30 years of dissociation from the U.S. He also presented a paper at the Kanazawa Institute in Japan in 1984 on the preservation of library materials. He was awarded the Henry Elias Howland Memorial Prize from Yale University in 1980. Wabash College conferred an honorary Doctor of Literature in 1983. The American Library Association awarded him the Melvil Dewey Medal in 1984. The citation says, in part: "Combining originality of method and vigorous leadership, Warren James Haas is invariably at the center of the most successful efforts to mould new information systems. A zealous amateur birdwatcher, he seems as perpetually airborne as his feathered friends, advancing projects in Los Angeles, New York, The Hague, Peking, and Tokyo . . . He is a spokesman with sensible solutions and an imaginative creator of the building blocks of the information systems of the future." After retiring from the CLR in 1991, Haas continued to work as a consultant to major foundation programs in the library and information fields.

FREDERICK DUDA

Haines, Helen
(1872–1951)

Helen Elizabeth Haines, American teacher, reviewer, and advocate of intellectual freedom, influenced generations of students of librarianship through her book

Living with Books: The Art of Book Selection (1935, 1950).

A native of New York City, Haines was born on February 9, 1872. Privately educated, she held only one degree, an honorary M.A. conferred by the University of Southern California in 1945.

After undertaking freelance work as an indexer and writing *The History of New Mexico from the Spanish Conquest to the Present Time, 1530–1890* (New Mexico Historical Publishing Company, 1891), Haines was employed by R. R. Bowker, publisher of library indexes and journals, in 1892 on the recommendation of Mary Wright Plummer, library educator and family friend. She held a number of editorial positions before she was appointed Managing Editor of *Library Journal* in 1896, a position she held until ill health forced her resignation in 1908.

The *Proceedings* of the American Library Association were published annually in *Library Journal,* and Haines became the Association's recorder. She served on the Council and the Executive Board; in 1906 she was elected Second Vice-President.

In Pasadena, California, where Haines moved in search of health, she began a career as book reviewer and activist in library affairs. She began a book review column, "The Library Table," in the *Pasadena News* in 1910 and continued it for 40 years. Her reviews appeared in other newspapers and periodicals, including the *New York Herald Tribune,* the *Nation,* and the *Saturday Review of Literature,* and she gave series of book talks for the Pasadena, Long Beach, and Los Angeles public libraries. Her articles on library legislation, book selection, and other topics appeared in state and national library journals.

Haines's advocacy of high literary standards in the selection of materials for libraries was brought to the attention of library educators, and in 1914 she began to teach book selection and the history of books and libraries at the training class of the Los Angeles Public Library. When the class became a library school and, in 1932, part of the University of Southern California, Haines became a full-time faculty member. She lectured to book selection classes at the University of California at Berkeley and prepared and conducted correspondence courses in book selection for the American Correspondence School of Librarianship and the Columbia University Home Study Department. She taught at Columbia University during summer sessions.

Columbia University Press gave Haines a grant that enabled her to write *Living with Books: The Art of Book Selection* (1935), which, published by Columbia, became a standard text in library schools and a reference tool in libraries. Appreciative of contemporary as well as traditional literature, comprehensive, liberal in outlook, and delightfully readable, it became the book-oriented librarian's bible. *What's in a Novel,* also published by Columbia (1942), an analysis and appreciation limited to contemporary literature, largely of the more or less popular mainstream, did not serve as broad a purpose.

By 1950, when a new edition of *Living with Books* was published, again by the Columbia University Press, the climate had changed. Haines, then 78 years old, again exhibited an open, liberal attitude toward the books of the period, including those on politics, religion, and science. It was inevitable that she should be accused of a pro-Soviet bias, and not surprising that many librarians should timidly reject the book. Long a defender of intellectual freedom, and one of the founders of the Committee on Intellectual Freedom of the California Library Association in 1940, Haines had foreseen and warned against censorship from within libraries.

Recognized as an outstanding library educator, a brilliant speaker and author, and a principal force in encouraging in librarians a love of books and high critical standards, Haines was given the Joseph W. Lippincott Award for outstanding achievement in librarianship by ALA in 1951. Her eloquent speech of acceptance measured the power of the book in the past and foretold its continuing influence in the future. Helen Haines died in Altadena, California, on August 26, 1951.

REFERENCES

Helen E. Haines, "Living with Books," *Library Journal* (1951).

Everett T. Moore, "Innocent Librarians," *ALA Bulletin* (1961), describes attacks on Haines as "a propagandist for the Stalinist way of life" by Oliver Carlson in *The Freeman* (1952), and the point-by-point answer given by Elinor S. Earle in *ALA Bulletin* (1952).

Everett T. Moore, "The Intellectual Freedom Saga in California," *California Librarian* (1974).

Robert D. Harlan, "Haines, Helen Elizabeth," *Dictionary of American Library Biography* (1978).

RUTH WARNCKE

Haiti

Haiti, a republic in the Caribbean Sea, occupies the western part of the island of Hispaniola, which lies between Puerto Rico and Cuba. It shares the island with the Dominican Republic on the east. Population (1990 est.) 5,963,000; area 27,750 sq.km. The official languages are Creole and French; the national language is Creole.

History. Haiti's first libraries were created during the French colonial period (1625–1803). Some private collections and a type of library called *cabinet de lecture* existed in Port-au-Prince, Cap-Haitien, and Cayes, but these books did not survive the war for independence. In 1825 a national library (with 444 books) was founded by President Jean-Pierre Boyer. In 1920 the library of l'Amicale du Lycée Pétion was established, followed by the library of the École Pratique de Damien (1926) and the Faculty of Medicine Library (1927). In 1940 the present National Library was built with branches in Jacmel, St-Marc, Jérémie, Cayes, and Port-de-Paix by President Sténio Vincent.

National Library. The National Library was organized in 1940. It was directed by Max Bissainthe, who published the Haitian current and retrospective bibliographies, compiled in his *Dictionnaire de bibliographie hiatienne (1804–1949)* and its *Supplement* covering the period 1950–70. After Bissainthe's administration (1942–57), the collection of 6,000 books was reduced to about 4,000.

The National Library was later reorganized under new legislation, with a new building and more modern equipment. Since 1984 it has received depository copies of Haitian imprints. It had no acquisition

Archives Nationales d'Haiti

National Library of Haiti.

budget as of the early 1990s. The Haitian Society of History and Geography gave it a deposit of 5,000 books and microfilm reels of Haitian colonial archives. The library was planned as the nucleus of a public libraries network under the Institut National Haitien de la Culture et des Arts (INAHCA). After INAHCA was dissolved in March 1986, the National Library became an autonomous institution reporting to the Ministry of Information, Culture, and Coordination.

The National Archives of Haiti has among its documents civil registers from 1793. Precious and rare documents were transferred to the present building in 1922. The bad conditions of conservation and management of those papers resulted in great losses. There are about 20 archival depositories in Port-au-Prince and many others in the provinces.

Academic Libraries. There are 17 schools of higher education in Haiti; in 1985, 9 of them had their own libraries. The best libraries were at the Faculty of Medicine (9,896 volumes), National Institute of Management and International Higher Studies (INAGHEI; 3,958 volumes), and Faculty of Agriculture (7,000 volumes). In the early 1990s, only the INAGHEI Library had an acquisition budget and had made a great part of its collections available on loan. Some collections for the period 1920–34 are available in the libraries of the faculties of Medicine and Agriculture.

Public Libraries. There are no state public libraries in Port-au-Prince. Small public libraries exist in seven towns in the country, supported by the National Library, which pays only for limited staff, some books, and elementary equipment.

The best public libraries are the French Institute Library (about 29,000 volumes) and the Haitian American Library (4,500 volumes), which provide free access to their bookstocks and make loans.

School Libraries and Media Centers. There is no school library service at the Ministry of National Education. Some public schools have small libraries. According to Ministry regulations, all private schools must have libraries, yet the requirement is met only in some of them. According to the latest data available in the early 1990s (published in 1975), schools with libraries numbered 21 public and 115 private; schools without libraries numbered 71 public and 332 private.

Special Libraries. Thirteen special libraries have between 500 and 4,000 volumes; managed in many cases by professionally unqualified employees, they offer services to small numbers of users. The most important is the Saint Louis Gonzague Library, with its 20,000 documents, the richest Haitian collection in the country, followed by the Jean Fouchard collection, owned by the Central Bank of Haiti (BRH). The Ministries of Commerce and Planning have many official documents and technical reports.

The Profession. There is no library school in Haiti. Courses in general librarianship are offered by the Faculty of Ethnology. Continuing education courses have been given by Haiti's section of the Association of French Caribbean Librarians, Archivists, and Documentalists, founded in 1979 at Fort-de-France (Martinique). It publishes *Notes bibliographiques Caraïbes* and *Bulletin d'Information de l'A.A.B.D.F.C. (section Haiti)*. Continuing education courses are now given by l'Association des Archivistes Haitiens (ASAH).

Haiti had 7 professional librarians, 22 paraprofessionals, and 14 archivist assistants in 1990.

REFERENCE

Association des Archivistes, bibliothécaires et documentalistes francophones de la Caraïbe (Section Haiti), *Répertoire commenté de la législation haitienne relative aux unités documentaires* (1983).

JEAN WILFRID BERTRAND

Libraries in Haiti (1987)

Type of library	Number of administrative units (main libraries)	Number of service points (branches, mobile stops, etc.)	Volumes in collections	Annual expenditures (gourde)	Population served	Professional staff (with certificate, diploma, etc.)	Total staff
National	1	14	35,000	Gdes:1,610,000	23,000	11	88
Academic	11	11	28,000	--	7,500	4	38
Public	3	4	37,900	--	9,500	4	11
School	9	9	--	--	--	1	11
Special	14	14	--	--	--	5	27
Other (describe)	--	--	--	--	--	--	--

Philip M. Hamer

Records of the National Archives

Hamer, Philip M.
(1891–1971)

U.S. Historian and teacher of history, librarian and archivist, Philip May Hamer served on the staff of the National Archives from 1935 and was Executive Director of the National Historical Publications Commission from 1951 to 1961.

Hamer was born in Marion, South Carolina, November 10, 1891. He received a B.A. from Wofford College in Spartanburg, South Carolina; an M.A. from Trinity College (now Duke University); and a Ph.D. in History (1918) from the University of Pennsylvania in Philadelphia. After a year as Professor of History at the University of Tennessee at Chattanooga, he went to the University of Tennessee at Knoxville, where he served as Associate Professor of History, 1920–26, Professor of History, 1926–35, and Chairman of the Graduate School, 1930–34.

Hamer was popular as a teacher, but he also loved research and writing history, and he published many articles on East Tennessee, the Revolutionary War, Indian relations, and the southwestern frontier, as well as a four-volume history of Tennessee (1933). He helped organize the East Tennessee Historical Society, of which he was President, 1926–28. Later, he was a founder of the Southern Historical Association, Editor of its *Journal of Southern History,* and in 1938 its President. His presidential address, delivered at New Orleans, "The Records of Southern History," was published in volume 5 of the Association's *Journal.*

Hamer joined the staff of the newly established National Archives in 1935 as a deputy examiner of records and was assigned to survey the records of the Interior Department, which had in its file rooms, basements, and attics much that intrigued him. But not only records in the District of Columbia were of interest to him. On January 1, 1936, he became the National Director of the Survey of Federal Records outside the District of Columbia, a project supported by Works Progress Administration funds. Hamer accepted this responsibility without special compensation, depending on the $3,500 a year he was receiving as Deputy Examiner. He prepared *The Manual of the Survey of Federal Archives,* a mimeographed pamphlet of 29 numbered leaves, which was sent to appointed regional directors, members of advisory committees, and some of the key workers.

When the Survey of Federal Records was legally terminated on June 30, 1937, most of the records of the federal government in the 48 states had been surveyed and reported, but the work of compiling and making available the information thus secured remained unfinished. Responsibility for such activity was transferred to the Historical Records Survey, of which Luther H. Evans was National Director, and members of the staff of the Survey of Federal Records both in the field and in Washington were also transferred. Hamer was appointed, again without pay, as Associate National Director. The intended *Inventory of Federal Records* in the states got out of hand because records of the federal agencies were stored in 58,840 rooms in 24,536 buildings and in volume amounted to 5,080,694 linear feet. By the end of 1940, 333 volumes with a total of 36,168 pages had been published in mimeograph form and distributed to libraries throughout the country. Hamer's interesting reports on the problems of the Survey of Federal Records from 1936 to 1940 may be found as appendices in the second to sixth Annual Reports of the Archivist of the United States. He also gave a number of speeches, one of them to the newly organized Society of American Archivists.

In April 1936 he was appointed Chief of the Division of the Library in the National Archives. It was expected that the Library would consist of some 50,000 or 60,000 volumes—mainly American history and biography—printed government documents, and many pamphlets and journals. Many older copies of printed documents could be secured from federal agencies that no longer needed them. His achievement—a good, working library—is still evident, for next to the Library of Congress the National Archives Library is the best and most convenient American history repository in the District of Columbia.

In 1938 Hamer was appointed Chief of the Reference Division, into which the Library Division had been merged, a position he held until 1944. During those years his staff members not only took care of the Library but also ran the central search room, requesting records from the custodial divisions for historians wishing to examine federal records.

From 1944 to 1951 Hamer was Director of Records Control. The change in title indicated that Hamer and his staff members, while still handling reference work, had become increasingly concerned with the preparation of guides, inventories, and other finding aids, and had taken over much of the work of the Classification and Cataloguing Divisions, which had been abolished in 1939 and 1941. The first adequate *Guide to the Records in the National Archives* (684 pages), published by the Government Printing Office in 1948, was "prepared under the immediate direction and editorial supervision of Philip M. Hamer." He was also responsible for planning and directing a special guide in two volumes to *Federal Records of World War II* (1950).

J.C.M. Hanson Collection Luther College Archives
J.C.M. Hanson

Hamer had also been serving as Secretary of a National Historical Publications Commission, 1946–51, established as part of the Act of 1934 creating the National Archives. Not much had been done before 1946 because of the demands of World War II, but Hamer, who had always been interested in making documentary sources more available, felt it was time to get that program going. He had the support of Solon J. Buck, the Archivist, who by law chaired the Commission. President Harry S. Truman, on being presented with volume one of Julian Boyd's *The Papers of Thomas Jefferson,* asked the Commission to canvass scholars and plan a similar program for publishing the papers of other American leaders. The Federal Records Act of 1950 gave the Commission additional authority, and in 1951 Hamer was made Executive Director, a full-time assignment that he held until his retirement in 1961.

In 1954 he transmitted to the President the Commission's *A National Program for the Publication of Historical Documents* (106 pages), which he had prepared after discussions with history teachers, historical societies, and others interested in the publication of source documents. The Commission also proposed the preparation of a guide to the archival and manuscript collections of the nation, which Hamer and his staff planned, prepared, and published in 1961. It describes the holdings of more than 1,000 archival agencies, historical societies, and libraries in the United States and is still a basic tool of the scholarly historian.

The Commission labeled as priority projects the publication of the papers of Benjamin Franklin, John and John Quincy Adams, Alexander Hamilton, and James Madison. Hamer helped to get all of them started, along with a project for the "Documentary History of the Ratification of the Constitution and First Ten Amendments." He worked with scholars and universities to start additional projects for John C. Calhoun, Henry Clay, John Jay, Andrew Johnson, John Marshall, James K. Polk, and Woodrow Wilson, among others.

In October 1960 Hamer was elected the 16th President of the Society of American Archivists, and in 1961 he gave the presidential address at the annual meeting in Kansas City. His subject was "Authentic Documents Tending to Elucidate Our History" (published in *The American Archivist,* volume 25).

Hamer wanted to see published the papers of Henry Laurens, who had represented South Carolina in the Continental Congress and served two years, 1777–78, as its President. Hamer felt that Laurens was a Revolutionary leader who had been all but forgotten. On retirement from the Commission on November 30, 1961, he continued to work on the project in the National Archives building, where the papers of the Continental Congress were preserved. He chose as his Associate Editor Professor George C. Rogers, Jr., of the University of South Carolina, which was another repository for many papers. Much collecting and editing had been done, and two volumes were published by the University of South Carolina Press, before Hamer died on April 10, 1971. A third volume, on which he had worked, was published in 1972; others followed.

OLIVER W. HOLMES
(d. 1981)

Hanson, J. C. M.
(1864–1943)

James Christian Meinich Hanson's was perhaps the greatest individual influence on the bibliographical organization of libraries in the United States during the first half of the 20th century. Hanson was born March 13, 1864, at Sørheim, his father's farm, in the district of Nord-Aurdal in the Valdres Valley of Norway. The sixth of eight children of Gunnerius (Gunnar) and Eleanore Adamine Röberg Hansen, he was christened Jens Christian Meinich Hansen. His boyhood friends in Iowa called him Jim, which he, to his later regret, formalized as James. He changed the spelling of his surname but was inconsistent in its use. By 1897 he had adopted "J. C. M. Hanson" as his signature, although he sometimes reverted to "Jens" or "J. C. M. Hansen" in his writings for the Norwegian-American press.

Hanson's father was a government official, *lensmand* for the district of Nord-Aurdal, and the family would not ordinarily have been among those considering emigration to the United States, but Hanson's mother's half-brother, Hans Röberg, had settled in Decorah, Iowa. He offered an education to one of the boys in the family, and in the summer of 1873 Hanson, who was then only nine, left Norway in the company of the Reverend Ove J. Hjort for the trip to Iowa. He could not enroll in the preparatory department of Luther College until the following year because of his age. In 1882, at the age of 18, he received a B.A. degree.

Hanson had no definite career plans and was persuaded by the Reverend Ulrich V. Koren, a member of the college Board of Trustees, that Concordia Seminary in St. Louis was the proper goal for a Luther graduate. Hanson stayed at Concordia for only two years. He felt no real call to the ministry, and the lack of adequate financial support would have made the third and final year exceedingly difficult even had he wished to remain. Instead he accepted a position in the fall of 1884 as Principal of Our Saviour's Church school in the Norwegian community in Chicago, *Klokker* (Deacon) for the church, and Superintendent of its Sunday School. He supplemented his income by teaching English to adult Scandinavians in the Montefiore Evening School and by pitching for several commercial baseball teams. After saving enough money for a year's graduate study, he enrolled at Cornell University in 1888.

In his second year at Cornell, Hanson was awarded the President White Fellowship in history and political science. His research required extensive use of the library, which was at the time undergoing reclassification. He became acquainted with the Acting Librarian, George William Harris, whose influence, according to Hanson, led him to decide on librarianship as his life's work. Accordingly, in September 1890 Hanson joined William Frederick Poole's prestigious training ground at the Newberry Library in Chicago. Among the many benefits gained there, the formation of his lifelong friendship with Charles Martel was not the least.

In 1893 Hanson was appointed Head Cataloguer at the University of Wisconsin. His experience in the planning and implementation of complete reclassification and recataloguing was to prove invaluable to him later at the Library of Congress.

Hanson was appointed Superintendent of the Catalogue Department at the Library of Congress in August 1897 by the newly appointed Librarian of Congress, John Russell Young. In beginning the new catalogue during Young's brief administration, Hanson laid the groundwork for the success of cooperative, later centralized, cataloguing by his carefully considered modifications of Charles A. Cutter's *Rules for a Printed Dictionary Catalogue* to conform to the best practice of the time and thereby "facilitate" the use by other libraries of the Library of Congress cataloguing. The resulting entries, printed for the copyright books in the subdivision "Books Proper" of the *Catalogue of the Register of Copyrights,* were welcomed enthusiastically in a *Library Journal* editorial.

The Montreal conference of the American Library Association in 1900 heralded an era of cooperation in cataloguing. The ALA Publishing Board established an Advisory Committee on Cataloging Rules with Hanson as Chairman. (The name of the committee, which became a special committee of the ALA in 1906, varies; the predominant form was Catalog Rules Committee.) The reconciliation of the numerous divergent views on the many disputed points of cataloguing was credited by William Warner Bishop to Hanson's "thoroughness and patience." His wholehearted commitment to cooperation in cataloguing, which is dependent on agreement on rules, was a major factor in his successful leadership.

This achievement was crowned by the further cooperation with the Library Association's Catalogue Rules Committee in the mutual acceptance, with only eight differences, of *Catalog Rules: Author and Title Entries,* commonly known as the Anglo-American code of 1908. The official ALA motion thanking the Catalog Rules Committee noted that thanks were due "especially" to Hanson, who "has done more to bring the English and American committees into harmony, and has borne the burden of the final editing of the Code." The catalogue cards produced at the Library of Congress under his direction were generally acclaimed for their excellence. Their quality and the general acceptance of the cataloguing rules were major factors in the success of the Library of Congress card distribution service. The card distribution service, in turn, led to an unprecedented national standardization in cataloguing practice.

Hanson's influence on subject cataloguing in the United States was equally powerful and long-lasting. Cutter's "dictionary" principle was radically modified for the new catalogue. Because of the anticipated size of the catalogue, Hanson thought the dispersion of related headings would be too great. Subject topics were therefore subordinated extensively, and independent headings were deliberately inverted to group the headings together. Although some of the principles underlying the system have been modified over the years, the *Library of Congress Subject Headings* remains virtually the standard list of subject headings in use in the United States today.

Within two months of his arrival at the Library of Congress, Hanson was able to bring Charles Martel from the Newberry Library as one of his two chief assistants. Hanson always accorded to Martel the credit for the Library of Congress Classification, but he himself had a major role in its beginnings, primarily in its conception and notation. Hanson, too, carried the responsibility for convincing both Young and Young's successor, Herbert Putnam, of the need for a new classification scheme.

In 1910 Hanson moved to the University of Chicago as Associate Director of the library. This was his third library reorganization, and he became one of the leading voices for cooperative cataloguing to supplement centralized cataloguing as the most efficient and economical means of bibliographical organization. He was appointed to the faculty of the newly established Graduate Library School of the University of Chicago in 1928.

That same year Hanson led the team of cataloguing experts sent by the Carnegie Endowment for International Peace to assist in the reorganization of the Vatican Library. The Vatican Library's *Norme per il catalogo degli stampati* ("rules for the cataloguing of printed books"), which reflected the influence of the Anglo-American code of 1908, was another step toward international agreement in cataloguing. Even after his retirement in 1934, Hanson continued to work for international cooperation in cataloguing as the only route for the future. In furtherance of this cause he compiled his monumental work, *A Comparative Study of Cataloging Rules Based on the Anglo-American Code of 1908; with Comments on the Rules and on the Prospects for a Further Extension of International Agreement and Co-operation* (1939).

Hanson was the author of numerous articles on technical library matters, book reviews, and frequent contributions to the Norwegian-American press. "Corporate Authorship versus Title Entry" (*Library Quarterly,* 1935) is perhaps his most frequently cited article, but his earlier paper on "Rules for Corporate Entry" (*Library Journal,* 1905) is especially valuable for its analysis of the problems.

Hanson's scholarship and the integrity of his character inspired respect; his kindliness, modesty, and generous spirit evoked the affection of his colleagues, staff, and students. His feeling for Luther College was strong. He was appointed to its Board of Trustees in 1920; in 1931 it bestowed on him the honorary LL.D. degree. In 1928 he was appointed Knight and Commander of the Order of Saint Olav by the Crown of Norway. Hanson died at Green Bay, Wisconsin, on November 8, 1943.

REFERENCES

The Hanson Festschrift issue of the *Library Quarterly* (1934) includes a chronological bibliography of Hanson's publications. The bibliography, with a continuation to May 1943, is also in Hanson's autobiography, *What Became of Jens?,* edited by Oivind M. Hovde (Luther College Press, 1974).

The largest collection of Hanson's papers is in the University of Chicago Libraries; a smaller collection of personal papers is in the Luther College Library, Decorah, Iowa.

The manuscript materials relating to Hanson's work at the Library of Congress are in the Library of Congress Archives. These sources, as well as secondary sources, are documented in Edith Scott, "J. C. M. Hanson and His Contribution to Twentieth-Century Cataloging" (Ph.D. dissertation, University of Chicago, 1970).

John Phillip Immroth, "Hanson, James Christian Meinich," *Dictionary of American Library Biography* (1978).

EDITH SCOTT
(d. 1983)

Photo by David Harrison
K. C. Harrison

Harrison, K. C.
(1915–)

Kenneth Cecil Harrison is not only an eminent British librarian, he is also a world traveller and library ambassador extraordinary. Few other librarians can have visited nearly 70 countries other than their own—many of them more than once—and have advised on local services, given lectures and addresses, and conducted study tours there.

Harrison was born at Hyde, Cheshire, near Manchester, April 29, 1915. He was educated at Hyde Grammar School and found his first post in Hyde Public Library, becoming Chief Librarian there at the age of 24. He served in the British Army from 1940 and was a company commander at the D-Day landing in France, where he was wounded. He was released with the rank of Major in 1946 and was awarded the MBE (Member of the Order of the British Empire, Military). His professional progress was rapid: he became Borough Librarian of Hove in 1947 and Borough Librarian of Eastbourne in 1950. He then left the Sussex coast and, moving to Greater London, became Borough Librarian of Hendon in 1958. His career was crowned by appointment as City Librarian of Westminster in 1961, succeeding Lionel McColvin. Westminster was regarded as one of the most senior posts in the United Kingdom and equal in status to those in such great provincial cities as Manchester and Liverpool. Harrison's responsibilities were much increased when his City was amalgamated, for administrative purposes, with two other large London boroughs, St. Marylebone and Paddington, following local government reorganization, in 1965.

He was active in the community life of the towns and city served, including, for example, holding the Vice-Presidency of the Westminster Arts Council and membership in local Rotary clubs. His interest in Rotary continued after he retired in 1980 and returned to Eastbourne, where he joined the Past Rotarians Club. He was appointed OBE (Officer of the Order of the British Empire) for his services to libraries and the arts and is one of the few who have received both the OBE and the MBE (Military). In 1976, for services to libraries and the arts in Finland, he was made a Knight First Class of the Order of the Lion of Finland.

Early in his career, Harrison qualified by examination as a Fellow of the Library Association. He became a member of the LA Council in 1953, was subsequently Chairman, in turn, of three of its standing committees and of its largest branch (London and the Home Counties), and was national President in 1973. He served as a member of the Executive Committee of the National Central Library (1958–73) and was its Chairman during the years before it merged with the British Library in 1973. He was also a prolific library and literary journalist, edited *The Library World* (1960–71), and chaired the National Library Week Joint Committee (1964–69).

Harrison's interests and activities extended far beyond the United Kingdom, as his *International Librarianship* (1989) makes clear. He introduced this anthology of the articles and addresses he had written for audiences outside Britain with "The Wider Librarianship," in which he pays tribute to those who have labored in the cause around the world and argues for untiring effort and a spirit of idealism. The references to visits to countries as distant from Britain as Fiji, Jamaica, Kenya, and the Seychelles present only an incomplete picture of an exceptional achievement. In his Foreword to the book, Lester Asheim refers to Harrison's

> direct and personal examination of libraries in other countries and in his participation in international organizations dedicated to the identification and improvement of the services they seek to perform, he is unfailingly aware of the factors outside of librarianship that shape and define the nature of the library's services.

One of the most important outcomes was formation of the Commonwealth Library Association (COMLA), which Harrison helped found and served as first President (1972–75) and as Executive Secretary (1980–83). He was Vice-President of the International Association of Metropolitan City Libraries (INTAMEL; 1974–81) and a member of the British Council's Libraries Advisory Committee (1974–80). He began serving as consultant to the Ranfurly Library Service in 1983. His Nordic friends called him "Mr. Scandinavia"; his Commonwealth colleagues dubbed him "Mr. COMLA."

Most of Harrison's books deal with British, and particularly public, libraries; some are aimed primarily at students and others at librarians or general readers. They include *First Steps in Librarianship: A Student's Guide* (1950), *Public Libraries Today* (1963), *The Library and the Community* (1963), *Libraries in Britain* (1969), and *Public Relations for Librarians* (1973); most went through several editions. He edited the volume celebrating the LA's centenary, *Prospects for British Librarianship* (1976) and three well-illustrated volumes on library buildings: *British Public Library Buildings* (with S. G. Berriman, 1966), *Public Library Buildings 1975–83* (1987), and *Library Buildings 1984–89* (1990). He had displayed similar concern for effective and aesthetically pleasing buildings in *Libraries in Scandinavia* (1961).

W. A. MUNFORD

Harvard University Library

Some books were no doubt present when a college was founded at Cambridge, Massachusetts, in 1636, but its library began in earnest in 1638, the year John Harvard bequeathed about 400 volumes, consisting of about 329 titles, to it. The number of books in the collection grew slowly, almost entirely by gift, until in 1764 it numbered about 5,000 volumes. Then, in January 1764, Harvard Hall burned down, and with it the library of Harvard College, the largest collection in the colonies. Only 404 volumes survived. Many donors responded to the need for books: the state of New Hampshire gave funds that made possible 700 acquisitions and the merchant John Hancock gave enough for 1,300 more. Many donations of money or books came from individuals and societies in the British Isles, for whom the college had been a favorite charity for some time. The purpose of the first printed catalogue of the library, published in 1723, was not so much to disseminate information about the collection as to stimulate gifts of books that were not already in it.

By 1766 the library was nearly as large as before, with 4,350 volumes. Gifts continued for nearly a

Harvard University Archives

Frontispiece of the sole surviving book from John Harvard's library, one of only 404 left after the disastrous fire of 1764. Like many of the other books saved, it was out at the time—and overdue.

century to be the major means for adding to the collection. College authorities appropriated funds mainly for reference works and a few periodicals. In the academic year 1806–07, the low point for acquisitions, only eleven titles and two maps were added. Major purchases did not begin until 1842, when college officials, realizing that a library could not rely on gifts in kind, asked for donations to the Donation Fund or Subscribed Fund. They raised $17,000 and spent it mainly on filling longstanding gaps identified by the faculty. When the fund was gone, the library returned to dependence on gifts. By 1856, the central library had about 100,000 volumes and pamphlets and the libraries of the Law School (begun in 1817), the Medical School (1819), and the Divinity School (1826) had several tens of thousands more.

College officials first articulated the idea that the growth of scholarship required regular purchases of newly published books in the late 1850s. A donor responded: in 1859, William Gray offered $5,000 a year for five years with the proviso that "the latest works be preferred to those of earlier date." The library returned to poverty after the five years, but a new President of Harvard set a new course. In 1869 Charles William Eliot began to transform Harvard into a university, with students free to choose their courses and with possibilities for graduate work under the direction of scholars who were themselves carrying out research and writing of the highest quality.

The library had to grow, and funds had to be acquired to make possible a library that could support such scholarship. Eliot sought endowed funds that could be invested to produce ongoing income. University endowment grew mightily, from less than $2,400,000 in 1869 to almost $6,800,000 in 1889, then to more than $22,700,000 in 1909. The library's first endowment, a bequest of $60,000 in 1870 for new books, was joined by others; by the late 1880s, it had nearly $200,000 in endowed funds for acquisitions and another $500,000 for other library purposes.

By the end of the 19th century, Harvard had 37 libraries, including those in scientific institutions such as the Arboretum, Astronomical Observatory, Herbarium, Museum of Comparative Zoology, and Peabody Museum, with holdings of more than 500,000 volumes. These collections were almost enough to make Harvard's one of the ten largest libraries in the world. Ainsworth Rand Spofford, in *A Book for All Readers* (1900), began his description of the collections with the word "select." For the previous 40 years purchases had indeed been selected, mainly by faculty members. But by 1900 the Harvard Library was beginning to go beyond carefully chosen volume-by-volume purchases—it was beginning to acquire collections of material of no immediate use, under the assumption that they would one day be essential in educating those who could lead the United States into a more important and influential role in the world.

The library director who built such international holdings was Archibald Cary Coolidge. Beginning in the 1890s, when he was a professor of history and not formally connected to the library, he used his own funds and those of family and friends to buy collections from various parts of the world. He became Director of the Library in 1910 and the pace of his acquisitions quickened; the effect lasted well beyond his death in 1928. His first gift, in 1895, was of 1,371 titles of Slavica from a catalog of the German bookseller Harrassowitz. In 1898–99 Coolidge or his family gave 322 volumes on Poland, 445 on Turkey, and the Riant Library of nearly 9,000 titles on the

Harvard University Archives

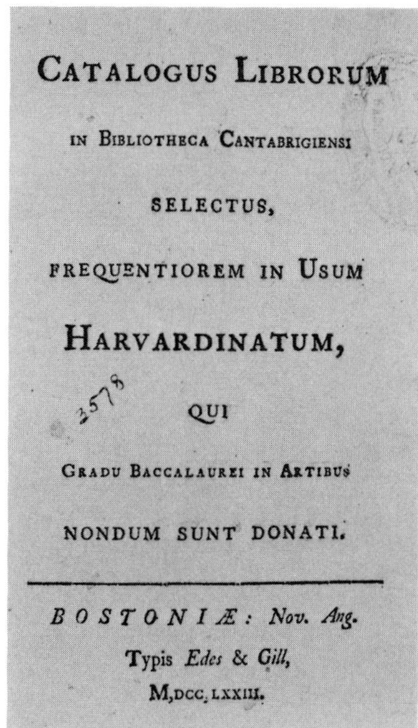
CATALOGUS LIBRORUM
IN BIBLIOTHECA CANTABRIGIENSI
SELECTUS,
FREQUENTIOREM IN USUM
HARVARDINATUM,
QUI
GRADU BACCALAUREI IN ARTIBUS
NONDUM SUNT DONATI.

BOSTONIÆ: Nov. Ang.
Typis *Edes* & *Gill*,
M,DCC,LXXIII.

In 1773, Harvard published the first list of books recommended for undergraduates. Sophomores were not allowed to borrow books until 1795; freshman not until 1814.

Harvard University Archives

Gore Hall, the first Harvard University Library building, later demolished to make space for Widener Library.

Crusades and the Latin East; in 1900, 2,000 titles from the library of the Slovak writer Lombardini of Sollein; in 1900–01, $3,750 for books on Poland and other Slavic countries, including 300 contemporary accounts of the Turkish wars of the 17th century; in 1901–02, a collection of Russian Nihilist pamphlets; in 1903, a pledge to purchase 10,000 volumes on German history; in 1903–04, the 10,000-volume library of Konrad von Maurer on Old Norse law and Scandinavian history; in 1906, $1,000 for books on French history; and, in 1913, several Latin American collections.

Others gave collections on Thomas à Kempis, Pope, Keats, Ronsard, and Molière. Mrs. William Hooper provided funds for Western Americana, including a library on Utah and Mormonism. Robert Gould Shaw gave a theatrical library; in 1918, Evert Jansen Wendell added 35,000 volumes on the theater, plus two million pieces of ephemera. Harvard acquired the Fernando Palha library of Portuguese history and literature in 1926 and 40,000 titles on the French Revolution the next year. After Coolidge's death, Harvard obtained a 10,000-item collection of Icelandica in 1930 and 40,000 books, pamphlets, serials, and broadsides on Italian history in the 19th century in 1932.

Harry Elkins Widener Memorial Library, opened in 1915.

Harvard University Archives

Coolidge worked with Roscoe Pound, Dean of the Harvard Law School, in such ventures as acquiring the 7,000-title Olivart collection on international law, plus 175 Italian statutes and a library on criminology, in 1912. Pound needed little encouragement to support library purchase and played a major role in creating the great international collections of the Harvard Law School Library.

Deans of the Graduate School of Business Administration (established 1908) emulated Coolidge and Pound in building a great library: Wallace B. Donham even signed a personal note for Herbert Somerton Foxwell's collection, which in 1939 became the foundation of the Kress Library of Business and Economics, one of the major collections of pre-1850 economic literature. Three other graduate schools founded in the 20th century—Design, Education, and Government—have led to expanded library holdings.

Coolidge's collection-building extended to Asian materials, and in 1927 he was instrumental in establishing the Harvard-Yenching Library, which is now one of the great collections of East Asian material in the West. The Coolidge tradition of expanding the geographical scope of the collections has continued. The Middle Eastern Department was established in 1954 and a separate Judaica Department in 1962, with the endowment of the post of Lee M. Friedman Bibliographer in Judaica.

Another kind of expansion of scope began in the late 1930s, when William A. Jackson took charge of the Treasure Room in the Widener Library. Changing Harvard's past policy of not acquiring the papers of individuals (with such exceptions as Senator Charles Sumner and the poet John Greenleaf Whittier), he succeeded in drawing to the Houghton Library (opened in 1942) the manuscripts, correspondence, and libraries of major New England figures, including the Alcotts, Thomas Bailey Aldrich, Emily Dickinson, Ralph Waldo Emerson, Nathaniel Hawthorne, Oliver Wendell Holmes, William Dean Howells, the Jameses, Henry Wadsworth Longfellow, Amy Lowell, James Russell Lowell, Herman Melville, and others.

The University Archives had long been collecting archival materials relating to the university, including the papers of eminent professors. The Business School Library in 1916 began gathering archives that document the industrial revolution in New England; the Law School collected the papers of alumni who went on to become eminent jurists. More recently, the Rare Books Department of the Countway Library of the Harvard Medical School attracted the papers of leading physicians and the archives of medical institutions. The various libraries have expanded the scope of their collecting beyond New England and beyond the 18th and 19th centuries to include such materials as the credit ledgers of Dun and Bradstreet, the papers of the financier Thomas Lamont, the poetical notebooks of Alfred Lord Tennyson, the papers of Leon Trotsky and of Thomas Wolfe, and many others. Collection-level descriptions for about 3,000 manuscript and archival collections are now in Harvard's online catalogue and in RLIN, the Research Libraries Information Network. In all, there are 4 to 5 million items in the Houghton Library, filling approximately 15,000 running feet of shelving. The Law School Library has 1.5 million items.

Great retrospective collections of printed books are less commonly received today than in the early 1900s, though they do continue, the most notable being the library of Philip Hofer, the founder of the Department of Printing and Graphic Arts, the first such department in a university library. Most growth takes place by purchase of new publications from around the world. The Annual Report for the year 1990–91 records that the libraries of the university added almost 403,000 volumes, for a net increase of more than 330,000. The total number of volumes is well over 12 million.

In addition to the printed material included in such statistics, the library's holdings of microforms exceed 5.5 million reels, microcards, microfiches, and microprints. To give some other examples of material not counted in the statistics in the annual report: The Theatre Collection contains more than 5 million items, including playbills and photographs; the Fine Arts Library has more than 1.5 million items in its Visual Collections; the Loeb Music Library has almost 38,000 sound recordings; and the Map Collection of the Harvard College Library and the Kummel Geological Sciences Library house more than 500,000 maps.

Expenditures for all these materials in the year 1990–91 totaled almost $11,900,000. Salaries, including retirement and health programs, came to almost $33,800,000. Total expenditures for the year were almost $58,500,000.

The fundamental work of the staff of the Harvard library is to process such material. Harvard has (using the function codes of the Association of Research Libraries) 17 heads of cataloguing departments, 72 cataloguers, 54 subject specialists, 11 heads of reference, and 39 reference librarians. The Harvard tradition that faculty and students should receive little assistance in using the library is gradually changing. More staff members provide assistance than in the past, mainly because access to information in nonprint media requires it.

The total number of full-time-equivalent employees is nearly 1,100, of whom 350 are professional librarians. Of that number, 14 percent have doctorates. Members of the staff have an average of almost 14 years of professional experience, averaging just over 13 years at Harvard.

The governance of this large library system, consisting of about 90 units, is not readily understood even by those in the university. The faculties of the university are financially independent, which means that their libraries constitute a federation whose administrative policy has been called "coordinated decentralization." The position of Librarian of Harvard College goes back to the 19th century; the position of Director of the University Library was established in 1910. Between then and 1979, the posts were sometimes held by two individuals, sometimes by one. Since 1979–80, the Director has been the holder of one of the most distinguished chairs in the university, the Carl H. Pforzheimer. Sidney Verba, a political scientist, became Director in 1985.

Harvard University Archives

Retrieving material from the state-of-the-art Harvard Depository.

The Director focuses on issues of long-term significance to scholarship and teaching, not the daily activities of the various library units. Those who report to the Director have university-wide responsibilities—for financial management, fund-raising, university-library personnel and university-wide personnel issues, preservation, publications, and systems planning and research, including the online catalogue HOLLIS. The University Archivist also reports to the Director. The Director, largely through that small but senior staff and through personal stature, fosters coordination, concerted action, and uniform policies. The Director reported to the President of the University until 1992, then to the newly created Provost.

The Director had major influence in the university's decision in the early 1980s to build the first unit of the state-of-the-art Harvard Depository on university-owned land in Southboro, Massachusetts. When the nine units are completed, total storage capacity in Southboro will be 20 million volumes or the equivalent. The Director gained the support of the librarians of the various faculties, then the approval of Harvard's governing body, for converting the card catalogues to electronic form. In these ways, the Director can play a crucial role, despite the fact that the librarians of the faculty libraries report to others.

The Librarian of Harvard College, the head of the largest unit of Harvard's library system, reports to the Dean of the Faculty of Arts and Sciences. The Librarian meets frequently with, but does not report to, the Director of the University Library. Similarly, the librarians of the other faculties—Business Administration, Design, Divinity, Education, Government, Law, and Medicine and Public Health—report directly or indirectly to their deans, but meet regularly as the University Library Council, a body established in 1970.

Changes in the ways in which the materials of scholarship and instruction become available will require new patterns in the relationships among the libraries at Harvard; and just as the outside world is placing new challenges before the Harvard Library, so are the same changes affecting the extent and nature of Harvard's contribution to the wider scholarly community. Harvard has always made available bibliographic data on its holdings, through participating in union catalogues and through publishing catalogues of collections or libraries in book form. It has also aided the wider scholarly community through interlibrary loan, but most scholars who want to use the materials, other than those available in microform, travel to Boston or Cambridge.

The nature of the contribution this non-governmental library makes to American scholarship is a keen question in this time of change. The university libraries have taken up the challenge posed by the strength of their retrospective collections and are participating fully in efforts to preserve deteriorating materials on microfilm, efforts whose overall success depends on shared responsibility and coordinated action. The Harvard libraries focused in the late 1980s and early 1990s on filming 19th-century Italian history, pre-Soviet Russian law, and American business literature. Converting the catalogues will be a major contribution reaching far beyond Harvard Yard.

Two units of the Harvard Library completed strategic plans in the early 1990s, the Countway Library of the Medical School and the Harvard College Library. These are signs that this private mega-library is changing to further the purpose it has always had—to support teaching and research.

KENNETH E. CARPENTER

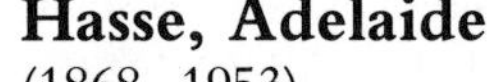

Hasse, Adelaide
(1868–1953)

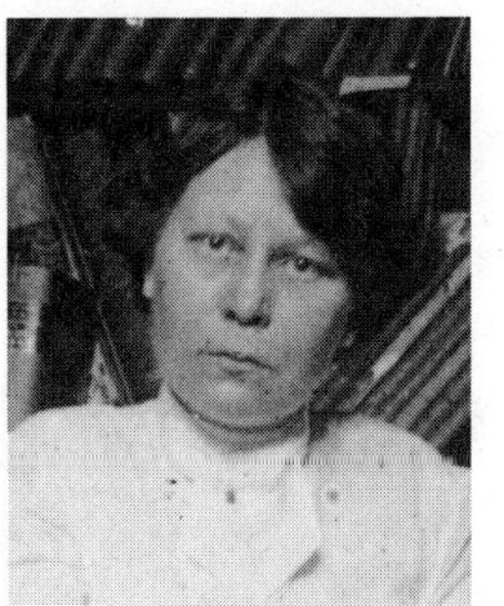

The New York Public Library
Adelaide Hasse

Indexer, writer, and bibliographer Adelaide Rosalie Hasse, during nearly 60 years in which she served in a variety of U.S. library and bibliographic positions, produced dozens of articles for the library and popular press and compiled a series of checklists and bibliographies that are unparalleled in their value and coverage.

Born in Milwaukee, Wisconsin, September 13, 1868, she was raised in an environment shaped by individuals who challenged both her mind and her ability to do unusual things in an unusual way. Her father, Hermann Edward Hasse, was a well-known physician, surgeon, and botanist who, with other members of a distinguished family, created a noteworthy learning environment for his five children. There is no evidence that Adelaide attended any private schools or attained a college education, but from childhood she was educated to think, to examine, to challenge the obvious and the easy. As a result, she developed analytical skills and a critical acumen that played an important role in her library career.

When her family moved to the West Coast, Adelaide Hasse began her library career in 1889 under the leadership of a woman of unique character, Tessa L. Kelso, of the Los Angeles Public Library. At that time, there was no school of library science other than the prototype Dewey enterprise in New York; those who came to the field learned by example and by doing. Several decades later Hasse recalled Kelso's tremendous impact on her life as one "which gave point and direction to my natural bent." At the Los Angeles Public Library, Kelso asked her apprentice to organize the library's collection of U.S. government publications. Since there were few guidelines or procedures, Hasse applied her own logical approach, devised a classification scheme, and began a checklist of items. The success of her methods, especially in a field where so little was known, quickly came to the attention of persons in key positions in Washington, D.C. Because of the requirements of the Printing Act of January 12, 1895, an office had been organized that, among other responsibilities, was to prepare and print an index to government publications. As a result of her pioneer work in Los Angeles, Hasse was invited to serve in Washington as the first Librarian of the Office of the Superintendent of Documents.

Washington, D.C.: 1895–97. Hasse arrived in the capital in May 1895; the following year the first of her major bibliographies was published by the Government Printing Office. *The List of Publications of the U.S. Department of Agriculture* initiated a life as an indexer and bibliographer that was not concluded until Hasse, in her 80s, came out of retirement to help edit a microfilm publication of records of the United States.

Among her works are two remarkable indexes that are still key resources. The first, published in 13 volumes from 1907 to 1922, is the *Index of Economic Material in Documents of the States of the United States.* Financed by the Carnegie Institution of Washington, it was, as R. R. Bowker noted in 1920, "a life work for any less persistent and industrious person." The second set, a three-volume *Index to United States Documents Relating to Foreign Affairs, 1828–1861,* was also funded by the Carnegie Institution and was published from 1914 to 1921.

Adelaide Hasse's arrival in Washington occasioned a burst of activity typical of her dedication and enthusiasm for her work. The duties of her position called for collecting existing documents from all government departments and then for organizing and housing them. She uncovered an amazing amount of material; in six weeks nearly 300,000 documents from all the government departments had been retrieved and roughly inventoried. Hasse's story of this experience, along with an autobiographical commentary on many aspects of her professional career, is contained in a privately published pamphlet, written in 1919, entitled "The Compensations of Librarianship."

Although Hasse remained in Washington for only two years, 1895–97, her efforts there are especially recognized because she developed a classification for government documents. The scheme was expanded in the *Checklist of United States Public Documents, 1789–1909,* and served as the structural basis for the *Monthly Catalog.* Her organization of the Library of the Superintendent of Documents so impressed John

Shaw Billings, Director of the New York Public Library, that she was offered a position "to build up what Dr. Billings wished to be a great document collection."

New York Public Library. Hasse's career in New York is divided into two distinct phases: (1) the period from 1897 until Billings's death in 1913, when she was able to develop a model public documents collection; and (2) the final six years during which, in her own eyes at least, her accomplishments and her position were destroyed. In both instances, the particular natures of her employers apparently were key factors.

John Shaw Billings was an outstanding librarian, even in an era of unusual library leaders; his vision and his administrative skills were instrumental in establishing the New York Public Library. In fact, only a man of his scholarship and achievements could have impressed Adelaide Hasse, who brought a special aptitude of her own to the library profession. Billings recognized her brilliance and dealt with her acerbic personality in such a way as to encourage and enhance her contributions. During the years of his administration, she was instrumental in building a collection of documents from an unorganized base of 10,000 items to nearly 300,000 catalogued volumes. Hasse's reputation as an expert on government publications was also evident in the contributions she made to the American Library Association; she served first as a member and later as Chair of the Committee on Public Documents, and she spoke and wrote often on the collection and administration of government publications. As life member number 779 of ALA, she regularly participated in conferences, was a member of the Committee on Library Schools, and was elected to ALA Council from 1908 through 1913.

In addition to her capable development of the documents collection, Hasse was also involved in serving the assorted publics of the Library. Her ability to retrieve specialized information from the vast resources of the government was extended to other databases as well. Since her perception of direct service to the business world predated that of many of her colleagues, Public Documents and then the Economics Division of the Library emerged as major service centers. During this productive period, the first decade of the 20th century, she also began a massive index of economic material and was able to uncover, during a trip to Europe, a copy of the "lost" *Bradford Journal,* which she later edited for publication.

Billings's death in 1913 marked the beginning of the end for much of Hasse's work in the New York Public Library, although six years elapsed before the Board of Trustees terminated her employment. The new director, E. H. Anderson, was not of the same mind and pursuits as his predecessor. Several personal and professional factors were involved, but before many months had passed, Hasse and Anderson were stubbornly set in a pattern of action and reaction that, given Anderson's power as Director, could only end in Hasse's removal. She made it clear that she considered Anderson incompetent and destructive of her work of 16 years; he, in turn, rallied the staff and the Board, charged her with insubordination, and asked for her resignation. Hasse refused and was fired in the fall of 1918.

The emotional character of the library conflict and the nature of the accusations leveled against Hasse, some of which involved rumors of pro-German sympathies in a traumatic war climate, might have debilitated a lesser personality. Hasse, however, was neither incapacitated nor silenced. "The Compensations of Librarianship" (1919) is a statement of professional interests, an accusatory and spirited explanation of the situation leading to her firing, and a credo of continuing dedication to library work. Moreover, she was able to provide positive evidence that the U.S. government perceived no treacherous tendencies, since she left New York in 1918, a few weeks after her termination, to work for the Department of State.

For the next 30 years, until she retired in 1941, Hasse was employed in a series of responsible positions in Washington including the War Labor Policies Board (1918–19), the War Industries Board (1919–21), the office of the Assistant Secretary of War (1921), the Brookings Institution (1923–32), the Works Progress Administration (1934–39), and the Temporary National Economics Committee (1939–41). After she retired, she continued to live in Washington until her death on July 29, 1953.

Appraisal. In reviewing Adelaide Hasse's long life, it is important to emphasize the amount of her publication, which includes nearly 24 monographs and some 50 articles. She was an incisive and perceptive commentator on numerous facets of library service as well as a compiler of excellent checklists and bibliographies, many of which identified difficult-to-locate government publications. Hasse was an early advocate of library service for special groups and, in Washington during the 1920s, helped to organize the local chapter of the Special Libraries Association, served as its first President, and edited the association journal, *Special Libraries.* She applied her expertise and organizational skill concerning government resources in her employment as a lecturer at George Washington University from 1933 to 1937 and, near the end of her career, at Catholic University.

Although Hasse's precise motivation and expectations cannot be interpreted exactly, it is well established that she had a confidence in the role of libraries and librarians that inspired a personal commitment that never wavered. Writing in the *New Republic* in January 1918, at a period in her life that for her was verging on the catastrophic, she posed the question to the library profession: "Why Not?" Hasse felt keenly the failure of the profession to function as a "public service organization." Yet beneath the critical question there existed a sense of that which might be. She asked then, and throughout her career, regardless of consequences, "What is there so very incongruous about taking just one more step and by so doing galvanizing the present inert mass into a pulsating service plant?" Her life was an example of that one more step.

REFERENCES

Laurel A. Grotzinger, "Hasse, Adelaide Rosalie," *Dictionary of American Library Biography* (1978).

Gail K. Nelson and John V. Richardson, "Adelaide Hasse and the Early History of the U.S. Superintendent of Documents Classification Scheme," *Government Publications Review* (1986).

LAUREL A. GROTZINGER

ALA

Frances E. Henne

Henne, Frances E.
(1906–1985)

Frances Elizabeth Henne, U.S. library educator who inspired thousands of students, drew on her critical and incisive mind to create books, articles, and addresses dedicated to excellence in service to children and youth. Always willing to break with tradition, she saw beyond the usual patterns to seek new and innovative ways to make learning a joy to children and to those who work with them.

Born in Springfield, Illinois, on October 11, 1906, she received her B.A. (1929) and M.A. (1934) in English from the University of Illinois, her B.S. from the School of Library Service, Columbia University (1935), and her Ph.D. from the University of Chicago Graduate Library School (1949). In 1942 she became the first woman appointed to the faculty of the Graduate Library School at the University of Chicago; from 1947 to 1950 she was Associate Dean and Dean of Students; and in 1951–52 she was Acting Dean. In 1954 she moved to the School of Library Service at Columbia.

While at the University of Chicago, Henne established the Center for Children's Books and its *Bulletin*. Her innovation was bringing children's books into one place for analysis and then producing a reviewing medium that related books to curriculum. It included reviews of books that were not recommended. *Time* magazine (May 5, 1952), describing the Center for Children's Books as unique in U.S. education, reported that she was worried that "there was no place where all books for children were being examined and reported on." Henne brought her concern to the attention of Robert M. Hutchins, then head of the University of Chicago, telling him that her juvenile books were just as important as his Great Books. The Center still contributes to education through its analysis of children's materials.

Book Selection and Evaluation Centers, including the Children's Book Council, were recipients of Henne's strong support and leadership. She acted as an adviser (1968–73) to the Educational Media Selection Centers Project, a joint program of the U.S. Office of Education and the National Book Committee. She established the annual Book Discussion Days at Columbia's School of Library Service, which served to influence similar activities elsewhere in the country; they offer opportunities for librarians to discuss children's books and to share their interpretations with others. In these ways her work continues to reach out to help bring children and books together.

Henne always grasped the significance of professional organizations and understood the internal dynamics of organizational life. She helped to found the American Association of School Librarians (AASL) and to define the role it could play in the lives of school librarians and in the lives of those they serve. As President of AASL (1948–49), she continued and expanded her influence. As a member of the School Library Standards Committee that prepared *School Libraries for Today and Tomorrow: Functions and Standards* (ALA, 1945) and Chairperson of the committee that prepared *Standards for School Library Programs* (ALA, 1960) and of the joint committee of AASL and the Department of Audio-Visual Instruction (DAVI) of the National Education Association that issued *Standards for School Media Programs* (ALA, 1969), Henne was a leading force in establishing criteria for excellence in school library programs in the United States.

Her research on school libraries in the U.S. contributed to the production of standards that formed the basis for most state evaluation programs in subsequent years. Very early Henne recognized the significance of nonprint media and the necessity to include all media in school library collections. She wrote prolifically on the role of standards in schooling and exerted influence far beyond what is usual for school librarianship with her coverage in national professional journals. Her special and unique contribution, however, was her ability to see the need for cooperative arrangements among all the institutions working with children and youth. She was the driving force, using the *Standards,* to forge the links of relationship with the Association for Educational Communications and Technology (AECT, then DAVI) and to win the recognition and support of many other national associations devoted to work with children and youth. She helped in the development of standards for school libraries for the deaf and aided individual states in their development of standards and guidelines. Her consistent belief in and championing of standards for school library media centers as a means to provide excellence in education was the most extraordinary achievement of her career; personal sacrifices and bitter attacks for her beliefs and vision never stopped her in her determination to make standards in school media programs critical to professional practice.

Henne served as a member of the Knapp School Library Development Project Advisory Board (1960–62) and was a member of the New York State Regents Advisory Council on Libraries (1965–74). She also served the U.S. Office of Education innumerable times as evaluator and consultant. She spoke to the profession not only through her lucid writing but also in speeches before professional meetings. She called all to follow her to the high path of quality, eschewing the path of mediocrity. The philosophy she set forth in *Youth Communication and Libraries* (ALA, 1949) was only a herald of what she was to continue to achieve in the years that followed.

Winner of the prestigious ALA Joseph W. Lippincott Award in 1963, an Honorary Citation during the Centennial of ALA (1976), and the Beta Phi Mu Award in 1978, Henne received many other national and regional awards for her outstanding scholarship and her contributions to work with children and youth. AASL gave her its President's Award in 1979 for her consistent and continuing efforts on behalf of children and schooling.

Henne recognized early in her career that the formal study of materials for children and youth is a scholarly discipline. Always a believer in interdisciplinary programs and ever hopeful of establishing a National Institute of Research on Children and Youth, she worked diligently to foster these goals. As a teacher she developed courses that met the vision and ideals she set forth. She taught one of the first courses in the history of children's literature and designed a course in the sociology of reading of children and youth. An avid book collector, particularly in the field of children's books, Henne gave her collections to the

Special Collections Department of the Columbia University Libraries (the Henne Collection).

Henne retired in June 1975 after 21 years at Columbia's School of Library Service. She died in Greenfield, Massachusetts, December 21, 1985.

A Festschrift, *Frontiers of Library Service for Youth* (Columbia University, 1979), completed by some of her students, contains their tribute to her through a continuation of her ideas and ideals and includes a bibliography of her publications.

In 1947 Henne wrote, "we must provide also the ideals, the force, the zeal, the spirit, the hard work, and yes, the toughness, that form the dynamics which turn visions and plans into workable realities."

JANE ANNE HANNIGAN

Henriot, Gabriel
(1880–1965)

Gabriel Henriot, French archivist and librarian and pioneer in library professional education, was a leader in international library cooperation and became known as the "spiritual father" of the International Federation of Library Associations (IFLA).

Henriot was born on January 18, 1880, in the Bellevue district of Paris. His grandfather was a peasant from Lorraine in the region of Domremy; his father worked for the Paris-Lyons-Mediterranean railway. The family moved to the Boulevard de Picpus shortly after the boy's birth, and he never moved from the Faubourg Saint-Antoine. He was enrolled in the neighborhood nursery school, then the communal primary school. A brilliant student singled out by his teachers, he easily obtained a scholarship to continue his studies at the Lycée Charlemagne. He then entered the École des Chartes (the national school for archivists) and at the same time attended classes at the École des Hautes Études. Thus he earned an advanced university degree (diplôme d'études supérieure) as well as an archivist's certificate (diplôme d'archiviste-paléographe).

In 1905 Henriot was named Librarian of the Bibliothèque Historique de la Ville de Paris (Historical Library of the City of Paris). He began working with Georges Bourgin on an edition of the proceedings of the Commune of 1871 (*Procès verbaux de la Commune de 1871*). World War I delayed the work, which was issued in parts beginning in 1924. Henriot, who had received officer training in 1901–02, was called to serve in the army in August 1914. He joined the 367th Infantry Regiment at Toul and fought for 52 months in dangerous posts (including Bois le Prêtre near Verdun, Alsace, and Picardy) without a single wound and without a day of sick leave. He became a major, with five citations and the Croix de Guerre, by the time of the Armistice. On his return to civilian life in 1920 he was named *Conservateur* (Director) at the Forney Library, a collection devoted to industrial design, arts, crafts, and related subjects. Henriot remained in this position until the general mobilization in September 1939.

The situation in the Forney Library was hardly brilliant. Since its foundation in 1886, the Library had functioned in antiquated quarters annexed to a school. Henriot refused to be discouraged by the material conditions of the Library and decided to make the Forney collection not just a resource for the artisans of the neighborhood but an arts and crafts institution for all of Paris.

At great personal effort, Henriot was able to carry out many kinds of activities with minimal funding. He opened the Library ten and a half hours a day, Monday through Saturday, and on Sunday morning. He put the telephone at the disposition of the readers. He published many reader aids; worked closely with vocational schools; participated in exhibits; and created the Society of Friends of the Library, interesting many noted individuals in the life of Forney.

Henriot preached by example, writing in journals (*Mobilier et decoration*) and publishing books (on furniture, wrought iron work, lighting, and wood carving) that were useful to those involved in contemporary arts and crafts. He also published a very beautiful book that captured the spirit of the Faubourg Saint-Antoine, where a hard-working population of artisans lovingly crafted the objects of daily life.

Gabriel Henriot

To carry out his innovative program, Henriot needed people, but library education was not organized in France until long after World War I. An archivist by training, he turned first to the École des Chartes. Elected President of its alumni society (1923), he unsuccessfully tried to persuade the group to promote library training. Henriot then approached the Association des Bibliothécaires Français (ABF, the French library association). First elected to the Executive Committee in 1923, Henriot was President from 1925 to 1927. During the first weeks of his presidency, he launched a survey of municipal libraries that became the basis for a report he drafted for the Minister of Public Instruction. His 1926 report was followed by a table with salaries for a proposed national corps of librarians. Published and discussed, that report finally began to bear fruit when Julien Cain became Director of the Bibliothèque Nationale.

Facing obstacles to the realization of the reforms he had specified, Henriot proposed using examples from abroad to make the French administration realize the importance of such changes. He made contact with the International Institute of Intellectual Cooperation and in 1924 undertook a survey of national library associations sponsored by ABF. At the International Congress of Librarians and Booklovers held in Prague in 1926, Henriot presented the proposal that led to the creation of a standing international library committee to serve as a liaison among library associations. Welcomed with enthusiasm, this initiative laid the foundations for IFLA. Three years later, at the first World Congress of Librarianship and Bibliography in Rome, IFLA became a reality.

Named President of the 11th section of IFLA in 1929, Henriot was charged with the task of drawing up a report on training and on library education. He took part in the IFLA Congress in Madrid in 1935, but three years earlier at the Berne Conference he had offered his resignation because of the neglect of professional education in France and because he believed that IFLA was more concerned with research libraries than with libraries for everyone. The latter were Henriot's chief preoccupation.

From 1924 on, at the same time that he was most active on the international level, Henriot also directed his efforts toward developing a specialty in library education. He in fact became an internationally known expert in this area. A meeting in Prague with Mary Parsons proved decisive for him. Parsons was the chief aide to Sarah Bogle, the Assistant Secretary of the American Library Association, who had been sent to Paris to organize a school for librarians. The school was funded for two years by the American Committee for Devastated France, a war relief agency that had set up small public libraries in Aisne and Paris. Bogle wished to adapt the American library school program to French needs. While the courses on cataloguing and classification were entrusted to Margaret Mann, then Vice-President of ALA, part of the training was delegated to French librarians such as Ernest Coyecque, Eugène Morel, and, of course, Henriot. He was entrusted with a course that covered the history of books and printing, book selection, and work with children. Henriot subsequently became chief French adviser to the school.

At the end of the second full-year course in 1926, Henriot persuaded his U.S. friends that the school should be continued. He cautioned: "If one abruptly withdraws the school's budget, it will be the end of the work for modern libraries. The Paris Library School and the libraries created through your aid will be a lost effort, without future." The school was to last for another three years. In all, 201 students from 25 countries enrolled in its program.

The Paris Library School had scarcely closed its doors when Henriot, with his characteristic tenacity, opened a municipal school for librarians. Because the national government had turned a deaf ear to his pleas, he cast his lot with the city of Paris.

In 1931 Henriot was named Inspector of Libraries for the city of Paris and the *département* of the Seine. During his inspection tours, he became aware of the urgent need to provide professional training for the haphazardly recruited, poorly paid personnel, most of whom only barely grasped the most elementary rudiments of librarianship. The new municipal library school that he created functioned for five years with no budget and without any quarters other than the reading room of the Forney Library. Classroom instruction, limited to just 24 hours, was complemented by practice work, visits to libraries, and short internships. The school was free and open not just to the municipal library staff but to anyone who wished to create popular libraries. The 200 students who benefited from this training were drawn from Paris and the provinces and from both the public and the private sector. The city, however, was indifferent to the effort. In December 1936, after failing to obtain for the instructors the modest salaries the city had promised them, Henriot decided to give up the school. A new possibility was then offered to him.

The Ligue féminine d'action catholique (Women's Catholic Action League) provided a grant enabling Henriot to create a library school at the private Institut Catholique. Although Henriot had long hoped for a national library school, he accepted the League's offer. He then set up a program of study that lasted two years and included practice work as well as a number of short internships and visits to institutions. After his second demobilization and his retirement from the Forney Library in 1940, Henriot devoted himself to teaching and to directing the school. When he died in Paris on April 21, 1965, the school had already trained 717 students from 45 countries. The creation of a national graduate library school did not overshadow the unique training program created by Henriot and adapted by his former students to meet the exigencies of modern librarianship.

COLETTE MEUVRET;
JACQUELINE VIAUX

Hewins, Caroline M.
(1846–1926)

ALA

Caroline M. Hewins

Caroline Maria Hewins was an American pioneer in children's library work and, for 50 years, Librarian of the Hartford (Connecticut) Public Library.

She was born October 10, 1846, in Roxbury, Massachusetts. Her paternal forebears had sailed from England to Sharon, Massachusetts, in 1656. Her father was a well-to-do Boston haberdasher. In her infancy the family moved to Jamaica Plain, and when she was seven to West Roxbury, where they occupied a five-acre estate, ample for their nine children, of whom she was the oldest.

A precocious, bookish child, Hewins was reading by the age of four and later enjoyed reading and telling stories to her younger sisters and brother. These experiences, which inculcated a lifelong love of children's books, were described in her memoir, *A Mid-Century Child and Her Books* (1926). Education at home and at private schools was followed by Eliot High School in Jamaica Plain and then the Girls' High and Normal School of Boston, which prepared her for teaching.

While at Normal School Hewins was much impressed with the Boston Athenaeum, where she was required to do some research. Upon graduation she arranged to work at that library in 1866 and 1867 under the guidance of its Librarian, William Frederick Poole. For a number of years thereafter she taught in private schools in the Boston area and took courses at Boston University.

In 1875, learning that the Young Men's Institute of Hartford, Connecticut, needed a librarian, she applied and was accepted. The Institute, a subscription library, served a membership of about 600 with a collection of some 20,000 volumes. It was absorbed by the older Hartford Library Association in 1878. Though few children used the library, Hewins sought by means of extensive discarding of objectionable books and purchase of desirable titles to improve the children's collection and raise reading standards. Without neglecting her other duties she became a pioneering specialist in work with children. An innovative administrator, she instituted many programs that later became standard practice in youth libraries, including clubs, book talks, storytelling, nature walks, a doll collection, and dramatics. She used the children's own book reviews as guides to book selection.

Membership in the library was opened to the schools; reading lists were provided for teachers; and eventually classroom libraries were sent out, making the Hartford Library a leader in the movement for cooperation between public and school libraries. A concern for disadvantaged youth led her to live for 12 years at the North Street Settlement House, where she founded a drama club and a branch library. On her frequent trips abroad Hewins wrote letters to her young patrons that were published in the *Hartford Courant* and later were published as a book, *A Traveller's Letters to Boys and Girls* (1923). Despite her prominence in the growing field of children's libraries, she was not able to persuade the trustees to establish a separate children's room until 1904, followed in 1907 by the appointment of a full-time children's librarian.

Hewins was nationally recognized as an authority on the selection of books for children. She started the quarterly *Bulletin of the Hartford Library Association,* primarily to list new acquisitions and including perhaps the first selected lists of children's books. These led in 1882 to the publication by Frederick Leypoldt of *Publishers' Weekly* of her *Books for the Young: A Guide for Parents and Children* (reprinted 1884) and later by the American Library Association of her *Books for Boys and Girls: A Selected List* (1897, rev. 1904, 1915). In these lists and elsewhere she expressed her philosophy of book selection for children. Her emphasis was heavily on the classics; modern books had to meet her exacting standards, and "series" books were rejected. She deplored an apparent tendency to denigrate the bookish child.

Although Hewins is remembered as a children's librarian, she also capably ran a growing city library. The Hartford Library Association became a free library in 1892 and the following year adopted the name of Hartford Public Library. By 1925, the last year of her administration, it had a collection of 150,000 volumes in the main library, branches, and deposit stations.

A founder in 1891 of the Connecticut Library Association, she served as President, 1912–13, and was also prominent in the Hartford Librarians' Club. In 1893 she was largely responsible for establishing the Connecticut Public Library Committee, for which she served as volunteer Executive Secretary and "library visitor" for many years. The Educational Association, later the Parent Teachers Association, occupied her organizational abilities in 1897. She lectured at library schools and educational workshops and taught children's literature to Hartford teachers and librarians.

Hewins probably joined the American Library Association at its third Conference in Boston in 1879. Recorded as the first woman to speak from the floor of an ALA Conference, she subsequently read many papers at those meetings. She was a Councilor from 1885 to 1888 and again from 1893 to 1902 and Vice-President in 1891. In 1897 she was one of two women in the American delegation who read papers at the second International Conference of Librarians in London; she spoke on children's books as seen by children themselves. A meeting of children's librarians that she called at the Montreal Conference of ALA in 1900 resulted ultimately in the establishment of its Children's Section. Hewins published extensively in library and educational periodicals, with well over half her writings on children's library work.

In 1911 Trinity College of Hartford awarded her an honorary Master's degree, the first woman to be so honored by this men's college. On February 15, 1926, at a celebration of her 50 years of service, the Hartford Librarians' Club gave her funds to establish the Caroline M. Hewins Scholarship Fund for Children's Librarians. During the same year, though retired, she remained active at the Library until she died in Hartford on November 4 after a brief illness.

Cheerful, energetic, intelligent, and capable, she had been one of the most eloquent supporters of the public library movement, particularly as it contributed toward a fuller life for children, and an exemplar of the increasing role of women in the professions. Her collection of children's books is now in the Connecticut Historical Society. The Caroline M. Hewins Lectureship, an annual presentation at New England Library Association meetings, was established by Frederick G. Melcher in 1946. When ALA celebrated its 75th anniversary, Hewins was one of 40 persons named to the "Library Hall of Fame."

REFERENCES

Jennie D. Lindquist, "Caroline Maria Hewins," in *Notable American Women, 1607–1950* (1971).

Mary E. Root, "Caroline Maria Hewins," in *Pioneering Leaders in Librarianship,* edited by Emily M. Danton (1953).

Budd L. Gambee, "Hewins, Caroline Maria," *Dictionary of American Library Biography* (1978).

BUDD L. GAMBEE

Holley, Edward G.
(1927-)

State University of New York
Edward G. Holley

Edward Gailon Holley contributed to the American library profession as a scholar (particularly in library history), university library administrator, library school dean and educator, past President of the American Library Association, and consultant.

He was born on November 26, 1927, in Pulaski (Giles County), Tennessee. His close contact with libraries began when he started working at the local public library on Sunday afternoons during high school. It continued at David Lipscomb College, where he worked as a library assistant. Indeed, Holley became de facto Librarian during his senior year, when there was no regular librarian. After his graduation in 1949 (B.A. in English, magna cum laude) Holley was persuaded by the Dean to stay on as Librarian. He also attended George Peabody College, where he earned a Master's in Library Science and English in 1951.

Holley then went on to the University of Illinois at Urbana-Champaign to a professional position at the Photo Reproduction Library and to begin work on a library science doctorate. From 1953 to 1956 he was called into active service from the U.S. Naval Reserve. Upon his return he served as a Graduate Assistant in the University of Illinois Library Science Library, 1956–57, and as Librarian of the Education, Philosophy, and Psychology Library from 1957 to 1962.

He was awarded the Ph.D. in Library Science at Illinois in 1961; his dissertation, *Charles Evans: American Bibliographer,* was published by the University of Illinois Press in 1963 and won the Scarecrow Press Award for Library Literature the same year.

From 1962 through 1971 Holley served as Director of Libraries at the University of Houston. During his tenure 126,000 sq.ft. were added to the existing 93,000 sq.ft. of library space and the collection grew from 300,000 to 665,000 volumes, with more than double the number of periodical subscriptions.

From 1972 to 1985 Holley was Dean and Professor at the School of Library Science of the University of North Carolina, where he strengthened the faculty with many outstanding appointments and inaugurated a doctoral program. After stepping down as dean, he remained on the faculty and in 1989 he was appointed to the William Kenan Rand Professorship.

His numerous activities included service as President of the Texas Library Association (1971); Chairperson of the ALA Publishing Board (1972–73); President of ALA (1975–76); President of Beta Phi Mu, the international library science honor society (1985–87); member of the Board of Trustees of the Online Computer Library Center (1985–) and its chair (1987–92); member of the Board of Governors of the University of North Carolina Press (1975–) and its chair (1988–); and member of the Chancellor's Advisory Committee at the University (1989–).

Among his major works are *Raking the Historical Coals: The ALA Scrapbook of 1876* (1967), *Resources of Texas Libraries* (with Donald Hendricks, 1968), *Resources of South Carolina Libraries* (with F. Roper and W. C. Sizemore, 1976), and *The Library Services and Construction Act: An Historical Overview from the Viewpoint of Major Participants* (with Robert Schremser, 1983). He also wrote more than 150 articles and 60 book reviews. He began work on a history of the emergence of the University of North Carolina as a major educational institution after World War II, with publication planned for 1995, when UNC celebrates its bicentennial.

Holley served as a consultant and accreditation site visitor in more than 60 instances, predominantly on library education, academic library buildings, or academic library collections.

In 1983 he was awarded the Melvil Dewey Medal by ALA. The citation paid tribute to his inspiring lifetime commitment to the education of librarians, to his distinguished service on numerous professional organizations, to his prolific contributions to library literature, and to his creative leadership in state, national, and international library organizations. Other awards and honors followed, including the ALA Joseph W. Lippincott Award (1987) for distinguished service to the profession of librarianship; the Distinguished Alumnus Award from the Peabody Library School of Vanderbilt University (1987); ACRL Academic Librarian of the Year Award (1988) for an outstanding national and international contribution to academic and research librarianship and library development; and the Distinguished Alumnus Award from the University of Illinois Graduate School of Library and Information Science (1988).

GEORGE S. BOBINSKI

Honduras

Honduras, a republic in Central America, is bounded by the Caribbean Sea on the north, Nicaragua on the east and south, El Salvador on the south and west, and Guatemala on the west. Population (1990 est.) 5,105,000; area 112,088 sq.km. The official language is Spanish.

National Library. Most of the major libraries in the country are government libraries. The Bibloteca Nacional de Honduras is in the capital city, Tegucigalpa. Founded in 1880, it has holdings of about 55,000 volumes. It shares with other libraries the legal deposit of three copies of each book published in Honduras, but enforcement of the law is not rigorous. From 1961 the National Library published an *Anuario Bibliografico Hondureno*.

Academic Libraries. In higher education, the library of the Universidad Nacional Autónoma de Honduras (founded 1847) has shown significant progress. The library has grown from 25,000 volumes early in the 1970s to 110,000 volumes, with 500 current periodicals, 2,000 dissertations, 1,000 microfilms, and 3,000 government documents. Its staff performs centralized cataloguing and other services for the University's two branch campus libraries as well as for the National Medical Library and its branch library, which are part of the University.

Public Libraries. Although 32 public libraries with a total holding of 50,000 volumes were reported in the early 1970s, some of these may in fact have been primary school libraries. The largest public library is the Romulo E. Durón in Tegucigalpa, with 20,000 volumes. However, the illiteracy rate is about 50 percent and the condition of public libraries is poor.

School Libraries. In the area of primary school libraries, Honduras showed its greatest initiative. In 1967 the government began the School Library Pilot Project in cooperation with Unesco. Under the direction of a librarian, the program was designed, among other things, to teach students the use of various kinds

Libraries in Honduras (1990)

Type of library	Number of administrative units (main libraries)	Number of service points (branches, mobile stops, etc.)	Volumes in collections	Population served	Professional staff (with certificate, diploma, etc.)	Total staff
National	1	1	35,000	500,000	0	24
Academic	12	17	500,000	100,000	16	150
Public	10	10	50,000	500,000	1	20
School	382	382	300,000	800,000	4	400
Special*	2	2	50,000	2,000	1	10
Other**	20	20	100,000	--	--	--

*Some are included as academic libraries
**Estimated data.

of library materials and to provide communities with public library facilities where none existed. The project was planned to have two stages. The first, from 1968 to 1972, was under the direction of Unesco, which provided extensive technical assistance. Schools were divided into four categories, depending on enrollment. Twenty-three libraries were opened before 1970. The second stage, beginning in 1973, was directed by the Ministry of Education. Unesco ended its participation in the project at the close of the first stage. After that, progress was slow.

Special Libraries. The government also maintains several special libraries, each with a collection of a few thousand volumes, emphasizing archaeology, art, law, administration, and the humanities.

The Profession. The Association of Librarians and Archivists has its headquarters in Tegucigalpa. It sponsors courses for its 53 members and seeks ways to improve organization and service in Honduran libraries. It also publishes the monthly *Catalogo de Prestamo* and keeps a small library of its own. It is affiliated with ACURIL.

Cooperation with librarians from other countries has centered mainly in the Primary School Pilot Project. Librarians from the National University have participated in the Consejo Superior Universitario Centroaméricano, a group made up of other national universities in Central America and designed to promote cooperation among them.

Overall, libraries in Honduras, where the system for publishing and distributing books is antiquated, and the political climate often stifled unapproved ideas, have been few, small, and poorly financed. They also lack professional staff. There has been little coordination among libraries, and librarians have not been well organized.

DANIEL W. BARTHELL

Hong Kong

Hong Kong, a British Dependent Territory off the southern coast of China, comprises Hong Kong Island and islets nearby; Kowloon Peninsula; and the mainland areas of the New Territories. Population (1990 est.) 5,801,000; area 1,045 sq.km. The official languages are English and Chinese.

History. The beginnings of library history in Hong Kong can be traced to a collection of books gathered at the English Factory in Canton in 1806. This collection later became part of the Morrison Education Society Library, which moved to Macao and then to Hong Kong in 1842.

National Services. Hong Kong has no national library or national bibliographical center. The Recreation and Cultural Branch of the Hong Kong Government Secretariat has assumed some of the functions of a national library in that it administers the Hong Kong Book Registration Ordinance. Under this Ordinance, publishers and printers submit five copies of every title published and printed locally to the Cultural Services Department of the Urban Services Department. Based on those deposits, *A Catalogue of Books Printed in Hong Kong* is issued quarterly.

The Public Records Office has the largest collection of official documents. Since 1972 that office has collected old documents and records from a number of the Government departments, some dating back to 1844.

Academic Libraries. The libraries of the University of Hong Kong, the Chinese University of Hong Kong, and the Hong Kong Polytechnic are the major academic libraries. Other academic libraries include those of the Baptist College, City Polytechnic, Lingnan College, and Open Learning Institute. The new Hong Kong University of Science and Technology opened a library in 1991. The collections at the two older universities each exceeded a million volumes. The University of Hong Kong Libraries system is the oldest (established in 1911) and most comprehensive library system in Hong Kong. Integrated library systems are used in or are being introduced into most of the academic libraries, including DRA, URICA, DOBIS, INNOVACQ, and various in-

University of Hong Kong Libraries

Interior view of the new wing of the University of Hong Kong's Main Library, opened in 1991. It more than doubles the library's usable space.

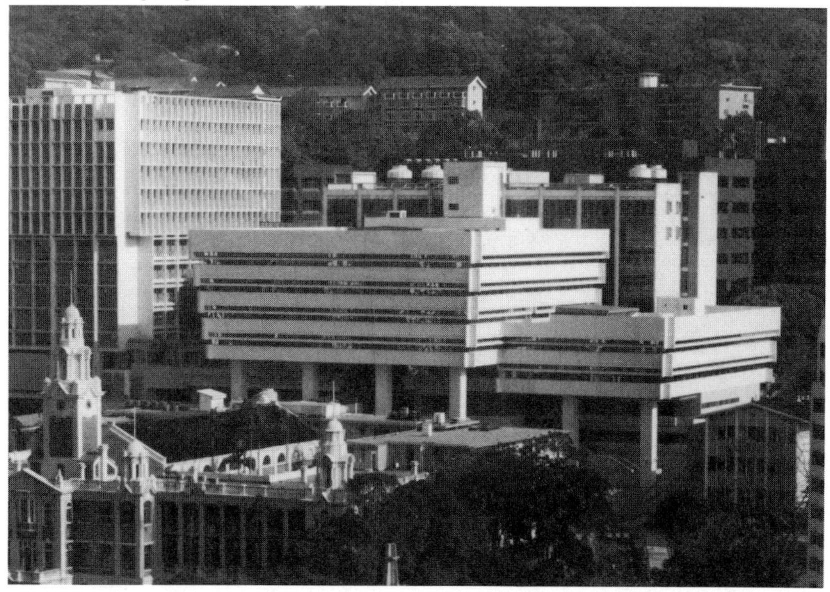

University of Hong Kong Libraries

Exterior view of the new wing of the University of Hong Kong's Main Library, opened in 1991. It more than doubles the library's usable space.

house systems. Online information services such as DIALOG and SDC and CD-ROMs are also available.

Public Libraries. The two public library systems of the Urban Council and Regional Council serve the general public of the urban and rural areas. The City Hall Library, opened in 1962, is the headquarters of the Urban Council Libraries. By 1990, the network of Urban Council Libraries comprised 30 libraries (including two mobile libraries) with a total of 2,300,000 volumes. The system administered by the Regional Council comprised 23 libraries (including two mobile libraries) with a total of 1,500,000 volumes. There are plans to continue opening more branch libraries in both systems.

School Libraries. School library service improved a great deal during the period from 1976 to 1990. Nearly 350 schools now employ teacher-librarians trained by the Education Department of the Hong Kong Government. Classroom libraries are provided for many primary schools by this Department.

Special Libraries. Many Government department libraries are specialized and serve primarily the staffs of their own departments. The Hong Kong Productivity Council, Hong Kong Trade Development Council, Federation of Hong Kong Industries, Hong Kong Management Associations, Management Development Center of Hong Kong, and Hong Kong Tourist Association, among others, maintain libraries and information services to serve the commercial and industry sectors. In addition, there are several medical libraries in hospitals, as well as special libraries in some business firms, factories, and learned societies.

The Profession. Approximately 170 professional librarians worked in the Hong Kong libraries in the early 1990s. From 1981 to 1989, the Department of Extramural Studies of the University of Hong Kong and the Hong Kong Library Association jointly offered a three-year part-time Diploma Course in Librarianship. A new joint three-year part-time Graduate Diploma of Arts in Library and Information Science is offered by the Department in cooperation with the new Charles Sturt University at Bathurst, N.S.W., in Australia. Established in 1958, the Hong Kong Library Association had a membership of more than 500 in 1990. The Association publishes a *Journal* and a *Newsletter*.

REFERENCE

L. B. Kan, Angela S. W. Yan, and Grace H. L. Chu, *Library and Information Services in Hong Kong* (1988).

KAN LAI-BING

Suzanne Honoré

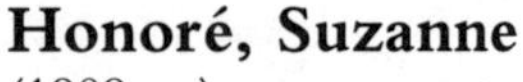

Honoré, Suzanne

(1909-)

During more than four decades of service at the Bibliothèque Nationale, Suzanne Duvergé Honoré became known both in France and abroad as a specialist in cataloguing and government publications. In addition to her administrative responsibilities at the national library, she continued her early interest in historical research, contributed to the standardization of French cataloguing practices, and promoted the international exchange of bibliographic data through her work in the International Federation of Library Associations (IFLA). She also played a key role in the Association des Bibliothécaires Français (ABF, the

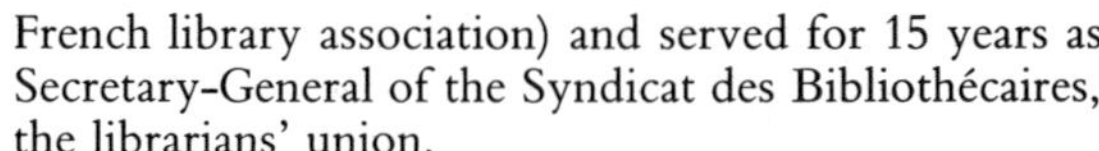

French library association) and served for 15 years as Secretary-General of the Syndicat des Bibliothécaires, the librarians' union.

Born on July 13, 1909, in Oloron-Sainte-Marie in southwestern France, Suzanne Duvergé grew up in a household where her interest in reading and travel were encouraged. Her father was a professor of mathematics. She took a degree in history from the University of Bordeaux and entered the École des Chartes in Paris, where she received training as an archivist-palaeographer. She graduated in 1932 as valedictorian of her class—a distinction that entitled her to a place at the École Française de Rome, a French institute for advanced research in medieval history. She remained in Rome from 1932 to 1934, when she was appointed to the École des Hautes Études Hispaniques in Madrid. There she continued scholarly work in medieval Spanish history. After two years in Madrid, she married Pierre Honoré, a French sculptor. They had three sons: Michel, Georges, and Olivier.

In 1936 she began her career at the Bibliothèque Nationale as a library assistant (auxiliaire). She was named Librarian (Bibliothécaire) six years later and subsequently served in the department of printed books and the department of official publications. In 1962 she prepared a comparative study of official publications from the perspective of their use in public relations. Her report on that topic was presented at the Congrès international des sciences administratives in 1962 and was published the following year. In 1963 Honoré became head of the department of international exchanges, which was reorganized and installed in new quarters under her direction. She left that post in 1967 to take charge of the Département des Entrées, the unit responsible for copyright deposit, the acquisition of books, and cataloguing.

In 1964 she was elected President of the ABF, the second woman to hold that office. She provided leadership at a time when the Association's statutes were being revised, and she was subsequently elected to the presidency for a second term, which expired in 1969.

In 1961 she participated in the International Conference on Cataloguing Principles held in Paris. She also took part in a second international cataloguing conference held in Copenhagen in 1969 under the sponsorship of IFLA and Unesco. Later she served as President of the Cataloguing Committee of the Association Française de Normalisation (AFNOR, the French national standards association) and participated in many meetings of the committee on documentation of the International Standards Organization (ISO). She was also active in other international bodies, serving as a member of the consultative committee of the International Office for Universal Bibliographic Control and also as Vice-President of the Association for International Libraries.

Honoré published about 35 articles and reports, ranging from scholarly studies in medieval history to the *International List of Approved Forms for Catalogue Entries of Names of States* (Unesco, 1964). She also taught cataloguing at the École des Chartes and gave courses on bibliography and on international library cooperation at the École Nationale Supérieure des Bibliothèques (the national library school).

Honoré retired from the Bibliothèque Nationale in 1978. In recognition of her many contributions, she was named to the Legion of Honor and later elevated to the rank of officer.

MARY NILES MAACK

Hookway, Sir Harry
(1921-)

In 1972 Parliament passed the British Library Act, which led to the establishment of the British Library in the following year. Prior to that time the national library of the United Kingdom was the British Museum Library, which was to form the centerpiece of the new British Library, together with the addition of the National Lending Library for Science and Technology, the National Central Library, and the *British National Bibliography*. The first Deputy Chairman and Chief Executive of the British Library was Harry Thurston Hookway, who occupied this signally important position from 1973 until he retired in 1984.

Hookway came to library organization rather late in life. Born in London on July 23, 1921, he obtained his B.Sc. (1941) and Ph.D. (1943) degrees from the University of London. From 1941 to 1949 he occupied several posts in industry, but from 1949 to 1965 he was with the Department of Scientific and Industrial Research (DSIR). From 1960 to 1964 he was seconded from the DSIR to direct the UK Scientific Mission (North America); during this time he was also Scientific Attaché at the British Embassy in Washington, D.C., and Scientific Adviser to the UK High Commission in Ottawa. In 1964 he returned to the DSIR and was Head of its Information Division in 1964–65. From 1966 to 1969 he was Chief Scientific Officer at the Department of Education and Science, becoming Assistant Under Secretary of State in that Department from 1969 to 1973.

The British Library was in gestation at that time, and Hookway formed an excellent working relationship with Lord Eccles, then the Minister responsible for Arts and Libraries. Hookway steeped himself in the history and problems of library organization in the United Kingdom, and with Lord Eccles he played an important role in preparing and steering through the legislation that led to the establishment of the British Library. He was careful to involve the Library Association, the National Central Library, and other interested bodies throughout this planning stage, giving them information on the broad intentions and allowing them to put forward their views to the Minister.

Although British librarians had naturally hoped that the first Chief Executive of the British Library would be a professional librarian, it came as no real surprise when Harry Hookway was named to the post. From the outset he cooperated closely with professional librarians and was accepted by them. Some preparatory work on the formation of the British Library had been carried out in advance of the official starting date of July 1, 1973, including the transfer of staff and stock from the National Central Library in London to the premises occupied by the National Lending Library for Science and Technology at Boston Spa in Yorkshire to form the British Library Lending Division (BLLD). But Hookway still had many difficult tasks facing him. He had to weld together personnel of varied experience, disciplines, and levels; in 1974 he had to arrange the formal inclusion of the *British National Bibliography* into the British Library organization; and he had to ensure that the British Library had a vigorous public relations policy so that people were kept fully informed about the problems and progress of Britain's national library. All this he did with conspicuous success.

Courtesy of the British Library
Sir Harry Hookway

But mostly he was concerned with the future of the British Library, and particularly with the provision of the much-needed new building in London to accommodate the Reference Division and the Central Administration. Thanks to the persistence of Hookway and the members of his Board, the government finally agreed that a new building would be erected on a site in the Euston Road next to St. Pancras railway station. Work began in 1982 but the date of completion could not be forecast because it was scheduled to be built in stages.

Hookway did much to further the cause of British librarianship. He chaired the Unesco Advisory Committee for Documentation, Libraries, and Archives, and from 1982 served as Chairman of the British Council Libraries Advisory Committee. He was Chairman of the Conference of Directors of National Libraries and a member of IFLA's Programme Management Committee. In 1984 he was awarded the IFLA Gold Medal.

He became an Honorary Fellow of the Institute of Information Scientists and was its President from 1973 to 1976. In 1982 he was made an Honorary Fellow of the Library Association and was its President in 1985. Meanwhile, in 1978, he was knighted by Queen Elizabeth II.

Hookway received honorary degrees from the Universities of Sheffield and Loughborough, and after his retirement from the British Library in 1983 he became Chairman of Publishers' Data Bases Ltd., a member of the Court and Common Council of Loughborough University, a Governor of Birkbeck College, and Vice-President of the National Book League.

K. C. HARRISON

Humphreys, K. W.
(1916-)

Kenneth William Humphreys, British university librarian and paleographer, became a major figure in the provision and development of academic library and information services, both nationally and internationally, in the years after 1950.

Birmingham University Library
K. W. Humphreys

Humphreys was born in Oxford on December 4, 1916. Obliged by family circumstances to leave school at 16, he became a junior library clerk in the Codrington Library, All Souls College, Oxford, in 1933. Three years later he joined the Bodleian Law Library as a member of "Extra Staff," an appointment which entailed some duties in the Bodleian Library itself. Studying in his free time, he obtained a B.A. degree in 1938 and was appointed an Assistant on the permanent staff of the Bodleian in the same year. With an interruption for war service in the army, he remained at the Bodleian until 1950, when he became Deputy Librarian at the Brotherton Library, University of Leeds. After only two years, Humphreys was appointed Librarian at the University of Birmingham, where he was to emerge as one of the leading librarians of his time.

In 1952 Humphreys inherited a library of 330,000 volumes housed in cramped conditions in elderly buildings and, as was the University itself, split between two sites some three miles apart. By the time he left Birmingham, the University had effectively been consolidated on one campus and the Library had grown to nearly a million volumes housed in new or completely refurbished accommodation. With its emphasis on open access for readers, full air-conditioning, and provision for a large bindery, the new building (opened in 1959) influenced subsequent university library planning in many parts of Europe; an extension was completed in 1970. A new Medical Library was also opened in 1959 and, in 1960, the Law Library was moved into the converted and renovated space formerly occupied by the Science Library.

By judicious purchases and by attracting gifts, Humphreys much improved the research capability of the bookstock. Attention was paid to official publications, older material was regularly acquired, and some valuable presentations were received, such as a collection of most of the books printed by Baskerville. The Library's status as a source of research material was enormously enhanced by the deposit of important literary and political manuscripts, the Brett Young, Galsworthy, and Harriet Martineau collections, and the papers of the Earl of Avon (Sir Anthony Eden) and the Chamberlains. At the same time, undergraduate services were improved by the introduction of a short loan collection and the duplication of titles in heavy demand.

Between 1967 and 1969 he established a small automation team; in collaboration with Birmingham's other university library at the University of Aston and with Birmingham Public Libraries, investigations were started into the cooperative use of tapes produced by the Library of Congress and the British National Bibliography (BNB), and the creation of a common machine-readable catalogue. From those beginnings, the Birmingham Libraries Cooperative Mechanization Project (BLCMP) evolved, financed by a government grant from the Office of Scientific and Technical Information (OSTI) and directed by committees representing the three libraries. BLCMP rapidly assumed national importance as other libraries became interested in its research; government financial support was extended, and there was increased collaboration with the BNB and, later, the British Library. The Project produced its first machine-generated catalogue in July 1973.

In 1975 Humphreys was appointed Librarian of the new European University Institute at Florence, where he confronted the opportunities and difficulties of building up a research library from nothing outside the Anglo-American library environment. Recruiting a multi-national staff from the countries of the European Communities, he planned a totally automated system providing online access to the Library database for staff and readers alike.

Humphreys was prominent in professional activities. He was Honorary Secretary of the Standing Conference of National and University Libraries (SCONUL) from 1954 to 1968 and Chairman from 1971 to 1973; he was a member of the Council of the Library Association from 1964 to 1975. He served on a number of committees connected with library cooperation; he was a member of the Library Advisory Council for England from 1966 to 1971 and, as a member of the Committee on Libraries set up by the University Grants Committee in 1963 to review the needs of universities for books and periodicals, made a large contribution to its *Report,* published in 1967.

In the International Federation of Library Associations (IFLA), Humphreys was President of the National and University Libraries Subsection from 1967 to 1973. He was closely associated with the formation and direction of the Ligue des Bibliothèques Européennes de Recherche (LIBER) in the 1970s and was Chairman of the British Council Books Panel from 1970 to 1975. In demand as a consultant, he advised on libraries in Europe, Africa, and Asia.

Alongside his professional duties as librarian and administrator, Humphreys maintained his scholarly interests in paleography. He was himself a collector of medieval manuscripts and for many years a member of the Comité International de Paléographie. He edited a series of studies on the history of libraries and librarianship and published a number of books and articles on medieval libraries and texts.

Humphreys became an Oxford M.A. in 1943 and obtained the degree of B.Litt. in 1949; in 1967 he was awarded a Birmingham Ph.D. and, in the same year, was made an honorary Litt.D. by Trinity College, Dublin. He also became a Fellow of the Library Association (F.L.A.) in 1967 and was made an Honorary F.L.A. in 1980.

Although he retired as a practicing librarian in 1981, Humphreys was Professor of Library Studies at the University of Haifa, Israel, in 1982. He delivered the British Library Panizzi Lectures in 1987 on "A National Library in Theory and in Practice." He continued to write on bibliographical and library history.

Humphreys' writings illustrate the national and international stretch of his conception of library services and, although primarily a university librarian, he comprehended all types of libraries. Yet he remained strictly practical in his ideas. He perceived that cooperation was essential to the successful development of national and international library and information networks, and practiced it from Birmingham to Tuscany. For Humphreys, academic librarianship had to be dynamic and adaptable, to take advantage of new technologies, but it also had to retain its links with scholarship if it was fully to achieve its purpose in serving education and research.

T. H. BOWYER

Hungary

A republic in Central Europe, Hungary is bounded by Czechoslovakia on the north, Ukraine and Romania on the east, Yugoslavia on the south, and Austria on the west. Population (1990 est.) 10,553,000 (98% Hungarian); area 93,032 sq.km. The language spoken is Hungarian, which is related only to Finnish and Estonian among European languages.

History. Hungarians, who migrated in the 9th century A.D. to their present country, used a runic script cut on wood. They soon adopted the Latin-language book hand of contemporary Europe. The first record to contain Hungarian words (the foundation deed of the Tihany Abbey) dates back to 1055. From 1190 to 1200 Hungarian history was written in Latin by an anonymous author in *Gesta Hungarorum*. The first coherent text in Hungarian, a funeral sermon, dates from about 1200.

The Library of the Benedictine Abbey in Pannonhalma was founded in 1001. The inventories of a few smaller monastery libraries remain from the end of the 11th century. One of the richest Humanist libraries of Europe, the Bibliotheca Corviniana, contained many richly decorated codices collected by King Mátyás Hunyadi (1458–1490). The library was destroyed during the 150 years of Turkish rule, and now only 168 codices are extant, 43 of them in Hungarian collections. The first printing office was established in Buda in 1473, the first Hungarian-language book was printed in 1533 in Cracow, and the first Hungarian translation of the New Testament was published at Sárvár in 1541.

The 16th century saw the foundation of Protestant college libraries (Sárospatak, 1531; Debrecen, 1538), followed by Catholic college libraries (Nagyszombat, 1561), which exist to this day. In the 18th century, academies of technology (Selmecbánya, 1735) and agriculture established their libraries. The private libraries of rich aristocrats became the bases of large public collections at the beginning of the 19th century. The endowment of Count Ferenc Széchényi laid the foundation of the national library; that of Count József Teleki played the same role for the Library of the Hungarian Academy of Sciences.

In the first decades of the 19th century, casinos and reading circles were established. Beginning in 1868 municipal libraries and popular libraries were set up; there were 53 municipal libraries by 1913. The first library authority, the National Council of Museums and Libraries, was formed in 1897.

Ervin Szabó (1887–1918), one of the greatest figures in Hungarian librarianship, established the first Anglo-Saxon-type public library at the beginning of the 20th century and introduced a number of innovations—Dewey Decimal Classification, bibliographical work, branch library service, and reference services.

The post–World War II period saw enormous development. Large libraries had to be modernized and public libraries newly organized. Work started in 1949 with libraries modeled on the Soviet system, but from the 1960s, as cultural policies became more liberal, Hungarian librarians drew on Western European and American models. The Council of Ministers issued a decree on librarianship in 1952 and the Presidential Council passed decrees on the subject in 1956 and 1976. Librarians held national conferences in 1952, 1955, 1970, and 1981 to define their tasks.

Municipal Library Szabo Ervin

National Széchényi Library, founded in 1802, largest Hungarian library.

Hungarian librarianship is administered by the Ministry of Culture, in cooperation with the Hungarian Council for Librarianship and the National Library. The library act of 1976 created a complicated system in which libraries were assigned both to cooperation circles on the one hand and to more than 100 systems on the other. Coordination centers tried to harmonize library work according to subject fields or regions. Changes in this system were under discussion in the radically changed society of the 1990s.

There are more than 15,000 libraries operating in Hungary, and the main problem of Hungarian librarianship is indicated by this figure itself. The number of libraries could not be reduced as needed and no adequate cooperation was established among them. In both public and special libraries, holdings are rather

Libraries in Hungary (1990)

Type of library	Number of administrative units (main libraries)	Number of service points (branches, mobile stops, etc.)	Volumes in collections	Annual expenditures[a] (in forint)	Population served	Professional staff (with certificate, diploma, etc.)	Total staff
National	1	1	7,040,916	461,791,000	10,375,323	428	874
Academic	29	n.a.	12,115,576	249,574,182	119,689	688	910
Public	2,390	4,960	52,988,443	222,014,757	10,375,323	3,976	4,950
School	3,897	--	27,179,176	99,127,550	1,757,372	964[a]	964[a]
Special	91	--	11,998,841	308,730,553	--	1,990	2,866
Church[a]	35	--	2,897,000	--	--	38	38

[a]1988 data

Sources: *Hungarian Statistical Pocket-book*. 1990. Statistical information of the Ministry of Culture, 1991. Annual report of the National Szechenyi Library, 1991.

fragmented and there are strong efforts toward self-sufficiency, leading to unnecessary duplication and wasted resources. The economic crisis of the early 1990s forced a number of libraries, especially trade union libraries, to close.

National Library. The National Széchényi Library, founded in 1802, is the largest Hungarian library, with a collection of almost 6,869,000 volumes (1988). Aiming at comprehensive coverage, it collects publications and phonograph records produced in Hungary, as well as works published abroad in Hungarian or pertaining to Hungary. (There are about 15,000,000 Hungarians in the world, more than 3,500,000 of them in neighboring countries and about 1,000,000 in North and South America.)

The responsibilities of the national library are to collect and distribute legal deposit copies; to maintain the national union catalogues of foreign books and periodicals; to serve as the center of interlibrary lending and to manage the international exchange of publications; to act as a central repository; to house the ISBN and ISSN bureaus; to maintain a central registry of libraries; to operate a central restoration laboratory; to perform research and development; to provide professional assistance for all Hungarian libraries through the Center for Library Science and Methodology (1959); and, last but not least, to compile and publish current and retrospective national bibliographies. The national library is also the coordination center for public library systems.

The *Magyar Nemzeti Bibliográfia Könyvek bibliográfiája* (Hungarian National Bibliography) lists Hungarian printed publications and phonograph records (UDC division) and, under the subtitle *Időszaki kiadványok repertóriuma* (Repertory of Serials), provides a list of articles in periodical publications. Its quarterly supplements are *Hungarika irodalmi szemle* (Hungarian Publications Published Abroad in Foreign Languages) and *Külföldi magyar nyelvü kiadványok* (Hungarian Publications Published Abroad in the Hungarian Language). The Időszaki kiadványok bibliográfiája (Hungarian National Bibliography of Serials) is published annually, the *A magyar bibliográfiák bibliográfiája* (Bibliography of Hungarian Bibliographies) every two years. Since 1961 annual cumulations of the Hungarian National Bibliography have been published. A group working on retrospective bibliographic ventures compiles the bibliographies of thus-far-uncovered periods and releases revised and enlarged editions of the great works from the last century. *Magyar könyvészet* (Hungarian National Bibliography) covers the period 1945 to 1960 in five volumes; the period 1921 to 1944 will be covered in nine volumes (five had been published by 1990). From the series of enlarged and updated bibliographies two volumes of *Régi magyarországi nyomtatványok* (Early Hungarian Printings) were published—for the periods 1473 to 1600 and 1601 to 1635, respectively—as well as supplements to the national bibliographies of the 18th and 19th centuries.

Since 1978 the current national bibliography for books has been processed by computer, but published only in printed form. The national serials database became accessible online in 1988.

The national library maintains two former church libraries, the old books of which have a historical value: the József Bajza Library in Gyöngyös (1473) and the Antal Reguly Library in Zirc (1720).

Archives. The Hungarian National Archives (1756) holds 35,167 linear meters of written documents and 47,000,000 film frames from the beginnings to 1945. The New Central Archives (1970), collecting material from 1945, contains 18,100 linear meters of records and 208,000 microfilm frames. Council or regional archives numbered 20 in 1988, and special archives included the archives of 12 state and social agencies and 37 churches. Holdings (1988) from all archives totaled 209,440 linear meters.

Academic Libraries. Each institution of higher education has a library system of its own, with a central library and institutional, faculty, clinical, and other designated libraries. University libraries generally serve as national switching centers. There are four academic library systems in science (Budapest, 1561; Debrecen, 1916; Pécs, 1774; and Szeged, 1921); three in technology (Budapest, 1848; Miskolc, 1735; and Veszprém, 1949); four in medicine (Budapest, 1828; Debrecen; Pécs; and Szeged); and nine in agriculture. The principal agricultural libraries are in veterinary science (1872) and in horticulture (1894) in Budapest; in forestry (1735) in Sopron, and further in Keszthely (1797), in Debrecen (1868), in Gödöllő (1945), and in Mosonmagyaróvár (1818). The holdings of these libraries range from 500,000 to 3,000,000 volumes.

Most colleges of arts and pedagogy, founded in the last century and having the rank of universities, have libraries with more than 100,000 volumes. The largest system serves the Loránd Eötvös University in Budapest. The main library has more than 1,300,000 items, the total system (130 libraries) 2,500,000. The system is particularly rich in old materials on the humanities.

Public Libraries. There are three types of public library systems in Hungary: council, trade union, and armed forces. There are council library systems in each of the 19 counties. Trade union library systems are also organized by counties, except in Budapest, where they are organized by trades. Council libraries play a dominant role in the delivery of local library services, holding an average of from 200,000 to 250,000 volumes. These institutions have been called county libraries since 1952. Council libraries also provide library services for hospital patients and minority nationalities, such as Germans and Slovaks. To serve the minorities better, 15 "basis libraries" supply materials in the communities where national minorities live. Trade union libraries serve workers at their factories and offices. In some industrial areas they serve the general population as well. In 1988, 6,388 council and trade union libraries contained almost 53,872,000 items; 2,127,000 registered readers borrowed more than 47,000,000 books a year. The number of registered readers is slowly declining. Public libraries have audiovisual materials, primarily phonograph records and cassettes. They operate more than 100 music departments.

The Metropolitan Szabó Ervin Library (1904) in Budapest, with 106 branches and total holdings of almost 4,300,000 volumes, is the leading public library system in the country. Its main library, the national clearinghouse for sociology, holds the largest local collection in Hungary. The Somogyi Library in

Szeged (1880) and the county libraries of Békéscsaba and Szombathely are famous not only for their rich collections but also for their modern buildings. The Gorky State Library collects literature in foreign languages and is a coordination center for basis libraries of the nationalities.

School Libraries. Since 1975, councils have spent considerable sums on school library acquisitions. Still, school libraries are the weakest links of Hungarian librarianship. There is a library in each of the more than 3,500 general schools and in about 1,000 secondary schools, but in most schools they have neither their own room nor specialized staff. School libraries belong to county and metropolitan systems headed by either the local continuing education institute or the county library. Their work is coordinated by the National Pedagogical Library and Museum, which also serves as the information center on teaching. The children's divisions of public libraries also serve school children.

Special Libraries. In 1978, 1,822 special libraries were reported in Hungary. Their number was not reduced thereafter, but statistics of the 1980s covered only those with at least one full-time librarian; thus their number was 860 in the early 1980s, academic libraries included. Together, they held more than 42,500,000 items. Statistical surveys after 1983 identify only the 123 main libraries, which are designated as national clearinghouses. They are authorized to organize cooperation circles in their subject fields and they hold 65 percent of the total stock of special libraries and provide most of their services. Hungarian special libraries are characterized first of all by traditional services; automation was at an initial stage in the first half of the 1980s. Some clearinghouses provide computerized SDI services from foreign databases. Automation of their own activities was started in the mid-1980s.

Special libraries are organized into systems according to their supervising authorities. So, for example, the Library of the Hungarian Academy of Sciences (1826) supervises the libraries of 51 research institutes. There are health, agricultural, museum, and other special library systems as well. The work of the various systems is coordinated by large special libraries. The National Technical Information Center and Library (1883), for example, coordinates the work of the libraries of more than 800 industrial firms and research institutes, the Information Center of the Ministry of Agriculture and Food (1951) that of 148 libraries, and the National Medical Information Institute and Library (1960) that of 197 libraries. Church libraries, especially those of the Roman Catholic and Reformed churches, have rich old collections.

The Profession. Librarians can graduate from universities or academies. Since 1949 librarians have been trained at the Loránd Eötvös University in Budapest. The program lasts five years for full-time students or six years for correspondence students. Graduates from other universities must take three-year post-graduate training or a one-year course on documentation. In three teachers' training colleges (Szombathely, Nyiregyháza, and Budapest), a librarian's diploma is granted in four years, with other courses in education. Large libraries organize 200-hour courses for library technicians. The system of continuing education, in the process of formation, relies primarily on the Center for Library Science and Methodology.

The Association of Hungarian Librarians (1935), a nongovernmental organization, is administered by an elected board. Its President and Secretary are also elected. The 3,500 members can participate in the work of several sections, including children's, technical, and music libraries and regional organizations. The Association promotes professional interests and organizes continuing education programs. A congress is held every year.

The Hungarian Academy of Sciences publishes the journal *Magyar Könyvszemle* (Hungarian Book Review) (1876) which includes mainly studies of a historical nature. The Hungarian Council for Librarianship and the Center for Library Science and Methodology compile the journal *Könyvtári Figyelő* (Library Review) (1955), which focuses more on current problems. Both provide summaries in English. Hungarian specialist literature is reviewed in English by the semi-annual publication *Hungarian Library and Information Science Abstracts,* edited by the Center for Library Science and Methodology.

REFERENCES

Jenő Kiss, *Libraries in Hungary* (1988).
The National Széchenyi Library (1985).
Peter Balázs, editor, *Guide to the Archives of Hungary* (1976).

JENŐ KISS

Huntington, Henry E.
(1850–1927)

Huntington Library
Henry E. Huntington

Henry Edwards Huntington was a leading North American businessman, a premier book collector, and the founder of the Henry E. Huntington Library, Art Gallery, and Botanical Gardens in San Marino, California. According to A. S. W. Rosenbach, Huntington was "the greatest figure in the history of American book-collecting." He and his legacy have had a profound influence on the development of research libraries in the United States.

Huntington was born February 27, 1850, in the village of Oneonta, in central New York state. His father's family had moved to New England from England in the early 17th century, and his father, Solon, moved west to Oneonta from Connecticut to open a general store. The fourth of seven children, the young "Ed" Huntington, as his boyhood friends knew him, worked in the family store, but set out on his own as soon as he had finished school. First he went to New York City, where he got a job in a hardware store, then to West Virginia to manage a sawmill (of which he soon became the sole owner), then to Tennessee and Kentucky to become construction superintendent for a railroad, and later to manage another railroad that was on the brink of failing. He was wonderfully successful in all his business dealings.

When he was 42, in 1892, he answered the call of his uncle, Collis P. Huntington (who had been a junior partner in the store in Oneonta), to go to San Francisco and share the management of the Southern Pacific Railway. Eight years later, in 1900, his uncle died and left him a large legacy. Two years later Huntington decided to move to southern California, where he developed the Pacific Electric Interurban

Railway for the Los Angeles area. That venture was especially successful because Huntington owned substantial amounts of land in the areas opened up, and the population tripled in a decade.

In 1910 Huntington retired at the age of 60. The Pacific Electric was transferred to the Southern Pacific, and Huntington gave up active business management. He retired to devote himself to his "other interests," which consisted mainly of books and manuscripts, along with paintings and other art objects, and the horticultural development of his ranch.

He was prepossessing in appearance but shy, retiring, and deferential in manner. He loved jokes and got his greatest pleasure from simple activities such as playing hearts and croquet. Business associates called him "H. E." In the family, he was "Uncle Edwards," or "Edwards," or "Edward." His dominant activity was reading.

The book-buying bug bit him in San Francisco. Soon after he arrived there, he began frequenting the bookshops, coming away first with one book, later with an armful. Often he spent his lunch hour in a bookshop. He was a reader by nature and by habit, and his principle was to buy things in which he had or could develop an interest. Through the 1890s he bought many books about the discovery of America and 19th-century fiction. In the first decade of this century, when Huntington was in Los Angeles and often in New York, his interests greatly increased, to writers such as Montaigne, Chaucer, and Izaak Walton. He began reading up on rare books and their prices and started buying first editions and small collections of rare books. He also collected such writers as Kipling, Conrad, and Wells in depth. "In depth" turned out to be the key to all his collecting.

In the great period of his collecting, from 1910 until his death in 1927, he bought dozens of large collections, important libraries, and choice rarities. These acquisitions included the E. Dwight Church Collection in 1911 (for $1,000,000), the cream of the Robert Hoe Collection (including the splendid copy of the Gutenberg Bible on vellum), the Beverly Chew Library of early English literature, the Kemble-Devonshire Collection of English plays, the Halsey Library, the Bridgewater House Library, many collections of Californiana and Americana, and many collections of English manuscripts (Loudoun, Abercromby, Battle Abbey, Hastings, and Stowe—the last alone containing some 350,000 manuscripts from the 12th century onward).

The result was a magnificent collection of great treasures (such as the Ellesmere manuscript of Chaucer and the manuscript of Franklin's *Autobiography*), but also a library of great depth (the largest collection of 15th-century printed books in the United States, for example, and firsts in many other areas). By concentrating on English and American literature and history, he was able to have strength in all periods from the medieval to the present.

Huntington early decided to found an independent institution so that his collections might continue to have useful value. In 1919 he established the Huntington Library and Art Gallery as a research institution for scholars and a cultural center for the public. The library building was completed in 1920; the collections were made freely available to qualified scholars, and exhibitions were open to the public. Huntington appointed a distinguished scholar as Director and made provision for a staff of scholars in residence in addition to the library staff.

Huntington was a builder by inclination. He built companies, and he built a Library. In addition, he built an Art Gallery and Botanical Gardens. He bought his ranch in 1903 and immediately started building gardens. In 1910 he began building a mansion to serve as an Art Gallery after his death. His first marriage, to Mary Alice Prentice in 1873, ended in divorce in 1906, and in 1913 he married Arabella Huntington, the widow since 1900 of his uncle Collis. Arabella (who was his own age) was an important art collector, and she guided him in collecting the most significant group of British paintings of the 18th and early 19th centuries outside London; it included such masterpieces as Gainsborough's *Blue Boy,* Reynolds' *Mrs. Siddons as the Tragic Muse,* Constable's *View on the Stour near Dedham,* and Lawrence's *Pinkie.* He also completed several important gardens, such as the Desert Garden, the Japanese Garden, and the North Vista.

The last book that Huntington examined before he died, in Philadelphia on May 23, 1927, was the *Short-Title Catalogue of Books Printed in England, Scotland and Ireland, 1475–1640.* At that time, his Library consisted of about 170,000 rare books and three-quarters of a million manuscripts. Since then, the rare book collection has more than doubled, the manuscript collection has grown fourfold, and there is a reference collection of nearly 300,000 volumes. Many new areas (such as 20th-century poetry) have been developed within the framework of English and American literature and history. The art collection has greatly increased (with more than 12,000 British drawings and watercolors, for example, and a new building for American art). There are now a dozen fully developed gardens, with 15,000 kinds of plants, occupying 130 acres.

One thousand five hundred scholars work at the Huntington every year, doing research in all of the divisions. Half a million visitors each year enjoy the cultural and educational activities. Thus the Huntington continues to fulfill the purposes that its founder set forth.

REFERENCE

Donald C. Dickinson, "Mr. Huntington and Mr. Smith" (the collector and his chief buyer), *The Book Collector* (1988).

JAMES THORPE

Hutchins, Margaret

(1884–1961)

Margaret Hutchins, library educator and reference specialist, made significant contributions to American librarianship through outstanding practice, teaching, and a seminal monograph, *Introduction to Reference Work.*

Born in Lancaster, New Hampshire, on September 21, 1884, Hutchins was graduated from Smith College in 1906 with a Bachelor of Arts degree. After receiving a Bachelor of Library Science from the University of Illinois in 1908, she became a reference librarian and lecturer in the library school there. Together with Alice S. Johnson, who held similar positions in the library and library school at Illinois, and Margaret S. Williams, an instructor in the New York State Library School, Hutchins wrote a text published by H. W. Wilson in 1922 as *Guide to the Use of Libraries: A Manual for College and University Students*. A revised edition was published in 1925.

Hutchins left Illinois in 1927 to become a reference specialist in the Queens Borough Public Library, New York. In 1931 she received an M.L.S. at the School of Library Service at Columbia University and joined the faculty there. She taught for many years, retiring as an Associate Professor in 1952. While at Columbia, Hutchins wrote the monograph that is her major contribution to librarianship—*Introduction to Reference Work* (1943). Dedicated to Francis Simpson, a teacher at Illinois, and Isadore Gilbert Mudge, a teacher at Columbia and Head of the Reference Department at its library, the book expressed its aim—"to describe and interpret reference work as the reference librarian sees it for the information of administrators of libraries and other librarians and library school students."

Hutchins's monograph bears some resemblance to James Wyer's *Reference Work* (1928) in that it describes the process of reference work rather than the contents of individual reference books. Wyer's work, however, had been based on a literature survey and visits to some 50 libraries; Hutchins did not repeat such an investigation. Instead she relied on her "thirty-five years' devotion to the subject, two thirds of which were spent in actual practice of reference work" to support "an attempt to interpret the essence of reference work in its universal aspects." The 28 chapters of the work are organized into seven sections: (1) the Scope of Reference Work as a Branch of Library Service, (2) Reference Questions, (3) Selection of Reference Material, (4) Organization of Reference Materials, (5) Organization and Administration of Reference Service, (6) the Less Common Functions of a Reference Librarian (including advising readers, teaching the use of books and libraries, reporting literature searches, work in connection with interlibrary loan, and participating in public relations), and (7) In Conclusion (Evaluating and Reporting Reference Work).

Recent developments in library service, ranging from the availability of databases for online searching to the establishment of information and referral services in public libraries, make Hutchins's *Introduction to Reference Work* seem very old-fashioned, but her comments on the reference interview are noticeably modern. Indeed, she was first to use the phrase "reference interview," and her chapter on that subject anticipates much that is currently discussed in articles and dissertations on the communication skills needed by reference librarians.

Hutchins died at Bayshore, Long Island, on January 4, 1961.

REFERENCE

Frances Neel Cheney, "Hutchins, Margaret," *Dictionary of American Library Biography* (1978).

MARY JO LYNCH

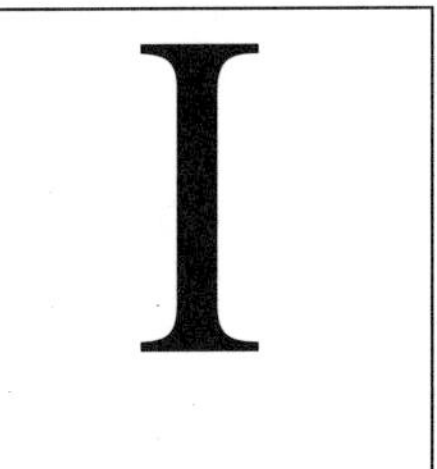

Iceland

Iceland, a republic, occupies an island in the North Atlantic Ocean near the Arctic Circle. Population (1990 est.) 255,000; area 103,000 sq.km. The official language is Icelandic.

History. Iceland was settled by Norsemen in the period from 874 to 930. In 930 the Icelanders founded a commonwealth and a general assembly (Althing) which is considered to be "the grandmother of parliaments." The country was under Norwegian and later Danish rule from the 13th century until independence in 1918; all ties with the Danish crown were cut in 1944.

Christianity was established by law in 1000. The Icelanders soon began writing on vellum their laws and their great treasury of poetry and saga, which until that time had been preserved only in oral form. The Golden Age of Saga literature covered the 11th to the 13th centuries. From 1000 to 1550 Iceland had nine Roman Catholic monasteries, where monks collected, copied, and preserved manuscripts before printing was introduced in 1534. The monasteries were destroyed during the Lutheran movement of the 16th century, resulting in the loss of many manuscripts. Little written literature survives from the following centuries, which were marked by volcanic devastation and epidemics. In 1971, the University of Copenhagen returned to Iceland the vast number of Icelandic manuscripts collected by the 18th-century scholar Árni Magnússon.

The first library in Iceland was founded in 1790 and named "the Icelandic Library and Reading Society in the South." Other reading societies (lestrarfélög) were founded, but all were short-lived, though some grew into modern public libraries. Their members were mainly priests and other professionals, and their collections were in foreign languages. The common people benefited little from them. The first truly public library was founded in 1828 in Akureyri. Until the Reykjavík City Library was founded in 1923, the National Library provided services for the people of Reykjavík.

National Library. Landsbókasafn Íslands was founded in 1818, instigated by members of the Icelandic Literary Society in Copenhagen. They collected money and books in Denmark, but space was not provided in the cathedral loft in Reykjavík until 1825. Through gifts, purchases, and a comprehensive exchange program, the Library grew. It moved first to the Althing (Parliament) building and then to its own home in 1909.

Since 1886 the National Library has received deposit copies of all works published in Iceland. The Library's holdings include an extensive collection of manuscripts and books, which in 1987 numbered about 406,000 (or about 1.6 volumes per capita). Since the founding of the University Library in 1940 and Iceland's full independence in 1944, the National Library has been responsible for acquiring materials in the humanities, while the University Library collects scientific books. In 1970 the Althing passed a resolution authorizing the building of a joint library and the eventual merging of the two collections. Work on the building began in 1978 and the exterior was completed by 1990. Construction has progressed slowly because of insufficient funding.

Among the National Library's activities are publication in Icelandic of *The Icelandic National Bibliography* since 1974, a *Union Catalog of Foreign Periodicals in Icelandic Libraries,* and a catalogue card distribution

National Library of Iceland, founded in 1818. It moved to this building in Reykjavík in 1909.

Kenneth C. Harrison

Libraries in Iceland (1990)

Type of library	Number of administrative units (main libraries)	Number of service points (branches, mobile stops, etc.)	Volumes in collections	Annual expenditures (krona/crown)	Population served	Professional staff (with certificate, diploma, etc.)	Total staff
National	1[a]	1[a]	406,000[a]		256,000	10[a]	31[a]
Academic	3	18	360,000	69,000,000	256,000	27	33
Public	233[b]	239[b]	7,574,000[b]	162,115,000[b]	256,000	--	--
School	ca. 50	--	--	--	--	--	--
Special	ca. 40	--	--	--	--	--	--

[a]1988 data
[b]1986 data

Sources: National Library of Iceland Annual Report, 1988. University Library Annual Report, 1990. University College of Education Annual Report, 1989–1990. Ministry of Culture and Education Annual Report, 1986.

service in collaboration with the Iceland Library Bureau, established in 1978.

Academic Libraries. Háskólabókasafn, the University Library, is the main academic library in the country, the others being the Library of the University College of Education (established 1908) and the Library of the University at Akureyri in North-Iceland (established 1988). In Reykjavík, the University Library held more than 392,000 volumes in 1987, including a large collection of materials on volcanology. On campus, the Stofnun Árna Magnússonar (Icelandic Manuscript Institute) houses the country's heritage of manuscripts. The Library of the University College of Education has the nation's largest collection of books on education and pedagogics (about 55,000 volumes in 1989).

Public Libraries. Iceland has a long-standing tradition of reading, and the literacy rate is almost 100 percent. The first public library act was passed in 1955; the current act was passed in 1976. There is a town or district library in each of the country's 43 districts. There are some 230 public libraries in the country, in all population centers. Reykjavík City Library has four branches, with bookmobile service in the suburbs. Per capita circulation in public libraries in 1986 was approximately 8.1 items. Services are provided to hospitals, asylums, and other institutions, and "bookboxes" are regularly prepared for ships in the country's fishing fleet. The state pays a small sum of money to Icelandic authors whose works have been acquired by libraries, to compensate for royalties not gained from direct sales.

School Libraries. In 1974 the Althing passed a law mandating libraries for all schools by 1984. Most schools in Reykjavík now have libraries, and a centralized service center in Reykjavík handles acquisitions, cataloguing, and other processes. Outside the Reykjavík area, there are few primary-school libraries and no service centers. In some of the smaller towns, school and public library functions are combined. Many secondary schools have developed libraries with professional librarians.

Special Libraries. Several small special libraries support research centers (such as the Agricultural Research Institute, the Institute for Industrial Technology, and the Marine Research Institute) and the specialized training schools (such as those in marine engineering and health-related professions). The Nordic House, a cultural center supported by the Nordic countries, holds an extensive collection of materials.

Icelandic Library for the Blind and Visually Handicapped. Blindrabókasafn Íslands was founded in 1982 and opened in 1983. It produces and distributes braille material and talking books. The Reykjavík City library and the Society for the Blind provided that service until 1983.

The Profession. The Icelandic Library Association was founded in 1960. By the late 1980s it had about 350 members. The Association of Professional Librarians, established in 1973, has about 155 members with university-level training, mostly from the University of Iceland, but also from the United States, Britain, or one of the Nordic countries. The University of Iceland provides professional training in combination with another study area in a three-year program. In May 1984 the Althing passed a Law on Professional Librarians defining the qualifications required to gain the right to the title of bókasafnsfræðingur (professional librarian).

ÁSGERDUR KJARTANSDÓTTIR

India

India, a federal republic in southern Asia, lies on a peninsula that juts out into the Indian Ocean; the Arabian Sea is on the west and the Bay of Bengal on the east. Pakistan lies to the northwest; China, Nepal, and Bhutan to the northeast; and Burma and Bangladesh to the east. Population (1990 est.) 827,057,000; area 3,287,590 sq.km. The national language is Hindi; English is an associate official language. Fifteen languages including Hindi are listed in the Eighth Schedule of the republic's constitution.

History. India has a long and rich tradition in education, the arts, culture, and scientific research. The significant contributions to human knowledge made by its poets, philosophers, religious leaders, mathematicians, medical experts, and thinkers such as Kalidasa, Adi Sankracharya, Buddha, Aryabhatt, and Charak are recognized worldwide. Universities such as those at Taxila and Nalanda were great centers of learning in ancient times. Education was also imparted in ashrams, temples, and other theological centers. These centers of learning had their libraries, some of which were quite large. But the present system of education and research has been largely influenced by the British system, which was introduced early in the 19th century.

The role libraries could play in the educational, scientific, industrial, and overall development of the country came to be recognized in the 1940s. The previous history of librarianship in India, as in several other countries in the East, put little emphasis on library service in the modern sense.

National Libraries and Archives. India has three named national libraries and one collection that is nationwide in scope.

National Library. The National Library of India came into existence in 1948 when the Constituent

Bombay University Library

Completed in 1878, the Rajabai Tower Building Library in Bombay.

Assembly passed the Imperial Library (Change of Name) Act. Soon afterward it moved to its 30-acre grounds at Belvedere, the former Viceregal Lodge in southeast Calcutta. It was opened to the public in 1953. It occupies a main building and three other buildings; work on a fifth building started in the late 1980s.

Its predecessor, the Imperial Library, was founded by Lord Curzon, then Viceroy and Governor-General of India, in 1902. It combined the holdings of the Calcutta Public Library (founded 1836) and the Imperial Secretariat Library (1891). Even today the National Library combines the functions of a public library for Calcutta and a permanent repository of all materials produced in or on India. Any Indian citizen aged 18 or older can use its services free of charge. It is one of four legally designated deposit libraries in the country, the others being the Connemara Public Library, Madras; the Central Library, Bombay; and the Delhi Public Library, Delhi.

The National Library had a total of almost 1,950,000 books in 1989, more than 430,000 of them in Indian languages. Its collection included almost 77,500 maps, 3,024 manuscripts, more than 107,000 bound volumes of serials, and 11,000 bound volumes of newspapers. Among its rare items are about 2,500 books in European languages published between the 15th and 18th centuries and another 3,500 rare titles published in India. The Library subscribes to almost 15,000 current serial titles and more than 800 newspapers. In 1987–88 it received nearly 17,000 books under the Delivery of Books and Newspapers (Public Libraries) Act, purchased 6,700 books, and received about 4,600 as gifts and 6,100 on exchange. During this year the Reading Room and Reference Division served almost 184,000 users, lent more than 97,000 items, and provided 85,000 more for consultation. Its reading rooms have almost 600 seats for its average of 1,000 daily readers. The Library is open 352 days a year. Accommodation is available for out-of-town users at the Readers' Hotel.

The Library has published *National Library Newsletter* since 1984. It also published several retrospective catalogues of some of its holdings. In the late 1980s, it began work on computerizing its operations and services. The Library is under the Department of Culture in the Union Ministry of Human Resource Development. Its work is divided into three main divisions: professional, conservation, and administrative. In 1989 the staff numbered 779, including 205 professionals.

National Medical Library. The National Medical Library (NML) was established in New Delhi in 1966. Formerly the Central Medical Library, created in 1961 from the Library of the Directorate General of Health Services, it moved in 1971 to its present building on the campus of the All India Institute of Medical Sciences. It functions as the focal point for collecting, processing, and disseminating biomedical information. The NML has a collection of more than 250,000 books, serials, technical reports, and nonbook materials, including a rich collection of 19th century medical literature. It receives about 2,300 serial titles annually. Its publications include a bimonthly accession list, *Library Bulletin*; a fortnightly service, *Selective Dissemination of Information*; a quarterly current awareness service, *Chetna*; and a quarterly *Index to Indian Medical Periodicals*. Work was underway in 1991 on the seventh edition of its *Union Catalogue of Medical Periodicals in Indian Libraries*. The NML is a national focal point for online access to databases such as MEDLINE. Since 1981 it has played an important role in training medical library professionals working in India and South Asia. The total staff of 87 includes 47 professionals.

National Science Library. The National Science Library was founded in 1964 as part of the Indian National Scientific Documentation Center (INSDOC). It occupies part of the INSDOC building in New Delhi. Its collection numbers some 200,000 items and receives about 5,000 current serials. Of its staff of 45, 32 are professionals.

Indian Agricultural Research Institute Library. This institution can rightly be called India's national agricultural library, although it is not so designated. Its collection consists of some 300,000 books, serials, and other materials; it receives about 5,000 current serials titles from 90 countries in 40 languages. It maintains a comprehensive collection of indexing and abstracting journals. Its publications include a monthly *Bibliography of Indian Agriculture* and a monthly press clipping service, *Development News in Agriculture*.

National Archives. The National Archives of India emerged from the former Imperial Record Department (founded 1891) when India achieved independence in 1947. In addition to the records of government ministries and departments, it has built a rich collection of the private papers of more than 75 eminent Indians. It publishes a scholarly biannual journal, *The Indian Archives,* and a quarterly newsletter, *The Archeion*. Its school of archival studies is an important center for training archivists from develop-

Libraries in India (1989)

Type of library	Number of administrative units (main libraries)	Number of service points (branches, mobile stops, etc.)	Volumes in collections	Annual expenditures (rupee)	Population served	Professional staff (with certificate, diploma, etc.)	Total staff
National	4	--	2,650,000	51,810,000	--	434	1,011
Academic	7,112	--	188,200,000	874,000,000	4,056,390	10,440	--
Public	7,180	18,000	35,900,000	359,000,000	--	12,000	--
School	62,240	--	64,240,000	1,606,000,000	--	25,000	--
Special	2,000	--	50,000,000	400,000,000	--	5,000	--

Sources: U.G.C. Annual Report, 1988–1989. India 1988–1989, a reference annual.

ing countries. It conducts research on improving and updating preservation techniques.

National Bibliography. The Indian National Bibliography has been compiled and published monthly by the Central Reference Library on the grounds of the National Library in Calcutta since 1958. The Central Reference Library also produces *Index Indiana,* a quarterly index of articles appearing in current periodicals in major Indian languages. The number of titles received per year in the late 1980s was almost 17,000.

Academic Libraries. The libraries of India's 150 universities, 22 institutions at university level, and 12 learned bodies recognized by the Union Government as institutions of national importance are the country's chief academic libraries. All these institutions have extensive collections and provide a wide range of services, as do the 6,800 colleges that offer educational and research facilities in various disciplines.

The real thrust in the development of academic libraries came after independence. The University Grants Commission (established 1953) provides financial assistance for collections, equipment, and buildings. It also helps formulate staffing norms and grants academic status to professional staff members.

Public Libraries. Provisions for developing public libraries have been included in the government's five-year plans since independence. In 1951, in cooperation with Unesco, the Delhi Public Library was established as a pilot project. It has grown into an impressive network for the Delhi metropolis. In 1958, the government-appointed Advisory Committee for Libraries outlined a plan for a country-wide system of state central libraries, district libraries, block libraries, and libraries at village level. By 1989 eight states had enacted public library laws and had made significant progress in public library service. Central libraries have been established in the other 18 states and 7 Union territories, and in some a fairly good infrastructure of district and rural libraries now exists. India had a literacy rate of about 35 percent in the late 1980s. The National Literacy Mission (established 1986) concentrates on setting up rural libraries and on the education of girls and women.

School Libraries. The states are responsible for primary and secondary schools, and the level of development varies widely from one to another. Many of the secondary and senior secondary schools in the country, numbering more than 64,200, have fairly good libraries, most of them manned by professionally qualified staff, though much remains to be achieved in this sector. Textbooks are generally available, but the lack of literature for general reading, particularly in local languages, greatly hampers development of these libraries.

Special Libraries. India has about 1,000 special libraries in the fields of science and technology. Organizations such as the Council of Scientific and Industrial Research, the Defense Research and Development Organization, the Indian Council of Medical Research, the Indian Council of Agricultural Research, the Indian Space Research Organization, the Electronics Commission, and the Atomic Energy Commission have developed good libraries. In addition, the Anthropological Survey of India, Botanical Survey of India, Geological Survey of India, and Zoological Survey of India (all located in Calcutta), the Indian Institute of Science (Bangalore), the Forest Research Institute (Dehradun), and Ahmedabad Textile Industries Research Association (Ahmedabad) have built large and rich collections.

This building houses the Indian National Scientific Documentation Centre (INSDOC) and the National Science Library. (New Delhi)

An estimated 600 social sciences libraries are attached to government departments, research institutes, and other organizations. The Indian Council of Social Science Research, established in the late 1960s in New Delhi as a funding agency, has helped develop libraries such as those at the A. N. Sinha Institute of Social Sciences (Patna), Sardar Patel Institute of Economic and Social Research (Ahmedabad), the Institute of Economic Growth (Delhi), and the National Council of Applied Economic Research (New Delhi).

Nearly all government ministries and departments have their own libraries, some quite extensive. There are several large libraries specializing in various areas of the humanities.

National Information Systems. The Indian National Scientific Documentation Center (INSDOC), New Delhi, set up in 1952 with assistance from Unesco, functions under the Council of Scientific and Industrial Research with regional centers at Bangalore, Calcutta, and Madras. Its services include providing documents, preparing specialized bibliographies, translation, reprography, printing, and selective dissemination of information. Its fortnightly, *Indian Science Abstracts,* scans some 700 periodicals for the contributions of Indian scientists. Other publications include a bimonthly, *Russian Scientific and Technical Publications,* and a monthly, *National Index of Translations.* Its *National Union Catalogue of Scientific Serials in India* lists 35,000 titles available in 800 scientific libraries in the country.

The National Information System in Science and Technology (NISSAT) has, since 1977, linked national information centers in various parts of the country and provided assistance to them. The Environment Information System (ENVIS), set up in 1982, has a network of 10 centers in areas such as pollution control, toxic chemicals, coastal and off-shore ecology, and occupational health. It publishes a quarterly journal, *Paryavaran Abstracts*.

The Profession. Librarianship as a profession has made great strides in India since the 1950s. There are about 75 library schools in universities conducting one-year Bachelor's-degree courses, two thirds of them offering additional one-year courses leading to the Master's degree. Delhi University conducts a one-year M.Phil. program. Its Library School, established on the advice of S. R. Ranganathan in 1946, has been the trend setter in the field. About 25 library schools register students for Ph.D. work.

Several library associations exist at the national level and each State and Union Territory has at least one. The Indian Library Association (ILA), founded in 1933, is the largest, with about 2,500 members. With headquarters in Delhi, it publishes the *ILA Bulletin*. The Indian Association of Special Libraries and Information Centers (IASLIC), founded in 1955 and headquartered in Calcutta, is the second largest library organization. It publishes the *IASLIC Bulletin*.

REFERENCE

S. R. Ranganathan, *Library Development Plan: Thirty-year Programme for India with Draft Library Bills for the Union and Constituent States* (1950).

PRAMOD B. MANGLA

Indonesia

Indonesia, a republic in Southeast Asia and part of the Malay archipelago, comprises thousands of islands over an area of 1,904,569 sq.km. The most densely populated island, Java (137,187 sq.km.), has 91,269,528 inhabitants (1980 census). Other principal islands are Sumatra, Kalimantan (Borneo), and Sulawesi (Celebes). Population (1990 est.) 179,300,000. The official language is Bahasa Indonesia, the government-sponsored form of Malay.

History. As in medieval Europe, scholarly activities in early Indonesia were intimately connected with religion. Besides writings about religion and ethics, treatises of a secular nature, such as belles-lettres and works on history, arts, and law, have been preserved. Like their medieval counterparts, however, these so-called secular works should also be seen against their cultural background, which was dominated by religions—first Hinduism and Buddhism, later by Islam (except in Bali and certain other areas).

Indonesia, with its thousands of islands, has a variety of social and cultural identities. A large number of local languages exist. Fortunately the Malay language was early accepted as a lingua franca. The language was used as a vehicle of communication for trade among the Chinese, the Hindus, the Arabs, the Portuguese, and later the Dutch, and also for the spread of religions. The Malay language grew to become the Indonesian language, and was later promoted to become the national language.

In the 19th century the Dutch colonial government introduced the Western style of education for the population, but it made reading available to the general public only in 1908 with the establishment of the Folk Program. About 1918 Balai Pustaka, the office in charge of promoting reading among the people, started operating mobile libraries. People were then able to read in their own local languages. During the Dutch colonial period, the special libraries to support colonial programs were better developed than the public libraries.

National Library. The National Library was established in 1980, merging four libraries in Jakarta: the National Museum Library (established in 1778), the Library of Social and Political History, the Provincial Library of Jakarta, and the Bibliographic and Deposit Division of the Center for Library Development.

The main functions are: to preserve national imprints, to collect publications on Indonesia and works written by Indonesians, wherever they are published; to publish the National Bibliography; and to act as a national center for library cooperation in the country and abroad. A draft Legal Deposit Act was submitted to the Parliament in the mid-1980s. The collection totaled 650,000 volumes in 1984. The Library was housed in temporary quarters while a new site for the National Library building was under discussion.

Academic Libraries. Most of the colleges and universities in Indonesia, and thus also their libraries, are comparatively young, especially those outside Java. Only the Faculty of Medicine of the University of Indonesia in Jakarta and the Institute of Technology in Bandung existed long before Indonesia gained its independence in 1945.

Most libraries in Indonesia are government-owned. Several private ones belong to the Islamic institutes, theological seminaries, and teachers' training colleges. More centralized university library services remained to be developed, as many universities still maintain departmental libraries. An integrated university library system is being managed by the Directorate of Higher Education, Department of Education and Culture.

In September 1984 an Open University System was opened, and it promised to give additional responsibilities and dimension to academic libraries.

Public Libraries. It is difficult to meet the demand of the reading needs of more than 150,000,000 people and to serve them properly because of the vastness of the country. An effective book publishing and distribution system was still needed in the late 1980s; programs are severely hampered by the inadequate transport and communication system.

Indonesia's 27 provincial capitals have provincial libraries. The public libraries are to be found in districts and villages.

About 275 public district libraries were in operation in 1984. The provincial and public libraries are managed centrally by the Center for Library Development in cooperation with the local governments. To reach people in faraway places, many of the provincial libraries started operating mobile libraries. In 1984, 104 mobile libraries were in operation.

School Libraries. Indonesia's school-age children make up 60 percent of the total population. The development of the state school libraries is the responsibility of the Center for Library Development. Effective school library service is handicapped by the shortage of available teacher-librarians.

Most of the services given are limited to borrowing and returning books during school breaks. Pilot projects were being set up in the mid-1980s to demonstrate models to teachers and parent-teacher associations.

Special Libraries. Categorized as special libraries are those with collections in a special field and also those rendering active information services. Most of the special libraries or information centers belong to research institutes or universities.

Many of the special libraries, in management and collections, are better off than the other types of libraries in the country because of their history. The *Directory of Special Libraries and Information Services in Indonesia 1981* reports a total of 295 libraries. National documentation and information centers, for example, in biology and agriculture, science and technology, and health and medicine, carry out national functions in their fields of specialization. National centers also become a training ground for staff from other libraries who are in need of improving management and technical capabilities.

In Indonesian library development, the special libraries could be considered the principal innovators in and advocates of library and information services. The system still faces financial and other handicaps in making the services effective for users in faraway places. Indonesia is still far from making all levels of the community information conscious.

The Profession. The Indonesian Library Association, founded in 1954, has undergone several changes of names and coverage of activities. At one time it was also an association for archivists. Later, between 1969 and 1973, workers in special libraries felt they needed their own association and formed the Indonesian Special Library Association. Although the small group flourished, many believed that the small number of professionals in the associations was not advantageous to the development of the profession and a new combined association was started in 1974. Many constraints work against making the Association strong with a voice to be heard.

REFERENCES

Central Bureau of Statistics, *Statistical Yearbook of Indonesia.*

Unesco, *Report on Survey. Indonesia National Survey of Scientific and Technological Information.* (1980).

LUWARSIH PRINGGOADISURJO

Information Science

The biological and behavioral sciences have long been concerned with how organisms process energy from the environment. Information science is interested in how this understanding can be applied to the analysis and design of systems—environments of people, technologies, and procedures—that serve to enhance the human capacity to deal with and utilize this energy.

Organisms in general possess a wide repertoire of mechanisms, the senses, that capture energy from the environment. With these mechanisms, the organisms can be aware of states and conditions that could influence their growth, development, and survival. This awareness represents the "what, where, when, and who" of experience. Systems that augment the human capacity for awareness are referred to as *information systems.* These systems may have various designations depending on their function and purpose. For example, there are information systems for such fields as business, law, and medicine. Regardless of their names, all these systems possess a structure from which the organization of the basic elements can be modelled. These models enable scientists to analyze and design such systems. Using these models, information science researchers can formulate theories about the structure of systems and can test the efficiency and effectiveness of various systems. Information science attempts to determine the principles and laws that pertain to the relationships that exist among the various components of these systems.

Information Science and Knowledge. For homo sapiens, just awareness, just information, is not enough in dealing with the complex nature of events and the requirements for action and adjustment to them. With greater neural endowment than other species, humankind has developed a need to derive meaning from awareness. The human search for new ideas (often called creativity) and the demand to solve problems, formulate decisions, and exercise judgment involves higher cognitive functions. We can refer to this process as a knowledge need or as an extension of awareness; whatever we call it, we can identify it as a requirement to know the *how* and *why* of experience.

Information science is an integral part of a large community of other sciences, including computer, library, and communication sciences, all of which can be subsumed under the term *knowledge sciences*—sciences that are directed to the advancement of human meaning and understanding through technology.

While information science is directed toward the design and development of systems that help increase human awareness, knowledge systems move toward the development of environments that strengthen the human capacity for dealing with matters of how and why. At present, such systems are referred to as *decision support systems* or *expert systems.* The field of studies for such systems is called *artificial intelligence* or *AI.* Long discussed and often derided, expert systems are now in use or under development in many fields.

Theories of Information Science. From the outset, information scientists have concentrated on how the record of human experience, encapsulated in such physical forms as books or written records, could best be accessed, retrieved, and distributed to others, enabling them to use this information to deal with the day-to-day demands of living. There are several bodies of knowledge that scientists and engineers can apply to the analysis and design of information systems that meet this purpose. Among these, three bodies of knowledge are particularly pertinent: logistics, cognition, and communication.

Logistics. Historically, logistics has referred to the acquisition, storage, and distribution of material and other resources needed to support military operations. But the principles governing logistics can be applied to non-military operations as well. Logistical principles are important to information scientists because they help in identifying, accessing, storing, retrieving, and distributing products generated by the human intellect.

Symbols are the basic tools that human beings have invented to help them to account for and manage objects and to identify their experiences. Letters and numbers, referred to collectively as *alphanumerics,* are examples of such symbols. Symbols are an important logistical tool. When symbols are put in a specific order to serve as designations for specific states of the environment or objects in it, the symbols so ordered constitute a datum. Numbers are such data. A number system is an aggregation of symbols, a language, that serves as a formally established means for dealing with objects and states in the environment.

An understanding of symbols is particularly important to both library and information science. Efficient use of symbols can ease the problems that arise from the growth of information and knowledge products. Symbols are an integral part of the machinery designed to facilitate accounting for objects or states. Such machinery increases our capacity for awareness, thereby increasing the potential for understanding. The design of such machinery is basically grounded in *automata theory,* formulated in the early 20th century by the British computer scientist Alvin Turing. The main notion underlying the theory is the postulate that any experience can be processed by a machine—an automaton—if the factors that relate to that experience can be identified and expressed quantitatively.

The power of a computer lies mainly in the generation of a set of procedures that drive the internal energizing elements. The computer executes these procedures, following an ordered set of instructions expressed in code or symbolic form—referred to as a programming language. New developments in programming languages continue to make possible new capabilities in processing data. The word *informatics* has been used as an inclusive term for the many efforts applied by several disciplines to increase the power of technology toward automating the handling of the products of the mind, such as documents and records. (It is difficult to find a consensus on the definition of informatics. Several encyclopedias include the term adjacent to the term *information science,* but without direct explication. Few recent English dictionaries include the term.)

Logistics is not solely restricted to locating objects. It is also concerned with the services that accompany the delivery of such objects. As such, the principles that govern logistics are relevant to the management of a library, an information center, and similar institutions.

Cognition. A whole host of theories address the biological, psychological, and sociological forces that impinge on a human being's ability to process information. *Cognitive theory* provides the framework for our understanding of such processes and related functions such as thinking, remembering, learning, and perceiving—functions directly attributed to human information processing.

All organisms are limited in their capacity to respond to stimulation, both present and potential. *Psychophysics* is a methodological approach to determining these limits. It derives from experiments conducted in the 18th, 19th, and 20th centuries that measured our ability to see, hear, smell, and respond to pressure and other sensory functions. Psychophysics is particularly pertinent to information scientists. It provides an understanding of the human ability to respond to the amount of data, information, and knowledge that is presented. Psychophysics can also provide ways for us to learn about how human beings search for objects that will satisfy their needs. This question is of interest to both librarians and information scientists. Further, psychophysics helps us understand how we can structure environments or systems that either help or impede the mental operations involved in dealing with information in both libraries and information systems—a process called "studying the human factors."

Communication. Like the circulatory system in living organisms, communication is the process that binds the various parts of a system and other related systems together. The basic elements of a system—the symbols and the data—flow through the various components of the system, enabling it to achieve its purpose or purposes. Communication is a vital element of interest to information science. Communication defines what librarians and information professionals do and what libraries do as both the custodians and agents in the transfer of information.

Communication is a generic term encompassing two major functions detailed in the following expression:

$$\text{communication} = \text{transmission} \times \text{signification}$$

Transmission refers to the movement of symbols or data among objects and organisms in time and space. The conveyer can be a physical medium that enables the presentation of the symbol. Such media include light, sound, parchment, film, smoke, odors, and the familiar media made possible by electronics, such as radio and television. The medium can also be the human voice, bodily expression by movement, or other signs. The structuring of systems and the means of tying them together for the purpose of conveying messages over time or distances is included in the term *telecommunications.* This term refers to a family of electronic technologies that enable the representation and movement of signal and symbols in space and time. It is an essential component of all information systems.

Shannon's *Information Theory* remains the preeminent statement accounting for measuring the actual physical content of a transmitted message, such as computer bits and bytes. One of the fundamental aspects of the theory is that the message serves to change the state of the receiver. The theory directly correlates the contents of the message with the probability of occurrence. Thus the message alters the state of uncertainty of the receiver. Several disciplines have utilized this concept in their attempt to understand human information processing.

Signification, or meaning and understanding, is both a necessary and a sufficient condition for communication to occur between sender and receiver. Shannon's theory of information does not include an acknowledgment of the meaning that is imparted in the content of the message. Understanding is derived from the language used in the message, the arrangement of the symbols in which it is conveyed. The meaning or understanding of the message is an extension of an information system and an integral part of a knowledge system.

A discipline that attempts to integrate the principles of logistics, cognition, and communication into a cohesive set of principles for the development of communication and control systems is *Cybernetics.*

Cyberneticians borrow principles from the physical, biological, and behavioral sciences. To the Cybernetician, time is the critical independent variable that demands acknowledgment in the understanding of the functions of communication and control systems. Variety in response is the variable on which the response of the system can be understood. Cyberneticians demand that the behavior of systems be expressed quantitatively. These measures then account for the dynamic properties and performance of systems in general.

Applications. Information scientists involved in field operations preponderantly direct their attention to analyzing and designing information systems that improve human awareness and provide the potential for facilitating the generation, use, and distribution of knowledge. In this task information scientists are, by and large, interdisciplinarians, varying considerably in their formal education and work experiences. The major focus of attention and the ultimate objective of these scientists is to improve the dissemination of recorded human experience, past and present. This process is not restricted to dissemination in the narrow sense—that is, the transfer or custody of the physical record of human experience. The broader context concerns the improvement in service—the human–technology interface. Information scientists are interested in how present and future information systems aid or can aid human beings in acquiring and using knowledge. They are interested in generating new procedures for accessing, storing, and retrieving information and knowledge through which institutions and individuals alike can achieve their highest potential. Information scientists are also interested in increasing the value of the information resource and in reducing the cost of providing access to it, in terms of both time and money.

Significant effort and advances have been made in these directions, particularly in the areas of storage and services. Advances in technology have probably contributed more to these aspects of information science than others. These advances have significantly influenced the services that institutions such as libraries provide.

Storage. Optical disks, compact disc–read only memory (CD-ROM), and videodiscs provide new ways for storing data. Since the early 1980s these technologies have gained new attention because of their ability to reduce costs, provide large storage capacity, and improve the effective use of personal computers in general. These technologies offer new opportunities for librarians to deal with the storage problem created by the rapid growth of information and knowledge.

Databases. An important element of information systems is the aggregation and management of *databases,* structured sets of related files. Developments since the late 1970s have attempted to integrate advances in computer technology with new database techniques in order to develop ways to combine databases to meet the advances in artificial intelligence, and specifically to meet the increasing needs of commercial interests. The main problems with databases include the user's lack of awareness of them, the user's lack of ability to use them, and the cost of access to them. But interest in online databases continues to grow. Users appreciate direct access to databases that interest them. Businesses contribute substantially to the generation and development of new databases. The continuing challenge is to increase individual awareness in terms of what databases exist, how they can be used to their maximum potential, and what can be expected in the future. This task is of central importance to information scientists.

Services. Libraries remain the main custodians of information and knowledge resources. At the local level, librarians seek to improve resource sharing, increase the efficiency and effectiveness of storage mechanisms made available through online databases, integrate new technology, and train both staff members and their patrons to use them. At the international level the picture is more complex because of social, cultural, and economic factors that serve to highlight the general difficulty encountered in developing a worldwide Data-Information-Knowledge System—that is, a World Brain.

For several decades, information scientists have attempted to frame policy on information- and knowledge-transfer practices in developing countries. At the international level, Unesco has been a major force in providing funds for studies done at the field level. These studies are aimed at establishing concepts and principles from which the analysis and design of such information systems for developing countries could be undertaken. Of particular interest is the effort to determine the gaps in information availability between developing and more developed countries.

At whatever level—individual, group, national, or international—the need for information professionals to act as intermediaries is emerging. The idea of an intermediary who serves as a broker, consultant, or counselor between the user and the vast ocean of information and knowledge has strong appeal. It is predicated on the expressed inability of many users to apply the technological resources at their disposal to specific tasks. Many users complain that they are flooded with information and knowledge in the form of printed products (such as books and papers) or presented to them electronically or orally. They desperately need some sense of organization in the abundant material available to them. From the evidence, the way people use information and knowledge is a matter of habit and cognitive style. Information scientists recognize this human aspect in designing information systems and the services they provide. Of course, reference and special librarians have played and will continue to play an important part in bridging the gap in question. What seems to be lacking is a body of theory on library service and information system interface that would account for the ways individuals receive, process, and interpret the information they seek. This theory would encompass the logistical dimensions covered previously as well as the cognitive styles of individual users.

Information and knowledge technologies now under development offer some promise in reducing the gap between people and machines through highly sophisticated programs that attempt to match the cognitive domains of individual users. The question remains: is a well-trained human intermediary in the final analysis an essential element in integrating the vast information power that exists with what is available through libraries and advanced data-processing technologies?

Library and Information Science. Since the introduction of the term information science and the redesignation of the American Documentation Institute as the American Society for Information Science in 1964, scholars have tried to differentiate the objectives and the boundaries of library and information science. Much debate and controversy surrounds the question of allocation and definition of domain. This debate is perhaps best demonstrated in the academic attempts to generate a coherent concept of the education and training of future information professionals and scientists. Attempts to delineate and identify specific areas of occupational activity and the skills to serve them have been made, but have not been totally successful because of a lack of consensus on policy and standards. This lack is particularly evident in information science, where most scholars and professionals have backgrounds and training in other formal disciplines. Extrapolations, interpolations, changes in ways of thinking, do not come easily!

Many of the perturbations that the library and information sciences experience in the 1990s may be considered as only a part of the dynamic changes that society and its cultures are now undergoing. The impact of rapid and significant advances in computer and communications technologies has changed the data-information-knowledge landscape, both as to role and function, but individuals, institutions, and society at large have not kept pace. As a result, the importance and value of these resources to the individual and collective welfare largely remain unrealized.

REFERENCES

James R. Beniger, *Control Revolution: Technological and Economic Origins of the Information Society* (1986).

Anthony Debons, "Foundations of Information Science," *Advances in Computers,* (1990).

Robert M. Hayes, "Education of the Information Professional: A Library School Perspective," *Journal of the American Society for Information Science* (1988).

ANTHONY DEBONS

Information Science Education

Information science has become an established discipline in the context of each of several related fields: librarianship, computer science, management, engineering, and others. This article defines information science and reviews the status of education for it, with special emphasis on its relevance to library education.

Definitions. First, it is essential to establish definitions of terms as they will be used in this article.

Information. The term "information" is used with a variety of meanings. Some identify it with communications over transmission lines, measured by the statistical properties of signals; some identify it with recorded facts; some with the content of text; some with the experience stored in the human mind. In this article, though, the following is the operational definition of the term:

> *Information* is a property of data resulting from or produced by a process performed on the data. The process may be simply data transmission (in which case the definition and measure used in communication theory are applicable); it may be data selection; it may be data organization; it may be data analysis.

It is important to note that, given this definition, information is dependent upon the processes that produce it. While some of the properties of information may be investigated independent of the means for performing these processes, the important and interesting ones cannot. That means that information can best be understood in the context of specific systems.

Information Systems. Any complex phenomenon encompasses a variety of aspects—physical structure, cybernetic responses to environment, chemical and metabolic balance, or information processing. Thus a person can be viewed as a physical organism made of bones and muscles, capable of performing mechanical tasks; as a chemical factory processing ingested food, water, and air and converting them to metabolic energy; or as a thinking human being, taking in sensory data, making decisions, and controlling its physical and chemical structure. A library can be viewed as a collection of physical books and records; as an administrative organization; or as an information processing system, taking in data and providing it in response to requests. If the aspects of specific interest are those that we identify as information processing, the phenomenon becomes an information system. Hence, the definition:

> An *information system* is that set of aspects of a general system (a natural phenomenon, a physical construct, or a logical construct) that are identified as information producing.

That leads then to the very natural definition of information science:

> *Information science* is the study of information producing processes in any information system in which they may occur.

This means that while information science may in principle be concerned with the analysis of pure process, it depends primarily upon the methodologies for studying phenomena in specific disciplines. For example, RNA and DNA can be studied for the information processes they embody and, as such, are information systems of vital interest to information science. But it would be impossible to study the means by which they transmit, select, organize, and analyze data (as represented by configurations of amino acids) without the methods of microbiology. It is therefore most appropriate to talk about information science in the context of specific disciplines—in genetics, in social theory, in documentation, in librarianship—instead of talking about it in isolation from specific systems.

Information Systems. What then are examples of systems with which information science is concerned?

The Computer. The computer has been an especially important context for information science, for very clear reasons. The *raison d'être* for the computer is data processing. Furthermore, those processes are well defined and measurable in precise ways; the computer is therefore a predictable system to study.

Computer-based Information Systems. The use of the computer in an ever increasing variety of applications has resulted in computer-based information systems that have been a major focus of information science. They embody information processes considerably more complex than those of the computer itself, since they function within organizations that provide many of the additional processes needed for people to acquire data and make decisions. Information science in this context has therefore needed to include the body of techniques by which such organizations are studied and by which alternative systems for information processing are designed and evaluated.

Libraries and Information Centers. These specific organizations exist, as institutions, for the information processing functions they provide. Those functions—cataloguing and indexing, for example—are relatively well formalized and serve as ideal subjects for study by information science. The results of such study can have direct value to the institutions, by improving their operations and extending their services. Indeed, the extent of mutual value has been so great that some have identified information science with library science.

Social Systems and Biological Systems. Each of these performs information processes. In governmental structures, the processes for selecting officials and for organizing bureaucracies all constitute information processes. Economics is concerned with processes upon symbols of capital. The genetic code, embodied in the amino acids of DNA and RNA, is transmitted and reorganized through information processes. Psychology is concerned with processes of the human mind. Each of these clearly relates to an example of an information system, which taken together have been called "living systems."

Information Science Education. Given the range of information systems within which information science must be important, it is not surprising that there is a parallel array of programs for education in information science. The result is a diversity that makes it impossible to extract a common curriculum.

The Range of Programs. Some educational programs include information science as part of computer science; in a few cases, they have even called themselves "computer and information science" programs. Some have focused on the use of computers in libraries for either internal operations or computer-based services; in a large number of cases, they have called themselves "library and information science" programs. Some have identified information science with "science information," focusing on documentation, indexing and abstracting, and mechanized information retrieval. Some have focused on the uses of computers for application to information needs in business and industry; typically, they call themselves "information management" programs.

Historical Development. The earliest identifiable recognition of the field as part of librarianship (not in name, but in fact) was at Western Reserve University, under the guidance of Dean Jesse Shera. In the mid-1950s, James W. Perry and Allen Kent established the Center for Documentation and Communication Research as an adjunct of that library school.

In the subsequent five to ten years, a number of short courses, workshops, conferences, and similar ad hoc means for instruction were launched by a number of other universities—at UCLA, American University, Drexel, Georgia Institute of Technology, and the University of Washington. In them, the several types of context listed above were thoroughly intermixed, with computer systems specialists, librarians, documentalists, and business data processing systems persons all working in all of them. The result was continuing confusion among the related fields—science information, computer science, information systems design, and information science.

The steadily increasing number of ad hoc programs, however, provided clear evidence of a real need for formal instruction. In 1961 and 1962, two conferences were held at Georgia Institute of Technology at which, for the first time, the various aspects of the field were identified and delineated and goals for formal curricula were defined.

Almost immediately, from 1964 to 1967, various schools initiated formal information science programs, but with foci representing the differing aspects of the field. The ones started at Georgia Institute of Technology (Vladimir Slamecka), Ohio State (Marshall Yovits), and Lehigh University (Robert Taylor and Donald Hillman) focused on the technological and theoretical aspects. The ones at the University of Chicago (Don Swanson), Case Western Reserve (Perry, Kent, and later Alan Goldwyn), UCLA (Robert Hayes and Harold Borko), and Pittsburgh (Allen Kent) were established as integral parts of library schools.

In the subsequent years, these programs developed variously. Those with a technological and theoretical orientation gradually became indistinguishable from computer science programs. Some of those in library schools became independent (as at the University of Pittsburgh), though with a tenuous connection to librarianship. Others associated with library schools (Chicago and UCLA, in particular) became increasingly integrated with librarianship.

In parallel, virtually every other library school in the United States added courses on one or another of the kinds of subject matter identified with information science—information retrieval, computer applications to libraries, indexing and abstracting, and so on. Many library schools changed their names to reflect the coverage of information science; some refer to "library and information science," others to "library and information studies," but all with the same intent of broadening the definition of the field.

By the mid-1970s, the importance of computer usage for information services in business and industry led several schools to take a new direction, related to information science and representing one of the more specific areas of interest—information management or, alternatively, information resource management. These programs (at Syracuse and the University of Southern California, for example) saw an increasing need for educated personnel to develop, manage, and serve in the information systems being created in corporate enterprises.

By the mid-1980s, there was a broad array of information science programs, with a substantial area of common concern, especially with respect to the computer, but also with substantial differences in curricula and focus.

Structure of Curricula. The curricula will to some extent include course work in six major areas: (1) core, introductory courses, (2) formal disciplines (mathematics and linguistics, for example), (3) applied disciplines (such as statistics and operations research), (4) computer-oriented courses (database management and computer retrieval, for example), (5) management-oriented courses (accounting and organization theory, for example), and (6) information organization and service courses (cataloguing and reference, for example, though frequently with differing names). These reflect the need for an educational program in information science to provide the student with the intellectual orientation and technical tools needed for professional and research work in the field. The student must learn about how information is used, how systems are designed and operated, and the technical tools needed for information work.

An effective information curriculum should provide a common core of technical knowledge, integrated into a framework of the total field. It should provide the basis for specialization in any one of the major components—the information specialist, concerned with utilization; the information manager, concerned with operations; the system designer, concerned with technical problems in implementation; and the theoretician, concerned with future research in the field. While any given curriculum will emphasize one or another of these specialty areas, each should be explicitly recognized if the curriculum is properly to be characterized as one in "information science."

Information Science in Library Education. Most library schools treat information science as a component of the M.L.S. degree program, with varying degrees of integration into the M.L.S. curriculum. While the broad range of specialties previously identified may be represented, the emphasis is likely to be on the operational and professional aspects, and there will be minimal attention to the other components. One crucial problem faced by every library school has been how best to integrate information science with the more traditional components of the M.L.S. curriculum. If not properly handled, the information science courses can become an isolated enclave, bearing little relationship to the remainder of the curriculum; the result is a loss for faculty and students in both library science and information science. Fortunately, the progress in the decade 1976–85 in developing computer-based systems and services in libraries made it easy to incorporate at least those aspects of information science into the M.L.S. curriculum. The more theoretical and technical course work, however, is difficult to encompass within the framework of one-year M.L.S. programs, and the coverage of it, if any, tends to be superficial.

Standards. As of the late 1980s, there were no established standards for education in information science, nor was there an accrediting body for the field. However, the American Library Association explicitly recognized information science in its *1972 Standards for Accreditation,* regarding it as an essential component of M.L.S. programs. In 1985 and 1986 the ALA Committee on Accreditation continued an investigation initiated by the Association of Library and Information Science Education (ALISE) aimed at determining how best to accommodate the needs of information science and other specialties in the field within the accreditation process.

ROBERT M. HAYES

International Association of Agricultural Librarians and Documentalists

The International Association of Agricultural Librarians and Documentalists (IAALD) was founded in 1955 to promote agricultural library science and documentation, internationally and nationally, as well as the professional interests of agricultural librarians and documentalists. The term agriculture is interpreted in its widest sense and includes forestry, agricultural engineering, veterinary science, fisheries, food and nutrition, and agricultural and food industries.

There are more than 700 members from some 80 countries. Membership is open to agricultural librarians and documentalists as individuals, corporate bodies (national and multinational associations of agricultural librarians and documentalists), and institutions (libraries, information or documentation centers, research and educational institutions, and official bodies).

In pursuing its objectives, IAALD encourages collaboration among agricultural libraries and documentation centers in various countries, including the loan and exchange of books, journals, and reports. This exchange has been formalized by the establishment of AGLINET, a cooperative document supply system supported by the major agricultural libraries of the world. The Association assists in coordinating activities and projects dealing with agricultural bibliographies and abstracting services. It cooperates with national, regional, and international organizations and networks in the field of agricultural information. In particular, IAALD supported and took part in the development of the FAO-sponsored international agricultural information system, AGRIS.

The organs of the Association are the General Assembly, the Executive Committee, and the Secretariat. The General Assembly of all members meets every five years in a World Congress at which it lays down general policy, amends the Constitution, appoints officers and members of the Executive Committee, and establishes membership fees. The Executive Committee consists of a President, two Vice-Presidents, a Secretary/Treasurer, at least six but not more than ten members, and a representative from each recognized national or multinational association of agricultural librarians and documentalists. The Executive Committee calls meetings of the General Assembly and directs the Association between them. The Secretariat handles current affairs of the Association under the direction of the Secretary/Treasurer. Additionally, a Working Group has been established on IAALD Education and Training.

IAALD holds a World Congress every five years. The eighth World Congress was held in 1990 in Budapest, Hungary, on the general theme of "Information and the End User." The 1985 Congress, in Ottawa, Canada, took up the theme of "Information for Food." Regional congresses are held at other times.

From 1956 the Association published a *Quarterly Bulletin of IAALD* and from 1980 the *IAALD News,* an occasional President's newsletter, both free to members. In addition to the *Proceedings* of the World Congresses, it published *World Directory of Agricultural Libraries and Documentation Centres* (1990), *Primer for Agricultural Libraries* (2nd edition, 1980), and the *Proceedings* of its regional conferences.

IAALD is affiliated with the International Federation of Library Associations and the International Federation for Documentation as an international member. It has close contact with regional and national associations in its field, which are represented on its Executive Committee.

D. J. VAN DER BURG

International Association of Metropolitan City Libraries

International Association of Metropolitan City Libraries (INTAMEL), founded in 1968, is open to all public libraries in cities (or counties) of more than 400,000. City librarians or directors represent their cities at INTAMEL general assemblies. In 1976, when INTAMEL became a Round Table of IFLA, the following statement of its purpose was approved:

> INTAMEL is a platform for professional communication and information for libraries of cities with 400,000 or more inhabitants. It is a Round Table of the Division of Libraries Serving the General Public.
>
> Every year INTAMEL organizes conferences where exchanges of experience and ideas take place on library systems, library buildings, and library activities. In the Medium-Term Programme period special attention will be given to:
>
> 1. Library networks in larger cities.
> 2. Library buildings.
> 3. The formation within city libraries of special subject departments with their own collections and services.
> 4. Catalogues in large city libraries: their use and organization.
> 5. The automation of catalogues and circulation.
> 6. The problems of library services to ethnic and linguistic minorities in large cities.
> 7. Research library work in city libraries.
> 8. The provision and use of online information services.

INTAMEL's inaugural meeting was held in Liverpool in 1968. Venues for general assemblies were, in 1969, Gothenburg, Sweden; 1970, Tokyo; 1971, Baltimore, Maryland; 1972, Milan; 1973, Delhi; 1974, Hamburg, Germany; 1975, Lagos, Nigeria; 1976, Paris; 1977, The Hague, Netherlands; 1978, Toronto; 1979, Vienna; 1980, Glasgow and Edinburgh, Scotland; 1981, Budapest; 1982, Mexico City; 1983 Berlin; 1984, Gothenburg; 1985, Cleveland, Ohio; 1986, Rotterdam; 1987, Paris; 1988, New York and Philadelphia; 1989, London and Birmingham; 1990, Hannover and Hamburg; 1991, Toulouse. An important part of the annual meetings is the study tours to major city libraries or other interesting libraries in the host city or neighboring cities. Over a period of several assemblies, regular attendees thus have the opportunity to visit scores of metropolitan city library systems in many countries.

Among themes treated in conferences were *Libraries and the Universal Availability of Information; Research Services; Services to Children; Budget Cuts; Library Services to Special Groups; Automation and the Future of Public Library Work; Visual Material in Libraries; Fundraising for Public Libraries; Public Libraries Against Illiteracy;* and *Library Service to Minorities.*

Host libraries or Presidents of INTAMEL succeeded in securing financial aid to ensure the participation of librarians from developing countries at several of the annual meetings.

By 1991 INTAMEL had about 110 members in 35 countries. Its president and secretary-treasurer are elected for three-year terms. At the inaugural meeting in 1968 George Chandler of Liverpool was elected as the first President of INTAMEL, with Godfrey Thompson of the City of London as Secretary and Lars Tynell of Stockholm as Treasurer. Vice-Presidents elected in Liverpool were Friedrich Andrae of Hamburg, Edwin Castagna of Baltimore, and Rudolf Malek of Prague. From 1974 to 1977, the President was Keith Doms (Philadelphia), with Kenneth F. Duchac (Brooklyn) serving as Secretary-Treasurer. During the next three years the President was Jürgen Eyssen (Hannover), and the Secretary-Treasurer was Friedrich Andrae (Hamburg). From 1980 to 1983, P. van Swigchem (The Hague) was President, with Piet Schoots (Rotterdam) serving as Secretary-Treasurer. From 1983 to 1986 Sten Cedergren (Gothenburg) served as President, with Andrew Miller (Glasgow) as Secretary-Treasurer. They were followed from 1986 to 1989 by Constance B. Cooke (New York) as President and Wim M. Renes (The Hague) as Secretary-Treasurer. In 1989 Melvyn Barnes (London) was elected President, with Christian Relly (Zürich) as Secretary-Treasurer.

One area of special attention for INTAMEL has been compiling and presenting comprehensive comparative statistics. They cover stocks of books, periodicals, audiovisual materials, loans, budgets, book funds, staff (professional and nonprofessional), branch libraries, mobile libraries, opening hours, and other statistical data from the member cities.

For several IFLA Conferences INTAMEL organized lectures and workshops dealing with subjects of general interest to public libraries. Some of these lectures have been published, including *Metropolitan Libraries on Their Way into the Eighties* (Marion Beaujean, 1982), *The Work of INTAMEL* (Constance B. Cooke, 1987), *Funding for Public Libraries in the Nineties* (Arthur Curtey, 1989), *Listening to the Culture: Librarianship for a New Age* (John S. Smith, 1990); and *The Development of Library Technicians: A Review of Experience in Selected Countries* (Ian M. Johnson, 1990).

STEN CEDERGREN;
CHRISTIAN RELLY

International Association of Music Libraries, Archives and Documentation Centres

The International Association of Music Libraries, Archives and Documentation Centres (IAML), also known as Association Internationale des Bibliothèques, Archives et Centres de Documentation Musicaux (AIBM), and Internationale Vereinigung der Musikbibliotheken, Musikarchive und Musikdokumentationszentren (IVMB), was formed shortly after World War II to promote worldwide cooperation in all aspects of music librarianship, bibliography, and documentation, such as cataloguing, interlibrary loan, training, and the creation of new tools for research. Meetings are held annually, every third year as international congresses.

In 1991 IAML had about 1,850 members, individuals and institutions, in 40 countries. It had national branches in 19 of those countries. National branches are entitled to send representatives to the IAML Council, the governing body. IAML is organized into Professional Branches and Subject Commissions, each also represented on the Council and each reflecting its primary concerns and areas of activity. The Professional Branches include Broadcasting and Orchestra Libraries, Public Libraries, Research Libraries, Libraries in Music Teaching Institutions, and Music Information Centres. There are Subject Commissions on Archives, Audio-Visual Material, Bibliography, Cataloguing, and Service and Training. Each commission has its own goals and projects and at the same time interacts with others to refine ideas and enhance productivity.

IAML has played a central role in the implementation and publication of the "four R's" of international musicology: Répertoire international des sources musicales (RISM); Répertoire international de littérature musicale (RILM); Répertoire international d'iconographie musicale (RIdIM); and Répertoire international de la presse musicale (RIPM).

RISM, founded in 1952, is concerned with gathering and publishing bibliographies of all sources in music and music literature to 1800—from the writings of the Hebrew and Greek theorists, through vast repertories of monophonic and polyphonic music and writings about music through the centuries, to extant printed editions and manuscripts of Dittersdorf, Boccherini, and Michael Haydn, among others.

RILM, founded in 1966, deals with current music literature. It sponsors *RILM Abstracts* (1967–), published quarterly in New York, which contains citations to literature on music published throughout the world, accompanied by a detailed computer-generated index. *RILM Abstracts* is also available online through the Dialog database and on CD-ROM. RILM has produced a series of annotated bibliographies entitled *RILM Retrospectives,* including *Thematic Catalogues in Music, French Dissertations in Music,* and *Congress Reports in Music.*

RIdIM, established in 1971, is concerned with accumulating, classifying, cataloguing, interpreting, and reproducing visual materials relating to music; training iconologists; and publishing checklists, bibliographies, iconographies, and scholarly studies. The Research Center for Musical Iconography, founded in 1972 at the City University of New York, serves as the international RIdIM center for collecting and classifying iconographical materials.

RIPM, established in 1983, works to provide access to information found in music periodicals from the 19th century. Core journals in English, French, German, Italian, Spanish, and Dutch, 65 in all, had been selected for indexing by the early 1990s. Each RIPM title contains an annotated table of contents, an alphabetical keyword and author index for cross-referencing, and a brief outline of the journal in its historical context. RIPM had published 14 titles by 1991. The Center for Studies in Nineteenth-Century Music at the University of Maryland at College Park is the base of operations for this international project.

Reports on the progress of the "four R's," as well as reports of IAML congresses, conferences, and meetings, and other IAML news, reviews, and communications, are published in *Fontes Artis Musicae,* the association's quarterly journal, founded in 1954 under the editorship of Vladimir Fédorov. Other IAML or IAML-assisted publications include *Documenta Musicologica; Catalogus Musicus; Terminorum Musicae Index Septum Linguis Redactus; The Guide for Dating Early Published Music;* the *Directories of Music Research Libraries* (RISM, Series C); the *RIdIM Newsletter;* the *RILM International Thesaurus;* the RIPM annual *Periodica Musica;* professional cataloguing manuals; and various national newsletters.

IAML cooperates with the International Musicological Society (IMS) on RISM, RILM, and RIdIM projects and with the International Council of Museums on RIdIM. In addition, it actively participates in projects with the International Federation of Library Associations (IFLA) and the Unesco-sponsored International Music Council (IMC) and is a member of the International Council on Archives. IAML became a member of IFLA in 1976 and is represented on several of IFLA's Standing Committees. Under the sponsorship of the IMC, IAML took the lead in collaboration with IMS, the International Society for Music Education, and the Music Information Centres Commission in implementing a new international documentation project, the *World Inventory of Sources of Music Information* (WISMI). In addition, IAML has spawned two sister organizations, the International Association of Sound Archives (IASA) and the International Association of Music Documentation Centres (IAMIC), and has served as a model for an international association of art libraries.

REFERENCE

Barry S. Brook, "Fontes at Twenty-five—IAML at Thirty," *Fontes Artis Musicae* (1978), covers the history of IAML.

BARRY S. BROOK;
NEIL RATLIFF;
VESLEMÖY HEINTZ

International Association of School Librarianship

The International Association of School Librarianship (IASL) was founded in 1971 in Kingston, Jamaica, at the annual conference of the World Confederation of Organizations of the Teaching Profession (WCOTP). By the late 1980s there were about 1,000 personal and 30 association members. Members include librarians, media specialists, educators, publishers, and interested lay persons.

During the early 1960s school librarians and educators interested in school library service who attended WCOTP meetings discussed the need for an international forum. In 1967 the American Library Association's International Relations Committee gave the American Association of School Librarians a small grant to bring together a group of 30 educators and librarians at the Vancouver WCOTP meeting. Those present decided to establish a committee and charged it to plan a program for the 1968 meeting in Dublin and to move toward formal committee status within WCOTP. An international steering committee representing Australia, Kenya, Malaysia, Paraguay, the United Kingdom, and the United States voted in Dublin (1968) to create an ad hoc committee for school library development. Program meetings were held in Abidjan, Ivory Coast (1969), and in Sydney, Australia (1970). At Sydney the concept of an independent organization was approved in principle. A charter was drawn up; IASL was incorporated in the state of Illinois and was inaugurated in 1971 in Jamaica. The new officers were installed by the Secretary General of WCOTP, John Thompson. The first leaders were

President, Jean E. Lowrie, U.S.A.; Vice-President, Margot Nilson, Sweden; Treasurer, Phyllis Hochstettler, U.S.A.; and directors representing Australia, Canada, Jamaica, Nigeria, Singapore, and the United Kingdom.

The objectives of the Association are (1) to encourage the development of school libraries and library programs throughout all countries; (2) to promote the professional preparation of school librarians; (3) to bring about close collaboration between school libraries in all countries, including the loan and exchange of literature; (4) to encourage the development of school library materials; and (5) to initiate and coordinate activities, conferences, and other projects in the field of school librarianship.

IASL has continued its pattern of growth and contact with school library/media center persons around the world. Personal and association memberships doubled. The growth of national school library associations indicates the value of support beyond the community while new program approaches are among the significant exchanges at annual conferences. The six-country Nordic School Library Association, a regional group within IASL, has become another forum for interchange. The number of Directors was expanded to include representation from East Africa as well as Southeast Asia. Membership on the board in the mid-1980s included Australia, Canada, Denmark, Japan, Kenya, Malaysia, Nigeria, the United Kingdom, the United States, and Venezuela.

The 1980s saw an expansion of the annual conference to five full days with an optional study-tour program to allow participants an opportunity for in-depth visits in the school libraries/media centers of the host country. The conference provides opportunities for discussion on such topics as school libraries and cultural involvement, crucial issues in school library development and professional education, and educational changes and their implications for quality library service.

A conference highlight is the Association Assembly. As more associations became interested in IASL, it became evident that a more formal sharing of programs, association needs, solutions, and activities was necessary. Association members send delegates to the conferences to represent their interests and participate in meetings where they are specifically discussed. The "assembly communique" is an annual publication and provides a mechanism for sharing among all member groups. The quarterly *Newsletter* was expanded in size and continues to be the only such international publication.

The conference proceedings increased in scope to embrace new areas of interest, such as school/community libraries, networking, and computer utilization. A third revised and enlarged edition of *People to Contact for Visiting School Libraries/Media Centers,* an updated *Directory of National School Library Associations, Getting Started* (an annotated bibliography of manuals and guidelines from 10 countries), *Library Services to Isolated Schools and Communities,* and *Indicators of Quality* (a joint publication with the Illinois Association of Media Educators on evaluation techniques), are publications that were in print in the mid-1980s.

IASL continues to be responsible for the Unesco Co-Action Program 554 (Books for School Libraries in Developing Countries). It maintained its affiliation with WCOTP and issued with it an official "Policy Statement on School Libraries." IASL maintains a liaison with the School Library section of the International Federation of Library Associations, of which it is a member, cooperating with it in preparing such documents as the international guidelines for school libraries/media centers, competencies for school librarians, and other projects. IASL works informally with the International Reading Association and the International Board on Books for Young People.

A five-year plan for the future of IASL, being developed by a task force in 1985, includes an analysis for program expansion, an evaluation of objectives, and a review of implementation needs.

JEAN E. LOWRIE

International Association of Technological University Libraries

The International Association of Technological University Libraries (IATUL) was founded in Dusseldorf in May 1955 as an international forum for the exchange of ideas relevant to librarianship in technological universities throughout the world. In September 1955 it was recognized as a subsection of the International Library Associations division of IFLA. It now works in close association with the IFLA Section of Science and Technology Libraries. In 1990 IATUL formally affiliated with Unesco.

Membership is open to the libraries of universities and other higher educational institutions of science and technology. There are four categories of membership: ordinary, official observer, sustaining, and non-voting associate. Ordinary membership is open to libraries of higher educational institutions that grant doctorates in science and technology. Official observer status is available to institutions such as national libraries, patent offices, or science museum libraries, whose collections in science and technology are of research calibre. By 1991 there were 198 member libraries from 41 countries. The first IATUL Regional Group was established in North America in 1985.

The Association is governed by a Board consisting of a President, Secretary, Treasurer, First and Second Vice-Presidents, and three Board Members elected by member libraries. The Board meets twice each year.

IATUL's main goal, the exchange of views on matters of current significance in university technological libraries, is accomplished through meetings, including conferences, seminars, and regional gatherings, and through publications. The 14th Biennial Conference was held at Massachusetts Institute of Technology in Cambridge, Massachusetts, in 1991 on the theme "New Technologies and Information Services—Evolution or Revolution." The 13th Conference was held in Ljubljana in 1989. International seminars are held in Europe and North America. The themes for these meetings have included various aspects of library management, the use of information resources in science and technology, user education, interaction between technological university libraries and industry, and the effects of new technology on information handling.

Through 1986, papers presented at biennial conferences appeared in *IATUL Conference Proceedings.* A parallel publication, *IATUL Proceedings,* included both general and specific articles. From 1987 through 1991, the two publications were merged to form the *IATUL Quarterly,* which brought together papers from conferences or seminars with articles on specific themes. Examples of these themes include libraries and the history of technology, measurement of library use, library buildings, and international library cooperation. Starting in 1992, IATUL issued two publications, the *IATUL Proceedings* (New Series) and the *IATUL News,* a quarterly newsletter.

REFERENCES

D. Schmidmaier, "The History of the International Association of Technological University Libraries," *IATUL Proceedings* (1976).

Dennis Shaw, "IATUL and Library Cooperation," *IATUL Quarterly* (1989).

NANCY FJÄLLBRANT

International Board on Books for Young People

The International Board on Books for Young People (IBBY) is the only international organization related to professional work in all disciplines concerned with the creation, promotion, study, and reading of children's literature.

Founded in Zurich in 1953 by Jella Lepman, then Director of the International Youth Library, it grew in membership from a few Western European sections to some 50 National Sections spread throughout the world by 1990. Individual members represent IBBY in countries where there is no National Section. The United States Board on Books for Young People, Inc., was established in 1984 to combine responsibilities that were formerly shared by the U.S. National Section of IBBY and the Friends of IBBY, Inc. The U.S. Board is a nonprofit, tax-exempt organization. It publishes a semi-annual *Newsletter.*

Purpose. IBBY's aims include (1) bringing together persons concerned about good books for young people; (2) promoting the availability of such books and access to them by encouraging their production to fit worldwide needs, associating them with communications media, such as radio, television, the press, films, and recordings, and encouraging the growth of libraries for the young; (3) encouraging translations and assisting in making available books of international quality; (4) initiating, encouraging, or advancing research in children's literature and its illustration and organizing the publication of the results of such research on an international scale; and (5) advising international or national individuals, groups, institutions, or organizations on books for the young and on the training of librarians, teachers, editors, writers, or illustrators.

Programs. *National Activities.* The National Sections present national awards, compile lists of best books of the year, organize exhibits, book weeks, seminars, and conferences, and celebrate IBBY's International Children's Book Day around April 2 (Hans Christian Andersen's birthday). For that day, National Sections serve in turn as sponsors, supplying an author's message and an artist's poster made available internationally.

International Activities. Of first significance on the international level are IBBY's biennial Hans Christian Andersen Medals, one for an author, presented first in 1956, and another for an illustrator, introduced in 1966. An IBBY Honour List presents books for a two-year period in three categories: text, illustration, and translation. The IBBY-Asahi Reading Promotion Award, co-sponsored by the Japanese newspaper publisher Asahi Shimbun since 1987, is presented every other year to a group or institution that is making a significant contribution in developing book programs for children and young adults. The award is endowed with the sum of one million yen.

IBBY participates in the publication of the quarterly *Bookbird,* edited at the International Institute for Children's Literature in Vienna and published by the Arnis Forlag in Denmark. It features articles, lists of outstanding books, reviews of professional works, and news of national and international conferences and prizes.

IBBY's biennial congress moves from country to country. In 1984 the Cypriot Section of IBBY hosted the 19th congress in Nicosia, dealing with children's book production and distribution in Third World countries. The theme for the 20th congress (Tokyo, 1986) was "Why do you write for children? Children, why do you read?" The 1988 congress in Oslo focused attention on the new media. The 1990 congress marked International Literacy Year: "Literacy through literature: Children's books make a difference." IBBY scheduled its 1992 congress for Berlin.

Supported by Unesco, IBBY organizes workshops on the writing and illustration, production, publishing, and distribution of children's books. Such workshops have been held in Costa Rica, Kenya, Argentina, Ghana, Mexico, and Colombia, and were planned for Mali and Egypt in the early 1990s.

IBBY has its own stand each year at the International Children's Book Fair in Bologna and exhibits at other international book fairs. IBBY representatives meet experts from all parts of the world at these fairs, creating interest in the Board's work and strengthening its visibility and influence.

IBBY has consultative relations with Unicef and Unesco. It is a member of the International Book Committee and the International Federation of Library Associations and cooperates with the International Reading Association in joint projects. Cooperation with the Norwegian Institute for Special Education resulted in three projects dealing with books for and about handicapped children, sponsored by Unesco.

LEENA MAISSEN

International Council of Scientific Unions

In 1931 the final Assembly of the International Research Council (IRC) became the first Assembly of the International Council of Scientific Unions (ICSU). The IRC had been founded in 1919 as an outgrowth of the earlier International Association of Academies, which had its first meeting in 1899. ICSU has two types of members, the International Scientific Unions, of which there were 20 in 1990; and the National Members, including academies of science and science research councils, among others, of which there were 75. There were also 29 Scientific Associates.

The principal objectives of the Council are (1) to encourage international scientific activity for the benefit of humankind; (2) to facilitate and coordinate the activities of the International Scientific Unions; (3) to stimulate, design, and coordinate international interdisciplinary scientific research projects; and (4) to facilitate the coordination of the international scientific activities of its National Members.

In addition to the International Scientific Unions, each of which has its own objectives and structure, ICSU functions through a series of Scientific and Special Committees, Inter-Union Commissions, Permanent Services, and other groups. These are concerned with interdisciplinary and inter-Union activities, such as the International Geophysical Year, launched by ICSU in 1957, and the International Biological Program (1964–74), the results of which were published in a series of 30 volumes.

The ICSU meets every three years in General Assembly with representatives of the National and Scientific Union Members and of all the subsidiary bodies. The General Committee—composed of 20 representatives from the Scientific Unions, 13 from the National Members, and the Officers—meets every year. The Secretariat of ICSU is at the Hôtel de Noailles, Paris, made available by the French Ministry of Education. Secretariats of six other ICSU bodies, including those of the Committee on Data for Science and Technology (CODATA) and of the International Council for Scientific and Technological Information (ICSTI) formerly the ICSU Abstracting Board, are also housed there. The other Secretariats, of the unions, committees, commissions, and others, are spread throughout the world.

From time to time ICSU organizes meetings of representatives of the members of the ICSU family involved in scientific information, documentation, libraries, and other activities, such as CODATA, ICSTI, the Federation of Astronomical and Geophysical Services, the World Data Centres Panel (WDC), several of the Scientific Associates, and a number of other such organizations to discuss future projects, ensure cooperation, and try to avoid unnecessary duplication.

ICSU in the mid-1980s had a joint Global Atmospheric Research Program and a joint World Climate Research Program with the World Meteorological Organization (WMO). In 1986 it set up the International Geosphere-Biosphere Program: A Study of Global Change (IGBP).

In cooperation with Unesco's PGI, the Third World Academy of Sciences, and other partners, including the American Association for the Advancement of Science, ICSU began working on an initiative to set up a joint network of scientific journal donation programs to enhance the availability of such literature to developing countries.

The ICSU *Year Book* provides information about the various members of the ICSU family and the addresses of the officers of these bodies. *Science International,* the ICSU newsletter, provides information about ongoing activities in the ICSU.

M. T. L. MILLWARD

International Council on Archives

The International Council on Archives (ICA) was founded in May 1948 at a meeting convened by Unesco to establish a worldwide organization of the archival profession. A provisional constitution was adopted, and the first International Congress on Archives met in Paris (1950) to establish the ICA formally.

ICA was created to improve the worldwide standards of archival administration and practice and to advance archival theory. The Council aids professional relations among archival institutions and organizations in order to stimulate the interchange of ideas and information, to solve archival problems, to ensure the physical preservation of mankind's archival heritage, and to support archival development and training in all countries.

The concerns and issues of the international archival community, as expressed in ICA publications and meetings, include the intellectual control of records, preservation, microreproduction, greater access to archives, and technological advances in the creation, control, and preservation of archives. The programs of the Council emanating from these goals are implemented by the ICA congresses, sections, regional branches, standing and ad hoc committees and working groups, and the Secretariat.

The membership of ICA is composed of public archival authorities on international, national, and subnational levels (category A members); professional associations (category B); state, local, and private institutions (category C); individuals (category D); and honorary members (category E).

In 1991 there were 1,105 members of ICA, including the national archival authorities of 132 countries. Sections have been established for professional associations (41 members), municipal archives (155 members), archivists of international organizations (53 members), archival education and training (70 members), and business and labor archives (85 members).

Nine regional branches of ICA in the Third World work to develop archival institutions and staff as integral parts of the information systems in those countries. The regional branches are Asociación Lationamericana de Archivos (ALA), Arab Regional Branch (ARBICA), Caribbean Regional Branch (CARBICA), Central African Regional Branch (CENARBICA), East and South African Regional Branch (ESARBICA), Pacific Regional Branch (PARBICA), Southeast Asian Regional Branch (SARBICA), South and West Asian Regional Branch (SWARBICA), and West African Regional Branch (WARBICA). These branch organizations sponsor conferences, seminars, and publications to make known the need for sound archival programs, to preserve the national heritages of the member countries, and to educate archivists, librarians, government officials, and the general public.

The governing bodies of the ICA are the General Assembly, the Executive Committee, and the Bureau of the Council. The General Assembly meets once every four years during the International Congresses on Archives to conduct the business activities of the Council, elect officers, and act on resolutions and recommendations concerning the professional interests of the worldwide archival community.

The Executive Committee is vested with governing powers for the years between General Assembly meetings. It is composed of the ICA officers, 14 elected members, and the chairmen of regional branches, who are ex officio members. The Bureau, a smaller governing body made up of the ICA officers, meets as often as necessary between the annual sessions of the Executive Committee to expedite the business of the Council and to advise the Secretariat of ICA. The Executive Director is in Paris and coordinates the programs of the Council and maintains liaison with Unesco and other international organizations.

ICA's development program is conducted and its development fund is managed by a Commission for Archival Development.

The ICA professional structure includes, in addition to the five Sections, committees on Automation, Current Records, Conservation, Reprography, Archives Buildings and Equipment, Sigillography, and Literature and Art Archives and Working Groups on Architectural Records and Archives of Science and Technology. Committees and sections hold annual meetings on topics of major professional interest. The papers produced through these activities are published in *Janus* or in the series of *ICA Studies*.

The International Congresses on Archives are the quadrennial meetings of ICA; subjects selected by the Executive Committee and the national organizing committee are discussed. Reports, prepared by specialists on the basis of original research and international inquiries, are presented at the plenary sessions and are followed by discussions and interventions. Congresses were held in London in 1980, in Bonn in 1984, and in Paris in 1988. The 1992 Congress was held in Montreal, with the overall theme of The Profession of the Archivist in the Information Age.

In 1954 the President of ICA, Charles Braibant (France), decided to convene an annual meeting of the leaders of the profession (directors of national archival institutions and presidents of national archival associations). These meetings, called the International Round Table Conferences on Archives, are held each year when an international congress is not held to study one or two major problems of archival administration. The 1990 Round Table Conference, held in Dresden, Germany, discussed "Archives and Archivists Serving the Protection of Cultural and National Heritages." The 1991 Conference met in Haarlem, the Netherlands, with the theme of "Financing Archival Services."

The International Council on Archives has associate and consultative relations with Unesco as a Category A international nongovernmental organization. ICA cooperates closely with the General Information Program of Unesco in implementing RAMP (Records and Archives Management Program) by preparing studies and guidelines, organizing international regional seminars, and carrying out consultant missions in developing countries. ICA cooperates with a number of international nongovernmental organizations operating in neighboring fields, among them IFLA, the International Federation for Documentation (FID), FIAF (for film archives), IFTA (for television archives), IASA (for sound archives), ICAM (for architectural museums), and CIBAL (for Balkan history).

The Council publishes a number of journals and volumes for the international community of archivists. *Archivum* is an annual journal devoted to special topics. The *ICA Bulletin* is a semiannual newsletter of ICA programs and meetings. The Council, with the assistance of Unesco, also publishes studies and handbooks on such topics as microfilming, archival buildings, access policies, professional training, and restoration techniques. ICA and Unesco have also cooperated in publishing a series of archival guides entitled *Guide to the Sources for the History of Nations*. By 1991, 39 volumes were published in three series: 12 volumes for Latin American, 14 volumes for Africa south of the Sahara, and 13 volumes for North Africa, Asia, and Oceania. These guides are intended to facilitate research in the histories of nations. The project of a General Guide to the Archives of Asia started in 1979 with the participation of twelve Asian countries. ICA cooperates with Unesco in organizing and implementing an international microfilming program for the reconstruction of the archival heritage of developing countries.

REFERENCES

F. B. Evans, "Archives and Research: a study in international cooperation," in *Miscellanea Carlos Wyffels* (1986).

J. B. Rhoads, "North American Contributions to International Archival Endeavors," ibid.

E. G. Franz, "Der Internationale Archivrat: Vergangenheit, Gegenwart, Zukunft," *Archivum* (1982).

JAMES B. RHOADS;
CHARLES KECSKEMETI

International Federation for Documentation

The Fédération Internationale de Documentation (FID), an international, not-for-profit, nongovernmental organization, was founded in September 1895 as the Institut International de Bibliographie (IIB). The IIB was one of the resolutions resulting from the Conférence Internationale de Bibliographie, assembled by Paul Otlet and Henri La Fontaine, the two persons regarded as the founders of FID. The objectives of that conference, held under the sponsorship of the Belgian government, were to establish the Institut, to create a Répertoire Bibliographique Universel (RBU) classified according to the Dewey Decimal Classification, and to form a Bibliographic Union among governments.

Membership. The members of IIB could be individuals, institutions, or associations, and there was no limit placed upon the size of the membership. This pattern of membership remained until after World War I. Today FID is composed of national members, only one being accepted from each country, and international members, international organizations active in the field of documentation. Apart from national and international members, FID accepts associates, interim members, and institutional and personal affiliates. The membership at the beginning of 1985 was 67 national members and 1 international member. In addition there were 234 affiliates from 59 countries (15 not represented by national members).

Purpose. When the IIB was founded, its essential functions were "to provide encouragement for the study of classification in general and to promote a uniform and international system of classification in particular." The purpose of FID has broadened in the ensuing years, and the original objectives of the IIB are now only a part of the Federation's purpose. Today the aim and nature of FID, as summarized in the preamble of its statutes, is "to promote, through international cooperation, research in and development of documentation, which includes inter alia the organization, storage, retrieval, dissemination, and evaluation of information, however recorded, in the fields of science, technology, social sciences, arts, and humanities.

"The nature of the Federation has been and should continue to be principally that of a federation of national members. This means that the principal responsibility in the government of the Federation remains in the hands of bodies representative of various countries, whereas it is agreed that individuals participate as specialists in the work of the Federation."

FID cannot handle the whole range of problems of documentation and information that call for study and action within that broad aim. Priority fields and activities are defined so that FID handles them effectively, taking into account information programs of related intergovernmental and nongovernmental organizations, such as Unesco and IFLA, among others.

History. The two major interests of the founders of the IIB were the development of the Decimal Classification and the Universal Bibliographic Repertory (RBU). The two were not developed independently, and the former resulted in the subsequent development of the Universal Decimal Classification (UDC). The first complete edition of the UDC was published in French in 1905 as IIB publication 63 and bore the title *Manuel du répertoire bibliographique universel.*

Because of World War I, the IIB remained stagnant for a number of years, but 1924 marked a turning point. The Institut was reorganized and became a federation with five national members: Belgium, France, Germany, the Netherlands, and Switzerland. Up to the time of the war the IIB had remained an international organization made up of individual and organizational members. The reorganization of the Institut changed its emphasis, and the UDC became only one of its tasks. At the same time, the UDC was recognized as having achieved an enhanced importance in the affairs of the IIB. The Classification Committee, which was formed in 1921, became in 1924 the official body through which the IIB exercised its control over the UDC. The Dutch national member, Nederlands Instituut voor Documentatie en Registratuur (NIDER), assumed the Secretariat for the Committee, and Frits Donker Duyvis, who was later to serve as FID Secretary General for many years, was appointed Secretary.

In 1931 the IIB became the Institut International de Documentation (IID), a name that continued until the present name was adopted in 1938. The 1931 name change, to incorporate the word *documentation,* signaled a clear separation from the word *bibliography* (work on the RBU had long since ceased) and an emphasis on practical aspects.

For almost 30 years the FID Secretariat was housed in Brussels with the Office International de Bibliographie, a semigovernmental Belgian organization. After 1924 the Netherlands and Belgium shared the Secretariat until 1938, when it was completely taken over by The Hague, and F. Donker Duyvis became the sole Secretary General—a position he had shared with the founders from 1924 to 1938.

Organization and Structure. By the end of World War II FID had added only three new national members to the first five of 1924. With the increased interest in documentation in the postwar years, membership gradually increased, and by 1958 there were 28 national members, including 7 outside Europe, making FID truly a world organization. The first committees other than the Classification Committee and its subcommittees were also established. Ten FID committees in 1985 helped to carry out the FID professional program: FID/CCC, Central Classification Committee, along with its 30 subcommittees for revising the UDC; FID/CR, Classification Research; FID/DT, Terminology of Information and Documentation; FID/ET, Education and Training; FID/II, Information for Industry; FID/IM, Informetrics; FID/LD, Linguistics in Documentation; FID/PD, Patent Information and Documentation; FID/RI, Research on the Theoretical Basis of Information; and FID/SD, Social Sciences Documentation. There are a Working Group, FID/BSO, Broad System of Ordering, and Task Forces on FID/IS/NW, Information Systems and Network Design and Management, and FID/SUN, Study of User Needs.

During 1984 FID commissioned a study of the management of the UDC by an external consultant, and in September 1984 appointed a UDC Management Group for the UDC.

FID established two regional commissions, FID/CLA, Latin American Commission (1960), and FID/CAO, Asia and Oceania (1968). The two commissions, in turn, have several of their own committees that assist in carrying out regional programs: in Latin America CLA/UDC Universal Decimal Classification, CLA/CCN National Union Catalogues, CLA/ET Education and Training, and CLA/II Information for Industry; in Asia CAO/II Information for Secondary Industry. In the mid-1980s FID was developing a program for the African region.

The highest authority of the FID is the General Assembly, which meets biennially and is composed of representatives of national and international members. The FID Council meets twice yearly to carry out the decisions of the General Assembly. The Council is composed of the President, 3 Vice-Presidents, the Treasurer, 14 Councillors (including the Presidents of regional commissions), and ex-officio the Secretary General. Between meetings of the Council the Executive Committee, made up of the officers and the Secretary General, may meet if there is a need. The daily operation of the Federation is handled through its Secretariat in The Hague and through the secretariats of the regional commissions.

Program. In 1978 the FID General Assembly meeting in Edinburgh accepted a new program structure for FID. Under it, the first Medium Term Program (MTP) was developed for the period 1981–84. Five priorities for action were identified in the Medium Term Program. They are: Theoretical and linguistic basis of information science (including terminology); information processing and technology; education and training of information specialists and information users; information system and network design and management; and information needs and habits of users.

A second Medium Term Program for the period 1983–86 was approved in 1982. A Program Planning Group was appointed by Council in 1984 to prepare the next MTP for the FID program up to 1990.

Publications. In addition to an active monograph publications program, FID publishes the monthly FID *News Bulletin,* the quarterly *International Forum on Information and Documentation* (in Russian and English), *R & D Projects in Documentation and Librarianship* (bimonthly), and *The Extensions and Corrections to the UDC* (annual). The *Bulletin* includes two special quarterly supplements: the "Document Delivery and Reproduction Survey" and the "Newsletter on Education and Training Programmes for Information Personnel." The biennial FID *Directory,* replacing the former *Yearbook,* provides information on membership, committees, and historical information on the Federation. Annual reports have been issued since 1983.

Relations with Other Organizations. FID cooperates with the programs of several other international organizations: the Unesco General Information Program (PGI), the World Intellectual Property Organization (WIPO), the International Federation of Library Associations (IFLA), the International Council of Archives (ICA), and the International Organization for Standardization (ISO).

REFERENCES

W. Boyd Rayward, *The Universe of Information: The Work of Paul Otlet for Documentation and International Organizations* (1975).

The ALA *Yearbook of Library and Information Services* and the FID *Annual Report* provide summaries of the activities of each year.

FID Publications: An 80-Year Bibliography 1895–1975 and the current list of FID's *Publications* provide a bibliographical survey of many publications.

STELLA KEENAN

International Federation of Library Associations and Institutions

History. The 50th anniversary Conference of the American Library Association in Atlantic City and Philadelphia in 1926 marked the beginning of the concept of an international library organization. Three months earlier, at the International Congress of Librarians and Bookmakers in Prague, Gabriel Henry, who has been called the spiritual father of IFLA (at that time President of the Association des bibliothècaires français and also professor at the American Library School in Paris), had voiced an appeal to set up an international committee to represent all the national library associations on a permanent basis. The idea materialized in Edinburgh on September 30, 1927, during the celebration of the 50th anniversary of the Library Association of the United Kingdom, when representatives of library associations from 15 countries signed a resolution that can be regarded as the founding of IFLA. Isak Collijn, the Swedish National Librarian, was elected first President. The most skillful negotiator was Carl H. Milam, Secretary of ALA, who agreed to draft the statutes. The first IFLA Constitution was approved in Rome in 1929 during the first World Congress of Librarianship and Bibliography, which took place under IFLA auspices.

The new organization was predominantly an association of library associations, aiming at the organization of regular world conferences. Originally, IFLA was a meeting point for leading librarians from Europe and America and continued as such for a long time. In the early years notable personalities—true representatives of their profession—defined IFLA's profile. It became a kind of "conference family," where personal friendships led to close cooperation in such areas as international loan and exchange, bibliographical standardization, and library education.

At the first IFLA session outside Europe (Chicago, 1933), the second IFLA President, William Warner Bishop, acted as host. During five years as President, he guided IFLA through the first years of economic crisis as membership reached 41 associations from 31 countries, including several library associations from outside Europe and the U.S. (China, India, Japan, Mexico, Philippines). IFLA could not yet boast of true universal international membership, however. That was not to be achieved for 40 years.

Marcel Godet, Director of the Swiss National Library at Berne, was IFLA's third President, from 1936 to 1947. Through Godet and Secretary A. C. Breycha-Vauthier, IFLA took part in the Advisory Committee on Literature for Prisoners-of-War and Internees, which distributed significant numbers of books to various camps. (Breycha-Vauthier also worked at the League of Nations Library at Geneva during the war.)

IFLA's first session following World War II was at Oslo in 1947. Funded by a grant from the Rockefeller Foundation, it was attended by 52 delegates from 18 countries. One important result of this conference was a formal agreement between IFLA and Unesco concerning future cooperation (IFLA has Consultative Status A with Unesco). In 1948 they organized an International Summer School on Public Library Practice in Manchester, attended by 50 librarians from 21 countries who from that time worked to better public librarianship (the first standards for public libraries were a result of this cooperation). Another Oslo resolution of lasting significance was the recommendation to accept an international format for catalogue cards.

In the postwar period IFLA developed slowly, perhaps too slowly, because its structure and lack of funds hampered effectiveness. Its profile was still defined by individuals who gave their time and expertise to IFLA during meetings, but who turned their attention between meetings to their national duties. From 1951 a series of proposals for reorganization was launched, based on a fundamental criticism about the lack of constructive programs, but they were too vague to lead to concrete results. By 1958 IFLA had grown to 64 member associations from 42 countries. The organization was basically similar to its prewar antecedent until the International Conference on Cataloguing Principles (Paris, 1961), for which the Council on Library Resources allotted a grant of $20,000, generated major activity for IFLA in the cataloguing field.

In 1962 IFLA's first permanent central secretariat was established by a Unesco grant; Anthony Thompson became the first full-time IFLA Secretary General. During this time IFLA began to exhibit real strength in the realm of programming; in 1963 the Federation published *Libraries in the World,* a long-term program for IFLA, which distinguished itself by an imaginative and realistic view of IFLA's future development. Attributed mainly to Leendert Brummel, it was also the work of Sir Frank Francis, F. G. B. Hutchings, and Herman Liebaers. Gradually the importance of sections for types of libraries and committees for types of library activity increased, enabling IFLA to react adequately to urgent library problems. IFLA's firmness of purpose became exemplary and resulted in steady growth. When Thompson resigned in 1970, the Federation had 250 members in 52 countries.

In 1971 an energetic President, Herman Liebaers, National Librarian of Belgium, moved the Secretariat to The Hague. As President he managed to interest several funding bodies in the work of IFLA. He launched the UBC (Universal Bibliographic Control) program and brought the librarians of the Third World into IFLA. With support from the Council on Library Resources, a small, effective Secretariat was strengthened at The Hague, and a permanent office for UBC was set up in London. A regional office at Kuala Lumpur in Malaysia was founded with assistance from the Canadian International Development Agency, and a program for the various world regions was developed.

When Liebaers left IFLA and the library profession in 1974, IFLA could claim virtually universal international membership with 600 members in 100 countries. Liebaers had the vision and drive necessary to adapt IFLA to the demands of modern society. He also had the foresight to use the services of a Program Development Group, a core of experts who paved the way for some major IFLA projects (such as Universal Availability of Publications and public library development) but who also had a keen eye for smaller, but nevertheless valuable, projects. This group would later develop into a statutory Professional Board.

In 1987 additional light was shed upon IFLA's early history when the archives (correspondence, minutes, financial records, and notes) belonging to the Federation and covering the period from 1926 to 1945 were discovered at the United Nations Library in Geneva. A French library student subsequently inventoried and catalogued the documents and based his Master's thesis on IFLA's activities during World War II.

Organization and Structure. After years of sometimes heated discussions, a new structure for IFLA was approved by the Council in Lausanne in 1976. The new Statutes define the purpose as follows:

> to promote international understanding, cooperation, discussion, research, and development in all fields of library activity, including bibliography, information services, and the education of personnel, and to provide a body through which librarianship can be represented in matters of international interest.

Membership. The name of the organization was expanded to include *institutions* (libraries, library schools, and bibliographic institutes). It became the International Federation of Library Associations and Institutions (IFLA). Since 1976 IFLA has had two main categories of members, Association and Institutional. Both have voting rights in all matters and meetings. However, in Council meetings Association Members have more votes than Institutional Members, at least 51 percent, with 7 to 35 votes for the joint Association Members in any one country. Relatively new categories are Personal Affiliate and Sustaining Affiliate, with no voting rights. There is also the opportunity for Consultative Status for related international organizations. Among those with Consultative Status are FID (International Federation for Documentation), ICA (International Council on Archives), ICAE (International Council on Adult Education), ISO (International Organization for Standardization), IPA (International Publishers Association), and ISDS (International Serials Data System). Other international organizations, mainly concerned with librarianship, tend to join IFLA as International Association Members with voting rights; for example, IAML (International Association of Music Libraries), IATUL (International Association of Technological University Libraries), COMLA (Commonwealth Library Association), LIBER (Ligue des Bibliothèques Européennes de Recherche), EFHIL (European Foundation for Health Information and Libraries), and ACURIL (Association of Caribbean University Research and Institutional Libraries). INTAMEL (International Association of Metropolitan Cities Libraries) functions as a Round Table in IFLA.

IFLA

IFLA commemorative stamp, issued on the occasion of its 50th anniversary, Brussels, 1977.

Steering Bodies. The main steering bodies as defined by the Statutes are the Executive and Professional boards; the first has full powers of administration and management and the second deals with coordinating and planning professional activities. The Executive Board consists of an elected President and seven elected members, with the Chairperson of the Professional Board serving as an ex-officio member. The Professional Board is composed of the Chairpersons of the eight Divisions, plus a Chairperson elected from the outgoing Professional Board by the incoming Board members.

In the 1970s and 1980s IFLA set up a number of subject-oriented Core Programs. These programs, explained in more detail below, are: Universal Biblio-

IFLA

Poster advertising IFLA's activities for prisoners-of-war during World War II.

graphic Control and International MARC (UBCIM), Universal Availability of Publications (UAP), Preservation and Conservation (PAC), Universal Dataflow and Telecommunications (UDT), and Advancement of Librarianship in the Third World (ALP). In May 1979 the Executive Board—at that time headed by Preben Kirkegaard—decided to establish a Program Management Committee to coordinate and manage IFLA's Core Programs, including their objectives, financing, and functions, and also to facilitate the liaison of those programs with the work of the Sections and Divisions.

In 1983 the Council (since 1977 convened in odd years only) approved the *IFLA Perspectives,* a document in which the Executive Board defined the Core Programs and their functioning. These Perspectives were the result of the deliberations of a Task Force convened by Else Granheim, IFLA President from 1979 to 1985.

In 1990, at the request of then-President Hans-Peter Geh, the Executive and Professional Boards set up a Task Force to carry out an examination of the steering, managerial, and advisory structures and coordination of IFLA's professional program, including the Professional Board, the Program Management Committee, Core Programs and their Advisory Committees, the Divisions, Sections, and Round Tables, ALP, and IFLA Headquarters. The Task Force was to look at these bodies and their relationship with the information profession at large, with a view to clarifying roles, simplifying and reducing administrative overheads, strengthening cooperation, and effectively integrating all the professional work of IFLA. The new structure, as approved by Council in 1991, is outlined in the accompanying diagram.

Subunits. In the new IFLA the Sections can be considered the grassroots of the organization; they are grouped together in Divisions for coordination. Members and affiliates register for the Sections of their choice and can nominate and elect persons for membership on Standing Committees, the core groups of experts that develop the program of the Section and ensure its execution. The Chairpersons and Secretaries of the Sections form the Coordinating Board of the Division to which they belong. The Chairpersons of the Divisional Coordinating Boards form the Professional Board.

In the professional field, IFLA has two other, less formal, means for the performance of professional tasks: Round Tables and Working Groups.

Headquarters. The Federation is headquartered in the Royal Library, The Hague, Netherlands. The staff consists of the Secretary General, the Coordinator of Professional Activities, an Executive Officer, and five administrative staff members. They are responsible for the daily management of the organization, liaison with related organizations, coordination of professional groups and units within IFLA, maintaining the secretariats of the Executive and Professional Boards, and issuing periodical publications.

Each Core Program is hosted by a national library that serves as the International Focal Point for it. The Core Program Focal Points can be found in Washington, D.C. (PAC), Boston Spa in the north of England (UAP), Frankfurt (UBCIM), Ottawa (UDT), and Uppsala (ALP). Regional offices, which serve as extensions of IFLA Headquarters, are maintained in Dakar, São Paulo, and Bangkok.

Programs. The Medium-Term Program 1992–1997 describes a variety of activities based on two approaches. Library operations can be looked at from two points of view, one treating all operations as elements in the functioning of an integrated whole—the library; the other viewing each operation as a separate activity with its own techniques. These approaches have been expressed in IFLA by the growth of two kinds of groups, one consisting of librarians responsible for a particular type of library and another consisting of librarians concerned with the techniques appropriate to a particular operation that is common to various types of libraries. The 32 Sections of IFLA, with the additional Round Tables and Working Groups, all have their own programs, ranging from sophisticated university library management studies to the professional training of school librarians, from the establishment of regional braille centers in the Third World to the availability of official publications, and from the improvement of the status and image of the library and information profession to the development of public library work. There are also Five Core Programs whose work cuts across the Sections, and IFLA actively encourages cooperation among Sections.

UBCIM. IFLA's international program for UBCIM (Universal Bibliographic Control and International MARC) has concentrated on the development of International Standard Bibliographic Descriptions (ISBDs), UNIMARC formats, and publications dealing with machine-readable cataloguing and the exchange of bibliographic records. Activities completed in the late 1980s and early 1990s include a study sponsored by the Commission of the European Community to facilitate the international exchange of bibliographic records and to establish the feasibility of using UNIMARC among the national libraries of the European Community, based on their present computer facilities; and a workshop to investigate the possibilities for the exchange of bibliographic data by conversion from CCF (Common Communication Format) records to UNIMARC or from UNIMARC records to CCF.

UAP. IFLA's international program for UAP (Universal Availability of Publications) has as its guiding principle that each country should be responsible for supplying its own publications by loan or photocopy on request to other countries. The program encompasses such matters as interlibrary lending systems, exchange of publications, legal deposit, copyright, and cooperative acquisition schemes. The scope of the program was extended to examining the barriers to making documents available in formats appropriate to the reader's needs. Publicity, research, and guidance and advice to others have played a large part in the initial development of the program. Additional research will include an extensive study of the role of national libraries in the new information environment—that is, examining the use of new technologies as well as their collection policies with regard to nonprint materials, ranging from sound and film to electronic publishing. The program is also taking an active interest in the role of copyright law and its effects on availability and is associated with an examination of copyright in electronic formats through a European Community initiative entitled CITED (Copyright in Electronically Transmitted Text).

IMP. The International MARC Program, established officially in 1983, consists of two main project components. The first, in the Deutsche Bibliothek in Frankfurt, is concerned mainly with International MARC applications, including technical feasibility studies and UNIMARC testing. The second, housed at the British Library in London, is primarily responsible for the continuous maintenance, revision, and development of the UNIMARC format on the basis of the *UNIMARC Handbook,* for feasibility studies for the most effective methods of international transfer of bibliographic data, and for the preparation of the third edition of the UNIMARC format.

PAC. The Preservation and Conservation core program was established with the aim of promoting solutions to the serious problems of physical deterioration of library and information materials. All facets of the program are oriented toward establishing an international milieu in which preservation activities can flourish and through which preservation information can flow. The program has established regional centers in Leipzig, Sable, Tokyo, Canberra, and Venezuela that work with the Library of Congress (the International Focal Point) by assisting with its projects, by publicizing its goals and activities, and by representing the preservation needs of the region to it.

UDT. The Universal Dataflow Telecommunications Program works to promote the electronic transfer of data between libraries and their users; to reduce telecommunications barriers; and to monitor development, provide information, and support the promotion, implementation, and use of compatible international standards for library-specific applications of electronic data communications.

ALP. Consultations on development of the Advancement of Librarianship in the Third World started during the 1984 IFLA Nairobi Conference. The ALP Core Program received new impetus with the establishment of an International Focal Point at Uppsala University in 1990. The objectives of ALP are to promote the progressive improvement of library and information services in developing countries so as to enable them to play an active role in national development. The most important program areas of ALP are: education and training; promotion of library and information services to the public, with particular attention to the needs of rural and urban marginal areas; and greater identification and involvement of libraries with literacy programs. The subject-oriented Core Programs and the Divisions, Sections, and Round Tables will continue to execute a substantial number of projects and other activities for developing countries.

Conferences and Meetings. To carry out IFLA's projects and activities, the importance of regular personal contact must not be underestimated. IFLA holds General Conferences each year, with more than 150 professional meetings during the conferences. Every second year (in odd years) such conferences are combined with Council meetings, where IFLA's business affairs (elections, budget, and rules) are dealt with. Venues were Brighton, 1987; Sydney, 1988; Paris, 1989; Stockholm, 1990; and Moscow, 1991. Conferences were scheduled for New Delhi, 1992; Barcelona, 1993; Havana, 1994; Istanbul, 1995; and Beijing, 1996. To celebrate IFLA's 75th anniversary, the year 2002 has been reserved for Edinburgh, the site of IFLA's first meeting in 1927.

Publications. Periodical publications of the Federation are the quarterly *IFLA Journal* and *International Cataloguing and Bibliographic Control; IFLA Annual,* issued yearly; and *IFLA Directory,* issued biennially.

IFLA Publications is a monograph series, published by K. G. Saur (Munich, London, New York, and Paris). Titles issued in this series included *World Guide to Library, Archive, and Information Science Associations; Education and Training for Conservation and Preservation; Reference Services for Publications of Intergovernmental Organizations; Managing the Preservation of Serial Literature;* and *Library Buildings: Preparations for Planning.*

A new series, *IFLA Professional Reports,* published by IFLA Headquarters under the auspices of the Professional Board, was started in 1984 to ensure that the results of IFLA professional projects reached the wider audience for which they were intended. Titles issued in this series included *Guidelines for Library Services to Deaf People, Guidelines for Children's Services, Guidelines for School Libraries,* and *Standards for University Libraries.*

Publications have also been issued under the auspices of the Core Programs. UBCIM's publications include the *International Standard Bibliographic Descriptions* (general, monographic publications, serials, nonbook materials, cartographic materials, computer files, antiquarian, and printed music) plus *Management and Use of Name Authority Files, International Guide to MARC Databases and Services, UNIMARC Manual,* and *Standard Practices in the Preparation of Bibliographic Records.* UAP's titles include: *The Impact of New Technology on Document Availability and Access* and *Guidelines for National Planning for the Availability of Publications.* UDT has begun a series on Data Communications Technologies and Standards for Libraries. Topics covered in the series are electronic document delivery, organizational aspects of OSI (Open Systems Interconnection) for libraries, and packet radio technology.

All Core Programs and many Divisions, Sections, and Round Tables issue newsletters to keep the library community regularly informed on new developments, activities, and projects they have undertaken or coordinated.

REFERENCES

IFLA's First Fifty years: Achievement and Challenge in International Librarianship, edited by W. R. H. Koops and J. Wieder (1977).

IFLA and Contemporary Library Problems, special issue of *IFLA Journal* (1977).

Frédéric Saby, "Le livre objet de liberté: aperçu sur l'activité pendant la seconde guerre mondiale, au sein du Comité consultatif de la Croix-Rouge pour la lecture des prisonniers et internés de guerre," *IFLA Journal* (1989).

CAROL HENRY

International Library and Bibliographical Organizations

International library and bibliographic organizations now fulfill a wide range of functions. Among these functions are: (1) regulating the loan or exchange of documentary materials; (2) regulating international commerce related to these materials (postal and tariff regulations, copyright agreements, publishing and distributing rights, and censorship); (3) generating, standardizing, exchanging, or publishing bibliographic data in various formats for books and non-book publications and indexing and abstracting data for journal articles and related materials; (4) creating, maintaining, and operating international information systems of various kinds; (5) providing moral, technical, and financial assistance to developing countries to help them improve their use of existing documentary materials and information systems; and (6) publishing reports, manuals, directories, monographs, and proceedings—a technical and general support literature about operations, systems, and procedures that represents the deliberations of expert bodies about problems of international interest.

Early History. Perhaps the first organizations to take on an international cast were the German book fairs of the 16th century, which drew buyers and sellers of books from all parts of Europe. The *Messkataloge,* begun in 1564 by Georg Willer, listed what was available and contained entries for books outside the German states, though, naturally enough, books published in them predominated. Various series of these catalogues were published until the late 19th century, though entries for non-German material began to decline in the 17th century. In 1617 John Bill began to publish an English edition of these catalogues; he soon added English titles (the catalogues already contained some), and from 1622 to 1626 these additions took the form of regular, separately titled supplements.

In the last half of the 17th century, the rise and increasingly rapid proliferation of journal literature added complexity to a bibliographic problem that, with the diffusion of printing and the widespread adoption of the vernacular, had already become serious. While much individual and later corporate effort was expended on the development of national bibliographic control, where the works created reached beyond national bounds, most of them tended to seek universality of scope. Among the enormous number of works of this kind, one of the first and greatest was Gesner's *Bibliotheca Universalis* (1545). Derived from the Frankfurt *Messkataloge* were Georg Draud's *Bibliotheca Classica, Bibliotheca Exotica,* and *Bibliotheca Librorum Germanicorum Classica* (1611–12, revised 1625). At the end of the 17th century, Raffaele Savanorola finished his *Orbis Litteraris.* Occupying some 40 folio volumes, it was never published and disappeared some time in the 19th century. Francesco Marucelli's *Mare Magnum,* a catalogue intended to list everything known to have been written, was compiled at about the same time; it, too, was never published but survives in 111 volumes copied sometime after 1751 from the now lost manuscript.

The idea of universal bibliographic control, of which these works are imperfect manifestations, exercised a potent fascination for bibliographers from the 17th through the 19th centuries. In 1631 Petrus Blanchot published his *Idea Bibliotheca Universalis,* a proposal for a universal subject index. In the 1840s and 1850s the idea sprang up more vigorously than ever, though apparently independently, in France, the United Kingdom, and the United States, in association with attempts to compile and publish library catalogues. Félix Danjou in France, Charles Wentworth Dilke, Andrea Crestadoro, and later Sir Henry Cole in the U.K., and Charles Coffin Jewett in the U.S., all had different schemes, to say nothing of the fin de siècle schemes of Ferdinand Bonnage in France and Vander Haeghen in Belgium.

In the latter half of the 17th century, with the publication of the *Journal des Sçavans* and the *Philosophical Transactions* of the Royal Society of London, the pattern of modern scholarly periodical publishing begins to emerge. As the century drew to a close, following experimentation with journals devoted to extracting and reviewing, an increasingly complex apparatus of abstracting and indexing publications gradually emerged in various major European languages. These publications were produced by individuals or by learned societies and aspired to varying degrees of internationalization in scope. By the first half of the 19th century a recognizably modern approach to the control of scientific, technical, and scholarly literature had emerged based in local and national institutions and the commercial publishing sector.

The 19th Century. A major development in the control of scientific literature in the 19th century was the publication of the Royal Society's *Catalogue of Scientific Papers.* Universal in scope, this catalogue was almost self-consciously national in execution, though foreign academies and learned societies were consulted for recommendations as to journals to be indexed. It was published in four series between 1867 and 1925, with a supplementary volume for the period 1800–83.

A little known attempt at international specialized scientific bibliography that seems to have had some success internationally was initiated in 1889 by the Société Mathématique de France through a Congrès

International de Bibliographies des Sciences Mathématiques in Paris. The *Répertoire Bibliographiques des Sciences Mathématiques* came into being in 1893 and had two forms: a simple retrospective bibliography published in Paris from 1893 to 1912 on cards and the *Revue Semestrielle des Publications Mathématiques d'Amsterdam.* This bibliography continued in the latter form until 1934, when it merged with the *Jahrbuch über die Fortschritte der Mathematik,* which ceased publication in 1942. Both the *Revue* and the *Jahrbuch* used the classification, revised from time to time, of the *Répertoire Bibliographique des Sciences Mathématiques.*

Such ventures are evidence of a growing, but incomplete, internationalism in bibliography. Two other 19th-century forms of bibliographical or bibliothecal internationalism should be mentioned: the first may be described as regulatory and involved governments; the second was essentially consultative and collegial. In 1817 a limited scheme was implemented for the exchange of dissertations among German universities, the Akademischer Tauschverein; by the early 1880s 50 European universities and academies had become involved in this venture. In the 1840s and 1850s Alexandre Vattemare, a ventriloquist and quick-change artist who desired to stimulate the exchange of publications between governments, set up an Agence Centrale des Échanges Internationaux in Paris to coordinate this work. He was eventually able, if only briefly, to interest many governments in his ideas, including 18 state legislatures and the Congress in the U.S. The major development in this area, however, was an international intergovernmental conference at Brussels in 1882. Here were signed two conventions governing the international exchange of documents: *Convention A* dealt with the exchange of government publications generally; *Convention B* dealt with parliamentary gazettes, journals, and annuals. These conventions remained in force and under scrutiny into the middle of the 20th century.

International copyright had been a subject of debate for much of the early part of the 19th century, and various bilateral agreements were concluded among European states in an attempt to protect the rights of authors internationally. As early as 1858 a major international congress in Brussels deliberated on the subject, and the movement then begun quickly gathered force, leading to a convention signed in Berne in 1886. A permanent bureau directed by Henri Morel and sponsored by the Swiss government was set up in 1888 to act as the headquarters for what has since become generally known as the Berne Copyright Union.

As the 19th century progressed and as literature proliferated and libraries grew, librarians and bibliographers began locally, nationally, and internationally to create formal associations. In 1868 a Société Bibliographique was created in Paris; in 1878 it held the first of three decennial international conferences that "in a series of reports would trace the scientific and literary movement of the ten-year period in order to provide ample materials and accurate information to all students." These gatherings, though strongly French, attracted some participants from Belgium, Italy, Luxembourg, the U.K., and elsewhere. Similar conferences were the International Conference of Librarians in London in 1877, which was enlivened by a large contingent of American librarians, and the 20th-anniversary conference of the Library Association of the U.K., which had been founded at the 1877 conference. Other international conferences were held, for example, on the occasion of the international exhibitions of Paris in 1900, San Francisco in 1904, and Brussels in 1910, but no permanent organization was created either to perpetuate the conferences themselves or to allow them to undertake some corporate activity of international value. Curiously, the 1900 conference had resolved that it should reconvene every five years (it did not), and the 1910 "Congrès de Bruxelles" was organized by an avowedly "Permanent Commission for the International Congresses of Archivists and Librarians," of which no more was heard.

Before World War I. For bibliographical organization, the year 1895 is a watershed. In that year the International Institute of Bibliography was created in Brussels by Paul Otlet and Henri LaFontaine; the Concilium Bibliographicum was in the process of being set up in Zurich by Herbert Haviland Field; and the consultations with foreign academies and learned societies undertaken by the Royal Society, prior to calling an international conference to explore the creation of an *International Catalogue of Scientific Literature,* were well advanced.

The International Conference on Bibliography, held in Brussels in 1895, created the International Institute of Bibliography (IIB), and the Belgian government undertook to support a headquarters organization for it, the International Office of Bibliography (OIB). The aim of the new organization was to create a universal bibliography or catalogue (Répertoire Bibliographique Universel), a database that would be organized both by author and, by means of a radical expansion of the Dewey Decimal Classification and a sophisticated development of the mechanics of the classification's notation, by subject.

The Concilium Bibliographicum's goal was to compile centrally and to distribute on cards or as supplements to major journals or reviews the current bibliography of zoology and related subjects. Agreements between the Concilium and the International Institute of Bibliography were made even as both organizations completed their initial arrangements. The latter adopted the three-by-five card as the basis for its work (it had originally proposed to use a card of a quite different size), promoted its use as an international standard, and confided to Field and his colleagues the development of the UDC in the areas of the Concilium's interest. In its turn, the Concilium undertook to develop the UDC, to use it in its bibliographical notices, and to send copies of its cards and other bibliographical publications to Brussels. As well as being published in card form, the zoological portion of the Concilium's work appeared as a supplement to the *Zoologischer Anzeiger,* the physiological portion as part of the *Zentralblatt für Physiologie,* and the protozoological portion in the *Archiv für Protistenkunde.* Support for the Concilium was provided by Field himself, by local sources (the Swiss Confederation and the city and canton of Zurich principally), and by international sponsors (the International Congress of Zoology and the French Zoological Society), and by revenues generated from the sale of its bibliographical services.

The first International Conference on a Catalogue of Scientific Literature was held in London in 1896, and others followed in 1898 and 1900. Sponsored by the Royal Society, these conferences led to the creation of a complex organization to oversee and produce the catalogue. It was governed by an International Convention that met in 1905, 1910, and 1922 and was administered by an International Council that met regularly at more frequent intervals. A Central Bureau, supervised by the Director of the Catalogue, Henry Forster Morely, prepared the work for publication. Regional bureaus in participating countries, such as the Smithsonian Institution in the U.S., transcribed references to their national scientific literature onto slips of a standard size and weight. Detailed specifications as to form of entry, content, punctuation, and abbreviation were followed in producing these slips. The first issue of the *International Catalogue of Scientific Publications,* divided into 17 subject areas, appeared in 22 volumes in 1901. Annual issues appeared until World War I.

Between the Two World Wars. The end of World War I marks a major turning point in the development of international bibliographic organization and control. A sustained period of development was abruptly terminated by the war. Prewar bibliographical ventures, overlapping each other to various degrees, had involved creating a formal mechanism to procure the international cooperation of scholars, the centralization of publishing and consultative activities in ambiguously supported, nationally based headquarters, and the provision of conventional enumerative bibliography.

The *International Catalogue of Scientific Publications* was not resumed after the war. The Royal Society looked into the usefulness of starting it again and found strong agreement in the scientific community against it. Scientists wanted specialized, up-to-date abstracting services rather than the cumbersome general indexing services the *Catalogue* offered. They found it too slow in appearing and offering limited information.

The work of the Concilium Bibliographicum was continued for a time, and a special grant from the Rockefeller Foundation assisted the Concilium's flagging finances. But it too fell rapidly into a decline from which it did not recover.

Despite the German occupation of Brussels during the war, the facilities and collections of the International Institute of Bibliography were unharmed, and for a short time its future seemed secure. Nevertheless, the Belgian government began to withdraw its support from the vast, overextended complex of organizations (Palais Mondial or Mundaneum) of which the IIB was part. In 1924 the IIB's members decided to reorganize the Institute, stressing its independence from the failing center in Brussels, the importance of national members to it, and the need to revise the UDC, now long out of print and out of date. The reorganizations begun in 1924 were continued under the presidencies of Allan Pollard, from the U.K. (1927–30), and J. Alingh Prins, from the Netherlands (1931–37). Emphasis was placed on decentralization of activity and federalism of organization. Annual congresses began in 1927, and the Institute in 1931 changed its name to International Institute of Documentation. It changed the name again in 1937, after the World Conference of International Documentation in Paris, to International Federation for Documentation (FID). Its work was limited to the continuous revision and translation into various languages of the UDC (the second full edition was issued in 1932), to the publication of the journal *Documentation Universalis* (1930–32) and its successor *IID Communicationes* (later *FID Communicationes*), and to the annual congresses. An effort was made to continue the Répertoire Bibliographique Universel in a decentralized form. A massive indexing project was intended to amplify the scope of the catalogue of the library of the Science Museum in London by creating a classified database for periodical literature. S. C. Bradford (of Bradford's "law of scatter"), director of the Science Museum, and A. F. C. Pollard, a professor at Imperial College and for a time President of the Institute, tried to interest H. G. Wells in the potential of the information service based on these catalogues and indexes in helping to bring to fruition his ideas about a "world brain." Bradford and Pollard, ardent exponents of the UDC, had created a British affiliate of the Institute at Brussels, the British Society for International Bibliography. Despite their work, universal bibliography as conceived before World War I declined.

Of doubtful utility, technically inadequate, and poorly supported, universal bibliography was subordinated first to the elaboration of a classification that, at least theoretically, could be used to bring a form of standardized access to any bibliography or catalogue anywhere, and then later, as the 1930s progressed, to the study of documentary reproduction, especially by microphotography, the techniques and uses of which the Institute had been exploring since 1906.

The League of Nations. The most important institution for the world of learning after the war took an organizational form different from any that had preceded it. Though at first not concerned with this area, the League of Nations in 1922 created an International Committee on Intellectual Cooperation and appointed to it 12 eminent scholars from a variety of disciplines and countries. Receiving inadequate financial support from the League from the start, the Committee was given permission in 1924 to appeal directly to governments for assistance. The French government then set up in Paris and partly funded an executive arm and headquarters organization for the Committee, the International Institute of Intellectual Cooperation, frequently referred to as the Paris Institute. The whole was called the League Organization of Intellectual Cooperation.

Among a wide range of tasks addressed by the International Committee on Intellectual Cooperation were the organization of relief for intellectual workers in central and eastern Europe, improvement in the international exchange of publications, improvement in international copyright, and the coordination of bibliography. Indeed, one of the first subcommittees set up by the Committee was for bibliography.

Over a period the League Organization of Intellectual Cooperation arranged consultations through the Subcommittee on Bibliography, and later its Committee of Library Experts, on how the bibliography of a diverse group of subjects might be improved; it proposed major modifications in the treaties governing the protection of intellectual property and the international exchange of publications; it held conferences, conducted surveys, and issued a great many publications. Some of these were directories and some bibliographies; some, such as the *Index Bibliographicus* and the *Index Translationem,* were continued after World War II by Unesco.

The League Organization of Intellectual Cooperation, as a matter of policy, did not attempt to carry out major projects. Rather, it sought to identify those that were of international importance and, whenever possible, sometimes by the provision of subsidies, to encourage other existing organizations to undertake them. From the start it had sought a viable relationship with the International Institute of Bibliography. But despite an agreement between the two bodies in 1924, their relationship, already delicate because of the personalities involved, deteriorated.

IFLA. League cooperation with the International Federation of Library Associations (IFLA) was more successful than with the International Institute of Bibliography, partly because there could be no clash of vested interests or organizational philosophy between the two. From its inception in 1927, IFLA was deeply influenced by the League Organization and by a long-held but unfulfilled hope in the Paris Institute of setting up as part of its Section on Scientific Relations an International Library Advisory Service. In 1926 a proposal to create a permanent professional library organization, one function of which would be to work with the Paris Institute, had been made at the International Conference of Librarians and Booklovers in Prague. In 1927, at the annual meeting of the Library Association of the United Kingdom, an International Library and Bibliographical Committee was formally created. This Committee became the International Federation of Library Associations in 1929, and in that year the first World Congress of Librarianship and Bibliography was held. According to the statutes of the new association, its executive committee was to be called the International Library Committee and was to meet annually, while the association as a whole was to assemble at least once every five years. IFLA cooperated closely with the League Organization in the publication of several directories and guides. The *Acts* of the International Library Committee and the *Proceedings* of the 1929 Rome-Venice conference and the 1935 Madrid-Barcelona conference provide evidence of the evolution from the limited, occasional prewar library conferences of a permanent international library community, characterized by continuous if fragile links between members, sustained formal communication, and some corporate activity.

The League Organization of Intellectual Cooperation also worked closely with the International Federation of National Standardizing Associations (ISA). The latter body was formed in 1926, and in 1938 a technical committee, ISA-46, was devoted to studying standardization in documentation. This technical committee was a direct forerunner of the present ISO/TC 46.

General cooperation between the League Organization and the International Research Council, set up in 1919, was a goal pursued by both over a period of years, though its achievement was hindered in part because of the relatively long intervals between meetings of the Council. A committee appointed by the Council in 1925 recommended in 1928 that a joint Council/League commission should be set up. In 1937 a formal agreement was reached for consultation and cooperation between the Council and the Paris Institute, which had, in any case, already referred matters to the Council for advice (including some matters of bibliography).

Thus by 1930 a pattern of international bibliographic and library organization had essentially emerged, the outlines of which can still be discerned beneath the increasing international complexity and activity characteristic of the period after World War II. At the center in the 1930s was the permanent international intergovernmental organization of the time, the League of Nations, as represented by the League Organization for Intellectual Cooperation. Its work took a number of forms. It published guides, directories, and bibliographies, often as the result of international surveys. It convened meetings of experts to consider issues of importance. And it tried to stimulate and coordinate the work of international nongovernmental organizations active in major areas of League interest: here lie the negotiations, successful and complete to varying degrees, between the League and IFLA, FID, ISA, and the forerunner of the International Council of Scientific Unions.

After World War II. As World War II drew to a close, there was no question that a new organization dealing with matters of education, culture, and science should be created as part of the United Nations family of organizations then being planned. Moreover, there was no doubt that part of the work of the new organization, which was to be called Unesco, should be concerned with libraries and bibliography. A rather grandiose plan put forward by Theodore Besterman for an International Library and Bibliographic Clearing House in the Unesco secretariat was soon abandoned as unrealistic. Unesco's program for libraries, bibliography, documentation, archives, and related subjects has grown over the years in strength, scope, and complexity. Its early conferences on science abstracting (1949) and the improvement of bibliographic services throughout the world (1950) culminated in the UNISIST (World Scientific and Technical Information) program adopted by an intergovernmental conference in 1971. In 1976 UNISIST was brought together with the related program for libraries and archives, NATIS (National Information Systems), in the General Information Program (PGI), an intersectoral program attached to the Office of the Directorate in order to facilitate coordination and development of work and to reduce duplication of effort and organizational conflict. The withdrawal of the U.S. from Unesco in 1985 diminished Unesco's work and the General Information Program, but by no means paralyzed the organization.

Unesco, like the League Organization before it, continued to rely on the help of other organizations. It convened an International Conference on Cataloguing Practices in Paris in 1961 with financial support from the Council on Library Resources, Inc. Following the conference, IFLA was able to bring about considerable international agreement in the areas of bibliographic description and control. In 1973 IFLA's work crystallized around two major programs, Universal Bibliographical Control (UBC) and the Universal Availability of Publications (UAP). The Council on Library Resources provided financial support for a secretariat for UBC; the British Library provided accommodation and in-kind support for UBC and UAP.

IFLA later organized its work into five core programs. The Universal Bibliographic Control and International Marc (UBCIM) program concentrated on preparing, developing, and maintaining UNIMARC. Its secretariat moved to Frankfurt in 1990. The UAP program remained at the British Library. The Universal Data flow and Telecommunications (UDT) program promotes the use of Open Systems Interconnection standards and applications; it is centered in the National Library of Canada. The Preservation and Conservation (PAC) program is centered at the Bibliothèque Nationale in Paris and has focal points in Australia, Germany, Japan, the U.S., and Venezuela. The Advancement of Librarianship in Developing Countries (ALP) program was promulgated in 1984 after a number of years of study. Its focal point was set up in the Uppsala University Library in 1991. In addition to these programs, IFLA's Divisions, Sections, and Round Tables continue their own programs of activities. In 1976 IFLA added the words "and Institutions" to its name to reflect its broadened membership base. IFLA's annual meetings, held in a different city each year, have become major international library events, and the organization issues an important body of monographic and periodical publications.

One of IFLA's major roles has been as a centralizing organization precipitating the emergence of specialist groups that become part of its federal structure. In 1955 the International Association of Agricultural Libraries and Documentalists (IAALD), the International Association of Theological Libraries (now the International Council of Associations of Theological Libraries), and the International Association of Technical (now Technological) University Libraries (IATUL) were created and sought affiliation with IFLA, the last becoming a Section. In 1959 the newly created International Association of Law Libraries (IALL) sought affiliation with IFLA. In 1968 the International Association of Metropolitan City Libraries (INTAMEL) was set up; it eventually became the equivalent of a Round Table of IFLA. One association, however, was created specifically to stand apart from IFLA. LIBER, the Ligue des Bibliothèques Européennes de Recherche, was constituted in 1971 with support from the Council of Europe to work outside the framework imposed by the IFLA Section on National and University Libraries, though it retains affiliate status with IFLA. Other regional library associations, notably the Association of Caribbean University, Research, and Institutional Libraries (ACURIL), created in 1969, and the Commonwealth Library Association (COMLA), inaugurated in 1972, are also affiliated with IFLA.

FID signed a contract with Unesco in 1947 that made it the major international body through which Unesco would deal with matters of international documentation. Because of organizational problems, FID has not been as effective as IFLA in its programs. It assumed responsibility for the ISORID program (International Information System on Research and Development in Documentation) in 1971, but closed it down in 1989. Also within the framework of Unesco's UNISIST program, FID oversaw the creation of a scheme called the Broad System of Ordering (BSO), intended to provide a means for switching among various indexing and classification systems in use in various countries. After more than a decade of development and discussion, the BSO seemed in the final analysis not to have come to anything.

A continuing task for FID has been maintenance and oversight of the development of the Universal Decimal Classification, which now exists in specialized and general editions in more than 20 languages. In 1992 a consortium of organizations took over management of UDC, with FID providing the chairman. Among basic concerns of the consortium is the development of a database that will serve as the equivalent of a base standard edition of UDC, from which other editions can be controlled.

Like IFLA, FID continues to hold a range of general and special meetings, issues publications, and acts jointly with other organizations in supporting workshops, conferences, seminars, and so on. It holds general conferences every two years. In 1986 it added the word "Information" to its name, becoming the International Federation for Information and Documentation, but retained its acronym.

The International Research Council evolved into the International Council of Scientific Unions, which created an Abstracting Board (ICSU-AB) in 1955. The Board operated at low key for many years, but gradually became an important forum for the major abstracting and indexing services in various parts of the world. In 1984 the Board became the International Council for Scientific and Technical Information (ICSTI). It worked to improve access to scientific and technical information by improving access tools and systems, especially exploiting technologies for electronic publishing and data transfer.

The advent of the computer as a major tool in information processing and the development of machine-readable bibliographic databases to some degree underlie aspects of UNISIST's program of systems interconnection. They have also led to the development of a number of international information systems, such as INIS (the International Nucelar Information System of the International Atomic Energy Agency) and AGRIS (Agriculture Information System of the Food and Agriculture Organization). Such systems are similar to the *International Catalogue of Scientific Publications;* their differences, however, are crucial. The subject and scope of the present systems are specific. The systems themselves constitute relatively minor parts of the work of major, broadly based intergovernmental organizations. And they can provide abstracts.

An important development in the last quarter of the 20th century has been the emergence of Europe as a bibliographical and bibliothecal region following the development of the European Community. An online network, Euronet/Diane (Direct Information Access Network for Europe), was launched in 1975 and was intended also to include Scandinavian countries that were not members of the European Community. It enjoyed only limited success, but led to the development of the idea of a market for access to data across borders. The desirability of a common market of this kind stimulated cooperation among the telecommunications agencies of the participating countries in developing common standards based on the OSI model. Directorate General XIII-B of the European

Community, in Luxembourg and Brussels, oversees developments in this area. It issued requirements for standards of data interchange and communication that became obligatory in 1987.

In 1984 the Community launched a program to revitalize European information technologies in relation to processing systems, office business systems, computer-integrated manufacturing, and basic research. It provided assistance to what are now called less favored regions in developing their communications infrastructures. In 1985 the Council of Ministers of Culture, recognizing that libraries were an important component in the information market (as well as traditional sources for disseminating knowledge and culture), called for collaboration among libraries in the fields of data processing. The Commission of the European Community in 1990 approved the Framework Program for Research and Technological Development. One of its subprograms, Telematic Systems of General Interest, includes a Libraries Program. Initial contracts for research and development projects related to the "action lines" of the program were announced in 1992. The European Community, with its record of work in developing infrastructure, creating an information services market that included libraries, and supporting a range of computer-based research and development projects, seemed certain to be a major source of international developments in librarianship well into the 21st century.

International library and bibliographic organization in the last years of the 20th century was complex. It involved a great many nongovernmental associations—some with fairly general goals and some with quite specific ones. It involved a number of intergovernmental organizations, some maintaining international systems and some, such as Unesco or ISO, responsible for developing, coordinating, and supporting the work of other organizations. It involved regional organizations and global ones. It involved international agreements of various degrees of formality, ranging from intergovernmental conventions on copyright, exchange of documents, and the international flow of educational and cultural materials to expressions of approval of vaguely formulated programs of international desiderata. It involved internationally drawn-up and maintained procedures and tools that are under constant scrutiny, development, and revision and that are accepted nationally with varying degrees of completeness. While much remains to be done, an established organizational basis, widespread international awareness, and rapidly developing technology suggest that we are moving ever closer to what Paul Otlet identified as necessary in the 19th century, a world network for universal documentation.

REFERENCES

Edward Carter, "The Birth of Unesco's Library Programmes," in *Med Boken Som Bakgrunn: Festkrift Til Harold L. Tveterås* (1964).

S. Steven Falk, "The International Committee on Intellectual Cooperation: Its Work for Bibliography" (unpublished M.A. thesis, University of Chicago Graduate Library School, 1977).

Katherine Oliver Murra, "Some Attempts to Organize Bibliography Internationally," in Jesse Shera and Margaret Egan, editors, *Bibliographic Organization* (1951).

W. Boyd Rayward, *The Universe of Information: The Work of Paul Otlet for Documentation and International Organization* (1975).

W. BOYD RAYWARD

International Organization for Standardization

The International Organization for Standardization (ISO) was established in 1947 following a meeting in London the previous year at which delegates from 25 countries decided to create a new international organization to "facilitate the international coordination and unification of industrial standards." ISO is a worldwide federation of national standards bodies which today comprises some 90 members representing more than 95 percent of the world's industrial production.

The object of ISO is to promote standardization and related activities in the world with a view to facilitating international exchange of goods and services and to developing cooperation in the spheres of intellectual, scientific, technological, and economic activity. Its scope covers standardization in all fields except electrical and electronic engineering, which is the responsibility of ISO's partner organization, the International Electrotechnical Commission (IEC).

ISO fulfills its objectives by developing and publishing international standards. The technical work is carried out in a hierarchy of some 2,600 technical committees, subcommittees, and working groups in which more than 20,000 experts from all parts of the world participate annually. The work of ISO is decentralized (committees are administered by the national standards bodies) and consensus-oriented (the broadest possible agreement must be obtained before an international standard can be published). By July 1991 there were 7,992 ISO standards listed in the ISO Catalogue, which amounted to 65,359 technical pages in a given language.

ISO standards are voluntary. That is, from ISO's point of view, they exist as agreements between competitors and their customers (market players) in non-regulated spheres of economic activity. However, because of the nature of the consensus-building process, voluntary standards are seen as sensible approaches to the need for rationalizing technological options in markets, and incentives for their use are normally market-driven. National voluntary standards such as the French (AFNOR), German (DIN), and Japanese (JISC) are often direct adoptions of ISO standards, even though such adoptions are also voluntary. It also happens, of course, that voluntary standards are used in regulated spheres of economic activity, at the discretion of the regulator involved.

There are three main phases in the ISO's standards development process once the need for an international standard has been recognized and formally agreed upon. The first phase involves defining the technical scope of the future standard. This phase is usually carried out in working groups which comprise technical experts from countries interested in the subject matter. During the second phase, a process of consensus-building, countries negotiate the detailed specifications in the standard. The final phase begins with formal approval of the draft standard. Acceptance criteria require approval by two-thirds of the ISO members that participated actively in the standards-development process and approval by three-fourths of all ISO members that vote. After approval, the accepted text is published as an ISO International Standard.

ISO/TC 46. Standardization of practices relating to libraries, documentation and information centers, indexing and abstracting services, archives, information science, and publishing is the subject of ISO Technical Committee 46 (ISO/TC 46). The committee had its origins in 1938, when the German Technical Committee of librarianship in the Deutscher Normenausschuss proposed that ISA-46 be set up and took over its secretariat. The secretariat was later held by NOBIN (Nederlands Orgaan voor de Bevordering fan de Intermatieverzorging) and was reallocated in 1966 to DNA (since 1975 DIN, Deutsches Institute für Normung). Twenty-six participating members and 36 observing members, who are nominees of the respective national standards institutions, carry out the standardization work. Eight other ISO technical committees and 43 international organizations also participate. Other technical committees working in the field of information and documentation are ISO/IEC Joint Technical Committee 1 (ISO/IEC JTC 1), Information Technology; ISO/TC 37, Terminology (principles and coordination); ISO/TC 154, Documents and Data Elements in Administration, Commerce, and Industry; and ISO/TC 171, Micrographics and optical memories for document and image recording, storage, and use.

ISO publishes numerous documents and periodicals, including the *ISO Catalogue,* an annual list of ISO standards that is updated quarterly, and the *ISO Technical Program,* a semiannual list of all draft ISO standards.

LAWRENCE D. EICHER

Iran

Iran, an Islamic republic in western Asia, is bounded by the Caspian Sea and Armenia, Azerbaijan, and Turkmenistan on the north, Afghanistan and Pakistan on the east, the Gulf of Oman and Persian Gulf on the south, and Iraq and Turkey on the west. Population (1991) 57,900,000; area 1,648,000 sq.km. The official language is Farsi (Persian), and the country was for years called Persia. Iran underwent two major revolutionary changes in the 20th century: the first, the constitutional revolution of 1906–09, the second, the Islamic revolution of 1977–78.

History. In spite of a long history of libraries dating to pre-Islamic times, such as the library of the University of Gondi-Shapur, the public library of Saruyeh-ye Ji in Esfahan, or the libraries of the Islamic period, modern librarianship is fairly new in Iran. In 1851 the highly intellectual Prime Minister, Amir Kabir, established Dar-al Fonun, a college similar to Western universities and colleges. Its library can be considered the first modern university library in Iran. Later, because of constant contact with the West and the expansion of education, the establishment of libraries became a necessity.

National Library. The National Library of Iran was established in 1937 in a small new building. The building has been enlarged, but has not grown to match the growth of the collection and staff, now housed in three locations. The national Plan and Budget Organization approved plans for a new building in the early 1990s. The National Library was not very active before the Islamic Revolution because it had few professionals on its staff. It became more active after 1983, when the Tehran Book Processing Center (TEBROC) and its qualified staff were transferred to it. The first step was to begin updating the *National Bibliography of Iran,* following the recommendations of Unesco; it is now published semi-annually.

Libraries in Iran (1990)

Type of library	Number of administrative units (main libraries)	Number of service points (branches, mobile stops, etc.)	Volumes in collections	Annual expenditures (rials)	Population served	Professional staff (with certificate, diploma, etc.)	Total staff
National	1	3	500,000†	343,000,000	1,487*	12	153
Academic	270	270	5,169,430†	559,914,000**	745,487*	336	1,784[(1)]
Public	501	501	4,274,585†	n.a.	601,421*	18	976[(2)]
School⁻	2,983	--	216,693†	n.a.	309,754°	n.a.	2,778[(3)]
Special	254	254	6,923,792†	311,557,000×+	159,607*⁻	114	1,172[(1)]
Children	250	250	2,700,000	n.a.	390,000	n.a.	n.a.

*Registered members in 1989
°Registered members in 1986
**159 out of 270 have not answered the budget
†All types of materials are included
⁻Data belongs to 1986
×+178 out of 254 have not answered the budget
*⁻Monthly use instances
1. Shirin Ta'avoni. *Directory of Documentation Centres, Special Libraries and University Libraries of Iran.* (under print by National Library) (Text in Persian)
2. *Shenāsnāmeh-ye Ketābkhānehā-ye 'Omumi-ye Keshvar.* (Tehrān: Office of the Board of Trustees of Public Libraries, 1370 (i.e., 1991)) (Text in Persian)
3. *Gozaresh-e Farhangi-ye Iran, 1365.* (Tehran: Ministry of Culture and Islamic Guidance, 1369 (i.e., 1990)) p. 60

The Library also publishes the *Directory of Iranian Periodicals* annually, as well as reference works and books and scholarly papers on Iranian librarianship, and produces catalogue cards.

The collection numbers about 500,000 volumes, including 12,000 outstanding manuscripts, 20,000 books on librarianship, and more than 30,000 books in Western languages on Iranology and Islamic studies. The Library owns one of the richest collections of Iranian periodicals (about 1,200 titles) dating back to the earliest newspapers published in Iran. The National Library is a depository for books and periodicals and has exchange programs with most national libraries of the world. It is a member of IFLA and FID.

In 1990 the parliament approved changes in the National Library Act, detaching the Library from the Ministry of Culture and Higher Education. It now has its own Board of Trustees, headed by the President of the Republic.

National Archives. The National Archive Organization, founded in 1970, is responsible for preserving historical documents. It has a separate department of restoration and preservation. The Archive of the Islamic Republic of Iran Broadcasting (IRIB) is the most important audiovisual center in the country. In addition to acquiring, organizing, and disseminating films, recordings, slides, and video materials, it also produces its own. It has a collection of 500,000 items, some dating from the time when Iran's first radio station was founded in 1939. Systematic organization of the collection began in 1979, and the collection was moved to a new building in 1989.

Academic Libraries. About 350 universities, colleges, and institutions of higher education exist in Iran, the University of Tehran (founded 1934) being the oldest. Most universities have central libraries and several faculty libraries, but the central libraries seldom function as such. The central libraries at the universities of Esfahan and Mash'had serve all members of their university communities. However, librarians at most of the central libraries collect and organize library materials for their own institutions, not for the whole university system. The older the faculty, the larger its collection. For example, the Faculty of Law and the Faculty of Letters at the University of Tehran have the largest collections. The Central Library of the University of Tehran has 228,000 volumes of printed books, nearly 88,000 items in its Documentation Center, and 15,000 manuscripts. It subscribes to more than a hundred periodicals and is equipped with microfilming and other duplicating equipment.

The National Library publishes statistics for 270 academic libraries, indicating that in the late 1980s they held more than 5,100,000 items (both books and audiovisual materials) and 26,700 manuscripts. They subscribed to almost 24,500 periodical titles.

Public Libraries. Iran has just over 500 public libraries, served by a total staff of less than a thousand, of whom only a few have some sort of library education. In 1989 these libraries held almost 4,000,000 volumes and more than 6,500 manuscripts. Tehran, with a population of more than 6,000,000, is served by 13 public libraries. Its Central Library has a collection of more than 78,000 volumes. Others have collections of from 3,000 to 22,000 volumes. On the whole, public libraries in Iran do not meet contemporary needs. The relevance of their collections, the services they offer, and the rate of growth of their holdings all leave much to be desired.

Religious Libraries. Most mosques have libraries that can be classified as public, because they serve public needs. Many of these libraries are fairly small and all concentrate on religious materials. Iran also has libraries, open to the public, for Islamic studies and research. The most famous is the Central Library and Documentation Center of the Astan-e Qods-e Razavi in Mash'had. Founded in the 15th century, it is the oldest functioning library in the country. It has a rich collection of more than 28,000 manuscripts and is renowned for its collection on the Koran. It also has more than 450,000 books and archival documents and 1,700 periodical titles. Its preservation office and binding department are active. The Library was scheduled to move into a large new building in the early 1990s. Its staff also supervises the holdings of several public libraries in Mash'had and elsewhere that have been donated to it.

A similar library is that of Ayatollah Mar'ashi in the holy city of Qom. Founded in 1938, it has 250,000 volumes of printed books and 25,000 manuscripts. After the Islamic Revolution, more libraries of this kind were established. The most important is the research library of the Great Islamic Encyclopedia. Founded in 1983, it already has 175,000 printed and 8,500 nonprint items. Its new building in Tehran is designed to hold 3,000,000 books.

School Libraries. With the exception of a few, school libraries are the weakest libraries in Iran. The country had more than 77,600 schools in 1989, but probably only about 3,000 of them had libraries, most of them with small collections. By law a certain amount of each school budget should be spent on

The National Library of Iran, Tehran, established in 1937.

Razi Institute Library

Periodicals section of the Razi State Institute Library, Tehran.

books, but that is seldom done. In many schools, most of the books were donated by students or their parents.

Children's Libraries. If Iran's school libraries are weak, at least the country has 250 good children's libraries. Established by the Institute for the Intellectual Development of Children and Young Adults (founded 1966), these libraries are not attached to schools under the Ministry of Education, nor to public libraries under the Ministry of Culture and Islamic Guidance. These libraries have good collections in part because the Institute itself publishes quality books. The Children's Book Council of Iran also has an important role in evaluating children's literature and influencing publishers. Many Iranian books have won international prizes.

Special Libraries. The establishment of special libraries, documentation centers, and information centers began in Iran in the 1950s. Many special libraries are quite small, with collections of as few as 400 volumes. Of the more than 250 special libraries surveyed in the late 1980s, only 25 had collections of more than 20,000 items. The Central Library of the Plan and Budget Organization, founded in 1982, is one of the best special libraries in the country. It holds almost 70,000 items and subscribes to more than 400 periodicals. Its well-qualified staff serves not only its parent organization but also students and researchers. The Central Library of the Iranian National Oil Company, founded in 1955, offers a high standard of service; much of its work is computerized. The Library and Documentation Center of the Atomic Energy Organization of Iran, founded in 1974, holds more than 72,500 items and subscribes to 700 periodicals.

The Profession. The first library school was established at Tehran University in 1966. It offered the Master of Library Science degree. Two other schools offer that degree, and eight universities offer the Higher Diploma in Librarianship to students who complete two years of work after the National High School Diploma. Because of the shortage of professionals, some government agencies offer short courses or diplomas in librarianship to their employees.

The Iranian Library Association was founded in 1966 and was active until the Islamic Revolution, when it died out. Some efforts were made to reestablish it in the late 1980s and early 1990s.

REFERENCES

Poori Soltani, "TEBROC: History and Influences on Iranian Librarianship," *Trends in International Librarianship: A Festschrift Honoring Anis Khurshid* (1991).

Poori Soltani, "National Library of Iran in Action," *International Cataloguing* (1985).

POORI SOLTANI

Iraq

The Republic of Iraq, an Arab state in the Middle East, is bounded by Turkey on the north, Iran on the east, Kuwait and Saudi Arabia on the south, and Jordan and Syria on the west. Almost one-fourth of the people live in the capital, Baghdad. Population (1990 est.) 18,920,000; area 438,317 sq.km. The official language is Arabic.

History. Cultural, scientific, and educational institutions have existed in Iraq since the early history of mankind. Libraries existed in ancient Iraq—which was known as Mesopotamia—as early as 4000 B.C. The earliest written records of the Sumerians, Assyrians, and Babylonians were excavated in the form of clay tablets from various locations in Iraq. In ancient Nippur, for example, near the city of Babylon (about 100 miles southeast of Baghdad), more than 60,000 clay tablets were excavated during the 1890s and early 1900s. These tablets dated partly from the Sumerian period (about 4000 B.C.) and partly from the Babylonian period (about 3000 B.C.). The tablets came from a huge temple collection that represents the library and archives center.

In the city of Nineveh, the Assyrian capital, in northern Iraq, another collection of clay tablets was uncovered. This collection represents a library known as the Royal Library of Assurbanipal (fl. 7th century

Libraries in Iraq (1990)

Type of library	Number of administrative units (main libraries)	Volumes in collections	Population served	Professional staff (with certificate, diploma, etc.)	Total staff
Academic	117	2,273,159	180,519	246	717

B.C.) (see Assurbanipal in this Encyclopedia).

During the Middle Ages, the Arab-Islamic civilization of the Abbasids flourished. In Baghdad, the capital of the Abbasids, there were 63 libraries that housed large collections of books and manuscripts. Most were open to scholars and the public. In addition, there were libraries in the cities of Basra and Kufa.

Iraqi libraries suffered considerable disruption during and after the 1991 war over Kuwait. The information given below reflects the condition of libraries before 1991.

National Library. The Iraqi National Library, established in 1920, was granted legal status as a depository library in 1961. In 1976 it moved to its new and modern building in the center of Baghdad. The building is designed to store more than a million volumes. The National Library publishes the National Bibliography as a quarterly serial.

The National Center of Archives, founded in 1963, was merged with the National Library in 1987 to form a new center called *Dar Al-Kutub Wal-Watha'iq* (Books and Archives House). The center is under the administrative supervision of the Ministry of Information. Some activities were merged, such as microfilming, but others, such as technical services and readers' services, are still provided separately.

The collection of the National Library numbers about 420,000 volumes, including about 40,000 volumes of periodicals. The collection of the National Center of Archives is about 5,000,000 items, organized into more than 40,000 files. The total staff numbers more than 180, of whom 40 are professionals.

Academic Libraries. Academic libraries are the best information centers in Iraq in terms of facilities, staff, and services. There are about 90 libraries in 11 universities and technical institutes.

The Central Library of the University of Baghdad, founded in 1959, and its 28 college libraries are the oldest and largest. Their total collections number about 750,000 volumes, about 5,700 periodical titles, and 49,000 other items, including maps, microforms, and audio recordings. The collection of this Library, like those of other Iraqi libraries and information centers, is mostly in Arabic or English. It has smaller collections in other languages.

The Central Library of Mosul University and its 14 college libraries hold the second largest academic collection—more than 250,000 books, 2,800 periodical titles, and 16,000 other items. It is the best-equipped university library in the country, with advanced information services such as CD-ROM and online searching capabilities.

Public Libraries. There are more than 70 public libraries in Iraq, with a total collection of about 1,000,000 volumes. These libraries are distributed throughout the country. Baghdad has 18 public libraries with a total of 242,000 volumes and a staff of 170, of whom 29 are professionals

Baghdad also has two children's public libraries, one (founded 1964) on the east bank of the Tigris River, the other (1985) on the west bank. They offer many activities for children aged 5 to 14, such as films, games, and storytelling, as well as offering collections of books and periodicals for children and young people.

Reading Room of the Central Library of Al-Mustansiriy University in Baghdad.

School Libraries. Of the 11,000 elementary, secondary, and technical schools in Iraq, nearly 9,000 have libraries, serving more than 4,300,000 students. More than 1,900 of the 2,600 secondary schools have libraries. Together, these libraries hold about 1,500,000 volumes. Iraq has only 130 full-time professional school librarians; the other school libraries are managed by school teachers on a part-time basis. For that reason, students at all levels are the chief users of public libraries.

Special Libraries. All Iraqi government ministries and most other government institutions have their own collections of books, periodicals, pamphlets, technical reports, and other library materials. For example, the Library of the Ministry of Planning (founded 1960) holds about 145,000 items. The Library of the Ministry of Foreign Affairs was founded in 1934 and holds more than 10,000 volumes, in addition to archival material, reports, and clippings.

The collections of both the Scientific Documentation Center and the Gulf States Information Documentation Center are of importance to researchers and Iraqi users. The first has a Library of 20,000 books and more than 1,300 titles of scientific and specialized periodicals and a collection of microforms and other audiovisual materials. The Gulf States Information Documentation Center, established in Baghdad in 1981 to serve Iraq and other Gulf Arab states, holds a large collection of clippings, about 800 titles of current periodicals, a large collection of microforms, audiovisual items, an information file (vertical file), and several thousand specialized books. Both centers offer various information services, such as indexing, bibliographies, abstracting, inquiry service, and other types of reference services. They also have access to computer services, using both local and international databases.

The Profession. Two universities offer formal courses in library and information science. In addition, the Iraqi Library Association and the Central Library of the University of Baghdad offer informal instruction.

The Department of Library Science at Al-Mustansiriya University in Baghdad (founded 1970) offers both graduate and undergraduate programs. It enrolls about 600 students a year. Many Iraqi professionals received Master's degrees there and hundreds of paraprofessonals earned Bachelor's degrees. Basra University started its own four-year undergraduate course in 1984. It has about 200 students enrolled each year.

The Iraqi Library Association was founded in Baghdad in 1968. It organizes annual professional meetings, short training courses, and other activities.

REFERENCE

Amer Ibrahim Kindilchie, "Libraries and Documentation Centers in Iraq" (in Arabic), *The Arab Magazine for Information Science* (Tunis) 1984.

AMER IBRAHIM KINDILCHIE

Ireland

The island of Ireland lies in the Atlantic Ocean west of Great Britain, northwest of the European mainland. Its 26 southern counties form the Republic of Ireland; 6 counties in the north are part of the United Kingdom. Population of the Republic (1990 est.) 3,503,000; area 70,284 sq.km. The official languages are Irish and English.

History. The early history of Irish libraries is bound up with the pursuit of learning carried out through countless monasteries and schools. The *scriptoria* or "houses of writing" of the monasteries, where the monks transcribed manuscripts, were the publishing houses of the Middle Ages. They were also the precursors of present-day interlibrary-loan centers, because the monks who traveled from monastery to monastery in Ireland and on the Continent carried their books with them, facilitating the international exchange of ideas. Norse invaders made devastating attacks on monasteries from A.D. 795 to 1014, causing widespread damage but not total destruction. A National Library microfilm project carried out in 1947 showed that large numbers of manuscripts salvaged from these early monastic libraries were lodged in the libraries and archives of Europe.

Development was further retarded from the 11th century to the 17th century by continuing internal strife and the Norman invasion. These difficulties led to the development of an oral tradition of passing on information through poetry and ballads, still an important aspect of Irish culture. But even in difficult circumstances, some important annals and compilations were produced, including the *Annals of the Four Masters* (written between 1632 and 1636), recording the history of Ireland to 1616.

The links between libraries and monasteries were finally cut with the Reformation, which brought about the closure of monasteries and the dispersal of their collections. After a long period in which there were few libraries in Ireland, the 19th century was notable for the foundation of some cathedral and subscription libraries.

The Mechanics' Institute libraries, founded in England during the later 18th and early 19th centuries to satisfy a demand for education, were the immediate predecessors of the public library system. With an underlying tradition of learning promoted through early monastic libraries, the retardation of library service caused by internal struggles is being overcome.

National Library. The National Library of Ireland is in Dublin, the capital. It was established under the terms of the Dublin Science and Museum Act of 1877, by which the state acquired the library of the Royal Dublin Society. The library has been greatly expanded by bequest and purchase, and it is now the major reference resource for material related to Ireland. It is a reference library only, but photocopying service is available. *The Guide to Collections in Dublin Libraries 1982* (worth consulting about a number of libraries mentioned in this article) lists some of its major holdings; they include works by and about Jonathan Swift, some early printed music, incunabula, and some 18th- and 19th-century Irish bindings. A former Director, Richard Hayes, published *Manuscript Sources for the History of Irish Civilisation* (1965).

The National Library Education Division promotes awareness of the resources available. Since 1976 it has produced a number of facsimile documents relating to aspects of Irish history and culture. The series includes folders on The Land War, 1879–1903; Daniel O'Connell, 19th-century Irish political leader; and James Joyce. With the assistance of the public library system and other organizations, the Division mounts exhibitions based on collections of the National Library in centers throughout the country.

Academic Libraries. The most important academic libraries in Ireland are those of the two universities—Dublin University (Trinity College) and the National University of Ireland, which has four

Libraries in Ireland (1990)

Type of library	Number of administrative units (main libraries)	Number of service points (branches, mobile stops, etc.)	Volumes in collections	Annual expenditures (Irish pound)	Population served	Professional staff (with certificate, diploma, etc.)	Total staff
National	1	3	550,000	1,000,000	--	--	49
Academic	7	56	4,893,000	17,300,000	43,000	126	415
Public	31	974	8,444,297	23,602,936	647,437	262	1,574
School	n.a.	--	--	--	--	--	
Special	62	--	--	--	--	--	194
Government	39	39	446,000	--	--	--	84

Sources: Library Association of Ireland, 1990. An Chomhairle Leabharlanna (The Library Council) Annual Statistics, 1988. Directory of Libraries and Information Services in Ireland, 1990.

constituent Colleges: Dublin, Cork, Galway, and Maynooth. Of these, the oldest and most important research library in Ireland is that of Trinity College, which was established by Royal Charter under Elizabeth I in 1591. It has been a legal deposit library since 1801; although now outside the United Kingdom, it still enjoys the right to claim all British publications under British copyright laws. The library also receives all Irish publications under Irish copyright laws, along with vast collections appropriate to the scholarly aims of the University. Trinity College Library also houses a priceless collection of ancient Irish manuscripts, chief of which is the Book of Kells. This transcription of the Four Gospels, executed by Irish monks, is considered by many experts to be the finest illuminated manuscript in the world. Trinity does not lend to individuals, but participates in interlibrary lending programs.

The libraries in the constituent Colleges of the National University of Ireland, established in 1908 under the Irish Universities Act, are of more recent origin. The collections at Dublin, Cork, and Galway are, in general, geared toward the courses taught at those Colleges. The library at University College, Dublin, the largest of the constituent Colleges, contains notable collections of archival material, including unpublished papers of Irish historical and political importance. The Dublin library also houses an extensive collection of books and periodicals on librarianship. Saint Patrick's College, Maynooth (County Kildare), a seminary for aspirants to the Roman Catholic priesthood, was recognized as a College of the National University in 1910. It now admits lay students who follow a variety of liberal arts courses. Its library has a heavy concentration of works on philosophy and theology.

Two new universities were constituted in 1989: Dublin City University, formerly the National Institute for Higher Education in Dublin (founded 1975) and the University of Limerick, formerly the National Institute for Higher Education, Limerick (founded 1968). Both universities offer a wide range of undergraduate and graduate courses, and their libraries reflect their strong technological orientation. Dublin City University Library has special collections in applied languages, communications, and international marketing; Limerick holds collections on Irish and European statistics and is a designated European Documentation Center. It has a full collection of Irish, British, and American Society for Testing Materials (ASTM) standards. There are major libraries at the Regional Technical Colleges in Athlone (Westmeath), Carlow, Dundalk (Louth), Galway, Letterkenny (Donegal), Sligo, and Waterford. Some of the Regional Technical College Libraries are organized and staffed by the local public library authorities. Libraries in the constituent colleges of the Dublin Institute of Technology are operated by staff from the Dublin Public Libraries.

Dublin has many specialist academic libraries, including that of the Royal Irish Academy (RIA), founded in 1785 to promote the study of science, belles lettres, and antiquities. The extensive collections of the RIA include part of the library of the Irish poet Thomas Moore (1779–1852). The Chester Beatty Library (Oriental arts) and the Franciscan Library, Dun Mhuire (Celtic studies and ecclesiastical history), also house material of research interest.

Public Libraries. Progress in public library development was slow, despite passage of the Public Library Ireland Act in 1855. The efforts of the Carnegie United Kingdom Trust, which from 1913 provided grants for public library development, proved to be an immense incentive. Until the founding of An Chomhairle Leabharlanna (The Library Council) under the Public Libraries Act, 1947, the Carnegie Trust was the most important motivating force for public library development.

There were 31 public library authorities in Ireland in the early 1990s, including one for each county. Four of the largest cities, Dublin, Cork, Limerick, and Waterford, and one small area within a county that retains a separate library identity, Dun Laoghaire (County Dublin), have independent library authorities.

The highest concentration of service is in Dublin, where nearly one-third of the total population lives. Service there is provided through 36 full-time branch libraries, 12 mobile library units, a business information center, a music library, a youth information center, and 5 prison libraries. The City Archive and Civic Museum also operate under the auspices of the Public Libraries. Professional assistance is available at all service points. Trends in Dublin in the 1990s include providing service to the disadvantaged and offering community information service. Outreach and extension activities are widely practiced.

Outside the capital, access to service and quality of service are subject to population and terrain factors. In rural areas most towns are too small to sustain full-time professionally operated libraries. Many rural areas have mobile library units or small centers operated on a part-time basis by locally recruited staff.

The government oversees library services through the Department of the Environment, advised by the Library Council. The Council advises local authorities on library matters and recommends grants for new projects, including buildings, bookstock, and library vehicles. The Council's Grants Scheme (1961) has been instrumental in encouraging major development in public library service. Other major influences have been the acceptance of professional qualifications for all executive posts and the introduction, in 1970, of a scholarship system of education based on full-time release for university study for public library staff members.

Alongside the publicly funded libraries established under the Public Library Ireland Act 1855 are a number of endowed public libraries. Marsh's Library, founded in 1701 and thus the first public library in the country, is by far the most important. The library contains incunabula and manuscripts and is of architectural interest.

School Libraries. At primary-school level, the public library service provides school libraries. In general, members of the professional staff have no direct involvement with students; instead, they advise teachers who are given special responsibility for library stock and organization. In Dublin library staffs organize special teacher in-service training courses. The state provides financial aid to local authorities on a per-capita basis for the national primary schools.

At higher levels, state funding is not available,

Marsh's Library

Archbishop Marsh's Library, founded in Dublin in 1702, the first public library in Ireland.

and library service is dependent on local initiatives. School children are encouraged to use their local public libraries, and there is extensive cooperation between school and library. The schools organize group visits and the libraries provide material for specific projects. In Dublin, a number of pilot projects involving public library staff in direct professional service to schools were monitored with the assistance of researchers from the Curriculum Development Unit of Trinity College. Dublin Public Libraries now maintains full service to two second-level schools as part of an ongoing research program.

Special Libraries. Ireland has a wide variety of special libraries. Most large organizations have libraries or information centers. A brief list, including the libraries of the Oireachtas (Parliament), Department of Education, Institute of Public Administration, Irish Management Institute, Irish Congress of Trade Unions, Federated Union of Employers, Economic and Social Research Institute, and A. Guinness Son & Co. Ltd., indicates that special libraries relate to all aspects of Irish life. There is extensive cooperation between these libraries and the university and public library systems.

The Profession. University College, Dublin, has a Department of Library and Information Studies. It offers a one-year post-graduate course leading to a diploma in Library and Information Science (DLIS) and a one-year (full-time) or two-year (part-time) course leading to a Master's degree in Library and Information Science (MLIS). It also offers a Bachelor of Social Science: Information Studies program and a research program leading to the Ph.D. degree. The Library Association of Ireland (LAI) offers some short seminars and workshops to provide opportunities for continuing education for those already qualified.

The LAI (founded in 1928) also offers regular programs on subjects of professional interest, such as audiovisual services, cataloguing and indexing, youth work, and university and special libraries, through a number of special interest groups. Fellowship of the Library Association of Ireland (FLAI) is open by thesis to those who possess recognized qualifications in librarianship. Associateship of the Library Association of Ireland (ALAI), introduced in 1989, is available to applicants who possess recognized professional qualifications and meet other criteria. The Association, which had a membership of some 650 in the early 1990s, publishes *An Leabharlann: The Irish Library* and *Directory of Libraries and Information Services in Ireland.*

Other professional associations include the Irish Association of Documentation and Information Services (IADIS), founded in 1967 to support special library and information work. IADIS published the *Union List of Current Periodicals in Irish Libraries* (1975). Cumann Leabharlannaithe Scoile (CLS; the Irish Association of School Libraries), founded in 1962, offers an annual summer course in school librarianship. Its official journal is the *CLS Bulletin.* Archivists further their professional interests through the Irish Association for Archives.

REFERENCES

Maura Neylon and Monica Henchy, *Public Libraries in Ireland* (1966).

The Library Association of Ireland and the Library Association, Northern Ireland Branch, *Directory of Libraries in Ireland* (1990).

DEIRDRE ELLIS-KING

Islamic Libraries

(7th to 17th centuries)

Islam evolved early in the 7th century A.D. from an Arabic civilization that was basically nomadic but one which in that century received a scripture. This development predisposed the Arabs to enrich their literary heritage with that of their Persian and Byzantine neighbors soon after they conquered them. The Qur'an (Koran), the Arabic revelation, encourages learning and knowledge. Although the word *knowledge* as used in the Qur'an has a religious connotation, later such sayings as "Seek ye knowledge from the cradle to the grave," "The search for knowledge is incumbent on every Muslim," "Seek ye knowledge even into China," and the like were broader and became commonplace. Since religion was the focal point in the Islamic state, the first library transaction can be observed in regard to the Qur'an—the deposit of a copy of this work with Hafsah, one of the Prophet Muhammad's widows.

The private library was the preponderant type of library in early Islam. Private libraries were owned mainly by scholars interested in those branches of knowledge that developed from the study of the Qur'an and the traditions of the Prophet, such as grammar, theology, law, and history. Eventually the collections of these libraries found their way into the mosques that had developed adjunct libraries rather early in their efforts to supplement religious instruction. The most famous mosque library is that of al-Azhar in Cairo, which was founded in the 9th century but gained university status in the 18th. It should also be noted that since in many instances the private libraries were accessible to other scholars and sometimes even the general public, there was a gradual transition from the private library to the later public libraries.

During the Umayyad Caliphate (661–750) scholarly interests extended to the natural sciences. This interest, particularly in mathematics, astronomy, and medicine, came to the fore during the Abbasid Caliphate (750–1258), when under al-Ma'mun (813–33) a *Dar al-Hikmah* (House of Wisdom) was established in Baghdad that was open to all. This academy contributed extensively to the understanding of Greek philosophy and science. Under its head and chief translator, Hunayn ibn Ishaq, Greek manuscripts were acquired and translated into Arabic, often through the Syriac medium. Many Greek works that were lost in the original were preserved only through these translations.

A similar institution was founded in Cairo during the Fatimid rule (909–1171). After the dissolution of this library at the end of the Fatimid reign, much of the collection was acquired by the Secretary of Saladin, Qadi al-Fadil, and was named al-Fadiliyah after him.

The third most important library of the Middle Ages in Islam was the court library of the Umayyad rulers of Cordova, Spain (750–1031). Although apparently less accessible to the public, it had extensive holdings.

These three libraries cannot be considered national libraries in the strict sense of the word, but they were the most outstanding central institutions in these countries and were—if indirectly—financed by public revenues. Unfortunately, these libraries were often short-lived because frequent political upheavals destroyed the libraries and their collections.

Under the Seljuks (1037–1300) the *madrasah* (colleges) came into prominence and with them college libraries. The wazir Nizam al-Mulk, who during a period of 20 years was the virtual ruler of the realm, built many colleges throughout the empire; the best-known one was in Baghdad and named al-Nizamiyah. The philosopher Al-Ghazzali was one of the outstanding teachers there. At that time monastic libraries also came into existence in conjunction with the rise of the dervish orders; their significance was minimal, however, compared with that of European monastic libraries.

The Ottoman Turks (1299–1923) made Constantinople their capital, and consequently the principal library activity followed to that city. Giambatista Toderini, visiting the city in the early 18th century, reported on 13 major libraries, many of them open to the public, and gave an insight into their holdings.

While the strength of the Islamic library collections was first measured in camel loads, numbers do exist for later periods; these, however, cannot always be taken at face value. Volume numbers up to half a million for major libraries during the Middle Ages are probably not exaggerated: most of these libraries had full-time manuscript copyists (*nassakh*) on their staffs. Other members of the library staff were the Superintendent (*sahib*), one or more Custodians (*khazin*), and Assistants (*farrash*). The scribes often belonged to the local guild and as such sometimes wielded considerable power; fearing for their jobs, they successfully opposed the introduction of printing into Constantinople until the beginning of the 18th century.

The arrangement of books was usually by subject, stored in compartments that could be locked. Since the books were stored on their sides, a practice that contributed to the deterioration of the outer covers and the title and colophon pages, the titles were written on labels attached to the spine and were written on the fore edge to facilitate identification. When catalogues existed, they were usually in book form. The lack of proper ventilation and the presence of vermin contributed to the damage of the manuscripts. The mosque libraries, not usually being equipped to forestall or repair deterioration, suffered most in this respect, while the caliphal libraries were financially best suited to house the collections in climate-controlled premises and to repair them when damage occurred. Unfortunately the latter libraries bore the brunt of attacks by human enemies—the thieves, sectarians, and Mongol invaders.

REFERENCES

O. Pinto, "The Libraries of the Arabs during the Time of the Addasids," *Islamic Culture* (1929).

Index Islamicus provides references under "Libraries."

MIROSLAV KREK

Bibliothèque Nationale

Interior of an Islamic library from an illuminated manuscript of al-Hariri in the Bibliothèque Nationale in Paris.

Israel

Israel, a republic in the Middle East, is bordered on the north by Lebanon, on the east by Syria and Jordan, and on the west by Egypt and the Mediterranean Sea. Population (1991 est.) 5,000,000; area (excluding occupied territory) 20,770 sq.km. The official languages are Hebrew and Arabic; English is widely known.

History. Books, reading, and study have always played a central part in Judaism. However, the "People of the Book" have not necessarily been the "People of the Library." On the one hand, the Jewish tradition of learning and book appreciation provides potentially fertile soil for the growth of libraries; in fact the institution of the *Beit Midrash* (House of Learning) attached to the synagogue in every community contained elements of a proto-public library, serving as it did as the cultural and social center of the community, with a book collection accessible to all. On the other hand, the strong need for books made individual acquisition and private borrowing a social norm, reducing the need for the library as an institution.

The late 19th century saw a resurgence of Jewish settlement in Palestine. The new settlers brought with them from the Diaspora the traditional library model of the Beit Midrash as well as other library models. In relatively short order a modest system of public libraries was established, including the library that later became the Jewish National and University Library (JNUL). With the subsequent development of the JNUL and the appointment of Hugo Bergmann as National Librarian, the foundations of the Israeli library scene were laid. Bergmann adopted the American tradition of a library open to all and responsive to a variety of interests. This reader-centered library model fitted the tradition of the Beit Midrash as the cultural center of the community as well as the egalitarian ideals of the democratic society being built in Palestine.

Until the early 1930s the Jewish population of Palestine numbered under 300,000 and was about 90 percent of European extraction, needing libraries mainly as an adjunct to private book acquisition. But in the 1930s a large wave of German Jewish immigrants brought with them the continental European library model of learned libraries for the intellectual elite and *volksbücherei* ("popular libraries") for the "common" people, which changed the face of librarianship in the country entirely. This model rapidly gained favor, appealing as it did to the respect for scholarship ingrained in the Jewish tradition. The ascendancy of the continental European model caused a change in the attitude toward librarianship as a profession: it began to be regarded as a technical-clerical occupation requiring minimal training. Only senior staff members in research and large libraries were expected to have academic degrees, and even then not necessarily in librarianship. Professional goals were soon replaced by an emphasis on techniques, a clerical approach, and an increasing disengagement of librarians from the role of bearing a social or cultural message.

Additional waves of immigration before 1948 brought with them the East European library tradition, which viewed the community library as a means of educating the public in the spirit of socialist ideology. This model was easily integrated with the prevailing continental-European model, since both aim at educating the masses. In this period the supply and the provision of books were still entirely adequate for the needs of the population (630,000 in 1947), which did not expect library services beyond those they were receiving.

When the great waves of immigration started to arrive after Israel became an independent state in 1948, the structure of society underwent drastic changes. It soon became clear that the library system would not be able to deal with such changes. During the first five years of statehood, when most institutions in the country made a concentrated effort to absorb more than a million immigrants, the libraries played no part.

The main reason for this inactivity was that the libraries were unable to function as community centers—the direct result of the changes in the profession in the 1930s. A second reason had to do with the demographic composition of the immigration: 800,000 were refugees from Arab countries. Jews of European background were interested in reading secular literature; that interest had been fostered throughout the 18th and 19th centuries by the influ-

Libraries in Israel (1990)

Type of library	Number of administrative units (main libraries)	Number of service points (branches, mobile stops, etc.)	Volumes in collections	Annual expenditures (new shekel)	Population served	Professional staff (with certificate, diploma, etc.)	Total staff
National	1	1	3,000,000	2,120,000	Open to all	100	150
Academic	7	80	6,300,000	45,000,000	71,190[1]	n.a.	n.a.
Public	--	983[a]	12,400,000[a]	26,476,800	4,240,000	1,200[a]	2,070[a]
School	1,735[b]	--	5,651,000[c]		1,461,282[2]	1,422[c]	1,940[c]
Special	400	--	--		--	--	--

[a]1985 data
[b]1987 data
[c]1983 data
1. Number of university students 1991
2. Number of pupils in all levels of schooling in 1991

Sources: Statistical Abstract of Israel, 1991. Monthly Bulletin of Statistics. Survey of School Libraries, 1987.

ence of the Haskalah (Enlightenment) movement and motivated the European Jews to apply religious norms of learning to secular learning as well. Jews from the Arab countries, on the other hand, had retained their love and respect for religious literature without necessarily extending it to secular literature. If the public libraries had religious literature in their collections, the refugees from the Arabic-speaking countries might well have been drawn to them, but such was not the case: the prestate immigrants, the pioneers, had been for the most part rebelling against religion, and the libraries they established were secular in nature.

In addition, the library collections did not meet the needs of large segments of the population in other ways. Many of the books were in German, a language unknown to both the eastern European Jews and the Jews from Arab countries. Even the Hebrew books were not readable by many people, because the language used was antiquated. The contents of the books reflected Central and East European Jewish culture, and as such were of little use to other cultural groups. In the absence of professional leadership, there was no initiative to refocus public library collections and activities.

Furthermore, in the first years of statehood, the money available for libraries went almost entirely to rebuilding the National and University Library, destroyed during the War of Independence. Only after the JNUL had been rebuilt was professional librarianship, with Curt Wormann (JNUL Director, 1947–68) at its head, ready to turn its attention to the state of the library system in the rest of Israel. In 1956 Wormann founded a library school at the Hebrew University, with the express intention of emphasizing the social and educational role of the librarian. This step, a landmark in the history of librarianship in Israel, was the beginning of a renewed professional approach.

The 1960s brought additional positive developments at a time when social integration was still one of the most pressing problems in Israeli society: C. I. Golan founded and became the first Director of the Public Library Section (later the Library Department) of the Ministry of Education and Culture. Golan saw the library as a tool for social integration; in his efforts to develop the library as an influential institution in each community, he adopted as a model the system prevalent in Denmark, where independent local libraries each receive government funding, but retain complete intellectual freedom. As a result of Golan's activities, libraries were founded in many settlements, especially in development towns populated by new immigrants.

In 1975 a Public Library Law was finally enacted. The law, designed to make mandatory the founding and maintenance of a public library by each local authority, is of central importance, although limited fiscal resources have since prevented its widespread enforcement. Public-library development slowed after the Yom Kippur War of 1973, Golan's retirement in the mid-1970s, and political changes in 1977. The government's share in financing public libraries declined sharply and was divided among more libraries. The Library Department began funding school libraries, decreasing the impact of both.

The law provided for a Council for Public Libraries to advise the Minister of Education. The Council required public-library workers to have an education similar to that of elementary-school teachers. After this positive development, the Council gradually lost influence.

New Social Science Library, Tel-Aviv University.

On the academic scene new universities were founded and older ones expanded; their libraries were given higher priority and began to offer new services. The new universities established libraries with centralized services and open shelves. Unfortunately, the new policies did not always work well in practice since many of the librarians, recent graduates of the Hebrew University Library School, did not have the experience to carry them out, and the new libraries did not live up to expectations. As a result, a regression to older norms took place, and faculty members in each institution began preempting responsibility for determining the nature of the library services. Also, many directors of university library were scholars in other disciplines who considered their library responsibilities subordinate to research in their specific fields. A tendency toward fragmentation of collection and services developed, with many departmental libraries in each university competing for limited funds.

In the short history of librarianship in Israel, during periods when the library was perceived as a potential agent for social change, the reader became the focus of attention and the librarian had an influential role. During periods when the library's main task was perceived as providing services to scholars and the academic elite, the book became the focus and the librarian was considered merely a clerk. The history of librarianship in Israel is, in effect, the history of the conflict between these two approaches, each of which in turn left its mark.

National Library. The Jewish National and University Library in Jerusalem serves a dual purpose as the National Library of Israel (and inherently of the entire Jewish people) and as the central library of the Hebrew University. The Library was begun in 1884 as a small collection mostly donated by European philanthropists, which merged with the library of the Bnei Brith Lodge in Jerusalem in 1892. In 1920 the World Zionist Organization took responsibility for its operation and named it "the Jewish National Library."

In 1925 the Library was incorporated into the newly founded Hebrew University and was renamed the Jewish National and University Library. The Library was destroyed during the War of Independence, then rebuilt on the campus of Hebrew University.

The Library, which grew to more than 3,000,000 volumes by the early 1990s, collects material about Israel, Palestine, Jews, and Judaism; material written by Jews regardless of the place of publication; and books written in Hebrew script or in a Jewish language. Priority is given to acquiring Hebrew and Jewish manuscripts, incunabula, and rare books. Private donors and organizations from all parts of the world have collected and sent books and archives to JNUL, and every effort was made to find and collect material salvaged from the Jewish communities annihilated by the Nazis in Europe during World War II. Since 1933, the JNUL has received two copies of any book published in Israel as legal deposit.

The JNUL's collection of Judaica and related subjects is one of the finest in the world. The Library also contains one of the largest and best-organized collections on Arabic and Islamic subjects in the Middle East. In its permanent collection, there are more than 200 incunabula, 11,000 original manuscripts, 47,000 reproductions of manuscripts, and 200,000 reproductions of fragments.

The JNUL's activities include publishing *Kiryat Sefer,* an annotated bibliography which includes entries for all imprints on Israel, Jews, and Judaica published in Israel and abroad; critical reviews of books; bibliographical research; and descriptive articles about important rare items in the JNUL's collections. The Library also publishes a bibliography of periodical literature called *Index of Articles on Jewish Studies,* which covers journals and serials from all parts of the world.

Academic Libraries. There are eight accredited universities, of which seven maintain full-fledged library services; the Open University has a small collection of its own, but it must supplement its services by making arrangements with the others. In the early 1990s the academic libraries' collections total some 9,300,000 books. Steady growth of collections in spite of severe budgetary restraints was ensured by the establishment of the University Grants Committee (1975).

Available funds are dispensed without interfering with matters of academic freedom. In the absence of formal acquisition policies in most academic libraries, however, collection development has been dictated by faculty demand, an ad hoc process often resulting in gaps in the collections. This problem was further aggravated by fragmentation of the collection and services between a central library and various departmental libraries, although that pattern has started to change. Economic pressures have placed a priority on internal cooperation and unification of resources. For example, at the Hebrew University, 25 of the 70 departmental libraries were united into one library on the social sciences and humanities in 1981 and 6 more were united into a science library in 1985.

In the late 1960s the government, which provides some 70 percent of the academic institutions' budgets, promoted interlibrary cooperation in order to achieve more efficient academic library services. The government established the Israel Standing Committee of National and University Libraries (SCONUL), a voluntary forum for discussing problems of policy and planning. A second forum, the Library Subcommittee of the Grants Committee, was formed in 1976; a third, the Steering Committee for the ALEPH Automation System, was formed in 1986. Library leaders began working in the early 1990s to coordinate, if not to unite, these organizations.

All academic libraries traditionally provide public library services to the community at large. Moreover, academic libraries fulfill national roles; for example, the Technion (Israel Institute of Technology) provides literature searches for scientific and research institutions and industrial companies; the Hebrew University houses the *Israel Union List of Serials;* the University of Haifa Library prepares one of Israel's main bibliographic tools, the computer-based annual *Index to Hebrew Periodicals,* as well as other computer-based bibliographic tools, and from 1981 to 1986 provided MARC-based automated cataloguing services to other universities. In 1989 the Haifa Library converted the Hebrew catalogue of the Center for Public Libraries into machine-readable form. The Center provides cataloguing services for Israel's public and school libraries.

Cooperation, Library Automation, and Networking. The first attempt at library automation for cooperation came in the early 1970s when the JNUL received a government grant to develop an automated cataloguing system, a project that failed. The next attempt to develop an automated cataloguing system suited to local conditions was deemed a complete technical success: MARCIS (MARC ISrael), an automated cataloguing service based on the MARC database. Created by the information division at one of the defense establishments, it became operational in 1974. In spite of its clear advantages, some university library directors decided not to use its services, mainly because they were unwilling to take responsibility for the required changes.

At the beginning of the 1980s formal cooperation was limited to a few undertakings such as the Israel Union List of Serials; an interlibrary loan system utilizing Telex; and MARCIS. Since then, cooperation in automation and networking has increased, mainly as a result of the Grants Committee's initiatives. In 1986 the Committee, following a recommendation from SCONUL, decided to subsidize university library participation in ALEPH. This library automation system was originally developed for the Hebrew University and then adapted to a distributed network (which the University of Haifa advocated). By the 1990s cooperation existed to a greater degree than ever before. All university libraries have automated and share an incipient network based on a union list of monographs; they all use online information systems such as Dialog and BRS; and they all use CD-ROM bibliographic tools. The first Israeli bibliography on CD-ROM is Haifa University Index to Hebrew periodicals; other bibliographies will be added to it.

Public Libraries. The traditional attitudes toward books and reading persist in modern Israel. There is a significantly high percentage of readers—surveys reveal that almost half the population reads at least one book a month—but only 23 percent of the population is registered at public libraries. It seems that the public satisfies most of its information needs by using alternatives to the public library system: private lending and borrowing of books and extensive use of university libraries. Public libraries in the south are aided by the Ben Gurion University Library and in the north by the University of Haifa Library. In addition to their direct service to the public, the university libraries "adopt" public libraries in their regions and advise them on the organization of collections, provide bibliographic service, and donate books to them.

Although Israelis were slow to recognize the importance of libraries as providers of information and as cultural and acculturation agencies, since the 1960s, when the library section of the Ministry of Education and Culture adopted measures for the active development and gradual upgrading of public library services, the trend has changed. The Library Law of 1975, although implemented slowly, provided for establishing and developing public libraries. By 1992 only 760 settlements out of 1,160 had "recognized" libraries provided under the supervision of the Ministry of Education and Culture, since "recognition" means help in funding. In the 1960s and early 1970s government funding provided about half the budget for recognized libraries; in 1974, 43 percent; in 1990, only about 11 percent.

The Center for Public Libraries (founded 1965) is another agent for public libraries, providing such services as a central cataloguing utility, centralized book acquisition, and book processing for libraries. The Center also publishes bibliographies, reference books, and a journal devoted to librarianship, *Yad la-Kore*. The Center's independence and service to public libraries seemed to decline in the early 1990s.

Kibbutz and Moshav Libraries. The *kibbutz* (collective settlement) and *moshav* (cooperative settlement) population has access to the highest proportion of library books per capita in Israel—284,000 people (6 percent of the entire population) had at their disposal about 6,000,000 volumes in the late 1980s. Some 37 percent of those residents are active readers and some 77 percent use settlement libraries. Until the late 1960s books were scattered throughout the settlements in small, often disorganized collections, but thereafter serious attempts were made to apply some method to their libraries. Also, an effort is being made to promote cooperation and sharing of resources between the settlement and the surrounding development towns and villages.

Arab Public Libraries. For the Arab minority in Israel, about 18 percent of the population, little local initiative was taken to provide adequate library service in the decades after 1948. Literacy in the Arab settlements was about 30 percent in Palestine in the 1940s, and many who spoke vernacular Arabic could not understand classical literary Arabic. Israeli newspapers and broadcast media contributed to the development of a literary language influenced by classical Arabic but rooted in the vernacular and thus comprehensible to a wider general reading public. Literacy rates grew steadily, reaching almost 85 percent by 1989.

From the late 1970s the Public Libraries Section of the Ministry of Education helped establish and finance new libraries in the Arab sector. Local leaders began working to establish community libraries or to develop the school libraries. Books in Arabic were published locally and imported through open bridges

Elyachar Library

Elyachar Central Library on the campus of the Technion, the Israel Institute of Technology in Haifa.

from Jordan and Lebanon and later directly from Egypt. Arab settlements send teachers and high school graduates to courses of study at a level below the university and comparable to that received by elementary school teachers.

The public library for Arabs in Israel emerged as a local community institution, receiving government support but relatively free from central government interference. By 1991 33 of the 64 Arab settlements had public libraries supported by the Ministry of Education, and an additional 11 were served by a bookmobile connected with Haifa Public Library. Others have libraries supported by foreign philanthropic organizations, presumed to be politically affiliated with Palestinian or Muslim fundamentalist organizations.

In towns of mixed Jewish and Arab population, the public libraries serve both Jewish and Arab readers. Arab students and teachers make use of the Arabic collections at the university libraries.

School Libraries. Since the 1970s there has been a growing awareness of the importance of school libraries and of their potential role in education and teaching. This newly acquired consciousness did not result in a formal decision to upgrade school libraries, but it did bring about improvement: by the early 1980s, only a handful of the elementary and high schools in the Jewish sector provided no library services whatsoever for their students. In the Arab sector a much larger share, about one in five of the elementary and high schools, had no library services.

School libraries still need much more attention: their collections are small and they offer only limited services. Children receive minimal encouragement and instruction to use libraries. Competition with public libraries for the resources of the Library Department of the Ministry of Education and Culture hampers improvement.

Special Libraries. Israel has some 400 special libraries connected to research institutions, hospitals, professional associations, government agencies, and industrial plants. They developed close ties and interlibrary loan arrangements on their own, and their readers' demand for constantly updated information brought to light the need for a central agency specifically dedicated to fostering cooperation and coordination in scientific and technical information services. The initiative for the establishment of such an agency again came from outside the profession, with the advent of government policy for industrialization in the 1960s. The National Council for Research and Development established the Center for Scientific and Technological Information (COSTI) in 1961.

COSTI initiated the use of new information technologies and provides central information services where needed. It offers selective dissemination of information from international databases it leases; online searching; clearinghouse services; and reference, training, and consultancy. Increasing use of international networking met much of the local need for scientific and technological information, rendering some local agencies redundant or even obsolete.

Other Libraries. *Parliamentary Library.* The Parliamentary Library holds a relatively small collection for the use of members of the Knesset (Israeli Parliament). It also receives deposit copies of Israeli publications, but unlike the JNUL it does not serve as a depository library; the books are distributed among other libraries.

Religious Libraries. Many Orthodox members of the public use libraries and book collections of a religious nature. The Jewish religious libraries are in synagogues, orthodox Jewish educational institutions, local religious councils, and rabbinical courts. There are also a number of private collections.

Christian religious libraries can be found in monasteries and missions and near churches. Although some serve the general public, many are limited to the use of researchers.

Muslim religious libraries have been founded and promoted mostly by the Muslim Religious Endowment (Waqf), although there are many private collections as well. There are libraries in mosques and others privately supported by Arab and Muslim philanthropic organizations outside Israel.

The Profession. Library education in Israel has always been influenced by changes in public opinion about the role of the library in society. Hugo Bergmann, who viewed librarians as filling a vital role in the community, saw to it that the senior librarians received appropriate professional training in library schools abroad, and that even librarians in small local libraries received training beyond the technical. He enabled them to be culture-bearers to the public. In the mid-1930s Bergmann's model of library education was replaced by a model of short, non-academic training courses that were purely technical.

Independence brought with it a shortage of professional library personnel, as the rapidly expanding economy provided many employment opportunities for academically trained people, all more lucrative than librarianship. In response to the shortage, the Library School at the Hebrew University was founded. The School adopted the framework of the American model of professional library education, although the content of the framework was frequently influenced by the continental European model.

In the 1970s additional academic library education programs were started. In response to the growing demand for academically trained librarians in northern Israel, the University of Haifa opened a graduate diploma course of library education in 1972 as part of the Faculty of the Humanities. The two-year course emphasizes principles rather than techniques and attempts to develop a comprehensive approach to librarianship, stressing the role of the library in society.

In 1973 Bar-Ilan University (the only Orthodox-oriented university in the country) opened a School of Library Education. The School offers a post-B.A. diploma course similar to those of other library schools and instituted a program of librarianship as a second major course of study for the undergraduate degree. In 1985 the University of Haifa instituted an undergraduate program, which is part of a general B.A. and does not lead to a professional degree; many students take the course as the main core of the university's communication courses.

In the 1980s many Israeli librarians realized that the non-academic training courses established in the 1960s were inadequate and that librarians, especially public librarians, should have a broader educational background. The Council for Public Libraries initiated changes in the non-academic courses, making their level equivalent to that of the training programs for elementary school teachers. The first such program, leading to the degree of chartered librarian, was put into effect at Haifa University School of Education of the kibbutz movement, Oranim, in 1976.

Associations. The Israel Library Association (ILA) is the professional organization for Israeli library personnel and archivists. Its membership grew from 150 at its foundation in 1952 to about 2,000, but many libraries chose not to join. The Israel Society of Special Libraries and Information Centers (ISLIC) was founded in 1966 to extend professional aid to special librarians and establish foreign and local contacts in the field of special librarianship. It publishes the *ISLIC Bulletin,* which deals with problems of special libraries.

REFERENCES

Irene Sever and Shmuel Sever, *The Library in Society* (1990), in Hebrew.

Shmuel Sever, "Library Education in Israel," *Journal of Education for Librarianship* (1981).

SHMUEL SEVER

Italy

Italy, a republic in southern Europe, comprises the Apennine Peninsula, Sicily, Sardinia, and various other islands. Italy juts out south into the Mediterranean Sea and is bordered on the north and west by France and Switzerland and on the north and east by Austria and Slovenia. Population (1990 est.) 57,062,000; area 301,268 sq.km. The official language is Italian.

History. Italy's first libraries were private collections started during the period of the Roman republic, which lasted from 510 to 30 B.C. (*See* Rome [Ancient].) Pliny describes the first major library, instituted by Asinio Pollione near the Temple of Liberty on the Aventine Hill. During the imperial era, which lasted from 30 B.C. until the barbarian invasions of the fifth century, the Ulpia library, situated near the column of Trajan, was the largest; others blossomed within the walls of various imperial palaces.

The invasion and destruction of the Roman Empire led to the virtual disappearance of libraries in Italy. Some monastic orders—notably the Benedictine Order, which placed much value on study and the copying of texts—saved many valuable manuscripts from vanishing. Monasteries at Bobbio, Grottaferrata, and Subiaco became famous for their libraries. Subiaco was the site of the first Italian printing works, in the 15th century.

During the Renaissance many noble families sought to make their courts centers of culture, founding palace libraries. Notable examples include the libraries of the Visconti and Sforza families of Pavia and the Aragonesi of Naples.

The 17th and 18th centuries mark the beginning of modern history for Italian libraries. Libraries opened their doors to the public and contributed to major scientific and cultural discoveries. The Biblioteca Ambrosiana, founded by Cardinal Federico Borromeo and named after St. Ambrose, the patron saint of Milan, was opened to the public in 1609. This library in Milan, which consisted of Borromeo's private collection, is considered the first public library in Italy. Major libraries grew up in many parts of the country, including the Gambalunghiana in Rimini.

A unified Italy in the 1860s faced the challenge of linking many regional libraries into an organized national system. Impeding this effort, undertaken between 1869 and 1967, was precisely the fragmented patchwork of administrations that governed each area library, resulting in a disorganization that not even the rigid totalitarian vision of fascism could conquer.

Recent years have seen improvements in the national library system. The launching of project SBN (National Library Service) was a major step toward establishing both a national union catalogue and a comprehensive national lending system. By 1990 more than 200 libraries had joined the effort, with current holdings of about 35 million volumes.

National Libraries. There are 10 institutions given the title of national libraries in Italy. The National Central Libraries in Rome and Florence are the most prominent, and both receive materials under the deposit laws of 1886 and subsequent modifications. The Library in Florence started with a donation from Antonio Magliabechi in the early 18th century. In 1935 it was moved to its present site, near the Church of Santa Croce, on the right bank of the River Arno. It suffered great damage from the flood of 1966. Today it holds nearly five million volumes and is completely automated.

The Library in Rome, officially known as the Biblioteca Nazionale Centrale Vittorio Emanuele II, collaborates with its sister Central Library in Florence to produce bibliographies of Italian and foreign materials. It has about 4.5 million volumes. The two libraries have different strengths: Rome specializes in lending; Florence serves as a major national archive.

Other national libraries are in Bari, Milan, Naples, Palermo, Turin, and Venice. The newest are those in Potenza (founded 1974) and Cosenza (founded 1990).

Academic Libraries. Nowhere is the administrative chaos that marks Italian libraries more evident than in the university library system. There are 12 such libraries, at Bologna, Cagliari, Catania, Genoa, Messina, Modena, Naples, Padova, Palermo, Pavia, Pisa, and Rome, and they come under the administrative rule of their universities. But, like the national libraries, they depend on the state for funding.

The university library in Rome is an example of the distinct historic value of these libraries. It was founded by Pope Alexander VII and opened to the public in 1670. Located initially in the Palazzo della Sapienza, seat of the ancient University of Rome, it was moved in 1935 to the university's new campus. The Library is—in Rome—second in size only to the city's national library and contains an important collection of rare and antique manuscripts.

Over the years academic libraries have faced problems, caused mainly by lack of resources, cooperation, and coordination, in obtaining materials for their collections and lending them out effectively. Progress in these areas became evident in the late 1980s, in part because of the modernization and automation of many branches. One of the major signs of progress is project SBN, designed to link university libraries not only with each other, but also with foreign libraries that have collections focused on similar subjects. In 1989 the government moved university administration from the Ministry of Public Instruction to the Ministry of University and Scientific

Libraries in Italy (1987)

Type of library	Number of administrative units (main libraries)°	Number of service points (branches, mobile stops, etc.)°	Volumes in collections°	Annual expenditures (lira)	Population served°	Professional staff (with certificate, diploma, etc.)	Total staff
National[a]	2	2	5,402,000	--	2,706	--	--
Academic[b]	11	11	4,581,000	1,861,776*	24,266	105	774
Public[c]	47	--	16,133,000	--	268,813	--	--
Non-specialized[a]	34	34	7,393,000	--	45,663	--	--

[a]1989 data
[b]1987 data
[c]1985 data; refer only to libraries of the Ministry of Culture & Environment
*refers to acquisition only

°Source: Unesco, *Statistical Yearbook,* 1991.

Columbia University

Italy's first public library, Biblioteca Ambrosiana (Milan), was opened to the public in 1609.

Research. Placing university libraries with research was designed to improve performance.

Public Libraries. The term "public library" is used in Italy to define libraries run by the national Ministero per i Beni Culturali e Ambientali. Included in this group are both national and university libraries, as well as the libraries of Cremona and of Lucca; the Marucelliana, Mediceo Laurenziana, and Riccardiana of Florence; the Isontina of Gorizia; the Estense of Modena; the Palatina of Parma; and the Angelica, Casanatense, and Vallicelliana of Rome; as well as the library of the Institute of Contemporary and Modern History in Rome.

A network of true public libraries did not exist in Italy until the 1970s. Some public libraries had existed over the years, thanks to either philanthropists or local socialist efforts. In 1861 Antonio Bruni founded a network of popular libraries that gave way in 1908 to a national federation of public libraries. The Fascist government of the 1930s broke up the federation, using libraries as instruments of political propaganda through censorship. Governments after World War II neglected public libraries, facing more serious problems in other spheres. Finally, between 1972 and 1977, the government gave regions control over their libraries. Not all regions felt compelled to invest, and the improvement in public libraries was uneven: the already varied cultural differences between northern and southern Italy were further accentuated.

The library system in Lombardy set the tone for the rest of the nation, promoting a sense of cooperation among branches. Each was assigned the job of buying, conserving, and evaluating books and documents, slowly building collections. The result: by 1988 more than two thirds of the cities in Lombardy had at least one library apiece, serving 93 percent of the population in the region. The libraries employ more than 1,400 personnel, with 363 having professional responsibilities.

Other noteworthy accomplishments in the field of public libraries include significant strides in intraprovincial cooperation and communication in Emilia Romagna. Ravenna was the first city in Italy to establish an SBN network, which connects public, specialized, and historic libraries in the area.

Southern Italy presents an entirely different picture. Regions such as Sicily, Sardinia, Puglia, and Campania do not have laws governing libraries and offer inadequate library systems for their people, with a few noteworthy exceptions. Foggia, for example, has a library noted for its efficient service and the quality of its collection.

School Libraries. Most Italian schools at all levels have collections of books available to students and teachers alike. There are about 45,000 of these collections, holding about 33 million volumes. But few of them can truly be called "libraries," because they have no catalogues, no financial resources, no adequate space for research, and no trained staffs. In one province, Emilia Romagna, only 52 of the 315 schools had libraries in 1986, most of them run by teachers rather than librarians. The post of "library coordinator" was established in 1989, specifying teachers who would run libraries and teach school librarianship. The basic problem for school libraries is that they are not recognized officially in law.

Special Libraries. Italy has many and varied special libraries. They include the Biblioteca dell'Instituto di Archeologia e Storia dell'Arte (Library of the Institute of Archaeology and the History of Art), the Biblioteca dell'Instituto di Storia Moderna e Contemporanea (Library of the Institute of Modern and Contemporary History), and the Biblioteca Medica Statale (State Medical Library), all in Rome. Government ministries have important special libraries, rich in documents related to government operation, with a collection of about 800,000 volumes and more than 3,000 current periodicals. Collections focusing on economics, history, law, and politics are also open to the public. Other special libraries belong to academies, cultural and scientific institutes, and local economic research centers. Under the SBN project, special libraries share their resources in specific academic areas.

Biblioteca Universitaria, Pavia

New information technologies have led to a vast improvement in the services of special libraries. They have also led to a blurring of the lines between a library and a document center, between a librarian and a documentalist. Databases on various subjects have developed over the years, especially in the fields of law and economics.

The Profession. Italian librarians come under the authority of administrations at every level—national, regional, provincial, and local—that have widely varying views of the importance of library service. Some of the nation's more prestigious libraries are staffed by professionals, but many others are in the hands of unqualified personnel. At the heart of this problem is the fact that the profession has no official recognition. Only some governments have specific roles for librarians, who have no national organization to set standards for hiring, conduct, and firing. Degrees in library science are fairly recent in Italian higher education, and those wishing to obtain them must first earn general university degrees.

There are moves under way to speed up the incorporation of librarians into the ranks of other professionals, especially because of the need for all professionals in the European Community to be at similar levels. A few universities have expanded their library offerings, adding courses in such topics as conservation.

The Associazione Italiana Biblioteche (AIB; Italian Library Association) was founded in 1930 and has about 3,000 members. It publishes *AIB Notizie,* a monthly newsletter; the *Bollettino d'Informazioni,* a quarterly; regional bulletins; and translations of various international studies. The Association oversees a library dedicated to the profession that is located near its headquarters in Rome.

The AIB organizes an annual conference to showcase products and services. In the 1980s and 1990s, it focused its efforts on making the field of library science a recognized profession and promoting laws to restructure the national library system.

REFERENCES

Enzo Bottasso, *Storia della biblioteca in Italia* (1984).

Mauro Caproni, *La formazione professionale del bibliotecario* (1989).

Giovanni Lazzari, *Libri e popolo: politica della biblioteca pubblica in Italia dall'Unità ad oggi* (1985).

Giovanni Solimine, *Gestione e innovazione della biblioteca* (1990).

GIOVANNI LAZZARI;
translated by MARCO R. DELLA CAVA

Ivory Coast

Ivory Coast, a republic in western Africa, is bordered by Mali and Burkina Faso on the north, Ghana on the east, the Gulf of Guinea on the south, and Liberia and Guinea on the west. Population (1990 est.) 11,998,000; area 322,463 sq.km. The official language is French.

National Library. The Bibliothèque Nationale in Abidjan, the capital of Ivory Coast, was begun in 1968 with the merger of the holdings of the former territorial library and those of the Institut Français d'Afrique Noir (IFAN) in Abidjan. A decree of 1971 defined its duties as collecting, conserving, and making available all materials printed in the country or concerning it; setting up a national documentation center and furnishing readers and researchers with documentation as varied and comprehensive as possible; establishing a general bibliographic center with information on all library collections in the country and publishing a national bibliography based on copyright deposit records; and coordinating activities in the development of libraries administered by the department of libraries and publications (now known as the book promotion department).

The Bibliothèque Nationale adjoins the national museum. These two institutions are part of the government center. The building, dedicated in January 1974, includes conference and lecture rooms, reading rooms, a film library and screening rooms, a popular circulating collection, and a noncirculating research collection. In 1965 the holdings of the former territorial library numbered 6,000 volumes. By 1981, according to Unesco, the Library held 65,000 volumes. And by the mid-1980s the holdings were estimated at 100,000 volumes and 2,000 periodical titles, including 700 current periodicals.

The Bibliothèque Nationale is administered by a chief librarian who also heads the book promotion department, which is part of the Directorate for Cultural Affairs. From August 1978 the institution was directed by Seydou Gueye.

Supplementing the Bibliothèque Nationale collection are the individual libraries maintained by the Assemblée Nationale and many cabinet ministries.

Academic Libraries. The principal academic library is the Bibliothèque Universitaire, on the main campus of the national university in a suburb of Abidjan. The Library is open only to students, faculty, and researchers affiliated with the university; however, students of other specialized colleges as well as individuals demonstrating a bona fide need may use the library after paying nominal fees. The library can arrange international interlibrary loans with the stipulation that borrowers pay shipping costs.

Bibliothèque Nationale

The National Library of the Ivory Coast, founded in Abidjan in 1968.

Some university research institutes maintain their own specialized libraries. Examples are the Library in the Institut d'Ethno-sociologie, specializing in sociology, ethnography, and economic development, and the Institut de Linguistique Appliqué, specializing in African linguistics and oral traditions. Additional libraries at the École Nationale Supérieure de Travaux Publiques, the École Nationale Supérieure Agronomique, and the École de Statistique also provide for specialized academic needs. The library of the École Nationale d'Administration, serving both students and members of the national government, contains more than 10,000 volumes and 100 serials as well as 500 documents and studies on Ivory Coast.

Public Libraries. In 1952 the Colonial government established a municipal library in Abidjan. By 1963 it contained more than 5,000 volumes. In 1964, as part of a Unesco pilot project, the government installed a public library in one of the busiest markets in the Abidjan area. Unesco reported 25,000 volumes in one public library by 1981. The only other public library is the collection of the Centre Culturel Jacques Aqua in Bouaké, the second largest city.

Special Libraries. The holdings of larger special libraries reflect the importance of agriculture for the development of Ivory Coast. The technical libraries of the Office de la Recherche Scientifique et Technique Outre-mer (ORSTOM) and those of the Institut de Recherche Agronomique Tropicale et Cultures Vivrières (IRAT) at Bouaké, the Institut Français du Café, du Cacao, et Autres Plantes Stimulantes, and the Centre Technique Forestier Tropicale de la Côte d'Ivoire contain important works on plant and soil sciences, geology, ecology, and tropical agriculture. There is also an important geology library in the Societé pour le Developpement Minier de la Côte d'Ivoire.

Other research institutes maintain smaller libraries having for the most part fewer than 500 volumes. The library of the Institut Africain pour le Developpement Economique et Sociale, however, includes more than 30,000 volumes and 250 serials focusing on the social sciences and economic development. Also concentrating on economic development is the collection of the Bureau National d'Études Techniques du Developpement (BNETD). Finally, the American, French, and German cultural centers in Abidjan established libraries on the history and culture of their respective countries.

School Libraries. With the stated objectives of helping students with classwork, stimulating thought, and encouraging reading for pleasure, the government set up libraries in secondary schools, though most of the libraries have fewer than 1,000 volumes. Volumes are distributed unequally among the secondary school libraries, with the lion's share going to the more prestigious, though not always larger, urban schools.

The Profession. The Association for the Development of Documentation, Libraries, and Archives of the Ivory Coast (connected with the Bibliothèque Nationale) was established in Abidjan. A decree of 1971 set rules for recruitment and training. Staffs are comparatively small, and most library employees received their training on the job.

ROBERT E. HANDLOFF;
SEYDOU GUEYE

J

Jamaica

Jamaica, a parliamentary state and member of the Commonwealth, lies in the Caribbean Sea south of Cuba. Population (1991 est.) 2,400,000; area 10,990 sq.km. The official language is English.

History. Jamaica was occupied by the Spaniards from 1509 to 1655, when the English captured it. In 1962 it was the first British colony in the West Indies to gain independence. Until 1948, it had no full-scale free public library. A subscription service was available from 1879 from the Institute of Jamaica. The territory's first free library, a separate junior center of the Institute library, opened for children in 1940. The Jamaica Library Service, established in 1948, now provides a comprehensive service throughout the island.

The National Council on Libraries, Archives, and Documentation Services (NACOLADS) was established in 1973 to plan and coordinate a national information network. It was responsible for the development of libraries and national standards. In 1991 its scope was broadened to reflect all aspects of information activities, including the communications media and informatics; it was renamed the National Council on Libraries, Archives, and Information Systems (NACOLAIS). Two of its major aims are to promote and to obtain increasing support for the libraries, archives, and documentation services of the nation.

National Library. The National Library of Jamaica (NLJ) was established by NACOLADS in 1979. Its primary responsibility is to collect, preserve, and make available all materials published in Jamaica, by Jamaicans, and about Jamaica. The Institute of Jamaica was founded in 1879 mainly for the encouragement of literature, science, and art. It established the West India Reference Library in 1894, and that collection forms the nucleus of the National Library. The library's collection of Caribbeana is extensive, with material dating back to the 16th century, and is constantly growing. Its holdings include more than 160,000 items of print, non-print, and audiovisual materials, as well as 50,000 ft. of audiotape and 5 million ft. of 16mm black and white archival film. It operates a National Referral Service and has made wide use of computer applications. Publications include the *Jamaica National Bibliography,* the *Gleaner Index,* an occasional bibliography series, and other works. NLJ is the national center for ISBN, ISSN, and Cataloguing-in-Publication data and has been designated as the legal deposit center; publishers are encouraged to deposit copies of their publications with the NLJ even before the country adopts a legal deposit law.

Academic Libraries. The libraries of the University of the West Indies, Mona, hold almost 450,000 volumes and nearly 12,500 serial titles, more than 7,500 of them current. They serve the main campus and, when necessary, programs at the other campuses of the regional university, Cave Hill in Barbados and St. Augustine in Trinidad. The Campus Librarian on the Mona Campus manages three branches: the Main Library, with a collection on the arts, the social sciences, general reference works, and library studies; the Science Library, covering physical and biological sciences and pre-clinical medicine; and the Medical Library, with a collection on clinical medicine. The Main Library is the primary academic library of Jamaica.

Other independent libraries at the Mona Campus serve specialized sections of the university community. These include the Institute of Social and Economic Research, the Documentation Center of the Faculty of Education, and other departmental libraries. Together they hold almost 60,000 volumes. Affiliated with the university are the libraries of the United Theological College (1967); St. Michael's Seminary (1952); the Norman Manley Law Library (1963); and the Caribbean Food and Nutrition Institute (1968). The Library of the College of Arts, Science, and Technology (CAST) is the focal point for the College Libraries Information Network (COLINET). The largest college library in the country, it has a collection of more than 30,000 items.

Public Libraries. The Jamaica Library Service is run by the Jamaica Library Board, established in 1948. The Service is based on local government areas known as *parishes.* Parish libraries are grouped in four regions, with the largest and most developed designated as regional headquarters. The regional network consists of 13 main libraries, one in each capital town, and more than 700 service points, including 153 branch libraries and more than 500 bookmobile stops. Services are provided to hospitals and correctional institutions, and a free postal service is provided for the elderly, the handicapped, and the homebound. Special collections include West Indian literature, the theatre, and foreign languages (French, Spanish, and German).

School Libraries. The Schools Library Service is based on a fleet of bookmobiles that rotate bookstocks regularly. It is administered by the Jamaica Library Service and served more than 820 primary schools and more than 90 secondary schools in the early 1990s. More than half the schools have separate library rooms and about a quarter of them have trained library staff. The service for primary schools began in 1952 and was extended to new secondary schools in 1969. The primary school stock in 1990 totaled almost

Jamaica Library Service

Main building of the National Library of Jamaica, Kingston, opened in 1978 as part of the Institute of Jamaica, established in 1879.

Libraries in Jamaica (1990)

Type of library	Number of administrative units (main libraries)	Number of service points (branches, mobile stops, etc.)	Volumes in collections	Population served	Professional staff (with certificate, diploma, etc.)	Total staff
National	1	1	41,615	National	21	89
Academic	7	9	676,688	8,336	37	108
Public	13	709	1,169,392	2,392,000	148	909
School	948	948	1,741,606	579,103	--	--
Primary						
New Secondary						
High						
Special	94	94	245,000	--	52	--
Other (describe)						
Tertiary/ College	14	14	195,000	26,000	12	87

1 million books and periodicals and served an enrollment of more than 400,000 pupils. The secondary school stock of some 420,000 served more than 100,000 students. In addition, the 30 traditional high schools had libraries of varying standards, some staffed by professionals, operated independently of the Schools Library Service.

Special Libraries. The libraries attached to government ministries, enterprises, corporations, and statutory bodies, as well as private-sector organizations, continue to improve their collections and facilities. In many instances the NLJ gives them assistance to strengthen the national information system. Special libraries in the public and private sector have been organized into subject-specific networks, including a Scientific and Technical Information Network (STIN), a Socio-Economic Information Network (SECIN), a Legal Information Network (LINET), and the College Libraries Information Network (COLINET). Each network has an advisory body.

The Profession. The Jamaica Library Association was established in 1950 and has full-time, associate, institutional, and student members. It seeks to strengthen libraries and the library profession by developing standards and promoting continuing education and training programs. The Ministry of Education accepted its standards for school libraries, developed in 1977. The Association has since developed standards for college libraries and special libraries. It is a member of the Commonwealth Library Association, the International Association of School Libraries, and the International Federation of Library Associations.

The Association has always been concerned with training and played a pivotal role in establishing the Department of Library Studies at the Mona campus of the University of the West Indies. The Department offers a three-year course toward the Bachelor of Arts degree and a fifteen-month course toward the Master's degree in Library Studies. The Jamaica Library Association has hosted international conferences and continuing education programs; its members have made important contributions to the activities of international professional associations.

STEPHNEY FERGUSON

Jameson, J. Franklin
(1859–1937)

John Franklin Jameson—historian, teacher, editor, manuscript librarian, and administrator—was present at the beginnings of the historical profession in the United States and later of the archival profession.

Born September 19, 1859, in Somerville, Massachusetts, Jameson early showed intellectual promise and habits of hard work. He was graduated from the Roxbury Latin School and, in 1879, as valedictorian from Amherst College. While in college he set course on becoming a historian. Unable to finance graduate study in Germany, he taught high school for a year before going to the newly established Johns Hopkins University. His Ph.D. in 1882 was the first history doctorate awarded there.

Jameson had the rare opportunity to found and shape important institutions. He was one of the founders in 1884 of the American Historical Association and in 1895 of the *American Historical Review,* which he edited with great distinction until 1928 (except for 1901–05).

For the two decades after taking his doctorate, Jameson held history professorships at Hopkins (1882–88), Brown University (1888–1901), and the University of Chicago (1901–05). But Jameson did not make his mark as a teacher.

On leaving Chicago, Jameson became the second Director of the Bureau of Historical Research of the recently founded (1902) Carnegie Institution of Washington. As an advisor to Carnegie's first President, Daniel Coit Gilman, Jameson had helped formulate Carnegie's historical programs, which centered on identifying, evaluating, and publishing guides to the archives of the federal government and of bodies of archival material abroad with bearing on American history. This work eventually made clear the abysmal state of the federal government's archival practices and the pressing need for an archives building and an appropriate agency to administer the whole enterprise. Jameson politicked actively for a quarter century for an archival establishment and was rewarded for his efforts by the construction of the National Archives building in 1934.

In 1927 Jameson became the first incumbent of a chair of American history at the Library of Congress as well as Chief of the Manuscript Division. He actively enlarged the division's role in fostering scholarship by expanding its program of photocopying records from foreign institutions (made possible by the guides he had published at Carnegie) and by acquiring many important new collections. Jameson was responsible for the policy formulation of the Division but also supervised closely all the routine work of his staff.

Although Jameson's bibliography is lengthy, most entries were edited pieces, reports, or reviews; this remarkable historical statesman was far more intent on administering great projects than in producing large-scale interpretive works himself. Still, two of his books, *The History of Historical Writing in America* (1891) and *The American Revolution Considered as a Social Movement* (1926), were of considerable influence in their day and for some years after.

Jameson died September 28, 1937, in Washington, D.C., while still occupying his posts at LC.

REFERENCES

Elizabeth Donnan and Leo F. Stock, editors, *An Historian's World: Selections from the Correspondence of John Franklin Jameson* (1956).

Ruth Anna Fisher and William Lloyd Fox, editors, *J. Franklin Jameson: A Tribute* (1965).

Victor Gondos, Jr., *J. Franklin Jameson and the Birth of the National Archives, 1906–1926* (1981).

The major collection of Jameson's papers is in the Manuscript Division of the Library of Congress.

JOHN B. HENCH

Japan

Japan, a constitutional monarchy, lies in the shape of a bow in eastern Asia and comprises an archipelago including four main islands: Hokkaido, Honshu, Shikoku, and Kyushu. Population (1990 est.) 123,537,000; area 377,801 sq.km. The official language is Japanese.

History. At the turn of the 3rd century A.D., Kanji (Chinese) characters were introduced to Japan by Korean scholars. In the 4th century, a number of political refugees from Korea were naturalized in Japan. Mostly Buddhists from the higher classes and well educated, the Koreans brought to Japanese society their continental culture and religion, which rapidly spread over the country.

As early as the 7th century, the Japanese government sent its first messenger to China to establish direct relations. That communication accelerated the flow of Chinese culture to Japan and the Japanese utilized Kanji as a means to express their native language.

The oldest book of Japanese history was compiled in Kanji in A.D. 712 and the copperplate or wood block prints of the Buddhist sutra of Hyakumanto ("A Million Pagodas") were printed in 770. Buddhist culture was accepted by the Emperor and his courtiers and noblemen, some of whom were interested in learning and began to collect scrolls for a library. Untei-in (Nara) of Isonokami no Yakatsugu (729–81) and Kobaiden (Kyoto) of Sugawara Michizane (845–903) were private collections on Buddhism and Confucianism available to scholars. The openness of the Nara collection is often cited as evidence that it was the first public library in Japan.

Samurai Rule. After a long period of civil war, the Samurai (warrior) class gained power, taking the place of the noblemen in the Kamakura period (1185–1333). Relations with China (Sung dynasty, 960–1279) were reopened and cultural and personal exchange began again. Many sutras and books on Buddhism and Confucianism were imported, stimulating the Japanese religious world. New sects, Zen and Nichiren, were born. Priests were eager to study and print sutras and books on Buddhism. Non-Buddhist books, however, were made by hand as in the past. Two great libraries of Samurai clans at the time still remain today.

Kanazawa Bunko (library) was the private collection set up by the Hojo clan in the latter half of the 13th century. The collection included Buddhist mate-

Libraries in Japan (1987)

Type of library	Number of administrative units (main libraries)	Number of service points (branches, mobile stops, etc.)	Volumes in collections	Annual expenditures (yen)	Population served	Professional staff (with certificate, diploma, etc.)	Total staff
National	1	38	9,667,401	12,573,410,000	122,335,000[a]	1,126[b]	1,259
Academic	926[c]	437	170,451,472	69,286,310,000	2,843,366	8,880[b]	13,808
Public	1,928[d]	635[e]	162,643,000	31,646,757,000	122,353,000	6,816	13,383
School	41,591	--	448,338,289	28,192,001,849	20,814,198	581	c.7,000
Special	2,116[f]	--	--	--	--	--	--

[a]data for 1989
[b] all full-time staffs; no distinction between professional and nonprofessional
[c]a number of junior colleges included
[d]branch libraries included
[e]a number of bookmobiles
[f]a number of special libraries only listed in the *Directory* published in 1988

Photograph by H. Urushibara

Annex to the National Diet Library, opened in 1986, features four stories above and eight stories below ground level and provides a stack capacity of 7,500,000 volumes.

rials in scrolled, folded, and printed forms numbering more than 10,000. The collection was heavily used by scholars.

Ashikaga Gakko (school) was rebuilt to educate boys of the Uesugi clan in 1432. Divination was the main subject taught, and the school's rich collection on the subject attracted scholars from all parts of the country.

The Shogun Tokugawa Ieyasu (1542–1616), who founded the last shogunate, moved the government from Kyoto to Edo (modern Tokyo) in 1590. He ruled a tranquil and prosperous country and encouraged learning to keep the country in peace. The Shogun, an enthusiastic scholar of Confucianism, invited scholars to print books, and he collected books and records that were scattered or thought lost during the civil war years. The Shogun had a private library called Momijiyama Bunko.

Library Center of Kanazawa Institute of Technology, opened in 1982.

The third Shogun of the Tokugawa dynasty, Tokugawa Iemitsu (1604–1651), appointed an official custodian for Momijiyama Bunko to collect books and compile a catalogue of the collection. The Bunko was kept by scholar-custodians under the sponsorship of the shogunate from generation to generation until 1868, when the shogunate fell. The Bunko was full of manuscripts and rare and important materials of the country. The collection is now divided and kept in the Library of the Imperial Household Agency and the Cabinet Library for use of scholars. The Library of the Imperial Household Agency inherited another collection, from the Shoheizaka School, which was a government school to educate Samurai in Edo.

There were more than 250 feudal provinces in Japan during the Edo period (1590–1868). Feudal lords, following the Shogun's policy, established provincial schools with libraries and printed books.

Many wajuku and terakoya (small private schools) gave basic education in reading, writing, and arithmetic to children of the non-Samurai classes. More than 800 terakoyas alone were reported in Edo in 1722.

In the latter part of the Edo period, the lending library became a business. Bookmen carried packs of books on their backs to customers at their homes and lent books for a fee. There were more than 2,000 publishers who had profitable businesses in Japan throughout the Edo period. Literacy of Samurai, merchants, their wives, and children appears to have been high.

Meiji Period. When the last shogun fell in 1868, the Imperial Government was restored to power. Japan opened its ports to trade with foreign countries for the first time since the 17th century. The government imported not only manufactured goods but also science, technology, and other knowledge from European countries and the United States in order to modernize and to catch up with Western civilization in those areas.

The government established the Imperial Library in 1872. It included the collections of Shoheizaka School and other Edo governmental institutions.

In 1872, when public education was enforced, organizations of school teachers were formed in each *ken* (prefecture or province). Those libraries would become the central libraries in kens in later years.

The Japan Library Association was formed by 35 librarians and book lovers in 1892. The first Library Act was issued in 1899. In commemoration of the new building of the Imperial Library, the first annual meeting of librarians was held in 1906. The next year the Japan Library Association began to publish its journal, *Toshokan Zasshi* ("Library Journal").

Taisho Period. During the Taisho period (1912–25), the number of public libraries rapidly grew. There were 445 in the first year and 4,337 in the last year of the Taisho period, but the average number of books was as small as 2,000 volumes per library.

The Librarian's Training Institute was founded under the control of the Ministry of Education in 1921. The Institute initially produced about 40 librarians at the high-school level annually, and later developed into the National University of Library and Information Science with graduate courses.

World War II. The number of public libraries grew steadily until there were 4,794 (1,500 private) at the outbreak of World War II in 1941. During the war, most of the large cities were swept by air-raid bombing and fire. More than half of the collections of central libraries in kens and 80 percent of those in municipal libraries were destroyed.

An Education Mission from the U.S. made recommendations on reform and democratization of education to the occupation authorities. As part of education reform, some recommendations and suggestions on improvements of libraries and library services were included. Japanese libraries have risen from the ashes to develop along the lines of those recommendations.

National Library. Kokuritsu Kokkai Toshokan—the National Diet Library (NDL)—was established by law in 1948. The NDL serves primarily members of the Diet, but also the general public. It is the only library and bibliographic center with the privilege of legal deposit of both civil and official publications in Japan. Its six-story building with basement (73,674 square meters) provide a stack capacity of 4,500,000 volumes. An annex, a four-story building with an eight-story basement, opened in 1986. Its 71,594 square meters provide a stack capacity of 7,500,000 volumes. The annex stores periodicals, newspapers, and materials on science and technology.

The NDL has six departments and a bureau. Its staff numbered 850 in the late 1980s. NDL has 38 branches, including the former Imperial Library, Toyo Bunko (Oriental Library), Library of the Supreme Court, libraries in the executive and judicial agencies of the government, and a detached library in the Diet building (a direct service point to Diet members).

The main collection totaled almost 5,100,000 volumes (almost 1,500,000 foreign), 115,500 periodical titles, 328,000 maps, 313,500 phonodisks, 170,000 reels of microfilms, 1,645,000 sheets of microfiches, 240,000 doctoral dissertations, and 5,100 braille books. More than 400,000 readers (1,600 a day) used the collection. The staff answered almost 279,000 reference questions by mail, by telephone, or in person in 1989.

There is no overall interlibrary loan system for the whole country. The NDL lends books to any library, whether it is a public, university, or special library. NDL loaned more than 4,000 books to its branches, 6,000 to university libraries, 5,000 to public libraries, 1,300 to special libraries, and almost 200 to libraries in foreign countries in a single year in the late 1980s.

In 1971 NDL installed a computer system to automate certain aspects of library work. The automated system's first publication was *The General Index to the Debates in Both Houses of the Diet*.

Bibliographic information on legal deposit publications is accumulated on magnetic tapes to form a central database, JAPAN MARC. The *Japanese National Bibliography*—weekly edition and quarterly index—are compiled and printed from JAPAN MARC. In 1989, 372 libraries subscribed to JAPAN MARC on CD-ROM, called J-Bisc, through the Japan Library Association.

NDL celebrated its 40th anniversary in November 1988, holding a symposium entitled "The Future of Librarianship."

Academic Libraries. Higher education in Japan faced great change under the Education Reform Act after World War II. A coeducational system was introduced, the number of university students greatly increased, and junior colleges for young women's education appeared as new institutions. Before reform, boys were educated for 16 years, from elementary school to university level, and girls for 11 years, from elementary school to girls' high schools. Girls who went on to colleges were the exception.

In 1988 there were 95 national universities, 38 prefectural and municipal universities, and 357 private universities. Together they served almost 2,000,000 students, of whom 34 percent were female. There were 344 national, 54 local, and 686 private university libraries, including departmental libraries and subject collections in faculty members' study rooms. They held more than 156,900,000 volumes, with 52.5 percent in private university, 42.5 percent in national,

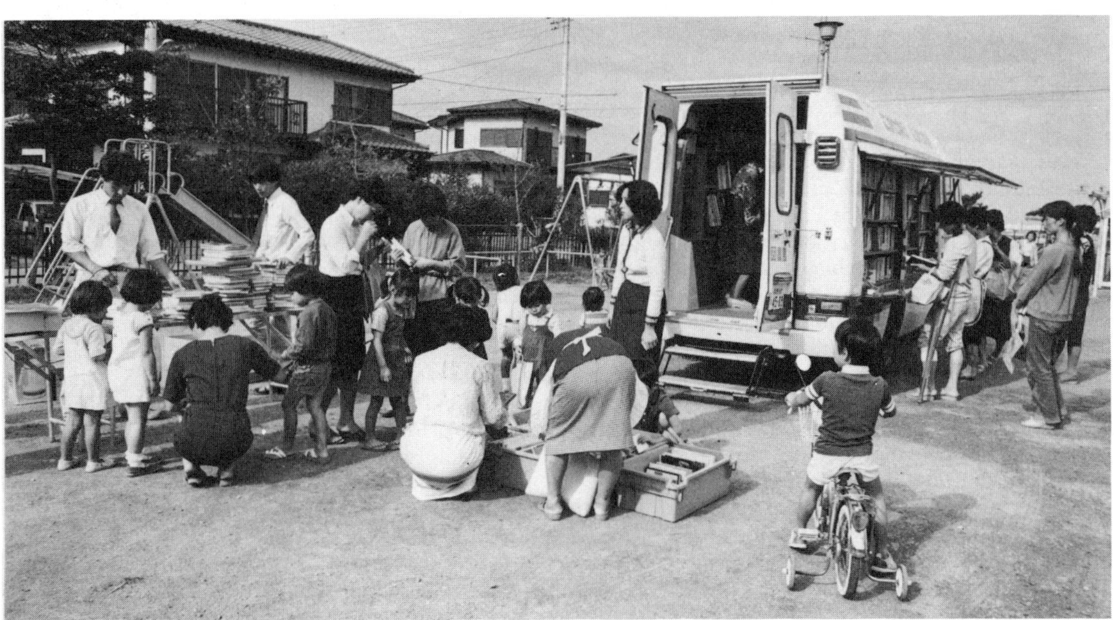

Bookmobile serving a prefecture.

Theodore F. Welch

Yumedono (Hall of Dreams), established on the grounds of the Horyuji Temple near Nara in A.D. 702, thought to be the earliest library in Japan.

and 5 percent in local libraries. The number of books per student ranged from almost 134 at national and almost 126 at local to almost 53 at private university libraries. Expenditures for library materials were almost 22,000 million yen at national, almost 1,800 million yen at local, and almost 33,000 million yen at private university libraries. Computerization of library services has reached 76 percent at national, 13 percent at local, and 27 percent at private universities.

The largest national university library is the University of Tokyo Library, founded in 1877. It comprises the general library and many libraries in faculties, departments, and research institutions. Keio University is the oldest private university. Its Library on the Mita campus, opened in 1983, provides open access to faculty members and students in all parts of the building. The Library Center of Kanazawa Institute of Technology (KIT), opened in 1982, attracted special attention because it installed a computer from the beginning to provide automated library services.

In 1980 the Ministry of Education accepted "The Report on Science Information Systems" submitted by the Science Council, which calls for setting up an information retrieval system based on computer technology that effectively utilizes library resources in universities. The Ministry subsidized national university libraries to cooperate in acquiring scientific periodicals, compiling union catalogues, and setting up interlibrary loan systems. By 1986 the university libraries established the National Center for Science Information System (NACSIS).

The number of university libraries that joined UTLAS (University of Toronto Library Automation Systems) or OCLC (Online Computer Library Center) for processing European and American books increased year by year.

Junior colleges, the comparatively new two- or three-year higher education institutions for females, appeared in 1950. There were 571 (40 national, 54 prefectural and municipal, and 477 private), with more than 450,000 students, by 1988. Junior college libraries, generally speaking, are small. The average number of books was 41,200, with 2.5 staff members in a library in 1988. About 80 percent allow open access.

Public Libraries. The concept of a public library as a tax-supported free institution whose purpose is to serve the community through books and other materials came into being after World War II. The concept was implemented in the enactment of the Public Library Law of April 30, 1950. The day has since been celebrated yearly as "Library Day."

There are two types of public libraries: the prefectural and the municipal (city, town, village, and ward). They have grown enormously since 1950, when 43 prefectures had libraries with total holdings of 3,678,000 volumes. By 1988, prefectural and municipal libraries numbered 1,873; their holdings reached 153,244,000 volumes and circulation reached 255,922,000 books.

Book loans for home use, reference services, audiovisual services, services for children, and bookmobiles started in the 1950s and expanded in the 1960s. Service to the handicapped began in the 1970s. Inspired by the IFLA Conference in Tokyo in 1986, services for minority groups started as a new challenge. Computers had been installed in about 30 percent of public libraries by the late 1980s.

School Libraries. The 6-3-3 system—six years primary, three middle, and three high school—was established under the postwar Education Reform Act. The first nine years of education are compulsory. After finishing compulsory education, 94.5 percent of middle school students go to high school.

Before the war, there were only a few school libraries, run by some enthusiastic teachers. The School Library Law was enacted in 1953 and now more than 98 percent of a total of 41,678 schools (24,901 primary, 11,265 middle, 5,512 high schools) have libraries. Although the School Library Law required schools to employ teacher-librarians, a supplementary provision of the law stated that "Schools may defer compliance concerning teacher-librarians for the present." The proviso was criticized for undermining sound development of school libraries. A new classification of librarian emerged: called "school librarians," they may or may not have teacher's licenses and librarian's certificates.

A school library survey done by the Japan School Library Association in 1988 showed that primary school libraries had an average of 5,811 books (14.6 volumes per pupil) and library expenditures of 365,000 yen (U.S. $2,400). In middle school libraries, the number of books averaged 6,496 (12.5 volumes per pupil) and library expenditures averaged 505,000 yen ($3,366). In high school libraries, the average book collection was 18,241 volumes (18.1 volumes per student); library expenditures were 1,635,000 yen ($10,900) for public high schools and 3,064,000 yen ($20,426) for private high schools. Public catalogues were available in 64.5 percent of the libraries. Full-time teacher–librarians were working in 68 percent of high school libraries.

Japanese schools face a marked decrease in the number of school-age children in the 1990s. Schools and their libraries are therefore likely to decrease.

Special Libraries and Information Centers. *A Directory of Special Libraries* (1988) listed 2,116 special libraries, of which 438 were established before 1945. Generally speaking, special libraries are small: the average was a collection of 32,000 Japanese and 17,000 foreign books and 328 Japanese and 225 foreign periodical titles and a full-time staff of six. Most of them are closed to the public. Special libraries may be categorized as libraries in private corporations, local government councils, research institutes attached to universities, government institutions, associations and societies, and foreign government institutions.

The Japan Information Center for Science and Technology (JICST) was established as a special nonprofit organization under a law passed in 1957. By 1988 it had approximately 15,000 titles of both Japanese and foreign periodicals, technical reports, conference proceedings, and other items. JICST's main work is to prepare abstracts in Japanese from both Japanese and foreign periodicals and to form the JICST database, from which twelve series of abstract journals are printed out monthly or semimonthly. JICST offers online search service for bibliographic data through JOIS (JICST Online Information Systems) and through STN International.

JICST compiles one database, JICST-E, to meet the increasing demands from abroad for bibliographic information on science and technology in Japan. JICST-E includes English-language titles of Japanese periodical literature and some English-language abstracts.

The Japan Medical Library Association (JMLA) includes 104 medical college libraries. The average medical library in the late 1980s had 64,400 books, 60,500 bound volumes of periodicals, 2,914 current periodical titles (1,307 Japanese, 1,607 foreign), and annual expenditures of 55,610,000 yen, with a full-time staff of 11.

Cooperation and interlibrary loan among medical libraries is well organized. JMLA works with NACSIS in compiling a union list of periodicals on medicine. Almost all medical libraries have computer terminals for online information services from JOIS, DIALOG, and BRS. CD-ROM technology is also becoming popular.

The Profession. *Education.* The Librarian's Training Institute was founded under the control of the Ministry of Education in 1921 in Ueno Park, Tokyo. It was the only institute to train librarians at the high school level before World War II. The Institute trained 1,530 librarians by 1964, when it was reorganized and became the National Junior College for Librarianship. The Junior College provided a two-year course in library science and a one-year course for university graduates with B.A. degrees. The junior college was reorganized again to become the National University of Library and Information Science when it moved from Tokyo to Tsukuba in Ibaraki Prefecture in 1980. Graduate courses were added in 1984.

The Japan Library School was established in the Faculty of Letters, Keio University, in 1951 with the assistance of the American Library Association and the Rockefeller Foundation. It was the first library school at the university level for professional education in Japan. During its early years, its curriculum emphasized American library science practices taught by American visiting professors with interpreters. When the grants ended, the School became part of Keio University as the Department of Library and Information Science. Graduate courses leading to the M.A. were added in 1967 and those leading to a Ph.D. in Letters in 1975.

Aichi Shukutoku (Women's) University in Nagoya set up a Department of Library and Information Science in 1984. It began offering graduate courses in 1988.

In addition, 97 universities and 87 junior colleges offered minors in library science in the late 1980s, with credits leading to public librarian's certificates. Ten universities offered two-month summer courses and five correspondence courses for public librarian's certificates in 1988.

A teacher-librarian's certificate is awarded after eight credits are earned in library science. Courses for teacher-librarians were offered in the late 1980s at 94 universities, 75 junior colleges, and 5 correspondence courses, together with courses for public librarians' certificates.

Associations. The Japan Library Association (JLA) is the only general association in the country that covers all types and subjects of libraries. It was founded in 1892, and its membership included more than 5,500 persons and almost 2,200 institutions in 1988; it is a member of IFLA. *Toshokan Zasshi* ("Library Journal") is published monthly. Other publications include "Nippon Cataloging Rules," "Nippon Decimal Classification," "Basic Subject Headings," "Library Yearbook," "Statistics on Libraries," and other books on librarianship.

Other associations include: the Association of Private University Libraries (1930); the Council on National University Libraries (1924); the Japan School Library Association (1950); the Japan Special Libraries Association (1952); the National Council of Public Libraries, Japan (1967); and the Private Junior College Library Association (1977). All issue newsletters or journals or both and many are members of IFLA.

There are other library associations in agriculture, hospitals, law, library science, music, and pharmaceutics. There also are regional and international associations such as Hokkaido Society of Library Science and La Société Franco-Japonaise des Bibliothècaires.

MADOKO KON

Jast, Louis Stanley

(1868–1944)

Louis Stanley Jast was one of the great pioneers in the development of the British public library service. He was an inventive practicing librarian, an engaging writer on librarianship, and the best speaker in the profession in his day.

Jast was born at Halifax, Yorkshire, August 20, 1868. He was the son of an exiled Polish army officer, and his family name, which he changed in 1895, was Jastrzebski. Jast began his library career in 1887 at the Halifax public library, where he was thoroughly grounded in all the pettifogging routines that were

Library Association

Louis Stanley Jast

then the very essence of public librarianship. Jast was unable to exercise his latent talents until he became his own master.

In 1892 Jast became Librarian of the small town of Peterborough. Soon afterward he discovered the Decimal Classification, which in later years he listed among the books that had most influenced his life. Under its spell he waged his first campaign, for the wider use of close classification in public libraries. He thereby gained the friendship of James Duff Brown, pioneer of open access in British public libraries. Jast joined forces with Brown not only on the platform in propagating the elements of "the new librarianship" but also in the pages of the *Library World,* the independent monthly journal that Brown had founded and also edited.

In 1898 Jast became Librarian of Croydon, a rapidly growing commuter town on the fringe of Greater London. There, with the backing of a sympathetic committee and a hard-working staff, Jast created a truly dynamic library service. Under his direction the Croydon libraries became a workshop for new ideas. Among the many novelties were the card catalogue, the reference information service, the library bulletin, lectures, reading circles, exhibitions of books and pictures, and liaison with the local schools.

Running the Croydon libraries was not enough to absorb Jast's boundless energy. From 1905 to 1915 he served as Honorary Secretary of the Library Association (LA). No one was better qualified for the post, but not even Jast's sparkle and enthusiasm could bring the LA prosperity. Its membership and resources remained obstinately small. The two major events during Jast's term of office were the inauguration in 1910 of a register of qualified librarians and the framing and publication, in collaboration with the American Library Association, of the well-known *Cataloguing Rules: Author and Title Entries* (1908).

In 1915 Jast became Deputy Librarian of Manchester and in 1920 Chief Librarian. His main preoccupation as Chief was the planning of the new central library, which was long overdue. Jast's contention that one could have a useful library "with books and brains and any sort of protection against the weather" was broadly true, but for him it was rather a sour truth. The new building he planned and longed for was not opened until July 1934, by which time he had been retired for two and a half years. Throughout his service at Manchester the central library was housed in "temporary" huts.

Apart from its circular shape, resulting from the nature of the site, and its great circular reading room—modeled on the reading room of the British Museum, which Jast greatly admired—the most interesting feature of the new Manchester Central Library was the book stack. This formed the core of the building, and the public rooms were grouped around it and above it. Jast called it "an integrated stack" and was very proud of it.

Jast had given much time to studying the design of large libraries in Britain and America. His mature thoughts on the subject, first presented in a lecture in December 1926, were published in pamphlet form as *The Planning of a Great Library* (1927). Jast enunciated four principles of library planning: (1) a properly designed library should not be a building containing books but books in an appropriate setting; (2) there are limits to the value of subject departmentalization; therefore, the stock should be kept as intact as possible; (3) the book stack should be "the central nerve ganglion of the whole building"; and (4) in the collaboration between librarian and architect, the premier role should be assigned to the librarian.

With regard to the second principle, Ernest A. Savage, a zealous advocate of subject departments and busy at the time forming as many as he could in his awkward Victorian central library at Edinburgh, said that in planning the new Manchester library Jast had "raised the standard of specialization without exposing it to too strong a wind." Jast, however, had played a significant part in the development of subject specialization in Britain; at Croydon he had given some attention to the collection of local materials and had made the central library the base for an elaborate photographic survey of the county. During World War I he had made nationally a strong plea for the creation of special public library services for businessmen. In 1917 he organized a commercial library at Manchester and in 1922 followed it with a technical library.

Jast's final practical contribution to librarianship was the mobile library. In 1931 he converted a former single-decker bus (he called it a "bibliobus") to provide a library service for Manchester's new housing projects.

Jast's interest in librarianship continued throughout his retirement, when his particular interests were library cooperation, professional education, and the need for a centralized cataloguing bureau. He died in Twickenham, Middlesex, on December 25, 1944.

Jast was a successful librarian who also had ambitions to become a successful author. His poetry and plays are of little merit, but he was an agreeable belletrist, and his professional writings were often spiced with genial witticisms.

Although Jast is undoubtedly an important figure in British library history, his achievements are not as fully appreciated as they should be. This is partly because the only biography of him is too slight to do him full justice and partly because he wrote no major work on librarianship and most of his best essays and speeches remain uncollected.

REFERENCES

W. G. Fry and W. A. Munford, *Louis Stanley Jast: A Biographical Sketch* (1966).

Numerous obituary appreciations appeared in the *Library World* (1945) and several in the *Library Association Record* (1945).

Ernest A. Savage, *A Librarian's Memories* (1952).

Charles Nowell, "Manchester Central Library," *Library Association Record* (1934).

JAMES G. OLLÉ

Jenkinson, Sir Hilary

(1882–1961)

Charles Hilary Jenkinson was founder and leader of the British archive profession.

He was born in London, November 2, 1882, and was educated at Dulwich College and at Pembroke College, Cambridge, being a Scholar of both. At

Cambridge he was placed in the First Class of the Classical Tripos. In 1905 he sat the entrance examination for the Home Civil Service and was placed in the Public Record Office.

During his earlier years in the Office, Jenkinson worked mainly on medieval records (in particular those of the Exchequer of Receipt), reducing their chaos to order and developing, from study of their vicissitudes, the principles that he was later to expound for the administration of both ancient and modern records. From 1916 to 1920 he served as an Artillery Officer and on the General Staff, then returned to the direction and reorganization of the Literary Search Room (the "Round Room") that he had undertaken in 1912 and was to continue until 1929.

In 1922 he took charge of Repairs and Binding and, relinquishing the Round Room in 1929, took charge of the Repository. In these closely related fields his most important work as an Assistant Keeper was done. Under his direction the physical care of records—not only the skilled repair of damage and decay but also their prevention through proper conditions of storage—was developed to a craft and a science, and the two departments became a center of study, experiment, and teaching.

In 1938 Jenkinson was appointed Secretary of the Public Record Office, and as its principal administrator he devised and directed the wartime program of ARP (air raid precautions), of dispersal of records and staff to improvised repositories in the country, and of their return after 1945. In 1947 he became head of the Office as Deputy Keeper; though postwar shortages frustrated many of his plans, he was able, by establishing the "intermediate repository" at Hayes, to lay the foundations for the Records Administration Division, the Office's most significant postwar development.

Though Jenkinson's official career was distinguished, his extracurricular activities gave him his unique standing and reputation. From 1911 until 1935, and again in 1938 and 1949, he was Maitland Lecturer at Cambridge. From 1920 he was Lecturer, and from 1925 to 1947 Reader, in Diplomatic and English Archives in the University of London. During the same period he published, as Charles Johnson's collaborator, *English Court Hand* (1915) and independently *Palaeography and Court Hand* (also in 1915) and *The Later Court Hands in England* (1927). These lectures and writings established Jenkinson as a leading authority on palaeography and diplomatic writings, and as the exponent of a new theme, already latent in his notable work for the Surrey Record Society, that the study of administrative history is the key to all work on records.

The establishment in 1932 of the British Records Association carried Jenkinson's influence and reputation into wider fields. Jenkinson was a founder of the Association and, as its joint Honorary Secretary for 15 years and thereafter as Chairman of its Records Preservation Section, he personally drafted most of the Association's influential *Reports* and *Memoranda* and led the campaigns that, among other achievements, established the *National Register of Archives* and, ultimately, a nationwide network of local record offices, besides saving countless archives from destruction.

All Jenkinson's extraofficial activities that related to archives (and few did not) were undertaken with the same boundless energy and conviction. Jenkinson was the original and most persistent advocate of the postgraduate diploma in Archive Studies at University College, London. Halfway between the official and the personal, and as important as either, was Jenkinson's appointment in 1943 as Archives Adviser to the War Office, in which capacity he planned and in part directed the rescue and preservation of archives in the war zones of Italy and Germany. In Italy the operation was successful, but in Germany a much more extensive program was less so; in both countries his work served as the basis of postwar reconstruction and greatly augmented his international reputation.

Jenkinson was a prolific writer for print, though few of his publications were in book form. The monograph upon which his fame securely rests is the *Manual of Archive Administration,* first published in 1922. This treatise, the first and the latest to be based upon English experience and practice, became at once the authoritative guide to all British archivists. Revised, reissued, and supplemented but still not superseded, the *Manual* remains required reading for archivists everywhere. Nor is it any disservice to Jenkinson's memory to recall that Charles Johnson's *The Care of Documents* preceded the *Manual* by three years and that C. G. Crump's magisterial article "Record" in the *Encylopaedia Britannica* was published in the Eleventh Edition of 1911. These men, with M. S. Giuseppi, were the young Jenkinson's mentors. Jenkinson was the youngest of the brilliant group who deduced and defined the principles of archival administration in England. He made it his task to examine these principles, to expound them with his own prophetic fervor, and to apply them in practice with a master's hand. No less he was the first of his English colleagues to perceive the relevance to native theory and practice of the manual of Müller, Feith, and Fruin, then accessible only in a French translation.

Jenkinson was a man abounding in energy, of mind and of body, most eloquent in all his causes and equally fertile of expedient. His Protean personality was not seen by all his contemporaries in the same guise; to an opponent Jenkinson could appear obstinate, unreasonable, devious. To those who enlisted under his banner Jenkinson was their most courageous, resourceful, and inspiring leader—able to evoke deep and lasting affection. In the years since his death in 1961 old differences have been laid to rest and his stature has steadily grown.

Jenkinson was made a Commander of the Order of the British Empire (CBE) in 1943 and was knighted as Sir Hilary in 1947. He was an Honorary Fellow of University College, London, and received the honorary degree of LL.D. from the University of Aberdeen, to whose library he left the greater part of his books. He was President of the Society of Archivists, of the Surrey Archaeological Society, of the Surrey Record Society, and of the Jewish Historical Society. He was a Vice-President of the British Records Association and an Honorary Member of the Society of American Archivists. From 1947 until his death he was a Commissioner of the Royal Commission on Historical Manuscripts.

Jenkinson died at Arun House, Horsham, Sussex, on March 15, 1961.

REFERENCES

A bibliography of Jenkinson's writings (1909–56) by Roger Ellis and William Kellaway is printed in *Studies Presented to Sir Hilary Jenkinson,* edited by J. Conway Davies (1957), which includes also an important *Memoir* (unsigned, by H. C. Johnson, later Keeper of Public Records). Further "Recollections of Sir Hilary Jenkinson," by Roger Ellis, are printed in *Journal of the Society of Archivists* (1971). Jenkinson's own small archive of personal papers is accessible at the Public Record Office.

ROGER ELLIS

Trustees of the Boston Public Library

Charles Coffin Jewett

Jewett, Charles Coffin

(1816–1868)

Charles Coffin Jewett's contributions to American librarianship are most durable. His career spanned the earliest days of the transition from the medieval to the modern in librarianship in America. Through his ingenuity and diligence, and his service in great institutions of national prominence in America, he was one of the founders of American librarianship. He was a logical thinker and was articulate in presenting his views. His perspicacity led to major innovations in librarianship that were proved of value in practice in three of the nation's leading libraries at their earliest period of modern growth. He helped crystallize the profession, and although he did not live to see the creation of the American Library Association in 1876, his support of the librarians' conference of 1853 was a catalyst for the permanent union.

Jewett was born in Lebanon, Maine, on August 12, 1816, one of several children of Paul Jewett, a New England minister. One of Jewett's brothers, John, achieved fame as the publisher of *Uncle Tom's Cabin.* Little is recorded about Jewett's early life, but following family influence and the normal route to education and employment, Jewett set out to gain a college education and to join the ministry. He entered Dartmouth College in 1831 but quickly transferred to Brown University, his father's alma mater, from which Charles Jewett graduated in 1835. He served briefly as preceptor at Uxbridge Academy in Massachusetts. In fall 1837 he entered Andover Seminary.

Jewett early evinced an interest in books and bibliography. While a student at Brown he and a classmate, William Lawton Brown, arranged, classified, and catalogued a collection of books belonging to one of the student societies. At Andover he assisted Oliver Alden Taylor, the Librarian, in the preparation and publication of the *Catalogue of the Library of the Theological Seminary*; as a result he was appointed Acting Librarian of the Seminary. Upon his graduation he became the Principal of Day's Academy in Wrentham, Massachusetts, but a few months later, in 1841, left to become Librarian at Brown.

Jewett was Brown's first full-time Librarian. Prior to his appointment it had been usual for a professor to hold that post. Brown's library program, however, had been expanded by its President, Francis Wayland. With an endowment of $25,000 for books and a new building, which the library shared with the University's chapel, the library program was too demanding to be managed as a part-time activity.

Jewett's first major task was to prepare and publish a new catalogue. It followed the plan of the Andover catalogue, being divided into two parts: (1) an author listing and (2) an alphabetical and classified subject index with cross references. It took two years to complete and was widely acclaimed for its arrangement and careful preparation.

The catalogue done, Jewett turned his attention to building the library collection. He traveled extensively in Europe, buying books and pamphlets and collections not only for the University but also for a few scholarly friends who entrusted him with funds to use at his discretion. Jewett was judicious and prescient in his selections, and the Brown University Library became one of the leading academic research libraries of its time.

Perhaps as important as book buying was Jewett's effort to learn more about bibliography. He spent time in England with Anthony Panizzi, Keeper of Printed Books in the British Museum. It is evident from his letters that Jewett formed important opinions about national libraries, bibliography, and all of the then-modern aspects of library science in this part of his trip.

Jewett returned to Brown in 1845. His book-buying feat placed him in the ranks of the leading scholar-bibliographers of his day. He joined the faculty at Brown and became a very popular professor of modern languages and literature.

All during Jewett's formative years as a librarian, events were transpiring in Washington, D.C., that would lead inevitably to his move to national prominence there. From 1835 to 1846 Congress had been arguing over the manner in which it could achieve the goal of the will of an English scientist, James Smithson, to operate an institution to "increase and diffuse knowledge among men." The opinion in Congress was strongly divided into two camps, one proposing the creation of a national library and the other the establishment of a scientific research and study agency. This division of opinion was transferred to the Regents of the agency, to be known as the Smithsonian Institution, when it was finally created in 1846.

The proponents of science seemed to prevail, and the Regents' choice for its Secretary and first chief operating officer of the Institution was Joseph Henry, a professor at Princeton University and then America's leading scientist. Several of the U.S. senators who were strong proponents of a national library, and who had been active in obtaining the legislation to establish the Smithsonian, served on its first Board of Regents. They kept the issue of the future of the Institution alive by promoting the appointment of an assistant secretary qualified to be the Institution's Librarian. As one of the best known and most energetic of American librarians, Jewett was the Regents' choice, and he entered their service in 1847.

The Regents were persuaded that they had full authority to spend the Institution's funds as they thought appropriate and never authorized the maximum budget for the library as allowed by congressional action. They devoted most of the funds in the early days to the construction of the first Smithsonian building, much to the dismay of both Henry and Jewett. With his usual devotion, Jewett managed to complete a list of the publications of the learned societies of the world; he established gift and exchange relationships with most of them, and by 1855, regardless of inner turmoil, the Smithsonian had thus acquired probably the finest library collection of these publications in the country.

Most of Jewett's attention, however, was focused on a novel and colossal plan for a national, centralized library catalogue production facility. In Jewett's time libraries generally printed their catalogues. Jewett devised a plan whereby the libraries could produce their catalogues from stereotype plates made and kept at the Smithsonian. Cataloguing copy would be provided by libraries, but duplicate cataloguing could be avoided by sharing the plates. The Smithsonian proposed to do the collating of entries and the printing of the catalogues.

An obvious requirement for the success of such a venture was a set of standard cataloguing rules. Here Jewett's acquaintance with Panizzi emerged, for Jewett's rules were based on Panizzi's own cataloguing rules. Along the way, in order to know his market, Jewett prepared the first major inventory of public libraries in the United States. The Smithsonian published his *Notices of Public Libraries,* prepared from descriptions provided by the libraries themselves, as an appendix to the 1851 *Annual Report* of the Regents of the Smithsonian.

Jewett described his cataloguing plan to the librarians of the United States at the 1853 librarians' conference, which he chaired. He noted that his plan could be carried out only by an agency at the national level, and that it could not be successful without the endorsement and cooperation of other libraries. The conference unanimously adopted resolutions acknowledging the need expressed by Jewett and supporting his national cataloguing plan.

His plan came to naught, however. The materials from which the stereotype plates were made warped and hence could not be made into a suitable printing surface. Of greater consequence, however, was the unwillingness of the Secretary of the Smithsonian to commit the Institution and its resources to the effort required to sustain a national library operation. In the end, with Jewett's departure from the Smithsonian, the chief advocate for a national library was without the national platform required for operating such an important national program. Still, every element of shared cataloguing and of national distribution of cataloguing copy from Washington, D.C., as it was finally put into place by the Library of Congress nearly 50 years later, was laid out in Jewett's plan.

The relationship between Jewett and Henry was never easy. Jewett assumed that he had been employed by the Regents as their direct assistant to head an independent library department. He refused to help Henry with any general duties and carried on a campaign among friends to overrule Henry's intent to make the Institution the national home for scientific research and publication. By 1854 Henry could no longer tolerate Jewett's actions, and with the Regents' approval he dismissed Jewett (January, 1855).

Jewett remained prominent in American librarianship even after leaving the Smithsonian. He was employed at the Boston Public Library, first as a cataloguer, then as an acquisitions librarian, and finally as the Library's first Superintendent from 1858 until his death 10 years later. At the Boston Public Library Jewett applied himself with his characteristic conscience, devoting his ingenuity to the problems of his library. As usual, his solutions to several key problems served as models for innovations in other libraries. Among other things he replaced the circulation record book with separate slips for each book circulated, thus introducing flexibility and management control of collections into what was formerly a cumbersome function. Under Jewett's direction the Library grew to over 150,000 volumes, second in size only to the Library of Congress. Jewett died in Braintree, Massachusetts, on January 9, 1868.

REFERENCES

Joseph A. Borome, *Charles Coffin Jewett* (1951).

Michael H. Harris, *The Age of Jewett: Charles Coffin Jewett and American Librarianship, 1841–1868* (1975).

Michael H. Harris, "Jewett, Charles Coffin," *Dictionary of American Library Biography* (1978).

Geoffrey Hellman, *The Smithsonian: Octopus on the Mall* (1967).

RUSSELL SHANK

Joeckel, Carleton B.
(1886–1960)

ALA

Carleton B. Joeckel

Carleton Bruns Joeckel, North American library educator, administrator, and scholar, was a unique blend of practitioner and theoretician. In his research he never lost touch with the realities of his profession. As a teacher, he was distinguished by his ability not only to impart knowledge but also to maintain fruitful contact with his students. Joeckel bequeathed a twofold legacy to the library profession: his published works, which stand as a monument to his productive scholarship, and a generation of librarians imbued with his philosophy of free public library service for everyone.

Joeckel was born in Lake Mills, Wisconsin, January 2, 1886, and attended the University of Wisconsin, obtaining his A.B. degree in 1908. Joeckel entered the New York State Library School in 1908 and completed the B.L.S. degree in 1910. His library career began in 1910 as secretary to the Librarian of the St. Louis Public Library. In 1911 he moved to Berkeley, California, where he was Assistant Reference Librarian and Superintendent of Circulation of the University of California until 1914. Writing in 1936, Sidney B. Mitchell, Founder-Director of the University of California School of Librarianship, remembered young Joeckel as leaving "a permanent impression of a quick, alert body and mind, of a habit of not talking unnecessarily and of intolerance of vague, dreamy ideas and of shams of any kind." So favorable was Joeckel's impression on the Head of the University Extension Division (who was also Chairman of the Board of the Berkeley Public Library) that in 1914 he was offered the post of Librarian. Except for a two-year leave of absence (1917–19) for service in the Army in the United States and overseas, Joeckel remained Librarian until 1927.

According to Mitchell, during Joeckel's tenure,

> he put his library on the map, built up a professional staff, made it easy for his younger untrained college graduates to go to library school, encouraged ambitious members to try out their ideas, made it evident that a humanized as well as an efficient service was to be expected by his public,

extended the service by new branches, built branch buildings, and secured the passage of a building fund for a main library building (since erected), even though a bond issue for new school buildings was defeated.

Joeckel's interest in the training of librarians developed during his years as Director of the Berkeley Public Library. In his first experience in teaching, he was a lecturer in public library administration in the unit that was to become the School of Librarianship of the University of California.

Joeckel's career took a new direction when in 1927 he left California for full-time teaching at the University of Michigan. Joining the faculty of the Department of Library Science as Associate Professor, he was promoted to Professor in 1930. He strengthened the teaching faculty, chiefly in the areas of library administration and book selection. His contract with the University included the opportunity to pursue advanced study in political science, which culminated with a Master's degree in 1928.

On receiving an ALA fellowship, Joeckel took a year's leave of absence for advanced study at the University of Chicago Graduate Library School (1933–34). After obtaining his doctorate in 1934, he resumed his teaching post at the University of Michigan for another year. In 1935 he joined the faculty of the Graduate Library School at Chicago, where he remained the next 10 years.

During his Chicago years Joeckel's career flourished. The University of Chicago was the only institution in the country offering a doctoral program in librarianship at that time, and Joeckel's dissertation, *The Government of the American Public Library* (1935), was the first comprehensive study of the public library and governmental relations. This trail-blazing treatise won for Joeckel the confidence and respect of the professional library community. It laid to rest the skepticism of some practitioners who maintained that librarianship was not a sufficiently comprehensive field in which to pursue doctoral study. A perceptive observer of the American library scene and a supporter of the Ph.D. program in librarianship, Wilhelm Munthe, Director of the University of Oslo Library, asserted, "This treatise alone is sufficient documentary evidence in justifying the existence of the [Graduate Library] school," since it "placed American library research on a higher plane."

Joeckel quickly became immersed in the spirit of research and publication that pervaded the University. Beginning in 1937 Joeckel, in collaboration with faculty colleague Leon Carnovsky, undertook a survey of the Chicago Public Library and documented the findings and recommendations in *A Metropolitan Library in Action* (1940). Their report was hailed as "a source book on the methodology of public library research" because it provided a framework for an objective approach to the study of problems in public libraries of all sizes. In 1938 Joeckel's report *Library Service,* prepared for President Franklin D. Roosevelt's Advisory Committee on Education, was released by the U.S. Government Printing Office.

Joeckel's expertise in the theory and practice of librarianship brought him in 1940 an invitation from the newly appointed Librarian of Congress, Archibald MacLeish, to serve as Chairman of the Librarian's Committee, whose charge was to make a comprehensive survey of the processing departments of the Library of Congress. MacLeish characterized the confidential report submitted by the Committee that Joeckel chaired as "one of the most important documents in the history of the Library." He used the recommendations of the Committee as the framework for a complete reorganization of the processing operations.

Of the many facets of librarianship to which Joeckel gave his attention there was none that he believed in more firmly or advocated more ardently that the concept of larger units of library service. As early as 1929 he had introduced this concept, an audacious one at that time, at the annual meeting of the Michigan Library Association. Three years later he put this perspective into sharp focus in a provocative address given before the ALA Council and published in the ALA *Bulletin* (1933):

> The typical public library unit is still so small and weak as to be seriously lacking in administrative efficiency, and the area it serves is unnecessarily circumscribed. . . . [The librarian] has been so absorbed in the library problems of his own town or city that he has overlooked the fascinating possibilities of expansion of the units of library service. . . . Sweeping changes in the complicated structure of local government are being recommended on all sides. The public library must adapt itself to them.

Throughout his career, Joeckel was actively involved in professional organizations. Recognition of his charismatic leadership came early in his career, as evidenced by the offices he held. He served as President of the California Library Association (1919–20) and of the Michigan Library Association (1930–31). He was a member of the Illinois Library Association's Executive Board (1935–45) and of the American Library Institute (1937–45). Joeckel joined the American Library Association in 1910, the year in which he graduated from the New York State Library School. Although he was to participate in many committee activities during the next 40 years, probably the most constructive were those of the Federal Relations Committee and of the Post-War Planning Committee, of which he was Chairman.

A staunch champion of federal aid to libraries, Joeckel advocated a nationwide program of library service to be funded jointly by the federal, state, and local governments. "Without federal aid," Joeckel wrote with characteristic forthrightness, "the establishment of a national minimum standard of library service is quite simply and literally impossible."

Joeckel played a major role in the establishment in 1937 of the Library Services Division in the Office of Education, the first federal agency established with the specific responsibility for fostering a national program of library development. He was the motivating force behind the passage of the Library Services Act in 1956.

As Chairman of the Post-War Planning Committee, Joeckel was the chief architect of the *ALA Post-War Standards for Public Libraries* (ALA, 1943) and (with Amy Winslow) the author of *A National Plan for Public Library Service* (ALA, 1948), prepared for the Committee on Post-War Planning.

Some of Joeckel's most significant writing appeared as papers in the proceedings of library institutes: "Realities of Regionalism" in *Library Trends* (papers presented before the GLS Institute, 1938);

"Library Extension Today" in *Library Extension: Problems and Solutions* (papers presented before the GLS Institute, 1946); and "Service Outlets as the Reader Sees Them" in *Reaching Readers: Techniques of Extending Library Services* (papers presented at the Library Institute sponsored by the University of California School of Librarianship and the ALA Library Extension Division, 1947). A noteworthy article entitled "National Leadership from Washington," written in collaboration with Willard O. Mishoff, appeared in *The Library of Tommorrow* (ALA, 1939).

Joeckel's editorial accomplishments were also impressive. They include: *Current Issues in Library Administration* (papers presented before the GLS Institute, 1938), *Library Extension, Reaching Readers, Post-War Standards for Public Libraries,* and his contributions to *The Library Quarterly* as Associate Editor from 1936 to 1945 and as Advisory Editor from 1946 to 1959.

Through his extensive writings and other professional activities, Joeckel made a notable impact on the American library scene in the 1930s and 1940s, but he contributed most significantly to the library profession through his teaching and his influence on his students. From his initial venture into teaching at the University of California in the 1920s to his return to the Berkeley campus in the mid-1940s, Joeckel concerned himself mainly with his students. His intellectual vigor and personal integrity earned their respect; his appealing and vibrant personality won their affection. A demanding professor, Joeckel expected his students to measure up to his standards. His seminars were stimulating experiences, challenging his students to critical thinking. Joeckel was major professor to many doctoral candidates who went out in all directions from Chicago to assume positions of high professional responsibility.

With the retirement of Louis Round Wilson in 1942, Joeckel was appointed Dean of the Graduate Library School, and Leon Carnovsky, a faculty colleague, was appointed Assistant Dean. In spite of war-born personnel shortages, Joeckel maintained the School's traditional strength in advanced seminars, research, and publishing. During his deanship he sponsored three summer institutes: The Library in the Community (1943); Library Extension: Problems and Solutions (1944); and Personnel Administration in Libraries (1945).

To carry out his plan of devoting some of his later years to research and writing, Joeckel resigned from his administrative post at GLS in 1945 and returned to Berkeley. Still vigorous in health, Joeckel resumed academic pursuits at the University of California by joining the faculty as Professor of Librarianship. Four years later ill health forced him to take a leave of absence, and one year later, in 1950, he retired for a second time.

Recognition of Joeckel's professional accomplishments came in the form of various honors. The American Library Association conferred upon him the first James Terry White Award for his notable professional writing (in 1938) and the Joseph W. Lippincott Award for his distinguished service to the profession (in 1958). Honorary life membership in the Association was conferred upon him in 1954. He died April 15, 1960, in Oakland, California.

REFERENCE

Thomas S. Harding, "Joeckel, Carleton Bruns," *Dictionary of American Library Biography* (1978).

MARY LUELLA POWERS
(d. 1983)

Jones, Virginia Lacy
(1912-1984)

Virginia Lacy Jones, library educator and professional leader, received many testimonies to her status in the field of library science, including the American Library Association's Melvil Dewey Award in 1973 and the Joseph W. Lippincott Award in 1977. Other recognitions indicate her profound influence on the profession as a whole. In August 1979 she was honored by the University of Michigan with a special citation for her contributions to library education. In 1980 she received the Beta Phi Mu Award and the Mary Rothrock Award. In 1981 she was cited by the Southeastern Library Association for her contributions to that organization and to the region.

Jones was born on June 25, 1912, in Cincinnati, Ohio, the daughter of Edward and Ellen Louise Parker Lacy. Her family moved shortly thereafter to Clarksburg, West Virginia, where she attended public schools. Her junior and senior high school years were spent in St. Louis, where she was sent to facilitate her entry into Stowe Teachers College. Instead of following that plan, she entered Hampton Institute in Virginia, from which she received the Bachelor of Science degree in Library Science (1933) and in Education (1936).

Her professional experience was begun at Louisville (Kentucky) Municipal College, the Negro branch of the University of Louisville. There she met Rufus E. Clement, President of the college, who was to have a significant influence on her career. In 1937 she received the first of two General Education Board fellowships which allowed her to complete her Master's degree at the University of Illinois (1938) and later her Ph.D. at the University of Chicago (1945). She was the second African-American to be awarded a doctor's degree in library science.

When Clement moved to Atlanta University (Georgia) as President, in 1938, he offered Jones a position as cataloguer if she would leave Louisville. She moved to Atlanta University and became a part of Clement's plan to replace the recently closed Hampton Institute Library School. Thus she became involved in the planning that led to the opening of the Atlanta University School of Library Service in 1941. She served on the faculty until 1945, when she was appointed Dean.

Her other positions included supervision of the Prairie View Regional Summer Training Center for Librarians, one of four sponsored by the General Education Board from 1936 to 1939. She was instrumental in spearheading, along with Ann Rucker, the establishment of the Library Section of the Kentucky Negro Education Association. Following her move to Atlanta, she worked in concert with Mollie Huston Lee of Raleigh, North Carolina, and Charlemae Rollins of the Chicago Public Library to raise the awareness of publishers about the negative images of African-Americans that appeared in many children's

Virginia Lacy Jones

University of Jordan Library, opened in 1962, is the major academic library in the country.

books. She also assisted in the establishment of a Field Service Program under the sponsorship of the Carnegie Corporation of New York that brought consultant services to libraries serving African-Americans in several southeastern states.

She served four terms as a member of the American Library Association Council and one term on its Executive Board. She also served as Secretary-Treasurer of the Association of American Library Schools (AALS) 1948–54, and as a member of its Board of Directors, 1960–64. She was AALS President in 1967. She became active with Beta Phi Mu (library science honorary society) and with other associations and projects related to library science. Other activities included work with the National Endowment for the Humanities, the Southern Association of Colleges and Schools, the Atlanta Area Teacher Education Service, and other professional and service organizations. She was a member of Delta Sigma Theta Sorority and of the NAACP.

On November 27, 1941, she was married to Edward Allen Jones, a professor of modern languages at Morehouse College.

She retired from the deanship of the Atlanta University School of Library Services in December 1981. From January 1982 through December 1983, she served as Director of the Robert W. Woodruff Library of Atlanta University Center. She died in Atlanta on December 3, 1984.

REFERENCES

Virginia Lacy Jones, "A Dean's Career," *The Black Librarian in America,* edited by E. J. Josey (1970); and "Reminiscences in Library and Library Education," a pamphlet published by the University of Michigan School of Library Science (1979) when she was awarded an honorary doctorate.

Obituaries were published in *American Libraries* (January 1985) and in *Black Caucus Newsletter* (December 1984).

ALBERT P. MARSHALL

Jordan

Jordan, a parliamentary constitutional monarchy in southwest Asia, lies between Syria on the north, Iraq on the east, Saudi Arabia on the east and south, the Gulf of Aqaba on the south, and Israel on the west. Population (1990 est.) 4,010,000; area 97,740 sq.km. The official language is Arabic.

History. Jordan was established under a British mandate after the collapse of the Ottoman Empire. The Emirate of Trans-Jordan, consisting of the East Bank of the River Jordan, was proclaimed the Hashemite Kingdom of Jordan after gaining independence in 1946. It included the West Bank from 1948 to 1967. Information given here relates to the East Bank only.

Until the 1950s libraries in Jordan were no more than small collections of books in some 15 school libraries. The first of these was established at al-Salt secondary school, then the only secondary school in the country, in 1926.

The modern library movement started during the late 1950s, after a Unesco mission visited the country in 1955. Three major events followed in the 1960s: Amman Public Library (APL) was founded in 1960, the University of Jordan in 1962, and the Jordan Library Association (JLA) in December 1963.

National Library. Strictly speaking, there is no national library in Jordan. A National Documentation Center was founded in 1975, then replaced in 1977 by the Directorate of National Documentation and Libraries, which was renamed the Department of Libraries and National Archives. This Department has a wide range of responsibilities, including the task of establishing and running a National Library. No legal deposit legislation is in place, but authors, publishers, and printing houses are officially asked to deliver two copies of each of their works to the Department. It has about 20,000 volumes in its library, as well as collections of documents, newspapers, and other printed materials. New legislation concerning a na-

Libraries in Jordan (1987)

Type of library	Number of administrative units (main libraries)	Number of service points (branches, mobile stops, etc.)	Volumes in collections	Annual expenditures (dinar)	Population served	Professional staff (with certificate, diploma, etc.)	Total staff
National (Dept. of Libraries)	1	1	20,000	25,000	--	5	22
Academic (Univ.)	4	4	846,000	650,000	40,000	45	227
Community Colleges	57	57	80,000	--	--	60	110
Public	39	45	410,000	--	--	20	95
School	479	479	1,134,200	--	--	119	553
Special	104	104	--	--	--	30	115

tional library and legal deposit is under consideration, and a National Information Service (NIS) is being established.

Academic Libraries. The major academic library is the University of Jordan Library (UJL), established in 1962. Its general collection numbers about 510,000 volumes and 1,300 current periodicals. Its collection of back issues exceeds 110,000 volumes. The UJL is a depository library for publications issued by the UN and other international agencies. Since 1986 it has been a depository library for theses submitted in all Arab universities. Online information services are available.

Yarmouk University Library, established in Irbid in 1976, has a collection of almost 210,000 volumes and 1,100 current periodicals, as well as about 12,000 non-book materials. It plays an important role in library development in the northern region of the country. Jordan University of Science and Technology Library, established in Irbid in 1986, has about 35,000 volumes and 940 current periodicals. Its collection is mainly in the fields of medicine and health sciences, engineering, and agriculture. Mu'ta University, near Karak in the south, established as a military academy in 1981, has a collection of 93,000 volumes and 310 current periodicals. The four university libraries coordinate their activities, especially in the area of subscription to periodicals. They also offer interlibrary loans and photocopying services.

Community colleges, providing post-secondary programs of two or three years duration, started in Jordan as early as 1952. There were more than 50 community colleges by the late 1980s, each with its own library. Collections and services vary from one institution to another; no college is accredited without meeting the standards set by the Ministry of Higher Education, which include eight volumes per student (with a minimum of 5,000 volumes) and a full-time librarian.

Public Libraries. Local authorities are responsible for public libraries. The first was established in Irbid in 1957 as a Unesco pilot project. The country had 39 public libraries by the late 1980s. The Amman Public Library has about 120,000 volumes, some 500 current periodicals, and a good collection of non-book materials. It houses a special collection for the blind. Abdel-Hameed Shouman Public Library and Information Center was established by a nonprofit organization in 1986. It has 24,500 titles and 1,500 periodicals and makes extensive use of new information technologies.

Children's libraries are found in many parts of the country, either as parts of public library systems or on their own. By the late 1980s there were 26 children's libraries, with 16 in the Amman governate alone.

School Libraries. The modern Jordanian library movement began in school libraries, which have seen a good deal of development. By 1987, the Ministry of Education reported 498 libraries in the schools under its control. No statistics are available for private schools or schools run by the military or the United Nations Relief and Works Administration (UNRWA).

Special Libraries. Libraries were established in the early 1950s at the Departments of Architecture and Antiquities, Statistics, and Agricultural Research and Guidance and at the Civil Aviation Authority. The JLA counted 104 special libraries attached to research and governmental institutions and agencies by the late 1980s. Chief among these is the Royal Scientific Society (founded in 1970), with a collection of books and periodicals, local and international reports and research papers, and CD-ROMs and online information services.

The Center of Documentation and Manuscripts at the University of Jordan is renowned for its valuable collections related to the history of the region. There are other documentation centers in the fields of agriculture, education, health, public administration, social development, and statistics.

The Profession. The Jordan Library Association (JLA) was founded in 1963. One of the most active professional library associations in the Arab world, it is a member of IFLA and the Arab Federation of Library and Information Specialists. JLA has had profound influence, especially through its training programs and publications. It publishes a quarterly library journal, *Rissalat Al-Maktaba,* started in 1965, and an annual *National Bibliography,* which appeared from 1980 to 1985.

REFERENCES

Mohammed Aman, *Documentation and Library Services of the Ministry of Information* (1980).

Farouq Mansour, "University and Research Libraries in Jordan: A Study of Users and Institutional Characteristics," Ph.D. dissertation, University of Sheffield (1983).

FAROUQ MANSOUR

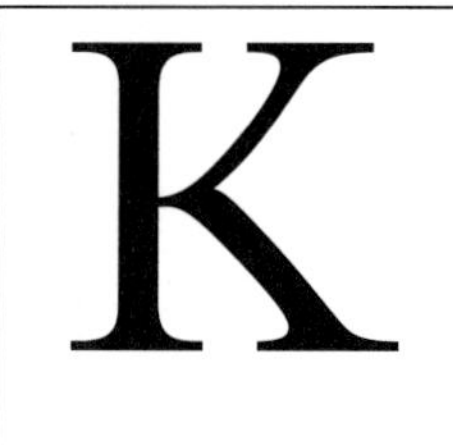

Kenya

Kenya, an independent republic, lies astride the Equator in eastern Africa. It is bounded by Sudan and Ethiopia on the north, Somalia and the Indian Ocean on the east, Tanzania on the south, and Uganda on the west. Population (1990 est.) 24,872,000; area 580,367 sq.km. The national language is Kiswahili, but English is the language of instruction beyond the primary school.

History. Library development followed the racial patterns of colonial Kenya. Philanthropic Asians founded the Seif Bin Salim Library and Free Reading Room in Mombasa in 1903. It was theoretically open to all, but collected only Indian literature. In 1931, Lady McMillan established a lending library for Nairobi's Europeans in memory of her husband, the Arctic explorer. Indians built the Desai Memorial Library in 1942, providing the third public library in Kenya, none of them serving Africans. In 1948 Elspeth Huxley proposed the East African Literature Bureau, with headquarters in Kenya, to produce and distribute literature in African languages. In 1960 the McMillan Memorial Library was handed over to the Nairobi City Council and opened to all, regardless of race.

Following recommendations by the East African Library Association and the report of Sydney Hockey, British Council library consultant, Parliament established the Kenya National Library Service (KNELLS) in 1965. When it opened in 1967, it inherited the programs and resources of the East African Literature Bureau. It took over the Seif Bin Salim Library in 1975 as its Mombasa area branch.

National Library. Several institutions share the functions of a national library: the KNELLS, the University of Nairobi Library, the National Archive, Kenyatta University Library, the McMillan Library, and the Documentation Center of the National Commission on Science and Technology. Several libraries have legal depository rights. The KNELLS produces the *Kenya National Bibliography* and represents the country in international organizations.

Academic Libraries. The University of Nairobi has the largest and most comprehensive library in the country, with the largest collection and the largest staff of professional librarians. Established in 1947 as a technical and commercial institute, it became the Royal Technical College of East Africa in 1951, the University College of Nairobi in 1963, and a full university in 1970. The University of Nairobi Library Service occupies the Jomo Kenyatta Memorial Library (completed in 1987), with a seating capacity of more than 1,300 readers. It has eight branches, including the Gandhi Memorial Library.

Moi University was established in 1984. Its library occupied five different spaces in its first five years, finally moving to a new building funded by the British government in 1992. Its collection had grown to 50,000 volumes and 300 current periodicals by 1990. Long-term plans call for a medical library at Eldoret, two branch libraries at the constituent Maseno University College, and one at Kuinet campus.

Kenyatta University was a constituent college of the University of Nairobi from 1970 to 1985, when it was established as a separate university offering programs in education. Its library complex, built in 1984 with British funds, seats 415 readers and houses 145,000 volumes and 1,000 journals.

Egerton University was established in 1939 as an agricultural school for European settlers. In 1960 Parliament formalized its structure and opened its courses to all Kenyans. In 1986 it became a university college and the next year a full university specializing in agriculture. Its library has 50,000 volumes and 780 periodicals in a building that seats 800 readers.

Of the 22 teacher training colleges, only the Kenya Science Teacher College and the Kenya Technical Teacher College have significant libraries and professional staffs—the first with 35,000 volumes and 120 periodicals, the second with 15,000 volumes and 100 periodicals. Elsewhere, library development depends on the initiative of individual principals and the support of local boards of governors, who are generally unable to attract professional librarians with the conditions of service they offer.

Kenya Polytechnic in Nairobi (40,500 volumes and 200 periodicals) and Mombasa Polytechnic (20,000 volumes and 40 periodicals) have long-established, professionally staffed libraries. Mombasa Polytechnic is hampered by a poorly planned and constructed library building. Eldoret Polytechnic, established in 1985, had no library of its own by the early 1990s.

Public Libraries. The KNELLS operates 14 area and district libraries with 8 mobile libraries, providing public library services throughout the country. Its collections in 1987 totaled about 500,000 volumes and its staff numbered more than 360, including 25 professional librarians and 50 paraprofessionals.

The Nairobi City Council operates the McMillan Memorial Library and two branches. In addition to a much-used children's section and a general reading collection, the McMillan is noted for its Africana holdings. Because of limited finances, it was forced in 1974–75 to reinstate nominal subscription fees for membership.

School Libraries. Library service in Kenya's almost 14,000 primary and 2,600 secondary schools is generally left to the initiative of heads and parents' associations, which means that only the wealthier schools have well-stocked libraries. The KNELLS supplies 200 books per term to any school able to pay a modest deposit. It also provides mobile library services to rural areas that schools can utilize. But its

Maridadi Photo Studio

McMillan Memorial Library, operated by the Nairobi City Council, stocks one of Kenya's major Africana collections.

Libraries in Kenya (1984)

Type of library	Number of administrative units (main libraries)	Number of service points (branches, mobile stops, etc.)	Volumes in collections	Annual expenditures (K. shilling × 1000)	Population served	Professional staff (with certificate, diploma, etc.)	Total staff
National	1	14 area libraries 6 mobiles	577,781	7,700	150,000	25	260
Academic	5	7	522,600	500,000	16,946	76	265
Public	12	4	700,250	21,520	300,000	10	70
School	26	--	180,300	65,740	17,733	0	0
Special	63	--	496,165	20,000,000	--	9	32
Other (describe)	148	--	52,604	2,000,000	--	11	160

Source: *Subject Guide to Information Sources in Kenya, 1984*

bookstock is geared to general reading and is not selected to support the curriculum.

Special Libraries. Special libraries are found in government departments, parastatal organizations, research institutes, private firms, and international organizations and embassies. One of the oldest and largest is that of the Ministry of Agriculture in Nairobi, with 100,000 volumes and 850 periodicals. Government agencies with important libraries include the Central Bureau of Statistics, High Court of Kenya, Mines and Geology Department, National Archives, National Council for Science and Technology, National Public Health Laboratories, and Veterinary Research Laboratories. Collections in the late 1980s ranged from 25,000 to more than 150,000 volumes plus journals. UN and OAU agencies with major special libraries in Kenya include the United Nations Environment Programme (UNEP), HABITAT, and the African Center for Animal Research.

The Profession. Librarians and archivists in Kenya are trained at two levels. For paraprofessionals, the one-year Library and Archives Certificate course at the Kenya Polytechnic has been replaced by a two-year diploma course. Moi University offers a first-degree course in Information Sciences through its Faculty of Information Sciences, with postgraduate courses planned for the 1990s. The program includes training for libraries, archives, publishing, and computer operations.

The East African Library Association was formed in 1956, with most members located in Nairobi. In 1962 it began publishing the *East African Library Association Bulletin,* and in 1964 formed branches in Uganda and Tanzania. At a 1972 conference the delegates decided that the East African Library Association should be disbanded and that each country should organize its own national association. The Kenya Library Association was founded in 1973. Regional cooperation is maintained through the Standing Conference of Eastern, Central, and Southern African Librarians (SCESAL), formed by the same conference that dissolved EALA. Biennial meetings rotate among Kenya, Tanzania, and Uganda.

REFERENCES

Kenya National Library Service Board, *Annual Report,* 1974– .

Guide to Information Sources in Kenya (1984).

JAFRED SHALIMBA MUSISI

Carnegie Corporation of New York

Frederick Paul Keppel

Keppel, Frederick Paul
(1875–1943)

Frederick Paul Keppel, foundation administrator, was a leading figure in the growth of American libraries.

Keppel was born July 2, 1875, in Staten Island, New York, and spent most of his early years in Yonkers, New York, where he attended the public schools. His parents, Frederick and Frances Keppel, were Irish immigrants. Upon completing high school, he worked for two years in his father's print-selling shop and then entered Columbia University, graduating with an outstanding academic record in 1898. He obtained a position with Harper and Brothers in the same year but thought himself unsuited for the publishing field.

In 1900 he took a position as Assistant Secretary at Columbia University, rapidly advancing to Secretary of the University in 1902 and then to the deanship of Columbia College in 1910. Wanting to serve his country in World War I but too old at 42 to volunteer for military service, Keppel went to Washington as a confidential clerk in the War Department. His administrative talents and ability to deal with people tactfully were quickly noticed by his superiors, and within a year he was made Third Assistant Secretary of War. After the war he held administrative posts with the American Red Cross (1919–20), in Paris with the

International Chamber of Commerce (1920–22), and for a brief period as Secretary of the Plan of New York. In December 1922 he was elected President of Carnegie Corporation of New York but did not actually assume his duties until October 1923.

Keppel was the fourth President of Carnegie Corporation of New York, an educational philanthropy whose name is closely associated with the early growth of libraries in the United States and abroad and with the nurturing and development of the library profession.

His earlier positions had given Keppel the understanding and skills to shape the foundation's policy, philosophy, and programs for the 18 years he was President, 1923–41. Because the Carnegie staff was quite small, he made extensive use of outside advisers and expertise. He was frank, but warm and courteous, concise, and a persuasive speaker, and he hated bores. He rarely put off decisions. His grantmaking was sometimes criticized for ranging too widely and not demonstrating any particular strategy, but he saw his role as being the administrator of a public trust, which made it incumbent upon him to dispense allocations in a variety of subject areas and projects and to do so fairly and representatively.

Libraries, particularly public libraries, he saw as among the major facilities for lifelong learning. Although he did not initiate the Corporation's relationship with the American Library Association, Keppel depended heavily on ALA to identify needs and to develop programs that would enhance librarianship and service to the public. Andrew Carnegie had started that relationship and actually gave the Association its original endowment grant of $100,000 in 1902. During Keppel's tenure $86,000,000 was given away; of that amount, approximately $30,000,000 went for library projects, and more than $3,000,000 of that went directly to ALA for its activities. Included in this sum were additional endowment grants of $2,000,000 (paid 1926–33). This kind of support for the Association and for a diverse group of library projects was part of the Corporation's long view regarding libraries.

Three commissioned evaluative reports, two by well-known and respected scholars Alvin S. Johnson and Charles C. Williamson and one by Carnegie staff member William S. Learned, contributed immeasurably to the Corporation's ultimate decision to revise its giving policy with respect to libraries. Johnson's 1919 report carried the recommendation that the Corporation cease providing assistance to communities for the construction of library buildings and that funds instead be made available for upgrading the training of librarians and for improving services. Williamson examined the training of librarians and concluded that they needed university training instead of that provided by public libraries, and that a library school should be established to offer graduate-level courses. Learned specifically recommended that the ALA expand its services to librarians and that the foundation finance demonstration projects that would represent innovations in library service, particularly to rural communities. Accordingly, the Corporation provided the funds to set up the first graduate school of library science, at the University of Chicago in 1926, with an endowment grant of $1,000,000. It made grants for training for librarianship, for book purchases to colleges and universities, for various kinds of experimental service projects, and for the development of other library schools. The ALA, assisted by Keppel, worked closely with the colleges and other organizations to implement many of these other programs and to strengthen the Association itself.

After retiring from the Corporation in 1941, Keppel became a member of the War Relief Control Board in Washington and still later a member of the Board of Appeals on Visa Cases at the Department of State. He remained as an educational consultant to the foundation.

Throughout his life Keppel gave innumerable speeches and lectures and wrote many books. His published works include *Columbia* (1914), *The Undergraduate and His College* (1917), *Education for Adults and Other Essays* (1926), *The Foundation* (1930), *The Arts in American Life,* with R. L. Duffus (1933), and *Philanthropy and Learning* (1936). He received honorary degrees from a number of distinguished colleges and universities, including Harvard, Columbia, Michigan, Pittsburgh, and Toronto.

Keppel died September 8, 1943, in New York City.

REFERENCES

Florence Anderson, *Carnegie Corporation Library Program, 1911–1961* (1963).

Peggy A. Sullivan, "Keppel, Frederick Paul," *Dictionary of American Library Biography* (1978).

GLORIA PRIMM BROWN

Kesavan, B. S.

(1909–)

Bellary Shamanna Kesavan, Indian library educator and administrator, was Librarian of the National Library, Calcutta, 1947–62, and first Director of the Indian National Scientific Documentation Centre (INSDOC), New Delhi, 1963–69.

Kesavan was born on May 10, 1909, in Mylapore, Madras, India. He was educated in Mysore and London, where he took an M.A. in English Literature at the University of London and earned a Diploma in Librarianship at the School of Librarianship and Archives, University College, London. He also had advanced training in Sanskrit and German.

Kesavan taught English at Mysore University (1929–44) and was Assistant Secretary of the Council of Scientific and Industrial Research (CSIR) in New Delhi, 1944–46. He served as educational adviser to the Ministry of Education in New Delhi in 1946 and 1947. Kesavan provided outstanding leadership to the Indian library and information community for more that two decades. The two national institutions he headed, the National Library in Calcutta and INSDOC, provide evidence of his skill for building and organization.

From 1947 to 1962 the National Library was developed from a mere storehouse of books to an active organization with national stature and international recognition. Apart from the tremendous growth of the document collection through purchase, gift, exchange, and deposit, and the generation of new services for users, the retrospective bibliographical projects of the National Library for such subjects as Indian anthropology, Indian botany, and Indian literature were significant contributions. Another important bibliographic project that was planned and brought out under the editorship of Kesavan for the Sahitya Akademi was the selective retrospective bibliography of books published from 1901 to 1953 on humanities in all the principal languages of India, including English.

Another achievement was the launching, in 1956, of the *Indian National Bibliography of Current Indian Publications,* a landmark in India's bibliographic history.

Kesavan's other major contribution was the development of INSDOC, which was established by CSIR with technical support from Unesco. In 1963 he became the first Director of INSDOC, which was until then under the administrative control of the National Physical Laboratory. Kesavan went about his new task with imagination and creativeness. The initiation of the National Science Library, the vigorous effort for the compilation of the *National Union Catalogue* of scientific serials to integrate and consolidate national resources and to create a computerized database, starting of an advanced training course in documentation and reprography, the publication of *Indian Science Abstracts,* development of programs to introduce computer-based information services, providing improved facilities for printing and reprographic services, building up translation potential, and setting up of the INSDOC Regional Centre at Bangalore were some of the major contributions during his tenure from 1963 to 1969.

He also gave leadership, direction, and advice to the development of library documentation and information services in CSIR laboratories and many research and development institutions, universities, and public sector undertakings. In effect he sowed seedlings for a national information system for science and technology.

Kesavan's international activities were also distinguished. He was the Vice-President of the International Federation of Documentation from 1964 to 1966, a member of the International Advisory Committee on Bibliography, Documentation, and Terminology of Unesco, and a member of the Expert Committee for Organizing the Library and Documentation Division in Unesco. He directed the Unesco Regional Seminar on the Development of National Libraries in Asia and the Pacific Area at Manila in February 1964.

Among his publications are a book on the national library (1961) and a small monograph on *Documentation in India* (1969), an abridged version of which was published in *Library Trends* (1969).

After retirement from his official career in 1969, Kesavan served international organizations such as the United Nations Development Programme and the World Health Organization. For publication by the National Book Trust of India, New Delhi, and under the auspices of the Indian Council of Social Science Research, New Delhi, he undertook preparation of a five-volume work, *The History of Printing and Publications in India: A Study of Cultural Reawakening*. The first volume was published in 1984.

T. N. RAJAN

Khurshid, Anis
(1926–)

University of Karachi, Pakistan
Anis Khurshid

Anis Khurshid, Pakistani librarian and educator, dominated the Pakistani library scene for more than 30 years and did much to promote and shape the development of Pakistani libraries.

He was born in Kamptee, India, on March 21, 1926. Khurshid started his career in librarianship in 1954 when he joined the Karachi University Library. He received a post-graduate diploma in library science from Karachi University and a Master's degree in Library Science from Rutgers University. He started teaching in the Department of Library Science, University of Karachi, in 1959 and served as Chairman of the Department from 1962 to 1964. He received an advanced certificate and a Ph.D. in Library and Information Science from the University of Pittsburgh in 1969. His dissertation ("Standards for Library Education in Burma, Ceylon, India and Pakistan") represents a landmark investigation in the field of librarianship.

From 1966 to 1969 he worked as Librarian of the International Library Information Center, University of Pittsburgh, an assignment that gave him an opportunity to learn more about librarianship in various parts of the world. On his return to Karachi, he put new life in the Library Science Department and served as Associate Professor from 1970 to 1979. From 1972 to 1975 he was Chairman of the Department. From 1979 he served Karachi University as Professor and Chairman of the Department of Library and Information Science.

Khurshid wrote several books dealing with various aspects of library science. They include *Cataloguing of Pakistani Names* (1964); *Standards for Library Education in Burma, Ceylon, India and Pakistan* (1969); *What Children Read: A Survey* (1976); and *The State of Library Resources in Pakistan* (1982). Khurshid edited many books, including reviews and *Shafi Dewey Decimal Expansions for Oriental Studies* (in Urdu; 1977); *Quaid-i-Azam Mohammad Ali Jinnah: An Annotated Bibliography* (1979); and *Library Education Across the Boundaries of Cultures: A Festschrift* (1981). Khurshid also contributed to various reference and professional publications.

Khurshid participated actively in the professional associations on local, national, and international levels. He was the founding chairman of the Karachi University Library Science Alumni Association (1957–58) and Editor of its journal, *Pakistan Library Review* (1958–62). He organized several annual conferences of the Pakistan Library Association and edited their proceedings. His other posts included Technical Chairman, Unesco Survey on Reading Habits in Pakistan (1972–73) and member, Standing Committee of Sind Educational Council (1973–); he chaired the University Grants Commission (UGC) Curriculum Revision Committee for Library Science (1979–80), the Intermediate Curriculum Committee for Library Science (1981), and the Technical Working Group for Development of a National Public Library System in Pakistan (1982–84). He also chaired the International Federation of Library Associations' Subgroup on South Asia (1976–78).

His wide range of contributions in library work,

teaching, research, and writing, including comparative librarianship, qualify him for consideration as one of the outstanding librarians of his generation in the world.

NAIMUDDIN QURESHI

Arthur Plotnik
Frederick G. Kilgour

Kilgour, Frederick G.
(1914–)

Frederick Gridley Kilgour, North American library administrator, lecturer, writer, and editor, is best known as the father of OCLC—the national shared cataloguing system that paved the way to a new era in library practice.

Born January 6, 1914, in Springfield, Massachusetts, Kilgour took his baccalaureate degree from Harvard College in 1931. While a student, he was appointed Circulation Assistant in the Widener Library; he eventually became Chief of the division. During this period he also did graduate work at Harvard and at the School of Library Service at Columbia University.

Called to war duty in 1942, Kilgour moved to Washington, D.C., where, except for overseas service, he remained for almost six years. Until 1945 he served in the Office of Strategic Services, attaining the naval rank of lieutenant (j.g.) and earning the Legion of Merit. For the following three years he was Deputy Director of the Office of Intelligence Collection and Dissemination in the U.S. Department of State.

In 1948 Kilgour was appointed Librarian of the Yale University School of Medicine, a position he held until 1965. During those years he wrote and lectured extensively in both librarianship and the history of science and technology and became active in the Medical Library Association (Secretary-Treasurer, 1950–52), the American Library Association, and other professional organizations. In 1961 he was a prime mover in one of the major early library automation efforts, the Columbia-Harvard-Yale Medical Libraries Computerization Project. As Yale's first Associate University Librarian for Research and Development (1965–67), he oversaw that library's entry into library automation.

OCLC. In 1967 Kilgour was called to what appeared to many at the time to be a most unprepossessing assignment but that later proved to be a development of great significance to American librarianship, the directorship of the Ohio College Library Center (OCLC). Technically a creature of the Ohio College Association (OCA), OCLC had actually been conceptualized by Kilgour and Ralph Parker as consultants to the OCA, and he now found himself brought to Columbus, Ohio, to implement his own recommendations.

Building on his successes and failures in automation at Yale, Kilgour was soon able to deliver batch-processed catalogue cards to his Ohio college library clients. By 1971 OCLC's shared cataloguing system was available online in the state of Ohio, and within two years after that it could be used elsewhere through other academic library consortia, first in the East, then the South, then the West. In 1978 it was reorganized as a national service. Despite some contemporary criticism, these developments brought about dramatic operational changes in libraries.

Kilgour served as the founding Editor of the *Journal of Library Automation,* published by ALA, and as author, lecturer, and international consultant. In 1974 he received the Margaret Mann Citation and in 1978 the Melvil Dewey Award from the ALA for his significant contributions to librarianship. In 1979 he was corecipient of ACRL's Academic Research Librarian of the Year Award. In subsequent years several colleges and universities conferred honorary degrees upon him in recognition of his distinguished career in public service.

In 1990 Kilgour and his wife, Eleanor Margaret Beach, who worked with him on many projects, moved to Chapel Hill, North Carolina. He was appointed Distinguished Research Professor at the University of North Carolina.

REFERENCES

Pamela S. Rogers, "Gathering Enemy Scientific Material in Wartime," *Libraries and Culture;* Proceedings of Library History Seminar VI (1981).

David L. Weisbrod, "Margaret Mann Citation, 1974: Frederick G. Kilgour," *Library Resources & Technical Services* (1974).

DAVID KASER

Kiribati

The Republic of Kiribati consists of 33 atolls in three groups in the central Pacific Ocean, 21 of them inhabited. With a very small land area (726 sq.km.) straddling a vast area of sea, Kiribati spans both the Equator and the International Date Line. One of the islands in the Gilbert group, Tarawa, is the center of government. Population (1990 est.) 66,000. The principal languages are I-Kiribati (Gilbertese) and English.

Kiribati once formed part of the British Gilbert and Ellice Islands Colony and became an independent republic in 1979. It does not have the same boundaries as the colony: the Ellice Islands gained independence separately as the Republic of Tuvalu. A government information library existed on Tarawa in 1946. Major development has been limited to three centers on South Tarawa: Bikenibeu, Bairik, and Besio. Libraries in these centers operated in the 1960s, though with limited hours and with collections based on donations.

The National Library and Archives Division of the Ministry of Education, Training, and Culture was set up in 1976. Since 1979, it has occupied a new Library and Archives building at Bariki. The building houses the Archives, which also has the National Library collection of Kiribati materials, and a public library for Bariki, as well as office space and an area for the distribution of donations. Donations are still a major source of books for the libraries. The first Librarian/Archivist, Richard Overy, deserves credit for guiding the National Library and Archives through its developmental stages.

The Tarawa Teachers College had a reasonable library by 1969. It was to have developed as a model collection, but did not flourish in the 1980s. The Library of the University of the South Pacific Extension Center moved into a new building in 1979. Two

Libraries in Kiribati (1987)

Type	Administrative units	Service points	Volumes	Expenditure
National	1		29,877	38,539#
Academic	5	5	--	
Public	2[a]		7,742	
School	--	--	--	--
–Other Data Not Available				

[a]This includes the public library which is a part of the National Library Building. There are also five Outer Island Libraries under development.

Source: Ministry of Education. *Digest of Education Statistics,* 1987.

other government tertiary institutions have small libraries.

There are two public libraries in Kiribati, one that forms part of the National Library at Bariki and one at Bikenibeu. Many people have worked to provide books to the Outer Islands since the 1960s, trying such plans as book boxes, village library units, collections at the schools, and collections at the Island Council offices. Starting in the 1980s, the government began building permanent structures for libraries on the Outer Islands whose people requested them. By 1990, five of these buildings had been completed.

Kiribati has eight secondary schools, but the government has provided books mainly for the more needy primary schools. The School Library Service, operating from the small Bikenibeu Public Library, worked to provide a stock of a hundred or so books for each of the primary and community high schools, distributing 55,000 books to 104 schools by the mid-1980s.

The few librarians in Kiribati do not have an association, and the only professional training in the country is through short, basic courses. Those seeking further training rely on the extension courses of the University of the South Pacific and the residential courses in Papua New Guinea.

REFERENCES

John Evans and Kunei Etikeria, "Rural Library Service in the Republic of Kiribati," *International Library Review* (1990).

John Evans and Kunei Etikeria, "Development of a Schools Library Service in the Republic of Kiribati," *Education Libraries Journal* (1990).

JOHN EVANS

Kirkegaard, Preben
(1913–)

Preben Kirkegaard, Danish library leader, may be considered the father of modern Danish librarianship. He was the founding head of the Royal School of Librarianship, Denmark's recognized center for professional education and training in library and information science. The foundation of the Danish Library School (1956) was Kirkegaard's *magnum opus*. He also left his stamp on practical librarianship through his work in public libraries in Jutland. At an early stage he entered the international library scene, became involved in consultancy work abroad, and was active in IFLA.

Preben Kirkegaard was born in Aarhus, Denmark, January 8, 1913. He passed a secondary school leaving exam in 1929, completed bookseller training in 1933, and was engaged as an assistant at the Aarhus Public Libraries on February 1, 1934. He became a trainee at the same library system on December 1 of that year. In 1936 Kirkegaard passed the final examination at the State Library School in Copenhagen. Kirkegaard was thus equipped with an all-round introduction to the book trade and to the basics of librarianship. Kirkegaard's time in Aarhus was characterized by his involvement with county-library-operated field work, especially assistance to the book selection process in the rural libraries, and library-based adult education seminars.

On January 1, 1945, Kirkegaard, at the age of 31, was appointed head of the Holstebro County Library. In 1946 he was appointed Chief Librarian of the County Library in Vejle. Vejle's emerging image as a "model library," which had an impact, even abroad, was largely due to Kirkegaard.

In 1956 Kirkegaard moved from practical librarianship into library education. The Ministry of Education appointed him Director of the newly established Royal School of Librarianship in Copenhagen, an independent institution set up through a special act. The new state college replaced the formal training program named the State Library School and operated by the State Inspection of Public Libraries. During the pioneering years of the school, the Director had his hands full in building a top-notch faculty and in taking care of curriculum development, planning, and administration. Yet Kirkegaard became the architect of a large-scale and impressive expansion of the educational activities and the institutional framework of the Royal School of Librarianship during the subsequent two decades. A new act on the Royal School of Librarianship was passed in June 1966 implying a reshaped public librarianship program as well as development of curricula oriented toward the education of professional library staff for the research and academic libraries sector. A new library school building on the island of Amager, near central Copenhagen, was converted into a well-functioning, working environment for some 50 full-time faculty members, technical and support staff, and more than 1,000 students. Thanks to Kirkegaard's dynamic efforts and negotiating skills, the financial support necessary to the operation of such a large institution was secured.

Preben Kirkegaard

In his many years as educator, planner, administrator, and negotiator, Kirkegaard never concealed his visions of an upgraded and consolidated library profession and his intention to enhance the level of library education and raise the status of his school. Kirkegaard took the view that library science is an academic discipline in its own right. It may well be that Kirkegaard's views of a philosophy of librarianship and his educational ideas were inspired by distinguished American library schools such as Chicago and Columbia.

He went to England, Canada, and the United States to study, joined IFLA as early as 1952, undertook a Unesco expert mission on library education in Greece (1962) and served on IACODLA (International Advisory Committee on Documentation, Libraries, and Archives) set up by Unesco, 1971–78. But Kirkegaard's work in IFLA constitutes the apex of his activities in the field of international library cooperation.

He became a dedicated worker for IFLA over many years, served on the sections of public libraries and library schools and the Executive Board of the organization (acting as Treasurer 1965–73), and served as President 1974–79. During his presidency Kirkegaard exerted a clear influence on the priorities and structure of IFLA. He had a key role to play in shaping a new organizational structure for the Federation. The constitution was blueprinted at the General Council in Lausanne, Switzerland, August 1976.

At the IFLA Council and General Conference in Oslo, Norway, August–September 1979, the title of Honorary President of IFLA was conferred on Kirkegaard in recognition of his untiring efforts. The selection of Kirkegaard as recipient of the Professor Kaula Gold Medal for the year 1982, "in recognition of his illustrious services for the cause of Library and information science," is another appreciation of his merits.

Kirkegaard's support of the library profession is also reflected in his contribution to the work of various organizations, committees, and bodies in Denmark, including the Danish Association and the Union for Public Librarians. He has served on the Executive Committee of the Danish Library Association. In 1983 he became a honorary member of the Association. From 1957 Kirkegaard was a co-editor of *Libri,* the international journal. Kirkegaard wrote numerous articles and reviews, and his monograph on Danish public libraries (1948) has been translated into several languages.

After his retirement in 1983, Kirkegaard worked as an active freelancer, contributing feature articles and book reviews to newspapers. He continued to keep an eye on developments in the library scene, and he studied selected library history themes.

REFERENCE

The Kirkegaard Festschrift *Biblioteket,* edited by Axel Andersen and Erland Munch-Petersen (1983), provides a bibliography of 291 of Kirkegaard's writings compiled through March 1982.

LEIF KAJBERG

Korea, Democratic People's Republic of

North Korea, officially the Democratic People's Republic of Korea, occupies the northern half of the Korean Peninsula in eastern Asia. It is bounded on the north by China and the former Soviet Union, on the east by the Sea of Japan, on the south by the Republic of Korea, and on the west by the Yellow Sea. Population (1990 est.) 21,773,000; area 120,538 sq.km. The official language is Korean.

The Central Library in Pyongyang, functioning as a national library, has a collection of about 1,500,000 volumes. Provincial libraries are in Chongjin, Hamhung, Shinniju, Haeju, Wonsan, Kangge, Pyonsong, Sariwon, and Hesan. The North Hwanghae Provincial Library in Sariwon is reported to have a collection of 60,000 volumes, the library in Hamhung 40,000, and the library in Haeju 33,000. In addition there are city libraries in Kaesong and Chongjin with collections of about 25,000 volumes.

The Academy of Sciences Publishing House, founded in 1953, publishes works on science, chemistry, geology, metallurgy, physics, biology, history, mathematics, meteorology, education, and economics. The Academy of Social Sciences and the Academy of Medical Sciences, both in Pyongyang, publish works in their respective fields.

The Kim Il Sung University in Pyongyang, founded in 1946, has faculties in history, philosophy, political economics, law, philology, foreign literature, geography, geology, physics, mathematics, chemistry, and biology. Its library has a collection of about 60,000 volumes. The Kim Chaek Polytechnic Institute and the Pyongyang Medical Institute are also in Pyongyang. There are institutions of higher and professional education in the main towns, including colleges of engineering, agriculture, fisheries, and teacher training. In addition, there are factory (engineering) colleges. Statistical and other detailed information was not available on library service in these institutions.

Special libraries are the Institute of Agricultural Sciences in Finjan and the Academy of Forestry, the Academy of Medical Science, and the Academy of Social Science, all in Pyongyang.

The Library Association of the Democratic People's Republic of Korea was established in 1953. The Association is affiliated with IFLA; its headquarters are in the Central Library at Pyongyang.

STAFF

Korea, Republic of

A densely populated mountainous country occupying the lower 99,016 sq.km. of the Korean peninsula, extending south from Manchuria between the Yellow Sea and the Korean Straits, the Republic of Korea is bounded on the north by the Democratic People's Republic of Korea. Population (1990 est.) 42,793,000. The official language is Korean.

History. Historical records prove that there were royal collections of books and collections in schools during the period of the Three Kingdoms (57 B.C.–A.D. 661). Papermaking and printing techniques, both woodblock and movable metallic type, reached their height during the thirteenth century, creating a good environment for bookmaking and, in turn, libraries. Fostered by the Buddhist religion and Confucian philosophy, temple libraries and private libraries of scholars also accumulated reading materials. Libraries attached to three levels of education—Seo-

Libraries in Republic of Korea (1990)

Type of library	Number of administrative units (main libraries)	Number of service points (branches, mobile stops, etc.)	Volumes in collections	Annual expenditures (jeon)	Population served	Professional staff (with certificate, diploma, etc.)	Total staff
National	2	1[a]	2,252,400	9,946,198	42,793,000*	254	500
Academic	305	39[b]	27,468,776	41,112,958	1,490,809	1,943	3,282
Public	231	17,828[c]	5,483,207	38,193,506	42,793,000*	1,104	3,133
School	6,468		27,675,092	4,461,801	9,353,266	993	7,889
Special	358		6,037,322	20,727,499	--	724	1,481
Other (describe)							

[a]branch
[b]mobil stops
[c]Saemaul Mungo (New Village Micro Library)

Sources: Statistics on Libraries in Korea, 1990. Seoul: Korea Library Association, 1990
Korea Statistical Yearbook, 1990. Seoul: National Bureau of Statistics, Economic Planning Board, 1990
(*1990 estimates)

Dang, Hyang-Kyo, and Seo-Won—opened their collections to authors, scholars, and individuals. More than 520 of these are preserved as local historical sites. Among early libraries, royal libraries remained dominant until the modern era. They were strengthened by succeeding rulers, storing archival materials, classics, and government documents. The Kyujangkak (Royal Library, established in 1776), with some 141,000 volumes of rare books and manuscripts in all fields, is one of the best sources for research in the Far East.

The Japanese modernized the library system a little during their rule (1910–1945), but wanted to use it for propaganda to assimilate Koreans into Japanese culture. They banned the use of the Korean language and prohibited all Korean publications, particularly scholarly works, handicapping the growth of modern libraries. Improvements after liberation in 1945 were stalled by the Korean War of 1950–53. The Korean Library Association was reorganized in 1955 and persuaded the government to enact a Library Law in 1963. The democratization of education, rapid progress in the publishing industry, and overall economic growth contributed to the development of Korean librarianship.

National Libraries. There are two national libraries, the National Central Library and the National Assembly Library. The forerunner of the National Central Library was opened in 1923 as a Japanese government library and went through reorganization in 1945 when Korea became independent. As a depository library, the National Central Library is charged with bibliographic and information services, including KOMARC (Korean MARC), bibliographic control of records related to the nation, international exchange services, and assistance to other libraries. It had almost 1,359,300 volumes in 1987, most of them Oriental, and almost 201,000 rare books. Its major publications are *Korean National Bibliography, Literary Information,* and *Bulletin of the National Central Library*. The National Central Library has six departments, one branch library, and mobile libraries. In 1988 the Library moved into a new modern building in South Seoul.

The National Assembly Library was founded in 1952. Its primary duty is to provide research services for members and committees of the Assembly. By necessity, its collection emphasizes politics, law, economics, and other fields of the social sciences. The Library also serves government officials and people from other research and educational institutions. As one of two depository libraries, it has exchange agreements with some 360 institutions in 83 countries. By 1987 the library had 585,600 volumes, including 10,600 rare books. Its collection is about 50 percent Korean, 25 percent English, and 20 percent Japanese. Its major publications are *Acquisitions List, Index to Korean-Language Periodicals, National Assembly Library Review,* and *Theses for the Doctor's and Master's Degrees Awarded in Korea.*

The Government Archives and Records Service (GARS), created in 1969, collects and preserves records from central and local government units and other affiliated offices. It also functions as the Government Reference Center and the agency for cooperation with foreign archival institutions. An agency of the Ministry of Government Administration with a staff of more than 100, it has a branch office in Pusan.

Academic Libraries. Despite rapid expansion of academic libraries after the Korean War, development of services and collections was hampered by the lack of library training in lower schools. Educational reforms beginning in the 1970s which stress independent study and higher standards created a strong demand for improved library services. Almost all areas of library operations improved, including the introduction of automated systems. Issues still requiring attention include strengthening reference and information services, upgrading the status of academic librarians from that of office staff, and reducing the disparity between the universities and four-year colleges and the junior and technical colleges. In 1987, more than 260 academic libraries served almost 1,426,000 users with some 21,640,000 volumes. Further improvement calls for close cooperation between the Association of National University and College Libraries and the Association of Private University and College Libraries.

The National Central Library, one of the country's two national libraries, moved into this new building in Seoul in 1988.

Seoul National University Library is the largest in Korea. The Kyujangkak, the Royal Library collection of classic literature, comprises part of the collection and is preserved in a specially designed section of the Library. Other national universities, one in each of the eight provinces, are active in promoting library development. Libraries at Ewha, Yonsei, Korea, Sogang, and Sungyunkwan universities are among the major ones on privately supported campuses.

Public Libraries. Modern public library development generally began with enactment of the Library Law of 1963. Still small in number and poor in materials and services 25 years later, public libraries eagerly awaited the effects of the first comprehensive amendment to that law, passed in 1987. The new law gave national and local governments mandatory responsibility for establishing and supporting public libraries. It created a Special Committee on Library Development to advise the Minister of Culture on important policies and overall operational matters affecting public libraries; encouraged the creation of a Library Promotion Fund; and differentiated further the status of librarians according to qualifications and experience. A Library Promotion Law passed in 1990 supplements previous library legislation. There were 175 public libraries in Korea in 1987, with approximately 237,500 users per library.

Micro Libraries. Started in 1960 as a private venture, the Micro Library movement has met the need for reading materials in remote and thinly populated villages and islands. The Korean Micro Library Association was inaugurated in 1961 and has helped to furnish half the cost of bookcases and books that ranged from 60 to 300 titles in accordance with the needs and interests of the people served. First operated under the auspices of the Ministry of Education, these successful mini-libraries are now subsidized by the Ministry of Home Affairs. The movement has spread steadily to factories and other workplaces, and Korea now has 33,000 Micro Libraries.

School Libraries. Modern school libraries also began with the end of the Korean War. The Library Law of 1963 recognizes the importance of school libraries under current teaching methods and curricula. But the lack of understanding, poor financial situation, increasing student population, and other competing educational needs have hampered the growth of school libraries as indispensable instructional media centers. Secondary-school students face fierce competition in national examinations for entrance to colleges and feel compelled to use their school libraries. But too many school libraries are nothing more than large study halls where students can use their own textbooks and notebooks. There were 3,309 elementary, 1,403 middle, and 1,343 high school libraries in Korea serving some 9,700,000 students in 1987.

Special Libraries. The need for rapid rehabilitation and industrial advancement gave added importance to special libraries. Today these libraries are the most advanced and the best supported in the country. Library and information services in science and technology are recognized as essential. Libraries in business and industry, government agencies and their affiliated institutions, research organizations, and other firms are growing rapidly in number and quality. The number of special libraries grew from 107 in 1977 to 262 in 1987, with 152, or 58 percent, in the Seoul area. The Science Park Complex in Seoul includes the libraries of KDI (Korea Development Institute), KIET (Korea Institute for Economics and Technology), and KIST (Korea Institute of Science and Technology). Others are those at the Academy of Korea Studies, Korea Educational Development Institute, and Korea Research Institute for Human Settlement.

The government has sponsored the Daeduk Science Complex in South Choong-Chung Province, which includes 17 government-subsidized research institutes, mostly in science and technology, along with private institutions. Specialized research libraries in Daeduk include those at the Electronics and Telecommunications Research Institute, Korea Institute of Energy and Resources, Korea Institute of Machinery and Metals, Korea Research Institute of Chemical Technology, and Korea Standards Research Institute. The Library at KAIST (Korean Advanced Institute of Science and Technology, a postgraduate institution), is headquarters for the Central Science Library Project, a plan to computerize and form a network among the libraries in the complex.

The Profession. *Education.* The first training program for librarians was offered by the Library School at the National Central Library in 1946. The one-year course concentrated on practical training, and the school produced only 77 librarians before it was suspended in 1950 because of the Korean War. In 1955 Ewha Woman's University offered undergraduate library courses as minor subjects. Full-fledged formal education in librarianship at the first degree level started in 1957 at Yonsei University in cooperation with George Peabody College for Teachers in the United States. In the 1970s more universities offered four-year programs and a number of junior colleges began offering two-year programs for assistant librarianship. The Ministry of Education grants certificates for both professional and assistant librarianship.

By 1987, Korea had 30 colleges and universities with library science departments. Among those, ten schools give Master's degrees and four universities offer Ph.D. programs. Six library science departments in junior colleges train assistant librarians and one one-year certificate program is offered in the form of in-service training. Library curricula have changed to adapt to the development of information technology, and many schools offer courses in information science or library automation.

Associations. Founded in 1945 and reorganized in 1955, the Korean Library Association (KLA) set out to achieve in a short period the development of modern libraries, professional growth of librarians, and international perspectives for Korean librarians. Headquartered in the compound of the National Central Library, the KLA sponsors activities such as the National Convention of Librarians and Library Week as well as workshops and seminars. It has a distribution center for reference materials. Along with its journal, *KLA Bulletin,* and *Statistics on Libraries in Korea,* it issues publications on library science, translations of foreign books, and library reference tools. In 1987 the KLA had 485 individual, 603 institutional, and 120 permanent members.

Faculty members and professional librarians interested in advanced studies in the field organized the Korean Library Science Society in 1970. Its main objective is to promote scholarly research through seminars, conferences, and publications. It publishes a journal.

In 1984 the Korean Society for Information Management was organized to emphasize information science and computer technology. The KSIM *Journal* is its research publication.

The Korean Bibliographical Society, founded in 1985, publishes *Research in Bibliographical Science.* Members include scholars and librarians generally concerned with the study of books and bibliographical and archival services.

REFERENCES

National Assembly, *Guide to the National Assembly Library: A Brief Description* (1990).

Pongsoon Lee, "Education for Librarianship in Korea," *Papers Presented at the FID/ET Workshop, 1982* (1983).

PONGSOON LEE

Krupskaya, Nadezhda
(1869–1939)

Nadezhda Konstantinovna Krupskaya Ulianova, the wife of Lenin, was prominent in Communist Party and Soviet state activities, one of the founders of the Soviet educational system, and a pioneer in the development of libraries during the Soviet period in Russia.

Krupskaya was born February 26, 1869, in St. Petersburg. She graduated from secondary school in 1887 and, in 1890, while a student of the Woman's College in St. Petersburg, she became a member of a Marxist circle. From 1891 to 1896 she taught at a Sunday evening school for workers and propagated revolutionary ideas.

She met V. I. Lenin in 1894, and soon they were married. With him she took part in the organization of the Revolution in Russia. In August 1896 Krupskaya was arrested and joined Lenin in his exile in the village of Shushenskoye and later in Ufa. At that time she wrote her first work, *The Woman-Worker.* From 1901 to 1905, together with Lenin, she lived in Germany, Great Britain, and Switzerland and was active in the revolutionary movement and the publishing of the Marxist newspapers *Iskra* and *Vperyod.* On her return to Russia in November 1905 she worked as the Secretary of the Central Committee of the Bolshevik Party. From the end of 1907 until April 1917 she again lived in exile with Lenin, continuing her revolutionary activities.

At the same time, she became interested in the study of popular education in Russia and in western European countries and in 1915–16 became a member of the Pestalozzi pedagogical society in Switzerland and the Berne and Fribourg pedagogical museums. In that period she also wrote one of her major works, *People's Education and Democracy,* which dealt with the development of popular education in the United States, a subject that she had examined in a number of her earlier works.

After the establishment of the Soviet government in Russia in November 1917, Krupskaya became one of the leaders of the Commissariat of People's Education (from 1929 serving as Deputy of the People's Commissar), where she took an active part in the preparation of the first legislative acts on people's education and became the chief organizer of cultural and educational work in the country. She taught at the Academy of Communist Education and was the founder of a number of voluntary societies, including "Away with Illiteracy" and "Children's Friend," and chaired the Society of Teachers-Marxists. She was a member of ruling bodies of the Communist Party and the Soviet government.

Krupskaya played a prominent role in activities directed toward the elimination of illiteracy, the organization of the Soviet school system, and the establishment of cultural foundations for a new society. She appreciably contributed to the formulation of the most important issues of Marxist education: the definition of the objectives of Communist education, preschool and primary education, the connection between the school and public life, professional and technical training, the content of curricula, and the education of the various nationalities of the Soviet Union. She was editor of a number of journals, including "Public Education," "People's Teacher," "Extra-Scholastic Education," and "School for Adults." Her literary production totals over 5,000 items, among which are a number of reminiscences of Lenin, representing significant primary sources for his biography.

Printed courtesy of *Soviet Life*
Nadezhda Krupskaya

She devoted much time to librarianship, to which she accorded an integral role in education and the development of public life. She had expert knowledge of bibliography in Russia, was acquainted with many western European libraries, and displayed a keen interest in U.S. libraries. She took part in the preparation of major legislative acts on libraries, including the decree "On the Centralization of Librarianship in the RSFSR" (1920) and the resolution of the Central Executive Committee, "On Librarianship in the USSR" (1934). The most significant meetings and conferences in the field were held under her guidance, and she gave speeches on book distribution, problems of library science, and bibliography. Such journals as "The Red Librarian," "In Aid of Self-Education," "BookBulletin," "What One Should Read," and others were founded on her initiative. She wrote hundreds of articles on librarianship, publishing, bibliography, lifelong education, and self-education.

The scope of her activities can be classified along three major lines. First, she was an ardent propagandist of the ideas of Lenin, who regarded the establishment of libraries as an inseparable part of the Socialist state policy in the field of culture and considered the establishment of an integrated system of various types of libraries, evenly distributed throughout the country and provided with all facilities required, as a necessity. Krupskaya's many speeches and articles, which were imbued with these ideas, and especially a widely known work, *What Lenin Wrote and Said about Libraries* (1929), helped to enhance the prestige of libraries in Soviet society.

Second, during the first two decades of Soviet power, Krupskaya headed the organization of a library system and the popularization of libraries and their use by wide sections of the public. She showed great concern for all aspects of librarianship, including the publication of needed materials and the most effective methods for their distribution according to the needs of various social and cultural groups. Krupskaya devoted much time to the development of children's literature and the organization of school and children's libraries. She encouraged the establishment of libraries in both cities and villages, supported the organization of reference and information services, encouraged the use of interlibrary loan, and supported the participation of all libraries in the country's economic, social, and cultural development. As early as 1918 Krupskaya initiated the opening of a number of library schools. She argued that raising the standards of librarianship was possible only if qualified personnel with sound training were available. She paid significant attention to the development of bibliography, especially to the compilation of recommendatory lists and indexes, and to the evaluation of books and the definition of their relevance for each category of reader—always, of course, with political criteria paramount in her thinking. She considered it important to teach broad sections of the population how to use libraries, choose books, and educate themselves.

Third, Krupskaya worked to elaborate fundamental principles of library science. The first library research institutions, such as the Research Institute of Library Science and Recommendatory Bibliography, were established on her initiative, as were the formulation of training programs in librarianship and bibliography for secondary schools and universities. She stressed the need for constant attention to the reading needs of the broad masses and for constant improvement of forms and methods for book publishing; the need for a purposeful policy in selecting book collections and servicing readers—a policy that would be in keeping with the objectives of building a new society; the need for combining the dissemination of professional and technical knowledge in library activities with efforts at developing a harmonious personality; and the need for understanding the cultural heritage of all the peoples of the world and for promoting humane qualities that would serve higher human ideals.

Krupskaya's writings are widely published and studied, and many books and articles have been written about her. Many libraries and educational and other institutions were named after her. An annual Krupskaya medal was awarded to the best teachers and librarians in the Soviet Union.

Krupskaya died in Moscow on February 27, 1939.

REFERENCES

The collected writings of Krupskaya are *Pedagogiheskie sochineniya* ("Pedagogical Works," in Russian) 11 volumes (Moscow, 1957–63); *O Bibliotechnom Dele* ("On Librarianship") (Moscow, 1st ed., 1957; 2nd ed., 1976); *Reminiscences of Lenin* translated by Bernard Isaacs (Moscow, 1959); *Memories of Lenin* translated by E. Verney, 2 volumes (London, 1930–32); *Memories of Lenin* (London, 1942).

A bibliography of her works and literature about her is *Nadezhda Konstantinovna Krupskaya: Bibliografia Trudov i Literatury o Zhizni i Deiatelnosti* ("Bibliography of Works and Literature about Life and Activities"), 2 volumes (Moscow, 1969–73); 4 volumes, 3rd ed., 1982–84).

Nadezhda Krupskaya, "Lenin's Work in Libraries," *Lenin and Library Organisation* (Moscow, 1983, pp. 156–164).

GEORGIJ FONOTOV

Kunze, Horst
(1909–)

Photo by Manfred Krause, 1988
Horst Kunze

Horst Kunze, one of the eminent figures of German librarianship in the 20th century, profoundly influenced the development of librarianship in the then German Democratic Republic and became one of the leading librarians there.

Born in Dresden September 22, 1909, Kunze studied modern languages and literature, especially German, and philosophy and completed those studies in 1935 with the Ph.D. The following two years he was educated as a subject specialist in academic and research libraries at the Sächsische Landesbibliothek in Dresden and the Deutsche Bücherei in Leipzig.

Kunze's library career started in 1937 at the Deutsche Bücherei and continued in 1939 at the Landesbibliothek in Darmstadt. In 1947 he was appointed Director of the Universitäts- und Landesbibliothek Halle. Three years later, he took over responsibility for the Öffentliche Wissenschaftliche Bibliothek in Berlin. This library, one of the two successors of the former Preussische Staatsbibliothek, was named Deutsche Staatsbibliothek in 1954. Until his retirement at the end of 1976, Kunze served as Director General of that distinguished library, which was incorporated into the the Stiftung Preussischer Kulturbesitz in 1990. After the founding of the Library Association of the German Democratic Republic in 1964, Kunze was elected its first President; this association united in 1991 with the Deutscher Bibliotheksverband.

Kunze taught library science in Halle from 1948, then in Berlin at the Humboldt University as Professor from 1953, and as Director of the Institute of Library Science and Scientific Information from 1955 for a decade and a half.

Kunze's international recognition as a scholar is based on his learned and methodology-oriented publications in library science, book science, literature, and librarianship. His textbook on library administration, *Grundzüge der Bibliothekslehre* ("Basic Library Management"; 1956; 4th edition, 1977), and the *Lexikon des Bibliothekswesens* ("Encyclopedia of Librarianship"; edited with Gotthard Rückl, 1969; 2nd edition, 1975) were outstanding publications in the field for many years.

His most significant contribution in the area of book science is his *Geschichte der Buchillustration in*

Deutschland ("History of Book Illustration in Germany"). Volume 1, covering the 15th Century, appeared in 1975; volume 2, on the 16th and 17th centuries, published in 1993. Specific interest in children's literature and in beautiful books of all ages is characteristic of his scholarly and popular writing. A number of his beautifully illustrated, designed, and printed books won prizes in the annual competitions for the best books in his country. Three collections of his articles on the book appeared, in 1974, 1980, and 1988. A selection of his works was published in Russian in 1983.

In Kunze's publications, which number more than 700, academic knowledge of the subjects treated is combined skillfully with historical developments and their impact on groups of people, especially the young, living in Germany and beyond. This general attitude gained Kunze many honorary positions not only in librarianship but also in publishing and bibliophily. As early as 1955, he was one of the co-founders of the Pirckheimer-Gesellschaft, the association of bibliophiles in the then German Democratic Republic.

Kunze was awarded many official decorations and medals and an honorary Ph.D. degree. He received the Gutenberg Prize from the city of Leipzig in 1972 and the P. N. Kaula Medal in 1983.

REFERENCES

Renate Gollmitz prepared a bibliography of Kunze's publications from 1935 to 1968 and published it in *Buch–Bibliothek–Leser* (1969); she was preparing an update in the early 1990s.

The latest Festschrift devoted to Kunze is the collection *Von der Wirkung des Buches* ("On the efficacy of the book"; 1990).

PAUL KAEGBEIN

Kuwait

Kuwait, an independent constitutional monarchy, lies on the northeast coast of the Arabian Peninsula, at the northwest end of the Persian Gulf. Kuwait is bordered by Iraq on the north and west and by Saudi Arabia on the south. Population (1990 est.) 2,143,000; area 17,818 sq.km. The official language is Arabic.

History. The first library in the country was established in 1922, but although it was the National Library and its stock rose to 1,500 volumes, neglect caused the collection to dwindle to 200. In 1936 the library was started up again and attached to the Ministry of Education. School libraries were started in the early 1960s, but the turning point came with the founding of Kuwait University in 1966. Its library opened with a collection of 20,000 volumes. Many libraries were damaged or destroyed during the brief occupation of Kuwait by Iraqi armed forces in 1990–91. The information given below relates to the situation before the war.

National Library. The National Library of Kuwait, the National Heritage Center, is closely affiliated with and supervised by Kuwait University Libraries Department. The Center was established in 1971 on a recommendation from the Kuwaiti Cabinet. Five copies of all printed publications issued in Kuwait must be deposited in the Center according to the legal deposit law of 1972. The functions of the Center are gathering and making available all printed and non-print materials concerning and issued in Kuwait, the Gulf States, and the Arabian Peninsula, as well as issuing national and specialized bibliographies. The library holdings of the Center total about 297,000 volumes.

Academic Libraries. The principal academic library in Kuwait is that of the Kuwait University, which was inaugurated in 1966. In the late 1970s its growing library system comprised the Central Library, six college libraries, a separate library for periodicals, and the National Heritage Center. By 1981 the number of its service points had risen to 11. The book collections in all libraries of Kuwait University total about 340,000 volumes. Acquisitions, cataloguing, classification, compiling bibliographies, audiovisual services, reference, and other functions are performed centrally by the Department of Libraries, which administers all libraries of the University. They serve about 17,000 students and a faculty of 600.

The Kuwait University Libraries Department

Libraries in Kuwait (1990)

Type of library	Number of administrative units (main libraries)	Number of service points (branches, mobile stops, etc.)	Volumes in collections	Population Served
National[a]	1	4	93,000	29,662
Academic[b]*	1	14	453,000	--
Public[c]	1	22	737,000	585,206
School[b]	570	--	3,127,000	748,053
Special[d]	13	16	137,000**	--

[a]1986 data
[b]1988 data
[c]1987 data
[d]1985 data
*main or central library only
**12 libraries only

Source: Unesco, *Statistical Yearbook*, 1991.

issued *Selected Bibliography on Kuwait and Arabian Gulf,* two volumes for foreign and Arabic sources (1969–70), the nucleus of the national bibliography; *A List of Books and Publications Received by the Kuwait University,* a computer printout from 1973; *Selected Bibliography on Arab Civilization* (1970); and other specialized bibliographies. The Kuwait Institute of Scientific Research issued editions of a union list of periodicals in the libraries of the Gulf States.

Public Libraries. Public library services in Kuwait came into existence with the establishment of the Central Public Library in 1936. The public library system consists of the Central Public Library and 23 branch libraries, mostly in the suburban shopping centers of the city of Kuwait. The public library system is administered by the Public Libraries Department of the Ministry of Education. All operations, such as acquisitions and technical processing, are done centrally by the Central Public Library. New books are distributed regularly to the branch libraries. Periodicals are acquired and processed separately. The book collections of the public library system total about 280,000 volumes.

School Libraries. The School Libraries Department of the Ministry of Education, established in 1954, is responsible for establishing and developing school libraries, providing them with library materials and personnel, and operating a book processing center for book distribution. The administration of individual school libraries is a responsibility assigned to each school principal. More than 325 school libraries serve elementary, intermediate, secondary, vocational, and technical schools.

Special Libraries. Government departments, research centers, banks, and other enterprises possess special libraries with sizable collections. Noteworthy among these libraries are those of the Ministry of Education, Ministry of Foreign Affairs, Ministry of Endowments, Kuwait Institute of Scientific Research, Arab Planning Institute, Planning Board, Kuwait Fund for Arab Economic Development, Central Bank of Kuwait, and Kuwait National Petroleum Company. The Documentation and Information Section of the Kuwait Institute of Scientific Research performs a leading role in scientific documentation, particularly in computerized bibliographies and specialized professional training.

MOHAMED M. EL HADI*

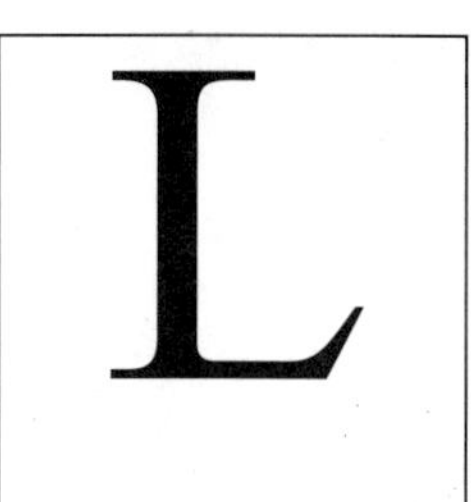

Lamb, W. Kaye
(1904–)

William Kaye Lamb, Canadian library administrator, archivist, scholarly editor, historian, and library association leader, was the first National Librarian of Canada.

Born in New Westminster, B.C., May 11, 1904, Lamb attended schools there and in Vancouver. In 1927 he earned a B.A. with first class honors in history from the University of British Columbia, followed by an M.A. in 1930. He spent the years 1928 to 1932 in France at the Sorbonne and the École Libre des Sciences Politiques. In England, at the London School of Economics, he obtained a doctorate in 1933 under the direction of Harold Laski. His appointment the next year in the dual role of Provincial Librarian and Archivist of British Columbia foreshadowed his later career and prepared him for it.

When, in two years' time, he was made the Superintendent of the British Columbia Public Library Commission, he found himself with a combination of responsibilities as unique as they were sweeping, attending to the development of the historical records of the province, serving the information requirements of the members of the Legislature and government officials, operating library services for citizens living in remote areas of a vast province, organizing regional library services in more settled areas, and generally coordinating public library services everywhere.

In 1940 he became the second Librarian of the University of British Columbia, succeeding John Ridington. The war and postwar years presented Lamb with formidable problems: the delivery of scholarly publications from Europe was disrupted; the cost of all imported journals and books was raised by special wartime taxes; budgets were lean; and at war's end the student body increased threefold in just two years, creating heavy demands for library materials, services, and study space. Nevertheless, collections grew significantly in that period, in large part as a result of Lamb's success in increasing private donations to the Library. Most notable among these gifts were the complementary collections of F. W. Howay and R. L. Reid, which established at the University one of the continent's finest collections of Canadian and Pacific Northwest history.

Responding to the Library's physical shortcomings—there had been no change to the building since its construction in 1925—Lamb obtained a commitment to build a north wing, which was opened in the fall of 1948. This event almost coincided with his appointment as Dominion Archivist. In that post, in 1950, he established the Canadian Bibliographic Center, which undertook the compilation of both a national union catalogue and a national bilingual bibliography, the first issue of which appeared in January 1951 under the title *Canadiana*.

Assigned special responsibility for the development of a national library, Lamb was instrumental in drafting legislation enacted by Parliament. The National Library came into official existence on January 1, 1953, with its creator as Canada's first National Librarian. Initially, the National Library had a statutory but not a separate physical existence. The Canadian Bibliographic Center, the core of the new institution, was housed in the Public Archives Building, a 30-year-old structure too small for current needs. Lamb set out promptly to alleviate space problems, and by 1956 a new and large Federal Records Center was constructed on the outskirts of Ottawa. The National Library was relocated there.

Planning had already commenced on a new building for the National Library and Public Archives of Canada; although plans were completed by 1954, changes in governments and their priorities delayed construction for more than a decade. By the time the National Library finally occupied its permanent home in June 1967, it had amassed a collection of more than 600,000 volumes through legal deposit, gift, and purchase; had compiled a union catalogue of more than 10,000,000 titles; was responding to more than 80,000 location requests a year; had published 16 annual cumulated volumes of *Canadiana;* had established a microfilming service for theses written at Canadian universities; had published since 1961–62 annual lists of theses; and had increased bibliographic and reference services in many other ways. While managing the developmental years of this new institution, Lamb was also guiding the expansion of the programs of the Public Archives of Canada, which assumed responsibility for the management of all federal government records in 1956.

As a historian, Lamb wrote monographs, edited nine major works, wrote more than 100 articles, contributed to encyclopedias, and wrote book reviews. For 10 years he was editor of the *British Columbia Historical Quarterly,* which he founded in 1937, and for 12 years he was President of the Champlain Society, a publisher of historical texts.

After retirement as Dominion Archivist and National Librarian in 1968, Lamb conducted further research, culminating in 1985 with his edition of Captain George Vancouver's *A Voyage of Discovery to the North Pacific Ocean and Round the World, 1791–1795,* published in London by the Hakluyt Society in four volumes. His 256-page introduction is the definitive biography of Vancouver.

Lamb served on the councils of scores of scholarly and professional organizations and as President of the British Columbia Library Association, the Canadian Library Association, the Pacific Northwest Library Association, the Canadian Historical Association, the Society of Archivists, and the Society of American Archivists. He received many honors, including doctorates from 10 Canadian universities. He was elected a Fellow of the Royal Society of Canada in 1949, served as its President in 1965–66, and was awarded its Tyrrell Medal for outstanding work in Canadian history in 1965. In 1969 he was appointed an officer of the Order of Canada.

REFERENCES

"Archives, Libraries, and the Canadian Heritage: Essays in Honour of W. Kaye Lamb," *Archivaria* (Winter 1982–83).

British Columbia, *Report of the Public Library Commission* (1936–39).

National Library of Canada, *Report of the National Librarian* (1953–67).

University of British Columbia, *Report of the Librarian to Senate* (1940–48).

BASIL STUART-STUBBS

Public Archives of Canada

W. K. Lamb

F. Wilfrid Lancaster

Lancaster, F. Wilfrid

(1933–)

Frederick Wilfrid Lancaster, British-born American library educator, became a major influence in the fields of information systems and the evaluation of library services. His work deals principally with the underlying intellectual problems and conceptual frameworks of information retrieval systems, rather than technical aspects of computing and systems design. His major contributions have been in the areas of vocabulary control, interaction between system and user, evaluation of systems effectiveness, and, in his later work, the implications of advanced information systems for the future of libraries in society.

Born September 4, 1933, in Durham, England, Lancaster studied at Newcastle-upon-Tyne School of Librarianship (1950–54) and became Fellow of the Library Association of Great Britain (by thesis) in 1969. Lancaster began his professional career in 1953 as Senior Assistant, Newcastle-upon-Tyne Public Libraries. His subsequent positions include Senior Librarian for Science and Technology, Akron (Ohio) Public Library; Resident Consultant and Head, Systems Evaluation Group, Herner and Company, Washington, D.C.; Information Systems Specialist, National Library of Medicine; and Director of Information Retrieval Services, Westat Research, Inc. From 1970 Lancaster served on the faculty of the University of Illinois, Graduate School of Library Science, with the rank of Professor from 1972.

Lancaster's contributions have been made through writing, teaching, and consulting. Major publications include *Indexing and Abstracting in Theory and Practice* (1991), *If You Want to Evaluate Your Library* (1988), *Libraries and Librarians in an Age of Electronics* (1983), *Investigative Methods in Library and Information Science* (1981), *Towards a Paperless Information System* (1978), *The Measurement and Evaluation of Library Services* (1977), Ralph Shaw Award (1978), *Information Retrieval Online* (1973), *Vocabulary Control for Information Retrieval* (1972), and *Information Retrieval Systems: Characteristics, Testing and Evaluation* (2nd edition, 1979). In addition, Lancaster edited a number of books and wrote many articles and technical reports.

His publications were recognized by the American Society for Information Science with best book awards in 1970 and 1975 and a best paper award in 1969. Other honors include University Scholar, University of Illinois, 1989–92; G. K. Hall Award of the American Library Association (1989); Award of Merit of the American Society for Information Science (1988); Outstanding Information Science Teacher Award, American Society for Information Science (1980); and Fulbright Fellowships in 1975 and 1985.

His consulting includes work for the Central Intelligence Agency, Center for Applied Linguistics, National Library of Medicine, various UN agencies, and the International Development Research Center. He prepared several reports and guidelines for Unesco.

Lancaster's strongest impact was on the development of criteria and procedures for the evaluation of systems performance, mainly through the extension, refinement, and application of concepts pioneered by the Cranfield studies, a series of investigations undertaken in the late 1950s at the College of Aeronautics, Cranfield, England, under the direction of C. W. Cleverdon. His *Evaluation of the MEDLARS Demand Search Service* (1968) represents a landmark investigation, not particularly for its influence on the later development of the MEDLARS system, but as a demonstration of the application of refined methods for testing, analyzing, and evaluating the performance of an operational information retrieval system.

The more general significance of Lancaster's work results from his ability to combine a rigorous and thorough approach with a clarity of expression that renders advanced concepts of information retrieval accessible to the student and the practicing librarian without oversimplification. Lancaster's work, therefore, might be viewed as an attempt to bridge several important divisions in the information professions. His early work on vocabulary control and systems evaluation provides a connection between practice and theory for the technically oriented designer of information systems. Subsequent work, particularly the *Measurement and Evaluation of Library Services,* serves to narrow the gap between the library profession at large and the growing body of research relevant to measurement and evaluation. Lancaster's most significant contribution to the literature of library and information science may well be his stimulation of interest in the possibility that theory and research may have some practical utility in the field.

JOE A. HEWITT

Laos

Laos, a people's democratic republic in southeast Asia, is bounded by Burma and China on the north, Vietnam on the east, Cambodia on the south, and Thailand on the west. Population (1990 est.) 4,139,000; area 236,800 sq.km. The official language is Lao.

National Library. The National Library of Laos in Vientiane includes the National Museum and National Archives. On the grounds of the School of Fine Arts, it is under the direction of the Ministry of Education. Its holdings are about 50,000 volumes in Lao, English, and French; the degree of continuity in its operations allowed by the government is uncertain. Prior to the declaration of a people's republic in 1975, the National Library received aid from the French and U.S. governments, private foundations, and Western scholars. For example, the Rockefeller Foundation presented 9,000 volumes, mainly in French, on a wide range of subjects; the Asia Foundation and the U.S. Library of Congress made other contributions. In 1974 the former Director of the National Library, Prachit Soulisak, told a representative of the U.S. Library of Congress that he had compiled a list of 84,000 titles available in Lao at various temples and libraries throughout the country; he said the list gave the location of each item.

The National Library of Laos published *Lao National Bibliography* in three volumes (1968–72). The Director of the National Library compiled *Bibliographie de Laos,* Institut Française d'Extreme Orient, with a supplement covering the years 1962–70.

Academic Libraries. Before 1975 the Buddhist Institute in Vientiane was one of the most important centers of scholarship in Laos. It maintained

Libraries in Laos (1987)

Type of library	Number of administrative units (main libraries)	Number of service points (branches, mobile stops, etc.)	Volumes in collections	Population served
Academic[a]				
Higher Education	5		121,000	8,370
School[a]	22		33,000	11,000
Other (describe)[b]				
Non-specialized	1	2	145,000	800

[a]1987 data
[b]1986 data

Source: Unesco, *Statistical Yearbook,* 1991.

a substantial collection of works, many in Pali and Sanskrit, for the use of its students and foreign scholars.

Sisavangvong University, in Vientiane, is the only university in Laos. It serves about 1,600 students. Library facilities of its faculties of medicine, law, and education were mainly provided by Western governments and foundations and are not extensive for research purposes. The libraries of the University's 10 institutes range in size from 800 to 4,200 volumes.

Public Libraries. There are not believed to be any public lending libraries, in the Western sense, in Laos. The library of at least one major temple, the Wat That in Luang Prabang, performed some of the functions of a public library, however. It reportedly has many contemporary works in Lao and Thai and circulated about 100 books a month to residents of Luang Prabang. Most temples have teaching functions and many serve as community centers; some of the larger ones have collections of manuscripts in Pali and Sanskrit.

Prior to the Pathet Lao takeover in 1975, a number of foreign governments, including France, the United Kingdom, and the United States, operated libraries and reading rooms in Vientiane and other major towns. These were often heavily patronized. With U.S. economic assistance, a program of providing modest library facilities in rural areas also enjoyed some success.

School Libraries. The French *lycées* and the normal and technical schools in Laos had relatively modest library facilities (mainly provided through foreign-aid programs). In most schools the libraries were reserved for the use of their own students and faculties.

Special Libraries. The Directorate of Archaeology in the Ministry of Culture developed a collection of manuscripts. The U.S. Agency for International Development also maintained collections of documents on foreign assistance to Laos. (AID was expelled from Laos in 1973.)

The Profession. The Lao Library Association was closely associated with its National Library and was physically housed in a building behind the library. Little is known about the ongoing work of the Association in later years, but prior to 1974 it published a considerable number of monographs. At that time the Siaw Savath Society was also associated with the National Library and published the theses of Lao students studying abroad. Unesco helped set up national document centers under assistance grants, and along with this has contributed to a number of training programs.

PETER A. POOLE

Lara, Juana Manrique de
(1899–1983)

Universidad Nacional Autónoma de Mexico

Juana Manrique de Lara

Juana Manrique de Lara, Mexican librarian, introduced modern librarianship to Mexico through teaching, writing, and official duties as Inspector General of Libraries.

Born in the village of El Cubo, Guanajuato, in Mexico, on March 12, 1899, she studied first in her native state and later in Puebla. A marked vocation toward teaching led her to graduate from the Normal School of Puebla. Inclined as well toward books, she enrolled in the first National School of Archivists and Librarians in Mexico City, studying there during the years of the Revolution, 1916–17.

She continued her studies in the United States to prepare as a professional librarian, one of the first Mexican women to do so. De Lara graduated from the School of the New York Public Library in 1924. Returning to Mexico, she dedicated herself to teaching library science. She taught at the early Library School of the Secretariat of Education and at the National School of Archivists and Librarians. The courses were many and the years were long, but her enthusiasm was contagious. For her pupils she published a number of valuable books such as the *Manual of the Mexican Librarian,* which she modestly described as advice for persons in charge of libraries, and which went through several editions. Other best-sellers for Mexican librarians, so lacking in tools, were her *Elementary Notions Concerning the Organization and Administration of a Small Library, Elements of the Organization and Administration of School Libraries,* and *Guide to Headings of Material for Dictionary Catalogues.* Another work supplied a need in Mexican literature, *School Libraries and Children's Literature*—lists of books for children in primary grades and youth in secondary schools. A valuable work written in collaboration with another distinguished librarian, Guadalupe Monroy Baigen, was *Pseudonyms, Anagrams, and Initials of Mexican Authors.* She wrote numerous articles in specialized magazines of the U.S., Mexico, and countries of Central America.

She was for many years Inspector General of Libraries, Director of Libraries of the Secretariat of Education, and other specialized branches, in all of which she left her impress of positive activity totally dedicated to the culture of her country.

Juana Manrique de Lara died in Mexico City, October 8, 1983.

ERNESTO DE LA TORRE VILLAR

Law Libraries

A law library is a specialized library defined by its subject matter. Its functions, collections, and services are determined by the nature of legal information and research.

PURPOSES AND OBJECTIVES

Law libraries differ as markedly as the publics they serve: academic or nonacademic, public or private. Public or government law libraries are funded by government entities; private ones are funded by attorneys or by business firms. But the source of a law library's funds does not adequately describe its public, because many types of users have access to nonacademic law libraries. Academic law libraries serving law schools primarily have characteristics of their own, depending especially on whether they are publicly or privately funded.

The nature and sources of law, legal authority, and the legal profession have affected the distinctive functions of law libraries, whether academic or nonacademic. The special characteristics of legal bibliography and legal research, how lawyers work, and what they do have also been influential in the development and administration of all types of libraries.

Academic Law Libraries. Known as law-school libraries, these institutions primarily serve the needs of a particular law school's faculty and students. They also serve faculty and students in other disciplines, members of the bench and the local bar, and the general public, especially when they are publicly funded. Because most of them are large libraries employing many professionals, there is considerable job specialization. Typically, a librarian will work in reference, circulation, cataloguing, or acquisition. In the larger libraries further subject specialization involving both reference and acquisition work also exists.

At the 176 law schools approved by the American Bar Association (ABA) in the early 1990s, the law libraries held, on average, about 310,000 volumes. Some 67 law-school libraries held more than 400,000 volumes, including Harvard, with nearly two million and Columbia, Michigan, New York, and Yale universities, with more than 800,000 volumes each. By contrast, about 35 law-school libraries had about 170,000 volumes each.

Government Law Libraries. In the United States, these libraries serve federal, state, and local agencies, all levels of the courts, and the bar. They range in size from the Law Library of Congress, with more than two million volumes, to small libraries with only basic working collections. Among other important U.S. government libraries are those of the Supreme Court, the Department of Justice, the Department of the Treasury, and the Federal Trade Commission.

Most state, county, and court libraries serve the general public as well as members of the local bar. The staffs of government libraries vary in size, as do their collections, from the very large, with many professional librarians, to units with one or two professionals and clerical support staff.

State law library service may be provided either by independent libraries or by divisions of other state agencies. Some provide legislative reference services and maintain collections of state legal materials, case reports, and statutes, both national and local. Their primary function is to serve officials in all departments of state government. Their collections range in size from 30,000 volumes to more than a million. The more important state law libraries are located in Massachusetts, Minnesota, New York, Rhode Island, New Jersey, and Wisconsin.

There are more than a hundred formally organized court libraries employing professional law librarians. Many more small court libraries are supervised by clerks rather than professional librarians. The largest numbers of court libraries, including those of the federal courts, are concentrated in the state of New York.

Private Law Libraries. Law firms, other businesses, and bar associations maintain libraries to serve their needs. Law office collections range from a few thousand volumes to more than 75,000, at one firm in New York City, or more than 60,000, at another firm in the same city. The largest numbers of law office libraries are in New York, California, and Illinois. In addition to acquiring the traditional types of library materials, these libraries invest heavily in new technologies, such as computer-assisted legal research (from such vendors as LEXIS and Westlaw), electronic online cataloguing, and computerized databases containing office records and briefs, legal memoranda, and legal forms of all types. They serve members of their own firms almost exclusively.

The legal departments of business firms maintain company law libraries of legal and law-related mate-

Main reference room at the Federal Trade Commission Library in Washington, D.C.

Federal Trade Commission

rials on various aspects of the businesses involved, such as communication, insurance, international business, and transportation. Some of the larger collections of this type are held by the Prudential Insurance Company in Newark, New Jersey, the American Telephone and Telegraph Company in New York City, and the General Motors Corporation in Detroit.

Bar associations maintain libraries to serve practicing lawyers, keyed to the research demands of litigation and client counseling. Among them are some of the leading law collections in the U.S., such as the Los Angeles County law library, with more than 700,000 volumes, and the Association of the Bar of the City of New York, with more than 500,000 volumes.

Functions. The tremendous growth of law book collections in the late 20th century, the increased dependence on new technologies in locating legal authority, and the need to provide interdisciplinary materials in legal research have changed the concept of the law library as merely a collection of books in which legal authority can be found. Technological developments will change that concept still further, to an information transfer network.

Actually, law librarians today already function as information specialists, coordinating the research activities of their institutions. They suggest sources of information lawyers can use and, even more significantly, locate such sources when they are initially unknown. Law librarians as trained legal information specialists typically provide efficient specialized reference service to attorneys, paralegals, and others; instruct and assist them in legal bibliography and research; structure and perform online searches of bibliographic and information databases; provide current-awareness service by previewing information in advance of publication, surveying current periodical literature, and acquisition; evaluate library materials and compile topical bibliographies; promote resource-sharing with other law libraries to augment their organization's resources; design and maintain control-and-retrieval systems for all types of materials in their care; assess the quality, depth, and scope of the existing collection and systematically tailor acquisitions of library materials; establish policies and procedures for preserving library materials; and prepare fiscal reports, budgets, and long-range information plans relative to library needs.

In actual research, law librarians can find legal citations or references, suggest sources of information, verify and translate citations, interpret abbreviations, assemble materials for specific projects, and prepare bibliographies. Law books are highly technical tools that may be difficult to use without guidance, and law librarians can explain their use. Actually, they provide significant assistance to legal researchers because of their knowledge of where to find the answers to questions involving business, medicine, history, the social services, economics, and the applied sciences. They are especially adept at using computers as research tools in law. As a result, the role of the law librarian as researcher and teacher in providing access to these sources has taken on more significance.

Because law librarians possess the legal background and judgment to anticipate the research needs of lawyers, as well as the resourcefulness to analyze legal materials and recognize their relevance to a particular subject or problem, they are considered the "silent partners" in the research activities of lawyers, judges, scholars, and other serious researchers in the field of law.

Minnesota State Law Library

The new Minnesota State Law Library, opened in 1990, houses one of the major state law library collections with over 200,000 volumes.

Education for Law Librarianship. This changing role of law librarianship has been reflected in rising demands on the educational and professional qualifications held not only by head law librarians but by the rank-and-file staff members as well. Although the education needed for law librarians varies according to the type of law library and the position to be held, there is still a commonly accepted core of professional and educational achievement prerequisite to success in law librarianship.

Basic educational preparation should include a four-year college or university degree and a graduate professional degree. A basic course in legal bibliography and research is necessary. Education should also include hands-on experience with computers and their application to law libraries; actually, a knowledge of computer science and electronic data processing is essential to law librarians. A reading knowledge of one or more foreign languages is desirable as well. Skills in personnel management, business administration, budgeting, and public relations may be significant in a law library. Professional librarians without legal training can function in technical and circulation services in a law library, but most director and assistant director positions in law-school libraries, large government libraries, and some large firm libraries require both law and library degrees in addition to a bachelor's degree. In large law-school libraries, the heads of public services may also be required to have both law and library degrees.

The American Bar Association (ABA) and the Association of American Law Schools (AALS), setting standards for accrediting law schools, have established criteria for qualifying law-school libraries and librari-

News and Information Services, the University of Michigan

Underground structure wired for computer terminals and built below the 60-year-old gothic walls of the University of Michigan Law Library in 1982.

ans. These criteria have been generally accepted as basic requirements for professional status.

The ABA standards for law librarians are part of its *Standards for the Approval of Law Schools* (1990). Standard 601 dictates that "the law school shall maintain and administer a library adequate for its program." Standard 602 (a) provides that "the law school library shall contain the Core Collection Library Schedule, attached as annex II." Standard 602 (b) provides that "the law school library shall contain or provide appropriate access to additional publications and information services reasonable and necessary for the proper conduct of the school's educational and research programs." Standard 605 provides that "the law library shall be administered by a full-time law librarian whose principal activities are the development and maintenance of the library and the furnishing of library assistance to faculty and students, and may include teaching courses in the law school." Standard 605 (a) adds that "the law librarian should have a degree in law or library science and shall have a sound knowledge of library administration and of the particular problems of a law library." Standard 605 (b) continues that "the law library shall have a competent staff, adequate to maintain library services, under the supervision of the law librarian."

AALS applies its own accreditation standards to law schools seeking membership, and membership contributes significantly to a law school's prestige. Its standards are more demanding than those of the ABA. AALS Executive Committee Regulation 8.2 (a) provides that "the director of the library should have both legal and library education." AALS Bylaws 6-10 adds, "A member school shall maintain a library adequate to support and encourage the instructions and research of its faculty and students. . . . A member school shall have a full-time librarian and a staff of sufficient number and with sufficient training to develop and maintain a high level of service to its program. The director of the library should be a full participating member of the faculty."

The impact of technological change has become so significant in legal research that it is now recognized even in the standards of the ABA. They are designed "to reflect current and prospective use of electronic and other technology in legal research." Law schools "should make reasonable provision for faculty access to automated information systems suitable for scholarly research." Annex II of its Standards states that law libraries are required to provide "computer-assisted legal research services of national scope and broad subject coverage." Although these standards apply only to law-school libraries, they should inevitably affect similar services and plans for bar libraries, court libraries, and private law firms.

The American Association of Law Libraries (AALL), founded in 1906, works to promote librarianship, develop and increase the usefulness of law libraries, cultivate the science of law librarianship, and foster a spirit of cooperation among its members. Its mission, as approved by its Executive Board in 1990, states: "Recognizing that the availability of legal information to all people is a necessary requirement for a just society, the AALL exists to promote and enhance the value of law libraries to the public, the legal community, and the world, to foster the profession of law librarianship, and to provide leadership in the field of legal information."

The AALL had more than 4,700 members representing most of the approximately 1,100 law libraries in the U.S. in the early 1990s. Of that total, more than 1,600 represented private law firm libraries; 1,400 law-school libraries; 500 government law libraries; 330 company law libraries; and 250 court, county, and bar libraries.

Membership in the AALL provides an opportunity to take advantage of the collective knowledge of the group through annual meetings, educational workshops, and institutes. Special-interest sections enable AALL members to participate in smaller groups that deal with specialized areas of law librarianship, such as automation and scientific development; contemporary social problems; foreign, comparative, and international law; legal history and rare books; and technical services.

The AALL publishes the quarterly *Law Library Journal*, which features scholarly articles and practical pieces on law, legal information, and law librarianship. The *AALL Newsletter* contains information about current professional developments. The annual *AALL Directory and Handbook* is a complete listing of AALL members and a description of all AALL operations. A *Minority Law Librarians Directory* is also available. The AALL offers placement information to members and employers.

Outside North America, formal organization of the profession of law librarianship has been slow to develop. The British and Irish Association of Law Libraries (BIALL) was founded in 1959, but the International Association of Law Libraries (IALL) did not come into being until 1969. Both organizations offer short courses and publish journals in addition to sponsoring conferences that provide an essential means for participants to confer on problems and prospects for the field.

REFERENCES

Julius J. Mark, and Richard Sloane, *Legal Research and Law Library Management* (1992, with semiannual supplements).

Heinz P. Mueller, Patrick E. Kehoe, and Louisa Hurtado, editors, *Law Librarianship: A Handbook* (1983).

JULIUS J. MARKE

SERVICES TO USERS

The effective law library was long known as a happy combination of books and people. Today the functional legal information center is a harmonious union of people, materials, and technology. This subtle change in nomenclature is important because it implies modern service to a demanding clientele.

The raison d'être for a legal information center is service to what are probably the most influential and powerful forces in society—the executive, legislative, and judicial branches of government and the advocates of the legal profession. The role of the legal information center is vital because the missions of its users are essential in the civil and criminal matters inherent in society. Without law there would be no order; without well-organized, readily accessible legal information, presidents and governors, legislators, judges, lawyers, and the public who must contend with law and regulation would be severely impeded in their activities.

The traditional law library selects and acquires legal materials for the use of its audience, catalogues and classifies those materials so that many individuals may benefit from their content, and answers questions on a variety of legal and other subjects. These functions constitute the traditional role, but in an era of demand for immediate access to rapidly changing information, they are not enough to satisfy legal professional needs properly.

Current Context. People must have information to survive in the world, and as the population increases it becomes necessary to find better ways of distributing needed information. Information is being produced faster by more people than in the past. In law this condition is reflected both in additional court decisions, because there are more people litigating, and in increased legislation, because society has become more complicated in human relationships and in scientific development. The number of specialized subjects is also increasing rapidly. For example, law must regulate space exploration, satellite communications, environmental pollution, toxic chemicals—areas for which there was little if any law a generation ago.

The library must become a media center that will allow its patrons communication with sources of information in various media—not only printed but also film, slides, videodiscs, and others—and in many locations. Information science is concerned with discovering better ways to get the right information quickly to the person who needs it and with finding information efficiently once it is stored in libraries and other centers of information.

The legal information system the law library profession envisions for the United States will deliver information to judges and lawyers, faculty and students, and the general public. To satisfy this objective it must meet three basic requirements: it should be able

Photo by Marco P. Zecchin/Image Center

Computer-assisted research has become the norm at Stanford Law School's Robert Crown Law Library.

to tell a user where to find information; it should be able to deliver that information; and it must respond within the time limits the user imposes.

A law library's operations will therefore be concerned with the way people create information, index or label it, store it, find it, analyze it, send and receive it, and use it. But the pressures of the information revolution present a significant challenge to law librarians, because the traditional means of supplying library service with printed media alone are rapidly shifting to a multimedia approach utilizing technology. The custodial librarian, long an anachronism, is now extinct, and has been replaced by a sophisticated specialist who must be a user of high-technology tools and an instructor in their use as well.

In responding to the mission of the legal information center, law librarians now utilize several tools: *computers,* because they can process information in the form of words as effectively as they compute numbers; *telecommunications,* because this technology is capable of distributing word and picture information at great speeds to widely dispersed places; *fax* (telefacsimile transmission) to send and receive written and illustrated communications over telephone lines, because the "library without walls" must tap myriad sources of information quickly; *micrographics,* because microform technology allows large quantities of information to be condensed into a small space; *CD-ROM,* because the discs can hold massive amounts of data—more than 600 megabytes of information, roughly equivalent to 500 high-density floppy disks—and the drives can retrieve the information in fractions of a second; *videodiscs,* because they provide instructional support utilizing such programs as CALI (computer-aided legal instruction) and Harvard's interactive video in a variety of legal specialties. These technologies complement one another: the marriage of CD-ROM indexes and micrographics speeds research, utilizing the great mass of information already on microforms and making possible full access to current and retrospective materials.

Law librarians seek to further their leadership in applying advanced technology to law by utilizing electronic retrieval systems such as LEXIS and Westlaw for reports of court decisions, statutes, and administrative law and by providing for the automation of library and bibliographic processes through RLIN (Research Libraries Information Network) and OCLC (Online Computer Library Center). The database systems developed by Lockheed, by Systems Development Corporation, and by others provide access to subjects related to law, such as energy and the environment. Leading law firms utilize computers and expect new lawyers to be knowledgeable in their operation. The law library is thus the true laboratory of the law where its patrons must experiment and learn to use the new tools of the profession.

Staff. Effective service requires a professionally qualified staff. The legal profession has been slow in grasping the advantages provided to law libraries by library-school graduates. Because there are no effective or enforceable standards for personnel in many county, court, and law-firm libraries, such libraries are sometimes quite poorly organized and maintained. With the advent of certification and accreditation procedures developed by professional associations, this situation may be expected to improve. Professional librarians are now typically the employees of choice in law-firm, government, and bar association libraries. In academic libraries the personnel may be lawyer-librarians with some training in information science.

The smaller a law library collection, the more important it is that the person in charge of the library have professional training, because, with a limited collection available, the librarian will need knowledge of sources of information off-premises. The law firm today is backing into the 20th century by discovering the value of professional librarians as information finders and organizers on both the legal and factual sides of legal causes.

Harvard Law Art Collection

Langdell Reading Room, Harvard Law School, Cambridge.

Services. Well-designed and -equipped physical facilities are critical to providing law library services and access to materials. On entering a library, the patron should see a directory on which all service elements are mapped. Next, by various architectural techniques, the patron should notice first an information outlet where he or she may inquire about a particular problem and be directed to the proper department. Typically, provision will be made for access to the collections through online, card, or microform catalogues, and additional standard bibliographic services and indexes will be provided in print form or, for example, by means of Wilson CD-ROM catalogues or InfoTrak. Copying and writing facilities are standard. Enclosed course-reserve materials areas in law-school libraries, reference rooms, audiovisual and computer instructional facilities, discussion rooms, rare- or restricted-book areas, and lounges are other features included in many modern libraries. Reference services will vary among law libraries according to the institutions they serve. Law-school libraries may provide more traditional academic library reference services, while in law-firm libraries the staff play an integral role in research.

Access to law libraries and their materials similarly varies according to institutional setting. By national policy, the courts of last resort in each jurisdiction and accredited law-school libraries with government depository status are urged to make their federal documents collections available to the general public. County law libraries are typically open to the public, while bar association and court libraries are often restricted to use by judges and attorneys. Special regulations may govern the use of law libraries in colleges and universities where space may be a factor in providing acceptable service to law students and faculty who will receive top priority. Firm law libraries are normally restricted to use by members of the firm. Relatively few public libraries maintain extensive collections of legal materials and, as library support in many communities is curtailed, this situation may be expected to continue. At the same time, however, there is a growing interest in providing access to legal materials for public library patrons.

Library personnel are not permitted to give legal advice, though they may point out standard reference sources. Legal materials may baffle the layman who has not been instructed in their use, so educational materials may be made readily available for self-instruction. There is a body of literature that shows the difficulty in refraining from giving legal advice while providing access to complex legal tools.

Interlibrary loans of legal materials may be restricted to secondary materials inasmuch as primary materials—statutes and cases—are essentially reference works in sets. The procedure for interlibrary loan would be the same as in general libraries, subject to the aforementioned restrictions.

DAN HENKE

COLLECTIONS

Law library collections reflect the characteristics of the clienteles they are designed to serve. While the core collections will be similar in libraries serving sole practitioners, law schools, or government agencies, the expanded collections will vary in accordance with the information expectations of the users. Even within the various types of legal communities served, vast differences may be observed in the collections assembled for use. For example, one law school may teach the rudiments of practice and require a library of the practitioners' primary tools, while another may emphasize research and scholarship in international law, requiring extensive resources in a number of languages. Law firm and corporate libraries collect books in the areas of their lawyers' specialities and, outside the core collection, may concentrate on highly specialized titles in limited fields of practice. Bar associations, courts, and governmental libraries acquire resources consistent with the interests of their patrons. The Law Library of Congress, for instance, acquires materials on a worldwide basis because of the demands for research materials and reports from Congress.

Materials. Law library collections differ from other types of special library collections in that serials comprise the largest proportion of primary materials, often as much as two-thirds of the collection. This fact results from the nature of the law itself. The state legislatures produce volumes of laws, known as *session laws,* which when codified become *codes* or *statutes* and when reproduced by commercial vendors along with cases and notes are called *annotated codes* or *annotated statutes*. Courts concurrently expound their opinions in *decisions* that are published as *reports* and are later consolidated into *annotated reports,* digests, encyclopedias, and eventually annotated codes or statutes. The magnitude of these serial publishing programs becomes evident: they emanate from 50 states and the federal systems' courts and agencies. Even the smallest library must maintain the current laws and court opinions in its state and federal law and opinions when applicable.

In addition to primary law books, indexing and finding tools are an essential part of legal research. As the scope of legal research activity increases, the library must parallel or exceed that activity by providing the information resources to support the demand. Growing collections may emphasize materials from the region in which they are located—the states around them or significant states with similar legal controversies—while the larger libraries will collect nationally and selectively in international fields. Ultimately, the largest libraries will amass collections that are worldwide in scope, although no single library could accumulate all of the world's legal output in print.

Libraries that support lawyers who write extensively must invest in research tools beyond the basics in laws and court reports. Law firms that have large appellate practices, corporate legal research units, law schools that emphasize research and writing and maintain student publications, bar associations, and courts and government agencies require secondary sources of the law to assist with formulating research products and preparing final written briefs and reports. Libraries will acquire some or all the secondary materials, depending upon their research requirements. Publications such as law reviews and periodicals, encyclopedias, dictionaries, and treatises fill this kind of need. Many professional associations publish legal journals and nearly every law school publishes at least one law review, edited by its students, with articles by leading practitioners, judges, faculty, and some students. The *American Bar Association Journal* and the *Harvard Law Review* are two of the approximately 550 periodicals indexed in the *Index to Legal Periodicals* and more than 700 in the *Current Legal Resources Index*.

York University Law Library (Toronto)

With over 200,000 volumes, York University Law Library in Toronto is the largest law school library in Canada.

Two national encyclopedias, the *American Jurisprudence 2nd* and *Corpus Juris Secundum,* cover basic American law principles, documented with cases that have enunciated them. Similarly, encyclopedias that treat local law are published for states. Law dictionaries define legal terms citing court opinions, among them *Black's Law Dictionary* and *Ballentine's Law Dictionary*. Books that exhaustively analyze a legal subject with supporting documentation are referred to as treatises; often their authors are authorities in their fields, and their works are frequently cited by name as the outstanding exposition on the law in a particular area, such as *Prosser on Torts*. *Shepard's Citations* has long served the legal profession by providing a "history" of each reported case (whether the case was affirmed, reversed, modified, or dismissed on appeal) and the "treatment" of each reported case (which indicates its value as authority by noting how other reported cases commented upon it by criticizing, distinguishing, explaining, following, limiting, overruling, or questioning its holding). The statutory divisions of *Shepard's* provide the legislative history of statutory law and show the reported state and federal court decisions and legislative enactments construing, applying, or affecting statutory law. In the natural sciences this method of research through citation is used in *Science Citation Index*.

Federal documents are another valuable source of legal information. The passage of Public Law 95–261 in 1978 afforded law-school libraries the opportunity to become depository libraries for U.S. government publications, and many have done so. Dramatic increases in information services and collection content enable law libraries to serve their patrons more effectively.

Notable Collections. Accumulation of law book collections has been an ongoing activity for many years. The first law library established in the U.S. was the Law Library Company of Philadelphia, formed in 1802 by a group of lawyers. Three years later the first law library book catalogue for this library listed 249 volumes. The Boston Social Law Library opened in 1804. Two state libraries that have excellent law collections were also established in this period, Pennsylvania in 1816 and New York in 1818. The Harvard Law School, founded in 1817, established a library with the nucleus from the college library, gifts, and some purchases; by 1826 the library had 1,752 volumes. One of the better-known American bar associations is the Association of the Bar of the City of New York, which was incorporated in 1869 and in two years had acquired 6,000 volumes. From these beginnings law libraries have increased exponentially both in quality and quantity of collections as well as in numbers of libraries. The Boston Social Law Library in the early 1990s contained more than 300,000 volumes. The largest law library in the world is the Law Library of Congress, with more than 2,000,000 volumes and many more when law titles in the Library of Congress are combined with the law collection.

The most spectacular growth in law library collections has occurred in law-school libraries. From its beginnings in 1817, the Harvard Law School Library collection has consistently ranked the largest among law schools over the years, numbering nearly two million volumes in hard copy and microform in the early 1990s. A span of at least a million volumes separates Harvard from those following in size: Columbia, Yale, and New York University.

Some early common-law collections were known to exist in England, but most law-school libraries were not independent of parent universities. The law collection at the Bodleian Library at Oxford was intermingled with the main collection until 1878, when a concession was made to shelve the law collection separately. A building completed in 1964 housed a separate Bodleian Law Library for the first time, holding nearly 200,000 volumes, the largest law library in the Commonwealth of Nations. A law library in London, part of the Institute for Advanced Legal Studies, enjoys a worldwide reputation for excellence. Under a cooperative acquisitions policy with four colleges of the University of London, it possesses an extensive common-law collection in addition to holdings in the law of Western European countries.

An outstanding library system with a world reputation is that of the Max Planck Institutes in Germany. The five Institutes, in five cities, are devoted to legal studies on foreign and international law, criminal, public, and private law, patents, copyrights, and unfair competition as well as legal history. Their combined libraries form a unique law collection.

Other libraries of excellence throughout the world that deserve mention are: York University Law Library (Toronto), the largest law-school library in Canada; the Law Courts Library of Sydney, Australia; the University of Singapore Law Library; the Faculty of Law Library, University of Tokyo; the Japanese Ministry of Justice Library; and the combined libraries of the Institute of Legal Studies and the Law School Library at the University of Lagos, Nigeria.

Collection Development. Ideally, a library should have every law title that its clientele could possibly desire at the time the need arises, but few, if any, libraries can operate in that kind of environment. Budgets and space are two significant delimiters to growth in law libraries. Some kind of judgment must be made in selecting legal materials to acquire. In libraries where each acquisition must be justified and approved, a committee of attorneys may make the selections for the library. In other libraries the librarian may have more freedom in selecting materials for the collection. In some government libraries a central purchasing agency must approve acquisitions. In law-school libraries, where nearly all librarians have both legal and library degrees, the selection of materials for the collection is largely at the discretion of the librarians.

Standards for the contents of law-school libraries are provided by the American Bar Association (ABA). The Association of American Law Schools (AALS) prescribes in more general terms. These libraries are expected to acquire the tools, books, microforms, and other information resources essential to support the teaching and research activities of the faculty and students. Jurisdictional materials for the federal government and for the state in which the law school is located are mandated. Additional flexibility permits acquisition of related materials to meet the specific interests of the faculty at each school.

Book selection aids include *Law Books in Print,* begun in 1957 and continuing in bound volumes and paper supplements. This series remains the primary for determining current editions and prices. As a further aid to book selection, the AALS in 1967 sponsored a series of 48 pamphlets of *Law Books Recommended for Libraries* in subject areas from Admiralty to Water Law and Foreign and International Law. Supplements were issued in 1974. Books are ranked in A, B, C order for priority in ordering. The "A" ranked books are recommended for purchase in all law-school libraries. Medium libraries should possess the "B" books, and only the largest law-school libraries would be expected to own the "C" books, which are primarily official government publications and materials in foreign languages. A survey conducted by the Special Networks Committee of the American Association of Law Libraries concluded that these rankings are largely valid, in accordance with the holdings of libraries in the various categories that checked their collections against the list. This title is continued as *Recommended Publications for Legal Research,* by Oscar J. Miller and Mortimer D. Schwartz.

Another aid in book selection, the *National Legal Bibliography,* by Peter D. Ward and Margaret A. Goldblatt, is a monthly compilation of current cataloguing of several dozen law libraries. It includes books, serials, government documents, theses, and dissertations. The contents are divided by jurisdictions and cover U.S. publications, international material, and foreign jurisdictions.

Other bibliographies cover book selection, and publishers and dealers, of course, provide advertisements, brochures, a sales slip service, and catalogues for examination. Emphasis in law-book buying is generally on the most current publications; interest in retrospective collections depends on the availability of funds beyond those required for the current collection. A survey conducted in a general university library indicated that the majority of its book buying consisted of titles more than one year on the market, whereas the vast majority of the law-book buying was prepublication or current-year publications. Law libraries are constantly under pressure to stay current with new publications.

Large law-book collections, while an asset for study and research, can become a liability where space is tight. A general rule of thumb in the academic world states that collections tend to double in 10 to 15 years. A building boom in law schools in the 1970s and 1980s seemed likely to give way to a trend toward making do in the 1990s. Law librarians will be challenged to cope with demands for access to more information and at the same time finding places to store it. Microforms and automated information may be solutions to this dilemma.

Despite mixed user reactions, law librarians are turning to alternative sources of information. In the past, microform was the only choice. An attractive market for microform encouraged publishers to provide major sets of law books in microfilm or microfiche. The entire set of state session laws from early times to the present is available in microfiche. State court reports are available in film or fiche. Congressional documents are produced in fiche, eliminating the storage and clerical chores involved in checking separate pamphlets. Many other titles are available from commercial sources to fill in sets that are impossible to obtain in complete form except in rare instances. Microform solves the problems of completeness, physical damage to books, and care and maintenance of aging collections. To illustrate their popularity among law-school librarians, in 1990 Harvard held almost 100,000 volume equivalents in microfilm reels and Georgetown and Minnesota each held more than a million sheets of microfiche.

Information in Computer Formats. Computers overtook libraries of all kinds, including law, in the 1980s and 1990s. While librarians are swept up in automating library processes, they are also focusing attention on enhancing information resources in online and CD-ROM formats. These rapidly growing technologies are popular media in law libraries. Major indexes and databases now available on CD-ROMs include *Index to Legal Periodicals* and other H. W. Wilson publications, *InfoTrak* and *LegalTrak,* and the *CIS Masterfile* of government documents.

Computerized online legal information systems are gaining acceptance and popularity in the legal field. In contrast to online systems available to other libraries, legal databases are searchable in full text, providing greater research capability and in-depth information. LEXIS and Westlaw are the two prominent systems offering access to vast stores of information. LEXIS, a product of Mead Data Central, went online in 1969 for Ohio and rapidly expanded. Westlaw is a product of the West Publishing Company, the largest law-book publisher in the world. Both offer federal and state laws and court decisions, agency regulations and decisions, texts and periodicals, and specialized materials. Mead also offers NEXIS for general information; West subscribers can access DIALOG.

Georgetown University Law Center

The five-story Edward Bennettt Williams Law Library at Georgetown University Law Center, opened in 1989. The library's international law collection occupies nearly one full floor.

Mead and West online products are available at commercial rates and at special academic rates. Virtually every law school in the U.S. considers access to these systems essential to the legal education process. In law schools, teaching the use of the systems occurs early in the curriculum and has become an integral part of the legal research and writing programs. In law firms, courts, and other law departments, only some lawyers may be proficient in using the systems to conduct their own searches; others may rely on librarians or designated professionals to frame the queries and search the databases.

Computer-assisted legal instruction is gaining in popularity in law-school libraries. Law courses are available primarily from the Center for Computer-Assisted Legal Instruction (CALI), in Minneapolis, Minnesota.

Audiovisual Materials. In addition to law books and information in microform or computer-based formats, many libraries are now expanding resources to include many kinds of audiovisual formats, including audio cassettes, video cassettes, films, and video and optical disks. Audio tapes on current topics of the law have become popular with those who have cassette players in their automobiles.

Videotapes are useful for group and self-instruction in trial tactics and other practical subjects. Videotaping for self-criticism is incorporated into trial practice instruction in law schools and in continuing legal education seminars for lawyers, faculty, and judges. Many law schools provide audiovisual services, either as a library function or through a separate department created for this purpose. The ABA, American Trial Lawyers Association, and National Institute for Trial Advocacy, among others, produce videotapes.

REFERENCE

Kathleen S. Grove, "1989–90 Statistical Survey of ABA Law School Libraries and Librarians," *Law Library Journal* (1991; published annually).

BETTY W. TAYLOR

ADMINISTRATION

The role of the law library administrator is to facilitate the library's ability to carry out its mission—organizing legal resources and materials to assist its clientele in understanding and interpreting the law and legal systems. The administrator oversees acquiring and organizing these materials and is responsible for making them available to patrons.

A law library is no different from any corporate unit in that its administration addresses the issues of governance, finance, budget, and personnel. The administrative structure of a particular library is tailored to that library's mission and clientele. The clientele of law libraries is composed of students, professors, lawyers, judges, scholars, and sometimes the lay public, either exclusively or in combination. It is easy to see how a library in a law firm serving 40 attorneys would be administered differently from an academic law library serving a thousand students and a faculty of 50.

The law library administrator is responsible for formulating and administering the library's strategic plan, a statement defining the library's mission, goals, objectives, and strategies. Beyond this, the administrator is charged with directing the creative energy of the staff to supporting the library's plan, encouraging individual contributions that will support the common good.

Administering a law library requires a broad range of skills. To be knowledgeable about the collection and to know how to access the materials in it requires a knowledge of the law and a knowledge of librarianship. In addition, a law library director must know enough about a variety of related fields to hire an effective staff and evaluate their efforts. Traditionally, these areas of expertise have included finance, architecture, and psychology, but the number and complexity of these fields are growing.

Personnel is the most complex and sensitive issue confronting a law library administrator. It does not matter how big the library's budget nor how long-standing its reputation, only a high-quality staff can ensure a high-quality library. No other administrative duty is as important as hiring, organizing, inspiring, educating, evaluating, and rewarding a good staff.

Most law libraries are organized into departments; at the very least, functions are separated into public services and technical services. The public services department may be organized by area of specialization, the number and character of these areas determined by the size and mission of the library. These subdivisions may include foreign law, rare books, media, computer resources, reserves, circulation, and reference. Each department is headed by a trained professional, all of them reporting to the head of public services.

In most law libraries, technical services include an acquisitions department and a cataloguing department that care for their respective duties. Continuation orders, such as serials, looseleaf publications, and supplemental monographs, account for the bulk of law library expenditures.

In academic settings, staff members with both library and law degrees work with the public in locating and disseminating information, although today some staff members with dual degrees work in technical services. Traditionally, professional law librarians were expected to have only qualifications in librarianship, but more frequently, particularly in academic settings, they have qualifications in law as well.

With resources becoming more expensive and budgets becoming tighter, the importance of the administrative staff has been highlighted. Perhaps the most dramatic changes in law library operations result from computer technology, which has put enormous demands on library budgets. Librarians, who are now trained information specialists, require higher salaries and benefits. To make the most efficient use of expensive resources, limited finances, and valuable personnel, the administrator must be a better informed and more careful manager than ever before.

The director turns to the administrative staff for support in overseeing the organization and operation of the library. The staff may include an associate director and a business manager. Together, they manage the financial and human resources, maintain the physical plant, and convey the concerns of the library to the governing body and to the patrons.

As policy decisions become more complicated, particularly those involving long-range planning, the administrator is likely to turn to the administrative staff for input and advice. For example, as information becomes increasingly available in a variety of formats, such as books, microform, and machine-readable databases, the administrator must be sure to invest in the information in the format that will be most cost-effective in the long run.

Governance. In almost all instances, the law librarian reports to the most important person in the unit, such as the dean of the law school, the managing partner of a law firm, or the senior judge responsible for administering the county law library. Because of the highly specific nature and uniqueness of the materials and services the law library provides, it is generally autonomous within the unit. In many cases a library committee of lawyers serves in an advisory capacity.

Finance. Sources of funding vary with the type of law library. Academic law libraries receive funds from tax revenues, tuition, gifts, and grants. A county law library receives money from earmarked portions of filing fees or from an appropriation from government funds. Associations rely on membership dues, investments, and fundraising efforts. The funds available to a law library in a law firm are determined by the governing members of the firm. All law libraries may supplement their funds with money-raising efforts such as publications programs or Friends of the Law Library groups.

Supplementary income has become particularly important for state institutions, which were affected by sharp budget cutbacks in the late 1980s and early 1990s. Increasingly, they have had to seek private funding from individuals, foundations, and the federal government. These law libraries may justify their requests for grants by demonstrating how the resources purchased with these funds will be used. In the past, it was sufficient to say that the money would be used for materials to be housed in the library and made available to patrons. But, beginning in the 1990s, administrators have had to develop and oversee outreach programs that would actively promote the use of materials by those who would benefit most from them. These programs include centers for criminal justice, centers that are clearinghouses for legal information on child abuse, and archives for the papers of prominent judges.

Budget. The administrator of a law library, like his or her counterpart in the corporate world, manages available resources to influence the future outcome of its operations. The administrator presents the budget and justifications for the proposed expenditures to the supervising person or body. The budget includes the following categories: personnel, supplies and equipment, and acquisition of materials.

Law library personnel are identified as professional staff (those holding positions that require both law and library degrees, as well as those holding positions that require only library degrees) and support staff or technicians. The usual formula for hiring staff is to hire two or three members of the support staff for every professional position.

The formula for acquisition of materials is to spend twice as much on material as on personnel. In most libraries, there is no budget for utilities, such as telephones and electricity, which are absorbed by the larger corporate unit. There are separate line items for expensive one-time appropriations, such as new computer systems, major renovations of the building, and furniture. Supplies and equipment include single computers, laser printers, audio and video equipment, and fax machines.

Contemporary Issues. Technology has made the law library a building without walls, and the library community is now a global one, but the role of the administrator remains fundamentally the same. This role is more demanding, however, because the administrator is expected to be knowledgeable in the variety of fields that have become increasingly important in the last few decades. In addition to computer technology and telecommunications, the administrator now must be educated in economics, history, international law, and social science methodology. While not necessarily an expert in all these fields, the director must know enough to be able to hire qualified specialists in them. Though the scope and complexities of law librarianship have increased, the function of the administrator is still to ensure that the mission of the law library is fulfilled.

ROY M. MERSKY

MEASUREMENT AND EVALUATION

Lawyers have special concerns about their libraries, because the common-law system, with its reliance on precedent and *stare decisis* ("let the decision stand"), its interconnected court reports, statutes, and administrative rules and decisions, has a unique need for easy access to written material. Law students, law professors, and practitioners daily subject their libraries to the most rigorous measurement and evaluation possible: the practical-use test. Perhaps because of these reasons, law librarians have been slower than others to develop written standards; those that exist have been written primarily by library users—the bar and the professorate—and not by librarians, although certainly librarians have been present and influential.

Methods of measurement and evaluation have been developed separately for each of the three major types of law libraries. Academic law libraries have the oldest and most systematic measurement techniques and standards. Libraries in the private sector and state, court, and county libraries have more recently developed measurement methods, but neither group has established a regular annual program.

Cook County Law Library, Chicago

Cook County Law Library, the second largest among county law libraries with 300,000 volumes, serves nearly 30,000 attorneys.

Standards that would provide the basis for performance evaluation are, for all types of libraries, primarily quantitative or prescriptive in terms of collections, rather than qualitative descriptions of professional skills or library services. The standards call for particular results, rather than prescribing methods to achieve the results. Although not labeled as standards, the two-volume *Law Librarianship: A Handbook,* edited by Heinz Peter Mueller and Patrick E. Kehoe (1983) has functioned as an authoritative description of the state of the profession's types of libraries and activities.

Academic Law Libraries. The American Bar Association (ABA), the accrediting agency authorized by the federal Department of Education to approve law schools, annually gathers statistics from law-school libraries and publishes the results in *Law Library Journal,* published by the American Association of Law Libraries (AALL) and, separately, as *Law Library Comprehensive Statistical Table Data from Fall [year] Annual Questionnaire.* This publication provides copious information and rankings for each library. In the early 1990s, the questionnaire included 73 questions and elicited more than 200 pieces of information from each library.

The information includes: volume and title counts, by physical format, for material added and withdrawn; numbers of pieces of microform and computer equipment; library functions automated, by type and by means; number and salaries of staff; expenditures for databases, books, serials, binding, preservation, equipment, salaries, fringe benefits, and staff development; measures of physical facilities in terms of net square feet, empty and occupied shelving, carrel and non-carrel seats; hours of operation and levels of staffing; and interlibrary loan activity.

Libraries may purchase from the ABA specialized

printouts for any desired group of respondents and data. The questionnaire has been fairly stable since it was first introduced in 1969, and the accumulated information provides a detailed picture of the development of academic law libraries since then. The results have been published annually in *Law Library Journal* after editing or additional manipulation by AALL members. In 1989, the ABA Office of the Consultant on Legal Education assumed primary responsibility for gathering and publishing the statistics, and AALL's role, through its Standing Committee on Statistics, became advisory.

Standards. The ABA promulgates standards through its Section on Legal Education and Admission to the Bar. As of 1991, there were 172 ABA-approved law schools. The ABA standards were published as *Standards for Approval of Law Schools and Interpretations; Rules of Procedure for Approval of Law Schools' Criteria for Approval of Semester Abroad Programs for Credit-Granting Foreign Segment of Approved J.D. Program and for Approval of Foreign Summer Programs of ABA-Approved Law Schools; Policies of the Council of the Section on Legal Education and Admission to the Bar and of the Accreditation Committee* in 1990. This publication includes a detailed description of the development of the standards. For earlier history, see Jerry L. Parsons, "Accreditation in Legal Education and in Education for Librarianship, 1878–1961," *Law Library Journal* (May 1975).

These standards include library administration, collections, employees, equipment, and physical facilities. The standards have evolved from being quite prescriptive—listing the specific titles a library should contain, for example—to being much more performance-based than quantitative, as a comparison of the version used in 1980 to that used in 1990 shows. The standards say nothing more about professional skills and library services than that they be those "reasonably necessary for the proper conduct of the school's educational and research programs" (Standard 602) and that "the law school library must be a responsive and active force within the educational life of the law school, [with] a direct, continuing, and informed relationship with the faculty and administration of the law school" (Standard 604).

A second source for academic law library standards is the membership requirements of the American Association of Law Schools (AALS). The Association, which includes 158 law schools, was founded in 1900 for "the improvement of the legal profession through legal education." It serves as the law teachers' learned society and is legal education's principal representative to the federal government and to other national higher education organizations and learned societies.

The AALS membership requirements for libraries can be found as Bylaw 6-10 and Executive Committee Regulations 8.1 to 8.6. As adopted in 1971 and amended through 1991, they are published in the annual *Association Handbook*. The bylaw and accompanying regulations are short, speaking in terms such as "adequate to support and encourage the instruction and research of its faculty and students," rather than more specific quantitative criteria. AALS made this change deliberately in the late 1980s to parallel similar changes in the ABA standards.

These two national organizations share a seven-year inspection cycle that sends a team of academics, practitioners, and a librarian to each school for a two- or three-day visit. Copious documentation, including a self-study, is gathered in advance and provided to the team. The results are made available to the appropriate evaluative groups in ABA and AALS, but are not made public. The accreditation and membership determination process applies to the whole law school, including the library.

Critics such as Martha J. K. Zachert ("Qualitative Evaluation of Law School Library Services," *Law Library Journal,* Spring 1989) argue that these standards do not evaluate qualitatively. Zachert encourages public services librarians to develop criteria for qualitative evaluation of staff and services. No such qualitative criteria have been established by the profession, nor has it attempted to adopt or modify those of other organizations, such as *Measuring Academic Library Performance: A Practical Approach,* prepared for the Association of College and Research Libraries in 1990.

Nonacademic Law Libraries. The State, Court, and County Law Library Special Interest Section of AALL periodically surveys the collections, serial subscriptions, salaries, and staffs of these law libraries. The sixth survey was published in *Law Library Journal* in 1991 and contained citations to earlier surveys.

The Private Law Libraries Special Interest Section of AALL compiled surveys in 1988 and 1990. Conducted by Altman & Weil, the surveys cover compensation, operations, and collections. Labeled "for confidential use of the purchaser only," these surveys are available only to libraries that participated in them. The reason: the competitive nature of the business of practicing law and the confidential nature of the salary and billing information disclosed. Constance P. Dickson provides more information about the 1988 survey in "Private Law Library Survey 1988" (*Law Library Journal,* 1990). The Private Law Libraries section also surveyed classification practices of its members and established a committee to work on standards for technical services.

Standards. The State, Court, and County Law Libraries Special Interest Section of AALL developed and published standards for its constituent groups. It has two committees that review and revise the standards about every ten years. For example, "Standards for Appellate Court and County Law Libraries" appeared in *Law Library Journal* in 1989. The standards cover governance, budget, personnel, physical plant and facilities, and the collection. As with standards for academic law libraries, these standards have no qualitative requirements for public services. These are official standards of the Section, approved by the Executive Board of the AALL, but they contain no mechanism for enforcement.

Prison law libraries received attention in Gene Teitelbaum's *Inspecting a Prison Law Library* (1989), which includes proposed standards based on the "adequate law libraries" provision of the U.S. Supreme Court's decision in Bounds v. Smith (1977). Arturo A. Flores provides an even more complete treatment in *Werner's Manual for Prison Law Libraries,* second edition (1990). Published under the auspices of AALL, this work describes in less than 200 pages how to create a collection and services that meet the needs of prisoners, including a recommended collection and a directory of law libraries offering services to prisoners.

Outside the United States, the British and Irish Association of Law Libraries (BIALL) publishes an annual survey in *The Law Librarian*. It sends the survey to more than 400 personal and institutional members in government, academic, and private law libraries in the United Kingdom and Ireland and elicits about 165 responses. BIALL also surveys university and polytechnic library expenditure on law materials. It published *Standards for Law Libraries* in 1981 and a revised "Statement of Minimum Holdings for Law Libraries in England and Wales" in *Legal Studies* (1987).

Education for Law Librarianship. The AALL participated in the American Library Association's process of developing new standards for accrediting library schools and was the first professional organization to provide ALA with guidelines for its area of specialization. "Guidelines for Graduate Programs in Law Librarianship," prepared by the Special Committee on Educational Policy of the AALL, appeared in *Law Library Journal* (1989). "The Controversy over Dual Degrees for Law Librarians," by Barbara B. Bonney, is both a description of the literature and an assessment of what the controversy means. It appeared in *Legal Reference Services Quarterly* (1991).

MARGARET A. LEARY

LAW LIBRARY COOPERATION

Cooperation among law libraries occurs in various ways. There are the traditional interlibrary loan procedures, which do not differ from those of other types of libraries. Most law libraries, especially those of university law schools, will lend materials to other libraries and will borrow as well, using standard interlibrary forms or online requests through major library networks for speed. Perhaps the only distinguishing feature in a law library is that more materials are of a reference nature and do not circulate under any circumstances. Increasingly, however, law libraries provide photocopies in lieu of lending the item itself.

But law libraries do participate in other forms of cooperation. Nearly all law school libraries at universities are administered as part of the law school rather than as a branch of the university library, but in many cases collection development is a cooperative matter, in part because of the commonality of interest among law professors and historians, political scientists, sociologists, economists, and criminologists. In some cases the university as a whole is better served by having most of these materials shelved in the law library, adjacent to sets, indices, and citators that supplement and complement them.

Cooperation may also occur on an interlibrary basis. In the past, large city law firm libraries in the same or nearby buildings would agree that one would buy one expensive set and the other another. With the prevalence of facsimile facilities in law firms of the 1990s, these agreements now stretch across cities and beyond. Additionally, large law firms now have offices in many cities, with law libraries in each office; fax ties these law libraries together as it does the rest of the firm. Many larger law libraries in an extended metropolitan area assume responsibility for sharing

Rhode Island State Law Library

Main Reading Room of the Rhode Island State Law Library in Providence, founded in 1827. Its holdings include a rare book collection with early English and American colonial law books dating back to 1490.

the acquisition of foreign law or special subject areas. One library may assume responsibility for legal materials of Latin America, for example, while one or more will collect European legal materials. Each library's patrons have open access for research use of these special collections or for free fax service in the instance of a specific citation. Along with this easy connectivity in the fax age have come hard concerns about copyright requirements.

Even so, several factors now point to an increased and more organized effort toward cooperation among law libraries. These factors are ongoing inflationary trends, an expanding growth in the subjects of law, and developing computer-based library networks. Prices for legal periodicals and other legal serials have increased more steeply than inflation generally in the U.S. since the late 1970s. Because of the nature of legal materials, serials and other continuations comprise a high percentage of law library collections. With economic constraints, the pressure for cooperation indeed becomes urgent.

The extent of the growth of the law in recent years is perhaps not generally realized, even by lawyers. Society seems to feel that any new societal problem can be solved by passing new laws. Some subject areas of the law developed after the mid-1960s, including computers, energy, the environment, fair employment practices, nuclear regulation, and pollution control. On the international scene, legal developments in the European Community and in the former socialist bloc have set law librarians scrambling to keep pace with the increasing globalization of legal issues. Growth in the law has by itself had a significant impact on the acquisitions policies of law libraries.

As regional and national computer networks became operational, law libraries were quick to participate. Many law-school libraries joined along with their university libraries, although usually arranging to keep their records separately identifiable. In a few instances a law-school library joined a network different from that of its university, judging that such a choice would better meet its needs. Unfortunately, law libraries have not all joined the same network, splitting their cataloguing data among several networks and impeding further development of shared acquisitions and cataloguing programs. Most law libraries, including some of the larger ones, such as those of Georgetown University and the universities of Florida and Illinois, joined the Online Computer Library Center (OCLC); about 20 percent, including those of Los Angeles County and New York and Stanford universities, joined the Research Library Information Network (RLIN); a few in the Pacific Northwest joined the Washington Library Network (WLN). In the late 1980s and early 1990s, a few law libraries, such as those at Northwestern and the University of Texas, switched networks. A very small number have regular access to at least two networks.

Many cooperative projects are developed to resolve a problem no one library could attempt on its own. For example, the Library of Congress had never finished its classification schedule for class K, which covers law. The Law Program Committee of the Research Libraries Group (RLG) agreed in 1990 to fund outside contracts for the work LC needed to maintain its timetable for completing class K. The RLG Law Program Committee was disbanded in 1991, but the Consortium for Law Classification continued the project. Under its auspices, about 30 of the larger law-school libraries contributed $3,000 each to assist in completing schedules for classes KL through KW, covering Asia, Africa, and Oceania. Both RLG and non-RLG law libraries shared a common interest in completing the foreign law schedules for use in their own institutions.

Unfortunately, work on revising schedule KZ, public international law, was not advanced enough to be included in the Consortium agreement. With the all but universal adoption of LC classification in major law libraries, the support of the American Association of Law Libraries for the project, and the enlightened self-interest of law libraries with international law collections, the Consortium expected to find even more assistance for the LC when work on KZ reached the same phase. AALL's backing was included in "Setting the Legal Information Agenda for the Year 2000: Preliminary Report of the National Legal Resources Committee," in *Law Library Journal* (1989).

Law Library Consortia. The Council of Law Library Consortia was established in 1984 to provide an effective exchange of information among its member consortia by means of regular annual meetings and a newsletter or quarterly report. The AALL recognized it as a caucus in 1991. Both the AALL and the American Bar Association encouraged its activities.

The constituent consortia range from almost amorphous groups with no officers or written documents to tightly-organized nonprofit corporate structures. Many have no dues or funds; others asses themselves several thousand dollars a year and administer substantial operating budgets, typically including personnel. The Chicago Legal Academic System (CLAS) pays the cost of a messenger service among metropolitan Chicago law libraries; its membership now extends to Indiana, Michigan, Wisconsin, and downstate Illinois. The New York Joint International Law Program enables three academic law libraries of various sizes to share the cost of an international bibliographer/reference librarian, which none could afford individually. The New England Law Library Consortium (NELLCO) has a salaried professional librarian coordinating its activities. The Law Library Microform Consortium (LLMC), started by the academic law libraries at Wayne State University in Michigan and the University of Hawaii, has no dues as such and supports its staff and micropublishing operations by selling its microfiche.

Some consortia are composed of a mix of academic, law firm, court, and government libraries, notably the Long-Range Planning Committee of Los Angeles and the Texas Association of Law Libraries Consortium (TALL). Others define themselves in terms of the types of member law libraries they include, such as the Council of California County Law Librarians, the Oregon Council of County Law Libraries, and the Conference of Law Libraries of the Association of Jesuit Colleges and Universities (AJCU) or in terms of the special interests that concern their member libraries, such as international law (JILP) or microforms (LLMC). In addition to the California, Oregon, and Texas consortia listed above, statewide consortia include the Arizona Law Library Consortium and Ohio Regional Consortium of Law Libraries (ORCLL). Several regional consortia exist, either characterized by a heavy emphasis on academic law libraries or limited to them: Chicago's CLAS, the Consortium of Southeastern Law Libraries (COSELL), Mid-America Law School Library Consortium, Mid-Atlantic Law Library Cooperative (MALLCO), and New England's NELLCO. The city-wide Columbia/Fordham/New York University Cooperative was extended to Yale and the University of Pennsylvania for joint foreign and international collection development only.

Shared Resources. What are the resources currently shared in these networks? Besides sharing the costs of personnel, the resources most often shared in metropolitan, state, and regional networks have been free interlibrary loan, free photocopying, and free faxing. Exchanges of free subscriptions to each other's law-school journals, newsletters, and other publications have gone beyond the law libraries' internal resources in an effort to lower subscription and administrative costs. Many young consortia have used union listing, whether online or in hard copy, to open access to each other's collections. Another inexpensive device has been exchanging each library's monthly acquisitions lists.

On a more sophisticated and expensive level, two regional consortia, Mid-America and NELLCO, implemented CD-ROM union catalogues for collection access in 1988 with the help of a Title II grant. Free faculty and student personal access to library collections began among the metropolitan law libraries and has spread to the regional consortia. A few academic law libraries have gone further and promised to provide additional services and appropriate workspace for visiting faculty from member law schools who are working on short-term projects. Cooperative storage agreements covering little-used large sets (such as the backfile of Martindale-Hubbel) ensure that the complete file is available in one place and open to all member library users in state-wide consortia. In some consortia cooperative staff development workshops and collaborative updating of library manuals have been features of low-cost/no-cost attempts at resource-sharing. Among regional academic law libraries, shared or compiled ABA annual statistical reports are circulated well in advance of the national compilation.

Many consortia have made some attempts at resource-sharing through coordinated collection development. Vehicles chosen have ranged from simply sharing plans or acquisition lists through coordinating plans for collecting super-expensive current sets, specialties such as international or foreign law, or state administrative codes or registers to sophisticated conspectus-based agreements. A CD-ROM union catalogue has an effect on regional or statewide collection development, because it is likely to include both OCLC and RLIN records. One consortium, NELLCO, developed a cooperative purchasing agreement with a single book jobber that provides substantial discounts for all members. Another, TALL, used its combined muscle (almost every law library in Texas is a member) to improve quality control of publishers' bindings, to publish a microfiche backfile of superseded Texas statutes, and to persuade publishers to index *The Texas Lawyer.* COSELL, the largest regional consortium, offered a picture and plan bank of law library buildings. Mid-America explored ways to share the expertise of its subject-specialist reference librarians or database searchers. Several consortia pursued private, state, or federal grants to support their resource sharing, and most succeeded.

Success for a consortium, short- or long-term, appears to rest not on the type of organization, the amount of funding, the character or quantity of projects, the size or monetary resources of members, or even the possession of an acronym, but rather on the quality of the commitment to shared goals, to perceived benefits, or to enlightened self-interest of the members. While most academic law libraries belong to at least one consortium, with some participation by court, government, and private libraries, the long-held dream of many law librarians—a national law library network—has yet to be achieved. (One obvious aspect of resource sharing that has not developed as much as it might have is the inter-consortium agreement.)

National Law Library Network. There have been several attempts in this direction, of which LAWNET was probably the most interesting. In order to measure the feasibility of a law network, the AALL, in cooperation with the AALS, engaged a consultant, Brett Butler, to advise on the matter. His 1978 report, *Toward a Law Network: Survey and Evaluation,* indicated that such a subject network is indeed feasible. His report recommends that the AALL sponsor the development of a law information network. This LAWNET would, among other things, assume the responsibility for developing standard subject headings for law libraries, standards for the format of bibliographic records, standards for the content of a law database, and other necessary standards. The report further recommends that LAWNET should proceed to build a composite database by merging selected machine-readable files gathered from those law libraries then inputting their records into a network. Once the database was created and procedures had been developed for maintaining and updating it, LAWNET was to make it available online and, for distribution to smaller law libraries, on microfiche. The report further recommended the development of a "LAWNET Location Guide" to provide listings by title, control number, and location code for all monographs and serials in the LAWNET database.

A first-phase computer-output microfiche (COM) union catalogue, representing the online holdings of more than 50 law libraries, resulted in 1981. Although LAWNET never completed this visionary project, it did provide the law library community with an intoxicating view of the probable automated future, a partially successful experience in nationwide resource sharing, and a measure of the difficulties and energy involved in such a large undertaking.

In 1988 the AALL National Legal Resources Committee tried to develop a national legal database under the auspices of OCLC. Apparently the major issue that prevented success was OCLC's demand that future tape loading by non-OCLC members should not be free. After this attempt failed, OCLC started Legend, which grouped all its law libraries and legal information services, such as the Minnesota Legislative Reference Service, under a group access symbol. Libraries need not be full members to join one of these *Inter-Library Loan* (ILL) groups. To prevent these "group" members from using the records for cataloguing, only enough of each record appears to be sufficient for ILL identification. This experience with the inability of networks to help in the cooperative law library spirit demonstrates again that nothing less than a great deal of selfless work will succeed, but that selfless work does not guarantee success.

A national law network, or even a confederated law network, could develop coordinated acquisitions programs to ensure that all necessary legal research materials will be available without unnecessary duplication. A great deal of attention will have to be given to document delivery.

The need for legal materials for the patrons of nonlaw libraries is growing. Citizens want to know their rights, want to know about environmental pollution control on municipal through international levels, or want to know which country is right according to international law. With law libraries struggling to provide an adequate level of collection for their primary patrons, access to legal materials for those outside the legal profession will become more difficult without some sort of nationally orchestrated program.

In summary, the fact that law libraries have not had a national law library comparable with the National Library of Medicine or the National Library of Agriculture has hindered the development of cooperation among law libraries. Some substitute for the sort of leadership and cooperation inherent in a national library would help all law libraries to be better able to meet the growing demand of the public for legal information.

EILEEN SEARLS

LAWS AND LEGISLATION

Any attempt to describe briefly the legislative foundation for U.S. law libraries is perilous indeed, for several reasons. First, the definition of what is a law library is subject to the criticism of being arbitrary; that criticism may be rebutted if the library is denominated a law library by its senior authority or governing rules. However, when the collection is an integral component of a larger administrative unit, or, although physically distinct, the collection is referred to as the "state library," "legislative library," or "department library," the definition of law library must be based on the nature of its collection, its services, and its primary clientele, and is necessarily subjective. Second, many law libraries cannot trace their birth to specific legislation. Rather, in many if not most instances libraries have evolved from informal office collections to major resources as an adjunct to the mission of the senior agency without initial statutory approbation. Third, the sovereignty of 50 states, as well as the federal government, results in a variety of approaches in the formulation of law library statutes that discourage their classification and the development of broad generalizations about them.

Federal Legislation. In 1832 direct statutory action was responsible for the creation of the paramount federal law library, the Law Library of Congress. It was established as one of the two administrative units of the Library of Congress, and the lawmakers intended to form a convenient collection of law books for the use of the Supreme Court, which at that time was also located in the Capitol. As activities of the Library of Congress and the Supreme Court evolved, however, particularly when the Supreme Court moved into its own building in 1935, the specific purpose of that early statute seemed to be lost. In 1977 the Librarian of Congress proposed a reorganization plan that would have taken away the law library's coequal status, making it just one of several subject departments. Focusing on the language of the 150-year-old statute, supporters of the Law Library of Congress argued strongly that the coequal status should be maintained. Faced with these strong representations, the Librarian withdrew the plan to reorganize insofar as the Law Library was concerned.

The Law Library of Congress continues to stand as a distinct unit in the LC. Through its specialized organization along worldwide regional lines, the Law Library serves its primary clientele, the members of Congress. Additionally, it offers an outstanding collection of legal materials on a global scale.

A separate department in the LC was created by statute in 1946 for the analysis, appraisal, and evaluation of legislative proposals. Originally called the Legislative Reference Service, it became in 1970 the Congressional Research Service. This unit does not manage large book collections, so it is not exactly a library; its interest ranges much more widely across the subject spectrum than merely the law in a narrow sense, so it is not exactly a law library. Yet, because it directly serves the legislative branch and because its enabling act specifically authorizes the appointment of American public law specialists, many argue that a law library was created. This institution serving the federal legislature exemplifies a type of legislative law library that is found in many state governments.

Two other significant congressional libraries, those of the House of Representatives and the Senate, although again not specifically law libraries, have a substantial legal content and are representative of libraries that began somewhat informally. Members of the House and Senate were no doubt collecting books, documents, and other material for their own use from the earliest days, but in the spring of 1792 both bodies passed resolutions charging the Secretary of the Senate and the Clerk of the House to procure library materials for their use. Subsequent legislative history provides ample evidence of legislative recognition of the existence of these libraries. Appropriations, debates about library space, and statutory provisions for appointment of librarians and administrative control all indicate the legislative support that has encouraged the development of the libraries, each with collections in excess of 200,000 volumes.

The Library of the U.S. Supreme Court similarly evolved over a period of time without benefit of specific statutory approval. The legal collection created in 1832 for the use of the Justices remained with the Law Library of Congress when the Court occupied the Supreme Court Building in 1935. The Court provided for its law book needs with a small collection that had served its Conference Room while it was in the Capitol, with duplicates from the Library of Congress, with gifts, and with purchases from supplemental appropriations. The Supreme Court Building, constructed with space for a major library, is indicative of legislative support for the nation's largest library devoted exclusively to the judiciary.

The libraries of the courts of appeals and district courts also developed both informally and by statute. When books were necessary to carry out the legal work of the judiciary, they were acquired as a function of regular court procurement. In 1948, however, possibly in reaction to the growth of these libraries and the need for appropriate supervision, to each court of appeals was given statutory authority to appoint a librarian and necessary library assistants. A companion statute authorized the appointment of a Marshal for the Court of Customs and Patent Appeals who would buy books and supplies and supervise its library. In 1954 the Tax Court was authorized to purchase library books and materials necessary to execute its functions.

Although no specific statutory authority seems to exist for the law libraries of the executive departments, they have no doubt come into being either, as in the Departments of Commerce and Interior, by virtue of the authority establishing the general libraries of those departments or, as in the Department of Justice, as concomitant resources to the department's meeting its larger statutory mission. Thus the combination of explicit statutory authority to establish libraries and the implicit authority to collect library books as part of required resources provided the framework for the law libraries of the federal government to grow and prosper since their early beginnings. By 1992 the American Association of Law Libraries (AALL) listed more than 50 government libraries in the District of Columbia alone.

Law libraries nationally have, of course, been affected by those laws that have an impact on libraries generally. Some law libraries have benefited from federal grants applicable to library building projects through the Library Services and Construction Act (LSCA). In 1988, for example, 15 Pennsylvania libraries, 14 of them law libraries, received an LSCA grant to install facsimile equipment. The consortium of Jesuit university law libraries received a similar grant. Law libraries feel the pressures of increased postal costs and limitations on the use of the "book rate." But in each of these instances the law library reacts to the legislation as a library and not in any particular way because it is a law library, and thus these laws have not had any unique meaning for law libraries.

Beginning in 1989, the AALL undertook to play a more prominent role in the debate about national library legislative policy. It established a Permanent Government Relations Committee to keep its members informed about legislative activity and to join other organizations in efforts to shape legislation affecting law libraries. In 1990 the Committee formulated an AALL "Government Relations Policy" statement that the Association approved. The Executive Board of AALL approved a strategic plan late that year that included the goal of influencing national and state information policies. As a consequence, law librarians supported or challenged every significant bill or proposed administrative action with implications for law librarianship, including the National Research and Education Network, the Government Printing Office's Wide Information Network Data Online (GPO WINDO), and proposed amendments to the Paperwork Reduction Act.

The Depository Library Act has been of immeasurable benefit to the general library community, and for many years it enabled state libraries and the highest state appellate court libraries to become depositories for U.S. government publications. As amended in 1978, it allows all approved law-school libraries to request depository status. A number of law-school libraries had become depositories in their own right under the original Act, but most law-school libraries, including several major research centers, had never been able to take advantage of depository benefits. Although other federal laws may have been more significant in the development of the library of a particular institution, the depository law has probably had the single greatest impact on law libraries nationally.

State Legislation. The laws that resulted in the formation of law libraries in the states generally follow the pattern outlined for the federal government. In general, librarians tend to classify these law libraries under three major heads: state law libraries, supreme court libraries, and county law libraries. Most state and supreme court libraries overlap in their functions and governance.

State and Supreme Court Libraries. The respondents to a 1974 survey of state and supreme court law libraries indicated a wide range of organizational structures. Two libraries were units of legislative or administrative departments; two were units of the state Attorney General's office; two were units of the legislative council; and four were parts of a larger, more comprehensive state library. In four instances the judicial branch shared a law library with a department of education; in six others the judicial and executive branches of government shared the same law library. Finally, 29 law libraries were units of the judicial branch exclusively. Statutory review supports the responses from the librarians themselves. The statutes of 37 states specifically establish either a state law library, a law department of a state library, or a law library for the supreme court. Twenty-one states, including 18 of these 37, have established legislative reference services that are also, in some instances, departments of the state library or the state law library.

With this variety of organizations, some resulting from statutes that are based on the earliest state administrative relationships and others from evolutionary development, it is difficult indeed to generalize about state law libraries. But most state statutes authorize law library service for the judicial branch and put superintending control in the hands of the state supreme court or a committee on which one or more members of the supreme court sit. Moreover, state structures are not immutable. In the 1980s Pennsylvania merged its State Library and its State Law Library in the hope of creating a more effective, more efficient, and less costly institution. Under the supervisory control of the Supreme Court, the Library provides both advice to county law libraries and service to the courts. Other states took similar action.

The University of Chicago Law School

The University of Chicago Law School Library, designed by Eero Saarinen. Five floors of stacks and reading space rise above a ground-floor lounge.

The method of financing state and court libraries is uneven, resulting in some libraries that are extremely strong, while others are of more modest circumstances. One library receives at least part of its financing from the sale of its court reports, another from a tax on newly admitted lawyers, a third from a fund composed of court fees, and a fourth from the proceeds of a state land grant. In most instances the laws are silent as to the specific services that the library is required to render, although several do specifically require that the library be open to the public.

Several libraries by statute and others (imitating the U.S. Supreme Court) by court rule prohibit the circulation of books from the court building. In one state the librarian is guilty of a misdemeanor if an unauthorized person borrows a book from the library! William B. Roalfe noted in his 1953 study, *The Libraries of the Legal Profession,* that "the service provided by state court libraries sometimes leaves a great deal to be desired and most of them operate on a level well below that maintained by the best examples." Four decades later, the statutory base of the state and court libraries had not changed substantially.

County Law Libraries are authorized by 35 states and represent, at least potentially, a major resource for providing legal materials. Once again the minds of legislators have conceived a plethora of methods to fund county law libraries. In 17 states systems of filing fees and fines support law libraries; 14 states have fixed appropriations; 5 states use a combination of filing fees and appropriations; the rest rely for funds on other miscellaneous fees.

There seems to be no particular advantage to the major types of funding in achieving a substantial level of library support. California uses fees; Ohio uses fines; New York relies on appropriations; yet each of these states has strong county law libraries, although Ohio with 44 county law libraries and California with 58 seem to provide more extensive county law library systems. In fact, the existence of substantial populations and the volume of litigation probably have a greater impact on law library development than the particular statutory method devised to support law library service. It is evident, however, that a financial support mechanism that is tied directly to litigation, such as filing fees or fines, will tend to provide a level of support that will automatically move upward as the demands increase. A survey of county law libraries in California indicates that a filing fee funding system has resulted in an array of law libraries roughly proportional to the general and lawyer populations in their respective counties. Legislative developments in most states have not matched, and probably, because of more limited means, cannot be expected to match, the superlative resources of the Los Angeles County Law Library, but the challenge of more generous funding for county law libraries in more populous counties in other jurisdictions still awaits the legislative ingenuity of many of the states.

Conflict has arisen over the imposition of surcharges on court fees to pay for library services. A report of the National Conference of Court Administrators recommended that these fees be frozen or even eliminated as an insidious form of taxation that threatens the democratic nature of the court system. But court librarians generally feel that reducing or eliminating these surcharges would jeopardize the very survival of their libraries.

ROGER F. JACOBS

REFERENCES

Richard A. Danner, *Strategic Planning: A Law Library Management Tool for the '90s* (1991).

Roy M. Mersky, "Everything You Always Wanted to Know about Law Libraries But Were Afraid to Ask . . .," *Journal of Legal Education* (1978).

Roy M. Mersky, "International Cooperation: A Critical Need for Bibliographic Control of Legal Materials," *International Journal of Law Libraries* (1977).

Bernard D. Reams, Jr., editor, *Reader in Law Librarianship* (1976).

Reference Section, Stotlzfus Library, Beirut University College.

Lebanon

Lebanon is a Middle Eastern republic on the eastern shore of the Mediterranean Sea. Syria lies to the north and east; Israel lies to the south. Population (1990 est.) 2,701,000; area 10,400 sq.km. The people, almost all Arabs, include Sunni and Shiite Muslims and Maronite, Greek Orthodox, and Greek Catholic Christians. The official language is Arabic, but most Lebanese also speak English or French.

History. Called Land of the Cedar in the Bible, Lebanon could also be called the land of the book. A Phoenician inscription at a tomb believed to be that of Ahiram, dated between the 13th and the 10th centuries B.C., is located at Jbail, which the Greeks translated as Byblos, from the word *biblio* (book). Such Lebanese archaeological sites as Baalbek, Tyre, Sidon, Tripoli, and Byblos show signs of libraries during the classical period. During the monastic period, almost every monastery had a library, but they were not organized. The best-known monastic libraries were the Holy Savior, founded in 1711 near Sidon, and the Salvatorian monastery at Khonshara, founded in 1696, both belonging to the Greek Catholic sect. A microfilming project in 1970 recorded the collections of all the monasteries; microfilms were deposited at the American University of Beirut (AUB).

Modern librarianship in Lebanon started in the 19th century with academic libraries. The Syrian Protestant College (which became the AUB) was established in 1866 and the French Saint Joseph College in 1881. Most of Lebanon's libraries were founded in the mid-1960s in Beirut, the capital, or its outskirts; rural areas had few services or nothing at all.

Civil war between Muslim and Christian Arabs broke out in 1975 and raged for more than a year. Many libraries were destroyed, burned, or looted. The heaviest losses were at the National Library and the Lebanese Center for Documentation and Research (CEDRE). Those remaining were indirectly affected by the loss of personnel; frozen or cut budgets; inflation; and the devaluation of the local currency. These factors halted library services or held advances to a minimum in more than 80 percent of the existing libraries. But the war brought some positive developments. The political parties involved in the conflict set up their own cultural centers, most including libraries, to promote their ideologies. Some cultural centers published bibliographies. Book exhibitions were common and frequent in large cities. Publishing continued to be active and highly productive. The Lebanese government established a Ministry of Culture in 1991 with promotion of libraries as one of its aims.

National Library. The Lebanese National Library, also a public library but without borrowing privileges, was placed under the Ministry of National Education in 1922. It started with the personal collection of Viscount Philippe de Tarazi at the National Museum. In 1937 it moved to the Parliament building. A copyright deposit law was passed in 1941 and amended in 1959, but the Library could never enforce it. The Library's aims and objectives were never defined, and it never had a qualified librarian. No recent inventory has been taken; some of its 100,000 volumes and 2,000 rare manuscripts were burned or stolen during the civil war. A National Library did not exist, except in name, in the early 1990s.

Academic Libraries. The AUB has four academic libraries on its campus with the richest collections in the Middle East. Its libraries hold 550,000 volumes, 1,350 manuscripts, and almost 4,000 current periodicals. Beirut University College has libraries on its three campuses, at Beirut, Byblos, and Sidon. Together they hold 115,000 volumes and about 500 periodicals; a Children's Library has 5,000 books and several hundred audiovisual materials. Beirut University College Library has a collection on Women in the Arab World that includes 5,000 volumes, 2,000 documents, and some specialized periodicals. Other academic libraries include those at Beirut Arab University, Haigazian College, Al-Balamand University, Lebanese University, Near East School of Theology, Université Saint Joseph, and Université Saint-Esprit de Kaslik.

Public Libraries. There are few public libraries in Lebanon. The Makassed Cultural Center (founded as the British Council Library) is the most active. Baakline Public Library was established during the war. There are 10 children's libraries in various cities, seven of them sponsored by the Lebanese Red Cross.

School Libraries. The law requiring every school to have a library has never been strictly enforced. Few schools have proper libraries except for shelves of books restricted to the use of teachers and administrative staff only. Among the best-equipped school libraries are those at the American Community School, International College, Collège Protestante, New Sidon School, and Makassed Secondary Schools.

Special Libraries. Many cultural centers and learned societies have their own libraries that are open to the public or to specialized clienteles. The most important include the Center for Arab Unity Studies, which specializes in all phases of Arab life, with 5,000 books and more than 600 periodicals, and the Institute for Palestine Studies, working to promote better understanding of the Palestine problem and the Arab-Israeli conflict, with 31,000 volumes, almost 400 current periodicals, 5,000 reels of film, and a large collection of private papers. Other important special libraries include those at the Centre d'Études et de Recherches sur le Moyen-Orient Contemporain; Centre de Documentation Economique sur le Proche-Orient; Institut Français d'Archéologie du Proche-Orient; and Orient-Institüt of the German Oriental Society.

Children's library in Beirut

The Profession. Library and information science is taught at three levels. Beirut University College offers a three-year academic program leading to a B.A. in Information Science. The Lebanese University's Faculty of Information and Documentation offers an academic program leading to a License in Library and Information Science. At the second level, Beirut University College offers a two-year program leading to an Associate of Arts and Science in Information Science. At the third level, government public schools and some private vocational institutes offer two-year vocational training programs leading to Technical Baccalaureates (BT I and BT II).

The Lebanese Library Association (LLA) was founded in 1960. Its activities declined because of the war, but it continued to send representatives to IFLA meetings and other international conferences. It resumed its activities on behalf of its members and the profession in the late 1980s and early 1990s.

REFERENCE

Helena Cobban, *The Making of Modern Lebanon* (1985).

AIDA SALMAN NAAMAN

Leibniz, Gottfried Wilhelm

(1646–1716)

A German philosopher, mathematician, scientist, jurist, historian, linguist, and librarian, Leibniz contrib-

Libraries in Lebanon (1991)

Type of library	Number of administrative units (main libraries)	Number of service points (branches, mobile stops, etc.)	Volumes in collections	Population served	Professional staff (with certificate, diploma, etc.)	Total staff
National[a]	--	--	100,000	--	--	--
Academic	10	37	1,500,000	110,000	40	200
Public	16	16	100,000	900,000	10	30
School[b]	10	10	70,000	13,000	8	15
Special	15	15	100,000	5,000	13	45

[a]Out of service now
[b]Major schools only

Gottfried Wilhelm Leibniz

Library of Congress

uted extensively in many disciplines; this article concentrates on his contributions to librarianship and information science.

Leibniz was born into a pious Lutheran family in Leipzig, July 1, 1646; his father was a professor and his mother the daughter of a professor at the University of Leipzig. A precocious boy, Leibniz learned to read early and widely; he taught himself Latin in the library of his father, who died when the boy was only six years old. From 1653 to 1661 he attended the local Nicolaischule, where among other subjects he acquired a knowledge of Greek and was impressed by the study of Aristotelian logic.

When he was nearly 15 he entered the University of Leipzig. He obtained a broad general education but concentrated on the study of philosophy and law. In 1662 he earned a Bachelor's degree and in 1664 a Master's degree of the Philosophical Faculty. A year later he obtained a Bachelor of Laws degree. Then he began to work on his doctoral dissertation, *Dissertatio de arte combinatoria* (Dissertation on the Art of Combination), which he published in 1666. His dissertation was influenced by the combinatorial logic of the Spanish mystic Raymond Lully. In this work he formulated a model that is a theoretical forerunner of modern computer logic; he saw his art of combination and permutation as a logical calculus and a logic of discovery that could lead to significant new insights. But when he wanted to obtain his Doctor of Laws degree during the same year, a majority of his faculty refused it because they felt he was still too young. Disappointed, he left his native city and moved to Altdorf, a university town close to Nürnberg, where at age 21 he earned a Doctor of Laws degree with distinction for his dissertation *On Perplexing Cases*. But he refused to accept a teaching position at the University of Altdorf.

In Nürnberg Leibniz met the retired statesman Johann Christian von Boineburg (1622–72), who had been the most prominent minister of Johann Philipp von Schönborn (1605–73), the ruling Archbishop and Elector of Mainz. With von Boineburg's recommendation, Leibniz obtained a position as legal counselor at this court and was assigned the task of revising and improving the German legal code. Von Boineburg owned a sizable private library and invited Leibniz to become his part-time librarian. Between 1668 and 1673 Leibniz had a classed catalogue prepared for this collection. The catalogue (rediscovered after World War II) consisted of four volumes with 9,840 main entries. Its major divisions corresponded to those that the German bibliographer and clergyman Georg Draud had used for his *Bibliotheca classica,* which had first appeared in 1611. A second edition was published in 1625, and both editions were available in von Boineburg's collection. The 15 main classes were further subdivided by many alphabetically arranged subject headings, several of which were sometimes used for the same work. But the death of von Boineburg brought the work to a halt; the catalogue is incomplete, and the syndetic devices are sparse. A general alphabetic author index has not been found.

In 1672 Leibniz was sent on a diplomatic mission to Paris, where he managed to stay for almost four years. In this vibrant metropolis he devoted himself to intensive studies and became acquainted with a number of the most renowned scientists. He also got to know the prominent librarians of the city, among them N. Clément, who introduced him to the rapidly growing Bibliothèque du Roi and its policies. His studies in Paris and visits to London in 1673 and 1676 broadened his intellectual horizons and established many scientific contacts for life. In 1673 he was elected a Member of the Royal Society.

Contributions to Librarianship. The need for a regular income forced Leibniz to accept a position as Counselor and Librarian at the court of Duke Johann Friedrich of Brunswick-Lüneburg, who owned in 1676 a private library of some 3,310 volumes, among them 158 manuscripts. Later Leibniz was also appointed Historiographer at the court, and he held these positions until his death in 1716. Unfortunately, the intellectual Johann Friedrich died in 1679, and his successor, Ernst August, did not appreciate libraries as much as his cosmopolitan brother. Leibniz was able to provide Ernst August with valuable historical and genealogical information that helped him to become Elector of Hanover in 1692. Nor did library support improve under Ernst August's son Georg Ludwig, who succeeded him in 1698 and became King George I of Great Britain in 1714.

In addition to his library duties at the Hanoverian Court, Leibniz was in 1690 appointed Librarian of the valuable Ducal Library at Wolfenbüttel, which was owned by another line of the Guelph dynasty. This library had been founded by the learned Duke August the Younger and held in 1661 some 28,000 volumes of printed works, including 2,000 incunabula, and about 2,000 manuscripts. Duke August had been his own librarian and had prepared a classed catalogue using 20 classes derived from Konrad Gesner's *Pandectae*. But here again the succeeding dukes did not share Duke August's enthusiasm for the library and provided little financial support for its upkeep and extension.

In Hanover and Wolfenbüttel Leibniz worked hard to extend and improve the collections through purchases of current works and advantageous auctions. The Hanoverian collection grew rapidly and served the princes and the court. At Wolfenbüttel he ordered the production of an alphabetical author catalogue, which was completed before 1700, and he was successful in having the first separate German baroque library building constructed. It was a rectangular library topped by a cupola and a dome light. Increased shelving space was provided by means of galleries and shelving that surrounded the supporting pillars. Against Leibniz's wishes it was built as a wooden structure, and no furnace was allowed in the building to provide heat in the winter.

More important than his actual achievements were Leibniz's novel ideas, which he spread in letters, memoranda, and petitions. As a leading scholar in several disciplines, he was fully aware of the importance of libraries for the advancement of knowledge. He advocated a universal library that would contain all the original ideas of mankind that have been recorded. Such a library was not to be measured by the number, rarity, or fancy bindings of its volumes but by the balance, accuracy, and up-to-dateness of the information contained in them. The main task of the librarian was to collect works with up-to-date information, organize them efficiently, and make them readily available for use. For speedy access good catalogues would be needed; while he himself favored classed catalogues, he also stressed the need for alphabetical author and subject catalogues. He personally designed two classification schemes for libraries.

Throughout his life he was most concerned with the research needs of scientists and scholars. In order to avoid needless duplication of efforts and to make results of research speedily available, he planned and promoted the construction of abstracting and indexing tools. The abstracted information was to be indexed and integrated into a demonstrative encyclopedia that was to be organized with the help of a detailed and complex universal classificatory language, his *characteristica universalis*. For this purpose he stressed the need for division of labor and sought the help of scientific societies. He himself was the founder and first President of an academy of sciences in Berlin and the moving spirit behind the founding of the academies in Vienna and Saint Petersburg.

Contributions to Information Science. Leibniz provided important ideas and techniques for information science. He developed binary arithmetic, demonstrated its use for addition, subtraction, multiplication, and division, and praised its advantages for computation. Binary arithmetic is now generally employed in digital computers.

He was also a pioneer in symbolic and mathematical logic. He invented and used diagrams that constitute iconic representations of standard-form categorical propositions, in which spatial inclusions and exclusions correspond to nonspatial inclusions and exclusions of classes. These diagrams provided not only an exceptionally clear method of notation, but also the simplest and most direct method for testing the validity of categorical syllogisms. Usually named after the Swiss mathematician Leonhard Euler (1707–83), who used them extensively, they were later improved by the British logician John Venn (1834–1923), whose logical diagrams are now most commonly used.

Leibniz was much interested in developing computers that could reduce tedious and repetitive computations to mechanical operations. While we know now that Wilhelm Schickard, an astronomer and associate of Johannes Kepler who died of the plague in 1635, was the first person to construct a working model of a computer that could add, subtract, multiply, and divide, Leibniz's computer that incorporated his invention of a stepped reckoner gained much wider renown and, in spite of serious mechanical defects, laid the foundation of the modern mechanical calculator.

Beyond that, Leibniz provided seminal ideas for cybernetics. He had plans for constructing a *machina combinatoria, sive analytica* ("combining or analytical machine") which could also handle logical operations involving letters. Norbert Wiener, in his landmark work *Cybernetics* (2nd edition, 1961) says: "The philosophy of Leibniz centers about two closely related concepts—that of a universal symbolism and that of a calculus of reasoning. From these are derived the mathematical notation and the symbolic logic of the present day. Now, just as the calculus of arithmetic lends itself to mechanization progressing through the abacus and the desk computing machine to the ultra-rapid computing machines of the present day, so the *calculus ratiocinator* of Leibniz contains the germs of the *machina ratiocinatrix,* the reasoning machine."

When Leibniz died on November 14, 1716, in Hanover, he had accomplished great tasks but was keenly aware of the tremendous work that still remained to be done.

REFERENCES

G. W. Leibniz, *Sämliche Schriften und Briefe* (1923).
Kurt Müller, *Leibniz-Bibliographie: Die Literatur über Leibniz* (1967).
Lindsay Mary Newman, *Leibniz (1646–1716) and the German Literary Scene* (1966).
Hans Georg Schulte-Albert, "Gottfried Wilhelm Leibniz and Library Classification," *Journal of Library History* (1971).
Hans Georg Schulte-Albert, "Leibniz's Plans for a World Encyclopaedia System," unpublished Ph.D. dissertation, Case Western Reserve University (1972).

HANS GEORG SCHULTE-ALBERT

Leland, Waldo Gifford
(1879–1966)

Waldo Gifford Leland, historian, archival advocate, and administrator, was a key figure in the creation of the U.S. National Archives.

Library of Congress
Waldo Gifford Leland

Leland was born in Newton, Massachusetts, July 17, 1879. He was graduated from Brown University in 1900 with a B.A. degree and membership in Phi Beta Kappa. Coming from a family of schoolteachers, Leland aimed at a career as a college professor. He leaned toward the social sciences, particularly sociology. Although he had studied little history at Brown, only part of a course taught by the great J. Franklin Jameson, he was persuaded by Jameson to do some graduate work in history before plunging into sociology. He went to Harvard for his advanced work, taking an M.A. in 1901 and beginning work on a Ph.D., and never did make the plunge into sociology.

Leland never completed his doctorate in history either; in 1903 one of his professors, Albert Bushnell Hart, persuaded him to go to Washington for six months to assist Claude H. Van Tyne in compiling a report for the recently established (1902) Carnegie Institution of Washington on the condition of the archives of the federal government. His decision to accept the post started him on a lifetime of work of the highest importance in the world of scholarship, history, and archives, but kept him from becoming the teacher he had set out to be.

The survey of the government's archives took the collaborators to basements and attics, warehouses and car barns, doorways and corridors in all parts of Washington—wherever neglectful or ignorant civil servants had placed federal records when they ceased to be current. File clerks and high officials, with few exceptions, welcomed them and were cooperative. The condition of the precious records they found varied considerably, but many were in advanced stages of deterioration. The immediate result of the research by Van Tyne and Leland was the publication in 1904 of the *Guide to the Archives of the Government of the United States in Washington,* which appeared in a revised and enlarged edition three years later. This assessment of the state of the federal archives had, in the long run, a profound influence on the course of archival development in the government.

After finishing the description of the archives, Leland stayed on with the Carnegie Institution's Department of Historical Research, of which his Brown history professor, Jameson, had become Director in 1905. One of the major projects Jameson directed was the compilation of a series of guides to source material for the study of American history in foreign archives and libraries. Leland's assignment was Paris, and he directed Carnegie's work there from 1907 to 1914 and again from 1922 to 1927. The published result was the two-volume *Guide to Materials for American History in the Libraries and Archives of Paris* (1923–43). In addition to being colleagues at the Carnegie Institution, Jameson and Leland were also close associates in the American Historical Association, Leland being the Association's Secretary (1909–20) and Jameson the Managing Editor of its journal, the *American Historical Review*.

Leland's work at the Carnegie Institution placed him center stage in the archival world, then just beginning the process of professionalization. In 1909 he spoke on "American Archival Problems" at the first American conference of archivists. Three years later he published in the *American Historical Review,* at Jameson's request, an article entitled "The National Archives: A Programme," which recited the litany of the government's neglect of and indifference to its own official records and set forth a bold plan of action to remedy the dismal situation. This article served as a public manifesto to accompany Jameson's backstage politicking for a national archives establishment. The creation of the National Archives in 1934 justified the quarter-century effort by Jameson, Leland, and others, though Leland modestly claimed no part of the credit for himself.

Many considered Leland the "dean of American archivists," but Leland confessed he was "somewhat embarrassed to find myself described as an archivist, a title to which I have no claim. I have never had charge of records, public or private." At most, he thought, he was an "archivist by association." Still, his colleagues in the new archival profession bestowed great honors on him. He served in 1940 as second President of the Society of American Archivists (founded in 1936, of which he was a charter member) and was made an Honorary Member in 1949 and a Fellow in 1958. Leland's portrait was hung in the National Archives building in Washington, D.C.

Throughout his long career, Leland maintained an active interest in the affairs and problems of libraries, especially the Library of Congress. When he first went to Washington in 1903 to be interviewed for the job with the Carnegie Institution, the site of the appointment was the Library of Congress building. His first meal in the capital city was at the famous Round Table presided over by the Librarian of Congress, Herbert Putnam. Leland noted years later, "I was impressed to the point of being awed." Putnam was one of the two most influential men in Leland's professional life, the other being Jameson. Putnam in fact asked Leland on the day after Jameson's funeral in 1937 to succeed Jameson as Chief of the LC Manuscript Division and as occupant of the library's chair of American history. Leland refused Putnam's invitation, which "was one of the hardest things I have ever had to do." Nevertheless, Leland served LC in a number of advisory capacities and sat on numerous committees, including the planning committee that, following World War II, examined the question of the future role of LC.

On leaving the Carnegie Institution in 1927, Leland became the Secretary, or chief administrative officer, of the American Council of Learned Societies (ACLS). He had been present as Secretary when the ACLS was founded in 1919 to provide United States representation in the newly established International Union of Academies. He remained the chief executive (the title was changed to Director in 1939) until 1946. One of the major achievements of his administration was the sponsorship of the *Dictionary of American Biography*.

Much of Leland's work was in the sphere of national and international cooperation in the humanities. This global concern led him to take a role as a U.S. delegate in the establishment of Unesco at the end of World War II, and he served as the U.S. representative to the third Unesco General Conference in Beirut in 1948.

Leland died in Washington on October 19, 1966.

REFERENCE

The major collection of Leland's papers is in the Manuscript Division, Library of Congress. He wrote a brief memoir, "Some Recollections of an Itinerant Historian," *Proceedings of the American Antiquarian Society* (1951).

JOHN B. HENCH

Lemaitre, Henri
(1881–1946)

Renée Lemaître
Henri Lemaître

The library historian Noë Richter described Henri Lemaître as the man who, at the beginning of the 20th century, best embodied the modern type of librarian in France. At the same time a scholar and a man of action, Lemaître was a pioneer in many domains: technical services, libraries for children, bookmobiles, library service in business firms and hospitals, documentation, and international cooperation.

Born in Valenciennes on February 17, 1881, he acquired a love for scholarship in the bookstore founded in that city by his grandfather. A brilliant student, Lemaître entered the École des Chartes (the national school for archivists) at the age of 18 and graduated in 1903. After becoming an archivist-palaeographer, he soon joined the staff of the Bibliothèque Nationale in the department of French history. Along with his library work he also pursued his scholarly studies and published medieval texts such as *Trente Noëls Poitevins* (1907) as well as articles and book reviews in scholarly journals, including the *Bibliothèque de l'École des Chartes*. His friendship with a Franciscan scholar led him to found and edit a journal entitled *Revue d'Histoire Franciscaine* (1924–31).

At the Bibliothèque Nationale, Lemaître became acquainted with Eugène Morel and willingly adopted Morel's innovative ideas on the development of "Free Public Libraries" in France and on the reform of copyright deposit. In 1910 he published a work on the history of copyright practices in France (*Histoire du Dépôt Légal en France*), and as a result he was sent to the United States the next year to observe the operation of the Copyright Office at the Library of Congress and to study the New York Public Library. On his return he participated in a series of lectures on modern libraries organized by Morel at l'École des Hautes Etudes Sociales (the Graduate School for the Social Sciences). There he discussed his experiences in the United States.

Mobilized in 1914 in a paramilitary unit of the army, Lemaître was sent to the French military mission in London, where he was assigned to the Cipher Service because of his knowledge of modern languages (English, German, Spanish, and Italian). On his return to France, he left the Bibliothèque Nationale to devote himself to working for the improvement of all types of libraries. For many years, his main source of support was an inheritance from the family bookstore.

During the period of reconstruction following World War I, Lemaître was an active member of the French Committee for the Modern Library, a group whose goal was to set up throughout France public libraries similar to the model libraries in Aisne that had been organized by the American Committee for Devastated France, a war relief agency. In the same spirit Lemaître welcomed the first library for children, l'Heure Joyeuse, which was given to the city of Paris by the Book Committee on Children's Libraries, another American philanthropic group. Lemaître wrote the first article on children's work in that library and published it in 1925 in the *Revue des Bibliothèques*. The previous year Lemaître had become Managing Editor of this journal, and under his impetus it became a mirror of library development throughout the world. After the *Revue des Bibliothèques* ceased publication in 1934, Lemaître became cofounder of a more ambitious journal, *Archives et Bibliothèques* (1935–38).

In 1928 Lemaître became President of l'Association des Bibliothécaires Français (ABF, the French Library Association), and in that capacity he represented France in Rome in 1929 at the first session of the International Library Committee (which was to become the International Federation of Library Associations). He represented France at all the following IFLA conferences until 1937 and directed the section on hospital libraries. Lemaître was named Honorary Vice President of IFLA at Cheltenham, England, in 1931. At the time he was the French librarian best known abroad.

That same year Lemaître launched an ambitious undertaking: organizing on behalf of ABF the Congrès International de la Lecture Publique, the first international congress on reading for the public. The term *lecture publique* was preferred over the word *bibliothèque* (library), which signified to French readers a dusty, outmoded institution. At the Congress, held in Algiers in 1931, Lemaître succeeded in attracting the interest of the Minister of Public Instruction, who promised to draft a law on public library service. This was the first success for the cause of public libraries, but unfortunately the law was never passed. The proceedings of that Congress, which Lemaître published under the title *La Lecture Publique* (1931), constitute a veritable textbook on the subject. That same year, out of a desire to see a bookmobile travel on the roads of France, Lemaître persuaded the Renault firm to construct a prototype that was exhibited at the ABF stand at the Colonial Exposition in Paris. Three years later the first French bookmobile was launched in Aisne. Following these successful undertakings, Lemaître was made a member of the Legion of Honor. He then began to turn toward another goal, documentation.

Named Assistant Director of l'Institut Scientifique de Recherches Économiques et Sociales (the Scientific Institute for Economic and Social Research), he soon set up a model documentation center for this organization. Lemaître also became President of l'Union Française des Organismes de Documentation (UFOD, the French association of organizations engaged in documentation), a group of which he had been an active member since its foundation in 1931. In addition he organized training in techniques of documentation for UFOD and taught courses himself (he was already teaching library science at the École des Chartes and in other institutions). He was also President of the Committee of l'Association Française de Normalization (AFNOR, the French national association for standardization), which elaborated the cataloguing code. In 1942, during World War II, he directed the Documentation Center for Scientific Research in the Colonies. Despite failing health, he gave many lectures to a diverse public, promoting the development of all kinds of libraries (in hospitals, in business enterprises, for the blind, and others).

The International Labor Bureau published *Bibliothèques Populaires et Loisirs Ouvriers,* his survey on popular libraries and leisure-time activities of workers, in 1933, and the French Ministry of National Education issued his monograph on librarians, *Les Bibliothécaires*. He devoted his remaining energy to completing a dictionary of technical library terms (in French, English, and German) sponsored by IFLA and published by Unesco as *Vocabularium Bibliothecarii*. Lemaître died in Sceaux, France, on November 8, 1946. He was a man with little interest in material rewards who enjoyed being surrounded by his wife and four children as well as artists and writers.

REFERENCES

Andre Martin, "Henri Lemaître," *Bibliothèque de l'École des Chartes* (1947).

Renée Lemaître, "La Lecture Publique aux Temps Héroiques," *Bulletin d'Information de l'Association des Bibliothécaires Français* (Spring, 1980).

RENÉE LEMAÎTRE;
translated by MARY NILES MAACK

Lesotho

Lesotho is a small monarchy entirely surrounded by South Africa. A British protectorate called Basutoland from 1868, the country became independent in 1966. Lesotho is a purely African country, the few European residents being government officials, traders, missionaries, and artisans. Population (1990 est.) 1,774,000; area 30,355 sq.km. The official languages are Sesotho and English.

History. The first colonial-period library was founded in 1886. It housed the National Archives. They were relocated several times and came under the jurisdiction of several authorities, but after independence they became the responsibility of the Ministry of Education. The first library offering any general services to readers was also established in 1886, in the High Commissioner's residence. By 1907 it had 3,000 volumes and was known as the Basutoland Public Library. However, it remained small and several times fell into decline. The Library at Catholic University was established in 1945. That university became the National University of Lesotho.

National Library. Work on the Lesotho National Library Service began in May 1976, and the Library opened its doors to the public in July 1978. The British Council provided £247,500 in initial funding for it through the Ministry of Overseas Development. The Library also serves as the center for the distribution of books to schools without collections of their own.

Public Library Service. A public library service is offered to residents of Maseru, and a free postal loan service is operated for persons outside Maseru. Books are also lent to secondary schools throughout the kingdom. Services provided include adult and children's lending and reference libraries, a magazine and newspaper reading room, and a collection of material on and about Lesotho. Premises for branch libraries were acquired in Mafeteng and Leribe, the old capital.

Academic and Other Libraries. Other libraries in Lesotho include that of the National University of Lesotho, which has 118,000 books and periodicals, and the library of the National Teachers Training College in Maseru (15,000 volumes). Smaller collections exist in government departments, educational and vocational training establishments such as the Lesotho Agricultural College (7,000 volumes) and Lesotho Institute of Public Administration, and foreign agencies such as the British Council (16,000 volumes) and U.S. Information Service (2,300 volumes).

The Profession. A professional body, the Lesotho Library Association, was formed in 1979.

VINCENT FORSHAW

LIBER

LIBER began at the 1968 conference of the International Federation of Library Associations and Institutions (IFLA), meeting in Frankfurt am Main, when a group of European university librarians agreed that IFLA itself could not meet the special needs for cooperation among European research libraries in an appropriate manner. The Ligue des Bibliothèques Européennes de Recherche (European Association of Research Libraries) was formally founded in 1971. It now has consultative status with the Council of Europe.

By the early 1990s some 300 libraries in 26 countries had become members of LIBER, having joined either the Council of Europe or its Council for Cultural Cooperation (CCC). Member institutions include both general research libraries, such as university and national libraries, and special research libraries at technological universities or research institutes. LIBER works closely with library-related organizations such as IFLA and the European Foundation for Library Cooperation (EFLC) and with political organizations such as the Commission of the European Communities (EC).

Library leaders from many countries have presided over LIBER. The presidents have been Jean-Pierre Clavel (Lausanne; 1971–74), Kenneth W. Humphreys (Birmingham; 1974–80), Gerhard Munthe (Oslo; 1980–83), Franz Kroller (Graz; 1983–89), and J. Michael Smethurst (British Library; 1989–).

The organization holds conferences as part of its annual general meetings and sponsors specialist seminars and workshops through a series of Working Groups. These Groups focus on Conspectus, Library Architecture, Library Automation, Library History, Library Management, Manuscripts and Rare Books, and Map Collections. The conferences and seminars have dealt with such subjects as Air Conditioning in Library Buildings, Conservation of Newspapers, Copyright of Manuscripts, European Conspectus Policy, Far Eastern Collections in European Libraries, Legal Deposit Laws (including legal deposit of new media), Management Implications of Library Auto-

Libraries in Lesotho (1987)

Type of library	Number of administrative units (main libraries)	Number of service points (branches, mobile stops, etc.)	Volumes in collections	Population served
National[a]	1	7	36,000	23
Public[b]	1	1	--	3,016

[a]1984 data
[b]1983 data

Source: Unesco, *Statistical Yearbook*, 1991.

mation, Map Collection Management, Reorganization of University Libraries, Retrospective Cataloguing, and Underground Stacks.

In 1986 LIBER and its national member delegations outlined a recommendation on behalf of the Council of Europe to improve European library cooperation. Both the CCC and the Council of Ministers adopted the recommendation, and all LIBER projects since then have followed it. For example, LIBER and the Center for Bibliographic Management at Bath in the United Kingdom compiled *Library Bibliographic Networks in Europe* (1988; 2nd edition, 1992) as a resource for those libraries, networks, associations, and national and international organizations interested in transborder flow of data.

In 1988 the Council of Europe set up a Working Party on Retrospective Cataloguing that consisted of delegates from ten countries and from EFLC, IFLA, and LIBER. The Working Party commissioned the LIBER Library Automation Group to draft the report, which comprises recommendations, a technical report, guidelines, and a study of bibliographical standards.

LIBER initiated the European Register of Microform Masters held by European research libraries (ERROM). It first conducted a study among member libraries to assess the feasibility of the idea, then gained the support of the Commission of the EC. The Göttingen State and University Library undertook the work.

The LIBER Conspectus Group worked in close cooperation with the National Librarians' Group on a European Conspectus in order to promote the use of Conspectus for resource-sharing in collection development, retrospective conversion, and conservation and preservation. The Group also worked on the need for European, national, regional, and local schedules for such a Conspectus and ways to ensure compatibility and common standards.

Other activities include cooperation between the Working Group on Library Management and the IFLA Section on Acquisition and Exchange to study a European Book Price Index and, for the Council of Europe, a comprehensive program of management improvement and training for research librarians in central and eastern Europe.

LIBER published *LIBER Bulletin* from 1972 and *LIBER News Sheet* from 1978. Both periodicals were replaced by the quarterly *European Research Libraries Cooperation* beginning in 1991.

HANS-ALBRECHT KOCH

Liberia

Liberia, a republic in western Africa, is bordered by Sierra Leone and Guinea on the north, Ivory Coast on the east, and the Atlantic Ocean on the south and west. Population (1990 est.) 2,607,000; area 11,369 sq.km. The official language is English.

History. Prior to the presence of books and recorded materials in Liberia, signs, symbols, palm kernels, and the making of rice farms were used for commercial purposes and determining births and deaths and keeping records among the people of the hinterland. The age of a person, for example, was determined by the number of rice farms made; story telling was the only way of preserving oral and traditional history.

The history of the Vai Tribe shows that in the 18th century Dawlu Bokele, who lived in the area of Grand Cape Mount County, one of the political subdivisions of Liberia, invented a form of syllabic writing for the transmission of messages between various ethnic groups. Carried by couriers, the messages were attached to sticks that indicated the urgency of the communications.

National Services. Liberia does not have a national library. In 1978 legislation was passed by the National Legislature creating a Center for National Documents and Records, which merged the Public Library System and Bureau of Archives. A newly constructed archival building was dedicated in April 1984. In the absence of a national library, the Center and academic libraries provide national leadership in library development.

Academic Libraries. The University of Liberia Libraries, established in 1862 in Monrovia, is a national institution operated by the government. Cuttington University College (1888), in Suacoco, Bong County, is a private institution operated by the Protestant Episcopal Church of Liberia.

The University of Liberia Library System maintains six professional library reading rooms for law, medicine, agriculture and forestry, engineering, regional planning, and science. It holds a collection of Africana and serves as depository center for the United Nations, Unesco, and other international organiza-

Libraries in Liberia (1983)

Type of library	Number of administrative units (main libraries)	Number of service points (branches, mobile stops, etc.)	Volumes in collections	Annual expenditures (Liberian dollar)	Population served	Professional staff (with certificate, diploma, etc.)	Total staff
National	--	--	--	--	--	--	--
Academic	2	6	200,526	552,718	406,833	11	75
Public	3	7	77,700	91,272	41,000	8	17
School	103	103	180,176	--	--	--	--
Special	1	1	6,000	--	--	2	4

Sources: Reports of Director of Libraries, University of Liberia; University Librarian, Cuttington University College; Deputy-Director General for Technical Services, Center for National Dcouments and Records; Director, Library Services, Liberian Institute of Public Administration Library, 1983.

Center for National Documents and Records, Monrovia, Liberia, dedicated in April, 1984. It was merged with the Public Library System and the Bureau of Archives.

University of Liberia Libraries, Monrovia

tions. Cuttington University College maintains a central library.

Public Libraries. Liberia's first public library system was organized in 1826 by the American Colonization Society, but little progress was made until 1937, when the National Legislature passed the act that gave birth to the public library movement. In the early 1950s, a national library committee was formed and charged with planning the system. In 1958 the first professionally trained public librarian was employed. The system's headquarters, in Monrovia, operates and coordinates a number of branch library reading rooms in counties and territories. In 1978 the public library system was placed under the administration of the Center for National Documents and Records.

School Libraries. By modern library standards and structure, Liberia's school library program has yet to be organized. Many schools suffer from an acute lack of funding. School librarians are not professionally trained. Few schools can afford trained library personnel, nor do they have adequate funds to build collections.

Special Libraries. Certain attempts by a few ministries and agencies of the government and private organizations have been made to organize special library services, but growth is relatively slow. Those services that exist are unstructured, because of lack of trained library personnel and funding.

The Liberian Institute of Public Administration Library (1975) provides source materials for instructors to prepare their lectures and provides collateral readings for trainees and civil servants. It had one professionally trained librarian in the mid-1980s and a number of semiprofessionals. Its collection totals approximately 6,000 volumes and contains about 1,500 government documents. The Library subscribes to some 70 specialized journals. Its subject strength is in the fields of public administration and management.

The Profession. The Liberian Library Association, organized in 1977, attempts to improve and develop library services and librarianship throughout the country. Its membership includes practicing as well as professional trained librarians.

From 1972 to 1982, the Institute of Librarianship operated a Certificate Program. It was the first formal training program of its kind to be organized in Liberia. The University of Liberia offered an Associate of Arts Degree in Library Science from 1982. Plans were under consideration in the mid-1980s for a Department of Library Science at the University of Liberia that would offer a Bachelor of Science degree in Library Science.

C. WESLEY ARMSTRONG

Librarianship, Philosophy of

EDITOR'S NOTE: This article, which originally appeared in the first edition of this Encyclopedia, is retained for its historical significance. Perhaps the last piece of writing finished before Jesse Shera's death, it stands as the final statement of a major thinker in the field.

The Retrospective View. "The Best Books for the Most People at the Least Cost" can hardly be called a philosophy of librarianship, but for many years it was, either implicitly or explicitly, all that the profession had. Terms were never defined nor cultural or social relationships examined. It was a creed rather than a philosophy, a dedication to a faith. Indeed, Oliver Garceau speaks at some length about "the library faith" in *The Public Library and the Political Process* (1949):

> Out of [the library's] past has come what we may call *the library faith.* It is a fundamental belief, so generally accepted as to be often left unsaid, in the virtue of the printed word, the reading of which is good in itself, and upon the preservation of which many basic values in our civilization rest. When culture is in question, the knowledge of books, the amount of reading, and the possession of a library—all become measures of value, not only of the individual, but also of the community.

Seen in the light of this faith, it may not be surprising that the present writer and his contemporaries in library school often observed that had all of us been born a generation earlier, we would likely have been ministers of the Gospel.

Pierce Butler remarked, in *The Reference Function of the Library* (1943), that librarians generally have been indifferent to a philosophical rationale for their profession:

> Some librarians dislike and distrust theory. They recognize clearly that the world needs efficient library service far more than it needs theoretical opinions. They fear, not without cause, that our quest for a professional philosophy may involve a neglect of practical values. Other librarians

> . . . are certain that the field of librarianship is amenable to rational analysis and that this analysis will reveal basic laws and principles. . . . They believe that a sound theory of librarianship can be developed without any sacrifice of practical efficiency. Moreover, they believe that such a sound theory must be established before librarians can become even reasonably competent in certain practical areas of their activity.

There are good historic reasons for the librarians' ambivalence, not to say indifference and neglect, concerning the philosophical raison d'etre of the library as a social organism. Over the millennia libraries created, by their very existence, their own rationale, their own philosophical justification. From the time of the ancient Sumerians and Egyptians libraries have been created because they are needed. Custody of the record of the culture was necessary for the transmission of that culture from generation to generation and beyond the reach of individual human memory—for training the priesthood, for documenting important commercial and other transactions, and for carrying on affairs of state. As the medieval universities arose, libraries were necessary because the book-centered educational system required them. The early librarians were scholars who not only gave the books in their custody the needed protective care but also worked with the texts themselves. The innovation of the modern public library created the philosophical need, not only for its justification, but also for its guidance as an institution.

Modern Public Library. The modern public library is rooted in those small voluntary associations of people who banded together in England and Colonial America to acquire the books they needed in their work and for their general stimulation but could not procure in sufficient quantity for themselves. Their collections were very similar to the personal library of the gentleman scholar. These social libraries, as they were called, spread along the east coast of Colonial America and were carried into the interior as it was opened by the pioneer settlers. Some, such as the Boston Athenaeum and the Redwood Library of Newport, Rhode Island, were sufficiently strong to survive periods of severe economic stringencies, but most of them fell by the wayside as their most enthusiastic supporters either died or moved away.

By the beginning of the 19th century it was apparent that voluntary support was inadequate for the book requirements of the new nation, and readers turned to municipal funds for support. Thus the public library was born and with it the need for a pragmatic justification to elicit public support. The *public* library as a new generic institutional form that was part of the public sector (of local government specifically) created a demand for its own justification. Edward Everett and George Ticknor found themselves in sharp disagreement about the kind of book collection the new Boston Public Library should have when they set themselves the task of writing the institution's first official report. Oliver Wendell Holmes asked, "What is a library but a nest to hatch scholars?" And Horace Mann saw the public library as "the crowning glory of our public schools." All of the early advocates of legislation in support of public libraries stressed that the institution was essential to an enlightened electorate, without which a democracy could not survive.

After the Civil War and the restabilization of the federal government, public libraries spread throughout the United States and, though few of them could be called opulent, many were enriched from, if not actually created by, Andrew Carnegie's generosity. That these libraries were desirable was readily acknowledged even by those who did not use them. They played important roles in the lives of many American young people, especially in the acculturation of the immigrants who at the turn of the 20th century were flocking to U.S. shores in increasing numbers. Not until the advent of the Great Depression in the 1930s did librarians suddenly awaken to the realization that they really were a part of the public sector, that they were created by society, and that what affected the social fabric of which they were a part also had serious implications for them. It was a rude awakening, but even then not many librarians struggling against economic misfortune thought it necessary to ask themselves, "What is our function in society, and why are we here?" Librarians, by temperament and training, have always been a pragmatic breed not much given to philosophical speculation.

As a result, librarians and their libraries in recent decades have assumed a wide variety of activities in the hope that by their very diversity they will attract increased public support: adult education, service to the aged, aid to the disadvantaged, programs for the physically handicapped, and many other social functions wholly admirable in themselves. But librarians failed to ask whether the library is really the best agency to be involved with such public services. Even in the sharply defined world of bibliography librarians have not been able to resolve the argument over the *quality* or *demand* theories of collection building. Over the centuries the library has been an elitist institution; can it, or should it, shed its heritage and strive to be as many things to as many people as possible? Questions like this are very stubborn, and no philosophical guides have evolved. The librarians talk glibly of library science, and indeed strive to endow it with scientific principles, but neglect the fact that librarianship emerged from a humanistic tradition.

Definition and Purpose. An assembly of books is not a library, nor is a library only a place where books are kept; a library in the sense we are concerned with here is an organization, a system designed to preserve and facilitate the use of graphic records. It is a social instrument created to form a link in the communication system that is essential to any society or culture. Without communication there can be no society, and without some form of graphic record and a means for the preservation of that record there can be no enduring culture. The library may from time to time assume certain marginal functions, but its basic purpose remains generically the same—a link in the communication chain that is concerned with the custody of recorded knowledge. Its fundamental concern is with the communication of knowledge, ideas, thought; but because those intangibles are embodied in physical objects—books and other graphic records—it is easy to mistake the physical object rather than its intellectual content as the reality. A book qua book is nothing more than a physical representation of what the author thought he said, and its utility varies directly with what the reader brings to it in understanding.

The modern library, in the Western world at least, is an integrated system of three interrelated and interdependent parts held together by an administrative authority, the purpose of which is to keep the triad in harmonious balance and to see that aims and objectives are adequately realized. The three parts, which may also be known as functions or operations, are: acquisition, organization, and interpretation or service.

Acquisition requires that the librarian should know what materials are to be procured to meet adequately the legitimate needs of the patron, or anticipated patron, and how these materials are to be acquired. Bibliography in the larger sense is the keystone of acquisition, because one learns about the materials to be acquired from bibliography.

Organization involves putting the materials, or the representation of those materials, together—in catalogues or other ordered files—in such a way as to make them available when needed. Organization also necessitates the analysis of the materials by subject or any other aspect that is believed to be useful to the patron. Order is essential, because the human mind can comprehend the intellectual or other aspects of the graphic record only through order and relationship. People cannot "think chaos"; order is heaven's first law, and nowhere is it more essential than in the organization of a library.

Interpretation, or service, is the rationale for the library; it is the goal for which acquisition and organization exist. Accumulating books and arranging them, no matter how expertly done, has little value if the system is not used. "Books are for use; every book its reader; and every reader his book" were the first three of S. R. Ranganathan's Five Laws of Library Science (*see* his biography in this volume). The fact that these are not really laws but precepts does not destroy their validity; they are the rationale of the library, no matter what kind, size, or type it happens to be.

Administration is necessary because there must be an operational focus, an authority to make decisions and impose standards. Administration is unproductive in that it does not "create" anything; it builds no collections, leaves behind it no taxonomic structures or analyses of the library's materials, and provides no direct apparent and tangible service to the user. Moreover, it should be held to a minimum. That administration is best that administers least, but this is not to say that administration is unimportant. At its best administration can achieve acceptable results under the most severe restrictions; at its worst it can leave the best library system in ruins. As libraries grow in size and complexity, the role of administration becomes increasingly important.

The library may also be viewed as operating in three spheres: the mechanistic, the one of maximum content, and the one of maximum context.

Mechanistic Sphere. This sphere encompasses all the physical operations involved in the total library process. Here are included all the "tools" the librarian uses in the performance of library tasks, including software and hardware, to borrow the terminology of the computer engineer. Such tools may be designed for either the librarian or the patron, or both.

Maximum Content. The sphere of maximum content includes the totality of the library's intellectual resources. The term maximum is used, not to suggest that the collections of the library should be as big as possible, but instead to suggest that the resources should be aligned to user needs to the greatest degree possible, given the library's available economic support. The term content also includes the resources of other libraries through various forms of interlibrary cooperation.

Maximum Context refers to the social and intellectual environment in which the library operates. The library's first responsibility is to its own culture, but this mandate does not exclude consideration of other cultures and other social goals. How far the library can or should go in stimulating alterations in its culture (that is, in the social context) is a philosophical question that has not yet been answered, if indeed it can be. A serious problem for the librarian is created when the goals of society itself are unclear or when the society is in a state of flux.

Society, Culture, and the Communication System. A society, as understood by the anthropologist, is composed of people working together to achieve common ends and to satisfy common needs. Culture is that body of knowledge, understandings, and beliefs held in common by a society. The culture is interpreted, nurtured, and enforced by institutions. Institutions are those large, powerful bodies in the society, such as those associated with family, religion, law, and education, that through their agencies, such as the church, courts, and schools, implement their power. Institutions set standards of conduct, grant rewards for adherence to the culture, and exact penalties for violations. Institutions in general dominate the society, and one departs from their dicta at one's peril. Libraries, then, are molded by the culture and kept in line by such institutions as the church, state, courts, and education. Libraries are generally thought of as an agency of the institution of education, and rightly so, but they are also subjects of the state, law, and even religion.

The culture is the totality of knowledge and beliefs of a society, maintained by a trinity: physical equipment, scholarship (in the broad sense of that which is known or believed), and social organization. The physical equipment is composed of tools of any kind, from stone axes to the most sophisticated computer or other mechanical or electronic mechanism. The scholarship is the totality of the products of thought, and the social organization is the system by which the whole is held together. Language is essential to a culture, and, indeed, many anthropologists consider language the essence of culture, without which cultures cannot exist. Language, either spoken, written, or kinesic, is a system of symbolic representations commonly understood and accepted by those in the culture. It is basic to the communication system in a culture, and the library is part of that system.

Because the library is an important agent in the communication system in society, how a society, or culture, acquires, absorbs, and disseminates knowledge must find accommodation in the librarian's professional philosophy. Douglas Waples was long convinced of the importance to librarianship of the study of the social effects of reading, and though he did not find the answers he sought, he at least opened the problem through his probing and did much to reveal its importance to the philosophy of the library profession. Information science, on the other hand, seems to concern itself primarily with the effectiveness of the communication channels in society and has not as yet addressed itself to the origins and growth of knowledge and the impact of that knowledge on its coeval culture. Moreover, information scientists seem to be aligning themselves with the natural sciences, which deal with physical phenomena, things, whereas the library and librarians deal with ideas and knowledge and their communication; hence librarianship is much closer to the humanities than to the "hard" sciences.

Thus there emerges a need for a new discipline, or science, of communication. This will emphatically not be a reworking of the old area of mass communication with which we have become, it must be admitted, rather tediously familiar. We are concerned here with a body of knowledge about knowledge itself. How knowledge has developed and been augmented has long been a subject of study, but how knowledge is coordinated, integrated, and put to work is yet an almost unrecognized field of investigation. We have, from the most ancient times, our systems of logic and our formulations of systematic scientific method. We know with some exactitude how knowledge of this kind is accumulated and transmitted from one generation to another. Philosophers have speculated for generations about the nature of knowledge, its sources and methods, and the limits of its validity. But the study of epistemology has always revolved about the intellectual processes of the *individual*. Psychologists carried the philosophers' speculations into the laboratory and made some progress in examining the mental abilities and behavior of the individual. But neither epistemologists nor psychologists have developed an orderly and comprehensive body of knowledge concerning intellectual differentiation and the integration of knowledge within a complex *social* structure. The sociologists, though they have directed their attention toward the behavior of people in groups, have paid scant heed to the *intellectual forces* shaping social structures.

The new discipline that we here envisage, which for want of a better name we have called "social epistemology," will provide a framework for the effective investigation of the whole complex problem of the intellectual processes of society—a study by which society as a whole seeks to achieve a perceptive or understanding relation to the total environment. It will lift the study of intellectual life from that of the individual to an inquiry into the means by which a society, nation, or culture achieves an understanding relationship with the totality of the environment, and its focus will be upon the production, flow, integration, and consumption of all forms of communication throughout the entire social pattern. From such a discipline should emerge a new body of knowledge about, and a new synthesis of the interaction between, knowledge and social activity.

But though social epistemology will have its own corpus of theoretical knowledge, it will be a very practical discipline, too.

Because of the emerging science of information, librarianship is, for the first time in its long history, compelled to formulate, self-consciously, its role in society, to examine critically its intellectual foundations, and to view itself holistically—as an integrated system that serves people, both as individuals and as members of society, throughout life. Despite the obvious relationship of librarianship to its coeval culture, the library has been recognized as a sociological entity only within the last half century. The rise of the public library in the U.S. coincided with important new developments in sociological theory, and the beginnings of a search for status encouraged all lines of inquiry that might help to establish the librarian's claim to being professional.

Public librarians are improving their skills in working effectively with other educational and social agencies in their service areas, and they are being called upon to participate in large-scale community programs for nonreaders, the functionally illiterate, the undereducated, and the culturally deprived. In recent decades, especially within the past few years, the public library has broadened and strengthened its role in the thinking and decision making of the community. In no way do these auxiliary functions diminish the library's independence, initiative, or social prestige. Programs for the professional education of the librarian have reflected changes in educational philosophy as well as in the theory of librarianship.

Personal Knowledge. Though the library is the creature of society, it does not reach the individual as do the mass media. Individuals must seek the library and its resources out for themselves, and the library achieves its social goals through them. Therefore, for the library, "the proper study of mankind is man."

It is important to librarians that they be supported as much as possible by an understanding of those psychological and other mental processes through which the individual receives and assimilates knowledge, that they know as much as can be known, given our present limitations, of the cognitive process. For the librarian the basic questions are: What is knowledge, how do we learn, and how does the assimilation of knowledge by whatever means influence behavior? What reading, in the generic sense, does to people was long ago addressed by Waples, but we are still ignorant of the influence that knowledge exerts on our behavior. Yet the problem of the nature of personal knowledge still eludes us. We are still unable to define a book other than to say that it deals in symbolic representations of what the originator intended to say.

Because most of our communication is carried out through symbolic representations—either written, oral, or through gestures and other forms of physical representations—the problem of communication, linguistics, and symbolization lies at the very heart of what the librarian is trying to do.

Thus librarians should remember that their primary concern is with ideas rather than physical objects. But because physical objects often embody or represent conceptualizations, the one is easily mistaken for the other. Librarianship touches all subject fields and is dependent on all of them for its intellectual and professional substance.

The philosophy of librarianship, as it is evolved, must encompass all forms of human activity, both physical and mental, not only because the library's shelves hold the record of the human adventure but also because those holdings represent and can respond to the needs of all human life.

All philosophy begins in an appreciation of our own ignorance—in asking ourselves the fundamental questions. "We have all the answers," Archibald MacLeish once told his staff when he was Librarian of Congress; "it is the questions we do not know."

REFERENCES

Pierce Butler, *An Introduction to Library Science* (1933).
Conrad H. Rawski, editor, *Toward a Theory of Librarianship* (1973).
Jesse H. Shera, *The Foundations of Education for Librarianship* (1972).
Jesse H. Shera, *Knowing Books and Men* (1976).

JESSE H. SHERA
(d. 1982)

Library and Information Science Research

Library and information science comprises an interdisciplinary field concerned with all phases of the information transfer process. Library science can trace its roots to the period 669–630 B.C. and to the cuneiform inscriptions on clay tablets collected in Nineveh by the Assyrian king Assurbanipal. Information science, although derived from and indebted to many fields, achieved an identity and image of its own after World War II, when many scientific and technological advances were put to peacetime use.

Definitions and Research Process. As an interdisciplinary field, it can be viewed as a spectrum of activities ranging from information theory through information technology to service-oriented functions, such as library and information center management. In fact, it is possible to visualize it through the use of a Venn diagram, a qualitative and descriptive technique for showing the logical relationships among sets within a universe or population. If we adopt a "hard" view of information science, we might state that it is defined by the intersection of all three sets in the diagram. A "softer" viewpoint might allow for logical union. Most information scientists would probably agree that some sort of compromise would be appropriate for an emerging field of this type, and therefore the diagram is shaded to suggest the various possibilities. In any case, contributions will come from many people with a wide diversity of backgrounds, and there is no point in making arbitrary distinctions. Moreover, in attempting to classify fields or people, it is important to avoid stereotyping them. Many people possess multiple skills, although few are qualified in all pertinent aspects of information science. And, unless we are "Renaissance men or women," we will have to specialize in some aspects of the field, while trying to remain sensitive to developments in the others.

With the exception of some historical work, scientific research is an empirical process that usually involves the following steps (the steps of the scientific method): (1) state the problem under consideration; (2) formulate a hypothesis; (3) test the hypothesis; (4) predict the results of the test; (5) compare observed and predicted results; and (6) draw conclusions from the comparison.

Problem statements are concise, expository statements of some perceived problem that requires further understanding, if not solution. The statement implies a hypothesis or conjecture and may even suggest an experiment to test the validity of the hypothesis. For this reason we must be careful to state the problem in clear and accurate terms and with correct scope.

Good hypotheses generally have the following characteristics: they are testable; they are in harmony with other hypotheses in the area of investigation; their logic is no more complex than necessary; they are relevant to the problem being considered; they are susceptible of quantification; and they are as general as possible (that is, they have a large number of consequences). We do not normally speak of "proving" hypotheses; rather, we seek support for them (that is, we try to confirm or refute them). In this sense science differs from pure mathematics, wherein we often deal with logical proofs. The difference lies between the analytical thought regarding mathematical abstractions and the synthetic thought employed when working with "real" objects or events. In the latter case we can never be certain about the interpretation of observations, but must be content to express relationships between objects or events inferred from these observations in terms of relative probabilities. This is true whether we are concerned with quantum mechanics or with the social and behavioral sciences, and unobtrusive and indirect methods of measurement must be employed along with approximations that are deemed adequate to describe the relations.

Subject Areas for Research. The true scope of library and information science is as yet unclear since the discipline is really in its emergent stage. Nevertheless, indications of the scope of library science may be given by enumerating the subject areas that have been addressed thus far. The following is a brief, representative, but certainly not exhaustive, list of subject areas; the list is derived from the index in Charles H. Davis's compilation, *Doctoral Dissertations in Library Science* (1976):

Academic and research libraries
Acquisition and book selection
Alphanumeric coding
Bibliography
Book storage
Cataloguing and classification
Dewey Decimal classification
Evaluation of library science
History of books and printing
Information analysis centers

A companion work, *Computer Science, a Dissertation Bibliography* (1977), yields an equally diverse sample of subjects.

To obtain a clear picture of related dissertation topics, we would need to study not only *Dissertation Abstracts* but *American Doctoral Dissertations* and then to add lists from individual universities that do not take part in these services. There is also *Master Abstracts* for the M.L.S. works. Other publications that report on thesis and dissertation research, such as *Library Quarterly, Library Research,* and *Journal of Librarianship,* provide insight into current research activity in the field. Research outside the library school is reported in publications of ERIC and NTIS.

Pure vs. Applied Research. Practicing librarians often think they have little or no time for research, and they are often right. But it is instructive to examine the history of scientific and technological discovery. Basic research has often come *after* technological discoveries, and the discoveries have often been made by practitioners. Archimedes came upon the famous principle that now bears his name while trying to satisfy a king's request to determine the relative amounts of gold and silver in a crown. Pasteur set forth the basic principles of bacteriology while working for the wine and silk industries. The steam engine was around long before the science of thermodynamics. And the telephone was quite well established by the time Shannon and Weaver developed a satisfactory theory of channel capacity in communication.

In a number of fields other than library and information science, there is an implicit understanding that professional and academic matters are inextricably intertwined and that they reinforce each other. In the sciences particularly, there is a substantial body of evidence suggesting that this is the case, even when we take care to differentiate properly between science and technology. But we are accustomed to thinking that basic research always precedes applications—a notion that is not discouraged by funding agencies such as the National Science Foundation. The evidence shows, however, that the converse is often true and that science is frequently the beneficiary of good technology. In fact, modern science has always been heavily dependent on instrumentation because of the need for precise and accurate measurement. High technology resulting from the space programs of the 1960s, 70s, and 80s transformed aspects of astronomy from an observational to an experimental science. Did technology arise from basic research in this instance, or is science merely along for the ride?

The point is that artificial distinctions between professional and academic concerns are not useful. They may even inhibit the growth of knowledge by erecting barriers to intelligent funding by agencies that view anything "applied" as beyond the scope of their responsibilities. In the case of science and technology, the issues are fairly clear; in librarianship and other professions and activities such as law, medicine, and business administration, the interdependence of theory and applications should be apparent too. What constitutes research, then? And how does it differ from management science, which often uses the same techniques and tools?

The difference seems to be the level of risk you are willing to take. Probability theory and statistics do not change from one arena to the other—that is, when you move from formal hypothesis testing to administrative decision making. What changes is the degree of risk, or the confidence level you wish to accept before moving ahead with a given task. In research, you must be as sure as possible that enough support has been found for a hypothesis. In administration or management, you need gather only enough evidence to improve the decision-making process over more arbitrary alternative procedures. Naturally, the better the evidence, the better the decision is likely to be; however, there is often insufficient time in administration to go through all the procedures that would constitute good research—work that is publishable and that can be expected to withstand the scrutiny of long-term peer review.

Perplexing Problems. Librarians and library researchers have been using the techniques of the social and behavioral sciences increasingly, particularly when trying to find out how people use libraries and information services. Studies of the interface between the user and the reference librarian are particularly difficult, and earlier textbooks in fact refer to "library mind-reading." In order to go beyond this mind-reading stage, so that we can determine how and why people use libraries and information services, we must do one of two things. Either we must alert the subjects of our study that we are going to try to find out about them, thereby running the risk of interfering with the experiment being conducted, or we must attempt to use unobtrusive methods, perhaps hidden microphones and videotape recorders, thereby running the risk of invading their privacy. Reconciling such problems is a difficult task.

On a deeper level, we need to look at how people associate symbols with their referents. Among other things, we need to study the semantics and semiotics associated with indexing and classification. In addition, artificial intelligence offers hope that we can make online retrieval systems more user-friendly by programming a certain amount of apparent quasi-intelligent behavior into them. This improvement would not obviate the need for a professional reference librarian or information specialist, but would help screen out straightforward questions that do not require professional intervention. Such "expert systems" would clearly be of use in traditional school, academic, and public library settings as well as in special libraries and information centers.

Areas such as these, which lend themselves to research and development, should make librarianship an increasingly interesting field, and they represent a welcome addition to the historical and bibliographic scholarship that has been going on for generations.

REFERENCES

Charles H. Busha and Stephen P. Harter, *Research Methods in Librarianship: Techniques and Interpretation* (1980).

Charles H. Davis, "Information Science and Libraries: A Note on the Contribution of Information Science to Librarianship," *The Bookmark* (1982).

Charles H. Davis, and James E. Rush, *Guide to Information Science* (1979).

Herbert Goldhor, *An Introduction to Scientific Research in Librarianship* (1972).

Mary Jo Lynch, "Research in Librarianship," *Library Trends* (1984).

Ronald R. Powell, *Basic Research Methods for Librarians* (1985).

CHARLES H. DAVIS;
JAMES E. RUSH

Library Association

The Library Association of the United Kingdom is the body that approves courses at British schools of librarianship and information science, awards professional qualifications, issues guidelines and sets standards, and, in short, acts as the voice of professional librarians in the United Kingdom. The Library Association (LA) was founded in 1877, the year following the formation of the American Library Association (ALA).

Early History. The Library Association was brought into existence for several reasons. First, there can be no doubt that the appearance of the ALA in 1876 acted as a spur; secondly, legislation permitting the establishment of public libraries in the U.K. was over 25 years old and had already resulted in a steady growth of libraries and librarians. But the immediate impulse came from E. W. B. Nicholson, who, early in

1877, had contributed an article to *The Academy* on the Philadelphia Conference of Librarians of 1876, and later wrote to *The Times* suggesting the need for an international conference of librarians in London. With remarkable speed, the idea was taken up and arrangements for such a conference were made; it was held at the London Institution in Finsbury Square, where Nicholson was Librarian.

The conference attracted 216, with 140 libraries represented. The international flavor was reflected by representatives from Australia, Belgium, Denmark, France, Germany, Greece, Italy, and the United States, as well as those from the UK itself. On the last day of the conference, October 5, 1877, those present resolved "That a Library Association of the United Kingdom be founded." The original LA constitution sought to encourage a wide membership. Its main object was "to unite all persons engaged in or interested in library work, for the purpose of promoting the best possible administration of existing libraries, and the formation of new ones where desirable. It shall also aim at the encouragement of bibliographical research." Membership was open not just to practicing librarians, but also to members of the governing bodies of libraries, as well as to those expressing an interest in the furtherance of the library movement. For this reason the LA could number among its early members such scholars as Benjamin Jowett, W. Stanley Jevons, Mark Pattison, Max Muller, and Alexandre Beljame.

The LA got off to a slow and tentative start, and its early years were tainted with serious differences rather than a unity of outlook. Membership was slow to gather momentum, and after 21 years' existence the total stood at a mere 582. The main cause was the paucity of library provision in the U.K. in the second half of the 19th century. Another reason was that, although the library movement could be said to be slowly growing, the profession of librarianship did not exist. To the credit of the early pioneers in the LA, they soon set about creating such a profession.

Schisms. The first two decades were dominated by an academic, bibliographical approach, but with the growth of the public library movement during the 1880s and 1890s, there was a natural reaction. Public librarians joining the LA wanted to see practical approaches, with more attention devoted to such topics as classification, cataloguing, and open access. Soon public librarians had virtually gained control of the Association. Between 1890 and 1930, the LA did not become a Public Library Association, though it nearly did so. The leading figures of those times—James Duff Brown, L. Stanley Jast, James D. Stewart, W. C. Berwick Sayers, and Ernest A. Savage, to name but a few—were all public librarians who saw to it that public library affairs were prominent in LA conferences, publications, and activities generally. The LA exhibited a noticeable lack of concern with nonpublic libraries, which did nothing to encourage academic and special librarians to join the Association. This public library bias on the part of the LA led directly to the formation of the Association of Special Libraries and Information Bureaux (Aslib) in 1926; of the School Library Association in 1937; and of the Standing Conference on National and University Libraries (SCONUL) in 1950.

By 1950 the LA had learned its lesson. After observing the centenary of the passage of the Public Libraries Act of 1850, the Association began to adopt a much more universal stance to encourage the unity of the profession. The formation of many more LA Groups to cater to specialist interests has resulted in dramatic increases in membership since 1945. Aslib, SCONUL, and the School Library Association still thrive, as do the Society of Archivists and the Institute of Information Scientists (IIS), but the LA cooperates with them all, and many people belong both to the LA and to other bodies appropriate to their needs. All these organizations endeavor to present a united front when making representations to the government on issues that concern librarians and information scientists.

Over the years there have been several moves to form a federation of all U.K. organizations concerned with library and information science and services, but none succeeded. In 1989 Wilfrid Saunders carried out an investigation on these lines and produced *Toward a Unified Professional Organization for Library and Information Science and Services: A Personal View,* a pamphlet strongly urging Aslib, the IIS, and the LA to unite. All three bodies gave the proposal serious consideration and the LA was prepared to follow the suggestion, but the others were lukewarm, and by 1991 the idea was dead.

Education Work. From 1880 onward the LA has been deeply interested in furthering the education and training of librarians and assistants. In that year a committee on the training of library assistants was set up. A syllabus was approved in 1884 and the first examination to be held under it took place in 1885. Correspondence courses were initiated, summer schools were held, and revisions of the syllabus occurred at intervals. During the 1920s the LA examinations consisted of six sections; passing four led to qualification as Associate of the Library Association (ALA); passing six to Fellowship (FLA). During the 1930s the LA adopted a three-stage syllabus—Elementary, Intermediate, and Final. Those completing the intermediate stage became Associate; those completing the final stage became Fellows.

In this period there was only one library school in the U.K., the graduate school established in 1919 at University College, London. The LA worked toward establishing other library schools. They would have emerged around 1940 but for the outbreak of World War II, and became a reality as soon as the war was over. Even so, the LA continued to hold examinations twice a year, and the library schools prepared their students for those examinations along the lines of the LA syllabus. The schools preferred to set their own qualifications, educational reforms were gradually instituted, and LA examinations were finally phased out in 1985. In 1991 the U.K. had 16 library schools. The Association nevertheless continues its interests in education and training by arranging courses for advanced students and practicing librarians, and by maintaining registers of Associates and Fellows.

Membership. LA membership was less than 400 in 1883 and by the end of the century it had grown only to 633; even in 1928, more than 50 years after its founding, LA membership was a mere 897. The next five years saw a phenomenal growth, which coincided with the appointment of the first paid full-time Secretary of the Association, Guy W. Keeling. He was active in stimulating a growth in membership, but there were other reasons for the increase as well. A Library Assistants' Association (LAA) had been formed in 1895; it changed its name to the Association of Assistant Librarians (AAL) in 1922. Over the years it had concerned itself with library education and training and it had developed a considerable membership. In 1929 the LA Council decided that after January 1, 1930, candidates for LA examinations must be members of the LA. In the following year, after protracted negotiations, AAL became a Section of the LA and brought its members into the Association.

These and other factors resulted in a membership increase from 897 in 1928 to 4,095 in 1932. The momentum continued until the outbreak of World War II in 1939, when the total had reached 6,167. Although there was a natural, though small, decline during the war, after 1945 there were more steady increases. The LA passed 10,000 members in 1950, 15,000 in 1965, and 20,000 in 1973. By 1980 the LA had just over 25,000 members, and although the total dropped slightly thereafter, it was still over 24,600 in 1990. The main reasons for the steady rise in membership after 1945 lie in the growth in number of all types of libraries in the U.K. and the more ecumenical approach of the Association toward all aspects of the profession.

In 1990 the LA established two new categories of members, Affiliated and Supporting members. Affiliated Members include persons working in library and information science who occupy nonprofessional or paraprofessional posts and do not intend to seek chartered status. Supporting Members include those who do not work in libraries or information service but have an interest in the aims and objectives of the Association. More than 400 Affiliated Members were enrolled by the end of 1990. Such members are represented on the LA Council and the LA now has an Affiliated Member Committee.

Presidents. The first President of the LA was J. Winter Jones, Director and Principal Librarian of the British Museum, and the second was H. O. Coxe, Bodley's Librarian. From the 1880s onward there was an increasing trend to nominate as President people outside the profession, such as noblemen, scholars, mayors, and chairmen of library governing bodies, although national and academic librarians continued to be chosen from time to time. The first public librarian to become President was Francis T. Barrett, City Librarian of Glasgow, in 1907. Among the many celebrities in the list of LA Presidents are Prince Philip, Duke of Edinburgh (1950), and Earl Attlee, former Prime Minister (1959). In 1961 the LA Council decided that in the future, except for special occasions, Presidents should come from the ranks of practicing librarians, a resolution that was honored thereafter with one exception. In 1977, the LA's centenary year, Sir Frederick (later Lord) Dainton was nominated; he had been Chairman of the Board of the British Library, which he had helped to bring into existence in 1973.

In more than a century, the LA has had only two women serve as President, Lorna V. Paulin in 1966 and Jean M. Plaister in 1988. The policy of nominating celebrities from outside the profession prevented many eminent women librarians from assuming the Presidency. Among them were Kate Pierce and A. M. Cooke. It seems certain that the LA, which is not and never has been anti-feminist, will elect many women Presidents in the future.

Secretaries. In its first 85 years the LA had a succession of noteworthy Honorary Secretaries, an office continued until 1961, when it was abolished after a reorganization. Well-known Honorary Secretaries of the past include Henry R. Tedder, J. Y. W. MacAlister, L. Stanley Jast, Lionel R. McColvin, and W. A. Munford. The LA had occasionally hired part-time secretarial assistance, but did not appoint its first full-time paid secretary, Guy W. Keeling, until 1928. He resigned because of ill health in 1931 and was succeeded by his deputy, Percy S. J. Welsford, who remained in office for 28 years. Welsford steered the LA through the war years and won credit for great advances in the size, influence, and work of the Association.

From 1959 to 1974 the Secretary was Hugh D. Barry, a barrister who quickly made his mark with proposals, which were mainly accepted, for reorganizing the Association. He also encouraged such activities as National Library Weeks in the late 1960s and the emergence of the Commonwealth Library Association (COMLA) in 1972. He helped to instigate joint meetings at top level between representatives of the LA and Aslib, SCONUL, IIS, and the Society of Archivists. Barry also had to resign on account of ill health, and R. P. Hilliard was secretary from 1974 to 1978, during which the LA celebrated its centenary year with an international conference and many other events. He was succeeded by Keith Lawrey (1978–84), George Cunningham, a former Member of Parliament (1984–92), and Ross Shimmon (1992–).

Headquarters. The LA did not have a central office until 1890; even then it was indebted to its Honorary Secretary, J. Y. W. MacAlister, for making available at low rent a basement office at the Royal Medical and Chirurgical Society, of which he was Librarian and Secretary, at 20 Hanover Square in the West End of London. There members of the Association held monthly meetings at which papers were read and discussed. Council, committee, and other meetings were held there until 1910. The LA moved offices four times between then and 1922, when Frank Pacy, then City Librarian of Westminster and Honorary Secretary of the LA, offered Buckingham Palace Road Library in Westminster as the Association headquarters. There it remained rent-free until the end of 1927. Early in the following year the LA operated from 26–27 Bedford Square, Bloomsbury, sharing the premises with Aslib and the Carnegie United Kingdom Trust (CUKT).

The year 1928 found the Association ready to expand and to settle in permanent headquarters. The CUKT, which had already given much financial help toward advancing libraries and librarianship in the U.K., was approached, and in 1931 the Trustees suggested that a property near the University of London be modernized and used partly for the National Central Library and partly for LA headquarters. The LA half of the building was opened as Chaucer House, Malet Place, in May 1933. It afforded generous office accommodation, a members' lounge, a Council chamber and committee room, and a library. Chaucer House became a mecca for librarians visiting London, and all Council, committee, and other meetings were held there. During World War II the headquarters moved for a time to Launceston in Cornwall. The adjacent National Central Library building suffered severe bomb damage and the LA's Chaucer House did not entirely escape.

Late in 1943 the LA office moved back to London. It continued to operate from Chaucer House for 20 years after the end of the war. In the early 1960s the University of London, whose premises practically surrounded the LA and NCL buildings in Malet Place, coveted the accommodation so much that it offered to erect a replacement building in Store Street, two blocks south of Malet Place. Agreement was reached, and toward the end of 1965 the LA moved to 7 Ridgmount Street, off Store Street. Council decided by a small majority not to retain the name Chaucer House, so the building is simply referred to as LAHQ. It was never officially opened, though Queen Elizabeth II inaugurated the neighboring National Central Library (now part of the British Library) in March 1966 to coincide with the first National Library Week ever celebrated in the UK.

The Ridgmount Street headquarters includes a members' lounge known as the Ewart Room, Council and committee rooms, and offices for the LA staff. It also has additional space on the upper floors for renting to appropriate organizations. There is also a library; it was originally the LA's own collection, but in 1974 the British Library assumed responsibility for it. The British Library staffs, maintains, and develops this collection, now known as BLISS (British Library Information Science Services) more ambitiously than the LA could hope to do. LA members lost no privileges in the transfer of power, and can use the library for reference or for borrowing either on the premises or by mail.

Conferences. The LA has staged an annual conference every year except 1914 and 1940 to 1945. World War I caused the 1914 conference at Oxford to be canceled, but conferences or annual meetings took place in London from 1915 through 1918. After World War I the first annual conference was that at Southport in September 1919, and the first after World War II was at Blackpool in May 1946. The format of conference has changed little over the years. Sometimes it has included the annual general meeting of members, which in other years has been held separately. Sometimes there have been joint conferences, such as that with the Library Association of Ireland in Dublin in 1967, or those held jointly with Aslib and other bodies in 1980 and some subsequent years. In the main, however, the LA annual conference has remained a domestic affair, including in its program general and sectional meetings, the Presidential Address (though recently this has been part of a separate Members' Day event), an exhibition of books and library furnishings and equipment, a conference dinner, related meetings, and social gatherings. The proceedings of each conference have invariably been published. Only twice has the LA annual conference been held outside the U.K.—in Paris in 1892 and in Dublin in 1967. (It was also held in Dublin in 1884, before Ireland became an independent republic.)

Publications. When the Association was founded, it adopted the *American Library Journal* as its official organ, with the word "American" dropped from the title. This arrangement lasted only from 1877 to 1882. A periodical called *Monthly Notes* had been started in 1880 and in 1883 it was the only LA journal. In 1884 a *Library Chronicle* was started, which ran until 1888; from 1889 to 1898 *The Library* was the official journal. There was much dissatisfaction with it and, impatient at the delay in producing a genuinely official periodical, James Duff Brown inaugurated his independent *Library World* in July 1898. But the LA was at work on its own publication, and in January 1899 the first issue of the *Library Association Record* appeared, with Henry Guppy as editor. It has been issued regularly ever since. Between 1899 and 1975 it had a distinguished series of librarian editors, including Arundell Esdaile, Lionel R. McColvin, and A. J. Walford. In January 1976 the *Record* appeared for the first time with a professional journalist as full-time paid Editor. Roger Walter, a former Fleet Street journalist, served until his death in 1984, followed by Jane Jenkins (1984–91) and Tony Mason (1991–).

As the *Record* became a more temporal and newsy journal, the LA decided that it also needed a more scholarly and staid approach, so in 1969 it launched the quarterly *Journal of Librarianship,* which has longer and more detailed articles than the *Record* and devotes more space to reviewing professional literature. The LA sold the quarterly, which is now published by Bowker-Saur Ltd., part of Reed International Books, under the title *Journal of Librarianship and Information Science*.

The first *LA Year Book* came out in 1892, but it did not actually appear annually until 1932; since then there has been an unbroken series. It lists names of members of Council and committees, details of Branches and Groups, gives the texts of the Royal Charter and the Bye-laws, and lists all members of the Association.

Since the mid-1930s the Association has pursued a vigorous publishing program. It has issued such serials as *Current Research, Library and Information Science Abstracts,* and *British Technology Index*. Among other publications with which the LA has been associated over the years are the *Anglo-American Cataloguing Rules* and Walford's *Guide to Reference Material*. Radical changes were made in 1990, when the LA sold its periodical titles to Bowker-Saur and transferred its book titles to Library Association Publishing Limited (LAPL), which published 29 new titles in 1990 compared with 21 in 1989.

Branches and Groups. Branches of the LA date back to 1896, when the North Western Branch came into being. Other district organizations followed, many based on such cities as Bristol and Birmingham; the largest branch, London and Home Counties, was inaugurated in 1923. The Scottish Library Association was founded in 1908 and became a Branch of the LA in 1931. With the formation of the Yorkshire and the South Western Branches in 1949, the entire U.K. was covered by LA branches. Wales is covered by the Welsh Library Association, a branch of the LA, and Northern Ireland by the Northern Ireland Branch. Members of the LA automatically become members of the branch in which they reside and work. The branches have proved themselves to be necessary adjuncts to the parent body. They arrange conferences, summer schools, and programs for meetings; they produce publications such as the *Scottish LA News* (SLAN), conference proceedings, and union catalogues of periodicals. There are 12 LA branches, each having an elected representative on the Council of the Association.

The history of the Groups could be said to have started in 1895 when the Library Assistants' Association was formed, but it was then an independent body and remained so for many years. As the AAL, it became a Section of the LA in 1930, just after the Association started Sections for university and research libraries and for county libraries. After 1945 the LA Council sought to attract into membership librarians from all types of libraries. More Sections were formed, those for Youth Libraries, Medical Libraries, and Reference and Special Libraries among them. In 1962, following the adoption of the Barry proposals, the Sections were renamed Groups. The radical changes at that time acted as spurs in the formation of other Groups. Groups were set up for Hospital Libraries and Handicapped Readers, Library History, Cataloguing and Indexing, Rare Books, and International Librarianship. Others followed until in 1991 there were 23 Groups in all. Like the Branches, they have been busy publishing journals such as *Public Library Journal, Library History,* and *Youth Library Review,* as well as arranging conferences and meetings in all parts of the country. Since 1988 each Group has been represented on the LA Council by a member elected by the Group.

International Work. Born at an international conference, and celebrating its 50th anniversary with a conference at Edinburgh (1927) that led to the founding of IFLA, the LA might seem always to have been internationally minded, but this is not so. Before the start of IFLA there appear to have been few attempts to give the LA a leading role in world librarianship, but since 1945 there has been a totally different approach, and the LA's contributions to IFLA have expanded to impressive proportions. Leaders include Sir Frank Francis, Lionel R. McColvin, Frank M. Gardner, Maurice Line, and others. LA has been host to numerous IFLA meetings, including the General Councils held in Cheltenham in 1931, in London in 1948 and again in 1950, in Edinburgh in 1961, in Liverpool in 1971, and in Brighton in 1987. Another international development after World War II was the expansion of the work of the British Council in providing and encouraging library development overseas, particularly in Commonwealth countries. Many British librarians went abroad to take charge of British Council libraries overseas or to advise developing countries on library affairs, and the LA advised on many of these appointments. The Association gave similar help and advice to Unesco from 1946 to 1985, when the British government withdrew from Unesco.

In 1971 the Commonwealth Foundation approached the LA to assist in setting up a Commonwealth Library Association (COMLA). Following an exploratory conference of librarians from 22 Commonwealth countries at LA headquarters in London, COMLA was inaugurated at Lagos, Nigeria, in 1972. Hugh D. Barry, LA Secretary and the first Acting Secretary of COMLA, drew up the original draft constitution. K. C. Harrison (LA President in 1973) was elected the first President of COMLA (1972–75) and was Executive Secretary (1980–83). LA continues to give full support to COMLA.

Since 1968, when it began, the International Group of the LA has thrived. It had nearly 1,500 members in 1991. It meets regularly and publishes the quarterly journal *Focus* for its members. All traces of isolationism have not yet been eradicated from the LA. There is still apathy, and sometimes downright opposition, toward international activities from some members. But since the mid-1940s LA involvement and influence in world librarianship has grown enormously, and the tide of activity is still rising.

Influence on Government. The LA was granted a Royal Charter in 1898 and its text includes such phrases as "to promote the better administration of libraries" and "to watch any legislation." True to its Royal Charter, the Association has lost few opportunities to make representations to government on library matters in the U.K., and has done so with varying degrees of success. It helped to secure passage of the 1919 law abolishing legal limits on public library expenditure in England and Wales and giving powers to establish county libraries. The LA also played an important part in finalizing the Net Books Agreements of 1929 and 1931, by which public libraries gained advantages. Over the years the Association has been represented on or has given evidence to many committees, both governmental and nongovernmental. These committees produced such important documents as the Kenyon Report of 1927, the Roberts Report of 1959, and the Dainton Report of 1969. Kenyon gave impetus to library cooperation in the U.K., Roberts led to the Public Libraries and Museums Act of 1964, and Dainton gave rise to the British Library Act of 1972.

The Association was also prominent in the protracted debates that preceded the Public Lending Right Act of 1979. The arguments had been going on since 1951, with the LA opposing several proposed PLR schemes. While the Association was not against reasonable compensation for authors, it consistently sought to ensure that library staffs would not be burdened with too much additional administrative work in connection with PLR, and also stressed that library book funds should not suffer because of the extra expenditure involved. The final legislation met those reservations, and PLR became operative in 1982.

Recent and Future Concerns. Over the years, as part of its efforts to live up to the high ideals of its founders, the LA has kept a watchful eye on such issues as censorship, copyright, and funding for libraries. While it is not a trade union, it has made recommendations on the salaries and service conditions of members at all levels. It has formulated guidelines and goals for public, school, hospital, and most other types of libraries and encourages governing bodies of libraries to meet these minimum standards of service. It has fought with some success such trends as libraries closing entirely or curtailing their opening hours on economic grounds. It has opposed, not always successfully, the trend to link public libraries with the arts, sport, and other leisure activities, with nonlibrarians as directors of these joint services.

The Association will have to face other challenges, among them the creeping trend to introduce charges for library services or to increase charges where they are already made. Some authorities are putting some services out to private contract, a trend the LA will have to watch. Librarians must also watch the effects on British libraries emanating from U.K. membership in the European Community. All these and many other issues are likely to concern members of the LA Council and staff in the coming years. One of the first of these concerns is to prepare a response to the Minister's invitation to the LA to draw up a model Library's Charter on "what the customer is entitled to and can reasonably expect within a reasonable budget."

REFERENCE

W. A. Munford, *A History of the Library Association, 1877–1977,* the Library Association Centenary Volume.

K. C. HARRISON

Library Automation

Throughout the 20th century, librarians have used technological devices to assist in their internal operations and to enhance service to their clientele. The term *library automation* has been applied both narrowly and broadly to the tools and activities that incorporate technologies into library operations and services. Some users of the term have equated it with what might more properly be called "library mechanization," encompassing practically every mechanical or electrical device used in libraries. Others have used the term only in close association with computers and their use in libraries.

Even without a universally accepted definition, most who have worked in the field of library automation would probably concur that the library mechanization perspective is too broad, and many would also argue that the requirement of computers in the equation may be slightly too narrow. What these two perspectives have in common is that their defining focus is on the equipment, or hardware, used in the processes of automation. In fact, while automation does imply the use of machines, what has actually distinguished the concept of library automation has not been the simple presence of machines in a process, but rather the form of the information that is acted upon by those machines. Ever since the term *library automation* came into use, it has referred to processing information that can be manipulated, rearranged, stored, or communicated in what has commonly been called *machine-readable* form, or what current usage calls *digitized* form.

Viewed in this light, devices such as typewriters, photocopy machines, and electronic security systems do not fall under the rubric of library automation, because none of these devices typically uses, generates, or communicates information in digitized form. On the other hand, computers clearly do meet this criterion, and in fact so do their precursors, such as punched-card readers and sorters, which came into use in libraries as early as the 1930s. Also included are communication devices such as TWX (TeletypeWriter eXchange), fax (telefacsimile) machines, modems, and other hardware that serves to facilitate encoding and transmitting data in digitized form.

The evolution of library automation has been one of an ongoing interaction between technologies, purposes, and applications. Simply put, libraries have attempted to use machine-readable data and the machines that manipulate it—the *technologies*—to assist in carrying out library operations and providing library service—the *applications*—in order to achieve certain *purposes*. The following sections examine first the purposes, as rationales and motivations, that have been the principal guiding forces behind decisions to automate in libraries. Then, with particular reference to North America and specifically the United States, the evolution of library automation is presented in terms of the interaction between technologies and applications.

PURPOSES OF AUTOMATION

The technologies used in library automation have changed dramatically since the first punched-card readers and sorters were introduced into libraries during the 1930s and 1940s, and there has even been an evolution in the types of library operations and services that have been automated during that span. Of the three points comprising the triad of library automation as described above, probably the most consistent over time has been the range of reasons and motivations for automating. With variations on the themes, there have been a handful of rationales and motivations that have served as the main impetus for library automation over the past several decades. Some arguably have not been as logical or noble as others, but all have been prominently used nevertheless, and, to greater or lesser degree, are likely to continue to be used in the future.

More Efficient Processing. Most internal library operations involve the multi-step processing of transactional information. The circulation of a book, for example, involves recording information about the book in conjunction with information about the individual borrowing it. When the book is returned, someone must retrieve the record indicating that it was on loan and to whom, then take some action that acknowledges that the item has been returned and that the individual to whom it had been charged is no longer responsible for its fate. In the interim between check-out and return, other library users may seek to confirm that the book is on loan and ask when it is due back. Further, the library may wish to have some way of tracking the book to ascertain that the patron returns it by the date it is due, and to notify that user if the item is indeed not returned on time. Many libraries allow patrons to "reserve" or place a "hold" on a specific item so that when it returns, the library can notify them and hold the item for them.

These fairly routine steps in a circulation procedure are all labor-intensive and file-intensive and require coordination. The same is true of most other technical processing functions in libraries, such as acquisitions, serials control, and catalogue maintenance. Computers, and even the electromechanical unit-record machines that were their precursors, have been a natural fit for such operations in libraries. They eliminate many of the rote tasks of manual file maintenance, yet at the same time provide more flexibility for accessing individual records, sorting them, and combining information on them in a variety of meaningful ways.

Improved Service to Library Users. One of the most sought-after goals in automating library operations is improvement in service to library users. Even in technical services operations where the user does not see the activities being performed, any way that automation helps to streamline procedures can result in improved service to the user. For example, books that are catalogued faster are available sooner; more access points to circulation files provide a greater number of ways to look up an item to see where it is.

Perhaps the library function in which increased flexibility for the user has been most visible is automation of the library catalogue and use of electronic indexing and abstracting services. Through features such as keyword searching, use of Boolean operators, expansion in the types of access points, use of search qualifiers such as publication date ranges, and automated treatment of alternative terminology and forms of headings, users can search online library catalogues and reference indexes in ways that card catalogues and manual indexes simply could not accommodate.

Saving Money and Containing Costs. If there is a single rationale for library automation that historically has been far more highly touted than experience has shown to be justified, it has been that automation is a way to reduce costs. Particularly in the early years of automation, in anticipating how computers might best be applied to library operations, there was a fairly widespread consensus that one of the benefits would be a dramatic reduction in costs, since so many of the rote manual-processing tasks could be performed by machines. Not long into the computer era, however, many realized that, as logical as it sounded, this expectation was in fact not borne out by experience. There certainly have been specific instances where automation has resulted either in a direct savings or in a slowing of cost increases, but these have been situation-specific and have probably been more the exception than the rule. What has happened more often is that eliminating certain tasks through automation has been accompanied by introducing new sets of tasks associated with new capabilities of the automated system over and above what was possible with its manual counterpart. In other cases, the response to elimination of tasks has simply been to reallocate personnel elsewhere.

Resource Sharing and Library Cooperation. One of the most underestimated factors in introducing automated systems and services into libraries since the 1960s has been the role of resource sharing and library cooperation. In some cases, this role has been visible and direct. For example, during the 1980s there were a number of instances, especially in metropolitan areas in the U.S., where several libraries that individually may not have been able to afford automated circulation or multi-purpose systems pooled their finances and purchased a system to share among themselves. In a few cases, this type of arrangement brought even some larger libraries into their first experience with large-scale automation.

Apart from these direct and more obvious cases, cooperative ventures such as the Online Computer Library Center (OCLC), the University of Toronto Library Automated System (UTLAS), and a number of state-supported efforts have also served an important if somewhat less dramatic role in laying the foundation for library automation, especially in smaller and medium-sized libraries in North America. For many libraries, OCLC terminals were the first computer terminals of any type ever installed, and the OCLC M100 IBM Personal Computer was the first microcomputer in the library. On the state level, projects such as LCS in Illinois took many of those same libraries a step further by introducing terminals over which statewide union catalogues could be accessed and circulation operations automated. A few states took databases online into libraries; many created union catalogues of holdings of libraries throughout the state using computer output microform (COM) or CD-ROM. While the smaller libraries invested little if any automated effort in creating these databases, they gained greater awareness of automation and its possibilities, fostering an atmosphere of receptiveness to the use of other automated systems and services.

Response to a Crisis. Though not necessarily desirable as a reason in itself, probably one of the most common motivations that has led libraries to abandon a manual way of doing things in favor of an automated one has been responding to a crisis. An increasingly large backlog in cataloguing, the lack of accurate or timely fund account reports in acquisitions, hopelessly disorganized circulation files, or a large measure of internal inconsistency in a public catalogue have long served as more convincing evidence of the need to automate than the most eloquent arguments about improving processing efficiency or service to the user.

Apart from a response to a visible breakdown in a manual system, automation has also at times been seen as an answer to other types of problems, such as organizational or structural ones. Under any type of administrative structure, policies, procedures, and patterns of interaction become so ingrained over time that change, even if desirable, may be extremely difficult to introduce. The introduction of automation can be carried out in such a way as to reinforce and even strengthen existing patterns, but it can also be carried out in a manner that totally disrupts existing patterns and requires administrative or workflow reorganization. This reason may not be among the most laudable motivations for automating, but there have been many cases where the main impetus to introduce automation sooner rather than later has been to create an opportunity to reorganize work patterns or even entire departments in a library.

Automation for Its Own Sake. Automation as an end in itself—to do it because it can be done—has generally been met with some measure of skepticism in the library field. The conventional wisdom has been that a more concrete purpose must be served or more serious problem solved. On the other hand, some have cast what seems like a self-fulfilling motivation for library automation in a different perspective; the spirit of this viewpoint was captured in the early 1980s by Richard Waters and V. F. Kralisz:

> We do not any longer decide to put telephones in our libraries. It would be a sad commentary if some day we were still debating the computer, videotext, and other electronic information delivery formats when they had become an essential element of the way society communicates.

Cast in this light, "automation for its own sake" in fact becomes automation for a purpose. To the extent that libraries want to portray themselves as playing an integral role in the information society and to keep pace with the norms and customs of their user communities, they must be seen as technologically abreast of other institutions and providers of information. While being cautious not to automate an operation or introduce a new technology simply for the sake of appearances, librarians should recognize the value of being perceived as fluent in the latest technologies.

TECHNOLOGIES AND APPLICATIONS

Though we cannot refer to *absolute* stages or phases in the evolution of library automation, progress has gone in cycles such that we can identify several relatively distinct periods since the 1930s. These periods have been distinguished by the technologies employed in combination with the applications they have addressed.

The Pre-Computer Era. In the first half of the 20th century, electromechanical systems called unit-record systems were based on some of the same general principles that later characterized computers. The revolutionary concept of this technology was that information could be entered onto a medium—punched cards in the case of unit-record systems—and then be repeatedly reused to perform the same or different calculations and be sorted and arranged according to instructions "programmed" into the machine performing the operations. A collection of punched cards in essence represented what later came to be recognized as data banks or databases. These cards comprised a store of data that could be easily added to, or withdrawn from, without having to recreate an entire body of information. Electromechanical machines were developed on which to record data, while others "processed" the cards and the data on them, performing calculations, sorting cards, integrating new ones, and so on.

The use of unit-record systems in libraries was not widespread. The first widely reported use of this technology in libraries was in the circulation department at the University of Texas in 1935, where Ralph Parker used punched cards and unit-record equipment to select cards for overdue materials from a single circulation file. This process obviated the traditional time-consuming practice of having to maintain multiple files in circulation, each arranged in a different order to accommodate different needs. Probably the most elaborate system based on unit-record technology in use in a single library was the benevolently named "Punchin' Judy" circulation system, designed by the International Business Machines Company (IBM) in 1942 for the Montclair, New Jersey, Public Library, as a showcase of how unit-record systems could facilitate circulation procedures in libraries.

In addition to circulation, early unit-record systems in libraries were applied to other internal processing functions, such as acquisitions and serials control. Their use was functionally specific, not necessarily taking advantage of the full capabilities of the equipment, limited as it was. Among the libraries that incorporated this equipment in acquisitions work, for example, most used it only as an aid in financial administration, leaving intact traditional manual procedures for processing and tracking order forms and maintaining files. In serials work, some libraries found unit-record equipment and punched cards useful and time saving in preparing lists of subscriptions at regular intervals for renewal review and as bidding lists to send to subscription agents. While a few libraries also employed unit-record equipment to generate serials lists for public use, hardly any attempted to incorporate this equipment into the serials check-in process.

Though mostly used for such operations, unit-record technology made a significant contribution in the area of public services during the 1950s when it served as the basis in several places for compiling, mass-producing, and distributing union catalogues. Traditionally, only a central library in a system would maintain a union card catalogue showing which materials were held where throughout the system; it would have been too costly to replicate the catalogue in all branches. Some librarians—usually in public, and typically county-wide, library systems—saw the capabilities of unit-record systems for automatically sorting and collating data, and printing it at what were then considered relatively high speeds, as an opportunity to abandon card catalogues in favor of a much more useful and far less labor-intensive tool—a union book catalogue showing the holdings of all branches. Though the number of libraries converting their catalogues in this manner was relatively small, it set the stage for the later adoption of the computer for this purpose, especially in combination with microfilm technology.

Offline Computerization. The decades of the 1960s, 70s, and 80s each saw a major transformation of the technologies used in library automation. The 1960s ushered in the use of large computers to process data such as daily library circulation transactions and acquisitions records. The earliest ventures involved *offline* processing, in which transactions were not recorded on the computer as they occurred, but collected over time and processed in what was called *batch mode*. A common scenario for a computerized offline circulation system, for example, involved the use of machine-readable punched book cards and patron identification cards. When a patron charged out a book, a library attendant used a machine that, though not connected to a computer, generated a computer-readable circulation transaction punched card that combined two vital pieces of information: the book's call number recorded from the punched book card, and patron identification information from the patron's identification card. The librarians held all such transaction cards throughout the day and—along with other transaction cards containing information about books returned that day, overdues processed, and so on—took them all to the computer center after the library closed. These transaction cards were processed against the entire circulation file to generate an updated printout of the circulation file for the librarians to pick up before the start of business the next day.

As with unit-record equipment, circulation was the leading target of batch-processing computerization in libraries; there were also efforts in the areas of acquisitions and serials control. Compared with the speed of unit-record technology, the enormous speed with which computers could process data made them useful in many more aspects of acquisitions work than had been possible previously. In serials control, the University of California at San Diego pioneered a computerized check-in function by designing a local serials system.

A highly publicized venture in library automation in Florida during the era of offline computerization came to symbolize the zeal with which some enthusiasts viewed the promise of the computer. In the early 1960s Florida Atlantic University was a new campus in the state university system, and librarians announced plans to embark on a bold experiment to computerize almost all processing and even some public services for the campus library. Acquisitions, cataloguing, serials control, and circulation would be automated in one integrated system. There would be no card catalogue; the catalogue would be in book form, printed by and maintained on computer. The significance of the Florida Atlantic experiment remained largely symbolic: the reality of the system fell far short of the goal, with the automated serials control, acquisitions, and book catalogue components abandoned within two years of their implementation.

In attempting to design an *integrated* automated system in which various library operations could use a single core machine-readable record for various purposes, Florida Atlantic undertook as one its tasks to attempt to devise a coding scheme to identify the bibliographic data elements that regularly appear in library records. Other libraries worked on similar schemes. At a time when the advantage of coordinating the codification of bibliographic data elements was becoming clear, the Library of Congress was also exploring possible methods for converting information on catalogue cards to machine-readable form. By 1965, the LC had issued a report entitled *A Proposed Format for a Standardized Machine-Readable Catalog Record*. What emerged in 1968, after a pilot project among 20 North American libraries and ongoing reworking of the code, was the MARC II format for coding and exchanging bibliographic information. To this day the MARC project and the resulting international MARC formats remain truly landmark accomplishments in library automation, setting a technical framework for many breakthrough developments.

Online Computerization. As the lead technology of the day, offline computerization of library operations lasted a relatively short time. By the late 1960s, when most librarians were still eagerly awaiting offline systems they could afford, some were already beginning to experiment with online library systems. The Illinois State Library, Midwestern University in Texas, and Eastern Illinois University all implemented online circulation systems between 1966 and 1968.

The early 1970s exploded with a series of developments that had long-lasting significance in the field of library automation. One was the local development at several major universities of large-scale online interactive systems. Three of the most significant of these designs emerged at Northwestern University (in Evanston, Illinois), the University of Chicago, and Stanford University. Though refined many times over since its inception, the Northwestern Online Total Integrated System (NOTIS) was eventually transformed under its acronym into one of the most successfully marketed commercial online library systems during the 1980s. Of all online systems developed in the early 1970s, the most sophisticated was Stanford University's technical processing system. Probably the most awkward part of the system was its name—Bibliographic Automation of Large Library Operations using a Time-sharing System—mercifully usually referred to by its initials, BALLOTS. The significance of BALLOTS extended well beyond Stanford, particularly after 1978 when several large research libraries in the U.S. formed the Research Libraries Group (RLG) and adopted BALLOTS as their common technical processing system, in the process renaming the system the Research Libraries Information Network (RLIN).

Another online development in the early 1970s that had a far-reaching impact on libraries was the emergence of the Online Computer Library Center (OCLC). Chartered in 1967 as the Ohio College Library Center and operating first in a batch-processing mode, OCLC went online in 1971 as a shared cataloguing system among 54 academic libraries in Ohio. The concept behind OCLC was simple: by sharing access to a common database of cataloguing records, all the libraries in the system could benefit, but only one library, the first to catalogue a book, would have to do the intellectual and basic data-entry work required to catalogue it. The benefits were so immediate and so clear that by 1973 OCLC lifted its geographic and type-of-library restrictions on participation and became the preeminent cataloguing system in use in libraries throughout the U.S. Each library that used an OCLC record for a title in its collection had its own identification code affixed to the record, so that OCLC came to be recognized not only as a source of cataloguing data but also as a source of locational data for interlibrary loan. In contrast to other major tools of the day, such as the *National Union Catalogue,* OCLC listed locations not just in the largest research libraries, but in libraries of all sizes and types, and this fact had a discernible impact on interlibrary lending. By 1979, OCLC's interlibrary loan role had become so well established that it implemented an online interlibrary loan messaging system, enabling members to transmit requests to one another virtually instantaneously. OCLC was the first of what came to be called the *bibliographic utilities,* with RLIN, the University of Toronto Library Automated System (UTLAS), and the Washington Library Network (WLN) all emerging as similar networks during the mid to late 1970s. None of these, nor any of several challengers in the commercial sector, ever came close to displacing OCLC, at least not in its first quarter century.

A third development of particular significance during the early 1970s was the emergence of commercially available online library systems. The technological development that enabled this industry to emerge was the minicomputer. Prior to the advent of the minicomputer, almost all offline and online library systems were run on large mainframe equipment housed in computer centers on campuses, in municipalities, or in corporations. The technical capabilities and radically more affordable pricing of minicomputers enabled libraries to purchase and house their own dedicated computers, and this approach gave rise to the commercial online library systems industry. The pioneer in this arena, Computer Library Systems, Inc. (CLSI), came to dominate the commercial market for online circulation systems well into the 1980s. Other vendors of online circulation systems began to emerge about 1977, and for several unstable years vendors left the business almost as quickly as they entered it. These commercial systems were often referred to as *turnkey,* implying that all the user had to do to implement such a system was to have it delivered, plug it in, and turn it on. While an attractive promotional concept, turnkey installation seldom proved so simple to implement.

These three developments had their primary impact in technical services operations in libraries. But public service activities also began to reap the benefits of computerization during the first half of the 1970s, primarily in the form of commercially available online indexing and abstracting services. During the 1960s, the Lockheed Corporation and the System Development Corporation (SDC) had won a series of government contracts to develop online interactive bibliographic retrieval systems. By the early 1970s, both companies had made a handful of databases available online on a commercial basis, Lockheed with its DIALOG system and SDC with its ORBIT system. The databases were mounted on computers at Lockheed and SDC; librarians accessed them by dialing into those computers. These electronic databases provided powerful alternatives to their equivalent print indexes because they provided sophisticated search features such as keyword searching, use of Boolean operators, and truncation. In 1971, there were some half dozen services such as DIALOG and ORBIT, though each offered access to three or fewer databases. By 1974, Lockheed and SDC were each offering access to more than ten databases; additional database vendors had appeared on the scene; and the number and range of databases had grown considerably.

During the 1970s and into the 1980s, the growth of online systems in libraries was significant. Some libraries continued to design in-house systems for handling circulation, acquisitions, and serials control functions, but many more turned to commercially available online library systems. For cataloguing and increasingly for interlibrary lending, the bibliographic utilities continued to prosper, and reference database services continued to grow impressively. The early 1980s saw a number of far-reaching changes. For one, that most venerable of public service institutions, the card catalogue, was challenged by online competitors. A few libraries developed quite sophisticated online catalogues during the mid and late 1970s, but the early 1980s saw a burst of activity with *online public access catalogues* (OPACs). Some individual libraries designed their own OPACs, and commercial vendors of online circulation systems offered off-the-shelf versions.

Coinciding with this increased level of activity in developing OPACs in the early 1980s was a trend toward expanding systems beyond single-library, single-purpose modes of operation. This trend could be seen in a number of OPACs in the early 1980s that were developed for a multi-institutional environment. Some were designed this way from the start, such as the Melvyl union catalogue of the nine campuses of the University of California and the CARL system in Colorado. In other cases, the core system was designed at a single institution and expanded to serve others, as with the Minnesota State University System Project for Automated Library Systems (PALS), developed at the Mankato State University campus.

While these large multi-institutional systems focused on the public-access catalogue, another trend at about the same time centered on expanding systems beyond their traditional single-purpose utility. The concept of a single integrated system providing circulation, acquisitions, serials control, and even public catalogue functions had been seen as a goal of automation in libraries even during the pre-computer era of unit-record systems, but development toward that end had always been slow. Some systems, such as NOTIS at Northwestern, were pretty close to realizing the truly integrated system during the 1970s; the leading commercial circulation system vendors set to work to introduce not only OPAC capabilities, but also acquisitions modules and, in a few cases, serials control modules in the early 1980s.

In yet another development, the Pikes Peak Library District in Colorado Springs, Colorado, looked beyond the single-purpose system in other ways; it began to provide access to community information databases and services through its public-access catalogue, while at the same time placing terminals in government buildings, grocery stores, and elsewhere, and allowing dial-in access from home and office microcomputers. Public libraries had a long tradition of being centers of community information and outreach, but none until Pikes Peak had so successfully brought this function into the online environment. The Pikes Peak experience illustrated just one more way that automation held a great deal of promise as a means of enhancing library service.

Microcomputers. Another major technological development was introduced in the early 1980s: the microcomputer. The earliest commercially available microcomputers were based on 4-bit processors, though 32-bit processors were introduced by 1984. In the early 1980s, 256 Kilobytes (256KB) of random-access memory (RAM) was considered fairly standard for microcomputers and 640KB was high end; few machines had hard disks for secondary storage, and among those that did, a 20 Megabyte (20MB) disk was considered large; and the machines processed data at an optimal speed of 4.7 Megahertz (4.7 MHz). By contrast, a decade later a microcomputer costing less money than its counterpart from the early 1980s would come with 4MB of RAM and more than 100MB of hard disk storage, and operate at speeds of 33MHz.

The significance of microcomputers for library automation proved to be threefold. First, they greatly expanded the range of libraries for which automation became affordable, providing an entirely new and previously untapped market for commercial vendors of online systems. While some of the providers of large systems eventually began to incorporate microcomputer-based systems into their product lines, a host of smaller companies created software packages to handle technical processing and public catalogues. The software ranged from simple catalogue-card production packages selling for less than $100 to more sophisticated integrated systems such as those offered early on by DataTrek and Inmagic.

Second, microcomputers could handle some process themselves, removing them from remotely located mainframes or minicomputers. This power created new and interesting possibilities and shifted some of the emphasis in library automation from a completely centralized environment to one where processing functions could be more decentralized, or *distributed*.

Third, microcomputers could be used as everyday tools for such administrative functions as word processing, budgeting, accounting, and so on. They had perhaps their broadest impact as standard tools, rather than remote, formidable, difficult machines only a few experts could deal with.

By the standards of the 1990s, the microcomputers of the 1980s were primitive in terms of speed and capacity, and indeed during the 1980s expectations and desires often outpaced performance. The resulting clash between promise and reality sometimes created disappointing results for libraries turning to microcomputer technology for automation of traditional library operations. But expectations and results were eventually brought more into line with one another and, in that better-matched context, microcomputers have proven themselves indispensable in libraries of all types and sizes, and that role is likely to continue to increase.

COM and CD-ROM. Cutting across the use of computers since the 1960s have been two technologies, computer-output microform (COM) and compact disc-read only memory (CD-ROM). What these two media have in common in libraries is that each has served dual purposes, both for storing data and for presenting data. Another feature they have in common is that the initial enthusiasm greeting each proved exaggerated when later viewed in terms of actual accomplishments.

Apart from its role for storage of full-text documents, COM came into use in libraries primarily as a medium for public-access catalogues during the 1960s. By this time, a number of public library systems in particular were generating union book catalogues of holdings by computer. Conversion from printed catalogues to COM versions preserved the advantage of relying on computers to sort, combine, manipulate, and maintain data in machine-readable form, while attempting to overcome the bulk and weight and sometimes poor print quality that characterized book catalogues. But COM catalogues brought with them their own problems, not the least of which was the need to install and maintain COM readers, a whole new set of machines in the library. The machines were slow and poorly designed, they broke down, and they produced poor images. Though the technology improved over the years, COM had a difficult time living down its early reputation. It remained in use, but on a limited scale, as more and more libraries eventually found online technology within their financial reach.

In the early 1970s there were predictions that an emerging technology, the optical disk, would revolutionize the storage and delivery of information in libraries. What came to pass in the 1980s, in fact, was that CD-ROM as a version of that technology found several important niche applications. A few library cataloguing systems incorporated the use of CD-ROM as the medium on which to distribute their core bibliographic databases; a handful of commercial vendors introduced CD-ROM-based public-access catalogues; and a number of statewide union catalogues were converted to CD-ROM. The greatest use of CD-ROM in libraries in the early 1990s, however, was for distributing bibliographic reference databases as alternatives to online search services such as DIALOG. SilverPlatter was the leading commercial innovator in this area. Some longtime indexing and abstracting services such as the H. W. Wilson Company also put their databases on CD-ROM, and DIALOG and some of the other online services also jumped into the fray. In theory, it made perfect sense: CD-ROM databases were an attractive alternative to online reference database searching, largely because the costs were fixed according to an annual subscription price, regardless of how heavily the databases were used. Libraries could make popular databases available directly to patrons rather than requiring intermediaries, as had normally been the practice with the online services that charged for access literally by the minute. A displacement did occur to some extent, but mostly with respect to some of the more commonly used academically oriented databases such as ERIC, PsychInfo, and Sociofile. Even at that, the late 1980s and early 1990s saw the emergence of another alternative to online database services: database producers offered *site licensing,* allowing libraries to mount the databases on their own local systems for fixed fees. The long-range possibilities of more sophisticated forms of optical disk have continued to attract attention, but it was clear in the early 1990s that this technology had met with only limited application in automating library work.

Communications Technologies. Libraries became involved in communicating digitized information, at least experimentally, as early as the 1950s. During the ascendancy of shared online systems and bibliographic networking in the 1970s and 1980s, telecommunications took on real meaning as the link that made those pursuits possible. In general, though, telecommunications for these purposes was seen as something for the technical experts to handle, and librarians seldom became more than tangentially involved in the mechanics of telecommunications.

One area where librarians have been more directly involved in electronic communication efforts for a long period of time has been in support of interlibrary loan operations. In the 1950s, some libraries installed teletype, or TWX, machines in order to communicate interlibrary loan requests and other messages among themselves. During the mid and late 1960s, a number of state libraries, with funds for resource-sharing under the federal Library Services and Construction Act, began to institute TWX communications networks among regional systems headquarters, strategic public libraries, and sometimes publicly supported universities in the state. Invariably the main use of these networks was transmitting interlibrary loan requests. Though eventually transferring from TWX to other communications media, many of these state networks continued, often in association with online or CD-ROM-based statewide union catalogues.

Libraries long showed an interest in another communications technology, fax transmission, as a substitute for mail in delivering full texts of documents, especially journal articles. The mid to late 1960s saw a flurry of experiments with fax, including two in the western U.S. sponsored by the Council on Library Resources (CLR). The larger-scale FACTS project in the New York State Interlibrary Loan Network (NYSILL) lasted for 14 months, during which more than 4,000 documents were delivered by fax. The findings in all these projects were similar: that neither fax technology nor the organization of interlibrary loan networks and departments were yet well-suited for a marriage between fax and interlibrary lending. The late 1970s saw another series of demonstration projects, but with most of the same conclusions as had been reached the previous decade. Suddenly in the late 1980s libraries in significant numbers began to install fax machines, but even so, there has been much evidence to show that, no matter how easy to use or fast fax might promise to become, it is likely to remain difficult for most interlibrary loan departments to use, because they are not organized to take full advantage of its capabilities. In the meantime, the search for more efficient ways to transmit copies of documents between libraries continued to be a focus of development efforts. In 1992, for example, the RLG announced the availability of Ariel, a document-transmission system that allowed for rapid transmission of high-quality images over electronic networks.

In the 1990s another form of communications began to capture the interest of librarians: electronic networking over a conglomeration of several thousand networks called the Internet. While electronic networking may have utility for some traditional library operations such as transmitting interlibrary loan requests, its real significance for librarians may be its potential to foster fundamentally different ways of seeking and sharing information, both in carrying out their duties and in altering patterns of professional communication and learning. The Internet environment of the early 1990s held a certain spirit of cooperation and enthusiasm not unlike that which has greeted most new technologies. It is difficult to determine the level or even direction of impact the Internet and its likely evolution into a publicly supported National Research and Education Network will have on libraries, their operations, services, and role in an information society. But if potential turns out to be a valid predictor of future performance, the impact will be great.

TRENDS

In terms of application to traditional library operations and services, librarianship in North America has probably progressed to what could be called a "post-automation" environment. This is not to say that all libraries have automated their operations or services, or that libraries will not continue to incorporate new operations and services using existing and new technologies. What it does mean is that librarians seldom debate any longer whether technologies should be applied to library operations and services; it has become a given that an intelligent and measured use of technology in libraries is a desirable means to an end.

Gradually since the 1930s, and even just since the advent of the computer, the trend in library automation has been toward greater direct interaction between library users and the technologies employed in the library. The earliest automation efforts centered on operations such as circulation control, acquisitions, cataloguing, and serials control, in which users had no hands-on interactive roles. Even with online reference database services, the pricing structure in particular led librarians to guard these resources closely and place themselves as intermediaries between the technology and the users. Users finally began to meet library technology hands-on with online public-access catalogues, and they went on easily to online union catalogues and reference databases on CD-ROM or on local systems. Increasing provision of dial-in access to the library from home and office microcomputers has further placed the emphasis on accommodating the user through technology.

Libraries of the early 1990s existed in an interesting environment. The media they collected and the technologies they employed were converging. Text, sound, and image were being integrated into single packages of information, while online access, distributed processing, optical media, and communications technology were coalescing to form new possibilities for the delivery, storage, and use of information. Librarians will continue to collect and lend books. They will also continue to purchase, upgrade, and replace automated systems that facilitate some traditional library functions. But they are also bound to be at the center of new ways of presenting and communicating knowledge, and their use of technology is likely to continue in the direction of increasingly serving the interactive needs of information users.

REFERENCES

Dennis Reynolds, *Library Automation: Issues and Applications* (1985).

Richard L. Waters and V. F. Kralisz, "Financing the Electronic Library: Models and Options," *Drexel Library Quarterly* (1981).

DENNIS J. REYNOLDS

Library Buildings

History. The earliest library or archive facilities were associated with temples or palaces. Examples of temple libraries from the third and second pre-Christian millennia are those at Heliopolis in Egypt and at Erech in Iraq. Palace libraries include those at Ebla in Syria and at Tel-el-Amarna in Egypt. Principal differences in their physical outfitting, however, resulted more from the format of the books and records they housed than from their locations. In Syria and Iraq cuneiform tablets were usually laid up on benches or shelves, sometimes in clay or wicker containers, with their opening texts displayed, whereas in Egypt leather or papyrus scrolls were kept either in chests, earthen jars, or wall bins with the identification tags visible.

The locations of libraries in temple or palace compounds have suggested to some scholars that, although they were primarily for proprietary use, they may have been occasionally used by the public as well. Certainly Assurbanipal's palace library at Nineveh and the library in the Temple of the Muses in Alexandria, both in the first millennium B.C., were available to the public.

In Greece and Rome public libraries came also to be built in other gathering places such as baths and forums. Usually rectangular in shape, with colonnades in the forecourts, most of these libraries had niches in the side and rear walls where scrolls were stacked in bins. This arrangement was sometimes duplicated in upper galleries, and in many cases statues of votive deities occupied apses facing the entry.

Information is scanty regarding early library buildings outside of Europe and the Middle East, but they too appear to have been primarily priestly or princely in origin. Written bamboo slips and silk scrolls were stored in the imperial libraries of China, and there were ancient temple collections in the Indian

Subcontinent. There are 10th- and 11th-century library buildings still standing at Angkor Wat and Banteai Srei in Cambodia, erected as adjuncts to shrines and temples to house sacred texts written on palm leaves. At Mandalay 729 extant three-by-five-foot alabaster slabs incised with the Tripitaka still stand sheltered under separate roofs, constituting a kind of decentralized library structure spread over 13 acres. Aztec priests in pre-Columbian Mexico had large collections of accordion-folded amate paper codices, but little is known of how they were housed.

By far the largest libraries anywhere during the Middle Ages were in the Muslim world, where collections comprising hundreds of thousands of volumes existed in university and public library buildings from Basra to Baghdad, Cairo, Cordova, and elsewhere. Manuscript codices, written on vellum or paper, were piled flat on wooden wall shelves, and some large libraries, such as the one at Bokhara, devoted certain rooms to specific topics in a kind of early subject divisional plan. European collections meanwhile were very small and until the 13th century were found almost solely in religious houses. Most of these libraries were stored in book presses, some of them freestanding, others built into the walls of cloister walks.

From the Renaissance to the present time Western libraries have been engaged in a continuing struggle to house growing numbers of books. It was standard early practice for a library to chain its few books in fixed locations, first singly on lecterns and later on shelves below and above reading surfaces. By the first decade of the 17th century these bookcases were commonly arrayed either at 90 degrees from the perimeter of the library room, as was done at Leiden, or along the perimeter walls, as in the Arts End of the Bodleian Library at Oxford. Because of their ability to accommodate large numbers of books, these two configurations came into wide use in university, cathedral, and other large libraries, where they continued to be fashionable into the late 19th century.

Perimeter shelves, many with galleries above, were especially favored in the Rococo era and were used in such 18th-century libraries as those at St. Gallen, Wiblingen, and the Imperial Library in Vienna. In the periods of Classical and Gothic Revival, architects found especially that they could dress the alcove arrangement felicitously in exteriors patterned on both Greek temples and medieval churches. The narthex could serve as the foyer, the nave as the reading room with clerestory windows above, and bookcases could range inward from the buttresses through the aisles. Lancet windows could illumine the bookcases, and columns at their interior ends could support one or more galleries and the vault above. There were some aberrations, such as the round library erected as the Radcliffe Camera at Oxford in 1749.

These were the models available when libraries first came to be constructed in British North America; thus the Library Company of Philadelphia (1791) shelved its books in perimeter bookcases with galleries, whereas the Redwood Library in Newport (1750) was designed to look like a Temple to Apollo. The first library at Harvard (1841) was patterned on a Gothic chapel with rows of bookcases in the aisles. The first library at the University of Virginia (1826), designed by Thomas Jefferson, was round.

By the 1870s, however, library practice was becoming more complex, architecture was coming increasingly to regard function as at least one factor in determining form, and new structural materials were coming into use, all of which resulted in experimentation in library building design. The multi-tier structural bookstack came into widespread use, resulting in a proliferation of large reading rooms with high ceilings to relieve summer heat and large north

Austrian National Library

Restoration of the 1773 Augustiner Lesesaal (baroque reading room) in the Austrian National Library, the former Imperial Court Library, was completed in 1989.

Restoration by Venturi, Scott Brown and Associates
Photo by Matt Wargo

Main Reading Room, Fine Arts Library of the University of Pennsylvania. Restoration of the century-old historic landmark, designed by Frank Furness, was completed in 1991.

Pittsburg, Pennsylvania

Carnegie Library Hazelwood Branch

Completed 1900

Cost, $37,000

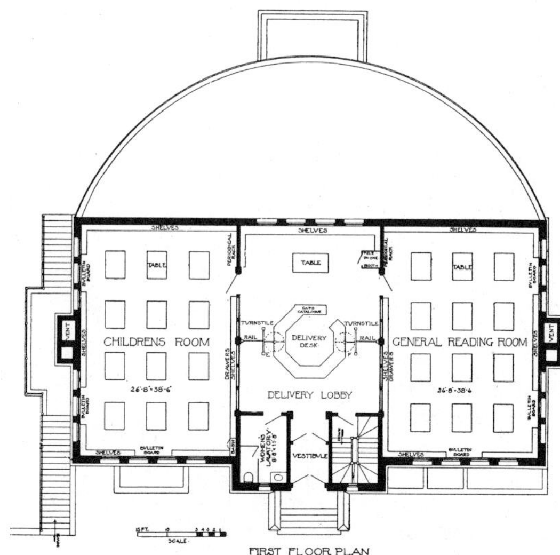

Material: brick, stone trimmings

Front, 80 feet. Depth, main floor, 40 feet

Depth, basement, 70 feet

Floor space, 3000 square feet

Book capacity, 12,000

Architects: Alden and Harlow, Pittsburg, Pa.

Books on wall shelves only. With growth a semicircular book room may be added to main floor.

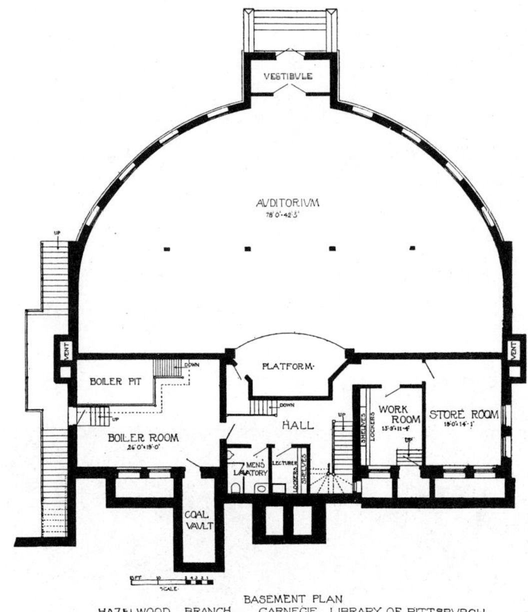

Basement auditorium to seat 500. Ground slopes to the rear.

windows to provide light and ventilation. Books were thus separated from readers in inflexible, fixed-function buildings, many of which, because of the great cost of their replacement, are still in use. The temple and palace origins of libraries are still evident in many of the buildings of this vintage; the Sterling Memorial Library at Yale (1931) is an example of the former and the Boston Public Library (1896) of the latter.

As the 20th century progressed, some voices began to protest that grandiose palace and temple models were inappropriate for libraries in modern democratic settings and to call instead for simpler and more utilitarian beauty in their appearance. Andrew Carnegie, influential because his philanthropy provided more than some 2,600 library buildings, insisted that the buildings he funded be functional and largely unadorned. This movement toward simplicity in American library building design accelerated during the Depression and came to fruition about mid-century with the advent of modular column-and-slab construction. Structural stacks gave way to free-standing shelving, and load-bearing walls gave way to curtain walls, allowing open shelves with adjacent seating to supersede closed stacks and reading rooms. Uniform lighting, floor-loading, and air treatment, made possible for the first time by modern technology, permitted inexpensive relocation of library activities as changing service needs demanded.

The period of simplicity in library building design did not last long. Although the concept of simplicity in interior layout continues today to dominate the aspirations of librarians, much new library architecture since about 1960 has tended to become increasingly complex. As a result, flexibility in the future use of much library space was reduced.

Planning and Construction Process. Every building is designed for a purpose. The more carefully that purpose is conceptualized beforehand, the more satisfactory the building is likely to be. Since most library and archive buildings serve for a half century or more, their probable use must be envisioned over a long future before their requirements can be defined. Community surveys, either formal or informal, are frequently used to this end. For public libraries population shifts and other demographic changes must be projected, and for academic libraries enrollments must be extrapolated and curriculum changes foreseen. Patterns of future information production and use must be considered and changing service needs anticipated.

A document, usually called a "program" or "brief," can then be prepared that delineates textually all the essential functional qualities and characteristics of the new building. It is usually considered good practice to write the same kind of building program whether the new structure is to be an expansion or a completely new building. In most cases the program is drafted either by the librarian or by a consultant with the counsel of a planning committee representing the owner. This document, which may run from 20 to more than 100 pages in length, is sometimes viewed as an extension of the architect's contract, since it defines what the owner wishes the architect to design into the building.

The building program normally comprises at least four essential components. An introduction attempts briefly to describe the history, service philosophy, and desired ambience of the institution. A second section enumerates assumptions regarding such matters as site and cost and identifies "functional criteria" used to determine the amount of seating, shelf capacity, and spatial calculations specified in the document. A third section defines every functional area or department in the building, giving for each its requisite proximities, structural qualities, room configuration, equipment inventory, and spatial needs. A fourth section contains notes on such matters as illumination levels, acoustics, keying systems, and ceiling heights. The preparation of a sound and thoughtful program is perhaps the most important thing the owner can do to assure a good building.

The owner must then select an architect. Questions often arise here as to the comparative advantages of local and national firms and of firms with and without previous library or archive experience. Any combination of these factors have resulted in both good and poor buildings, and such issues should not determine final selection. Selection should rather be based on the architect's previous work on buildings of all kinds, the firm's communication skills, its ability to keep on schedule and within budget, its experience in adhering to program, and other professional factors. The fee for architectural services is normally related to the cost of construction.

Missouri Historical Society

The ornate 40-foot Greco-Byzantine dome crowns the Reading Room of the Missouri Historical Society, formerly the sanctuary of the United Hebrew Temple in St. Louis. The society moved into the renovated complex in December 1991.

The architect then converts the program's textual description of the required building into graphic representations which, together with design specifications, instruct the contractor in what is to be built. This process involves first the general articulation of the building's requisite areas into functional proximities, then aggregating them into an aesthetically pleasing mass that will grace the site in harmony with its surroundings. Through a series of interchanges between the architect and the planning committee, sketches are then developed laying out individual activity areas in efficient interrelationships, and necessary furniture and equipment is configured into these areas. Construction and other related costs are estimated and a budget is prepared.

When these matters are agreed to, the owner authorizes the architect to prepare working drawings and building specifications. In this stage all details must be determined, construction and finishing materials must be specified, and bid documents prepared. During this phase the architect must often draw upon a wide range of supporting expertise, including perhaps those of illumination and acoustical consultants, structural as well as heating and ventilating engineers, interior designers, and others. Fulfillment of building code and other legal requirements must also be assured at this time.

By now a full year or more may have been spent just in planning the project. Although such planning is seldom begun unless the owner has some reason to expect that necessary funding will be available when needed, the owner should spend this period by completing financial arrangements for the project. Depending in part on the nature of the institution, this process may involve obtaining bonding authority, seeking appropriations from a government agency, soliciting assistance from philanthropic foundations,

Facade, Technical University Library, Vienna, completed in 1987.

Photo by Micha Erben

seeking the participation of private or corporate donors, or indeed any combination of these.

When planning and funding preparations are complete, the building can be bid and construction begun. Careful planning and good architecture will facilitate these processes by keeping expensive snags and change orders minimal and by reducing unnecessary delays in the project schedule. The owner's interest during construction is protected not only by the architect but also by the continuous oversight of a "clerk of the works" who stays on the site, checking for adherence to drawings and specifications. Payment to the contractor is normally made monthly during construction upon certification by the clerk and the architect.

Careful planning can also assure ease and efficiency in occupying the building after its completion. Many details must be resolved just in moving the books and documents themselves and in locating them properly in the new facility. The cost of moving must be budgeted. If public service is to be maintained during the move, it must be planned. Many schedules will need to be coordinated. If additional staff members will be required to operate the new facility, they should be recruited and trained beforehand.

In developing new space for archives or libraries, the training needed not only for new and old staff members but also for patrons is often overlooked. Library use often rises considerably when a new building is opened. Orientation to the new building will be needed, and many questions will require answering. Many visitors will come to see the new building, some of them architects and librarians wishing to discuss in detail many aspects of the project. The staff must arrange dedication ceremonies and plan appropriate honors for donors. Occupying a new building will be much easier if all of these demands on staff time are anticipated and budgeted.

Design Considerations. From the standpoint of librarians and archivists, the most significant building design considerations may be grouped under the three elements of efficiency, economy, and effectiveness. From the standpoint of the user, the most important is no doubt efficiency, the degree to which the design of the building enhances the ease with which its contents and services can be utilized.

Efficiency. The layout of a building can facilitate the movement of patrons through it, or it can impair that movement. There are natural locations for many library activities, and a well-designed building respects these natural dispositions. In nations where people habitually keep to the right, for example, circulation desks serve best when they are situated on the right of the exit, so that departing patrons may stop to check out books without crossing the flow of people entering the building. There are other "natural" locations for such things as the public catalogue and reference service which must be similarly taken into account in the placement of library functions.

Attention to layout can also accomplish efficiencies within departments as well as among them. The layout of the general stack, for example, is of great importance; much of a patron's time in seeking a book will be saved if he or she can immediately sense on entering a stack area exactly where the volume is likely to be shelved, instead of having to seek ranges distributed haphazardly or secluded in cul-de-sacs and behind stairwells. The placement of tables and chairs close to all book ranges can also save time for readers. If only ten readers a day have to go a half-dozen steps out of their way because of poor layout, they will walk more than 1,200 miles unnecessarily in the 50-year lifetime of the building.

Efficiency of layout is also important to library operation. If these ten walkers happen to be staff members, then the library will pay wages for the 1,200 unnecessary miles walked. Attention to traditional time-and-motion principles as well as to systems analysis should precede both the layout of departments and the deployment of furniture and equipment in departments.

Economy. Two kinds of economy should be considered in planning a building: the economy with which it can be constructed and the economy with which it can be operated during its lifetime. Economy of construction can result from many factors. Obviously, the selection of building materials will impinge upon construction costs. Some new libraries still use sumptuous materials and finishes reminiscent of their palace and temple origins rather than cheaper, more modest materials, driving up the cost of the building.

Simplicity of design can also be a factor in the economy of construction. Rectangular structures are generally cheaper to construct than complex designs, and, since the true basic "module" of a library is the rectangular book, rectangular spaces are easier to

Photo by Micha Erben

Entry hall, Technical University Library, Vienna, completed in 1987.

utilize. Irregular shapes moreover usually result in larger areas of exterior wall surface requiring expensive cosmetic treatment. Buildings with balanced ratios of height to width and depth are ordinarily cheaper to construct, and they are certainly more economical to use, than buildings that are disproportionately tall or squat. Site considerations sometimes mitigate these principles, but almost always at a cost.

The "efficiency ratio" in a design, or the relationship between its net assignable and gross areas, is also a factor in the economy of construction. This applies not only to floor area where it is ordinarily calculated, but also to vertical space. Atria and unnecessarily high ceilings, which may themselves also be vestiges of the palatial age in libraries, enlarge buildings and result in greater cubage to be maintained, heated, and cooled during the occupancy of the building. Open wells and high ceilings also create acoustical problems, increase the cost of ceiling-mounted illumination, and reduce flexibility in the future use of space. As with irregular shapes, these added costs must be evaluated when their use is being considered.

The role of design in the operating economies of library buildings has already been cited. A well-designed building will be economical to staff, and the costs of its physical maintenance will be reasonable. A good building will also be "energy efficient," so that unnecessarily high expenditures will not be required to keep it adequately lighted and at comfortable temperature and humidity levels throughout its period of use.

Effectiveness. The effectiveness of a library or archives building can be of several kinds, but the most basic of these is as shelter. Even an effective shelter, however, must do more than just protect materials, readers, and services from the wind and weather; it must also aid in the preservation of the books and documents it houses. Water damage to materials, for example, is more likely to result from poorly drained sites, inadequately sealed walls below grade, or bad plumbing than from leaky roofs. Water security of all kinds should therefore be considered in building planning.

Windows, important though they may be to the aesthetics of a building, can reduce the effectiveness of libraries and archives as shelter if they are not sensitively handled. Direct sunlight is difficult to read by and bleaches the spines of books, so it should be avoided wherever possible. The ultraviolet rays of even indirect natural light can also cause deterioration of paper and should be filtered out of areas where preservation is important. Care should also be taken to screen ultraviolet rays out of the artificial illumination used in such areas.

Since fire security is important in virtually all kinds of buildings, it is almost always well covered in basic building code requirements. Nonetheless, because of the unusual susceptibility of books and documents to damage from combinations of fire and water, fire security should receive special attention in libraries and archives. Likewise securing materials from theft and mutilation must also be considered in the effectiveness of a library building as shelter. Although no building can be fully theft-proof, such factors as the layout of services and equipment, the location and design of windows, and the kind and number of exits from a library building will figure in the security of its contents against theft.

University of Toronto Library

Architecture of the Robarts Research Library at the University of Toronto has attracted international attention.

REFERENCES

Aaron and Elaine Cohen, *Designing and Space Planning for Libraries* (1979)

Ralph E. Ellsworth, *Planning Manual for Academic Libraries* (1973).

Raymond M. Holt, *Planning Library Buildings and Facilities* (1989).

Keyes D. Metcalf, *Planning Academic and Research Library Buildings* (1965); 2nd edition by David Weber (1986).

Rolf Myller, *The Design of the Small Public Library* (1966).

Godfrey Thompson, *Planning and Design of Library Buildings,* 3rd edition (1989).

DAVID KASER

Library Cooperative Systems

The first example of library cooperation is impossible to identify. Joe W. Kraus reports that "catalogs of manuscripts in more than one monastery library existed in the first half of the 13th century. Manuscripts in 138 English and Scottish monasteries were listed in the *Registrum Librorum Angliae.*" Curt D. Wormann cites examples of an exchange agreement among the universities of Lund, Abo, and Greifswald as early as 1740, a projected union catalogue of the libraries of Weimar and Jean, a proposal for a coordinated acquisitions scheme for Wolfenbüttel and Göttingen, and the ambitious attempt to establish a *Bibliographie générale* based on the millions of books confiscated during the French Revolution and gathered in the *depots littéraires.*

Suggestions for cooperative activities in the U.S. appeared in the 1846 Annual Report of the Board of Regents of the Smithsonian Institution, whose Committee on Organization proposed that the institution "become a centre of literary and bibliographical reference for the entire country . . . to procure catalogs of all the important works of bibliography so that they might be consulted by the scholar, the student, the author, the historian, from every section of the Union, and . . . inform them whether any works they may desire to examine are to be found in the United States; and if so in what library; or if in Europe only, in what country of Europe they must be sought." On September 15, 1853, Charles Coffin

Jewett, the first Librarian of the Smithsonian Institution, was elected President of the first meeting of librarians ever held in the United States. The next day he spoke about the Smithsonian Catalogue System and his proposal to make general catalogues with the use of stereotype plates and his hope to publish a general catalogue of all the libraries in the country. His plan failed, not because the idea was faulty but because of inadequate technology (the impermanence of the stereotype process), inadequate financial support, and lack of an organization to support the project (the three factors necessary for any successful cooperative venture). In an 1876 *Library Journal* article Samuel Swett Green proposed that librarians enter into agreements to share resources.

The first major national union list in the U.S. was Henry C. Bolton's *A Catalogue of Scientific and Technical Periodicals,* published in 1885. By 1901 the Library of Congress initiated cooperative cataloguing and began building the first National Union Catalog by collecting catalogue cards from government libraries in Washington, D.C., the New York Public Library, the Boston Public Library, Harvard University, the John Crerar Library, and several others. The first interlibrary lending code was drawn up by an ALA Committee on Coordination of College Libraries in 1917. The Code suggested photoreproduction in place of lending the original publications. The earliest regional union catalogue in the U.S., a card catalogue of books in public libraries in California, was developed by the California State Library in 1909. The first edition of the *Union List of Serials* (1927) located 75,000 titles in 225 libraries and in a bibliography listed 179 examples of union lists.

Major union catalogues increased in number between 1932 and 1940, when 17 catalogues were established, many through the assistance of the Works Progress Administration (WPA). A number of these regional catalogues were added to the National Union Catalog so that by 1968 it contained more than 16,000,000 cards, representing about 10,000,000 titles and editions. Since that time, bibliographic cooperatives and networks have accelerated in pace to such an extent that resource-sharing, cooperative bibliographic systems, and the formalized development of library systems, consortia, and networks are commonly accepted.

National Library of Medicine

Canadian Institute for Scientific and Technical Information, site of the Canadian MEDLARS Center, Ottawa.

Definitions. The terms cooperative, consortium, and network are usually used interchangeably. The National Center for Education Statistics (NCES) defined the terms as follows:

> Cooperative: . . . a group of independent and autonomous libraries banded together by informal or formal agreements or contracts which stipulate the common services to be planned and coordinated by the directors of the cooperative systems.
>
> Consortium: . . . a formal arrangement of two or more libraries not under the same institutional control for joint activities to improve the library service of the participants by cooperation extending beyond traditional interlibrary loan as defined in the National Interlibrary Loan Code of 1968.
>
> Network: . . . a formal organization among libraries for cooperation and sharing of resources, usually with an explicitly hierarchical structure, in which the group as a whole is organized into subgroups with the expectation that most of the needs of a library will be satisfied within the subgroups of which it is a member [Alphonse F. Trezza, "Networks," *The ALA Yearbook* (1977)].

Raynard C. Swank defines networks as a "concept that includes the development of cooperative systems of libraries on geographical, subject, or other lines, each with some kind of center that not only coordinates the internal activities of the system but also serves as the system's outlet to, and inlet from, the centers of other systems. The concept is also hierarchical . . . ." The U.S. National Commission on Libraries and Information Science (NCLIS) in its National Program (1975) defines a network in its glossary as

> Two or more libraries and/or other organizations engaged in a common pattern of information exchange, through communications, for some functional purpose. A network usually consists of a formal arrangement whereby materials, information, and services provided by a variety of types of libraries and/or other organizations are made available to all potential users. (Libraries may be in different jurisdictions but agree to serve one another on the same basis as each serves its own constituents. Computers and telecommunications may be among the tools used for facilitating communication among them.)

Types of Networks. The earlier and more traditional cooperatives and network activity were between like types of libraries. Networking among different types of libraries in the U.S. received long-overdue stimulus with the passage of the Library Services and Construction Act, Title III (LSCA), and the Higher Education Act, Title II–B (HEA), which provided funds, specifically in LSCA and permissively in HEA, for intertype or multitype library cooperation. Most multitype library cooperation occurs between public libraries and academic libraries, although some experimentation and activity with school and special libraries have developed and are gradually accelerating.

Networks in the U.S. have developed at the local, state, intrastate and interstate, regional, and national levels. Local cooperatives or networks tend to be in metropolitan or urban areas, are voluntary, loosely organized, and minimally funded. Local networks generally consist of one single type of library—such as academic—or of two types—academic and public. In some urban areas metropolitan multitype library organizations have developed; New York City, Cleveland, and Milwaukee are examples of successful efforts. Reciprocal borrowing, interlibrary loan (ILL), local delivery services, cooperative collection development, and telephone reference services are the major activities undertaken.

State networks have traditionally been in a single type of library—public, with major university collections serving as backup resources. Funding came from state and federal sources. Services include resource sharing—ILL (books, periodicals, audiovisual materials)—reference, delivery service, cooperative cataloguing, collection development, and consulting.

One of the most significant national trends in library development since 1970 is the creation of statewide multitype library systems. Many states regard public library systems as transitional, expanding to become multitype systems/networks by adding university, college, junior and community college libraries, elementary and secondary school library/media centers, residential institutions, and special libraries in corporations and nonprofit organizations. Multitype library systems were first established in Illinois in 1972, in California and Colorado in 1976, in Connecticut in 1977, in Minnesota in 1983, and in Kentucky, Kansas, and New Jersey in 1984. Pilot projects also began in the early 1980s in Wisconsin, Alabama, and New York.

The first multi-state regional network was established in 1966. Six New England land-grant university libraries joined together to form the New England Library and Information Network (NELINET) whose primary purpose was to supply its members with offline computerized bibliographic sources, a machine-readable catalogue data file, catalogue data file searching, catalogue cards, and book pockets and labels. By the mid-1970s three major bibliographic utilities were established as the direct result of computerized library operations. (The utilities provide computer-based services organized by and for libraries whereby members contribute to and modify the resource databases as needed to provide various library and information services.) The Online Computer Library Center, Inc. (OCLC), began as the Ohio College Library Center. The Research Libraries Group (RLG) first consisted of the New York Public Library and the libraries of Columbia, Harvard, and Yale universities and did not have its own network computer facilities; the entity that became RLG's Research Libraries Information Network (RLIN) was under the control of Stanford University—not an RLG member at the time—as BALLOTS (Bibliographic Automation of Large Library Operations Using a Time-Sharing System). BALLOTS was also accessible to other libraries for shared cataloguing and searching functions. The Western Library Network (WLN), formerly the Washington Library Network, had been established, although it had not yet begun full implementation of its online system.

In the next 10 years, a number of other regional networks were established. Some of the major ones are:

- AMIGOS Bibliographic Council (in the Southwest)
- California Library Authority for Systems and Services (CLASS), now the Cooperative Library Agency for Systems and Services
- New England Library and Information Network (NELINET)
- Pennsylvania Area Library Network (PALINET)
- Pittsburgh Regional Library Center (PRLC)
- Southeastern Library Network (SOLINET)
- State University of New York (SUNY)

They all serve as brokers for libraries of OCLC cooperative cataloguing services as well as of the many new services developed in the 1980s.

Two major subject-oriented networks at the national level developed in the 1960s when the National Library of Medicine (NLM) mechanized its indexing service. NLM stored citations in its computer for use in the Medical Literature Analysis and Retrieval Systems (MEDLARS), which produced 21 major indexes, including *Index Medicus,* a monthly index to more than 2,500 of the world's biomedical journals. By the early 1980s more than 1,300 universities, medical schools, hospitals, government agencies, commercial organizations, and other libraries had access to MEDLARS III's 4,500,000-plus references to journal articles and books published in the health sciences since 1965. The National Library of Medicine now offers more than 15 databases online through its Medline online database service, which by 1990 included 6,200,000 records. NLM sponsored the planning and development of Integrated Academic Information Management Systems (IAIMS), designed to use computer and communications technologies to unify varied health information resources into an easily accessible system. Its goal is to integrate library systems with the multitude of individual and institutional working information files, such as clinical, administrative, research, and educational databases.

In 1962 the Department of Agricultural Library was designated as the National Agricultural Library (NAL). NAL developed network services with the Department's various branches and field services. Its online agricultural database, AGRICOLA, includes indexes to worldwide journals and monographic literature and U.S. government reports on general agriculture, food, nutrition, agricultural economics, and many related scientific and sociological subject fields. It has also established seven USDA Regional Document Delivery Systems serving 35 land-grant university libraries.

At the national level two major events provided both an initial impetus and lasting impact and influence on networking. In 1969 the LC began distributing MARC data in machine-readable form, and in 1975 NCLIS's National Program provided national policy direction. The MARC database provided the resource for establishing and developing cooperative cataloguing services by OCLC, WLN, BALLOTS (later RLIN), and other institutionally and commercially based services. NCLIS called for a nationwide library and information services network to provide access to information for all, using the best in technology and telecommunications, building on existing local, state, and national resources, and raising, but not trying to resolve, the issue of governance. It provided a challenge and a framework for action. The Commission continued its efforts by engaging the library community in discussing, reviewing, and recommending actions in resource sharing, copyright issues and revision of the copyright law, and the role of government and the private sector in providing information services. It funded studies on the role of the LC in networking activity and, in cooperation with the National Bureau of Standards, initial development of computer network protocols; in addition the Commission planned and implemented the 1979 White House Conference on Libraries and Information Services, which stressed access, cooperation, sharing, network development, and effective use of technology and telecommunications. The 1991 White House Conference on Library and Information Services concentrated on literacy, productivity, and democracy.

The LC in 1976 established a Network Advisory Committee. It provides a forum for discussing the issues involved in nationwide networking by officers and directors of state, regional, and national networks, consortia, and cooperatives. LC, with the strong support of the Council on Library Resources (CLR), developed the mechanisms for linking the major utilities—OCLC, RLIN, and WLN.

Organizational Structures, Governance, and Finance. Local cooperatives or consortia in most cases are informal, voluntary institutional membership organizations. They develop bylaws providing for officers, boards of directors, and committees. Members may withdraw and in many cases participate in only those cooperative services they choose. Financial support comes from modest local dues and from fees for services provided. Grants from state library agencies, foundations, or federal sources may fund feasibility studies of new services, the purchase of equipment, or studies and surveys. In a few cases—mainly in urban areas—a small paid staff is responsible for operating the cooperative, but ordinarily the staff is voluntary and part-time.

Intrastate regional systems or networks have their organizational structures defined by state statute. They encompass the entire state, their number varying from state to state. The law provides for a formal organization and a board, makes provisions for paid staff, and specifies the system's purpose and major services. The law also usually indicates both the rights and responsibilities of the participants. The board may be a lay board representative of the member libraries of the organization, or it may include both librarians and lay members. Funding comes primarily from state appropriations and usually according to a formula, such as per capita and area grants. The member libraries may contribute funding from their own budgets for specific services or general purposes. Additional funds from LSCA and other federal sources are available through the grant process. The state library agency is the administrator of the intrastate regional systems and the major funding source and can exert a strong influence on statewide directions and services. However, the state library agencies rely on various advisory groups to assure user input in the decision-making process.

Statewide networks are also established by law and administered by a state agency, almost always the state library agency. The network may be regionally organized as described previously, with the added provision of back-up resources from major research libraries, large public libraries and, in most cases, the state library agency library. This resource sharing is hierarchical. Funding for the backup centers may be an annual fixed sum, or be based on a formula and applied on the basis of actual use of the collection. New York, Illinois, and Texas are examples of this latter type of network structure. Overall administration of the network is the responsibility of the state agency and always includes an advisory board and user committees that address service, evaluation, financing, relationships, management, and other matters. The funding of statewide multitype networks, although primarily from state sources, is supplemented by LSCA Title III funds.

At the interstate regional level, networks are strictly membership organizations. The networks are chartered as not-for-profit agencies, have bylaws, plans of service, paid staff, governing boards, and advisory committees. The basic goals and objectives of the organization are included in its organizational documents. Funding comes from membership dues and service fees, although some additional support may be available from grants by foundations or state or federal agencies. The regionals offer brokered services of the utilities, training, retrospective conversion, development of area union catalogues, and access to bibliographic databases, among other services.

National-level networks' organization, governance, and financing differ with each network. The Regional Medical Library Network is organized and administered by the NLM, with funds appropriated by the federal government to support the network. NLM provides opportunities for institutions and librarians to offer recommendations concerning its services at both the national and regional levels.

Each of the three national utilities has its own organizational structure. OCLC started as the Ohio College Library Center primarily to serve Ohio academic institutions, and its structure included a board of trustees composed of librarians elected by Ohio libraries. Its governance was restructured in 1978 to include a new board of trustees and a Users' Council; the board is partially self-perpetuating and partially elected by members of the Users' Council. Users' Council members are elected by the regional network members participating in the OCLC system. Financing is primarily through fees for service, with additional funds from foundation and government grants. OCLC is a not-for-profit corporation and is a vendor of services to libraries.

RLIN, founded in 1974 by the RLG, operates as a corporation owned by its members, with a board of governors composed of one representative from each institution. RLG derives its income from three principal sources: partnership dues, RLIN service charges, and grants or loans from foundations and other sources.

WLN was originally a state-owned operation established and operated by the Washington State Library. In 1985 it became a not-for-profit membership organization with a board of trustees and user committees. It is supported principally by service fees and grants.

Services and Functions. A bibliographic utility is an organization that maintains online bibliographic databases, enabling it to offer computer-based support to any interested users. A bibliographic utility maintains components of a national library network data store and provides a standard interface through which bibliographic source centers and individual participants may gain access to the nationwide network. OCLC, RLIN, and WLN are considered bibliographic utilities. The bibliographic source centers serve as brokers or distributors of computer-based bibliographic processing services. A source center gains access to network resources through the facilities of a bibliographic utility; it does not necessarily contribute records directly to or maintain portions of the national library network database. AMIGOS, CLASS, NELINET, PALINET, PRLC, and SOLINET are examples of bibliographic source centers.

Although resource sharing in its broadest definition includes all types of library materials, services, and staff expertise, the principal type of resource sharing is in library materials available through ILL or reciprocal borrowing. Identification of bibliographic information and location can be derived from the online bibliographic services of the utilities, and requests for materials may also be placed through them. Actual delivery of material may be by mail, commercial delivery services, or local—and in some cases statewide—delivery services. Many statewide resource networks provide both identification and delivery of resources with a success rate over 80 percent. Examples of effective statewide networks that have been operating for many years are ILLINET (Illinois), NYSILL (New York), and FLIN (Florida).

Network Developments in Europe are so diverse that generalization is difficult. European networks offer a diversity of structures, sizes, and objectives. They differ from one another in many aspects, such as geographic scope (regional or national), funding (private or public), age (older or newer), structure (centralized or decentralized), and primary emphasis or applications (shared cataloguing, ILL, bibliographic information, or library automation).

One of the major purposes for library cooperatives is resource sharing through cooperative cataloguing and ILL. In the late 1980s the development of online catalogues became an important incentive for cooperation. A major impetus for cooperation was and continues to be sharing costs, which contribute to the reduction of operational costs for individual libraries.

In Austria and France, librarians concentrate their networking activities on serials and ILL through centralized national planning. In Belgium and the Netherlands, emphasis is on local online cataloguing systems and online public access catalogues. Germany, which has a long tradition of union cataloguing, has one national system, a union catalogue of serials. Regional networks in Germany, based on the states of the federal structure, are supported and run by government agencies. These are bibliographic networks used primarily for shared cataloguing and ILL. Italian librarians are developing decentralized distributed databases with computer-to-computer links. Most Scandinavian networks are national. Denmark, Norway, and Sweden have academic networks; Norway and Sweden also have public library networks. Networking in the United Kingdom is based on the British Library (BL), which produces and makes available national and international bibliographic data. It provides online access through a dial-up connection to the corresponding databases for subscribers registered with the BL-owned BLASE-LINE.

Trends and Issues. The 1980s saw rapid and widespread use of microcomputers in cooperative library functions. The way ILL requests were communicated changed markedly with computerized circulation and interfaces between automated circulation systems, integrated online catalogues and union catalogues, CD-ROMs, and electronic mail and fax transmissions. The increase in the number of requests was somewhat offset by the reduction in the time needed to determine the availability of an item and transmit the request to the lending institution, making ILL more attractive as a supplement to an institution's collection. Document delivery times were still longer than desirable, but full-text databases and electronic document delivery offered viable solutions.

The impact of improved resource sharing on an individual library's collection development policy cannot be underestimated. Size of collection may not be as important a criterion for excellence as availability and access through resource sharing. Issues and problems must be considered carefully—responsibility for collection development at the local level cannot be replaced by resource sharing, no matter how efficient the services. Reproduction of documents and journal articles raises copyright issues, and new technologies involve new players, such as the carriers, gateway operators, systems licensors, and database producers. All of these concerns are manageable if librarians, information scientists, publishers, and information entrepreneurs work toward the same goal of equal opportunity of access for all who desire it regardless of the individual's location, social, economic, or physical condition, or level of intellectual achievement.

The trend from the 1970s on was toward networking for mutual benefit, whereby each participant in the cooperative effort contributed not equally but fairly and to the best of its ability. Its contribution might take the form of skill, knowledge, money, resources, or technology. A successful network depended on a clear focus on the problems and issues to be addressed, on a commitment to cooperation by its participants, and on leadership by its governing authority, staff, and user groups.

Shortly after the introduction of laser disks the then-Executive Director of NCLIS, Alphonse F. Trezza, in a talk on a national periodical system, speculated that the trend in the 1970s and 80s would definitely be in favor of cooperation, networking, and sharing resources, but that, because of dramatic changes in technologies, the trend could easily shift in the 90s from centralization to decentralization. He predicted that large amounts of books, journals, and audiovisual materials would be available on laser disks at a modest cost, giving individual libraries the opportunity to enhance their on-site collections. The development of value-added compact-disk union catalogues in the 90s bore out the prediction, providing virtual research library resources for users at the local level.

By the 1990s many library users expected electronic access to information. Librarians, fiscally constrained, remained hopeful that development of the National Research and Education Network (NREN) would enable them to provide effective information systems for the electronic scholar. NREN, added to the bibliographic and online catalogue capabilities smaller networks supplied, offered the ability to share information resources nationwide.

Another trend of the late 1980s and early 1990s involved links among existing networks. The Linked Systems Project established network links among OCLC, RLIN, and other bibliographic utilities that had previously operated as independent, dedicated networks. OCLC formed a link with LC to exchange records over the Linked System using *open systems interface* (OSI) protocols; in 1987 OCLC extended its mission statement to include providing expanded information services to libraries and other information users. In addition to its own vast information resources, OCLC provided access to ERIC, NTIS, AGRICOLA, and other databases in an effort to supply easier, cost-effective access to a broad range of information.

The concept of computer networks has evolved from simple links among a few machines to move digital information around to complete environments in which many users can communicate and share information resources. As with any major advance, this change results in changes in policy and practice at individual institutions and on a national level. A thorough review and evaluation of the problems and benefits of networks will be in order. As technologies develop, librarians will continue to face tough decisions on how to harness new potentials in ways that best serve their patrons. Just what are the cost benefits and trade-offs? Are the library director's time and resources better used in operating the library or in devoting many hours and days to discussing cooperative programs and trying to work out the jurisdictional, programmatic, and financial problems? Is access to electronic databases a viable alternative to traditional collection development based on printed materials?

Cooperative systems and resulting service levels can and do solve some kinds of problems, but it can be argued that the field has gone too far, looking to networking as a solution for deficiencies and problems it cannot cure. Creative use of the latest technology may make libraries less dependent on others and make them more self-sufficient, but it would be a mistake to take self-sufficiency to the extreme. Interaction, mutual cooperation, and sharing and working together are essential for the survival of society; libraries and librarians are part of that process. The trend in the future, therefore, may be toward more selective networking, toward more methodical use of and interfacing among technologies, and toward a different balance between the traditional, the current, and the future. Consistent commitments are needed to preserve the knowledge of the past, serve the present, and plan for the future.

REFERENCES

Henriette D. Avram, "LSP and Library Network Services in the Future," *EDUCOM Bulletin* (1988).

Jack Burkett, *Library and Information Networks in Western Europe* (1983).

Joe W. Kraus, "Prologue to Library Cooperation," *Library Trends* (1975).

Pat Molholt, "Library Networking: The Interface of Ideas and Actions," Office of Library Programs, U.S. Department of Education (1988).

Karl Wilhelm Neubauer and Esther R. Dyer, *European Library Networks* (1990).

U.S. National Commission on Libraries and Information Science, *Towards a National Program for Library and Information Services: Goals for Action* (1975).

Curt D. Wormann, "Aspects of International Library Cooperation, Historical and Contemporary," *Library Quarterly* (1968).

ALPHONSE F. TREZZA

Library Education

For several decades, library education as reflected through curricula changed at a sluggish pace, with only minor adjustments to content and structure; however, fundamental and more rapid curricular revision has been characteristic of the period after 1975. Several factors precipitated curriculum change in North America:

(1) The revision adopted in 1972 by the American Library Association of its *Standards for Accreditation* of library education programs leading to the first professional degree, the Master's degree. The previous standards had been in effect since 1952. The new standards, which encourage flexibility, are more guidelines than standards; therefore, each school has great latitude in curriculum development, and most curricula reflect the predominant philosophy of librarianship at the institutions that offer them.

(2) The notable influx into library schools of library educators holding doctorates. This development resulted in large part from fellowships available for doctoral study in librarianship through the Higher Education Act of 1965. Approximately three-quarters of the full-time faculty teaching in schools holding membership in the Association for Library and Information Science Education (ALISE) have completed their doctorates. While these library educators agree that Master's education is fundamentally professional education, they bring to education for librarianship concerns and experience that encompass more than the day-to-day operational concerns of library institutions.

(3) The increasing number of undergraduate, joint-degree, sixth-year certificate, and Ph.D. programs as important components of library education programs. In the institutions where these programs exist, they affect the curriculum available to Master's degree students.

(4) The far-reaching developments in society, in technology, and in bibliography since the 1960s. One indication of the recognition of the great changes in the library environment is the trend toward changing library school names to include the broader term "information." Of the 61 American and Canadian schools admitting students and holding full accreditation from the ALA in 1985, 42 had changed their names to add in the word information.

In order to accommodate these and many other factors, change in curricular content and structure has come to characterize contemporary library education programs. Some Master's programs contain specially structured required curriculum components and some extended the number of required credit hours. While the modal number of graduate-level academic credits required to complete the degree remains 36 semester hours or its equivalent in quarter hours, required courses vary from as few as 28 to more than 50 semester hours; nineteen schools require more than 36 semester-equivalent credits for award of the Master's degree. Because most library educators and many practitioners agree that the basic knowledge now required for librarianship has expanded and, to a lesser degree, concur that librarians should develop a certain (although as yet undetermined) level of competence in an area of specialization prior to receiving the Master's degree, it is understandable that there appears to be a desire for, if not a trend toward, increasing the number of credit hours required for the first professional degree. The question of program length is probably the key harbinger of fundamental curriculum change taking place in library education today.

Fundamentals in Library Education. The ALA's Committee on Accreditation (COA) gives the following as the basic content areas that all Master's programs must cover: (1) an understanding of the role of the library as an educational and informational agency; (2) an understanding of the theories of collecting, building, and organizing library materials for use; (3) a knowledge of information sources and an ability to assist the user of library materials in locating and interpreting desired items; and (4) knowledge of the principles of administration and organization to provide information services. Translated into curriculum structure in Master's programs, these four content areas constitute what has come to be known as the "core." Of 51 schools reporting for the *ALISE Statistical Report,* no school reported fewer than eight hours of course work required of all students; one school reported 24 required hours; and the typical requirement is from 12 to 15 hours (21 schools).

Because curriculum revision, especially at the level of the core, is so characteristic of today's schools, it has become difficult to describe a typical core curriculum. The required hours seem to be principally devoted to the traditional content area of librarianship that came into acceptance in the 1940s and 1950s, including courses covering reference, materials selection, cataloguing and classification, and administration. Courses or course components dealing with the library as a societal institution were introduced in the late 1960s and early 1970s and remain in the typical required core. The limitations imposed by this largely library institution-focused curriculum have come under careful scrutiny, however. Integration and expansion of core content to add course components in information science appears to be the present direction; even though there is no agreement as to the basis for an *integrated* core in librarianship, a significant number of schools are creating and implementing such curricular structures.

The first attempt at offering an integrated core curriculum was undertaken in the 1960s under the leadership of Jesse Shera at Case Western Reserve University. Since then, many schools have introduced and revised variations of an integrated core. Some include a required "foundations of librarianship" course, coupled with a small number of separate, largely skill-based courses. Another approach is a totally integrated core, usually consisting of 9 to 12 credit hours that may be taken either in a block or in a sequence of a primary 6 hours followed by 3 to 6 additional hours. These integrated core curricula subsume substantial parts of the traditional core of reference, cataloguing, materials selection, and administration and add significant components dealing with foundations, communications, the research process, media, and most notably information science. The integrated core emphasizes the view that there are elements common to all types of libraries and other information services that include both theoretical and philosophical fundamentals, as well as skill. The central institutional focus remains the library, but other institutional and independent work settings and roles are included.

A class in bibliography at Pennsylvania State University, c. 1894.

In those schools with the longest experience with integrated core curricula, notably Drexel University and the universities of North and South Carolina, the integrated core approach has had influence on the entire curriculum, especially in reducing redundancy and providing individual faculty with a shared knowledge base of those students who have completed the core.

An abbreviated, generalized outline for a hypothetical integrated core curriculum is an follows:

I. Libraries and Society

  A. Communications
     Information—its meaning, interpretation, dissemination
  B. Library role in the communication process
     User needs; comparison with other information agencies; library and information science as a profession.
  C. Social role of information institutions
     Meeting the needs of clients
  D. Political and economic context of information institutions
     Library in its institutional setting, its administrative structure, means of support, legal base
  E. Freedom of information, intellectual freedom, and copyright
  F. Forms of communication media
     Film, audio tape, telecommunications, other media

II. Library Services and Materials

  A. Information institutions as service systems
  B. Mechanization of library services
     Computer usage; computer languages and programming
  C. Types of materials; types of collections; types of libraries and users; technique and principles of selection; selection tools; collection maintenance

D. Collection access
 Bibliographic descriptions; subject analysis and description; physical access

E. Information seeking
 Reference services; materials and automated services; reference interview

III. Research (as a means of studying concerns in library and information science)

Problem identification, research techniques, design, data collection and treatment. Communication of research results.

IV. Management

A. Planning, organizing, staffing, directing, controlling
B. Systems analysis
C. Effectiveness measurement
D. Interlibrary cooperation and organization

Returning to the traditional core of reference, cataloguing and classification, administration, and selection, it can easily be seen that the integrated core does indeed subsume these topics, but important elements emphasizing conceptual and methodological concerns are added. Especially noteworthy are (1) the comparison of libraries and librarians with other institutions, professions, and occupations that provide information services; (2) identification of user needs and behaviors and the roles of information professionals in identifying and responding to them; (3) introduction of technology and information science to all who will become professional librarians; (4) recognition that knowledge of the content and process of research is essential to all library professionals; and (5) acknowledgment of the increasing responsibility of all professional librarians in the management of library operations.

The emphasis on the core curriculum in library education, especially the inclusion in the core of the concerns and contributions of information science and other disciplines, indicates the strong desire of library educators to maintain the traditional generalist curriculum and to head off a possible breakup of first professional degree education into specializations. However, holding together education for the information professions may well be beyond the capacity of most library education programs as they are presently structured in relatively autonomous graduate schools. It may be that mergers of related departments, as had been accomplished at Rutgers University in its School of Communications, Information, and Library Studies, will be necessary to integrate education for the information professions. The 1984 ALISE/ALA initiative to bring together professionals interested in accreditation of information-related education programs may indicate whether it will be possible to integrate education for the information professions, or whether education for librarianship will remain principally education for those preparing to work in libraries.

The curriculum of librarianship, which through the 1960s had been focused almost exclusively on the library, in most cases continues to emphasize specialization in the profession by the type of institution in which the professional might expect to work—in school, public, academic, or special libraries. There are indications from curricular changes that this emphasis is declining and that specialization in the field could better focus on type of client served (such as student, researcher, or recreational user) or information function pursued (such as indexer/abstracter, collection developer, information interpreter, or information manager), disregarding the institutional setting of the professional. The development of integrated core curricula is one of the key indicators of this shift.

Specialist Areas. So long as the vast majority of Master's degree holders continue to find employment in library institutions, and so long as these institutions require only that their beginning professionals possess the degree—without much regard to the courses taken to obtain that degree—true educational specialization will be concentrated in on-the-job experience and post-Master's programs. (School/media librarianship is the only type of clearly developed library specialization offered in most schools.) Regardless of the many reasons given for continued reliance on the generalist curriculum, a growing number of

University of Iowa Archives

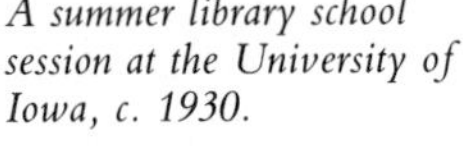

A summer library school session at the University of Iowa, c. 1930.

library educators and practitioners concur that specialist preparation is needed. They agree that the 36-hour Master's curriculum is insufficient for the education of "real" specialists; however, if a school elects to educate only one or two types of information professional, with all courses after the core curriculum focused on selected institutional, subject, or functional areas, then specialization may be possible. Even then 36 hours may be too limited. Some library educators and employers believe that more library education programs should declare a specialty or perhaps small groups of specialty curricula. For example, a school might state that its single purpose is the education of public librarians, and perhaps include tracks for urban and rural public librarians. This type of specialization in a school might have in the curriculum, in addition to its core, such course offerings and distribution as the following:

Required of all students

Political Environment of the Public Library (3)
Economics of Public Service (3)
Systems of Libraries (3)
Administration of Public Libraries (3)

Rural Track	*Urban Track*
Rural Sociology (3)	The City (3)
Regional Planning (3)	Urban Planning (3)
Rural Libraries (3)	Metropolitan and Suburban Libraries (3)
Rural Economics (3)	Urban Economics (3)
Resources for Small Public Libraries (3)	Resources for Large Public Libraries (3)
Rural Library Research (3)	Urban Library Research (3)

This type of specialist program offered totally within the library school could also be developed for academic librarianship to include tracks for university, college, and community college librarians.

Another type of single-purpose curriculum that could be developed in the offerings of a single-purpose school might be the reference specialist. As in the past, many generalist librarians still decide to concentrate in reference service without regard to the type of library in which they might find employment. These students take courses in reference, totaling at least 15 semester hours, which would probably include

Introduction to Reference Service (3)
Resources for the Humanities (3)
Resources for the Social Sciences (3)
Resources for Science and Technology (3)
Government Publications (3)

In today's complex information environment, a single-purpose curriculum of some depth for a reference specialist might well include

Introduction to Reference (3)
Resources for the Humanities (3)
Resources for the Behavioral Sciences (3)
Resources for the Social Sciences (3)
Resources for the Sciences (3)
Resources for Technology (3)
U.S. Government Publications (3)
Government Publications (outside the U.S.) (3)
Serial Publications (3)
Nonprint Media (3)

The Unesco Regional Office for Education in Asia and the Pacific

Library/documentation internship courses being conducted at the Unesco Regional Office for Education, Bangkok.

Online Bibliographic Resources and Services (3)
Information User Studies (3)
Administration of Reference Services (3)

This hypothetical curriculum represents a total of 39 semester hours, of which only 3, Introduction to Reference, might be concentrated in the core. Additional single-subject resource courses could well be added, boosting the number of credits to well over 40. Indeed, a school that chooses to be a reference specialist school could reasonably develop tracks for social science specialists, humanities specialists, and others.

Another route to specialist preparation is through cooperation with other academic departments. While the specialization program by type of library could be pursued in this manner—for example, by having those pursuing academic librarianship taking courses

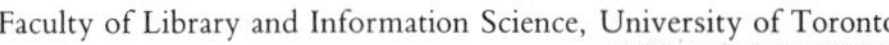

Faculty of Library and Information Science, University of Toronto

A colloquium for doctoral students, Faculty of Library and Information Science, University of Toronto.

A course in classification at the School of Library and Information Science, The University of Western Ontario.

Jerry Golab/The University of Western Ontario Photographic Services

in schools of education and public administration—this path to specialization is especially appropriate for subject specialists. Prospective art librarians might profitably take a variety of courses in art history and fine arts as well as specific courses in the library school. While many students might choose dual Master's degree programs, it would be possible to gain appropriate preparation for a specialty with fewer hours than those needed for a dual degree, provided, of course, that the specialist program is well designed.

The principal reason specializations are not more widely pursued is that library education programs continue to draw their students mainly from their local areas. The largest number of students demand education that is generalist in nature so that they can apply for a wide variety of beginning library positions. There is no national recruiting program for the field and no developed consensus on what specialization consists of; therefore, there is no clear demand for specialization except that created by state regulations for school library/media certification.

Training school for children's librarians, Springfield School station, Pittsburgh, Pennsylvania, 1917.

Carnegie Library of Pittsburgh

While programs of specialization are available in library schools, only a few students choose them and they vary greatly in structure. In reporting to ALISE, 26 schools indicated that they offered a total of more than 64 specialization programs. Twelve schools reported specializations in history; seven reported programs in law or business; many reported the availability of multiple specializations.

One area of specialization in the Master's curriculum that has been demanded especially by library practitioners is management. It is unclear whether practitioners are calling for an actual specialization or for an extension of the curriculum for all librarians in the area of management. There is considerable evidence, based on research studies, continuing education needs assessments, and programs held at professional meetings, that professional librarians are increasingly being used in management and supervisory positions. Traditionally, library schools offered only the core course in general library administration and taught additional administrative knowledge through type-of-library courses. A number of library schools, responding to the need to provide additional administrative knowledge, have introduced advanced general administration courses, and many offer courses in such skills as systems analysis. Courses in the administration of specific library functions such as technical services and public services are also offered at some schools, and many courses dealing with library networking or cooperative systems emphasize administrative aspects. The most prevalent means for providing concentration in administrative aspects of librarianship is through cooperation with other academic departments. Master's students may be encouraged to take courses such as personnel management or organizational behavior in schools of business or public administration.

Only the schools with the largest number of faculty can hope to provide more than one or two specialization programs, although many can offer single-specialized courses such as law, map, music, or archival librarianship. The individual specialized courses do not amount to specialization in the opinion of most concerned people, and these courses are typical in most traditional library education curricula because they are offered based on the expertise available from a particular full-time or adjunct faculty member.

The future development of specialization programs in the 36-hour Master's degree is problematic. Because the COA has approved of the concept of single-purpose programs, there seems to be little compelling argument against them as long as a market exists for such specialists. However, except for some as yet not clearly defined indications from the academic library community, there does not appear to be a market for specialization at the first professional degree level. It is especially difficult for publicly supported library schools to abandon the generalist library education program, because they are expected to train librarians for all types of libraries in their states. Further, the development of specialized library education programs would best be accomplished through a national plan for library education; although a number of writers have called for such a national plan, none is on the horizon.

Trends. It appears that the most likely changes to occur in the education of librarians are that (1) curriculum content will continue to be expanded to emphasize development of competence in the technologically-oriented aspects of the information environment; (2) the number of credit hours required for the first professional degree will increase slightly; and (3) undergraduate education for information professionals, including education for library support staff, will be further developed and more closely articulated with first professional degree programs.

Library education curricula in the 1980s were in a period of scrutiny and change, and curricular change will continue to be the most characteristic element of library education. The inclusion of flexible course structures, such as Issues in Librarianship or Resources in Special Literatures, which will allow library educators to respond rapidly to changes in library and information science, will become essential elements in the curriculum.

ALISE. The Association for Library and Information Science Education was founded in 1915. Its mission is to promote excellence in education for library and information science as a means of increasing the effectiveness of library and information services. ALISE's goals are (1) to provide a forum for the active interchange of ideas and information among library educators; (2) to promote, conduct, and demonstrate research related to teaching and to library and information science; (3) to formulate and promulgate positions on matters of mutual interest to library education; and (4) to cooperate with other organizations on matters of mutual interest.

Membership in the Association is open to both institutions and personal members. Institutional memberships are granted on request to any school in an accredited institution that offers degrees in librarianship or cognate fields; personal membership is open to anyone interested in the goals of the Association.

The curriculum of library education programs is of vital concern to the membership of ALISE. Because this membership is principally made up of faculty of ALA-accredited schools and schools that plan to seek accreditation, the emphasis is greatest on curriculum at the Master's level. ALISE devoted its 1977 annual meeting to the core curriculum and its 1984 annual meeting to undergraduate preparation for the information professions. The Association supports both a general Curriculum Interest Group and several interest groups that emphasize specific curricular components such as online bibliographic services, library history, and research methods. The membership of the ALA Council's Standing Committee on Library Education (SCOLE) is largely composed of members of ALISE. Of chief concern to both SCOLE and ALISE are the continued development and availability to potential information professionals of excellent programs of library education.

REFERENCES

Association for Library and Information Science Education, *Library and Information Science Education Statistical Report* (1980–).

Richard L. Darling and Terry Belanger, editors, *Extended Library Education Programs* (1980).

Arlene T. Dowell, "The Two-Year Master's: Perspectives and Prospects," *Journal of Education for Librarianship* (1978).

King Research, Inc., *Library Human Resources: A Study of Supply and Demand* (1983).

Charles A. Seavey, editor, "Accreditation Conference," *Journal of Education for Library and Information Science* (1984).

JANE ROBBINS-CARTER

Library Education: Continuing Professional Education

Commitment to lifelong learning is important to the library and information science profession because its professionals must themselves participate in lifelong learning in order to perform competently their evolving roles in society. Further, they must be prepared to assist adults in creating a learning society.

IN THE UNITED STATES

Since the early 1960s many professions, including library and information services, have come to realize that continuing professional education (CPE) is an important way to sustain professional competence. See, for example, B. V. Dryer's plan for a comprehensive system for "Lifetime Learning for Physicians" in *Journal of Medical Education* (1962) and the landmark work of Cyril O. Houle, *Continuing Learning in the Professions* (1980).

Unfortunately, despite the recognition of the need for and the importance of CPE, a comprehensive system for CPE has yet to be developed that is accepted by the library and information services profession. Such a system is defined by R. M. Cervero and J. F. Azzaretto in their *Visions of the Future of Continuing Professional Education* as "a complex unity formed of many diverse parts and serving a common purpose."

Rather, the library and information services profession has a host of providers competing for what they believe the market wants without attempting to develop an overall, comprehensive national direction for lifelong professional learning that would best serve society in the information age.

W. J. Haas in a 1992 planning paper for the W. K. Kellogg Foundation entitled "Human Resources for the Management of Information Systems" stated: "Information specialists, by whatever name, are growing in numbers, but they still lack a shared sense of purpose and the kind of cohesion that is required if the information age is to deliver on its promise of supporting substantial public progress."

Definitions. The term *continuing education* (CE) means different things to different people. The definition presented here was included in the American Library Association's "Guidelines for Quality in Continuing Education for Information, Library, and Media Personnel" (1988):

> Continuing education is a learning process which builds on and updates previously acquired knowledge, skills, and attitudes of the individual. Continuing education comes after the preparatory education necessary for involvement in or with information, library, and media services. It is usually self-initiated learning in which individuals assume responsibility for their own development and for fulfilling their need to learn. It is broader than staff development, which is usually initiated by an organization for the growth of its own human resources.

The document goes on to identify goals and benefits in these terms:

> Continuous learning is an obligation of all those who work to identify, select, organize, retrieve, disseminate, and make accessible the record of human thought and actions. The goal of continuing education is to improve information, library, and media services by maintaining or improving the competence of practitioners. Regular participation in continuing education activities enables the practitioners to: refresh basic education by mastering new concepts in a constantly changing environment; keep up with the new knowledge and skills required to perform their roles responsibly; prepare for specialization in a new area; enjoy the intrinsic satisfaction resulting from learning.

CPE, therefore, is concerned with the development of competent persons—those who can apply knowledge, understanding, and skills in performance at some level of proficiency. Continuing education, these statements imply, is more than listening to a lecture, attending a workshop, or using a new device; the learner must be able to demonstrate increased competency in actual performance.

The Need. A critical issue facing the social system of the U.S.—the impending obsolescence of the nation's work force, particularly in the professional sector—was underscored in the 1983 report of the National Commission on Excellence in Education, *A Nation at Risk: The Imperative for Educational Reform,* which included identification of the problems affecting American leaders in CPE and retraining programs. The library/information community responded in 1984 with the publication *Alliance for Excellence,* which presented 13 recommendations for the alliance of home, school, and library as essential to attaining excellence in education and in attaining a learning society. It offered a sound and persuasive vision of what the library of the near future could and should be as a center of the learning society. In the area of CPE, the report recommended: "Everyone in the library community—librarians, their employers, their graduate schools, funding agencies, membership organizations—should accept the precept that professional development is a continuing responsibility shared by them all. Every library and library system should budget annually to cover continuing education costs for professionals and other staff."

In 1991 the White House Conference on Library and Information Services requested that the President and Congress "formally recognize all libraries as educational institutions for lifelong learning by specifically including libraries in all relevant legislation, regulations, and policy statements" and asked "that libraries be designated as educational agencies and that the President include members of the library community in implementing *America 2000.*"

Assessing CPE Needs. Three areas of analysis are essential for effective CPE needs assessment: (1) The work setting, which changes continually through the input of new knowledge, new technologies, and new service expectations of the public. The environment is the motivating and directing force for CPE. (2) Prospective learner needs, interests, and characteristics. P. O'Donnell gives a comprehensive but succinct survey of ways to conduct audience CE needs assessments in the March-April 1991 issue of *Library Personnel News.* (3) Determining the provider's capability to design and deliver quality CPE experiences. Criteria include: organization and management capabilities; expertise of the presenters vis-à-vis programs offered; adequate facilities conducive to good learning; appropriate learning methods and tools; targeted levels of competence identified; involvement of targeted learners in the planning process; effective delivery systems; honest marketing; accurate record keeping; and provision for recognition.

Target Groups. The 1973 study *Continuing Library and Information Science Education,* sponsored by the National Commission on Libraries and Information Service (NCLIS), found that there was considerable concern throughout the profession for the CE needs not only of professionals, but also of all levels of personnel—including support staffs and all those associated with libraries. It therefore underscored the importance of all CE providers identifying accurately the target audience for which a particular offering is developed and to indicate the level of difficulty of each offering—beginning, intermediary, or advanced.

Paraprofessionals. By 1992 a vigorous trend existed among paraprofessionals (defined as employees, regardless of title, who do not hold Master's degrees in Library Science) to push for CE opportunities and to organize themselves to achieve this goal. Before this trend emerged, up to the mid or late 1980s, most people involved in CPE assumed that the education of paraprofessionals was the responsibility of the local library or library system, rather than an issue of national concern. But programs in conferences for paraprofessionals have become common. As paraprofessionals take on more and more library functions at increasingly responsible levels, formal provisions for continued learning are becoming a necessity to assure high-quality library operations and services.

Throughout the profession there are growing numbers of CE providers targeting programs for paraprofessionals. The first national conference directed toward paraprofessionals, in 1990, was sponsored by the School of Library and Information Studies at the University of Wisconsin–Madison. Attendees came from all parts of the U.S. and the enthusiastic response led to provision for large biannual conferences. Major issues of the profession were addressed; the chief difference between this meeting and CPE conferences was the target audience.

Providers of CPE. From the bombardment of literature sent by mail and the thick catalogues produced by a wide range of CPE providers, there might seem to be an overabundance of learning opportunities for library/information practitioners. Houle cautions against such a belief: "Too few professionals continue to learn throughout their lives, and the opportunities provided to aid and encourage them to do so are far less abundant than they should be." The major providers of CE opportunities in library and information studies are associations; library education programs in colleges and universities; employing institutions; state library agencies; the federal government; vendors; foundations; and autonomous groups.

Associations. In general associations, by playing a central role in the profession for CPE, have heeded the advice of Malcolm Knowles to serve as "learning communities for their members, providing research, support, and excitement to foster their members' growth, development, and adaptation to change." They are expected to identify needs and coming trends in the field; provide CPE publications; identify CPE resources; and set standards and guidelines for CPE. Unfortunately, associations have not collaborated more to provide opportunities with less overlap and more systematic coverage of knowledge and skills; they have made only minimal effort to work with other disciplines in developing cooperative programs.

An inquiry into professional associations in library and information science in 1987 indicated that CPE showed some general trends, including a gain in priority ranking as a major function of associations; deep involvement in making practitioners at all levels comfortable with technology; recognition of the effectiveness and efficiency of having paid professional CPE directors; and increased concern for quality assurance of CPE.

The 11 Divisions and 16 Round Tables of the *American Library Association* (ALA), in cooperation with its Office for Library Personnel Resources (OLPR), issue each year a brochure entitled "ALA Is Continuing Education" that gives an overview of the scores of CPE activities available to members, in addition to the wealth of programs at the Annual Conference, the development of learning centers, clearing-house functions, and learning programs in publications, poster sessions, and the ALA Library Video Network.

ALA's interest in CPE issues increased markedly in the 1980s. In 1984 the Council voted to incorporate the Continuing Library Education Network and Exchange (CLENE) into ALA as a Round Table (CLENERT). Established in 1975 at the School of Library and Information Science at the Catholic University of America with a grant from the U.S. Office of Education, CLENE was the only association in the profession that had CE as its sole mission. It used federal funds to develop the National Council on Quality Continuing Education, which prepared "Criteria for Quality." In 1987 the Continuing Education Subcommittee of ALA's Standing Committee on Library Education (SCOLE) adapted the "Criteria for Quality" into "Guidelines for Quality in Continuing Education for Information, Library, and Media Personnel." The ALA Council adopted these guidelines in 1988.

Members of the *American Association of Law Libraries* (AALL) took a major step toward CPE when the Association hired its first professional CE staff member. The Professional Development Officer is charged with providing administrative support for the AALL's CPE programs, including its summer institutes and workshops.

Darlene Weingand prepared the 1992 CPE report for the *Association for Library and Information Science Education* (ALISE), one of a series of annual reports on the topic. Of the 59 schools accredited by the ALA in the period covered (1990–91), 45 offered CPE in some form, 13 reported no activity, and 1 claimed to "define CE differently." The survey tabulated only events targeted for non-degree-seeking participants; it tabulated events with academic credit separately from events without academic credit.

In the non-credit category, overall attendance increased by 1 percent over the preceding year, but the number of events decreased by 2 percent—the lowest number in five years. The survey found a dramatic increase in "institute/symposium/conference/forum" events, up 105 percent; short courses, up 125 percent; and "other formats," up 233 percent. The author commented, "The explosive increase in 'Other Formats' underscores the trend toward alternative delivery systems, as this category includes study tours, correspondence, and telecommunications opportunities. In addition, some of the 'Short Courses' also were delivered via teleconferencing networks." The number of workshops rose 10 percent; seminars decreased by 23 percent; and colloquia held steady. Conference attendance rose 72 percent; more events were held on campuses; and many more programs were offered for CEU.

In the for-credit category (but not for degree-seeking students), the number of one- or two-week short courses for one credit went up 42 percent and evening courses for one credit went up 230 percent. The total enrollment for one- or two-week courses went up 49 percent; for three- or four-week courses, 38 percent; for five- or six-week courses, 233 percent; for seven-week courses, up 78 percent; for evening courses, up 60 percent; and for "other" (one-day) events, up a huge 421 percent. These figures show a dramatic increase in the number interested in continuing their education. The survey also found an increase in the number of faculty members teaching non-credit offerings as part of their teaching load.

The University of Wisconsin–Madison offered the largest number of CE events in the year surveyed: 93 events, serving more than 2,700 students. Columbia University followed with 54 events that served more than 1,600 students. The survey concluded that CPE courses attracted large audiences in spite of the economic constraints of the year.

For academic libraries, the *Association of Research Libraries* (ARL), through its Office of Management Services, conducts a Training Skills Institute throughout the U.S. and Canada. It is designed to aid in developing in-house training programs by improving the training competencies of those who participate. Its programs include basic and advanced management skills institutes, management skills institutes for directors, special focus workshops, and management training films.

In 1957 the *Medical Library Association* (MLA) began a series of national seminars on CE; by the late 1970s, it had a full-scale national program in operation. The Association maintains a competency-based certification system for medical librarians, with credentials issued by MLA state agencies based on specific educational credentials and experience. Some state certificates last five years, others for life; some states require periodic relicensure or recertification, in most cases based on mandatory CE. The MLA has a full-time Director of CPE to administer its program. In its strategic plan, it places CE programs at the forefront of its priorities. Its policies are greatly influenced by the shift from knowledge-oriented to performance-oriented CPE programs. The Association develops self-study courses for its members.

After 1984, when it identified CPE as its first priority, the *Special Libraries Association* (SLA) initiated a wide array of CE opportunities under a full-time Professional Education Director. It offers courses at its annual meeting, a Winter Education Conference, and regional programs in six to ten locations in the U.S. and Canada. An annual two-day State-of-the-Art Institute in Washington, D.C., features issues that have not been explored in a conference setting. SLA's most advanced CPE offering is a two-day Executive Management Program. The Association offers a self-study program, "Education to Go," covering business and library-related topics. And in 1992 SLA began a Japan Information Access Project to guide business leaders, scientists, educators, and other professionals through Japan's linguistic and cultural information.

At the state library association level, almost all have either CE or professional development (PD) goals. Many have written guidelines for CE and PD; others rely on close ties with academic institutions to assist in reaching these goals. They turn to library school faculty, consultants outside the library profession, and the ALA to provide CE and PD.

Professional Schools. Houle made a persuasive case for the continuum of library education when he urged that a professional school's chief responsibility relative to its alumni was to develop a "lifelong student body." He outlined specific steps to make this concept a reality, pointing out that the school, after investing heavily in its graduates, should help them keep on the cutting edge of new developments. Accepting this challenge and using a variety of delivery systems would seem to be one way for a school to build a potential market, fulfilling the needs of alumni and earning needed revenue during tight economic times. But library schools were slow to accept the concept.

Employing Institutions have the most to gain when members of their staffs improve their abilities through CPE. In an essay in *American Libraries* (May 1992), Patricia Glass Schuman, then President of ALA, asked why the profession pays so little attention to education, training, job design, and career development for the majority of library workers. "Whatever the reason," she wrote, "it's time to recognize that the fate of all library workers is intertwined." She concluded: "Americans count on libraries for their right to know, but it is people, not places, who make the right to know a reality. It will take all of us, focusing less on what we did yesterday and more on what we can do together tomorrow, to make sure it happens!"

State Library Agencies. The goal of the agencies is to promote and provide a program of continuing education for library personnel at all levels, including trustees. They work to achieve this goal by cooperating with library schools and professional associations and by sponsoring CPE opportunities such as meetings and workshops. Their influence reaches to all residents in each state and determines both qualitatively and quantitatively the level of library resources and services in the state. A survey of the Chief Officers of State Library Agencies in 1989 found that they thought the greatest needs for CE were in (1) applying new technologies used in libraries, (2) management and administration, (3) budgeting, including grantsmanship, and (4) strategic planning. In that survey they listed ethics for the first time as an area needing CE. State librarians expressed concern that their professional staffs had a heavy workload in helping paraprofessionals learn the core activities of reference work.

The Federal Government supports professional education for librarians through many programs, but only two are targeted specifically for library and information science education, the Higher Education Act (HEA) and the Library Services and Construction Act (LSCA). The Department of Education oversees these programs through the Division of Library Programs in the Office of Educational Research and Improvement. The purpose of the Library Career Training Program, Title II-B of HEA, is to provide grants to train librarians and to establish, develop, and expand library programs. In the first 25 years of the program, starting in 1966, almost 21,000 individuals received HEA assistance in training or retraining for library service. Most of the funds appropriated under LSCA go directly to state library agencies to meet the needs identified in their long-range plans.

Delivery Systems. The approach to education for adults that emerged in the 1970s and continued in the 1990s embraces the concepts that CPE can be achieved effectively only by understanding the prodigious lifelong learning ability of adults, their need to be self-directed, and their need for CPE throughout their careers. New patterns of learning and a host of alternative delivery systems have developed from the recognition that school is only one provider of professional education. New delivery systems have been called such names as "open learning," "independent study," "self-directed learning," "competency-based learning," "home study," "non-traditional education," "contract learning," and "distance learning."

The workshop, where people can interact with others in solving problems, is still the most used delivery system for CPE in the profession. But distance learning enables people to learn at their own pace, place, and time and provides those in remote areas with learning options they would not otherwise have. The basic concepts of distance learning have been practiced for more than a hundred years, and many models have been developed. Distance learning involves a courses system, for creating, producing, and distributing learning materials, and a student system, for enrollment, support, and evaluation. The essential features of distance learning include curricula designed around a modular course structure; highly centralized development of multimedia course materials; and learning based on independent study by people working at a distance from, and not normally meeting, those organizing or providing the materials. A wide range of media may be used, including books, radio and television broadcasts, audio- and videocassettes, films, computer-assisted learning, and teleconferencing.

Delivery systems in use today include videotapes, such as those produced by the ALA Library Video Network (LVN) to provide high-quality informational and staff training programs. LVN also produces *Library Video Magazine,* which contains video coverage of significant library news and trends.

A delivery system used increasingly by library associations, first popularized by the MLA (which put quality control measures into its design, implementation, and evaluation), is a packaged series of CPE programs administered first in conjunction with annual conferences and then offered separately wherever there is a demand.

"Motivation: A Vital Force in the Organization," a five-module home study course from CLENE, includes narrative text, self-tests, exercises, readings, selected materials for further study, forms for evaluation of each module, and final examinations. Students send their exercises to assigned faculty advisors, who have personal student profiles to aid in counseling students. Catholic University markets the program, and students can take it for academic credit or CEU.

The University of Wisconsin–Madison offers about 20 short courses and four semester-length courses in both teleconferencing and correspondence/tape formats. The North Carolina Department of Public Instruction saved about $34,000 in staff time, travel, and other costs by presenting a three-hour satellite staff development workshop for all library media personnel in 1991. The program provided classroom instruction for students and staff development for teachers and librarians in remote areas of the state.

Poster sessions for information exchange were introduced at the 1982 ALA Annual Conference. They proved so valuable that they became a regular feature of ALA Conferences.

Credit and Recognition. The Continuing Education Unit (CEU) was developed to give recognition for participation in the noncredit, nontraditional forms of learning in the profession. A uniform measure to assist in the accumulation and exchange of standardized credit for participation in CE activities, one CEU is defined as "ten contact hours of participation in an organized continuing education activity under responsible sponsorship, capable direction, and qualified instruction." The International Association for Continuing Education and Training (IACET) published *Continuing Education Unit Guidelines,* which explains the administrative and program criteria that must be satisfied. For example, an institution awarding CEU must keep a permanent record for each individual who receives one and must provide transcripts on request.

Starting in 1976, associations, state library agencies, and universities used the CEU to give credit for nontraditional learning experiences. For many years members of the ALA debated it. In early 1991 OLPR surveyed state library agencies to learn the standing of and need for the CEU. The Subcommittee on Continuing Education presented a poster session at the 1991 ALA Conference to learn whether members wanted the Association to offer the CEU for attendance at appropriate ALA events. As a result of these surveys, SCOLE recommended that the ALA revise its 1979 policy, "The American Library Association and Continuing Education," to include ALA-awarded CEU and to establish a central CEU registry for ALA members.

Concern for accountability at both professional and paraprofessional levels led the ALA to begin studies in 1992 on certification for librarians. Certification for support staff has been proposed as a means of recognizing those who have attained a level of knowledge or skill and of encouraging others to reach that level.

Criteria for Quality. In 1984 IACET (then called the Council on the Continuing Education Unit) issued *Principles of Good Practice in Continuing Education,* the result of a three-year project to promote standards in the field. *Principles,* which consists of 18 principles and 70 statements of amplification and interpretation, provides a reference document for organizations developing their own CE standards and criteria.

The ALA's "Guidelines for Quality in Continuing Education for Information, Library, and Media Personnel" include criteria for five kinds of CE strategies: group programs and activities, individualized programs and activities, instructional materials and technologies, continuing education providers, and learning consultants for individualized continuing education programs. In each area, assessment factors are presented after each criterion listed. For example, under continuing education providers, criteria are administration, human resources, facilities, and resources. Specific assessment factors are presented in the form of questions.

Development of the "Guidelines" is a major step forward for the ALA. If it is to provide direction for profession-wide CPE, it must have in place formal written documentation that speaks to the critical issue of quality.

INTERNATIONAL PERSPECTIVES

International Organizations. Many international organizations have been active in CPE in the field of library and information science, especially in developing countries. They have spread awareness of the value of CPE by organizing short courses, supporting fledgling CPE programs, providing for faculty development, developing educational guidelines, providing funds for students, organizing conferences with CPE components, and publishing proceedings for wide distribution. For example:

The *Commonwealth Library Association* (COMLA) has contributed to CPE in developing countries by encouraging the preparation of papers for workshops and seminars and through its regular quarterly newsletter, which records developments in the field of education and training.

The *International Federation for Documentation* (FID) has an active Education and Training Committee (FID/ET) that organizes international meetings and publishes proceedings, plans, proposals, and differences of opinion. It publishes a *Newsletter on Education and Training Programs for Information Personnel* and maintains a Clearinghouse of Information Education Training Materials at Syracuse University. Its regional commission for Latin America regularly includes in its journal, *Revista Latinoamericana de Documentación,* announcements about courses and discussions of CPE activities.

The *International Federation of Library Associations and Institutions* (IFLA) includes in the objectives of all five of its core programs items relevant to the education and training of library and information personnel. For example, "Advancement of Librarianship in the Third World" stated that its top goal for the period 1992–97 was "to assist library staff, library schools, and library associations in education and training." IFLA has a Section on Education and Training in its Division of Education and Research.

Following the 1985 World Conference on Continuing Professional Education for the Library and Information Science Professions, held at Palos Hills, Illinois, under the direction of Brooke E. Sheldon and

Elizabeth W. Stone, IFLA accepted a recommendation from the delegates (from 31 countries and as many U.S. states) and in 1986 established the *Continuing Professional Education Round Table* (CPERT). This Round Table has promoted CPE-related programs at each annual IFLA Conference since 1986, created the *CPERT Newsletter* and an international network of volunteers who provide news of CPE activities in their areas, published *Continuing Professional Education: An IFLA Guidebook* (1991), prepared three bibliographies on distance learning worldwide, and maintained an up-to-date mailing list of more than 600 people in more than 60 countries who have shown an interest in its activities.

Africa. The root causes of the poor performance of African librarianship are not external, but the internal weaknesses of the system, according to Kingo Mchombu. He presented a paper at the 1990 IFLA Conference in Stockholm, published as "Which Way African Librarianship?" *IFLA Journal* (1991), that makes interesting background reading for studying CPE in Africa.

Mchombu, affiliated with the Department of Library and Information Studies at the University of Botswana, urges reform of African librarianship using a reference framework different from that of the Anglo-American model. The crucial problems to be addressed are failure of librarianship to adapt to African conditions, inadequate on-the-job training in libraries, weak library associations, and weak library-school programs. "Relevant training whether offered in a library school or as part of continuing education should be doing at least two things: first, suffusing the entire programme with a consciousness of the African information environment as the foundation on which present libraries are created; second, developing an in-depth programme of specialization to include repackaging of information, indigenous knowledge resources, and development librarianship."

A few library schools are emerging that do not slavishly follow overseas models but provide an education in the context of the social, political, and economic environment in which the graduates will work. Two examples are Kenya's Moi University and the University of Botswana, where formulating a curriculum is preceded by surveying the education and training needs of library and information workers. Many students take courses abroad that are designed for a totally different information environment.

Mchombu's suggestions for reform include providing management training for Africa's top librarians as part of a CE program; recognizing that Africa's information needs cannot be fully satisfied by importing information products from overseas; bridging the information gap by using desktop publishing to produce small-scale information resources; and reforming African librarianship into "development librarianship," capable of making a major contribution to the development of Africa.

Sub-Saharan Africa. According to librarians from five African nations attending the 1985 Palos Hills CPE conference, barriers to developing CPE include lack of funding, lack of adequate leadership to teach courses (especially in information science and technology), poor coordination of the array of offerings, absence of national policies on CE, and inadequate materials, facilities, and equipment. Other problems are disruptive political conditions, lack of publicity for the programs developed, the apathy of administrators, poor support for library schools, too heavy reliance on foreign technology and foreign-published texts and syllabi, and the problems librarians have in adapting what they learn abroad to the totally different context at home.

South Africa. South Africa's setting in both the First and Third Worlds presents situations and problems different from those of most other African nations. The chief providers of CPE are library schools, library associations, and employing institutions. The South African Institute for Librarianship and Information Science (SAILIS) promotes CPE on a national scale, especially through its Committee for Non-Formal Training. Its functions are identifying training needs, sharing information about available opportunities, initiating new programs, preparing guidelines for organizing courses, evaluating requests for funding, and gathering reports on programs presented. A network of individuals in the regional branches of SAILIS promotes, encourages, and assists with non-formal training and CPE. Presentation of courses, symposia, and training is done chiefly by libraries and departments of librarianship. SAILIS publishes a monthly newsletter that includes a calendar of forthcoming CPE opportunities.

The University of South Africa, Pretoria, one of the largest correspondence universities in the world, offers parts of its library and information program to practitioners throughout the continent (and abroad) who wish to update their knowledge without seeking a degree. A major setback at the university level was the discontinuance of the Department of Library and Information Science at the University of Witwatersrand, Johannesburg, which offered CPE opportunities as well as advanced degrees.

Among the chief barriers to CPE in South Africa are the great distances to travel and lack of sufficient funding. Increased use of teleconferencing reduces costs and enables individuals to maintain contact with others that would otherwise be impossible.

Asia and the Pacific. In a paper at the 1991 IFLA Conference, Maxine K. Rochester of the School of Information Studies at the Charles Sturt University in Australia pointed out that library and information services, as part of the high-priority emphasis on education, are seen as one of the prerequisites for development in the region. In addition to giving many examples of government and non-government agencies and international organizations already active in the area, she described how the Asian and Pacific countries have joined together to solve their own problems with organizations such as the Congress of Southeast Asian Librarians (CONSAL). She mentioned that Indonesia needed to train 150 professional librarians and 450 library technicians each year, and even more if the government carried out its plans to create village libraries. The country's present schools could not meet this staggering need, but the Indonesian Library Association was gaining strength.

The challenge throughout Asia is to find and encourage leaders who will develop innovative services the local people need and use, as well as curriculum and teaching materials designed for the local social, political, and economic environment. IFLA members could help achieve these goals by encouraging informal communication on a person-to-person basis, making twinning arrangements between library schools in various countries, exchanging staff and students between individual libraries, and providing funds so colleagues from developing countries can attend international conferences.

Australia. The Australian Library and Information Association (ALIA), formerly the Library Association of Australia, has long placed a high priority on CPE and considers it one of its major services to its members. Priorities include advanced management studies, technology updates, in-depth study in special areas, marketing and lobbying, preservation and conservation, and providing information for special groups. Initiatives include developing a database of all CE activities in each state to enable managers to plan CPE more effectively for members of their staffs. ALIA's Board of Education identified four areas of need and invited information providers to develop self-paced accredited packages for individuals to use in four areas: making the most of a teleconference, choosing a system to automate a small library, how to approach AACR2, and promoting library services to minority groups. The federal government, in industrial agreements it supervises, planned to guarantee training for workers in the form of training leave, CPE, or modules (building-block credits) that would add up to a specific qualification or level of achievement.

China. Ministry of Culture statistics for 1986 list more than 32,000 libraries and some 275,000 staff members, but few of the library personnel are professional. Writing in 1992, Dong Xiaoying of the Department of Library and Information Science at Beijing University found that the proportion had risen sharply from 1980 to 1989. At the beginning of the decade, only 2 to 5 percent had formal or informal education; by its end, between 30 and 50 percent had. Sun Yun-chou of the Department of Library and Information Science, Huyadong Teachers University, Shanghai, explains that in China "professional education" means formal education to which students are admitted through uniform national examinations. CPE is viewed as supplementary or spare-time education. It includes on-the-job training, vocational schooling sponsored by national or regional libraries, radio and television programs for college studies, adult education, secondary specialized schools, short-term workshops or seminars, and correspondence courses. The advantage of correspondence education in China is great. It makes maximum use of existing faculties, equipment, and facilities, and helps the central government achieve its goal of greatest output for the least cost. Also, correspondence students can correlate on-the-job experience with text materials and apply theory to library practice while learning.

The many programs offered are viewed as an effective way to meet the urgent need for library personnel. Dong Xiaoying wrote that the trend of CPE in China would be to give priority training to all levels of personnel based on their working categories and updating the knowledge of middle-level librarians without MLS degrees, especially in the areas of library management, reference service, material conservation, and application of computers and modern technologies. Until 1978 there were only two library schools in China; by 1989 50 more had been added; even with them, the professional schools could not provide anything like the number needed, and CPE appeared to be part of the answer to the problem.

Fiji. The University of the South Pacific introduced a sub-graduate Diploma program based on distance learning in the early 1990s, its highest-level program in librarianship at the time. Canada's International Development Research Center (IDRC) began helping the University in developing a CPE program in 1991.

India. The government's National Policy on Education 1986 resulted in programs for CPE for academic librarians and teachers in library and information schools through Academic Staff Colleges (ASCs) in all parts of the country. The ASCs offer both orientation and refresher courses for those with more than eight years of service. The senior staff member of the appropriate department determines focus areas, draws up a detailed syllabus for each area, schedules sessions, identifies resource persons, and monitors the progress of the course. The ten courses developed were academic librarianship aims and objectives; policy perspectives; management issues; collection development; physical and bibliographic control; academic library services; resource sharing and networking; library buildings and equipment; library automation; and visits to libraries and information centers.

Japan. Because of the great diversity in qualifications for those entering the profession, CPE is regarded as in-service education for those in library and information positions, regardless of their professional education. Most universities offer CPE opportunities. For example, the Ministry of Education, Science, and Culture founded the University of Library and Information Science (ULIS) in 1980 in response to the growing need for upgrading the professional education of library and information specialists. It has offered annual workshops on various subjects for practicing librarians and information specialists. It joined with other universities in offering three-week workshops for librarians who have worked more than 10 years in university libraries. The Department of Library and Information Science at Keio University offers training for in-service librarians anywhere in Japan, one specifically for biomedical librarians. Japan's Science Information System, a nationwide interuniversity network, covers all fields of knowledge. Its Science Information Center provides annual CPE seminars for practitioners in university and research institutions.

Librarianship and information science are not firmly established in Japan as professions, partly because of the diversity of educational qualifications required, and the permanent employment system gives little incentive for CPE. The subject needs more study and new approaches, such as prototype packages for home study.

New Zealand. Librarians have recognized for many years that the country has a serious and continuing gap in providing CPE. Hindrances to progress included deciding what should be part of the first professional qualification, what should be on-the-job training, and what would be appropriate as CPE. In 1989 a report commissioned by the Continuing Education Committee of the New Zealand Library Association (NZLA) outlined a three-year plan for CE and recommended that the Association train CE facilitators. Despite lack of funds, some courses were offered and information was shared throughout the country, laying a foundation for future courses. The Wellington Branch of the NZLA, working with the Center for Continuing Education at Victoria University of Wellington, organized a refresher course on cataloguing and planned to develop further courses.

Papua New Guinea. With help from Canada's IDRC, the Department of Library and Information Studies at the University of Papua New Guinea developed CPE programs based on surveys of library workers. Definitions of what should be part of the Bachelor's degree and what should be CPE have arisen, even though the Bachelor's program at the University has been available only since 1989. The University expects to use distance education methods and other innovations appropriate to local conditions.

Taiwan in 1989 had four universities and a college offering undergraduate programs in library and information science; one university offered graduate programs. The Library Association of China (LAC), library schools, and major public libraries provide CPE through workshops, seminars, institutes, and similar programs. LAC in 1956 began offering summer workshops for both professional and nonprofessional librarians, teaching almost 3,300 library workers in the first 30 years of the programs. The most popular subjects were cataloguing and classification, reference services, acquisition techniques, and an introduction to library science. The library schools offer a wide range of opportunities, chiefly during the summer. In cooperation with LAC, the Department of Library Science at National Taiwan University began offering seminars in library automation for professionals in 1979. The seminars covered more than a dozen areas of automation, including artificial intelligence, Chinese MARC, and online searching.

Caribbean Area. The chief providers of CPE are library associations in the individual islands, regional associations, the Library School of the University of the West Indies (UWI), and employing institutions. Most countries in the region have library associations that provide CPE mainly through workshops and seminars, many in cooperation with other agencies. The outstanding CE activity in the region is the annual week-long conference of the Association of Caribbean University Research and Institution Libraries (ACURIL). The conferences are held in various countries and include pre- and post-conference workshops. Themes are determined by the needs of the area and influence the direction of the profession across language and administrative barriers. Some smaller countries send nearly half their professionals to the conferences and workshops; most larger countries send eight to ten percent of theirs. Many librarians see the future of CPE in distance learning programs carried by satellite.

The Library School of UWI at the Mona campus in Jamaica takes an active part in CPE, supporting seminars, workshops, and short courses, usually with participants from several countries and with funding help from international agencies. The School also provides opportunities for professionals to audit courses. It launched a Distance Teaching Experiment, linking three campuses and three Extra-Mural Centers.

Librarians in public, school, and government libraries in many Caribbean countries have found benefit in studying with colleagues from other fields of public service. The Central Library of Trinidad and Tobago convenes regular bimonthly meetings devoted entirely to professional development, chaired by younger staff and scheduled a year in advance, with participants choosing the topics for study and publishing the proceedings.

Europe. A potential force for CPE came into being in 1992 with an organization linking all library, information, and documentation associations in the member states of the European Community. Professional associations in the Community will be full members, with associate membership open to associations from other European countries.

Finland has CE centers in institutions of higher education charged with organizing CPE and Open University teaching. The Center at the University of Tampere organizes CPE for librarians. The Center organized a workshop on the "Management of Change" that included some innovative concepts. For example, in six five-day sessions spread across an academic year, reference librarians were challenged to consider and evaluate their own professional role and work practices. Each participating library sent two staff members, a "principal," who took part in the whole program and prepared any written work, and an "auxiliary" who only attended lectures; this device enabled participants to study how to make ideas heard throughout an organization. Each library also had to designate a current change that would be implemented during the year. Much of the instruction came from professionals outside library work; this device enabled participants to reflect on how processes could be adapted to libraries. The participants concluded that the carryover into the workplace was more effective than in other courses, in part because of the involvement of more than one professional from each library.

Germany. The Fachhochschule für Bibliotheks- und Dokumentationswesen (FHBD; Professional University for Library and Documentation Studies), long the preeminent provider of CPE programs for librarians, had to reduce its program because of staffing difficulties. CPE is provided primarily by professional schools and associations, but also by private commercial agencies. Members of the profession have asked for a central agency to coordinate plans for CPE, but the voluntary Fortbildungskommission des Deutschen Bibliotheksinstituts of the former Federal Republic was the only agency in the early 1990s. Its members exchange information, serve as regional representatives for CPE, and try to ensure that courses are given in various regions. The Commission developed guidelines for carrying out in-service education.

Russia. The Training Center of the Lenin State Library provides postgraduate CPE to enable specialists to fulfill their professional functions in a technological society by improving their ability to perform required tasks, leveling the professional structures of libraries, and preparing management staff reserves. In addition, many libraries plan and teach their own CPE programs. The Moscow State Institute of Culture has provided CPE since 1979 in an effort to increase the efficiency of library specialists. It seeks to provide a comprehensive program that ensures knowledge of the newest information, integration of theory and practice, stimulation of student thinking, and enhancement of skills for continuing self-education.

Slovakia. The Continuing Education Center for Slovak librarians at Matica Slovenská, the Slovak National Library, was founded in 1978. In its first ten years, it retrained some 1,500 librarians in 31 educational cycles. The state required volunteers and nonprofessionals in part-time library jobs to take part in CE programs for at least eight hours a year. After the collapse of the Communist government, library schools introduced new courses of study. Students had greater access to information as part of their greater freedom, but also had to accept greater responsibility for making the most of their education.

United Kingdom. Long known for its innovative teaching methods, the Department of Librarianship and Information Studies at Newcastle upon Tyne Polytechnic has developed postgraduate courses in a modular structure that allows professionals in the field to take one or more six-hour modules. The program was designed to help practitioners prepare to return to work, upgrade their knowledge in a particular area, gain specialist knowledge, prepare for a change of career, or study for personal development. Under an Associate Student plan, CPE students work alongside regular students, but may choose whether or not to take examinations.

The opportunities available in further education expanded in the 1980s, and uncertified learning can now be assessed and given credit for a wide range of higher-education qualifications. The Council for National Academic Awards set up a Credit Accumulation and Transfer (CAT) Registry in 1985. In addition, the Learning from Experience Trust (LET), established in 1986, recognizes knowledge gained through day-to-day experiences at work. Schools such as Newcastle Polytechnic incorporated CAT into their programs, enabling practitioners to build their own lifelong learning programs.

The Open University offered no courses specifically in librarianship in the early 1990s, but courses for librarians were being considered for development. Distance learning opportunities were available from a number of schools. Local libraries are actively involved in distance learning, helping students by preparing supplementary resources

Latin America. All the nations of Latin America have national professional associations that are the chief sources for CPE. The scarcity of professional literature in Spanish and Portuguese has led to excessive dependence on resources in English, but many associations are affiliated with IFLA, which now has Spanish as one of its official languages.

Brazil. A wide array of agencies supports CE, which in Brazil is also called permanent education. Professional associations offer short and long courses, promote seminars and meetings, offer distance teaching, and produce professional publications. The Brazilian Institute for Information Science and Technology (IBICT) develops courses in cooperation with universities. Library schools offer specialized courses and work with the associations and the government in developing CPE opportunities. Some research has been done in teaching methods, curriculum development, and professional requirements.

TRENDS

Although the meaning of the terms "professional" and "continuing professional education" may be blurred and may vary from one country to another, almost all involved in library and information work recognize that learning must occur throughout the lifespan of the individual if the profession is to serve the needs of a changing society effectively. Library performance is directly related to the quality of the library staff, so it is encouraging to see practitioners at all levels demanding CE opportunities and professionals taking leadership roles in providing such opportunities. Many now recognize that the extent to which human resources will be developed in any given library or library system will depend largely on the management perspective and leadership style of the chief administrator, who, more than anyone else, sets the tone and philosophy of a library and is responsible for allocating resources and time for CPE throughout the system.

As practitioners demand greater flexibility in fulfilling their learning needs, they will cause a dramatic increase in the use of distance education and the development of many new modalities for CE. Greater emphasis must be placed on independent learning activities, such as projects that capitalize on the resources of the learner's own community, rather than on processes that simply transfer information as presented in classrooms by way of the new technologies. If lifelong learning means that students guide and direct their own learning and acquire the skills to learn how to learn, then distance teachers will need training to understand the differences between distance education and on-campus instruction.

Growth in the use of distance education in other professions and in the public at large places new pressures on librarians and library support services. Libraries become vital resources for independent learning systems. Research is needed to identify ways in which libraries, especially public libraries, might make more effective provision of information materials and collaborate with professionals in other disciplines, relevant community agencies, and the media, to ensure that independent learners receive appropriate backup for their lifelong learning endeavors. The methods chosen must fit local circumstances, instead of copying wholesale what may have been successful somewhere else.

There seems to be a need for a curriculum for library-oriented CPE coordinators and planners working with people from other professions. Access to interprofessional CE would enable those in library and information work to place their own problems in perspective and help them recognize that many societal issues span many professions.

All reports from the field testify to the important role professional associations play in CPE by providing workshops, seminars, conferences, and publications, by setting and monitoring standards for quality of CE offerings, by providing for accreditation and certification, by recognizing individuals for their CE activities, and by putting pressure on legislative bodies to improve standards, provide funding for CPE, require employers to invest in CE, to recognize the value of lifelong learning, and to offer incentives to those who pursue it. In addition, the associations provide zest, excitement, and stimulation for participating in lifelong learning.

Unfortunately, reports worldwide indicate a serious lack of collaboration among providers of CE. Building collaboration and communication among providers in a country is essential if the profession is to develop and endorse a concept of national direction. The gap between libraries and schools of library and information work could well be closed if the schools were as interested in providing quality activities, products, and services for CPE as in providing pre-service education. A positive, visible working relationship among all the providers in a country would enable the public to see more clearly the key role libraries play for the public good—a role no other institution is equipped to play.

Perhaps consideration should be given to forming a group of dedicated leaders representing all the major providers in a nation to focus on how, in collaboration, they might find some solutions to major issues, such as ways to balance the demand for learning "high-tech" applications with the need for learning "high-touch" techniques for dealing with individuals. The greatest demands for CE in almost all countries are for learning how to use the latest technologies and how to manage human resources.

Perhaps instead of speaking of "continuing professional education" we should, more positively and more realistically, say "continuing education for the profession," thereby recognizing that all those who serve in libraries need to be engaged in lifelong learning. Continuing education is a never-ending pilgrimage, but an urgent pilgrimage that demands that the best in human, material, and technical resources be integrated to serve the fundamental needs of society.

REFERENCES

R. M. Cervero and J. F. Azzaretto, *Visions of the Future of Continuing Professional Education* (1990).

"Continuing Professional Education," in *The ALA Yearbook of Library and Information Services* (1976–).

Continuing Professional Education Round Table, International Federation of Library Associations and Institutions, *Continuing Professional Education: An IFLA Guidebook* (1991).

G. E. Gorman, editor, *The Education and Training of Information Professionals* (1990).

Cyril O. Houle, *Continuing Learning in the Professions* (1980).

ELIZABETH W. STONE

Library Education: Education and Training for Library Employees

People who work in libraries can be divided into two groups: librarians and people who are not librarians but work under the direction of librarians. For this article, all members of the second group are classified as *library employees*. Library employees need special knowledge in order to do their work, a need met through vocational instruction. This article recognizes three types of instruction: work experience, training, and education.

Work Experience. The simplest way to learn a job is by doing it, with exposure to the work itself, to remnants of prior work, and to the example of co-workers, and with casual instruction by colleagues and superiors. This type of instruction, long used in libraries, can be effective, but it is unreliable and inefficient because the order of instruction is dictated by the workplace rather than by the needs of the learner. It is most appropriate for teaching simple tasks, whenever inept or incorrect performance cannot inconvenience a library user or embarrass the library.

Training. Planned instruction by the library is superior to work experience as a teaching method. It may range from classroom instruction by a training officer to one-on-one instruction by a supervisor. When properly conducted, it is purposeful and combines teaching with testing and practice; job assignments are deferred until the employee attains an adequate level of proficiency. Training programs are costly to develop and administer but are more efficient and more reliable means of staff development than experience alone. Through training, employees can attain higher levels of proficiency than most can reach through work experience, and training can teach procedures that are too complex to master through work experience. In fact, there is no library technique, be it manual, mechanical, interpersonal, or bibliographic, that employees cannot learn through training programs.

Education. In this article, *education* means instruction administered by professional educators outside libraries, usually in scholastic or academic settings. It is most useful for teaching knowledge that is not library-specific, such as that needed to discharge the professional responsibilities of librarians. Knowledge that is library-specific, such as knowledge of a circulation system or filing system, can usually be taught better through training, but in special cases superior facilities or teaching skills may make education more efficient than training, even in teaching library-specific subjects.

CLASSES OF WORK

Library work can be classified as routine or not routine; as "unskilled," skilled, or professional; and as "library work" or "not library work."

Routine or Not Routine. Any work that can be done by following a prescribed procedure is routine work. Procedures may be simple, such as the process of shelving books, or they may be intricate, such as the procedure for cataloguing books—but they are all routine.

Most work in libraries is routine. Apart from professional work (defined below) the only work that is not routine (or potentially so) is responding to the unexpected, something rather rare in libraries. (Even emergencies can be anticipated, and procedures developed for responding to them.) Generally speaking, work that is not routine is the responsibility of librarians, and only routine work should be assigned to employees.

"Unskilled" or Skilled. Work that is simple enough to be learned quickly through work experience, and the employees hired to do such work, are both described as "unskilled" (in quotation marks because the true meaning is "simple-skill" rather than "no-skill"). Skilled work can be learned only through education, special training, or extensive work experience. Many librarians do skilled work themselves, to avoid the costs of hiring and training employees to do it. Consequently, many people mistakenly classify work that requires a technical skill (such as classifying books) as professional work, and reserve it for librarians only. Actually, any routine work can be assigned to an employee, no matter what level or type of skill it may require, if the employee possesses that requisite skill.

Professional Work. The work of all professionals is exemplified in that of physicians, who diagnose their patients' illnesses, prescribe treatment, and then administer their prescriptions, either with their own hands or through subordinates. Physicians decide what needs to be done, decide how it is to be done, and get it done. In the business world and increasingly elsewhere, these activities are called planning and direction and are classified as managerial work, in contrast to the technical work through which plans are implemented.

Librarians are the professionals of librarianship. They "diagnose" information needs, "prescribe" library service to meet those needs, and build and operate libraries to provide that service. Library employees differ from librarians in four ways: (1) With rare exceptions, they are not members of any learned profession; they are responsible only for carrying out specific tasks assigned by librarians. (2) They are not all members of a single vocational class; they belong to various classes. Since different classes need different skills, it is inappropriate to impose a single educational program (such as the librarian's professional education) on all library employees. (3) Skills required of employees must be job-related. Librarians must be able to evaluate many services or methods that they may never provide or use, but an employee needs only the knowledge actually to be used on the job. (4) Librarians' knowledge is applicable in many library activities and in many libraries, but much of an employee's vocational knowledge applies only to the library in which he or she is employed. Consequently, while librarians are prepared better for their work by education than by training (though every librarian needs orientation training at least), employees usually can be prepared better for their work by training.

"Library Work" and "Not Library Work." Any work done in or for a library is, of course, library work, but only some work, such as repairing or cataloguing books, is peculiar to librarianship. The rest (such as typing and running a computer) is not peculiar to librarianship; skills that are specific to librarianship must be taught in libraries or in library schools, while those that are not should be acquired through vocational education outside librarianship.

INSTRUCTION FACTORS

Since employees' jobs determine what they need to know, any factor that affects those jobs may also affect employee training. Four factors that do are change in libraries, library growth, the division of work between librarians and the support staff, and the division of work within the support staff.

Change in Libraries. Libraries are not static institutions. Their environments change, the resources and technologies available to them change, and the needs and other library-related characteristics of the people they serve change. In response to these changes, libraries themselves must change, providing new services, employing new methods, and adopting new forms of organization with different jobs and different skill requirements. These changes must always be accompanied by corresponding changes in vocational instruction. Since the direction of change in libraries is, almost invariably, from the simpler to the more complex, which requires more staff expertise, vocational instruction tends to move away from dependence on work experience toward increasing reliance on training and education.

Library Growth. Growth is a special form of change common to all libraries. As a library grows, its workload increases, and it must change its methods to secure economies. Its employees must not only increase in number, but also learn new techniques and assume new responsibilities. Consequently, a library's vocational instruction must change as it grows. An instructional procedure that is satisfactory when a library is small will be less so as it grows larger.

Division of Work. As managers, librarians may choose to do technical work themselves or assign it to employees but, especially as libraries grow, they are pressed to assign such work, and increasing shares of supervisory and administrative duties too, to employees. This pressure comes from four sources, all associated with growth: (1) An increasing professional workload, inevitable as libraries become more complex, forces librarians to withdraw from technical roles. (2) A broadening range of technical duties must inevitably exceed the range of librarians' technical skills and force them to depend on employees with the skills they lack. (3) The pursuit of efficiency (a determining factor in libraries' ability to compete against other agencies for resources) demands use of cheaper or more cost-effective methods, which often require use of employees rather than librarians. (4) Recognition that having librarians do technical work reinforces their popular image as technicians (or clerks) rather than as professionals adds impetus to dividing work between librarians and other employees.

In small libraries, librarians must do technical work (this is perhaps the origin of the librarians' non-professional image), but as libraries grow their options increase. In small libraries employees usually are employed only in "unskilled" tasks, which they learn through work experience. As librarians progressively assign more skilled work to them, training and education must supplant work experience in the vocational instruction of employees.

Division of Work among Employees. There are two basic ways to divide work among employees. One is to give each employee a share of every task that is assigned to all; the employees must then be generalists. This approach is most appropriate where flexibility is considered more important than a high volume of output, and where only "unskilled" work is assigned to employees. It is usually found in small libraries and is the conventional way of dividing work among library employees. It is not appropriate for large libraries, however, where employees may be limited to work in a single department, or even to a single task; such employees are de facto specialists.

The second way to divide work is to assign each employee a special group of tasks, that is, to use them as specialists rather than generalists. Generalists, all sharing the same duties and having the same skills, form a single vocational class. Specialists, with different duties, divide into many classes, each with its own instructional requirements. Specialists, if they are to be used properly, must be trained to a high degree of expertise, each one in the special skills required by his or her own job. Since any employee assigned to a specific job must be specially trained for it, use of specialists imposes a heavy training burden on the library, but one offset by a key advantage: performance improves when specialists are used. When they are employed in the same work, specialists will outperform generalist employees and librarians. (Since librarians' education in technical methods is extensive rather than intensive, they are inherently generalists with respect to technical work.) In any case, specialists must be employed when the range of tasks becomes too great or the tasks themselves too complex to be mastered by generalists.

IN U.S. LIBRARIES

Five modes of vocational instruction have prepared employees for work in libraries in the United States: apprenticeship, apprentice-schools, training classes, academic schools, and library technology training programs.

Apprenticeship. Before Melvil Dewey founded the first library school in 1887, all librarians and library employees (then called *library assistants*) learned their jobs through apprenticeship in large libraries, under the direction of the librarians. (In those days, *librarian* meant the person in charge, and no library had more than one.) Librarians were promoted from the ranks of the assistants, and small libraries with no assistants were expected to recruit their librarians from the staffs of large libraries.

Apprentice-Schools. Dewey's school was founded because the number of libraries training assistants was too small to satisfy a growing demand for librarians. That school and any others before World War I are called apprentice-schools here because they resembled apprenticeship programs more than conventional schools. Many of their graduates began their careers as library assistants.

Training Classes. In 1891 the Los Angeles Public Library began a formal apprentice program for library assistants, and during the next 25 years other large libraries followed its example. The programs, called training classes, were much like the contemporary library schools, but were intended to produce assistants rather than librarians.

Academic Schools. After World War I C. C. Williamson's study of library schools identified two types of library personnel, which he called librarians and clerks. He recommended academic preparation for the librarians and training programs in large libraries for the clerks. The latter recommendation was ignored, but with support from the Carnegie Corporation and the American Library Association, the library schools and some training classes were gradually converted into academic institutions, each becoming part of a university and accepting only college graduates into its program.

Library school graduates were then so much preferred over employees trained by apprenticeship or in training classes that those two methods all but ceased to be used. From 1930, when economic depression reduced demand for library personnel, until after World War II, library positions that required any special skill or knowledge were reserved for library-school graduates. Employees who were not library-school graduates were restricted to "unskilled" tasks. Library-school graduates called themselves librarians and professionals, but most actually were employed as skilled technicians—not true librarians, but library employees. The library schools, ostensibly professional schools, actually functioned primarily as technical schools. Libraries, assuming erroneously that all library-school graduates were qualified for any library work, stopped training almost entirely. And they restricted themselves unnecessarily to an artificially small pool of potential employees.

Library Technology Training Programs. After World War II demand for skilled library employees far exceeded the supply of library-school graduates. A few undergraduate schools then began programs to teach library skills to help meet that demand. Two or three schools began to offer such programs before 1950. Seven schools were doing so in 1960, 20 in 1965, and more than 100 in 1970. In 1975, according to a directory published by COLT (the Council on Library Media Technical Assistants), library technology programs were offered by 130 schools in the United States, 23 schools in Canada, and three more schools in American Samoa, Puerto Rico, and the Panama Canal Zone. The 1980 edition of *American Library Directory* listed 112 schools offering such programs and the 1985 edition 63 schools. (The decline in number reflects both a decline in all types of library schools and the impact of an increase in the relative number of library school graduates.)

Most of these schools are community colleges. At first their programs varied widely in quality and utility, but they have become a valuable adjunct to librarianship, teaching skills useful in libraries, in many cases with emphasis on machine skills. Beginning with audiovisual equipment, they came to include instruction in use of computers and computer-based library systems.

The contrast that these schools and their graduates offer has helped to define the professional images of graduate library schools and their graduates, and their impact on librarianship during the 1960s helped inspire the ALA to develop and to publish in 1970 its policy statement on *Library Education and Personnel Utilization* (originally *Library Education and Manpower*), which recognized again the value—obscured since 1930—of library employees without graduate library school degrees.

TRAINING THE LIBRARY STAFF

Primary responsibility for the competence of library employees does not rest on schools or even on the employees, but on libraries, because they alone know exactly what their needs are. Libraries are responsible for testing the competencies of job applicants and choosing the most competent. They are responsible for developing competencies as needed in those they employ, through either training or education programs. Training is usually the more practical choice.

Training has been so little used in libraries since 1930 that it is not part of the common image of librarianship. But in a changing world common images are always out of date and should never be used as models for planning. Training is necessary in librarianship, and will be even more necessary in the future, so much so that its absence seems prima facie evidence of poor management.

Training is required to orient new employees (and new librarians) to their library, its environment, and the people it serves. Training is necessary to teach job skills, to upgrade skills, to prepare employees for promotion or transfer, and to replace current methods with new ones. Training may be a necessary response to change or a way to refresh skills.

Well-planned training programs convey knowledge rather than specific job information, but that knowledge is always job related. They must be based on job descriptions and job specifications, which specify knowledge needs. They employ testing to find out what employees know and teach employees to apply knowledge. They also set performance standards. Ideally, employees who are unable to meet a standard are assigned to other work; thus training programs also screen employees and help to fit them into the library staff.

Education is an alternative to training if a school is accessible and has the resources that a library education program requires. Reliance on education programs rather than training can be more efficient when the needed resources are available and the number of students sufficient to make education economically feasible. Libraries near a school might elect to standardize their methods, so that their employees could be educated in a single program. But libraries cannot discharge their responsibility for staff development merely by sending employees to a school; they must participate actively in developing the educational program and monitor it to make sure that it meets their needs.

Like other organizations, libraries are becoming more dependent on skilled employees, and on the education and training through which they become skilled. Librarians too are changing, becoming more like other managers who get work done through other people. Success in this art depends very much on teaching those people what their work requires them to know.

REFERENCES

Brooke E. Sheldon, *Planning and Evaluating Library Training Programs* (1976).

Charles W. Evans, "The Evolution of Paraprofessional Library Employees," *Advances in Librarianship* (1979).

Robert D. Stueart and John Taylor Eastlick, *Library Management* (1981).

William R. Tracey, *Designing Training and Development Systems* (1984).

CHARLES W. EVANS

Library Education: History

Education for work in libraries began with the first libraries; formal education began in the second half of the 19th century, primarily in North America. Ideas and methods developed there gradually spread to other parts of the world.

NORTH AMERICA

Formal library education began in North America in 1887 with the first classes at the School of Library Economy, Columbia University, under the direction of Melvil Dewey. Dewey had been an advocate of full-time education for a number of years, using the American Library Association (ALA) as a forum to gain support for this new approach. Dewey's appointment as Librarian at Columbia in 1883 gave him the opportunity he sought. He persuaded the Annual Conference of ALA that year to endorse the concept, although some prominent members of the Association opposed the idea, notably William Frederick Poole, John Shaw Billings, and Justin Winsor. Essentially, they held that experience in a good library would provide all that was needed to become a librarian, provided a person had a sound general education. At the 1877 International Conference in London, Winsor noted that libraries in the United States offered good career prospects for women and urged British librarians to train women for library work.

From 1884 to 1886 Dewey held preliminary classes at Columbia to try out his ideas. In January 1887, the School opened officially with a class of 20—17 women and 3 men—and a staff of 7, all part-time instructors, including Dewey himself. The President of Columbia, Frederick A. P. Barnard (1809–89), supported the admission of women, although the Trustees opposed it; they were relieved when, in January 1889, Dewey moved to Albany as the New York State Librarian and took the Library School with him. The School did not return to Columbia until 1926, at which time it was combined with the New York Public Library School.

While the initial programs at Columbia and Albany tended to emphasize the practical aspects of librarianship, they did offer systematic training and an opportunity to look beyond one library system. Their influence was great in that eight of the schools established in later years were founded by Dewey's graduates. Apart from Columbia, the early schools were not located in universities but in institutes of technology, such as Pratt, Drexel, and Armour (later moved to the University of Illinois), and in such large public libraries as the Los Angeles Public Library. ALA maintained a keen interest in the work of these new schools by establishing a series of committees and other units. The first committee, in 1883, was intended to serve as a liaison with Columbia but it was followed by Committees on Library Examinations and Credentials (1900), on Professional Instruction and Bibliography (1901), on Library Training (1903), and on Professional Training for Librarianship (1909), and a Round Table of Library School Instructors (1911). Four years later that Round Table separated from ALA to become the Association of American Library Schools (AALS), renamed in 1983 the Association for Library and Information Science Education (ALISE).

20th Century. Over these early years, three ideas emerged that were to influence American library education as it developed in the 20th century—library schools should be affiliated with universities; college graduation should be required for admission; and an examining board with clearly defined authority should be established. While these points were still being discussed by the schools, ALA, and AALS, the influence of an outside agency provided a much needed impetus. In 1916 the Trustees of the Carnegie Corporation of New York had commissioned a report from Alvin S. Johnson, an economist, on its policy of providing funding for public library buildings. Johnson's *Report* focused on the need to be more concerned with the low quality of many of those staffing these libraries. He was also critical of the low standards of the library schools. The Trustees sought a follow-up report from C. C. Williamson, an economist who also taught at the New York Public Library School. In his recommendations, Williamson favored the development of a coordinated plan for library education. The Carnegie Trustees then hired Williamson to undertake a major survey of library education, which he did from 1919 to 1921.

The subsequent Williamson *Report* is generally regarded as the most important document to have appeared in the history of library education. It was critical of current library education. Among its proposals were that library schools should distinguish between clerical and professional work and only teach the latter; such schools should be located in universities; more financial support should be provided for schools, their faculty members, and students; courses should run for two years—one year for general principles and one for specializations; a national system of certification should be adopted; and schools should be accredited. Prior to the publication of the Williamson *Report,* ALA had established a Temporary Library Training Board drawn from all sections of the membership to look into library training, standards, and an accrediting plan. In 1924 ALA replaced that temporary body with the Board of Education for Librarianship (BEL), later the Committee on Accreditation (COA). Williamson's proposal for a national examining body was not accepted but accreditation of schools was. To carry out the accreditation process, *Standards* were developed by the BEL, and later the COA, and adopted by ALA Council in 1925, 1933, 1951, 1972, and 1992. (*See* Accreditation.)

The Ten-Year Program in Library Service, initiated by the Carnegie Corporation under its President F. P. Keppel as follow-up to the Williamson *Report,* provided generous support for ALA and for individual library schools. The program was based on a staff report by William S. Learned. The most significant Carnegie Corporation benefaction was to the University of Chicago to enable it to establish a Graduate Library School (GLS) in 1926, designed to be librarianship's equivalent of the Johns Hopkins Medical School and the Harvard Law School. Historian Donald G. Davis, Jr., notes that its foundation "was perhaps of greater significance to education for librarianship than was the founding 40 years earlier of the Columbia school." Its faculty was drawn from cognate disciplines in which the scholars held doctorates, and in 1928 Chicago introduced the first doctoral program in the field. The GLS emphasis on research and publications had a major impact on the program and its graduates and on library education itself.

In the years following the Williamson *Report,* library education did become the responsibility of universities as schools affiliated with large public libraries closed. Admission to the program now called for an undergraduate degree, whereas before 1924 only the New York State Library School and that at the University of Illinois required a bachelor's degree for admission. The qualifications of the faculty were improved, and more and better textbooks became available. Later reports on library education, published between 1936 and 1952 by various authors, presented varying perspectives on library education, but all tended to emphasize perceived deficiencies in the curriculum. Special conferences focused on library education, especially in the period 1940–48, and the ideas discussed and proposals made all contributed to the ferment of the times. However, the profession had recognized that the growing and increasing complexity of libraries did justify the education of its librarians at the graduate level.

The M.L.S. Matters came to a head in 1951 when the ALA Council adopted new *Standards for Accreditation.* These had the effect of ensuring that professional librarians were those obtaining the "fifth-year" degree (that is, one year of professional study after four years of undergraduate preparation) at graduate library schools whose programs were accredited by ALA. An unanticipated change came in the early 1950s when this fifth-year degree became a Master's degree (M.L.S.) replacing the former B.L.S. as U.S. schools strengthened and, in some cases slightly lengthened, their programs.

Canada. The BLS as the first professional degree remained longer in Canada, where a similar but slightly different pattern of education for librarianship developed. Dewey's influence was seen in the earliest formal instruction when his friend Charles Gould, Librarian at McGill University, offered a three-week summer school there in 1904. Short courses were offered in other years at McGill and later by the Ontario Department of Education, which established the Ontario Library School in 1919. The first full-year programs were instituted at McGill in 1927 and at the University of Toronto (taking over from the Ontario Library School) in 1928. Both schools subsequently sought and received ALA accreditation for their programs, thus setting a precedent for virtually all other library schools later established in Canada. The Canadian Library Association (CLA) was not established until 1946. (Although Provincial associations existed from 1900 onward, national gatherings of Canadian librarians were held at ALA conferences until 1946.) In the late 1960s, all but one of the Canadian schools agreed to adopt the M.L.S. as the first professional degree to be offered after four terms of study. This lengthened program became the norm for all seven Canadian schools. Periodically, since 1955, the Canadian Library Association has considered the question of a Canadian system of accreditation.

One of the seven Canadian schools (Montreal) is Francophone and CLA is an English-speaking-only organization. This alone would complicate but not be an insuperable barrier to a Canadian system of accreditation in what is officially a bilingual country. In 1985, even before the CLA Committee reported in 1986, there had already been strong support expressed for continuation of the ALA accreditation process from six of the seven schools.

Other Developments affected library education in the U.S. in the 1950s apart from the adoption of new *Standards* and the introduction of the M.L.S. as the first professional degree. In 1956 the BEL was replaced by COA for accreditation matters, with the Library Education Division (LED) serving as a forum for the broader participation of ALA members, whether library educators or not. In 1959 ALA

Council approved *Standards* for undergraduate training that have served to guide programs seeking to prepare those in teacher-training institutions. In addition, by then, several Schools had joined Chicago in offering doctoral programs.

The 1960s saw a boom in library education in the U.S. as enrollments grew and the number of library schools increased to meet the growing demands of the field. Four of Canada's seven schools opened in the 1960s. Much of the growth in the U.S. was the result of increased federal and state funding for libraries at all levels. Funding was made available to support potential faculty members in doctoral programs. Recruitment of minority group students also became a more active concern. The U.S. Office of Education and its Library Service Branch proved to be a catalyst; an institute it sponsored at Western Reserve University led to ALA's establishment of a Commission on a National Plan for Library Education in 1963. It led to the creation of an Office for Library Education in ALA in 1966 for which the H. W. Wilson Foundation provided matching funds. That Office, under Lester Asheim, produced the *Library Education and Manpower* statement designed to respond to library staffing needs at various levels. In addition to the expansion of M.L.S., Ph.D., and undergraduate teacher certification programs, the 1960s also saw the creation of library technician programs in community colleges and the introduction of sixth-year programs for post-Master's work.

From 1970 the picture for library education was much less bright. In 1971 ALA closed its Office for Library Education. ALA's LED was next to go when it was unable to attract enough members to ensure its financial survival. It was replaced by a lesser unit, the Standing Committee on Library Education (SCOLE), with some of the former staff services of LED now provided by the Office for Library Personnel Resources, although its main interest lies elsewhere.

ALA initiated and the H. W. Wilson Foundation funded a major study of library education by an academic investigator, Ralph W. Conant, over the period 1972–77. When ALA released the draft report for publication, however, it stated that neither the Association nor its Advisory Committee "endorses, sanctions, or otherwise approves of the study." Conant's recommendations were not regarded as contributing greatly to the field and his research methodology was widely criticized.

There has been much enthusiasm shown in recent years in both the U.S. and Canada for changing the names of the schools in which the degree is offered. The words "information science" or "information studies" are being added to or, in some instances, replacing the more traditional "library science" or "library service." This is being done to reflect the changing nature of what is being offered in these schools; indeed, a few schools have introduced undergraduate degrees in information science that do not seem to be designed for those who will later seek the M.L.S. Many schools now offer an array of joint degrees with library science linked with another subject, such as law, or programs in information science or archives alongside the M.L.S. degree. Schools are also involved to varying degrees with continuing education offerings. A 1980 conference at Columbia University examined the case for extending the length of the M.L.S. program and generally found it wanting; only the Canadian schools and a handful of U.S. schools called in the mid-1980s for a period of study beyond one calendar year for the M.L.S. degree.

The October 1985 listing of accredited programs issued by COA included 63 schools, of which 7 were in Canada. Doctoral programs were offered at 23 schools, of which 2 were in Canada. Many schools closed and the status of some others was threatened by the turbulent economic conditions from the late 1970s through the early 1990s. The annual statistical reports issued by ALISE tell their story of an overall drop in enrollments, dwindling faculty numbers, and declining financial support. Canada's schools have largely regional affiliations that may assist their survival.

UNITED KINGDOM

Education for librarianship in the United Kingdom has followed a course different from that in North America. In so doing, it has been influenced by the society in which its libraries operate and in which the pattern of higher education also differs. Until after World War II, when the number of universities increased markedly, vocational education for professional groups such as librarians, architects, and accountants had been largely the responsibility of national professional associations rather than of universities. In addition, much higher education in the U.K. is still carried out in colleges and polytechnics, which are tertiary-level institutions with a different structure for the awarding of qualifications. When library education began in the U.K. in the late 19th century, the few universities that then existed—which catered to a small, largely elite section of the population—were not considered appropriate training agencies.

The Library Association. Three years after its establishment in 1877, the Library Association of the U.K. (LA) carried a motion that "it is desirable that the Council of the Association should consider how library assistants may be aided in their training in the general principles of their profession." What evolved was a system of nationwide examinations, starting in London and Nottingham in 1885, administered by the LA. Initially, the examinations sought to test both librarianship and the general education of the candidates—which was not high. Gradually the emphasis was placed almost entirely on the practical aspects of librarianship.

In 1898 the LA received its Royal Charter, which conveys certain privileges and powers on a body of persons for some specific purposes. In the LA's Charter were two important clauses that authorized the LA "To promote whatever may tend to the improvement of the position and qualifications of librarians" and "To hold examinations in librarianship and issue certificates of efficiency." This was followed in 1909 by the LA's setting up a Register of qualified librarians known as Chartered Librarians. To qualify for admission to the Register, a library worker would have to join the LA, complete its examination requirements, and then remain in membership by paying annual dues. This system was favored by Williamson in his 1921 *Report* as a means of funding the proposed national certification system for the U.S.

Although initial interest in taking the LA examinations was limited, the establishment of the Register and a greater awareness of the need for trained staff led to an increased number of candidates. In the absence of any system of full-time library education, the LA encouraged the holding of summer schools, evening classes in larger centers of population generally held in public libraries or colleges, advice columns in the library press, and correspondence courses. In the largely urban public libraries, whose staffs were serving virtual apprenticeships, the LA examination system flourished as staff members sought to qualify for admission to the Register.

The London School. As in the U.S., the report of an outside surveyor to the Carnegie trustees affected the development of library education in the U.K. Following the 1915 *Report on Library Provision and Policy to the Carnegie United Kingdom Trust* by W. G. S. Adams, the Carnegie United Kingdom Trust (CUKT) provided initial funding for starting a full-time library school at the University of London. As a university school, London offered its own diploma, which was recognized by the LA as admitting its holders to the Register. This surrender of the LA's monopoly as an examining body was resented by many of those in the urban public libraries who had to work long hours and then were expected to study part-time for their professional qualifications. There was also unhappiness in the 1930s that too many Chartered Librarians were being produced as the LA examination system was increasingly accepted. The London School admitted both graduate and non-graduate students. Many of those completing its program found employment in academic and special libraries and also in the then newly developing county (that is, rural) public libraries. The few university graduates entering the library profession in the years up to World War II tended to be employed in the small number of academic and national libraries where professional library qualifications were not considered essential. The London School with its largely part-time teaching staff never had the impact on the British scene that the Chicago School had in the U.S. Yet when it closed in 1939 at the outbreak of war, it had at least shown that a full-time school could exist in a British university environment.

Postwar Developments. During the years 1939–45, much postwar planning took place in the U.K. involving both educational institutions and the various professional associations. In 1942 the LA considered a report by its Honorary Secretary, Lionel R. McColvin, *The Public Library System of Great Britain*, funded by the CUKT. In it he proposed a national system of library schools to provide full-time education for the ex-servicemen and -women whose careers had been interrupted. Although these schools would be small in size, McColvin foresaw that they might continue in existence to provide full-time education for new recruits to the profession. McColvin, supported by the LA Council, felt it essential that the Association remain in control of the examination system, thereby enforcing national standards. Given the many pressures on university education immediately after the war, it was unlikely that, apart from London, the university authorities would have welcomed courses in librarianship, but the LA's insistence on controlling the syllabus settled the matter. Nonetheless, the LA did succeed in having seven full-time schools opened by 1947 in colleges of commerce and similar institutions of tertiary education. All prepared their students for the LA examinations which at the time offered two tiers of qualification, first the Associateship (A.L.A.) and second, the Fellowship (F.L.A.). The schools admitted both graduates and non-graduates, with the latter numerically much larger. The introduction of these full-time schools did not mean the elimination of either part-time study or correspondence courses, although the superior success rate of those attending the schools could clearly be demonstrated.

By 1955, the LA and the schools realized that a major overhaul of the system of education for librarianship was needed. From a postwar program largely designed to update ex-service people, the schools were becoming permanent fixtures seeking to control the examination of their students, providing for career paths for new recruits, and wishing to revise the syllabus which was still controlled by the LA. It took almost ten years before the various segments of the profession, which by now involved the Association of British library schools and Aslib, could come to agreement. By this time other factors had entered the picture, leading to an increasing diversity in British library education.

The year 1964 may be taken as crucial; the LA introduced a new syllabus calling for a full-time two-year program for non-graduates and a one-year postgraduate diploma for those already holding a university degree leading to the first professional qualification, the Associateship. The Fellowship now became available by thesis rather than examination. With part-time study eliminated, the schools were able to increase their staffing numbers to prepare for this expanded instructional program. At the same time, in 1964, the Council on National Academic Awards (CNAA) received its Royal Charter, which authorized it to grant degrees to those completing approved programs at colleges and polytechnics that were not themselves universities. Library schools, with their expanded staffs, were not slow to see the implications of this and soon moved to develop programs leading to first degrees in librarianship to be approved by CNAA or in one instance by a nearby university. Some of these schools now offer Master's and Doctoral degrees. Meanwhile in addition to the school at the University of London, five other schools were located in universities, all preparing for their own qualifications. As a result the LA changed from being an examining body in its own right to an agency that recognizes existing qualifications for admission to its Register.

Current Status. There were 17 schools in the U.K. in the late 1980s. Most schools offer first degrees in librarianship of three or four years' duration. Postgraduate diplomas and degrees at the Master's level are available at many schools, mostly after one year of full-time study, although it is possible to study part-time in some situations. Some schools offer higher research degrees that may be at Master's or Doctoral level. The great majority of the courses qualify for admission to the Register of the LA. However, the LA has long required a period of supervised work experience as well as successful completion of examinations, whether its own or others. It later introduced a three-tier structure. After successful completion of an approved course, candidates for admission to the Register have to complete one year of training supervised by a Chartered Librarian, after which they may apply to become Licentiates of the LA. A further period of not less than two years as a Licentiate, again under the supervision of a Chartered Librarian, is required for the Associateship. After five years on the Register, an Associate may submit work of various kinds for election to the Fellowship.

Beginning in 1986 the LA agreed to recognize courses taken at programs accredited by the American and Australian library association as equivalent to those taken at programs approved by the LA insofar as gaining admission to the Register is concerned. The other requirements concerning membership of the LA and its Licentiateship scheme still have to be met. The lengthy period of licentiateship before being admitted to the Register as a Chartered Librarian engendered much discussion in the LA; it is believed that an increasing number of the holders of university degrees are not persuaded of the need to follow this route. The implications to the LA are significant as there is a loss of membership and dues from those who chose not to join the Association and its Register. The Association in the mid-1980s was considering expanding its membership to seek to attract those from related professional groups. How they would be accommodated by the existing Register requirements remained to be determined. The LA also was considering a change of name to the Library and Information Association. (See also Library Association.)

At the same time the central government in the U.K., which funds virtually all undergraduate students and many graduate students, has been concerned for some time with the number of librarians being produced by this system. In 1985 it established the Transbinary Study Group on Librarianship and Information Studies, which for the first time was to look at library education in the U.K. as taught by the "public" sector (colleges and polytechnics) and the "independent" sector (the universities). Its mandate appeared to cover not only the content of library education but also the question of supply and demand. As in North America, schools in the U.K. have programs to reflect what they see as the changing nature of the field. As examples, Leeds in the 1980s offered a B.A. in Librarianship and a B.Sc. in Information Science, Sheffield changed the title of its School to the Department of Information Studies, and Strathclyde became a Department of Information Science as part of the Strathclyde Business School.

SCHOOL LIBRARIANSHIP

In general, both North American and British library schools have sought to provide a general system of education for librarians in all types of library work and now in related fields. The exception to this in both systems has been the generally limited success in providing appropriate educational experiences for those seeking employment as school- or teacher-librarians. This calls for recognition as both a teacher and a librarian, and despite efforts over many years it seems fair to say that the ideal mix has not yet been achieved. In the U.S. many states have certification requirements for employment in the school system that favor qualifications obtained from state colleges rather than ALA-accredited programs. In Canada the Canadian School Library Association has sought to establish nationwide qualifications but here again Provincial requirements complicate the picture. In the U.K. school librarianship has traditionally had even greater difficulties in gaining recognition.

INTERNATIONAL MAIN CURRENTS

Commonwealth. The monopolistic control of library education by the LA in the U.K. has been dramatically changed by the events outlined above. One additional aspect is the international influence of the LA through its examination system, which did not necessarily require attendance at a full-time library school. From its early days, the LA has been receptive to enabling overseas students to sit for its examinations and has made the necessary arrangements, enabling librarians in many parts of the world to obtain recognized library qualifications when no library school or in some cases no library association existed in their home countries. The 1964 decision to require two years of full-time attendance at library school led effectively to the cessation of this system of overseas examinations.

Some early library schools established in Commonwealth countries also prepared their students for the LA examinations before moving to their own indigenous systems. In the years after World War II, many Commonwealth countries sent their students to the U.K. to obtain professional library qualifications. The fact that these were offered at first-degree level was more attractive in some cases where those being sent lacked the first degree necessary for admission to North American schools. As a result of these two approaches, some 10 percent of the LA's Register of Chartered Librarians are resident overseas, although a proportion of these are British librarians who have emigrated to other countries. In any case this percentage is likely to decline. However, British influence on library education overseas shows no sign of abating as the steady stream of faculty members serving and advising library schools in many countries, especially those of developing nations in the Commonwealth, continues with the financial support of the government, largely through the British Council.

U.S. Influence. U.S. influence on library education overseas has also a long and historic tradition. While ALA has been involved in many cases, it has not held the same position as that of the LA because of ALA's decision to accredit individual programs according to its *Standards*. As a result, much U.S. aid has come through foundations such as the Carnegie Corporation of New York, Rockefeller Foundation, Ford Foundation, and governmental bodies such as the U.S. Information Agency, the Agency for International Development, and Fulbright lecturers. Writing in *Library Trends* (1972), Robert S. Burgess noted that "New library schools have been established or existing ones strengthened with U.S. assistance in, among other places, Columbia, Japan, Korea, Mexico, Nigeria, Puerto Rico, the Philippines, Thailand, Iran, Turkey, and Uruguay." An earlier example was the foundation of the Boone Library School in China in 1920 by Mary Elizabeth Wood, who graduated from Simmons. Although foundation and government aid for overseas library education dwindled in the 1980s, the U.S. influence remains strong as many overseas faculty members hold advanced degrees from U.S.

schools. U.S. faculty have held visiting appointments at overseas schools but for a variety of reasons, among them lack of external funding and development of local trained staff, fewer did so in the 1980s.

International Cooperation. An international library school was talked about as early as 1904, when Guido Biagi wrote about the idea in *Library Journal*. More recent discussion has taken place in the International Federation of Library Associations and Institutions (IFLA) and the International Federation for Documentation (FID), but there had been no really concrete progress by 1993. Unesco has been suggested as a sponsoring agency, but the location of the proposed school, language of instruction, curriculum, and recruitment of faculty present problems that so far have been and may continue to be insurmountable. On a more modest scale, a successful example of international cooperation has been the International Graduate Summer School (IGSS) held annually at the College of Librarianship Wales (CLW) in Aberystwyth, also the home of the National Library of Wales. CLW is a residential college devoted exclusively to librarianship. The faculty of the summer school changes from year to year, although there is some degree of continuity. The majority are drawn from North American schools and CLW itself, with a few from other European countries and further afield. To increase its appeal to students from North America, the IGSS is cosponsored by the School of Library and Information Science of the University of Pittsburgh. Pittsburgh issues transcripts for courses completed, thus facilitating transfer of credit to M.L.S. programs in the U.S. and Canada. The international flavor of the school was further enhanced by students from other overseas countries, many specially funded by the British Council.

Other examples of international cooperation in formal education for librarianship can be found in the establishment of regional schools serving more than one country. Regional schools would seem to have much to commend them, especially in those areas where resources are limited. They enable faculty and institutional support to come together to meet the needs of a student body drawn in the main, although not exclusively, from the host region. The language of instruction may also be a unifying factor, as is the case of the Interamerican Library School, Medellín, Colombia, established in 1956 for Spanish-speaking countries, or the University of Dakar's School for Librarians, Archivists, and Documentalists, founded in 1963 to meet the needs of French-speaking countries in Africa. It has had strong support from the French government and Unesco; its founding Director came from France.

Other regional schools are those in Uganda and the West Indies. The East African School of Librarianship, established in 1963 at Makerere University College, Kampala, Uganda, aims to train librarians from Kenya, Tanzania, and Uganda. It has had support from Unesco, various foundations, and Scandinavia, which provided its first Director, Knud Larsen. The difficult political situation in Uganda starting in the 1970s was not conducive to its development.

The West Indies School began in 1971 at the Mona campus, Kingston, Jamaica, to serve Jamaica, Trinidad and Tobago, Barbados, Grenada, Guyana, and the British Associated States and Colonies in the Caribbean. Its first two directors were supported by Unesco, as have been other staff appointments. Additional support came from Canada through governmental agencies and with the cooperation of the library schools at Western Ontario and Dalhousie, which made faculty members available to teach at the West Indies School.

European Patterns. Most countries of the world have adopted either the North American model of graduate education or the British multi-level approach for types of librarianship. One region that is largely an exception is Continental Europe, in which a stratification for library education can be seen. Most European countries have academic education at university level; training at a lesser level of institution for those to be employed in what might be termed subprofessional positions; and training for support staff at a third type of institution. As Donald E. Davinson makes clear in a survey published in 1976, it is difficult to categorize when dealing with countries as diverse and as small as Denmark with its monolithic Royal Danish School providing "programs at all levels, from advanced to those for part-time library assistants" and as vast as Russia, with its legacy of a tightly controlled system designed to accord with its manpower plan.

Although library schools worldwide may teach the international standards for cataloguing, there are no such standards for library education programs. The IFLA Section of Library Schools resolved in 1974 to follow up earlier work in this field by seeking to formulate global standards for library education programs.

Equivalency. The question of equivalency and reciprocity of qualifications remains. The LED of ALA had a committee to advise on these matters. It set up Country Resource Panels consisting of two North American members of ALA knowledgeable about the educational system in the country concerned, together with one national resident in that country. These panels, which exist in ALA's Standing Committee on Library Education (SCOLE), give opinions on the equivalency and relationship of foreign library qualifications to those offered in North America. In late 1985 the LA decided it too would establish resource panels as it began to recognize courses from overseas schools as qualifying for admission to its Register. The LA also moved ahead on developing a system of equivalence of qualifications to permit the employment of non-nationals in member countries of the European Community.

REFERENCES

Robert S. Burgess, "Education for Librarianship: U.S. Assistance," *Library Trends* (1972).

Ralph W. Conant, *The Conant Report: A Study of the Education of Librarians* (1980).

J. Periam Danton, *Between M.L.S. and Ph.D.: A Study of Sixth-Year Specialist Programs in Accredited Library Schools* (1970).

Richard L. Darling and Terry Belanger, editors, *Extended Library Education Programs; Proceedings of a Conference Held at the School of Library Service, Columbia University, March 13–14, 1980* (1980).

Donald E. Davinson, "Trends in Library Education—Europe," *Advances in Librarianship* (1976).

Donald G. Davis, Jr., "Education for Librarianship," *Library Trends* (1976).

Alvin S. Johnson, *A Report to the Carnegie Corporation of New York on the Policy of Donations to Free Public Libraries* (1917).
William A. Learned, *The American Public Library and the Diffusion of Knowledge* (1924).
John Richardson, Jr., *The Spirit of Inquiry: The Graduate Library School at Chicago, 1921–1951* (1982).
Sarah K. Vann, *The Williamson Reports of 1921 and 1923: A Study* (1971).

NORMAN HORROCKS

Library Management and Administration

Libraries have existed since the dawn of history, and their initial functions of acquiring materials, arranging them, facilitating their circulation, and providing some aid to those using them are still represented among the organizational activities of present-day libraries. But if the administration of the modern library is to be defined in the framework of contemporary institutional life, the 19th century seems a more logical place to begin this account of library management.

The 19th Century proved a hospitable climate for the birth of the modern library movement for several reasons. Reading matter became more widely available as significant changes in the publishing industry facilitated the manufacture of cheaper and larger editions of books. Major cities in Europe and the United States, already important centers of commercial and mercantile interests, became appropriate sites for governments to support libraries open to the general public. Reforms in the German universities early in the century led to the increased prominence of their university collections; the subsequent adoption of the German university model in the U.S., with its emphasis on research as a prerequisite for faculty appointment, resulted in the great growth of university libraries there as the century drew to a close. And, as skilled work forces came to be in great demand, they needed a managerial cadre capable of supervising them, with the result that training and education for managers began in the private sector, a development that also influenced concomitant reforms in public administration and in the extension of the civil service.

Two important theorists, both born in the 19th century, made great contributions to managerial change: Max Weber (1864–1920) in Europe and Frederick W. Taylor (1856–1915) in the United States. Their writings on the organization of work and the administration of the enterprise proved to be seminal. To Weber we owe the conceptualization of bureaucracy, the bureaucratic organization being one that is operated along hierarchical lines, requires merit as the criterion for recruitment and promotion, is governed by organizational rules and regulations for the uniform conduct of affairs, and is divided into functional units characterized on the one hand by likeness of work responsibilities and on the other by similarities in staff abilities and skills. To Taylor we owe the development of the principles of scientific management aimed at procuring maximum efficiency and maximum prosperity for both employer and employee. It is widely held that Taylor's work served as the precursor of modern organization and decision theory.

Northeast Document Conservation Center, Andover, Massachusetts

Members of the Association of College and Research Libraries discuss the development of management strategies for mass deacidification pilot programs with Northeast Document Conservation Center staff at a two day roundtable.

Organization. In Weber's terms, libraries are bureaucracies. As units of larger organizational structures, such as government departments, academic institutions, schools, municipalities or other local jurisdictions, and corporations in the private sector, they are governed by the rules and regulations of their parent institutions. This adherence to universally held norms, affecting working conditions, classification and pay plans, benefit packages, and other perquisites of modern employment, is the primary way an organization provides for employee equity. Then, too, libraries, especially those of significant size, are in themselves functionally organized. Their departmentalization follows widely accepted practices in both the public and private sectors. Departmentalization results from a response to distinctive client needs; territorial considerations; and the particular properties of the products or services involved, whether they are inherent in their intellectual content or in their format. Distinctive client groups include, among others, children, the blind and physically handicapped, undergraduates, and the elderly. Branches of public libraries are obvious examples of territorial subdivision, although departmental libraries of universities and decentralized collections attached to specific research laboratories are just as good examples. Librarians recognized in the 19th century that readers would find the physical arrangement of materials by intellectual content, as characterized by the subject departmentalized library, more useful than arrangement by such criteria as size. They also recognized format subdivisions, establishing departments devoted to pictures and prints, music, maps, and other materials having unique physical properties. Departments oriented toward the needs of specific equipment were a later development as film and microfilm were added to library holdings. The advent of computers for bibliographic control and patron use contributes to further departmentalization in response to the need for specific equipment.

Management. Although Weber's ideation could extend to many organizations and enterprises throughout the world, Taylor specifically addressed the industrial and business communities with his writings, most importantly *The Principles of Scientific Management* (1911). Here he synthesized some of his early work, promulgating his theory that rule-of-thumb methods should be replaced by explicitly stated laws, rules, and principles, thus making of management a science. One of Taylor's disciples, the French industrialist Henri Fayol (1841–1925), made his own contribution to management thought when in his treatise on industrial and general administration he became the first writer to classify the study of management into specific functional areas, such as planning, organizing, commanding, coordinating, and controlling.

Adding to these functions became the contribution of a later management pioneer, Luther H. Gulick (1892–1993), who invented the acronym POSDCORB to represent seven distinctive managerial elements: planning, organizing, staffing, directing, coordinating, reporting, and budgeting. Gulick, a professor of public administration at Columbia University, came up with this device while serving as a member of the President's Committee on Administrative Management, appointed by Franklin D. Roosevelt in 1936 to advise on new directions for managing the executive branch of the U.S. government.

The writings of Taylor and his followers particularly influenced librarianship in the U.S. Taylor's application of scientific principles to management came at a time when people expressed great concern over the pursuit of efficiency and economy in the workplace. His principles were considered particularly appropriate for such routinized library operations as ordering, cataloguing, circulation, shelving, and binding. Although Taylor's approach was not adopted wholesale in the U.S., his thinking did influence some of its leading librarians, most notably Ralph Shaw (1907–72), a director of the library of the U.S. Department of Agriculture and later a prominent library school educator and dean. Taylor and Gulick were also influential in the career of academic librarian Donald Coney (1901–73), whose treatise on scientific management in university libraries was published in 1930.

Systems Analysis. A revival of scientific management occurred after World War II as operations research, an outgrowth of British endeavors to mobilize scientific manpower in rendering more effective military decisions, gained recognition as an academic discipline and an accepted tool for undergirding managerial decisions. Since operations research was dependent on a systematic analysis of the flow of employee activities, it became the forerunner of a new discipline, systems analysis, which the scientific and technical community hailed as an important breakthrough in the development of management thought. The trajectory of systems analysis in the conduct of libraries in the U.S. and the United Kingdom is a somewhat uneven one. Including in its armamentarium such devices as mathematical modeling, tactical gaming, scenario construction, and probability theory, systems analysis was early on applied to library operations in a variety of technologically oriented institutions, including the Case Institute of Technology, the University of California at Berkeley, the Johns Hopkins University, the Massachusetts Institute of Technology, and Purdue University in the U.S. and the University of Lancaster in the U.K.

Although widely credited for contributing greater understanding to such varied aspects of library work as storage of materials, allocation of book and periodical budgets, loan policies, and document delivery, systems analysis was later faulted on two grounds. First, it often resulted in considering library operations only at a suboptimized level, without paying sufficient attention to the more complex whole of which the analyzed activities were only a part. Second, it eschewed many of the political variables affecting modern decision making that result from the demands of key actors in the policy process, such as the faculty affecting an academic library or a special-interest group affecting the conduct of a public library.

The systems analysis approach may have reached its apogee in the mid-1960s, when PPBS (Planning, Programming, and Budgeting System) was adopted as the base of all managerial activities in the U.S. government. Because of its widespread use and the amount of attention paid to it in public-administration circles, it was widely imitated at state and local levels of government, with the result that many U.S. libraries, whether school, academic, or public, employed it for projecting current and longer-term budgetary needs. Its paper requirements and undeniable complexities hampered its effective use over the long term, but it did focus attention on determining planned objectives and applying appropriate funding levels to accomplish them. PPBS was discontinued in the federal government in 1971, but its influence can still be perceived in further efforts to prioritize government objectives, such as MBO (management by objectives) in the Nixon administration or ZBB (zero-based budgeting) in the Carter administration.

Strategic Planning. All these control systems place great importance on delineating specific objectives, an important component in scientific management's latest development, strategic planning and, by extension, strategic management. Emphasizing the futurity of current decisions, strategic planning is usually considered the province of the higher executive levels of line management, in contrast to the operating plans of middle or lower management. It is expected to deal substantively with difficult policy questions regarding the specifics of organizational mission when weighed against considerations of future market economies and environmental forecasts. A number of leading libraries have attempted strategic planning, and it has also been applied to the development of professional library associations.

Although strategic planning may have begun in the private sector of an advanced capitalist country, the process of planning library service has been a characteristic of mid- and late-20th century socioeconomic life throughout the world. Even though there are distinctions between those nations in which a national library and information science infrastructure already exists and those in which such a structure is being developed, the idea of library service as basic to the achievement of national literacy and economic productivity became a constant after World War II. In part this development was brought about by the work of Unesco, which in 1974 sponsored an intergovernmental conference in Paris on planning national documentation, library, and archives infrastructures. This NATIS (national information systems) conference was the culmination of the work of four regional meetings of experts in the area of national library planning that had begun in 1966.

Automation. The more developed countries have recognized that one of their principal management problems is furthering synergistic relations among already established and functioning libraries, such as links between those serving higher education and those used by the general public. Anticipating that advances in computer and telecommunications technology will stimulate resource sharing, the industrial and post-industrial societies in Europe and North America have placed great emphasis on library automation. Originally limited to managing internal library records in such matters as serials control, circulation, and cataloguing, automation brought the end user much more into focus, with the result that workstations, teleconferencing, and teaching tutorials are becoming more commonplace. Other nations, lacking in some cases the financial resources or technological infrastructure for electronic development, have placed considerable emphasis on establishing traditional services and on encouraging a national planning structure through a designated national library or other government mechanism.

Education for Management. Relevant to both these spheres of library operations is the need for an educational program to train administrators in managing organizations that may in the future bear little resemblance to what we now know as libraries. Central to this question is whether the library will continue as a centralized unit with satellite branches or departments or will be transformed into a decentralized service outlet, making its resources available through a wide variety of locations, including dormitory rooms, faculty offices, industrial plants, and even private residences. Portents of home delivery of information services are already evident, and the technology exists to enhance this development. The administrator of the future will require not only a consummate understanding of the technology but also an ability to create and improve a far more customized service than has been required. Although the desiderata for such administrators are complex, several attempts have been made to arrive at a common definition of managerial responsibility.

Among other organizations, the International Federation of Library Associations and Institutions (IFLA) has exhibited considerable concern over the creation of a core curriculum that would permit a greater degree of harmonization in educating those working in the three major information professions, librarianship, archival management, and information science. Management was prominent among the fields of endeavor that were believed susceptible to such integration. Activities in this area date back to the mid-1970s; the subject received primary attention at a conference in Vienna in 1983 on "Management for the Information Professions: Implications for Education and Training" that attracted 22 participants from 13 countries. During the meeting, Edward Evans, author of a well-known library management textbook published in the U.S., listed 18 topics that could be subsumed under the broad rubric of management/administration. The participants then drafted a working paper detailing various components of the management process and divided them into two categories: the theoretical and the practical. One outcome of this workshop was that Miriam Tees of the Graduate School of Library and Information Studies at McGill University undertook to develop a core curriculum in the area. She designed an eight-module study program dealing with an introduction to management, planning, organization, staffing, leading, controlling, marketing, and operations. A second conference, held in Varna, Bulgaria, in 1985, further highlighted this activity.

Educational harmonization of the three information professions was prominently featured at a conference in London in 1987, but little was done after that to continue the effort. Part of the reason, Tees suggests, is the state of flux in education for the information professions. Schools in some countries were closed or merged with other academic units teaching information science, computer science, or information management. She writes, "Widespread rethinking of the mission of the information professional, debate over standards of education for librarianship in North America, and discussion of the academic level at which librarians, information scientists, and archivists should be educated, all point to changes in the way information professionals will be taught in the future." Whatever the outcome of these deliberations may be, it is doubtful that training for the administrators of modern information enterprises will revert to the apprenticeship mode of earlier periods of library development. What may be more to the point is that the rate of technological change will force administrators and middle managers of the future to avail themselves repeatedly of opportunities for continuous reeducation and retraining. Change may be the only constant in the management function of the future.

REFERENCES

Richard M. Dougherty and Fred J. Heinritz, *Scientific Management of Library Operations,* 2nd edition (1982).

Ian M. Johnson, et al., editors, *Harmonization of Education and Training Programs for Library, Information, and Archival Personnel,* Proceedings of an International Colloquium, London, August 9–15, 1987 (1989).

F. F. Leimkuhler, "Systems Approach to Library Management," in Ching-chih Chen, editor, *Quantitative Measurement and Dynamic Library Service* (1978).

Beverly P. Lynch, "Libraries as Bureaucracies," *Library Trends* (1979).

R. Kathleen Molz, *Library Planning and Policy Making: The Legacy of the Public and Private Sectors* (1990).

Miriam Tees, "Harmonization of Education and Training for Information Professionals," *IFLA Journal* (1991).

R. KATHLEEN MOLZ

Library of Congress

The Library of Congress, in Washington, D.C., is regarded as the national library of the United States. Its vast collections constitute an unparalleled treasure of the American democratic experience. Its services extend not only to members of Congress, but also to members of the executive and judicial branches of the government, to libraries throughout the world, and to individual scholars, researchers, artists, and scientists who use its resources.

The LC is the most open and accessible major national library in the world. It serves its readers through 22 public reading rooms in the three-building Library complex on Capitol Hill and the Performing Arts Library at the John F. Kennedy Center for the Performing Arts. In addition, it has two separate reading rooms for members of Congress and their staffs, and the Congressional Research Service operates reference centers in several House and Senate office buildings.

Today's LC is very different from the library Congress created in 1800. The act that provided for moving the seat of government to the new capital city of Washington provided, among other items, $5,000 "for the purchase of such books as may be necessary for the use of Congress . . . and for fitting up a suitable apartment for containing them . . . ." The reference library was clearly intended for Congress only.

The Library was established as part of the legislative, rather than executive, branch of the government. It remains a legislative branch agency today, which means that it reports to the Congress rather than to the President. But the President appoints the Librarian of Congress and the Senate confirms the nomination.

HISTORY

The First Hundred Years. The first books for the Library were ordered from London booksellers Cadell & Davies and shipped across the Atlantic in 1801 in 11 trunks and a map case. They were housed in a room in the Capitol until August 1814, when British troops set fire to the building. The collection of some 3,000 volumes was lost in the flames.

Within a month Thomas Jefferson, living in retirement at Monticello, offered his personal library, accumulated over a span of 50 years, as a replacement. It was considered one of the finest libraries in the U.S. In offering the library to the Congress, Jefferson wrote, "I do not know that it contains any branch of science which Congress would wish to exclude from their collection; there is, in fact, no subject to which a Member of Congress may not have occasion to refer." After considerable debate, Congress in January 1815 accepted Jefferson's offer, appropriating $23,950 for the collection of 6,487 books.

Two other fires influenced the development of the Library. In 1825 a small fire in the Library (housed once again in the Capitol) burned some duplicate volumes. A more serious fire in 1851 destroyed two-thirds of the accumulated holdings of 55,000 volumes, including a substantial portion of the collection purchased from Jefferson. Within three weeks, President Millard Fillmore approved an emergency appropriation of $10,000 to begin to replace the books lost in the fire. The following year, Congress voted almost $150,000 to buy new books and to construct a large, multigalleried series of rooms across the west side of the Capitol for the exclusive use of the Library.

By the end of the Civil War, the collections of the LC, popularly called "the Congressional Library," had grown to 82,000 volumes. They were used primarily by members of Congress, justices of the Supreme Court, the diplomatic corps, and members of the Cabinet.

Expanding the Collections. In 1864 President Lincoln appointed as Librarian of Congress a man who was to transform the Library over the next 30 years. Ainsworth Rand Spofford greatly expanded the LC's collections and gave the institution a new national role.

Spofford successfully advocated a change in the copyright law so that the LC would receive two free copies of every book, map, chart, dramatic or musical composition, engraving, print, or photograph submitted for copyright. Through an agreement with the

Library of Congress

Library of Congress under construction, November 25, 1892.

Smithsonian Institution, he also began to acquire American scientific materials and foreign exchange documents on a regular basis. Another law enabled the Library to receive free copies of the *Congressional Record* and all U.S. statutes; Spofford used them to begin document exchanges with all foreign countries that had diplomatic relations with the U.S.

Predictably, Spofford soon filled the Library's rooms, attics, and hallways in the Capitol with his flood of new acquisitions. He won another lobbying effort in 1873—for a new building to be the permanent home of the nation's growing collection, with reading rooms to serve scholars and the reading public. He thus assured the transformation of the Congressional Library into the nation's library.

Housing the Collections. Two Washington architects, John L. Smithmeyer and Paul J. Pelz, designed the Library's Thomas Jefferson Building in a modified Italian Renaissance style. It was completed in 1897. A celebration of the arts, the building has murals, mosaics, and statues produced by scores of painters, sculptors, and stonecutters. Crowning the structure is the dome of the Main Reading Room, 125 feet high and 100 feet wide, supported by marble columns and 11-foot statues characterizing "civilized life and thought."

As the collections and staff grew, Congress added two more buildings to the Library complex on Capitol Hill: the John Adams Building, designed at the height of the art deco period and opened in 1939, and the James Madison Memorial Building, enclosing almost 35 acres, the third largest federal government building when it opened in 1980. (Only the Pentagon and the J. Edgar Hoover Building of the Federal Bureau of Investigation were larger.)

Cataloguing the Collections. The first Librarian of Congress in the new building in 1897 was a newspaperman with no library experience, John Russell Young. He quickly realized that the LC had to get control of collections that had been piling up and overflowing the rooms in the Capitol. Young set up new organizational units and programs that changed the Library from an acquisitions and storage operation into an efficient processing factory that organized the materials and made them useful.

Librarians of the 20th Century. Young was succeeded after only two years by Herbert Putnam, previously head of the Boston Public Library, who served from 1899 to 1939.

The Legacy of Putnam. The LC came of age under Putnam. Spofford had collected the materials and Young had made a start on organizing them, but Putnam set out to ensure that they would be used. One of his first major tasks was to develop a new system for classifying books; the one then in use was based on the scheme devised by Jefferson, woefully inadequate for a collection of the size and scope of the LC. The result was a totally new LC classification schedule, a system that is generally acknowledged to be the best for very large libraries.

In 1901 Congress authorized the LC to lend books outside the District of Columbia for the first time, thus establishing an interlibrary loan program. Putnam initiated steps that led to printing the familiar three-by-five-inch library catalogue cards so libraries in all parts of the country could purchase them. His idea was to catalogue books as quickly as the LC received them by copyright deposit, exchange, or purchase, then to sell the printed catalogue cards to local libraries at cost; smaller institutions would be spared the trouble and expense of doing the cataloguing work themselves when they bought the same book. Thus the LC assumed a leadership role in standardizing cataloguing practices. The Library's cataloguing records are now provided for the most part through MARC (machine-readable cataloguing) tapes rather than printed cards, but the same principle applies today. U.S. libraries saved an estimated $387 million in cataloguing costs in 1991 alone by relying on the LC's cataloguing services.

Library of Congress

Herbert Putnam, Librarian of Congress (3rd from right, front row) and the officers of the Library of Congress, 1914.

In 1914, following the example of a number of state legislatures, Putnam asked Congress to create a new unit in the Library to serve the legislature and to respond quickly to questions that arose in the course of the legislative process. Called the Legislative Reference Service, it started out by preparing indexes, digests, and compilations of law that the Congress might need, but it quickly became a specialized reference unit for information transfer and research.

Putnam forged alliances with two patrons of music whose generosity broadened the scope of the Library and enriched its collections immeasurably: Elizabeth Sprague Coolidge and Gertrude Clarke Whittall. Mrs. Coolidge created the Coolidge Foundation at the LC for "the study, composition, and appreciation of music" and provided funds to construct the Coolidge Auditorium for chamber music; the first concert was given there in 1925. Mrs. Whittall gave five Stradivarius instruments to the Library in 1935, along with an endowment for concerts at which the instruments could be played. These gifts led to the acquisition of thousands of musical manuscript masterpieces and made the LC an unrivaled center for studying music.

Other highlights of Putnam's 40 years at the LC include establishing a number of divisions devoted to the literatures and languages of other cultures; creating a program "for the acquisition of American folksong," now part of the Library's American Folklife

Fish eye view of the Main Reading Room of the Library of Congress after its renovation in 1991.

Jim Higgins/Library of Congress

Center; naming a Consultant in Poetry; acquiring the now-priceless Vollbehr collection of 15th-century books, which included one of three existing perfect copies on vellum of the Gutenberg Bible; and the gift of the magnificent Hispanic Division Reading Room through the Hispanic Society of America and its president, Archer M. Huntington.

After Putnam. The poet Archibald MacLeish, who served as Librarian of Congress from 1939 to 1945, saw as his first task designing a modern fiscal and administrative structure for the LC. He wrote that "The principal difficulty with the old Library, from my point of view, as the unexpected and unexpectant heir, was the fact that the whole fabric depended from the Librarian as the miraculous architecture of the paper wasp hangs from a single anchor." The structure MacLeish created lasted for 30 years. He also wrote the first policy statement setting out the Library's objectives, incorporating his "Canons of Service" and "Canons of Selection." In effect, they defined the priorities of the institution, and they are, in the main, still in force today.

Luther Evans, who had been director of the Legislative Reference Service, succeeded MacLeish, serving from 1945 to 1953. He expanded the Library's international role, widening international exchange agreements and sending members of the LC staff to developing countries to help in establishing library systems.

L. Quincy Mumford served as Librarian of Congress from 1954 to 1975—the first person with a professional library degree to hold the office. He oversaw a revolution in library technology during his term. Cataloguing was automated and converted to digital format, bibliographic data was distributed on MARC tapes rather than printed cards, and researchers became accustomed to searching the vast collections by computer instead of flipping through catalogue cards. Foreign acquisitions increased exponentially under Mumford, largely as a result of Congressional concern that the U.S. keep up with other nations in the race for scientific and technological information that began when the U.S.S.R. launched its Sputnik satellite in 1957. Mumford also persuaded Congress that the LC needed another building on Capitol Hill to house its staff and its growing collections.

The noted historian Daniel J. Boorstin served as Librarian from 1975 to 1987. A scholar with strong links to the national and international world of scholarship, he sought to make the LC better known to scholars. He sponsored seminars, created a Council of Scholars, invited eminent figures from the scholarly and cultural worlds for stimulating conversations over lunch, and staged festive dinners in the Library's Great Hall to honor creative Americans. All these efforts brought positive publicity to the institution.

James H. Billington was appointed to succeed Boorstin in 1987. Also a historian, Billington shared many of Boorstin's concerns about making the LC better known to scholars and researchers. With changing technologies, he also saw an opportunity to make the LC a vital force in the nation's educational life. He sought to make its collections accessible to people in all parts of the country without requiring them to travel to Washington to use them. Testifying before Congress in 1990, he said that "technology—the electronic storage, selection, and transmission of information—will make it possible for the Library of Congress to become a library without walls. This library will increasingly serve the American people nationwide through a sophisticated network of local libraries which will be the community outlets funnelling knowledge from the Library of Congress to local users."

THE LIBRARY OF CONGRESS TODAY

The Library's Constituencies. Today's Library of Congress serves many constituencies. The first, of course, is the Congress, served primarily by the Library's Congressional Research Service (CRS), created in 1970 to replace the Legislative Reference Service. With a staff of almost 850 employees, CRS answers some 500,000 requests for information, research, and analysis every year from members and committees of Congress.

Another specialized constituency is blind and physically handicapped citizens. The National Library Service for the Blind and Physically Handicapped (NLS) administers a free national library program of brailled and recorded materials for anyone who cannot read a printed book. Created originally in 1931, the NLS served nearly 760,000 readers with more than 20 million recorded and braille books in 1991 through a network of some 160 regional and local libraries.

The American artistic and creative community, including artists, authors, composers, and publishers, is served by the Copyright Office. This LC agency registered 660,000 claims for copyright in 1991.

And the LC assists the library community in many ways, including establishing and maintaining national and international cataloguing standards; cataloguing books, maps, and other materials in forms all libraries can use and distributing cataloguing data; cataloguing in cooperation with other research institutions; acquiring foreign publications in cooperation with other institutions; coordinating activities with other federal libraries through the Federal Library Information Center Committee (FLICC) and its computer link, the Federal Library and Information Network (FEDLINK); and searching for new methods of preserving books in large quantities to halt the disintegration of acidic paper.

The Library's Collections. The LC abounds in superlatives. It is the largest library in the world, with more than a hundred million items in its collections. Less than 20 percent of that total is made up of books in the classified collections; the rest, more than 83 million items, includes more than 12,580,000 books in large type or raised characters, incunabula, monographs and serials, music, bound newspapers, pamphlets, technical reports, and other printed material; more than 1,870,000 audio materials, such as discs, tapes, and other recorded formats; almost 40,000,000 manuscripts; almost 4,100,000 maps; almost 8,700,000 microforms; more than 500,000 motion pictures; almost 14,000,000 photographs; more than 80,000 posters; almost 350,000 fine prints and drawings; more than 130,000 videotapes and videodiscs; and almost 1,240,000 other visual materials.

The LC has a staff of more than 5,000 employees to manage these collections; it received appropriations of more than $328 million a year in the early 1990s. Its computer system holds 12,600,000 records in its databases and serves some 3,000 terminals in the three buildings and on Capitol Hill. The LC has overseas offices in Cairo, Jakarta, Karachi, Nairobi, New Delhi, and Rio de Janeiro and an acquisitions office in Moscow.

The Library's Treasures. In the course of accumulating the world's knowledge, the Library also acquired many rare and precious examples of human intellectual efforts. In fact, through the generosity of individual donors, the LC has become a museum celebrating the creative genius. But, unlike a museum, the Library acquired its collections so they could be used, not just displayed—so they could be studied, compared, and analyzed in order to enrich and inform our understanding of ourselves and our heritage.

Along with its incunabula, the LC takes equal pride in such less likely pieces as the earliest motion picture print, *Fred Ott's Sneeze,* made by Thomas Edison in 1893; the original manuscripts of such musical theater classics as *Oklahoma!, Porgy and Bess, Show Boat,* and *West Side Story* in their composers' own hands; and the world's most comprehensive collection of commercial and noncommercial recordings made by jazz giant Duke Ellington.

For Americans, probably the Library's greatest treasure is Thomas Jefferson's Rough Draft of the Declaration of Independence. The four pen-and-ink pages were Jefferson's original working copy and show changes made by Benjamin Franklin, John Adams, and others. The Library has thousands of other items relating to the Revolutionary War and the founding of the republic, including the Articles of Capitulation at Yorktown, signed by both Lord Cornwallis and George Washington, and James Madison's "Notes of Debates in the Federal Convention," a handwritten record of the proceedings of the Constitutional Convention in 1787. The Library owns the personal papers of most of the presidents from Washington to Coolidge and has great quantities of memorabilia from such figures as Lincoln, Theodore Roosevelt, and Woodrow Wilson. It owns the handwritten draft of the Emancipation Proclamation and two handwritten copies of the Gettysburg Address.

Library of Congress

The book conveyor system beneath the Main Reading Room of the Library of Congress.

Pictorial treasures come from many places and most times. The LC owns the earliest known photograph of the Capitol, taken in 1846. It has all the original photographs the Wright Brothers took to record their first successful powered flights at Kitty Hawk. And it has the earliest known map of Manhattan Island, a watercolor prepared for the Dutch West India Company in 1639.

The Lessing J. Rosenwald collection of the illustrated book from the 15th century to the 20th probably contains the most extensive group of rarities. Made up of more than 2,500 precious items, it includes the Giant Bible of Mainz (1453), one of the two known copies of the *Epistolae et Evangelia*(1495), and rare products from William Caxton's press.

The Library's music collection contains both rare instruments and rare manuscripts. It owns more than 1,600 flutes from cultures around the world (including Frederick the Great's own flute in its handmade porcelain case) in the Dayton C. Miller flute collection.

Using the Library of Congress. The general reading rooms are open to any adult who presents

Library of Congress

Conservation specialist at work in the Library of Congress.

Visually handicapped patron with tape recorder made available through the reading program coordinated by the National Library Service for the Blind and Physically Handicapped, Library of Congress.

Library of Congress

identification that includes a photo and requests a user card. Users can access the Library's bibliographic databases by using touch-screen computer terminals. Readers in the Main Reading Room can search a number of other standard bibliographic reference sources easily at CD-ROM workstations that are all linked to a common "jukebox."

The Library's special-format reading rooms, such as those for manuscripts, maps, motion pictures, and music, are also open to the general adult public, although users may have to make appointments to use materials that are stored at remote sites. For example, an optical-disk workstation allows users in the Prints and Photographs Reading Room to search quickly through images of thousands of posters to find the one they want, and even to print copies of the desired image for reference. A Machine-Readable Collections Reading Room is stocked with a great variety of computer software programs for users to study.

The LC also welcomes thousands of visitors from all parts of the world every year who come just to see its buildings. A major renovation of the two older buildings began in 1986 and was scheduled for completion by the mid-1990s. The buildings remain open for researchers, and visitors may view the Main Reading Room of the Thomas Jefferson Building from an overhead enclosed gallery on one of the Library's regularly scheduled public tours. Free literary programs and concerts of chamber music are held regularly throughout the year. During the summer the American Folklife Center sponsors noontime concerts outside the main entrance of the Jefferson Building.

A LIBRARY WITHOUT WALLS

The LC sought in the late 1980s and early 1990s to make its collections more accessible to researchers, scholars, and students in all parts of the U.S. It explored a number of means to achieve this goal, including a pilot subscription service called LC DIRECT that gave state library agencies direct online access to the LC's bibliographic databases. Another experimental program, American Memory, used computer technologies to disseminate electronic copies of archival photographs, manuscripts, music, motion pictures, books, and sound recordings, providing access to unique materials that previously could be used only at the LC.

The Library began work on a new Science and Technology Center with two main purposes. One was to increase its own collection of foreign scientific materials. The second was, in James Billington's words, to "provide a kind of electronic 'yellow pages' guide to networks and databases of scientific and technological information around the world."

The Center for the Book at the Library of Congress, established in 1977 to promote reading and literacy programs, is another example of the Library reaching out beyond its own walls. Since 1984, more than half the states have established their own Centers for the Book to work with the LC in developing activities that promote their own state's book culture and literary heritage, sponsoring projects and hosting events that call attention to the importance of books, reading, literacy, and libraries.

REFERENCES

John Y. Cole, *For Congress and the Nation: A Chronological History of the Library of Congress* (1979).

Charles A. Goodrum and Helen W. Dalrymple, *The Library of Congress* (1982).

Charles A. Goodrum, *Treasures of the Library of Congress,* revised edition (1991).

Josephus Nelson and Judith Farley, *Full Circle: Ninety Years of Service in the Main Reading Room* (1991).

Herbert Small, *The Library of Congress: Its Architecture and Decoration* (1982).

HELEN DALRYMPLE

Libya

Libya, officially the Socialist People's Libyan Arab Jamahiriya, is in northern Africa, bordered by the Mediterranean Sea on the north, Egypt on the east, Sudan on the southeast, Chad and Niger on the south, and Algeria and Tunisia on the west. Population (1990 est.) 4,000,000; area 1,749,000 sq.km. The language is Arabic.

History. Libya was a center of some of the outstanding civilizations of ancient times. In the Eastern Region the Greeks established a large public library in Cyrene. By Roman times many other libraries had been introduced. During Islamic rule the country benefited from the educated people who crossed the territory, traveling from one end of the Islamic world to the other. The people began to engage in scientific and literary activities. The largest library, started in Jaghboub, contained about 40,000 volumes, the great majority of which were in manuscript; remains of that collection (over 1,000 manuscripts) are now in the Central Library of Garyounis University.

An antiquities library was founded in the capital city, Tripoli, in 1911. It is the richest library of rare books, documents, and archives in the country. Another was established in Cyrene in 1914; it holds more than 10,000 rare books in various languages. Many other libraries were founded throughout the country to serve religious and social groups where there were no public libraries. The collections of these libraries are mixed, but they cover mostly Arabic literature and Islamic interests.

National Library. From 1955, the university library acted as a national library, but in response to the need for a national library the Ministry of Education decided to establish one in Benghazi City.

Construction now completed, it has been furnished and equipped. The book, manuscript, document, and periodical collections are quickly growing, and in 1984 a proclamation was issued to establish it as a depository library. Plans called for it to be open to the public.

Academic Libraries. The Central Library of Garyounis University, Benghazi, was founded in 1955. It started with a collection of 300 volumes and grew at a fast rate in print and nonprint materials, reaching more than 260,000 volumes by the late 1980s. The building consists of four air-conditioned floors, with a capacity of 3,000 seats plus facilities for a million volumes. The library has four main departments: Readers' Services, Branch Libraries, Technical Services, and Administration. It uses the Dewey Decimal Classification for non-Arabic books. An amended system is used for the Arabic collection. The Audiovisual Division is well equipped with good facilities. There are six branch libraries.

The first library in the University of El-Fateh, Tripoli, was established in 1957 when the Faculty of Science was opened. There are seven libraries, each with a rich collection mainly in the field of the faculty. The collection totals about 155,800 volumes in addition to 3,510 periodicals and a large number of back issues. Audiovisual departments with large collections function in each library. In 1970 a decision was made to erect a new Central Library building, but the project was delayed. The basic book collection of the Central Library is temporarily located in a part of the Faculty of Science. The Library School at this university gives good support to the faculty libraries, mainly in providing them with professional staff and technical services. The Dewey Decimal System and Anglo-American Cataloguing Rules are used.

Bright Star University of Technology was opened in Brega, 280 km. west of Benghazi, in 1981. A Central Library building was erected on the campus. The book collection totals about 35,000 volumes, mostly in English. It subscribes to 415 periodicals and has a small collection of back issues. A small audiovisual section has been established. Several departmental libraries offer quick service to the faculty, staff, and students. The library applies the technical system used in the University of Garyounis libraries.

The University of Sebha was founded in 1983. Its library was established in 1977 for the Faculty of Education that was part of the University of El-Fateh in Tripoli. The book collection is over 35,000 volumes in various languages. The Library subscribes to 410 periodicals. It publishes a quarterly bulletin to notify readers of new additions and other news. It uses the same technical system as the other university libraries. In spite of shortages in technical manpower and other difficulties, it promised to become a dependable library serving the educated people in the southern part of Libya.

Higher Technical Institutes. Five higher institutes for technical education were founded in various parts of the country between 1972 and 1977. Each institute has its own library; each contains about 10,000 volumes. The institutes cooperate to cover any needs that may arise among them.

Public Libraries. Public library service in the modern sense was started in the country in 1953. These libraries were under the Minister of Education. In 1960 the Minister of Information and Culture introduced a new service at the people's cultural centers. Both public libraries and cultural centers cooperate to provide their clientele with new books, magazines, newspapers, and government publications. They numbered more than 160 in the late 1980s. Technical services, acquisitions, and budget control are centralized in a department of the Secretary of Information.

School Libraries. From 1960 considerable efforts were made to establish libraries in secondary, preparatory, and vocational schools. By the end of 1978 almost all of them had small libraries. Services of those libraries improved when the Secretary of Education provided better support with more adequate budgets. They are still in need of proper facilities and sufficient trained personnel.

Special Libraries. These libraries have become indispensable for the main secretariats, organizations, and other establishments. Special libraries up to 1970 numbered only eight in the whole country. That number had increased to 29 by the end of 1982. Each library maintains material relating to its special activities.

AHMED M. GALLAL

Liebaers, Herman
(1919–)

EUROPALIA
Herman Liebaers

Herman Liebaers, Librarian on the staff of the Royal Library of Belgium (1943–54), Director of the Library (1956–73), and Grand Marshal of the Court of Belgium (1974–81), led in strengthening IFLA and international librarianship.

Born at Tienen, Belgium, February 1, 1919, Herman Liebaers was educated in Brussels and at the University of Ghent; like many Europeans of his generation, he was caught up in World War II. During the German occupation of Belgium, he spent most of 1943 in German captivity. On return to Brussels he came into librarianship and into his eminent career at the Royal Library by mere chance when that Library needed a staff member who had academic training in Germanic language and literature but who was, obviously, not pro-German. During his early career in the Royal Library, where his first task was to translate the existing French subject catalogue into Dutch, he not only achieved his library certification in 1944 but also continued his scholarly studies, receiving his Ph.D. from the University of Ghent in 1955. His study of the 19th-century Dutch poet Hélène Swarth, together with her correspondence, was subsequently published by the Royal Flemish Academy of Language and Literature.

Another significant element in his early career came by way of a five-month visit to the United States during 1950–51, when he was a consultant at the Library of Congress and visited many U.S. libraries, museums, and art galleries. During the next few years he conducted summer courses in Flemish art for foreign art historians under a program sponsored by the Belgian-American Educational Foundation.

In 1954 Liebaers left the Royal Library, spent half a year as Librarian of the European Council for Nuclear Research (CERN), and then returned to the U.S. until 1956 as a Fellow and Associate Secretary of the Belgian-American Educational Foundation. He returned to the Royal Library in 1956 as Director.

The Royal Library set high standards for the other ancient national libraries of western Europe in many ways under his forceful leadership. A new building, dedicated in 1959, not only functions efficiently but is also an appropriate component of the national cultural center of Brussels. In establishing an effective modern scientific and technical documentation service, Liebaers dispatched the Chief of the new facility to Kansas City to spend a term under the tutelage of Joseph Shipman at the Linda Hall Library. On quite another front, he extended the Library's rich Burgundian heritage of rare books, manuscripts, coins, and prints and brought it into public view and scholarly use through an impressive and handsome series of exhibitions and catalogs. Under his direction legal deposit was established for the Library, and the national bibliography was modernized.

In 1973 Liebaers took a leave of absence from the Royal Library and returned to the U.S. as Consultant to the Council on Library Resources with the intention, at least in the minds of his friends, of producing an analysis of American research libraries—sort of an update of Wilhelm Munthe's *American Librarianship from a European Angle* (1939). But before the year was out his career took a decided change of course when King Baudouin appointed him Grand Marshal of the Court of Belgium. Thus he left the Royal Library and moved, metaphorically at least, across the way to the Royal Palace. The new royal appointment, which Liebaers held until 1981, recognized his crucial role in Belgian cultural and intellectual life, his extensive international experience, and his notable diplomatic talents.

Liebaers's library career reached far beyond Belgium and the U.S., through the agency of the International Federation of Library Associations and Institutions (IFLA), to which he gave increasing attention in the years following 1956. He was Chairman of its National and University Libraries Section from 1959 to 1964, joined the IFLA Executive Board in 1963, was elected a Vice-President in 1964, became First Vice-President in 1967, and then in 1969 was elected President for the term 1969–72, succeeding Sir Frank Francis. He was elected to a second term in 1972, but it ended prematurely when he resigned in 1974 to take up his new post at the Belgian Court. At that point he was elected Honorary President of IFLA.

During his presidency IFLA was enabled to establish a permanent Secretariat in The Hague and to solidify its fiscal position, with generous support from the Council on Library Resources. It was thereby able to mount a succession of aggressive projects, notably the Universal Bibliographic Control (UBC) program and more recently that for Universal Availability of Publications.

Sir Frank Francis had grasped the international significance of the American Shared Cataloguing Program, which led to the National Program for Acquisitions and Cataloguing (NPAC); under Liebaers's leadership, this development was crystallized into the powerful UBC program. Similarly, Liebaers sensed the symbolic importance of Unesco's International Book Year Project of 1972 and saw to it that IFLA was the prime mover in the worldwide success of the Unesco project. For that service the Association of the German Book Trade awarded him its Interprofessional Award at the Frankfurt Book Fair in 1973. During his IFLA tenure Liebaers traveled extensively, particularly in the Third World, taking the message of books and libraries wherever he went. In these years Third World membership in IFLA expanded rapidly, and IFLA entered into an active regionalization program in order to take the IFLA program into all corners of the world.

For these and other efforts Herman Liebaers was widely honored. In 1956 he was named a Laureate of the Royal Flemish Academy of Language and Literature and in 1970 a Professor of Librarianship and Bibliography in the Free University of Brussels; the University of Liverpool awarded him an honorary doctorate in 1971, and in 1973 the Library Association of the United Kingdom named him an Honorary Vice-President; he became an Honorary Member of the Special Libraries Association in 1974 and of the American Library Association at its Centennial Conference in 1976. He continued to be active in international work as a member of the Board of Directors of the Council on Library Resources.

REFERENCES

A bibliography of Herman Liebaers, by Robert Gabriel, appeared in the Belgian journal *Mens en Taak* (1975).

A volume of Liebaers's reminiscences, *Mostly in the Line of Duty: Thirty Years with Books,* was published by Nijhoff in 1980.

ROBERT VOSPER

Liechtenstein

The principality of Liechtenstein, lying between Switzerland and Austria, is one of the smallest countries in the world. It has an area of 160 sq.km. and a population of about 28,000 (1988) in 11 *Gemeinden* (communities). Its national territory comprises the dominions of Vaduz and Schellenberg, which stood directly under the Holy Roman emperor in the late Middle Ages. The official language is German.

For centuries Liechtenstein was a desperately poor country, with poor land that was often flooded by the Rhine River. It also suffered from the dislocations of war and economic isolation. But industrialization began in the 19th century, and increased commercial activity brought gradual economic improvement. The material and intellectual foundations for the emergence of libraries were lacking until the end of the 19th century. The *Leservereine* (reading societies) established at that time served the literary and social needs of their members and may be seen as the predecessors of *Volksbibliotheken* (public libraries).

The *Historischer Verein für das Fürstentum Liechtenstein* (Historical Society for the Principality of Liechtenstein), founded in 1901, initiated an immense number of historical and regional works and published them in its annual volumes, which have appeared since 1901. The Library of the Historical Society collects mainly Liechtenstein publications, as well as works in the areas of history and historical sciences.

The members of the princely House of Liechtenstein, creators of the largest and most valuable private art galleries in the world, also collected books and

Libraries in Liechtenstein (1990)

Type of library	Number of administrative units (main libraries)	Number of service points (branches, mobile stops, etc.)	Volumes in collections	Annual expenditures (Swiss francs)	Population served	Professional staff (with certificate, diploma, etc.)	Total staff
National	1	1	130,000	980,000	29,000	3.5	7.5 Vollstellen
Public[a]	3	3	24,000	100,000	12,000	--	3 Teilzeitstellen
School[b]	7	223	28,000	--	2,550	--	--

[a]1989 data
[b]1987 data

Source: Unesco, *Statistical Yearbook,* 1991

maintained libraries. The beginnings of the *Fürstlich Liechtensteinischer Bibliothek* (Princely Liechtenstein Library), in Vienna, go back to the 16th century. Large parts of its rich collection were lost during and after World War II or were sold.

The *Liechtenstein Landesbibliothek* was established by law in 1961 as an independent, state-supported foundation with its seat in Vaduz. The Library's purpose is to collect the publications of Liechtenstein as completely as possible, to provide essential subject literature for citizens engaged in scientific research, and to promote books in Liechtenstein for education and entertainment. In its goals the Library functions as the national library, a scientific library, and a public library at the same time.

In its first 30 years the Library became a true center for information in Liechtenstein. Its collection numbered 120,000 volumes in the early 1990s. In 1974 it began publishing *Liechtensteinische Bibliographie* annually, listing materials published in Liechtenstein. The Library worked to close the existing gaps in the record of Liechtenstein's literature.

A few new school and community libraries were developed in the 1970s and 1980s. They supplement the Landesbibliothek in its function as a public library.

Liechtenstein has no significant special libraries, nor any professional library organizations. As a very small country, Liechtenstein is dependent in cultural and scientific matters on access to the corresponding institutions of neighboring Switzerland and Austria.

ALOIS OSPELT;
translated by JOHN FELBINGER

Lippincott, J. B.
(1813–1886)

Joshua Ballinger Lippincott's business life as a printer, binder, publisher, bookseller, and distributor was conducted in such a way that his publishing peers in the United States referred to him as "the Napoleon of the book trade." His business philosophy is reflected in the motto of his old-line house, *Droit et Avant* ("Right and forward," or roughly, "Be sure you are right and then go ahead").

An only child, Lippincott was born in Juliustown, Burlington County, New Jersey, March 18, 1813. Little is known of his childhood years. He had a common school education and began working at the age of 13. Little is recorded concerning his nonbusiness life, other than noting that the business, banking, and educational community of Philadelphia benefited from his leadership as a member of the boards of directors of the Philadelphia and Reading Railroad, the Farmers' and Mechanics' Bank of Philadelphia, the Philadelphia Saving Fund Society, the Pennsylvania Company for Insurance on Lives and Granting Annuities, and the Board of Trustees of the University of Pennsylvania.

Lippincott began his book-oriented career in 1827 as a clerk in a Philadelphia store owned by a bookseller named Clarke. Creditors subsequently closed on Clarke, and in 1832 Lippincott was designated as the store's manager. He paid close attention to the business and to his personal finances and by 1836 had saved enough from his earnings to purchase the business, thus launching J. B. Lippincott and Company.

Lippincott was energetic and increasingly successful. He was fast making his mark as a substantial publisher of bibles, prayer books, and general literature. Lippincott gave special attention to the manufacturing aspects of the book, and his interest in elegant bindings made his books popular with booksellers. He also retailed books and did contract printing.

In 1850 he made the major decision to purchase the entire stock of books and stationery of Grigg and Elliott, Philadelphia—at that time the country's largest wholesalers in the field. Although many in the trade considered it an unwise purchase, Lippincott meant it to help him become the foremost publisher in Philadelphia. This transaction more than any other occasioned people to call him "the Naopleon of the book trade."

An early business practice followed by Lippincott was to take in his assistants as partners, resulting in such imprints as Lippincott, Grambo, and Company in the first part of the 1850s. During the period 1855–85 he used the imprint J. B. Lippincott & Company.

Lippincott's early catalogue was distinguished by its comprehensiveness. Its notable works ranged from bibles, religious books, and tracts to major reference titles. In 1855 the first edition of *Lippincott's Pronouncing Gazetteer of the World* was published; subsequent editions continued in print for almost a century. In 1858 the firm began publishing Webster's *Blue-Back Speller.* Other successes under Lippincott's direction were *Allibone's Dictionary of Authors* (beginning with

J. B. Lippincott Company
J. B. Lippincott

the second volume in 1870), a number of excellent editions of the *Unabridged Dictionary* by Webster, which the firm gave up in 1876 when it began publication of *Worcester's Dictionary,* and *Lippincott's Pronouncing Dictionary of Biography and Mythology.*

Lippincott was also a publisher of periodicals. In 1857 he began the *Medico-Chirugical Review,* edited by Samuel D. Gross. Other periodicals included *The Medical Times* and *Annals of Surgery.* In 1868, under the editorship of Lloyd Smith, Librarian of the Library Company of Philadelphia, Lippincott launched *Lippincott's Magazine.* In the years immediately following the Civil War, Lippincott expanded in the medical field, publishing textbooks and handbooks. Early examples of his success were Da Costa's three-volume *Medical Diagnosis, Principles and Practice of Surgery* by Agnew, and the *Photographic Atlas of Diseases of the Skin* by Fox. A widely used handbook is *The Dispensatory of the United States of America;* with the 27th edition in 1985 it remains the oldest continuously published reference work under private ownership in the world. He is also credited with the publication of *A Handbook of Nursing* (1878), the first nursing textbook in the U.S.

Another of Lippincott's noteworthy contributions was the massive Chambers' *Cyclopaedia of English Literature.* He was the first American publisher of this title, and this nine-volume facsimile edition, illustrated with wood engravings and original maps, was important in establishing Lippincott's business with publishers in Europe.

While Lippincott was especially strong in books of reference and medicine, he also issued a sizable list of general books. Included were standard and deluxe editions of the works of Bulwer-Lytton, Scott, Thackeray, and Dickens, as well as Foster's three-volume biography of Charles Dickens. In 1871, under the editorship of Horace H. Furness, Lippincott published *Romeo and Juliet,* the first volume in its outstanding *Variorum Edition of Shakespeare.*

He executed important government-sponsored works, most notably Henry Schoolcraft's *History of the Indian Tribes,* published in six folio volumes and costing nearly $100,000. Lippincott's business acumen was displayed in his securing the copyright and plates for the 15 volumes of Prescott's historical works from the Boston firm of Phillips, Sampson and Company, and from Prescott's heirs.

Some of the important works Lippincott published were the romances of Marie Louise de la Ramé, better known by her nom de plume, Ouida; an edition of Scott's Waverley novels; *The Life of John Quincy Adams,* edited by his son Charles Francis Adams; and Bigelow's life of Benjamin Franklin. Other noteworthy publications were *The Writings of Albert Gallatin* and an accompanying title, *Life of Gallatin,* by Henry Adams. During Lippincott's time the idea of a series of books on a common nonfiction theme was being developed. In 1869 Lippincott produced the "Reason Why Series."

The panic of 1873 was devastating to a number of publishers and booksellers and resulted in demands for a national trade association that would regulate the retail price of books based on the cost of production. A national convention was held July 21–23, 1874, at the summer resort of Put-in-Bay on Lake Erie, and J. B. Lippincott was represented at this first American Book Trade Association (ABTA) convention at which the historic "20 percent rule" was made. The rule provided that publishers and booksellers would agree not to sell at a discount greater than 20 percent on miscellaneous books and schoolbooks to libraries, large book buyers outside the trade, professional people, and teachers, or of more than 10 percent on medical books.

Although the Lippincott firm was in attendance at Put-in-Bay, it opposed the rule, fearing that so sudden and drastic a marketing decision would adversely affect its trade. Lippincott's position subsequently moderated in objection to being called "the only holdout in the industry." Its condition for signing was that all books must be sold at the published retail price, except for a maximum discount of 20 percent to libraries, school teachers, and buyers outside the trade who purchased more than $100 net at any one time. This proposal caused much argument over a number of months, but at the second ABTA convention in July 1875 it was announced that Lippincott had finally signed the agreement. By this time Lippincott shared the distinction with Appleton of owning one of the two largest bookstores in the U.S.

In order to supply his vast empire, Lippincott developed an outstanding physical plant, moving to various locations in Philadelphia. In 1861 the firm erected a magnificent new marble building on Market Street, between Seventh and Eighth streets. Subsequent additions were built until it was the largest book publishing, distributing, and manufacturing office in the world.

In December 1879 Lippincott discussed his business with *Publishers' Weekly:*

> Twenty-nine presses are kept constantly running to meet the demands of our business. The average number of books printed by them is 2,000. Our business extends from the Atlantic to the Pacific, from Newfoundland to Texas. From 25,000 to 30,000 boxes of books are annually shipped to our various customers, and about 100,000 express packages. A manuscript is brought into the establishment and comes out a bound volume. The entire book is manufactured under this roof. Here it is printed, bound, published, sold, and distributed.

In 1884 Lippincott's health began to fail. Realizing this, he reorganized the firm in February 1885. It was incorporated with a capital of $1,000,000, and he personally held 9,970 of the 10,000 shares of stock. The new name of the firm was J. B. Lippincott Company; he was the president and owner and the first publisher to incorporate in the U.S. On January 5, 1886, Lippincott died at his home in Philadelphia.

REFERENCES

Stuart Freeman, *Centennial Reflections: J. B. Lippincott Company in the 1870's* (1976).

J. B. Lippincott Company, *The Author and His Audience; With a Chronology of Major Events in the Publishing History of J. B. Lippincott Company* (1967).

Charles A. Madison, *Book Publishing in America* (1966).

John Tebbel, *A History of Book Publishing in the United States,* 2 volumes (1972, 1975).

RICHARD FITZSIMMONS

Li Ta-chao

(1888–1927)

Li Ta-chao, a founder of the Chinese Communist Party, honored as China's first revolutionary martyr, is considered the father of modern Chinese librarianship.

Born October 6, 1888, in the village of Ta-hei-t'o, Hopei Province, Li was raised in an upper-middle-class environment. Between 1907 and 1913 he studied at the Peiyang College of Law and Political Science in Tientsin, concentrating on political economy and foreign languages. Upon graduation Li furthered his schooling at Waseda University in Tokyo.

Returning from Japan in 1916, he began several years of political activism in Peking and Shanghai. The two greatest concerns of the young Chinese intellectuals in the early 20th century were the encroachment of foreign interests, on the one hand, and the inevitable transition of a nation from the Middle Kingdom to a modern industrialized state on the other. A leading voice of the intelligentsia was *Hsin Ch'ing-nien* ("New Youth"), for which Li wrote extensively and became a member of the editorial board in 1918. Soon after his appointment Li was asked to assume the position of Head Librarian at Peking University.

Li's career as Librarian of one of China's leading universities was to have a tremendous impact on modern history. During his tenure, from 1918 to the mid-1920s, he utilized to its fullest measure the library's potential as a center for political activism. By directing the traditional functions of a university library (such as systematic acquisition and distribution of materials and utilizing space for private study and small discussions) toward the promulgation of the philosophies of Marxism, Li Ta-chao organized enough support to begin China's journey toward revolution.

Li's office was the center of much research and study. He collected and translated a major corpus of Marxist and Leninist works and made them available to students and faculty. His Marxist Research Society attracted many individuals to his office, which became known as the *hung-lou* (Red Chamber). Among his early followers was a young library assistant named Mao Tse-tung, who worked with him and attended many sessions in the Red Chamber. Years later Mao would credit Li with his initial introduction to Marxism and the beginning of his own political development.

In 1919 a series of events known as the May Fourth Movement indicate the far-reaching importance of Li's work. For several weeks intensive riots and demonstrations occurred in several major cities as the Chinese voiced their opposition to foreign presence on their native soil. Li and the Peking University Library served a unique role during this politically volatile time, directing the earliest activities of the Marxist leaders of modern China.

Li's career, although vitally important, was brief. By the mid-1920s Li and other faculty members had been forced to leave the University, because the government was becoming increasingly hostile to Communists. Eventually Li was arrested in Peking and, on April 28, 1927, was executed.

The political activism of Chinese libraries in the decades following the founding of the People's Republic was strongly influenced by the work of Li Ta-chao. It has been written that if Chinese librarians study political and cultural materials, work diligently to improve their knowledge, and actively impart this information to the people, the profession will approach Li's ideal of the library after the Marxist revolution. The example of the Red Chamber, according to this view, places a responsibility upon Chinese librarians that is unique in the history of the profession.

Courtesy of The Harvard University Press

Li Ta-chao

REFERENCES

Nearly all writing on Li Ta-chao's career in librarianship is in Chinese and untranslated as of the late 1980s. Two works that address this subject and draw from the original materials are:

Maurice Meisner, *Li Ta-chao and the Origins of Chinese Marxism* (1967).

Diane M. Nelson and Robert B. Nelson, "The Red Chamber: Li Ta-chao and the Sources of Radicalism in Modern Chinese Librarianship," *Journal of Library History, Philosophy and Comparative Librarianship* (Spring 1979).

DIANE M. NELSON;
ROBERT B. NELSON

Lithuania

Lithuania, one of the Baltic states, broke away from the U.S.S.R. to reclaim its independence on March 11, 1990. It had been an independent republic from 1918 to 1940. Latvia lies to the north, Belarus to the east and south, Poland to the southwest, and the Baltic Sea to the west. Population (1990 est.) 3,723,000; area 65,200 sq.km. The official language is Lithuanian.

History. Lithuanian library history dates back to the 14th and 15th centuries, when noblemen, monasteries, and churches collected books. Among the important collections dating from the 16th century were those of King Sigismund Augustus, the nobleman Mikalojus Pacas, bishop Merkelis Giedraitis, the priest Mikalojus Daukša, and scholars Abraomas Kulvietis and Motiejust Strijkoyskis. The earliest university and secondary-school libraries also emerged in this period, including that of Vilnius University (founded 1570).

At the end of the 18th century Russia annexed Lithuania and tried to suppress Lithuanian language and culture. The Russians closed Vilnius University (1832) and banned the Lithuanian press, schools, libraries, and use of the language. Underground efforts to preserve books and culture led to a national renaissance that started in 1904 and culminated in independence in 1918. The National Library was founded in 1919, the Kaunas University Library in 1922, the Bibliographical Institute, and a network of public libraries in apskritis (rural) centers. The development of primary-school and public libraries became a matter of national priority in the 1930s.

All or parts of Lithuania were occupied by Poland in 1937–38, by Germany in 1939, by the Soviet Union in 1940–41, by Germany again in 1941–44, and by the Soviet Union again in 1944. Each occupying power sought to supplant Lithuanian culture with its own. The devastation of World War included bombed libraries and burned or looted collections. As a republic of the Soviet Union, Lithuania developed a

U.S.S.R. Ministry of Culture

Map collection in the Vilnius State Library, Lithuania.

Soviet-style library system with collections emphasizing Soviet ideology and eliminating works considered unacceptable. Library development was impressive, with more than 5,000 libraries organized in 11 networks by 1985, but they remained isolated from the non-Soviet world. Emphasis since independence has been on developing national library collections and international ties.

National Library. Martynas Mažvydas National Library of Lithuania (founded 1919) is the primary scholarly library open to the public; since 1991 it has also served as the Parliamentary library. It collects books, manuscripts, microforms, and audiovisual materials of humanistic interest, with total holdings of five million volumes. It receives on deposit all Lithuanian printed works and collects material on Lithuanian subjects published abroad. The Library provides reference and interlibrary loan services and organizes exhibitions, seminars, symposia, and scientific conferences. It serves about 30,000 readers, with 1,500 visitors a day and a circulation of 1,800,000 volumes.

In cooperation with other libraries and bibliographic institutions, the National Library compiles the national bibliography, both retrospective and current, as well as reference indexes in various subjects and union catalogues of foreign literature. It coordinates research on libraries, bibliography, and library history, theory, and practice. It publishes a professional monthly, begun in 1946 as *Biblioteku Darbas* and renamed *Tarp Knygu* ("Among Books") in 1990.

Academic Libraries. Lithuanian universities, academies, and educational institutes form a network of 13 libraries with 12 million volumes and other documents used by more than 97,000 readers. Among the largest libraries in the network is that of Vilnius University, with present holdings of almost five million items. It has a rich collection of rare books and manuscripts and is a depository library of UN publications.

Public Libraries. Intensive development of local public libraries began in 1950; by 1978 a centralized network of district and local libraries was completed, with common collections, staff lists, and technical services. Libraries were linked hierarchically, with the National Library providing overall supervision. In 1992 the country had 1,700 libraries organized into 44 district and five city systems. Together they held some 23 million volumes and served 800,000 readers. Some libraries, particularly in resort towns, had not been centralized.

School Libraries serve students and teachers in 44 specialized secondary schools (37,000 readers and more than two million items), 56 professional-technical schools (23,000 readers and 1,700,000 items), and more than 2,000 general secondary schools (435,000 readers and 19 million items). The collections are geared to each school's curriculum and provide general reading material as well. On the Soviet model, they provided methodological and pedagogical material for teachers. When the Schools Pedagogical Library was dissolved in 1989, the National Library took over guidance of the school library network.

Special Libraries. The Academy of Sciences of Lithuania maintains a network with a Central Library and eight branches attached to specialized institutes. In 1941 the Central Library took over the collections of the Wroblewski Library, the Evangelical Synod Library (founded 1557), the Lithuanian Learned Society Library, and other collections in Vilnius and Kaunas. Its 3,800,000 books and other documents include many rare publications, maps, and manuscripts. The Central Library maintains exchange ties with institutions in 41 countries.

The Technical Library of Lithuania (founded 1957) supervises a network of almost 150 technical libraries with total holdings of 5.6 million items. These libraries serve the professional needs of institutions in such fields as building, transportation, and scientific research. For example, the health-care library system has 93 libraries, of which the most important is the State Scientific Medical Library (founded 1941). More than 80 agricultural libraries form an independent network, as do the libraries of professional unions. Highly centralized in the past, these library systems began reorganizing on simpler lines in 1989.

Other Libraries. Lithuania has a network of libraries for the Lithuanian of the Blind and those with poor eyesight. With four branches in cities and 42 service points in rural areas, the libraries provide print, braille, and recorded material for 5,000 users. The network holds 450,000 items and has a recording studio for producing additional materials.

The Profession. The Lithuanian Librarians Association was founded in 1931 and became a member of the International Federation of Library Associations (IFLA) in 1936. Primary support for professional development and research comes from the National Library.

ELENA KOŠINSKIENE

American Library Association
George Locke

Locke, George
(1870–1937)

George Herbert Locke, educator and librarian, was one of two Canadians elected President of the American Library Association. He directed the fortunes of the Toronto Public Library for nearly 30 years (1908–37), during which it expanded from a small system with a staff of 26 to a major institution boasting a large central building, 16 branches, and a staff of 232.

Locke was born in Beamsville, Ontario, March 29, 1870. Educated at Victoria College, University of Toronto, he received the B.A. and M.A. degrees in classics. He then did graduate study and teaching in educational theory, first at the University of Chicago, later at Harvard. From 1899 to 1903 he was Associate Professor at Chicago, then was appointed Dean of the College of Education. He was Editor of the *School Review* (1900–06), a prestigious journal of American secondary education. After a year in Boston as an Assistant Editor with the publishing firm of Ginn & Co., Locke returned to Canada as Dean of the School of Education at McGill University, Montreal. From McGill he was invited to the Toronto Public Library in 1908.

Locke brought neither formal training nor prior library experience to his new position, but he had a personal concept of the public library as a social institution. Probably developed from his work in education, Locke's concept of the library contained two major components: the library should bring the pleasures of literature to the general public for recreation, and it should play a major role in continuing adult education. For him, librarianship was as educational in character as the teaching profession, although it offered no specific formal instruction and served a more varied clientele.

He used his term as ALA President (1926–27) to reiterate his conviction that the public library was an intellectual public utility that would help preserve and inspire the democratic state. Its resources, properly interpreted by librarians, would allow citizens to prepare for intelligent service to society and to become informed about workings of the democratic process. His years on the ALA Executive Board produced definite views concerning the most desirable role for the Association. Librarians served a social institution, and Locke felt their professional association needed strong personal leadership. The membership exceeded 10,000 by the mid-1920s and Locke urged alternating full membership meetings with regional meetings every second year. He also urged a two-year term for the ALA presidency to prevent erosion of the office's power by the permanent general staff.

Furthering an active professional life, Locke produced a substantial body of publications for both educational and library journals and works for the general public. He wrote two works of popular Canadian history and a study of English history for the ALA's "Reading with a Purpose" series. He was a member of the American Association for the Advancement of Science, the Dominion Education Association, and several Canadian and American library associations. For his services to the community the University of Toronto awarded him an LL.D. in 1927. He died in Toronto on January 28, 1937, and was mourned in three countries—Canada, the United States, and the United Kingdom—and most of all by the city of Toronto.

REFERENCE

Margaret Anderson, "Locke, George Herbert," *Dictionary of American Library Biography* (1978).

MARGARET ANDERSON

Lubetzky, Seymour
(1898–)

Seymour Lubetzky, the greatest theoretician of descriptive cataloguing in the 20th century, was born around 1898 in Zelwa, a town then part of Russia, later of Poland, and now of Belarus. After being a teacher in his native land, he went to Los Angeles, California, where in 1927 he became a student at the University of California at Los Angeles, majoring in German. Graduating in 1931, he attended the University of California at Berkeley, gaining a teaching certificate and an M.A. in German in 1932 and, finally, a Certificate in Librarianship from the School of Librarianship in 1934.

In 1936 Lubetzky started work at the UCLA Library, eventually becoming a cataloguer. While there he wrote articles questioning then-current library practices with respect to capitalization, the use of unnecessary title-added entries, and the division of library catalogues. These articles displayed the talent that caused the Library of Congress to hire him in 1943 to look into current cataloguing practices.

In 1942 Lubetzky worked in a shipyard in the San Francisco Bay area so that he might contribute to the war effort in a tangible fashion. By creating a uniform set of parts descriptions in a fully-referenced card catalogue, he was able to reorganize the shipyard's stock and thereby save many thousands of dollars.

Although Lubetzky's first assignment at LC in 1943 was temporary only, he was later appointed Chief of the LC Catalog Maintenance Division, where he was responsible for planning for the publication of the ongoing *National Union Catalog* (then the closest equivalent to an American national bibliography). Finally, he became Consultant (later Specialist) in Bibliographic and Cataloging Policy, the position in which he made his most important theoretical contributions.

Lubetzky's first major endeavor at LC was simplification of the rules for description. His studies led to the 1949 publication of *Rules for Descriptive Cataloging in the Library of Congress (Adopted by the American Library Association),* a code based on explicitly stated objectives. He next turned his attention to the rules for entry found in the *A.L.A. Cataloging Rules for Author and Title Entries, Second Edition* (1949). His analysis and critique of those rules is found in his *Cataloging Rules and Principles,* published by LC in 1953. *Cataloging Rules and Principles,* one of the classics of library literature, questions previous practice with respect to the form of heading for both personal and corporate authors as well as the very structure of previous cataloguing codes. In addition, it provides the outline for a future code.

As a result of the favorable reaction to *Cataloging Rules and Principles,* Lubetzky was appointed editor for a revised cataloguing code. The revision he contemplated is found in two major drafts—*Code of Cataloging Rules: Bibliographic Entry and Description* was issued in 1958; *Code of Cataloging Rules: Author and Title Entry* was issued in 1960, with its appendant *Additions, Revisions and Changes* appearing in 1961. These drafts are characterized by the clear statement of the objectives of cataloguing and the rigorous pursuit of those objectives in the form of rules addressed to bibliographic conditions, instead of the unsystematic, case-by-case approach found in previous cataloguing codes.

Lubetzky was unable to finish work on the revised code because of the press of duties connected with his appointment in 1960 as professor at the new School of Library Service at UCLA, as well as unwillingness to compromise on important points in the new code. Many of Lubetzky's major findings, however, were incorporated in the "Statement of Principles" formulated at the International Conference on Cataloguing Principles held in Paris in 1961. These principles are at the base of all modern cataloguing codes.

Probably the most definitive statement of Lubetzky's views is to be found in his 1969 report, *Principles of Cataloging; Final Report, Phase I: Descriptive Cataloging*. Among other major points, Lubetzky insists that a catalogue must deal with *works*, not books, as the fundamental objects to be catalogued, that main entry is designed to represent a *book* as an edition of a particular *work* and thus bring together the various editions of a work, and that corporate bodies are authors of their publications. Lubetzky further notes that a catalogue is an instrument communicating much more than a mere finding list: a catalogue is an aid to users in exploiting the resources of a library. These points are part of what Lubetzky calls the ideological bases of a catalogue, and they do not vary in the face of changing technology used in the display of a catalogue. These and other conclusions have permanent value although they have not been consistently observed in the Second Edition of the *Anglo-American Cataloguing Rules* (AACR2).

Lubetzky was awarded the ALA Margaret Mann Citation in 1955, the Beta Phi Mu Award for Good Teaching in 1964, the Doctor of Laws degree by UCLA in 1968, and the ALA Melvil Dewey Award in 1977. The citation for the Dewey Award states that Lubetzky's achievements assure recognition of his "position as the greatest influence on cataloging theory since Cutter."

MICHAEL CARPENTER

Luhn, Hans Peter
(1896–1964)

Hans Peter Luhn, a German-born American, was one of the early information scientists. He came to information science by way of engineering. His interest was in the use of machines to aid in the retrieval and dissemination of information and the use of devices for the preparation of indexes and abstracts. Luhn's name will always be associated with Key Word in Context (KWIC) indexes and Selective Dissemination of Information (SDI), but beyond these two methods he pioneered in the use of mechanical—and later electronic—devices for processing textual material.

Luhn, known to his friends as Pete, was born in Barmen, Germany, July 1, 1896. He completed secondary school (gymnasium) in Germany and then went to Sankt Gallen, Switzerland, to learn the printing business. His father was a well-known printer in Germany, and he was expected to join the business. At this early age, Luhn already showed an inventive mind and took great interest in technical matters, physics, and statistics.

His stay in Sankt Gallen was interrupted by World War I, in which he served in the German Army as a communications officer in France, Turkey, Romania, and Bulgaria. After the war Luhn continued his studies in Switzerland but also found time to invent a double-entry bookkeeping machine to record both debits and credits on ledger cards. In connection with that work he first became acquainted with Hollerith machines, the punched card equipment then coming increasingly into use.

In the early 1920s Luhn switched to the textile field, first as a freelance designer and then as an agent for a German textile firm, which he represented in 1924 in the United States with the hope of establishing textile plants there. Because of financial problems the mission failed, and Luhn was forced to look for a job. After working in a bank, he again joined the textile business as Assistant to the President of a company in Pennsylvania. It offered him the opportunity to show his inventiveness, and from 1927 to 1930 he was able to obtain 10 patents. One of these, the Lunometer, a device used to count threads in fabrics, is still marketed.

In 1933 Luhn established himself as an engineering consultant. The number and types of patents granted him during this period demonstrate the scope of interests and the inventiveness of the man: foldable raincoat, game table, recipe guide, apparatus to determine thickness of thread, and many others.

The recipe guide was Luhn's first invention related to information retrieval. Marketed as the Cocktail Oracle, it enables users of this "optical coincidence" system to determine quickly which cocktails they could prepare with the ingredients available on their shelves.

Luhn's interest in documentation, now called information retrieval, began in the late 1940s when he was asked by IBM to find a solution to the problem of searching chemical compounds that could be represented in coded form. Luhn's solution was to record the codes on punched cards, and he developed a machine (which became known as the Luhn Scanner) to search files of these specially encoded cards. Luhn soon recognized the limited capacity of the punched card and of the equipment used to process it if it were to be used in searching files of textual information or index terms, for example. His inventiveness was demonstrated over and over again as he came up with new schemes, such as "Super-imposed Coding" and "Row by Row Searching" to overcome the limitations of the available equipment.

With the beginning of the computer age in the early 1950s Luhn was able to find solutions to the problems he encountered in the storage and retrieval of information by using computer software, rather than having to invent machines to overcome the limitations of conventional punched-card equipment. He saw the great potential offered by computers to solve the problems created by the rapidly growing volume of scientific and technical literature. He wanted to understand these problems in depth and so participated in many meetings and conferences of librarians and documentalists.

One of the highlights of Luhn's career was his participation in the 1958 International Conference on Scientific Information in Washington, D.C. At that conference he discussed and demonstrated a method of automatically preparing abstracts of documents. Actual conference papers, the texts of which were available on Monotype tape as a byproduct of publication in the conference proceedings, were abstracted automatically by a computer using a program he developed.

In 1958 Luhn wrote a paper entitled "A Business Intelligence System" in which he proposed an automatic method to provide current awareness services to scientists and engineers faced with the ever-growing volume of literature. Luhn's techniques assumed that the text would be available in machine-readable form; his system would make abstracts automatically and match them against interest profiles of users, which he called action points. The result of a match would be a notice containing the abstract and relevant bibliographic information sent to a subscriber. Such systems of disseminating information on a selective basis, known as SDI systems, are in use today.

Another professional triumph for Luhn was the adoption by the American Chemical Society in 1960 of the Key Word in Context (KWIC) method of indexing and the publication of *Chemical Titles* by this method. Luhn had been advocating the use of computers for the preparation of permuted indexes to cut the costs and delays inherent in conventional indexing methods.

Luhn died August 19, 1964, in Armonk, New York. Throughout his career, but especially as an information scientist, Luhn always searched for the simple solution.

REFERENCES

Claire K. Schultz, editor, *H. P. Luhn: Pioneer of Information Science, Selected Works* (1968), with bibliography of Luhn's papers related to information science.

John F. Harvey, "Luhn, Hans Peter," *Dictionary of American Library Biography* (1978).

STEPHEN E. FURTH

Luxembourg

A small independent state in western Europe, the Grand Duchy of Luxembourg lies between Germany on the east, France on the south, and Belgium on the west and north. Population (1990 est.) 380,000; area 2,586 sq.km. The national language is Letzebuergesch, but parallel education in French and German makes Luxembourgers trilingual. French carries legislative authority in administrative matters. The language situation has given birth to a literature in three languages.

History. An ancient county, Luxembourg was destined by its geographical location to be fought over for centuries. The Luxembourg dynasty, founded by Count Sigefroy in 963, included four rulers of the Holy Roman Empire. One of them, Charles IV, raised Luxembourg to the rank of duchy in 1354. This duchy was united with Burgundy in 1443. After three hundred years of hard sieges and bloody battles, the fortress of Luxembourg was ceded to Austria under the Treaty of Utrecht (1713), then annexed to France under the Peace of Campo Formio (1797). After the Congress of Vienna (1815), Luxembourg was given as a personal possession to William I, King of Holland. It became independent in 1839; at that time, the western part of the ancient county was given to Belgium. The Treaty of London of 1867 proclaimed the duchy perpetually neutral, a neutrality German troops violated in 1914 and 1940. After World War II, Luxembourg took a leading part in founding Benelux, Nato, and the European Community.

Natonal Library. Cultural life centered around the large abbeys founded during the Middle Ages at such places as Echternach, Muenster, and Orval. In

Bibliothèque Nationale de Luxembourg

South facade with main entrance to the National Library of Luxembourg, built in 1611, standing next to the Cathedral of Our Lady of Luxembourg, built in 1936.

Libraries in Luxembourg (1987)*

Type of library	Number of administrative units (main libraries)	Volumes in collections	Annual expenditures (Luxifranc)	Population served	Professional staff (with certificate, diploma, etc.)	Total staff
National	1	700,000	60,000,000	150,000	20	38
Academic	2	150,000	40,000,000	50,000	8	16
Public	4	150,000	32,000,000	200,000	8	15
School	50	400,000	25,000,000	60,000	10	20(part-time)
Special	10	320,000	35,000,000	40,000	20	40

*All figures are estimations.

1603 the Jesuits began building a college in the center of the town of Luxembourg. There was no public library under the old regime. The first public library was made part of the École Centrale de Luxembourg in 1798. It took the name of National Library in 1899. After some 30 years spent in temporary quarters, the National Library in 1972 opened its doors on the site of the old Jesuit College. Since then it has played a dominant role in the intellectual life of the country.

In 1990 the National Library's general holdings were estimated at 700,000 volumes, 2,300 foreign periodicals, and 1,000 Luxembourg periodicals. Its annual growth rate is estimated at 10,000 volumes. Special collections include 140 incunabula, 700 manuscripts (from the 9th to the 20th centuries), 14,000 illustrated postal cards, 14,000 artistic posters, 2,000 maps (prior to 1850), 200 atlases, and 200 art bindings. The Luxembourg national bibliography, compiled by the National Library, lists about 2,200 references, including about 450 books and significant periodical articles. There is no interlibrary loan network in Luxembourg.

The National Archives in Luxembourg store mainly historic and administrative archives on about 50 linear km. of shelving.

Other Libraries. Academic libraries include the Centre Universitaire, the Grand Seminaire de Luxembourg, and the libraries of various sections of the Institut Grand-Ducal, a learned society. Among public libraries, foremost are the municipal libraries of Esch-sur-Alzette (60,000 volumes) and of Luxembourg (40,000 volumes). About ten high schools have important libraries for their students.

Interesting special libraries accessible to the general public are located at the cultural centers of the French, German, and Russian embassies, at Miami University's European Center, and at the offices of various European Community institutions, including the European Commission, the European Parliament, the Court of Justice, and the European Investment Bank.

The Profession. There is no training school for librarians in Luxembourg, nor is there an association of librarians. Qualified staff are recruited after training at specialized institutions in neighboring countries.

JUL CHRISTOPHORY

MacAlister, Sir John Young Walker
(1856–1925)

John Young Walker MacAlister was the best known British medical librarian of his day, and he was immensely influential as a leader of others. He drove the infant Library Association (LA) at a pace comparable to Melvil Dewey's during the early years of the American Library Association.

MacAlister was born in Perth, Scotland, May 10, 1856. He had served an appropriate double apprenticeship prior to his appointment as Librarian and Secretary of the Royal Medical and Chirurgical Society in London in 1887. He had abandoned his early medical training at Edinburgh because of illness and had instead obtained library posts in Liverpool and Leeds. From 1887 until his retirement he built up his employing society into the great Royal Society of Medicine, an achievement appropriately recognized by his Sovereign, who conferred a knighthood on him in 1919. But in 1887 he was appointed Honorary Secretary of the Library Association, and he is best remembered in this capacity and in that of Proprietor and Editor of its official organ, *The Library,* from its inception in 1889 until its supersession by *The Library Association Record* in 1899.

He provided the LA with offices and a meeting place in his employing society's headquarters in Hanover Square, London, and stimulated its members, and particularly its younger members, with ambitious ideas and untiring encouragement, both in person and through the pages of *The Library*. He was a prominent clubman at a time when the London clubs were at the height of their power and importance and persuaded his extensive and influential acquaintances to do all possible to help and support the LA. "Mac," as he was always known to his contemporaries, was almost too ambitious for the LA, since its very small membership and limited financial resources proved discouragingly restrictive. But the recollections of such prominent librarians as James Duff Brown, L. Stanley Jast, and Ernest Savage leave a later generation in no doubt as to his standing with them.

MacAlister was largely instrumental in gaining for the Library Association its Royal Charter of incorporation in 1898 but took a lesser part in its activities after his resignation from the Honorary Secretaryship in the same year. His interest and active participation in professional affairs were renewed during the years of World War I when serving as LA President from 1915 until 1919. He died in London on December 1, 1925.

REFERENCE

Shane Godbolt and W. A. Munford, *The Incomparable Mac: A Biographical Study of Sir J. Y. W. MacAlister* (1983).

W. A. MUNFORD

McCarthy, Stephen
(1908–1990)

Stephen Anthony McCarthy, American university library director, headed the Cornell University Libraries for 21 years and was Executive Director of the Association of Research Libraries, 1967–74.

Born in Eden Valley, Minnesota, McCarthy attended Saint Thomas College in Saint Paul and Gonzaga University in Spokane, Washington, where he received his baccalaureate degree in 1929. After completing a Master's degree in literature at Gonzaga in 1931, McCarthy taught high school. Returning to the Midwest, he enrolled in a classics course at the University of Chicago and later enrolled at McGill University in Montreal, receiving a library degree in 1932.

He moved back to Chicago in 1934 and joined the staff of the Northwestern University Library. He also began doctoral studies at the Graduate Library School of the University of Chicago (Ph.D., 1941), then headed by Louis Round Wilson. The influence of Wilson and other faculty members and friendships with fellow students, including Ralph Ellsworth, Robert Miller, G. Flint Purdy, Benjamin Powell, and J. Periam Danton, proved important throughout McCarthy's career.

In 1937 McCarthy took the position of Assistant Director at the University of Nebraska Library, in Lincoln, then under the directorship of Robert Miller. Miller and McCarthy found a university and a library system suffering from the ravages of a prolonged depression. A small and antiquated building had forced the creation of too many small departmental libraries. McCarthy worked for seven years to improve salaries, services, and facilities. A union catalogue was created, a backlog of books was processed, and plans were made for a new building.

On the recommendation of Wilson, McCarthy was appointed one of the three Assistant Directors of the Columbia University library in 1944. His major duties included business affairs, personnel, and service as Acting Director when Carl White, the Director, was away on government assignments. The Columbia years were marked by staff shortages and frequent turnovers because of the war, but included plans for a rapid expansion of acquisitions and services after the war.

McCarthy became a candidate for the directorship of the Cornell University Libraries in 1946. However, when he visited the campus at Ithaca, New York, he was appalled at the conditions of the library system. During a second visit, McCarthy was persuaded by the President of Cornell that the conditions in the library would be improved as quickly as possible. Fall 1946 found McCarthy in Ithaca.

During the next 21 years, McCarthy, his associates, and their staff transformed a group of poorly housed libraries with meager collections and inadequate services into one of the outstanding university library systems in the country. Cornell University was an unusual combination of endowed private colleges and state-supported professional schools. The separate colleges and schools operated almost independently of central administrative controls. It took McCarthy more than a decade to bring about a system of coordinated libraries with more central control and budget authority.

One of McCarthy's lasting contributions to Cornell was the legacy of the Olin Library building and the other improvements made to all library facilities during his tenure. He considered replacing the 1891 library one of his most urgent goals on arriving in Ithaca. More than a decade of university committee deliberations and staff planning was frustrated by changes in both the presidency and the membership of

Department of Manuscripts and University Archives, Cornell University Libraries

Stephen McCarthy

the board of trustees, but a major commitment by a donor and the university administration after 1955 pushed the Olin Library to a successful conclusion by 1961.

In 1967 McCarthy became the Executive Director of the Association of Research Libraries (ARL) in Washington, D.C., a position he held for seven years. While at ARL he created the Office of Management Studies, presented testimony to Congress on matters affecting higher education and libraries, and advised a congressional committee on revising the "fair use" section of the 1976 Copyright law. McCarthy retired from ARL in November 1974.

In 1940 McCarthy served as President of the Nebraska Library Association. Later he served as President of the New York Library Association. In 1953 he spent a year in Cairo as a Fulbright lecturer and adviser to several Egyptian university libraries. He spent part of 1967 in Great Britain surveying resources for the study of American culture. After retiring from ARL, he served as a consultant to the Council on Library Resources. McCarthy also made a dozen or more surveys of college and university libraries during the 1950s and 1960s.

McCarthy died in 1990.

DONALD E. OEHLERTS

Library Association

Lionel R. McColvin

McColvin, Lionel R.
(1896–1976)

Lionel Roy McColvin was the outstanding public librarian of his generation in Britain. From the mid-1930s until his retirement in 1961, he dominated the public library scene, not just in his own country but internationally as well.

Born in Newcastle upon Tyne on November 30, 1896, McColvin was the son of an artist. His first library post was at Croydon, a borough of Greater London, where he worked as Reference Librarian under W. C. Berwick Sayers. He was appointed Deputy Librarian of Wigan Public Libraries in 1921 and Chief Librarian of Ipswich, in eastern England, in 1924. He earned both these appointments before his 28th birthday, an early age to become a chief librarian in Britain. After seven years at Ipswich he became Chief Librarian of Hampstead, a northern suburb of London, and remained there until 1938, when he was appointed City Librarian of Westminster, one of the most important posts in British public librarianship.

Westminster was to be McColvin's final position; indeed it would have been difficult if not impossible for him to have advanced further. He was due to retire at the end of 1961, but in December 1960 he suffered a series of strokes that left him with loss of memory. He remained City Librarian of Westminster until his official retirement date on November 30, 1961, but was on sick leave for most of that year. He died in London on January 16, 1976.

McColvin was active in the Library Association (LA) all his life. He was elected to the LA Council in 1925 at the early age of 29, and it would not be far from the truth to say that he dedicated his life to the Association. He was Honorary Secretary from 1934 to 1951, a title that no longer exists but that was akin to being Prime Minister of the Association. During these years McColvin established a rapport with Percy Welsford, the full-time paid Secretary of LA, a working relationship that was to be extremely fruitful for British librarianship.

The LA Council soon recognized that it possessed an outstanding person in McColvin, and in 1936 he was sent to the United States to study library administration on behalf of the Association. At that time most public library systems in Britain had been in existence for 50 or more years, and many could be described only as Augean stables more than ready for a cleanup. To draw attention to this state of affairs, the LA sent a number of senior librarians, including McColvin, on tours of Britain with the object of investigating libraries and making recommendations for improvements.

World War II put an end to thoughts of radical improvements in libraries. McColvin, who had served in the British Army during the latter part of World War I, was too old to be called for active service in the second conflict, but he could still look after LA affairs, and he remained in close touch with Percy Welsford. During the darkest days of the war, the LA asked McColvin to undertake a one-man survey of public libraries in Britain, and to its credit the Westminster City Council agreed to release the City Librarian for that assignment.

The result of McColvin's tours, undertaken in bombed wartime Britain, often in conditions fraught with discomfort and danger, was the publication in 1942 of his report *The Public Library System of Great Britain.* It soon became known as the McColvin Report and was immediately debated at great length both inside and outside the profession.

McColvin's investigations convinced him that there were too many public library authorities in Britain and that the majority of them were too small to function efficiently, being without the financial resources necessary for effective service. His answer was to redraw the local government map of the country, creating fewer but larger authorities, and in this respect he was years ahead of his time. Reorganization of local government finally took place in London in 1965, with similar moves in England, Wales, and Scotland in 1974 and 1975. The result of these changes was a reduction in the number of public library authorities from more than 500, as there were in McColvin's day, to 170. In this way, McColvin's dream came true nearly 40 years after his report. Furthermore, the new local government boundaries bore some striking resemblances to McColvin's suggestions in 1942.

After World War II McColvin became a great library traveler, performing missions for Unesco, the British Council, and other agencies. He visited Australia, New Zealand, the Middle East, the U.S., Germany, Turkey, Scandinavia, and elsewhere. With Bengt Hjelmqvist he founded the Anglo-Scandinavian Public Library Conference, held triennially from 1958. He attended IFLA General Council meetings and in 1953 was elected Chairman of its Public Libraries Section. Alone and unaided, he drafted standards for public library service, which were printed in *Libri* in 1958; these formed the basis for the IFLA *Standards for Public Libraries,* which were published in 1973.

Meanwhile, back in Britain, he still continued to serve on the LA Council, on the Executive Committee of the National Central Library, and on the British

Council Advisory Panel on Libraries. A great advocate of the principle of free access to public libraries, he successfully campaigned against library charges as a member of the Roberts Committee. He was elected President of the LA in 1952 and became an Honorary Fellow in 1961.

McColvin wrote 20 books. The first, *Music in Public Libraries* (1924), was followed by works on book selection, assistance to readers, children's libraries, and other topics. Among his best works were *Music Libraries* (with Harold Reeves, 1937–38), *The Personal Library* (1953), and *The Chance to Read* (1956). In addition to his books he was a prolific contributor to conferences and to professional journals.

Festschrift. In 1971 the LA published a Festschrift for McColvin entitled *Libraries for the People,* edited by his former Deputy at Westminster, R. F. Vollans, and including contributions from a formidable array of international librarians such as Louis Shores, Helle Kannila, Bengt Hjelmqvist, E. Allerslev Jensen, and Anders Andreassen. It was a tribute that McColvin richly deserved.

REFERENCE

Robert L. Collison, "Lionel Roy McColvin: A Bibliography of His Writings," in *Libraries for the People: International Studies in Librarianship in Honour of Lionel R. McColvin* (1968).

K. C. HARRISON

MacLeish, Archibald
(1892–1982)

Writer and poet Archibald MacLeish was the first well-known figure from outside the library profession to be nominated and confirmed as Librarian of Congress. The controversy surrounding his nomination, especially the bitter opposition of the American Library Association, has obscured his achievements from 1939 to 1944 as Librarian of Congress and his unique role as an eloquent spokesman on behalf of libraries and librarianship. MacLeish's chief administrative accomplishments were a thorough reorganization, development of the first explicit statements of the institution's objectives (the "Canons of Selection" and a statement of reference and research objectives), and a concern for procedures and morale that brought the administration and the staff of the Library of Congress into accord for the first time in many years. Furthermore, he permanently enlarged the role of the Library of Congress as a repository of the American intellectual and cultural tradition. His contribution to the profession centered on his frequently expressed belief that librarians must play an active role in American life, particularly in educating the American public to the value of the democratic experience.

MacLeish entered public life for the first time at the age of 47 when, on July 10, 1939, the local postmaster in Conway, Massachusetts, administered his oath of office as Librarian of Congress. He was already a man of several successful careers. Born in Glencoe, Illinois, on May 7, 1892, he attended Hotchkiss preparatory school in Connecticut before entering Yale in 1911. A star athlete at Yale, he also was elected to Phi Beta Kappa. After entering Harvard Law School, he served in the U.S. Army in France during World War I, then returned to Harvard, where he was an editor of the *Harvard Law Review* before graduating in 1919. He gave up law practice with a prominent Boston firm in 1923 for Paris, where he established close ties with the American writers living on the Left Bank and published several collections of verse. He returned to the United States in 1929, joining Henry Luce's new *Fortune* magazine, for which he wrote articles on political and cultural subjects for the next nine years. During that period he continued to write verse and drama, the subjects reflecting his liberal social and political views. Such opinions consolidated MacLeish's intellectual sympathy with the New Deal and contributed to his departure from the Luce organization. They also paved the road to his nomination as Librarian of Congress.

Library of Congress
Archibald MacLeish

From the start President Franklin D. Roosevelt looked outside the profession for a successor to Librarian of Congress Herbert Putnam. In choosing MacLeish, Roosevelt followed the advice of his friend Felix Frankfurter, the Supreme Court justice, who informed him that "only a scholarly man of letters can make a great national library a general place of habitation for scholars." The nomination was announced at a press conference on June 6, 1939, at which Roosevelt proclaimed that the job of Librarian of Congress required not a professional librarian but "a gentleman and a scholar."

The American Library Association was shocked. Roosevelt had not only ignored its own candidate for the job, the ALA Executive Secretary, Carl H. Milam, but also ignored all offers of ALA assistance. Even worse, in the ALA view, his nominee had no library experience. At its annual meeting in San Francisco on June 18, the ALA adopted a resolution opposing the nomination because "the Congress and the American people should have as a Librarian . . . one who is not only a gentleman and a scholar but who is also the ablest Library administrator available." The ALA testified unsuccessfully against the nomination in the Senate hearings. On June 29, 1939, by a vote of 63 to 8, the Senate confirmed the President's choice, and MacLeish became the ninth Librarian of Congress.

When the new Librarian officially began work on October 2, the Library had a book collection of approximately 6,000,000 volumes, a staff of about 1,100, and, in fiscal year 1939, a direct appropriation of approximately $3,000,000.

The new Librarian immediately tackled the most pressing internal problems left behind by Putnam. He launched studies of the Library's cataloguing, acquisitions, personnel, and budget policies. The results were distressing, and MacLeish and his senior staff asked for a substantial increase in the Library's budget request to remedy the many problems. The request was for $4,200,000 and included 287 additional positions. The Appropriations Committee approved 130 of the new positions and encouraged the new Librarian to continue his "industrious and intelligent" beginning. In response to the Appropriations Committee's report and to carry on the investigations already begun, MacLeish appointed on April 10, 1940, a special Librarian's Committee to analyze the operations of the Library—especially its processing activities. The report of the Committee, headed by Carleton B. Joeckel of the University of Chicago Graduate Library School, served as a catalyst for MacLeish's reorganization—a functional restructuring that served as the basis of the Library's administrative structure for the next three decades.

While the administrative reorganization was probably MacLeish's single most significant achievement, it was only one of his accomplishments. He also enhanced the Library's reputation as a major cultural institution, not only because of his own prominence as a poet but also by inaugurating the first series of poetry readings. He brought many prominent writers and poets to the Library, including the war refugees Aléxis Saint-Léger Léger (who wrote under the name Saint-John Perse) and Thomas Mann. They also included the U.S. poet Allen Tate, who served both as Poetry Consultant and as the first Editor of the newly established *Quarterly Journal of Current Acquisitions*. Relationships between the Library and scholarly and literary communities were improved through a new program of resident fellowships for young scholars and the formation of the Fellows of the Library of Congress, a group of prominent writers and poets.

MacLeish, a wartime librarian, quickly became a leading spokesman for the cause of democracy. Speaking before the ALA on May 31, 1940, he asserted that librarians "must become active and not passive agents of the democratic process." People who had bitterly opposed his nomination a year earlier applauded vigorously, and relations between the Library of Congress and ALA were on the mend. At the annual conference of the Association in June 1942, ALA President Charles H. Brown introduced MacLeish as "a man of whom we librarians are very proud," and the Librarian received a thunderous ovation before delivering his address, "Towards an Intellectual Offensive."

MacLeish and Luther H. Evans, his Chief Assistant Librarian, inaugurated a staff *Information Bulletin* and created a staff advisory committee. In April 1942 MacLeish announced the formation of the Librarian's Council, composed of distinguished librarians, scholars, and book collectors who would make recommendations about collection development and reference service. Weekly meetings with department directors were started, and in 1943 the Library administration began holding informal monthly meetings with the professional staff.

During the war MacLeish helped Roosevelt in many ways. Those activities meant that he served only part-time as Librarian of Congress, which makes the many achievements of his administration especially remarkable. In October 1941 the President directed him to assume, in addition to his duties as Librarian, supervision of the government's newly established Office of Facts and Figures. The appointment was controversial, both because of the publications produced by the new office and because the Librarian's additional duties often kept him away from the Library. In June 1942 the Office of Facts and Figures was combined with other agencies to form the Office of War Information, which MacLeish served part-time as an Assistant Director. The Librarian also drafted speeches for the President and represented the government at various meetings, as in March 1944 when he went to London as a delegate to the Conference of Allied Ministers of Education, a forerunner of the United Nations. MacLeish apparently indicated a wish to leave the Library of Congress as early as the summer of 1943, but he stayed in office until December 19, 1944, when he resigned to become an Assistant Secretary of State, in charge of public and cultural relations.

MacLeish's relatively brief administration was one of the most fruitful in the history of the Library of Congress. The accomplishments were not his alone; in fact, as he was the first to acknowledge, his colleagues Luther H. Evans, Verner Clapp, and David C. Mearns played major roles. The style, tone, and motivation, however, came directly from the Librarian. He provided the Library of Congress and the library profession with inspiration and a badly needed sense of perspective. His succinct statement of the purpose of the Library in the first issue of the *Quarterly Journal of Current Acquisitions* (1943), for example, stands today as both a summary and a challenge: "The first duty of the Library of Congress is to serve the Congress and the officers and agencies of government. Its second duty is to serve the world of scholarship and letters. Through both it endeavors to serve the American people to whom it belongs and for whom it exists."

MacLeish died in Boston on April 20, 1982.

REFERENCES

Nancy L. Benco, "Archibald MacLeish: The Poet as Librarian," *Quarterly Journal of the Library of Congress* (1976).

Edward J. Mullaly, *Archibald MacLeish: A Checklist* (1973).

Dennis Thomison, "F. D. R., the ALA, and Mr. MacLeish: The Selection of the Librarian of Congress, 1939," *Library Quarterly* (1972).

JOHN Y. COLE

Madagascar

Madagascar (Madagasikara), an island republic, lies in the Indian Ocean off the southeastern coast of Africa. Population (1990 est.) 11,197,000; area 587,041 sq.km. The official languages are Malagasy and French.

History. Madagascar's indigenous culture is essentially Indonesian, with Arabic and Islamic contributions. The London Missionary Society introduced printing in the 1820s, and the Merina dialect, in the Roman alphabet, became the official language. There is a rich written literature in the Malagasy language, which is of the Malyo-Polynesian stock, with borrowings from Bantu and Arabic as well as French and English.

Manuscripts in Arabic script have been preserved by the peoples of the southeast. The main libraries and other cultural institutions are in the capital, Tananarive (Antananarivo), where they reflect the influence of the French. Madagascar was a French colony, 1896–1945, and a member of the French Union 1946–58.

National Library. The National Library, instituted in 1961 following the country's independence in 1960, inherited the collection of 80,000 volumes from the Library of the former General Government, created in Tananarive in 1920. The Library received its works thanks to legal deposit while acting as a public library for the capital as well as a documentation center for research. From 1961 to 1973 the National Library, while fulfilling its former roles, served as national center for the promotion of books and reading and libraries. The extension of these activities led to the creation of the National Library Service in 1973. The Library Service consists of a division for the promotion of books and reading whose main role is promoting the art of writing, the rights of authors, publishing, and the pleasure of reading. It also publishes the national bibliography. The National Library is the other element; it has a collection of 170,000 printed books, manuscripts, periodicals, photos, and maps. It continues to receive printed works thanks to legal deposit; it assures the conservation of national patrimony; and it plays an important role as a public and research library because of its extensive collection on Madagascar. A new building for the service was inaugurated in 1982.

University Library. The University of Madagascar in Tananarive has a Library that specializes in the disciplines of the University. It was created in 1960 and has a collection of 180,000 works. Following decentralization of the University, five regional centers were attached to it, the oldest being the Toliara Center.

Public and School Libraries. A program to promote public libraries in the Fivondronana (subregional constituencies grouping several former communes) was launched in 1978 and was to proceed gradually over several years. It consists of stimulating the former municipal libraries and former information centers and creating new libraries: 57 small units operated in 1984. The Library Service ensures the technical training of personnel.

Furthermore, about 300 units of small libraries operate through the country. They are school libraries supported by funds from school cooperatives or private funds, or firm and association libraries. Their collections vary: most range between 1,000 and 6,000 volumes.

Special Libraries. The Malagasy Academy Library in Tananarive, created in 1905, is a specialized library in language, literature, art, social and political sciences, and fundamental and applied sciences. It had a collection of 33,000 works in the mid-1980s and received 30 periodicals. It also exchanges materials with other library systems.

Research institutions, such as the National Center of Oceanographic Research, the National Center of Pharmacological Research, and the National Center of Applied Research in Rural Development, offer studies, reports, and results of research concerning the country.

Government ministries and departments, such as Education, Agriculture, Information, Health, Justice, Industry, Economy, Telecommunication, Public Works, Development Planning, and Defense also have special libraries; most consist of 2,000 to 7,000 volumes.

The Profession. The Malagasy Books Office in Tananarive, an association created in 1971 by a few librarians, publishes and diffuses works tending to develop the pleasure of reading, promotes a book policy on a national scale, and serves as a center of information concerning books and as a resource for writers.

The Association of Archivists, Librarians, Documentalists, and Musicologists was formed in September 1976.

JULIETTE RATSIMANDRAVA

Malawi

Malawi, known as Nyasaland before its independence from Great Britain in 1964, is a republic in southeastern Africa. It is bordered by Tanzania on the north, Mozambique on the east and south, and Zambia on the west. Population (1990 est.) 8,289,000; area 118,484 sq.km. The official language is English; Chichewa is the lingua franca.

History. Although some rock paintings are known to exist and to have been used in the early years of human settlement, the traditional means of communication among the Maravi peoples was oral. The missionaries who settled in the area in the 1860s used books and printing to help spread the Gospel. The first mission library was created in 1890 at the Free Church Mission station in Bandawe, followed by that of the Universities' Mission to Central Africa at Likoma. A government library is known to have existed in 1890, but there was no public library until 1950.

When it opened in 1964, the University of Malawi Library System became the largest library in the country and the first to be organized along professional lines, under Wilfred Plumbe, its first Librarian. The Malawi National Library Service was established in 1968. A good road network and an inexpensive internal postal rate for books have promoted excellent library cooperation.

National Libraries and Archives. The functions of a national library are performed by the National Archives of Malawi, official repository of the country's official documents and historical manuscripts. Under the Printed Publications Act, the National Archives is the country's only legal deposit library and contains the most comprehensive collec-

Libraries in Malawi (1990)

Type of library	Number of administrative units (main libraries)	Number of service points (branches, mobile stops, etc.)	Volumes in collections	Annual expenditures (kwacha)	Population served	Professional staff (with certificate, diploma, etc.)	Total staff
National	1	--	25,000	60,000	1,000	2	3
Academic	6	--	300,000	1,700,000	4,000	48	96
Public	7	780	200,000	1,300,000	3,400,000	32	106
School	72	--	333,000	175,000	28,000	10	80
Special	26	--	60,000	80,000	1,500	15	39

The National Library Service of Malawi

Headquarters of the Malawi National Library Service in Lilongwe, established by an act of Parliament in 1967.

tion of Malawiana in existence. It publishes an annual cumulation, *The Malawi National Bibliography*.

Academic Libraries. The University of Malawi Library System is a federation of five college libraries scattered in three of the country's largest cities: Bunda College of Agriculture Library, Chancellor College Library, Kamuzu College of Nursing Library, the Polytechnic Library, and Medical School Library in Blantyre. The holdings of the Libraries have grown steadily since the mid-1960s. By 1987 the total bookstock including periodical titles stood at more than 240,000. Outside borrowers are permitted to use the libraries on payment of token fees.

Public Libraries. The National Library Service was created by an act of Parliament in 1967 to operate free library services throughout Malawi. It has seven major service points, in Blantyre, Limbe, Zomba, Lilongwe, Mzuzu, and Karonga. These stations, which in 1988–89 circulated almost 373,000 books to readers, are augmented by the School Services Department, which provides library services to primary, secondary, and higher education institutions. A parallel Rural Services Department operates 244 Rural Community Information Centers throughout the country. This service, with the nationwide postal service, ensures that users in remote areas can have access to books. The National Library Service boasts a bookstock of more than 173,000 volumes.

Other public libraries include those operated by foreign governments or organizations, such as the British Council, the United States Information Service, and the French Cultural Center. All have highly regarded book collections and popular collections of nonprint media.

School Libraries. Malawi has a network of school libraries in secondary schools, technical colleges, and teacher training colleges in all three regions of the country. The largest school library is that of the Malawi Institute of Education at Domasi.

Special Libraries. Government departments, statutory organizations, and private firms operate a wide range of special libraries, with varied strengths in book and human resources. The Library of the Department of Agricultural Research, which receives World Bank funding, remains Malawi's best-known special library. Other major special libraries are those of the Forestry Research Institute of Malawi, the Malawi Broadcasting Corporation, the Malawi Bureau of Standards, and the Malawi Export Promotions Council.

The Profession. The Malawi Library Association was inaugurated on April 30, 1977. Since 1979 it has organized Malawi Library Assistant Certificate Courses to train library paraprofessionals. It also holds occasional short seminars and workshops. All of the 27 professional librarians (in 1987) were trained abroad, mainly in the United Kingdom and Botswana. The Malawi Library Association publishes the *MALA Bulletin*. At the instigation of the Association, the government is evolving a national information policy with a view to harmonizing the country's library, documentation, and archives services into one national information system. Already, with support from the government and the United Nations Development Program, the Department of Research and Environmental Affairs has undertaken to establish a National Documentation Center and a Central Microfilming Bureau.

STEVE S. MWIYERIWA

Malaysia

Malaysia, a federation of 13 states in Southeast Asia, comprises two distinct land areas—Peninsular Malaysia and the states of Sabah and Sarawak on the island of Borneo. It gained its independence from Great Britain in 1957 and achieved its present form in 1963. Malaysia is a member of ASEAN (the Association of South East Asian Nations) and of the Commonwealth. Population (1990 est.) 17,861,000; area 329,749 sq.km. Bahasa Malaysia, the Malay language, is the official language of the country.

History. Although monastic and temple collections and state archives existed in the Indianized empires of Southeast Asia, there is little evidence of their existence in the Malay states. The earliest libraries in Malaysia were subscription libraries estab-

Libraries in Malaysia (1989)

Type of library	Number of administrative units (main libraries)	Volumes in collections	Professional staff (with certificate, diploma, etc.)	Total staff
National	1	719,971	78	256
Academic	111	4,584,358	238	1,325
Public	70	4,259,191	73	793
Special	265	2,098,913	83	783

Source: *Directory of Libraries in Malaysia.* Kuala Lampur, National Library of Malaysia, 1991.

lished by the British in the 19th and early 20th centuries to serve the needs of the European community. The planned development of libraries in Malaysia began only in the late 1960s. In that early period, the Malaysian Library Association played a leading role by initiating and submitting to the Government a *Blueprint for Public Library Development in Malaysia (1968),* prepared by Hedwig Anuar, which provided a plan for the development of public libraries and outlined the role of the National Library.

National Library. The National Library, established under provisions of the National Library Act of 1972, formed part of the Federal Department of Archives and National Library until 1977, when it was separated from the Archives and established as a Federal Department under the Ministry of Housing and Local Government. In 1982 it was placed under the Ministry of Culture, Youth, and Sport. The National Library Act was amended in 1987 with particular reference to the objectives and functions of the National Library. Under the 1987 amendments, the functions of the National Library were "to make available for the use of present and future generations a national collection of library resources; to facilitate nationwide access to library resources available within the country and abroad; [and] to provide leadership on matters pertaining to libraries." Based on these objectives, the National Library has wide-ranging functions, including advising the Minister on national policy pertaining to libraries; advising and assisting in the national planning and development of libraries; functioning as the national focal point for the national information system; promoting and facilitating the establishment of a nationwide system of public libraries; promoting the establishment of a network of special libraries; establishing a national bibliographic center, the national bibliographic network, and the national center for Malay manuscripts; and a host of other duties.

The Deposit of Library Materials Act of 1986 repealed the Preservation of Books Act of 1966 and made the National Library the sole legal depository for the country. With a collection of 603,000 volumes by 1987, acquired through purchase, exchange, donation, and legal deposit, it ranks as one of the country's major libraries. It publishes the *Bibliografi Negara Malaysia* ("Malaysian National Bibliography"), issued quarterly from 1967 with annual cumulations; *Indeks Suratkhabar Malaysia* ("Malaysian Newspaper Index") from 1976 (quarterly); and *Indeks Persidangan Malaysia* ("Malaysian Conference Index") from 1984 (annual).

Public Libraries. The National Library plays an advisory and coordinating role in the development of public libraries in the country. Public library services in Peninsular Malaysia, in accordance with *Blueprint* recommendations, are provided by state public library corporations established under state laws. These corporations function in all the Peninsular states. The National Library and the Malaysian Library Association are represented on these corporations. In Sabah, public library services are constituted as a department of the state government, and in Sarawak they are provided by state and local government authorities. While the federal government provides funds through the National Library for public library development in Peninsular Malaysia, all recurrent expenditures are met by state governments.

National Library of Malaysia

University Pertanian Malaysia Library, founded in 1971.

Although public library services are now provided in all states, services are largely urban-oriented but are being actively extended to the rural areas. However, the use of public library services was still minimal in the late 1980s, only 13 percent of the literate population being regularly served as members of the public library system. In 1987 approximately 3,920,000 books were borrowed through the country's public libraries.

Academic Libraries. There are libraries in the country's seven universities, technical colleges, colleges of further education, and teacher training colleges. Particularly outstanding are some of the university libraries. These include the University of Malaya (established 1959), University Sains Malaysia (1969), University Kebangsaan Malaysia (1970), University Pertanian Malaysia (1971), and University Teknoloji Malaysia (1972). Two newer universities are the University Utara Malaysia (1984) and the International Islamic University (1983), which is co-sponsored by a number of countries. On the whole, university libraries are better funded and staffed than other libraries in the country. University library collections vary considerably in size and ranged in the late 1980s from 932,000 volumes in the University of Malaya, 485,000 in University Sains Malaysia, and 500,000 in University Kebangsaan Malaysia, to 233,000 in University Pertanian Malaysia and 212,000 in University Teknoloji Malaysia. The collections in the two newer universities are still relatively small. Of the technical colleges, the more outstanding were the Mara Institute of Technology with 191,500 volumes and the Tungku Abdul Rahman College with 87,000 volumes. The 16 teacher training college libraries vary in size, with collections ranging from 15,000 to 21,000 volumes.

Cooperation between the university libraries and the National Library is well established. The National Library and most of the university libraries are active participants in the MALMARC (Malaysian MARC) System with University Sains Malaysia functioning as coordinating center. The MALMARC database contains more than 200,000 records, and the system generates institutional catalogues (in COM) and accession lists as well as the union catalogue. A serials database called PERPUNET with wider institutional participation is also maintained. Planning for online access to national databases began after the introduction of a public data network by the Telecommunications Department at the end of 1984. University libraries and the National Library are also linked by telex.

School Libraries. There are over 7,900 schools in Malaysia, many with their own libraries. School library collections on the whole are relatively small and do not exceed 3,000 volumes. Malaysian school libraries are managed by teacher-librarians who have basic educational qualifications with some library training. School libraries receive annual grants based on student enrollment; they also charge library fees. Overall supervision of school libraries is provided through school library organizers, many with both teaching and library qualifications, who are attached to state departments of education. National coordination and supervision is provided by the School Library Unit in the Schools Division of the Ministry of Education. In 1979 the Malaysian Library Association submitted to the government its *Blueprint for School Library Development in Malaysia*. The major recommendations of the *Blueprint* have been progressively implemented.

Special Libraries. Special libraries represent one of the fastest-growing library sectors in the country. There were nearly 165 special libraries in the late 1980s, although many are relatively small. About 65 percent of special libraries have collections of fewer than 5,000 volumes. The largest special libraries are found in research institutes. They include the Rubber Research Institute (97,000 volumes), the Forest Research Institute (60,000), the Malaysian Agricultural Research and Development Institute (40,000), and the Institute for Medical Research (20,000). Other large special libraries include the Ministry of Agriculture (80,000), the Dewan Bahasa dan Perpustaka (Language and Literary Agency; 58,000), the Bank Negara Malaysia (26,000), the Asian and Pacific Development Center (25,000), and the National Institute of Public Administration (16,000). Special libraries are largely staffed by professionally qualified librarians. Special librarians in government libraries serve in a Common User Library Service under the purview of the National Library.

The Profession. The Malaysian Library Association, established in 1955 as the Malayan Library Group, is the only association for professional librarians in the country. Professional education for librarians is provided by the School of Library and Information Studies, Mara Institute of Technology.

REFERENCES

Hedwig Anuar, *Blueprint for Public Library Development in Malaysia*(1968).

D. E. K. Wijasuriya and others, *The Barefoot Librarian: Library Developments in Southeast Asia with Special Reference to Malaysia* (1975).

B. A. J. Winslade, *Rancangan pembangunan perpustakaan sekolah di Malaysia; Blueprint for school library development in Malaysia* (1979).

D. E. K. WIJASURIYA

Malclès, Louise-Noëlle

(1899–1977)

The career of Louise-Noëlle Malclès as a French bibliographer embraced the three elements of practicing, teaching, and writing. They did not, however, fall into separate or even overlapping periods of her life, but were for the most part carried on simultaneously in Paris. There is no doubt that Malclès stands as one of the most distinguished practitioners and teachers of bibliography in 20th-century Europe.

Born in the south of France on September 20, 1899, she was the daughter of a professor of physics at the Faculty of Sciences of the University of Clermont-Ferrand, where she later received her university training. Her long association with the library of the Sorbonne (now designated one of the Inter-University Libraries in the Réunion des Bibliothèques Universitaires de Paris, reflecting the restructuring of the old University of Paris) began in 1928 and lasted until 1962. Working first under the Hispanist Louis Barrau-Dihigo and later Germain Calmette, Malclès established the Salle de Bibliographie (Bibliography Room) and presided over its collections and services to students, faculty, and scholars for many years. Separate from the main reading room of the Sorbonne Library and not a main reference/reading room as found in American university libraries, this room, accommodating perhaps 20 readers, contains a carefully selected but wide-ranging group of bibliographical tools (such as bibliographies, published library catalogues, guides to the literature, and periodical indexes) both of general nature and of individual disciplines, which Malclès and her small staff used in helping a generation of persons doing research. This high-level service was geared primarily to bibliographical and documentation needs rather than to general reference questions, although the distinction often blurred in the interest of providing help. Here, too, in the 1950s—as time permitted—Malclès did some of the work on the successive volumes of *Les Sources du travail bibliographique*.

In the 1930s she spent time in Germany (Leipzig and Berlin) studying German national bibliography and union catalogues. In the 1950s she visited a number of European cities (Rome, Lisbon, Madrid, Brussels, Amsterdam, and The Hague) prior to preparing the reports on bibliographical activities for Unesco.

Attached to the Direction des Bibliothèques de France in the last years of her professional career, she had responsibility for special projects for strengthening bibliographical collections and services in French scholarly libraries. She retired in 1969 with the rank of *conservateur en chef* and returned to the south of France, spending some years in Avignon, where she died on March 27, 1977.

Her most important contribution to the field of bibliography is the monumental *Les Sources du travail bibliographique* (*Sources for Bibliographical Work*), published in Geneva by Droz from 1950 to 1958. This work is not a guide to reference materials in the usual sense, but rather to all works useful in bibliographical work: bibliographies themselves, library catalogues, indexing and abstracting services, historical sets, descriptions of library resources, journals carrying reviews, and so on. Published in four physical volumes, the work consists of two parts: general bibliographies and specialized bibliographies, the latter in turn subdivided into *sciences humaines* (humanities and social sciences) and pure sciences, medicine and pharmacy. The conception, planning, style, and majority of the text remain the work of Malclès herself, although collaborators contributed some of the sections on the sciences and on countries outside western Europe. Remarkable for clarity of exposition, precision of comments, and wealth of detail, the work nevertheless avoids the pitfall of becoming simply an elaboration of important titles. The user who still finds it helpful many years after its completion can only regret that this guide was followed by neither supplement nor later editions. It stands, however, as one of the most important syntheses of the bibliographical control achieved by the mid-20th century and assures Malclès of a permanent place in the history of the discipline to which she was so passionately devoted.

Another publication is closely related to *Les Sources:* the *Cours de bibliographie,* written primarily as a textbook for students preparing for careers in libraries and documentation centers. Published first by Droz in 1954 (before the completion of *Les Sources*), it later appeared under the title *Manuel de bibliographie.* Malclès herself prepared the first (1963) and second (1969) editions of the *Manuel;* revisions for the third (1976) and fourth (1985) were done by Andrée Lhéritier, to whom Malclès had entrusted the continuation of this work, confident that her former student and later colleague and friend would maintain her high standards for bibliographical work. The *Manuel* follows the arrangement of *Les Sources,* but has—as might be expected in a textbook—more limited coverage and greater emphasis on French titles.

In both *Les Sources* and the *Cours* Malclès had traced the history of bibliography, but full development of her ideas came several years later, when *La Bibliographie* appeared (1956) as volume 708 in the "Que sais-je" series. Three editions (1960, 1962, and 1977) followed, reaching a total of 32,000 copies sold and in print (a large number for a work in this field). There are translations in several languages.

Among Malclès's publications were two reports on *Bibliographical Services throughout the World* (1951–52 and 1952–53), published on the recommendation of Unesco's International Advisory Committee on Bibliography. The first attempt to report on such activities in the member states of Unesco, the series was continued by others at five-year intervals.

Malclès's third, and probably least known, activity was her teaching, begun at the Sorbonne in 1933. There is no doubt that her abilities in the classroom soon led to recognition as *the* teacher of bibliography to a generation of French students. Her teaching career spanned more than three decades, most of it concurrent with her work at the Sorbonne; during that period she was also concerned with improving education for librarianship. When the École Supérieure des Bibliothèques was created in 1964 to provide higher level training, Malclès gave the first course on bibliography.

Malclès was named to the Legion d'honneur in France and was known beyond its borders (especially after the publication of *Les Sources*), but many feel that she never received the full recognition and appreciation she deserved.

REFERENCES

Richard K. Gardner, *Education for Librarianship in France: An Historical Survey* (Ph.D. dissertation, Case Western Reserve University, 1968).

Andrée Lhéritier, "Necrologie. Louise-Noëlle Malclès (1899–1977)," *Bulletin des Bibliothèques de France* (1977).

H. J. de Vleeschauwer, *L'oeuvre bibiographique de L.-N. Malclès* (1957).

WILLIAM VERNON JACKSON

Maldives

The Republic of Maldives, located 650 kilometers south of the tip of India, stretches 753.6 kilometers across the equator and is 118 kilometers wide. Its 1,190 coral islands have a combined land mass of 298 sq.km. and a maximum elevation of less than two meters. Nearly all are clustered in the shallow lagoons of atolls enclosed by protective reefs. Pop. (1990 census) 214,000, on 202 islands; 58,000 (27 percent) live in Male, the capital. Dhivehi is the official language, but English and Arabic are used in schools as well.

People from India or Sri Lanka settled the islands before recorded history. The islands form a coral barrier across major trade routes, and shipwrecked people added to the population. The people accepted Islam in 1153 and began calling their rulers sultans and sultanas, rather than kings and queens. The Portuguese ruled the islands in the mid-1500s, followed by the Dutch. The British established a protectorate in 1881. The people founded a republic in 1953 and gained full independence from Britain in 1965.

The official literacy rate has climbed continuously from 49 percent in 1921 to more than 93 percent in 1986, but supportive library services began only in the 1940s. The Majeedee Library in Male was founded in 1945 by Amir Mohamed Didi, head of the Department of Education, as the state library of the Maldives.

Libraries in The Republic of Maldives (1989)

Type of library	Number of administrative units (main libraries)	Number of service points (branches, mobile stops, etc.)	Volumes in collections	Annual expenditures (rufiyaa)	Population served	Professional staff (with certificate, diploma, etc.)	Total staff
National	1	0	19,107	75,000	58,000	7	12
Public	12	0	--	--	--	--	--
School	17	0	71,243[a]	--	--	--	--
Special			10,400[b]	--	--	--	--
Other (describe)							
Archives	2	0	legal and international documents	--	--	0	3

[a]for 13 schools
[b]for 4 libraries

Reading Room, the National Library of Maldives.

It is the only major Maldivian public library. Various personal collections, as well as the Royal Air Force library from the southernmost atoll, were added to it over the years. It was renamed the National Library in 1982. Its collection includes books in Dhivehi, Arabic, Urdu, and English. Anyone may use books at the library, but only members may take them out on loan. The library has 250 adult members and 1,000 temporary members (students and those under 15).

Many of the 17 school libraries for students and teachers are housed in classrooms. The oldest was founded in the mid-1960s; the youngest in 1989. The largest has more than 19,000 volumes; the smallest has fewer than 1,000.

A dozen libraries are registered in the atolls outside of Male. Classification in Maldives is by the Dewey Decimal System. All the libraries face inadequate funding, inadequate space, and shortages of trained personnel. To improve staff quality, the National Library, with support from the Asia Foundation, has sponsored a training program and sent some personnel overseas for training and experience.

The Library Association, formed in 1989, encourages cooperation among the libraries in Male. Its goals include raising standards, encouraging librarianship, and fostering reading habits.

IBRAHIM SABIR

Mali

The Republic of Mali, formerly the French Sudan, is bounded on the north by Mauritania and Algeria, on the east by Niger, on the south by Burkina Faso, the Ivory Coast, and Guinea, and on the west by Sénégal. Population (1990 est.) 8,156,000; area 1,240,192 sq.km. The official language is French; more that 15 indigenous languages are spoken, but only six of them are written.

History. Mali traces its origins to great empires and kingdoms that flourished in West Africa between the 12th and 19th centuries, after which French colonial penetration began. After gaining independence in 1960, Mali was ruled by a socialist government (1960–68) and a military regime (1968–91).

Mali's oldest libraries are those in Timbuktu and Djenné, both centers of Islamic culture since the Middle Ages. The colonial government established the Institut Fondamental d'Afrique Noire (IFAN; Institute for the Study of Black Africa) and other academic libraries.

National Library. Created in 1962, the Bibliothèque Nationale inherited collections from the IFAN library. Its collection reached 15,000 volumes by 1985 and included many periodicals. It serves as the copyright center for all national publications. It is open to all residents of Bamako. The Bibliothèque Nationale publishes works by Malian students in Mali and abroad.

Academic Libraries. Higher education is available at large specialized schools, each with a library that reflects the subjects being taught. The largest of these is the library of the École Normale Supérieure, a school for training secondary school teachers created in 1962, with more than 30,000 books. Others include the Library of the National School for Administration (1966), with more than 10,000 volumes; the Library of the Rural Polytechnic

Libraries in Mali (1990)

Type of library	Number of administrative units (main libraries)	Number of service points (branches, mobile stops, etc.)	Volumes in collections	Annual expenditures (CFA franc)	Population served	Professional staff (with certificate, diploma, etc.)	Total staff
National	1	0	22,500	600,000	800,000*	3	25
Academic	8	0	65,000	--	8,500**	5	28
Public[a]	55	15	115,000	--	1,500,000	8	82
School	36	0	120,000	--	17,500***	0	95
Special	64[b]	0	130,000	--	n.a.	--	--

*Population of Bamako
**Students
***Pupils
[a]1991 data
[b]1988 data

Institute of Katibougou (1966), with about 3,000 items; the Library of the National School for Medicine and Pharmacy (1968), with 15,000 items; the Library of the Institut Supérieur de Formation et de Recherche Appliquée (1973), with about 6,000 books; the Library of the École des Hautes Études Pratiques (1979), with about 2,000 items; and the Library of the National School for Engineers (1983), with more than 5,000 books. All these libraries contain theses and *mémoires* prepared by their students.

Public Libraries. L'Operation Lecture Publique (the Campaign for Public Reading), created by the government in 1977, set up 46 public libraries, each containing about 1,500 volumes. It also set up five libraries for adults and one for children in the district of Bamako. It operates a railway-car library that serves 11 communities between Bamako and the border with Sénégal.

In addition, the libraries and documentation centers belonging to national and foreign cultural centers are open to the public. Among these are the Cultural Palace, the Youth Center, and the French, American, Russian, and Libyan cultural centers. The Catholic mission manages an important library at the Djoliba Cultural Center in Bamako and libraries in rural areas.

School Libraries. About 40 school libraries, half in high schools and the other half in vocational schools, participated in the Campaign for Public Reading starting in 1984. Collections in school libraries range from about a thousand books to five thousand or so. These libraries are staffed by nonprofessionals.

Special Libraries. Providing statistics on special libraries is not easy, in that nearly all public and private agencies have libraries. Important examples include the libraries of l'Institut d'Économie Rurale, l'Institut du Sahel, the Humanities Institute, the Ahmed Baba Study and Research Center, the National Institute for Pedagogy, and the National Museum. There are also a large number of private family libraries.

The Profession. The Association Malienne des Bibliothécaires, Archivistes et Documentalistes (AMBAD; the Malian Association of Librarians, Archivists and Documentalists) was created in 1978. It worked to create standards for librarians, archivists, and documentalists and to establish a school for professional training. Most librarians in Mali travel to Sénégal or to France for training.

The National Library of Mali, Bamako.

AL HADY KOITA;
translated by MIRKA DELLA CAVA

Malta

The Republic of Malta, comprising the islands of Malta, Gozo, and Comino, lies in the middle of the Mediterranean Sea, about 90 km. southwest of Sicily. Population (1990 est.) 354,000; area 316 sq.km. Official languages are Maltese and English.

History. The first documented institutional libraries, all belonging to religious bodies, date back to the 16th century. In 1687 Giuseppe Zammit founded a medical library at the recently established medical school in Valletta; early in the 18th century a library was set up at the Bishop's Palace, Valletta. Much more important was the founding in 1776 of the Public Library in Valletta by the Knights of St. John, then the rulers of Malta. This institution was the forerunner of today's National Library of Malta and of the public library system.

Early in the 19th century, officers in the service of the new British rulers of Malta set up a subscription library, known as the Garrison Library. It flourished until the country became independent in 1964.

Staff and students at the University of Malta, founded in 1769, tended to rely on the Public Library

Libraries in Malta (1990)

Type of library	Number of administrative units (main libraries)	Number of service points (branches, mobile stops, etc.)	Volumes in collections	Annual expenditures (Maltese pound)	Population served	Professional staff (with certificate, diploma, etc.)	Total staff
National	1	2	402,000[a]	170,000[b]	--	2	42
Academic[c]	2	3	355,000	259,341	4,000	4	30
Public	2	56	426,000	27,000	330,000	2	65[d]
School	1	32	128,000	9,000	24,000	--	34[d]
Special[e]	4	4	90,000	--	--	4	8

[a]estimated
[b]Books & Salaries
[c]Including Foundation for International Studies
[d]Including part-timers
[e]Data based on 3 special libraries

for most of their requirements; no professional librarian attempted to organize the University's modest collection of books as a library until 1954. It moved into its own building in 1967—the first purpose-built library building put up in Malta since the late 18th century. In the 1980s, Maltese librarians worked to establish librarianship as a profession and took the first tentative steps in library automation.

National Library and Archives. Valletta's Public Library became the Royal Malta Library and then, in 1976, the National Library of Malta (NLM). Housed in a handsome late 18th century building, it has a large collection of books, serials, and maps relating to Malta. Its collection of Maltese newspapers and other periodicals is comprehensive. Also noteworthy are the archives of the Order of St. John from the 12th to the 18th centuries.

The NLM, a legal deposit library (together with the Gozo Public Library) since 1925, has published the annual *Bibliografija Nazzjonali ta' Malta* ("Malta National Bibliography") since 1984. It has had a book restoration laboratory since 1981.

The Libraries Department was renamed the Libraries and Archives Department under the National Archives Act of 1990 and became responsible for the NLM, the National Archives, and the public library system. The National Archives are housed mainly in a medieval building in Rabat that has been specially renovated.

Academic Libraries. The two major academic libraries are the University of Malta Library and the Foundation for Theological Studies Library in Rabat. The University has its Main Library on its Msida campus and a Medical Library at its Medical School in G'Mangia. The total stock now comprises around 320,000 volumes of books, pamphlets, and bound periodicals. It has a fine Maltese studies collection which includes important literary manuscripts. Other areas of strength include law, Mediterranean culture and history, English literature, sociology of education, and immunology. A leader in Maltese librarianship, the University library introduced CD-ROM databases in 1988 and automation of its serials control in 1990.

The Foundation for Theological Studies was the University's Faculty of Theology, but became an autonomous institution from 1978 to 1987. Its Library, at Rabat, specializes in theological and philosophical materials. A new academic library is that of the Foundation for International Studies, established in 1986 and housed in the Old University building in Valletta.

Public Libraries. The public library system has its headquarters at Beltissebh, outside Valletta, and includes the Gozo Public Library and a full-time regional branch library at Paola. By 1990 it had 57 branch libraries, open to the public four hours weekly and also serving as school libraries. From 1978 the branch libraries replaced a number of poorly-stocked "District Libraries," set up from 1922 onwards.

Since it opened in 1974, the Beltissebh library has had a large readership, especially among the young, with impressive annual circulation figures. It has a reference reading room, provides a talking books for the blind service, and cooperates closely with the Library Association in organizing annual Book Week activities.

The Gozo Public Library, which originated as a subscription library in 1839, is both a public library and an extension of the NLM. Besides its large collection of material received on legal deposit, it houses the archives of Gozo's administration and courts. It has separate lending and reference departments, both of them in Victoria, the main town of the island of Gozo.

School Libraries. Teacher-librarians staff the branch libraries that serve as school libraries in State schools, serving on a part-time basis. These libraries include basic reference and lending collections. They are serviced by the Schools Library Service at the Public Library, Beltissebh, which provides centralized ordering, classification, and cataloguing; supplies filmstrips, slides, and multi-media kits for school projects; and organizes basic library training and in-service courses for teacher-librarians. The libraries in private schools do not have the benefit of this service and cooperate little among themselves. There are no accepted standards of library provision in these schools.

Special Libraries. Apart from libraries in a number of religious institutions, special libraries are not widespread. Many Government offices have collections of books looked after by clerks, but not organized libraries. The one notable exception is the Central Bank of Malta, which has had a well-equipped and professionally staffed library and information service almost since it was founded in 1968. It provides selective dissemination of information to the bank staff and issues weekly digests of local and foreign news and regular lists of the foreign documentation it receives. It cooperates with other Maltese libraries and offers its services to economists, businessmen, and university students. The Trade Documentation Unit formerly housed in this library is now at the Malta Trade Export Corporation (METCO). In 1990 the Central Bank of Malta Library became the first Maltese library to purchase an integrated software system.

The Centru ta' Ricerka u Dokumentazzjoni ("Research and Documentation Center") of the Nationalist party, one of the main political parties, deals mainly with local current events and has an automated database. Other libraries in the same field are those belonging to Allied Malta Newspapers and the General Workers' Union Research Department, both in Valletta. Also in Valletta are the libraries of the Moviment Azzjoni Socjali ("Social Action Movement"), specializing in industrial relations and cooperatives, and that of the Teachers' Institute.

The International Ocean Institute (Valletta), which trains managers and conservators of marine resources, has a library covering this area of studies. The European Documentation Center (Valletta) maintains documentation on the European Communities. Air Malta, the national airline, has a technical library run by a professional librarian.

Of the religious libraries, those of the Franciscan Friars (Valletta) and the Capuchins (Floriana) date back to the 16th century. The Capuchin library is notable for its holdings of rare 16th and 17th century editions. Most influential is the John XXIII Memorial Library (Valletta), the provincial library for the Maltese Jesuits, specializing in contemporary theology, which has initiated a number of cooperative projects among religious libraries.

The Profession. The Ghaqda Bibljotekarji (GhB), as the Malta Library Association was renamed in 1978, accepts as members both professional and non-professional library staff, including teacher-librarians. It organizes an annual Book Week and short and long courses for subprofessionals and teacher-librarians. From 1986 to 1988, it organized a diploma course at the professional level. Some courses are run independently, others in conjunction with the State Department of Education or the University of Malta's Faculty of Education. The GhB maintains a Register of Professional Librarians. It has been a member of IFLA since its creation in 1969 and helped to found the Commonwealth Library Association (COMLA) in 1972.

REFERENCE

Paul Xuereb, *Promoters of Information: The first twenty years of the Ghaqda Bibljotekarji, 1969–1989* (1989).

PAUL XUEREB

Mamiya, Fujio
(1890–1970)

Fujio Mamiya made contributions to the Japanese library world that have much in common with some of Melvil Dewey's contributions to the American library world, and he has been called the Dewey of Japan.

Born July 26, 1890, in Tokyo, Mamiya finished his higher primary school in 1902 and joined, as an apprentice, the Book Division of Maruzen Co., Ltd., the oldest and largest import trader of foreign books and stationery in Japan. Although his formal school education was short, he felt strongly the importance of reading as a method of self-education, and he was devoted to improvement of Japanese libraries in his later years.

In the days he worked for Maruzen, he came to the attention of a businessman in the typewriter trade who made possible a trip to the United States, a long-cherished desire. In 1915 Mamiya attended training classes of typewriter corporations in New York. He returned to Japan in 1916 and worked in the Kurosawa typewriter shop for five years.

In 1921 he left the Kurosawa shop and opened his own shop in Osaka, producing and selling library supplies. His shop developed successfully. In 1927 the League of Young Librarians, a research group for libraries, was organized under his leadership. The Japan Library Association had existed long before the League started, but the League emphasized "the standardization of norms and forms." From 1928 *Toshokan Kenkyu* ("Library Study") was published quarterly as a bulletin of the League and as the only research journal for libraries in Japan. It was forced to cease in 1943 by increasingly severe war limitations.

Mamiya made efforts to promote international standard-size cards through his library supply business. In addition, he established at his office the Mamiya Library, consisting of about 3,000 volumes of foreign books on library science. Unfortunately, the Library was destroyed by fire during an air raid in May 1945 with the whole Mamiya shop. In 1950 Mamiya founded the Japan Library Bureau in Tokyo. The Japanese government recognized his long distinguished service for the Japanese library world with formal awards in 1961 and 1966. Another of Mamiya's interests was the movement to promote romanization of the Japanese alphabet, to which he devoted efforts all his life. Mamiya died on October 24, 1970.

TOSHIO IWASARU

National Diet Library

Fujio Mamiya

Mann, Margaret
(1873–1960)

A brilliant and imaginative American teacher, Margaret Mann revolutionized instruction in cataloguing. In an obituary, the *Australian Library Journal* described her as "one of the most outstanding librarians of the twentieth century."

She was born April 9, 1873, in Cedar Rapids, Iowa. After graduating from Chicago's Englewood High School in 1893, she entered the Department of Library Economy at Armour Institute, Chicago, under the direction of Katharine Sharp. Armour was one of four library schools founded between 1887 and 1893 and the first in the Middle West. Entering students were at least 20 years of age and had to have a high school education; the entrance examination stressed a knowledge of authors and their works (in French, German, Latin, Greek, and English), some background in history, and a familiarity with current events. Students put in 40 hours a week during their year's study and were awarded certificates if successful. In addition to attending classes, they worked for various members of the library staff and gave some hours each week to the Institute.

Mann was one of 12 applicants (22 tried) to pass Armour's entrance examination. She finished the first-year course with superior grades and was employed as a cataloguer for the Institute's new 10,000-volume library. At the same time, she began a second year of study in the Armour Library School, and by 1896 she was teaching cataloguing at Armour and summer courses at the University of Wisconsin.

In September 1897 Armour moved to the University of Illinois (as the University of Illinois State Library School) with Katharine Sharp as Director of the School and Librarian of the University. Mann became an instructor; her course in the cataloguing and reference use of public documents was the first of its kind to be offered anywhere. She organized and supervised the Catalog Department in the university library and in 1900 was named Assistant Librarian.

In 1903 Mann became Head of the Cataloguing Department at the Carnegie Library of Pittsburgh, where she prepared for publication the Library's classified catalogue, a monument of its kind and a valued reference tool for many years. During her years in Pittsburgh, Mann taught cataloguing regularly in the Library's training school; offered courses at Western Reserve (Cleveland) and in Riverside, California; lectured; wrote; and began serving the American Library Association. She had become ALA member number 1,527 in 1896, when Katharine Sharp was a member of Council. In 1909 and 1910 she was Chairman of ALA's Catalog Section; from 1910 to 1913 she was a member of the Committee on Catalog Rules for Small Libraries; and she was elected to Council for the first of three five-year terms beginning in 1912. In 1914 she was appointed by the Executive Board to a Special Committee to Study Cost and Methods of Cataloging, in 1917 to the Decimal

School of Library Science, University of Michigan

Margaret Mann

Classification Advisory Committee (for one year), and also in 1917 to the Catalog Rules Committee, where she served—except for one three-year lapse—until 1932. ALA published her *List of Subject Headings for a Juvenile Catalog* in 1916.

In 1919 Harrison Craver, under whose directorship Mann had worked in Pittsburgh, employed her again in New York at the United Engineering Societies Library. From the separate catalogues and collections that had merged to form the Library, Mann created one collection arranged by a relatively brief Dewey number and a classified catalogue arranged by the Universal Decimal classification. During these years she was instrumental in organizing a system of regional cataloguing groups that became ALA's Council of Regional Groups. She was active on the Committee on Library Training from 1920 to 1924, was appointed to the Executive Board of ALA to fill a vacancy in 1921–22, and served on the Fiftieth Anniversary Committee in 1923–24.

In 1923 the ALA set up a library school in Paris as an outgrowth of reconstruction work with war-damaged libraries in France carried on by the American Committee for Devastated France. Sarah C. N. Bogle, Director of the École des Bibliothècaires and Mann's friend from the Pittsburgh days, asked Mann to teach in the Paris Library School in 1924. The School's international student body was taught in French and took courses for eight months, followed by a six-week summer course. Subjects were not taught in discrete parts, as in most American schools at the time, but in large groups. Mann's cataloguing course, for example, included work with the ALA and French cataloguing codes; Dewey Decimal, Brunet, Cutter, Library of Congress, and Universal Decimal classifications; shelflisting; and the making of dictionary and classified catalogues.

By the time Mann returned to the U.S. in 1926, William Warner Bishop had formed a new library school at the University of Michigan, Ann Arbor. They had met at Armour, where he was an instructor. Years later they served together on ALA Council and on the Catalog Rules Committee, where Bishop found Mann an ally against the proponents of constant change in the code. In 1923, when he left the chairmanship of the Committee (then called the Committee on Cataloging), she was appointed in his place.

Bishop's concern to find capable instructors for the school led him to Mann. By 1926 she was internationally recognized both as cataloguer and as teacher of cataloguing. Reporting to Michigan's President on Mann's qualifications, Bishop wrote: "Without exception every one in the country says that Miss Margaret Mann, now teaching cataloguing and classification . . . in Paris, . . . is the best teacher of these subjects to be found anywhere. In this opinion I heartily concur. There are certain obstacles to her appointment . . . chief of which is the fact that she has had no college work whatever. . . . Personally, I think the University of Michigan is big enough to employ the best teachers irrespective of their academic preparation. . . . Despite her lack of academic study, she is one of the best-read people I have ever met in my life." Later she was offered one of three full-time positions in the new school.

Inasmuch as Mann's fame rests chiefly on her excellence as a teacher of cataloguing, her views on the subject and methods of communicating it are worthy of attention. The organization of her Paris course does not seem unusual today until it is contrasted with other styles of teaching cataloguing. The three schools that followed Dewey's at Albany—Pratt, Drexel, and Armour— were connected with circulating public libraries. While they could not offer students the resources of a large academic library, they could offer actual practice in library routines. Following the first plan of Dewey's school, they emphasized technique almost to the exclusion of principle. In contrast to an emphasis on activities she felt were largely clerical in nature, Mann insisted that cataloguers needed to develop critical judgment and executive ability; "emphasis on technical details," she wrote, "will never make a good cataloger." She saw the library catalogue as a service instrument for library staff and users and attempted to teach every facet of the subject in its relation to the needs of users.

In 1926 the Board of Education for Librarianship asked Mann to write the cataloguing volume in a series of seven basic textbooks sponsored by ALA and funded by the Carnegie Corporation. ALA published *Introduction to Cataloguing and the Classification of Books* in mimeograph form in 1928 and in bound form in 1930; a second edition came out in 1943. Regarded as a classic in its own time, it won an influence that still continues.

Mann's book followed the organization of her course. She felt cataloguing training should begin with a study of books, since students would have some familiarity with them while they lacked techniques of librarianship. Next she covered subject approach, and students learned classification and the use of subject headings. These topics were followed by cataloguing and then by subjects related to the administration of a catalogue department. Although Mann believed in laboratory practice for students, she felt card sets should be made by typists. Apparently she was one of the first library school instructors to use audiovisuals as an aid to the teaching of cataloguing: she used a reflectoscope to display title pages on a screen.

When Bishop was immersed in problems of cataloguing the Vatican Library in the late 1920s, Mann served as an adviser on cataloguing and trained several cataloguers sent to Michigan from the Vatican. She surveyed cataloguing and classification conditions at the library of Teachers College, Columbia University; this survey led to a revision of its catalogue.

The ALA Executive Board in 1931 appointed her to a committee to study the possibilities for cooperative cataloguing among research libraries; the project begun as a result of this work was funded by the General Education Board. In 1932 she shared in a Carnegie Corporation grant and spent her sabbatical year studying library education in Europe.

Mann retired from teaching in 1938 when she was 65, although she continued to be active on ALA's Catalog Code Revision Committee until 1942. In 1945 she moved to Chula Vista, California, where she died on August 22, 1960.

REFERENCE

Laurel A. Grotzinger, "Mann, Margaret," *Dictionary of American Library Biography* (1978).

CONSTANCE RINEHART

MARC

Library of Congress

Bibliographic information available on diskette and CD–ROM.

As editors, printers, and publishers began experimenting with using computers in producing books in the early 1960s, librarians began considering ways to store bibliographic information in forms computers could read. From the first efforts to "save the keystrokes" required to produce catalogue cards for later use in producing printed catalogues, pioneers in the field soon went on to consider ways to exchange bibliographic information in machine-readable form with others who could also avoid typing.

An initial study of recording cataloguing data in machine-readable form began when the Council on Library Resources awarded a contract that resulted in a report, *The Recording of Library of Congress Bibliographical Data in Machine-Readable Form* (1964). This report concentrated on producing printed products from cataloguing data in machine-readable form. The Library of Congress (LC), the Council on Library Resources (CLR), and the Committee on Automation of the Association of Research Libraries (ARL) sponsored a conference at the Library in January 1965. The purpose of the meeting was to determine the requirements for a machine-readable record. Conferees concluded that LC should distribute bibliographic data for current materials in machine-readable form and that probably the best means of achieving standardization would be to have LC design such a machine-readable record. As a result of this meeting, three LC staff members were assigned the task of analyzing cataloguing data from a machine processing point of view. The results of this study, issued in June 1965 as *A Proposed Format for a Standardized Machine-Readable Catalog Card: A Preliminary Draft,* suggested the contents of a machine-readable record, the manner of representing the data, and the concept of fixed and variable fields. Many people reviewed the proposed machine-readable record and submitted their comments to LC. A second conference, concentrating on the data element content of the bibliographic record, was held at LC in November 1965, drawing together representatives from various types of libraries. As a result, LC sought a grant from CLR to conduct a pilot project to test the feasibility and utility of producing and distributing LC cataloguing data in machine-readable form to user libraries. The project was named the Machine Readable Cataloging Project, or MARC, for *MA*chine-*R*eadable *C*ataloging.

From November 1966 until the pilot project ended in June 1968, LC distributed approximately 50,000 records for English-language monographs on magnetic tape to 16 participating libraries. *The MARC Pilot Project: Final Report on a Project Sponsored by the Council on Library Resources, Inc.* (1968) includes descriptions of the work at LC and the reports of the participating libraries. This final report is a useful document not only for the history of MARC through 1968 but also for its description of this pioneering effort in cooperative library automation, which would have wide implications for the library community and the future of automated library systems. The positive results of the pilot project encouraged LC to implement the MARC Distribution Service in March 1969 to distribute machine-readable cataloguing records to subscribing libraries and institutions.

Part of the rationale for the pilot project was to test a machine format under operational conditions in order to design an improved second format based on the experience gained. The substantive evaluation of the format used during the pilot project, called MARC I, provided the input required to design what became known as MARC II. The philosophy of the MARC format was the design of one format structure (the physical representation on a machine-readable medium) capable of containing bibliographic information for all forms of materials (such as books, serials, and maps) and related records (including name and subject authority records). The MARC formats, which were later called LC MARC and eventually USMARC, are standards for representing and communicating bibliographic and related information in machine-readable form and are currently defined for bibliographic, holdings, authority, and classification data.

Each USMARC record involves three elements: the record structure, the content designation, and the data content of the record. The structure of USMARC records is an implementation of national and international standards: the national standard is ANSI Z39.2-1985, *American National Standard for Bibliographic Information Interchange on Magnetic Tape,* adopted in 1971; the international equivalent is ISO 2709-1981, *Documentation—Format for Bibliographic Information Interchange on Magnetic Tape,* adopted in 1973. Both the ANSI and the ISO standards for information interchange describe a framework designed specifically for exchange of data between systems (rather than for processing data in a system) for all material capable of receiving bibliographic description and related information. As an implementation of these structure standards, the USMARC formats define application-specific content designation (such as tags and codes). In addition to the format, the MARC project included the design of an extended character set for roman-alphabet languages as well as codes for languages and countries. The impetus MARC gave to standardization is doubtless one of its most important results.

From the outset, MARC and standardization have been complementary activities. As members of the library community have recognized the importance of standardization for effective resource sharing, they have become increasingly involved in various standards activities. These activities have involved not only the appropriate national and international standards organizations but the International Federation of Library Associations and Institutions (IFLA) and other related organizations as well. LC continues to play a major role in maintaining MARC formats in the United States by assuming responsibility for (1) making any necessary changes to established formats and designing new formats with the advice and assistance of the library community; (2) compiling and distributing all MARC documentation; (3) maintaining liaison with the ALA Machine-Readable Bibliographic Information Committee (MARBI); and (4) representing the U.S. library community in international MARC standardization activities.

The development of MARC in the U.S. was closely followed by the development of national MARC projects by national bibliographic agencies in countries worldwide. During the course of the pilot project, staff from the British National Bibliography visited LC to investigate the possibility of a UK/MARC Pilot Project. Its staff worked with LC's MARC staff on the MARC II format to satisfy the requirements of both institutions. This cooperation has had long-term effects. Both institutions recognized the future implications of an interchange format and the importance of agreement by two major publishing countries on a standard for information interchange. Thus the same format structure was adopted, although content designation has in some instances taken different paths. The way was now open for other countries to follow the lead and to develop their own MARC projects. Since 1969 many national bibliographic agencies have developed similar MARC services, assuming responsibility for creating MARC records representing the publishing output of their countries. By 1986, 19 countries reported the existence of national MARC services and another 25 were at various stages of planning for distribution or online services.

International exchange of data, however, has remained problematic. Although the national format structures are identical, differences exist among MARC implementations because of differences in cataloguing codes that influence the content, and thus the content designation, of each record. As a result, each national agency must prepare tailor-made computer programs to process the MARC data of every other national agency. To overcome this problem, UNIMARC (Universal MARC) was developed under the auspices of IFLA to provide a communications format for exchanging bibliographic data among national libraries or bibliographic agencies. UNIMARC enables each national agency to write and maintain only two conversion programs, one from the national format to UNIMARC and the other from UNIMARC to the national format.

Library of Congress
Charles Martel

The UNIMARC format, under design since 1973, was originally published in 1977 and has the benefit of years of experience in using various national MARC formats. Adoption of the format for international exchange started slowly, but picked up speed in the late 1980s and early 1990s. In addition, it is being considered as the format for use among the countries of the European Community.

At the international level, the IFLA Universal Bibliographic Control and International MARC (UBCIM) Core Program is responsible for MARC-related matters. The aim of UBCIM is "to promote

the exchange and use of compatible bibliographic records among libraries in general and national bibliographic agencies in particular, and to create, maintain, and promote the use of standards for the exchange of bibliographic data in machine-readable form." UNIMARC has been a particular focus of the UBCIM Program since the late 1980s. The *UNIMARC Manual* has been translated into several languages for the widest possible dissemination and an update to the *International Guide to MARC Databases* was published in 1991. UBCIM work is in progress on specific International Standard Bibliographic Descriptions (ISBDs) for general books, antiquarian books, computer files, and printed music; a manual on the application of ISBDs; the UNIMARC format for authorities; and the management and use of name authority files. UBCIM's work reflects the international library community's continued support of MARC and related matters.

MARC has been operational since 1969. Technology made great strides in that period, and a high-speed gigabit U.S. National Research and Education Network was well on its way to becoming a reality. In addition to bibliographic records, users will be able to access the content of the items the records represent. New standards will be required to access this information, and MARC and all the standards encompassed by that term will be the building blocks for a system of far greater potential than exists today.

REFERENCES

Henriette D. Avram, *The MARC Pilot Project: Final Report on a Project Sponsored by the Council on Library Resources, Inc.* (1968).

Henriette D. Avram, *MARC: Its History and Implications* (1975).

Walt Crawford, *MARC for Library Use: Understanding Integrated USMARC,* 2nd ed. (1987).

Brian P. Holt, editor, *UNIMARC Manual* (1987).

HENRIETTE D. AVRAM

Martel, Charles
(1860–1945)

Charles Martel, the chief architect of the Library of Congress classification, was born March 5, 1860, in Zürich, Switzerland. James Bennett Childs has stated that Martel's name was originally Karl David Hanke and that he was the son of Franz and Maria Gertrud Strässle Hanke. Franz Hanke was a publisher and antiquarian bookseller, and Martel credited his education to his association with the bookstore, but he also completed the Gymnasium course in 1876 and attended the University of Zürich in 1876–77. In 1876 Martel spent five months visiting the United States. He returned to the U.S. in either late 1879 or early 1880 and became a citizen in 1887 under the name of Charles Martel. From 1880 to 1892 he taught in schools in Missouri and Nebraska and was employed in a law office in Council Bluffs, Iowa.

Martel had served as a volunteer in various libraries, and he chose librarianship as a full-time career in February 1892 when he joined the staff of the Newberry Library in Chicago. Eight months later Librarian William Frederick Poole recommended an increase in salary "because of his very great ability and enthusiasm." Poole's further evaluation in a report in

October 1892 would be confirmed by others: "a quiet, scholarly man, indefatigable, and working in season and out of season." Martel was involved in both cataloguing and classification and was in charge of the Department of Arts and Letters (1893–96) and of early printed books and manuscripts (1896–97).

While at the Newberry, Martel formed a lifelong friendship with his colleague J. C. M. Hanson. Within two months after Hanson's arrival to head the bibliographical reorganization of the Library of Congress consequent to its move from the Capitol, Librarian John Russell Young appointed Charles Martel as Assistant in the Catalogue Department, one of the two top-salaried positions, effective December 1, 1897. When Martel joined Hanson, the Library of Congress acquired "a team which has never been equaled anywhere," according to William Warner Bishop (*Library Quarterly,* January 1948).

Martel's analysis of the existing classification, his first assignment, was submitted to Young by the end of the month. Although it included an outline of a new scheme, it emphasized the notation, not the scheme itself. He described the new scheme merely as an eclectic one "combining the best features of those in use in other reference libraries." Moreover, the arrangement for class Z (Bibliography and Library Science) had been "modified so as to disturb as little as possible the existing order" of the collection. These emphases may have been made in deference to the Assistant Librarian, Ainsworth Rand Spofford, an articulate foe of close classification.

Hanson always rejected any credit for the classification, as he reminded Herbert Putnam:

> Aside from some preliminary planning of the notation, I am afraid that my claims to association in the construction of the Library of Congress classification are very slight. Soon after 1898 I was forced to give almost all my time to the cataloguing, leaving the details of the classification very largely to Mr. Martel (March 25, 1915; University of Chicago Library Archives).

Work on the reclassification began in January 1898 but was suspended when, after Young's death in January 1899, Herbert Putnam was appointed to succeed him. The project was not resumed until January 18, 1901, when the reclassification of U.S. history into classes E and F, prepared by Martel in 1898–1900, was undertaken with an enlarged staff. A number of subject specialists worked with Martel in developing the other schedules.

In 1901, beginning with classes D (Universal and Old World History) and Q (Science), and in subsequent classes, a second letter for the major subdivisions was introduced to permit "the beginning of operations simultaneously at various points in the system" (Report of the Librarian of Congress . . . June 30, 1902). In 1911 Martel introduced another notational modification in subdivisions needing provision for many names, by incorporating the initial letter in the number for the subdivision and assigning the Cutter author number from the second letter in the name.

The pressure to complete and publish the classification schedules was so great that a detailed description of the philosophical basis of the system could not be written for publication until 1911. Martel first wrote it as part of a larger paper, "Classification: A Brief Conspectus of Present Day Practice," read at a meeting of the New Zealand Library Association in April 1911. The part on the Library of Congress scheme was sent for reading at the Pasadena meeting of the American Library Association in May of the same year.

Martel also made a major contribution in descriptive cataloguing. For 28 years after he was appointed Chief of the Catalog Division in October 1912 (to succeed Charles H. Hastings, who had served during the interregnum following Hanson's resignation in October 1910), Martel guided Library of Congress cataloguing on a level generally accepted as authoritative. When he reached the statutory retirement age of 70 in 1930, he filled the specially created position of Consultant in Cataloging, Classification, and Bibliography. On June 30, 1932, President Herbert Hoover, on Putnam's recommendation, exempted Martel from the provisions of the Retirement Act by Executive Order, citing Martel's "irreplaceable knowledge of the collections of the Library of Congress and his rich bibliographical and technical expertise."

In 1928 William Warner Bishop asked Martel to head a commission of cataloguers to assist in the reorganization of the Vatican Library, a project supported by the Carnegie Endowment for International Peace. Martel at first refused, but he reconsidered when Hanson, who was next approached, refused to go without him. The cataloguing rules they worked out with the Monsignors Tisserant and Mercati constituted the original draft of the Vatican Library's *Norme per il catalogo degli stampati* ("rules for the cataloguing of printed books"), a major step in international library cooperation. Martel also assisted in the translation into Italian of the needed parts of the Library of Congress Classification. Martel retired on May 1, 1945, and died two weeks later, on May 15.

REFERENCES

James Bennett Childs, "Martel, Charles," *Encyclopedia of Library and Information Science,* and the *Dictionary of American Biography* (3rd Supplement), volume 17 (1976).

Leo E. LaMontagne, *American Library Classification with Special Reference to the Library of Congress* (1961).

Edith Scott, "J. C. M. Hanson and His Contribution to Twentieth-Century Cataloging" (Ph.D. dissertation, University of Chicago, 1970).

Harriet Wheeler Pierson, "Charles Martel," *Catalogers' and Classifiers' Yearbook* no. 9 (1941).

James Bennett Childs and John Y. Cole, "Martel, Charles," *Dictionary of American Library Biography* (1978).

EDITH SCOTT
(d. 1983)

Martin, Allie Beth
(1914–1976)

Allie Beth Martin was an outstanding American educator, a skillful politician, a talented writer, a respected leader, and a dedicated librarian. She headed the Tulsa Public Library for 13 years, and under her leadership it became well known throughout the United States for innovative and forward-looking programs.

She was born in the small town of Annieville, Arkansas, on June 28, 1914, to Carleton Gayle Dent and Ethel McCaleb Dent. She attended public schools in Seattle, Washington, and Batesville, Arkansas. While attending Batesville's high school, Martin lived

Tulsa City—County Library
Allie Beth Martin

with her grandfather, who had a primary influence on her life and the course it would later take. It has been said that she decided as a child that she wanted to become a librarian.

Following her graduation from high school in 1932, Martin enrolled at Arkansas College in Batesville, where she majored in foreign languages and English while working part-time in the college library. She graduated in 1935 with a B.A. and became the first Librarian of the Batesville Public Library. A year later she moved to Little Rock, where she was in charge of the junior college library. The following year she joined the Arkansas Library Commission as Assistant to the Executive Secretary. She married Ralph F. Martin, a journalist, on October 6, 1937, and later resigned from the Commission. In 1939 she received a B.S. in Library Science from George Peabody College for Teachers in Nashville, Tennessee. She moved with her husband to Arkansas when he entered medical school, and she served as Director of the Mississippi County Library in Osceola, Arkansas, and later, from 1942 to 1947, returned again to the staff of the Arkansas Library Commission. In 1945 she was elected President of the Arkansas Library Association, and she served as Editor of *Arkansas Libraries* until 1947. During her husband's internship and residency in New York, she attended Columbia University School of Library Science and received her Master's degree in 1949.

In 1949 the Martins moved to Tulsa, Oklahoma, where Dr. Martin practiced medicine until his death in 1968. She joined the Tulsa Public Library and spent her first year serving in various departments. In 1950 she worked as a children's librarian, following that with the position of extension librarian, in which she served until 1961. Martin edited *Oklahoma Librarian* in 1953 and 1954 and was elected President of the Oklahoma Library Association in 1955. She was later honored by OLA with the Distinguished Service Award.

The condition of the Tulsa Public Library in the late 1950s was typical of many libraries of that time. The Central Library, built with Carnegie funds in 1916, was overcrowded and in a state of disrepair, as were the four branch libraries. Martin became actively involved in persuading the community of the need for new and improved facilities. A first bond issue failed, only to be overwhelmingly approved when presented the second time on November 14, 1961. The bond issue included $3,800,000 for construction of a new Central Library and building and renovation of 20 branch libraries and an annually recurring levy for the operation of the Tulsa City–County Library System. In 1963 Martin was named Director of the library system she was instrumental in creating.

Martin served as President of the Southwestern Library Association (1969–70) and led the regional association into an active role in continuing education and cooperative projects.

A member of the American Library Association from 1935, she served in many capacities: on the executive boards of the Public Libraries and Children's Services Divisions, and as Chairperson of the ALA Membership Committee. *Strategy for Public Library Change: Proposed Public Library Goals* was published by ALA in 1972. She was elected to the ALA Council for the term 1972–1976 and to the Executive Board in 1973. She was inaugurated President of ALA in July 1975 at the San Francisco Conference. Three months later she underwent surgery for cancer. She continued with her work as President and as Library Director until her death in Tulsa on April 11, 1976.

Martin received many awards and honors during her lifetime and following her death; a regional library of the Tulsa System was named for her, as was a national library award and a lecture series.

REFERENCE

Frances Kennedy, "Martin, Allie Beth," *Dictionary of American Library Biography* (1978).

PAT WOODRUM

Maunsell, Andrew

(d.1595)

Andrew Maunsell, a member of the Drapers' Company in London, is remembered today almost entirely for his bibliographical work. As compiler of the first effective national bibliography on scientific principles, Maunsell is a figure of considerable importance.

Though not a member of the Stationers' Company, he obtained a license as early as 1578 to publish *The State of Swearinge and Swearers,* and thereafter until 1595 was active as a bookseller and publisher, particularly of theological works. At that time there was no general printed catalogue of English works, with the partial exception of the *Scriptorum illustrium majoris Britanniae . . . catalogus* of John Bale (Wesel, 1548; another edition Basel, 1557–59) In the *Catalogue of English Printed Books,* which occupied Maunsell in the last years of his life, he tried to prepare a true national bibliography, and in a form that presented many advances in bibliographical technique.

In *The First Part of the Catalogue of English printed Books: which concerneth such matters of Divinitie, as have bin either written in our owne Tongue, or translated out of anie other language,* published by Maunsell from his shop in Lothbury in 1595, he explained his purpose and method in the prefatory address to the Master of the Stationers' Company. He justified his work on the ground that it was as necessary for the bookseller to have such a catalogue "as the Apothecarie his *Dispensatorium,* or the Schoolemaster his *Dictionarie.*" In distinction to Bale and other earlier compilers, he pointed out that he was including only printed works and only works that he had personally examined, and he had arranged his entries so that books on the same subject were grouped together. Another advance was that alphabetical arrangement was by surnames, not forenames; anonymous works were listed by title and by subject. He took care to record translators, printers and publishers, date of publication, and format. Deliberate exclusions were noted: "The auncient Popish Books that have been Printed heere, I have also inserted among the rest, but the Bookes written by the fugitive Papistes, as also those that are written against the present government, I doe not thinke meete for me to meddle withall."

The First Part (which was arranged on the dictionary principle, with author, title, and subject entries in a single alphabet) was followed later in the same year by *The Second Part,* which listed works on "the Sciences Mathematicall, as Arithmetick, Geometrie,

Astronomie, Astrologie, Musick, the Arte of Warre, and Navigation: And also, of Phisick and Surgerie" arranged on the same general principles. A third part was promised in the preface to this volume. It was to deal with "Humanitie," which Maunsell defined as "Grammer, Logick, Rethoricke, Lawe, Historie, Poetrie, Policie, &c. which will for the most parte concerne matters of Delight and Pleasure." However, since it was difficult to collect information, and "so tedious to digest into any good methode," Maunsell had thought it wise to publish the first two parts to test public reaction before completing his work. We must be grateful that he did so: though public reaction was favorable, Maunsell's death late in 1595 prevented the completion of his labors. His *Catalogue* was reprinted in 1962 as part of the Gregg/Archive Press series on English Bibliographical Sources.

RODERICK CAVE

Mauritania

Mauritania, an Islamic republic in West Africa, is bounded by Western (Spanish) Sahara on the northwest, Algeria on the north, Mali on the east and southeast, Senegal on the southwest, and the Atlantic Ocean on the west. Population (1990 est.) 2,025,000; area 1,025,520 sq.km. The official languages are Arabic and French.

The national library system in Mauritania was instituted by a law of July 10, 1962, which foresaw, in particular, the establishment of an integrated system comprised of (1) a national conservation library of all works on or printed in Mauritania and the essentials of the written civilization; (2) public and school libraries; and (3) study libraries for the use of universities, institutes, laboratories, and others.

National Library. The National Library of Mauritania in Nouakchott, the capital, was created on January 27, 1965, by decree. It comprises a conservation library, a documentation center on Mauritania, and a study and research library. The country is weak in resources, and the National Library also provides school libraries and public reading programs. It is responsible for policies on the development of libraries and documentation throughout the country. Its collection totaled 10,000 volumes and 4,000 manuscripts in the mid-1980s. The manuscript department, which had 3,500 works in 1975, was attached in 1979 to the Mauritanian Institute of Scientific Research, which had nearly 2,500 others.

Academic Libraries. Until the 1980s there was no university in Mauritania, but many schools of higher learning existed with the status of university institutes. Each had its own library. They included a School of Education (created in 1970), which had a library with nearly 10,000 volumes; a national School of Administration (1966) with a library of approximately 12,000 volumes; and a School of Elementary Education Training (1965), which had a library of more than 8,000 volumes. In 1982 the École Nationale d'Administration and the École Nationale des Sciences in Nouakchott began offering degree courses, and in 1983 the nation's first university, the University of Nouakchott, opened.

Public Library Service. The department of public reading of the National Library provides public library services, as does the Bibliothèque Publique Centrale in Nouakchott. Other libraries open to the public were those of the cultural centers of several accredited embassies in Mauritania, including Egypt, France, Libya, Russia, and Syria, among others.

School Libraries. There is a library in each secondary school for the use of its teachers and students, but they were underdeveloped as of the mid-1980s. The 26 school libraries contain a total of some 112,000 volumes.

Special Libraries. Several special libraries or documentation centers serve various government ministries or semiprivate organizations. Among examples are the documentation services of the National Society of Mine Imports (SNIM, which has a collection of close to 13,000 titles); the National Society of Rural Development (SONADER); the Administration of Studies and Programming of the Ministry in Charge of Special Projects; the National Pedagogical Institute; the documentation division of the Administration of Mines and Geology; the documentation project of the Ministry of Rural Development; and the Mauritanian Institute of Scientific Research Library. There are Arab libraries at Chinguetti, Kaedi, and other towns.

The Profession. The Mauritanian section of the International Association for the Development of Libraries and Archives in Africa (AIDBA) formerly existed in the country. In May 1979 a new association was created. Continuing the work of the AIDBA and named the Mauritanian Association of Librarians, Archivists, and Documentalists (AMBAD), it established headquarters in Nouakchott; a Directory Committee included the Director of the National Library, who served as President.

OUMAR DIOUWARA

Mauritius

Mauritius, a parliamentary state, lies east of the island of Madagascar in the Indian Ocean. It includes the island of Mauritius and the dependencies of Agalega, Cargados Carajos Shoals, and Rodrigues. Population (1990 est.) 1,082,000; area 2,040 sq.km. The official language is English, but French and many oriental languages are widely used.

History. In the early 19th century Mauritius had a few subscription libraries in bookshops; patrons could buy books or borrow them for low subscription fees. The Librairie Baron had about 10,000 books by 1807 and Baron and Sauvignec owned "reading halls" in 1816. The Mauritius Literary Association sponsored a subscription lending library in the early 1800s and later opened it to the public. The Municipality of Port Louis Library, the first public library of note in the capital, was created in 1851.

National Library and Archives. No library bears the official designation of national library. The Mauritius Archives is the official repository of archives, notary deeds, and copies of all books, periodicals, and newspapers printed and published in Mauritius. It also has collections of maps, postage stamps, portraits, photographs, seals, and private archives. It publishes a quarterly memorandum of all books

Libraries in Mauritius (1991)

Type of library	Number of administrative units (main libraries)	Number of service points (branches, mobile stops, etc.)	Volumes in collections	Annual expenditures (rupee)*	Population served	Professional staff (with certificate, diploma, etc.)	Total staff
National & Archives	1	0	46,430	25,000	2,000	2	18
Academic	4	2	182,000	3,495,000	6,500	11	62
Public	16		362,709	2,755,000	223,889	10	100
School**	26		170,000	1,200,000	31,852	2	52
Special	13	53	237,708	1,290,000	11,715	4	102

*Books and periodicals
**Government secondary schools only

deposited and maintains an annual supplement to the Bibliography of Mauritius (1502–1954).

The Mauritius Institute, which has a natural history museum, started a public library in 1901 after it received a collection of about 9,000 books from Sir Virgil Naz. The Library has the right of legal deposit for books; it shares with the Mauritius Archives and the University Library certain national library functions. The Mauritius Institute is also the depository library for Unesco publications. It holds about 65,000 volumes, with a section on Mauritius and nearby islands.

Academic Libraries. The University of Mauritius Library (founded 1968) occupies a functional building of about 33,000 sq.ft. with seats for 350. It serves the information, research, and teaching needs of the four constituent schools of the University: Agriculture; Engineering; Law, Management, and Social Studies; and Science. It also serves the island community at large. The Library contains about 90,000 volumes. It is a partial depository for United Nations documents and shares legal deposit. The Law Collection and the Mauritiana collection house some of the earliest local newspapers and government documents.

The Mauritius Institute in Port Louis, opened to the public in 1901, fulfills some functions of a national library.

The Library runs a printing, binding, and microfilming unit and provides centralized audiovisual service for the University.

The Mauritius Institute of Education (1975) has a main library in Reduit and a branch library (formerly the Mauritius College of Education library) at Beau Bassin. The collections total about 40,000 volumes.

The Mahatma Gandhi Institute Library functions as a public, school, and research library with a stock of about 40,000 volumes. It also serves the School of Oriental, African, and Mauritian Studies. It houses documents on early Indian immigration and an extensive literature collection in Indian and Chinese languages.

Public Libraries. Public library service in Port-Louis is provided by the Mauritius Institute, the Indian High Commission, and the Port-Louis city library. The city library, established in 1851, opened its doors to the public in 1933. It has a collection of about 100,000 volumes. There are four other municipal libraries in the district of Plaines Wilhems: the libraries of the municipalities of Beau Bassin and Rose Hill, Quatre Bornes, Vacoas Phoenix, and Curepipe.

School Libraries. Most of the more than 125 secondary schools have libraries, although fewer than half the 280 primary schools do. One in five of the government's secondary schools has full-fledged library services, with bookstocks totaling more than 155,000.

Special Libraries. The Mauritius Sugar Industry Research Institute, at Reduit, promotes the technical progress and efficiency of the sugar industry in Mauritius. Its library (1953) has about 23,000 volumes. Several government departments and ministries have libraries or documentation centers.

The Profession. The Mauritius Library Association, founded in 1974, numbers about 70 members of the library profession, including about 20 who have had professional training abroad.

The National Council for Libraries, Documentation, and Archives Services was set up in 1987 under the aegis of the Ministry of Education and Cultural Affairs. It includes members from various government ministries, parastatal library bodies, and the Mauritius Library Association. Its purpose is to advise on policy matters concerning the maintenance and development of libraries, archives, and documentation services. It began discussing the proposed framework for a national library and information service in the early 1990s.

B. R. GOORDYAL

Measurement and Evaluation in Libraries

Measurement is the process by which numbers are assigned to describe some object or phenomenon in a standardized manner. As Kaplan has written, it "is a device for standardization, by which we are assured of equivalences among objects of diverse origin." Furthermore, it "allows us to know what quantity we are getting, and to get and give just what is called for." Measurement may or may not lead to evaluation; evaluation often requires measurement.

Evaluation is the process of identifying and collecting data about specific services or activities, establishing criteria to assess their success, and determining the degree to which the service or activity accomplishes stated goals and objectives. As such, evaluation is a decision-making tool intended primarily to assist library staff in allocating necessary resources to those activities and services that best accomplish organizational goals and objectives.

This article defines and describes aspects of measurement and evaluation in the context of libraries and information centers. Some researchers continue to develop, refine, and validate the processes of describing and assessing library and information services, but much work related to measurement and evaluation remains to be done. Generally, measurement and evaluation are concepts in search of wide practice in managing libraries and information centers.

Difficulties with Measurement. Reliable and valid measurement in the social sciences is extremely difficult. All measurements are based on a range of assumptions. The more complicated the phenomenon for measurement, the more limiting are the assumptions allowing that phenomenon to be measured. Key concepts in measurement are identifying and defining *indicators* of the phenomenon to be measured and developing standardized *rules* that produce numbers representing the indicator of the phenomenon to be measured.

For example, someone wishing to measure "user satisfaction with reference service" must first determine which indicator might be used. One such indicator might be "number of reference questions asked per capita," while another might be assessment of the service by users on a Likert scale ranging from 1 (unsatisfactory) to 5 (very satisfactory).

But this example is fraught with difficulties. The indicator "number of reference questions asked per capita" may not be a valid representation of "satisfaction"; or different users may assess the same level of reference services differently on the Likert scale. Furthermore, the development of and adherence to standardized rules and procedures should ensure the collection of reliable data, but, even if such data are collected, they still may not be valid, because they may not measure what they purport to measure.

Measurement results in the collection of data that can be described as nominal, ordinal, interval, or ratio. Nominal data allow the least flexibility for the researcher to use various statistical techniques, while ratio data allow the most. Most measurement data in library and information science studies are nominal or ordinal. If researchers cannot conceptualize and operationalize complex phenomena in these studies, they may have to measure at the nominal or ordinal levels, or adopt qualitative research designs.

Performance Measures. Performance measures represent a broad managerial concept that encompasses measurement of both input (indicators of the resources essential to library services) and output (indicators of the services resulting from library activities). Performance measures can assess the extent, effectiveness, and efficiency of library operations, services, and programs. Simply stated, performance measures ask library decision makers to consider "How well is the library doing what it claims to be doing?"

The primary utility of a performance measure is for internal self-diagnosis of a library's services and activities. Managers must select and use measures having value to their institutions and meeting the information needs of their clientele. When managers compare the performance of one library to that of another library, they may be distorting the mission, goals, and objectives of each library. They must also recognize the limitations and weaknesses of a sampling frame, self-reported questionnaires, circulation records, and other methods of data collection. Furthermore, they might question the extent to which evaluators collected reliable and valid data.

Consequently, "specific local decisions about measurement methods may make data noncomparable across libraries, so external comparisons can be made only with extreme caution and with a detailed understanding of how each library implemented these measures" (*Measuring Academic Library Performance*).

There may be trade-off relationships between specific performance measures. In other words, increasing the score on one measure may decrease that on another. In addition, a number of other factors must be remembered when using performance measures (as listed in *Measuring Academic Library Performance*):

- Each measure emphasizes only one facet of library activity; measures are best used in conjunction with each other;
- Conditions can be manipulated to improve the performance on a particular measure without always improving the quality of the service or operation (for example, increase the turnover rate simply by heavily weeding the collection);
- There are no "right" or "wrong" scores on a performance measure; the scores are tied to specific library goals and objectives and provide benchmarks to assess the effectiveness of library activities;
- A primary use of a performance measure is to identify areas where change is desired, to determine whether change has occurred, and to identify areas where additional research is required;
- Performance measures should suggest not only what is happening in the library but also the quality of what is occurring, without going into the details of how those outputs were produced. Performance measures do not in themselves diagnose the causes of inadequate performance;
- "Output measures reflect services delivered, uses made of the library. The archival function of the library's collection

is not fully reflected. In some libraries, this is a major consideration";

- Measures "reflect user success in the library, not simply library performance. The final outcome is a function of the library, the user, and the library's success in anticipating user needs and assisting in the user's search"; and
- Measures "reflect the interaction of users and library resources, constrained by the environment in which they operate. The meaning of a specific score on any measure depends on a broad range of factors including the library's goals, the current circumstances of the library and its environment, the users, the manner in which the measure was constructed, and how the data were collected."

Output Measures for Public Libraries (2nd ed.), which standardized a core set of measures for public library use, offered step-by-step procedures to guide data collection. *Measuring Academic Library Performance* has a similar purpose for academic and research libraries. This manual identifies diverse areas subject to measurement (overall user success, materials availability and use, facilities and equipment availability and use, and information services). While these manuals mark a major advance in evaluation and in applying performance measures, much work remains to be done to refine, apply, and use such techniques.

Evaluation. In one sense, evaluation is primarily an information gathering, analysis, and reporting process. Librarians identify specific activities, questions, or areas as appropriate for evaluation, then develop research designs and methodologies to guide the evaluation. In addition, library decision makers collect data that specifically assess the service activity to be evaluated, then analyze the data in such a way that they can describe and compare the quality and performance of the service or activity against appropriate criteria. Then they report and implement the results to change or improve the service or activity.

Evaluation may require measurement but is not dependent on it. In other words, evaluation may employ research designs and methods of data collection that reduce data to numbers and report the findings in terms of descriptive and inferential statistics. Some evaluation studies involve *quantification*. Others might encompass *qualitative research* and use focus groups, heuristic research, naturalistic inquiry, or other methods to collect data that might not lend themselves to meaningful summarization in quantifiable form.

Because evaluation is part of decision making and encourages organizational change, library staff who embark on an ongoing evaluation process should recognize that:

- Evaluation reflects value judgments about what the library *should* be doing, *adequate* levels of performance, and criteria that describe *success* or organizational *effectiveness;*
- Evaluation requires a clearly stated and carefully thought-out set of organizational goals and objectives;
- Evaluation is tantamount to saying that change is both possible and desirable for the organization; and
- The availability of adequate staff time and organizational resources is essential for evaluation research to be done successfully.

Thus, to engage in an ongoing evaluation process is to question what the library *should* be doing, develop methods to accomplish those objectives, and encourage constant change to occur.

Libraries constantly respond to changing internal and external conditions. Policies emanating from federal, state, and local governments, technological developments, institutional mandates for library actions, changing demographics of the constituencies, and new or different competitors providing information services are only some of the external environmental factors that could affect library services and activities.

Internal conditions include budgetary increases or decreases, the addition of new personnel, changing or revised organizational or institutional missions, and new methods to access information resources and services. Thus, a library may have to change its services and activities just to maintain its current level of effectiveness. Determining what to change, and how to change it, is an important component of evaluation.

Evaluation Concepts. Evaluation includes five key concepts:

Extensiveness, the amount of a service provided in relation to the population served—generally a measure of quantity;

Effectiveness, the extent to which a service or activity accomplishes stated objectives or the extent to which it satisfies the demands that users place on it;

Efficiency, the appropriateness of resource allocations, possibly judged in the context of stated objectives;

Cost-effectiveness, the accomplishment of objectives expressed in terms of costs; and

Cost-benefit, the justification for the expense of providing a service or program in terms of the benefits derived from it.

To conduct a cost-effectiveness or cost-benefit study, librarians determine all costs (direct or indirect, immediate or long-term) related to a specific activity or service. The difference between cost-effectiveness and cost-benefit studies is that the former compares costs to the actual impact of a service or activity and the latter requires the assignment of a monetary value to that service or activity.

Traditionally, library managers have tended to concentrate on efficiency criteria, such as the number of items catalogued or the number of reference transactions completed per day. However, library managers must also consider effectiveness-related questions such as: Is the library performing activities and offering services that should be provided?

Confusion between effectiveness and efficiency may result in doing things well (efficiency) that need not be done (ineffectiveness).

Limited attention to the evaluation of library activities and services may result in continuing many library services and activities that are ineffective and/or inefficient; a blind faith that governing bodies accept the overall "goodness" of libraries and fund them at least at current levels; failure to set priorities and improve mediocre services; an inability to demonstrate to outside agencies the excellence of those services and activities that are of high quality; and limited understanding of what evaluation is, why it is important, and how librarians can accomplish it. Library staff members often make decisions about existing services and activities based on untested assumptions.

Attention to efficiency rather than effectiveness

fails to consider the likely trade-off relationships between the two types of measures. Efficiency of an activity or service cannot be improved beyond a certain critical point without injuring the effectiveness of that activity or service, and vice versa. Thus continued attention to increasing the efficiency of various activities and services may become dysfunctional or counterproductive to effectiveness criteria. For example, having reference staff drastically increase the number of transactions completed (efficiency) will reach a point at which additional transactions will not be answered correctly (ineffectiveness), if for no other reason than that the staff is dealing with an overload of questions asked and answered.

Levels of Evaluation. Evaluation research occurs at four primary levels of analysis: societal, organizational, programs, and individuals. At a societal level, evaluation is concerned with changes that have occurred in a society or community of individuals as a result of regulations; legislation; cultural values; or economic, political, or sociological factors. At this level, evaluators exercise limited control over the research design, and their findings tend to be general.

At the organizational level, evaluators have greater control over the variables to assess. Furthermore, organizational goals and objectives are likely to be more concrete than those at a societal level, and specific measures of organizational effectiveness can be established. The time for such evaluation to occur can be shorter, and intervention strategies to change organizational behavior can be more easily established than at a societal level.

At a program level, evaluators are concerned about specific services and activities. Evaluation at this level is more straightforward than evaluation at an organizational level because activities and services can be closely defined, variables better controlled, and the time for evaluation limited.

Evaluation of individual performance is better known as personnel evaluation. The purpose of such evaluation is to determine the quality and quantity of work performed; offer guidance and strategies for how the individual can be more creative, productive, and effective; and assist the organization to accomplish stated objectives better in the future.

Each level of evaluation is dependent on the others, and an individual's performance affects the quality of programs and organizations. For most libraries, assessment of organizational and program performance provides a mechanism by which individual performance can be improved. Focusing on organizational and program evaluation can enhance the quality of library services as well as the competitive edge of libraries in relation to other information providers and safety nets.

Basic Evaluation Approaches. There are two basic approaches to evaluation. *Formative* evaluation is an ongoing assessment that provides information to monitor and improve an activity or service in progress. *Summative* evaluation determines the level of program success or failure. Formative evaluation improves, while summative evaluation proves.

One purpose of evaluation is to monitor the degree to which an organization or program meets stated goals and objectives and to readjust the program to accomplish these goals better. As such, the approach is effectiveness-oriented and conducted on a formative basis.

A second purpose is to provide a "once-only" assessment of how well the organization or program meets stated goals and objectives. In this instance, the evaluation, though effectiveness-oriented, is concerned with whether the program or activity should be continued or discontinued.

A third purpose is to monitor the allocation of organizational resources. This approach is efficiency-oriented and assesses how the organization uses standard resource categories (personnel, equipment, books and other information resources, supplies, and other budgeted items). Another type of efficiency criterion includes time. For instance, the number of books catalogued per day is an efficiency assessment; if evaluators conduct such an assessment on an ongoing basis, they can identify and monitor delays in the cataloguing process.

In terms of the ease of effort required for each of these evaluation purposes, summative evaluation of resource allocation takes less effort than formative evaluation of resource allocation, which in turn takes less effort than summative evaluation of organizational/program effectiveness. Formative evaluation of organizational/program effectiveness may require the greatest effort, because the evaluation of effectiveness criteria requires the existence of clearly stated library goals and objectives, and formative evaluation involves continuous monitoring of an activity and requires the establishment of regular data collection and analysis procedures. In contrast, summative evaluation is a "one-shot" activity. Thus the greater use of effectiveness-oriented evaluation that relies on formative assessment procedures, the greater is the evaluation effort in terms of planning, staff time, commitment, and resource support. The greatest benefits in terms of meeting the information needs of the library's clientele, competing successfully against other information providers, and offering improved access to information sources and services come from the use of formative and effectiveness-oriented evaluation.

Obstacles to Measurement and Evaluation. Organizational, philosophical, and individual obstacles to evaluation may exist in any library. Perhaps the most deadly and insidious obstacle is the belief that "everything is fine in my library." In the vast majority of instances, librarians do not know how well their activities and services meet the information needs of their users, whether specific services and programs are effective and efficient, or whether resources could be better spent on supporting other activities or services.

One set of obstacles related to evaluation efforts is that the library could apply evaluation inappropriately or use it merely to serve organizational or administrative self-interests. In some instances, librarians really fear evaluating their services and activities. They may recognize that evaluation will show that the library is, in fact, ineffective or inefficient; that existing resources are poorly allocated to activities that do not fulfill patrons' information needs; or that individuals in the library may be incompetent, inadequately trained, or lacking specific knowledge and skills necessary to do their jobs effectively.

The attitude that measurement and evaluation are not really necessary, that the librarians really know what is happening in their library, and that the librarians have a good feel for knowing when a service or activity is effective or ineffective is an obstacle to the completion of successful library evaluation. Faith in common-sense approaches to organizational effectiveness is simplistic and unrealistic in these times of complex organizations, innovative technologies, and limited resources.

Some other obstacles to the conduct of successful evaluation include the perceived lack of resources to support the evaluation process and, on completion of the study, an unwillingness on the part of decision makers to implement the recommendations arising from it. Implementation requires a knowledge of basic planning techniques and an ability to develop practical strategies and recommendations.

The comment that there is not enough time to measure and evaluate simply means that the library and the profession do not regard such efforts as important. The comment that "we don't know how to produce valid measures or conduct evaluations" means that decision makers do not encourage staff to develop evaluation skills, do not perceive a need for them to do so, and may not recognize the complexity of decision making in today's library/information center.

Politics of Evaluation. Just because an activity has high quality and displays excellent measures of effectiveness or efficiency is not the same as saying that activity has value. The value of a library service or activity depends on a host of factors, most of which have to do with politics at some level.

Evaluation is conducted in a complex political context, and many evaluators may not be well prepared to guard against political ramifications or to exploit these ramifications to advantage. Considering evaluation within the political realities of libraries defies easy description and explanation. At the minimum, however, evaluators should be aware of (1) which individuals initiated or supported the evaluation; (2) what the individuals involved in the area under evaluation have to gain or lose as a result of the process; (3) how the operation of this particular area in the library relates to organizational priorities and goals; (4) how external officials or agencies such as the state library regard the library; and (5) how the results of an evaluation relate to the interests of powerful individuals in the organization. Finally, those conducting evaluations in an organization that employs them should clearly understand their own political power base, status, and authority before they take on evaluation responsibilities.

This brief description of the politics of evaluation is not intended to discourage people from conducting evaluation research. Rather, it raises an issue that, in itself, can account for a study's success or failure. Indeed, the evaluation process is simply an aspect of organizational planning and decision making, and the political considerations at work in those activities are much the same as those affecting the evaluation process.

The Need for Measurement and Evaluation. The complexity of operating effective and efficient libraries requires greater knowledge about measuring those processes and evaluating how they influence library decision making and planning. An excellent investigation that carefully combined developing new measures with evaluating library operations is detailed in *The Public Library Effectiveness Study* (1989).

Such studies suggest that progress can be made in both measurement and evaluation in libraries and information science services. Knowing how to conduct an evaluation can only increase in importance as more opportunities and challenges (such as diminished funding) emerge. In order for libraries to maintain or increase their share of information-related markets, librarians must be both producers and consumers of evaluation research that develops valid and reliable measures, collects information useful for local decision making, and uses data to improve information services, programs, and operations.

The essence of measurement and evaluation is constantly to question, study, and improve the effectiveness of library information services and operations. Evaluation embraces change and encourages libraries to treat change as a positive force. By engaging in planning and evaluation research, librarians have a better idea of the future. They can meet that future with effective, efficient services that will play an important and positive role in the information society.

REFERENCES

Thomas Childers and Nancy A. Van House, *The Public Library Effectiveness Study* (1989).

Peter Hernon and Charles R. McClure, *Evaluation and Library Decision Making* (1990).

Abraham Kaplan, *The Conduct of Inquiry* (1964).

F. W. Lancaster, *The Measurement and Evaluation of Library Services* (1977).

F. W. Lancaster, *If You Want to Evaluate Your Library* (1988).

Charles R. McClure, Douglas L. Zweizig, Mary Jo Lynch, and Nancy A. Van House, "Output Measures: Myths, Realities, and Prospects," *Public Libraries* (1986).

Peter H. Rossi and Howard E. Freeman, *Evaluation: A Systematic Approach* (1989).

James E. Rush Associates, *Library Systems Evaluation Guide,* 8 volumes (1983–84).

Nancy A. Van House, Mary Jo Lynch, Charles R. McClure, Douglas L. Zweizig, and Eleanor Jo Rodger, *Output Measures for Public Libraries* (1987).

Nancy A. Van House, Beth Weil, and Charles R. McClure, *Measuring Academic Library Performance* (1990).

PETER HERNON;
CHARLES R. MCCLURE

Medical Libraries

PURPOSES AND OBJECTIVES

Medical libraries (or "health sciences" libraries, as they are now frequently designated) are united by common subject matter collections, clientele, and service goals. For these reasons they fall within the general category of special libraries that support the broad goals of institutions in the health field: teaching (education), research, and patient care, including health maintenance. For those supporting for-profit hospitals or industries such as insurance or pharmaceuticals, contributing to company profits may be another major goal. Depending on the institution's mission, the library's collections or services may emphasize all these goals, or only one or two. Medical libraries are also distinguished by the emphasis they place on innovative and timely user services and for their leadership in library automation and resource sharing through networks.

The clientele served are primarily professionals: research scientists and university faculty, physicians, dentists, nurses, pharmacists, veterinarians, health administrators, and students working toward careers in the health sciences and services. This primary user group determines not only the subject scope and coverage of the collections, but also the format of the materials and time periods covered. The current serial literature forms the bulk of most collections because it carries the record of clinical and basic research and the most up-to-date information on diagnosis and treatment of patients. Where teaching is a primary goal, audiovisual and computer-aided instruction programs will also be actively collected.

Since the mid-1970s most medical libraries in the United States (especially those in non-profit hospitals and public universities) have also faced growing pressure to meet the health information needs of patients and the general lay public. Alliances continue to be formed with public libraries to meet this need, and medical librarians from larger academic libraries are helping to educate public librarians about materials aimed at the consumer and about appropriate uses of materials aimed at health professionals. Many health sciences libraries that were once closed to the general public now make special efforts to acquire nontechnical health information and to serve lay users.

The subject scope of medical library collections has been traditionally focused in the basic biomedical sciences and in the clinical disciplines of medicine, surgery, nursing, pharmacy, and dentistry. With the growing recognition that health is strongly affected by individual behavior and the environment, most medical libraries have collections spanning a broad range of subjects and disciplines. They may even hold materials in the arts and humanities to support patient recovery and rehabilitation through bibliotherapy, music therapy, and art therapy. Public health (including environmental sciences and engineering), health economics and policy analysis, medical ethics, and the social sciences also compete for a share of the acquisition budgets of health sciences libraries.

Three major subgroups of medical libraries can be distinguished: academic health sciences libraries; hospital libraries; and special libraries serving societies or associations, commercial or industrial companies, or government agencies. *Academic medical libraries* typically serve either a single professional school or a number of schools and clinical facilities in an academic health sciences center. The size of the combined user population for these libraries typically justifies a sizable staff (ranging to 60 or more), a large budget (some over $3 million), and a wide range of services. *Hospital libraries* serve institutions ranging from small community hospitals with fewer than 50 beds to large teaching hospitals with well over 1,000 beds. Their average staff levels, budgets, and services tend to be much smaller, but they vary widely. *Society or association libraries* (a much larger and stronger subcategory of medical libraries in the early to mid-1900s) serve local, state, or national health organizations or associations of health professionals, such as the American Hospital Association or the American Medical Association. Commercial and industrial health sciences libraries exist in companies specializing in biotechnology products, health insurance, hospital supplies, medical devices, and pharmaceuticals. They typically support research and marketing activities and place greater emphasis on information retrieval than on collection building. Many health-related local, state, and national government agencies also support health sciences libraries. They are typically located in government research centers, military installations, and public health laboratories. Hospital libraries far outnumber the two other categories.

National Library of Medicine

National Library of Medicine. At left is the Library's Lister Hill National Center for Biomedical Communications.

The largest and most important medical library in the world is the U.S. National Library of Medicine (NLM), located on the campus of the National Institutes of Health in Bethesda, Maryland. The NLM, with more than 5 million items (including extensive collections of manuscripts, illustrations, and other special materials) serves as the hub and apex of a national and increasingly international network of biomedical libraries linked through interlibrary loan agreements, access to computerized bibliographic databases, and online document retrieval systems. The NLM has also been a major source of support for growth and innovation in U.S. medical libraries through its extramural grant programs and for innovations in the use of information technologies through its intramural research and development activities. Donald A. B. Lindberg became Director of NLM in 1984. His long and distinguished career in the field of medical informatics was instrumental in shaping NLM's emphasis on research, training, and services designed to improve the information processing and communication tasks of the health professions and the use of technology to support these tasks.

The Medical Library Association (MLA) serves as the primary professional association for most U.S. and Canadian health sciences librarians and also attracts a large contingent of members from other parts of the world. MLA is the second-oldest U.S. national library association (founded in 1898), with membership in the early 1990s of slightly over 5,000. It is particularly noted for its strong continuing education programs, offered each year in conjunction with its annual conference and at regional and local meetings of medical librarians. Since 1979 MLA has also offered courses at international conferences, including the Section of Biological and Medical Sciences Libraries of the International Federation of Library Associations and Institutions (IFLA) and the quinquennial International Congress on Medical Librarianship (ICML).

A formal means for ensuring the competence of health sciences librarians has been a major concern of MLA since 1949, when it implemented its first formal certification program. Since that time, the program has been under continuous review to accommodate changes in the profession. The certification program established by vote of the membership in 1988 recognizes competence based on educational qualifications and documented knowledge in core areas of medical information science as well as professional experience and activities. Medical librarians can apply for five-year renewable memberships in the Academy of Health Information Professionals at one of four levels: Associate, Member, Senior Member, and Distinguished Member. The application process includes completing a Portfolio of Professional Progress and review by a committee of peers. By 1992 more than 1,700 individuals had become certified members of the Academy.

MLA's professional development efforts also include an extensive program of honors, awards, scholarships, and fellowships to recognize and promote excellence in health science librarianship. Of particular note are the annual Janet Doe Lectureship on the History or Philosophy of Medical Librarianship and the Association's highest professional distinction, the Marcia C. Noyes Award.

Professional associations of medical librarians have been organized in many other parts of the world, especially since 1980. Strong national associations are active in Canada, Finland, Germany, India, Japan, New Zealand, and the United Kingdom. A multinational association serves medical librarians in Africa. The Biological and Medical Sciences Libraries Section of IFLA brings medical librarians together from all parts of the world every five years for an International Congress on Medical Librarianship.

Health sciences libraries play a major role in biomedical information transfer. In the U.S., and increasingly throughout the world, they work together in a highly structured network to provide health researchers, students, and professionals from a variety of health disciplines with access to the world's health information resources. As leaders in library automation, medical librarians recognize the vital role computers and telecommunications technologies will play in controlling, disseminating, and ensuring the effective use of information for the improvement of world health.

Consumer Health Information Program and Services (CHIPS), of the Los Angeles County Public Library and the Harbor-UCLA Medical Center, uses bilingual volunteers to answer or refer health questions from the community.

Los Angeles County Public Library

REFERENCES

Prudence W. Dalrymple, editor, "Libraries and Information Services in the Health Sciences," *Library Trends* (scheduled for publication in 1993).

Michael E. DeBakey, "The National Library of Medicine: Evolution of a Premier Information Center," *JAMA* (1991).

Erich Meyerhoff, "Foundations of Medical Librarianship," *Bulletin of the Medical Library Association* (1977).

Irwin H. Pizer, "The International Congresses on Medical Librarianship—Thirty Years of Evolutionary Change," *IFLA Journal* (1985).

GARY D. BYRD

SERVICES TO USERS

The growth of science and technology following World War II brought about unprecedented changes and advances in both biomedicine and information science. Today's health sciences library must respond to the needs of practitioners, educators, students, and scientists working to improve the health of citizens by providing both print and electronic access to information as well as the variety of resources that form the biomedical literature. The range of services includes information retrieval through computer or CD-ROM information systems, expert systems, bibliographic and knowledge databases, resource sharing networks, instruction for end-user searchers, interactive computer programs, audiovisual services, and outreach programs. In addition, many libraries have expanded their clientele to include health consumers.

Online Services. Health sciences librarians have an array of resources and access systems to assist the user. Databases are mounted on in-house computers or CD-ROM network systems, requests for resources are sent and received over electronic mail, and library information systems may be linked to patient information systems, library online catalogues, and diagnostic systems.

Technology has made this electronic access possible. Before the development of online databases in the 1960s, librarians relied on printed resources such as indexes and abstracts which they had to search manually. With the rapid expansion of scientific research in the 1940s and 1950s, the production of information derived from that research resulted in an explosion of biomedical literature. Health sciences libraries were ill prepared to handle and house the volume of this literature. Two events changed the status of health sciences libraries and the ability of health professionals and scientists to identify and locate needed information and resources: passage of the Medical Library Assistance Act (MLAA) and the emergence of the computer and its application in information services.

The MLAA, passed in 1965, authorized the National Library of Medicine (NLM) to award grants for research, resources, training, construction, and publication, and established the Regional Medical Library Network. The impact of the MLAA is fully outlined later in this article, but it should be noted here that it provided the impetus to build and improve health sciences libraries across the U.S. and in many other countries.

Computers were used in information services as

early as the late 1950s. The ways in which information professionals could use them grew at the same time the machines increased in power and shrank in size. When the volume of literature threatened to overwhelm both libraries and users, the electronic control and retrieval of information provided a solution.

To treat patients and to carry out biomedical research require that practitioners and scientists have access to the literature of the past. It is fortunate that one man, John Shaw Billings, recognized the significance of access to the literature and determined that he would index the collection of the Surgeon General's Library, forerunner of the NLM. He created the monumental *Index-Catalogue of the Library of the Surgeon General's Office,* publishing the first volume in 1880. To complement this massive work, he instituted the monthly *Index Medicus* in 1879 as a source of current bibliographic access to the biomedical literature. Health sciences libraries are fortunate to have these printed tools to identify the works of the past. The printed *Index Medicus* continues today, but its computer counterpart, MEDLINE, with coverage from 1966 on, has revolutionized the way both librarians and users find current literature.

Health sciences libraries were the first to have access to literature online for a number of reasons. In the early 1960s the NLM, which was struggling to keep up with the production of the printed *Index Medicus,* began to explore automation as a way to cope with the explosive growth of biomedical literature. In addition, the demands and resources of the biomedical community supported and encouraged the development of better and faster ways to retrieve information. The urgency of medical research gave medical libraries high priority in the competition for special project funds.

NLM's experiments led to MEDLARS (Medical Literature Analysis and Retrieval System), and by 1964 this system made possible not only automated production of *Index Medicus,* but also production of bibliographies in batch mode. By 1968 the State University of New York Biomedical Communications Network made the database available online for the first time; by 1971 NLM's MEDLINE (MEDLARS online) became operational nationwide. The success of searching bibliographic databases online was phenomenal, and health sciences librarians found their users both enthusiastic and receptive.

What started in a few large health sciences libraries soon spread to even the smallest hospital libraries. Today health sciences searchers have dozens of databases available covering such fields as medicine, nursing, psychology, biology, and toxicology. Two dozen institutions used MEDLINE in 1971; by 1985 some 4,000 registered users had access to it, primarily libraries; and by 1992 the NLM had issued more than 50,000 access codes to both individual and institutional users of its databases. The NLM and a number of commercial vendors make MEDLINE available in 75 countries.

The primary use of online database services has been producing bibliographies tailored to the exact needs of specific users, but researchers have found other valuable uses of online searching. Many databases include abstracts of articles, providing users with brief résumés of the contents of the articles cited. Such abstracts are especially important to researchers and residents needing specific answers. Searchers can retrieve citations by age group, by institution, by country of origin, by language, or by a variety of other criteria, as well as by combining a number of search topics. Some systems make the full text of articles from selected journals available for immediate retrieval.

Arabian Gulf University

Arabian Gulf University College of Medicine and Medical Sciences Library, where Bahrain's first library computer was installed in September 1985.

Starting in the mid-1980s, improvements in the effectiveness and user-friendliness of search software encouraged a growing number of users to do their own searching. The widespread availability of personal computers and increasing number of databases helpful to health professionals provided an impetus to libraries to offer training in how to search.

Most often using CD-ROM technology, libraries offer single workstations or multiple-station networks that provide local direct access to databases, textbooks, and reference resources, all with the advantage that the user does not incur online charges. In addition, many textbooks, clinical trials, or full-text journals may be accessed using *hypertext* search software, electronic systems for dynamically cross-referencing words, phrases, or concepts. Knowledge bases, compiled with the help of subject experts in many areas of the health sciences, distill the information known about a particular subject from many sources. In order to facilitate retrieving and integrating information from these diverse resources, the NLM has begun work on a Unified Medical Language System (UMLS). This project is not an attempt to impose a single standard vocabulary, record format, or knowledge base on the biomedical community; rather, it is an attempt to provide products that can compensate for differences in the vocabularies or coding schemes used in various systems and by various user groups.

Keeping up with the medical literature has always been a concern for medical practitioners, students, and scientists, as Billings's intent more than a hundred years ago indicates. He envisioned a way to control the published record by compiling author and subject indexes in a printed format. Technology has provided faster and more powerful ways to make retrieval of citations or information more current and comprehensive. Libraries continue to offer the medical literature in traditional print formats and through mediated and end-user searching. New technologies have made available a growing variety of resources—a natural continuation of the basic goal Billings described, to ensure that health professionals and scientists have the most accurate and most current information and knowledge possible to treat their patients and to advance the art and science of medicine.

Selective Dissemination of Information. Up until about 1950, scientists could identify the few important journals in their field of science or medicine and feel confident that they were seeing the important papers and reports. Today the volume of literature in the biomedical sciences is enormous, and reviewing a few standard journals is no longer a guarantee of seeing even most of the major articles in the field.

The advent of online databases made possible an automatic method for keeping current. Database vendors now offer Selective Dissemination of Information (SDI) services that provide relevant searches at regular and frequent intervals. A library or database vendor begins by establishing a profile of each individual's specific subject interests. The profile includes, in addition to the combination of topics, restrictions such as age group, human or animal, language, countries or regions, and time period to be covered. With the profile completed, the librarian or vendor can deliver search results to the user, usually monthly, as the database is updated. Another useful method of keeping abreast of the literature on a regular basis is to review the weekly issues of *Current Contents,* published by the Institute for Scientific Information. This publication is an early alerting service that contains the tables of contents of journals, often before they are available to readers. *Current Contents* is available commercially not only in print, but online and in CD-ROM versions that can be accessed by author, subject, or journal title.

User Instruction. Medical librarians have always instructed users in how to find information and how to work effectively in a library. Many health sciences libraries now offer formal courses in library use, teaching users about the range of reference materials available, ways to review the literature, and ways to enhance library skills. Many medical librarians also give guest lectures on literature resources and searching in courses taught in the schools they serve and in more general medical informatics training programs.

National Library of Medicine

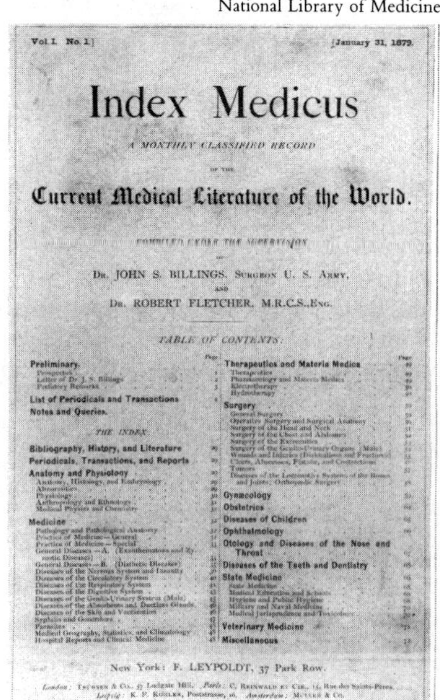

Vol. I. No. 1.] [January 31, 1879.

Index Medicus

A MONTHLY CLASSIFIED RECORD

OF THE

Current Medical Literature of the World.

COMPILED UNDER THE SUPERVISION

OF

Dr. JOHN S. BILLINGS, Surgeon U. S. Army,

AND

Dr. ROBERT FLETCHER, M.R.C.S., Eng.

TABLE OF CONTENTS.

Preliminary.

List of Periodicals and Transactions

Notes and Queries.

THE INDEX.

Bibliography, History, and Literature

Periodicals, Transactions, and Reports

Anatomy and Physiology

Medicine

Therapeutics and Materia Medica

Surgery

Gynæcology

Obstetrics

Diseases of Children

Ophthalmology

Otology and Diseases of the Nose and Throat

Diseases of the Teeth and Dentistry

State Medicine

Veterinary Medicine

Miscellaneous

New York: F. LEYPOLDT, 37 Park Row.

Title page from the first volume of Index Medicus, *January 31, 1879.*

With the introduction of user-friendly software in the mid-1980s, medical librarians received frequent requests for courses on how to search biomedical databases. Already highly skilled in searching a variety of databases for users, librarians responded by designing and teaching courses for end-users. In many libraries these courses include hands-on training using electronic classroom and microcomputer laboratory facilities.

Many users assume that one search can cover all the literature they need. Librarians emphasize how to formulate a search strategy, how to use Boolean and keyword strategies, and how to select from the various databases available the ones most likely to contain the subject sought. They also teach users how to select likely databases using such criteria as title coverage and time-span coverage. And they teach users how to limit their searches to terms likely to be used. For example, a major part of MEDLINE training focuses on the use of Medical Subject Headings (MeSH), the controlled vocabulary NLM developed for *Index Medicus* and MEDLINE.

Audiovisual Services. Health sciences libraries have long included non-print resources as well as the traditional printed materials in their collections to support instruction and continuing education in their institutions. Many libraries, both large and small, offer an array of audiovisual items such as models, slides, audio- and videotapes, videodiscs, and interactive computer software. These materials are particularly effective in demonstrating techniques used in surgery, listening to heart sounds, or reinforcing the subjects presented in computer-assisted instruction programs. Medical audiovisuals help students and health professionals to measure their comprehension of new subjects and to sharpen their decision-making skills.

Circulation. The computer has also changed circulation activities. Many libraries use automated systems to facilitate lending books, journals, and other materials to users. Automated systems usually link a barcode on the item requested to another barcode on a user's identification card to complete the transaction. Users no longer need to fill out forms or sign cards when borrowing items. Librarians have accurate online records and need not maintain card files. Automated systems also provide sophisticated management reports, overdue notices, and fine records, all formerly maintained manually. In addition, these systems can produce analyses of circulation records indicating the categories of borrowers, the subjects most frequently circulated, and the journal titles most in demand. This information is important in building collections and providing services that respond to user needs.

Borrowing materials for use outside the library is only one aspect of circulation. Most health science library users prefer to photocopy items rather than borrow the books or journals that contain them. An accurate record of use of resources must include statistics on in-house use as well as borrowing totals. Some medical libraries are experimenting with devices to scan barcode labels on the volumes reshelved after photocopying to provide this kind of statistic on usage.

REFERENCES

Scott Adams, *Medical Bibliography in an Age of Discontinuity* (1981).

National Institutes of Health, *Communication in the Service of American Health: A Bicentennial Report from the National Library of Medicine* (1976).

R. Brian Haynes et al., "How to Keep Up with the Medical Literature: III: Expanding the Number of Journals You Read Regularly," *Annals of Internal Medicine* (1986).

Jerome P. Kassirer, "Journals in Bits and Bytes: Electronic Medical Journals," *New England Journal of Medicine* (1992).

LUCRETIA W. MCCLURE

COLLECTIONS AND COLLECTION DEVELOPMENT

In a review of collection development in health sciences libraries, Dottie Eakin observed that through its services a library can link its users to a vast world of information resources, but the library is most often judged by its own collections. The collections in medical and health sciences libraries vary in size, depth, and complexity, in general reflecting the characteristics of their parent organizations.

The collection in a medical or health sciences library is a central focus of the library's information program, but several factors, principally economic, have converged to change the base for collection development from buying in anticipation of demand to buying in response to demonstrated need. Information in electronic formats, too, has changed the character of collections in these libraries and has introduced an array of new criteria that must be considered in making selection decisions. The concept of the medical library has changed from that of an archive or place to that of an information center and coordinator of access to information. Each of these factors is having a profound effect on collection development. The challenge to medical and health sciences librarians is to ensure that collections continue to be responsive to users' changing information needs.

Collection development as a specialized, discrete function in health sciences libraries is a relatively recent phenomenon, though the concept and the rubric have been generally employed in academic libraries for some time. Until the 1980s selection activities in medical libraries have usually been subsumed under the title "acquisitions librarian" or have been regarded as the exclusive responsibility of the library director.

Among the factors that hastened the maturation of collection development in the health sciences were increasing institutional complexity coupled with greater accountability for large sums of institutional dollars; tightening budgets coupled with a seemingly uncontrollably burgeoning output from the medical publishing industry; and a heightened distinction between the two principal aspects of acquisitions, selection and procurement.

Libraries exist in institutional contexts, and librarians must identify the purposes of the institution and keep them at the forefront of the collection development program. Health sciences library collections, in general, are developed to support five basic functions: (1) clinical practice and health care services; (2) research by faculty, staff, and students; (3) education and training of health care professionals; (4) administration of health care services and educational programs; and (5) preservation of institutional publications or related materials.

Organizational Models. Collection development in health sciences libraries is characterized as *distributed* where several staff members share the work and *centralized* where one person has primary responsibility. In most academic health sciences libraries, one person is responsible for both collection development and purchasing. Health sciences bibliographers or subject specialists are rare and are usually found in settings where the library is a unit or branch of a large institution.

Policies and Selection Criteria. In general, financial support for health sciences libraries has declined at the same time that the number of in-scope titles published has continued to increase. These two factors together have caused librarians to develop more rigorous selection methodologies and to define more closely the criteria by which decisions are made. A decision to acquire a journal title, for example, carries with it a future commitment of funds for binding and staff time for processing; such mortgages on the future require that librarians adhere to a systematic and rigorous set of policies on journal selection.

The most commonly applied selection criterion in medical and health sciences libraries is the relevance of the individual item to the actual or potential needs of the research, clinical, and educational programs of the institution. Other characteristics of the item to be scrutinized include its scope and content; the quality of the content and the technical aspects of the item; the depth of the existing collection in the subject; the availability of the item through consortial arrangements; and the bibliographic accessibility of the item—whether it is indexed in major abstracting and indexing services. Other formats, such as audiovisuals, rare books, electronic formats, and reference materials, have additional criteria to be considered.

Collection development in hospital libraries is different from collection development in academic or other types of medical libraries. Hospital librarians generally have a keener knowledge of their library's collection, as well as a more detailed knowledge of the user group. The financial resources available for collection development are more restricted and the library must rely more on resource sharing in responding to users' information needs. Errors in selection are relatively more costly and certainly more obvious than in a large medical center library. Hospital librarians tend to involve library users in the selection process, in many cases in the form of a library committee to provide input. An intimate knowledge of the clinical and research programs of the hospital is critical to the process.

Serials Review and Cancellation Projects. Since early in the 1980s, the growth in the volume of health sciences serial literature and the rising costs of that literature have caused health sciences librarians to assess their serials collections. The approaches they have taken have varied, depending on the institution

National Library of Medicine

Chinese Institute for Medical Information in Beijing—the opening of the China MEDLARS Center, June 6, 1987.

and the urgency with which they have undertaken the projects. The length of time they devote to this type of analysis has a direct relationship to the reliability of the information that results and the use to which it can be put.

Many smaller libraries, especially in hospitals, review their subscription lists each year and are able to respond to budget pressures in a fairly systematic way. Larger libraries, in recognition of the continued upward spiral of both new titles and costs, have implemented long-term projects to rationalize selection decisions through prioritization and consideration of factors in addition to subscription cost. Utilizing subject-based reviews, librarians divide the journal lists into broad subject areas and submit them to review by the primary users in each discipline. If they choose not to use subject reviews, librarians may list their journal titles in order of subscription price.

In addition to use and cost, librarians consider institutional duplication of the title, especially in academic medical libraries that are parts of university library systems. Other criteria that figure prominently in review processes include interlibrary lending statistics, whether a particular journal is indexed in major abstracting and indexing tools, and the "impact factor" listed in the *Science Citation Index*. The net result of these efforts in medical and health sciences libraries is a homogenization of collections, because many libraries are removing the esoteric and the expensive titles from their collections.

Cooperation. Cooperative collection development occurs when two or more libraries coordinate their collection-building activities in some agreed way. The history of resource sharing is a long and distinguished one among health sciences libraries. Productive resource-sharing arrangements among health sciences librarians began with the creation of the Medical Library Association Exchange in the late 19th century. But cooperative collection development has grown primarily in the late 20th century, generally as a consequence of budget constraints and a growing awareness that libraries are more and more dependent on one another for materials

Cooperative programs with a large geographic base have developed in the Regional Medical Library (RML) network. Some ensure retention of important serial titles in a specific region; others expand the monographs available among health sciences libraries. These programs tend to include libraries of varying types and sizes. Even though the number of cooperative collection development arrangements is not particularly high, the administrative and bibliographic structures they have developed to support interlibrary loan and exchange of duplicates provide an excellent basis for further work in this area. These structures provide health science librarians with a solid base on which to build and refine more comprehensive collection development agreements.

The future for cooperation in resource building and sharing among health sciences libraries appears to be bright. Many of the factors that prescribe cooperation will only increase, and there seems no likelihood of a drop in the volume of materials in the information base. As health sciences librarians face greater difficulty in affording secondary and tertiary materials their users need, they will find the benefits of expanding cooperative agreements with other libraries ever more apparent.

The Biomedical Literature. The controversial 17th-century English chemist and physiologist John Mayow observed that "as a rule, disease can scarcely keep pace with the itch to scribble about it." John Shaw Billings stated more than two centuries later that "the proportion of what is both new and true is not much greater in medicine than it is in theology." These statements illustrate the dilemma that faces medical librarians in developing collections that are responsive to the multitude of information needs of their users.

Both health science librarians and medical library users agree that the true journal literature represents the most important format for published biomedical literature, with books assuming a subordinate place. Many medical and health sciences libraries make distinctions among types of books as well, especially between textbooks and monographs. Most textbooks appear in large editions that are intended to be superseded by later editions. They tend to be general treatments of a discipline, definitive for teaching at a given time, but not for the discipline as a whole for all time. They have a fairly short life, affected by trends in education, by the popularity of specific teaching methods, and by the changing importance of disciplines.

Monographs, by contrast, are relatively ageless and thorough presentations on narrow subjects. They have a permanent usefulness because they try to be comprehensive within their restricted areas. In general, the more specific and the more specialized the topic of a medical book, the longer the book is likely to be valuable in a library collection. Books in medical specialties are likely to have a longer life than general titles issued in large editions.

The visual record too is of great importance in the health sciences literature. It is present in journals, monographs, and textbooks in such forms as plates, portraits, photomicrographs, and radiographs. Only in art is the visual as important to the scholarly record.

According to book publishing statistics, between 3,000 and 3,500 newly published books in medicine appear in the U.S. each year, including some English-language imports. Worldwide, at least 13,000 to 14,000 new medical books appear, based on the acquisition rates listed in the 1990 Annual Report of the NLM. Analyzed by discipline, however, these gross figures show widely varying growth rates. Psychiatry grows at a rate of about 250 titles a year in the U.S., whereas human anatomy grows at a relatively modest rate of about 40 titles a year.

In 1992 there were about 25,000 active periodical publications in the health sciences, and new titles continue to appear each month. This continuing rapid growth results both from the splintering of disciplines and more interdisciplinary approaches to health sciences research.

The Scholarly Record for medicine is vast. The NLM collection in the early 1990s held nearly 2 million book items and another 3 million non-book items. These figures include nearly 700,000 monographs, approximately 1,000,000 periodical volumes, 300,000 theses, and 50,000 audiovisual items. NLM maintains approximately 23,000 subscriptions and more than 150,000 pieces arrive annually.

The Library of Congress and the National Agricultural Library each have collections in the health sciences that do not duplicate those at the NLM. Most notable are LC's coverage of the popular medical literature and its comprehensive collections of related medical subjects such as anthropology and biology. The NAL collects some areas of veterinary medicine more comprehensively than the NLM and houses large collections of relevant documents and foreign government reports complementary to those held at the NLM.

Beyond the NLM and the other national libraries, a large network of medical libraries, both in the U.S. and abroad, holds varying percentages of unique materials. Mammoth collections of medical records exist outside libraries in museums and archives, in patient file rooms in medical centers, and in the files of practicing physicians and other health care providers. Actual numbers of items in these categories are impossible to estimate, but the numbers are significant. All of these collections combined result in a scholarly record for biomedicine that comprises many millions of items.

Preservation. A growing concern in health sciences libraries, as in libraries of other types, is preserving the collections. The NLM has assumed a principal responsibility for preserving the literature of biomedicine and has led the way for other libraries by developing and promulgating its plan for "Preservation of the Biomedical Literature" (1985). This seminal report provides a framework in which the NLM will preserve its own collection and will assist other U.S. institutions in preserving the important biomedical literature they hold. Principal elements of the preservation program include an extensive microfilming schedule, a research component exploring alternatives to microfilming such as digitization, and an aggressive campaign to persuade medical publishers to use acid-free paper.

Western Psychiatric Institute and Clinic, University of Pittsburgh School of Medicine

Viewer consults video presentation on mental health at the Western Psychiatric Institute and Clinic Library, University of Pittsburgh School of Medicine.

REFERENCES

Margaret Byrnes, "Preservation of the Biomedical Literature: An Overview," *Bulletin of the Medical Library Association* (1989).

Dottie Eakin, "Health Sciences Library Materials: Collection Development," in Louise Darling et al., editors, *Handbook of Medical Library Practice,* 4th ed. (1983).

Daniel T. Richards and Dottie Eakin, *Collection Development and Assessment in Health Sciences Libraries* (scheduled for publication as one volume of *Current Practice in Health Sciences Librarianship,* 1993).

DANIEL T. RICHARDS

GOVERNANCE, FINANCE, AND MANAGEMENT

Governance. Health sciences libraries play significant roles in patient care, education, and clinical and basic sciences research. They also act as a community health information resource for commercial companies, law enforcement agencies, local and state health departments, and the public. Their governance is a function of the role they play in their parent organizations.

Hospital libraries make up the largest group of medical libraries. In most hospitals the hospital librarian reports to the hospital administration, but may report to the Chief of Staff, who is an ex officio member of the library committee. This committee normally includes representatives of the various professional groups on the staff, such as medical doctors, nurses, pharmacists, laboratory technicians, and members of the education department. The committee offers advice and guidance to the librarian on selection, library policy, development, maintenance of standards, and effectiveness of services. The hospital administration, not the committee, confers with the librarian on matters of budget, personnel, and daily operations.

Libraries in health-related associations such as medical societies and academies are among the oldest medical libraries in the United States. Such libraries function within the governance structure of their associations, and their librarians ordinarily report to the chief executive officer or the chairman of the board.

Corporate medical libraries are most often found in pharmaceutical and insurance companies. These libraries are well funded and support the mission of the company. The governance structure normally reflects overall corporate structure. The librarian usually reports to a senior executive in charge of research support. Library committees, if they exist, are advisory in function.

Academic medical libraries in medical schools rank among the largest medical libraries in the world and are major employers of professional medical librarians. Most such libraries, though located in medical centers, are parts of university systems, and they fall under one of two governance structures: (1) integral parts of the university library systems; or (2) independent of the university library system but under the administration of the medical school or medical center. Of the 138 medical libraries in the U.S. and Canada in 1992, 13 were freestanding (not part of a university), 10 were independent libraries providing service to a medical school, 69 were under the governance of a medical school, and 46 were part of a university library system.

If under the governance of a university library system, the medical library director normally reports to the university librarian or to an associate director in the university library system. If under the governance of a medical school, the medical library director normally reports to the chief executive officer, either the dean or, in a multi-health-program campus, to a vice-chancellor for health affairs. In some instances the library director reports to a senior administrator in information, informatics, or health research policy. The precise position to which a director reports usually reflects the organizational structure of the medical center. It is important, however, that the director report to someone at a senior level, an individual who is representative of the broad community of users on a medical campus, to ensure that the library's resources and services will indeed serve all interests on campus and be free from the influence of special interest groups. Reporting to a senior administrator also ensures that the library's budget, personnel, and other needs are given an adequate hearing. There is general agreement that a medical school is better served when the library director reports to the medical center administration rather than to the university library administration. Parker (1977) raises several points in favor of this arrangement, including the speed of processing acquired materials, wider latitude in recruiting personnel to meet special needs, and setting priorities that reflect the needs of the medical center.

The governance structure of a medical school library establishes its policy-making structure. The functions and goals of its advisory structure, on the other hand, are often unfocused and less understood. A library committee can advise the medical librarian in setting policies, procedures, and goals. It can act as a sounding board that assists the librarian in determining policy. On the other hand, there are library committees, most of them in hospital settings, that actually determine policy and procedures and expect the library staff to implement them. An advisory committee can play a significant role in the overall direction of the library, in contrast to a policy-making committee, which can prove to be a liability, especially in the presence of a competent library administrator and staff. The medical librarian must continue to assume responsibility for all of the library's policies, the committee notwithstanding.

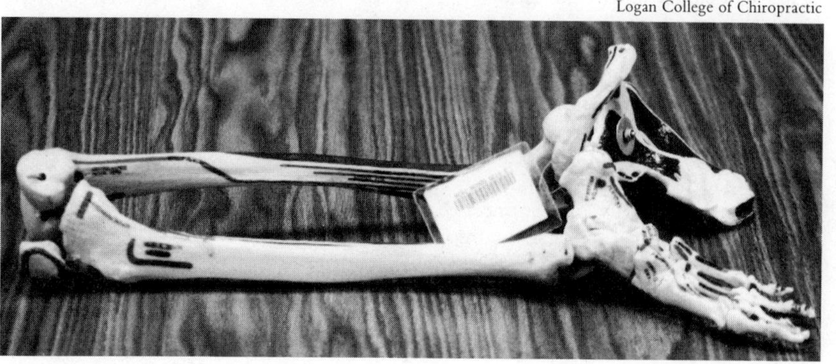
Logan College of Chiropractic

Barcoded bones are among the non-print resources that circulate in medical libraries.

Finance. Medical librarians of the 1990s are acutely aware of the conflicting demands placed on medical centers for high-quality medical care in an era where funding from public and private sources is decreasing. Government agencies and the medical community are experiencing growing political and social pressures to provide comprehensive "free" medical care for all segments of society, but within costs acceptable to the consumers. Most of the cost increases in medical care result from new and expensive developments in electronic medical devices, costs associated with computers and information technology, salary demands from physicians and other health care personnel, energy costs, construction costs for replacing outdated or outgrown facilities, costs for health insurance and retirement benefits for employees, and costs for pharmaceuticals, all of them rising. The demand for high-quality health care in a cost-constrained environment will be the major challenge facing medical centers well past the year 2000.

The medical library is directly affected by the social, political, and economic factors that affect its parent institution. These factors impact directly on the resources and services of the library. Medical librarians most often defend their budget requirements through the use of such performance indicators as circulation statistics. These indicators are essential, but librarians also need to adopt the practice of budgeting for the programs needed to meet the information requirements of the institution.

The medical library's budget is prepared by the library director, along with others on the library staff, and is submitted to the person to whom the director reports for final approval. A budget request normally includes all expected operational costs for the library for the year, including personnel, acquisitions, cataloguing, public services, supplies, communications, travel, automation, and equipment. In a typical medical library approximately 60 percent of the budget goes for personnel costs and the rest for operational costs. Most medical school libraries use institutional funds for their base budgets, though more and more rely on grants, contracts, and revenue-generating programs. Hospital medical libraries receive most of their funds from the hospital budget and perhaps some funds from the medical staff.

Management. A joint report by the Association of Academic Health Sciences Library Directors and the Medical Library Association in 1987 saw good management as providing well-documented, user-based proposals for cost-effective solutions in providing optimal information services. It described management as a partnership in which the library shares common goals with the parent institution. It also stated the need for ongoing, user-based planning to set priorities and evaluate programs through cost-benefit analyses of the services provided.

The 1982 Matheson/Cooper Report describing the now familiar "integrated academic information management system" (IAIMS) concept has also played a major role in shaping the way medical libraries are viewed and in the way they are now managed. Matheson and Cooper outlined a future in which technology would profoundly affect the way libraries are managed. The ongoing adoption of such technology since 1982 is influencing the way medical libraries interact with education, patient care, research, and community service programs, affecting the substance and style of library management.

Publication of the *Annual Statistics of Medical School Libraries in the United States and Canada,* beginning in 1978, provides comparative performance statistics that can be used to gauge effectiveness. A next step for medical libraries will be to create management information systems designed to monitor performance effectiveness. Before a medical library will be able to do this, it must first clearly define its organizational direction, a somewhat difficult task in the 1990s, given the transitional technological state in which it operates. By the year 2000 it will have had to face pressures from academic programs in medical informatics, medical center management information systems, scientific computing centers, health information technology centers, and similar developments in technology. All these external forces have the potential to affect the medical library adversely, setting it adrift in the administrative milieu of the medical center with an unfocused and often misunderstood mission. The library director of the future will need to be alert to these problems and continue to refocus and redirect the energies of the library and to reassert the library's leadership role as the primary provider of information services to the institution. The director can do this only if the library interacts with and is responsive to the institutional mission and goals.

Most hospital libraries are small and staffed by one librarian, often with volunteer assistance. The management of such a library is simple, with the librarian performing all the traditional professional functions and often the clerical functions as well. The medical school library, larger medical society library or corporate library, and major medical center library, on the other hand, will have an internal structure differing little from that of a general academic library. The separation into divisions of technical and public services is routine, with further subdivision when warranted. Special function areas such as audiovisual services, archives, collections on the history of medicine, computer support services, and microcomputer laboratories are present in many large medical libraries. There are typically many variations in organizational structure, based on the size and complexity of the library in question. For example, many larger libraries have two or more associate directors, a financial administrator, and a personnel officer. Some directors do not adopt the divisional structure at all, preferring a flat organizational structure with each department head reporting directly to the top.

Because the average medical library is small relative to a general academic library or a large public library system, most professional medical librarians find themselves functioning as generalists. For instance, in many medical libraries, all professionals are expected to help staff the reference desk each week. Many believe that this generalist approach to library services provides the most comprehensive level of service to the user. Others believe that this approach dilutes the quality of service by leaving the medical library with no true subject content expertise on the staff. Many medical libraries would benefit from a combination of both approaches to user services.

REFERENCES

Jana Bradley et al., editors, *Hospital Library Management* (1983); 2nd edition edited by Ruth Holst scheduled for publication in 1993.

Erika Love, editor, *Challenge to Action: Planning and Evaluation Guidelines for Academic Health Sciences Libraries* (1987).

Nina Matheson and John A. D. Cooper, "Academic Information in the Academic Health Sciences Center: Roles for the Library in Information Management," *Journal of Medical Education* (1982).

Virginia Parker, "The Relationships of Medical School Libraries to University Library Systems," *Bulletin of the Medical Library Association* (1977).

PATRICK W. BRENNEN

MEASUREMENT AND EVALUATION

Measurement and evaluation play important roles in health science library management. Managers of health information libraries of all kinds—academic, hospital, and special—like their counterparts in other disciplines, struggle with the discontinuities of our times. These include more information, and more demand for it, coupled with a tendency toward reduced support; the strong persistence of some traditional information storage and transfer media, especially print on paper, as complementary media of many kinds emerge and compete for the information dollar; a time-driven user group, hungry for high-tech information systems promoted in the press and other media but stalled by issues of standardization, policy, technology, legal status, or cost; and a lack of stability in some basic information handling systems at a time when links to exciting new peripheral systems are being designed.

These and other trends require the stabilizing influence of planning to establish overall directions and continuous, evaluative feedback loops to determine whether planning and implementation are on course. In an environment of rapid change, all of these must themselves be dynamic processes.

Standards. The importance, development, and use of standards vary considerably between two of the major groups of health science libraries, those in hospitals and those in academic institutions. There is considerable crossover, especially in gray areas such as the one including large freestanding teaching hospitals and hospitals affiliated with major academic institutions. But the trend in all cases is to move away from a recipe for what an ideal library should contain and toward a set of measures of what a library should do.

Management expectations of hospital libraries can be substantially affected by the requirements the Joint Commission on Accreditation of Healthcare Organizations (JCAHO) includes in its accreditation manual. The agency's "Agenda for Change" in the early 1990s gave new emphasis to the importance of better information management in improving patient care.

Photo by Nita Winter

Medical Library, St. Mary's Hospital and Medical Center, San Francisco, California.

Its standards for accreditation identify the provision of library service as a key indicator, one that carries special weight in evaluation. In the standards it developed for implementation in the mid-1990s, the JCAHO planned to concentrate in one chapter all information-related functions, including libraries, patient records, and the data-gathering and -manipulation functions related to management information systems and continuous quality improvement efforts. Substantial work on the part of the Hospital Library Section of the Medical Library Association (MLA), including a paper by Chris Jones, "The Health Sciences Librarian's Contribution to Continuous Quality Improvement," influenced this effort.

Academic medical libraries moved away from prescriptive standards with the publication of *Challenge to Action: Planning and Evaluation Guidelines for Academic Health Sciences Libraries* (1987), the product of a joint task force of the Association of Academic Health Sciences Library Directors (AAHSLD) and the MLA. It recognizes the continuing value of the fundamental concepts expressed in the *Guidelines for Medical Libraries* (1965), but goes on to treat the library less as a freestanding entity in the academic setting and more as a partner, affected by and responsive to the needs and fortunes of its parent institution. The 1987 guidelines encourage libraries to use and supplement the standards in ways appropriate to their own institutional settings.

Statistics. All types of health science libraries use statistics to document their functions, resources, and performance on an individual basis. A regular compilation, *Annual Statistics of Medical School Libraries in the United States and Canada,* has been especially influential in academic health science librarianship. Produced since 1978 by the Houston Academy of Medicine–Texas Medical Center Library, this publication received financial and editorial support from AAHSLD, which now fully supports it. An active editorial board is responsible for reviewing the data-collection instrument and for editing the responses to ensure consistent reporting. Efforts have been made to use the data to categorize libraries and to use certain cross-tabulated data to establish performance measures. This tool has provided a source of comparative data for librarians seeking information or trends in libraries of similar complexity and size. An article by Leatherbury and Lyders in the *Bulletin of the Medical Library Association* (January 1992) reports trends derived from 10 years of data available from this publication and its electronic databases.

In individual libraries, the automation of various library functions has produced a great deal of data as a by-product. Librarians in institutions of all sizes are learning to use this information in productive ways. They, like others, are having to strike a balance between reporting what is easily reportable and reporting what is meaningful. The easy availability of so much data has, if anything, refocused attention on the importance of deciding what questions need answering before collecting the answers.

Management information systems are being developed in a number of health science libraries. These systems identify recurring decision points and the data or information needed to support those decisions, as well as providing the tools to collect and analyze the data on a regular basis.

Evaluation. Critical evaluation is taking place at all levels in medical librarianship. Library administrators are concerned about such issues as demonstrating the effective use of scarce resources to meet user needs and institutional expectations. It has become increasingly important to have long- and short-range goals institutionally internalized and validated. These goals then, ideally, become the anchor-pins of evaluation in the institution. Evaluation on a broader level often takes the form of comparing programs or performance within peer groups of institutions, because there is considerable variability even within broad groups such as academic, special, or hospital health science libraries.

Surveys continue to be popular instruments for collecting information from peer institutions for comparative evaluation in specific areas. There are perhaps fewer of these surveys than there were in the late 1970s, now that there are some regularly available data compilations in important areas. MLA's recurrent salary survey is a good example. It provides salary lows, highs, means, and medians in a variety of tables based on geography, type of library or institution, position, and a number of other variables.

A current variation on the survey has blossomed with the advent of electronic mail. Those with ready access to peer libraries on a communications network can conduct impromptu polls of peer groups or institutions about issues or practices of immediate concern.

Intra-library surveys of users, their needs and habits, continue to be useful instruments in gauging satisfaction, needs, and concerns. But these surveys are seldom consistent enough in content and method from one library to another to allow for meaningful comparison.

Overall, the planning, evaluation, data collection, and analysis efforts of health sciences libraries are more sophisticated than ever before. The new emphasis in standards is on quality and performance. The new focus in statistics is on output measures. The increased importance of evaluation results from the need for accountability in a time of scarce resources and mounting demands.

REFERENCES

Association of Academic Health Sciences Library Directors, *Annual Statistics of Medical School Libraries in the United States and Canada,* 12th edition (1990).

Maurice Leatherbury and Richard Lyders, "Trends in Medical School Library Statistics in the 1980s," *Bulletin of the Medical Library Association* (1992).

Erika Love, editor, *Challenge to Action: Planning and Evaluation Guidelines for Academic Health Sciences Libraries* (1987).

VIRGINIA H. HOLTZ

McGill University

McIntyre Medical Sciences Building, home of McGill University's Medical Library in Montreal, Canada.

LIBRARY COOPERATION

Cooperation among medical libraries is a continually evolving process driven increasingly by the enormous effort of coping with the exponential expansion of published biomedical information and the spiraling cost of acquiring this information. Many health sciences libraries are also reaching the physical limits of maintaining on-site print resources.

At the same time, medical librarians have been able to use sophisticated information technologies to meet these challenges in new ways. Advanced technology enables them not only to share resources in ways not previously feasible, but to develop electronic networks on a worldwide scale.

Networks and Organizations. Modern medical library cooperation is expressed through a variety of networks, organizations, and linkages that are not always mutually exclusive. Their common goal is expanded access to greater amounts of health information with a minimum of effort and expense.

United States. The preeminent medical library network in the United States is the National Network of Libraries of Medicine (NN/LM), officially introduced in May 1991 by its parent institution, the National Library of Medicine (NLM). The NN/LM replaces the Regional Medical Library (RML) Network, created in 1965. The goals of the NN/LM are (1) to promote awareness of and equal access to biomedical information resources for all U.S. health professionals and (2) to develop and improve biomedical information resources and support sharing these resources in the regions and throughout the nation.

To carry out this mission, the NN/LM operates through a network of eight regions covering the entire nation. Reconfigured from eleven regions in 1983 and again from seven regions in 1991, the eight regions collaborate to provide document delivery and other information services to health professionals and to strengthen library resources and cooperation. More than 3,600 academic, hospital, and special health science libraries are members of the NN/LM.

The NN/LM has a hierarchical structure, with the NLM at the top. Each region has a *Regional Medical Library* (RML) which contracts with the NLM to perform specific functions relating to network goals. *Resource Libraries* in each state agree to provide designated services in their areas for the RML. Initially Resource Libraries were those with major medical collections, usually academic. Later they included other selected libraries that could enhance the network with their resources or services.

In utilizing the NN/LM, a health professional can make an information request to a local Primary Access Library (PAL). If that library cannot supply the service or resource, it may refer the request to another PAL in a local consortium. If the second PAL cannot satisfy the request, the first PAL refers the request to a Resource Library in the region or to the RML. The referral point beyond the RML is usually the NLM. Thus, through the NN/LM, local health professionals have access to national resources. As a last resort, NLM maintains a lending agreement with the British Library Document Supply Center.

Each RML operates through a Management Office and has an Advisory Board to provide input from network members. The Board is composed of librarians from Resource Libraries and Primary Access Libraries and professionals from various health fields.

Funding for the NN/LM comes primarily through the Medical Library Assistance Act (MLAA) which, from its inception in 1965, has included grants and contracts to assist medical libraries and to facilitate the dissemination and use of health science information. In its first fiscal year, 1967, the RML network budget was $105,000. By 1992 the budget totalled $5,500,000. In addition, network members make contributions from their own budgets to further network goals.

Although not a medical library network, the Online Computer Library Center, Inc. (OCLC), offers services and maintains a union list that are widely used by medical libraries. Its cataloguing subsystem allows medical libraries to reduce labor-intensive efforts by sharing cataloguing records, including those contributed by the NLM. Libraries employing Medical Subject Headings (MeSH) and the NLM Classification find this service especially valuable. OCLC also provides an interlibrary loan service, produces tailored serials union lists, and offers gateway access to many bibliographic databases, and medical libraries use all these services for cooperation and resource sharing. U.S. medical librarians have a strong voice in OCLC policy making through the Health Sciences OCLC Users Group (HSOCLCUG).

National Library of Medicine

Library at the World Health Organization Headquarters, Geneva.

Professional organizations also play an instrumental role in medical library cooperation. In the U.S., the Medical Library Association (MLA) fosters cooperation through its 24 interest sections and 14 geographic chapters. MLA is represented on many library and health science associations, among them the American Library Association, the Association of Academic Health Science Library Directors, the North American Serials Interest Group, and the annual Symposium on Computer Applications in Medical Care (SCAMC).

MLA also plays a role in international cooperation. In addition to programs such as its longstanding duplicate serials exchange service, its International Cooperation Committee advises the Board of Directors on international matters, maintains international representation, and assists sponsoring agencies in making arrangements for visiting foreign librarians. MLA is represented on a number of international library organizations, such as the European Association for Health Information and Libraries and the International Federation of Library Associations and Institutions (IFLA).

Each year the Cunningham Memorial International Fellowship enables a medical librarian from outside the U.S. or Canada to spend six months working and learning in North America. It provides a stipend of approximately $3,000, with an extra $500 for travel in North America. Named for Eileen Roach Cunningham, the Fellowship was established in 1965 to replace the MLA's International Fellowship program, which operated from 1948 to 1963. As of 1991, 24 librarians from 20 countries had received Cunningham Fellowships.

International. A number of associations of medical librarians promote cooperation among countries and regions of the world. One of the foremost of these is IFLA. Its Biological and Medical Sciences Libraries Section assists in developing mutually supportive regional groupings and producing world and regional directories.

IFLA also organizes the International Congress on Medical Librarianship (ICML). The ICML is the principal forum where medical librarians from all parts of the world can meet and exchange ideas. The ICML met in 1953 and 1963, then every five years from 1980. Programs for presenting research, discussing plans for cooperation, and getting to know colleagues from other countries comprise the week-long meetings. At the fifth ICML in New Delhi in 1990, delegates proposed the creation of a World Health Libraries Organization. The idea was slated for discussion in depth at the sixth ICML, scheduled for Washington, D.C., in 1995, in conjunction with the annual conference of the MLA.

The World Health Organization (WHO) has a significant impact on international medical library cooperation. Its Health Literature Services Program focuses on strengthening health libraries and literature services on national levels as well as fostering cooperation between neighboring countries. WHO provides financial assistance for medical librarians from third world countries to attend ICMLs.

Other networks have taken on important roles in medical library cooperation for large parts of the world. They produce regional union lists, strengthen local libraries, and index a large body of "fugitive" literature. A prime example is the Southeast Asian Medical Information Center (SEAMIC), founded in 1972 to encourage and develop cooperative efforts in southeast Asia. Another is BIREME, the Biblioteca Regional de Medicine, the Pan American Health Organization's regional library of medicine. Founded in 1967 and based in Brazil, BIREME serves as a resource-sharing network for Latin America. It publishes a Latin American *Index Medicus* and handles about 60,000 requests a year, filling about 90 percent of the requests from its own or network member collections.

International organizations such as Unesco and the International Federation for Documentation (FID) and regional associations such as the European Association for Health Information and Libraries, the African Medical Library Association, and others contribute greatly to the improvement of medical library resource sharing, particularly for underdeveloped parts of the world.

Consortia. On a local level, consortium development has played a large part in cooperative networking among medical libraries. In the U.S. most RML programs support consortium development, and funding is still available from the NLM through its Information Access and Information Systems Resource Grants. The Greater Midwest Region of the NN/LM counted 59 consortia among its 10 states in the early 1990s, a number of them established with NLM grant funding.

The advent of library computerization has broadened consortium networking by facilitating more effective groupings. These electronic consortia allow users at each member library to search the collections of other libraries. Many consortia provide joint access to MEDLINE or other bibliographic databases and employ a subsystem for requesting interlibrary loans. Electronic consortia also offer the potential for better cooperative collection development programs.

In some cases, sophisticated computerization allows medical libraries to form discrete homogenous consortia within a larger multi-type online network that includes academic, public, school, and special libraries. One example is THOR (Teaching Hospital Online Resources), a group of medical libraries that share their own database and common loan policies but also function as individual members of ODIN (Online Dakota Information Network), a statewide multi-type library network in North Dakota.

Resource Sharing among medical libraries includes both lending original items and providing non-returnable photocopies of book chapters, periodical articles, or other documents. For medical libraries, the periodical article is the most frequently shared resource and photocopies are the most widely used medium for this activity.

Microprocessors and telecommunications are changing the landscape for library resource sharing. Librarians, publishers, and researchers can now share information in a wide variety of ways, including direct access to published materials in digital formats, downloading for local storage or manipulation, and transmission of single documents to many individuals on a network.

Electronic mail networks, such as the higher education community's BITNET, are now being used to transmit documents and research results and to publish online. They also provide gateways to databases and to online library systems. For example, INTERNET, the U.S. government's network of networks, provides access to more than 200 library systems. Its replacement, the high-speed and high-capacity National Research and Education Network (NREN), is designed to connect institutions in higher education, government, and industry with a far-reaching impact on library resource sharing.

For U.S. medical libraries, resource sharing has been organized primarily under the leadership of the NLM. In addition to building the NN/LM structure, the NLM has enhanced resource sharing through a number of technological advances. The SERHOLD (Serials Holding online) database, for example, has enabled many medical librarians to computerize their periodical holdings. The database can also accept holdings data from OCLC's Union List and merge them with those of other libraries to create union lists for the RMLs. DOCLINE, the NLM's automatic interlibrary loan request routing system, greatly speeds loan requests by computer. The system uses the SERHOLD database to identify holding libraries and then randomly routes the request to one of them, thus allocating the loan burden among participating holders so that no one of them is overwhelmed. The system is organized in increasingly broad tiers, starting at the local level, to facilitate the routing.

The resource-sharing tool with the largest single impact has been the NLM's MEDLARS (Medical Literature Analysis and Retrieval System). This system contains more than 20 bibliographic and information databases, of which MEDLINE (Medical Literature Online) is the most frequently used. MEDLINE is the online version of the *Index Medicus,* covering more than 3,000 biomedical periodicals from all parts of the world since 1966.

MEDLINE is available in a variety of formats: online through national or international networks and locally on proprietary mainframes or minicomputers, or on desktop microcomputers on compact discs in CD-ROM format. The NLM makes the database or subsets of it available to international organizations such as WHO or BIREME for processing and online retrieval and to commercial vendors such as DIALOG and BRS for online retrieval or searching on CD-ROM.

Local MEDLINE access can be extended to individuals dispersed about an institution by network cabling and to individuals outside using dial-up communications equipment. Depending on the hardware and search software used, the advantages of a local system can include wider access for a lower price, easier searching for unsophisticated users, and retrieval sets tailored to local periodical holdings. The disadvantages usually include a less powerful search engine and a limit on the number of simultaneous users.

The NLM in the early 1990s provided an advance in resource sharing called GRATEFUL MED/LOANSOME DOC. This combination of software programs enables individual health professionals to access both the MEDLINE database and the DOCLINE interlibrary loan network without extensive training. Employing microcomputer communications software, GRATEFUL MED helps the user to formulate MEDLINE searches and automatically sends the search to the appropriate database and downloads the search results. The user can then request the citations retrieved through LOANSOME DOC, which sends them to the DOCLINE system of the local medical library to which he or she has access.

Facsimile transmission, usually shortened to *fax,* has had a profound impact on medical resource sharing. Copies of documents, photographs, or drawings can be transmitted over telephone lines between fax machines or microcomputers with fax hardware and software. The technology has been available since the 1950s and 1960s, but only became widespread, efficient, and affordable when incorporated with microprocessors in the late 1980s. Its impact has been tremendous. Nearly all U.S. medical libraries use fax to make almost instantaneous interlibrary loans and to transmit other documents, especially for patient care.

In the early 1990s the NLM worked on a Unified Medical Language System, service linkages for biotechnology information, and more RML network enhancements. These, combined with the develop-

Pan American Health Organization's Regional Library of Medicine, São Paulo, Brazil.

ment of the NREN, rapid advances in information technologies, and continued refinement of library networking, will be key components in the further development of medical library cooperation and resource sharing.

REFERENCES

Patrick W. Brennen and Marilyn B. Gorman Sullivan, "Work/Training Programs for International Health Science Librarians in American Medical School Libraries," *Bulletin of the Medical Library Association* (1989).

Alison Bunting, "The Nation's Health Information Network: History of the Regional Medical Library Program, 1965–1985," *Bulletin of the Medical Library Association* (1987).

Alexander Y. Mychko-Megrin, "A Comparison of Biomedical Databases," *Bulletin of the Medical Library Association* (1991).

National Library of Medicine Board of Regents, *Long Range Plan,* a series of seven reports (1986).

DAVID W. BOILARD

LAWS AND LEGISLATION

International Issues. The challenges faced by medical librarians in developing countries differ only in degree from those of the industrialized world. Breinich (1991) identifies several factors affecting the development and progress of medical libraries in those countries, chief of which he believes is the economic factor. Currency exchange rates and lack of foreign currency (especially U.S. dollars) have a powerful effect on these libraries. Political turmoil affects their ability to maintain their collections and services, as shown by the near impossibility of obtaining western journals in the People's Republic of China during the Cultural Revolution. The recognition of international copyright law has certainly imposed at least temporary barriers to the free flow of health sciences information. Breinich also identifies geography, the expense of maintaining roads and telephone service, and a country's traditions and willingness to spend money for information as possible impediments to medical information exchange. And, in spite of new technologies, the costs associated with their use are high, especially when payment is required in U.S. dollars. CD-ROM technology is a positive exception which should provide MEDLINE and other databases at fixed costs without telecommunications charges.

A study of the information policies and practices in 17 countries (1989) documents the degree to which the world's industrialized nations differ in developing national information policies. Officials in some countries replied simply that "we have no information policy," while others had clearly defined policies. In most cases current policies are formulated or changed in reaction to the progress of information technology. In most countries, including the United States, governments have been reluctant to invest a single agency with sole authority for national information management. In the U.S., a report to the President in 1976 recommended establishing a White House office with responsibility for information policy, and the Office of Management and Budget eagerly sought such authority, but a broad range of issues continues to be dealt with legislatively and piecemeal. These issues, all of concern to medical libraries, include telecommunications, transborder data flow, intellectual freedom, and copyright, among others.

Formulation of a national information policy is generally a reaction to circumstances and the result of investigation by a legislative committee or government agency. A primary determinant today appears to continue to be economics, as exemplified by the trend toward privatization and the development of commercial markets for government health information services.

General Legislation. Medical librarians expect the Government to continue to provide funding for the National Institutes of Health and the National Library of Medicine and hope that it will continue funding begun with the Medical Library Assistance Act (1965). Beyond these financial matters, U.S. medical librarians share the concerns of most librarians about information transfer in today's technological environment. In the early 1990s, legislative policymakers worked on technological issues of information transfer and the legality of downloading electronic data.

White House Conferences on national library issues in 1979 and 1991 addressed items that concern medical libraries either directly or indirectly. The Conference in 1991 concentrated mainly on the needs of public and school libraries, but its preliminary report, "Information 2000: Library and Information Services for the 21st Century," contained 95 policy recommendations. They included creating and funding a National Research and Education Network (NREN); developing a network to connect small urban, rural, and tribal libraries; and amending copyright legislation to support access to new and emerging information technologies.

Passage of the High Performance Computing Act of 1991 moved the NREN closer to establishment. The NREN was designed to link research and educational institutions, government agencies, and industries in every state with a high-speed, high-performance computer and telecommunications network. The National Science Foundation was scheduled to coordinate the NREN, with libraries, including the NLM, playing significant roles. Resolution of the issues of governance, financing, standards, data privacy, and copyright pose at least as much of a challenge as the technical issues. The Coalition for Networked Information was established in 1990 to monitor and promote the provision of information resources throughout the network.

All segments of the library community actively discussed a legislative proposal in 1992 to create a Government Printing Office Wide Information Network for Data Online (WINDO). By establishing online access to government information through the GPO, WINDO could become a single-account, "one-stop shopping" way to access and query federal databases. Planners described a system in which the least costly and technologically simplest services would be made available first, but with a goal of providing online access to as many federal databases as possible.

The medical library community continued to be concerned with two separate but related issues arising from the federal government's attempts to cut costs—the Paperwork Reduction Act and the possibility of privatizing the National Technical Information Service (NTIS). Passed in 1980 and amended in 1986, the

Paperwork Reduction Act sought to improve information resources management in the federal government to maximize the usefulness and minimize the costs of collecting, maintaining, and disseminating federal information, including medical information. The NTIS provides at least two functions vital for health sciences libraries: (1) the continued permanent availability of reports on federally funded science and technology projects, without copyright restrictions, preferably from a centralized service, at a reasonable price; and (2) comprehensive bibliographic access to these reports. Medical librarians viewed attempts to privatize NTIS as a threat to full access to government information.

Copyright issues relating to downloading data from online searches or extracting data from CD-ROMs caused great concern in the early 1990s. However, most medical librarians continued to provide services, on the assumption that rights and privileges are assured by analogy to printed materials under U.S. copyright laws. In the absence of provisions in copyright law specifically covering databases, legal scholars generally agreed that the practice was permissible, providing that "fair use" criteria are met. A complicating factor was that database vendors sought to stipulate further licensing restrictions. Lawyers considered the conflict between the terms of restrictive contracts and the rights accorded to individuals under copyright law unresolved. All agreed that only by a combination of new legislative and case law could a clear and appropriate legal balance be established between the rights of database vendors or producers and the needs of health sciences database users.

The Office of Technology Assessment issued a report in 1988 on federal information in an electronic age. This report made clear the extent to which new information technologies affected the way the government collects and disseminates information. Magnetic and electronic media have overtaken microfiche and paper, requiring government information agencies such as the GPO and the NTIS to adopt new standards and practices. Issues of concern to medical librarians include equity for persons without an electronic means of access and competition with the private sector information industry. The report emphasized the need for government leadership in effecting the changes needed by today's information-driven society.

Medical Library Legislation. More than 150 years of federal support for medical libraries, beginning with an appropriation of $150 for books for the Army Surgeon General's Office, led the National Library of Medicine (NLM) to inaugurate the National Network of Libraries of Medicine in 1991. Today the NLM houses the world's largest collection of health sciences literature. With funding support through the Medical Library Assistance Act since 1966, the NLM has provided important national and international leadership in the development of information and library services in the health sciences.

The NLM launched a long-range planning project in 1985 that proved to be extremely important to the nation's medical library community and its users. A national panel of medical librarians and health care professionals identified NLM's responsibilities in five areas: (1) building and organizing the NLM's collections; (2) locating and gaining access to medical and scientific literature; (3) building factual databases; (4) studying medical informatics (that is, the application of computers and information technologies to medical problem-solving and information transfer); and (5) assisting in educating health professionals through information technology. The panel gave particular emphasis to the urgent need for improved access by health care professionals and scientists to the rapidly growing scientific literature. It urged the NLM to move quickly to translate raw information into products and services that can improve health care, particularly in the field of molecular biology and biotechnology.

Congress, recognizing that individual health practitioners need ready access to the NLM's information services, specifically encouraged the NLM to develop an outreach program aimed toward health professionals practicing outside academic medical centers and to publicize the availability of its products and services. In 1989 an Outreach Planning Panel chaired by Michael DeBakey identified four major challenges and opportunities for the NLM: (1) to reach individual health professionals and include them in the activities of the National Network of Libraries of Medicine; (2) to strengthen access to national biomedical information services for hospitals and local institutions; (3) to increase substantially the number of medical informatics training centers; and (4) to accelerate intramural research and development of products and services that are optimally responsive to the information needs of individual health professionals. The NLM modified its resource grant program to simplify the application process and offer greater flexibility for support of technology-based proposals.

The Medical Library Association, through its Government Relations Committee, provided strong assistance to the NLM in communicating its budget needs to Congress. MLA's interest and involvement in legislative issues dates from the 1960s, when the first Legislative Committee was appointed. Renamed the Government Relations Committee in the mid-1980s, it strove through this period to raise the awareness of MLA members about issues of national policy and to involve members in determining national information policy. By the 1990s the MLA felt a growing need to define its legislative strategies more clearly.

In 1985 the MLA and the Association of Academic Health Sciences Library Directors formed a joint task force to create a federal legislative agenda for health sciences libraries. Its initial strategy included an education program aimed at key federal administrators, legislators, and Congressional committee staff members. The task force quickly recognized the value of regular communication with legislators.

Computerization of information transfer is now at the forefront of medical librarianship. Two national legislative issues faced medical librarians in the 1990s: the distribution of information technology to all levels of the biomedical community, and the legal constraints on access to electronic health sciences information and data.

REFERENCES

John A. Breinich, "Libraries in Developing Countries Face Challenges," *MLA News* (1991).

Domestic Council Committee on the Right of Privacy, *National Information Policy* (1976).
Michael W. Hill, compiler, on behalf of the International Federation for Documentation at the request of the Unesco General Information Program, *National Information Policies* (1989).
Charles McClure et al., *The National Research and Education Network (NREN): Research and Policy Perspectives* (1991).
National Library of Medicine Board of Regents, *Improving Health Professionals' Access to Information* (1989).
Office of Technology Assessment, *Informing the Nation: Federal Information in an Electronic Age* (1988).

SARA JEAN JACKSON

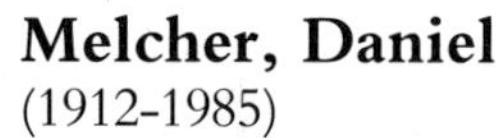

Melcher, Daniel
(1912-1985)

Daniel Melcher

Daniel Melcher, North American publishing executive, contributed to library service as an innovator in developing professional publications, reference services, and methods for improving book production and distribution.

Melcher was born July 10, 1912, at Newton Center, Massachusetts, the son of Marguerite Fellows Melcher and Frederic Gershom Melcher (later President of R. R. Bowker Company). Daniel Melcher was graduated from Harvard College (A.B.) in 1934. In 1934 and 1935 Melcher was a publicity assistant at the London publishing house of George Allen and Unwin and an assistant and student of publishing methods at other houses in London and Leipzig, Germany. From 1936 to 1942 he worked in a variety of sales promotion and management capacities at Henry Holt and Company, Oxford University Press, Alliance Book Corporation, and Viking Press, all in New York City. During World War II he worked in Washington, D.C., with the U.S. Treasury Department's War Finance Division, first as publishing consultant and then as National Director of its education section. In 1946 he was Director of the National Committee on Atomic Information, also in Washington.

When he joined the R. R. Bowker Company, New York, in 1947, Melcher was appointed Publisher of the firm's *Library Journal.* He quickly began developing the 70-year-old magazine into a major publication dealing with every aspect of the library profession, and in 1954 he founded, as an adjunct, *Junior Libraries (School Library Journal,* beginning 1961).

At the same time, Melcher had been working on the idea of a series of current in-print directories of American books. He devised the procedures by which the directories could be edited and produced, and in 1948 the firm launched the annual *Books in Print,* with author and title indexes. There followed, also under Melcher's vigorous direction, *Paperbound Books in Print* (1956), *Subject Guide to Books in Print* (1957), *Forthcoming Books* (advance listings), and *American Book Publishing Record* (catalogue listings, current and cumulative, in Dewey cataloguing sequence, 1961).

Meanwhile, Melcher was writing articles on library questions for *LJ* and on book distribution and book manufacturing for *Publishers' Weekly*. He contributed to the automated "belt press" concept of book manufacturing. His concern for distribution made him a major force in the mid-1960s in establishing the International Standard Book Numbering System.

Melcher became a Director and General Manager of Bowker in 1956; Vice-President, 1959; and President, 1963–68. After Bowker acquired Jacques Cattell Press, biographical directory publisher, Melcher was its Board Chairman, 1961–67. He took part in the Bowker stockholders' decision to sell the firm to the Xerox Corporation January 1, 1968, and was then Bowker Chairman under Xerox but resigned early in 1969.

He was Board Chairman of Gale Research Corporation, 1971–73, and thereafter an independent consultant. He was a member of the ALA Council, 1972–74, and from 1969 a board member of Institutes for Achievement of Human Potentials, with a special interest in the ways by which very young children can learn to read.

With Nancy Larrick, Melcher wrote a basic guide, *Printing and Promotion Handbook* (1949, 1956, 1967), and, with Margaret Saul Melcher, *Melcher on Acquisitions* (1971).

In 1937 he married Peggy Zimmerman, later a children's librarian; they had one son, Frederic G. Melcher II. After her death (1967), he married Margaret Saul, who had been editor of *School Library Journal.* Daniel Melcher died July 22, 1985, in Charlottesville, Virginia.

CHANDLER B. GRANNIS

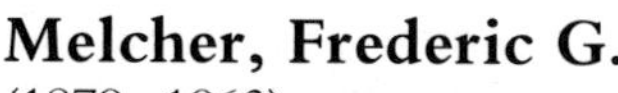

Melcher, Frederic G.
(1879–1963)

Frederic Gershom Melcher, editor, publisher, bookseller, and book collector, became one of the most influential and respected figures in the world of books not only in the United States but throughout the world during his 45 years with the R. R. Bowker Company. Rarely has a single person had such familiarity with all the aspects of bookmaking, bookselling, and book acquisition. Melcher's devotion to books began early when as a child he read in the public libraries of Newton, Massachusetts; later, in 1947, he honored a pioneer children's librarian, Caroline M. Hewins, by establishing a lectureship on New England children's literature and naming it for her.

Born April 12, 1879, in Malden, Massachusetts, the son of Edwin Forrest Melcher and Alice Jane Bartlett Melcher, he grew up in Newton Center and graduated from high school in 1895. He took the "Institute course," to prepare for the Massachusetts Institute of Technology, but the illness of his father and the difficult times following the depression of 1893 (combined with his own disinclination to become, as he put it, "a chemist or a civil engineer") made it necessary for him to seek a job instead.

Through the influence of his maternal grandfather, he obtained a position in the mailroom at Lauriat's bookstore in Boston. He remained at Lauriat's 18 years and handled its large library business for a time, built up its children's department, and eventually became one of its most successful salesmen. His discernment in judging and recommending current books earned him a reputation that began to spread beyond the Boston area; Arnold Bennett, for example, credited him with initiating the demand that led to the American success of *The Old Wives' Tale* in 1908.

His activity in professional organizations fostered his growing reputation: he was President in 1912 of the Boston Booksellers' League and delivered some rousing remarks at both the 1911 and 1912 American Booksellers Association conventions. One member of the audience, W. K. Stewart, soon after asked him to be manager of his Indianapolis store, and in March 1913 Melcher and his family (he had married Marguerite Fellows June 2, 1910) moved to Indianapolis.

The store served as the heart of Indiana's thriving literary activity. Melcher not only met Riley, Tarkington, Ade, Nicholson, Hubbard, and other writers and artists but also discussed book design and fine printing with Edwin Grabhorn, who set up his Studio Press in Indianapolis in 1915. During these years Melcher was becoming active in local and state library associations and speaking before library groups as well as writing for *Publishers' Weekly* and addressing the 1918 ABA convention. He was therefore widely known, and his knowledge of the book trade was thorough, when in 1918 an editorship of *Publishers' Weekly* became available. He joined the Bowker Company, publisher of the journal, in May 1918 as Vice-President and was associated with *Publishers' Weekly* for the next 40 years, first as Managing Editor and then, after Bowker's death in 1933, as Co-editor with Mildred C. Smith.

His intense interest in all aspects of the book and his belief in the interdependence of all parts of the book world were reflected in his handling of *PW*. One of his first actions was to institute a column on bookmaking and book design; another was to devote certain issues each year to children's books. He kept abreast of new developments and maintained personal contact with hundreds of people in the field through extensive travel, both in the U.S. and abroad, serving as a delegate to the International Publishers' Congresses and, following World War II, making trips to Europe and Japan for the State Department and the War Department. His editorials over the years amount to a compendium of informed and sensible commentary on all that was taking place.

In 1934 he succeeded R. R. Bowker as President of the company; under his direction the Bowker lists, while continuing to offer basic book trade tools for libraries and booksellers, increased their attention to bibliophilic books and works of scholarly bibliography. Bowker became the American publisher of Michael Sadleir's "Bibliographia" series, issued a series of state imprint bibliographies for the Bibliographical Society of America, and published John Carter's great *Taste and Technique in Book-Collecting* (1948—dedicated to Melcher in its 1970 printing), as well as important books on collecting by Mary Benjamin, Jacob Blanck, Howard Peckham, and Colton Storm, and *American Book-Prices Current*. The distinction of this list underlies the comment made by John Carter, one of Melcher's many English friends in the trade, in his 50th-anniversary address to the Bibliographical Society of America, when he singled out three firms, Bowker in New York and Constable and Hart-Davis in London, as having been particularly hospitable to bibliography.

In these years Melcher continued to be tireless in his professional service for such groups as the American Booksellers Association (Secretary, 1918–20), National Association of Book Publishers (Executive Secretary, 1920–24), New York Booksellers' League (President, 1924–25), American Institute of Graphic Arts (President, 1927–28), and New York Library Association (President, 1935–36) and in his work in connection with the Copyright Committee, the NRA code, the Council on Books in Wartime, and the American Civil Liberties Union, among others. As of 1959 Melcher, approaching his 80th birthday, gave up his long editorship of *PW* and presidency of Bowker and became Chairman of the Board; he remained active, however, and attended the International Publishers' Congress in Spain in 1962, the year before he died, on March 9, 1963, in Montclair, New Jersey.

Melcher's influence, through *PW* and the Bowker Company and through his wide acquaintance, was pervasive during the second quarter of the 20th century. But his influence has been and will continue to be felt in another way—through his generosity in establishing awards and disposing of his own collections. Children's books were always one of his special interests: besides being a founder in 1919 of Children's Book Week, he set up in 1922 an annual award for excellence in children's books, the Newbery Medal, and in 1937 added to it the Caldecott Medal for children's book illustration. He commissioned and donated these medals, but with characteristic modesty he did not wish his name attached to them. As the most prestigious awards in their field, however, they will remain one of his best memorials.

ALA

Frederic G. Melcher

Among the other awards indicative of his temperament and aims are one he established in 1940 for the Indiana library most active in promoting regional history or literature and another that he set up in 1943 for creative publishing (named after Mathew Carey and Isaiah Thomas).

His name will also be remembered for his collecting, and he often expressed his delight in the feel of a well-made book. The many friends who had the pleasure of examining his books at his house in Montclair, New Jersey, would be glad to know that much of the collection can still be consulted in libraries: his private press books are in the university libraries at Princeton and Syracuse; his Vachel Lindsay collection is in the Lilly Library at Indiana University; and his extensive collection of books about books is handsomely housed and effectively maintained (and kept up to date) in the library named for him at the R. R. Bowker Company.

A bestower of awards, he sought none for himself, but they inevitably came to him as the premier ambassador of the book world. In 1945 he was given the medal of the American Institute of Graphic Arts (in addition to being its President in 1927–28, he helped organize its Book Clinic in 1931) and in 1950 a plaque from the Children's Library Association; in 1955 at the Newbery-Caldecott dinner he was informed that a Melcher Scholarship has been established in the field of library service for children; in 1958 he was awarded an Honorary Litt.D. from Rutgers (New Brunswick, New Jersey) and the following year one from Syracuse in New York; and in 1962 the Regina Medal was presented to him by the Catholic Library Association for his work with children's literature.

Contributors to the book published in connection with the May 1945 dinner commemorating his first 50 years in the book trade were in agreement about the position he occupied; B. W. Huebsch, for instance, called him the leader "by tacit consent," and Marion E. Dodd labeled him the "number one liaison man to all the branches of the book world." The London *Bookseller* in 1954 referred to him as "the dean of the *corps diplomatique* of the American book-trade," and after his death it pronounced him "without doubt the greatest all-round bookman the English-speaking world has produced." His broad knowledge, his engaging personality and sense of humor, his infectious enthusiasm for books, his encouragement of newcomers in the field, his skill in bringing together people of diverse interests, and his vigorous championship of professional and humanitarian causes all have combined to make him a legendary figure.

REFERENCES

Mildred C. Smith, editor, *Frederic G. Melcher: Friendly Reminiscences of a Half Century among Books and Bookmen* (1945).

"Frederick G. Melcher—1879–1963," *Publishers' Weekly* (March 18, 1963).

Helen Adams Masten, editor, "Frederic G. Melcher Memorial Issue," *Top of the News* (March 1964).

Daniel Melcher, "Fred Melcher as I Knew Him," *ALA Bulletin* (January 1967).

Irene Smith, *A History of the Newbery and Caldecott Medals* (1957).

Chandler B. Grannis, "Melcher, Frederick Gershom," *Dictionary of American Library Biography* (1978).

G. THOMAS TANSELLE

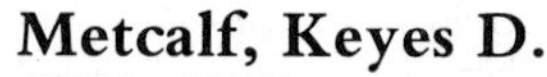

Metcalf, Keyes D.

(1889–1983)

ALA

Keyes D. Metcalf

Keyes Dewitt Metcalf achieved international recognition for his contributions as a library administrator at the New York Public Library, as Director of University Libraries at Harvard during a period of vigorous growth, and as consultant to the library world at large. He became a leader of the profession who won the admiration of generations of American librarians.

Metcalf was born April 13, 1889, in Elyria, Ohio, the son of a railroad engineer. One of 17 children, he went to work while still in high school as a page in the nearby Oberlin College Library, where his brother-in-law, Azariah Root, was Librarian. As a student at Oberlin between 1907 and 1911, he continued his work in the Library as well as playing on the college football and track teams. After graduation he served for a time as Root's Executive Assistant.

Metcalf enrolled in 1911 in the first class of the New York Public Library School, earning its certificate in 1913 and its diploma in 1915. While a student there he worked in the main reading room of the then new and still palatial building at Fifth Avenue and 42nd Street, beginning a relationship with that institution that was to extend over the next quarter-century. He served successively as its Chief of Stacks, Chief of the Order Division, and Executive Assistant, and finally—from 1928 to 1937—was in charge of the entire massive operation as Chief of the Reference Department.

Metcalf's accomplishments at the NYPL alone would have been enough to assure him illustrious recognition in the annals of American librarianship. Together with its Director, Harry M. Lydenberg, he furnished a substantial measure of leadership to the library profession through his increasing involvement in the work of the American Library Association. Also during this period he married Martha Gerrish; they had two children. Widowed in 1938, he later married Elinor Gregory.

Metcalf began the second portion of his tripartite career when President James B. Conant of Harvard persuaded him in 1937 to go to Cambridge, Massachusetts, as Librarian of Harvard College and Director of University Libraries. The first person ever to fill that post who was not himself a Harvard graduate, and the first trained librarian, Metcalf instituted many significant changes in library operations between that time and his retirement 18 years later.

Faced early in his incumbency with a worsening space situation in the Widener Library, then only two decades old, Metcalf soon conceived a multifaceted library plant development program calculated to accommodate Harvard's extensive collections for almost a half-century. The program included construction of a special building for rare books and manuscripts, completed as the Houghton Library in 1942; a remote facility for joint storage of seldom-used materials, the New England Deposit Library, completed in the same year; a library for undergraduates, the Lamont Library, opened in 1949; and a structure for additional stacks and services beneath the southeast corner of the Harvard Yard, added as the Pusey Library in 1977. This network of libraries, interconnected above and below grade with Widener, created in effect a library campus within a university campus.

Another integral part of Metcalf's plan for meeting the University's spatial requirements was a calculated move toward intentional but controlled physical decentralization of libraries. All of these developments were implemented during and after Metcalf's administration in accord with the concepts described in his annual report for the year 1939–40.

Metcalf's program for housing the collections was one of many major accomplishments that took place during his tenure. Among other things, he altered markedly the character of Harvard's library staff by bringing in large numbers of men and women trained in library schools, a change that brought the library system closer to the mainstream of American librarianship and gave it a more professional, cosmopolitan cast. His concern for the collections themselves manifested itself in the remarkable accessions of rare materials, the vast increase in general holdings (from 4,000,000 to 6,000,000 volumes), and the establishment of a strong library book selection program. He also elicited important modifications in the way in which the University administered and funded its library affairs, in keeping with the needs of contemporary scholarship.

As head of the world's largest university library during this period of vigorous library growth, Metcalf thus experienced first—and frequently solved—many of the problems of sheer size that would later plague other institutions. Other libraries found it always to their benefit, when faced by a problem resulting from size, to look first at how Harvard had responded to it. In this way Metcalf and his associates, whom he was particularly adept at selecting and developing, came deservedly to be viewed as a principal fountainhead of creativity and innovation in the field of research librarianship.

In 1955 Harvard University conferred emeritus status upon Metcalf, but this meant only that he could then embark full-time upon a third career—one already well established—as adviser and consultant extraordinary to the library world at large. Especially active in the field of planning library buildings, Metcalf traveled in the next quarter-century to all the continents on the globe save Antarctica, and worked on a phenomenal 600 assignments. In 1965 he produced his landmark work, *Planning Academic and Research Library Buildings,* which brought the impress of his expertise to bear upon hundreds of additional buildings.

Metcalf remained professionally active throughout his long career. He served on innumerable boards and committees of ALA and was President, 1942–43. The historian of the Association of Research Libraries, of which Metcalf was for five years Executive Secretary, rates him that Association's all-time most influential participant. He was a founding member and President of the American Documentation Institute, later the American Society for Information Science. He was Adjunct Professor of Library Service at Rutgers from 1955 to 1958. His bibliography of published writings extends to more than 180 items. These accomplishments brought him many prestigious awards and recognitions, including 13 honorary doctor's degrees and the unique 50th Anniversary Medal of Achievement from the New York Public Library in 1971.

Great industry, boundless energy, and enviable endurance pervaded his work at every point. He also became well known for his unexampled humanity, his patience, his humility, and his gentleness. A gregarious but slightly shy man, quick to smile and easy to know, Keyes Metcalf continued in the tenth decade of his life to fulfill a felicitous father-image for generations of American librarians. He died in Cambridge, Massachusetts, on November 3, 1983.

REFERENCES

Peter Hernon, "Keyes DeWitt Metcalf," *Leaders in American Academic Librarianship: 1925–1975,* edited by Wayne A. Wiegand (1983).

Keyes D. Metcalf, *Random Recollections of an Anachronism: or, Seventy-Five Years of Library Work* (1980).

Keyes D. Metcalf, "Six Influential Academic and Research Libraries," *College and Research Libraries* (1976).

Edwin E. Williams, "The Metcalf Administration, 1937–1955" and "Keyes D. Metcalf, a Bibliography of Published Writings," *Harvard Library Bulletin* (1969).

DAVID KASER

Metcalfe, John Wallace
(1901–1982)

John Wallace Metcalfe, Australian library leader and educator, won an international reputation for his contributions to the history and theory of cataloguing and classification. He was born in Blackburn, Lancashire, England, on May 16, 1901. When he was six, the family moved to New Zealand, then moved again three years later to Adelaide, South Australia. When Metcalfe was 11, they moved yet again, to Sydney, New South Wales. There Metcalfe remained for the rest of his professional life, destined to play an important role in the intellectual life of the city and state.

Metcalfe attended a state school in Marrickville, a Sydney suburb, and took his first library position at the age of 16 as an Assistant in the Fisher Library of the University of Sydney. He graduated from the University with First Class Honours in History in 1923 and on December 1 of that year was appointed an Assistant in the Public Library of New South Wales, the oldest and then probably the largest and most influential reference and research library in the Australian Commonwealth. Nine years later he had risen to the position of Deputy Principal Librarian. In 1942 he was appointed Principal Librarian, a position he was to hold until 1959, when he became Librarian of the University of New South Wales.

During his years in the Public Library of New South Wales, Metcalfe was active in creating and supporting the Free Library Movement. Established in 1935 as an organization for lay persons, the Free Library Movement had as a major aim the creation of free public libraries in municipalities and shires throughout the country, supported partly by local taxes and partly by state subsidy. It was founded by Geoffrey Remington and others after the results of the Munn-Pitt survey of Australian libraries were published. Metcalfe's involvement was also intensified by his experience (1934–35) of studying libraries in Great Britain, other countries of Europe, and the United States on a grant from the Carnegie Corporation. Largely as a result of the activity of the Free Library Movement, the New South Wales Minister for Education set up a Library Advisory Committee in 1937 with Metcalfe as member and Secretary. He was responsible for much of the Committee's report and for the attached draft bill that became the basis for the Library Act of 1939. Because of the war, the provisions of the Act were not fully implemented until 1944, and in that year Metcalfe, as Principal Librarian of the Public Library of New South Wales, became ex officio Executive Member of the Library Board of New South Wales. Created under that act, the Board was to encourage and oversee the development of public libraries throughout the state and to recommend the disbursement of state subsidies to them.

In 1935 Metcalfe became the first Australian to be admitted by examination as a Fellow of the Library Association (FLA) of the United Kingdom. His interest in the education of librarians, the systematic provision of whom was also an aim of the Free Library Movement, led him to set up training classes in the Public Library of New South Wales in 1937 or 1938. The library school thus created continued for many years and enabled Metcalfe and his associates to put their stamp on a whole generation of Australian librarians. His *General Introduction to Library Practice,* part of which was prepared in collaboration with others, formed the basis for instruction in the library school and went through three editions (1940, 1943, and 1955) with various formats and supplements.

In 1937 Metcalfe organized the Australian Institute of Librarians, which became the Library Association of Australia in 1949 and which was granted a Royal Charter in 1963. A major function of the Association was that of a professional examining body for librarians, and Metcalfe served as Chairman of its Board of Examiners from 1943 to 1958. He was General Secretary of the Association in 1937 and 1938 and again from 1950 to 1953, President from 1946 to 1948, and again President from 1957 to 1959. He was the first Editor of the Association's journal, *The*

T. Dobrovits

John Wallace Metcalfe

Australian Library Journal, and wrote most if not all of the unsigned copy for many of the early issues.

After 35 years of service with the state government in the Public Library of New South Wales, Metcalfe resigned in 1959 to become the first Librarian of the University of New South Wales, a position he accepted partly because of the opportunity it gave him of creating a postgraduate School of Librarianship in the University. The School was opened in 1960 and initiated a new pattern of education for librarians in Australia.

Metcalfe wrote widely on a variety of professional subjects. His major books are *Information Indexing and Subject Cataloging: Alphabetical, Classified, Coordinate, Mechanical* (1957), *Subject Classifying and Indexing of Libraries and Literature* (1959), *Alphabetical Subject Indication of Information* (Rutgers Series on Systems for the Intellectual Organization of Information, vol 3, 1965) and *Information Retrieval, British and American, 1876–1976* (1976). He also wrote voluminously on many educational, cultural, and community matters in Australian local and national journals and newspapers, the latter of which, in his heyday in the Public Library of New South Wales, consulted him frequently for or reported his forceful, pithy, sometimes controversial views.

In 1947 Metcalfe was appointed to the Australian delegation to the Unesco General Conference in Mexico City, and upon its conclusion, at the invitation of the Carnegie Corporation and the British Council, was once again able to visit libraries in the U.S. and Great Britain. In 1956 he was a consultant to the Fisher Library at the University of Sydney. Metcalfe retired from the University of New South Wales and from professional life in 1968. He died in Sydney on February 7, 1982.

REFERENCE

W. Boyd Rayward, editor, *The Variety of Librarianship: Essays in Honour of John Wallace Metcalfe* (1976), contains a full bibliography of Metcalfe's writing together with a list of published items about him in the *Australian Library Journal.*

W. BOYD RAYWARD

Mexico

The United States of Mexico, the northernmost country of Middle America, is bounded on the north by the United States, on the east by the Gulf of Mexico, on the south by Belize and Guatemala, and on the west by the Pacific Ocean. Population (1990 est.) 86,154,000; area 1,958,201 sq.km. The official language is Spanish.

History. Documentary evidence about pre-Columbian Mexico is recorded in codexes written on amate paper, deerskin, and, possibly, jaguar skin. These manuscripts were used in schools for the nobility and the clergy, known as *Calmecac,* and in schools for the people, known as *Telpochcalli.* The codexes were stored in special areas called *Amocalli.* Spanish conquerors carried books with them. Fray Juan de Zumárraga, Bishop of New Spain, petitioned King Charles I of Spain and was given permission to open the first library in Mexico in 1534.

Only those who belonged to the church and were educated had access to the clerical libraries. The collections were continually enriched by the books that arrived from Europe, all of which had to be approved by the Inquisition. But people in New Spain found ways to import clandestine books that greatly contributed to increased liberal thinking and made possible the War of Independence (1810–21). The Biblioteca Nacional was founded in 1833.

Improving education became a priority after the Mexican Revolution (1910–11) and the civil wars that followed it. In the early 1920s, under President Alvaro Obregón, José Vasconcelos, his Secretary of Education, established a far-reaching program for *bibliotecas populares,* a considerable achievement given the conditions of Mexico at the time.

National Library. The Biblioteca Nacional de Mexico (National Library of Mexico) and the Hemeroteca Nacional de Mexico (National Library of Periodicals of Mexico) are part of and are coordinated by the Instituto de Investigaciones Bibliográficas (Bibliographical Research Institute) of the Universidad Nacional Autónoma de México (UNAM).

The Biblioteca Nacional was founded by a decree of President Benito Juárez in 1867 in Mexico City, the capital. It is a depository library for all material published in Mexico and offers information and research services to all kinds of users. Among its great cultural treasures are two collections of old and rare books comprising 500,000 volumes. It is rich in historical material and offers a vast amount of primary source material on Mexico. The bibliography section has some 20,000 volumes of bibliographies from all parts of the world.

The Library published the *Anuario Bibliográfico* (Bibliographic Annual), which covers all material published in Mexico, from 1958 to 1964. Thereafter the bibliography was published irregularly as *Bibliografía Mexicana.*

Libraries in Mexico (1990)

Type of library	Number of administrative units (main libraries)	Volumes in collections	Annual expenditures (peso)	Population served	Professional staff (with certificate, diploma, etc.)	Total staff
National	1	2,069,065	5,611,633,074	270,000	22	458
Academic	853	8,037,507	--	1,097,141	1,164	5,384
Public	3,594	13,933,937	--	80,027,090	1,423	7,906
School	3,261	9,037,967	--	7,793,284	1,228	6,572
Special	130	2,878,070	--	45,899	241	831

The Hemeroteca Nacional is for periodical publications what the Biblioteca Nacional is for books. The collection of newspapers and journals is an important resource, especially notable for Mexico City newspapers, some of which date from the 17th century. The materials are available for internal use or through interlibrary loan. Other services available include reference, research, photocopying, and microfilming.

For many years the files of newspapers and periodicals were part of the Biblioteca Nacional. As the collection grew, it outgrew its space, and in 1944 the Hemeroteca Nacional was established. A project to house both libraries under the same roof was begun in the late 1970s and finished by the mid-1980s.

Academic Libraries. Even though many university libraries still lack the collections, facilities, and professional staff necessary to offer adequate library service, such libraries showed important tendencies toward development starting in the 1970s. Collections grew and improved considerably as institutions realized the importance of libraries and allowed larger budgets for acquisitions and for better-paid professional librarians. The Escuela Nacional de Agricultura (National School of Agriculture), Instituto Tecnológico y de Estudios Superiores de Monterrey (Technological Institute of Monterrey), Universidad Autónoma Metropolitana, and particularly UNAM were among those that designed and built new library buildings in the 1970s. UNAM now has 164 libraries housing a total of 2,350,000 volumes, with a catalogue on CD-ROM.

Public Libraries. Since the end of the Mexican Revolution the development of public libraries has gone through three stages. The first stage began in 1921 with the creation of the Departamento de Bibliotecas in the Secretaria de Educación Pública. The department set up many bibliotecas populares, particularly in the Federal District. The second stage began in 1940, when the Secretaria shifted its support from libraries to sorely needed literacy programs. The third stage began with the Programa Nacional de Bibliotecas Públicas (National Program of Public Libraries) in 1983. The program established for the first time a Red Nacional de Bibliotecas Públicas (national network of public libraries). By the early 1990s the country had almost 3,200 public libraries, serving nearly 2,100 of the almost 2,400 municipalities. In the early 1980s, these libraries held 1,321,000 volumes; by the early 1990s, they held more than 12,200,000 volumes. Catalogues for all the collections are on CD-ROM. User inquiries rose from 4,000,000 in 1983 to 61,000,000 in 1989.

Central to the effort to develop the Red Nacional was an intense effort to train the personnel in charge of services. In addition, the national government worked to improve collection development and management. At the same time, it continued an extensive program to teach reading to people of all ages. For the young, the Programa de Computación Gratuíta para todos los niños teaches children to use computers provided free at their public libraries. And in 1989 public libraries began offering access to film classics and cultural programs on videocassettes.

School Libraries. Few schools at the elementary and secondary levels have their own libraries. The Programa Nacional created specific areas in public libraries for children. In most public libraries in Mexico, children can find assistance for their daily homework and participate in workshops, games, literary clubs, and guided visits. The public libraries provide qualified staff to work with children.

Biblioteca Nacional (Mexico)

Ciudad Universitaria, addition to the National Library of Mexico (1979).

Special Libraries. There are almost 800 special libraries and information centers in Mexico. Special libraries and information centers grew in the 1970s in response to the needs of developing technology and industry. Financial institutions, government offices dealing with scientific and technological developments, and centers of higher education and technology throughout the country have collections pertinent to their fields.

The Profession. The Asociación Mexicana de Bibliotecarios, Asociación Civil (AMBAC; Mexican Association of Librarians) was founded in 1954 and had 520 members by the early 1990s. Two of its main objectives are to enhance the professional development of its members and to promote libraries and library services throughout the country.

AMBAC has several regional associations and an affiliate, the Asociación de Bibliotecarios en Instituciones de Enseñanza Superior e Investigación (ABIESI; Association of Librarians in Higher Education and Research Institutions), founded in 1957. ABIESI had 60 institutional members and 120 personal members in 1992. It sets the standards for interlibrary loan in the country and organizes courses and seminars for library professionals.

Several institutions teach librarianship. The oldest is the Escuela Nacional de Biblioteconomía y Archivología (ENBA; National School of Librarians and Archivists, founded in 1945 and under the Secretary of Public Education). UNAM, through the Faculty of Philosophy and Letters, also offers a degree for librarians. Both are in Mexico City. ENBA stresses the administrative side of the profession while UNAM emphasizes its technical side. Several universities outside the capital grant degrees in library science: the

Biblioteca Central Estatal "Mauricio Magdaleno" (Zacatecas), one of Mexico's 3192 public libraries.

Autonomous University of Guadalajara, one in Nuevo León, one in San Luis Potosí, and one in Guanajuato. UNAM, Guanajuato, and Nuevo León offer Master's degrees in library science.

ANA MARÍA MAGALONI DE BUSTAMANTE

Middle Ages, Libraries in the

The period from the extinction of the Roman Empire in the West to the discovery of America and the rise of European nation-states—from 476 to 1492—is on the whole one of the darkest in the history of culture, books, and libraries. But a tenuous connection survived between the great libraries of the ancient world and the beginning of libraries as they are understood today. This great extent of time was far from being uniform and can be subdivided into four periods that showed different characteristics of library development.

The first period, up to the end of the 6th century, witnessed the final collapse of the ancient classical heritage. The second period, up to the 9th century, saw its replacement by the Christian institution of monasticism as the refuge of a tradition of letters. The third period commenced with the slow growth of medieval cultural institutions after the devastations of the last phase of the barbarian invasions—the raids of the Vikings, the Saracens, and the Hungarians in the 9th and 10th centuries—which gravely impaired social institutions and destroyed many monasteries and their libraries. It closed with the rise of the universities in an age of increased clerical literacy in the service of church and state.

The final period of the Middle Ages showed a rapid increase in the production of books in manuscript and, at the end, in printed form, as well as rapidly growing literacy among the middle-class laity, the beginning of the new learning of the Renaissance, and the physical development of libraries in the older institutions.

Dom David Knowles, in his *Religious Orders in England* (1955), gives a relevant definition: "A library is to our thinking a large and comprehensive collection of books, gathered together according to a carefully prepared scheme to serve determined purposes, and housed from the beginning in a building designed to accommodate both the books and those who wish to consult or study them." If we are to understand the history of libraries as instruments of scholarly work or preservers of the intellectual heritage at this early period, it is necessary to put together all scraps of information that survive relating to the provision of books. Evidence is available in literary and historical references and archaeology, as well as in catalogues of medieval collections and in the books themselves that have survived the devastations caused by negligent or intentional destruction. With the caveat that literacy—even literacy in Latin—is not learning, and that learning does not predicate the existence of libraries, the thread can then be traced. There is a single constant throughout the library history of the Middle Ages: the universality of the manuscript in codex format, written on folded leaves of vellum and bound between stout wooden boards, the physical form common to the earliest liturgical manuscripts and some incunabula printed after the age of paper had begun. Provision for storage and use of the codex explains the origin of library architecture.

The format of classical pagan literature had been the papyrus roll, whose physical survival necessitated repeated copying. Neglect and damp, even more than deliberate or accidental destruction by Christians and barbarians, had probably reduced the stock of Roman literature before the beginning of the medieval period, although the tradition of collecting the classics survived among wealthy Romans and provincials in Italy and Gaul into the 6th century. Nevertheless, one of the most vital cultural services of Christian institutions throughout the Middle Ages was the preservation of pagan literary works by copying texts from decaying papyrus to permanent vellum. Christian hostility to pagan writings had been tempered even before the institution of the Christian Roman Empire by Constantine in the 4th century, through the habit of regarding them as in some sense precursors of Christian revelation, and later they were viewed as sources for grammatical teaching. Boethius (480–524), the last Roman philosopher and a Christian, furnished a link between the pagan and Christian traditions, since he studied in the library of his father-in-law, Symmachus, heir of the last great pagan family of Rome. His *De consolatione philosophiae* describes the glazed bookcases ornamented with ivory in his own library. Boethius's career as minister to the conquering Gothic king Theodoric is paralleled by that of a more significant figure in the history of libraries, Cassiodorus (502–597).

Monastery Libraries. After his retirement from the court of Ravenna and the siege of Rome in 546, Cassiodorus founded the monastery of Vivarium in southern Italy, where he established a *scriptorium* and a library. His *Institutiones* was to serve as a bibliographical guide for future monastic collections and included a detailed account of the making of books. He describes the arrangement of the library, contained in nine *armaria,* or bookcases, the majority of which held theological works and the remainder liberal arts and sciences. The *Etymologiae* of a Spanish bishop, Saint Isidore (c. 560–636), was even more influential in the organization of knowledge in the Middle Ages. This encyclopedia cites over 150 pagan and Christian writers and contains chapters on libraries, librarians, and their duties. His poem *Versus titulis bibliothecae* indicates that his private library occupied 14 to 16 cases containing from 400 to 500 volumes.

Saint Benedict (c. 480–547?) provided the key to the development of the monastic orders. His *Regula,* on which all later monastic rules were based, secured the place of writing and literacy in the Latin language. Chapter 48 mentions the word *bibliotheca,* though it is uncertain whether it means a room or a collection of books; more significant was the ample provision of time for reading sacred writings and the insistence on manual labor, later to be interpreted as including the work of the scriptorium. In the 500 years after Benedict, the copying of books inspired by his Rule—and consequently the survival of learning—was confined almost exclusively to monastic institutions. The root of the Benedictine traditions did not come from the schools of Christian learning in the later Roman Empire but rather from the Eastern monasticism that developed in Egypt. Originally communities of ascetic and usually illiterate hermits, Coptic monasteries, by the time of Saint Pachomius in the 4th century, had codified the place of cloistral reading of the Scriptures, the Fathers, and works of devotion. Archaeological evidence of their use of books can be traced through as late as the 13th century.

The most significant advance of Christianity in the Middle Ages was the tide of conversion that flowed from Rome to England and from the British Isles back to the pagan German lands. Its leaders, devoted to monasticism, regarded books as the lifeblood of Christianity, and the monasteries they founded developed a vital library tradition of incalculable importance in preserving and transmitting European culture. The missionaries and monasteries can be placed in a family tree that reached to and from the north of England and returned to Italy. Pope Gregory the Great dispatched Saint Augustine to the Kentish kingdom in 597. Saint Augustine, the Easterner Theodore of Tarsus, his successor as Archbishop, and Hadrian, an African monk who had been Abbot of a south Italian monastery, carried books from Rome to Canterbury. The cathedral monastery of Christ Church and the abbey of Saints Peter and Paul, later Saint Augustine's, both established libraries that existed until their destruction in the 16th century. The Northumbrian Benedict Biscop, pupil and successor of Hadrian as Abbot of Saint Peter's, journeyed to Rome several times collecting books and founded the twin monasteries of Wearmouth (674) and Jarrow (681).

Saint Ceolfrid, Abbot of both monasteries, also traveled to Rome, where he probably acquired the *Codex Grandior* that may have belonged to Cassiodorus. The *Codex Amiatinus,* written under his direction for presentation to the Pope, copied its frontispiece, a unique pictorial record of an early library bookcase. The Venerable Bede (673–735) composed his many scriptural, historical, and scientific works at Jarrow, which indicates the richness of the book collection available to him. His pupil Egbert, Archbishop of York from 732 to 766, founded a cathedral school and library, and this collection served as a source of copies made for monasteries of the Frankish Empire.

Christianity came to Northern England not only from Rome but also from the Celtic church of Ireland. Little can be conjectured about the book collections of Irish monasteries, but Saint Columbanus (543–615) provided books to the monasteries he founded in his missionary journeys to the Continent. Luxeuil in Burgundy (founded 590) and Bobbio in northern Italy (founded 612) developed great scriptoria and libraries, as did the houses founded by his disciples—Saint Gall, in Switzerland (founded 614), and Saint Riquier, in northern France (founded 625–645). A 9th-century plan of Saint Gall indicates a bookroom connected with a scriptorium, and the abbey today has one of the most magnificent of monastic libraries. The library at Bobbio transmitted some of the most ancient books of the Western world to modern times.

The Englishman Boniface, the apostle of Germany (680–755), founded the bishoprics and monasteries in the pagan areas east of the Frankish kingdom. When he was martyred by the Frisians, books were in his baggage. The sees of Mainz, Wurzburg, and Salzburg became centers of religious and political influence with schools and libraries. Boniface's monastery of Fulda (founded 744) became the most

Courtesy of the Newberry Library

The Cloisters, Gloucester, western England.

powerful in Germany, housing a scriptorium famous for illuminated manuscripts and a great library, of which an 8th-century catalogue survives. Charlemagne, the first of the Frankish emperors, called Alcuin of York to be master of his palace school, and Alcuin became his trusted minister. As the Abbot of Tours, he sent for books from England to add to the library. Alcuin revived Frankish monasticism under his royal patronage. Monasteries such as Fleury (7th century) and Corbie (founded 657) created collections of manuscripts that were to be matched by those in German lands, such as Reichenau (founded 724), Lorsch (founded 763), and Corvey (founded 822).

Classics copied in the Carolingian minuscule hand were to transmit their clear calligraphy to the scholars of the Renaissance. The letters of Lupus, Abbot of Ferrieres (842–860), an indefatigable collector of both classical and Christian titles, document the bibliographical cooperation between monasteries in the period before the devastation inflicted by the Northmen eliminated learning in most of the British Isles and gravely affected it on the Continent.

The period from the 10th to the 12th centuries witnessed first a slow and then a rapid recovery that brought about a rebirth of monastic institutions and their libraries. In England the efforts of Saint Dunstan (924–988) were succeeded by those of Lanfranc (1005–1089), teacher, Prior of Bec in Normandy, and Archbishop of Canterbury. His influential recension of the Benedictine Rule made specific references to the lending and reading of books. Norman prelates rebuilt English abbeys and renewed their collections. After the Saracen sack of Monte Cassino, Abbot Desiderius in the 11th century raised its library and scriptorium to its highest level.

The greatest age of monasticism was ushered in by the foundation of the new orders of reformed Benedictinism, the "Black Monks" of Cluny (founded 910) and the "White Monks" of Citeaux (founded 1098); both evolved international systems of daughter houses that spread over Europe. The primary concern of their monastic life was not learning but a communal spiritual life in isolation from the world. The Cluniacs placed emphasis on liturgical worship, and the early Cistercians restricted on principle the collecting and reading of books to devotional requirements. These monks regarded copying manuscripts as religious work prescribed by the Rule, rather than as a method of building up holdings, but along with their great building and economic activities, they created libraries. The first catalogue of Cluny itself in the 13th century enumerated nearly 600 works, and by this time most of the important houses of Black Monks also had sizable collections. Cistercian foundations, such as Fountains in England and Fossa Nuova in Italy, made careful architectural provision for protecting their books, and these developed over the centuries.

The fundamental unit of monastic book storage remained the classical *armarium,* a large wooden cupboard with shelves on which the bindings were laid flat. Sometimes it was recessed into stonework, which has survived. It was usually in the east walk of the cloister, between the chapter house (where books were distributed on an annual basis during Lent for the monks' private reading) and the side door of the church. The usual location for study and writing was under the windows of the north walk of the cloister, which in many places in the later Middle Ages was glazed and fitted with wooden carrels. When space became inadequate, storage rooms were built adjoining the chapter house. The book regulations of other orders, such as the Carthusians (founded 1084) and the Premonstratensians (founded 1120), were generally similar to those of the Benedictines. The Carthusians, who lived in detached cells, were allowed to borrow two books at a time. Supervision of books and readers was the responsibility of the precentor, the official primarily responsible for the maintenance of church services, which included the care of the liturgical books used in the choir. By the end of the 12th century, the provision of libraries in large and small monastic houses was so close to universal practice that an epigram was coined: "A cloister without books is like a castle without an armory."

Episcopal establishments were frequently centers of learning throughout the Middle Ages, and the teaching of famous scholars encouraged the accumulation of books. This was particularly true in cities of northern Italy. A catalogue of the library of Cremona was made shortly after the death of Bishop Liutprand (902–972), diplomat and classicist, and other early records refer to collections at Novara, Vercelli, Monza, and Ivrea. At Verona the Capitular Library can claim lineal descent back to the 5th century, when manuscripts were written that survive to the present. North of the Alps, Archbishop Hincmar of Reims (805–822) and Gerbert, a teacher in the cathedral school there who became Pope Sylvester II (999–1003), acquired notable collections. The latter's pupil Fulbert created a library at Chartres; Beauvais and Rouen also possessed rich libraries. The see of Bamberg (founded 1007) maintained a famous school and inherited the library of the Emperor Henry II in 1024. Prior to the rise of the universities, the educational influence of the cathedral schools and their libraries had outstripped that of the monasteries. Thus when Peter Lombard, the authority on canon law, died in 1160, he bequeathed his books to the cathedral of Notre Dame in Paris.

University Libraries. Before the end of the 12th century, the University of Paris, which had its roots in the cathedral school, had become the center of the scholastic philosophy that generated a new professional literature for the clergy and largely outmoded older medieval writings. The need for books for thousands of students became pressing. The primary response of university authorities was to regulate the book trade by controlling the *stationarii* who supplied the textbooks. The many professional scribes, principally laymen, copied an *exemplar,* writing by the *pecia* for fixed prices. Public library facilities were a secondary growth. The many student hostels in Paris and the daughter university of Oxford were for the most part too small and poor to assume such a function. The growth of larger residences for masters and students, such as the Sorbonne (founded 1257), with substantial buildings and a regulated community life, made the formation of libraries possible. The Sorbonne library was organized and catalogued in 1289, and library rules exist from 1321. The collection, as was customary in monastic as well as academic institutions, was divided into two parts: books constantly referred to were chained in the great library, those available for loan or rarely used being secured in a separate room. By 1338 more than 300 volumes were in the first location and more than 1,000 in the second.

At Oxford and Cambridge during the 14th and 15th centuries, the smaller halls were gradually squeezed out by endowed colleges, which erected library facilities of a pattern that has survived to the present day. Libraries common to the university as a whole were of less importance and were founded at a relatively late date. Oxford's collection, bequeathed by Thomas de Cobham in 1327, was housed in a room above the University Church. At Cambridge a university library did not exist until the first half of the 15th century.

The new mendicant orders of friars quickly assumed a dominant role in the universities. The Dominicans (founded 1215) produced famous teachers of philosophy and were soon followed by the Franciscans (founded 1210). Their convents established working collections of books, largely academic and pastoral in content. Dominican instructions of the 1250s include precise library regulations, as do Franciscan constitutions of 1260. The catalogue of the Franciscan motherhouse at Assisi in 1381 describes a large collection carefully classified, labeled, and shelved. Substantial libraries were established by the friars in other urban centers. In England the Augustinian collection in York numbered more than 600 works in 1372, and in 1429 Sir Richard Whittington built the Greyfriars' convent in London with a substantial library.

Other Libraries. Throughout the Middle Ages the popes of Rome must always have acquired books and archives, but the history of the papal library is fragmented and puzzling. Earlier collections of books and archives probably suffered destruction during the repeated sacking of the city—by the Vandals in 455, the Saracens in 846, and the Normans in 1084. The

Courtesy of Newberry Library

Medieval Scribe

exile of the papacy to Avignon during the 14th and 15th centuries dispersed the library described in the earliest surviving catalogue of 1295, but records of the existence of libraries go back as far as Pope Damasus (366–84). Archaeological excavation has revealed remains of the building used as a library by Pope Agapetus (535–36), an associate of Cassiodorus. Gregory the Great (590–604) complained of an inadequate library, though the collection may have increased when Pope Zacharias (741–52) transferred it to the Lateran. The title of librarian existed from the time of Hadrian I (722–95), and names are known for librarians of the 11th century.

Eastern Empire. The separation between Western and Eastern forms of Christianity was a concomitant of the division of the Roman Empire. The Eastern or Byzantine Empire, Greek in language and Orthodox in religion, maintained in isolation from the West a continuity of both cultural tradition and imperial authority. Evidence of Eastern libraries exists intermittently over the whole period. Many emperors, from Theodosius II at the end of the 5th century through the Nicaean rulers after the Latin conquest, maintained libraries that may have afforded a degree of public access. A traveler's reference of 1437 gives a glimpse of stone benches and tables used in consulting the palace collection. The contents can be presumed to have included, besides law and theology, works of Greek literature and science. Byzantine encyclopedic works and digests refer to classical works now lost. Higher educational institutions, both theological and secular, such as the academy established by Theodosius II (408–50) and those founded by the Emperors Leo the Philosopher in the 9th century and Constantine Monomachus in the 10th, must have had extensive book collections. The Patriarchate maintained schools and libraries. Monastic collections, such as those at the Lavra on Mount Athos and Saint Catherine's on Mount Sinai, were widely distributed, though usually small. About 825 Saint Theodore, Abbot of Studium, regulated his monks' reading and copying. A Greek monastery that can be singled out because its library still survives in situ and largely intact is one founded by the monk Christodoulos in 1088 on Saint John's island of Patmos in the Aegean. The looting of Constantinople by the Latins in 1204 began the flow of Greek manuscripts to Italy, and the pace accelerated until the final conquest of the city by the Turks in 1453. The acquisitions of Western travelers were supplemented by books brought by emigré Greeks, such as Cardinal Bessarion, who bequeathed his library to the Republic of Venice in 1472. Italian libraries became the home of Greek literature and philosophy, which transformed the culture of the Renaissance and superseded the medieval tradition of learning.

14th and 15th Centuries. The last two centuries of the Middle Ages witnessed greatly increased production of books and a corresponding growth in accommodation for them among collegiate and monastic institutions. The latter declined drastically in intellectual influence but maintained economic power that enabled them to erect buildings to house, not the products of their own scriptoria, but rather scholastic works coming to them by gift or bequest, often from their members who had attended university. At Oxford, the great abbeys of Gloucester and Durham maintained their own halls of residence. The latter was bequeathed but apparently did not receive the rich collection of Richard de Bury (1287–1345), royal civil servant and Bishop of Durham. His *Philobiblon* gives valuable insight as to the state of contemporary learning and libraries. At Canterbury, Archbishop Henry Chichele erected a library building in the early 15th century, and other English cathedral foundations did likewise, a development that was matched in France, as at Rouen. An exceptional 15th-century monastic collection was formed by John Tritheim (1462–1516), Abbot of Sponheim, who acquired 2,000 volumes, many of them printed. Incunabula from other south German monasteries have reached many modern collections, a large proportion of them having found their way into the Bavarian State Library as the result of confiscation during the Napoleonic period.

Oxford colleges had relatively small collections up to the beginning of the 14th century. Later foundations, such as New College (founded 1379), All Souls (founded 1437), and Magdalen (founded 1458), all included libraries in their building plans. These long, narrow rooms had equidistant windows on both sides between which were set lecterns, with the volumes resting on the sloping tops, either at standing height or at sitting height with benches placed between, under the windows. The books were customarily chained, and the length of the desks and the narrow shelf below limited the number of books. This system became universal in larger libraries throughout western Europe. It is exemplified in the library built by the University of Oxford over the Divinity School between 1444 and 1487 and named in honor of its benefactor, Duke Humphrey of Gloucester.

The universities had trained many clerics who possessed private libraries—Chaucer's Clerk of Oxenford, with his 20 books, must have been typical of many thousands. But country gentlemen and lawyers, too, began in the 14th and 15th centuries to acquire considerable collections, evidence of which is found in wills, inventories, and records of gifts. Like other valuables, the books were habitually stored in the stout wooden chests universally used throughout the period. Culturally, the laymen's holdings were significant because of the high proportion of books in vernacular languages, only occasionally present in institutional libraries. An outstanding German private collection was formed by the physicians Hermann (1410–85) and Hartman (1440–1514) Schedel, burghers of the wealthy free city of Nuremberg, most of which survives in the Bavarian State Library. A number of German cities established public libraries for their citizens during the 15th century, Brunswick being the earliest in 1413.

The greatest lay libraries were in the hands of royalty, and these were to become predecessors of the national collections of the future, although bequest, sale, or plunder destroyed their continuity. Kings and emperors throughout the Middle Ages had occasionally been patrons of learning. Charlemagne installed two libraries in his capital of Aachen—as recorded by his biographer Einhard, himself a book collector—and his example was followed by his son, Louis the Pious (814–40), and his grandson, Charles the Bald (840–77). Regrettably, there is no trace of the books of the brilliant Emperor Frederick II, which must have reflected his contacts with the Greek and Muslim cultures of Sicily and southern Italy.

In the later Middle Ages kings became less peripatetic, and residence in fixed centers of government made the establishment of royal libraries feasible. Foremost among these were the collections of the French royal house, a good part of whose holdings were literary and historical works written in or translated into French. John II (1350–64) bequeathed his taste for books to both branches of his descendants—the Kings of France and the Dukes of Burgundy. His eldest son, Charles V (1364–70), installed a library of three floors in the Louvre with a resident librarian. His third son, John, Duke of Berry (1340–1416), was a munificent patron of scribes and illuminators. His fourth son, Philip the Bold (1363–1404), commenced the collection of the Dukes of Burgundy, augmented by his successors. Partially dispersed after the Netherlands passed under Hapsburg rule, the remainder became the nucleus of the Belgian Royal Library.

Two English princes of the House of Lancaster amassed book collections. John, Duke of Bedford and Regent of France (1389–1435), in 1424 bought the library formed by Charles V. Humphrey, Duke of Gloucester (1391–1447), an early patron of Humanist learning north of the Alps, gave hundreds of volumes to the University of Oxford, and after his death King Henry VI gave some of the remainder of his library to King's College in Cambridge, although only a few of his books survived the Reformation. A unique royal library was formed by Matthias Corvinus, King of Hungary (1440–90), allied by marriage with the royal house of Naples, also great collectors. His magnificent Renaissance manuscripts were looted by the Turks after the capture of Buda in 1526, and all but a tiny proportion perished through neglect.

Renaissance Italy. The libraries established by the princes of Italy were of the greatest cultural significance because their collections reflected the new learning of the Renaissance. City tyrants cooperated with the passionate enthusiasm of Humanist scholars in discovering and copying manuscripts of the Latin and Greek classical writers and in preserving them in libraries. Princely families, such as the Este of Ferrara and Modena, the Gonzaga of Mantua, and the Visconti and Sforza of Milan, formed sumptuous collections that had a propaganda value in reflecting the liberality and culture of the ruling house. Typical were the manuscripts of Federigo da Montefeltro, Lord of Urbino (1444–82), commissioned from the Florentine dealer Vespasiano da Bisticci. The earliest of the great Humanists, the poet Petrarch (1304–74), possessed a library that he intended to, but never did, bequeath to form a public library in Venice.

The leading center of Renaissance learning was Florence. At the beginning of the 15th century two friaries maintained libraries accessible to the citizens, the Carmelites and the Augustinians of San Spirito, to which Petrarch's disciple Boccaccio (1313–75) bequeathed his books. The first citizen and de facto ruler of Florence, Cosimo de Medici, founded the Dominican house of San Marco, and in 1444 built a library in it designed for public use. He arranged for his donations to be supplemented by the bequest of the many classical manuscripts of the scholar and bibliophile Niccolo Niccoli (1363–1437). His fellow Humanist, Poggio Bracciolini (1380–1459), traveled in southern Germany and France from 1415 to 1417, buying, borrowing, or stealing manuscripts of classic authors from the most ancient monastic libraries. The private library of the Medici, greatly increased by Lorenzo the Magnificent (1449–92), did not find a permanent home in San Marco, but most of it—after a sojourn in Rome in the early part of the 16th century with the Medici popes, Leo X and Clement VII—returned to Florence to be incorporated in the Biblioteca Medicea-Laurentiana. It is worth noting that the library's fittings, designed by Michelangelo before 1571, are a final example of the medieval lectern system. The example of San Marco was copied by Malatesta Novella, Lord of Cesena, in a library he had built in the Franciscan convent in 1447, which survives with the original collection, desks, and benches intact.

The most magnificent Renaissance library housed the papal collection, recreated by the Humanist Pope Nicholas V (1447–55) and enlarged by Sixtus IV (1471–84), who installed the Humanist Bartolomeo Platina as Librarian in 1475 and provided appropriate quarters and fittings. Though these were replaced by the present building in the 16th century, the continuity of the collection extends to the Vatican Library of today.

Reformation Losses. The libraries of Italy were to have a happier destiny than the medieval libraries north of the Alps. During the Reformation, people came to regard many libraries as representatives of an outmoded philosophy of learning and a hostile religion; some libraries fell into neglect and many others were destroyed. In England hundreds of monasteries were destroyed with the loss of almost all their books between 1536 and 1540—Durham Cathedral alone retaining an appreciable percentage—and from 1549 to 1551 the university collections were purged. In France and Germany, many libraries suffered similar dispersal and loss in the popular tumults and wars of the 16th and 17th centuries. The social and political upheavals of the French revolutionary era were hardly less destructive. While contemporaries rarely cared, posterity was to mourn the irreplaceable loss of a thousand years of cultural achievement.

REFERENCES

Anthony R. A. Hobson, *Great Libraries* (1970).
Raymond Irwin, *The Heritage of the English Library* (1964).
Burnett Hillman Streeter, *The Chained Library* (1970).
James Westfall Thompson, *The Medieval Library* (1957).
Francis Wormald and Cyril E. Wright, editors, *The English Library before 1700* (1958).
Medieval Scribes, Manuscripts and Libraries: Essays Presented to N. R. Ker (1978).

JOHN R. T. ETTLINGER

Milam, Carl H.
(1884–1963)

ALA
Carl H. Milam

Carl Hastings Milam held the principal executive position of the American Library Association from 1920 to 1948, first as Secretary and later as Executive Secretary. It may be difficult for anyone who was not involved closely with him during a considerable period of his career to appreciate his abilities as a librarian and administrator. His tenure at ALA spanned the 28 years from the end of World War I to the end of World War II and covered the period of rapid growth and change in both the Association and the profession of librarianship.

Milam was born in Harper County, Kansas, October 22, 1884. Although a native of Kansas and resident of Illinois during most of his adult years, Milam considered himself an Oklahoman, having lived there from 1893 to 1907. He attended the University of Oklahoma, where he worked as one of two student assistants to Milton Ferguson, then the only professional librarian on the staff of the University Library. He joined the ALA and, through Ferguson's influence, decided on a career in librarianship, entering the New York State Library School after his graduation from Oklahoma in 1907. After completing his studies, he worked as a cataloguer at Purdue University (1908–09).

When Chalmers Hadley resigned in September 1909 as Secretary and organizer of the Indiana Public Library Commission to become Secretary and Executive Officer of ALA, Milam followed him at the Commission. As Secretary at a time when many public libraries were being organized and needed Commission assistance, he provided advice both in his travels throughout the state and from headquarters in Indianapolis. He prepared reports and forms, spoke to various groups on behalf of libraries, developed programs for continuing education of librarians, and initiated the founding of the first state organization of public library trustees.

Milam resigned late in 1913 to accept the post of Librarian of the Public Library of Birmingham, Alabama, the largest in the state. In 1917 he took leave to work with the Library War Service in Washington,

D.C., but returned to Birmingham several times during his leave, finally resigning in 1919.

Milam was one of several assistants to Herbert Putnam, Director of the Library War Service, financed initially by the Carnegie Corporation of New York and by contributions to ALA of $50,000 from libraries and individuals. When Putnam went overseas after the Armistice in 1918, Milam became Acting Director; he succeeded Putnam as Director in 1919. Before and after the Armistice Milam worked long hours and showed his administrative abilities in recruiting, selecting, and assigning personnel, planning, policymaking, and public relations. He negotiated skillfully with army officers, government officials, nongovernmental agencies, and other representatives concerned with library service to armed service personnel in the United States and abroad.

Work with the Library War Service led Milam directly into ALA's Enlarged Program, of which he was named Director in 1919 and was thus at the same time Director of both the Library War Service, which was terminating its activities, and the Enlarged Program, which was just beginning. At its March 1920 meeting, the ALA Executive Board considered, among other matters, the resignation of George B. Utley as Secretary and a report by Milam as Director of both the Library War Service and the Enlarged Program. In his report Milam suggested the feasibility of consolidating the two programs in Chicago. The Board abolished the Enlarged Program directorship, merged the responsibilities of that program with those of the Secretary of ALA, and offered the new post to Milam. He became the 12th Secretary but only the 4th paid, full-time executive officer of the Association.

ALA membership grew from 4,460 in 1920 when Milam took office to 18,280 when he resigned in 1948. He served under 29 Presidents of ALA and was involved in many major reorganizations of the Association—beginning in 1923, through the first three Activities Committees, and through part of the changes that resulted from the investigations and reports of the Fourth Activities Committee (*see* American Library Association).

Milam had to organize a growing, diverse, and increasingly specialized staff to match the growth and diversification of ALA interests and activities. His energies were also directed toward the substantive matters that concerned the Association: improved library services; welfare, salaries, and annuities for librarians; technical bibliographical improvements; publishing; education for librarianship; international relations; better statistical measurements of effectiveness of libraries; federal aid for libraries; and a host of other concerns. In pursuit of the Association's interests, Milam developed strong working relationships with many foundations, including the Carnegie Corporation of New York, Carnegie Endowment for International Peace, Laura Spelman Rockefeller Memorial, Julius Rosenwald Foundation, General Education Board, and Rockefeller Foundation, as well as with federal agencies and congressional representatives. These relationships bore fruit in support for a wide range of large and small projects, including such major ones as endowment funds for ALA, federal aid for libraries, aid for foreign libraries affected by World War II, establishment of U.S. libraries abroad, and experimentation with microfilm and cooperative cataloguing. Milam also maintained a rapport with other national associations, including the Adult Education Association, the Special Libraries Association, and the Canadian Library Council and its successor, the Canadian Library Association.

Milam left his ALA post in 1948 to become Librarian of the United Nations Library. As Librarian from 1948 to 1950, he was responsible for its development from its early beginnings at Hunter College and Lake Success to its move to new quarters at the new UN headquarters in New York City. Milam believed that a legislative reference type of service should be developed primarily for the UN Secretariat and staff but that the Library might also serve other agencies, the communications media, international governmental agencies, and affiliated nongovernmental organizations, as well as educational institutions, scholars, and writers.

In 1950 Milam and his wife, the former Nell Robinson, whom he had married in 1910, retired to their farm near Barrington, Illinois. He grew irises and Christmas trees and engaged in some professional work, but the care of his wife, who died in 1956 of a progressively debilitating disease, came to require his constant attention.

In late 1961 he returned to New York for the dedication of the new UN Library building on the invitation of UN Secretary-General Dag Hammarskjöld. Milam was praised for his contributions to the organization, functioning, and continuing direction of the UN Library, then renamed the Dag Hammarskjöld Library.

Milam died in Barrington on August 26, 1963. The Carl H. Milam Memorial Lecture was established by ALA in 1971. Visiting foreign lecturers were invited to the U.S. to speak at library schools.

REFERENCES

Doris Cruger Dale, editor, *Carl H. Milam and the United Nations Library* (1976).

Peggy A. Sullivan, *Carl H. Milam and the American Library Association* (1976).

Peggy A. Sullivan, "Milam, Carl Hastings," *Dictionary of American Biography* (1978).

MARION A. MILCZEWSKI
(d. 1981)

Milkau, Fritz
(1859–1934)

Prussian—and German—librarianship since the end of the 19th century has been shaped considerably by Fritz Milkau, leading and representative librarian, library politician, and scholar.

Milkau was born in Lötzen, in eastern Prussia, September 28, 1859. He finished his university studies in classical, German, and Sanskrit philology with the Ph.D. in 1888. In the same year he started a highly successful library career in the University Library in Königsberg. His career led him later to Berlin, Bonn, Greifswald, Breslau, and Berlin again. His outstanding capacities as librarian were recommended early to Friedrich Althoff in the Prussian Ministry of Cultural Affairs, who at that time (1882–1907) was reforming the Prussian universities (including their libraries) and high schools. Althoff passed on to Milkau in 1895 the task of planning methods for organizing a union catalogue of Prussian libraries.

Milkau's publication *Zentralkataloge und Titeldrucke* ("Union Catalogues and Printed Catalogue Cards," 1898) presented the theoretical basis for that enormous undertaking. The *Instruktionen für die alphabetischen Kataloge der preussischen Bibliotheken und für den Preussischen Gesamtkatalog* ("Instructions for the Alphabetic Catalogue of Prussian Libraries and the Prussian Union Catalogue," 1899, the so-called Prussian Instructions) were substantially influenced by Milkau's ideas. They formed for many decades the frame not only for cataloguing principles in Germany and beyond but also for the description of titles in bibliographies—until they were replaced by the *Regeln für die alphabetische Katalogisierung* ("Rules for Alphabetic Cataloguing," 1977, called RAK).

From 1897 Milkau had to manage the Prussian Union Catalogue worked out on the basis of the catalogue of the Royal Library in Berlin. After three years of organizational work in the Prussian Ministry of Cultural Affairs, he was appointed Director of the University Library Greifswald in 1902 and in 1907 Director of the University Library Breslau. Both libraries flourished under his guidance and special collections for Lower German literature (in Greifswald) and Slavic literature (in Breslau) were started and enlarged under his direction. During and just after World War I, Milkau was sent to Belgium to deal with the protection of libraries from the consequences of war.

When Adolf von Harnack left office as Director General of the Prussian State Library (the former Royal Library) in Berlin in 1921, Milkau succeeded him. This was the leading position in Prussian academic and research libraries, and Milkau used it for manifold activities.

From 1911 he had been a member of the Prussian Beirat für Bibliotheksangelegenheiten (Advisory Council for Library Affairs); as its Chairman, after World War I, Milkau was in a position to strengthen considerably the central position of the Prussian State Library in Germany. Among the results was the decision to publish the Prussian Union Catalogue (1925), the manuscript of which had been completed in 1922. Milkau's *Denkschrift vom 30. Juli 1913 betr. die Kataloge der Preussischen Bibliotheken und ihre Reform durch den Druck des Gesamtkatalogs* ("Memorandum of July 30, 1913, regarding the Catalogues of the Prussian Libraries and their Reformation through the Printing of the Union Catalogue," 1925) was followed for this project. Milkau also began publishing the *Gesamtkatalog der Wiegendrucke* ("Union Catalogue of Incunabula"), in preparation since 1904; the first volume appeared in 1925.

In 1920 the Notgemeinschaft der deutschen Wissenschaft (Emergency Community for German Academic Research) was founded and Milkau became the first Chairman of its Library Committee. During and after the period of devastating inflation in the 1920s, that institution provided additional funds for the purchase of foreign publications, at first for the state libraries in Berlin and Munich and later also for German university libraries.

Milkau's responsibilities thus extended beyond the borders of Prussian libraries. He expanded the Prussian interlibrary loan system to other parts of Germany on the basis of the first German *Leihverkehrsordnung* ("Regulations for Interlibrary Loan"), put into operation in 1924.

In 1925 Milkau retired from his position in the Prussian State Library. The Faculty of Arts at the University of Berlin nominated him Honorary Professor of Library Science. Milkau's lectures concentrated on library history, which he considered, together with book history, as the core of library science. Engaged for many years in the reform of the librarian's theoretical education in Prussia, he achieved in 1928 the foundation of an Institute of Library Science connected with that Faculty and stayed as its Head until 1933. The courses given there were intended especially for library candidates for the Prussian state examination, preparing them as subject specialists. New state regulations for this purpose based on Milkau's ideas were issued in 1930. But it was not possible in those years to include those studies in the regular university curricula.

Milkau laid the theoretical foundations of the discipline he taught in the *Handbuch der Bibliothekswissenschaft* ("Handbook of Library Science," 1931–42, 2nd edition 1952–65). He edited the first two volumes, on script and book (1931) and on library management (1933); the third volume, on library history, did not appear until 1940. In this huge monument of scholarship, Milkau did not intend to analyze and define library science in detail but to present in clear order knowledge of the subject from the historical and philological points of view. His emphasis on book and library history as the best way to approach library science did not survive to the present, but the "Handbook" can be considered one of the important cornerstones of the discipline.

To library history, Milkau contributed especially with a comprehensive study on libraries in the collection *Die Kultur der Gegenwart* ("The Contemporary Culture," 1906, 2nd edition 1912), in which he stressed the coherence of their history with general cultural developments. His *Geschichte der Bibliotheken im alten Orient* ("History of Libraries in the Ancient Orient," 1935) was later included in a revised version in the second edition of the "Handbook" (1953).

He died in Berlin on January 23, 1934. A lover of the book as a work of art, he had a deep sense of duty, order, thoroughness, and self-discipline. Milkau was a representative of the traditional, conservative ideas of his time. But, engaged actively in pursuing new and important developments in academic and research libraries, he was successful in achieving remarkable results through his talent to convince people with striking arguments. His eloquence and ingenious formulations gave force and authority to his writing. Milkau also stressed the importance to the public of libraries as cultural and national institutions, a result of his personal engagement. His contributions were perceived and appreciated outside Germany.

REFERENCES

Fritz Milkau zum Gedächtnis. Ansprachen, Vorträge und Verzeichnis seiner Schriften, edited by Gustav Abb (1934).

Handbuch der Bibliothekswissenschaft, 2nd edition, edited by Georg Leyh, vol. 2 (1961).

Zeitschrift für Bibliothekswesen und Bibliographie (1984). *Zentralblatt für Bibliothekswesen* (1934, 1979, 1985).

PAUL KAEGBEIN

Foster E. Mohrhardt

Mohrhardt, Foster E.

(1907–1992)

Foster E. Mohrhardt, American librarian and administrator, national library director, and officer in national and international library and documentation associations, whose career stretched from junior college libraries to national and international library planning, has been called the premier librarian-diplomat of the United States.

He was born in Lansing, Michigan, March 7, 1907. His higher education began at Michigan State University with a B.A. in 1929, as well as with student assistance experience that led him to Columbia for a B.S. in library science the next year. He returned for an M.A. from the University of Michigan in 1933. There he found a role model and mentor in the University's distinguished Librarian, William Warner Bishop, who had been President of ALA and of IFLA. Mohrhardt later wrote of Bishop as "our first international librarian."

In 1935 the Carnegie Corporation of New York appointed Bishop chairman of an Advisory Group on Junior College Libraries. The junior college at that time was fairly new in higher education, and the Corporation proposed to stimulate interest in its proper development by a series of support grants for book purchases. Bishop recalled Mohrhardt from a brief stint on the library and teaching staff of Colorado State College at Greeley to become his assistant on the project. Mohrhardt was involved in site visits across the country and became compiler of the Group's enduring work, *List of Books for Junior College Libraries,* published by ALA in 1937.

This task led to his appointment as Librarian of Washington and Lee University in 1938. He remained there until 1946, with an interlude of wartime service. During his tenure at Lexington the new Cyrus Hall McCormick Library was completed, and in 1942 the Trustees established the Robert E. Lee Archives Division to enhance the Library's existing collections of Lee materials. A dramatic development occurred in 1941 when the Library of Congress was seeking safe hostelry, against possible war damage, for its more valuable holdings. Washington and Lee had excess stack space which Mohrhardt made available for this evacuation service. A key LC officer at the time was Verner Clapp, and this emergency experience led to a long and close friendship between the two, who later had parallel careers as officials of national libraries, as Council on Library Resources officers, and as library advisers to the Japanese government.

Following on a 1947–48 visiting professorship at Columbia's library school, Mohrhardt began his productive Washington career. From 1948 to 1954 he was Director of Library Services for the far-flung Veterans Administration, with responsibility for 450 separate collections serving both patients and professional staff in the U.S. and abroad. There he streamlined book procurement and cataloguing systems and gained such skill in the federal service that in 1954 he succeeded the redoubtable Ralph Shaw as Director of the U.S. Department of Agriculture Library, a position Mohrhardt held until 1968.

In 1962, its centennial year, this library was rechristened as the National Agricultural Library. To some extent the change was related to developments generally in the country; the former Army Medical Library had become the National Library of Medicine (NLM) in 1956. More significant in this shift of title was Mohrhardt's successful vision of the library as serving a national, even an international, role in providing bibliographic information and library services to the bio-agricultural community.

Reflecting in a 1967 lecture at Louisiana State University on his aspirations for NAL, he listed: national library coordination with LC and NLM; development of a national library network with the land-grant colleges; a systems study, as well as the design of an agricultural-biological thesaurus, looking toward the automation of library functions, including bibliographic services; and the establishment of intensive specialized information centers. By the time he left NAL those aspirations had been realized. One of his visible monuments is the multi-volume *Dictionary Catalog* of NAL holdings 1862–1965, with the newly automated *Bibliography of Agriculture* carrying on from that point; another is the Pesticide Information Center; and towering above all this activity is the NAL building in Beltsville, Maryland, opened in 1969.

Mohrhardt's vision and forum were worldwide. In 1955 he was central to the founding of the International Association of Agricultural Librarians and Documentalists, and he became its first President, serving until 1969. Thereby he was instrumental in launching *World Agricultural Economics and Sociology Abstracts,* and in 1965 the third World Congress of Agricultural Librarians and Documentalists was held in Washington with Mohrhardt in the Chair.

For services of this order he was granted USDA's Distinguished Service Award in 1963 "for unusual vision, competence and accomplishment in evolving and promoting a dynamic agricultural library program for the department and the nation, and for exceptional leadership." In the same year he became the first librarian to serve as a Vice-President of the American Association for the Advancement of Science. Then in 1977 an International Symposium was convened at NAL in Mohrhardt's honor, resulting in the Festschrift volume *International Agricultural Librarianship: Continuity and Change* (Greenwood Press, 1979).

During those fruitful NAL years he served the profession with equal distinction: President of ARL 1966; President of ALA 1967–68, Vice-President of IFLA 1965–71, President of the National Federation of Scientific Abstracting and Indexing Services 1964–65, and Chairman of the U.S. National Commission for FID in 1965.

Early on, this librarian-diplomat's focus of international service was in Asia, especially Japan. During his tenure NAL published catalogues of its Japanese, Korean, and Chinese holdings, and he was a key figure at a number of conferences focusing on higher education, library development, and scientific and publications exchange with Japan. In consequence the Japanese government in 1980 awarded him the Order of the Rising Sun, and later he was named Honorary Librarian of the highly experimental new library of Kanazawa Institute of Technology.

Mohrhardt's diplomatic skill proved evident as well in his uncommon ability to build bridges of understanding and creative activity between the often disparate fields of librarianship and documentation. He may be the only librarian to have served as a high officer in both IFLA and FID.

In 1968 Fred C. Cole, then the new President of the Council on Library Resources, tapped Mohrhardt for appointment as Senior Program Officer, later Consultant, for the Council, a post well suited for his notable understanding of national and international library development, as well as of research and higher education.

A charming and effective American emissary to world librarianship, Mohrhardt won admiration for a sparkling manner and personal warmth and public grace, spiced with what some styled a delightfully Pickwickian appearance. Mohrhardt died in June 1992.

ROBERT VOSPER

Moore, Anne Carroll

(1871–1961)

The New York Public Library
Anne Carroll Moore

Anne Carroll Moore, children's librarian, author, editor, and critic, formed the Children's Department of the New York Public Library, made many contributions to a new profession, and had significant influence on the creation and publishing of children's literature in the United States.

She was born July 12, 1871, in Limerick, Maine, and was christened Annie. Years later, at the suggestion of her editor, she changed Annie to Anne in order to avoid confusion with Annie E. Moore, who was engaged in a related field of work. In *Roads to Childhood* (1920) she wrote about her parents, her seven older brothers, and especially the influence her father had on her childhood and youth. In her home her lawyer-father read aloud, there were vigorous family discussions, she had her own books, and there always seemed to be a family celebration. When she was ten years old, she was sent to Limerick Academy; "No doubt it was the Academy that gave Anne early control of a lucid style in speaking and writing that was to make her a distinctive critic and essayist in her day," according to her biographer, Frances Clarke Sayers. Moore entered Bradford Academy in 1889, completed her courses in two years, and graduated in 1891. She returned to Limerick to read law with her father, but the death of both parents brought that plan to an end.

In 1895 she entered Pratt Institute in Brooklyn, New York, for library training. At the end of this period Mary Wright Plummer, Director of the Pratt Institute Free Library, asked her to become Librarian of the Children's Room—"the first in the country to be included in an architect's plan, and the first to make the circulation of books subordinate to familiar acquaintance with books and pictures in a free library" (*Horn Book,* January-February 1942). Her years there were marked by bringing together children, books, and pictures. Moore was not content to know the children who came to the library; she went where they were—to the schools, settlement houses, streets. She established the Children's Library as a focal part of the community. When the room was closed to circulation, she read aloud to the children. Reading aroused an interest in storytelling and, though she never attempted to tell a story herself, she recognized its value in introducing children to stories. She was convinced of it when she heard Marie Shedlock, the great English storyteller, tell Andersen's stories.

Moore took storytelling to the New York Public Library when she was asked to form a children's department there. She reported to work on September 1, 1906. Her first responsibility was to bring together under her leadership all those who in any way had been assigned to work with children. At the same time she visited the 36 branches in Manhattan, the Bronx, and Staten Island. She began immediately to train those working with children, lecturing on such subjects as open shelves, reading aloud, book selection, and administration—all pioneering in children's work. Five years later, May 23, 1911, the main library at 5th Avenue and 42nd Street was opened, and in it was a Central Children's Room. Over the years this room was to become nationally and internationally known for its collections, staff, programs, and influence on authors and illustrators. Meanwhile, Moore was also guiding the growth of work in the branches so that upon her retirement she had one of the strongest children's departments in the U.S.

Her contributions to the profession were many. In 1900 she was chosen as President of the first Round Table organization of librarians actually in charge of children's work at the American Library Association's Annual Conference in Montreal, and in 1901, at the invitation of ALA, the Round Table became a section of ALA and Moore was its first Chairman. She had been active since her first ALA Conference in 1896. In the fall of 1918 Franklin K. Mathiews of the Boy Scouts of America and Frederic Melcher, Editor of *Publisher's Weekly,* went to Moore's office to discuss a plan to encourage authors of children's books and to interest others in the children's book world. Children's Book Week, later known as Book Week, was devised in order to celebrate books and reading. There followed the Caldecott and Newbery medals, which Frederic Melcher established under ALA auspices. In 1918 Ben W. Huebsch, a prominent publisher, asked Moore to prepare and deliver a series of lectures to a group of distinguished book people—heads of publishing firms, editors, booksellers, writers, artists—on the subject of children's books. Also in 1918 Macmillan announced the first separate department for publishing children's books under Louise Seaman Bechtel, a close associate of Moore. In the years that followed, Moore worked closely with children's editors and their authors and illustrators. She exposed her staff, through meetings and branch library visits, to many of the great literary figures of the day. Her staff and exhibits in Central Children's Room represented many nations, and she had enduring friendships with such book people as Beatrix Potter, Leslie Brooke, Walter de la Mare, Padraic Colum, and Ruth Sawyer Durand.

In 1918 *The Bookman,* the chief American literary journal of its day, asked Moore to contribute articles and reviews of children's books at regular intervals. There had been frequent but sporadic reviewing of children's books by distinguished writers and illustrators, but, up to that time, there had been a lack of sustained criticism of children's books. She did so from 1918 to 1926. From 1924 to 1930 Moore edited a weekly page of criticism of children's books in *Books* of the *New York Herald Tribune*. Its logo was "The Three Owls," and subsequent books by her carried that title. In 1936 she offered "The Three Owls Notebook" as well as her editorial advice to the *Horn Book*. Her page was last published in 1960, but she continued as one of the Associate Editors. She also contributed lists and articles to journals and publications too numerous to name here. It would be difficult to measure the stimulating effect of such criticism upon the writing, illustrating, and publishing of children's books.

Moore retired from the New York Public Library on October 1, 1941. She died on January 20, 1961, in New York City. According to Frances Clarke Sayers, "One person more than any other gave shape and content to the new profession, to the greatest degree and in the fullest measure: Anne Carroll Moore, of Brooklyn's Pratt Institute and the New York Public Library. To be sure, confluence of period and place set the stage for her achievement, but the color and character of her accomplishment derived from the quality of her imagination; her courage and stubborn determination; her shrewd, New England practicality; her logical, analytical mind, which, like a pyrotechnical display, could turn and light up the sky with its rocketing commitment to joy."

Moore's books include *Nicholas: A Manhattan Christmas Story,* with drawings by Jay Van Everen (1924); *Nicholas and the Golden Goose,* with drawings by Van Everen (1932); and an Introduction to *The Art of Beatrix Potter* (1954).

Moore edited *Roads to Childhood* (1920); *New Roads to Childhood* (1923); *Cross Roads to Childhood (1926);* and *My Roads to Childhood: Views and Reviews of Children's Books* (1939). Others include *The Three Owls: A Book about Children's Books* (1925); *The Three Owls, Second Book* (1928); *The Three Owls, Third Book* (1931); *Knickerbocker's History of New York,* by Washington Irving, illustrated by Daugherty (1928); and *The Bold Dragoon and Other Ghostly Tales,* by Washington Irving, illustrated by Daugherty (1930). "Children's Books Suggested as Holiday Gifts," published by the New York Public Library as an annual list, was edited by Anne Carroll Moore from 1918 to 1941. She issued other lists and wrote many articles.

Moore received honorary degrees (Pratt, 1955; University of Maine, 1940), the Regina Medal of the Catholic Library Association (1960), and other honors, including the first Constance Lindsay Skinner Gold Medal from the Women's National Book Association (1940).

REFERENCES

Frances Clarke Sayers, *Anne Carroll Moore* (1972).

Adele M. Fasick, "Moore, Anne Carroll," *Dictionary of American Library Biography* (1978).

AUGUSTA BAKER

Rubens Borba Alves de Moraes

Moraes, Rubens Borba Alves de

(1899–1986)

Rubens Borba Alves de Moraes, General Director of the National Library of Brazil, Director of the UN Library in New York, educator, author, and editor, was responsible for significant innovations and development in Brazilian libraries.

Moraes was born in Araraquara, in the state of São Paulo, January 23, 1899. He studied at the Collège de l'Université de Genève, Switzerland, where he received the degree of *licencié en lettres* in 1919. His first work was written in French and published in Switzerland. When he returned to São Paulo, Moraes associated himself with a group of avant-garde writers and artists. He participated in the celebrated Week of Modern Art in 1922 and collaborated in journals of the Brazilian Modernist movement. He was one of the founders of the futurist periodical *Klaxon* (1922–23). In 1932 he participated in the constitutionalist revolution against the federal government.

In 1934, with a fellowship from the Rockefeller Foundation, he studied library organization and operation in the United States. Returning to São Paulo in 1935, he was appointed Director of the Municipal Public Library, and in 1936 he established the first university course in library science, with a U.S. orientation. In 1938 he founded the São Paulo Librarians Association. He reorganized São Paulo's public library in a modern building, planned and built under his guidance, and directed its opening in 1942. A year later he published *O problema das bibliotecas brasileiras* (1943), a comparative essay on European, American, and Brazilian libraries in which he introduced the concept of the library network as a solution to the problems of Brazilian libraries.

From 1945 to 1947 he was the General Director of the National Library in Rio de Janeiro. He introduced the dictionary catalogue, the Dewey Decimal Classification, free access by readers to reference collections, and a more liberal philosophy in relations with the public. During this same period, he was Professor of Bibliography and Reference in the National Library course.

In 1947 he was invited by the United Nations to direct the UN Information Service in Paris, where he remained until 1951. During this time he published the *Manual bibliográfico de estudos brasileiros* (1949), which he edited with William Berrien. This collective work was the first critical survey of Brazilian studies in the fields of humanities and social sciences and contained contributions by Brazilian and foreign experts. He then became the Director of the UN Library in New York City, a position he held until 1959. From 1963 to 1970 he was a professor at the University of Brasilia, teaching the history of books and libraries and Brazilian bibliography. During his teaching career he published *Bibliografia brasileira do periodo colonial* (1969), a critical bibliography of Brazilian works published before 1808. In 1971 the University awarded him the title of Professor Emeritus. In 1975 he was elected Honorary President of the 8th Brazilian Congress of Librarianship and Documentation, held in Brasilia.

Moraes' other major publications include the *Bibliographia brasiliana* (1958–59; 2nd edition revised, 1979), a bibliographical essay written in English on rare books about Brazil, and *O bibliofilo aprendiz* (1965), an introductory guide for those who wish to collect rare books, ancient or modern. In addition to his important contributions to Brazilian librarianship and bibliography, Moraes translated, introduced, and edited a number of works by foreign authors about Brazil and São Paulo in two serials, the *Biblioteca Historica Brasileira* and the *Biblioteca Historica Paulista.*

His *Livros e bibliotecas no Brasil colonial* (1979) covers libraries, book printing, and commerce in colonial Brazil. Moraes died on September 11, 1986 at Itapira, São Paulo, Brazil.

EDSON NERY DA FONSECA

Morel, Eugène
(1869–1934)

Best known for his untiring efforts to promote free public libraries in France, Eugène Morel was a versatile leader whose contributions touched virtually every aspect of librarianship. His most notable achievements included the first application of the Dewey Decimal Classification in a French public library, the organization of the first course of lectures on modern librarianship, and the reform of the French copyright deposit law in 1925. He was also an ardent advocate of information services in libraries, a promoter of children's work, and one of the first French librarians to call for the employment of women in public libraries. Morel's innovative ideas extended to library mechanization, and he was always eager to experiment with the new technology of his time, from filmstrips and microphotographic film to mechanical processes that would facilitate research work or duplicate catalogue cards.

Born in Paris June 21, 1869, Morel grew up in a milieu where his artistic and literary interests were encouraged. While a student at the Lycée Charlemagne, he showed a great talent for literature and for foreign languages, particularly German. At an early age he had begun to study English with his mother, who had grown up in London. In search of a profession that would allow him a certain amount of leisure to devote to writing, Morel was encouraged by his mother to study law. Just 20 when he began his law career, Morel had already published his first novel and was becoming known for his contributions to literary journals. In 1892 he abandoned law for a post at the Bibliothèque Nationale that allowed him time to continue his literary pursuits. By 1905 he had already published nine novels, and had served as Editor of the *Revue d'Art Dramatique* (1900–03). He also wrote plays for the popular theater. His potential as a writer was appreciated by such contemporaries as Romain Rolland and his work was encouraged by established authors, including Jules Verne. When an interviewer reported that Leo Tolstoy had cited Eugène Morel as "one of the most original" French novelists, the young man's literary success seemed assured. In the meantime, Morel began to turn his energies toward a new goal—the establishment of free public libraries in France.

Morel later recalled his first unpremeditated visit to a London public library on a rainy night in 1895 when a sudden storm forced him to take shelter. On his return to Paris, Morel was disappointed to find that his enthusiasm for free public libraries was not shared by his colleagues, who were either indifferent or skeptical that France would ever provide enough funding to offer the kinds of library services available in Britain. For more than a decade Morel systematically gathered data on library development abroad, which he published to stimulate public interest in improving French libraries. After publishing articles in several influential journals, he finally issued his famous and highly polemical work entitled *Bibliothèques* in 1908. This two-volume comparative "essay" dealt with all aspects of library development in France, Great Britain, and the United States. Despite the caustic style of the work, it was unquestionably well documented, with many tables, statistics, and budgets. The biting tone of Morel's work ensured that its content could not be ignored. One leading librarian charged that Morel's brilliant imagination as a novelist led him to champion reforms that were "pure utopias" while another conservative colleague described Morel's book as "passionate, highly colored, brutal and shocking."

Eugène Morel

Other library leaders were much more sympathetic to Morel's views, and he soon attracted a few colleagues, educators, and writers who were also eager to promote free public libraries. At the urging of these supporters and enthusiasts, Morel began to condense his study, eliminating discussion of academic and research libraries. The result of these efforts was *La Librarie Publique* (1910), later described as the first book in France to be devoted entirely to public libraries. In his choice of title for this pioneering work, Morel intentionally avoided the word *bibliothèque* with its scholarly connotations and attempted to repatriate the word *librairie,* which had been adopted by the English. Although Morel discussed many British libraries, which he knew firsthand, he did not hesitate to affirm that *la librarie publique* was "an American invention." Caught up by the missionary fervor of his U.S. colleagues, Morel painted an idealistic portrait of American libraries—"free, absolutely free, open all day, every day and evening . . . not waiting for the public to come, going out to [the public] . . . they are for the grown man what the school is for the child."

In order to create such libraries in France, Morel felt that propaganda was essential. He therefore organized a series of conferences aimed at the general public as well as librarians, booksellers, scholars, and bibliophiles. This lecture series, held at the École des Hautes Études Sociales each year from 1910 to 1914, was cosponsored by the French library association and by the publishers' society. Much to Morel's satisfaction, the conferences also attracted the interest of certain municipalities, and in 1911 he received an invitation to recatalogue the municipal library of Levallois-Perret. This working-class, industrial community on the northern outskirts of Paris offered Morel the first opportunity to introduce France to the Dewey Decimal Classification, which had been "rejected without being known." Morel's classified catalogue was published in 1913; six months after it appeared, both consultation of books and circulation figures had doubled, while the loan of nonfiction works rose from 3 to 40 percent of all books borrowed. This change—which was all the more impressive considering that the public did not have open access to the shelves—further convinced Morel that American library methods could be successfully adapted in France. Because Morel and many of his colleagues were mobilized in 1914, experimentation with open-access public libraries did not begin in earnest until after World War I. Morel's election as President of the Association des Bibliothécaires Français (French library association) in 1918 marked a softening of old antagonisms in the field at a time when there was growing public interest in modernizing and democratizing French libraries as a part of postwar reconstruction.

In 1920 when an American war relief agency, the Comité Américaine pour des Régions Devastées (CARD), prepared to inaugurate its most important model public library in Aisne, Morel was invited to participate in the ceremonies. From that point on, Morel was instrumental in publicizing the success of the American model libraries; he also served on the French Committee for the Modern Library, gained support to send young French women to study in U.S. library schools, and later became a lecturer at the Paris Library School, run by ALA from 1923 to 1929.

The Pierpont Morgan Library
J. Pierpont Morgan

Morel passed more than four decades of his professional career at the Bibliothèque Nationale, where his work on the reform of the copyright deposit law was considered his most important accomplishment. Morel's influences however, extended beyond the national library, and his leadership was especially valued by an energetic cadre of public librarians who were attempting to put his ideas into practice in a handful of Parisian and provincial municipal libraries. Unfortunately, Morel did not live to see this movement extended throughout France following the creation of a national library directorate in 1945. Although not alone in the reforms he advocated, Morel was frequently ahead of his time. In a comparative study of public library development, the French scholar Jean Hassenforder remarked:

> In vitality and stature Eugène Morel of France was the equal of the great British and American pioneers, Edward Edwards and Melvil Dewey, and it was he who introduced to France the principles of modern librarianship. In all probability the reason these three were not equally influential was ascribable to the milieu more than personality. Eugène Morel was up against the French mentality of his time.

During Morel's lifetime, his reputation abroad was equal to or greater than his influence in France. In 1912 he was named an Honorary Fellow by the British Library Assistants' Association, and in 1926 he was designated the official French delegate to ALA's 50th anniversary conference. His ideas were also widely discussed in Belgium, where his book *Bibliothèques* was the inspiration for the passage of a 1921 law (*Loi Destrée*) described as the first compulsory library law on the continent. Morel was also an active member of the French affiliate of the International Institute of Bibliography created by Otlet and LaFontaine. Always interested in bibliographic control and scholarly communication, Morel submitted proposals for the improvement of international publishing and library statistics at the first IFLA conference in Rome in 1929. He further developed those ideas at the 10th Annual Conference on Bibliography in 1931 in The Hague, where he presented an important report warning against the misuse of statistics in bibliometric analysis.

When Morel died in Paris on March 23, 1934, his loss was keenly felt by a small but dynamic group of "modernist" librarians and documentalists in France and abroad.

REFERENCES

Gaetan Benoit, "Eugène Morel: 1869–1934: His Life and Work," *Libri* (1980).

Jean Hassenforder, *Développement comparé des bibliothèques publiques en France, en Grande-Bretagne et aux Etats-Unis dans la seconde moitié du XIXe siècle (1850–1914)* (1967).

MARY NILES MAACK

Morgan, J. Pierpont
(1837–1913)

One of the outstanding 19th-century American collectors of rare books and manuscripts, John Pierpont Morgan created one of the major research libraries in the U.S. His role as collector evolved from several fortuitous circumstances—a well-to-do father, an international education, and a time of economic expansion. In Morgan's time, big American corporations needed capital funds; the House of Morgan arranged capital for railroad, steel, banking, and insurance companies. Morgan was an aristocrat who dominated every situation with his powerful personality.

Morgan was born in Hartford, Connecticut, April 17, 1837, and studied in Germany at the University of Göttingen. His first acquisition was typical for a 14-year-old—a presidential signature, that of President Millard Fillmore. The collection grew slowly during Morgan's first 45 years. On the death of his father, Junius Spencer Morgan (1890), and the formation of the firm of J. P. Morgan & Company in 1895, Morgan began to buy on a grand scale.

Junius Morgan had been a collector and owned a George Washington letter as well as the original manuscript of Sir Walter Scott's *Guy Mannering*. Pierpont Morgan's interest was probably stimulated by his father's possessions. That interest was further enhanced by the efforts of his nephew, another Junius Morgan, who was an ardent collector of books, prints, and manuscripts, including an unequaled collection of Virgil. Over the next several decades, the collection grew apace, with group and individual purchases, each adhering to the principle of selectivity first established.

Examples of the acquisitions include a Gutenberg Bible on vellum, the 1459 Mainz Psalter (for many years the only copy in the U.S.), the four Shakespeare Folios, and the original autograph manuscripts of Keats's *Endymion* and Dickens's *A Christmas Carol*. Collections purchased en bloc included a fine run of Aldine imprints in hand-tooled leather bindings. Several collections of manuscripts were acquired, including the Duke of Hamilton's famous "Golden Gospels" and a choice group of 270 Rembrandt etchings. By 1905 Morgan had purchased some 700 incunabula, among them 40 from the press of William Caxton. The collection now holds more than 60 Caxtons, five of them unique. Besides the printed works and manuscripts, the Morgan collections include outstanding early written records such as seals, tablets, and papyri. The collections are unusual—a high percentage of the holdings are unique copies.

In 1906 Morgan had a library building constructed adjacent to his New York home at 36th Street and Madison Avenue in New York City. Designed by the noted architectural firm of McKim, Mead, and White, it is styled as a Renaissance palazzo. With a grandiose interior that has been carefully preserved, the J. Pierpont Morgan Library has become a noted landmark. The original building was expanded with a large annex in 1928, and additions were built in 1962 and 1977.

After the books and manuscripts were moved into the new building, Morgan seemed determined to increase the scale and depth of his collection. Joining him in this effort was a talented librarian, Belle DaCosta Greene, who became a model as a private collector's librarian. She served 43 years in the post, guiding the growth of the library during the time of the transition from a private collection to an invaluable research resource. Morgan died in Rome on March 31, 1913.

The Library sponsors many publications and exhibits and supports an active research program; its vast resources are available at the Library to scholars. The success of the Morgan Library probably far exceeded the founder's vision of its usefulness.

REFERENCES

An Introduction to the Pierpont Morgan Library (1974).

Francis Henry Taylor, *Pierpont Morgan as Collector and Patron, 1837–1913* (1957).

DONALD D. HENDRICKS

Morocco

Morocco, a constitutional monarchy in northwestern Africa, is bounded on the north by the Mediterranean Sea, on the east by Algeria, on the south by Mauritania, and on the west by the Atlantic Ocean. Population (1990 est.) 25,061,000; area 446,550 sq.km. The official language is Arabic, but French is widely spoken.

History and National Library Services. Morocco was a major center of medieval Islamic culture, but modern library services began only in the 20th century. Parts of what are now Morocco were ruled by the French and by Spanish authorities until the monarchy gained independence in 1956. Founded in Rabat in 1920, the Bibliothèque Générale et Archives de Maroc (BGA) played an important part in the development of the country's libraries. Based initially on the collections of the Moroccan Institute of Higher Studies, it has developed special strengths in studies of the Maghreb and Muslim west. Over time it also developed a collection of humanities, science, and general interest material, primarily for European readers. Established in 1926, it gradually acquired the functions of a national library, serving as an administrative archive and supervising public libraries. By the early 1990s its holdings had reached 300,000 volumes, 7,400 periodicals, and 30,000 manuscripts. The BGA publishes the national bibliography.

The Spanish-language equivalent of the BGA, the Tétouan General Library, was founded in 1939. Its specialized collection on the area, mostly in Spanish and Arabic, totals more than 60,000 volumes, 2,200 periodicals, and 1,500 manuscripts. Its archives hold some 80,000 historic and administrative documents and 35,000 photographs. It supervises the public libraries in Asilah, Larache, Ksar el Kebir, and Tangier.

After independence, the Ministry of Cultural Affairs assumed responsibility for library services. In 1990 it conducted a study on establishing a national library separate from the BGA.

National Documentation Center. The Centre Nationale de Documentation (CND) was established in 1968 as the first step toward a Moroccan national information system under the Unesco NATIS program. Supervised by the Ministry of Planning, the CND gradually expanded its role from an agricultural documentation center to coordinator of all national

Libraries in Morocco (1987)

Type of library	Number of administrative units (main libraries)	Volumes in collections	Professional staff (with certificate, diploma, etc.)	Total staff
National	+ CND 2	500,000* 6,000** 24,500***	+ CND 32	189
Academic	107	18,760* 598** 2,680***	51	668
Public	68	11,066* 81** 1,070***	4	335
School	474	6,570* 2** 1,261***	0	581
Special	190	2,217* 101** 5,794***	115	739
Other[a]	49	41,320* 673** 6,854***	19	442

[a]Any library having a collection of documents that isn't included in the series of libraries given above
*Monographs
**Periodicals
***Plans, maps, archives files, microfiches, films, slides, sound recordings, etc.

and international documentation services in the country dealing with economic and social development, especially in science and technology. Since 1982 the CND has created seven online access points at regional branches of the Ministry of Planning to permit decentralized access to its information sources. It maintains databases covering bibliographic references, periodical indexes, libraries and documentation centers in Morocco, documents, full-text items, and an ISSN index to periodical articles. It is linked to 160 international databases. The CND annually codes 150,000 references onto electronic media and conducts about 3,500 searches. Its collection includes 6,900 volumes and 620 periodicals. It is a founding member of ARISNET and MAGHREBNET and is responsible for the North Africa Regional Technical Committee of PADIS.

Academic Libraries. A survey by the École des Sciences de l'Information (ESI) and the CND in 1986 indicated that the universities, faculties, and institutes of higher education in the country had 107 libraries. Service is decentralized, with each faculty having its own library. The most famous is the Kairouyyin (Quarouine) University in Fez, founded in 1400 and now attached to the Ministry of Cultural Affairs. Its collections in the early 1990s totaled about 17,000 volumes, 450 periodicals, 2,000 manuscripts, and 5,600 microforms. Newer universities include the Université Mohammed V, the Université Sidi Mohammed Ben Abdellah, the Université Mohammed I, the Université Cado Ayyad, and the Université Hassan II. Altogether the academic libraries serve about 140,000 students and 5,800 faculty members.

Public Libraries. The 1986 survey by ESI and CND identified 68 public libraries throughout the country, run by the Ministry of Cultural Affairs, municipalities, other government bodies, foreign agencies, and cultural associations. Only 10 date to the period before independence; the first three were opened in Casablanca in 1918, in Fez in 1920, and in Marrakesh in 1923, then two in Tétouan in 1937 and 1939.

The books and periodicals in government-supported libraries are almost all in Arabic; those in the foreign cultural centers are mainly in the languages associated with them (French, English, Spanish, German, and Russian). The French cultural centers in Rabat and Fez organize programs for children.

School Libraries. Of the more than 470 school libraries identified in 1986, only five were in elementary schools, serving 2,200,000 pupils and 83,000 teachers. The secondary-school libraries serve 1,200,000 pupils and 77,000 teachers and administrative employees. In Rabat, where 80 percent of the secondary schools have libraries, the collections averaged 1,300 works, chiefly schoolbooks.

Special Libraries. Morocco has 190 special libraries and 49 archives centers. They have a vital place in the national information system, serving decision makers in agriculture, mining, industry, education, and social services. Only about 30 of them date to the period before independence. The oldest, a private library, was founded in 1917 by the Association of Public Works and Buildings. Government agencies have set up many of the newer special libraries.

The Royal Library contains a collection of historic archives and Arabic manuscripts and the Libraries of

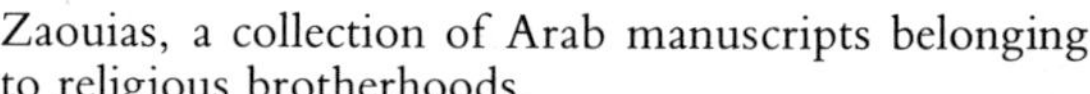

Zaouias, a collection of Arab manuscripts belonging to religious brotherhoods.

The Profession. The École des Sciences de l'Information (ESI) was founded in 1974 to train professionals for service in libraries, documentation centers, and archives. The ESI offers programs at both undergraduate and graduate levels. The four-year undergraduate program in information science, related disciplines, and languages, with field work in information and documentation institutions, leads to the degree of *Informatiste.* The two-year graduate program, designed for students holding a first degree in information science or some other discipline, includes a final research paper and leads to the degree of *Informatiste Specialisé.* The ESI works with the Association Nationale des Informatistes (ANI; National Association of Information Specialists), formed in 1973, to provide continuing professional education for its graduates.

The ESI is noted for its model library, with 10,000 monographs, 300 periodicals, and audiovisual and electronic data materials in information science and related fields. As part of its automation program, which emphasizes the use of microcomputers, the library has an online connection to the CND. The ESI is an active member of several international associations and has cooperative study agreements with schools of library and information sciences in Canada, France, Saudi Arabia, Sweden, the United Kingdom, and the United States.

LOLA SOUAD

Morton, Elizabeth Homer
(1903–1977)

Canadian Library Association
Elizabeth Homer Morton

Elizabeth Homer Morton was the founding Executive Director of the Canadian Library Association. She was the best-known Canadian librarian of her generation and perhaps the most esteemed, as much for her qualities of heart and mind as for her formal achievements.

Born February 3, 1903, in Tunapuna, Trinidad, of Canadian parentage, Morton was privately educated until 1919. She did her high school studies in Saint John, New Brunswick, and then took an arts degree (1926) at Dalhousie University in Halifax, Nova Scotia. Brief service as a teacher in Cape Breton, Nova Scotia, convinced Morton of Canada's urgent need for better library service, and she decided to become a librarian. She took the librarian's course given by the Ontario Department of Education and then worked in the Cataloguing Department of the Toronto Public Library. Returning to New Brunswick, she was employed as a teacher and school librarian and then as Secretary of the New Brunswick Library Commission. In 1931 she rejoined the staff of the Toronto Public Library, this time as a member of the Reference Department, where she remained until 1944. From 1936 to 1943 she also served as Secretary of the Ontario Library Association.

The decisive step in Morton's career came in 1944 when she left the security of library employment to become the full-time Secretary of the Canadian Library Council, a struggling organization whose main purpose was to pave the way for the formation of a national library association. When the Canadian Library Association/Association Canadienne des Bibliothèques was actually established in 1946 (in good part because of her efforts), it was wholly logical that Morton be selected as its initial Executive Director. She held that position until her retirement in 1968.

In the fledgling years of the CLA, Morton was in effect the one-person team on whom the continued existence of the Association depended. The Association had large ambitions, a small membership, and precarious funding, and it had to accommodate itself to a taxing diversity of regional, cultural, and professional interests. Aided by a tiny staff, Morton served as initiator, organizer, lobbyist, counselor, convener, and editor. Her most visible accomplishments were the establishment and continued supervision of the *Canadian Periodical Index* (the first major index of Canadian periodicals), the *Canadian Newspaper Microfilm Project,* and the Association's two journals, *Canadian Library Association Bulletin* (now *Canadian Library Journal*) and *Feliciter.* She also edited the *C.L.A. Occasional Papers* series.

Less visible but perhaps even more important was the influence she wielded behind the scenes. Her excellent contacts in governmental and educational circles did much to muster support for the formation of Canada's National Library (1950). Her advice was sought in many library appointments and policy decisions. She was, unobtrusively, the originator as well as the executor of major developments in the Canadian Library Association itself.

To mark her retirement from the CLA in 1968, the Association published an impressive book of essays on Canadian librarianship. She was made a member of the Order of Canada in 1968 and was awarded honorary doctorates by the University of Alberta (1969) and Sir George Williams University (1970).

After leaving the CLA, Morton continued to be active for a decade. She took a Master's degree from the Graduate Library School of the University of Chicago (1969), operated her own consulting firm, assisted in the National Library's survey of resources, and acted as library consultant for Unesco in Trinidad. She lectured at various library schools and worked on several books.

Elizabeth Morton died in Ottawa on July 6, 1977.

SAMUEL ROTHSTEIN;
MARION GILROY (d. 1981)

Mozambique

Mozambique, an independent republic on the southeast coast of Africa, is bordered on the north by Tanzania, on the east by the Indian Ocean, on the south by Swaziland and South Africa, and on the west by Zimbabwe, Zambia, and Malawi. Population (1990 est.) 15,656,000; area 801,590 sq.km. The official language is Portuguese; Bantu languages are widely spoken.

The National Library of Mozambique, founded in Maputo in 1961, houses about 110,000 volumes. Mozambique does not issue a national bibliography of its own, but bibliographical references to publications of or about Mozambique are listed in the *Boletim de la Bibliografia Portuguesa.* The journal *Documentario trimestral,* issued in Mozambique from 1935, lists publications deposited under copyright law during the previous four-month period. Archival materials are kept at the Arquivo Histórico de Moçambique, Maputo, founded in 1934. The collection consists of almost 12,000 volumes. There is one university in Mozambique, the Universidade Eduardo Mondlane (formerly the Universidade de Lourenço Marques), founded in Maputo in 1962. The language of instruction is Portuguese. There are approximately 80,000 volumes in the general and departmental libraries of the university, plus 8,600 periodicals. Educational facilities in Mozambique are not highly developed. There is a city library in Maputo, the Biblioteca Municipal, which holds approximately 8,000 volumes.

The Mozambique Institute of Scientific Research, founded in Maputo in 1955, houses a library and documentation center, the Biblioteca e Centro de Documentação e Informação, established in 1977 under the Ministry of Education. The library's collection consists of approximately 3,000 scientific volumes. The Institute publishes works on ecology, natural sciences, earth sciences, and social sciences, particularly on Mozambique history. There are two other notable libraries in Maputo. The Direcção dos Serviços de Geologia e Minas, founded in 1930, specializes in mining research and geological studies. The collection consists of about 16,000 books. Research findings are published in the society's *Boletim.* The Instituto de Algodão de Moçambique (Cotton Research Institute), founded in 1962, houses 2,500 volumes and 210 journals.

STAFF

Mudge, Isadore Gilbert
(1875–1957)

ALA
Isadore Gilbert Mudge

Isadore Gilbert Mudge was America's foremost reference librarian and for many years the author of the standard *Guide to Reference Books.* Under Mudge's editorship, the *Guide* became so well known that, as her biographer John Waddell pointed out, "'Mudge' became not merely a woman's name, but a noun, an adjective, and a verb upon the lips of librarians and students in the entire English-speaking world."

Born in Brooklyn, New York, March 14, 1875, Mudge was the daughter of well-educated parents. Her father, Alfred Eugene Mudge, was a respected Brooklyn lawyer and the stepson of Charles Kendall Adams, who served as President of Cornell University and the University of Wisconsin and was instrumental in building important libraries at each institution. Mudge's mother, Mary Ten Brook, was the daughter of Andrew Ten Brook, a noted historian and at one time the Librarian at the University of Michigan.

Mudge was named in memory of her aunt, the name Isadore having come originally from a popular romance. Nothing is known about her early years. In 1889 she enrolled in the Adelphi Academy in Brooklyn; graduating at the top of her class in spring 1893, Mudge entered "Grandfather's university" the following fall, though by then Charles Kendall Adams had moved from Ithaca to Madison.

At Cornell, Mudge excelled in her studies and was elected to Phi Beta Kappa in her junior year. She majored in history and took classes with some of the most distinguished professors in the country, including Moses Coit Tyler and George Lincoln Burr. Of the two, Burr was the more influential. She enrolled in every course he offered and later revealed that the training she received from him started her on her career as a reference librarian.

In September 1898, 15 months after she graduated from Cornell, she enrolled in the New York State Library School at Albany, the famous school established by Melvil Dewey at the time he became State Librarian. She excelled at the Library School, completing the two-year program in 1900 and receiving the B.L.S. degree with distinction.

Mudge seems to have made a favorable impression on Dewey during her residence in Albany. Although there is no evidence of a close friendship between the two, Dewey—at the peak of his career—does appear to have recommended Mudge for her first two library positions. The first of these was at the University of Illinois, where Dewey's close friend and former star pupil, Katharine Lucinda Sharp, was the Director of the new library and the founder of an important library school in Urbana. Mudge arrived on the Urbana campus in 1900 and was put in charge of the Reference Department and made Assistant Professor in the library school. She stayed for three years, working hard to develop the reference collection and provide services for researchers. She also met Minnie Earl Sears of the Cataloguing Department, a woman who would be her companion and collaborator for several decades.

In 1903 Mudge resigned her position at Illinois to accept the directorship of the Bryn Mawr (Pennsylvania) College library. Dewey recommended her for this job as well, just as he had trained and recommended the previous two directors of the library. Accompanied by Sears, who would become Head of the Cataloguing Department there, Mudge took charge of an entire library for the only time in her life. It was a responsibility she may not have enjoyed; nothing is known about the work she did there, and she was always reticent about the details of her Bryn Mawr experience. In 1907 she took a one-year leave of absence from the position but did not return when the year was over.

After seven years of library work, Mudge went to Europe accompanied by Sears. They traveled and worked on their *Thackeray Dictionary* (1910). After they returned to the United States they found a number of projects and part-time appointments: Mudge taught in the library school at Simmons College in Boston in 1910 and 1911, reviewed reference books for *Library Journal,* and assisted William D. Johnston in compiling *Special Collections in Libraries in the United States* (1912). Johnston was the Director of the Columbia University library, and her association with him on this project led to her eventual appointment at Columbia in 1911. She spent the rest of her professional career there.

The year before that appointment, however, Mudge began another association that would also occupy the rest of her career and would make her the best-known librarian of her generation. At the 1910 conference of the American Library Association, Mudge was asked to take over the editorship of Alice Bertha Kroeger's *Guide to the Study and Use of Reference Books.* Kroeger had brought out editions of this work in 1902 and 1908 before she died in 1909. Mudge began her editorial work by preparing a two-year supplement to the 1908 edition. Under her editorship, the *Guide* became the standard book of librarianship, and Mudge was to see it through four editions.

Columbia University. While preparing that first supplement, she was appointed to the Columbia University library by Johnston. Her first position as Gifts and Exchange Librarian (February 6, 1911) was followed a few months later by the appointment as Reference Librarian, and she remained in that position for the next 30 years. Mudge said that she had "set her mind on wanting Columbia from the days that I was at Cornell." By the time she arrived on the Morningside Heights campus, Columbia had already established itself as a university of the highest quality. Under the direction of President Nicholas Murray Butler, its graduate faculties were producing more Ph.D.s than any other university in the country. But the library at Columbia was woefully inadequate to support so much advanced scholarship.

Mudge began at once to develop the reference collection and quickly won the support of Butler himself. He discovered her resourcefulness in satisfying his own bibliographical needs, and with his help Mudge was able to build the finest reference collection in existence. Moreover, she provided thorough and expert guidance to that collection for students and faculty alike. The reference service she had begun at Columbia was unique at that time. It took several years for these services to gain recognition in the Library, but gradually more and more scholars realized how helpful her knowledge could be in their research. In fact, it became clear with the passing years that her methods contributed significantly to the research and instruction at Columbia.

Throughout her years at Columbia, Mudge had the ongoing project of preparing editions and supplements to her *Guide to Reference Books,* a work that has had a distinguished history. Mudge's first edition (but the third edition since 1902) appeared in 1917, and it became the most frequently used reference book in every research library; it greatly enhanced every reference library by providing a guide to all kinds of reference books in many languages. Other editions of the *Guide* appeared in 1923, 1929, and 1936, and the tradition established by Mudge at Columbia was continued by her successors Constance Winchell and Eugene Sheehy.

During the 1920s and 1930s Mudge was the undisputed authority on reference books, and the Columbia reference department served as a model for reference departments at other institutions. Mudge-trained librarians were eagerly sought to fill newly created reference positions throughout the country. Some neophyte librarians studied with Mudge at Simmons College, where she continued to teach from time to time, and at the New York Public Library's Library School, where she also occasionally offered courses. Others studied with Mudge at Columbia after a merger in 1926 of the Albany Library School and the New York Public Library School formed the School of Library Service at Columbia. Mudge became Associate Professor there and from 1927 on regularly taught Bibliography and Bibliographical Methods, a course that made lasting impressions on the many students, who in turn spread Mudge's methods far and wide.

With Minnie Sears's death in 1933, Mudge's life began to slow down. The 1936 edition of the *Guide* was the last one she edited, and it was extremely difficult for her to complete. She had never honored deadlines, and as she grew older her habits became impossible for her publisher. Finally, ALA decided that a new editor should be sought to prepare the next edition of the *Guide*. Constance Winchell became the new editor, and Mudge retired from the Reference Department in 1941, continuing her teaching just one year longer. She moved to the Westchester home that she and Sears had purchased years before. She died on May 16, 1957, in Baltimore, Maryland.

REFERENCES

The only full study of Mudge is John Neal Waddell, "The Career of Isadore G. Mudge: A Chapter in the History of Reference Librarianship." (unpublished Ph.D. dissertation, Columbia University, 1973).

Laurel L. Grotzinger, "Women Who 'Spoke for Themselves,'" *College and Research Libraries* (1978).

John N. Waddell and Laurel A. Grotzinger, "Mudge, Isadore Gilbert," *Dictionary of American Library Biography* (1978).

PAUL COHEN

Laurentian University/Université Larentienné

J. N. Desmarais Library/ Bibliothèque J.N. Desmarais, Sadbury, Ontario. The new library serves Laurentian's bilingual campus.

Multicultural Populations, Services to

Earlier editions of this work carried this material under the title of "Bilingual and Ethnic Groups, Services to." The growth and development of this type of library service has moved well beyond the identification of specific literatures aimed at populations with special linguistic and ethnic origins. While language and ethnicity remain at the heart of the service, recognition of broader cultural differences has been proven necessary in order to reach various groups of users with library and information services appropriate to their needs and interests.

Immigrant populations of Europe, North America, and Australia and New Zealand since the 1960s, together with established linguistic and ethnic minorities of African, Asian, and European nations have generated new types of library outreach services that extend the breadth of social services and contribute to a rich diversity of cultural life. At the same time, the larger effort to acculturate immigrant and established minority populations has strained resources and raised new questions about national identity in Canada, Germany, and the United States.

In Europe and North America, libraries for a long time provided their services solely in the official language or languages of their own countries, and providing for other language groups was an acknowledged concern in relatively few countries. On the assumption that all citizens should know the national language, such service as was provided seldom went beyond a small collection of "foreign" books. An understanding that the responsibility to provide library service equally to all involves going beyond the official languages developed only recently. In examining the services offered today, a distinction has been made, therefore, between countries where a mixed population goes back far into history (the established multilingual countries) and those where the traditional composition of population was changed by immigration or influx of migrant workers in more recent years.

Established Multilingual Countries. In Europe most of the countries with more than one language group have been created over the centuries by wars and peace agreements. The degree of cultural and language amalgamation varies considerably and so consequently do their libraries' services, as the following examples illustrate.

Belgium is home to two culturally, linguistically different groups that are also territorially separated, the Dutch-speaking Flemings in the north and the French-speaking Walloons in the south, with both languages spoken only in Brussels; this strict division is also followed in the libraries.

Switzerland. Less rigidity is exercised in Switzerland, where in various areas French, German, Italian, and Romansch are spoken. In each area public libraries, while organized for service to the dominant group, also provide a reasonable quantity of books in the other languages.

South Africa. Two official languages, Afrikaans and English, are taught in schools and are used in all spheres of life. Library personnel must be bilingual in them as a condition of employment in most if not all provincial and municipal institutions, and the collections reflect language policy as well as reading needs. There are also about eight other large language groups, both African and Asian, in South Africa, but they are regarded as "nonofficial." Limited library service is available to their groups.

Finland is an example of how the language of a larger and dominant nation persists even after political ties have been broken. Besides the Finnish language, Swedish is spoken and read by a large minority, and, accordingly, public libraries in large centers, such as Helsinki, provide material in both languages.

North America. The history of bilingualism in North America is of more recent date. Canada is often described as a bilingual country, but the description is

Indian Library Services Project, San Diego County Library

Kapsala Community Library, Viejas Indian Reservation, one of eight public libraries on Indian reservations in San Diego County, California.

not entirely accurate, since French is spoken primarily in the province of Quebec. The Official Languages Act accords equal status to English and French in Parliament and in the federal civil service. Public libraries, while intent on meeting the needs of the majority groups in their environment, also provide books in the other language. Many libraries in the English-speaking provinces consider it a patriotic as well as a cultural duty to promote the reading of French, especially works by French Canadian authors.

Although the U.S. is officially unilingual in practice, no law establishes English as the official language; efforts to enact such a law have found only limited support. However, many local ordinances require that official documents be printed in Spanish or other main minority languages as well as English, and many federal documents appear in both English and Spanish. Cultural pluralism has been a fact for a long time, with local celebrations highlighting the specific origins of population groups each summer in many parts of the country. Although concerns for bilingual instruction and English as a second language (ESL) originated to serve the population with Spanish-language origins, it has grown to serve Chinese, Japanese, Korean, Thai, and other language groups as well. However, Spanish is the dominant second language in the U.S., where one resident in ten is of Hispanic origin. Government policy and funding since the 1950s have supported the growth and development of library services to Spanish-speaking users and to African-American and Native American users as well. The need of Chicanos and other Spanish-speaking groups for service in their own language resulted in the demand for and eventually the creation of library positions for bilingual personnel, and many libraries owe their success to their Spanish-speaking staff. Since the 1970s broader definitions of minority populations have extended federal funding to support library services to other groups.

Multinational Minorities after World War II. World War II and its aftermath caused massive demographic changes in many countries and presented libraries with new and difficult tasks. Two variants of the population movement are clearly distinguishable and should be treated separately because they impinge somewhat differently on the functions of libraries. They are migrant workers, more common in Europe, and immigrants who move to a country to live there permanently.

Migrant Workers have had profound impact in many central and western European countries. When the postwar expansion of industry in Belgium, Denmark, Germany, Sweden, and Switzerland—to name the countries most affected—depleted the reservoir of indigenous labor, workers were recruited from the Mediterranean area, notably Algeria, Greece, Italy, Spain, Turkey, and Yugoslavia.

The theory was that *Gastarbeiter* (guest workers) would stay a few years in the host country and then return home. This theory also served as an excuse for withholding cultural, educational, and some social services from them. Contrary to expectations, though a certain number of workers went home when their contracts expired, others arrived to take their place, and a growing number remained when immigration regulations permitted. Eventually libraries took notice of the new challenge, for which most if not all were largely unprepared. The newcomers did not at first know the indigenous languages, were in many cases illiterate, and were in most cases ignorant or distrustful of the public library as an institution. Most libraries, on the other hand, lacked bilingual or multilingual staff and lacked books in foreign languages and the means of getting them. Faced with such difficulties, they had to look for good reasons for providing materials and services for foreign readers, and they had to instill motivation in staffs.

Support for special services was not difficult to justify. Migrant workers contributed to the national wealth not only through their work but also through taxes and therefore had a claim on public services. In the interest of general economic and social welfare, they needed help in adapting to prevailing circumstances; through knowledge of the national language, the newcomers could not only better understand their daily work and living conditions but also improve their vocational knowledge and their participation as citizens. Furthermore, it was unavoidable that families followed or were started by the workers. Children who went to school and were taught in the indigenous language could become estranged from their parents. When the time came to return to their home country, both old and young might have become completely assimilated and unable to resume, or, in the case of children born abroad, to enter into the prevailing way of life there.

Immigrants must be considered in most cases as permanent additions to a nation, although again exceptions are possible. The types of immigrants—and consequently the role of libraries—vary from country to country, and from one period to another. The largest group of immigrants to the United Kingdom arrived after World War II from countries of the Commonwealth—India, Pakistan, the West Indies—but that immigration had virtually stopped by the late 1970s. Immigrants to France came from northern and western Africa and most had at least some speaking knowledge of French or English. The U.S. has always attracted immigrants from Europe. After the wars in Korea and Vietnam, immigrants to the U.S. from Southeast Asia became more numerous. Canada has accepted immigrants from non-English, non-French backgrounds for 300 years. Recently many West Indians have immigrated to Canada. Only after World War II did Australia relax its preference for immigrants from Europe, mainly northern Europe.

BEGINNINGS

In North America at the turn of the 19th century, librarians made honest attempts to provide books to immigrants in non-English languages. The American Library Association established in 1917 the Committee on Work for the Foreign Born, which published in 1929 a handbook, *Reading Services for the Foreign Born.* In 1948 the Committee was renamed Committee on Intercultural Relations and nothing more was heard of it. At the same time, the long and honorable history of services to ethnic groups, as exemplified by the public libraries of Cleveland, Detroit, and New York, showed signs of stagnation, caused in part by declining immigration, better-educated immigrants with greater demands on library material, and declining circulation. The emphasis then shifted to the "disadvantaged," meaning African-Americans, Latinos, and Native Americans. The influx of immigrants after World War II, greater in Canada than in the U.S., revived consciousness of the centuries-old ties between the Old and the New World.

The so-called melting-pot theory never reached fruition; immigrant communities were transformed into ethnic communities in the U.S., while in Canada the government declared a policy of multiculturalism, that is, one nation based on cultural pluralism.

U.S. libraries began in the 1970s to concern themselves with ethnic reading needs once more, a decade after their Canadian counterparts. When Congress passed the Educational Amendment of 1972, which provided for an Ethnic Heritage Studies Program, it noted that "in a multiethnic society a greater understanding of the contribution of one's own heritage and those of one's fellow citizens can contribute to a more harmonious, patriotic, and committed populace."

More and more public libraries provide funds, either from their own budgets or from grants, for selecting and purchasing books in *community* languages. (This term is preferred to *foreign,* which is imprecise and may be offensive to many citizens.) Encouraging signs of deepening concern for the objectives as much as for the difficulties have been noted in the literature as well as in personal communications to the author from many countries. Even so, the difficulties are enormous: problems of selection and bibliographic aids; problems of acquisition from faraway countries; problems of processing; and, finally, problems of promoting the resources to the intended user groups. Library associations in France, Germany, Sweden, and the U.K., among others, are grappling with the problem. In 1975 the ALA's Public Library Association constituted a Multilingual Services Committee, which met for the first time during ALA's Midwinter Meeting in Chicago in 1978.

SERVICES IN INDIVIDUAL LIBRARIES

Objectives and Standards. Even before the practical problems are tackled, philosophy for service should be stated and goals set. It is not enough merely to start a "foreign" or "multilingual" collection; some thought must be given to general library objectives, reading habits of the target groups, and the extent to which special (and invariably costly) resources for minority readers should be developed. Are they to be helped to assimilate? They would need language manuals and books descriptive of their new country. Are they to be helped to maintain and hand down their cultural traditions through judiciously selected works by their national authors? Or will the whole point be "books in your language," irrespective of author and content? Other issues include literacy of new citizens and attitudes toward institutions such as libraries, toward book buying, and toward book borrowing habits, and personal preference for or against retention of the mother tongue.

Ron Davies. Courtesy Dyfed County Library

Bookmobile in Dyfed County, Wales, offering materials in Welsh and English.

Selection. The implication for careful selection is obvious. It is difficult, if not impossible, to plan a complete, effective service to minority groups from scratch. Census figures are inadequate guides; one has to proceed by educated guesses, trial and error.

Standards for bibliographic records and book reviewing and reporting vary considerably from country to country. As a general rule, however, one feature is almost universal: most of them are written in the language of the country of production. Knowledge of that language is, to say the least, helpful in order to consider titles for ordering. Failing that, one has to rely on booksellers at home and abroad or, worse, restrict purchases to translations of easily identified titles.

Booklists are relatively easy to obtain from publishers and booksellers; occasionally they are annotated. Critical reviews can be found in many literary or general magazines, but it is doubtful, given the language problem, whether the average library would subscribe to them except for the use of their ethnic readers. The ALA *Booklist* carries annotated lists of

The Newark Public Library Photo by Bill May

The art of "origami" being taught at the 1991 International Cultural Festival, Newark Public Library, New Jersey.

foreign books with addresses of some appropriate booksellers in the U.S. Some libraries issue acquisition lists at regular or irregular intervals, with or without annotations in English and vernacular (Cumberland County Library System, New York Public Library, Cleveland Public Libraries, and others). A comprehensive guide to selection aids and suppliers was published in 1979 by the Canadian Library Association and K. G. Saur as *Books in Other Languages*.

The frequently asked question "How many volumes?" is more difficult to answer. It depends on many factors, such as number of readers, rate of adoption of the host country's language, rate of retention of their own language, and limits on bookstock imposed by budget or library policy. IFLA standards recommend distinction between national minorities with fixed residence who should have "adequate quantity of their national literature" and nonresident groups, who should have service when they number at least 500. It is suggested that for a population of 2,000, 1 volume per migrant worker is appropriate; for over 2,000, 1 for 10. There should be a minimum of 100 volumes.

Acquisition. It is axiomatic that the best source of supply is in the country of production, and the source gets poorer in direct proportion to distance from that country. Immigrants, unless heavily concentrated in a particular area or town, do not offer a lucrative market for bookshops, but those shops that do exist have stocks that are usually limited in quality and quantity; nevertheless, librarians should not bypass them entirely. An alert and knowledgeable bookseller can provide valuable guidance on books and take orders for transmission to publishers abroad, who often are not equipped to deal with customers from other countries.

Conversely, many librarians cannot deal with booksellers and publishers in foreign countries and in foreign languages. The language problem can be aggravated by unusual local commercial practices concerning, for example, terms of payment or means of conveyance. In some countries publishing is carried on by many small enterprises, each of which sells only its own product. Only a capable jobber on the spot or a staff member on a buying trip can ensure timely purchase, for the press runs are usually limited and there is no reprinting. By far the best, reliable, and under ideal circumstances even the most economical way to purchase foreign books in other languages is to buy them personally in the country of publication; an adequate volume of ordering is necessary to justify the expense of a buying trip. This suggests cooperation on regional, national, and international levels.

Processing. Books in foreign languages, many in non-Roman alphabets, find most librarians unprepared. The difficulty begins when checking the bill against the consignment, especially when the bill is in another language *and* in a non-Roman script. When non-Roman material is catalogued and classified, the standard aids for checking authors and authorities and for interpreting content may be inadequate or unavailable.

Staff. Mere knowledge of a language is not in itself sufficient qualification; of course, it is important when assisting those ethnic users who do not as yet speak the language of the country. In order to select books, a good education and cultural background are essential. This does not mean that the staff member must be a native of the country whose cultural heritage is to be promoted, but it helps. In the promotion of books and contact with users, the employment of members of ethnic groups is useful and frequently recommended.

Service Patterns. In North America local public libraries have long experience in providing services to cultural minorities and have received support from the Canadian and U.S. federal governments to recruit and train staff, develop special collections, and sponsor community cultural programs. Public Libraries in Montreal, New York City, San Francisco, and Toronto have developed guidelines and shared booklists with smaller institutions with similar needs but fewer resources. The Canadian government in 1973 began funding a national library service for ethnocultural communities based in the National Library of Canada.

The countries of Scandinavia since the mid-1970s have developed a centralized concept of library services to multicultural populations built around national collections of specific language and cultural materials that are made available to local libraries to supplement their collections. The largest of these is in Sweden, where public libraries in the early 1990s had collections in which more than 150 languages were represented, numbering more than one and a half million volumes. Advisory bodies representative of the groups served have brought extensive experience not available on local library staffs.

After examining various centralized models, New Zealand librarians planned to follow the lead of Australia in using a regional cooperative model to deliver services primarily to the resident Chinese population. The "Chinatown" branch library found in many North American cities was not considered appropriate for New Zealand.

Regardless of the pattern of service to multicultural populations, experience since the 1970s has indicated the need to recognize the subtle cultural differences that make even the introduction of specific library services difficult. There is clear recognition of the library as a cultural broker, in many cases providing access to information on business, literature, and current affairs that would not be available even in the country of origin for the target group of users.

Service to Children. Children of ethnocultural minorities present a somewhat different task to libraries. Again, there is a distinction between children of migrant workers and those of immigrants or their descendants and between children arriving in the host country at preschool age or at schoolgoing age. In the latter case, learning of language, culture, and way of life comes easily, more so than for children who during the primary years of growth are confined to their home, where that knowledge is inadequate.

In most cases children receive a good education in the country where their parents work but are then expected to return with their parents to their home country when the work contract expires. It is essential, then, that they be educated in their native tongue and learn about the history and culture of their native country in order to ease social and psychological problems they might face in the host country or at their repatriation. An additional reason for all children, whether temporary or permanent residents, to retain language and feeling of identity of their ethnic group is the need to prevent estrangement between parent and children, which can and does occur easily when children assimilate completely into the society of the host country while their parents alone retain language and way of life to which they have been accustomed.

Awareness of the need for library services to ethnic and cultural minorities in many countries has led to earnest investigation of ethnicity and of acquisition problems, and in many cases to the development of interesting projects. Given the uncertainty of human mobility in the future and the inevitable consequences of acculturation, the possibility and desirability of long-term plans cannot be taken for granted. For the present, however, most libraries have still much inducement to develop, even create, a useful service to ethnic groups.

REFERENCES

New Methods and New Media in Library Services to Multicultural Populations, proceedings of an IFLA seminar (1990).

Birgitta Hellman, "Library Services to Refugees and Immigrants," *Scandinavian Public Library Quarterly* (1990).

Cheng Yu, "Library Needs of the Chinese Community," *New Zealand Libraries* (1992).

LEONARD WERTHEIMER

Mumford, L. Quincy

(1903–1982)

Lawrence Quincy Mumford, 11th Librarian of Congress, directed the U.S. Library of Congress (LC) during a period of great growth, from 1954 to 1974.

Mumford was born on a farm in Ayden, North Carolina, December 11, 1903. From Duke University he received his A.B. in 1925 and his M.A. in 1928. His library career began when he was a student assistant in the Duke University Library; in 1926 he became Head of its circulation department, and in 1928 the Acting Chief of Reference and Circulation. While at Columbia University (1928–29), where he earned a graduate degree in library science, Mumford was an assistant in the library.

In 1929 he joined the staff of the New York Public Library as a reference assistant. There he served as General Assistant in charge of the Director's Office (1932–35), Executive Assistant and Chief of the Preparation Division (1936–43), and Executive Assistant and Coordinator of the General Service Divisions (1943–45). In 1940, at the request of the then Librarian of Congress, Archibald MacLeish, Mumford was granted a leave of absence to organize the Processing Department of the Library of Congress and to serve a year as its Director. In 1945 he was appointed Assistant Director of the Cleveland Public Library and in 1950 became its Director, a position he held until his appointment as Librarian of Congress in 1954 by President Dwight D. Eisenhower. He was the first Librarian to have a professional degree in librarianship. In an editorial headed "Librarians' Librarian" the *Washington Post* on April 28, 1954, applauded the selection.

Arthur Plotnik

L. Quincy Mumford

The Library of Congress made remarkable progress during Mumford's 20 years as Librarian. Congressional appropriations increased from about $10 million to almost $100 million. In 1958 the Library was authorized to use U.S.-owned foreign currencies (under the Agricultural Trade Development and Assistance Act) to acquire books for itself and other U.S. libraries and to establish acquisition offices in foreign countries such as Egypt, India, Indonesia, Israel, and Pakistan. In 1965 the Higher Education Act authorized the establishment of the National Program for Acquisitions and Cataloging (NPAC), which greatly expanded the Library's foreign procurement program and inaugurated a system to speed up the acquisition, cataloguing, and dissemination of cataloguing data for "all library materials currently published throughout the world which are of value to scholarship." Under that program the Library established additional overseas offices in Austria, Brazil, France, Germany, Japan, Kenya, Norway, Poland, Spain, the United Kingdom, and Yugoslavia. This improved service to the nation's libraries resulted in great savings in cataloguing costs nationally and improved access to research materials.

As a result of studies of space requirements for the Library, which began during Mumford's administration, Congress in 1965 authorized the construction of the Library's third major building, the James Madison Memorial Building. It more than doubled the space available for the Library's services and collections when it came into use in 1979.

The application of automation to the Library's processes and services began and made substantial progress under Mumford. Following the publication in 1964 of a feasibility study, *Automation and the Library of Congress,* the Information Systems Office was established. In 1965 the Machine Readable Cataloging (MARC) project began. It became the basis for the revolution in the rapid distribution of cataloguing information utilizing computers and communication technology (*see* MARC).

Other notable advances at LC under Mumford include the organization of the papers of the Presidents; the beginning publication of the *National Union Catalog of Manuscript Collections* and the *National Register of Microform Masters;* the establishment with the cooperation of the Bureau of the Budget of the Federal Library Committee; the tremendous expansion of the National Books for the Blind program to include the physically handicapped; the establishment of a separate Preservation Office and expansion of preservation research and services, including motion picture preservation in cooperation with the American Film Institute; the beginning of the *Pre-1956 National Union Catalog* project, scheduled to exceed 600 volumes; the huge expansion of the Congressional Research Service under the Legislative Reorganization Act; and the establishment of the Cataloging-In-Publication program in cooperation with publishers.

Under Mumford, collections grew from about 33,000,000 items in 1954 to almost 74,000,000 in 1974, and the staff grew by more than 50 percent, to a total of more than 4,500 by 1974.

Mumford served as President of the Ohio Library Association, 1947–48, and of the American Library Association, 1954–55. He also was President of the Manuscript Society (1968–70), a member of the Lincoln Sesquicentennial Commission (1958–60), and a member on the President's Committee on Libraries (1966–68), named to review the recommendations of the temporary National Advisory Commission on Libraries. During his service as Librarian of Congress, he was a member of the Board of Advisors of the Dumbarton Oaks Research Library and Collection, the Sponsors Committee of the *Papers of Woodrow Wilson,* the U.S. National Book Committee, the National Trust for Historic Preservation, and a number of other advisory boards. He received several honorary degrees. Mumford died in Washington, D.C., August 15, 1982. On December 13, 1983, the Assembly Room on the sixth floor of the James Madison Memorial Building was named the L. Quincy Mumford Room.

REFERENCE

L. Quincy Mumford, "Twenty Years as Librarian of Congress, September 1, 1954–September 1, 1974: A Record of Progress" (1974).

JOHN G. LORENZ

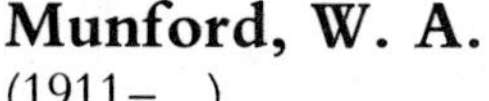

Munford, W. A.
(1911–)

K. C. Harrison/
Library of Westminister

W. A. Munford

When Britain's Library Association (LA) planned its centenary celebrations for 1977, it was inevitable that W. A. Munford should be invited to become a member of the committee responsible for planning the events. It also went without saying that he was asked to write the history of the LA, designed to be published as one of several LA centenary volumes. Munford had already carved a niche for himself as a library historian par excellence and had been the founder of the Association's Library History Group. Add to these the further qualifications of the executive positions he had held in British librarianship, plus services as a former Honorary Secretary of the LA, and it will be obvious why he was the perfect and natural choice to advise on centenary events and to write the LA's history. He completed the book in time for publication just prior to the start of the LA centenary year.

William Arthur Munford was born in Islington, north London, April 27, 1911. Educated first at a high school in nearby Hornsey, he later obtained the degrees of B.Sc. (Econ.) and Ph.D., both gained in leisure hours, at the London School of Economics. He received his early experience in public libraries at Hornsey and at Ilford in east London before becoming the borough librarian of Dover in 1934 at the early age of 23. He remained in that post until 1945. Dover, only 21 miles from the French coast, was in the firing line for most of World War II, from June 1940 to September 1944, suffering much damage from air raids and heavy artillery shelling. Munford was Food Executive Officer for Dover from 1939 to 1945, and in 1946 he was appointed M.B.E. (Member of the Order of the British Empire) for his war services. He was City Librarian of Cambridge from 1945 to 1953.

Even before the war, Munford had evinced a deep interest in professional affairs, contributing articles to the *Library Association Record* and the *Times Literary Supplement* and chapters to issues of *The Year's Work in Librarianship*. But in the postwar years his professional work burgeoned. A strong LA supporter, he became a member of its Council and in 1947 was responsible for forming the Eastern Branch of the LA, thus ensuring the unity of the profession in the counties of Cambridge, Norfolk, and Suffolk. From 1952 to 1955 he was Honorary Secretary of the LA, a position that no longer exists but was at that time regarded as the most prominent job in the Association. If the President of the LA could be regarded as the head of state, then the Honorary Secretary was the prime minister.

In those years he formed a close friendship and working relationship with Percy Welsford, the paid secretary of the LA from 1931 to 1959, and one of those responsible for the rapid expansion of the Association during those years. Meanwhile, Munford was still working as City Librarian of Cambridge, where he did much to improve the standing of the Cambridge Public Libraries in the eyes of both town and gown. He associated with many of the academics in the Cambridge colleges, one of his particular friends being Dr. (later Sir) Sydney C. Roberts, Master of Pembroke College, Cambridge. In 1953 Roberts served as President of the LA. Munford's persuasiveness was an obvious factor, both in selling Roberts to the LA and, perhaps more important, selling the LA to Roberts. Roberts chaired in 1957 a Ministry of Education Committee charged with investigating the structure of the public library service in England and Wales. The Roberts Committee's report, published in 1959, led to the passing of the Public Libraries and Museums Act of 1964, which remains the current legislation for public libraries in England and Wales.

Munford's first book was a bibliography called *Books for Basic Stock,* published in 1939. But in 1951 he made his name as a library historian with a book published by the Library Association called *Penny Rate: Aspects of British Public Library History*. It was rapidly taken up by the library schools as a textbook. But it was not just a textbook: it possessed readability as well. In it Munford explored the events that led to the passing of the first Public Libraries Act of 1850 and brought to life such personalities as Edward Edwards and William Ewart, both protagonists for public libraries, as well as Colonel Sibthorp, a member of Parliament notorious for his opposition to the movement.

Munford made additional contributions to library history later, with his biography *William Ewart, M.P.,* and his studies of *Edward Edwards* (1963), *Louis Stanley Jast* (1966), *James Duff Brown* (1968), and *Sir John MacAlister* (1983). The study of Jast was written in collaboration with W. G. Fry, and that of MacAlister with S. Godbolt. In 1976 Munford completed *A History of the Library Association, 1877–1977.* He next compiled *Who Was Who in British Librarianship* (1987).

In 1954 Munford was appointed Director-General of the National Library for the Blind, which at that time was centered in Great Smith Street, Westminster, London, with a northern branch in Deansgate, Manchester. He held that post until his retirement in 1982. During his 28 years' service he initiated many improvements, notably in the braille bookstock, and culminating in the fusion of the Westminster and Manchester libraries for the blind in new premises at Bredbury, near Stockport, Cheshire. He handled the inevitable staffing problems of such an amalgamation with admirable tact and diplomacy. Munford also became an active supporter of the provision of books in large print for the hard-of-seeing, becoming a Trustee of the Ulverscroft Foundation, set up to mark the work of Frederick A. Thorpe, the founder of large-print book publishing in Britain. Profits from the sales of Ulverscoft LP books are added to the funds of the Foundation, which supports hospitals, schools, and libraries. Munford's work for the Ulverscroft Foundation and for the LA was commemorated in 1989 by the establishment of the Ulverscroft Munford research fellowship, funded by the Foundation and awarded by the LA in alternate years.

Munford was a prolific library journalist. He contributed steadily for nearly 60 years to all the British library periodicals and to some overseas as well. He served as a regional adviser to the *ALA World Encyclopedia of Library and Information Services* as well as being a contributor to Thomas Landau's *Encyclopedia of Librarianship* (1958; 3rd. ed. 1966) and to the *Encyclopedia of Library and Information Science* published by Marcel Dekker, Inc. An omnivorous reader with wide-ranging tastes, though with a preference for history, biography, literature, and detective stories, Munford writes engagingly, frequently skeptically, with a literary turn of phrase and a decided sense of humor.

In 1977 the Library Association made him an Honorary Fellow. Earlier, his concern for and interest in library cooperation had led to his becoming Chairman of the Executive Committee and the Regional Council of the East Midlands Regional Library System.

K. C. HARRISON

Munn, Ralph
(1894–1975)

ALA
Ralph Munn

Ralph Munn was an American library administrator and educator, consultant, author, and leader in professional organizations.

Munn was born in Aurora, Illinois, September 19, 1894, grew up in Colorado, and attended the University of Denver, where he earned an A.B. degree in 1916 and an LL.B. degree in 1917. After service with the U.S. Army in France from April 1917 to July 1919, he attended the New York State Library School at Albany, from which he received the B.L.S. degree in 1921. He was married to Anne Shepard, also a librarian, on June 6, 1922.

His first professional position was in the Seattle Public Library, where he served as Reference Librarian, 1921–25, and Assistant Librarian, 1925–26. He then became Librarian of the Flint (Michigan) Public Library, 1926–28. From 1928 to 1964 he served as Director of the Carnegie Library of Pittsburgh. He served also as Director, and later Dean, of the Carnegie Library School of Carnegie Institute of Technology, 1928–62, when the school was transferred to the University of Pittsburgh.

Throughout his long and distinguished career, Munn was actively involved in international interests and concerns as a professional librarian and citizen. In 1934, commissioned by the Carnegie Corporation, he surveyed the libraries of Australia and New Zealand and made recommendations for their development and for the selections of librarians to study library practice in the United States. As a result, he became known as the "father of the modern library movement in Australia and New Zealand."

Nine years later, in 1943, he was retained by the City Planning Commission of New York City to survey library needs and select sites for new branch libraries in New York's five boroughs.

In 1947 he undertook a goodwill tour of libraries of Central and South America for the U.S. Department of State and as a representative of the American Library Association. While on that mission, he spoke in Lima, Peru, on the occasion of a presentation of 10,000 American books given to the Peru National Library, which had been rebuilt following a fire. For his work in behalf of the reconstruction of the Library, the Peruvian government awarded him the degree of Knight of the Order El Sol del Peru. In 1950 he served as Chairman of the U.S. delegation to a Unesco Library Seminar in Malmo, Sweden, to determine the needs of public libraries throughout the world.

Throughout his career Munn never deviated from his conviction that the public library's primary role was educational, informational, and cultural. This conviction brought into clear focus the issue of demand versus quality. In 1938 he implemented a revised book selection policy that sharply defined and limited the purchase of light, recreational fiction and effectively eliminated the acquisition of books that he categorized as "shopping bag fiction." As a result, the Carnegie Library of Pittsburgh gained remarkable status as a distinguished local institution, widely recognized for the quality of its collections and services.

Under his administration Carnegie Library expanded its services significantly. He frequently appeared before governmental bodies to seek necessary funds for library facilities, collections, and services. Munn sought to make libraries more responsive to the needs of young people, who, he once said, "are required to read books I never heard of until I got to college."

Through his leadership, unified library services were established in Pittsburgh with the merger of the Carnegie Free Library of Allegheny and Carnegie Library of Pittsburgh in 1956. Also in 1956 Carnegie Library contracted with the County Commissioners of Allegheny County to give service to county residents. Free borrowing privileges were extended, and bookmobile services were operated in parts of the county not served by local libraries. In his judgment, achievement of the difficult merger with the Carnegie Library of Allegheny and implementation of contractual services with the county were the most significant innovations of his administration. Previously he had established the Downtown Branch and Business Branch, and in 1958 he published his *Plan for the Federation of Libraries in Allegheny County*.

Munn was persistent in his efforts to improve public library service throughout Pennsylvania. In 1930 and 1931 and again in 1958 he served on the Governor's Commission on Public Library Development. His participation in the work of the 1958 Commission contributed to the formation of a state library system under which Pennsylvania was divided into 29 districts, with Carnegie Library of Pittsburgh as the headquarters for all of Allegheny County and parts of Butler and Westmoreland counties. As a result of its outstanding science and technology collections, the Carnegie Library became designated the resource in that field for the entire state. In 1959 he was the first recipient of the Distinguished Service Award given by the Pennsylvania Library Association for outstanding service by a Pennsylvania librarian to library development in the state.

His longtime associate, Elizabeth Nesbitt, observed that as Dean of the Carnegie Library School, Munn "insisted upon maintenance of standards in admission and performance of students, and upon honesty and fairness to employer and employee in placement of students." In 1936 the Carnegie Corporation published his *Conditions and Trends in Training for Librarianship*.

Munn was constant in his advocacy of cooperation among libraries. Cost and space factors, community needs, and the interdependence of libraries caused him to assume leadership in 1942 in coordinating the acquisition of costly research materials by the University of Pittsburgh, Carnegie Institute of Technology, and Carnegie Library. The results of this early work provided a foundation that led to the formation of the Pittsburgh Regional Library Center nearly 25 years later.

Always conscious of cost effectiveness in his management of Carnegie Library, he sought to keep overhead costs as low as possible in order to make available maximum funding for collection development and informational services. He introduced labor-saving devices and employed management techniques and principles of financial administration that were sensible and effective. He was one of a small cluster of progressive library administrators who established public relations offices in the mid-1940s.

Munn was respected universally for his professional as well as personal integrity. His unusually well-balanced judgment was combined with an unerring sense of timing that contributed greatly to his effectiveness as an administrator, planner, and strategist. His lifelong interest in young people inspired him in his work and enriched his personal life. Through his international activities, and long before the Fulbright Program was implemented, he welcomed many young librarians from abroad, including Australia, the Netherlands, and Scandinavia. They were added to the staff of the Carnegie Library, where they received the same salaries, benefits, and opportunities as their American colleagues. He took great interest in their professional development and provided many opportunities to participate in staff activities and community cultural events.

Whether writing or speaking, he had an extraordinary gift for clarity and grace. He was a keen observer, responsive, and always interested in others. His commanding and courtly presence was temporized by inner warmth and a fine sense of humor. Munn was forthright, perceptive, considerate, and kind. He possessed the qualities of a master teacher who willingly shared his insights and experience with many younger librarians.

He felt strongly that able women were too often denied equal opportunity to advance in a profession where women predominated. His concern was deepened in the years following World War II, when men were actively recruited into library schools.

A much respected leader in the American library movement throughout his long and distinguished career, he maintained active membership in professional organizations. He was the president of the American Library Association, 1939–40, and of the Pennsylvania Library Association, 1930–31. He made key addresses on many auspicious occasions, including the dedicatory address for the new ALA Headquarters building during the Association's 1963 Conference in Chicago.

Munn was honored by the University of Pittsburgh, which conferred upon him the honorary degree of Doctor of Laws in 1940. In 1960 Waynesburg College in Pennsylvania bestowed upon him the honorary degree of Doctor of Laws.

Upon his retirement, effective October 1, 1964, he was appointed Director Emeritus by the Board of Trustees of the Carnegie Library of Pittsburgh. Shortly thereafter a fund was established to support the Ralph Munn Lecture Series, subsequently a program for precollege students of the Greater Pittsburgh area. Following his death in Pittsburgh, January 2, 1975, the American Library Association adopted a resolution expressing its sense of loss and appreciation for his contribution to the library profession. The resolution characterized Munn as exemplifying "the highest ideals of the library profession in his activities as Association official, library administrator and educator, author, consultant and citizen."

REFRENCE

Regina F. Berneis, "Munn, Ralph," *Dictionary of American Library Biography* (1978).

KEITH DOMS

Munthe, Wilhelm
(1883–1965)

American Library Association
Wilhelm Munthe

Abraham Wilhelm Støren Munthe, Norwegian library director, devoted his whole life to the world of libraries. Munthe brought new ideas and stimulated professional development on the national scene in Norway; he also built bridges among the various parts of the library profession on the international level.

Born October 20, 1883, in Oslo, he passed the student's examination for the university in 1902 and, while a student at the University of Oslo, he also entered the Royal University Library as an apprentice in 1903, thus starting a career that was to last for 50 years. He went through the ranks in the library, becoming Library Assistant in 1909 and Amanuensis in 1910. In 1920 he took over as Head of the Manuscript Department. In 1922 he became Director of the Royal University Library, a position in which he remained until 1953.

In the years 1913 to 1916 he studied in Berlin, Copenhagen, Stockholm, and Uppsala. He developed a lasting interest in library developments on the international scene. He also developed a keen interest in all sorts of organizational matters concerning libraries, from the very practical housekeeping details to the more general levels of library planning and library buildings. In his time Munthe came to be regarded as a specialist in library planning, called upon as consultant for a number of library projects abroad.

As the Director of Norway's largest and most important library for more than 30 years, Munthe had great influence on the whole of the Norwegian library community. He was instrumental in setting up the annual Norwegian Library Meetings, joint meetings with librarians from both the academic libraries and the public libraries. He encouraged the staff of the Royal University Library to take part in these meetings, and he pressed for programs for the meetings that included items of appeal for all types of librarians.

The Royal University Library had since 1815 served a dual function as a University Library for the University of Oslo and as the National Library for the Kingdom of Norway. In 1925 Munthe raised the question of separating the library from the University of Oslo and making it an independent national library. The time was not ready for such a change, and the suggestion created wide debate. The result was that the library remained in the University of Oslo and continued serving as the national library. It so lasted until 1985, when the Ministry of Culture finally decided to create a separate and independent national library.

Munthe developed particularly good relations with the library community in the United States. In 1936 the Carnegie Corporation wanted a European librarian to give a critical appraisal of American librarianship, and he was given the task. From his extensive traveling in the U.S. emerged a book, *American Librarianship from a European Angle* (1939). An observant and outspoken account of the American library scene as viewed by an outsider, the book was used in American library schools for many years.

Munthe was active in the work of IFLA, and in the years after World War II he was the President of that organization, 1947–51.

His ability as a scholar and a writer can be observed, among other places, in the books *Litteraere Falsknerier* ("Literary Frauds," 1942) and *Essays for Bokvenner* ("Essays for Book Lovers," 1943).

A number of organizations and activities outside his professional field benefited from his knowledge and enthusiasm over the years, in particular the Norwegian Tourist Association (Den Norske Turistforening). His love for nature directed a lot of his energy toward work for nature preservation and the pleasures of mountain hiking and outdoor life.

Munthe was given honorary doctorates at the universities of Uppsala, Toronto, and Hamburg, and the Library Association made him an Honorary Member. On his 50th birthday celebration in 1933 he was given a large Festschrift with contributions from colleagues in all parts of the world. In his time the Royal University Library twice had extensions added to the original building, which made it among the more advanced and modern of the old European libraries.

Munthe died in Oslo on December 18, 1965.

BENDIK RUGAAS

Myanmar

Myanmar, a republic of southeast Asia, is bounded by China, Laos, and Thailand on the east and the Bay of Begal, Bangladesh, and India on the west. It was known as Burma until the late 1980s. Population (1990 est.) 41,675,000; area 676,578 sq.km. The official language is Burmese.

History. The history of Myanmar's libraries begins with King Anawrahta's violent seizure of Buddhist texts from Thaton in the late 11th century. This act established Pagan as a center for Buddhism over many centuries, and monastery libraries grew up around it. The collection of scriptures, in palm-leaf manuscript form, was housed in the Pitaka Taik. In 1795 a British envoy estimated that the Royal Library in Amarapura was the largest royal library between the Danube and China. And in Mandalay a library of 729 alabaster tablets, each 5 feet by 3 feet, was erected in 1857. It has been called "the most permanent library in the world."

National Libraries. There are two national libraries in Myanmar, one in the capital city, Rangoon, the other in Mandalay. Their combined strength approximated 100,000 volumes, with about a third of the materials in English. The library in Rangoon provides author and title indexes to leading Burmese periodicals from their dates of publication. The strength of holdings lies predominantly in primary source materials on colonial Burma; however, both libraries receive books and periodicals under the Press Registration Act of 1962 and are thus depository libraries. In addition to periodicals and newspapers, the libraries also contain several thousand books in manuscript form. Although open access is not allowed, spacious reading rooms are available. The rate of acquisition exceeds several thousand titles a year and is primarily reflective of the quantity of publications in Myanmar. Myanmar also has its National Archives, whose holdings include the entire run of the *Burma Gazette*.

Academic Libraries. Major academic libraries are those of Rangoon University, Mandalay University, and Moulmein College. At Rangoon the Central Universities Library is responsible for acquisition of foreign materials except for medical literature, acquired by the Department of Medicine Research Library. The Central Universities Library has a collection of about 250,000 volumes. The three Institute of Medicine libraries (in Rangoon and Mandalay) house about 45,000 volumes among them. The libraries conduct literature searches, maintain union catalogues of holdings on campuses, and prepare and publish bibliographies. A notable activity is the library orientation program at Rangoon Institute of Technology (about 35,000 volumes), where library training has also been incorporated into the curriculum. A major research library is the Library of the Central Research Institute, which completed a Union List of Scientific Serials covering some 20 libraries. The Library has an exchange program with the British Library Lending Division. Myanmar's academic libraries are decentralized; there are several departmental and institute libraries such as the Library of the Institute of Veterinary Science. The Arts and Science University Library in Mandalay (103,000 volumes) should also be mentioned, as well as the Institute of Economics Library and the Institute of Education Library. Both are in Rangoon and both have collections of about 35,000 volumes. The college libraries in Bassain, Magwe, and Moulmein are somewhat smaller.

Public Libraries. Three or four major state libraries provide the bulk of library service to the general populace. Perhaps the most outstanding public library is the Sarpay Beikman ("House of Literature") Institute Library in Rangoon, which has its own publishing house and which administers reading rooms in many Burmese villages. It has about 74,000 volumes, 17,670 of them in English. The bulk of Myanmar's domestic interlibrary loan activities are carried out by this library.

Special Libraries. Special libraries are found in the industries and institutes of various ministries. A special library of significance is the Research Library of Buddhistic Studies, whose holdings are world renowned.

Myanmar's libraries receive high-level government understanding and available support but are faced with the common problem of a shortage of funds.

REFERENCES

G. Miller, "Notes on Libraries in Burma," *International Library Review* (July 1978).

G. Raymond Nunn, "Libraries in Burma," *International Library Review* (October 1975).

THEIN SWE

Namibia

Namibia, formerly South West Africa, lies in southwestern Africa, with Angola and Zambia to the north, Botswana to the east, South Africa to the south, and the Atlantic Ocean to the west. Almost all the land—92 percent—is classified as extremely arid to semi-arid. The capital and only city is Windhoek. Population (1990 est.) 1,781,000; area 824,292 sq.km. The population is a mixture of many distinct ethnic groups. The official language is English, but Afrikaans, Oshivambo, Otjiherero, Nama/Damara, and German are used.

History. The indigenous peoples of Namibia are nomadic Bushmen and Hottentots. Starting in the 16th century both African and European groups moved into the area. The Germans ruled from 1884 to 1915; the League of Nations gave South Africa a mandate to rule from 1920, but the UN refused to allow it to annex the area in 1946. In 1968 the UN General Assembly gave the area the name Namibia, and the International Court of Justice declared in 1971 that South Africa was occupying it illegally. After a long liberation struggle, the UN supervised elections in 1989 and Namibia became independent in 1990.

National Library and Archives. The Estorff Reference Library performs some of the functions of a national library. It started in 1926 as the Legislative Assembly Library with a collection of books inherited from the German colonial administration. In 1957 it became part of the South West Africa Library Service, which fell under the Administration for Whites in 1980. Closed in 1981, it was reopened in 1984 as the Estorff Reference Library in one of the oldest buildings in Windhoek. After independence it came under the Ministry of Education and Culture.

The Library provides reference and interlibrary loan facilities for people of all races. It compiles union catalogues such as "Periodicals in Namibian Libraries" and is building a Namibiana collection through its legal deposit privileges. It is a depository for UN publications. Its collection comprises general reference materials, items published in Namibia, on Namibia, or by Namibians outside the country, an extensive newspaper collection, and a microfilm collection of theses on Namibia.

By the early 1990s the Library had 41,000 volumes and 300 periodical titles. It offers online search facilities for databases in South Africa, the United Kingdom, and the United States.

A retrospective Namibian national bibliography was published commercially overseas in 1978 and 1979 as *Namibian National Bibliography* (NNB). Its three volumes covered 1971–75, 1976–77, and 1978–79. NAMLIT, a comprehensive bibliographical database incorporating more than 30,000 items published from 1884 on, was being prepared for publication in the early 1990s.

The National Archives was established in 1939 as the repository for all government records. It also has a library serving researchers and less serious readers. Its holdings include records of government offices dating from 1884; some 600 collections from individuals, institutions, or associations; more than 10,000 photographs depicting all aspects of Namibian life since the 1860s; more than 5,500 maps; all Namibian newspapers, the earlier ones in microform; more than 600 films on Namibia; and oral history tapes made since 1984. The Archives provides efficient finding aids and a *List of Archivalia* and has published a number of archival source publications.

Academic Libraries. The Academy is the main tertiary institution in Namibia, comprising the University, Technikon, and Out-of-School College. Its two branches have 40,000 books, 600 periodical titles, and an audiovisual collection. The Library was started in 1980 with a collection from the University of South Africa for use by external students in Namibia. The Library of the Windhoek College of Education opened in 1979. It has 32,000 books and audiovisual items and 240 periodical titles. The government proposed to build a library as part of its plans for a National University of Namibia in the early 1990s.

Public Libraries. The first public library was established in Lüderitzbucht in 1914 with a collection of donated books and periodicals and a volunteer staff. Several other libraries developed along the same lines until 1968, when the Library Service of South West Africa was established to provide a professional library service for the public and for schools. Public libraries served whites only until 1980, when non-white local authorities opened libraries. Libraries in the smaller communities served as few as 68 readers. By the 1990s, 22 service points had a total collection of more than 300,000 volumes.

The largest public library, in Windhoek, was established in 1924, mainly through the work of Lisa Gebhardt. She ran the library from 1926 to 1967 and died in September 1984 at the age of 89. Library service is scant outside the capital, with only one church-run library in the north. Accommodation, staff shortages, and inadequate financing are major problems.

Libraries in Namibia (1990)

Type of library	Number of administrative units (main libraries)	Number of service points (branches, mobile stops, etc.)	Volumes in collections	Annual expenditures (rand)	Population served	Professional staff (with certificate, diploma, etc.)	Total staff
National	1	1	41,300	320,000	1,500	2	8
Academic	2	4	72,000	2,300,000	3,500	12	21
Public	1	22	300,623	850,000	1,500	9	76
School	1	230	420,500	600,000	161,000	87	230
Special	12	12	73,000	--	2,400	5	17

Namibia Library Service

Estorff Reference Library of Windhoek, Namibia's national library. It is housed in one of Windhoek's oldest buildings, constructed in 1891 during German colonial times.

School Libraries. The apartheid practices of colonial times resulted in unequal distribution of school libraries between formerly all-white schools and other schools. Three of every four Namibian schools have no school libraries, book collections, or media centers. With the exception of 63 formerly all-white schools, some of which have good libraries, school libraries are in a deplorable state in terms of collections, accommodations, staffing, and other facilities.

Special Libraries. Many companies, government agencies, and parastatal organizations have special libraries, including the Department of Agriculture and Nature Conservation, the Bank of Namibia, the National Broadcasting Corporation, and the Supreme Court. The State Museum Library in Windhoek has a collection of 5,000 books and a Namibiana collection; it subscribes to 400 periodicals. Since 1962 it has published *Cimbebasia,* a periodical reporting on research in the social sciences and natural history.

The former Museum Library in Swakopmund, founded in 1951, was incorporated into the Sam Cohen Library, a private library opened in 1977 and managed by the Society for Scientific Development. The Library contains 7,000 volumes, including the Ferdinand Stich collection of more than 2,000 volumes, a special collection of Namibian newspapers covering the period since 1898, and many historical photographs.

The Namibian Scientific Society Library, established in Windhoek in 1924, has a collection of 7,800 books and almost 4,000 volumes of periodicals, with 425 current titles. It inherited several thousand titles from the Landesmuseum of German colonial times.

The American Cultural Center Library was opened in 1991. Its reading room can seat 50. The Library, run by a professional, has 4,500 books, 200 periodicals, and 500 tapes.

The Profession. Soon after independence in 1990, the Namibian Information Workers Association (NIWA) was formed. With almost 70 members, it provides a forum for discussing professional issues and advises the government and employers on service conditions. It is a member of IFLA, COMLA, and the Namibian Professional Association, and produces a newsletter.

Education for teacher-librarians is offered at the University of Namibia and Windhoek Teachers College. The regional library school at the University of Botswana offers professional-level education.

REFERENCES

A. J. Totemeyer, *Namibian Public Libraries* (1991).

Kalervo Jarvelin, Ann Hakari, and Jaana Kaki, *Library and Information Work and Its Requirements in Namibia* (1991).

KWAMI E. AVAFIA

National Bibliographies

The following list of 100 current national bibliographies was compiled from the catalogues and collections, and with assistance from the staff, of the Library of Congress. It is as exhaustive as possible, but no claim for completeness can be put forward. Some national bibliographies that are said to exist could not be traced in any of the library catalogues or holdings lists that were examined.

For this article the editors decided to regard as "current" any national bibliography known to be active since 1984, even if its coverage lagged considerably behind the imprint date. Some of the bibliographies included on this basis may have suspended or ceased publication recently because of political changes in various parts of the world. To keep entries relatively short, each country has been limited to one title, with the exception of Czechoslovakia, which issues separate bibliographies for its two major languages. In cases where the national bibliography is issued in several parts covering various types of publications, only the part dealing with trade books is listed. With few exceptions, details about frequency, cumulations, title changes, subseries, and bibliographies that antedate the establishment of the current national bibliography have been omitted. Additional information of this kind can be found in the published sources listed under *References*. In the absence of a bona fide national bibliography, an entry is provided for the next best available source produced by local agencies (such as individual booksellers, book trade organizations, university or public libraries, or learned societies). Some of these substitutes, especially in the cases of the smaller territories, include writings published elsewhere about the area in addition to items published locally. The current title and imprint are given in the vernacular, and, in most cases, a starting date is given. Titles in non-Roman alphabets have been transliterated. If the issuing agency does not appear as corporate author, as publisher, or in an "at head of title" note, its name is supplied in a drop note.

Although many countries do not produce separate national bibliographies, good coverage of their publications may be found through regional bibliographies such as *The CARICOM Bibliography, Boletin Bibliografico, The Arab Bulletin of Publications, South Pacific Bibliography,* and the regional *Accessions Lists* published by the Library of Congress. Complete descriptions of these and other regional bibliographies may be found in the Bell and Gorman and Mills books listed under *References*.

Consideration of national bibliographies in the

1990s is not complete without a mention of automation. The following countries produce national bibliographies in machine-readable form on tapes, CD-ROMs, or both: Australia, Brazil, Canada, Chile, Denmark, Finland, France, Germany, Indonesia, Italy, Japan, The Netherlands, New Zealand, Norway, Russia, South Africa, Spain, Sweden, United Kingdom, United States, and Venezuela. Czechoslovakia, Malaysia, Mexico, and Yugoslavia—and undoubtedly other countries—are in the process of developing machine-readable bibliographies.

ALBANIA

Bibliografia kombëtare e Republikës Popullore të Shqipërisë: libri shqip. Bibliographie nationale de la R. P. A.: les livres albanais. 1958+ Tiranë, Botim i Bibliotekës Kombëtare.

ALGERIA

al-Bībliyūghrāfyā al-Jazā'irīyah. 1. + année; 1. oct. 1963+ Alger, al-Maktabah al-Waṭanīyah [Bibliothèque Nationale].

Added title page: *Bibliographie de l'Algérie.*

ARGENTINA

Libros Argentinos: ISBN. 1984+ Buenos Aires, Camara Argentina del Libro.

AUSTRALIA

Australian National Bibliography. Jan. 1961+ Canberra, National Library of Australia.

AUSTRIA

Oesterreichische Bibliographie; Verzeichnis der österreichischen Neuerscheinungen. Bearb. von der Österreichischen Nationalbibliothek. 1945+ Wien, Hauptverband des österreichischen Buchhandels, 1946+

BANGLADESH

Bāmlādeśa jātīya granthapañjī. Bangladesh National Bibliography. 1+ 1972+ Dhākā, Bāmlādeśa Árakāibhs o Granthāgāra Paridaptara, Śikshā, Samskṛti, o Krīṛā Mantranālaya, Gaṇaprajātantrī Bāmlādeśa Sarakāra [Directorate of Archives and Libraries, National Library of Bangladesh].

BARBADOS

The National Bibliography of Barbados. Jan./Mar. 1975+ Bridgetown, Public Library.

BELGIUM

Bibliographie de Belgique. Belgische bibliografie. 1. + année; jan. 1875+ Bruxelles, Bibliothèque royale Albert Ier.

BERMUDA

Bermuda National Bibliography. v. 1+ 1983+ Hamilton, The Bermuda Library.

BOLIVIA

Bio-bibliografía boliviana. 1975+ La Paz, Editorial Los Amigos del Libro, 1977+

Compiled by W. Guttentag Tichauer.

Supersedes *Bibliografía boliviana.*

BOTSWANA

The National Bibliography of Botswana. v. 1+ 1969+ [Gaberones] Botswana National Library Service.

BRAZIL

Bibliografia brasileira. jan./jun. 1983+ [Rio de Janeiro] Biblioteca Nacional, 1984+

Supersedes *Boletim bibliográfico da Biblioteca Nacional.*

BULGARIA

Natsionalna biblografiia na NR Bulgariia. Seriia 1, Bŭlgarski knigopis: knigi, notni, graficheski i kartografski izdaniia. no. 78+ ian 1974+ Sofiia, Narodna biblioteka Kiril i Metodiĭ.

Supersedes in part *Bŭlgarski knigopis* (1897–1973) and continues its numbering.

CANADA

Canadiana. Jan. 15, 1951+ Ottawa.

Compiled and edited by the Cataloguing Branch, National Library of Canada.

CARIBBEAN AREA

The CARICOM Bibliography. v. 1+ 1977+ Georgetown, Guyana, Caribbean Community Secretariat Library, 1977+

This is a cumulated subject list of current national imprints of the Caribbean Community member countries (Barbados, Guyana, Jamaica, and Trinidad and Tobago) and areas not yet producing national bibliographies, such as the Bahamas and Belize.

CHILE

Bibliografía chilena. 1980+ Santiago, Biblioteca Nacional, 1982+

Retrospective volume covering 1976–79 was published in 1981.

Supersedes *Anuario de la prensa chilena.*

CHINA, PEOPLE'S REPUBLIC OF

Ch'uan kuo hsin shu mu. Quan-guo xinshumu. National Bibliography. 1950+ Pei-ching, Wen hua pu, Ch'u pan shih-yeh kuan li chu, Pan-pent'u shu kuan, 1951+

CHINA, REPUBLIC OF (TAIWAN)

Chung-hua min-kuo ch'u pan t'u shu mu lu. 1970+ T'ai-pei, Kuo li chung yang t'u shu kuan.

Supersedes *The Monthly List of Chinese Books* (1960–69).

COLOMBIA

Anuario bibliográfico colombiano "Rubén Pérez Ortiz." 1951+ Bogotá.

At head of title: Instituto Caro y Cuervo. Departamento de Bibliographía.

CUBA

Bibliografía Cubano. 1937+ La Habana, Consejo Nacional de Cultura.

From 1937 to 1952 title was *Anuario bibliográfico cubano.*

CZECHOSLOVAKIA

České knihy. 1951+ Praha, Statni Knihovna CSR.

Supersedes *Bibliografický katalog,* pt. A, *Knihy české* (1933–50).

Slovenská národná bibliografia. Séria A: knihy. roč., 21+ 1970+ Martin, Matica slovenská.

Continues *Slovenské knihy* (1951–69), which superseded *Bibliografický katalog* pt. B, *Knihy slovenské* (1946–50).

DENMARK

Dansk bogfortegnelse. The Danish National Bibliography. Books. 1841/58+ Udarb. af Bilbiotekscentralen. Ballerup, Bibliotekscentralens Forlag, 1861+

Det dansk bogmarked contains a weekly alphabetical list of new books.

DOMINICAN REPUBLIC

Anuario bibliográfico dominicano. 1980/82+ Santo Domingo, Biblioteca Nacional, 1984+

Supersedes *Boletin bibliográfico dominicano.*

ECUADOR

Bibliografía ecuatoriana. 1975+ Quito, Biblioteca General de las Universidad Central del Ecuador.

Annual cumulation title is *Annuario bibliográfico Ecuatoriana y Bibliografía Ecuatoriana.*

Continues *Ecuador, Bibliografía Analítica.*

EGYPT

Nashrat al-īdā'. [al-Qahirah] Dar al-Kutub wa-al-Watha'iqal-Qawmiyah.

Added title page: *Legal Deposit Bulletin.*

ETHIOPIA

Ethiopian Publications. 1963/64+ Addis Ababa, Haile Selassie I University, Institute of Ethiopian Studies, 1965+

FIJI

Fiji National Bibliography v. 1+ 1970–78+ Lautoka, Fiji, Library Service of Fiji, Ministry of Social Welfare, Dec. 1979+

FINLAND

Suomen kirjallisuus. Finlands litteratur. The Finnish National Bibliography. 1544/1877+ [Helsinki] Helsingin Yliopiston Kirjasto, 1878+

FRANCE

Bibliographie de la France. 1. + année; nov. 1811+ Paris, Cercle de la Librarie.

THE GAMBIA

National Bibliography of The Gambia. v. 1+ Jan./June 1977+ Banjul, National Library of The Gambia, 1980+

GERMANY, FEDERAL REPUBLIC OF

Deutsche Bibliographie. Wöchentliches Verzeichnis. Amtsblatt der Deutschen Bibliothek. A: *Erscheinungen des Verlagsbuchhandels.* 1. März 1947+ Frankfurt am Main, Buchhändler-Vereinigung.

As a result of reunification, the national bibliography for the German Democratic Republic was discontinued in 1991:

Deutsche Nationalbibliographie und Bibliographie des im Ausland erschienenen deutschspraghigen Schrifttums. Bearb. und hrsg. von der Deutschen Bücherei. *Reihe A: Neuerscheinungen des Buchhandels.* 3. Jan. 1931+ Leipzig, VEB Verlag für Buch- und Bibliothekswesen.

GHANA

Ghana National Bibliography. 1965+ Accra, Ghana Library Board, 1968+

GUYANA

Guyanese National Bibliography. Jan./Mar. 1973+ Georgetown, National Library.

HONDURAS

Anuario bibliográfico hondureno (Tegucigalpa, Honduras). 1980+ Tegucigalpa, El Sistema, 1982+

At head of title: Universidad Nacional Autonoma de Honduras. Sistema Bibliotecario.

HONG KONG

A Catalogue of Books Printed in Hong Kong. In *Hong Kong Government Gazette.* Compiled by the Chief Librarian, New Territories Public Libraries, Cultural Services Department, Hong Kong.

Published quarterly as special supplement no. 4.

HUNGARY

Magyar nemzeti bibliográfia: könyvek bibliográfiája. 32. evf. + aug. 15, 1977+ Budapest, Országos Széchényi Könyvtár.

Continues *Magyar nemzeti bibliográfia,* which began publication jan./márc. 1946.

ICELAND

Íslensk bókaskrá. The Icelandic National Bibliography. 1974+ Reykjavík, Landsbókasafn Íslands, 1975+

A continuation of "Íslenzk rit," which appeared in *Árbok Landsbókasafns Íslands,* 1945–75, and *Bókaskrá Bóksalafélags Íslands,* 1937–73.

INDIA

Indian National Bibliography. v. 1+ Jan./Mar. 1958+ [Calcutta] Central Reference Library.

INDONESIA

Bibliografi nasional Indonesia. Okt. 1975+ Jakarta, Proyek Pengembangan Perpustakaan, Departemen Pendidikan den Kebudayaan, Apr. 1978+

Continues Indonesia. Kantor Bibliografi Nasional. *Bibliografi nasional Indonesia.*

IRAN

Teheran. Kitabkhanah-i Milli. *Kitabshinasi-i milli.* 1+ [1963]+ Tihran.

Added title page: *National Bibliography, Iranian Publications.*

IRAQ

al-Fihris al-watani lil-matbu'at al-'Iraqiyah. al-sanah 7+ al-adad 17/18+ [Baghdad] Wizarat al-I'lam, Mudiriyat al-Thaqafah al-Ammah, al-Maktabah al-Wataniyah, 1977+

Added title page: *National Bibliography of Iraq.*

Continues *al-Bibliyughrafiyah al-wataniyah al-'Iraqiyah.*

IRELAND

Irish Publishing Record. 1967+ [Dublin] School of Librarianship, University College Dublin.

ISRAEL

Kiryat sefer, rive'on le-bibliografyah shel bet ha-sefarim a-le'umi veha-'universita'i bi-Yerushalayim. shanah 1+ [Jerusalem, 1924]+

Added title page: *Kiryat Sefer, Bibliographical Quarterly of the Jewish National and University Library, Jerusalem.*

ITALY

Bibliografia nazionale italiana. anno 1+ genn. 1958+ Firenze, Biblioteca nazionale centrale.

IVORY COAST

Bibliographie de la Côte d'Ivoire. 1969+ [Abidjan] Bibliothèque nationale [1970]+

JAMAICA

Jamaican National Bibliography. v. 1+ Jan.–Mar. 1975+ Kingston, Institute of Jamaica, West India Reference Library, Jan.–Mar. 1976+

Continues Institute of Jamaica, Kingston, West India Reference Library. *Jamaican National Bibliography.*

A cumulation covering 1964–1974 was published in 1981 by Kraus Thomson.

JAPAN

Nihon zenkoku shoshi. 1977+ Tokyo, Kokuitsu Kokkai Toshokan.

Continues *Zen Nihon shuppanbutsu somokuroku.*

JORDAN

al-Bibliyughrafiya al-wataniyah al-Urduniyah. 1979+ Amman, al-Jamiyah, 1980+ The Jordan Library Association.

KENYA

Kenya National Bibliography. 1980+ Nairobi, Kenya National Library Service, National Reference & Bibliographic Department, 1983+

Works published in 1979 and before constitute materials for the retrospective *Kenya National Bibliography*.

KOREA, REPUBLIC OF

Taehan Min'guk ch'ulp'anmul ch'ongmongnok. 1945/62+ [Seoul] Kungnip Chungang Tosogwan.

Added title page: *Korean National Bibliography*.

LESOTHO

Lesotho index: an annotated bibliography of new and newly located Lesotho materials. 1989+ Roma, Documentation Centre, Institute of Southern African Studies, National University of Lesotho.

Continues *Lesothana*. 1982+

LIECHTENSTEIN

Liechtensteinische Bibliographie. 1. + Jahrg. 1974+ Vaduz, Liechtensteinische Landesbibliothek.

LUXEMBOURG

Bibliographie luxembourgeoise. [1.] + année; 1944/45+ Luxembourg, P. Linden.

At head of title: Bibliothèque nationale, Luxembourg.

MADAGASCAR

Raki-tahirinkevi-pirenen'i madagasikara. Bibliographie nationale de Madagascar. 1970/71+ Antananarivo, Bibliothèque Universitaire; 1983 + Bibliothèque Nationale.

Continues *Bibliographie annuelle de Madagascar*.

MALAWI

Malawi National Bibliography: List of Publications Deposited in the Library of the National Archives. 1965+ Zomba, National Archives of Malawi.

MALAYSIA

Bibliografi negara Malaysia. Malaysian National Bibliography. 1967+ Kuala Lumpur, Perkhidmatan Perpustakaan Negara, Arkib Negara Malaysia.

MALTA

Bibljografija nazzjonali ta Malta. Malta national bibliography. 1983+ Valetta, National Library of Malta.

MAURITIUS

Mauritius. Archives Dept. *Annual Report* (includes *Bibliography of Mauritius*) 1955+ Port Louis,

Continues *Memorandum of Books Printed in Mauritius and Registered in the Archives Office*.

MEXICO

Bibliografia mexicana. enero/feb. 1967+ [México] Biblioteca Nacional de México, Instituto de Investigaciones Bibliograficas.

At head of title: Universidad Nacional Autónoma de México.

MOROCCO

Bibliyughrafiya al-wataniyah al-Maghribiyah. al-ida: al-qanuni li-sanat. 1961+ Rabat, Morocco. Khizanah al-Ammah lil-Kutub wa-al-Watha'iq [Bibliothèque Générale et Archives].

Added title page: *Bibliographie nationale marocaine*.

Continues *Bibliographie nationale marocaine*.

NEPAL

Nepalese national bibliography in *Journal of the Nepal Research Centre*. 1981/82+ Wiesbaden, Franz Steiner.

Compiled by staff of the Tribhuvan University Central Library.

THE NETHERLANDS

Brinkman's cumulatieve catalogus van boeken. 1. + jaarg. 1846+ Alphen aan den Rijn, A. U. Sijthoff.

NEW ZEALAND

New Zealand National Bibliography. Feb. 1967+ Wellington, National Library of New Zealand.

Supersedes in part the *Index to New Zealand Periodicals, and Current National Bibliography* (1950–65).

NICARAGUA

Nicaraguan national bibliography, 1800–1978. Bibliografia nacional nicaraguense, 1800–1978. 1986, Redlands, Calif., Latin American Bibliographic Foundation; Managua, Biblioteca Nacional Rubén Darío.

Supplements are planned.

NIGERIA

National Bibliography of Nigeria. 1973+ Lagos, National Library of Nigeria.

Continues *Nigerian Publications: Current National Bibliography* (1950–72).

NORWAY

Norsk bokfortegnelse. The Norwegian National Bibliography. 1814/47+ Oslo, Norsk Bokhandlerforening, 1848+

PAKISTAN

The Pakistan National Bibliography. 1962+ Karachi, Govt. of Pakistan, Directorate of Archives & Libraries, National Bibliographical Unit.

PALESTINE

Palestine Local Bibliography. 1981+ East Jerusalem, Arab Studies Society.

PAPUA NEW GUINEA

Papua New Guinea National Bibliography. Mar. 1981+ Waigan, National Library Service of Papua New Guinea, 1981+

Continues *New Guinea Bibliography*.

PARAGUAY

Paraguay . . . anos de bibliografia. 1986+ Asuncion, Cromos.

Began with *Paraguay, cinco anos de bibliografia, 1980–1984*, followed by *Paraguay, un ano de bibliografia, 1987* and *Paraguay, dos anos de bibliographia, 1988–1989*.

PHILIPPINES

Philippines National Bibliography. Jan./Feb. 1974+ Manila, National Library of the Philippines.

Preceded by *Philippine Bibliography* (1963/64–70/72), issued 1965–73 by the University of the Philippines Library in Quezon City.

POLAND

Przewodnik bibliograficzny: urzedowy wykaz druków wydawnych w Rzeczpospolitej Polskiej. [rocz. 1]+ 1944/45+ Warszawa, Biblioteka narodowa.

Supersedes *Urzedowy wykaz druków* (1928–39) and its predecessor, *Przewodnik bibliograficzny* (1878–1933).

PORTUGAL

Boletim de bibliografia portugesa. Monografias; Boletim de bibliografia portugesa. Publicões em série; Boletim de bibliografia portugesa. Documentos não textuals. 1981+ Lisbon, Biblioteca Nacional.

Continues *Boletim de bibliografia portuguesa*. v. 1+ ano de 1935+ Lisboa, 1937+ Biblioteca Nacional.

QATAR

Qā'imat al-intāj al-fikrī al-Qatarī li-'ām [National Bibliography of Qatar]. 1971+ Doha, Dār al-kutub al-Qaṭarīyah [Qatar National Library].

ROMANIA

Bibliografia Republicii Socialiste România: cărţi, albume, hărţi. 1952+ Bucharest, Biblioteca Centrală de Stat.

RUSSIA

Knizhnaia letopis, organ gosudarstvennoi bibliografii SSSR. g. 1+ 14 iiulia 1907+ Moskva, Izd-vo "Kniga."

Issued by Vsesoiuznaia knizhnaia palata.

SENEGAL

Bibliographie du Sénégal. no. 40+ 1972+ [Dakar, Archives du Sénégal]

Continues *Bulletin bibliographique des Archives du Sénégal* (1963–71).

SIERRA LEONE

Sierra Leone Publications. 1962/63+ Freetown, 1964+ Sierra Leone. Library Board.

SINGAPORE

Singapore National Bibliography. 1967+ Singapore, National Library.

SOUTH AFRICA

South African National Bibliography. Suid-Afrikaanse nasionale bibliografie. 1959+ Pretoria, State Library [1960]+

Continues *Publications Received in Terms of Copyright Act no. 9 of 1916,* issued by the State Library, Apr. 1933–1958.

SPAIN

Bibliografía española. 1958+ Madrid, Ministerio de Educación Nacional, Dirección General de Archivos y Bibliotecas.

SRI LANKA

Śrī Laṅkā jātika grantha nāmāvaliya = Ilaṅkait tēcīya nūrpaṭṭiyal = Sri Lanka natinal bibliography. 1963+ Kolamba, Śrī Laṅkā Jātika Pustakāla Sēvā Maṇḍalaya [Sri Lanka National Library Services Board].

Continues *Ceylon national bibliography,* 1964–1972, Kolamba, National Bibliography Division of the National Archives.

SWAZILAND

Swaziland National Bibliography. 1973/76+ Kwaluseni University of Botswana and Swaziland.

SWEDEN

Svensk bokförteckning. The Swedish National Bibliography. jan. 1953+ Redigerad av Bibliografiska Institutet vid Kungl. Biblioteket i Stockholm. Stockholm, Svensk bokhandel.

SWITZERLAND

Das Schweizer Buch. Le livre suisse. Il libro svizzero. Hrsg. von der Schweizerischen Landesbibliothek. 1. + Jahrg.; Jan./Feb. 1901+ Zürich, Schweizerischer Buchhändler- und Verleger Verband.

SYRIA

al-Bibliyūjrāfiyā al-waṭanīyah al-Sūrīyah. [Dimashq] al-Jumhuriyah al-'Arabiyah al-Suriyah, Wizarat al-Thaqafah, Maktabat al-Asad [Bibliographical Section, Assad Library].

Continues *al-Nashrah al-maktabiyah bi-al-kutub al-sadirah fi al-Jumhuriyah al-'Arabiyah al-Suriyah.*

TANZANIA

Tanzania National Bibliography. 1974/75+ Dar es Salaam, Tanzania Library Service.

Continues *Printed in Tanzania.*

TRINIDAD AND TOBAGO

Trinidad and Tobago National Bibliography. v. 1+ Jan./June 1975+ [Port of Spain] Central Library of Trinidad and Tobago.

TUNISIA

Bibliographie nationale de Tunisie. 1. + année; 1 semestre 1969+ Tunis, Bibliothèque nationale, 1970+

Added title page: *al-Bībliyūghrāfiyā al-qawmīyah al-Tūnisyah.*

Retrospective coverage is provided by *Bibliographie Nationale; Publications non-officielles, 1956–1968,* compiled by the Bibliothèque Nationale (Dar al Kutab al-Qawmiyah) and published in Tunis by Service documentaire (1974. 167, 165 leaves).

TURKEY

Türkiye bibliyografyasi. 1934+ Ankara, Turk Tarih Kurumu Basimevi.

UNITED KINGDOM

British National Bibliography. 1950+ London, British Library, Bibliographic Services Division.

UNITED STATES

Cumulative Book Index. 1898/99+ New York, H. W. Wilson Co.

URUGUAY

Anuario bibliográfico uruguayo. 1946–49; 1968+ Montevideo, Biblioteca Nacional, 1947–51; 1969+

Bibliografía uruguaya, which began publication in 1962, is still being issued by the Biblioteca del Poder Legislativo, but its coverage is now about eight years behind.

VENEZUELA

Bibliografía venezolano. v. 1+ 1980–81+ Caracas, Instituto Autonomo Biblioteca Nacional y de Servicios de Bibliotecas, 1982+

Continues *Anuario bibliográfico venezolano.*

VIETNAM

Thu'muc quoc gia Viet Nam. Ha-Noi.

At head of title: Cong Hoa Xa Hoi Chu Nghia Viet Nam, Thu'-Vien Quoc Gia.

Publications of South Vietnam were formerly covered by *Thu'tich quoc-gia Vietnam; National Bibliography of Vietnam,* issued in Saigon beginning June 1968 by Nha Van-Kho va Thu'-Vien Quoc-Gia, Bo Van-Hoa Giao-Duc va Thanh-Nien.

YUGOSLAVIA

Bibliografija Jugoslavije: knjige, brošure i muzikalije. The Bibliography of Yugoslavia: Books, Pamphlets and Music. god 1+ 1950+ Beograd.

Bibliografija Jugoslavije: knjige, brošure i muzikalije, 1950–1980, compiled by Nevenka Skendzic and edited by Venceslav Glisic, was published in Belgrade in 1981 by the Jugoslovenski bibliografski institut as part of its *Bibliografske informacije* series.

ZAIRE

Bibliographie du Zaïre. 1987+ Kinshasa, Bibliothèque nationale.

Continues *Bibliographie nationale.* no. 5+ 1974+ Kinshasa/Gombe, Direction des Arts et Culture, République du Zaïre (suspended 1975), which continued *Bibliographie nationale retrospective des publications zaïroises ou relatives à la République du Zaïre, acquises par la Bibliothèque nationale.*

ZAMBIA
The National Bibliography of Zambia. 1970/71+ Lusaka, National Archives of Zambia.

ZIMBABWE
Zimbabwe National Bibliography. 1979+ Salisbury, National Archives, 1980+
Continues *Rhodesia National Bibliography.*

REFERENCES
Barbara L. Bell, *An Annotated Guide to Current National Bibliographies* (1986).
G. E. Gorman, "African National Bibliographies as Selection Resources," *International Library Review* (1989).
G. E. Gorman and J. J. Mills, *Guide to Current National Bibliographies in the Third World,* 2nd rev. ed. (1987).
Cecily Johns, editor, *Selection of Library Materials for Area Studies. Pt. 1 Asia, Iberia, the Caribbean and Latin America, Eastern Europe and the Soviet Union, and the South Pacific* (1990).
D. W. Kummel, "Guides to National Bibliographies: A Review Essay," *Libraries & Culture* (1989).
Annemarie Nilges, *Nationalbibliographien Lateinamerikas* (1983).

ABBY YOCHELSON

National Libraries

HISTORY

The earliest national libraries date back to the 15th and 16th centuries—the Biblioteca Marciana in Venice (1468), the Bibliothèque Nationale of France (1537), the Österreichische Bibliothek in Vienna, the Bayerische Staatsbibliothek in Munich (1558), and the Bibliothèque Royale in Brussels (1559)—but there is disagreement on dates of foundation. Two of these institutions are now provincial or regional rather than national libraries; it is extremely difficult to define a national library precisely. By the year 1800 more than 20 countries had national libraries, though not all had that status at the time. Nearly all traced their origins to royal collections or large private collections. Most were in Europe, but they included the Library of Congress in the United States and the national libraries of Colombia and Ecuador.

In the 19th century nearly all the remaining countries of Europe established national libraries, as did most countries in Latin America. The national library became not only a source of national pride but also a symbol of nationhood, especially for newly emergent countries. Prestigious buildings were planned, though often only partly executed. Many libraries of this period were created, if not from nothing, from small existing collections, and although they had high ambitions they were (and are) often seriously under-resourced. Relatively few of them were able to accumulate great collections.

A third wave of national libraries in the later 19th and 20th centuries appeared in various parts of the world, notably Asia and Africa, though Africa has several countries without them. This group of national libraries is more varied. In several less developed countries, especially in Africa, the national library is the organizational center of the nation's library system, often the center of its public library services, and sometimes the site of its library school. In several developed countries, such as Canada and New Zealand, the national libraries have concentrated on collections of national material and on giving bibliographic and other services.

National Library of India

The National Library of India, Belvedere, southeast Calcutta. It stands on 30-acre grounds.

One or two older libraries have undergone major reorganizations since World War II. The largest transformation has been the creation in 1973 of the British Library from the Library of the British Museum, the National Lending Library for Science and Technology, and four other national bodies, making it one of the most wide-ranging of national libraries. In France, the new Bibliothèque de France, which will coexist with the Bibliothèque Nationale, will also bring about great changes.

Few new national libraries have been created since the 1970s, partly because of costs and partly because library leaders believe that national library objectives can be achieved more economically in other ways. However, statements of objectives (such as those for the National Library of Sri Lanka) may be no less ambitious than those of the big traditional national libraries.

PRESENT STATUS

Legal deposit regulations, originally linked with copyright protection, were used to ensure that national libraries receive the nation's printed book production; these regulations were of varying effectiveness, but in the more developed countries they resulted in a steady flow of material. In the older libraries, rich collections of foreign books were expanded by extensive purchases and occasional donations. The size of these collections demanded catalogues far better than what had gone before. At a time when there were no public libraries in the modern sense, and most academic libraries served only restricted groups, national libraries assumed pre-eminent status. If any lead was to be given to librarianship, it was likely to come from them. They set standards, attracted some of the best librarians, produced various innovations, and played a major role in establishing national library associations. In some countries they introduced library education. National libraries created since World War II still perform these functions, or try to do so. But the period since about 1960 has seen a change of emphasis from service to individuals to service to libraries.

Numbers. No one can say how many national libraries exist in the world, because the number depends on how a national library is defined. About 100 institutions are actually designated as national libraries, but many more libraries have some recognized national functions. Some countries (including Japan and the United States) have libraries that actually serve as national libraries in a wide sense, although their titles indicate other functions (in both cases service to the legislature). Some nations have more than one national library, for historical reasons or because collections are divided by subject, by format, or by function. For historical reasons, Canada and the United Kingdom, which once consisted of several independent entities, have several national libraries. Division by subject is exemplified by the National Agricultural Library and the National Library of Medicine in the United States. Division by format appears in the National Film Archives in Finland and the U.K. and in France's Département de la Phonothèque Nationale et de l'Audiovisuel. Division by function is shown in South Africa, where the State Library in Pretoria offers bibliographic services and provides books and the South Africa Library in Cape Town is the national reference collection. Some institutions (such as the six in Italy that are not Bibliotechi Nazionali Centrali) are little different in status from state libraries in Australia or the U.S.

In several countries the role of national library is combined with that of university or public library (the latter almost exclusively in less developed countries), while in others national functions are distributed by subject among several libraries with other primary roles. Scandinavia provides examples of both. For example, the University Library of Helsinki is designated as the National Library of Finland, but subjects other than the humanities are the responsibility of various other designated libraries. In a few countries (including Bolivia, Kampuchea, and Zambia) the national library and the national archives are combined in one institution. Some countries such as Botswana, Kenya, and Malawi have a "national library service" rather than, and possibly as a preliminary to, a national library. On somewhat similar lines, Denmark and Norway have National Librarians with national planning responsibilities but no libraries directly under them; these countries have distributed national libraries, with the Royal Library of Denmark and the University of Oslo Library carrying out many major national library functions.

Cyril and Methodius National Library of Bulgaria in Sofia.

These examples show how complex the situation is and why it is impossible to say precisely how many national libraries exist: there are fully national, semi-national, paranational, sub-national, pseudo-national, and, perhaps, in the case of the biggest, supernational libraries. It is almost equally difficult to compare them for size, because statistics are kept in many ways, but it is clear that the five largest are the Library of Congress in the U.S., the Russian State Library (formerly the Lenin State Library), the British Library, the National Library of China, and the Bibliothèque Nationale of France. As for quality, in general the oldest have the richest and most valuable historical collections, but not all have good collections for all periods.

Much cooperation between national libraries is bilateral, but the period since 1970 has seen the creation of the Conference of Directors of National Libraries (CDNL) and smaller bodies such as the Conference of European National Libraries (CENL). National librarians in regions such as southeast Asia and Latin America have met; these bodies and meetings have shown that national libraries can achieve much progress by agreeing among themselves on such matters as common record formats.

FUNCTIONS

Many people have compiled lists of functions of national libraries, based largely on the main common features of existing ones. But national libraries exhibit more variety than any other kinds of libraries, and the only feature they all have in common is that they seek to collect and conserve printed publications produced in the country; this was the final definition arrived at after much discussion at an IFLA colloquium in 1973. Even it is imperfect: in nearly every country patents are the responsibility of a separate body, an exception being the U.K.

Other frequently found functions can be divided into four groups: national production, national services, national planning and control, and national leadership.

National Production involves such functions as collecting works written by national authors or works written on the country; collecting manuscripts of national interest; and creating the national bibliography (*see* National Bibliographies). How widely the term "national publications" is interpreted varies. In some countries, such as Norway, the national library has legal deposit of all kinds of published material, from print through audiovisual to electronic, including broadcast material. In many countries, the national library collects only one or two forms, usually sound recordings and print. The extent to which "nationalia" are collected depends partly on the size and historical significance of the country: it is much easier in Iceland, for example, than in the U.S.

National Services include providing catalogue records to libraries, providing documents to libraries, and managing international (and occasionally national) exchange of publications. These services may be narrow or broad, according to the material collected; a national library in a small country that collected only national imprints could not supply many documents or records.

Services to individuals can be considered a subset of national services: consultation, direct loans (other than through interlibrary loan), and photocopying.

National Planning, Coordination, and Control include such items as a national acquisitions policy, an interlibrary loan system, a national bibliographic database, library education and training, and library and information research. Most national libraries serve as the main library links with other countries and provide national representation to international bodies. In some countries the national library has a statutory duty to plan the national system and oversee other libraries, as in Venezuela, where the Instituto Autónomo Biblioteca Nacional y de Servicios de Bibliotecas has responsibility for the whole public library system.

National Leadership involves building up and maintaining a major research collection of the world's literature and offering services based on such a collection. The first national libraries were, or intended to be, the biggest and best in the country. In many if not most countries today some university and occasionally public libraries are bigger than the national library.

Changing Functions. The huge changes since World War II have affected all libraries, but their influence on national libraries is more fundamental, affecting their very nature and functions. The vast increase in the volume of printed matter has been accompanied by a still more rapid growth in other media, including publications produced and stored electronically. Money for publicly funded libraries has run short. National libraries have felt political as well as economic pressures to cut costs, earn money, or transfer activities to the private information sector. Many activities and services that were best performed by a national library can now be performed equally if not more satisfactorily in other ways: cooperatively by other libraries or commercially by private firms. Every one of the functions carried out by national libraries, including collecting the nation's literature, can be done in other ways and is being so done in one country or another.

As a result of financial restrictions, many national libraries have reduced their collecting effort and curtailed their services or are now charging for some services. The services are still needed, and the search for alternatives continues. Lists of national library functions, whether descriptive or prescriptive, are beginning to give way to analyses of national functions and possible ways in which they might be carried out. Collecting is coming to be shared with other libraries in the country (as in "distributed national collections") and with libraries in other countries. The comprehensive national library, on the lines of the Bibliothèque Nationale and the British Library, was never more than a distant aim for most countries; it is now an impossible and probably unnecessary one. Indeed, these two libraries are not comprehensive—neither collects all types of published media, for example.

Administration of Information Affairs, Ministry of Education, Qatar

Preservation of rare manuscripts at the National Library of Qatar in Doha.

In eastern Europe a different model of national library operated between the end of World War II and the end of the Cold War. Instruments of the state, these libraries were well funded and staffed, but had to select and display stock, issue catalogues, and advise readers in ways that served the purposes of the state. Large portions of their bookstocks were not only kept in tightly restricted areas but also excluded from public catalogues. The libraries were responsible for carrying out state decrees relating to libraries; they set up "methodological centers" to set rules and promote their observance. These libraries faced enormous problems in the 1990s as they moved from centralized control to local management, problems made worse by much reduced funding.

National libraries are essentially conservative institutions, and for good reason. They are geared to collecting and conserving printed materials, but less able to deal with the other media that account for an increasing proportion of the nation's published output. Most of them are also overwhelmingly concerned with humanistic literature; they serve the social sciences less well, and science and technology poorly. Other institutions have arisen to serve these enormous areas, bodies such as the Canada Institute for Scientific and Technical Information (CISTI) or the documentation centers such as INSDOC in India and TURDOC in Turkey. The reasons are partly historical: the humanities dominated literature until the 20th century, a far cry from today, when three out of four publications are in science or technology. Also, scientists demand the latest publications and more service than humanities scholars do, and national libraries had neither the traditions, the systems, nor the staff to provide what they asked. New institutions were set up to fill the need, usually with more funds than the national library, leaving national libraries with a relatively smaller national role.

Some national libraries do cover a wide range of formats, as in Norway, and some have purchase policies covering all subjects, as in the National Library of Australia and the British Library. But in

National Library of Austria

National Library of Austria in Vienna.

general national libraries are restricted in their coverage, and this restriction will become relatively greater unless radical steps are taken to change it.

ORGANIZATION

One thing all national libraries have in common is that they receive all or most of their funds from the state and are directly accountable to it. Unlike most public and academic libraries, they have no buffer between them and the government. They have the advantage of better access to government departments, but are more directly exposed to government policies and decisions, including financial restrictions. A change in government can have a dramatic effect on a national library, as in Iran, where the Islamic Revolution forced librarians to abandon extremely ambitious plans for a new Pahlavi National Library. Most national libraries report to ministries or departments of Culture, Arts, or Education; a few report to Research or some other area. Many national libraries have Boards of Directors or Trustees to oversee general policy matters; most have advisory machinery of one kind or another.

Organizational structures vary greatly. The main divisions may be based on types of materials (such as printed books and maps), major functions (reference and conservation), subject, or site (in cases where there are two or more sites). Various other kinds of divisions are possible. Division by type of material is most common in the older libraries, but division by function is becoming more popular.

Many national libraries, because of their leadership role, size, range of stock, and range of functions, have large staffs that include a wide range of professional, academic, and technical expertise. Many now require skills that are not confined to libraries: information technology, marketing, public relations, and assorted management skills.

A mobile library used in the National Library of Malaysia's extension services.

SERVICES

All national libraries offer consultation facilities, but some of them are highly restricted, limiting access to scholars who can prove their status and their need, whether because of tradition, the value or nature of the collection, limited seating space, or volume of demand. Nearly all lend books to other libraries, if only as a last resort and on stringent conditions; the British Library is unique in having a massive separate collection devoted entirely to document supply. Lending books directly to readers is rare in older libraries, though quite common in newer ones in less developed countries.

Many national libraries, whether or not they lend their own materials, maintain national union catalogues, most of them confined to foreign publications. Such catalogues are rarely printed, because it is much more efficient in terms of both construction and use to maintain them as machine-readable databases.

Bibliographic services, largely based on the records prepared for the national bibliography, are almost universal. Automation has greatly enhanced these services in recent years, including the retrospective conversion of existing catalogues. All major catalogues will not be converted for a long time, but a signal event was the appearance in 1991 of the complete British Library catalogue on CD-ROM. The current bibliographies of France, Germany, and the U.K. are regularly issued as a single package on CD-ROMs. In some countries, such as the Netherlands, the national bibliography is prepared by a private or semi-private organization, and in one or two, such as India, by other libraries; some countries, including the U.S., have no national bibliographies.

Many bibliographic services are linked with national bibliographic networks, as in Australia and New Zealand (ABN and NZBN). In these cases the national libraries have taken responsibility for developing and managing them, but networks may be quite independent of the national library, as the OCLC network is in the U.S.

Information services other than reference are a relatively new departure. In some cases these are charged services, aimed at scientific and technical research or industry; examples are SATIS in the National Library of New Zealand and the Business Information Services of the British Library and the National Library of Scotland.

Some national libraries, such as those in Australia and the U.S., provide special services for the handicapped.

STOCK MAINTENANCE AND CONSERVATION

National libraries have a responsibility both to retain their stock and to keep it in good condition, especially national imprints. They cannot easily discard less used or unused materials, as all other types of libraries can. However, the old assumption that all national imprints should be acquired and kept is now being challenged, largely on the grounds that the volume of production in many countries makes such collection impracticable.

As for keeping stock in good condition, librarians realized only about 1980 the full scope of the problem of deteriorating printed matter, caused mainly by poor quality acid-bleached paper and worsened by environmental conditions. Huge proportions of the stock of major libraries are decaying at a rate faster than can be remedied by present methods. Efforts to solve the problem include mass deacidification and converting the information contents to microform or digital optical disks, but the cost of all methods is extremely high.

OTHER ACTIVITIES

Nearly all national libraries publish a good deal of material, mainly but not exclusively relating to the material in their collections; bibliographic publications, in addition to the national bibliography, are common. Almost all national libraries sponsor or organize exhibitions of their own materials or materials from other sources.

Some librarians sense a danger that electronic technologies may distract attention from the traditional book, the dominant carrier of knowledge of the last five hundred years and the heart of national library collections. To celebrate and promote books, Centers for the Book have been set up in at least two national libraries, in the U.K. and the U.S.

BUILDINGS

Most national libraries have purpose-designed buildings, but they range from the monumental and architecturally important to the small and insignificant; in their design, aesthetics has often prevailed over function. Few national libraries can dispose of their stock, and the inexorable growth of the collections is a continual problem.

Major buildings completed since the mid-1980s include those for the national libraries of China and New Zealand (1987), Indonesia (1989), and Malaysia and Sri Lanka (1990). Most of these new buildings replace old ones; in addition, there have been many extensions. The new National Library of China, with space for 20 million volumes and 3,000 seats, is reputed to be the largest single library building in the world. Librarians at the national libraries of Poland and Venezuela began using new buildings in the early 1990s, even before the structures were completed. New buildings were planned or under way for the

Biblioteca Nacional

National Library of Peru

British Library, the Österreichische Bibliothek, and the Bibliothèque de France.

Almost all national libraries are situated in national capitals, even where, as in the cases of Australia and Canada, there are much larger centers of population in the country. However, there are several striking exceptions. Norway has established a large "branch" in the northern town of Mo i Rana, and half of the British Library is now at Boston Spa in the north of England; in both cases these sites are the centers of bibliographic processing and document supply, while the reference collections remain in Oslo and London. There is a similar division between the two national libraries in South Africa and, though less clear, between the Bibliotechi Nazionali Centrali of Rome and Florence. In Japan a new highly automated institution for bibliographic and document supply services, Kansai-Kan, National Diet Library, is planned for a site some distance from Tokyo. Some Scandinavian national libraries have set up centers in fairly remote locations for repository collections (storing material disposed of by other libraries), microfilming, or conservation. This trend may be expected to continue.

TRENDS

Improved access to the catalogues and hence the stock of libraries in other countries is calling into question the need to accumulate huge collections of foreign publications, whether in national libraries or by other national means. The need—and the ability—to collect everything national will also be more and more questioned, especially in view of the increasing amount of material issued or made available in electronic form; legal deposit will need to be redefined, as may the concept of "publication" itself.

Circulation desk, National Library of Iran, Tehran.

There has been a strong move in most countries for libraries to be judged in terms of services rather than collections. This move has affected national libraries less than other types of libraries, because of their role in collecting and preserving the nation's archive of published material, but it has had an influence nonetheless. There is also an increasing emphasis on services to other libraries rather than to individuals. The balance between collections and services varies; services tend to receive more attention in relatively recently founded national libraries, but some older national libraries have also become service-oriented.

National libraries have not been immune to the increasing emphasis on the market, though their situation is different from that of other kinds of libraries. Most other libraries have fairly clearly defined clienteles and do not need to spend much effort on identifying their markets, though they do have to find out what their markets need. National libraries have to do both, because they do not belong to any institution and so have no core users. Yet they have to determine whom they are serving before they can establish how to serve them, just as they have to decide what business they are in. Such a determination is essential if, as is generally the case, restricted budgets force them to establish priorities among their existing and possible activities, but it is by no means easy. The size and age of many national libraries—the sheer weight of tradition and the effort required to undertake major changes—make the task more difficult.

Biblioteca Nacional José Martí in Havana.

Also being demanded, at least in the western world, is value for money, a clear return on the resources invested. To satisfy this demand, national libraries have to determine clear objectives and targets and assess what progress they have made in attaining them. The development of valid and reliable performance indicators, difficult in any library, is often particularly hard in national libraries, because national objectives are harder to establish and data harder to collect. In some cases, such as conservation, the success of actions cannot be established for decades.

Some national libraries have been subjected to external scrutinies (as in Australia and France) or have conducted radical reviews themselves (as in Denmark, Norway, and the U.S.). As a result of such reviews, or in parallel with them, the librarians have prepared several strategic plans (perhaps called corporate or business plans). This process is an increasingly popular way to approach the whole set of issues mentioned, in both large and small national libraries.

National libraries face pressures to earn money, for both ideological and hard economic reasons. Many libraries now charge for such services as bibliographic access and document supply; many have long charged for publications. Few earn more than ten percent of their expenditure, although two (the National Library of Australia and the British Library) earn as much as a quarter; it is no accident that these are the two libraries that cover all subjects and offer a wide range of services. To clarify the issue, it is becoming necessary to divide services into "basic" and "value-added," though there is dispute as to which services fall into each category.

The future of national libraries seems to be less as massive central collections and more as centers of coordination and service to libraries. This shift will both strengthen and weaken their position. They may no longer be (if they ever were) the pre-eminent collection in the country, but they should be in a position to exert great influence on the country's library and information development. If they do not take the opportunity, others will.

REFERENCES

Abdulaziz Mohamed Al-Nahari, *The Role of National Libraries in Developing Countries* (1984).

K. W. Humphreys, *A National Library in Theory and Practice* (1988).

Maurice B. Line and Joyce Line, editors, *National Libraries* (1979); *National Libraries 2: 1977–85* (1987): two collec-

tions of articles on national libraries.
Maurice B. Line, "National Libraries in a Time of Change," *IFLA Journal* (1988).
Maurice B. Line, "Do We Need National Libraries, and If So What Sort?" *Alexandria* (1990).
Alexandria (1989–), a journal that is specially concerned with national libraries, includes an annual review of the literature on national libraries and articles on general issues and on individual national libraries.

MAURICE B. LINE

Naudé, Gabriel
(1600–1653)

The French librarian Gabriel Naudé was one of the first men to attain distinction as a professional librarian. He achieved this feat partly through his labors in assembling and organizing the library of Cardinal Mazarin but mainly through his celebrated treatise on library economy, *Advis pour dresser une bibliothèque (Advice on Establishing a Library)*. Strangely, the *Advis* was published when Naudé was quite young and his library experience fairly small. It was first published in Paris (1627) and dedicated to Naudé's first employer, Henri de Mesme, *President a Mortier* in the Parliament of Paris.

Naudé was born in Paris, February 2, 1600. For several years he studied medicine, but apparently he never practiced. Having become Librarian to de Mesme, he remained one—serving a succession of illustrious bibliophiles, including, for a short period, Cardinal Richelieu, and also Queen Christina of Sweden. But his most important appointment and most ambitious assignment was as Librarian to Cardinal Mazarin, for whom he assembled a magnificent and unusually large library of 40,000 volumes, which he collected himself from all parts of Europe. Mazarin fell from power in 1652, and his library was ruthlessly dispersed; some years later it was reconstituted, but Naudé did not live to see it, having died at Abbeville July 29, 1653.

The Mazarine Library reflected exactly Naudé's own enlightened views on how the library of a wealthy private collector should be organized and administered, views that he had already expressed with boldness and clarity in his *Advis*. Naudé believed that such a library should include books valuable for their content, rather than their rarity or beauty; that they should be housed with due attention to natural lighting and freedom from dampness and household noises; and that they should be arranged by subject and made freely accessible to deserving scholars with few books of their own. These were the particular characteristics of the Mazarine Library, which was dedicated *a tous ceux qui y vouloient aller estudier* ("to all those who wish to go there to study").

Although the *Advis* was reprinted, and translated into Latin and English—the English edition (London, 1661) was a translation by scholar-diarist John Evelyn—its circulation was small. All the same, it is probable that it was of some influence in library development. It is generally agreed that it influenced the library career of Leibniz.

To be ahead of one's time may be a disadvantage, as well as a distinction. Naudé belonged, in spirit, to the modern world of freely accessible public libraries and was, in the limitations of his day, an ideal librarian.

REFERENCES

The best modern editions of Naudé's pioneer treatise are, in French, *Advis pour dresser une bibliothèque* (Leipzig, 1963), and, in English, *Advice on Establishing a Library* (1950).
Jack A. Clarke, *Gabriel Naudé 1600–1653* (1970), a full biography that is readable and scholarly.

JAMES G. OLLÉ

Near East, Ancient

The principal Babylonian sites where written records have been found are all in southern and southeastern Iraq: Uruk (now Warka) and the ancient city of Ur (now El-Mukajjar) in southern Babylonia; Shuruppak (now Farah), almost in the middle of the area; and present-day Jamdat Nasr (ancient name unknown), north of Babylon. Oldest, heralding the new role of writing, are the tablets of the so-called Uruk-Jamdat Nasr period (3100–2700 B.C.), whose messages are clear to us about very little so far. Somewhat later are those of Ur level III, 400 tablets and many more fragments of varied content. Nikolaus Schneider studied the economic items among them, concluding (1940) that the tablets had been distributed among clay containers by subject and date and that the clay containers had tags indicating their respective contents. It is hypothesized that literary and religious texts may have been handled likewise and that the edifice in which the tablets were found had housed a school associated with the nearby temple. The temple area proper yielded religious and astronomical texts; they are ascribed to the 3rd millennium B.C., but exact dates have not been fixed.

A little later than Ur, in turn, are the Early Dynasty II and III (mid-3rd millennium) tablets recovered at Shuruppak (now Farah), some 40 miles southeast of Nippur. The numbered series among them contain lists of commodities, quantities, and persons in connection with either temple accounts or school exercises; included are lexicons and incantation texts. There are also unnumbered lists of things like writing signs, for study, and tablets bearing early examples of known Sumerian literature and lexical texts. Neither the temple nor the school tablets demonstrate the existence of a library, but they do testify to preservation of older written materials and to the development of at least rudimentary organizational devices.

Furthermore, the temple records raise the distinction between archives and libraries. Probably most widely accepted are the criteria of Mogens Weitmeyer (1955–56) that archival materials were stored by their nature and date; library materials were gathered into subject-related series, bore colophons including regulations of a library character, and were listed in separate catalogues.

Nearer the close of the 3rd millennium, it appears, are the thousands of tablets surviving from Lagash (present-day Tello), numerous enough for the site to be called "Tablet Hill" since G. C. Ernest de Sarzec found it in 1894. They are organized in individual rooms, which had plastered walls, containers along the walls, and surfaces on which to place tablets (for reading?). Of particular interest is the evidence that each room had tablets in only one corner, perhaps leaving space for additions. Access to any one of the rooms was provided only through a hole in the ceiling, which brings to mind storerooms or even graves rather than library facilities.

Second Millennium. Surviving from Ur and Nippur, particularly, and other sites are numerous tablets documenting the culture of the age of Hammurabi (18th century B.C.). The subjects were from the past: legends of ancient Sumerian gods, kings, and heroes such as Gilgamesh. The literary forms similarly derived from long practice, polished in a scholastic style. The script was cuneiform and mainly in Sumerian, but use of vernaculars was beginning, notably the Akkadian used by the Babylonians, into which Sumerian writings were increasingly being translated. Sumerian remained, like Latin in a later day, preferred for learning and literature. Serving religion were Sumerian myths, hymns, and psalms praising gods and kings; incantations and prayers of a private sort; and, most important, divination—primarily haruspicy, or prediction from entrails. Equally prominent were mathematics texts. The significance of scribes, moreover, is evident from writings about their education—both serious and humorous.

Mari, on the Euphrates, is revealed as a commercial center that flourished early in the 2nd millennium, until crushed by Hammurabi about 1750 B.C. Presently on the Syrian-Iraqi border, it is still important to the nomads. Its ancient remains cover more than 100 acres. The palace is believed to have occupied more than 6 acres, and more than 260 chambers, courtyards, and corridors have been identified. Scholars are satisfied that the building was both the king's residence and an administrative center with workshops and archives. The surviving 20,000 tablets bear mainly diplomatic and household economic records of three unconnected periods of Assyrian rule, and it is considered definite that they were shelved in separate groups.

At ancient Alalakh, a few miles northeast of Antioch, were found tablets in a western dialect of Akkadian constituting an archive of a state of consequence for perhaps 75 years soon after the fall of Mari. It seems to have benefited from trade between the sea and Aleppo, some 50 miles to the east, and the timber of the Amanus mountains north of the town. Most of the extant tablets are administrative, a few lexicographical and literary, throwing much light on Hurrian activities; but, as at Mari, nothing of a library nature has been established to date.

The world of tablets in cuneiform apparently included also, by the 16th century B.C., archives at the Hittite capitals in Anatolia. The extant data revealing bilingual dictionaries—documents such as the Hittite and Akkadian testament of Hattusili I and facilities much like those at Lagash—are interpreted by some to indicate a temple or state library. The degree to which the organized resources included known Hittite historical writings and supernatural or anecdotal literature is not established. Yet there are historical-critical evidences that Assyrian, biblical, and Greco-Roman historiography were influenced by the novel separation from mythology of the "Ten-Year Annals" of a 14th-century Hittite ruler, Mursili. The apparatus for such influence seems likely to have included "book" collections.

The expansion of the Hittite Empire and growing complexity of Near Eastern commercial and diplomatic activity signaled by the Amarna letters are among the events reflected in the 14th- and 13th-century tablets excavated at Ras Shamra, a Syrian coastal town about seven miles north of Latakia. Their contents encompass administrative, economic, ritual, and literary themes, often in more than one language and supported by bilingual word lists. They were found in buildings, both public and private, of ancient Ugarit, not just in the center but at various locations. The Baal temple is held to have had a library, not just archives. The nearby house of the chief priest possessed mythological and religious texts not only in the official North Canaanite dialect but also in Hurrian, the language of an important minority; also on hand were vocabularies and other items suggesting that the establishment performed also the functions of a seminary for training temple scribes. Not far from the palace were spacious homes of high officials, at least one of whom owned a library; the variety of its contents is perhaps implied by a surviving lexicographical tablet with equivalents linking Ugaratic and Hurrian with Sumerian and Babylonian. Conspicuous in the artisans' quarter was an imposing stone edifice that had housed a library of texts in Babylonian cuneiform, some astrological and some literary, perhaps used for teaching.

Fairly well documented is the 14th-century activity in Assyria-Babylonia of the Middle Kassite period. The Babylonian heritage of religious hero-poems, wisdom literature, theology, philology, prognostication, medicine, and astronomy was collected, edited, translated, and arranged by learned Babylonian scribes in series of numbered tablets. From the traditions of the Kassite rulers came additional cults and cult literature, magic, and demonology. It seems likely that library collections played an important part in that work, which anticipates the later achievements at Alexandria.

In any case, "omens" (predictions), hymns, prayers, and lexicographical texts from the mid-13th-century reign of Shalmaneser I of Assyria became part of a collection expanded by the conquests of Tukulti-Ninurta, the great Assyrian king of the late 13th century. According to a Sumerian-Akkadian epic, indeed, the latter carried off the tablets that distinguished the libraries of Babylonia. Involved were the usual omens, prayers, and incantations, as well as medical texts. Some of them appear to have turned up among the remains of the library established at the Assur temple early in the 11th century by Tiglath-Pileser during his days as Crown Prince.

Assurbanipal's Library. For the most impressive legacy, testifying beyond serious challenge to a library, one jumps five centuries to Assurbanipal, "King of the World, King of Assyria" (668–c. 631). In 1850 Austen Henry Layard crowned several years' labor at Nineveh sites near Mosul, in far northern Iraq, by identifying "Chambers of Records." In 1854 Hormudz Rassam found an important portion of a library in a nearby structure. The subsequent half-century of excavations added more enlightenment. Some 20,000 tablets and fragments, preserved in the British Museum, owed their remarkable condition to the destruction of Nineveh in 612 by the Medes, so thorough that the sites had lain virtually undisturbed for more than 2,400 years. It is clear from the huge assemblage of Assyro-Babylonian and Sumerian writings and his own correspondence that Assurbanipal built his library partly by welcoming copies from any possible source. Those sources may include the temples, whose plundering by his soldiers is noted in the records of his reign.

The library included the main works of Akkadian literature. More particularly, Leo Oppenheim inventoried the tablets as follows: more than 300, each of which bears from 80 to 200 individual omen texts; 200 with lists of cuneiform signs and combinations, including Sumerian-Akkadian dictionaries; more than 100 Sumerian incantations with interlinear Akkadian translations; 100-plus with proverbs, cycles of conjuration, and others; 200 miscellaneous, including reference works for court diviners and magicians and handbooks for education, research, and the training of scribes; and some 35 or 40 with epic literature. King Assurbanipal himself could read, and it may be assumed that, as elsewhere in the ancient Orient, writings could be used by priests, officials, and merchants, but that was probably all.

Assurbanipal's concerns presumably explain in part the directions that led to stocking his library with exceptional tablets. By comparison with many other Assyro-Babylonian survivals, they consist of notably finer and better baked clay than the usual, and the script achieved marked elegance and clarity by means of physically tight inscribing. The correcting and editing was of matching quality.

How the tablets were stored is not known, not from any direct evidence at the library, at any rate. Layard reported in 1853 that he had found two small rooms whose floors were piled a foot or more high with broken clay tablets and cylinders, most of which had probably fallen there from a higher room, and adjoining chambers with similar but slighter remains. Nothing further can be inferred from Rassam's narrative; we hear that additional fragments of the same tablets or belonging to the same series have been found scattered in various places, but thanks to the inexperience and carelessness of excavators or local handlers and arrangers we do not know from which of the two palaces involved any given fragment came. It can hardly be doubted that there were once a definite order and supervision, but we have neither knowledge of them nor any basis for reconstructing them.

Extraordinary care led to the discovery of subscripts on the tablets. Besides the ownership stamp, "Palace of Assurbanipal, King of the World, King of Assyria," precise data were furnished, the equivalent of book or manuscript description. It is now agreed that they were not created by Assurbanipal or his staff but borrowed from available models. These practices had been known at the state library of the Hittites at Boghazköi, and it is no longer doubted that the seeds were planted in oldest Babylon.

That Assurbanipal was collecting systematically is plain from the tablet and series indexes, indexes that furnish at the beginning of each tablet in a series the number of lines on each tablet, and series indexes that bring together the titles of various series whose contents are related. The extant collections do not include index tablets of a bibliographical character or catalogues.

For indicators there were plain, oddly shaped little clay markers, which bear nothing but a series title, perhaps to facilitate finding the series, and which lay on the pile of series items or on the reed or clay receptacles that contained them. Such a receptacle was called *girginakku,* a designation that seems to have carried over to the whole library-like *biblio-theke;* at least the chief was called *rab girginakku,* or supervisor thereof. It may be that the scion of an old scholarly family, whose tablet collection Assurbanipal apparently acquired, was the actual organizer and first director of the royal library.

REFERENCE

Ernst Posner, *Archives in the Ancient World* (1973).

SIDNEY L. JACKSON
(d. 1979)

Nepal

Nepal, the only Hindu kingdom in the world, is a landlocked country in the Himalaya Mountains, shaped like a rectangle about 800 km. long and 200 km. wide. It lies between two powerful nations of Asia, China on the north and India on the south. Population (1990 est.) 18,916,000; area 140,797 sq.km. More than 93 percent of the total population live in rural areas and are engaged in agriculture, the backbone of Nepal's economy. The official language is Nepali.

History. Nepal has been a center of learning since ancient times. The low rate of literacy (25 percent) shows Nepal's lack of development, but education is mentioned in ancient stone inscriptions and early records preserved in the monasteries and temples. Sanskrit education flourished in Nepal before the 6th century, and Nepal is believed to have been a repository of untold treasures of manuscripts on Tantrism, philosophy, Sanskrit grammar, astrology, rituals, religion, medicine, and Vedic literature.

Nepal can be called a country with ancient library traditions, yet education and libraries could not develop in Nepal under the autocratic Rana rule from 1846 to 1951. Books, magazines, newspapers, the

Libraries in Nepal (1990)

Type of library	Number of administrative units (main libraries)	Volumes in collections	Annual expenditures (rupee)	Population served	Professional staff (with certificate, diploma, etc.)	Total staff
National	1	71,000	541,400	--	4	20
Academic	142	1,023,996	4,390,250	92,058	110	478
Public	465	--	--	--	--	--
Special	71	293,944	872,000	--	13	157

Tribhuvan University Library

Tribhuvan University Library in Kirtipur. It is Nepal's principal academic library, and the country's only library in a separate building of its own.

radio, and other media of communication and academic study were banned for the majority. Even expressing the need for a library was forbidden and could lead to punishment. In 1929 a great Nepali poet, Laxmi Prasad Devkota, and some of his friends were punished for their decision to establish a public library in Nepal. Nevertheless, public libraries came into existence in various places in Nepal as forerunners of the revolution of 1950.

After 1950, many schools and colleges were opened and so-called public libraries were established in the hope of providing free access to knowledge. But library services in a modern sense were introduced in Nepal only in 1959 with the establishment of a Central Library under an agreement between the governments of Nepal and the United States; unfortunately the agreement came to an end in a short time.

Tribhuvan University Central Library was established in Kirtipur, Kathmandu, and the whole collection of the Central Library was handed over to it in 1962. Tribhuvan University Central Library played a leading role in the library movement in Nepal from 1963.

National Library and Archives. The Nepal National Library was established in 1955, after the royal government bought the private collection of the royal priest Pandit Hemraj Pandey. It is located at Pulchok, Patan, in Kathmandu Valley. It contains 70,000 books in 11 languages. The library has not been able to function as a national library should. It is more like a museum than a library.

The Nepal National Archive has a long history. It began in the time of the Malla kings more than two centuries ago. The Bir Library, the oldest library of Nepal, was renamed the Nepal National Archive. Located at Thapathali, Kathmandu, it has 65,750 manuscripts; of these, 12,000 are on palm leaves. It has many valuable manuscripts that are not available in any other part of the world. These manuscripts were microfilmed under a joint Nepal–German Manuscript Preservation Project.

Academic Libraries. There are libraries at the technical institutes for medicine in Kathmandu, for engineering at Patan, for agriculture at Rampur, and for forestry at Hetauda. Collections of a few hundred or a few thousand books can be found at some institutions, but without much organization. Trichandra Multiple Campus Library, established in 1918, is the oldest academic library. It has more than 30,500 volumes. Nepal has two universities, Tribhuvan and Mahandra Sanskrit, and two royal academies, the Royal Nepal Academy of Science and Technology (RONAST) and the Royal Nepal Academy. Tribhuvan University has five technical institutes and four research centers. Its 142 campuses all have some sort of library service. Their collections consist of from 3,000 to 39,000 volumes. With foreign aid projects, appreciable attention has been given to library services on technical campuses. The research centers have documentation centers.

Tribhuvan University Central Library in Kathmandu is the biggest and best organized library in the country. Starting from a 1,200-book collection in 1959, it had almost 163,000 volumes by the late 1980s. It functions as a national library, promoting library development at all levels, serving as the depository library for UN documents, and cooperating in other international activities. The Library has published the *Nepalese National Bibliography* since 1981. It also issues occasional bibliographies on various topics of interest. It is a member of IFLA.

School Libraries and Media Centers. Most of the schools do not have libraries. The few that exist cannot be called school libraries in any real sense. Schoolchildren buy textbooks for their own use. Some foreign-aided schools, such as Budhanilkantha School, St. Xavier's, and St. Mary's, have better developed school library services.

Special Libraries. There are more than 70 libraries and documentation centers in government departments, research centers, and other organizations. Notable among them are Madan Puraskar Pustakalaya, the Library of the Agricultural Projects Services Center (APROSC), the Department of Botany Library, the Rastra Bank Library, the Library of the Trade Promotion Center, Bir Hospital Library, and the Asha Saphukuthi. Madan Puraskar Pustakalaya is well known for its collection on Nepali literature and languages. Asha Saphukuthi has a good collection on Newari literature. APROSC Library serves as the National Agricultural Documentation Center. RONAST worked to develop a science and technology information network.

The Profession. The library profession has not been fully recognized in the country. Nepal has no library school. Tribhuvan University Central Library has organized training courses for working librarians since 1974. In 1976, the University began sponsoring training for professionals at library schools in India. By the early 1990s Nepal had 110 professional and 310 paraprofessional librarians. The country had library associations for brief periods in the 1950s and 1970s before the Nepal Library Association was established in 1980. It publishes *Nepali Awaj* (Journal of NLA).

REFERENCE

Shanti Mishra, "Library Movement in Nepal," *Unesco Bulletin for Libraries* (1974).

SHANTI MISHRA

Netherlands

The Kingdom of the Netherlands lies on the North Sea, bounded by Germany on the east and Belgium on the south. Population (1990 est.) 14,943,000; area 40,844 sq.km. Part of the country is below sea level. The official language is Dutch.

History. The contents of the many medieval monastery libraries are widely scattered and mostly known only by their contemporary catalogues; a notable exception is the library of the Carthusian monastery at Utrecht, now in the local University Library. The only late medieval library still extant is the Librije at Zutphen, built as an annex of the Walburgis church in 1563. The number of Dutch, mostly late medieval, manuscripts described in the Bibliotheca Neerlandica Manuscripta, a central catalogue in the University Library at Leiden, totals more than 12,000. The products of the earliest printing presses set up in Holland, 1566–72, are known as "prototypography." The first dated book was printed in Utrecht in 1473. As many as 1,500 Dutch presses produced 2,100 editions. The postincunabula (1501–40) are well documented.

With the coming of Protestantism, secularization of the properties of the monasteries gave rise to city libraries that in Amsterdam, Utrecht, and Groningen developed into university libraries. In the 17th century the firms of Blaeu, Elsevier, and others were the printers for the whole of Europe, specializing in scientific and cartographic works.

A national library was founded in 1798 after a political revolution. Two of its librarians, J. W. Holtrop (1806–70) and M. F. A. G. Campbell (1819–90), laid the foundations of incunabular studies. The number of incunabula in Dutch libraries is about 8,000. P. A. Tiele (1834–89), who worked in the university libraries of Amsterdam, Leiden, and Utrecht, was important as a bibliographer and cataloguer. H. E. Greve (1878–1957) was the leader of the public library movement in the Netherlands. F. Donker Duyvis (1894–1961), Secretary-General of the International Federation for Documentation (FID), was a pioneer in the fields of documentation, standardization, and efficiency.

The Dutch library landscape can be characterized as a complex of cooperative bodies, each serving its specific group but with a long tradition of service outside its own domain.

National Library. The Koninklijke Bibliotheek (Royal Library) at The Hague functions as the national library. Its starting collection was the confiscated library of Prince-Stadholder William V, which was amalgamated in 1798 with some other libraries considered as public property. In 1814, after the restoration of the House of Orange, King William I renounced all claims to the confiscated collections and took great interest in the Library. It was enriched during the 19th century by the acquisition of many private collections. A representative collection of Dutch manuscripts, early editions, pamphlets, and songbooks was built. Complete coverage of Dutch literature and Dutch newspapers is attempted.

In 1982 the Royal Library moved into a new building next to that of the General State Archives. In its closed stacks it has a capacity for 5,000,000 volumes; there are 350 reading tables and 227 tables for consulting reference works. Also housed in the building are the Museum and Documentation Center for Dutch Literature, Bureau of the National Committee for Dutch History, National Bureau for the Documentation of the History of Art, Bureau of the Library Council, Headquarters of IFLA and of FID, and some other institutions.

The Royal Library is not a copyright library. To compensate for the lack of a legal deposit system, a voluntary deposit scheme was adopted in 1974. In 1990 the depositary received 35,000 books, 12,000 periodical publications, and 4,000 maps. On the basis of these materials the Dutch Bibliography has been published. *Brinkman's Cumulative Catalogue of Books published in the Netherlands and Flanders* (since 1858) was renamed in 1983; it is now the official Dutch national bibliography. Next to it six series are published: for trade publications, for noncommercial publications, for governmental publications, for maps, for translations, and the Cataloguing-in-Publication list. In 1983 the Dutch Bibliographical Center (NBC) was created as a consortium of the Royal Library, publishers, booksellers, and other parties; the National Bibliography is produced under its auspices. The holdings of the Library comprise about 1,800,000 printed volumes (including 6,000 printed before 1540), 1,500 medieval manuscripts, 5,000 other manuscripts, and 120,000 letters. There are many special collections, including a chess collection of 15,000 volumes. The scope of the collection of foreign publications is limited to the

Libraries in The Netherlands (1987)

Type of library	Number of administrative units (main libraries)	Number of service points (branches, mobile stops, etc.)	Volumes in collections	Annual expenditures (Dutch florin)[a]	Population served	Professional staff (with certificate, diploma, etc.)	Total staff
National	1	1	2,182,000	9,816,000	--	84	270
Academic	22	287	19,325,000	48,021,000	--	1,324	1,608
Public[b]	484	2,974	42,098,000	280,000,000[c]	4,182,000	4,164	8,995
School	8,100	--	--	--	--	--	--
Special	691	--	15,453,000	69,667,000	--	1,885	2,207
Vocational Training Colleges	252	--	2,852,000	5,048,000	300,000	292	305

[a]Excludes salaries and housing.
[b]Data for 1986.
[c]Salaries included.

Sources: Centraal Bureau voor de Statistiek, *Wetenschappelijke en Speciale Bibliotheken 1987.* Den Haag: SDU, 1989. Idem, *Openbure Bibliotheken 1986.* Ibid., 1988.

Royal Library

Royal Library at The Hague, which functions as the national library.

humanities and the social sciences; the responsibility for the other domains is the task of other libraries, especially the Library of the Royal Netherlands Academy of Sciences (biomedical sciences), the Library of the Technical University of Delft (technical sciences), and the Library of the Agricultural University of Wageningen (agricultural sciences). Two large retrospective bibliographical projects are based in the Royal Library: the Short Title Catalogue Netherlands (STCN), covering book production in the period 1540–1800 (about 300,000 titles), and the pre-Brinkman project, covering the period 1801–32. Since 1922 the Royal Library has maintained the Union Catalogue.

In 1983 the Netherlands Central Catalogue (NCC) became operational; it is the online version of the machine-readable parts of the Union Catalogue of the Royal Library (with input from the university libraries and other research libraries and of the libraries of the ministries), of the Central Technical Catalogue, maintained by the Technical University at Delft, and of the Central Agricultural Catalogue, maintained by the Agricultural University at Wageningen. This system is one of the facilities of PICA (Project for Integrated Catalogue Automation), originally a cooperative organization of the Royal Library and the university libraries, but gradually embracing all types of libraries, the public libraries as well. PICA evolved from a project for shared cataloguing to a truly national information network. PICA has its headquarters and its technical equipment in Leiden.

Academic Libraries. There are 13 universities in the country, including three technical and one agricultural. The library collections reflect to a high degree the disciplines represented in the institutions. The State Universities (Leiden, founded 1575; Groningen, 1614; Utrecht, 1636); the Municipal University of Amsterdam (1877); the Free (Calvinist) University at Amsterdam, (1880); and the Catholic University at Nijmegen (1923) are complete universities with all faculties, whereas the others are more specialized. Autonomous in their administration, all universities are fully supported by the State. Collections and services are integrated in the national library services at large. The university libraries provide 40 percent of all interlibrary loans, and their collections add up to 47 percent of the total volumes outside the domain of the public libraries. There are nine institutes for higher learning, mainly theological schools.

In principle the central libraries form one system or network with the libraries of the faculties and the departments. The head librarians are united in a consultative, coordinating, and cooperating body, together with the librarians of the Royal Library and of the Library of the Royal Netherlands Academy of Sciences.

Public Libraries. Popular reading libraries were common from an early date, although a public library system was fully developed only in the 20th century. The first public library in the modern sense of the word opened in Utrecht in 1892. The denominational rift in Dutch society also split the public library world: apart from the general public libraries, both Protestants and Catholics started public library systems of their own. All received government subsidies and held the same ideal of educating the people through reading. They all gave priority to books for study and did not attract the large groups of people who wanted to read for recreation. But whereas the general libraries did not wish to select their books by other standards than inherent quality, Protestant and Catholic leaders resisted an indiscriminate supply of books. During the 1960s such segregation was relaxed and finally disappeared, uniting public libraries in the Nederlands Bibliotheek en Lektuur Centrum (NBLC: Dutch Center for [public] Libraries and Literature). Popular works were acquired in large quantities, branch libraries multiplied, and the reading public came to the libraries in previously unknown numbers. An annual fee is required, except for those under 18. The Public Library Act of 1975 provided that the central government was to pay all costs of staff and 20 percent of all other expenditure, the remaining 80 percent to be supplied by the provincial and local authorities. In 1983 the Library Act was withdrawn and public library work was included in a broad act on social welfare. In the framework of decentralized responsibilities, provincial and local authorities receive lump sums yearly for public library work. Those authorities can decide for themselves how much they wish to pay from their own means for this work.

Until comparatively recently, research libraries were able to cope with the demand for books for study; but the increase in numbers of students, both at the universities and at the vocational colleges, required some extension of the library system. So 13 libraries were designated as regional supporting libraries; most are large public libraries, others provincial or municipal libraries. Additional government grants enabled them to buy bibliographical tools and to equip reading rooms.

School Libraries. The development of school libraries depends to a large degree on the pedagogical insights of the local school authorities. Paid professional school librarians are an exception; mostly the school libraries are managed by volunteers. But funds are available for equipment and materials. A large measure of support is given by the NBLC, the provincial library centers, or the local public libraries. This support consists of a number of special bibliographical publications, training for volunteers, and distribution of tools (such as an adapted classification scheme, derived from the scheme used by the public libraries). In many primary schools informative materials and audiovisual items are organized in so-called documentation centers, separated from narrative literature; in the secondary schools both categories are found in single units.

Special Libraries. At least four groups can be distinguished: (1) libraries of learned societies and scientific institutes; (2) provincial and municipal libraries; (3) libraries of vocational colleges; and (4) special libraries in a more restricted sense.

Of the learned societies the Royal Netherlands Academy of Science in Amsterdam takes first place. It was founded in 1808 by Napoleon's brother, then King of Holland. Its importance now lies primarily in its collection of scientific and medical journals. All journals indexed by *Excerpta Medica* are kept in microfiche form. The library of the Teyler Foundation in Haarlem (1778) is celebrated for its collection in the natural sciences. An important library for the study of modern history is that of the International Institute for Social History in Amsterdam, founded in 1935, which documents the history of the labor movement, socialism, and anarchism with its archives, 550,000 books and 2,400 periodicals. The Library of the Peace Palace in The Hague, founded in 1913 by the Carnegie Endowment for International Peace, has a comprehensive collection in the fields of international law, international organizations, and diplomatic history. It has also a fine collection of works by and about the Dutch political scientist Hugo Grotius (1583–1645). It serves the International Court of Justice, a body of the United Nations, as well as the Académie de Droit Internationale. The library of the Royal Tropical Institute in Amsterdam (founded 1910) focused from 1950 on problems of Third World countries. It consists of 400,000 volumes and 5,000 current periodicals.

The provincial libraries of Friesland, Zeeland, and Gelderland, all dating from the middle of the 19th century, play an important role in library service for their regions. They possess important research collections, especially on local history, but some of national importance. The same applies to city libraries. The oldest is the Athenaeum Library in Deventer (1560). The City Library of Haarlem dates from 1596; it has a fine collection on the history of typesetting. The Municipal Library of Rotterdam (1604) has a collection of works by and about the Rotterdam-born Humanist Desiderius Erasmus (1469–1536). The City Library of Maastricht was founded in 1662.

The libraries of the vocational colleges serve primarily their own students and staff. There were 25 technical colleges, 7 agricultural, 36 economic, 23 health care, 26 socio-pedagogic, 20 fine arts, and 43 pedagogic colleges in 1991.

The special libraries in a narrower sense vary enormously in scope and volume. There were 13 ministerial libraries and 234 libraries of governmental agencies and institutions, 128 business/industrial libraries, 115 libraries of foundations or associations, 85 hospital libraries, 26 museum libraries, and 28 libraries of religious organizations in 1991. Most of them participate in the interlibrary loan system with the effect that they delivered 34 percent of all interlibrary loans in the country in 1989. Some of these libraries build databases, of which some are of more than national importance, such as *Economics Abstracts International,* produced by the library of the Ministry for Economic Affairs. Also the use of online searching is heaviest in this category.

The Profession. Library and documentation/information education is offered by three types of institutions: at the University of Amsterdam; at six Library and Documentation Academies (undergraduate courses); and through various part-time courses by the Stichting Gemeenschappelijke Opleiding (GO), which vary from the basic to a postgraduate level.

Librarians of all library types have had their professional organization, since 1912, in the Nederlandse Vereniging van Bibliothecarissen (NVB; Dutch Association of Librarians). Public librarians in 1972 organized themselves under the NBLC, but returned to the NVB in 1989. The NVB from 1974 incorporated documentalists and information specialists. It has sections for special, research, and vocational college libraries, a section for information specialists, and groups for law librarians, medical librarians, and agricultural librarians. To provide the necessary unity the Federatie van Organisaties op het gebied van het Bibliotheek-, Informatie- en Documentatiewezen (FOBID; Federation of Organizations in the Fields of Library, Information and Documentation Services) was created in 1974. Theological librarians organized their own association in 1949. Diversification in the profession led to a number of new groupings: map librarians working group (1975), patent librarians (1976), and Association of Online Users (1977).

The Dutch library journal *Open* is published under the auspices of FOBID. The public libraries have *Bibliotheek en Samenleving* as their journal.

An Act of Parliament created the Netherlands Council for Libraries and Information Services in 1987 to advise the government. It replaces and greatly expands the work of the Library Council. The Netherlands Organization for Libraries and Information Services was founded at the same time to improve the infrastructure of providing information in the public domain.

A. H. H. M. MATHIJSEN

Netherlands Antilles

The Netherlands Antilles, part of the Leeward Islands in the Caribbean, consists of Curaçao, Aruba, Bonaire, Saint Eustatius, Saba, and the southern part of Saint Martin. Population (1990 est.) 189,000; area 800 sq.km. The official language is Dutch.

National Library Services. The Willemstad Public Library (Openbare Bibliotheek), established in Curaçao in 1922, functions as a national library for the Netherlands Antilles. There are two branch libraries, plus a bookmobile that serves suburbs. Although there is no legal deposit law, the library tries to purchase all works about, or printed in, the six islands. Its collection of Caribbeana consists of approximately 6,000 volumes. These are the only noncirculating volumes in the accumulation of more than 100,000 volumes. Holdings are mainly in Dutch, although the Library has some works in English and in Spanish.

There are only a few titles in Papiamento, the patois spoken by most people in the Netherlands Antilles.

The Centraal Historisch Archief (Central Historical Archives), founded in Willemstad in 1969, contains all archival publications of the Netherlands Antilles, concentrating on government documents. The library is in close contact with the National Library in The Hague and makes copies of all documents there that relate to the Netherlands Antilles.

Only government officials may borrow materials, but the collection is accessible to students and others during restricted hours. The library collects periodicals related to archival matters, publishes two newsletters describing old and new acquisitions, and restores and laminates Caribbeana documents.

Public Libraries. The Public Library of Aruba opened in 1944 in Oranjestad and houses approximately 140,450 books. Holdings are in Dutch, English, Spanish, French, and Papiamento. Another branch in the suburb of Saint Nicholas has been in operation for many years. The Caribbeana collection is a noteworthy feature of the Oranjestad main library. Most of the collection circulates, although a deposit is required for some of the older works. Only the rarest items must be used on the premises. Adults must pay a membership fee to join these public libraries; membership is free to children.

The main public libraries at Oranjestad and Willemstad both have special collections on music, including musical scores and works related to music, particularly that of the Netherlands Antilles.

Academic Libraries. The University of Aruba, founded in 1970, comprises colleges of liberal arts and sciences, business administration, languages, preprofession sciences, and education. The library houses more than 3,000 volumes.

The Institute of Higher Studies of the Netherlands Antilles became the University of the Netherlands Antilles in 1979. Its library was opened in 1970 and houses approximately 100,000 volumes, mainly books on law, economics, business administration, and sociology. Students are allowed to borrow books, the number of titles dependent on their class standing. The library subscribes to approximately 100 periodicals and has an active interlibrary loan operation. In addition, the library maintains a union catalogue of all library holdings in the Netherlands Antilles.

There are some special libraries in the Netherlands Antilles. The Oranjestad Sportburo was established in Aruba in 1978 as an outgrowth of a new government bureau in charge of coordinating physical activities in the schools. This circulating library has about 600 books on sports-related topics, half in English and the rest in Dutch.

The Stichting Wetenschappelijke Bibliotheek (Scientific Library Foundation), founded in 1950 in Willemstad, holds some 16,500 volumes, with an extensive music collection in addition to works on the pure and applied sciences. Holdings include musical scores, printed music, and books on music of the Netherlands Antilles, with a special collection of music by Curaçao composers. Publications of the foundation include a union catalogue of all nonfiction books in the Netherlands Antilles, plus *Curaçao Folklore, Curaçao Music,* and *Nansi Stories.*

Other special libraries connected to research institutes in Curaçao include those of the Caraibisch Marien-Biologisch Instituut, with more than 3,000 volumes, and the Meteorologische Dienst van de Nederlandse Antillen (Meteorological Service of the Netherlands Antilles).

The Association di Biblioteka i Archivo di Korsow (ABAK: Association of Libraries and Archives of Curaçao) was established in 1972 and is affiliated with IFLA. The association is housed in temporary headquarters in Willemstad, Curaçao. It has no official publication.

BARBARA FOSTER

New York Public Library

The New York Public Library is unique among libraries in combining under a single corporation four research facilities of international distinction, known as the Research Libraries, and one of the most extensive city branch library systems in the United States, the Branch Libraries. It is a private, nonprofit educational corporation chartered by the Regents of the University of the State of New York. The Corporation is headed by a President and guided by a 42-member Board of Trustees; each of its two components is managed by a Director.

The Research Libraries date back to the formal creation of the New York Public Library on May 24, 1895, when two private libraries were consolidated with a trust of $2,500,000 left by Samuel J. Tilden. The two institutions were the Astor Library, a public reference library founded in 1849 through the generosity of American entrepreneur John Jacob Astor (1763–1848), and the Lenox Library, a private collection of rare books and manuscripts formed by the book collector James Lenox (1800–80). The Branch Libraries developed through the merger of eleven already extant free circulating libraries with the New York Public Library in 1901. That same year, Andrew

Libraries in Netherlands Antilles (1987)

Type of library	Number of administrative units (main libraries)	Number of service points (branches, mobile stops, etc.)	Volumes in collections	Annual expenditures (Dutch florin)	Population served	Professional staff (with certificate, diploma, etc.)	Total staff
Academic	1	--	>100,000	149,000	1,000	4	9
Public	5	27	271,414	114,375	187,087	26	99
School	41	--	24,600	--	12,000	--	--
Special	9	--	35,000	80,700	10,000	5	15

Carnegie gave the City of New York $5,200,000 for the construction of new branch libraries. The City supplied the sites for the new buildings and agreed to support their maintenance and operations from public funds.

In 1911, the large marble building at Fifth Avenue and 42nd Street opened to the public with 1,200,000 volumes. It has since become one of the most familiar landmarks in the United States and a symbol of the Library as a whole. Designed in the classical style by John Carrère and Thomas Hastings, and guarded by two stone lions, the building was constructed on the site of the former Croton Reservoir to house the Central Research Library. President William Howard Taft indicated the special character of the New York Public Library in his speech at the opening of the building, eliciting support for the new institution from the city and the nation:

> This day crowns a work of national importance. The dedication of this beautiful structure for the spread of knowledge among the people marks not only the consummation of a noteworthy plan for bringing within the grasp of the humblest and poorest citizen the opportunity for acquiring information on every subject of every kind, but it furnishes a model and example for other cities which have been struggling with the same problem . . . .

The Library's Board of Trustees presides over 86 facilities, an annual operating budget of $131,000,000 (in fiscal year 1991), and a staff of more than 3,000. In fiscal year 1990, the Research and Branch libraries together contained collections numbering some 46,000,000 items, served more than 7,800,000 users, and circulated more than 10,000,000 items to 1,122,000 cardholders.

The Research Libraries rely on a combination of public and private funds for support of their operations. New York State contributes to the Research Libraries' operating costs, and facilities are maintained with the support of City funds. Matching and outright grants from federal agencies have stimulated private giving and supported costs in some operations. Annual fund-raising drives, individual supporters, and the business community contribute to operating costs.

Photo by Peter A. Juley

The New York Public Library's Public Catalog Room in 1911.

Foundation grants make possible special initiatives in a variety of areas. The total annual budget for the Research Libraries for fiscal year 1991 was $53,700,000.

The Branch Libraries are primarily funded by tax dollars. About 80 percent of the Branch Libraries' budget is provided by New York City; 11 percent comes from New York State; 1 percent comes from federal funds; and 2.6 percent is received from private gifts. The total annual budget for the Branches for fiscal year 1991 was $72,500,000.

THE RESEARCH LIBRARIES

Collections. The research collections of the New York Public Library rank in size, scope, and quality with the world's great national and university libraries; in the United States, only the collections of the Library of Congress and the Harvard University Libraries are larger. Organized into four research centers, the Research Libraries' collections in 1990 contained more than 10,000,000 noncirculating books and book-like materials (volumes, microforms, playscripts, scores, and scrapbooks) and over 26,000,000 "nonbooks" (including sound recordings, broadsides, motion pictures, videotapes, manuscripts, maps, pho-

The New York Public Library

A 1907 view of the uncompleted New York Public Library at Fifth Avenue and 42nd Street, designed by John Carrère and Thomas Hastings.

tographs, posters, prints, and sheet music) in more than 3,000 languages and dialects. The Research Libraries receive more than 100,000 serial titles, of which more than 30,000 are current periodicals.

With the exception of law, medicine, theology, and education, which are collected on a limited basis, the Research Libraries have developed collections of excellence in most subject fields, and in several areas—American history, language and linguistics, literature, music, Judaica, Slavica, genealogy, local history, rare books, maps, prints, and recorded sound—the collections are in the front rank of American library resources. In some areas not collected by most research libraries—notably theater, dance, and Black studies—the collections are unmatched anywhere in the world. The Research Libraries hold many unique resources, including the most extensive pamphlet collection in the United States and more than 20,000 linear feet of manuscripts.

As a founding member of the Research Libraries Group (RLG), a consortium of 31 major research libraries, the Research Libraries of the New York Public Library has assumed national collecting responsibility for 80 subjects in recognition of the preeminent strength of its holdings in those areas. Only the Library of Congress has collecting responsibility for more areas.

Organization. The subject and language divisions of the Research Libraries are organized in four centers: the Humanities, Social Sciences, and Special Collections Research Center; the Science, Industry, and Business Library; the Schomburg Center for Research in Black Culture; and the New York Public Library for the Performing Arts.

Photo by Casey Cronin

The landmark New York Public Library building, guarded by two stone lions, was opened to the public in 1911 with holdings of 1,200,000 volumes.

The Humanities, Social Sciences, and Special Collections Research Center. Housed in the landmark Central Research Library building at Fifth Avenue and 42nd Street, this research center is comprised of the Libraries' oldest, and some of its most distinguished, general and special collections: the General Research Division; the Map Division; the Slavic and Baltic, Oriental, and Jewish divisions; the Miriam and Ira D. Wallach Art, Prints, and Photographs Division; the Berg Collection of English and American Literature; the Rare Books and Manuscripts Division; and the Spencer, Arents, and Pforzheimer collections. The collections that make up the Science, Industry, and Business Library were scheduled to move to a new facility by the mid-1990s, leaving the Central Research Library devoted entirely to humanities, social sciences, and special collections, providing new reading, service, and storage space.

The Science, Industry, and Business Library (SIBL). A single administrative unit, SIBL was slated to move from the Central Research Library building to a separate facility with enhanced services, state-of-the-art technology, and expanded access to its considerable resources (some 2,500,000 volumes) by 1995. Formed by the merger of the Science and Technology Research Center and the Economic and Public Affairs Division in 1990, SIBL in its new quarters is expected to be the largest publicly accessible business and science information center in the world. It is to have new services targeted to the special needs of an international clientele in the fields of business and science.

The Schomburg Center for Research in Black Culture. Located in a modern complex at Lenox Avenue and 135th Street in Harlem, the Schomburg Center is one of the leading repositories in the world devoted exclusively to collecting, preserving, interpreting, and providing free public access to materials documenting Black life, with holdings in excess of 5,000,000 items. The Center's collections are organized into a General Research and Reference unit and four special collections units—Art and Artifacts; Moving Image and Recorded Sound; Photographs and Prints; and Rare Books, Manuscripts, and Archives.

The New York Public Library for the Performing Arts. A unique administrative unit, combining under a single director both the circulating and research collections of NYPL in theater, dance, and music, this Library is located next to the Metropolitan Opera House at Lincoln Center. Each of the four units that comprise the research collections—the Dance Collection, the Music Division, the Rodgers and Hammerstein Archives of Recorded Sound, and the Billy Rose Theatre Collection—stands on its own as a collection of international importance. Together, they serve a clientele of performing artists—dancers and musicians, actors and playwrights, scene and costume designers, composers and conductors, choreographers and cinematographers—as well as scholars, critics, and students.

Catalogues. The bibliographic tools available for determining the Library's holdings are extensive. The Library's pre-1972 holdings are recorded in several printed catalogues, but primarily in the 800-volume *Dictionary Catalog of the Research Libraries,* a resource which despite its great size is owned by many of the world's major research libraries. For materials added to the collections from 1971 onwards, computerized bibliographic records are available locally on the Libraries' online public access catalogue, CATNYP, and nationally on the Research Libraries Information Network and the Online Computer Library Center database.

Other materials not listed in these central catalogues are found in a variety of other printed catalogues, including the *Dictionary Catalog of the Schomburg Collection, Dictionary Catalog of the Slavonic Collection, Dictionary Catalog of the Oriental Collection, Catalog of the Henry W. and Albert A. Berg Collection of English and American Literature, Dictionary Catalog of the Map Division, Dictionary Catalog of the Rodgers and Hammerstein Archives of Recorded Sound, Dictionary Catalog of the Dance Collection,* and *Catalog of the Theatre and Drama Collections, Part III, Non-Book Collection,* among others. All of these catalogues are rendered more valuable by the fact that the Research Libraries made extensive analytics for many works catalogued during the first half of the 1900s.

Services. The services provided by the Research Libraries for access to its non-circulating collections are national and international in scope and freely available onsite. In 1990, the four centers served an average of 3,500 readers a day. In addition, the Libraries extend their services by photocopy, mail, telefacsimile, and telephone reference service and by limited interlibrary loan. More than 300,000 inquiries were answered by these means in 1990 alone.

The NYPL is a major participant in a number of cooperative library endeavors. Through interlibrary loan agreements with the RLG and the United Nations, the NYPL makes books available to other institutions and borrows books requested by readers. Chartered as a non-circulating library and committed to remaining a national library of last resort, the NYPL limits its loans to other institutions and maintains an unusually low not-on-shelf rate of two to three percent. But, through the work of the Copy Services Division and the microfilming laboratory, the NYPL's materials are widely shared. In 1989, the Library filmed 13,752 feet of microfilm in response to mail and phone orders and made 163,131 photocopies.

Preservation. Conservation of library materials is of compelling concern to the Research Libraries. The New York Public Library was among the pioneers of preservation planning and technology. As early as 1914, it conducted experiments to determine the best method of preserving newsprint; in the 1930s it was an early advocate of the use of preservation microfilming. In 1972, the Library established a Conservation Division, one of the first preservation programs to be established in a research library. Today the Division has five components: the Shelf and Binding Preparation Office, the Preservation Microfilming Office, the Preservation Microfilming Laboratory, the Conservation Laboratory, and the Collections Maintenance Office.

While preservation is a problem for all research libraries, it is especially urgent at the NYPL. Several factors in combination contribute to this special sense of urgency: the large size of the collections and the Library's significance as a national resource and a library of record; the policy of acquiring a single copy

The New York Public Library

The eighty-two branch sites of the New York Public Library form one of the largest circulating libraries in the world.

of any item, making the collection particularly vulnerable to the loss of materials through deterioration; and the Research Libraries's policy of unrestricted public access, which results in heavy wear on the collections. The age, frequent use, and diversity of materials in the collections require that preservation activities consist of diverse approaches, techniques, procedures, and staff skills. A full range of treatment options—including microfilming, deacidification, mylar encapsulation, protective enclosures, photocopying, binding and rebinding, and selective restoration—is used in order to achieve the most appropriate, cost-effective preservation program. The Libraries' collection of master microform negatives of research materials is the second largest repository in the United States. While microfilming has constituted the bulk of the preservation effort, the Research Libraries have also received restricted funds for special conservation projects, such as the restoration of important historical manuscripts.

The Research Libraries and the Library of Congress have cooperated in many joint conservation programs, such as the ongoing project to microfilm the official gazettes of governments throughout the world. This project is of such dimensions that it would not be feasible for any single library to undertake alone. The Libraries have also engaged in joint conservation programs with other members of the RLG and with other institutions throughout the United States. The Libraries participate in the brittle books program of the National Endowment for the Humanities and in the United States Newspaper Project, among others.

Peter Aaron/Esto

The Edna Barnes Salomon Room of the New York Public Library.

THE BRANCH LIBRARIES

Sometimes called "a great free university," the Branch Libraries of the NYPL form one of the largest circulating libraries in the world, with 82 locations in three of the City's five boroughs. The NYPL entered into an agreement with the City of New York in 1901 to establish and operate branch libraries in the Bronx, Manhattan, and Staten Island, three of the most populous counties in the United States. The result was the development of a model public library system which has set standards for specialized services for children, young adults, and the elderly; pioneered the use of audiovisual and non-book materials; and developed an extensive range of programs to encourage reading and literacy. All of its collections are available to anyone who lives, works, or goes to school in the state of New York.

The Branch Libraries are organized to be responsive to the needs of local communities. Local service is provided through 77 neighborhood libraries, 14 of which are designated regional libraries and have larger collections. In addition, more comprehensive collections of circulating and current research materials are located at two borough library centers (Fordham in the Bronx and St. George in Staten Island). The most extensive collections are available at the central libraries of the Branch Library system, which consist of the Mid-Manhattan Library, the Donnell Library Center, and the circulating library of the New York Public Library for the Performing Arts. Hours of service vary from branch to branch.

Collections. The collections of the Branch Libraries total nearly 10,000,000 items, including more than 5,900,000 available for circulation. They include not only books, but also periodicals, pamphlets, films, recordings, audio- and videocassettes, pictures, and materials for the blind in recorded and braille formats. Many branches carry materials in foreign languages familiar to local residents; four ethnic heritage collections offer materials on Afro-Americans and Africans, Chinese-Americans and Chinese, Hispanic history and culture, and the Italian heritage. NYPL's Library for the Blind and Physically Handicapped is one of the largest in the country and serves the five boroughs of New York City and all of Long Island. The circulating library of the New York Public Library for the Performing Arts is the largest circulating collection in this specialized area—indeed, one of the few in existence.

Recent acquisitions and the entire collection of the Mid-Manhattan Library are included in computer-generated book catalogues available throughout the NYPL and in other libraries, and Branch Libraries holdings are available for interbranch loan and interbranch referral through online computer displays. Installation of an automated circulation system was scheduled to be completed in all branches in the early 1990s.

Services. In addition to reference services available through the librarian at each branch, two special telephone services provide rapid access to information. The Union Catalog staff directs callers to the nearest branch location for the material they're looking for, and the Telephone Reference Service handles calls from some 1,000 patrons a day, answering questions that can be quickly researched. The Branch Libraries have always been leaders in educational programming: free literacy and English-as-a-Second-Language classes are heavily in demand, as are job information and learner's advisory services. In 1990, the Branch Libraries offered nearly 26,500 programs for people of all ages, and more than 570,300 people took advantage of them.

The Branch Libraries cooperate with 21 other public library systems in New York State on interlibrary loan and on statewide services.

Despite reductions in hours because of declines in government funding, the Branch Libraries continue to be heavily used. More than one million people held borrower's cards in the year ending June 30, 1990. In the same period, circulation, which has grown steadily, reached 10,400,000, of which 2,700,000 represented circulation of children's books. The Branch Libraries answered 4,700,000 reference inquiries in person and by telephone that year, during which 6,300,000 people walked through their doors.

REFERENCES

Bulletin of the New York Public Library. Monthly, 1897–1977.

Phyllis Dain, *The New York Public Library: A History of Its Founding and Early Years* (1972).

Marshall B. Davidson and Bernard McTigue, *Treasures of the New York Public Library* (1988).

Harry Miller Lydenberg, *History of the New York Public Library: Astor, Lenox, and Tilden Foundations* (1923).

New York Public Library, *Report*. Annual, 1896– .

Henry Hope Reed, *The New York Public Library: Its Architecture and Decoration* (1986).

Sam P. Williams, *Guide to the Research Collections of the New York Public Library* (1975).

TIMOTHY S. HEALY
(d. 1992)

New Zealand

New Zealand, a parliamentary state and member of the Commonwealth, lies in the South Pacific Ocean; the Tasman Sea separates the country from Australia. New Zealand comprises the North and South islands and Chatham and Stewart, among other islands. Population (1990 est.) 3,346,000; area 270,986 sq.km. The official language is English.

History. The earliest libraries in New Zealand were established by European settlers at the beginning of the 19th century. The first library for public use was the Port Nicholson Exchange and Public Library, set up in Wellington in 1840.

The first European visitors to New Zealand in the 18th century found an indigenous culture which had not devised a system of writing. The Maori had an extensive unwritten literature; the records of the people were passed from generation to generation through songs, recited genealogies, stories, and proverbs; they were inscribed in the painted and carved decorations of their wooden buildings and in cave paintings. The missionaries who worked in the country from 1814 onward established the first printing presses and endeavored to record and publish these unwritten texts.

Books were among the household items brought to the new land by European settlers. They established libraries on the model of those in England and Scotland. The development of library services owed much initially to the influence of the English scholarly and public library systems, but American and Scandinavian practices have also been introduced as a result of overseas training and travel by New Zealand librarians.

Libraries experienced slow and uneven development up to the mid-1930s. Public libraries were established by local councils but public access was not free; university libraries were poorly funded and not adequately housed; and there was no national library.

Impetus was provided by the reformation of the Libraries Association in 1935, by the activities of the Carnegie Corporation in sponsoring surveys and providing fellowships, and by the establishment of a government library agency, the Country Library Service, in 1938. The following 30 years saw the establishment of systems for training librarians, the modernization of public library service, a better distribution of service, the establishment of strong university libraries, and the formation of a national library.

Despite the small size of its population, New Zealand has the reputation of being among the best-read countries in the world, a characteristic which owes much to the liveliness of local publishing, the large number of bookshops, and not least the quality of the library service.

University of Canterbury Library

University of Canterbury Library in Christchurch (opened in 1975).

National Library. The National Library was established by an act of Parliament in 1965 and came into being in 1966 by a merging of the existing National Library Service, the Alexander Turnbull Library, and the General Assembly Library. The National Librarian is an officer of the Crown, responsible to the Minister of Education. A statutory Board of Trustees advises the Minister on the state and development of the National Library and promotes the development of library services in New Zealand. The Library is financed by an annual appropriation from Parliament.

The Library provides the normal national bibliographical and interlibrary loan services and manages the national collections. Its Regional Services Division provides book loans, information services, and technical assistance to public libraries and other agencies. The School Library Service provides advisory and loan services to elementary and secondary schools. The New Zealand Bibliographic Network, established in 1982, provides a comprehensive national database of holdings and publications data. It is being expanded from an in-house system to a full nationwide cooperative network coordinated by the National Library.

The Alexander Turnbull Library, an institution for scholarly research, was founded in 1918 as the

Libraries in New Zealand (1990)

Type of library	Number of administrative units (main libraries)	Number of service points (branches, mobile stops, etc.)	Volumes in collections
National	1[a]	33[a]	5,335,000[a]
Academic	7[b]	33[b]	5,228,000[b]

[a]1984
[b]1987

Source: Unesco, *Statistical Yearbook,* 1991.

result of a bequest; its collection reflects the interests of its donor—the Pacific, New Zealand history and literature, English literature (particularly the mid-17th century and the work of John Milton)—with additional strengths in early printed books and the development of the art of printing. The General Assembly Library, established in 1858 as the library of Parliament, was for a time a library of historical research because of the strength of its holdings, but by the mid-1980s, through transfer of stock and internal reorganization, it returned to its primary role as a parliamentary information service.

The National Archives in Wellington selects, preserves, and makes available the records of central government. It may advise and assist other organizations and arrange for the preservation of specified categories of local authority records. The main record centers are in Wellington and Auckland, but some repositories of regional records also exist in nongovernmental institutions in other parts of the country. The National Archives holds 15,000 linear meters of documents, 400,000 maps and plans, and photographs and pictures.

Academic Libraries. The six universities, at Auckland, Hamilton, Palmerston North, Wellington, Christchurch, and Dunedin, and the agricultural college at Lincoln, finance their libraries from their government grants. The libraries have developed rapidly since 1960, following the report in 1959 by a Government Committee of Inquiry on Universities (the Parry Report). All libraries are housed in buildings erected since 1964; research collections have been built up, and salaries and conditions of employment for professional staff are competitive with those in other sectors. At the time of the Parry inquiry the holdings of all the university libraries together were some 818,000 volumes; by 1981 they held 4,120,000 volumes.

No New Zealand university library collection can match the collections of major universities in larger countries, but each library is now much more adequate for the support of postgraduate studies and research, the development of which became official policy following the Parry Report. Surveys of university library resources were carried out in 1972 and 1982 and their reports published (McEldowney, 1973 and 1983).

There are libraries in the six colleges for training elementary and secondary school teachers, financed by central government through the Department of Education.

In the 14 technical institutes and 8 community colleges (which provide education for technicians, the trades, and some professions), funding comes from central government and is based on a Department of Education formula that is not generous by overseas standards. But the holdings of these libraries (430,000 volumes in all) form a useful contribution to national resources, particularly in the area of health sciences.

Public Libraries. Public library service, other than that supplied to some isolated settlements and rural communities, is exclusively the responsibility of local government—boroughs or counties. Finance for the service is derived from a local land tax. The period of most rapid development of public libraries, 1945 onward, coincided with or was a consequence of the abandonment of the subscription and rental library systems. In 1938, local bodies operated 104 libraries; by 1959, 164; and by 1979, 276. This period has also seen the replacement of most library buildings.

All libraries in cities, most of those in boroughs, and a few in counties provide free lending and reference services to their residents. Special services in light fiction, sound recordings, and art reproductions are normally operated on a rental basis. There is a strong emphasis on lending, but increasing attention is being given to information and reference work and to services directed at particular groups, such as housebound readers, literacy students, and businesses. Services to children are strong.

The standards of public library service vary widely in various parts of the country. Local autonomy and funding and the absence of public library legislation and central government funding explain the wide disparities. The National Library and the Library Association tried to promote the reorganization of service into larger units through pilot schemes or cooperative ventures, but with little success. It was clear in the mid-1980s that the reorganization of public library service would have to await the reorganization of local government in general.

School Libraries. Formal education at the elementary and secondary stages is the responsibility of central government, financed by annual appropriations through the Department of Education.

Most primary and secondary schools have library buildings or rooms. In many cases the library collections are improving and their scope is being widened to include a range of book and other library resources, but the emphasis continues to be on the library as a book storage area. Programs and services are very limited. The Department of Education makes no provision for the employment of professional staff in the school library resource centers, and that continues to be a major inhibiting factor.

The School Library Service, a division of the National Library of New Zealand, provides library support services to schools. Its reference services supplement the collections of school libraries and its advisory services assist and encourage the development of school-based library services.

Special Libraries. The number of special libraries has grown at a high rate since World War II. In 1959, 98 special libraries were recorded in the Census of Libraries; by 1979 the number was 241, and the development continues. The strength of this group was such that a Special Libraries Section was formed in the New Zealand Library Association in 1971.

These libraries exist to meet the information needs of their parent bodies, but some of them—by virtue of the extent of their resources—function as national collections in their subject fields, as with the libraries of the Ministry of Works and Development, the Ministry of Agriculture and Fisheries, the Department of Scientific and Industrial Research, and the Department of Health.

The Profession. The New Zealand Library Association was founded as an association of libraries in 1910. It adopted its present name and admitted personal members in 1935, after which it became a wider forum for discussion and cultivation of library matters. It has been a powerful force in the development of library service, initiating or stimulating a wide range of activities—bibliographical projects, library training, the introduction of free library service, promotion of the National Library, interlibrary loan, publication of standards, promotion of regional library service, and sponsorship of surveys. Most recently it has been active in pressing the Government for improved school libraries, in promoting the national bibliographic network, and in developing contacts with library associations in Australia and the South Pacific. The Association publishes the monthly newsletter *Library Life* and the quarterly journal *New Zealand Libraries*.

Librarians are trained in two institutions—Victoria University of Wellington and the Wellington Teachers College. The University confers a Diploma in Librarianship, a Master of Arts degree in Librarianship, and Certificates of Proficiency in individual diploma subjects. Entrants for the diploma course must normally have university degrees. The diploma course runs for an academic year. Forty-five full-time students and five part-time students were admitted each year in the mid-1980s.

The Teachers' College confers the New Zealand Library Studies Certificate. Students at the course must have the University Entrance qualification and must be working in a library throughout the course. The certificate course comprises 18 weeks of full-time studies, split into three sections over a period of approximately 18 months. Each course admitted 120 students in the mid-1980s.

Most continuing education is organized by the branches and sections of the Association. It takes the form of local and national courses or seminars linked with the Association's annual conference.

REFERENCES

New Zealand Department of Statistics, *Census of Libraries 1979* (1981).

Sara Innis Fenwick, *Library Services for Children in New Zealand Schools and Public Libraries: A Report to the New Zealand Library Association* (1975).

Walter John McEldowney, *New Zealand Library Association 1910–1960* (1962).

Walter John McEldowney, *New Zealand University Library Resources 1982: Report of a Survey Carried Out for the Committee of New Zealand University Libraries* (1983).

Report of the Trustees of the National Library of New Zealand and of the National Librarian. (Annual report presented to the House of Representatives).

Wilfrid Smith, *Archives in New Zealand: A Report* (1978).

BRIAN McKEON

Nicaragua

Nicaragua, a republic and the largest country of Central America, lies between the Pacific Ocean on the west and the Caribbean Sea on the east; it is bounded by Honduras on the north and Costa Rica on the south. Population (1990 est.) 3,871,000; area 130,000 sq.km. The official language is Spanish.

National Library. The National Library of Nicaragua was founded in 1882. At its inception it occupied the National Palace; it later transferred to its own building in the western sector of Managua, the capital. After the earthquake of 1972 it was transferred again, to the National Cultural Center in the northeastern section of the capital. The National Library originally contained approximately 5,000 volumes; in the mid-1980s it held 70,000, consisting of Nicaraguan bibliography, works of reference, textbooks, and other items, including works for leisure reading. The Library was named after Rubén Dario (1867–1916), the great Hispanic-American poet who in his earlier years was employed in it as Assistant Librarian. With the goal of eventually fulfilling the objectives of a truly national library, it attended in the meantime to the immediate needs of the student body of Managua. Costs of defense and economic stringency under the Sandinista government in the early 1980s led to rationing of many basic goods and deterioration in many public services, including library services.

Academic Libraries. Six major institutions have academic libraries: the Autonomous National University of Nicaragua, Central American University, National Educational Center, Polytechnic University, Autonomous Private University, and National School of Agriculture and Cattle Breeding. The principal academic libraries, in stock, organization, and function, are those of the National University in Managua and León, the Central American University, and the National Educational Center in Managua.

Public Libraries. From 1968 efforts were made to augment the quality and quantity of public libraries. They were established in the departments of Managua, Chinandega, Esteli, León, Jinotega, Bluefields, Corinto, Masaya, Ocotal, Matagalpa, Granada, and Carazo.

The public libraries in the cities of Jinotepe, Jinotega, and Chinandega were established by Rotarians and became preeminent. Others are the product of the joint efforts of municipalities, the Ministry of Education, and some citizens aware of the importance

Libraries in Nicaragua (1990)

Type of library	Number of administrative units (main libraries)	Number of service points (branches, mobile stops, etc.)	Volumes in collections	Population served
Academic[a]	13	18	281,000	6,962
School[a]	412	412	595,000	71,948

[a]1987 figures

Source: Unesco, *Statistical Yearbook*, 1991.

of libraries in the development of nations. All of them are in urban areas and are used largely by students at lower, intermediate, and higher levels of learning.

School Libraries. From the mid-1960s much effort went into the improvement of the libraries in educational centers. Several organizations and agencies donated books and so aided in the enlargement of those libraries—the International Development Agency, the National Institute of Spanish Books, the Central Bank of Nicaragua, and, particularly, the Organization of American States.

Special Libraries. Nicaragua's special libraries are in the capital at Managua. They include the Central American Institute of Business Administration, the Central Bank, the Supreme Court, the Ministry of Education, the National Bank, and the Bank of America. The library at the Central American Institute was established in 1968 with fewer than 500 volumes; it later acquired more than 25,000 volumes and about 500 periodicals, films, and other audiovisual items. The Library at the Central Bank, founded in 1961, was damaged in the earthquake of 1972 but thereafter largely recovered. The Library of the Ministry of Education was created in 1966; it has more than 6,000 volumes, specializing in teaching. It is used by teachers, officials of the institution, and law students. The Library of the Supreme Court was founded in 1950. The earthquake of 1972 destroyed a great portion of its books, documents, and facilities.

The Profession. The Association of University and Special Libraries of Nicaragua was created in 1969 and has some 45 personal and 20 institutional members. The Association of Librarians was established in 1965. Both associations endeavor to motivate librarians to improve service to the public within their limited financial means by offering lectures and courses, expositions, professional meetings, and workshops.

LUISA CARDENAS PEREZ

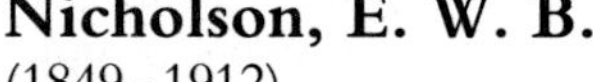

Nicholson, E. W. B.
(1849–1912)

Library Association

E. W. B. Nicholson

British librarian Edward Williams Byron Nicholson was founder of the Library Association and Librarian of the Bodleian Library.

Nicholson was born in St. Helier, Jersey, March 16, 1849, and educated at Tonbridge School, Kent. He published a catalogue of the school library in 1866. At Oxford he studied classics but spent much time writing for undergraduate journals. He graduated B.A. in 1871 and M.A. in 1874. His involvement in Oxford Union debates revealed an excitable character, while his duties as Librarian of the union introduced him to the practical problems of librarianship.

By accepting the post of Superintendent and Librarian of the London Institution in 1873, Nicholson hoped to gain a foothold in literary circles. He completely reorganized this moribund proprietary institution; the reference library of 60,000 volumes was recatalogued and classified according to a decimal scheme, while the circulating library was increased, issues rising sixfold in five years. A letter from Nicholson to *The Times* in 1875 produced a flood of new members (and income). Popular guest lecturers were secured; in February 1876, 700 people heard John Ruskin, while 200 had to be turned away.

In 1876 the Philadelphia Conference of Librarians, resulting in the organization of the American Library Association, impelled Nicholson—aged 27 and completely unknown—to invite British librarians to support a similar venture, with the aim of establishing a Library Association of the United Kingdom. The International Conference of Librarians, held at the London Institution on October 2–5, 1877, and attended by 216, was a great success, particularly because of the American librarians present.

Nicholson and Henry R. Tedder were the main forces behind the Metropolitan Free Libraries Association, whose aim was promoting public libraries in London. Several violent public meetings discouraged them from continuing direct action, and Nicholson and Tedder instead drafted a public libraries bill to make the provision of libraries easier. This bill was introduced in Parliament in 1881, with the support of the Library Association Council, but unsuccessfully. Provincial public librarians resented the fact that the LA was run mainly by London-based nonpublic librarians. The provincial librarians drafted a rival bill, which also failed. These events and the growing belief that the LA was too indolent to encourage new developments in librarianship made Nicholson resign from its Council in 1881. He was never suited to work with people of opposing views.

Bodleian Library. Nicholson's election as Bodley's Librarian in 1882—which forced him to abandon his literary plans—was unexpected, since he lacked scholarship and experience. Although the Curators wanted an energetic person capable of undertaking a large-scale reorganization, their choice of an outsider was ill-received, especially by Sublibrarians Adolf Neubauer and Falconer Madan. However hard Nicholson worked at improving the Bodleian, he worked even harder at arguing against their continual opposition.

Nicholson found the Bodleian in a depressing state: "Always undermanned as it had been, always undermoneyed, and almost always underroomed, its organization, fairly advanced at some points, was in most respects absolutely rudimentary or non-existent" (Bodleian Curators papers, untitled fly-sheet by Nicholson, February 8, 1899). For years the annual income never exceeded £59,000, with expenditure only a little less. Nicholson complained about the Bodleian's poverty to the London *Daily News* in 1894 and at the Bodleian Tercentenary in 1902. His public appeals were vindicated when, from 1907, the Library was aided by Lord Brassey's Oxford University Endowment Fund.

The Bodleian's stock increased from approximately 500,000 to 1,000,000 items under Nicholson, mainly because of rigid enforcement of the legal deposit privilege (he even claimed Valentine cards and tram tickets). He was more parsimonious about purchasing books and manuscripts. Nicholson's weakness was in trying to be a perfectionist; he spent large sums on unnecessary binding and catalogued all acquisitions in detail. Notable accessions included the Saint Margaret's Gospel Book, bought for £56, and a First Folio Shakespeare, acquired after Nicholson raised a public subscription, despite opposition from Library Curators.

Nicholson's most obvious achievements were the underground bookstore—the first constructed on such a scale—and the conversion of the Picture Gallery into the Upper Reading Room, amid tremendous dissension. Nicholson published a cataloguing code in 1883 and devised an elaborate classification scheme. The latter provided the basis for producing "the greatest subject-index the world has ever seen," according to Nicholson (memorandum to the Curators, February 13, 1909), but lack of money and staff thwarted Nicholson's hopes. Much to Nicholson's mortification, his deputy, Falconer Madan, was authorized in 1890 to commence the abbreviated *Summary Catalogue of Western Manuscripts.* The Bodleian's Oriental catalogues show Nicholson's desire for detailed cataloguing.

Nicholson formed a "Select Library" of open-access reference books, exhibited manuscripts, established a photographic department, and published facsimiles. Yet he encountered opposition over minor matters, such as extending opening hours or the seating and heating arrangements. He employed boys for routine duties and undergraduates for cataloguing. Despite ingrained prejudice, he appointed a female assistant librarian. Duties were recorded in the *Staff-Kalendar,* the first published library manual of its kind.

Nicholson's tenure was marred by perpetual animosity between himself and Madan, who thought that the Library's scholarly calm had been replaced by continual disorganization. The Curators tried to "fetter" Nicholson, as he was fond of saying, but he would not be muzzled. In 1898 he threatened to take them to law if they persisted in persecuting him. Nicholson suffered his first nervous breakdown in 1901 and became increasingly incapable of administration, though he would not admit it. He died in Oxford on March 17, 1912.

REFERENCES

Henry R. Tedder, "E. W. B. Nicholson. . . In Memoriam," *Library Association Record* (March 1914).

Strickland Gibson, "E. W. B. Nicholson (1849–1912): Some Impressions," *Library Association Record* (May 1949).

Sir Edmund Craster, *History of the Bodleian Library, 1845–1945* (1952; reprinted 1981), pp. 152–245.

K. A. Manley, "Edward Williams Byron Nicholson," *Encyclopedia of Library and Information Science,* volume 19 (1976), includes bibliography of Nicholson's major writings.

K. A. Manley, "E. W. B. Nicholson and the London Institution," *Journal of Librarianship* (1973).

K. A. Manley, "E. W. B. Nicholson and the Bodleian Facsimile Series," *Bodleian Library Record* (1977).

K. A. MANLEY

Niger

Niger, a republic of north central Africa, is bordered on the north by Algeria and Libya, on the east by Chad, on the south by Nigeria and Benin, and on the west by Burkina Faso and Mali. Population (1990 est.) 7,732,000; area 1,267,000 sq.km. The official language is French, but Sudanic languages are widely spoken.

Niger as of the mid-1980s did not have a national library, a national bibliography, or a legal deposit system, and there was no library system. There are few libraries in the country.

The Ministère du Plan, founded in 1976 in Niamey, took over the functions of the Centre de Documentation, which was under the Commissariat Général au Développement. Its primary function is to gather and conserve documents on Niger, as well as the documents of other countries. Its holdings include some 23,000 items, mainly periodicals and documents. Strongest subjects in the collection are economics, statistics, technical reports of ministries and public and private organizations, and social affairs. The Centre publishes bibliographies and catalogues, but does not function as a national library.

The Archives Nationales in Niamey, founded in 1913, houses a collection of documents through the 19th century.

The Institut de Recherches en Sciences Humaines (IRSH), founded as the Centre IFAN de Niamey in 1944 and later called the Centre Nigérien de Recherches en Sciences Humaines (CNRSH), was integrated with the Université de Niamey in 1973. The Institut has a limited scholarly library of about 14,000 volumes. Approximately 60 percent of the collection is in French, and the remainder is in English, Arabic, or African languages. The Institut issues the *Études Nigériennes* on an irregular basis, approximately three times a year.

The educational system has not been adequately developed. The Ministry of National Education is responsible for primary schools, secondary schools, and teacher training colleges. Literacy programs are conducted in the major African languages of the country.

There is one university. The Université de Niamey was founded in 1971 and attained university status in 1973. Its Library is that of the IRSH. In addition, it houses about 15,000 volumes.

Libraries in Niger (1990)

Type of library	Number of administrative units (main libraries)	Number of service points (branches, mobile stops, etc.)	Volumes in collections
Academic	1[a]	1[a]	21,000[a]

[a]1987

Source: Unesco, *Statistical Yearbook,* 1991.

Chuck Hutchinson, University of Arizona

The Documentation Center for the Ministry of Planning in Niamey, Niger, was completed in 1989.

The École Nationale d'Administration du Niger was founded in Niamey in 1963 to train civil servants and other officials. Its Library consists of approximately 18,000 volumes and 100 current periodicals.

Special Libraries. Two notable special libraries are those of the Centre Régional de Recherche et de Documentation pour la Tradition Orale, founded in 1968 in Niamey in cooperation with Unesco, with a collection of approximately 5,000 tape recordings of songs, tales, fables, and other records in the major African languages spoken in Niger; and of the Commission du Fleuve Niger (Niger River Commission), founded in 1971 in Niamey. Its documentation center provides abstracting services in agricultural production, stock farming, fish breeding, soil science and geology, and hydrology.

STAFF

Nigeria

Nigeria, a republic and federation of 21 states and its Federal Capital Territory (Abuja) in West Africa, is bordered by Niger on the north, Chad and Cameroon on the east, the Bights of Benin and Biafra on the south, and Benin on the west. Population (1990 est.) 108,542,000; area 923,768 sq.km. The official language is English, but there are more than 250 indigenous languages.

History. Nigeria as a political entity emerged in 1914 from the union of Northern and Southern Protectorates. It gained independence from Britain in 1960. Libraries are a relatively recent phenomenon in Nigeria. A few, mostly special and school, libraries date from the late 1800s, but the first modern public and academic libraries were founded shortly before independence. The first library school was established in 1961; the first indigenous librarian graduated in the 1950s. Unesco and British Council assistance, as well as sizable grants from the Carnegie and Ford foundations, served as catalysts in introducing modern libraries in Nigeria.

Natonal Library. Established under the National Library Act of 1964 (superseded by the National Library Act of 1970), the National Library of Nigeria (NLN) has headquarters in Lagos and branches so far in 14 states. It holds approximately 666,600 volumes, including monographs, rare publications of the colonial period, and old Nigerian newspaper files, as well as official government publications and national periodicals. A reference library, it is the nation's service center for receipt of legal deposits. The NLN publishes the *National Bibliography of Nigeria* and maintains, on cards, the *National Union Catalogue.* In 1971 it published the *National Union List of Serials in Nigerian Libraries.* A magnificent multi-million-dollar National Library headquarters complex in Abuja is planned for completion in the early 1990s.

National Archives. The Nigerian Records Office was created in 1954 to preserve national records, thanks in part to the work of historian and educator Kenneth Onwuka Dike. The Public Archives Act was passed in 1957 and the records office was renamed. With headquarters at Ibadan and branches at Enugu and Kaduna, the National Archives began a program in the late 1980s to set up a branch in each state. Its headquarters will move to the new capital, Abuja, along with the NLN. *A Bibliography of the National Archives Library,* compiled by L. C. Gwam, was published in 1964.

Academic Libraries. The nation's main academic libraries in the late 1980s included those at 21 federal universities and a defense college, 8 state-financed universities, 28 polytechnics or colleges of technology, and 52 colleges of education or advanced teachers colleges. The university libraries hold about three million volumes, with the premier University of Ibadan stocking about 440,000 volumes. The college libraries hold about a million volumes. Federal policy

Libraries in Nigeria (1990)

Type of library	Number of administrative units (main libraries)	Number of service points (branches, mobile stops, etc.)	Volumes in collections	Annual expenditures (naira)	Population served	Professional staff (with certificate, diploma, etc.)	Total staff
National[a]	1	15	558,000	3,693,067[b]	29,906	91[c]	563[c]
Academic[b]	110	144	4,098,777	25,819,727[c]	157,965[c]	795[c]	2,982[c]
Public[a]	12	92	1,108,000	2,835,156[c]	46,728	136[c]	1,054[c]
Special[c]	71	103	827,762	2,958,301[c]	75,462	151	777

[a]1989 data; source: Unesco, *Statistical Yearbook,* 1991
[b]1986 data
[c]1987 data

specifies that institutions of higher learning spend five percent of their recurrent budgets on library services.

The Academic and Research Libraries Section is one of the largest and most active sections of the Nigerian Library Association (NLA). It publishes the proceedings of its annual seminars. The chief librarians of the three types of academic libraries have standing committees which serve as forums for exchanging ideas and promoting common professional interests.

Public Libraries. The oldest public libraries in Nigeria are the Lagos Island Local Government Library, still functioning, and the Lagos Subscription Library. The real awakening in public library establishment in Nigeria occurred in 1955 with the promulgation of the Eastern Regional Library Act and the construction of the Unesco-funded model public library building in Enugu. About two thirds of the states have library service laws setting up governing boards; all states and the Federal Capital Territory have one form or another of public library system.

Some local governments have initiated public library services of varying sizes and quality. Mobile library systems are the exception rather than the rule; the boatmobile library service operated in the Rivers State is noteworthy. Services to patrons in prisons, hospitals, institutions for the blind, and other special locations are rare. Some public libraries have established book depots run on a commercial basis in an effort to ensure good supplies of library materials. Largely because of the low literacy rate in the country (about 35 percent in the late 1980s), public library service reaches only a small part of the nation's population. As a result, many people have studied how information could be provided to the non-literate members of the population, possibly by libraries structurally quite different from Western models. One such study is the RUDIS (Rural Development Information Service) project by Olabimpe Aboyade at Badeku.

School Libraries. Few of Nigeria's nearly 5,500 primary and more than 5,500 secondary schools maintain collections that qualify as libraries, despite the fact that the government adopted a national policy on education in 1981 that states: "Government will establish a school library service and ensure that teachers are given in-service training in the management and organization of school libraries."

In the early 1960s the federal government inaugurated a school library service which it later handed on to the Lagos State Library Service. In 1970 the University of Ibadan Department of Education founded the Abadina Media Resource Center, a model school library. Current efforts are aimed at getting the state library services to assume statutory responsibility for providing libraries in schools, as in Bendel State.

Enthusiastic librarians and teacher-librarians founded the Nigerian School Library Association in 1977. It publishes a semi-annual *Nigerian School Library Journal*.

Special Libraries. There are about 70 special libraries owned by both government and private organizations. Their collections and services range from the grossly inadequate to the excellent, the latter including the libraries of about 22 research institutes operating under the aegis of the Federal Ministry of Science and Technology. For example, the library at the Federal Institute of Industrial Research, Oshodi, has computerized several of its processes. Other noteworthy special libraries, some of which have become research libraries in their own right, include those at the Nigerian Institute of International Affairs, Lagos; International Institute of Tropical Agriculture, Ibadan; National Institute of Policy and Strategic Studies, Kuru; National Veterinary Research Institute, Vom; Central Bank of Nigeria, Lagos; Administrative Staff College of Nigeria, Badagry; Center for Management Development, Lagos; and Nigerian National Petroleum Corporation, Lagos. A union list of serial holdings of agricultural libraries was published in 1985. The libraries of such foreign agencies as the British Council and the United States Information Service can be found in some state capitals.

United Nations

Students in the library of the Federal Advanced Teacher's College in Lagos.

The Profession. The Nigerian Library Association (NLA) was founded in 1962. Governed by a Council headed by its President, it operates a chapter in each state. Special interest and subject groups form sections, such as Cataloguing and Classification. The NLA publishes *Nigerian Libraries* and *NLA Newsletter*. Some chapters put out such publications as *Bendel Library Journal*.

Nigeria's earliest indigenous librarians received their training in Britain or the United States. The Carnegie Foundation in 1961 funded the establishment of the Institute of Librarianship at the University of Ibadan (now its Department of Library, Information, and Archival Studies). Other institutions offering training include Ahmadu Bello University, Zaria; Bayero University, Kano; University of Maiduguri, Maiduguri; University of Nigeria, Nsukka; Imo State University, Okigwe; Anambra State University of

Technology, Enugu; Kaduna Polytechnic, Kaduna; and The Polytechnic, Nekede. Some colleges of education offer courses in library science, mainly for teacher-librarians. The programs at these institutions are at sub-degree, first degree, and graduate degree levels. Only the University of Ibadan and Ahmadu Bello University offer courses at the doctoral level.

The NLN published the now-dated *Nominal List of Practising Librarians in Nigeria* in 1981. It still provides an insight into the number of local and foreign librarians working in Nigeria.

B. U. NWAFOR

Illinois State Archives
Margaret Cross Norton

Norton, Margaret
(1891–1984)

Margaret Cross Norton, Illinois State Archivist, during a career of more than 35 years, played a leading role in redirecting an emerging U.S. archival profession toward public service, entitled to public support, and important for public administration, at a time when many saw care of public records as an adjunct to the primary concerns of the historical profession.

Born in Rockford, Illinois, to Samuel and Jennie Adams Norton, July 7, 1891, Margaret Norton attended Rockford College and the University of Chicago, where she received a Ph.B. in History in 1913, followed by an M.A. in History in 1914. She then enrolled in the New York State Library School at Albany; after her graduation in 1915, she became a cataloguer at the Vassar College Library. Norton became a cataloguer in the Department of History and Archives of the Indiana State Library in 1918, although she spent the early part of 1919 and the 1919–20 academic year working on a Ph.D. in History at the University of Chicago. Late in 1920 she became Cataloguer for the State Historical Society of Missouri, a position she held until April 1922.

At that time few states had archival programs, although Alabama, Delaware, Mississippi, North Carolina, and South Carolina had established state agencies with archival responsibilities. Several quasi-public state historical societies, including Minnesota and Wisconsin, served as repositories for archival materials; and some state libraries, including Pennsylvania, Texas, and Virginia, had begun to acquire and store permanently valuable public records of their states. In Illinois the Secretary of State had long been legal custodian of the state's records; a Division of Archives and Index was established in his office in 1873, but it became concerned principally with current matters and did not develop along archival lines. In 1921 the legislature created three divisions in the Illinois State Library; on April 1, 1922, Norton became Archivist of Illinois when she was designated Head of the Archives Division.

Using storage space in the state library stacks in the Centennial Building, Norton began to bring together the state's valuable records. Searching through steam tunnels, under the Capitol steps, and in attics, she acquired much of the material. During that period she contributed two volumes of *Illinois Census Returns,* published in 1934 and 1935 as volumes 14 and 16 of the *Collections of the Illinois State Historical Library*.

Norton first attended a meeting of the Public Archives Commission of the American Historical Association in 1923. Established in 1899, the Commission had as its goal the establishment of a national archives to facilitate historical research. Seven years later she became a member of the Commission, continuing until it was replaced by the Society of American Archivists (SAA) in 1936. A charter member of the SAA, she served as its first Vice-President, and in 1937 she became a Council member. She was elected fourth President of SAA, serving from 1943 to 1945, and in 1946 she began a two-year term as Editor of *American Archivist.*

At the same time, she became active in the National Association of State Libraries; she served as Secretary-Treasurer for five years beginning in 1933. She had served earlier as Chairman of an Archives Committee with members Charles B. Galbreath (Ohio) and George S. Godard (Connecticut). That Committee soon became inactive, and in 1935 an Archives and Libraries Committee was created with Norton first as a member and then as Chairman for 1942. Thus, for a period of more than 10 years, she was one of the links between the National Association of State Libraries and the ALA on the one hand and the Public Archives Commission of the American Historical Association and the Society of American Archivists on the other.

As early as 1930, Norton warned against allowing historians to preempt the field of archival care and preservation. She pointed out that public records were the product of governmental activity and were primarily designed to serve governmental needs. Speaking before the National Association of State Librarians in 1930, she asserted that the proper care of archives was an administrative concern of state government and not merely an adjunct to the historical field. "The archivist," she maintained, "should be a public official whose first interest is business efficiency, and only secondarily should he be interested in history. If the public records are cared for in a way that preserves their proper provenance, the historian not only of today but also of tomorrow will be as well served as the public official."

Seven years later she repeated the principle of the value of archives for administrative purposes: "An archives department is the governmental agency charged with the duty of planning and supervising the preservation of all those records of the business transactions of its government required by law or other legal implication to be preserved indefinitely."

The 1930s were doubly important to Norton's professional career. First, the state arsenal adjacent to the Capitol grounds in Springfield burned in 1934; responding to the outcry of patriotic and veterans organizations, the 1935 General Assembly appropriated money for a state archives building, and additional funds were obtained from the Public Works Administration. The building was dedicated during the Second Annual Meeting of the SAA in 1938. In the same year, the reorganization of the Illinois State Library began; it was completed in 1939 with the revision of the State Library Act. As a result of the reorganization, *Illinois Libraries,* formerly a publication of the Library Extension Division, became the official publication of the state library, and Norton became a regular contributor. The section initially entitled "The Archives of Illinois" and, after March 1942, "Illinois Archival Information" comprised what Ernst Posner called "the first American manual of archives administration." Articles were appearing elsewhere, but Norton's writings in *Illinois Libraries* specifically addressed the problems of the state archivist. Although devoted to the principles and philosophy of archival administration, they were based to a large extent on her own practical experience. She wrote at a time when the only discussions of archival practice originated in European experience, and her articles made *Illinois Libraries* essential reading for archivists. Norton also published articles in the *American Archivist* and in publications of the National Association of State Libraries and ALA.

After 1947 Norton wrote infrequently for *Illinois Libraries*. Her last article appeared in October 1956, when she discussed the relationship between the archivist and the records manager—a discussion that raised certain questions that are still debated.

Margaret Cross Norton retired as Illinois State Archivist on April 15, 1957. Her career spanned more than 35 years, the climax of which was a successful statewide records management survey. She died on May 21, 1984.

REFERENCE

Maynard J. Brichford, "Margaret Cross Norton: A Tribute," *Illinois Libraries* (1987) Thornton W. Mitchell, editor, *Norton on Archives: The Writings of Margaret Cross Norton on Archival and Records Management* (1975).

THORNTON W. MITCHELL

Norway

The Kingdom of Norway lies in the western part of the Scandinavian Peninsula in northern Europe. The Arctic Ocean lies to the north, Finland and Russia to the extreme northeast, Sweden to the east, the North Sea to the south, and the Atlantic Ocean to the west. Population (1990 est.) 4,242,000; area 323,895 sq.km. The official language is Norwegian, but the language of the Lapp minority is also spoken in the north.

History. In the 17th and 18th centuries the influence of the Age of Enlightenment spurred the first library activities in Norway. Reading associations were established in many towns, and dedicated priests and schoolteachers in rural areas organized book collections that would later develop into libraries. The Kongelige Norske Videnskapers Selskap (Royal Norwegian Society of Sciences and Letters) was founded in 1760, and its book collection is the foundation of the oldest scientific library in Norway. The University of Oslo Library was founded in 1811 and became the country's largest and most important scientific library.

In 1814 Norway went from a union with Denmark into a union with Sweden, and throughout the 19th century strong nationalistic forces strove for an independent Norway. Nationalism was accompanied by creation of a new university and development of reading associations and public libraries in rural areas. The poet Henrik Wergeland was among the eager supporters of public libraries as a foundation for the new Norwegian state.

Academic and special libraries in Norway tended to follow European models, especially German ones, but public libraries were profoundly influenced by the public library movement in the United States. The Norwegian public library pioneer was Haakon Nyhuus, who developed the Deichmanske Bibliotek, the Oslo City Library, into a modern public library from 1897 to 1913. The library reform of 1902 laid down guidelines and standards for public libraries. That reform led to the A/L Biblioteksentralen, the Norwegian Library Bureau. The first Public Library Act came into force in 1935, but public libraries were not required in all municipalities until 1947. The government appointed a commission in 1988 to look into the whole area of librarianship in Norway and set new directions for library development for the 1990s.

National Libraries and Archives. Since its founding in 1811 the Universitets-Biblioteket i Oslo (University of Oslo Library) has served as a national library for Norway. For most of its existence it had the right of legal deposit. The law covering legal deposit was passed in 1882, revised in 1939, and revised again to take effect in 1990. In 1989 the government decided to create a new independent National Library of Norway with a main library in Oslo. It set up a branch of the new library in the small town of Mo i Rana in northern Norway, a little south of the Arctic Circle, to

Libraries in Norway (1987)

Type of library	Number of administrative units (main libraries)	Number of service points (branches, mobile stops, etc.)	Volumes in collections	Annual expenditures (krone)	Population served	Professional staff (with certificate, diploma, etc.)	Total staff
National	1	2	2,213,000	10,582,000	--	96	160
Academic	113	200	8,374,000	57,420,000	--	397	550
Public	465	1,373	19,103,000	107,099,000	4,174,544	965 personer (ca. 800 årsverk)	1805[2]
School[1]	3,383	3,383	6,501,000	23,145,000	486,294	--	--
Special							
public	109	118	2,996,000	22,277,000	--	172	262
private	50	54	801,000	8,101,000	--	58	92

[1]secondary schools *not* included
[2]årsverk

Vestre Toten Public Library

Vestre Toten Public Library, Raufoss.

handle all legal deposit material. The new law on legal deposit, probably one of the most advanced in the world, covers printed material, pictures, films, videotapes, sound recordings, broadcast material, databases, and other types of electronically and optically stored materials—in principle, every information format available to the public. The branch in Rana is to develop a national depository library, national lending services, a newspaper microfilming program, and a unit for converting old catalogue cards into machine-readable data. The branch will also have a laboratory for visual media and will handle restoration of older films and photographs.

The *Norsk Bokfortegnelse* (Norwegian national bibliography) is published by the University of Oslo Library and is available on microfilm and on CD-ROM (for the period 1962–89).

The National Archives consists of the main National Archive in Oslo and seven state archives throughout the country. There are also private archives, such as the Archive of the Labor Movement.

Academic Libraries. Norway has four universities, in Oslo, Trondheim, Bergen, and Tromsø. Together the four university libraries constitute the largest collections of research material in the country. They have developed a common computerized library system, BIBSYS, that is also used by some other colleges and by the National Library branch in Mo i Rana.

The University of Oslo Library is the oldest and the largest, with a collection of well over 4 million volumes in the early 1990s. The Library serves a wider public than just the 28,000 students at the University. While not officially designated as a clearinghouse, the Library handles a large number of international interlibrary loans. The Medical Library and the Science Library are part of a group of Norwegian academic and special libraries (ansvarsbibliotek) that carry particular responsibility for their subject areas. The main library is today quite a distance from the university campus, and a number of faculties and institutes have their own branches.

The University of Trondheim Library shows the effects of bringing together the old Trondheim University of Technology and several other institutions, including the Museum of the old Royal Norwegian Society of Sciences and Letters. The University Library in Bergen is based on the Bergen Museum collections, founded in 1825, although the University itself was founded in 1948. The youngest and smallest is the University of Tromsø. Its Library, founded in 1971, is the northernmost university library in the world.

There are academic libraries at a number of colleges that deal with such subjects as agriculture, commerce, and veterinary medicine. Since the early 1970s a system of regional colleges has developed in all the counties of Norway.

Public Libraries. Since 1947 all municipalities have been required to have public libraries. The Library Act of 1971 required municipalities to support the libraries if they met certain requirements. The Act was revised in 1984 to fit a new financial system for the municipalities, under which the government makes lump-sum grants to the municipalities and counties, instead of special-purpose grants.

County Libraries. There are 20 county libraries to supplement the public and school libraries in their districts with books either from their own collections or from other libraries through an interlibrary loan scheme. They also give professional advice to the libraries, many of which are run by part-time librarians.

School Libraries. Libraries are required in elementary schools and are covered by laws governing primary education. State grants for school libraries are included in the lump-sum grants for education.

Special Libraries. There are about 400 public and private special libraries. Among the better known are the Stortingsbiblioteket (Library of the Parliament), the Library of the Nobel Institute, and the Library of the Central Bureau of Statistics. Most of these libraries report their holdings to the National Union Catalogue, operated by the University of Oslo Library. Since 1983 this union catalogue has been available as an online service.

Library Institutions. The Riksbibliotektjenesten (National Office for Research and Special Libraries) was established in 1969 to coordinate the functions of academic and special libraries and to advise government ministries on these matters. It is headed by the National Librarian. It faced as a major task for the 1990s creating the independent National Library.

The main tasks of the Statens Bibliotektilsyn (State Directorate for Public and School Libraries) are to supervise, control, and advise public and school libraries in accordance with the Library Act; to assist and advise the Ministry of Culture in matters concerning public and school libraries; and to strengthen library activities.

The A/L Biblioteksentralen (Norwegian Library Bureau) was founded in 1952 and is jointly owned by the state, the local authorities, and the Norwegian Library Association. It was created to serve the public by providing books, binding and library material and equipment, and bibliographic services.

The Profession. The Norwegian School of Library and Information Science gives a three-year course of study at the university level. It also offers an advanced two-year program in computer applications and information management, leading to the title of *Diplom-bibliotekar*. The school also has an extensive program of short courses on a wide range of topics.

BRODD, a special unit for consultancy and research, serves the Norwegian library and archives community, as well as institutions in other sectors needing assistance in information planning and systems design.

The Norsk Bibliotekforening (Norwegian Library Association), founded in 1913, functions as an umbrella organization for a number of smaller associations and special groups. It had about 3,000 individual members and 600 institutional members in the early 1990s. It is an active member of IFLA, and Else Granheim, director of the State Directorate for Public and School Libraries, was the first woman president of IFLA.

REFERENCES

Jostein H. Hauge and Maurice B. Line, *National Library Services in Norway* (1990).

Bendik Rugaas, "Developing a New National Library in Norway," *Alexandria* (1990).

BENDIK RUGAAS

Official Publications

The answer to the question of what is an official publication determines what one country agrees to send to its international exchange partners, which publications are provided through domestic depository programs, which publications are included in official publications collections and bibliographies, which publications are identified as official on national cataloguing tapes, and what comprises the contents of professional courses of study on official publications. But the question is not easy to answer. In 1983, after considerable study and discussion, the International Federation of Library Associations and Institutions (IFLA) adopted the following definition of official publications:

1. An official publication is any item produced by reprographic or any other method, issued by an organization that is an official body, and available to an audience wider than that body.

2. An official body is:

(i) any legislature of a state or federation of states; or of a province (state) or regional, local, or other administrative subdivision;

(ii) any executive agency of the central government of such a state or federation of states or of a province (state) or regional, local, or other administrative subdivision; or

(iii) any court or judicial organ; or

(iv) any other organization which was set up by an official body as in (i), (ii), and (iii) above and maintains continuing links with that body, whether through direct funding or through its reporting mechanism or its accountability; or

(v) any organization of which the members belong to any of the four categories above, including intergovernmental organizations.

3. An official publication is defined by the status of the issuing source, regardless of the subject matter, content, or physical form.

Notes

(1) For the purposes of this definition, the term "official publication" is comparable to terms used in some countries, such as "government publication" and "government document."

(2) The following bodies—universities; learned societies and academies; industrial and trade associations and chambers of commerce; libraries, museums, and art galleries; and independent research institutes not direct recipients of public funds—will be included as official bodies according to the practice of their individual countries.

(3) Political parties will not normally be considered official bodies unless in the practice or constitution of a particular country there is reason to do so.

(4) Nationalized enterprises and banks, public corporations, and other statutory bodies set up to carry out industrial or other productive activity will be considered official bodies according to the practice of the individual countries. However, state majority ownership of capital and heavy direct subsidy in enterprises that are otherwise nominally independent will not cause those enterprises to be considered official bodies.

(5) Publications originating in official bodies but published by or with the cooperation of commercial firms, universities, or independent research institutes, or any other non-official bodies, will normally be considered official publications.

Universal Bibliographic Control. IFLA has worked for years, along with national libraries and national library associations, to promote the universal bibliographic control of official publications. That is, agencies in each country work to catalogue all the official publications issued in that country according to international standards and to share that cataloguing information with other countries. IFLA has made great efforts to persuade all the government agencies responsible for cataloguing to adopt international cataloguing and format standards. Agencies in some countries have made good progress. For example, the U.S. Government Printing Office (GPO), in cooperation with the Library of Congress, catalogues thousands of official publications each year according to international standards. A growing number of U.S. libraries incorporate these electronic records into their public catalogues. As a result, the use of U.S. official publications is growing.

The IFLA Section on Government Information and Official Publications, in cooperation with the Section on Bibliography, asked Sylvie Jacques of the United Nations to conduct a survey of librarians about the bibliographic services of intergovernmental organizations. The results of the survey, published as *Reference Service for Publications of Intergovernmental Organizations* (1991), indicate a universal desire to have international organizations adopt the international standards and formats for cataloguing. The survey also shows that librarians would like to have this information available electronically as well as on paper.

It would not be possible to describe the bibliographic programs in all countries, but the program used in one government agency, the U.S. GPO, can serve as an example. GPO publishes a *Monthly Catalog of U.S. Government Publications,* which lists some 50,000 publications a year from the legislative, executive, and judicial branches of the federal government. The catalogue, available in paper and microfiche forms and online through library and commercial networks, follows international bibliographic standards. Each cataloguing record indicates whether the publication listed has been sent to depository libraries.

GPO also publishes the *Publications Reference File,* which lists only those titles GPO has for sale. This catalogue, available in microfiche and on computer tape, is available online in a commercial network and online at GPO for staff filling orders.

In order to reach the nonlibrary public, GPO publishes *U.S. Government Books,* a catalogue listing the most popular books it has for sale.

Universal Availability. One of the major goals of those involved with official publications is to encourage librarians and government publishers to work together to share government information with the people in their own countries and with the rest of the world. An IFLA resolution urges all governments to work out ways to provide copies of government publications to libraries in their countries. In most countries the publications are housed at national and parliamentary libraries. Treaties and intergovernmental agreements cover the exchange of official publications between or among governments.

Government agencies inform the public about available publications through catalogues, fliers, marketing, exhibits, and meetings. For example, in the

U.S. a number of agencies have as their sole purpose promoting the public's access to official publications. Those agencies include GPO, CIC (the Consumer Information Center of the General Services Administration), ERIC (the Educational Research Information Center), and NTIS (the National Technical Information Service). Many agencies also have information centers and libraries that provide access to the public as well as to their own staffs.

GPO operates a large mail-order business and 20 bookstores throughout the U.S. It also operates the federal depository library program, which includes 1,400 libraries and the international exchange service for the Library of Congress. GPO arranges marketing, often in conjunction with the publishing agencies, and produces public service announcements for use on radio and television and in newspapers and journals.

CIC provides consumer publications free or for low prices and advertises them through public service announcements and its own catalogue. One of the free items it offers is the *Directory of Depository Libraries* from the Joint Committee on Printing. ERIC collects, indexes, and sells materials in education, and NTIS does the same in the areas of science, technology, and business.

Fugitive Official Publications. Many users of official publications complain that the information they need is not available at all or is not available when they need it, even if it eventually gets to libraries. Much of this information appears in what are called fugitive documents in some countries and gray literature in others. There are several reasons for this situation.

In many cases, the publications are produced in agency printing plants because the information is perishable, is sensitive until released, or must be published quickly and therefore cannot wait to be printed by a national printer. By the time this information is available in paper or microfiche for libraries, it is so old that its only value is historical.

In some cases, the publishing agency does its own printing but refuses to provide enough paper copies to fill library needs. The national agency responsible for acquiring and distributing them cannot persuade the publishing agency to go back to press or agree to pay for the national printer to reprint.

In other cases, the national printers do the printing, but do not print extra copies for libraries. Or the publications no longer appear in paper at all and are available only in electronic form.

The agency responsible for acquiring copies for libraries may not have an automated tracking system and may not know that a publication has not been acquired. By the time the acquiring agency learns of a missing publication, it may be unable to find or to afford copies for distribution to libraries.

Finally, the publishing agency may have declared the publications exempt from depository distribution because it considers them sensitive, internal, or controversial, or it may have privatized the publications, which then become available only through a private vendor, who may or may not be the agency's contractor.

New Technologies. The increased use of electronic technologies has dramatically changed the role government agencies play in disseminating the public's information. Governments around the world are using or planning to use electronic means to collect, publish, and disseminate official publications. A number of international organizations, such as the Pan American Health Organization, have decided that librarians in developing countries face great difficulties in accessing data online, such as the lack of reliable communications and the cost of accessing what is available. Such organizations have developed CD-ROM publications and have provided the libraries with the equipment needed to use them.

Introducing the *Improvement of Information Access Act* of 1991 in the U.S. House of Representatives, Major Owens could have been speaking for librarians and library users in all parts of the world when he stated:

> As more and more Government records become automated, new and exciting questions should be asked about the information products and services that should be available from Federal agencies. These new technologies should lead to new ways of looking at information, because more will be possible. Not only will it be cheaper and easier to produce new information products and services, but the staggering drop in the costs of computing and data storage have made it possible to manipulate these data in ways that were unthinkable a decade ago.

The Profession. Most countries have national associations of librarians and many associations of librarians have units concerned with official publications. Most national associations are members of IFLA, which has a Section on Government Information and Official Publications. This Section encourages official publications librarians around the world to organize themselves in their geographic areas and to form interest groups in their national associations so they can develop strategies and programs to improve the production, organization, dissemination, and access to official publications.

The IFLA Section on Government Information promotes the inclusion of librarians from the Third World in IFLA activities by recruiting them for its standing committee and by using funds raised through its projects and seminars to bring librarians to IFLA conferences and the Section's seminars. The attendees at the seminar in Canberra, Australia, in 1988 passed the following resolution:

> that the information professionals in each of the countries in the South Pacific Area take steps to establish or expand a group within a national professional body to promote communication and education in the area of government information and to provide a mechanism for monitoring and advising government publishers and policy makers [and] that these national groups establish a Government Information Users Council composed of at least two representatives from each national government information group to identify, discuss, and take appropriate action in areas of common interest.

In the U.S. the largest and most active organization of official publications librarians is the Government Documents Round Table of the American Library Association. In a number of countries, government publishers have established advisory groups, such as Her Majesty's Stationery Office Services Working Party in the United Kingdom and the Depository Library Council to the Public Printer in the U.S.

More and more library schools offer courses in official publications and many official publications groups around the world conduct workshops and seminars. In addition, the IFLA Section on Government Information organizes seminars in connection with annual IFLA meetings. The first seminar was held in Saratoga Springs, New York, in 1982 and attracted librarians and publishers from 16 countries. The Section then held seminars in Chicago (1985) on "Social Sciences and Electronic Technology in the Area of Government Information," in London (1987) on "Official Government Publications Collections: Their Contribution to Making Official Government Information Accessible," and in Paris (1989) on "Reference Service for Publications of Intergovernmental Organizations."

The IFLA Section also organizes seminars for developing countries. The first, for French-speaking African librarians, was held in Rabat, Morocco, in 1987. The seminar was organized by Laydia Bachr of Morocco, Pierre Pelou of France, and Oumar Diallo of Senegal. Unesco provided a grant to enable a librarian from each of the French-speaking countries of Africa to attend the seminar. La Documentation Français published the proceedings, *La Question des Publications Officielles*. This Francophone seminar was so successful that a second one was held in Tunis in 1991.

The second seminar for developing countries was held for the island nations of the South Pacific in Canberra, Australia, in 1988 and was organized by Ann Miller of Australia. Funds from such sources as the Association of South-East Asian Nations enabled a librarian from each of the small nations of the South Pacific to attend the seminar.

The third seminar for developing countries was held in Mexico City, Mexico, in 1991 for librarians from Latin America. Rosa Ma. Fernandez de Zamora of Mexico organized the seminar with the assistance of Bernadine Abbott Hoduski, Barbara Ford, and Al Kagan of the U.S. and Anna Flavia Fonseca of Brazil. IFLA provided funds to enable one librarian from each Latin American country to attend the seminar.

REFERENCE

U.S. Government Printing Office, *GPO/2001: Vision for a New Millennium* (1991).

BERNADINE E. ABBOTT HODUSKI

Damel Bernstein, Waltham, MA
Felicia Adetowun Ogunsheye

Ogunsheye, Felicia Adetowun
(1926–)

Felicia Adetowun Ogunsheye, educator and author, became the first Nigerian head of a library school.

She was born December 5, 1926, in Nigeria, attended elementary school in various parts of the country, and took her secondary school education in Queen's College, Lagos, from 1939 to 1945. She proceeded to the Higher College, Lagos, where she obtained a Teaching Diploma in 1949. She attended Newham College, Cambridge, where she was graduated with a B.A. with honors in Geography in 1952, followed by an M.A. at the same university in 1956.

She married Ayo Ogunsheye, an economist and at one time a faculty member of the University of Ibadan, and started her working life as a teacher, first in high schools for girls and later in the Nigerian 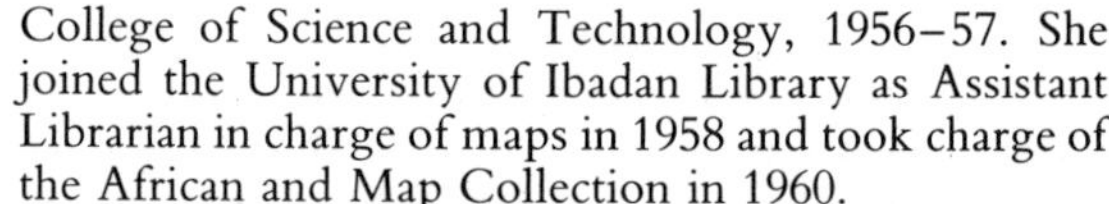 College of Science and Technology, 1956–57. She joined the University of Ibadan Library as Assistant Librarian in charge of maps in 1958 and took charge of the African and Map Collection in 1960.

At Simmons College, Boston, Massachusetts, she earned a Master's degree in Library Science in 1962. She returned to her post, finding time to lecture in a new Institute of Librarianship. In 1963 she became a full-time lecturer and was named Senior Lecturer. Ogunsheye was appointed Acting Director in 1970. When the Institute was redesignated the Department of Library Studies, she became the first Head, rising in rank to Professor in 1973. From 1977 she served as Dean of the Faculty of Education of the University.

In the field of bibliography, her studies and publications are extensive. She initiated the Abadina Media Research Project, a pilot library set up on the campus of Ibadan University for the children of Abadina, a satellite village created for the low-income, nonacademic staff of the University, providing direct library services and facilities for the children and offering research facilities. The center is headquarters of the Nigerian School Library Association, of which Ogunsheye became President.

A member of the Council of the Nigerian Library Association, she was Vice-President, Acting President, and President in succession in the years 1966 to 1971, which included the Nigerian Civil War years of 1967 to 1970.

She served on many committees, panels, and boards, including the National Library Board of Nigeria, and from 1971 participated regularly in the activities of IFLA, serving on some of the Standing Advisory Committees.

A tireless organizer, she played a key role in making the Department of Library Studies of the University of Ibadan an active center of the pursuit of knowledge in librarianship. She also became President of the Association of African Library Schools. She was first Secretary of the Nigerian Council of Women Societies and West African Council of Women Societies. She served as President of the Women's Improvement Society and the Nigerian Society of University Women. Simmons College awarded her an honorary doctoral degree, and she received the International Alumni Award (1979).

S. B. AJE;
VIRGINIA W. DIKE

Oman

The Sultanate of Oman occupies the southeast corner of the Arabian Peninsula and is the second largest country in that area. Population (1990 est.) 2,000,000; area 212,547 sq.km. Arabic is the official language, but English is widely understood.

History. The interior of the country remains a source of traditional cultural influence, but the coastal regions reflect the diversified and cosmopolitan interests of a mercantile people. Social and economic development became government priorities with the accession of Sultan Qaboos bin Said in 1970. Many of the country's mosques contain religious books deposited as endowments.

In 1977 a royal decree promoted the recovery and

preservation of the estimated 35,000 manuscripts in private collections. About 4,500 had been collected by 1985. They are being carefully conserved and catalogued in the Ministry of National Heritage and Culture, which also contains a Documentation Center dedicated to preserving current sources of information about the Sultanate.

There is no designated National Library, but a 1984 royal decree promulgating a Press and Publications Law requires those who issue or import printed matter to deposit copies with the Ministry of Information.

Academic Libraries. The Main Library of Sultan Qaboos University near Muscat is the largest in the country. In 1989 it had 38,000 monograph volumes and 2,300 current periodical subscriptions in English and Arabic. This Library also includes works in a variety of media. It was designed as a completely automated facility, and has commenced using an online public access catalogue. Several training colleges have substantial collections of academic interest.

Public Library Services. The main public library is the Islamic Library in the capital area. It has a collection of more than 20,000 volumes and includes a children's section. Also in the capital area is a recently completed public technical library built under the instructions of the Sultan to commemorate the 20th National day. Many government libraries are also open to the public.

School Libraries. By 1989 there were 721 schools with almost 298,500 students. The Ministry of Education and Youth distributes books to school libraries.

Special Libraries. These exist in more than 20 government ministries and agencies.

The Profession. There is no library association in Oman because there are few professionally trained librarians working in the country. A degree course in librarianship has been introduced at Sultan Qaboos University as part of Oman's drive toward full development of its resources.

REFERENCES

Frank A. Clements, *Oman* (1981), issued as volume 29 in the World Bibliographical Series.

Donald Hawley, *Oman and Its Renaissance* (1987).

"Oman," an illustrated pamphlet issued annually by the Ministry of Information.

Omani Library Directory (Sultan Qaboos University Main Library, 1989).

IAN SIMONS

The Main Library of Sultan Qaboos University near Muscat is Oman's largest library.

Organization of American States

The Organization of American States (OAS), headquartered in Washington, D.C., includes 32 member countries from the Western Hemisphere. The oldest international regional organization, it was called the Pan American Union (PAU) when it was created in 1890.

The OAS has political and technical functions. Political functions involve settling border disputes, monitoring human rights, and establishing international treaties. Technical branches of the OAS are concerned with problems basic to development in the fields of education, science, culture, economic, and social affairs. These include a wide range of projects concerned with libraries, archives, documentation centers, publishing, conservation and microfilming, and related advanced information technologies.

Background. Linked to the OAS is the world's oldest international communications association, the Inter-American Conference on Telecommunications (CITEL), which sets policies and establishes the norms for air rights. It deals with problems related to telecommunications that must be overcome for the countries to take advantage of the newer information technologies. CITEL evolved from the Inter-American Electrical Communications Commission, created in 1923. During the following decades, ideas about the

Libraries in Oman (1990)

Type of library	Number of administrative units (main libraries)	Volumes in collections	Population served	Professional staff (with certificate, diploma, etc.)	Total staff
Academic	11	105,400	--	36	71
Public	4	41,700	--	7	22
School	134	252,900	341,200	4	134
Special	30	98,700	--	23	55

Sources: *Omani Library Directory*, 1990. Ministry of Education. *The status of school libraries in the Sultanate of Oman*, 1990.

Inter-American Telecommunications Network (ITN) and the Inter-American Telecommunications Satellite Network (SARIT) were formulated. In 1961–62 the infrastructure of ITN was developed, and a study was undertaken of the policies and problems of the Americas in telecommunications. CITEL became a permanent Specialized Conference in 1971.

The Columbus Memorial Library (endowed by Andrew Carnegie) serves the reference needs of the various OAS programs and of the public. It is also responsible for developing catalogues of official OAS documents and publishing related bibliographic works. In the 1940s and early 1950s it began to assist the member countries. These services were separated from it when the Library Development Program (LDP) was created in the Department of Cultural Affairs under Marietta Daniels Shepard (1913–1984).

In the late 1940s and the 1950s, the PAU carried out activities related to copyright legislation and legal deposit, international exchange of publications, and free circulation of books among the members. These concerns became the responsibility of the Regional Center for Development of the Book in Latin America and the Caribbean (CERLAL), in Bogotá, Colombia.

In the 1960s the Library Development Program began assisting library schools and libraries in Latin America. To serve a large region that had little access to technical information, it also granted graduate level fellowships and published important series including: *Inter-American Library Relations* in English and Spanish, *Manuales del Bibliotecario, Estudios Bibliotecarios, Reuniones Bibliotecologicas,* and *Cuadernos Bibliotecologicos.* By the 1970s, responsibility for providing technical publications shifted to projects in various countries.

Two OAS secretariats cover a broad range of subject areas dedicated to pooling regional resources for development: the Executive Secretariat for Economic and Social Affairs and the Executive Secretariat for Education, Science, and Culture; the second is most concerned with development of libraries, archives, publishing, and information systems, and this article is primarily concerned with the projects of its departments.

Libraries and Information Systems. It is difficult to generalize about Latin America and the Caribbean because of the wide diversity, but a summary of the situation and problems of the region is important to understand the context of the OAS projects.

Most governments of the region, especially the legislative and executive branches, make comparatively little use of information services, much less those delivered electronically. Almost all of the countries have serious foreign exchange problems that make purchase of computers and information (whether in book or electronic form) not only expensive but unreliable—an institution may be receiving the monthly data from a service only to miss six months for lack of foreign exchange. A greater problem is the shortage of trained personnel, especially at the mid-level in the library profession. The highly trained people in key positions do not have the support staffs they need. Research techniques and terminology are not taught widely. Librarians lack training opportunities in abstracting, indexing, and analysis, which hinders creation of national databases.

There is a great desire for exchange of information within and between countries of the region, but the means to do so are weak. On the other hand, the means for sale and distribution of information from the United States, European nations, and Japan are strong. In the Information Age, as in the Industrial, the information-rich are getting richer and the information-poor are getting poorer. There is also frequently an imbalance within a country whereby one institution or series of institutions (such as a central bank library) commands information facilities far better than the rest. The imbalance makes collaboration within a country difficult because the inadequate institutions are seen as a drag on the advancement of the developed. In some countries, such as Brazil, Venezuela, Mexico, and Jamaica, there are several strong institutions that cover a variety of disciplines. In such countries national systems and important national databases in various fields are being developed. The OAS uses the resources of these countries to help the others.

Users are not experienced with traditional library use, much less with electronically delivered information, and so do not demand the services, even though their need for information might be great. Most people have never used a library—school and public libraries are not common, and paper and most books are imported and expensive. Reading materials suitable for low-level readers, new literates, and children are few and poorly distributed. Large rural populations scattered throughout the region are isolated from doctors, priests, schools, books, and libraries.

Much of the OAS assistance to libraries aims to develop library staffs to the point where they can control national information, not just process data from abroad. The OAS has worked on a variety of ways to promote standardization of technical processes. It published the Spanish versions of *Anglo-American Cataloging Rules,* both 1 and 2, and translated the MARC format into Spanish. It supported the updating of the Rovira List of Subject Headings, *Lista de Encabezamientos de Materias para Bibliotecas,* which provides a common vocabulary for Spanish-speaking countries. In these efforts it collaborated with the University of Costa Rica Library, the University of Mexico and the National Council on Science and Technology of Mexico, and the Institute for Promotion of Higher Education of Colombia. The experts who worked on these projects were from many parts of Latin America.

Many library school professors received advanced training with OAS fellowships, and OAS worked to help improve the curriculum of library schools. In 1984–85, for example, it formed with the Center of Library Research at the University of Mexico a documentation center on Latin American library research and training. It supported courses for library school faculty on research techniques, abstracting, indexing, and information analysis so they could incorporate those skills in their curricula. It assisted the Department of Library Studies of the University of the West Indies (UWI) over many years by training faculty, paying for travel to professional meetings, and providing bibliographic materials and equipment. It also helps the UWI offer extension courses in the 10 English-speaking Caribbean member states. For many years it supported the Inter-American Library School of Medellín, Colombia, by providing fellowships to students from other countries, by sponsoring advanced training to faculty, and by supporting its publishing program. It helps the University of Costa Rica to train Latin Americans in school librarianship. In the 1980s it developed a series of modules to train paraprofessionals in the Caribbean that allow library assistants to take basic training without having to go abroad.

OAS also worked with university libraries on both basic library processes and advanced technologies. Help to one is frequently applied to others. For example, the OAS helped the Library of the University of Costa Rica to develop computer facilities that in turn are used to train librarians from other Central American institutions. National libraries run the gamut from highly advanced centers of national information systems, as in Venezuela, to sadly neglected repositories of ragged out-of-date collections. The projects try to deal with the particular problems of each so they can assume more important roles in national information systems.

The newer OAS member states in the Eastern Caribbean have populations of under 250,000. Many have only one or two trained librarians who must serve all of the information needs of the country, with low budgets and few qualified paraprofessionals to support them. To help them, the OAS in the 1980s worked to develop new curricula, training, and assistance tailored to the special needs of countries. It works with them to develop different and more adequate systems than models from the larger countries can provide. OAS works in these countries with libraries of all kinds, documentation centers, archives, and publishers, to maximize the use of limited resources. A committee of librarians and archivists from each country meets every two years to set priorities for OAS activities.

The fields of agriculture and science are the most advanced in use of electronic technology for information, thanks in part to the Inter-American Institute for Cooperation on Agriculture (IICA), an OAS specialized organization created in 1942. Within it is the Agricultural Documentation and Information Center (CIDIA) in Costa Rica, which supports research and technology transfer. CIDIA serves governments, the academic community, and farmers. It effectively helped create an Inter-American system with subsystems on agriculture, rural well-being, and related production, marketing, statistical, and socio-economic information that operates throughout the Hemisphere. It set up the AGRINTER information system, which is part of the AGRIS global data network. From 1972 AGRINTER worked to establish national documentation centers in most member countries. It promotes not only dissemination of information and creation of databases on many subjects, but also planning and preparation of basic bibliographic works and training.

Banks and industries such as the petroleum industry are perhaps the institutions making most sophisticated use of advanced technology for their own needs. The OAS project Scientific and Technological Information Services for Industry, which began in 1974, developed an Inter-American network of centers moving toward use of advanced information technology. The Caribbean Industrial Research Institute (CARIRI) in Trinidad and Tobago, which the OAS assists to provide information to industry, and the Scientific Research Council in Jamaica were the only English-speaking participants as of 1986.

Using the resources of ICAITI in Guatemala (the Central American Research Institute for Industry, which is assisted by the OAS), a series of workshops began in 1985 that brought many English-speaking countries into the network. The first workshop provided an overview of techniques to establish and maintain a technical information center, identify user needs, market technical information services, establish documentation centers, use online access to computerized databases, and apply microcomputer technology in libraries and information centers. This introductory seminar was to be followed by more in-depth courses.

School libraries are becoming more widespread through a program to train teacher-librarians and to train teachers in use of books. Working through the ministries of education, many national projects in both Latin America and the English-speaking countries are helping establish basic media centers. *Flexible Model for a National System of School Libraries,* published in Spanish (1983), Portuguese (1985), and English (1986), is used by educators throughout the Hemisphere. It reflects with its practical low-cost solutions the years of experience in many countries.

Most of the people of the region are poor and half of the poor are under 15 years of age. Information services to them have been negligible and dispersed. Public libraries have not reached many. Literacy programs have had an insignificant impact because the new readers often lapse into illiteracy within months for lack of materials to read. Few writers of fiction or of information materials in the fields of sciences, health, technology, or culture know the techniques of writing for the new reader. Few institutions such as public libraries and community cultural centers effectively reach the new reader. Not only do they lack the necessary variety and quality of culturally relevant materials at the new reader's level, they are not constituted to facilitate communication *from* the low income communities as well as *to* them.

The OAS made efforts to organize the services necessary to create and maintain an ambience of reading in rural and urban communities that have achieved bare literacy. Its projects in this field deal with the creation, production, and dissemination of printed materials to and from the new reader through channels independent of the formal education system. The OAS builds on existing literacy and community development projects to make use of activities that have begun and to provide the essential follow-up. Efforts are made to improve coordination between and organization of a variety of existing cultural, economic, and technical institutions at the community level as well as at the national and regional levels. Cores of people in each country are trained to write for the new reader, including journalists, fiction writers, librarians, cultural administrators, and specialists from technical, agricultural, health, science, and cultural fields. These same people are also trained in community research techniques and in distribution of information. New readers are trained in use and construction of mimeographs and in communication techniques so they can produce their own materials. Community participation in design and implementation of the projects is an important feature. Projects in Central America and the Andean countries are working together to share expertise and materials through an Inter-American network.

Publishing and Mass Media. A large potential market for children's books in Spanish is being served by publishers in Spain and Mexico whose publishing industries are well organized. Most Latin American publishers produce small editions and do not promote their books vigorously, with the result that the books are unnecessarily expensive, the writers and illustrators of Latin America have no market for their work, and Latin Americans have little access to books published in their own countries or elsewhere in Latin America. The same can be said of radio and television production for children. Between 1980 and 1985 the Proyecto Interamericano de Literatura Infantil (PILI), headquartered in Venezuela, built up 12 national documentation centers on children's literature as part of the Inter-American Network on Children's Literature, which collects and disseminates information about national publishers, writers and illustrators abroad and within each country. More are being created. These centers send information to the Banco del Libro in Venezuela. It in turn sends them relevant information. The Banco publishes current notices of recent books in catalogue format and sends this information to the countries so that potential buyers can have access to the latest Latin American publishing. The centers met in Bolivia as a group for the first time in 1984 to plan how each could help the others improve their work. With Radio Nederland and the Inter-American Center for Advanced Journalism Studies for Latin America (CIESPAL), the OAS established in 1986 a similar means for exchange and production of radio and television programs for children as well as for training of producers, actors, and writers. PILI promotes Latin American materials abroad through exhibits and participation in world book fairs, particularly the Bologna Book Fair, where the OAS exhibits from 1980 gave many Latin American publishers their first broad exposure. It also trains writers, illustrators, publishers, and journalists.

Archives. The member states of the OAS comprise two main archival traditions, the Hispanic and the British. The Spanish-speaking countries inherited a sophisticated, highly advanced system of record keeping from Spain that fell into disuse but that left the countries with valuable colonial archives. The English-speaking members are new countries. Many are beginning to establish national archives. (Jamaica, the Bahamas, and Barbados have well-established archives.) Their colonial records are largely in England. Their national history is short. In the Spanish-speaking countries, OAS assistance is devoted largely to improving the education level of archives staff through fellowships for basic training at the OAS Inter-American Center for Archives in Argentina, and for advanced studies in Spain, and to helping countries develop effective archives networks. In the newest English-speaking member countries, OAS helps to establish archives legislation, devise records management, and train the new staffs in archives management. Assistance to archives is closely tied with that to libraries.

Conservation. Through an Inter-American project and national projects, the OAS helps libraries and archives with storage, repair, microfilming, and architectural planning. It provides training, advice, and equipment. OAS emphasizes prevention of damage through proper storage and cleaning and provides assistance simultaneously in each country to policy makers, administrators, and "bench" people. Because the conservators of Europe and the United States are largely technicians with advanced formal education, many of their manuals and techniques are not applicable in countries where the person doing the repair probably has not finished secondary school. In these countries, unlike the richer countries, manual labor is low cost and highly skilled, while advanced mechanized methods are prohibitively expensive. The OAS therefore tries to adapt basic technical publications to appropriate levels. It emphasizes the lower-cost manual techniques that do not require expensive equipment that is frequently impossible to maintain.

SUSAN SHATTUCK BENSON

Osborn, Andrew D.
(1902–)

Andrew Delbridge Osborn, Australian-born university librarian, author on library cataloguing practice, and library educator, wrote the standard treatise for librarians on serial publications.

Osborn was born in Launceston, Tasmania, Australia, June 14, 1902. When, at the age of 17, he joined the Australian Commonwealth Parliamentary Library, it was still in Melbourne. He rose in its ranks to be Senior Cataloguer, a post he held for eight years.

In 1925 Osborn received his B.A. degree in psychology and philosophy from the University of Melbourne, and in 1927 his M.A. degree. January 1928, however, found him no longer in Australia. Looking for new professional and academic opportunities, he presented himself for employment at the Director's office in the New York Public Library. He was given a job at the information desk under the direction of Frank A. Waite, whose daughter he was to marry. At the New York Public Library he rubbed shoulders with Robert Downs, Quincy Mumford, and David Clift, among others, who were to become, like Osborn himself, luminaries of American librarianship.

Repeating a pattern begun in Melbourne, he entered Columbia University. There he completed his Ph.D. in 1934. His dissertation was published in that same year as *The Philosophy of Edmund Husserl in Its Development from His Mathematical Interests to His First Conception of Phenomenology in Logical Investigations*. A second edition, more simply titled *Edmund Husserl and His Logical Investigations,* was issued in 1949, and this edition was reprinted by Garland Publishing in 1980. During the mid- to late 1930s, Osborn wrote a number of philosophical articles for the *Journal of Philosophy*.

But his career was to be that of librarian, not philosopher. While working at the New York Public Library, he wrote an article on the Prussian Union Catalogue for *Library Journal*. It was perhaps to plant an idea that bore fruit a few years later. In 1935–36, on a leave of absence from the Library, he completed the requirements for the A.M.L.S. degree at the University of Michigan, where his mentors were William Warner Bishop and Margaret Mann.

At the suggestion of Keyes Metcalfe, he was invited to spend the academic year 1936–37 organizing a new library school at the University of Southern California. Bishop persuaded him to spend the following academic year teaching in the Michigan Library School. There Osborn completed his masterful translation of the German cataloguing rules. His *The Prussian Instructions: Rules for the Alphabetical Catalogs of the Prussian Library* was published by the University of Michigan Press in 1938. For this work Osborn provided a comprehensive and scholarly introduction and useful footnotes to the text. Like his Husserl book, his translation of the *Prussian Instructions* was something of a tour de force in its mastery of German and in its grasp of the scholarship of its subject.

In 1938 Osborn followed Metcalfe to Harvard and began what might be called the first of his three major careers. He served at Harvard until 1958. He became Chief of the Serials Division, Assistant Librarian in Charge of Cataloguing, and eventually Associate Librarian. His work at Harvard was amplified by various consulting and writing assignments. He was appointed to the important committee Archibald MacLeish, Librarian of Congress, created under the chairmanship of Carleton B. Joeckel to study reorganizing the processing operations of the Library of Congress. The committee reported in 1940. Osborn's participation in this work was followed by a number of surveys, both in collaboration with others and alone, of a variety of libraries—public, state, and university—and of the Library School of the University of Illinois (1943). In 1948–49 he took a leave of absence to head the processing section of the United Nations Library in New York and continued as a consultant to that library through 1951.

His experience during this period crystallized into a number of major publications. Chief among these was his celebrated though relatively short paper, "The Crisis in Cataloging," which was published in *The Library Quarterly* in 1931. In it, Osborn describes and condemns what he calls the legalistic, perfectionist, and bibliographic approaches to cataloguing and calls for a pragmatic approach emphasizing economy, efficiency, and common sense. Not only should catalogue codes become clearer and simpler, in Osborn's view, but library administrators should take a firm stand to ensure cost-effective, streamlined processing in catalogue departments. Osborn dealt equally bluntly with the problems of classification and subject headings, concluding that systems for intellectual access to library materials had become too cumbersome and complex to be effective. The paper was widely reviewed, reprinted, and translated. Osborn followed it up over the years with other thoughtful commentaries on and surveys of current cataloguing practice.

In 1942 and 1943 he helped with the revision of Margaret Mann's *Introduction to Cataloging and the Classification of Books*. Osborn had dedicated his translation of the *Prussian Instructions* to Mann in 1938. He was to receive the American Library Association's Margaret Mann citation in 1959.

Osborn's *Serial Publications: Their Place and Treatment in Libraries* was published by ALA in 1955. Widely reviewed, it remains the standard treatise in its field.

In 1958 Osborn began his second major career. He returned to Australia as Associate Librarian of the University of Sydney, where he soon became Librarian. He remained in Sydney four years. During that time he almost doubled the University Library's collection; created an undergraduate library; and planned and oversaw the erection of the new Fisher Library—remarkable for its design both as a library and as a building. Upon completion, it immediately won several major architectural prizes.

Osborn operated on a scale and with an energy hitherto unprecedented in Australian librarianship. Though he created considerable consternation and eventually strong criticism among academic administrators and some of his more conservative professional colleagues, he helped to dramatize the paucity of library resources throughout the country and the need for aggressive expansion if the needs of modern scholarship were to be met. Thus he was instrumental in enlarging the horizons of librarianship as a profession in Australia. Whatever difficulties his drive and style of action caused in the University of Sydney, his achievements were ultimately recognized by the University itself when it awarded him an honorary LL.D. degree in 1978. (He was the first librarian to be so honored by an Australian university.)

Osborn left Australia in 1962. After a stint of teaching at the Library School at the University of Pittsburgh, he began his third major career in 1966 when he undertook the challenge of creating a new school of library and information science at the University of Western Ontario in Canada. The rapidity of development and outstanding success of that venture are remarkable. In a period of four years, he developed the School, assembled an international faculty, indoctrinated the faculty with a philosophy of instruction based on the repudiation of the lecture method and the use of a seminar method that he devised, organized a large experimentally arranged library with a major rare-books and bibliography collection to serve as the School's laboratory, secured accreditation for the School, and populated it with a student body that had grown to 200 by 1970. The resonance of his powerful personality and of his educational philosophy for the new school remained perceptible within its walls for many years after his departure.

In 1970 Osborn retired to Sydney. He set up there as a bookseller, though he continued to travel, to teach occasionally, and to write (a second edition of *Serial Publications* appeared in 1973). Indomitable and indefatigable, Osborn continued his work. He brought out the third edition of *Serial Publications* in 1980.

REFERENCES

Serials Librarian (Spring 1982) is devoted to Osborn. Of special note are Keyes Metcalfe, "Andrew D. Osborn"; Harrison Bryan, "The Three Careers of Andrew Osborn"; Constantine M. Hotinsky, "Andrew D. Osborn and Education for Librarianship in Canada"; and Perry D. Morrison and Elizabeth B. Cooksey, "Andrew D. Osborn: A Bio-Bibliography."

W. BOYD RAYWARD

W. Boyd Rayward
Paul-Marie-Ghislain Otlet

Otlet, Paul-Marie-Ghislain
(1868–1944)

Paul-Marie-Ghislain Otlet, Belgian lawyer, bibliographer, and internationalist, in a lifelong collaboration with Henri LaFontaine, gave life to the International Federation for Documentation (FID), the Union of International Associations (UIA), and a major bibliographical tool still in widespread international use, the Universal Decimal Classification (UDC). He also initiated in Europe the formal study of documentation, a term he popularized and gave its specialized contemporary meaning. His work and that of friends and followers had considerable influence in the United States, especially in the founding of the American Documentation Institute, now the American Society for Information Science.

He was born in Brussels, August 23, 1868, to a family of wealth and some social importance; as he grew up, he was surrounded by notable figures in the literary, artistic, and intellectual circles of Brussels. His education was at first private and then in the hands of the Jesuits until he transferred in 1866 from the Université de Louvain to the Université Libre de Bruxelles, where he earned a law degree in 1890. He then married his cousin Fernande Gloner and joined an old family friend, Emile Picard, as a *stagiaire* (trainee) at the Palais de Justice.

But the law was of no vital interest to him, and he longed for some inspirational work of social and intellectual value. In 1891 he was to find both in the recently formed Société des Études Sociales et Politiques. At this time he began his collaboration with Henri LaFontaine, a former stagiaire of Picard's, now an international jurist of some reputation, and 15 years Otlet's senior. LaFontaine had directed a section for bibliography in the Society, and the disciplines of bibliography seemed to fire Otlet's imagination. In a seminal paper, "Un Peu de Bibliographie" ("Something About Bibliography," 1892), he addressed the question: "How can the social sciences be given the positive and documentary character of the natural sciences?" Some of the answers, he believed, could be found in new forms of bibliography practiced on an international scale.

In 1893 the two friends expanded their work and became codirectors of what they now called the International Institute of Sociological Bibliography. Otlet's discovery of Melvil Dewey's Decimal Classification in 1895 led them to seek yet further expansion. Under the sponsorship of the Belgian government and with financial support from Ernest Solvay, industrialist and social theorist, they convened the first International Conference on Bibliography to discuss the problems involved in this expansion. The conference resolved that a catalogue truly universal in scope should be attempted, that an International Institute of Bibliography (IIB) should be formed to further the work, that the Decimal Classification should be adopted en bloc as the basis for the subject arrangement of the catalogue, and that a documentary union of governments should be created to support it. The Belgian government provided a headquarters for the Institute, and an International Office of Bibliography (OIB) was established by royal decree, September 17, 1895 (an official documentary union was never achieved, though the idea was raised again in 1908, 1910, and 1919).

The Universal Bibliographic Repertory (RBU) grew rapidly. By 1903 its various parts together contained more than six million notices; the number in the 1930s was variously estimated as between twelve and fifteen million. An on-demand search service was instituted, and the service gradually expanded in the number and variety of consultations made of it. The Office began bibliographical publications of its own, directed others, and persuaded many bibliographical publishers to adapt their publications to meet minimum requirements for easy incorporation of entries into the RBU (thus becoming what were called "contributions" to the "Bibliographia Universalis").

The classification was to provide subject access to the RBU and was developed as the repertory grew. For Otlet and LaFontaine the Decimal Classification and the three-by-five-inch card, with its promise of indefinite intercalation, constituted a modern technology that for the first time in history made possible the creation of an up-to-date universal subject catalogue of infinite extensibility and correctability. On the one hand, they interested a cadre of prominent European scholars and scientists in developing the tables of the classification; on the other, Otlet gradually elaborated those technical features that were to make it distinctive and the first "faceted" classification. These features were a series of common subdivisions and methods for extending or elaborating classification numbers using combinatorial symbols of a prescribed function and order. The sophistication of the system was to enable it to express what Otlet called "all the nuances of ideologico-bibliographical analysis" of documents. The first full edition of the classification with a detailed description of principles, rules, and practices appeared in 1905 under the title *Manuel du Répertoire Bibliographique Universel* ("Manual of the Repertoire of Universal Bibliography").

The process of expansion and revision in Belgium of the American edition of the classification was conducted in close consultation with Melvil Dewey and his assistants in the United States in Otlet's rather one-sided hope that concordance between the two versions might be maintained. As the years passed, however, divergences inevitably increased: the purposes of the two classifications and the philosophies guiding their elaboration were too different for much mutual understanding or for accommodation to be achieved.

The first decade of the 20th century brought many developments in the IIB's work. The Institute held conferences in 1897, 1900, 1908, and 1910. In 1905 a Universal Iconographic Repertory, a "documentary repertory of pictorial material," arranged by UDC, was begun, and was intended to provide an illustrative supplement to the RBU. In 1907 came an Encyclopedic Repertory of Dossiers, in which brochures, pamphlets, and periodical and newspaper articles were assembled; its purpose was to give the RBU a substantive component, to constitute a kind of encyclopedia for which the RBU could theoretically act as a table of contents, its essential function for knowledge as a whole in Otlet's view. Also in 1907 a Collective Library of Learned Associations was opened, bringing together the libraries of a variety of national and international associations and societies, the number of which grew rapidly with the years, their collections as a whole providing a kind of documentary backup for the RBU.

Paralleling Otlet and LaFontaine's widening concern with the international organization of knowledge was their increasing interest in the problems of international organizations themselves, for, as Otlet observed, "The proper organization of documentation considered in the widest sense of the term is today one of the foremost functions to have devolved on international associations." In 1906 the two friends founded a Central Office of International Associations and mounted first a survey of those having headquarters in Belgium and then, in collaboration with Cyril Van Overbergh and the Belgian Sociological Society, a survey of international organizations more generally. In 1909 they coedited with Alfred Fried the *Annuaire de la Vie Internationale;* this directory, begun by Fried in 1904, was enormously expanded and was prefaced by a long, comprehensive analysis by Otlet of the structure, government, and functions of international organizations. They published a subsequent edition of the directory independently of Fried in 1910–11. Above all, in 1910 they organized the first World Congress of International Associations, a highly successful affair at which the Union of International Associations (UIA) was founded and for which the Central Office henceforth acted as headquarters.

A number of the associations taking part in the Congress in 1910 supported Otlet's proposal that the left wing of the Palais du Cinquantenaire should become an international museum. The Belgian government approved, and Otlet conceived of the huge building as a preliminary location for a Palais Mondial, a vast center of internationalism. In this were to be conjoined the bibliographic services of the IIB, the international library, the international museum, secretarial and publishing services for the associations, and ultimately an international university. Here, Otlet hoped, they would be developed as an integral whole with the support of governments and associations. The organization, rationalization, and propaganda for the Palais Mondial became the major preoccupations of the rest of Otlet's life. A second, even larger World Congress of International Associations was held in 1913, and plans for a third in San Francisco in 1915 were also begun. The museum had grown vigorously in the interim, and some attempt to consolidate in the Palais Mondial the collections and services originating with the RBU in 1895 was made before the outbreak of World War I put an end to such efforts.

During these prewar years Otlet had grown in importance internationally and in Belgian official and intellectual circles. The course of his personal life, however, had not been smooth. He had two sons, Marcel and Jean, the latter killed in the war, but his marriage eventually failed, and in 1908 he and Fernande were divorced. In the early years of the new century, after a series of crises, the Otlet family fortune was almost wholly lost, and Otlet was to be plagued by legal and family problems associated with its dissolution. He married in 1912 a wealthy Dutchwoman, Cato Van Nederhasselt, whose income helped support him and his institutes for the rest of his life.

During the war he lived mostly in Paris and was an active member of the European movement for a League of Nations (Société des Nations). An integral part of the international order Otlet hoped to see established after the war was the creation by the League of an organization for intellectual relations with the Palais Mondial at its center. Otlet and LaFontaine had some influence on the League's eventual creation of an International Committee on Intellectual Cooperation.

After the war the primary task confronting the two friends was to resume their work in Brussels. They found that their institutes and collections had been unharmed by the occupation government and carefully maintained by a small, devoted staff. In 1920 they held the first of what were called Quinzaines Internationales, or International Fortnights (others were held in 1921, 1922, and 1924), during which meetings of the IIB, the UIA, and other international associations were held. Otlet now called for the creation of an International University and sought for it the patronage of the League of Nations. The League, however, impoverished, politically insecure, and only recently established in Geneva, was prepared to offer no more than sympathy and encouragement for the new enterprise.

Otlet and LaFontaine's various undertakings, now increasingly identified with Otlet, at first seemed successfully recovered after the war, and they had been completed by the foundation in 1920 of what was rather extravagantly named an International University. They fell fairly soon, however, on difficult times. Otlet could not interest the League in offering them any concrete support; its Committee on Intellectual Cooperation, created in 1922, soon went in directions that he regarded as inimical to the Palais Mondial and all it stood for. Efforts to collaborate with the Committee and with its executive arm, the International Institute for Intellectual Cooperation in Paris, failed and led to bitterness on Otlet's part and suspicion of him on that of League officials. The support of the Belgian government became increasingly uncertain until, in 1924, for a short period it actually resumed occupancy of the Palais Mondial for a trade fair.

It became clear that something needed to be done for the IIB lest it be lost and buried in the Palais Mondial. Assisted by LaFontaine, the Institute gradually began to assume an independent existence. New personalities began to move it in new directions, even changing its name in 1932 to the International Institute of Documentation. Otlet disliked and resisted all of the changes that this essentially new generation of supporters effected. He restored the Palais Mondial, which he now began to call the "Mundaneum," as best he could after the dislocations of 1924, and continued to seek support for it. His opposition to the trends in the Institute toward decentralization and federalism was silenced in 1934 when the Belgian government once more closed the Palais Mondial, this time effectively for good. The UIA's last meeting was held in 1924, though Otlet continued to issue publications in its name, and the Germans tried to use it for their purposes during the occupation of Brussels in World War II.

In all of these interwar years of struggle and

disappointment, Otlet continued to act as one of the Secretaries-General of the IIB along with LaFontaine and eventually Frits Donker Duyvis. While it was open, he regularly lectured at the Palais Mondial. He worked rather ineffectively and controversially on the revision of the UDC, the completed second edition of which finally appeared in 1932. He gave courses in librarianship and documentation in Brussels and wrote ceaselessly on the broad international questions that interested him. As grand old men of European documentation, he and LaFontaine were much feted at the World Congress of Universal Documentation held in Paris in 1937 jointly with the International Institute for Intellectual Cooperation. Here the IIB's name was again changed, to the International Federation for Documentation. Otlet, however, continued to speak of it as part of that vast intellectual edifice, the Mundaneum, to the elaboration of which so much of his life had been devoted, and in protest against the changes that had occurred in the IIB he cut it out of his will.

A lifetime of research and writing culminated in the publication in 1934 of *Traité de la Documentation* ("Treatise on Documentation") and in 1935 of *Monde: Essai d'Universalisme* ("The World: an Essay on Universalism"). These are large, slightly absurd encyclopedic works from which little insight seems possible because they contain no theories and offer no arguments, positions, or proof. Earlier writings, however, remain landmarks in the formal study of documentation and internationalism and have been too much neglected.

Otlet died in Brussels on December 10, 1944, a year after LaFontaine. After World War II both the FID and the UIA were resurrected. The FID still issues the UDC in a variety of translations and editions though allowing it no exclusively central place in its work; the UIA has taken up the *Yearbook of International Organizations* as a major task and has made of it an indispensable reference tool.

REFERENCES

Otlet's manuscript diary and the archives of the IIB are preserved in the Mundaneum in Brussels.

Samuel Bradford, "Fifty Years of Documentation," in his *Documentation* (1948).

F. Donker Duyvis, "International Federation for Documentation," *Journal of Documentary Reproduction* (1940).

W. Boyd Rayward, "The Case of Paul Otlet, Pioneer of Information Science, Internationalist, Visionary," *Journal of Librarianship and Information Science* (1991).

W. BOYD RAYWARD

P

Pakistan

The Islamic Republic of Pakistan is bounded by China on the northeast, India on the east, the Arabian Sea on the south, and Iran and Afghanistan on the west and northwest. It was established as a federal republic on August 14, 1947, as a result of partition of the Indian subcontinent. Its four provinces are Balochistan, North-West Frontier Province, Punjab, and Sind; the province of East Pakistan broke away to form Bangladesh in 1971. Population (1990 est.) 112,049,000; area 796,095 sq.km. The national language is Urdu, but English continues to be the official language.

History. Before partition the great libraries of Lahore, capital of Punjab, held a preeminent position on the subcontinent. In 1915 the Punjab University inaugurated the first library course at university level in the then British Empire, directed by an American, Asa Don Dickinson (1876–1960), a student of Melvil Dewey. But the disruption caused by partition crippled existing services to such an extent that the new nation had to start its library development virtually from scratch.

The founding of the Karachi Library Association (1949) and the Pakistan Bibliographical Working Group (1950), and the revival of Dickinson's school in Lahore in 1950, led to noticeable changes in attitudes to library service in the mid-1950s. Abdul Moid (1920–84), Librarian of the University of Karachi, started the first postgraduate diploma course in library science there in 1956 and helped to found the Pakistan Library Association in 1957. He served as its founding Secretary General.

National Library. The National Library of Pakistan occupies a new building, completed in the late 1980s, on Constitution Avenue in Islamabad, the capital. It has an auditorium, 15 research rooms, seats for 500 readers, and microfilming and computing services; its collection had reached 80,000 volumes by the late 1980s. It is also the temporary home of the federal government's Department of Libraries, which publishes the *Pakistan National Bibliography*.

Archival materials are maintained at the federal and provincial government levels. The National Archives of Pakistan also holds private collections and will house the Freedom Movement Archives, some 100,000 documents pertaining to the All-India Muslim League. The Ministry of Foreign Affairs maintains its archives independently.

Academic Libraries. University libraries are among the most advanced in the country. The 10 universities existing in 1981 grew to 23 in 1989; their more than 140 libraries held almost 2,900,000 volumes, more than a fifth of all books in Pakistani libraries. They grew at more than 60,000 volumes a year in the 1980s, keeping pace with the growth of the student population. The government's University Grants Commission funds libraries at all public universities. It organized local workshops for librarians from 1980 to 1987 in cooperation with the British Council, with follow-up courses in the United Kingdom.

Notable central university collections are at the University of Punjab Library (opened 1906; 769,000 volumes); the Mahmud Husain Library, Karachi (founded 1952; 255,000 volumes); Peshawar University (1951; 200,000 volumes); Qaid-e-Azam University (1965; 150,000 volumes); and Sind University (opened 1949; 137,800 volumes). The Lahore University of Management Sciences (8,000 volumes) and Shah Abdul Latif University, Khairpur (19,200 volumes) opened in 1985; the Hamdard University (80,000) volumes opened at Madinat al-Hikmat in 1989. The University of Punjab Library has a collection of almost 20,000 manuscripts in Arabic, Gurmukhi, Persian, Sanskrit, and Urdu. The special collections of the library are renowned equally for their rarity and richness.

The libraries of Pakistan's 680 colleges hold more than 3,640,000 volumes. They include some of the oldest libraries in the country: King Edward Medical

The new National Library of Pakistan, Islamabad.

Libraries in Pakistan (1990)

Type of library	Number of administrative units (main libraries)	Number of service points (branches, mobile stops, etc.)	Volumes in collections	Professional staff (with certificate, diploma, etc.)	Total staff
Academic	452	452	3,961,500	--	--
School	481 (includes 16 polytechnic institutes)	481	980,800	30	35
Other**	1				

**Mobile Library inaugurated in October 1990 in Lahore Division visits 7/8 places in the suburban areas of Lahore. The Library is fully equipped with television and audio system. The mobile library has been built at a cost of RS. 1.6 million (eq: $1.00 = over RS. 24.00).

Liaquat Memorial Library, Provincial Library-designate of Sindh, Pakistan.

College, Lahore (1860; 42,000 volumes); Government College, Lahore (1864; 91,000 volumes); Forman Christian College, Lahore (1866; 67,000 volumes); College of Veterinary Sciences, Lahore (1882; 30,000 volumes); D. J. Sindh Government Science College, Karachi (1887; 35,000 volumes); and Government Gordon College, Rawalpindi (1898; 55,000 volumes).

Public Libraries grew from just 21 in 1951 to more than 280 by 1989. The Punjab Public Library, Lahore (founded 1884), holds the country's third largest collection (215,000 volumes) with 1,200 manuscripts in Arabic, Gurmukhi, Persian, and Urdu. The Dayal Singh Trust Library, Lahore (founded 1908), holds 122,000 volumes. Others include the Liaquat Memorial Library, Karachi (1950; 120,000 volumes), and the Central Public Library, Bahawalpur (1948; 100,000 volumes, including a children's collection of almost 8,000 volumes). The Children's Academy, Quetta, has a children's library of 8,100 books; the Children's Complex in Lahore includes a library of 8,100 books, a gymnasium, and a center for handicapped children. The Qaid-e-Azam Reference and Research Library (1981; 68,000 volumes) opened to the public in Lahore's beautiful gardens, Bagh-e-Jinnah, in 1984. Among the oldest libraries in the country are the Karachi Metropolitan City Library (founded in 1851 as the Frere Hall Library; 43,300 volumes) and Sandeman Public Library, Quetta (1856; 16,700 volumes).

The Dr. Mahmud Husain Library, University of Karachi.

University of Karachi

School Libraries. With few exceptions school libraries, where they exist, remain at a rudimentary level.

Special Libraries. There are more than 330 special libraries in Pakistan, holding some 2,500,000 volumes. Mostly well-organized, they cover such fields as agriculture, banking, children, medicine, the military, science and technology, and the social sciences. Many are attached to universities or colleges. Some were established in the 1800s, including the Punjab Civil Secretariat Library, Lahore (founded in 1885; 60,000 volumes) and the Punjab Textbook Board Library, Lahore (1892; 32,000 volumes). The Hatim Alavi Memorial Braille Library in Karachi (1977) provides valuable library services for the blind. The Pakistan Scientific and Technological Information Center (PASTIC), in Islamabad, computerized its bibliographic services in the mid-1980s, publishing in 1987 the *Union Catalogue of Scientific Periodicals in the Libraries of Rawalpindi—Islamabad.*

Other Libraries. Rental or vending libraries, popularly known as *anna* libraries, continue to grow, largely because of the absence of public libraries at easily reachable locations in cities and, more importantly, because most of the libraries that do exist have few reading materials that appeal to popular tastes.

The Profession. The University of Karachi offered the first post-graduate Diploma course (now called Bachelor in Library and Information Science), in 1956, and the first M.A. in Library Science, in 1962. It offered the Ph.D. in Library Science from 1967. Six other library schools offer courses at the university level, four government-supported (Punjab, Sind, Peshawar, and Balochistan) and two private (Islamia University at Bahawalpur and the Allam Iqbal Open University at Islamabad).

The Pakistan Library Association (founded 1967) is the only association in the country still active in the profession, organizing conferences and publishing proceedings.

REFERENCES

Akhtar Hanif et al., editors, *University Librarianship in Pakistan* (1986).

Zahiruddin Khurshid, *Ten Years' Work in Librarianship in Pakistan, 1973–1982* (1983).

Technical Working Group (Anis Khurshid, Chairman), *Public Library Facilities in Pakistan: A Survey Report* (1985).

ANIS KHURSHID

Panama

Panama, a republic of Central America, is bounded by the Caribbean Sea on the north, the Pacific Ocean on the south, Colombia in South America on the east, and Costa Rica on the west. The Canal Zone bisects the Isthmus of Panama. Population (1990 est.) 2,418,000; area 77,082 sq.km. The official language is Spanish, but English is widely spoken.

History and National Library. A decree of January 31, 1942, authorized the establishment of the National Library of Panama. With initial holdings of 10,000 volumes originally at the Cólón Library, which had been donated by the Municipal Council of the Ministry of Education, it was founded on July 11,

1942. The Cólón Library of the Municipality of Panama, dating from October 12, 1892, was discontinued in 1941 by disposition of the District Council. The National Library serves as a repository of the nation's bibliographic production, including all the literature relating to the history of Panama. Its newspaper section contains the most complete collection of the dailies of the country. The collection totals 200,000 volumes.

Academic Libraries. Academic libraries are under the aegis of the country's two universities—the University of Panama, the national university, and the Santa María la Antigua University, a private institution. The University of Panama has two libraries—the Central Library and the Simón Bolívar Inter-American Library, the latter with sections on medicine and law. Three others are independent of the Central Library—the Library of Dentistry, another at the Institute of Criminology, and a third at the Central American Institute of Administration and Supervision of Education (ICASE).

Simón Bolívar Inter-American Library was established immediately after the founding of the University of Panama in October 1935. The Library was reorganized in 1941 under the direction of Gastón Lyton. In 1951 it was transferred to La Colina, now part of University City. In 1978 it was moved again, to new facilities on the campus. The new Library was given responsibility for the acquisition and organization of material from the Libraries of Medicine, Law, and five Regional University Centers at Cólón, Penome, Chitre, Santiago, and Chiriqui. The Library of ICASE was established May 11, 1970. Its collection consists of 5,000 volumes and 100 periodicals.

The Library of the University of Santa María la Antigua was established when the University was founded on April 27, 1965. The collection consists of 50,000 volumes, including imported magazines. It publishes an annual *Boletín Informativo* and bibliographies of existing material.

Public Municipal Libraries. Supported by the municipalities, these libraries are named for their sustaining organizations and not for their primary purpose or services. All offer mostly material for primary school students. There were 18, with a total of some 100,000 volumes, in 1980. The Mayor's Department of Education is in charge of the libraries of the Municipality of Panama.

School Libraries. These serve primary and middle-grade students in their own schools or groups of schools. In Panama City are libraries of the José Dolores Moscote Institute, founded in 1959 (more than 10,000 volumes), and the Octavio Méndez Pereira Library, part of the Isabel Herrera Obaldía Professional School in Paitilla (more than 10,000 books). A Unesco pilot project was organized with the cooperation and technical advice of the National Library and the Association of Librarians of Panama. It serves the following schools: Republic of Cuba, Republic of the Argentine, Republic of Peru, and Chorrillo Community.

Special Libraries. The Library of the Department of the Census and Statistics of the Comptroller General of the Republic was founded in 1914. It serves the public interested in the statistics of Panama as well as other countries and is equipped to reproduce documents. Its collection totals some 55,000 volumes.

University of Panama

The Simón Bolívar Inter-American Library, opened on the campus of the University of Panama in 1978.

The Medical Library of the Social Security General Hospital, established March 31, 1969, contains medical information available to medical personnel working in the social security hospitals, in the city, and in the interior. Its collection consists of 600 books.

The Bio-Medical Library of the Commemorative Gorgas Laboratory is in the City of Panama. The Institute maintains an office in Washington, D.C. Its collection embraces more than 10,000 volumes and some 500 periodical titles. The contents consists of books and reviews covering preventive tropical medicine and certain facets of biology that result from investigations conducted in the laboratory. It serves the requirements of its scientific personnel and collaborators and the scientific community of the area, in particular of the medical doctors of Saint Thomas and Children's Hospitals. It receives photocopies of articles from the U.S. National Library of Medicine and bibliographies prepared under the MEDLARS and GRACE systems.

Gorgas Hospital Medical Library, founded in 1918, concentrates on clinical medicine, with 30,000 books and periodicals.

The Smithsonian Tropical Research Institute, established in 1925, is near the Canal. It has a fairly complete collection of 22,000 volumes. It serves all persons in Panama and the Canal Zone. It is much used by patrons from the University of Panama.

The Amador Washington Library of the International Communication Agency (ICA) was created in 1952. In 1964 a fire destroyed its physical plant and its collection, and in that year it was recreated with the same staff and new books under its present name. It has a collection of 10,000 volumes and 17,000 microforms. It offers all readers service concerning books published in the U.S.

The Profession. The Panamanian Association of Librarians was established on March 6, 1951. A law approved by the National Assembly in 1956 regulated the profession of librarian and established the National Service throughout the country. Librarians created a guild. The Association participated in national and international activities contributing to the organization and improvement of the libraries in Panama. The Association publishes an annual bulletin. It has also published a bibliography of literature by Panamanian women. It addresses issues concerning the recognition of librarians' professional stature within the sanction of law; the law of 1956 was considered to have failed to achieve its goals.

VICTOR U. MENDIETA ORTIZ

British Museum
Sir Anthony Panizzi

Panizzi, Sir Anthony
(1797–1879)

Antonio Panizzi (knighted as Sir Anthony in 1869) is one of the greatest figures in library history. Posthumously, Panizzi's reputation has grown ever more lustrous. To Arundell Esdaile he was the most creative force in the history of the British Museum; to Albert Predeek he was "the greatest lawgiver the library world has known"; to Edward Miller, his biographer, he was "a librarian of librarians, perhaps the greatest we have yet seen."

He was born September 16, 1797, at Brescello, a small town in the Duchy of Modena in northern Italy. After studying at the University of Parma, he practiced law for a while at Brescello. Unfortunately, the Duchy was then under Austrian domination and virtually a police state; when it became known that Panizzi was a member of a secret society working against the government, he was obliged to flee the country. For a short time he lived in Switzerland, but in 1823, like a number of his compatriots, he found refuge in the United Kingdom.

For several years Panizzi eked out a living as a teacher of Italian at Liverpool. In 1828 he was appointed first Professor of Italian Language and Literature at the new University of London, but since students were few and the remuneration small, the appointment turned out to be a barren honor. In 1831 he joined the staff of the British Museum (BM).

Although the British Museum had been founded by an act of Parliament in 1753, in 1831 it was still a random miscellany of museum specimens, books, and manuscripts, in the care of scholarly but unenterprising officials who enjoyed a peaceful but pensionless service. The Museum lacked a vital sense of purpose and its income was slender. The Department of Printed Books, which Panizzi joined as an extra assistant, was among the least regarded of the departments, even though it embraced several former private collections of considerable importance. Among them were the Old Royal Library and the King's Library. The latter, the magnificent private library of George III, was given to the BM in 1823, forcing the Trustees to provide a new building, and work had just begun on it when Panizzi joined the staff.

Although his knowledge of libraries was then slight, by dint of travel and correspondence he had become well informed by 1836, when he was called upon to give evidence to the Parliamentary Select Committee on the condition and management of the Museum.

In 1837 Panizzi was appointed Keeper of the Department of Printed Books. In this capacity he not only did most of the things for which he is best remembered but had to endure the strongest attacks from his enemies, both in the Museum and outside it. In 1856 Panizzi was appointed Principal Librarian (i.e., Chief Officer) of the BM, but because of ill health he had to resign in 1866. He died in London, April 8, 1879.

Although Panizzi was not lacking in friends, he had to suffer virulent criticism and hatred throughout most of his career at the BM, partly because he was regarded as a foreign upstart and partly because he refused to budge an inch when he believed he was right—as he usually was.

Some librarians are remembered for the work they did for their own libraries; others are remembered for their contribution to librarianship at large. Panizzi belongs squarely to the former group. By the end of the 20th century, the great circular Reading Room of the British Museum, which to many people was Panizzi's finest achievement, probably will be vacated when the British Library, of which the former BM Library is now part, takes over its elaborate new headquarters at Somers Town, near London's Saint Pancras Station. No longer, then, will one be able to say, in a literal sense, *Si monumentum requiris circumspice* ("If you seek a monument, look around"). But this was never an altogether satisfactory verdict on Panizzi's achievement, which may be more profitably considered under five headings: bookstock, building, staff, service, and cataloguing.

Bookstock. The vast increase in the bookstock of the BM Library since the 1850s has been due mainly to the action taken by Panizzi, as Keeper of the Department of Printed Books, to enforce the law of legal deposit, under which the Museum was entitled to receive one copy of every new British publication. In recent years it has several times been suggested that deposit at the British Library should be selective, to prevent the acquisition of "rubbish." Panizzi, however, was unwilling to speculate on the probable needs of scholars of the future; he insisted on receiving everything. On the other hand, he recognized the disadvantage to scholars of having a national library with a stock based almost entirely on deposited publications and random donations. By securing regular and generous book funds and using them largely to acquire European and American publications, he gave the stock of the BM Library proper dimensions.

Building. Panizzi's reputation as a library planner rests securely on his successful advocacy (the conception was not entirely his own) of a great circular reading room with extensive surrounding stacks, all fabricated of cast iron, at that time little used in building construction. The addition of these desirable amenities meant the sacrifice of the Museum's inner quadrangle, but the result was accommodation for readers and books without parallel in any other library in the world.

Staff. Panizzi's particular solution to the staffing problems of the BM was to secure for its personnel civil service conditions of employment, including security of tenure. The benefits to the Library were clear toward the end of the century, when there were several outstanding men in its service who were quite willing to make their work at the BM a lifelong career.

Cataloguing. A large part of the history of the BM Library during Panizzi's service there is concerned with his troubles with the catalogue. When Panizzi joined the BM staff, the main catalogue was urgently in need of revision; the task of preparing a new one was still in hand when Panizzi became Keeper seven years later. The problems that this catalogue generated bothered Panizzi almost continuously for the next 13 years. The main difficulty was that Panizzi and the Trustees could not agree on what kind of catalogue should be provided, but close behind it was the fact that the Trustees interfered with the day-to-day work of the cataloguers.

When he was an assistant librarian, Panizzi had

made up his mind as to what was desirable and feasible: an alphabetical name catalogue in manuscript form, compiled throughout by the application of a new, comprehensive code of cataloguing rules. In the end Panizzi achieved this kind of catalogue, but only after long, bitter, and widely publicized wrangling.

The first step was to convince the Trustees that an alphabetical catalogue was preferable to a classed one; the second was to get them to approve a new catalogue code, the famous *91 Catalogue Rules,* which Panizzi drew up with the help of his colleagues. The most difficult step was the third. Panizzi realized that printing the alphabetical catalogue would be inadvisable until the entire stock had been catalogued. This proposition the Trustees would not accept, even after Panizzi had demonstrated the folly of premature printing by actually having one specimen volume printed. Panizzi won in the end, but under the worst possible conditions. The Royal Commission, which was appointed in 1847 ostensibly to "examine the constitution and government of the British Museum," was, in effect, an ill-advised attempt to impeach Panizzi for incompetence and insubordination. Unable to prove his inefficiency on any other count, Panizzi's accusers turned to his long-standing quarrel with the Trustees over the catalogue. In their final report (1850) the Commissioners accepted all Panizzi's arguments and agreed that his refusal to print the catalogue was justified. The eventual benefits of this fortunate end to a disagreeable episode were the compilation of an incomparable reading room catalogue and following it, at the end of the century, the publication of the world-famous BM *Catalogue of Printed Books.*

Service. The standard of service built up by Panizzi was, for its day, very high. One aspect of it, by itself, indicated the kind of man Panizzi was—his refusal to favor some readers more than others. His statement to the Select Committee in 1836 on this matter is his most familiar pronouncement:

> I want a poor student to have the same means of indulging his learned curiosity, of following his rational pursuits, of consulting the same authorities, of fathoming the most intricate enquiry, as the richest man in the kingdom, as far as books go, and I contend that Government is bound to give him the most liberal and unlimited assistance in this respect.

Rather less familiar is Panizzi's observation to the Royal Commission, in 1849: "I never felt the skin of any reader and they are all treated alike."

One of Panizzi's archenemies outside the BM was the author Thomas Carlyle. Carlyle played a major role in founding the London Library in 1841, in part because Panizzi would not grant him special privileges as a reader at the BM. This quarrel therefore had the beneficial effect of enriching the metropolis with one of the finest learned subscription libraries in the world.

Evaluation. Panizzi could not have done all that he did alone. Although he was a hard taskmaster (one member of his staff described him as "a thorough-going tyrant"), he inspired in most of his lieutenants loyalty and willing cooperation. Prominent among those who helped him in all his endeavors was Thomas Watts, his right-hand man; outstanding among those who hindered him was Sir Frederic Madden, the brilliant but querulous Keeper of the Department of Manuscripts. The story of Panizzi's ceaseless arguments with Madden and the Museum's Trustees would make a volume in itself. It is a part of Panizzi's life that cannot be ignored, because the progress he made in spite of it is all the more remarkable. Furthermore, the existence of this powerful opposition led Panizzi to explain and defend his actions as he might never have done otherwise. Although he published a fair amount on language and literature, he published hardly anything on librarianship.

Most people now generally accept that the British national library should be the apex of the British library system, which is precisely what the new British Library is. But in Panizzi's day there was no national public library network; there were not even many academic libraries. Edward Edwards, who worked with Panizzi for a while, visualized a nationwide public library service and helped to prepare the way for it. Panizzi was not a protagonist in the public library movement, but this was not to his discredit; the BM's affairs absorbed him utterly.

Panizzi's name is more familiar than the names of most librarians of the past; that may be due, in some measure, to his friendship with many of the leading political figures of his day and the role he played in the struggle for the unification of Italy. Nevertheless, it is undeniable that his work for the British Museum Library was of seminal importance. He took over several valuable but static collections and left behind him a large, coherent, working library, so organized and so sustained that its continuance as a great national library was scarcely in doubt.

REFERENCES

Miller, Edward, *Prince of Librarians: The Life and Times of Antonio Panizzi of the British Museum* (1967).

Arundell, Esdaile. *The British Museum Library: A Short History and Survey* (1946).

Because Panizzi himself published little on the BM Library and his work for it, the evidence he gave to the Select Committee and the Royal Commission, which was published verbatim in their respective reports, is particularly useful. Complete facsimiles of both reports were published by the Irish University Press in its British Parliamentary Papers series, *Report from the Select Committee on the Condition, Management and Affairs of the British Museum, 1836* (1968) and *Report of the Commissioners on the Constitution and Government of the British Museum, 1850* (1969).

See also the excellent symposium on Panizzi in *British Library Journal* (1979).

JAMES G. OLLÉ

Papua New Guinea

A parliamentary state in the western South Pacific to the north of Australia, Papua New Guinea includes the eastern section of the island of New Guinea and nearby islands. Independent since 1978, it was formerly the Australian Territory of Papua and New Guinea, formed in 1949 from the Territory of Papua and the Trust Territory of New Guinea. Population (1990 est.) 3,699,000; area 462,840 sq.km. There are more than 700 local languages, but the official language is English.

History. Books have a limited history in this country of rich oral traditions. Printing began with the advent of Christian missions when William Lawes, a missionary, produced a printed sheet in 1875. A Government Printing Office was established in 1888.

Photo by Jim Jiki/University of Papua New Guinea

Michael Somare Library, University of Papua New Guinea, the country's largest library.

In 1936 Australia's National Library began providing public library service.

National Library and Archives. The National Library Service (NLS) was established in 1975 in the capital, Port Moresby. Under the Copyright Act of 1978 and the Statutory Deposit Act of 1979, it constitutes one of the country's three depository libraries. In 1978 the NLS moved into the new National Library building, an independence gift from Australia, where some 45,000 volumes are housed.

The NLS incorporates the National Film Library, which had 4,000 films and 600 videos in 1985, the School Libraries Service, and the three public libraries in the National Capital District. It provides centralized processing and advisory services to public, school, and government libraries. The NLS houses a notable New Guinea collection and produces the *Papua New Guinea National Bibliography*. Development of the NLS has been hindered by its limited budget. The Library Council of Papua New Guinea promotes cooperation and exchange of views among the nation's librarians.

The National Archives, originally established in 1962, is a branch of the NLS. It moved into a new building next to the National Library in Waigani in 1988.

Academic Libraries. Major libraries are those at the University of Papua New Guinea (UPNG) and the Papua New Guinea University of Technology (Unitech). At UPNG the main Michael Somare Library (Waigani Campus), established in 1965, had 350,000 volumes in 1986, the Medical Library (Taurama Campus) 44,500, and the Goroka Teachers' College 48,000 volumes, up from a combined total of 331,000 in 1980. Stock at the Unitech Library rose from about 56,600 volumes in 1983 to 75,700 in 1985. Both major libraries have developed substantial New Guinea collections and both are depository libraries. Both are heavily involved in computerization of services. Audiovisual service is a notable activity at Unitech's Matheson Library.

Public Libraries. The National Library of Australia established a Public Library Service in 1936. Devolution of national government powers in 1978 transferred responsibility for library service to the 19 provincial governments. The libraries in Rabaul, Kavieng, and the National Capital District are not in dire straits, but most other libraries are: their resources are so limited that they can afford only part-time staff for their small, outdated collections. All 22 public libraries are in urban areas, which have only 15 percent of the population. Even after considerable discussion about providing rural service and a few experiments with community libraries, there has been no overall plan for library service to rural areas since the Village Library plan was tried unsuccessfully between 1949 and 1962. The national literacy rate in English is about 32 percent.

School Libraries. In 1986 the 100 libraries in high schools (provincial, national, and international) stocked 456,000 volumes, up from the 210,000 volumes in 56 libraries in 1977. Growth of these libraries has been encouraged by the national School Libraries Service and a World Bank project that supplied funds for books. But development of school libraries is hampered by a lack of training opportunities, particularly for high-school teachers. Each school is responsible for its own funding. The 2,000 community (primary) schools have few books.

Special Libraries. There were 71 special libraries in 1985, up from 10 in 1973. Some 30 serve government departments, principally the Parliament, Department of Justice, and Office of Forests. The Library of the Prime Minister's Department has an extensive collection of rare historical documents, and the Research Library of the Department of Education

Libraries in Papua New Guinea (1986)

Type of library	Number of administrative units (main libraries)	Number of service points (branches, mobile stops, etc.)	Volumes in collections	Annual expenditures (kina)	Total staff
National	1	43++	85,000	60,000*	79
Academic	50	--	845,000	1,366,010	174
Public	25**	25	183,211	60,620*	48
School	100+		456,000	243,000*	82
Special	70	94	183,000	175,000*	108

*Book fund only
**These are in addition at least five small community libraries.
+High schools only; one also serves as a public library. Small libraries exist in some community schools.
++Includes the National Archives (with 1 branch) and 2 public libraries; a third public library is within the National Library building.

provides a postal loan service to teachers throughout the country. The Papua New Guinea Institute of Public Administration, established in 1961, has special collections in government, New Guineana, and library science.

The Profession. The Papua New Guinea Library Association (PNGLA) replaced the Papua New Guinea Branch of the Library Association of Australia in 1974. Its activities include an annual conference and production of a quarterly journal, *Tok Tok Bilong Haus Buk,* among other publications. Education for librarianship began with courses at the Administrative College in 1968. Responsibility for these courses moved to the Department of Library and Information Studies at UPNG in 1988.

REFERENCES

Kwami Avafia, "Library Development in Papua New Guinea," *Libri* (1975).

Leigh Baker, *Development of University Libraries in Papua New Guinea,* Master of Philosophy thesis, PNGUT (1978), includes survey of libraries and librarianship.

Harold Holdsworth, *The Development of Library Services in Papua New Guinea* (1976).

Miles M. Jackson, "Library and Information Services in the Pacific Islands," *International Library Review* (1981), includes a section on Papua New Guinea.

JOHN EVANS

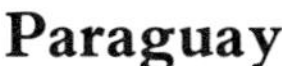

Paraguay

The Republic of Paraguay lies in the center of South America, bounded by Bolivia on the north, Brazil on the east, and Argentina on the south and west. Population (1990 est.) 4,277,000; area 406,752 sq.km. Its official languages are Spanish and Guaraní.

History. The Guaraní and other indigenous inhabitants of the area were nomads. For generations their method of communication was oral, not written, and the folklore of the Guaraní is rich with stories, myths, and legends. Spaniards under Juan de Salazar y Espinosa reached the area and founded Asunción in 1537. The Spaniards ruled Paraguay as a colony until it gained independence in 1811. For much of that time, they restricted the flow of books into the area.

The Junta Superior Gubernativa, which ruled from 1811 to 1813, founded the first public library in Paraguay. Books were imported from Buenos Aires, Montevideo, and several cities in Brazil. The dictator Gaspar Rodríguez de Francia, who ruled from 1817 to 1840, again restricted the importation of books. During that period a xylographic press was set up to print books from engraved wooden blocks. It was best suited to producing A-B-Cs and primers because of the short sentences involved. After his death, the Public Library was reopened on October 16, 1840, a day celebrated annually as the "Dia del Bibliotecario Paraguayo." Printing from movable type began during the presidency of Carlos Antonio López, who ruled from 1841 to 1862; he allowed books to be imported again and made education free and compulsory. But his son, who succeeded him, involved the country in war with Brazil, Argentina, and Uruguay. The War of the Triple Alliance (1864–70) devastated Paraguay. As the people tried to rebuild their country, a group of young men founded a public library, sometimes called the Biblioteca Municipal and sometimes the Biblioteca Nacional. It received government support from 1874.

Information Office, PNGUT

Matheson Library, Papua New Guinea University of Technology. Local artists created the mural and sculpture.

The National Library. The Biblioteca Nacional in Asunción (BN) was probably an outgrowth of the Municipal Library. Exactly when it was founded is subject to conjecture, but the legislature passed a bill establishing and supporting it in 1897. In 1904 it acquired the Biblioteca Americana of Juan Silvano Godoy, about 15,000 volumes that form the most complete collection of Americana in the Rio de la Plata region. Two years later it acquired the Biblioteca Paraguaya of Enrique Solano López. Its periodicals room holds some of the most important newspapers from the 18th and 19th centuries to the present. The BN now has about 40,000 books. It also has its first professional librarian, Carlos Fernández Caballero, appointed in 1989.

The BN faces many problems, including the poor condition of its building, the need for better relations between professionals and nonprofessionals, and the need for coordinated acquisition of materials. The government adopted a deposit law in 1985, requiring all authors and printers to provide five copies of every work published in Paraguay, but the law did not include any provisions for enforcement.

Academic Libraries. University libraries in Paraguay can be classified into two administrative systems: those that belong to the Universidad Nacional de Asunción (UNA; National University of Asunción) and those that belong to the Universidad Católica Nuestra Señora de la Asunción (UC; Catholic University).

National Library of Paraguay, Asunción.

Library of the Faculty of Agronomic Engineering, National University of Asunción.

Most libraries in the UNA are well developed, thanks to a major development project and a loan from the Interamerican Development Bank. Several schools moved into larger buildings at the university campus in San Lorenzo, just outside Asunción, in the late 1980s, including the faculties of Agronomic Engineering and of Economics, Administration, and Accounting. The Library of the Faculty of Veterinary Sciences moved into a modern building in 1983. The Central Library moved into a large building on the campus in 1989. It is engaged in introducing automation and building a network of university libraries.

The Pope Paul VI Central Library of the UC continues to improve its collections and services, including microfilming magazines and newspapers from 1870 on. The faculties of Accounting, Computing, Engineering, and Technology moved to a new university campus just outside Asunción beginning in 1985, each with its own library.

Public Libraries are not well developed in Paraguay. Few have lending services. Only the Biblioteca Roosevelt del Centro Cultural Paraguayo-Americano (sponsored by the United States), the Biblioteca Municipal in San Lorenzo (20 kilometers from Asunción), and the Librería Filadelfia de la Colonia Menonita del Chaco Paraguayo (the Mennonite settlement) lend books. About half the public libraries are directed by professional librarians; in 1990 the city of Asunción appointed a graduate of UNA as director of its municipal library.

School Libraries. As in all developing countries, school libraries have grown slowly. A study by the UNA School of Library Science, with the help of Nanako Takase, a volunteer member of the Servicio de Voluntarios Japoneses para la Cooperación con el Extranjero, showed that few schools have libraries and fewer still have libraries with more than a thousand volumes. Some school libraries in the city have professional librarians; in other parts of the country, most staff are not adequately trained. Some have taken short courses offered for school librarians by nonuniversity institutions.

Special Libraries. Beginning in the 1960s, special libraries attracted increasing support and gained importance. About 85 percent of the country's special libraries were founded after 1960. The major subjects covered are agriculture, economics, education, employment, hydroelectricity, livestock, population, and sociology. Most special libraries are in Asunción.

In 1984, with the help of the Comisión Económica para la América Latina y el Caribe/Centro Latinoamericano de Documentación Económica y Social (CEPAL/CLADES), 35 public and private institutions in Paraguay set up the Red Nacional de Información para la Planificación (RED NAPLAN; National Network for Planning Information). It is coordinated by the Secretaría Técnica de Planificación, immediately under the President of the Republic.

The Biblioteca Nacional de Agricultura (BINA; National Agricultural Library) and the Library of the Faculty of Veterinary Sciences at UNA have library cooperation programs and serve rural areas through small library branches.

Paraguayan librarians have little experience in using computers for information retrieval and automating routine library tasks. The government's Centro de Promoción de las Exportaciones began automating its information system in 1983 and began extending the work to its outlying units in 1988. Other institutions experimenting with new technologies include the Secretaría Técnica de Planificación, the National Atomic Energy Commission, the Faculty of Agronomic Engineering at UNA, and the Paraguayan Center for Sociological Studies.

The Profession. Library education in Paraguay began in the 1960s. The Centro Cultural Juan de Salazar offers short courses every year and the Escuela

Libraries in Paraguay (1990)

Type of library	Number of administrative units (main libraries)	Number of service points (branches, mobile stops, etc.)	Volumes in collections	Annual expenditures (guarani)	Population served	Professional staff (with certificate, diploma, etc.)	Total staff
National	1	--	40,000	--	3,000	6	18
Academic	26	4	178,540	211,604,800	274,702	44	125
Public	20	--	101,944	78,220,000	71,729	11	49
School[a]	86	1	324,825	250,398,750	101,451	32	168
Special	46	5	156,612	331,548,600	50,492	44	135

[a]1988 data

Sources: Survey by the author, bibliographical investigation (see Bibliografía consultada)

de Bibliotecología (EB; School of Librarianship) of UNA offers a full training program. The EB was created in 1971 and until 1988 reported directly to the head of UNA. It was incorporated into the Polytechnic Faculty and, in 1989, moved to the UNA campus in San Lorenzo. It offers two levels of training: a four-year course leading to the degree of licenciado en bibliotecología (licenciate in librarianship) and a two-year course for técnico en bibliotecología (library technician). It also offers some permanent special programs and some intensive extracurricular courses for persons without professional library education. It works with other agencies on developing library networks and promoting reading among children and youth. Since 1983 it has operated bookmobiles to provide books for young people during the winter months.

Two library associations are active in Paraguay: the Asociación de Bibliotecarios de Paraguay (ABIPAR; Association of Librarians of Paraguay), founded in 1961, and the Asociación de Bibliotecarios Graduados de Paraguay (ABIGRAP; Association of Graduate Librarians of Paraguay), founded in 1974 as the Asociación de Bibliotecarios de la Universidad de Paraguay and renamed in 1986. Both associations offer some professional activities, but neither had a publishing program in the early 1990s.

REFERENCES

Petrona Francisca Díaz de Santacruz, *Situación de las Bibliotecas de los Institutos de Formación Docente del Paraguay* (Asunción, 1988).

Yoshiko Moriya de Freundorfer, *Formación de los Bibliotecarios Profesionales y el Mercado Ocupacional* (Asunción, 1990).

Nanako Takase, *Bibliotecas Públicas y Escolares del Paraguay, 1988* (Asunción, 1990).

Alfredo Viola, *La Biblioteca Nacional* (Asunción, 1987)

YOSHIKO MORIYA DE FREUNDORFER;
translated by JOSEFINA TRELLES-SOLOMON
and GLADYS MARKOFF-SOTOMAYOR

Partaningrat, Winarti
(1922–1978)

PDIN-LIPI
Winarti Partaningrat

Winarti Partaningrat, Indonesian librarian and government official, was one of the prominent figures who worked for the establishment and early development of special librarianship and documentation services in Indonesia.

Born September 21, 1922, at Sragen, Central Java, she was educated at schools in Indonesia, including a medical school. From 1946 to 1951, she worked for the English Section of the Foreign Broadcasting of Radio Republik Indonesia in Jakarta. In New York City she worked at the Voice of America of the U.S. Information Service and United Nations Radio at UN Headquarters from 1951 to 1958 while studying at Columbia University. She obtained a B.S. in Latin American Studies in 1957 and a Master's degree in Library Service in 1958, then worked for a year in the Science and Technology Department at the Queensborough Public Library, Jamaica, N.Y.

She returned to Indonesia in late 1959. In early 1960 she was appointed Head of the Bureau of Documentation of the Madjelis Ilmu Pengetahuan Indonesia (MIPI; Council of Sciences of Indonesia) in Jakarta. Later, in 1965, she became the first Director of the Pusat Dokumentasi Ilmiah Nasional–Lembaga Ilmu Pengetahuan Indonesia (PDIN-LIPI; Indonesian National Scientific Documentation Center–Indonesian Institute of Sciences). That Center, officially established on June 1, 1965, was formerly the Bureau of Documentation of MIPI.

She was an active member of the Himpunan Pustakawan Chusus Indonesia (HPCI; Indonesian Special Library Association), which was merged in 1973 with the Asosiasi Perpustakaan, Arsip dan Dokumentasi Indonesia (APADI; Association of Libraries, Archives and Documentation of Indonesia) to form a new association, the Ikatan Pustakawan Indonesia (IPI; Indonesian Library Association).

Partaningrat was a leader in organizing a workshop on a National Network System of Library, Documentation and Information Services in Indonesia, held in 1971. That workshop laid basic foundations for the early development of library services of the country covering the following fields: scientific and technical information, coordinated by the PDIN-LIPI; biology and agriculture, coordinated by the PUSTAKA, the Central Library for Biology and Agriculture of the Ministry of Agriculture; health, medicine, and pharmacy, coordinated by the Ministry of Health; and social sciences and humanities, coordinated by the National Library of Indonesia.

She actively participated at several international meetings. Among them were the Unesco Seminar on Scientific Documentation in South and Southeast Asia, held in New Delhi, March 1961, where she submitted a working paper on "Scientific Information Facilities in Indonesia;" the 10th Pacific Science Congress, in Tokyo, 1966, where she presented "Characteristics and History of Indonesian Scientific Periodicals;" and the Conference on Southeast Asian Research Materials, at Puncak, Indonesia, 1969. She also wrote several articles in the fields of library and documentation services. She also edited *Masterlist of Southeast Asian Microforms* (Singapore University Press, 1978), a joint project of SARBICA (Southeast Asian Regional Branch of the International Council on Archives) and CONSAL (Conference of Southeast Asian Librarians), started in the mid-1970s.

Partaningrat retired from work as a government official in 1974. She died on May 8, 1978, in Jakarta.

HERNANDONO

Paulin, Lorna V.
(1914–)

The Library Association
Lorna V. Paulin

Lorna Paulin, English public librarian, was elected president of the Library Association and awarded the Order of the British Empire, only two indications of significant contributions to librarianship by an outstanding librarian. She was the first woman to hold the office of President of the LA.

Born in Bexley, Kent, in 1914, she spent her childhood in what was then the country but is now almost engulfed in London's outer suburbs. Even at the early age of 11 she had made up her mind as to her profession, the height of which was to be the Chief Librarian of the neighboring borough.

After leaving the Grammar School for girls at

Dedication of the Lorna Paulin Seminar Room in the Headquarters of the Library Association, 1990.

Dartford, she took a B.A. degree in English in 1934 and an M.A. in English in 1936 at University College, London. The M.A. degree was combined with part-time study at the School of Librarianship, resulting initially in a Diploma in Librarianship and then, in 1938, Fellowship of the Library Association.

She held various posts in Kent County Library from 1936 to 1948, through responsibility for student services to Branch Librarian and Deputy County Librarian. In Nottinghamshire, as County Librarian from 1948 to 1952, she saw rapid postwar library improvements in schools and in mobile services to rural areas. But she significantly influenced the librarianship of her time as County Librarian of Hertfordshire from 1952 to 1976. With enormous energy and clarity of purpose, she developed all aspects of the county's public library service, including work with schools and developing other library services for children; setting up mobile library services for rural and suburban areas; instituting professionally run hospital library services, medical and general; a large program of providing new branch library holdings; technical library and information services in cooperation with the libraries of the colleges in the county; cooperative schemes with libraries of all types in the county; and instituting a training scheme for staff.

Carlos Victor Penna

Paulin worked assiduously for the library profession throughout her career. She was a member of the Council of the LA from 1948 to 1978 and holder of successive offices in the County Libraries Section, culminating in becoming Honorary Secretary and subsequently Chairman. In the LA, because of her strong commitment to the education of librarians, she was for many years Chairman of the Education Committee. Later she was Chairman of the Executive Committee and Chairman of Council, becoming President in 1966. Unquestionably she will be most remembered for sterling work on professional qualifications. The report on that work, known as the Paulin Report, was implemented by a Board of which she was Chairman. It introduced far-reaching changes into the system for British professional library qualifications.

Her consistent attention to education for librarianship led her to be involved in setting up the School of Librarianship at Queen's University, Belfast. She then became an external examiner for this and other schools.

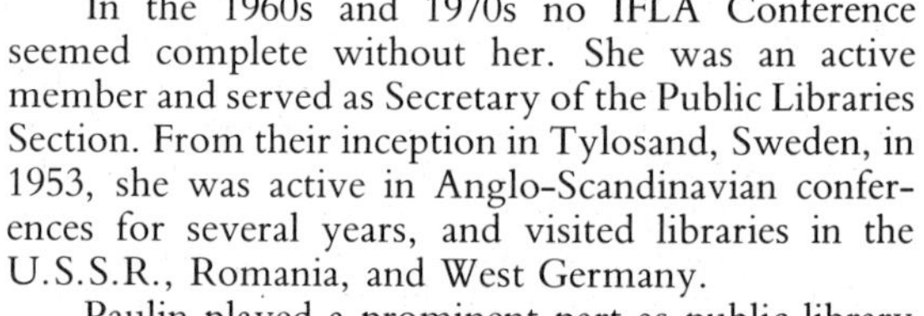

In the 1960s and 1970s no IFLA Conference seemed complete without her. She was an active member and served as Secretary of the Public Libraries Section. From their inception in Tylosand, Sweden, in 1953, she was active in Anglo-Scandinavian conferences for several years, and visited libraries in the U.S.S.R., Romania, and West Germany.

Paulin played a prominent part as public library legislation loomed in developing standards of service. She was a member of the Ministry of Education Working Party on Standards for Public Library Services in England and Wales, set up in 1961. She appended her own reservation to the published report in 1962 because she did not consider the recommended standards to be high enough in some respects. She was one of the first members of the Library Advisory Council (England), formed in 1966, and for six years served on it and its working parties and subcommittees.

In later years Paulin chaired the Board of Trustees of the Library Association Benevolent Fund. She was awarded the O.B.E. in 1970 for service to libraries, and the highest distinction of the LA, Honorary Fellowship, was bestowed in 1980. Ten years later the LA inaugurated the Lorna Paulin Seminar Room in its Headquarters to honor her contribution to library education policies and practices.

Paulin was a leader of librarians with authority, integrity, and vision, charm, and humanity, with a delightful sense of humor never far away.

R. G. SURRIDGE

Penna, Carlos Victor
(1911–)

Carlos Victor Penna, Argentinian library educator and administrator, wrote extensively, worked for library advancement in Latin America as a Unesco specialist, and contributed concepts of library and information service planning that led to the Unesco NATIS program.

He was born in Bahia Blanca, Buenos Aires Province, Argentina, October 1, 1911. He attended school in Cayupán and Maza, small towns in the provinces of Buenos Aires and Pampa, and in 1927 he began studies at the Escuela de Mecánica de la Armada (Fleet School of Mechanics), which he left in 1931, unwilling to adapt to the military regimen required there.

In 1933 he began work at the Library of the Estado Mayor de la Marina (Department of the Navy) as a page in charge of stack maintenance. When he was promoted to the position of Cataloguer, he applied modern cataloguing techniques for the first time in Argentina, having translated and experimented with some of the Vatican "Rules for the Cataloguing of Book Materials" and the Universal Decimal System. He later organized the centralized cataloguing of the books of more than 100 libraries in Marina—the first cooperative venture of this nature practiced in Latin America.

Penna also pioneered in the introduction of microphotographic techniques applied to the organization of the Central Catalogue of the University of Buenos Aires, which he directed in 1943 after returning from library studies at Columbia University in New York City in 1941.

Penna organized the Library School of the Social Museum of Argentina and introduced modern information management methods into the curriculum. The School had a great impact not only in Argentina but on a continental scale, and the text materials written by the faculty have been utilized by library schools in all parts of Latin America.

In 1945 Penna began traveling in a way that later enabled him to participate fully in information work on an international level. First he visited La Paz, Bolivia, together with Augusto Raúl Cortázar, to reorganize the Mariscal Santa Cruz Library. In 1947 he participated in the Assembly of American Librarians. In 1950 he traveled to Cuba to teach courses at the Library School of the Friends Society of Cuba and also made several visits to Uruguay to assist A. Gropp in the development of the Library School that the North American had organized in Montevideo. In 1951 Penna became a Unesco specialist, first assigned to the Western Hemisphere Regional Center in Havana, Cuba. From Havana, as a specialist in the area of library development, Penna worked hard for the betterment of libraries throughout Latin America. In 1964 he was transferred to the main offices of Unesco, from which he retired in 1971 as Director of the Division for the Development of Documentation, Libraries, and Archives.

On leaving Unesco, Penna made his home in Palma de Mallorca, Spain, serving as an expert of the Iberoamerican Education Office. In 1974 he moved again, this time to the United States, where he taught subjects such as library and information services planning at Pratt Institute and acted in an advisory capacity with the Coordinating Commission of the National System of Library and Information Services of Venezuela.

Penna published more than 120 journal articles and professional papers. Among his many books and projects are *Catalogación y Clasificación de Libros* (1st ed., 1949; 2nd ed., 1964); direction of the translation of *Sears List of Subject Headings for Small Libraries* (1949); *Manual de Bibliotecología* ("Manual of Librarianship"), in collaboration with other authors (1968); direction of the Kapelusz Editorial Series, together with E. J. Sabor, *Bibliotecología: Planeamiento de Servicios Bibliotecarios* ("Librarianship: The Planning of Library Services"; 1968), also published in English, French, Japanese, Arabic, and Turkish; *Planeamiento de Servicios Bibliotecarios y de Documentación* ("Planning Library and Documentation Services"; 2nd ed., by Sewell and Liebaers, 1970), also published in English and French; and *Servicios de Bibliotecas e Información: Nueva Concepción Latinoamericana* ("Library and Information Services: A New Latin American Concept"; 1972).

REFERENCE

Horacio Becco, *La Obra Bibliotecologica de Carlos Victor Penna* (1981), covers his works and contributions to universal librarianship.

EMMA LINARES

Peru

Peru, a republic in western South America, is bordered by Ecuador and Colombia on the north, Brazil and Bolivia on the east, Chile on the south, and the Pacific Ocean on the west. Population (1990 est.) 22,232,000; area 1,285,216 sq.km. The official languages are Spanish and Quechua.

History. The Biblioteca Nacional, the National Library of Peru, was founded in 1821 by José de San Martín. Although it was partially destroyed by fire in 1943, it was reopened in 1947, and copies of the first publications printed in Peru and the Americas are still among its most prized possessions. Public libraries in Peru were generally not developed as lending libraries, as is true in the majority of Latin American countries. In many cases public library services have been merged with the functions of the National Library, and only comparatively recently have these two types of service begun to be separate in practice. Some significant collections of manuscripts and valuable historical materials are found in convents and monasteries.

National Library. The National Library contains 706,000 volumes, 263,600 manuscripts, 11,800 maps, and almost two million issues of periodical publications and newspapers. It is especially strong in Peruvian history, literature, and law.

The National Library was once called the Biblioteca Publica, or public library. However, although open to the general public, it is not permitted by law to allow borrowing privileges. It publishes the *Annuario Bibliográfico Peruano* ("Annual Bibliography of Peru"), as well as the *Boletín de la Biblioteca Nacional* ("National Library Bulletin"), the *Gaceta Bibliotecaria del Perú* ("Peruvian Librarian's Gazette"), and other publications.

The Archivo General de la Nación, founded in 1861, and the Biblioteca del Instituto Nacional both complement the National Library's activities, the latter having participated closely in the identification and classification of Peruvian publications.

Academic Libraries. Academic libraries in

Libraries in Peru (1987)

Type of library	Number of administrative units (main libraries)	Number of service points (branches, mobile stops, etc.)	Volumes in collections	Population served	Professional staff (with certificate, diploma, etc.)	Total staff
National	1	8	3,205,989	121,416	38	312
Academic	6	8	860,000	--	--	--
Public	1,314	--	6,500,000	--	--	--
School	1,621	--	--	--	--	--
Special	130	--	--	--	--	--

Photo Archive of *El Comercio*, Lima

National Library of Peru in Lima.

Peru exist in almost every institution of higher learning, these numbering at least 200. They are generally closed collections offering access only through card catalogues and limiting borrowing privileges to registered students. Required text materials are usually available in multiple copies and constitute the most heavily used portions of these collections.

The Biblioteca Central of the Universidad Nacional Mayor de San Marcos (San Marcos National Higher University) was founded in Lima during the 16th century and possesses more than 450,000 volumes. It originally owned a large portion of the colonial collection presently housed in the National Library.

The Biblioteca Central of the Pontificia Universidad Nacional Católica del Perú (National Peruvian Pontifical Catholic University), although founded as recently as 1917, possesses an ample collection of more than 250,000 volumes, many of a recent, technical nature.

The Biblioteca de la Universidad Nacional de San Augustin in Arequipa is an example of the decentralization trend taking place in many Latin American academic libraries. The central library coordinates 12 specialized libraries that possess some 100,000 volumes above and beyond the basic collection of monographs, pamphlets, and periodical publications.

In many cases academic libraries function more as study halls than as information centers. Libraries are slowly becoming equipped to handle new demands of modern library research on their collections, services, and personnel.

Public Libraries. Public libraries in Peru are generally referred to as *bibliotecas publicas municipales* (municipal public libraries). There were about 445 such libraries in Peru in 1982, with total holdings of some 4,100,000 volumes. The majority possess small collections of donated materials and are directed by staff members with little or no formal training in modern library methods.

Several exceptions to this broad generalization exist, principally in the major urban centers. The Lima Municipal Library, founded in 1935, has a collection of about 16,000 volumes, relatively small because of the role played by the National Library in Lima.

The Arequipa Public Municipal Library was, on the other hand, founded earlier than the Lima Public and contains more than 28,000 volumes. The Casa de la Cultura (Cultural Institute) of Peru is housed in that library, giving an indication of the humanistic nature of the collection.

The largest public library in Peru is in Callao. The Biblioteca Publica Municipal Piloto (Callao Municipal Pilot Public Library) was founded as recently as 1936 and reorganized in 1957. It offers a broad collection of some 48,000 volumes to the general public.

Public libraries in Peru receive technical assistance from the Oficina Nacional de Bibliotecas Populares Municipales, located in the National Library.

School Libraries. The majority of school libraries in Peru are found in private schools and in large public primary and secondary schools, mainly in the major cities. Most are directed by untrained personnel, in many cases teachers with full class schedules. These factors generally lead to less than adequate collections and services and even affect access to the libraries, given usually irregular and insufficient working hours.

Audiovisual aids are generally underutilized or unavailable and many times are not considered the responsibility of the school libraries. The Dewey Decimal System is generally used for classification, but a number of school libraries are uncatalogued and unclassified because they lack trained personnel.

Special Libraries. The *Directorio de Bibliotecas Especializadas del Peru* ("Directory of Peruvian Special Libraries") was published by ABIISE (Agrupación de Bibliotecas para la Integración de la Información socioeconomica; Consortia of Libraries for the Integration of Socioeconomic Information) in 1972, serving as an update of the Peruvian Library Association's 1969 *Guia de Bibliotecas Especializadas*. The Directory lists 100 special libraries out of a total of 130 identified during the survey period. The libraries included are of three types, one-third each being in the social sciences, the applied and basic sciences, and the humanities, or geared to the broad concerns of a particular institution. About a third of the total, drawn from all three categories, were directly related to government offices, such as ministries.

Special libraries in Peru include INTINTEC (Instituto de Investigación Tecnológica Industrial y de Normas Tecnicas; Industrial Technology and Standards Research Institute), a fine hard-technology information and documentation center, while ESAP (Escuela Superior de Administración Publica; School of Public Administration) and ESAN (Escuela de Administración de Negocios para Graduados; Graduate School of Business Management) have specialized in the area of soft technology. Socioeconomic information sources are by far the most developed and coordinated in Peru, thanks to the efforts of ABIISE. A number of the monasteries with collections of historical interest are open to researchers and to the public.

The Profession. The two major professional associations are the APB (Asociación Peruana de Bibliotecarios; Peruvian Library Association) and ABIISE. Both have played a vital role in the development of libraries and librarianship in Peru.

A trade group, the Asociación de Empleados de la Biblioteca Nacional, was established for the employees of the National Library. The Cámara Peruana del Libro (Peruvian Book Council) worked closely with the Library Association in a number of areas and made important donations to various libraries.

MARTHA GORMAN

Petherick, Edward Augustus

(1847–1917)

Edward Augustus Petherick, bookseller, publisher, bibliographer, and book collector, provided a collection that formed the basis of what is now the National Library of Australia's large and important body of materials relating to Australia, New Zealand, and the Pacific Islands.

Petherick was born March 6, 1847, at Burnham, Somerset, England, the eldest of nine surviving children of Peter John Petherick, stationer-librarian, and his wife, Ann. The family sailed from Bristol to Melbourne, Australia, landing in March 1853 with, among other things, 400 books to sell. Edward attended Alfred Brunton's Public School in Melbourne part-time while working for his father. He soon began work in the bookselling and stationery firm of George Robertson, who was impressed by his precocious knowledge of books and enthusiastic application to his duties.

After 10 years with the firm, Petherick was chosen in 1870 to reorganize its London office, which he quickly transformed and continued to manage until Robertson retired in 1887. That year Petherick set up his own business in London. His Colonial Booksellers' Agency at 33 Paternoster Row had a capital of $800 and was backed by a number of publishers and assisted by Australian banks supporting distributing branches in Sydney, Melbourne, and Adelaide. At this time he began publishing, issuing quarterly the *Colonial Book Circular and Bibliographical Record,* later changing its title to *The Torch,* and in 1889 launched his *Collection of Favourite and Approved Authors.*

As early as 1865 Petherick had collected titles for a catalogue or bibliography of Australiana but put it aside when he went to England in 1870. In 1878 he made a fresh start with it, commenting, "The business of the London department being well organised, I took up the work again; but finding I could do little without the books, I began to collect them—as they came within my grasp, and the savings of a limited salary." In 1882 he won public recognition as a bibliographer by publishing the *Catalogue of the York Gate Geographical and Colonial Library.* Its success prompted William Silver, the owner, to enlarge his collection with help from Petherick, whom he commissioned to prepare a second edition, subtitled *An Index to the Literature of Geography, Maritime and Inland Discovery, Commerce and Colonisation;* it was published by John Murray in 1886. When Silver died in 1905, Petherick arranged the sale of the York Gate Library to the South Australian Branch of the Royal Geographical Society of Australasia. With tireless industry, inexhaustible energy, and bachelor freedom, he became involved with many learned societies and corporate activities—from the Royal Geographical, Hakluyt, and Linnean Societies to the Royal Colonial Institute and the Library Association—becoming a life member of all. He wrote numerous reviews, letters, and articles, many of which remain unpublished.

National Library of Australia
Edward Augustus Petherick

Petherick's publishing venture continued until 1894, when the Australian bank crisis and his own lack of financial reserves forced him into bankruptcy with debts of about $50,000. His book stocks were sold to E. W. Cole, a Melbourne bookseller, and his *Collection of Favourite and Approved Authors* was taken over by the London publishers George Bell & Sons. On March 1, 1892, in Dorset, Petherick had married a widow, Mary Agatha Annear Skeats, and mainly with her help met his financial difficulties and succeeded in saving his own collection of Australiana. Broken by business failure, he became a cataloguer with the antiquarian booksellers Francis Edwards & Co. and between 1895 and 1908 produced a series of outstanding catalogues of Australasian material. As means permitted, he continued collecting and devoted great effort to completing his *Bibliography of Australia and Polynesia;* he prepared a printed prospectus of it in 1898 but was unable to arrange publication.

As his collection grew, Petherick became anxious that it should pass to the Australian people and, even before the federation of the Australian states in 1901, he approached two premiers with an offer to present his collection to "Federated Australia," but no action resulted. Nor did anything result when he wrote to Prime Minister Barton in March 1901, his approach at that time being premature. In 1908, however, he and his wife took the collection to Australia and soon negotiated with the Federal Parliament. Its Library Committee on May 27, 1909, recommended acquisition of the collection "in consideration of an annuity of $500 a year, Mr. Petherick to render during the currency of the annuity such services in the Commonwealth Library as the Committee may from time to time prescribe." The Collection consisted of some 10,000 volumes, 232 boxes of pamphlets, and some manuscripts, maps, and pictures. It was accompanied by the sheets of the still unpublished *Bibliography* of about 100,000 entries.

Petherick tended his collection from 1909 to 1917, distressed by the casual recognition that Australians made of his overseas achievements and the small encouragement they gave him to develop his collection further, compensated only by a belated appointment as C.M.G. in 1916. Predeceased by his wife on May 10, 1915, Petherick died in Melbourne on September 17, 1917. He is commemorated today in the Petherick Reading Room of the National Library of Australia.

REFERENCE

The papers and correspondence of E. A. Petherick are held in the National Library of Australia, Canberra.

C. A. BURMESTER

Philippines

The Philippines, on the western rim of the Pacific Ocean, is an island republic of 7,107 islands. Population (1990 est.) 61,480,000; area about 300,000 sq.km. English and Filipino are the official languages, but there are more than 120 Philippine languages.

History. Philippine script can be found in specimens of writings used by the Tagbanwa of Palawan and the Mangyans of Mindoro, in early Spanish works published in the country, and in pre-Spanish artifacts such as clay pots and burial jars dating from the 14th and 15th centuries. The Filipino alphabet and script have a Hindu-Buddhist affinity but there is no extant pre-Hispanic written body of literature. Epics, poems, and songs were transmitted by oral tradition. Ancient Filipinos wrote on bamboo and other plant materials, using knives to scratch the characters.

Printing was introduced in Manila in 1593. Father Francisco de San José was the first to use a printing press in the provinces, in 1610, with Tomás Pinpin as his first Filipino printer.

The earliest libraries were the convent libraries of the Spanish missionaries, built from 1565 when the Augustinian friars began to arrive in the islands. By 1593 the Augustinian Francisco de Ortega reported a total of 72 convents and monasteries; probably all carried on the European tradition of having books and libraries in their religious houses. The Dominicans had the greatest number of books, with some 10,000 volumes besides their archives. Academic libraries began with the founding of the University of Santo Tomás in 1611. Acquisition of books for its library commenced in 1610 with the donation of volumes made by the Archbishop of Manila, Miguel de Benavides, and Diego de Soria, Bishop of Nueva Segovia. Among other libraries established were the Colegio de San Felipe de Austria, Colegio de San José, and Colegio de San Ignacio.

Nonreligious libraries were established toward the end of the 18th century. The first was the Real Sociedad Económica de Amigo del País library in 1781, the Biblioteca Militar in 1846 for the use of the Spanish soldiers, and much later the Museo Biblioteca de Filipinas in 1887 and the small library of the School of Arts and Trades in 1889. The Museo Biblioteca was in essence a national library with a scanty collection of about a thousand volumes and with only 74 Philippine titles. Don Pedro A. Paterno, its first Director, also published the first library periodical, *Boletín del Museo Biblioteca de Filipinas,* in 1895. Paterno, a lawyer, poet, and statesman, is also the author of the law creating the Philippine Library which consolidated all government libraries.

The first library established during the American period was public in nature: a subscription library whose objective was "to create a source of instruction and profitable entertainment for the residents of Manila." The book collection of the American Circulating Library was donated to the Philippine government to become the nucleus of a public library system and a national library through a law approved in 1901. By 1903 the book collection had grown to 21,750 volumes; Nelly Young Egbert served as Librarian and James Alexander Robertson as Director. The first public school library was established in 1907 by Lois Stewart Osborn, an American teacher assigned to the Pampanga High School.

Libraries today vary widely in size, services, resources, and staff. Most libraries continue traditional library methods, but others are rapidly adopting new technology. In the late 1970s computerized information services began to appear, notably at the University of the Philippines at Los Baños (UPLB), the National Science Development Board (NSDB), and the National Library. Still, the rapid development of libraries was hindered by budget cuts, freezing of promotions and appointments, retrenchments, and other measures to combat inflation. In Central Philippines ALBASA (Academic Libraries Book Acquisition Systems Association Inc.) is a cooperative acquisitions project among 56 libraries. In metropolitan Manila the Inter-Institutional Consortium of Southern Manila Area composed of six government and private educa-

Libraries in Philippines (1987)

Type of library	Number of administrative units (main libraries)	Number of service points (branches, mobile stops, etc.)	Volumes in collections	Population served
National[a]	1	1	33,000	216,663
Public[a]	1	517	5,756,000	1,595,194
Special[b]	224	--	35,118,000	--
Non-specialized[c]	1	1	--	232

[a]1989 data
[b]1985 data
[c]1986 data

Source: Unesco, *Statistical Yearbook,* 1991.

tional institutions embarked on a shared cataloguing project.

National Library and Archives. The National Library of the Philippines serves both as a repository of the nation's recorded cultural heritage and as a public library through its 493 branch libraries in various cities and towns in the country. It provides leadership among the nation's libraries; serves as a permanent depository of all publications issued in the country; maintains an up-to-date *Philippine National Bibliography,* a *National Union Catalogue,* and other bibliographical services; acquires and makes available other types of reference materials; serves as a coordinating center for cooperative activities; and provides library and information services to government agencies.

The *Philippine National Bibliography,* begun in 1974, is a current listing of books published in the Philippines by Filipino authors and of books relating to the Philippines even if published abroad. It lists books, first issues of periodicals, theses and dissertations, government publications, music scores, and conference proceedings. It is published quarterly and cumulated annually.

The Decree on Intellectual Property (the copyright law of the Philippines) and two other presidential decrees are the bases of the national bibliography. The Decree on Intellectual Property (presidential decree 49) requires the deposit of at least two copies of each work published if the copyright claimant wants the work registered with the copyright office of the National Library. Presidential decree 812, known as the Decree on Legal and Cultural Deposit, designates the National Library as the prime depository library for all publications issued in the country, together with four other state institutions. The law requires each publisher to deposit at least two copies of each work at the National Library, as well as a copy each to the University of the Philippines Library in Diliman, Quezon City; the Cultural Center of the Philippines in Manila; the University of the Philippines–Cebu in Cebu City, Central Philippines; and Mindanao State University in Marawi City in Mindanao. Presidential decree 285, aimed at reducing costs and making reading materials available to the broader masses for research and study, requires the deposit of two copies of each textbook or reference book of foreign imprint intended by a publisher to be reprinted and distributed in the Philippines.

Among notable possessions in the National Library are books and manuscripts in the Rizaliana collection, by and about the national hero, José Rizal y Alonso; and original records of the Filipino-American war of 1898–1903 in Spanish and Tagalog, turned over by the United States government to the Philippine government in 1955. The President Manuel L. Quezon papers comprise an estimated 180,000 items, and the President Carlos P. Garcia papers consist of 162,000 items.

The National Archives was a division of the National Library until it was transferred to the Bureau of Records Management in 1958 as the Division of Archives. In 1982 it was renamed Records Management and Archives Office. The archival records consist of Spanish and American documents: naturalization papers, citizenship records, civil service records, notarial records, cattle brands, public works contracts, court records, and civil registers. Altogether there are about 13,321,000 items.

Theodore F. Welch

The Asian Development Bank Library in Manila, an extensive book and pamphlet collection on finance and economics.

Academic Libraries. The Ministry of Education, Culture, and Sports requires each of the 942 institutions of higher learning to have library facilities; 75 are state-supported colleges and universities. There is, however, wide disparity in both human and financial resources as well as in facilities and book collections.

The University of the Philippines Library System, established in 1908, is the largest of the state-supported academic institutions, with a total book collection of 1,141,000 volumes, more than 19,000 serial titles, and almost 40,000 pieces of nonprint materials as of 1984. The UPLB Library is the national center for AGRIS (Agricultural Information System); the UP Law Center is the largest and most comprehensive in law library in Southeast Asia.

The University of Santo Tomás (UST) Library is the oldest university library. It has one of the largest book collections, consisting of 280,000 books, 30,000 serials, and almost 9,000 nonprint materials. The Ateneo de Manila University Library, founded in 1859 by the Jesuits, also has excellent book and microform collections.

Other notable library buildings and collections are those of the De La Salle University in Manila, the St. Louis University in Baguio, the Silliman University in Dumaguete City, the University of the East in Manila and the Mindanao State University. The University of San Carlos possesses outstanding collections of Filipiniana, Cebuano materials, and the humanities. Generally, private college and university libraries are supported mainly from matriculation and library fees, gifts, and endowments from foreign agencies. The Fund for Assistance to Private Education (FAPE) also gives training grants to libraries in the private educational institutions and provides books to libraries through its Filipiniana Book Enhancement Program.

Libraries of state colleges and universities are minimal because a large portion of their budgets goes to personnel for wages and is spent on other maintenance services. Donations are also a source of funding for the libraries.

Public Libraries. In the Philippines, public libraries rely almost entirely on the financial support of their respective local governments, whether city, municipal, or provincial. There were more than 500 public libraries in the mid-1980s, of which 493 were under the supervision and control of the National Library through its Extension Division. Some 97 public libraries are located in metropolitan Manila; the rest are scattered in the various cities and towns of the country. However, only 35 of the 72 provinces and 31 of the 61 cities have public libraries. Bookmobiles are available in seven provinces as part of the countryside development program. Yet library services to urban and rural communities are still inadequate.

School Libraries and Media Centers. School libraries and media centers both at the secondary and elementary level generally remain neglected despite the requirement that each school provide adequate library services to its students. Most are one-room affairs, others only a few shelves of discarded American books and textbooks. The national government launched in 1984 a book enhancement program wherein 77 high school libraries, chosen on the basis of population density and central location from each province and the four cities of the national capital region, were to receive 10,000 books over a four-year period from 1985 to 1988. The program was provided an annual budget of 30,000,000 pesos.

The private school libraries have some of the better resources. They include those of St. Scholastica's College in Malate, Manila; Xavier School; Ateneo de Manila; De La Salle; and the International School. They have up-to-date and excellent collections.

Special Libraries. This type of library grew from 51 special libraries in 1961 to almost 500 by the first half of the 1980s.

The International Center for Living and Aquatic Resources Management (ICLARM) was established in 1978. Its resources as of 1984 covered more than 4,000 books and almost 500 periodical titles and 2,000 nonprint materials dealing with fisheries and aquaculture. Philippine Aquatic Science and Fisheries Information System (PASFIS) is a networking activity of ICLARM. ICLARM has a link with the Dialog information system.

The Southeast Asian Fisheries Development Center (SEAFDEC) in Tigbauan, Iloilo City, has an excellent collection in fisheries. Its resources consist of 6,500 books, 400 periodical and serial titles, and 8,300 nonprint materials. The Aquaculture Information System became operational in 1982.

The International Rice Research Institute (IRRI) Library and Documentation Center in Los Baños, Laguna, was established in 1960 with total resources of almost 62,500 books and monographs, more than 2,600 periodical and serial titles, and nearly 5,700 nonprint materials in the field of rice research.

The National Scientific Clearinghouse and Documentation Service Division of the National Science and Technology Authority (NSTA) was established in 1906. Its resources consist of 26,000 books, 7,000 pamphlets, 5,000 periodical and serial titles, and 6,700 nonprint materials. The agency provides computerized information services to the science community through National Information System for Science and Technology (NISST), Current Awareness Service (CAS), and Selective Dissemination of Information (SDI).

The Philippine Council for Agriculture and Resources Research (PCARR) Library in Los Baños, Laguna, was established in 1972. Its resources consist of 4,400 books, 1,100 periodical and serial titles, and 3,000 nonprint materials in the field of agriculture and allied disciplines.

The Energy Research and Development Center (ERDC) Library and Information Center of the Philippine National Oil Company was established in 1981. It has total holdings of 1,500 books.

The Dansalan Research Center in Marawi City has an extensive collection of Islamic literature, and the Cebuano Studies Center at the University of San Carlos in Cebu City has a strong collection of Bisayan literature, history, languages, and anthropology.

Other special libraries have outstanding collections in banking, management, business, and industry, including those of the Asian Development Bank (ADB), Asian Institute of Management (AIM), and San Miguel Corporation (SMC) Human Resources Library Division.

The Profession. As early as 1914, a library science course was offered at the University of the Philippines with American library pioneers such as Mary Polk and James Alexander Robertson as teachers. The U.P. Institute of Library Science offers library science course at the Master's level. Other library schools offering graduate library science courses are the University of Santo Tomás, University of the East, Philippine Women's University (all in Manila), and University of San Carlos in Cebu City.

The Philippine Library Association, founded on October 22, 1923, by Trinidad H. Pardo de Tavera, former Director of the National Library, is the umbrella organization of some 24 sectoral and local library associations. It publishes the quarterly *Bulletin of the Philippine Library Association* and the *PLA Newsletter*. The Association of Special Libraries in the Philippines publishes the quarterly ASLP Bulletin; the Philippine Association of Academic and Research Libraries, its quarterly *PAARL Newsletter*; and the Agricultural Libraries Association of the Philippines, its *ALAP News*, irregularly published.

REFERENCES

Concordia Sanchez, *Philippine School Libraries: Their Organization and Management* (1972).

Filomena Tann, *Philippine Librarianship: The Past and the Future* (1982).

Rosa M. Vallejo, *Philippine Librarianship: A Historical Perspective* (1981).

SERAFIN QUIASON

Platina, Bartolomeo

(1421–1481)

Italian librarian and Humanist Bartolomeo Platina was Vatican Librarian under Pope Sixtus IV.

Born into the Sacchi family in 1421 at Piadena (thus "Platina") near Mantua, he was, in his earlier years, a tutor for the children of Marquis Ludovico Gonzaga at Mantua. From 1457 to 1461 Platina studied

Greek at Florence, and the following year he became Secretary to Cardinal Francesco Gonzaga in Rome.

Two years later Platina was one of the Humanist scholars employed by the papacy to draft social letters and documents in an elegant calligraphic hand, on a staff that generally consisted of 70 "abbreviators." When Pope Paul (1464–71), dissatisfied with their work, abolished the office, the 70 picketed the papal residence for 20 days in formal protest. As organizer and leader, Platina further offended the Pope by insisting upon arbitration and drew a three-month prison sentence when he threatened to appeal before kings and princes for a public hearing of the abbreviators' problems.

Shortly after his release, Platina and other dismissed scholars formed a study group to read Latin writers, as opposed to the Greek. The Pope, however, favored the study of early Christian writers, or at least such classics as did not breathe an air of immorality and paganism, and claimed that the writings of Juvenal, Ovid, Plautus, and Terence could only corrupt children. For his contrary opinions Platina and other scholars were arrested, and he was sentenced to a year in prison.

The Vatican library at Rome was in many ways the most important of Renaissance libraries. Fifteenth-century popes were not only spiritual leaders of the world but secular rulers of territorial states. Other princes in Italy encouraged and developed manuscript and book collections; some popes also felt it a civic duty to become library patrons.

In 1474 Platina published the first part of his *Lives of the Popes,* a readable book that achieved wide circulation, and the following year Pope Sixtus IV appointed him Vatican Librarian. Pope Nicholas V (d. 1453) had initiated the idea of a library, but Platina's administrative genius made the plan feasible, causing the Pope to create an annual library budget to support book purchases, regular salaries for the librarian, two assistants, and three copyists, and the operation of a book bindery.

The Pope aspired to create in Rome the foremost library anywhere. He authorized Platina to plan a library building to hold writings collected by earlier popes and to accommodate future acquisitions, giving him a free hand in construction and in the selection of artists and craftsmen. The library, occupying the ground floor of the papal palace, consisted of four halls for books and readers: one for Latin writings; another for Greek works; a third, the *Secreta,* for valuable manuscripts; and a fourth, the *Pontificia,* for papal archives and registers. Renowned painters, such as the Ghirlandaio brothers and A. Romano, decorated walls and ceilings with paintings, while the talents of Melozzo da Forli resulted in the fresco "Pope Sixtus IV Appoints Platina as Vatican Librarian." Special efforts were made to accommodate patrons, including portable heating devices for their convenience during chilly Italian winters. The originality of posted regulations in Latin requesting silence and order prompted one patron in 1513 to make a copy: "When in the Library let no one speak vociferously with another nor be troublesome; and when he is going from place to place, let him not climb the steps and scrape them with his feet. Let him close the books and replace them in their proper places. Everyone may read whatever he wishes wherever he wishes. Whosoever acts otherwise will be ejected in dishonor and will henceforth be denied entrance to this place."

Three *scriptores* (copyists) were hired to reproduce Latin, Greek, and Hebrew manuscripts, and Platina also had regular funds to dispatch book agents outside Italy in what a contemporary writer, Vespasiano, viewed as a new epoch in the manuscript book trade. Platina's success in developing the holdings may be measured by noting the library's growth. When he assumed his duties in 1475, his inventory listed 2,527 volumes. The materials were Latin or Greek, with none in the Italian vernacular. Though there was increasing emphasis on theology and philosophy, one-fourth of the holdings were ancient classics. Six years later, in a report prepared eight days before Platina's death, the number had increased to 3,499, an annual increase of 162 volumes. The library's only rival was the 3,000-volume collection of Matthias Corvinus of Hungary.

REFERENCE

J. W. Clark, "On the Vatican Library of Sixtus IV," *Cambridge Antiquarian Society Proceedings and Communications* (1899).

REDMOND A. BURKE

ALA

Mary Wright Plummer

Plummer, Mary Wright
(1856–1916)

Mary Wright Plummer, U.S. library educator and leader, attempted throughout her professional life to communicate her enthusiasm for broadly based liberal education and cultural experience and for practical professional training.

She was born March 8, 1856, in Richmond, Indiana, to Jonathan W. and Hannah Ballard Plummer, who valued their Quaker heritage and passed it on to their children. Attending the Friends Academy in Richmond until she was 17, she moved about 1873 with her family to Chicago, where her father was employed as a wholesale druggist. Except for attending Wellesley College, 1881–82, she spent her early adulthood with her family—teaching, writing poetry, and generally educating herself, including mastering several modern languages.

In January 1887 she enrolled in the first class of

Melvil Dewey's new library school at Columbia College, where she first made her mark. At the September 1887 conference of the American Library Association she reported on the school to curious members in a talk that was later published in *Library Journal* as "The Columbia College School of Library Economy from a Student's Standpoint." On completing the program at Columbia she worked as cataloguer at the St. Louis Public Library for two years.

In the fall of 1890 she went to Pratt Institute Free Library in Brooklyn as both a librarian and an instructor for the training class. Following a year's tour of European libraries she became head of both operations in 1895—a demanding joint position she filled until 1904, when at her request she concentrated on directing the developing library school. In 1911 she became the first Principal of the new library school of the New York Public Library, where she served until her death in 1916.

Active in state and local library organizations, she was enthusiastic about the early planning that led to the establishment of the Association of American Library Schools in 1915. She had previously chaired the ALA's Committee on Library Training (1903–10). Elected the Association's second woman President for 1915–16, she did not live much beyond the end of her term; she became ill, and her presidential address of June 26, 1916, had to be read to the Conference at Asbury Park, New Jersey, in her absence. She died September 21, 1916, in Dixon, Illinois.

At both Pratt and the New York Public Library Plummer attempted to help the schools respond to the contemporary and unique needs of students and institutions, rather than to the uniform patterns of the emerging university schools. She insisted on flexible admission requirements and a greater emphasis on practice work. All the while, she hoped that the esteem in which scholarly librarianship was held in Europe could be approached in her homeland. Concerned about the status of women in librarianship, she was nevertheless patient in temperament and preferred to work for change slowly by encouraging individual achievements in the conventional manner.

During her years at Pratt, she published a book of poetry and several children's titles. Her *Hints to Small Libraries,* originally published in 1894, appeared in its fourth edition in 1911. She contributed to *Library Journal, Pratt Institute Monthly,* and the *ALA Bulletin,* as well as the "Training for Librarianship" chapter to the ALA *Manual of Library Economy* (1913). Her 1909 talk before the New York State Library Association appeared in the *Sewanee Review* (1910) as "The Seven Joys of Reading" and has been reprinted several times. Her 1916 presidential address to the ALA, "The Public Library and the Pursuit of Truth," appeared in *Library Journal* and in the conference proceedings.

REFERENCE

Robert A. Karlowich and Nasser Sharify, "Plummer, Mary Wright," *Dictionary of American Library Biography* (1978).

DONALD G. DAVIS, JR.

Poland

Poland, a republic in eastern Europe, borders the Baltic Sea and Lithuania on the north, Belarus and Ukraine on the east, the Czech Republic and Slovakia on the south, and Germany on the west. Population (1990 est.) 38,180,000; area 312,677 sq.km. The official language is Polish.

History. A Polish state has existed since the mid-tenth century, except for the years 1795–1918, when its territory was partitioned and absorbed by neighboring Russia, Prussia, and Austria. The earliest books in the country were manuscript volumes imported for missionary work by Catholic clergy after the country's conversion to Christianity in 966. The first Polish scriptoria, as well as cathedral, chapter, and monastic libraries, appeared at the beginning of the 11th century at Gniezno, Poznan, and Cracow. The library of the Jagiellonian University in Cracow was founded along with the university itself in 1364. The first printing house was established in Cracow in 1473, and the first printed book in Polish came out in 1513 (most earlier printed works had been in Latin). The first city libraries were founded in Poznan in 1523 and in Gdansk (Danzig) in 1596.

In the 16th century, printing houses appeared in Wroclaw (Breslau), Gdansk, and Malbork (Marienburg). Printing spread throughout the country in conjunction with the Reformation and, later, the Counter-Reformation. Also in the 16th century, private princely and professional libraries began springing up, first in Cracow and then in other centers. A flowering of libraries, like that of printing, coincided with the Renaissance, Reformation, and Counter-Reformation. In the 17th century, however, wars brought a halt to the development of the country and its libraries. The second half of the 18th century witnessed a revival, particularly after the creation of the *Komisja Edukacji Narodowej* (Commission of National Education), the first ministry of education in Europe. In 1780 the parliament decreed the obligatory deposit of copies of newly published works in the Zaiuski Library in Warsaw and the library of the Wilno Academy, and in 1783 the first legal statutes regulating the professional status of librarians were promulgated.

Following the partition of Poland and the disappearance of the Polish state, great aristocratic and foundation libraries played an important role. Their founders brought together collections of Polish writing and monuments of the nation's past. After independence in 1918, a host of academic, school, special, and public libraries were created or reopened. The academic libraries of this period achieved a particularly high level of professionalism. Both World Wars, the second in particular, inflicted enormous losses on Polish libraries. The 1946 Library Decree (superseded by the 1968 Library Statute) created the legal basis for the establishment of thousands of new school, public, special, trade-union, academy, and pedagogical libraries, as well as centers for training librarians and a state system of library administration.

National Library. The idea of a Polish national library was espoused in the 18th century by the brothers Zaiuski, who used their personal collections as the basis for a public library bringing together the whole body of Polish writing. Opened in Warsaw in 1747, it was presented as a gift to the nation. With holdings of approximately 400,000 volumes, it was one of the largest collections in Europe. After the loss of independence, its collections were confiscated and transported to St. Petersburg.

After the restoration of Polish independence, a new *Biblioteka Narodowa* (National Library) was created in Warsaw in 1928. Its resources included part of the repatriated holdings of the Zaiuski Library as well as other historic collections. During World War II the National Library was bombed and its collections were put to the torch by Nazi troops. Among the irreplaceable losses were the treasures of the Rapperswil and Batignolles collections, and indeed almost all of the library's special collections, amounting to some 20,000 manuscripts, 2,200 incunabula, 80,000 early books, and 100,000 pieces of graphic art.

The Biblioteka Narodowa in Warsaw, the central library of the state, functions today as a national book depository for all Polish publications and literature related to Poland, as a general research library specializing in the humanities, as a national bibliographic agency, as the country's chief collection of works on library, information, book, and archival science, as a center for information on the Polish and foreign-language holdings of the nation's libraries, and as a research center in the fields of library science, reading, information science, bibliography, and the history of the book and libraries. This wide range of activities places the National Library at a strategic point in the national information system and makes it an important partner in international cooperative schemes.

The National Library employs a staff of 950. Its collections, totalling more than 4,500,000 volumes and other items in 1991, were transferred to a new building with a capacity of 62,000 sq.m. Its resources include more than 1,627,000 books published since 1800, more than 522,000 serial volumes from the same period, and more than 1,406,000 documents from the 19th and 20th centuries; almost 13,400 manuscripts and more than 170,300 books published before 1800; more than 93,000 pieces of music, 23,700 recordings, 321,400 prints and drawings, 65,200 maps, and 143,800 microfilms.

The National Library compiles and publishes (in its own printing house) current and retrospective national bibliographies, specialized bibliographies, catalogues of foreign-language publications in Polish libraries, statistics on publishing and on the activities of public libraries, and printed library catalogue cards. It also provides in-publication cataloguing; establishes bibliographic and library norms; offers consulting services; and produces research on reading, library science, scholarly information, bibliography, and the history of books and libraries. The majority of these activities are carried out by the Library's *Instytut Bibliograficzny* (Bibliographic Institute) and *Instytut Książki i Czytelnictwa* (Institute of the Book and Reading).

Academic Libraries. There are 91 institutions of higher learning in Poland, each with a central library and most with several departmental and institute libraries, with a combined total of about 41,000,000 volumes. The network of 11 university central libraries includes some 300 departmental libraries; that of the technical universities has 19 central and about 290 departmental libraries. There are libraries at the 10 medical academies, 9 agricultural academies, 10 higher pedagogical schools, 5 academies of economics, 6 higher schools of physical education, 16 art, music, and theatrical academies, 7 theological schools, and 2 higher maritime schools.

National Library of Poland

Historic Palace of the Republic, which houses special collections of the National Library.

The Library of the Jagiellonian University, founded in 1364, is among the oldest academic libraries in Europe and has the country's richest collection of pre-1800 Polish imprints. Its resources, amounting to 2,646,000 volumes (1987), include 1,312,000 books, 460,200 serial volumes, and 873,900 items in special collections (21,400 manuscripts, almost 1,800 incunabula, 100,800 works published before 1800, 40,700 graphic works, and 11,500 cartographic items). The university's library system comprises 41 branches. Rich collections are also found in the university libraries of Poznan, Warsaw (founded in 1817), and Wroclaw.

Public Libraries. In 1990 there were more than 10,300 public libraries (including branches), with collections of more than 136,783,000 volumes and 2,541,000 items in special collections. Public libraries in Poland include 49 *województwo* (province), city, and rural community libraries and their branches. There are almost 19,000 *punkty biblioteczne* (library outlets), mainly in rural areas, staffed by volunteers. On average, the country has one library or branch for every 3,500 inhabitants and every 604 library users, with a supply of 20 books per user. More than 20 percent of the people make use of public libraries.

Special Libraries. There are libraries in a variety of research, pedagogical, enterprise, and scholarly institutions. Among the leading research collections are the 75 libraries of the Polish Academy of Sciences, which hold a total of 5,122,000 volumes, as well as special collections. They include libraries in Wroclaw (the National Ossolinski Foundation), Gdansk, Kornik, Cracow, and Warsaw. Other important collections include the Chief Medical Library of Warsaw, the Central Agricultural Library, the Central Army Library, the Library of the Sejm (Parliament), and the libraries of 28 scientific research institutes. There are more than 3,800 technical libraries in economic enterprises and 232 libraries in research institutions. The holdings of this group as a whole amount to about 103,000,000 volumes and other items.

The Profession. The Polish Librarians' Association, founded in 1917 and a founding member of IFLA in 1929, has long played a guiding role, both through its publishing and training activities and through its formulation of policy statements on issues relating to librarianship in Poland. It publishes works on the theory and practice of librarianship and on bibliography, the quarterly *Przegląd Biblioteczny* (The Library Review), and two monthlies, *Bibliotekarz* (The

Librarian) and *Poradnik Bibliotekarza* (The Librarian's Advisor). The professional status of librarians is regulated by the Library Statute of 1968. Education for librarians is provided in 14 institutions of higher learning and in secondary schools on both a full-time and part-time basis. The University of Wroclaw awards an advanced doctorate in library science and several other universities offer regular doctoral programs in library and information science.

REFERENCES

Encyklopedia Wiedzy o Książce (Encyclopedia of the Book) (1971).

Encyklopedia Wspóiczesnego Bibliotekarstwa Polskiego (Encyclopedia of Modern Polish Librarianship) (1976).

Rocznik Statystyczny 1990 (Statistical Yearbook for 1990) (1990).

Polish Libraries Today, vol. 1 (1991).

JAN WOLOSZ

Pollard, A. W.

(1859–1944)

Alfred William Pollard, British librarian and bibliographer of early printed books, produced with G. R. Redgrave the *Short-Title Catalogue* for the period 1475–1640.

Pollard was born in London, August 14, 1859, and was educated at an excellent London school. Taught by John Wesley Hales, he studied English literature, notably Chaucer and Shakespeare, whose texts he later reexamined and edited. His admission to the University of Oxford was a natural progression; he entered Saint John's College in 1877 with an open scholarship and earned a B.A. Honours degree in Classical Studies and Philosophy.

Pollard proved to be a brilliant addition to the staff of the Printed Books Department of the British Museum Library when he went to work there in 1883. He married a graduate of Cambridge University in 1887, who, with her own intellectual interests, constantly inspired and stimulated his work. They had two sons and a daughter; both sons were killed in World War I, a loss for which Pollard's solace was intensive scholarship and bibliographical research. He became Keeper of Printed Books in the British Museum in 1919 and in the same year was appointed honorary Professor of Bibliography at the University of London. He retired from the Museum in 1924 but remained mentally active and productive until 1935, when he suffered some brain damage after an accident.

He was associated with a bibliographical journal, *The Library,* for nearly 46 years and was officially recognized as co-editor in 1899. In the London Bibliographical Society, founded in 1892, Pollard was appointed Secretary in 1893, and under his guidance it became a prestigious organization. Eventually, *The Library* became the official publication of the London Bibliographical Society.

The high quality of Pollard's work was recognized by various institutions. In 1907 he became a Fellow of King's College, London, and in 1921 received the honorary degree of Doctor of Letters from the University of Durham. He was made a Fellow of the British Academy in 1922, and that year he was invested as a Companion of the Order of the Bath by King George V. He was also known and admired by scholars and librarians in the United States and collaborated, by mail, with the scholar Henrietta Bartlett in the compilation of a *Census of Shakespeare's Plays in Quarto* (1916). During his only visit to the U.S. he catalogued the rich library of an eccentric bibliophile, General Rush C. Hawkins, in Providence, Rhode Island. In 1921 he was elected an Honorary Foreign Corresponding Member of the Bibliographical Society of America.

All his awards cannot be listed but even those named here prove that he had a great reputation as a bibliographer. His work, however, must be assessed in historical perspective and his aims analyzed in the light of his performance. Most of his early research into 15th-century printing was done in collaboration with Robert Proctor, who joined the British Museum Library's staff in 1893. Both were keenly interested in incunabula—"fifteeners," as they were sometimes known, books produced before 1500, during printing's infancy. Proctor and Pollard cooperated in an ideal partnership. Proctor possessed the meticulous assiduity and patient precision necessary for the measurement and identification of typefaces, and Pollard concentrated on early book illustration.

Pollard condoned his partner's obsession with fifteeners but also, characteristically, saw the other side of the picture. Of Proctor's work at Oxford with J. G. Milne in the library of Corpus Christi he said, "I gather that the responsible librarian was a little alarmed at the enthusiasm with which the fragments of printers' or binders' waste were extracted from the old bindings, and despite the extraordinarily interesting finds which have been made in book-covers, there is much to be said on the librarian's side." Proctor had, according to Pollard, an enormous ability to labor and concentrate on bibliographical detail, but he was not an innovator. He "had one of the brains which require some outside influence to kindle them into activity."

Pollard regarded himself as a journalistic bibliographer while recognizing the importance of the work undertaken by men of the caliber of Proctor. When Proctor died suddenly in 1903, Pollard reluctantly but dutifully took on the burden of compiling a full-scale catalogue of the early printed books in the British Museum Library. Curiously, but not unnaturally, the section concerning the incunabula of the United Kingdom has not yet been completed. Pollard's ambivalent attitude toward bibliographical tasks of this nature preserved a sense of balance in the undertaking. In the words of his colleague at the Museum, Victor Scholderer, Pollard's "precision with which he kept the wood in focus could prove uncommonly disconcerting to a disciple bemused with the multitude of trees."

Although Pollard was bored by the tedious processes involved in the recognition of typefaces, he saw their importance in training beginners to catalogue early printed books. His sense of humor was such that he could not take minutiae too seriously, and he was keenly aware of humanity. It is significant that his presidential address to the Edinburgh Bibliographical Society in 1923 was entitled *The Human Factor in Bibliography*.

Pollard was in a lighthearted mood at a meeting of the London Bibliographical Society in January 1918 when he proposed publication of the work that became his chief contribution to bibliography: *A*

Short-Title Catalogue of Books Printed in England, Scotland, and Ireland and of English Books Printed Abroad, 1475–1640, produced in collaboration with G. R. Redgrave. The vast compilation of over 26,000 items took about nine years to prepare. Pollard received the assistance of many bibliographers, but in the last resort he was the editor and did much of the work himself. He believed that in the extensive bibliographical field, speed and production were more important than detail. The "S.T.C.," as it is now known, was not intended as a final product. Pollard makes this clear in his preface:

> One object of this preface is to warn all users of this book that from the mixed character of its sources, it is a dangerous work for any one to handle lazily, that is, without verification. The main workers on it on the average are septuagenarians.

Pollard's view of bibliography's function was succinctly expressed as the enumeration of books and the provision of a basis for textual criticism. Because he had an open mind, he did not expect his judgments and conclusions to be regarded as final and irrevocable, but he did expect other scholars to be stimulated by his work and to undertake further investigations. All bibliographers are indebted to him for his scientific approach to an occupation formerly regarded as a bibliophilic hobby.

Pollard died in Wimbledon, South London, March 8, 1944.

REFERENCES

G. Murphy, *A Select Bibliography of the Writings of A. W. Pollard* (1938), includes notes and an autobiographical essay, "My First Fifty Years."

J. Dover Wilson, *Alfred William Pollard, 1859–1944* (1948).

MARGARET WRIGHT

Poole, William Frederick
(1821–1894)

William Frederick Poole was Librarian of the Boston Athenaeum, of the Chicago Public Library, and of the Newberry Library. He was one of the outstanding U.S. librarians of the 19th century.

He was born in Salem, Massachusetts, December 24, 1821, the son of working-class parents and was compelled to abandon his studies at 12 and seek employment in a variety of occupations. Through his mother's encouragement, at the age of 17 he was able to enroll in the Leicester Academy while at the same time teaching in the local schools. He entered Yale University in 1842 but after a year was obliged to suspend his education again for financial reasons. He turned to teaching a second time and three years later resumed his college career at Yale, from which he graduated in 1849 with election to Phi Beta Kappa.

To supplement his income, during his junior year at Yale he became the Assistant Librarian of the Society of Brothers in Unity, a student literary and debating organization. The Society provided its members with a collection of books and periodicals to help them find material for their debates and other forensic exercises. Although the library maintained a catalogue of the book collection, there was no similar key to the contents of periodicals. In his desire to assist the students, Poole decided to compile an index to the periodical collection. He promptly undertook the task of preparing an index in manuscript form of some 200 volumes of magazines. Since there was only one copy of the index, Poole soon realized that it would need to be published. Through the efforts of Henry Stevens, a former Librarian of the Society, he was able to persuade G. P. Putnam to publish it. As a result of this work he received considerable recognition both at home and abroad. The first edition of the index was quickly sold out, and Poole began to compile a second edition, which was issued in 1853.

ALA
William Frederick Poole

In the interim, although he indicated some leanings toward the legal profession, Poole decided to pursue librarianship as a life career. In 1851 he received a temporary appointment as Assistant Librarian of the Boston Athenaeum and shortly thereafter became the Librarian of the Mercantile Library Association of Boston, one of the leading social libraries in the country. Poole threw himself into his new responsibilities with vigor. He managed the moving of the library to new quarters, enlarged the book collection, and published a printed catalogue of its holdings. In issuing the catalogue, he introduced an innovation in that the author, title, and subject entries were listed in a single alphabetical sequence, setting a precedent that became a standard practice for many libraries to follow, popularly referred to as the dictionary catalogue. During his tenure at the Mercantile Library, he attended the first library conference, which was held in New York in 1853. Poole was treated as one of the important delegates at the conference. An advance copy of the second edition of his periodical index was on display at the meeting, and a resolution approving it was adopted by the members present.

In 1856 Poole was offered the position of Librarian of the Boston Athenaeum. The Athenaeum was one of the prestigious libraries of the country, and this appointment offered Poole considerable visibility. He remained at the Athenaeum for 13 years and was responsible for a number of important improvements in the physical quarters of the Library as well as in its services. He expanded the book collection and devised a classification scheme that was pragmatic in nature. Poole did not advocate strict subject classification, nor did he believe that it was possible. He also enlarged and trained the professional staff. Several of his assistants, among whom were Caroline M. Hewins, William I. Fletcher, and Charles Evans, later became nationally prominent librarians. In his leisure moments Poole was engaged in working on his periodical index and in writing, particularly in the field of early New England history. He published a new edition of Edward Johnson's *Wonder-Working Providence of Sion's Saviour in New England* together with a lengthy scholarly introduction that afforded him recognition as a historian. From 1858 to 1870, he served as a member of the Visiting Committee for the Harvard Library.

Serving the reading and research needs of the intellectual elite of Boston, who were members of the Athenaeum, was doubtless an enriching experience for Poole. Nevertheless in 1869 he felt the need for greater professional opportunities and tendered his resignation to the proprietors of the Athenaeum. For the next few years he served as a consultant and adviser to a number of libraries throughout the country. In some instances his services were limited to the selection of books; in other cases he was involved in complete reorganization of the library, as in the case of the Naval Academy library in Annapolis and the Cincinnati Public Library. His work in Cincinnati led to a full-time appointment as Librarian in 1871. In a short period of time he transformed a feeble institution into a strong and vibrant organization second only to the Boston Public Library. Under Poole, the Cincinnati Public Library opened its reading room on Sundays, increased the circulation of books significantly, and organized a room for fine arts and decoration to serve commercial designers. This may well be the first subject department to have been established in a public library.

His tenure in Cincinnati was brief: in January 1874 he became Librarian of the newly established Chicago Public Library. Even before he accepted the position in Chicago, he had advised library leaders in Peoria on legislation on the legal structure of public libraries for Illinois. Poole was familiar with Ohio and Indiana library legislation, which placed public libraries under the jurisdiction of public school boards of education. He found this governing authority unsatisfactory, and he proposed the concept of a library board appointed by the mayor of a municipality that would be free from excessive political interference. The Illinois Public Library Act of 1872 , under which the Chicago Public Library was established, bore the fruits of Poole's advice.

Poole's first task on assuming his duties was to organize a book collection and to provide suitable quarters for the Library. The people of Great Britain had sent some 8,000 volumes following the Chicago fire of 1871, but they were largely reference and scholarly works. Poole knew he needed a large collection of books to meet the reading needs of the average user. With the assistance of his staff, Poole promptly began acquiring, cataloguing, and classifying the initial collection. Since Poole was essentially a pragmatist rather than a purist or a perfectionist on issues relating to cataloguing and classification, the work proceeded with dispatch. Poole designed a classification scheme that was based on utility rather than theory. It was divided into 20 major subjects or classes. Each class was assigned a letter of the alphabet. His book notation system consisted of a single letter followed by a serial number. Books in each class were numbered serially beginning with one and running continuously as books were added. Provision was made for subclasses by reserving in advance blocks of numbers for each subclass. With his characteristic flair for producing results, Poole managed to have an ample collection of circulating books ready for use within four months after he took office.

Since a printed catalogue was not possible, Poole decided on a device that he called a "finding list." This printed publication contained a sampling of the collection, with the titles arranged by subject and with the call number included. For a time the Library charged a small fee for the finding list. In later years the lists were published by a commercial firm, carried some advertising, and were distributed free.

Poole was a firm believer that the public library was an important educational institution, and he strove to make its influence felt in the community. In 1884 he expanded library service to the outlying areas of the city through a system called "station delivery." Neighborhood stores whose proprietors agreed to accept orders for library books were designated as stations. Orders were picked up by library messengers each day and the books delivered as promptly as the service would permit. The storekeepers were paid a small fee for the service they performed. Under Poole's strong leadership, the Chicago Public Library became the largest circulating library in the United States.

At this period in his professional career, Poole was undoubtedly one of the outstanding librarians of the day, if not the most eminent, second only to Justin Winsor. In 1876 he served on the organizing committee to form the American Library Association at a meeting held in Philadelphia. He was elected Vice-President of the newly established association at that historic conference, served in that capacity for eight years, then served two terms as President. Poole's proposal for the cooperative preparation of his index to periodicals was adopted at the 1876 meeting. Under his plan, librarians from both the U.S. and United Kingdom would participate in the indexing project, to be coordinated by Poole and William I. Fletcher. This project came to a successful conclusion with the publication of the third edition of *Poole's Index to Periodical Literature* in 1882, receiving wide applause.

During America's centennial year Poole was also invited to contribute an article to the U.S. Bureau of Education Report on *Public Libraries in the United States of America*. His paper was entitled "The Organization and Management of Public Libraries" and can be described as a distillation of the principles and practices of library administration at that time. In 1877 he attended the International Conference of Librarians in London and served as Vice-President for the meeting.

In 1887 Poole resigned from the Chicago Public Library to become the first Librarian of the Newberry Library, which came into being under a munificent bequest of Walter L. Newberry, an early business giant of Chicago. The Newberry was to be a reference library, and Poole, at what would be retirement age for many, accepted a new challenge. Poole's contribution to this institution lay in developing its rich collection and in his architectural plan for the building. Although this was his first opportunity to plan a completely new building, he had become a specialist in library architecture. Poole was an innovator in the field since he believed that a library building should be functional rather than monumental. Instead of the traditional large hall with a high vaulted ceiling, Poole advocated a number of large rooms, each 50 feet in width, which could accommodate a number of subject departments to be administered by subject specialists. With the use of steel beams, which were coming into general use as a result of the new Chicago school of architecture, such a building was possible. Despite the opposition of the architect, Henry Ives Cobb, the Board adopted Poole's plan. To assist him in the operation of the Library, Poole recruited an impressive array of assistants who laid the professional groundwork for the future development of the famous Library.

Poole was a dynamic person and found time to pursue the writing of history in addition to his full-time responsibilities as a librarian. He studied two major areas, Colonial New England and the early West. His writings were based on deep research into original sources and exhibited the highest degree of scholarship. For his historical studies he was elected President of the American Historical Association in 1888. Poole was also active in the literary life of Chicago. He was a founding member of the Chicago Literary Club, and his historical bent furnished him with material for a number of papers delivered at meetings of this organization.

Poole died on March 1, 1894, in Evanston, Illinois, leaving a legacy of professional accomplishments and attainments that would be difficult to match.

REFERENCES

Annual Reports of the Board of Directors of the Chicago Public Library (1874–86).

William Landrum Williamson, *William Frederick Poole and the Modern Library Movement* (1963).

William Landrum Williamson, "Poole, William Frederick," *Dictionary of American Library Biography* (1978).

ALEX LADENSON

Portugal

Portugal, a republic on the western coast of the Iberian Peninsula, lies between Spain on the north and east and the Atlantic Ocean. Population (1990 est.) 10,525,000; area 92,389 sq.km. The official language is Portuguese.

History. Queen Mary I created the Royal Public Library in 1796 with initial holdings from the Real Mesa Censória (Royal Censoring Board), the government institution responsible for book censorship after the Inquisition. This library became the National Library. Its collections were enriched in 1834 and 1910 with holdings from extinct monasteries and further enlarged after enactment of the legal deposit law in 1931.

National Library. In 1969, the National Library moved from the ancient Convent of São Francisco to a specially built new home in Lisbon, where some 1,000,000 titles are housed in 27 km. of stacks with seating for 395. The Library also holds codified manuscripts, incunabula, collections of miscellaneous manuscripts, prints, maps, geographic charts, and periodicals. It has a valuable collection of medallions, coins, and other ancient items. Of special significance is its music section. Collections in the National Library are mainly in the arts and humanities; the country has no science library as such.

Jorge Alves

Formerly the Royal Public Library of the Court created in 1796, the National Library in Lisbon moved to this building in 1969.

The National Library is responsible for publishing the National Bibliography, coordinating and maintaining the Union Catalogue of Portuguese Libraries, and assigning bibliographic control code designations. It also runs the Portuguese Bibliographic Database (PORBASE), a cooperative network that held 350,000 records by 1991 and was designed to become a nationwide reference database. Records are being input from 55 academic and special libraries. News about the database is published regularly in a PORBASE newsletter. The National Library has begun a program for preservation and conservation, focusing initially on microfilming the extensive newspaper and journal collections. The library subscribes to 6,000 current titles, of which newspapers published in Africa are an important component.

Archives. The important *distritais* (county) archives are coordinated by the Instituto Português de Arquivos. Archival collections are being reorganized under a program named ARQbase. The Arquivo Nacional da Torre do Tombo, created in the 14th century and remarkable for its vast historical collections, was scheduled to move from an old monastery in Lisbon to a new building in the early 1990s.

Academic Libraries. Among academic libraries the most famous is the Biblioteca General da

Libraries in Portugal (1989)

Type of library	Number of administrative units (main libraries)	Number of service points (branches, mobile stops, etc.)	Volumes in collections	Annual expenditures (escudo)	Population served	Professional staff (with certificate, diploma, etc.)	Total staff
National	1	1	2,241,056	477,324	65,099	57	273
Academic	229	320	4,070,291	752,410	313,232	300	853
Public	173	239	4,852,133	821,400	952,281	280[a]	857[a]
School	768	892	3,357,831	--	735,146	--	--
Special	275	405	4,265,048	1,239,537	203,525	234	1,167
Other (describe)	8	8	2,848,719	216,260	94,620	58	185

[a] 1986 data

Source: *Estatísticas da Cultura, Desporto e Recreio,* 1989. Lisboa, Instituto Nacional de Estatística, 1991.

National Library of Portugal, Lisbson

Main Reading Room, National Library of Portugal.

Universidade de Coimbra (General Library of the University of Coimbra), dating from the 16th century. A portion of its collection is still housed in a magnificent 18th century baroque edifice; the main administrative area is in a modern building on the university campus. Primarily a reference library, it holds about 700,000 titles, including manuscripts, incunabula, and rare books of great value, as well as contemporary publications. Its collections, like those of the National Library, are mainly in the area of the humanities.

Public Libraries. The most important Municipal Library is in Oporto, with a collection of approximately 1,325,000 volumes. It was founded in 1833 with books from convents abandoned during the political wars of the period. It was made a Municipal Library in 1896. Evora and Braga also have important collections of ancient books. The Instituto Português do Livro e da Leitura, a government agency, launched a Project on Public Reading in 1988 to modernize public libraries.

School Libraries. Some secondary schools have libraries with rich collections; an example is the one at the secondary school of Passos Manuel, in Lisbon, which inherited the library of the Convent of Jesus. Overall, the management and development of school libraries need coordination.

Special Libraries. Notable are the Portuguese Academy of History, the Scientific Academic Library of Lisbon, and the libraries of the Geographic Society and the National Academy of Belas Artes. The Ajuda Library in Lisbon and the library of the Mafra Convent are rich in old and rare books. Significant special libraries include those associated with the Calouste Gulbenkian Foundation (art history); National Institute of Statistics; Camara Pestana Institute (biology and toxicology); Center of Philological Studies (linguistics); National Laboratory of Civil Engineering; and Laboratory of Nuclear Physics and Engineering (nuclear energy).

The Profession. The Portuguese Association of Librarians, Archivists, and Documentalists has served professionals in these fields since 1973. Its publications are *Cadernos* and *Noticia BAD*. The National Library publishes *Revista da Biblioteca Nacional*.

MARIA LUISA CABRAL

Posner, Ernst
(1892–1980)

Ernst Posner, often affectionately referred to as the Dean of American Archivists, was a major influence on the development of archival education and administration in the United States. Many archivists practicing today studied with him. But he achieved success as an archivist in Germany long before he migrated to the U.S. with his wife, Katherina, in July 1939.

Posner was born August 9, 1892, the youngest of three children, into a cultivated, liberal German family. His father was a doctor of philosophy as well as an M.D. who practiced and taught as a urologist at the University of Berlin while he was coeditor of a journal of urology. His uncle Max, a historian recognized for his contributions to 18th-century intellectual history, was also an archivist. All family members wrote, enjoyed music and literature, and spoke and read several languages. Posner grew to manhood in this intellectual and challenging atmosphere.

He attended the University of Berlin, where he graduated in 1910. After two years of required military service in 1911 and 1912, he left the Army as a reserve noncommissioned officer to reenter the university for graduate study in auxiliary historical science and in comparative administration. World War I interrupted his studies, and he returned to the German Army to serve from 1914 to 1918, when he was mustered out as a reserve lieutenant and awarded the Iron Cross, First Class. He resumed his studies again, and in 1920 he received two degrees, one for the teaching licentiate and one for the doctorate. He was now prepared to become either a teacher or an archivist. While he eventually became both, initially he chose to pursue his career as an archivist.

In November 1920 Posner became a professional archivist at the Prussian Geheime Staatsarchiv. From the beginning he was highly regarded. Soon he became the administrative assistant to the director in charge of building and personnel. He discharged this responsibility so ably that in 1930, as a 37-year-old archivist and scholar, he was among those mentioned for the position of Director.

Posner also found time to write and edit. Between 1922 and 1934 he published four papers and reports and contributed to a comprehensive bibliography of German history. He also wrote annual review articles about new literature on the history of Prussia. From 1922 to 1938 he served on behalf of the Prussian Academy of Sciences as the editor of Volumes 11 through 15 of the *Acta Borussica,* continuing the documentary publication dealing with the internal history of Prussia during the 18th century. During this period Posner became a teacher, serving from 1930 to 1935 as a faculty member of the Institute for Archival Science and Advanced Historical Studies connected with the Geheime Staatsarchiv. January 30, 1933, the date on which Adolf Hitler came to power, was the beginning of the end of Posner's archival career in Germany. As a Jew, he was gradually made to resign all of his archival, editing, and teaching positions. Posner was arrested during the Krystallnacht pogrom in November 1938 and spent six weeks in Sachsenhausen concentration camp. His archival career in Germany was over.

With the help of several American historians, among them Eugene Anderson, Waldo Leland, Merle Curti, and Solon Buck, Posner and his wife made their way to the U.S. They settled in Washington, D.C., where Posner joined Buck at the American University to teach one of the first courses offered in the U.S. on the history and administration of archives. In 1942, when Buck succeeded R. D. W. Connor as Archivist of the United States, Posner was made solely responsible for teaching the course. Over the next several years he designed and added other courses to develop a major archival education curriculum. By 1957 American University could boast a certificate and degree program in archival administration and records management. The curriculum Posner developed became a model for archival education programs in other institutions throughout the U.S.

Posner's summers were busy, too. In 1945 he began the summer Institutes on Archives Administration, directing them for the next 16 years. They were designed as introductory or continuing education courses primarily for prospective archivists or for those who had on-the-job archival experience but no formal schooling in archival administration. In 1950 Posner started a summer Institute on Genealogical Research; in 1954, the Institutes in Records Management. With the cooperation of Colonial Williamsburg and the National Park Service, Posner presented summer Institutes on the Interpretation of Historic Sites during 1949 and 1950.

From 1939 to 1945 Posner served as a part-time member of the American University faculty, first as a Lecturer and after 1940 as an Adjunct Professor. In 1945 he became Professor of History and Archives Administration and was made Dean of the Graduate Division. Two years later he became Director of the School of Social Sciences and Public Affairs and in 1955 was appointed Dean of the Graduate School. He took time off in 1957 when he was awarded a Guggenheim Fellowship and Fulbright research grant to work on his history of archival development in the ancient world. After he returned from his leave in Rome, he resumed his chairmanship of the history department, which he retained until he retired from academic life in 1961.

While pursuing his career as academician, Posner also had time to participate in other professional activities. For many he was uniquely qualified by virtue of his German background and experience. In 1943 and 1944 he served, consecutively, two bodies concerned with protecting cultural treasure in countries torn by World War II. The first was the Dinsmore Committee of the American Council of Learned Societies; the second, an official body, the American Commission for the Protection and Salvage of Artistic and Historic Monuments in Europe (the Roberts Commission). For the first time he wrote a number of reports on archival establishments in Europe and Asia. He also prepared manuals on German and Italian record practices for the U.S. War Department.

A member of the Society of American Archivists from 1939 and an honorary member from 1965, Posner served the organization long and ably. He was a member of its Council, 1947–51; Vice-President, 1953–54; and President, 1955–56. He was Chairman of several of its important committees as well as a member of the editorial board of its scholarly journal, *The American Archivist.* He often represented the Society in international archival meetings. From 1958 he served intermittently as lecturer on American archival administration and practices at the German Archives School at Marburg.

The last few years of Posner's life were marred by ill health. He and his family settled in Europe, where he continued his researches in archival history. He worked at the Vatican Archives, lived in Switzerland, and later moved to Wiesbaden. He died April 18, 1980.

In the U.S. one of his most famous works, researched and written on behalf of the Society of American Archivists between 1961 and 1964 and supported by a grant to the Society from the Council on Library Resources, was *American State Archives,* published by the University of Chicago Press in 1964. This signal work was an examination and evaluation of archival agencies throughout the United States and Puerto Rico. *Archives and the Public Interest: Selected Essays by Ernst Posner,* edited by Ken Munden, was published by the Public Affairs Press in 1967. Posner's major work *Archives in the Ancient World,* a study of the development of archives from the Tigris-Euphrates civilization to the division of the Roman Empire into eastern and western halves, appeared to acclaim in 1972.

Posner received wide recognition for his accomplishments. In 1958 he became a Fellow of the Society of American Archivists. The American Association for State and Local History honored him in 1963 by presenting him with its first Award of Distinction. The Society of American Archivists gave him a Certificate of Appreciation in 1964, and in 1965 *American State Archives* won the Waldo Gifford Leland Prize. Posner won his second Leland Prize for *Archives in the Ancient World* in 1973.

MARY LYNN McCREE BRYAN

Society of American Archivists
Ernst Posner

Powell, Lawrence Clark

(1906–)

American Lawrence Clark Powell may be the last of a small but significant minority—directors of major libraries who are also bookmen. In the autobiography he wrote when he took early retirement, he characterized himself as having "a personal, autobiographical, egocentric, didactic, flamboyant, hyperbolic manner." Others have called him "the Picasso of librarianship," "one of the great eccentrics," and a "demigod." When one of his detractors, a proponent of scientific management, called him a "biblio-simpleton," he responded with "library housekeeper!"

Although he served as President of the Bibliographical Society of America (BSA), 1954–56, he was impatient with the ponderous bureaucracy of library associations. The American Library Association nonetheless gave him the Clarence Day Award (1960) and made him an honorary member (1981)—its highest award. He was elected President of the California Library Association (1950), was a Guggenheim Fellow twice (1950–51 and 1966–67), and received, in his words, "various honorary doctorates."

© Cynthia Farah 1985
Lawrence Clark Powell

Powell was born in Washington, D.C., September 3, 1906, to Quaker parents. When he was five, the family moved to South Pasadena, California, where the public librarian waived the rules for this already voracious reader: card 3089 was good for as many books as the boy could carry.

His friend Ward Ritchie, later to be one of America's most distinguished book designers and printers, decided to enroll at nearby Occidental College. Powell also applied, but was admitted only after his mother persuaded his high school teachers to recommend him despite some low grades. There Powell came under the influence of Carlyle F. MacIntyre and Benjamin Franklin Stelter. The latter "prepared me for graduate work," he later wrote, "as Mac's courses prepared me for life and literature."

After graduation in 1929, Powell did a stint as shipping clerk in Vroman's Bookstore in Pasadena. Meantime, Ritchie's admiration for the poetry of Robinson Jeffers bolstered Powell's resolve to write a dissertation on that California poet. Few universities then considered living poets fit topics for doctoral study, so he decided to enroll at the University of Dijon. After successfully defending his dissertation, he used a legacy from his grandmother to finance his *wanderjahre* in Europe. He returned to California in 1933 and was married to Fay Ellen Shoemaker, whom he had met at Occidental.

He worked at Jake Zeitlin's bookstore in Los Angeles for the next couple of years, laying the groundwork for his life's career. To make ends meet, he found after-hours work with Primavera Press—billing, wrapping, and shipping books. During a visit to the Los Angeles Public Library with the latest offerings from Zeitlin's shop, he was surprised to have the head of the order department declare, "You should be buying for, not selling to, libraries." This man introduced Powell to the dynamic Althea Warren, LAPL's Chief Librarian, who promptly sent him to the library school at the University of California in Berkeley. Dean Sydney B. Mitchell was away on sabbatical, and Powell found the library school instructors "not inspiring."

A year later, now equipped to begin his library career, Powell found himself again in Los Angeles looking for work. Althea Warren helped out with a substitute position, and in January 1938 Dean Mitchell alerted Powell to a beginning position at the University of California at Los Angeles. Director John E. Goodwin had noted his book reviews for *Westways,* his work on Robinson Jeffers, and his experience with Zeitlin—all of which qualified Powell for an immediate task: accessioning the Robert Ernest Cowan collection of Californiana.

Over the next six years Powell made his presence known at UCLA. The work on the Cowan collection had revealed that the library's technical processing staff had spoiled much of it by routine treatment. Powell wrote a paper deploring insensitivity to valuable documents that caught the attention of Randolph G. Adams, Director of the University of Michigan's Clements Library and author of a controversial article, "Librarians as Enemies of Books." Further, the exhibits and book displays that Powell designed and promoted gained him powerful friends on the faculty.

In spring 1943 Powell learned that he had been recommended for the post of Librarian at Northwestern University in Evanston, Illinois. Characteristically, he dropped his resignation in the mailbox at Union Station when he left for Evanston. On his return, he found that the president of UCLA, Robert Gordon Sproul, had a flood of letters from the faculty urging that Powell be retained. Sproul offered Powell a choice: head the university library or direct the William Andrews Clark Memorial Library, UCLA's rare book collection, housed in its own elegant building some miles from campus. Powell suggested that he take both jobs. Sproul was persuaded by the rationale of coordination—and perhaps by the thought of filling two posts with less than two salaries. So it was done: Powell became Director of the Clark on January 1, 1944, and University Librarian six months later.

The University of California had achieved distinction as the best state university in the country on the basis of Berkeley's faculty alone. The regents took a bold step in deciding that UCLA would be built to the same strength, and rapidly. The "Southern Branch," as UCLA was then designated, was to grow from what the Berkeley folk called "a twig" to a full-sized tree. Powell's Assistant Librarian, Everett Moore, recalls:

> Larry was conscious of the remarkable role he was playing in building a library that would contribute greatly to the development of a university campus that would be a worthy part of UC. He had fought hard for the job, and he strained every nerve to make a strong library that could give appropriate support to an ambitious undertaking by this brash young campus. With the establishment of one major school or program after another, Larry in most instances was in on the ground floor in pressing for and planning new library resources. (Louise Darling's appointment as Biomedical Librarian was second only to that of Stafford Warren as dean of the new Medical School.)

During Powell's 17 years as University Librarian, he drew able people to substantiate his vision. A number went on to important careers elsewhere (Neal Harlow, Gordon Williams, Robert Vosper, Andrew Horn, H. Richard Archer, John E. Smith); some returned; others (Page Ackerman, Everett Moore, Miriam Dudley) stayed to make national reputations at UCLA.

Powell's administrative style was "getting things done through people." It was highly personalized. Staff members got the kudos, although often he had laid the groundwork. When things went awry, Powell publicly took the blame.

The book collections Powell amassed (including the Michael Sadleir, C. K. Odgen, and Isaac Foot) raised the UCLA library from the bottom quartile to fourth in the nation. The intellectual camaraderie Powell maintained with faculty and such writers as Aldous Huxley, Henry Miller, and Lawrence Durrell helped him transform the Clark Library from a mausoleum into a research institution with seminars and publications. Other strengths were his own voluminous writing and speechmaking. "Books are basic" was his theme and he spun infinite variations on it. Telephoned by a panicky program planner for the title of his upcoming speech, he said, "Oh, it's just a literary cocktail—'Shake Well and Speak.'" When introducing Powell to the audience, the same person gaily announced that he would speak on "Shakespeare and Keats." And he did.

A study by Robert D. Leigh in 1952 recommended expansion of the library schools at Berkeley and at UCLA's crosstown rival, the University of Southern California, but not a new one at UCLA. The Master Plan for Higher Education in California (1955) called for no action until 1960. With his unfailing sense of timing, Powell decided to push ahead. He pressed prominent librarians and library organizations into service, and the lobbying effort was successful: the regents approved a new library school for UCLA on August 14, 1958.

The faculty Senate, displeased that the school had been approved without its usual committee process, showed its power by insisting that Powell could be either Dean of the new school or University Librarian but not both, as Powell had anticipated. Powell moved to the library school, leaving the librarian's position open on July 1, 1961, for Robert Vosper.

As Dean, Powell drew around him an exemplary faculty (Seymour Lubetzsky, Frances Clark Sayers, Betty Rosenberg) and brightened every semester with a galaxy of visiting scholars, bookmen, and librarians. Andy Horn as Assistant Dean established and maintained liaison with the Graduate Division, organized the thrust for accreditation, and set up a printer's chapel for the students. Rosenberg says, "The school was a humanistic dream. The emphasis was on books and reading and service to readers and the creation of new librarians full of zeal and enthusiasm. It was an amazing library school and still is, but not as he dreamt! The machines caught up with him and he retired while his dream still held."

When the new Research Library was completed, the collections were largely moved there, leaving the undergraduate library and the library school in the original library building. On Powell's retirement on his sixtieth birthday in 1966, the regents named the building after him.

After a few years of travel and writing, Powell began still another career in 1971 as consultant to Presidents Richard A. Harvill and John P. Schaefer of the University of Arizona. There he initiated a survey of the library, which resulted in the appointment of a new young librarian (W. David Laird, UCLA M.L.S., 1966) and the construction of a new building. He also helped to get the library school staffed and accredited.

Drawing new strength from his beloved Southwest, he continued writing and speaking. In Arizona, in his third career, he had written four novels by 1986, published a long piece on Ansel Adams, and worked on a "Portrait of My Father." John David Marshall planned and edited a collection of Powell quotations.

In addition to scores of articles and reviews in the library press and such journals as the *Pacific Historical Review, Southwest Review,* and the *Papers* of the Bibliographical Society of America, Powell contributed regularly to *Westways, Arizona Highways,* and *Hoja Volante*. Many of these writings were gathered in such collections as *Islands of Books* (1951), *Books West Southwest* (1957), *A Passion for Books,* (1959), *Books in My Baggage* (1960), and *The Little Package* (1964). Other titles are *Robinson Jeffers* (1932; 1934; 1940), *Philosopher Pickett* (1942), *The Alchemy of Books* (1954), and his novels, *The Blue Train* (1977), *The River Between* (1979), *El Morro* (1984), and *Portrait of My Father* (1986). The four novels were collected in one volume, *The Evening Redness* (1991). This is only a sampling of Powell's published works.

To understand Powell, one must see him as a Humanist, steeped in literature, music, history, and art. Sensitive and emotional on the one hand, he could also be practical, realistic, and sometimes ruthless on the other. Ahead of his time in fair treatment of women and in encouragement of ethnic minorities, he proved fiercely loyal to old friends and to institutions. His countless speeches, lectures, and writings drew many to the profession and confirmed others in their practice of it. A patron of the arts and frequent commissioner of fine printing, Powell stands as a veritable Renaissance man.

REFERENCES

Lawrence Clark Powell, *Fortune and Friendship: An Autobiography* (1968).

Lawrence Clark Powell, *Life Goes On: Twenty More Years of Fortune and Friendship* (1986).

Lawrence Clark Powell, "Notes on My Writing, 1930–1990," in *The Evening Redness* (1991).

Lawrence Clark Powell and William Everson, *Take Hold Upon the Future: Letters on Writing and Writers, 1938–1946* (1992).

Wayne A. Wiegand, editor, *Leaders in American Academic Librarianship: 1925–1975,* pp. 262–287 (Beta Phi Mu, 1983).

Betty Rosenberg *Checklist of the Published Writings of LCP* (1966).

Donald C. Dickinson, et al., *Voices from the Southwest* (1976).

WILLIAM R. ESHELMAN

Power, Effie Louise
(1873–1969)

ALA

Effie Louise Power

Effie Louise Power, pioneer American children's librarian, educator, and author, directly influenced the development of services to children in three major U.S. cities, Cleveland, St. Louis, and Pittsburgh.

She was born February 12, 1873, near Conneautville, Pennsylvania. When she was 13, her family moved to Cleveland, where she graduated from Central High School. William Howard Brett, a neighbor of the Power family, invited her to take the Cleveland Public Library's entrance examination and thus brought to library service a protégée who caught his inspirational spark. Throughout her career, Power kindled it in others.

Power began her library work as an apprentice in autumn 1895, then left for about three months to be school librarian at her former high school. Returning to the Public Library, she took charge of the "Junior Alcove" under Brett's supervision. His plans for a children's room materialized in 1898, and Power became the first children's librarian in the Cleveland system, a post she filled until 1902. One of her first contributions was to change the handling of nonfiction books for children. Such books had been kept out of the children's alcove on the theory that children read nonfiction only under coercion from adults. Each day Power went through the library gathering up biography, history, and nature books suited to children and arranging them on the counters in the children's alcove. Each day the books disappeared, and so did the assumption that children would check out only fiction.

Service to children profited when in late 1901 the Cleveland Library moved to new but temporary quarters that provided a large and pleasant basement room for the children's department. For the first time, Power and her two assistants had sufficient space to bring the children together for storytelling. The following year, having established the children's room on firm principles and practices, Power decided to add to her practical experience a more formal foundation of knowledge and technique. Brett noted in his annual report for 1902 that she was spending the school year studying work for children in the training program for children's librarians at the Carnegie Library in Pittsburgh. She received her diploma in 1904.

Power returned to Cleveland after a year's study only to direct her talents in new directions. Brett had long advocated that the Cleveland City Normal School introduce a course in children's literature and the use of books. At the last moment, the candidate selected to teach the course refused the invitation, and Power was given a leave of absence to fill the position. She taught at City Normal School from 1903 to 1908. During summer 1906, she earned a teaching certificate at Columbia University. Although accounts differ, some claiming she did not return to the Cleveland Public Library until 1920, certain information indicates that she returned to the Library in 1908 and stayed for a year as the children's librarian.

Power became first assistant in the children's department of the Carnegie Library of Pittsburgh in 1909 and also taught in the library school there. In March 1911 she was appointed Supervisor of Children's Work in the Saint Louis Public Library. Less than a year later, when the Library was moved to a new building, she demonstrated her belief in preparing the young to take civic pride in their library. After the general public had inspected the new building, she held a special opening; 1,000 children were taken in groups on tours of inspection and heard short talks by members of all departments.

Power stated her principles in *How the Children of a Great City Get Their Books,* first published as part of the annual report of the Saint Louis Public Library for 1913–14. Her standards for book selection were high. After being approved by the librarians, a book had to win the approval of the children before it was duplicated to any great extent. Stating the library's responsibility for books placed on open shelves, and recognizing the dependence of parents and librarians in smaller libraries on the lists put out by the Saint Louis Library, Power expressed her conviction that children's librarians must know not only "a good book but the best book for each particular need."

About this time, Power's leadership took on a national character. A member of the American Library Association since 1906, she chaired the Children's Section in 1912–13 and again in 1929–30 and served on Council (1914–19). She joined the National Education Association in 1896, serving as President of the Library Department (1916–17), and she also chaired the Committee on Elementary School Libraries from 1914 to 1918.

Power returned to Pittsburgh in 1914 as Supervisor of the Carnegie Library's schools division and later as Head of the Children's Department (1917–20). During her years in Pittsburgh, she worked for the introduction of libraries in the city's high schools and for courses in the use of books and libraries in the Teacher's Training School.

In 1920 she again returned to the Cleveland Public Library as director of work with children. She also taught at Western Reserve University, as Instructor until 1925 and as Assistant Professor (1925–29), and continued her practice begun in 1918 of teaching in library schools throughout the country. One of her contributions in these teaching stints was to help develop cooperative programs between the public library and the schools.

The ALA asked her to write a textbook on library work with children; this first authoritative text on the subject, *Library Service for Children* (1930), was widely used in the United States. The ALA published her revision of the work in 1943 under the title *Work with Children in Public Libraries*. In addition, she wrote many professional articles that reveal both a sense of history and a sense of humor and was the co-author, author, or compiler of several other works. In 1928 she collaborated with a Cleveland teacher, Florence Everson, in writing a collection of stories about pioneer life, *Early Days in Ohio*. In an attempt to bring to storytellers the best of world literature, she compiled four collections of stories for children: *Bag o' Tales* (1934), *Blue Caravan Tales* (1935), *Stories to Shorten the Road* (1936), and *From Umar's Pack* (1937). After her retirement, she wrote another book for children, *Osceola Buddy, a Florida Farm Mule* (1941).

Allegheny College awarded Power an honorary Master's degree in 1934. Three years later, when she retired from the Cleveland Public Library, Columbia University offered her a position as Instructor in the School of Library Service; she taught there until 1939. Moving to Pompano Beach, Florida, she succeeded in inspiring the citizens to raise funds for a new library to replace one destroyed by a hurricane 20 years earlier.

Power seems in retrospect to have been the ideal librarian. In addition to her work as an influential practitioner, she, as an educator and author of professional books and articles, indirectly influenced the libraries in which her students and readers worked. She always held to essentials. Children's work would develop in direct proportion to the support given by knowledgeable administrators to well-trained and dedicated children's librarians determined to maintain the highest standards in services and collections. Throughout her long and varied career, she demonstrated a willingness to leave a comfortable position in order to meet the challenge of a new situation. Never could it be said of Effie Louise Power that she stopped growing professionally. She retired to Pompano Beach, Florida, in 1940. She died on October 8, 1969.

REFERENCE

Regina F. Berneis, "Power, Effie Louise," *Dictionary of American Library Biography* (1978).

MARY E. KINGSBURY

Prasad, S. N.

(1921–)

Sri Nandan Prasad, archivist and historian, was Director of the National Archives of India.

Prasad was born September 18, 1921, in Varanasi, Uttar Pradesh. He obtained M.A. (History, 1944) and

D.Phil. (1948) degrees from Allahabad University and entered the field of archives in 1949 as Senior Research Officer, Historical Section, in the Indian Ministry of Defence; he was later its Director (1964–69). He administered and utilized confidential military records of the government of India in those capacities.

In 1969 he was selected to head the National Archives of India as its Director. During the decade of his stewardship (1969–79) he was chiefly responsible for setting up an Institute of Archival Training and new record centers at Jaipur and Pondicherry. He also contributed to framing and implementing archival policy by the government of India for better records management, accelerated acquisition of documentary materials in India and abroad, better conservation, greater facilities for users by way of reference aids, publication development, easier access, and improved techniques of reproduction. As Secretary of the Indian Historical Records Commission, he provided effective leadership to Indian archivists. The expansion of the National Archives reflected his able guidance.

He joined the International Council on Archives, first as a member of its Executive Committee (1969–76), later as the only Asian member of the Committee on Archival Development (1972–76) and Vice-President (1976–80). He acted as a rapporteur at the Moscow Congress of ICA (1972) and presented a comprehensive report on "Technical Assistance: Viewpoint of Developing Countries." He represented India, the Third World, and the ICA at many meetings and provided expertise to Unesco as well. He took the lead in setting up the South and West Asian Regional Branch of the ICA (SWARBICA) in 1976.

Noted as a military historian, Prasad wrote *Expansion of Armed Forces and Defence Organization* (1956), *Reconquest of Burma* (1958), *Paramountcy under Dalhousie* (1964), and *Survey of Work Done on the Military History of India* (1976). Articles in professional journals cover a wide range of subjects.

N. H. KULKARNEE

PRECIS

The impetus for developing PRECIS, the *PRE*served Context *I*ndex *S*ystem, was a decision in 1971 to begin producing the *British National Bibliography* automatically from MARC-coded data. It soon became evident that acceptable entries and indexes for this printed project could be generated from all parts of MARC records except the subject field. A subject indexing system compatible with automated data manipulation was therefore required.

The new system was to be precoordinate, using a controlled vocabulary. The criteria for its development required that it must be capable of generating entries under all searchable terms used to express a subject; that each entry must be meaningful and coextensive with the subject; and that full use should be made of the computer technology then available, demanding of indexers only those conceptual tasks where human intelligence was required.

Derek Austin developed PRECIS at the British Library in the early 1970s, immediately after he had served with the Classification Research Group. The two assignments can be seen as a creative continuum; PRECIS is an alphabetical, rather than a notational, analytico-synthetic system. In PRECIS, however, the analytico-synthetic principles of concept organization and citation order evolved beyond those of "relative significance" (as in Ranganathan's PMEST formula and chain indexing, for example). The notion of "relative significance," similar to that of "main entry," is necessary in manual systems and in systems where shelf location is a factor. Austin saw very early that machine-readable records signalled the death of main entry as an organizing concept—*all* coded data could now be manipulated into accessible positions. Freed from considerations of fixed term position, searchers could think simply of terms and their relationships. PRECIS is thus an *indexing language,* explainable in terms of semantic categories and syntactic rules.

PRECIS indexers analyze documents with the objective of formulating short abstracts or précis, called subject statements. They analyze each statement linguistically. Is there a term in the statement that denotes action? If so, does the action have an object? Is there an agent or performer? Is time and/or location a significant factor? Indexers ask these and other questions, using the PRECIS operators and codes as their analytic guide. They then place the analyzed terms in a subject "string," the order of the terms in the string determined by the operators assigned. When the indexers have finished their work, the fully coded input strings contain the operators, identification of searchable terms to be placed in a "lead" position, and all other instructions to the computer for generating index entries.

An example of subject analysis in PRECIS is as follows:

Subject statement:	This document is about *the conservation of forests in Canada*	
Linguistic analysis:	conservation	action
	forests	object of action
	Canada	location
PRECIS operators: (appear as third character in string)	(0) Canada (1) forests (2) conservation	
Coded input string: (fourth character marks all terms as "lead")	$z01030$d Canada $z11030$a forests $z21030$a conservation	

Entries are generated for printed indexes from machine-readable strings according to a two-line format with three positions:

LEAD. QUALIFIER
DISPLAY

There must of course always be a lead term. Terms in the qualifier position, when present, automatically qualify (modify) the lead term. Terms in the display position further specify the subject; in grammatical terms, the display is the predicate.

The two-line entry format ensures that, as the computer manipulates the terms to "shunt" each one into the lead and other positions, the contextual relationship remains constant among all the terms comprising a string. This "preserved context" is necessary to avoid ambiguity in any of the entries.

With the sample string given above as input, the computer would generate the following entries and interfile them appropriately in a printed index:

Canada. Forests
Conservation

Forests. Canada
Conservation

Conservation. Forests
Canada

In addition to the syntactic part of the PRECIS software, an equally important part governs the creation of a supporting thesaurus. The two parts of PRECIS, the syntactic and the thesaural, mirror the two aspects of all language systems: the syntactic and the paradigmatic. For printed indexes, the thesaural part of the PRECIS software generates the cross-references. Online, the ability to search terms in paradigms creates cognitive pathways for further retrieval. The PRECIS machine-readable thesaurus conforms fully to the guidelines of the British Standards Institution and the International Organization for Standardization.

With the development of interactive systems and CD-ROM products, many of the syntactic operators and codes necessary for printed products in PRECIS have become redundant. Online, for example, each term in an entry is accessible without manipulation into a "lead" position. All that is required in response to a search is the capacity to generate a single meaningful subject display. Yet because it is a rule-based system for terms and their relationships, PRECIS has adapted well to online environments with Boolean and other searching capabilities.

The British Library has responded to the growing domination of its BLAISE online service and CD-ROM products by simplifying and restructuring PRECIS. In 1990 the system was renamed and introduced as COMPASS (Computer-Aided Subject System). PRECIS continues unchanged in Canada's FORMAT, a national network of bilingual information on audiovisual products. Several printed catalogues, including *Film/Video Canadiana,* are generated from the FORMAT database, in addition to online access provided by the National Film Board of Canada and QL Systems Ltd. The National Film Board has also developed PC-PRECIS, a microcomputer software product for indexers.

Experimental PRECIS projects have been conducted in various languages around the world. In the PRECIS Translingual Project funded by the British Library from 1976 to 1979, algorithms were developed for automatic translation of index entries in English, French, and German from a single input string.

PRECIS is a sophisticated rule-based system, in which single-concept terms form the building blocks for the construction of both syntactic expressions and cognitive networks. It is too soon to judge the system's lasting significance, particularly in a time of radical change. With the vast expansion of intelligence in retrieval systems, however, the contribution of PRECIS to our understanding of textual analysis and synthesis could be significant indeed.

REFERENCES

Derek Austin, *PRECIS: A Manual of Concept Analysis and Subject Indexing*. 2nd ed., with assistance from Mary Dykstra (1984).

Mary Dykstra, *PRECIS: A Primer* (1987).

MARY DYKSTRA

Public Libraries

PURPOSES AND OBJECTIVES

Since the mid-1960s the objectives of public libraries and library systems in many parts of the world have been the subject of regular review, and they have been examined and reexamined by users and librarians alike to determine whether they respond adequately to the particular needs of their communities. Concern about objectives of service can be found in countries with well-established library systems as well as in those with few public libraries. That reexamination should be carried on in various parts of the globe is not surprising. The tide of social change that has swept through a wide variety of countries generated increased demand from citizens for improved access to information and education. So also have technological advances in the production and distribution of information.

The public library has traditionally been in the forefront of the institutions that have responded to such a demand. In the 1990s the question is not "Should the public library respond?" but rather, "How can it best contribute to social change and economic development, and how can it meet the needs of diverse users?" Public libraries today represent a focal point for the aspirations of many citizens and are vital to many governments and public agencies.

Changes in the goals and objectives of public libraries, which have accelerated in recent decades, have been constant throughout their history. The objectives set for a public library system by one generation are normally revised and altered by the next in light of changing conditions. Particular forms of library service have disappeared and new services and new forms of organization have replaced them. The library has been the initiator of activities later taken over by other institutions, and it has left these in their care and gone on to develop fresh approaches. Many mercantile, special, technical, and business collections, community reference information services, continuing education courses for adults, and local history collections had their beginnings in the public library. Along with the evolution of these and other services, there has been a constant transformation of the library's collection of resources.

Public library collections evolved through many phases, from being the private possession of a few persons to being owned by a group or private association and eventually becoming the public possession of an entire nation. Public libraries' materials have been alternatively hoarded and divided, fought over and bartered, suppressed and exhibited, warehoused and disseminated. Public library administrations have had to take into account the policies set through changing social conditions in the libraries' communities. The public library will continue in this manner as long as it operates as a public agency. In this it is unlike its progenitor, the private library, which had often been able to maintain a fixed policy for decades.

It is not known how many public library systems exist today, and no single list of their goals and objectives can be prepared. The 1.1 billion people of China are served by 2,400 public libraries; the 252 million people of the United States have access to more than 9,000 public library systems, plus an additional 6,000 branches; the 5 million people of Finland have access to 11,150 library systems and 1,400 additional service points. With such wide differences in distribution, financial support, and population characteristics, there can be no general statement of public library purposes and goals that applies universally.

The Unesco Public Library Manifesto, first issued in 1949 and included in *Guidelines for Public Libraries* published in 1986 by the International Federation of Library Associations and Institutions (IFLA), is a broad charter of public library goals. It does not cover the full variety of purposes and activities that a public library can serve, but it does identify the most fundamental and common:

To contribute to lifelong universal education

To facilitate appreciation of the achievement of humanity in knowledge and culture

To be the principal means whereby the record of man's thought and ideas, and the expression of his creative imagination, are made freely available to all

To refresh the human spirit by the provision of books and other media for relaxation and pleasure

To assist students

To provide up-to-date technical, scientific, and sociological information.

The Public Library Research Group of the London and Home Countries Branch of the Library Association of the United Kingdom (LA) set out in 1971 the following objectives for public library services in that country:

Education: To foster and provide means for self-development of the individual/group at whatever stage of education, closing the gap between the individual and recorded knowledge.

Information: To bring to the individual/group accurate information quickly and in depth, particularly on topics of current concern.

Culture: To be one of the principal centres of cultural life and promote a keener participation, enjoyment and appreciation of all the arts.

Leisure: To play a part in encouraging the positive use of leisure and providing material for change and relaxation.

In 1977 the Public Library Association of the American Library Association (ALA), after conducting a review over a number of years of the standards set out a decade earlier, issued in its "Mission Statement for Public Libraries" the following statement of public library objectives:

Provide access to the human record of the past—factual, imaginative, scientific, and humanistic—partly through its own collections and partly through an effective network linking all collections in the region, state, nation, and the world.

Albany Public Library

The first readers' bureau in a U.S. public library was begun at Albany, New York (early 1920s).

Organize this human record so that access can be made to it from a myriad of directions allowing not only the facts but also the wisdom in the record to be retrieved.

Collect, translate, and organize the human record on all intellectual levels in many packages, print and nonprint.

Conduct a vigorous program of dissemination dramatizing the relevance of the record of past and present human experience in resolving today's problems.

Develop, in cooperation with other information agencies and libraries, a responsible policy for preserving and erasing portions of humankind's voluminous current record as described in the section dealing with the exponential increase of records.

Take leadership in defining a new statement of professional ethics and in creating new structures to protect intellectual freedom in the light of the responsibility to preserve or erase.

Take a leadership role in coordinating the acquisition policies of other libraries and information agencies, because no one agency can preserve all significant and representative materials in all forms at all levels.

Having developed policies for shared acquisition, assume leadership in creating and maintaining an effective network so that all citizens would have easy access to any record, no matter where stored.

Not only select, collect, organize, and preserve the human record, but also become expert in using flexible procedures for allowing citizens to inform themselves uniquely.

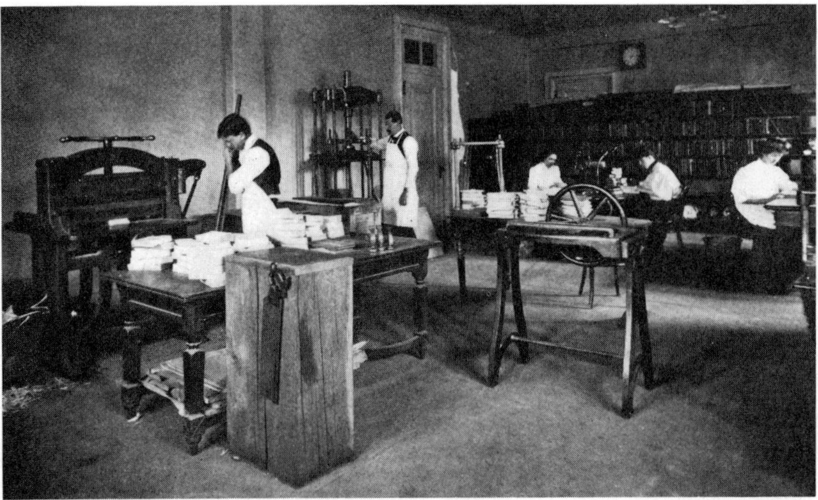

Columbia University

Book bindery in the basement of a public library in Washington, D.C., 1907.

Package and present the human record to allow easy access for people previously excluded by lack of education, lack of language facility, ethnic or cultural backgrounds, age, physical or mental handicaps, and apathy.

Many countries in all parts of the world have similar declarations adopted by their library profession, their governing body for library development, or their national association of librarians. One of the main requirements of any active library development group is that it update and review on a regular basis both the statement of the purposes of public libraries and the ways in which these purposes are being carried out.

SERVICES TO USERS

The specific services that any particular public library offers may constitute a relatively short list, but the range of possibilities is extremely broad because the public library has a broad charge, subject to multiple interpretations, and it serves, potentially at least, everyone. In general, statements of purpose of a public library say that a public library supplies materials and services to its community in order to support the community's educational, information, cultural, and recreational needs. To all residents of an area, and to all on an equal basis, the public library offers "library services"—not the mere provision of a circulating collection of books but many different things, ranging from story hours for children to database searches for business.

San Diego (California) Public Library, one of the buildings funded by Andrew Carnegie.

San Diego Public Library

Statistics have been available for many years describing the number of public libraries in the U.S., their holdings, budgets, and personnel. Counts of items circulated have also been recorded, but the range of items available is not known on a national scale. In addition, no national data exist that describe the number of other services (that is, besides circulation) available from public libraries and the use of these services. Statistics on public library services in other countries are similarly scarce. The Unesco *Statistical Yearbook* records holdings, budgets, and personnel for public libraries in each nation but says nothing about services.

From one perspective, everything a library does is a service, but it is also possible to think of services as those activities that library staff perform in direct response to patron requests or in anticipation of patron interest. Services in this second sense are listed in Table 1, an adaptation of a list that the U.S. National Center for Educational Statistics devised in 1979 as part of a study on public library service.

From this broad array of service activities a particular library can choose to emphasize a specific menu, which can be more broadly understood under the rubric of a library's "role." Once deliberately selected and articulated, these role statements will define whom the library serves, what it is trying to accomplish, and what resources it needs to fulfill its roles. In 1987 the ALA published *Planning and Role Setting for Public Libraries,* a manual devised by the Public Library Association to help public libraries identify their priority roles and plan, measure, and evaluate services to suit those roles. The standard public library roles identified are:

Community Activities Center: The library is a central focus point for community activities, meetings, and services.

Community Information Center: The library is a clearinghouse for current information on community organizations, issues, and services.

Formal Education Support Center: The library assists students of all ages in meeting educational objectives established during their formal courses of study.

Independent Learning Center: The library supports individuals of all ages pursuing sustained programs of learning independent of any educational provider.

Popular Materials Library: The library features current, high-demand, high-interest materials in a variety of formats for persons of all ages.

Preschoolers' Door to Learning: The library encourages young children to develop an interest in reading and learning through services for children, and for parents and children together.

Reference Library: The library actively provides timely, accurate, and useful information for community residents.

Research Center: The library assists scholars and researchers to conduct in-depth studies, investigate specific areas of knowledge, and create new knowledge.

Since no public library can offer all the service activities mentioned, nor adequately fulfill all library roles, a more specific focus on a set of selected roles that are most appropriate to a community's needs will result in more effective library service for the public.

COLLECTIONS AND MATERIALS

Collections in public libraries in the U.S. range in size from the New York Public's 9,000,000 or more volumes to Elk Township, Michigan's 900 volumes. They range in form from books, periodicals, reports, and clippings through recordings, films, and videocassettes to compact discs and CD-ROMs, microforms, and databases on magnetic tape. They range in content from the most scholarly to those in basic English for the functionally illiterate. They range in focus from materials for preschool children to materials for the aged. They include special materials for the handicapped, such as talking books or braille titles. They are as diverse as public libraries themselves, but always collections are at the heart of all public library service.

Collections are the concrete expressions of the public library's mission. In the words of the *Public Library Mission Statement and Its Imperatives for Service* endorsed by the ALA's Public Library Association (1979):

> Materials should be selected according to a written policy to support the library's program of services which have been designed to meet the unique cultural, informational, educational, and rehabilitative needs of the community. Relative emphases on these four needs should be determined by analysis of the individual community and by the availability of resources in all types of libraries within the community.
>
> Materials should be selected to meet the needs of as wide a variety of target groups as live within the community, including the literate, the illiterate, the educated, the undereducated, children, adults, aged people, hearing-impaired, visually and physically handicapped, and majority and minority cultures.

These imperatives reemphasize the position on collections expressed by the ALA's *Minimum Standards for Public Library Systems* (1966):

> The public library as an institution exists to provide materials which communicate experience and ideas from one person to another. The function is to assemble, organize, preserve, and make easily and freely available to all people the printed and nonprinted material that will assist them to:
>
> Educate themselves continually
> Keep pace with progress in all fields of knowledge
> Become better members of home and community
> Discharge political and social obligations
> Be more capable in their daily occupations
> Develop their creative and spiritual capacities
> Appreciate and enjoy the works of art and literature
> Use leisure time to promote personal and social well-being
> Contribute to the growth of knowledge.

Although the centrality of materials to the library's mission seems philosophically obvious, its importance is not always reflected in budget allocations. Funds for purchasing library materials take from 3 to 30 percent of total public library expenditures, with the average at about 15 percent (from reports compiled annually by the Public Library Data Service). The ever-increasing costs of library materials, both print and nonprint, and the escalating range of materials available make this statistic even more ominous.

Materials Selection and Collection Management. Theories of materials selection vary among public libraries from the "demand" position of the Baltimore County Public Library ("BCPL is committed to collecting, not a broad array of materials that librarians feel users should read or use, but those materials which most users do read or use") to the "should" position of many public librarians who base selection on principles of quality, authenticity, and social value. On this continuum most public libraries attempt to find a middle ground.

All public librarians agree however—in theory, if not in practice—that selection of materials should be made in the context of a written policy that articulates the objectives of the individual library or library system. The ALA Standards describe this policy statement as follows:

> This statement should be approved and supported by the governing body. It sets forth the purposes, levels of quality, and community needs to be reflected in acquiring materials. It describes the scope and emphasis and defines the limits of the collection; it affirms the institution's position on supplying resources on controversial subjects; and records the policies which govern withdrawals.

The materials selection policy is perceived by the library profession to be a guideline for the day-to-day selection and maintenance of the collections, a bulwark against attacks on intellectual freedom by community groups and individuals, and a statement to the library's public about what it can expect. The ALA Standards enunciate the broad principles that should underlie materials selection policy, such as:

> Materials acquired should meet high standards of quality in content, expression, and form.

Theodore F. Welch

Kyoto Prefectural Library

Gothenberg City Library

A bookboat from the county library in Gothenberg, Sweden, visiting islands off Sweden's west coast.

> Within Standards of purpose and quality, collections should be built to meet the needs and interests of people.
>
> Library collections should contain opposite views on controversial topics.

Collection management entails more than the articulation of general principles, however. The current emphasis in library planning on community assessment requires a careful analysis and response to both the stated and perceived needs of the public. Aging and expanding collections demand attentiveness to issues of preservation, deaccessioning, and efficient use of space. The impact of advances in technology and library automation on collection development has also been far-reaching. Public libraries can now use computer-generated collection analysis reports and use studies to make purchasing decisions. The development of regional, statewide, and national networks to link bibliographic records and process interlibrary loans provides the opportunity for cooperative coordinated collection development and use. The proliferation of CD-ROM resources presents both the advantage of enhanced access and the challenge of yet another pressure on dwindling financial resources as libraries struggle to encompass a universe of information that is no longer recorded only in print.

Carnegie Library of Pittsburgh. Photo by Ray Fleming

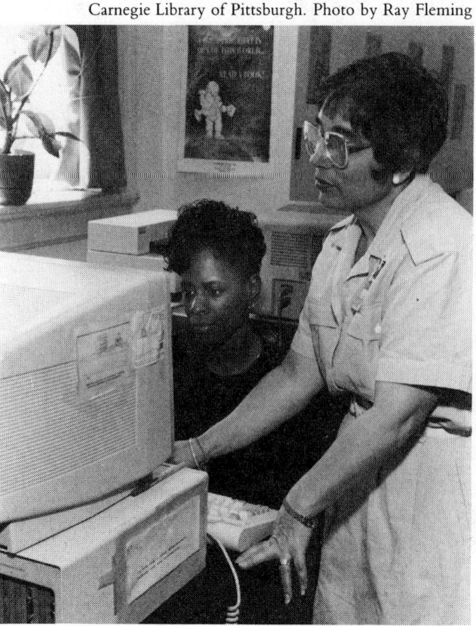

Librarian assists patron writing a resume at the Job and Career Education Center, Carnegie Library of Pittsburgh, Pennsylvania.

Materials Other than Print. Most libraries agree that public library collections should include more than print materials, although it must be acknowledged that the vast bulk of the human record is still in print and that extensive nonprint collections are probably the exception rather than the rule, especially among smaller public libraries.

The ALA Standards proposed that:

> To provide a reservoir of knowledge and aesthetic enjoyment which supplies inquiring minds, library materials [should] include a variety of forms:
>
> Books — Films, slides, filmstrips
> Periodicals — Music scores
> Pamphlets — Maps
> Newspapers — Recordings
> Pictures — Various forms of microreproduction

Books	Films, slides, filmstrips
Periodicals	Music scores
Pamphlets	Maps
Newspapers	Recordings
Pictures	Various forms of microreproduction

The later Guidelines are even more explicit and extensive in their concept of library resources:

> Library resources should include multiple forms—print, non-print, audio, visual, magnetic tape, etc.
>
> Human information resources in the community, as well as recorded experience should be considered part of the library's material. Community resource files, including information on organizations and agencies, their officers, activities, services, speakers, etc., should be maintained in all public libraries. Hardware to make use of microforms, audio and visual tapes, and slides, films and filmstrips, videocassettes, etc., should be available for community use.

The Audiovisual Committee of the Public Library Association published in 1975 *Guidelines for Audiovisual Materials and Services for Large Public Libraries* and *Recommendations for Audiovisual Materials and Services for Small and Medium Sized Public Libraries.* These are quantitative guidelines, proposed in the context of the following assumptions, stated in the former document:

1. Librarians are concerned with the products of imagination, intellect, and spirit.
2. All formalized communication formats are of interest to librarians.
3. Audiovisual materials and services should have equal weight, concern, familiarity, and support of library administrations and staff as those of printed materials. Integration of planning and programs, regardless of subject, format, or age level served, is required for the library to continue as a relevant agency.

These guidelines recommend that all public libraries, regardless of size,

> offer a variety of audiovisual resources [whether from their own collections or through a regional system], a minimum of 10–15 percent of the library's resources budget for

audiovisual resources, and that once an audiovisual department is established and operative, 10–15 percent of its materials budget be allocated for repair and replacements. Variables affecting basic staff and materials requirements recognized by the guidelines are:

a. population served
b. area of service in square miles
c. number of 16mm titles
d. hours open per week
e. accessibility
f. range of media

Although these guidelines would meet with little or no disagreement in principle from public libraries, the degree to which the specific, quantitative recommendations are being met is uncertain. The comment made by Lowell Martin in 1969 when he surveyed the Chicago Public Library in *Library Response to Urban Change* is probably still relevant today:

> One of the shortcomings of public libraries is a concept of resources limited to the book or at most to the book and the magazine rather than to the full range of communication media.

Increasingly, however, as Kathleen Molz has pointed out, public libraries are confronting the realities of a public who no longer depend upon print as the primary medium for news and information, who no longer have the leisure and education necessary for serious reading, and who indeed may not have mastered even basic reading skills needed for day-to-day coping. In this environment nonprint materials are certain to become increasingly emphasized in public library collections.

Intellectual Freedom and Public Library Materials. Issues relating to the preservation of intellectual freedom and guaranteeing the right to read are central to collection development in the public library. At first glance it would seem that the basic policies of materials selection are clear as enunciated in the Library Bill of Rights, first adopted by the ALA Council in 1948 and last amended in 1980:

1. Books and other library materials selected should be provided for the interest, information, and enlightenment of all people of the community the library serves. Materials should not be excluded because of the origin, background, or views of those contributing to their creation.
2. Libraries should provide materials and information presenting all points of view on current and historical issues. Materials should not be proscribed or removed because of partisan and doctrinal disapproval.
3. Libraries should challenge censorship in the fulfillment of their responsibility to provide information and enlightenment.
4. Libraries should cooperate with all persons and groups concerned with resisting abridgment of free expression and free access to ideas.
5. A person's right to use of a library should not be denied or abridged because of his origin, age, background, or views.
6. Libraries which make exhibit spaces and meeting rooms available to the public they serve should make such facilities available on an equitable basis, regardless of the beliefs or affiliations of individuals or groups requesting their use.

Despite the apparent clarity of the Library Bill of Rights, it has become necessary over the years to define its application in library practice by a series of "interpretations," also adopted by the ALA Council at

San Diego County Library (California)

Kapsala Community Library at the Viejas Education Center, Viejas Indian Reservation is maintained through the San Deigo County Library's Outreach Services program.

the recommendation of ALA's Intellectual Freedom Committee. A summary of the interpretations pertinent to collection development follows.

The statement of *Free Access to Libraries for Minors,* approved in 1972 and revised in 1981, affirms that a parent may restrict *only his or her* child from access to library materials, and that the librarian does not function as a parent. The statement opposes library procedures, such as restricted reading rooms for adults only, closed collections for adults only, and interlibrary loans for adults only, that limit access of minors to library materials. The statement affirms the *right* of children to *all* library materials rather than to only a part of a library's collection and sources.

The *Statement on Labeling,* first adopted in 1951 and amended in 1971 and 1981, opposed the techniques of labeling as "a 'censor tool,' a means of prejudicing readers against library materials." "Libraries," the statement declares, "do not advocate the ideas found in their collections, nor does the presence of books indicate endorsement of their contents."

The statement on *Expurgation of Library Materials,* adopted in 1973 and revised in 1981, defines *expurgation* as "deletion, excision, alteration, or obliteration" of any portion of any document or literary work (or

Biblioteca Central Estatal "Jaime Torres Bodet," Aguascalientes.

Bibliothèque Nationale, Paris

Municipal Library, Montreuil, France.

film). Such expurgation is declared a violation of the Library Bill of Rights because it imposes a restriction on the rights of library users to the full ideas the work was intended to express.

The statement on *Reevaluating Library Collections,* adopted in 1973 and revised in 1981, while endorsing the "continuous review of library collections to remove physically deteriorated or obsolete materials," warns against the abuse of this procedure as a kind of "silent censorship" of those materials considered too controversial or disapproved of by segments of the community.

The statement on *Challenged Materials,* adopted by ALA in 1971 and revised in 1981, declares that

> challenged materials which meet the materials selection policy of the library should not be removed under any legal or extralegal pressure.

The statement on *Restricted Access to Library Material,* adopted in 1973 and revised in 1981, opposes such library practices as closed shelves, locked cases, and "adults only" collections. While the statement recognizes that these limitations differ from direct censorship activities such as refusal to purchase or subsequent withdrawal of controversial publications, they do constitute a form of "subtle" censorship and should be avoided.

The statement on *Circulation of Motion Pictures and Video Productions,* adopted in 1984, advises libraries to

> apply the same standards for circulation (of these materials) as are applied to books. Just as labelling of books is deemed "an attempt to prejudice attitudes," so is affixing the MPAA rating codes to motion pictures and video productions.

McMillan Memorial Library, located in the center of Nairobi, Kenya.

The statement on *Diversity in Collection Development,* adopted in 1982, replaced a policy on Racism, Sexism, and Other -Isms adopted in 1973. That document had attempted to clarify the meaning of the Library Bill of Rights as it pertains to attempts to censor library materials because of alleged racism, sexism, or other isms. By the early 1980s it became clear that a broader statement covering the influence of conflicting values, philosophies, and points of view on library collections would be more appropriate. Hence

> Libraries have a professional responsibility to be inclusive, not exclusive, in collection development and . . . should not unjustly exclude materials offensive to the librarian or user. . . . Librarians have an obligation to protect library collections from removal of materials based on personal bias or prejudice.

Recognizing that maintaining principles of the Library Bill of Rights can be complicated, if not hazardous, the ALA, as early as 1962, adopted the statement *How Libraries Can Resist Censorship.* This statement recommends that public libraries as a matter of standard operating procedures:

1. Maintain a definite materials selection policy. It should be in written form and approved by the appropriate regents or other governing authority. It should apply to all library materials equally.
2. Maintain a clearly defined method for handling complaints. Basic requirements should be that the complaint be filed in writing and the complainant be properly identified before his request is considered. Action should be deferred until full consideration by appropriate administrative authority.
3. Maintain lines of communication with civic, religious, educational, and political bodies of the community. Participation in local organizations and in community affairs is desirable. Because the library and the school are key centers of the community, the librarian should be known publicly as a community leader.
4. Maintain a vigorous public relations program on behalf of intellectual freedom. Newspapers, radio, and television should be informed of policies governing materials selection and use, and of any special activities pertaining to intellectual freedom.

The public library profession recognizes its responsibilities: (1) to meet the general library and information needs of all users, actual and potential, young and old, educated and undereducated, handicapped or well; (2) to consider materials selection in the context of total available resources in a community, since no one library can provide access to the whole human record; (3) to defend the free flow of ideas against all censorship by means of a responsible, defensible selection policy; and (4) to provide materials in whatever form is appropriate to the ideas expressed and to the users to whom the ideas are disseminated.

The Library Bill of Rights and its interpretations were written and now function in a North American context. The general principles expressed are consistent with Unesco's Article 19 of the Universal Declaration of Human Rights, which IFLA adopted as its policy in 1989.

FINANCE AND ADMINISTRATION

The public library in the U.S. has since its beginnings adapted to the changing social environment because it sprang from democratic idealism and not from autocratic condescension. As a voluntary institution with no mandate in law, it flourishes on the goodwill of the citizen but for the same reason often lacks the scholarly aspirations of academic libraries. The quality of a public library's performance in the U.S. may be closely related to amount of financial support it receives; financial support and library excellence vary greatly across the nation. In the 1990s annual per capita support ranged from less than $1 in the poorest jurisdictions to well over $50 in others.

Finance. The key distinguishing feature of the public library in the U.S. is its local governance, mirrored in the shift to local governance in libraries in the U.K. since the 1970s. In the absence of federally imposed standards, state and local standards set the performance levels; even so, most state library boards lack legal authority to impose penalties and are resigned to an advisory role, leaving the local library to succeed or fail as it will. Of the 50 states only Hawaii has made the public library a function of state government. Beginning in 1986, Ohio set aside 6.3 percent of the state income tax to provide basic support for local public libraries, but without disturbing traditional local government. Elsewhere the library is a creation of county, city, town, or village as permitted by state law. The diversity thus spawned by decentralization is representative of the American preference for local decision making for human service. Reliance on local autonomy leads to an occasional jewel, but more often local poverty nurtures inadequate libraries and in some sparsely populated areas none at all. Local pride, however, may succeed in overcoming poverty to help local leaders form strong libraries. Some declining cities of the northeastern U.S. still boast superior institutions and support them well from shrinking tax bases.

The fiscal mainstay of the local public library has long been the property tax, while taxes other than those on real property are tapped in some states. (These exceptions will not be described here, since in general about 90 percent of library tax support originates in real estate, the remainder in grants from state or federal sources.) For most cities the property tax began to lose its reliability in the mid-1960s as taxpayers offered resistance to the mounting cost of local government. The changing climate manifested itself dramatically in California, where in 1978 a statewide referendum placed a ceiling on property tax rates. The economic problems and budget shortfalls at all levels of government in the late 1980s and early 1990s led to a decline in support of public libraries. Reports of service reductions because of budgetary stringency became numerous not just in all regions of the U.S., but in many parts of the world.

Not all the developments in public library finance were negative in this period; the mid-1980s saw some impressive gains in state aid to libraries, although some of those gains were eroded by the early 1990s. When given the opportunity to vote directly on library issues, citizens in many areas approved bond issues for library construction and renovation. Although fiscal instability was not the only challenge public libraries faced in the early 1990s, it was certainly the most serious, because it fundamentally affects their ability to achieve their purposes.

La Trobe Collection/State Library of Victoria

Melbourne (Australia) Public Library's great domed reading room, built in 1913.

Administration. Another feature of public libraries in the U.S. is their historical dependence on lay boards of governors, commonly designated as trustees, even though most such boards have only nominal or advisory authority. Library boards symbolize the democratic character of the library, and they exemplify the original motive of founders: to keep the library at some distance from politics. The public library is analogous to the public school with respect to its governance, for both sprang from the same generous social impulse and both developed complementary missions to educate the masses. Local lay control may be somewhat anachronistic in a management-oriented society where the professional overrides the proprietor, as it were; yet the library board can provide stability and continuity during changing times. Some boards had their origins in the private libraries that were the antecedents of contemporary public libraries, and it is not unusual today to find self-perpetuating boards with memberships largely confined to local elites. More commonly, boards are appointed by publicly elected officers; a few are elected by popular vote at the polls. Boards may possess taxing and budgetary authority, but just as often their control over money is nominal.

While a library board theoretically functions as a

Photograph by Carole Talan

Children and parents enjoy Storytime at Colusa County Library, an activity sponsored by the Families For Literacy program of the California State Library.

Metropolitan Toronto Library

Five-story Metropolitan Toronto Library, opened in 1977, one of the largest libraries in North America in seating capacity.

policy-setting authority, a director is responsible for implementing policy and administering the library day to day, managing the services, staff, collections, and facilities. Most public libraries in the U.S. function as departments of municipal or local governments and may share common personnel, purchasing, or maintenance procedures.

Libraries have traditionally tended to develop organizational structures along functional lines: materials selection, acquisitions, cataloguing, reference and information services, and circulation. Larger libraries and library systems add additional layers of services: public information, development, programs, and exhibits. As collection size grows, subject specializations proliferate and separate collections, service points, and staffs are maintained. As the geographic area and size of population served increase, a system of branch libraries may develop. The appropriate degree of complexity of an individual library's administrative structure, subject specialization, and branch configuration is a perennial challenge to public library leaders, who must strive to achieve the proper fit of the organization to the needs of the clientele it serves and to the resources available to serve those needs.

The quality and capabilities of library staff are another concern of public library administrators. In the past, major city libraries established in-house training schools for librarians before there was an adequate supply of graduates in the academic market. Many library schools had their origins in public libraries, and over the years public library administrators have championed high-quality academic preparation for librarianship. In the 1960s and 1970s, when professional were in short supply, some public libraries turned to training paraprofessionals.

While the supply of and demand for professional librarians have waxed and waned over the years, so too has the effort to enhance the stature and image of the librarians. Recruitment of capable candidates to the profession is hampered by the profession's relatively low pay scale and the perception of librarianship as a lower-status female profession and of the public librarian as a public servant. Professional associations and graduate schools worked to enhance the stature of librarianship by promoting a more positive image to the public, by working to upgrade salaries, and by encouraging increasing diversity in the race, age, and sex of potential library staff.

Library workers formed labor unions to enhance their working conditions. These unions grew rapidly in the 1960s and 1970s, but reached a plateau and then declined as the total number of library employees declined.

The managerial skills required to administer today's public library are complex and varied: political acumen, expertise in automation, skill in public relations, leadership ability, financial skills, and, most important, a keen commitment to service to the public.

Urban Libraries. The large urban library or the regional library system in a populous suburban area is a complex organization. Many diverse services may flourish in the large library. Literacy activities, cultural programs, art exhibits, assistance with English as a second language—all are representative of what may be found in a major institution. The urban library is normally characterized by an ample—sometimes monumental—building housing a major book collection located at the center of the commercial area of the city, accompanied by a system of smaller branches designed to serve residents in their neighborhoods. These outlying units are ordinarily further augmented by mobile services and outreach efforts in housing projects, day-care centers, and hospitals. A typical urban library is likely to invest more than half its annual budget in its central library. In the largest cities that central library may, in the range and complexity of its collections, achieve the stature of a strong university library. The chief characteristic that distinguishes the city library from an equally complex suburban library system is the central building itself. While suburban systems perform extremely well in meeting citizens' reading demands by many standard measures, the urban central library remains a unique institution. A few of the finest research libraries in the U.S. are in fact public central libraries: New York, Boston, Philadelphia, and Cleveland, for example.

The uniqueness of the urban central library has inadvertently established an urban-suburban rivalry for tax dollars. Suburban libraries do not have to maintain massive research collections in large, monumental buildings. They can perform more efficiently

Children participate in a group chess match at a public library in Cienfuegos, Cuba.

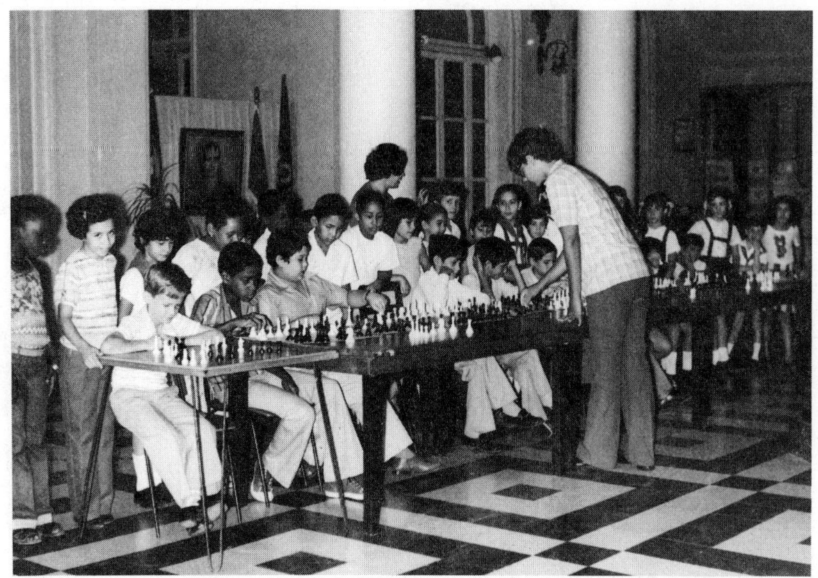

and operate at lower cost by focusing on circulating books, their chief activity. The flight of the middle class to the suburbs caused urban libraries to serve the same people who, after leaving the taxing area, no longer contributed to their support but continued to use them for materials and services their local libraries did not provide. The stress caused by these demographic and service patterns is not unique to library services, but it poses extremely serious problems for library boards and directors faced with providing high volumes of service and access to expensive collections primarily for nonresidents. The imbalance between the tax support and library patronage has been rectified constructively in some jurisdictions through contracts designed to divert suburban tax revenues into the city. Mergers between urban libraries and adjacent suburban systems have also been successful. Despite isolated examples of success, many cities continued to struggle with this issue. Evidence of interest in a totally different solution is beginning to appear—the designation of urban central libraries as state resources, giving the state government a stake in the maintenance of a city's intellectual treasures.

Long before the central library became too heavy a burden for cities to carry, New York City by historical accident created a dual library system: a publicly funded popular service system of branches, and a privately funded main research center. In 1976 Toronto, starting from altogether different premises, divided its main library from its branch system and created a new board representing the entire district to control the main and now independent unit. The branch system continues as before under its separate board. New York City and Toronto may not be typical, but one way or another library leaders are emphasizing the distinction between main and branch libraries.

The tension created by the need to serve both the local population, represented by the branches, and a wider constituency, represented by the main library, is one of the many pressing challenges facing today's urban libraries. The critical special needs of urban populations—illiteracy, substandard health care, poverty, poor schools—demand innovative service solutions. In attempting to grapple with these issues, even in a time of declining financial support, urban public libraries are pioneering services that are vital to the educational and economic advancement of the people they serve. Nowhere is this more evident than in their response to the changing demographics of urban populations. Migrations of populations worldwide have precipitated ambitious efforts to provide services relevant to a multicultural populace composed of significant "majority" minority populations. Librarians in California have led the way in their broad offerings of collections, staff, and services specifically suited to their increasingly diverse constituents. Such new initiatives are continuing evidence of urban public libraries' vital involvement with and adaptability to changing public needs.

The Future. The last years of the 20th century will put heavy pressure on library managers. The destabilizing forces of poverty and resource depletion that agitate all institutions pose a particularly unsettling challenge to libraries. As reading declines, as illiteracy spreads, as computers, video, and telecommunications make inroads on the library's traditional clientele, how will the profession respond? Problems appear now where all was thought to be safe and secure. In the U.S. children's use of public libraries, once the staple of public library services, has been halved since the mid-1950s; in most cities children's circulation is now only about one-third of the total. Americans are using their libraries more heavily as information sources rather than as reading centers, a phenomenon also reported elsewhere in the world.

Libraries now have the capability of answering reference questions by means of access to remote databases in preference to using printed sources. While faster, the service is more expensive, and it can drive the cost of reference service to prohibitive levels. This phenomenon is bringing into question the validity of the "free" public library. Increasingly, the "free" library is being challenged by economists and politicians, many of whom advocate placing the cost burden on the beneficiary of the service rather than on the tax rolls. Such political opinions generate strong resistance among traditionalists who hold to egalitarian standards. This battleground will be fought over in the decades ahead, and in the dust of conflict the library director will require diplomatic arts to maintain a stable and safe institution. Whatever the outcome in this conflict, or any of the others, one point is indisputable: the tempo of change is speeding up, and the pressures on the managers are growing. Yet library administrators who delay decisions while awaiting a clearer view of the field will not serve their institutions well. A flexible posture is required, a willingness to move with emerging forces and still retain inviolate the fundamental principles of librarianship. It is not an easy period in public librarianship, but it may yet be the most fertile in ideas.

MEASUREMENT AND EVALUATION

If a library cannot provide evidence of its accomplishments, it will generate little support from its funding sources. As public library systems throughout the world become more sophisticated, more time is spent on measuring and evaluating their performance. In the 1960s and early 1970s there was a tendency to centralize work in each country and to rely on ever more detailed quantitative measures. Beginning in the 1980s the emphasis moved to decentralization and to

National Library of Poland

Municipal library of Zielona Góra, Poland. It features mosaics and billboard-high signs for identification.

Bulawayo and District Publicity Association

Mzilikazi Memorial Library, Bulawayo, Zimbabwe.

qualitative rather than quantitative measures of performance.

Standards. The tendency toward qualitative measures is particularly noticeable with the development of new public library standards. Traditionally, standards have been devised centrally by a professional association or a government agency. They have been expressed in numerical terms and related to inputs—that is, the number of staff, number of books, and number and size of service points. Furthermore, they have been compiled with the implicit assumption that what was appropriate to a library in one kind of community was appropriate to other libraries serving very different communities.

The newer forms of standards tend to reject this assumption and accordingly are framed in rather different ways. Modern standards start from the proposition that public library systems should themselves determine what is appropriate in their particular circumstances. There is much more emphasis on providing a framework or methodology that can be used to calculate the number and proportion of inputs required for a given output or level of service. The end results of this approach are standards that are more difficult to apply in individual circumstances but that take much more account of local variations.

A good example of the traditional form of library standards is the *Standards for Public Libraries* issued by IFLA in 1973. These were formulated to provide "guidance as to the levels of provision needed to maintain efficient library services . . . and should provide a basis for the formulation of national standards." They are expressed in terms of the various quantities of each input thought to be required to meet the needs of given levels of population. The standards were framed in the specific belief that "separate standards were not desirable, since the general objectives in all countries are the same."

In direct contrast to the IFLA Standards are those concerning the *Staffing of Public Libraries,* published by the U.K. Department of Education and Science in 1976. These standards were calculated on the basis of detailed work study exercises that examined the various tasks undertaken in a modern public library. The result is a series of formulas that can be applied to produce information on the number of staff needed to provide a given level of service in the light of particular local circumstances.

Other examples of the new way of thinking about standards are *A Planning Process for Public Libraries* (1980) and *Output Measures for Public Libraries* (1982), published by the ALA's Public Library Association. The purpose of this project was to formulate library standards based on library services (outputs) rather than library resources (inputs) based on a review of goals, objectives, and performance. Many libraries used the process outlined in these manuals and incorporated output measures and planning into their administrative efforts. In doing so, they discovered that they needed assistance in articulating priorities for service roles and that they needed comparative quantitative data. In response to these needs, *A Planning Process* was revised (1987) to include the role-setting process and *Output Measures* was revised (1987) to integrate more closely with the planning process. Further, the Public Library Data Service (PLDS) was established to collect and make accessible data from libraries across the U.S.

The development of these programs has replaced the move for prescriptive national standards, leaving the impetus for such efforts to state and local agencies if deemed appropriate. While these new evaluation methods have been widely used, questions have arisen as to their applicability to all library communities. Some have questioned the appropriateness of drawing comparisons and judging the quality of library service among libraries that have selected fundamentally different roles and that serve communities with very different social, educational, and economic characteristics. Qualitative comparative judgments can have a serious impact if they are used as a basis for funding decisions, because they will serve to justify rewarding the "good" output producers and penalizing the "bad." At the same time, since libraries are held accountable by the agencies that fund them for measuring and evaluating their own performance, the continued use of this program, and perhaps its continued revision, seems assured.

Research. In addition to the largely unpublished research of individual libraries initiated during the planning process, there is also a rich body of published research on the library's public, both users and nonusers. From the 1940s on, many researchers have polled, surveyed, and sampled the public's opinion on libraries and their uses, library users' characteristics, and the factors that influence use. An example is the 1990 Louis Harris survey, "Consumers in the Information Age," which found that six out of ten people reported using the library during the previous year. The survey also reported increased use of almost all specific library services since the previous national survey, conducted by George Gallup in 1978. The Harris survey corroborated the consistent increase in measurements of use reported by libraries—more than 45 percent increase in circulation per capita in the decade of the 1980s.

In 1991 the University of Illinois Library Research Center conducted the first annual survey of library service, materials, governance, and financial support. This survey polled both librarians and the general public and found a wide discrepancy between public and professional opinions on libraries. In general the public perceives a broader social and educational role for libraries than librarians do, but a more conservative attitude toward the collections. National research of this kind provides a cogent context for local decision making based on local concerns.

PUBLIC LIBRARY LEGISLATION IN THE UNITED STATES

The earliest legislative measure in the U.S. dealing with public libraries was enacted in 1848 as a special act of the General Court of Massachusetts, authorizing the establishment of the Boston Public Library. A year later a general act was adopted by the legislature of New Hampshire authorizing cities and towns to establish free tax-supported public libraries. The other New England states adopted similar laws between 1851 and 1869. In 1872 Illinois approved a public library act that for the first time provided for separate boards to govern public libraries; the Illinois law was more comprehensive than the New Hampshire act and served as a model for many of the western states to follow.

Public Library Acts. Every state in the U.S. has a public library act that provides the legal basis for the establishment, governance, administration, and tax support of public libraries.

One of the major provisions in a public library act is a grant of authority from the legislature to the municipality empowering it to establish a public library. There are three such types of grants. In most states the grant is extended to the corporate authority—that is, the city council, village board, or county board of commissioners. In some states the law provides for a referendum of the voters to decide whether a public library is to be established. And in a few states the statute permits the establishment of a public library initiated by a petition addressed to a municipal body and containing the signatures of a requisite number or percentage of the legal residents.

Another vital provision in a public library act is the grant of power to levy taxes for library purposes. This authorization is made to the corporate body and not to the library board, except in certain district libraries that are expressly granted such power. Funding is made available in one of two ways: (1) through a special library tax on property, usually expressed in terms of a millage rate as, for example, one mill or more on each dollar of the assessed valuation of property; or (2) through a lump sum appropriation from the general revenue of the municipality.

A third important provision in a public library act relates to the governmental structure of the library. The law usually provides for a board of a specified number of directors, appointed or elected for a given term of years, and enumerates the powers and duties of the board.

There are a variety of other provisions. Almost all public library acts provide that use of the library shall be forever free to the inhabitants of the municipality. A provision authorizing the corporate authorities to provide suitable penalties for persons committing injury to library property or for failure to return books belonging to the library is also included. An extremely significant provision is the requirement that the proceeds from the library tax must be kept in a separate fund, designated as the "library fund," and must not be intermingled with other funds of the corporate authority. A common provision requires the library board to submit an annual report to the corporate authority as well as to the state library agency. Finally, a large number of the laws provide for joint library service between two or more governmental units.

Newark Public Library

The Newark (New Jersey) Public Library celebrates Kwanzaa, an African harvest festival.

Federal Legislation. The federal government was a latecomer in the field of public library legislation. More than a century and a half elapsed before Congress took any legislative recognition of public libraries. In 1956 Congress passed the Library Services Act. Designed to promote the extension of library services to rural areas, it was in essence a library demonstration program for rural communities. To participate in the program, a state was required to submit a plan for extension of library service that had to be approved by the U.S. Commissioner of Education. In 1964 the Library Services Act was amended, making it applicable to all public libraries, urban as well as rural, and it became known as the Library Services and Construction Act (LSCA).

LSCA now consists of six titles: Services; Construction; Interlibrary Cooperation; Older Readers Services; Foreign Language Materials; and Library Literacy Programs. Over the years the proportions spent on various titles have varied: in 1979 Congress appropriated $62,500,000 for services, $5,000,000 for interlibrary cooperation, and nothing for the other titles; in 1992 Congress appropriated almost $130,000,000 for services, nearly $84,000,000 for construction, almost $17,000,000 for interlibrary cooperation, more than $8,000,000 for library literacy programs, and less than $1,000,000 for foreign language materials.

LIBRARY COOPERATION

A basic principle of public libraries is equal access to information. Economic necessity and the need to increase the effectiveness of individual libraries have spurred cooperative efforts among groups of libraries to achieve equity of access, at least, for individual library users. Small libraries are particularly threatened by the complexity and cost of automated systems and their inability to purchase the full range of resources their patrons need. Large libraries have difficulty managing the acquisition, storage, and maintenance of complex collections because their operating costs tend to rise, regardless of increases or decreases in the amount of public service rendered. Library administrators in both large and small libraries try to substi-

Qaid-e-Azam Library in Lahore, the main reference and research library for Punjab Province, Pakistan.

tute sharing for endless growth. Initial cooperative efforts tended to be joint projects to accomplish routine library functions: to catalogue, process, or store materials, for example. Other cooperative activities have entailed building joint bibliographic records, such as indexes, catalogues, and union lists. The most common form of cooperation has been interlibrary lending of monographs and serials. Traditionally these arrangements were voluntary and informal, and the largest libraries bore a high proportion of the administrative costs, as well as the costs of being heavy net lenders.

Recent experience in a more cost-conscious age has shown the limitations of the older systems of voluntary cooperation. The small members tend to contribute little of significance; the administrative costs of maintaining union location lists are considerable. There is a tendency to abuse the facilities of the cooperative to compensate for basic weakness, ultimately hindering pressure for real improvement through consolidation of nonviable libraries and more adequate funding for units with a potential to be largely self-sufficient. Critics doubt whether such cooperatives really achieve improvement in access to resources. There is a further problem in the metropolitan areas that are served by the greatest concentration of public libraries in that the new multibranch suburban systems, serving mainly the prosperous communities, make no contribution to the major reference collections in the declining urban centers.

The new generation of cooperatives and networks (cooperatives based on computers and telecommunications, and necessarily formal in their procedures) has to be cost-effective, not so much extending equity as offering a more economic trade-off between building up local resources and buying services or obtaining them at the expense of a higher level of government. This approach requires a wider definition of cooperation, perhaps as contractual services. Many new library networks are multitype and broker remote commercial or fee-charging public services providing bibliographic processing of information. Another characteristic, in the U.S. and Canada, is the use of cooperatives as a means of applying federal or state/provincial funds so as to reorganize and strengthen a group of autonomous public libraries, inherited from an earlier period, when the aim was for each town or city to provide itself with a general cultural facility, on a scale determined by local means and willingness to pay.

The complaint about "localism," that is, jealous preservation of autonomy, so often heard from network planners, derives from a conflict between the traditional view that the local library, with its permanent collections, is largely self-sufficient, and the planners' view that local libraries should serve primarily as public service outlets, with technical services support coming from a central service elsewhere and distributed to libraries as needed. The planners are unlikely to prevail in isolated towns and small cities unless they can "buy themselves in" with funding from other sources. Here is the fundamental structural weakness that faces public libraries in the Anglo-American and Scandinavian countries that pioneered the type. In Canada public libraries outside the metropolitan areas are inadequately funded and organized and are too small. Similar problems affect countries such as Germany, trying to build public library networks side by side with outmoded types, and such socialist countries as China, where public libraries have been established as widespread community services.

In the U.S., where more than 350 consortia are already in existence, the trend seems to be best illustrated by Illinois, where regional networks based on major public libraries are being merged into a multitype state and interstate network, which, while limiting the growth of the powers of the public library systems, also provides a highly efficient service delivery mechanism. A general prediction has been made that the future public library will serve primarily for face-to-face public services and as a switching point or broker between users and information, regardless of location. Illinois shows the logical result of such thinking in a statement on collection management policy that envisages that every library unit will concentrate its local resources on satisfying expressed demand, without constraints of quality or literary merit—a qualification clearly aimed at the public library sector. Others have argued the dangers of systematic shedding of less-used material, among them a loss of browsing value and of demand derived from immediate availability. In other countries different methods for getting around administrative fragmentation are used; for example, in Germany the Einkaufzentral in Reittlingen functions as a purchasing and servicing agency for public libraries and for two research and planning bodies. In developing countries such as Malaysia and Singapore public libraries are being built up on a planned basis with strong direction by the national library.

The U.K. provides the prime example of the corporate approach. The various libraries at the national level have been integrated under the British Library Board with its divisions for reference, lending and bibliographic services, and research and development. At the local level most people in England and Wales are now served by county libraries for an average 600,000 population, with library authorities in the metropolitan areas serving populations between 250,000 and 350,000, or rather less in London. The British Library Board has a specific duty to provide support to the whole library and information community and is thus creating networks of service that are modifying existing cooperatives. The Lending Division (BLLD) serves as an example. It dominates the national interlibrary lending of serials through mass photocopying and is in the process of establishing similar preeminence in monograph loans. A recent development is the establishment of a national delivery service, achieving more than 80 percent success in document delivery in 24 hours and almost complete success in 48 hours. The individual library is still able to borrow directly from others in the region using an ISBN list of holdings or can go directly to BLLD or indirectly through the regional bureau.

Cooperation between public and school libraries had left much to be desired in the past. In the U.S., where school libraries have been professionally staffed for generations, school and public library relations were still being defined as a problem in 1972 because of poor communications with teachers on study assignments and a lack of role definition. The school-public library seems at first sight to have much promise for giving rural areas improved library services. Promising developments were reported from New Zealand, but Newfoundland abandoned the practice. In the U.K. dual-use libraries are growing in number after a slow start. In Adelaide, Australia, the experimental use of school audiovisual materials by the general community is one positive gain from such cooperation.

Jurisdictional boundaries between public libraries and other social agencies that have library and information needs, especially at the metropolitan and regional level, form a barrier to developing the full potential of the public library. Of 300 Regional Councils of Government (COG) in the U.S., only three had library components; Denver is cited as an admirable exception to the rule. In the U.K. the Department of Education and Science saw opportunities in the local government reorganization of 1974 for a corporate library and information service reaching out to schools, social service establishments, hospitals, and prisons, and also a special library service to local government. This was made simpler by the concurrency of powers of the new local authorities. The original British impetus in multitype cooperatives was to provide a serials lending service, a declining need with the arrival of BLLD. Major British research-type public libraries do not have the advantages of metropolitan Toronto in that services to their region generally are supported by the local taxpayers in the core city.

The literature of cooperation tends to ignore the role of the public library as a cultural agency. In Bulgaria public libraries are housed in cultural centers; in France a public library is an important function in a *Maison de la Culture;* in the U.K. most metropolitan public libraries are administered as part of a leisure or cultural directorate, although the library profession does not support this practice.

Participation in automated networks is of two kinds: to support internal operations and to provide user services. The latter are easily assessed, as they provide additional resources at an established cost, but participation in joint cataloguing, processing, and collection management involves in addition a partial loss of control of standards and performance.

Given a choice between centralized shared cataloguing and working with a regional consortium, public librarians prefer the latter because they normally have a voice in policymaking. Critics of OCLC and similar systems argue that they are based on an obsolescent configuration of a remote mainframe computer, with heavy line costs, and that the new networks will be based on chains of local microcomputers linked to one another to give a distributed national database. One side effect of using automated cataloguing is the long delayed abandonment by North American libraries of expensive card catalogues in favor of online systems and CD-ROM catalogues. The real gains in public library applications of automation lie in an integrated approach to all internal operations. Small public libraries, in particular, may always find it better to delegate as much as possible of their internal systems to a remote agency, where standards will be superior, and where costs will probably be lower because of subsidies. There are cooperative examples of practically every library operation from preselection of stock to staff placement, which are often substitutes for consolidating small library units.

Diechmanske Public Library, Oslo

Diechmanske Public Library in Oslo, which provides listening facilities, and sound circulating collections.

Social, technological, and communications advances of the late 20th century are having an impact on a public library sector still structured on a 19th-century model. One of the responses of public libraries has been to create larger units of administration and to fund coordinating mechanisms, of which the fast-growing library and information networks are an example. The involvement of public librarians in the activities of these networks is key to their future development and to the future of public libraries.

REFERENCES

Goals, Guidelines, and Standards Committee of the Public Library Association, *The Public Library Mission Statement and Its Imperatives for Service,* (1979).

Lowell A. Martin, *Organizational Structure of Libraries* (1984)

Charles R. McClure et al., *Planning and Role Setting for Public Libraries* (1987).

Office for Intellectual Freedom of the American Library Association, *Intellectual Freedom Manual* (1989).

Ann E. Prentice, *Financial Planning for Libraries* (1983).

Section of Public Libraries of the International Federation of Library Associations and Institutions, *Guidelines for Public Libraries* (1986).

Nancy A. Van House et al., *Output Measures for Public Libraries,* 2nd edition (1987).

ALEX BOYD

Public Relations

Public relations as a professional skill is a late-20th-century development, the outgrowth of mass communication, mass marketing, and the coupling of both to stimulate action. Simply defined, public relations is a planned and sustained effort to establish mutual understanding between an organization and its public.

The practice of public relations involves researching the attitudes and opinions of the many publics an organization serves, advising management on attitudes and responses, helping set policy that demonstrates responsiveness, communicating information about the organization, and constantly evaluating the effectiveness of all programs.

Ironically, public relations has an image problem. It is often seen as simple publicity, which is just one of its tools, or friendly public manners. There is also a tinge of suspicion and distrust that may be associated with aggressive press agentry. Yet in spite of these misconceptions, public relations has become a powerful and indispensable tool of management. PR practitioners insist that they do not create images; a good reputation must be earned.

A public relations program may include merchandising, press agentry, promotion, publicity—rarely just one of these. PR is notably different from advertising alone, which uses paid space and time, while public relations depends on free editorial space and news or public service time.

History. Public relations was "invented" in the early 20th century when big business was forced to abandon its "public be damned" attitude. Such muckrakers as Ida M. Tarbell and Upton Sinclair were fighting corruption in business and government, and the public was reading, listening, and demanding reform. In response to their attacks, business produced a whitewash of words, one-sided communication, and little action.

In the first decades of the 20th century, both business and government learned that words could be used to shape public opinion in supporting institutions or actions. Ivy L. Lee demonstrated before World War I the value of cooperating with the press, instead of viewing it as a nuisance or, worse, an enemy. During the war, Woodrow Wilson's Committee on Public Information, headed by journalist George Creel conducted an "educational" campaign that sent American propaganda around the world; according to some historians, words won the war. Another pioneer, Edward L. Bernays, who wrote the first book on the subject, *Crystallizing Public Opinion* (1922), developed the theory of specialized publics, stressing that messages should be targeted to specific audiences.

Although public relations was not defined in standard dictionaries until 1946, it has since become part of everyday vocabulary and is an accepted management function. Few business or government organizations are without a public relations department, and two of the largest public relations firms in the late 1980s had more than 1,500 employees and annual billings that approached $85,000,000. Most PR practitioners entered the field through training or experience as journalists, but more than 175 colleges have student chapters of the Public Relations Society of America and offer a minimum of five courses in public relations.

Library Use. Libraries have made use of the philosophy and technique of public relations vigorously but inconsistently. As early as 1910 John Cotton Dana horrified some of his more staid library colleagues by using a billboard to advertise the library. He identified local interests and developed accordingly the libraries he directed in Denver, Colorado, Springfield, Massachusetts, and Newark, New Jersey, and he believed in telling the community what the library had and did. A major section of his practical guide, *Modern American Library Economy as Illustrated by the Newark, N.J., Free Public Library* (1910), was devoted to advertising and is still a useful tool. He asserts:

> Nothing is better for a public institution than publicity. The people who pay for its support are entitled to know—it is part of their education to know—all its ins and outs, its receipts, its expenditures, its methods, its plans and ambitions. Newspapers are almost invariably willing to print notes of these things. They feel that about the management of a public library there should not be, toward the public, the slightest intimation of a desire for secrecy.

His guide outlines many ways a library can involve its community and communicate effectively, from stories for the newspaper to working with local schools. His tradition of public relations has been continued by a profession that gives an annual John Cotton Dana Library Public Relations Award. Excellence in public relations in all types of libraries is recognized by this award program, established in 1946 by the H. W. Wilson Company and the American Library Association.

The Library Public Relations Council (LPRC) was founded in 1939, a decade ahead of similar organizations for colleges and schools. LPRC is devoted to investigation, discussion, and promotion of every phase of library public relations. "Public relations of libraries" first appeared as a subject heading in *Library Literature* in the 1943–45 volume, and the articles on the subject have been numerous.

In spite of early and enthusiastic interest in public

Library of Congress

Librarian of Congress, James H. Billington, heads a rally for libraries during the White House Conference on Libraries and Information Services, Washington, D.C., 1991.

relations, librarians have been uneasy about PR and have long debated its merits. A January 1974 *Library Journal* editorial, for example, protested the "selling of the public library." The writer objected to aggressive PR messages, holding that people need and will use the public library just as they use hospitals, schools, and other essential services:

> This commercial pap, when applied to an institution like the public library, may be effective to a degree, if we want to pack 'em in, but beyond its lack of dignity, it overlooks the basic justification for all public services—that people need them. No other essential public service finds it necessary to peddle its wares as if they were new appliances for a consumer public that is tired of washing dishes, preparing food from scratch, or having hair with split ends.

The editorial inspired a flurry of letters and articles on both sides of the issue. Confusion between public relations and publicity continues, and both are seen by some as undignified hucksterism. Billboards advertising libraries are still just as shocking to many librarians as they were to Dana's colleagues. A basic text on administration of the college library prefers the term *interpretation* to *public relations* "for reasons less of logic than of sensibility."

The 1980s saw major growth in the numbers of libraries—even academic libraries—that use public relations techniques. For example, in 1979 PR consultant Alice Norton found only three U.S. college libraries with full-time PR positions. In contrast, *College and Research Libraries* (September 1985) includes a PR survey by Vikki Ford of 48 library directors at universities with student enrollments of 9,000 to 12,000; the response rate of 85 percent suggests a high interest in public relations. Forty of the 41 respondents said their academic libraries conduct some form of publicity, and 17 reported planned PR programs assigned to individual staff members. Five directors rated their programs as highly effective in helping to protect funds during budget crises. Yet Ford noted that academic librarians had still not adopted PR programs wholeheartedly, and the majority saw their programs as only moderately effective.

In the late 1980s the library profession began focusing on development and fundraising, as the competition for public-sector funds became more intense. The use of public relations techniques became more sophisticated, more focused on planned communications strategies—more a necessity than a frill.

While public relations has growing recognition as an important and legitimate tool of library management, many library administrators are becoming even more interested in "marketing." As defined by Philip Kotler, an expert in marketing for nonprofit organizations, marketing is "that function of the organization that can keep in constant touch with the organization's consumers, read their needs, develop products that meet these needs, and build a program of communications to express the organization's purposes." In theory, marketing goes beyond public relations, in turning to the consumer for information about the products and services to be developed. Selling focuses on the needs of the seller, marketing on the needs of the buyer.

Should libraries make use of "business" skills such as public relations and marketing? A business produces goods and services, and its bottom line is profit; a nonprofit organization such as the library provides services, and its bottom line is "quality of life"; such a concept is considerably more difficult to measure than profit. A marketing approach can help a library develop a clear statement of its services and concrete plans for delivering them.

In his keynote address to the combined 1978 conference of the Southeast and Southwest library associations, O. B. Hardison, Jr., Director of the Folger Shakespeare Library, stressed the "imperative of responsiveness" and described the funding realities that make research libraries "ivory towers in the arena." Referring to lunchtime folk concerts designed to make the Library of Congress more open, less forbidding, he continued:

> The problem is not whether to enter the arena but, having entered, to plot a course that is compatible with the institution's long-range interests. This situation creates stress, but I think it is basically good. It is an adjustment to current realities. The alternative is—or seems to me to be—withdrawal and decline.

The question now should not be *whether* public relations is appropriate to libraries but rather *how* every public, school, academic, and special library can best use the techniques and skills of PR to assure that its services are well defined, understood, used, and supported.

U.S. library symbol, adopted by ALA in 1982.

Four Basic Steps. There are four basic steps in public relations: research, planning, communication, and evaluation. These are steps in a process that can be applied to any type and size of library. They are functions of good management.

Research involves identifying the library's publics and their attitudes toward the library. These publics may include the staff, governing board, volunteer or friends group, users and nonusers, and booksellers or other suppliers. Research should begin inside the library to determine how the staff and trustees view the library, how well they understand its goals and policies, what they see as its major strengths and weaknesses, and how they feel about their relationship with the library administration. The evaluation of the library should also include an objective view of its physical appearance, from the cold realities of access, signage, and lighting to the warmer considerations of welcoming comfort and ambiance.

Beyond the library, research involves gathering all available demographic information about its community: age, income, ethnic background, occupation, religion, interests, community groups, and whatever other formal or informal data are available. Original research should be undertaken to discern attitudes toward the library and information needs. Librarians have used many survey techniques to gather such information, among them mail questionnaires and telephone surveys of population samples and personal contact with and responses from clubs, churches, and other local institutions. The goal is constant sensitivity to public opinion.

Planning should make the PR process an integral part of the total library program. There should be a written PR plan with short- and long-range goals, a clear idea of the specific publics to be reached, a timetable and reporting schedule, lists of resources such as printing facilities, artists, and volunteers, a staffing plan, and a budget. Although most libraries are not in a position to afford the large public relations staff employed by major businesses, PR does require special expertise, and it cannot be done well without sufficient funding.

In 1983 Frank Wylie, Director of Public Affairs at California State University and former President of the Public Relations Society of America, completed a national survey of U.S. library PR programs. The results were presented to the Public Relations Section of ALA's Library Administration and Management Association at the 1983 ALA Conference. The national sample included 34 percent academic libraries and 66 percent public libraries. Of all libraries surveyed, 58 percent had PR programs, but only 19 percent claimed to have formal PR plans. Wylie commented, "librarians should insist on, and participate in, the development of a formal plan for the public relations program. You need the organization and focus that a plan can contribute. You also need to reassess your institutional mission and establish priorities and objectives for the library before you begin to develop a PR program to help you achieve those objectives."

Communication. The communication element of the public relations process comprises the outreach, programming, and publicity for which the research and planning prepared. One of the first steps toward communication for the library is building a media or press list of all available publications and broadcast channels, including daily and weekly newspapers, radio and television stations, community group newsletters, school newspapers, and any other media that may reach the target audience. Personal contact with the people on the press list is especially important. Libraries in the U.S. are eligible for free public service advertising time on radio and television stations, but must compete with many other community agencies and services.

Beyond mass media, there are many other publicity tools regularly used by libraries, including newsletters (internal and external), annual reports, posters, booklists and bibliographies, exhibits and displays, special programs, audiovisual presentations, speakers bureaus, and more. Some libraries prepare newsletters for specific groups, such as expectant parents and senior citizens. The Elmer Holmes Bobst Library at New York University introduced its new online catalogue with a mascot, "Bob Cat," that appeared on posters, T-shirts, and bookbags; it was even chosen to represent the NYU varsity basketball team. The Northwest Regional Library System in Panama City, Florida, reaches out to potential adult users with a series of special radio messages, including a bilingual 30-minute weekly program to help Vietnamese residents adapt to life in the United States.

Special Libraries Association

International Special Librarians Day was scrolled in lights across the top of the Philadelphia Electric Company buildings on April 9, 1992.

Evaluation, the final step of the PR process, requires that the public relations staff determine whether the communications program meets its stated objectives. One objective may have been media coverage, and a tally on how often radio and television stations carried the library messages along with a description of their audience is proof of achievement. Other means to evaluate a specific aspect of the PR program might include clips of newspaper coverage, use of evaluation forms at programs, or surveys in the library to determine how users found out about various services. It may be difficult to prove a direct cause-and-effect relationship between a communications program and increased library usage, but an attempt should be made to measure the impact of the public relations investment.

U.S. National Programs. There is a growing national effort in the U.S. to increase citizen use and support of libraries. Since 1945 the Children's Book Council has created posters and other promotional materials for Children's Book Week, observed each year since 1919. In 1958 publishers and librarians initiated National Library Week, the first and only national promotion program to increase use and support of libraries. The National Library Week program mobilized prominent citizens and librarians at the national and local levels to focus public and media attention on libraries. Workshops, handbooks, promotional materials, and national public relations support have made National Library Week a means to inform the public about library services, as well as an important public relations teaching tool for the profession.

ALA. After assuming responsibility for National Library Week in 1975, the American Library Association's Public Information Office (PIO) took a leading role in library public relations in the U.S. PIO expanded the scope of National Library Week to include Library Legislative Day, as a way to focus attention on the need for continued funding for libraries, and the highly successful "Night of a Thousand Stars—The Great American Read Aloud," featuring celebrities reading aloud from their favorite books in libraries in all parts of the country on the Wednesday of National Library Week.

ALA has continued to produce posters and other graphic materials that generate income for support of year-round PR efforts. It places radio and television public service announcements with the networks, feature stories and print public service ads in national magazines, wire service stories, and other national publicity.

In 1981 ALA launched a targeted campaign, "Call Your Library," to increase public awareness of telephone information services provided by public libraries. ALA also successfully lobbied the U.S. Postal Service for a commemorative stamp honoring America's libraries, introduced a national library symbol that has since received approval from the Federal

Highway Administration for use on highway signs, and collected and published *68 Great Ideas,* a book of promotion ideas for all types of libraries. In 1987 ALA and the National Commission for Libraries and Information Science announced a joint program, funded by the Reader's Digest Foundation, to provide every child in the U.S. with a library card. Libraries concentrate on this program each September as a back-to-school promotion. In 1983 the Gale Research Company began contributing a $2,500 annual award to recognize the most creative and successful library development projects.

The Public Relations Section of the Library Administration and Management Association, a Division of ALA, provides further national leadership in public relations. The 1,600-member section engages PR specialists from libraries across the country who work together to produce active and effective continuing education programs, workshops, and publications. Their annual "PR Swap 'n' Shop" has become one of the best-attended ALA conference programs and offers librarians a chance to sample promotional materials from libraries across the country and get expert counseling on PR matters. The Public Relations Section administers the John Cotton Dana Library Public Relations Awards.

Other Activities. The Library of Congress Center for the Book was established in 1977. Introducing the new Center, Librarian of Congress Daniel J. Boorstin said, "It is to organize, focus, and dramatize our nation's interest and attention on the book, to marshall the nation's support—spiritual, physical, and fiscal—for the book." Among its many successful programs, the Center for the Book established "Read More About It," a joint endeavor of the Library of Congress and CBS Television that has recruited hundreds of television stars to present 30-second messages promoting books and reading on their shows. The Center spawned state centers in more than half the states by 1992

At the grass roots, thousands of citizen delegates participating in the state pre-White House Conferences in 1978 and 1979 asked libraries to do a better job of informing the public of their services. Almost every state conference produced a resolution similar to this one from Ohio:

> Develop an aggressive, consistent, and better organized marketing, advertising, and public relations program using all available media and other agencies to increase public awareness of library and information services and their value to daily life, destroy stigmas, and improve the image of all libraries.

At the White House Conference on Library and Information Services held in Washington, D.C., in 1979, the delegates adopted as one of their major resolutions a statement on public awareness calling for "an aggressive, comprehensive national public awareness campaign coordinated at the federal level." Some of their specific recommendations, such as development of a national library symbol, were accomplished. Delegates at a second White House Conference in 1991 recommended "that model programs be created to market libraries to their publics, emphasizing the library as a resource to meet educational, business, and personal needs. The models should promote all elements and components of the library community."

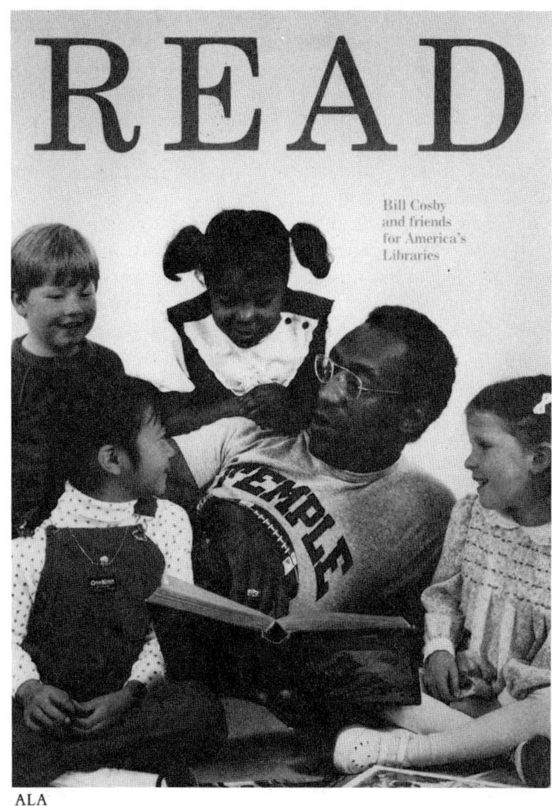

ALA

ALA celebrity poster promoting libraries and reading.

Citizen support of libraries is the concern of another U.S. national group, Friends of Libraries U.S.A. (FOLUSA), founded in 1980. With more than 2,000 individual and organization members, FOLUSA works to develop and support local Friends of Library groups throughout the country.

The special, medical, and law library associations also increased their interest in public relations, as evidenced by their publications and conference programs. A growing number of jobs advertised in their publications require communications and marketing skills.

Other Countries. U.S. libraries were pioneers in library public relations, but some of the same techniques have been used effectively elsewhere. National Library Weeks have been observed in Australia, Canada, Denmark, New Zealand, the United Kingdom, and other countries, though they are usually conducted on a more occasional basis than in the U.S. In the late 1970s, the Australian Library Promotion Council adapted the U.S. National Library Week graphics for its own week. Children's Book Week is a tradition known in the U.K. and Scandinavia. In Sweden the Library Service Ltd., started in 1951, produces a great variety of public relations materials such as posters, pamphlets, and booklists. Dutch libraries have an outstanding array of well-designed graphic materials, including a national library logo. In 1985 the Library Association in the U.K. launched its first nationwide library public relations contest, sponsored jointly with a library supplier, T. C. Farries.

In connection with the 1985 conference of the International Federation of Library Associations and Institutions held in Chicago, ALA and the Department of Library Science at Northern Illinois University sponsored an International Library Poster competition that generated more than 100 entries from 60 libraries and library associations in 22 countries. The judges selected posters from the Goethe Institute in London and the Australian Library Promotion Council as top winners. The overall response to the call for posters suggests a growing interest in library promotion worldwide.

How will librarians meet the growing demand for public relations programs? More and more library schools are offering seminars and short courses in public relations and marketing, as suggested in Unesco's "Guidelines for the Teaching of Marketing in the Training of Librarians, Documentalists and Archivists" (1988). Many include PR in a general library management course, and there are many programs and workshops offered at ALA Conferences and state and regional library association meetings.

A planned communication program is a necessity for passing a bond issue, competing effectively for funds, and generating the support needed to keep the library doors open and service flowing. Libraries will have a future as primary information resources if librarians use public relations principles and techniques to find political allies and build positive public opinion. It may well be a matter of survival. Abraham Lincoln said, "With public sentiment nothing can fail; without it nothing can succeed." Lee Brawner, director of the Metropolitan Library System in Oklahoma City, observed, "People are usually down on what they ain't up on!"

REFERENCES

Marian Edsall, *Library Promotion Handbook* (1980).

Philip Kotler, *Marketing for Nonprofit Organizations,* 2nd edition (1982).

American Library Association Public Information Office, *Campaign Book* (annual), a complete and inexpensive primer on the latest library PR ideas and opportunities.

PEGGY BARBER

Puerto Rico

Puerto Rico, since 1952 a self-governing commonwealth in association with the United States, is the smallest and most easterly of the Greater Antilles islands of the West Indies. It is bounded by the Atlantic Ocean on the north, the Lesser Antilles on the east, the Caribbean Sea on the south, and the Dominican Republic on the west. Population (1990 est.) 3,599,000; area (including the islands of Culebra and Vieques) 8,897 sq.km. Spanish is the language spoken in the island, with English and Spanish as official languages.

History. Priests who accompanied the early Spanish settlers brought collections of books to Puerto Rico. The island's first bishop, Alonso Manso, had a collection that is considered the first Puerto Rican library. It was burned in 1513 when Carib Indians destroyed the Spanish settlement. Two outstanding 17th century libraries were those of Bishop Bernardo de Balbuena (destroyed during a Dutch attack in 1625) and the Dominican Monastery. Termites and pirates were the main enemies of early libraries in the island.

The first printing press was established in Puerto Rico in 1806. The Sociedad Económica de Amigos del País (Society of Friends of the Island), founded in 1813, included a library that by 1835 started the first periodical and newspaper collection in Puerto Rico. A lawyers' association, El Ilustre Colegio de Abogados de Puerto Rico, founded in 1840, maintained a celebrated Law Library. The Ateneo Puertorriqueño, a cultural group founded in 1876, started its own library in 1883. That library absorbed much of the collection when the Sociedad Económica was abolished in 1899. Two important libraries outside San Juan were the Gabinete de Lectura de Ponce (1869) and the Biblioteca Popular de Mayaguez (1874).

The change from Spanish to U.S. rule in 1898 brought changes in institutions and associations, but not in interest in libraries. The Biblioteca Insular de Puerto Rico (1903) became the Carnegie Library when the governor obtained a Carnegie grant in 1916. Soon after, the Department of Education was given full control of public and school libraries. The 20th century saw the growth of all types of libraries, particularly academic libraries.

National Library. The Biblioteca General de Puerto Rico (General Library of Puerto Rico), established in the 1970s under the Institute of Puerto Rican Culture, has yet to assume the functions of a national library. Researchers of Puerto Rican subjects must turn to the Puerto Rican Collection of the José M. Lázaro Library at the Río Piedras Campus of the University of Puerto Rico, the General Archives, and other libraries. Various institutional libraries and professional groups perform other functions of a national library.

Academic Libraries. The University of Puerto Rico (UPR) is the public university and comprises 11 units in various parts of the island. There are three campuses: Río Piedras, the oldest and largest; May-

Libraries in Puerto Rico (1990)

Type of library	Number of administrative units (main libraries)	Number of service points (branches, mobile stops, etc.)	Volumes in collections	Annual expenditures (dollar)	Population served	Professional staff (with certificate, diploma, etc.)	Total staff
Academic	35	65	6,000,000	25,000,000	230,000	255	810
Public	132	139	800,000	3,500,000	3,200,000	5	235
School*	825	825	3,100,000	9,136,000	662,000	124	776

*Statistics for Department of Education System. Not available for private school libraries.

aguez, for many years an engineering and agricultural college; and Medical Sciences; university colleges at Humacao and Cayey; and six regional colleges. The Río Piedras Library System started as a small campus library in 1905 and grew to 18 units comprising libraries and special collections with holdings of more than three million items, including printed volumes, audiovisual materials, and microforms, and 6,000 periodical subscriptions. Among its units are the private collection of the Spanish poet Juan Ramón Jiménez, a Law School Library (134,000 volumes), an Architecture Library (25,000 volumes and 101,000 slides), and facilities for the physically handicapped.

The Mayaguez campus has a library with one main building and four smaller units (260,000 books and 2,600 periodical subscriptions), including its Agricultural Experiment Station Library. The Medical Sciences Campus (260,800 volumes and 1,500 periodical subscriptions) serves faculty and students and the island's medical community.

The Interamerican University and the Catholic University, two private institutions, have autonomous units in various parts of the island, each with a library. The Interamerican University has two campuses, in San Juan and in San Germán, and nine smaller units, with total holdings of 600,000 volumes. The Catholic University's main library, the Encarnación Valdés Library, and the Law School Library are in Ponce. The Ana G. Méndez Educational Foundation, a nonprofit organization, has three autonomous academic institutions, each with a library: Turabo University, Puerto Rico Junior College, and Metropolitan University. Together, their libraries hold 185,000 volumes.

All academic libraries in Puerto Rico have undertaken or are studying automation for library processes, records, and services. The Mayaguez campus library adopted the ATLAS system from Data Research Associates; the other libraries of the UPR are converting to the integrated NOTIS system from Northwestern University. General librarians conduct bibliographic searches using DIALOG or individual databases on CD-ROM; medical and law librarians utilize both North American law databases and Spanish-language services such as Compuley, for Spanish laws and jurisprudence, and Compuclerk, for Puerto Rican jurisprudence.

Puerto Rican academic libraries have a tradition of serving the general public, functioning as public reference libraries for the communities in which they are located, in part because of the inadequacies of the public library system. The José Lázaro Library of the UPR and the Encarnación Valdés Library of the Catholic University are heavily used by schoolchildren and the general public.

Public Libraries. The Public Libraries System is a division of the Educational Extension Area of the Commonwealth Department of Education. The System includes 67 public libraries in 63 municipalities, 29 small libraries in public housing projects, 25 in correctional institutions, and 7 bookmobiles to serve isolated and rural areas. It also administers the Regional Library for the Blind and Physically Handicapped in San Juan. The System is developing literacy programs, services to the elderly and to persons of limited English-speaking ability, and community information referral centers. The island also has 10 other public libraries under municipal administration.

Puerto Rico Public Library Services

Patrons at the Villalba Public Library in Puerto Rico.

School Libraries. The School Libraries Program of the Department of Education has 825 libraries. These libraries serve all high schools in the public school system, 85 percent of the junior high schools, and 63 percent of the elementary schools. Their collections include audiovisual and microform materials. The libraries offer bibliographic instruction, develop projects to motivate students to read and do research, and offer orientation programs for parents so they can be tutors for their children.

There are 14 pilot public-school libraries with microcomputers and educational software, fax machines, and other resources, including participation in the cooperative Library Involvement for Education Network (LIFENET). In addition, the island's private schools, religious and secular, have libraries, some with excellent resources and facilities.

Special Libraries. The San Juan area has special libraries serving a variety of needs and interests, including the Legislative Library, in the Capitol, for legislators and researchers; law libraries such as the Supreme Court Library; hospital libraries such as the one at the Veterans Hospital; and libraries in private brokerage and law firms. A library-museum specializing in Spanish incunabula is La Casa del Libro in Old San Juan.

The Profession. The number of professional librarians in Puerto Rico increased dramatically, starting in the 1960s, and professional activity and awareness grew with it. The School of Library and Information Science of the UPR, founded in 1969, was instrumental in this development. Its M.L.S. program was accredited by ALA in 1990. The Interamerican University has an M.L.S. program at its San Germán campus. The UPR Library School, the professional associations, and individual libraries offer continuing education programs.

The Sociedad de Bibliotecarios de Puerto Rico (Puerto Rico Librarians Society), founded in 1961, is the largest of four professional organizations. The others are the Asociación de Bibliotecarios Escolares de Puerto Rico (ABESPRI; School Librarians Association), the Asociación de Bibliotecas de Derecho de Puerto Rico (Association of Law Librarians), and the Asociación de Egresados de la Escuela Graduada de Bibliotecología (ASEGRAB; Alumni Association of the UPR Library School). Puerto Rican librarians participate in regional professional activities, particularly through the Association of Caribbean University, Research and Institutional Libraries (ACURIL).

REFERENCES

Arturo Morales Carrión, "Reflexiones sobre la Biblioteca en Puerto Rico," *Revista del Colegio de Abogados de Puerto Rico* (May 1972).

Public Library Services Program of the Department of Education of Puerto Rico, "Long-Range Program, 1990–94, of the Public Library Service for the U.S. Department of Education, Office of Educational Research and Improvement, Division of Library Programs," n.d.

EMILIA BERNAL-ROSA

ALA

Herbert Putnam

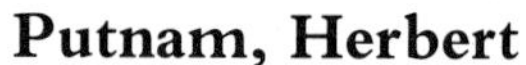

Putnam, Herbert
(1861–1955)

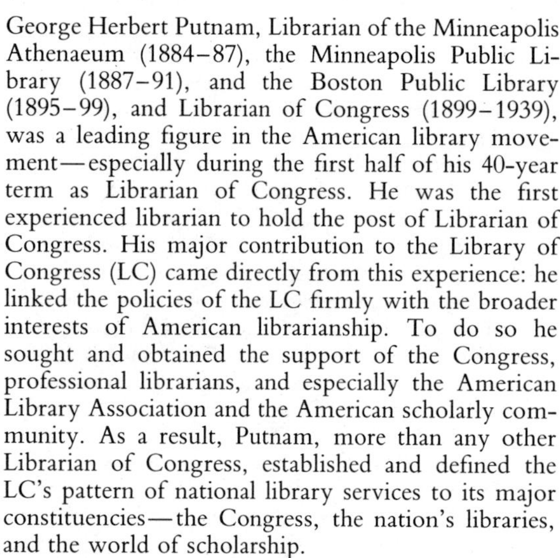

George Herbert Putnam, Librarian of the Minneapolis Athenaeum (1884–87), the Minneapolis Public Library (1887–91), and the Boston Public Library (1895–99), and Librarian of Congress (1899–1939), was a leading figure in the American library movement—especially during the first half of his 40-year term as Librarian of Congress. He was the first experienced librarian to hold the post of Librarian of Congress. His major contribution to the Library of Congress (LC) came directly from this experience: he linked the policies of the LC firmly with the broader interests of American librarianship. To do so he sought and obtained the support of the Congress, professional librarians, and especially the American Library Association and the American scholarly community. As a result, Putnam, more than any other Librarian of Congress, established and defined the LC's pattern of national library services to its major constituencies—the Congress, the nation's libraries, and the world of scholarship.

Putnam was born in New York City, September 20, 1861, the tenth child of Victorine Putnam and George Palmer Putnam, the founder of the Putnam publishing house. Herbert attended private schools and received his B.A. from Harvard in 1883, graduating magna cum laude. The next year he attended Columbia University Law School but was soon enticed by friends to Minneapolis as the head of the library at the Minneapolis Athenaeum. While successfully responding to the problems facing that institution, he pursued his legal studies and was admitted to the Minnesota bar. In 1887 he became Librarian of the new Minneapolis Public Library, which had absorbed the Athenaeum. After vigorously leading the Minneapolis Public Library through its fledgling years, Putnam resigned in late 1891 and returned with his family to Massachusetts to be near his ailing mother. He practiced law until he was persuaded to return to librarianship—as Superintendent of the Boston Public Library, the nation's largest public library. He assumed those duties in February 1895.

Putnam's leadership abilities and his new position quickly involved him in the American Library Association. From November 16 to December 7, 1896, the Congressional Joint Committee on the Library held hearings on the "condition" of the LC on the eve of its move into its new building, and Putnam was one of the ALA witnesses.

The Librarian of Congress at the time, Ainsworth Rand Spofford, had served for more than 30 years and was personally responsible for the rapid growth of the Library into an institution of national significance. The ALA sent six witnesses to the hearings. Putnam and Melvil Dewey dominated, each advocating an expanded national role for the LC—a role that extended far beyond Spofford's basic concept or his accomplishments. The two library leaders offered many specific suggestions for national library service.

The 1896 hearings marked a turning point in the relations between the LC and the American library movement. For the first time ALA offered its advice to Congress, albeit cautiously, about the purpose and functions of the LC. Moreover, Congress listened; the testimony at the hearings, along with a report filed by Spofford on January 18, 1897, were major influences on the reorganization of the Library that was contained in the legislative appropriations act for fiscal year 1898, approved by President Grover Cleveland on February 19, 1897. The restructuring and expansion of the Library simply could not wait for the report on the hearing held by the Joint Committee on the Library. Because the changes were part of the appropriations act, they became effective July 1, 1897, the beginning of the new fiscal year. On June 30, 1897, President William McKinley nominated his friend John Russell Young, a journalist and former diplomat, to be Librarian of Congress. The Senate confirmed the nomination on the same day, and Young was sworn in on July 1, the day the reorganization became effective.

Young did a remarkable job in the year and a half that he served as Librarian. After presiding over the move from the Capitol into the new building, which opened to great public acclaim on November 1, 1897, he concerned himself with organizational matters and new appointments. The new law authorized an increase in the staff of the Library proper from 42 to 108; Young was flooded with applications, and he chose well. Never a healthy man, Young did not recover from two severe falls during the winter of 1898–99, and he died on January 17, 1899. The newspapers were immediately filled with speculation regarding his successor. This time the ALA, through R. R. Bowker and William Coolidge Lane, ALA President and Librarian of Harvard University, took the lead. Two of Young's appointees, Thorvald Solberg and J. C. M. Hanson, worked closely with the librarians. On January 23, less than a week after Young's death, Lane wrote a letter to President McKinley, printed in the *Library Journal,* urging the appointment of an experienced library administrator as the next Librarian of Congress since that library—as the national library—should "stand at the head of American libraries as the best organized and the best equipped of all."

In the next few days, the ALA leaders settled on Herbert Putnam as their candidate. The story of how Putnam was finally nominated is complicated, but there is no doubt that without the intervention of the ALA he would not have become Librarian. William Coolidge Lane not only persuaded President McKinley; it appears that in the end he also persuaded Putnam. On March 13, 1899, during the congressional recess, McKinley appointed Putnam to be the eighth Librarian of Congress. Putnam took the oath of office on April 5 and was confirmed by the U.S. Senate, somewhat after the fact, on December 12.

With Putnam's appointment, the relationship between the LC and the ALA truly entered a new era. Putnam was not only a librarian's librarian but also an association spokesman. Twice he served as ALA President: from January to August, 1898, when he completed the unexpired term of the late Justin Winsor, and again in 1903–04. From 1900 to 1905, the critical years of his administration, he served on the ALA Council.

As Librarian of Congress Putnam moved quickly to expand the LC into the type of national library put forward in his 1896 testimony before the Joint Committee on the Library. He initiated a new classification scheme, the sale and distribution of printed catalogue cards, interlibrary loan, and a national union catalogue. In an appendix to his annual report for 1901, he described the organization and collection of the LC in a "manual" that came to be regarded as a model for libraries. Other Putnam actions during the first two decades of the 20th century included obtaining the support of President Theodore Roosevelt for the expansion of the LC's activities, perhaps most dramatically through an executive order transferring presidential and other state papers to the Library; revision of the 1870 copyright law, begun in 1905 and completed in 1909; the acquisition, in 1907, of collections of Russian and Japanese books, thereby establishing the foundation of the LC's Slavic and Oriental collections; and direction of the ALA's Library War Service Committee (1917–19), which was a model of efficiency and a triumph of American librarianship.

During the first half of Putnam's administration, lasting roughly from 1899 through World War I, the Librarian had, by and large, the full support of professional librarians and the ALA. The next 20 years were not so harmonious, and the LC and the American library movement drifted apart.

One reason was that Putnam gave increasing attention to matters that did not directly concern the American library community. A separate Legislative Reference Service was created in 1914. In 1921 the Declaration of Independence and the Constitution of the United States were transferred from the State Department to the LC, enhancing the image of the Library of Congress as a symbol of American democracy. In the mid-1920s, through Putnam's efforts, the LC became a national patron of the arts; a gift from Elizabeth Sprague Coolidge provided an auditorium for the performance of chamber music, and a generous endowment from Mrs. Coolidge shortly thereafter led to the creation in 1925 of the Library of Congress Trust Fund Board, an instrument that enabled the LC, for the first time, to accept, hold, and invest gifts and bequests.

Furthermore, Putnam's personal interest in library cooperation and related technical matters was replaced with an increasing concern for the "interpretation" of the collections. Putnam had always viewed the use of the LC's collections as the prime object of the administration; in the 1896 hearings, for example, he described the national library as, ideally, the library "which stands foremost as a model and example of assisting forward the work of scholarship in the United States." After the establishment of the Library of Congress Trust Fund Board, he began to obtain private funds to support "chairs" and consultantships for subject specialists who could aid scholars in their use of the collections.

In sum, as Putnam focused on other activities, his interest in the role of the LC as a leader among American libraries lessened. For example, in 1935, in a letter to ALA Secretary Carl H. Milam, the Librarian flatly rejected the notion of locating a federal library bureau in the Library of Congress, contending that the functions of such an agency "would tend to confuse and impede the service to learning which should be the primary duty of our National Library." In Putnam's opinion, the bureau instead "should be associated with one of the executive departments of the government."

Putnam's authoritarian style presented further difficulties. He was a stern administrator, both venerated and feared. Apparently no associate ever called him by his first name, and it appears that there was no one, either inside or outside the LC, who was able to influence him to any significant degree.

By the late 1930s the LC was suffering from administrative stagnation, intensified by low staff morale and operational problems such as a large cataloguing backlog. These problems were compounded by Putnam's refusal, or inability, to delegate responsibility. By 1939 there were 35 divisions, each reporting directly to the Librarian, compared to the 16 listed in his 1901 annual report. Even Putnam, with all his gifts, could not successfully oversee 35 diverse units and 1,100 employees. In the late 1930s there were many librarians and politicians who were waiting for Putnam to decide to retire. Apparently even President Franklin D. Roosevelt chose to wait.

Such difficulties aside, Putnam was enormously respected by scholars and librarians alike. When he did retire to become, on October 1, 1939, Librarian Emeritus of Congress, his friends in the American Library Association paid him tribute as "dean of our profession" who had led LC to "its present proud position as the world's largest bibliographical institution." He continued to contribute to the LC, keeping regular office hours, for the next 15 years. He died at Woods Hole, Massachusetts, on August 14, 1955. Putnam wrote no memoirs; his 40 annual reports between 1899 and 1939 serve as the record of his achievements at the Library of Congress.

REFERENCES

John Y. Cole, "Herbert Putnam and the National Library," *Milestones to the Present: Papers from Library History Seminar V* (1978).

John Y. Cole, "Putnam, George Herbert," *Dictionary of American Library Biography* (1978).

Wayne A. Wiegand, "Herbert Putnam's Appointment as Librarian of Congress," *Library Quarterly* (1979).

JOHN Y. COLE

Qatar

Qatar, an independent state, juts out from the Arabian Peninsula into the Persian Gulf. The Gulf lies to the west, north, and east; the United Arab Emirates and Saudi Arabia lie to the south. Population (1990 est.) 368,000; area 11,000 sq.km. The official language is Arabic.

National Library. The National Library in the capital city of Doha was founded in 1962 as a merger of two existing libraries: Doha Public Library (founded in 1956) and the Educational Library (1954). Modern librarianship in Qatar dates from this merger. With six branches, the National Library also functions as a public library. Operating from a new building, its staff started recataloguing and reclassifying the collections to produce a central catalogue for itself and the branches.

The National Library of Qatar has been a legal deposit center since 1982. It has issued the annual *Qatar National Bibliography* since 1970. The Library also has a center for exchanging publications with Arab national and university libraries, as well as with libraries in America, Europe, and other parts of Asia. Its book collection totals some 56,500 volumes in Arabic, 9,400 volumes in English, and approximately 1,300 Arabic and Persian manuscripts. It published on microfilm a catalogue of illustrated manuscripts, 1962–83.

Main Reading Room, National Library of Qatar, Doha. The National Library also serves as the main public library.

Administration of Information Affairs, Ministry of Education, Qatar

Public Libraries. Public libraries were established as branches of the National Library, following the Egyptian model. The first was opened in al-Khur in 1979 and the sixth in al-Wakra in 1985.

Academic Libraries. The University of Qatar, founded in 1973 as the College of Education, had more than 4,900 students in 1987, two-thirds of whom were women. In 1985 it moved into two complete campuses, one for men and one for women, with two separate libraries. By 1990 the libraries together held 259,000 books, almost 1,600 periodical subscriptions, and more than 6,500 microfiche, representing 137 titles.

With the help of the University Computing Center, the libraries started work on an automated system, beginning with acquisitions. The University Libraries provide retrieval service through DIALOG, interlibrary loan with other libraries of the region, and access to the British Library Lending Service.

School Libraries. The Ministry of Education has embarked on a plan for establishing and developing school libraries and making them an integral part of the curriculum. There are 167 libraries in Qatari schools, the largest of them in the secondary schools, the Religious Institute, the Institute of Administration, and the Institute of Languages. Together, the school libraries hold almost 350,000 volumes in Arabic and almost 40,000 books in other languages.

Special Libraries. The Ministry of Information and Culture has two special libraries, the Doha Culture Center Library (with almost 7,000 volumes and 200 periodicals) and the Cultural Library at the broadcasting station (with more than 5,500 volumes). The Hamad Medical Library holds almost 10,000 volumes and almost 700 periodicals. Government agencies such as the Advisory Council also have special libraries.

Doha has a number of private libraries. The Sheikh Faleh Library has 11,000 volumes in Arabic, many of them rare. The Sheikh Ansary Library holds about 25,000 volumes in Arabic, including many first editions and some works more than a hundred years old.

M. H. AL NASSR

Libraries in Qatar (1990)

Type of library	Number of administrative units (main libraries)	Volumes in collections	Annual expenditures (Qatar riyal)	Population served	Professional staff (with certificate, diploma, etc.)	Total staff
National	1	173,810	500,000	200,000	9	31
Academic	2	259,000(1987)	--	6,143	60	90
Public	6	158,415	--	100,000	9	37
School	173	427,672	--	60,987	--	150
Special	6	32,677	--	--	--	--
Other	2	36,000	--	--	--	--

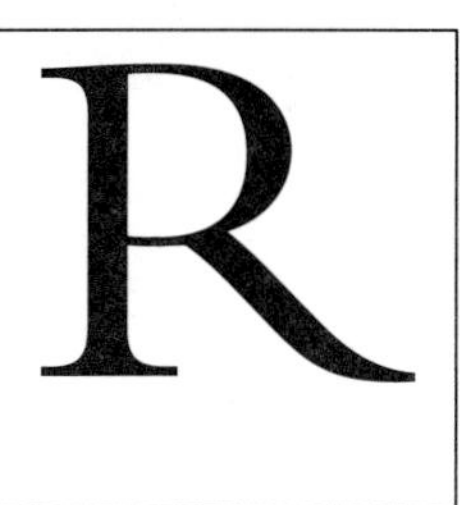

Ranganathan, S. R.
(1892–1972)

The author of *Colon Classification,* of many books and papers on classification, and of the Five Laws of Library Science, Shiyali Ramamrita Ranganathan of India stands as one of the immortals of library science.

Ranganathan was born August 9, 1892, into the Brahman community at Shiyali in the Tanjur District of Madras State. He was educated at Sabhanayaka Mudaliar's Hindu High School, Shiyali, from 1897 to 1908 and at Madras Christian College, where he majored in mathematics, from 1909 to 1916. He took a teaching diploma at the Teachers' College, Saidapet, Madras, in 1917 and became Assistant Lecturer in Mathematics at Government College (later Presidency College), Bangalore. In 1921 he was appointed Assistant Professor of Mathematics there.

In 1924 Ranganathan began a new career when he was appointed the first Librarian of the University of Madras. He was required to study for his new profession in Britain and went to University College, London, where he met and was considerably influenced by W. C. Berwick Sayers. During his two years in Britain (1924–25) he visited about a hundred libraries and was confirmed in his new vocation. He received an Honours Certificate from the School of Librarianship at University College in 1925 and was elected a Fellow of the (British) Library Association in 1930.

He remained Librarian of the University of Madras until 1944, later becoming University Librarian and Professor of Library Science at Banaras Hindu University (1945–47), Professor of Library Science at the University of Delhi (1947–54), and Visiting Professor of Library Science at Vikram University, Ujjain (1957–59). He was appointed Honorary Professor and Head of the Documentation Research and Training Centre, Bangalore, which he had founded under the auspices of the Indian Statistical Institute, in 1962; in 1965 the Indian government appointed him National Research Professor in Library Science.

Contributions. Ranganathan will almost certainly be best remembered by librarians for his *Colon Classification;* had he achieved nothing else, this pioneer faceted classification would have been sufficient to place him among the giants of librarianship. The classification is hardly used outside India, though at least two quite different British libraries (at Metal Box Limited and Christ's College, Cambridge) have used it, but its influence has been tremendous: on successive editions of the Dewey Decimal Classification, the Universal Decimal Classification, and, more recently, the Bliss Bibliographic Classification; on many specialist classifications; on various indexing methods; and on bibliographies such as *The British National Bibliography.* Chain indexing, developed by Ranganathan as a demonstration of the "symbiosis" between classification and subject indexing and as a technique for ensuring that aspects of a subject separated by a classification scheme are collocated in the index, is a method of subject indexing widely used in British libraries.

Apart from the *Colon Classification,* Ranganathan wrote many books and papers on classification, ranging from the introductory *Elements of Library Classification* to the monumental *Prolegomena to Library Classification.* Douglas Foskett has said that "in his writings, Ranganathan sometimes gave the impression that he was difficult or abstruse." To some extent this is true, but the *Elements* is not difficult to master, and the *Prolegomena* will repay considerable effort on the part of the reader.

But classification was only one of Ranganathan's interests, if a major one. His contributions to cataloguing include codes of rules for dictionary and classified catalogues, *Theory of Library Catalogue,* and a stimulating comparative study of catalogue codes, *Heading and Canons,* which K. G. B. Bakewell rates second only to Lubetzky's *Cataloguing Rules and Principles* as the outstanding contribution to cataloguing thought in the 20th century. As S. S. Agraval points out, Ranganathan's influence on the *Anglo-American Cataloging Rules* of 1967 was not inconsiderable, his canons of "sought heading" and "ascertainability" being particularly relevant.

Before any of these works came his analytical study of the purpose of libraries, resulting in the Five Laws of Library Science that formed the basis of his first published books on librarianship: books are for use; every book its reader; every reader his book; save the time of the reader; a library is a growing organism. Although many today would substitute "documents" or "library materials" for "books" (and say "every reader his/her document"), these laws are as valid today as they were when first enunciated. They seem—and are—simple, but they remain fundamental objectives of the library profession; Pauline Atherton said, "these words stir students to think of and believe in library *service* above library *work* as their life goal."

Some of Ranganathan's works were specifically concerned with the development of libraries in India. Following a request from the Punjab Library Association, he produced a pamphlet in 1944 on the postwar reconstruction of libraries in India, in which he proposed a national library network of national, state, university, public, and school libraries. This was followed in 1950 by a more detailed work, *Library Development Plan,* outlining a 30-year program. Library development in India was considerably influenced by these two publications, which were followed by library development plans and draft legislation for other Indian states.

There is scarcely an area of librarianship to which Ranganathan did not turn his attention: library management, school and college libraries, the broader aspects of libraries and education, book selection, reference service, and bibliography. In addition to his own writings, he edited many works and shared with others in the authorship of more books and papers. He founded *Annals of Library Science* in 1956 and *Library Science with a Slant to Documentation* in 1965 and edited both journals until they had become firmly established. Jesse Shera said, "That one cannot properly judge the work of S. R. Ranganathan without reference to the totality of librarianship is a tribute to the breadth and depth of his contribution to the profession."

International Library Scene. V. V. Giri, then Governor of Mysore and later President of India, described Ranganathan as "the father of library science in India" when presenting him with a copy of the Ranganathan Festschrift at Bangalore on December

Shiyali Ramamrita Ranganathan

18, 1965. This was an apt description, for Ranganathan had done more than anyone to further library development in India, but his work transcended national barriers. As Girja Kumar said, "He was universal because his work was not confined to any geographical boundary."

H. Coblans has written about Ranganathan's contributions to international librarianship: his influence on the development of the United Nations Library; his foundation of the International Federation for Documentation (FID) Committee on General Classification and his work as Secretary and Chairman of this committee; and his work for Unesco, the International Federation of Library Associations, and the International Organization for Standardization. His fervent belief in international standardization is well known.

Offices and Honors. Ranganathan had been a librarian for only four years when he was elected the first Secretary of the Madras Library Association, which he had founded in 1928; he held that office for 25 years. Such was his energy that he managed also to hold the office of Treasurer of the Indian Mathematical Society for six of those years (1928–34). He was President of the Indian Library Association, 1944–53, and of the Madras Library Association, 1958–67.

His other offices included: Chairman of the Documentation Committee of the Indian Standards Institution (1947–66); Vice-President of the Madras Library Association (1948–57); Secretary of the Indian Adult Education Association (1949–53); Vice-President of FID (1953–56 and 1958–61); Secretary and Chairman of the FID Committee on General Classification (1954–64). He was an Honorary Fellow of FID and an Honorary Vice-President of the LA.

Among his many awards are two of special distinction that he received from the government of his country in recognition of his achievements: the title *Rao Sahib* and the distinction of *Padmashree.* He was given an Honorary Doctorate of Literature by the University of Delhi and the University of Pittsburgh. In 1970 he was awarded the Margaret Mann Citation in Cataloging and Classification by the American Library Association. His contributions to library science were recognized in 1965 by the publication of a Ranganathan Festschrift to mark his 71st birthday. He died in Bangalore on September 27, 1972, at the age of 80. After his death the FID Committee on Classification Research further recognized his achievements by establishing a Ranganathan Award for Classification Research.

The Man. What kind of man was this energetic genius who was so immersed in his work? P. N. Kaula tells us that Ranganathan never took a single day's leave during the 20 years he spent as University Librarian at Madras. The Ranganathan Memorial Number of *Herald of Library Science* contains many personal anecdotes about Ranganathan and 14 obituaries, not only containing references to his analytical mind and consideration but also noting that he could be frank, intolerant, uncompromising, and selfish. Girja Kumar refers to his sense of humor, optimism, and interest in mysticism. V. V. Giri, when presenting the Ranganathan Festschrift to him, mentioned his humility and philanthropy but said that what struck him most about Ranganathan was "his enthusiasm and ebullient spirit which even many a youth in the country could envy."

Perhaps the most moving accounts of Ranganathan as a person have come from English Librarian Bernard Palmer, who told how, inspired by reading the *Prolegomena* when he began to teach classification in 1940, he made a vow that if ever he had the money, he would go to Madras to meet the author. The opportunity came only a year later when, serving in the Royal Air Force, Palmer found himself at a camp on the outskirts of Madras. On his first free afternoon he went to the University Library and introduced himself to Ranganathan, thus laying the foundations of a friendship that lasted until Ranganathan's death. Like others, Palmer referred to Ranganathan's analytical mind, his enthusiasm, his good humor, his kindliness, and his genial personality (though admitting that he could be cold and offhand with those he believed to be fools or opponents). Palmer stated that although conscious of his unique position in Indian librarianship, Ranganathan was modest and unassuming and welcomed him, then "a quite humble member of the profession," as though he were his intellectual and cultural equal.

Ranganathan was married in 1907 and, after his wife died 21 years later, married again in 1929. In honor of his second wife and at her suggestion, he endowed all his property to the Sarada Ranganathan Chair of Library Science in the University of Madras in 1957. He also established the Sarada Ranganathan Lectures on Library Science, the first of which was given by Palmer in 1965.

Ranganthan was passionately concerned about library science, which he saw as a vital tool for "the development of an atmosphere of peaceful co-existence among nations . . . and the evolution of One-World."

REFERENCES

Edward Dudley, editor, *S. R. Ranganathan, 1892–1972: Papers Given at a Memorial Meeting on Thursday 25th January 1973* (1974).

P. N. Kaula, "Some Less Known Facts about Ranganathan," *Herald of Library Science* (1973).

T. S. Rajagopalan, editor, *Ranganathan's Philosophy: Assessment, Impact, and Relevance* (1986); *Relevance of Ranganathan's Contributions to Library Science* (1988).

Ravindra Nath Sharma, *Indian Academic Libraries and Dr. S. R. Ranganathan: A Critical Study* (1986).

K. G. B. BAKEWELL

Rare Books and Special Collections

Departments of rare books and special collections exist in libraries to gather together, preserve, and make accessible the primary materials of research in the historical humanities. The particular genius of North American librarianship has been to develop a library network whose essential value is democratization of *access* to sources of information, knowledge, and entertainment. Librarians in American special collections by and large share this value. To it, however, they add a second imperative, *preservation* of the material embodiments of these sources in conditions as close as possible to the conditions in which they were issued. Balancing these two values—often harmonious, sometimes in conflict—is, in one sense, the story of American special collections librarianship.

Contents. The materials gathered and made accessible in special collections may be handwritten or printed, old or new. The primary materials collected include manuscripts, early printed books, first editions, and unusually expensive books.

Manuscripts. Librarians in most North American institutions automatically place manuscripts in special collections departments for a number of reasons. The items are by definition unique; many are fragile and most are expensive; they are historically significant or, at the least, have some evidentiary value; and they are literally irreplaceable. Most manuscripts require special treatment in order to be made accessible to users and may require unusual storage or supervision as well. Manuscripts may be four-thousand-year-old cylinder seals from ancient Mesopotamia, 9th-century fragments of Jewish sacred texts from the Cairo Genizah, bound anthologies of 14th-century French poetry written on vellum for royal patrons, 17th-century commentaries on Aristotle's works written on paper for students, diplomatic correspondence by Thomas Jefferson, Lord Byron's will, longhand drafts or typescripts of the works, diaries, and letters of 20th-century novelists or 20th-century physicists, records of a corporation or public agency, or the varied remains of a political or journalistic career. Because of their uniqueness, many manuscripts have pride of place in special collections.

Early Printed Books. Librarians almost always place *incunabula* or incunables—books printed between the beginnings of printing from movable type (which occurred about 1455 in the West) and the end of the year 1500—in special collections departments. They almost always place 16th-century imprints there, usually put 17th-century imprints there, and more and more place 18th-century imprints there. They are likely to put exemplars of early Oriental printing in such collections.

First Editions. First or early editions of great or influential works in the history of literature or thought—whether good or bad, old or new—are commonly located in special collections. For example, the *editio princeps* (the first appearance in print) of Horace's poetry (about 1741–42), the first edition of Cervantes' *Don Quixote* (1605–15), the first 1859 printing of Darwin's *On the Origin of Species,* or the first edition of *Mein Kampf* (1925–27) will all be equally at home in such a department. At many institutions, policies dictate that special collections will include *all* books printed before a certain date, regardless of their price or significance. That date may be 1801 for European books or a slightly later year for North American imprints. Special collections may include early exemplars of printing from a specific place, even though they may not specialize in materials of such relatively recent vintage. For example, libraries may collect British printing in Calcutta from the 18th century on, evangelical printing from mission presses in the South Pacific during the mid-19th century, or the first imprints from Wyoming from the later 19th century.

Other Rare Books. Exceptionally expensive books, when they are known to be expensive, are usually placed in special collections. So are books known to be absolutely rare because only a few copies still exist or because only a few copies were ever printed. Some librarians refer to the "iconic" value of some books as the reason for placing them in special collections. Two examples are the King James Bible (1611) and the First Folio of Shakespeare's plays (1623). Other collections may include books illustrated by famous artists; books covered in spectacularly beautiful or historically significant bindings; books with a famous provenance—once owned, for example, by Isaac Newton or King Louis XVI; or books presented by their authors to friends or lovers, or signed by their authors, or annotated or corrected by their authors or their authors' friends or contemporaries. The fragility of a book thought to have some merit as an intellectual entity in its original physical condition may justify its inclusion in a special collection. Sometimes the presence of a dustwrapper, map, or illustration will justify that location.

Detroit Public Library

Detroit (Michigan) Public Library's Rare Book Room, which preserves historical materials and examples of fine printing.

Other Items. Special collections may also include playbills, promptbooks, drawings, prints, maps, or

Huntington Library, San Marino, California

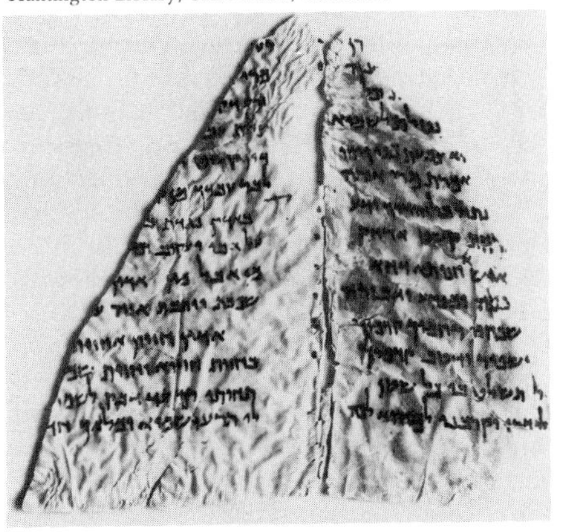

Fragment of the Dead Sea Scrolls from the testament of Levi. The fragment is one of over 3,000 images of the Dead Sea Scrolls in the Huntington Library special collection.

Boston Athenaeum. Washington Collection

Early American bindings from the library of George Washington. The one on the left bears the inscription, "George Washington Esquire President of the United States of America."

photographs. Under some circumstances, they may even include microforms or other reproductions. Such collections also house *objets* such as portraits of the individuals represented in them, a lock of a poet's hair, a writer's desk or a grandfather clock, or the gun with which a statesman was assassinated.

Some current reference books may be necessary to make a special collection fully usable. Librarians may place ordinary modern books with a special collection devoted to the manuscripts or printed output of a single writer or on a single subject. Ordinary books from the library of a writer or scientist whose literary remains constitute a special collection may similarly become part of a special collection.

Supervision. These varied materials are brought together for use under supervision. The very concept of "supervision" is anathema in most American libraries, where respect for readers' privacy is one of the profession's paramount values. Any readers with permission to use a library assume that they may use its materials without supervision, perhaps outside the physical premises of the library itself. During most of the time when materials are actually in use, neither they nor their users receive any supervision at all. By contrast, users of special collections have access to materials only in the precincts of the special collections department or rare book room. Readers know that they are under the observation of staff while in those areas; normally, they can take notes only with pencils or laptop computers, not pens; they cannot photograph, photocopy, or trace the pages, or drop fluids on them for chemical tests, without curatorial intervention. They also know that members of the staff carefully maintain records of all the materials they use.

Tight supervision of the use of special collections materials is justified, despite considerable aversion to it from both readers and librarians, for a variety of reasons. The basic reason is the belief that the objects themselves are important and that their physical existence should be prolonged as much as possible. Without such a concept, special collections would not have come into being in the first place.

The age of some materials is perhaps the most common justification for supervising their use. The fact that manuscripts and archival materials are unique and irreplaceable justifies supervising their use. When it is known, the absolute rarity of certain printed books provides similar justification for locating them in special collections—even when they are modern, not old—so their use can be supervised. The price (or the projected replacement cost) of materials can also mandate their use under supervision. It really makes no difference that Shakespeare's First Folio is not especially rare: many copies are placed in special collections because they have an iconic value as an embodiment of English literature. The First Folio is expensive, with a price in the high six figures (in U.S. dollars) in the early 1990s. Most librarians would feel that they were abandoning their fiduciary responsibilities to their institutions if they allowed the book to circulate like a modern novel or university press publication.

Fragility—often associated with age, of course—may also require supervising the use of materials. Bindings may disintegrate or be on the verge of doing so; the acid used in making the paper may make it brittle or cause it to crumble; the paper or the ink may become discolored if handled too much or if exposed to too much light; and illustrations may be vulnerable to damage from overexposure to light. In addition, a binding may be not only fragile, but also fine; a playscript may have been marked up for theatrical presentation by a famous director; the illustrations may be the work of an illustrator collectible in their own right, which might all too easily be cut out and stolen.

Preservation. All of the primary materials in a special collection may at some time require, and presumably have been judged to deserve, conservatorial attention. Tight supervision as these materials are used improves the chances that they will receive such attention while they can still benefit from it. (*See* Conservation and Preservation of Library Materials.)

Access. Materials in special collections are brought together in part so that they may be made accessible in other than normal, dictionary-catalogue ways. Author, title, and subject certainly suffice for the majority of readers almost all the time. But some forms of research require learning about and perhaps actually examining, for example, all books known to have been in a famous person's library; known to have been printed in the city of Mainz between 1455 and 1501; printed anywhere in the world in the year 1789; or written by a particular author and with marginal annotations by another. Other topics may require access to books bound in vellum before 1700; or with metal clasps; or with gauffered edges; or with fore-edge paintings; or with covers by a specific binder. Rare-book or special-collections librarians attempt to provide such highly specialized forms of access to their holdings by creating files (for provenance, imprint, chronology, or bindings, for example) or guides to large and complex manuscript archival collections, or by annotating published reference tools to indicate their own holdings in particular authors or subjects. They thereby work to make access to special collections through non-standard as well as standard approaches as easy as possible. Because they cannot allow users to browse in stack or storage areas, they have to provide additional access points if their collections are to be truly useful to and usable by the readers they hope to serve.

Institutional Setting. All of these generalizations are complicated by the varied natures of the institutional contexts in which special-collections departments exist. Rare books in one library may be gathered in a special collection alongside perfectly commonplace materials that would not be brought together in such a unified way elsewhere. A special collection at another library may be housed with the general, perhaps even circulating, collections, even though it includes materials rarely found in other libraries. Both extremes, and most possible variations on them, can be found somewhere in North America at the present time. Because special collections are found in academic research, academic teaching, public, governmental, independent, and even some special libraries, each with its own distinctive mission and programs, and in giant libraries as well as small ones, generalizations must always be qualified by exceptions.

History. Most collections of rare printed books and *codex* (bound) manuscripts do share some elements of a common history. They are likely to have developed from small *reserve* collections of materials moved away from public access for safekeeping. Many libraries attracted private philanthropic funds to augment their reserve collections; some received donations of collections created by private individuals. Modern special collections developed from these two bases.

Many librarians had rare books to care for long before they had departments of special collections. In many libraries they stored these books in closets in the director's office for safekeeping. As the number of rare materials grew and public interest in them increased, librarians found it expedient to show them off to potential supporters. In some instances they created *treasure rooms* to house these works—the first administrative structures devoted to their care. Gradually, particularly in larger institutions with clearly-defined missions to support research, treasure rooms became *rare book departments*. Strong pressures to add such departments where they did not already exist, or to expand those that did, came after World War II. During this period, North American research institutions expanded to take on intellectual leadership in many areas of the historical humanities. At the same time, weakened European and Asian economies enabled American librarians to acquire enormous quantities of research materials relatively inexpensively. As the definition of topics on which research could profitably be undertaken exfoliated to include more recent as well as older subjects and authors, large and comprehensive collections of materials not intrinsically rare began to seem of sufficient intellectual (and sometimes monetary) value to warrant location in separate departments. Rare book departments thus expanded to become *special collections,* that is, congeries of old books, rare books, and various more or less distinct author, subject, and reference collections that could include printed books, periodicals, and related or separate codices and archival collections of modern manuscripts.

Meanwhile, North American collectors had long gathered their own collections of printed or manuscript materials, supporting their own scholarship, or curiosity, or vanity, or sense of public need. These private collections tended over time to gravitate towards or become the basis for public institutions. As early as the 18th century, James Logan established such a library in Philadelphia; it is now one of the bases of the strength of the Library Company of Philadelphia. He was among the first of a long and distinguished line of benefactors of public libraries, and there was a comparable line of benefactors of university and college collections.

Non-collectors also assisted the growth of special collections. Some, such as Walter Newberry in Chicago, gave money to establish libraries where there were none. Others founded research libraries to augment the programs of existing libraries, as Mrs. Kenneth Spencer did in establishing the Kenneth Spencer Research Library at the University of Kansas. Still others gave materials they possessed not because they were collectors but because they had been creators of, or participants in, the subjects of their collections. Examples include Harriet Monroe, who gave her collection of poetry to the University of Chicago, and H. L. Mencken, who gave some of his manuscripts and books to Baltimore's Enoch Pratt and the New York Public libraries.

Undirected and uncoordinated, these patterns of growth yielded many different kinds of institutions with special collections. Universities and colleges, independent research libraries, great public institutions such as the Library of Congress and the New York Public Library, smaller public libraries, historical societies, local, state, and national public and private archives, some business and foundation archives, art, history, and natural history museums, and genealogical societies all actively collect materials and make them accessible through special collections departments. Some of these institutions are use- and program-driven; they may exist solely to support research and teaching. Others may view themselves as repositories only, rigorously restricting access to their collections. Still others must balance individual research needs against broad educational objectives. Librarians at some institutions periodically display

Staff working with 19th century Puerto Rican periodicals in the Rare Book Room of the Puerto Rican Collection, José M. Lázaro Library.

Library of Congress

Four Japanese dharani, *passages from a Buddhist sutre used as prayer charms,* A.D. *770.*

selections from their collections in public exhibitions that show off the materials, but keep them from being used. Librarians at other institutions, although they may tolerate research, regard special collections as merely ancillary to their main collecting needs, assuming that most of their readers require modern books and periodicals to support their teaching and studies. In their institutions, special collections materials may function only as exhibition materials or as objects that will impress visiting dignitaries. Some librarians make almost no use of such materials at all, keeping them simply because they regard possession as somehow contributing to their institution's image or prestige, because retention is mandated by some outside authority, or because divestiture seems legally impossible, intimidatingly difficult, or bad for public relations.

How an institution defines its mission is central to the use it makes of its special collections. Indeed, redefinition of that mission may occasionally lead to the dispersal of all or parts of such collections. Divestiture is more than a theoretical possibility: the John Carter Brown Library at Brown University deaccessioned early manuscripts deemed out of scope in a library primarily concerned with other subjects, and Philadelphia's Franklin Institute divested itself almost entirely of major collections in the history of science and technology after a prolonged period of institutional reconceptualization.

Staff. In general, special collections are expensive to operate. The spaces they occupy may need environmental and security controls beyond those ordinary elsewhere in a library. They tend to be staff-intensive departments, especially relative to the number of users they normally receive. The main library at a large university may serve several thousand readers on a single day; its special collections department may serve far fewer readers in an entire year. Yet the staff of such a department may include specialists in reader services, preservation and conservation, exhibitions, acquisitions and processing, cataloguing, and, perhaps, any number of subspecialties. Members of the staff may need language skills and the ability to serve the needs of scholars and specialists.

As the kinds of materials collected in such departments become increasingly specialized, staff with correspondingly specialized educational backgrounds become necessary both to interpret collections to their potential users and to build collections knowledgeably rather than impressionistically. Such staff tend to command somewhat higher salaries than staff in other departments, a sign not only of the complexity of special collections but also of the growing professionalism of the field itself. Originally handled by private collectors, with or without hired librarians, or by librarians who cared for them with one hand, so to speak, while reserving the other hand for their "real" work, many special collections became the purview of gentlemen librarians, dollar-a-year men—and "men" is the right word here—able to treat institutional collections as extensions of or analogues to their own. Occasionally such collections became dumping grounds for staff unable to function well in other areas of library service. Now, however, staffing in special collections reflects a growing emphasis on both librarianship (methodology) and subject expertise (substantive knowledge). Professional degrees in librarianship or archival practice and advanced degrees in academic subject fields relevant to those represented in the collections are now commonly demanded of aspirants to work in special collections. This emphasis on credentials is complemented by the creation of specialized organizations, such as the Society of American Archivists and the Rare Books and Manuscripts Section of the Association of College and Research Libraries, and the establishment of professional journals such as *American Archivist* and *Rare Book and Manuscript Librarianship*.

The Future of Special Collections. As the century and the millennium draw to a close, electronic and other forms of high-technology communication threaten, if they have not already displaced, the dominance of printed books. Libraries and higher education are both simultaneously approaching a period of significant change. Speculation about the future of special collections in such times is a doubtful venture. But preservation of shards from the past and significant monuments from the printed and manuscript records of the present will continue to appeal to many people, not only scholars but also collectors. Many of the impulses that have brought about the varied characteristics of special collections will prove to have staying power. Antiquarian and historical research may become a less significant priority among scholars than it was in the first 90 years of the 20th century. Nonetheless, barring large-scale reversals in both research practices and the institutional bases (both academic and library) of special collections, they seem an entrenched part of the academic and library landscape. Some institutions will surely retrench. Some that entered the field relatively late, are uncertain in their commitments, or lack sufficient financial resources, will leave it. But tradition and bureaucratic inertia, on the one hand, and a persistent interest in charting the past, on the other, will likely provide for the growth, perhaps even the strengthening, of those special collections that weather the intellectual changes and economic difficulties likely to characterize the last decade of the 20th century.

REFERENCES
Roderick Cave, *Rare Book Librarianship,* 2nd edition (1982).
Michèle Valerie Cloonan, editor, "Recent Trends in Rare Book Librarianship," *Library Trends* (1987).

DANIEL TRAISTER

Reference and Information Services

Reference and information services exist in libraries because the many means of access to information in library collections are complex and are not intuitively self-evident. Although the organization of library collections has an inner logic readily intelligible to librarians, that organization often seems arbitrary and confusing to library users. Furthermore, despite the existence of some universal principles (mostly inherent in widely used classification schemes), the organization of each library includes variations on these principles. To mediate between library users' information needs and the information resources of the library, libraries offer reference and information services.

The dual concept of reference *and* information services is a relatively new one. Although information service—meaning the provision of specific facts and information to library users—has always been implicit in reference service, libraries initially offered reference service for didactic reasons as a part of their broad educational role. Many definitions of reference service have been offered over the years, all of them illustrative, none definitive; part art, part science, it is better described than defined. The purpose of reference service is to help a library's clientele use its collections and external resources effectively to meet their information needs. The distinguishing features of reference service are a staff designated to provide the service; a collection of reference works accessible to the public in an area set aside for the provision of the service; adequate guides to the library's resources (such as a classification scheme, a catalogue, and indexes); and a high degree of interaction between the staff and the clientele. During its history in North American libraries, reference service has included reader's advisory service, bibliographic instruction, and information and referral service. These represent different developments of the service's basic purpose.

Historical Development and Definitions. The convenient and obvious place to begin any description of the history of reference service is Samuel Swett Green's article, "Personal Relations between Librarians and Readers," published in the November 30, 1876, issue of *Library Journal.* Green argued that librarians have an obligation to do more than provide a collection for their clientele, that they must also provide personal service and help readers select appropriate books from the collection. Green was most concerned with increasing use of the Worcester Public Library's "reference" collection. The term's connotation then differed from its connotation today; then it meant any work of serious nonfiction, regardless of its internal structure or organization. In Green's day, reference works of the sort that fill today's reference collections—works offering guidance to other bibliographic works and their contents or providing easy access to factual information—were few in number. Green believed that many library users lacked the sophistication to make the best selections from serious nonfiction themselves. The purpose of reference service was to elevate their taste and improve their minds. Although this ostensible purpose included neither provision of specific bits of information nor instruction in the use of the library, Green's many examples illustrate both of these as implicit possibilities in reference service.

Minneapolis Public Library

Readers' advisory services at the Minneapolis Public Library in 1940.

Green's idea found favor in many libraries. As librarians moved beyond their original makeshift quarters in former school buildings and mansions, they designed new library buildings that included reference rooms. A paper presented at the American Library Association (ALA) conference in 1882 demonstrates that public libraries were preparing special reading lists and catalogues of children's books for schools in their areas. By 1883 many libraries were giving assistant librarians special training in the techniques of reference work. The ALA Annual Conferences included reports on "Aids and Guides to Readers," and by 1891 the term "reference work" was being used in the annual index to *Library Journal;* that same year "reference work" appeared for the first time in the title of an article.

Librarians of the day wished to improve their readers' taste in fiction—or, better yet in the view of the day, wean them away from fiction—and reference service developed most rapidly in the large urban public libraries. The public libraries of Boston, Brooklyn, Chicago, Detroit, Milwaukee, Newark, Providence, and Saint Louis were among the first to give particular staff members responsibility for reference service. The staff member so charged at the Saint Louis Public Library was called the "library hostess."

The textbook-based instructional methods used by colleges in the late 19th century placed the college library on the periphery of the academic program. In 1885 Melvil Dewey announced that at Columbia he was applying the "modern library idea" of reference work to the university library. He appointed two reference librarians to aid inquirers. Despite this example, academic libraries, especially in the state universities and colleges, were slower than public libraries to adopt the modern idea. Reference service did not become a regular service of academic libraries until World War I.

The purpose of reference work later broadened to include specific fact retrieval and instruction in the use of library resources. Librarians did not plan these services; they responded to needs expressed by their clients. Out of this broadening of services grew a debate about the purpose and proper function of reference work, a debate not yet resolved. Some librarians have argued that the purpose of reference service is to teach library users how to use the library independently; others have argued that the librarian should provide as much service as possible to the user, illustrated by Green's example of the librarian finding appropriate books and bringing them to a patron open to pertinent pages.

The first position has been labeled "conservative" or "minimum" service; the second position has been called "liberal" or "maximum" service. They have been discussed as "theories" of reference; however, rather than being theories, they are attitudes about or philosophies of service. Opinion about these philosophies has been most sharply divided in academic libraries. Because of the educational role of the academic library within its parent institution, many college and university librarians believe that they have an obligation to teach students how to use library resources. It is doubtful that any library or any individual librarian applies either of these philosophies consistently.

For the sake of both the librarian's and the patron's convenience, it is simpler to give one level of service at one time and the other level at another, depending on the patron's need. For example, when a patron needs only a fact such as the latitude and longitude of a particular town or the birthplace of a particular author, it is most efficient for both parties for the librarian simply to look up the answer in an appropriate reference source, rather than attempt to explain the complicated process to be followed to arrive at the same source. The librarian's superior knowledge of reference works and their contents and the organization of the library's collections makes this the preferred mode of service in such cases. On the other hand, if sources on a particular topic must be selected and judged for their relevance, it is more practical for the librarian to instruct the person needing those sources how to use the catalogue and periodical indexes, leaving the judgments to the patron. The patron's knowledge of his or her own needs makes this the preferred mode of service in such cases.

Out of these apparent inconsistencies librarians have identified a third so-called "theory" of reference service, "moderate" service, meaning that both the conservative and the liberal levels are offered in varying circumstances. Because of its obvious relation to the expressed original educational purpose of reference service, the conservative level operates more commonly in academic and school libraries than in public and special libraries.

Regardless of the type of library, the level of service, or the age of the patron, reference work possesses certain constants. When a patron asks a question, the reference librarian must clarify what the person needs. People generally ask questions too broad or too narrow to convey their needs clearly. The librarian must usually ask a series of open-ended questions until both patron and librarian are in agreement on what the patron wants. This process is called the "reference interview" or "question negotiation." It demands patience and good interpersonal communication skills on the part of the reference librarian. After determining the nature of the patron's need, the librarian must match that need with the information sources available by drawing on what Green called "the habit of mental classification." In other words, the librarian categorizes the question by its subject and by the type of reference work which answers that sort of question, then identifies specific works of that type and consults them for an answer. If a question is complicated, the librarian will formulate a search strategy involving a series of reference works to be used in a particular order. After the search is completed, the patron may still not be satisfied, and further interviewing then becomes necessary until together the librarian and patron find a satisfactory answer or the librarian must make a professional judgment that the needed source is not available. In such cases the librarian recommends other approaches and may refer the patron to likely sources outside the library, including other libraries.

Some libraries participate in formalized networks for referring questions that cannot be answered in one library to another library in the network or to a headquarters reference center. The degree of formality of these arrangements varies. The ALA's Reference and Adult Services Division (RASD) produced its Information Request Form in 1984 and issued guidelines for its use three years later, so libraries, especially those not participating in such networks, can make information requests and referrals in a uniform way.

A class receiving bibliographic instruction at the University of Tennessee Library in Knoxville.

University of Tennessee, Knoxville

Information services (as defined above) first flourished in special libraries. Just as the conservative philosophy agrees with the purpose of school and academic libraries' parent institutions, the liberal philosophy agrees with the purpose of special libraries' sponsors. Legislative reference libraries developed the techniques of amplified service which characterize special libraries. Melvil Dewey created the New York State Library's legislative reference section in 1890, but Charles McCarthy of the Legislative Reference Department in Wisconsin created the model of the special library, drawing information from sources outside the library, preparing digests of relevant information, and becoming a partner in the legislators' work. Both world wars further spurred the development of special libraries in business and industry.

Applications of the techniques of special libraries have been attempted in academic and public libraries. In the early 1930s the Carnegie Corporation funded two experimental "research librarianships," one at Cornell and one at the University of Pennsylvania. At each university a designated librarian was given full-time responsibility for assisting faculty in major research projects in the humanities and social sciences. The experiment, despite initial skepticism among the faculty that a librarian could understand their research needs, was an unqualified success, but no other institution imitated it, and when funding ran out both Cornell and Pennsylvania discontinued the program. In the early 1980s both public and academic libraries experimented with offering in-depth reference and information service to business and industry. Well-known services developed at Rice University, the University of Michigan, Long Island University, and the Cleveland and Indianapolis public libraries. However, these services have stepped outside the tradition of free information service and charge fees for their labors. Several companies, such as Information on Demand, have also entered the information service business for profit. Often called "information brokers," these firms offer comprehensive, speedy information and document delivery services, exemplifying the liberal philosophy at its fullest.

Through union catalogues, union lists, and periodical indexes, librarians have for decades been able to identify pertinent information sources to satisfy individual users' needs. This ability increased with the application of computer and telecommunications technology to such tools in the late 1960s and early 1970s with the development of bibliographic databases and utilities such as DIALOG and OCLC. However, given the inevitability that no library collection is self-sufficient, libraries' ability to deliver the information in the sources catalogued in these systems has lagged far behind. During the late 1980s the gap began to narrow, thanks to widespread use of facsimile machines for document delivery and the availability of full-text databases online and in CD-ROM. The development of services such as UnCover by CARL Systems, Inc., and the Faxon Finder and Faxon Xpress services through OCLC have begun to integrate the document identification and the document delivery functions. Today the main barriers to more rapid, more effective document delivery are economic rather than technological.

Reference service developed its distinguishing characteristics during its first quarter century. It

Westinghouse Electric Corp.

Information services first flourished in special libraries. The Westinghouse Technical Library provides service to over 30,000 patrons annually.

acquired the trappings of a mature professional field starting about 1960. In that year the Reference Services Division of ALA began publishing *RQ*, a quarterly journal devoted to issues in the field. Other quarterlies, *Reference Services Review* and *The Reference Librarian*, followed in 1973 and 1981 respectively. Since 1959 ALA's Reference and Adult Services Division has annually presented the Isadore Mudge Citation "to an individual who has made a distinguished contribution to reference librarianship." In 1976 RASD issued "A Commitment to Information Services: Developmental Guidelines." Revised in 1990 and issued as "Information Services for Information Consumers: Guidelines for Providers," these guidelines state ideals for reference and information services and are the closest thing to standards for reference service in existence.

Reader Guidance. From the earliest days reference service was concerned with improving readers' taste in reading, especially in fiction. This function was formalized in many public libraries in the 1920s through the creation of readers' advisory services, or readers' bureaus, separate from the libraries' reference departments. Readers' advisory service was the libraries' response to the adult education movement. The first readers' bureau was established at the Chicago Public Library in 1923. Others were created at the public libraries of Akron, Albany, Boston, Cincinnati, Detroit, Minneapolis, New York City, and Oklahoma City.

The purpose of the readers' bureaus was to assist individual adult readers in planning systematic reading programs relating to their interests, to help casual readers select the best books, to compile lists of recommended books, and to work with adult education groups, including those concerned with adult literacy as well as those concerned with general personal improvement. The readers' advisor would meet with a patron and conduct an extensive interview to identify his or her interests, needs, and capabilities. The advisor would then draw up a bibliography of books suited to the patron's purposes. The advisor would also do follow-up work with the patron to monitor progress and to learn about changes in the patron's interests or the growth of those interests in new directions. Such changes would, of course, require new recommendations. Many bureaus maintained extensive card files of patrons' interests and notified them when new books relating to their interests arrived; the books would be held for the patrons to examine.

The heyday of readers' advisory service was the 1930s. During that decade the big cities expanded their service from the central libraries into the branches, and many small town libraries made readers' advisory work a routine part of their reference activities. It was, however, a labor-intensive service that reached relatively few people. During the 1940s the focus of adult education efforts shifted from individuals to groups, and the service began to fade as a separate operation in libraries. The decentralization of reference service into subject departments in main libraries later dispersed the readers' advisory function. Although by 1960 nearly all formal readers' advisory services had been disbanded, the function had not disappeared, and readers' advisory service is carried on to varying degrees in reference departments in all types of libraries.

Information and Referral. Another service intended to help people improve their lives has been information and referral centers, often called I & R centers, in public libraries. They enjoyed their greatest popularity during the 1970s. The purpose of an I & R center is to bring people with legal, medical, or personal problems into contact with social agencies that can help them solve those problems. An I & R center differs from a traditional reference department in that it makes little use of such traditional reference tools as the library's catalogue. Instead it depends heavily on in-depth directories, often developed locally, of social service providers. The librarian interviews a client, determines that person's need, deals with appropriate agencies to determine which ones will help, and then directs the client to the proper office at each agency. Some proponents of I & R service have said that the librarian should also furnish transportation to the agency offices and follow up on the client's progress, staying with the case until it is resolved to the client's satisfaction. Nearly every public library has a directory of local social service agencies, and many keep in-house files to supplement these directories, but few support I & R centers. In 1979 only 13 percent of public libraries surveyed in the United States offered true I & R service.

The Detroit (Michigan) Public Library was one of the first to designate staff responsible for reference service (1928).

Detroit Public Library

Reference Tools. Concomitant with the development of reference service has been the development of reference works. When Green developed the idea of reference service in 1876, the universe of reference works in English consisted of little more than several general-purpose encyclopedias, a few almanacs, Bartlett's *Familiar Quotations,* the *Annual Register of World Events,* and several general-purpose dictionaries. By the end of the 19th century, all of the essential features of reference service had been developed; at the same time, reference book publishing began to grow. The relationship between reference service and reference works was synergistic. As reference service became more common, the need for reference works increased; as reference works became more common, librarians' ability to do reference work improved. Many significant reference works, still being published and in use today, date from this period. R. R. Bowker's *Publishers' Trade List Annual* has appeared since 1873. H. W. Wilson began publishing the monthly *Cumulative Book Index* in 1898; his *Reader's Guide to Periodical Literature* began three years later. The ALA promoted reference publishing with its *A.L.A. Index to General Literature* in 1901. In 1902 ALA published Alice B. Kroeger's *Guide to the Study and Use of Reference Books;* after her death in 1909, editorship of the guide passed to Isadore G. Mudge. Later editions were prepared by Constance M. Winchell and Eugene P. Sheehy. Sheehy's tenth edition of the *Guide to Reference Books,* often called "the reference librarian's bible," appeared in 1986 and was kept up-to-date thereafter by the editorial staff of *Choice* magazine.

By 1928 the volume of reference publishing was such that librarians desired authoritative evaluations to guide their purchasing decisions. In response, ALA created the Subscription Books Review Committee. Two years later it published its first evaluations of subscription books and encyclopedias in the quarterly *Subscription Books Bulletin.* The committee's scope broadened to include reviews of single-volume reference works. Though the committee's name and the name of its journal have changed several times, its basic purpose of evaluating reference works is still carried out in the *Reference Book Bulletin,* published in the pages of *Booklist.* Other important sources of reviews of new reference books are the *Wilson Library Bulletin, RQ, Library Journal, Choice,* and *American Reference Books Annual.*

In addition to books, reference librarians since the mid-1970s have made extensive use of online databases that offer speed, convenience, and multiple access points. Most of these databases are indexes, including abstracts, to the journals of specialized fields. Some have printed counterparts; others exist only in machine-readable form. As noted above, full-text databases have become increasingly important. Many patrons found the protocols and commands for searching these databases intimidating, leaving them to librarians to master. Some vendors, however, developed simpler menu-driven interfaces to encourage patrons to do their own searching. Because the cost of searching an online database cannot be predicted beforehand—let alone accurately budgeted for a year or more in advance—online searching has in many libraries been regarded as a source of last resort; or the library's policy of passing along to the user charges for online searches has been cause for many users to consider this service a source of last resort.

In the mid-1980s many of the most heavily used online databases became available on CD-ROM. Compact-disc technology has been as big a hit in libraries as it originally was in the music industry. It is popular with librarians because they can budget for its one-time annual cost, and it is popular with users because they can interact directly with the contents of the database, usually at no cost to themselves. Part of the public popularity of CD-ROMs is surely that they are much more visible than online services. A microcomputer with a monitor continuously announcing the presence of an information source is, apparently, more compelling advertising than any of the various outreach efforts tried for promoting online services.

National cultural values regarding access to information will inevitably always color philosophies of reference service and its practice around the world. The traditions of individual freedom and the wealth of information sources in the vernacular have allowed reference and information services to reach their apex in the English-speaking world. Yet, as in other matters, advances in technology have promoted global homogeneity and reference services, at least among developed nations, are becoming more like those long offered in the United States. Transborder technology transfer and information flow will accelerate this trend.

Research. Research in reference service has addressed several key questions. These are: What is the quality of reference service? Who can do reference work? What are the interpersonal dynamics of the reference encounter? And what precisely *is* reference work? Over a number of years investigators have conducted unobtrusive tests of reference service in many types of libraries, especially public and academic libraries, to measure the quality of reference service. In an unobtrusive test, a trained surrogate poses as a library patron asking a reference question; the accuracy of librarians' answers yield the test results. Results of these tests show considerable uniformity: in most unobtrusive tests, reference departments answer simple factual questions correctly only a little more than half the time. Because the results among individual libraries tested vary widely, further unobtrusive testing conducted with the purpose of isolating variables could prove fruitful in explaining what makes for quality reference service. Tests comparing librarians and nonprofessional trained library workers have shown little difference in the results of their reference work, but have indicated that the professionals answer questions in less time.

A number of researchers in reference work, particularly during the 1970s, borrowed models and methods from such fields as counseling psychology, anthropology, and sociology to elucidate what happens during the interaction between an inquirer and a reference librarian. Out of these efforts has come a good deal of practical advice on how to conduct an effective reference interview.

Family History Library of the Church of the Latter-Day Saints, Salt Lake City, Utah

Librarian at the British Reference Desk of the Family History Library (Salt Lake City, Utah) assists patron conducting genealogical research.

Many writers have attempted to define reference work. Some have depended upon a great deal of data collection and analysis; others have drawn on less formal observation and reflection on personal experience. If a definitive explanation of what reference work is should ever be developed and accepted by the profession, it will most likely result from an amalgam of personal reflection and formal research into the diverse aspects of reference service.

Issues and Trends. A number of issues face reference librarianship. As alternative information providers have grown up, they have offered their wares directly to the public. Services such as America Online, CompuServe, GEnie, and Prodigy offer people the convenience of obtaining information by computer and phone line from the comfort of their own homes. Many libraries provide some information over the telephone, but few of their information services offer the convenience of a system such as Prodigy. Yet only libraries offer the depth and breadth of information held in their rich print collections. Reference librarians must devise new organizational paradigms and delivery systems if they are to make these riches available to people with the same convenience that competing services have begun to make their limited range of information available.

The debate about conservative versus liberal service has not received much attention in the reference press in recent years, but it is played out daily in every reference encounter in every library. It can still rouse passionate argument in staff meetings and classrooms. Perhaps this issue will never be laid to rest. The development of more user-friendly information systems that shift responsibility for the mechanics of information retrieval from the user to system software may influence the course of the debate. If users have less "how-to" to learn about systems, they can concentrate their effort on judging the value of the information these systems retrieve for them. The role of the reference librarian will not be the teacher of system mechanics valued by the conservative view, but rather a counselor to users about system selection and an intermediary.

Perhaps the biggest issue facing reference librarianship is evaluation. No truly useful way of evaluating reference service has ever been devised. Unobtrusive tests can indicate something about the results of reference service, but few have attempted to deal simultaneously with the process that delivers those results. Evaluation, always impressionistic, will necessarily remain so until a significant breakthrough is achieved in this area. This is the area in greatest need of an intense research effort. It is encouraging that it has received increased attention since the mid-1980s.

Much of the literature regarding reference librarianship is impressionistic and anecdotal. Other areas requiring research are collection development and core collection desiderata, user behavior and expectations, referral effectiveness, personnel utilization and evaluation, and factors affecting reference librarians' job satisfaction. Because each of these issues is related in some way to each of the others, researchers must face the challenge of isolating and controlling variables.

Reference and information service has changed considerably since Green first proposed its core concept or Dewey introduced it to academe. As societal values change, as information products and delivery systems change, and as the environment in which libraries function changes, reference and information service will have to change to continue to meet individuals' information needs in a timely, complete, and accurate way.

REFERENCES

Richard E. Bopp and Linda C. Smith, *Reference and Information Services: An Introduction* (1991).

William A. Katz, *Introduction to Reference Work* (1982).

Marjorie E. Murfin and Lubomyr R. Wynar, *Reference Service: An Annotated Bibliographic Guide* (1977); *Supplement 1976–1982* (1984).

JAMES R. RETTIG

Renaissance Books and Libraries

The history of the Renaissance is inseparable from the history of its books and libraries. The expansion of knowledge within the scholastic tradition, the secularization of society, and the rekindling of interest in ancient history, literature, and art, both in Italy and in Northern Europe, placed new demands on both books and libraries from 1400 to 1700.

The intellectual achievements of the Renaissance were as complex and varied as the kinds of books and libraries that the Renaissance produced. Renaissance libraries included university libraries, since the universities founded in the Middle Ages greatly expanded during the Renaissance, and new universities with new libraries of scholastic texts were created. Other Renaissance libraries were religious libraries, many of which were established to serve the new reformed orders that spread during the period. These libraries also contained rich collections of scholastic literature. Still other Renaissance libraries were courtly libraries, assembled to preserve the new corpus of vernacular literature that expanded particularly in France under the patronage of Charles V and great noblemen such as Jean, Duke of Berry and in England under the patronage of Edward IV. Other Renaissance libraries were Humanist libraries, assembled by Italian Humanists and their lay and ecclesiastical patrons to preserve the manuscripts of newly recovered ancient texts. Finally, Renaissance libraries can be said to have included theological libraries formed chiefly from printed books to serve the Protestant Reformation and the Catholic Counter-Reformation.

Rise in Literacy. Despite their remarkable variety, Renaissance libraries reflected a single and common phenomenon: a rise in the rate of literacy that, when set in the context of a moderate increase in population, yielded a dramatic increase in the number of people who were able to read and write and therefore sought to use books and to avail themselves of libraries. In the 12th century only a small, chiefly monastic, elite were able to read and write, and literate people constituted a tiny fraction of the general population. By 1533 Thomas More estimated that over half the population of England was literate in the vernacular. The rate of increase in literacy accelerated at the end of the 14th and during the 15th century. During the Renaissance, Europe was transformed from an oral culture, with a population primarily of listeners, to a population that included significant numbers of readers.

Manuscript Book Production. Monasteries had been the major centers of book production in the Middle Ages, when they also served as the major libraries. (*See* Middle Ages, Libraries in the.) Although monastic book production continued after 1300, book production generally became the domain of professional scribes, who served a varied clientele of schoolmen and lay aristocracy. Beginning in the mid-13th century Europe witnessed a growth in demand for scholastic textbooks, which stimulated a remarkable series of innovations in the way in which these books were produced. The first of these was the *pecia* system employed in the universities of Naples, Bologna, Padua, Paris, Oxford, Cambridge, and Uppsala from the 13th through the 15th centuries. Fundamental to the operation of the pecia system was the creation of exemplars—model manuscripts certified for their textual accuracy which were subdivided into their component quires or *pecia* of six or eight folios and rented to licensed scribes. Whereas previously a given manuscript could be copied only by one scribe at a time, the pecia system allowed a number of scribes to make copies of the same text simultaneously. The result was an increase in manuscript production combined with greater control of textual uniformity, for the quality of the exemplars was under the control of the university. The awareness of the need for accurate textual transmission reflected in the pecia system was to become a hallmark of Renaissance book production.

Innovations: Imposition and Cursive Handwriting. Succeeding centuries brought continued innovation, reflecting the desire to produce standardized manuscripts with great speed. In France, the Low Countries, and England in the 14th century, scribes developed the practice of imposition, the significance of which is still being assessed by manuscript scholars. Imposition meant that texts were written on uncut quires before folding and thus out of narrative sequence, in a manner similar to the uncut pages produced by later printing presses. Another innovation that began throughout Europe in the 14th century was the adaptation of cursive handwriting to book production. Cursive scripts could be written with fewer liftings of the pen, allowing books to be made more swiftly and thus sold at lower prices.

Impact of Paper. The use of paper was also a major development. It was first introduced to book production in the 14th century but took firm hold only in the course of the 15th century when paper played a more important role in lowering the cost of books than did the introduction of printing from movable type. Paper books, written in cursive scripts, became the first truly cheap books, easily within the means of townspeople, gentry, and poor students in Italy, England, and France. In the early 1400s ordinary school manuals were being produced by *scriptoria* in editions of 200 to 300 copies, numbers comparable to the runs of printed editions a century later.

Early Standardization. While some changes in technical procedures allowed the production of cheap manuscript books, other changes increased the supply of deluxe books, which in the 15th century were becoming more uniform as they were produced in larger and larger quantities. The use of a form of tracing paper permitted the exact reproduction of miniatures and thus the standardization of iconography. Some miniatures intended for books of hours were mass-produced separately from the text. Increasing division of labor separated the copying, illustration, and decoration of the manuscript. As a result, deluxe manuscript books of the 15th century showed increased uniformity in appearance, dimensions, and length.

Impact of Printing. The invention of printing from movable type must be viewed in the light of the growing appetite in Western Europe for standardized books. The invention has traditionally been attributed to Johann Gutenberg of Mainz in 1444. Before Gutenberg, block printing was used in textile decoration, illustrations, and short texts. These processes did not play a major role in book production, however, and are of importance only insofar as they may have stimulated printers to think of the possibility of using movable type cast in molds to produce books.

The earliest printers came from *outside* the group of artisans directly concerned with manuscript book production. Gutenberg was a goldsmith, as were apparently early printers in Avignon and Basle. The secret method of *artificialiter scribere,* like other skills of goldsmiths, was initially meant to be applied to works of beauty and high cost. Many of the first printed books were printed on vellum, an indication of the luxury market to which early printers most often sought to cater. Many early printed books were illustrated with hand-painted miniatures and decorated with floral borders identical to those in contemporary manuscript codices.

Only after 1480 did printers, many of whom were former scribes, begin to produce cheap books. By 1500 printing had become an important source of cheap university textbooks, and most of the titles printed were works of proven value that had been previously disseminated in manuscript. In the first third of the 16th century, however, a new kind of author emerged who wrote with the press and its potentially wide audience in mind. Printing played an especially important role in spreading the new ideas of the Protestant Reformation and was probably a decisive factor in making Protestantism a different phenomenon from the 14th-century heresies of Wyclifism and Hussitism, which lacked a comparable means of mass communication. During the Wars of Religion in France (1562–98), printing became an important medium for the expression of political theory.

Printing had an enormous impact on the content of Renaissance libraries, since standardized and uniform books ultimately led to standardized collections. Before printing, Jerome's *De Viribus Illustribus* had on occasion been used as a model for library catalogues, but manuscript collections had remained incredibly diverse. Printing led to standardization of the texts and the definition of the corpus of ancient and medieval authors. Bibliographies such as those prepared by Conrad Gesner (1516–1565), Swiss Humanist scholar, were meant by their authors to serve as standardized catalogues of libraries of printed texts (*see* Gesner, Conrad). By the mid-16th century the corpus of cited literature was increasingly defined by what had been printed. Works that for whatever reason had escaped the press fell from the tradition of learned discourse. Whereas printing standardized the bibliographical base of 16th-century culture, it did not immediately lead to libraries larger than those of the previous century, which had been composed exclusively of manuscripts. Many printed book libraries were in fact smaller than important manuscript collections; for example, under Louis XIII the royal library of France had only 400 more printed books than the library of Charles V had manuscript books two and a half centuries earlier. Most printed books found their way into the increasing number of small personal libraries.

The Renaissance Book. In addition to changes in techniques and technology, intellectual and social changes played a major role in determining the physical appearance and content of Renaissance books and libraries. In Italy Humanism was of enormous import. Humanism developed outside the universities, which had been responsible for the greater portion of Italian book production in the 13th and 14th centuries. In general, early Humanists were not the university-trained doctors of theology, medicine, and law but laymen, often notaries, trained in the tradition of the "ars dictanimis" (the art of eloquent written expression). The early Humanists shared a common goal: the restoration of eloquence in Latin prose. To achieve this end Petrarch, Boccaccio, and Salutati assembled collections remarkable for their richness in ancient Latin literature. The Humanists avidly collected the oldest possible manuscripts of classical authors and had them copied in order to build libraries of ancient texts in their original form, free from the corruptions in orthography and grammar introduced by medieval scribes.

For the books that they themselves copied and for their libraries, the first Humanists used the highly legible Gothic textual scripts favored in courtly and bourgeois Italian circles of the 14th century. In the first decade of the Quattrocento (1400s), however, Florentine Humanists began to produce books whose scripts and decoration were based on older manuscripts, particularly Tuscan manuscripts of the 10th to 12th centuries, which were characteristically written in Caroline script and decorated with white ivy stem motifs. Whether the Humanists really believed these manuscripts to have resembled those of the age of Cicero is not clear; nevertheless, it is certain that the Humanists believed that *littera antiqua* was the appro-

Biblioteca Comunale Malatestiana (Cesena, Italy), founded in 1452, lays claim to being the only early Renaissance library which preserves its original building, furniture and books.

priate script for the classical texts. During the 15th century these scripts came to be used for other materials, including vernacular literature, and even for scholastic treatises and papal bulls. When printing was introduced into Italy in 1458, the dominant type fonts—Roman and Italic—were modeled on two varieties of Humanistic script.

In the second half of the 15th century, Humanists exhibited an increasing interest in epigraphy (ancient inscriptions), with particular emphasis on the inscriptions of the Roman Empire; capital letters of the Imperial period became the models for the capital letters of manuscript books and ultimately of printed books.

The link between Humanism and the physical appearance of the book, so strong in Italy, was weak in Northern Europe. In 15th-century France Humanistic script was not popular, and Humanistic texts were frequently copied in scripts wholly un-Humanistic in appearance. The major force in forming scripts and secular libraries in the early Northern Renaissance was the growth in vernacular and courtly literature under aristocratic patronage. Beginning with Charles V of France, the French-speaking aristocracy in France, the Low Countries, and England began forming libraries of vernacular texts equal in size (roughly 400 to 1,000 volumes) to those of the bibliophilic Italian Humanists. In earlier centuries princes had been read to by professional readers, who were at ease with the Gothic textual script of the universities; however, as lay readership increased, a new and more legible script became popular in aristocratic circles. *Lettre batarde,* termed *hybrida* by some modern paleographers, achieved a dominance for the vernacular literature of Northern Europe equal to that of the forms for Humanistic texts in Italy. The vernacular chronicles, chivalric romances, and books of devotion so popular in aristocratic circles were written and printed in lettre batarde until the first third of the 16th century. In France Humanistic type fonts then replaced lettre batarde, but in Germany lettre batarde prevailed and became the model for the *fractura* type font, which remained the standard German type font until the 20th century.

Renaissance Libraries. Throughout the Renaissance the largest libraries remained university libraries; the Sorbonne, for example, in 1338 already possessed over 1,700 volumes. The holdings of university libraries were divided into reference collections, which were chained to desks for consultation only in the library, and general collections, which circulated to both students and masters. The reference collections were often freely open for consultation, and the circulating collections were, in some cases, available to even the poorest students. The university libraries were therefore the early Renaissance forerunners of public libraries. In architecture they differed greatly from the smaller monastic libraries, which had been installed in cloisters. The university libraries were centralized in halls equipped with benches and tables. They became the models for the libraries of religious houses as well as for the great princely collections of the 14th and 15th centuries.

Pope Urban V in Avignon and King Charles V in Paris founded the first of the great princely libraries in the mid-14th century. Subsequently, other important libraries were formed by Gian Galeazzo Visconti, Jean Duke of Berry, Philip Duke of Burgundy, King Alfonso the Magnanimous of Naples, and King Matthias Corvinus of Hungary. Pope Nicholas V founded the Vatican Library in Rome to take the place of the Avignon library lost during the Great Schism.

In contrast to university collections, princely libraries were considered private possessions, and admission was accorded only to the favorites of the prince. The books in princely libraries were more luxurious than those in university libraries, and new standards of cataloguing—with emphasis on description of decoration and script—were developed, in part, to prevent theft.

Princes did not always think only of themselves. Cosimo de'Medici in the mid-15th century purchased volumes and donated them, along with selected items from his own collection, to the Dominican convent of San Marco to establish a public library for the use of the citizens of Florence. Cosimo's grandson, Lorenzo the Magnificent, established the Biblioteca Medicea-Laurentiana with similar intent. Pope Sixtus IV in 1475 opened the Vatican Library to the public. During the reign of Charles IX, public access was permitted to the French Royal Library. By the 17th century many of the private libraries of the 14th and 15th centuries had become the possession, through inheritance and purchase, of the libraries of sovereign princes who permitted consultation to the public.

In the mid-16th century Europe's largest and oldest libraries still were manuscript collections. Federigo Duke of Urbino (1422–1482) was said to have been proud that he had only handwritten books and no printed books. While Paul II and Sixtus IV were patrons of printing, the Vatican appears to have retained its preference for manuscripts until the middle of the 16th century. Under Louis XIII in 1643, the Royal Library still had twice as many manuscripts as printed books.

By contrast, the new libraries of Protestant institutions were composed principally of printed volumes. Protestants, alienated from their society, built some of the first comprehensive collections of exclusively printed materials to compensate for their lack of access to the older royal and ecclesiastical collections with their great manuscript holdings. The destruction of monastic libraries during the Reformation added to the dependency of Protestants on printed sources. In Geneva the Academy of Calvin was composed entirely of printed works, as was the library of the Protestant University of Leiden at its foundation.

Protestants, who used the printing press so effectively to communicate their ideas, frequently presented copies of their works to libraries. Gifts were not the only source, however; in Geneva the law of copyright deposit of 1530 was an important aid in building the library of the Academy of Calvin.

Among Catholics the Jesuits, leaders in the Counter-Reformation, had no manuscript collection of their own and were particularly active in building large libraries of printed books and in increasing the level of bibliographic expertise. The Jesuit Library of Paris at the end of the 16th century is said to have numbered 20,000 volumes, an astounding figure when compared with libraries of the previous century.

Librarians. In the monasteries of the Middle Ages, the functions of Librarian were regularly performed by the *precentor,* who had general responsibility for liturgy, of which reading was seen as an extension. In the universities the formal office of Librarian was created, but it did not have great importance as a position of erudition, although some scholastics of note at times performed its functions. Similarly, librarians of the kings and princes of France in the 14th and 15th centuries were not known as scholars.

The first scholar-librarians in the modern sense appeared in Italy in the 15th century, when Humanist scholars such as Niccolò Niccoli built their own extensive collections. In the second half of the 15th century the Popes consistently placed scholars in charge of the Vatican Library. In the early 16th century Pope Julius II chose the renowned Humanist Tomasso Ingherami as his second Librarian; Pope Leo X chose as his Librarian Filippo Beroaldo, who in 1515 prepared the first edition of the *Annales* of Tacitus. The custom of placing libraries in the charge of scholars was emulated in France under Francis I, who chose Guillaume Budé as *maitre de la librarie du Roy* and Jacques Lefevre d'Étaples as one of his librarians. The collection of Greek manuscripts flourished under their care, and both men were responsible for a significant revival of interest in the Greek language and literature.

The modern connection between scholar-librarians and the editing of texts became clearly established in the 16th century. Marguerin de la Bigne, the first great editor of the Western Church Fathers, was Librarian of the Sorbonne and founded a tradition of entrusting the editing of patristic texts to librarians. This practice was maintained in the 17th century by Jean Mabillon and the Congrégation de Saint-Maur, to which he belonged. Under the administration of eminent scholar-librarians, libraries at the end of the Renaissance also showed an increased interest in the preservation of books, with particular emphasis on binding, which with the support of wealthy patrons evolved into an art form in its own right. With their interest in editions and textual problems, scholar-librarians also established the tradition—which endured until the 19th century—of maintaining a corps of scribes in the service of great libraries for the preparation of accurate copies for the library itself and for the benefit of scholars personally unable to consult the library's collections.

REFERENCES

Hanna H. Gray, "Renaissance Humanism: The Pursuit of Eloquence," *Journal of the History of Ideas* (1963), reprinted in Paul Oskar Kristeller and Philip P. Wiener, *Renaissance Essays* (1968).

Paul Oskar Kristeller, *Renaissance Thought: The Classic, Scholastic and Humanistic Strains* (1961).

Paul Oskar Kristeller, *Renaissance Thought II: Papers on Humanism and the Arts* (1965).

Curt Ferdinand Bühler, *The Fifteenth Century Book* (1960).

John Willis Clark, *The Care of Books: An Essay on the Development of Libraries and Their Fittings, from Earliest Times to the End of the Eighteenth Century* (1909).

Lucian Febvre and Henri-Jean Martin, *The Impact of Printing, 1450-1860,* translated by David Gerard (1976).

Sandra Hindman and James Douglas Farquhar, *Pen to Press: Illustrated Manuscripts and Printed Books in the First Century of Printing* (1977).

Malcolm Parkes, "The Literacy of the Laity," in *Literature and Western Civilization,* edited by David Daiches and Anthony Thorlby (1972–76), volume II.

Sigfrid Heinrich Steinberg, *Five Hundred Years of Printing* (1955; revised ed. 1974).

Berthold L. Ullman, *The Origin and Development of Humanistic Script* (1960).

Berthold L. Ullman and Philip A. Stadter, *The Public Library of Renaissance Florence* (1972).

Francis Wormald and C. E. Wright, *The English Library before 1700* (1958).

PAUL SAENGER

Reprography

During the 1950s a new word, "reprography," came to be used to describe the technology of reproducing two-dimensional items in administrative, business, and institutional settings. The term appeared sporadically in the library literature of the 1960s and entered the working vocabulary of librarians in the mid-1970s, gradually replacing photoduplication, document copying, documentary reproduction, and, to some extent, photocopying, although that term is still very much in use.

A reprographic program in a library is usually designed to meet one or more of the following objectives: *acquisition,* or collection building; *preservation,* including disaster protection and recovery; and *use* by patrons in that library or another institution. For centuries, the only method of reproducing library materials was to copy the items by hand. With technological advances since the 1950s, librarians have many reprographic options available. These options tend to revolve around three major media: paper, micrographics, and optical formats.

Paper. Options for reproducing library materials on paper fall into two broad categories: direct processes and transfer processes. A *direct process* produces a copy immediately on the final piece of material, with no intervening step. A *transfer process* produces an image on sensitized material that transfers the image to another piece of material, the final copy. The sensitized material may be exposed to energy (heat or light, depending on the process) through a lens or while in direct contact with the original. Thus the method of exposure may be called *contact* or *optical*.

Mechanical means of reproduction are primarily a 20th century phenomenon. At an exhibition in Paris in 1900, an inventor demonstrated a camera, equipped with a reversing prism, designed to make copies from books on rolls of paper; it was awarded a prize. In 1910 a similar machine, the Photostat camera, entered the American market. The Photostat system (and similar apparatus made by other manufacturers) combines a copyboard, a prism-equipped camera capable of making prints up to 18 by 24 inches, a large-capacity paper supply, and developing and fixing trays in one machine. The user has no need for a darkroom. The first copy is negative; its size may be varied from 50 to 200 percent of the original. The user can exercise various photographic controls during exposure and processing. As a result, the quality of the product is potentially very high.

Introduction of the photostat-type camera, which is well suited to copying library materials, greatly expanded the use of reprography for acquisition and preservation, as well as for patrons' use. By 1912, photostat-type cameras were installed in the Library of Congress, Chicago's John Crerar Library, and the New York Public Library; by 1929, 42 libraries had such machines. Until the mid-1930s, when librarians turned to microfilm for such tasks, they used photostats to reprint rare books in small editions and to preserve deteriorating newspaper collections. By 1946 the public demand for copies had increased so much that the New York Public Library produced almost half a million photostat copies in one year.

Photostat services proved valuable to libraries and library users. Yet they required relatively large investments and, in order to be economically efficient, consistently high production levels; only a few dozen libraries could afford them. Most libraries had to wait for simpler and cheaper copying methods. These methods became available when some major manufacturers decided to concentrate on the one segment of the copying market that had the highest sales potential, office records.

The new processes of the 1950s were conceived as office systems, for an input (business letters and records) that was of standard size and of fairly uniform graphic quality, and for an output that satisfied rather modest functional requirements in terms of appearance, legibility, and permanence. Since the machines were cheap and the process simple, any library could afford them. Most did acquire them, in spite of the serious shortcomings of the equipment and materials for library purposes. Copying from bound volumes was difficult and wasted much time and material. Books were subject to far more wear and tear than in Photostatting or microfilming. Larger books and other "difficult" items could not be handled at all, and the results from even routine materials were normally quite inferior to photostats. But copies were readily available and affordable; "convenience copying" had begun.

Photostat Department, Connecticut State Library, ca. 1925.

One important reprographic system introduced in the 1950s was a new silver halide process: *diffusion-transfer-reversal* (DTR). It produces a positive copy in one step. Thanks to the speedy and simple processing, inexpensive equipment, and many fiercely competitive suppliers, DTR became the dominant copying method of the time. A second innovation of the 1950s was *Verifax,* a gelatin-dye-transfer process, which achieves the same result as DTR by different means; it was also popular for a time. A third reprographic novelty of the 1950s was *Thermo-Fax,* the first practical imaging process operating by the action of heat rather than light. The process is simple, clean, convenient, and very fast. It has two main disadvantages. The text of the original must be written, typed, or printed with heat-absorbing (carbon content) ink, because dyes do not absorb heat. More seriously, unexposed parts of the material retain their sensitivity to heat and are subject to deterioration. In the *dual spectrum process,* a combined photographic and thermographic process introduced a few years later, the original need not absorb heat and, like the Thermo-Fax process it largely replaced, does not need chemicals for processing.

A direct electrophotographic process, *Electrofax,* became commercially available in 1954. In this process the latent image is formed on a thin photoconductive layer coated on the paper itself. The coating, zinc oxide, is readily available, inexpensive, non-toxic, and stable. The sensitivity of zinc-oxide paper can be modified and controlled by the addition of dyes to the coating and, with pigment suspended in liquid, can produce copies with very high resolution.

Xerography, an electrophotographic transfer process, was also introduced in the 1950s. After a relatively slow start, it has had a more far-reaching effect in the long run than either DTR or thermography. Xerography is based on the behavior of certain materials, called *photoconductors,* that retain an electrostatic charge in the dark, but dissipate it upon exposure to light. If the photoconductor (such as a selenium-coated plate or cylinder) is given an electrostatic charge before being exposed to light, it retains the charge or dissipates it, forming a latent image, according to the pattern of light reflected from the original. Pigment particles (called *toner*) attracted by the retained charge make the latent image visible. The pigment is transferred from the plate or cylinder to some material, such as uncoated paper, and fused by heat or pressure.

In 1959 the Xerox Corporation introduced its model 914 automated copier. This machine made copying easier and faster than at any time previously, and the copies it produced, made on inexpensive plain paper, were usually better. The machine was complex and expensive, but the company leased it, instead of selling it, with charges based on usage. Under those circumstances, many libraries were able to install the machines and offer a copying service that was faster, cheaper, and for the most part better than before. By the end of the 1960s, the highly developed self-contained, automated equipment made for office copying with the electrophotographic method made almost all previous copying processes look obsolete.

Because of the ease and speed of their operation, and because they were effectively marketed, the Xerox and other electrostatic machines quickly established themselves in libraries. Low prices and fast service led to such a great expansion in demand that patrons not only kept staff-operated copy services busy, but also turned to coin-operated self-service copiers when they became common in libraries by the mid-1960s. With the advent of these machines, convenience copying increased significantly.

When the price of copies fell to a few cents, many library users stopped taking notes and copied the entire text of their reading instead. Low-cost instant copying has thus changed study habits and has been instrumental in the partial conversion of the circulating library into a duplicating library. There have been several consequences of this development for libraries. First, by the early 1970s self-service copying had lowered the volume of work in staff-operated services to the point that some were no longer economically justifiable. Second, electrostatic copying added to the preservation problems in the library because of wear and tear. Third, some members of the public seem to have developed a sense of unquestionable right to uninterrupted copying in the library. These library users often copy from originals that are relatively difficult to handle, yet many lack the elementary skills required to operate the copiers and seem not to understand the frailties of the machines. They break the machines, interrupting service to others, or complain about poor-quality copies that result from their failure to use the machines correctly.

Legally, it may be argued, most copying in libraries seems to constitute "fair use"; the legitimate rights of publishers or authors do not appear to be violated by the practice. Nevertheless, the implications of the large expansion of copying, especially for interlibrary loan, were among the hotly debated issues in writing the U.S. Copyright Act of 1976. This law attempts to balance the private interests of authors and publishers with the rights of the public, a basic feature of U.S. copyright law from the beginning.

A refinement to plain paper reprography is the *laser copier,* introduced in 1985. This copier resembles medium-volume electrostatic copiers in appearance and size; the copies it produces look identical to those made on standard high-quality copy equipment. Instead of imaging optically, however, the laser copier scans the original document and prints the copy from digital signals, using a process developed for computer page printers.

The laser copier can do more, however, than just duplicate the product of conventional optical copiers. It can create new images; change the dimensions of the image differentially—that is, to a greater or lesser degree horizontally than vertically; selectively copy part of an image; delete part of an image; automatically center the image on the copy, regardless of the position of the original document on the copy glass; shift an image to any position on the copy; and reverse images from positive to negative or vice versa. The laser copier can also act as an input device: its digitized image may be sent to a word processor or to computer memory. As an output device, it can receive and print images from external storage or from a transmission line. The laser copier combines the functions of an optical copier with those of a graphic arts image manipulator, a digital image processor, and a versatile computer peripheral device.

Micrographics. Micrographics is the science of producing images in microfilm. It was first demonstrated in 1839, the same year that photography was introduced. Microfilm is nothing more than fine-grain, high-resolution photographic film capable of reproducing images greatly reduced in size. As with any photographic medium, microfilm is composed of two major parts: a light-sensitive *emulsion* and a *base* or substrate used as a carrier for the emulsion. There are two principal bases for microfilm: *acetate,* the common "safety film" made from cotton; and *polyester,* a petroleum derivative known for its strength. Polyester film can have a thinner base, allowing greater packing of information on the same size carrier.

Most librarians considering implementing a micrographics system will choose among three main emulsions or film types: silver gelatin, diazo, and vesicular.

Silver gelatin film consists of a light-sensitive emulsion of silver halide crystals suspended in gelatin. It is processed using chemicals and water and is the only film type considered to be "archival." (When discussing archival-quality microfilm, "silver gelatin" is a more accurate term than "silver halide," because some non-permanent dry-silver films can also be called "silver halide.")

There are five steps in producing an image on silver gelatin film: light modifies the silver crystals exposed to it; a developer converts the latent (invisible) image to metallic silver; a fixer, ammonium thiosulphate, dissolves unexposed silver halide crystals so they will not be exposed in the future; washing removes the chemicals from the film; and drying resolidifies the emulsion. Silver gelatin film is the only one considered "fast" enough by photographic standards to be a camera film. It may also serve as a duplicating film.

Various standards-setting organizations have sought to refine the terms "archival" or "permanent" because of the increasing use of these terms to denote short- as well as long-term storage. (For example, saving a computer file overnight on a diskette is often called "archiving" it.) In the United States, the American National Standards Institute promotes the concept of "life expectancy" rather than "permanence." With silver gelatin microfilm on a polyester base, the maximum life expectancy is defined as 500 years.

Diazo is the second major film type. The diazo process was discovered toward the end of the 19th century and became commercially available in the 1920s for engineering drawings. The emulsion of diazo film is composed of three elements: *diazonium salts,* which constitute the photosensitive part; *dye couplers,* which join with the salts to form a colored dye; and a *stabilizer* that prevents coupling until the

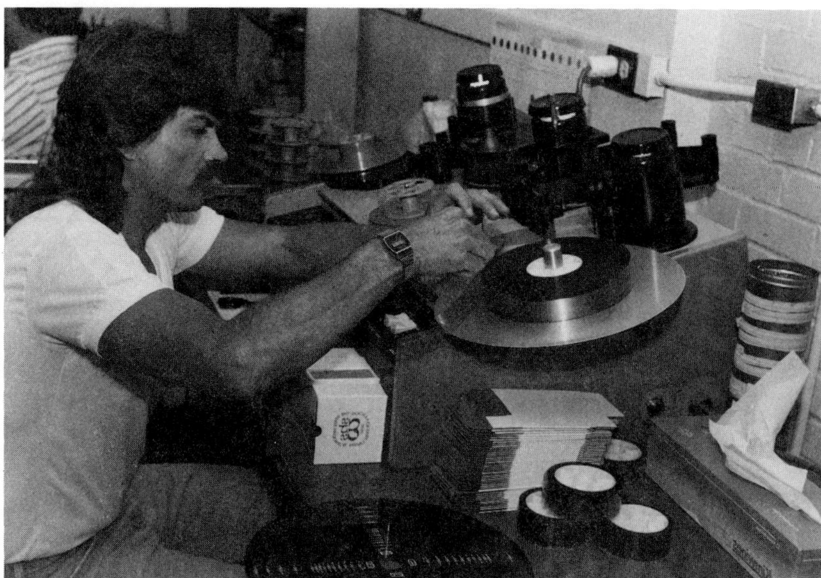

State Historical Society of Wisconsin. Photo by Robert Granflaten

A microfilm technician at the State Historical Society of Wisconsin threads a printer to make a positive working copy from an original negative to be used for interlibrary loan.

desired conditions are present. When this three-part emulsion is exposed to ultraviolet light transmitted through a master microform, the diazonium salts are dispersed in the areas of the microfilm corresponding to light areas of the original image. Areas on the diazo film corresponding to dark areas of the master microform are protected from exposure and remain unchanged, forming a latent image. When the exposed but latent diazo film is treated with ammonia, the alkaline neutralizes the stabilizer, allowing the coupling process to occur, forming a dye in the areas unaffected by the ultraviolet radiation (the dark areas of the master). Diazo film is dark blue or black. It is a durable film that is resistant to scratches, and is a good choice for user (or "service") copies. Diazo film is not intended for long-term preservation and should never be stored with silver film, because it may give of ammonia gas that would damage the silver emulsion.

Vesicular film, the third major type, is a system of dry duplication involving exposure to ultraviolet light and development by heat. The vesicular process was first demonstrated in Germany in 1932. Vesicular film also uses diazonium salts as the photosensitive element suspended in a thermoplastic resin on a polyester base. When exposed to ultraviolet light transmitted through a master microform, the diazonium salts decompose, forming nitrogen gas and colorless photolytic products. Because of the nature of the polymer, the nitrogen gas remains entrapped, constituting the latent image. The latent image is developed by heat which softens the polymer, allowing the trapped nitrogen to expand and form microscopic *vesicles* (bubbles) that become stable and rigid when the film cools. The vesicles form an image by virtue of their light-scattering (as opposed to light-transmitting) nature. After development, the film is fixed by reexposure to decompose the diazonium salts remaining in the unexposed areas. It is important to avoid subsequent applications of heat; the temperature at the reader film plate should not exceed 167 degrees Fahrenheit. The vesicular process requires no chemicals—it is convenient, fast, and odorless. Vesicular film has a gray, beige, or light blue color.

Preservation Quality. Only silver gelatin film is suitable for creating a preservation-quality microfilm master. Most preservation microfilming of library materials is done on 35mm microfilm, because of the size of the original items and the desire not to reduce the original more than is absolutely necessary. There is nothing magical about 35mm microfilm, however: preservation-quality microfilm can also be 16mm or even 105mm, the size of microfiche.

No matter what its size, the silver gelatin preservation microfilm should meet standards in three areas: density, resolution, and archival quality. *Density* is a measure of the opaqueness of the film, or how much light it blocks. Density is important for reproducing the film or generating paper copies from it. *Resolution* is a measure of the film's capacity to distinguish fine detail. It helps to determine the sharpness of the image. *Archival quality* is a measure of how long the film may be expected to last. The test of archival quality, called the methyline blue test, gives an objective measure of how much fixer (residual thiosulfate) remains on the film. Even properly processed silver gelatin film will not meet its life expectancy unless it is stored under proper conditions. People handling archival film must establish procedures for systematic random sampling of stored microfilm to detect any deterioration. In the early 1990s, researchers at the Image Permanence Institute at the Rochester Institute of Technology and other institutions sought ways to improve archival quality. The results of their work may refine the way we create, test, store, and monitor preservation-quality microfilm.

Optical Storage. Optical storage technology is a new medium that records large amounts of information in a digital, and therefore computer-manageable, format. It can be integrated with other computer and telecommunications technologies to form a totally digital information network. As the name implies, optics and a laser light source are used to record and store information; the heat generated by the laser modifies the properties of the recording surface.

A librarian considering optical storage will face a number of choices. There are both erasable and non-erasable media for storing information. However, most library applications, as well as archival applications, will involve non-erasable media.

An optical disk consists of several layers: a substrate, a reflective layer, one or two sensitive recording layers, and a transparent top layer that protects the disk and provides the final focus for the laser light source. In making an optical disk, unlike the process for making magnetic media, such as computer disks or videotape, the optical *read-write head* never touches the disk, thereby reducing wear and tear on the disk and preventing damaging head crashes.

Non-erasable optical storage systems alter the reflective properties of the disk in one of three ways: by forming a *pit,* by forming a *bubble,* or by changing the *alloy structure* of the layers just above the reflective layer. Erasable optical storage systems currently consist of two types: *magneto-optic,* which uses a combination of an external magnetic field and a laser light source, and *phase change,* which uses only laser heat to change the physical properties of a point on the disk or change it back again.

The first major library application of optical technology was the CD-ROM (compact disk-read only memory), containing prerecorded information. In particular, databases on CD-ROM have saved libraries a great deal of money in online charges while at the same time making information more widely available to patrons. Records managers have begun using WORM (write once, read many) systems as substitutes for other reprographic technologies, especially microfilm.

In archival and preservation circles, three unresolved areas of optical disk electronic imaging systems—compatibility, permanence, and legal admissibility—have slowed acceptance of this new medium. In places where archivists and preservation librarians have begun using optical disk systems, they have used the technology more for access than for preservation. As the three troublesome areas are resolved, we may expect to see digital optical disk systems implemented more widely in libraries and archives. One scenario involves microfilming items to ensure preservation and then digitizing (either from the original item or from the microfilm) to promote access and use. Some libraries are already experimenting with this hybrid of micrographics and optical storage. This experimentation is in keeping with the tradition of 20th century librarians in using emerging reprographic technologies to fulfill the mission of acquisition, preservation, and use of library materials.

REFERENCES

Association for Information and Image Management, *Micrographic Film Technology* (1983).

F. C. Crix, *Reprographic Management Handbook* (1975).

William R. Hawken, *Copying Methods Manual* (1966).

Charles LaHood and Robert C. Sullivan, *Reprographic Services in Libraries: Organization and Administration* (1975).

William Saffady, *Micrographics* (1985).

Robert Williams, editor, *Legality of Optical Storage* (1987).

GREGORY S. HUNTER

Resource Sharing

Any study of the library literature reveals many concepts of resource sharing and indicates that the range of resource sharing activities encompasses virtually all the functions of a library. At the heart of most uses of the term, however, is a view that, whatever resource is being considered, the sharing of it means not only that a library gives and receives a part of it, but also that the library is involved in the process of determining how the resource should be shared and in the work of its distribution. Resources to be shared may be objects, persons, or funds, and include library materials, library records, staff expertise, storage facilities, and equipment such as computers.

Two definitions, from the American and British library literature, will provide a clearer idea of the concept. First, Allen Kent states:

> Resource sharing denotes a mode of operation whereby library functions are shared in common by a number of libraries. The goals are to provide a positive net effect: (*a*) on the library user in terms of access to more materials or services, and/or (*b*) on the library budget in terms of providing level service at less cost, increased service at level cost, or much more service at less cost than if undertaken individually. (*Encyclopedia of Library and Information Science* [1978], vol. 25, p. 295)

Second, Philip Sewell writes:

> Resource sharing may appear to be nothing more than a new term for the familiar concept of library cooperation. True, many of the same activities are included, but there is a significant difference in approach. The earlier term takes the existence of libraries for granted and describes how they can achieve their objectives better by working together. The new term appears rather to assume a range of physical, intellectual and conceptual resources on the one hand and a body of people on the other, and covers the activities involved in organizing the one into a set of optimum relationships to meet the needs of the other. (*Resource Sharing* [1981], p. 9)

This second definition particularly emphasizes that resource sharing is not an end in itself, but rather a means to improve the services provided to information users.

The need for resource sharing activity is the result of three underlying trends in 20th-century society: (1) the growth of all forms of literature; (2) stemming from this, society's increasing reliance on information to enable it to function effectively; (3) inflation in the cost of materials coupled with increasing availability of technology, which have made it economically imperative to consider sharing resources.

Resource Sharing Activities. The oldest and most common resource sharing activity is almost certainly the provision of access to library materials. Indeed, interlibrary lending of material has been practiced for many years, although the scale of such activity has expanded greatly since the mid-1950s. Interlibrary loan (ILL) arrangements have inherent weaknesses; they fail to extend the total provision of available material unless accompanied by a cooperative acquisition policy. Additionally, they require the construction of union lists of holdings and/or possibly time-consuming and staff-intensive procedures for processing ILL requests. Interlibrary lending may also conflict with a library's obligations to its own users, and in the larger decentralized systems the stage has been reached where the demands imposed on those libraries with richer collections have spawned restrictions and punitive charges. The net results of these weaknesses are low satisfaction rates, delays, high costs, and low confidence.

An alternative is to provide a centralized collection dedicated to the provision of services to other libraries. This is the approach adopted in the United Kingdom, where 75 percent of all interlibrary lending demand is channeled through the British Library Lending Division (BLLD). Such an arrangement avoids some of the weaknesses of decentralized interlending and can result in better provision and more efficient access. However, the crucial factor is whether such an arrangement is a sensible use of funds. Maurice Line asserted (1984) that government funding of centralized collections can be justified:

> If the volume of demand is large enough to result in low unit costs; at least 1,500,000 requests a year need to be

> received to make a system based on a comprehensive central stock more economic than a co-operative one, though it might be decided to operate with fewer requests than this on the grounds that the better service is worth paying for.

This is in effect a shared resource.

Another means for providing access to materials through resource sharing is the referral of readers themselves to collections likely to be able to supply their particular information needs, a process that may be assisted by the compilation of directories of resources. Other activities may include joint provision of transport arrangements for document supply; co-operative indexing, abstracting, or translation of material; and joint provision of online services to assist exploitation of collections.

Cooperative Acquisition Policies within Groups of Libraries. These feature prominently in many resource sharing arrangements. In some cases, as in the Research Libraries Group, an analysis of existing collection strengths and development policies may be the starting point. Other schemes, such as the British Regional Library Systems subject specialization schemes, may fund cooperative acquisition arrangements to ensure adequate coverage of particular material. Such arrangements, however, are frequently in conflict with the primary responsibility of a library to its own clientele, in that in order to satisfy its obligation to the resource sharing policy the library is purchasing some material of less importance to its own readers, with funds that could otherwise be spent on more relevant material. It is therefore not surprising that cooperative acquisition programs have a checkered history. Both cooperative acquisition and deacquisition—cooperative decisions as to which monographs should be discarded to ensure that adequate coverage is maintained, or which less-used serials each partner should cancel to ensure that at least one copy of each title is held—also rely on union lists and catalogues as do interlending arrangements.

Other extensions of resource sharing to support collection development include the provision of cooperative storage facilities for lesser-used material and a cooperative approach to preservation and binding policies. Both require as much coordination as cooperative acquisition and deacquisition policies, and suffer from the same drawbacks, but the looming preservation crisis will result in greater attention to this aspect of resource sharing.

Record Creation Activities. These comprise a further set of objectives in many resource sharing arrangements. Indeed, despite the establishment of national bibliographies throughout all the developed and much of the developing world, many resource sharing arrangements have their origin in shared cataloguing, largely assisted by the increasing availability of suitable computer technology since the mid-1960s. We have already noted how cooperative collection development policies and interlending may be facilitated by the availability of union listings, but there is a conflict between the needs for successful interlending on the one hand and shared record creation on the other. The latter's efficiency is enhanced by a large overlap of acquisitions between member libraries, whereas interlending is aiming at providing access to as many different titles as possible within the resource sharing arrangement. One extension of cooperative record creation that does facilitate interlending is the sharing of circulation data; information about a particular title's availability on the shelf in another library may be a valuable addition to the services a library can offer to its users.

Staff; Management Information. Finally, two other activities amenable to resource sharing involve staff resources and management information. Resource sharing may incorporate arrangements for cooperative staff training ventures and exchanges of staff, while most successful resource sharing requires a sharing of information for monitoring its activities, including levels of provision and use within each of the cooperating libraries.

Organization and Administration of Programs. Resource sharing can be carried out at any level, from the international to the local, and can be arranged in a variety of ways. Work by Unesco in the 1970s, in cooperation with organizations such as the International Federation of Library Associations and Institutions (IFLA), led to the establishment of two complementary programs later merged: UNISIST, concentrating on the development of a world science information system, and NATIS, identifying the structures required to enable library and information services to play an effective role in national plans for economic and social development. IFLA conducts two major programs, Universal Bibliographic Control (UBC), which seeks to make available basic bibliographic data on all publications issued in all countries, and Universal Availability of Publications (UAP), which aims to improve availability of materials at all levels, including access to new publications and retention of last copies, and which is based on the principle that every country should be able to provide access to its own publications. Both are programs that, if fully developed, will have profound resource sharing implications.

At the national level, the centralized approach to interlibrary lending in the United Kingdom has been described. Plans for the establishment of a National Periodicals Center in the U.S. foundered largely because of disagreement among librarians as to how it should operate, because of the tradition of state autonomy, and because of a lack of federal funding. Resource sharing in the U.S. is largely characterized by privately funded networks such as RLG's Research Libraries Information Network (RLIN), OCLC, and state or regional networks such as the Washington Library Network (WLN) and the Minnesota Interlibrary Telecommunications Exchange (MINITEX). Many local resource sharing ventures have operated for long periods, based on particular cities or conurbations, one such example being the Sheffield Interchange Organization (SINTO) in the U.K.

In developing countries the need for resource sharing may be obvious, but the lack of resources to share may be a fundamental obstacle. Experience suggests that an evolutionary progression, from exchange of accessions lists and compilation of directories of resources to formal establishment of union lists and interlibrary loans (perhaps restricted to particular subject fields) is likely to prove more successful than broader, centralized schemes, such as the Standing Conference of African University Librarians (SCAUL), that have attempted to be comprehensive both in functions and subject coverage.

The arrangements between partners in a resource sharing venture can often be categorized into star, hierarchical, and distributed networks. If most of the funds of the venture are spent on maintaining one or a few major centers it will probably be a highly centralized or "star" network. If requests for information are expected to be routed through particular stages, for example, through a regional center and, if failed, to a larger state library, inherent delays result from such a hierarchical structure. A distributed network of partners of equal status is now becoming a more effective option because of developments in telecommunications and computing, but it is still complex to organize such a network effectively.

Impact on Individual Libraries. Resource sharing activities affect the autonomy of the libraries involved. Dangers arising from that factor can be minimized only by firm and unambiguous arrangements with partners and a clear understanding of the roles of each of the participating libraries. Librarians need to consider responsibilities to their primary clientele and the ways in which resource sharing can enhance their services. Successful sharing will occur only where there is no conflict between obligations made by the resource sharing arrangement and the objectives of the institutions involved.

Membership of networks that involve the sharing of records may have a profound effect on the record creation and automation activities of member libraries. While local discretion is possible in such matters as cataloguing standards, deviations will of themselves consume resources and libraries will reap the maximum benefits only by conforming to agreed standards. The problems of transitional arrangements between new and existing record creation practices may receive attention and retrospective conversion of older records may require consideration. The costs involved in such arrangements should be defined, compared with those of the existing practices, and weighed against the benefit resource sharing is expected to bring.

Resource sharing will require a willingness on the part of those involved to adapt to change and to come to terms with the realization that libraries can no longer be self-sufficient. Users must be educated and consulted in order to build an understanding of the types of material that can be expected to be provided locally and of how to gain access to the resources of other libraries.

Users must also be convinced that they can live with the delays inherent in resource sharing, or special arrangements must be made to meet the extra costs of rapid delivery of documents by such means as facsimile transmission. Sensible predictions about trends in users' needs have to be made so that acquisitions are reduced only in those areas where demands are likely to remain slight. Users will still expect that their primary needs will be met from their own libraries' resources, and large increases in interlending and document supply transactions may adversely affect both the standard and the costs of the service offered.

The effectiveness of any resource sharing arrangement will depend upon efficient and reliable communications and delivery systems between members. Resource sharing is not an end in itself, and there would be more success stories to report in this field if librarians regarded cooperation not only altruistically, but also realistically as a means for the library to improve its standards of services to its users.

University of Tennessee, Knoxville

Researchers receiving assistance in using the Inter-University Consortium for Political and Social Research (ICPSR) data tapes at their member institution. ICPSR, located at the University of Michigan, is the world's largest repository of machine-readable social data.

Trends and Issues. Many trends will be significant in the development of resource sharing activities in the next decade, but the effects of *technology* are likely to be more profound than all others. The impetus for increased resource sharing has often come in the past from particular technical developments, and this pattern is likely to continue. The first such impetus came from the introduction of cheap and reliable photocoyping equipment, which provided an alternative to interlibrary loan for shorter items such as serial articles. Document supply, a term which has been developed to cover both the loan of originals and the supply of surrogates or copies for retention, will undergo a further transformation when it becomes economic and reliable to transmit images digitally over telecommunication networks. Facsimile transmission (fax) has been available to libraries for many years but numerous studies and practical experience have shown that facsimile is unsuitable for the mass transmission of library documents; however, there is hope that the forthcoming generation of equipment will change this situation. Telecommunication facilities, including satellites, which enable massive amounts of data, including digital images of documents, to be transmitted from continent to continent are already available and becoming cheaper. Even the existing telecommunication networks of major library networks such as RLG and OCLC have capacity at quiet periods, especially overnight, to transmit images of documents, once the problems of rapidly digitizing the originals and storing them for later transmission have been overcome.

Developments in the technology for storing data are also likely to have a powerful impact on resource sharing networks. Present bibliographic networks have become possible only because of advances already made in the storage of large quantities of machine-readable data on magnetic media. The development of optical disk technology appears to offer the prospect of libraries being able to hold far more data on their own computer equipment than at present. It is possible to predict that within only a few years a database of the size of RLIN's can be copied onto optical disks and distributed to member libraries for mounting on their own computers. Such technology also enables libraries to store complete texts online.

Copyright. Publishers throughout the world have argued, with varying degrees of conviction, that library photocopying is damaging their interests and have pressed for legislation to control such activities. Although in the U.S. libraries are now obliged by law to limit their photocopying and a Copyright Clearance Center was established, there has been no change in the legal position in the U.K. or in many other countries. Publishers have not been slow to appreciate the potential benefits of new technology, however, in particular optical disks. Although a consortium of major scientific, technical, and medical publishers known as ADONIS did not proceed with its initial plans, it was indicative of likely future development. The ADONIS system was originally envisaged as a cooperative venture to store on optical disks the full texts of current and recent issues of the approximately 5,000 journals most frequently requested on interlibrary loan. A service for copies of single articles would then be offered by the publishers, possibly bypassing libraries altogether, but more likely using existing document suppliers as agents. The revenues to be gained from such a service might yet tempt the publishers to exploit the single-article market directly, although such activity in the late 1980s was mainly restricted to licensing commercial document suppliers to provide copies of articles.

The development of electronic publishing, particularly where there is no hardcopy or microform equivalent, may also have a significant effect on resource sharing during the next decade. Publishers will have far greater control over the use made of these texts and are likely to ensure that library users pay royalties.

Conservation. Richard De Gennaro highlighted the issue of conservation in a resource sharing context thus (1980):

> A vast majority of the books printed between 1850 and 1950 will be unusable by the end of this century as a result of the destructive effects of air pollution and the presence of acid and other harmful chemicals in their paper and binding. When we add to this the destructive effects of careless use, repeated photocopying, and frequent shipment through the mails, we are facing a crisis of monumental proportions.

Clearly, conservation is going to play a more prominent role in resource sharing considerations in the future. On the one hand, libraries will become more cautious about loaning originals, but, on the other, conservation by microfilming, deacidification, or digital storage may all be activities undertaken by resource sharing networks to enable surrogates of fragile material to continue to be used.

Evaluation and Research. Resource sharing will clearly be a continuing element in the provision of library services. It is already one of the topics most written about in library literature, and now has a journal devoted entirely to the subject, *Resource Sharing and Library Networks* (1981–). Yet there has been little evaluation of the results of resource sharing that is useful for professional guidance. There is clearly a

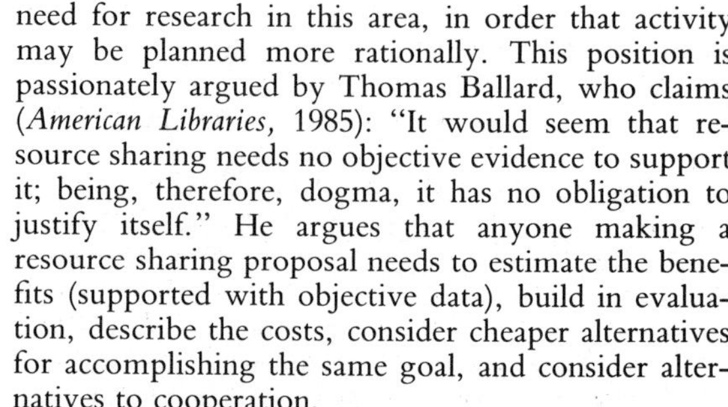

need for research in this area, in order that activity may be planned more rationally. This position is passionately argued by Thomas Ballard, who claims (*American Libraries,* 1985): "It would seem that resource sharing needs no objective evidence to support it; being, therefore, dogma, it has no obligation to justify itself." He argues that anyone making a resource sharing proposal needs to estimate the benefits (supported with objective data), build in evaluation, describe the costs, consider cheaper alternatives for accomplishing the same goal, and consider alternatives to cooperation.

While technological developments may have a substantial effect on resource sharing in the Western Hemisphere, it is not realistic to assume that progress in library provision will be made at the same pace throughout the world. The international dimension of resource sharing, however, will assume greater importance in the future because of current developments in telecommunications. Resource sharing should not be seen as an end in itself. All such activities still need to be assessed in light of overall benefit to the library user.

REFERENCES

Richard De Gennaro, "Resource Sharing in a Network Environment," *Library Journal* (1980).

Maurice Line, "Resource Sharing: The Present Situation and the Likely Effect of Electronic Technology." *The Future of Serials: Publication, Automation, and Management* (1984).

Rose Mary Magrill, "The Concept of Resource Sharing," *Canadian Library Journal* (1978).

Philip Sewell, *Resource Sharing* (1981).

H. D. L. Vervliet, *Resource Sharing of Libraries in Developing Countries* (1979).

MALCOLM SMITH

Richardson, Ernest C.

(1860–1939)

Ernest C. Richardson

Exemplar of the scholar-librarian tradition, Ernest Cushing Richardson made enduring contributions to American librarianship. Among his notable accomplishments may be counted the directorship of the Princeton University Library (1890–1920), the development of a classification scheme, the pursuit of cooperative bibliographic arrangements, and the publication of nearly 200 items covering an impressive range of library topics and other scholarly subjects.

Richardson was born February 9, 1860, in Woburn, Massachusetts. His early years were devoted to school, athletic activities, and frequent use of the local public library. He entered Amherst College in 1876 at 16, the last year of Melvil Dewey's term as Assistant Librarian. Although Richardson became a library student assistant during his freshman year, it is not known whether he was captivated by the charismatic Dewey. Richardson's apprenticeship under Dewey's brilliant successor, Walter S. Biscoe, was a decisive influence on the selection of a career in librarianship.

Deeply religious and committed to a life of scholarship, Richardson entered the Hartford Theological Seminary in 1880. He worked as a student assistant, became Assistant Librarian in 1882, and accepted the position of Director in 1884. During 1884 Richardson traveled to Europe and studied at various university libraries, a journey that he repeated many times in the ensuing years. The European visit marked the beginning of a lifetime concern with international library cooperation. At the Hartford Seminary, Richardson devised and implemented a classification scheme and completed many learned studies. In 1888 he was awarded an honorary doctorate from Washington and Jefferson College for preparation of the *Bibliographical Synopsis of the Ante-Nicene Fathers* (1887), a guide to the literature relating to early Christian leaders.

Although Richardson enjoyed the congenial atmosphere at the Hartford Seminary, the need for salary improvement and the challenge of managing a distinguished research library persuaded him to accept the Librarian's position at Princeton University in 1890. One year after his appointment, Richardson married Grace Duncan Ely, a woman of above-average financial means.

For 30 years Richardson struggled to provide the collections, facilities, and services that he believed Princeton needed. By 1900 Princeton had adopted a decimal classification scheme devised by Richardson, and in 1901 the Library became one of the early subscribers to the Library of Congress catalogue cards. That momentous decision was reached in a meeting which included such luminaries as Woodrow Wilson, Grover Cleveland, and John S. Billings. Richardson was perhaps most successful with the acquisitions program; the collection grew from 81,000 volumes in 1890 to approximately 450,000 volumes in 1920.

The reduction of bibliographic complexity was one of Richardson's many crusades that found application at Princeton. He believed in abbreviated cataloguing, an approach that provided the minimum information needed to identify and locate library materials. Richardson's "title-a-bar" theory involved the use of a Linotype machine to print one-line entries for each book in the form of a printed catalogue. That type of catalogue was not uniformly endorsed by the Princeton faculty. Beginning in 1913 the Princeton Library experienced reduced financial support, and salary levels declined. Faculty demands for more services and various complaints led to the appointment of an investigatory committee in 1920. An Associate Librarian, James Gerould, was employed with special authority to institute changes. He immediately abandoned the printed catalogues and began to reclassify portions of the collection. Administratively dethroned and elevated to figurehead status, Richardson argued bitterly with the university until 1925, when he accepted a position as honorary consultant in bibliography at the Library of Congress. Neither side was without fault, but Richardson was clearly stubborn, unwilling to compromise or concede shortcomings. This unfortunate propensity to pursue a collision course would occur again.

At the Library of Congress Richardson continued to teach as he had done at Princeton and initiated one of the most significant bibliographic projects of that era. For 20 years Richardson had been writing and speaking, primarily through the American Library Institute, a deliberative body affiliated with the American Library Association, about the paucity of resources in research libraries and the lack of systematic bibliographic organization. As Chairman of ALA's Committee on Bibliography, Richardson had laid the groundwork for "Project B," a cooperative cataloguing program to augment and revitalize the national union catalogue at the Library of Congress. Richardson and his staff succeeded in enlarging the union catalogue file from 1,500,000 titles in 1927 to approximately 7,000,000 titles in 1932. Unhappily, Richardson became enmeshed in a debate with the ALA Executive Board over the jurisdiction of another committee, the Cooperative Cataloguing Committee. After a protracted controversy, which erupted in the professional journals, Richardson resigned in 1934 to pursue his many scholarly interests. His commitment to bibliographic control and cooperative arrangements exceeded that of most contemporaries, and "Project B" may be considered the unheralded predecessor of the better-known Farmington Plan of the 1940s.

Foremost a scholar, Richardson published extensively in the fields of librarianship, history, and theology. Significant contributions to the library field included *Classification, Theoretical and Practical* (1901), which influenced such classificationists as England's W. C. Berwick Sayers, *Some Aspects of International Library Cooperation* (1928), *General Library Cooperation and American Research Books* (1930), and *Some Aspects of Cooperative Cataloging* (1934). His writings in library history reveal a serious as well as a whimsical side: *Some Old Egyptian Librarians* (1911), *Biblical Libraries* (1914), and *The Beginnings of Libraries* (1914). Historians remain indebted to his pioneering editorial work on the first volume of *Writings on American History* (1904).

Richardson was an active member and officer of many learned societies and professional groups: American Library Association (President, 1904–05); councillor of the Bibliographical Society of America (1917–37); Chairman of the Bibliography Committee of the American Historical Association (1902–15); and Chairman of the ALA Committee on Bibliography (1922–34). Following World War I his service extended beyond the academy to participation on the United States House Inquiry Commission, a group designated to select and transport documents for the peace conference at Versailles.

After the death of his wife in 1933 and the confrontation with the Executive Board in 1934, Richardson withdrew from library affairs and moved to a cottage near Old Lyme, Connecticut. His scholarly work continued, especially in theology, and he remained actively associated with several institutions of higher education. He died in Old Lyme, Connecticut, June 3, 1939, while engaged in a study of rare books.

Although Richardson does not today enjoy the reputation accorded some early library leaders, his accomplishments were impressive. Few librarians have surpassed his scholarly attainments or pursued more vigorously the goal of bibliographic interdependence. Fittingly, Richardson defined and exemplified the object of library science as the need "to connect a reader, surely and promptly, with the book that he wants to use."

REFERENCES

Lewis C. Branscomb, *A Bio-Bibliographical Study of Ernest Cushing Richardson, 1860–1939.*

Primary sources are in the Princeton University Library, the Library of Congress, and the Hartford Seminary Foundation Library.

Lewis C. Branscomb, "Richardson, Ernest Cushing," *Dictionary of American Library Biography* (1978).

ARTHUR P. YOUNG

Godfrey Memorial Library
Arthur Fremont Rider

Rider, Arthur Fremont
(1885–1962)

Arthur Fremont Rider, self-described as inquisitive, introverted, and principled, was one of the American library profession's most versatile figures. He was an editor, publisher, and writer, associate of Dewey, university librarian, and early microform advocate. Blending the conceptual with the practical was his forte. Rider's bequest to library scholarship is confirmed by the frequent citations to his seminal writings.

Rider was born in Trenton, New Jersey, May 25, 1885. His childhood years were spent in Middletown, Connecticut, where he first used the Wesleyan University Library, a library he would later direct. Rider graduated from Syracuse University in 1905 and enrolled in the New York State Library School (class of 1907). Before graduating he was invited by Melvil Dewey, a lifelong influence, to work on a revision of the Decimal Classification at the Lake Placid Club. Rider met his first wife, Grace Godfrey, a relative of Dewey, at Lake Placid, and they were married in 1908. Rider was married to Marie Gallup Ambrose in 1951.

Rider began in 1907 the first of many often overlapping careers. Between 1907 and 1917 he served as Associate Editor of *The Delineator* and Editor of *Monthly Book Review, Publishers' Weekly,* and *Library Journal.* From 1914 to 1932 he was President of Rider Press, a periodical press that printed most of the R. R. Bowker publications. The press failed at the depth of the Depression following a debilitating struggle with a union and the withdrawal of Bowker's patronage. During that period Rider published a series of well-received guidebooks to New York City, Washington, Bermuda, and California. Still not content with those accomplishments, he wrote numerous short stories for popular magazines and dabbled in poetry, drama, and real estate.

Rider's early association with Dewey and library publishing together with business acumen and literary inclinations were valuable assets for the next phase of his career. He was invited to become Librarian of Wesleyan University's Olin Library in 1933, and for the next two decades Rider challenged tradition, experimented, and proselytized new concepts. The results of these reappraisals and other pertinent information about the Wesleyan Library were reported in the Rider-edited periodical, *About Books.* The collection more than doubled during his tenure, largely through en bloc purchases. New cost accounting procedures were introduced; catalogue cards for Wesleyan titles not listed in the Library of Congress catalogue were printed and distributed to many libraries; and cooperative relationships with neighboring libraries were pursued. Faced with limited shelving, Rider initiated a compact shelving program for seldom-used books. The books were shelved, after cropping, on their foreedges. His controversial ideas on compact shelving were published in *Compact Book Storage* (1949). Because of his provocative writings and practical adaptations at Wesleyan, Rider was in con-

National Library of Jamaica
Joyce Robinson

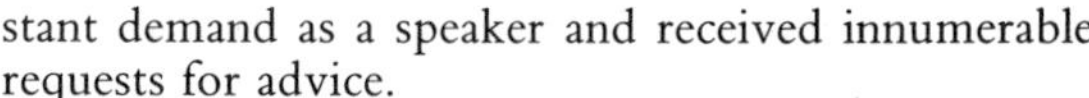

stant demand as a speaker and received innumerable requests for advice.

Of his numerous achievements, perhaps his enduring legacy remains his analysis of research library growth and advocacy of microcards espoused in *The Scholar and the Future of the Research Library* (1944). By studying collection growth patterns, Rider concluded that the collections of research libraries double approximately every 16 years. This observation, startling in its time, coupled with the infrequent use of research-level materials, led Rider to propose the microcard as a cost-effective, space-saving solution. Ingeniously, the catalogue card and the relevant document were combined to form a single card with bibliographic description on the front and microtext on the back. His book was reviewed extensively in the library literature and in such nonlibrary journals as the *Columbia Law Review* and the *New England Quarterly.* He invariably received high marks for his trenchant analysis and concise style, but many reviewers questioned the immediate practicability of the idea; however, all would have concurred with William Warner Bishop's remark that Rider had "given librarians much to think about and to think about furiously." Unselfish about the microcard, Rider never patented the concept. Years later, in 1961, he was awarded the annual medal of the National Microfilm Association for his distinguished contribution to microform technology.

Near the end of his library career, in 1951, Rider built the Godfrey Memorial Library, a noncirculating library for the study and promotion of genealogical research. Of major importance to historians and genealogists is the *American Genealogical-Biographical Index* (100+ volumes), issued by that research facility. In 1961, one year before his death, Rider published *Rider's International Classification for the Arrangement of Books on the Shelves of General Libraries.* Reviewers were impressed with the brave attempt but decidedly lukewarm over the results.

Rider's multidimensional career is flamboyantly reconstructed in an often vainglorious autobiography, *And Master of None* (1955), a mine of information, especially about his nonlibrary activities. His contribution to library history was *Melvil Dewey: A Biography* (ALA, 1944); although expectedly favorable toward Dewey, Rider's study was a refreshing corrective to Grosvenor Dawes's earlier deification of the great pioneer.

Rider died October 26, 1962, in Middletown, Connecticut. His intellect, vision, and creative applications place him in the front rank of library forebears.

REFERENCE

Wyman W. Parker, "Rider, Arthur Fremont," *Dictionary of American Library Biography* (1978).

ARTHUR P. YOUNG

Robinson, Joyce
(1925–)

Joyce Lilieth Robinson, first Jamaican Director of the Jamaica Library Service, gained an impressive record of professional achievement and made an indelible mark on the fields of librarianship and adult education at national, regional, and international levels.

Born in Saint James, Jamaica, July 2, 1925,

Robinson was educated in Jamaica and in London. Appointed Director of the Jamaica Library Service in 1957, she served in that post until 1976. She provided effective leadership in developing an island-wide public library service by significantly expanding public libraries, introducing the use of bookmobiles, and vigorously expanding a library building program. She also worked to expand school libraries.

A founding member of the Jamaica Library Association, Robinson served it in many offices, including two terms as President, in 1964 and 1973. She contributed advice and expertise in shaping Jamaica's National Information System through her work as Chairman of the Board of Management of the National Library of Jamaica (1978–) and as a founding member of the National Council on Libraries, Archives, and Documentation Services, on which she served as Chairman from 1980 to 1990. She became Vice-Chairman of the restructured National Council on Libraries, Archives, and Information Systems, which advises the government on the coordination of policies and plans for further development of the entire information sector, including publishing, information technology, media, and communication, as well as statistical and numerical databases.

From 1973 to 1981, as Executive Director of the Jamaica Movement for the Advancement of Literacy (JAMAL), she piloted a comprehensive community-centered national literacy program for persons 15 years and older. This program, which won international recognition for its innovative approach and its use of locally developed materials, attracted more than 13,000 volunteer teachers in 8,000 classes throughout the island. Using a curriculum based on 400 instruction hours, 2,000 adults achieved literacy during this period.

Robinson served as the first woman General Manager of the Jamaica Broadcasting Corporation (1981–82), continuing her work in information and adult education. She then served (1982–91 as Managing Director of the Human Employment and Research Training program (HEART), an island-wide skills training program for school leavers and adults. HEART includes vocational training based on eight residential academies, on-the-job training in 1,500 firms in the private sector, and a self-help entrepreneurship program comprising 3,500 projects in crafts, vending, and agriculture.

On the international scene, Robinson distinguished herself as Vice-Chairman of Unesco's International Committee on Documentation, Libraries, and Archives (1975–77 and 1979–81), and as Vice-President of the International Council on Adult Education (1986–90). She played leading roles in many conferences, seminars, and training courses. Her many publications in national and international journals reflect her commitment to the advancement of librarianship and literacy.

Robinson's outstanding achievements won for her many accolades. The (British) Library Association named her an Honorary Vice-President for life (1973); the American Library Association selected her as its Carl Milam International Lecturer (1979). She was awarded honorary doctorates by Dalhousie University (1979) and the University of the West Indies (1990) in recognition of her outstanding work in the fields of librarianship, literacy, and adult education. The British Government named her a Member of the Order of the British Empire (M.B.E.) in 1959 and the Government of Jamaica conferred on her the Order of Jamaica (O.J.) in 1978.

Retired since 1991, she continues to contribute her time and expertise in the service of several social, educational, cultural, and professional organizations.

REFERENCES

Jamaica Movement for the Advancement of Literacy, "JAMAL Foundation Five-Year Plan, 1978–1983" (1978).

The HEART Trust, "The Solidarity Programme, November 1985 – August 1988" (1988).

STEPHNEY FERGUSON

Rogers, Frank Bradway
(1914–1987)

ALA

Frank Bradway Rogers

Frank Bradway Rogers, military surgeon, trained librarian, and Director of the National Library of Medicine in a crucial period, became one of the developers of the first automated database for scientific literature (MEDLARS) and supervised its transfer to medical libraries and hospitals, conceiving a national system for strengthening the provision of biomedical information to health professionals.

Frank "Brad" Rogers was born December 31, 1914, in Norwood, Ohio. He returned there for his medical training after obtaining an undergraduate degree from Yale University and working for several years at various jobs in New York City and the Midwest. He was private secretary to a professor-turned-congressman (an experience that stood him in good stead later in life when he was trying to persuade Congress to pass the Medical Library Assistance Act), advertising agent for a soap firm, and clerk in a food store, all to obtain enough money to see him through medical school, like John Shaw Billings. Rogers joined the Army Medical Corps after graduation from medical school. He took his internship at Letterman General Hospital near San Francisco; later he served in the campaigns in Luzon in the Philippines and in the American Occupation in Japan.

After World War II Rogers accepted a residency in surgery at Walter Reed Army Medical Center. While there he learned that the Army was looking for a physician to be Director of what was then called the Army Medical Library. When the position was offered to him in 1948, he accepted—and thus changed the whole direction of his life.

At that time the Army Medical Library had just undergone a thorough reevaluation, after a long period when it had been allowed to disintegrate to a remarkable degree. Billings, its founder, had given it momentum in the late 19th century through his vision and sense of purpose (aided greatly by the backing and fiscal care bestowed on the Library by the various earlier Surgeons-General of the Army), but the momentum had gradually declined or been halted. When World War II erupted and the armed forces began fighting in exotic areas of the world, encountering exotic diseases, it became obvious that the Army Medical Library could not help the medical officers in their struggles against blackwater fever, jungle rot, tsutsugamushi disease, and unusual tick and bacterial fevers unknown to the physicians in America and western Europe.

Perhaps the most serious example of the inadequacies of the then Army Medical Library was its failure to keep up regular publication of the *Index-Catalogue of the Library of the Surgeon General's Office, Army Medical Library*. Billings had founded the *Index-Catalogue* in the 1870s as a list of the books and journal articles in the Library, the largest medical library in the world. It was arranged and issued alphabetically in a 15- to 20-year cycle—volume 1, for example, contained all the authors and subjects beginning with the letters A to Be; volume 2 went on to Ch; and so on. By 1936 three complete series had been published, but the fourth series was stuck in the middle of the alphabet.

The *Index-Catalogue* had always had a companion publication, the *Index Medicus,* which appeared monthly and brought the alphabetical volumes up to date. By using the two works together, a biomedical worker could obtain a conspectus of some 15 to 20 years of the literature on a topic in one place (the *Index-Catalogue*), then bring it up to date year by year by use of the *Index Medicus*.

This systematic approach to the knowledge of medicine was destroyed when the *Index-Catalogue* was not published on a regular basis and when the *Index Medicus* (after uniting with the American Medical Association's *Quarterly Cumulative Index Medicus*) was not published at all in the 1940s. Neither the older writings of those who had experience with these diseases nor the newer knowledge that was being uncovered in the vast laboratory of World War II medicine was available to military physicians, and it is estimated that, as a result, endemic diseases may have been as lethal to the troops as enemy gunfire.

The need was so obvious, something had to be done. The Surgeon-General asked a committee of distinguished librarians from the American Library Association to survey the Library and to recommend needed action. One of their recommendations was for a professionally trained Director of the Library who would be assigned long enough to be able to carry out the needed reforms. Rogers was appointed to this post; he was sent to the library school at Columbia University for a year (1948–49) and then took office. He remained as Director of the Library until August 1963, when he left to become the Librarian of the University of Colorado Medical Center in Denver.

During his term in Washington, Rogers oversaw the transformation of the Library from a sleepy and almost moribund institution to perhaps the most dynamic library, not only for medicine, but for information science as well. He helped transfer the Library from the Army alone to the armed forces as a whole, then from military control to the U.S. Public Health Service, which understood its mission as being central to the purpose of the agency itself. Not surprisingly, Rogers was able to obtain from so understanding an agency a much-needed new Library building, whose form has made it an architectural delight. As the Director of the National Library of Medicine, Rogers defined its role; planned and carried out its reorganization into a Library using 20th-century methods; reinvigorated its classic mission of producing indexes to the medical literature that were extensive in scope and that appeared on time; and began a series of experiments with modern technology (such as time-lapse photography and computer-assisted printing) that has made medicine the best-served field bibliographically speaking, and which has become the model for many other fields and endeavors. The extent of its influence is shown in such achievements as the MEDLARS/MEDLINE system (the precursor to all the automated databases now in use) and the Medical Library Assistance Act, which provided the U.S. for the first time with a national network of medical information centers available to its citizens generally, and which encouraged research and development in this subject fiscally in many national and international centers.

Rogers also saw and acted on the responsibilities of the United States in a period when it had become a world leader. Whether he was co-chairing the First International Congress on Medical Librarianship, in London in 1953, seeing to the myriad details of the Second Congress, held at the new building of the NLM in Bethesda in 1963, or arranging to bring foreign medical librarians to NLM for observation or training, Rogers always had international purposes in mind. He carried out consulting missions in Nigeria and Korea for the Ford and other foundations. When the occasion presented itself, he took over from the National Institutes of Health responsibility for running the medical portion of the translation program under Public Law 480, which used blocked currency from U.S. debtor nations to purchase translations of Russian- and other-language medical research works. He published them in sizable editions and distributed them free to appropriate American institutions.

Rogers was a student of medical history, which he enjoyed examining by himself and which he helped to put on a sound footing again at NLM. He was a craftsman who delighted in the well-bound book, and fitted up a bindery for himself, in which he continued to work after his retirement. His sense of words and their use made all of his writings exact, fitting, and musical. His honors and awards include election to the presidency of the Medical Library Association (which also bestowed on him its Marcia C. Noyes Award) and the American Association of the History of Medicine; the award of the Cyril Barnard Memorial Prize for outstanding service to medical librarianship in 1954; the Melvil Dewey medal of the American Library Association; the U.S. Public Service Distinguished Service Award; and the Horace Hart Award of the Education Council of the Graphic Arts Industry. In 1983 the Frank B. Rogers Information Advancement Award was established by the Institute for Scientific Information in the Medical Library Association.

Rogers's place in the history of the transmission of biomedical information is safe for all time. He came at the right time with Pasteur's "mind prepared," and he left this field immeasurably ahead of where he had found it. A colleague who worked with him for many years described him admiringly as "the civil servant the citizens of the United States don't deserve"; indeed, it was on the basis of Rogers's work there that the later history of NLM has developed.

REFERENCES

Estelle Brodman, "Frank Bradway Rogers, M.D., President, Medical Library Association, 1962–63," *Bulletin of the Medical Library Association* (1962).

Wyndham D. Miles, *A History of the National Library of Medicine, The Nation's Treasury of Medical Knowledge* (1982).

ESTELLE BRODMAN

Romania

Romania, a republic of the Balkan Peninsula in southeastern Europe, is bounded by Ukraine on the north, Moldova and the Black Sea on the east, Bulgaria on the south, and Yugoslavia and Hungary on the west. Population (1990 est.) 23,200,000; area 237,500 sq.km. The official language is Romanian.

History. The first libraries in Romania, as elsewhere in Europe, were linked with churches, monasteries, and princely courts. The princes amassed collections of books mainly in the capitals of Wallachia and Moldavia. Starting in the 16th century, when printing became an important cultural and political reality (the first book printed in Romania came off the press in 1508), books began to circulate widely and the foundations for libraries were laid in all areas inhabited by Romanians.

Before 1859, when the modern Romanian state was founded, the most important libraries were connected with universities at Bucharest in Wallachia and at Jassy in Moldavia. The first modern public libraries, the Central State Library in Bucharest and the Central State Library in Jassy, were founded in 1864. Library services continued to grow until World War II. Between the war and the Revolution of 1989, Romanian libraries followed patterns laid down by Soviet authorities.

National Libraries. Romania has two libraries recognized as national in scope, the National Library and the Library of the Romanian Academy.

National Library. The National Library was founded in 1935 as the Central State Library. It continues the traditions of earlier libraries in Bucharest, but administrative structures changed greatly over time. The collections are encyclopedic in character, and by the late 1980s they totaled more than 15,800,000 volumes. The National Library has the right of central legal deposit and publishes national current bibliographies and the National Bibliography; makes up the national union catalogue on cards; and publishes directories and union catalogues of foreign books and serials, among other activities.

The National Library has a nucleus of documentation in librarianship and a center of methodological guidance for public libraries. It also houses an agency for international exchange of publications and manages international interlibrary loans. It has several reading rooms specialized by fields of knowledge and by categories of publications and media (such as manuscripts and letters, Romanian bibliophilic books, foreign bibliophilic books, maps, loose sheets, and newspapers); there is also a department for official publications and offices for Unesco publications and publications of other international bodies. Educational activities include organizing exhibitions, meetings with writers and scholars, musical programs, and other events.

Library of the Romanian Academy. The second national library of the country was founded in 1867. Its early growth owed much to private donations and to legal deposit privileges (since 1885). Until 1948 the Library covered almost exclusively humanities and social sciences, but after the reorganization of the Romanian Academy, the Library started collecting works in scientific and technical fields as well. Holdings total some 9,800,000 volumes; in addition there are thousands of manuscripts, rare books, engravings, maps, about 300,000 letters, archives of important personalities, records, and various categories of other items.

The Library of the Academy is concerned with the publication of the Romanian national retrospective bibliography of books and periodicals from the 16th century. It provides various bibliographic tools and services for its collections. It also administers a major exchange program with publications issued by the Publishing House of the Academy, which are sent to about 10,000 exchange partners in more than 100 countries and fulfill interlibrary loan requests.

The Library of the Academy has branch libraries in all parts of the country. The branch libraries in Cluj and Jassy have particularly rich and valuable collections.

Academic Libraries. There are three central university libraries, in Bucharest (founded in 1891), Jassy (1640), and Cluj (1872). Together they have

Libraries in Romania (1990)

Type of library	Number of administrative units (main libraries)	Volumes in collections	Population served	Total staff
National	2	15,820,000*	500,000*	570
Academic	44	23,100,000*	1,500,000*	2,850
Public	6,900**	72,200,000*	7,300,000*	3,200*
School	10,987	61,000,000*	13,800,000*	2,100
Special	2,908	21,920,000*	3,600,000*	3,206*
Other (describe)	--	--	--	--

*Estimate
**Library supported by the public authorities only

Source: Anuarul statistic al României 1990

National Library of Romania, formerly the Central State Library

National Library of Romania, formerly the Central State Library.

more than 10,000,000 volumes and include in their holdings Romanian works of great cultural value, outstanding works of the world cultural heritage, works by Romanian personalities in manuscript form, private collections of books with dedications, and autographed books. They have the right of legal deposit. These three libraries are directly subordinated to the Ministry of Education and Science and each serves the entire university community on its campus, providing support for library activities and for refresher courses for librarians in the university libraries.

The Central University Library in Bucharest acquires domestic publications (books and periodicals) for libraries in the academic network and maintains holdings for the departments of Romanian language, literature, and civilization created abroad.

There are 42 other academic libraries, such as those in the fields of technical sciences, medicine, and agronomy, with collections ranging from 500,000 to 1,500,000 volumes. They are expected to meet not only the requirements of education and research but also the requirements of study and documentation for the specialists on the university campuses they serve. They issue information bulletins, bibliographies, indexes of journals, bibliographic studies on subjects, directories, and other information sources and instruments. They contribute—on the local and national level—to bibliographic and documentary information works and instruct students in library use.

Public Libraries. Romania has public libraries at the county, city, town, and village level. Their collections vary greatly in size and importance. Some, in centers such as Jassy, Galaţi, Craiova, and Sibiu, have valuable historical and cultural collections. Some rural areas have few library services. County libraries draw up local bibliographies and provide guidance to other public libraries; they organize some branch libraries, provide mobile lending centers, and develop special sections for children.

School Libraries. In Romania school libraries are organized in each elementary school, gymnasium, secondary school, and vocational school, sponsored by the local educational bodies or by the corresponding ministries (the technical and vocational schools). They receive guidance from the Ministry of Education and Science and the Central Pedagogical Library in Bucharest. Their holdings contain materials that support the educational program. In some areas without public libraries, school libraries provide library materials for adults as well as children.

Special Libraries. Special libraries in Romania form a category of library service insufficiently defined as yet. Some are branches of such institutions as the Central Pedagogical Library; others are independent entities such as the Library of the National Institute for Information and Documentation; still others belong to research institutes, institutes of higher education, academies, scientific and cultural associations, cultural institutions, institutions of the state administration, industrial units, documentation centers, and offices. Their holdings reflect the specialized character of the fields they serve.

The Profession. Training for librarianship in Romania takes place through the Section of library and information science in Bucharest University (a four-year course) or through colleges of librarianship at the universities in Bucharest and Sibiu (a three-year course). Training in both courses is designed for both specialization and a solid cultural background.

Romania has two library associations with a total membership of 4,000 professionals: Asociaţa bibliotecarilor din Invatamînt (ABIR; Association of Librarians in Education) and Asociaţa bibliotecarilor din bibliotecile publice (ABBPR; Association of Librarians in Public Libraries). Both associations are members of IFLA and both work for the growth of professional standards and for strengthening relations with the international librarianship movement.

ION STOICA

Rome (Ancient)

There is considerable literary evidence of the private book collections assembled in the latter days of the Republic, thanks successively to Greek stimulation, Roman pride, and military conquest. Much less is known about libraries of a public sort because the archaeological testimony becomes more critical and very little has survived. It is possible that M. T. Varro, a leading Roman of the 1st century B.C., composed a treatise on libraries, but it is established only that Caesar asked him to take charge of a project to build a grand public library, Rome's first, and that nothing came of it directly after Caesar's assassination. Caesar's friend, C. Asinius Pollio, did found near the Forum ("Atrium Libertatis") in the 30s B.C. a library apparently of the sort Caesar had wanted. Reportedly it comprised mainly book booty from the Illyrian campaign of 39 B.C. Latin and Greek sister libraries were formed; the premises were decorated with likenesses of the outstanding writers, Varro being the only living author among those so honored. What became of it is not known.

Several libraries were organized in the imperial capital to memorialize past achievement and nourish national pride. When in 28 B.C. Augustus dedicated a temple of Apollo on the Palatine, Latin and Greek libraries were attached to it. This pairing, as well as the temple nexus, had precedent, but this occasion may have been the first time a practical advantage was manifest, inasmuch as the Latin division was strong in

Roman law and the Senate met there occasionally. The Palatine library story is further marked by severe losses from fire, some rebuilding, and leadership by a number of learned men appointed by the emperor; the fire of 363 was apparently the end. The same career and fate seem to have been the lot of the paired libraries begun by Augustus about 25 B.C. on the Campus Martius, named in honor of his sister Octavia. Later emperors also founded libraries, some of which endured: 28 in Constantine's day, it is said (reasonably, although only 10 names are known).

Noteworthy is the Pantheon Library, founded by Emperor Alexander Severus around 230, perhaps the first public library in Rome to have held Eastern religious materials, especially Christian and Jewish writings. It is interesting, and possibly of critical significance, that Julius Africanus, appointed Director, was not only a career soldier and engineer but also a scholar in Christian church chronology and a man of broad enough interests to compile an encyclopedia.

The royal example was followed almost from the start by individuals prominent in letters and well enough off to endow a library—or wealthy and desiring to be remembered as friendly to the world of intellect. We know of a library for the Musicians and Actors Association, and it seems likely that various other associations and institutions had book collections too, whether endowed or not. Were they, like the imperial gifts, placed at temples, public baths, or colonnades?

When chronicler Ammianus Marcellinus complained late in the 4th century that the libraries of Rome were shut up like tombs, he, a Syrian Greek defending Rome against the declining tone in upper-crust Roman life, may well have taken comfort from the vigor outside Rome. From the early 3rd century until the empire's collapse, public libraries were a fairly standard feature of Roman centers in western Europe and North Africa, scattered details being available in the literary records and occasionally from archaeology. Verified information about such institutions in the East is similarly fragmentary, but many of them played a part in the rise and 4th-century triumph of Christianity; of course they were often ecclesiastical rather than really "public." Also, the leading library at Constantinople is apparently the first to have drawn attention in public law, a decree of 372 incorporated in the Theodosian Code.

The first books in a Roman library were most likely to have arrived by arrangement with whoever had donated the building. Such a donation was one recognized means of winning honorable notice, perhaps even from the emperor; it often led to the erection of a statue. The sovereign did not hesitate to ban from these libraries books he considered objectionable, but the general practice was reportedly rather generous, admitting Christian and non-Roman philosophy. Proscription first of Christian and then of anti-Christian materials did not begin until the struggles of the 4th century.

The book trade could be counted on only for ordinary current works, and the copies supplied by dealers were held in low esteem. Libraries tended to make their own, insofar as they could not fill gaps with the help of auctions or other special opportunities; besides, papyrus exposed to the air lasted no more than 200 years. Many libraries public and private, not just the very largest, operated copying rooms. Regulations sometimes called for annual fresh copies of certain works, and there must have been great dependence on a cadre of skilled copyists. We know that in late-4th-century Constantinople the copyists (*antiquarii*) were important individuals, reminiscent of the scribes 2,500 years earlier.

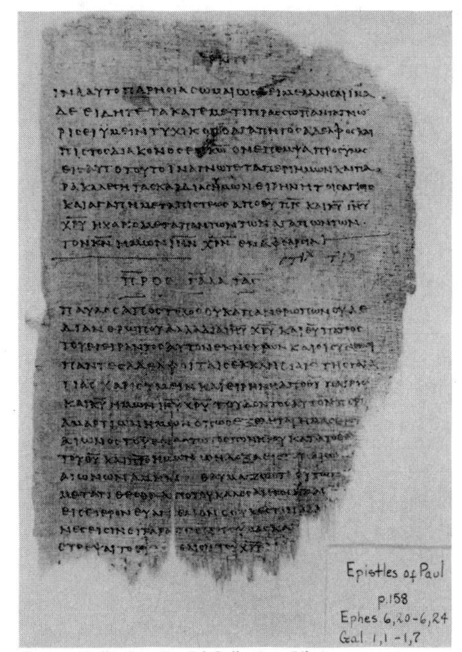

Papyrus Collection, Special Collections Library, The University of Michigan

Leaf of a papyrus codex of the Epistles of Saint Paul displays the concluding paragraphs of Ephesians and the beginning of Galatians. Dating from ca. 200 A.D., it is the oldest known copy of the Epistles.

Extant catalogue information indicates beyond serious doubt that titles were listed in subject groups. It seems almost as clear that the shelving of rolls followed the same plan; at least the recorded placement of likenesses of writers also argues for that conclusion. In each cabinet (*armarium*), the rolls were arranged in author-alphabetical order, individually identified by a small stick projecting from the center of the roll (*titulus*). No location number has been found for an individual work. Cabinet doors were kept closed to protect the rolls from light.

For a book owner to allow friends to read on the premises was common, but to loan a book for use elsewhere called for unusual friendship. The public libraries were essentially limited to reading on the premises. Evidence has survived of an oath required of readers in an Athenian library that they would not walk off with the book entrusted to them. Now as then, of course, permission to borrow was granted to a person of known scholarship or exceptional influence.

The daylight hours were obviously of prime importance. Architect Vitruvius urged that a library be arranged so that its windows maximized the availability of sunlight. The Athenian library just mentioned was open, according to an inscription, from sunrise to 6 P.M.

The would-be reader in a public library went first to the catalogue, then applied to the staff for the desired item; only the latter were supposed to go to the book-cabinets. Literary testimony suggests that this procedure was reasonably satisfactory. Some moments were remembered because the catalogue generated either frustration or a pleasant surprise.

Some staff members were imperial slaves assigned to the leading libraries founded in the 1st century A.D.; these are noted, with their library relationship, in many tomb inscriptions. Anonymity absorbed their successors, perhaps in connection with the civil service reforms begun under Hadrian. Library direction was customarily in the hands of scholars: they were among the procurators in the 1st century, but the latter category gradually became transformed primarily into performer of fiscal and other external functions—by the 4th century part of the duties of the city prefect—and the scholars tended to be limited to internal affairs such as book selection.

The division of library labor had by empire days reached the stage of establishing perhaps a dozen Latin verbs for specifically library functions. They included special meanings for terms used in other ways too, such as *disponere* ("organize"), and terms peculiar to the library, for example, *commutare* ("replace a poor copy with a better one").

Librarianship as a set of skills attracted some thoughtful attention, but the extant records give greatly varying support on various issues. Least questioned is the tradition of scholarly management and purpose well established in Hellenistic days, especially at Alexandria; the testimony is almost entirely literary. That Varro could have said many useful things in his treatise on libraries, with known ideas and practices to back them up from Hellenistic data, is quite plausible. Unfortunately, not one scrap survives; we cannot be certain that he ever wrote that treatise. Widely accepted as likely, though impossible to prove with archaeological evidence, is the debt of Rome's noted library buildings to whatever the Ptolemaic architects devised at Alexandria. Indications are available from the physical remains at other sites, such as Pergamum. In any case, architect Vitruvius, writing in the late 1st century B.C., advised on library design as an expected topic. The same applies to library catalogues, for whose existence the literary testimony from at least the 1st century A.D. is noticeable though neither routine nor detailed. If the Alexandrian customs were known, they would apparently have been associated with Callimachus's *Pinakes*. The sole regular allusions to libraries surviving from Roman times are those in Suetonius, who names sponsoring emperors, librarians, and the writers of consequence represented in those libraries. The data are scientific materials only in the sense that they give us a proximate source for Aulus Gellius's and Isidor of Seville's passages on libraries.

Christian books also first appeared during the Roman Empire, but the story of Christian libraries falls more naturally with the information on the Middle Ages (*See* Middle Ages, Libraries in the).

SIDNEY L. JACKSON
(d. 1979)

Rovira, Carmen
(1919–)

Carmen Rovira's experience and pioneering scholarship in the bibliography, classification, and cataloguing of Spanish-language materials, together with many related and significant organizational activities, made her a figure of central importance in Latin American librarianship.

Rovira was born in Santiago de Cuba on June 13, 1919, and her early life was spent in both Spain and Cuba. She received a doctoral degree in Philosophy and Letters from the University of Havana in 1946 and graduated from its Library School in 1952. In 1969 Rovira received a Master's degree in Library Science from the Graduate Library School of the Catholic University of America in Washington, D.C.

In 1942 Rovira began her professional career as Librarian of the Art History Department of the University of Havana. She was appointed library cataloguer at the Catholic University of Saint Thomas of Villanova in 1952; in 1953 she was made head of the library, a post she held until she left Cuba in 1960 after the revolution. Between 1951 and 1960 she gave numerous courses in librarianship in both the summer school and regular sessions of the University of Havana's Library School, most frequently on the subjects of cataloguing and classification.

From 1960 Rovira worked in the Library Development Program of the Organization of American States, which she headed from 1978 until 1982, when she retired.

Between 1961 and 1966 she compiled, together with Jorge Aguayo, the *Lista de Encabezamientos de Materia para Bibliotecas* ("Subject Heading List for Libraries"), a milestone work that has served the entire Spanish-speaking world since its publication in 1967 as the basic subject-heading list for library materials in Spanish. She also served as a consultant to Forest Press on the Spanish translation of the 18th edition of the Dewey Decimal Classification. After her retirement from the OAS, she translated the 12th edition of the *Sears List of Subject Headings* into Spanish for the H. W. Wilson Company. It appeared in 1984 as *Sears: Lista de Encabezamientos de Materia*. Then, with Caroline Reyes, she compiled the 13th edition of the *Sears List of Subject Headings* (1986).

Carmen Rovira's other major publication is *Los Epígrafes en el Catálogo Diccionario* ("Titles in a Dictionary Catalogue," 1953; 2nd edition, 1966), the first Spanish-language work on the theory of subject headings. She also served as Director of the professional journal *Cuba Bibliotecológica* ("Cuban Librarianship") in 1953 and again between 1955 and 1957.

MARTHA TOMÉ

Rudomino, Margarita Ivanovna
(1900–1989)

Margarita Ivanovna Rudomino founded the All-Union State Library of Foreign Literature in Moscow in 1921, remained its Director for more than 50 years, and had a broad international experience, mainly through the International Federation of Library Associations. She became the principal ambassador of Soviet librarianship abroad.

She was born July 3, 1900, in Bialystok, in what is now Poland, and although orphaned at an early age, she was able to finish secondary school in Saratov, Russia. She was Librarian in the school for foreign studies in the same city four years before being entrusted with the library of foreign literature—known at the time as the Neophilological Library.

The All-Union State Library of Foreign Literature had a modest start in 1921. Initially on the fifth floor of a 19th-century building in the center of Moscow, it moved four times among several buildings before it finally occupied a large modern building, designed as a library by the architect V. Sitnov (1967). At the time of the dedication it had 700 staff members, 55,000 registered readers, and a collection of about 4,000,000 volumes in 128 languages. It became one of the important libraries in the world, while its objective gives it a unique character. It has a number of unusual features, foreign languages being fundamental to the entire operation: language courses in laboratories with sophisticated audiovisual equipment, readings by foreign authors, exhibitions of foreign books, bibliographic control of foreign literatures, and guidance to Soviet libraries with foreign language departments and departments of foreign library literature.

At the dedication ceremonies Rudomino said, "All about this building—both its exterior view and its light reading rooms—create that atmosphere of peace and joy which is so important for thoughtful, thorough study of a book or a manuscript." The architecture contributes to the urban landscape of Moscow both a local ponderousness and an imported elegance, Scandinavian influence being most obvious in the interior design and furniture.

The collections come mainly, but not exclusively, from the West. They are organized according to Western patterns, and an American or European librarian can easily understand its structure. Catalogues and other tools match familiar standards and traditions. Rudomino carefully studied European library techniques, particularly in Denmark.

The founder of the library was still in charge at the celebration of its 50th anniversary in 1972. Rudomino could look back on a brilliant achievement both at home and abroad. She took most of her professional, political, and philological training after she had started the All-Union Library of Foreign Literature. In 1926 she graduated from Moscow University, Philological Department, Romanic-Germanic division, and in 1939 she finished work at the University of Marxism-Leninism. As late as 1955 she completed a postgraduate course at the Moscow State Library Institute. In the meantime she had married a physician, Vasili Moskalienko, and had two children. She retired in 1973.

The many publications the Library issued over the years are linked to the overall purpose of the Institution: opening up foreign literature, classical and new, in all fields, to the Soviet reader—whether expert or beginner—through indexes, reference tools, bio-bibliographic monographs, union catalogues, and so forth. Rudomino took responsibility for them all. The long list of her own writings shows an unfailing interest in Western librarianship. Her articles appeared in Russian and foreign professional journals. She was mainly responsible for introducing Western ideas into Soviet librarianship; now foreign library literature is acquired, analyzed, indexed, summarized, and, when needed, translated into Russian. For many years she edited the Russian version of the *Unesco Bulletin for Libraries*.

Rudomino always believed in two-way traffic, from abroad toward the Soviet Union but also from her home country to the rest of the world. She often officially represented the U.S.S.R. abroad. From the early 1950s she was an active member of the International Federation of Library Associations and was elected Vice-President in 1967, First Vice-President in 1971, and Honorary Vice-President in 1973. She took part in all annual general council meetings of the Federation and was the key figure of the one organized in Moscow in 1970. Several times she was the Soviet representative at library meetings organized by Unesco—such as the Brussels meeting in 1958 on the exchange agreements of library materials and, at Unesco headquarters in Paris, of the International Advisory Committee on Libraries, Archives, and Documentation.

R. Wedgeworth

Plaster bust of Margarita Ivanovna Rudomino

Her leadership position made her a member or chair of domestic professional committees, organizations, or editorial boards. She was close to the Lenin Library, the State Committee on Public Libraries, the Council for Library Service, and many other government agencies. Through her professional interest abroad she played an important role in the Council of Societies for Friendship with Foreign Countries, the U.S.S.R.-Denmark Society, the U.S.S.R.-France Society, and the National Unesco Commission.

Rudomino, interested in the contents of the books that she handled as a librarian, read widely, and although the choice of her authors—mainly foreign—reflected the social system to which she belonged, her critical sense always remained alert. She had friendly relations with many foreign writers, whom she always tried to meet during her numerous trips abroad. She traveled widely in Eastern and Western Europe, the United States, Canada, and the East. Like many of her countrymen, she demonstrated an outspoken leaning toward a theoretical foundation of all professional and intellectual activities, favoring a view of major issues in a wide historical and methodological perspective. This did not, however, prevent her interest in human influences; biographies of leading figures, in professional and other fields, remained close to her heart. She would have been happy to be the editor of a Russian counterpart of a work like this *Encyclopedia*. In her *dacha,* near Moscow, she worked on a history of her own library and of the International Federation of Library Associations.

HERMAN LIEBAERS

Rwanda

Rwanda, a republic in central Africa, is bordered by Uganda on the north, Tanzania on the east, Burundi on the south, and Zaire on the west. Population (1990 est.) 7,181,000; area 26,338 sq.km. The official languages are Kinyarwanda and French.

History. Long before Europeans introduced writing, Rwandans devised various means of communicating messages. Ancient Rwandans evolved several kinds of oral traditions. They included a popular tradition; a sapient tradition of proverbs and riddles; and a dynastic tradition, including an esoteric code, a dynastic genealogy, pastoral poetry, war songs, and harp music. Most of these traditions were written down after missionaries arrived in Rwanda and created schools for local peoples. Their work was continued

Athanase Hakizimana

National University of Rwanda Library, Butare campus.

by the colonial administration of Germany and then by that of Belgium in 1916.

The Documentation Center of the Kabgayi Bishopric, one of the oldest libraries in Rwanda, can be traced to 1900. The Groupe Scolaire of Butare (founded 1929) strove to set up a library collecting both general and technical material. The Library of the Rwandan Institute of Agronomic Sciences (ISAR) dates back to 1932. In 1936 the Major Catholic Seminary of Nyakibanda, which had just been transferred from Kabgayi, opened its Library. The Governor-General of the Belgian Congo, to which Rwanda was attached, was charged in 1931 with organizing public libraries in the colony. A library for Europeans was created in Kigali between 1932 and 1940. From 1947 to 1952 a public library was opened for local people in each of the 10 administrative districts. The most important library, in Kigali, had 2,623 books in 1960. In most of those libraries, at least half the members of the administration boards had to be Rwandans.

From 1959 to 1962, operations of district libraries were disrupted by the Rwandan Revolution. After the country became a republic in 1961 and gained independence in 1962, libraries were founded by private or semi-private institutions. The Association Caritas Rwanda played a considerable role in promoting national culture by granting books to newly founded reading clubs, certain prisons, and other institutions. The Ministry of Education Library for Pedagogic Documentation was opened in Kigali in 1963 with the help of Unesco. The Library of the National University of Rwanda was founded in 1964 and that of the National Pedagogic Institute in 1966. The National Archives Service was established in 1978. An act establishing copyright was promulgated in 1984. The National Library was established in 1989 and placed under the Ministry of Higher Education and Scientific Research. The National Archives Service was transferred to the same Ministry in 1991.

Two Canadian librarians did great pioneering work both at the National University and throughout the country. Albert Lévesque was the first to head the National University Library (1964–69) and the first Director of the Center of Rwandan Bibliography (1970–72). Paulette Trudeau-Lévesque served at the National University Library and then headed it (1969–72). They were the first professionals to run a well-organized library in Rwanda.

National Library and Archives. The National Library, in Kigali, acquires and preserves materials on Rwanda and those published by Rwandans. It also acquires reference and general works, emphasizing Africana and works dealing with Rwanda's neighbors. It operates interlibrary loans and creates and promotes public reading centers. It has departments dealing with acquisitions, monographs, periodicals, and official publications. By 1990 it contained about 6,000 volumes.

The Information and National Archives Service includes the Central Archives Repository and the Pre-archiving Section. The Repository preserves public archives from the pre-independence period. There are also some small private archives deposits, most of them belonging to religious communities, that are considered to be well kept. The Archives of the Kabgayi Bishopric, for example, deal mainly with the history of the Catholic Church in Rwanda.

Academic Libraries. The Libraries of the National University of Rwanda constitute the most important system of academic libraries in the country. After the National University of Rwanda merged with the National Pedagogic Institute in 1981, the two university campuses each had its own library. The library on the main campus at Butare held about 60,000 books in 1974; by 1990 it had 130,000 books and 440 periodical titles. It consists of the Central Library, Medical Library, Documentation Center, and Rwandan Bibliographic Center, all on the Butare campus, and the Law Library, in Kigali. The University Library on the Ruhengeri campus serves teachers and students of the Arts Faculty and the Educational Sciences Faculty. It held about 65,000 books and 70

Libraries in Rwanda (1990)

Type of library	Number of administrative units (main libraries)	Number of service points (branches, mobile stops, etc.)	Volumes in collections	Population served
Academic[a]	9	9	157,000	7,806
Special[b]	5	13	30,000	270

[a]1984 data
[b]1983 data

Source: Unesco, *Statistical Yearbook,* 1991.

periodicals in 1989. The University Library on the campus at Butare occupies a modern functional building; the one on the Ruhengeri campus is housed in a fairly adequate building.

Public Libraries. After Rwanda became independent in 1962, libraries serving the public were opened by embassies, religious institutions, associations, and towns and villages, and by the National University Extension Service. The most important of these, the French–Rwandan Cultural Exchange Center Library, opened at Kigali in 1967. By 1989 it had more than 24,000 books, collected periodicals in French and Kinyarwanda, and had a good collection of films and slides. It opened branch libraries at Ruhengeri and Butare. Public libraries in general have few trained workers, and most of their materials are in French; a few are in English.

Other libraries include the American Cultural Center Library, built in Kigali in 1965; the Club Rafiki Library, opened by the Dominican Fathers at Nyamirambo in 1975; the Public Library of Rwandan Social Funds; and the Library of the Islamic Cultural Center in Kigali. The Public Library of the National University Extension Service at Butare had 16,000 books in 1988; the one in Ruhengeri had more than 5,500.

School Libraries and Media Centers. Secondary schools generally have very small libraries. Much of the material in their collections comes from donations. One of the best-known school libraries in the country is part of the Groupe Scolaire in Butare. By 1990 it had almost 28,000 volumes and 65 periodical titles. Secondary schools benefit from the mobile library and educational films made available by the National University Extension Service of Butare. In 1987 the mobile library service had 14,000 books and was able to meet the needs of only 40 schools. Few primary schools had libraries as of the early 1990s.

Special Libraries. The Library of the Institute of Scientific Research and Technology (IRST) in Butare owns some precious works on the natural sciences. The Rwandan Institute of Agronomy at Rubona (Butare) is building a collection in agriculture, breeding, and botany. The Cooperative Research and Formation Center (IWACU) began a library in Kigali on how to run cooperatives.

The National Development Council (Parliament) and most ministries and public institutions have libraries or documentation services of various sizes. Examples include the Ministry of Primary and Secondary Education (10,500 books in 1988); the Ministry of Planning; the Ministry of Public Works, Energy, and Water; the Ministry of Agriculture and Breeding and of Forests; the Ministry of Industry and Crafts; the Rwandan Office of Information; and the National Bank of Rwanda.

Many libraries belong to religious communities and dioceses. The best known are the Library of the Archbishopric of Kigali, the Library of the Monastery at Gihindamuyaga, and the Library of the Dominican Fathers in Kigali, whose collection contained nearly 30,000 books and 60 periodicals in 1983. This library deals primarily with theology, philosophy, and literacy training.

The Profession. Rwandan professional librarians are trained abroad, especially in Senegal, Russia, France, or Canada. Their number, however, is still small, although some foreign librarians lend their services to libraries in the country. In the 1980s, the government sponsored six- to nine-month training programs intended for those taking positions in libraries, archives, and documentation centers. Opportunities for professional education are still limited, and the country often resorts to sending librarians abroad for short-term training programs.

REFERENCES

Jean Brock, "Les bibliothèques en Afrique centrale," *Archives et Bibliothèques de Belgique* (1972).

André Guitard, "Etre bibliothécaire au coeur de l'Afrique," *Argus* (July–August 1974).

Grégoire Hategekimana, "L'information scientifique et technique, la politique de développement et la circulation de l'information nécessaire à l'application de la science et la technique au Rwanda," *Education et Culture* (April–June 1980).

EMMANUEL SERUGENDO

S

Sabin, Joseph

(1821–1881)

British-born American Joseph Sabin ranks among the preeminent booksellers, auctioneers, and bibliographers of the mid-19th century. His reputation and lasting importance rest upon his *Dictionary of Books Relating to America from Its Discovery to the Present Time,* also known as *Bibliotheca Americana,* or simply, "Sabin." It is an alphabetical list by author of books and pamphlets, in any language, that in some way relate to the New World.

Sabin was born in Braunston, Northamptonshire, England, in December 1821. At 14, he was apprenticed to Charles Richards, an Oxford bookseller, to learn bookbinding. Within a few months, Richards saw that Sabin's abilities were better suited to the sales room, and he was instead trained as a bookseller. In 1842, after completing his seven-year apprenticeship, Sabin and a partner set up on their own as booksellers and auctioneers in Oxford. Sabin's first book, *The Thirty-Nine Articles of the Church of England with Scripture Proof and References,* was anonymously published by his firm in 1844.

Sabin emigrated to the United States with his wife and two sons in 1848. He landed in New York, but soon went to Philadelphia, where he took a position with George S. Appleton. Sabin is said to have introduced there the English binding style known as half-leather: a binding with paper-covered sides and leather on the spine and corners. After about two years, Sabin returned to New York to work as a cataloguer for the auction firm of Cooley and Keese, which was sold in 1851 to Lyman and Rawdon. For one of their first auctions, Sabin compiled a large, detailed catalogue of the library of Samuel Farmer Jarvis. A dispute regarding Sabin's payment for the work followed, and Sabin left in 1852 for the rival firm of Bangs, Brother & Co., then becoming one of the most active auction houses in New York. While there, Sabin not only catalogued many large libraries, but also began to see much Americana. He was thus inspired to begin collecting notes and references that would eventually become the *Bibliotheca Americana.* One of the last catalogues Sabin prepared for Bangs was of the library of Edward B. Corwin (sold November 10, 1856), consisting exclusively of Americana.

Early in 1857, Sabin opened a bookshop in New York, but within a year moved it to Philadelphia. There he began to prosper—particularly with customers from the South. As the Civil War approached, however, the book trade in general, and Sabin's in particular, became severely weakened. He moved back to New York, and in partnership with H. A. Jennings set up an auction firm in 1860. It failed after one auction, that of the library of William E. Burton, in which more than 6,000 lots sold for next to nothing. Sabin spent the next few years preparing catalogues of private libraries and freelancing for various auction houses, a practice continued (though more selectively) after he established a bookshop, J. Sabin and Sons, on Nassau Street in 1864.

Courtesy Grolier Club Library/ Jay Cantor, New York City

Joseph Sabin

Nassau Street was the center of the New York book trade, and 1864 marked the beginning of a revival in book collecting. The signal event of the revival was the auction of the library of John Allan in May 1864; it resulted in the highest sales total in the U.S. to that date. In following years, Sabin would be involved in the sales of other important collections, such as that of John A. Rice (March 1870), who had acquired many books through Sabin; Thomas W. Field (May 1875), rich in material on American Indians and the basis of a bibliography on the subject; and William Menzies (November 1876), a notable collection of Americana. Sabin wrote the catalogues and was auctioneer for all of these sales.

In the midst of this activity, in December 1866, Sabin issued a prospectus announcing the publication of the work for which he is now remembered: his *Dictionary of Books Relating to America.* The first four parts appeared in 1867, and six parts each year thereafter until his death. (The edition totaled 635 copies, with 110 on large paper.) Sabin also published a monthly journal called *The American Bibliopolist* from 1869 until 1877. It featured news of the book trade and auctions, general articles on book collecting and other bookish subjects, and a section of advertising—both lists of books from Sabin's stock and display advertisements from other dealers. Here one can see the broad range of material that Sabin handled—recent English acquisitions (a son had opened the firm's London branch in 1871), prints, portraits, and illustrated books, as well as Americana and literature.

A trend of the 1860s and 70s was the reprinting of rare historical texts. Sabin published more than a dozen such works, among them *The Journal of Major George Washington,* and William Smith's *History of the First Discovery and Settlement of Virginia.* In 1877 Sabin's *Bibliography of Bibliography, or a Handy Book About Books which Relate to Books* was published separately after appearing serially in *The American Bibliopolist.*

In 1879 Sabin retired from the daily operation of his business. The firm changed its name to J. Sabin's Sons and was run by several members of his family. Sabin, however, continued to work on his *Dictionary* and still did some auctioneering. His last auction was Part Three of the library of George Brinley, an Americana collection that rivalled those of John Carter Brown and James Lenox. The sale was scheduled for March 1881 but was postponed until April because of Sabin's poor health. Lot 5839 was Brinley's copy of the Gutenberg Bible, the second Gutenberg Bible brought to the U.S. and the first to be sold in an American auction.

Sabin died in Brooklyn, N.Y., June 5, 1881. His *Bibliotheca Americana,* however, did not cease. By the time of his death, Sabin had completed 82 parts. (The last two were published posthumously.) From 1884 to 1892, Wilberforce Eames edited parts 83-116. Publication was then suspended for 35 years. When it resumed in 1927, Eames was still the editor and he continued until 1930 when succeeded by R. W. G. Vail. The final part (no. 172) appeared in 1936. (From 1929 the work was published by the Bibliographical Society of America.) Eames and Vail refined Sabin's all-encompassing definition of Americana; they eliminated ephemeral items and many government publications; they set a cut-off date of 1860 (later changed to 1840), and provided more bibliographically thorough descriptions. At its completion, the *Dictionary* numbered 106,413 entries, many of which include references to more than one work or edition. Vail estimated that more than a quarter of a million publications are included in it.

Although it took 70 years to complete, and the work is not without flaws, the *Bibliotheca Americana* remains an invaluable guide to books about America. It certifies Sabin's place in bibliographical history. That he also made important contributions to the book trade, book collecting, and publishing only confirm it.

REFERENCES

Frederick R. Goff, *Joseph Sabin, Bibliographer (1821–1881),* (1963).

Adolph Growell, *Book-Trade Bibliography in the United States in the XIXth Century* (New York, The Dibdin Club, 1898).

New York Times obituary, June 6, 1881.

William S. Reese, "Joseph Sabin," *American Book Collector* (1984).

R. W. G. Vail, "Sabin's 'Dictionary,'" *Papers of the Bibliographical Society of America* (1937).

ALLEN ASAF

Sabor, Josefa
(1916–)

Josefa Sabor

Josefa Emilia Sabor, Spanish-born Argentine library educator, administrator, and author, attended many international conferences, lectured in and outside Argentina, and studied libraries, documentation centers, and schools for librarians in Europe and the three Americas.

Born November 23, 1916, in Villanueva de Arosa, Spain, she became an Argentine citizen in 1937. She was a high school and normal school teacher, specializing in history in the Faculty of Philosophy and Letters of the University of Buenos Aires and a librarian of the same faculty. She was granted a scholarship by Unesco and the Office of Ibero-American Education to study documentation in Spain, France, Italy, West Germany, and Brazil and received another scholarship from the U.S. State Department's Bureau of Educational and Cultural Affairs to study the teaching of library techniques in 10 U.S. universities.

In 1938 Sabor became a library assistant in the Teaching Institute of the Faculty of Philosophy and Letters of the University of Buenos Aires. She served as Director of the Library and of Bibliography, Library Institute, University of Buenos Aires, from 1943 to 1946, and Director of the Library, Argentine Museum of Natural Sciences, from 1948 until 1952, when she was dismissed for political reasons. From 1955 to 1964 she served as Director of the Central Library of the Faculty of Philosophy and Letters, University of Buenos Aires.

Her teaching activities in Argentina included service from 1947 to 1951 as Professor of Reference in the School for Librarians of the Argentine Social Museum, from 1955 to 1970 as Director of the School for Librarians, Faculty of Philosophy and Letters, University of Buenos Aires, and from 1963 as Associate—later full—Professor of Bibliography, Reference Services, and Documentation in that faculty. She became Titular Professor in 1969. From 1965 to 1970 she reorganized and directed the Career of Librarianship program in the Faculty of Philosophy and Letters. From 1955 to 1957 she directed and organized the National School of Librarians for the Ministry of Justice and Education, and from 1963 to 1973 she served as founding Director of the Center for Library Research of the Faculty of Philosophy and Letters in collaboration with Unesco.

She retired from active teaching in 1980 and thereafter dedicated herself to research. She worked in the National Council of Scientific and Technical Research on the origins of Argentine bibliography.

Her international activities included contributions as Director of the Library and Publications Department of the Inter-American Living Center, Bogotá, Colombia, for the Organization of American States (1952–53); Unesco expert, consultant, and Professor at the Central Library of the University of Costa Rica (1962); member of the International Consulting Committee for Librarians, Unesco, Paris (1965–69); OAS Visiting Professor at the Inter-American School of Librarianship in Medellín, Colombia (1973–74); and Visiting Professor at the School of Librarianship, National University of Asunción, Paraguay (1975). For the OAS she presented two programs for teachers in the Master's Program in Librarianship, University of Guanajuato, Mexico (1977).

Her publications include *Manual de Bibliotecología* ("Manual of Librarianship," with Juan Albani, J. Federico Finó, Carlos Victor Penna, and Emilio Ruiz, 1951, 2nd edition, 1984), *Manual de Fuentes de Información* ("Manual of Information Sources," 1957, 3rd edition, 1979), *Bibliografía Básica de Obras de Referencia de Artes y Letras para la Argentina* ("Basic Bibliography of Reference Works in Arts and Letters for Argentina," 1969), *Methods of Teaching Librarianship* (1969), *Las Normas y Conclusiones de Medellín y la Formación de Bibliotecarios en América Latina* ("The Medellín Standards and Conclusions and the Training of Librarians in Latin America," 1974), *El Planeamiento Bibliotecario a Través de los Congresos y Reuniones Celebrados en América Latina* ("Library Planning Through Congresses and Meetings in Latin America," 1974), *Desarrollo del Planeamiento Bibliotecario en América Latina* ("Development of Library Planning in Latin America," 1975), and many articles in library journals.

EMMA LINARES;
revised and translated by EDWIN S. GLEAVES

St. John, Francis R.
(1908–1971)

Brooklyn Public Library, Brooklyn Collection

Francis R. St. John

American Francis Regis St. John was Director of the Brooklyn (New York) Public Library, the position for which he is best known and remembered, from 1949 to 1963.

His life and career were centered in the East from his birth in Northampton, Massachusetts, June 16, 1908, until his death in Manchester, New Hampshire, July 19, 1971. His association with libraries began as page and desk assistant at the Northampton Public Library when he was 11 years old and continued through his student years at Amherst (Massachusetts) College (A.B., 1931). Professional education at Catholic University, Washington D.C., followed immediately (B.S., 1932).

His professional career began at the New York Public Library, where he held several professional positions, the last of which was Chief of the Circulation Department. In 1939 he became Assistant Librarian at the Enoch Pratt Free Library under Joseph L. Wheeler.

During World War II, St. John organized the Army Medical Library (1943–45), which later became the National Library of Medicine. Following the war he was the first Director of Library Services for the Veterans Administration. In 1949 he left the VA for the Brooklyn Public Library, where he was to earn his national reputation.

The St. John years at Brooklyn were a time of enormous change and growth for the system. Circulation of materials doubled from over 5,000,000 to more than 10,000,000 annually. The number of branches increased from 38 to 55. There were innovations in service programs as well. The District Library concept, which put strong subject collections and specialists closer to the people, was inaugurated, and the Community Coordinator program, which placed librarians on detached duty in the community to form linkages with agencies and organizations, was begun.

St. John quickly became identified as a manager. The introduction of assembly-line book processing and other management innovations held down operating costs, freeing funds for expanded service programs.

Personal professional activities were diverse and extensive. He was a founding member of the National Book Committee and initiator of the Franklin Books program. His *Survey of Library Service to the Blind, 1956* (1957) is a major document in the development of library services.

Following his retirement from Brooklyn in 1963, St. John opened a private consulting firm. Among the projects undertaken was a statewide library survey for the state of Oklahoma. In the years before his death he served as Consultant to the New Hampshire College and University Council and was also Librarian at Saint Anselm's College in Manchester, New Hampshire.

REFEENCE

Milton S. Byam, "St. John, Francis Regis," *Dictionary of American Library Biography* (1978).

F. WILLIAM SUMMERS

Samper Ortega, Daniel

(1895–1943)

Daniel Samper Ortega, educator, historian, and writer, was the leading promoter of library development in Colombia.

Samper was born in Bogotá, Colombia, November 28, 1895. After graduation from the Military Academy, he wrote four novels, two plays, and several essays. Later he went to Spain to do research for a historical novel and to lecture at a Spanish university. He taught also in the Gimnasio Moderno, a progressive, independent, and private high school founded by his father, one of his uncles, and other businessmen with Agustín Nieto Caballero, an outstanding educator trained in Europe.

In 1930, during the Depression, the Liberal Party came to power after 50 years of Conservative rule in Colombia. There was a spirit of renewal in the country, and in February 1931 Samper Ortega was called by President Olaya Herrera and his Minister of Education to become the Director of the National Public Library in Bogotá, a position given traditionally to men of letters who took little serious interest in library development.

The state in which he received the Library was appalling. It was in a dilapidated old colonial house near Plaza de Bolívar, the main square. Books, magazines, and newspapers were thrown on the floors; the rest, unreachable, were piled on dusty shelves. Eighty-seven boxes of exchange publications, sent not only for the National Library but for other institutions in the country, remained unopened; some dated as far back as 1898. In the main room 52,000 volumes were uncatalogued except for a few private collections donated to the Library. Sixteen thousand valuable incunabula and parchment books were found, piled on shelves three volumes deep or on the floor. The final search yielded a total of 85,355 volumes, of which 60 percent were unreachable for lack of shelves.

He undertook a thorough reorganization of the National Library and despite financial limitations turned it into one of the most modern and efficient public libraries of Latin America at that time. By 1934 a total of 192,914 additional reference cards had been made; the exchange system had been organized and 15,898 volumes had been sent to other libraries; the National Archives were incorporated into the Library and 290,000 historical documents had been organized; and readers had increased to 9,362 a month, an increase of 358 percent from the time the reorganization was started.

Samper organized with Janeiro Brooks (later Schmidt) the first Library School of Colombia. Librarians were trained for the other ministries, the National University, the Central Bank (Banco de la República, which today has the best economics library in the country), and other institutions. By 1938 the National Library had in operation a children's library and theater, which was used as a model for the future satellite libraries.

He conceived the National Library as a dynamic center for the diffusion of education and culture, capable of breaking down provincial and national boundaries. He did not want to wait for the readers to come to the Library; he went out to the readers. The books, to him, were only one of the means to serve the readers. Early in the reorganization he started the National Radio Station, as part of the Library, and a section to produce educational films. He compiled a 100-volume selection of Colombian literature (*Selección Samper Ortega*), a titanic effort, unparalleled in Colombia and in the rest of Latin America. He started the *Biblioteca Aldeana de Cultura Popular,* a series of manuals prepared for farmers on subjects such as cultivation of various crops, health, care of children, and food, to take culture and education to the rural regions, through the National Library. Finally, in 1934 he started the publication of a monthly journal, *Senderos* ("Paths"), finely designed and printed, for the diffusion of ideas and knowledge as well as of information about the National Library. Later the Ministry of Education assumed those educational services.

The culmination of his seven years of service as Director of the National Library was the inauguration, in August 1938, of a magnificent, large, functional, and complete new building, in a corner of the Park of Independence, planned for a growth of at least a century. The inauguration of the new building was one of the main events with which Colombia celebrated the 400th anniversary of the founding of the city of Bogotá. Samper was at that time a Founding Member of the Academy of Arts, the Permanent Secretary of the Academy of Letters, and the President of the Academy of History. He resigned and became Cultural Counselor of the Colombian embassy in the United States. In Washington, D.C., he displayed his boundless energy for two years, making known the cultural achievements of Colombia, lecturing at the universities, and keeping in touch with educational and professional groups, among them the American Library Association.

He resigned his diplomatic post in 1941 to return to Colombia as Director of the Gimnasio Moderno, a school with which he had sentimental ties. There, with renewed energy, he undertook the task of turning it into a private university. With assistance from the Business School of Harvard University he opened the first College of Business Administration and Economics in Colombia, where the new business executives and economists of the country were trained.

He died in Bogotá on November 3, 1943.

In 1977, at the initiative of the historian Pilar Moreno de Angel, then Director of the National Library, and on the occasion of the 200th anniversary of the library, the Colombian Institute of Culture (Colcultura) of the Ministry of Education remodeled the new building, inaugurated in 1938, and introduced new services. The main reading room was named after Samper.

REFERENCE

Guillermo Hernandez de Alba and Juan Carrasquilla Botero, *Historia de la Biblioteca Nacional de Colombia* (1977), a complete and concise history of the National Library of Colombia. Chapter 24 is dedicated to "Daniel Samper Ortega, the Restorer" and chapter 25 to "Daniel Samper and the new building of the Library."

ARMANDO SAMPER

Sarmiento, Domingo Faustino

(1811–1888)

A man whose activities embraced many interests, including public education, politics, diplomacy, literature, and librarianship, Domingo Faustino Sarmiento has been termed a "universal man" and a "father of public education." He was President of his country, the Argentine Republic, 1868–74. To his own passion for books and popular education he added lessons learned from years of travel and study abroad, and he took advantage of the opportunity to act offered by political office.

Born in San Juan City, province of San Juan, Argentina, February 14, 1811, Sarmiento rose quickly in local and national politics, serving in provincial and cabinet posts. In 1840, as a consequence of political events, he was forced to flee. He settled in Chile, involving himself in politics and devoting himself to putting his ideas on public education into practice.

Sarmiento was an indefatigable traveler and a born journalist. In 1845 the Chilean government commissioned him to study the organization of schooling in Europe and the United States. He visited France, Spain, Germany, Switzerland, Holland, Belgium, and Great Britain on the European leg of his tour. Before returning home by way of Cuba, Panama, and Peru, he conducted a survey of educational innovations in the U.S. While in the U.S. he cultivated the friendship of Horace Mann. Sarmiento thereafter spread Mann's ideas on education throughout South America.

Photo Archive of *La Nación*, Buenos Aires

Domingo Faustino Sarmiento

Sarmiento returned to Chile in February 1848. He founded a well-equipped printing house directed by Julio Belin, who later married Sarmiento's daughter, Faustina, in 1850. Throughout his exile, Sarmiento remained a prolific writer on matters of education, culture, and intellectual interests. His collected works would ultimately amount to 52 volumes. He played a significant role in the overthrow of the Rosas government in 1852, and in December 1863 the President of Argentina appointed Sarmiento Ambassador to the United States. He returned to the U.S. in May 1865. Sarmiento displayed remarkable energy, constantly traveling throughout the land in order to acquaint himself with subjects of practical interest to the development of Argentina. In 1866 he published a biography of his personal hero, Abraham Lincoln, and *Las Escuelas Como Base de la Prosperidad de la República en los EEUU* ("Schools as the Basis of Prosperity in the U.S."). He attended an international conference of teachers, and in June 1868 the University of Michigan awarded him an honorary doctorate. Horace Mann's widow, Mary, translated his *Recuerdos de Provincia* (*Reminiscences of a Province*) and introduced Sarmiento in North America.

Sarmiento remained in the U.S. until July 1868, when he was elected President of the Argentine republic, a post he held until 1874. Under his leadership, the first nationally financed schools for the training of teachers were founded in Argentina. He arranged for 65 professional teachers from Mann's state of Massachusetts to establish normal and primary schools in his country and train personnel for them.

Sarmiento quickly acted to assure the parallel development of popular libraries. On September 23, 1870, he signed into law legislation creating the Comisión Protectora de Bibliotecas Populares (Protective Commission of Popular Libraries). Sarmiento later said in reference to this major cornerstone of his education program that "the need for libraries is everywhere felt. It is necessary to create the school library to complement the school and enliven it, serving as an aid to the teacher and an incentive to the child's curiosity." He also noted that it is "not without reason that we include schools and libraries within the same function. The latter complement the former; and as education becomes more generally available so will the number of libraries, occupying the position due them within the scheme of public instruction. Now the library is an integral part of the social organization, just like the free and compulsory schools—something not so before."

He died in Asunción, Paraguay, on September 11, 1888. Though Sarmiento's goals are far from realization in the countries of South America, his ideal remains true.

REINALDO JOSÉ SUÁREZ

Saudi Arabia

Saudi Arabia, a monarchy in southwest Asia, comprises most of the Arabian Peninsula. It is surrounded by Jordan, Iraq, and Kuwait on the north; the Persian Gulf, Qatar, and the United Arab Emirates on the east; Oman and Yemen on the south; and the Red Sea on the west. Population (1990 est.) 14,870,000; area 2,149,690 sq.km. The official language is Arabic.

History. The early libraries of Arabia developed mainly in two holy cities, Mecca and Medina, notably the collections of the Great Mosque of Mecca and the Prophet's Mosque in Medina. Other types of libraries—public, academic, school, and special—were not established until after World War II. The Dar al-Kutub al-Watani'yah (National Book House) was founded in Riyadh, the capital, in 1968; it functioned as a public library.

National Library. The King Fahd National Library opened in 1989 with an area of 23,000 sq.m., nearly 150 employees, and collections totalling almost 225,000 items. Its staff planned to carry out the normal work of a national library, including pressing for a deposit law, developing a national bibliography, and leading and coordinating library activities in the country.

Academic Libraries. Modern academic libraries have been established with the emergence of higher education in the country. The universities that have developed in the kingdom since the 1950s have shown special interest in developing their libraries as focal points for teaching. There are seven universities in various parts of the country. King Sa'ud University in Riyadh (founded in 1957), King Abdulaziz University in Jeddah (1965), King Fahd University for Petroleum and Minerals in Dhahran (1963), and King Faisal University in Dammam and al-Hasa (1975) specialize mainly in sciences and general studies. Imam Muhammad ibn Sa'ud Islamic University in Riyadh (1974), the Islamic University in Medina (1961), and Umm al-Qura University in Mecca (1981) specialize in Islamic studies, the Arabic language, humanities, and social sciences. The university libraries hold large collections of books, periodicals, manuscripts, government publications, and audiovisual materials. They are well organized, with automated information systems. The King Sa'ud University Library, for example, was established to serve only one college in 1957. It now serves 12 colleges and a number of research centers. The Central Library of the University occupies an ultra-modern building at the center of the campus, with space for 4,000 readers and 400 researchers. Its collection in 1990 included almost 600,000 titles in more than 1,400,000 volumes.

King Saud University Libraries

Main entrance to King Saud University Central Library, Riyadh.

King Saud University Libraries

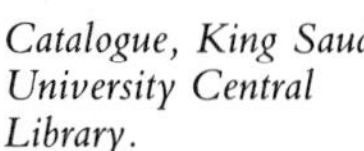

Catalogue, King Saud University Central Library.

Public Libraries. The Ministry of Education founded 60 public libraries in various parts of the country. The Ministry of Hajj and Awqaf is the custodian of a few public libraries, mainly in Mecca and Medina. Public libraries are generally not as fast growing or as well organized as academic and special libraries in the country. An exception is the King Abdulaziz Public Library in Riyadh (1985), a modern library holding 102,000 Arabic volumes, more than 15,000 non-Arabic volumes, more than 700 periodicals, and other materials.

School Libraries. Saudi Arabia is paying great attention to education, founding thousands of schools and providing libraries for almost all of them. They vary widely in collections, staff, organization, and services. The Department of School Libraries of the Ministry of Education is responsible for centralized acquisition and technical processing of library materials. Most school libraries have part-time teacher-librarians in charge. Compared with other libraries, school libraries need better organization and larger collections to provide better service.

Special Libraries. Saudi Arabian ministries, government agencies, organizations, companies, and research centers have shown interest in establishing special libraries to serve their users. More than 100 special libraries have been founded since the mid-1950s. Institutions with well-organized special libraries include government ministries of Petroleum and Mineral Resources, Agriculture and Water, Industry and Electricity, and Municipal and Rural Affairs; and such institutions as the Arab Saudi Standards Organization, Saudi Consulting House, Saudi Monetary Agency, Arab-American Oil Company, and Saudia Airlines. The Ministry of Education has a major Documentation Center. The Library and Documents Institute of Public Administration (1960), fully automated, holds nearly 180,000 items and 44,000 administrative documents. The National Center for Financial and Economic Information (1977) offers access to its computerized bibliographic and statistical databases by satellite telecommunications. The King Faisal Center for Research and Islamic Studies (1984) also has specialized databases.

The Profession. Since the 1960s the profession has grown rapidly. Four library departments offer graduate studies and the Institute of Public Administration offers training courses. In addition to graduates of universities in the U.K. and U.S., some with doctorates, active professionals include hundreds of graduates holding local B.A. and M.L.S. degrees and specialized diplomas. They have made increasing use of information technology, especially in academic and information centers, enabling the profession to gain greater respect.

NASSER M. SWAYDAN

Savage, Ernest A.
(1877–1966)

Ernest Albert Savage had one of the most original minds and was one of the most vigorous personalities in the history of the British public library service.

He was born at Croydon, Surrey, March 30, 1877, and began his library career at the recently established Croydon public library at the age of 13. By a fortunate chance he rejoined the Croydon staff, after two years at Watford Public Library, just before the Croydon libraries came under the direction of Louis Stanley Jast. Jast was not only a bold experimenter; he was infectiously enthusiastic. He perceived that Savage was of more than average ability and made him his deputy. As Savage later realized, working closely with Jast was a better professional education than going to a library school.

In 1904 Savage became Librarian of Bromley, Kent, and in 1906 Librarian of Wallasey, Cheshire. At each of these towns he planned a Carnegie library, but he did not have a major opportunity to prove his mettle until he became Librarian of Coventry in 1915. As a versatile industrial city of high repute, Coventry was then much concerned with war contracts. It seemed to Savage that its industrial efficiency would be all the greater if its factories had the benefit of a public technical information service. He therefore set about providing one at the central library. Following the success of this novel enterprise, Savage persuaded the Library Association to appoint a committee to discuss means of improving the supply of technical information throughout the country. Although this committee, of which Savage was Secretary, failed to secure government support for its ambitious plan for a national technical information service (in suggesting the establishment of a National Lending Library of Science and Technology it was over 30 years ahead of its time), it did encourage the public libraries of several of the larger British industrial cities to provide out of their own resources special library and information services for local industrial and commercial firms.

Savage was also one of the first British librarians to recognize the value of local studies and perceive how public libraries might assist and stimulate them. The Coventry and Warwickshire Collection, which Savage organized and for which he devised a special classification scheme still in use today, was far ahead of the average local collection at that time.

In 1922 Savage was appointed Principal Librarian of Edinburgh city libraries. He took over a library system that, like too many others in the United Kingdom, was suffering from old-fashioned administration, unimaginative policies, and the unavoidable restrictions imposed by World War I.

Savage's career at Edinburgh spanned two decades. During the first he brought the city libraries up to the level of the best in the country; during the second he raised them above it, although not as far as he wished. Lack of resources prevented him from making Edinburgh Central Library the first completely subject departmentalized public library in Britain. The conversion of the city libraries to open access during the first decade was not in itself novel. The adoption of the Library of Congress Classification, which Savage greatly admired, instead of the ubiquitous Decimal Classification, was.

ALA

Ernest A. Savage

The partial reorganization of the central library into subject departments, during the 1930s, was inspired by the pioneering divisional organization of the U.S. public libraries of Cleveland, Los Angeles, and Baltimore. While Jast was planning a new and unusually large central library at Manchester, which would have offered ample capacity for subject departmentalization had Jast favored it, Savage was struggling with the restrictions of an existing Carnegie library. His establishment of an Edinburgh Historical and Topographical Library, an Economics and Commercial Library, a Music Library, and a Fine Arts Library were steps in the right direction. A more sophisticated pattern of subject specialization was not established in any British public library until after World War II, when George Chandler reorganized the Liverpool Central Library.

Savage's 20 years at Edinburgh were notable also for his outside activities. Early in 1933, at the request of the Carnegie Corporation, Savage went to the West Indies to report on the various libraries available to the public. Most of the libraries Savage visited were subscription libraries; he recommended the establishment of a public library service modeled after English county libraries. Although Savage's recommendations could not be adopted in their entirety, a public library service was eventually inaugurated at Trinidad and Tobago with the help of the Carnegie Corporation.

Savage believed in the need for the Library Association; though he was always its most vehement critic, he was also its savior. In 1926 Savage attended the jubilee meeting of the American Library Association in Atlantic City. Impressed by the ALA's resources, activities, and status in the library profession, he felt that the ALA was "the powerful driving force of the library movement in the States and Canada." He returned to the U.K. resolved to bring the Library Association out of the doldrums, where it had been becalmed for many years, with a small membership and negligible resources.

The essence of Savage's plan was to engineer amalgamation with the Association of Assistant Librarians and the other independent library associations and to obtain financial aid from the Carnegie United Kingdom Trust (CUKT). When Savage became Honorary Secretary of the LA in 1928, he was in a good position to further his plan. With CUKT funds and the cooperation of the other library associations, the LA was transformed in a few years. By the early 1930s it had a paid secretary, its own headquarters building, and a library. Having piloted the LA through a crucial period in its history, Savage resigned from the honorary secretaryship in February 1934. In 1936 he served as President and for the rest of his life told the LA what it should do.

Savage's retirement in 1942 was purely nominal. Over the next 20 years he published several books and many articles, all of them written in his uniquely pungent, didactic, aphoristic style. Usually he was wise; often he was farsighted. Only in his opposition to the McColvin Report (*The Public Library System of Great Britain,* 1942), which advocated fewer and larger public library authorities, did Savage join forces with the reactionaries. For the most part, his contributions to the *Library Association Record,* the *Library World,* and the *Library Review* during the 1940s and 1950s rank high in the annals of library literature.

Among his books the most notable is *Special Librarianship in General Libraries and Other Papers* (1939). This collection of published and unpublished papers was the most original and stimulating book on librarianship published in the U.K. before World War II. Savage attacked the traditional pattern of public library organization in Britain (the common division of the stock into a general reference library and a general home reading library) and offered sound advice on how to replace it with subject departments. Even more striking, however, was the long essay on "The Training of Librarians," which foreshadowed the establishment of the postwar library schools in the U.K. and their eventual emancipation from the Library Association's unsatisfactory examination system.

Special Librarianship also included two of Savage's best contributions to library history, yet another area in which he excelled. When he was Librarian of Wallasey, he had somehow found time to write an impressive treatise called *Old English Libraries* (1911), which is still in use. In his retirement Savage wrote a fascinating professional autobiography, *A Librarian's Memories: Portraits and Reflections* (1952), which, despite its omissions and its occasional unfair judgments on some of his contemporaries, is likely to survive longer than any of his writings. When Savage published his last essay, in October 1963, he brought to a close a period of 73 years devoted almost entirely to librarianship.

In his day Savage was not appreciated as much as he deserved. His abiding and ill-concealed dissatisfaction with so many things in the library world gave him the reputation of a captious schoolmaster, which was not altogether fair. Savage's criticism was always constructive, and he never suggested anything should be done that he was incapable of doing himself. Jast was more endearing as a critic of library practice, and W. C. Berwick Sayers was a more patient mentor, but Savage was the most versatile and, in the end, the most influential public librarian of his day. He died at Edinburgh, February 4, 1966.

REFERENCES

James G. Ollé, *Ernest A. Savage: Librarian Extraordinary,* 2nd rev. ed. (1978).

Ernest A. Savage, *A Librarian's Memoirs: Portraits and Reflections* (1952).

JAMES G. OLLÉ

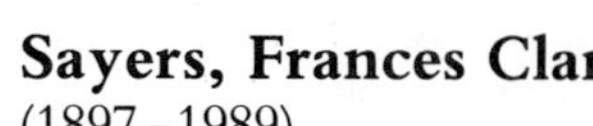

Sayers, Frances Clarke
(1897–1989)

ALA

Frances Clarke Sayers

Frances Clarke Sayers, an American, contributed to the world of children's literature as author, critic, lecturer, storyteller, and teacher. Perhaps her major contributions were sharing a sense of celebration and enthusiasm for good children's books and demonstrating that children's literature can be not only the lifelong occupation but the object of passionate advocacy of a mature and thinking individual.

Born in Topeka, Kansas, September 4, 1897, she spent her childhood in Galveston, Texas. Summers on the forested shore of Lake Michigan left permanent impressions of the pleasures of reading, the beauties of the natural setting, and the intensity of early experiences. When she was 12 years old, she read an article in *St. Nicholas Magazine* on service to children in the New York Public Library—and determined immediately that she would someday be a children's librarian.

After two years at the University of Texas, she entered Carnegie Library School in Pittsburgh, noted for its devoted staff and belief in taking books to children wherever they were. Anne Carroll Moore, the energetic and stimulating pioneer of library service to children in the United States, invited the young Frances Clarke to join the children's staff at the New York Public Library. This heady environment, with its outstanding personnel and direct access to authors, illustrators, and publishers of children's books, as well as New York's other intellectual and cultural influences, played an important role in developing her abilities as critic, storyteller, and teacher.

After five years' service at the New York Public Library, Frances Clarke left in 1923 to live with her family in California. Two years later she married Alfred H. P. Sayers, an old friend from her New York days. They lived for seven years in Chicago and then in Sausalito, California, near the Golden Gate. During this period she not only retained her close association with children's literature and children's library service, but began to write children's books. In *Bluebonnets for Lucinda,* published by Viking and illustrated by Helen Sewell (1932), a little girl who lived on an offshore Texas island saw for the first time miles of Texas bluebonnets brightening the earth of the mainland. *Mr. Tidy Paws,* with lithographs by Zhenya Gay (1934), told in a mixture of realism and fantasy how a boy's changeling cat made badly needed money for the boy's grandmother by performing in a dog and pony show. *Tag-Along Tooloo,* illustrated by Helen Sewell (1941), described five-year-old Talluluh's dependence upon her big sister until she became something of a heroine at the circus.

Frances Sayers also began to lecture. Beginning in 1936 she offered a course in children's literature at the Library School of the University of California, Berkeley, where she emphasized high standards of criticism, respect for children and children's books, and delight in storytelling. At the same time, she took her enthusiasm and knowledge of books to schools throughout California.

In 1941 she was named Superintendent of Work with Children at the New York Public Library, succeeding Anne Carroll Moore, a powerful figure to follow; but the new Superintendent "brought to the direction of the room not only first-hand familiarity with its life and tradition, but a vision of her own for a future in which artists and children continue to flourish" (*Illustrators of Children's Books 1744–1945,* The Horn Book, 1947, p. 125). Staff members looked forward to their monthly meetings with her because she always provided something to surprise them and lift their spirits.

During her tenure at the New York Public Library, she wrote two children's books: *Sally Tait,* illustrated by Eileen Evans (1948), an account of the ninth year of a Texas girl, 1912–13, and *Ginny and Custard,* illustrated by Eileen Evans (1951), in which a young New York girl, her parents, and her beloved cat spent a year exploring the country and urban sights in the Los Angeles area.

She also taught a course in writing for children at the New School for Social Research, wrote the script for *The Impressionable Years,* a U.S. State Department film on library service to children, and served as a Consultant to the Library of Congress for the reorganization of its Children's Book Collection. Eleven years before it came into being, she recommended the establishment of a Children's Book Section at the LC.

She retired from the New York Public Library in 1952. *Compton's Pictured Encyclopedia* then sponsored her visits to 25 colleges and universities with library schools or courses in children's literature for teachers. From February 1953 to May 1954, she lectured on the importance and joys of reading for children and told stories as well, leaving "a trail of enthusiasm behind her" (*The Horn Book,* April 1954, p. 81).

By that time she had moved to Los Angeles, where she lived with her sister, Marie Clarke, a librarian at the University of California, Los Angeles. In addition to writing and editing, Frances Sayers was teaching yet again—this time as Senior Lecturer in the English Department of UCLA. When the UCLA School of Library Service opened in 1960, she was invited to offer the course in children's literature there also.

She collaborated with Edna Johnson and Evelyn H. Sickels in producing the third edition of *Anthology of Children's Literature* (1959), a collection of more than 700 stories and poems, divided into approximately 15 categories, each introduced by a critical and historical essay. She later collaborated on a fourth, revised edition.

Summoned by Books (1965), a collection of Sayers's speeches and essays from 1937 through 1961, was edited by a former library school student, Marjeanne Jensen Blinn, with an introduction by Lawrence Clark Powell. The intent of this publication was to preserve for those who had not known her work personally or read her articles in professional periodicals some of Sayers's best contributions to the philosophy of children's library service and to the criticism of children's literature.

In 1965 Sayers retired from UCLA and moved to Ojai, California. She continued to write for professional journals and wrote a children's book, *Oscar Lincoln Busby Stokes,* illustrated by Gunnar Anderson (1970), in which a contemporary boy learned to be proud of his unusual name. She completed a major work, *Anne Carroll Moore: A Biography* (1972), a project that occupied her for 10 years.

During Sayers's long and productive professional life—she was present when Frederick Melcher opened the first Book Week Celebration in 1919—she was honored with many awards, including the Joseph W. Lippincott Award for Distinguished Service in the Profession of Librarianship (1965); the Clarence Day Award for *Summoned by Books* (1966); a Southern California Council on Literature for Children and Young People's Award (1969); and the Catholic Library Association's Regina Medal (1973).

Her love of books, music, fine art, animals, good food, and all forms of nature are evident throughout her writings. She attributed her eagerness to reach out for new insights and new friendships to the influence of her mother and railroad-official father. All these characteristics she synthesized over the years in becoming a spellbinding storyteller and a Pied Piper of a speaker.

Sayers's professional work was always characterized by a crusading spirit. She continuously spoke forthrightly against shoddiness, faddishness, and didacticism in children's literature, trusting the power of art to give children wisdom. "The awakened and aware spirit is best served by subtlety and indirection—in short, by the arts" (*The Horn Book,* 1972, p. 446), she said. She proved a strong defender of the freedom of ideas.

Frances Clarke Sayers died at her home August 24, 1989.

WINIFRED RAGSDALE

Sayers, W. C. Berwick
(1881–1960)

Library Association

W. C. Berwick Sayers

William Charles Berwick Sayers was one of the most prominent public librarians of his generation in the United Kingdom. Indeed, through his textbooks, he influenced the library education of at least two generations after him. His influence was not confined to the development of public librarianship, since as an editor and writer on such pervasive topics as classification he had an important hand in the progress of all types of librarianship during his life. Furthermore, he can be described as a Library Association man. He was a Council member for nearly 50 years, President in 1938, and one of the great figures in the Association's history.

Born on December 23, 1881, at Mitcham, England, he received his early education in Bournemouth and began his career at Bournemouth Public Libraries. He was Sublibrarian there for four years from 1900, and then at the age of 23 he was appointed Deputy Librarian of Croydon under the great Louis Stanley Jast. Jast helped most in the molding of Sayers as a professional librarian. From the viewpoint of his future career, Sayers could not have been at a better age, in a better place, or under a better guide.

Education for librarians was at that time in an embryonic stage in the U.K., and aspirants had to enlarge their knowledge as best they could, since there were no library schools. Before going to Croydon, Sayers had already demonstrated his professional ambitions by winning the Greenwood prize in librarianship, and with Jast's encouragement he widened his knowledge by attending lectures organized by the London School of Economics from 1905 to 1908.

At about this time Sayers became interested in the activities of the Library Assistants' Association, which had been formed in 1895. For 10 years, until he became a chief librarian, he worked heart and soul for the LAA, being Honorary Secretary from 1912 to 1915. At the same time his interest in the LA was growing. In 1908 he became a Fellow by honors diploma, and in 1912 he was elected to the Council and also became one of the Association's examiners.

In 1915 he was appointed Chief Librarian of

Wallasey, where he succeeded Ernest A. Savage. But Sayers was destined to hold his new position for less than a year. Jast, his erstwhile chief at Croydon, was leaving to go to Manchester, and the Croydon authorities, no doubt on Jast's advice, invited Sayers to return to Croydon as chief.

Sayers remained Chief Librarian of Croydon until his retirement in 1947. Although his term of office was affected by two world wars, he instigated the provision of several new branch libraries for the rapidly expanding suburban population. Sayers also saw to it that Croydon remained the professional powerhouse of British librarianship created by Jast. Sayers in his time brought along such later notables as Lionel R. McColvin, Clifford Musgrave, Henry A. Sharp, and L. Montague Harrod.

But Sayers is remembered even more for his influential writings and for his work for the LA and for the National Central Library. In addition to writing hundreds of articles, he was the author of a dozen books and edited four editions of Brown's *Manual of Library Economy*. It was also an open secret that for many years he was the anonymous editor of *The Library World,* the monthly journal Brown had founded in 1898. His first book appeared in 1912; entitled *The Children's Library,* it was later described by Munford as a pioneer British book on the subject. Twenty years after, Sayers was to return to the same theme with a more mature book called *Children's Libraries*.

Sayers was not merely an author on library topics. He wrote books about Croydon and in 1913 published *Over Some Alpine Passes*. He was also a poet and musician. He composed many songs and wrote the definitive biography of the British composer Samuel Coleridge-Taylor, which appeared in 1915, with a later edition in 1927.

Classification was, however, the topic always associated with the name of Sayers. His earliest book on this subject was the *Canons of Classification,* issued in 1915, followed by *An Introduction to Library Classification* in 1918. This latter title achieved no fewer than nine editions in the ensuing 40 years. His magnum opus was undoubtedly the *Manual of Classification,* which appeared in 1926, with second and third editions in 1944 and 1955. Arthur Maltby produced a fourth completely revised edition in 1967 and a fifth edition in 1975.

Sayers added much to our knowledge of the history of classification, and he was a judicious if sometimes biased assessor of modern bibliographical schemes. He favored the enumerative schemes of Dewey, Cutter, the Library of Congress, and Brown, but was much less at home with Bliss and with faceted schemes such as that of Ranganathan, his former pupil. Nevertheless, he was an inspiring writer on classification, and lectured on the subject for 32 years at the University of London School of Librarianship.

Although he retired from practicing librarianship in 1947, he remained active and influential until his death in Croydon on October 7, 1960. He had been Chairman of the LA Executive Committee throughout World War II and received the accolade of the Honorary Fellowship in 1947. He continued to serve on the LA Council, being a particularly valuable member of the Education and the Publications Committee and later a Trustee of the National Central Library.

Memorial Volume. The profession was preparing to celebrate Sayers' 80th birthday with a Festschrift edited by D. J. Foskett and B. I. Palmer when Sayers died shortly before his 79th birthday. Work went ahead on the proposed tribute, which eventually appeared in 1961, published by the LA as the *Sayers Memorial Volume*. It contains 16 chapters by various writers, mainly on classification themes, and it proved a fitting tribute to a man who was a tower of strength to the libraries he served, to the LA, and to library education and library cooperation in his country. He is still remembered as a gentlemanly librarian, urbane of speech, and possessed of a Churchillian turn of phrase suitable for the big occasion.

K. C. HARRISON

Scandinavian Federation of Research Librarians

The Nordiska Vetenskapliga Bibliotekarieförbundet (NVBF); (Scandinavian Federation of Research Librarians) was established on August 15, 1947, in Copenhagen. Its purpose was to promote cooperation among research libraries in the Nordic countries and stimulate the exchange of ideas and experiences of their research librarians.

At the start, the Federation launched two important projects with great impact on Scandinavian library life, the Scandia Plan and the Nordic Union Catalogue for Periodicals (NOSP). The exchange of ideas was also taken into account: a general handbook on librarianship appeared in two editions and the Federation initiated and arranged a number of Round Table conferences on various subjects.

As time went by the Scandia Plan and NOSP proved to be too heavy a load on the Federation, which was run primarily by unpaid volunteers. During the 1970s library life was more and more professionalized, and official bodies advising on library matters were established in all Scandinavian countries. In 1967 a Nordic Council for Scientific and Technical Information, NORDINFO, was established and, with some relief, NVBF handed over its two great projects—the Scandia Plan and NOSP—to this organization. Since then the question has many times been raised whether the NVBF still has a raison d'être. It is still important as the source of inspiration and ideas for NORDINFO and of mutual benefit for its member organizations as a forum for exchange of knowledge and experiences. The Federation is still strong, issuing publications and arranging Round Table conferences and general meetings.

The members of the Federation are the following research library associations in the Nordic countries: Foreningen af Medarbejdere ved Danmarks Forskningsbiblioteker (Denmark), Finlands Ventenskapliga Bibliotekssamfund (Suomen tieteellinen kirjastoseura, Finland), Deild Bókavaróa Í Íslenskum Rannsóknarbókasfnum (Iceland), Norsk Fagbiblioteksforening (Norway), and Svenska Bibliotekariesamfundet (Sweden). These member associations nominate two members each to the NVBF board, except the Icelandic association, which nominates one. The chairmanship rotates among the countries on a two-year basis and the custom is for the country next in turn to provide the vice-chairman/treasurer. NVBF is financed by fees from the member associations, sale of publications, and grants for special projects given by NORDINFO.

The individual members of the member associations convene at general meetings every second year. The general meeting comprises a relatively modest part of the general Nordic library meeting, which is arranged every fourth year; in other alternate years NVBF has its own three- or four-day meeting. These meetings are the most important, with invited keynote speakers and opportunities for the individual members to gather in groups of interests. Round Table conferences are held once or twice a year on diverse topics, such as collection and preservation of manuscripts, collection management, marketing of the library, and other issues.

NVBF published during the 1950s a Nordic library handbook, which used to be a cornerstone in Nordic library education. In many parts it is still valid, though it became dated in other parts. A revision was not undertaken, however, as publications issued took on a more specialized character—special handbooks (for example, on library questions about developing countries) and proceedings of meetings and Round Table conferences.

NVBF withdrew as a member association of IFLA, partly for financial reasons, partly because the member associations by themselves are members of IFLA. As to NORDINFO, NVBF takes a role comparable to that IFLA takes with Unesco: NVBF initiates and in many cases executes projects financed by NORDINFO.

LARS-ERIK SANNER

Schellenberg, Theodore R.

(1903–1970)

Theodore R. Schellenberg was an American archivist whose major influence was less as an archival administrator than as a theoretician, author, and teacher.

Schellenberg was born February 24, 1903, in Harvey County, Kansas. He received his undergraduate degree from Kansas State University and earned a Ph.D. in history at the University of Pennsylvania. In 1934 he moved to Washington to serve as Secretary of the Joint Committee on Materials for Research of the American Council of Learned Societies and the Social Science Research Council, a position that involved him in the early application of microfilm to documentary materials. He then served briefly as Associate National Director of the Survey of Federal Archives before joining the staff of the recently established National Archives in 1935.

Schellenberg began his archival career as a Deputy Examiner, one of a small group of academically trained professionals who advised the Archivist of the United States on the appraisal and disposition of noncurrent government records, determining whether records no longer needed for conducting current business should be preserved in the Archives or destroyed. A concern with this most difficult responsibility of the Archivist became a central theme in Schellenberg's writings and teaching for the next 30 years, and one of his most important contributions to archival theory and practice was his elaboration of the "evidential" and "informational" criteria to be applied in the collective appraisal of institutional records. Schellenberg rose rapidly in the National Archives to the position of Chief of the Agriculture Department Archives, where he contributed to the development of records disposition schedules for federal agencies, which identified and authorized, on a continuing basis, the destruction of those recurring record series without archival value.

University of Wisconsin-Madison Archives

Theodore R. Schellenberg

After World War II Schellenberg became Records Officer of the Office of Price Administration, where he could participate directly in the development of the subdiscipline of records management. Emphasizing the life-cycle concept of records—from creation or receipt through maintenance and use to preservation as archives or destruction when noncurrent—records management attempts to reduce the quantity and improve the quality of records in their creation-receipt phase, to achieve greater economy and efficiency in the maintenance and use of current records, and to assure an orderly and timely retirement and disposition when records become semicurrent, including their intermediate storage in records centers. In 1948 Schellenberg returned to the National Archives as Program Adviser to the Archivist. He became Director of Archival Management the following year when the National Archives was reorganized as the National Archives and Records Service and in 1962 was appointed Assistant Archivist for a newly established Office of Records Appraisal, a position he held until his retirement from the federal service at the end of 1963.

He prepared the first comprehensive handbook of procedures for the National Archives—covering all professional activities—and wrote a number of staff information papers, bulletins, and journal articles on archival theory and practice. He organized and taught training courses for staff members of the National Archives; together with Ernst Posner of the American University, he taught credit courses and short intensive institutes on the preservation and administration of modern archives. In 1954 he was a Fulbright Lecturer in Australia and New Zealand; these lectures were the basis of the manual *Modern Archives: Principles and Techniques,* published in 1956. The work became the most widely known and influential American publication in the field and formed the basis for Schellenberg's international reputation and influence with its eventual translation into Spanish, Portuguese, German, and Hebrew.

Having provided a theoretical and methodological foundation for the administration of modern public records and archives, Schellenberg then turned to bridging the gaps that had developed between archivists, manuscript curators, and librarians in their increasing specialization. After his retirement he lectured widely and taught courses at several universities. In 1965 he published his second major work, *Management of Archives,* which was based on the conviction that the principles and techniques of administering modern public records and archives are also applicable to those of private institutions and to accumulations of personal papers. He also proposed that chief responsibility for the training of archivists be placed with graduate library schools. Although the book did not have the widespread acceptance and impact of his earlier treatise, it has had a continuing influence on the relations between archivists, manuscript curators, and librarians.

Schellenberg continued to teach and write until shortly before his death on January 14, 1970. In addition to his travels throughout the U.S., he was also active internationally, particularly in the Caribbean and Latin America. In 1961 he organized and directed the first Inter-American Archival Council and continued to serve as an adviser on the development of archival programs in this region. In recognition of his contributions to the archival profession worldwide, he was the first American to be elected to honorary membership in the International Council on Archives.

FRANK B. EVANS

Scholarly and Research Services

The archetypal scholarly library, the lost library at Alexandria, was a total scholarly enterprise: all the knowledge of the known (Mediterranean) world was said to have been gathered there and systematically organized; copyists reproduced books; and scholars edited and translated texts, studied old works, and produced new knowledge. Today's great comprehensive libraries—such as the Bibliothèque Nationale in Paris, the British Library in London, the Library of Congress in Washington, and the New York Public Library—along with specialized research collections, can be seen as a species of learned academy through their sustained commitment to preserving and disseminating the human record and through the scholarly knowledge and attainments of their librarians. Research libraries undertake such scholarly endeavors as carefully assembled exhibitions, detailed library catalogues and bibliographies, lecture series and seminars, translation services, oral history projects, special curatorships and scholar-in-residence programs, and other interpretive services. And, to the extent that they are open freely to the public, such libraries have been instruments in the democratization of knowledge. In the milieu of higher education, libraries have been for centuries seen as symbols of intellectual life and, more recently, as tools for research whose librarians participate in the scholar's quests. Librarians have also been active in studying the history of the book in its various aspects, especially in France, Germany, the United Kingdom, and the United States. The major U.S. institutional centers for such study are the Center for the Book in the Library of Congress and the Program in the History of the Book in American Culture at the American Antiquarian Society.

American Antiquarian Society

American Antiquarian Society, Worcester, Massachusetts.

Collections and ways to provide access to them have traditionally been the prime contribution of libraries to scholarship and research. Library holdings have been nodes in the process of communication without which modern scholarship, dependent on awareness of what is already known and thought, could not flourish. By the mid-20th century American research resources, after years of remarkable growth, could finally compare favorably with the great European research holdings, and American libraries continued to strengthen their collections in support of research, aided by microform publishing projects and programs to acquire materials from abroad.

European librarians who built modern collections, most notably Antonio Panizzi, creator of the Library of the British Museum in the Victorian Age, and German university librarians of the same era, developed policies to guide collecting. In most U.S. libraries such policies tended until the 20th century to be implicit and to some extent inconsistent rather than explicit and systematic, although there were notable exceptions. Written collection development guidelines became common in the 1970s, along with specialist bibliographers to carry them out. Current ideal practice is for libraries to develop (with the advice of faculty members in academic institutions) detailed policies in standardized format and with provisions for review in light of new conditions or changing scholarly interests.

A major current trend among scholars has been the broadening of interests in virtually every way—geographical, chronological, linguistic, cultural, societal, and topical. Scholars as a result need to see many more so-called unconventional or nontraditional sources. Many libraries, although popularly conceived as holding primarily print materials (books and serial publications), have for years undertaken to preserve the documentation of human culture through collections in varied formats: manuscripts, maps, slides, printed music, posters, prints, photographs, plans, memorabilia, and, more recently, sound recordings, motion picture reels, videotapes, and digitized files. They also have "gray" literature—publications that do not flow through established distribution channels, including artifacts of popular culture. Attention to such acquisitions, however, and bibliographic descriptions of them have been somewhat uneven and inconsistent; university libraries on the whole were slow to collect the newer media.

Another trend is the growth of interdisciplinary

and multidisciplinary studies and research, superimposed on conventional scholarly disciplines or representing a synergy of such disciplines. Such intellectual interests present challenges to libraries, not only in acquiring relevant materials, but also in organizing and presenting them in useful ways. Traditional schemes of access—shelf classification and standard cataloguing—are based on older and to some extent obsolete concepts and constructs that will have to be rethought and reconfigured. At issue also is the balance in allocating resources between current research interests and potential future interests.

The widening of scholars' information needs occurred concomitantly with extraordinary increases in the production, and the cost, of publications, especially of scientific journals. The so-called information explosion, combined with sharply rising prices and the fiscal stringencies of universities and other nonprofit institutions, beginning in the 1970s, have limited any one institution's ability to satisfy local scholars' demands, much less to acquire more than a fraction of the world's output of documents. It is no longer possible, if it ever really was, for an individual library to have a self-contained comprehensive collection. Indeed, by the late 1980s many libraries were forced either to sacrifice purchases of monographic publications in favor of journals, or to cancel journal subscriptions.

Resource Sharing and Technology. Leaders of the research library community have seen interinstitutional collaboration as one solution: resource sharing was the watchword of the 1980s. Resource sharing encompasses several components: merging bibliographic records of holdings, effective systems for accessing the holdings themselves, and cooperative collection development programs to distribute responsibility for collecting (and preserving) research materials, in the interests of comprehensive coverage. Involved as well is the role of structures, such as the British Library Document Supply Center in the U.K. and the Center for Research Libraries in the U.S., containing central collections that scholars can use.

Resource sharing, neither a new idea nor a new practice, has been made possible on an unprecedented scale and with unprecedented efficiency by computer and telecommunications technologies. By the 1980s, almost all North American scholarly libraries of consequence, and many national and university libraries on other continents, were entering bibliographic records into regional or national electronic databases or bibliographic utilities (such as OCLC or RLIN in the U.S. and UTLAS in Canada). These databases also contain records of manuscript and other special collections, specialized bibliographies and files, and materials in non-Roman alphabets, and they offer international connections as well. When merged or linked databases are a reality, there will be in effect a dynamic universal bibliography of millions of items, the knowledge of whose existence and location can ideally be at the fingertips of all scholars, either directly through their own electronic workstations or indirectly through the help of librarians at their local libraries. Many research libraries, in addition, have launched online public access catalogues (OPACs) that can be accessed from a distance. For at least recent publications, bibliographic information and in many cases circulation status are electronically available to

Elmer Holmes Bobst Library, New York University

A centralized switcher controls 28 VCRs at the Avery Fisher Center for Music and Media, Elmer Holmes Bobst Library, New York University. Opened in 1986, the Center has more than one hundred separate audio/video stations and houses a large and varied collection of resources.

users, albeit with as yet less than full authority control (consistency among entries and indication of relationships among works). A problem for scholars needing older works remains the uneven levels of conversion of records of retrospective materials to machine-readable form.

The major mode of obtaining the documents themselves from locations other than the home library is traditional interlibrary loan, though for certain materials reprographic and telefacsimile technologies enable users to buy copies rather than borrow originals. The new electronic technology facilitates document delivery through the bibliographic utilities or other networks, local or regional, a process that has immensely broadened access to research materials and reduced considerably the time for items to reach the user.

Easier and faster interlibrary loan and reprography notwithstanding, scholars will still need to visit particular libraries. Certain materials are available only at the holding institution, including rare or unique books and manuscripts, reference works, fragile items, and nonbook materials such as maps that cannot readily travel. In any case, scholars may need to see originals rather than copies, and they may need to examine groups of materials rather than only specified works on loan. Various reciprocal use arrangements exist. The problem of providing for on-site use of materials also exists at home libraries as administrators, pressed for space, consign little-used materials to remote storage.

The Research Libraries Group (RLG) developed the Conspectus to asses past and present collection strengths, organized by LC classification. Beginning in 1983, the Conspectus was expanded under the aegis of the Association of Research Libraries (ARL) into the North American Collection Inventory Project (NCIP). Some Canadian and British libraries have adopted the conspectus concept, and there is interest in it in Australia and other countries of Europe. Such standardized, comparative information in computerized form can serve as a basis for cooperative collection development and help advise researchers about the existence of collections of interest to them. Among RLG members there have been assignments for primary collecting responsibility in certain subjects, and in many parts of the U.S. there is some division of collecting responsibilities among neighboring institutions. Systematic national or regional cooperative collection development is not yet a reality, however, and questions remain about the balance and possible conflicts of interest between local needs and resource-sharing policies based on interdependence among libraries.

Another way of extending access to information and materials derives from the proliferation of electronic databases external to libraries. First, in the late 1960s and the 1970s, came computerized periodical indexes and abstracts and other current bibliographies, eventually combined with systems to deliver the actual documents; then compilations of statistical and other nonbibliographic information; and, more recently, full texts of documents, current and retrospective, as well as hypertext. Electronic publishing, which might replace print and hence preclude library acquisition of certain materials, is growing but not yet widespread, and its future extent and impact are still speculative.

Much of the digitized information is online; some, increasingly, is in CD-ROM form; some systems combine the two; and certain of these files are available through the bibliographic utilities. These developments, occurring first in science and technology and then in the social sciences and humanities, have for the most part come out of developments in the private sector or nonprofit scholarly and scientific publishing. In libraries these databases tended initially to be made available to scholars through the mediation of librarians trained in database selection and searching. One problem has been the cost of such on-demand service. Fee policies are inconsistent from institution to institution, and the issue remains alive as universities and other institutions supporting research establish local telecommunication networks and external electronic linkages enabling users at personal computers to call up an immense variety of digitized information sources, including data and texts. Also involved is the fee for access to public depository libraries of data in digitized form. In general, the efforts begun in the U.S. during the 1980s to privatize information sources have raised questions of cost and equity in obtaining public information. Librarians fear that imbalance or inequity in access to the expensive and sophisticated new technologies that are transforming modes of conducting research will exacerbate existing disparities.

Harvard University

Staff member in Research and Bibliographic Services, Harvard University Libraries, prepares to use a CD-ROM database.

Libraries, Technology, and Scholars. Although the pace of development is uneven and institutional variations exist, there seems to be consensus among research librarians that libraries and librarians, with their traditional service orientation, knowledge of the research literature and of research needs, and experience in organizing intellectual records, should play a key role in organizing and administering automated systems for scholars. Librarians have sought to define and articulate the concept of the scholarly workstation through which scholars would have before them, in user-friendly systems, the panoply of databases, library catalogues, descriptions of archives, full texts, and other information in digitized form. Librarians are extending their traditional role as intermediaries, instructors, and consultants—fulfilled in the past through reference and instructional services—to helping scholars find their way through the daunting complexities of computerized information. Librarians' vision of the future, which still includes libraries (that is, collections, albeit in more varied formats and differently organized and administered), involves close ties with scholars and close attention to their needs.

In this concern, a new initiative in aid of humanistic scholarship is the Center for Electronic Texts in the Humanities at Rutgers University Libraries (New Brunswick, New Jersey), a collaborative effort of Rutgers and Princeton universities. Launched in 1991, the project was designed to serve as a national node in an international network to provide access to humanities datafiles and as an international information and education center for scholars, students, and librarians involved in creating, disseminating, using, and preserving such files.

In the U.S. all these activities have developed incrementally and variously, in the private for-profit and nonprofit sectors, with some government support and with some standardization. In 1990 ARL, CAUSE (Association for the Management of Information and Technology in Higher Education), and EDUCOM (a consortium of higher education institutions involved in campus networking) created the Coalition for Networked Information to advance scholarship and intellectual productivity through networks, including libraries, and aiming to address the implications—economic, legal, technical, and organizational—of a national electronic information infrastructure. Also in 1990 the National Information Standards Organization began work on standards for storing, transmitting, and using electronic information.

Library organizations and consortia and the chief foundation in the field, the Council on Library Resources, Inc. (CLR), have been active in interpreting, utilizing, and controlling the new world of information in the interests of scholarship and research, and with particular concern for the quality and potential instability of electronic information being increasingly produced and controlled by the private, market-driven sector. Librarians' groups have also been working with scientific and scholarly organizations to deal with the crisis in journal pricing. Among scholarly organizations, the American Council of Learned Societies (ACLS) has been perhaps most concerned with scholarly communication and libraries. It was a chief participant in the National Enquiry into Scholarly Communication, whose report was published in 1979 and from which came the ACLS Office for Scholarly Communication. The Office was discontinued in 1987, but the ACLS maintained its interest in scholarly communication and the role of libraries. In 1988 the ACLS, together with the Association of American Universities and the Social Science Research Council, co-sponsored a Research Library Committee established by the CLR to consider the problems and possibilities of libraries in support of humanistic and historical studies in the next century. The Committee's *Statement,* issued in May 1990, urged that the research library be redefined in light of new information technologies, changes in scholarship and teaching, and the problems and transformations of universities; the Committee dissolved in June 1990.

Preservation. A crucial aspect of research library service is preserving collections, which is of particular interest to humanistic and historical scholars, with their heavy use of retrospective materials. Great strides were made from the mid-1960s on in raising consciousness and discovering facts about the physical care of collections. Catalysts in this process were the effects of the flood of the Arno River in Florence in 1966 and the earlier discovery that paper produced from woodpulp since the mid-19th century was rapidly deteriorating, mainly because of its acid content. The result was activity in various fronts: research and development by national libraries, national archives, and private firms into modes of deacidifying paper, efforts that are not yet standardized, scientifically validated, or fully operational; creation of local and regional preservation service centers; installation in many research libraries of preservation officers and programs; endorsement of the use of acid-free paper; support for preservation projects, including the first and only postgraduate degree program to educate preservation administrators and conservation specialists, begun in 1981 at the Columbia University School of Library Service and transferred in 1992 to the University of Texas at Austin; extensive preservation microfilming programs, some with the active participation of scholars; establishment of standards for preservation microfilming and for environmental controls; and bibliographic control of microform copies.

In 1986 CLR formed the Commission on Preservation and Access, which, with ties to the scholarly and higher education establishment, has been a leader in promoting research, national planning, and policy formation in preservation and in the public relations and political aspects of the field. Reflecting the increased internationalization of preservation efforts is the Commission's interest in creating a machine-readable database for sharing preservation records across national boundaries. Progress in preservation research worldwide was the subject of an international conference hosted by Columbia's School of Library Service in 1991.

Preservation activity has concentrated more on retrospective collections, on saving endangered existing material, than on prospective preservation to ensure that materials currently produced and acquired will be intact for use by future scholars. Prospective preservation involves not only print on paper, but also materials that are evanescent, subject to continual change, and accessible only through machines, whose hardware and software are always changing. The contemporary scholarly interest in nontraditional sources, many of them ephemeral and in fragile form, presents challenges to libraries in preservation as well as in acquisition. Preventive measures to protect materials from theft and vandalism as well as decay may also include limitations on the open access to stacks typical of libraries in North America.

International Developments. Advances in telecommunication make possible international information networks. Such collaboration exists, for example, between the U.S., Canada, and the U.K., and international library interests have as their goal universal access to bibliographic information and library materials. In general, however, the development of new technology in aid of scholarship has been a feature of the developed world—mainly North America and Western Europe—and, even there, political and economic barriers can inhibit communication across borders, and systems are quite diverse. In the developing world, with its deepening economic problems and weak technological, bibliographic, and publishing infrastructures, library progress has seriously slowed and utilization of computer and telecommunications technology is problematical. However, telefacsimile communication and the use of CD-ROM products are increasing. The major tasks there are to develop regional cooperation and indigenous systems with appropriate technology.

A major project of Unesco's World Decade for Cultural Development (which began in 1988), supported by the Egyptian government and promoted by an international commission, is the revival of the Bibliotheca Alexandrina. The project aimed to rebuild Alexandria as a seat of learning through building a modern library-museum-planetarium, with a center for preserving old books and manuscripts and an international school of information studies (*see* Bibliotheca Alexandrina). The new Bibliotheca Alexandrina was designed to emphasize the cultural heritage of northern Africa, the Mediterranean region, and the Arab world. The bibliothecal tradition symbolized by the library of ancient Alexandria will have come full circle at Alexandria itself, just as computer and telecommunication technologies are enabling the fulfillment in the modern world of the Alexandrine concept of access to universal knowledge.

REFERENCES

Phyllis Dain and John Y. Cole, editors, *Libraries and Scholarly Communication in the United States: The Historical Dimension* (1990).

Constance C. Gould, *Information Needs in the Humanities: An Assessment* (1988).

Constance C. Gould and Mark Handler, *Information Needs in the Social Sciences: An Assessment* (1989).

Herbert C. Morton et al., *Writings on Scholarly Communication: An Annotated Bibliography of Books and Articles on Publishing, Libraries, Scholarly Research, and Related Issues* (1988).

PHYLLIS DAIN

School Libraries/Media Centers

BACKGROUND AND OBJECTIVES

School libraries can be traced back to the mid-1800s or early 1900s in such countries as Canada, Japan, the Nordic countries, the United Kingdom, and the

Prince George's County Public Schools, Maryland

Poetry reading in public school, Prince George's County, Maryland.

United States. The objectives of these early libraries were to provide supplementary materials to support classroom instruction and to encourage reading and the enjoyment of literature. In most cases they represented isolated efforts, with systematic development delayed until the second half of the 20th century.

In the U.S. school library development was first promoted in the late 1800s. Around 1895 farsighted high-school principals and directors of public libraries in various communities began to create school libraries. There was a steady expansion of high-school libraries, but elementary-school libraries were slower to develop, gaining prominence only after World War II.

The move to establish school libraries had strong professional support. In the U.S. the National Education Association (NEA) through its Library Department, the Library Section of the National Council of Teachers of English (NCTE), and the American Library Association (ALA) supported the development of the concept. These professional bodies had a clear vision of what school library service could become long before school libraries were a widespread reality. The NEA *Proceedings* for 1912 stated that "the school library will be the proof of the educational value of the new curriculum. . . . the library will be the open door to the opportunity of the present."

Changing ideas in education often provided the impetus for school library development. New ideas about children's education and reading initiated a move to introduce elementary-school libraries in Sweden around 1900. Many school libraries were established in Japan as a result of the New Education Movement of the 1920s. Even in rural areas, progressive elementary-school teachers led a movement to set up classroom libraries.

An understanding of the educational importance of school libraries sometimes gave rise to legislative support, as early as 1724 in Finland. In 1891 the Norwegian Parliament voted to provide money for elementary-school libraries in rural areas. Denmark made important provisions for state support of elementary-school libraries in 1931 and followed up with a 1937 school act incorporating library work into the educational plan.

Systematic and widespread development of school libraries took place in many countries after World War II, a period of economic growth and relative prosperity in which school systems expanded because of increasing population. Development was also spurred by the attainment of independence by many Asian and African nations. Educational expansion and reorientation leading to school library development took place in countries as diverse as Jordan, Malaysia, Nigeria, and Tanzania in the years following independence.

But the most important factor leading to the achievements of this period was educational change. The educational ferment characteristic of the 1960s and 1970s resulted from a combination of factors: pressures for more democratic and culturally relevant education, the effects of rapid change and the knowledge explosion, and the insights gained through educational research. These factors provided the impetus for basic changes in educational objectives and practices and helped spur reform movements in many countries.

The new education focused on the learner and the learning process, with a consequent emphasis on self-directed learning and individualized instruction. Education became resource-based, the aim being to provide the combination of resources most appropriate to various learners in particular learning situations. In a rapidly changing world, emphasis shifted from mastering a body of knowledge to acquiring the skills for handling information throughout life. Modern life also increased the need for adaptability and critical thinking. Education was to be functional, tailored to the needs of the individual and the society and aiming for wholeness in development.

These reforms turned new attention to the school library, already known in many countries as a resource center and learning laboratory. The school library was seen as offering the variety of materials required to meet individual needs. It could provide the learning opportunities and resources to support inquiry, the development of learning skills, and critical thinking. The move toward learner-centered and resource-based education brought the school library to the center of the educational process.

This new perception of the school library was reflected in educational policy and legislation. Hong Kong's Education Commission Report of 1965 and the Swedish senior high-school reform of the same year both recommended school libraries as essential for the development of an inquiring mind and independent study. School or library legislation, taking the form of standards, establishment of school library units, or special funding, laid the foundation for school library development in countries around the world.

By the 1980s school libraries were well established in many places. Such countries as Australia, Denmark, Japan, Sweden, and the U.S. had libraries in virtually every school. Others, such as Hong Kong, Israel, Malaysia, and New Zealand, had made good progress in developing school library systems. Still others showed growing awareness and active efforts on behalf of school libraries. The impact of school library media and services, and their role and function in education, seemed destined to grow in all countries.

The 1980s, however, brought some disappointments and a consequent reevaluation. The economic difficulties experienced in many countries in the decade meant less money for established school libraries and threatened to halt school library progress in poorer countries. In many countries the noble objectives enunciated in educational policy were not achieved in practice, and school libraries were still far from being the educational heart of their schools. Librarians who assumed that the curriculum was enough to secure provision of school libraries (as with elementary schools in the U.S. and high schools in Norway) discovered that without legal obligations, development was uncertain, especially when hard times hit. In other places school librarians felt they had not done enough to put across the value of school libraries, rendering them vulnerable to cutbacks. School libraries had made impressive progress, but many challenges remained for the 1990s.

Education. Dual qualification in education and librarianship is widely held to be the ideal for professional school library personnel. In most parts of the U.S. certification codes specify minimum standards in both education and librarianship for school library/media specialists at the secondary level and, in some states, at the elementary level. In the U.S., *Information Power,* published by the American Association of School Librarians (AASL) and Association for Educational Communications and Technology (AECT) in 1988, recommends a library qualification at the Master's degree level on top of a strong liberal arts background and teaching certification as the entry-level qualification for the building school library/media specialist. Similarly, the Canadian School Library Association recommended a graduate library qualification added to a first degree in education, teaching certificate, and classroom teaching experience. In Australia teacher-librarians prepare through four-year Bachelor of Education programs or first degrees plus one-year graduate diplomas in education, librarianship, or teacher-librarianship. In Denmark and Nigeria teacher-librarians study in teacher training institutions. Likewise, standards for Iceland (1984) and Israel (1988) recommend as elementary-school librarians either qualified teachers with some training in librarianship or qualified librarians with additional studies in education.

While dual qualification is a widely accepted ideal, it is realized in relatively few countries, especially at the elementary-school level. Controversy has arisen in several countries over who, in the absence of personnel with dual qualifications, should have responsibility for school libraries. Should it be a school librarian, commonly denoting someone who is first a librarian and who may not have teaching qualifications, or a teacher-librarian, whose first profession is teaching and who may not have library qualifications?

Those who favor appointing qualified teachers to run school libraries point to the need for teaching competencies and for an understanding of educational principles and practice. They also argue that a teacher-librarian will more easily be included as a member of the teaching team and will be better placed to integrate the library with the curriculum. The problem is compounded where librarians have a lower status, lower wages, and fewer benefits than teachers, as is the case in Israel, Japan, and Sweden.

On the other hand, librarians argue for the importance of library competencies, since this is an area where other school personnel lack expertise. Library competencies become especially important where the libraries have no central support services, such as acquisitions and cataloguing. In addition librarians argue against the tendency to see teacher-librarians primarily as teachers. In many countries library duties are simply added to normal teaching loads. While this is more likely to happen to those without library training, qualified teacher-librarians are not exempt. This problem led the Nigerian School Library Association to resolve in 1991 that full-time school librarians rather than qualified teacher-librarians be posted to Nigerian school libraries.

Prince George's County Public Schools, Maryland

Learning how to make books—in a Maryland junior high school library.

A working group set up by the International Federation of Library Associations and Institutions (IFLA) on the education and training of school librarians concluded that, whatever their professional background or level of qualification, school librarians require competencies in three areas: librarianship, education, and management.

The fact that teachers without library training are appointed to run school libraries indicates a large role for in-service courses. Teachers so appointed in Hong Kong are required to take two-year part-time day release programs in school librarianship. The University of Iceland offers one-year programs for teachers who want certification as school librarians, as do library schools in Israel. New Zealand and Norway have introduced successful programs to produce initiators in the field, selecting teachers with special interest or from schools that have shown a commitment to school library programs.

In many countries library associations, higher institutions, education departments, or public libraries offer school library personnel short in-service courses ranging from one week to three months. These courses help motivate and guide teachers who have ben assigned responsibility for school libraries.

However, it is not enough to train a few teachers to take care of school libraries. Classroom teachers lack understanding of the role of the library in education and lack experience in using its resources,

Leisure reading corner, G. Karaslavov Secondary School in Sofia, Bulgaria.

impeding students in effective use of the library. Librarians argue that aspects of library education must be incorporated into the training of all teachers. To further this end, IFLA set up a working group on instruction for teachers on the educational and curricular use of school libraries. The working group reported on the subject in 1986.

Professional Associations. School libraries link education and librarianship, and professional associations concerned with them reflect this dual background at both international and national levels. There are two prominent international associations dealing with school libraries, the International Association of School Librarianship (IASL) and the School Libraries Section of IFLA.

IASL, founded in 1971, grew out of the World Confederation of Organizations of the Teaching Profession (WCOTP). Its aims are to provide an international forum for school librarianship and to encourage worldwide school library development. Major themes emerging from IASL conferences in the late 1980s and early 1990s included school libraries and society, the integration of school libraries into the curriculum, new technologies, library cooperation, literacy, and the uses of literature. IASL published *School Libraries: International Developments* (2nd edition, 1991), comparing school libraries in 24 countries: three from Africa, nine from Asia, seven from Europe, two from North America, and three from Oceania.

The School Libraries Section of IFLA was founded in 1976. It has been especially concerned with integrating effective school library use into teaching and learning. Early projects related to establishing school libraries, teachers' promotion of voluntary reading, and teaching information concepts and skills. A seminar on the education of school librarians (held in Costa Rica in 1978) led to projects on the competencies required by school librarians and instruction for teachers on the use of school libraries.

Active national associations for school librarians have grown up in recent years. In the U.S., school librarians first organized as a section in the ALA in 1914; the section became an autonomous division, the AASL, in 1951. The ALA and AASL have been responsible for a series of guidelines and standards defining the direction for school libraries in the U.S.

The Japan School Library Association provides awards for distinguished school library activities and research and runs contests for picture books and book reviews prepared by school pupils. It conducts an annual sampling survey, offers training for school library staff, and publishes handbooks and textbooks.

The Nigerian School Library Association has worked with the government to promote implementation of school library provisions in the National Policy on Education. At state level, the Anambra State School Libraries Association worked in active partnership with state library and education authorities to promote school library development, winning government acceptance of minimum standards, a library fee for secondary schools, and training programs for teacher-librarians in colleges of education.

The Thai Library Association holds an annual school library contest, awarding prizes to librarians and administrators of winning schools at kindergarten, primary, and secondary levels.

Professional associations play a valuable role in promoting standards and legislation, in conducting research and training, and in encouraging reading and library awareness. Their active presence has stimulated school library development in many countries.

SERVICES TO USERS

The revolutionary changes in education dating from the mid-1950s have expanded school library services to users. Early school libraries concentrated on enriching textbook teaching with supplementary materials and introducing children to the wonderful world of imaginative literature; reforms precipitated by the

Hamsters and gerbils keeping students company in library of a St. Paul, Minnesota, elementary school.

Highwood Hills Elementary School, St. Paul School District

extraordinary increase in knowledge, proliferation of communication technologies, and findings of educational research changed education and with it the nature and focus of services to users. Libraries emerged as the places where students would learn from a range of information sources and media, using "discovery" and problem-solving learning procedures. The result has been to move the school library and the librarian from the periphery of the instructional program into the mainstream of educational effort.

Reference and Information Services. The school library is the information center of the school, with a collection of basic reference sources and assistance in locating information. In the U.S. the National Center for Educational Statistics (NCES) carried out a study in 1985–86 that found reference assistance to be the most common service provided to students and teachers: 91 percent of library media specialists from elementary and secondary schools responded that they assist students in locating information and resources; 75 percent reported that they provide reference assistance to teachers. Information service in connection with assignments was identified as one of four most common services offered in Iceland's elementary schools and as second among services offered by secondary school teachers in Nigeria.

Reading Guidance and Promotion. Encouraging reading has been an enduring role of the school library. In country after country, school librarians list the promotion of reading and literature as among their most important services to users. Many elementary-school teachers see it as the basic service of the school library. Almost a third of the papers presented at IASL conferences in the late 1980s dealt with reading and the role of literature.

Activities used to promote reading include storytelling, book talks, visits from authors, compilation of bibliographies, displays, and reading clubs. School libraries also serve as reading guidance centers, in which school librarians help students, as individuals or in groups, to find books for information or pleasure.

Concerns over the high level of functional illiteracy in the Nordic countries, the U.K., and the U.S. became pronounced in the 1970s and 1980s, leading to renewed emphasis on reading promotion in school libraries. Improving reading habits and skills is no less important in developing countries, where literacy is seen as crucial to national growth, yet children from nonliterate backgrounds encounter books and reading only in school and, in many cases, in a second language.

The role of school libraries in introducing children to the world of imaginative literature has also been reaffirmed in recent years. There is a long association between school libraries and the development of children's literature in countries such as Norway and Sweden. Faced with the huge volume of mediocre books flooding the market, school librarians have reasserted the importance of reading guidance in fostering encounters with the best in national and international literature for children and youth. In the U.S., reading guidance programs are used to promote understanding and acceptance of ethnic diversity.

Information Skills Instruction. School libraries/media centers help students learn how to learn. This teaching role is basic to an education aimed at developing inquiring minds and information skills for lifelong education. The ALA, in connection with the Presidential Committee on Information Literacy, defined "information literacy" in 1989 as the ability to recognize when information is needed and to be able to locate, evaluate, and use the needed information effectively.

M. Marland summed up the specific skills required in nine steps:

What do I need to do? (formulation and analysis of need)

Where could I go? (identification and appraisal of likely sources)

How do I get information? (tracing and locating individual resources)

Which resources shall I use? (examining, selecting, and rejecting individual resources)

How shall I use resources? (interrogating resources)

What should I make a record of? (recording and storing information)

Have I got the information I need? (interpretation, analysis, synthesis, evaluation)

How should I present it? (presentation, communication, shape)

What have I achieved? (evaluation)

Mary Holloway has described the applications of an online catalogue to information skills instruction, pointing out its advantages in developing higher-level thinking skills in synthesis, organization, and presentation of data.

User education—teaching library and learning skills—is a traditional service that has acquired a new focus. It may still take the form of simple lessons in how to use the library, but many school librarians are moving toward informal instruction through project work or with individual students as the need arises. This approach promotes the integration of the school library into the educational program of the school.

Greenwich Public Schools

Students construct a set and prepare to film a movie at Western Junior High School in Greenwich, Connecticut.

Greenwich Public Schools

Students at Julian Curtiss School, Greenwich, Connecticut, locating their town on a library globe.

New Technologies. Recent years have seen a vast expansion in the resources available in the school library/media center. From being primarily a collection of books, the library is now seen as a resource center or media center housing an array of audiovisual materials and equipment, computers, and learning machines. Much of the responsibility for integrating the new communications media into the fabric of instruction falls upon the school librarian, who identifies, selects, organizes, and makes these resources available to teachers and students.

Audiovisual Media. The increasing influence of picture-based information has made visual literacy and mastery of audiovisual media key educational objectives and a priority in service to users. Some of the new technologies are not only sources of information, but also themselves media for communication and vehicles for artistic expression. Some school library/media centers provide facilities for production and staff for teaching the technology-related communication arts.

Computers have become increasingly common in school libraries/media centers, and many librarians have had to give instruction in their use. Skill in searching for information and references by accessing specific databases is becoming an integral part of student competencies in Australia, Canada, Sweden, the U.K., and the U.S. However, in spite of their widespread use in school library operations, computers have not yet caused a revolution in education, primarily because teachers are reluctant and lack training in computer use. Providing assistance and training to teachers, therefore, becomes a necessary service of media center staff.

Learning Centers. The supervision of skill development or "prescriptive" learning centers is yet another service of school library/media centers. Using programmed instruction, media center staff work with teachers in providing remedial experiences for problem learners, principally in reading, language, and mathematics.

Curriculum Planning and Implementation. School librarians can contribute their professional expertise as media specialists in planning and implementing the curriculum. In Canada the development of resource-based programs integrated with the school's instructional programs is seen to be the most important responsibility of the teacher-librarian. Units of study drawing on a variety of library resources and integrating appropriate information skills are developed jointly by teachers and teacher-librarians. In Norway as well, the expectation that elementary-school teachers will develop learning material connected with the local community and students' experiences provides opportunities for individualizing instruction and including the school library in the educational process.

J. Gordon Coleman, Jr., and Rebecca Allan Condon have suggested "curriculum mapping" as a technique for integrating library resources into information skills instruction. By this method, teachers and librarians select certain courses each year and analyze their curricular content. The school librarian can then base information skills instruction and curriculum development on units receiving emphasis, utilizing a variety of resources and methods of teaching and evaluation.

In spite of lofty aims, many schools have made little progress in fully integrating the school library into the curriculum, causing widespread disappointment. Marilyn L. Miller and Marilyn Shantz found that U.S. media specialists do not do serious planning with teachers. Experience in New Zealand and Norway, among other countries, indicates that the school library's educational potential is not realized, partly because of deficiencies in teacher training. Moreover, school librarians in countries such as Germany, India, Nigeria, and Tanzania are still struggling to change an education focused on teacher and textbook and dominated by examinations. School librarians still face the challenge of bringing the school library to the center of the school's educational program and fully integrating it with classroom instruction.

COLLECTIONS

Changing trends in education have also affected school library collections. The book collection of the traditional library has given way to the multimedia collection of the school library/media center. While books are still the mainstay of the collection, a range of audiovisual resources and equipment, and other new technologies such as microforms and computers, have become increasingly important. The new school library/media center collection includes reference materials, nonfiction, fiction, periodicals, vertical-file materials such as pamphlets and clippings, audiovisual resources in old forms (pictures, charts, maps, models, and specimens) and new (sound recordings, slides and filmstrips, transparencies, motion pictures, and videotapes), microforms, programmed instruction materials, and computer programs.

The size and content of the collection depend on the level of school library development. Many countries are still working to establish school libraries and build up basic book collections. While virtually every school in Japan has a library, with book collections averaging more than 5,000 for elementary schools, almost 6,000 for junior high schools, and nearly

18,000 for senior high schools, only about 41 percent of recognized schools in India have libraries, and these few have collections ranging from fewer than 100 to a maximum of about 5,000 books.

Audiovisual collections are a reality in the well-established libraries of developed countries. Elsewhere, there is growing awareness of their value. School library authorities in Hong Kong, Malaysia, and Singapore have embraced the concept of the school library as a resource center, even while still building up their book collections. Use of resources requiring equipment is limited in many countries by lack of funds, lack of electrical power to schools, and lack of maintenance facilities. Schools and regional resource centers may, however, produce teaching aids such as charts, pictures, and models with restricted facilities.

Computers are a common feature of school libraries in Australia, Canada, Denmark, Sweden, the U.K., and the U.S. A few other countries, among them Finland, Iceland, Japan, New Zealand, and Norway, are beginning to explore their use in schools.

Organization. An integrated approach in organizing materials results in a collection in which all materials, regardless of format, are classified and catalogued according to a single system. The complete index to the collection (whether in card or book form or on a computer terminal) indicates all book and nonbook materials in a single listing, enabling users to identify and locate the library's entire holdings on a given subject.

With the publication of the Second Edition of the *Anglo-American Cataloguing Rules* (AACR2) in 1978, a standard for cataloguing nonbook materials was established. Many of the changes consolidated in the 1988 revision of AACR2 reflect further progress toward the goal of fully integrated cataloguing. Book and nonbook materials can be processed with uniformity, facilitating integrated collections. Whether the various types of media are placed together on the shelves, stored in separate areas in the library, or housed throughout the school depends on the facilities available and the policy of the individual school library. Uniformity in processing and an integrated catalogue also increase the potential for sharing resources through systems and networks, thus offering a greater wealth of material to students and teachers.

Collection Building. Development of the collection is guided by the needs of the users: the students and teachers of the school. Attention must be given to user needs relating to the educational program and to personal enrichment. Quantitative analysis is applied to the collection by dividing the total number of items in a category by the enrollment of the school. For qualitative analysis, librarians and teachers rate the collection in terms of variety of media, currency of materials, relevance of materials, range of ability levels, and range of opinions represented. These analyses enable school librarians to identify gaps and guide future collection development.

An important consideration in the selection process is the need for a balanced collection. Balance is aimed at meeting the various objectives of the school library program and the needs of students. The collection should include materials for various ages, interests, and levels of reading ability. The school library should strive to maintain balance between print and nonprint, fiction and nonfiction, arts and science subjects, curricular and recreational materials, and various viewpoints.

IASL and WCOTP issued a joint policy statement on school libraries in 1983–84 that addressed the issue of criteria for selection in terms of the appropriateness of materials. The statement identified seven aspects of "appropriateness":

1. an awareness of the total range of information and communication technology;
2. variety concerning many fields of knowledge and recreational activities;
3. materials devised to serve children within the range of their cognitive, affective, and psychomotor skills;
4. appeal to children's interests;
5. utilization of the student's primary language;
6. reflection of the cultural interests valued by the children's families; and
7. application to the economic environment.

Some of these aspects have particular relevance to developing countries, where school librarians can find few books in local languages or reflecting local environment and culture.

In many countries collection development is complicated by "book famine," where books are not available because local ones are scarce and foreign ones are almost impossible to obtain. As in the Nordic countries in an earlier period, so today there is a close association between school libraries and the promotion of local children's books in Thailand, Venezuela, and other developing countries.

Continuous evaluation of the collection for accuracy of information, current interests, and changing curriculum content is important if the collection is to be meaningful and useful. As library materials are added to the collection, so they must be weeded. Otherwise the integrity of the collection will be compromised by out-of-date or inaccurate materials. Weeding as well as selection should be an ongoing process governed by regular procedures.

Collection Policy. Each school should have a written policy statement regarding selection. Such a statement helps guide the selection process toward a collection of high quality that reflects the needs and interests of the users. The policy statement may be

Irmo Middle School Complex, Irmo, South Carolina

Library media center in Irmo, South Carolina. It provides equipment and guidance for various productions, including video news spots.

St. Paul School District, St. Paul, Minnesota

Students sharing a story on tape in a school library in St. Paul, Minnesota.

prepared at the school, district, or higher level, depending on the system. Professional library staff, administrators, teachers, parents, and school board members may participate in developing such a statement, which may include the philosophy of the school's educational program, the types of materials to be ordered, criteria for their evaluation, and procedures for handling problems that may arise when material selected is questioned.

Many school libraries in the U.S. have encountered problems with censorship arising from parental or community objections to particular library materials. The incidence of such objections was high throughout the 1980s, with a focus on ideas as well as "dirty" books. A report by the National Commission on Libraries and Information Science (NCLIS) indicated that school library materials were more likely to be challenged than either classroom materials or public library materials. In 1986 the ALA responded to this problem by adopting an interpretation of the Library Bill of Rights for school library/media programs. The statement emphasized the need for selection policies and procedures that were board-approved and used on a daily basis in order to counter infringement on students' rights to have access to information.

ADMINISTRATION

School libraries have various patterns of governance, depending on the division of governmental responsibility for education. Some countries, among them Denmark, Israel, Japan, and Malaysia, have strong central control of education. Policies and legislation for school libraries are set at the center. At the other end of the spectrum are countries such as Australia, Canada, and the U.S., where states or provinces are responsible for education, including school library service, although the federal governments may provide leadership through special programs or funding. Other countries, including Nigeria, Sweden, and the U.K., follow a middle way, in which the central government sets educational policy and states or local governments implement policy and finance education. Many countries have strong traditions of local autonomy in education, and the level of school library provision depends on local priorities and circumstances, whatever the national policy or governance pattern.

In Malaysia, as an example of central control, education is the responsibility of the national government, with all schools following a central curriculum. Implementation of policy and supervision of schools are carried out by state education departments and district education offices. School library development throughout the country is the responsibility of the School Library Unit of the Ministry of Education; Educational Technology Units coordinate services at state level.

The Malaysian government introduced a number of school library provisions in the 1970s, including annual library book grants for all schools, establishment of library rooms and basic collections in all newly built schools, a specialist course for teacher-librarians, and periodic surveys to monitor school library development in the country. With these measures school libraries developed rapidly, to the point where by 1977 almost all secondary schools and four out of five primary schools had central libraries.

In the U.S., an example of a decentralized system, state governments have responsibility for education. Legislatures set policy for schools through state boards of education and state departments of public instruction. Many states employ school library supervisors to develop programs in the schools. The degree of local community control over the curriculum, textbook selection, and funding for personnel, learning resources, and buildings varies from state to state.

The federal government may enact laws that affect public education, with the Department of Education administering federal programs for public and private schools. In the 1960s and 1970s Congress passed a number of such laws, vastly increasing funding for school libraries. Prominent among them was the Elementary and Secondary Education Act (ESEA) of 1965. ESEA funding was especially important in developing the nation's primary-school libraries. By the mid-1980s, 93 percent of the public schools in the U.S. had school library/media centers, although the figure drops to 75 percent for private schools.

Personnel. Administration of the school library/media center at the building level is usually the responsibility of the principal, who delegates authority to the school librarian or a teacher. Personnel is one of the most serious problems facing school library service. School libraries in many countries lack adequate staff, because of the small size of elementary schools, the few library facilities to administer, and economic constraints. Many school libraries, especially at the elementary-school level, have no library staff positions or at best half-time ones. This situation is understandable in countries where schools are small, as in Finland, in which most primary schools have fewer than five teaching units, and Norway, where a third of the basic schools have fewer than 50 pupils. Even where full-time or half-time library positions exist, many people designated as "school librarians" or "teacher-librarians" are without any professional library qualifications or training.

Professionally qualified school librarians or teacher-librarians are most often found in countries with well-developed school library services, such as Australia and the U.S. Even in such countries, they are more likely to be found in large high schools than in smaller or lower-level schools. In Canada most full-time teacher-librarians work in high schools with more than a thousand students. Most Swedish senior high schools have qualified school librarians, with 50 percent working half-time.

The most common practice is for a teacher to be assigned responsibility for the library in addition to normal teaching duties. This is the pattern even in some countries with fairly well-established systems, such as Japan, the U.K., and Nordic and Southeast Asian countries, as well as in the developing systems of African and Latin American nations. In some cases these teachers are given a small allowance or reduction in teaching load. In some cases, also, they are given opportunities for training.

The strength of support staff also varies widely. Some school libraries have library assistants, audiovisual technicians, and clerical staff, while others have only an aide, student helpers, or parent volunteers.

The lack of adequate personnel, in terms of both number and qualification, is a major hindrance to effective school library service. The establishment of library staff positions and training of school library personnel remain priorities in many countries.

Facilities. To render effective service, school libraries need adequate resources, staff, and facilities. The facilities available for school libraries range from large and well-equipped special-purpose buildings containing rooms for various purposes and a wide variety of resources and equipment, to small cupboards of books in offices. Many elementary schools have only small classroom collections or book corners.

Accommodation is a major obstacle to library development in some countries. Either the school population is too small to support a separate library, as in the case of rural schools in sparsely populated areas, or a rapid expansion of the school population has led to a shortage of classrooms. In Nigeria, for example, accommodation is perhaps the greatest obstacle to the establishment of primary-school libraries. The introduction of free universal primary education in 1976, while it did not last, brought such rapid increases in enrollment that many schools went on double shift and even held classes under the trees. Coupled with this lack of space is the style of building: many primary schools are long halls with open doors and windows. There is no classroom to be converted to library use, and the only securable space may be a locked cupboard in the headmaster's office.

Portable libraries have been used to provide library service to schools without any library accommodation. Thailand's Portable Libraries Project, winner of the Rising Sun Prize for reading promotion in 1989, carries or donates book boxes to schools in rural areas. The boxes, about the size of a suitcase, open into trisectioned display units holding 200 to 250 books. They can be locked and stored each night or carried from school to school. In Venezuela the Banco del Libro (Book Bank), winner of the 1988 Rising Sun Prize, distributes portable libraries in the form of hanging canvas showcases that hold about 30 books in transparent book pockets. Teachers can take these portable libraries home at night and bring them back each day to set up mini-libraries in schools.

Josephine Riss Fang

Nankai Middle School Library in Tianjing (Tientsin) China.

Aware of the importance of accommodation to an effective school library service, ministries of education in Jordan, Malaysia, and Tanzania, among others, have regulations incorporating purpose-built libraries into all new schools, at least at secondary level. In other schools, they direct that one or more classrooms be converted to library use. Parent-teacher organizations and individual donors in some countries have also provided library facilities for schools.

LIBRARY COOPERATION

Library cooperation in the form of resource sharing and networks is a major theme in school librarianship.

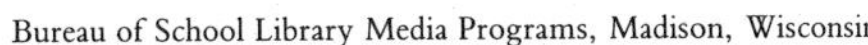

Bureau of School Library Media Programs, Madison, Wisconsin

Media equipment in use in school library in Madison, Wisconsin.

Frances Laverne Carroll identified cooperation as one of three major advances in school librarianship in the 1960s and 1970s. Cooperation was the theme of IASL conferences in Australia (1978) and Honolulu (1984). School/public library cooperation was featured at the 1990 IFLA conference in Stockholm.

The high level of interest in library cooperation derives from the fact that no one library, however fine its resources, can meet all the needs of all its users. Yet school libraries aspire to the goal of the U.S. National Commission on Libraries and Information Science, that every person should have equal opportunity of access to the total information resources that will satisfy the individual's educational, working, cultural, and leisure-time needs and interests. Only through cooperation and networks can school libraries hope to come close to this goal.

Cooperation takes a number of forms. Resource sharing among school libraries can be in the form of sharing materials, as in interlibrary loans; sharing personnel, as when one librarian takes care of both school and children's services in a community; or sharing facilities, as in the case of combined libraries. Cooperation may also formalize into single-type networks, involving only school libraries, or multitype networks, bringing school libraries together with public or other libraries. The two most common forms of cooperation for school libraries are cooperation with public libraries and networks of school libraries with centralized services.

School/Public Library Cooperation. There has always been a close relationship between the two types of libraries serving children and youth. In the early years of development, many libraries serving adults and children were located in schools and run by teachers, or school services were provided by the better-equipped and -staffed public libraries. Cooperation between school and public libraries has continued over the years and may even be mandated by law, as in Finland, Norway, and Sweden.

The joint ALA/NEA statement of 1941, *Schools and Public Libraries Working Together in School Library Service,* saw cooperation as a way of coordinating efforts to provide the best possible service to children while avoiding unnecessary duplication. Cooperation also enables school libraries to draw on the greater resources of the public libraries, while at the same time creating future public library users and supporters.

Library of St. Neophytos Gymnasium, Paphos, Cyprus.

Public library services to schools take a number of forms. In Sweden public librarians give book talks in schools, arrange school visits to public libraries, and offer teachers training on children's literature and information skills. In Australia state libraries provide interlibrary loans, tours of the library, and curriculum-related resource kits.

Public libraries play an even greater role in countries such as Germany, where they have been given responsibility for building up the school library system, or New Zealand, where the Department of Education and the National Library have joint responsibility. The Tanzania Library Service has assisted school libraries by training personnel, preparing standards and manuals, advising on organization and management, and providing mobile library services. The Jamaica Library Service through its Schools Library Service is responsible for acquisition and distribution of books to schools, supervision of service to schools, and training courses and seminars for principals and teacher-librarians. State libraries in Nigeria organize selection and central purchasing through book depots, provide in-service training, and increase library awareness through school library competitions.

Combining school and public library services in the same facility is another form of cooperation. Combined libraries are common in Australia, Canada, Finland, Germany, Iceland, Israel, and Sweden. Interest has increased in recent years as a result of broader acceptance of the community school concept, the desire to increase access to information, and decreasing financial resources. Combined libraries have been most successful in rural communities with low population density, where separate library services for schools and the general public would not be feasible.

Networks. Many centralized services are provided through networks of libraries at a particular administrative level (municipality, district, state, or nation). The 1975 ALA standards, *Media Programs: District and School,* focused attention on the need for district-level services to school libraries in the U.S., and the findings of the Miller and Shantz study of expenditures indicates that such services do improve school library collections and services. Nationwide networks offering centralized services have been instrumental in developing school libraries in Jordan, Malaysia, Singapore, and the countries of Latin America.

The Australian Schools Catalogue Information Service (ASCIS), introduced in 1984, is another example of networking. The world's first national database designed for school libraries, it had grown to more than 250,000 cataloguing records by 1987.

Multitype library networks including school libraries are also becoming more common. An example is the agreement among the Chicago Board of Education, Chicago Public Library, and Illinois State Library in the late 1980s that enables 113,000 high-school students to participate in resource sharing through ILLINET, the Illinois Library and Information Network.

Even with the progress described, few are satisfied with the level of cooperation reached so far. The economic recession of the 1980s, by slowing growth and necessitating cutbacks in staff and funding, led to even greater awareness of the need for cooperation, resource sharing, and networking. This awareness must be translated into reality.

STANDARDS AND LEGISLATION

School library standards and legislation vary in type with the pattern of governance in various countries. Professional associations have played an active role in formulating standards for school libraries in many countries, including Australia, Canada, Nigeria, and the U.S.

In the U.S. the ALA and AASL, often in cooperation with other professional bodies, have been responsible for a series of standards defining the direction of school library development over the years. A joint effort of the AASL and the Association for Educational Communications and Technology (AECT), *Information Power* (1988) describes the ideal library/media program in qualitative terms, emphasizing the need for a commitment both to traditional media and services and to technology and innovation. It stresses the need for the school librarian to work in partnership with teachers and administrators to integrate the school library fully into the curriculum of the school.

National legislation on school libraries is common in countries with centralized systems of education. Denmark, Israel, Japan, and Norway are examples of countries with national laws governing school libraries, in some cases making them mandatory. Legal support in other countries takes the form of directives and regulations issued by the ministry of education.

Legislation supporting school library development may provide special funding and programs. Examples include federal spending for school libraries in the U.S. under the Elementary and Secondary Education Act (1965), the Australian Commonwealth School Library Program (1969), and the Singapore School Library Development Project (1983).

As school libraries move toward the 21st century, those in the field can look back on several decades of great accomplishment. School library systems are established or being developed in many countries of the world, supported by an educational philosophy that places the school library at the center of education. Challenges remain in overcoming the economic problems that threaten to slow or halt progress, extending cooperation for greater access and more effective use of library resources, training qualified school library personnel and teachers who understand the library's role in education, and finding ways to integrate school libraries fully into the curriculum.

REFERENCES

Frances Laverne Carroll, *Recent Advances in School Librarianship* (1981).

Noelene Hall, *Teachers, Information, and School Libraries* (1986).

James E. Herring, *School Librarianship*, 2nd edition (1988).

Jean E. Lowrie and Mieko Nagakura, editors, *School Libraries: International Developments,* 2nd edition (1991).

Marilyn L. Miller and Marilyn Shantz, "Expenditures for Resources in School Library/Media Centers, Fiscal Year 1989–90," *School Library Journal* (1991).

VIRGINIA W. DIKE

Scoggin, Margaret C.

(1905–1968)

The New York Public Library

Margaret C. Scoggin

Margaret Clara Scoggin was a pioneer in the establishment of young adult (YA) services in American public libraries. She designed, opened, and supervised the Nathan Straus Branch of the New York Public Library (NYPL), which was devoted exclusively to patrons 21 and under. As a result of her experience there, the American Library Association invited her to help organize the International Youth Library in Munich, Germany, and she toured other European libraries in an advisory capacity for Unesco. As successor to Mabel Williams, Scoggin served as Superintendent of Work with Young People for the New York Public Library from 1952 until 1967. She was the recipient of many awards and honors, most notably the ALA Grolier Award for outstanding service to young people.

Born in Caruthersville, Missouri, April 14, 1905, Margaret Scoggin graduated as high school valedictorian with a record-setting average; she then finished Radcliffe magna cum laude and was elected to Phi Beta Kappa. Her interest in youth work may have started with the classes she taught in a local settlement house during college. In July 1926 Scoggin worked as a summer replacement at NYPL, starting at the Mott Haven Branch and moving around in various branches to gain experience, under the encouraging supervision of Mabel Williams, Supervisor of Work with Schools. Young people's opinions were important to her; she believed that libraries would serve young people best through identifying their interests and listening carefully to what they had to say. She wrote, "True reading guidance lies in discovering in each boy and girl the interests he has. . . . It calls for tolerance of young people's choices—listening instead of telling." She saw this communication process as one that enhanced the growth of critical judgment in young people through the testing of their ideas in a supportive environment. She created this environment at that time in two ways—through library-based clubs in which young adults discussed books and produced plays and puppet shows, and through skilled one-to-one reading guidance.

After completing a degree at the School of Librarianship at the University of London, Scoggin returned to NYPL to continue her YA work and introduced a teen book review booklet, called *Back Talk,* which included articles on topics of interest to young people as well as reviews. She said, "In school only the best is taken, but the public library takes everything." This attitude continues to distinguish public library YA work from school-related activities.

Although she started a Master's program at Columbia University, Scoggin never completed the degree because of pressures of time and money. In 1935 she was named systemwide Librarian in Charge of Vocational and Industrial Schools of NYPL. In this capacity she spoke at assemblies and arranged class visits and presentations in all parts of the city. She also compiled bibliographies of simple technical books for vocational-school students, because she identified their great need for books on a level they could comprehend. NYPL published *Simple Technical Books* in 1939.

In April 1940, having completed her work with the vocational schools, Scoggin began work with designers on the Nathan Straus Branch Library for Children and Young People. She insisted on good light, bright colors, a welcoming atmosphere, a collection built around youth interests, and a specially trained staff. The branch opened in 1941, and its success can be measured, in Scoggin's own terms, by comments from patrons of 1943:

> I can get the kind of books I want without wading through a mess of junk that's way over my head.
>
> The librarians LIKE to help you in any problem you have and they are all very nice.
>
> You feel as you come in that you are going into your own home.
>
> I guess I don't dislike anything or anyone in this library.

While supervising Nathan Straus, which quickly became a professional demonstration library in addition to its other mission of service to young people, Scoggin lectured at Saint John's University, served on local agency councils and ALA committees, and was consulted by innumerable literary, publishing, and youthwork groups. During her time at Nathan Straus she also pioneered music library programs for young adults and was a leading advocate of recordings as part of YA collections. The Nathan Straus branch continued from 1941 until 1955, when the YA services and collection were moved to their present location at the Donnell Library Center on 53rd Street.

In 1945, after an interview on New York radio station WMCA, owned by Mrs. Nathan Straus, wife of the philanthropist who gave money for the branch bearing his name, Scoggin was invited to organize a young people's radio review program. The enormously successful program continues on WNYC today. The quality of "The Young Book Reviewers" program was recognized by awards from the Institute of Education by Radio and Television at Ohio State University. When the program moved to WNYC as the library-sponsored "Teen Age Book Talk," it won the George Foster Peabody Broadcasting Award of the Henry W. Grady School of Journalism at the University of Georgia. In 1965 the radio program was judged "Best Radio Program for Youth" as one of the Thomas Alva Edison Foundation's National Mass Media Award Winners.

With her good sense of what really interested young adults, Scoggin produced six anthologies of stories for young people taken primarily from adult books. Two featured humor—*Chucklebait* (1945) and *More Chucklebait* (1949); three adventure—*Lure of Danger* (1945), *Edge of Danger* (1951), and *Escapes and Rescues* (1960); and one true stories from World War II—*Battle Stations* (1953).

Scoggin left a rich body of professional writings. In 1947 she presented "The Library as a Center for Young People in the Community" at the University of Chicago's Symposium, *Youth, Communication, and Libraries.* In 1948 she originated "Outlook Tower" in *Horn Book,* a review column of recommended adult books for YA's of which she was editor for almost 20 years. In 1952 Scoggin coedited *Gateways to Readable Books,* a graded, annotated list of books for slow readers in high schools. Her articles were as eloquent as they were entertaining, as this 1952 quote from *ALA Bulletin* shows:

> Young readers need an adult mind to challenge their ideas of books and authors. Let us be sure that the minds we provide as the challenge are both adult and functioning.

Scoggin continued to be a "Renaissance Woman" as Superintendent of Work with Young People. Even in that demanding position, she still managed to find time to teach a weekly course at the Simmons library school. During this period she also initiated annotations as Editor of *Books for the Teenage,* an annual list started in NYPL in 1929.

In postwar Germany the success of an International Book Exhibition organized by Hella Lepman under the American military government led to the idea of a permanent International Youth Library. Such a library would collect the best children's books of the world to help foster international understanding through books. With funds from the Rockefeller Foundation and the Bavarian government, ALA chose Scoggin as its representative because of her work at Nathan Straus. Scoggin spent six gruelling months weeding and classifying 8,000 books from 24 countries and developing programs to lure and keep the young interested in the library. In addition, she toured other European libraries for Unesco and persuaded authorities to include books in CARE packages. After much effort and encouragement, the International Youth Library opened in 1949, and Scoggin continued soliciting materials and equipment for it after she returned home. Because of her work with the Library, the Children's Book Council established the Margaret Scoggin Memorial Collection there. It includes all the titles on the annual ALA Notable Children's Books and Best Books for Young Adults lists.

Scoggin was active in professional associations in many capacities. She was the first Chair of the newly formed Children's and Young Adult Services Division of the New York Library Association in 1951–52. In ALA she chaired the International Relations Committee and the Young People's Reading Round Table, was elected an ALA Councilor, and received the Grolier Award. From the Women's National Book Association she received the Constance Lindsay Skinner Award.

The full measure of her outstanding contributions to librarianship may be measured, and remembered, by two comments. The first is from "some of her grateful young book reviewers" on a scroll they presented to her:

> To Margaret Scoggin, who has opened the door to the wonderful world of books for many who might not have found the way themselves.

The second is a tribute written after her death in New York City on July 11, 1968, by Dorothy L. Cromien, formerly her assistant at Nathan Straus:

> The professional world is served today in many places by those whom Miss Scoggin encouraged and inspired. The most lasting tribute we can give Margaret Scoggin is to turn with her generosity to the generations we may have scarcely noticed coming up behind us.

REFERENCE

Beverly Lowy, "Margaret C. Scoggin (1905–1968): Her Professional Life and Work in Young Adult Librarianship"

(unpublished M.A. thesis, Palmer Graduate Library School, Long Island University, May 1970.)

MARY K. CHELTON

Sears, Minnie Earl
(1873–1933)

Minnie Earl Sears, cataloguer, reference librarian, bibliographer, teacher, and editor of reference books, is best known for her *List of Subject Headings for Small Libraries*.

Sears was born November 17, 1873, in Lafayette, Indiana, and received the B.S. degree from Purdue University in 1891, at the age of 18, the youngest member of her class. Two years later she received the M.S. degree from the same university, and in 1900 she received the B.L.S. degree from the University of Illinois.

Her particular interest was cataloguing. She served as Head Cataloguer at Bryn Mawr College Library, 1903–07, Head Cataloguer at the University of Minnesota Library, 1909–14, and First Assistant of the Reference-Catalogue Division of the New York Public Library, 1914–20.

Isadore Gilbert Mudge, colleague, friend, and co-editor of several works, described her in the January 1934 issue of *Wilson Bulletin for Librarians* as follows: "She had an unusual ability for research work of a high order and, had her tastes turned in that direction, would have made one of the great reference librarians of the country, but from the beginning she was interested especially in the scholarly side of cataloging and cataloging research, and in the problems of subject cataloging."

She also had a strong interest in bibliographic and literary research, evident in the *Thackeray Dictionary* (1910) and the *George Eliot Dictionary* (1924), which she wrote with Mudge.

In 1923 she joined the editorial staff of the H. W. Wilson Company, where she combined her cataloguing expertise with her research ability. In this capacity she was able to use her knowledge and understanding of libraries to assist not just one library but many libraries throughout the country. She edited the third edition of *Children's Catalog* in 1925 and the fourth edition in 1930. Because of her interest and care, this selection tool for juvenile books became a cataloguing and reference tool and also a useful source for teaching in library schools. She edited other similar reference works: the second edition of the ALA *Standard Catalog for High School Libraries* (1932) and the ALA *Standard Catalog for Public Libraries* (1927–33).

One of her goals in compiling the *George Eliot Dictionary* was to identify the songs and musical compositions referred to in George Eliot's works. This task required the use of the resources of the three largest music libraries in the country at that time, as well as foreign correspondence. When Sears accepted the task of editing the *Song Index,* she did so with a practical knowledge of the problems involved and an appreciation of the need for such a tool. The *Song Index* was published in 1926.

The plan for *Essay and General Literature Index* (1931–33), which Sears edited with Marion Shaw, "was based on one of the points of her cataloguing creed upon which she always felt very strongly, that is, the economic waste of analyzing in individual card catalogues material which could be analyzed once for all in a printed catalogue or index," according to Mudge (*Wilson Bulletin for Librarians,* January 1934). Thus the basis for describing titles included in such works as *Essay and General Literature Index* and *Standard Catalog for Public Libraries* was careful cataloguing and the availability of cooperative cataloguing to libraries everywhere.

Columbia University
Minnie Earl Sears

Her *List of Subject Headings for Small Libraries,* first published in 1923 (14th edition, *Sears List of Subject Headings,* 1991) filled a long-felt need among smaller libraries and soon became a tool for teaching subject heading work in library schools. In the 3rd edition, published in 1933, the last one she edited, she added a chapter entitled "Practical Suggestions for the Beginner in Subject Heading Work." Also published as a separate pamphlet, it contained simple rules with logical explanations about how to assign subject headings, told how new subject headings are established, and gave advice on how to handle subject heading changes. From the start Sears used the Library of Congress form for subject headings. As a result, cataloguers could easily add Library of Congress headings when a subject was not included in the Sears *List*. One exception to this practice was the use of hyphens; in the *Wilson Bulletin* (vol. 2, 1922–26), Sears commented on her preference in the *Sears List* for the more modern usage of less hyphenation.

In a talk to the New York Regional Catalogers Group on "The Teaching of Cataloging" (*Library Journal,* June 1, 1927), she discussed several issues about elementary and advanced cataloguing courses and the continuation of learning about cataloguing that needs to follow library school graduation. One issue that she discussed seems to summarize the essence of her purpose as cataloguer and reference librarian: "Can not more be done to make [cataloguers] realize that there is no difference between the research work often demanded in cataloging, especially in a large library, and the work that is done as pure reference work? . . . Could something more be done in reference courses to connect practical reference with cataloging and vice versa?"

Sears joined the faculty of the Columbia University School of Library Service in 1927 and served there until 1931. She organized the first graduate course in cataloguing for the Master's degree. She served as Chairman of the ALA Catalog Section, 1927–28, and Chairman of the New York Regional Catalog Group, 1931–32; from 1932 until her death on November 28, 1933, she was a member of the ALA committee advising on the revision of the *ALA Catalog Rules*.

BARBARA GATES

Seminar on the Acquisition of Latin American Library Materials

The Seminar on the Acquisition of Latin American Library Materials (SALALM) was born out of a 1956 meeting to consider the challenges of acquiring Latin American imprints for North American research libraries. Additional annual meetings were held in the ensuing years, and SALALM was incorporated as a nonprofit organization in January 1968.

Membership. The organization's international membership combines a range of Latin Americanist constituencies. Selectors, publishers, and bookdealers work together to address overlapping concerns. Scholars and librarians are also represented. The needs of a discipline—and area—characterized by diffuse and often idiosyncratic patterns of research and publication have mandated close collaboration among all the affected parties. This alliance has, in turn, enriched each of them.

The membership includes about 325 individuals (1991). Approximately 70 percent are from North America, and the rest divide fairly evenly between Latin America and the rest of the world. There are also about 150 institutional members.

Purpose. SALALM's name denotes one of the organization's primary purposes. Its constitution enumerates the following goals:

> to promote the improvement of library services in support of study and research activities in Latin American and inter-American affairs; to provide an association for study programs in which scholars, librarians, and others interested in book and library resources relating to Latin American and inter-American studies can discuss problems and carry out programs of common interest; and to promote cooperative efforts to achieve better library services as a means of encouraging and advancing international understanding in the Western Hemisphere.

SALALM's conference programs, publications, and committee structure illuminate its purposes and concerns more fully than any formal statement. All have shifted over time, in an evolution reflecting changes in the Latin American book trade, the organization's successes in improving acquisitions possibilities, an ongoing dialogue with scholars, and the opportunities and demands of new technology.

History. SALALM originated at a meeting at Chinsegut Hill, Florida, June 14–15, 1956. Until its formal incorporation, in 1968, the organization was administered through an Executive Secretary and a Steering Committee. The annual conferences were self-supporting (as they for the most part remain), and the Executive Secretariat was unofficially maintained in the Library Development Program of the Organization of American States, under the tutelage of Marietta Daniels Shepard. After 1968, SALALM gradually constructed a more elaborate governmental apparatus, as mandated by its constitution and bylaws.

Organization. SALALM's Executive Board includes both elected and ex officio members. The President is elected to a one-year term, and serves as Vice-President/President-elect for one year before assuming the presidency. The Executive Board normally meets once or twice a year. The organization is self-supporting. Most income is derived from dues, conference fees, and publication sales. Expenses include Secretariat costs (usually shared by the institution hosting the secretariat), conference charges, and printing and editorial work.

SALALM's committees are the principal locus for the organization's activities. The eight Executive Board Committees are concerned with maintaining the organization per se. The Substantive Committees, with their affiliated subcommittees, have been responsible for most of SALALM's more public accomplishments. Participation on substantive committees is open without restriction to the entire membership. More than 40 percent of SALALM's personal members serve on committees or subcommittees. Committee chairs, one-third of whom change each year, are appointed to three-year terms by the incoming President.

SALALM includes six substantive committees and a host of affiliated subcommittees. The Acquisitions Committee thus oversees the Subcommittee on Gifts and Exchanges, which maintains a heavily utilized guide to exchange sources in Latin America. The Library-Bookdealer-Publisher Relations Subcommittee addresses the difficulties of international and intercultural business relationships. The Subcommittee on Marginalized Peoples and Ideas particularly focuses on the representations of groups outside the social, scholarly, and library mainstream. The Serials Subcommittee addresses a format as volatile as it is essential. The Acquisitions Committee also oversees the ongoing annual compilation of book cost statistics for Latin Americana.

The Bibliography Committee prepares the annual *Bibliography of Latin American Bibliographies,* which is periodically cumulated as supplements to Arthur Gropp's *A Bibliography of Latin American Bibliographies.* The Committee also addresses techniques for Latin Americanist bibliographic instruction through its similarly named subcommittee. Its Subcommittee on Cuban Bibliography has produced a number of definitive specialized bibliographies. And the Subcommittee on Non-Print Media grapples with the special problems of acquiring and controlling materials in nontraditional formats. The Subcommittee on Special Bibliographic Projects is planning introductory bibliographies for topics of particular timeliness.

The Committee on Library Operations and Services oversees the Subcommittee on Reference Services, which addresses a host of public service concerns. The Subcommittee on Cataloguing and Bibliographic Technology focuses on general issues of processing support.

The Joint Committee on Official Publications was formed in response to the bibliographic and acquisitions complexities associated with these crucial materials. The Outreach/Enlace Committee has pursued closer relationships with librarians from Latin America by administering competitive travel grants to SALALM meetings, publicizing the organization in Latin America, and strengthening personal networks. It also collaborates with Latin American libraries. The Marietta Daniels Shepard scholarship for a Latin American library school student at the University of Texas, while a project of the organization as a whole, similarly reflects SALALM's continuing commitment to Latin American librarianship.

Finally, the Committee on Interlibrary Cooperation oversees three subcommittees. The Subcommittee on National-Level Cooperation has focused on philosophies, tools, and specific projects to enhance coordinated collection development, processing, and preservation. Major Latin American collections in the United States remain divided about evenly between institutions using OCLC as their bibliographic utility and those belonging to the Research Libraries Group. The SALALM Subcommittees for OCLC Users and RLG Members provide forums for the constituents of these utilities.

Programs. SALALM's annual programs, for which the President is responsible, are one of the organization's most substantial manifestations. The meetings last for four or five days and are usually held at centers for Latin American research. SALALM meets outside the U.S. about once every three or four years. The conferences combine sessions based on formal papers with workshops and committee meetings. In most years the substantive committees play a major role in organizing specific sessions.

During SALALM's early years, most conferences emphasized the bibliographic and acquisitions problems of specific countries or subregions. Shifts toward issue-oriented scholarship, in conjunction with improved bibliographic control and dealer service throughout much of Latin America, have more recently resulted in themes that emphasize particular issues or sets of issues. The second conference (1957), for example, dealt with acquiring materials from Mexico; the third (1958), with Chile and Argentina; the fifth (1960), with the Caribbean. By contrast, the 33rd meeting (1988) addressed "Latin American Frontiers, Borders, and Hinterlands: Research Needs and Resources"; the 34th (1989), "Artistic Representation of Latin American Diversity: Sources and Collections"; and the 36th (1991), "Latin American Studies into the Twenty-First Century: New Focus, New Formats, New Challenges." SALALM has paid increasing attention to the twin contexts of Latin American Studies in the academic community and Latin American collections in research libraries. Expensive area-related academic and acquisitions programs sometimes seem peripheral to national research priorities; SALALM thus intensified its efforts to understand the area's present and to anticipate its future.

Publications. SALALM's most prominent publications have always been the collected working papers of its conferences. They summarize findings, list sources, and outline strategies for acquisitions, collection development, and reference service. SALALM has also, through its "Bibliography and Reference Series," published many specific compilations. It prepares the annual *Bibliography of Latin American Bibliographies,* and its *Microfilming Projects Newsletter* records Latin Americanist microfilming. Current announcements and news are disseminated through a bimonthly *Newsletter*. SALALM encourages publications of its members through the José Toribio Medina Award, available annually for outstanding article- and book-length bibliographies or reference sources.

Relations with Other Organizations. SALALM has avoided formal alliances with other bodies, but it places a high value on collaborative working relationships. SALALM's 1982 meeting was held jointly with the Latin American Studies Association (LASA), and its 1987 meeting was held in tandem with the Association of Caribbean University and Research Libraries (ACURIL). The President of SALALM attends LASA Executive Board meetings, and LASA in 1990 appointed a Task Force on Scholarly Resources that works closely with SALALM.

SALALM recognizes other significant endeavors by providing meeting time and program support during its annual conferences. The Latin American Microform Project (LAMP), a voluntary association of institutions administered through the Center for Research Libraries, conducts specific microfilming projects throughout the hemisphere. The *Hispanic American Periodicals Index* (HAPI) relies almost exclusively on SALALM volunteers as indexers. Both enterprises meet in conjunction with SALALM.

SALALM's primary concern remains that which inspired its formation: to make necessary resources available to Latin Americanist students and scholars throughout the world. Many of the materials essential for current scholarship remain elusive. The balance of forces in North American libraries and academic institutions likewise continues to change, as a result of both new technologies and political and intellectual dynamics. These shifting contexts will continue to challenge and stimulate SALALM.

DAN C. HAZEN

Senegal

Senegal, a republic of West Africa, lies on the Atlantic Ocean and is bounded by Mauritania on the north, Mali on the east, and Guinea and Guinea-Bissau on the south. Population (1990 est.) 7,327,000; area 196,722 sq.km. The official language is French.

History. The history of libraries in Senegal is recent in comparison with that of developed countries. Like most African nations, Senegal is a country of oral traditions. They have a certain documentary value because they convey the social and cultural heritage of peoples, but this source of information was not conserved in a methodical manner. Oral traditions are fragile and perishable, leading Hampaté Bą to declare that "in Africa when an old man dies, it is a whole library that burns." On the other hand, although these traditions were the monopoly of the *griots* (a caste of

Libraries in Senegal (1990)

Type of library	Number of administrative units (main libraries)	Number of service points (branches, mobile stops, etc.)	Volumes in collections	Annual expenditures (CFA franc)	Population served	Professional staff (with certificate, diploma, etc.)	Total staff
National	1	1	26,000	--	--	8	15
Academic	2	2	588,724	111,413,000	20,000	54	76
Public	8	19	121,050	--	--	8	39
School	6	6	69,845	--	--	6	--
Special	58	58	189,304	38,703,404	--	55	113

The Central Library of the University of Dakar, Senegal.

praise singers), who acted as guardians of the values of the past by transmitting their knowledge from father to son, the process of transmission was not exempt from alteration.

Aware of the importance of oral tradition as a firsthand source of information, the Senegalese government set up the Direction des Archives Culturelles (Directorate for Cultural Archives, a multimedia archival agency), responsible for collecting, conserving, and studying various forms of cultural expression of the various ethnic groups in the country. Publishers have also gathered oral traditions and have published them in historical novels and in collections of folktales.

With the coming of the printed word, oral traditions had to compete with written sources introduced during colonization. The first libraries established in Senegal made their appearance with the French conquest in Africa. In an effort to promote the French language and to respond to the needs of colonial administrators, the French established the first public, administrative, municipal, and teachers' libraries in Senegal.

With the goal of developing a test for reading by providing the inhabitants of the two largest communes (cities with voting rights) with books for their instruction and entertainment, two public libraries were created in Senegal: the first in Saint-Louis in 1849 and the second in Dakar in 1905.

National Library Services. Three libraries perform the functions of a national library. The Library of the Institut Fondamental d'Afrique Noire (IFAN; Fundamental Institute of Black Africa) was established in 1938, when it inherited more than 6,000 works from the Library of the government of French West Africa. It later increased its collections more than tenfold and owns manuscripts, rare books, and newspapers dating back to Colonial times. It received copyright privileges on July 17, 1946. A decree on legal deposit requirements was adopted April 9, 1976. The Library of the Archives Nationales du Sénégal was founded in 1913 and is housed in Dakar. From 1962 it published a bibliographical bulletin (Bibliographie du Sénégal), a first draft toward a national bibliography. From its founding it received official state publications for deposit. The Library of the Centre de Recherche et de Documentation du Sénégal (Center for Research and Documentation of Senegal) in Saint-Louis was founded in 1944 when it acquired the former IFAN Center of Senegal.

Academic Libraries. There is a central library at the University of Dakar, founded in 1952. In addition, there are a number of other institutional and professional school libraries.

Administrative Libraries. After 1904 administrative libraries were created in the *cercles* in order to meet the immediate needs of the colonial administrators who presided over the district tribunals. These libraries contained works on both French and Islamic law. In Dakar, the capital of French West Africa, there was also an administrative library composed mainly of legal works to aid the administrators in governing the colony. This library also contained the first important scientific collection in the region.

Teachers' Libraries. After 1904 pedagogical or teachers' libraries were set up in the capitals of colonies that were part of French West Africa. Two of these were in Senegal, one in Dakar and one in Saint-Louis. They were established to enable teachers to learn more about the colony and prepare their courses.

Public and Other Library Service. A Municipal Library was created in Louga in 1915. Senegal benefited by acquiring some libraries created during French rule. But the system was not consolidated after Senegal became independent. Many small municipal libraries from the Colonial period disappeared or lost their effectiveness as a result of lack of follow-through and of funding. The Senegalese government was obliged to start anew in creating new, better adapted services, such as the national documentation center, the directorate for public reading (Direction de la Lecture Publique), the directorate for archives, and other services; however, other collections inherited by Senegal (such as the University Library, the IFAN Library, the Library at the National Archives, and the basic administrative structure and collections of the archives themselves) placed Senegalese library resources far ahead of those in any other country in Francophone Africa.

The Profession. Since 1967 the training of information professionals has been offered at the University of Dakar by the École des Bibliothécaires, Archivistes et Documentalistes (EBAD; the School for Librarians, Archivists, and Documentalists). This school replaced the Centre Régional de Formation des Bibliothécaires (CRFB), a regional center created to train qualified library personnel in Africa and for Africa. Broader in conception than CRFB (which concentrated solely on library education), EBAD includes two other sections, one for archivists and one for documentalists. Like CRFB, EBAD has a regional vocation because it welcomes students from many countries in Francophone Africa.

EBAD includes two levels of training: an undergraduate program for training intermediate-level personnel in two years; and a graduate program for training higher-level personnel in two years. Admission to the graduate program is gained by competitive examination, reserved for those holding *licences* (university degrees), or professional examination, reserved for those holding undergraduate diplomas from EBAD who have completed at least three years of library or information work. An advanced diploma of information science and communication is awarded on completion of two years of training.

Besides the training offered at EBAD, students may obtain professional education abroad, notably in

France (at the École Nationale Supérieure des Bibliothécaires in Lyon or the Institut National des Techniques de la Documentation in Paris) or in Canada (at the University of Montreal). After the creation of the graduate program at EBAD, the Senegalese government accorded fewer scholarships for graduate study in librarianship abroad.

REFERENCES

Mary Niles Maack, *Libraries in Senegal: Continuity and Change in an Emerging Nation* (1981).

"The A.O.F. Archives and the Study of African History," *Bulletin de l'Institut Fondamental d'Afrique Noire, Série B* (1980).

"Libraries for the General Public in French-Speaking Africa: Their Cultural Role," *Journal of Library History* (1981).

"The Colonial Legacy in West African Libraries: A Comparative Analysis," *Advances in Librarianship* (1982).

WALY NDIAYE;
translated by MARY NILES MAACK

Serials

The definition of a serial has become accepted. In the words of Harrod's *Librarian's Glossary,* a serial is "any publication issued in successive parts, appearing at intervals, usually regular ones, and, as a rule, intended to be continued indefinitely. The term includes periodicals, newspapers, annuals, numbered monographic series, and the proceedings, transactions, and memoirs of societies." While the definition has been standardized, the vagaries of classification and format and the problems of price and use of serials have been a challenge for librarians throughout the 20th century.

Serials represent the most current information in what are often the most important topics. They are the media through which scientists officially communicate theories, experiments, and results. Because access to their contents is critical to researchers and students alike, they have become a measure of an institution's support of research. However, as their role in research has become more central, their impact on library budgets has become more critical. In institutions that support strong scientific research programs, they have become the single most costly part of the acquisitions budget, posing a constant problem for evaluation of cost and use.

Acquisition. In general, librarians obtain serials by purchasing them either from publishers, in direct orders, or from vendors. Less often they receive them on exchange or as gifts. They use vendors or subscription agents in order to reduce paperwork in the library by dealing with a smaller number of sources, by drawing on the vendor's expertise in handling claims and invoice problems with publishers, and by using the vendor's management data, such as multiple-year price histories, lists of a library's serials by call number, and so on, and other financially oriented information—all this for a fee. Vendors derive their income from the discounts they receive from publishers, from the service charges they assess customers, and from other revenue-producing activities, including fund management. Some vendors serve as distributors of publications and as account managers and marketers for some titles; others have created auxiliary services such as document delivery and publication programs of their own. While vendors serve their customer libraries as agents, they traditionally derive the bulk of their income from publisher discounts; they are in the position of serving the needs of both publishers and libraries.

Athanase Hakizimana

Serials Division, National University of Rwanda Library, Butare campus.

The Boom in Serials Publication. In the 1920s and 1930s German scientists were preeminent in many fields, and access to their writings was critical for worldwide advances. German scientific, technical, and medical (STM) serials became the most expensive items in many research collections; protests against pricing, price gouging, and publication patterns were common up to the beginning of World War II. After the war, the subsequent boom in research made STM journals essential for newly emerging scientific disciplines. Both commercial and academic-society publications experienced rapid growth. Demand for new journals to cover new fields was tremendous. Several commercial publishers began to dominate the field of international publications, forming peer review systems and editorial boards that crossed national boundaries.

Since the 1950s, large numbers of new titles have been introduced. One of the most successful marketing techniques has been "twigging," starting new journals based on ongoing successful ones. In addition interdisciplinary studies opened up whole new fields of exploration and journals that both reported and supported those fields were created. Both proliferation and twigging of journal titles have been management problems for librarians.

Funding Concerns. Because serials represent a long-term purchasing commitment on the part of libraries, there has been a gradual but discernible increase in the percentage of research library acquisitions budgets committed to their support. For example, members of the Association of Research Libraries (ARL) spent approximately 49 percent of their materials budgets for serials in 1979–80. By 1990–91, they spent 63 percent of their materials budgets on serials.

In 1989 the ARL distributed a major report on the impact of the prices of a few publishers on the journals collections of most research libraries. The report provided an overview of the trends in average prices and costs of certain serials over time, described and analyzed the impact of serial pricing, and made recommendations for dealing with the systemic crisis in STM journals. Many publishers and librarians began implementing its recommendations in the early 1990s.

Education and Activism. The late 1970s and early

80s saw several developments in serials education and activism. First was the formation of the United Kingdom Serials Group (UKSG) in 1978. It had its beginnings in Blackwell's periodicals conferences in 1975 and 1977. Then, in 1986, the North American Serials Interest Group (NASIG) held its first meeting. Both groups focused on concerns of the professional serialist, whether employed in the commercial or academic sector. Through their yearly conferences, they have explored the whole range of serials concerns: cataloguing and pricing, vendor evaluation, peer review, and editing. They have become a valuable forum for professionals in the serials information chain to learn from each other and stay current on trends in the field. In 1989 the *Newsletter on Serials Pricing Issues,* the first electronic publication on serials issues, was initiated. It became a vehicle for rapid dissemination of information on issues related to pricing and publication. More than 900 subscribers worldwide receive it, representing all the varied constituencies of the serials field: scholars, societies and associations, vendors, commercial and noncommercial publishers, academic administrators, and librarians. Similar ventures in electronic publication of important information for serials include *Serialist,* a moderated list-serve, and *Acqnet,* a more formal publication primarily directed toward acquisitions librarians.

Because of the cost-control crisis, librarians have begun to conduct regular reviews of serial collections, a practice that in the past was honored more in theory than in action. In studying their serial collections, research librarians have learned that a few publishers have established dominant positions in their cost structures. In a moderate to large academic collection, as few as 10 percent of the serial titles may absorb 50 percent of the total budget. A fairly small number of international scientific publishers have been dominant in these cost patterns, and the trend has grown more serious because of a wave of consolidations in commercial publishing. In 1991 Elsevier, based in the Netherlands, the world's largest publisher of STM journals, acquired the third-largest STM publisher, Pergamon Press, based in the U.K. Other major commercial STM publishers include Springer in Germany, Blackwell in the U.K., and Academic, Wiley, and Plenum in the U.S.

Automated Serials Systems. Librarians have turned away from card files to automated systems for recording receipt and payment information. These systems can stand alone or be part of a library's integrated system, which can provide access to current serials information through an online public-access catalogue (OPAC). Automated systems provide some, if not all, the following features: predictive check-in, claims identification, order creation, tapeloading of invoice data, links to the institution's accounting system, and holdings listed in MARC (machine-readable) format.

Formats and Standards. The potential of publications in electronic format became great with the commercial development of CD-ROM. Indexes to serials literature, which had previously been limited to paper subscriptions or expensive online search services, became commonplace on CD-ROM. Regularly updated indexes were also mounted on local computer systems and networks. Many of these indexes came from commercial sources. Electronic publication reached another milestone in 1992 when the American Academy for the Advancement of Science, in cooperation with the Online Computer Library Center, began production of the *Online Journal of Current Clinical Trials,* a peer-reviewed medical journal.

Standards development has kept pace with other areas in serials. The International Standard Serial Number (ISSN), a unique identifier for every serial title published, was given official sanction by the International Organization for Standardization in 1975. The ISSN provides a standard numeric identification code for titles and aids interlibrary loan, citation, and communication in the trade distribution system. In the U.S., in addition, the U.S. Postal Service uses the ISSN to provide second-class and controlled-circulation rates.

The Serials Industry Advisory Committee (SISAC) was founded in 1982 with a goal of providing a method of uniquely identifying serials issues in machine-readable form. The first SISAC symbol was tested in 1986. The Board of Standards Review of the American National Standards Institute (ANSI) approved the Serial Item and Contribution Identifier (SICI) in 1991. The SISAC standard was developed for machine-readable bar-coding of individual serial titles. The SICI code provides issue-specific, article-level identification. The SICI standard can be used for machine-scannable check-in systems and automated ordering of individual articles.

In the area of electronic holdings information, the MARC holdings format was approved to communicate issue-level holdings information. Potential uses include support of predictive check-in and claiming. Several groups and individuals have suggested establishing a U.S. national pattern database, but no plan had been adopted by the early 1990s.

A development that promises greater flexibility in electronic data interchange (EDI) between librarians and publishers or vendors is the emergence of the ANSI standard X-12 for EDI transmission. It will allow information to be passed seamlessly among

The EBSCONET Control Center at Ebsco Subscription Services International Headquarters. Librarians worldwide can order, claim, or research serials any time of day. EBSCONET also provides gateway access to the CARL System and Internet.

EBSCO Subscription Services

publishers, vendors, and librarians. It can provide real-time publication and shipping notification to subscribers; expeditious transfer of claiming information through the vendor to the publisher and back to the librarian; and easy transfer of invoicing and other financial data in a cost-effective manner.

As the cost of providing access to the world's serial literature has grown at phenomenal rates, several document delivery services have developed and are reaching a level of acceptance and maturity. Commercial document delivery services have been available for some time, and the British Library Document Supply Center at Boston Spa in the U.K. provides access to a wide range of serials literature for librarians worldwide. In the U.S., suppliers such as UMI, RLG, CARL, and Faxon have joined document supply with indexes, providing end-users with article-level identification and delivery. More competitors are entering this field, and some publishers now supply copies of articles from their own journals on demand.

Cooperative Efforts. Major cooperative efforts are prominent in the field. CONSER (Cooperative CONversion of SERials) is a massive project to provide current and updated MARC cataloguing for serials, an international database for cataloguing and union list maintenance. It started out as a U.S.-Canadian effort to catalogue two million serials held by American libraries. Discussions leading to the establishment of CONSER began at the annual American Library Association conference in 1973. A full CONSER record includes information that is critical not only for uniform cataloguing, but for evaluation as well. Updated information about coverage of a title by abstracting or indexing services in Canada or the U.S. is particularly important and is as necessary for evaluation as uniform bibliographic description.

Another major cooperative effort has been the U.S. Newspaper Program, funded by the National Endowment for the Humanities. The Library of Congress provides technical coordination, including monitoring and training. Funding has been provided on a competitive-grant basis for surveying, cataloguing, and microfilming U.S. newspapers.

After an emergency cooperative serials identification project in 1987, the Research Libraries Group (RLG) began the Long-Term Serials Project, a cooperative activity of bibliographers at RLG member libraries to identify, monitor, and maintain subject-based serials acquisitions projects in such fields as business, chemistry, geology, German, law, mathematics, and physics. The intent is to identify an international research core collection in each area and assure maintenance of the titles by at least one member of the group by means of a three-year commitment to each title. It was designed as a safety net as libraries began serious and potentially deep cancellation projects.

The Future of Serials. The cost of maintaining a current collection of serials has become so serious that both publishers and librarians have had to reconsider the problem. Both institutions and publishers have made preliminary efforts to provide the next step in the evolution of the scholarly journal. Because electronic publications can be forwarded from their original recipient to other readers, publishers fear that easy access to their information in electronic format will eliminate their profits or even the fiscal sustainability of their publications. Libraries have a primary concern not only for immediate access to serial publications, but also for the long-term archival survival of the record of research and civilization. These three needs—for financial viability of publications, for preservation, and for access—seem to be on a collision course at present. The battlegrounds are technology and the courts. The courts will define limitations on copyright and protection of the publisher's right to a profit, while technology will revolutionize distribution and access to information.

Austrian National Library

Periodicals reading area, Technical University Library, Vienna, Austria.

Some observers predict that the ultimate losers in this confrontation will be libraries. Their role, it is thought, will disappear as end-users strengthen their connection directly to the publisher. Tied to this view is the feeling that libraries cannot afford to continue to support the system financially. Funding will have to shift to the end-user and research system directly, rather than having libraries as intermediaries. Whatever the outcome, the original need that prompted the creation of the scientific serial will continue. The need for verification of research through peer review, the need to communicate that research, and the need to archive it for future use will continue.

One line of argument speculates that individual articles will be "unbundled" from the issues of the journals in which they appear. The existence of indexes and abstracts in fact already provides identification of the article as the defining level for distribution of information to the individual. The issue or volume is just the package, the means we use for acquiring a set of articles. As long as distribution of a subset of information has no foreseeable end, whatever the format, and the publishing function is recognizable, serials will continue to exist.

REFERENCES

Association of Research Libraries, *Report of the ARL Serials Prices Project* (1989).

N. Bernard Basch, *Buying Serials: A How-to-Do-It Manual for Librarians* (1990).

Marcia Tuttle, *Introduction to Serials Management* (1983).

CHARLES A. HAMAKER;
DEANA L. ASTLE

Services for Users with Disabilities

The promise of the Age of Information has brought substantial change to the lives of individuals whose vision, hearing, or physical mobility or dexterity is impaired. The importance of communications in contemporary daily life underscores the need for library and information services to those with disabilities. Because access to the printed word is impossible for the blind and limited for persons with other disabilities, they must depend on the assistance or intervention of others to gain access to educational and occupational information.

As the number of persons with various disabilities increases, particularly among the elderly, the need to provide appropriate assistance and intervention becomes even more critical. In the United States, the government recognized this need and passed the Americans with Disabilities Act (ADA), which requires businesses and institutions to prepare to meet the needs of all disabled people. ADA mandates the removal of architectural barriers, making buildings and offices physically accessible, and the removal of communication barriers, providing the disabled with routine access to various devices that assist them in overcoming the isolation in their lives.

This article deals with several aspects of efforts in the U.S. and other countries to increase access to information for persons with disabilities. In the mid to late 1980s public librarians, who are most frequently involved in these services to their communities, became more aware of the needs of these special users and initiated a number of activities to assist them. Libraries have made encouraging accommodations, ranging from staff members learning sign language to having buildings designed or remodeled to provide barrier-free access. Libraries have become deposit stations to house and circulate books in special format (for example, braille, spoken word recordings, and large print) and have installed a variety of reading machines. Library schools have instituted classes to acquaint future librarians with library service for disabled persons, and library associations are lending support and assistance to the development of standards in this field of library service. The work of the American Library Association (ALA) and the International Federation of Library Associations (IFLA) has been particularly noteworthy.

Outstanding advances have also been made in technology. For example, computers and miniaturization can now provide a direct reading of a page through synthesized speech, and technology is also helping improve the timeliness of the circulation of reading materials and related equipment. Technology is helping those with disabilities meet the demands and challenges of an industrialized society and is facilitating their participation in community life.

Readers with Disabilities. The terms *handicap, impairment,* and *disability* have no legal or medical definition. For the library, however, they do indicate persons in the community who usually or obviously need special assistance or special equipment and who must meet eligibility or certification requirements not usually sought from others.

National statistics can give some indication of the extent and prevalence of various disabling conditions. For example, the U.S. National Center for Health Statistics regularly surveys the population with regard to certain health conditions. Data from 1988 indicate that 8,365,000 persons had visual impairments, 21,869,000 had hearing impairments, and more than 26,878,000 suffered from orthopedic problems affecting their mobility or dexterity. In 1987 Canada reported almost 3,317,000 persons with some type of disability, 6 percent of whom were under the age of 14.

Few countries fail to provide some kind of library or reading service for their disabled citizens. Such service varies widely depending on whether it is centralized solely under the auspices of the central or federal government or is decentralized among public libraries and charitable organizations. A trend also exists toward more cooperation among libraries in sharing resources that are scarce and expensive to produce. Following are a few examples of library service in various countries on the continents of Asia, Australia, Europe, and North America.

United States. The Americans with Disabilities Act was only one of a long line of actions designed to aid persons with special needs.

National Library Service is a free service authorized by Congress for residents, as well as eligible American citizens living abroad, who are certified by competent authority as being unable to see a page of print, hold a book, or turn its pages. Examples of disabling conditions that may make a person eligible include cerebral palsy, blindness, severe arthritis, multiple sclerosis, muscular dystrophy, and quadriplegia. Mailing to and from the cooperating network of 56 regional libraries and more than 100 subregionals is free. The cooperating network, made up largely of state and local public libraries, serves persons who are blind or otherwise disabled in its service area. Four multistate service centers (MSCs) provide backup, such as duplicating services, interlibrary loan coordination, storage for publication and equipment reserves, and housing for multiple copies of books in all media. Each MSC serves regional libraries in 13 to 15 contiguous states.

Full-length books and magazines of general interest are produced by the Library of Congress, National Library Service for the Blind and Physically Handicapped (LC-NLS), in braille as well as on disk and cassette tapes. This material, along with related equipment to play the recordings, is provided to the regional libraries as a basic collection. Magazines are a large proportion of the material circulated in recorded form. More than 70 popular titles are recorded on flexible disks and mailed directly from the producer to the readers. In one five-year period, 1980 to 1984, the number of blind or otherwise disabled readers throughout the country grew from more than 605,000 to almost 635,000 and circulation from fewer than 17 million units (volumes and containers) to more than 19 million. The network collection is supplemented by single-copy transcriptions and recordings by local volunteers. The music collection at NLS is the major national resource for music scores, textbooks, and instructional materials in a format usable by disabled persons.

Other Programs. NLS cooperates with educational, vocational, and nonprofit organizations that provide materials to disabled persons. One such organization, Recording for the Blind (RFB), with headquarters in Princeton, New Jersey, lends free textbooks on cassettes to medically certified visually, physically, or perceptually disabled students and professional persons. By 1992 the RFB Master Tape Collection contained more than 80,000 titles covering all educational levels, from elementary school through the university level.

Public libraries in the U.S. have taken initiatives to provide easier access to the buildings and to printed collections so that disabled persons can take their place in the cultural and social life of their communities on equal terms with everyone else.

The Phoenix, Arizona, Public Library, while not typical, nevertheless illustrates a public library's extensive use of technology to benefit handicapped persons without dependence on sighted people. It has a Special Needs Center where the staff can communicate with deaf persons in sign language. Equipment in the Center includes a Versabraille computer for telephone communication with deaf-blind persons and a Kurzweil reading machine, a computer-assisted device that scans a printed page through an optical character recognition system and reads the page aloud in synthesized speech. The Kurzweil machine, coupled with a paperless braille machine, a computer with synthetic speech, and a letter-quality printer, enables blind persons to read and write braille or printed material electronically, edit manuscripts, and print out corrected copies. The center also has a TDD (a telephone device for the deaf), a video print enlarger, a microfiche enlarger, and a braille fingerspelling program.

Versabraille, the trade name for one of several machines known as "cassette braille" or "paperless braille," is a specially designed cassette recorder/player that receives and stores braille characters on a cassette tape. The user reads the braille displayed as a line of metal pins that are advanced on command. This machine and others, such as the Optacon, which converts letters into vibrating points that can be felt on the fingertips, are in use in many libraries.

Librarians and others, such as those in educational and rehabilitation agencies and volunteer organizations, bring newspapers and other timely and topical information to disabled persons through radio reading services. Using both paid professionals and volunteers, FM stations broadcast news and interpretive reports, often from daily and weekly newspapers, to disabled persons who listen over specially adapted receivers. Some libraries and volunteer groups record selected articles from newspapers onto cassettes. These papers are not usually recorded in their entirety because of the cost and time involved, but they are usually recorded on a weekly basis.

Tactile maps, often called "braille maps," convey geographic location information through the use of raised lines and braille notation. Such maps are receiving increased attention in the U.S. and abroad. The first International Symposium on Maps and Graphics for the Visually Handicapped was held in Washington, D.C., in March 1983 and was attended by more than 100 cartographers, geographers, and educators working with blind persons. In April 1984 more than 200 persons from 40 countries gathered in what was then called East Berlin to discuss international cooperation and technological advances in tactile map production. IFLA's Section of Libraries for the Blind developed an international registry of maps to be located in the Netherlands Library for the Blind. In 1984 the NLS published a bibliography with more than 475 entries relating to maps and graphics and covering such diverse topics as spatial perception and map design.

Library of Congress

Daniel J. Boorstin, 12th Librarian of Congress, narrating his book An American Primer *in a studio of the National Library Service for the Blind and Physically Handicapped. When completed, the book was made available in 1,500 copies for the thousands of users of the LC program.*

Video is being used for deaf persons the same way audio tapes are used for the blind—that is, to make already existing print material available in another medium. The videotapes are also used for sign-language training. Some libraries, through grants under the Library Services and Construction Act, have purchased telecaption decoders. Such decoders enable deaf persons to view some 30 hours of educational and commercial television programs a week.

Until comparatively recently, public libraries had not made special attempts to serve mentally retarded individuals adequately. The term *mentally retarded* covers those with a wide range of abilities. Some of the more severely retarded may have difficulty reading and be able to speak only with difficulty. Changes in

Photo by Bob Rink

The Special Needs Center at Phoenix Public Library (Arizona) is equipped with TDD (Text Telephone Device for the Deaf), Super Phone and Telebraille to assist patrons with hearing impairments.

A variety of enabling technologies, such as synthetic speech, print enlargement on CRT screens, and braille printers and displays assist blind and visually impaired patrons in using the resources of M.C. Migel Memorial Library and Information Center, American Foundation for the Blind.

M.C. Migel Memorial Library and Information Center, American Foundation for the Blind, New York City

public attitudes and improved and enlightened care, training, and psychological evaluation have led to greater efforts to bring mentally retarded people into community life. These efforts include library service as well. According to some librarians, mentally retarded children have problems in book selection common also to dyslexic children. Libraries have been stocking toys for both groups on the theory that toys can lead to improved interaction between handicapped and nonhandicapped children.

For dyslexics, therapists in the U.S. found the combination of printed text with accompanying cassettes spoken at slow speed to be effective. The same combination was in use in Australia and the Netherlands in the early 1990s. Dutch researchers began developing a recorded book in the mid-1980s that could turn out to be an important reading and teaching aid for dyslexic children. Each word in the book has below it a combination of black and white marks making up a bar code, much like those used on products in supermarkets. A computer analyzes the binary sequence that the scanner reads and converts it into speech sounds that emerge from a speaker. The project is a joint effort of Eindhoven's Technical University and the Phillips Language Laboratory.

Scandinavia. In Scandinavian countries, service to disabled persons has in the past been the responsibility of charitable associations for the blind operating through centralized services. With the growth of public libraries and increased concern for the welfare of the disabled, however, conditions favorable to decentralization are present.

Denmark. In Denmark, service is entirely the responsibility of the state. Until 1976, it was centralized in the Statens Bibliotek og Trykkeri for Blinde (State Library and Printing House for the Blind, SBTB). Decentralization began in 1976, the year that marked the beginning of production of talking books for Denmark's public libraries as well as the entry of commercial publishers into the talking book business.

Proposed legislative changes led to the formation of the Committee on Library Servicing of the Blind and Sight Impaired to assist in transferring talking book circulation from the government agency for the blind to local public libraries. By 1982, 205 of 247 public libraries were lending talking books, and the Danish government and private publishers had each produced 500 titles for public library distribution. Individual blind and visually impaired users were to have the option of selecting books from either source during the changeover period when public libraries expand their capabilities for service.

Sweden. As in most Scandinavian countries, library service for blind persons in Sweden was originally created on philanthropic initiative. The Society for the Blind began service as early as 1892 and began lending recorded books in 1955, two years before the society had received its first state grant for library activities. The Library for Talking Books and Braille (TPB) was established in 1980. Cassette tapes are the dominant medium. TPB, a state authority under the auspices of the Ministry of Education, is responsible for almost all braille-related activity. Visually handicapped persons in Sweden obtain braille books directly from TPB and borrow talking books, produced by TPB and the Swedish Library Service, Ltd., through public libraries. Recorded books are made available to local and regional libraries through deposit collections and interlibrary loans.

Visually impaired students at universities and colleges and professional persons have access to academic material in braille or recorded-book form through TPB's Section for Course Material. About 300 to 400 recorded book titles are produced for these readers yearly. TPB initiates the production of the majority of the 1,600 titles recorded for library use each year. The Swedish Library Service, Ltd., arranges for the recording of about 150 recorded titles a year. Along with approximately 500 of TPB's recordings, these titles are sold to public libraries.

In recent years, the public libraries have been building up their collections of recorded books using grants from county councils. About two-thirds of the 279 municipalities have recorded books. The loan of these books represents about one percent of the total annual circulation in Sweden.

Iceland. An act of Parliament in 1982 created the Icelandic Library for the Blind, bringing together the resources and services formerly provided by the Reykjavik Public Library and the Icelandic Association for the Blind. The Icelandic Association for the Blind serves blind and visually handicapped persons as well as anyone unable to read normal print. Materials are available in braille and on cassettes.

The Icelandic Library for the Blind is governed by a 10-member board appointed by the Ministry of Education and is divided into three departments. The Educational Materials Department provides students past the elementary grades with textbook support. During 1983, the library's first year of operation, it served about 1,000 people, circulated 23,000 items, and added 100 titles to its collection.

The braille collection contains 600 uncatalogued titles, mostly in Danish, which were contributed to the library by the Icelandic Association for the Blind. Danish is the first foreign language Icelandic students learn in school. For recordings, all narration (for example, reading a book onto cassette tape) is done by volunteers. Cassette readers buy their own machines. Members of the Association for the Blind are able to purchase theirs duty-free; other readers buy theirs commercially. The cassette collection contained approximately 1,300 titles in 1985, with three cassette copies each. An agreement between the Library and the Author's Association restricts the library to recording and duplicating only three copies of each title.

Poland. Although braille libraries existed in Poland before World War II, more extensive services have been organized since then under social organizations such as the Section for the Propagation of Reading Programs for Invalids and Physically Handicapped Persons. In 1952 the Central Library of the Polish Association for the Blind was established in Warsaw to provide training assistance and library materials to six branch libraries in large city centers and nearly 20 libraries in cooperatives, schools, and community centers. Services to those with visual and physical impairments are also offered by public libraries, although on a more limited scale. These services have begun to increase, especially for persons with physical disabilities and for nonhospitalized invalids. Reading programs for the blind and physically disabled were introduced in public libraries in 1975 as a result of an agreement between the Polish Association for the Blind and the Ministry of Culture and Art. Of the 49 regional branches of the Association of Polish Librarians, 35 have sections for recorded books, and some of them have recording studios. The Ministry of Culture and Art has steadily increased funds to purchase tape-recorded books and related equipment. All the libraries have cassette players for cassette readers on a loan basis. By the end of 1981, 35 libraries had recorded book collections amounting to just over 12,000 titles, not including titles purchased for the libraries by the Polish Association for the War on Disability, which are deposited in the libraries but not listed in the catalogues.

Japan. Of the 83 braille libraries throughout Japan, the Japan Braille Library has the largest collection. It was established in 1940 with a collection of 700 braille books; 40 years later it contained about 104,000 braille volumes. Recorded books were added in 1958 and by the 1980s numbered 182,000 tapes. The Japan Braille Library lent more than 64,000 braille volumes and 424,000 tapes to its 12,750 registered borrowers. The library produced both press-braille and single-copy, transcribed braille books.

Facilities and services vary greatly among the other 82 libraries. Some concentrate on braille books, while others focus on recorded books, personal reader or reference services, aides, training classes for daily living, or braille classes. Nineteen main braille-publishing centers provide most of the braille books for the braille libraries, and some have small publishing departments for special items. The Japanese Red Cross loans braille books and provides volunteer braille transcription services. Lions Clubs also provide braille and recorded books.

In Japan, volunteer narrators are an important part of the increasing reader preference for talking books. Such recording requires less training than do braille transcribers, who train from 16 to 36 months. Most braille libraries in Japan are governed by elected boards of directors. Organizations are entitled to national government funding if they are registered under the Social Welfare Law of 1963. The balance of funds comes from local and prefectural governments and fund-raising activities. The Ueda Braille Library is the only one in Japan that is government-operated.

Experts meeting in Osaka in 1992 concluded that visually impaired persons in Japan were not gaining greater access to the large volume of information available to the sighted, since most services concentrate on braille books. Of the 37,000 visually impaired persons in Japan, only 1,300 have access to computers.

BiFolkal Productions, Inc., Madison, Wisconsin

Librarian and Activities Director at the Pennsylvania State Hospital, Danville, coordinate programs using multimedia theme kits.

Australia. The Royal Blind Society (RBS) of New South Wales provides reader services, audio production, music, and student and special request materials. Full-time and part-time employees are assisted by about 300 volunteers who do reading, proofreading, and clerical work in addition to helping with brailling.

As a braille library, RBS dates back to the early years of the 20th century. In 1961 it took over the production and distribution of recorded books, which had been a separate operation of the Blind Book Society up to that time. The Blind Book Society then became the RBS Talking Book Auxiliary. Through its Reader Services Section, RBS lends braille, recorded books, line-embossed system (Moon Type) books, and large print; it also has a circulating library of magazines. The Department of Social Security under-

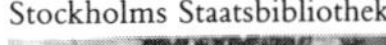

Stockholms Staatsbibliothek

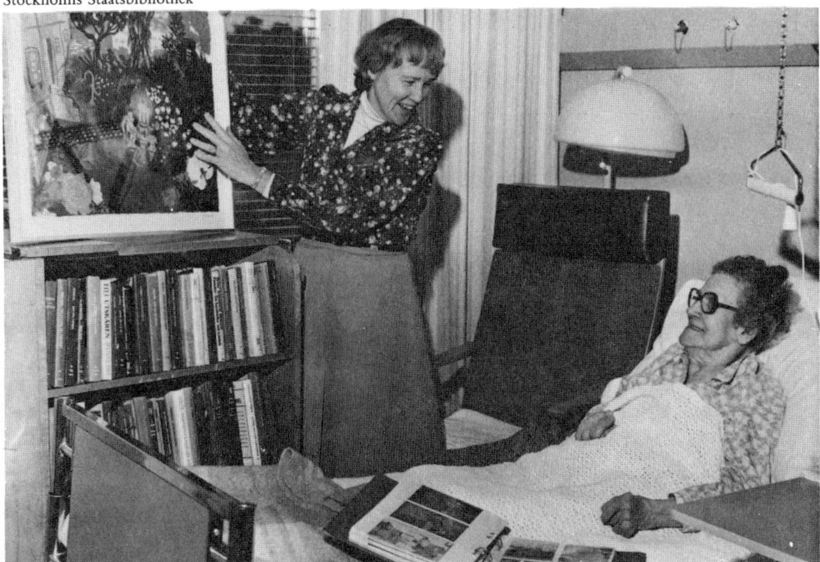

Book-truck delivery of library materials to patients in a Swedish hospital.

Institute for Perception Research

At the Institute for Perception Research in the Netherlands, a boy scanning a barcode with a light pen. The barcode indicates which word is to be produced by the sound synthesizer.

writes the cost of one-third of the audio and braille productions that meet certain production standards. Visually impaired persons in Australia are not directly served by RBS; instead, the society supplies recorded cassettes at cost to public libraries serving both visually impaired and blind readers. Submaster tapes are made available to similar agencies in Victoria and Western Australia on the same basis. In 1982 more than 2,100 titles were sold. A survey conducted by the National Library of Australia and a higher education policy study in 1988 both suggested that support for extending services to the disabled was likely to grow in the 1990s.

International Cooperation. Librarians from a number of countries have worked together to share resources and materials for blind persons that are both scarce and expensive to produce. IFLA has been important in the field. In 1977, at the IFLA meeting in Brussels, Belgium, a Working Group was established by the Hospital Library Section. In 1979 it was renamed the Round Table of Libraries for the Blind and later the Section of Libraries for the Blind. The many and varied activities and interests of the Section include consideration of international standards for talking book formats, recommendations on national standards for talking book formats, recommendations on national standards of library service for the blind, copyright exemption for materials for the disabled, and international cooperation and exchange of bibliographic information.

Library of Congress

The recorded books project began at the Library of Congress in 1931.

The Section published two useful directories: the *International Directory of Libraries and Production Facilities for the Blind* and the *International Directory of Braille Music Collections.* The first lists sources for braille and recorded materials throughout the world and provides pertinent information, such as the languages in which the materials are produced. The music directory lists sources for braille music along with detailed information on the nature of the collections. Its purpose is to locate needed braille music and also to encourage future bibliographic research, to foster international cooperation among braille music organizations, and to conserve limited resources by avoiding unnecessary duplication of braille music.

Section members work with international organizations, such as the Universal Postal Union and the International Transport Association, to improve the movement of library materials among countries. They devised a self-adhesive label bearing the word *Blindpost.* The label has black letters on an orange background for maximum visibility and is intended to help speed packages through international postal depots and customs by identifying them as materials for the blind. Certain materials for the blind, particularly braille, can now be mailed free across international borders using surface (but often slow) mail.

New IFLA Guidelines for Library Services for the Deaf, covering services, personnel, communications, collections, and promotion, were reported in 1991 after adoption by IFLA and the World Federation of the Deaf.

Standards. The *Approved Recommendations on Working Out National Standards of Library Service for the Blind* (August 1983), compiled and edited by the Standards Development Committee of the Section of Libraries for the Blind, IFLA, has received international support. It was compiled by Frank Kurt Cylke (U.S.), Henry Fidder (The Netherlands), William C. Byrne (Australia), and D. S. Zharkov (Soviet Union). These standards cover a wide variety of essential topics, including library administration, resource development, lending policies, and response to users.

The IFLA standards and those published under the auspices of the ALA, the revised *Standards and Guidelines for the Library of Congress Network Libraries for the Blind and Physically Handicapped, 1984,* indicate an important trend in upgrading the quality of library service for disabled individuals. It should be noted that important progress has been made in this area of service since the mid-1960s. That progress can most likely be attributed to concentration on certain objectives: (1) continuity of service, so that users can request and rely on quality service at any entry point in the system; (2) fullest use of the bookstock, each title and volume of which is more expensive to produce and more limited in quantity than what is available to members of the general public; (3) increase in the use of professional personnel at all service points and the elevation of professional librarians in charge of libraries for the disabled to administrative, policy-making positions, along with a more flexible approach to the whole organization of the service; and (4) increase in accessibility of books and information for the users of the collections, together with an increase in the breadth and range of titles and subjects from which the disabled reader may choose.

The ALA standards were the first comprehensive review related to libraries serving blind and disabled persons. Begun in 1977 with a contract between the NLS and the ALA Health and Rehabilitative Services Division, the standards were approved in 1979. They were developed for service to blind and disabled individuals provided by regional, subregional, state, public, school, academic, and institutional libraries. Subsequently, Battelle's Columbus Laboratories evaluated the NLS regional and subregional network, including NLS itself, through data collected from questionnaires, from interviews, and from site visits. Each component in the network received a detailed report on its performance as measured against the standards. Also, a comprehensive state-of-the-network report, with comparative data for libraries of similar size and scope, was issued. The study indicates an improved understanding of library services in this network. The standards were scheduled for revision again in 1989, when the network libraries, their parent agencies and organizations, state libraries, and administering and funding agencies would be provided with an excellent means of assessing the current status of library service for disabled individuals.

Book Production and Distribution. The objectives of producing materials for use by disabled individuals are to decrease costs, increase timeliness, and maintain quality. The increase in the use of computers foreshadows revolutionary developments in braille production—particularly in increasing speed, which would in turn shorten the time between the book's publication in print and its availability to the disabled reader. Computers have been assisting publishers of braille and are also helping to increase the efficiency of transcribers. For example, complex braille codes can be input so that less transcriber training is required, and the text can be edited before it is committed to paper. Master copies can be stored on diskettes rather than on bulky paper or metal plates, so more material can be kept in a given amount of storage space.

The timeliness of braille production has improved with the use of compositor tapes, the storage medium that drives typesetting equipment for print materials. Compositor tapes can be employed to operate braille presses automatically. They eliminate the need for time-consuming manual stereographing and provide readers with braille versions of books and periodicals nearer to the time the print version is published. *National Geographic,* for example, is published using such tapes. The braille edition of Joseph Lash's *Helen and Teacher,* a biography of Helen Keller and Anne Sullivan Macy, was available to blind individuals at about the same time the print edition became available for the sighted. Except for experiments with compositor tapes in braille production in 1969, it was the first time in the U.S. that

Photo by Bob Rink

Closed-caption television and video for the hearing impaired at the Special Needs Center, Phoenix Public Library, Phoenix, Arizona.

a book of that length—786 pages, or eight braille volumes—had been produced in that manner.

Further improvements in the quality and speed of braille production may be expected. A cooperative project was begun in 1980 between the Library of Congress and the American Foundation for the Blind (AFB) in New York. AFB contributed significantly to the development of talking books in the 1930s and became one of two major producers of sound recordings for blind and disabled people. The project calls for the establishment of a production center and a developmental laboratory to examine technology in relation to the use of computers in producing high-quality braille.

Voice Indexing. Technological advances have made reference material, not previously available in recorded form, accessible to blind and disabled individuals through voice indexing. This technique uses key words to locate specific information. Index words are audible when the cassette is played in the fast-forward mode. When the desired word or name is located, the reader stops the tape and resumes play at regular speed to hear the full entry under that heading. Recorded voice-indexed reference material includes *Access National Parks: A Guide for Handicapped Visitors;* the *Concise Heritage Dictionary,* recorded in the studios of the NLS on 55 cassettes; and the 1980 *World Book Encyclopedia,* recorded on 219 cassettes at the American Printing House for the Blind in Louisville, Kentucky.

Computer Technology. Computers now perform many of the centralized functions of NLS. For example, the NLS Comprehensive Mailing List System (CMLS) is used to accomplish the massive job of mailing periodicals and catalogues to thousands of individuals. A recent development in the use of computer technology is the Reader Enrollment and Delivery System (READS), a computer-based circulation system designed for long-term growth. And READS is designed to be compatible with NLSNET, a planned information system linking NLS, its multistate service centers (MSCs), and automated network libraries by computer for intercommunication and data transfer. READS was designed to handle four functions: (1) maintenance of patron records, (2) circulation, (3) inventory control, and (4) information exchange. The system was in the test phase at pilot locations in 1985 and was designed to take advantage of local area network architecture, using computer workstations performing a variety of tasks including optical scanning. One of READS' objectives is to operate on as wide a range of devices as are available in the computer marketplace. The READS system will contain data to support activities related to book circulation, magazine subscriptions, inventory of sound reproduction equipment, and patron record-keeping. Modifications in the system will be made as required.

FRANK KURT CYLKE;
ALFRED D. HAGLE

Sevensma, T. P.

(1879–1966)

ALA

T. P. Sevensma

Founder and first President of the Nederlandse Vereiniging van Bibliothecarissen (NVB; Dutch Library Association), and the first General Secretary of the International Federation of Library Associations (IFLA), Tiestse Pieter Sevensma gave distinguished leadership to the international library world for more than 30 years.

Born in 1879 in Sneek, in the northern province of Friesland in the Netherlands, Sevensma gained his principal education at the University of Amsterdam, where he went to take doctoral degrees in both theology and political science. After a brief period as a lecturer in Hebrew at a Rotterdam grammar school, he began his library career in 1908 at the University of Amsterdam. He also compiled booksellers' catalogues for Martinus Nijhoff of The Hague.

In 1913 Sevensma was appointed Librarian of the Commercial University Library in Rotterdam, where he organized the library in a new building. After three years he moved back to Amsterdam as Librarian of the Public Library. This responsibility was combined with that of Librarian of the University of Amsterdam Library in 1929. Sevensma founded and served as the first President of the NVB (1912–23).

His academic library experience and impressive linguistic skills made him a natural choice to succeed Florence Wilson of Columbia University as the Librarian of the League of Nations Library in 1927. A new library building in Geneva was completed, with the assistance of an international committee of library experts appointed by the Secretariat. Sevensma directed the transition to the new facility with only one day without service to readers. Geneva and the League were considered the heart of international influence, and the International Federation of Library Associations invited Sevensma to become its first Secretary in June 1929.

Although Sevensma left the League of Nations in 1938 to become Librarian of the oldest university library in the Netherlands, Leiden, he remained Secretary of IFLA until 1958. Appointing Arthur C. Breycha-Vauthier as Assistant Secretary and Sevensma's successor at the League, IFLA continued to benefit from office subvention by the League. Through the years of World War II Sevensma held fast to the idea of IFLA.

Sevensma maintained an active scholarly life as one of the editors of the fourth edition of Winkler Prins's *Encyclopedia* and as chief editor of a newly created Dutch encyclopedia, *Zoecklicht* ("Searchlight").

Sevensma's colleagues honored him at 60 by establishing the Sevensma prize, offered annually by IFLA for the best essay on a selected topic. Active until an advanced age, he died in Hilversum at 87.

ROBERT WEDGEWORTH

Seychelles

Seychelles, a republic in the Indian Ocean off the east coast of Africa, comprises a group of 115 islands. Population (1990 est.) 67,378; land area, 280 sq.km. The population is of mixed European, African, and Asian origin. The people speak mostly Creole; English, French, and Creole are the official languages.

The Seychelles were settled by the French in 1770 and remained a French colony until 1814, when they passed under British rule and became a dependency of Mauritius. They became a colony in their own right in 1903 and gained independence from Britain in 1976.

Public libraries in the Seychelles date from 1910, when the Carnegie Library was founded. Administered by a board of directors, the library progressed or lagged behind, depending on the enthusiasm of those in office. In the period following independence, new policies in education and culture resulted in an expansion of library services. In 1978, the Carnegie Library moved to a more spacious building and became the National Library. It offers only public library services. It is situated on the main island, Mahé, and operates a Mobile Library service to fifteen rural areas and one National Youth Service Village. It also administers three branch libraries, two on the island of Praslin and one on the island of La Digue.

Libraries in Seychelles (1990)

Type of library	Number of administrative units (main libraries)	Number of service points (branches, mobile stops, etc.)	Volumes in collections	Annual expenditures (rupee)	Population served	Professional staff (with certificate, diploma, etc.)	Total staff
Academic	1	4	35,000	301,000	15,000	1 degree 1 diploma 3 certificate	10
Public	1	18	42,000	741,800	50,702	2 diploma 1 certificate	16
School		22	93,859	544,600	8,520	2 diploma	23
Special	12	--	--	--	--	1 diploma	18
French Cultural Centre	1	--	21,000	--	400	--	2

The need for a new National Library that would offer the services appropriate to such an institution and that would keep pace with development in the country was felt as early as 1980. Construction of such a library began in the late 1980s and was scheduled for completion by 1992. The new National Library planned to offer both national and public library services, as well as facilities for cultural and literary activities.

The Seychelles National Archives was scheduled to occupy a section of the new National Library building. The Archives was opened to the public in 1964. It had the right of legal deposit and planned to relinquish it to the new National Library.

The School Library Service is administered by the Ministry of Education. Each of the 27 schools has a library, with collections ranging from 2,000 to 6,000 volumes. The schools receive additional reading materials both from the National Library and its Mobile Library service. The Mobile Library serves 14 schools in rural areas. The Ministry of Education also administers academic libraries, which support programs at the Seychelles Polytechnic, the only institution providing academic study at ordinary and advanced levels, as well as vocational training.

Rapid development in the social and economic sectors has resulted in creation of a number of special libraries in ministries and parastatal organizations. By 1991, 12 such libraries were in operation, the most advanced being the Scientific and Technical Documentation Center in the Department of Industry. The French Embassy Cultural Center provides reference and reading services, but its lending services are restricted.

The Ministry of Information, Culture, and Sports works in close liaison with ministries and parastatal organizations to develop library services in the country. The Seychelles Library Association was formed in 1991 to unite those working in libraries, documentation centers, and the archives, and to promote the profession.

REFERENCES

Jean-Michel Filiot, *Histoire des Seychelles* (1982).
Seychelles in Figures (1991).

LINA ERNESTA

National Library Trust Fund
Photo by Kingsley Pouponneau/National Audio Visual Centre

Architectural model of the new Seychelles National Library, completed in 1992.

Shackleton, Robert

(1919–)

Robert Shackleton, Librarian of the Bodleian Library and author of work of outstanding originality and perception in French 18th-century studies over many years, was Chairman of the Committee on Oxford University Libraries in England. He resolved the managerial anomalies of the departmental, faculty, and museum collections that had grown up independently over centuries, reconciled local and knowledgeable supervision, selection, and spending, under individual committees, with fiscal common sense as enunciated by a Libraries Board, and guided the largest unit, the Bodleian Library, into extension, automation, and shared acquisition policies for materials published abroad.

Shackleton was born in Yorkshire, England, November 25, 1919. He was an undergraduate at Oriel College (graduated 1940), and his early academic appointments were at Trinity College (Lecturer, 1946–49) and Brasenose College (Fellow, 1946–79; Vice-Principal, 1963–66). From 1948 to 1966 he was Librarian. From University Lecturer in French he proceeded to the Readership in 1965, the year of his heaviest activity as Chairman of the Committee appointed to consider what might be done to exact the greatest utility, scholarly and economic, from the University Libraries, especially those not under the authority of the Curators of the Bodleian Library. "The importance of these may be demonstrated," to quote the report (known generally as the *Parry Report*) of the Committee on Libraries of the University Grants Committee, 1967 "by comparing the book resources of Oxford with one of the larger libraries in a provincial university. If the Bodleian complex and all college libraries were destroyed, the remaining libraries would still have a larger stock than that of the largest English university libraries, for example Birmingham or Leeds or Liverpool or Manchester."

The recommendations for common standards and policies and collaboration set forth by Shackleton's committee, published as the *Report of the Committee on University Libraries,* (Supplement No. 1 to the *Oxford University Gazette,* XCVII), appeared in November 1966. It was a model of industry, historical and economic analysis, and tact, and it gained early and, in an Oxford context, surprisingly unacrimonious acceptance. In the year of its publication Shackleton became Bodley's Librarian. Much of the tolerance by faculties and departments of a mildly directive system for library management, which was philosophically at variance with academic self-government and the notion of independence in the university's parts, was owed to the new Librarian's political sense and modest but firm persuasiveness.

By virtue of his office, Shackleton became a member of the Libraries Board, and his quiet reasonableness and avoidance of partisanship helped to set the tone of the new body, and of the meetings of librarians from the extra-Bodleian libraries which rounded the consultative system. For 13 years, within and without the central Library, he guided, thoughtfully and unabrasively, the policies and practice of acquisition, proliferation, funding, and common storage of library materials in Oxford. He saw to a successful conclusion such essential new construction as the underground area of the Radcliffe Science Library and such happy refurbishment as the splendid exterior of Gibbs's Radcliffe Camera. These and like improvements were wholly within the Bodleian op-

Bodleian Library

Robert Shackleton

eration; to some extent outside it, and to the benefit of the University Libraries at large, were cooperative ventures such as the book repository at Nuneham Courtenay with delivery at a speed held by some librarians if not by their readers to be unseemly. In 1979 Shackleton retired.

The circumstances of his retirement were felicitous. In the Preface to *Montesquieu: A Critical Biography* (1961), Shackleton had disclaimed for himself the universal competence of his subject. His prudence was a mark of integrity; it was Oxford's fortune that he was able to discard the restraints of specialization in his office as Bodley's Librarian. From the early Brasenose conference on library automation to the increasingly intricate conventions, in the later 1970s, of the International Federation of Library Associations, with little visible diminution of his work in French literature or in Enlightenment studies, Shackleton found his way surely through the technological mazes of innovative and administrative librarianship and was honored not only by learned societies but also by professional bodies for librarians. Yet the highest honor was in his recall to the plow. With a Fellowship at All Souls College, Oxford, he was elected Marshal Foch Professor of French, the first Englishman so appointed.

In this chair, long held by his admired Jean Seznec, and in sustained industry, Shackleton rounded off with distinction the career in letters in which Bodley's librarianship was an equally distinguished intervention.

Shackleton assembled a superb Montesquieu collection; his wider taste in rare books resulted in his election to the Grolier Club of New York in 1967 and to its pantheon of Honorary Foreign Corresponding Members three years later. As he drew the reader into his work on Montesquieu, Shackleton confessed his unfitness, as he saw it, to discuss the springs of thought and action in one whose mind could still be open to all the sciences and all the arts; but the attempt secured to him a treasury of understanding.

Distinctions conferred on Shackleton include the Fellowships of the British Academy, the Society of Antiquaries, and the Royal Society of Literature, the Presidency of the Society for French Studies, a Visiting Fellowship of the Humanities Research Centre of the Australian National University, the Foreign Honorary Membership of the American Academy of Arts and Sciences, the Lyell Readership and the Zaharoff Lectureship in the University of Oxford, various American visiting professorships, the office of Delegate (board member) of the Oxford University Press, the Presidency of the International Society for 18th-Century Studies, a Directorship of the Voltaire Foundation, corresponding membership of the Académie de Bordeaux, and many honorary fellowships in Oxford and honorary doctorates in English-speaking countries. Honors also include the Honorary Doctorate of the University of Bordeaux, the Médaille de la Ville de Paris, the John Brademas Inaugural Award at New York University, and appointment as Chevalier de la Légion d'Honneur.

CLIFFORD CURRIE

Shamurin, E. I.

(1889–1962)

Evgenii Ivanovich Shamurin was one of the most erudite Soviet scholars in librarianship and bibliography. He distinguished himself with excellence in research, prolific writing, and outstanding teaching. Many students and peers were touched by his vast knowledge.

He was born October 28, 1889, in Erevan, Armenia. After his father, an attorney, died in 1904, the young Shamurin settled in an orphanage in Tambov, where he finished his secondary education in 1908. Following anti-government demonstrations during the Russo-Japanese War (1905), Shamurin was jailed and placed on probation. Soon after that he went to live with his maternal uncle, N. P. Zagoskin, a professor of law at the University of Kazan. He enrolled in the law school there, but also took advantage of broad curricular offerings. In addition to law, he took a program in the humanities and the social sciences. This background led him to pursue his interests in the fine arts and literature rather than the practice of law. After graduation he fulfilled the required military service in 1912.

Virtually penniless, he left Kazan for Moscow, where he took some additional training in the arts and music. He began to write for various papers and journals, often using pseudonyms. His activities were interrupted by World War I. He served in the imperial army and was demobilized after the outbreak of the October Revolution.

He served as a jurist and a law lecturer until 1920 in the city of Tomsk. In early 1921 Shamurin began to work in the Bibliography Section of the Tartar State Publishing enterprise. In September 1921 he secured a job at the Russian Central Book Chamber in Moscow. This was a turning point in his career. The next 40 years he devoted to the field of bibliography and librarianship.

In the Book Chamber he held positions of steadily increasing responsibility dealing with such tasks as editorial work, organization of catalogues, descriptive cataloguing, classification, and the problems of terminology. He was active in the organization of two significant all-Russian bibliographic conferences, holding important official posts. He demonstrated his competence at the first conference, delivering papers "On the Application of the Anglo-American Code in the Russian Bibliographic Practice" and "On the Measures toward the Standard Title Page," both published in the 1926 conference proceedings.

During the 1920s he joined many professional groups, such as the Russian Bibliographic Society, Russian Society of Decimalists, Society of Friends of the Book, and the Ukrainian Bibliological Society. During the 1930s he played many leading roles in the growth, development, and reorganization of the Book Chamber. He was instrumental in launching the journal *Bibliography,* later titled *Soviet Bibliography.*

In 1937 he left the Book Chamber but retained the role of a learned consultant. He participated in the advanced work of the Interlibrary Cataloguing Commission and many other official assignments. During this decade he gathered a wealth of knowledge and materials in the field of classification. His intention was to complete his doctoral studies. In 1943 he defended his 865-page dissertation, "The Library and Bibliographic Classification Abroad and in Pre-Revolutionary Russia." In 1944 he was awarded the degree of doctor of pedagogical sciences with the rank of full professor and named chairman of the Department of

Collections and Catalogues at the Moscow State Library Institute, where he served from 1940 to 1950.

He steered the project on the new Soviet library-bibliographic classification under the aegis of the Lenin State Library. He also guided the scholarly work of the Book Chamber in retrospective bibliography, editorial work, and the restoration of fire-damaged catalogues.

In 1950 he was sent into early retirement at the age of 61. But the last 12 years of his life proved to be his most productive period. Three of his chief works were published: the monumental *Essays on the History of the Library—Bibliographic Classification* (vol. 1, 1955, vol. 2, 1959; translated into German, 1964–67); *Dictionary of Library Terminology* (1958); and *Methods in the Preparation of Annotations* (1959).

Shamurin died in Moscow, December 1, 1962. A biography was started by Y. I. Masanov and completed by I. B. Gracheva (1970). A definitive bibliography (1911–62) was prepared by his daughter, Sofiia E. Shamurina, also a librarian. It lists 34 monographs, most of them accompanied by references to book reviews. It also lists 93 of his journal articles, book reviews, contributions to other works, lectures, and speeches. And it lists 49 works edited by him or under his editorial supervision. For his achievements, Shamurin was awarded the Order of the Red Banner of Labor and a privileged personal pension on retirement. Sidney L. Jackson said: "When every doctor of library science can show some knowledge of Shamurin's achievement, education for librarianship will have taken a long step towards truly professional education."

REFERENCES

Sidney L. Jackson, "In Review," *Journal of Education for Librarianship* (1968).

Y. I. Masanov and I. B. Gracheva, *E. I. Shamurin, 1889–1962* (1970).

Ray R. Suput, *The Contribution of E. I. Shamurin to Soviet Librarianship* (dissertation, Case Western Reserve University, 1972).

RAY R. SUPUT

Sharp, Katharine

(1865–1914)

One of the outstanding U.S. library leaders of the late 19th and early 20th centuries, Katharine Lucinda Sharp built the cornerstone of the University of Illinois research libraries and contributed to the acceptance of graduate education for librarianship in the Midwest.

She was born in Elgin, Illinois, May 21, 1865. The details of her childhood years are largely unrecorded; her mother's death, when Katharine was seven, led to her being housed with relatives while she attained her basic education at the Elgin Academy from 1872 to 1880. She enrolled in 1881 at Northwestern University, Evanston, Illinois, and graduated in 1885 with a Bachelor of Philosophy degree with honors. At the New York State Library School, Albany, she earned a Bachelor's degree in 1892 and a Master's degree in 1907. Sharp also, in 1899, received a Master of Philosophy degree from Northwestern.

She spent the years from 1888 to 1907 devoted to studying, practicing, and living the profession of librarianship. Until her death at Saranac Lake, New York, June 1, 1914, caused by injuries suffered in an automobile accident May 28 at Lake Placid, she was

ALA

Katharine Lucinda Sharp

closely associated with other 19th-century library pioneers, particularly her mentor and friend Melvil Dewey. Sharp studied with Dewey at Albany, and when she left the University of Illinois, in 1907, she found a close circle of friends at his Lake Placid Club in New York, where she served as Vice-President until her death.

Three years after her graduation from Northwestern she accepted her first library position, as Assistant Librarian at the public library at Oak Park, Illinois. During the intervening years she had taught at the Elgin Academy. Her first exposure to library work quickly led her to the conclusion that she should enroll in the country's first library school; Dewey later noted that she "was so easily first" there. His recommendation to Frank W. Gunsaulus, President of the newly established Armour Institute in Chicago, brought her appointment, in 1893, as Director of both the Library and the Department of Library Economy. Of special note was the establishment of the library training class, the fourth opened in the United States and the first in the Midwest.

In 1897 she moved to the Champaign/Urbana campus of the University of Illinois; the Armour library class was transferred with her. She was already recognized for her ability and leadership in the emerging library profession. Her students at Armour included other future leaders such as Margaret Mann, Cornelia Marvin Pierce, and Alice Tyler. Sharp also was perceived as a national figure through her activities in the American Library Association and her vibrant advocacy of state library organizations, extension work, and cooperative information systems. At Illinois Sharp was named Head Librarian and Director of the Library School, and she also served as Professor of Library Economy.

In the 10 years of her work at the University of Illinois, Sharp's life was dominated by three concerns: the Illinois State Library School, now the Graduate School of Library and Information Science; the University library itself; and the development of a strong library organization and information network in Illinois. In each area she had extraordinary successes, but in each area she also had many disappointments.

The main interest of Sharp's professional career rested in her personal belief in education for librarianship housed in an academic setting. Dewey had broken the pattern of "learning by experience" in his prototype school; Sharp, his protégée, accepted the philosophy that Dewey promulgated and carried it as far as she could at the University of Illinois. The classes at the Armour Institute and at the University of Illinois were founded to provide a specialization taught in an institution of higher education. At Illinois a combination of three elements, faculty, curriculum, and students, was brought together in such a way as to set a standard of achievement essential to the continuation of formal education for librarianship. The School, under her leadership, moved steadily from a B.L.S. based on a junior and senior year of college work toward acceptance of a graduate program. Although she did not completely achieve that objective, the curriculum evolved from routine "economy" courses in cataloguing, classification, and library "techniques" to administration, the study of various kinds of resources such as public documents, library extension, special services, research methods, and new technology.

Sharp arrived at Illinois at a critical period in its history; the University Library was disorganized and lacked a professional perception. Sharp imposed her own distinctive conception of library service on the institution. A logical order and arrangement of the collection was basic; this was followed by expansion of the services, including reference (which was directed by Isadore Gilbert Mudge) and modernization of procedures. She enlarged the staff from three in 1897 to 15 in 1907, while the number of volumes increased from 37,000 to 96,000—all catalogued, classified, and accessible. She left a sound foundation for her successors.

Sharp's third, closely linked professional concern lay in the extension of the library into the community and the development of an effective political body that could work for the betterment of library services for all citizens. In this larger arena she did attain certain goals but also failed, since her efforts in Illinois to provide a strong authority for the promotion of library interests were not rewarded. An effective state library association was founded and set firmly on its way, but she and her colleagues did not initiate successful legislation to establish a state library commission. Her efforts to centralize library extension at the University also failed, although she did leave behind dedicated followers who continued to stress her philosophy and who mustered library supporters throughout the state.

Although she was not a prolific writer, she published nearly two dozen articles and a monumental compilation on the condition of libraries in Illinois, *Illinois Libraries* (1906–08), a multivolume survey of the current status of public, school, academic, and special libraries. It contained an exhaustive historical study.

Throughout her life Sharp was active in library and professional associations. In each organization she was a major officer, including ALA; she was active on many ALA committees, served 10 years on the Council, and was twice elected Vice-President.

REFERENCES

Laurel A. Grotzinger, *The Power and the Dignity: Librarianship and Katharine Sharp* (1966), the only book-length treatment of Katharine Sharp.

Harriet E. Howe, "Katharine Lucinda Sharp, 1865–1914," in *Pioneering Leaders in Librarianship,* edited by Emily Miller Danton (1953), a memoir prepared by a former student.

Laurel A. Grotzinger, "Sharp, Katharine Lucinda," *Dictionary of American Library Biography* (1978).

LAUREL A. GROTZINGER

Shaw, Ralph
(1907–1972)

Ralph Robert Shaw, internationally known library administrator, researcher, educator, and inventor, was one of the most creative librarians to have worked in the United States. He was considered a radical in his early years and a conservative, by some of his colleagues, in his later years. His brilliant mind had the capacity to see a problem, create a solution, then turn it over to colleagues to perfect and implement.

Shaw was born in Detroit, Michigan, May 18, 1907. He secured an A.B. degree from Western Reserve University in 1928, the B.S. and M.S. at Columbia in 1929 and 1931, and the Ph.D. at the University of Chicago in 1950. His early professional experience included the New York Public Library (1928–29), Engineering Societies Library (1929–36), and service as Chief Librarian, Gary (Indiana) Public Library (1936–40). In 1940 he became Director of Libraries, U.S. Department of Agriculture, a position that he held (with time out to serve in the U.S. armed forces) until 1954, when he went to Rutgers, the State University of New Jersey. There he served as Professor in the newly established Graduate School of Library Service, becoming Dean, 1959–61, and Distinguished Service Professor, 1961–64. Finally he became Professor, Dean of Library Activities, and Professor Emeritus at the University of Hawaii in Honolulu until his retirement in 1969, although he continued to lecture occasionally at Rutgers until 1968.

Everywhere Shaw worked, his keen mind attacked the problems of the institution and produced innovative solutions, showing special interest in the scientific and efficient management of libraries. In Gary he instituted transaction charging, the use of photography in circulation control, and the use of truck cabs coupled with trailers as bookmobiles, which could be left on location for several days or longer. His invention of the rapid selector came during this period, as well as his translation of Georg Schneider's *Theory and History of Bibliography* (1934). His dissertation at Chicago, revised and published as *Literary Property in the United States* (1950), marked the beginning of a continuing concern with copyright problems, evidenced again in one of his last works, "Williams and Wilkins v. the U.S.: A Review of the Commissioner's Report" (*American Libraries,* October 1972).

His work at the U.S. Department of Agriculture offered ample opportunity to continue his interest in the use of machines as tools of management. There he initiated the first study of scientific management as applied to libraries of that department, and later he carried this to Rutgers, where one of the first courses on this subject was introduced in the regular library school curriculum. His concern with bibliography brought his attention to the development of the *Bibliography of Agriculture,* which became a major tool for the dissemination of agricultural information on a worldwide basis.

His interest in international problems was also shown at this time and continued throughout his career. He was active on numerous committees for the American Library Association and Unesco and served as a consultant on major library studies for a variety of governmental agencies. For example, he advised the Department of State, the National Science Foundation, and the Veterans Administration, to name only a few. He planned a network of agencies to distribute agricultural information in India (1957), developed the information component of the International Rice Research Institute at Los Baños, Philippines (1962), and worked as well in many Latin American countries through his membership on the advisory committee of the Inter-American Institute of Agricultural Science.

Shaw's continuing service to public libraries was shown through a survey for the Toronto Public Library (*Libraries of Metropolitan Toronto,* 1960); a feasibility study for the Boards of Trustees of the Brooklyn Public Library, New York Public Library, and Queens Borough Public Library (*A Study of the Advantages and Disadvantages of Consolidation,* 1957); and work at the local level to establish new public libraries, such as the one in Woodbridge, New Jersey. To all of these projects, and many more, he brought enthusiastic commitment, positive support, and expertise seldom matched in an individual librarian.

Publishing, as the other side of the coin of library development, received his attention in 1950 when he established the Scarecrow Press, Inc., on the principle of producing scholarly works and bibliographies in librarianship for which only a small market could be anticipated at a reasonable price, usually printing by offset from plates made from typewritten copy, yet always paying a royalty to authors. Among other experiments he tried miniprint, published especially to meet the needs of scholars in developing countries. With the help of Viola Leff Shaw, whom he had married in 1929 and who died in 1968, he worked from the basement of their homes in Alexandria, Virginia, and New Brunswick, New Jersey, and built a business until it became too large to manage at home and then sold a controlling interest in 1955 to Albert Daub, Sr.; in 1968 it was sold outright to Grolier Educational Corporation. Other similar publishers have used Scarecrow as a model for their operations. In 1969 he was married to Mary McChesney Andrews in Honolulu.

Few who knew Shaw during his days in Washington would have thought of him as having potential as a university professor, and yet when he was interviewed at Rutgers by Mason Gross, the President phoned the Dean and said, "We *must* have that man." When Shaw joined the small group of faculty who established the school in 1954, he quickly made an impact as an excellent instructor, an effective colleague in the development of curriculum, and a person deeply sympathetic to students, even though he was tough-minded and frequently dogmatic, could seldom suffer fools gladly, and had a special gift for stirring controversy. He initiated courses new to the library field, was influential in developing the doctoral curriculum, was tireless in seeking support for students and generous to colleagues, but brooked no delay on the part of faculty in responding to deadlines for dissertations and other related responsibilities.

A major contribution to the School and to the profession at this time was his editorship of the State of the Library Art series (5 volumes, 1960–61), published under a grant from the Council on Library Resources. He also initiated the Shaw/Shoemaker project *American Bibliography: A Preliminary Checklist for 1801–1819* (22 volumes, 1958–66) in order to cover the final 20 years originally proposed in Charles Evans's pioneering work, which had finally ended with 1800 imprints. It was typical of a Shaw project that he conceived the idea of using the "WPA shoe boxes" of cards plus photocopying as a method of expediting the work; as a result he was successful in producing, from a variety of secondary sources, a tool that has a remarkably high record of accuracy. Another contribution to librarianship was his development, as adviser to doctoral students, of a number of related research studies in the field of management as a means of "growing the field," in his words.

In 1964, when he was invited to go to the University of Hawaii, he carried much of the Rutgers curriculum and some of the faculty and doctoral students to establish a new library school there and to breathe new life into its library system. True to form, he experimented there too, particularly using his "visiting professor" idea, begun at Rutgers when such luminaries as Ranganathan, Joseph Wheeler, and Keyes Metcalfe visited and lectured to library school students. At Honolulu he applied this idea to undergraduate students with some success, though limited by the economics of the situation.

Shaw was also always active in professional associations, although he questioned the effectiveness of library meetings. He was President of the Indiana Library Association (1938–39), the New Jersey Library Association (1962–63), and the ALA (1956–57), becoming an Honorary Member of that Association in 1971. He was active in committees related to all his many, varied interests but in the ALA especially in association reorganization. It is difficult to set priorities for a presidential year and equally difficult to assess the impact of an ALA President. In Shaw's case, his report to Council at the 1957 Midwinter Conference reflects both his expectations and his frustrations. He criticized ALA at that time for "not approaching its goals, . . . in fact, appearing to go in the opposite direction" ("The President's Report," *ALA Bulletin,* March 1957). In his year as President, however, Shaw could take satisfaction in having eliminated a considerable amount of work from membership record-keeping and in bringing about the consolidation of *Booklist* and *Subscription Books Bulletin.*

One of his colleagues at that time, looking back on his presidency, has stated that "Shaw maintained that A.L.A. was a sprawling, inefficient, wasteful, non-productive organization, badly in need of effective business procedures and more democratic mem-

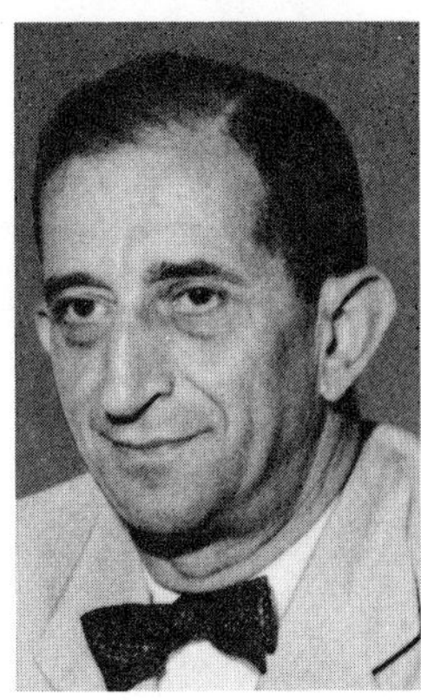

ALA

Ralph Shaw

bership control," typical of Shaw's usual incisive analysis. Some of his criticisms are still true today; others have been ameliorated by recent activists.

Shaw's printed publications make up a list of more than a hundred references from 1932 to 1972, with many more unpublished speeches, in-house reports, and the like remaining to be sorted and organized. In addition to those publications already mentioned, a few of his more significant contributions are worthy of special mention. As he was never averse to controversy, one of the more interesting examples arose as a result of Jesse Shera's article "Beyond 1984" (*ALA Bulletin,* March 1967). This exchange on the role of machines in libraries provided an opportunity for Shaw to reiterate his position that "it is just as stupid to hate machines as it is to love them. They are tools which may, used properly, help us to do the library and bibliographical jobs that we are supposed to do, and if used improperly can waste our resources." Shaw's *Pilot Study on the Use of Scientific Literature by Scientists* (1971), originally published in 1956, was constantly referred to in his teaching as a model for services by librarians and information scientists. His "CATCALL: Completely Automated Technique [for] Cataloging [and] Acquisition [of] Literature [for] Libraries" (*College & Research Libraries,* March 1970), in addition to illustrating his addiction to acronyms, also illustrates his forward-looking ability to advocate new and more economic ways of carrying out library procedures, in this case through cooperation with publishers and the book trade; some of the recommendations he made have since been realized, but others still await fulfillment.

Finally, almost on his deathbed, Shaw completed the translation and editing of the monumental work by Richard Muther, *German Book Illustration of the Gothic Period and the Early Renaissance (1460–1530)* (1972). In his own words, Shaw's work on this book was intended to illustrate how such early works—"verbose, using various German languages, and tough even if you are a German scholar"—can be reorganized with integrity to the original.

Shaw died in Honolulu on October 14, 1972. Until the end this amazing and unique scholar-librarian continued experimenting and breaking new ground. His greatest impact, however, will be felt through his students, especially those in his doctoral classes, who treasured his Shavian witticisms and aphorisms, crowded his classes to catch every word, and carry on his ideals of research and experimentation. A colleague, Lawrence Thompson, characterized him as "a globe-trotter, raconteur, wit, host, and in some dozens of other capacities . . . approaching the ideal of the Renaissance man" (*College & Research Libraries,* October 1954).

REFERENCES

Norman D. Stevens, editor, *Essays for Ralph Shaw* (1975), contains a tribute to Ralph Shaw (Lowell Martin), "Shaw and the Machine" (Theodore C. Hines), and an "Afterword: The Aphorisms of Ralph Shaw."

Mary V. Gaver, "Ralph Shaw at Rutgers," *Wilson Library Bulletin* (February 1973).

Stanley L. West, "Ralph R. Shaw: The Hawaiian Years," *Hawaii Library Association Journal* (December 1973).

Norman D. Stevens, "Shaw, Ralph Robert," *Dictionary of American Library Biography* (1978).

MARY V. GAVER

ALA

Jesse Shera

Shera, Jesse H.
(1903–1982)

Jesse Hauk Shera, U.S. educator, philosopher, and theoretician, considered that perhaps his most significant contribution to librarianship was not a "thing" but a concept—"the concept of librarianship as a totality, a unity in which all the facts are interrelated and interdependent." He consistently held that documentation and information science are an integral part of the totality of librarianship, that librarianship is the generic term, and information science contributes to the theoretical and intellectual base for the librarian's operations. The role of the librarian, he felt, is to act as mediator between users and graphic records, and "the goal of the librarian is to maximize the social utility of graphic records for the benefit of humanity."

Shera was born December 8, 1903, in Oxford, Ohio. He attended William McGuffey High School in Oxford and went on to Miami University, where he earned an A.B. with honors in English (1925). His graduate work at Yale culminated with an A.M. in English Literature (1927). He received a Ph.D. in Library Science from the University of Chicago in 1944.

Initially, Shera wanted to become a professor of English, but signs of the Depression were already visible when he completed his work at Yale. Opportunities to teach—especially English—were diminishing drastically; Shera felt even more restricted because of his somewhat impaired vision. Thus, when Librarian Edgar King offered him a job in Miami University's Library, he took it. Later King urged him to apply to library school. Shera was accepted at Columbia (King's school) in 1928 but instead decided to work as Bibliographer and Research Assistant of the Scripps Foundation for Population Research at Miami, a position he held until 1938.

Shera's glimmer of interest in the sociological aspects of librarianship—reflected in his master's thesis at Yale and subsequent doctoral work at the Graduate School of the University of Chicago from 1938 to 1940—grew more ardent through his association with Warren S. Thompson, Director of the Scripps Foundation, who held a Ph.D. in sociology from Columbia and had already made a name for himself in demography. So without professional training and education, Shera "backed into library work," as he put it.

At Chicago he encountered ideas about the breadth of librarianship that underscored and affirmed his own thinking. GLS offered a philosophical, theoretical, and interdisciplinary approach to library service. Louis Round Wilson, Douglas Waples, Carleton Joeckel, Ralph Beals, and Pierce Butler, to mention only a few, were among the library leaders he met there.

For several years after Shera completed his course work at GLS and before his degree was conferred, he worked in Washington: first as Chief of the Census Library Project at the Library of Congress, 1940–41, later as Deputy Chief, Central Information Division, Research and Analysis Branch, Office of Strategic Services (OSS), 1941–44. His first year in Washington was frustrating because of the lack of a clear charge in his assignment, but the experience at OSS was significant. In addition to supervising a conventional library, picture collection, and "intelligence documents" (reports from various armed services), there was something called "censorship intercepts" (taken from the mail by the Office of Censorship). This amorphous mass of material had to be organized to provide easy access, necessitating experimenting with methods of retrieving information. Having had exposure at Scripps to tabulating machines, punched cards, and the like, Shera utilized these devices for recording, storing, searching, and retrieving information through a system of assigning subject headings (or descriptors). Besides experimenting with these aspects of mechanization, Shera gained valuable experience in administration and an insight into government libraries.

While in Washington, Shera continued to work on his dissertation (which was later published) and solidified his friendship with Ralph Beals—a colleague from GLS who was Assistant Director of the Public Library in Washington, D.C., and who helped strengthen and widen Shera's grasp of librarianship. In March 1944 Beals became Director of the University of Chicago libraries and invited Shera to be Associate Director, first in charge of technical services, then of public services; when Beals was appointed Dean of GLS, he asked Shera to teach on a part-time basis. So Shera found his teaching career—though not in English literature—and in 1947 was appointed to the faculty of GLS on a full-time basis. There he taught courses on academic libraries, administration, cataloguing, American library history, and the theory of classification.

With his colleagues at GLS, he pondered the implications of the new technology on library service but would wait a few years before he did anything more concrete with his ideas than to attend conferences, to organize with Margaret Egan in 1950 a conference on bibliographic organization, and to become a charter member of the revived American Documentation Institute (ADI) early in 1952. Later that year Shera was appointed Dean of Western Reserve's School of Library Science (SLS) in Cleveland.

Shera's deanship was one of the most felicitous and fruitful of appointments, for both the individual and the institution. For Shera, Western Reserve provided a setting where he had strong moral support and had time to write and speak. For Western Reserve, especially the SLS, Shera initiated a new era. Probably Shera's greatest single contribution was the establishment of the Center for Documentation and Communication Research (CDCR), which developed a program of teaching and research in the emerging field of information retrieval. In 1952 Shera and James Perry, then at Battelle Memorial Institute in Columbus, agreed to work jointly in the new field and later proposed an international conference to be sponsored by Battelle and Western Reserve, held at the latter institution. When conditions changed at Battelle and Perry left, Shera persuaded him and his associate, Allen Kent, to join Western Reserve, and the CDCR was established in spring 1955.

The CDCR prospered. A three-day International Conference held in January 1956 and known as the PURK Conference (Practical Utilization of Recorded Knowledge) was a huge success, gathering some 700 attendees who represented business, industry, government, and academe, as well as the library world. This was the first in a series of significant conferences, international and interdisciplinary in their appeal, held in the following decade. Perry designed and constructed at Western Reserve a "searching selector," and early in 1959 the University signed a contract with General Electric to build a high-speed electronic counterpart of it for the CDCR (delivered in 1961). Research contracts were made with various scientific societies and government agencies, notably the American Society for Metals to organize and abstract the literature of metallurgy. With all those successes in various operations, the original purpose of the CDCR to promote research in the development and evaluation of new and unconventional methods in information storage and retrieval was greatly diminished, although the educational program was enriched through new courses and seminars. Perry left Western Reserve in 1960 and Kent in 1962. In 1963 Shera appointed A. J. Goldwyn, a senior member of the CDCR staff, Executive Director, and a reorganization of the work of the Center freed the staff from the burden of operations and made possible the creation of a Comparative Systems Laboratory.

In addition to guiding the work of the CDCR and participating actively in its conferences, Shera continued not only to carry the responsibilities of Dean and administrative head of the SLS but also to teach; to plan and execute the observances in connection with the 50th anniversary of the School in 1954; to participate in professional affairs, including holding important offices and making significant addresses; to serve as Editor of the official journal of ADI (1953–60) and of the Western Reserve Press (1954–59); and to write a monthly column for the *Wilson Library Bulletin* (1961–68). Verner Clapp said, "Shera is too many for us." As Dean, Shera increased the number of full-time faculty and made it possible for graduates holding the Bachelor's in Library Science to earn the Master's through additional study and the writing of a master's paper. He also initiated a doctoral program that strengthened work in library and information science with emphasis on research.

Greatly concerned with the foundations of education for librarianship, he held a series of meetings with the faculty on the philosophy and theory of librarianship. In February 1956 he received funding from the Carnegie Corporation for a three-year study. In 1972 the book resulting from this study was published as *Foundations of Education for Librarianship*. It was delayed because of his many activities and other difficulties, but Shera said, "It is by the quality of the finished study that the wisdom of the original investment will be eventually judged." The book was awarded the Scarecrow Press Award in 1974.

Other activities in which Shera engaged during these years were many and varied. His contribution to the Ohio Library Association, for example, was substantial—helping to avert the closing of the State Library, establishing the Office of Executive Secretary for the Association, and initiating a Library Development Committee.

Shera retired as Dean of what was then the Case Western Reserve University's School of Library Science in June 1970. His first year thereafter was spent teaching in the Graduate Library School of the University of Texas, and the next year he returned to Western Reserve to teach. He continued to teach, both at Western Reserve and at a number of other schools, sometimes for a week or two, sometimes for a quarter or semester. He continued to write—"It gets in your blood," he said—and to take an active part in professional affairs. [For this Encyclopedia, he contributed "Librarianship, Philosophy of," a fixture since the First Edition.] He continued to be in demand as speaker, editor, contributor, and consultant.

Shera became known for his wide range of interests and for his ability to talk with all kinds of people, on all kinds of topics, ranging from football and television to social epistemology and classical music. He won notice for his wit. When Alan Rees told Shera he had been asked to write a personality portrait of him for *Science Information News,* Shera replied, "It seems most appropriate that a publication known as SIN should take some notice of my retirement."

Shera died in Cleveland, Ohio, on March 8, 1982. The Jesse H. Shera Memorial Endowment Fund was established at CWRU to support an assistant professorship in library science education. After the closing of the School in June 1985, the assistant professorship no longer carried library science in its name but rather humanities. Thus Shera's name was perpetuated at CWRU and his broad interests and humanistic concerns recognized.

REFERENCE

The Shera Festschrift, *Toward a Theory of Librarianship: Papers in Honor of Jesse Hauk Shera,* edited by Conrad H. Rawski (1973), provides a bibliography of 381 of Shera's writings compiled through December 1971. Rawski later revised and updated it for publication in the *Encyclopedia of Information and Library Science.*

MARGARET KALTENBACH

Sierra Leone

Sierra Leone, a republic in West Africa, is bounded by Guinea on the north and east, Liberia on the south, and the Atlantic Ocean on the west. Population (1990 est.) 4,151,000; area 71,740 sq.km. The people use various national languages, with Krio as the lingua franca; the official language is English.

The Sierra Leone Library Association

Central Library in Freetown, Sierra Leone, which performs certain national library functions.

National Library. There is no national library in Sierra Leone. In its absence, the Sierra Leone Library Board performs certain national library functions. The Publications Ordinance of 1962 designated the library operated by the Library Board as one of two copyright libraries (the other is Fourah Bay College Library in Freetown, the capital), and it produces an annual list of publications. Though not a national bibliography, since it is not a comprehensive list of titles published in Sierra Leone, the list is useful in providing information mostly on titles published by the Government Printing Office.

The Sierra Leone Government Archives preserves and manages the country's important historical documents. It makes these records accessible to researchers, government officials, and the general public.

Public Library. The Sierra Leone Library Board operates the main public library, founded in 1959. It has a central library in Freetown, three regional branches, and nine sub-branches in various parts of the country. The Library functions as a national library service, providing interlibrary loan and other services. It also offers a wide range of cultural activities, including storytelling and film screenings, especially for children.

Academic Libraries. The principal academic library is the University of Sierra Leone Library. The university was established in 1966, bringing together Fourah Bay College (founded 1827), Njala University College (1964), the College of Medicine and Health Sciences (1988), and two university institutes. Fourah Bay houses the general collections, covering the arts, economic and social studies, engineering, law, and science (110,000 volumes); Njala specializes in agriculture and education (45,000 volumes); Medicine and Health has 2,000 volumes; the Institute of Library and Information Studies, 500 volumes; and the Institute of Public Administration and Management, 2,000 volumes.

School Libraries. The British Council provides books and periodicals through its Book Presentation Program for Secondary Schools. To ensure that materials provided under this program are maintained, the local British Council office encourages the appointment of library assistants who serve as the paraprofessional staff. The Ministry of Education provides the salaries of library assistants who have acquired educational qualification and have participated in one of the University's library training courses.

Many secondary schools place teacher/librarians in charge of their libraries. These are qualified teachers, many of them graduates, who are required to attend short library courses organized annually by the University.

The Sierra Leone School Library Association produced minimum standards for secondary school libraries, which were endorsed and accepted by the National Conference of Principals of Secondary Schools.

Special Libraries. The establishment of special libraries is based on the provision of library facilities in government administrative departments and ministries. After the country's independence in 1961, foreign embassies and other parastatal institutions were established, many of which have libraries or information centers serving their individual needs. There are about 20 special libraries in addition to those in ministries. The British Council Library constitutes one of the largest special libraries in the country in terms of both bookstock and numbers of users. The Library has been a major source of books and materials for other libraries and institutions in all parts of the country.

The Profession. The Institute of Library and Information Studies at the University of Sierra Leone was established in 1989 to provide education and training for librarians, archivists, and information workers at a variety of levels, professional and paraprofessional. It offers Certificates and Diplomas in Library and Information Studies, as well as postgraduate Diplomas and Master's degrees in Library and Information Studies.

Sierra Leone has a number of professional associations, including the Sierra Leone Association of Library and Information Scientists (founded in 1970 as the Sierra Leone Library Association and renamed in 1987) and the Sierra Leone School Library Association (1975). These associations hold workshops, seminars, and conferences to further the general development of libraries in Sierra Leone. The larger association publishes *The Sierra Leone Library Journal* (1974; two issues a year) and a *Directory of Libraries and Information Services in Sierra Leone.*

GLADYS M. JUSU-SHERIFF

Singapore

Singapore, a republic on the southern tip of the Malay Peninsula in Southeast Asia, includes the island of Singapore and 50 islets. Population (1990 est.) 3,003,000; area 618 sq.km. The national language is Malay; official languages include Chinese, English, and Tamil as well as Malay.

History. The earliest records are presumed to have been printed on palm leaf, bark, clay, sandstone, and other such materials, but few examples have survived, the most notable being fragments of the undeciphered *Singapore Stone,* from about the 13th or 14th century and now in the National Museum.

The history of Singapore libraries began soon after the founding of modern Singapore by Sir Stamford Raffles in 1819 as a trading post of the East India Company. In 1823 Raffles founded the Singapore Institution as a school for promising students, with a library open to parents, teachers, and students. It became the forerunner of the Raffles Library, a subscription library that was eventually reconstituted in 1958 as the National and Public Library of Singapore. The earliest special library was that of the Botanic Gardens, founded in 1859. The earliest academic libraries were those of the King Edward VII Medical College (founded in 1905) and Raffles College (founded in 1928), which later formed part of the University of Malaya (founded in 1949).

The greatest incentive to the development of all types of libraries was the attainment of internal self-government in 1959, followed by incorporation in Malaysia in 1963 and full independence in 1965. With the expansion of primary, secondary, and tertiary education since 1959, the literacy rate increased from about 50 percent in 1957 to 87.2 percent by 1988. Existing libraries were expanded and new libraries set up to meet educational, informational, and cultural needs.

National Library. The National Library of Singapore was established in 1958 following the passage of the Raffles Library Ordinance of 1957 under which the Raffles Library, a subscription library, became a public and national library. It was called the Raffles National Library until 1960. The National Library inherited the legal deposit functions that had been in force since 1886 as well as archival functions that had been added in 1938. With the National Archives and Records Center Act of 1967, the archives were separated from the Library and administered as a separate department but continued to be housed in the National Library until 1970 and headed by the same Director until 1978. The National Library provides reference services, interlibrary loans and exchanges, reprographic services, and bibliographic services, including the compilation of the national bibliography, periodicals index, and various union catalogues. Its research collection on Southeast Asia is open to local and overseas scholars and researchers.

The National Library is the central agency for

Libraries in Singapore (1989)

Type of library	Number of administrative units (main libraries)	Number of service points (branches, mobile stops, etc.)	Volumes in collections	Annual expenditures (Singapore dollars)	Population served	Professional staff (with certificate, diploma, etc.)	Total staff
National and Public	1	15	2,379,657	15,220,425	2,647,100[a]	95	385[b]
Academic	6	18	2,127,085	21,105,527[c]	71,659	106	404
School	373	373	4,688,146	4,924,372[d]	458,862	16	2,686
Special	84	91	13,164,672[e]	4,615,970[f]	235,832[g]	82	408

[a]1988 data
[b]March 1990 data
[c]No expense data available for 1 academic library. All libraries exclude personnel expenses
[d]1988 expense data given. All school data were obtained from the School Library Unit, Ministry of Education
[e]No data available for 2 special libraries
[f]No data available for 19 special libraries
[g]No data available for 1 special library

National Library of Singapore

National Library of Singapore, established in 1958.

the Singapore Integrated Library Automation Service (SILAS), a national bibliographic network with a union catalogue for its participating libraries. Its collection totaled almost 2,370,000 volumes in Malay, Chinese, Tamil, and English in 1990, plus nearly 190,000 items of special materials, including sheet music and scores, microforms, films, slides, tapes, and sound and video recordings.

Academic Libraries. The University of Singapore was founded in 1949 as the University of Malaya, incorporating the former King Edward VII Medical College (1905) and Raffles College (1928). Nanyang University (1956), founded as a Chinese-language institution, gradually included English as the medium of instruction for some courses. Its policy of having first-year students undergo courses jointly with University of Singapore students at the Bukit Timah campus took effect in 1978. In 1980 the two universities were merged to form the National University of Singapore (NUS). The NUS Library has more than 1,500,000 volumes in six constituent libraries—the Main Library; Chinese Library; Hon Sui Sen Memorial Library; Law Library and Science Library at the Kent Ridge Campus; and Medical Library in the Faculty of Medicine building at Sepoy Lines.

The Nanyang Technological University (1991) was founded as a technological institute in 1981. Its Library has more than 150,000 volumes and 2,000 other items. Other academic institutions with libraries include the Singapore Polytechnic, the Ngee Ann Polytechnic, the Institute of Education, and the private Trinity Theological College.

Public Libraries. The National Library operates the public library system, which includes a central library, eight full-time branches, and six bookmobile points. Loan services are fully computerized. Loans of books and periodicals totaled more than 9,000,000 in 1989, including bulk loans to social welfare homes, community centers, and other agencies. The total number of registered users in 1989 was estimated at 23.9 percent of the total population. Adults formed the largest group, with 39 percent of total membership, followed by young people (aged 12 to 19 years), with 34 percent, and children under 12 (27 percent).

School Libraries. All primary and secondary schools, including 14 junior colleges (offering two years of preuniversity education) and two centralized institutes (three years of preuniversity education), have centralized libraries. Some also have classroom libraries. All new schools are equipped with libraries, including furniture, equipment, and initial bookstock. School libraries are also developing into resource centers with audiovisual resources and facilities as well as printed materials. An Instructional Materials Library provides additional audiovisual resources on loan to schools. School library development is handicapped by the lack of trained staff.

Special Libraries. There are 34 special libraries attached to government departments, including 17 staffed by professionals and a few others with subprofessional staff. Most serve only the staffs of their agencies, but the Department of Statistics Library is open to the public. In addition there are 21 libraries of statutory bodies, including the Institute of Southeast Asian Studies, most with professional staffs. There are 29 libraries attached to such foreign agencies as the American Resource Center, the British Council, the Goethe Institute, and banks, newspapers, and other firms in the private sector.

The Profession. Professional librarianship began in Singapore after World War II. The Malayan Library Group was founded in 1955 and succeeded by the Library Association of Singapore (LAS). At that time, there were only about a half dozen qualified librarians in Singapore, most of them expatriates from Britain, Australia and New Zealand, working mainly at the University of Malaya Library. By 1990 the LAS had 169 qualified librarians out of a total of 256 members, most of them Singapore citizens. Most of them have also been trained abroad, in Australia, Britain, Canada, New Zealand, and the United States. The largest number are employed by the government.

Singapore lacks a library school. The continued shortage of librarians led the National Library and the LAS in 1982 to provide a basic part-time Postgraduate Course in Library and Information Science. They also organize continuing education courses.

The LAS publishes *Singapore Libraries,* its annual official journal, as well as a quarterly *Newsletter,* a *Directory of Libraries in Singapore* (latest edition, 1989), and other occasional publications such as conference proceedings. The Association works closely with the PPM (Library Association of Malaysia), with which it shares a common origin in the Malayan Library Group. Cooperation is fostered through a joint liaison council of the two associations as well as work in various bibliographical and other projects. The LAS and the PPM were also joint sponsors of the Congress of Southeast Asian Librarians (CONSAL).

HEDWIG ANUAR

National Library of Singapore

Arts Resource Center, Reference Services Division, National Library of Singapore.

Solomon Islands

A scattered Melanesian archipelago east of Papua New Guinea in the southwestern Pacific Ocean, the Solomon Islands gained independence from Britain in 1978. Population (1990 est.) 321,000; area 28,896 sq.km. Honiara, on the island of Guadalcanal, is the capital. The people use some 80 languages; while pidgin English is of considerable importance, standard English is the official language.

History. The British set up the British Solomon Islands Protectorate in 1893. Some books were available at District Commissioners' offices, and this scheme was expanded after 1958. A Solomon Islands Public Library was established at Honiara in 1968 and renamed the Honiara Public Library when the town council took responsibility for it in 1973. The National Library Service was established in 1974.

National Library Service. Pioneers of the National Library Service were Sally Edridge and Sidney Hockey, expatriate library advisors; local personnel have continued their work. The Service has focused on library development and service to schools. It has linked library development to government policy and has succeeded in supplying books to schools despite limited resources and in establishing provincial and community libraries. Aid schemes and book donations have been important sources of materials, and volunteer personnel have been active in library development.

Academic Libraries. The Solomon Islands College of Higher Education (1983) brings several distributed service points together in a unified system with a Headquarters Library at Panatina Campus. The Library has the best resources in the country, including an Audio-Visual Resource Center. The Extension Center of the University of the South Pacific, at Honiara, has another important academic library.

Public Libraries. With the support of the National Library Service, public libraries have spread beyond Honiara to seven provinces. These small units, despite many problems, are interesting examples of a partnership between central and provincial authorities. Provincial libraries have small standard buildings and contain at most 4,000 volumes each. The country has more than a dozen community libraries, very small but in remote locations, and their number is growing.

School Libraries. There are 22 secondary schools with basic library facilities, all supported by the Schools Library Service. There is little documentation on the situation in these libraries and less on the situation in the primary schools.

Special Libraries include those at the Forum Fisheries Agency and the Dodo Creek Research Station at Honiara. As the country develops, its special libraries will grow as well.

The Profession. Libraries and librarianship are new to the Solomon Islands; the first national received training in the 1960s. Library training in the country is dependent on courses provided in Papua New Guinea and extension courses at the University of the South Pacific. A core group of young local professionals was emerging in the early 1990s.

REFERENCES

John Evans, "Development of Rural Libraries in the Solomon Islands," *International Library and Information Review* (1992).

Peter Williams, "Library Training in the Solomon Islands," *Focus on International and Comparative Librarianship* (1992).

JOHN EVANS

Somalia

Somalia is a republic on the Horn of Africa. It lies in the northeastern corner of Africa, bounded by the Gulf of Aden on the north, the Indian Ocean on the east, and Kenya, Ethiopia, and Djibouti on the west. It has the longest coastline in Africa, 3,000 km. Population (1990 est.) 7,497,000; area 637,657 sq.km. The official languages are Somali and Arabic, but English and Italian are also used in communication.

History. British and Italian authorities governed northern and southern Somaliland until 1960, when the two colonies united as the Somali Republic. A dictator ruled the country from 1969 to 1990, when warring factions began a fierce civil war that left thousands to die of starvation. The UN intervened in 1992 and worked to establish a stable government.

Somali became a written language only in 1972, and written Somali literature is not yet abundant, in spite of the language's rich cultural past. Also, book

Libraries in Solomon Islands (1990)

Type of library	Number of administrative units (main libraries)	Number of service points (branches, mobile stops, etc.)	Volumes in collections	Annual expenditures (SI dollar)	Population served	Professional staff (with certificate, diploma, etc.)
National	1	(support public & school libraries)	20,000	12,000		5
Academic	3	5	43,500	72,000	4,100	8
Public	8	+	--	--	--	--
School	22*	22	--	--	--	--
Special (major)	2	2**	22,000(approx)	$127,000*** (one library only)	399 (approx)	3

+There are also more than 12 community libraries
*Secondary schools
**Within S. Islands
***CAN $; one library only

Libraries in Somalia (1990)

Type of library	Number of administrative units (main libraries)	Number of service points (branches, mobile stops, etc.)	Volumes in collections	Population served
Academic*	1	3	40,000	1,162

*1983 data

Source: Unesco, *Statistical Yearbook,* 1991.

development is of comparatively recent origin, and adequate printing and production facilities had yet to be organized in the early 1990s.

Library facilities in Somalia are in an early stage of development. Formal education and literacy training did not receive much attention in colonial times, and reading has been of little interest to the 80 percent of the population who are nomads. The lack of qualified staff is a serious barrier to the systematic organization of libraries. The importance of library and information services for supporting national development programs is recognized. Many government departments and agencies worked to set up library and documentation centers with the help of international organizations such as Unesco, the World Health Organization, and the World Bank. Other countries, among them the United States, Germany, Italy, and India, provided technical assistance in the field of librarianship and documentation.

There were no public libraries in the early 1990s; at the most there were a few reading rooms in some regions of the country.

National Library Services. Plans for a national library were begun in 1976 on the initiative provided by Unesco. Proposals were made from time to time to construct a permanent building. The National Library holdings comprised only a few thousand items in the early 1990s. Under library legislation of 1976, the Ministry of Higher Education and Culture was given responsibility for library development. In spite of the enactment of library legislation and formulation of guidelines for evolving a national library system, there was no strong commitment on the part of the country to undertake development of libraries. Under a five-year development plan (1982–86), a permanent building for a National Library was under construction; it was badly damaged during the civil war.

Academic Libraries. Before the civil war, the university library system under the Somali National University consisted of a central library and seven faculty libraries. The central library, organized largely with Italian technical assistance, had a collection of about 28,000 volumes. Among the faculty libraries, the library of the College of Education had good facilities and resources, a result of Indian technical assistance and U.S. AID assistance to the college. The Library of the College of Education had 37,500 volumes, and it included textbooks in multiple copies. The library of the Faculty of Medicine had 6,000 volumes. The library of the Faculty of Agriculture was also fairly well equipped. Little is known of the conditions of these libraries since the civil war.

School Libraries. School libraries hardly exist. The Women's Education School Library had a collection of 3,000 volumes set up with UN assistance. The library of the American School had excellent facilities, but it is not a Somali institution.

Special Libraries. A few government agencies and ministries had libraries. The Documentation Center of the Ministry of National Planning, formerly the State Planning Commission, was developed in 1976 as a UN Development Program/Unesco project. It was the only documentation center well established and organized to meet the documentation and information needs of the country. It served the needs of development planners, consultants, missions, ministry staff, and students and faculty of the National Institute of Statistics and Applied Economics, run by the Ministry of National Planning. The center was recognized by the Pan-African Documentation and Information System (PADIS) as a National Information and Documentation Center.

The Somali Institute for Development Administration and Management, a UN and World Bank project, had a fairly well established library. The Ministry of Foreign Affairs had good physical facilities but lacked qualified staff. The Ministry of Industry developed a technical library in 1983 with the assistance of a United Nations Volunteer (UNV) Librarian.

The reading public used the libraries of foreign missions such as those of the U.S., Italy, France, and India. The Library of the United Nations Development Program had a collection of publications on international organizations. The active role of UN Volunteer programs and bilateral assistance in the field of librarianship led to establishment of several ministry and agency libraries in the country.

The Profession. Efforts were made in the early 1980s to establish a library association and a training center to meet the immediate problems of staffing. Under UN and Unesco auspices a few short-term training programs were conducted in 1979 and in 1980 and 1982. In-service training was conducted regularly, but there remained a pressing demand for regular training, especially for middle-level staff.

G. THIMME GOWDA

South Africa

South Africa is a republic on the southern tip of Africa. It lies between the Atlantic and Indian oceans; Namibia, Botswana, and Zimbabwe lie to the north, and Mozambique and Swaziland lie to the northeast. Population (1990 est.) 35,282,000; area 1,221,037 sq.km. The official languages are Afrikaans and

English; nine or more major indigenous African languages are spoken.

History. Libraries in South Africa have been in existence since the second half of the 18th century. The history of libraries throughout the 18th and 19th centuries is largely that of public libraries. In 1818 the South African Library, now a national library, was founded as one of the world's first free tax-supported libraries. Eight South African university libraries and more than 70 subscription libraries were established in the 19th century, as well as a number of school libraries, the latter mostly in the Cape Colony, and six major special libraries.

The modern library movement in South Africa effectively dates from 1928, following the visit of two Carnegie Corporation commissioners, Milton Ferguson (State Librarian of California) and Septimus A. Pitt (City Librarian of Glasgow); the first national conference on library affairs was held that year. It was followed in 1930 by the establishment of the South African Library Association and in 1937 by the Report of the Government's Interdepartmental Committee on the Libraries of the Union of South Africa.

Rural library services were developed in the 1940s following the establishment of provincial library services in each of the four provinces. After World War II there was considerable growth in university libraries, school libraries, and special libraries and information centers. In 1983 the South African Bibliographic and Information Network (SABINET) launched its computerized bibliographic database, created because librarians became increasingly aware that no single library or information service had the resources to cope adequately with the dramatic escalation of information sources for its members. Librarians can discover from their own terminals whether new acquisitions have catalogue entries in the database.

Until 1990 the government rigidly enforced a policy of *apartheid* (racial separation), designating non-whites as Black, Coloured, or Indian. In that year the government scrapped the Separate Amenities Act, ending apartheid in all public services, including public libraries. The 1990 *Directory of Southern African Libraries* listed 1,836 libraries. Prior to 1990 a few were open to all people, regardless of race, but most were closed to blacks.

National Libraries. South Africa has three national libraries: the South African Library (Cape Town), the State Library (Pretoria), and the National Library for the Blind (Grahamstown). The South African Library and the State Library have deposit privileges, as do the Library of Parliament (Cape Town), the Natal Society Library (Pietermaritzburg), and the Bloemfontein Public Library.

South African Library

South African Library, Capetown, established in 1818.

The South African Library, founded in 1818, is the national center for collecting and preserving legal deposit material, as well as rare or unique material, and is the national center for compiling retrospective bibliographies and indexes of Southern African materials. It established a Center for the Book in 1990 to stimulate interest in the book and reading and to provide a forum for publishers, booksellers, and libraries.

The State Library, founded in 1887, is responsible for coordinating the national bookstock, exchange programs with other countries, interlibrary loans, redistributing surplus materials, and compiling the *South African National Bibliography*. It coordinates the exchange of bibliographic records and national and international bibliographic standards.

The South African Library for the Blind was founded in 1919 and became a national library for the print handicapped in 1969. It produces and provides books in braille and on tape and offers a service for blind students throughout the country.

Academic Libraries. Library services to academic staff and students are provided at all 22 universities and nine technikons in South Africa. The university libraries vary enormously in size between the older and newer universities and between universities traditionally white and traditionally black (although formal restrictions based on race were lifted in 1986). The older university libraries house important research and special collections, such as the Africana collections at the University of Natal, the University

Libraries in South Africa (1990)

Type of library	Number of administrative units (main libraries)	Number of service points (branches, mobile stops, etc.)	Volumes in collections	Annual expenditures (rand)	Professional staff (with certificate, diploma, etc.)	Total staff
National	2	5	1,376,943	5,834,000	79	253
Academic	84	166	7,513,127	20,051,000	801	1,827
Public	675	1,858	32,027,345	122,777,000	1,063	4,122
Special	381	657	3,646,782	26,978,000	560	1,484
Government	91	112	1,494,497	5,666,000	228	348

of the Witwatersrand, the University of Stellenbosch, Rhodes University, and the University of the Orange Free State. Because of their resources, the university libraries are major links in the interlibrary loan system.

The Inter-University Library Committee coordinates the services of university libraries, addressing such issues as finance, collection development, document delivery, and bibliographic aids. It works to promote the efficiency and effectiveness of services at university libraries and advises the Committee of University Principals on improving library services.

Public Libraries. The South African public library system is organized according to two parameters: the size of the community and its racial composition. Outside the main urban centers, library services for whites, Indians, and Coloureds are provided by provincial library services in the four provinces, working with the local authorities.

A local authority can establish and run a public library as part of a provincial library service as long as it provides the building and appoints and pays the staff. The provincial library service then provides a stock of materials, including books, periodicals, art prints, films, and audio media; processing services; centralized reference services; professional guidance and technical assistance; financial assistance; and staff training courses. The provincial library services bind isolated public libraries into a strong network, enabling the smallest rural community to gain access to the stock of materials of the country as a whole.

Three provinces stipulate the sizes of towns eligible to affiliate with provincial library services. The Cape Province limits affiliation to towns with white populations below 25,000; Natal sets the limit at 10,000; and the Transvaal, 50,000. (The fourth province, the Orange Free State, sets no limit.) As a result of the limit, the city libraries of Cape Town, East London, and Port Elizabeth do not form part of the provincial system. Cape Town City Library has a membership of 210,000 and 31 branch libraries; East London almost 45,000 members and eight branch libraries; and Port Elizabeth more than 96,000 members and 11 branch libraries.

The black population's library facilities are the responsibility of the black local authorities; depending on whether they are in urban areas, they may affiliate with their provincial library services. Black library services are notoriously impoverished, with inadequate buildings, poorly qualified staff, and a policy of book selection that pays little attention to the readers' interests.

All the larger cities have free, tax-supported public libraries. Some are quite highly developed, such as the Johannesburg Public Library, with a central reference library and suburban branch libraries and important subject libraries for Africana, art, music, and local government. One of the largest and most important public libraries, it pioneered in opening its doors to people of all races.

School Libraries. Schools fall under the jurisdiction of different authorities, depending on whether they serve white, Coloured, Indian, or black children. Educational authorities since 1950 have been aware of the impact of school libraries on education. Because of the government's racial policies, school libraries have developed in an uncoordinated manner.

Schools for whites are controlled by the Department of National Education but administered by provincial education departments. The Cape and Transvaal have well-equipped school libraries; Natal and Orange Free State school library services are less developed. Schools for Coloureds and Indians are run by the Department of Education and Culture; those for Coloureds follow the Cape and Transvaal models; those for Indians follow the pattern of Transvaal provincial schools. Schools for blacks are administered by the Department of Education and Training, and their libraries lag far behind those in other schools.

An independent nonprofit organization, READ (Read, Educate, and Develop), was established in the private sector in 1979 to improve the quality of education and to remove barriers based on race, socio-economic, and sex differentiation. READ plays an important role in providing school libraries for blacks in all parts of the country. It selects core books for libraries and supplies them fully catalogued and ready to put on the shelves. It also develops and tests educational materials that address the specific reading-related needs of the communities in which it operates. READ sponsors various activities, such as festivals of books, poetry readings, and storytelling, to promote reading and the use of books.

Special Libraries. South Africa boasts a plethora of special libraries in both the private and public sectors. Major research organizations such as the Atomic Energy Corporation, Council for Scientific and Industrial Research (CSIR), Council for Mineral Technology, Human Science Research Council (HSRC), and Medical Research Council (MRC), as well as large industrial corporations such as the African Explosives and Chemical Industries (AECI), Anglo-American Corporation, and Iron and Steel Corporation (ISCOR) have large special libraries and information centers. The central government has more than 200 special libraries coordinated by the Division of Library Services of the Department of National Education. Museums, semi-governmental industrial organizations, private industry, and private professional research bodies have special libraries. The majority of special libraries in South Africa are located in the Pretoria-Witwatersrand-Vaal Triangle area.

The Profession. The South African Institute for Librarianship and Information Science (SAILIS) was founded in 1979 as a professional body with membership open to all qualified librarians and information scientists, regardless of race. In 1990, it opened its membership to all who work in libraries and information services. By 1990 it had a total membership of almost 2,750. SAILIS replaced the South African Library Association (SALA), founded in 1930, which the government made an all-white organization in 1962 in keeping with its apartheid policies. SAILIS works to safeguard and advance the interests of its members; promotes scholarly exchange of information, professional training, and an ethical code for librarians and information scientists; publicizes the importance of libraries to the public; and produces a quarterly journal, the *South African Journal of Library and Information Science,* and a monthly newsletter.

The African Library Association of South Africa (ALASA) was formed in 1964 for black library workers, most of them untrained. It works to promote reading among blacks and to promote libraries in predominantly black residential areas. It is affiliated with SAILIS.

Library and information science is a well-established discipline in South African higher education. It is offered as a subject in 14 universities and four technikons. Courses lead to the Diploma in Librarianship, the Diploma in School Librarianship (paraprofessional qualification), the post-graduate Higher Diploma in Librarianship, and Bachelor's, Honours, Master's, and Doctoral degrees.

SETH MANAKA

Spain

Spain, a monarchy in southwestern Europe, is bordered by the Bay of Biscay, France, and Andorra on the north, the Mediterranean Sea on the east and southeast, the Atlantic Ocean on the northwest and southwest, and Portugal on the west. Its territory includes the Balearic Islands (off the east coast) and the Canary Islands (off the west). Population (1990 est.) 38,959,000; area 504,782 sq. km. The official language is Spanish.

History. The first Spanish libraries were those of Visigoth Spain (5th–8th centuries), the best known of which was that of the Sevillian archbishops San Leandro and San Isidoro. In his book *Etimologías* ("Etymologies"), San Isidoro devoted a section to books and libraries. During the High Middle Ages, libraries, most of them with few books, were found predominantly in monasteries, although in Córdoba in Muslim Spain the Caliph al-Hakem II maintained a collection of 400,000 volumes. In the Late Middle Ages, the best libraries were found in universities, especially the University of Salamanca, where King Alfonso the Wise, who had established a large private library, provided library and research services. In the 16th century Cardinal Cisneros, after creating the University of Alcalá de Henares, provided the university with an important library; in Seville, Fernando Colón, son of Christopher Columbus, willed his library, the Biblioteca Colombina, to the city's cathedral; and King Felipe II founded his famous library in the Escorial.

The National Library of Spain was founded in Madrid in 1712 by Felipe V as a public library; it belonged to the Crown until 1836, when it was nationalized and became a governmental unit. In 1896 it was moved to a beautiful and centrally located building covering some 40,000 square meters. In 1856 the School of Diplomacy was founded for training those with responsibility for the state libraries and archives; and in 1858 the Faculty of Archivists and Librarians was established, which still maintains responsibility for this area.

The General Board of Archivists and Librarians was created in the Ministry of Education in 1939, but dissolved in 1972. Archives now belong to the General Board of Fine Arts and Archives, while libraries are under the General Board of Books and Libraries; both report to the Ministry of Culture. The General Board of Books and Libraries has administrative responsibility for the National Library, the Copyright Office, the International Exchange Center, and the National Documentary and Bibliographic Treasury, which inventories the collections and assures that materials are purchased as they appear on the market. The Hispanic Bibliographic Center oversees legal deposit and prepares the Spanish national bibliography. The Center for Bibliographic and Documentary Studies is primarily a center for training professionals. Provincial public libraries also report to the General Board of Books and Libraries, as did the public libraries associated with the National Reading Center until the approval of the new constitution in 1978. Those libraries, along with the 48 Provincial Coordinating Centers for Libraries and other governmental agencies, have been transferred to the 17 autonomous governments in the country.

National Library. The National Library of Spain contains the largest and richest collection in the country and provides the greatest number of services. It specializes in the humanities, most notably in Spanish culture. The Manuscript Section possesses more than 2,000 medieval codices, some of them dating from the 10th century. In addition to the many Latin and Castillian codices, there are also many excellent ones in Greek, Arabic, and Hebrew. Two outstanding collections include codices adorned with miniature paintings, as well as manuscripts of Spanish comedies of the Golden Age (16th–17th centuries), including original manuscripts of great dramatists such as Lope de Vega and Calderón de la Barca. The Cervantes Collection contains 14,000 books and 3,000 pamphlets. The Incunabula and Rare Books Section maintains a collection of more than 2,900 incunabula and 40,000 valuable, rare, and unique items. The African Section is important for its holdings on the modern history of North Africa. The Prints and Fine Arts Section features 200,000 prints and engravings and 14,000 drawings of special interest because of their themes or their artists: Dürer, Velásquez, Rubens,

Libraries in Spain (1990)

Type of library	Number of administrative units (main libraries)	Number of service points (branches, mobile stops, etc.)	Volumes in collections	Professional staff (with certificate, diploma, etc.)	Total staff
National	1	2	3,039,271	271	694
Academic	567	1,028	15,182,738	1,020	3,390
Public	3,285	3,635	26,381,507	755	7,289
Special	1,196	1,375	15,694,423	615	3,193
Other	13	19	634,337	22	149

Biblioteca del Palacio

Library of the National Palace, where 300,000 volumes, including manuscripts and incunabula, are preserved.

Titian, Rembrandt, and Goya. The Music Section holds 100,000 musical scores and 170,000 records and cassettes; the Map Section, 100,000 maps and plans; and the Periodicals Section, 30,000 titles, of which about 15,000 are currently published.

In all, the National Library possesses more than 3,000,000 volumes. Each year a half million readers utilize more than a million works. More than 130,000 items are loaned annually, and the library's laboratories produce 1,300,000 photocopies and 400,000 microfilms for its readers. Half of the works acquired come in through legal deposit, an advantage the National Library has had since its creation.

Academic Libraries. Great differences exist among Spanish academic libraries in collections, annual acquisitions, financial resources, personnel, and services. The libraries of the country's 30 universities occupy a special place among academic libraries. Although each library is considered a unit in its university and has a director, in reality the libraries are fragmented into school and departmental libraries; some serve professors exclusively. Even the libraries at the school level are more oriented to meeting the needs of the teachers than the interests of students, who usually lack places for study. Personnel are scarce in all these libraries, although the number has grown in recent years. Of special interest are the libraries of the Complutense in Madrid, with more than 700,000 volumes, the Central University in Barcelona, and the universities in Valencia, Zaragoza, Vallodolid, and Salamanca. Vallodolid and Salamanca, established in the 13th century, are notable not only for the number of books acquired annually but also for the richness of their historical collections, including valuable medieval manuscripts and incunabula.

Public Libraries. Public libraries are organized into systems called Provincial Coordinating Library Centers, with a central library in the capital of the province and branch libraries in other towns. The centers are regulated by boards of trustees and are supported by donations from three sources: the autonomous government, the provincial government, and the municipality. It was difficult in the late 1980s to obtain reliable data from the autonomous governments concerning the 48 provinces that have Library Centers, but in 1977, according to information provided by the General Board of Books and Libraries, there were 1,245 libraries containing a total of 6,500,000 volumes, with 13,000,000 readers using 18,300,000 volumes. The provincial governments of Navarra and Barcelona maintain their own systems; Barcelona's is the more important. The central library contains more than 500,000 books, and its network of 75 branch libraries serves both the neighborhoods of Barcelona and the other towns in the province. In addition to the independent municipal libraries, there are networks of public libraries in a number of provinces supported by savings banks, the most notable of which is the library network of the Old Age and Savings Fund of Catalonia.

School Libraries. There are no school libraries in Spain worthy of the name, although in the Centers for Basic General Education and in the Spanish equivalents of American high schools some collections of books are sufficiently strong to qualify as libraries. The reason is simply that as of the late 1980s there were no standards to govern their operations, nor were there personnel or financial resources. The books that make up these collections consist of occasional gifts from the Ministry of Education.

Special Libraries. The libraries that support research in government offices and private firms are many and diverse. One of the most important special libraries is the consortium of the Superior Council of Scientific Research, with a total of 1,500,000 volumes distributed across two general libraries and 50 others that serve specialized centers in various fields of the sciences, technology, and humanities.

In the field of the humanities, the National Palace Library is especially notable, containing more than 300,000 volumes, among them valuable manuscripts, incunabula, and collections of fine bindings and drawings. Equally important are the libraries of the Royal Academies, especially the History Library, which contains 200,000 volumes and a large collection of historical manuscripts, and the Language Library, with 80,000 volumes. The Military Center Library has a collection of 300,000 specialized works on Spanish history. The libraries of the Church, especially the cathedral libraries, are particularly rich, although specific information on such libraries is scarce.

The Profession. Since the early years of the 20th century, library education has taken place at the University of Madrid, which assumed instructional responsibilities when the School of Diplomacy closed in 1900. Instruction was later offered in other universities. In 1915 the School of Librarians of Barcelona was established; it has been incorporated into the main university of that city. Professional education is also offered at the University of Granada and at the School of Bibliographic and Documentary Studies in Madrid; the latter is a continuation of the courses begun in 1952 by the General Board of Archives and Libraries.

A professional association for archivists, librarians, and museum curators (ANABA) was founded in 1949. New statutes provide memberships for documentalists and accordingly revise the name to Asociación des Archiveros, Bibliotecarios, Conservadores de Museos y Documentalistas (ANABAD). The Association organizes conventions and working meetings and publishes some books and a bulletin. It had about 1,500 members in the late 1980s.

REFERENCES
Hipólito Escolar Sobrino, *Historia del Libro* (1984).
Escolar Sobrino, *Historia de las Bibliotecas* (1985).

HIPOLITO ESCOLAR-SOBRINO;
translated by EDWIN S. GLEAVES

Special Libraries

PURPOSES AND OBJECTIVES

Information service is the raison d'être of special libraries. While other types of libraries may encompass multiple objectives—education, recreation, aesthetic appreciation, and scholarly research—the major, and usually only, objective of a special library is to provide information in support of the objectives of its parent organization. In 1916 John A. Lapp, a pioneer special librarian, wrote that "Undoubtedly one of the greatest problems of the time is to put the knowledge which we possess at work." From Lapp's statement came the motto of the Special Libraries Association (SLA), "Putting Knowledge to Work," a phrase that succinctly describes the purpose and objectives of the special library. SLA reaffirmed this purpose in 1989 in its strategic plan, which defines a special library as "an organization that provides focused, working information to a special clientele on an ongoing basis to further the mission and goals of the parent company/organization."

A special library may have its own goals and objectives regarding the resources and services needed or desired to serve its clientele, but these goals are internal to the library. The parent organization usually has little interest in library service as an end in itself; rather, it is interested in the library and supports it as the means of getting the information it needs. If the special library is to exist, it must provide information more efficiently and economically than could be provided by alternate methods, and it must continually demonstrate to the management of its parent organization that it is doing so. If it does not accomplish this goal, it will not thrive; it may even cease to exist. The ultimate decision as to the practicability, efficiency, and value of the special library and the resources that will be allocated to it is made by the parent organization. Such a decision is not based on how well the library is meeting its own goals; it is based on how well the library is providing needed information service.

Special libraries exist in a wide variety of organizational settings. They are units of larger organizations whose purposes are usually other than the provision of education or library service. Special libraries are found in private business and industrial organizations such as banks, insurance companies, advertising agencies, public utilities, publishers, chemical and pharmaceutical manufacturers, petroleum producers, engineering firms, and the aerospace and automotive industries, to name a few. Others serve government agencies at every level, national, regional, or municipal. A significant number of special libraries are in nonprofit institutions such as hospitals and health agencies, social and welfare organizations, and museums, or are parts of trade and professional associations and societies.

Special libraries are often described (and usually associated or organized) along subject lines because they are limited in scope and oriented to a single subject or, more often, a group of related subjects that comprise a field of activity. Their scope is determined by the interests of their parent organizations. The library collects and organizes intensively in its primary subject areas, often at a depth impossible for other types of libraries. While the special library may collect some information peripheral to its primary interests, it depends on resources outside the library and parent organization for material that is little used or out of scope.

Most special libraries serve a limited and well-defined clientele. Most frequently, the special library's clientele is limited to its parent organization, and may range from the personnel of a single department to employees throughout the organization, sometimes to employees in other geographic locations. When the clientele is limited to a particular organization, special libraries often develop close working relationships with their users and are able to identify, not only on an organizational basis but also on an individual basis, the type of information needed and how it should be delivered. Thus services can be closely tailored to fit the needs and working habits of the users. Some special libraries, such as those maintained by societies and associations, consider the group's membership or anyone with a serious interest in the subject as their clientele. Most special libraries admit outsiders who have a need to use their resources, although such access is usually within the constraints of organizational and library policy and confidentiality of unpublished or internal materials in the collection.

The special librarian is viewed by some as a distinguishing characteristic of the special library, on

Columbia University

Library of the Milwaukee Journal, *1923.*

National Association of Realtors

Library of the National Association of Realtors, Chicago, Illinois.

the grounds that the special librarian's active role in information service is the main working asset of the library. The special librarian serves as a specialist in the literature of the subject, bringing to the organization professional expertise in identifying, acquiring, organizing, evaluating, and interpreting information. Without the expertise of the special librarian, the organization might have a library, but it would not have information service.

Another characteristic of special libraries that adds to the frame of reference in discussing their nature is size. Some special libraries have scores of employees and hundreds of thousands of volumes in their collections, but most are small in staff, space occupied, and size of collection. More than half of all special libraries are estimated to be one- or two-person operations.

Problems of Definition. The precise definition of special library is one of the unresolved issues of librarianship. The literature is littered with definitions ranging from those based on the logic that the term fits all libraries that are specialized in some way (clientele, collection, form, ownership, or purpose) and therefore may include all libraries, through definitions based on the presence of a combination of characteristics (special collection, special form, and/or ownership), to definitions that attempt a pragmatic, discrete delineation of a type of library. Even within a relatively narrow definition of the special library as distinct from a public, academic, or school library, special libraries display such diversity and individuality that descriptions of characteristics and activities must be broad rather than specific.

Another issues arises with nomenclature. While many special libraries use the word "library," others use "information center" or "information service" to identify the unit's purpose more clearly or to avoid what some regard as a passive connotation of the word "library." In Europe the preferred term has been "documentation center," and the professional staff are called "documentalists." In theory, "information center" indicates a greater range and depth of services and more advanced technology, but in practice one organization's library may be more sophisticated than another's information center. Whatever the parent organization calls its information unit, it is likely to add a modifier to the name to clarify the unit's scope or its primary clientele: "technical library," "business information center," and "research information service" are typical examples.

U.S. Growth. Special libraries first began to appear in significant numbers in the United States in the first decades of the 20th century. They were a new form of library, sharply differentiated from the mainstream of American librarianship at that time in their singleness of purpose and in their departure from traditional methods of collecting and organizing materials. The early special libraries were largely isolated from each other and invisible to the library community until the founding of the SLA in 1909. SLA provided a focal point for the emerging special libraries and their leadership as the modern special library movement gained momentum.

Vast changes had begun to take place in American business and industry in the late 19th century. Organizations increased in size and complexity as business and industry evolved from smaller enterprises into larger corporations. Governmental units proliferated and increased in size and jurisdiction. In business and industry, interest in efficiency and scientific management developed. In government there was a strong move toward legislative and social reform. Professional and trade associations and societies with strong interests in standards and education were formed. All of these interests required information to support their activities. An entirely new business and technical literature, much of it in nontraditional and ephemeral formats, began to develop along with increases in collecting and publishing statistics, issuing government regulations, publishing financial reports, and disseminating business records.

Legislative reference libraries serving state and municipal governments were among the earliest modern special libraries, becoming models for intensive or "amplified" reference service. Special libraries in business and financial organizations next emerged to "manage" business and financial material and also developed high levels of information service for a clientele relatively unfamiliar with literature-based research.

The exigencies of World Wars I and II and the "information explosion" of the post-World War II years contributed to the continuation of an environment hospitable to special libraries. Each war stimulated an expansion in scientific and technical research; research and development became increasingly institutionalized; and the number and size of research departments and organizations grew as team research supplanted individual investigation. This growth was paralleled by the increase and expansion of scientific and technical libraries to support the research and to cope with the ever-increasing flow of published results.

Although efforts have been under way since the late 1950s to develop census statistics for special libraries, there has never been an accurate count of their number. Problems of definition, diversity, and poor visibility because of small size or lack of participation in the library community form strong barriers to compiling accurate statistics for special libraries. Although some segments of the field—medical, law, and government libraries—have been surveyed, a large segment of the special library universe remains unexplored.

Such figures as are available are derived as byproducts of directories. For example, the *American Library Directory* (44th edition, 1991–92) reports more than 9,000 special libraries, including government, law, medical, and religious libraries not affiliated with colleges and universities in the U.S. and another 1,200 special libraries in Canada. The other principal North American directory, *Directory of Special Libraries and Information Centers* (15th edition, 1992), lists more than 20,200 special libraries, including those affiliated with public and university libraries in the U.S. and Canada.

Despite the inability to document the exact number of special libraries, growth has been one of their outstanding characteristics in the past, and all evidence points to continued growth. The factors that gave rise to the emergence of special libraries in the past have not disappeared; indeed, they are stronger than ever before and spreading in influence as new industries and new organizations evolve. The challenge of putting information to work continues to grow.

Other Countries. The pattern of the U.S. special library movement has been repeated around the world. In France, Germany, the United Kingdom, and other industrialized nations, special libraries were established in the first decades of the 20th century, and their rate of growth, particularly in the scientific and technical fields, increased to meet the demand for support of postwar research activities. As nations have continued to industrialize and increase their research efforts, special libraries have been established in government ministries and agencies, research institutes, and private business and industry in nations around the world, including the developing countries. Many U.S. corporations with international facilities have libraries in their foreign subsidiaries and affiliates. The interest in special libraries around the world is illustrated in the International Federation of Library Associations (IFLA) where, in 1976, the Special Libraries Section was elevated to Divisional status. The Division of Special Libraries currently comprises six sections—administrative libraries, art libraries, biological and medical sciences libraries, geography and map libraries, science and technology libraries, and social science libraries.

Statistics on special libraries in other countries may be found in this Encyclopedia. Articles on individual countries include in tabular form statistics reported by the countries and by Unesco on the number of special libraries as the countries define them.

SERVICES TO USERS

A special library provides two basic types of information service. The first is that provided in response to requests for information and encompasses reference and research services. The second is information service in anticipation of need and encompasses services designed to keep the library's clientele up to date on new and current information—usually described as current awareness services.

The major effort in the special library is devoted to disseminating information through these services; all other functions support information services. Decisions about allocation of the library's resources, particularly staff resources, between acquiring and organizing materials and information service must take this fact into account.

Reference Services. Reference and research services range from answering simple reference questions to undertaking complex research and literature searches. The special librarian may assist users who wish to pursue their own search, but often the librarian, as an information expert whose function is to save the inquirer's time, is the primary user of the library, locating requested information and transmitting it in the most useful form.

The special librarian's expertise in information handling may be applied to a reference question that requires a specific answer—a name, an address, a report, article, or book. Most special libraries devote a good deal of time to literature searches, either comprehensive or limited by time period, language, or other parameter. Unless the inquirer requests the information in a certain form, the librarian decides, on the basis of the results of the search and knowledge of the inquirer's preferences, how best to present the information—in a bibliography, copies of relevant materials, a memorandum, or a report.

Some special libraries offer translations, providing in-house service or obtaining them from outside sources. Many serve as centralized sources for ordering publications, subscriptions, and databases for the organization to eliminate duplication of resources.

Special librarians, particularly those whose primary clientele is located in an organization, develop close working relationships with their users. They learn users' ongoing information needs and interests; they learn how to negotiate requests effectively; they learn how the inquirer wants the information delivered. The alert special librarian also tries to anticipate

Logo for International Special Librarians Day, 1992.

Missouri Historical Society

Library and Collections Center, Missouri Historical Society, St. Louis.

need so that information can be collected and, when desirable, disseminated in advance of need.

Current Awareness Service. Special libraries have developed a wide range of services to keep their clientele informed of new and current developments. Such services may be directed to the organization as a whole or tailored to specific groups or individuals. Some also make their current awareness services available to a secondary clientele—other offices or libraries in the organization, special libraries in other organizations, or fee-paying subscribers.

Routing current periodicals is one of the most common functions of the special library. The library periodically surveys its clientele as to which periodicals they wish to see on a regular basis, then circulates them to readers as issues arrive. Acquisition bulletins, another common service, may be simple lists of new materials or may include annotations or abstracts. Subject-oriented abstract bulletins, news summaries, and digests in print or electronic format are other current awareness services offered by the special library. They may be based on the library's own abstracting or obtained from commercial services or databases. The indexes some libraries prepare to cover unindexed periodicals may be used in the library or may be published as bulletins, combining citations with order forms so users can request indexed materials.

In addition to general distribution in the organization, current awareness may be targeted to individual users through selective dissemination of information (SDI). In SDI systems, librarians compile interest profiles for individual users on index cards or in computer databases and match incoming information with the profiles. The result is a personalized service closely tailored to each user's needs and interests. SDI may operate in-house or be obtained from online databases or outside SDI services.

Bibliographic Instruction. While there is little emphasis on bibliographic instruction in most special libraries, it may be offered where there is a demand, as in searching chemical literature in chemical and pharmaceutical libraries or in searching legal literature in law libraries. Some special libraries coordinate online database searching in their organizations; the library staff provides end-user training for those who want to do their own searching.

Levels of Function. The nature and extent of information services offered by the individual special library varies according to the working habits and needs of its primary clientele and according to its own resources in staff and collections. If the clientele is large in proportion to library staff, or if the clientele is made up of users who as part of their jobs perform their own research, then the library staff is generally engaged in ready reference, fact checking, advising on research problems, or conducting research involving unfamiliar subjects or databases or use of outside resources. On the other hand, if the library itself has primary responsibility for documentary research and the provision of information, then the librarians themselves become the library's primary users and function at a more intensive level of service.

Three functional levels are sometimes used to describe the range of information services provided by the special librarian. At the minimum level, the librarian disseminates information and materials, answers reference questions, directs users needing detailed or research information to appropriate sources, and handles such simple current awareness services as periodical routing. At the intermediate level, the special librarian also offers literature searches, either manual or online; prepares bibliographies; selects and transmits research materials; and provides additional current awareness services such as acquisition bulletins. At the maximum level, the special librarian adds to or substitutes for the activities already described synthesizing and evaluating information in written form; preparing critical bibliographies; conducting evaluative, comprehensive literature searches; and providing more complex current awareness services such as SDI. The information center concept is best exemplified at the maximum level of service.

Most special libraries do not function at a single level of service. The individual library operates at various levels, depending on the varying needs of its clientele. Nevertheless, the special library's ultimate goal is to function at the maximum level of service when given the opportunity and resources to do so.

COLLECTIONS

Special library collections are working collections to support information services, with emphasis on current information. The extent of retrospective material held is determined by need and use patterns and available outside resources. While some collections may concentrate on a single format such as pictures, clippings, or maps, special library collections typically include a wide variety of formats. Some, particularly those in scientific and technical areas, have collections that are largely in the traditional formats of books, journals, and technical reports. Other special libraries' collections are significant for their files of information from business records and ephemeral material. Although it may be physically small, the special library collects in great depth in its primary areas of interest and includes materials that may not be found in other types of libraries.

Some of the larger subject groupings of special library collections include: advertising and marketing, aerospace, biological sciences, business and finance, chemistry, education, engineering, environmental sciences, food and nutrition, health care and medicine, insurance, law, legislative reference, metals and materials, nuclear science, petroleum, pharmaceuticals, physics, public utilities, social welfare, telecommunication, and transportation. Even within these broad groups, individual libraries display a wide diversity; a transportation library, for example, may cover all forms of transportation, or focus on automotive, air, railroad, or urban transportation, and further specialize by technical, business, or consumer aspects. Insurance libraries may concentrate on one or more branches of insurance—life, property, health, or casualty—and such related areas as actuarial science, insurance law, marketing, and insurance education for employees.

Libraries that serve such organizations as accounting firms, advertising agencies, banks and other financial institutions, law firms, and consultants in many fields encompass not only accounting, advertising, banking, or law but also the subject areas represented by present and prospective clients.

The subject scope of the collection is not static; it is dynamic and changing. As new products or services, mergers, or the extension of interdisciplinary methods affect the parent organization, they also affect the subject scope of the special library. The special librarian must therefore be constantly alert to possible new areas and the changing interests of the organization so that the library's collection can respond to changing demands for information.

Special library collections have three major components: the first is published information, the second internally generated information, and the third the information available from sources outside the organization.

Published Information. Published information includes both print and electronically stored information that is considered publicly available. In most special libraries, periodicals provide the most up-to-date information; in some, they provide the only information. Although books are important in some special libraries, periodicals often form a large and important segment of the collection. Periodical collections include not only research journals but also the many business and trade magazines and newsletters published for specialized audiences.

Special (or "vertical") file materials are another major special library resource. These collections bring together large and small bits of information from such varied sources as clippings, pamphlets, speeches, statistical compilations, advertising brochures, sales literature and samples, trade catalogues, annual reports and financial statements, patents, and government documents.

Technical reports—the results of public and private research and development—are an important and sometimes overwhelming part of the special library collection, especially in scientific and technical fields. Such reports figured largely in the information explosion after World War II, when special libraries had to scramble frantically to impose some sort of order on the acquisition and control of technical reports. Special indexing and cataloguing techniques were developed, with many special librarians using their organizations' computers to assist them in this effort. The situation improved after the mid-1960s when various commissions studied the need for bibliographic control and information transfer and a number of federal, contract, and private technical information centers and abstracting and indexing services were established to improve control of and access to these reports. A notable development in the control of reports was the creation in 1970 of the National Technical Information Service (NTIS), an agency of the U.S. Department of Commerce. The National Aeronautics and Space Administration's Scientific and Technical Information Facility (NASA/

National Archives of Japan

Underground stacks area of the Japanese Cabinet Library.

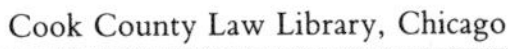

Cook County Law Library, Chicago

Cook County Law Library, Chicago, one of the busiest law libraries in the country.

Family History Library of the Church of the Latter-Day Saints, Salt Lake City, Utah

Family History Library (Salt Lake City) is the premier library for genealogical research.

STIF), the Defense Technical Information Center (DTIC), and the Department of Energy's Technical Information Center (DOE/TIC) are other major federal document centers. The Educational Resources Information Center (ERIC) acts as a clearinghouse for the literature of education, including library and information science.

Other formats are also found in special library collections, including maps, pictures, audiovisual materials, patents, technical standards and specifications, and realia. Microforms may be used to add retrospective resources and to conserve space. Databases, both online and CD-ROM, are available in almost all special libraries. A survey of technology being used in special libraries in 1989 showed that 87.8 percent of special libraries subscribed to external databases.

Internal Information. The second major component of the collection is information generated internally: research reports, technical memoranda, laboratory notebooks, working papers, correspondence, house organs and newsletters, sales literature, and company and competitive advertising. The library usually makes a conscious decision either to be responsible for managing all or part of the organization's internal material or to collect only such information as is germane to its primary clientele. The library in a research department may be responsible for that department's complete file of research reports and working papers but may collect only selected material from other departments. Some special libraries maintain the corporate archives and some are responsible for records (or information resource) management, the supervision and control of all internal records. Some special libraries also manage internal databases.

The presence of internal and proprietary material in the special library is sometimes a barrier to outside use. Such material is either removed before access to the file is granted to outside users or is completely isolated from the general collection and thereby kept confidential.

Outside Resources. Use of resources outside the organization is the third component of the special library collection. While the library may strive to be self-sufficient in its primary subject area or in heavily used materials, it depends on outside resources for information and materials outside its scope. It is said that a special librarian's best friend is the local directory of special libraries; indeed, informal cooperation with other special libraries is a long-standing tradition in special librarianship. Special libraries also use public, academic, and research libraries through more formal interlibrary loan procedures, purchasing memberships or company registrations, paying user fees, and participating in multitype library cooperatives and networks. Document delivery services are also used to extend the library's own resources. Special libraries also seek information from research organizations, professional and trade associations, individual subject experts, and commercial information firms, the so-called information brokers.

Organization. Special libraries employ a wide spectrum of methods of organization, with an emphasis on flexibility and adaptability to changing needs. Though simple methods of organization are used wherever possible, special libraries also develop complex and specialized systems where needed. Organization may be the key to efficient use of the collection, but it must also be balanced against the priorities of information service.

Special libraries with small collections and limited staff usually operate at a minimal level of organization. Material is arranged in a simple, logical order—books by author or subject, periodicals by title and date, vertical file materials under broad subject headings, and other material similarly. The catalogue, if there is one, may be limited to one or two entries per item. As collections grow and the need dictates, more formal methods of organization may be employed. The print or online catalogue may become more complex; catalogue records may be obtained from online bibliographic utilities.

Some special libraries adopt or adapt one of the major classification systems, the Dewey Decimal or Library of Congress Classification. Others may use a classification designed for their subject area. Although some special libraries have developed their own classification systems, most find an existing system, with adaptation or expansion, to be suitable.

For subject analysis, special libraries can select from one of the large, general subject heading lists or from the many specialized subject heading lists and thesauri, or, again, develop their own. However, even when a thesaurus is available in their subject field, individual special libraries generally choose to adapt and supplement it in order to achieve maximum effectiveness for their areas of interest and to coordinate with their own organization's terminology.

As in information service, special libraries seldom function at a single level of organization, nor do they process each item to the same degree; rather, the maximum organizational effort is devoted to the in-depth subject analysis of the most important information. Any one item, no matter what its form, will be given precisely the amount of processing it needs to be retrieved most efficiently, according to the importance of the information it contains, its probable use, the length of time it will be retained, and the availability of published guides to it. The decision as to what to retain and process is as important as what to acquire. Weeding of outdated, nonessential information goes on constantly, and retention policies are used to control the size of the collection. In spite of such measures, however, collections do tend to grow rapidly; one estimate suggests that a newly established special library will double in size and space requirements in five years.

Another consideration that affects the special library's organization is who actually uses it. If most of the actual physical use is by the library staff itself, many organizational shortcuts can be taken. On the other hand, if a large number of users come to the library, the organization must facilitate their access. Although some adopt an overall organization for the entire collection, most special libraries consist of separate segments, each arranged according to the need and use factors described above.

Retrieval. Abstracting and indexing are of paramount importance in the special library. Special libraries have a long tradition of indexing, first because there were no indexing or abstracting services in their areas of interest and later, as indexes became available, to supplement commercially produced coverage and to cover internal information. Special librarians were among the first to develop newer information retrieval methods in both manual and computer-based applications.

Today, commercial abstracting and indexing services, particularly in database form, have brought some degree of coverage to most subjects. However, many special libraries continue their own indexing and abstracting and use computers to construct databases to meet their needs more specifically than external sources can. The purpose of these databases may be to provide deep analysis of important information, to focus on a new subject of vital interest to the organization, or to track material in publications important to the organization but not covered by commercial indexes. Much internal material is indexed in depth, and while reports are most often treated in this way, the library may also index memoranda, minutes, house organs, and other internal documents. A few special libraries make their indexes and databases available outside their parent organizations on a subscription basis.

ADMINISTRATION

Special library administration has two major aspects. One is the library's administrative relationship to its parent organization; the other is its internal administration.

The special library's place in the structure of its parent organization varies according to what part of the organization it serves and how the organization is structured. If the library was established to serve the entire organization, its optimal location is one directly accessible to its clientele, from which it can build and maintain effective, direct communication with all departments. Personnel thus have direct access to the library and need not go through administrative channels to request service. If, on the other hand, the library was set up to serve a single department or division, it would typically be located with that department.

The special library may be directly under the cognizance of top management, with the librarian reporting directly to the chief executive officer or an administrative assistant to that officer. More often, whether it is a separate department or a subunit of a larger department, the library is part of a division such as research and development, administrative services, public relations or public information, editorial, or information services, reporting to the senior executive in charge of that area.

In addition to the significance that organizational location holds for effective service and communication, the library's place in the hierarchy and its reporting channel are important for facilitating general communication with decision makers in the organization. The special library must not only provide an effective information service, but also be able to demonstrate to management that it is doing so and, further, must educate management about the resources required to provide such service. While its users may be in the best position to appreciate and understand the library and its needs, in many cases they are not among those who determine its support.

The special library within the research and development, editorial, or management information services area operates in a close relationship with those who use information, appreciate its value, and recognize the library as a tool in their work; the executive in charge is likely to be in a good position to understand and endorse the library's needs. On the other hand, the library that is under administrative services (along with the mail room and the cafeteria), or that reports to an administrative assistant, may have direct access to the decision-making level but may be reporting to an executive who has little direct experience with library service and only a vague idea of its contribution to the organization.

Although the practice is not widespread, some special libraries have an advisory committee drawn from the organization's personnel or membership. Advisory committee functions vary; some aid in

United Nations

Information desk at the National Agricultural Institute's library, Chapingo, Mexico.

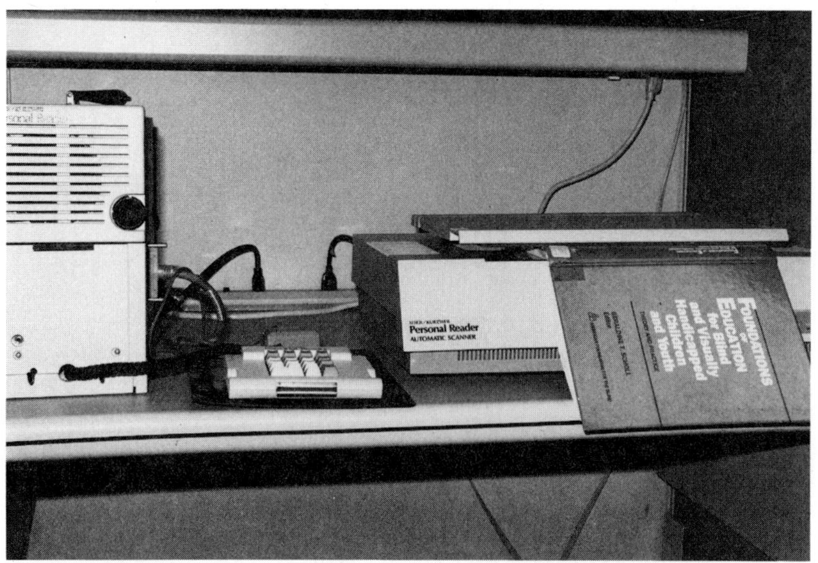

M.C. Migel Memorial Library and Information Center, American Foundation for the Blind, New York City

M.C. Migel Memorial Library, American Foundation for the Blind, houses one of the largest collections in the world on the subject of blindness and visual impairment.

selecting materials while others may advise on policies, objectives, and administrative matters.

Although most organizations maintain one library, some large organizations have two or more separate libraries. When divisions of an organization are geographically separate, libraries may be established in the various locations. Some organizations consolidate business, technical, legal, and other subjects in one library, but a more common pattern is to provide separate libraries, conveniently located near the appropriate departments. These intraorganizational libraries may operate autonomously, cooperating with each other on an informal basis, or they may be formally coordinated by a senior information officer. A large corporation may have a dozen or more libraries; some of the largest have more than 30 libraries of various sizes. When libraries remain centralized, they use electronic mail and facsimile transmission to reach distant users quickly and efficiently.

Finance. In a few cases, the parent organization may qualify for a grant or other outside assistance, and the special library may obtain some outside funding. In general and for the vast majority of libraries, however, funding comes from the library's parent organization, and accounting and budgeting procedures are set by the organization. Although special librarians widely discuss budgeting and costs, concrete cost figures for establishing and maintaining special libraries have not been gathered on a regular basis. The great diversity of budgeting procedures and differing levels of service make standardized reporting difficult, and most private-sector organizations regard such financial information as confidential.

Virtually all organizations classify the cost of the library as an overhead or indirect expense, making the library budget vulnerable to pressures to reduce overhead. A common method of distributing library costs is to allocate library expenses to departments or budgetary units in the organization. The special library may allocate or charge some of its expenses directly; the library in a service organization, for example, may be able to charge project research time to a client, transforming part of the overhead to a direct cost. Such charges may include library overhead or may be limited to staff time or computer costs. While this practice results in a reduction of the cost of the library as an overhead expense, it also increases pressure on the library to bill as much of its time as possible and, correspondingly, to spend less time on nonbillable but still important activities. A few libraries are able to recover some costs by marketing their research services, publications, or databases to outside users.

A special library's operating budget includes the categories of personnel, books, journals and database fees, equipment and supplies, and professional dues and meetings. The library may or may not also be responsible for such overhead costs as space, utilities, and other office services. Personnel may represent anywhere from 30 to 60 percent of the special library budget; materials and computer resources, the major part of the rest.

Staff. The special librarian is at once a manager, a librarian, and a subject specialist. In addition to library and subject skills, the special librarian must have a strong motivation toward service, flexibility in procedures, and aggressiveness in promoting the library to the organization. Managerial skills are needed because the librarian functions both as an executive in the organization and as a manager of the library staff. One of the continuing debates in the field is whether the special librarian should be primarily a subject specialist, a librarian, or both. Ideally, the librarian should have a library degree and some education or experience in the organization's areas of interest. Although the special librarian is equipped through a library education to obtain a working knowledge of a subject and its literature, many organizations feel more comfortable with a subject specialist. The organization understands what the subject specialist knows; it is less likely to understand what the librarian knows. The issue of professional staffing commonly arises in organizations seeking to establish a new library, in some smaller special libraries, and sometimes in larger libraries adding professional staff.

The minimum staffing level for a special library is considered to be one professional and one clerical person. In larger libraries, a ratio of one professional to two clerical assistants may be found, but the ratio varies considerably, depending on the nature of the library's services. In the small special library, the librarian must assume all professional responsibilities. As staff size increases, specialization becomes possible: additional professional staff may include reference personnel, cataloguers, indexers, abstractors, literature specialists, or translators. The assistant in the small special library works closely with the librarian and frequently gets considerable on-the-job training in reference work, in addition to performing clerical duties. As the staff grows, specialization at the clerical level may evolve into such positions as secretary, acquisitions clerk, file clerk, or typist. Technicians or paraprofessionals may also be added.

Space. The special library's physical facilities depend on the space the organization itself occupies, and there is often considerable competition in the organization for what may be expensive floor space. The library's physical facilities should be designed in relation to its role, how it achieves its goals, how its staff operates, and what the future is likely to hold. The contents of the library have a direct bearing on space and furniture requirements, as does the amount of time devoted to the various administrative, bibliographic, information, and clerical functions. The library's space must be physically contiguous and separate from other office uses. While the special library may occupy only a few thousand square feet of floor space, the not infrequent practice of scattering shelving down hallways or in conference and storage rooms ultimately serves to reduce efficiency, accessibility, and control. (An exception is found in records management, where active records may be located throughout the organization and little-used records may be stored in less expensive off-site warehouse space.) A major factor in space allocation is the nature of use; the library that is primarily used by its staff will allocate less space for browsing and study areas than will the library in which users frequently come in to do research or reading. Finally, space for growth must be provided. Even though the special library weeds its collection of unused, outdated materials and may turn to compact shelving or microforms to conserve space, its collection still grows, and adequate space for expansion must be allowed.

MEASUREMENT AND EVALUATION

The ultimate measure of the special library's value is its continued existence. In profit making and nonprofit organizations alike, there are competitive pressures for available resources. The library, along with other overhead services, is particularly vulnerable to such pressures, and the special library is continually challenged to demonstrate its contributions. This challenge is made even more difficult in light of the fact that while the lingua franca of many organizations is economic, the economics of information are still but dimly understood. The major concern of both the special library and management has been to evaluate the library and its services according to its effectiveness in meeting its clientele's information needs.

Statistics. Traditional statistical measures of library activity gathered by some special libraries include collection size, processing volume, number of users, and reference questions answered; they are useful measures of library efficiency and workload, but do not reflect the depth, quality, relevance, or effectiveness of information service. Because such statistics are time-consuming to collect, they are given relatively low priority in the special library with only limited staff time.

Special library collections do not lend themselves well to statistical description. Although some may have significant book collections, in many the journal is predominant, so the size of the periodical collection is far more significant. For many special libraries the number of special file drawers, technical reports, pictures, maps, or clippings may be more significant. In any case, size of the collection and growth rate are not as important as the relevance of the materials and the use made of them. Counts of books catalogued, material processed, or number of items indexed or abstracted may indicate that the library is busy but mean little to management. Similarly circulation statistics (where there is a formal circulation system) do not reflect either use of materials in the library or the output of information in the form of spoken messages, written memoranda, or reports, all of which may be more significant means of information transfer.

Statistics on the number of users and of reference and research requests do relate more directly to information service and, to some extent, indicate who is using the library and what type of information is being sought. The special library can usually identify its potential user population as the total number of employees or members of the organization to whom library services are available. User statistics are somewhat more difficult to collect since few special libraries have any type of registration and the count of users must take into account on-site use, telephone or written requests, those on routing and distributions lists, and possibly electronic mail or database use. Statistics of use, to be meaningful, must be based on the relative levels of service provided—what proportion is ready reference, what proportion is intensive research, and how much involves evaluating and summarizing information or repackaging it into bibliographies, reports, or other more useful forms.

User Surveys. Through day-to-day interaction with users, special librarians can informally evaluate how well the library is meeting the information needs of the users and thereby adjust services to meet changing needs. Formal user surveys are undertaken from time to time; such surveys may be conducted by the library itself, management, or an outside consultant, using personal interviews or questionnaires. A typical survey covers services used and satisfaction with the quality, relevance, and promptness of service.

Surveys of user attitudes combined with selected use statistics are the most common methods used by special librarians to evaluate the effectiveness of library services and to demonstrate to management the library's contribution to the goals of the organization.

Objectives. Although the diversity of special libraries all but precludes comparison among libraries and development of standards, it has long been

Center for Migration Studies, Staten Island, New York
Photo by Rocco Galatiato

A team researching immigration policy begins work at the Center for Migration Studies Library, a specialized library focusing on international migration and refugees.

recognized that successful special libraries do have certain elements in common. These elements are described in the SLA publication *Objectives for Special Libraries,* first issued in 1964. The *Objectives,* designed to serve as guidelines for both management and librarians, describe the qualities found in the objectives, staff, collection, services, physical facilities, and budgets of successful special libraries. Qualitative rather than quantitative, the *Objectives* provide a conceptual framework for both the design and the evaluation of special library services.

Valuing Library Services. Special librarians have also been concerned with defining the economic value of information and information services and the value added by the information professional. Cost effectiveness, which focuses on the relationship between level of performance and the costs of achieving that level, has become a useful tool in evaluating alternatives in information systems and services.

Cost-benefit analysis has also received considerable attention. Cost benefit refers to the relationship between the benefits of a particular product or service and the costs of providing it. While it is possible to identify the costs of providing library service, it has not yet been demonstrated that it is possible to identify total benefit in economic terms. It is difficult to place a monetary value on such benefits as information's general contribution to the knowledge of its users, the improvement in productivity resulting from this knowledge, or the time and resources library service frees for its users to spend on other activities.

In 1987 the SLA President's Task Force on the Value of the Information Professional issued a report summarizing possible approaches to measuring value (published in *From the Top: Profiles of U.S. and Canadian Corporate Libraries and Information Centers* [1989]). One approach is to collect instances of specific impacts of library service. For example, an $11 search provided information that saved 200 hours of original research time. The specific impact approach, however, is limited in that it covers single instances rather than total service. Another approach is to measure and place a monetary value on the amount of users' time saved. A third approach is to base value on users' estimates of their willingness to pay for information provided by the library, of the cost of alternative methods of obtaining the information, and of what benefits would be lost if the library did not exist. Studies using these approaches have shown that library services do save time and money and offer a significant return on investment.

COOPERATION

Cooperation is one of the cornerstones of special librarianship. Pioneer special librarians at the turn of the century recognized that effective and efficient information service depended on extending an individual library's resources through cooperation with other libraries. The specialized library associations proved to be a strong force in facilitating cooperation and in providing leadership in cooperative projects. The SLA, its geographic Chapters, and its subject Divisions engage in various resource-sharing activities; the most common are exchanging materials and preparing directories of special libraries. Within six months of its founding, the SLA had published its first directory of special libraries (April 1910); over the next 40 years, it published four more editions. Although after the mid-1950s other directories began to serve as national inventories of special libraries, the SLA membership directory continues to be a valuable resource. Local and regional directories of special libraries and their subject specializations are still an important part of Chapter activities. Boston special librarians produced the first regional directory in 1920, and since then most SLA Chapters have done likewise. A number of Chapters have produced local and regional union lists of serial holdings in special libraries, and many coordinate the exchange of materials through duplicate exchanges.

In the United Kingdom, functions and activities comparable to those of SLA are conducted by Aslib, founded in 1924 as the Association of Special Libraries and Information Bureaux. With more than 2,000 institutional and individual members, Aslib publishes several journals and a variety of monographic and reference works. It sponsors frequent seminars, workshops, and training courses.

The need for bibliographic access and control of technical, nontraditional, and specialized subject literature has also been the focus of cooperative efforts. The *Industrial Arts Index* (predecessor of the *Applied Science & Technology Index*) and *Public Affairs Information Service* both had their genesis as cooperative efforts of special librarians. SLA's Insurance and Employee Benefits Division publishes *Insurance Periodicals Index* and the Engineering-Aeronautical Section began an index of translations in 1946 that evolved into the Translations Center now at the Library of Congress. SLA units also initiated such publications as *Unlisted Drugs, Technical Book Review Index, Scientific Meetings, Dictionary of Report Series Codes,* and countless bibliographies published in *Special Libraries* and as monographs.

Traditionally, informality has been the predominant characteristic of special library cooperation in resource sharing. Such informality has been possible because local groups of special librarians have tended to be small and closely knit networks. Within these networks special librarians can operate, with some discretion, even though their parent organizations may be in competition. Despite the development of more formal single and multitype networks, informality will probably continue to characterize the cooperative relationships special librarians maintain among themselves, simply because informal cooperation has worked so well.

At the most basic level, cooperation in resource sharing is on an ad hoc basis, with no long-term commitments. In a number of instances, however, special libraries in physical proximity, ranging from a region of several counties to an area as small as a complex of office buildings, may develop more lasting relationships that are usually based on union lists, sharing responsibility for long-term retention of journals, or forming bibliographic utility user groups.

Cooperative relationships have also been initiated by special libraries in a single company. Although some large organizations with multiple special libraries in various locations sometimes provide a centralized organizational structure for their library and information services, more often they do not. In such instances the special libraries serving the various units develop cooperative relationships to share resources and coordinate activities.

Subject-oriented networks have also emerged. An example is the Textile Information Users Council, which works to develop and improve information services related to the textile industry. Its members represent fiber producers, chemical and dyestuff manufacturers, textile companies, textile machinery manufacturers, trade associations, research institutes, and academic textile schools.

Special libraries, despite their contributions to librarianship and access to specialized literature, were for a long time a little known and poorly understood resource, separated from the mainstream of librarianship. They were often bypassed, except in the role of users, as active contributors to national information resources. In the 1970s, as multitype library networks and consortia emerged, significant moves were made to include special libraries and to show them to be effective parts of the library community. While networks have proven to be valuable for special libraries in gaining access to additional resources, as was expected, special libraries have contributed to networks unique resources and a willingness to lend them, service on governing bodies, and "advanced thinking."

Some predicted barriers to special library participation in networks have been overcome. Many feared that concern for confidentiality and an unwillingness to standardize would hinder special library participation in shared cataloguing. However, the number of special libraries joining bibliographic utilities indicates that these barriers are not insurmountable.

Possible legal problems in including libraries in for-profit organizations were identified early in multitype network planning. In order to mobilize total library resources, federal and state laws have, by and large, implicitly if not explicitly, enabled special libraries to be included in multitype cooperatives and networks. Individual cooperatives and networks have used various strategies, restricting for-profit membership to a certain percentage or setting up nonvoting or associate membership categories, and no serious challenges have arisen.

Barriers or constraints to special library participation in networks come from special libraries themselves. Although their participation in networking is substantial, some special libraries do not participate at all. Many of these libraries are in highly competitive sectors—business and finance, newspapers, engineering, petroleum, chemicals, and insurance—where the parent companies regard information resources as competitive advantages and therefore confidential. Cost is another barrier. Some libraries are simply too small, have neither the time or resources to contribute, and will always be too small for networking. Finally, many special libraries find that their long-term informal cooperative efforts are comfortable and are reluctant to replace them with the more complex or different methods required by formal networks.

LAWS AND LEGISLATION

Special libraries, nestled within parent organizations that provide financial support, are seldom directly involved in or affected by legislation. There are, of course, exceptions. There are instances of involvement in government regulations and funding among groups of special libraries, notably those in the public sector, government libraries, medical libraries, and libraries whose parent organizations hold government contracts. But until the mid-1970s most special librarians in the U.S. had not been involved with laws and legislation to the same degree as had their colleagues in other types of libraries. Change came from two directions: legislation concerning multitype cooperatives and networks (mentioned earlier) and the Copyright Law of 1976.

As revision of copyright moved toward passage in Congress, special librarians become deeply involved in the legislative process as they, individually and through the SLA, joined with five other major U.S. library associations (American Association of Law Libraries, American Library Association, Association of Research Libraries, Medical Library Association, and Music Library Association) in a unified effort to ensure equitable treatment for libraries. After enactment of the copyright law, SLA continued to represent the special library community on copyright matters and to disseminate information on copyright law implementation and compliance to special librarians.

For all libraries a significant part of the U.S. copyright law has been library reprography and photocopying, specifically Sections 107, governing fair use, and 108, governing reproductions by libraries and archives. Special libraries, particularly those in for-profit organizations, have had some specific problems with Section 108 and with the interpretation of "direct or indirect commercial advantage" and "systematic" reproduction.

In implementing provisions of the law, special libraries were faced with the same problems of interlibrary loan procedures, interpretation of fair use, and warning notices as were other types of libraries. The prohibitions against "multiple" and "systematic" photocopying, however, meant that special librarians had to review carefully their current awareness services for possible infringements. Many special librarians, naturally reluctant to embroil their parent organizations in legal difficulties, turned to their firms' lawyers for advice, with the result that each special library developed its own policies, reflecting the varying opinions of legal counsel. In some cases alternative methods have been adopted for disseminating information or copyright clearance has been obtained; some services have simply been dropped, either because of possible infringement or because an efficient, effective alternative could not be found.

In recognition of special libraries' increasing interest in legislation, the SLA in 1980 abandoned its deliberate policy of noninvolvement and established a standing Government Relations Committee. This committee developed legislative programs for SLA, focusing on legislation and policies that advance library and information services in the public and private sectors, including copyright, network legislation, government information policies, and telecommunications.

REFERENCES

Elin B. Christianson, David E. King, and Janet L. Ahrensfeld, *Special Libraries: A Guide for Management,* 3rd edition (1991).

Ellis Mount, *Special Libraries and Information Centers: An Introductory Text,* 2nd edition (1991).

ELIN B. CHRISTIANSON

Library of Congress
Ainsworth Rand Spofford

Spofford, Ainsworth Rand

(1825–1908)

The modern history of the Library of Congress (LC) began when Ainsworth Rand Spofford became Librarian: during his 32-year administration (1865–97) he transformed the LC into an institution of national significance. Spofford permanently joined the legislative and national functions of the Library, first in practice and then, through the 1897 reorganization of the Library, in law. He provided his successors as Librarian with four essential prerequisites for the development of an American national library: (1) firm congressional support for the notion of the LC as both a legislative and a national library; (2) the beginning of a comprehensive collection of Americana; (3) a magnificent new building, itself a national monument; and (4) a strong and independent office of Librarian of Congress. Spofford had the interest, skill, and perseverance to capitalize on the LC's claim to a national role. Each Librarian of Congress since Spofford has shaped the institution in a different manner, but none has wavered from Spofford's fundamental assertion that the Library was both a legislative and a national institution.

Spofford was born in Gilmanton, New Hampshire, September 12, 1825. He was tutored at home and developed into an avid reader and student. In 1845 he moved West to Cincinnati and found a job in a bookstore that soon became, thanks to his efforts, the city's leading importer of the books of the New England transcendentalists. From the book business he moved, in 1859, to a new career as Associate Editor of Cincinnati's leading newspaper, the *Daily Commercial;* his first editorial, titled "A Bibliologist," attacked the naive book-buying practices of the city librarian. Two years later the newspaper sent Spofford to Washington, D.C., to report on President Abraham Lincoln's inauguration, a trip that led to his accepting, in the autumn of 1861, the position of Assistant Librarian of Congress. On December 31, 1864, President Lincoln named the knowledgeable, industrious, and ambitious Spofford to the post of Librarian of Congress. Located in the west front of the U.S. Capitol, the Library had a staff of seven and a book collection of approximately 82,000 volumes.

Spofford soon proved to be a skilled politician as well as an energetic librarian. Congressmen liked him and the nonpartisan manner in which he administered the Library. As one result, between 1865 and 1870 he obtained support for several legislative acts that ensured the growth of the collections and made the LC the largest library in the United States. The most important new measure was the copyright law of 1870, which centralized all U.S. copyright registration and deposit activities at the Library. The new law brought books, pamphlets, maps, prints, photographs, and music into the institution without substantial cost, thus assuring the future growth of the Americana collections and providing the LC with an essential and unique national function.

In his annual reports to Congress, Spofford continually emphasized that a national library should be a permanent, comprehensive collection of national literature "representing the complete product of the American mind in every department of science and literature." Comprehensiveness was essential, for in his view the American national library should serve both the American citizenry and its elected representatives. Books and information were needed about all subjects and, as the library of the American government, the LC was the natural site for such a comprehensive collection.

In 1874, for the first time, the copyright law brought in more books than were obtained through purchase, and three years later Spofford's already cramped library was out of space and more than 70,000 books were "piled on the floor in all directions." The Librarian's struggle for a separate building, which began in 1871, was a crucial part of his national library effort. A separate structure would ensure, once and for all, the unique status of the LC among American libraries—and would give the U.S. a national library that would equal if not surpass the great national libraries of Europe. The latter argument was a particularly popular one with the Congress. Spofford personally wanted a national monument that would also serve as an efficient, well-functioning building. The new building, however, was not authorized until 1886 and not completed for another decade. Spofford's dream was fulfilled in 1897 when the doors to the ornate new structure across the east plaza from the Capitol, at the time the "largest, safest, and costliest" library building in the world, were finally opened to an admiring public.

For the most part Spofford operated quite independently of the American library movement and the American Library Association. By 1876, when ALA was founded, Spofford's LC was already the leading library in the country, and he was completely absorbed in his struggle for a new building. His independence from other libraries and librarians was accentuated by his idea of a national library as well as by his personal temperament. The national library was a single, enormous accumulation of the nation's literature. He did not view it as a focal point for cooperative library activities and was not inclined to exert leadership in that direction.

From November 16 to December 7, 1896, the Joint Committee on the Library held hearings about the LC, its "condition," and its organization. Although Spofford was the principal witness, ALA sent six librarians to testify. The testimony of Melvil Dewey and Herbert Putnam on the desirable features of the LC was of special interest; both men avoided direct criticism of Spofford, but it was obvious that their view of the proper functions of the Library differed from that of the aging Librarian. Putnam wholeheartedly endorsed Dewey's description of the necessary role of a national library: "a center to which the libraries of the whole country can turn for inspiration, guidance, and practical help." Centralized cataloguing, interlibrary loan, and a national union catalogue were among the services described.

Immediately after the hearings, Putnam supplemented his comments in a letter in which he summarized the testimony of the ALA witnesses and stated, tactfully, that the time had come for the LC to modernize and to expand its services far beyond those offered by the Library under Spofford.

The hearings resulted in a major reorganization and expansion, effective July 1, 1897. Spofford became Chief Assistant Librarian under a new Librarian of Congress, John Russell Young, and he continued as Chief Assistant under Herbert Putnam, who became the Librarian of Congress in April 1899. Spofford died in Holderness, New Hampshire, on August 11, 1908.

Spofford's professional and personal interests were perhaps most accurately described in the formidable title of his *A Book for All Readers, Designed as an Aid to the Collection, Use, and Preservation of Books and Formation of Public and Private Libraries* (1900). He was respected by librarians, politicians, and the general public, not only because of his accomplishments at the LC, but also because of his fair-mindedness and his continual delight in sharing his views about his favorite subjects—reading, bibliography, and collection building.

REFERENCES

John Y. Cole, editor, *Ainsworth Rand Spofford: Bookman and Librarian* (1975).

John Y. Cole, "Spofford, Ainsworth Rand," *Dictionary of American Library Biography* (1978).

JOHN Y. COLE

Sri Lanka

Sri Lanka, an island republic in the Indian Ocean, lies off the southeastern coast of India. It was earlier known as Ceylon. Population (1990 est.) 16,993,000; area 65,610 sq.km. The official languages are Sinhala and Tamil; the lingua franca is English.

History. Libraries, research, and learning have been a part of Sri Lanka's heritage, with records that date as far back as the 3rd century B.C. Several ancient kings encouraged the development of literature by providing royal patronage. Temple libraries called *Pothgul* contained both religious and secular works. English-speaking readers during the period of British rule used subscription libraries, such as the United Services Library in Colombo, founded in 1813. The Colombo Library was founded in 1824, and the two were merged in 1874. The Royal Asiatic Society of Sri Lanka Library was established in 1845.

Establishment of the Government Oriental Library, as early as 1870, can be considered the first step in setting up a library at the national level. Subsequently the Museum Library was established in 1877. Its collections numbered approximately 600,000 volumes, including manuscripts, and it served as a legal deposit library from 1885. It is the principal state reference library. The Colombo Municipal Council established the Colombo Public Library in 1925, merging the Colombo Library and the Pettah Library, founded in 1829. Ceylon was granted independence from British rule in 1948. The state-sponsored free education system helped in achieving a literacy rate of 85 percent.

National Library and Archives. The National Library of Sri Lanka opened in 1990, fulfilling a long-felt need in the country. It was one product of the work of the Sri Lanka National Library Services Board, set up by an act of Parliament in 1970. The Board's primary objectives are to formulate a national library policy, to promote and assist the development of all types of libraries, especially those maintained by state funds, and to manage the National Library. The National Library functions as the central coordinating agency for all aspects of national and international library and information services. It is responsible for producing the Sri Lanka *National Bibliography,* begun in 1962, and has had legal deposit privileges since 1974.

The Department of National Archives is also a legal deposit library, and the Director of National Archives is the Registrar of Books, Periodicals, Newspapers, and Printing Presses. With the passage of the National Archives Law in 1973, the scope of the Archives was extended. It now houses both public and private records of archival value.

Academic Libraries. The oldest academic library in Sri Lanka, founded in 1921 as the University

Libraries in Sri Lanka (1988)

Type of library	Number of administrative units (main libraries)	Number of service points (branches, mobile stops, etc.)	Volumes in collections	Annual expenditures (rupee)	Professional staff (with certificate, diploma, etc.)	Total staff
National	1	1	44,000	18,923,880	20	126
Academic[a]	52	60	1,461,025	18,000,000	35	310
Pirivena Libraries (libraries attached to Temples)	428	428	--			
Public	580	700	--	10,996,000	30	1,200
School	3,700	3,700	2,846,000	1,320,000	61	825
Special	150	155	627,483	4,200,000	74	370
(Voluntary organization libraries)	300	300				

[a]University Libraries only.

Source: information received by the Research and Development Division of the Sri Lanka National Library Services Board.

National Library of Sri Lanka, opened in 1990.

College Library, became the University of Ceylon Library in 1942. It was moved to Peradeniya in 1952. Another important Library is the Medical College Library, founded in 1870 and now part of the University of Colombo Library. The Library of the University of Ceylon at Peradeniya has one of the largest collections in the country, numbering more than 500,000 volumes. The other nine state university libraries also have significant collections. There are special collections on Sri Lanka and Oriental subjects in the larger universities. The universities have the best libraries in the country. There are libraries at the teacher training colleges, colleges of education, and technical colleges.

Public Libraries. Public libraries in Sri Lanka developed from subscription libraries such as the United Services Library. The quality of public library service varies greatly from region to region, because local governments are not required to maintain libraries. The country had 580 public libraries in 1990, but changes in local government indicated a possible restructuring of public libraries into provincial systems.

School Libraries. Despite the rapid growth of public education since independence, school libraries are less well developed than other educational facilities. Modern methods of teaching have increased the demand for school library services. There are now about 3,700 school libraries at all levels, providing literature in Sinhala, Tamil, and English.

Special Libraries. Special libraries and documentation centers are located in state corporations, government departments, and private organizations. They cover industry, commerce, scientific research, technology, agriculture, and allied subjects. The National Resources, Energy, and Science Authority of Sri Lanka (NARESA) is the body chiefly responsible for science information services. It operates a Science and Technology Information Center and coordinates information networks among science and technology libraries. Set up in 1981, it replaced the National Science Council of Sri Lanka.

The Profession. The Sri Lanka Library Association was established in 1960. It conducts part-time courses in librarianship and information studies at various levels. A Department of Library and Information Science was established in the University of Kelaniya in 1972. The Sri Lanka National Library Services Board conducts short-term training programs for practicing librarians.

REFERENCES

M. S. U. Amarasiri, editor, *The National Library of Sri Lanka, 1990,* a commemorative volume. Ishvari Corea, editor, *Libraries and People* (1975).

Population Statistics of Sri Lanka (1991).

ISHVARI COREA

Standing Conference of African University Libraries

The Standing Conference of African University Librarians (SCAUL) was formed as a result of discussions at the Leverhulme Inter-University Conference on the Needs and Problems of University Librarians in Tropical Africa, held in Salisbury, Rhodesia, September 14–23, 1964. At the end of the Conference, a Continuation Committee was appointed and charged with the responsibility of implementing the conference resolutions, one of which recommended that further conferences be held periodically.

Members of the Continuation Committee took the opportunity of the Conference of Librarians from Commonwealth Universities in Africa, sponsored by the Commonwealth Foundation and held in Lusaka, Zambia, August 24–29, 1969, to discuss further the organization of the Standing Conference of African University Librarians. At this conference, the non-Commonwealth Committee members, Ethiopia and Senegal, took part as observers. Some important recommendations concerning the organization of SCAUL were made, and a draft constitution was drawn up.

According to this constitution, full membership in SCAUL would be open to heads of libraries of universities eligible for membership in the Association of African Universities, with associate membership open to university libraries in other parts of the world, SCAUL activities would be developed mainly within Area Organizations of SCAUL. A Central Committee, comprising the Convener/Secretary (Chairman), representatives of Area Organizations, and the Editor of the *Newsletter,* would meet periodically to coordinate the work of the Areas. Each member of SCAUL would be free to choose the Area that it would join and would be allowed to attend as an observer the conferences in the Areas to which it did not belong. Each Area would determine its own membership requirements and draft its own constitution based on that of SCAUL. The *Newsletter* was to be published as the official organ of SCAUL. The name of the organization was changed to Standing Conference of African University Libraries.

These recommendations were subsequently approved in a postal ballot, and the draft constitution was fully discussed at Area meetings in 1971 and 1972 and subsequently approved.

SCAUL now operates through two Area Organizations: the Eastern Area (SCAULEA) and the Western Area (SCAULWA). The headquarters rotates with the post of Chairman. Each Area Organization has both anglophone and francophone countries as members. SCAULEA has held conferences in Addis Ababa (1971), Mauritius (1973), and Nairobi (1977). SCAULWA held conferences in Dakar (1974), Accra (1976), Kinshasha (1978), Monrovia (1980), Yaoundé (1982), Lagos (1984), Lomé (1986), Freetown (1988), and Benin City (1990).

The aims of SCAUL are (1) to keep members informed of each other's activities and, whenever possible, to correlate such activities in the common interest; and (2) to support and develop university library services in Africa.

SCAUL seeks to advance the development of university libraries by organizing conferences as a forum for discussing the problems of university librarianship in Africa. Topics covered have included the problems of management in university libraries, education for library staff, and managing libraries in an era of scarce resources. SCAUL sponsors individual research activities and projects and meetings of specialists on African bibliography, cataloguing, classification, and other library topics.

SCAUL publications include proceedings of the conferences of SCAULEA and SCAULWA and the SCAUL *Newsletter*. SCAULWA also publishes *African Journal of Academic Librarianship*, established in 1983 under the editorship of E. Bejide Bankole.

E. BEJIDE BANKOLE;
VIRGINIA W. DIKE

Sudan

The Democratic Republic of the Sudan, in northeastern Africa, is bounded by Egypt on the north, the Red Sea and Ethiopia on the east, Kenya, Uganda, and Zaire on the south, and the Central African Republic, Chad, and Libya on the west. Population (1990 est.) 25,204,000; area 2,505,813 sq.km. The official language is Arabic; English is widely spoken and is considered the first European language in the school system.

History. The word "Sudan" was used for hundreds of years to refer to the land south of the Great Desert. Its use was first limited to the area of the present Democratic Republic of the Sudan in 1899, at the beginning of the dual role played by Egypt and Britain in that part of Africa.

In 1903 Gordon's Memorial College was set up to train qualified personnel to serve in the government and to teach in schools. The first public library was established in 1947 at Wadmedani. Two comprehensive reports on Sudanese libraries, in 1960 and in 1972, revealed that responsibility for establishing libraries and training librarians was distributed among several authorities. The National Commission of Unesco, which examined the two reports, recommended the establishment of a National Council for Libraries. The Council consists of representatives from various ministries and educational institutions interested in library development.

National Library Service. There is no national library in the Sudan. The University of Khartoum Central Library functions as a national library, receiving publications through legal deposit and maintaining the Sudan Collection. The Collection was established in 1962 to serve scholars and researchers involved in Sudanese studies.

Academic Libraries. There are several university and college libraries in the Sudan. The development of Gordon's Memorial College into Gordon's University College in 1945 underscored the need for establishing a good library with a comprehensive collection to support advanced studies and to continue to provide students and faculty with adequate reference and reading materials. A new library was established around the collection of Sir Douglas Newbold, who was the Administrative Secretary of the Sudanese government. The Library was named after him until 1956.

In 1956 the University College became the University of Khartoum, with the addition of new colleges. The Library of the new University acquired collections from various sources, totaling about 3,000 titles and covering such subjects as the history and topology of the Sudan, African history, agriculture, and medicine. Two more universities and several university colleges were later established and equipped with fairly good libraries.

The University of Khartoum Library is the largest and richest in the country. It uses the Bliss Classification System; some of the college libraries use the Colon Classification. Prior to 1978 the Central Library supervised the various faculty libraries technically and administratively. After 1978 the faculties of Agriculture, Engineering, Law, and Medicine developed their own acquisition and cataloguing programs. These libraries submit catalogue cards to the Central Library for its union catalogue. The Library uses the University's computer center for computerizing its classified catalogue and serials files.

Circulation statistics at the University of Khartoum show that the Central Library has the highest circulation, followed by Medicine and Agriculture.

Libraries in Sudan (1987)

Type of library	Number of administrative units (main libraries)	Number of service points (branches, mobile stops, etc.)	Volumes in collections	Population served
Academic[a]	1	5	500,000	20,000

[a]1987 data

Source: Unesco, *Statistical Yearbook*, 1991.

Omdurman Islamic University was established in 1917 as the Omdurman Religious Institution to teach Islamic jurisprudence. Through various contributions, from charitable societies and individuals, the institution's Library was developed and its collection augmented. In 1965 the Institution achieved the status of an Islamic university and the old collection formed the core of the University Library's collection. The Library uses the Dewey Decimal Classification.

Public Libraries. Public libraries were introduced in the Sudan at the end of World War II, under the jurisdiction of the Ministry of Local Government. They were known as municipal libraries because they were directly administered by the municipalities set up by the Ministry of Local Government. Supervision was later transferred to the Public Libraries Department in the Ministry of Culture and Information.

Public libraries were established in Wadmedani, Atbara, Port Sudan, Khartoum, and many other towns. They have poor and small collections compared to the size of the population to be served, mainly because of financial constraints, high rates of theft, and loss of borrowed books. Their collections tend to emphasize literature and fiction, and little if any attention is paid to the sciences or social sciences. Borrowers are mainly government employees, teachers, and students. There is a marked absence in these libraries of registers of borrowers and books loaned. Most catalogues are outdated.

Several foreign cultural centers have opened their libraries to the Sudanese public, but the majority of titles in those libraries are in foreign languages and require a fair knowledge of those languages by the Sudanese users. Some centers are heavily used by university students, particularly in medicine and sciences and other related fields in which American and European texts are heavily used.

School Libraries and Media Centers. The first primary schools in the Sudan were established in 1863 in Khartoum, Barbar, Dongola, and Kassala and a few years later at Swaken and Sinnar. Preparatory schools were established in 1906 in Barbar, Omdurman, Wadmedani, Khartoum, Swaken, and Halfa. It is not known whether school libraries existed before; there are no references to the existence of such libraries. In 1974 the Ministry of Education established a department to plan for and develop school libraries.

At the primary and preparatory school levels, school libraries are no more than collections of books under the control of a particular teacher. However, there are libraries in secondary schools in compliance with a regulation that every secondary school should have a room designated as a library and every school with more than 640 pupils should have a full-time librarian.

In spite of this regulation, the school libraries situation was still poor not only in physical location and facilities but also in collections, as indicated by the ratio of 89,000 volumes against 4,686 schools or only 19 books per school.

Special Libraries. Special libraries have been established in the ministries, banks, research centers, and other sectors in order to meet the objectives of the respective organizations and to serve the needs of their staffs.

The National Documentation Center began as the main documentation center for the National Council for Research (in Science and Technology). It became an autonomous body and took its present name in 1972. The Center publishes abstract bulletins. It has microfiche and microfilm readers and printers but they are not heavily used. As part of an agreement with Unesco, the Center received a minicomputer for processing information and creating a local database utilizing MINISIS software.

The Sudan News Agency (SUNA) maintains an active Information and Research Department. The Department is divided into two units: the Information and Library Section and the Research Statistics and Follow-up Section. The former compiles data on a variety of topics, including ministries and other governmental departments, corporations, and institutions. The Department also maintains biographical files on all prominent Sudanese and international figures. Its library has more than 1,000 volumes and published a number of research works on oil in the Sudan, regional government in the Sudan, the Western Sahara, and other topics.

Mosque libraries are administered by the Ministry of Religious Affairs and Endowments. The Ministry aims at setting up a library in every large mosque in the country.

The Profession. Sudan launched the first library training courses in 1961, when the University of Khartoum's Department of General Studies organized two permanent training courses for employees in libraries and archives centers. A preliminary training program dealt with acquisition, cataloguing, circulation, and readers' advisory services, followed by advanced training in library administration, classification, and bibliography. Lecturers for these courses were recruited from the University Library and the Institute of Public Administration. Although the course was for one academic year, it did not lead to a formal degree or certification.

In 1966–67 the Department of Librarianship and Archives was established at Omdurman Islamic University. The undergraduate program lasts four years. In the first year, students are offered general courses in the humanities and in the social sciences; the other three years are devoted to library and archival studies.

Library training in the southern part of the Sudan began at the University of Juba in 1978 when regional ministries and other institutions were seeking to establish libraries. Short courses in basic librarianship were organized.

The certificate course for paraprofessionals began in 1981 and lasts a year. The objective of the program at the University of Juba is to train library assistants to run small libraries or to work under the guidance of professional librarians.

The Sudan Library Association, established in 1971, held its first conference in January 1972. The Association ceased to be active in 1979. Both the British Council and the U.S. Information Center maintain close liaison with practicing Sudanese librarians, who are usually invited to attend meetings or colloquia hosted by those active centers.

M. M. AMAN;
SHA'BAN A. KHALIFA

Suriname

Suriname, a republic in northern South America, is bounded by the Atlantic Ocean on the north, French Guiana on the east, Brazil on the south, and Guyana on the west. Population (1990 est.) 422,000; area 163,265 sq.km. The official language is Dutch.

History. Suriname has had a tradition of libraries since the 18th century, when the capital of Paramaribo had a large scientific library comparable to similar libraries in Western Europe and the United States. The library was destroyed in the 19th century by a fire set by the freedom fighters of the time, the Maroons. Various private libraries also date from this period, as do personal libraries. The so-called Volksbibliotheek (People's Library) was set up at the end of the 18th century under the influence of the Maatchappij tot Nut van het Algemeen (Public Benefit Company) in the Netherlands, but that library was also destroyed by fire in 1821.

Between 1821 and 1856 some brief attempts were made to establish loan associations for books on a commercial basis. In 1856 two medical doctors, F. A. G. Dumontier and C. Landré, proposed a plan to set up a library in Paramaribo. Their plan was successful, and on December 1, 1857, the Colonial Library was established under the jurisdiction of the Inspector of Education. This was the first attempt to found a national library, which had to serve as both public and research library. A lack of expert personnel and poor facilities caused the National Library to close in 1957. The collection was distributed among a number of libraries in the Netherlands, including the library of the Royal Institute for the Tropics and the Royal Library. In 1950 the collections for adults and children had already been turned over to the Public Library of the Cultural Centre of Suriname (CCS), which had begun operating in 1949.

Academic Libraries. At the University of Suriname, libraries were established at the Faculty of Law (with holdings of about 10,000 publications), the Faculty of Medicine (10,000), the Faculty of Social and Economic Sciences (3,000), the Engineering Faculty (10,000), the Faculty of Natural Resource Studies (10,000), and the International Law library (2,000). These faculty libraries primarily serve the university's 1,000 students.

Public Libraries. The Public Library of the CCS was set up on the initiative of the Cultural Committee for Suriname. Pioneering work was performed by M. Nassy, the first Librarian of this institution. It quickly became apparent that an organization of the existing libraries was necessary. From 1950 to 1957 the National Library functioned as a center for reference works and scientific literature, while the CCS library covered belles lettres and services to youth.

The CCS library operates as a central public library and works to set up public libraries in other regions. Until 1975 it was subsidized by STICUSA (Foundation for Cultural Cooperation between the Netherlands, Suriname, and the Netherlands Antilles), but after Suriname's independence in 1975 it was supported by the state. The central library and its six branches and two bookmobiles have a total collection of about 225,000 volumes.

School Libraries. The Ministry of Education and Community Development is largely responsible for school libraries; a Library Affairs Section was attached to the Ministry in 1968. The first library it established was the General Educational Library (1969), a central library for all the school libraries, where expensive research material may be consulted. The Library also provides materials for evening school courses. The Library Affairs Section founded 60 school libraries, with estimated total collections of about 60,000 items. The General Educational Library has about 35,000 publications, with some 75,000 annual loans and visitors.

Special Libraries. Most of the special libraries in Suriname are in ministries. They include the Ministry of Agriculture, Animal Husbandry, and Fisheries (37,000 volumes), the Ministry of Justice and Police Affairs, the State Forest Administration, and the Central Bank. Other libraries that are open to a larger public are the library of the Suriname Museum Foundation, which has the largest collection of writings on Suriname (12,000 publications), the Institute for Advanced Teacher Training, and the Scientific Institute Foundation.

The Profession. Most workers in school libraries are teachers who have taken three-week in-service training courses at the Library Affairs Section. The staff at the Library Affairs Section must have at least four years of practical experience and one year of professional training. There is also a two-year library course at the CCS.

R. CH. W. LONT

Swaziland

Swaziland, a monarchy based on tribal tradition in southwestern Africa, is bounded on the east by Mozambique and on the north, west, and south by South Africa. Population (1990 est.) 768,000; area 17,364 sq.km. The official languages are English and Swazi.

National Library Services. The functions of a national library, in the absence of such an institution, were assigned to the Swaziland National Library Service and the University of Swaziland Library, which enjoy legal deposit status.

Academic Library. The only academic library is the University of Swaziland Library, founded in 1971 at the dissolution of the University of Botswana, Lesotho, and Swaziland and incorporating the Swaziland Agricultural College and University Center. It consists of the Main Library at Kwaluseni, with 55,000 volumes, and the Faculty of Agriculture Library at Luyengo, with 15,000 volumes. In addition to undergraduate material, the Library has a collection of Swaziana and compiles the *Swaziland National Bibliography* (1976–). It also has deposit status for documents of the Food and Agriculture Organization and the World Bank.

Public Libraries. The Swaziland National Library Service provides public library services, operating a public library in Manzini with several branches, depots, and mobile unit stops. It has holdings of 55,000 volumes and 1,000 current periodicals and an annual circulation of around 120,000; it reaches more than 20 percent of the country's literate population.

School Libraries. The Ministry of Education operates some 500 schools for about 125,000 pupils and distributes books among 48 school libraries, while the Swaziland National Library Service lends books to the schools. A number of secondary and high school libraries operate on their own budgets. The Swaziland College of Technology, the Swaziland Institute of Management and Public Administration, and two teacher training colleges have libraries with more than 10,000 volumes.

Special Libraries. The Malkerns Research Station and the Lowveld Experimental Farm have libraries with a joint stock of more than 6,000 volumes and more than 200 agricultural journals. There is a 2,500-volume library at the Mananga Agricultural Management Center, run by the Commonwealth Development Corporation, which provides training for junior and middle level management and extension workers from developing countries of the Commonwealth. A few ministries of government have departmental libraries for their staffs. The Attorney General's Chambers Library serves the Ministry of Justice and the Central Statistical Office Library serves the Government Statistician. The Monetary Authority and the Ministry of Agriculture operate libraries; the National Archives contains a library section devoted to Swaziana. The British High Commission Office and the American embassy run libraries with open membership, while the Mbabane Library Association is a subscription library.

REFERENCES

A. W. Z. Kuzwayo, *Information Systems and National Information Services in Swaziland* (University College of Swaziland Library, 1978).

Wallace Van Jackson, "Library Development in Swaziland," *International Library Review* (1976).

A. W. Z. KUZWAYO

Sweden

Sweden, a constitutional monarchy, lies on the eastern part of the Scandinavian Peninsula in northern Europe. It is bounded by Norway on the west, Finland on the northeast, the Gulf of Bothnia and the Baltic Sea on the east, and the North Sea on the southwest. Population (1990 est.) 8,559,000; area 449,964 sq.km. The official language is Swedish.

History. Around 3,000 years ago the ancestors of present Swedes left extensive rock carvings in granite as a pictorial script of events occurring in shipping, hunting, and agriculture, and in association with religion and magic. The oral traditions behind these events have been lost, and we can only guess at their meaning. The most famous ones are found in Tanum, Bohuslän. A large megalith calendar can be seen at Kåseberga, Skåne.

Contacts with writing later took place in encounters with the Mediterranean peoples. Ancient Greek cursive characters were taken over or readjusted so that they could be carved on wooden objects as "runes," which first appeared in the 4th century A.D. Runes are also found in the fragments of the Codex Argenteus, a vellum manuscript now in the Uppsala University Library. Most visible are about 3,000 memorial runestones scattered around the country. One runestone four meters tall is now in the hall of Lund University Library. The Swedish Vikings left behind "graffiti" of carved runes and dragon ornaments on the Lion of Piraeus, which has stood since 1687 in front of the Armory of Venice, and in the large mosque of Istanbul. Even though there are numerous runes inscribed on such useful objects as weapons, rings, and coins, runes do not constitute a Swedish book culture.

Books came with the Catholic monks who from the 9th century on traveled to the distant North in their zeal to convert Scandinavian believers in the Aesir (a group of deities) to Christianity. The first libraries were founded in churches and monasteries to serve the needs of the ecclesiastics. The oldest Nordic manuscript, Necrologium Lundense, now in the Lund University Library, started in 1123 as a registry of the dates of deaths of persons associated with the Diocesan Chapter of the Saint Laurentii Church, Lund. It contains the first library instruction in Sweden, proving that the Chapter at that time had an extant "library in the custody of the Cantor" (in Latin).

Besides cathedral libraries in Linköping, Skara, Strängnäs, and Uppsala, wealthy libraries were found in monasteries. The library of the Abbey of St. Bridget, Vadstena, grew during the Middle Ages to be the largest library in the Nordic countries, holding more than 1,400 manuscripts and books. The Abbey in 1495 set up the first printshop.

The first book printed in Sweden was made by Johan Snell, who in 1483 was called from Lübeck, Germany, to Stockholm to print *Dialogus Creaturarum Moralizatus,* a collection of sermons and fables. Before the end of the century another 11 incunabula were printed.

Libraries in Sweden (1990)

Type of library	Number of administrative units (main libraries)	Number of service points (branches, mobile stops, etc.)	Volumes in collections	Annual expenditures (Swedish krona)	Population served	Professional staff (with certificate, diploma, etc.)	Total staff
National	1	4	3,300,000	58,500,000	c. 25,000	77	194
Academic	10	76	14,700,000	218,700,000	c. 150,000	364	867
Public	284	c. 2,000	46,160,000	2,231,973,000	c. 8,500,000	2,564	6,189
School	--	--	33,000,000		1,200,000	--	--
Special	43	74	6,200,000	96,200,000	30,000	156	290

Sources: *Statistisk årsbok 1991,* Stockholm 1990, *Statistiska meddelanden,* Ku 11, 12, 13, Stockholm, 1988/89

The judicial arm also needed books, and the oldest manuscript in Swedish, *Västgötalagen,* dates back to the beginning of the 13th century, followed by many similar editions for the law of various lands. Parchment of sheep, goat, or calf played the main role for book material. Paper documents first appeared in Sweden in 1345, but paper manufacturing there did not start until two hundred years later.

The Protestant Reformation that Luther started in 1527 turned out to be a catastrophe for many libraries. They were deprived of most of their collections, and many Latin manuscripts were torn up and used as material in making tax lists and in binding records of the emerging national state. Others were placed in the Court library, schools, and private collections.

In contrast to the decline in the 16th century, lively collection building occurred in the 17th. Sweden as a great power enriched its libraries with booty from royal libraries and monasteries in Northern Europe. Universities were founded with libraries—Uppsala Library in 1620 and Lund Library in 1666. Queen Christina (reigned 1632–54) opened the Royal Library to scholars. In spite of the early government contributions in support of these libraries, the 18th and 19th centuries marked slow progress for them. A new university library was founded in Göteborg in 1861. The 20th century saw a rapid establishment of new universities and colleges with libraries—Umeå (1964), Linköping (1969), Stockholm (1971), and other institutions.

In a long, narrow, sparsely populated country, the state had difficulty in developing adequate library services for the general public. Toward the end of the 18th century a public library movement was begun with the establishment of parish libraries. In 1842 the public school law stated that the vicars "should encourage the setting up and usage of parish libraries and also propose books for that end." In 1868 a total of 1,437 such libraries were recorded; then came a period of decline. Instead, with industrialization there was a swing toward the establishment of town libraries, of which the Dicksonska, Göteborg, founded in 1861, was the most important. These libraries were seen as complements to elementary education in order to promote the general educational level. Workmen's association libraries were started in Stockholm in 1882. Many of the parish, town, and workmen's libraries were later merged with public libraries established in each community.

For long the government was reluctant to support that movement. In 1905 the public libraries were acknowledged by a government grant for their activities. In the 1920s other forms of public libraries, such as hospital and seamen's libraries, got such funding. The Public Library Act of 1930 recognized only one library in each county as eligible for funding, considering it central in assisting the local libraries in their book demands; the municipalities, in the meantime, had to support all of their public and school libraries. A government commission in 1984 submitted a proposal to the Parliament to upgrade the poorest libraries in the municipalities.

National Libraries. The Kungliga Biblioteket (Royal Library) is the national library of Sweden. Originally the private collection of the Swedish kings, it became a deposit library in 1661 and has had the status of a national library since then. In 1978 Lund University Library became the national lending library for Swedish materials, but it had been receiving copyright materials since 1698. Deposit copies of films and sound and video recordings are preserved by the Arkivet för Ljud och Bild (Archive for the Preservation of Films and Recordings), established in 1977.

The Royal Library G.A. Dahl/Architect

Main entrance to Kungliga Biblioteket (Royal Library), Sweden's national library.

The Royal Library also collects foreign publications in the humanities and the social sciences. Its collection of manuscripts, occupying more than 2,100 meters of shelving, concentrates on Swedish authors such as August Strindberg and Nobel Prize authors Selma Lagerlöf and Pär Lagerqvist. The Rare Books Collection is of high quality.

The Royal Library is responsible for the annual *Svensk Bokförteckning* and the five-year cumulations of the *Svensk Bokkatalog.* A joint union catalogue was created as early as 1886. The National Bibliography and the union catalogue are computerized in a network, the LIBRIS (LIBRary Information System), started in the early 1970s and now the responsibility of the Royal Library. Through cooperative input, by 1990 the database held more than 2,100,000 bibliographic records accessible by terminals. Many libraries download their own records and use them in local networks.

In 1988 the Royal Library became responsible for program coordination among research libraries at the national level, providing financial support for research projects, promoting the use of new technology, giving grants, and overseeing the system of ansvarsbibliotek (subject-oriented central libraries) established in 1984. The goal of the subject-oriented program is to develop libraries with substantial expertise and large media collections in various disciplines to meet national demands for modern research. By the early 1990s there were subject centers for agriculture, economics, medicine, psychology and education, and technology.

The Royal Library is a government agency directly under the Ministry of Education and Cultural Affairs. It has four divisions and a remote deposit library, Statens Biblioteksbyrå. Its collections amount to more than three million volumes.

The Riksarkivet (national archive, 1618), holds earlier medieval archives (about 13,000 parchment documents). Since 1906, it has been the central authority for all archives of government bodies.

Academic Libraries. The general research libraries are located at six universities and ten university colleges. There are university libraries in Göteborg (1861), Linköping (1969), Lund (1671), Stockholm (1877, 1971), Umeå (1964), and Uppsala (1620). All of them have legal deposit rights. With the exception of the university library in Stockholm, which has no sections for medicine and technology, the libraries are cross-disciplinary. The university libraries constitute the most important part of the Swedish research library system. In addition to serving their own institutions, they also have responsibilities in their regions and, through interlibrary loan, throughout the country. They are open to the public in that everyone is allowed access to the reference collections and can order books to read in the reading rooms.

Uppsala University Library, Carolina Rediviva, is the oldest and most renowned academic library, with more than four million volumes. It was founded in 1620, but integrated earlier monastic libraries such as that of St. Bridget's monastery. It owns the most valuable book in Sweden, the Codex Argenteus (Silver Bible), a Gothic manuscript probably originating in northern Italy during the 6th century. It also has a good collection of rare books, beautiful bindings, books on the history of medicine, illustrated manuscripts, and other remarkable books.

The University Library of Lund, founded in 1671, actually dates to medieval times, because it houses books and manuscripts from the former Danish cathedral chapter.

Public Libraries. Most public libraries in Sweden date back to the popular movements that built libraries for their own general educational purposes in the 19th century. From the mid-1930s to the mid-1970s the municipalities gradually took over these libraries, and each now has public library service. There are about 2,000 library units with some 46,000,000 volumes.

According to a parliamentary decision, public libraries are instruments of public educational policy and constitute an integral part of the democratic process. The mission of public libraries is to stimulate people to seek knowledge and cultural experiences and to provide a wide range of good-quality media and cultural activities. Public libraries are open to all free of charge.

Through its cultural committee, each local municipality, not the central government, decides how to develop its public library services. The activities of Sweden's public libraries are not regulated by law as they are in other Nordic countries. The standards of library service vary a little from one municipality to another, depending on local priorities. Many municipalities in Sweden are small: more than half have fewer than 20,000 inhabitants. In such places, the library may be the only venue for general cultural activities. Municipal governments cover 95 percent of library costs, county councils 2 percent, and the government 3 percent.

Swedish authors and foreign authors resident in Sweden receive compensation for library loans under an agreement between the government and the Swedish Writers' Union. Half of this library-loan compensation goes directly to the authors; the other half goes to the Swedish Authors' Fund, which distributes the money mainly in the form of stipends for writers.

School Libraries. The municipalities are responsible for school libraries, but until 1989 teachers were employees of the national government. Most schools have libraries with out-of-date stocks, and 6 percent of schools have no libraries at all. The number of loans dropped from 28,000,000 in the early 1980s to 19,000,000 at the end of the decade; bookstocks decreased from 36,000,000 to 33,000,000 in the same period. Almost two thirds of the smallest school libraries are staffed for only one hour a week, and the librarians in the schools are in most cases teachers.

Special Libraries. The large central medical library at the Karolinska Institute (KIBIC, 1810) is responsible for a large portion of the interlibrary loans in its field. Noteworthy are the libraries at the Royal Institute of Technology in Stockholm (1826), the Chalmers University of Technology in Göteborg (1829), and the University of Agricultural Sciences in Uppsala, which, unlike the others, is under the Ministry of Agriculture rather than the Ministry of Education and Cultural Affairs. The National Library for Psychology and Education (SPPB, 1885) is an independent research library with national responsibility for the behavioral sciences. The Stockholm School of Economics has the nation's best collection of books and other publications in the field of economics. Other official special libraries are at the larger museums, such as the art library at the National Museum of Fine Arts, the ethnology library at the Nordic Museum, and the libraries at the Royal Academy of Letters, Historical Museum, and Royal Academy of Music.

Many larger authorities outside the educational system have good libraries and information services in their fields. These libraries primarily serve their organizations, although some are open to the public, such as the libraries of the National Board of Occupational Safety and Health and the National Environmental Protection Agency. The Riksdagsbiblioteket (Parliamentary Library) serves both members of Parliament and civil servants in the central government.

Uppsala University Library. Founded in 1620, it is the most renowned of Sweden's academic libraries. Collections date from early monastic libraries.

Uppsala-Bild

Since 1931 it has been responsible for the current bibliography of government publications, *Årsbibliografi över Sveriges Statliga Publikationer.*

Large companies that carry out research have good libraries. Examples include the pharmaceutical manufacturers Astra, Pharmacia, and Kabi, automobile makers Volvo and Saab, and electronics giants Ericsson and ABB. These libraries are not open to the public.

The Profession. The Bibliotekshögskolan Borås (BHS; Swedish School of Library and Information Sciences), formed in 1972, is responsible for the academic preparation of public and research librarians. The curriculum spans four terms; for a bachelor's degree, a student must also study two terms in other subjects. The school admits 110 students each term, or 220 in a year. From 1985, students with doctorates in other subjects could graduate from a two-term course. The school offers a one-term course for library assistants and continuing education courses.

A program in Informatik (information science) was established at Stockholm University in 1981; a Center for Library Research at the University of Göteborg in 1987; and an Institute for Book and Library History at the University of Lund in 1990. These institutions have different purposes, but they provide librarians of all kinds with opportunities to study library and information science up to the doctoral level.

The Tekniska Litteratursällskapet (TLS; Swedish Society for Technical Documentation) and the Svenska Bibliotekariesamfundet (SBF; Swedish Association for University and Research Librarians) offer courses for staff in academic and special libraries dealing with literature searches, acquisition methods, special collections, and related topics. Fellowships for studies abroad in the library information field are given by the Forskningsrådsnämnden (Council for Planning and Coordination of Research) and the Royal Library.

The Sveriges Allmänna Biblioteksförening (SAB; Swedish Library Association), founded in 1915, has mainly institutional members and is organized in five sections, each representing one kind of library. It publishes *Biblioteksbladet* eight times a year. The SBF, founded in 1921, is a professional organization for librarians in this sector. Librarians from the industrial sector belong to TLS (1936), which has a membership of 1,300. It publishes *Tidskrift för dokumentation* four times a year. These three organizations belong to IFLA. The Royal Library is the national member of FID.

REFERENCES

Tomas Lidman, *Libraries in Sweden* (Stockholm, 1990).

Magnus Torstensson, "Library History Research in Sweden: A Field in Development," *Svensk Biblioteksforskning* (1988).

Scientific and Technical Information Provision in Sweden: Proposal for New Organization (Report submitted by two Swedish government commissions) (1977; Summary, Stockholm, 1978).

TOMAS LIDMAN

Switzerland

Switzerland, a federal republic in western Europe, is bounded by Germany on the north, Austria and Liechtenstein on the east, Italy on the south, and France on the west. Population (1990 est.) 6,712,000, area 41,293 sq.km. The official languages are French, German, and Italian. The 26 cantons and semi-cantons are responsible for matters of cultural and educational policy. Therefore the historical background and the structure of the public authorities have both exerted a strong influence on the development and organization of Swiss libraries.

History. One of the oldest libraries in the world, the library of the Abbey of St. Gall (Stiftsbibliothek) in Switzerland, was founded at the beginning of the 7th century. Around the year 820, the abbot Gozbert gave the order to draw up a plan of the Abbey. The manuscript has been preserved in the archives of the Abbey, and the collections have remained intact for nearly 1,300 years. Some of the most important Swiss libraries date back to the Renaissance (Basel, 1460), the Reformation (Bern, 1529, 1537; Geneva, 1559), or the 17th century (Zurich, 1629).

Under the influence of the economic institutions originating from the Enlightenment, which developed in Switzerland during the second half of the 18th century, many libraries were built in less important towns such as Morges, Yverdon, Zofingen, and Neuchâtel.

One of the most beautiful creations in Swiss library history is the Bibliotheca Bodmeriana, founded by Martin Bodmer (1899–1971). He reassembled 150,000 rare and precious books and manuscripts, including the only known manuscripts of the Greek poet Menander, the oldest papyri of the New Testament (2nd century), and the valuable autographs of the poet Rainer Maria Rilke (1875–1926). The collection is organized around five poles: Homer, the Bible, Dante, Shakespeare, and Goethe. This fascinating collection was given to the Bodmer

Libraries in Switzerland (1990)

Type of library	Number of administrative units (main libraries)	Number of service points (branches, mobile stops, etc.)	Volumes in collections	Annual expenditures (Swiss franc)	Population served	Professional staff (with certificate, diploma, etc.)	Total staff
National	1	1	2,922,000	6,662,000	6,800,000	35	75
Academic	12	--	16,000,000	100,000,000	133,000	450	900
Public	1,948	--	--	1,612,000,000	6,800,000	--	--
School	2,764	--	--	--	365,000	--	--
Special	1,276	--	--	--	--	--	--

The National Library of Switzerland, Bern, founded in 1895.

National Library of Switzerland

foundation after the death of Martin Bodmer, and is open to the public.

National Library. The Swiss National Library shows the influence of historical factors through several characteristics. It was not founded until 1895, and initially its role was limited to acquiring *Helvetica* (works concerning Switzerland and those of Swiss authorship, as well as works printed in Switzerland) after 1848. Since legal deposit had not been adopted, "free deposit" was established in 1915 between the Library and the two associations of Swiss booksellers and editors, under which the associations submit one copy of each new publication to the Library. Any Swiss national or any person over 15 years of age residing in Switzerland can borrow books.

Over the years the Library's functions have been augmented. It manages a bookstock of about three million items, including publications of official Swiss, as well as international, organizations. It administers the Swiss Union Catalogue, which indexes more than seven million foreign publications held in 300 libraries. In order to exploit these resources, the Library has produced a series of publications: *Das Schweizer Buch; Das Schweizer Bücherverzeichnis,* the cumulative edition published quinquennially; *Das Schweizer Zeitschriftenverzeichnis; Bibliographie der Schweizergeschichte; Bibliographia Scientiae Naturalis Helvetica; Jahresverzeichnis des Schweizerischen Hochschulschriften;* and *Bibliographie der Schweizer Familiengeschichte.* The library also houses an office responsible for publishing the *Statistische Quellenwerke der Schweiz.*

Academic Libraries. Most of the 10 Swiss university libraries were founded between 1460 (Basel) and 1629 (Zurich). The Fribourg Library was founded in 1848 through the fusion of the old libraries of the dissolved convents—Collège Saint-Michel. The Zurich Federal Polytechnic, founded in 1855, has developed considerably; it possesses a bookstock of about four million items. Swiss academic libraries possess a total of 15 million volumes and approximately 6,000 incunabula. Several of these libraries have a second function. As canton libraries they serve the local population's needs in scientific literature.

Automation. The Bibliothèque Cantonale et Universitaire of Lausanne (BCU/L) developed a computerized system (SIBIL) (Système Informatisé de Bibliothèques) based on a format derived from MARC II. It serves the needs of lending scheduling by bar code, acquisitions, and online cataloguing. The database acquires nearly 100,000 records a year, originating from about 20 libraries of Fribourg, Geneva, Lausanne, and Neuchâtel. The database (more than 900,000 titles in 1987) is a mainstay of REBUS.

REBUS (Réseau des Bibliothèques Utilisant SIBIL) is a network of four databases utilizing the SIBIL system: Lausanne (connecting more than 20 libraries of four universities), Basel (University Library and Law library), Sankt Gallen (cantonal libraries, including the National Library of Liechtenstein), and—in France—Montpellier (university libraries including also the university libraries of Bordeaux, Pau, and Grenoble, and the École Polytechnique of Paris). REBUS is designed to connect the four databases and to extend the network to other libraries in France, Belgium, Luxembourg, Spain, and Switzerland. The library of the Swiss Federal Institute of Technology in Zurich developed its own computerized system, ETHICS.

Building. The university library building in Lausanne (150,000 square feet) opened its doors in 1982; it was built according to an American model. It holds 200,000 volumes in an open-access system.

Public Libraries. The earliest public libraries in Switzerland were originally theological libraries established during the Reformation (Bern, 1528; Sankt Gallen, 1551). The first public libraries without theological antecedents were at Berthoud (1729) and Glarus (1758). The development of public libraries gained momentum, however, principally in the 19th century. From 1868 to 1911 the number of these libraries almost tripled.

There are approximately 2,000 public libraries. Those canton libraries not controlled by a university acquire scientific and bibliographic reference works and additionally conserve the local printed production, which is incorporated in its entirety.

Public library networks have been created, notably in Geneva, Zurich (Bibliothek der Pestalozzi-Gesellschaft), and Bern (Berner Volksbücherei). The Schweizerische Volksbibliothek, founded in 1920, has seven regional branches housing 200,000 volumes, which may be lent either to organizations or to individuals.

School Libraries. There are approximately 3,000 school libraries of varying size and importance.

Special Libraries. Approximately 1,300 special libraries may be divided into four categories: (1) 15 libraries of international organizations, among them the United Nations Library (700,000 volumes, 12,000 periodicals), the International Bureau of Education Library/Unesco (60,000 volumes, 800 periodicals), and the International Labour Office Library (300,000 volumes, 10,000 periodicals); (2) 200 libraries belonging to public societies and associations; (3) approximately 100 libraries belonging to private enterprise (industry, banks, and insurance companies), with collections totaling more than 1,200,000 volumes; and (4) 118 archival libraries.

Monastic Libraries. Among many libraries meriting citation the following are especially important: the Stiftsbibliothek Sankt Gallen (100,000 volumes, 2,000 manuscripts, 1,650 incunabula) and the libraries of Einsiedeln and Engelberg.

Associations. There are three library associations in Switzerland: the Vereinigung Schweizerischer Bibliothekare (VSB) (200 corporate members and 1,000 individual members), the Schweizerische Vereinigung für Dokumentation (SVI) (425 individual members), and the Vereinigung Schweizerischer Archivare (VSA) (35 corporate members and 124 individual members).

JEAN-PIERRE CLAVEL;
J. MÉDIONI

Sylvestre, Guy
(1918–)

Jean-Guy Sylvestre was the second National Librarian of Canada and under him the National Library experienced remarkable growth and development. He reorganized and expanded the institution, took major initiatives in the areas of collection development, bibliographic control, and systems, and created a consultative approach to policy formulation.

Sylvestre was born in Sorel, Quebec, May 17, 1918. He graduated from the University of Ottawa with a B.A. in 1939, a L.Ph. in 1940, and an M.A. in 1941. Following several years of government service, he became the private secretary to the Prime Minister of Canada, Louis St. Laurent, in 1945. In 1953 he was appointed Assistant Parliamentary Librarian, and in 1956 Associate. He succeeded W. Kaye Lamb as National Librarian in 1968, serving until November 17, 1983. He was Chairman of the Board and Executive Director of the Canadian Institute for Historical Microreproductions from 1984 to 1986 and became chairman of the Ottawa Valley Book Festival in 1989.

Sylvestre was the architect of the revised National Library Act (1969), which expanded the mandate of the library by giving it a role as coordinator of federal library services and enabling it to enter into formal agreements with other libraries and educational institutions in respect to library services. Through this device, the National Library was able to pursue the goal of a nationwide library network.

Because the National Library was a relatively new institution, established in 1952, its collections were not comprehensive, and consisted mainly of materials received through legal deposit and transferred from the Library of Parliament and other federal libraries. Sylvestre created a Collection Development Branch in 1972 and, a year later, a Rare Books and Manuscripts Division. These agencies accelerated the systematic development of a retrospective collection of Canadiana and of literature in the humanities and social sciences, with the objectives of supporting research and interlibrary loan. Sylvestre's initiative led to the acquisition of many notable private collections and the papers of several major Canadian authors, composers, and musicians. In 1968 Sylvestre established a Resources Survey Office to assess and monitor the development of collections in other Canadian libraries. To facilitate sharing these resources, he took several measures to improve interlibrary loan in Canada, including establishing a Resource Network Committee in 1980.

Guy Sylvestre

Having responsibility for the compilation of the national bibliography *Canadiana,* Sylvestre understood the importance of the principles of Universal Bibliographic Control. He moved aggressively to establish and implement national and international standards in the context of developing computer-based systems. Special task forces were established in the early 1970s to develop Canadian cataloguing standards and a Canadian MARC format that would accommodate the two official languages, English and French. These and subsequent committees led to the definition and publication of Canadian MARC formats, authorities, and subject headings. The National Library assumed responsibility for the assignment of ISBNs and ISSNs and developed a decentralized system of Cataloguing-In-Publication.

The appointment of a Systems Development Team in 1968 and the establishment of a Research and Planning Branch in 1970 (later reorganized as the Library Systems Center and the Office for Network Development) led to the acquisition and modification of DOBIS software in 1976 and its subsequent application to producing the national bibliography, to creating an online cataloguing system for federal libraries, and to implementing an automated union catalogue in 1980. In 1982 the National Library was a key participant in a successful experiment in interchanging bibliographic data between autonomous computer systems.

Sylvestre also moved to improve public services, for example by establishing in 1972 a selective dissemination of information service and in 1973 a multilingual biblioservice which provides loan collections to public libraries for the use of Canada's many ethnic groups. Much attention was devoted to the future of the union catalogue location services: location requests shot up from 58,000 in 1968 to 183,000 in 1983. The National Library provides locations for about 78 percent of these requests and fills about 27 percent of them from its own enlarged collections.

Sylvestre made a particular effort to establish liaison with the library community nationally and internationally. He expanded the National Library's publishing program, launching the *National Library News* in 1979 as a vehicle for the regular provision of information. He exploited consultative mechanisms to the fullest extent, involving hundreds of librarians in the work of the National Library Advisory Board and many committees and task forces. He called upon all librarians in Canada to contribute to the development of a long-range plan for the National Library, which was published in 1979. On the international front, he initiated the practice of regular administrative meetings with the Library of Congress, was prominent in the affairs of the International Federation of Library Associations, and was the founder and first Chairman (in 1974) of the Conference of Directors of National Libraries.

Sylvestre was at the same time an active scholar and a man of letters, having published extensively in the fields of French- and English-Canadian literature. He was elected a Fellow of the Royal Society of Canada in 1951, serving as its President in 1973, and was appointed an Officer of the Order of Canada in 1982. He received many honorary degrees and awards, including, in 1983, the government's highest form of recognition, the Outstanding Public Service Award.

REFERENCES

F. Dolores Donnelley, *The National Library of Canada* (1973).
National Library of Canada, *The Future of the National Library of Canada* (1979).
Ian Wees, *The National Library of Canada: Twenty-Five Years After* (1978).

BASIL STUART-STUBBS

Syria

Syria, a republic in southwest Asia, is bounded by Turkey on the north, Iraq on the east, Jordan on the south, and Israel, Lebanon, and the Mediterranean Sea on the west. Population (1990 est.) 12,116,000; area 185,180 sq.km. The official language is Arabic.

National Library. The Assad National Library is the national library of Syria. Established in 1984, it is the official legal deposit library, receiving five copies of every publication produced in Syria or by Syrians in other countries. By 1990 the provisions of a new legal deposit law for all book and nonbook materials were already being applied, and the Library held nearly 133,000 volumes. Its modern nine-story building has a total area of 22,000 sq.m. and space for two million volumes. It has eight main reference rooms, with seats for 500 readers; a reading room for the blind; an auditorium; a seminar room; and two reception rooms.

The Library's holdings cover everything published in Syria, including books, periodicals, printed music, cultural and commercial films, and slides of the works of Syrian plastic artists. Nonbook holdings total almost 12,500 items. The Library also holds 19,000 Arabic manuscripts, Syrian dissertations, and selected publications from other countries, acquired by purchase, legal deposit, exchange, and donation.

The Library holds training courses throughout the year for those working in the fields of libraries, archives, and preserving documents. It supervises the annual Arabic book fair, in which many Syrian and Arab publishers participate. It publishes the annual *Syrian National Bibliography* (1984–), the *National Bibliography of pre-1984 Syrian Publications* (issued irregularly), the *Analytical Index of Syrian Periodicals* (quarterly since 1985), and Masters' and Doctoral Dissertations by Syrian students in Syrian and foreign universities. By 1990 it was completing a database of the text of all legislation issued in Syria after 1918 and several other computer databases.

Academic Libraries. Damascus University (founded in 1919) has a central library and 26 branch libraries with total holdings of 290,000 volumes and almost 5,500 periodicals. Aleppo University (1960) has a central library and 20 branch libraries holding 250,000 volumes, nearly 1,400 periodicals, and 6,000 items of nonbook material. Teshrin University in Latakia (1971) has a total of 26,000 volumes in its central library and six branch libraries. Al-Baath University (1980) has a central library and seven branch libraries holding a total of 10,000 volumes. The Center for Scientific and Research Studies (1970) holds 20,000 volumes, more than 1,200 periodicals, 5,300 reports and pamphlets, and 3,500 nonbook items.

Public Libraries. The Ministry of Culture supervises Syrian public libraries. They include the National Library in Aleppo and Cultural Centers throughout the country, as well as Al-Zaheria Library in Damascus, which is administered by the Arab Academy of the Ministry of Higher Education. The country has more than 90 Cultural Centers that offer, in addition to collections of books in the humanities and social sciences, such cultural activities as lectures, symposia, musical recitals, exhibitions, and film shows. The Centers hold a total of more than a million books and periodicals. The Ministry of Culture also operates 40 mobile libraries, seeking to extend library

Libraries in Syria (1987)

Type of library	Number of administrative units (main libraries)	Number of service points (branches, mobile stops, etc.)	Volumes in collections	Annual expenditures (pound)	Population served	Professional staff (with certificate, diploma, etc.)	Total staff
National	1	--	151,600	15,000,000	--	24	260
Academic	5	59	596,000	6,000,000	158,880	10	114
Public	92	40	1,000,000	--	--	--	370
School	903	--	800,000	--	--	--	903

services to all residential districts in cities and rural areas.

The Al-Zaheria Library (1882) served as a national library until 1984. It contained Arabic manuscripts collected from private libraries; the manuscripts and rare books were transferred to the Assad National Library, and the Al-Zaheria Library now holds 140,000 volumes of books and periodicals in the humanities and social sciences.

School Libraries. Syria has more than 900 school libraries at all educational levels, the majority administered by full-time teachers trained in courses run by the Ministry of Education. Total holdings number 800,000 volumes in all subjects.

Special Libraries. Government ministries and most institutes and administrative bodies have collections to support research by their staffs. These libraries hold from 500 to 20,000 volumes. Some also hold periodicals and nonbook materials, provide photocopying services, and use personal computers in their work. No precise statistics are available for the total number of special libraries or their holdings.

The Profession. Until 1984, Syrian librarians received their training abroad, because Syria had no school of librarianship. In that year, when the country had 75 trained professional librarians, the Faculty of Literature of Damascus University opened a section for library education. By 1990 it had 40 graduates and had enrolled 450 students.

Assad National Library

GHASSAN LAHHAM

Taiwan

Taiwan, an island in eastern Asia off the southeast coast of the People's Republic of China, became the seat of the Republic of China in 1949. Population (1991 est.) 20,536,233; area 35,742 sq.km. The official language is Chinese. Some people on the island preserve the Taiwanese language.

History. When the nationalist Chinese moved their government to Taiwan in 1949, there were only about 100 libraries on the island. The library profession developed rapidly. By 1988 there were more than 3,300 libraries in Taiwan, according to the *Library Survey of the Republic of China* (1988). These include a national Library, a branch national library, more than 250 public libraries, 120 university and college libraries, 2,400 school libraries, and almost 500 special libraries and information centers.

National Library. The National Central Library (NCL), under the jurisdiction of the Ministry of Education, renders national library services, serves as a research library, and leads and coordinates all library-related activities in the Republic of China. The NCL was established in 1933 at Nanking. At the time of its relocation to Taiwan in 1948, its collection numbered 140,000 volumes. The NCL main library moved to a new building in 1986 and offers extended services. The new building has an area of 431,500 sq.ft. and accommodates 2,500,000 volumes and 3,000 readers.

In October 1973 the Provincial Taipei Library was converted into a branch of the NCL. The Branch Library has almost 515,000 volumes in its holdings, including an outstanding collection on Taiwan and southeastern Asia, such as gazetteers and other works published during the time Taiwan was governed by the Dutch and Spaniards.

By 1990 the NCL and its branch held a total of more than 1,875,000 volumes.

National Central Library, Republic of China (Taiwan), opened in 1986.

Public Libraries. Public libraries can be found throughout Taiwan. There are 2 municipal libraries, 1 provincial library, and 21 libraries in Taiwan's county and cultural centers. The county libraries are dispersed throughout the island. In addition, there are 95 private public libraries and 137 town and branch libraries.

University Libraries. At the beginning of Taiwan's restoration under the Republic of China, one university and three colleges existed, with a total of 2,022 students. As a result of the government's promotion of higher education, there were 127 public and private universities and colleges in 1988. Most of the universities and the better-equipped colleges have independent libraries reporting directly to the presidents of the institutions.

School Libraries. Approximately 99 percent of school-age children are enrolled in schools. There are 2,444 school libraries, including 345 senior high school libraries, 566 junior high school libraries, and 1,533 elementary school libraries.

Special Libraries. Special libraries form an important segment of the republic's library services. There are a number of organizations or groups that collect materials to support their business or research. Currently there are well over 490 special libraries in Taiwan. They include the Academia Sinica, with 14 departmental libraries and some of the best collections in their subject fields; the National Palace Museum, with one of the largest collections of archives and a collection of rare books second only to that of the NCL; and the Agricultural Science Information Center, devoted to editing an agricultural thesaurus and processing agricultural information.

The Profession. The rapid development of libraries in Taiwan has elicited a demand for qualified librarians. They have been trained by six universities and colleges in Taiwan, as well as two graduate library studies programs. There are approximately 350 library science graduates every year. In addition, the NCL and the Library Association of China (LAC) annually sponsor a summer workshop for librarians.

Libraries in Taiwan (Republic of China) (1991)

Type of library	Number of administrative units (main libraries)	Number of service points (branches, mobile stops, etc.)	Volumes in collections	Annual expenditures (NT dollar)	Population served	Professional staff (with certificate, diploma, etc.)	Total staff
National	1	3	1,875,284	222,406,000[a]	650,350	287	359
Academic	122	245	14,646,632	425,124,999	580,041	703	1,914
Public	256	313	6,639,161	584,854,331	19,725,010	384	1,647
School	2,444	2,464	20,463,761	116,020,678	3,261,364	1,783[b]	4,069
Special	491	499	5,547,171	252,929,740	1,577,105	753	1,645

[a]1990 data
[b]1,346 with some training in library science

There has been no shortage of professional librarians at any level in Taiwan; moreover, the quality of library service has been continually upgraded, and many professional librarians have been sent abroad for advanced studies under various exchange programs and with government grants.

The LAC was incorporated in 1953. Membership is open to everyone who has studied library science or who is interested in library work. Major accomplishments of the LAC include the summer workshops, formulation of library standards, and the annual publication of the *Bulletin of the Library Association of China* (since 1954), as well as the quarterly *Library Association of China Newsletter* (since 1975).

The Library Automation Planning Committee, created by the LAC and the NCL in 1980, formulated the National Library Automation Project. This project in turn organized the Chinese MARC Working Group, the Chinese Cataloguing Working Group, and the Chinese Subject Heading Working Group. The Chinese MARC format was completed in 1982 and made available to libraries both locally and abroad as a basis for processing Chinese-language data, and also as a reference for processing data in other languages. *Chinese Cataloguing Rules* and *Chinese Subject Headings* are in print.

The NCL has provided strong leadership, too, in the development of library automation. Together with seven large academic libraries in Taiwan, the NCL has established a Chinese bibliographical database. By 1988 it consisted of 480,000 entries for Chinese publications. Work continued in the late 1980s on the *Union List of Chinese Serials in the Republic of China* to make it compatible with the new Chinese bibliographic database.

In addition, several university libraries and information centers have undertaken their own automation projects. National Taiwan Normal University developed the Chinese Educational Resource Information System, the Agricultural Science Information Center developed the Agricultural Science and Technology Information Management System, and the Science and Technology Information Center developed the Domestic Science and Technology System (which includes a *Union List of Scientific and Technical Serials in the Republic of China* and *Sci-Tech Research Reports*). Other universities have created Western-language control projects, serial control and acquisition packages, and circulation systems. For foreign information searching, some libraries have opened online information retrieval services over the satellite communications network to complement conventional reference services.

The Taiwan government launched a Cultural Development Project to build a cultural center for each county or city and to include in each a library, museum, and music hall. More than 20 such cultural centers had been established by 1986, and were open to the public.

Utilizing the Chinese MARC format and the Chinese Cataloging Rules, the Library Automation Committee developed the NCL Automated Information Service system. A library and information network was under study, and eventually that network was to include the public and academic library systems and the information center system.

CHEN-KU WANG

National Chengchi University Library

Chung-Cheng Library, founded in 1977, the main library of National Chengchi University in Taipei.

Tanodi, Aurelio Zlatko
(1914–)

Aurelio Zlatko Tanodi, leading Argentine scholar associated with the development of various scholarly pursuits, including historical research, paleography, and archival studies, conducted many research projects. His work in the organization of archival materials, together with the training of high-level personnel in the discipline, won him special recognition.

Tanodi was born September 1, 1914, in Hum, Zagreb, Croatia. He studied at the National College of Varazdin and in 1937 received a degree in Universal History from the Faculty of Philosophy of Zagreb University.

His work at the Colegio Clasico de Varazdin (Classic College of Varazdin) began with historical research based on medieval documents deposited in the municipal archives of the city. He worked at the National Archive of Croatia in Zagreb and, commissioned by the government of his country, studied at the Secret Archive of the Vatican and the National Archive of Hungary in Budapest. During this period he worked at the National Academy of Arts and Sciences of Croatia, obtaining the title Doctor of History at the University of Zagreb; his thesis, "Bula de Oro de Zagreb" (The Golden Papal Bull of Zagreb) won highest honors.

In 1945 he moved to Austria, continuing studies at the University of Graz. During 1947–48 he worked at the Biblioteca Mayor of the Antonianum University in Rome, simultaneously studying archival management at the Vatican Archive and librarianship at the Vatican Library. Having established residence in Argentina in 1948, Tanodi began a teaching career at the National University of Córdoba in 1953.

Aurelio Zlatko Tanodi

He published the *Manual de Archivología Hispanoamericana: teorías y principios* ("Manual of Hispanoamerican Archives: Theories and Principles") in 1961 in the Collectanea Archivistica series. During 1972–73 he visited various Latin American countries under the auspices of the International Archival Council and the Department of Cultural Affairs of the OAS, demonstrating the urgent need for professional training in this area.

Tanodi's work in Argentina was centered at the Escuela de Archiveros (School of Archival Management), part of the National University of Córdoba, of which he became Director in 1959. He also directed the Centro Interamericano de Desarrollo de Archivos (Interamerican Center for the Development of Archives), part of the School of Archival Management, under the auspices of the OAS, from 1972. Aside from administrative and teaching activities, Tanodi also did advisory and consulting work in the area of archival management in various Latin American countries and edited the *Anuario Interamericano de Archivos*. He participated in a number of national and international congresses and conferences.

REFERENCES

Oganización de los Estados Americanos, *De Archivos y Archivistas: Homenaje a Aurelio Tanodi* (1987).

Branka M. Tanodi de Chiapero, *Anuario Interamericano de Archivos* (1989). Includes a "Bibliografía de Aurelio Tanodi."

REINALDO J. SUAREZ;
Translated by JOSEFINA TRELLES-SOLOMON
and GLADYS MARKOFF

Tanzania

Tanzania, a republic in southeast Africa, comprises two distinct areas. Tanganyika, bordering the Indian Ocean, is surrounded by Kenya, Uganda, Rwanda, Burundi, Zaire, Zambia, Malawi, and Mozambique. Zanzibar, including Pemba Island, Zanzibar Island, and various small islets, is off the coast. Population (1990 est.) 25,635,000; area 945,087 sq.km. The official languages are English and Swahili.

History. The genesis of a nationwide library system in Tanzania dates to 1960, when Sidney Hockey was invited by the governments of Uganda, Kenya, Tanganyika, and Zanzibar to carry out a survey of their existing library facilities and make recommendations on services to be offered. Tanganyika was the first country to adopt the Hockey report. In 1963 the Tanganyika Library Services Board Act was passed, empowering the Board to promote, establish, equip, manage, maintain, and develop libraries in mainland Tanzania. In 1975 a new act repealed that of 1963. Enacted in the framework of Unesco's NATIS concept, the act empowers the Board to coordinate library and documentation services, arrange facilities for library training, promote literacy campaigns and the development of indigenous literature, and supervise all types of libraries in Tanzania.

National Library. There was no separate national library in the late 1980s. The National Central Library operates as both a national and a public library. Plans were under way to establish a separate national library in the new capital, Dodoma. The National Central Library was founded in 1965 as a pilot library in temporary premises with a collection of 30,000 books from the East African Literature Bureau and 20,000 from the British Council. The new building was opened by President Mwalimu Julius K. Nyerere in 1967 and is the headquarters of a nationwide library service. It has public reference and lending service for both adults and children, a central book processing and supply unit, and a central advisory service. Since 1969 Tanzania Library Service has compiled the national bibliography of Tanzania, and it enjoys legal deposit status.

The Service is responsible for the promotion, establishment, and management of all public libraries in the country in both urban and rural areas. By the mid-1980s 15 branch (regional) libraries had been established in major towns in mainland Tanzania, and rural library services were being offered to several areas by bookmobiles and village libraries.

The National Central Library also operates (1) the Tanzania National Documentation Centre (TANDOC), which produces, among other things, *Agricultural Abstracts, Industrial Abstracts,* and *Education Abstracts;* and (2) the National Bibliographic Agency (NBA), which, apart from producing *Tanzania National Bibliography* (TNB), allocates International Standard Book Numbers (ISBNs) and International Standard Serial Numbers (ISSNs) to local publishers and institutions.

With Unesco's assistance, plans were underway in 1985 to automate the National Bibliographic Agency using a microcomputer.

Academic Libraries. Although there are several libraries in teacher training colleges and other institutions of higher education, they are not well developed. The most important academic library is that of the University of Dar es Salaam. The University College, Dar es Salaam, was founded by the Tanganyika Africa National Union (TANU) in October 1961. The College at first was downtown in the building that now houses the Institute of Adult Education. In 1963 it became a constituent College of the University College and Nairobi University College. The University of East Africa was initially affiliated with the University of London. In 1964 the College moved to its present campus on

National Central Library in Dar Es Salaam, founded in 1965.

Tanzania Library Service

Observation Hill overlooking the city of Dar es Salaam.

On July 1, 1970, an act of Parliament revoked the 1962 Act of the East African Common Service Organization (EACSO), which linked the three constituent Colleges, and consequently the University College of Dar es Salaam ceased to exist. The University of East Africa also terminated activities, and on August 29, 1970, the University of Dar es Salaam was formally inaugurated as an independent university. The University Library was established downtown at the same time as its parent institution in 1961 and moved to its present building in July 1965.

A large quantity of materials, particularly Tanzanian government documents, were acquired under the Library (Deposit of Books) Act of 1962. Also placed in the library are publications of major international organizations. There are other special collections on law and East Africana; of particular importance is the East African Bibliography on punched cards, which includes entries from libraries at Makerere and Nairobi universities. The library has also an excellent collection of maps, mainly of East African countries, and manuscripts. In addition to the main library, branch libraries serve the faculty of medicine at Muhimbili Hospital in Dar es Salaam and the faculty of agriculture and veterinary science at Morogoro.

School Libraries. The Education Libraries Department at the National Central Library provides services to schools and teacher training colleges, including advice on book selection, design and planning of library buildings, library seminars, and actual visits to schools and colleges. There is, in addition, a school mobile library service with a van specially designed for this purpose. Visits are made to secondary schools where books are distributed to libraries to supplement their educational needs.

Special Libraries. The Tanzania Library Service is also responsible for special libraries. Many requests are received from government ministries and from other organizations and institutions for assistance in the organization of their libraries. The Tanzania Library Service gives professional advice and, wherever possible, sends librarians to these institutions.

The Profession. The Tanzania Library Association (TLA) was formed in 1965 as a branch of the East African Library Association (EALA), established in 1956. In 1971–72 the TLA became an autonomous national association. Since 1968 the TLA has published *Someni* as its official journal. The Association's main functions are: to unite all people working or interested in library work; to encourage the promotion, establishment, and improvement of libraries and library services; and to improve the standard of librarianship.

REFERENCE

E. E. Kaungamno, "The Functions and Activities of Tanzania Library Services within the NATIS Concept," *Unesco Bulletin for Libraries* (1975).

E. E. KAUNGAMNO

Taube, Mortimer

(1910–1965)

Mortimer Taube, an American information scientist and library consultant, was an innovator and inventor, as well as scholar and business executive. He is widely credited with the implementation of *coordinate indexing* through the application of "uniterms," a concept that, although initially applied to manual retrieval systems, forms the basis of a significant amount of computerized search strategy.

He was born in Jersey City, New Jersey, December 6, 1910. He received an A.B. degree from the University of Chicago and was elected to Phi Beta Kappa. He did graduate work at Harvard University in philosophy under Alfred North Whitehead, received a Ph.D. from the University of California at Berkeley in 1935, and followed with a certificate in librarianship at Berkeley in 1936.

Starting in 1936 he held a variety of academic library positions: circulation librarian at Mills College (Oakland, California), cataloguer at Rutgers University (New Brunswick, New Jersey), and Head of the Acquisitions Department at Duke University (Durham, North Carolina) from 1940 to 1944. He joined the Library of Congress in 1944 and served for five years as Assistant Chief of the General Reference and Bibliography Division, Assistant Director of the Acquisitions Department, and Chief of the Science and Technology Project. He left LC to serve, from 1949 to 1952, as Deputy Chief of the Atomic Energy Commission's Technical Information Service.

Taube founded Documentation, Inc., in 1952 and served as its Board Chairman and leader until his death. Documentation, Inc., was the first (and for a long time only) information science corporation in existence. Starting with only a handful of associates, Taube built an organization that, by 1965, numbered over 500. Under his guidance the corporation engaged in a large number of innovative studies for government agencies—including the U.S. Air Force and the National Institutes of Health—and pioneered in the field of information facilities management. The organization administered the first contract-operated national information program, the NASA Scientific and Technical Information Facility, from 1962 to 1968. Those who worked with and for Taube in the pioneering days at Documentation, Inc., came to comprise a Who's Who of the information science profession.

Throughout his career Taube found time to lecture and write. He taught at the University of Chicago and Columbia University and flew to New York weekly for seminars at Columbia. He wrote many articles and several significant books, including *Studies in Coordinate Indexing,* volumes 1–6 (1953–65) and *Computers and Common Sense: The Myth of Thinking Machines* (1961). He was Editor of *American Documentation,* 1951–52. The Special Libraries Association presented him its Professional Award in 1952, and the American Society for Information Science presented its Award of Merit to him posthumously in 1966.

Taube was indefatigable in his search for truth and honesty. He was often controversial, usually because his ideas were well ahead of their time. A natural teacher and brilliant and witty lecturer, Taube had strong convictions and was not afraid to express them, but he had abiding respect for other opinions if he felt they were honestly and intelligently derived. He was the outspoken foe of shoddy scholarship, meaningless studies, and twisted logic to support predetermined conclusions.

Taube was particularly concerned lest practices designed for manual library systems simply be moved to computers. He feared the library profession would miss the opportunity to reexamine its premises in light of the opportunities computer technology would offer in bibliographic control and analysis.

A person of many talents and interests, Taube worked tirelessly on behalf of religious, political, and many charitable interests. He died September 3, 1965, at the age of 54. At the time of his death he was engaged in one of the many activities that involved him passionately: he was sailing on Chesapeake Bay.

REFERENCE

Jesse H. Shera, "Taube, Mortimer," *Dictionary of American Library Biography* (1978).

HERBERT S. WHITE

Tauber, Maurice
(1908–1980)

ALA

Maurice Tauber

Maurice Falcom Tauber was an international leader in library and information science—a prolific American writer, biographer, editor, critic, researcher, scholar, educator, administrator, and expert in technical services and library buildings.

He was born February 14, 1908, in Norfolk, Virginia. In 1925 his family moved to Philadelphia. He studied at Temple University, Philadelphia, where he majored in English and education and earned a Master's degree in sociology (1929). In 1932, while working in the Library of Temple University, he commuted to New York City to take courses at Columbia University School of Library Service. He completed the school's Bachelor of Science program in 1934.

In 1935 he was appointed Head of the Cataloguing Department of Temple University. While there he undertook the reclassification of the Library's holdings from Dewey to Library of Congress. He enrolled in the Graduate Library School of the University of Chicago (Ph.D., 1941), and in 1941 he joined the University Library at Chicago as Head of its Cataloguing Department. Soon after, he was appointed to the faculty of the Graduate Library School as Assistant Professor.

In 1944 Tauber returned to Columbia University as Assistant Director of its Library, in charge of Technical Services, and Assistant Professor at the School of Library Service. He gave up his position at the Library to become a full-time member of the School of Library Service faculty with the rank of Associate Professor in 1946. Tauber was finally able to fulfill his dream of fully dedicating his time to teaching and research. He was awarded a full professorship three years later. In 1954 he was named Melvil Dewey Professor of Library Service. He held that post until his retirement from Columbia in 1976, but it did not make him favor the Dewey Decimal Classification—he spent a lifetime promoting the LC classification and influenced many academic libraries to shift from Dewey to LC.

As a researcher and consultant, Tauber was asked to conduct surveys by a great number of institutions. A bibliography (Marion C. Szigethy, 1974) cites 75 survey reports, of which 5 were on a national level (libraries in Australia); 45 on university, college, and research libraries; 5 on public and school libraries; 11 on special libraries; and 9 on state libraries and library systems. Among the institutions he surveyed were Columbia University (1943 and 1957); Cornell (1947); Dartmouth (1952); Barnard College Library (1954); Boston University (1956); Manhattanville College (1958); University of South Carolina (1958); Montana State University (1959); and Australian libraries (1964).

Szigethy also credits Tauber with 20 monographs; 25 conference papers, proceedings, and reports; and 85 articles and essays. Tauber was Editor of *College and Research Libraries* for 18 years. He was also on the editorial advisory boards of *Library Sources and Technical Services,* the *Journal of Cataloging and Classification,* the *Journal of Documentation,* the *Journal of Higher Education,* and others.

Tauber's first publication was a 17-page monograph, *Brief History of the Library of Temple University* (1934). Among his many publications, *The University Library* (1945), on which he collaborated with Louis Round Wilson, and *Technical Services in Libraries* (1954), stand out as classics. Tauber was interested in all aspects of the library and information profession but distinguished himself as a champion in the specific areas of reclassification and recataloguing.

In technical services, he loudly and clearly sang his song in favor of centralization of services. Academic and research libraries became his main platform. He also became deeply interested in the planning and design of library buildings. Sixteen of his surveys were primarily concerned with design of library buildings. Tauber's interests were not limited to American institutions. In Australia he visited 162 libraries in 1964; his report included approximately 300.

His service to ALA and other professional associations was extensive. He received many national awards, among them the Margaret Mann Citation (1953) and the Melvil Dewey Award and Medal (1955).

As a teacher he won the affection and admiration of many of his students; he opened his house to them, especially to those from foreign lands.

In 1981 the Maurice F. Tauber Foundation was established in New York. It sponsors an annual memorial lecture hosted by library schools throughout the United States, publication of appropriate scholarly works, and an annual award for excellence in library and information science. The first memorial lecture was delivered by Lowell A. Martin at Columbia University, December 12, 1981, on "The Library Surveyor—Innovator or Intruder?"

REFERENCES

Richard L. Darling, "Maurice F. Tauber, 1908–1980," *Library Service News* 41 (Fall, 1980).

Kurt S. Maier, "Maurice F. Tauber," *Leaders in American Academic Librarianship 1925–1975,* edited by Wayne A. Wiegand (Beta Phi Mu, 1983).

Marion C. Szigethy, *Maurice Falcom Tauber: A Bibliography 1934–1973* (1974).

NASSER SHARIFY

Thailand

Thailand, an independent constitutional monarchy in southeastern Asia, is bounded by Laos on the northeast, Kampuchea on the southeast, the South China Sea on the south, and Burma on the west; a section of Thailand extends down the Malay Peninsula to Malaysia on the south and the Indian Ocean on the west. Population (1990 est.) 57,196,000; area 513,115 sq.km. The official language is Thai.

National Library. The National Library of Thailand is composed of three libraries: the Vajirayana Library, Vajiravudh Library, and Damrongrajanupharb Library. Established in 1950, the National Library is a division in the Department of Fine Arts of the Ministry of Education. The Library has 11 branches in provincial towns.

The present National Library building was opened in May 1966. Its printed book collection is strong in the history and geography of Thailand and totals about 1,470,800 volumes in Thai and other languages. The National Library also holds more than 184,000 Thai manuscripts. Written on palm leaves and Thai paper folded in accordion pleats, they are mainly copies of Buddhist sacred books and other Buddhist literature, literary compositions, and works on medicine, law, history, arts, and astrology. There are 87 stone inscriptions in various ancient languages and scripts of the Southeast Asian region. The Library is entitled by law to receive two copies of every book published in Thailand, but this law has not been well enforced. Thailand signed the treaty on copyright law at Berne in 1886. Copyright registration at present follows a revised law passed in 1983. The government is considering an amendment on enforcement and punishment to include computer software and other electronic media.

Audiovisual materials include a collection of tapes and Thai folklore, important lectures and discussions, and parliamentary debates and speeches. The library compiles various bibliographies.

Two libraries in addition to the National Library are the Phya Anuman Rajadhon Memorial Library and the Library of King Rama VI. The National Archives was developed along with the National Library and has its own building.

Academic Libraries. Thailand has 16 state universities and 22 private universities. All have their own libraries, many with more than 200,000 books, most in foreign languages. Financial support for university libraries varies from one institution to another. In most universities, faculty libraries are run as branches of the main libraries, with acquisition done by the central library staff.

Computer applications in library and information services are particularly prevalent in university libraries. In 1988 the Computer Network Project of the Ministry of Science, Technology, and Energy conducted a survey of databases and computing facilities at 11 state university libraries that have strong collections in science and technology. University libraries have a total of more than 70 microcomputers and four mainframe computers; the majority use the ISIS software developed by Unesco. The survey found 78 databases containing almost 134,000 bibliographic records in subject fields offered by those universities. About half of the records are in English. None of the databases are linked yet, but the Computer Network Project has plans for linking them. About 10 libraries, mainly university libraries, have access to databases in North America and Europe. No library has an integrated computer library system.

CD-ROM databases play an important role in affording access to world literature for the academic community. Online search services through 15 CD-ROM databases are available at 16 libraries. Facsimile machines are used for interlibrary loan services; telex machines are used mainly for library administration and acquisition.

Public Libraries. Public library services are being developed. The government began these services in 1949. By 1990 there were 519 public libraries throughout the country. Most have small reading rooms with about 2,000 volumes. The Department of Non-Formal Education in the Ministry of Education began a five-year plan in the late 1980s for developing trained personnel for all public libraries, especially those in the provinces. Other government agencies responsible for public libraries are the Bangkok Metropolitan Administration, the Community Development Department of the National Security Command, and the Ministry of the Interior. Budgets for running the libraries are too small to bring the collections and services up to standard.

School Libraries. The Ministry of Education supervises the almost 45,000 school and college libraries under nine departments, including the Department of General Education, Office of the National Primary Education Commission, Rajmangla Institute of Technology, and Department of Fine Arts. The Book

Libraries in Thailand (1990)

Type of library	Number of administrative units (main libraries)	Number of service points (branches, mobile stops, etc.)	Volumes in collections	Annual expenditures (baht)	Population served	Professional staff (with certificate, diploma, etc.)	Total staff
National	1	15	36,384,412	31,755,800	1,540,962	58	326
Academic:							
State	18	105	3,743,395	248,705,521	13,765,446	595	1,666
Private	22	26	--	--	--	--	--
Public	4	519	--	--	--	--	--
School & Colleges	9	44,876	--	--	--	--	--
Special	277	281	2,781,000	--	--	--	--

The Thai National Library building, Bangkok.

Development Committee under the Department of Technical and Curriculum Development helps in producing textbooks and supplementary reading books for school libraries, which raises the standards of their book collections. Most school and college libraries have trained librarians, some with teaching qualifications. The Thai Library Association organizes awards for the best school and public libraries every year, which also encourages improved standards.

Special Libraries. Special libraries in Thailand are found in research institutes, government agencies, professional and trade associations, learned societies, and business firms. Among the libraries that have special resources in the field of science and technology are those at the Division of Scientific and Technological Information, Department of Science Service, Ministry of Science, Technology, and Energy; the Petroleum Authority of Thailand; and the Electricity Generating Authority of Thailand. The faculty libraries at all state universities have specialized collections on their relevant subjects and have adequate facilities. The Thai National Documentation Center supplies scientific and technical information and publishes Thai abstracts for scientific and technical research.

Other special libraries include the Siam Society Library of Southeast Asian materials, the Bank of Thailand Library, the Highway Department Library, and the Department of Technical and Economic Cooperation Library. All foreign embassies and nearly all international organizations in Thailand, such as United Nations offices, have their own special libraries.

The Profession. The Thai Library Association was founded in 1954 with the help of the Asia Foundation. The Association holds annual meetings for more than 900 members as of 1990. Its Executive Board, elected every two years at an annual meeting, arranges workshops, conferences and seminars, radio and television programs, publications, and other activities. The Association's work has played an important role in the development of the library and information profession in Thailand. The Association hosted the IFLA Regional Office for Asia and Oceania after it was relocated from Kuala Lumpur in 1989.

PONGPAN RATTANBUSIT

Thorpe, Frederick A.

(1913–)

Frederick A. Thorpe, British publisher, founded large-print book publishing in Britain.

Thorpe was born October 22, 1913, in Leicester, one of the major English provincial cities, and brought up there. His initial experience in publishing was interrupted by war service in the Royal Air Force from 1940 to 1946. On his return to Leicester he resumed his publishing interests, which developed and expanded to become a highly successful business. In it he gained the experience in every aspect of the book trade and publishing that, like the contacts he made with agents and distributors worldwide, was to prove an apprenticeship for his second career, that of pioneering the publication of books in large print.

In 1963, when he was about to retire from his business, Thorpe was approached by a committee set up in response to the concern expressed by the British Government for the cultural well-being of elderly people. There were books available in abundance, but many elderly people could not easily read normal-size print. The committee sought Thorpe's advice, and he applied his experience in printing and publishing to the problem. He discussed it with the Library Association and learned of the results of earlier investigations into this and similar problems, none of which had produced a solution. He decided that the technical difficulties of printing and producing books in print twice as large as that in normal books, and with an ink density and paper quality that would ensure a sharp contrast, could be solved; he founded the nonprofit publishing house of Ulverscroft Large Print Books to produce them.

In selecting the first titles for publication, Thorpe found publishers reluctant to allow their authors' work to appear in a new and untried format from an unknown publisher. His market for large-print books was mainly the elderly who looked for established authors and well-written books. After some initial disappointments he approached Dame Agatha Christie, who gave the project her full support and encouraged other well-known authors to allow their books to appear in the new series. Four thousand copies of each of the first four titles were published in September 1964: *Pocketful of Rye* by Agatha Christie, *I Brought a Mountain* by Thomas Firbank, *The Avenger* by Edgar Wallace, and *The Fettered Past* by Netta Muskett. They established a precedent both in the careful selection of titles that is a hallmark of the firm and in their format. They were printed by offset lithography from photographic enlargements of the normal-size editions. Their size, eleven by eight inches, and their distinctive book jackets (blue for romances and historical and romantic suspense; orange for westerns; black for mystery; red for general fiction, adventure, and suspense; green for nonfiction; and, later, purple for specialist series and brown for individual specialist titles) made them immediately recognizable.

Thorpe decided that the books should be sold directly to libraries and other institutions, not through the book trade, which helped to keep the selling price low. The Library Association sent one book, with a letter supporting the venture, to each library. While orders from libraries reached the expected level, there were few from hospitals and welfare institutions, which had been expected to purchase half the copies. Thorpe therefore sought overseas markets. Through his own international contacts, and others made through the American and Canadian Library Associations, Rotary International, and a number of interested individuals, the sale of Ulverscroft Large Print Books spread throughout the English-speaking world. Thorpe's personal interest, his visits to libraries, and his presence at conference exhibitions made him an internationally recognized figure in librarianship.

The development of large-print books from 1963 to 1969 was one of technical experiment to improve quality and overcome the difficulties caused by the photographic enlargement of existing typesetting, especially broken type and uneven inking, which are much more noticeable when enlarged. The solution was to reset the books in large print; this decision, along with the production of a thinner but opaque paper, led in 1969 to a new nine-by-six-inch format, easier for the reader to enjoy and the library to shelve. The new format was greatly appreciated, and Thorpe went on to newer, still thinner papers, producing even longer books in the series that are not uncomfortable to handle.

The 500th title appeared in 1971 and the 1,000th in 1976, an event marked by the publication of a five-volume edition of *War and Peace*. Thorpe introduced the Charnwood Series in 1981 in order to include a wider range of titles to meet the needs of a new generation of large-print readers and began the Linford Series of paperback books in 1983 to help frail elderly readers. By 1984 the number of titles published had reached more than 2,400, and Thorpe had plans for further developments.

The profits from Ulverscroft Large Print Books are covenanted to the Ulverscroft Foundation, a charity that also receives donations from individuals, including many readers of Ulverscroft books. The Foundation is administered by trustees and assists hospitals, schools, and libraries.

The importance of Thorpe's work has been recognized in several ways. In 1969 he was awarded the Order of the British Empire (OBE) by the Queen, in 1972 the ALA's Francis Joseph Campbell Award, in 1973 the Queen's Award to Industry and the Grimshaw Memorial Award from the National Federation of the Blind, in 1976 an ALA Centennial Citation, and in 1984 an engrossed resolution of the Council of the Library Association.

Thorpe's achievement is expressed in the title of the book he chose as the 500th Ulverscroft large-print title *A Many-Splendoured Thing*. He had made reading possible for many people by bringing unbounded energy and business experience to the creation of a new and now essential part of the resources of libraries in meeting the needs of the disadvantaged.

REFERENCES

F. A. Thorpe, "Large Print: An Assessment of its Development and Potential," *Library Association Record* (March 1972).

W. A. Munford, "Books for the Partially Sighted," *British Book News* (April 1976).

GEOFFREY SMITH

Togo

Togo, a West African republic, is bounded on the north by Upper Volta, on the east by Benin, on the south by the Gulf of Guinea, and on the west by Ghana. Population (1990 est.) 3,531,000; area 56,785 sq.km. The official language is French.

National Library. The Bibliothèque Nationale in Lomé was decreed a national library on October 1, 1969. Under the directorship of the Ministère de l'Éducation Nationale, the library originally was established in 1937 as the Service de la Documentation Générale, a documentation center to study documentation concerns in museums, archives, and libraries. In 1945 it was taken over by the local IFAN Centre (Institut Fondamental de l'Afrique Noire), and in 1960 that center become the Institut Togolais des Sciences Humaines. The Institut has departments of anthropology, archaeology, ethnography, geography, history, linguistics, and sociology. In the mid-1980s the Library's collection housed approximately 6,000 volumes and 1,000 periodicals; 85 percent of all holdings are in French.

The functions of a national archives are performed by the Institut Togolais des Sciences Humaines and the Archives de la Présidence de la République. Although Togo has some laws relating to legal deposit, they have never been systematically enforced.

Academic Libraries. Togo has one university, the Université du Bénin, which was founded as a college in Lomé in 1965 and attained university status in 1970. All higher education institutions throughout the country are part of the University. The language of instruction is French. The University's libraries are decentralized. Holdings include 50,000 volumes and pamphlets, 90 percent of which are in French. Another institution of higher education is the École Nationale d'Administration (ENA), founded in Lomé in 1958 to provide a training center for Togolese civil servants. The library has more than 1,000 volumes. There are government-sponsored technical colleges at Lomé and at Sokodé and an agricultural school in Kpalimé with a library of about 3,500 volumes. The library of the teacher training college at Atakpamé holds some 6,000 volumes.

Other Services. Togo does not have an organized public library system.

Important collections of specialized research institutes include those of the Institut National de la Recherche Scientifique and the Office de la Recherche Scientifique et Technique Outre-Mer (ORSTOM). The Institut National de la Recherche Scientifique, Lomé, was founded in 1965 as a coordination center for scientific research. Its library currently holds 6,000 volumes; findings of research activity are published in its quarterly, *Études Togolaises*. The Library of ORSTOM, founded in 1948, has more than 2,000 volumes.

The library has holdings on child development, geography, sociology, and geophysics.

The Library of the Centre Regional d'Études et de Documentation Économiques, founded in 1972 in Lomé, houses more than 3,500 volumes and 100 current periodicals, specializing in economics, labor, and unionism. It publishes *African Trade Union News* in English and French editions.

There are two cultural center libraries in Lomé, the American Cultural Center Library and the Library of the Centre Culturel Français. The American collection consists of approximately 3,700 volumes; the French, more than 20,000 volumes.

The documentation center of the Institut Pédagogique National houses more than 3,000 volumes, specializing in education and educational psychology.

The Profession. A Togo branch of the Association Internationale pour le Développement de la Documentation, des Bibliothèques et des Archives en Afrique was established in 1959. It has its headquarters at the Library of the Université du Bénin in Lomé. It is affiliated with IFLA.

STAFF

Trinidad and Tobago

The republic of Trinidad and Tobago comprises two islands off the coast of Venezuela. Population (1990 est.) 1,227,000; area 5,130 sq.km. A former British colony, the country gained independence in 1962 and has retained an education system based on the British pattern. The official language is English.

National Library. There is no officially designated national library. Plans for the development of a national library service, including national library functions, were outlined in the government's Draft Plan for Educational Development published in 1968. Approval was subsequently given for the development of an integrated national network, the headquarters of the system to be known as NALIAS—the National Library Information and Archives Service. It was to consist of seven major units: Archives and Heritage Library, Bibliographic Services, Public Libraries, School Libraries, Special Libraries Information Network, Planning and Development, and Administration. These plans have not been carried out, in part because of a change of government and policy in 1986.

Main Library of The University of the West Indies at St. Augustine, Trinidad.

The University of the West Indies Photo by Neil Hokan

The National Archives continues to operate independently and some national library functions are distributed between the Central Library of Trinidad and Tobago and the University of the West Indies Library, which jointly produce the Trinidad and Tobago National Bibliography. The University Library, drawing on the British Library and its own resources, coordinates interlibrary loan services.

Academic Libraries. The country is one of 14 in the Caribbean served by the regional University of the West Indies. The University Campus in Trinidad was established in 1960 by merger with the former Imperial College of Tropical Agriculture (ICTA). Its main library has strong collections supporting faculties in agriculture, arts, engineering, and the natural and social sciences It also has a collection of West Indiana and beginning collections in the medical sciences for a new facility to be opened in this field. Other academic libraries are those of the Faculty of Education (15,000 volumes), the Hugh Wooding Law School (almost 21,000 volumes), and the Institute of International Relations (15,000 volumes).

Public Libraries. Local leaders founded the Trinidad Public Library in 1851 by buying a former circulating library. It was supported partly by the colonial government and partly by a small subscription from its members. It became a free library in 1951. It serves workers and residents of the capital city, Port-of-Spain, and operates three suburban branches. It is now one of three independent public library services in the country, two of which work in close collaboration. The Carnegie Free Library opened in 1919 and the Central Library of Trinidad and Tobago was established in 1949. The government proposed full integration of these three services.

School Libraries. A School Libraries Division of the Central Library was established in 1977 to coordinate service to schools. Initial efforts concentrated on the secondary level and on developing suitable collections for senior pupils (aged 16 and above). By 1987 there were 97 such libraries with 44 professionals among the trained school librarians. Services for primary schools are slowly being developed.

Special Libraries. In 1960 only 13 well-organized special libraries responded to a survey questionnaire. By 1986, 124 were identified in a survey sponsored by the NALIAS Interim Board, although only 84 responded. This steep increase paralleled the economic and industrial growth of the country. Some cooperation already exists, but the NALIAS plan envisages two broad networks, one in science and technology and one in the social sciences.

The Profession. The Department of Library Studies at the University of the West Indies in Jamaica offers a Postgraduate Diploma in Library Studies (one year) and a Bachelor's Degree (three years), but training facilities in North America and the United Kingdom are also used.

The Library Association of Trinidad and Tobago provides some opportunity for continuing education by sponsoring workshops, some of them jointly with the Department of Library Studies. The Association, founded in 1960, provides a useful channel of communication for the body of professionals in the country. Its membership is open to all persons interested in

Libraries in Trinidad and Tobago (1990)

Type of library	Number of administrative units (main libraries)	Number of service points (branches, mobile stops, etc.)	Volumes in collections	Annual expenditures (TT dollar)	Population served	Professional staff (with certificate, diploma, etc.)	Total staff
National	--	--	--	--	--	--	--
Academic	6	15	345,627	11,971,351	5,752	29	124
Public	5	66	390,868	7,468,931	1,235,400	34	270
School	147	565	365,200	--	285,930	51	147
Special*	104	127	400,000	--	--	53	125
Other (describe)	--	--	--	--	--	--	--

*Includes tertiary education institutes and colleges

promoting its objectives. The Association publishes a bulletin on an irregular basis.

ALMA JORDAN;
BARBARA COMISSIONG

Tropovsky, Lev
(1885–1944)

Lev Naumovich Tropovsky was a Soviet specialist in library science and bibliography noted especially for his work in library classification.

He was born in Kremenchug February 12 (old style; February 25, new style), 1885. On graduating from secondary school he entered the Faculty of Natural Sciences at Warsaw University. Later he was expelled for taking part in a students' meeting and strike. In 1904 he joined the Polish Socialist-Democratic Party and in 1905 he became a member of the Warsaw Committee of the Military and Revolutionary Organization of the Socialist-Democrats. He was arrested, then emigrated.

While living in Paris, Tropovsky graduated from the Faculty of Natural Sciences of the Sorbonne. In 1917 he returned to Russia, where in 1920 he became a member of the Communist Party of the Soviet Union (Bolsheviks). From 1923 he was chief of the Bibliographic Department of the Central Board of Political and Educational Activities (Glavpolitprosvet), where he worked under the direct guidance of N. K. Krupskaya. In that period he delivered a number of reports at important scientific conferences dealing with party spirit in bibliography. From 1932 he was Director of the Research Institute of Library Science and Recommendatory Bibliography and Head of the Bibliographic Department of the Moscow State Library Institute. He wrote such educational works as *Library Classification* and *Bibliography of Natural History*. Tropovsky was a member of the editorial board of leading specialized journals and helped make possible collections of articles such as *Bibliography, Bibliography and Library Science,* and *Soviet Bibliography*. He was also a member of the Learned Councils of the State Lenin Library, the All-Union Book Chamber, and the Moscow Library Institute. He died in Moscow October 26, 1944.

With other library specialists and bibliographers he worked at modifying the UDC in keeping with the needs of Soviet libraries. Glavpolitprosvet introduced a version of the UDC in 1921; the work was the responsibility of a committee headed by Tropovsky. He substantially revised the decimal classification and introduced a number of amendments and additions into some of its classes, particularly those dealing with questions of philosophy, ideology, and sociopolitical activities. He introduced a new class in the classification—"Marxism-Leninism," in which works by Marx, Engels, Lenin, and leaders of the Communist Party and government were reflected. He also worked out geographical subdivisions for the U.S.S.R. and edited all the classes and subdivisions.

Lenin State Library

Lev Tropovsky

The tables of library classification worked out by Tropovsky were popular and widely used in scientific and public libraries of the Soviet Union. Shortly before his death he also took part in the preparation of a new Soviet classification for books. The work was carried out in the late 1930s and early 1940s under the guidance of the State Lenin Library. In postwar years this work was continued by Tropovsky's pupil, Z. N. Ambartsumian (1903–70). The most important editions of this classification are *Library Classification Tables for Public Libraries,* which ran into three editions (1959, 1961, and 1968), and *Library Classification Tables for Children's Libraries* (1960, 1964, 1974).

The activities of Tropovsky and other Soviet library specialists advanced the preparation of the original Soviet library classification (BBK), separate issues of which were published beginning in 1960. The BBK is a universal classification that embraces all branches of knowledge and areas of human practical activity reflected in printed matter. The BBK was published in 25 issues (30 volumes), the abbreviated version in 5 issues (7 volumes). The version for small public libraries and tables for children's libraries were worked out and published on the basis of the abbreviated tables. The BBK tables are used by more than 300 scientific and special libraries, and they were introduced widely in public library practice.

In Tropovsky's working-out of theoretical and practical problems of bibliography, "recommendatory" bibliography in particular was especially great. He emphasized the importance of giving an estimate of a book in the annotations of bibliographic indexes. Tropovsky showed a marked interest in recommendatory bibliography all his life, and he paid special attention to its political and social role in the Soviet Union.

C. I. ABRAMOV

Tunisia

Tunisia, a republic of North Africa in the easternmost part of the Maghreb, faces the Mediterranean Sea on the north and east and is bounded on the south by Libya and on the west by Algeria. Population (1990 est.) 8,180,000; area 163,610 sq.km. The official language is Arabic; French is widely spoken.

History. Libraries in Tunisia were founded in great number, especially during the Aghlabid and Fatimid ages (800–1171) when they were located in mosques and also in schools. Among the most famous libraries are the Ibdilliyya Library (1393), the Al-Ahmadiyya Library (1840), and the Sadiqiyya Library (1885). Before independence in 1956, library services were administered by cultural institutions such as the Khalduniyya Library (1909) and Al-Lakmiyya library in Sfax (1931). There are also a limited number of foreign libraries, notably that of the British Council (1943) and the Library of the American Cultural Center (1948).

The concept of modern library service emerged after independence in 1956. Libraries were given greater attention, and since 1963 the persistent need for raising the standard of library services moved the authorities to plan for libraries in the "Fourth Plan: 1972–1976." As a result of the Fourth and Fifth Plans, several types of libraries are found in Tunisia.

National Library. Known as the French Library and later as the Public Library, the National Library in Tunis was established by law in 1885 under French government sponsorship. Its collection was gathered in individual sporadic efforts and by gifts.

The concept of Dâr Al-Kutub Al-Wataniyya, the National Library, however, emerged only after independence in 1956. In 1970 the Tunisian National Library published the first issue of the *Tunisian National Bibliography,* a booklet covering the first period in 1969. From then on the National Library has tried to fulfill the enormous task of publishing current and retrospective bibliographies at the same time, ensuring the link between the past and the present and tracing every single document produced in the area from the introduction of printing in Tunisia (1881) up to independence. By 1983, 13 bibliographies had been issued covering the years from 1956 through 1982.

The *Tunisian National Bibliography* is issued quarterly with an annual cumulation. It covers all documents published in Tunisia and deposited at the National Library. These documents include government and nongovernment publications, university theses, textbooks, and new periodicals. Nonbook material is not covered. The National Library also compiles current bibliographies on special Tunisian and Arabic subjects.

The National Library's collection of manuscripts, which includes some that date from the 5th century, totals 25,000. The National Library also has a collection of about 10,000 current periodicals, more than two-thirds of them in Arabic.

The Library's collection reached about 750,000 volumes by 1984. It suffers from lack of space for users. It serves about 27,000 users a year, even though the number of seats is just 160. The collection is primarily in Arabic and French, but there are considerable holdings in English, and volumes are collected in 12 languages.

The National Library is a depository for Tunisian publications and has an accession rate of about 10,000 volumes a year. The Library's Documentary Department is responsible for legal deposit, but it did not officially have copyright deposit privilege in the mid-1980s.

In December 1984 the government started building a modern library to serve as a National Library. Modern processes and operations will be used for computer applications, nonbook materials, and bibliographic and other services.

Tunisia is one of the few African countries to have an International Serials Data System (ISDS) national center.

Academic Libraries. The University of Tunis was founded in 1960 and academic libraries were established later in the various parts of the republic—Sfax, Sousse, Monastir, Gabès, Gafsa, and Bizerte. The University of Tunis has no central library. Every school, institute, and faculty has its own library. Each functions separately from the others. The Library of the Zitouna mosque (now the Faculty of Theology of the University of Tunis) was established in the 8th century. It was considered important for its Arabic and Islamic collections, attracting students and scholars from various Muslim countries.

There are two types of academic collections: the European and American collections and the Arabic collections. The most important and the largest library of the University of Tunis is the Library of the Faculty of Law, Political Science, and Economics, which had a collection of about 128,180 volumes in the mid-1980s, two-thirds in French and the remainder evenly divided into Arabic and other languages, and 800 current periodicals. The library of the Faculty of Letters and Humanities had a collection of more than 124,000 volumes and 1,140 periodicals. The Faculty of Sciences (Mathematics, Physics, and Natural Sciences) had a collection of more than 37,000 volumes and almost 450 periodicals. The Library of the Faculty of Medicine of Tunis had a collection of 12,700 volumes, 600 periodicals, 39,000 foreign theses, and 1,600 Tunisian theses by the mid-1980s.

The National School of Administration, founded in 1949 and reorganized in 1964, is run by the Prime Minister and has a collection of 50,000 volumes and 400 periodicals. The Bourguiba Institute of Modern Languages, founded in 1961, has a library created in 1966 with aid from the Ford Foundation; its collection covers linguistics and translation.

Problems affecting library development include lack of professional staff, inadequacy of collections, shortcomings in technical services, and difficulties concerning library automation. Academic libraries in Tunisia are in a state of transition. In the mid-1980s the number of students had grown far more quickly (to almost 30,000 students) than the university libraries, which numbered 27.

Public Libraries. Public libraries in Tunisia have developed during the years since independence, and their administration is fully centralized in the Ministry of Cultural Affairs. The public libraries do not, in general, possess large book collections, although as early as 1968 they had a total of 330,000 volumes. By 1970 the circulating stock was nearly 600,000 volumes, 65 percent in Arabic and 35 percent in French. Efforts are being made to develop the collections. Public libraries had a collection of books totaling more than 1,300,000 in the mid-1980s.

The Central library is in Tunis. Branches are operated throughout the country and are distributed as follows: 63 public libraries for adults, 62 public libraries for children, 76 public libraries for youth, 8 municipal libraries, 46 popular and community libraries, 21 bookmobiles, and 4 regional libraries.

School Libraries. In 1956 the distinction between state schools and religious schools was eliminated, and free education was made available to all pupils of Tunisia. Enrollment increased dramatically in the years following independence: between 1956 and 1985 the number of pupils in primary schools increased from 225,000 to almost 1,120,000. In secondary schools, the number of students increased from 30,000 in 1956 to approximately almost 365,000 in 1985. In addition, students were enrolled in vocational schools and in teacher-training programs. The languages of instruction are Arabic and French.

In Tunisia all school libraries are administered by the Minister of Education. The Division of School Libraries is responsible for operating school libraries, including selecting and acquiring library materials. School libraries in Tunisia are still in an early stage of development. There are a few school libraries in primary schools, and the collections of books in secondary schools are limited principally to textbooks.

Special Libraries. Tunisia has a large number of special libraries and specialized documentation centers. More than 25 special libraries and documentation centers are attached to ministries and government departments. Among the important special libraries are those of the Prime Minister, Justice Ministry, and Health Ministry and the Documentation Center of Cultural Development. Two specialized institutions that should be mentioned are the National Documentation Center and the Agricultural National Documentation Center.

The Tunisian National Documentation Center was established in 1966 to collect, catalogue, analyze, and preserve all government documents, mainly documents on economics, political and social sciences, and cultural affairs, published in Tunisia and abroad. In 1975 a terminal was installed with the database called TANIT.

The Agricultural National Documentation Center was established in 1975 to lay out a modern system to collect data on agriculture in Tunisia and analyze it for dissemination. The Center accommodates two automated information systems. One is the National Tunisian Documentation System for Agriculture (TUNAGRI), consisting of a database of analyzed agricultural documents. It has direct communication with the International System for Agriculture (AGRIS), and data are exchanged between the two systems. Current Tunisian Research in Agriculture (CARIST) consists of a database covering subjects, places of current research, and names of researchers in the field of agriculture in all parts of Tunisia.

The Profession. The Tunisian Association of Documentalists, Librarians, and Archivists was established on June 10, 1965, at the Institut Bach Hamba, its headquarters in Tunis. The Association started activities in January 1966. The *Bulletin de l'A.T.D.* (1966–), its official journal, is issued approximately four times a year. The A.T.D. is a member of IFLA and the Tunisian Committee of Unesco and UNISIST.

Professional education in the field of library science in Tunisia has undergone several developments since independence in 1956. The origins of these educational programs can be traced to the Institut Bach Hamba in Tunis, which in 1964 offered a six-month study program for 50 students of librarianship. The persistent need for raising the standard of personnel working in libraries prompted the Ministry of Cultural Affairs to plan in 1965 for an educational and training program at the National Library. In fewer than five years two groups of assistant librarians and four groups of clerical secretaries benefitted from programs offered by the National Library.

Responsibility for educational programs in library science were in 1971 transferred to the National School of Administration under the sponsorship of the Prime Minister's Office. In 1979 the responsibility for professional education in library science was transferred once again, this time to the Institute of Journalism and Information Sciences, which was under the jurisdiction of the Ministry of Higher Education and Scientific Research. In 1981 that program was replaced by a course of studies directed to graduate students with first university degrees in any subject who could pass an entrance examination. The students followed a two-year professional program, graduating with bachelor's degrees.

Since 1982 two institutions have taught documentation, library science, and archives subjects. The Institut de Presse et des Sciences de l'Information is affiliated with the University of Tunis and offers a graduate program in library science. As of 1985, there were 100 students enrolled, with 24 staff members. L'Institut Supérieur de Documentation" (ISD) is also affiliated with the University of Tunis; it offers an undergraduate program for students of library science. Students in the latter institution enter upon the successful completion of a secondary school leaving exam, and after two years of professional instruction are graduated as assistant librarians. In 1985, there were 150 students and 10 staff members.

During the academic year 1984–85, the IPSI started a new postgraduate program open to students with B.A. degrees in any subject. They undertake a two-year program leading to a Diplôme de Conservateur.

School libraries face many difficulties. There are shortages of qualified university teachers capable of teaching in the Arabic language and of Arabic teaching manuals and materials. There are also serious shortcomings in technical services.

REFERENCES

Mohammed Abdeljaouad, "La situation des B.U. de Tunisie en 1984," *A.T.D. Bulletin* (1984).

Ridha Attia, "National Bibliographies in the Maghreb: A Survey of Their Contents and Perspectives," *IFLA Council* (1984).

Douglas W. Cooper, "Libraries of Tunisia," *Wilson Library Bulletin* (June, 1979).

Hussein Habaili, "Development of Libraries and Information Services in Tunisia" *The Arab Magazine for Information Sciences* (ALESCO, Tunis, 1984).

HUSSEIN HABAILI

Turkey

Turkey, a republic in southeastern Europe and Asia Minor, is bordered by the Black Sea on the north; Georgia, Armenia, and Iran on the east; Iraq, Syria, and the Mediterranean Sea on the south; the Aegean Sea on the west; and Greece and Bulgaria on the northwest. Population (1990 est.) 58,687,000; area 779,452 sq.km. The official language is Turkish.

National Library. The National Library of Turkey, in Ankara, was officially opened in 1948. After spending 34 years in a temporary building, it finally moved into new quarters in 1983. The National Library, which played a leadership role in modern librarianship in Turkey for many years, lost this role during the 1970s and 1980s, largely because it lacked administrative support, personnel, finance, and space. With its move to new quarters, it renewed its claim to that role. Its major effort in the early 1990s was to automate its catalogue (covering approximately 1,500,000 volumes) and its two important bibliographical publications, *Türkiye Bibliyografyası* (Turkish National Bibliography, published since 1939) and *Türkiye Makaleler Bibliyografyası* (bibliography of articles published in Turkish periodicals, published since 1952). The third important publication of the National Library is *Türkiye Cumhuriyeti Devlet Yayınları Bibliyografyası* (bibliography of government publications, published since 1971).

The National Archives, which is separate from the National Library, moved to a new site in Ankara in 1988. In this modern building, it works to collect the official records of Turkey and give service to its multinational users. It also began automating its records and services.

Another pioneer in library automation in Turkey is the Parliament Library, established in 1923. Many of its records and services are computerized. It maintains connections with other parliamentary libraries around the world.

TÜRDOK, the Turkish Documentation Center, was established in 1966 to disseminate scientific and technical documents and to promote and coordinate library and information systems. Yükseköğretim Kurulu (the Documentation Center of the Higher Education Council) was established in 1981; in 1983 it took over most of the tasks of TÜRDOK for the academic community. As the largest periodical center in the Middle East (with about 15,000 title subscriptions), this Documentation Center serves not only university members, but also researchers from all parts of Turkey. It collects theses, microforms, and other types of documents. It provides online search services and offers its own databases of journal titles and Turkish theses through the Turkish academic network, TÜVEKA. Largely automated in its services, the Center plays an important coordinating role among the university libraries.

Academic Libraries. There were 29 universities in Turkey in 1991, including one private one, Bilkent. The libraries of these institutions vary greatly. In 1982, the Higher Education Council began trying to unify and centralize the unit and departmental libraries in the universities. There are automated libraries at some universities, such as Bilkent, but most are still traditional in their appearance and services. There is, however, a great impetus for automation in these libraries, even though they are largely devoid of plans that might enforce adherence to international standards. Almost all have some type of automation; some are even doing online or CD-ROM literature searching. By 1991, 16 universities were part of the academic network.

Older universities such as İstanbul and Ankara are decentralized, with many smaller libraries serving various schools and departments. Newer universities, such as Middle East Technical University and Hacettepe University in Ankara and Boğaziçi University (formerly Roberts College) in İstanbul have central campuses and better library facilities.

Public Libraries. Turkish people were traditionally interested in books and built many libraries under Ottoman rule, before 1923. Many were mosque-affiliated libraries; public libraries were developed and governed by individual foundations. In 1924 the Unity of Education Act brought public libraries

Libraries in Turkey (1990)

Type of library	Number of administrative units (main libraries)	Number of service points (branches, mobile stops, etc.)	Volumes in collections	Annual expenditures (lire) (1991)	Population served	Professional staff (with certificate, diploma, etc.)	Total staff
National	1	1	1,500,000	11,412,000,000	56,000,000	36	244
Academic	29	200	5,327,000	41,359,000,000	739,800	224	1188
Public	938	989	7,880,000	44,450,000,000	56,000,000	216	3524
School	4915	4915	9,303,000	--	10,470,000	--	2331
Special* (1989)	375	375	1,839,000	--	--	76	1068
Other Documentation Center	11	11	578,000	14,000,000,000	--	45	160

*Türkiye Kütüphaneleri: Kültür Bakanliği, 1989
Resmi Gazete (Official Gazette), 1991
DIE (State Institution of Statistics)
MEB (Ministry of Education)

together under state control. All public libraries (which numbered 938, with 51 bookmobiles, in 1991), fall administratively under the General Directorate of Libraries in the Ministry of Culture. Their collections grew from 660,000 in 1945 to 7,880,000 in 1990. However, the quality of these collections and services is far behind that of most university or special libraries. Their services are still traditional, and they have problems with physical facilities, lack of funds, and lack of professionals. Turkey has no union catalogue for these libraries.

In Turkey almost any library has a collection of manuscripts, small or large. The manuscripts may be in Turkish, Persian, or Arabic. The most famous of these is the Süleymaniye (Suleiman the Magnificent) Library in İstanbul, with nearly 66,000 invaluable manuscripts. This Library has a book conservation division. The total number of manuscripts held in public and manuscript libraries is about 182,000.

The Directorate of Libraries pioneered in establishing the International Standard Book Number system (ISBN) in Turkey in 1987. It is now promoting the International Standard Serial Number system (ISSN).

School Libraries. School libraries are the most neglected type in Turkey. According to 1991 figures of the Ministry of Education, which is responsible for them, there are about 4,900 school libraries in Turkey with collections totalling more than 9,333,600 volumes. Insufficient funds, lack of suitable space, and, most important, lack of professional personnel are the main causes for this underdevelopment. The Ministry sponsors summer training courses in order to improve the library situation.

Special Libraries. These libraries display a paradox in Turkey. Most of them are small, traditional, and in need of financial support or professional staff. But Turkey also has well-developed, well-organized libraries and documentation centers that apply international standards and reflect the latest developments. Some of these are: Turkish Historical Society, Ankara; Chamber of Commerce, İstanbul; State Planning Organization, Ankara; Marmara Scientific and Industrial Research Institute, Gebze, Kocaeli; Ankara Nuclear Research and Training Center (which is also the liaison center for INIS, International Nuclear Information System); Çekmece Nuclear Research and Training Center, İstanbul; YARPET (Petroleum Research Center), Yarımca, Kocaeli; and Şişe-Cam Frabrikası (glassware factory), İstanbul.

The number of special libraries can only be estimated, because there is no central authority for them. Turkey probably has about 375 special libraries. There is a trend in the private sector and in governmental and semigovernmental institutions toward establishing automated documentation centers.

The National Library of Turkey, officially opened in 1948, moved to these new quarters in 1983.

The Profession. There are three undergraduate library science departments in Turkey: two in Ankara (Ankara University, established in 1954, and Hacettepe University, established in 1974) and one in İstanbul (İstanbul University, established in 1964). Altogether 150 to 170 students graduate from these departments yearly. The departments have been restructured to include archives and documentation/information in addition to traditional librarianship and to reflect the latest developments in library science. Graduate training at the Master's and Doctoral level is possible at all three schools.

The professional association, Türk Kütüphaneciler Derneği (TKD; Turkish Librarians' Association) was founded in 1949 in Ankara. It has 28 branches and 1,100 members. Its quarterly, *Türk Kütüphaneciler Derneği Bülteni* (Bulletin of the Turkish Library Association), was renamed *Türk Kütüphaneciliği* (Turkish Librarianship) in 1987. The Association plans a Library Week each year and publishes professional materials.

An association for academic and research libraries, Üniversite ve Araştırma Kütüphanecileri Derneği (ÜNAK) was founded in 1991.

REFERENCES

Irfan Çakın, "Turkish Libraries: Historical Context," *International Library Review* (1984).

Yaşar A. Tonta, "Turkish Librarianship: An annotated bibliography (1950–1984)," *International Library Review* (1986).

Nilüfer Tuncer, "Experience with Online Search in Turkey," *International Library Review* (1987).

NILÜFER TUNCER

Uganda

Uganda, a land-locked republic in eastern Africa, is bounded by Sudan on the north, Kenya on the east, Tanzania and Rwanda on the south, and Zaire on the west. It was a British protectorate from 1900 to 1962 and became a republic in 1967. Population (1990 est.) 18,795,000; area 235,880 sq.km. The official language is English.

History. There are more than 50 ethnic groups in Uganda, speaking distinct dialects or languages. The indigenous languages have been allowed to sink into oblivion, both by the British and by successive Ugandan governments. There are not enough reading materials in indigenous languages, and the number of indigenous people who have mastered Swahili, English, or French has remained small. At the same time, library materials favored foreign languages and cultures. Between 60 and 80 percent of adult and potential readers cannot comprehend foreign language library materials in Uganda. Library service for all remains an illusory goal until either sufficient indigenous reading materials are produced or a greater proportion of Ugandans master foreign languages, unlikely in the foreseeable future.

Uganda's library services thus differ from those in developed countries but are comparable with those in many developing countries in Africa. First, there is no national library as such. Some of the conventional functions of a national library are performed by the large academic or special libraries. Second, most library services are funded by the central government, and few libraries have developed as a result of local initiative. This fact partly explains the marked concentration of large libraries in the capital city of Kampala and other towns where readers have a functional knowledge of English. Rural areas remain hardly touched by public library development.

In 1973 a dark period began for libraries. Traditional users of the existing libraries (Asians, Europeans, academicians, research fellows, and associates) fled the oppressive military rule. A shortage of foreign exchange and a lack of appreciation of the role of libraries in the priorities of funding authorities, moreover, meant that a considerable number of periodical subscriptions could not be renewed. For example, the Makerere University library system had more than 2,000 exchange partners and regular donors outside Uganda in 1973, mainly in Britain and the United States. These exchange agreements were cancelled as libraries in Uganda failed to reciprocate. Library budgets dwindled and development almost came to a standstill. Ugandan libraries in the early 1990s were still trying to recover from their decline and revert to the pre-1973 conditions.

Academic Libraries. The largest academic libraries have been associated with Makerere University. The origins of the university can be traced as far back as 1922, when it started as a technical school. It was affiliated with the University of London (1948–63), then was a College of the University of East Africa (1964–70). In 1970 it became a full-fledged university. It has a British-style system of organization with 11 faculties, 2 associated schools, and 2 institutes. Its library system includes the Main Library, founded in 1940, seven sublibraries, and small department collections. In 1985 some University departments were transferred to Kyambogo (site of Uganda Technical College and National Teachers College) and to Nakawa (site of Uganda College of Commerce). Makerere University acquired campuses in both places. According to 1977 estimates, the system had a stock of 400,000 volumes. With assistance from foreign governments, its staff hopes to double the stock in the 1990s.

The Main Library is one of the legal depository libraries in the country under the Deposit Library Act of 1964. The sublibraries benefit from deposits according to their fields of specialization. The Main Library also has a special collection of Africana with concentration on eastern Africa. The sublibraries include the Albert Cook Medical Library; the Faculty of Education Library; the Faculty of Agriculture Library at Kabanyolo; the East African School of Librarianship Library; and the Faculty of Veterinary Medicine Library. They all enjoy a certain degree of autonomy from the Main Library in their fields of specialization.

The oldest and most important is the Albert Cook Medical Library, founded in 1960. It serves the Mulago Hospital Medical School, with a strong concentration on tropical medicine and research literature on medical problems in eastern Africa. It is a depository of World Health Organization publications. The Education Library, founded in 1962 as a separate unit under the auspices of Unesco, periodically issues *Education in East Africa: A Selected Bibliography*. The Makerere Institute of Social Research Library, founded in 1958 as the East African Institute of Social Research Library, is a center of interdisciplinary and cross-cultural research with a strong regional

Libraries in Uganda (1990)

Type of library	Number of administrative units (main libraries)	Number of service points (branches, mobile stops, etc.)	Volumes in collections	Annual expenditures (shilling)	Population served	Professional staff (with certificate, diploma, etc.)	Total staff
Academic	3	9 branches	600,000	1,500,000	10,000	40	150
Public	1	20 branches	150,000	30,000	5,000,000	27	87
School	350	--	6,250,000	--	300,000*	30	400
Special	30	--	100,000	--	--	--	60

*Excluding private

Several religious institutions such as Seminaries and Theological Colleges have libraries which are so seclusive that they may be classified as private ones.

commitment to eastern Africa. The university library system extends its services to serious readers throughout Uganda. With no comparable libraries in the country, it serves as the de facto, though not de jure, national reference library.

Public Libraries. Early attempts to provide a public library service were made in the late 1940s as part of postwar efforts to improve conditions in the country. As early as 1923, however, the Uganda Society Library provided services for the reading needs of expatriates in Kampala and Entebbe, who at that time were almost the only people literate in English. Under the 10-year development plan (1946–56), social services were emphasized, among them lending libraries, but the project lasted only a few years before it was abandoned. In 1948 the East African Literature Bureau, serving Kenya, Uganda, and Tanzania, started a public libraries program based at Kampala. It was composed of two services: circulating book boxes to subscribing institutions and a postal loan service to subscribing individuals. The East African Literature innovation should be viewed as a venture to reach more of the English-language readers throughout the country who did not have access to Kampala Public Library. That Library was founded in 1964 as a branch of the Uganda Library Service. It had originally been known as Kampala Municipal Library and was under the Kampala Municipal Council.

The 1964 Public Library Act provided for a national headquarters and regional libraries under a Public Libraries Board. By 1973 the Board had a stock of more than 100,000 books, local newspapers, and periodicals intended for circulation throughout its 32 branch libraries in the country. It also had a postal lending service to individuals, a book box loan scheme to institutions, and mobile library service. Public library service has yet to recover from the devastation of the mid-1970s.

School Libraries. Since the mid-1960s the central government has gradually taken control of the large schools in the country, so that by 1976 all the major schools were either fully or partly financed by the government; that support led to more emphasis on the development of school libraries. Capital funds from foreign loans were used to establish or equip libraries. With funds from the World Bank, a number of new secondary schools were built, and old ones were improved under an Agency for International Development (AID) project; all AID project schools were planned to include libraries. With the phasing out of loan agreements for such projects, however, those libraries often found it difficult to continue their progress.

A study conducted in 1975 and 1976 found that the average high school library contained about 2,000 to 3,000 books. However, because of shortages of funds, many schools cannot buy new editions fast enough to have current collections. Primary schools have less funds, and some do not have libraries of any sort. The 1970s and 1980s saw little improvement in this situation.

Special Libraries. The Uganda Technical College Library is considered the leading special library in the country. Although its basic role is to serve the Uganda Technical College, it is also an important technical information source for practicing engineers in the country. It houses the Uganda Technical Information Service (UTIS), to which several consulting firms subscribe. It has a stock of more than 16,000 volumes, more than 240 journals, and collections of standards. Practically all government departments and parastatal bodies have established working libraries, but private firms, especially international corporations such as the oil and tobacco companies, have not usually established libraries in Uganda. They have instead relied on services from their overseas headquarters.

Africana Publishing Corporation

The Main Library of Makerere University.

The Institute of Public Administration Library, founded in 1968 at Kololo under the Ministry of Public Service and Cabinet Affairs, was accorded legal depository rights. It is also the base of the Uganda National Documentation Center. The Institute is responsible for in-service training for all Uganda government cadres, the main users of the library. Other notable special libraries include those of the Bank of Uganda, East African Development Bank, the Geological Survey of Uganda at Entebbe, Kawanda Agricultural Research Station, and Law Development Center at Makerere.

Many of the special libraries are not professionally staffed because of a shortage of trained personnel and money at all levels. There are also examples of qualified librarians not having sufficient books or facilities. "The Directory of East African Libraries" (1969), although outdated, gives an almost complete list of these libraries and their addresses.

The Profession. The East African School of Librarianship was founded at Makerere in 1962 with the assistance of Kenya, Uganda, and Tanzania. When the countries agreed to dissolve the University of East Africa in 1970 and to create independent national universities, they also agreed to support the School of Librarianship as a regional institution. The Council for Library Training in East Africa supervises the School. It is the only one of its kind in the region dedicated to the education of library personnel for professional and nonprofessional careers in the field of librarianship.

The Uganda Library Association (ULA) was formed in 1972. Earlier it had been the regional branch of the East African Library Association (EALA), created in 1958. Under normal circumstances, such as those prevailing before 1973, the Uganda Library Association holds national seminars. It also collaborates with such international organizations as IFLA, the Commonwealth Library Association (COMLA), the International Federation for Documentation (FID), and the Standing Conference of Eastern, Central, and Southern Africa Librarians (SCECSAL). Its journal, *Uganda Libraries,* is published by the East African School of Librarianship. ULA membership in the late 1980s was about 60 individuals and a few institutions.

REFERENCES

Margaret Macpherson, *They Built for the Future: A Chronicle of Makerere University College, 1922–1962* (1964).

B. W. K. Matogo, "Leading Issues in Developing Public Libraries in Emergent Uganda 1960–1970," *Libri* (1975).

"Directory of East African Libraries," 2nd revised edition (1969).

BONIFACE M. KAWESA

Ukraine

An independent democratic republic, Ukraine was a constituent of the Union of Soviet Socialist Republics for most of the 20th century. A member of the United Nations since 1945, it gained its independence on August 24, 1991. Belarus lies to the north, Russia to the north and east, the Black Sea, Moldova, and Romania to the south, and Slovakia and Poland to the west. Population (1990 est.) 52,000,000; area 603,700 sq.km. The official language is Ukrainian, but Russian is also widely used.

History. Ukraine has a rich and varied library tradition that dates from the times of Kievan Rus. The Kievan prince Yaroslav Mudryj (Yaroslav the Wise, *c.* 987–1054) established the first library in Ukraine in 1037. From the 11th to the 14th centuries libraries were established throughout Kievan Rus, principally affiliated with monasteries and churches. The most prominent is the library of the Kievo-Pechersk monastery in the heart of the capital, Kiev. Other early libraries are located in the cities of Chernihiv, Pereyaslav, and Polotsk and in the regions of Halychyna and Volyn in western Ukraine. In the late 14th and early 15th centuries the first schools were established: schools run by associations of lay religious personnel, the so-called brotherhood schools, and the Greek-Slavic-Latin Academy in the town of Ostrih, all of which operated their own libraries.

In the 17th century the Kiev-Mohyla Academy was established in Kiev, the first institution of higher learning in Ukraine and the cultural center of eastern Europe. Ukrainian philosophical thought and the Ukrainian literary language were developed there. The Academy supported a magnificent library that contained books and manuscripts from all parts of the world. Its collection included Ukrainian and international scientific and artistic works, rare manuscripts, and periodicals.

The libraries of the Kiev, Odessa, and Chernihiv universities and other institutions of higher learning played an important part in the development of national culture in Ukraine in the 19th century. At the same time, the process of establishing public libraries began throughout Ukraine. Several prominent Ukrainian scholars and writers of the time, such as I. Franko, L. Ukrainka, and M. Lysenko, were instrumental in developing libraries.

The All-National Library of Ukraine (now the Central Scientific Library of Ukraine) was established in 1918 and a network of local, public, school, children's, and workers' libraries developed. During the 1920s a number of journals dedicated to books and libraries appeared. The 1930s brought famine, then political and ethnic repression initiated by Josef Stalin. The 1940s brought World War II, which included the destruction of many libraries along with much else in Ukraine. The government library system was restored and centralized after the war.

National Library. The V. I. Vernadsky Central Scientific Library, the research library of the Ukrainian Academy of Sciences, is the largest library in Ukraine and the de facto National Library. It houses more than 12,500,000 volumes and receives more than 200,000 new publications annually, among them some 23,000 foreign volumes. It offers international interlibrary loan, access to electronic mail, and computerized bibliographic databases and plans an online union

Libraries in Ukraine (1992)

Type of library	Number of administrative units (main libraries)	Number of service points (branches, mobile stops, etc.)	Volumes in collections	Professional staff (with certificate, diploma, etc.)	Total staff
National	1	1	12,500,000	478	686
Academic	153	--	--	--	6,500
Public*	22,300	22,300	--	43,000	--
School	17,000	--	--	17,200	--
Scientific/technical	2,500	--	--	--	--
Special: medical	1,035	--	--	2,600	--
agricultural	250	--	--	--	--
professional union	3,000	--	--	--	--
academy/research	93	--	12,500,000	--	1,100

*Under the Ministry of Culture

Source: Statistics provided by author

catalogue. The Library is a scientific research center in library science, bibliography, the history of books, and the computerization of library and information services.

The Library moved into a new building in 1989. Its priceless collection of old and rare manuscripts includes the "Assyrian-Babylonian book list" from the third century B.C. The Library also owns one of two existing copies of the "History of Animals" by Aristotle published in Venice in 1476.

Academic Libraries. The Taras Shevchenko Kiev State University was established in 1834. Its library was based on the collection of the Volyn Lyceum (1805–32), but received gifts and bequests from graduates, professors, and patrons of the arts, including Mykola Kostomarov, I. Sikorsky, and O. Lazarevsky. By 1900 it had become one of the best libraries in the country, with an extensive collection of old and rare books, autographed works, and works by Ukrainian and foreign writers. It now has nearly 3,530,000 volumes and serves about 69,000 visitors yearly. It also functions as the methodological and coordinating center for more than 150 libraries affiliated with institutions of higher learning in Ukraine.

The State Scientific-Technical Library of Ukraine was founded in 1935 and is a main contributor to the development of science and manufacturing and to the spread and popularization of new technologies and innovations. The Library, which houses more than 20,000,000 volumes, coordinates the work of scientific libraries throughout Ukraine. It has a database for the scientific-technical information system for the country, including all categories of Ukrainian and foreign standards, technical specifications, and manufacturing catalogues for Ukrainian and foreign products, as well as patent information from more than 60 countries.

Public Libraries. The Ministry of Culture operates 22,300 libraries. The most important of these is the State Library of the Ukraine in Kiev, founded in 1866. It holds 4,000,000 books, periodicals, musical scores, maps, newspapers, and other documents in 66 languages. One of the most precious items in its collection is the *Ostrih Bible,* printed in 1581 by Ivan Fedorov. The library serves 4,000 users annually.

The M. Ostrovsky National Library for the Blind serves the sight-impaired and plays a direct role in determining their social, medical, and professional rehabilitation. It has more than 160,000 volumes, both braille and flat type, as well as books on tape, sound recordings, and periodicals. It works with the Ukrainian House of Sound Recording and the printing house of the Ukrainian Society for the Blind to ensure that adequate materials are available. It serves more than 2,000 patrons annually, most of them on an individual basis. It also arranges readers' conferences, radio journals, and thematic and literary evenings. The Library serves as a methodological center for 78 specialty libraries that serve more than 40,000 sight-impaired citizens a year. It publishes 10 to 12 methodological works and 20 to 40 bibliographic materials annually, among them such works as "Sight-Impaired Writers of Ukraine" and "Sight-Impaired Artists of Ukraine."

The Profession. There are more than 83,200 professional librarians in Ukraine, including 43,000 with higher specialized education who work in librar-

Marco della Cava

Central Research Library of the Academy of Sciences of Ukraine in Kiev.

ies administered by the Ministry of Culture. Universities and other institutions of higher learning have 6,500 professional librarians; academies have 1,100; medical libraries have 2,600; and secondary trade schools have 17,200.

Training is available in the library science departments of the Institutes of Culture of Kiev, Kharkív, and Pivne, and in 26 pre-professional training institutes. Immediately after independence in 1991, Ukrainian library educators initiated reforms modeled on library education in North America.

TETIANA ARSEENKO
translated by MARTA ZIELYK

Unesco

Unesco, the United Nations Educational, Scientific and Cultural Organization, a specialized agency of the UN, was founded in London on November 16, 1946, by representatives of 44 nations. It has its headquarters in Paris. The Preamble to its Constitution, which was largely inspired by British Prime Minister Clement Attlee and the American poet Archibald MacLeish, states that "Since wars begin in the minds of men, it is in the minds of men that the defences of peace must be constructed."

"The Purpose of the Organization is to contribute to peace and security by promoting collaboration among nations through education, science and culture in order to further universal respect for justice, for the rule of law and for the human rights and fundamental

Unesco/D. Roger

Unesco literacy training program in Ethiopia.

freedoms which are affirmed for the peoples of the world, without distinction of race, sex, language or religion by the Charter of the United Nations" (Article 1, paragraph 1 of the Constitution).

Unesco is committed to: "(a) collaborate in the work of advancing the mutual knowledge and understanding of peoples through all means of mass communication and, to that end, recommend such international agreements as may be necessary to promote the free flow of ideas by word and image . . . (b) give fresh impulse to popular education and to the spread of culture . . . (c) maintain, increase and diffuse knowledge" (Article 1, paragraph 2 of the Constitution).

To these ends, Unesco's activities, as defined in its Third Medium Term Plan (1990–95), are carried out in five main sectors: Education; Natural Sciences; Social and Human Sciences; Culture; and Communication, Information, and Informatics. It operates liaison offices around the world and regional offices in four regions: (1) Africa, (2) Latin America and the Caribbean, (3) the Arab states, and (4) Asia and the Pacific.

Structure. Unesco had a membership of 163 states in 1991. In most of them a Unesco National Commission provides a link between institutions concerned with educational, scientific, cultural, and communication matters and the work of Unesco as a whole.

The supreme body of Unesco is the General Conference, which meets every two years to decide policy and approve a program and budget for the next two years. The General Conference, at its 26th session in 1991, voted a regular budget of $444,704,000 for the 1992–93 biennium. Between general conferences, the program is implemented by the Secretariat under the supervision of the Executive Board, whose members are elected by the General Conference from among regional groupings. The Director-General is elected by the General Conference for a period of six years. Federico Mayor, formerly Spain's Minister of Education, was elected Director-General in 1987.

The Unesco staff numbered more than 2,700 in 1991, almost 2,000 at Headquarters in Paris and more than 700 in the field and in regional offices. All Unesco activities are implemented within the framework of its Third Medium Term Plan (1990–95), approved by the General Conference. The Plan is based on an analysis of contemporary world problems. It presents the major programs designed to facilitate the discharge of the Organization's five "essential tasks." These tasks are defined as follows: "(1) To contribute to a continuing study of present world problems so as to create a greater awareness of the common destiny which now unites individuals and peoples alike. (2) To help pave the way for the widest participation by individuals and groups in the life of the societies to which they belong and in that of the world community. (3) To assist in strengthening problem-solving capability by fostering the development and democratization of education and the advancement of science, by increasing and developing the creative potential, both scientific and technological, of all peoples by reinforcing aptitudes and abilities, by developing research and training infrastructures and by promoting the free flow of knowledge and know-how. (4) To help to facilitate the changes and transitions that are now recognized as necessary by the international community as a whole, in fields where the convergence of aspirations gives rise to a broad consensus. (5) To arouse and encourage a renewal of values within a context of genuine understanding among peoples, thereby advancing the cause of peace and human rights."

PGI. The Division of the General Information Program, often called PGI, the initials of its name in French—Programme Général d'Information—was established in 1976 to provide a focus for Unesco's activities in the fields of specialized information systems, documentation, libraries, and archives. It is committed to promote the dissemination of specialized information of use to economic and social development, especially in the Third World. PGI incorporates the previously launched Unesco/UNISIST program for cooperation in the field of scientific and technological information. Under the UNISIST program, standards, rules, methods, principles, and techniques for the processing and transfer of information are now adopted and applied internationally. The scope of PGI and UNISIST has been extended beyond science and technology to include all fields of specialized information.

An Intergovernmental Council of 30 members, elected by the General Conference, guides the implementation of each biennial program.

PGI helps member states to strengthen their national capabilities for handling information by offering assistance in setting up and managing national and regional information systems. It conducts activities designed to help them in: elaborating and implementing national information policies and plans;

promoting the use of standards and software for information systems (including extension of the Common Communication Format and development of the CDS/ISIS and IDAMS programs); strengthening the training of information specialists and developing computer-assisted instruction material; encouraging the implementation of regional information strategies; promoting the use of information systems and services for decision making in environmental management and in some areas in the social sciences; strengthening the roles of libraries in promoting literacy, education, and community development through creating school and public libraries, completing a worldwide survey of school libraries, promoting guidelines for preserving the printed world heritage, and extending the Unesco Network of Associated Libraries; and promoting the safeguarding of and access to the archival heritage through advisory services on establishing regional audiovisual archival development plans, reconstituting the archival heritage through microfilming, training archival workers in modernizing archival infrastructures, and evaluating the Records and Archives Management Program (RAMP).

PGI works in close cooperation with member states, intergovernmental and nongovernmental organizations, other Unesco programs, and the United Nations and its other specialized agencies. PGI convenes meetings, consultations, and conferences; sponsors, organizes, or supports education and training courses and seminars; launches projects and organizes consultancy missions; offers study fellowships and equipment grants; conducts research; and issues studies and publications. It issues a bibliography of its publications.

The work of PGI is financed from a variety of sources, including the United Nations Development Program (UNDP), Funds-in-Trust, and development banks, as well as its regular budget and the Unesco participation program. Its total budget from all sources for the 1992–93 biennium was approximately $9,100,000.

During the early 1990s emphasis was placed on operational activities; promoting new technology applications in information handling; setting up the systems needed for numerical, statistical, and other factual data; and information analysis, consolidation, and repackaging, required in order to meet the needs of a variety of user groups.

The applications of information technology in developing countries include library and archive applications, information service applications, setting up local databases, and online access to remote databases using national and international telecommunication networks. Successful experiments have been carried out with computer messaging systems, electronic mail, teleconferencing, and videotex.

A feature of the activities proposed under this program is the balance that has been achieved between innovative pursuits that take technological changes into account and seek to introduce modern information systems and create databases using computers—particularly microcomputers—and the continuing efforts made to establish and consolidate essential traditional information services. While it is vital to foster the introduction of new informatics and telecommunication technologies on which rapid access to information in fundamental areas now depends, traditional archive and library services (national, university, public, and school libraries) still constitute the irreplaceable means of acquiring knowledge and safeguarding the intellectual heritage of all nations.

Information Policies and Plans. PGI organizes and participates in consultations on existing and planned information systems, contributes to study and research on the exchange and transfer of information, both inside and outside the United Nations system. At the national level, liaison between PGI and member states is maintained through 59 Focal Points and 45 UNISIST National Committees. A National Focal Point is a government agency responsible for overall information policy and coordination of national activities; a UNISIST National Committee is a consultative body designated to advise on all aspects of information exchange and to work in liaison with PGI. Working contacts are maintained with existing information networks and programs, such as those of the European Community.

Member states are assisted in reviewing their information needs so they can make the best possible use of existing information sources. To this end, surveys were undertaken in member states to study innovations in planning information policies and removing obstacles to the flow of information. On the basis of these surveys, PGI held seminars on the analysis and evaluation of national information policies and plans.

In the early 1990s PGI sought to improve information resources at national, subregional, and regional levels in terms of planning, management, and integration into communication and information strategies, mainly through training about a hundred leading information specialists and decision-makers, and including information components in the national development plans of some five to eight member states. It offered advisory services on coordinating national information services and systems, on harmonizing information policies and the implications of transborder flow, and on regional and interregional agreements and information resource sharing.

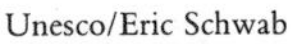
Unesco/Eric Schwab

Unesco-sponsored primary school in Douala, Cameroon, attended by Europeans and Africans.

Unesco/Carracciolo and Banoun

Students in New Delhi, India, participating in a Unesco-sponsored Institute of Film and Television.

Norms and Standards and Developing Software. In drawing up and disseminating standards and norms relevant to information work, PGI cooperates closely with the International Organization for Standardization (ISO), which is responsible for the ultimate adoption of international standards; with the International Center for Terminology (Infoterm); and with professional organizations. PGI concentrates on the application of international standards and only to a lesser extent on their elaboration. Promotion of existing standards is ensured by a number of methods, including updating such documents as the *ISO Standards Handbook on Information Transfer* and the *UNISIST Guide to Standards for Information Handling,* which was broadened to include standards relating to archives administration and records management systems and services. PGI has produced many educational materials and made them available to member states in order to promote the adoption of standards.

The Common Communication Format (CCF) was developed to make communication of bibliographic data practicable among computer-based systems throughout the world. PGI planned to extend CCF to include related conversion programs and to apply it in the online environment. It also planned to assist the International Serials Data System (ISDS) to achieve self-reliance in 1994–95, to prepare guidelines for decision support information systems (in cooperation with the United Nations University), and to develop international standards for archival descriptions.

To achieve widespread use of its information resources, Unesco reviewed users' requirements and studied the feasibility of developing a clearinghouse for information. It plans to support users by promoting and using modern dissemination techniques (including both microcomputer and mainframe versions of CDS/ISIS and IDAMS software); maintaining the micro version of CDS/ISIS and documenting it in English, French, and Spanish; organizing regional teacher-training seminars in its use; supporting regional meetings of CDS/ISIS software distributors; and publishing the *CDS/ISIS Technical Newsletter.*

Training Information Specialists. PGI promotes in member states and at the regional level the creation and reinforcement of educational programs designed to prepare the information scientists, librarians, archivists, and other technical staff required to staff a full range of information systems and services and promote the improvement of information use by a wide range of user groups. It fosters the establishment of new regional or national education and training institutions or the reinforcement of existing ones. It organizes intensive courses in areas such as new technologies, establishing nonconventional information services, and management, with a view to updating the knowledge of practicing teachers, managers, information scientists, and archivists. PGI also prepares and disseminates teaching packages, textbooks, and curricula on a variety of topics including microcomputer use, restoration and preservation, information analysis, numerical data services, and referral services with a view to training information professionals. In order to increase public awareness of the value of information and its proper use in pilot sectors, PGI also prepares model user training materials for introduction into the study programs of educational institutions at various levels. It conducts activities designed to improve harmonization of specialized training programs in the information sciences and collects and disseminates information on training opportunities and materials.

As examples of some of these activities, PGI planned an expert meeting in the Arab region to devise a strategy for adapting the education of information professionals, including women, to the information society. It also organized international seminars with such nongovernmental organizations as the International Federation of Library Associations and Institutions (IFLA), the International Federation for Documentation (FID), and the International Council on Archives (ICA) for training educators. PGI worked to develop computer-assisted instruction materials for use in schools of library and information sciences in francophone member states and to establish an archival training program in Latin America.

Development of Regional Information Strategies and Networks. PGI works with established regional and subregional coordinating mechanisms in Latin America and the Caribbean such as INFOLAC and CARSTIN and in Asia and the Pacific such as ASTINFO, the Regional Network for the Exchange of Information and Experience in Science and Technology in Asia and the Pacific. In addition to providing some funds, PGI helps regional information and documentation programs seek help from UNDP and other sources.

For Latin America and the Caribbean, the activities include advice on developing national referral centers or clearinghouses, such as the Amazonian Information System and the Andean Parliament Information System; a pilot project on a regional document delivery system; four national and two subregional seminars on information use; and ways to develop commercial services and products.

For Asia and the Pacific, the activities include advice and financial assistance for members of ASTINFO, especially on linking the network to other information systems; technical and financial support for the Asian Pacific Information Network for Medicinal and Aromatic Plants (APINMAP); pilot projects on community information services to support basic education in two member states; and consultation on human resource development and appropriate regional training facilities in four member states, with special attention to participation by women.

In Africa, PGI promotes information services to support research and decision making on environmental and natural resources management and on some areas of social sciences. Its activities include publishing guidelines for exchanging and using environmental information; training some 75 decision makers and key scientists, including women, in establishing and using environmental information systems; establishing a prototype documentation center for women (in Cameroon); and conducting a feasibility study on a subregional African network for information in the social sciences. PGI worked to consolidate the Pan-African Network for a Geological Information System (PANGIS), sought to develop links and common methodologies between it and the International Hydrological Program, and hoped to help it achieve self-reliance by the mid-1990s.

In the Arab states, PGI promotes the flow of information through collaboration with the Arab League Educational, Cultural and Scientific Organization (ALECSO).

Libraries and Documentation Units. PGI plays a major role in developing libraries and documentation units worldwide. It seeks to strengthen community information services in support of post-literacy and continuing education (especially in rural areas through the development of public library and rural community information services in five African member states) by offering guidance and technical assistance to member states in planning and running library services and by providing advice on fund-raising for library projects.

To cite some examples, PGI prepared a worldwide survey of library and information systems in cooperation with IFLA. It cooperates with IFLA in many other projects and provides it with some funds to promote library services and raise professional standards. In close cooperation with the Unesco Associated School Project, PGI worked to strengthen the Unesco Network of Associated Libraries (UNAL) and organized seminars on the role of libraries in serving international understanding and peace.

In addition, PGI provides a document procurement service in scientific literature for 20 to 30 institutions in developing countries. It provides training for 100 librarians, mainly women, in four member states in planning and running document delivery services and in using CD-ROM technology. It works with the Third World Academy of Sciences, the International Council of Scientific Unions, and the UNITWIN project to achieve better coordination and streamlining of book and journal donation programs. And it was a sponsor of the International Workshop on Book Donation Programs presented by the Canadian Organization for the Development of Education and the International Book Bank.

The Archival Heritage and RAMP. One of PGI's major objectives is to increase awareness of the fragility of archival materials, the memory of mankind. It works to safeguard and reconstitute the national archival heritage through transferring technical know-how to developing countries and through a microfilming program.

Safeguarding the archival heritage includes advisory services for creating regional audiovisual technical laboratories; preparing audiovisual development plans in four member states, most of them in Africa; reconstituting and providing access to archival materials through microfilms; and bilateral arrangements for reproducing archival collections and acquiring the necessary equipment and training. PGI provides advice on improving archival infrastructure and training in the use of new technologies, in particular on the basis of the project "Automation of the General Archives of the Indies." It provides funds for the ICA and helps member states find funding for archival work.

PGI is responsible for the Records and Archives Management Program (RAMP). Implemented in consultation with ICA, RAMP covers policies, standards, infrastructures, training, research, and other aspects of archival development at the national, regional, and international level. It is being developed on a long-term basis in recognition of the growing importance of records and archives in member states.

Studies are conducted and guidelines prepared with ICA; they include work on records surveys and schedules and the archival appraisal of motion pictures and related records, machine-readable records, and still pictures. Other studies deal with archival records management, legislation, and regulations, and the preservation and restoration of paper records and publications and of photographic materials. PGI prepared model classification standards and job descriptions for personnel in archival and records management services, with particular reference to developing countries.

WOLFGANG LÖHNER

Union of Soviet Socialist Republics

EDITOR'S NOTE: The Union of Soviet Socialist Republics no longer exists. It disintegrated during the months when the editors were preparing this edition, and the political and economic turmoil eventually produced a loose grouping of republics known as the Commonwealth of Independent States. Detailed information about libraries and information services in these republics was all but impossible to obtain. Therefore, rather than provide no information on Russia and the 14 other successor republics, the editors decided to reprint material from the Second Edition under the old title, much of it about Russia, the principal component of the U.S.S.R. and of the C.I.S. We did receive information in time to include separate articles on Estonia, Lithuania, and Ukraine.

The U.S.S.R. comprised 15 Union Republics, including the largest, the Russian Soviet Federated Socialist Republic (R.S.F.S.R.), now known as Russia, and the Armenian Soviet Socialist Republic (S.S.R.), now Armenia; the Azerbaidzhan S.S.R., now Azerbaijan; the Belorussian S.S.R., now Belarus; the Estonian S.S.R., now Estonia; the Georgian S.S.R., now Georgia; the Kazakh S.S.R., now Kazakhstan; the Kirgiz S.S.R., now Kyrgyzstan; the Latvian S.S.R., now Latvia; the Lithuanian S.S.R., now Lithuania; the Moldavian S.S.R., now Moldova; the

Tadzhik S.S.R., now Tajikistan; the Turkmen S.S.R., now Turkmenistan; the Ukrainian S.S.R., now Ukraine; and the Uzbek S.S.R., now Uzbekistan. Population (1988 est.) 286,435,000; area 22,402,200 sq. km. More than 90 languages are spoken. Russian is the official language.

History. The first famous Russian book repository was founded about 1037 in the Sofia Cathedral in Kiev. It was the most complete collection of written monuments and government documents of ancient Rus. In the earliest development of oral and written works, the high point of cultural and economic connections of the Russian principalities led to the appearance of libraries in the large Troitse-Sergiev, Solovetsk, and Belozersk monasteries. In the 12th century, book repositories also appeared in Vladimir, Riazan, Chernigov, Suzdal, Rostov, Murom, Polotsk, Smolensk, Pekov, and other cities. In Novgorod, as archaeological excavations show, there were many written collections on birch bark, made from thin layers of birch-tree bark. Many valuable Slavic manuscripts were preserved there, among which was the first dated, written monument—the celebrated "Ostromir Gospel" (1057).

The invasion of Rus by numerous enemies—from the East the Mongol Horde, from the West the Teutonic Knights—conflagration and civil war, accompanied by the destruction of cities and monasteries, in which were concentrated the written treasures, destroyed thousands of priceless written documents of the past.

The first printing press in Russia appeared in Moscow in the middle of the 16th century, and I. Fedorov printed the first Russian book, *Apostol,* in 1564. Only then did favorable conditions arise for the development of libraries. From the beginning of book printing to the beginning of the 18th century, only about 1,000 books were produced in Russia. In the epoch of Peter I (reigned 1682–1725) more than 600 books were printed.

That promoted the appearance of the first large private book collections. For example, the library of Field Marshal B. P. Sheremet'ev numbered more than 25,000 volumes. In 1714 in the capital of the country, St. Petersburg, the first library was born (now the Library of the Academy of Sciences of the U.S.S.R.) and 40 years later the first library appeared in Moscow (now the Lomonosov Library of Moscow State University).

In St. Petersburg in 1795 the beginning of another prominent library was laid—the Imperial (now the Saltykov-Shchedrin State Public Library [renamed the Russian National Library in the early 1990s]), which opened to visitors in 1814. Almost a half-century later, in 1862 in the Rumiantsev Museum in Moscow, a public library was also founded (now the Lenin State Library of the U.S.S.R. [renamed the Russian State Library in the early 1990s]). Up to that time public libraries were arising in other district towns also, and on the national frontiers of Russia—in Riga, Tallinn, Kishinev, Erevan, Tblisi, Kazan, and Tashkent. They preserved in various circumstances the best monuments of the written culture of the peoples of the Baltic, Transcaucasia, and Central Asia.

In prerevolutionary Russia there were altogether no more than 76,000 libraries, of which the vast majority offered small book collections, full of loyal literature permitted for reading by the tsarist censors. At the same time those libraries also held works of A. S. Pushkin, M. I. Lermontov, N. V. Gogol, N. A. Nekrasov, F. M. Dostoevsky, L. N. Tolstoy, A. P. Chekhov, and others who enjoyed great popularity.

The Great October Socialist Revolution of October 25, 1917 (O.S.), opened a new stage of development for library work. V. I. Lenin gave libraries special meaning as the most popular and accessible centers for the diffusion of knowledge and the enlightenment of the people. "He considered the elevation of library work to be one of the indicators of the cultural level of a country," wrote N. K. Krupskaya, Lenin's wife and a leader in Soviet library development. On the initiative of Lenin, the Soviet administration issued a series of fundamental directives and decrees, aimed at a basic reorganization of library work on new Socialist principles. The following decrees, among others, were issued: "On the Preservation of Libraries and Book Repositories of the R.S.F.S.R." (1918), "On the Centralization of Library Work in the R.S.F.S.R." (1920), and "On the Transfer of Library Work in the R.S.F.S.R. to the National Commissariat for Education" (1920).

An important event was the reorganization in 1925 of the Library of the Rumiantsev Museum as the Lenin State Library of the U.S.S.R., which helped the process of organizing a unified library system. The first Soviet library law, issued in 1934, "On Library Work in the U.S.S.R.," noted significant successes in libraries: the growth of a network of libraries, the opening of new libraries in factories, construction projects, and collectives; and a significant increase in library holdings and numbers of readers.

At the beginning of 1941, there were 277,000 libraries of all types and forms in the U.S.S.R. with book holdings of 520,000,000 items. The readers in libraries overall numbered 55,000,000. There was one public library for every 2,000 people, and for every 100 people there were 96.5 books.

In the years of World War II, 1941–45, called in the Soviet Union the Great Patriotic War, Hitler's troops, while in occupied regions of the U.S.S.R., completely destroyed 43,000 public and hundreds of large libraries and plundered more than 100,000,000 books. In the postwar period special attention was given to the restoration of the network of libraries and their collections. By 1950 the number of libraries surpassed prewar records by 12 percent.

In 1959 the Central Committee of the Communist Party (CPSU) issued a directive "On the Condition and Measures for Improvement of Library Work in the Country," and in 1974 one titled "On the Promotion of the Role of Libraries in Communist Education of the Workers and Scientific-Technical Progress."

The implementation of these party documents involved widening the sphere of influence of libraries, increasing the number of readers and of books lent, and strengthening interdepartmental connections and reinforcing coordination of the activities of various libraries.

In the Soviet Union there were about 329,000 libraries (1985) with book collections of 4,717,000,000 items, used by 224,000,000 readers.

On March 13, 1984, the Presidium of the Supreme Soviet of the U.S.S.R. ratified by decree "The

Regulation of Library Work in the U.S.S.R.," a new law regulating various aspects and activities of Soviet libraries. This document established the social function of libraries as ideological, cultural-educational, and scientific-informational institutions whose activity is guided toward the realization of the constitutional rights of the citizens of the U.S.S.R. to an education and to make use of the achievements of culture, recreation, and the freedom of scientific, technical, and artistic creation.

"The Regulation of Library Work in the U.S.S.R." thus set out to strengthen Lenin's principles of organization of library work in the U.S.S.R.: joining libraries into a single system, planned development and the spread of the system, the guarantee of unity of organization and methodological leadership, government planning of the training of library staff, general accessibility, and cost-free library services for the population.

National, All-Union, Republic, Regional, and District Libraries. *Lenin State Library*. In accordance with "the Regulation of Library Work in the U.S.S.R.," the Lenin State Library of the U.S.S.R. (founded in 1862 [and renamed the Russian State Library in the 1990s]) functions as the main national library of the country.

The Statute of the Library, ratified in 1985, defines its functions in the system of libraries of the Soviet Union as the overall state universal book repository, the all-union coordination center for scientific research work in the area of librarianship, bibliographic control, and book processing, the primary all-union scientific-methodological center for all libraries, regardless of their position in the hierarchy, the center for selected bibliographies and interlibrary loan, and a museum of the book.

The overall size of the collections of the Lenin State Library of the U.S.S.R. (mid-1980s) is 32,345,000 items in 247 languages, of which 20,960,400 (64.8 percent) are in Russian and other languages of the peoples of the U.S.S.R. 11,384,560 (35.2 percent) are in foreign languages. The annual receipts exceed 1,000,000 items. The exchange of literature involves approximately 3,415 libraries and organizations in 105 countries of the world.

The number of readers exceeds 220,000. At their service is a system of reading halls with 2,500 seats. Every day from 9 AM to 10 PM, from 8,000 to 10,000 people visit the library. Annual visits exceed 2,175,000, and book loans 12,000,000, including 335,000 through interlibrary loan.

The library administers various bibliographic projects for display and information (up to 100,000 inquiries are handled annually), provides service for the inquiries of party and government agencies, fulfills the functions of an information center for culture and art, issues reference and review and analysis publications, compiles advisory and retrospective bibliographic sources, and develops standards for various library-bibliographic processes.

Book Chamber. The current national bibliography in the U.S.S.R. is handled by the All-Union Book Chamber (founded in 1917), which registers all kinds of publications: books and brochures, periodical publications, playbills, posters, postcards, music scores, and maps in *Knizhnaia letopis* ("Book Annual") and other annuals, in *Ezhegodnik knigi* ("Annual of the Book"), and also in categorized sets of catalogue cards. The holdings of the Chamber total some 61,000,000 items (mid- 1980s). Every year the Chamber receives several hundred thousand newly printed publications, since after appropriate bibliographic preparation, one copy of every type of publication is sent to the State Archive of Publication of the U.S.S.R. for permanent preservation. The Chamber provides centralized cataloguing and statistics of publications, and fulfills the functions of a scientific center in the area of book processing and publishing activities.

State Library of Foreign Literature. The All-Union State Library of Foreign Literature (founded in 1922 [and renamed the Rudomino All-Russian Library of Foreign Literature in the early 1990s]) in accordance with the statute ratified in 1985, serves in the single system of libraries of the U.S.S.R. the functions of a library of broad humanistic services, satisfying inquiries about foreign literature from scientific research institutions; conducting work in the area of foreign librarianship and book processing; and serving as the center for interlibrary loan of literature in foreign languages. The holdings of the library total 4,394,600 items. The number of readers is 50,000. The annual book loans total 2,500,000. Book exchanges are conducted with more than 1,275 partners in 97 countries of the world.

Saltykov-Shchedrin State Public Library. This library in Leningrad (founded in 1814 [and renamed the Russian National Library in the early 1990s]) became, because it was one of the first to receive an obligatory copy of the printed works in Russia, the holder of a priceless collection of publications in the Russian language. The Library's collections number 25,044,653 items. Annual additions total 280,000 items, book loans 8,882,900. The number of readers is 185,000.

Public Libraries. The leading place in the system of library service to the people of the U.S.S.R. is held by the 133,200 public libraries (in the mid-1980s) with book collections of 1,945,100,000 items, which are used by 148,000,000 people, or more than half the population of the country. Readers annually borrow 3,170,000,000 items, 22 books and journals per person in a year. Toward the end of 1980, in accordance with the decree of the Central Committee of the CPSU "On the Promotion of the Role of Libraries in the Communist Education of the Workers and Scientific-Technical Progress" (1974), a reorganization of the work of these libraries was completed on the principles of centralization. Isolated libraries were brought into a system with almost 4,000 strong library associations affiliated with separate cities and administrative regions.

The reorganization of the network of public libraries permitted the spread of the sphere of influence of libraries, and satisfied more than half of the population's requirements for books. This development was facilitated by many things, including the publication in a special library series of 5,000 titles of the most popular books in a total quantity of 170,000,000 copies, which helped to build up collections of the public libraries.

Children's Libraries and School Libraries. To serve the rising generation of the U.S.S.R. with books, more than 10,000 libraries were created for children and young people, including republic, regional, district, and urban libraries, as well as 144,000 school libraries. Their combined book holdings exceed 862,000,000 items, which are regularly replenished with publications of school series, which include the best works of classic and current domestic and foreign literature. The readership of these libraries consists of the 40,000,000 pupils of general-education schools.

Scientific, Technical, and Other Specialized Libraries. There are 53,000 scientific, technical, and other specialized libraries with book holdings of 2,031,000,000 items. These libraries are an integral part of the State Automated System of Scientific-Technical Information (GASNTI) headed by the All-Union Institute of Scientific and Technical Information (VINITI), which works on an immense flow of documents on natural and technical sciences, received from 130 countries of the world in 66 languages.

The most diverse network of scientific-technical libraries exists in such branches of the national economy as the automobile industry, heavy and transport machine construction, rail transport, non-ferrous and ferrous metallurgy, the chemical and coal industry, and others. These libraries possess large numbers of scientific and technical works, periodical publications, special forms, and other documents, the use of which serves the advance of scientific and technical progress, the achievement of entire complex programs of development of the national economy, and the realization of economic experiments in various branches of industry.

The main scientific-technical library of the country is the State Public Scientific-Technical Library of the U.S.S.R. (founded in 1958). It carries out library bibliographic and information services for ministries and departments of the U.S.S.R. and Union Republics, enterprises, institutions, and organizations, as well as for individual users of information. It conducts analysis and preservation of domestic and foreign sources of information and searches for information in them. The holdings of the library approach 10,000,000 items, readership is 170,000, and book loans total 7,000,000 items. Every year the holdings are increased by more than 300,000 publications of various kinds.

The Library coordinates subscriptions to foreign literature on science and technology; from 1964 it annually issued "A List of Foreign Journals Subscribed to by Organizations of the U.S.S.R." It publishes lists of "New Foreign Books" and "New Foreign Journals" and prepares advanced information about the contents of the most important foreign journals on science and technology. Since 1968 an information-computer center has existed in the library, provided with new equipment and machines.

The other large scientific-technical library of the country is the State Public Scientific-Technical Library of the Siberian Division of the Academy of Sciences of the U.S.S.R. in Novosibirsk (founded in 1918). The holdings of the library exceed 9,000,000 items, annual additions number 220,000 items.

Academy Libraries. In the system of academic libraries there are the Library of the Academy of Sciences of the U.S.S.R. in Leningrad (founded in 1714), the Library for the Natural Sciences of the Academy of Sciences in Moscow (founded in 1973), and the Library of the Institute of Scientific Information for the Social Sciences (founded in 1969), whose basic direction of activity is the preparation of bibliographic and reference information. The holdings of the Library of this institute exceed 10,000,000 items, more than half of which are foreign publications. The number of readers is 31,000; book loans number 3,000,000.

A central library is in operation in each of the 15 Union Republics. The holdings of the Library of the Academy of Sciences of the Latvian S.S.R. (founded in 1524), as one example, exceed 3,000,000 items. The number of readers is 15,000 and book loans total 1,300,000 items.

Agricultural Libraries. The leader is the Central Scientific Agricultural Library of the Lenin All-Union Academy of Agricultural Sciences (founded in 1930). The holdings of the library exceed 3,000,000 items; its readers number 40,000 and book loans, 2,000,000. From 1948 the library issued a monthly bibliographic list, "Agricultural Literature of the U.S.S.R.," and from 1961 "New Works in Agricultural Science and Practice." The library is the methodological center for 1,300 libraries of scientific-research institutions, colleges, and technical schools with an agricultural emphasis, and experiment stations with a total holdings of 90,000,000 items, used by 2,000,000 readers.

Medical Libraries. In order to serve the medical workers and specialists in health services, a network of medical libraries was created, headed by the State Central Scientific Medical Library (founded in 1919), the holdings of which equal 2,500,000 items.

Educational Institutions. The students and teachers of nearly 900 universities and higher educational institutions and 4,400 middle-level specialist educational institutions of the country have special libraries at their disposal. Among them the oldest are the Library of Lvov University (founded in 1661), Moscow (1755), Tartu (1802), Vilnius (1803), and Kazan (1804). The overall number of reader-students (mid-1980s) is 9,833,000. The Gorky Research Library of Lomonosov Moscow State University is the All-Union scientific-methodological center, carrying out the leadership of the network of libraries of higher and middle-level specialist educational institutions.

I. NAZMUTDINOV
translated by THOMAS L. MANN

United Arab Emirates

The United Arab Emirates, a union of seven former Trucial sheikdoms (Abu Dhabi, Ajman, Dubai, Fujairah, Ras al-Khaimah, Sharjah, and Umm al-Qaiwain), lies on the eastern coast of the Arabian Peninsula in the Persian Gulf. Population (1990 est.) 1,589,000; area 83,600 sq.km. The official language is Arabic.

National Library. There is no national library in the country. The book production is negligible. In 1968 the Center for Documentation and Research was founded. Attached to the Presidential Court, it collects manuscripts, documents, books, maps, and articles relevant to the Gulf States and Arabian Peninsula. The Center also conducts research on subjects related to those areas. Its library contains more than 5,000 volumes in Arabic and foreign languages.

Academic Library. The University of the United Arab Emirates, at Al Ain, founded in 1978, established a central library with its Teachers College

Libraries in United Arab Emirates (1987)

Type of library	Number of administrative units (main libraries)	Number of service points (branches, mobile stops, etc.)	Volumes in collections	Population served
Academic	3	3	144,000	7,335

Source: Unesco, *Statistical Yearbook,* 1991

as its primary focus. The Library has some 28,000 volumes. The University established colleges of Art, Political and Administrative Sciences, Natural Sciences, and Law and Jurisprudence.

Public Libraries. There is a public library in each of the seven emirates. Noteworthy is the Dubai Public Library, with a collection of about 15,000 volumes, mostly in Arabic. The public libraries support adult education in the country.

Special Libraries. Four ministerial libraries contain small collections of books, periodicals, reports, and newspapers. A Gulf Documentation Center in Abu Dhabi is under the supervision of the Ministry of Information and Tourism. The Center collects, processes, and disseminates communications information for the Gulf States and the Arabian Peninsula.

MOHAMED M. EL HADI

United Kingdom

The United Kingdom, a constitutional monarchy, comprises the island of Great Britain (England, Scotland, and Wales), Northern Ireland, and various islands. Population (1991 census) 55,500,000; area 244,100 sq.km. The official language is English.

History. The oldest libraries in Britain can trace their origins back a thousand years. They are the ecclesiastical collections, some of which still exist. The next oldest are those of colleges at the universities of Oxford, Cambridge, and St. Andrews. From 1753 to 1973 the national library was the Library of the British Museum, but copyright deposit actually dates back to 1666 in England. After the union with Scotland in 1707, a Copyright Act of 1709 became the first to extend the practice to Great Britain as a whole. That act required nine copies of every printed publication to be delivered to Stationers' Hall, these being destined for the Royal Library, the two English and four Scottish university libraries, Sion College Library, and the Advocates' Library in Edinburgh.

From the 17th century a few libraries were open to the public, examples being Chetham's Library in Manchester and Archbishop Tenison's Library in Westminster, but public libraries as we know them date only from an act of Parliament passed in 1850. Since the 1930s the whole of Britain has enjoyed a comprehensive public library service, while libraries in other institutions, universities, colleges, polytechnics, schools, and hospitals have steadily expanded. Since 1877 the Library Association (LA) has had a great and continuing influence on library progress. Full-time education for librarianship may be said to have begun in Britain in 1919.

NATIONAL LIBRARIES

The British Library. Britain's national library until 1973 was the Library of the British Museum, which could trace its origins back to 1753, when Sir Hans Sloane bequeathed his outstanding collection of books and manuscripts to the nation. In 1969, however, the Dainton Committee Report drew attention to the need to rationalize the British Museum Library

Libraries in United Kingdom (1991)

Type of library	Number of administrative units (main libraries)	Number of service points (branches, mobile stops, etc.)	Volumes in collections	Annual expenditures (pounds)	Population served	Professional staff (with certificate, diploma, etc.)	Total staff
National							
British Library[1]	4	12*	c. 18,000,000	80,493,000	57,000,000[7]	834	2,344
Scotland[2]	2	3	c. 6,000,000	5,201,000	--	26	278
Wales[3]	1	1	c. 5,000,000	3,906,032	--	78	153
Academic							
Universities[4]	52**	--	--	107,295,000	380,265	--	--
Polytechnics[5]	36	135	10,975,214	41,139,100	340,914	764	1,868
Public[6]	167	6,057	156,755,000	642,200,000	57,000,000[7]	9,280	33,584

*Reading rooms.
**Universities comprising a number of colleges (i.e., Oxford, Cambridge, London) each counted as one.

Sources: 1. British Library, 18th Annual Report 1990–91.
2. National Library of Scotland, Annual Report 1990–91.
3. National Library of Wales, Annual Report 1990–91.
4. Universities' Statistical Record. University Statistics 1988–89. Vol. 3. Finance.
5. Council of Polytechnic Librarians (COPOL). COPOL Annual Statistics 1989–90.
6. Chartered Institute of Public Finance and Accountancy. Public Library Statistics 1989–90. Actuals.
7. Population of UK according to *Britain 1991: an official handbook*. London. HMSO. (Does not cover large numbers of foreign visitors using libraries or participation in international loan service.)

Theodore F. Welch

England's oldest surviving college library building is at Oxford University's Merton College, which was founded in 1264.

and other related collections. The LA strongly urged the Government to act on the Dainton Committee Report; in 1972 Parliament passed the British Library Act, and on July 2, 1973, the British Library (BL) came into being. It was formed from the British Museum Library, the Science Reference Library, the Patent Office Library, the National Lending Library for Science and Technology, the National Central Library, and the *British National Bibliography* (BNB). The BNB had been formed in 1950, the British Museum and the LA being among the partners that had initiated and supported it.

The British Library is the subject of a separate article in this volume. Reference to that article and to the Annual Reports of the BL will give readers more comprehensive details of the BL and its services. The BL planned a major move for the early 1990s, merging its scattered London operations in a new building at St. Pancras. Builders planned to open the first phase of the new structure in 1993, with a gross area of more than 80,000 sq.m., affording 579 reader seats, 12.7 km. of open-access shelving, and 292 km. of closed-access shelving. The final phase, scheduled to open in 1996 with a gross area of almost 35,000 sq.m., was designed to add 627 reader seats, 10.5 km. of open-access shelving, and 23 km. of closed-access seating. The architects for the new building are Colin St John Wilson and Partners. While the building was under construction, the lending functions of the BL remained at the British Library Document Supply Center (BLDSC) at Boston Spa in Yorkshire, some 200 miles north of London.

Other National Libraries. In addition to the British Library there are two other national libraries in the United Kingdom—the National Library of Scotland, which can trace its origins back to the 17th century, and the more recent National Library of Wales.

Scotland. The National Library of Scotland was founded in 1682 as the Advocates' Library; the Faculty of Advocates presented its collections to the nation in 1925 and Parliament set them up as the National Library. Since 1709 it has been a copyright library; it contains a notable collection of Scottish books and manuscripts. Housed in a building on George IV Bridge, Edinburgh, it includes a fine Reading Room and imposing Exhibition Rooms; the printed accessions number more than 100,000 annually. A Board of Trustees directs the Library's activities.

Wales. The National Library of Wales is at Aberystwyth, where its building was begun in 1911 and finally completed in 1955. It has three departments: Manuscripts and Records; Printed Books; and Prints, Drawings, and Maps. Classification is by the Library of Congress system. The Library has benefited under the Copyright Act since 1911, but it may demand only certain material, mainly Welsh, under the legal deposit system. It possesses more than 2,000,000 printed books and large collections of other materials. It is the headquarters of the Regional Library System for Wales.

ACADEMIC LIBRARIES

Universities. Britain is well equipped with academic libraries, headed by those of the older universities of Oxford and Cambridge. Oxford is served by the Bodleian Library, which was actually begun in the 14th century but reorganized by Sir Thomas Bodley in 1598. The building was expanded in 1946; it houses well over 2,000,000 volumes and substantial collections of other materials. Like the Cambridge University Library, the Bodleian Library has enjoyed copyright deposit privileges since the inception of legal deposit. Cambridge University Library also has collections dating from the 14th century and is of similar size. Its distinctive building was opened in 1934.

Next in importance are the libraries of the University of London. In addition to the Central University of London Library in Malet Street, London, are some 44 other libraries in the group. As a whole, the University of London libraries possess more than 6,000,000 volumes and seat more than 10,000 readers. The main controlling body is the Library Resources Co-ordinating Committee of the University.

Many of the 44 degree-granting universities in Britain are of more recent origin. The so-called "red-brick" universities, such as Nottingham and Southampton, emerged in the early part of the 20th century, but most of the county universities—such as those of Kent, Lancaster, Sussex, York, and others—were formed after 1945. The University Grants Committee has provided funds for libraries for these newer institutions. Some notable university library buildings have resulted, including those of the universities of Edinburgh, Dundee, Loughborough, and Nottingham. An outstanding building of the late 1980s is that of Queen Mary College of the University of London, in the East End of London.

College and Institute Libraries. These also add much luster and value to the British academic library scene, good examples being some of the university college libraries at Oxford, Cambridge, London, Durham, St. Andrews, Belfast, Coleraine, and elsewhere. England's oldest surviving college library building is at Oxford University's Merton College, which was founded in 1264.

The many institute libraries in the University of London are also worthy of mention. Britain has many university extramural libraries, as well as libraries in colleges of education. In addition there are 30 polytechnics in England, Wales, and Northern Ireland, all of which have libraries of growing importance. Just as British university and national librarians have formed themselves into a body known as the Standing Conference of National and University Libraries (SCONUL), so the polytechnic librarians started the Council of Polytechnic Librarians (COPOL). The LA has also been active in producing and revising minimum standards for college and other types of academic libraries.

PUBLIC LIBRARIES

History. In 1850 Parliament passed the first Public Libraries Act—a weak, tentative law, permissive and not mandatory. The Act left almost everything to local initiative in cities and towns. County councils did not then exist; they came into being in 1888, and they were not permitted to operate public library services until 1919. The duty to provide public libraries was imposed on city, town, and county councils in 1964, but by that time coverage of the country was virtually complete.

After 1850 public library progress at first was slow, but from the 1880s it began to accelerate, favorable factors being the grants offered by Andrew Carnegie and the increasing professional influence of the LA. British public libraries really began to burgeon in the 1930s. By that time financial limitations had been relaxed, county libraries had been set up, and the library cooperative networks based on the National Central Library and the Regional Library Systems were working more effectively. Attracted by the more efficient services and in many cases the new, purpose-planned buildings, new readers began to flock to Britain's public libraries in the days before World War II. Improved salaries and working conditions also had their effect, attracting better recruits to the staffs of public libraries.

During the war years, in spite of reduced staffs and often in the face of enemy bombardments, the country's public libraries were used more than ever before; their role as purveyors of reference work and information was increasingly recognized. After the war the profession began to build upon its newfound confidence. As soon as conditions permitted, existing services were expanded and new ones started, such as the provision of audiovisual materials and the estab-
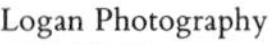
lishment of services to the disadvantaged.

Until the mid-1960s, however, public library development in Britain was hampered by the fact that too many local authorities existed. They varied greatly in size and financial resources, and too many unacceptable inequalities in the service resulted. Lionel R. McColvin had drawn attention to this problem in his *Report on Public Library Systems in Great Britain (1942),* which had been endorsed by the LA. There were more than 600 separate public library authorities in McColvin's time, but a succession of new laws—the London Government Act of 1963, the Public Libraries and Museums Act of 1964, and the Local Government Act of 1973, along with separate legislation for Scotland and Northern Ireland—reduced the number of local library authorities to 167 (172 with the Channel Islands and the Isle of Man).

Inequalities still persist but are much less noticeable than before; the larger authorities created by mergers and combinations of the older ones are financially more viable and capable of sustaining better all-round provision for ever-widening public library responsibilities and services. Since the dawn of the 1980s, budget cuts have begun to make themselves felt, especially in the industrial areas, and inequalities of service were beginning once again to be apparent in the late 1980s. Nevertheless, many public library systems continued to develop through the provision of new library buildings and by the adoption of automated systems integrating the ordering of materials, cataloguing, and loan methods.

Buildings. From 1958 there was a welcome renaissance of public library building. Hundreds of new branch libraries were erected in cities, towns, and

Joel Lee

Samuel Pepy's Library, dating from the 17th century, preserved at Magdalene College, Cambridge.

Logan Photography

British Library Lending Division (BL Document Supply Centre from December 1985) building at Boston Spa, Yorkshire, formerly site of the National Lending Library for Science and Technology.

© The British Library

Reading Room of the British Library, inside the quadrangle of the British Museum, was completed in 1857. Since 1973, the British Library has been independent of the British Museum.

counties. Reflecting the best influences of Scandinavian architecture and design, the attractive buildings appeared throughout the 1960s and the first half of the 1970s. There was a short pause in the late 1970s because of fiscal restrictions, but the program by no means came to a halt. New main libraries for the cities and larger towns and new headquarters for county libraries were at first not as common as the smaller branches, but many major public library buildings emerged during the two decades from the mid-1960s. These include the great extensions to the Mitchell Library in Glasgow (making it the largest public library in Europe) and new central libraries in such cities and towns as Birmingham, Bradford, Cardiff, and Carlisle; in the Channel Islands at St. Helier in Jersey; in the London area at Ilford, Uxbridge, and the City of London; and county library headquarters in Kent and elsewhere.

Free Principle. Members of the reading public were not slow to use these facilities. Public library services in Britain have been, and remain, free, both for those borrowing books and for those consulting reference material. A loophole in the 1964 Act, however, did permit library authorities to charge for borrowing phonograph records and cassettes, and most do so. From time to time the idea of making charges for borrowing books is mooted but so far it has been effectively resisted. All the main political parties have supported the free principle, but Conservative governments from 1979 to 1992 have threatened it from time to time, and the LA is ready to resist any proposal to abandon it.

Public Lending Right. From 1951 onwards the idea of a public lending right (PLR) was debated in the United Kingdom. The LA agreed that authors should be fairly compensated for their work, but it opposed some of the early schemes that would have thrown much extra work upon library staffs and could have had depressing effects upon book funds. After studies by various governments, Parliament passed the Public Lending Right Act in 1982. The first payments were made to authors in 1984.

The LA's arguments were taken into account when the law was prepared; calculations are based on samplings from a limited number of libraries in various parts of the country, and the money, both for the authors' compensation and for the scheme's administration, comes from central government and not the local library authorities. The first decade's working of PLR confirmed the suspicions of librarians—that it does little or nothing for the vast majority of authors of modest standing; it only adds to the income of the already well-off, best-selling writers. In 1990–91, fewer than a hundred authors reached the £6,000 maximum payment, but more than 11,600 writers received less than £100.

Circulation and Special Services. British public libraries are among the most fully used in the world; the loan figure has been as high as 650,000,000 volumes a year, about 12 per capita. The PLR reports in the early 1990s quoted a figure of 568,000,000 loans, just over 10 per capita. In addition to providing comprehensive lending departments for both adults and children, most lend sound and video recordings, with borrowing fees for these audiovisual materials. Reference and information work is generally well developed, and there are special services for the housebound, immigrant communities, slow readers, and other special groups. Some, but not all, British public libraries also operate the school, hospital, and prison libraries in their areas. Where that is not done, school libraries are organized by the education authority, hospital libraries either by the Regional Hospital Boards or by voluntary effort, and prison libraries by the Home Office. School, hospital, and prison libraries in the United Kingdom still need a more rational organization.

The larger British public libraries, especially those of the big cities, often have more in common with research libraries than with smaller public libraries. Many operate important special collections, such as the Shakespeare collection of Birmingham City Libraries, the International Library of Liverpool City Libraries, the Business Library of the City of London Libraries, and the Central Music Library of Westminster City Libraries.

Most British public libraries emphasize children's and youth library work. Branch and mobile libraries are generally well provided and relatively few people in the country live more than a mile away from their nearest library service point. Computerized methods of cataloguing and charging are in common use; and public relations programs—oral, visual, and printed—are being developed within limitations of staff and finances.

SPECIAL AND INDUSTRIAL LIBRARIES

Although earlier examples can be cited, most British special and industrial libraries developed after the 1920s. Indeed, World War I probably first drew attention to the need for libraries catering to the needs of those concerned with technology, industry, commerce, and statistics. Steady increases in the appearance of such libraries took place between the two world wars. They were sponsored by Government departments; industrial, commercial, and professional organizations; public authorities; research associations;

and other bodies. To aid and encourage their development, the Association of Special Libraries and Information Bureaux (Aslib) was formed in 1924, and the LA later formed a Reference, Special and Information Libraries Section, as well as an Industrial Group, a Government Libraries Group, and a Medical, Health and Welfare Libraries Group.

World War II gave further impetus to the need for more special and industrial libraries in the United Kingdom, and another fillip was added in 1948 when the Royal Society sponsored a Scientific Information Conference that proved influential in Government circles. Aslib's *Handbook of Special Librarianship* has run to many editions and has fostered developments in this field.

Some of the biggest and most important special libraries are Government owned, examples being those of the Department of Trade and Industry and of the Department of Education and Science. Important public authority libraries include the many collections owned by the BBC and the libraries of the National Coal Board and the UK Atomic Energy Authority. Outstanding among industrial and commercial libraries are those belonging to the Metal Box Company, ICI Limited, and the Wellcome Research Laboratories. Professional libraries also abound; important ones include those of the British Medical Association and the Royal Institute of British Architects. There are also collections of great significance belonging to private societies and clubs: among these are the libraries of the Zoological Society of London and the MCC (Marylebone Cricket Club) at Lord's Cricket Ground in London. Such libraries are invariably made available to bona-fide researchers, even if they are not members of the society or club.

THE PROFESSION

Associations. For many years only one organization was devoted to the development of British libraries and librarianship—the LA, founded in 1877, only a year after the formation of the American Library Association. *See* Library Association.

Aslib was formed as an association for special libraries and information bureaux and changed its name to Aslib, the Association for Information Management. It consists almost entirely of institutional members, of which there are more than 2,000 in 70 countries, mostly in the Commonwealth. Like the LA, it is organized into Branches and Groups; it arranges conferences, meetings, and courses; and it has an active publishing program, including the monthly *Aslib Proceedings,* the quarterly *Journal of Documentation,* as well as the *Aslib Directory* and the *Aslib Year Book.* Aslib publishes *Current Awareness Bulletin* monthly and *Network and Information Management Today* quarterly. Aslib maintains a library and information service, a consultancy service for its members, a staff employment register, a register of specialist translators and indexers, and an online resources center offering advice on online data management matters. It conducts searches for a fee. Aslib also has a research function funded partly by the British Library.

There are many other bodies devoted to developing various aspects of British library and information science. Among them are SCONUL and COPOL, already mentioned, and the Association of British Library and Information Science Schools (ABLISS), to name just a few.

Professional Education. For the first 90 years of its existence, the LA was virtually the only body in the United Kingdom concerned with education in librarianship. From its earliest years it organized courses for aspiring librarians, planned a syllabus, conducted examinations, and maintained, as it still does, a professional register. It also encouraged the formation of library schools, of which there were 16 in the country in the early 1990s.

Although the LA's role as an examining body steadily diminished, and disappeared entirely in 1985, the Association still plays an important part in continuing professional education and training. It organizes an increasing number of short courses on the latest developments in library and information science, and carries on a continuing dialogue with the heads of the library schools.

Of the library schools, the oldest is that of University College, London, founded in 1919. The remaining schools did not begin to function until 1946 and succeeding years. Seven are attached to universities, seven are part of polytechnics, and the other two are attached to colleges or institutes of technology or higher education. All the library schools offer graduate or postgraduate courses in library and information science, documentation, and archival work. Most offer special courses for external students, and some have arranged international seminars and have published occasional papers. Many professors and lecturers from British library schools have had international experience as consultants overseas sponsored by Unesco, the British Council, and other bodies.

International Librarianship. Britain has exercised considerable influence on world librarianship. British librarians have traditionally played important

Theodore F. Welch

Cambridge University Library traces its origins to the 14th century. This building opened in 1934.

Joel Lee

National Library of Wales Aberystwyth.

parts in developing IFLA, itself formed after the LA's 50th Anniversary Conference in Edinburgh in 1927. Both the British Council and the LA helped to start library movements in the developing countries of the Commonwealth and have had particular successes in Ghana, India, Jamaica, Kenya, Singapore, and Sri Lanka. The LA also gave invaluable help and encouragement in establishing the Commonwealth Library Association (COMLA) in 1972. Large amounts of money have been fed into many of the developing countries by the Overseas Development Administration and the British Council, and many British librarians have acted as consultants or library advisers for Unesco, the British Council, and other bodies in such countries as Mauritius, Seychelles, Sudan, Tanzania, and the United Arab Emirates. Other members of the profession have given their services through Voluntary Service Overseas, the British equivalent of the U.S. Peace Corps.

Library Press. Library journalism has flourished in the United Kingdom since the 1880s. Soon after its foundation the LA communicated with its membership through a publication known as *Monthly Notes.* It lasted from 1880 to 1884, then from that year until 1888 it was succeeded by *The Library Chronicle.* From 1889 to 1898, a monthly journal, *The Library,* was adopted as the official organ of the LA, although it was owned and edited by J. Y. W. MacAlister. Finally, in 1899, the *Library Association Record* became the Association's official journal, and has remained so ever since. Its first editor was Henry Guppy, and it has had many distinguished librarian-editors, including Arundell Esdaile, A. J. Walford, W. B. Stevenson, J. D. Reynolds, and Edward Dudley. From 1976 it was edited by full-time professional journalists. In 1969 the LA established the *Journal of Librarianship,* but since 1990 the quarterly has been published by Bowker-Saur Ltd. as the *Journal of Librarianship and Information Science.*

There have also been several independent library journals in Britain. One of these, *The Library World,* was founded by James Duff Brown in July 1898, and it thus predates the *Library Association Record* by six months. It has appeared monthly ever since that date, though it changed its title to *New Library World* when it was purchased by the publisher Clive Bingley in 1971. After Duff Brown, its editors have included J. D. Stewart, W. C. Berwick Sayers, K. C. Harrison, and Edward Dudley. In October 1983 it issued its 1,000th number, with suitable celebratory articles.

Another British independent journal was *The Librarian and Book World,* a monthly started by Alex J. Philip in 1911 and carried on bravely until the 1960s, being taken over after Philip's death by the publishing firm of James Clarke and Company. In 1927 yet another independent publication appeared, the *Library Review,* published in Glasgow and edited by the Scottish librarian R. D. Macleod. It began as a quarterly devoted to libraries and literature, and throughout its existence it has tended to give prominence to the literary and historical side of librarianship. It devotes much space to book reviews in depth, both of professional and general literature, and it frequently features articles on aspects of library history and biography. It is edited under the direction of a collective of librarians and a board of consultants.

REFERENCES

David Bromley and Angela Allott, editors, *British Librarianship and Information Work, 1981–85.* 2 volumes (1988).

K. C. Harrison, editor, *Library Buildings, 1984–89* (1990).

Thomas Kelly, *A History of Public Libraries in Great Britain, 1847–1975* (1977).

W. A. Munford, *A History of the Library Association, 1877–1977* (1976).

Annual reports published since 1975 by the British Library.

K. C. HARRISON

United States

The United States of America is a federal republic of 50 states; 48 of them, the coterminous states, are bordered by Canada on the north, the Atlantic Ocean on the east, Mexico on the south, and the Pacific Ocean on the west; Alaska is bordered by Canada on the east and the Pacific on the west, and Hawaii is in the mid-Pacific. Population (1990 census) 248,709,873; area 9,372,614 sq.km.

HISTORY

Colonial Period: Oral Culture. For many years after their arrival in 1607, New World colonists had little time for books and reading. With homes to build, forests to clear, and crops to plant and harvest, these immigrants had to spend most of their energy surviving a new environment and adapting to its unique demands. Any immediate, practical information needs they had were answered most often by the experience of trial and error, on occasion by native Americans, or perhaps not at all. The colonists lived in an oral culture. Literacy was not essential for daily living, and intellectual needs naturally received a low priority. The population—though growing—was neither large nor wealthy enough to support a literary class. The New World lacked prominent aristocrats to patronize authors and artists; and although some members of the medical and theological professions possessed a score or more of books they felt necessary for their vocations, the small minority of colonists who could read required little print information beyond their Bibles, hymnals, and prayer books. Others managed to get themselves through church services by committing favorite verses to memory, or to interpret important documents by trusting a friend who could read.

Private Collections. Despite the dominance of an oral culture, literacy was more widely diffused among the New World populations than in Europe, and eventually libraries began to take root and grow. At first, most collections were private. Until the turn of the 18th century, personal libraries characteristically consisted of 50 to 100 volumes held by ministers or doctors. But several stood apart. By 1639, Connecticut's Governor John Winthrop, Jr., had accumulated more than a thousand volumes in his personal library. Six decades later, Cotton Mather of Massachusetts and William Byrd of Virginia each boasted collections of more than 4,000 volumes.

Several attempts were made during the late 17th century to expand access to print materials beyond private libraries. In 1656 Captain Robert Keayne, a Massachusetts merchant, willed part of his personal collection to establish a public library in Boston, provided that the city construct a suitable building to house it.

Thomas Bray's Libraries. At the turn of the 18th century, Thomas Bray, an Anglican clergyman, made more serious efforts to create literary centers for colonists. Operating from England, Bray set up more than 70 libraries in the Colonies between 1695 and 1704. Five were located in large cities to serve entire provinces; 40 were given for use by the parishioners of specific churches; the remainder were controlled by ministers of the Anglican church and designed to serve laymen. Several colonial legislatures passed laws to maintain and staff the Bray libraries, but they made little provision to add new volumes to the original collections. As a result, the libraries fell into disuse shortly after their sponsor died in 1730.

By that time, the New World was changing. Within a century of the landing at Plymouth Rock, the brush had been cleared from the Eastern seaboard, the forests pushed back, and the threat of Indian raids reduced. Colonists began to find time to reflect on their current situation. European intellectuals, among them Newton, Locke, and Rousseau, were asking significant questions and offering important observations about human nature and the social and political environment. Literate colonists found themselves thinking less about their religious needs and more about their secular and vocational goals. They desired to expand their interests, and they hungered for access to more information sources that would help them answer questions unique to their New World environment.

The Library Company of Philadelphia

Library and Surgeons' Hall, home of the Library Company of Philadelphia, 1790–1880. Founded by Benjamin Franklin in 1731, the Library Company is the oldest subscription library in the United States.

Benjamin Franklin and Social Libraries. In 1728 an enterprising Pennsylvania printer named Benjamin Franklin joined in organizing the Philadelphia Junto, a group of 12 men seeking intellectual stimuli. Franklin suggested that members pool their book holdings and locate them in one place for the benefit of all. Although that scheme failed, the resourceful Franklin did not give up. In 1731 he organized the Library Company of Philadelphia. He asked members to purchase shares of stock (which

Libraries in the United States (1989)

Type of library	Number of administrative units (main libraries)	Number of service points (branches, mobile stops, etc.)	Volumes in collections	Annual expenditures (dollar)	Population served	Professional staff (with certificate, diploma, etc.)	Total staff
National[a]	3	--	29,277,384	--	--	--	--
Academic[b]	4,607	--	633,848,000	2,416,998,000	--	21,919	88,842
Public[b]	9,068	5,930	600,000,000	3,700,000,000	--	35,000	105,000
School[c]	102,538	--	923,025,222	633,301,000[d]	48,700,000[b,e]	68,391	112,952
Special[b,f]	11,146	--	--	--	--	--	--

[a]Library of Congress, National Library of Medicine, National Agriculture Library
[b]*Statistical Abstract of the United States, 1991*
[c]*Statistics of Public and Private School Library Media Centers, 1985–1986*
[d]Excludes salaries and wages
[e]Public and private school (elementary and secondary education) pupils and teachers
[f]Also includes medical, government, religious, armed forces, and law libraries

Columbia University

The nation's first local library supported by public taxes and opened to all its citizens was established in Peterborough, New Hampshire, in 1834.

could be subsequently traded or sold) and promised to use the money they invested to acquire books of interest to all. The newly acquired collections demonstrated the continued trend away from religious reading interests. The Library Company eagerly accumulated volumes on such topics as philosophy, travel, and biography.

The Company's proprietary structure served as a prototype for other kinds of social libraries. Some expanded their holdings by inviting nonshareholders to pay a "subscription" price to utilize library services, thus introducing the "subscription library." Others acquired newspapers and magazines for their collections and, by charging large stock prices and fostering other cultural activities, became known as "athenaeums." A fourth type of social library—the "mechanics" or "mercantile" library—resulted from the philanthropic inclinations of prosperous businessmen and industrialists who wanted to provide white-collar clerks and blue-collar mechanics with opportunities to advance themselves through self-education.

Other Public Library Precursors. Other types of libraries existed along with the social library, but served different purposes. Collections in Sunday school libraries emphasized religious themes designed to provide inspirational messages. Some industries sponsored "apprentice" libraries to foster educational and recreational reading among their employees. The "circulating" library also served those who sought recreational reading; for a small fee, patrons could withdraw books from a library (usually in a printshop or bookstore) whose collection consisted mainly of fiction.

Braddock's Field Historical Society

The Carnegie Free Library in Braddock, Pennsylvania, erected in 1889, was the first Carnegie library in America.

In 1835 the New York state legislature passed a law authorizing school districts to impose taxes on citizens to fund libraries. The legislature approved matching funds three years later, and these library collections contained some 1,500,000 volumes by 1850. Although several other states passed similar legislation, the success of school district libraries was short-lived. Legislators usually neglected to provide additional funds for staff and quarters, and the book selection procedures were haphazard. Most school district libraries died for lack of interest and attention.

Public Libraries. The changes libraries experienced in the United States mirrored changes in America's rapidly diversifying socioeconomic structure. By 1850, the United States began to suffer new growing pains. As the nation neared its 100th birthday, it was becoming less dependent on foreign manufactures to fulfill industrial needs. New industries, which clustered in or near major urban areas, struggled to meet demands created by growing populations. In the process, they created jobs that attracted workers from rural areas and held ever-growing numbers of immigrants who had fled the static and often depressing economic and social conditions of their native lands for the promise of a new life in the United States. At the same time, farms were becoming increasingly mechanized and required fewer laborers. Industrialization and urbanization also stimulated the growth of a professional middle class. Its members sought to perpetuate the country's growth patterns and to remove obstacles that threatened to alter radically the socioeconomic structure supporting their endeavors. As members of this class looked upon the manifestations of their nation's growing pains with increased anxiety, they began to search for solutions to perceived problems.

One solution they advocated transformed the nation from an oral to a written culture. Mid-century proponents of universal literacy promised that the United States could correct its social ills only if all its citizens could read and write. They were persuasive enough to persuade most states to mandate school attendance; their efforts led to the establishment of institutions that had significant potential for socializing the nation's youth. The American library community was eager to tie itself to this new force. Melvil Dewey, who helped organize the American Library Association and establish the *Library Journal* in 1876, echoed the sentiments of many ALA peers by arguing repeatedly that more tax-supported libraries were needed, and each of these ought to become a "people's university," a place citizens could turn to for self-paced education after the conclusion of their formal schooling. Of course, he noted, librarians would provide the proper direction for this mass educational venture by developing and organizing high-quality collections and supplementing them with valuable personal assistance. The ideology emerging from this perspective helped spark the library movement in the last quarter of the 19th century. In their rush to help educate America, librarians took the institutions for which they held responsibility into new directions.

The transition from the social to the public library that characterized one major direction in the late 19th century traced its roots to Thomas Jefferson's firm belief that a democratic government could not function properly without an informed public. Peterbor-

L.C. Scarborough

Rear view of the Walter Royal Davis Library, the University of North Carolina at Chapel Hill.

ough, New Hampshire, established the nation's first local library supported by public taxes and open to all its citizens (1834). By the middle of the 19th century, several state legislatures passed laws giving local governments the authority to tax their citizens to support public libraries. New Hampshire was first in 1849, but Massachusetts's 1851 law led directly to the 1854 opening of the Boston Public Library, which became the model for most urban libraries (and many smaller ones) for the remainder of the 19th century.

While city after city established and funded urban public libraries that were developing innovative methods to serve the newer populations flocking to their cities, state after state established library commissions to ensure that similar information services were extended to rural populations by traveling libraries or through small-town public libraries.

Carnegie Libraries. Much of this activity was fueled by the philanthropic benefactions of Andrew Carnegie (1835–1919), the steel magnate and philanthropist who perceived the public library as a self-help mechanism particularly well suited to nurturing American democratic ideals. After retiring from industry in 1901, he accelerated his philanthropy, and by 1920 he had dispensed more than $50,000,000 in the construction of about 2,500 library buildings in various parts of the world. To merit consideration for a grant, municipalities had only to guarantee an annual appropriation of 10 percent of the sum given in order to support the library.

World War I. The war and its effects significantly influenced the American public library. While the American Library Association directed efforts to provide a Library War Service for American troops at home and abroad, public libraries also assisted in obtaining gift books and donating staff services. In addition, they encouraged patriotic organizations to use their facilities, reached out to the new arrivals to their towns who had come to work in war-related industries, and eagerly served as channels for information that the federal government wished to pass along to citizens. Many of them also destroyed or withdrew from circulation materials considered seditious or pacifistic. By the end of the war in 1918, the public library had matured into a bona fide social service institution.

The 1920s and 1930s. The 1920s contrasted sharply with the previous two decades. Resolution of the social problems that seemed so important and received so much attention during the first two decades of the 20th century appeared to dissipate in an overriding desire to accumulate more personal and corporate wealth. Just as individuals turned more attention to personal concerns, so the public library focused more attention on its internal mechanisms. Some public libraries attempted to reach out to nonuser populations and to harness the momentum of the adult education movement, but the nation was not ripe for social crusades.

The next decade brought significant change, however. First, the Great Depression threw millions out of work. Partly to relieve their boredom, partly to improve their chances at reentering the labor market through vocational self-education, Americans began to use libraries more frequently. Circulation increased, and librarians found themselves called upon to meet increasing demands with decreasing budgets for staff and materials. Then, as European and Asian totalitarian governments posed an apparent ever-increasing threat to world stability through a variety of aggressive actions (including such activities as book-burnings), American public libraries promoted themselves as "guardians of the people's right to know." This theme persisted through the World War II years, the McCarthy era of the 1950s, and down to the present day.

Later History. By the mid-1950s, the public library augmented its focus on wider service, especially by reaching out to traditional nonuser groups. Fed by the Great Society programs of the mid- and late 1960s, outreach and rural services once again received increased attention. Public libraries reattached themselves to the adult education movement and used the influx of new federal dollars to spur more efforts at cooperation and new activities such as information and referral services. Federal dollars also contributed significantly to the construction of new libraries, many of which replaced old Carnegie buildings.

Independent Research Libraries. The late 19th-century public library movement also sparked the birth of several unanticipated offspring. A few wealthy men with bibliophilic propensities donated vast sums of money for the construction and maintenance of private research libraries to answer the needs of a clientele not directly addressed by the new objectives public and academic libraries had defined for themselves. Chicago received a major share of attention in the 1890s when money left by Walter L. Newberry and John Crerar created research libraries that now bear their names. The Lenox and John J. Astor Libraries had performed similar functions for New York City in the mid-19th century, until they were merged into the New York Public Library system during the same decade. In 1919 Henry Huntington founded a library bearing his name in San Marino, California, which built on his substantial rare book collection. The Folger Shakespeare Library was founded in 1932 in Washington, D.C., as a result of the Shakespeare collections and fortune of Henry Clay Folger. Other prominent endowed research libraries established before 1970 include the Hoover Library on War, Revolution, and Peace at Stanford University (1919), the Pierpont Morgan Library in New York City (1924), and the Marshall Research Library in Lexington, Virginia (1964).

United Press Photo

Main Reading Room of the Library of Congress.

Academic Libraries. The nation's transformation from an oral to a written culture, coupled with the effects of immigration, urbanization, and industrialization, pressed American academic libraries at the turn of the 20th century into a direction different from that of public libraries. Previously, academic libraries had had a quiet history dating back to 1638, when John Harvard donated nearly 300 books—three-fourths of which dealt with theological topics—to establish a New World institution of higher learning. The well-intentioned clergyman did not realize that his gift would reflect three problems that plagued academic libraries for the next two-and-a-half centuries. First, academic institutions struggling to survive were reluctant to commit money for books for their libraries, forcing college librarians to augment their collections largely through donations. Second, the gift books themselves badly skewed the collections; many donated texts were discards that owners no longer wanted, and most were in the subject areas of theology and the classics. As long as the institution's curriculum demonstrated a theological-classical emphasis, the college library could at least render lip service to supporting it, but once college curricula began changing during the mid-19th century, the utility of academic library collections became even more marginal. Third, the attitude that characterized college library administrators augmented the libraries' inherent problems. Academic librarians were often faculty members whose library duties were simply added to their regular classroom duties, and the institutions' trustees and administrators normally looked to these caretakers for library security and careful record-keeping. Librarians extended borrowing privileges mostly to faculty, infrequently to upperclassmen, and almost never to undergraduates. They opened their libraries as little as possible and often at inconvenient times. Understandably, students shied away from academic libraries and began to develop their own alternative—the literary society library. Between the American Revolution and 1850, for example, literary society libraries at Ivy League colleges were more accessible, contained more books, were broader in scope, and were much more comfortable than their institutional counterparts.

By the mid-19th century, the situation began to change. Charles W. Eliot, President of Harvard from 1869 to 1909, endorsed an elective system that gave students more options, and other institutions followed Harvard's lead. In addition, many American scholars had been trained in German universities that emphasized research; as they took faculty positions in American colleges and universities, they began to demand that academic libraries provide better research facilities for themselves and their students. Finally, members of a new professional middle class demanded that colleges offer courses designed to introduce students to the special knowledge of particular professions.

All of these factors served to persuade college administrators that they needed to provide more funds to alter the traditional patterns of academic library service. Academic libraries began to push for longer hours, services to all members of the academic community, and better catalogues to record their holdings. Most literary society libraries had been absorbed into regular academic library collections by the turn of the 20th century, a fact that suggests that academic libraries were responding more directly to student and faculty needs. The proliferation of seminars, graduate education, and honors and independent study programs all had significant impact on the patterns of academic library use. Librarians instituted closed reserve systems to address the problem of circulating heavily used class-related materials. In the 1930s, several academic library directors began dividing their holdings and service into subject collections, and scholars began to acknowledge that intellectual content worthy of preservation might be found in formats other than print.

Post-World War II. The years after World War II brought changes that, although not as significant as the late 19th century in changes of service, were much more impressive in numbers. The G.I. Bill provided a tempting invitation to returning veterans to undertake college education, and institutional enrollments expanded. As veterans and their offspring progressed through the American educational system in the 1950s and 1960s, academic libraries found their collection resources and service capacities sorely tested. The federal government supplied some help; the Higher Education Act of 1965 awarded acquisition grants directly to academic institutions, while other federal acts funded the construction of many new academic library buildings in the 1960s. Standards created by various national, regional, and local accrediting agencies also had significant impact on the development of modern academic library services.

School Libraries. School-library development is largely a 20th-century phenomenon. Although some school libraries had early 18th-century beginnings, significant movement to provide library services to school children did not occur until the last two decades of the 19th century, when many public libraries attempted to serve school curricula by making the schools branch public library stations. While these efforts proved helpful, many members of the National Education Association (NEA) looked for more direct control over school library collections. NEA began seeking more autonomy for the libraries and pressed for acceptance of the concept of separate school libraries that were acquired, staffed, and organized solely for the use of school faculty and students and designed to support the school curriculum. In the 1920s the Association developed standards for elementary and secondary school libraries. State and local governments encouraged this trend by funding school library supervisors and recommended booklists and specially developed handbooks.

The Great Depression of the 1930s temporarily stayed school library development, but the years after World War II saw the growth patterns restored and several new trends. One was more use of nonprint media for instruction. Since someone had to acquire, store, maintain, and circulate media equipment and materials, the school library was gradually transformed into an instructional materials center. Another trend after World War II reflected efforts to establish more elementary school libraries. The movement received tremendous impetus with the passage of the

Theodore F. Welch

National Agricultural Library.

Elementary and Secondary Education Act of 1965. School libraries used the influx of federal dollars to emulate successful demonstration projects that had been supported by the Knapp Foundation and a School Library Development Project organized by the American Library Association and funded by the Council on Library Resources. The Higher Education Acts of 1965 and 1966 also promoted school librarian training.

Overview. Until the mid-19th century, libraries in the United States experienced slow, sometimes lethargic growth in the midst of a predominantly oral culture. Library development was affected only infrequently by strong individuals of moderate to high means who perceived the institution's value to a society they helped to control. Only after government intervened to supplement or replace private funding with public tax dollars in the last half of the 19th century did library growth accelerate. By the turn of the 20th century the push for universal literacy had produced a momentum that librarians willingly tapped in order to motivate their institutions to improve collections and services. That momentum slowed for several decades following World War I, but received a significant new impetus when Congress authorized President Lyndon B. Johnson's Great Society programs in the mid-1960s. A contemporaneous yet coincidental development—the growth of computer technology and accessibility—combined with this new impetus to launch libraries into the new Information Age.

NATIONAL LIBRARIES

Library of Congress. The United States sponsors many governmental libraries, but three qualify as national because of the constituencies they serve. The largest is the Library of Congress (88,300,000 items in 1988), created by law in 1800 to serve the information needs of the Congress. The British destroyed the Library during the War of 1812, but Thomas Jefferson offered to revive it by selling his personal library to the federal government in 1816. After some political haggling, Congress decided to accept Jefferson's offer, subsuming not only his collection but also his classification scheme. The Library of Congress limped along for several decades on minimal budgets and in inadequate quarters, but space needs accelerated when the Smithsonian Institution gave its scientific periodicals collections to the Library in 1866 and Congress authorized the purchase of Peter Force's collection of Americana in 1867. Then, when Congress passed the Copyright Law of 1870, mandating that two copies of any work copyrighted in the United States be deposited in the Library, the collection really began to swell. Ainsworth Rand Spofford, Librarian of Congress from 1865 to 1897, argued that the Library needed a separate building and, after nearly two decades of constant pressure, finally persuaded Congress of the Library's critical situation. Workmen completed the new structure in 1897, and two major additions followed in the 20th century—the Thomas Jefferson Building in 1939 and the James Madison Building in 1983.

Herbert Putnam became Librarian of Congress in 1899, and under his direction the Library began to flex its muscle as a national library by spearheading efforts to centralize cataloguing processes. What started in the first decade of the 20th century as a service to distribute catalogue cards grew to the printing of the *National Union Catalog* in the fourth decade and ultimately led to Machine Readable Cataloguing (MARC) tapes in the sixth (*see* MARC). The Library also plays a role in other national library activities; it is actively involved in investigating better methods for preserving print materials, in sponsoring book exchanges, and in acting as a center for the National Library Services for the Blind and Physically Handicapped. In addition, in 1977 Congress authorized the Library to establish a Center for the Book to focus attention on that medium's traditionally important role.

Medicine and Agriculture. The federal government also supports two other important national libraries. The National Library of Medicine (NLM) emerged in the 1950s directly from its predecessor, the Army Medical Library, and serves America's physicians and medical scientists through MEDLARS (Medical Literature Analysis and Retrieval System), an intricate and sophisticated computerized storage and retrieval system that grew from *Index Medicus*, the Library's paper-copy index to current medical literature. Holdings of the NLM surpassed 4,750,000 catalogued items by 1990.

John Fitzgerald Kennedy Library

The John F. Kennedy Library, designed by I.M. Pei, is one of nine presidential libraries operated by the National Archives.

The National Agricultural Library grew out of the Department of Agriculture Library. It, too, has led in the development of computerized storage and retrieval of information in its field.

Other Government Libraries. Many federal government agencies have acquired impressive collections. The Department of State began building its library when President George Washington created the cabinet post in 1789, and libraries at other cabinet-level agencies have followed State's lead. The National Archives established its own library in 1934 to facilitate use of the millions of documents it houses. Libraries serve both faculty and students at each of the nation's military academies, and the United States supports a presidential library for every Chief Executive since Herbert Hoover; each collects manuscript materials and memorabilia about the president's life and term in office.

STATE LIBRARY AGENCIES AND LOCAL SYSTEMS

Services and collections among state library agencies vary greatly. Although some state libraries were established in the early 1800s, state-supported library services did not expand significantly until the turn of the 20th century when new agencies, often public library commissions, were established outside state library control. Many states consolidated commission and state library functions after World War I, and by 1940 services commonly offered by surviving state library agencies included legislative reference, provisions for traveling libraries, and library promotion. From there, however, functions differ markedly. Some have developed into large research libraries (as in California and New York), while others act as the center of the state's public library system and serve city and county public libraries through interlibrary loans and traveling exhibits. Since 1956, state library agencies have also acted as conduits for federal library funds.

Local Systems. At the beginning of the 20th century, municipal and local library systems established branch libraries, book stations, bookmobiles, and books-by-mail programs. Later emphasis was placed on the development of local consortia designed to pool resources, distribute costs, share in acquisition, and cooperate in weeding.

ACADEMIC LIBRARIES

Academic libraries have developed individual growth patterns. Harvard's library system represents the largest of the privately supported institutions, whose collections and inter-institutional responsibilities have grown geometrically. The University of Wisconsin library system demonstrates a pattern of support by an individual state that looked to the major publicly supported institution within its borders for leadership. Many land-grant institutions of higher education provided indifferently for their libraries until the press of increasing numbers of students and the demand for new services forced changes in the 1960s. Small libraries at institutions such as Earlham College in Richmond, Indiana, have been among the most consistent performers since the 1940s. Although their collections and services have grown to meet the varied needs of more students, such institutions continue to place great emphasis on individualized services. The same may be said of outstanding community college libraries that survived the impact of sporadic periods of growth in the decades from the mid-1950s through the mid-1980s. Many made significant contributions to their students' intellectual and vocational development.

The combination of shrinking budgets and concern for better service sparked several cooperative ventures. In 1942 several Boston libraries pooled little-used materials into the New England Depository Library. The Center for Research Libraries, founded in 1949 by 10 Midwestern universities, has large holdings from which its 169 institutional members can withdraw by interlibrary loan. The Online Computer Library Center (OCLC), started originally in 1968 as a cooperative cataloguing effort among a number of academic libraries in Ohio, grew into a national system serving more than 6,000 libraries of all types. The Research Libraries Group (consisting in 1990 of more than 100 U.S. research institutions) was organized in 1974 to identify collection strengths and minimize wasteful duplication.

PUBLIC LIBRARIES

The 1970s brought a shrinking of federal financial support to public libraries in the United States. Inflation seriously weakened budgets, programs were cancelled, and many services were either curtailed or cut off altogether. The growth patterns characteristic of the 1960s appeared to have been arrested. Despite these difficulties, however, public libraries have continued to provide essential information services to their constituent communities.

For more than a century the local public library has benefited from the widely held Jeffersonian belief that a democracy can survive and prosper only in a society of citizens educated and informed enough to make prudent choices. That citizens in the United States adhere to that belief is evident from their willingness to be taxed (mostly on the basis of real estate ownership) in order to support public libraries. In return, all citizens residing in the taxed community are free to use the public library's services. Traditionally these services fall into four broad categories: basic education (such as computer and reading literacy programs and story hours); culture (exhibits, lectures, and public forums); information (ready reference queries, referral services for community agencies, and database searches); and leisure (films, concerts, and crafts demonstrations). The distinctions among these categories have tended to blur.

More than 15,000 public libraries (including branches) serve U.S. citizens. They range in size from the Boston Public Library (established in 1854, holding more than 6,000,000 volumes, and circulating almost 1,900,000 items a year in the late 1980s) to the Chandler Public Library in Chandler, Oklahoma (founded in 1987, holding almost 9,000 volumes, and circulating more than 3,600 items a year in the late 1980s). Like most public libraries, the Boston and the Chandler Public Libraries answer to local governing boards whose structure and composition are determined by state laws authorizing localities to establish public libraries and impose taxes to support them.

The future holds many challenges for American public libraries. Automation has altered the way traditional services are delivered, and in the future may

Huntington Library, San Marino, California

Founded by Henry Edwards Huntington in 1919, the Huntington Library in San Marino is one of the country's finest independent research libraries.

eliminate a few and create some new ones. These changes, among others, are forcing the public library community to address several knotty questions brought by new technological developments. The dilemma of "fee-based" versus "free" database searches with promising but costly technologies demonstrates only one of the more pressing problems. Local systems are also exploring ways to cooperate on a regional basis to increase efficiency and control costs.

SCHOOL LIBRARIES AND MEDIA CENTERS

More than 75,000 library and media centers can now be found in public and private elementary and secondary schools in the United States. Since World War II their establishment and growth have been stimulated by the development and regular revision of standards defined by the American Association of School Librarians (AASL) and the Association for Educational Communication and Technology (AECT) and endorsed by the NEA and ALA. Even more significant, however, were the federal dollars funneled into the development of libraries and media centers by the National Defense Education Act (1958), the Library Services and Construction Acts (1964, 1965), the Elementary and Secondary Education Act (1965), and the Higher Education Act (1965).

The infusion of federal support, coupled with standards developed by professional associations, allowed libraries and media centers to improve traditional services in the areas of reading, reference, and teaching, and to augment their role in supplying schools with additional instructional support. In many cases they are also participating actively in computer literacy programs in the nation's elementary and secondary schools.

SPECIAL LIBRARIES

Special libraries exist to serve specific clienteles. Because they do not concern themselves with the information needs of larger populations, their collections are usually smaller, many are staffed by library and information science professionals with special training, they offer tailored hours and types of

The Boston Public Library

Courtyard of the Boston (Massachusetts) Public Library's historic McKim Building in Copley Square, completed in 1854.

services, and they reflect different patterns of organization. Some are affiliated with larger library systems (such as medical libraries in university systems), but most are attached to specific industries or services that have developed a need for quick access to specific kinds of information. The special libraries at AT&T's Bell Laboratories, International Business Machines, and Westinghouse Electric Corporation are examples. Newspapers, advertising agencies, and other businesses need special libraries for staff research use. Special libraries also serve educational and professional associations and institutions: the ALA Headquarters Library in Chicago and the Engineering Societies Library in New York City are examples.

Most special libraries receive their support from private sources. They include those at historical and philosophical societies, private schools, hospitals, and banking, investment, law, publishing, research, and scientific institutions. Special libraries at federal, state, and local mental and correctional institutions receive most of their funding from taxes. Most special libraries have developed in the 20th century.

THE PROFESSION

American Library Association. One hundred and three people sharing an interest in libraries met in Philadelphia in the fall of 1876 as part of the nation's centennial celebration in that city. Near the end of the meeting, Melvil Dewey moved that the group form the American Library Association (ALA) and, after his motion was approved, signed himself "No. 1."

In the early years, ALA concerned itself primarily with matters such as cooperative activities, standardization of library procedures and forms, and debating the merits and demerits of stocking fiction. In 1886 the Association established a section to oversee the publication of bibliographical aids, and a $100,000 gift from Andrew Carnegie in 1902 permitted the Publishing Section to expand its program significantly. By the beginning of World War I, the Association had become the national voice for library interests. The war provided ALA with an opportunity it had never before experienced. In organizing the Library War Service under Herbert Putnam's direction, ALA willingly sought to supply the reading needs of U.S. soldiers and sailors at home and abroad. Association members helped to set up camp libraries and to collect books for shipment overseas. After the war ended in 1918, some members of ALA sought to capitalize on the Association's positive wartime experiences and push for an enlarged program designed to expand its activities. But funding agencies and the membership failed to support it, and the proposed program died for lack of interest.

By the end of the war the Association, like the profession it represented, had become highly feminized. In 1870 the Bureau of the Census could locate only 43 female library workers; in 1910 the Bureau found 8,621. A decade later women comprised more than 90 percent of total library employees, a proportion larger than that of social work or teaching. As a female culture based on the Victorian ideal of domesticity began to lose its grip in the late 19th century, women looking for expanded career opportunities beyond the relatively few open to them were attracted to library work. Library trustees and employers welcomed them into the profession, in part because they thought a "mother" image and a "domestic touch" promised increased benefits for library services, in part because they realized women provided cheaper labor than men. But most of the prestigious posts in librarianship—and in ALA—continued to go to men. Women's contributions and leadership in American librarianship would remain in the historical shadows for decades.

Carl Milam (1884–1963) served as ALA Executive Secretary from 1920 to 1948. He consolidated ALA programs and activities at ALA's Chicago Headquarters (where it continues to reside, despite periodic suggestions that it move elsewhere). He saw ALA through the 1920s, when the Association concerned itself with the adult education movement, the status of library education, and librarians' welfare, and through the 1930s, when many ALA members questioned its management as "undemocratic." He still led its staff in the 1940s, when ALA took up the banner of intellectual freedom. Milam's successor, David Clift (1907–1973), carried that banner through the McCarthy era and into the late 1950s, when the federal government began to provide funds for library services. Robert Wedgeworth, Executive Director from 1972 to 1985, directed his attention toward implementing changes in the dues and organizational structure, controlling budget deficits, rebuilding staff morale at Headquarters, and expanding facilities in a new building. Membership increased significantly under Thomas Galvin, Executive Director from 1985 to 1989, when he was succeeded by Linda Crismond, who resigned in 1992. The Association grew significantly from a membership of 69 in 1876 to 1,152 in 1902, 8,848 in 1926, 19,701 in 1951, and more than

50,000 by 1985. (*See also* American Library Association.)

Other Associations. The American Association of Law Libraries, established in 1906, had more than 4,100 members in 1990. The American Theological Library Association was organized in 1947 to foster cooperation and understanding of a special library's function in a school of theology; membership was more than 600 in 1990. The Art Libraries Society of North America, begun in 1972, provides a forum for art librarians. Institutional and personal members numbered 1,300 in 1990. The Catholic Library Association, organized in 1921, had more than 3,250 members in 1990. The Medical Library Association, begun in 1898, served more than 5,000 institutional and individual members in 1990. The Music Library Association, founded in 1931, had nearly 1,700 members. The Special Libraries Association, established in 1909, served 12,500 members. The Theatre Library Association, established in 1937, had nearly 500 institutional and personal members in 1990.

The Association of Research Libraries, organized in 1932, represents a different type of library association. It consists of 119 member institutions that seek to address problems common to the needs of large research libraries.

U.S. librarians are also served by regional, state, and local library associations. The Pacific Northwest Library Association (with more than 900 members in 1990) began in 1909, the Southeastern Library Association in 1920 (with more than 2,000 members in 1990). Nearly every state in the Union has its own library association, ranging from the largest in New York (3,200 members) to the smallest in Nevada (250 members).

Other associations and agencies heavily involved in library and information activities include the American Society for Information Science (ASIS), born of the American Documentation Institute (founded in 1937; more than 4,300 members in 1990), and the Society of American Archivists, established in 1936 (membership more than 4,300 in 1990). Beta Phi Mu, the international library science honor society founded in 1948, has more than 22,500 members in more than 50 chapters in library schools across the country. The Continuing Library Education Network and Exchange (CLENE) was organized in 1975 to provide a forum for the discussion of the continuing education needs of library personnel. The National Commission on Library and Information Science (NCLIS), the Council on Library Resources, and the Urban Libraries Council are among organizations that deserve mention for their efforts to facilitate and improve library services.

The Library Press. Members of the library community in the United States enjoy many avenues of communication with their professional colleagues. The library press in the United States can trace its roots to 1876, when the *American Library Journal* published its first issue. Shortly thereafter, it dropped "American" from its title and now acts as an independent voice in library affairs. The *Wilson Library Bulletin* is in the same category. The *Journal of Academic Librarianship* serves an audience with more specific interests.

ALA and its divisions publish important journals. *American Libraries* is ALA's principal publication for

The Westinghouse Electric Corp.

An online catalogue and CD-ROM workstation in the Westinghouse Technical Library, Pittsburgh, Pennsylvania.

communicating with its members and the public. *College and Research Libraries* is published by the Association of College and Research Libraries, a division of ALA. *RQ* is a quarterly sponsored by the Reference and Adult Services Division. Other ALA journals and newsletters also make important contributions to the profession. Most regional, state, and national library and information science associations issue journals, many of which started publication with the founding of their parent organization. Periodicals such as *Library Quarterly* (University of Chicago Press), *Libraries & Culture* (University of Texas Press), and *Library and Information Science Research* (Ablex Publishing) provide forums for professionals of scholarly bent.

Commercial publishers, such as the R. R. Bowker Company, McFarland & Co., Scarecrow Press, and the H. W. Wilson Company, issue monographs and reference tools that often prove important and even essential to library services, as does ALA Publishing Services. *Library Trends* (University of Illinois Graduate School of Library and Information Science) devotes whole issues to specific topics of current interest.

REFERENCES

Useful surveys include Michael Harris, *History of Libraries in the Western World* (1984), and Howard Winger, editor, "American Library History: 1876–1976," *Library Trends* (1976).

Jesse Shera, *Foundations of the Public Library: The Origins of the Public Library Movement in New England, 1629–1855* (1949).

Dee Garrison, *Apostles of Culture: The Public Librarian and American Society, 1876–1920* (1979).

Evelyn Geller, *Forbidden Books in American Public Libraries, 1876–1939: A Study in Cultural Change* (1984).

Arthur T. Hamlin, *The University Library in the United States: Its Origins and Development* (1981).

Orvin Lee Shiflett, *Origins of American Academic Librarianship* (1981).

Wayne A. Wiegand, *Politics of an Emerging Profession: The American Library Association, 1876–1917* (1986).

Bohdan S. Wynar, editor, *Dictionary of American Library Biography* (1978); Wayne A. Wiegand, *Supplement to the Dictionary of American Library Biography* (1990).

WAYNE A. WIEGAND

Library Association

Donald John Urquhart

Urquhart, Donald John
(1909–)

Donald John Urquhart, British librarian, administrator, and information expert, won worldwide recognition for the practical success of his ideas for the National Lending Library in Boston Spa, Yorkshire.

Born November 27, 1909, he was reared in the northeast of England, brought up in Whitley Bay, and educated at Barnard Castle School and Sheffield University. He showed the qualities of determination, directness, and independence of mind that characterize the sons of that part of England and that in his case have marked his approach to librarianship and the work of the librarian.

After taking his B.Sc. and Ph.D. degrees at Sheffield, Urquhart worked from 1934 to 1937 in the Research Department of the English Steel Corporation. In 1938 he joined the library staff of the Science Museum, then under the directorship of S. C. Bradford, the active supporter of the Universal Decimal Classification and one of the founders of the British Society for International Bibliography. Bradford's work and that of his successor, Lancaster-Jones, was of great significance in the library field and in the new field of documentation. During World War II Urquhart worked in several government departments, most importantly in the Ministry of Supply, all of which were crucially concerned with the supply of scientific and industrial information and were grievously embarrassed by the consequences of past neglect of this vital aspect of library information work. The war had brought home to scientists and industrialists the significance of information in the day-to-day activities of an industrial society, and it was becoming clear that the speed at which new knowledge and ideas were made available was governed by the effectiveness of information services. Management also needed up-to-date assessments of raw materials, supply and production processes, and equipment design.

These problems prompted several conferences at which scientific information services were discussed in considerable detail, notably the Royal Society Empire Scientific Conference (1946), the Royal Society Scientific Information Conference (1948), and the 27th annual conference of Aslib, the Association of Special Libraries and Information Bureaux (1952). At this last meeting Urquhart, who by this time had become attached to the Department of Scientific and Industrial Research (DSIR) and was thereby much concerned with the results of the Scientific Information Conference, reviewed the results of the conference with special reference to the part played by DSIR in implementing them. He was able to point to the publication of a number of guides to sources of information, but the most important question to be resolved was how to ensure that the United Kingdom would have an adequate system of scientific libraries.

The first attempt at solving this problem centered on the possibility of extending the Patent Office Library and the Science Museum Library to include every publication containing material of value to science and technology. The final answer, however, was to establish and develop in DSIR itself, under Urquhart's direction, a so-called Lending Library Unit, which afterward became the National Lending Library for Science and Technology. As a division of the British Library, it was named the British Library Document Supply Center.

The National Lending Library embodies many of the ideas that Urquhart had strenuously advocated during the years of discussion after the Royal Society Conference in 1948. For example, the location of the Library at Boston Spa in Yorkshire was to a considerable extent conditioned by his belief that such a library should be a purely practical institution without elaborate architectural features or adornment, that it should be within easy postal reach of all parts of the country, and that it should have space to enable it to respond to all requests by return mail.

REFERENCE

Donald Urquhart, *Mr Boston Spa* (1990).

SIR FRANK FRANCIS

Uruguay

Uruguay, a republic in southern South America, is bounded by Brazil on the north and east, the Atlantic Ocean on the southeast, the Rio de la Plata on the south, and Argentina on the west. Population (1990 est.) 3,094,000; area 177,414 sq.km. The official language is Spanish.

National Library and Archives. The first public library, founded in Montevideo in 1816, was the antecedent of the National Library. Invading Portuguese forces destroyed its collections eight months after it opened; it finally reopened in 1838, assuming simultaneously the roles of a national, research, and public library. The Copyright Law of 1970 requires publishers to deposit two copies of all printed materials in the National Library and one in the library of the Palacio Legislativo. The collection consists of 900,000 books, 800,000 manuscripts and related items, 35,000 pamphlets, and 20,000 serial titles. The Library serves more than 150,000 readers annually. It has published the national bibliography, *Anuario Bibliográfico Uruguayo,* since 1946. The Centro Nacional de Documentación Científica, Técnica y Económica (Center for Scientific, Technical, and Economic Documentation) is attached to the National Library.

Libraries in Uruguay (1990)

Type of library	Number of administrative units (main libraries)	Volumes in collections	Annual expenditures (peso)	Population served	Professional staff (with certificate, diploma, etc.)	Total staff
National	1	890,000	510,000,000	150,000[a]	48	190
Academic	18[c]	1,117,524[d]	--	60,514[b]	100	--
Public	87[c]	237,969[d]	--	--	22	--
School	69[c]	187,835[d]	--	--	--	--
Special	138[c]	1,189,524[d]	--	--	150	--

[a]users/year
[b]Universidad de la República 1988
[c]1989 data
[d]1987 data

The General National Archive collects all inactive documents emanating from public offices, as well as relevant historical documents.

Academic Libraries. Uruguay has two universities. The Catholic University, which is private, has a central library. The University of the Republic, a public institution, has faculties, schools, and institutes located throughout the capital, Montevideo, each with its own library. These autonomous libraries are quite advanced in their organization and in acquiring bibliographic material in their fields. Some are connected to international databases, such as MEDLARS. Holdings are estimated at close to 1,000,000. The University has a union catalogue of serials and began work in the late 1980s on an automated system, SIBUR, connecting all its libraries.

Public Libraries. Most public libraries are administered by local municipalities, without a centralized system. In rural areas, few libraries have professional staffs. Most public libraries have special programs for children and for the elderly. But most libraries serve less than half the people in their areas. Montevideo has a network of 15 libraries with book-box service. Since 1988 students at the School of Librarianship have provided a popular service called "books in the sun." Riding tricycles, they take books to the people on the beaches during the summer and in the public squares during the winter.

School Libraries. In general, schools lack libraries. Some maintain small "Biblioteca de Aula," classroom libraries, overseen by teachers. The Government has approved a system of libraries for secondary schools, but implementation has been delayed because of inadequate funding. The schools that do have libraries run by professionals seek support from parent associations for them.

Special Libraries. In most special libraries in Uruguay, qualified personnel use advanced information management techniques and up-to-date technology. Most are small, forming parts of larger organizations such as banks and private businesses, embassies, and regional and international organizations. The first national database appeared in 1980; within five years, about one in four information centers was using it. Most special libraries use CDS/ISIS software, in part because it is made available by the Unesco Regional Office in Montevideo.

The Profession. The Escuela Universitaria de Bibliotecología y Ciencias Afines (School of Librarianship) was originally established as part of the Faculty of Economics in 1943, but became an independent University school in 1945. Its curriculum has been revised several times; the revision of 1985 aimed to bring it into line with the real needs of the country. A four-year course leads to the degree of Licenciado en Bibliotecologia. The School of Librarianship began offering a specialization in Archivología (archives management) in 1983. Offered irregularly at first, the program is now standard.

The Library Association of Uruguay is the professional organization for librarians. It seeks to promote the scientific, technical, cultural, and ethical interests of the profession. The Association is a member of IFLA. The Uruguayan Institute of Library Research, founded in 1977, has organized courses related to librarianship and promotes technical standards and cooperation.

REFERENCES

Centro Nacional de Documentación Científica, Técnica y Económica, *Directorio de Servicios de Información y Documentación en el Uruguay* (1988).

Ana María Cherro y Alberto Gonzalez, *Situación del Uruguay en Materia de Información: Breve Informe del Análisis Estadístico en DATINFUR* (1990).

GLORIA A. GASPERINI

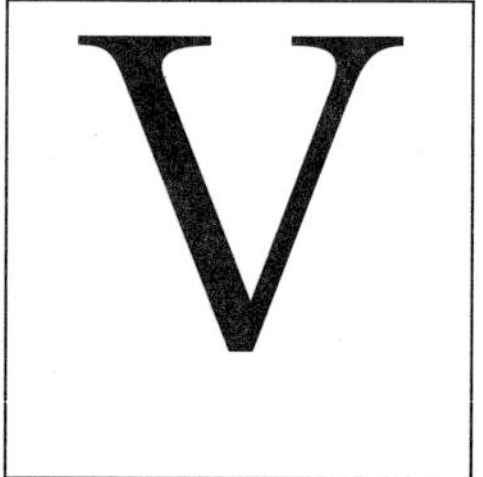

Vatican Library

Vatican City is one of the world's smallest independent states, covering 0.44 sq.km. in the heart of Rome, the capital of Italy. The see of the Roman pontiffs, it is entirely independent from Italy and is one of the world's oldest governments. Its library and museums hold some of the great treasures of Western culture. Population (1990 est.) 1,000. The Church uses Latin; the spoken language is Italian.

History. There is evidence that a papal library, known as a *scrinium* or case for books and papers, existed as early as the 4th century. It served not only as a library but also as archives. Unfortunately, for unknown reasons, this collection was dispersed during the first half of the 13th century. Traditionally Pope Nicholas V (reigned 1447–55) has been regarded as the founder of the Vatican Library, but Sixtus IV (reigned 1471–84) actually provided for buildings, personnel, and endowments in the bull *Ad decorum* (1475). He appointed Bartolomeo Platina as the first librarian. Sixtus V (reigned 1585–90) built the structure within the Vatican walls expressly for the Library between 1587 and 1589.

Vera Fotografia

The Vatican Library in Rome dates from the 13th century and is open to the public, but collections are restricted to use by qualified scholars.

Vatican Library

The Manuscripts Reading Room of the Vatican Library.

Over the centuries, the library has consistently grown in size and in variety of collections. Under Leo XIII (reigned 1878–1903) and under the direction of Franz Ehrle, who served as prefect from 1895 to 1913, the Library began three major projects: establishing a conservation department, one of the first in Europe; opening a reference room, complete with some 50,000 volumes on open shelves; and publishing *Studi e Testi,* a series including photographic reproductions of the more famous codices. Further improvements were made under Pius XI (reigned 1922–39) and John Paul II (1978–). In 1984 technical services were transferred to a new building adjoining the original and the collection of manuscripts was moved to an underground, climate-controlled environment.

Collections. The Library is divided into three sections: printed materials, manuscript materials, and art. The printed section includes approximately 1,500,000 titles, made up of reference books and the *fondi chiusi* (entire libraries belonging to eminent families and scholars), which include about 8,500 incunabula. The manuscript section includes some 75,000 codices, from the 2nd century to the present, as well as 65,000 units of archival documents in 23 record groups. The art section houses more than 100,000 prints, engravings, maps, and drawings; 330,000 Greek, Roman, and papal coins and medals; and a small but valuable assemblage of sacred and secular artifacts in the library museum.

Catalogues. The problem of providing and publishing catalogues of the manuscript holdings was tackled at the beginning of the 20th century. The academic staff of the Library, with the help of outside collaborators, has produced a series of exhaustive catalogues covering about one third of the entire collection. For the rest of the manuscripts, users have many old handwritten and some modern typewritten inventories at their disposal. In the case of printed books, an excellent card catalogue with perhaps 2,000,000 main entries is available in the reference room. It was started with the help of the Carnegie Institution and the Library of Congress between 1927 and 1939.

Automation. An automated system was introduced in 1985 for the internal convenience of the Library staff. It handles accessions, serials management, and the catalogues of the various collections. The database is accessible from several external sites.

School. The Library houses the Vatican School of Librarianship, founded in 1934 by Pius XI. It has an international student body.

REFERENCES

Bibliotheca Vaticana (1987).

J. Bignami-Odier, *La Bibliothèque Vaticane de Sixte IV à Pie XI* (*Studi e Testi* 272, 1972).

P. G. Weston and A. Pernigotti, "Automated Access to the Vatican Library Collections," *International Cataloguing and Bibliographic Control* (1989).

PAUL GABRIELLE WESTON

Venezuela

Venezuela, a republic of northern South America, is bordered on the north by the Caribbean Sea and the Atlantic Ocean, on the east by Guyana, on the south by Brazil, and on the southwest and west by Colombia. Population (1990 est.) 19,735,000; area 912,050 sq.km. The official language is Spanish.

History. The country won its independence from Spain in 1821 under Simón Bolívar, who was born in Caracas in 1783. The first imprint in Caracas, the capital, was dated October 24, 1808; the book was printed on a press acquired from Trinidad. The discovery of oil at Maracaibo in 1917 brought new prosperity to what had been an agrarian country with limited public services. Library services in urban areas greatly improved.

In the years following adoption of the Unesco NATIS Program in 1974, the National Commission for Library and Information Services (SINASBI) was created by presidential decree in 1976 and reformed in 1978. Structured to coordinate all aspects of library, archival, and information services in the country, it had ceased to exist for all practical purposes by the mid-1980s and many of its functions were absorbed by the National Library.

National Library. The Biblioteca Nacional de Venezuela was founded by decree in 1833. Its scope of responsibilities was expanded by law in 1977 to encompass the public library system and a broad array of information services. Its full name is Instituto Autónomo Biblioteca Nacional y de Servicios de Bibliotecas.

Under the leadership of Virginia Betancourt, Director from 1974, this institution has developed library and information services in the country, reaching out to a population new to library services. It is organized around four main programs: the National Library as such, the National Public Library System, and a Technical Services support program covering all holdings, and an administrative program.

By 1987 the National Library housed more than 1,000,000 books, almost 1,000,000 periodicals (mostly on Venezuelan topics), almost 500,000 audiovisual items, and a microfilm collection of 10,000 frames of official publications.

The Venezuelan Legal Deposit Law was amended in 1982 to broaden its scope to include audiovisual material. A Decree of September 1982 requires each government body to allocate 25 percent of its publications to the National Library. The law and decree proved an effective means of enriching holdings.

Publications of the National Library include the *Bibliografía Venezolana,* which lists books and pamphlets, official publications, academic theses and dissertations, and musical scores published from approximately 1942, and the *Boletin Bibliotecnico,* a periodical devoted to technical subjects in library science and standardization.

In 1978 the National Library signed an agreement with Northwestern University of Evanston, Illinois, for the use in Venezuela of its NOTIS computerized library system. From 1981 services were extended with the use of DocuMaster software to the Supreme Court of Justice, Ministry of Foreign Affairs, Center for Legislative Information and Documentation of the National Congress, and Public Prosecutor's Office and the main library of the Central University, all of them in Caracas.

Construction of a new National Library building began in the mid-1980s at the Foro Libertador in Caracas, where 80,000 sq.m. of space will provide an excellent opportunity to improve services for a broad patron base. The first units moved into the new building in 1990.

The Archivo General de la Nación, founded in 1888, is responsible for historical, religious, and public administration archives. Its collections are divided into three sections: La Colonia (1535–1810), La Revolución (1810–1830), and La República (1830 to about 1950). It was given legal standing in 1945, but updating did not follow and its role remains largely historical. However, a new building of 20,000 sq.m. was also under construction at the Foro Libertador site in the mid-1980s. The National Archives publishes a biannual bulletin.

Public Libraries. The Public library system in Venezuela experienced a period of sustained growth in the early 1980s. For administrative purposes the country was divided into nine geographic regions, the most extensive services being provided for the Metropolitan Caracas and Federal District System, which serves the capital city. Each state has a central public library that follows the technical directives of the National Library, although all personnel and expenses are covered by the individual states. By 1987 there were more than 550 public libraries throughout the

Libraries in Venezuela (1987)

Type of library	Number of administrative units (main libraries)	Number of service points (branches, mobile stops, etc.)	Volumes in collections	Annual expenditures (bolivar)	Population served	Professional staff (with certificate, diploma, etc.)	Total staff
National	1	3	1,975,000	150,273,406	19,725,000	51	748
Academic	70	--	--	--	--	--	--
Public	465	67	2,081,292	24,490,582	--	--	1,722
School	--	--	--	--	--	--	--
Special	83	--	--	--	--	--	--

Sources: Unesco Demographic Yearbook 1990 and 1991

Theodore F. Welch

National Library of Venezuela, Caracas, established in 1833 and expanded in 1977.

nation, covering 85 percent of all districts. Additionally, all states except one enjoyed bookmobile service. Patron requests increased from fewer than 3,000,000 in 1980 to more than 8,750,000 in 1987.

Another important institution, the Banco del Libro, originally created in 1960 to provide a textbook exchange facility, has been expanded into a research center for public library services directed toward children. It promotes reading techniques and materials. It maintains Ediciónes Ekare, a children's book publishing house started in 1978 and known for its beautiful illustrations and dissemination of folktales and poems of Venezuelan origin. It also trains schoolteachers in library services. The National Library designated it to select children's books for all public libraries in the country.

Starting in 1980, Banco del Libro published *Parapara,* the only journal on children's literature in all of Latin America. It is also the center for the Interamerican Project on Children's Literature sponsored by the Organization of American States. The Banco del Libro operates two libraries in Caracas and four in Ciudad Guayana, Bolívar state, as testing grounds for its research.

School Libraries. The school library system covers primary and secondary schools. A typical collection comprises 45 percent texts, 20 percent recreational literature, 5 percent reference works, 5 percent teaching materials, and the remaining 25 percent titles complementary to the scholastic program. Coordination, planning, and follow-up are managed through the education authorities in each state, who are accountable to the Ministry of Education.

Special Libraries. The Consejo Nacional de Investigaciónes Científicas y Tecnológicas (CONICIT, the National Scientific and Technological Research Council), created in 1967, coordinates scientific and technological information networks. Cooperative information networks in the early 1990s included Biomedical Information, Agricultural Sciences (REDIAGRO), Engineering and Architecture (REDINARA), Social and Economic (REDINSE), Housing and Urban Planning, and Technology and Industry.

CONICIT authorized a feasibility study on a countrywide automated data transmission information system called Sistema Automatizado de Información Científica y Tecnológica (SAYCIT). Strategically placed nodes would link most heavily industrialized regions, and the Caracas node would connect to an international network. Emphasis was placed on providing training on database searching, mainly in conjunction with U.S. vendors, and developing expertise in creating local databases and indexing systems. Venezuela participates in the Andean Technological Information System (SAIT) and the Latin-American Technological Information Network (RITLA).

In addition, there are many institutions with specialized libraries in science and technology. The Venezuelan Institute of Scientific Research (IVIC) has the largest holdings of scientific periodicals in the country, some 4,500 titles. INTEVEP, the Center for Research and Development of the Venezuelan nationalized oil industry, organized the first automated information network with national coverage, linking information centers in the oil industry to a centralized database resident at the company's Los Teques headquarters. This system is MARC compatible, as is the one at the National Library, thus creating a de facto national standard.

The Petroleum and Petrochemical Information Network (RIPPET) covered more than 30 oil industry information centers, most of them connected to the automated library system. The Periodicals Union Catalogue listed 1,800 titles, 131,000 technical reports, 82,000 books, and 213,500 other items such as microforms, maps, and industrial drawings. INTEVEP's Technological Information Center (CIT), the coordinating body of RIPPET, was the first Venezuelan information center to offer access to international database searching (1978).

The Profession. The Colegio de Bibliotecologos y Archivologos de Venezuela is the main national organization for professional librarians and archivists. It was founded in 1952 to promote the welfare and professional competency of its members, who number more than 600. The library community is represented in many international organizations and participates in Unesco's General Information Program, FID, IFLA, and ACURIL, and attends the yearly ALA Convention.

GUADALUPE LÓPEZ

Verona, Eva

Eva Verona, Yugoslav university librarian, has been highly influential in the areas of international bibliographic control in general and of the role of corporate entry in cataloguing in particular. With a background in mathematics and physics, she brought to the field a logical mind, a disciplined scholarship, and the ability to communicate, not only in her own country but in international circles as well.

She first appeared in meetings of the International Federation of Library Associations in 1952; for the ensuing 25 years she was an active member, eventually serving both as member and chairman of the Association's Committee on Cataloguing. During that time, she had become head of two departments in the National and University Library in Zagreb, and in 1966 she held the position of Senior Lecturer in the Postgraduate Study of Librarianship, Documentation, and Information Sciences at the University of Zagreb.

For a long time she had been keenly interested in the area of corporate entry in cataloguing, particularly in logical aspects of the formats developed in this area. A lengthy article entitled "A historical approach to corporate entries," appeared in *LIBRI* in 1957. It was followed by a series of books and articles in Croatian.

The major part of those contributions came about as a result of involvement in the international discussions about codes for descriptive cataloguing taking place in the 1960s and 1970s. Verona's most significant work prior to 1975 was the *Statement of Principles Adopted at the International Conference on Cataloguing Principles, Paris, 1961* (Annotated Edition, with Commentary and Examples, IFLA Committee on Cataloguing, 1971). In preparing that monograph she was assisted by Franz Georg Kaltwasser, P. R. Lewis, and Roger Pierrot. At that time she was also caught up in the general movement toward the creation of a means for achieving international bibliographic control. This movement produced the successful International Standard Description for Monographs (ISBD–M) as a means for obtaining a standardized format suitable for both acquisitions and cataloguing. An International Standard Book Number had already been developed in Britain. Other similar standards followed, but these were the most freely adopted.

The 1970s in particular saw much discussion of the principles of authorship, in particular the notion of corporate authorship. This had been controversial in the past and probably will continue to be in the future. Nevertheless, Verona, who had been interested in the problems involved in considering a corporate body as the *author* of its works, now produced highly significant research on the topic, entitled *Corporate Headings: Their Use in Library Catalogues and National Bibliographies* (1971). This major work strongly influenced the treatment of corporate bodies in the second edition of *Anglo-American Cataloguing Rules* (1978).

Verona's *Corporate Headings* defines corporate authorship as follows:

> A work should be considered to be of corporate authorship if it may be concluded by its character or nature that it is the result of creative and/or organizational activity of a corporate body as a whole, and not the result of an independent creative activity of the individual(s) who drafted it.

The 1970s witnessed a rethinking of the principles of authorship and much serious discussion of corporate authorship. The 1978 Anglo-American code greatly altered the interpretation of "the result of creative and/or organizational activity of a corporate body as a whole." In fact, the limitations described in its 21st chapter are more organizational than creative activity.

The advent of the computer, it has been argued, has made the concept of *main entry* obsolete and in that respect much of the argument over entry (any kind of entry) is unnecessary because one can now use as many entries as the topic requires—something that was impossible with card catalogues and very difficult with book catalogues. While Verona's argument is significant, a dissertation by Michael Carpenter (published 1981) suggests that, philosophically speaking, one can still make a fair argument for corporate entry, under limited conditions.

In 1976 Verona received the Margaret Mann Citation from the ALA's Resources and Technical Services Division, a well-deserved award for what clearly has become a definitive work on the subject.

REFERENCES

Eva Verona, "A Historical Approach to Corporate Entries," *LIBRI* (1957).

Eva Verona, *Corporate Headings: Their Use in Library Catalogues and National Bibliographies: a Comparative and Critical Study*. (IFLA Committee on Cataloguing, 1971).

PHYLLIS A. RICHMOND

Vickery, Brian
(1918–)

Brian Campbell Vickery, British information scientist, is known—particularly to those outside the United Kingdom—as an accomplished theoretician of information retrieval.

Vickery was born in Sydney, Australia, on September 11, 1918. He was educated in England at the King's School, Canterbury, and Oxford University, where he majored in chemistry. During World War II he worked at the Royal Ordnance Factory in Somerset.

After a brief period as a technical journalist, Vickery joined the Ackers Research Laboratory of Imperial Chemical Industries (ICI) as its Librarian in 1946, and he remained there for 14 years. As an active member of the (UK) Classification Research Group, he began his investigations in classification and indexing and the newly emerging discipline of information retrieval. Two major monographs emerged, both early recognized as significant contributions and now considered classics: *Classification and Indexing in Science* (1958) and *On Retrieval System Theory* (1970). Both works have been translated into other languages and both have been reissued.

Vickery gained an international reputation as a theoretician. While such a reputation is wholly justified, his undoubted abilities as a practitioner of information science are perhaps less appreciated. In fact, his career demonstrated a perhaps unusual capacity to contribute both to the fundamental understanding of the nature of information science and to the development of practical services as a result of such insights. His early appreciation of Bradford's Law of scattering led, for example, to one of the first recorded applications of it in an industrial special library.

Vickery's wide-ranging abilities were recognized by D. J. Urquhart, who recruited him as Principal Scientific Officer to the newly created National Lending Library for Science and Technology (later to be absorbed into the British Library as its Lending Division). From 1960 to 1964 he worked there, during the formative years of that unique and universally respected institution, and served subsequently on its Advisory Committee.

From 1964 to 1966 he was the Librarian of the Manchester Institute of Science and Technology, an institution with a formidable international reputation in the development of computer technology. Two major monographs were to emerge during his period as Director of Research at Aslib, London, from 1966 to 1973: *Techniques of Information Retrieval* (1970) and *Information Systems* (1973). These reflected an increasing involvement in research and consultancy on systems development and evaluation, and particularly on automated systems. Two major development studies at that time were concerned with the Commonwealth Agricultural Bureaux and the House of Commons Library.

In 1973 he was appointed Professor and Director of the School of Library, Archives, and Information Studies at University College, London, where he remained until his retirement in 1983. There he expanded teaching in the areas of computer applications and communications technology, and also in techniques for the investigation and evaluation of libraries and information services. With his second wife, Alina, the Director of the Central Information Services at London University (Senate House), he formed an axis for the rational development of library and information services within the University. He remained an active Honorary Research Fellow of the College.

His more than 100 publications in the professional literature cover a wide variety of topics—information retrieval, systems development and management, information systems dynamic modeling, library procedures, online search services, microcomputers, and the social aspects of information—and reflect his breadth of interests and experience. He was also much sought after as a reviewer because of his authority and fairness, qualities consistent with his lack of identification with any particular faction or school of thought. He became a Fellow both of the Library Association and of the Institute of Information Scientists.

HARRY EAST

Vietnam

Vietnam, a socialist republic of southeast Asia, is bounded by China on the north, the South China Sea on the east, and Cambodia and Laos on the west. Population (1990 est.) 66,200,000; area 331,689 sq.km. Vietnamese is the official language; English, French, and Russian are also spoken.

History and National Library. The National Library, in the capital city, Hanoi, was established by the French in 1919 as the Bibliothèque Centrale of Indochina, which they then ruled. From 1921 until about 1941 it was the legal deposit library and officially received one copy of each publication produced in Indochina. By the 1950s its collections included 150,000 books and 2,300 periodicals. In 1954 the French took a portion of the collection to Saigon and Paris (approximately 50,000 books and 400 periodicals) as they withdrew from Vietnam. Civil war led to intervention by the United States from the early 1960s until the Vietnam War ended in 1976.

The Vietnamese began to rebuild the central collections in the 1960s, adding more than 20,000 items. The National Library has legal deposit rights to 10 copies of all new publications. By the 1970s the Library possessed more than 1,200,000 books and 70,000 bound volumes of periodicals. Besides the growing Vietnamese collection, it has good French, Russian, Chinese, English, and German collections. Special collections include Asian languages, ethnic minority material, maps, engravings, photographs, recordings, and children's books. It produces a national bibliography, bibliographies of periodical and newspaper articles, and lists of recommended reading.

The National Library in the former Saigon is now the General Scientific Library of Ho Chi Minh City, attached to the city's cultural office; it holds some 600,000 volumes.

Academic Libraries. The main research library is the Central Scientific Library in Hanoi, founded in 1959 and based on and located in the old library of the École Française d'Extrême Orient (1898). Holdings total some 320,000 volumes and 5,000 periodicals. In addition, all universities and colleges have their own libraries. For example, Hanoi University has a library containing about 80,000 volumes. The book collections in more than 30 university libraries and 200 research libraries total about 4,200,000 volumes.

Public Libraries. The provincial libraries, the largest in Hanoi, Hue, and Ho Chi Minh City, were set up to coordinate the use of written materials in their areas. By the 1980s there were 44 libraries in cities and provinces, 482 city or town reading rooms, and more than 20,000 libraries across the

Libraries in Vietnam (1987)

Type of library	Number of administrative units (main libraries)	Number of service points (branches, mobile stops, etc.)	Volumes in collections	Annual expenditures (dong)	Population served	Professional staff (with certificate diploma, etc.)	Total staff
National	1	1	1,800,000	--	--	70	185
Academic	--	230	4,200,000	--	--	284	760
Public	--	20,044	8,000,000	--	--	--	--
School	--	6,637	--	--	--	--	--
Special	--	276	1,393,000	268,000,000*	--	320	828
Other (describe)							

*For thirty-five libraries of STI institutes and centres

countryside. Their holdings totaled more than 8,000,000 volumes.

School Libraries. Somewhat over half the 10,000 secondary schools have libraries. In primary schools, the proportion is probably a little lower. Local governments have sought the aid of parents and school cooperatives to build small collections.

Special Libraries. The Central Institute for Scientific and Technological Information (CISTI) was founded in 1972 to collect, process, and provide information for decision makers, managers, and various other workers. It also manages a national network of 35 institutes and centers belonging to various Ministries. For example, the Institute for Information on the Social Sciences, founded in 1976, holds about a million items; the Central Institute for Medical Science Information (1979), part of the Ministry of Health, has a collection of more than 50,000 volumes and 450 periodical titles.

The Profession. Before the Vietnam War ended in 1976, most of the 1,000 documentalists and librarians had training only through short courses. Beginning in the 1980s such organizations as CISTI and the UN Development Program sponsored postgraduate courses in Hanoi, Hue, Da Nang, and Ho Chi Minh City. The Ministry of Culture, Communication, Sport, and Tourism set up a Cultural College in 1981. It offers four-year courses leading to Bachelor's degrees in librarianship.

Two library associations are active in Vietnam, the Scientific Information, Documentation, and Library Association of Ho Chi Minh City and the Library Association of Universities and Colleges in Hanoi.

REFERENCES

Final Report of the National Seminar on Information Policy of Vietnam (1987).

Nguyen Van Dung, "L'Activité de l'Information Scientifique et Technologique au Vietnam," *L'Ecluse* (1989).

Vu Van Son, "Central Library for Science and Technology through 30 Years of Activity, *Hoat Dong Khoa Hoc,* (1990).

DANG NGOC DINH;
NGUYEN VAN DUNG;
and TRUONG THAI DUNG

Vosper, Robert G.

(1913–)

Robert Gordon Vosper, university librarian and educator, gained recognition as a force in general support of librarianship in the United States and throughout the world.

Born in Portland, Oregon, June 21, 1913, he early set a goal of pursuing scholarship in the classics. After finishing his B.A. (1937) and M.A. degrees (1939) at the University of Oregon, he enrolled in the School of Librarianship at the University of California, Berkeley, as a logical next step when the pressures of the Depression foreclosed his first option. With an offer of a job as a student employee at the University Library, Vosper was successful in winning admission to the School.

After completing his library studies at Berkeley in 1940, Vosper served as a Reference Librarian there, then as an Assistant Reference Librarian at Stanford, 1940–44. There he was associated with Nathan van Patten, Director of the Library and an outstanding expert in the field of acquisitions for academic libraries. With van Patten's encouragement and assistance, Vosper moved to the University of California at Los Angeles in 1944 to head the acquisitions department under the direction of University Librarian Lawrence Clark Powell. He was closely involved in building research library collections as UCLA grew from the status of the southern branch of the University of California to that of a leading research institution.

Robert G. Vosper

Vosper rose to the rank of Assistant, then Associate, Librarian under Powell before becoming the head of the University of Kansas Library in 1952. Franklin Murphy, the University's new President, was the chief advocate of the Library as an indispensable resource in building a first-rate research institution. With Vosper, he toured the state and persuaded the legislators to provide funds for the Library, with great success. Vosper enlisted the faculty's help in selecting materials and began to build a core of specialists in the Library to guide the development of the collections. In this manner, Vosper may be considered the agent who gave credibility and visibility to the position of "bibliographer" in libraries.

Murphy moved to become Chancellor at UCLA in 1960. The regents of the University of California had decided that UCLA's library should reach parity with Berkeley, and once again Murphy turned to Vosper to guide the Library's development. Vosper became University Librarian at UCLA in 1961, succeeding Powell, who was devoting his time to the establishment of a library school.

Vosper directed the UCLA library as it grew by nearly 2,000,000 volumes. He also supervised construction of a new research library building and its first addition. He retired as University Librarian in 1973 and assumed full-time teaching duties as professor in the UCLA Graduate School of Library and Information Science. At the same time he continued to serve as Director of UCLA's Clark Library, a prestigious segment of the system, devoted to many aspects of English literature, including the works of John Dryden and Oscar Wilde. He retired from active University service in 1984, with the rank of University Librarian and Professor Emeritus. He continued his contribution to university work by serving as President of the UCLA Emeriti Association and on various committees in the University. He remained active as a writer and speaker on research library development and continued to serve as a member of the Board of the Council on Library Resources.

Vosper was President of the Association of College and Research Libraries, 1955–56, and of the American Library Association, 1965–66. As Chairman of the Association of Research Libraries Board of Directors in 1963–64, he opened membership to the many schools then achieving research status. The libraries at these schools had problems in common, and ARL became a logical agent for developing programs to build strength through cooperative solutions. Vosper also led the way to section status for the rare books and manuscripts librarians in ACRL. His commanding view led to his membership on the Board of Directors of the Council on Library Resources (1968–). He also served as a consultant, external reviewer, and member of the boards of many prominent agencies, including the Center for Research Libraries, the American Chemical Society, the National Library of Medicine, and Stanford University.

Vosper proved always an advocate for recognizing the rights of librarians as partners in a scholarly enterprise. While he was in library school, and through his leadership, students from the school employed at the library were recognized as professionals. While he was at Kansas, librarians gained faculty status, although Vosper believed that status as librarians was reward in itself and should not be confused with that of traditional faculty members. Even in a position which accrues power such as he had at UCLA, he was able to recruit managers who could give evidence of faith in the abilities of librarians to apply their own judgment in conducting the work of the library.

Vosper's work in international librarianship earned him high honors. Foreign acquisitions are major elements of academic research libraries, hence his interest was elicited early in his career. He attended the Princeton Conference on International Cultural, Educational, and Scientific Exchanges in 1946. The conference led to the formation of the Farmington Plan, administered by the Association of Research Libraries, to increase the foreign holdings of academic libraries. In 1957 Vosper conducted a study of the Plan, leading to important changes in its administration nationwide.

Following a Guggenheim tour of Europe in 1959, Vosper arranged for a meeting of the Association of Research Libraries with its British counterpart. He became interested in the work of the International Federation of Library Associations, a tie he strengthened during a Fulbright tour in Italy. He was IFLA Vice-President from 1971 to 1976, Chairman of the Steering Committee for Universal Bibliographic Control, and Chairman of the program committee for the 50th anniversary celebration in Brussels in 1977. He received the Order of the Belgian Crown for that work, and was honored with the rank of Fellow of IFLA. He was a member of the U.S. State Department's Government Advisory Committee on Overseas Book and Library Programs from 1970 to 1975. From 1968 to 1973 he was a member of the U.S. National Commission on Unesco.

During the years of student unrest on university campuses in the late 1960s his commitment to libraries was a beacon for campus guidance. His words were posted in the library:

> The Library is an open intellectual sanctuary. It is devoted to individual intellectual inquiry. Its function is to provide free access to ideas and information. It is a calm and peaceful haven of privacy, a source of both cultural and intellectual sustenance for the individual reader. Since it is thus committed to free and open inquiry on a personal basis, the Library must remain open, with access to it always guaranteed.

This view gave staff the strength it needed, not only to deal with crises, but also to develop new programs of service to the University. His influence on individuals was extended through his teaching career, not only on the faculty at UCLA, but also as a faculty member and lecturer at Columbia University and the Universities of Minnesota and Tennessee.

When he retired as University Librarian, a quotation from his writings was engraved for permanent display in the Library:

> If we mean, as we do, to support creative, imaginative research and inspired scholarship, UCLA must have a library rich in the whole history of man's intellectual and cultural life as it is crystallized and presented in books.

Vosper was given the LL.D. degree by Hofstra University in 1967 and was honored with the Joseph D. Lippincott Award by the American Library Association in 1985. His citation reads: "Through his patient and quiet leadership in the belief that libraries are collections and people, not systems, Robert G. Vosper has had a major impact on our profession."

REFERENCES

Alexandra Mason, "Rare Books in the Great American Desert," *Antiquarian Bookman* (1982).

Betty Milum, "Robert G. Vosper," *Leaders in American Academic Librarianship: 1925–1975* (1983).

Robert G. Vosper, *International Library Horizons: Some Personal Observations* (1989).

RUSSELL SHANK

Walford, A. J.
(1906–)

Albert John Walford, English reference librarian and editor, is known primarily as compiler and editor of various widely used bibliographical publications, especially the *Guide to Reference Material,* the British reference librarian's bible.

Born August 3, 1906, in Bermondsey, he spent his early years in the southeastern part of Greater London and graduated from London University. He began his library career as a senior assistant at Stoke Newington Public Library and continued it at Lambeth Public Libraries, where he was chief assistant from 1932 to 1946, apart from the period when he was on war service. When, toward the end of World War II, the War Office inaugurated a network of libraries to support the Army's educational activities, Walford became supervisor of the command libraries in North Africa and Italy. Soon after demobilization he became one of the first librarians to leave the public library service for senior posts in the expanding libraries of the central government departments, which were in need of reorganization by qualified and experienced staff. From 1946 to 1973 he was employed at the Ministry of Defence.

Walford's retirement from the Ministry proved to be purely nominal. In various ways he contrived to remain active in matters bibliographical and bibliothecal. His particular concern was the preparation of new editions of his well-known *Guide to Reference Material.*

From the 1930s he was at pains to communicate his wide-ranging knowledge of classification, reference techniques, and subject bibliography to others. He first became known in the profession for his articles and pamphlets on problems encountered by students of librarianship, guidance particularly welcome when attendance at a library school was available to only a few students in the U.K. The 1950s saw him engaged simultaneously on two of his major part-time activities. During the period 1953–59 he edited the monthly *Library Association Record* and planned and compiled the first edition of his *Guide to Reference Material,* published by the LA in 1959.

The *Guide* was not an entirely new kind of subject bibliography. The American Library Association's classic *Guide to Reference Books*—which *Walford* complements more than it rivals—had first appeared in 1902. The LA itself had published *Reference Books: A Classified and Annotated Guide,* compiled by John Minto, in 1929. Unfortunately, through lack of support from British libraries, for whom it had been expressly compiled, Minto's bibliography faded away after the publication of one supplement. The new LA *Guide,* published when reference and special libraries had become more numerous and active, was cordially received. Although, like the earlier *Guide,* it favored British publications, its scope was wide and every title listed was given a helpful descriptive annotation. Walford's declared purpose, which remains unchanged, was "to provide a signpost to reference books and bibliographies published mainly in recent years . . . for librarians, in the building up and revision of reference library stock; for use in general and special enquiry work; as an aid to students taking examinations in librarianship; and for research workers, in the initial stages of research" (Introduction).

The second edition of the *Guide* was in three volumes. Volume 1 covered *Science and Technology;* volume 2, *Social and Historical Sciences, Philosophy and Religion;* and volume 3, *Generalities, Languages, the Arts and Literature.* They appeared between 1966 and 1970, and a third edition appeared in the 1970s. In the fourth edition the title was changed to *Walford's Guide to Reference Material.* The fifth edition, still in three volumes, appeared from 1985 to 1991.

Walford won a reputation as a librarian whose knowledge was matched by his energy, both prodigious. In the compilation of the *Guide* he had the cooperation of many colleagues in the library profession who had specialized knowledge. But in the planning and routine of compilation, his was the mastermind, even though the editorial labors were later shared.

REFERENCE

A. J. Walford, "Compiling the *Guide to Reference Material,*" *Journal of Librarianship* (1978).

JAMES G. OLLÉ

Waples, Douglas
(1893–1978)

Douglas Waples was an American whose roots were in literature, culture, research, and educational psychology, and who grew with and contributed to the growth of theory in the field of communications, the central core of his professional attention. His work in army intelligence and psychological warfare while serving in the U.S. Army during two world wars and as a consultant to the U.S. Department of State was tied closely to his interest in international communications. Recruited to library education as a specialist in educational method and in research, Waples studied librarianship and library education with a fine glass and saw librarianship as having high potential, but never thought of himself as a librarian. Critical and stimulating in his objective clarity, Waples was always an outsider in relation to the field he served so well. He was not only an interdisciplinary scholar but also an exemplar of the post–World War II international perspective.

Born March 3, 1893, in Philadelphia, Douglas Waples was the only child of Rufus Waples and Christine Beach Isham Waples; his mother, who suffered from tuberculosis, took him with her to Colorado Springs, Mexico City, and El Paso for the first five years of his life. Upon his mother's death in 1898, he returned to Pennsylvania, living in Wayne and attending Miss Miel's school. With his father's marriage in 1901, Douglas entered Radnor public school and sang in the Saint Mary's Protestant Episcopal Church boys' choir. In 1904 he entered Haverford School and became enamored of athletics, English, Latin, and Greek. Vacationing in New England and Michigan meant sports and the out-of-doors over the years, with a three-week canoe trip on the French River in Canada a memorable highlight. Thus early in life Waples established his devotion to music, sports, and literature. A bassoonist, Waples later played with equal pleasure in the university orchestra and in a woodwind quartet in Chicago. Former students recall him jogging regularly around the Midway in his later years on the Chicago campus.

Four years at Haverford College culminated in 1914 with election to Phi Beta Kappa, some literary prizes, and a bid to the 1914 Olympics. Teaching English and athletics in the Gilman School in Baltimore led him back to study, this time at Harvard, from which he earned an M.A. in June 1917, the same month he married Eleanor Cary. His doctorate came three years and a world war later, a Ph.D. degree in Educational Psychology from the University of Pennsylvania in 1920, the same spring as the birth of his first child.

His family and his career were launched with a position as Assistant Professor of Psychology and Education at Tufts in Boston, from which he continued studies at Harvard. In 1923 Waples moved to the University of Pittsburgh, where W. W. Charters was a colleague. Charters moved to the University of Chicago in 1925 and saw to it that Waples also was added to that faculty. When Waples retired in 1957, Washington Island, Wisconsin, become home base for him and Dorothy (Blake) Waples, his wife since 1947. Their Fulbright research trips to India and Peru sustained Waples's activity in public communication research until a debilitating stroke in 1960 severely limited his activity. He died on Washington Island April 25, 1978.

University of Chicago. Waples's 15 years (1928–42) on the faculty of the Graduate Library School of the University of Chicago spread his influence among his students and brought three of his major interests to bear on librarianship: scholarship, research, and reading behavior—all related to his central focus on public communication.

Waples's writings in the area of scholarship dealt often with the international exchange of ideas. *National Libraries and Foreign Scholarship,* written with Harold D. Lasswell (1936), and Waples's later article "Belgian Scholars and Their Libraries" (*Library Quarterly,* 1940), described the interaction between political nationalism and the importation of foreign social science literature and detailed the significance of broad general research collections in the development of scholarship.

Research was central to Waples's professional life. Each of his five important contributions to secondary education published between 1924 and 1930 made the research orientation central to curriculum evaluation, teaching methods, or supervision. Waples wrote with Ralph W. Tyler (1930) a textbook for teachers on the use of research methods that was precursor to his later volume on research methods applied to librarianship, *Investigating Library Problems* (1939), which stressed the importance of building a research-based body of knowledge for librarianship. This emphasis made Waples, equally with Pierce Butler (*Introduction to Library Science,* 1934), spokesman for the unique research orientation of the Graduate Library School from 1928 to 1942.

Waples's studies of reading behavior, however, were then and remain his most substantive contribution to librarianship. He provided insight into the "hierarchy" of choices of reading materials: accessibility, readability, and subject interest in "The Relation of Subject Interests to Actual Reading" (*Library Quarterly,* 1932). "People versus Print," in L. R. Wilson's *Library Trends* (1936), with its corollary perspective on the library's role in making accessible the socially significant materials of an era, has had strong impact on American librarianship.

Waples's sheer intellectual power in grouping and analyzing data, in generating hypotheses, and in giving order to the chaos of perceived significance in reading studies is demonstrated in the unmatched series of publications that use sociological research strategies to explore his psychological hypotheses in the area of adult reading. *What People Want to Read About,* written with Ralph W. Tyler (1931), was even more significant for its methodology and its analysis of the field of reading research problems than it was for its findings on the subject interests of a wide range of adult groups. Similarly, his monograph *People and Print* (1936) studies the "social aspects of reading in the depression," opening research into the relationship of the larger trends and critical events in society and the use of library resources. He explored market analysis, special publics, advertising, and cost efficiency in various types of book service. But he still saw the compelling problem as that of effective description of readers "to present why they read as they do." Waples always sought methods of investigation that would allow penetration of this problem below the superficial level, and this search represents his major contribution. *Libraries and Readers in the State of New York,* which he wrote with Leon Carnovsky (1939), was the first study of research in total communities in an experimental design.

His research report, with Bernard Berelson and Franklyn R. Bradshaw, *What Reading Does to People* (1940), was notable not only for his full statement of "the five effects of reading," the record of reading as social history; it was also notable for a summation of the field of research in the social effects of reading and for recommendations on the methodology of content analysis and case studies. A brilliant conceptualizer, and skilled practitioner in research design, Waples has not had his equal in the area of adult reading studies.

Following World War II, Waples devoted himself to his public-communications studies outside the context of the Graduate Library School. He was Chairman of the University's Committee in Communication from 1951 to his retirement in 1957. Waples was one of that small group of major figures at GLS who shared in establishing a base for library science and a research orientation to library education.

REFERENCE

John V. Richardson, Jr., "Waples, Douglas (1893–1978)," *Dictionary of American Library Biography* (Suppl. 1990).

MARGARET E. MONROE

Wheeler, Joseph L.

(1884–1970)

When the Enoch Pratt Free Library of Baltimore celebrated the 30th anniversary of its famous central building on February 15, 1963, the American librarian responsible for making it a model of its kind was present. He saw carved on the marble entrance to the auditorium named in his honor, "Joseph L. Wheeler, 1926–1945. Under His Leadership the Enoch Pratt Free Library Became One of the Notable Libraries of the World." A skilled publicist, he had an eye for potential talent and the ability to inspire his staff, many of whom went on to major positions.

Wheeler was born March 16, 1884, in Dorchester, Massachusetts. After public schooling in Bridgewater and frequent visits to the local library, he studied engineering at Brown University and worked at the Providence Public Library. He switched courses, taking a Bachelor of Philosophy degree and a Master's degree in Social and Political Science from Brown. Later he completed the course at the New York State Library School in Albany.

Wheeler's professional progress was rapid and steady. Beginning at the Washington, D.C., Public Library, he held positions of increasing responsibility in public libraries of Jacksonville, Florida; Los Angeles; and Youngstown, Ohio.

Wheeler was 42 years old, energetic, seasoned, and boiling with ideas when he took over as Librarian of Baltimore's unexciting public library in 1926. He breathed life into the institution, using his skills in publicity and personnel development. He motivated and prodded trustees, staff, and officials of the city. The Pratt quickly earned a reputation for being in the van of public library organization and service.

Service to the public was Wheeler's obsession, as shown in the Pratt's building design. It was the first large public library with a street-level entrance, big display windows, and collections easily accessible to the public. Staff stations were strategically placed for assistance to readers.

Recognition of the Pratt Library for excellence and the proven efficiency of the central library created a nationwide demand for Wheeler's services as a consultant. After leaving Baltimore in 1944, he advised many libraries. He had completed more that 225 studies and surveys by the time of his death in Benson, Vermont, December 3, 1970.

REFERENCE

Lee H. Warner, "Wheeler, Joseph Lewis," *Dictionary of American Library Biography* (1978).

EDWIN CASTAGNA
(d. 1983)

The Baltimore Sun Papers

Joseph Lewis Wheeler

Wijasuriya, D. E. K.

(1934–)

Donald Earlian Kingsley Wijasuriya, a pioneer of the library profession in Malaysia, was born in Kuala Lumpur, Malaysia, on November 22, 1934. In Sri Lanka he obtained a B.A. degree from the University of Ceylon in Paradeniya in 1959. He joined the University of Malaya Library as a library assistant and after spending a year there was sent by the University to the North-Western Polytechnic in London for professional studies in library science, 1961–63. He was admitted as an Associate of the Library Association, London, in 1962. Three years later, he was admitted by examination as a Fellow of the Library Association. In 1980 he received a doctorate from Loughborough University in the United Kingdom. In 1984 he was admitted as an Associate of the Australian Library Association.

He served the University of Malaya Library for more than 13 years, as Head of the Readers Services Division, Head of the Serials Division, and Deputy Librarian. At times he was Acting Librarian (1970–72). In 1972 Wijasuriya left the premier university library of the country to take a position with the young national library, still in its formative years. He was seconded from the University of Malaya Library and became the Deputy Director General of the National Library of Malaysia. It was the highest professional position in the National Library; the position of the Director General was traditionally filled by a senior civil servant from the administrative or diplomatic service. From May 1983, however, he acted as the Director General of the National Library.

He served on the Council of the Library Association of Malaysia from 1964 to 1979, during which time he was Secretary (1964–65), Vice-President (1970–71), and President (1972, 1973, 1975) of the Library Association of Malaysia. He also served on several committees of the Association in various capacities.

Public library service in Malaysia came to owe much to the efforts of Wijasuriya. In the 1970s he worked unceasingly with state library committees and provided valuable advice and guidelines in formulating the laws setting up the state public library services. The Sultan of the State of Kedah awarded him the Kedah Distinguished Service Star in 1979 in recognition of his public library contributions. In the same year the King of Malaysia made him an Officer of the Most Distinguished Order of the Defender of the Realm for his services to the nation.

D. E. K. Wijasuriya

Under Wijasuriya's leadership, the National Library, from humble beginnings as a section of the National Archives with a collection of about 4,000 volumes, went through a period of spectacular growth and development after 1972. In 1977 it was established as an independent department of the federal government with its own identity, and by the mid-1980s had a collection of more than half a million volumes and a staff of about 240, of whom more than a quarter were professionals. The operational budget of the National Library increased by about twenty-fold. Wijasuriya was the moving force behind most of the services developed in the National Library, including the *National Bibliography, Index to Malaysian Periodicals, The Malaysian Newspaper Index,* and *The Malaysian Conference Index* as well as a national postal loan service and the branch and mobile library services in the Federal Territory.

Wijasuriya initiated the establishment of a network of the four university libraries in the country and the national library to ensure optimum resource-sharing. With the assistance of Unesco, that project led to the development of the MALMARC database, which had about 250,000 records of holdings of all the participating libraries in the mid-1980s.

Active in the Conference of South East Asian Librarians (CONSAL), he served on its Board from 1974 and was Chairman of the Board, 1979–81, when Malaysia was host to CONSAL.

In 1984 Wijasuriya chaired a government commission to formulate national policies for information services and library development in Malaysia. The commission's recommendations were enacted as a National Policy on Library and Information Services in 1988. Wijasuriya retired from the National Library of Malaysia in 1990.

J. S. SOOSAI

Margreet Wijnstroom

Wijnstroom, Margreet
(1922–)

Margreet Wijnstroom, Dutch librarian and association leader, became known to the international library world as the Secretary General of IFLA (the International Federation of Library Associations and Institutions) from 1971 to 1987.

She was born August 26, 1922, in Bloemendaal, the Netherlands. For her as well as many others of the same generation, World War II caused changes in the plans for a future career. She had decided to study law, but during the war students who wanted to enter a university had to sign a declaration of loyalty decreed by the Nazis. She, like many others, found that unacceptable. Instead, she took up librarianship, which was taught in courses organized by the Dutch Library Association, and received her practical training in the City Library in Haarlem. For a short period thereafter she worked in The Hague Public Library. For the rest of the war she worked illegally in Haarlem, because official jobs were reserved for those friendly to the occupation forces.

In 1945–46 she followed the course for future directors of public libraries in The Hague. She could not, however, completely give up the idea of studying law and started her studies at the University of Amsterdam in 1947. She obtained her degree in 1954 but nevertheless continued in the library field as a public relations librarian at the Public Library in Amsterdam, 1954–57.

Margreet Wijnstroom stood up for women's rights to an extent hard to credit today, but the need was urgent in the 1950s. Thus she could not resist applying for the job as Secretary of the Dutch Public Library Association, although the position was advertised for men only. She received the job, luckily for the library world at large, and soon revealed her outstanding ability to run a professional organization. During the period that she was in charge, 1954–1971, the staff of the Association increased from 6 to 80 and a number of new activities were launched, so that the Association also became what in many other countries is known as a library center. She was asked to join IFLA as its first full-time Secretary General in 1971. Her experience in the library field as well as her background in law proved an excellent combination. Her citizenship in a small country, where people are known for their international interests and contacts, was of equal importance. To make an international organization prosper is not merely a question of increasing the membership, but also requires the person in charge to be able to create an atmosphere of trust among members from all parts of the world.

IFLA's growth after 1971 soon made it necessary for the Federation to revise its statutes. This was far from a painless operation. The proposal put forward to the Council in 1975 was found unacceptable by the membership and for a time IFLA's future situation was unclear. That the new statutes were eventually adopted in the following year was to a great extent due to the Secretary General, who, in addition to being familiar with the juridical formalities governing such an international organization, also had a feeling for what might be accepted by the members, who based themselves on their national organization systems. The former "gentlemen's club" then really changed into a workable organization, inspiring new generations of librarians to take an interest in joining IFLA and working in specialized areas toward the common goal of promoting librarianship.

Though the membership grew continuously, this does not necessarily mean that more money could be put at the disposal of the Secretariat, because of the differentiated fee system. The Secretary General, delighted that so many new members from the Third World joined IFLA, thereby making it a truly global organization, came to face a constant challenge for finding ways to make ends meet. Wijnstroom retired from IFLA in 1987, following the IFLA Council and General Conference in Brighton, England.

Wijnstroom was active in a number of areas. In her youth she was an international field hockey player, captaining the Dutch team for a decade. She assisted the Dutch Field Hockey Association as member or chair of various committees and designed a new legal penalty system for the Association. She is well known in Holland as a critical reviewer of Dutch and foreign mystery literature. Not content with criticism, she published her first mystery, *Steekspel in de Bibliotheek Arena* ("Murder in the Library Stacks") in 1990, then wrote a second.

Professionally, Wijnstroom wrote *De Openbare Bibliotheek in Europe* ("The Public Library in Europe") and contributed many articles in library journals. Her various activities brought many honors, including Officer in the Order of Oranje Nassau (Netherlands), Officer in the Crown Order of Belgium, and a Special Citation from the U.S. National Commission on Library and Information Science.

ELSE GRANHEIM

Williamson, Charles C.
(1877–1965)

Charles Clarence Williamson, U.S. librarian, is most widely known for his landmark study, *Training for Library Service,* yet his many achievements as a special librarian, academic librarian, and dean were also major contributions to the emerging field of librarianship.

Williamson was born in Salem, Ohio, January 26, 1877. In June 1897 he graduated from the Salem high school first in his class. He had to work while studying for his A.B. degree and, after one year of study at Ohio Wesleyan University, he returned to Salem in

1899 and became a first grade teacher; he later became principal as well. In 1901 Williamson, anxious to resume his college education, accepted a part-time job from the President of Western Reserve University, Charles F. Thwing. The job provided an opportunity for Williamson to resume his college education at Western Reserve. He majored in economics and graduated in 1903 magna cum laude and was elected to Phi Beta Kappa. He then assisted and studied under Richard T. Ely at the University of Wisconsin, checking bibliographies and making recommendations for the purchase of books in economics and related subjects. In 1906, at the end of the academic year, Ely went to Columbia University in New York City, and Williamson, who had been awarded a fellowship, also transferred to Columbia, from which he received his Ph.D. degree in 1907.

Williamson demonstrated, for almost four decades, that "he was a man of many interests and possessed an innate interest in almost every thing. This is revealed in his life, work, writings, and contributions; support of professional and scholarly groups; bibliographical activities; activities in professional library associations; and a career which included work as a teacher, principal, secretary, economist, associate professor, political scientist, librarian, statistician, foundation executive, library director, dean, library educator, professor, author, editor, bibliographer, compiler, surveyor, and consultant." (Paul Winckler).

John Shaw Billings, acting on the advice of Edwin R. Seligman, one of Williamson's former professors, appointed him Chief of the new Division of Economics and Sociology at the New York Public Library with the understanding that it would be available to the public on the opening day of the new building at Fifth Avenue and 42nd Street. Williamson was then a professor at Bryn Mawr College (Pennsylvania). The new library opened May 23, 1911, before Williamson could leave Bryn Mawr. He nonetheless completed all the planning and organization required for the Division of Economics and Sociology to open as scheduled.

The Economics Division quickly became one of the library's most important and heavily used centers of research and scholarship. Williamson and his staff provided a wide range of information services and aggressive promotion; they also added more than 100,000 volumes to the collection by 1914. Williamson then took on a second major challenge: he became the Municipal Reference Librarian of New York City on October 19, 1914. The relatively new library was in disarray because of the poor performance of the previous head librarian, who had been dismissed. In fewer than four years, Williamson developed the Municipal Reference Library into a model of efficiency and effectiveness in the delivery of information and reference services to the city's employees and officials. He established the practice of aggressively supplying city employees and officials with pertinent data. He started *Municipal Reference Notes,* which was sent to city employees and policymakers to alert them to recent useful information. Thus from Williamson came a forerunner of today's selective dissemination of information.

Williamson also acted to provide facts about the entire government of New York City; he did so by compiling and publishing the *Municipal Year Book of the City of New York*; later he described the need and helped to secure funding for the publication of the *Minutes of the Common Council of the City of New York, 1784–1831*; he further contributed to this work by serving as Secretary to the Publications Committee. But perhaps of even greater importance, Williamson envisioned a greater role for *Public Affairs Information Service* and worked to make it a reality. Williamson's landmark achievements at the Municipal Reference Library were all the more remarkable considering that the political environment in which he accomplished so much was only minimally hospitable to him. With no small relief, he accepted a new and entirely different assignment with the Carnegie Corporation in 1918. One year later, after he had completed his part of the Corporation's "Study of the Methods of Americanization," Williamson returned to his position as Chief of the Division of Economics and Sociology at the NYPL in 1919.

During his second tenure at the NYPL, Williamson began to focus his attention on education for librarianship. The Carnegie Corporation commissioned him to do his pioneering study of the institutions that were preparing librarians to operate the nation's libraries. As early as 1914, Henry S. Pritchett, President of the Board of the Carnegie Corporation, had expressed his uneasiness ". . . about the activities of the corporation in planting libraries" around the country, and he had obtained the services of Alvin Johnson to survey the Corporation's library building program. Johnson stated his belief that "Not buildings nor even book collections, but trained, intelligent, enterprising library service makes a real library." Hence he recommended that the Corporation ". . . divert as much as practicable of available library funds to the promotion and support of library training." Following World War I, the Corporation's and Williamson's interests in library training matched; the result was *Training for Library Service, A Report Prepared for the Carnegie Corporation of New York* (1923). This report laid the foundation for today's strong library schools. The Report also assured Williamson a prominent place in the history of professional education along with Abraham Flexner, who had submitted a set of recommendations that revolutionized medical education in America almost two decades earlier.

In 1921 Williamson left the NYPL and joined the staff of the Rockefeller Foundation. He became its Information Officer and had administrative responsibility for its library. Williamson managed the Library and the Foundation's public relations with his usual care and thoroughness until 1926.

On May 1, 1926, he was appointed Director of the Libraries and of the School of Library Service at Columbia University. Williamson's performance became further testimony of his uncommon skills as a planner and organizer. By the time he retired in 1943, Columbia was ranked among the top library schools in the nation; Williamson had carried out the decision to merge the Library School of the New York Public Library and the New York State Library School. The libraries, which were scattered around Columbia University's campus, were operating in a well-coordinated system before he retired. The Library Administration and the Library School were both housed in a handsome new library building Williamson had planned. Of the building Keyes Metcalf said: "It was a great university library building; and, in spite of monumental features, it cost just about one-half as much as Yale's Sterling Library, which was built at the same time, had the same number of square feet, and was designed by the same architect." Later named Butler Library, it contained the forerunner of undergraduate libraries that were later popular.

Williamson found time to play key roles in a wide range of other interests. He was a leader for many years of the Conference of Eastern Librarians; the French government named him a Chevalier of the Legion of Honor for the important part he played in the publication of the printed catalogue of the Bibliothèque Nationale; he also served as an officer of the Special Libraries Association, the American Library Association, the Association of American Library Schools, and the American Library Institute. And he was an active member of the Association of Research Libraries. Williamson was, moreover, a participant in other associations, among them the Bibliographical Society of America, the American Economic Association, the American Political Science Association, and the American Sociological Society.

Few librarians have been able to make so many important contributions directly to the advancement of librarianship and in many other areas of service as Williamson did. He died January 11, 1965, in Greenwich, Connecticut.

REFERENCES

Paul A. Winckler, "Charles Clarence Williamson (1877–1965): His Professional Life and Work in Librarianship and Library Education in the United States" (Ph.D. dissertation, New York University, 1968).

Keyes D. Metcalf, "Six Influential Academic and Research Librarians," *College and Research Libraries* (July 1976).

CHARLES D. CHURCHWELL

ALA

H. W. Wilson

Wilson, H. W.
(1868–1954)

Halsey William Wilson's contributions to librarianship cannot easily be overstated. It is hardly possible to imagine American libraries without the indexes and bibliographies he created as bookseller, publisher, and founder of the company that bears his name.

Son of Althea Dunnell Wilson and John Thompson Wilson, a stonecutter, H. W. Wilson was born in Wilmington, Vermont, May 12, 1868. He was a descendant of Roger Williams, Anne Hutchinson, and Mary Dyer, the Quaker martyr. Orphaned before the age of three, Wilson was brought up by his maternal grandparents in rural Massachusetts and later by an aunt and uncle in Iowa. He soon developed his legendary capacity for work and began to exercise his talent for simultaneous activity. He gained his formal education at a Beloit, Wisconsin, boarding school and the University of Minnesota. While attending the university intermittently between 1885 and 1892, he delivered newspapers, worked as a church custodian, ran a small job-printing business, studied music in hope of becoming an organist, worked weekends at the Minneapolis Public Library, and, with his roommate, Henry S. Morris, acted as book agent for faculty and students.

In December 1889 the two young men pooled their modest resources, $200, and opened a campus bookstore in the main university building. The firm of Morris and Wilson began on a small scale, furnishing textbooks and supplies and printing syllabuses. After Morris's graduation in 1891, Wilson bought out his partner, continued the business, and soon built it up into the best bookstore in Minneapolis. At one period the store had a bicycle section and managed the university post office, ensuring that everyone on campus made a daily visit to the bookstore. The success of the business enabled Wilson to marry, on August 12, 1895, Justine Leavitt, a graduate student. She was closely associated with the bookstore and the publishing firm until about 1913, when she turned her full attention to civic matters, especially the women's suffrage movement.

As a bookseller, Wilson became aware of the need for an accurate, up-to-date source for locating books in print. *Publishers Weekly* had published semiannual cumulations of its weekly lists, but discontinued them in 1897 because of rising costs. Wilson, spurred on by what he later called the "bibliographic urge," conceived the idea of a monthly listing of new books, to be cumulated into a permanent record of American book publishing. Thus was born *Cumulative Book Index* (CBI), which first appeared in February 1898. CBI embodied the now familiar Wilson bibliographical features: author, title, and subject entries arranged in one alphabet. The success of CBI, limited at first, led Wilson to produce the first *United States Catalog, Books in Print,* in 1899. Hard on the heels of this came the most familiar of all the Wilson publications, *Readers' Guide to Periodical Literature,* which first appeared in 1901, indexing the contents of 20 general periodicals. These early publications were cumulated by another Wilson innovation: bibliographic entries on Linotype slugs that could be kept and rearranged at will before each printing.

In 1903 Wilson incorporated his bookstore-publishing firm, offering stock in the H. W. Wilson Company to friends in the academic, bookselling, and library communities. Thus began the company's continuing association with librarians. The first product of the new firm was the *Book Review Digest* (1905), edited by Mrs. Wilson. Over the next several years, some half-dozen periodical indexes, forerunners of now standard titles, appeared under the Wilson imprint, as well as two cumulative editions of *Readers' Guide,* two revisions of the *United States Catalog,* and a number of other library-oriented publications. The firm also issued dozens of titles as the unofficial University of Minnesota Press.

Early in his career, Wilson evolved a method of pricing *Readers' Guide* on a sliding scale, the "service basis," which made it possible for almost all libraries to afford this valuable reference source. He conceived the index as a *service:* the price depended upon a library's periodical holdings and thus the index's usefulness to that library. The more titles indexed for a library, the more useful *Readers' Guide* was; and each library was charged accordingly. Similar but more complex scales were developed for the specialized Wilson indexes, involving not only the number of periodical titles held but also the number of indexing entries per title. The service basis, though criticized from time to time, has served both the company and its subscribers well.

As the firm flourished, Wilson recognized the need to be located on the East Coast, closer to the publishing world and the majority of his subscribers. In 1913 he moved the firm to White Plains, New York. From White Plains came *Industrial Arts Index* (1913), *Agricultural Index* (1916), and still more library-oriented reference books. A house organ begun in this period evolved into *Wilson Library Bulletin*. After four years in White Plains, Wilson moved the firm even closer to New York City. In 1917, on a site in the Bronx overlooking the Hudson River, he built the first building of a complex that ultimately included four large structures. He also built the 30-foot lighthouse that became the company's colophon.

From the familiar 950 University Avenue address, the Wilson Company developed additional specialized periodical indexes, among them *Art Index* (1929), *Education Index* (1929), *Library Literature* (1936), and *Bibliographic Index* (1938). Other specialized reference guides from this period are *Essay and General Literature Index* (1934), *Vertical File Index* (1932), *Current Biography* (1940), and *Biography Index* (1946). The Standard Catalog series was developed fully in this period. The first *Union List of Serials in Libraries of the United States and Canada* (1928) was the result of cooperation between the Wilson Company, the American Library Association, and participating libraries. Wilson later provided a feasibility study for the continuation of the Library of Congress's *Catalog of Books Represented by Library of Congress Printed Cards, issue to July 31, 1942,* which contributed in large measure to its continuation as the *National Union Catalog*.

Wilson realized quite early that the success of his firm, with its market limited mostly to libraries, depended upon close cooperation with librarians. The firm employed many librarians in its indexing operations. Practicing librarians were consulted at every step about the company's services and activities, even to the point of making decisions about the scope and content of many Wilson publications. To facilitate cooperation, Wilson attended more than 40 American Library Association national meetings, as many Midwinter meetings, and hundreds of regional, state, and local meetings of librarians. He also participated in and sponsored national and international bibliographical projects, created library awards, and placed librarians on his board of directors. The Wilson staff was encouraged to participate in library association activities and allowed generous time for committee work. Over the years these close ties to the library community led to a steady stream of Wilson publications, each geared to some specific library need.

In 1948 Wilson summed up his method of creating new publications, emphasizing the importance of listening to and talking with librarians:

> First, listen to the advice of prospective supporters of a project. If the project is important it will be discussed in librarians' meetings and journals. Then scan the field and study what has been done and why there may have been successes and failures. Consult and secure advice from librarians who may be expected to have an interest in the project. Then the final question: "If this is a good plan and if we proceed with it, will you plan to subscribe for it?"

While Wilson's business methods and bibliographical innovations were quite modern, his managerial approach was that of the paternalistic Yankee individualist. Though he grew to manhood in the age of Rockefeller, Carnegie, Gould, and Fisk, he became a Wilsonian Democrat in his middle years. An admirer of Henry Ford, he disliked the income tax, loathed Franklin D. Roosevelt and the New Deal, and unsuccessfully resisted unions in the firm. From the beginning, the staff of the Wilson Company was like a family, and this feeling never entirely disappeared as the firm grew. Though salaries were skimpy, Wilson provided such fringe benefits as stock sharing, pensions for older employees, cumulative sick leave, and hospitalization at a time when few American business firms did so. He encouraged vacations, though rarely taking them himself; employed women and placed them in positions of responsibility; and pioneered in the hiring of the physically handicapped.

Wilson began developing his publications at a time when the need for bibliographical control of an expanding world of print was becoming acute. Extension of secondary and higher education, growth of the book and periodical publishing industry, the Carnegie-inspired revolution in library expansion, the rise of scholarly and scientific publication and research, all had created a flood of information and generated a need for indexes to make this information easily accessible. Wilson's knowledge of the needs of libraries, his high standards of indexing, his pricing systems to make his indexes widely available, his publication of a broad range of indexes and services, and his continuing modernization of his publications ultimately made for a unique, satisfying, and profitable bibliographical publishing career.

In person Wilson was a stocky, robust figure. His round features and a twinkle in the eye relieved an otherwise stolid but not forbidding appearance. Though personally abstemious (he neither smoked nor drank alcohol), he did indulge a stupendous sweet tooth and a wry sense of humor. He was addicted to puns, and the wary soon learned to spot the signs that a particularly horrendous one was on the way. Fond of after-dinner stories, he published, under the transparent pseudonym Harold Workman Williams, three collections of jokes, stories, and quotations for all occasions.

Wilson was much honored in his lifetime. Brown University presented him an honorary Doctor of Letters degree in 1939; in 1948 the University of Minnesota honored him with its first Outstanding Achievement award. The American Library Association and the Special Libraries Association made special presentations on the 50th anniversary of the Wilson Company in 1948. In 1950 he received the American Library Association's Joseph W. Lippincott Award. In his turn, Wilson honored the library community. In 1946 the firm began to sponsor library awards, the most prestigious of which is the annual John Cotton Dana Library Publicity Award.

Wilson resigned as President of the firm in December, 1952, but continued as Chairman of the Board until his death at his home in Yorktown Heights, New York, March 1, 1954. He died 60 years to the day after the death of an earlier bibliographer and periodical indexer, William Frederick Poole. After Mrs. Wilson's death in 1955, the Wilson estate was turned over to the H. W. Wilson Foundation, to be used primarily for the benefit of former employees. Grants were made for such purposes as library school scholarships, National Library Week, the activities of several library associations, and programs for the blind and physically handicapped.

REFERENCE

Arthur Plotnik, "Wilson, Halsey William," *Dictionary of American Library Biography* (1978).

A. E. SKINNER

ALA

Louis Round Wilson

Wilson, Louis Round

(1876–1979)

Louis Round Wilson, a leader of American librarianship, was Librarian of the University of North Carolina at Chapel Hill, 1901–32, and Dean of the Graduate Library School of the University of Chicago, 1932–42. His career as librarian, teacher, writer, and editor and his active and influential participation in library associations exemplify the emergence of the professional university library administrator in the United States.

Born in Lenoir, North Carolina, December 27, 1876, Wilson was educated in Lenoir schools, attended Haverford (Pennsylvania) College, and was graduated from the University of North Carolina at Chapel Hill in 1899. He taught in private academies in North Carolina for two years before returning to Chapel Hill as University Librarian in 1901. He also pursued graduate study and received a Master's degree in English in 1902 and a Ph.D. in 1905. Though Wilson had expected to become a professor of English, he decided instead to remain with the University of North Carolina as its Librarian, a decision that influenced his own life and made an indelible impact on the library profession.

Wilson foresaw the growth and development of the University of North Carolina into one of the major universities in the United States and endeavored to build a library collection that would support graduate study and research. Working with the university's academic departments, he acquired books, periodicals, and bibliographic materials that greatly expanded the holdings of the main library. Wilson was especially interested in the special collections of the library; acknowledging the regional quality of the University, he envisioned a manuscript collection that would serve historians of the South. He lived to see the Southern Historical Collection take its place among the major manuscript repositories in the U.S. He encouraged the development of a collection of North Caroliniana and sought and gained financial support from friends and alumni of the University for the purchase and preservation of rare books and incunabula.

Wilson supervised the construction of two library buildings. A Carnegie building was completed in 1907, and the present special collections library, which bears his name, was dedicated in 1929. With the growth of the collections and the expanded physical facilities came an increase in the number of trained librarians on Wilson's staff. In 1907, when the Carnegie library was opened, Wilson ran the library with the aid of only one trained librarian and a few student assistants; by 1932 there were 23 librarians on the staff.

Wilson taught his first course in librarianship in the summer session of 1904. In 1907 courses in library administration were offered in the regular session, and Wilson was made an Assistant Professor of Library Administration. In 1920 Wilson was made a Kenan Professor of Library Science; the Kenan professorships are the University of North Carolina's oldest and most distinguished endowed chairs. Wilson taught courses in library science until he left the University and was vigorous and successful in campaigning for a School of Library Science, which opened in 1931 with Wilson as its first Dean.

As a member of the faculty of the University, Wilson assumed many additional duties. As Chairman of the Committee on Extension from 1912 to 1920, he drew the library heavily into extension work; through the Library Extension Department books were circulated to the people of North Carolina for more than 40 years. Wilson was Editor of the *Alumni Review*, 1912–24, and co-founder and Director of the University Press, 1922–32.

In 1932 Wilson accepted the position of Dean of the Graduate Library School of the University of Chicago. As Dean of the seven-year-old school, he led the faculty in developing a curriculum designed to produce librarians who would be specialists in administration of various types of libraries. Wilson taught courses in university library administration and library trends. He organized teams of students and faculty members to study current problems in librarianship and began institutes that explored new directions for the profession. Many of these studies resulted in books that were published as part of the University of Chicago Studies in Library Science series, of which Wilson was General Editor.

Wilson's own volume in the series, *The Geography of Reading* (1938), reflects his long-standing interest in the phenomenon of reading. As early as 1922 he was studying the reading habits of North Carolinians, and in the 1930s he extended this interest in reading and public libraries to the entire country.

In 1942 Wilson returned to North Carolina, where he rejoined the faculty of the School of Library Science. In 1945 he and Maurice F. Tauber published *The University Library*, a significant addition to the literature of library administration. After retiring from the faculty at 83 in 1959, Wilson continued in service to the University as a consultant to the President of the university system until 1969.

Throughout his career Wilson served as a library consultant and surveyor. His opinions on academic libraries, library buildings, and possible sites for library schools were sought by the Carnegie Corporation, the General Education Board, and the Board of Education for Librarianship of the American Library Association. In the mid-1930s Wilson and Edgar A. Wight surveyed county libraries in the Southeast, and in 1941 and 1946 Wilson conducted surveys for the Tennessee Valley Authority and the Tennessee Valley Library Council, with a view to increasing library service to the Tennessee Valley region under the aegis of the Tennessee Valley Authority.

Wilson's participation in professional associations began when he joined ALA in 1904. As President of ALA, 1935–36, he led a successful campaign for adoption of a statement in support of federal aid to libraries. He helped to found the North Carolina Library Association in 1904 and was its President in 1910 and again in 1930–31. Wilson was President of the Southeast Library Association (SELA), 1924–26, and endeavored to join the efforts of SELA and the Southern Association of Colleges and Secondary Schools in providing standards for school and college libraries. Always mindful of the needs of the people of the state, Wilson helped to draft the legislation that created the North Carolina Library Commission in 1909 and served as Chairman of the Commission from 1909 until 1916. He was active in the Citizen's Library Movement in 1927.

Wilson's career demonstrates his belief in the role of the library as a service organization. He saw the library as an active force in American society and never ceased in his efforts to bring the library into active service to the people. He knew that the library was a vital and necessary adjunct to the school and college, but he also believed that the librarian must reach out beyond the walls of the library in bringing the materials of the library to the people.

Wilson was married in 1909 to Penelope Bryan Wright. They had four children. He built a house in Chapel Hill in 1911. His oldest two daughters lived with him until his death in Chapel Hill, December 10, 1979, at the age of 102.

REFERENCES

Louis Round Wilson Bibliography: A Chronological List of Works and Editorial Activities (1976).

Maurice F. Tauber, *Louis Round Wilson: Librarian and Administrator* (1967).

Frances A. Weaver, *Louis Round Wilson, The Years since 1955* (1976).

Edward G. Holley, "The Centenary of a Giant of Librarianship: Louis Round Wilson" (illustrated), *The ALA Yearbook* (1977).

John V. Richardson, Jr., "Louis Round Wilson," *Leaders in American Academic Librarianship* (1983).

FRANCES A. WEAVER

Winchell, Constance M.
(1896–1984)

Constance Mabel Winchell, American librarian, a member of the reference staff at Columbia University Library for 38 years, was responsible for the seventh and eighth editions of *A Guide to Reference Books.*

Winchell was born November 2, 1896, in Northampton, Massachusetts, where her aunt was a librarian in the historic Forbes Library directed by Charles Ammi Cutter. Winchell earned a Bachelor of Arts degree from the University of Michigan, where she "filed her way through college" with a job in the university library. Upon graduation Winchell began her career as a librarian at the Central High School in Duluth, Minnesota. She had prepared for such a post by attending the "library summer school" sessions conducted at Michigan by the Director of the University Library, William Warner Bishop, following her junior and senior years. Unlike many who become librarians after trying some other profession, Winchell wanted that career from the beginning. In an interview she once remarked: "It never entered my mind that I was not going to be a librarian. I had always intended to be a librarian, always."

On Bishop's advice, she attended the Library School at New York Public Library and received a certificate in 1920. She then worked for the U.S. Merchant Marine in New York City and was responsible for libraries in lighthouses. Five months later

ALA

Constance M. Winchell

Winchell returned to Ann Arbor, where she worked first as a reviser in the catalogue department of the university library and then as a reference assistant. She wanted to do reference work immediately, but Bishop advised that any reference librarian should have cataloguing experience.

In 1924 Winchell went to the American Library in Paris as Head Cataloguer. Bishop disapproved, but Winchell wanted the experience of life in another country. She returned to the United States in 1925 and joined the reference staff of the Columbia University Library. Winchell stayed there for 38 years, rising from Reference Assistant to Assistant Reference Librarian to Reference Librarian—taking that post when Isadore Gilbert Mudge retired in 1941.

Mudge was Head of the Reference Department during Winchell's early years at Columbia and was also Winchell's teacher in the Columbia School of Library Service, where Winchell earned an M.S. in 1930. Mudge suggested and then supervised the preparation of Winchell's Master's essay, published as *Locating Books for Interlibrary Loan* (H. W. Wilson, 1930). The work incorporates many of the techniques and concepts Mudge had developed through 20 years of work with interlibrary loan problems. Winchell's lucid explication of practices at Columbia stood for many years as the standard guide for interlibrary loan operations, which were then expanding in all parts of the country.

The value of this work was noted when Winchell received the Isadore Gilbert Mudge Citation for distinguished contributions to reference librarianship in 1960. Winchell was the second person to receive this award, established by the Reference Services Division of ALA in 1959. Winchell received it for "her constructive service to the Library of Columbia University in building its reference collection and . . . her trail-blazing book, *Locating Books for Interlibrary Loan,* which has been an effective aid to the development of interlibrary loan in this country and which continues to be useful as a systematic guide to finding the location of a needed book [and for] . . . that bible of the librarian, *A Guide to Reference Books.*"

A Guide to Reference Books was started by Alice Bertha Kroeger, who was responsible for the first edition in 1902, the five annual supplements that were published in *Library Journal,* and the second edition published in 1908. Isadore Gilbert Mudge prepared supplements to the second edition and was responsible for the third, fourth, fifth, and sixth editions and all the supplements in between. When Mudge retired in 1941, she turned over the *Guide* to Winchell, who had been involved in it ever since she helped with *Reference Books of 1929,* a supplement to the fifth edition. After Mudge's retirement, Winchell produced supplements to the sixth edition and both the seventh and eighth editions—the last published five years after her own retirement from Columbia. Reviewers of these volumes have praised Winchell's skill in making good use of the work of her predecessors while introducing significant and useful changes in the *Guide.*

Winchell not only knew the contents of reference books; she also understood what good reference service should be. When she retired in 1962, the Director of Libraries at Columbia, Richard Logdson, wrote a brief tribute in *College and Research Libraries:*

> Miss Winchell's standards of excellence, her almost uncanny skill in unraveling bibliographic snarls, her zeal in learning new tools to improve existing techniques, and her thorough training of younger assistants have characterized her work through the years. She possessed these qualities, desired in all good reference chiefs, to the highest degree, but beyond these were two deserving special mention. The first is Miss Winchell's concept of a university library as part of the university, not as an island alone. . . . Finally there is Miss Winchell's devotion to duty nurtured by such a profoundly kind heart that she had found it impossible to appear impatient, or bored, or irritated with a reader. . . .

Before she retired, Winchell took a four-month leave of absence for an extensive tour of Asia. Her interest in faraway places was reflected in the many post cards that decorated the home in New Paltz, in upstate New York, where she moved after completion of the eighth edition of the *Guide.* She died there on May 23, 1984.

REFERENCES

Mary Jo Lynch, "Women in Reference Service," in *Women in the Library Profession: Leadership Roles and Contributions* (1971).

Constance M. Winchell, "The Reminiscences of Constance Mabel Winchell," transcript of an interview with Elizabeth Rumics in 1963, on file in the Oral History Collection, Columbia University Library.

MARY JO LYNCH

Wing, Donald Goddard
(1904–1972)

Yale University Archives, Manuscripts and Archives, Yale University Library

Donald G. Wing

Donald Goddard Wing, who was associated for over 40 years with the Yale University Library, compiled an indispensable tool for librarians and the book trade, the *Short-Title Catalogue* of books printed in English in the 17th century.

Wing was born in Athol, Massachusetts, August 18, 1904. His interest in literature and books developed early; while in school in Athol he read and collected the *Smart Set* and other "little magazines." From Athol he went to Yale, where he studied English, added a book a day to his collection, and was elected to the Elizabethan Club. After graduating in 1926, he spent a year at Trinity College, Cambridge, tutored by George Rylands. A member of the Bloomsbury group, Rylands confirmed Wing's passion for contemporary poetry and literature. Wing traveled widely during his year abroad, and when he returned to the United States he had his copy of the still-banned *Ulysses* hidden in his laundry bag. After a year at Harvard to earn his M.A., Wing returned to Yale, remaining there until the end of his life. He received his Ph.D. in English from Yale in 1932 for his dissertation on "Origins of the Comedy of Humours."

At Yale, Wing served as Head of Accessions (1939–45), Associate Librarian (1945–65), and Associate Librarian for Collections of the Libraries (1966–70). The Yale Library grew tremendously during those years and gained international prominence. Wing's remarkable memory and intimate knowledge of the Yale collections, combined with his diverse intellectual interests, significantly contributed to the Library's expansion. He loved books and delighted in American libraries' "delirious, exhilarating race toward adequacy."

Wing's great and enduring contribution to bibliography is his *Short-Title Catalogue of Books Printed in England, Scotland, Ireland, Wales, and British America and of English Books Printed in Other Countries, 1641–1700.* It was issued in three volumes by the Index Society from 1945 to 1951. His work served as a continuation of Pollard and Redgrave's *Short-Title Catalogue of Books . . . 1475–1640.* Wing surveyed a greater range of libraries than Pollard and Redgrave had; he provided more cross references, gave longer imprints, and indicated by ellipsis the shortening of titles. In addition, he dealt with about 90,000 titles, about three times as many as the earlier STC. Remarkably, Wing compiled his STC during his spare time, except for a year in England in 1936 on a Guggenheim Fellowship.

Yale's acquisition of Falconer Madan's personal collection of Oxford books, and the need to make sense of Yale's holdings of early English books, provided Wing with reason to begin collecting notes while still in his 20s. He wrote out a slip for each title; on it he noted author, short-title, imprint, format, edition, and number of pages. He listed the location of copies, giving the British Museum and Yale shelf numbers and noting unusual provenance. He examined bibliographical reference works and added specific citations for each book. He searched sale catalogues from the 19th century for rare titles and noted the appearance of uncommon items at auction or in booksellers' catalogues in his own day. He not only looked at each tract in the Thomason Collection at the British Museum but also examined at least one copy of the great majority of the titles he listed. To fill in details, he corresponded with librarians and scholars.

Wing's achievement was astonishing. In little over a decade, he produced what quickly became an indispensable tool. Soon librarians and booksellers spoke of "Wing books," and many used "Wing numbers" for identifying, selling, cataloguing, and shelving "Wing period" titles. Librarians were able to measure the strength of their collections and to plot acquisition policy; booksellers could determine at a glance relative rarity and set prices accordingly; and scholars could refer to lists of an author's work or search for pamphlets on a similar theme or subject.

During the remainder of his career, Wing kept his slips up to date with the goal of preparing a revised edition. His *A Gallery of Ghosts* (1967) was based on his search list for 5,000 titles or editions that had appeared at auction or in a bookseller's catalogue or were listed in a previous bibliographer's work but for which no copy was found. Wing received a gratifying response; over half of his ghosts were quickly identified or laid to rest. With the benefit of a sabbatical year, the first granted to a Yale librarian, Wing prepared his revision of the first volume for publication in 1972.

The period 1641 to 1700 comprised only part of Wing's interests. Although he put together an excellent collection of the works of James Howell, a prolific Wing period author, he also collected and read Henry James, Ronald Firbank, Marcel Proust, Edith Wharton, Ezra Pound (whom he first met, appropriately, in the Laurentian library in Florence), Ellen Glasgow, Wyndham Lewis, E. M. Forster, André Gide, all the Sitwells, and Virginia Woolf.

Wing was a member of the Grolier Club and of the Bibliographical Societies of America, London, Cambridge, Oxford, and Edinburgh. He wrote articles and reviews for the *Yale University Library Gazette,* the *Yale Review,* the *Saturday Review of Literature,* and the *William and Mary Quarterly*. He died in Woodbridge, Connecticut, October 8, 1972.

His research notes are available to scholars in the Yale Library; they form the basis of the revision of his STC, sponsored by the Modern Language Association of America.

REFERENCE

Katherine Cveljo, "Wing, Donald Goddard," *Dictionary of American Library Biography* (1978).

TIMOTHY J. CRIST

Winsor, Justin

(1831–1897)

Justin Winsor, American librarian and historian, is probably best remembered for his efforts to make libraries more accessible to their users. He was a founder and first President of the American Library Association.

Winsor was born in Boston, Massachusetts, January 2, 1831, one of five children of Nathaniel Winsor, a prosperous merchant. Descendants of English settlers, the Winsor family had lived in the Boston area since the early 1700s. As a child Justin was somewhat introverted and very fond of reading; he was also quite independent and inclined to rebel against authority. As a result, he was often in difficulty at school and was sent to a boarding school at the age of 10 with the hope that a more structured situation would benefit him.

Winsor, however, intensely disliked the uniformity that prevailed there and enjoyed neither his boarding school days nor his later studies at the Boston Latin School. Although intelligent, he was judged a poor student because he preferred to concentrate on his own projects rather than school assignments. He developed an aversion to memorization from textbooks that lasted throughout his life. Similarly, Winsor's student days at Harvard College were not distinguished. His rejection of the prescribed curriculum led to his leaving in January 1852 without graduating, though 15 years later he was awarded a degree in recognition of his scholarly writings.

His career as a historian began in 1849 with the publication, during his freshman year at Harvard, of *A History of the Town of Duxbury, Massachusetts . . . .* The material for this work had been collected on family trips to Duxbury while visiting relatives. On those visits Winsor not only gathered information but also drew maps of the town to scale. He showed an early interest in cartography, a field in which he later became a recognized authority.

After leaving Harvard, Winsor traveled and studied in Europe for almost a year. He settled in Boston, devoting his time to writing poetry, short pieces of fiction, and literary criticism. Upon his return from Europe, Winsor became engaged to Caroline Tufts Barker, of his Harvard class of 1853; they were married on December 18, 1855. Marriage tended to expand his somewhat limited social contacts, and although he had never enjoyed churchgoing in his youth, he began to attend the Church of the Unity (Unitarian) in Boston and even compiled a small volume of hymns to be used by the congregation.

ALA

Justin Winsor

Boston Public Library. Rejected for military service during the Civil War because of poor eyesight, Winsor continued to spend most of his time in literary pursuits, becoming well known in Boston and New York for his critical writing, which appeared regularly in leading newspapers and periodicals. In large part because of this prominence, he was appointed to the Board of Trustees of the Boston Public Library in 1867; at 36, he was its youngest member.

The Boston Public Library, founded 12 years earlier, was the first large American library wholly supported by city taxes. It was then the yearly practice of the Board to appoint an Examining Committee of five city residents, chaired by a Trustee, to analyze and make recommendations on the operations of the library. Winsor was chosen to head the 1867 Committee.

Always a forthright person, Winsor presented clearly and concisely what he felt were the positive and negative aspects of the library operations. He commended the staff on the size of the collection and rate of accessions but noted the crowded conditions in the building, the lack of proper workrooms, and poor ventilation and insufficient lighting. Winsor also was greatly concerned over the circulation of books, which he felt was too low, and over the nature of the collection as compared with the nature of the reading public. Whereas fiction constituted only one-fourth of the collection, it accounted for two-thirds of the circulation at the time. He recommended setting up branch libraries to increase circulation and purchasing more and better fiction titles to satisfy patron needs.

Charles Coffin Jewett, then Superintendent of the Library, died suddenly in January 1868; since the Assistant Superintendent was in poor health and could not assume control, the Trustees appointed Winsor as Temporary Superintendent. He took over the library administration so energetically and effectively, however, that they confirmed a regular appointment in February.

Winsor was by education a historian, with no experience or training as a librarian, but he had learned much in his few months as a Trustee. Always a humble person, he realized that he had risen rapidly considering his lack of training. The Trustees, however, had obtained a man with great administrative and executive talents, and the Boston Public Library expanded its services extensively during his leadership.

Among the innovations he brought to the library were the initiation of studies to identify the readers and what they read, in order to serve their needs better. Interlibrary loan procedures were instituted to obtain additional materials. He also supervised the repair and renovation of the existing building and established six branches.

Winsor's creation of a "shelf list" in card form in place of an accession ledger was widely adopted by other libraries, as was his system of "continuous inventory," which made unnecessary the closing of the library for a one-month inventory, as had been the earlier practice. He also opened the library on Sundays and reduced the age limit for borrowers. His guiding principle was always more and better service for the readers.

Harvard. Winsor's career as Superintendent came to an abrupt end when the City Council, exceeding its authority, reduced the salaries of all library staff members, including Winsor's. Winsor had received an offer of the post of Librarian at Harvard to replace the retiring John Langdon Sibley, and when some of the Boston City Council members reneged on the terms of a proposed salary designed to keep him at the Public Library, he resigned, annoyed, and accepted the Harvard position on July 11, 1877.

In his first annual report at Harvard, Winsor stated the principle that was to guide his work for the next 20 years: "I consider nothing more important than the provision of large classes of books to which unrestricted access can be had." Accordingly, he opened the stacks to students, an unusual practice at the time, and greatly extended the reserved-book system begun by Sibley.

He began to keep precise records of circulation, including them in his annual reports to the President. He had studies made of book use by the students and in 1887, ten years after he had become Librarian, could report that nine out of ten students were using the library, in contrast to five out of ten in 1876. Winsor pioneered in that kind of statistical analysis in library administration.

Other notable accomplishments at Harvard included designing call slips to be filled out by borrowers, thus speeding up circulation; initiating instruction in library use; devising a compact metal stack storage plan for the collections; promoting more effective participation of the faculty in book selection; exchanging serials holdings lists with other libraries; and reorganizing the administrative structure of the library to delegate more responsibility to each staff member.

An early advocate of the employment of women in libraries, Winsor, at a conference in 1877, urged his British colleagues to train more women for library work. He stated that graduates of Vassar and Wellesley, skilled in languages, were finding challenging positions in the American library system.

Winsor believed a university librarian should be both an administrator and a scholar, and his own career illustrated his philosophy. He continued to do historical research and to write and was considered a leading cartographer. While at Harvard he edited two important historical works: *The Memorial History of Boston* (four volumes, 1880–81) and *A Narrative and Critical History of America* (eight volumes, 1889). The more important of his own works include *Reader's Handbook of the American Revolution* (1879); *Christopher Columbus and How He Received and Imparted the Spirit of Discovery* (1891); *Cartier to Frontenac: Geographical Discovery in the Interior of North America in Its Historical Relations, 1534–1700* (1894); *The Mississippi Basin* (1895); and *The Westward Movement* (1897).

Always active in professional organizations, Winsor was the American Library Assocation's first President, from 1876 to 1885, and President again in 1897, the year he died. He also helped found the *Library Journal.* Winsor foresaw a future in which librarians would be purveyors as well as preservers of knowledge, and his work in the profession was always directed toward that end.

Winsor died in Boston on October 22, 1897.

REFERENCES

Joseph A. Borome, "The Life and Letters of Justin Winsor" (Ph.D. dissertation, Columbia University, 1950).

Kenneth J. Brough, *Scholar's Workshop: Evolving Conceptions of Library Service* (1953).

Robert E. Brundin, "Justin Winsor and the Liberalizing of the College Library," *Journal of Library History* (January 1975).

Wayne Cutler and Michael H. Harris, "Winsor, Justin," *Dictionary of American Library Biography* (1978).

Walter Muir Whitehill, *Boston Public Library: A Centennial History* (1956).

Winsor, Justin, *Justin Winsor: Scholar-Librarian* (1980).

ROBERT E. BRUNDIN

Yemen

Yemen, a republic in the Arabian Peninsula, is bounded by Saudi Arabia on the north, Oman on the east, the Gulf of Aden and the Arabian Sea on the south, and the Red Sea on the west. Population (1990 est.) 11,656,000; area 527,968 sq.km. The official language is Arabic.

History. Nominally governed by the Ottoman Turks until 1918, northeastern Yemen was actually ruled by competing imams until a coup in 1962 established a republican government in Sana'a. Southwestern Yemen was ruled by the British and called Aden from the 1830s until it gained independence in 1967 as a people's republic. The two states fought a prolonged war and finally formed a united republic in 1990.

National Library. The National Library in Sana'a was founded in 1968 with the establishment of the General Organization for Antiquities and National Library. All printed books that were found in the palaces of the deposed kingdom were transferred to this library, while the Arabic manuscripts remained in the Library of the Great Mosque in Sana'a (not open to the public). The Yemeni Center for Cultural Research in Aden (established 1976) is organized into sections for manuscripts, microfilming, publishing, printing, museums, and the library. The Center's Library holds about 2,000 volumes on Yemeni affairs. The country lacked a deposit law and a national bibliography; the publishing industry was almost nonexistent in the early 1990s.

Academic Libraries. The Sana'a University was established in 1971 with financial aid from the Kuwaiti government. Its Central Library and college libraries are being developed. A few recruited personnel from other Arab countries direct and organize the book collections in these libraries. Aden University has five college libraries and a central library in an early stage of development. The Central Library has a collection of about 2,000 volumes. The Library of the Higher College of Education, founded in 1970, holds about 15,000 volumes, of which 10,000 are in Arabic. The Library of the College of Medicine, established in 1975, has 5,000 volumes, mostly in Spanish, a language not spoken in the country. The Library of the Higher Technical Institute, established in 1952, maintains a collection of some 10,000 volumes that are mostly duplicate copies. The Library of Nasser College for Agricultural Sciences, founded in 1972, possesses about 6,000 volumes. The Library of the College of Economics and Administration contains 2,000 volumes. The academic libraries in Aden University are staffed by nonprofessional personnel. Most of the library holdings are not processed; its collections are not catalogued but only registered. The libraries began to reclassify their collections according to the Dewey Decimal Classification.

Public Libraries. The public library system is not well enough developed to support the adult education campaign in the country. The Miswat Public Library in Aden and the People's Library at Al-Mukalla, Hadramawt, are the largest public libraries. The Miswat Public Library, with a collection of about 30,000 volumes, was established in 1953 and is administered by Aden Municipality. The People's Library of Hadramawt, established in 1930, is administered by the Ministry of Culture. The General Organization of Antiquities and National Library is responsible for public libraries. The Library of the Great Mosque, founded by Imam Ahmed in 1925, was known as Al-Awqaf Library. The Library's manuscripts number about 10,000; a microfilming project began, sponsored by the Arab League with the aid of Unesco.

School Libraries. Although some secondary schools possess sizable collections of books, they are not well organized because of the lack of qualified school librarians in the country.

Special Libraries. The Central Library of the Ministry of Education, the Library of the Central Planning Agency (founded 1976), and the Library of the National Institute of Public Administration (founded 1973) offer library services to their employees and to all those interested in their collections.

MOHAMED M. EL HADI

Young Adult Services

History. The first viable young adult (YA) public library program probably began at the New York Public Library under the direction of Mabel Williams. Williams, a former reference librarian, initially worked with schools to see that the instructional needs of high school students were met in the adult sections of the New York Public Library. She also introduced teachers and students to the resources available in the Library.

One of Williams's protégées, Margaret A. Edwards, organized the YA department at the Enoch Pratt Free Library in Baltimore. Edwards described her philosophy of service and techniques to encourage reading in her book *The Fair Garden and the Swarm of Beasts* (1974); the philosophy and techniques are still used in work with today's young adults.

High school libraries were available to young adults in the early 20th century. The first high school

Administration of Information Affairs, Ministry of Education, Qatar

Students gathering information for school reports at Qatar National Library, Doha.

Brookhaven National Laboratory
Photo by Roger Stoutenburgh

Through the Partners in Science Program, a joint project of the School Library Systems (Suffolk County, New York) and the Brookhaven National Laboratory, students learn the special skills needed to use a research library.

librarian, Mary Kingsbury, was appointed in Brooklyn, New York, in 1900. Although educators were primarily interested in curriculum support for classes, they also envisioned a school library as a source of inspiration and recreation for young adults.

The development of YA services has been sporadic and uneven. In the 1960s YA services in both school and public libraries in the United States and Canada experienced a period of vitality and growth, mainly because of increased funding. This infusion of money led to additional staff members, larger collections, and more programming. The economic constraints of the 1970s and 1980s caused cutbacks in school and public libraries. In 1988 the U.S. government reported that one of every four public library patrons was a young adult, but only about one in ten of the libraries had YA librarians.

Student at G. Karaslavov Secondary School (Sofia, Bulgaria) receives assistance with an online information search.

Definitions. Young adults are generally defined as persons between the ages of 12 and 18. The terms "adolescents," "kids," "teenagers," "teens," and "youth" are used interchangeably with "young adults" in the professional literature.

Young adult services is a specialized service in public libraries; in many libraries it is organized as a department. Specialization is characterized by (1) specialists serving young adults; (2) a separate association or division; (3) separate YA collections and budgets; and (4) separate YA programs and services.

The phrase "service to young adults" implies a broader application of the specialization. Librarians who are specialists in other areas of the profession or who are generalists in any type of library may also serve young adults. All library professionals serving youth must accept and apply the philosophy, techniques, and competencies that are the basic tenets of YA services in this wider view.

Resources. The resources today's young adults use must be up-to-date, attractive, appealing, and accessible. Young adults use resources to fulfill recreational, informational, and educational needs. Television, magazines, video games, books, music, newspapers, and movies all compete for a share of the teenager's attention.

When YA services began, most materials collections consisted of hardcover books. The challenge for librarians was to identify books written for adults that would appeal to teens. Early choices included *The Adventures of Huckleberry Finn, Little Women,* and the stories of Jack London and Arthur Conan Doyle. Maureen Daly's *Seventeenth Summer,* published in the 1940s, is generally considered the first young adult novel. Because it represented an adolescent's experiences from the sympathetic yet realistic view of an adolescent, the book was not only unique, but also popular. S. E. Hinton's *The Outsiders* and Paul Zindel's *The Pigman* were published in the 1960s, and their popularity led to other books written primarily for a young adult audience. Adolescent literature became a separate genre and an accepted part of the publishing and reviewing world in the U.S. and Canada. Although literature in the United Kingdom is rich in its appeal to young adults, specialized services to this group developed slowly.

Young adult literature is the term used to describe the broader reading interests of this age group. Young adult literature means anything that readers between the approximate ages of 12 and 20 choose to read. Favorite authors in the early 1990s include a mix of fiction and nonfiction writers for adults and young adults. They include V. C. Andrews, Tom Clancy, Mary Higgins Clark, Chris Crutcher, Torey Hayden, S. E. Hinton, Stephen King, Christopher Pike, and Danielle Steele.

Although reviewers concentrate on hardcover books and libraries purchase them in large numbers, young adults prefer the paperback format for their reading choices. The books are more portable, more attractive, and less expensive to buy or replace. If young adult collections in school and public libraries contain a large percentage of paperback books, teenagers may still choose another type of reading material. An examination of reading surveys revealed that young adults prefer magazines over books. Magazines are more timely, are probably easier to read, cover interesting subjects, and are acceptable to others in the reader's peer group.

A relevant, up-to-date collection of resources for young adults must include a variety of nonprint materials. Compact discs are the current preferred format for music. All kinds of music, especially rock and rap music by currently popular artists, may be included. Teens play cassette tapes in their cars and on personal stereos; they use books on tape for school assignments and for recreation. Videos are also popular. A video collection will appeal to young adults if it includes popular movies, curriculum-related titles, how-to-do-it items, and educational films on subjects of interest to them.

Computer software for home or library use is important in a collection of nonprint materials for young adults. Teens will request arcade-style computer games, but will also use many other types of programs when they are available for circulation.

Materials, both print and nonprint, have never been more plentiful. Many of the resources require specific equipment for access. Videocassette recorders, compact-disc players, and computers are necessary components in any modern-day collection of resources for young adults. Electronic searching is a part of the instructional program in many schools; students learn to search for information using indexes available from information services or on CD-ROM. Access to electronic sources of information should be available to young adults in any libraries that offer them to adult patrons.

Facilities. Teens need an area they can use for study or recreation. The area should be inviting, accessible, comfortable, and manageable, and it should be located closer to the adult area than to the children's area. The area should have furnishings, resources, and technology organized for individuals or groups.

A school library reflects the integrated instructional program of the school. The arrangement of school libraries should create an environment that encourages the use of various media, facilitates inquiry, and helps motivate students to use the materials and services necessary for learning. It should also provide the design flexibility needed to accommodate new technologies.

Services. Services to young adults cover a range of informational, educational, recreational, and cultural activities inside and outside the library. The extent to which each service is provided will depend on local priorities, resources, and needs. If service is to be effective, a library's policies and procedures must encourage young people to use the library. Policies should reflect the needs of young adults, especially in the areas of equality of service, access to information, and intellectual freedom.

If there are no YA specialists on the staff, one staff member may be appointed to look after the interests and needs of young adults and to coordinate services.

Ninth-grade students preparing a social studies report using microfilmed resources.

Many public libraries appoint coordinators of youth services. Unfortunately, children's services take up most of their time because of the large numbers of clients and the heavy programming demands for children. A staff member from adult services will better serve the interests of young adults.

The range of YA services offered should include (1) information services, (2) readers' advisory services, (3) programs, (4) outreach and interagency cooperation, and (5) public relations.

Historically, YA services were first seen as predominantly readers' advisory services—the right book for the right teen at the right time—preferably something more enriching and more adult than what the teen had been reading previously. A variety of promotional techniques, including booktalking, book discussion groups, reading lists, displays, and programs about books and authors support the librarians' efforts to encourage reading and literacy to this day.

Since the time when secondary schooling became compulsory, public libraries have offered school-related services including class visits, individual and group instruction, bibliographies for frequently re-

A public librarian helping students use a periodical index.

quested topics, and more recently homework hotlines, tutoring, literacy classes, and programs that addressed various youth issues and problems.

With the emergence of alternative services for troubled youths in the 1960s, libraries became involved in offering specialized information and referral services to relatively small numbers of adolescents. By the 1990s, troubled youth had become at-risk youth and their numbers had grown. There was a growing consensus that libraries were an invaluable resource for teenagers and that libraries needed to be more involved in responding to the needs of at-risk youth.

The Bay Area Youth at Risk Project in the San Francisco area is a model for planning and expanding YA services to youth at risk in particular and to young adults in general. After a period of training, coalition-building, and needs assessment, nine libraries in the San Francisco area began a series of innovative programs to improve services to youth at risk. The needs assessment revealed common concerns among young adults in the area. They were (1) doing well in school, (2) staying in school, (3) improving literacy skills, (4) multicultural relations, (5) a need for information about life skills and problems, and (6) accessing information if English is the second language. In response to these concerns, librarians planned strategies ranging from special collections to programs dealing with study skills. Some used young adults as active participants in planning or implementing new collections or programs.

School libraries offered many of the same types of services in addition to curriculum support and instruction in library skills. During the 1960s an emphasis on audiovisual instruction led to more services dealing with the use and production of nonprint materials. Since 1988, decisions about services in school libraries are influenced by guidelines for school library media programs. The mission of the guidelines is to ensure that students and staff are effective users of ideas and information.

Education and Research. In 1937 there were no courses offered for young adult librarians at library schools in the U.S. Such courses are now offered, mainly as electives, but schools accredited by the American Library Association (ALA) continue to emphasize the general body of knowledge any librarian needs. School library media certification requirements vary widely by state and may be awarded by non-ALA-accredited schools.

In 1991 ALA's Young Adult Services Division (YASD) became the Young Adult Library Services Association to reflect its mission more clearly. YALSA's mission is to advocate, promote, and strengthen service to young adults as part of the continuum of total library services.

YALSA has a list of competencies that librarians working with young adults in any type of information agency should be able to demonstrate. The document, *Young Adults Deserve the Best: Competencies for Librarians Serving Youth* (1991) emphasizes the necessity of a broad general library science background, but lists specific skills also needed for successful work with this age group.

The Journal of Young Adult Services in Librarianship is now a refereed publication, an indication of the renewed commitment to research by librarians in youth services.

Trends and Issues. Challenges to library resources for young adults continue to occur, especially in the schools, in the U.S. People for the American Way, a liberal advocacy group, reports less emphasis on banning some of the traditional targets, such as *Catcher in the Rye, The Adventures of Huckleberry Finn,* and *Forever,* and more emphasis on banning anti-Christian materials that deal with New Age philosophy, the occult, and satanism.

Another type of challenge for YA librarians is the increasing cultural diversity of their clientele. Various ethnic groups that form minorities in many countries will become significant targets for multicultural library services in the next century.

Libraries are networking with other youth-serving agencies to deal more effectively with the problems young adults face today. Libraries can provide information to help young adults cope with their problems and are a vital part of any networking effort.

The top vote-getter at the 1992 U.S. White House Conference on Library and Information Services was the Omnibus Children and Youth Literacy through Libraries Act. Delegates at the conference recognized the importance of services to children and young adults. Any resulting legislation will strengthen the library community's ability to provide these much-needed services.

REFERENCES

Patrick Jones, *Connecting Young Adults and Libraries* (1992).

Kathy Latrobe and Mildred Laughlin, *Multicultural Aspects of Library Media Programs* (1992).

National Center for Educational Statistics, *Services and Resources for Young Adults in Public Libraries* (1988).

Young Adult Library Services Association, *Young Adults Deserve the Best: Competencies for Librarians Serving Youth* (1991).

LINDA WADDLE

Yuan, T'ung-li
(1895–1965)

Yuan T'ung-li, Chinese librarian, educator, and library administrator, was a pioneer in the modern library movement and an exponent of closer cultural ties between East and West. He proposed large-scale exchange programs not only for librarians but also for students.

Yuan T'ung-li was born in 1895, the second son of a government official in Hsushui, Hebei, China. At an early age Yuan showed an avid interest in books and scholarship. He graduated from National Beijing (then Peking) University in 1916 and immediately began work as Assistant Librarian at Tsinghua College. He became Acting Librarian the following year and was largely responsible for construction of the College's new library building.

In 1920 Yuan went to the United States for advanced studies; he received the A.B. degree from Columbia University in 1922 and the B.L.S. degree in 1923 from New York State Library School in Albany. He also spent a year doing postgraduate work at the University of London's Institute of Historical Research. During this period he spent three summers at the Library of Congress helping to catalogue its Chinese collections. In 1924 he returned to China to become Librarian of Guandong (then Kwangtung)

University. He became Librarian and Professor of Bibliography at Beijing University in 1925, and when the Beijing National Library was organized in 1926, he became its Librarian, with Liang Ch'i-ch'ao as Director. In 1929 the Metropolitan Library and the old National Library were merged to form the National Library of Beijing, and Ts'ai Yuan-p'ei was made its Director, with Yuan as Associate Director. Later Yuan served successively as Acting Director and Director, helping to build it into the largest library in China and one of the largest in the world.

Many library activities in China were disrupted by the Sino-Japanese War, and in 1942 Yuan T'ung-li moved to China's wartime capital, Chongqing (then Chungking), where he set up an office of the National Library of Beijing. There he also engaged in many cultural cooperation projects with the United Kingdom and the U.S. on behalf of the Chinese government. In 1945 he was an adviser to the Chinese delegation to the United Nations Conference on International Organization in San Francisco, and in May of that year he received an honorary degree from the University of Pittsburgh.

During the 1920s and 1930s he was credited with the discovery of rare works and manuscripts of Chinese literature, including the remains of a vast encyclopedia from the Ming Dynasty, the *Yung lo ta tien*, long thought to have been destroyed, but of which he compiled successive censuses of surviving extant volumes. Among his most important contributions to the library profession was his introduction to China of such Western practices as interlibrary loan, a photocopying service, exchange of materials with foreign countries, and the compilation of union catalogues and serial lists.

In 1949 Yuan went to the United States, and from 1951 to 1953 he served as Chief Bibliographer of Stanford Research Institute. He rejoined the Library of Congress in 1957 in the Descriptive Cataloging Division and served in the Subject Cataloging Division from 1958 to the time of his retirement on January 15, 1965. His service with the Library of Congress totaled eight and a half years but spanned more than 43. He died in Washington, D.C., February 6, 1965.

Among his more significant publications are *China in Western Literature* (1958), *Russian Works on China, 1918–1960, in American Libraries* (1961), and various guides to doctoral dissertations by Chinese students.

CHI WANG

Yugoslavia

EDITOR'S NOTE : As this volume goes to press, the dissolution of the Yugoslav republic into several independent states has not been resolved. For purposes of reference, we are reprinting below the article on Yugoslavia from the Second Edition of this work.

Yugoslavia, a socialist federal republic in eastern Europe, is bordered by Austria and Hungary on the north, Romania on the northeast, Bulgaria on the east, Greece on the south, Albania and the Adriatic Sea on the southwest, and Italy on the west. Population (1990 est.) 23,809,000; area 255,804 sq.km. Yugoslavia comprises six republics: Bosnia-Hercegovina, Croatia, Macedonia, Montenegro, Serbia, and Slovenia. The official languages are Serbo-Croatian, Slovenian, and Macedonian.

History. In Yugoslavia, as in other European nations, the development of libraries came under the aegis of the church during the Middle Ages. In monasteries and bishoprics books were written, copied, and illuminated primarily for the church and then for secular purposes. Many monasteries existed in Serbia, among them Studenica, which was founded in the second half of the 12th century, Žiča dating from the first half of the 13th century, Dečani (1327–35), where a remainder of the library still exists, and Manasija (1407–18). In Croatia there was the famous Benedictine Abbey in Zadar (986). In Slovenia the Cistercian convents at Stična (1136), Konstajevica (1234), and Bistra (1260) served as libraries in the Middle Ages. Among medieval bishoprics in Croatia, the Zagreb See with its old Chapter library is still in existence. The Turkish invaders of the 15th century greatly limited the growth of libraries in areas under their domination. In Bosnia, where some of the people embraced Islam, Muslim cultural institutions appeared. In 1537 Gazi Husrevbeg set up a library for the medresa (school) he had founded in Sarajevo.

During the 19th century the Southern Slavs experienced a national revival and with it a new growth in libraries. In 1832 the Serbs founded the National Library in Beograd (Belgrade). By 1816 the Academy Library in Zagreb, Croatia, was taking on the role of a national library. In Slovenia the Ljubljana Library had already developed into the main and central library for Carniola, acquiring the right to legal deposit under Napoleon's rule. In Montenegro the State Library was founded in 1896 at Cetinje.

National Libraries. Each of the six republics has a national library. These are: in Bosnia-Hercegovina, the National and University Library of Bosnia-Hercegovina, Sarajevo; Croatia, the National and University Library, Zagreb; Macedonia, the National and University Library Kliment Ohridski, Skopje; Montenegro, the Central National Library Djordje Crnojević, Cetinje; Serbia, the National Library of Serbia, Beograd; Slovenia, the National and University Library, Ljubljana. The two autonomous provinces also have national libraries: Kosovo, the National Library of Kosovo, in Priština, and Vojvodina, the Matica Srpska Library, Novi Sad.

All the national libraries build up their collections by legal deposits of all works published throughout the country. The national library of each republic or province takes special responsibility for materials from its own area as well as materials referring to its area found in libraries of other republics and abroad. National libraries also purchase the outstanding works of world literature and sources in all branches of science.

National libraries provide complete coverage of the library-information network in their territories, assuming the function of central library promotion centers in the system and taking care of training. All the national libraries, together with the Yugoslav Bibliographical Institute and some university libraries, are involved in building a shared catalogue. It has been available online since 1988.

The Yugoslav Bibliographical Institute develops the bibliography of Yugoslavia, covering books, pamphlets, and music from 1950 and serial publications from 1956. Series A includes articles from the social sciences; Series B, natural, applied, medical, and technical sciences; and Series C, arts, philology, and literature. The national libraries of all republics and provinces deal with bibliography, producing mainly national retrospective bibliographies. For example, the National and University Library in Ljubljana, Slovenia, issues the "Slovenian Bibliography of Journals and Books."

Academic Libraries. National libraries are also central university libraries except in Serbia, Vojvodina, and Montenegro. There are a large number of academic libraries in each of the republics: central faculty libraries, seminar libraries, and libraries at research institutions with extensive book holdings of domestic and foreign scientific literature. Scientific libraries include those under the scope of republican academies of sciences, such as the Library of the Serbian Academy of Sciences and Arts in Belgrade, Library of the Yugoslav Academy of Sciences and Arts in Zagreb, Library of the Academy of Sciences and Arts of Slovenia in Ljubljana, Library of the Macedonian Academy of Sciences and Arts in Skopje, Library of the Association of Science and Arts of Montenegro in Titograd, and Library of the Academy of Sciences and Arts of Bosnia-Hercegovina in Sarajevo. These libraries collect publications issued by academies of sciences, universities, and scientific and professional associations in all parts of the world.

Public Libraries. Public libraries provide basic library service in the areas they serve—in regions, provinces, and local communities. These libraries provide at the same time the institutional support for educational and cultural activities. More than 2,000 public libraries held more than 24,000,000 volumes in the mid-1980s.

Special Libraries. Special libraries are attached to industrial, social, scientific, and cultural institutions and organizations. In Yugoslavia in the mid-1980s there were more than 1,000 special libraries collecting scientific and technical literature from all branches of science. They also provide online access to foreign databases.

The Profession. There are eight library associations in Yugoslavia. The three major ones are: Hrvatsko Bibliotekarsko Društvo (Croatian Library Association), in Zagreb, Zveza Bibliotekarskih Društev Slovenij (Library Association of Slovenia) in Ljubljana, and Društvo Bibliotečkih Radnika Srbije (Union of Serbian Library Workers), in Belgrade. Librarians from all republic and provincial libraries are through their associations members of the Savez Društava Bibliotečkih Radnika Jugoslavije (Union of Librarians Associations of Yugoslavia), which moves its headquarters from one capital to another every two years. National libraries of all the republics and provinces together with the Yugoslav Bibliographical Institute are associated in the League of Yugoslav National Libraries.

RICHARD L. KORT

Zaire

Zaire, a republic of equatorial Africa (formerly the Democratic Republic of the Congo, which was a Belgian colony until 1960), is bordered on the north by the Central African Republic and Sudan, on the east by Uganda, Rwanda, Burundi, and Tanzania, on the south by Zambia and Angola, and on the west by the Congo, the Cabinda enclave of Angola, and the Atlantic Ocean. Population (1990 est.) 35,562,000; area 2,345,409 sq.km. Although the official language is French, four national languages are recognized: Swahili, Tshiluba, Lingala, and Kikongo. More than 200 Pygmy, Bantu, and Nilo-Saharan languages and dialects are spoken within the country.

National Library. The Bibliothèque Centrale du Congo, founded in 1949, became the Bibliothèque Nationale after independence in 1960. The National Library, in Kinshasa-Gombe, is both a governmental library and a public library. Works published in or about Zaire are required by law to be deposited there. In addition, as of 1950, two copies of all government publications had to be deposited. Although government publications comprise a large share of the total number of volumes, the Library also has an important Africana collection and extensive holdings in economics, social sciences, and law. During fighting in the area, many libraries lost much of their stock. In 1980 holdings totaled some 146,000 volumes. The Archives Nationales, a section connected to the national library, attempts to acquire all administrative and historical archives relating to Zaire. In 1955 the Library began a monthly accessions list, which later become the *Bibliographie Nationale.* The Library also issued a retrospective national bibliography of its acquisitions that had been published between 1871 and 1960. Efforts were begun to establish a union catalogue of all the libraries of Zaire, but political turmoil curtailed such library activities. Book publishing in Zaire is limited.

Academic Libraries. In 1971 the three universities of Zaire were incorporated into the Université Nationale du Zaire (UNAZA): the Université Lovanium in Kinshasa, founded in 1949; the Université Libre du Congo in Kisangani (1963); and the Université Officielle du Congo in Lubumbashi (1956). Each campus has a central library; those at Kinshasa and Lubumbashi also have many departmental libraries. The library at Kisangani has, in addition to its central library, faculty libraries of Science and Education. The Bibliothèque Centrale, Kinshasa, holds approximately 300,000 volumes; the Bibliothèque Centrale, Kisangani, 46,000 volumes; and the Bibliothèque Centrale, Lubumbashi, 93,000 volumes. Holdings are primarily in French, with a considerably smaller number of volumes in English and in African languages and Arabic. The many departmental libraries are of varying sizes and are all catalogued at the central libraries. Interlibrary loans are available among the university libraries, research centers, and specialized libraries.

Public Libraries. There is no centralized public library system in Zaire. Individual public libraries throughout the provinces are administered through the local offices of the Ministry of Fine Arts and Cultural Affairs, which is actually a division of the Bibliothèque Nationale. Most of these libraries are subscription libraries, which require a fee for use of their materials. Holdings are very limited and, for the most part, are not widely used. The illiteracy rate is high. The Ministry published a *Liste des bibliothèques publiques* (list of public libraries) in 1971. The size of the country and limited communication systems, as well as political unrest, worked against the establishment of effective public library service.

School Libraries. Most schools in Zaire have been established through the missions, particularly the Catholic missions. Statistical and detailed information concerning existing libraries for school students was not available in the early 1990s. Most schools did not have libraries.

Special Libraries. Most special libraries were established prior to independence in 1960. Many government ministries have their own libraries, with collections of works on Africa and on Zaire in particular. These libraries are especially important to researchers, as are those attached to major research centers, such as the Institut National pour l'Étude et la Recherche Agronomique (INERA) at Yangambi, founded in 1933. The Library's holdings consist of approximately 44,000 technical and scientific volumes, 2,300 current periodicals, and about 3,000 maps and photographs. That library serves the agriculture department at the Kisangani campus. The Institut maintains several regional libraries. Also of importance are the libraries of the Institut de Recherche Scientifique. The Library, Documentation, and Publications section of the Institut Makanda Kabobi (IMK), established in 1974 in Kinshasa, houses approximately 10,000 volumes and has extensive newspaper clippings that relate to the Institute's work. The IMK was founded to train executive personnel, but its library is open to the public. Its collection is particularly strong in the humanities. Many of the institutes connected with the universities have extensive libraries. The central library of the Institut Pedagogique National (IPN), founded in Kinshasa in 1961, houses approximately 37,000 volumes, primarily in French and English. The Instituts Supérieurs Pédagogiques (ISP) have libraries in at least ten provinces, many of which were established in the late 1960s. In addition, many libraries are affiliated with private companies, independent research institutes, and cultural centers of embassies and consulates.

The Profession. The Zairian Association of Archivists, Librarians, and Documentalists was established in Kinshasa on October 5, 1968. Its purpose is to promote library and documentation centers throughout the country and to establish technology and information science centers in Zaire. It is affiliated with IFLA, AIDBA, and FID. Meetings are held every three years. The Association publishes an official journal, *Mukanda: Bulletin des Archives, Bibliothèques et Documentation du Zaire* (1975–), and issues proceedings of seminars and conferences.

Zambia

Zambia, a republic in south-central Africa, is bounded on the north by Zaire and Tanzania, on the east by Malawi, on the southeast by Mozambique, on the south by Mozambique, Zimbabwe, Botswana, and Namibia, and on the west by Zaire. Population (1990 est.) 8,073,000; area 752,614 sq.km. Many Bantu languages are spoken. Four major languages are

National Archives of Zambia

Library of the National Archives of Zambia, Lusaka.

Tonga, Bemba, Nyanja, and Lozi. The language of the administration is English.

History. The history of libraries in Zambia is linked with the colonial history of the country. Cultural traditions and beliefs of various ethnic groups were preserved through memory and repeated orally from generation to generation. The changeover from oral traditions to the written word came with the arrival of missionaries who introduced Western education with its emphasis on reading and writing skills. The first missionary to arrive in Zambia, David Livingstone, introduced the first prototype library. Known as the "tin-truck" portable library, it was carried around during his travels in Zambia between 1853 and 1873.

The Livingstone subscription library was one among the first libraries established in Livingstone about 1908; and in the 1920s a number of small subscription libraries were set up in the townships such as Chipata, Kasama, Mongu, Mansa, Lusaka, Luanshya, Choma, and Ndola. Those libraries were used mostly by Europeans who could afford to pay membership and subscription fees.

The British South Africa Company, founded by Cecil Rhodes in 1889, ruled Zambia (then called Northern Rhodesia) until 1924, and did almost nothing to provide and develop library services for the Africans. Similarly, the British colonial government, which ruled Zambia from 1924 to 1964, did not do much either except that some money from its Colonial Development and Welfare Fund was used to establish the Northern Rhodesia Publications Bureau in 1947. The Bureau, renamed Joint Publications Bureau of Northern Rhodesia and Nyasaland in 1948, introduced a country book-box library scheme in 1959 that provided the majority of Africans their first access to library services. In 1960 the Joint Publications Bureau received a grant-in-aid from the Ford Foundation toward the development of country-wide public library service in Zambia. This grant led to the establishment in 1962 of the Northern Rhodesia Library Service, which was subsequently renamed the Zambia Library Service.

Public library service in Zambia received little government support and suffered from lack of public library legislation. Further contributing factors to disappointing development were unfavorable economic and environmental conditions, resulting in falling prices for exports and rising costs for imports; inadequate transport facilities; unproductive farming; lack of foreign exchange; and mounting inflation.

National Library and Archives. Although no national library was established by legislation, the University of Zambia (UNZA) Library serves the functions of a national library. Wherever possible, it extends its facilities and services to scientists and researchers beyond the University community from its holdings of 300,000 volumes. It is a depository for government and international publications and repository of printed official documents of the United Nations and its agencies. The Library has extensive collections of East African government publications, Zambiana (including oral history and archival materials), Africana, Livingstoniana, and material on former Portuguese territories in Southern and Central Africa, the Simon's Collection on African law, and University theses.

The Library of the National Archives of Zambia in Lusaka was developed into a relatively advanced reference and research center for the country. It has record centers in the nine provinces of the country. Its origin can be traced back to 1935 when the Archives of Zimbabwe was inaugurated and its services extended to Malawi and Zambia in 1946. An act establishing the National Archives of Zambia was passed in 1969.

The Archives Library has almost 13,500 books, 360 foreign periodicals, 310 Zambian periodicals, and more than 20,000 archival files. The historical manuscripts in the archives include private papers of explorers, missionaries, administrators, and political figures dating back to 1877. Among the important collections are the papers and diaries of President Kenneth David Kaunda of the Republic of Zambia.

The Library has legal deposit rights and all the books and periodicals so received are registered and compiled annually into a *National Bibliography of Zambia,* published since 1970.

Academic Libraries. Almost all academic libraries of note are financed by the government of Zambia. The largest is that attached to the University of Zambia, established by an act of Parliament in 1965. The UNZA library system consists of the Main Library in Lusaka (250,000 volumes and 2,170 serials); the Medical Library, also in Lusaka (21,000 volumes and 283 periodicals); and the Ndola Campus Library, established in 1978 some 320 kilometers from Lusaka (10,000 volumes and 200 serials) specializing in business, industrial, and environmental collections. A new library was established in the mid-1980s at UNZA School of Veterinary Medicine in Lusaka.

Other academic libraries are those attached to institutions of higher learning, such as the Natural Resources Development College, founded in Lusaka in 1964 (20,000 volumes, 1,500 serials, and 10,000 technical reports); Nkrumah Teachers College, established in 1967 in Kabwe (19,000 volumes and 12 serials); Dag Hammarskjold Memorial Library, established in 1963 at Mindolo Ecumenical Foundation in Kitwe (18,000 volumes and 60 serials); Zambia Institute of Technology, also in Kitwe, established in 1970 (17,000 volumes, 150 serials, and 800 technical reports); and David Livingstone Teachers College Resource Center, established in 1978 in Livingstone (14,600 volumes, 16 serials, and 75 technical reports).

Public Libraries. The birth of the Zambia Library Service (ZLS) in 1962 marks the rise and development of nationwide public Library service in Zambia. Its Headquarters Library is in Lusaka; there are seven regional libraries, in Chipata, Monze, Mansa, Kasama, Solwezi, Choma, and Mongu, and a branch library at Solwezi. The Headquarters Library contains 150,000 volumes and 200 serials. The average stock in each of the regional (provincial) libraries is 37,500 volumes and 10 serials. ZLS serves 931 centers, each with a collection ranging from 100 to 250 books, in schools, governmental, and parastatal organizations in urban and rural areas.

Despite shortcomings in the development of public libraries, the ZLS through a network of provincial libraries, district libraries, and library centers makes books freely available on loan wherever possible in urban and rural areas.

Zambia also has municipal public libraries that operate autonomously, serving the residents of the urban areas of Lusaka, Kabwe, Livingstone, Luanshya, and Chingola. Although the municipal libraries are administered and operated separately from the ZLS, they both receive funds from the central government. The municipal libraries are financed by the Ministry of Local Government and the ZLS by the Ministry of Education. The services of both are available to all in the country.

The services of the municipal libraries and the ZLS are supplemented by the libraries run by the U.S. Information Service in Lusaka (15,000 volumes and 100 serials) and the British Council libraries in Lusaka and Ndola (25,000 volumes and 200 serials). These libraries are administered and financed separately by their respective governments and serve as both public and special libraries. They are popular with schoolchildren and with professional men and women.

School Libraries and Media Centers. The 931 centers served by the ZLS provide library services to elementary and secondary schools. The municipal libraries in urban areas link their services to schools by providing mobile libraries, and the city of Lusaka Public Library has branches in the residential areas to attract schoolchildren to their libraries. In a survey carried out in 1977, questionnaires were sent to 119 schools, out of which only 81 replied, probably because 38 out of 119 schools did not have school libraries. Just over 51 percent (41) out of 78 responding schools had between 500 and 1,000 pupils. Almost the same number (39) had between 1,000 and 3,000 books. Taking the mean of both sets of figures would indicate approximately three times as many books as pupils. This situation has not changed much.

Special Libraries. Most of Zambia's 65 special libraries are owned and financed by the various government ministries. They enjoy good informal interlibrary cooperation with the University of Zambia libraries. They specialize in subjects such as natural sciences, agriculture, law, education, banking, and mining, all of great economic importance to the country. The Library of the National Council for Scientific Research and Documentation (10,000 volumes), established in 1967 in Lusaka, specializes in natural sciences, and in the mid-1980s had the potential for becoming the principal documentation and information center for the country. The Department of Agriculture Library, established in 1953 at Mount Makulu Research Station, has service points at 11 regional stations and contains special collections in agriculture and related sciences (10,000 volumes, 200 serials, 2,000 FAO Reports). Livingstone Museum Research Library, established in 1951 in Livingstone (22,000 volumes and 400 reports), produces a museum journal and museum guide and contains materials on archaeology, ethnography, history, anthropology, and Africana. The Geological Survey library in Lusaka (34,645 volumes) has publications on geology, mining, metallurgy, and allied scientific and engineering subjects. In the Copperbelt, the mining industries maintain special libraries in Kitwe and Ndola that contain materials on all aspects of mining in Zambia. The Bank of Zambia Library, established in 1967 in Lusaka (2,500 volumes, 468 serials), has materials on economics, the International Monetary Fund, the World Bank, the United Nations, and financial and nonfinancial institutions of Zambia.

Other libraries with special collections are the Parliamentary Information and Research library of the National Assembly (23,000 volumes); the Library at Highcourt in Zambia (7,000 volumes, 30 serials); Radio Zambia Record and Reference Library in Lusaka with branch at Kitwe studios (75,000 discs, 23,000 tapes); Zambia Information Service Film Library (7,000 films); Zambia Standard Institute Technical Reference Library (8,000 volumes); United National Independence Party (UNIP) Library, established in 1975 (5,000 volumes, 70 serials); and Civil Aviation Technical Library (1,300 volumes). Libraries with religious collections are found at the United Church of Zambia Theological College Library in Kitwe and Jesuit Theological Library and Islamic Library in Lusaka.

The Profession. The Department of Library Studies in the University of Zambia offers a four-year B.A. in Library Studies (B.A.L.S.) and a two-year nongraduate Diploma in Librarianship (Dip. Lib.). From its inception in 1967 until 1984 the Department trained 115 graduates with the B.A.L.S. and 59 with the Dip. Lib. In addition, the Department offers a course in School Librarianship to fourth-year B.A. and B.Sc. education students who wish to become teacher-librarians in schools. Plans were under way in the mid-1980s to introduce a Master's degree in Library Science. The publications of the Department include its *Handbook,* published annually, and *Zambian Libraries,* a journal whose first issue came out in 1984.

The Posts and Telecommunication Training College in Ndola offers a six-month subprofessional course called the Certificate Course in Librarianship.

The Zambia Library Association (ZLA) was established in 1967 with the Zambia Library Association Council as its governing body. Separate committees in the ZLA make recommendations on topics such as establishing the National Information System (NATIS), compiling a National Union Catalogue, and employment of librarians in Zambia. ZLA takes an active interest in the development of regional information and documentation services for the countries in Eastern, Central, and Southern Africa. The *Zambian Library Association Journal* was issued quarterly from 1968, but changed to biannual publication in 1979. The *Zambia Library Association Newsletter,* a bimonthly, was inaugurated in April 1979. From 1983, however, the frequency of publication and appearance of those publications were irregular.

O. N. MOHAMEDALI

Zimbabwe

Zimbabwe, a republic in southern Africa, is bordered by Zambia on the north, Mozambique on the northeast and east, South Africa on the south, and Botswana on the southwest and west. Population (1990 est.) 9,369,000; area 390,580 sq.km. The official language is English and the principal national languages are Shona and Ndebele.

History. Writing was introduced into what is now Zimbabwe by missionaries in the 19th century, and libraries were first established by colonists in the mid-1890s. After an initial pioneer phase, development was slow.

National Libraries. The Library of the National Archives of Zimbabwe, founded in the capital city of Salisbury (now Harare) in 1935 as a department of the Central African Archives, is the principal legal deposit library, the foremost center for research on South-Central Africa and its history, and the chief bibliographical services center. In 1987 its collections, which comprise all works published in Zimbabwe, works by Zimbabwean authors, and works on Zimbabwe published elsewhere, totaled 43,000 monographs, 36,000 audiovisual materials, and 6,000 current serials in 1984. The Library publishes the *Zimbabwe National Bibliography,* maintains the *Directory of Zimbabwean Libraries,* administers the allocation of international standard book numbers, and is the Unesco deposit library for Zimbabwe.

The National Free Library of Zimbabwe, founded at Bulawayo in 1944, is the national lending library, national center for interlibrary loans, and central library for students. It maintains a national union catalogue of monographs published between 1956 and 1972 and coordinates the incorporation of the records of Zimbabwean library holdings into Southern African union catalogues published on microfiche since 1972. Its collections, which in 1987 totaled more than 90,000 monographs, 15,000 technical specifications, and 500 current periodicals, supplement public library services in providing academic, scientific, technical, and cultural books and information.

University Library. The largest library in Zimbabwe is the Library of the University of Zimbabwe at Harare, founded in 1957 as the University College of Rhodesia and Nyasaland. It lends generously through interlibrary loan from its collections, which totaled 400,000 monographs and 5,000 current periodicals in 1987. It comprises a main library, extended in 1983–84 to accommodate a rapidly expanding student body, and law, medical, education, map, and veterinary science libraries, with special collections of Zimbabweana and African languages.

Public Libraries. Zimbabwe inherited from the colonial era (1890–1980) a dual system of grant-aided public subscription libraries and municipal libraries. The largest public libraries are the Harare City Library, founded in 1902 as the Queen Victoria Memorial Library, with 80,000 volumes and five branch libraries; the Bulawayo Public Library, founded in 1896, with 85,000 volumes, three branch libraries, and a mobile library service; and the Bulawayo Municipal Libraries, with 75,000 volumes and seven branch libraries (1984). The Bulawayo Public Library is the country's second legal deposit library; it maintains a Historic Reference Collection at the Bulawayo City Hall.

Moves sponsored by the Carnegie Corporation of New York to foster a free public library system failed in 1929 for want of finance, but resulted in the foundation of the National Free Library in 1944. The Varley Report (1951), commissioned by the Central African Branch of the South African Library Association, recommended a national library service for the two Rhodesias and Nyasaland. The Rhodesia Library Commission (1970) reported serious deficiencies in the public library system and proposed the establishment of a nationwide free public library service. Neither report was implemented.

The coming of independence in 1980 brought with it a new impetus for library planning. At government request, the British Council sponsored a survey by W. A. G. Alison, Director of Libraries of the City of Glasgow, Scotland. He recommended in 1981 the establishment of a national library service uniting government, academic, school, and public libraries. In 1982 a Swedish library mission recommended the inclusion of a national information and documentation center and supplied a blueprint for a library school. Ground was broken in 1984 for a new National Library and Documentation Service headquarters at Harare. Parliament passed a national library development law in 1985. It calls for a central administration, 8 regional centers, and rural library service by bookmobile and through 55 district libraries. The National Free Library has been incorporated as a constituent library and urban public libraries have been invited to join on an affiliate basis.

National Archives of Zimbabwe

National Archives of Zimbabwe, Harare.

School and College Libraries. School libraries, coordinated by the School Libraries Section of the Ministry of Education and supported by a per capita grant from the Ministry, are provided in most secondary schools. College libraries are established at teachers' colleges, technical colleges, and agricultural colleges.

Special Libraries. Most special libraries are in government departments and state-related bodies. Libraries are coordinated by the National Library and Documentation Service. Foremost is the Library of Parliament in Harare, founded in 1897 as the Library of the Legislative Council, with collections that totaled 55,000 monographs and 196 current periodicals in 1987. The Central Library of the Ministry of Agriculture, which had collections totaling 3,170 monographs, 3,900 microforms, and 500 current periodicals in 1987, was strengthened to become a resource for the Southern African Development Coordination Conference (SADCC). The British Council and the U.S. Information Service operate lending and study libraries in Harare. Notable libraries of international standing are those of the National Museums and Monuments of Zimbabwe and the Tobacco Research Board.

The Profession. The Zimbabwe Library Association was founded in 1959 as the Library Association of Rhodesia and Nyasaland. It publishes *The Zimbabwe Librarian*. Its membership in 1987 was about 220 institutional and 200 personal members.

REFERENCES

Norman Johnson, "Library Development in Rhodesia," *Give the People Light: Essays in Honour of Matthew Miller Stirling* (1972).

William A. G. Alison, *A National Library Service for Zimbabwe: A Report to the British Council* (1981).

National Archives of Zimbabwe, *Directory of Zimbabwean Libraries* (1981). Chagan Lalloo, Kerstin Jonsson, and Nina Bergstrom. *Zimbabwe: National Library and Documentation Service: Report of the Swedish Library Mission* (1982).

Michael Wise, *Aspects of African Librarianship: A Collection of Writings* (1985).

STAN MADE

Index

NOTE: *Index entries in boldface print indicate that these entries are also articles in the encyclopedia.*

A Portfolio of Great Libraries

Main entrance, Rue de Richelieu,
Bibliothèque Nationale

Main Reading Room,
Bibliothèque Nationale

BIBLIOTHÈQUE NATIONALE
Paris

Domed ceiling of the
Main Reading Room,
Bibliothèque Nationale

Bibliographic search being conducted on
BN/OPAL, Bibliothèque Nationale's
dedicated online catalogue

Department of Medals and Antiques, Bibliothèque Nationale, originally the Medals Chamber of Louis XV

Reading Room, Department of Manuscripts, Bibliothèque Nationale

Ceiling of Galerie Mazarin, Bibliothèque Nationale, executed in 1641 by Romanelli and Grimaldi

Rare books and manuscripts,
Bibliothèque Nationale

Conservator at work in the Department of Restoration, Bibliothèque Nationale

Illuminated manuscript on parchment, *Livre de la Chasse,* by Gaston Phoebus, early 15th century, Department of Manuscripts, Bibliothèque Nationale

Carte du Tendre, illustration in 17th century romance, *L'Astre,* by Honore d'Urfe, Department of Printed Books, Bibliothèque Nationale

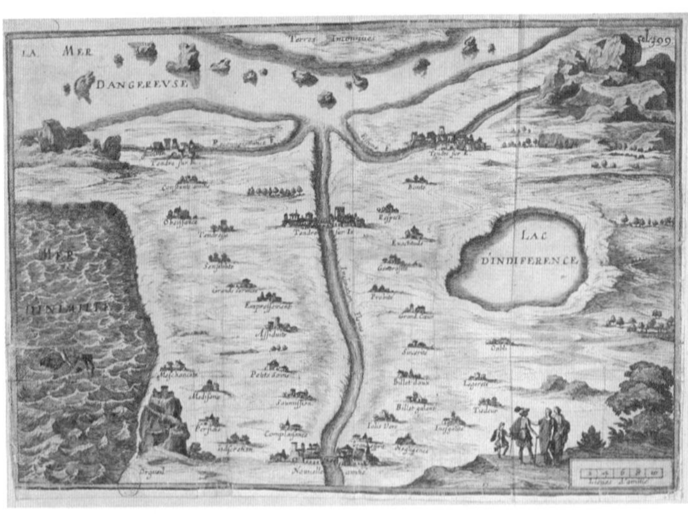

Greek gold coin bearing the head of Perseus, Department of Medals and Antiques, Bibliothèque Nationale

Slides were provided by Bibliothèque Nationale.

THE BRITISH LIBRARY
London

The British Library Round Reading Room

The British Library Newspaper Library at Colindale, north London

The British Library Document Supply Centre at Boston Spa

Reading Room, the Science Reference and Information Service, London

Artist's rendition of the new British Library building at St. Pancras, showing cut-away views of reading room and basements. Rendering by Robbie Polley

Artist's rendition of the King's Library in the new British Library building at St. Pancras. Rendering by Carl Laubin

Artist's rendition of the Rare Books Reading Room in the new British Library building at St. Pancras. Rendering by Robbie Polley

Researchers and staff consult the Eighteenth Century Short Title Catalogue (ECST) at the British Library. ECST, the largest retrospective cataloguing project in the world, is recording the output of British and British colonial presses in any language, and English language printing wherever it was produced, 1701–1800.

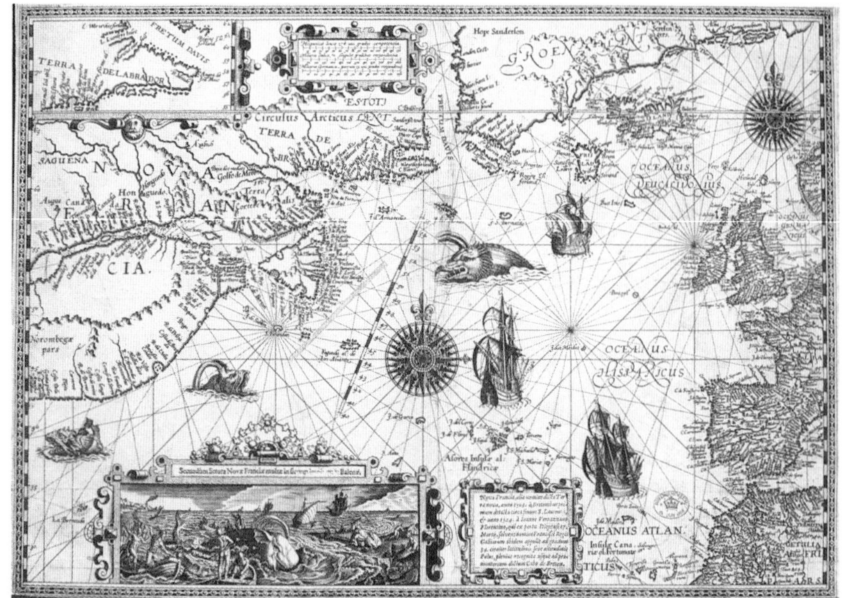

Map of the North Atlantic, ca. 1594, one of the earliest masterpieces of Dutch cartography, Map Library, British Library

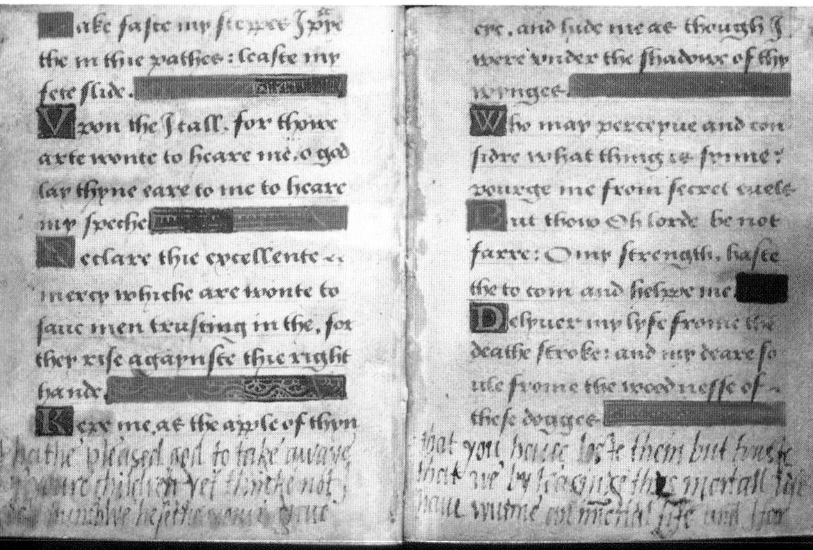
Make faste my steppes in thi pathes: leaste my fete slide. Upon the I call, for thou arte wonte to heare me, o god lay thyne eare to me to heare my speche. Declare thie excellente mercy which are wonte to saue men trusting in the, for ther rise agaynste thie right hande. Kepe me as the apple of thyn eye, and hide me as though I were under the shadowe of thy wynges. Who may perceyue and consider what thing is synne? Pourge me from secret euels. But thow Oh lorde be not farre: O my strength, haste the to com and helpe me. Delyuer my lyfe frome the deathe stroke: and my deare sowle frome the woodnesse of these dogges.

Manual of Prayers, thought to be the one carried to the scaffold by Lady Jane Grey on 12 February 1554. Her message of farewell to her father, the Duke of Suffolk, appears in the lower margins. Department of Manuscripts, British Library

Book binding at the British Library's Preservation Service

The slides are provided by The British Library Board. Artists and photographers are identified under the captions.

THE LIBRARY OF CONGRESS
Washington, D.C.

Thomas Jefferson Building, Library of Congress

Neptune Fountain in front of the Thomas Jefferson Building, Library of Congress

Great Hall of the Library of Congress, Thomas Jefferson Building

Main Reading Room of the Library of Congress, now equipped with outlets so that personal computers may be used at the Reading Room desks

Hispanic Reading Room, Thomas Jefferson Building, Library of Congress

James Madison Memorial Building, Library of Congress

Reading Room, John Adams Building, Library of Congress

Congressional Research Service Inquiry Unit of the Library of Congress logs approximately 1,000 telephone calls a day from congressional offices

American Memory project, Library of Congress, a computerized multi-media documentary history of the United States

Executive Mansion,

Washington, ..., 186 .

Four score and seven years ago our fathers brought forth, upon this continent, a new nation, conceived in liberty, and dedicated to the proposition that "all men are created equal"

Now we are engaged in a great civil war, testing whether that nation, or any nation so conceived, and so dedicated, can long endure. We are met on a great battle field of that war. We have come to dedicate a portion of it, as a final rest-

Gettysburg Address in Abraham Lincoln's hand, Manuscript Division, Library of Congress

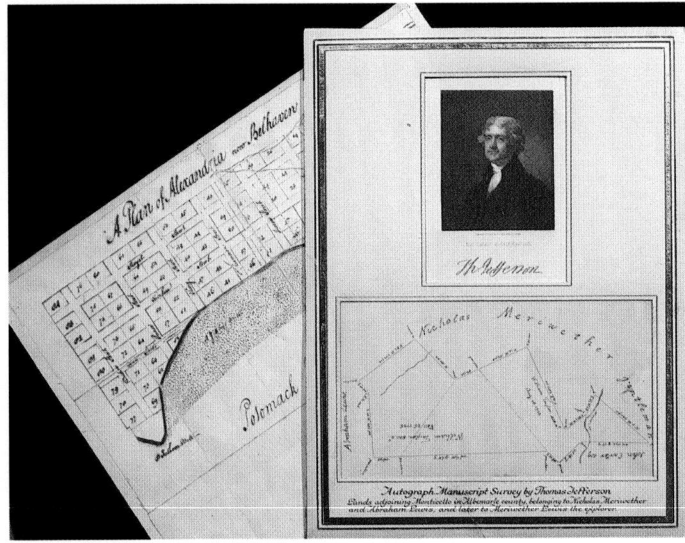

Surveys by George Washington and Thomas Jefferson, Geography and Map Division, Library of Congress

Cataloguer at work, Library of Congress

Slides were provided by The Library of Congress.

THE HARVARD UNIVERSITY LIBRARIES
Cambridge, Massachusetts

Widener Library,
the heart of the Harvard
University library system
Photo by John Nordell

Main Reading Room, Widener
Library, Harvard University
Photo by John Nordell

The Harry Elkins Widener
Memorial Room, Widener
Library, Harvard University
Photo by John Nordell

A reader in the stacks at Widener Library, Harvard University

HOLLIS (Harvard On-Line Library Information System) terminals outside the Main Reading Room of Widener Library. Photo by John Nordell

Leverett House Library. At Harvard College, upperclassmen live in Houses, and each House has its own library. Photo by William Mercer

Houghton Library (above ground) and Pusey Library (below ground), Harvard University. Houghton Library was the first academic library in the United States expressly constructed for rare books and manuscripts. Photo by John Nordell

Houghton Library Exhibition Room with Gutenberg Bible in left foreground (Harvard University). Photo by John Nordell

The Harvard-Yenching Library, housing East Asian materials

The visual collections of the Fine Arts Library at Harvard University include over 1.3 million items. Photo by John Nordell

Harvard University Archives, located below ground in Pusey Library. Photo by John Nordell

Reading Room, Law School Library, Harvard University

Slides and negatives were provided by Harvard University. Photographers are identified under the captions.

THE NEW YORK PUBLIC LIBRARY
New York City

The New York Public Library, Fifth Avenue and 42nd Street, New York City

Astor Hall (entrance foyer), New York Public Library, Fifth Avenue and 42nd Street, New York City

Public Catalog Room, New York Public Library, Fifth Avenue and 42nd Street, New York City

Main Reading Room, New York Public Library, Fifth Avenue and 42nd Street, New York City

Computerized catalogue (CATNYP) of New York Public Library, listing all holdings since 1972

D. Samuel and Jeane H. Gottesman Exhibition Hall, New York Public Library, Fifth Avenue and 42nd Street, New York City

Celeste Bartos Forum, New York Public Library, Fifth Avenue and 42nd Street, New York City

The New York Public Library for the Performing Arts, Lincoln Center Plaza, New York City

The Schomburg Center for Research in Black Culture, New York Public Library, New York City

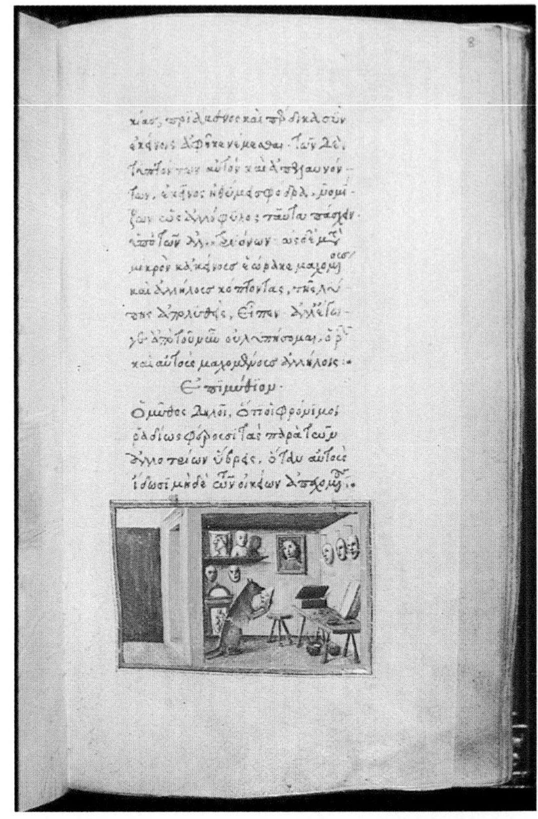

Greek manuscript of *Aesop's Fables,* Italy, ca. 1480, Spenser Collection, New York Public Library

Carolingian manuscript, ca. 850, New York Public Library

Conservation and Preservation Department, New York Public Library

The slides were provided by the New York Public Library.